Standard & Poor's MidCap 400 Guide

1996 Edition

Standard & Poor's

McGraw-Hill

New York San Francisco Washington, D.C. Auckland Bogotá
Caracas Lisbon London Madrid Mexico City Milan
Montreal New Delhi San Juan Singapore
Sydney Tokyo Toronto

FOR STANDARD & POOR'S
Vice President, Index Products & Services: Elliott Shurgin
Managing Editor: Shauna Morrison
Business Manager: Richard Albanese

McGraw-Hill

*A Division of The **McGraw-Hill** Companies*

1 2 3 4 5 6 7 8 9 0 AGM/AGM 9 0 0 9 8 7 6 5

ISBN 0-07-052153-0

The sponsoring editor for this book was David Conti, and the production supervisor was Thomas G. Kowalczyk. The front matter and introduction were set by North Market Street Graphics.

Printed and bound by Quebecor Printing.

This book is printed on acid-free paper.

The companies contained in this handbook represented the components of the S&P MidCap 400 Index as of October 20, 1995. Additions to or deletions from the Index will cause its composition to change over time. Company additions and company deletions from the S&P equity indexes do not in any way reflect an opinion on the investment merits of the company.

ABOUT THE AUTHOR

Standard & Poor's, a division of The McGraw-Hill Companies, Inc., is the nation's leading securities information company. It provides a broad range of financial services, including the respected debt ratings and stock rankings, advisory services, data guides, and the most closely watched and widely reported gauges of stock market activity—the S&P 500, S&P MidCap 400, S&P SmallCap 600, and the S&P Super Composite 1500 stock price indexes. S&P products are marketed around the world and used extensively by financial professionals and individual investors.

Introduction

by Alan J. Miller, C.F.A.

Most serious investors have heard of the Standard & Poor's 500 Composite Stock Index. Together with the Dow Jones Industrial Average, it is one of the two oldest stock market indices around (the DJIA having started in 1884 and the predecessor to the S&P 500 in 1923). It is the index of choice for measuring the performance of most professionally managed investment portfolios. And it is the basis upon which upwards of $320 billion in passive index funds are managed.

Moreover, there are few investors who have not at least heard of the most prominent components of the S&P 500. Their names read like a veritable "Who's Who" of American industry: AT&T, Aetna Life & Casualty, Exxon, Philip Morris, Sears, Roebuck & Co., Wal-Mart Stores—and that's just a handful of the components! Little wonder when the "average" S&P 500 company had a market value of $8.6 billion at the end of 1995's third quarter.

The S&P MidCap 400 Index, however, is not yet as well known. It has been around for less than five years, having been introduced in June 1991, and the companies which comprise it are not nearly as famous as their S&P 500 counterparts. Some of the companies in this lesser-known group include Analog Devices, Chiron Corp., Loctite Corp., Shaw Industries, Tidewater Inc., and Witco Corp. How many have you heard of?

This lack of recognition is unfortunate for several reasons:

1. Today's S&P MidCap 400 may well be the precursor of the S&P 500 of our grandchildren's time. The average market capitalization of companies in the S&P MidCap 400 is only about $1.5 billion (about one-sixth of the $8.6 billion average for companies in the S&P 500). But while companies in the S&P MidCap 400 are much smaller than their S&P 500 counterparts today, they well may grow to be the giants of tomorrow.

   That is because many mid-capitalization stocks are in relatively fast-growing industries, offering superior earnings growth potential and boasting strong balance sheets and high returns on equity. So investors who are willing to assume the incremental risk of investing in somewhat smaller and newer companies than the bluest of the blue chips in the S&P 500, in an attempt at realizing better than

S&P 500 market returns, well might be advised to take a look at the stocks in this index.

2. The S&P 500 is probably the best equity index benchmark for the entire U.S. equities market. At year-end 1994, it represented approximately 68% of the total market value of all domestic stocks. However, it is largely dominated by large capitalization stocks, with over 50% of its total market value accounted for by the 60 largest stocks in the index. And it is the skewness toward large capitalization stocks which created a need for other means of indexing to capture the equity performance of the remaining U.S. equity market segments.

   That's where the S&P MidCap 400 came in. From a universe of 1,700 securities with 1990 year-end values ranging from $5 billion down to $200 million, Standard & Poor's selected the 400 stock sample that came to comprise the S&P MidCap 400 Index, in order to better reflect the performance of the mid-sized market capitalization segment.

3. Prior to the creation of the S&P MidCap 400 Index, investors in mid-sized capitalization companies didn't really have a good benchmark against which to measure their investment managers' performance. The S&P MidCap 400 Index filled that void.

4. Investors who wish to invest in the mid-sized capitalization market without incurring the company-specific risk inherent in choosing individual stocks now can invest in passively managed index funds pegged to the S&P MidCap 400 Index. To be sure, such passively managed funds now amount to only about $8.2 billion (compared to 39 times as much currently indexed to the S&P 500), but remember that five years ago the opportunity to index a portfolio of mid-sized capitalization stocks didn't exist at all.

   Alternatively, investors who wish to invest in the mid-sized capitalization market without incurring specific company risk can invest directly in S&P MidCap 400 futures contracts or options on S&P MidCap 400 futures contracts. Futures on the S&P MidCap 400 and options on those futures contracts are traded on the Chicago Mercantile Exchange. Options on the S&P MidCap 400 Index are traded on the American Stock Exchange.

5. Finally, there are those who may not even be investors, but who have all sorts of other reasons for needing to know how individual mid-sized capitalization companies are doing. Perhaps they are job hunters, seeking employment in companies like these which offer above-average career opportunities. Perhaps they are salespeople or marketers, searching for new clients in rapidly growing industries. Perhaps they are the owners or managers of private or public companies who need to know how their competitors are doing. All of

these people will find the companies which comprise the S&P MidCap 400 of interest to them.

How to Use This Book

In the pages that follow, you will find a wealth of information on each of the 400 companies which comprise the S&P MidCap 400 Index, information which will allow you to make reasoned investment, business, and personal judgments regarding these companies. But to get the most value from this book, you should take a few moments to familiarize yourself with just what you'll find on these pages.

Please note that during 1995, Standard & Poor's greatly improved the Stock Reports by adding a variety of new features to help you in making investment decisions. At the time this handbook was being prepared, some companies were not yet converted to the enhanced format and are presented in this book in their existing format.

Following is a glossary of terms and definitions used throughout this book. Please refer to this section as you encounter terms which need further clarification.

Enhanced Stock Report Terms

Quantitative Evaluations

S&P Opinion—Buy, hold or sell recommendations are provided using S&P's unique STARS (Stock Appreciation Ranking System), which measures short-term (six- to 12-month) appreciation potential of stocks. STARS performance is measured against the performance of the S&P 500 Index.

STARS Rankings are as follows:

- ***** Buy—Expected to be among the best performers over the next 12 months.
- **** Accumulate—Expected to be an above-average performer.
- *** Hold—Expected to be an average performer.
- ** Avoid—Likely to be a below-average performer.
- * Sell—Expected to be a well-below-average performer and fall in price.

Outlook—Using S&P's exclusive proprietary quantitative model, stocks are ranked in one of five Outlook Groups—ranging from Group 5, listing the most undervalued stocks, to Group 1, the most overvalued issues. Group 5 stocks are expected to generally outperform all others. To identify a stock that is in a strengthening or weakening position, a positive (+) or negative (–) Timing Index is placed next to the Outlook ranking. Using these rankings, here's what action should be taken:

5+ = Buy	3– = Sell
5 = Hold if in portfolio	2+ = Hold if in portfolio
4+ = Hold if in portfolio	2– = Sell
4– = Sell	1+ = Hold if in portfolio
3+ = Hold if in portfolio	1– = Sell

The Timing Index helps identify the right time to buy stocks, but its most important function is to indicate when it is time to sell. Because Group 5 stocks have historically produced the best results, S&P recommends buying only Group 5 stocks with a positive Timing Index. Then, hold onto each one for as long as it remains in a positive trend (positive Timing Index), even if the ranking falls as the stock appreciates toward overvalued status. This will reduce transaction costs and substantially raise your chances of outperforming the market in the long run. It will also raise the number of transactions which qualify as long-term capital gains for tax purposes.

Fair Value—The price at which a stock should sell today as calculated by S&P's computers using our quantitative model based on the company's earnings, growth potential, return on equity relative to the S&P 500 and its industry group, price to book ratio history, current yield relative to the S&P 500, and other factors. The current fair price is shown given today's S&P 500 level.

Risk—Rates the volatility of the stock's price over the past year.

Technical Evaluation—In researching the past market history of prices and trading volume for each company, S&P's computer models apply special technical methods and formulas to identify and project price trends for the stock. They analyze how the price of the stock is moving and evaluate the interrelationships between the moving averages to ultimately determine buy or sell signals—and to decide whether they're bullish, neutral or bearish for the stock. The date the signals were initiated is also provided so you can take advantage of a recent or ongoing uptrend in price, or see how a stock has performed over time since our last technical signal was generated.

Relative Strength Rank—Shows, on a scale of 1 to 99, how the stock has performed compared with all other companies in S&P's universe of companies on a rolling 13-week basis.

Insider Activity—Gives an insight as to insider sentiment by showing whether directors, officers and key employees—who may have proprietary information not available to the general public—are buying or selling the company's stock during the most recent six months.

Key Stock Statistics

Avg. Daily Vol.—The average daily trading volume of the stock for the past 20 days on a rolling basis, shown in millions.

Market Cap.—The price of the stock multiplied by the number of shares outstanding, shown in billions.

Insider Holdings—The percentage of outstanding shares held by directors, officers and key employees of the company, and others who hold a minimum of 10% of the outstanding shares.

Value of $10,000 Invested 5 years ago—The value today of a $10,000 investment in the stock made five years ago, assuming year-end reinvestment of dividends.

S&P Ranking

The investment process involves assessment of various factors—such as products and industry position, company resources and financial policy—with results that make some common stocks more highly esteemed than others. In this assessment, Standard & Poor's believes that earnings and dividend performance is the end result of the interplay of these factors and that, over the long run, the record of this performance has a considerable bearing on relative quality. The rankings, however, do not reflect all of the factors that may bear on stock quality.

Growth and stability of earnings and dividends are the key elements in Standard & Poor's earnings and dividend rankings for common stocks, which are designed to capsulize the nature of this record in a single symbol. It should be noted, however, that the process also takes into consideration certain adjustments and modifications deemed desirable in establishing such rankings.

These rankings are derived by means of a computerized scoring system based on per share earnings and dividend records of the most recent ten years. Basic scores are computed for earnings and dividends and then adjusted by a set of predetermined modifiers for growth, stability, and cyclicality. Adjusted scores for earnings and dividends are then combined to yield a final score.

The ranking system also makes allowance for the fact that, in general, corporate size imparts certain recognized advantages from an investment standpoint. Minimum size limits (in terms of corporate sales) are set for the various rankings, but exceptions may be made where a score reflects an outstanding earnings-dividend record.

The final score is then translated into one of the following rankings:

A+ Highest
A High
A− Above Average
B+ Average
B Below Average
B− Lower
C Lowest
D In Reorganization
NR No Ranking

In some instances, rankings may be modified by special considerations, such as natural disasters, massive strikes, or nonrecurring accounting adjustments.

It is important to note that a ranking is not a forecast of future market price performance, but is basically an appraisal of past performance of earnings and dividends and relative current standing. Consequently, rankings should not be used as market recommendations: a high-score stock may at times be so overpriced as to justify its sale while a low-score stock may be attractively priced for purchase. Rankings based upon earnings and dividend records are no substitute for complete analysis. They cannot take into account the potential effects of management changes, internal company policies not yet fully reflected in the earnings and dividend record, public relations standings, recent competitive shifts, and a host of other factors that may be relevant in investment decision making.

Beta

The beta coefficient is a measure of the volatility of a stock's price relative to the S&P 500 Index (a proxy for the overall market). An issue with a beta of 1.5 for example, tends to move 50% more than the overall market, in the same direction. An issue with a beta of 0.5 tends to move 50% less. If a stock moved exactly as the market moved, it would have a beta of 1.0. A stock with a negative beta tends to move in a direction opposite to that of the overall market.

Per Share Data ($) Tables

Tangible Book Value; Book Value (See also: "Common Equity" under Industrial)—Indicates the theoretical dollar amount per common share one might expect to receive from a company's tangible "book" assets should liquidation take place. Generally, book value is determined by adding the stated value of the common stock, paid-in capital and retained earnings and then subtracting intangible assets (excess cost over equity of acquired companies, goodwill, and patents), preferred stock at liquidating value and unamortized debt discount. Divide that amount by the outstanding shares to get book value per common share.

Cash Flow—Net income plus depreciation, depletion, and amortization, divided by shares used to calculate earnings per common share. (Also see: "Cash Flow" for Industrial Companies)

Earnings—The amount a company reports as having been earned for the year on its common stock based on generally accepted accounting standards. Earnings may be indicated in terms of *primary* (common stock and common stock equivalents such as stock options and warrants) and *fully diluted* (reflecting dilution in earnings resulting if all contingent issuances of common stock materialized at the outset of the year), and are generally reported from continuing operations, before extraordinary items. INSURANCE companies report *operating earnings* before gains/losses on security transactions and *earnings* after such transactions.

Dividends—Generally total cash payments per share based on the ex-dividend dates over a twelve-month period. May also be reported on a declared basis where this has been established to be a company's payout policy.

Payout Ratio—Indicates the percentage of earnings paid out in dividends. It is calculated by dividing the annual dividend by the earnings. For INSURANCE companies *earnings* after gains/losses on security transactions are used.

Prices High/Low—Shows the calendar year high and low of a stock's market price.

P/E Ratio High/Low—The ratio of market price to earnings—essentially indicates the valuation investors place on a company's earnings. Obtained by dividing the annual earnings into the high and low market price for the year. For INSURANCE companies *operating earnings* before gains/losses on security transactions are used.

Net Asset Value—Appears on investment company reports and reflects the market value of stocks, bonds, and net cash divided by outstanding shares. The % DIFFERENCE indicates the percentage premium or discount of the market price over the net asset value.

Portfolio Turnover—Appears on investment company reports and indicates percentage of total security purchases and sales for the year to overall investment assets. Primarily mirrors trading aggressiveness.

Income/Balance Sheet Data Tables

Banks

Net Interest Income—Interest and dividend income, minus interest expense.

Loan Loss Provision—Amount charged to operating expenses to provide an adequate reserve to cover anticipated losses in the loan portfolio.

Taxable Equivalent Adjustment—Increase to render income from tax-exempt loans and securities comparable to fully taxed income.

Noninterest Income—Service fees, trading and other income, excluding gains/losses on securities transactions.

% Expenses/Op. Revenues—Noninterest expense as a percentage of taxable equivalent net interest income plus noninterest income (before securities gains/losses). A measure of cost control.

Commercial Loans—Commercial, industrial, financial, agricultural loans and leases, gross.

Other Loans—Gross consumer, real estate and foreign loans.

% Loan Loss Reserve—Contra-account to loan assets, built through provisions for loan losses, which serves as a cushion for possible future loan charge-offs.

% Loans/Deposits—Proportion of loans funded by deposits. A measure of liquidity and an indication of bank's ability to write more loans.

Earning Assets—Assets on which interest is earned.

Money Market Assets—Interest-bearing interbank deposits, federal funds sold, trading account securities.

Investment Securities—Federal, state, and local government bonds and other securities.

Gains/Losses on Securities Transactions—Realized losses on sales of securities, usually bonds.

Net Before Taxes—Amount remaining after operating expenses are deducted from income, including gains or losses on security transactions.

Effective Tax Rate—Actual income tax expense divided by net before taxes.

Net Income—The final profit before dividends (common/preferred) from all sources after deduction of expenses, taxes, and fixed charges, but before any discontinued operations or extraordinary items.

Net Interest Margin—A percentage computed by dividing net interest income, on a taxable equivalent basis, by average earning assets. Used as an analytical tool to measure profit margins from providing credit services.

% Return on Revenues—Net income divided by gross revenues.

% Return on Assets—Net income divided by average total assets. An analytical measure of asset-use efficiency and industry comparison.

% Return on Equity—Net income (minus preferred dividend requirements) divided by average common equity. Generally used to measure performance.

Total Assets—Includes interest-earning financial instruments—principally commercial, real estate, consumer loans and leases; investment securities/trading accounts; cash/money market investments; other owned assets.

Cash—Mainly vault cash, interest-bearing deposits placed with banks, reserves required by the Federal Reserve and items in the process of collection—generally referred to as float.

Government Securities—Includes United States Treasury securities and securities of other U.S. government agencies at book or carrying value. A bank's major "liquid asset."

State and Municipal Securities—State and municipal securities owned at book value.

Loans—All domestic and foreign loans (excluding leases), less unearned discount and reserve for possible losses. Generally considered a bank's principal asset.

Deposits—Primarily classified as either *demand* (payable at any time upon demand of depositor) or *time* (not payable within thirty days).

Deposits/Capital Funds—Average deposits divided by average capital funds. Capital funds include capital notes/debentures, other long-term debt, capital stock, surplus, and undivided profits. May be used as a "leverage" measure.

Long-Term Debt—Total borrowings for terms beyond one year including notes payable, mortgages, debentures, term loans, and capitalized lease obligations.

Common Equity—Includes common/capital surplus, undivided profits, reserve for contingencies and other capital reserves.

% Equity to Assets—Average common equity divided by average total assets. Used as a measure of capital adequacy.

% Equity to Loans—Average common equity divided by average loans. Reflects the degree of equity coverage to loans outstanding.

Industrial Companies

Following data is based on Form 10K Annual Report data as filed with SEC.

Revenues—Net sales and other operating revenues. Includes franchise/leased department income for retailers, and royalties for publishers and oil and mining companies. Excludes excise taxes for tobacco, liquor, and oil companies.

Operating Income—Net sales and operating revenues less cost of goods sold and operating expenses (including research and development, profit sharing, exploration and bad debt, but excluding depreciation and amortization).

% Operating Income of Revenues—Net sales and operating revenues divided into operating income. Used as a measure of operating profitability.

Capital Expenditures—The sum of additions at cost to property, plant and equipment and leaseholds, generally excluding amounts arising from acquisitions.

Depreciation—Includes noncash charges for obsolescence, wear on property, current portion of capitalized expenses (intangibles), and depletion charges.

Interest Expense—Includes all interest expense on short/long-term debt, amortization of debt discount/premium and deferred expenses (e.g., financing costs).

Net Before Taxes—Includes operating and nonoperating revenues (including extraordinary items not net of taxes), less all operating and nonoperating expenses, except income taxes and minority interest, but including equity in nonconsolidated subsidiaries.

Effective Tax Rate—Actual income tax charges divided by net before taxes.

Net Income—Profits derived from all sources after deduction of expenses, taxes, and fixed charges, but before any discontinued operations, extraordinary items, and dividends (preferred/common).

% Net Income of Revenues—Net income divided by sales/operating revenues.

Cash Flow—Net income (before extraordinary items and discontinued operations, and after preferred dividends) plus depreciation, depletion, and amortization.

Cash—Includes all cash and government and other marketable securities.

Current Assets—Those assets expected to be realized in cash or used up in the production of revenue within one year.

Current Liabilities—Generally includes all debts/obligations falling due within one year.

Current Ratio—Current assets divided by current liabilities. A measure of liquidity.

Total Assets—Current assets plus net plant and other noncurrent assets (intangibles and deferred items).

% Return on Assets—Net income divided by average total assets on a per common share basis. Used in industry analysis and as a measure of asset-use efficiency.

Long-Term Debt—Debts/obligations due after one year. Includes bonds, notes payable, mortgages, lease obligations, and industrial revenue bonds. Other Long-Term Debt, when reported as a separate account, is excluded. This account generally includes pension and retirement benefits.

Common Equity (See also: "Book Value" under Per Share Data Table)—Common stock plus capital surplus and retained earnings, less any difference between the carrying value and liquidating value of preferred stock.

Total Invested Capital—The sum of stockholders' equity plus long-term debt, capital lease obligations, deferred income taxes, investment credits, and minority interest.

% Long-Term Debt of Invested Capital—Long-term debt divided by total invested capital. Indicates how highly "leveraged" a business might be.

% Return on Equity—Net income less preferred dividend requirements divided by average common shareholders' equity on a per common share basis. Generally used to measure performance and industry comparisons.

Utilities

Operating Revenues—Represents the amount billed to customers by the utility.

Depreciation—Amounts charged to income to compensate for the decline in useful value of plant and equipment.

Maintenance—Amounts spent to keep plants in good operating condition.

Operating Ratio—Ratio of operating costs to operating revenues or the proportion of revenues absorbed by expenses. Obtained by dividing operating expenses including depreciation, maintenance, and taxes by revenues.

Fixed Charges Coverage—The number of times income before interest charges (operating income plus other income) after taxes covers total interest charges and preferred dividend requirements.

Construction Credits—Credits for interest charged to the cost of constructing new plant. A combination of allowance for equity funds used during construction and allowance for borrowed funds used during construction—credit.

Effective Tax Rate—Actual income tax expense divided by the total of net income and actual income tax expense.

Net Income—Amount of earnings for the year which is available for preferred and common dividend payments.

% Return on Revenues—Obtained by dividing net income for the year by revenues.

% Return on Invested Capital—Percentage obtained by dividing income available for fixed charges by average total invested capital.

% Return on Common Equity—Percentage obtained by dividing income available for common stock (net income less preferred dividend requirements) by average common equity.

Gross Property—Includes utility plant at cost, plant work in progress, and nuclear fuel.

Capital Expenditures—Represents the amounts spent on capital improvements to plant and funds for construction programs.

Net Property—Includes items in gross property less provision for depreciation.

% Earned on Net Property—Percentage obtained by dividing operating income by average net property for the year. A measure of plant efficiency.

Total Invested Capital—Sum of total capitalization (common-preferred-debt), accumulated deferred income taxes, accumulated investment tax credits, minority interest, contingency reserves, and contributions in aid of construction.

Total Capitalization—Combined sum of total common equity, preferred stock, and long-term debt.

Long-Term Debt—Debt obligations due beyond one year from balance sheet date.

Capitalization Ratios—Reflect the percentage of each type of debt/equity issues outstanding to total capitalization. % DEBT is obtained by dividing total debt by the sum of debt, preferred, common, paid-in capital and retained earnings. % PREFERRED is obtained by dividing the preferred stocks outstanding by total capitalization. % COMMON, divide the sum of common stocks, paid-in capital and retained earnings by total capitalization.

Finally, at the very bottom of the right-hand page, you'll find general information about the company: its address and telephone number, the names of its senior executive officers and directors (usually including the name of the investor contact), the transfer agent and registrar for the stock, and the state in which the company is incorporated.

How to Use This Book to Select Investments

And so, at last, we come to the most important question: given this vast array of data, how might a businessperson seeking to find out about her competition, a marketing manager looking for clients, a job seeker, or an investor use it to best serve their respective purposes?

If you fall into one of the first three of these categories—a businessperson seeking to find out information about her competition, a marketing manager looking for clients, or a job seeker—your task will be arduous, to be sure, but this book will provide you with an excellent starting point and your payoff can make it all worthwhile. You will have to go through this book page by page, looking for those companies that are in the industries in which you are interested, that are of the size and financial strength that appeal to you, that are located geographically in your territory or where you're willing to relocate, that have been profitable and growing, and so forth. And then you will have to read about just what's going on at those companies by referring to the appropriate "Business Summary" and "Important Developments" comments in these reports. But the companies you end up with can be those high-growth entities with the greatest potential.

Of course, this book won't do it *all* for you. It is, after all, just a starting point, not a conclusive summary of everything you might need to know. It is designed to educate, not to render advice or provide recommendations. But it will get you pointed in the right direction.

Finally, what about the investor who wants to use this book to find good individual investments from among the stocks in the S&P MidCap 400 Index? If you fall into that category, what should you do?

Well, you can approach your quest the same way that the businesswoman looking for information about her competitors, the marketing manager, and the job seeker approached theirs—by thumbing through this book page by page, looking for companies with high historic growth rates, generous dividend payout policies, wide profit margins, A+ S&P Rankings, or whatever other characteristics you consider desirable in stocks in which you might invest. In this case, however, we have made your job just a little bit easier.

We have already prescreened the 400 companies in this book for several of the stock characteristics in which investors generally are most interested, including S&P Earnings and Dividend Rankings, growth records, and dividend payment histories, and we're pleased to present on the next five pages lists of those companies which score highest on the basis of these criteria. So if you, like most investors, find these characteristics important in potential investments, you might want to turn first to the companies on these lists in your search for attractive investments.

One final thought: since many of these companies are less closely followed by Wall Street analysts, they may not be as efficiently priced as the better-known blue chips. Hence, they could include some interesting "hidden values" for those investors willing to accept some degree of incremental risk.

Good luck and happy investment returns!

Stocks With A+ or A Rankings

Based on the issues in this handbook, this screen shows stocks of all companies with Standard & Poor's earnings and dividend rankings of A+ or A.

Company	Business
Issues Ranked A+	
Cintas Corp	Sales & rental of uniforms
Crompton & Knowles	Spec chemicals,ind'l mchy
Donaldson Co	Engine air cleaners, mufflers
Federal Signal	Special trucks,tools,signals
Fifth Third Bancorp	Comm'l bkg,Cincinnati,Ohio
Hannaford Bros	Food dstr: partner supermkts
Heilig–Meyers	Retail furniture stores
Regions Financial	Commercial bkg,Alabama
RPM, Inc	Protective coatings: fabrics
State Str Boston	Comml bkg,Boston,Mass
Teleflex Inc	Aerospace ctrls: medical prod
Wilmington Trust Corp	Commercial bkg,Delaware
Issues Ranked A	
AFLAC Inc	Insurance & broadcasting
Arnold Indus	Trucking–gen'l commodities
Avnet, Inc	Distributor elec components
Bancorp Hawaii	Commercial bkg,Hawaii
Betz Laboratories	Water treatment chemicals
Black Hills Corp	Electric utility:coal mining
Bob Evans Farms	Restaurants sausage prod
Central Fidelity Banks	Commercial bkg,Virginia
Century Tel Enterp	Tel svc in parts of 14 states
Church & Dwight	Arm&Hammer,sodium bicarb
Cracker Brl Old Ctry	Restaurant & gift stores
Dauphin Deposit	Comm'l bkg,Pennsylvania
Dean Foods	Milk & dairy: food items
Dollar General	Self–service discount stores
Edwards(AG)Inc	Security broker: inv banker
First Security	Comm'l bkg,UT,ID,WY,OR

Company	Business
First Virginia Banks	Commercial bkg,Virginia
Flightsafety Intl	Aircraft & marine training
Franklin Resources	Mut'l fd inv advisory & svcs
Hubbell Inc Cl'B'	Electrical wiring devices:
Kelly Services'A'	Temporary help services
Lancaster Colony	Mfr food/auto prod
Leggett & Platt	Mfr springs,etc for furn,bed
Lincoln Telecommun	Telephone serv, Nebraska
Loctite Corp	Chemical sealants, adhesives
McCormick & Co	Spices, flavoring, tea, mixes
Mercantile Bankshares	Comm'l bkg,Baltimore, MD
Modine Mfg	Auto parts: heating: air–cond
Molex Inc	Terminals,connectors,switch
Morrison Restaurants	Public & contract food svcs
Nordson Corp	Industrial application eqp
Omnicom Group	Major int'l advertising co
Ruddick Corp	Food supermkts,thread/yarn
Schulman (A.)	Plastic mfr/merchant resins
Shaw Indus	Carpet manufacturer
Smucker (J.M.) Cl'A'	Preserves: jellies & fillings
SouthTrust Corp	Commercial bkg,Alabama
Standard Register	Business forms & handl'g eq
Superior Indus Intl	Custom auto accessories
TECO Energy	Hldg co:Tampa Electric
Tyson Foods Cl'A'	Integrated poultry business
Univl Foods	Yeast, cheese: spec food prod
Wallace Computer Svc	Business forms:comm'l print
Washington Gas Lt	Natural gas:D.C.,Md,Va
Wisconsin EnergyCorp	Hdlg:El & gas utility
WPL Holdings	Utility hldg:Wisconsin Pwr/Lt

Chart based on October 20, 1995 prices and data.

Companies With Five Consecutive Years of Earnings Increases

This table, compiled from a computer screen of the stocks in this handbook, shows companies that have recorded rising per-share earnings for five consecutive years, have a minimum 10% five-year EPS growth rate based on trailing 12-month earnings, have estimated 1995 EPS at least 10% above those reported for 1994, and pay dividends. The list is sorted by the five-year EPS growth rate.

Company	Business	Fiscal Year End	5 Yr. EPS Growth Rate %	— EPS $— 1994 Act.	1995 Est.	S&P Stock Rank	Price	P/E on 1995 Est.	% Yield
Linear Technology Corp	Mfrs integrated circuits	Jun#	41	0.75	1.11	B+	43.50	39.2	0.3
Green Tree Finl	Purchases hous'g contracts	Dec	40	1.30	1.77	B+	29.50	16.7	0.8
Dollar General	Self–service discount stores	Jan*	39	1.07	1.32	A	25.63	19.4	0.7
Mylan Labs	Pharmaceutical products	Mar*	31	1.01	1.15	A–	18.75	16.3	0.8
Cracker Brl Old Ctry	Restaurant & gift stores	Jul#	28	0.94	1.09	A	18.50	17.0	0.1
Stryker Corp	Specialty medical devices	Dec	28	1.50	1.80	A–	48.00	26.7	0.1
AFLAC Inc	Insurance & broadcasting	Dec	23	2.84	3.50	A	44.00	12.6	1.1
Clayton Homes	Produces/finances mfrd hms	Jun#	20	0.94	1.15	B+	26.25	22.8	0.3
Illinois Central Corp	Major freight railroad sys	Dec	18	2.67	3.10	NR	38.38	12.4	2.6
Fifth Third Bancorp	Comm'l bkg,Cincinnati,Ohio	Dec	16	3.80	4.30	A+	65.00	15.1	2.1
Molex Inc	Terminals,connectors,switch	Jun#	16	0.96	1.24	A	35.00	28.2	0.1
Cintas Corp	Sales & rental of uniforms	May#	15	1.12	1.34	A+	43.00	32.1	0.4
Donaldson Co	Engine air cleaners, mufflers	Jul#	13	1.17	1.45	A+	24.50	16.9	1.1
Transatlantic Holdings	Reinsur: property/casualty	Dec	13	4.44	5.20	NR	69.50	13.4	0.5
Federal Signal	Special trucks,tools,signals	Dec	12	1.02	1.20	A+	22.50	18.8	2.2
Omnicom Group	Major int'l advertising co	Dec	12	3.15	3.67	A	65.38	17.8	2.1
Arnold Indus	Trucking–gen'l commodities	Dec	10	1.16	1.45	A	18.75	12.9	2.3
RPM, Inc	Protective coatings: fabrics	May#	10	0.93	1.07	A+	19.81	18.5	3.0

*Actual 1995 EPS & estimated 1996 EPS; P/E based on estimated 1996 EPS. #Actual 1995 EPS; P/E based on 1995 actual EPS.

Chart based on October 20, 1995 prices and data.

NOTE: All earnings estimates are Standard & Poor's projections.

Rapid Growth Stocks

The stocks listed below have shown strong and consistent earnings growth. Issues of rapidly growing companies tend to carry high price-earnings ratios and offer potential for substantial appreciation. At the same time, though, the stocks are subject to strong selling pressures should growth in earnings slow. Five-year earnings growth rates have been calculated for fiscal years 1990 through 1994 and the most current 12-month earnings.

Company	Business	S&P Stock Rank	Fiscal Year End	— EPS $ — 1994 Act.	1995 Est.	5 Yr. EPS % Growth	Price	P/E on 1995 Est.	% Yield
AFLAC Inc	Insurance & broadcasting	A	Dec	2.84	3.50	23	44.00	12.6	1.1
Amer Power Conversion	Mfr constant pwr supply prod	B	Dec	0.77	0.93	55	12.81	13.8	....
BMC Software	Dvlp IBM compatible softwr	B+	Mar*	1.52	2.40	22	34.00	14.2	....
Brinker Intl	Limited menu restaurants	B+	Jun#	0.83	0.98	19	12.63	12.9	....
Buffets Inc	Operates buffet–style rest'ts	B+	Dec	0.71	0.80	22	12.00	15.0	....
Cintas Corp	Sales & rental of uniforms	A+	May#	1.12	1.34	15	43.00	32.1	0.4
Clayton Homes	Produces/finances mfrd hms	B+	Jun#	0.94	1.15	20	26.25	22.8	0.3
Cracker Brl Old Ctry	Restaurant & gift stores	A	Jul#	0.94	1.09	28	18.50	17.0	0.1
Dollar General	Self–service discount stores	A	Jan*	1.07	1.32	39	25.63	19.4	0.7
Forest Labs	Pharmaceutical mfr & dstr	B+	Mar*	2.15	2.55	21	41.75	16.4	....
Green Tree Finl	Purchases hous'g contracts	B+	Dec	1.30	1.77	40	29.50	16.7	0.8
HealthCare COMPARE	Hlthcare utiliz'n review svc	B	Dec	1.45	1.88	48	39.75	21.1	....
Linear Technology Corp	Mfrs integrated circuits	B+	Jun#	0.75	1.11	41	43.50	39.2	0.3
PacifiCare Health Sys'B'	Health maintenance svcs	B+	Sep	3.02	3.60	36	72.25	20.1	....
Sealed Air	Protective packaging mtl	A–	Dec	0.93	1.20	28	25.38	21.1	....
Stryker Corp	Specialty medical devices	A–	Dec	1.50	1.80	28	48.00	26.7	0.1
Thermo Electron	Eng'd ind'l pr: environ instr	B+	Dec	1.40	1.60	16	44.50	27.8	....

*Actual 1995 EPS & estimated 1996 EPS; P/E based on estimated 1996 EPS. #Actual 1995 EPS; P/E based on 1995 actual EPS.

Chart based on October 20, 1995 prices and data.

NOTE: All earnings estimates are Standard & Poor's projections.

Fast-Rising Dividends

Using the companies in this handbook, the issues below were chosen on the basis of their five-year annual growth rate in dividends from 1990 to the current 12-month indicated rate. All have increased their dividend payments each calendar year from 1990 to their current 12-month indicated rate.

Company	\$ Divd. Paid 1990	\$ Divd. Paid 1994	†Ind. Divd. Rate	* Divd. Growth Rate %	Price	% Yield
Schwab(Chas)Corp	0.02	0.09	0.16	51.32	22.63	0.7
Paychex,Inc	0.05	0.18	0.36	46.79	45.50	0.7
Dollar General	0.06	0.15	0.20	29.62	25.63	0.7
Stewart & Stevenson	0.10	0.26	0.32	25.23	27.75	1.1
Mylan Labs	0.05	0.11	0.16	24.33	18.75	0.8
Cardinal Health	0.04	0.11	0.12	23.50	56.38	0.2
Crompton & Knowles	0.20	0.46	0.54	22.65	12.75	4.2
Cintas Corp	0.08	0.17	0.20	21.42	43.00	0.4
Flightsafety Intl	0.21	0.42	0.56	20.99	46.25	1.2
Watts Industries'A'	0.10	0.22	0.25	20.93	21.75	1.1
Superior Indus Intl	0.08	0.15	0.20	19.80	28.63	0.6
McCormick & Co	0.23	0.48	0.52	18.17	26.13	1.9
Federal Signal	0.21	0.41	0.50	18.03	22.50	2.2
Heilig–Meyers	0.13	0.23	0.28	17.42	20.50	1.3
Kaydon Corp	0.20	0.40	0.44	17.13	28.38	1.5
Atlantic So'east Air	0.16	0.32	0.34	16.67	25.88	1.3
First Security	0.57	1.04	1.12	16.27	35.63	3.1
Schulman (A.)	0.16	0.30	0.34	16.05	20.00	1.7
Varian Associates	0.13	0.23	0.28	15.94	51.50	0.5
Fifth Third Bancorp	0.66	1.16	1.40	15.92	65.00	2.1
State Str Boston	0.33	0.58	0.68	15.73	43.13	1.5
Northern Trust	0.51	0.88	1.04	15.68	48.00	2.1
Central Fidelity Banks	0.59	1.09	1.20	15.55	32.63	3.6
Family Dollar Stores	0.20	0.33	0.40	15.44	16.88	2.3
TCA Cable TV	0.24	0.44	0.48	15.30	30.00	1.6
Reynolds & Reynolds'A'	0.20	0.33	0.40	15.25	36.63	1.0
AFLAC Inc	0.26	0.45	0.52	14.48	44.00	1.1
Franklin Resources	0.20	0.32	0.40	13.82	53.88	0.7
Hannaford Bros	0.22	0.38	0.42	13.71	26.50	1.5
Amer Finl Group	0.48	0.88	1.00	13.69	29.88	3.3
First Tenn Natl	1.07	1.68	1.88	12.86	56.88	3.3
Modine Mfg	0.33	0.51	0.60	12.16	28.00	2.1
Wausau Paper Mills	0.14	0.22	0.25	12.13	24.75	1.0
Arnold Indus	0.25	0.41	0.44	12.10	18.75	2.3
Nordson Corp	0.36	0.56	0.64	12.02	55.25	1.1
SouthTrust Corp	0.45	0.66	0.80	11.98	25.75	3.1
Wallace Computer Svc	0.47	0.67	0.86	11.77	58.00	1.4
Teleflex Inc	0.35	0.52	0.62	11.48	40.13	1.5
Marshall & Ilsley	0.39	0.59	0.66	11.16	25.00	2.6
Bob Evans Farms	0.20	0.28	0.32	10.77	17.00	1.8
Fuller (HB)	0.40	0.57	0.64	10.71	31.25	2.0
First Virginia Banks	0.84	1.26	1.36	10.70	43.63	3.1
Wilmington Trust Corp	0.72	1.06	1.20	10.58	31.50	3.8
Mercantile Bankshares	0.54	0.74	0.92	10.51	27.88	3.3
Comerica Inc	0.85	1.20	1.40	10.37	37.25	3.7
Regions Financial	0.82	1.16	1.32	10.27	41.50	3.1
Loctite Corp	0.58	0.81	1.00	10.26	46.25	2.1
Smucker (J.M.) Cl'A'	0.32	0.49	0.52	10.09	20.63	2.5
Tambrands Inc	1.11	1.70	1.76	10.07	45.63	3.8

†12-month indicated rate. *Five-year annual compounded growth rate.

Chart based on October 20, 1995 prices and data.

Higher Dividends For Ten Years

These companies have all paid higher cash dividends in each of the past ten calendar years and currently yield at least 2%. To be able to increase dividends under the difficult economic conditions that were experienced at times over the past ten years, indicates healthy finances and capable management.

Company	Price	†Ind. Divd. Rate	% Yield	Company	Price	†Ind. Divd. Rate	% Yield
Angelica Corp	22.88	0.96	4.1	Keystone Intl	23.00	0.74	3.2
Aon Corp	42.88	1.36	3.1	Lee Enterprises	41.50	0.88	2.1
Arnold Indus	18.75	0.44	2.3	LG&E Energy	42.13	2.22	5.2
Betz Laboratories	41.38	1.48	3.5	Loctite Corp	46.25	1.00	2.1
Black Hills Corp	25.50	1.34	5.2	Marshall & Ilsley	25.00	0.66	2.6
Brooklyn Union Gas	25.75	1.39	5.3	Mercantile Bankshares	27.88	0.92	3.3
Carlisle Cos	41.50	0.88	2.1	Minnesota Pwr & Lt	28.88	2.04	7.0
Central Fidelity Banks	32.63	1.20	3.6	Modine Mfg	28.00	0.60	2.1
Central La Elec	27.25	1.50	5.5	Natl Fuel Gas	30.75	1.62	5.2
Comerica Inc	37.25	1.40	3.7	Northern Trust	48.00	1.04	2.1
Crompton & Knowles	12.75	0.54	4.2	Questar Corp	30.63	1.18	3.8
Dauphin Deposit	29.75	1.06	3.5	Regions Financial	41.50	1.32	3.1
Family Dollar Stores	16.88	0.40	2.3	RPM, Inc	19.81	0.60	3.0
Fifth Third Bancorp	65.00	1.40	2.1	SCANA Corp	25.75	1.44	5.5
First of America Bk	45.25	1.76	3.8	Smucker (J.M.) Cl'A'	20.63	0.52	2.5
First Tenn Natl	56.88	1.88	3.3	Sonoco Products	26.75	0.60	2.2
First Virginia Banks	43.63	1.36	3.1	SouthTrust Corp	25.75	0.80	3.1
Florida Progress	34.00	2.02	5.9	Stanhome Inc	31.88	1.06	3.3
Flowers Indus	22.63	0.86	3.8	Tambrands Inc	45.63	1.76	3.8
Frontier Corp	27.88	0.83	2.9	TECO Energy	24.50	1.06	4.3
Fuller (HB)	31.25	0.64	2.0	Univl Corp	22.00	1.00	4.5
GATX Corp	50.75	1.60	3.1	Univl Foods	35.25	1.00	2.8
Hartford Stm Boiler Ins	46.38	2.28	4.9	UtiliCorp United	29.13	1.72	5.9
Hawaiian Elec Indus	38.63	2.40	6.2	Washington Gas Lt	20.00	1.12	5.6
Houghton Mifflin	43.63	0.96	2.2	Wilmington Trust Corp	31.50	1.20	3.8
Hubbell Inc Cl'B'	60.88	1.88	3.0	Wisconsin EnergyCorp	29.38	1.47	5.0
Indiana Energy	21.50	1.10	5.1	Witco Corp	32.00	1.12	3.5
Kelly Services'A'	25.25	0.80	3.1	WPL Holdings	30.50	1.94	6.3

†12-month indicated rate

Chart based on October 20, 1995 prices and data.

Stock Reports

In using the Stock Reports in this handbook, please pay particular attention to the dates attached to each evaluation, recommendation, or analysis section. Opinions rendered are as of that date and may change often. It is strongly suggested that before investing in any security you should obtain the current analysis on that issue.

To order the latest Standard & Poor's Stock Report on a company, for as little as $2.00 per report, please call:

S&P Reports On-Demand at 1-800-292-0808.

STANDARD & POOR'S

ADC Telecommunications

STOCK REPORTS

NASDAQ Symbol **ADCT**
In S&P MidCap 400

26-SEP-95

Industry: Telecommunications

Summary: ADC provides a broad range of transmission and networking systems and products for broadband telecommunications networks using copper and fiberoptic transmission media.

S&P Opinion: Accumulate (★★★★)

Recent Price • 46¼
52 Wk Range • 49⅜-18¾
Yield • Nil
12-Mo. P/E • 53.2

Quantitative Evaluations

Outlook (1 Lowest—5 Highest)
• **1+**

Fair Value
• **38⅞**

Risk
• **High**

Earn./Div. Rank
• **B**

Technical Eval.
• **Bullish** since 5/92

Rel. Strength Rank (1 Lowest—99 Highest)
• **88**

Insider Activity
• **Neutral**

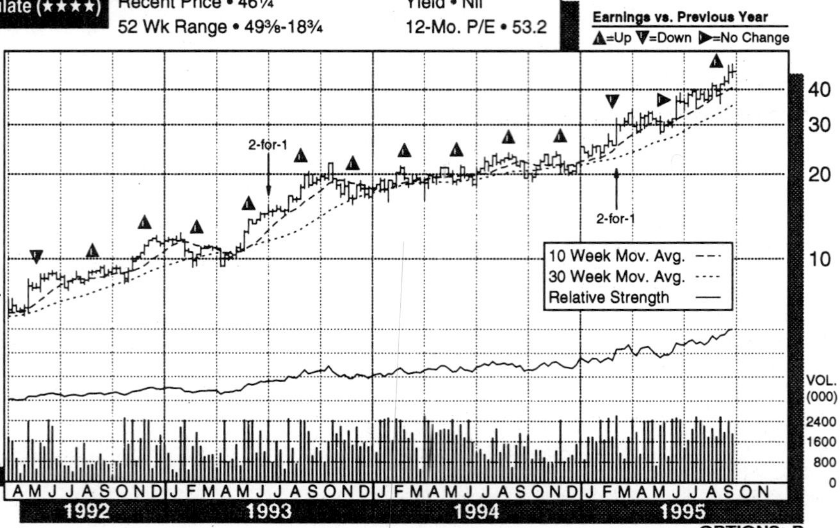

OPTIONS: P

Overview - 26-SEP-95

Revenues should grow strongly again in fiscal 1995, as public telephone companies continue to upgrade their networks. A contract to provide Ameritech with the Homeworx access platform and DV6000 supertrunking transmission system is expected to add $75 million to $100 million in revenues over the next five years. The customer base also includes cable television operators, with aggressive plans to offer telephone service to their customers. Gross margins are expected to narrow as ADC continues to roll out new products. The company is well positioned to benefit from the emergence of fiberoptics and from a shift in networking traffic to more data and video. Future results should also be bolstered by the company's entry into the wireless equipment market.

Valuation - 26-SEP-95

The shares, which have risen sharply thus far in 1995, were recently trading near the high end of their 52-week range. As local telephone companies, long-distance carriers and cable television operators race to construct the information superhighway, ADC should benefit by providing needed equipment to each group. As competition among carriers intensifies, ADC's earnings should accelerate. The shares provide good potential for long-term capital appreciation.

Key Stock Statistics

S&P EPS Est. 1995	0.95	Tang. Bk. Value/Share	5.11
P/E on S&P Est. 1995	48.7	Beta	1.48
S&P EPS Est. 1996	1.14	Shareholders	1,600
Dividend Rate/Share	Nil	Market cap. (B)	$ 2.8
Shs. outstg. (M)	61.6	Inst. holdings	76%
Avg. daily vol. (M)	0.548	Insider holdings	NA

Value of $10,000 invested 5 years ago: $ 100,674

Fiscal Year Ending Oct. 31

	1995	% Change	1994	% Change	1993	% Change
Revenues (Million $)						
1Q	121.8	34%	91.18	16%	78.60	21%
2Q	140.3	24%	113.6	28%	89.00	13%
3Q	150.4	30%	115.7	24%	93.35	11%
4Q	—	—	128.3	22%	105.1	18%
Yr.	—	—	448.7	23%	366.1	16%
Income (Million $)						
1Q	10.47	56%	6.70	27%	5.26	NM
2Q	10.39	3%	10.09	43%	7.06	13%
3Q	15.67	42%	11.00	20%	9.18	21%
4Q	—	—	12.74	26%	10.13	20%
Yr.	—	—	40.52	28%	31.64	50%
Earnings Per Share ($)						
1Q	0.09	-25%	0.12	26%	0.09	NM
2Q	0.18	NM	0.18	38%	0.13	13%
3Q	0.26	30%	0.20	21%	0.17	18%
4Q	E0.42	83%	0.23	24%	0.19	19%
Yr.	E0.95	30%	0.73	27%	0.57	47%

Next earnings report expected: mid December

ADC Telecommunications

Business Summary - 26-SEP-95

ADC Telecommunications, Inc. provides products that are used in public telecommunciations networks by telephone operating companies, interexchange carriers, other telecommunications carriers and broadcast and cable television networks and in private telecommunications networks by large businesses and government agencies. Sales in recent fiscal years were derived as follows:

	1994	1993
Broadband connectivity products	49%	55%
Networking products	28%	26%
Transmission products	23%	19%

Broadband connectivity products provide contact points to connect telecommunications system components and gain access to system circuits by electromechanical means, to test, monitor or reconfigure such circuits. Most products are designed for copper-based transmission systems.

Networking products provide interconnection and transportation of voice, data and video signals in a single building or campus and access to the public network. The Kentrox unit makes digital public network access equipment. Products interconnect digitally the common carrier network and the customer network. Fibermux manufactures internetworking products, including the Crossbow multi-LAN hub family of products, which interconnect workstations, personal computers and terminals. The Fibermux Magnum 100 family of products transports multiple voice, data and video signals simultaneously over a 100-megabit fiber-optic backbone. ADC also offers a patch/switch system to gain access to, monitor, test and reconfigure digital circuits.

Transmission products support the generation of electronic signals and optical signals over a telecommunications circuit. Products include digital repeaters, which regenerate digital signals that have degraded because of transmission over long distances, and test and monitoring systems.

Important Developments

Aug. '95—China's Hunan Post & Telecommunications Administration will purchase ADC's DV6000 digital transmission system from Shanghai ADC Telecommunications Equipment Co., a joint venture.
Jun. '95—In a public stock offering, 6,325,000 ADC common shares were sold at $30 each.
Feb. '95—The company received a contract valued at up to $185 million to supply advanced broadband technology to an Australian consortium developing a combined telephony and home entertainment service.

Capitalization

Long Term Debt: None (7/95).

Per Share Data ($)

(Year Ended Oct. 31)

	1994	1993	1992	1991	1990	1989
Tangible Bk. Val.	4.74	3.98	3.35	2.95	2.52	2.09
Cash Flow	1.12	0.87	0.68	0.68	0.66	0.50
Earnings	0.73	0.57	0.39	0.42	0.43	0.32
Dividends	Nil	Nil	Nil	Nil	Nil	Nil
Payout Ratio	Nil	Nil	Nil	Nil	Nil	Nil
Prices - High	25⅜	22	12⅛	10⅞	6½	4¾
- Low	15⅞	9⅜	5¾	5⅛	3⅞	2⅞
P/E Ratio - High	35	38	31	26	15	15
- Low	22	16	16	12	9	9

Income Statement Analysis (Million $)

	1994	%Chg	1993	%Chg	1992	%Chg	1991
Revs.	449	23%	366	16%	316	7%	294
Oper. Inc.	86.0	24%	69.6	20%	58.0	9%	53.0
Depr.	21.7	33%	16.3	4%	15.6	8%	14.5
Int. Exp.	NA	—	NA	—	0.9	-48%	1.8
Pretax Inc.	64.3	29%	49.7	43%	34.7	-5%	36.4
Eff. Tax Rate	37%	—	36%	—	40%	—	40%
Net Inc.	40.5	28%	31.6	50%	21.0	-5%	22.0

Balance Sheet & Other Fin. Data (Million $)

	1994	1993	1992	1991	1990	1989
Cash	49.5	16.3	20.5	30.1	26.0	17.6
Curr. Assets	199	143	115	120	103	76.0
Total Assets	335	280	241	247	182	144
Curr. Liab.	67.4	54.9	40.1	40.5	37.3	23.9
LT Debt	0.4	0.8	14.1	43.6	4.8	4.7
Common Eqty.	265	220	182	158	134	110
Total Cap.	267	225	201	207	144	120
Cap. Exp.	23.4	21.5	16.6	27.1	15.3	15.9
Cash Flow	62.2	47.9	36.7	36.5	34.9	26.3

Ratio Analysis

	1994	1993	1992	1991	1990	1989
Curr. Ratio	3.0	2.6	2.9	2.9	2.7	3.2
% LT Debt of Cap.	0.2	0.4	7.0	21.1	3.4	3.9
% Net Inc.of Revs.	9.0	8.6	6.6	7.5	8.8	8.4
% Ret. on Assets	13.1	12.1	8.6	10.2	14.0	12.4
% Ret. on Equity	16.7	15.6	12.3	15.0	18.7	16.0

Dividend Data —No cash has been paid. Two-for-one stock splits were effected in June 1993 and February 1995.

Amt. of Div. $	Date Decl.	Ex-Div. Date	Stock of Record	Payment Date
2-for-1	Jan. 25	Mar. 01	Feb. 15	Feb. 28 '95

Data as orig. reptd.; bef. results of disc. opers. and/or spec. items. Per share data adj. for stk. divs. as of ex-div. date. E-Estimated. NA-Not Available. NM-Not Meaningful. NR-Not Ranked.

Office—4900 W. 78th St., Minneapolis, MN 55435. **Tel**—(612) 938-8080. **Chrmn, Pres & CEO**—W. J. Cadogan. **VP & CFO**—R. E. Switz. **Treas & Investor Contact**—Aimee L. Gallogly (612) 946-3338. **Dirs**—W. J. Cadogan, J. C. Castle, T. E. Holloran, B. K. Johnson, C. W. Oswald, A. E. Ross, J. Rosso, D. M. Sullivan, W. F. Wheaton, J. D. Wunsch. **Transfer Agent & Registrar**—Norwest Bank Minnesota, South St. Paul. **Incorporated** in Minnesota in 1953. **Empl**-2,644. **S&P Analyst:** Kevin J. Gooley

STANDARD & POOR'S

STOCK REPORTS

AES Corp.

NASDAQ Symbol **AESC**
In S&P MidCap 400

26-SEP-95

Industry: Services

Summary: This major developer and operator of electric generating facilities supplies electricity to public utilities and steam to industrial companies in over 25 countries.

Quantitative Evaluations

Outlook (1 Lowest—5 Highest) • **5**

Fair Value • **23⅜**

Risk • **Average**

Earn./Div. Rank • **NR**

Technical Eval. • **Bearish** since 10/94

Rel. Strength Rank (1 Lowest—99 Highest) • **33**

Insider Activity • **Unfavorable**

Recent Price • 19
52 Wk Range • 21¾-16
Yield • Nil
12-Mo. P/E • 14.0

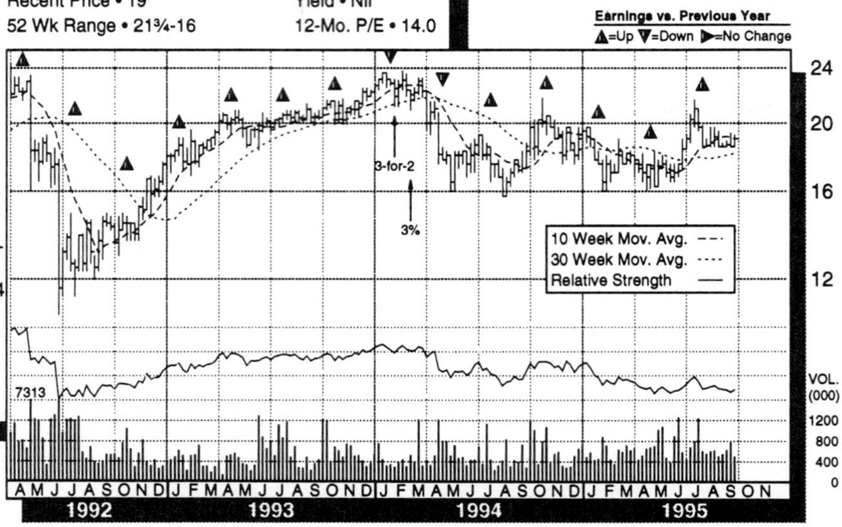

Business Profile - 25-SEP-95

AES owns and operates independent power generation facilities, supplying electricity to public utilities and steam to industrial companies. AES currently has over 3,000 megawatts of capacity in operation or under construction in the United States, Argentina, and the United Kingdom, and has projects under development in Pakistan, India, Puerto Rico, and in the U.S., in Maryland and San Francisco. The chairman and the CEO, founders of the company in 1981, own over 28% of the common stock.

Operational Review - 25-SEP-95

Revenues for the six months ended June 30, 1995, climbed 29%, as the company expanded its ownership of AES Deepwater, Texas, and Central Termica San Nicolas S.A., Argentina, leading to consolidation of these operations. Margins narrowed following a 54% jump in the cost of sales. Higher interest income on larger cash balances and improved earnings from affiliates led to a 10% increase in net income, excluding an extraordinary gain in 1994.

Stock Performance - 22-SEP-95

In the past 30 trading days, AESC's shares have increased 1%, compared to a 5% rise in the S&P 500. Average trading volume for the past five days was 97,400 shares, compared with the 40-day moving average of 118,464 shares.

Key Stock Statistics

Dividend Rate/Share	Nil	Shareholders	800
Shs. outstg. (M)	75.0	Market cap. (B)	$ 1.4
Avg. daily vol. (M)	0.124	Inst. holdings	38%
Tang. Bk. Value/Share	5.36	Insider holdings	NA
Beta	NA		

Value of $10,000 invested 5 years ago: NA

Fiscal Year Ending Dec. 31

	1995	% Change	1994	% Change	1993	% Change
Revenues (Million $)						
1Q	137.5	10%	125.2	-3%	129.5	46%
2Q	167.3	23%	136.0	6%	128.8	48%
3Q	—	—	136.4	6%	129.2	20%
4Q	—	—	135.1	3%	131.1	12%
Yr.	—	—	532.7	3%	518.7	29%
Income (Million $)						
1Q	24.80	18%	20.94	NM	21.07	76%
2Q	26.50	3%	25.64	18%	21.81	83%
3Q	—	—	25.56	11%	23.12	38%
4Q	—	—	26.20	NM	5.40	-64%
Yr.	—	—	98.30	38%	71.27	28%
Earnings Per Share ($)						
1Q	0.33	18%	0.28	-7%	0.30	72%
2Q	0.35	3%	0.34	10%	0.31	77%
3Q	—	—	0.34	10%	0.31	29%
4Q	—	—	0.35	NM	0.07	-67%
Yr.	—	—	1.30	33%	0.98	22%

Next earnings report expected: late October

AES Corp.

Business Summary - 25-SEP-95

AES Corp. (formerly Applied Energy Services, Inc.) develops, owns and operates independent (non-utility) electric power generation facilities. All of its domestic plants are cogeneration facilities -- a power generation technology that provides for the sequential generation of two or more forms of energy (electricity and steam) from a single primary fuel source, such as coal or natural gas.

Through its subsidiaries, AESC currently operates and manages plants totaling 3,126 megawatts (mw) and has ownership interests of 1,645 mw of capacity in operation or under construction in the U.S., the U.K. and Argentina. In the U.S., the company owns and operates facilities in Pennsylvania (125 mw), California (110 mw), Connecticut (181 mw), Oklahoma (320 mw), Hawaii (180 mw), and Texas (140 mw).

In March 1994, AESC spun off AES China Generating Co., Ltd. in an initial public offering. AESC maintained a 42% equity interest. In May 1993, AES San Nicolas S.A., an Argentine subsidiary of AESC, acquired part ownership and management interest in a company that owns a 650 mw power plant in the region. AESC increased its ownership interest from 34%, to 70%, in the second quarter of 1995.

A wholly owned U.K. subsidiary, AES Medway Electric Limited, completed financial closing for a 660 mw combined cycle gas-fired power plant in England in April 1992. This joint venture is 25% owned by AES Medway Electric, Ltd., and operated by AES Medway Operations Ltd. Construction should be completed and commercial operations should begin in the first quarter of 1996. AESC is actively pursuing additional projects that are in various stages of development in the U.S., Europe, Mexico, Pakistan, India, Southeast Asia, South America and Africa.

The company's project subsidiaries sell electricity to utilities under long-term power sales contracts, and purchase fuel under long-term supply agreements. AESC attempts to hedge the effects of changes in energy prices by structuring payments in its sales contracts to adjust with the same price indices as do its contracts with companies supplying fuel for the same projects.

Important Developments

Aug. '95—AES was the winning bidder for a 112 mw hydroelectric system in Argentina, which has been in operation since 1978. The company also announced that financing was attained for development of a 337 mw power plant in Pakistan, which is expected to be operational by late 1997.

Capitalization

Long Term Debt: $1,010,800,000 (6/95), incl. $50,000,000 of 6.5% sub. debs. due 2002, conv. into com. at $40.50 a sh.
Minority Interest: $64,500,000.

Per Share Data ($) (Year Ended Dec. 31)

	1994	1993	1992	1991	1990	1989
Tangible Bk. Val.	5.37	4.15	2.59	2.12	0.59	0.30
Cash Flow	1.87	1.55	1.29	1.11	0.50	0.21
Earnings	1.30	0.98	0.80	0.66	0.26	0.07
Dividends	Nil	0.58	0.39	0.13	Nil	0.01
Payout Ratio	Nil	59%	48%	20%	Nil	9%
Prices - High	23¾	22⅝	24⅜	22⅛	NA	NA
- Low	15¾	16⅞	10⅝	12¼	NA	NA
P/E Ratio - High	18	23	30	34	NA	NA
- Low	12	17	13	19	NA	NA

Income Statement Analysis (Million $)

	1994	%Chg	1993	%Chg	1992	%Chg	1991
Revs.	533	3%	519	29%	401	20%	334
Oper. Inc.	276	7%	257	38%	186	16%	161
Depr.	43.4	4%	41.7	24%	33.7	15%	29.2
Int. Exp.	124	-2%	126	7%	118	9%	108
Pretax Inc.	145	62%	89.4	36%	65.9	28%	51.3
Eff. Tax Rate	30%	—	20%	—	14%	—	15%
Net Inc.	98.3	38%	71.3	28%	55.8	31%	42.6

Balance Sheet & Other Fin. Data (Million $)

	1994	1993	1992	1991	1990	1989
Cash	349	156	76.4	70.2	20.1	20.1
Curr. Assets	436	231	144	112	56.0	56.0
Total Assets	1,915	1,687	1,552	1,440	1,128	1,128
Curr. Liab.	108	132	127	115	69.0	69.0
LT Debt	1,144	1,200	1,196	1,160	1,008	1,008
Common Eqty.	401	309	177	141	34.4	34.4
Total Cap.	1,802	1,551	1,405	1,324	1,058	1,046
Cap. Exp.	10.0	14.0	123	236	210	291
Cash Flow	142	113	89.5	71.8	30.7	12.4

Ratio Analysis

	1994	1993	1992	1991	1990	1989
Curr. Ratio	4.1	1.8	1.1	1.0	0.8	0.8
% LT Debt of Cap.	63.5	77.3	85.1	87.6	95.2	96.3
% Net Inc.of Revs.	18.5	13.7	13.9	12.8	8.2	4.2
% Ret. on Assets	5.4	4.2	3.7	3.1	3.3	1.6
% Ret. on Equity	27.6	28.4	34.6	47.4	48.6	60.0

Dividend Data —An annual 3% stock dividend, initiated in March 1994, was discontinued in February 1995.

Data as orig. reptd.; bef. results of disc. opers. and/or spec. items. Per share data adj. for stk. divs. as of ex-div. date. E-Estimated. NA-Not Available. NM-Not Meaningful. NR-Not Ranked.

Office—1001 North 19th St., Arlington, VA 22209. **Tel**—(703) 522-1315. **Chrmn**—R. W. Sant. **Pres & CEO**—D. W. Bakke. **VP-CFO & Secy**—B. J. Sharp. **Dirs**—V. Assevero, D. W. Bakke, A. F. Emerson, F. Jungers, H. R. Linden, R. W. Sant, R. E. Train, T. I. Unterberg, R. H. Waterman, Jr. **Transfer Agent & Registrar**—Chemical Bank, NYC. **Incorporated** in Delaware in 1981. **Empl**-680. **S&P Analyst:** J. Santoriello

STANDARD & POOR'S

STOCK REPORTS

AST Research

NASDAQ Symbol **ASTA**
In S&P MidCap 400

16-SEP-95 **Industry:** Data Processing

Summary: AST is a leading manufacturer of desktop, file server and notebook computers. In July 1995, Korea-based Samsung Electronics purchased a 40.25% stake.

S&P Opinion: Avoid (★★)

Recent Price • 11⅜ | 52 Wk Range • 19⅛-10⅝ | Yield • Nil | 12-Mo. P/E • NM

Quantitative Evaluations

Outlook
(1 Lowest—5 Highest)
• **3+**

Fair Value
• **13**

Risk
• **High**

Earn./Div. Rank
• **C**

Technical Eval.
• **Bearish** since 2/95

Rel. Strength Rank
(1 Lowest—99 Highest)
• **1**

Insider Activity
• **Unfavorable**

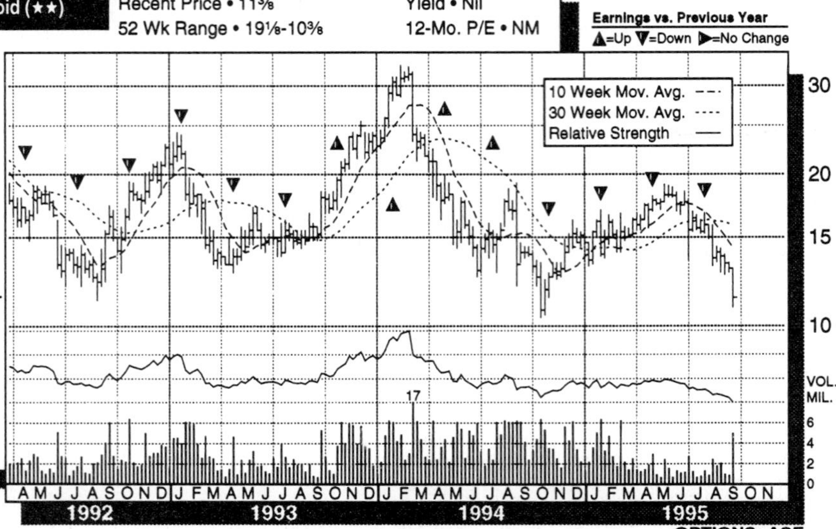

OPTIONS: ASE

Overview - 15-SEP-95

We do not expect AST to earn a profit until fiscal 1997, although it is considering operational changes that could push the timetable up to the first half of calendar 1996. AST continues to be outmanuevered in the U.S. marketplace by top tier PC vendors such as Compaq, Hewlett Packard and Packard Bell, which have superior execution, manufacturing and distribution capabilities. AST is well positioned internationally, but growth overseas is not expected to offset the U.S. weakness. Overall, we see flat to slightly lower sales for the year. Gross margins are likely to remain in the single digit range until the company improves its manufacturing execution and product mix. Expense cuts may partially offset this weakness, but losses will persist until AST rejuvenates its reputation and sales growth.

Valuation - 15-SEP-95

We have lowered our opinion on the shares to avoid from neutral after the company disclosed that results in fiscal 1996's first quarter will be much worse than expected. The magnitude of the expected losses and the resultant management changes suggest that this is not a one quarter problem. Furthermore, we are troubled that the company is having profitability problems of this magnitude in a very strong market. As a result, we believe the company will need several quarters to remedy these substantial problems. Therefore, we recommend that investors avoid the shares until there are clearer signs that the company can execute profitably in this highly competitive industry.

Key Stock Statistics

S&P EPS Est. 1996	-2.45	Tang. Bk. Value/Share	9.96
P/E on S&P Est. 1996	NM	Beta	2.21
S&P EPS Est. 1997	0.65	Shareholders	1,200
Dividend Rate/Share	Nil	Market cap. (B)	$0.506
Shs. outstg. (M)	44.4	Inst. holdings	45%
Avg. daily vol. (M)	0.445	Insider holdings	NA

Value of $10,000 invested 5 years ago: $ 21,925

Fiscal Year Ending Jun. 30

	1995	% Change	1994	% Change	1993	% Change
Revenues (Million $)						
1Q	495.5	-4%	514.4	80%	286.0	45%
2Q	640.2	-5%	677.0	96%	346.0	45%
3Q	670.2	13%	591.3	60%	370.3	53%
4Q	662.0	13%	584.5	43%	409.2	54%
Yr.	2,468	4%	2,367	68%	1,412	50%
Income (Million $)						
1Q	-39.89	NM	8.23	—	—	—
2Q	-22.32	NM	17.93	23%	14.58	-13%
3Q	-7.23	NM	13.21	20%	11.05	-34%
4Q	-31.63	NM	14.12	NM	-87.01	NM
Yr.	-99.3	NM	53.50	NM	-53.74	NM
Earnings Per Share ($)						
1Q	-1.23	NM	0.26	8%	0.24	-54%
2Q	-0.69	NM	0.55	20%	0.46	-12%
3Q	-0.22	NM	0.40	14%	0.35	-34%
4Q	-0.98	NM	0.43	NM	-2.76	NM
Yr.	-3.07	NM	1.64	NM	-1.72	NM

Next earnings report expected: late October

AST Research

Business Summary - 15-SEP-95

AST Research designs, manufactures and markets a broad line of IBM-compatible personal computers, including desktop, notebook and network server systems. International business contributed 45% of total revenues in fiscal 1995, up from 36% in fiscal 1994.

AST has developed multiple brands targeting a variety of price points and user requirements. These include the Advantage! product line, designed for the consumer retail market, the value-oriented Bravo product line, the high-end Premmia desktop product line, and the high performance Ascentia notebook line, the successor to the PowerExec line of notebook computers. AST also sells a complete line of servers under the Premmia and Manhattan labels, including symmetric multiprocessing (SMP) systems targeted for LAN and multiuser UNIX environments.

In June 1993, AST purchased Tandy Corp.'s PC manufacturing operations and the GRiD North American and GRiD/Victor European sales divisions for $15 million cash and a $90 million three-year promissory note. During fiscal 1994's fourth quarter, AST discontinued all manufacturing, marketing and sales efforts related to the Tandy/GRiD acquisition. The GRiD product line includes handheld and pen-based systems as well as a full line of GRiD and Victor desktop and notebook products.

The company's manufacturing and warehousing facilities include over 1.5 million of sq. ft. and are located in Fort Worth, Tex., Hong Kong, People's Republic of China, Taiwan and Lizmerick, Ireland. The company's Fountain Valley, Calif., manufacturing facility was closed in February 1995.

Important Developments

Sep. '95—AST said it will post a loss in fiscal 1996's first quarter significantly higher than the $40 million loss recorded in the year earlier period. The company cited continued weakness in the U.S. market and seasonal softness in Europe. AST also indicated that it is considering operational changes that may warrant additional charges and result in a higher loss for the quarter.

Jul. '95—Korea-based Samsung Electronics Co. completed its investment in AST On July 31. Under terms of the agreement, Samsung purchased a 40.25% stake in AST that included a tender offer for 5.82 million shares (18%) of AST common at $22 a share, 6.44 million newly issued AST shares at $19.50 a share and 5.53 million newly issued ASTA shares at $22 a share. Samsung will also provide a letter of credit to support AST's existing $96.7 million note to Tandy Corp. and satisfy $75 million of the note obligation in July 1996. The companies also entered into other strategic relationships, including component supply and joint procurement agreements.

Capitalization

Long Term Debt: $219,224,000 (7/1/95).

Per Share Data ($)

(Year Ended Jun. 30)

	1995	1994	1993	1992	1991	1990
Tangible Bk. Val.	NA	9.96	9.46	11.80	9.33	6.30
Cash Flow	NA	2.47	-1.29	2.53	2.50	1.89
Earnings	-3.07	1.64	-1.72	2.16	2.13	1.43
Dividends	Nil	Nil	Nil	Nil	Nil	Nil
Payout Ratio	Nil	Nil	Nil	Nil	Nil	Nil
Prices - High	19⅛	33	24¼	24½	32¾	18⅞
- Low	13⅛	10⅜	12¾	11¼	14½	5¼
P/E Ratio - High	NM	20	NM	11	15	13
- Low	NM	6	NM	5	7	4

Income Statement Analysis (Million $)

	1994	%Chg	1993	%Chg	1992	%Chg	1991
Revs.	2,367	68%	1,412	50%	944	37%	688
Oper. Inc.	101	36%	74.0	-32%	109	4%	105
Depr.	26.8	103%	13.2	12%	11.8	4%	11.3
Int. Exp.	9.9	NM	1.3	-48%	2.4	-34%	3.7
Pretax Inc.	79.0	NM	-65.0	NM	100	2%	98.0
Eff. Tax Rate	32%	—	NM	—	32%	—	34%
Net Inc.	53.5	NM	-53.7	NM	68.5	6%	64.7

Balance Sheet & Other Fin. Data (Million $)

	1994	1993	1992	1991	1990	1989
Cash	153	122	141	153	92.0	18.0
Curr. Assets	866	761	515	424	262	200
Total Assets	1,038	886	581	485	324	261
Curr. Liab.	431	460	182	141	77.0	58.0
LT Debt	215	92.3	2.4	30.1	30.1	81.0
Common Eqty.	384	319	363	282	193	109
Total Cap.	599	411	366	312	223	190
Cap. Exp.	30.0	20.9	15.9	8.9	11.1	11.8
Cash Flow	80.3	-40.5	80.3	76.0	46.4	3.9

Ratio Analysis

	1994	1993	1992	1991	1990	1989
Curr. Ratio	2.0	1.7	2.8	3.0	3.4	3.4
% LT Debt of Cap.	35.9	22.4	0.7	9.6	13.5	42.7
% Net Inc.of Revs.	2.3	NM	7.3	9.4	6.6	NM
% Ret. on Assets	5.6	NM	12.7	16.0	10.5	NM
% Ret. on Equity	15.2	NM	21.1	27.3	20.9	NM

Dividend Data —No cash has been paid. A two-for-one stock split was effected in 1991.

Data as orig. reptd.; bef. results of disc. opers. and/or spec. items. Per share data adj. for stk. divs. as of ex-div. date. E-Estimated. NA-Not Available. NM-Not Meaningful. NR-Not Ranked.

Office—16215 Alton Parkway, Irvine, CA 92718. **Tel**—(714) 727-4141. **Chrmn & CEO**—S. U. Qureshey. **EVP-Fin & CFO**—B. C. Edwards. **Secy**—D. R. Leibel. **Investor Contact**—Misty Omhart (714-727-7728). **Dirs**—B. C. Edwards, R. J. Goeglein, J. W. Peltason, S. U. Qureshey, C. J. Santoro, D. W. Yocam. **Transfer Agent & Registrar**—American Stock Transfer & Trust Co., NYC. **Incorporated** in California in 1980; reincorporated in Delaware in 1987. **Empl**- 6,977. **S&P Analyst:** John D. Coyle, CFA

STANDARD & POOR'S

STOCK REPORTS

Acuson Corp.

NYSE Symbol **ACN**
In S&P MidCap 400

31-AUG-95 **Industry:** Medical equipment/ supply

Summary: Acuson manufactures, markets and services medical diagnostic ultrasound systems and image management products.

S&P Opinion: Avoid (★★) | Recent Price • 13 | 52 Wk Range • 18⅜-10⅛ | Yield • Nil | 12-Mo. P/E • 36.1

Quantitative Evaluations
Outlook
(1 Lowest—5 Highest)
• **1−**
Fair Value
• **9½**
Risk
• **Average**
Earn./Div. Rank
• **B**

Technical Eval.
• **Bearish** since 7/95
Rel. Strength Rank
(1 Lowest—99 Highest)
• **70**
Insider Activity
• **Neutral**

Earnings vs. Previous Year
▲=Up ▼=Down ▶=No Change

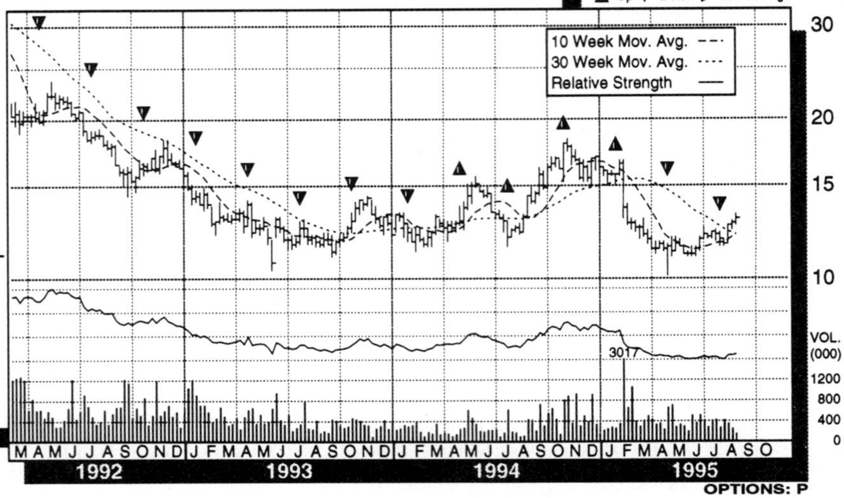

OPTIONS: P

Overview - 28-AUG-95

Revenues may decline further during the remainder of 1995, as demand for ultrasound systems in the U.S. continues to deteriorate amid increased consolidation among healthcare providers and lower capital spending by hospitals. International sales, however, which are expected to rise 20% annually, should partly offset weak domestic demand. Margins will remain under pressure due to the highly competitive market conditions. Despite an expected decline in profits, per-share earnings comparisons will be aided by stock repurchases.

Valuation - 28-AUG-95

Acuson's shares plunged in early 1995, reaching levels not seen since mid-1993, reflecting poor results and prevailing difficult conditions in the medical equipment market. The shares have since partially recovered some of the loss, aided by an active share repurchase program. Regardless, the shares are still trading at a relatively high valuation based on expected earnings. Although further sharp EPS declines may be averted as the company continues its share repurchase program, near term appreciation is not likely, given the lack of an encouraging outlook for demand for Acuson's products.

Key Stock Statistics

S&P EPS Est. 1995	0.30	Tang. Bk. Value/Share	7.16
P/E on S&P Est. 1995	43.3	Beta	0.98
S&P EPS Est. 1996	0.55	Shareholders	1,800
Dividend Rate/Share	Nil	Market cap. (B)	$0.363
Shs. outstg. (M)	27.9	Inst. holdings	47%
Avg. daily vol. (M)	0.049	Insider holdings	NA

Value of $10,000 invested 5 years ago: $ 6,093

Fiscal Year Ending Dec. 31

	1995	% Change	1994	% Change	1993	% Change
Revenues (Million $)						
1Q	87.97	-5%	92.83	13%	82.30	-5%
2Q	81.94	-7%	88.01	22%	72.10	-18%
3Q	—	—	86.39	29%	67.07	-21%
4Q	—	—	83.26	13%	73.83	-12%
Yr.	—	—	350.5	19%	295.3	-14%
Income (Million $)						
1Q	2.24	-66%	6.58	31%	5.02	-61%
2Q	1.01	-75%	4.09	NM	-6.72	NM
3Q	—	—	3.73	64%	2.28	-68%
4Q	—	—	3.86	23%	3.14	-47%
Yr.	—	—	18.27	NM	3.71	-90%
Earnings Per Share ($)						
1Q	0.08	-65%	0.23	35%	0.17	-51%
2Q	0.04	-71%	0.14	NM	-0.23	NM
3Q	E0.08	-38%	0.13	63%	0.08	-64%
4Q	E0.10	-23%	0.13	18%	0.11	-45%
Yr.	E0.30	-52%	0.62	NM	0.13	-88%

Next earnings report expected: late October

Acuson Corp.

Business Summary - 31-AUG-95

Acuson Corp. is a leader in the design, manufacture, and marketing of premium quality medical diagnostic ultrasound imaging systems. Such systems use low power, high-frequency sound waves to noninvasively generate real-time moving images of soft tissues, internal body organs and blood flows. Ultrasound is often the imaging technique of choice for many soft tissues and has common cardiac, abdominal (liver, kidney, spleen and gallbladder), gynecological, obstetrical, urological (prostate), and peripheral vascular applications.

The company's systems use a hybrid analog/digital computer architecture designed to electronically form high resolution, real-time ultrasound images under software control. This basic architecture was utilized in the Acuson 128 system (introduced for radiology applications in 1983) and also forms the basis for its second generation 128XP system (launched in 1990 with expanded radiology capabilities). The 128XP systems can operate in all high resolution imaging formats, which include sector, Vector Array, linear array and High Performace Curved Array. ACN's systems can provide all of the major operating modalities, including B-mode, spectral Doppler and color Doppler.

In 1993, ACN introduced Acoustic Response Technology (ART) as an upgrade to the 128XP platform. ART incorporates new imaging processing techniques that increase the amount of imaging and Doppler information that the system provides. It also unveiled the 128XP/4, a lower cost configuration of the 128XP product. In addition, it began shipments of the AEGIS Sonography Management System, which digitizes, stores, and organizes images. The company believes that AEGIS netwoks represent the largest installed base of ultrasound image management systems.

In November 1994, Acuson acquired Sound Technology, Inc., a producer of ultrasound transducers and a supplier to the company for several years.

The company sells its products primarily to hospitals, private and government institutions, and healthcare agencies, medical equipment distributors, and doctors' offices. It employs a full-time sales, service and applications staff in North America, selected European countries, Australia, and Japan, and sells through independent distributors in a number of countries. Foreign sales represented 20% of total sales in 1994.

Important Developments

Jul. '95—The company said that as of July 1, 1995, it had repurchased 1,693,500 shares of common stock under a 1993 authorization to buy back up to four million shares over an unspecified period of time.

Capitalization

Long Term Debt: None (7/1/95).

Per Share Data ($)

(Year Ended Dec. 31)

	1994	1993	1992	1991	1990	1989
Tangible Bk. Val.	7.19	6.48	6.75	7.69	5.75	4.23
Cash Flow	1.29	0.85	1.67	1.98	1.67	1.35
Earnings	0.62	0.13	1.08	1.59	1.33	1.07
Dividends	Nil	Nil	Nil	Nil	Nil	Nil
Payout Ratio	Nil	Nil	Nil	Nil	Nil	Nil
Prices - High	18⅜	16	33⅜	40	32¾	25¾
- Low	11¼	10⅜	14⅜	22¾	18⅞	14¾
P/E Ratio - High	30	NM	31	25	25	24
- Low	18	NM	13	14	14	14

Income Statement Analysis (Million $)

	1994	%Chg	1993	%Chg	1992	%Chg	1991
Revs.	350	19%	295	-14%	343	2%	336
Oper. Inc.	41.7	31%	31.8	-55%	71.3	-28%	99
Depr.	19.7	-6%	21.0	3%	20.4	42%	14.4
Int. Exp.	NA	—	0.1	-50%	0.1	20%	0.1
Pretax Inc.	25.6	NM	3.4	-94%	58.3	-37%	93.2
Eff. Tax Rate	29%	—	NM	—	37%	—	37%
Net Inc.	18.3	NM	3.7	-90%	36.8	-37%	58.5

Balance Sheet & Other Fin. Data (Million $)

	1994	1993	1992	1991	1990	1989
Cash	67.0	59.0	65.0	154	98.0	67.0
Curr. Assets	235	201	209	287	212	154
Total Assets	305	271	279	336	249	184
Curr. Liab.	96.9	87.8	77.4	59.9	49.3	39.1
LT Debt	Nil	Nil	Nil	Nil	Nil	Nil
Common Eqty.	208	183	201	272	200	145
Total Cap.	208	183	201	276	200	145
Cap. Exp.	23.7	15.0	35.2	18.9	19.1	13.8
Cash Flow	37.9	24.7	57.3	72.9	60.2	48.2

Ratio Analysis

	1994	1993	1992	1991	1990	1989
Curr. Ratio	2.4	2.3	2.7	4.8	4.3	3.9
% LT Debt of Cap.	Nil	Nil	Nil	Nil	Nil	Nil
% Net Inc.of Revs.	5.2	1.3	10.7	17.4	16.9	16.7
% Ret. on Assets	6.3	1.4	13.1	19.8	22.0	23.8
% Ret. on Equity	9.2	2.0	17.1	24.6	27.6	30.7

Dividend Data —The company has never paid a cash dividend.

Data as orig. reptd.; bef. results of disc. opers. and/or spec. items. Per share data adj. for stk. divs. as of ex-div. date. E-Estimated. NA-Not Available. NM-Not Meaningful. NR-Not Ranked.

Office—1220 Charleston Rd. (PO Box 7393), Mountain View, CA 94039-7393. **Tel**—(415) 969-9112. **Chrmn & CEO**—S. H. Maslak. **Pres & COO**—R. J. Gallagher. **VP, CFO & Treas**—S. T. Johnson. **Secy**—C. H. Dearborn. **Dirs**—R. Diener, R. J. Gallagher, A. L. Greene, K.H Johannsmeier, S. H. Maslak, A. C. Mendelson. **Transfer Agent & Registrar**—First National Bank of Boston. **Incorporated** in California in 1981; reincorporated in Delaware in 1986. **Empl**-1,652. **S&P Analyst:** Philip J. Birbara

STANDARD & POOR'S

STOCK REPORTS

Adobe Systems

NASDAQ Symbol **ADBE**

In S&P MidCap 400

17-OCT-95 **Industry:** Data Processing

Summary: Adobe's software is used to create and print integrated text and graphics for electronic printing and publishing.

S&P Opinion: Hold (★★★)

Recent Price • 49¼
52 Wk Range • 66½-27¼

Yield • 0.4%
12-Mo. P/E • 70.4

Quantitative Evaluations

Outlook
(1 Lowest—5 Highest)
• **4-**

Fair Value
• **56⅛**

Risk
• **High**

Earn./Div. Rank
• **B**

Technical Eval.
• **Bullish** since 9/95

Rel. Strength Rank
(1 Lowest—99 Highest)
• **13**

Insider Activity
• **Neutral**

Earnings vs. Previous Year
▲=Up ▼=Down ▶=No Change

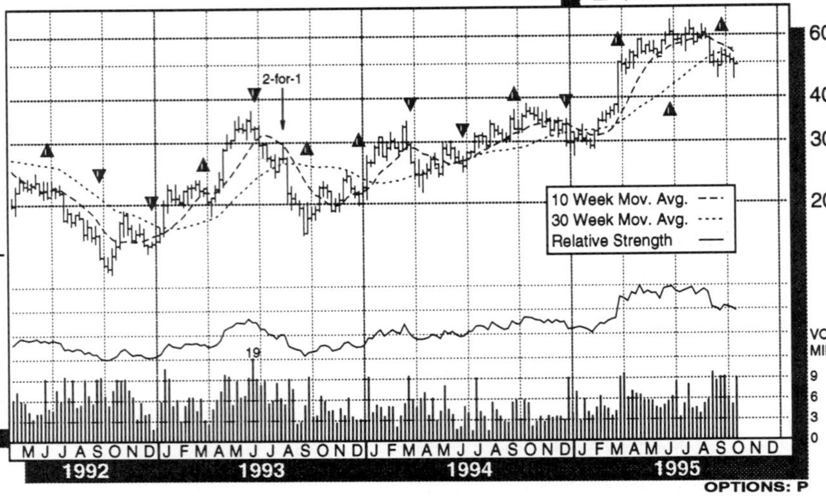

OPTIONS: P

Overview - 17-OCT-95

Revenues should rise strongly through fiscal 1996, reflecting continued demand for Photoshop, Illustrator, Premiere and other graphics and video products, gains by PageMaker, the leading desktop publishing product, continued market acceptance of Acrobat (a document interchange product), contributions from the acquisition of Frame Technology, and the introduction of new printers incorporating Adobe's PostScript page description language. Margins are expected to be maintained as the higher volume and merger-related synergies offset ongoing pricing pressure in the page description market.

Valuation - 17-OCT-95

The shares shot sharply higher in March of this year and have held much of their gains since then on signs the company has successfully integrated Aldus into its operations and is beginning to realize synergies from the merger. Earnings in recent periods have been aided by the successful leveraging of Aldus' international distribution channel. The acquisition of Frame Technology should solidify and expand Adobe's position as a leader in document creation and publishing. The shares trade at a premium to the market, reflecting expectations of strong earnings gains. While the company remains well positioned, we believe the shares are fairly valued, especially in light of uncertainties related to the acquisition of Frame Technology. The stock is expected to move in line with the market over the next 12 months.

Key Stock Statistics

S&P EPS Est. 1995	2.05	Tang. Bk. Value/Share	8.99
P/E on S&P Est. 1995	24.0	Beta	2.33
S&P EPS Est. 1996	2.50	Shareholders	2,200
Dividend Rate/Share	0.20	Market cap. (B)	$ 3.0
Shs. outstg. (M)	63.3	Inst. holdings	87%
Avg. daily vol. (M)	1.500	Insider holdings	NA

Value of $10,000 invested 5 years ago: $ 50,718

Fiscal Year Ending Nov. 30

	1995	% Change	1994	% Change	1993	% Change
Revenues (Million $)						
1Q	168.6	24%	135.9	98%	68.50	9%
2Q	168.0	12%	149.8	88%	79.63	14%
3Q	156.6	7%	146.6	86%	78.76	25%
4Q	—	—	165.4	91%	86.53	22%
Yr.	—	—	597.8	91%	313.5	18%
Income (Million $)						
1Q	34.35	80%	19.09	23%	15.46	16%
2Q	33.90	96%	17.31	20%	14.45	-5%
3Q	29.45	63%	18.06	59%	11.35	70%
4Q	—	—	-48.15	NM	15.76	87%
Yr.	—	—	6.31	-89%	57.03	31%
Earnings Per Share ($)						
1Q	0.54	74%	0.31	-7%	0.33	18%
2Q	0.51	82%	0.28	-10%	0.31	-5%
3Q	0.44	52%	0.29	21%	0.24	66%
4Q	E0.56	NM	-0.79	NM	0.34	84%
Yr.	E2.05	NM	0.10	-92%	1.22	31%

Next earnings report expected: early January

Adobe Systems

Business Summary - 17-OCT-95

Adobe Systems develops and supports computer software used to create, display, print and communicate all forms of electronic documents. Products are delivered through two divisions: the System Products Division (SPD), which develops technology for information distribution; and the Application Products Division (APD), which develops packaged applications for information authoring.

The SPD supports system level software tools and technologies which are embeded within the branded products of OEMs. The division is organized into five product groups: prepress (PressWise; PrePrint and TrapWise), information (including Acrobat, a document interchange product), display (the Display Postscript Level 2 system), imaging systems (the configurable Postscript interpreter) and printer (Postscript).

The primary offering within the SPD is the PostScript interpreter, which executes page descriptions generated from applications that support the PostScript language to produce documents containing multiple typefaces and graphics, including charts, diagrams, drawings and photographic images. Royalties from licensing system products, primarily the PostScript interpreter, accounted for 26% of fiscal 1994 revenues, down from 28% in fiscal 1993, both adjusted for the acquisition of Aldus.

The APD is divided into three product units: graphics and video, print publishing, and consumer products. Graphics and video products include Photoshop, an image enhancement tool; Illustrator, a leading illustration and page design tool; and Persuasion, a desktop presentations program. Print publishing products include PageMaker, a leading desktop publishing product. Consumer products include software designed for personal use. Application product sales accounted for 74% of fiscal 1994 revenues, up from 72% in fiscal 1993 (as adjusted).

Important Developments

Oct. '95—Revenues for the quarter ended September 1, 1995, rose 18% from those of the prior year's interim when 1994 revenues were adjusted for the absence of Freehand and Photostyler, which Adobe no longer offers.

Jun. '95—The company signed a definitive agreement to acquire Frame Technology, a leading provider of document creation, management and distribution software, for stock valued at about $500 million. The transaction is expected to close in late October.

Jan. '95—In the fiscal 1994 fourth quarter, a $72,183,000 charge was recorded, related to the acquisition of Aldus Corp., the maker of the PageMaker desktop publishing program. In addition, Adobe recorded a $12,424,000 charge associated with the purchase of LaserTools Corp.

Capitalization

Long Term Debt: None (9/1/95).

Per Share Data ($)

(Year Ended Nov. 30)

	1994	1993	1992	1991	1990	1989
Tangible Bk. Val.	7.47	6.18	5.06	4.13	2.57	1.46
Cash Flow	0.97	1.51	1.13	1.27	1.02	0.86
Earnings	0.10	1.22	0.93	1.13	0.91	0.77
Dividends	0.20	0.19	0.16	0.15	0.11	0.09
Payout Ratio	NM	15%	17%	13%	13%	11%
Prices - High	38½	37	34¼	33⅞	25⅝	15
- Low	20½	15⅝	12⅝	13⅜	8½	7
P/E Ratio - High	NM	30	37	30	28	19
- Low	NM	13	14	12	9	9

Income Statement Analysis (Million $)

	1994	%Chg	1993	%Chg	1992	%Chg	1991
Revs.	598	91%	313	18%	266	16%	230
Oper. Inc.	182	93%	94.5	13%	83.5	-1%	84.6
Depr.	53.2	NM	13.6	55%	8.8	32%	6.7
Int. Exp.	Nil	—	Nil	—	Nil	—	NA
Pretax Inc.	40.0	-56%	91.1	31%	69.5	-17%	83.6
Eff. Tax Rate	84%	—	37%	—	37%	—	38%
Net Inc.	6.3	-89%	57.0	31%	43.6	-16%	51.6

Balance Sheet & Other Fin. Data (Million $)

	1994	1993	1992	1991	1990	1989
Cash	400	236	160	116	70.0	50.0
Curr. Assets	532	304	224	162	109	77.0
Total Assets	626	353	281	221	146	94.0
Curr. Liab.	169	73.7	56.8	36.9	37.0	34.1
LT Debt	Nil	Nil	Nil	Nil	0.3	0.5
Common Eqty.	457	279	225	183	108	59.0
Total Cap.	457	279	225	184	109	60.0
Cap. Exp.	28.5	14.4	11.9	12.2	7.4	5.2
Cash Flow	59.5	70.6	52.4	58.3	44.9	37.4

Ratio Analysis

	1994	1993	1992	1991	1990	1989
Curr. Ratio	3.2	4.1	4.0	4.4	2.9	2.3
% LT Debt of Cap.	Nil	Nil	Nil	Nil	0.2	0.8
% Net Inc.of Revs.	1.1	18.2	16.4	22.5	23.7	27.8
% Ret. on Assets	1.1	17.9	17.3	27.5	32.9	42.7
% Ret. on Equity	1.5	22.5	21.4	34.8	47.4	66.2

Dividend Data —A shareholder rights plan was adopted in 1990.

Amt. of Div. $	Date Decl.	Ex-Div. Date	Stock of Record	Payment Date
0.050	Sep. 19	Sep. 29	Oct. 05	Oct. 19 '94
0.050	Dec. 21	Jan. 12	Jan. 19	Feb. 03 '95
0.050	Mar. 20	Mar. 31	Apr. 06	Apr. 20 '95
0.050	Jun. 21	Jul. 05	Jul. 07	Jul. 21 '95
0.050	Sep. 18	Oct. 04	Oct. 06	Oct. 20 '95

Data as orig. reptd.; bef. results of disc. opers. and/or spec. items. Per share data adj. for stk. divs. as of ex-div. date. E-Estimated. NA-Not Available. NM-Not Meaningful. NR-Not Ranked.

Office—1585 Charleston Rd., Mountain View, CA 94043-1225. **Tel**—(415) 961-4400. **Chrmn & CEO**—J. E. Warnock. **Pres & COO**—C. M. Geschke. **SVP-Fin, CFO, Treas & Investor Contact**—M. Bruce Nakao. **Secy**—C. M. Pouliot. **Dirs**—P. Brainerd, G. P. Carter, C. M. Geschke, W. R. Hambrecht, R. Sedgewick, W. J. Spencer, J. E. Warnock, D. W. Yocam. **Transfer Agent & Registrar**—Chemical Bank, SF. **Incorporated** in California in 1983. **Empl**-904. **S&P Analyst:** Peter C. Wood, CFA

STANDARD & POOR'S

STOCK REPORTS

Advanced Technology Labs.

NASDAQ Symbol **ATLI**

In S&P MidCap 400

27-AUG-95

Industry: Medical equipment/ supply

Summary: ATLI is a leading developer, producer, marketer and servicer of diagnostic medical ultrasound systems used in radiology, cardiology, OB/GYN and vascular clinical markets.

Quantitative Evaluations

Outlook
(1 Lowest—5 Highest)
• **3-**

Fair Value
• **17½**

Risk
• **Average**

Earn./Div. Rank
• **C**

Technical Eval.
• **Bullish** since 7/95

Rel. Strength Rank
(1 Lowest—99 Highest)
• **67**

Insider Activity
• **Neutral**

Recent Price • 17½
52 Wk Range • 19½-13

Yield • Nil
12-Mo. P/E • NM

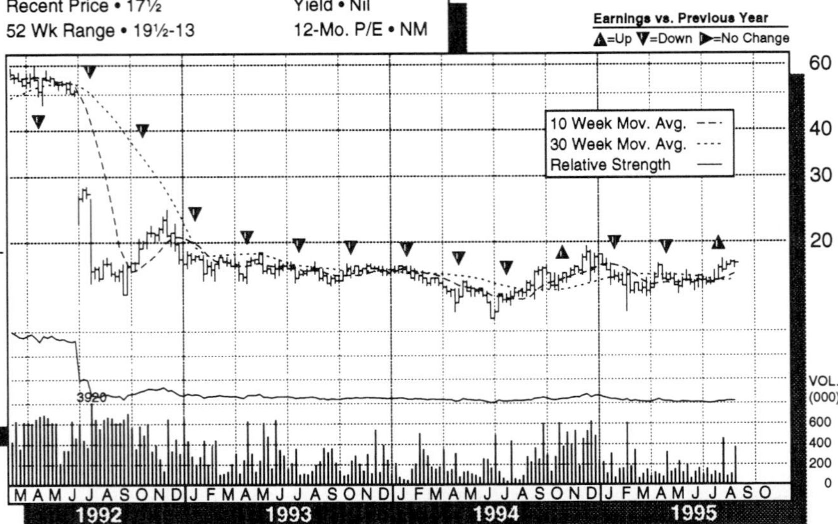

OPTIONS: Ph

Business Profile - 27-AUG-95

ATLI greatly expanded its presence in the cardiology market via the acquisition of Interspec in 1994. Despite its strong industry position, ATLI must cope with an increasingly competitive health care market. Demand for new ultrasound equipment is not expected to rise substantially in the near term, and revenue growth is being driven by product upgrades and service to the installed base. These trends are likely to persist in 1995, as health care providers seek to offer quality care at lower cost.

Operational Review - 27-AUG-95

Revenues have advanced in recent periods (as restated for the acquisition of Interspec Inc.), reflecting the introduction of new ultrasound systems and higher service revenues. Margins widened on an improved product mix and cost reduction programs. Results were hurt by a nonrecurring charge of $1.2 million for consolidation of Interspec operations, partly offset by an operating expense credit from a favorable Washington State tax audit.

Stock Performance - 25-AUG-95

In the past 30 trading days, ATLI's shares have increased 13%, compared to a 0.04% rise in the S&P 500. Average trading volume for the past five days was 72,620 shares, compared with the 40-day moving average of 37,215 shares.

Key Stock Statistics

Dividend Rate/Share	Nil	Shareholders	9,300
Shs. outstg. (M)	13.4	Market cap. (B)	$0.234
Avg. daily vol. (M)	0.050	Inst. holdings	72%
Tang. Bk. Value/Share	17.50	Insider holdings	NA
Beta	1.38		

Value of $10,000 invested 5 years ago: $ 3,804

Fiscal Year Ending Dec. 31

	1995	% Change	1994	% Change	1993	% Change
Revenues (Million $)						
1Q	94.36	6%	89.40	10%	81.40	7%
2Q	91.28	8%	84.80	12%	75.41	-2%
3Q	—	—	87.35	33%	65.69	-16%
4Q	—	—	104.7	28%	82.01	-11%
Yr.	—	—	366.1	20%	304.5	-6%
Income (Million $)						
1Q	-0.27	NM	0.30	-84%	1.92	-30%
2Q	0.84	NM	-9.95	NM	-1.79	NM
3Q	—	—	-4.76	NM	-8.73	NM
4Q	—	—	-5.80	NM	3.50	-32%
Yr.	—	—	-20.20	NM	-5.11	NM
Earnings Per Share ($)						
1Q	-0.02	NM	0.02	-88%	0.17	-32%
2Q	0.06	NM	-0.76	NM	-0.16	NM
3Q	—	—	-0.36	NM	-0.80	NM
4Q	—	—	-0.44	NM	0.33	-27%
Yr.	—	—	-1.53	NM	-0.46	NM

Next earnings report expected: early November

Advanced Technology Labs.

Business Summary - 27-AUG-95

Advanced Technology Laboratories Inc. (ATL) is a global supplier of diagnostic ultrasound medical equipment. The company believes it has become a leader in ultrasound technology through its proprietary position in digital, broad bandwidth beamforming and scanhead technologies.

Ultrasound systems provide a safe, noninvasive and painless means of observing soft tissues and internal body organs and assessing blood flow through the heart and vessels. High-frequency sound waves are focused at internal structures, and the resulting echoes are gathered and electronically processed. Repeated scannings of the body interior at very high speeds produce moving, two-dimensional video images in real time. Ultrasound systems can also analyze blood flow characteristics using the Doppler principle. The company's High Definition Imaging (HDI), Apogee and Ultramark product lines serve all major diagnostic ultrasound clinical markets, including radiology, cardiology, OB/GYN and vascular medicine. These product lines span a range of system prices from mid to premium priced ultrasound products.

ATL has pioneered the development of digital beamformers, which digitize the signals returning from the body prior to processing, and broad-bandwidth scanhead technologies, which complement the capability of its digital beamforming technology and allow physicians to see more of the tissue signature with greater clarity.

The company's HDI-3000 system was designed to address the economic imperatives of the evolving health care environment in the U.S. and international markets. ATL's highest-performing system, the Ultramark 9 with High Definition Imaging, contains an ASIC-based digital beamformer that allows high resolution images and captures a broad bandwidth of tissue signatures.

With the 1994 acquisition of Interspec Inc., ATL now sells the Apogee line of ultrasound systems to the radiology and cardiology mid-range markets.

Important Developments

Feb. '95—ATL said it plans to consolidate the Pennsylvania operations of Interspec Inc. into its Washington headquarters, and will close the Interspec facility during the second half of 1995. The consolidation should save about $8 million annually; ATL anticipates related charges of $5 million in 1995.

Dec. '94—A U.S. Court of Appeals upheld a lower court ruling that ATL infringed a U.S. patent of SRI International Inc. allegedly related to an electrical circuit used in the Ultramark 4, as well as two other discontinued products. SRI is seeking damages of over $5 million. The patent expired in April 1994, and product shipments are thus not affected.

Capitalization

Long Term Debt: $15,665,000 (6/95).

Per Share Data ($) (Year Ended Dec. 31)

	1994	1993	1992	1991	1990	1989
Tangible Bk. Val.	14.34	17.68	18.04	30.17	27.71	26.18
Cash Flow	-0.32	0.62	1.66	3.61	3.00	2.99
Earnings	-1.53	-0.46	0.67	2.09	1.61	1.85
Dividends	Nil	Nil	Nil	Nil	Nil	Nil
Payout Ratio	Nil	Nil	Nil	Nil	Nil	Nil
Prices - High	19½	19	63	54¼	52¼	51½
- Low	12½	15¼	14½	21½	16¾	26½
P/E Ratio - High	NM	NM	94	26	32	28
- Low	NM	NM	22	10	10	14

Income Statement Analysis (Million $)

	1994	%Chg	1993	%Chg	1992	%Chg	1991
Revs.	366	20%	305	-6%	324	-36%	505
Oper. Inc.	6.7	-43%	11.7	-54%	25.3	-36%	39.4
Depr.	15.9	34%	11.9	8%	11.0	-29%	15.5
Int. Exp.	1.4	99%	0.7	-13%	0.8	-51%	1.6
Pretax Inc.	-20.9	NM	-3.6	NM	9.5	-72%	34.0
Eff. Tax Rate	NM	—	NM	—	22%	—	37%
Net Inc.	-20.2	NM	-5.1	NM	7.4	-65%	21.4

Balance Sheet & Other Fin. Data (Million $)

	1994	1993	1992	1991	1990	1989
Cash	22.9	54.6	77.4	74.8	36.8	48.7
Curr. Assets	246	225	249	350	311	292
Total Assets	332	277	296	452	396	365
Curr. Liab.	118	87.0	89.0	119	114	92.0
LT Debt	17.7	Nil	NA	13.3	Nil	Nil
Common Eqty.	191	186	204	314	277	268
Total Cap.	213	189	207	333	282	274
Cap. Exp.	15.0	14.2	10.2	24.0	19.1	14.0
Cash Flow	-4.3	6.8	18.4	36.9	30.7	30.9

Ratio Analysis

	1994	1993	1992	1991	1990	1989
Curr. Ratio	2.1	2.6	2.8	2.9	2.7	3.2
% LT Debt of Cap.	8.3	Nil	NA	4.0	Nil	Nil
% Net Inc.of Revs.	NM	NM	2.3	4.2	3.4	4.3
% Ret. on Assets	NM	NM	1.8	4.9	4.4	5.5
% Ret. on Equity	NM	NM	2.6	7.1	6.2	7.5

Dividend Data —No cash has been paid.

Data as orig. reptd.; bef. results of disc. opers. and/or spec. items. Per share data adj. for stk. divs. as of ex-div. date. E-Estimated. NA-Not Available. NM-Not Meaningful. NR-Not Ranked.

Office—22100 Bothell-Everett Highway, P. O. Box 3003, Bothell, WA 98041-3003. **Tel**—(206) 487-7000. **Chrmn, Pres & CEO**—D. C. Fill. **SVP-Fin & CFO**—H. N. Gillis. **VP & Investor Contact**—Anne Marie Bugge (206-487-7081). **Dirs**—K. L. Cramer, H. Feigenbaum, D. C. Fill, E. A. Larson, J. Miller, P. M. Nudelman, D. M. Perozek, E. Ray, H. Woolf. **Transfer Agent & Registrar**—First Chicago Trust Co. of New York, NYC. **Incorporated** in Delaware in 1983. **Empl**-2,630. **S&P Analyst:** Philip J. Birbara

STANDARD & POOR'S

STOCK REPORTS

AFLAC Inc.

NYSE Symbol **AFL**
In S&P MidCap 400

18-OCT-95 **Industry:** Insurance

Summary: This holding company offers supplemental cancer insurance and other individual health coverages, and also owns TV stations. During 1994, AFL derived 84% of its revenues from Japan.

S&P Opinion: Accumulate (★★★★)

Recent Price • 42¼
52 Wk Range • 44¾-31⅞
Yield • 1.2%
12-Mo. P/E • 13.0

Quantitative Evaluations

Outlook
(1 Lowest—5 Highest)
• **2+**

Fair Value
• **40⅞**

Risk
• **Low**

Earn./Div. Rank
• **A**

Technical Eval.
• **Bullish** since 12/94

Rel. Strength Rank
(1 Lowest—99 Highest)
• **79**

Insider Activity
• **Neutral**

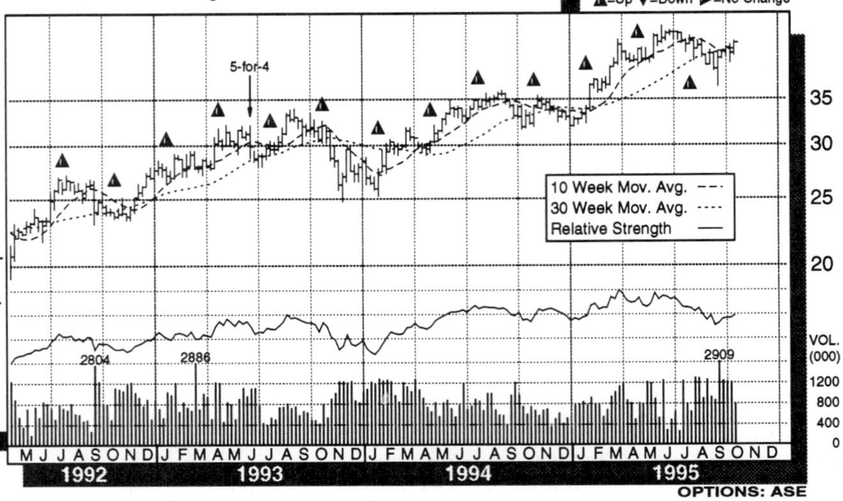

Overview - 18-OCT-95

Our forecast for higher earnings is predicated upon continued favorable persistency rates. AFL is the dominant underwriter of supplemental cancer insurance in Japan and has capitalized on that strength to exploit new market and product niches. In the U.S., a product expansion program away from solely cancer coverage, combined with stepped-up marketing efforts, aids the long-term premium growth outlook. Increased persistency rates and a maturing book of business will aid growth in margins. Investment income growth will be aided by the attendant increase in cash flow, though lower interest rates could reduce yields. Writedowns to the high quality portfolio are unlikely. Broadcast earnings may improve on cost controls and an uptick in advertising expenditures. Share repurchases, such as the 5 million authorization announced in August 1995, will aid per-share comparisons.

Valuation - 18-OCT-95

These interest-sensitive shares have appreciated almost 30% since year-end 1994 and now trade close to their 52-week high. AFL's strong earnings growth, the positive effects of a weaker U.S. dollar (versus the yen) and prospects for lower interest rates have fueled the shares' recent rise. Trading at 12 times our conservative 1995 operating earnings estimate, the shares are attractively valued, long term. Near term, we would look for a pullback of about 10% from current levels before adding to positions.

Key Stock Statistics

S&P EPS Est. 1995	3.50	Tang. Bk. Value/Share	19.91
P/E on S&P Est. 1995	12.1	Beta	0.99
S&P EPS Est. 1996	4.00	Shareholders	27,900
Dividend Rate/Share	0.52	Market cap. (B)	$ 4.2
Shs. outstg. (M)	96.3	Inst. holdings	54%
Avg. daily vol. (M)	0.230	Insider holdings	NA

Value of $10,000 invested 5 years ago: $ 31,719

Fiscal Year Ending Dec. 31

	1995	% Change	1994	% Change	1993	% Change
Revenues (Million $)						
1Q	1,714	23%	1,392	24%	1,121	20%
2Q	1,933	30%	1,481	20%	1,237	29%
3Q	—	—	1,602	22%	1,308	28%
4Q	—	—	1,636	23%	1,334	25%
Yr.	—	—	6,111	22%	5,001	25%
Income (Million $)						
1Q	84.87	21%	69.96	30%	53.75	27%
2Q	92.92	34%	69.38	18%	58.74	33%
3Q	—	—	76.06	18%	64.54	35%
4Q	—	—	77.40	16%	66.86	37%
Yr.	—	—	292.8	20%	243.9	33%
Earnings Per Share ($)						
1Q	0.83	24%	0.67	31%	0.51	21%
2Q	0.92	37%	0.67	20%	0.56	30%
3Q	—	—	0.74	21%	0.61	33%
4Q	—	—	0.76	19%	0.64	33%
Yr.	E3.50	23%	2.84	22%	2.32	30%

Next earnings report expected: late January

AFLAC Inc.

Business Summary - 18-OCT-95

AFLAC Inc. is a holding company with insurance and broadcasting interests. Segment contributions to pretax profits (before intercompany eliminations) in recent years were:

	1994	1993
Insurance-foreign	81%	82%
Insurance-U.S.	16%	16%
Broadcasting & other	3%	2%

Foreign insurance operations consist primarily of the underwriting and sale of cancer insurance in Japan. AFL's policy pays cash directly to the policyholder to help defray certain out-of-pocket expenses (like private or at-home nursing care or non-covered medicines) incurred in the treatment of cancer. The majority of new cancer policy sales are made on a payroll-deduction basis through corporate-sponsored agencies. Super-Care, a long term care/disability policy introduced in 1992 as part of a product broadening plan, equaled 18% of new policy sales in 1994. AFL plans to offer two new policies -- a living benefits life policy and a hospital indemnity policy -- in 1995.

In the U.S., AFL has expanded its product line away from solely cancer insurance (which still remains a core offering) to an array of supplemental health insurance products, including hospital intensive care, home health care, accident and disability, Medicare supplemental and long-term care protection. During 1994, supplemental health products (other than cancer protection) accounted for 63% of new premium sales.

Broadcast properties consist of seven network-affiliated television stations located primarily in the southeastern U.S.

Important Developments

Aug. '95—AFL's directors authorized the repurchase of up to 5 million common shares. This follows a 4.6 million share buyback authorization made in February 1995. Separately, AFL's new annualized premium sales in Japan rose 14% (in yen), year to year, during the first half of 1995. Growth was aided by strong sales of care policies. In the U.S., new annualized premium sales increased 12%, as contributions from new product offerings offset a slowdown in Medicare supplemental sales. Excluding Medicare supplemental sales, new policy sales rose 19%. A stronger yen versus the dollar added $0.21 a share to earnings in 1995's first half.

Capitalization

Notes Payable: $269,521,000 (6/95).

Per Share Data ($) (Year Ended Dec. 31)

	1994	1993	1992	1991	1990	1989
Tangible Bk. Val.	16.48	12.09	9.35	7.86	6.54	5.63
Oper. Earnings	2.84	2.30	1.79	1.46	1.15	0.76
Earnings	2.84	2.32	1.79	1.46	1.15	0.80
Dividends	0.44	0.39	0.34	0.30	0.26	0.23
Payout Ratio	16%	17%	19%	20%	23%	29%
Prices - High	36⅛	34	27⅞	24⅞	15⅜	18
- Low	25¼	24¾	19¼	14⅜	9¾	10¾
P/E Ratio - High	13	15	16	17	13	23
- Low	9	11	11	10	8	13

Income Statement Analysis (Million $)

	1994	%Chg	1993	%Chg	1992	%Chg	1991
Life Ins. In Force	NA	—	NA	—	10,553	7%	9,839
Premium Income Life	NA	—	NA	—	16.7	-2%	17.0
Prem.Inc A & H	5,181	23%	4,225	26%	3,353	22%	2,748
Premium Income Other	Nil	—	Nil	—	Nil	—	Nil
Net Invest. Inc.	839	22%	689	29%	533	24%	431
Total Revs.	6,111	22%	5,001	25%	3,986	21%	3,283
Pretax Inc.	504	18%	428	32%	325	23%	265
Net Oper. Inc.	293	21%	242	32%	183	24%	148
Net Inc.	293	20%	244	33%	183	23%	149

Balance Sheet & Other Fin. Data (Million $)

	1994	1993	1992	1991	1990	1989
Cash & Equiv.	238	208	185	184	136	109
Premiums Due	304	232	180	160	144	120
Inv Assets Bonds	15,862	12,304	9,267	7,861	6,105	4,891
Inv. Assets Stock	84.4	82.1	68.0	61.0	55.0	49.0
Inv. Assets Loans	25.1	57.5	89.9	88.6	83.1	36.4
Inv. Assets Total	15,976	12,446	9,425	8,010	6,243	4,976
Deferred Policy Cost	2,403	1,953	1,614	1,407	1,164	967
Total Assets	20,287	15,443	11,901	10,145	8,035	6,515
Debt	185	122	126	139	158	214
Common Eqty.	1,752	1,366	1,082	923	791	702

Ratio Analysis

	1994	1993	1992	1991	1990	1989
% Ret. on Revs.	4.8	4.9	4.6	4.5	4.4	3.3
% Ret. on Assets	1.6	1.8	1.7	1.6	1.6	1.3
% Ret. on Equity	18.8	19.9	18.3	17.3	15.7	12.0
% Invest. Yield	5.9	6.3	6.1	6.1	6.1	6.2

Dividend Data —Cash dividends have been paid since 1973. A dividend reinvestment plan is available.

Amt. of Div. $	Date Decl.	Ex-Div. Date	Stock of Record	Payment Date
0.115	Oct. 26	Nov. 14	Nov. 18	Dec. 01 '94
0.115	Jan. 30	Feb. 13	Feb. 17	Mar. 01 '95
0.130	Apr. 25	May. 15	May. 19	Jun. 01 '95
0.130	Jul. 26	Aug. 16	Aug. 18	Sep. 01 '95

Data as orig. reptd.; bef. results of disc. opers. and/or spec. items. Per share data adj. for stk. divs. as of ex-div. date. E-Estimated. NA-Not Available. NM-Not Meaningful. NR-Not Ranked.

Office—1932 Wynnton Rd., Columbus, GA 31999. **Tel**—(706) 323-3431; (800) 235-2667. **Chrmn**—P. S. Amos. **Pres & CEO**—D. P. Amos. **SVP-Secy**—J. M. Loudermilk. **EVP-CFO**—K. Cloninger III. **SVP & Investor Contact**—Kenneth S. Janke Jr. **Dirs**—D. P. Amos, J. S. Amos II, P. S. Amos, M. H. Armacost, M. D. Edwards, G. W. Ford Jr., C. E. Garcia, J. F. Harris, E. J. Hudson, K. S. Janke Sr., C. B. Knapp, H. Kobayashi, P. D. Morrow, Y. Otake, J. M. Pope, E. S. Purdom, H. C. Schwob, J. K. Spencer, G. Vaughn Jr. **Transfer Agent**—Company's office. **Registrar**—Columbus Bank & Trust Co. **Incorporated** in Georgia in 1955; reincorporated in 1973. **Empl**-4,000. **S&P Analyst:** Catherine A. Seifert

Air & Water Technologies

ASE Symbol **AWT**
In S&P MidCap 400

17-OCT-95

Industry:
Pollution Control

Summary: This company provides a wide range of environmental services and technologies in the areas of air pollution control, water resources management and the reuse of waste by-products.

Quantitative Evaluations
Outlook
(1 Lowest—5 Highest)
• **1**
Fair Value
• **3¼**
Risk
• **High**
Earn./Div. Rank
• **NR**

Technical Eval.
• **Bullish** since 9/95
Rel. Strength Rank
(1 Lowest—99 Highest)
• **18**
Insider Activity
• **NA**

Recent Price • 5¼
52 Wk Range • 7⅜-4⅛

Yield • Nil
12-Mo. P/E • NM

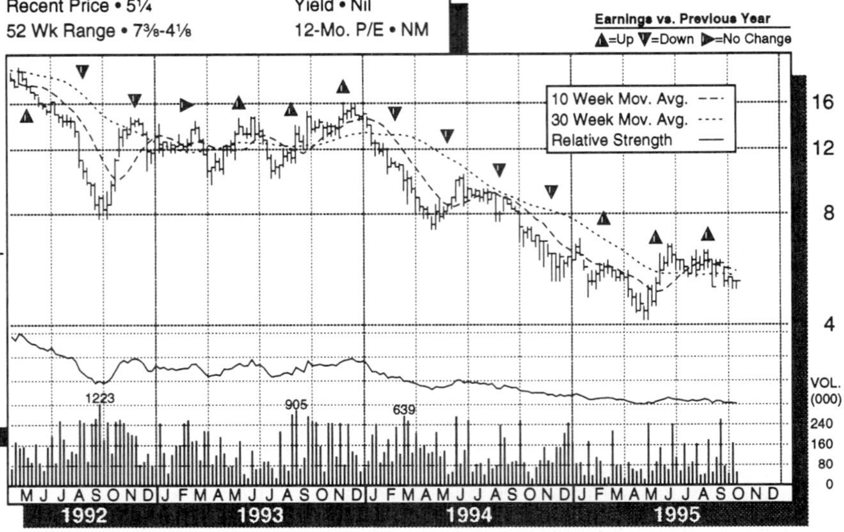

Business Profile - 17-OCT-95

After incurring a large loss in fiscal 1994, this provider of environmental services and products continued to post losses in fiscal 1995, although the nine-month deficit narrowed considerably. Besides controlling costs, AWT's strategy includes building on strengths of professional services, restoring Metcalf & Eddy to a higher level of profitability and aggressively overhaulng its air pollution control business. Important contracts received in May and July 1995 should benefit future revenues.

Operational Review - 17-OCT-95

Sales for the nine months ended July 31, 1995, advanced 19%, year to year. The higher sales, cost controls and the absence of unusual charges led to operating profit of $9.2 million, which contrasted with a loss of $147.2 million. Total other expenses exceeded operating profit, and the loss from continuing operations was $10.9 million ($0.42 a share), versus a loss of $168.4 million ($6.44, before a $1.63 loss from discontinued operations and a $0.30 special charge).

Stock Performance - 13-OCT-95

In the past 30 trading days, AWT's shares have increased 4%, compared to a 4% rise in the S&P 500. Average trading volume for the past five days was 9,560 shares, compared with the 40-day moving average of 28,508 shares.

Key Stock Statistics

Dividend Rate/Share	Nil	Shareholders	700
Shs. outstg. (M)	32.0	Market cap. (B)	$0.164
Avg. daily vol. (M)	0.016	Inst. holdings	50%
Tang. Bk. Value/Share	NM	Insider holdings	NA
Beta	1.19		

Value of $10,000 invested 5 years ago: $ 2,441

Fiscal Year Ending Oct. 31

	1995	% Change	1994	% Change	1993	% Change
Revenues (Million $)						
1Q	148.4	21%	122.8	-24%	161.1	5%
2Q	155.8	30%	119.7	-31%	172.4	NM
3Q	146.2	8%	135.8	-4%	140.8	-23%
4Q	—	—	144.4	-8%	156.2	-25%
Yr.	—	—	522.6	-17%	630.4	-12%
Income (Million $)						
1Q	-7.39	NM	-30.77	NM	0.28	87%
2Q	-3.58	NM	-18.79	NM	1.51	NM
3Q	0.10	NM	-118.8	NM	0.60	NM
4Q	—	—	-42.64	NM	2.17	NM
Yr.	—	—	-211.0	NM	4.55	NM
Earnings Per Share ($)						
1Q	-0.26	NM	-1.24	NM	0.01	NM
2Q	-0.14	NM	-0.75	NM	0.06	NM
3Q	-0.02	NM	-4.15	NM	0.02	NM
4Q	—	—	-1.36	NM	0.09	NM
Yr.	—	—	-7.68	NM	0.18	NM

Next earnings report expected: early February

Air & Water Technologies

Business Summary - 17-OCT-95

Air & Water Technologies Corporation, through its subsidiaries, provides a broad range of environmental services--water resource management, air pollution control, and operations and maintenance services--and technologies to utility, industrial and government clients. Sales contributions by division in recent fiscal years were:

	1994	1993
Research-Cottrell	41%	48%
Metcalf & Eddy	42%	43%
Professional Services	16%	8%
Other	1%	1%

The Research-Cottrell unit provides products and services for the reduction, control and monitoring of air pollution from power generation and industrial process sources. Products include electrostatic precipitators, fabric filters and dust collectors, scrubbers, chimneys, monitors and cooling towers. Services include equipment design, engineering, fabrication and startup; repair, upgrade, rebuild and preventive maintenance; and construction and project management.

The Metcalf & Eddy unit provides environmental treatment and services to industry and government, specializing in water, wastewater, solid waste, hazardous waste and air quality. Activities include protection, collection, treatment and distribution of drinking water; collection, treatment and disposal of wastewater and wastewater by-products; treatment of industrial wastewater; remediation of hazardous waste; and monitoring, expansion and closure of solid-waste facilities.

The Professional Services Group provides services for the operation, maintenance and management of treatment facilities in the water, wastewater, sludge and biosolid-waste management markets. Services range from addressing individual operating needs to the assumption of complete responsibility for operating treatment facilities.

Important Developments

Jul. '95—AWT was granted a contract by the EPA, valued at a maximum of $400 million over 10 years, to provide remedial investigations and feasibility studies, design of remedial actions and construction management. Separately, in June, AWT said it would receive a $17.5 million litigation settlement.

May '95—AWT said it was granted a five-year $500 million contract to operate, maintain and manage water and wastewater treatment facilities, collection and distribution systems and billing collections for the island of Puerto Rico.

Capitalization

Long Term Debt: $313,206,000 (7/95), incl. $115,000,000 of 8% sub. debs. due 2015 & conv. into com. at $30 a sh.

5.5% Ser. A Pfd. Stock: 1,200,000 shs. ($0.01 par); ea. sh. conv. into four Cl. A shs.

Per Share Data ($) (Year Ended Oct. 31)

	1994	1993	1992	1991	1990	1989
Tangible Bk. Val.	-6.54	-1.08	8.72	9.12	8.96	3.45
Cash Flow	-7.01	0.77	0.27	-0.48	1.01	-0.11
Earnings	-7.68	0.18	-0.40	-1.15	0.35	-0.87
Dividends	Nil	Nil	Nil	Nil	Nil	Nil
Payout Ratio	Nil	Nil	Nil	Nil	Nil	Nil
Prices - High	$14\frac{3}{4}$	$16\frac{1}{8}$	$24\frac{1}{8}$	$25\frac{7}{8}$	$30\frac{3}{8}$	$21\frac{1}{2}$
- Low	$5\frac{1}{4}$	$9\frac{5}{8}$	$7\frac{3}{4}$	$15\frac{7}{8}$	$11\frac{3}{4}$	$15\frac{1}{4}$
P/E Ratio - High	NM	90	NM	NM	87	NM
- Low	NM	53	NM	NM	34	NM

Income Statement Analysis (Million $)

	1994	%Chg	1993	%Chg	1992	%Chg	1991
Revs.	523	-17%	630	-12%	719	9%	657
Oper. Inc.	-18.8	NM	45.2	15%	39.3	42%	27.7
Depr.	18.5	27%	14.6	-14%	16.9	12%	15.1
Int. Exp.	24.4	NM	24.6	6%	23.1	5%	22.0
Pretax Inc.	-209	NM	4.6	-47%	8.7	NM	-23.9
Eff. Tax Rate	NM	—	1.50%	—	NM	—	NM
Net Inc.	-210	NM	4.6	NM	-10.0	NM	-25.9

Balance Sheet & Other Fin. Data (Million $)

	1994	1993	1992	1991	1990	1989
Cash	11.0	7.6	10.1	20.0	66.3	27.2
Curr. Assets	188	271	293	278	319	213
Total Assets	603	602	619	601	600	478
Curr. Liab.	240	169	180	150	143	143
LT Debt	246	222	222	225	226	254
Common Eqty.	74.0	210	216	226	201	55.0
Total Cap.	321	433	439	451	458	335
Cap. Exp.	5.5	5.2	9.2	12.0	14.1	7.9
Cash Flow	-193	19.2	6.8	-10.8	19.0	-1.4

Ratio Analysis

	1994	1993	1992	1991	1990	1989
Curr. Ratio	0.8	1.6	1.6	1.9	2.2	1.5
% LT Debt of Cap.	76.7	51.3	50.6	49.9	49.4	76.0
% Net Inc.of Revs.	NM	0.7	NM	NM	1.1	NM
% Ret. on Assets	NM	0.7	NM	NM	1.0	NM
% Ret. on Equity	NM	2.1	NM	NM	4.7	NM

Dividend Data —No cash dividends have been paid.

Data as orig. reptd.; bef. results of disc. opers. and/or spec. items. Per share data adj. for stk. divs. as of ex-div. date. E-Estimated. NA-Not Available. NM-Not Meaningful. NR-Not Ranked.

Office—U.S. Highway 22 West and Station Rd., Branchburg, NJ 08876. **Tel**—(908) 685-4600. **Chrmn & CEO**—C. Elia. **Pres**—A. L. Glenn. **VP & CFO**—A. Brunais. **VP & Secy**—D. A. Satzger. **VP & Investor Contact**—Robert S. Volland. **Dirs**—D. M. Costle, J. David, N. DeBenedictis, J. Deschamps, C. Elia, C. L. Green, W. Kriegel, J. W. Morris, E. F. Senior. **Transfer Agent & Registrar**—First Chicago Trust Company of New York. **Incorporated** in Delaware in 1987. **Empl**-3,600. **S&P Analyst:** N.J. DeVita

STANDARD & POOR'S

STOCK REPORTS

Airborne Freight

NYSE Symbol **ABF**

In S&P MidCap 400

17-AUG-95 **Industry:** Air Transport

Summary: This company is an integrated air express delivery company, specializing in door-to-door, overnight and second-day deliveries of small packages and documents.

S&P Opinion: Avoid (★★)

Recent Price • 21 | Yield • 1.5%
52 Wk Range • 30⅞-18 | 12-Mo. P/E • 19.6

Quantitative Evaluations

Outlook (1 Lowest—5 Highest)
• **3-**

Fair Value
• **20⅝**

Risk
• **High**

Earn./Div. Rank
• **B**

Technical Eval.
• **Bullish** since 8/94

Rel. Strength Rank (1 Lowest—99 Highest)
• **20**

Insider Activity
• **NA**

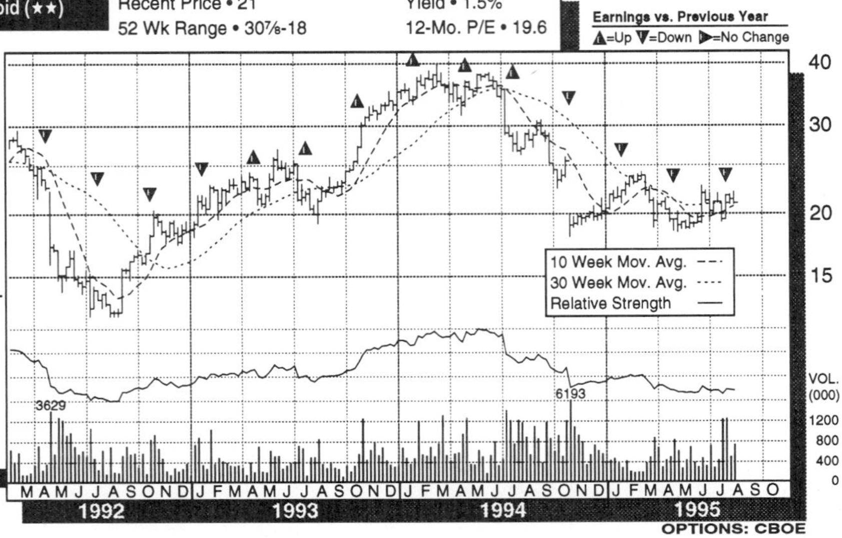

OPTIONS: CBOE

Overview - 17-AUG-95

Revenues for 1995 are projected to advance more than 10% from those of 1994. Domestic shipment growth is forecast to stay robust as customers shift to this low priced transporter in the face of a slowing U.S. economy. However, most of the increase will be in the lower-priced second day service. In addition, average shipment weight will see a decline. International revenues will benefit from the strengthening worldwide economies. The trend towards greater foreign trade should also boost international revenues. Margins will narrow, given the relative importance of the lower domestic shipments yield. Revenue management actions in the second half of 1995 are expected to minimize the margin erosion.

Valuation - 17-AUG-95

Earnings of air freight carriers have been restricted in recent periods by a customer trend to purchase less expensive (and less profitable) services, such as second day delivery. ABF has been hit particularly hard given the decline in its average weight per shipment. Presumably, the shipper has been acquiring the low profit customers that Federal Express and UPS have been turning away. Accordingly, the carrier will be initiating another round of price increases to offset margin erosion. Although shares are reasonably priced based on our forecast of 1996 earnings, we recommend waiting for evidence of improved earnings.

Key Stock Statistics

S&P EPS Est. 1995	0.80	Tang. Bk. Value/Share	18.48
P/E on S&P Est. 1995	26.3	Beta	1.64
S&P EPS Est. 1996	1.50	Shareholders	1,400
Dividend Rate/Share	0.30	Market cap. (B)	$0.426
Shs. outstg. (M)	21.0	Inst. holdings	93%
Avg. daily vol. (M)	0.187	Insider holdings	NA

Value of $10,000 invested 5 years ago: $ 12,854

Fiscal Year Ending Dec. 31

	1995	% Change	1994	% Change	1993	% Change
Revenues (Million $)						
1Q	529.9	14%	466.5	17%	398.8	11%
2Q	545.9	13%	484.5	15%	419.9	17%
3Q	—	—	489.7	13%	434.2	17%
4Q	—	—	529.9	13%	467.1	19%
Yr.	—	—	1,971	15%	1,720	16%
Income (Million $)						
1Q	1.88	-73%	7.00	93%	3.63	NM
2Q	2.26	-83%	13.06	108%	6.28	NM
3Q	—	—	8.15	-26%	11.07	NM
4Q	—	—	10.63	-26%	14.32	159%
Yr.	—	—	38.84	10%	35.29	NM
Earnings Per Share ($)						
1Q	0.09	-72%	0.32	113%	0.15	NM
2Q	0.10	-84%	0.61	110%	0.29	NM
3Q	E0.26	-32%	0.38	-28%	0.53	NM
4Q	E0.35	-30%	0.50	-28%	0.69	176%
Yr.	E0.80	-56%	1.81	9%	1.66	NM

Next earnings report expected: late October

Airborne Freight

Business Summary - 17-AUG-95

Airborne Freight is an integrated air express transportation company operating under the name Airborne Express. Revenue and profit contributions in 1994 were:

	Revs.	Profits
Domestic	84%	94%
International	16%	6%

Domestic operations consist primarily of express door-to-door delivery of packages weighing less than 100 lbs. Also available to attract less frequent shippers were approximately 8,500 drop boxes. The majority of shipments flow through ABF's airport and central sorting facility in Wilmington, Ohio. Ten regional hubs, which handled about 23% of shipment weight in 1994, are operated at high-traffic areas.

In 1994, approximately 63% of the company's domestic shipments were for overnight express delivery (generally for delivery before noon on the next business day). The remaining 37% of shipment were for a deferred service product, which provide for next afternoon or second day delivery.

Most shipments are carried on the company's own aircraft fleet, which as of December 31, 1994, consisted of 97 aircraft: 29 DC-8s, 57 DC-9s, and 11 YS-11 turboprop aircraft. Pickup and delivery is handled by a fleet of approximately 11,300 radio-dispatched vans and trucks.

ABF provides international express door-to-door delivery and a variety of freight services. It uses commercial airlines for international services. In 1994, the company began offering ocean service capabilities for customers who wanted a lower cost shipping option. A joint venture with Mitsui & Co. and Tonami Transportation conducts operations in Japan.

Important Developments

Jul. '95—Airborne reported a 20% rise in total shipments in the second quarter of 1995. However, the quarter experienced the same pressures on average weight and revenue per domestic shipment experienced in the first qurter of 1995, but the downward trend stabilized in the second quarter. Although productivity gains continued, the increase was not enough to offset drops in revenue per shipment. Consequently, the company said it intends to take a more aggressive approach to enhancing domestic revenue yields and to decreasing unit costs.

Capitalization

Long Term Debt: $449,397,000 (6/95), incl. $115 million of debs. conv. into com. at $35.50 a sh.
$3.45 Conv. Preferred Stock: 100,000 shs. ($50 par); conv. into 2.14 com. Held by Mitsui & Co. & Tonami Transportation.

Per Share Data ($)

(Year Ended Dec. 31)

	1994	1993	1992	1991	1990	1989
Tangible Bk. Val.	18.47	16.46	14.88	15.11	13.99	10.65
Cash Flow	8.36	8.50	6.33	6.49	5.61	5.14
Earnings	1.81	1.66	0.12	1.40	1.76	1.34
Dividends	0.30	0.30	0.30	0.30	0.30	0.30
Payout Ratio	17%	18%	NM	21%	18%	25%
Prices - High	39⅞	35¼	29¾	30	27	19⅞
- Low	18	18	12½	16⅝	13½	10½
P/E Ratio - High	22	21	NM	21	15	15
- Low	10	11	NM	12	8	8

Income Statement Analysis (Million $)

	1994	%Chg	1993	%Chg	1992	%Chg	1991
Revs.	1,971	15%	1,720	16%	1,484	9%	1,367
Oper. Inc.	227	5%	217	47%	148	-6%	158
Depr.	138	3%	134	11%	121	22%	99
Int. Exp.	26.8	2%	26.2	24%	21.2	39%	15.3
Pretax Inc.	64.3	9%	59.0	NM	9.1	-81%	48.4
Eff. Tax Rate	40%	—	40%	—	43%	—	38%
Net Inc.	38.8	10%	35.3	NM	5.2	-83%	30.0

Balance Sheet & Other Fin. Data (Million $)

	1994	1993	1992	1991	1990	1989
Cash	10.3	7.1	10.2	8.0	8.8	8.6
Curr. Assets	293	259	219	195	176	150
Total Assets	1,079	1,007	965	824	614	471
Curr. Liab.	226	199	168	177	152	125
LT Debt	398	391	429	283	124	144
Common Eqty.	387	319	286	287	263	168
Total Cap.	821	778	773	610	428	312
Cap. Exp.	177	143	255	253	225	164
Cash Flow	176	166	123	126	106	74.0

Ratio Analysis

	1994	1993	1992	1991	1990	1989
Curr. Ratio	1.3	1.3	1.3	1.1	1.2	1.2
% LT Debt of Cap.	48.5	50.3	55.5	46.3	29.0	46.2
% Net Inc.of Revs.	2.0	2.1	0.3	2.2	2.8	2.0
% Ret. on Assets	3.6	3.6	0.6	4.2	5.7	4.0
% Ret. on Equity	10.4	10.7	0.8	9.8	13.4	12.2

Dividend Data —Dividends were initiated in 1974. A "poison pill" stock purchase rights plan was adopted in 1986.

Amt. of Div. $	Date Decl.	Ex-Div. Date	Stock of Record	Payment Date
0.075	Aug. 09	Aug. 17	Aug. 23	Sep. 06 '94
0.075	Nov. 01	Nov. 08	Nov. 15	Nov. 29 '94
0.075	Feb. 07	Feb. 14	Feb. 21	Mar. 07 '95
0.075	Apr. 25	May. 03	May. 09	May. 23 '95
0.075	Aug. 08	Aug. 18	Aug. 22	Sep. 05 '95

Data as orig. reptd.; bef. results of disc. opers. and/or spec. items. Per share data adj. for stk. divs. as of ex-div. date. E-Estimated. NA-Not Available. NM-Not Meaningful. NR-Not Ranked.

Office—3101 Western Ave., P.O. Box 662, Seattle, WA 98111-0662. **Tel**—(206) 285-4600. **Chrmn & CEO**—R. S. Cline. **Pres**—R. G. Brazier. **Secy**—D. C. Anderson. **EVP-CFO & Investor Contact**—Roy C. Liljebeck (206-281-1003). **Dirs**—R. G. Brazier, A. F. Brimmer, J. H. Carey, R. S. Cline, A. B. Kim, H. M. Messmer Jr., R. M. Rosenberg, A. V. Smith, W. Swindells. **Transfer Agent & Registrar**—First Interstate Bank of Washington, Seattle. **Incorporated** in Delaware in 1968. **Empl**-10,400. **S&P Analyst:** Joe Victor Shammas

STANDARD & POOR'S
STOCK REPORTS

Alaska Air Group

NYSE Symbol **ALK**
In S&P MidCap 400

02-AUG-95 **Industry:** Air Transport

Summary: ALK operates two passenger airlines, Alaska Airlines, the leading carrier between Alaska and the lower 48 states, and Horizon Air, which serves small cities in the Northwest.

S&P Opinion: Hold (★★★)

Recent Price • 19⅝ | Yield • Nil
52 Wk Range • 20⅛-13⅛ | 12-Mo. P/E • 26.9

Quantitative Evaluations

Outlook (1 Lowest—5 Highest)
• **2-**

Fair Value
• **17⅜**

Risk
• **Average**

Earn./Div. Rank
• **C**

Technical Eval.
• **Bullish** since 7/95

Rel. Strength Rank (1 Lowest—99 Highest)
• **76**

Insider Activity
• **Neutral**

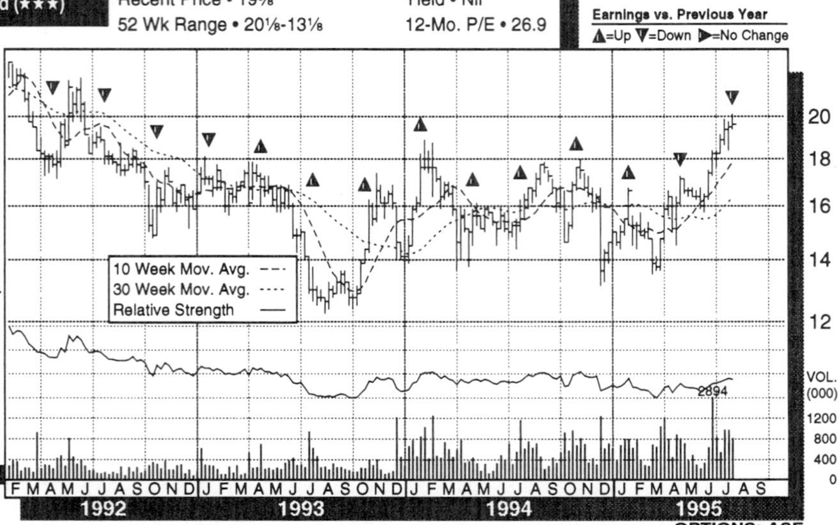

OPTIONS: ASE

Overview - 02-AUG-95

Revenues for 1995 are forecast to rise 8%-10% from those of 1994. Spurring sales growth will be additional capacity from several new aircraft brought into service and more efficient aircraft utilization. Although industry traffic is up, competitive pricing will result in lower average fares. Unit costs should decline, reflecting a more efficient fleet and continued cost reduction programs. Nonetheless, margins are forecast to narrow slightly. Net income is projected to benefit from a recent debt exchange, to less costly debentures; however, share earnings comparisons will be penalized by more shares outstanding.

Valuation - 02-AUG-95

ALK's shares rebounded in the first half of 1995, similar to other airline stocks, in part, reflecting improved industry conditions. Alaska Airlines has been particularly hard hit by competition from Southwest Airlines and United's new discount shuttle operations. The company must establish a solid position in its markets before these competitors further expand into its territory. Moreover, Alaska must continue slashing costs and upgrading to more efficient aircraft. The shares seem reasonably priced, but upside potential may be limited with debt comprising over 70% of total capital. We expect the stock to move on indications, one way or another, of how Alaska Air is dealing with these conditions.

Key Stock Statistics

S&P EPS Est. 1995	1.40	Tang. Bk. Value/Share	8.22
P/E on S&P Est. 1995	14.0	Beta	1.57
S&P EPS Est. 1996	2.00	Shareholders	6,200
Dividend Rate/Share	Nil	Market cap. (B)	$0.256
Shs. outstg. (M)	13.4	Inst. holdings	64%
Avg. daily vol. (M)	0.173	Insider holdings	NA

Value of $10,000 invested 5 years ago: $ 9,830

Fiscal Year Ending Dec. 31

	1995	% Change	1994	% Change	1993	% Change
Revenues (Million $)						
1Q	294.6	5%	280.4	12%	250.2	-3%
2Q	362.2	10%	330.5	19%	277.5	NM
3Q	—	—	386.8	20%	323.4	NM
4Q	—	—	318.0	15%	277.2	7%
Yr.	—	—	1,316	17%	1,128	1%
Income (Million $)						
1Q	-16.34	NM	-6.31	NM	-15.03	-4%
2Q	7.02	-27%	9.68	NM	-3.59	-80%
3Q	—	—	24.26	NM	8.03	NM
4Q	—	—	-5.10	NM	-20.32	-54%
Yr.	—	—	22.53	NM	-30.92	NM
Earnings Per Share ($)						
1Q	-1.22	NM	-0.47	NM	-1.25	NM
2Q	0.52	-28%	0.72	NM	-0.33	NM
3Q	E1.40	—	1.81	NM	0.60	NM
4Q	E0.70	—	-0.38	NM	-1.52	NM
Yr.	E1.40	—	1.68	NM	-2.51	NM

Next earnings report expected: mid October

Alaska Air Group

Business Summary - 02-AUG-95

Alaska Air Group, Inc. is the holding company for Alaska Airlines and Horizon Air Industries. Contributions by carrier in 1994 were:

	Sales	Profits
Alaska Airlines	81%	83%
Horizon Air	19%	17%

Alaska Airlines, a national airline, operates an all jet fleet. It is the leading airline between Alaska and the lower 48 states. As of December 31, 1994, the carrier provided service to 43 cities in Alaska, Arizona, California, Nevada, Oregon, and Washington, and six destinations in Mexico and Russia. Its major hubs are Seattle, Portland and Anchorage.

Horizon Air, a regional airline, operates a turboprop fleet. As of December 31, 1994, it served 38 destinations in Washington, Oregon, California, Idaho, Montana, Utah, and Canada. Its major hubs are Seattle, Portland, Spokane and Boise.

Consolidated operating data in recent years (passenger and seat miles in billions):

	1994	1993	1992
Rev. pass. miles	8.32	6.07	6.02
Avail. seat miles	13.25	10.41	10.52
Load factor	62.8%	58.3%	57.2%
Breakeven load factor	60.0%	60.3%	63.7%
Rev. per RPM (cents)	14.1	16.5	16.6
Cost per ASM (cents)	9.4	11.0	11.5

As of December 31, 1994, the Alaska Airlines fleet included 72 aircraft: eight Boeing 737-200s, 22 Boeing 737-400s, and 42 McDonnell Douglas-80s. On order were six McDonnell Douglas 80s. Horizon's fleet comprised 65 aircraft: 23 Metroliner IIIs, 23 de Havilland Dash 8s, 10 Fokker F-28s, and 9 Dornier 328s. On order were 51 Dornier 328s.

Important Developments

Jul. '95—Alaska Airline's passenger traffic for the first six months of 1995 climbed 17%, year to year. Capacity increased 22%, and the load factor fell to 58.9%, from 61.4%. At Horizon Air, traffic jumped 25% on a 32% rise in capacity. Load factor fell to 57.5%, from 60.5%.

Jun. '95—The company sold $132,250,000 principal amount of convertible senior debentures due 2005. The bonds, bearing interest at 6.5%, are convertible into common stock at $21.50 a share.

Capitalization

Long Term Debt: $579,236,000 (3/95).

Per Share Data ($)

(Year Ended Dec. 31)

	1994	1993	1992	1991	1990	1989
Tangible Bk. Val.	8.32	6.16	7.62	13.78	13.02	16.51
Cash Flow	7.48	2.81	-1.14	5.05	5.09	5.89
Earnings	1.68	-2.51	-6.53	0.27	0.82	2.71
Dividends	Nil	Nil	0.20	0.20	0.20	0.20
Payout Ratio	Nil	Nil	NM	74%	24%	7%
Prices - High	18⅞	18⅛	23⅞	25⅜	26	30½
- Low	13⅛	12¼	14¾	17½	13⅞	19⅞
P/E Ratio - High	11	NM	NM	94	32	11
- Low	8	NM	NM	65	17	7

Income Statement Analysis (Million $)

	1994	%Chg	1993	%Chg	1992	%Chg	1991
Revs.	1,316	17%	1,128	1%	1,115	NM	1,104
Oper. Inc.	153	122%	69.0	NM	3.0	-97%	99
Depr.	77.5	9%	70.9	-1%	71.8	12%	64.0
Int. Exp.	47.0	25%	37.6	-13%	43.2	7%	40.2
Pretax Inc.	41.0	NM	-46.0	NM	-125	NM	16.2
Eff. Tax Rate	45%	—	NM	—	NM	—	36%
Net Inc.	22.5	NM	-30.9	NM	-80.3	NM	10.3

Balance Sheet & Other Fin. Data (Million $)

	1994	1993	1992	1991	1990	1989
Cash	105	101	83.0	103	52.0	111
Curr. Assets	273	274	250	226	168	220
Total Assets	13.6	1,135	1,208	1,212	1,021	874
Curr. Liab.	420	336	336	250	296	211
LT Debt	5.9	525	488	500	282	227
Common Eqty.	191	167	195	283	278	342
Total Cap.	810	713	775	889	665	611
Cap. Exp.	189	30.0	278	213	249	144
Cash Flow	100	37.4	-15.1	67.7	69.6	93.4

Ratio Analysis

	1994	1993	1992	1991	1990	1989
Curr. Ratio	0.6	0.8	0.7	0.9	0.6	1.0
% LT Debt of Cap.	72.8	73.7	63.0	56.2	42.4	37.1
% Net Inc.of Revs.	1.7	NM	NM	0.9	1.6	4.7
% Ret. on Assets	1.8	NM	NM	0.9	1.9	5.4
% Ret. on Equity	12.6	NM	NM	1.3	3.9	13.3

Dividend Data (Dividends, resumed in 1982 after a three-year hiatus, were omitted in December 1992. A "poison pill" stock purchase right was adopted in 1986.)

Data as orig. reptd.; bef. results of disc. opers. and/or spec. items. Per share data adj. for stk. divs. as of ex-div. date. E-Estimated. NA-Not Available. NM-Not Meaningful. NR-Not Ranked.

Office—19300 Pacific Highway South, Seattle, WA 98188. **Tel**—(206) 431-7040. **Chrmn, Pres & CEO**—J. F. Kelly. **VP-Fin**—H. G. Lehr. **VP & Secy**—M. E. Laws. **Dirs**—W. H. Clapp, R. F. Cosgrave, M. J. Fate, J. F. Kelly, B. R. Kennedy, R. M. Langland, B. I. Mallott, B. R. McCaw, R. L. Parker, Jr., R. A. Wien. **Transfer Agent & Registrar**—First National Bank of Boston. **Incorporated** in Alaska in 1937; reincorporated in Delaware in 1985. **Empl**-9,852. **S&P Analyst:** Joe Victor Shammas

STANDARD & POOR'S

STOCK REPORTS

Albany International

NYSE Symbol **AIN**

In S&P MidCap 400

07-SEP-95 **Industry:** Manufacturing/Distr

Summary: This company is the world's largest producer of paper machine clothing -- custom-designed, engineered fabrics essential to the paper-making process.

Quantitative Evaluations

Outlook (1 Lowest—5 Highest) • **3+**

Fair Value • **24**

Risk • **Average**

Earn./Div. Rank • **B**

Technical Eval. • **Bullish** since 8/94

Rel. Strength Rank (1 Lowest—99 Highest) • **49**

Insider Activity • **Neutral**

Recent Price • 24⅜ | Yield • 1.6%

52 Wk Range • 26½-16¼ | 12-Mo. P/E • 21.8

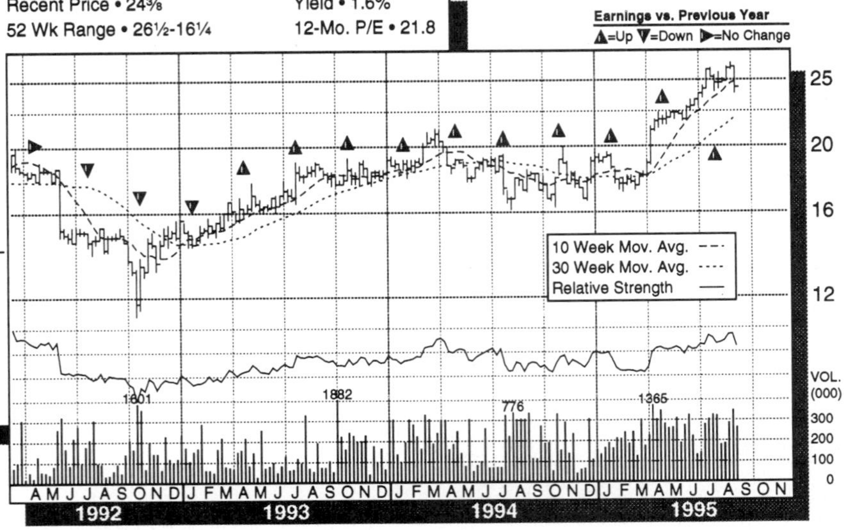

Business Profile - 06-SEP-95

With the paper industry expected to grow at a rate equal to or better than the overall economy, AIN should benefit from being the largest producer of paper machine clothing in the world. A favorable pricing environment, combined with cost reductions and improved operating efficiencies, should increase profitability. New products have added to market share, particularly in forming fabrics, and will strengthen AIN's position within a consolidating and highly competitive industry.

Operational Review - 07-SEP-95

Revenues advanced 18% in the first half of 1995, aided by a weaker dollar and strength in Europe. Price increases contributed to wider margins and, despite higher interest and other expenses (net), pretax income surged 92%. Following lower taxes, net income doubled to $0.64 a share. Although sales for the rest of 1995 are expected to grow at a somewhat slower pace, results should continue to benefit as price increases will have a greater impact in the second half.

Stock Performance - 01-SEP-95

In the past 30 trading days, AIN's shares have declined 3%, compared to a 2% rise in the S&P 500. Average trading volume for the past five days was 52,360 shares, compared with the 40-day moving average of 83,045 shares.

Key Stock Statistics

Dividend Rate/Share	0.40	Shareholders	5,200
Shs. outstg. (M)	30.2	Market cap. (B)	$0.758
Avg. daily vol. (M)	0.092	Inst. holdings	69%
Tang. Bk. Value/Share	9.13	Insider holdings	NA
Beta	0.76		

Value of $10,000 invested 5 years ago: $ 14,685

Fiscal Year Ending Dec. 31

	1995	% Change	1994	% Change	1993	% Change
Revenues (Million $)						
1Q	154.1	17%	131.4	-4%	137.0	NM
2Q	166.8	19%	139.6	-7%	149.6	7%
3Q	—	—	145.1	16%	125.6	-12%
4Q	—	—	151.4	13%	133.8	-5%
Yr.	—	—	567.6	4%	546.1	-3%
Income (Million $)						
1Q	7.69	111%	3.65	NM	0.13	NM
2Q	11.63	96%	5.93	30%	4.57	NM
3Q	—	—	5.98	35%	4.42	92%
4Q	—	—	8.38	31%	6.40	NM
Yr.	—	—	23.95	54%	15.52	NM
Earnings Per Share ($)						
1Q	0.26	117%	0.12	NM	0.01	—
2Q	0.38	90%	0.20	18%	0.17	NM
3Q	—	—	0.20	11%	0.18	100%
4Q	—	—	0.28	27%	0.22	NM
Yr.	—	—	0.80	38%	0.58	NM

Next earnings report expected: late October

Albany International

Business Summary - 07-SEP-95

Albany International designs, manufactures and markets paper machine clothing, of which it is the world's largest producer. AIN believes it has a market share of 27% in the U.S. and Canada and 17% in the rest of the world. Contributions by geographic area in 1994 were:

	Revs.	Income
United States	42%	50%
Europe	34%	24%
Canada	10%	12%
Rest of world	14%	14%

Paper machine clothing consists of large continuous belts of custom-designed, engineered fabrics that are installed on paper machines and carry the paper stock through the three primary stages of the paper production process: the forming of paperstock into a continuous sheet as it is being carried on the forming fabric; the pressing of the paper sheet between rollers as it is transported on the press fabrics to partially reduce its water content; and the evaporation of most of the remaining water content as the sheet is held against a series of heated cylinders by the dryer fabrics.

The design and material composition of paper machine clothing can have a considerable effect on the quality of paper products produced and the efficiency of the paper machines on which it is used. AIN also makes other engineered fabrics, which include fabrics for the non-woven industry, corrugator belts, filtration media and rapid roll doors.

Company R & D centers have introduced a broad range of new products that include Dynatex, a multiaxial press fabric with more crossover points than traditional base fabrics, producing an improved uniformity and moisture profile; Dri-Plane III, a dryer fabric that is made with contaminant-resistant monofilament yarns; and InnerDri, a fabric within a fabric that provides complete protection against seam wear, with no seam marking on the paper sheet.

Over the past few years, paper manufacturers have reduced the number of suppliers of paper machine clothing. The company believes this trend has increased opportunities for market leaders, of which only six compete on a global basis. AIN maintains wholly owned manufacturing facilities in 11 countries, as well as a 50% interest in a partnership in South Africa.

Important Developments

Sep. '95—AIN acquired Technical Service Industries, a supplier of engineered fabrics to the non-woven industry, for approximately $9 million.

Capitalization

Long Term Debt: $243,731,000 (6/95).
Class A Com. Stk.: 24,529,151 shs. ($0.001 par).
Class B Com. Stk.: 5,633,427 shs. ($0.001 par).
10 votes per sh.; conv. sh.-for-sh. into Cl. A.
J.S. Standish owns 86%.

Per Share Data ($)

(Year Ended Dec. 31)

	1994	1993	1992	1991	1990	1989
Tangible Bk. Val.	8.37	7.33	6.35	8.73	8.66	8.27
Cash Flow	2.08	2.16	1.89	2.06	1.66	2.84
Earnings	0.80	0.58	0.11	0.41	0.30	1.75
Dividends	0.35	0.35	0.35	0.35	0.35	0.31
Payout Ratio	44%	60%	334%	87%	116%	18%
Prices - High	21¼	19¼	21¼	20	19⅜	23½
- Low	16⅛	14¼	11¼	10	8	15¾
P/E Ratio - High	27	33	NM	49	65	13
- Low	20	25	NM	24	27	9

Income Statement Analysis (Million $)

	1994	%Chg	1993	%Chg	1992	%Chg	1991
Revs.	568	2%	555	-3%	570	2%	560
Oper. Inc.	101	7%	94.0	9%	86.0	-9%	95.0
Depr.	38.2	-9%	42.0	-8%	45.5	8%	42.0
Int. Exp.	17.9	3%	17.3	-16%	20.6	-7%	22.2
Pretax Inc.	41.9	64%	25.5	NM	2.7	-86%	19.4
Eff. Tax Rate	43%	—	39%	—	36%	—	53%
Net Inc.	24.0	55%	15.5	NM	2.7	-74%	10.3

Balance Sheet & Other Fin. Data (Million $)

	1994	1993	1992	1991	1990	1989
Cash	0.2	1.4	4.0	5.1	4.2	11.7
Curr. Assets	314	264	250	254	273	243
Total Assets	721	655	646	675	703	566
Curr. Liab.	113	98.0	109	103	104	99
LT Debt	233	209	240	250	262	145
Common Eqty.	272	244	191	244	243	239
Total Cap.	505	453	431	495	506	421
Cap. Exp.	36.0	66.0	20.0	42.0	111	90.0
Cash Flow	62.2	57.5	48.2	52.3	42.1	72.1

Ratio Analysis

	1994	1993	1992	1991	1990	1989
Curr. Ratio	2.8	2.7	2.3	2.5	2.6	2.5
% LT Debt of Cap.	46.1	46.0	55.7	50.6	47.4	34.6
% Net Inc.of Revs.	4.2	2.8	0.5	1.8	1.4	8.7
% Ret. on Assets	3.5	2.2	0.4	1.5	1.2	8.4
% Ret. on Equity	9.3	6.7	1.2	4.2	3.2	21.1

Dividend Data —Cash dividends on the Class A common were resumed in 1987. Since September 1991, Class A and B have equal rights to dividends.

Amt. of Div. $	Date Decl.	Ex-Div. Date	Stock of Record	Payment Date
0.087	Aug. 09	Aug. 29	Sep. 02	Oct. 03 '94
0.087	Nov. 01	Nov. 28	Dec. 02	Jan. 02 '95
0.087	Feb. 14	Mar. 14	Mar. 20	Apr. 03 '95
0.100	May. 18	May. 26	Jun. 02	Jul. 03 '95
0.100	Aug. 08	Aug. 30	Sep. 01	Oct. 02 '95

Data as orig. reptd.; bef. results of disc. opers. and/or spec. items. Per share data adj. for stk. divs. as of ex-div. date. E-Estimated. NA-Not Available. NM-Not Meaningful. NR-Not Ranked.

Office—1373 Broadway, Albany, NY 12204. **Tel**—(518) 445-2200. **Chrmn**—J.S. Standish. **Pres & CEO**—F.L. McKone. **SVP-CFO**—M.C. Nahl. **VP-Secy & Investor Contact**—Charles B. Buchanan. **Dirs**—P. Bancroft III, T.R. Beecher Jr., C.B. Buchanan, S.I. Landgraf, F.L. McKone, J.S. Standish, A. Stenshamn, B.P. Wright. **Transfer Agent & Registrar**—Harris Trust and Savings Bank, Chicago. **Incorporated** in New York in 1895; reincorporated in Delaware in 1987. **Empl**-5,404. **S&P Analyst:** Justin McCann

STANDARD & POOR'S

STOCK REPORTS

Albemarle Corp.

NYSE Symbol **ALB**

In S&P MidCap 400

11-AUG-95 **Industry:** Chemicals

Summary: This early 1994 Ethyl Corp. spinoff makes specialty chemicals and intermediates for detergents, polymers, electronics, agricultural chemicals and pharmaceuticals.

S&P Opinion: Hold (★★★)

Recent Price • 16⅛ | Yield • 1.4%

52 Wk Range • 16¾-12¼ | 12-Mo. P/E • 20.4

Quantitative Evaluations

Outlook (1 Lowest—5 Highest)
• **NA**

Fair Value
• **NA**

Risk
• **Low**

Earn./Div. Rank
• **NR**

Technical Eval.
• **Bearish** since 5/95

Rel. Strength Rank (1 Lowest—99 Highest)
• **57**

Insider Activity
• **Neutral**

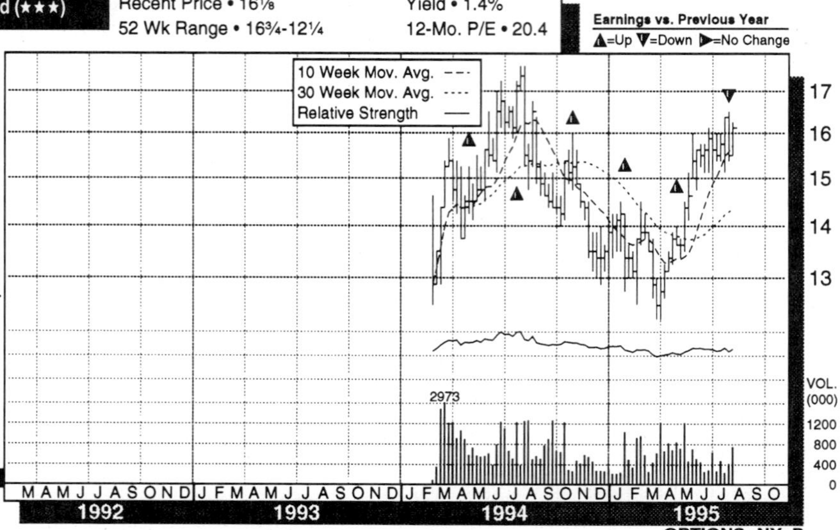

OPTIONS: NY, P

Overview - 11-AUG-95

S&P estimates that sales for Albemarle in 1995 will climb to over $1.2 billion, on continued volume gains and price increases for key intermediate products. Flame retardants will also be boosted by a recently completed capacity expansion and growth of newer products. Although sales of ibuprofen should remain healthy, FDA approval of a new enhanced version may not be received until 1996. Second half earnings will improve from the 1995 first half on the absence of unusual negatives in olefins including a strike at the Belgium plant during April and a plant maintenance shutdown at the Houston facility in June. Lower ethylene costs will also help margins in alpha olefins. However, the French electrolysis business may remain unprofitable due to poor selling prices.

Valuation - 11-AUG-95

This stock has rebounded since the 1995 first quarter on the prospects of better EPS comparisons in the second half. We now project that the company's margins will benefit from ethylene's recent price decline following the price surge since mid-1994. Ethylene is the key raw material for ALB's alpha olefins product line. ALB consumes about 1 billion pounds per year of ethylene, with a 50% exposure to market prices. The stock appears fully valued at a P/E multiple slightly higher than other major specialty chemical companies.

Key Stock Statistics

S&P EPS Est. 1995	0.85	Tang. Bk. Value/Share	8.16
P/E on S&P Est. 1995	19.0	Beta	NA
S&P EPS Est. 1996	1.00	Shareholders	12,500
Dividend Rate/Share	0.22	Market cap. (B)	$ 1.1
Shs. outstg. (M)	66.1	Inst. holdings	46%
Avg. daily vol. (M)	0.090	Insider holdings	NA

Value of $10,000 invested 5 years ago: NA

Fiscal Year Ending Dec. 31

	1995	% Change	1994	% Change	1993	% Change
Revenues (Million $)						
1Q	313.3	29%	242.0	12%	216.0	—
2Q	319.7	18%	269.9	19%	227.0	—
3Q	—	—	282.6	25%	226.0	—
4Q	—	—	286.6	22%	235.0	—
Yr.	—	—	1,081	20%	903.4	-1%
Income (Million $)						
1Q	14.61	49%	9.78	84%	5.31	—
2Q	12.47	-19%	15.33	NM	4.05	—
3Q	—	—	19.50	NM	4.54	—
4Q	—	—	5.70	194%	1.94	—
Yr.	—	—	50.30	NM	15.85	-61%
Earnings Per Share ($)						
1Q	0.22	38%	0.16	78%	0.09	—
2Q	0.19	-24%	0.25	NM	0.06	—
3Q	E0.22	—	0.30	NM	0.08	—
4Q	E0.22	—	0.08	100%	0.04	—
Yr.	E0.85	—	0.79	193%	0.27	-60%

Next earnings report expected: mid October

Albemarle Corp.

Business Summary - 11-AUG-95

Albemarle Corp. is a producer of olefins and derivatives, bromine chemicals and specialty chemicals, serving the polymers, detergent, personal care, petroleum, electronics, pharmaceutical and agricultural markets. The company was spun off to shareholders of Ethyl Corp. in February 1994. Contributions by geographic segment in 1994 (profits in $ million) were:

	Sales	Profits
U.S.	74%	$124.0
Foreign	26%	-15.3

The olefins and derivatives business (45% of 1994 sales) provides intermediates used primarily in the production of plastic polymers, detergent intermediates, synthetic lubricants and fluids.

The specialty chemicals business (28%) produces pharmaceutical intermediates (primarily ibuprofen), agricultural intermediates (pesticides and herbicides), polymer curatives for polyurethane and epoxy polymers, and catalysts (aluminum alkyls) for the production of thermoplastic resins and for chemical synthesis. ALB sold its polysilicon business in July 1994 and the polyimide foams business in September 1994.

Bromine chemicals (27%) include elemental bromine, flame retardants, alkyl bromide and inorganic bromides with applications in chemical synthesis, polymer products, oil and gas well drilling and completion, water purification, soil fumigation and chemical intermediates. ALB operates an electrolysis unit in France that produces caustic potash and potassium carbonates used in the glass, water treatment, detergent and food industries.

Important Developments

Jul. '95—ALB said high ethylene prices continued to suppress earnings from alpha olefins in the second quarter, while there were also the costs of a strike at its Belgium plant in April and a two-week plant maintenance turnaround at its Houston facility in June. Flame retardants continued to post strong performance in all major markets. ALB was experiencing overall good peformances from its businesses and was optimistic that it will see an improvement in the second half of 1995 versus the first half. Separately, ALB sold its electronics materials business (sales of $35 million in 1994) to MEMC Electronics Materials Inc., for an undisclosed amount.

Jan. '95—Results in 1994 included a net gain of $6.7 milion ($0.11 a share) from the sale of ALB's solimide business, while 1993 included net charges of $7.1 million ($0.12 a share).

Capitalization

Long Term Debt: $253,468,000 (6/95).

Per Share Data ($) (Year Ended Dec. 31)

	1994	1993	1992	1991	1990	1989
Tangible Bk. Val.	7.78	NA	6.54	NA	NA	NA
Cash Flow	2.27	NA	NA	NA	NA	NA
Earnings	0.79	0.27	0.68	NA	NA	NA
Dividends	0.15	NA	NA	NA	NA	NA
Payout Ratio	19%	NA	NA	NA	NA	NA
Prices - High	17⅞	NA	NA	NA	NA	NA
- Low	12½	NA	NA	NA	NA	NA
P/E Ratio - High	22	NA	NA	NA	NA	NA
- Low	16	NA	NA	NA	NA	NA

Income Statement Analysis (Million $)

	1994	%Chg	1993	%Chg	1992	%Chg	1991
Revs.	1,081	20%	903	-1%	914	—	NA
Oper. Inc.	187	30%	144	—	NA	—	NA
Depr.	93.3	5%	88.5	—	NA	—	NA
Int. Exp.	15.5	99%	7.8	-52%	16.3	—	NA
Pretax Inc.	89.4	110%	42.5	-25%	56.6	—	NA
Eff. Tax Rate	43%	—	49%	—	29%	—	NA
Net Inc.	51.3	135%	21.8	-46%	40.4	—	NA

Balance Sheet & Other Fin. Data (Million $)

	1994	1993	1992	1991	1990	1989
Cash	32.1	32.5	46.6	NA	NA	NA
Curr. Assets	390	327	340	NA	NA	NA
Total Assets	1,130	1,085	1,110	NA	NA	NA
Curr. Liab.	181	146	146	NA	NA	NA
LT Debt	238	81.0	382	NA	NA	NA
Common Eqty.	545	700	424	NA	NA	NA
Total Cap.	907	899	923	NA	NA	NA
Cap. Exp.	70.4	88.1	NA	NA	NA	NA
Cash Flow	145	110	NA	NA	NA	NA

Ratio Analysis

	1994	1993	1992	1991	1990	1989
Curr. Ratio	2.2	2.2	2.3	NA	NA	NA
% LT Debt of Cap.	26.2	9.1	41.4	NA	NA	NA
% Net Inc.of Revs.	4.7	2.4	4.4	NA	NA	NA
% Ret. on Assets	NA	NA	NA	NA	NA	NA
% Ret. on Equity	NA	NA	NA	NA	NA	NA

Dividend Data (Dividends were initiated in April 1994. A dividend reinvestment plan is available.)

Amt. of Div. $	Date Decl.	Ex-Div. Date	Stock of Record	Payment Date
0.050	Jul. 28	Sep. 09	Sep. 15	Oct. 01 '94
0.050	Nov. 22	Dec. 09	Dec. 15	Jan. 01 '95
0.050	Feb. 23	Mar. 09	Mar. 15	Apr. 01 '95
0.050	Apr. 12	Jun. 13	Jun. 15	Jul. 01 '95
0.055	Jul. 27	Sep. 13	Sep. 15	Oct. 01 '95

Data as orig. reptd.; bef. results of disc. opers. and/or spec. items. Per share data adj. for stk. divs. as of ex-div. date. E-Estimated. NA-Not Available. NM-Not Meaningful. NR-Not Ranked. Quarterly data pro forma.

Office—330 South Fourth St., Richmond, VA 23219. **Tel**—(804) 788-6000. **Chrmn & CEO**—F. D. Gottwald Jr. **Pres**—E. G. Cook. **Vice Chrmn & CFO**—C. B. Walker. **SVP & Secy**—E. W. Elmore. **Investor Contact**—Michael J. Zobrist (504-388-8180). **Dirs**—L. B. Andrew, W. W. Berry, J. C. Carter, Jr., E. G. Cook, E. W. Elmore, B. C. Gottwald, B. C. Gottwald Jr., F. D. Gottwald Jr., J. D. Gottwald, W. M. Gottwald, G. M. Grosvenor, A. W. Helwig, A. B. Lacy, E. J. Rice, S. B. Scott, C. B. Walker. **Transfer Agent & Registrar**—Harris Trust & Savings Bank, Chicago. **Incorporated** in Virginia in 1993. **Empl**-3,700. **S&P Analyst:** Richard O'Reilly, CFA.

STANDARD & POOR'S

STOCK REPORTS

Alexander & Baldwin

NASDAQ Symbol **ALEX**

In S&P MidCap 400

07-AUG-95

Industry: Conglomerate/diversified

Summary: This company provides ocean shipping services between Hawaii and the U.S. Pacific Coast, has interests in real estate, and produces coffee, raw sugar and refined sugar products.

S&P Opinion: Hold (★★★)

Recent Price • 23⅝

52 Wk Range • 26¼-20½

Yield • 3.7%

12-Mo. P/E • 15.8

Quantitative Evaluations

Outlook (1 Lowest—5 Highest)
• **1−**

Fair Value
• **17½**

Risk
• **Low**

Earn./Div. Rank
• **A-**

Technical Eval.
• **Bearish** since 5/95

Rel. Strength Rank (1 Lowest—99 Highest)
• **39**

Insider Activity
• **Neutral**

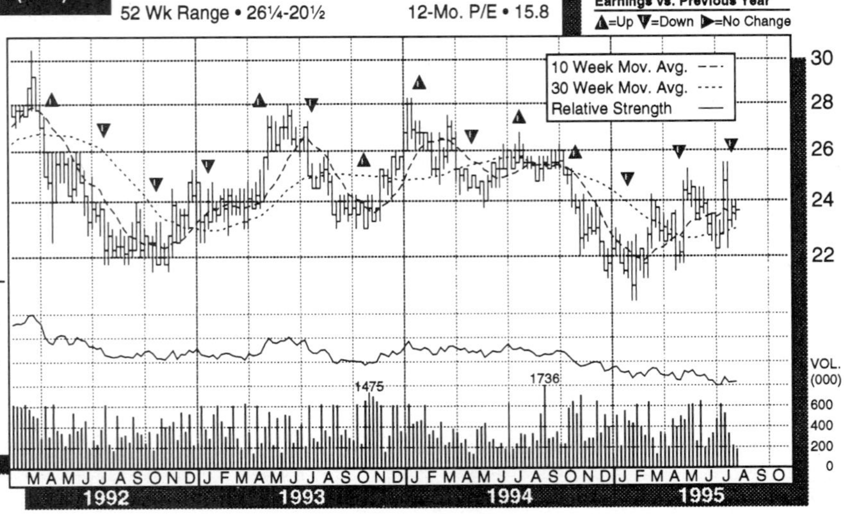

Overview - 07-AUG-95

Shipping profits in 1995 may slip, despite January's rate hike and increased Capital Construction Fund income. Profits are being hampered by lower container volumes, reflecting a sluggish Hawaiian economy and absence of 1994's strike-related windfall. Profits also will be hurt by continued start up losses at Matson's Pacific Coast shuttle and higher fuel costs. Real estate lease income may slip, as ALEX did not replace the Arapahoe Marketplace property (sold at 1994 year-end) with new properties until mid-1995. Income from property sales may decline. Additional losses are anticipated for the food products group, reflecting a continued margin squeeze in sugar refining. Sugar plantation profits (excluding charges) should increase, reflecting better yields on Maui. The absence of container leasing profits will be balanced by reduced interest costs.

Valuation - 07-AUG-95

ALEX's shares have underperformed the stock market for the past few years. A weak Hawaiian economy, a poor performance at ALEX's food products group and fewer property sales have restrained profits. The planned closing of the McBryde sugar plantation in 1996, a vessel-sharing plan with American President Lines, and sale of its container leasing unit at a high price all should help ALEX report sharply higher profits in 1996. Despite these developments, we think ALEX will only be an average market performer near term since, at current prices, the shares amply discount the improvement seen for 1996.

Key Stock Statistics

S&P EPS Est. 1995	1.00	Tang. Bk. Value/Share	13.83
P/E on S&P Est. 1995	23.6	Beta	0.65
S&P EPS Est. 1996	1.90	Shareholders	6,700
Dividend Rate/Share	0.88	Market cap. (B)	$ 1.1
Shs. outstg. (M)	45.5	Inst. holdings	54%
Avg. daily vol. (M)	0.062	Insider holdings	NA

Value of $10,000 invested 5 years ago: $ 7,712

Fiscal Year Ending Dec. 31

	1995	% Change	1994	% Change	1993	% Change
Revenues (Million $)						
1Q	245.7	-3%	254.4	36%	186.4	10%
2Q	270.3	-7%	291.1	37%	212.7	16%
3Q	—	—	301.1	6%	282.8	45%
4Q	—	—	361.5	21%	297.6	45%
Yr.	—	—	1,208	23%	979.5	30%
Income (Million $)						
1Q	5.95	-65%	16.91	-6%	18.05	20%
2Q	3.54	-83%	20.93	21%	17.36	-16%
3Q	—	—	13.81	76%	7.86	101%
4Q	—	—	22.95	-3%	23.72	14%
Yr.	—	—	74.61	11%	66.99	11%
Earnings Per Share ($)						
1Q	0.13	-65%	0.37	-5%	0.39	18%
2Q	0.08	-82%	0.45	22%	0.37	-18%
3Q	E0.30	—	0.30	76%	0.17	113%
4Q	E0.49	—	0.50	-4%	0.52	16%
Yr.	E1.00	—	1.62	12%	1.45	11%

Next earnings report expected: mid October

Alexander & Baldwin

Business Summary - 07-AUG-95

Contributions to operating profits (in $ millions) by business segment in recent years were:

	1994	1993	1992
Shipping	$97.3	$91.2	$97.2
Container leasing	16.6	13.0	12.5
Property leasing	21.2	23.0	21.4
Property sales	18.5	18.6	17.7
Food products	-0.4	12.7	-2.3
Other	3.1	2.4	4.3

Matson Navigation Co. is the principal ocean carrier operating between Hawaii and the U.S. Pacific Coast. Service is also provided to Johnston Island and the Marshall Islands. Matson's fleet at 1994 year-end consisted of 13 ships or barges, two tugs, 17,900 containers and 6,800 chassis. In 1994, Matson transported 240,612 containers (24-foot equivalent units), versus 232,539 units in 1993, and 116,762 automobiles against 109,221.

In June 1995, ALEX sold its Matson Leasing Co. for $360 million. Matson manages a fleet of 112,000 containers through a network of 92 depots.

Through A&B Hawaii, Inc. ALEX manages 92,854 acres of land of which 98% are in Hawaii and used primarily for agricultural purposes or watershed and conservation lands. Some 1,350 acres of Hawaiian lands are zoned for urban use with another 9,800 acres seen having development potential. On the U.S. mainland, ALEX owns 2,068 acres, primarily in California. ALEX's rental portfolio consists of 2,550,000 sq. ft. of commercial and industrial properties (75% on the U.S. mainland) and ground leases on 11,000 acres.

ALEX is the largest producer of raw sugar in Hawaii. In 1994 ALEX produced 223,490 tons of sugar at two plantations. ALEX also grows coffee on 4,000 acres in Hawaii. California and Hawaiian Sugar Co. is the leading refiner and marketer of sugar products in the western U.S.

Important Developments

Jul. '95—Profits for 1995's second quarter included a $17.2 million ($0.38 a share) net gain on the sale of ALEX's Matson Leasing Co. unit. ALEX sold Matson to XTRA Corp. for $360 million. Profits from continuing operations for the second quarter were reduced by $5.1 million ($0.11) to reflect costs related to the planned phase out of sugar production at McBryde Sugar Co. on Kauai by September 1996. McBryde accounted for some 8% of sugar production in 1994.

Apr. '95—Matson Navigation agreed to buy six containerships from American President Lines (APL) and other assets for $166 million. Additionally, Matson plans to launch a vessel sharing arrangement with APL beginning early 1996.

Capitalization

Long Term Debt: $518,000,000 (6/95).

Per Share Data ($)

(Year Ended Dec. 31)

	1994	1993	1992	1991	1990	1989
Tangible Bk. Val.	13.85	12.65	12.07	15.90	14.75	13.12
Cash Flow	3.90	3.56	3.15	3.66	3.88	5.54
Earnings	1.62	1.45	1.31	2.00	2.50	4.38
Dividends	0.88	0.88	0.88	0.88	0.86	0.80
Payout Ratio	54%	61%	67%	44%	34%	18%
Prices - High	28¼	28	30½	29½	38	39½
- Low	21¼	22½	21½	21	19	31¼
P/E Ratio - High	17	19	23	15	15	9
- Low	13	16	16	11	8	7

Income Statement Analysis (Million $)

	1994	%Chg	1993	%Chg	1992	%Chg	1991
Revs.	1,185	23%	962	32%	731	1%	721
Oper. Inc.	223	NM	222	14%	195	-6%	207
Depr.	105	7%	97.8	15%	85.4	11%	76.7
Int. Exp.	31.4	NM	31.4	NM	31.6	-4%	32.8
Pretax Inc.	113	NM	113	35%	84.0	-37%	133
Eff. Tax Rate	34%	—	41%	—	28%	—	31%
Net Inc.	75.0	12%	67.0	10%	61.0	-34%	92.0

Balance Sheet & Other Fin. Data (Million $)

	1994	1993	1992	1991	1990	1989
Cash	9.6	32.7	21.1	18.9	47.5	23.6
Curr. Assets	277	285	162	144	170	127
Total Assets	1,933	1,912	1,686	1,555	1,371	1,139
Curr. Liab.	205	212	116	118	119	93.0
LT Debt	562	627	615	527	407	296
Common Eqty.	633	587	559	735	683	605
Total Cap.	1,544	1,512	1,456	1,395	1,211	1,004
Cap. Exp.	104	152	234	273	266	250
Cash Flow	180	165	146	169	179	257

Ratio Analysis

	1994	1993	1992	1991	1990	1989
Curr. Ratio	1.4	1.3	1.4	1.2	1.4	1.4
% LT Debt of Cap.	36.4	41.5	42.3	37.8	33.6	29.5
% Net Inc.of Revs.	6.3	7.0	8.3	12.8	17.1	32.7
% Ret. on Assets	3.9	3.7	3.7	6.3	9.2	19.1
% Ret. on Equity	12.3	11.7	9.3	13.0	17.9	35.1

Dividend Data (Cash has been paid each year since 1903. A "poison pill" stock purchase rights plan was adopted in 1989. A dividend reinvestment plan is available.)

Amt. of Div. $	Date Decl.	Ex-Div. Date	Stock of Record	Payment Date
0.220	Oct. 27	Nov. 04	Nov. 10	Dec. 01 '94
0.220	Jan. 26	Feb. 13	Feb. 17	Mar. 02 '95
0.220	Apr. 27	May. 05	May. 11	Jun. 01 '95
0.220	Jun. 22	Aug. 01	Aug. 03	Sep. 07 '95

Data as orig. reptd.; bef. results of disc. opers. and/or spec. items. Per share data adj. for stk. divs. as of ex-div. date. E-Estimated. NA-Not Available. NM-Not Meaningful. NR-Not Ranked.

Office—822 Bishop St., P.O. Box 3440, Honolulu, HI 96801. **Tel**—(808) 525-6611. **Chrmn & CEO**—J. C. Couch. **VP & Secy**—M. J. Marks. **VP-Treas & CFO**—G. R. Rogers. **VP & Investor Contact**—John B. Kelley (808-525-8422). **Dirs**—M. J. Chun, J. C. Couch, L. E. Denlea Jr., W. A. Dods Jr., C. G. King, C. R. McKissick, C. B. Mulholland, R. G. Reed III, M. G. Shaw, C. M. Stockholm. **Transfer Agents & Registrars**—Chemical Trust Co. of California, San Francisco; Chemical Bank, NYC. **Incorporated** in Hawaii in 1900. **Empl**-3,581. **S&P Analyst:** Stephen R. Klein

STANDARD & POOR'S

STOCK REPORTS

Allegheny Ludlum

NYSE Symbol **ALS**
In S&P MidCap 400

29-SEP-95 **Industry:** Steel-Iron

Summary: This company is the leading producer of stainless steel in the U. S. and also manufactures silicon electrical and specialty steel alloy.

S&P Opinion: Hold (★★★)

Recent Price • 20⅝
52 Wk Range • 23-18
Yield • 2.4%
12-Mo. P/E • 15.7

Quantitative Evaluations
Outlook (1 Lowest—5 Highest)
• 5⁻
Fair Value
• 24⅛
Risk
• Average
Earn./Div. Rank
• NR

Technical Eval.
• **Bullish** since 7/95
Rel. Strength Rank (1 Lowest—99 Highest)
• 23
Insider Activity
• Neutral

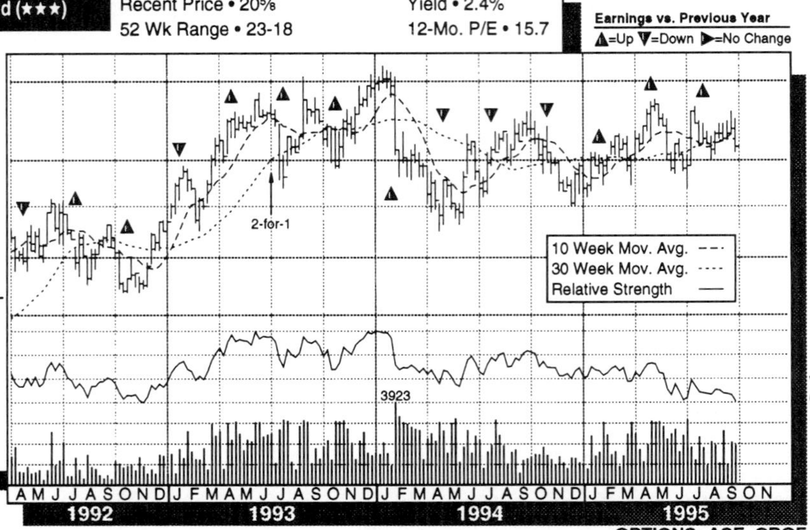

OPTIONS: ASE, CBOE

Overview - 29-SEP-95

Assuming 2.6% GDP growth in 1996 and a lower level of imports, we anticipate an 11% sales gain in 1996. Most of the increase will reflect a 10% rise in revenue per ton; volume will probably rise by just 1.0%. Continued high operating rates, an improved product mix, higher prices and only a moderate increase in raw material costs should offset increased depreciation and permit an expansion of margins. The improved product mix will result from greater sales of specialty strip and less emphasis on sales of 409. Aided by flat or lower interest expense and a flat tax rate, earnings should increase again in 1996. The company's ongoing efforts to increase sales of value-added products together with strong secular growth prospects for stainless steel will boost long-term sales and earnings prospects.

Valuation - 29-SEP-95

Despite its strong near term earnings outlook we are maintaining our hold rating on Allegheny Ludlum. We remain concerned that service centers have not completed paring inventories and that this could cause prices and volume to level off. While the company's more positive assessment of inventories may prove us wrong, we prefer to err on the side of caution. Through late September ALS was up 9.3%, versus a 24% gain in the S&P 500. The shares have performed in line with its peers. Longer term we view ALS as a strong buy based on its very strong sales and earnings prospects as well as its rock solid finances.

Key Stock Statistics

S&P EPS Est. 1995	1.60	Tang. Bk. Value/Share	3.59
P/E on S&P Est. 1995	12.9	Beta	1.21
S&P EPS Est. 1996	1.85	Shareholders	2,800
Dividend Rate/Share	0.48	Market cap. (B)	$ 1.4
Shs. outstg. (M)	69.1	Inst. holdings	47%
Avg. daily vol. (M)	0.160	Insider holdings	NA

Value of $10,000 invested 5 years ago: $ 17,883

Fiscal Year Ending Dec. 31

	1995	% Change	1994	% Change	1993	% Change
Revenues (Million $)						
1Q	395.3	26%	313.9	8%	289.9	10%
2Q	390.5	127%	172.2	-38%	279.5	7%
3Q	—	—	262.3	NM	262.3	3%
4Q	—	—	328.5	22%	268.4	4%
Yr.	—	—	1,077	-2%	1,100	6%
Income (Million $)						
1Q	28.85	59%	18.12	NM	18.27	61%
2Q	34.47	NM	-29.18	NM	18.60	61%
3Q	—	—	10.33	-38%	16.56	30%
4Q	—	—	18.95	9%	17.33	54%
Yr.	—	—	18.21	-74%	70.76	51%
Earnings Per Share ($)						
1Q	0.41	58%	0.26	-7%	0.28	65%
2Q	0.49	NM	-0.41	NM	0.28	60%
3Q	E0.32	129%	0.14	-44%	0.25	32%
4Q	E0.38	41%	0.27	8%	0.25	47%
Yr.	E1.60	NM	0.26	-75%	1.06	49%

Next earnings report expected: late October

Allegheny Ludlum

Business Summary - 29-SEP-95

Allegheny Ludlum is one of the largest U.S. producers of stainless steel, and a major producer of silicon electrical steels and other high technology alloys. Contributions in recent years:

	1994	1993	1992	1991
Stainless	78%	81%	80%	77%
Silicon electrical	13%	14%	16%	17%
Other specialty steel alloys	9%	5%	4%	6%

Stainless steel products are sold in the form of sheet, strip and plate, as well as stampings and welded tubing. Stainless steel sheet is used in commercial kitchens, fast food restaurants, food processing equipment, chemical processing equipment, and storage tanks. Stainless steel strip is used in flatware, cookware, dishwashers, ranges, vacuum bottles, and automotive components. Stainless steel plate is used primarily in industrial equipment that requires cleanliness or corrosion-resistant capabilities, including food processing equipment, pulp and paper equipment, chemical equipment, and power generation equipment.

Silicon electrical steel products are used primarily in applications in which electrical conductivity and magnetic properties are important. Users of ALS's silicon electrical steel products include manufacturers of transformers, motors, generators and communications equipment.

ALS produces tool steel, high temperature alloys, electronic and thermostatic alloys, and other spcial alloys in flat-rolled form. These alloys are used primarily in applications that require high strength, hardness, heat resistance and special magnetic, electronic or expansion characteristics.

Principal markets in 1994 included steel service centers (43%), energy (14%), transportation (12%), converters (8%), commercial and domestic products (7%), exports (7%), industrial machinery and equipment (3%), construction and contractor products (3%), communications and electronic equipment (1%), and other (2%).

Important Developments

Sep. '95—ALS said that it expected that 1995's third quarter earnings would be the best since 1989's third quarter when the company earned $0.50. The company noted the earnings for the second half of the year are generally weaker that the first but said that strong first half momenutm was continuing into the second half.

Jul. '95—ALS repurchased 1.7 million of its shares through July 21 as part of its expanded buyback program. A total of 4.6 million shares of the 8.0 million authorized have been repurchased to date.

Capitalization

Long Term Debt: $131,807,000 (7/2/95), incl. $100 million of 5.875% debs. due 2002, conv. into com. at $20.25 a sh.

Per Share Data ($) (Year Ended Dec. 31)

	1994	1993	1992	1991	1990	1989
Tangible Bk. Val.	3.22	3.65	3.91	5.55	5.36	4.90
Cash Flow	0.80	1.51	1.13	1.02	1.38	2.29
Earnings	0.26	1.06	0.71	0.63	1.04	1.98
Dividends	0.48	0.47	0.44	0.44	0.43	0.35
Payout Ratio	185%	44%	62%	70%	41%	18%
Prices - High	24⅞	24⅜	18⅜	14⅝	17⅛	13⅞
- Low	17	17	13¾	10⅛	9⅛	9¾
P/E Ratio - High	96	23	26	23	17	7
- Low	65	16	19	16	9	5

Income Statement Analysis (Million $)

	1994	%Chg	1993	%Chg	1992	%Chg	1991
Revs.	1,077	-2%	1,100	6%	1,036	3%	1,005
Oper. Inc.	80.0	-40%	134	29%	104	4%	100
Depr.	38.2	27%	30.0	9%	27.6	5%	26.2
Int. Exp.	8.5	-2%	8.7	9%	8.0	48%	5.4
Pretax Inc.	33.0	-72%	119	51%	79.0	10%	72.0
Eff. Tax Rate	45%	—	41%	—	41%	—	43%
Net Inc.	18.0	-75%	71.0	51%	47.0	15%	41.0

Balance Sheet & Other Fin. Data (Million $)

	1994	1993	1992	1991	1990	1989
Cash	11.0	99	124	2.6	5.7	79.1
Curr. Assets	396	470	460	385	427	458
Total Assets	1,095	1,174	871	764	793	785
Curr. Liab.	170	211	160	192	229	220
LT Debt	133	139	138	48.5	52.8	67.8
Common Eqty.	362	403	257	364	352	329
Total Cap.	495	542	395	476	463	449
Cap. Exp.	NA	50.4	26.0	36.5	57.0	35.4
Cash Flow	56.0	101	74.0	67.0	92.0	155

Ratio Analysis

	1994	1993	1992	1991	1990	1989
Curr. Ratio	2.3	2.2	2.9	2.0	1.9	2.1
% LT Debt of Cap.	26.9	25.6	35.0	10.2	11.4	15.2
% Net Inc.of Revs.	1.7	6.4	4.5	4.1	6.4	11.3
% Ret. on Assets	1.6	6.7	5.7	5.3	8.8	18.0
% Ret. on Equity	4.8	20.8	15.1	11.5	20.4	48.4

Dividend Data —Dividends were initiated in 1987.

Amt. of Div. $	Date Decl.	Ex-Div. Date	Stock of Record	Payment Date
0.120	Aug. 11	Aug. 25	Aug. 31	Sep. 30 '94
0.120	Nov. 11	Nov. 23	Nov. 30	Dec. 30 '94
0.120	Feb. 02	Feb. 22	Feb. 28	Apr. 03 '95
0.120	May. 19	May. 24	May. 31	Jul. 03 '95
0.120	Aug. 10	Aug. 29	Aug. 31	Oct. 02 '95

Data as orig. reptd.; bef. results of disc. opers. and/or spec. items. Per share data adj. for stk. divs. as of ex-div. date. E-Estimated. NA-Not Available. NM-Not Meaningful. NR-Not Ranked.

Office—1000 Six PPG Place, Pittsburgh, PA 15222-5479. **Tel**—(412) 394-2800. **Chrmn**—R. P. Simmons. **Pres & CEO**—A. H Aronson. **SVP-CFO**—J. L. Murdy. **Secy**— J. D. Walton. **Investor Contact**—Hubert W. Delano. **Dirs**—A. H. Aronson, R. P. Bozzone, P. S. Brentlinger, C. F. Fetterolf, T. Marshall, W. C. McClelland, J. L. Murdy, R. K. Pitler, A. Pol. C. J. Queenan, J. E. Rohr, R. P. Simmons, G. W. Tippins, S. C. Wheelwright. **Transfer Agent & Registrar**—Mellon Bank, Pittsburgh. **Incorporated** in Pennsylvania in 1979. **Empl**-6,000. **S&P Analyst:** Leo Larkin

STANDARD & POOR'S

STOCK REPORTS

Allegheny Power System

NYSE Symbol **AYP**

In S&P MidCap 400

20-OCT-95 **Industry:** Utilities-Electric

Summary: This integrated coal-based electric utility system serves contiguous areas primarily in Pennsylvania, West Virginia and Maryland.

S&P Opinion: Hold (★★★)

Recent Price • 26⅜ | 52 Wk Range • 26⅝-20¼ | Yield • 6.2% | 12-Mo. P/E • 13.6

Quantitative Evaluations

Outlook (1 Lowest—5 Highest)
• 1-

Fair Value
• 23⅜

Risk
• Low

Earn./Div. Rank
• A-

Technical Eval.
• Bearish since 2/95

Rel. Strength Rank (1 Lowest—99 Highest)
• 76

Insider Activity
• Neutral

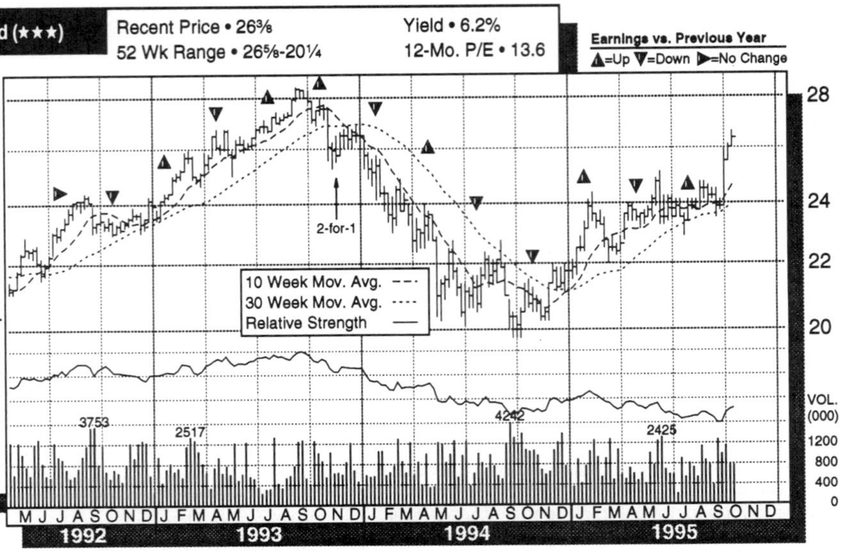

Overview - 20-OCT-95

Higher earnings in 1995 and beyond should reflect rate orders received in May, August and November 1994, as well as pending rate increases. Favorable conclusions by state regulatory commissions for each utility subsidiary regarding AYP's strategy to comply with Phase I of the Clean Air Act Amendments of 1990 removed major uncertainty concerning extensive cost recovery. Although regulatory lags may cause short delays in recovering compliance costs, they should not materially hurt 1995 revenues or earnings. The first nine months of 1995 have already seen an upturn in income, as retail revenues rose. Annual interest expense will be reduced as a result of a 1993 debt refinancing program. The company has also moved to become more competitive, and is actively seeking opportunities for its investment subsidiary.

Valuation - 20-OCT-95

The shares appear adequately valued, with limited upside potential. The yield and P/E are about average for the industry. Recent rate increases should assure an ongoing, attractive revenue stream, as evidenced by current income growth. Utilities have been a traditional proxy for interest rates, but this may be altered in the new environment of competition mandated by the National Energy Policy Act of 1992. Although AYP is not exempt from change, it has made efforts to keep costs low and is diversifying through its AYP Capital unit. Future growth will hinge on these twin efforts.

Key Stock Statistics

S&P EPS Est. 1995	1.96	Tang. Bk. Value/Share	17.48
P/E on S&P Est. 1995	13.5	Beta	0.32
S&P EPS Est. 1996	2.00	Shareholders	66,800
Dividend Rate/Share	1.64	Market cap. (B)	$ 3.2
Shs. outstg. (M)	120.0	Inst. holdings	41%
Avg. daily vol. (M)	0.172	Insider holdings	NA

Value of $10,000 invested 5 years ago: $ 18,677

Fiscal Year Ending Dec. 31

	1995	% Change	1994	% Change	1993	% Change
Revenues (Million $)						
1Q	700.0	NM	697.3	13%	614.7	-1%
2Q	603.1	7%	561.2	2%	552.4	NM
3Q	672.1	14%	591.1	1%	583.3	6%
4Q	—	—	602.1	4%	581.2	NM
Yr.	—	—	2,452	5%	2,332	1%
Income (Million $)						
1Q	76.13	NM	75.90	12%	67.61	NM
2Q	42.69	8%	39.40	-11%	44.36	4%
3Q	58.24	17%	49.80	-9%	54.53	23%
4Q	—	—	54.70	11%	49.26	NM
Yr.	—	—	219.8	2%	215.8	6%
Earnings Per Share ($)						
1Q	0.64	-2%	0.65	9%	0.60	-4%
2Q	0.36	9%	0.33	-15%	0.39	1%
3Q	0.49	17%	0.42	-10%	0.46	19%
4Q	E0.47	2%	0.46	10%	0.42	-3%
Yr.	E1.96	5%	1.86	-1%	1.88	3%

Next earnings report expected: mid February

Allegheny Power System

Business Summary - 18-OCT-95

Allegheny Power System, Inc. is an electric utility holding company that derives substantially all of its income from the electric utility operations of its subsidiaries, Monongahela Power Co., The Potomac Edison Co., and West Penn Power Co. These subsidiaries jointly own Allegheny Generating Co., which owns and sells to its parents 840 mw of pumped-storage generating capacity. The properties of the subsidiaries are located in Maryland (20.5% of 1994 revenues), Ohio (1.6%), Pennsylvania (44.5%), Virginia (5.4%) and West Virginia (28.0%), are interconnected, and are operated as a single integrated electric utility system, which is interconnected with all neighboring utility sysytems. The subsidiaries serve more than 1.3 million customers in an area of 29,100 sq. mi. with a population of 2.9 million. The 23 largest communities served have populations ranging from about 10,900 to 40,100. Electric revenues in recent years were derived as follows:

	1994	1993	1992	1991
Residential	35%	35%	32%	31%
Commercial	19%	18%	17%	17%
Industrial	30%	29%	28%	26%
Other	16%	18%	23%	26%

The system has generating capacity totaling 8,369 mw, of which 8,070 is owned. Owned capacity is 88% coal fired, 10% pumped-storage, and 1% hydroelectric. The weighted average age of the coal-fired stations at December 31, 1994, was 24.6 years. The system's all-time peak load of 7,280 mw occured on February 6, 1995. The peak load in 1994 was 7,153 mw and in 1993, it was 6,678 mw. No additional generating capacity should be needed until the late 1990s or beyond.

Construction spending in 1994 totaled $508 million, and is put at $341 million and $284 million for 1995 and 1996, respectively. AYP has budgeted these funds for major pollution control and transmission projects.

To meet the challenges of a newly competitive utility market, AYP Capital, Inc. was formed in 1994. An unregulated, wholly owned subsidiary, it is to pursue opportunities that are directly related to the company's core utility business.

Important Developments

Oct. '95—Revenues advanced in the nine months ending September 30, 1995, year to year, reflecting previously reported rate increases and, in the summer, extreme weather conditions. Net income was impacted by a $0.07 per share restructuring charge for separation costs associated with staff reductions related to ongoing company re-engineering efforts.

Capitalization

Long Term Debt: $2,258,250,000 (6/95).
Subsidiary Pfd. Stk.: $170,086,000.

Per Share Data ($) (Year Ended Dec. 31)

	1994	1993	1992	1991	1990	1989
Tangible Bk. Val.	17.11	16.49	15.58	15.32	15.07	14.80
Earnings	1.86	1.88	1.83	1.80	1.80	1.86
Dividends	1.64	1.63	1.61	1.58	1.58	1.55
Payout Ratio	88%	87%	88%	88%	88%	83%
Prices - High	26½	28⅜	24⅜	23¼	21⅛	21¼
- Low	19¾	23⅜	20¾	17½	17	17⅞
P/E Ratio - High	14	15	13	13	12	11
- Low	11	12	11	10	9	10

Income Statement Analysis (Million $)

	1994	%Chg	1993	%Chg	1992	%Chg	1991
Revs.	2,452	5%	2,332	1%	2,307	1%	2,282
Depr.	224	7%	210	6%	198	4%	190
Maint.	242	5%	231	9%	211	3%	204
Fxd. Chgs. Cov.	3.0	7%	2.8	1%	2.8	-6%	3.0
Constr. Credits	19.6	-9%	21.5	22%	17.6	123%	7.9
Eff. Tax Rate	35%	—	37%	—	34%	—	36%
Net Inc.	220	2%	216	6%	204	5%	194

Balance Sheet & Other Fin. Data (Million $)

	1994	1993	1992	1991	1990	1989
Gross Prop.	7,587	7,177	6,680	6,256	5,986	5,721
Cap. Exp.	508	574	488	338	322	303
Net Prop.	5,057	4,788	4,440	4,162	4,040	3,914
Capitalization:						
LT Debt	2,178	2,008	1,952	1,748	1,642	1,578
% LT Debt	48	47	48	47	46	46
Pfd.	325	276	278	264	266	266
% Pfd.	7.10	6.50	6.90	7.10	7.50	7.70
Common	2,059	1,956	1,828	1,686	1,632	1,582
% Common	45	46	45	46	46	46
Total Cap.	5,693	5,280	4,645	4,271	4,103	3,998

Ratio Analysis

	1994	1993	1992	1991	1990	1989
Oper. Ratio	84.2	83.9	84.6	84.7	85.1	85.1
% Earn. on Net Prop.	7.9	8.1	8.3	8.5	8.6	8.7
% Ret. on Revs.	9.0	9.3	8.8	8.5	8.3	8.6
% Ret. On Invest.Cap	7.2	7.8	8.2	8.5	8.6	8.7
% Return On Com.Eqty	10.9	11.4	11.6	11.7	11.9	12.5

Dividend Data —Dividends have been paid since 1935. A dividend reinvestment plan is available.

Amt. of Div. $	Date Decl.	Ex-Div. Date	Stock of Record	Payment Date
0.410	Dec. 01	Dec. 06	Dec. 12	Dec. 30 '94
0.410	Mar. 02	Mar. 07	Mar. 13	Mar. 31 '95
0.410	Jun. 01	Jun. 08	Jun. 12	Jun. 30 '95
0.410	Sep. 07	Sep. 14	Sep. 18	Sep. 29 '95

Data as orig. reptd.; bef. results of disc opers. and/or spec. items. Per share data adj. for stk. divs. as of ex-div. date. E-Estimated. NA-Not Available. NM-Not Meaningful. NR-Not Ranked.

Office—12 East 49th St., New York, NY 10017. **Tel**—(212) 752-2121. **Chrmn & CEO**—K. Bergman. **Pres & COO**—A. J. Noia. **Secy**—E. M. Beck. **SVP-Fin**—S. I. Garnett. **VP, Treas & Investor Contact**—Nancy Campbell (212-836-4305). **Dirs**—E. Baum, W. L. Bennett, K. Bergman, W. F. Holland, P. E. Lint, E. H. Malone, F. A. Metz, Jr., A. J. Noia, S. H. Rice, G. E. Sarsten, P. L. Shea. **Transfer Agents & Registrars**—Chemical Bank, NYC; Chemical Trust Co. of California. **Incorporated** in Maryland in 1925. **Empl-**6,061. **S&P Analyst:** Michael C. Barr

STANDARD & POOR'S

STOCK REPORTS

Altera Corp.

NASDAQ Symbol **ALTR**

In S&P MidCap 400

01-SEP-95

Industry: Electronics/Electric

Summary: Altera is a leader in high-performance, high-density programmable logic devices (HPLDs) and associated computer-aided engineering logic development tools.

S&P Opinion: Accumulate (★★★★)

Recent Price • 63⅛

52 Wk Range • 64¾-13⅛

Yield • Nil

12-Mo. P/E • 85.3

Quantitative Evaluations

Outlook (1 Lowest—5 Highest)

• **1+**

Fair Value

• **53⅝**

Risk

• **High**

Earn./Div. Rank

• **B-**

Technical Eval.

• **Bullish** since 10/94

Rel. Strength Rank (1 Lowest—99 Highest)

• **94**

Insider Activity

• **Neutral**

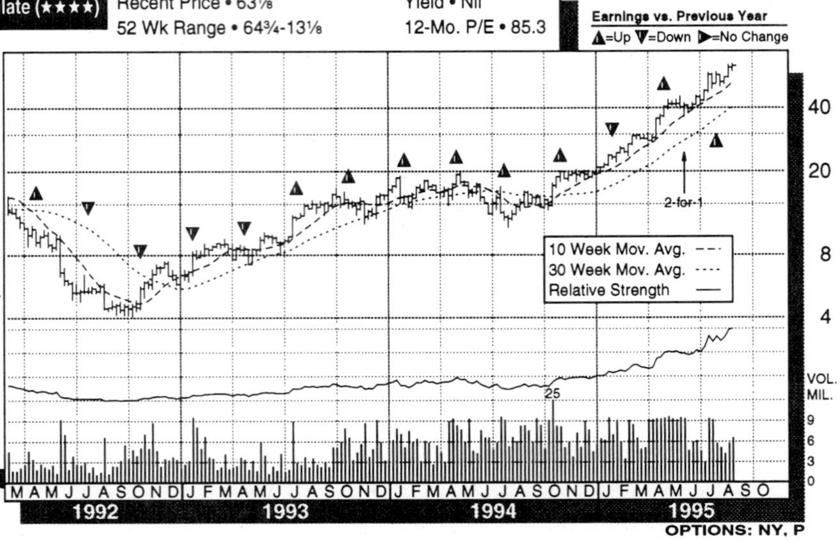

OPTIONS: NY, P

Overview - 20-JUL-95

Sales for 1995 are expected to increase more than 30%, aided by the acquisition of Intel's programmable logic business and an aggressive new product introduction program. The gain should also be assisted by continued industry growth, which, although likely to slow from 1994's projected growth rate of close to 30%, is still expected to exceed 15%. Continued strong growth in the United States and in most Asian markets should be complemented by a rebound in the Japanese market, which has been depressed for a prolonged period. Capacity is not an immediate problem as Altera's long-term relationship with wafer suppliers has made it a priority customer.

Valuation - 01-SEP-95

We recommend accumulation of Altera on the continued bright outlook for semiconductor manufacturers. Second quarter sales were up 96%, year to year, and 23% sequentially. We believe the company can maintain 30%+ earnings growth in the coming years as HPLDs encroach on gate arrays and Altera continues to boost its market share in the HPLD sector. Future results will benefit from the growing demand for the Flex 8000 and Max 7000 products, which accounted for 68% of incoming orders in the latest period, up from 54% in the first quarter. We have increased our 1996 estimate $0.25 to $2.50 a share due to an incease in capacity stemming from the expansion of Altera's agreement with a major supplier and the company's shift to 8-inch wafers and 0.5 micron linewidths.

Key Stock Statistics

S&P EPS Est. 1995	1.75	Tang. Bk. Value/Share	4.51
P/E on S&P Est. 1995	36.1	Beta	2.35
S&P EPS Est. 1996	2.50	Shareholders	400
Dividend Rate/Share	Nil	Market cap. (B)	$ 2.7
Shs. outstg. (M)	43.3	Inst. holdings	90%
Avg. daily vol. (M)	1.109	Insider holdings	NA

Value of $10,000 invested 5 years ago: $ 183,636

Fiscal Year Ending Dec. 31

	1995	% Change	1994	% Change	1993	% Change
Revenues (Million $)						
1Q	75.04	72%	43.51	50%	29.10	-2%
2Q	92.16	96%	47.06	42%	33.07	44%
3Q	—	—	49.05	32%	37.07	64%
4Q	—	—	59.17	44%	41.08	58%
Yr.	—	—	198.8	42%	140.3	38%
Income (Million $)						
1Q	15.10	97%	7.66	144%	3.14	-41%
2Q	19.63	137%	8.29	80%	4.61	53%
3Q	—	—	8.45	35%	6.27	NM
4Q	—	—	-9.79	NM	7.18	NM
Yr.	—	—	14.61	-31%	21.20	84%
Earnings Per Share ($)						
1Q	0.33	86%	0.18	140%	0.08	-40%
2Q	0.43	121%	0.19	77%	0.11	47%
3Q	E0.46	130%	0.20	33%	0.15	NM
4Q	E0.53	NM	-0.22	NM	0.17	NM
Yr.	E1.75	NM	0.34	-33%	0.51	80%

Next earnings report expected: mid October

Altera Corp.

Business Summary - 01-SEP-95

Altera Corporation designs, develops and markets programmable logic integrated circuits and associated computer engineering development software and hardware.

The company's semiconductor products, generally known as Complex Programmable Logic Devices (CPLDs), are standard logic chips that customers configure for specific end-use applications using the company's proprietary software. The company's customers enjoy the benefits of low development costs, short lead times and standard product inventories when compared to application-specific integrated circuits (ASICs) and high density and low power consumption when compared to transistor transistor logic (TTL).

Altera currently markets seven families of CMOS programmable logic in over 500 package/chip combinations. The use of low power CMOS technology, in contrast to the older bipolar technology, permits higher chip densities and allows system designers to use programmable logic chips to address applications that had previously required ASICs.

A cornerstone of the company's strategy is the market penetration of its low-cost (beginning at under $5,000) proprietary software design tools in order to achieve an installed base of design sites that may generate future chip orders.

The company does not manufacture semiconductor wafers, but has them made by leading producers pursuant to technology exchange and foundry agreements. This eliminates the expense and inflexibility of in-house wafer fabrication.

Customers are in a broad range of market segments, including telecommunications (49% of 1994 sales), industrial (17%), computers (18%) and military (9%).

In 1994, exports accounted for approximately 48% of sales, with Europe representing 21% and Japan 19%.

R&D spending totaled $45.9 million (including $23.7 million of R&D in process related to the acquisition of Intels' programmable logic device division) in 1994 which represented 23% of sales.

Important Developments

Jul. '95—ALTR noted that the largest sales increase in its record second quarter occurred in the international arena, with the Japanese and European markets particularly strong.

Jun. '95—The company completed a $230 million private placement of convertble subordinated notes due in 2002. The notes are non-callable for three years and represent a maximum of 4,494,821 of common shares. Net proceeds of $224.8 million are earmarked for expansion.

Capitalization

Long Term Debt: $230,000,000 of conv. sub. debt due 2002 and convert. at $51.17 per share. (6/95).

Per Share Data ($)

(Year Ended Dec. 31)

	1994	1993	1992	1991	1990	1989
Tangible Bk. Val.	3.67	2.98	2.38	2.05	1.57	1.23
Cash Flow	0.50	0.69	0.46	0.57	0.45	0.36
Earnings	0.34	0.51	0.28	0.43	0.33	0.28
Dividends	Nil	Nil	Nil	Nil	Nil	Nil
Payout Ratio	Nil	Nil	Nil	Nil	Nil	Nil
Prices - High	$21\frac{5}{8}$	$16\frac{7}{8}$	18	$14\frac{1}{4}$	$7\frac{1}{2}$	$4\frac{3}{4}$
- Low	$10\frac{7}{8}$	6	$4\frac{1}{8}$	$4\frac{5}{8}$	$3\frac{3}{8}$	$2\frac{3}{8}$
P/E Ratio - High	63	33	64	33	22	17
- Low	32	12	15	10	10	9

Income Statement Analysis (Million $)

	1994	%Chg	1993	%Chg	1992	%Chg	1991
Revs.	199	42%	140	39%	101	-6%	107
Oper. Inc.	60.1	51%	39.7	66%	23.9	-25%	32.0
Depr.	7.0	-10%	7.8	6%	7.3	27%	5.8
Int. Exp.	Nil	—	Nil	—	Nil	—	Nil
Pretax Inc.	31.5	NM	31.4	74%	18.0	-35%	27.8
Eff. Tax Rate	54%	—	33%	—	36%	—	36%
Net Inc.	14.6	-31%	21.2	84%	11.5	-35%	17.8

Balance Sheet & Other Fin. Data (Million $)

	1994	1993	1992	1991	1990	1989
Cash	92.6	81.6	50.6	40.1	23.3	26.0
Curr. Assets	177	129	85.6	72.2	51.9	45.8
Total Assets	214	156	115	102	75.0	56.0
Curr. Liab.	559	34.1	19.1	20.8	13.9	8.8
LT Debt	Nil	Nil	Nil	Nil	Nil	Nil
Common Eqty.	158	122	95.6	81.5	61.0	46.6
Total Cap.	158	122	95.6	81.5	61.0	46.6
Cap. Exp.	10.5	5.5	6.0	7.8	8.1	5.6
Cash Flow	21.6	29.0	18.9	23.6	18.0	14.2

Ratio Analysis

	1994	1993	1992	1991	1990	1989
Curr. Ratio	3.2	3.8	4.5	3.5	3.7	5.2
% LT Debt of Cap.	Nil	Nil	Nil	Nil	Nil	Nil
% Net Inc.of Revs.	7.3	15.1	11.4	16.7	17.1	18.3
% Ret. on Assets	7.7	15.6	10.6	19.9	20.3	21.2
% Ret. on Equity	10.2	19.4	12.9	24.8	24.6	27.2

Dividend Data —No cash dividends have been paid on the common shares. A 2-for-1 common stock split was paid in May 1995.

Amt. of Div. $	Date Decl.	Ex-Div. Date	Stock of Record	Payment Date
2-for-1	Apr. 26	Jun. 01	May. 10	May. 31 '95

Data as orig. reptd.; bef. results of disc. opers. and/or spec. items. Per share data adj. for stk. divs. as of ex-div. date. E-Estimated. NA-Not Available. NM-Not Meaningful. NR-Not Ranked.

Office—2610 Orchard Pkwy., San Jose, CA 95134-2020. **Tel**—(408) 894-7000. **Chrmn, Pres & CEO**—R. Smith. **VP-Fin & CFO**—N. Sarkisian. **VP & Investor Contact**—Thomas Nicoletti. **Dirs**—M. A. Ellison, P. Newhagen, R. W. Reed, R. Smith, W. Terry. **Transfer Agent & Registrar**—Bank of Boston, Boston, MA. **Incorporated** in California in 1984. **Empl**-667. **S&P Analyst:** Steven A. Jaworski

Alumax Inc.

NYSE Symbol AMX Options on ASE, Phil (Jan-Apr-Jul-Oct) In S&P MidCap 400

Price	Range	P–E Ratio	Dividend	Yield	S&P Ranking	Beta
Aug. 10'95	1995					
34¼	37⅞–23¾	8	None	None	NR	NA

Summary

The third largest U.S. aluminum company, Alumax produces and markets primary aluminum ingot and billet and is a major fabricator of value-added aluminum products used in the architectural, building and construction, transportation, container and packaging, and consumer durables industries. Earnings will advance substantially in 1995, reflecting higher average annual aluminum prices, cost savings on consolidation of operations and a more profitable product mix.

Current Outlook

Earnings for 1996 are projected at $5.25 a share, versus 1995's estimated earnings of $4.90, which includes an unusual gain of $1.99.

Initiation of common dividends is not expected.

Sales for 1995 should increase as lower aluminum shipments due to closure of some operations are offset by higher average aluminum prices. Strong U.S. and European demand and a recovery in Japanese demand will absorb a continued heavy level of Russian aluminum exports and a gradual reopening of idled industry capacity. Aided by higher prices, cost savings and a more favorable product mix, margins are likely to expand. Sales and earnings should advance again in 1996.

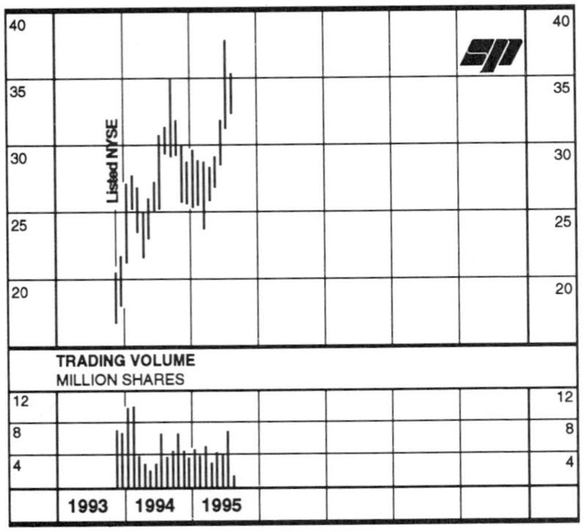

Net Sales (Million $)

Quarter:	1995	1994	1993	[1]1992
Mar.	699	597	566	548
Jun.	721	687	598	599
Sep.		698	591	642
Dec.		772	592	642
		2,755	2,347	2,431

Sales in the six months ended June 30, 1995, rose 11%, year to year, as higher prices outweighed a decline in shipments. Margins widened, and with a $128.8 million gain on the sale of assets, pretax income of $227.7 million replaced a $4.8 million pretax loss. After taxes at 34.3%, versus tax credits of $1.4 million, there was net income of $149.6 million versus a $6.2 million net loss. After preferred dividends, share earnings were $3.22, versus a share loss of $0.24.

Common Share Earnings ($)

Quarter:	1995	1994	1993	[1]1992
Mar.	2.41	d0.25	d0.52	---
Jun.	0.82	0.01	d0.40	---
Sep.	E0.75	0.17	d0.48	---
Dec.	E0.92	0.90	d1.84	---
	E4.90	0.84	d3.24	d1.56

Important Developments

Aug. '95— AMX announced that it will build a $26 million aluminum plate production plant in Lancaster, Pa. The new plant will increase production of its MIC-6 cast aluminum plate by more than 50% and enable the company to expand its markets in Europe and enter Asian markets.

Jul. '95— AMX reported earnings of $0.82 on a 5.0% increase in sales for 1995's second quarter, versus $0.01 a year ago. AMX attributed the gain to improved market conditions. It noted, however, that it had experienced a slowdown in metal shipments in the latter part of the second quarter as a result of customers reducing inventories. It added that current world market prospects suggest that demand for aluminum in 1995 and beyond will be strong.

Next earnings report expected in mid-October.

Per Share Data ($)

Yr. End Dec. 31	1994	1993	[1]1992
Tangible Bk. Val.	**23.45**	22.16	[2]27.74
Cash Flow	**3.28**	d0.86	0.97
Earnings[3]	**0.84**	d3.24	d1.56
Dividends	**Nil**	Nil	NA
Payout Ratio	**Nil**	Nil	NA
Prices—High	**35**	21¾	NA
Low	**21¼**	16¾	NA
P/E Ratio—	**42–25**	NM	NA

Data as orig. reptd.; prior to 1993 data as reptd. in joint proxy statement-prospectus dated Sep. 24, 1993. **1.** Pro forma. **2.** As of Jun. 30, 1993. **3.** Bef. spec. item(s) of -0.09 in 1993. d-Deficit. E-Estimated. NM-Not Meaningful. NA-Not Available.

Income Data (Million $)

Year Ended Dec. 31	Revs.	Oper. Inc.	% Oper. Inc. of Revs.	Cap. Exp.	Depr.	Int. Exp.	Net Bef. Taxes	Eff. Tax Rate	[5]Net Inc.	% Net Inc. of Revs.	Cash Flow
1994	**2,755**	**243.0**	**8.8**	**80**	**109**	**78.2**	**[4]72.0**	**35.5%**	**47.0**	**1.7**	**147.0**
1993	2,347	88.1	3.8	58	[3]107	79.2	[4]d187.0	NM	d135.0	NM	d36.4
[1]1992	2,431	78.5	3.2	181	112	[2]49.8	d81.3	NM	d68.8	NM	42.6

Balance Sheet Data (Million $)

Dec. 31	Cash	Curr. Assets	Curr. Liab.	Curr. Ratio	Total Assets	% Ret. on Assets	Long Term Debt	Common Equity	Total Cap.	% LT Debt of Cap.	% Ret. on Equity
1994	**93.0**	**1,171**	**501**	**2.3**	**2,923**	**1.6**	**852**	**1,045**	**2,086**	**40.8**	**3.7**
1993	128.0	1,103	531	2.1	2,959	NM	925	983	2,090	44.3	NM
[6]1992	57.6	953	520	1.8	2,837	NA	805	1,224	2,031	39.6	NA

Data as reptd. in joint proxy statement-prospectus dated Sep. 24, 1993. **1.** Pro forma. **2.** Net of int. inc. **3.** Refl. acctg. change. **4.** Incl. equity in earns. of nonconsol. subs. **5.** Bef. spec. item(s). **6.** As of Jun. 30, 1993, pro forma. d-Deficit. NM-Not Meaningful. NA-Not Available.

Business Summary

Alumax is an integrated aluminum company engaged in the production and sale of primary aluminum, semi-fabricated products such as sheet, plate, extrusions and foil, and diverse fabricated products. It is the third largest U.S. aluminum company and operates over 100 plants and other facilities in 30 states, Canada and Western Europe. Segment contributions in 1994:

	Sales	Profits
Primary & semi–fabricated...	64%	81%
Fabricated products............	36%	19%

International sales (excluding Canada) accounted for 13% of total sales and 21% of operating profit in 1994.

Primary aluminum is produced by the reduction of alumina through an electrolytic process. Aluminum reduction facilities produce t-ingot, extrusion billet, slab and a variety of additional products. These are consumed by both the company's downstream operations and third-party customers, in rolling mills, extrusion plants, foundries and remelt operations. Alumax has interests in five reduction plants: wholly owned Lauralco (Quebec), 75%-owned Intalco (Washington) and Eastalco (Maryland), 73.33%-owned Mt. Holly (South Carolina) and 24.95%-owned ABI (Quebec). Alumax's share of 1994 output was 680,674 metric tons, or 88% of its share of 773,000 tons of annual capacity.

Semi-fabricated products include sheet, plate, circles and blanks, which are used for building products, transportation products, consumer durables, machinery and equipment and in other industrial applications, as well as non-heat treatable sheet to the automotive, truck and marine markets, all of which are produced by Alumax Mill Products; extrusions for the building and construction, transportation, machinery and equipment and electrical markets, manufactured by Alumax Extrusions; and aluminum foil for the flexible packaging, converter, foodservice and pharmaceutical markets, produced by Alumax Foils.

Fabricated products consist of architectural aluminum products and a wide range of products for the manufactured housing, recreational vehicle, agricultural and utility building, residential construction and home improvement markets. Architectural aluminum products designed, manufactured and marketed by the Kawneer subsidiary include curtainwall, store front and entrance systems, windows and facings, as well as decorative aluminum products that are anodized or painted. Alumax's fabricated product operations are co nducted on a worldwide basis, with facilities and service centers located in the U.S., Canada, Western Europe and North Africa.

Alumax holds interests in the Rosario Companies, which own several Mexican mining operations involving principally silver, gold, lead and zinc. In March 1994, Alumax sold for $75 million its 37% of Aztec Mining Co. Ltd., which owns interests in various mining operations in Australia involving gold, zinc, lead, copper and coal.

Finances

In December 1994, Alumax filed a shelf registration with the SEC in lieu of a proposed public offering of eight million shares of its common stock. AMX attributed its decision to convert the offering to a shelf registration to the significant improvement in its operating performance in 1994 and in part to then depressed market conditions.

Alumax expects that capital spending will be about $270 million in 1995.

Dividend Data

In December 1994, Alumax said it does not intend to pay any cash dividends on its common stock until industry fundamentals and the company's earnings improve significantly.

Capitalization

Long Term Debt: $830,900,000 (3/95).

$4 Series A Cum. Preferred Stock: 2,333,320 shs. ($50 liquid. pref.); ea. conv. into 4.1148 com.; privately held.

Common Stock: 44,646,756 shs. ($0.01 par). Institutions hold about 86%. Shareholders of record: 11,632.

Office—5655 Peachtree Parkway, Norcross, GA 30092-2812. **Tel**—(404) 246-6600. **Chrmn & CEO**—A. Born. **Sr VP, CFO & Treas**—L. B. Frost. **VP-Secy**—H. M. Feeney. **Investor Contact**—R. Daniel Loh. **Dirs**—A. Born, H. Brown, L. D. Brown, P. Des Marais II, A. P. Gammie, J. C. Huntington Jr., T. G. Labrecque, W. L. Landau, P. W. MacAvoy, A. Wexler. **Transfer Agent & Registrar**—Chemical Bank, NYC. **Incorporated** in Delaware in 1973. **Empl**—14,000.

 Leo J. Larkin

American Financial Group

NYSE Symbol AFG Options on Phila In S&P MidCap 400

Price	Range	P–E Ratio	Dividend	Yield	S&P Ranking	Beta
Oct. 10'95	1995					
29	32⅛–22⅞	16	1.00	3.4%	B	1.25

Summary

American Financial Group (formerly American Premier Group) was formed as a holding company for both American Premier Underwriters (APU) and American Financial Corp. (AFC), and completed the acquisition of AFC and APU in April 1995. American Financial Group provides specialty and multi-line property and casualty insurance, and sells tax-deferred annuities. Entities controlled by Carl Lindner hold about 51%.

Business Summary

American Financial Group, Inc. (formerly American Premier Group, Inc.), was formed in December 1994, and in April 1995, became the holding company for American Premier Underwriters (APU) and American Financial Corp. (AFC). Following a restructuring effort which began in late 1992, American Premier Underwriters, Inc., formerly Penn Central Corp., underwrites automobile insurance for high-risk individuals, as well as workers' compensation insurance, through subsidiaries.

American Financial Corp. manages and operates property and casualty insurance businesses as three major sectors: specialty lines, non-standard automobile, and mainstreet personal and commercial insurance. AFC conducts the majority of its property and casualty insurance business through its wholly-owned subsidiary, Great American Insurance Company, while its other major operating business is conducted through its 81%-owned subsidiary American Annuity Group, Inc., which issues tax-deferred annuities. AFG also holds significant minority ownership interests in Chiquita Brands International, Inc., a leading international marketer of quality fresh and processed food products; and Citicasters Inc., which owns and operates radio and television broadcast stations.

On a pro forma basis, total invested assets at December 31, 1994, amounted to $9.7 billion, of which 88% were insurance company investments. The majority, approximately $8.3 billion, derive from American Financial's investment portfolio, three-fifths of which were invested in marketable securities. The company seeks to optimize investment income while building the value of its portfolio, placing empashis on long-term performance. Significant portions of equity, and to a lesser extent, fixed income investments are concentrated in a relatively limited number of major positions. Approximately 95% of the bonds and redeemable preferred stocks held by AFG were rated "investment grade" at June 30, 1995.

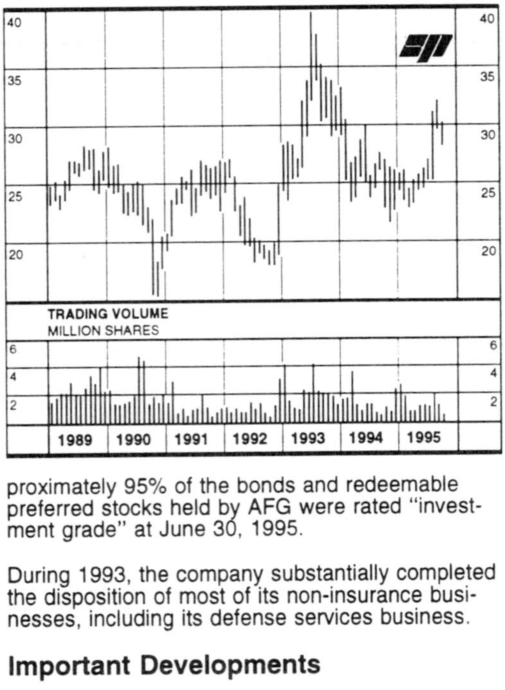

During 1993, the company substantially completed the disposition of most of its non-insurance businesses, including its defense services business.

Important Developments

Jun. '95— Since AFG began operations as a holding company in April, over $500 million of debt of American Premier Underwriters and American Financial Corp., has been retired, primarily from internal funds. This has resulted in a reduction of the company's overall debt by approximately one-third. The Lindner family holds approximately 50.9% of AFG's outstanding common shares.

Next earnings report expected in late October.

Per Share Data ($)

Yr. End Dec. 31	1994	1993	1992	1991	[1]1990	[1]1989	[1]1988	1987	[1]1986	[1]1985
Tangible Bk. Val.	**24.94**	27.73	23.85	22.59	20.97	22.76	23.78	21.58	24.20	18.87
Earnings[2]	**0.02**	5.03	1.32	1.30	1.60	2.48	1.33	0.45	1.93	1.38
Dividends	**0.910**	0.850	0.810	0.710	0.530	0.420	0.100	0.025	0.025	Nil
Payout Ratio	**46%**	17%	60%	53%	29%	16%	8%	5%	1%	Nil
Prices—High	**33¼**	39¾	27⅛	27	28¼	28⅜	24⅜	34¼	31⅜	29⅜
Low	**21⅝**	23½	18	19¼	15⅜	22⅞	19⅞	18½	25⅜	22½
P/E Ratio—	**NM**	8–5	21–14	21–15	18–10	11–9	18–15	77–42	16–13	21–16

Data as orig. reptd. Adj. for stk. div(s). of 100% Mar. 1988. **1.** Reflects merger or acquisition. **2.** Bef. results of disc. opers. of -0.01 in 1994, -0.22 in 1993, -0.04 in 1992, -1.25 in 1991, +0.13 in 1988, +0.02 in 1987 and spec. item(s) of +5.20 in 1992. NA-Not Available. NM-Not Meaningful.

Income Data (Million $)

Year Ended Dec. 31	Premium Income	Net Invest. Inc.	Oth. Revs.	Total Revs.	Property & Casualty Underwriting Ratios Loss	Expense	Comb.	Net Bef. Taxes	Net Oper. Inc.	[6]Net Inc.	—% Return On— Revs.	Equity
1994	**1,557**	**130**	**80**	**[4]1,767**	**75.9**	**23.9**	**99.8**	**41**	**NA**	**0.8**	**NM**	**NM**
[1]1993	NA	NA	NA	[4]1,763	NA	NA	NA	189	NA	243.0	NA	NA
1992	NA	NA	NA	1,797	NA	NA	NA	[5]102	NA	62.0	NA	NA
[2]1991	NA	NA	NA	1,669	NA	NA	NA	[5]105	NA	63.0	NA	NA
[3]1990	NA	NA	NA	2,154	NA	NA	NA	[5]155	NA	98.0	NA	NA
[3]1989	NA	NA	NA	1,725	NA	NA	NA	[5]241	NA	174.0	NA	NA
[1]1988	NA	NA	NA	1,547	NA	NA	NA	[5]146	NA	94.0	NA	NA
[2]1987	NA	NA	NA	1,421	NA	NA	NA	[5]78	NA	35.0	NA	NA
[1]1986	NA	NA	NA	2,388	NA	NA	NA	[5]292	NA	154.0	NA	NA
[1]1985	NA	NA	NA	2,527	NA	NA	NA	[5]213	NA	111.0	NA	NA

Balance Sheet Data (Million $)

Dec. 31	Cash & Equiv.	Premiums Due	Investment Assets Bonds	Stocks	Loans	Total	% Invest. Yield	Deferred Policy Costs	Total Assets	Debt	Common Equity
1994	**83**	**344**	**2,421**	**Nil**	**Nil**	**2,684**	**NA**	**92.1**	**4,194**	**507**	**1,549**
1993	477	NA	NA	NA	NA	NA	NA	NA	4,050	NA	1,722
1992	294	NA	NA	NA	NA	NA	NA	NA	3,531	NA	1,503
1991	15	NA	NA	NA	NA	NA	NA	NA	3,383	NA	1,479
1990	35	NA	NA	NA	NA	NA	NA	NA	3,547	NA	1,634
1989	969	NA	NA	NA	NA	NA	NA	NA	3,178	NA	1,827
1988	758	NA	NA	NA	NA	NA	NA	NA	2,400	NA	1,770
1987	1,072	NA	NA	NA	NA	NA	NA	NA	2,493	NA	1,657
1986	1,079	NA	NA	NA	NA	NA	NA	NA	2,933	NA	2,092
1985	193	NA	NA	NA	NA	NA	NA	NA	2,874	NA	1,826

Data as orig. reptd. **1.** Excludes discontinued operations and reflects merger or acquisition. **2.** Excludes discontinued operations. **3.** Reflects merger or acquisition. **4.** Incl. other inc. **5.** Incl. equity in earns. of nonconsol. subs. **6.** Bef. results of disc. opers and spec. item(s). NA-Not Available. NM-Not Meaningful.

Revenues (Million $)

Quarter:	1995	1994	1993	1992
Mar.	433	358	370	432
Jun.	1,006	470	427	450
Sep.		477	444	449
Dec.		463	523	467
		1,767	1,763	1,797

On a pro forma basis, revenues in the six months ended June 30, 1995 rose 6.5%, year to year, to $2.0 billion. Earnings before extraordinary items were $86.0 million, compared to $19.0 million. After an extraordinary gain of $1.0 million, versus a charge of $16.0 million, net earnings of $87.0 million were significantly higher than the $3.0 million earned in the prior year.

Common Share Earnings ($)

Quarter:	1995	1994	1993	1992
Mar.	0.37	d1.16	0.67	0.28
Jun.	0.63	0.35	1.60	0.30
Sep.		0.52	1.77	0.30
Dec.		0.31	1.03	0.43
		0.02	5.03	1.32

d-Deficit.

Dividend Data

Dividends were initiated in 1986 on an annual basis and were put on a quarterly basis in 1988.

Amt. of Divd. $	Date Decl.	Ex-divd. Date	Stock of Record	Payment Date
0.25	Dec. 12	Dec. 23	Dec. 30	Jan. 13'95
0.25	Mar. 23	Mar. 27	Mar. 31	Apr. 14'95
0.25	Jun. 15	Jun. 28	Jun. 30	Jul. 14'95
0.25	Sep. 18	Sep. 27	Sep. 29	Oct. 13'95

Finances

In mergers completed in April 1995, AFG issued 71.4 million of its common shares to acquire both American Financial Corp. and American Premier Underwriters.

Capitalization

Total Debt: $1,234,898,000 (6/95).

Minority Interest: $294,442,000.

Common Stock: 52,738,000 shs. ($1 par).
Institutions hold approximately 20%; the Lindner family holds about 51%.
Shareholders: 13,563 of record (3/94).

Office—One East Fourth St., Cincinnati, OH 45202. **Tel**—(513) 579-6600. **Chrmn & CEO**—C. H. Lindner. **Pres**—C. H. Lindner III. **SVP & Investor Contact**—Neil Hahl. **SVP-Treas**—F. J. Runk. **SVP-Secy**—R. W. Olson. **Dirs**—T. H. Emmerich, J. E. Evans, T. M. Hunt, C. H. Lindner, C. H. Lindner III, K. E. Lindner, S. C. Lindner, W. R. Martin, A. W. Martinelli. **Transfer Agent & Registrar**—Co. itself. **Incorporated** in Pennsylvania in 1846; reincorporated in Pennsylvania in 1987. **Empl**—5,100.

 Thomas C. Ferguson

STANDARD & POOR'S

STOCK REPORTS

American Power Conversion

NASDAQ Symbol **APCC**

In S&P MidCap 400

30-AUG-95

Industry: Electronics/Electric

Summary: APCC manufactures uninterruptible power supply (UPS) products that protect data in personal computers and other electronic devices from disruptions or surges in electric power.

S&P Opinion: Avoid (★★)

Recent Price • 16½
52 Wk Range • 25⅞-14⅜

Yield • Nil
12-Mo. P/E • 19.6

Quantitative Evaluations

Outlook
(1 Lowest—5 Highest)
• **5-**

Fair Value
• **30⅛**

Risk
• **High**

Earn./Div. Rank
• **B**

Technical Eval.
• **Bearish** since 8/95

Rel. Strength Rank
(1 Lowest—99 Highest)
• **4**

Insider Activity
• **Unfavorable**

Earnings vs. Previous Year
▲=Up ▼=Down ▶=No Change

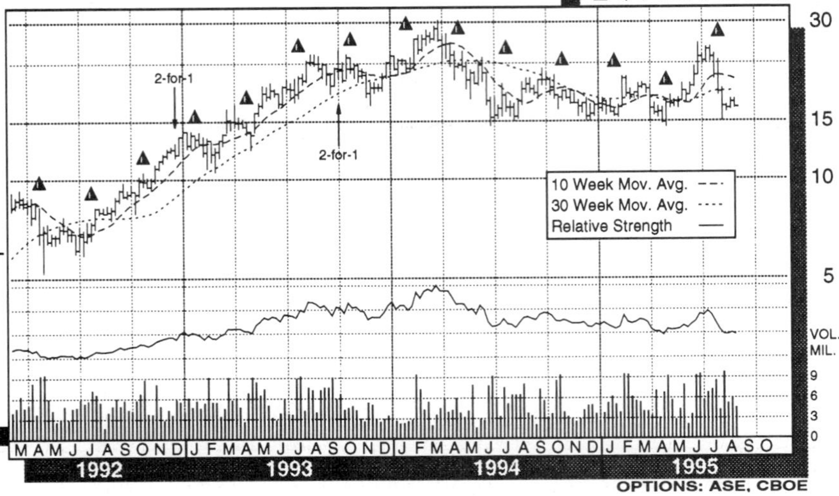

OPTIONS: ASE, CBOE

Overview - 29-JUN-95

Demand for the company's UPS products continues to be driven by the domestic proliferation of local area networks (LANs) and related equipment. This trend is expected to continue in 1995, supplemented by expansion into the European and Latin American markets. A new domestic facility, located in Florida, will roughly double U.S. manufacturing capacity and act as a supply source for Latin America. Although there is competition for UPS products in the marketplace, the favorable reputation and popularity of the company's products have allowed it, up untill now, to solidify its market position without heavy sales price discounts.

Valuation - 23-AUG-95

In previous reports we cited sagging gross margins as a point of concern. In reporting second quarter results, APCC noted that margins slid once again. Expenses related to a defective component were reported as the primary culprit for the decline. In previous periods, the company noted the negative effect of start-up costs and producton efficiencies in its two recently opened plants. We believe that lower margins will likely be recorded at these facilities in the immediate future until the top of the learning curve is reached. Another area of concern is the sharp rise in inventory levels. The buildup appears excessive despite the seasonally strong second half and could cause problems in the weak winter months. Another point of note is the fact that insiders sold almost $10 million of stock in June.

Key Stock Statistics

S&P EPS Est. 1995	0.93	Tang. Bk. Value/Share	2.72
P/E on S&P Est. 1995	17.7	Beta	2.20
S&P EPS Est. 1996	1.15	Shareholders	3,900
Dividend Rate/Share	Nil	Market cap. (B)	$ 1.5
Shs. outstg. (M)	93.0	Inst. holdings	55%
Avg. daily vol. (M)	1.445	Insider holdings	NA

Value of $10,000 invested 5 years ago: $ 229,485

Fiscal Year Ending Dec. 31

	1995	% Change	1994	% Change	1993	% Change
Revenues (Million $)						
1Q	109.2	46%	74.62	55%	48.13	56%
2Q	122.6	42%	86.36	52%	56.99	71%
3Q	—	—	103.8	48%	70.11	58%
4Q	—	—	113.5	51%	75.06	53%
Yr.	—	—	378.3	51%	250.3	59%
Income (Million $)						
1Q	18.27	35%	13.56	65%	8.20	78%
2Q	17.38	11%	15.59	48%	10.52	86%
3Q	—	—	19.19	42%	13.51	80%
4Q	—	—	22.93	40%	16.33	63%
Yr.	—	—	71.27	47%	48.56	75%
Earnings Per Share ($)						
1Q	0.20	33%	0.15	67%	0.09	80%
2Q	0.19	12%	0.17	48%	0.11	77%
3Q	E0.25	19%	0.21	40%	0.15	76%
4Q	E0.29	16%	0.25	39%	0.18	64%
Yr.	E0.93	21%	0.77	45%	0.53	71%

Next earnings report expected: late October

American Power Conversion

Business Summary - 22-AUG-95

American Power Conversion Corp. designs, develops, manufactures and markets a line of uninterruptible power supply (UPS) products, electrical surge protection devices, power conditioning products and associated software and interface cables that are used with personal computers, engineering workstations, file servers, communications and internetworking equipment and other sensitive electronic devices that rely on electric utility power.

As microcomputers have become increasingly important to the business strategy of many organizations, it has become necessary to ensure that data stored in, and operating instructions for, microcomputers are protected from fluctuations in utility power. A UPS protects against these disturbances by providing continuous power automatically and virtually instantaneously after the electric power supply is interrupted or sags, as well as line filtering and protection against surges while the electric utility is operating.

The company's strategy has been to design and manufacture products that incorporate high performance and quality at competitive prices. In addition, its products are designed to be aesthetically pleasing and appropriate for use in an office environment. Products are engineered and extensively tested for compatibility with nearly all common microcomputers and small minicomputers. Over 50 different UPS models are offered, ranging in capacity from 200 to 5,000 volt-amps and in end-user list price from $119 to $6,499.

APCC markets its products through a domestic and international network of computer distributors, computer dealers and catalog merchandisers. It also sells directly to some large value-added resellers, which integrate the company's products into specialized microcomputer systems and then market turnkey systems to selected vertical markets, and to manufacturers. Ingram Micro D Corp. accounted for about 11% of sales in 1994 and 1993. Sales outside of North America accounted for 35% of the company's net sales in 1994, up from 31% in 1993.

Important Developments

Jul. '95—APCC said that it expects sales to PC users to increase in the near future as the Windows 95 launch delivers multitasking to PCs, allowing users to open several applications at once, multiplying the risk of data loss or disruption. Such losses are relatively small in older DOS-based systems.

Capitalization

Long Term Debt: None (6/95).

Per Share Data ($) (Year Ended Dec. 31)

	1994	1993	1992	1991	1990	1989
Tangible Bk. Val.	2.29	1.45	0.87	0.51	0.31	0.19
Cash Flow	0.83	0.56	0.32	0.19	0.11	0.08
Earnings	0.77	0.53	0.31	0.17	0.11	0.08
Dividends	Nil	Nil	Nil	Nil	Nil	Nil
Payout Ratio	Nil	Nil	Nil	Nil	Nil	Nil
Prices - High	30½	24¾	14⅜	7⅛	2 7/16	1 1/16
- Low	14½	10½	5¼	1 13/16	⅝	5/16
P/E Ratio - High	40	47	47	41	23	15
- Low	19	20	17	10	6	4

Income Statement Analysis (Million $)

	1994	%Chg	1993	%Chg	1992	%Chg	1991
Revs.	378	51%	250	59%	157	68%	93.6
Oper. Inc.	112	44%	77.9	74%	44.7	78%	25.1
Depr.	6.1	104%	3.0	64%	1.8	102%	0.9
Int. Exp.	Nil	—	Nil	—	0.1	-82%	0.4
Pretax Inc.	109	44%	75.9	76%	43.1	78%	24.2
Eff. Tax Rate	35%	—	36%	—	36%	—	36%
Net Inc.	71.3	47%	48.6	75%	27.8	78%	15.6

Balance Sheet & Other Fin. Data (Million $)

	1994	1993	1992	1991	1990	1989
Cash	41.5	47.8	21.0	12.2	3.0	6.1
Curr. Assets	211	135	82.7	46.9	29.5	20.7
Total Assets	265	159	99	58.2	35.9	24.7
Curr. Liab.	50.3	25.4	21.5	14.0	7.1	6.0
LT Debt	Nil	Nil	Nil	Nil	3.0	3.5
Common Eqty.	212	132	76.0	43.7	25.6	15.1
Total Cap.	215	134	77.0	44.2	28.7	18.6
Cap. Exp.	35.9	10.9	6.4	5.9	3.2	2.9
Cash Flow	77.4	51.5	29.6	16.5	10.0	6.5

Ratio Analysis

	1994	1993	1992	1991	1990	1989
Curr. Ratio	4.2	5.3	3.9	3.3	4.1	3.4
% LT Debt of Cap.	Nil	Nil	Nil	Nil	10.6	18.9
% Net Inc.of Revs.	18.8	19.4	17.6	16.6	15.8	17.0
% Ret. on Assets	33.4	37.2	35.2	32.9	30.7	31.3
% Ret. on Equity	41.2	46.1	46.1	44.7	45.7	50.2

Dividend Data —No cash dividends have been paid on the public shares. A two-for-one stock split was effected September 24, 1993. The shares were split two-for-one in December 1992 and December 1991, three-for-one in October 1990, five-for-four in 1989, and five-for-one in 1988.

Data as orig. reptd.; bef. results of disc. opers. and/or spec. items. Per share data adj. for stk. divs. as of ex-div. date. E-Estimated. NA-Not Available. NM-Not Meaningful. NR-Not Ranked.

Office—132 Fairgrounds Rd., West Kingston, RI 02892. **Tel**—(401) 789-5735. **Chrmn, Pres & CEO**—R. B. Dowdell, Jr. **CFO**—D. Muir. **VP & Secy**—E. E. Landsman. **Investor Contact**—Debbie Grey. **Dirs**—R. B. Dowdell, Jr., J. D. Gerson, E. E. Landsman, E. F. Lyon, N. E. Rasmussen. **Transfer Agent & Registrar**—Bank of Boston. **Incorporated** in Massachusetts in 1981. **Empl**-914. **S&P Analyst:** Steven A. Jaworski

STANDARD & POOR'S

STOCK REPORTS

American President

NYSE Symbol **APS**
In S&P MidCap 400

18-OCT-95 **Industry:** Shipping/shipbuilding

Summary: This leading containership operator serves trans-Pacific and intra-Asia routes and provides doublestack service in the US. Limited service between Europe and Asia began in 1995.

S&P Opinion: Accumulate (★★★★) Recent Price • 25½ 52 Wk Range • 31¾-21 Yield • 1.5% 12-Mo. P/E • 11.4

Quantitative Evaluations
Outlook (1 Lowest—5 Highest) • **4+**
Fair Value • **27**
Risk • **Average**
Earn./Div. Rank • **B**

Technical Eval. • **Bullish** since 4/94
Rel. Strength Rank (1 Lowest—99 Highest) • **23**
Insider Activity • **Neutral**

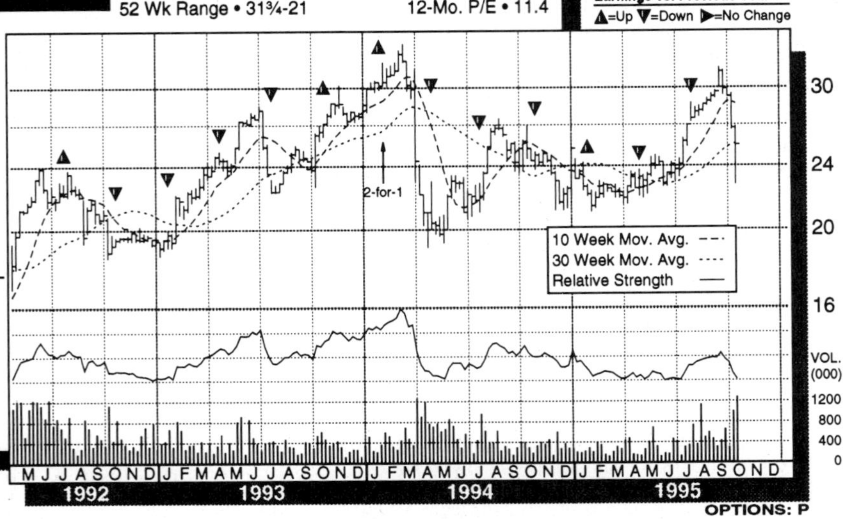

Overview - 18-OCT-95

Container volumes in 1996 will benefit from continued good gains in the Pacific Rim, and the ramp up of new services between Europe and Asia and Asia and the U.S. East coast. Despite some rate pressure on certain trans-Pacific cargo, margins should widen reflecting improved operating efficiency of new vessels and vessel sharing arrangements under the Global Alliance and with Matson Navigation. Savings also will be realized from the reflagging of certain vessels and staff reductions following the overhaul of financial and operating systems. Aiding comparisons will be the absence of disruptions due to the Kobe earthquake in 1995. Doublestack will benefit from increased demand from motor carriers. High interest and depreciation charges should be offset by some 5.6% fewer shares and absence of preferred dividends.

Valuation - 18-OCT-95

Shares of this shipping line have gyrated like a runaway rollercoaster in 1995. APS soared during the summer as it bought 4,820,00 of its shares at an average cost of $28.75. These purchases offset the issuance of 4,000,000 new APS shares when a preferred issue was converted. By October APS had slumped to near its yearly low as the firm launched a rate war for certain cargo moving between Japan and the U.S. A strong third quarter performance should get the rollercoaster back on the upwswing. Despite the volatility we believe APS is well-positioned to participate in the long-term expansion of trade between the U.S., Asia and Europe.

Key Stock Statistics

S&P EPS Est. 1995	2.30	Tang. Bk. Value/Share	19.69
P/E on S&P Est. 1995	11.1	Beta	2.51
S&P EPS Est. 1996	3.10	Shareholders	3,900
Dividend Rate/Share	0.40	Market cap. (B)	$0.696
Shs. outstg. (M)	26.6	Inst. holdings	75%
Avg. daily vol. (M)	0.218	Insider holdings	NA

Value of $10,000 invested 5 years ago: $ 20,152

Fiscal Year Ending Dec. 31

	1995	% Change	1994	% Change	1993	% Change
Revenues (Million $)						
1Q	740.7	5%	703.0	12%	629.0	-5%
2Q	674.3	3%	654.0	12%	582.0	NM
3Q	711.1	6%	672.1	8%	622.0	5%
4Q	—	—	764.7	NM	762.0	14%
Yr.	—	—	2,794	8%	2,594	4%
Income (Million $)						
1Q	1.06	-90%	10.17	-16%	12.13	-32%
2Q	14.26	-25%	18.99	-11%	21.30	-19%
3Q	30.90	37%	22.56	-12%	25.50	141%
4Q	—	—	22.50	6%	21.20	100%
Yr.	—	—	74.20	-7%	80.11	3%
Earnings Per Share ($)						
1Q	-0.02	NM	0.30	-23%	0.39	-26%
2Q	0.45	-27%	0.62	-13%	0.71	-12%
3Q	1.02	38%	0.74	-14%	0.86	15%
4Q	E0.81	9%	0.74	7%	0.69	116%
Yr.	E2.30	-3%	2.38	-10%	2.65	9%

Next earnings report expected: early February

Business Summary - 18-OCT-95

American President Companies is a leading containership operator and provides doublestack rail service in North America. APS disposed of its remaining real estate holdings in 1994. Contributions to revenues in recent years were:

	1994	1993	1992
Shipping	72.2%	73.9%	74.6%
Land transportation	27.2%	25.4%	25.2%
Real estate	0.6%	0.7%	0.2%

American President Lines (APL) operates a fleet of 19 containerships serving trans-Pacific and intra-Asia markets through a network of 183 agents in 45 nations. Trans-Pacific service, coordinated under an arrangement with Orient Overseas Container Line (OOCL) since 1991, will be expanded in late 1995 to include Mitsui O.S.K. Lines (MOL). In March 1995 APL launched a Europe to Asia service; in early 1996 APL's presence in that market will be greatly expanded through an alliance with OOCL, MOL, Nedlloyd Lines and Malaysia International Shipping.

In 1994, APL derived 80% of its shipping revenues from trans-Pacific service, handling 373,300 40-foot equivalents (FEUs), versus 369,800 units in 1993. Intra-Asia service (20%) generated 184,600 FEUs in 1994, compared with 173,300 units in 1993.

APS provides integrated rail/motor carrier transportation to more than 30 cities in North America. Operating a fleet of 930 railcars (transportation is performed by various railroads under contract), APS handled 594,000 FEUs in 1994, versus 538,200 FEUs in 1993. APS also provides domestic freight brokerage services, arranges transportation for time-sensitive freight for the automobile industry and consolidates small international shipments into full containerloads.

Important Developments

Sep. '95—APS repurchased 2,820,499 of its common shares at $30 each through a "Dutch Auction" self-tender for up to 4,000,000 shares. In August APS bought 2,000,000 of its common shares at $27 each through a private transaction. In July holders of $75 face amount of APS' 9% Series C Prefered Stock converted their securities for 3,960,000 APS common shares. Following these transactions APS had 26.6 million common shares outstanding.
Sep. '95—APS sold six vessels and certain assets on Guam to Matson Navigation for $164 million. Concurrently, APS and Matson agreed to forma a 10-year vessel sharing plan on certain trans-Pacific routes.

Capitalization

Long Term Debt: $436,278,000 (6/95), incl. $4.0 million of lease obligs.

Per Share Data ($) (Year Ended Dec. 31)

	1994	1993	1992	1991	1990	1989
Tangible Bk. Val.	19.54	17.44	14.97	15.17	13.04	14.68
Cash Flow	6.14	6.55	6.05	5.20	1.09	2.96
Earnings	2.38	2.65	2.43	1.83	-1.73	-0.02
Dividends	0.40	0.30	0.30	0.30	0.30	0.29
Payout Ratio	17%	11%	12%	15%	NM	NM
Prices - High	34	30¼	24	21¾	14⅝	19⅜
- Low	19	18⅝	15⅛	7⅞	5¼	13⅜
P/E Ratio - High	14	11	10	12	NM	NM
- Low	8	7	6	4	NM	NM

Income Statement Analysis (Million $)

	1994	%Chg	1993	%Chg	1992	%Chg	1991
Revs.	2,854	7%	2,659	3%	2,574	2%	2,518
Oper. Inc.	229	-5%	241	-2%	246	-4%	256
Depr.	106	-2%	108	2%	106	NM	106
Int. Exp.	35.3	84%	19.2	-50%	38.7	-12%	44.0
Pretax Inc.	110	-16%	131	7%	122	14%	107
Eff. Tax Rate	33%	—	39%	—	36%	—	40%
Net Inc.	74.2	-7%	80.0	3%	78.0	22%	64.0

Balance Sheet & Other Fin. Data (Million $)

	1994	1993	1992	1991	1990	1989
Cash	255	84.0	132	179	118	127
Curr. Assets	609	439	459	473	467	421
Total Assets	1,664	1,454	1,436	1,514	1,590	1,661
Curr. Liab.	403	387	475	338	373	315
LT Debt	386	267	242	444	481	511
Common Eqty.	534	468	390	446	481	587
Total Cap.	1,143	948	850	1,065	1,134	1,298
Cap. Exp.	128	160	66.0	20.0	39.0	111
Cash Flow	174	182	177	163	42.0	103

Ratio Analysis

	1994	1993	1992	1991	1990	1989
Curr. Ratio	1.5	1.1	1.0	1.4	1.3	1.3
% LT Debt of Cap.	33.8	28.2	28.5	41.7	42.4	39.4
% Net Inc.of Revs.	2.6	3.0	3.0	2.5	NM	0.5
% Ret. on Assets	4.7	5.5	5.6	4.6	NM	0.6
% Ret. on Equity	13.4	16.9	18.2	13.8	NM	NM

Dividend Data —Dividends, which are subject to restrictions by the Maritime Administration and various loan agreements, were initiated in 1985.

Amt. of Div. $	Date Decl.	Ex-Div. Date	Stock of Record	Payment Date
0.100	Oct. 07	Nov. 08	Nov. 15	Nov. 30 '94
0.100	Jan. 31	Feb. 09	Feb. 15	Feb. 28 '95
0.100	May. 02	May. 09	May. 15	May. 31 '95
0.100	Jul. 21	Aug. 11	Aug. 15	Aug. 31 '95
0.100	Oct. 16	Nov. 13	Nov. 15	Nov. 30 '95

Data as orig. reptd.; bef. results of disc. opers. and/or spec. items. Per share data adj. for stk. divs. as of ex-div. date. E-Estimated. NA-Not Available. NM-Not Meaningful. NR-Not Ranked.

Office—1111 Broadway, Oakland, CA 94607. **Tel**—(510) 272-8000. **Chrmn**—J. Hayashi. **Pres & CEO**—T. Rhein. **EVP & CFO**—L. D. Crandall. **VP & Secy**—M. B. Cattani. **Investor Contact**—Tom Meier. **Dirs**—C. S. Arledge, J. H. Barr, T. M. Friedman, J. Hayashi, F. W. Hellman, T. Rembe, T. J. Rhein, F. N. Shumway, G. C. Sullivan, B. L. Williams. **Transfer Agent & Registrar**—Bank of Boston. **Incorporated** in Delaware in 1983. **Empl**-5,434. **S&P Analyst:** Stephen R. Klein

STANDARD & POOR'S
STOCK REPORTS

AMETEK, Inc.

NYSE Symbol **AME**
In S&P MidCap 400

11-OCT-95 **Industry:** Machinery

Summary: This diversified industrial company makes precision instruments, electro-mechanical products, and industrial materials.

S&P Opinion: Accumulate (★★★★)

Recent Price • 17 | 52 Wk Range • 19½-15¾ | Yield • 1.4% | 12-Mo. P/E • 10.9

Quantitative Evaluations

Outlook
(1 Lowest—5 Highest)
• **5⁻**

Fair Value
• **20½**

Risk
• **Low**

Earn./Div. Rank
• **B**

Technical Eval.
• **Bearish** since 7/95

Rel. Strength Rank
(1 Lowest—99 Highest)
• **36**

Insider Activity
• **Neutral**

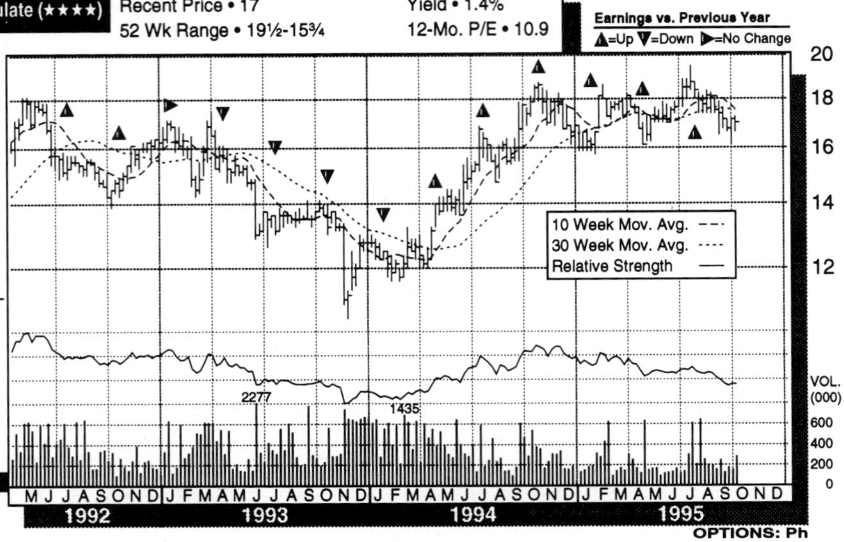

Overview - 08-OCT-95

Sales should rise moderately in 1995, building on 1994 gains stemming from realignment of operations and recovery in European and Pacific Rim markets. We expect precision instruments to continue to rebound from soft aerospace and process industry markets near-term. Long-term results are more likely to benefit from investment in Europe and Asia, resized operations, a move into the growing heavy vehicle instrumentation business, and the acquisition of Dixson. Electromechanical results should improve on new plant efficiencies, increased capacity, and improved worldwide demand. Earnings from industrial materials may also grow, on continued strong results at Specialty Metals. EPS comparisons will benefit from 24% fewer shares outstanding, and a recent authorization to repurchase an additional $25 million of stock.

Valuation - 08-OCT-95

The shares of this diversified industrial company have traded in a narrow range since late in the 1994 third quarter. Beginning in April 1994, when the effects of a shareholder value enhancement plan began to be seen, strong EPS gains have been recorded. All three operating units continue to produce excellent results, and, as demand in the U.S. grows and European and Pacific Rim economies improve, earnings gains predicted for 1995 should serve to push the shares higher again soon.

Key Stock Statistics

S&P EPS Est. 1995	1.30	Tang. Bk. Value/Share	1.26
P/E on S&P Est. 1995	13.1	Beta	0.73
S&P EPS Est. 1996	1.55	Shareholders	6,000
Dividend Rate/Share	0.24	Market cap. (B)	$0.552
Shs. outstg. (M)	32.9	Inst. holdings	56%
Avg. daily vol. (M)	0.038	Insider holdings	NA

Value of $10,000 invested 5 years ago: $ 15,720

Fiscal Year Ending Dec. 31

	1995	% Change	1994	% Change	1993	% Change
Revenues (Million $)						
1Q	219.6	10%	199.3	7%	187.1	-5%
2Q	219.1	4%	209.7	12%	186.8	-4%
3Q	—	—	198.7	14%	175.0	-6%
4Q	—	—	200.3	9%	183.3	-4%
Yr.	—	—	808.0	10%	732.2	-5%
Income (Million $)						
1Q	10.66	21%	8.81	44%	6.10	-46%
2Q	11.93	23%	9.67	55%	6.22	-47%
3Q	—	—	10.23	NM	1.98	-82%
4Q	—	—	10.29	NM	-21.63	NM
Yr.	—	—	38.99	NM	-7.33	NM
Earnings Per Share ($)						
1Q	0.31	48%	0.21	50%	0.14	-46%
2Q	0.36	33%	0.27	93%	0.14	-46%
3Q	E0.31	7%	0.29	NM	0.05	-80%
4Q	E0.33	10%	0.30	NM	-0.50	NM
Yr.	E1.30	24%	1.05	NM	-0.17	NM

Next earnings report expected: mid October

AMETEK, Inc.

Business Summary - 08-OCT-95

AMETEK is a diversified multi-product manufacturer. Segment contributions in 1994 (profits in millions) were:

	Sales	Profits
Electro-mechanical	42%	$46.2
Precision instruments	35%	29.2
Industrial materials	23%	27.3

International business accounted for about one-third of 1994's sales.

Electro-mechanical has a leading market share in electric motors for vacuum cleaners and floor care products. Products include motor-blower systems and injection-molded components (for manufacturers of floor care appliances) and electric and brushless D.C. fractional horsepower motors and motor blowers (used in computers, business machines, medical equipment, and high efficiency gas furnaces).

Precision Instruments (PI) products consist primarily of aircraft cockpit instruments and displays; pressure, temperature, fuel and liquid level sensors (for aircraft jet engine manufacturers and for airlines); and airborne electronics systems (to monitor and record flight and engine data). Other products include instruments and complete instrument panels (for heavy truck builders); process monitoring and display systems; combustion, gas analysis, moisture and emissions monitoring systems; force and speed measuring instruments; air and noise monitors; pressure and temperature calibrators; pressure-indicating and digital manometers; and general gauge products. PI has been selected by Boeing to manufacture an engine vibration monitoring system and sensor system for Boeing's new 777 aircraft.

Industrial materials products include high temperature resistant materials and textiles; lightweight foam sheet packaging material; filters for drinking water and other liquids; filter housings; high-purity metals and alloys in powder, strip and wire form for high performance applications; and specialty resins and thermoplastic compounds.

Important Developments

May '95—AME sold its Microfoam division to Astro Valcour, Inc., for about $37 million. The division, which makes and sells MICROFOAM, a low-density polypropylene foam sheeting for interior packaging and laminates, had 1994 sales of about $34 million.

Mar. '95—The company acquired the heavy vehicle instrumentation business of Dixson, Inc., a maker of high-quality electronic instrumentation products. Dixson's 1995 sales are projected at $27 million. AME expects its heavy vehicle business, including Dixson, to grow to about $100 million in annual sales over the next four to five years.

Capitalization

Long Term Debt: $185,506,000 (6/95).

Per Share Data ($) (Year Ended Dec. 31)

	1994	1993	1992	1991	1990	1989
Tangible Bk. Val.	1.26	2.92	3.69	3.54	3.30	3.03
Cash Flow	1.86	0.48	1.67	1.51	1.39	1.26
Earnings	1.05	-0.17	1.01	0.87	0.85	0.87
Dividends	0.24	0.57	0.68	0.66	0.64	0.62
Payout Ratio	23%	NM	67%	76%	75%	72%
Prices - High	18¾	17½	18⅛	14	14½	15⅞
- Low	11⅝	10⅝	13⅛	8½	8¼	12
P/E Ratio - High	18	NM	18	16	17	18
- Low	11	NM	13	10	10	14

Income Statement Analysis (Million $)

	1994	%Chg	1993	%Chg	1992	%Chg	1991
Revs.	808	10%	732	-5%	770	8%	715
Oper. Inc.	109	49%	73.0	-33%	109	15%	94.6
Depr.	30.0	6%	28.3	-4%	29.4	4%	28.3
Int. Exp.	21.6	23%	17.6	-11%	19.7	-11%	22.1
Pretax Inc.	61.8	NM	-11.2	NM	66.7	27%	52.4
Eff. Tax Rate	37%	—	NM	—	34%	—	28%
Net Inc.	39.0	NM	-7.3	NM	44.4	17%	38.0

Balance Sheet & Other Fin. Data (Million $)

	1994	1993	1992	1991	1990	1989
Cash	18.0	85.0	116	107	111	116
Curr. Assets	254	302	319	319	318	316
Total Assets	502	563	595	612	615	563
Curr. Liab.	183	168	138	138	133	101
LT Debt	190	172	187	205	224	220
Common Eqty.	73.0	165	210	211	199	195
Total Cap.	292	366	432	452	459	447
Cap. Exp.	23.1	41.1	24.0	18.8	35.7	53.1
Cash Flow	69.0	20.9	73.7	66.3	61.4	55.9

Ratio Analysis

	1994	1993	1992	1991	1990	1989
Curr. Ratio	1.4	1.8	2.3	2.3	2.4	3.1
% LT Debt of Cap.	65.2	47.2	43.3	45.3	48.7	49.2
% Net Inc.of Revs.	4.8	NM	5.8	5.3	5.7	6.5
% Ret. on Assets	8.2	NM	7.3	6.2	6.4	7.6
% Ret. on Equity	38.1	NM	21.0	18.4	19.1	20.3

Dividend Data —Dividends have been paid since 1942.

Amt. of Div. $	Date Decl.	Ex-Div. Date	Stock of Record	Payment Date
0.060	Nov. 16	Dec. 05	Dec. 09	Dec. 23 '94
0.060	Feb. 22	Mar. 13	Mar. 17	Mar. 31 '95
0.060	May. 24	Jun. 14	Jun. 16	Jun. 30 '95
0.060	Aug. 23	Sep. 13	Sep. 15	Sep. 29 '95

Data as orig. reptd.; bef. results of disc. opers. and/or spec. items; incl. merger or acquisition in 1991, 1990. Per share data adj. for stk. divs. as of ex-div. date. E-Estimated. NA-Not Available. NM-Not Meaningful. NR-Not Ran

Office—Station Square, Paoli, PA 19301. **Tel**—(610) 647-2121. **Chrmn & CEO**—W. E. Blankely. **SVP & CFO**—J. J. Molinelli. **Secy**—R. W. Yannarell. **Treas**—Deirdre D. Saunders. **VP & Investor Contact**—William F. Cleary. **Dirs**—W. E. Blankely, L. G. Cole, H. N. Friedlaender, S. S. Gordon, C. D. Klein, J. R. Malone, D. P. Steinmann, E. R. Varet. **Transfer Agent & Registrar**—American Stock Transfer & Trust Co., NYC. **Incorporated** in Delaware in 1930. **Empl**-6,100. **S&P Analyst:** Robert E. Friedman

STANDARD & POOR'S

STOCK REPORTS

Anadarko Petroleum

NYSE Symbol **APC**
In S&P MidCap 400

24-AUG-95 **Industry:** Oil and Gas

Summary: Anadarko is one of the leading independent natural gas and crude oil production companies in the U.S.

S&P Opinion: Hold (★★★) | Recent Price • 44 3/8 | 52 Wk Range • 50 5/8-35 5/8 | Yield • 0.7% | 12-Mo. P/E • NM

Quantitative Evaluations
Outlook
(1 Lowest—5 Highest)
• **1-**
Fair Value
• **31 3/8**
Risk
• **Average**
Earn./Div. Rank
• **B**

Technical Eval.
• **Bearish** since 6/95
Rel. Strength Rank
(1 Lowest—99 Highest)
• **63**
Insider Activity
• **NA**

OPTIONS: CBOE

Overview - 24-AUG-95

Revenues will advance near term, as greater volumes should offset lower gas prices. However, profits in 1995 will be restrained if weak prices persist. APC's strategy of integrating natural gas production with gas marketing will aid long-term prospects, as natural gas usage is expected to increase. The company's aggressive exploration program in Algeria, conducted in partnership with Sonatrach (which owns 12% of APC), the state-owned oil company of Algeria, should provide a major boost to earnings beyond 1996, though considerable political risk is present in Algeria at the moment. Subsalt exploration in the Gulf of Mexico, being pioneered by Anadarko, should also boost earnings in 1995 and 1996. APC plans to drill four wildcat subsalt wells in 1995.

Valuation - 24-AUG-95

The shares have been in a downtrend over the past several weeks, with gas prices moving lower and oil fundamentals being shaken by OPEC's handwringing over lost market share. An anticipated rise in gas prices and improved results from exploration should help the shares move up over the next two years. Further successes in finding additional reserves in the subsalt of the Gulf of Mexico would boost the shares in the short and long term. Investors will need to be watchful of developments in Algeria, where APC is looking for much of its future growth. Petroleum revenues represent Algeria's largest source of export revenues, and we believe the government will seek to preserve stable conditions for the oil industry.

Key Stock Statistics

S&P EPS Est. 1995	0.55	Tang. Bk. Value/Share	15.30
P/E on S&P Est. 1995	80.7	Beta	0.47
S&P EPS Est. 1996	1.10	Shareholders	7,800
Dividend Rate/Share	0.30	Market cap. (B)	$ 2.7
Shs. outstg. (M)	58.9	Inst. holdings	76%
Avg. daily vol. (M)	0.226	Insider holdings	NA

Value of $10,000 invested 5 years ago: $ 12,634

Fiscal Year Ending Dec. 31

	1996	% Change	1995	% Change	1994	% Change
Revenues (Million $)						
1Q	—	—	102.8	-22%	132.0	2%
2Q	—	—	113.9	-5%	119.5	6%
3Q	—	—	—	—	111.4	8%
4Q	—	—	—	—	115.3	-12%
Yr.	—	—	—	—	482.5	1%
Income (Million $)						
1Q	—	—	4.08	-76%	17.06	12%
2Q	—	—	9.10	-22%	11.68	-6%
3Q	—	—	—	—	10.31	NM
4Q	—	—	—	—	2.00	-86%
Yr.	—	—	—	—	41.10	3%
Earnings Per Share ($)						
1Q	—	—	0.07	-76%	0.29	4%
2Q	—	—	0.15	-25%	0.20	-9%
3Q	—	—	0.14	-22%	0.18	NM
4Q	—	—	0.19	NM	0.03	-88%
Yr.	E1.10	100%	E0.55	-21%	0.70	NM

Next earnings report expected: late October

Anadarko Petroleum

Business Summary - 24-AUG-95

Anadarko Petroleum Corporation is engaged in crude oil and natural gas exploration, development and production. Production in 1994 amounted to 8,303,000 bbl. of oil (7,910,000 bbl. in 1993), 175.8 Bcf of natural gas (161.9 Bcf) and 3,512,000 bbl. of natural gas liquids (3,320,000 bbl.). At December 31, 1994, estimated proved reserves amounted to 157,400,000 bbl. of oil and condensate (78,500,000 bbl. in 1993) and 1,910 Bcf of natural gas (1,875 Bcf).

The company's drilling program focuses on known petroleum and natural gas areas onshore in North America, primarily in the Anadarko Basin of Oklahoma, the Mid-continent region (Arkoma and Golden Trend Basins) of Arkansas and Oklahoma, the Permian Basin of West Texas and New Mexico, the Rocky Mountain regions of Nevada and Wyoming, and southern Alberta. APC also drills offshore in the Gulf of Mexico. The company is also exploring in selected joint-venture projects overseas in Algeria, Indonesia and China. A significant portion of APC's reserves is located in the Hugoton natural gas field, the largest natural gas field in the U.S.To enhance recovery and marketability of its natural gas reserves, Anadarko owns interests in 15 gas gathering systems and eight gas processing plants in the Mid-continent area.

During 1994, APC replaced 308% of total production with reserves of oil and natural gas, on an energy equivalent barrel (EEB) basis. The company's worldwide finding cost in 1994 was $2.76 per EEB, down from $4.07, mainly as a result of the initial success of the Algerian exploration program.

The capital budget for 1995 was initially set at $314 million, down from $423 million in 1994, primarily in anticipation of lower gas prices.

Important Developments

Jul. '95—The company reported that second-quarter results suffered as U.S. natural gas prices fell 16%, year to prior year, while oil volumes fell about 9%. Gas volumes produced amounted to 479 million cubic feet per day (MMcf/d), up from 472 MMcf/d, though APC "shut-in" some gas production as a result of low prices. Crude oil average prices rose 11%, year to year. Previously, in July, Anadarko said test results from the Hassi Berkine East No. 2 well located in the Ghadames Basin on Block 404 in Algeria's Sahara Desert tested at a rate of 17,309 barrels of oil per day and 3.9 MMcf/d. APC expects inital gross production perhaps by late 1996 of about 30,000 barrels/day, with substantial increases from additional fields within two years.

Capitalization

Long Term Debt: $629,281,000 (3/95).

Per Share Data ($) (Year Ended Dec. 31)

	1994	1993	1992	1991	1990	1989
Tangible Bk. Val.	15.28	14.73	11.88	11.62	11.25	9.47
Cash Flow	3.64	3.63	2.90	2.79	3.52	3.35
Earnings	0.70	0.70	0.49	0.59	1.04	0.92
Dividends	0.30	0.30	0.30	0.30	0.30	0.30
Payout Ratio	43%	43%	61%	51%	30%	33%
Prices - High	58½	51¾	32⅞	33⅛	39⅞	38½
- Low	37	25⅝	18½	21½	28⅝	24½
P/E Ratio - High	84	74	67	56	38	42
- Low	53	37	38	36	28	27

Income Statement Analysis (Million $)

	1994	%Chg	1993	%Chg	1992	%Chg	1991
Revs.	482	1%	476	27%	375	11%	337
Oper. Inc.	267	-2%	272	35%	201	4%	194
Depr. Depl. & Amort.	173	3%	168	26%	133	10%	121
Int. Exp.	41.6	9%	38.0	4%	36.6	NM	36.8
Pretax Inc.	64.7	-16%	77.4	94%	40.0	-17%	48.0
Eff. Tax Rate	36%	—	48%	—	32%	—	33%
Net Inc.	41.1	3%	40.0	47%	27.3	-16%	32.4

Balance Sheet & Other Fin. Data (Million $)

	1994	1993	1992	1991	1990	1989
Cash	6.5	17.8	14.8	15.0	13.0	9.5
Curr. Assets	139	141	139	107	120	103
Total Assets	2,142	2,023	1,905	1,676	1,647	1,553
Curr. Liab.	128	126	107	104	118	97.0
LT Debt	629	543	647	440	427	493
Common Eqty.	900	864	657	641	618	495
Total Cap.	1,968	1,831	1,783	1,556	1,512	1,441
Cap. Exp.	423	265	362	170	213	203
Cash Flow	214	208	160	154	187	175

Ratio Analysis

	1994	1993	1992	1991	1990	1989
Curr. Ratio	1.1	1.1	1.3	1.0	1.0	1.1
% LT Debt of Cap.	32.0	29.6	36.3	28.2	28.2	34.2
% Ret. on Assets	2.0	2.0	1.5	1.9	3.4	3.1
% Ret. on Equity	4.7	5.1	4.2	5.1	9.7	10.1

Dividend Data —Dividends were initiated in 1986. A new "poison pill" stock purchase rights plan was adopted in 1988.

Amt. of Div. $	Date Decl.	Ex-Div. Date	Stock of Record	Payment Date
0.075	Aug. 02	Sep. 08	Sep. 14	Sep. 28 '94
0.075	Oct. 28	Dec. 08	Dec. 14	Dec. 28 '94
0.075	Jan. 26	Mar. 02	Mar. 08	Mar. 22 '95
0.075	Apr. 27	Jun. 12	Jun. 14	Jun. 28 '95
0.075	Jul. 31	Sep. 11	Sep. 13	Sep. 27 '95

Data as orig. reptd.; bef. results of disc opers. and/or spec. items. Per share data adj. for stk. divs. as of ex-div. date. E-Estimated. NA-Not Available. NM-Not Meaningful. NR-Not Ranked.

Office—Anadarko Tower, 17001 Northchase Dr., P.O. Box 1330, Houston, TX 77060. **Tel**—(713) 875-1101. **Chrmn, Pres & CEO**—R. J. Allison Jr. **Sr VP-Fin & CFO**—M. E. Rose. **Secy**—Suzanne Suter. **VP & Investor Contact**—A. Paul Taylor Jr. **Dirs**—C. P. Albert, R. J. Allison Jr., L. Barcus, R. Brown, J. L. Bryan, J. R. Gordon, C. M. Simmons. **Transfer Agent & Registrar**—Chemical Bank, NYC. **Incorporated** in Delaware in 1985. **Empl**-1,085. **S&P Analyst:** Raymond J. Deacon

STANDARD & POOR'S

STOCK REPORTS

Analog Devices

NYSE Symbol **ADI**
In S&P MidCap 400

24-AUG-95 **Industry:** Electronics/Electric

Summary: ADI manufactures high-performance integrated circuits used in analog and digital signal processing applications.

S&P Opinion: Hold (★★★) | Recent Price • 36⅝ | 52 Wk Range • 39½-19½ | Yield • Nil | 12-Mo. P/E • 27.1

Quantitative Evaluations

Outlook (1 Lowest—5 Highest)
• 5^+

Fair Value
• 41⅝

Risk
• **Average**

Earn./Div. Rank
• **B-**

Technical Eval.
• **Bullish** since 1/92

Rel. Strength Rank (1 Lowest—99 Highest)
• **54**

Insider Activity
• **Unfavorable**

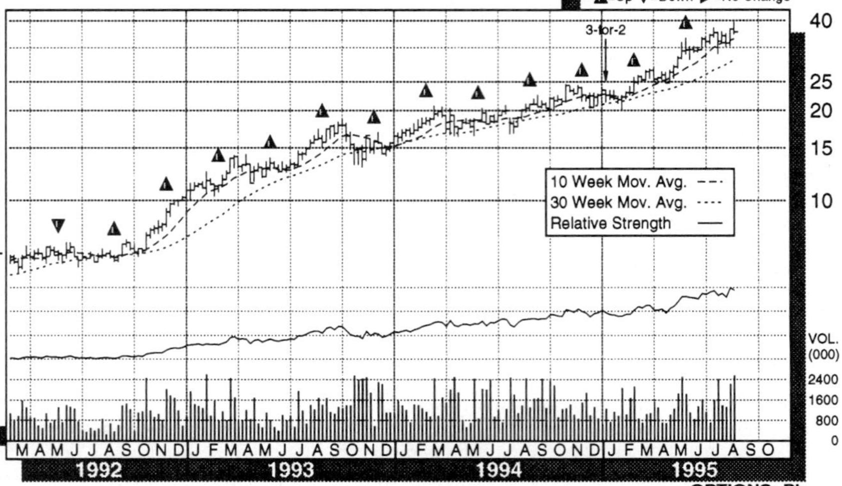

OPTIONS: Ph

Overview - 24-AUG-95

We project sales gains of 25% to 30% for fiscal 1996, on continued strong industry growth and new product launches. The fastest growing area should be system level ICs, including digital signal processing (DSP) ICs. The DSP market, currently estimated at about $1 billion, is expected to grow over 35% annually for the foreseeable future. Third quarter gross margins of 50.8% are likely to dip modestly in the next few periods, as ADI ramps up new production facilities. Long-term prospects are enhanced by additional capacity that should start to come on line in the first half of calender 1996, and by a focus on higher-margin product introductions.

Valuation - 24-AUG-95

We are upgrading the shares to hold, reflecting expected strong demand for system ICs. The major PC, communications and automatic test equipment markets are likely to remain strong in the near-term. However, capacity constraits restricted sales growth in the past two quarters. ADI is addressing this problem by conversion of current linear capacity from 4" to 6" wafers; acquisition of a 6" foundry; joint investment with an outside source; and expansion of an existing relationship with a major supplier. Despite these actions, the capacity issue is not expected to be fully resolved until the second half of fiscal 1996. As a result, despite favorable long-term prospects, we believe that short-term upside could be limited.

Key Stock Statistics

S&P EPS Est. 1995	1.47	Tang. Bk. Value/Share	7.43
P/E on S&P Est. 1995	24.9	Beta	1.63
S&P EPS Est. 1996	2.05	Shareholders	4,400
Dividend Rate/Share	Nil	Market cap. (B)	$ 2.6
Shs. outstg. (M)	75.7	Inst. holdings	76%
Avg. daily vol. (M)	0.470	Insider holdings	NA

Value of $10,000 invested 5 years ago: $ 56,346

Fiscal Year Ending Oct. 31

	1995	% Change	1994	% Change	1993	% Change
Revenues (Million $)						
1Q	208.0	15%	181.1	20%	151.3	15%
2Q	230.1	20%	192.0	18%	162.9	14%
3Q	246.3	25%	197.1	14%	173.1	20%
4Q	—	—	203.3	14%	179.0	20%
Yr.	—	—	773.5	16%	666.3	17%
Income (Million $)						
1Q	23.65	55%	15.26	88%	8.13	NM
2Q	28.71	61%	17.88	76%	10.15	160%
3Q	31.78	61%	19.68	62%	12.16	145%
4Q	—	—	21.67	55%	14.02	99%
Yr.	—	—	74.50	68%	44.46	198%
Earnings Per Share ($)						
1Q	0.30	50%	0.20	87%	0.11	NM
2Q	0.30	29%	0.23	75%	0.13	150%
3Q	0.36	42%	0.25	58%	0.16	140%
4Q	E0.41	46%	0.28	50%	0.19	87%
Yr.	E1.47	53%	0.96	63%	0.59	185%

Next earnings report expected: late November

Analog Devices

Business Summary - 24-AUG-95

Analog Devices designs, makes and markets a broad line of standard-function linear and mixed-signal integrated circuits (SLICs), special-purpose linear and mixed signal integrated circuits (SPLICs) and digital signal processing integrated circuits (DSP ICs), and assembled products.

Contributions by product category in the recent years were:

Products	1993-4	1992-3	1991-2
SLICs	59%	60%	64%
SPLICs and DSP ICs	30%	26%	18%
Assembled products	11%	14%	18%

The company believes that it is one of the world's largest suppliers of SLIC products. Its SLIC products are primarily high-performance, single function devices. The majority of SLIC revenues come from data converters (analog-to-digital and digital-to-analog) and amplifiers. Other products in this category with significant sales are analog signal-processing devices (such as analog multipliers), voltage references and comparators.

SPLICs and DSP ICs, collectively referred to as system level integrated circuits (ICs), are multi-function devices that feature high levels of functional integration on a single chip. Just one of these devices typically replaces 5 to 20 (or more) simpler ICs used to perform the same or similar functions in a prior generation of equipment.

The company's assembled products consist primarily of hybrid products (devices with several IC chips mounted and wired together on a substrate) and modules (ICs and other components soldered to a small printed circuit board, which is mounted inside a small plastic case).

Foreign operations accounted for 43% of sales and 48% of operating income in fiscal 1994.

R&D spending totaled $106.9 million (13.3% of sales) in fiscal 1994, versus $94.1 million (13.5%) in fiscal 1993.

In October 1992, ADI sold its MicroMac product line of measurement, data acquisition and control system products.

Important Developments

Aug. '95—ADI said bookings in the fiscal 1995 third quarter increased to $280 million, up 37% from the level of the fiscal 1994 quarter and 7% from the fiscal 1995 second quarter. The company added that sales in the quarter could have been higher if more manufacturing capacity had been available. Several capacity expansion programs currently in progress will provide substantially higher production capability in fiscal 1996.

Capitalization

Long Term Debt: $80,000,000 (7/95).

Per Share Data ($)

(Year Ended Oct. 31)

	1994	1993	1992	1991	1990	1989
Tangible Bk. Val.	6.68	5.57	4.87	4.61	4.51	5.04
Cash Flow	1.76	1.35	0.95	0.83	0.47	0.95
Earnings	0.96	0.59	0.21	0.11	-0.19	0.39
Dividends	Nil	Nil	Nil	Nil	Nil	Nil
Payout Ratio	Nil	Nil	Nil	Nil	Nil	Nil
Prices - High	24½	18⅝	10⅞	8⅜	6⅝	8⅝
- Low	15⅝	10⅛	5¾	4⅜	3⅝	5⅜
P/E Ratio - High	26	32	52	74	NM	22
- Low	16	17	28	38	NM	14

Income Statement Analysis (Million $)

	1994	%Chg	1993	%Chg	1992	%Chg	1991
Revs.	773	16%	666	17%	567	5%	538
Oper. Inc.	163	36%	120	52%	79.0	6%	74.4
Depr.	61.3	6%	57.7	9%	52.9	6%	50.0
Int. Exp.	7.2	NM	7.2	20%	6.0	25%	4.8
Pretax Inc.	96.9	75%	55.5	192%	19.0	102%	9.4
Eff. Tax Rate	23%	—	20%	—	21%	—	13%
Net Inc.	74.5	67%	44.5	199%	14.9	82%	8.2

Balance Sheet & Other Fin. Data (Million $)

	1994	1993	1992	1991	1990	1989
Cash	182	80.7	17.7	16.5	8.3	30.1
Curr. Assets	505	403	297	249	232	223
Total Assets	816	678	562	503	487	453
Curr. Liab.	206	133	100	97.0	106	63.0
LT Debt	80.0	100	70.6	36.8	24.1	12.2
Common Eqty.	522	432	375	354	343	361
Total Cap.	605	541	458	403	378	388
Cap. Exp.	90.9	70.3	67.1	57.9	59.4	51.7
Cash Flow	136	102	67.8	58.2	32.8	68.8

Ratio Analysis

	1994	1993	1992	1991	1990	1989
Curr. Ratio	2.5	3.0	3.0	2.6	2.2	3.5
% LT Debt of Cap.	13.2	18.5	15.4	9.1	6.4	3.1
% Net Inc.of Revs.	9.6	6.7	2.6	1.5	NM	6.1
% Ret. on Assets	9.9	7.1	2.8	1.6	NM	6.1
% Ret. on Equity	15.5	10.9	4.1	2.3	NM	8.0

Dividend Data —No cash dividends have ever been paid. A poison pill stock purchase rights plan was adopted in 1988. A three-for-two stock split was effected in January 1995.

Amt. of Div. $	Date Decl.	Ex-Div. Date	Stock of Record	Payment Date
3-for-2	Nov. 30	Jan. 05	Dec. 12	Jan. 04 '95

Data as orig. reptd.; bef. results of disc. opers. and/or spec. items. Per share data adj. for stk. divs. as of ex-div. date. E-Estimated. NA-Not Available. NM-Not Meaningful. NR-Not Ranked.

Office—One Technology Way, Norwood, MA 02062-9106. **Tel**—(617) 329-4700. **Chrmn & CEO**—R. Stata. **Pres**—J. G. Fishman. **VP-Fin**—J. E. McDonough. **Clerk**—P. P. Brountas. **Investor Contact**—James Fishbeck (617-461-3282). **Dirs**—M. Chang, J. D. Doyle, J. G. Fishman, S. H. Fuller, P. L. Lowe, G. C. McKeague, J. Moses, R. Stata, L. C. Thurow. **Transfer Agent**—Bank of Boston. **Registrar**—Co.'s office. **Incorporated** in Massachusetts in 1965. **Empl**-5,700. **S&P Analyst:** Steven A. Jaworski

STANDARD & POOR'S

STOCK REPORTS

Angelica Corp.

NYSE Symbol **AGL**
In S&P MidCap 400

18-OCT-95 **Industry:** Textiles

Summary: AGL provides textile rental and laundry services to health care institutions, manufactures uniforms, and operates a national chain of specialty retail stores.

Quantitative Evaluations

Outlook
(1 Lowest—5 Highest)
• **2-**
Fair Value
• **23⅛**
Risk
• **Low**
Earn./Div. Rank
• **B+**

Technical Eval.
• **Bearish** since 12/93
Rel. Strength Rank
(1 Lowest—99 Highest)
• **27**
Insider Activity
• **NA**

Recent Price • 24⅝
52 Wk Range • 27⅝-24¼
Yield • 4.0%
12-Mo. P/E • 17.5

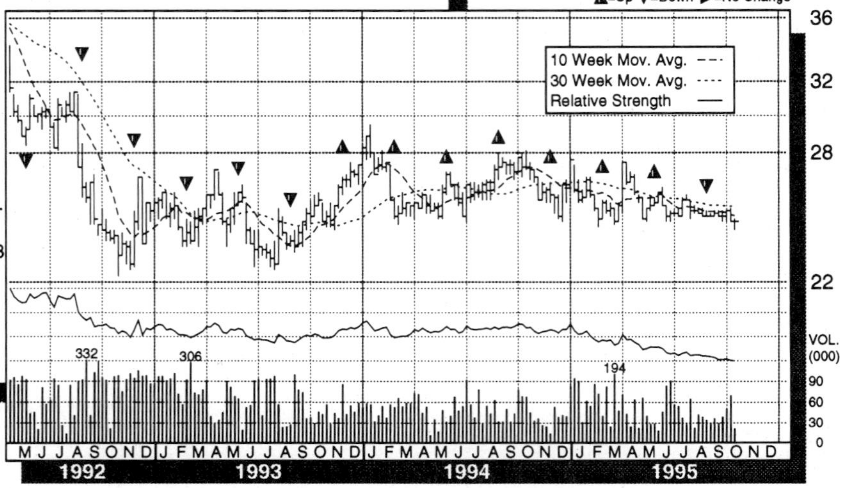

Business Profile - 17-OCT-95

This provider of textile rental and laundry services has been purchasing privately-owned and hospital cooperative laundry businesses across the U.S. Hospitals have been shifting from on-premise and cooperative laundries to contract laundry services such as those operated by AGL in order to to reduce their textile and laundry processing costs. The recent acquisition of HLA Services enabled Angelica to expand its textile rental and laundry services into the Boston market.

Operational Review - 17-OCT-95

Revenues in the six months ended July 29, 1995, rose 4.4%, year to year, primarily reflecting the inclusion of acquisitions in the rental services and retail sales segments. Excluding acquisitions made in the first quarter of 1994-95, sales and revenues were essentially flat. The company said it believes that recent actions taken in its key segments will produce improved results in the second half of 1995-96, with full-year results increasing slightly over 1994-95.

Stock Performance - 13-OCT-95

In the past 30 trading days, AGL's shares have declined 1%, compared to a 4% rise in the S&P 500. Average trading volume for the past five days was 4,080 shares, compared with the 40-day moving average of 7,736 shares.

Key Stock Statistics

Dividend Rate/Share	0.96	Shareholders	1,900
Shs. outstg. (M)	9.1	Market cap. (B)	$0.218
Avg. daily vol. (M)	0.009	Inst. holdings	81%
Tang. Bk. Value/Share	20.97	Insider holdings	NA
Beta	0.57		

Value of $10,000 invested 5 years ago: $ 9,786

Fiscal Year Ending Jan. 31

	1996	% Change	1995	% Change	1994	% Change
Revenues (Million $)						
1Q	123.8	6%	117.0	12%	104.1	-6%
2Q	121.9	3%	118.2	14%	104.0	-4%
3Q	—	—	120.1	9%	110.5	1%
4Q	—	—	117.5	8%	108.5	6%
Yr.	—	—	472.8	11%	427.1	NM
Income (Million $)						
1Q	3.44	9%	3.15	25%	2.52	-50%
2Q	2.65	-17%	3.18	35%	2.35	-38%
3Q	—	—	4.20	8%	3.90	2%
4Q	—	—	2.54	6%	2.39	108%
Yr.	—	—	13.07	17%	11.15	-19%
Earnings Per Share ($)						
1Q	0.38	9%	0.35	25%	0.28	-48%
2Q	0.29	-17%	0.35	35%	0.26	-37%
3Q	—	—	0.46	7%	0.43	2%
4Q	—	—	0.28	8%	0.26	100%
Yr.	—	—	1.44	17%	1.23	-18%

Next earnings report expected: mid November

Angelica Corp.

Business Summary - 18-OCT-95

Angelica Corp. provides textile rental and laundry services to health care institutions; is a leading manufacturer and marketer of uniforms and business career apparel for a wide variety of institutions and businesses; and is the largest operator of specialty retail stores offering uniforms and duty shoes primarily for nurses and other health care professionals. Contributions in 1994-95 were:

	Sales	Profits
Rental services	50%	60%
Manufacturing & marketing	36%	21%
Retail sales	14%	19%

The Rental Services division, with 37 plants in or near major U.S. metropolitan areas, provides textile rental and laundry services for health care institutions. It also provides general linen services in selected areas, principally to hotels, motels and restaurants.

The company's manufacturing and marketing operations consist of the Angelica Uniform Group in the U.S. and companies in Canada and the U.K., all of which are involved in the production of uniforms and business career apparel for a wide variety of institutions and businesses.

The Life Retail Stores division is a specialty retailer offering uniforms and duty shoes primarily for nurses and other health care professionals. As of 1994-95 year end, it was operating in excess of 260 stores, primarily in malls and strip shopping centers.

Customers in the health services market include health service networks and institutions (hospitals, nursing homes, outpatient service centers, HMOs, medical clinics and laboratories) and health service personnel (doctors, dentists and nurses). Hospitality market customers include lodging, gaming and food service establishments and amusement parks. The company also serves other service industry markets including retailers, financial institutions, transportation companies, manufacturers, law enforcement and security companies, and educational and government institutions.

Important Developments

Oct. '95—The company acquired HLA Services, Inc. ($10 million of annual revenues), a hospital cooperative laundry in Boston, Mass., for an undisclosed amount of cash and the assumption of debt. Angelica said the transaction is part of a nationwide trend of hospitals shifting from on-premise and cooperative laundries to contract laundry service.

Capitalization

Long Term Debt: $98,512,000 (7/29/95).

Per Share Data ($) (Year Ended Jan. 31)

	1995	1994	1993	1992	1991	1990
Tangible Bk. Val.	20.77	20.49	20.87	20.43	18.92	17.01
Cash Flow	2.90	2.64	2.86	3.68	3.47	3.08
Earnings	1.44	1.23	1.50	2.43	2.37	2.06
Dividends	0.94	0.93	0.92	0.89	0.84	0.77
Payout Ratio	65%	76%	60%	37%	35%	37%
Cal. Yrs.	1994	1993	1992	1991	1990	1989
Prices - High	29½	28⅜	40	40¼	33⅞	30⅜
- Low	24½	22½	22¼	29⅝	27	22
P/E Ratio - High	20	23	27	17	14	15
- Low	17	18	15	12	11	11

Income Statement Analysis (Million $)

	1995	%Chg	1994	%Chg	1993	%Chg	1992
Revs.	473	11%	427	NM	431	NM	434
Oper. Inc.	45.5	9%	41.9	-7%	45.0	-21%	57.2
Depr.	13.3	3%	12.9	2%	12.6	8%	11.7
Int. Exp.	7.9	6%	7.4	-1%	7.5	8%	7.0
Pretax Inc.	21.3	18%	18.1	-19%	22.3	-39%	36.5
Eff. Tax Rate	39%	—	38%	—	38%	—	38%
Net Inc.	13.1	17%	11.2	-19%	13.8	-39%	22.7

Balance Sheet & Other Fin. Data (Million $)

	1995	1994	1993	1992	1991	1990
Cash	2.2	2.0	2.7	6.1	2.0	6.9
Curr. Assets	220	210	205	211	205	184
Total Assets	354	333	327	335	316	279
Curr. Liab.	69.2	53.1	43.7	50.4	70.4	53.7
LT Debt	69.7	72.3	78.2	80.5	57.8	50.6
Common Eqty.	197	192	189	190	176	161
Total Cap.	270	269	273	275	238	218
Cap. Exp.	11.5	12.2	11.8	13.3	14.1	13.6
Cash Flow	26.4	24.0	26.4	34.4	32.4	28.6

Ratio Analysis

	1995	1994	1993	1992	1991	1990
Curr. Ratio	3.2	4.0	4.7	4.2	2.9	3.4
% LT Debt of Cap.	25.8	26.9	28.7	29.3	24.3	23.2
% Net Inc.of Revs.	2.8	2.6	3.2	5.2	5.3	5.2
% Ret. on Assets	3.8	3.4	4.2	6.9	7.4	7.5
% Ret. on Equity	6.7	5.8	7.4	12.4	13.1	12.4

Dividend Data —Dividends have been paid since 1954. A "poison pill" stock purchase rights plan was adopted in 1988.

Amt. of Div. $	Date Decl.	Ex-Div. Date	Stock of Record	Payment Date
0.235	Nov. 29	Dec. 09	Dec. 15	Jan. 01 '95
0.235	Mar. 01	Mar. 09	Mar. 15	Apr. 01 '95
0.235	May. 23	Jun. 13	Jun. 15	Jul. 01 '95
0.240	Aug. 29	Sep. 13	Sep. 15	Oct. 01 '95

Data as orig. reptd.; bef. results of disc. opers. and/or spec. items. Per share data adj. for stk. divs. as of ex-div. date. E-Estimated. NA-Not Available. NM-Not Meaningful. NR-Not Ranked.

Office—424 S. Woods Mill Rd., Chesterfield, MO 63017. **Tel**—(314) 854-3800. **Chrmn, Pres & CEO**—L. J. Young. **Sr VP-Fin, CFO & Investor Contact**—Theodore M. Armstrong. **Treas**—T. M. Degnan. **VP-Secy**—J. Witter. **Dirs**—E. H. Harbison Jr., L. M. Liberman, L. F. Loewe, M. Sneider, E. H. Stein, W. P. Stiritz, H. E. Trusheim, L. J. Young. **Transfer Agent & Registrar**—Boatmen's Trust Co., St. Louis. **Incorporated** in Missouri in 1904; reincorporated in Missouri in 1968. **Empl**-9,800. **S&P Analyst:** Philip D. Wohl

STANDARD & POOR'S

STOCK REPORTS

AnnTaylor Stores

NYSE Symbol **ANN**
In S&P MidCap 400

10-OCT-95 **Industry:** Retail Stores

Summary: This leading specialty retailer of women's better-quality apparel, shoes, and accessories operates 289 stores in 38 states and the District of Columbia.

S&P Opinion: Hold (★★★) | Recent Price • 13¾ | 52 Wk Range • 44⅞-13⅜ | Yield • Nil | 12-Mo. P/E • 19.9

Earnings vs. Previous Year
▲=Up ▼=Down ▶=No Change

Quantitative Evaluations

Outlook
(1 Lowest—5 Highest)
• **NA**

Fair Value
• **NA**

Risk
• **High**

Earn./Div. Rank
• **NR**

Technical Eval.
• **Bullish** since 5/95

Rel. Strength Rank
(1 Lowest—99 Highest)
• **1**

Insider Activity
• **NA**

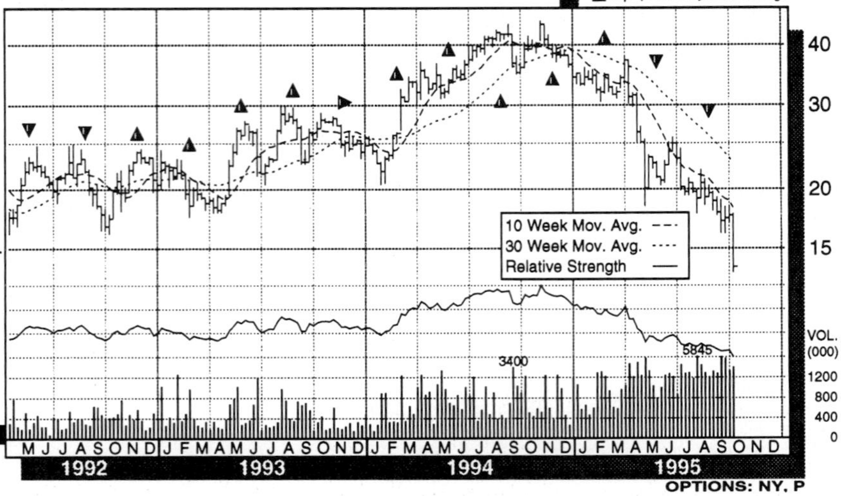

OPTIONS: NY, P

Overview - 27-SEP-95

Sales gains in 1995-6 will come mostly from new stores, with modest declines in same-store sales. Gross margins should narrow, on weaker volume and sharply competitive pricing. Expense ratios may rise as a result of higher occupancy costs of new stores and a lack of sales leverage to cover costs. Interest expense should increase, as a result of higher capital spending for new stores. In light of weak sales gains thus far in 1995, and lack of management depth, the company plans to slow its new store expansion in 1996, and to focus on achieving the right merchandise mix to boost sales. Over time, product line extensions, such as freestanding shoe stores, fragrances, and the Ann Taylor Loft stores (a new format geared toward less expensive merchandise) should boost earnings growth.

Valuation - 27-SEP-95

The shares fell sharply following the announcement of a 10.3% drop in June 1995 same-store sales, despite heavy promotions. As a result, earnings estimates have been revised downward. We anticipate that over time the company will be able to make up some of the sales shortfall through improved merchandise assortments, and that consumer spending will pickup modestly. A renewed focus on core AnnTaylor stores should boost profitability in 1996-7.

Key Stock Statistics

S&P EPS Est. 1996	0.35	Tang. Bk. Value/Share	0.23
P/E on S&P Est. 1996	39.3	Beta	NA
S&P EPS Est. 1997	1.05	Shareholders	500
Dividend Rate/Share	Nil	Market cap. (B)	$0.288
Shs. outstg. (M)	23.1	Inst. holdings	79%
Avg. daily vol. (M)	0.839	Insider holdings	NA

Value of $10,000 invested 5 years ago: NA

Fiscal Year Ending Jan. 31

	1996	% Change	1995	% Change	1994	% Change
Revenues (Million $)						
1Q	168.3	16%	145.0	21%	120.2	5%
2Q	183.7	15%	159.9	28%	124.8	11%
3Q	—	—	164.6	35%	122.0	6%
4Q	—	—	188.9	40%	134.6	7%
Yr.	—	—	658.8	31%	501.6	7%
Income (Million $)						
1Q	3.49	-57%	8.06	145%	3.29	54%
2Q	-3.81	NM	7.92	118%	3.63	NM
3Q	—	—	8.28	92%	4.32	1%
4Q	—	—	8.35	NM	2.46	NM
Yr.	—	—	32.62	128%	14.33	142%
Earnings Per Share ($)						
1Q	0.15	-58%	0.36	140%	0.15	50%
2Q	-0.16	NM	0.34	113%	0.16	NM
3Q	E0.08	-77%	0.35	75%	0.20	NM
4Q	E0.28	-20%	0.35	150%	0.14	NM
Yr.	E0.35	-75%	1.40	112%	0.66	136%

Next earnings report expected: mid November

AnnTaylor Stores

Business Summary - 28-SEP-95

AnnTaylor Stores is a leading specialty retailer of women's better-quality apparel, shoes and accessories. Its stores offer a distinctive collection of ready-to-wear sportswear, dresses and suits, consisting primarily of private-label fashions complemented by a selection of designer and brandname goods.

At January 28, 1995, the company operated 262 stores in 38 states and the District of Columbia. The stores were located primarily in malls (113 units); 25 were in downtown locations. Of the remaining stores, 37 in villages, and 61 in specialty centers. There were 21 outlet stores and five AnnTaylor Studio shoe and accessory stores. During 1992, two store prototypes were designed. The first is a store model of about 5,500 sq. ft., on which most new and expanded stores will be based. A larger prototype of 10,000 to 12,000 sq. ft. has been designed for certain premier markets.

AnnTaylor believes that its customer base is made up primarily of relatively affluent, fashion- conscious women who prefer classic styles, updated to reflect current fasion trends. Stores offer a variety of coordinated apparel and an assortment of shoes and accessories to enable customers to assemble complete outfits. The company has also been introducing product line extensions, such as its own line of denim jeans and petite sizes; fragrances and related products. A new moderate priced stores is being tested under the name Ann Taylor Loft.

The company publishes a catalog four times a year, mailed primarily to AnnTaylor credit card holders. Although catalog merchandise is available by mail or phone order, the catalog is used primarily to increase in-store sales. At January 28, 1995, more than 480,000 credit accounts had been used in the preceding 18 months.

Important Developments

Sep. '95—ANN received a committment from one of its banker lenders to provide an additional $25 million in financing. The loan increases the amount the company can access from $125 million to $150 million. The company agreed to amendments to its credit agreements that revised certain financial covenants required by the agreements to be met for the second quarter and the remainder of the year. The company attributed disappointing second quarter results to weak customer response to its spring merchandise offerings and continued overall weak demand for women's apparel. Same store sales fell 5.6% and net sales rose 14.9%. The company cut expansion plans for 1996-7 to about 250,000 sq. ft., from the 500,000 sq. ft. seen for 1995-6. Inventories per square foot were up 0.7% from a year earlier at the end of the second quarter.

Capitalization

Long Term Debt: $249,300,000 (7/95).
Options: To buy 1,398,006 shs. at $6.80 to $42.75 ea. (1/95).

Per Share Data ($) (Year Ended Jan. 31)

	1995	1994	1993	1992	1991	1990
Tangible Bk. Val.	0.13	-3.42	-4.69	-6.24	-21.14	-21.91
Cash Flow	2.32	1.47	1.08	0.87	1.08	0.26
Earnings	1.40	0.66	0.28	0.05	0.08	-0.91
Dividends	Nil	Nil	Nil	Nil	Nil	Nil
Payout Ratio	Nil	Nil	Nil	Nil	Nil	Nil
Cal. Yrs.	1994	1993	1992	1991	1990	1989
Prices - High	44⅞	30	25	36½	NA	NA
- Low	20½	17½	14½	12	NA	NA
P/E Ratio - High	32	45	89	NM	NA	NA
- Low	15	27	52	NA	NA	NA

Income Statement Analysis (Million $)

	1995	%Chg	1994	%Chg	1993	%Chg	1992
Revs.	666	31%	508	7%	474	7%	444
Oper. Inc.	99	43%	69.0	16%	59.5	1%	58.9
Depr.	21.3	18%	18.0	6%	17.0	8%	15.7
Int. Exp.	14.2	-20%	17.7	-17%	21.3	-37%	34.0
Pretax Inc.	62.9	100%	31.5	84%	17.1	97%	8.7
Eff. Tax Rate	48%	—	55%	—	65%	—	88%
Net Inc.	32.6	128%	14.3	142%	5.9	NM	1.0

Balance Sheet & Other Fin. Data (Million $)

	1995	1994	1993	1992	1991	1990
Cash	1.5	0.3	0.2	0.2	0.2	0.1
Curr. Assets	168	121	108	99	104	82.0
Total Assets	598	513	488	492	511	493
Curr. Liab.	65.9	68.1	78.5	72.4	61.9	58.3
LT Debt	200	180	158	186	367	356
Common Eqty.	326	259	245	229	58.0	58.0
Total Cap.	526	440	404	415	446	433
Cap. Exp.	61.3	25.1	4.3	10.0	11.8	6.1
Cash Flow	53.9	32.3	22.9	16.7	15.2	3.5

Ratio Analysis

	1995	1994	1993	1992	1991	1990
Curr. Ratio	2.6	1.8	1.4	1.4	1.7	1.4
% LT Debt of Cap.	38.0	41.0	39.2	44.8	82.4	82.1
% Net Inc.of Revs.	4.9	2.8	1.2	0.2	0.3	NM
% Ret. on Assets	5.7	2.8	1.2	0.1	0.2	NM
% Ret. on Equity	10.8	5.6	2.4	0.6	2.1	NM

Dividend Data —No dividends have been paid.

Data as orig. reptd.; bef. results of disc. opers. and/or spec. items. Per share data adj. for stk. divs. as of ex-div. date. E-Estimated. NA-Not Available. NM-Not Meaningful. NR-Not Ranked.

Office—142 West 57th St., New York, NY 10019. **Tel**—(212) 541-3300. **Chrmn & CEO**—Sally F. Kasaks. **EVP-Fin & Admin**—P. E. Francis. **VP, Secy & Investor Contact**—Jocelyn F. L. Barandiaran. **Dirs**—G. S. Armstrong, J. J. Burke, Jr., P. E. Francis, R. C. Grayson, S. F. Kasaks, R. B. Lazarus, H. M. Merriman. **Transfer Agent & Registrar**—Continental Stock Transfer & Trust Co. NYC. **Incorporated** in Delaware in 1988. **Empl**-5,258. **S&P Analyst:** Karen J. Sack, CFA

STANDARD & POOR'S

STOCK REPORTS

Aon Corp.

NYSE Symbol **AOC**
In S&P MidCap 400

18-OCT-95 **Industry:** Insurance

Summary: This life, accident/health, and property/casualty insurer has expanded its insurance brokerage unit through acquisitions, and is now the second largest insurance broker in the U.S.

S&P Opinion: Accumulate (★★★★)

Recent Price • 43⅛
52 Wk Range • 43⅞-29¼
Yield • 3.1%
12-Mo. P/E • 13.1

Quantitative Evaluations
Outlook
(1 Lowest—5 Highest)
• **3+**
Fair Value
• **42½**
Risk
• **Low**
Earn./Div. Rank
• **A-**

Technical Eval.
• **Bullish** since 10/94
Rel. Strength Rank
(1 Lowest—99 Highest)
• **88**
Insider Activity
• **NA**

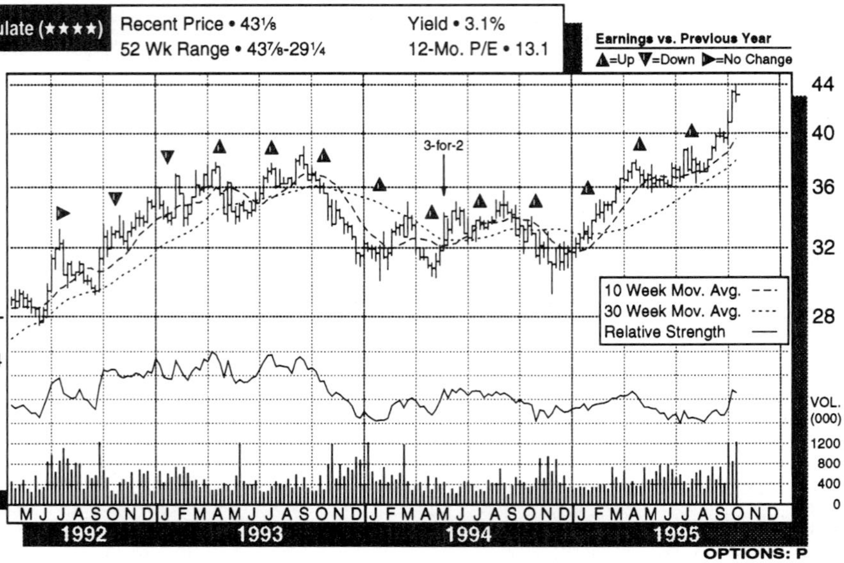

Overview - 18-OCT-95

Revenue and earnings growth in most segments is likely in coming periods. Having integrated the Frank B. Hall acquisition, the brokerage division is poised to reap the benefits of firmer insurance rates (in selected areas). Reinsurance and wholesale broking have exhibited the strongest growth, while competitive premium pricing has limited growth in the retail broking sector. Margin expansion is predicated on AOC's ability to reign in costs here. Demand for investment-oriented products, the positive impact of expense controls, and stable to lower interest rates will aid life profits. Accident and health results are expected to be mixed. Specialty property-casualty premiums may decline amid a curtailment of certain writings, but this move will aid underwriting results. The proposed sale of two insurance units will free up capital that might be used to further expand the brokerage unit.

Valuation - 18-OCT-95

After trending downward along with most other interest-sensitive issues during the latter half of 1994, Aon shares have rebounded nicely so far in 1995. Multi-line insurance stocks (like Aon) tend to trade at relatively low P/E multiples. However, Aon's growing participation in the insurance brokerage market (and its attendant higher market valuations) is not fully reflected in the current valuation. Hence, at only 11 times our 1996 operating earnings estimate, additional upside potential exists.

Key Stock Statistics

S&P EPS Est. 1995	3.50	Tang. Bk. Value/Share	9.46
P/E on S&P Est. 1995	12.3	Beta	0.68
S&P EPS Est. 1996	3.90	Shareholders	14,700
Dividend Rate/Share	1.36	Market cap. (B)	$ 4.7
Shs. outstg. (M)	107.1	Inst. holdings	46%
Avg. daily vol. (M)	0.206	Insider holdings	NA

Value of $10,000 invested 5 years ago: $ 19,011

Fiscal Year Ending Dec. 31

	1995	% Change	1994	% Change	1993	% Change
Revenues (Million $)						
1Q	1,139	12%	1,020	7%	950.3	17%
2Q	1,141	11%	1,026	7%	963.0	20%
3Q	—	—	1,031	8%	954.2	17%
4Q	—	—	1,080	11%	977.0	8%
Yr.	—	—	4,157	8%	3,844	15%
Income (Million $)						
1Q	111.2	12%	99.1	11%	89.00	19%
2Q	98.70	12%	88.20	12%	79.10	19%
3Q	—	—	86.70	11%	77.80	22%
4Q	—	—	86.00	10%	77.90	NM
Yr.	—	—	360.0	11%	323.8	57%
Earnings Per Share ($)						
1Q	0.96	9%	0.88	12%	0.79	9%
2Q	0.85	10%	0.77	12%	0.69	8%
3Q	—	—	0.76	13%	0.67	11%
4Q	—	—	0.74	10%	0.67	NM
Yr.	E3.50	11%	3.14	12%	2.81	46%

Next earnings report expected: early November

Aon Corp.

Business Summary - 18-OCT-95

Aon Corp. (formerly Combined International) is a holding company whose subsidiaries write accident and health, life and specialty property-casualty insurance. Other operations include insurance brokerage and related services. Pretax income by segment:

	1994	1993	1992
Accident & health	36%	35%	43%
Life insurance	23%	22%	25%
Spec. prop.-cas.	10%	9%	10%
Brokerage services	24%	27%	18%
Corp. & other	7%	7%	4%

Accident and health products (underwritten by Combined Insurance, Union Fidelity, Credit Life and Ryan Insurance Group) include Medicare supplemental insurance, disability, credit, cancer and accident and health supplemental insurance.

Life insurance, which is offered by Life of Virginia, Combined Insurance, and Union Fidelity consists of capital accumulation products (such as universal life and annuities), ordinary life products and credit insurance.

Specialty property-casualty lines include automobile and appliance extended-warranty coverage and reinsurance.

Insurance brokerage and related services, conducted by Rollins Hudig Hall (formerly Rollins Burdick Hunter Co.) and affiliates (Aon Risk Services, Aon Specialty group, Godwins, Nicholson Chamberlain Colls Ltd. and Leslie Godwin Ltd.), provide clients with risk management, reinsurance services and employee benefit consulting.

Important Developments

Sep. '95—AOC said that it plans to explore the sale of two of its insurance subsidiaries, The Life Insurance Company of Virginia and Union Fidelity Life Insurance Company. This decision is part of AOC's plan to concentrate its efforts in two core segments: insurance brokerage and life, accident/health, and extended warranty insurance coverage. No timetable for the sale was set. Life of Virginia underwrites capital accumulation, life insurance, and annuity products. Union Fidelity offers life, health, and accident insurance.

Capitalization

Notes Payable: $496,200,000 (6/95).
Redeem. Preferred Stock: $50,000,000.
Preferred Stock: $11,100,000 (par value).

Per Share Data ($)

(Year Ended Dec. 31)

	1994	1993	1992	1991	1990	1989
Tangible Bk. Val.	6.48	7.33	13.62	13.37	12.16	12.33
Oper. Earnings	3.10	2.71	1.90	2.44	2.37	2.33
Earnings	3.14	2.81	1.93	2.47	2.41	2.36
Dividends	1.26	1.18	1.11	1.05	0.99	0.91
Relative Payout	40%	42%	57%	43%	41%	39%
Prices - High	35¾	39	36	27⅞	28⅜	28⅞
- Low	29¼	30⅞	26⅛	19⅞	17⅞	18
P/E Ratio - High	11	14	19	11	12	12
- Low	9	11	14	8	7	8

Income Statement Analysis (Million $)

	1994	%Chg	1993	%Chg	1992	%Chg	1991
Life Ins. In Force	75,222	4%	72,161	NM	71,851	NM	71,900
Prem.Inc Life A&H	1,684	8%	1,562	NM	1,548	4%	1,487
Prem.Inc Cas/Prop	250	-4%	261	-6%	278	13%	247
Net Invest. Inc.	760	2%	745	1%	737	3%	713
Oth. Revs.	1,464	15%	1,277	65%	773	60%	484
Total Revs.	4,157	8%	3,845	15%	3,337	14%	2,931
Pretax Inc.	538	12%	479	65%	291	-12%	332
Net Oper. Inc.	NA	—	312	54%	203	-15%	239
Net Inc.	360	11%	324	57%	206	-15%	242

Balance Sheet & Other Fin. Data (Million $)

	1994	1993	1992	1991	1990	1989
Cash & Equiv.	642	292	229	183	224	162
Premiums Due	2,520	2,101	1,720	822	594	529
Inv Assets Bonds	7,927	7,858	7,366	6,774	6,038	4,903
Inv. Assets Stock	939	933	830	610	628	811
Inv. Assets Loans	782	767	797	852	894	884
Inv. Assets Total	9,783	9,652	9,088	8,360	7,704	6,665
Deferred Policy Cost	1,182	1,005	948	911	868	761
Total Assets	17,922	16,279	14,290	11,633	10,432	9,156
Debt	496	521	478	418	430	438
Common Eqty.	2,246	2,274	2,089	1,771	1,457	1,421

Ratio Analysis

	1994	1993	1992	1991	1990	1989
Comb. Loss-Exp.Ratio	NA	NA	NA	NA	NA	NA
% Ret. on Revs.	8.7	8.4	6.2	8.3	9.1	10.0
% Ret. on Equity	14.5	14.8	9.9	15.0	16.6	17.2
% Invest. Yield	7.8	8.0	8.4	8.9	9.2	9.3

Dividend Data —Cash dividends have been paid since 1950. A dividend reinvestment plan is available.

Amt. of Div. $	Date Decl.	Ex-Div. Date	Stock of Record	Payment Date
0.320	Sep. 16	Oct. 26	Nov. 01	Nov. 14 '94
0.320	Jan. 20	Feb. 03	Feb. 09	Feb. 23 '95
0.340	Mar. 17	Apr. 26	May. 02	May. 15 '95
0.340	Jul. 13	Jul. 28	Aug. 01	Aug. 14 '95
0.340	Sep. 15	Oct. 31	Nov. 02	Nov. 15 '95

Data as orig. reptd.; bef. results of disc. opers. and/or spec. items. Per share data adj. for stk. divs. as of ex-div. date. E-Estimate. NA-Not Available. NM-Not Meaningful. NR-Not Ranked.

Office—123 North Wacker Drive, Chicago, IL 60606. **Tel**—(312) 701-3000. **Chrmn & Pres**—P. G. Ryan. **EVP-CFO & Treas**—H. N. Medvin. **Sr VP-Secy**—A. F. Quern. **VP-Investor Contact**—Joan E. Steel. **Dirs**—D. T. Carroll, F. A. Cole, P. J. Lewis, J. D. Manley, A. J. McKenna, N. N. Minow, P. Pedersen, D. S. Perkins, J. W. Rogers, Jr., P. G. Ryan, G. A. Schaefer, R. I. Skilling, J. E. Swearingen, F. L. Turner, A. R. Weber. **Transfer Agent & Registrar**—First Chicago Trust Co. of New York, NYC. **Incorporated** in Illinois in 1949; reincorporated in Delaware in 1980. **Empl**-27,000. **S&P Analyst:** Catherine A. Seifert

STANDARD & POOR'S

STOCK REPORTS

Apache Corp.

NYSE Symbol **APA**
In S&P MidCap 400

23-SEP-95

Industry:
Oil and Gas

Summary: Apache is an independent energy company engaged in the exploration for and production and marketing of oil and natural gas.

S&P Opinion: Accumulate (★★★★)

Recent Price • 27
52 Wk Range • 31-22¼

Yield • 1.0%
12-Mo. P/E • 57.4

Quantitative Evaluations

Outlook
(1 Lowest—5 Highest)
• **1−**

Fair Value
• **18⅝**

Risk
• **Average**

Earn./Div. Rank
• **B-**

Technical Eval.
• **Bearish** since 9/95

Rel. Strength Rank
(1 Lowest—99 Highest)
• **20**

Insider Activity
• **NA**

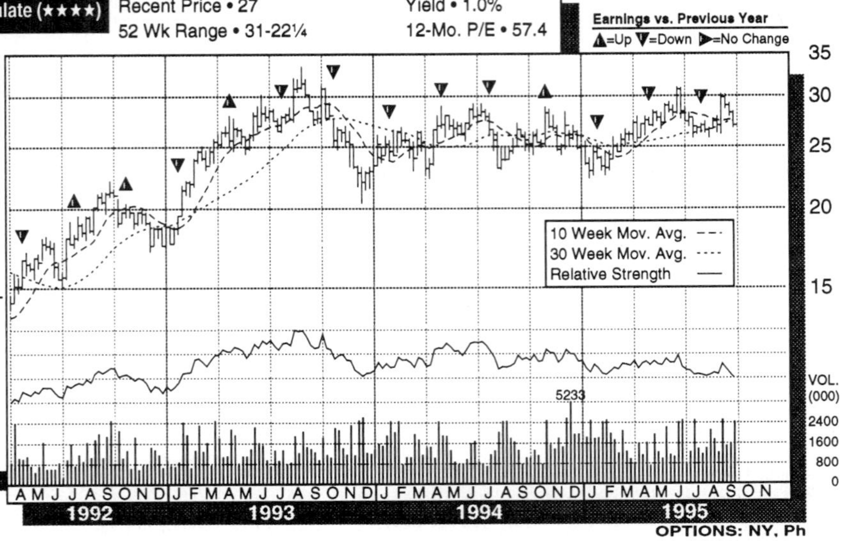

OPTIONS: NY, Ph

Overview - 22-SEP-95

Share earnings in 1995 are projected to decline to $0.40 (including a $0.12 a share charge for DEKALB merger), as depressed gas prices will negatively impact earnings. However, the company's acquisition program together with efforts to increase production from properties should lead to continued growth in both natural gas and oil production. APA should benefit from the acquisition of certain Texaco properties, its merger with DEKALB Energy, and its recently announced agreement to purchase Aquila Energy Resources from UtiliCorp. The divestiture of certain non-core oil and gas properties should help to improve APA's balance sheet by reducing the inflated debt levels caused by acquisition activity. 1996 results should benefit from increases in gas prices and expansion of Apache's international presence.

Valuation - 22-SEP-95

Decreasing oil and gas prices in 1994 have led to a deterioration in the oil and natural gas markets, translating into depressed earnings and relatively weak stock prices across the industry. Although Apache's shares did lose some of their value in 1994, the stock is up about 12% since the beginning of 1995. The shares are currently trading at about 29 times estimated 1996 share earnings of $0.95. Apache's share price should benefit from key acquisitions and divestitures of low-margin, non-strategic assets. Therefore, based on Apache's near-term outlook, these shares should outperform in the next six to 12 months.

Key Stock Statistics

S&P EPS Est. 1995	0.40	Tang. Bk. Value/Share	13.28
P/E on S&P Est. 1995	67.5	Beta	0.66
S&P EPS Est. 1996	0.95	Shareholders	10,400
Dividend Rate/Share	0.28	Market cap. (B)	$ 1.9
Shs. outstg. (M)	69.9	Inst. holdings	71%
Avg. daily vol. (M)	0.464	Insider holdings	NA

Value of $10,000 invested 5 years ago: $ 15,991

Fiscal Year Ending Dec. 31

	1995	% Change	1994	% Change	1993	% Change
Revenues (Million $)						
1Q	158.6	30%	121.6	12%	108.6	18%
2Q	206.1	53%	134.9	21%	111.3	-15%
3Q	—	—	140.8	15%	122.0	10%
4Q	—	—	148.3	19%	124.8	4%
Yr.	—	—	545.6	17%	466.6	3%
Income (Million $)						
1Q	5.99	-36%	9.41	-19%	11.59	186%
2Q	0.54	-95%	10.20	-11%	11.50	-52%
3Q	—	—	10.58	NM	1.08	-87%
4Q	—	—	12.66	-4%	13.17	17%
Yr.	—	—	42.84	15%	37.33	-22%
Earnings Per Share ($)						
1Q	0.10	-33%	0.15	-38%	0.24	167%
2Q	0.01	-94%	0.17	-23%	0.22	-57%
3Q	E0.10	-41%	0.17	NM	0.02	-89%
4Q	E0.19	-10%	0.21	-5%	0.22	-8%
Yr.	E0.40	-43%	0.70	NM	0.70	-31%

Next earnings report expected: late October

Apache Corp.

Business Summary - 22-SEP-95

Apache Corp. is an independent energy company engaged in the exploration for and development, production, processing and marketing of natural gas and oil, mostly on- and offshore in the continental U.S. Through a subsidiary, the company holds international exploration interests.

At December 31, 1994, proved reserves aggregated 99,908,000 bbl. of crude oil (90% developed) and 1,016.3 Bcf of natural gas (90%), compared with 89,723,000 bbl. of oil (88%) and 848.2 Bcf of gas (85%) at year-end 1993.

Acreage held under domestic leases and international production and exploration rights at year-end 1994 totaled 1,852,448 gross (781,336 net) developed acres, and 11,206,235 gross (4,843,092 net) undeveloped acres. At December 31, 1994, APA had 3,275 gross productive gas wells (1,262 net wells) and 4,819 gross productive oil wells (2,415 net). During 1994, it drilled 52 exploratory wells, of which 27 were productive, and 264 development wells, with 225 productive.

Production in 1994 totaled 13,084,000 bbl. of oil and 155.9 Bcf of gas, versus 12,294,000 bbl. and 110.6 Bcf in 1993. The average price of oil was $15.66 per bbl. ($16.78 in 1993) and of gas $1.81 per Mcf ($2.03).

In March 1995, Apache purchased certain oil and gas properties from Texaco Exploration and Production Inc. for an adjusted purchase price of $571 million. In December 1994, Apache entered into a merger agreement with DEKALB Energy Co. under which DEKLAB shareholders will receive between 8.0 and 9.0 million shares of Apache common stock and DEKALB will become a wholly-owned subsidiary of Apache. Also in December 1994, APA purchased the U.S. oil and gas properties of Crystal Oil Co. for approximately $95.8 million.

Important Developments

Sep. '95—APA completed the sale of certain Rocky Mountain properties to Houston-based Citation Oil & Gas Corp. for $155 million. After adjustments, Apache and its net-profit-interest partners will receive about $151 million, of which Apache's share is about $143 million.

Aug. '95—APA agreed to purchase substantially all of the assets of Aquila Energy Resources from UtiliCorp United for about $198 million. Assets to be purchased include proved and probable reserves estimated by Apache to total 236 Bcf of gas equivalent on about 115,000 developed and 26,000 undeveloped net acres in western Oklahoma's Anadarko Basin and offshore in the Gulf of Mexico. The transaction is expected to close in late September 1995.

Capitalization

Long Term Debt: $1,207,913,000 (6/95).

Per Share Data ($)

(Year Ended Dec. 31)

	1994	1993	1992	1991	1990	1989
Tangible Bk. Val.	13.28	12.86	10.12	9.39	8.65	7.97
Cash Flow	4.61	4.42	4.63	3.72	3.52	3.41
Earnings	0.70	0.70	1.02	0.76	0.90	0.64
Dividends	0.28	0.28	0.28	0.28	0.28	0.28
Payout Ratio	40%	40%	27%	38%	31%	56%
Prices - High	29¼	33½	22⅛	20¾	20¾	18⅜
- Low	22¼	17⅝	12	12	13⅜	7⅞
P/E Ratio - High	42	48	22	27	23	29
- Low	32	25	12	16	15	12

Income Statement Analysis (Million $)

	1994	%Chg	1993	%Chg	1992	%Chg	1991
Revs.	538	16%	463	9%	423	24%	342
Oper. Inc.	327	16%	281	15%	244	21%	201
Depr. Depl. & Amort.	240	21%	199	18%	169	24%	136
Int. Exp.	36.0	13%	32.0	-18%	39.2	20%	32.7
Pretax Inc.	64.0	10%	58.0	-17%	70.0	59%	44.0
Eff. Tax Rate	34%	—	36%	—	32%	—	22%
Net Inc.	42.8	15%	37.3	-22%	47.8	38%	34.6

Balance Sheet & Other Fin. Data (Million $)

	1994	1993	1992	1991	1990	1989
Cash	15.1	17.1	26.1	6.4	85.2	75.2
Curr. Assets	135	123	114	91.0	138	133
Total Assets	1,879	1,592	1,219	1,209	830	764
Curr. Liab.	148	185	158	146	123	108
LT Debt	657	453	454	491	195	196
Common Eqty.	816	786	475	440	387	350
Total Cap.	1,630	1,367	1,013	996	648	599
Cap. Exp.	494	583	207	686	191	134
Cash Flow	283	237	217	170	157	118

Ratio Analysis

	1994	1993	1992	1991	1990	1989
Curr. Ratio	0.9	0.7	0.7	0.6	1.1	1.2
% LT Debt of Cap.	40.3	33.1	44.9	49.3	30.1	32.7
% Ret. on Assets	2.5	2.3	3.9	3.3	5.0	2.6
% Ret. on Equity	5.3	5.3	10.4	8.2	10.8	7.1

Dividend Data —Dividends have been paid since 1965. A dividend reinvestment plan is available. A "poison pill" stock purchase rights plan was adopted in 1986.

Amt. of Div. $	Date Decl.	Ex-Div. Date	Stock of Record	Payment Date
0.070	Aug. 01	Sep. 26	Sep. 30	Oct. 31 '94
0.070	Dec. 13	Dec. 23	Dec. 30	Jan. 31 '95
0.070	Mar. 01	Mar. 27	Mar. 31	Apr. 28 '95
0.070	May. 04	Jun. 28	Jun. 30	Jul. 31 '95
0.070	Jul. 14	Sep. 27	Sep. 29	Oct. 31 '95

Data as orig. reptd.; bef. results of disc opers. and/or spec. items. Per share data adj. for stk. divs. as of ex-div. date. Revs. in Income Statement Analysis excl. other income. E-Estimated. NA-Not Available. NM-Not Meaningful. NR-Not Ranked.

Office—2000 Post Oak Blvd., Houston, TX 77056-4400. **Tel**—(713) 296-6000. **Chrmn & CEO**—R. Plank. **Pres & COO**—G. S. Farris. **VP & Secy**—Z. S. Kobiashvili. **VP & Treas**—C. E. McKenzie. **Investor Contact**—Paul Korus. **Dirs**—F. M. Bohen, V. B. Day, G. S. Farris, R. M. Ferlic, E. C. Fiedorek, W. B. Fields, R. V. Gisselbeck, S. K. Hathaway, J. A. Kocur, R. Plank, J. A. Precourt, J. A. Rice. **Transfer Agent & Registar**—Norwest Bank Minnesota, South St. Paul. **Incorporated** in Delaware in 1954. **Empl-** 1,086. **S&P Analyst:** Ronald J. Gross

STANDARD & POOR'S
STOCK REPORTS

Applied Bioscience Int'l

NASDAQ Symbol **APBI**
In S&P MidCap 400

26-SEP-95 **Industry:** Health Care Centers

Summary: This company provides research and consulting services to clients in the pharmaceutical, chemical, agrochemical, biotechnology and other industries worldwide.

Quantitative Evaluations
Outlook (1 Lowest—5 Highest) • **1⁻**
Fair Value • **6½**
Risk • **Average**
Earn./Div. Rank • **NR**

Technical Eval. • **Bullish** since 8/95
Rel. Strength Rank (1 Lowest—99 Highest) • **63**
Insider Activity • **NA**

Recent Price • 6⅝
52 Wk Range • 7⅞-4⅛
Yield • Nil
12-Mo. P/E • NM

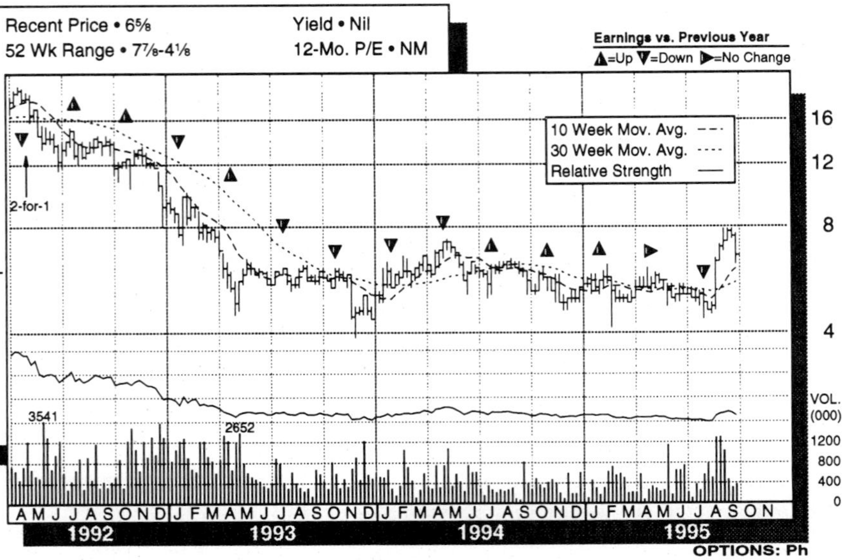

OPTIONS: Ph

Business Profile - 26-SEP-95

This scientific research/consulting company has been reorganizing and refocusing its strategic efforts since 1993. Over the last two years it has divested two divisions from its environmental sciences group (Paragon and ETC), sold its toxicology business and disposed of its Astrix subsidiary. APBI is investing significant capital in its high margin biostatistics business of Pharmaco LSR and facility expansion. Results from continuing operations have been profitable since the 1993 restructuring.

Operational Review - 26-SEP-95

Total revenues in the six months ended June 30, 1995, rose 10%, year to year, attributable to gains in the life sciences (8.9% growth) and environmental sciences (13%) divisions. Margins narrowed and operating income declined slightly to $3.4 million from $3.5 million. After taxes at 43.0% versus 32.7%, income from continuing operations fell 30% to $1.2 million ($0.04 a share) from $1.8 million ($0.06). Results in the 1994 period exclude losses of $0.03 a share from discontinued operations.

Stock Performance - 22-SEP-95

In the past 30 trading days, APBI's shares have increased 39%, compared to a 5% rise in the S&P 500. Average trading volume for the past five days was 70,500 shares, compared with the 40-day moving average of 197,256 shares.

Key Stock Statistics

Dividend Rate/Share	Nil	Shareholders	5,100
Shs. outstg. (M)	28.1	Market cap. (B)	$0.183
Avg. daily vol. (M)	0.108	Inst. holdings	67%
Tang. Bk. Value/Share	2.25	Insider holdings	NA
Beta	1.27		

Value of $10,000 invested 5 years ago: $ 8,548

Fiscal Year Ending Dec. 31

	1995	% Change	1994	% Change	1993	% Change
Revenues (Million $)						
1Q	45.77	14%	40.20	-4%	41.80	NM
2Q	47.89	7%	44.94	3%	43.60	NM
3Q	—	—	44.23	24%	35.76	-23%
4Q	—	—	45.50	20%	37.78	-23%
Yr.	—	—	174.9	10%	158.9	-12%
Income (Million $)						
1Q	0.44	-21%	0.56	-66%	1.64	NM
2Q	0.78	-35%	1.20	186%	0.42	-91%
3Q	—	—	1.36	NM	-13.31	NM
4Q	—	—	-0.25	NM	-6.09	NM
Yr.	—	—	2.86	NM	-17.33	NM
Earnings Per Share ($)						
1Q	0.02	NM	0.02	-67%	0.06	NM
2Q	0.03	-25%	0.04	100%	0.02	-87%
3Q	—	—	0.05	NM	-0.47	NM
4Q	—	—	-0.01	NM	-0.22	NM
Yr.	—	—	0.10	NM	-0.61	NM

Next earnings report expected: late October

Applied Bioscience Int'l

Business Summary - 26-SEP-95

Applied Bioscience International Inc. provides a broad range of services, including biological safety testing; clinical research and development; chemical risk assessment and risk management; and analytical laboratory services. Clients are engaged in pharmaceutical, general chemical, biotechnology and other industries worldwide. Operating revenues (net of subcontractor costs) in recent years were divided:

	1994	1993	1992
Life sciences	74%	72%	63%
Environmental sciences	26%	28%	37%

In 1992, following the acquisition of Pharmaco, the company reorganized its Life Sciences operations into Pharmaco LSR. Pharmaco LSR provides contract biological safety (toxicological) testing services on a worldwide basis through two laboratories, located in the U.K. and the U.S. The toxicology divisions conduct studies designed to produce the data needed to identify, quantify and evaluate the risks to humans and the environment resulting from the manufacture or use of pharmaceutical, chemical, biotechnology and other products. Pharmaco LSR generated approximately 64% of the net revenues in the Life Sciences Group during 1994.

Pharmaco LSR's clinical services division provides clinical research and development services primarily to the pharmaceutical industry. It is engaged in most aspects of the clinical development process, including analytical chemistry, evaluation of clinical data, data processing, biostatistical analysis and the preparation of supporting documentation for compliance with regulatory requirements.

APBI's Environmental Sciences Group provides environmental and health sciences consulting services under the name Environ. Environ generated virtually all of the revenues from APBI's environmental sciences group. Consulting services include chemical risk assessment, litigation support, product safety regulation and others. In 1993, the group formed a new division, Astrix Software, which develops software for laboratories. Astrix was sold in August 1995. During mid-1994, the group sold its agrochemicals unit, Paragon Global Services.

In August 1994, APBI merged its Environmental Testing and Certification (ETC) division with Pace, Inc. and Coast-to-Coast Analytical Services Inc., two leading laboratories. The new environmental services firm, 35% owned by APBI, is known as Pace Inc.

Important Developments

Aug. '95—The company agreed to sell its two toxicology laboratories to Huntingdon International Holdings for $32.5 million in cash. Separately, the company sold its Astrix software division to Astrix management.

Capitalization

Long Term Debt: $35,761,000 (6/95).

Per Share Data ($) (Year Ended Dec. 31)

	1994	1993	1992	1991	1990	1989
Tangible Bk. Val.	2.21	2.48	3.28	3.50	2.23	2.13
Cash Flow	0.49	-0.30	0.55	0.81	0.54	0.58
Earnings	0.10	-0.61	0.22	0.54	0.31	0.37
Dividends	Nil	Nil	Nil	Nil	Nil	Nil
Payout Ratio	Nil	Nil	Nil	Nil	Nil	Nil
Prices - High	7³/₈	10	20¹/₈	19⁵/₈	10¹/₄	8³/₈
- Low	4⁵/₈	3⁷/₈	8	9³/₈	6¹/₂	4¹/₂
P/E Ratio - High	74	NM	91	36	33	23
- Low	46	NM	36	17	21	12

Income Statement Analysis (Million $)

	1994	%Chg	1993	%Chg	1992	%Chg	1991
Revs.	175	10%	159	-12%	181	59%	114
Oper. Inc.	18.4	NM	-1.6	NM	33.9	36%	24.9
Depr.	11.0	25%	8.8	-11%	9.9	60%	6.2
Int. Exp.	3.2	62%	2.0	89%	1.0	60%	0.6
Pretax Inc.	4.7	NM	-21.0	NM	12.4	-37%	19.7
Eff. Tax Rate	40%	—	NM	—	48%	—	37%
Net Inc.	2.9	NM	-17.3	NM	6.5	-48%	12.5

Balance Sheet & Other Fin. Data (Million $)

	1994	1993	1992	1991	1990	1989
Cash	7.9	10.5	12.9	15.3	8.5	6.3
Curr. Assets	81.1	77.2	94.0	63.6	46.7	24.7
Total Assets	182	183	196	139	110	70.0
Curr. Liab.	57.4	80.1	57.4	36.7	42.1	24.9
LT Debt	42.9	14.4	14.0	4.2	3.0	2.3
Common Eqty.	69.0	77.0	112	84.2	50.4	32.9
Total Cap.	123	101	137	101	65.0	45.0
Cap. Exp.	14.5	15.8	17.8	8.8	10.6	6.6
Cash Flow	13.8	-8.6	16.4	18.6	11.4	7.8

Ratio Analysis

	1994	1993	1992	1991	1990	1989
Curr. Ratio	1.4	1.0	1.6	1.7	1.1	1.0
% LT Debt of Cap.	34.9	14.2	10.2	4.1	4.7	5.2
% Net Inc.of Revs.	1.6	NM	3.6	11.0	6.6	8.6
% Ret. on Assets	1.6	NM	3.3	9.6	6.0	7.5
% Ret. on Equity	3.9	NM	6.3	17.9	13.0	16.2

Dividend Data —No cash dividends have been paid. Two-for-one stock splits were effected in April 1992 and January 1991.

Data as orig. reptd.; bef. results of disc. opers. and/or spec. items. Per share data adj. for stk. divs. as of ex-div. date. E-Estimated. NA-Not Available. NM-Not Meaningful. NR-Not Ranked.

Tel—(703) 516-2490. **Chrmn, Pres & CEO**—K. H. Harper. **SVP, CFO & Treas**—S. L. Waechter. **Secy**—C. E. Chason. **SVP & Investor Contact**—John H. Timoney (609-951-9090). **Dirs**—J. D. Bryer, J. G. Donelan, S. A. Fleckman, F. Frank, K. H. Harper, M. L. Hendrix, J. H. Highland, F. E. Loy, L. C. McQuade, T. J. Russell, Jr., J. H. Timoney, S. L. Waechter. **Transfer Agent & Registrar**—Midlantic National Bank, Edison, N.J. **Incorporated** in Delaware in 1986. **Empl**-1,912. **S&P Analyst:** Thomas Tirney

STANDARD & POOR'S

STOCK REPORTS

Arnold Industries

NASDAQ Symbol **AIND**
In S&P MidCap 400

02-AUG-95 **Industry:** Trucking

Summary: Arnold Industries is a trucking company that provides less-than-truckload (LTL), truckload and warehouse services primarily in the northeastern U.S.

S&P Opinion: Hold (★★★)

Recent Price • 18½ | Yield • 2.4%
52 Wk Range • 23½-16¼ | 12-Mo. P/E • 14.0

Quantitative Evaluations

Outlook
(1 Lowest—5 Highest)
• **5⁻**

Fair Value
• **19⅜**

Risk
• **Average**

Earn./Div. Rank
• **A**

Technical Eval.
• **Bullish** since 6/95

Rel. Strength Rank
(1 Lowest—99 Highest)
• **44**

Insider Activity
• **NA**

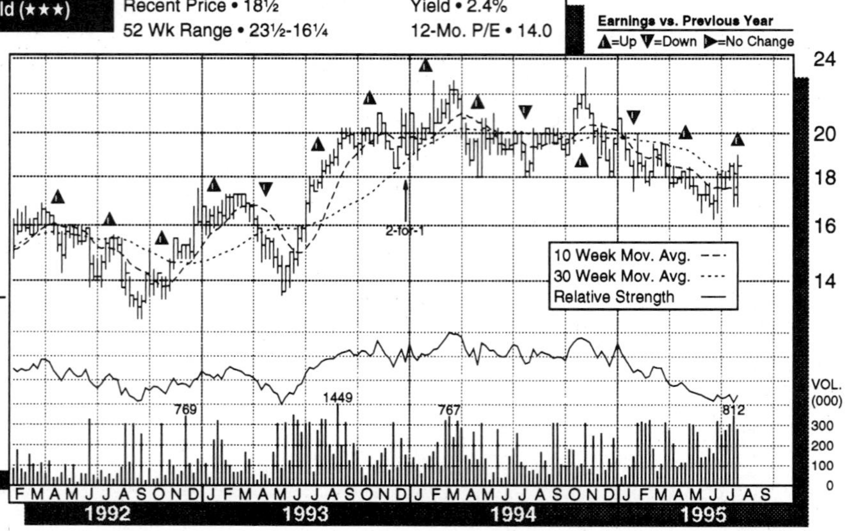

Overview - 02-AUG-95

Revenues for 1995 should increase at least 10% from those of 1994, reflecting the bankruptcy and exit of major competitor St. Johnsbury Trucking Co., the largest LTL carrier in the Northeast, as well as gains from continued internal growth and an expanding economy. However, revenues must continue to pick up at New Penn, which saw operating revenues decline slightly in the first quarter of 1995, but rise 42% in the second quarter. Profitability should improve on the higher volumes and efficiencies resulting from implementation of better management systems--including management information and costing systems--at DW Freight and SilverEagle (both acquired in 1992). Arnold's long-term strategy includes expanding its services into contiguous geographic areas and increasing efficiencies.

Valuation - 02-AUG-95

The shares of this trucking company have traded in a narrow range since the middle of 1993 and are down about 13% from their January 1995 high. Revenues and earnings have grown steadily over the last few years, though most of these gains can be attributed to recent acquisitions. However, earnings for 1995 are expected to advance 25%, principally reflecting additional acquisitions, rate increases and higher volumes. These factors, in combination with an expected economic recovery in the second half of 1995, should help the shares rebound from their recent lows.

Key Stock Statistics

S&P EPS Est. 1995	1.45	Tang. Bk. Value/Share	6.48
P/E on S&P Est. 1995	12.8	Beta	0.81
S&P EPS Est. 1996	1.60	Shareholders	1,100
Dividend Rate/Share	0.44	Market cap. (B)	$0.479
Shs. outstg. (M)	26.6	Inst. holdings	58%
Avg. daily vol. (M)	0.087	Insider holdings	NA

Value of $10,000 invested 5 years ago: $ 25,869

Fiscal Year Ending Dec. 31

	1995	% Change	1994	% Change	1993	% Change
Revenues (Million $)						
1Q	83.42	11%	75.03	25%	59.91	17%
2Q	83.38	26%	65.98	-1%	66.87	12%
3Q	—	—	80.87	12%	72.32	18%
4Q	—	—	80.51	9%	73.59	21%
Yr.	—	—	302.4	11%	272.7	17%
Income (Million $)						
1Q	8.51	15%	7.42	30%	5.70	-6%
2Q	8.52	60%	5.31	-30%	7.56	15%
3Q	—	—	8.96	21%	7.43	23%
4Q	—	—	9.05	-2%	9.21	29%
Yr.	—	—	30.74	3%	29.90	16%
Earnings Per Share ($)						
1Q	0.32	14%	0.28	27%	0.22	-4%
2Q	0.32	60%	0.20	-29%	0.28	14%
3Q	E0.39	—	0.34	21%	0.28	22%
4Q	E0.42	—	0.34	-3%	0.35	30%
Yr.	E1.45	—	1.16	3%	1.13	16%

Next earnings report expected: late October

Arnold Industries

Business Summary - 02-AUG-95

Arnold Industries is engaged in the trucking and warehousing business. Operations are conducted through four subsidiaries--one less-than-truckload (LTL) carrier, New Penn Motor Express, and three truckload (TL) carriers, Lebarnold, DW Freight and SilverEagle Transport. Revenue contributions in recent years:

	1994	1993	1992
LTL	53%	57%	59%
Truckload	42%	37%	33%
Warehousing/Related trucking	5%	6%	8%

New Penn, a less-than-truckload carrier, transports commodities primarily in interstate commerce in New England and the Middle Atlantic states, and areas of Canada, with extensive intrastate carriage in Pennsylvania and New York. Southeastern Atlantic states, Florida and Puerto Rico are serviced by a specific carrier in each area that is on-line with New Penn's computer system. Commodities transported include food; textiles and apparel; building, metal and paper products; office equipment and supplies; and pharmaceuticals.

Arnold Logistic Services includes regional truckload carriers Lebarnold, Inc., SilverEagle Transport, Inc. and DW Freight, Inc., and ADW (Lebarnold's specialty warehouse division). Lebarnold is a Northeast TL carrier. In 1992, after closing its pier container operation, Lebarnold expanded its local Northeast and Charlotte, N.C., operations. ADW serves the assembly, distribution and warehousing needs of its customers from five warehouses in two Pennsylvania locations. SilverEagle is a regional dry freight TL carrier based in Jacksonville, Florida, serving primarily food industry participants, from terminals located in Florida, Georgia, North Carolina, New York and Ohio. In January 1995, the company, through SilverEagle, acquired T.W. Owens & Sons Trucking, Inc., a truckload carrier located in Georgia, for approximately $12 million.

DW Freight's primary operating unit is TL carrier Dalworth Trucking Co., based in Fort Worth, Tex. DW serves mostly container business participants, and operates primarily in Texas and Oklahoma. In March 1994, DW acquired H.R. Hill, an Oklahoma-based truckload carrier that serves points the Midwest.

Important Developments

Jul. '95—In reporting results for the second quarter of 1995, the company said that operating revenues for New Penn advanced 42%, as comparisons were aided by the absence of the Teamsters strike which hampered results in 1994;net operating income soared 120%. However, operating revenues for the Arnold Logistics Companies climbed only 13% and the gain in net operating income was limited to 8.6%.

Capitalization

Long Term Debt: None (3/95).

Per Share Data ($)

(Year Ended Dec. 31)

	1994	1993	1992	1991	1990	1989
Tangible Bk. Val.	6.30	5.52	4.73	4.42	3.82	3.26
Cash Flow	1.95	1.78	1.49	1.22	1.14	1.01
Earnings	1.16	1.13	0.98	0.88	0.81	0.70
Dividends	0.41	0.35	0.16	0.29	0.25	0.22
Payout Ratio	35%	31%	32%	33%	31%	31%
Prices - High	23½	21¼	17½	16⅞	9½	8½
- Low	18	13½	12¾	8½	6¾	7
P/E Ratio - High	20	19	18	19	12	12
- Low	16	12	13	10	8	10

Income Statement Analysis (Million $)

	1994	%Chg	1993	%Chg	1992	%Chg	1991
Revs.	302	11%	273	17%	234	42%	165
Oper. Inc.	70.6	10%	64.2	18%	54.2	26%	43.0
Depr.	21.1	22%	17.3	25%	13.8	58%	8.7
Int. Exp.	1.3	15%	1.2	-30%	1.7	NM	0.2
Pretax Inc.	49.1	1%	48.6	20%	40.5	11%	36.4
Eff. Tax Rate	37%	—	38%	—	36%	—	37%
Net Inc.	30.7	3%	29.9	16%	25.8	12%	23.1

Balance Sheet & Other Fin. Data (Million $)

	1994	1993	1992	1991	1990	1989
Cash	41.6	38.3	45.2	56.4	43.6	27.7
Curr. Assets	78.7	72.0	73.7	71.3	59.9	43.4
Total Assets	260	228	197	146	137	113
Curr. Liab.	53.8	47.9	43.8	16.4	30.2	20.5
LT Debt	Nil	Nil	0.5	2.0	2.3	2.4
Common Eqty.	176	157	136	116	100	86.0
Total Cap.	195	169	143	121	107	93.0
Cap. Exp.	49.9	55.6	39.0	6.7	17.2	20.1
Cash Flow	51.9	47.2	39.7	31.9	29.7	26.3

Ratio Analysis

	1994	1993	1992	1991	1990	1989
Curr. Ratio	1.5	1.5	1.7	4.3	2.0	2.1
% LT Debt of Cap.	Nil	Nil	0.3	1.7	2.1	2.6
% Net Inc.of Revs.	10.2	11.0	11.1	14.0	13.4	12.7
% Ret. on Assets	12.6	14.0	15.0	16.3	17.0	17.1
% Ret. on Equity	18.4	20.4	20.3	21.3	22.8	23.1

Dividend Data (Cash has been paid each year since 1972.)

Amt. of Div. $	Date Decl.	Ex-Div. Date	Stock of Record	Payment Date
0.100	Jul. 28	Aug. 09	Aug. 15	Sep. 01 '94
0.110	Oct. 31	Nov. 09	Nov. 16	Dec. 01 '94
0.110	Feb. 03	Feb. 13	Feb. 17	Mar. 01 '95
0.110	Apr. 28	May. 12	May. 18	Jun. 02 '95
0.110	Jul. 21	Aug. 11	Aug. 15	Sep. 01 '95

Data as orig. reptd.; bef. results of disc. opers. and/or spec. items. Per share data adj. for stk. divs. as of ex-div. date. E-Estimated. NA-Not Available. NM-Not Meaningful. NR-Not Ranked.

Office—625 South Fifth Ave., Lebanon, PA 17042. **Tel**—(717) 274-2521. **Chrmn & Pres**—E. H. Arnold. **CFO**—P. L. Shiffler. **Treas & Investor Contact**—Ronald E. Walborn (717-236-7912). **Secy**—H. L. Allen. **Dirs**—H. L. Allen, E. H. Arnold, C. E. Hughes, K. F. Leedy, A. L. Peterson, R. E. Walborn. **Transfer Agent & Registrar**—Registrar & Transfer Co., Cranford, NJ. **Incorporated** in Pennsylvania in 1982. **Empl**-3,000. **S&P Analyst:** Alan Aaron

STANDARD & POOR'S

STOCK REPORTS

Arrow Electronics

NYSE Symbol **ARW**
In S&P MidCap 400

20-SEP-95 **Industry:** Electronics/Electric

Summary: This company is the world's largest distributor of electronic components and computer products to industrial and commercial customers.

S&P Opinion: Hold (★★★)

Recent Price • 54¾ | Yield • Nil
52 Wk Range • 59¾-33¾ | 12-Mo. P/E • 18.1

Quantitative Evaluations

Outlook
(1 Lowest—5 Highest)
• **5+**

Fair Value
• **62⅛**

Risk
• **Low**

Earn./Div. Rank
• **B-**

Technical Eval.
• **Bullish** since 2/95

Rel. Strength Rank
(1 Lowest—99 Highest)
• **45**

Insider Activity
• **Unfavorable**

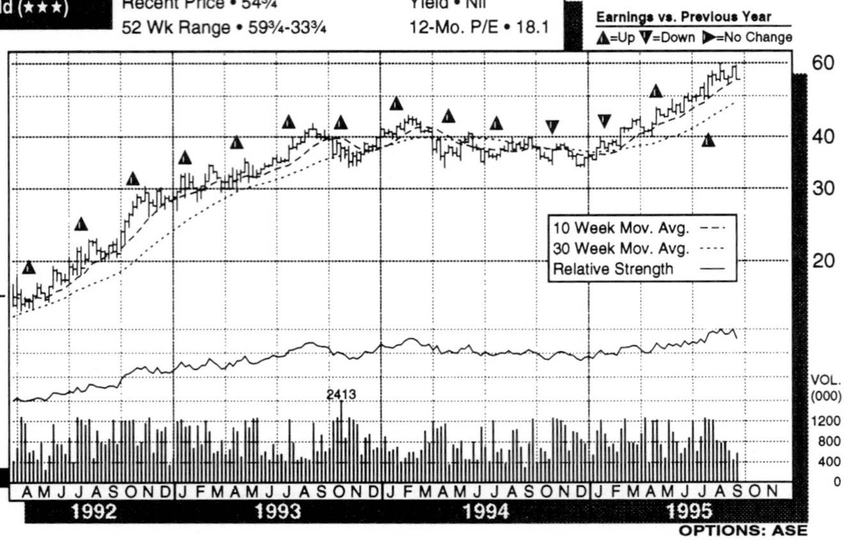

OPTIONS: ASE

Overview - 20-SEP-95

Sales are expected to rise about 20% for the balance of 1995 and into 1996, as restated for the acquisitions of Gates/FA Distributing and Anthem Electronics. Growth will be led by strength in the semiconductor industry, with sales gains likely for all geographic regions and product lines. Gross margins may narrow slightly, reflecting an increased proprotion of lower-margin Gates/FA Distributing and other computer-related businesses, but should be outweighed by well controlled expenses. The company should benefit in the long-term from its leading market positions, broad product line and strong finances.

Valuation - 20-SEP-95

We are upgrading the shares to hold, based on Arrow's earnings gains thus far in 1995. The shares reached a new high recently, in line with strength in other electronics stocks. We believe that well-balanced growth will continue as long as the rest of the technology sector continues to thrive. Costs have been well controlled, and the company successfully integrated two recent acquisitions (Gates/FA and Anthem), which are proving to be beneficial to operations. In light of its fundamentals, we believe that the stock will be a market performer for the near-term. We have raised our 1995 EPS estimate to $3.95, with $4.60 seen for 1996.

Key Stock Statistics

S&P EPS Est. 1995	3.95	Tang. Bk. Value/Share	12.35
P/E on S&P Est. 1995	13.9	Beta	0.95
S&P EPS Est. 1996	4.60	Shareholders	4,500
Dividend Rate/Share	Nil	Market cap. (B)	$ 2.6
Shs. outstg. (M)	46.7	Inst. holdings	90%
Avg. daily vol. (M)	0.137	Insider holdings	NA

Value of $10,000 invested 5 years ago: $ 141,290

Fiscal Year Ending Dec. 31

	1995	% Change	1994	% Change	1993	% Change
Revenues (Million $)						
1Q	1,440	29%	1,118	103%	551.4	45%
2Q	1,458	31%	1,114	91%	584.1	53%
3Q	—	—	1,161	66%	697.8	71%
4Q	—	—	1,256	79%	702.3	55%
Yr.	—	—	4,649	83%	2,536	56%
Income (Million $)						
1Q	44.85	34%	33.38	86%	17.98	94%
2Q	51.75	57%	32.90	72%	19.11	66%
3Q	—	—	21.78	NM	21.73	63%
4Q	—	—	23.83	5%	22.73	41%
Yr.	—	—	111.9	37%	81.56	62%
Earnings Per Share ($)						
1Q	0.96	33%	0.72	22%	0.59	55%
2Q	1.09	54%	0.71	15%	0.62	51%
3Q	E0.95	102%	0.47	-32%	0.69	47%
4Q	E0.95	86%	0.51	-29%	0.72	36%
Yr.	E3.95	65%	2.40	-8%	2.62	45%

Next earnings report expected: late October

Arrow Electronics

Business Summary - 20-SEP-95

Arrow Electronics is the world's largest distributor of electronic components and computer products to industrial and commercial customers.

The company's electronics distribution networks, spanning North America, Europe and Asia, incorporate 160 selling locations and 15 distribution centers in 28 countries, serving 350 suppliers and over 140,000 customers worldwide.

About two-thirds of consolidated sales are semiconductor products; industrial and commercial computer products account for 25%; the remaining sales are passive, electromechanical and connector products.

Foreign operations accounted for 28% of sales and 30% of operating income in 1994. These operations have been expanded through acquisitions in recent years.

The company has pursued an aggressive policy of acquisitions in recent period. In November 1994, it purchased Anthem Electronics, Inc., the sixth largest U.S. distributor, in exchange for 10,803,000 common shares. Anthem earned $20.2 million on revenues of $622.4 million in 1994. Also in November, Arrow acquired an Australian electronics distribution group. In October 1994, it acquired Megachip SA and its subsidiaries (a group of French distribution companies). In August 1994, the company purchased Gates/FA Distributing, Inc., a leading commercial distributor of microcomputers with annual sales of $450 million. The price consisted of about 3.7 million common shares. In early, the company acquired an additional 15% interest in Spoerle Electronic, Germany's largest electronics distributor, bringing its holdings to 70%, and increased its holdings in Silverstar Ltd. S.p.A., Italy's largest distributor, to a majority share. Several acquisitions were also made in 1993.

Important Developments

Jul. '95—Arrow completed an agreement with NMB Technologies Inc., the world's largest maker of axial cooling fans. The company will distribute NMB's full line of AC and DC fans. Separately, Arrow reached an agreement to distribute to resellers products of Lantronix, a maker of Ethernet connectivity products.

Capitalization

Long Term Debt: $337,354,000 (6/95).
Minority Interest: $94,970,000.

Per Share Data ($)

(Year Ended Dec. 31)

	1994	1993	1992	1991	1990	1989
Tangible Bk. Val.	10.91	8.23	8.09	4.23	3.41	2.18
Cash Flow	2.99	3.19	2.29	0.93	1.21	0.71
Earnings	2.40	2.62	1.81	0.28	0.44	-0.19
Dividends	Nil	Nil	Nil	Nil	Nil	Nil
Payout Ratio	Nil	Nil	Nil	Nil	Nil	Nil
Prices - High	45⅛	43⅛	30½	16½	7	6¾
- Low	33⅝	26½	14⅜	3⅝	3⅝	3⅛
P/E Ratio - High	19	16	17	59	16	NM
- Low	14	10	8	13	8	NM

Income Statement Analysis (Million $)

	1994	%Chg	1993	%Chg	1992	%Chg	1991
Revs.	4,649	83%	2,536	56%	1,622	55%	1,044
Oper. Inc.	329	65%	199	72%	116	116%	53.7
Depr.	27.8	59%	17.5	42%	12.3	29%	9.5
Int. Exp.	36.2	45%	25.0	-17%	30.1	3%	29.1
Pretax Inc.	220	39%	158	97%	80.3	NM	10.9
Eff. Tax Rate	42%	—	41%	—	37%	—	20%
Net Inc.	112	37%	81.6	63%	50.2	NM	8.7

Balance Sheet & Other Fin. Data (Million $)

	1994	1993	1992	1991	1990	1989
Cash	106	60.7	3.4	1.5	0.9	4.6
Curr. Assets	1,558	870	549	512	327	357
Total Assets	2,039	1,191	781	745	478	498
Curr. Liab.	689	341	180	186	96.0	110
LT Debt	349	279	225	304	207	216
Common Eqty.	838	457	335	167	92.0	78.0
Total Cap.	1,313	807	577	530	358	363
Cap. Exp.	22.8	16.8	3.5	3.8	6.0	3.9
Cash Flow	140	98.1	58.6	13.5	14.4	8.3

Ratio Analysis

	1994	1993	1992	1991	1990	1989
Curr. Ratio	2.3	2.6	3.1	2.8	3.4	3.2
% LT Debt of Cap.	26.6	34.5	39.1	57.4	57.8	59.3
% Net Inc.of Revs.	2.4	3.2	3.1	0.8	1.0	0.3
% Ret. on Assets	5.9	8.1	5.4	1.1	2.1	0.6
% Ret. on Equity	14.8	19.8	16.0	2.6	6.1	NM

Dividend Data —Dividends, initiated in 1977, were omitted in December 1986. A poison pill stock purchase rights plan was adopted in 1988.

Data as orig. reptd.; bef. results of disc. opers. and/or spec. items. Per share data adj. for stk. divs. as of ex-div. date. E-Estimated. NA-Not Available. NM-Not Meaningful. NR-Not Ranked.

Office—25 Hub Drive, Melville, NY 11747. **Tel**—(516) 391-1300. **Chrmn & CEO**—S. P. Kaufman. **Vice-Chrmn**—J. C. Waddell. **SVP, CFO & Investor Contact**—Robert E. Klatell. **Dirs**—D. W. Duval, C. Giersch, J. S. Gould, S. P. Kaufman, L. R. Kem, R. E. Klatell, S. W. Menefee, K. G. Mills, A. Pol, R. S. Rosenbloom, R. S. Throop, J. C. Waddell. **Transfer Agent & Registrar**—Chemical Bank, NYC. **Incorporated** in New York in 1946. **Empl**-6,500. **S&P Analyst:** Mike Cavanaugh

STANDARD & POOR'S

STOCK REPORTS

Arvin Industries

NYSE Symbol **ARV**
In S&P MidCap 400

22-SEP-95 **Industry:** Auto parts/equipment

Summary: Arvin manufactures a broad line of automotive exhaust and ride control products, coated metals and other industrial products and services in the U.S. and Europe.

S&P Opinion: Sell (★)

Recent Price • 22⅞
52 Wk Range • 25⅞-19¾
Yield • 3.4%
12-Mo. P/E • NM

Quantitative Evaluations

Outlook
(1 Lowest—5 Highest)
• **1⁻**

Fair Value
• **20¼**

Risk
• **Low**

Earn./Div. Rank
• **B-**

Technical Eval.
• **Bullish** since 9/95

Rel. Strength Rank
(1 Lowest—99 Highest)
• **32**

Insider Activity
• **NA**

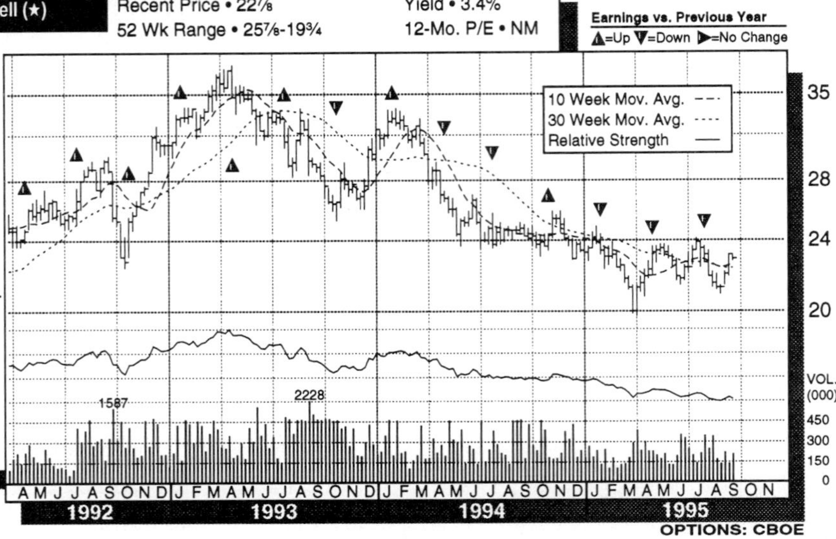

OPTIONS: CBOE

Overview - 22-SEP-95

Reductions in production of motor vehicles in North America and only slow growth in Europe have tempered the outlook for original equipment exhaust and ride control products for the second half of 1995 and for 1996. Aftermarket sales are also falling, with particularly weak demand in North America. Concurrently, ARV's margins are being squeezed by sharp increases in raw materials costs. ARV is instituting price increases in the replacement market and is negotiating raw materials cost pass-throughs with its original equipment (OEM) customers. However, we expect only gradual restoration of margins, assuming demand remains at present levels or increases. Continued decline in demand would likely result in further pressures on margins and lower earnings.

Valuation - 22-SEP-95

We downgraded the shares to sell after weak second quarter earnings and indications that it would take a while to restore margins after the recent rapid rise in raw materials costs. We view the reliance on price increases to restore margins as tenuous in a mature low technology business such as exhaust products. We also think that changing fundamentals may be contributing to lower demand for repair parts. The largest factor is the improved quality of new parts which are not being replaced as frequently as in the past. We believe the shares are overpriced at 22 times our 1995 estimate and 18 times our 1996 estimate, versus a normal multiple of about 12 for parts companies.

Key Stock Statistics

S&P EPS Est. 1995	1.05	Tang. Bk. Value/Share	11.11
P/E on S&P Est. 1995	21.8	Beta	1.46
S&P EPS Est. 1996	1.25	Shareholders	5,300
Dividend Rate/Share	0.76	Market cap. (B)	$0.500
Shs. outstg. (M)	22.3	Inst. holdings	56%
Avg. daily vol. (M)	0.037	Insider holdings	NA

Value of $10,000 invested 5 years ago: $ 17,257

Fiscal Year Ending Dec. 31

	1995	% Change	1994	% Change	1993	% Change
Revenues (Million $)						
1Q	553.4	15%	479.2	NM	476.0	4%
2Q	566.6	5%	539.3	4%	520.5	4%
3Q	—	—	505.7	7%	474.2	NM
4Q	—	—	515.6	10%	468.7	3%
Yr.	—	—	2,040	5%	1,939	3%
Income (Million $)						
1Q	4.40	-14%	5.10	-17%	6.15	69%
2Q	5.60	-60%	14.00	-15%	16.52	11%
3Q	—	—	9.80	33%	7.38	-38%
4Q	—	—	-46.30	NM	10.30	10%
Yr.	—	—	-17.40	NM	40.34	1%
Earnings Per Share ($)						
1Q	0.20	-13%	0.23	-18%	0.28	NM
2Q	0.25	-60%	0.63	-15%	0.74	10%
3Q	E0.25	-43%	0.44	33%	0.33	-35%
4Q	E0.35	NM	-2.07	NM	0.46	7%
Yr.	E1.05	NM	-0.78	NM	1.81	6%

Next earnings report expected: mid October

Arvin Industries

Business Summary - 22-SEP-95

Arvin Industries is primarily a manufacturer of automotive products. Segment contributions in 1994 (profits in $ millions) were as follows:

	Sales	Profits
Automotive		
Original equipment	59%	$70.9
Replacement	32%	33.2
Technology	9%	-54.3

ARV supplies parts to the worldwide original equipment automotive market, including mufflers, exhaust pipes, catalytic converters, tubular manifolds, fuel filler tubes, tubeless tire valves, shock absorbers, MacPherson struts, gas springs, decorative trim parts, and coated coil steel for fabricating into body parts. Shipments to the automotive replacement market include mufflers, exhaust pipes, catalytic converters, shock absorbers, MacPherson struts, gas springs, brake and front end parts, and accessories. Automotive original equipment also includes the Roll Coater division, which provides precoated coils of steel and aluminum. Schrader Automotive, which produces valves for tires and other commercial purposes, was sold in February 1995.

The technology unit consists of a 70% interest in Space Industries Intl., formed in 1993 by combining the company's Calspan unit with Space Industries. The unit provides R&D and testing services to government and industry in such areas as aerodynamics, automobile crash testing and accident research, aircraft systems, electronic systems analysis, and surface and laser chemistry, and designs aerospace products. (See Important Dewvelopment.)

In 1994, two large automotive customers accounted for 16.0% and 9.9%, respectively, of sales. Foreign operations accounted for 35% of sales and $40.3 million of profits in 1994.

Important Developments

Aug. '95—ARV agreed to sell 70%-owned Space Industries International (SIII) to the unit's management for $42.6 million. ARV will guarantee $22.9 million of the new owners' debt. SIII had sales of $65.7 million and income of $4.6 million for the 1995 first half. ARV's investment in SIII totals $30.8 million.

Jul. '95—Second quarter profits were hurt by lower OEM operating margins, reflecting unrecovered materials cost increases and reductions in build schedules due to the mild slowdown in vehicle demand. The replacement parts business was hurt by lower demand in North America. ARV expects price increases and cost pass-throughs to the OEMs to restore margins over several quarters.

Capitalization

Long Term Debt: $358,000,000 (6/95), incl. $89.7 million of debs. conv. into com. stock.

Minority Interest: $63,700,000.

Per Share Data ($) (Year Ended Dec. 31)

	1994	1993	1992	1991	1990	1989
Tangible Bk. Val.	11.02	10.65	9.95	10.44	10.22	8.34
Cash Flow	2.72	4.94	5.14	4.02	4.58	3.55
Earnings	-0.78	1.81	1.70	0.75	1.35	0.70
Dividends	0.76	0.76	0.70	0.68	0.68	0.68
Payout Ratio	NM	42%	44%	90%	50%	97%
Prices - High	33¾	37¾	32¼	26⅜	19	26¾
- Low	22¾	25¼	20⅜	16¼	13⅜	14½
P/E Ratio - High	NM	21	19	35	14	38
- Low	NM	14	12	22	10	21

Income Statement Analysis (Million $)

	1994	%Chg	1993	%Chg	1992	%Chg	1991
Revs.	2,040	5%	1,939	3%	1,890	13%	1,676
Oper. Inc.	190	9%	174	-4%	181	25%	145
Depr.	78.2	12%	70.0	2%	68.9	10%	62.6
Int. Exp.	43.6	13%	38.5	-6%	40.8	-8%	44.3
Pretax Inc.	-12.5	NM	64.9	-2%	66.5	66%	40.0
Eff. Tax Rate	NM	—	39%	—	40%	—	45%
Net Inc.	-17.4	NM	40.3	1%	39.9	81%	22.0

Balance Sheet & Other Fin. Data (Million $)

	1994	1993	1992	1991	1990	1989
Cash	17.6	39.1	14.6	7.6	17.2	12.9
Curr. Assets	502	491	469	474	541	524
Total Assets	1,275	1,246	1,152	1,125	1,193	1,130
Curr. Liab.	339	255	284	252	338	302
LT Debt	416	434	390	335	321	334
Common Eqty.	396	421	398	387	386	355
Total Cap.	858	914	794	835	851	828
Cap. Exp.	107	93.0	101	74.6	86.7	85.6
Cash Flow	61.0	110	103	76.8	86.3	66.9

Ratio Analysis

	1994	1993	1992	1991	1990	1989
Curr. Ratio	1.5	1.9	1.6	1.9	1.6	1.7
% LT Debt of Cap.	48.5	47.5	49.1	40.1	37.7	40.3
% Net Inc.of Revs.	NM	2.1	2.1	1.3	2.0	1.3
% Ret. on Assets	NM	3.3	3.3	1.9	2.9	1.8
% Ret. on Equity	NM	9.7	8.1	3.7	6.9	3.7

Dividend Data —Dividends have been paid since 1925.

Amt. of Div. $	Date Decl.	Ex-Div. Date	Stock of Record	Payment Date
0.190	Sep. 08	Sep. 13	Sep. 19	Sep. 30 '94
0.190	Nov. 10	Nov. 28	Dec. 02	Dec. 30 '94
0.190	Feb. 09	Mar. 06	Mar. 10	Mar. 31 '95
0.190	Apr. 14	Jun. 06	Jun. 09	Jun. 30 '95
0.190	Jun. 15	Sep. 06	Sep. 08	Sep. 29 '95

Data as orig. reptd.; bef. results of disc. opers. and/or spec. items. Per share data adj. for stk. divs. as of ex-div. date. E-Estimated. NA-Not Available. NM-Not Meaningful. NR-Not Ranked.

Office—One Noblitt Plaza, Columbus, IN 47202-3000. **Tel**—(812) 379-3000. **Chrmn**—J. K. Baker. **Pres & CEO**—B. O. Pond. **VP & Secy**—R. R. Snyder. **VP-Fin & CFO**—R. A. Smith **Investor Contact**—John W. Brown. **Dirs**—J. P. Allen, J. K. Baker, S. C. Beering, J. P. Flannery, W. D. George, Jr., I. W. Gorr, R. W. Hanselman, W. Hunt, D. J. Kacek, F. R. Meyer, B. O. Pond, R. A. Smith, A. R. Velasquez. **Transfer Agent & Registrar**—Harris Trust & Savings Bank, Chicago. **Incorporated** in Indiana in 1921. **Empl**-13,298. **S&P Analyst:** Joshua M. Harari, CFA

Atlanta Gas Light

NYSE Symbol ATG In S&P MidCap 400

Price	Range	P-E Ratio	Dividend	Yield	S&P Ranking	Beta
Aug. 7'95	1995					
34⅝	36¾–29¾	34	2.08	6.0%	A–	0.37

Summary

This natural gas utility serves the principal industrial and metropolitan areas of Georgia, including Atlanta and Savannah, distributing about 75% of the natural gas consumed in the state. In November 1994, the company announced a restructuring plan that will consolidate field offices, payment centers and offices, as well as personnel. Charges for the restructuring reduced earnings per share by $1.64. ATG expects the resulting cost savings to help improve its competitive position.

Business Summary

Atlanta Gas Light Company is the largest gas distribution utility in the Southeast, serving more than 1.3 million customers in 229 cities and communities in Georgia and, through its Chattanooga Gas Co. subsidiary, more than 45,000 customers in Chattanooga and Cleveland, Tenn. Operating revenues by customer group in recent fiscal years were:

	1994	1993	1992
Residential	58%	58%	58%
Commercial	24%	24%	23%
Industrial	14%	14%	14%
Transportation/other	4%	4%	5%

Gas transported and sold in fiscal 1994 totaled 2,604 million therms, down from 2,664 million therms in fiscal 1993. An average of 1,315,700 customers were served during fiscal 1994, compared with 1,280,900 in fiscal 1993.

The company's major gas suppliers, Southern Natural Gas Co., Transcontinental Gas Pipe Line, South Georgia Natural Gas and East Tennessee Natural Gas, provide for total daily supply of 940,233 Mcf of pipeline gas. Supplemental gas supplies include underground storage and liquefied natural gas. Total send-out on ATG's system during fiscal 1994 consisted of 55% natural gas purchased, 19% natural gas withdrawn from storage and 26% transportation of customer-owned gas.

Other activities include the sale of gas appliances and gas appliance parts; gas production; the sale of propane; real estate development; and natural gas vehicle conversions.

Variations in revenues due to abnormal weather during the heating season are largely offset by a weather normalization adjustment in rates.

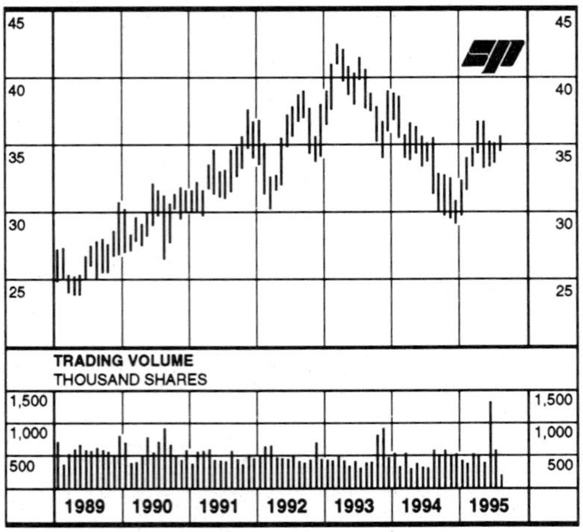

Important Developments

Aug. '95— In a Gas Supply Plan recently filed with the Georgia Public Service Commission, ATG proposed to lower gas costs to 30.84 cents per therm from 37.82 cents and to refund $38.5 million to customers.

May '95— The company announced an agreement in principle to purchase a 35% interest in Sonat Marketing Co., a subsidiary of Sonat Inc., for $43 million. One of the largest natural gas marketing firms in the U.S., with daily average sales at 1.9 billion cubic feet, the unit offers natural gas sales, transportation, risk management and storage services to natural gas users in key markets in the U.S.

Next earnings report expected in early November.

Per Share Data ($)

Yr. End Sep. 30	1994	1993	1992	1991	1990	1989	1988	1987	1986	1985
Tangible Bk. Val.	**20.15**	19.84	19.43	20.27	19.26	18.75	18.30	16.47	16.74	15.89
Earnings[2]	**2.34**	2.16	2.26	2.07	2.02	1.90	2.25	2.04	1.66	1.82
Dividends	**2.08**	2.08	2.06	2.04	1.96	1.88	1.76	1.60	1.40	1.26
Payout Ratio	**89%**	96%	91%	99%	97%	99%	78%	78%	84%	69%
Prices[1]—High	**38⅞**	42½	39	37⅝	32⅛	30¾	28	26⅜	24¼	19
Low	**29⅛**	34	30¼	29¾	26½	23⅞	21½	19⅜	18½	14
P/E Ratio—	**17–12**	20–16	17–13	18–14	16–13	16–13	12–10	13–9	15–11	10–8

Data as orig. reptd. Adj. for stk. div. of 100% Dec. 1986. **1.** Cal. yr. **2.** Bef. spec. item of +0.15 in 1988.

Atlanta Gas Light Company

Income Data (Million $)

Year Ended Sep. 30	Revs.	Depr.	Maint.	Oper. Ratio	[1]Fxd. Chgs. Cover.	Constr. Credits	Eff. Tax Rate	[2]Net Inc.	% Return On Revs.	% Return On [3]Invest. Capital	% Return On [4]Com. Equity
1994	**1,200**	**55.4**	**32.8**	**91.0%**	**2.81**	**0.40**	**36.5%**	**63.2**	**5.3**	**8.9**	**11.6**
1993	1,130	58.8	30.9	91.2%	2.60	0.90	34.7%	57.5	5.1	9.6	11.0
1992	995	54.9	29.5	89.9%	2.66	2.90	31.8%	55.4	5.6	9.6	11.8
1991	964	50.2	28.6	90.2%	2.55	2.98	34.8%	49.4	5.1	9.1	11.4
1990	1,001	46.3	28.1	90.7%	2.47	1.25	31.7%	45.6	4.6	9.2	11.4
1989	939	43.2	25.3	91.7%	1.94	0.87	27.7%	42.1	4.5	8.9	10.8
1988	976	36.1	24.0	92.5%	2.30	4.98	31.8%	46.0	4.7	9.3	14.2
1987	983	31.2	22.4	93.3%	2.18	4.45	47.6%	39.4	4.0	9.3	13.2
1986	1,008	28.1	21.3	94.0%	1.76	1.11	46.0%	29.2	2.9	9.4	11.0
1985	1,165	24.9	18.0	95.2%	1.86	1.26	46.7%	29.7	2.5	10.6	13.7

Balance Sheet Data (Million $)

Sep. 30	[5]Gross Prop.	Capital Expend.	Net Prop.	% Earn. on Net Prop.	Total Cap.	Capitalization LT Debt	Capitalization % LT Debt	Capitalization Pfd.	Capitalization % Pfd.	Capitalization Com.	Capitalization % Com.
1994	**1,833**	**122**	**1,280**	**8.6**	**1,323**	**555**	**49.0**	**58.5**	**5.2**	**519**	**45.8**
1993	1,786	122	1,264	8.1	1,153	375	40.5	58.7	6.3	492	53.2
1992	1,679	132	1,202	8.6	1,019	326	40.2	14.2	1.7	472	58.1
1991	1,559	141	1,123	8.8	1,113	456	49.6	14.5	1.6	448	48.8
1990	1,433	122	1,033	9.3	1,013	418	50.2	16.8	2.0	397	47.8
1989	1,331	162	962	8.7	950	369	47.9	18.0	2.3	383	49.8
1988	1,156	126	845	9.1	945	379	49.3	19.3	2.5	370	48.2
1987	1,036	139	758	9.4	756	271	46.2	20.5	3.5	296	50.3
1986	905	121	652	10.0	736	292	49.4	21.8	3.7	277	47.9
1985	790	95	561	10.7	616	243	49.8	23.1	4.7	222	45.5

Data as orig. reptd. **1.** Times int. exp. & pfd. divs. covered. **2.** Bef. spec. item in 1988. **3.** Based on inc. bef. int. charges. **4.** As reptd. by co. **5.** Utility plant.

Operating Revenues (Million $)

Quarter:	1994–95	1993–94	1992–93	1991–92
Dec.	329	362	334	300
Mar.	448	500	448	395
Jun.	178	191	198	176
Sep.		147	150	123
		1,200	1,130	995

Revenues for the nine months ended June 30, 1995, fell 9.4%, year to year, reflecting weak volume due to unusually warm weather and reduced recoveries from customers under purchased gas provisions of rate schedules for the cost of gas supply contracts. Cost of gas fell 18% and, due to weather normalization adjustment riders, the weather did not have a significant impact on the comparability of earnings for the quarter or the year to date. A $1.64 restructuring charge hurt results; earnings available to common fell to $1.44 a share, from $2.78.

Common Share Earnings ($)

Quarter:	1994–95	1993–94	1992–93	1991–92
Dec.	0.03	1.01	0.87	0.88
Mar.	1.41	1.97	1.79	1.79
Jun.	0.01	d0.19	d0.14	d0.08
Sep.		d0.43	d0.34	d0.31
		2.34	2.16	2.26

Dividend Data

Dividends have been paid in each year since 1939. A dividend reinvestment plan is available.

Amt. of Divd. $	Date Decl.	Ex–divd. Date	Stock of Record	Payment Date
0.52	Nov. 4	Nov. 14	Nov. 18	Dec. 1'94
0.52	Feb. 3	Feb. 13	Feb. 17	Mar. 1'95
0.52	May 5	May 15	May 19	Jun. 1'95
0.52	Aug. 4	Aug. 16	Aug. 18	Sep. 1'95

Finances

In June 1995, ATG offered publicly, through underwriters led by Merrill Lynch & Co., 1.3 million common shares at $33.625 each. Proceeds will be used primarily to fund the company's capital expenditure program. Capital expenditures for 1994 totaled $122.5 million and are expected to be $340 million from 1995 through 1997. The outlays are largely for equipment to provide service to new customers.

Capitalization

Long Term Debt: $554,500,000 (6/95).

Preferred Stock: $58,500,000.

Common Stock: 27,400,000 shs. ($5 par).
Institutions hold about 19%.
Shareholders of record: 17,400 (6/95).

d-Deficit.

Office—303 Peachtree St., N.E., P.O. Box 4569, Atlanta, GA 30302. **Tel**—(404) 584-4000. **Pres & CEO**—D. R. Jones. **Exec VP, CFO, Secy & Investor Contact**—Robert L. Goocher. **Treas**—C. C. Moore Jr. **Dirs**—F. Barron Jr., W. W. Bradley, O. A. Brumby Jr., L. L. Gellerstedt Jr., D. R. Jones, K. D. Lewis, A. G. Norman Jr., D. R. Riddle, B. L. Siegel, B. J. Tarbutton Jr., C. M. Taylor, F. W. Ward Jr. **Transfer Agent & Registrar**—Wachovia Bank of North Carolina, Winston-Salem. **Incorporated** in Georgia in 1856. **Empl**—3,764.

 Jane Collin

STANDARD & POOR'S

STOCK REPORTS

Atlantic Energy

NYSE Symbol **ATE**
In S&P MidCap 400

28-SEP-95

Industry:
Utilities-Electric

Summary: This utility holding company owns Atlantic City Electric, which supplies electricity to more than 455,000 customers in a 2,700 square mile area in the southern third of New Jersey.

Quantitative Evaluations

Recent Price • 19
52 Wk Range • 19⅝-16
Yield • 7.8%
12-Mo. P/E • 17.4

Outlook
(1 Lowest—5 Highest)
• 1⁻

Fair Value
• 15⅜

Risk
• Low

Earn./Div. Rank
• A-

Technical Eval.
• Bullish since 9/94

Rel. Strength Rank
(1 Lowest—99 Highest)
• 67

Insider Activity
• Neutral

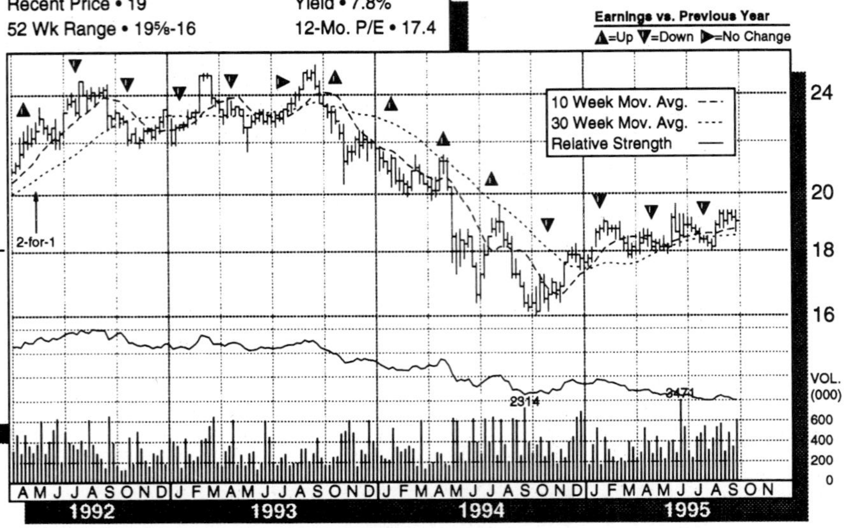

Business Profile - 28-SEP-95

This utility holding company owns Atlantic City Electric, which supplies electricity to a 2,700 square mile area in southern New Jersey. ATE's strategic plan includes the redesign of key operations to improve efficiency, the development of new products and services to enhance revenue, and the reduction of capital spending and operations and maintenance expenses. As part of the plan, a voluntary severance program in the 1995 first quarter eliminated about 20% of the work force.

Operational Review - 28-SEP-95

Earnings fell sharply in the 1995 first half. A decline in sales for resale reflected a decrease in supplemental excess energy sources available to ATE as a result of the expiration of a 200 mw capacity arrangement in May 1994. The drop also reflected a decline demands of the regional power pool, as a result of relatively mild weather. Results were also penalized by ATE's Southern New Jersey Economic Initiative, because of which the company did not recover otherwise eligible energy costs.

Stock Performance - 22-SEP-95

In the past 30 trading days, ATE's shares have increased 5%, compared to a 5% rise in the S&P 500. Average trading volume for the past five days was 127,640 shares, compared with the 40-day moving average of 91,692 shares.

Key Stock Statistics

Dividend Rate/Share	1.54	Shareholders	47,800
Shs. outstg. (M)	52.6	Market cap. (B)	$ 1.0
Avg. daily vol. (M)	0.107	Inst. holdings	23%
Tang. Bk. Value/Share	14.43	Insider holdings	NA
Beta	0.34		

Value of $10,000 invested 5 years ago: $ 15,414

Fiscal Year Ending Dec. 31

	1995	% Change	1994	% Change	1993	% Change
Revenues (Million $)						
1Q	218.6	-6%	232.1	14%	203.7	3%
2Q	206.2	NM	205.8	7%	192.5	3%
3Q	—	—	272.7	1%	268.9	13%
4Q	—	—	202.4	NM	200.6	3%
Yr.	—	—	913.0	5%	865.7	6%
Income (Million $)						
1Q	11.47	-50%	22.86	14%	20.00	-28%
2Q	10.57	-37%	16.80	51%	11.09	2%
3Q	—	—	46.32	-11%	52.33	32%
4Q	—	—	-9.87	NM	11.88	52%
Yr.	—	—	76.11	-20%	95.30	11%
Earnings Per Share ($)						
1Q	0.21	-51%	0.43	13%	0.38	-31%
2Q	0.20	-35%	0.31	48%	0.21	NM
3Q	—	—	0.85	-14%	0.99	30%
4Q	—	—	-0.18	NM	0.22	47%
Yr.	—	—	1.41	-22%	1.80	8%

Next earnings report expected: late October

Atlantic Energy

Business Summary - 28-SEP-95

Atlantic Energy is the holding company formed in 1987 by Atlantic City Electric to facilitate diversification into nonutility businesses. Atlantic City Electric (ACE) supplies electricity in a 2,700 square mile area in southern New Jersey with a population of about 1,000,000. The territory includes a resort area along the Atlantic Seaboard and an industrial section in the Delaware River Valley, separated by an agricultural belt. Contributions by class of customers in recent years:

	1994	1993	1992	1991
Residential	48%	48%	47%	47%
Commercial	39%	39%	39%	38%
Industrial	12%	12%	13%	14%
Other	1%	1%	1%	1%

In 1994, ACE sold 8,167,856 mwh of electricity, up 1.3% from 1993. Coal and nuclear energy together provided about 66% of the utility's energy requirements in 1993. ACE is a co-owner of the Hope Creek (5.0% interest), Salem (7.41%), and Peach Bottom (7.51%) nuclear stations and the Keystone (2.47%) and Conemaugh (3.83%) coal facilities.

Atlantic Generation, Inc. is engaged in the development of cogeneration power projects. ATE Investment, Inc. manages capital investments for the company. Atlantic Southern Properties owns, develops and manages commercial real estate. Other subsidiaries include Atlantic Thermal Systems and Atlantic Energy Technology.

In November 1994, the company announced staff reductions of 350 employees at its utility subsidiary. The reduction included a voluntary separation program that took place in the first quarter of 1995. During the last five years, Atlantic Electric's work force has been reduced from more than 2,000 employees to its current level of about 1,500 employees. The majority of charges associated with the staff reduction plan was incurred in the 1994 fourth quarter.

Construction spending, estimated at $268 million for 1995-7, will be used for improvements to distribution and transmission facilities and compliance with the Clean Air Act Amendments of 1990.

Important Developments

Jul. '95—The New Jersey Board of Public Utilities (BPU) approved ACE's provisional $37 million increase in the annual levelized energy clause revenues effective for service rendered to customers on and after July 7, 1995. A final BPU decision is expected in the 1995 fourth quarter.

Capitalization

Long Term Debt: $791,100,000 (6/95).
Subsid. Red. Cum. Preferred Stock: $149,250,000.
Subsid. Cum. Preferred Stock: $40,000,000.

Per Share Data ($) (Year Ended Dec. 31)

	1994	1993	1992	1991	1990	1989
Tangible Bk. Val.	14.78	14.83	14.50	14.15	13.57	13.43
Earnings	1.41	1.80	1.67	1.75	1.51	1.87
Dividends	1.54	1.54	1.52	1.49	1.47	1.42
Payout Ratio	109%	85%	91%	86%	97%	76%
Prices - High	21¾	25⅜	24⅝	21	19¼	19⅞
- Low	16	20⅜	19½	16	16	16¼
P/E Ratio - High	15	14	15	12	13	11
- Low	11	11	12	9	11	9

Income Statement Analysis (Million $)

	1994	%Chg	1993	%Chg	1992	%Chg	1991
Revs.	913	5%	866	6%	817	5%	778
Depr.	73.0	7%	68.0	-2%	69.4	5%	66.0
Maint.	37.6	-17%	45.4	-9%	49.8	-4%	52.0
Fxd. Chgs. Cov.	2.6	-7%	2.8	5%	2.7	-3%	2.8
Constr. Credits	6.4	68%	3.8	NM	3.8	-22%	4.9
Eff. Tax Rate	29%	—	29%	—	30%	—	27%
Net Inc.	76.1	-20%	95.3	11%	86.2	NM	85.6

Balance Sheet & Other Fin. Data (Million $)

	1994	1993	1992	1991	1990	1989
Gross Prop.	2,508	2,402	2,281	2,176	2,027	1,846
Cap. Exp.	120	138	131	172	167	145
Net Prop.	1,782	1,734	1,682	1,630	1,523	1,387
Capitalization:						
LT Debt	819	811	680	618	633	639
% LT Debt	44	44	40	39	44	46
Pfd.	189	214	230	231	162	113
% Pfd.	10	12	14	14	11	8.10
Common	843	836	792	755	660	643
% Common	46	45	47	47	45	46
Total Cap.	2,316	2,298	2,036	1,919	1,753	1,668

Ratio Analysis

	1994	1993	1992	1991	1990	1989
Oper. Ratio	83.2	81.6	83.2	81.4	82.6	80.9
% Earn. on Net Prop.	8.7	9.4	8.3	9.2	8.6	10.1
% Ret. on Revs.	8.3	11.0	10.6	11.0	9.6	11.5
% Ret. On Invest.Cap	6.4	8.0	8.0	8.4	7.8	9.0
% Return On Com.Eqty	9.1	11.7	11.1	12.1	10.6	13.6

Dividend Data —Dividends have been paid since 1919. A dividend reinvestment plan is available.

Amt. of Div. $	Date Decl.	Ex-Div. Date	Stock of Record	Payment Date
0.385	Sep. 08	Sep. 13	Sep. 19	Oct. 17 '94
0.385	Dec. 08	Dec. 13	Dec. 19	Jan. 16 '95
0.385	Mar. 09	Mar. 14	Mar. 20	Apr. 17 '95
0.385	Jun. 01	Jun. 15	Jun. 19	Jul. 17 '95
0.385	Sep. 14	Sep. 21	Sep. 25	Oct. 16 '95

Data as orig. reptd.; bef. results of disc opers. and/or spec. items. Per share data adj. for stk. divs. as of ex-div. date. E-Estimated. NA-Not Available. NM-Not Meaningful. NR-Not Ranked.

Office—6801 Black Horse Pike, Pleasantville, NJ 08232. **Tel**—(609) 645-4500. **Chrmn, Pres & CEO**—J. L. Jacobs. **VP, Treas & Secy**—J. G. Salomone. **Investor Contact**—R. K. Marshall. **Dirs**—J. M. Galvin Jr., G. A. Hale, M. Holden, Jr., C. H. Holley, E. D. Huggard, J. L. Jacobs, K. MacDonnell, R. B. McGlynn, B. J. Morgan, H. J. Ravache. **Transfer Agent & Registrar**—Co.'s office. **Incorporated** in New Jersey in 1907. **Empl**-1,500. **S&P Analyst:** Ronald J. Gross

STANDARD & POOR'S

STOCK REPORTS

Atlantic Southeast Airlines

NASDAQ Symbol **ASAI**

In S&P MidCap 400

03-AUG-95 **Industry:** Air Transport

Summary: This regional air carrier provides regularly scheduled, high-frequency commuter service from hubs in Atlanta and Dallas/Ft. Worth. It is a member of the "Delta Connection" program.

S&P Opinion: Hold (★★★)

Recent Price • 26⅜ | 52 Wk Range • 34¼-12¾ | Yield • 1.3% | 12-Mo. P/E • 17.9

Quantitative Evaluations

Outlook (1 Lowest—5 Highest)
• **4**

Fair Value
• **28⅝**

Risk
• **High**

Earn./Div. Rank
• **B+**

Technical Eval.
• **Bearish** since 7/95

Rel. Strength Rank (1 Lowest—99 Highest)
• **31**

Insider Activity
• **Neutral**

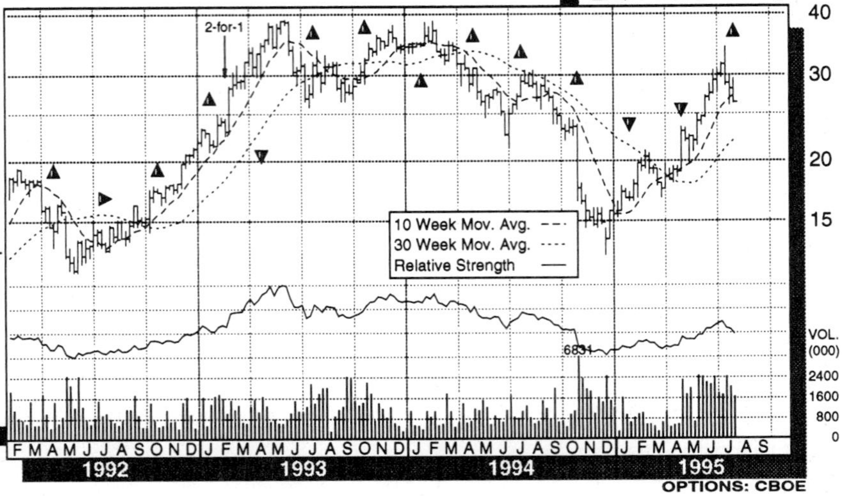

OPTIONS: CBOE

Overview - 03-AUG-95

Revenues for 1995 are expected to be about the same as those of 1994. Traffic is projected to benefit from continued regional economic strength. However, yields are likely to decline moderately, reflecting an expected lower average ticket price. Available seat miles (capacity) are forecast to increase 4-5%, due to the addition of new aircraft (primarily those purchased in 1994). Units costs are expected to decline slightly from the greater efficiency of the new aircraft and from improved aircraft utilization. Accordingly, margins will widen fractionally. Share earnings should benefit from fewer shares outstanding. Unfavorable publicity regarding the safety of ATRs, which had a slightly negative impact on results earlier in the year, has diminished, and is not expected to have a significant impact on the rest of 1995.

Valuation - 03-AUG-95

ASAI shares have soared in the first half of 1995, beyond those of other major regional carriers, recovering from poor 1994 performance. The stock also benefited from indications that severe competitive fare discounting was ending. Recent fare increases implemented by USAir (with which the company has a substantial overlap in service) and others will certainly add to earnings. However, trading at around 16 to 17 times our estimate of 1995 earnings, we consider the shares to be fairly valued.

Key Stock Statistics

S&P EPS Est. 1995	1.65	Tang. Bk. Value/Share	7.51
P/E on S&P Est. 1995	16.0	Beta	1.85
S&P EPS Est. 1996	1.80	Shareholders	1,400
Dividend Rate/Share	0.34	Market cap. (B)	$0.904
Shs. outstg. (M)	33.0	Inst. holdings	54%
Avg. daily vol. (M)	0.442	Insider holdings	NA

Value of $10,000 invested 5 years ago: $ 51,138

Fiscal Year Ending Dec. 31

	1995	% Change	1994	% Change	1993	% Change
Revenues (Million $)						
1Q	71.89	-4%	75.02	16%	64.50	12%
2Q	90.05	10%	82.03	17%	69.85	21%
3Q	—	—	80.08	7%	74.60	28%
4Q	—	—	74.96	-6%	79.54	28%
Yr.	—	—	312.1	8%	288.5	22%
Income (Million $)						
1Q	9.56	-23%	12.35	75%	7.07	-15%
2Q	14.98	-10%	16.58	27%	13.06	34%
3Q	—	—	12.51	NM	12.40	36%
4Q	—	—	11.22	-19%	13.80	39%
Yr.	—	—	52.66	14%	46.33	25%
Earnings Per Share ($)						
1Q	0.29	-19%	0.36	71%	0.21	-13%
2Q	0.45	-6%	0.48	26%	0.38	31%
3Q	E0.47	—	0.37	3%	0.36	33%
4Q	E0.44	—	0.33	-18%	0.40	38%
Yr.	E1.65	—	1.54	14%	1.35	24%

Next earnings report expected: late October

Atlantic Southeast Airlines

Business Summary - 03-AUG-95

Atlantic Southeast Airlines (ASA) is a regional air carrier that provides scheduled, high-frequency commuter service from hubs in Atlanta and Dallas/Ft. Worth.

As part of the "Delta Connection" program, ASA is able to offer passengers cost savings inherent in through-fares, coordinated schedules for timely connections, and mileage for the Delta Frequent Flyer Program.

As of March 1995, service was provided between Hartsfield Atlanta International Airport in Atlanta, Ga., and 39 other airports in Alabama, Florida, Georgia, Indiana, Kentucky, Mississippi, North Carolina, South Carolina, Tennessee, Virginia and West Virginia. A similar hub-and-spoke operation from the Dallas/Ft. Worth International Airport served 26 other airports in Arkansas, Kansas, Louisiana, Missouri, Oklahoma and Texas.

Operating data for recent years (passenger and seat miles in millions):

	1994	1993	1992
Rev. pass. miles	780	641	547
Avail. seat miles	1,654	1,367	1,077
Load factor	47.2%	46.9%	50.8%
Breakeven load factor	34.2%	34.3%	38.0%
Rev. per RPM (cents)	39.2	44.2	42.2
Cost per ASM (cents)	13.8	15.4	16.2

The operations at the Atlanta and Dallas/Ft. Worth hubs are primarily dependent upon business, government and military related travel. The company estimates that pleasure travel accounted for approximately 20% of the passengers during 1994.

As of March 1995, the fleet consisted of 83 turboprop aircraft: 12 ATR-72s (66-passenger capacity), 60 Embraer Brasilias (30-passenger), and 11 Embraer Bandeirantes (15-passenger). On order were six additional Brasilias to serve as replacement aircraft for the company's Bandeirante fleet.

At February 15, 1995, Delta Air Lines held a 24% stake in ASA.

Important Developments

Jul. '95—ASA said that second quarter share earnings would have increased to $0.49, from $0.43, were it not for unusual items. While a litigation settlement contributed $0.04 to earnings, ASA's Stock Appreciation Rights plan resulted in an after-tax charge of $0.08 a share, versus a benefit of $0.05.

Jul. '95—For the first six months of 1995, passenger traffic was down 1.3%, year to year. Capacity was up 4.0%, and the load factor fell to 44.6%, from 47.0%.

Jul. '95—Atlantic announced plans to acquire five BAe 146-200 jet aircraft, with options to acquire 15 more. The five jets, with an 88-passenger configuration, are scheduled for delivery in late 1995 and early 1996.

Capitalization

Long Term Debt: $143,879,000 (4/95).

Per Share Data ($) (Year Ended Dec. 31)

	1994	1993	1992	1991	1990	1989
Tangible Bk. Val.	7.46	6.47	5.14	4.25	3.47	2.97
Cash Flow	2.51	2.20	1.86	1.70	1.38	1.29
Earnings	1.54	1.35	1.09	0.95	0.73	0.76
Dividends	0.32	0.28	0.24	0.20	0.16	0.08
Payout Ratio	21%	21%	22%	21%	21%	11%
Prices - High	38¾	39	22⅜	15¾	7¼	6⅝
- Low	12¾	20⅞	11¾	5½	4	2⅞
P/E Ratio - High	25	29	21	16	10	9
- Low	8	15	11	6	6	4

Income Statement Analysis (Million $)

	1994	%Chg	1993	%Chg	1992	%Chg	1991
Revs.	312	8%	288	22%	236	6%	222
Oper. Inc.	117	9%	107	23%	87.2	12%	78.0
Depr.	33.2	14%	29.2	11%	26.4	4%	25.4
Int. Exp.	6.2	20%	5.2	-18%	6.3	-10%	7.0
Pretax Inc.	85.6	11%	77.4	31%	59.3	15%	51.6
Eff. Tax Rate	39%	—	40%	—	38%	—	37%
Net Inc.	52.7	14%	46.3	25%	37.1	14%	32.5

Balance Sheet & Other Fin. Data (Million $)

	1994	1993	1992	1991	1990	1989
Cash	176	166	133	111	88.0	80.0
Curr. Assets	194	182	146	124	99	91.0
Total Assets	520	475	431	378	325	288
Curr. Liab.	53.2	55.4	52.5	45.3	39.1	35.9
LT Debt	153	136	146	139	128	112
Common Eqty.	247	225	179	148	120	108
Total Cap.	466	419	378	332	286	252
Cap. Exp.	67.9	35.8	57.9	52.1	52.6	53.2
Cash Flow	85.8	75.5	63.4	57.9	48.1	46.9

Ratio Analysis

	1994	1993	1992	1991	1990	1989
Curr. Ratio	3.6	3.3	2.8	2.7	2.5	2.5
% LT Debt of Cap.	32.8	32.5	38.6	42.0	44.6	44.3
% Net Inc.of Revs.	16.9	16.1	15.7	14.6	13.6	15.3
% Ret. on Assets	10.8	10.2	9.2	9.2	8.5	10.9
% Ret. on Equity	22.6	22.9	22.7	24.1	22.7	28.2

Dividend Data (Cash payments were initiated in 1989.)

Amt. of Div. $	Date Decl.	Ex-Div. Date	Stock of Record	Payment Date
0.080	Jul. 27	Aug. 26	Sep. 01	Sep. 15 '94
0.080	Oct. 26	Nov. 25	Dec. 01	Dec. 15 '94
0.085	Feb. 01	Feb. 23	Mar. 01	Mar. 15 '95
0.085	May. 24	May. 25	Jun. 01	Jun. 15 '95

Data as orig. reptd.; bef. results of disc. opers. and/or spec. items. Per share data adj. for stk. divs. as of ex-div. date. E-Estimated. NA-Not Available. NM-Not Meaningful. NR-Not Ranked.

Office—100 Hartsfield Centre Parkway, Suite 800, Atlanta, GA 30354-1356. **Tel**—(404) 766-1400. **Chrmn & CEO**—G. F. Pickett, Jr. **Pres & Secy**—J. W. Beiser. **VP, Treas, CFO & Investor Contact**—Ronald V. Sapp. **Dirs**—J. W. Beiser, J. P. Gwin, R. H. Heil, J. A. Mori, P. H. Petit, G. F. Pickett, Jr., A. M. Voorhees, R. W. Voorhees. **Transfer Agent & Registrar**—Trust Co. Bank, Atlanta. **Incorporated** in Georgia in 1979. **Empl**-2,191. **S&P Analyst:** Joe Victor Shammas

STANDARD & POOR'S

STOCK REPORTS

Atmel Corp.

NASDAQ Symbol **ATML**
In S&P MidCap 400

16-OCT-95 **Industry:** Data Processing

Summary: This company makes and markets a broad range of high-performance memory and logic integrated circuits.

S&P Opinion: Buy (★★★★★) Recent Price • 30⅛ | 52 Wk Range • 36¾-15⅛ | Yield • Nil | 12-Mo. P/E • 31.1

Quantitative Evaluations
Outlook (1 Lowest—5 Highest)
• **5**
Fair Value
• **44⅝**
Risk
• **Average**
Earn./Div. Rank
• **NR**

Technical Eval.
• **Bullish** since 12/93
Rel. Strength Rank (1 Lowest—99 Highest)
• **25**
Insider Activity
• **Neutral**

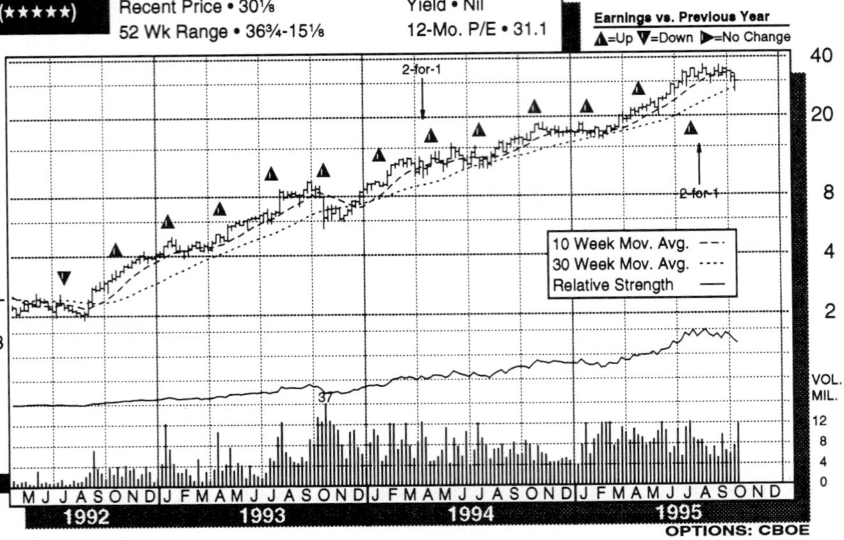

OPTIONS: CBOE

Overview - 13-OCT-95

We estimate that sales will increase 40-45% in 1996, driven by demand from the high growth consumer electronics and telecommunications sectors. New product introductions, including SRAM devices, will also assist sales growth. Gross margins should remain stable as yield improvements from upgraded facilities and a shift to smaller linewidths help offset any weakness in pricing. The company continues to aggressively add capacity. Atmel expects to spend about 40% of its sales, approximately double the industry average, on capacity expansion in the near future. Despite plans to add 10-15% more capacity in the next several quarters, the company will remain capacity constrained until early 1997 when a new fabrication facility is scheduled to begin operations.

Valuation - 16-OCT-95

Despite the recent slide in the technology sector, we are still bullish on Atmel. Sales remain strong, with the company reporting a 16% sequential rise in the third quarter. Counter to the notion that orders for chips are softening, we see Atmel's products experiencing increased demand. Factors supporting our outlook are: a sequential increase of over 10% in bookings, a decline in days of inventory on hand to 44 days from 49 days (2nd quarter), and an increase in customer order lead time. Currently, capacity appears to be the limiting factor in top-line growth. Additionally, prices for the fast growing Flash and EEPROM memory products are trending upward. We believe EPS growth will top 30% in the foreseeable future, making ATML attractive at 21x estimated 1996 earnings.

Key Stock Statistics

S&P EPS Est. 1995	1.12	Tang. Bk. Value/Share	3.95
P/E on S&P Est. 1995	26.9	Beta	NA
S&P EPS Est. 1996	1.55	Shareholders	600
Dividend Rate/Share	Nil	Market cap. (B)	$ 2.9
Shs. outstg. (M)	96.7	Inst. holdings	75%
Avg. daily vol. (M)	1.553	Insider holdings	NA

Value of $10,000 invested 5 years ago: NA

Fiscal Year Ending Dec. 31

	1995	% Change	1994	% Change	1993	% Change
Revenues (Million $)						
1Q	119.3	50%	79.29	81%	43.92	53%
2Q	145.9	64%	89.18	76%	50.66	54%
3Q	168.8	71%	98.62	67%	59.02	60%
4Q	—	—	108.0	59%	68.13	67%
Yr.	—	—	375.1	69%	221.7	59%
Income (Million $)						
1Q	19.83	63%	12.17	139%	5.10	107%
2Q	24.53	75%	14.03	124%	6.26	111%
3Q	31.21	101%	15.52	87%	8.29	119%
4Q	—	—	17.73	71%	10.37	120%
Yr.	—	—	59.45	98%	30.02	116%
Earnings Per Share ($)						
1Q	0.21	50%	0.14	107%	0.07	93%
2Q	0.26	63%	0.16	100%	0.08	88%
3Q	0.31	77%	0.17	75%	0.10	90%
4Q	E0.34	79%	0.19	58%	0.12	92%
Yr.	E1.12	70%	0.66	81%	0.36	90%

Next earnings report expected: mid January

Atmel Corp.

Business Summary - 13-OCT-95

Atmel Corporation designs, develops, manufactures and markets a broad range of high-performance memory and logic integrated circuits using its proprietary CMOS (complementary metal-oxide-silicon) technologies.

Atmel's memory devices include EPROMs (erasable programmable read-only memories), EEPROMs (electronically erasable programmable ROMs) and Flash memories.

Logic products include user-configurable EPLDs (erasable programmable logic devices), FPGAs (field programmable gate arrays), both of which are semicustom devices that can be configured into complex specialized circuits according to customer specification. It also produces ASICs (application specific integrated circuits) and microcontrollers.

Atmel's products are used in a range of applications in computing, telecommunications, industrial control and instrumentation, consumer electronics, and commercial and military avionics markets.

The company markets its products to large OEMs through manufacturers' representatives and to others through independent distributors. The company believes that systems manufacturers are increasingly seeking to reduce the number of qualified suppliers, and that the breadth of Atmel's products lines provides customers with a source for multiple product needs.

Atmel's strategy is to offer products that provide the enabling technology and features to allow its customers to develop and bring to market high value-added systems and products. Atmel's strategy is to focus on high performance applications where its integrated circuits can be differentiated by speed, density, power usage or specialty packaging. The company's products are critical elements of complex electronic systems and typically command higher average selling prices compared to integrated circuits sold for commodity applications. For example, Atmel believes that the low power usage of its Flash memories and EEPROMs better positions the company to supply memory integrated circuits for use in portable systems such as cellular telephones, notebook computers and consumer electronic products, where battery life is critical.

Foreign product sales represented approximately 48% and 46% of total revenues in 1994 and 1993, respectively.

Important Developments

Oct. '95—Commenting on the exposure to the cellular phone market, through its relationship with Motorola (about 20% of sales), Atmel noted that while demand for analog phones may be weakening, it supplies components used in the fast growing digital (high-end) cellular phone market.

Capitalization

Long Term Debt: $82,015,000 (9/95).

Per Share Data ($)

(Year Ended Dec. 31)

	1994	1993	1992	1991	1990	1989
Tangible Bk. Val.	3.95	2.63	1.88	1.71	0.91	0.80
Cash Flow	1.05	0.55	0.30	0.27	0.21	0.18
Earnings	0.66	0.37	0.19	0.15	0.09	0.16
Dividends	Nil	Nil	Nil	Nil	Nil	Nil
Payout Ratio	Nil	Nil	Nil	Nil	Nil	Nil
Prices - High	18 7/8	9 5/8	4 1/4	4 3/4	NA	NA
- Low	8 1/4	3 7/8	1 15/16	1 11/16	NA	NA
P/E Ratio - High	28	26	22	31	NA	NA
- Low	12	10	10	11	NA	NA

Income Statement Analysis (Million $)

	1994	%Chg	1993	%Chg	1992	%Chg	1991
Revs.	375	69%	222	59%	140	17%	120
Oper. Inc.	122	105%	59.4	122%	26.8	14%	23.6
Depr.	34.1	123%	15.3	98%	7.7	-5%	8.2
Int. Exp.	2.8	-2%	2.9	-8%	3.1	-25%	4.1
Pretax Inc.	90.1	101%	44.8	125%	19.9	34%	14.9
Eff. Tax Rate	34%	—	33%	—	30%	—	31%
Net Inc.	59.5	98%	30.0	116%	13.9	35%	10.3

Balance Sheet & Other Fin. Data (Million $)

	1994	1993	1992	1991	1990	1989
Cash	79.3	67.6	24.9	45.3	21.7	28.6
Curr. Assets	188	144	100	110	77.0	75.0
Total Assets	541	301	183	160	101	93.0
Curr. Liab.	124	54.8	27.9	23.6	29.6	38.8
LT Debt	46.5	24.0	23.0	21.2	34.4	21.9
Common Eqty.	358	218	132	115	37.0	32.0
Total Cap.	417	246	156	136	72.0	54.0
Cap. Exp.	183	73.9	14.2	7.3	2.2	6.1
Cash Flow	93.5	45.3	21.7	18.5	10.3	8.3

Ratio Analysis

	1994	1993	1992	1991	1990	1989
Curr. Ratio	1.5	2.6	3.6	4.7	2.6	1.9
% LT Debt of Cap.	11.2	9.7	14.8	15.6	47.9	40.3
% Net Inc.of Revs.	15.8	13.5	10.0	8.6	5.5	12.3
% Ret. on Assets	13.7	11.6	8.0	7.9	4.4	10.9
% Ret. on Equity	19.9	16.1	11.1	13.6	12.3	26.1

Dividend Data —No cash has been paid. A two-for-one stock split was effected in April 1994.

Amt. of Div. $	Date Decl.	Ex-Div. Date	Stock of Record	Payment Date
2-for-1	Jul. 13	Aug. 09	Jul. 24	Aug. 08 '95

Data as orig. reptd.; bef. results of disc. opers. and/or spec. items. Per share data adj. for stk. divs. as of ex-div. date. E-Estimated. NA-Not Available. NM-Not Meaningful. NR-Not Ranked.

Office—2125 O'Nel Dr., San Jose, CA 95131. **Tel**—(408) 441-0311. **Fax**—(408) 436-4200. **Chrmn, Pres & CEO**—George Perlegos. **VP-Fin & CFO**—K. Chellam. **Dirs**—N. Hall, George Perlegos, Gust Perlegos, T. P. Thomas, T. Wu. **Transfer Agent & Registrar**—Chemical Trust Co. of California. **Incorporated** in California in 1984. **Empl**-1,907. **S&P Analyst:** Steven A. Jaworski

Avnet, Inc.

NYSE Symbol **AVT**
In S&P MidCap 400

21-SEP-95 **Industry:** Electronics/Electric

Summary: Avnet is one of the world's largest distributors of electronic components and computer products.

S&P Opinion: Accumulate (★★★★) Recent Price • 54¼ Yield • 1.1%
52 Wk Range • 55⅝-33¾ 12-Mo. P/E • 16.3

Quantitative Evaluations

Outlook
(1 Lowest—5 Highest)
• **4+**

Fair Value
• **54⅞**

Risk
• **Low**

Earn./Div. Rank
• **A**

Technical Eval.
• **Bearish** since 8/94

Rel. Strength Rank
(1 Lowest—99 Highest)
• **59**

Insider Activity
• **Neutral**

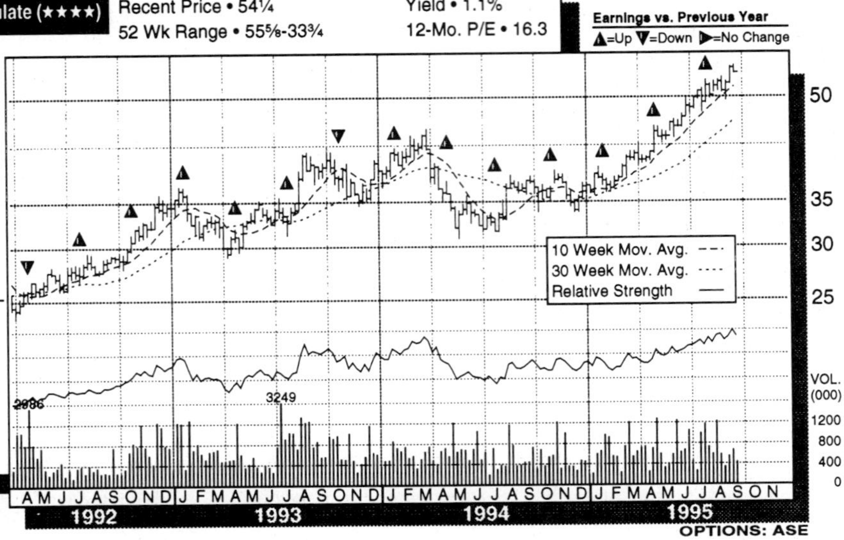

OPTIONS: ASE

Overview - 21-SEP-95

Fiscal 1996 sales are likely to increase significantly, as a solid economy allows the electronics industry to expand further. In addition, the company made eight acquisitions during fiscal 1995. Electronic marketing is benefiting as suppliers place more sales through distributors, especially those like Avnet with technical abilities to provide field service. Recent acquisitions strengthened the company's position in the wireless communication distributin market, and it has entered the Asian market as well. Despite pressure on gross profit margins from a shift to lower-margin products and services, well controlled operating costs should be an offset.

Valuation - 21-SEP-95

The shares have climbed over 50% since late 1994, reflecting strong computer and electronics markets. The company, already one of the world's largest electronics distributors, has aggressively expanded its market presence through acquisitions. We believe that continued strength in the electronics sector and the benefits of acquisitions will drive revenues and earnings up over 15% in fiscal 1996. Based on these strong fundamentals, and with the shares trading at only 13X our fiscal 1996 EPS estimate of $4.15, we consider the shares attractive for accumulation.

Key Stock Statistics

S&P EPS Est. 1996	4.15	Tang. Bk. Value/Share	15.57
P/E on S&P Est. 1996	13.1	Beta	1.12
S&P EPS Est. 1997	4.85	Shareholders	6,700
Dividend Rate/Share	0.60	Market cap. (B)	$ 2.2
Shs. outstg. (M)	40.8	Inst. holdings	81%
Avg. daily vol. (M)	0.101	Insider holdings	NA

Value of $10,000 invested 5 years ago: $ 19,425

Fiscal Year Ending Jun. 30

	1995	% Change	1994	% Change	1993	% Change
Revenues (Million $)						
1Q	953.8	9%	878.0	65%	533.0	29%
2Q	1,040	22%	850.5	61%	526.8	27%
3Q	1,130	26%	900.0	55%	582.5	37%
4Q	1,178	28%	919.2	54%	595.5	18%
Yr.	4,300	21%	3,548	59%	2,238	27%
Income (Million $)						
1Q	28.93	186%	10.11	-40%	16.90	54%
2Q	31.06	32%	23.60	52%	15.50	32%
3Q	36.40	44%	25.34	39%	18.19	47%
4Q	43.90	51%	29.10	57%	18.50	20%
Yr.	140.3	59%	88.11	28%	69.06	37%
Earnings Per Share ($)						
1Q	0.69	176%	0.25	-47%	0.47	52%
2Q	0.74	28%	0.58	35%	0.43	30%
3Q	0.86	39%	0.62	24%	0.50	43%
4Q	1.03	45%	0.71	39%	0.51	19%
Yr.	3.32	54%	2.16	13%	1.91	35%

Next earnings report expected: late October

Avnet, Inc.

Business Summary - 21-SEP-95

Avnet distributes electronic components and computer products. It also makes other electronic products. Contributions to sales and operating profit by segment in fiscal 1994 were:

	Sales	Profits
Electronic marketing	89%	93%
Electrical & industrial	6%	6%
Video communications	5%	1%

International operations accounted for 17% of sales and 16% of operating profits in fiscal 1994.

The Electronic Marketing Group is engaged in the marketing, assembly, and/or processing of electronic and electromechanical components and computer products. The principal products its distributes are semiconductors for industrial, commercial and military use. It is also a distributor of computer products. Lastly, the group is the world's leading distributor of interconnect products including value-added connectors, electro-mechanical and passive components and cable assembly services.

The electrical and industrial group distributes electrical insulation, magnet wire, electric motors and supply parts. Industrial maintenance and factory supplies are also distributed.

The video communications group principally designs, develops and manufactures TV signal processing and audio equipment. Other products include private-label CD players and turntables.

Important Developments

Sep. '95—Avnet said it had acquired Germany-based Setron-Schiffer-Elektronik GmbH & Co. KG, a limited partnership engaged in the distribution of electronics. Setron, which operates in 20 European countries, projects 1995 sales at about $130 million.
Jul. '95—The company acquired VSI Electronics (Australia) PTY Ltd., an Australian electronics distributor, and VSI Electronics (NZ) Ltd., a New Zealand-based electronics distributor, from Electron House PLC. The two companies had sales of about $43 million in the fiscal year ended May 31, 1995. Terms were not disclosed. In May, Avnet purchased Sertek Inc., a technical specialist distributor of microwave and radio frequency products in the Southwest. Sertek had sales of over $9 million in the fiscal year ended June 30, 1994.

Capitalization

Long Term Debt: $419,016,000 (6/95).

Per Share Data ($) (Year Ended Jun. 30)

	1995	1994	1993	1992	1991	1990
Tangible Bk. Val.	NA	17.80	23.19	22.60	21.83	20.93
Cash Flow	NA	2.94	2.40	2.09	2.25	2.20
Earnings	3.32	2.16	1.91	1.42	1.72	1.57
Dividends	0.75	0.60	0.60	0.60	0.60	0.60
Payout Ratio	23%	28%	31%	42%	35%	38%
Prices - High	53	45	42¼	36	30	33½
- Low	35¾	30¾	29	23½	23¼	21½
P/E Ratio - High	16	21	22	25	17	21
- Low	11	14	15	17	14	14

Income Statement Analysis (Million $)

	1994	%Chg	1993	%Chg	1992	%Chg	1991
Revs.	3,548	59%	2,238	27%	1,759	1%	1,741
Oper. Inc.	22.0	-83%	126	34%	94.0	-15%	111
Depr.	31.8	39%	22.8	-5%	24.0	-3%	24.8
Int. Exp.	15.0	67%	9.0	-33%	13.4	NM	13.3
Pretax Inc.	155	36%	114	37%	83.0	-17%	100
Eff. Tax Rate	43%	—	40%	—	39%	—	38%
Net Inc.	88.1	27%	69.1	37%	50.5	-18%	61.6

Balance Sheet & Other Fin. Data (Million $)

	1994	1993	1992	1991	1990	1989
Cash	54.0	220	305	341	344	237
Curr. Assets	1,264	1,076	1,079	1,038	1,030	983
Total Assets	1,788	1,247	1,243	1,181	1,158	1,126
Curr. Liab.	376	273	230	179	186	179
LT Debt	303	107	175	201	202	211
Common Eqty.	1,109	868	837	801	770	735
Total Cap.	1,412	975	1,013	1,002	972	947
Cap. Exp.	21.4	15.1	25.1	20.4	17.4	22.6
Cash Flow	120	92.0	75.0	86.0	85.0	84.0

Ratio Analysis

	1994	1993	1992	1991	1990	1989
Curr. Ratio	3.4	3.9	4.7	5.8	5.5	5.5
% LT Debt of Cap.	21.5	10.9	17.3	20.1	20.8	22.3
% Net Inc.of Revs.	2.5	3.1	2.9	3.5	3.2	2.8
% Ret. on Assets	5.8	5.5	4.2	5.3	4.9	4.7
% Ret. on Equity	8.9	8.1	6.2	7.9	7.5	7.5

Dividend Data —Dividends have been paid since 1961. A dividend reinvestment plan is available.

Amt. of Div. $	Date Decl.	Ex-Div. Date	Stock of Record	Payment Date
0.150	Jul. 27	Sep. 02	Sep. 09	Oct. 03 '94
0.150	Nov. 16	Dec. 05	Dec. 09	Jan. 03 '95
0.150	Jan. 25	Mar. 06	Mar. 10	Apr. 03 '95
0.150	May. 31	Jun. 14	Jun. 16	Jul. 03 '95
0.150	Jul. 26	Sep. 13	Sep. 15	Oct. 02 '95

Data as orig. reptd.; bef. results of disc. opers. and/or spec. items. Per share data adj. for stk. divs. as of ex-div. date. E-Estimated. NA-Not Available. NM-Not Meaningful. NR-Not Ranked.

Office—80 Cutter Mill Rd., Great Neck, NY 11021. **Tel**—(516) 466-7000. **Chrmn & CEO**—L. Machiz. **Pres**—R. Vallee. **VP & Secy**—S. D. Herlihy. **SVP, CFO & Assistant Secy**—R. Sadowski. **Investor Contact**—Stephanie Wagoner. **Dirs**— E. Baum, G. J. Berkman, J. F. Caligiuri, S. D. Herlihy, E. Houminer, L. Machiz, S. J. Nuzzo, F. Salerno, D. Shaw, H. Stein, R. Vallee, F. S. Wood. **Transfer Agent & Registrar**—Bank of New York, NYC. **Incorporated** in New York in 1955. **Empl**-8,000. **S&P Analyst:** Mike Cavanaugh

BJ Services

NYSE Symbol BJS Options on CBOE In S&P MidCap 400

Price	Range	P–E Ratio	Dividend	Yield	S&P Ranking	Beta
Oct. 16'95	1995					
24¼	27⅜–15½	78	None	None	NR	0.49

Summary

This company is a leading participant in the pressure pumping business, serving the petroleum industry worldwide. Its principal activities consist of well cementing and stimulation services and casing and tubing services for the drilling and completion of oil and natural gas wells. Operations were substantially expanded by the April 1995 acquisition of Western Co. of North America, another leading provider of oilfield services, for more than $510 million.

Business Summary

BJ Services Company provides pressure pumping services to the petroleum industry on a worldwide basis. Its principal activities consist of well cementing and stimulation services and casing and tubing services for drilling and completion of oil and natural gas wells, both onshore and offshore. BJS also provides commissioning and leak detection services on offshore platforms and pipelines. BJS was a subsidiary of Baker Hughes Inc. prior to its initial public offering in July 1990.

BJS's cementing services are utilized in a number of specific applications in oilfield operations, the most important of which is the cementing between the casing pipe and the wellbore during the drilling and completion phase of the well ("primary cementing"). Primary cementing provides structural support for the protective casing, prevents migration of fluids between productive formations, allows selective production among formations and seals the casing from corrosive formation fluids. Cementing services are also utilized when a well is to be plugged and abandoned or when existing wells require remedial work.

Stimulation services consist of hydraulic fracturing, acidizing and nitrogen services to improve the flow of oil or natural gas from producing formations. Hydraulic fracturing is applied in formations and reservoirs with relatively low or impaired productive capabilities. Acidizing services are used to repair and unblock formations whose productivity has been lessened by damage or buildup over time of various materials in the formation. Nitrogen services are used to support cement and fracturing services.

BJS's services are provided to customers in the major oil and gas producing regions of the U.S. (48% of fiscal 1994 revenues), Latin America and Canada (17%), Europe (22%) and other areas (13%). BJS downsized its North American operations during fiscal 1992 and fiscal 1993 and focused its expansion efforts on international markets.

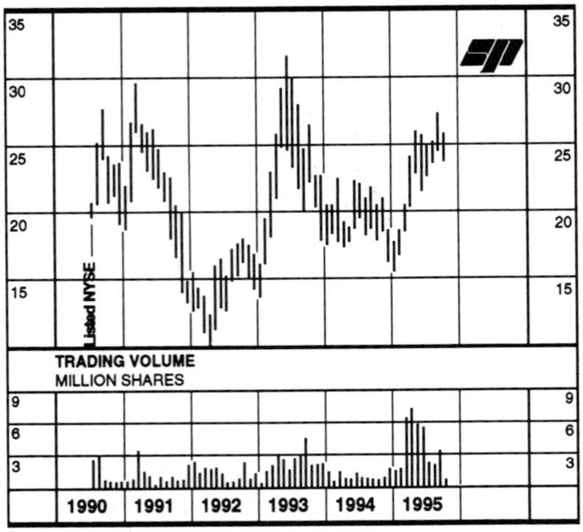

Important Developments

Apr. '95— BJS acquired The Western Co. of North America for total consideration of $511.4 million, consisting of $247.4 million in cash, $240.0 million in common stock (12,036,393 shares) and $24.0 million in warrants to purchase common stock (4,800,037 warrants). Western, another leading provider of oilfield services, had revenues for the 12 months ended September 30, 1994, of $353.5 million.

Next earnings report expected in November.

Per Share Data ($)

Yr. End Sep. 30	1994	1993	[4]1992	1991	1990	[1]1989
Tangible Bk. Val.	**10.78**	10.67	8.99	10.41	8.57	[2]7.33
Cash Flow	**2.30**	2.46	0.89	2.99	2.39	NA
Earnings[5]	**0.69**	0.94	d0.08	1.88	1.42	0.45
Dividends	**Nil**	Nil	Nil	Nil	Nil	Nil
Payout Ratio	**Nil**	Nil	Nil	Nil	Nil	Nil
Prices[3]—High	**22½**	31⅝	18	29⅝	27¾	NA
Low	**16¼**	13⅝	10	13¼	19⅛	NA
P/E Ratio—	**33–24**	34–14	NM	16–7	20–13	NA

Data as orig. reptd. **1.** Pro forma. **2.** As of Mar. 31, 1990. **3.** Cal. yr. **4.** Refl. merger or acq. **5.** Bef. spec. item of -0.67 in 1994. d-Deficit. NM-Not Meaningful. NA-Not Available.

Income Data (Million $)

Year Ended Sep. 30	Revs.	Oper. Inc.	% Oper. Inc. of Revs.	Cap. Exp.	Depr.	Int. Exp.	Net Bef. Taxes	Eff. Tax Rate	[6]Net Inc.	% Net Inc. of Revs.	Cash Flow
1994	**434**	**44.8**	**10.3**	**39.3**	**25.3**	**7.92**	[2]**12.9**	**15.5%**	[5]**10.8**	**2.5**	**36.1**
1993	394	43.7	11.1	37.4	23.5	[4]5.41	[2]16.8	9.5%	14.6	3.7	38.0
[3]1992	330	26.2	7.9	26.2	12.7	3.78	[2]d4.2	NM	d1.1	NM	11.6
1991	390	44.8	11.5	34.6	14.5	3.89	[2]31.1	16.6%	24.4	6.3	38.9
1990	350	41.8	11.9	20.1	12.6	1.37	[2]28.8	31.9%	18.5	5.3	31.1
[1]1989	317	35.6	11.2	NA	13.7	3.87	15.7	56.4%	5.9	1.9	NA

Balance Sheet Data (Million $)

Sep. 30	Cash	Assets	Curr. Liab.	Ratio	Total Assets	% Ret. on Assets	Long Term Debt	Common Equity	Total Cap.	% LT Debt of Cap.	% Ret. on Equity
1994	**3.22**	**158**	**121**	**1.3**	**410**	**2.8**	**74.7**	**190**	**272**	**27.5**	**5.7**
1993	1.62	146	90	1.6	370	3.8	84.5	187	277	30.6	8.4
1992	1.48	130	129	1.0	329	NM	55.5	135	200	27.8	NM
1991	5.41	121	86	1.4	266	9.7	31.0	135	179	17.3	19.8
1990	3.09	112	90	1.2	239	NA	24.0	111	148	16.3	NA
[7]1989	0.05	91	74	1.2	211	NA	27.4	95	136	20.2	NA

Data as orig. reptd. **1.** Pro forma. **2.** Incl. equity in earns. of nonconsol. subs. **3.** Refl. merger or acq. **4.** Net of int. inc. **5.** Refl. acctg. change. **6.** Bef. spec. item in 1994. **7.** As of Mar. 31, 1990, pro forma. d-Deficit. NM-Not Meaningful. NA-Not Available.

Revenues (Million $)

Quarter:	1994–5	1993–4	1992–3	1991–2
Dec.	106.7	104.8	94.4	88.7
Mar.	199.4	98.5	100.1	78.1
Jun.	199.5	106.3	96.7	79.4
Sep.		125.0	103.1	83.9
		434.5	394.4	330.0

Revenues for the nine months ended June 30, 1995, rose 38%, year to year, largely reflecting the inclusion of Western Co. of North America from April 1, 1995. Results were penalized by higher interest expense and by an unusual charge of $16 million in connection with a consolidation program. Aftertax income fell to $274,000 ($0.01 a share, based on 22% more shares), from $6,084,000 ($0.39). Results for the 1993-4 period exclude a $0.66-a-share charge from the cumulative effect of an accounting change.

Common Share Earnings ($)

Quarter:	1994–5	1993–4	1992–3	1991–2
Dec.	0.15	0.23	0.21	0.17
Mar.	0.09	0.03	0.15	d0.75
Jun.	d0.23	0.13	0.21	0.20
Sep.		0.30	0.38	0.30
		0.69	0.94	d0.08

Finances

Capital expenditures for the first nine months of fiscal 1995 were $24.3 million, or $7.8 million below spending in the year-earlier period that included about $12 million used to construct two offshore stimulation vessels.

In April 1995, the company arranged a committed unsecured credit facility that consists of a five-year $175 million revolving credit facility and a six-year $225 million term loan.

Effective February 9, 1994, BJS acquired the remaining 50% ownership of its previously unconsolidated joint venture in Egypt, Hughes Services C.I., Ltd., for $2.0 million.

At September 30, 1994, BJS had about $112 million of U.S. tax net operating loss carryforwards expiring between 2004 and 2009.

In October 1992, BJS sold publicly 2.5 million common shares at $17.375 per share. Net proceeds of $40.8 million were used to repay debt, including $24.8 million of notes related to the Salvesen acquisition.

In September 1992, the company acquired Salvesen Ltd. (since renamed BJS Oilfield Technology Limited) for about $52 million. Salvesen provides services primarily in the U.K. North Sea.

In July 1990, BJ Services Co., a wholly owned subsidiary of Baker Hughes Inc., offered 9,000,000 common shares at $20 each in its initial public offering.

Dividend Data

The company does not currently intend to pay dividends on its common shares. Any earnings, for the foreseeable future, will be retained for use in BJS's business. Also, the company's credit facilities restrict dividends.

Capitalization

Long Term Debt: $274,666,000 (6/95).

Common Shares: 27,942,154 shs. ($0.10 par). Institutions hold about 89%. Shareholders of record: 276 (12/94).

d-Deficit.

Office—5500 Northwest Central Drive, Houston, TX 77092; P.O. Box 4442, Houston, TX 77210-4442. **Tel**—(713) 462-4239. **Chrmn, Pres & CEO**—J. W. Stewart. **VP-Fin, CFO & Investor Contact**—Michael McShane. **VP-Secy**—Margaret B. Shannon. **Treas**—T. M. Whichard. **Dirs**—L. W. Heiligbrodt, J. R. Huff, D. D. Jordan, R. A. LeBlanc, J. E. McCormick, M. McShane, J. W. Stewart. **Transfer Agent & Registrar**—First Chicago Shareholders Services Trust Co., NYC. **Incorporated** in Delaware in 1990. **Empl**—2,780.

STANDARD & POOR'S
STOCK REPORTS

BMC Software

NASDAQ Symbol **BMCS**
In S&P MidCap 400

17-OCT-95 **Industry:** Data Processing

Summary: BMC markets software to enhance IBM's database management and data communications products, principally IMS, DB2 and CISC. It also offers applications management products.

S&P Opinion: Accumulate (★★★★) Recent Price • 33⅜ Yield • Nil
52 Wk Range • 51½-20⅛ 12-Mo. P/E • 20.6

Quantitative Evaluations
Outlook (1 Lowest—5 Highest)
• **5⁻**
Fair Value
• **56⅝**
Risk
• **Average**
Earn./Div. Rank
• **B+**

Technical Eval.
• **Bearish** since 3/95
Rel. Strength Rank (1 Lowest—99 Highest)
• **4**
Insider Activity
• **Neutral**

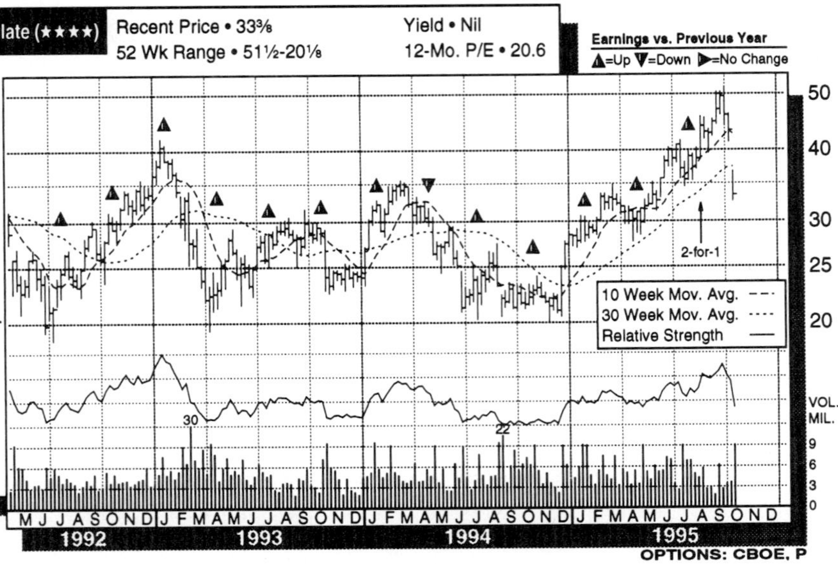

OPTIONS: CBOE, P

Overview - 17-OCT-95

Revenues should continue to advance in 1995-6, aided by demand for IMS and DB2 mainframe database enhancement software programs and by the introduction of new products that integrate and improve the performance of computer networks. The September quarter notwithstanding, the backlog of prospective new business remains healthy and international business is again showing growth, aided by strengthening economies and a more focused sales effort. Maintenance revenues should advance at double-digit rates. Margins for the full fiscal year are expected to widen slightly, on volume efficiencies and cost controls, despite continued investments in R&D.

Valuation - 17-OCT-95

The shares have fluctuated widely in the past three years, driven lower by concern about the future of the company's mainframe software business and pushed higher by a steady stream of solid financial results. The recent October decline stems from a company announcement of lower than expected revenues in the September 1995 quarter. However, we expect BMC to generate annual share earnings growth of about 20% over the next several years, reflecting continued gains in core mainframe database utility, tool and connectivity products and new products that increase the usefulness of computer networks. We believe that the price more than discounts potential uncertainties and feel that the shares should outperform the market, driven by earnings growth and potential expansion of the P/E multiple.

Key Stock Statistics

S&P EPS Est. 1996	2.40	Tang. Bk. Value/Share	6.54
P/E on S&P Est. 1996	13.9	Beta	1.04
Dividend Rate/Share	Nil	Shareholders	300
Shs. outstg. (M)	50.5	Market cap. (B)	$ 1.7
Avg. daily vol. (M)	0.941	Inst. holdings	101%
		Insider holdings	NA

Value of $10,000 invested 5 years ago: $ 33,098

Fiscal Year Ending Mar. 31

	1996	% Change	1995	% Change	1994	% Change
Revenues (Million $)						
1Q	93.30	20%	78.00	20%	65.00	29%
2Q	—	—	80.00	18%	68.00	18%
3Q	—	—	90.70	20%	75.50	16%
4Q	—	—	96.30	20%	80.00	22%
Yr.	—	—	345.0	20%	288.5	21%
Income (Million $)						
1Q	27.47	24%	22.10	21%	18.20	38%
2Q	—	—	24.28	20%	20.19	33%
3Q	—	—	27.71	20%	23.08	34%
4Q	—	—	3.43	NM	-4.99	NM
Yr.	—	—	77.52	37%	56.49	-14%
Earnings Per Share ($)						
1Q	0.53	23%	0.43	25%	0.35	35%
2Q	E0.50	4%	0.48	25%	0.39	33%
3Q	E0.65	18%	0.55	24%	0.44	35%
4Q	E0.72	NM	0.07	NM	-0.09	NM
Yr.	E2.40	58%	1.52	41%	1.08	-14%

Next earnings report expected: late October

BMC Software

Business Summary - 17-OCT-95

BMC Software, Inc. develops, markets and supports standard systems software products to enhance and increase the performance of large-scale (mainframe) computer database management and data communications software systems.

Revenues by major product group in recent fiscal years were as follows:

	1994-5	1993-4	1992-3
IMS products	37%	38%	39%
DB2 products	34%	33%	33%
Network Performance Series	7%	8%	9%
Other	22%	21%	19%

BMC offers about 75 systems software products for use on IBM's primary mainframe operating system, MVS, MVS-based DBMSs and data communications systems. Its products aid database management and maintenance, boost data network communications speed and efficiency, and compress data stored in direct access storage devices.

Core products (tools and utilities) generated 71% of total revenues and 73% of license revenues in 1994-5. IMS database utilities products contributed 37% of total revenues and 34% of license revenues, while tools and utilities for DB2, IBM's second-generation DBMS, contributed 34% and 39%, respectively.

Offerings also include network performance products, data communications enhancements and data compression products. In addition, the company sells Patrol, a database monitoring and application management product.

International marketing is conducted through ten wholly owned subsidiaries in Europe, Japan and Australia and through some 37 independent agents worldwide. Customers outside North America accounted for 39% of revenues in both 1994-5 and 1993-4.

Important Developments

Oct. '95—The company said that it expected revenues for its second quarter ended September 30, 1995,to approximate $88,250,000 with earnings per share in the range of $0.49 and $0.51. The results were lower than consensus analysts' estimates; product transition issues and delays in closing several large license transactions contributed to the shortfall.

May '95—In the fourth quarter of 1994-5, the company recorded nonrecurring charges totaling $29,260,000 ($25,701,000, or $1.00 a share, after tax) for the writeoff of in-process R&D. Also in the fourth quarter, the company announced Cooperative Enterprise Management Solutions, its strategy for application and data management of open systems.

Capitalization

Long Term Debt: None (6/95).

Per Share Data ($)

(Year Ended Mar. 31)

	1995	1994	1993	1992	1991	1990
Tangible Bk. Val.	6.06	4.86	4.26	2.91	1.77	1.26
Cash Flow	1.84	1.21	1.33	1.03	0.57	0.46
Earnings	1.52	1.08	1.25	0.94	0.51	0.42
Dividends	Nil	Nil	Nil	Nil	Nil	Nil
Payout Ratio	Nil	Nil	Nil	Nil	Nil	Nil
Cal. Yrs.	1994	1993	1992	1991	1990	1989
Prices - High	35½	42⅛	39½	37⅜	15⅛	10¼
- Low	20⅛	19⅜	18⅝	13½	8⅞	4⅝
P/E Ratio - High	23	39	32	40	30	25
- Low	13	18	15	14	17	11

Income Statement Analysis (Million $)

	1995	%Chg	1994	%Chg	1993	%Chg	1992
Revs.	345	19%	289	21%	239	26%	189
Oper. Inc.	127	7%	119	32%	90.4	28%	70.8
Depr.	18.8	176%	6.8	59%	4.3	-9%	4.7
Int. Exp.	Nil	—	NM	—	Nil	—	Nil
Pretax Inc.	120	33%	90.6	-3%	93.4	32%	70.5
Eff. Tax Rate	36%	—	38%	—	30%	—	31%
Net Inc.	77.5	37%	56.5	-14%	65.4	35%	48.6

Balance Sheet & Other Fin. Data (Million $)

	1995	1994	1993	1992	1991	1990
Cash	93.8	80.0	131	138	92.0	53.0
Curr. Assets	183	161	198	191	120	68.0
Total Assets	503	418	379	242	148	87.0
Curr. Liab.	148	127	123	74.5	50.9	20.8
LT Debt	Nil	Nil	Nil	Nil	Nil	0.0
Common Eqty.	306	250	223	150	86.0	58.0
Total Cap.	306	250	223	150	86.0	58.0
Cap. Exp.	20.2	38.1	39.6	19.0	9.0	4.1
Cash Flow	96.3	63.3	69.7	53.3	29.0	22.1

Ratio Analysis

	1995	1994	1993	1992	1991	1990
Curr. Ratio	1.2	1.3	1.6	2.6	2.3	3.3
% LT Debt of Cap.	Nil	Nil	Nil	NM	NM	NM
% Net Inc.of Revs.	22.5	19.6	27.4	25.8	19.6	21.8
% Ret. on Assets	16.9	14.3	20.7	24.5	21.2	30.1
% Ret. on Equity	27.9	24.1	35.6	40.5	34.6	45.5

Dividend Data —No cash dividends have been paid. A "poison pill" stockholder rights plan was adopted in May 1995. A 2-for-1 stock split was effected in August 1995.

Amt. of Div. $	Date Decl.	Ex-Div. Date	Stock of Record	Payment Date
2-for-1	Jul. 19	Aug. 15	Aug. 04	Aug. 14 '95

Data as orig. reptd.; bef. results of disc. opers. and/or spec. items. Per share data adj. for stk. divs. as of ex-div. date. E-Estimated. NA-Not Available. NM-Not Meaningful. NR-Not Ranked.

Office—2102 CityWest Blvd., Houston, TX 77042-2827. **Tel**—(713) 918-8800. **Fax**—(713) 918-8000. **Chrmn, Pres & CEO**—M. P. Watson Jr. **VP & Secy**—M. B. Morse. **Investor Contact**—John Cox. **Dirs**—J. W. Barter, B. G. Cupp, M. K. Gafner, L. W. Gray, G. F. Raymond, M. P. Watson Jr. **Transfer Agent**—First National Bank of Boston. **Incorporated** in Texas in 1980; reincorporated in Delaware in 1988. **Empl**-1,185. **S&P Analyst:** Peter C. Wood, CFA

STANDARD & POOR'S

STOCK REPORTS

Bancorp Hawaii

NYSE Symbol **BOH**
In S&P MidCap 400

27-SEP-95 **Industry:** Banking

Summary: This regional bank holding company has more than 115 offices throughout Hawaii, Arizona, Asia and the Pacific.

S&P Opinion: Avoid (★★)

Recent Price • 34
52 Wk Range • 36¾-24⅛
Yield • 3.3%
12-Mo. P/E • 13.5

Quantitative Evaluations
Outlook (1 Lowest—5 Highest) • **3-**
Fair Value • **33⅛**
Risk • **Low**
Earn./Div. Rank • **A**

Technical Eval. • **Bearish** since 2/93
Rel. Strength Rank (1 Lowest—99 Highest) • **57**
Insider Activity • **Favorable**

Earnings vs. Previous Year
▲=Up ▼=Down ▶=No Change

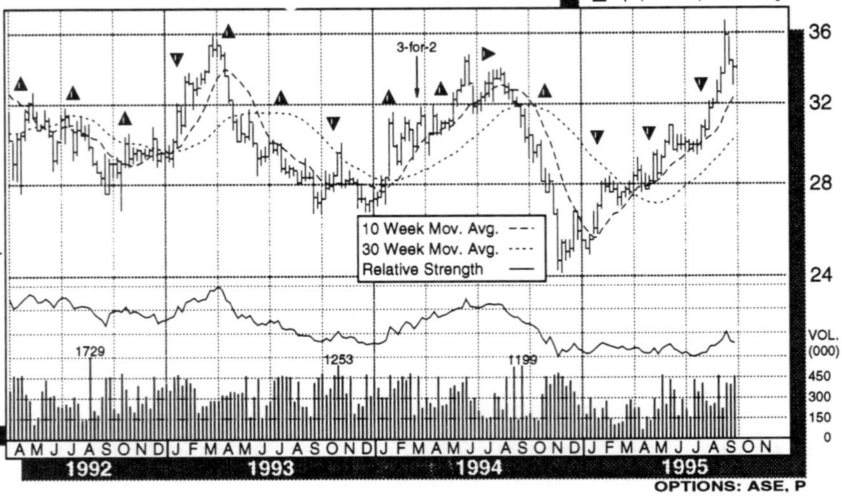

OPTIONS: ASE, P

Overview - 27-SEP-95

Recent results were penalized by sluggish growth of the Hawaiian economy, which, with visitor arrivals and private construction gaining only modestly, is expected to continue to lag the U.S. economy over the next year. In the first half of 1995, net income fell 17%, year to year; EPs were down 15%. Lower net interest income offset 7.7% higher noninterest income. Net interest margins widened in the second quarter from the level in the first quarter, but remained below those of the 1994 period. Asset quality improved; nonperforming assets at June 30, 1995, declined to 0.66% of total loans outstanding, from 0.71% a year earlier. During the 1994 fourth quarter, BOH restructured its securities portfolio to reduce its liability sensitivity. It has begun a strategic realignment away from product-driven operations, toward a relationship-driven approach.

Valuation - 27-SEP-95

The shares have climbed 35% thus far in 1995, slightly less than the bank indices, but better than the broader market. However, in anticipation of only modest near-term growth, principally because of continued weakness in the Hawaiian economy, we maintain our avoid rating. Despite fundamentals that show signs of improvement, with a current P/E of 12X our 1995 EPs estimate, and with EPS growth projected at about 5% for 1996, the stock appears overvalued at current levels.

Key Stock Statistics

S&P EPS Est. 1995	2.90	Tang. Bk. Value/Share	22.38
P/E on S&P Est. 1995	11.7	Beta	1.33
S&P EPS Est. 1996	3.05	Shareholders	6,900
Dividend Rate/Share	1.09	Market cap. (B)	$ 1.4
Shs. outstg. (M)	41.5	Inst. holdings	58%
Avg. daily vol. (M)	0.074	Insider holdings	NA

Value of $10,000 invested 5 years ago: $ 18,684

Fiscal Year Ending Dec. 31

	1995	% Change	1994	% Change	1993	% Change
Revenues (Million $)						
1Q	254.4	11%	229.6	-1%	233.0	-3%
2Q	257.8	9%	235.9	2%	232.2	-2%
3Q	—	—	240.1	NM	241.7	5%
4Q	—	—	235.8	2%	231.2	NM
Yr.	—	—	941.4	NM	938.1	NM
Income (Million $)						
1Q	28.25	-18%	34.39	4%	32.98	8%
2Q	28.55	-16%	34.16	1%	33.76	5%
3Q	—	—	31.96	6%	30.14	-5%
4Q	—	—	17.22	-52%	35.69	59%
Yr.	—	—	117.7	-11%	132.6	14%
Earnings Per Share ($)						
1Q	0.67	-16%	0.80	4%	0.77	7%
2Q	0.68	-14%	0.79	NM	0.79	5%
3Q	E0.75	NM	0.75	7%	0.70	-6%
4Q	E0.80	95%	0.41	-50%	0.83	57%
Yr.	E2.90	5%	2.75	-11%	3.09	12%

Next earnings report expected: mid October

Bancorp Hawaii

Business Summary - 27-SEP-95

Bancorp Hawaii owns Bank of Hawaii, the largest commercial bank in that state, Bancorp Pacific, Inc. (formerly FirstFed America, Inc.), a savings and loan holding company, and First National Bank of Arizona, a commercial bank that operates four branches in that state. Bank of Hawaii provides all customary commercial bank services. It has offices in Hawaii, and branch or representative offices in 14 South Pacific island areas, plus locations in Tokyo, Seoul, Hong Kong, Singapore and Nassau, as well as affiliates in six other South Pacific locations. Gross loans totaled $7.89 billion at year-end 1994 and were divided:

	1994
Residential mortgage	36.4%
Commercial/Industrial	23.2%
Commercial mortgage	15.7%
Installment	9.4%
Foreign	8.8%
Lease financing	4.8%
Real estate-construction	1.7%

The reserve for possible loan losses was $148.5 million at 1994 year-end (1.88% of gross loans outstanding), versus $125.3 million (1.72%) a year earlier. There were no net loan chargeoffs during 1994, versus chargeoffs of $57.5 million (0.82% of average loans) during 1993. Nonperforming assets at December 31, 1994, totaled $53.2 million (0.67% of total loans), down from $68.8 million (0.95%) a year earlier.

Average deposits of $7.29 billion in 1994 were apportioned: interest-bearing demand 26.0%, noninterest-bearing demand 19.0%, regular savings accounts 16.9%, foreign 17.0%, private time CDs of $100,000 or more 6.5%, public time CDs of $100,000 or more 0.9% and all other time and savings certificates 13.7%. On a tax-equivalent basis, the average yield on interest-earning assets was 6.90% in 1994 (6.77% in 1993), while the average rate paid on interest-bearing liabilities was 3.62% (3.29%), for a net spread of 3.28% (3.48%).

Important Developments

Jun. '95—During the first half of 1995, BOH repurchased 313,000 common shares, bringing to about 540,000 the number of shares purchased under a December 1994 plan to buy back up to 2 million shares.

Capitalization

Long Term Debt: $877,640,000 (6/95).

Per Share Data ($) (Year Ended Dec. 31)

	1994	1993	1992	1991	1990	1989
Tangible Bk. Val.	20.84	19.59	18.43	16.37	13.85	12.83
Earnings	2.75	3.09	2.75	2.69	2.45	2.19
Dividends	1.04	0.90	0.85	0.78	0.70	0.59
Payout Ratio	38%	29%	31%	29%	29%	27%
Prices - High	34¾	35⅞	34⅝	31⅞	24⅝	25¼
- Low	24⅛	26⅝	26⅞	18⅞	14	15½
P/E Ratio - High	13	12	13	12	10	12
- Low	9	9	10	7	6	7

Income Statement Analysis (Million $)

	1994	%Chg	1993	%Chg	1992	%Chg	1991
Net Int. Inc.	449	-5%	473	7%	441	8%	408
Tax Equiv. Adj.	1.8	-18%	2.2	-33%	3.3	-28%	4.6
Non Int. Inc.	128	8%	119	9%	109	20%	91.0
Loan Loss Prov.	21.9	-60%	54.2	8%	50.1	69%	29.6
% Exp/Op Revs.	62%	—	57%	—	57%	—	57%
Pretax Inc.	195	-8%	212	12%	189	3%	184
Eff. Tax Rate	40%	—	38%	—	38%	—	39%
Net Inc.	118	-11%	133	14%	117	4%	113
% Net Int. Marg.	3.82%	—	4.00%	—	4.06%	—	4.05%

Balance Sheet & Other Fin. Data (Million $)

	1994	1993	1992	1991	1990	1989
Earning Assets:						
Money Mkt.	781	970	2,037	1,472	1,511	1,471
Inv. Securities	3,151	3,647	3,036	2,545	2,036	1,364
Com'l Loans	2,209	2,111	2,257	2,104	1,981	1,826
Other Loans	5,683	5,148	4,707	4,655	4,532	3,150
Total Assets	12,586	12,462	12,713	11,409	10,699	8,317
Demand Deposits	1,437	1,406	1,257	1,251	1,236	1,127
Time Deposits	5,678	5,599	6,633	7,416	7,549	5,897
LT Debt	704	358	84.1	75.5	117	47.6
Common Eqty.	967	938	828	724	630	483

Ratio Analysis

	1994	1993	1992	1991	1990	1989
% Ret. on Assets	0.9	1.0	1.0	1.0	1.0	1.1
% Ret. on Equity	12.1	14.9	15.6	16.5	17.0	17.6
% Loan Loss Resv.	1.9	1.8	1.9	1.7	1.6	1.7
% Loans/Deposits	100.9	101.5	86.6	76.5	72.7	69.6
% Equity to Assets	7.7	7.1	6.7	6.3	6.1	6.3

Dividend Data —Cash has been paid each year since 1899. A dividend reinvestment plan is available.

Amt. of Div. $	Date Decl.	Ex-Div. Date	Stock of Record	Payment Date
0.260	Oct. 28	Nov. 15	Nov. 21	Dec. 14 '94
0.260	Jan. 25	Feb. 14	Feb. 21	Mar. 14 '95
0.272	May. 02	May. 16	May. 22	Jun. 14 '95
0.272	Jul. 28	Aug. 17	Aug. 21	Sep. 15 '95

Data as orig. reptd.; bef. results of disc opers. and/or spec. items. Per share data adj. for stk. divs. as of ex-div. date. E-Estimated. NA-Not Available. NM-Not Meaningful. NR-Not Ranked.

Office—130 Merchant St., Honolulu, HI 96813. **Tel**—(808) 537-8111. **Chrmn & CEO**—L. M. Johnson. **SVP, Treas & CFO**—D. A. Houle. **Secy**—C. C. Weston. **Investor Contact**—Sharlene K. Bliss (808-537-8037). **Dirs**—P. D. Baldwin, M. G. F. Bitterman, R. J. Dahl, T. B. Hayward, D. A. Heenan, S. T. K. Ho, D. A. Houle, D. K. Isono, L. M. Johnson, H. M. Richards, Jr., H. H. Stephenson, F. E. Trotter, C. R. Wichman, K. T. Yee. **Transfer Agents & Registrars**—Bank of New York, NYC; Hawaiian Trust Co., Ltd., Honolulu. **Incorporated** in Hawaii in 1972; bank organized in 1897. **Empl**-4,488. **S&P Analyst:** Thomas C. Ferguson

STANDARD & POOR'S

STOCK REPORTS

Banta Corp.

NASDAQ Symbol **BNTA**

In S&P MidCap 400

24-OCT-95 **Industry:** Graphic Arts

Summary: Banta is a leading provider of printing and digital imaging services, multimedia and software packages, interactive media, point-of-purchase products and software packages.

S&P Opinion: Hold (★★★)

Recent Price • 39¾ | Yield • 1.4%
52 Wk Range • 43¼-27 | 12-Mo. P/E • 16.3

Quantitative Evaluations

Outlook (1 Lowest—5 Highest)
• **5⁻**

Fair Value
• **47⅞**

Risk
• **Low**

Earn./Div. Rank
• **A-**

Technical Eval.
• **Bullish** since 3/95

Rel. Strength Rank (1 Lowest—99 Highest)
• **51**

Insider Activity
• **NA**

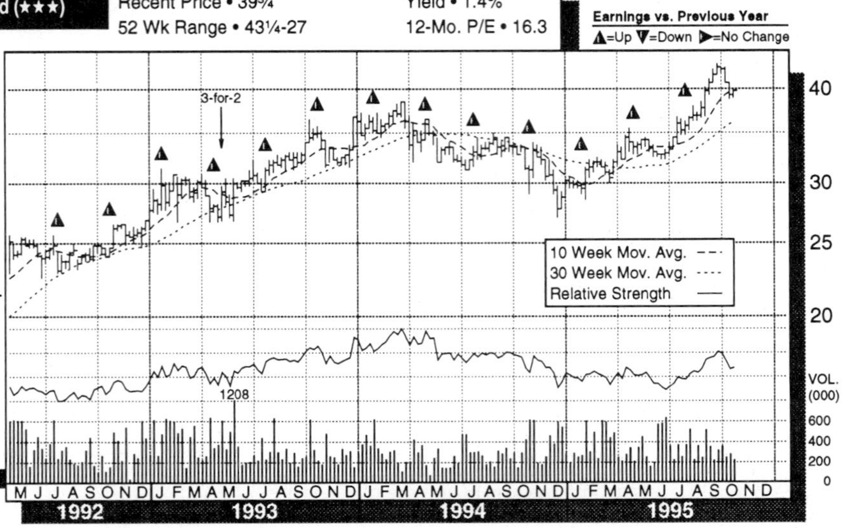

Overview - 19-OCT-95

Revenues in 1995 will advance, boosted by recent acquisitions, plus the full-year inclusion of Danbury Printing and United Graphics, as well as ongoing gains in most other areas. Since Banta supplies much of its customers' paper, sharply rising paper prices will also boost revenues beyond normal levels. Profit margins will be pressured by the higher raw materials costs, and development spending. Interest expenses will also be higher, reflecting borrowings for acquisitions. In 1996, favorable economic conditions, acquisitions, and gains in market share should contribute to higher revenues and earnings. A promising business environment along with Banta's continued emphasis on new markets and advanced technologies enhance the longer term outlook for growth and profitability.

Valuation - 23-OCT-95

After a rather sluggish first half when Banta did not quite keep up with the market, the stock climbed in the third quarter to a new high. The market reacted favorably to Banta's announcement in August of a major acquisition that will significantly widen the company's reach in Europe and provide additional growth opportunities in the U.S. as well. Earnings are expected to continue to rise at a percentage rate in the mid teens over the next several years, with dividend increases keeping pace, but after the stock's third-quarter 1995 advance, the shares appear reasonably valued for now.

Key Stock Statistics

S&P EPS Est. 1995	2.60	Tang. Bk. Value/Share	16.07
P/E on S&P Est. 1995	15.3	Beta	0.95
S&P EPS Est. 1996	2.90	Shareholders	2,100
Dividend Rate/Share	0.56	Market cap. (B)	$0.793
Shs. outstg. (M)	20.2	Inst. holdings	72%
Avg. daily vol. (M)	0.054	Insider holdings	NA

Value of $10,000 invested 5 years ago: $ 28,385

Fiscal Year Ending Dec. 31

	1995	% Change	1994	% Change	1993	% Change
Revenues (Million $)						
1Q	232.9	24%	187.5	16%	162.0	6%
2Q	235.4	27%	185.8	12%	165.9	9%
3Q	—	—	207.7	13%	184.4	11%
4Q	—	—	230.3	29%	178.9	7%
Yr.	—	—	811.3	17%	691.2	8%
Income (Million $)						
1Q	11.00	15%	9.57	16%	8.27	13%
2Q	12.75	7%	11.96	14%	10.48	22%
3Q	—	—	13.31	15%	11.56	8%
4Q	—	—	12.40	16%	10.68	18%
Yr.	—	—	47.23	15%	40.99	15%
Earnings Per Share ($)						
1Q	0.54	15%	0.47	15%	0.41	12%
2Q	0.63	7%	0.59	13%	0.52	20%
3Q	E0.74	12%	0.66	16%	0.57	7%
4Q	E0.69	13%	0.61	15%	0.53	17%
Yr.	E2.60	12%	2.33	15%	2.03	13%

Next earnings report expected: early November

Banta Corp.

Business Summary - 23-OCT-95

Banta Corporation, a leading U.S. printer, provides a broad range of printing and graphic arts services to a variety of customers.

Products for the commercial market (46% of net sales in 1994) include catalogs and direct marketing materials. Bindery services provide ink-jet labeling and demographic binding. Healthcare products include plastic garment covers, gloves, stretcher sheets and examination table paper.

Book publishing (32%) is largely comprised of consumable grade-school workbooks. Other products include textbooks (primarily soft-cover), testing materials and paperbound books. Banta Information Services Group serves the computer and software industries, printing manuals and offering complete turnkey servces. Multimedia products are also produced for educational publishers and industry, professional and trade associations. Other customers include publishers of religious books, trade books, cookbooks, manuals and fiction and nonfiction books.

The magazine publishing segment (12%) prints, sorts and mails magazines representing more than 500 different titles. These magazines are primarily short- to medium-run publications (usually less than 350,000 copies), generally distributed to subscribers by mail.

Other operations (10%) include traditional prepress services and the processing, distribution and storing of digital information; and KCS Industries, which produces point-of-purchase products.

Important Developments

Oct. '95—Banta expanded its on-line marketing services by acquiring New Frontier Information Corp., a software company specializing in commercial interactive applications for the Internet and World Wide Web. Terms were not disclosed.

Oct. '95—Banta completed the acquisition of BG Turnkey Services Ltd. and its affiliated companies, headquartered in Cork, Ireland. BG Turnkey, with annual sales of about US$160 million, is a major European supplier of project management, procurement, packaging, duplication, localization, assembly and fulfillment services for computer software publishers and hardware manufacturers. The purchase price, which includes the issuance of common stock and debt, was not disclosed, but Banta said the acquisition will have a moderately positive impact on earnings per share.

Jun. '95—Banta acquired Applied Technology Corp., a specialty products supplier to the health care industry which had 1994 sales of about $5 million. Terms were not disclosed.

Capitalization

Long Term Debt: $107,299,000 (7/1/95).

Per Share Data ($) (Year Ended Dec. 31)

	1994	1993	1992	1991	1990	1989
Tangible Bk. Val.	15.27	13.73	12.10	10.64	9.83	8.74
Cash Flow	4.38	3.71	3.33	2.89	2.91	2.90
Earnings	2.33	2.03	1.79	1.44	1.53	1.24
Dividends	0.52	0.64	0.41	0.41	0.37	0.35
Payout Ratio	22%	32%	23%	29%	24%	28%
Prices - High	38½	37	27⅞	21⅛	17⅜	17
- Low	27	26⅝	18½	13½	13	14½
P/E Ratio - High	17	18	16	15	11	14
- Low	12	13	10	9	9	12

Income Statement Analysis (Million $)

	1994	%Chg	1993	%Chg	1992	%Chg	1991
Revs.	811	17%	691	8%	637	13%	565
Oper. Inc.	125	18%	106	13%	94.0	17%	80.1
Depr.	41.5	23%	33.7	9%	30.8	8%	28.6
Int. Exp.	7.6	17%	6.5	NM	6.5	14%	5.7
Pretax Inc.	78.7	15%	68.7	17%	58.5	27%	46.2
Eff. Tax Rate	40%	—	40%	—	39%	—	39%
Net Inc.	47.2	15%	41.0	15%	35.7	27%	28.2

Balance Sheet & Other Fin. Data (Million $)

	1994	1993	1992	1991	1990	1989
Cash	0.4	8.2	13.3	4.8	1.5	5.0
Curr. Assets	248	198	175	176	181	153
Total Assets	578	457	410	397	398	383
Curr. Liab.	147	92.0	73.0	81.0	91.0	93.0
LT Debt	67.8	45.6	52.5	64.1	75.4	70.0
Common Eqty.	332	292	258	227	207	195
Total Cap.	419	356	329	312	302	286
Cap. Exp.	87.0	63.0	33.0	32.0	51.0	56.0
Cash Flow	88.7	74.7	66.5	56.8	55.8	55.5

Ratio Analysis

	1994	1993	1992	1991	1990	1989
Curr. Ratio	1.7	2.2	2.4	2.2	2.0	1.7
% LT Debt of Cap.	16.2	12.8	16.0	20.5	25.0	24.5
% Net Inc.of Revs.	5.8	5.9	5.6	5.0	5.1	4.2
% Ret. on Assets	9.1	9.4	8.8	7.0	7.5	6.3
% Ret. on Equity	15.1	14.8	14.6	12.8	14.6	13.1

Dividend Data —Cash has been paid each year since 1927. A dividend reinvestment plan is available.

Amt. of Div. $	Date Decl.	Ex-Div. Date	Stock of Record	Payment Date
0.130	Jul. 26	Oct. 07	Oct. 14	Oct. 28 '94
0.140	Dec. 06	Jan. 09	Jan. 13	Feb. 01 '95
0.140	Jan. 31	Apr. 10	Apr. 14	May. 01 '95
0.140	Apr. 25	Jul. 12	Jul. 14	Aug. 01 '95
0.140	Jul. 25	Oct. 11	Oct. 13	Nov. 01 '95

Data as orig. reptd.; bef. results of disc. opers. and/or spec. items. Per share data adj. for stk. divs. as of ex-div. date. E-Estimated. NA-Not Available. NM-Not Meaningful. NR-Not Ranked.

Office—225 Main St., Box 8003, Menasha, WI 54952-8003. **Tel**—(414) 751-7777. **Chrmn, Pres & CEO**—D. D. Belcher. **VP & Secy**—R. D. Kneezel. **Exec VP & CFO**—Gerald A. Henseler. **Treas**—R. A. Kreider. **Investor Contact**—Mark Fleming. **Dirs**—B. K. Allen, C. W. Aurand Jr., J. A. Baxter, D. D. Belcher, G. T. Brophy, W. J. Cadogan, R. L. Gunderson, G. A. Henseler, B. S. Kubale, C. W. Tarr, D. Taylor, A. J. Williamson. **Transfer Agent**—Firstar Trust Co., Milwaukee. **Registrar**—Co.'s office. **Incorporated** in Wisconsin in 1901. **Empl**-4,908. **S&P Analyst:** William H. Donald

STANDARD & POOR'S

STOCK REPORTS

Battle Mountain Gold

NYSE Symbol **BMG**

In S&P MidCap 400

15-AUG-95

Industry: Mining/Diversified

Summary: Battle Mountain Gold is a worldwide producer of precious metals with about half of its production derived from the Kori Kollo mine in Bolivia.

S&P Opinion: Hold (★★★)

Recent Price • 9 5/8

52 Wk Range • 13-8 7/8

Yield • 0.5%

12-Mo. P/E • NM

Quantitative Evaluations

Outlook (1 Lowest—5 Highest)
• **1-**

Fair Value
• **4 7/8**

Risk
• **Average**

Earn./Div. Rank
• **B-**

Technical Eval.
• **Bullish** since 1/95

Rel. Strength Rank (1 Lowest—99 Highest)
• **37**

Insider Activity
• **Neutral**

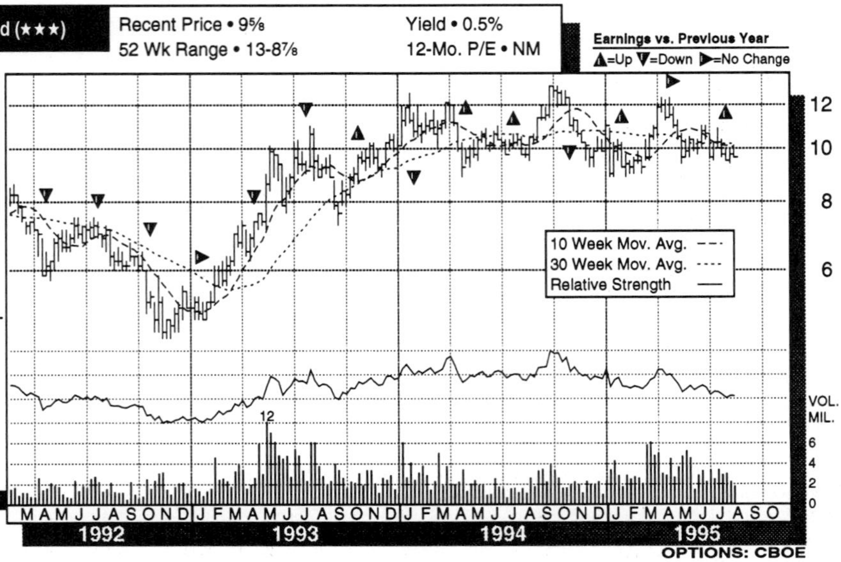

OPTIONS: CBOE

Overview - 15-AUG-95

Gold volumes are expected to increase about 17% in 1995 reflecting full-year contributions from the Reona heap leach mine at Battle Mountain, sharply higher output at Red Dome after deepening the pit to access higher-grade ore and increased output at Kori Kollo following the implementation of new recovery enhancement techniques. Silver and copper volumes also should be higher. The average price of gold realized during 1995's first half was $382/oz., versus $384/oz. Operating costs are likely to increase, reflecting higher stripping ratios at Kori Kollo and the shift to production of more expensive sulfide ore. Tax rates will be sharply lower reflecting the recognition of deferred foreign tax credits. Higher depletion and depreciation charges will outweigh lower interest costs.

Valuation - 15-AUG-95

Shares of this international precious metals producer have traded in a narrow range since early 1994 partly reflecting flat gold prices. Though BMG appears to be headed for its second consecutive year of profits, its valuation is fair considering the high level of reserve concentration in Bolivia where new environmental regulations may add to costs. Additionally, with low rates of inflation, the argument for higher gold prices at this time is weak. Longer-term BMG has some interesting projects coming on line in 1997 and 1998 located in Washington and Papua New Guinea.

Key Stock Statistics

S&P EPS Est. 1995	0.10	Tang. Bk. Value/Share	3.27
P/E on S&P Est. 1995	96.3	Beta	0.11
S&P EPS Est. 1996	0.15	Shareholders	30,300
Dividend Rate/Share	0.05	Market cap. (B)	$0.820
Shs. outstg. (M)	81.0	Inst. holdings	52%
Avg. daily vol. (M)	0.498	Insider holdings	NA

Value of $10,000 invested 5 years ago: $ 6,149

Fiscal Year Ending Dec. 31

	1995	% Change	1994	% Change	1993	% Change
Revenues (Million $)						
1Q	54.08	6%	50.92	-6%	53.90	22%
2Q	81.26	42%	57.04	41%	40.52	-6%
3Q	—	—	55.83	12%	50.02	16%
4Q	—	—	65.89	35%	48.93	-5%
Yr.	—	—	229.7	19%	193.4	6%
Income (Million $)						
1Q	2.48	-13%	2.85	NM	-3.17	NM
2Q	6.30	105%	3.08	NM	-2.59	-56%
3Q	—	—	1.45	-19%	1.80	NM
4Q	—	—	2.19	NM	-0.45	NM
Yr.	—	—	9.57	NM	-4.41	NM
Earnings Per Share ($)						
1Q	0.01	NM	0.01	NM	-0.04	NM
2Q	0.05	NM	0.01	NM	-0.03	NM
3Q	E0.02	NM	-0.01	—	Nil	—
4Q	E0.02	100%	0.01	NM	-0.03	—
Yr.	E0.10	NM	0.02	NM	-0.10	NM

Next earnings report expected: early November

Battle Mountain Gold

Business Summary - 15-AUG-95

Battle Mountain Gold operates precious metals mines in the U.S. Bolivia, Chile and Australia and has important interests in properties under development in Papua New Guinea. Contribution to net revenues in recent years:

	1994	1993
Gold	90%	89%
Silver	5%	5%
Copper	5%	6%

BMG's wholly-owned producing properties include Battle Mountain (Nevada), San Luis (Colorado) and Pajingo (Australia). Empresa Minera Inti Raymi (88%-owned) operates the Kori Kollo mine in Bolivia which generated 52% of total revenues in 1994. Niugini Mining Ltd. (50.5%-owned) operates the Red Dome mine in Australia and San Cristobal in Chile.

Gold production (net of minority interests) in 1994 was 486,000 ounces, versus 400,000 ounces in 1993. The average realized price of gold was $385/oz. in 1994, compared with $363/oz. in 1993. The average cost to produce gold in 1994 was $281/oz., versus $308/oz, in 1993. Silver production (net) in 1994 was 1,724,000 ounces ($5.33/oz.) versus 1,783,000 ounces in 1993 ($4.30/oz.) Copper production in 1994 was 6,546,000 lbs. ($1.05/lb.), versus 5,374,000 lbs. ($0.98/lb.).

Total contained gold reserves at 1994 year-end were 8,070,000 ounces including 2,340,000 ounces from the partially developed Lhir project in Papua New Guinea and Crown Jewel project in Washington. BMG expects Lihir (30%-owned by Niugini Mining) to commence production in 1998. Crown Jewel (54%-owned) is expected to start up in 1997.

Important Developments

Aug. '95—Pretax income for 1995's second quarter included a $4.2 million gain from the sale of BMG's interest in the Plutonic Bore project in western Australia to Resolute Resources. Offsetting the gain was a $2.2 million writedown of milling assets at the depleted Fortitude mine in Nveada.

Jun. '95—Niugini Mining (50.5%-owned) lifted its holdings in the Lihir project in Papua New Guinea to 30% with the purchase of a 16% stake from RTZ Corp. for $54.1 million. Lihir is expected to commence gold production by early 1998.

Capitalization

Long Term Debt: $158,837,000 (6/95), incl. $100 million of 6% debs. conv. into com. at $20

Per Share Data ($) (Year Ended Dec. 31)

	1994	1993	1992	1991	1990	1989
Tangible Bk. Val.	3.22	3.17	3.37	3.94	3.58	3.08
Cash Flow	0.62	0.42	0.07	0.36	0.45	0.79
Earnings	0.02	-0.10	-0.44	-0.02	0.21	0.40
Dividends	0.05	0.05	0.10	0.10	0.10	0.10
Payout Ratio	250%	NM	NM	NM	44%	25%
Prices - High	13	11	8⅝	10⅝	19	18¼
- Low	8⅞	4⅞	4½	5¾	5½	13
P/E Ratio - High	NM	NM	NM	NM	90	46
- Low	NM	NM	NM	NM	26	33

Income Statement Analysis (Million $)

	1994	%Chg	1993	%Chg	1992	%Chg	1991
Revs.	230	19%	193	6%	182	7%	170
Oper. Inc.	72.1	101%	35.8	NM	-5.1	NM	22.3
Depr.	51.3	24%	41.5	3%	40.2	40%	28.7
Int. Exp.	13.7	-9%	15.1	47%	10.3	24%	8.3
Pretax Inc.	16.5	NM	-3.8	NM	-46.0	NM	-5.5
Eff. Tax Rate	15%	—	NM	—	NM	—	NM
Net Inc.	9.6	NM	-4.4	NM	-34.9	NM	-1.2

Balance Sheet & Other Fin. Data (Million $)

	1994	1993	1992	1991	1990	1989
Cash	76.0	115	45.4	28.7	100	39.6
Curr. Assets	139	181	86.0	58.0	120	56.0
Total Assets	680	668	577	525	449	351
Curr. Liab.	42.3	40.3	50.1	31.9	28.5	9.7
LT Debt	166	179	199	125	111	50.0
Common Eqty.	261	255	270	315	255	204
Total Cap.	605	603	505	479	414	338
Cap. Exp.	92.0	52.0	114	110	130	173
Cash Flow	53.4	33.4	5.2	27.5	33.5	51.7

Ratio Analysis

	1994	1993	1992	1991	1990	1989
Curr. Ratio	3.3	4.5	1.7	1.8	4.2	5.8
% LT Debt of Cap.	27.4	29.7	39.4	26.2	26.9	14.8
% Net Inc.of Revs.	4.2	NM	NM	NM	11.2	20.2
% Ret. on Assets	1.4	NM	NM	NM	3.9	9.5
% Ret. on Equity	0.8	NM	NM	NM	6.7	13.8

Dividend Data —Dividends were initiated in 1985. A "poison pill" stock purchase rights plan was adopted in 1988.

Amt. of Div. $	Date Decl.	Ex-Div. Date	Stock of Record	Payment Date
0.025	Jul. 12	Jul. 27	Aug. 02	Aug. 16 '93
0.025	Dec. 01	Jan. 26	Feb. 01	Feb. 15 '94
0.025	Jul. 06	Jul. 26	Aug. 01	Aug. 15 '94
0.025	Jan. 04	Jan. 26	Feb. 01	Feb. 15 '95
0.025	Jul. 05	Jul. 28	Aug. 01	Aug. 15 '95

Data as orig. reptd.; bef. results of disc. opers. and/or spec. items. Per share data adj. for stk. divs. as of ex-div. date. E-Estimated. NA-Not Available. NM-Not Meaningful. NR-Not Ranked.

Office—333 Clay St., 42nd Floor, Houston, TX 77002. **Tel**—(713) 650-6400. **Chrmn & CEO**—K. E. Elers. **Pres & COO**—K. R. Werneburg. **VP-Fin & CFO**—R. D. O'Connell. **VP & Secy**—R. J. Quinn. **VP & Investor Contact**—Les Van Dyke. **Dirs**—D. J. Bourne, D. H. Caspary, C. E. Childers, J. R. Crosby, K. E. Elers, R. L. Gray, T. H. Pate, Jr., K. R. Werneburg, W. A. Wise. **Transfer Agent & Registrar**—Bank of New York, NYC. **Incorporated** in Nevada in 1985. **Empl**-1,261. **S&P Analyst:** Stephen R. Klein

STANDARD & POOR'S

STOCK REPORTS

Bay Networks

NASDAQ Symbol **BNET**

In S&P MidCap 400

11-SEP-95 **Industry:** Data Processing

Summary: Bay Networks manufactures a complete line of networking products, including high-speed routers, LAN switches, intelligent hubs and management products.

S&P Opinion: Hold (★★★)

Recent Price • 50¼ | 52 Wk Range • 51-18⅝ | Yield • Nil | 12-Mo. P/E • 45.7

Quantitative Evaluations

Outlook (1 Lowest—5 Highest)
• **NA**

Fair Value
• **NA**

Risk
• **Average**

Earn./Div. Rank
• **NR**

Technical Eval.
• **Bullish** since 11/94

Rel. Strength Rank (1 Lowest—99 Highest)
• **84**

Insider Activity
• **Unfavorable**

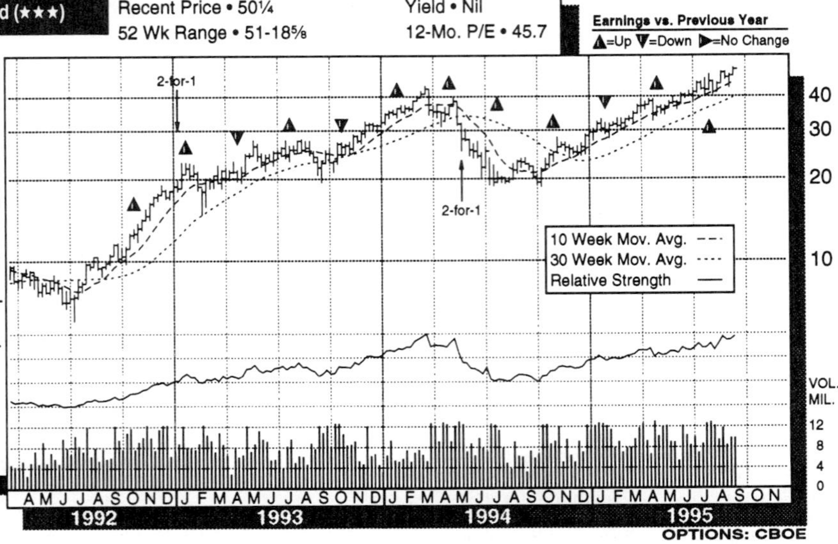

OPTIONS: CBOE

Overview - 11-SEP-95

Revenues in fiscal 1996 are expected to grow 35%, reflecting continued strong demand for hubs, routers and switching products. BNET is in the early stages of several new product cycles, which should fuel demand. In addition, the recent acquisition of Centillion, the pending acquisition of Xylogics and the emerging switching marketplace should provide explosive revenue growth opportunities. Gross margins are likely to narrow further, owing to competitive pressures, a product mix shift to low-end routers, and the greater use of less profitable indirect selling channels. Well controlled R&D and sales and marketing expense should lead to perating profit margins above 20%. Our $2.00 estimate for fiscal 1996 is a 39% gain from the $1.44 of fiscal 1995, excluding a one-time charge, and assuming minimal dilution from Xylogics.

Valuation - 11-SEP-95

The shares are up sharply in 1995, reflecting the flawless merger execution of the old Synoptics and WellFleet entities and an increasingly improved financial performance. Originally, we were skeptical about the merger prospects as well as the ongoing health of the router business, a segment that was expected to have a diminished role in the emerging switched internetworks. However, we have been proven wrong on both fronts and now expect BNET to enjoy the fruits of the strengthening networking industry. Nevertheless, the current valuation already reflects these positive developments and we recommend holding the shares, versus our previous avoid opinion.

Key Stock Statistics

S&P EPS Est. 1996	2.00	Tang. Bk. Value/Share	3.10
P/E on S&P Est. 1996	25.1	Beta	NA
S&P EPS Est. 1997	2.50	Shareholders	3,600
Dividend Rate/Share	Nil	Market cap. (B)	$ 5.8
Shs. outstg. (M)	116.3	Inst. holdings	73%
Avg. daily vol. (M)	2.020	Insider holdings	NA

Value of $10,000 invested 5 years ago: NA

Fiscal Year Ending Jun. 30

	1995	% Change	1994	% Change	1993	% Change
Revenues (Million $)						
1Q	300.0	17%	256.0	38%	185.0	120%
2Q	314.2	14%	276.0	25%	220.0	118%
3Q	337.1	27%	265.0	15%	231.0	77%
4Q	390.7	35%	289.0	17%	248.0	57%
Yr.	1,342	24%	1,086	23%	885.0	87%
Income (Million $)						
1Q	38.37	125%	17.07	-35%	26.10	NM
2Q	-3.65	NM	37.02	22%	30.23	181%
3Q	46.04	44%	31.94	156%	12.46	-26%
4Q	54.40	56%	34.90	9%	32.14	54%
Yr.	131.0	8%	120.9	20%	100.9	80%
Earnings Per Share ($)						
1Q	0.34	127%	0.15	-35%	0.23	NM
2Q	-0.03	NM	0.32	19%	0.27	170%
3Q	0.39	39%	0.28	155%	0.11	-27%
4Q	0.44	42%	0.31	11%	0.28	47%
Yr.	1.10	4%	1.06	19%	0.89	71%

Next earnings report expected: mid October

Bay Networks

Business Summary - 11-SEP-95

Bay Networks is the surviving entity of the merger on October 20, 1994, between SynOptics Communications, a leading supplier of intelligent hubs, and Wellfleet Communications, a major manufacturer of internetworking products. BNET features a full line of products for high-performance networks, including high-end routers, wide area network access devices, local area network switches and sophisticated management software.

Intelligent hubs reside at the center of networks and serve as control and consolidation points for network activity. Hub products are both modular, offering a variety of configuration and growth options, and non-modular, optimized for particular network requirements.

Internetworking products allow multiple types of local area networks (LANs), comprised of multi-vendor computer equipment, to form an internetworked system. Wellfleet's products connect LANs located in a single facility and, through wide area network (WAN) connections, may connect LANs dispersed around the world. The internetworking of the networks allows computer users operating different types of equipment in different locations to communicate, exchange data and share other computing resources.

A major rationale for the merger was the growing convergence of hub and router technology. New alternative technologies, such as switching, are increasingly incorporating both hub and routing capabilities.

International sales accounted for 28% and 23% of Wellfleet's net sales in fiscal 1994 and 1993, respectively, and 31% of SynOptics' revenue in both fiscal 1993 and 1992.

In May 1995, BNET acquired Centillion Networks, Inc., a leading provider of Token Ring and Token Ring-to-ATM switching products, for 3,928,822 shares ($140 million market value).

Important Developments

Sep. '95—BNET agreed to acquire Mass.-based Xylogics, Inc (NASDAQ, XLGX), a provider of remote access products for corporate networks, for about 5,623,000 common shares. The transaction had an indicated value of $330 million based on the $50.25 price of BNET's stock on September 5. XLGX had sales of some $47 million in the first nine months of 1995.

Jul. '95—BNET entered into a joint development, support and marketing alliance with Microsoft Corp. that will embed its Routing Services into the latter's Windows NT Server.

Apr. '95—Directors authorized the repurchase of up to $100 million of BNET stock over the next 18 months.

Capitalization

Long Term Debt: $110,000,000 (6/95).

Per Share Data ($)

(Year Ended Jun. 30)

	1995	1994	1993	1992	1991	1990
Tangible Bk. Val.	NA	4.69	NA	NA	NA	NA
Cash Flow	NA	NA	NA	NA	NA	NA
Earnings	1.10	1.06	0.89	0.52	NA	NA
Dividends	Nil	Nil	Nil	Nil	NA	NA
Payout Ratio	Nil	Nil	Nil	Nil	NA	NA
Prices - High	51	28⅜	NA	NA	NA	NA
- Low	27½	23	NA	NA	NA	NA
P/E Ratio - High	46	27	NA	NA	NA	NA
- Low	25	22	NA	NA	NA	NA

Income Statement Analysis (Million $)

	1994	%Chg	1993	%Chg	1992	%Chg	1991
Revs.	1,086	23%	885	87%	474	—	NA
Oper. Inc.	196	20%	164	102%	81.0	—	NA
Depr.	NA	—	NA	—	NA	—	NA
Int. Exp.	NA	—	NA	—	NA	—	NA
Pretax Inc.	203	19%	170	102%	84.0	—	NA
Eff. Tax Rate	40%	—	41%	—	34%	—	NA
Net Inc.	121	20%	101	80%	56.0	—	NA

Balance Sheet & Other Fin. Data (Million $)

	1994	1993	1992	1991	1990	1989
Cash	428	NA	NA	NA	NA	NA
Curr. Assets	719	NA	NA	NA	NA	NA
Total Assets	818	NA	NA	NA	NA	NA
Curr. Liab.	199	NA	NA	NA	NA	NA
LT Debt	110	NA	NA	NA	NA	NA
Common Eqty.	509	NA	NA	NA	NA	NA
Total Cap.	619	NA	NA	NA	NA	NA
Cap. Exp.	NA	NA	NA	NA	NA	NA
Cash Flow	NA	NA	NA	NA	NA	NA

Ratio Analysis

	1994	1993	1992	1991	1990	1989
Curr. Ratio	3.6	NA	NA	NA	NA	NA
% LT Debt of Cap.	17.8	NA	NA	NA	NA	NA
% Net Inc.of Revs.	11.1	11.4	11.8	NA	NA	NA
% Ret. on Assets	NA	NA	NA	NA	NA	NA
% Ret. on Equity	NA	NA	NA	NA	NA	NA

Dividend Data —No cash dividends have been paid, and the company has no plans to pay any in the foreseeable future.

Data as orig. reptd.; bef. results of disc. opers. and/or spec. items. Per share data adj. for stk. divs. as of ex-div. date. E-Estimated. NA-Not Available. NM-Not Meaningful. NR-Not Ranked.

Offices—Western Operations: 4401 Great American Pkwy., Santa Clara, CA 95054; Eastern Operations: 8 Federal St., Billerica, MA 01821 **Tels**—(408) 988-2400; (508) 670-8888. **Chrmn**—P. J. Severino. **Pres & CEO**—A. K. Ludwick. **Exec VP & CFO**—W. J. Ruehle. **Investor Contact**—John Delea (508-436-3540). **Dirs**—A. Carr, S. H. Carter Jr., J. S. Lewis, A. K. Ludwick, B. F. Robelen, P. J. Severino. **Transfer Agent & Registrar**—Bank of Boston. **Incorporated** in Delaware in 1994. **Empl**-3,096. **S&P Analyst:** John D. Coyle, CFA

STANDARD & POOR'S

STOCK REPORTS

Bear Stearns

NYSE Symbol **BSC**
In S&P MidCap 400

25-AUG-95 **Industry:** Securities

Summary: This company's Bear Stearns & Co. unit is a leading investment bank and broker, and is ranked as one of the largest NYSE member firms as measured by total capital.

S&P Opinion: No Opinion

Recent Price • 21¾ | Yield • 2.9%
52 Wk Range • 23⅜-14 | 12-Mo. P/E • 12.8

Quantitative Evaluations

Outlook
(1 Lowest—5 Highest)
• 3+

Fair Value
• 21½

Risk
• Low

Earn./Div. Rank
• B+

Technical Eval.
• Bearish since 8/95

Rel. Strength Rank
(1 Lowest—99 Highest)
• 19

Insider Activity
• Unfavorable

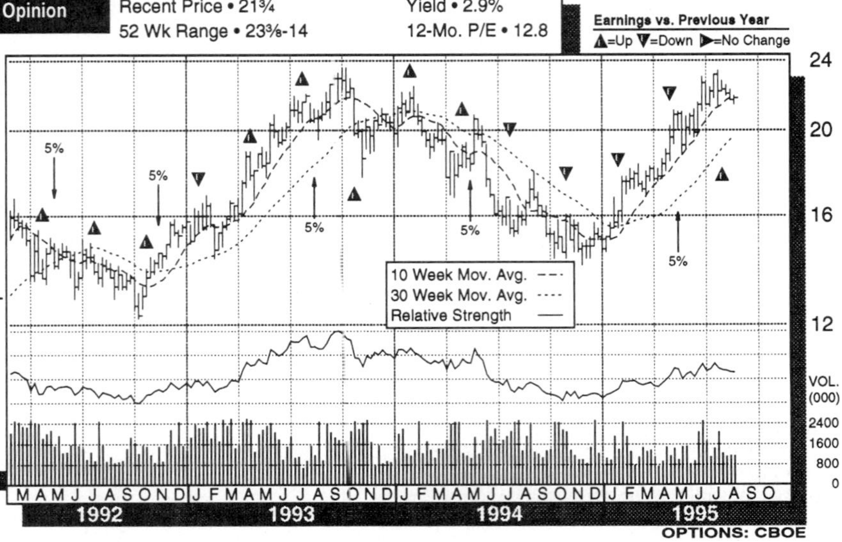

Overview - 25-AUG-95

Profits for the fiscal year ending June 30, 1996, are expected to increase from the fiscal 1995 level. One important positive factor is anticipated improved trading results in a more favorable interest rate environment. Investment banking fees should advance, spurred by increased issuer activity, although equity offerings have lagged debt transactions. Merger and acquisition advisory work has been strong, aided by a trend toward consolidation in many industries. Commission revenues will remain robust. Interest and dividends should continue to rise, with increased customer order flow and lower financing costs. Asset management fees, a relatively small contributor, are expected to increase.

Valuation - 25-AUG-95

The shares have rebounded sharply, together with other brokerage issues, reflecting a general market advance, a decline in interest rates, and encouraging earnings reports. Book value is the preferred method for valuing brokers, because their highly liquid balance sheets are marked to market on a daily basis. The traditional P/E ratio is subject to several distortions: it makes the stocks look undervalued at market tops and overvalued at market bottoms. At slightly more than a one-third premium to book value, the stock is near the high end of its price to book range over the past several years.

Key Stock Statistics

S&P EPS Est. 1996	2.70	Tang. Bk. Value/Share	15.80
P/E on S&P Est. 1996	8.1	Beta	1.75
Dividend Rate/Share	0.60	Shareholders	4,000
Shs. outstg. (M)	112.1	Market cap. (B)	$ 2.3
Avg. daily vol. (M)	0.239	Inst. holdings	79%
		Insider holdings	NA

Value of $10,000 invested 5 years ago: $ 32,324

Fiscal Year Ending Jun. 30

	1995	% Change	1994	% Change	1993	% Change
Revenues (Million $)						
1Q	809.8	5%	769.4	27%	604.0	1%
2Q	826.7	-18%	1,003	59%	631.1	-10%
3Q	1,027	14%	899.0	22%	734.1	3%
4Q	1,091	42%	770.2	-13%	885.3	32%
Yr.	3,754	9%	3,441	20%	2,857	7%
Income (Million $)						
1Q	35.46	-66%	104.3	66%	62.96	34%
2Q	32.93	-76%	134.8	110%	64.29	-17%
3Q	82.74	-28%	115.4	5%	110.4	21%
4Q	89.48	176%	32.40	-74%	124.8	58%
Yr.	240.6	-38%	387.0	7%	362.5	23%
Earnings Per Share ($)						
1Q	0.24	-68%	0.73	47%	0.50	45%
2Q	0.21	-78%	0.95	100%	0.48	-18%
3Q	0.60	-29%	0.84	NM	0.84	21%
4Q	0.65	NM	0.20	-78%	0.92	51%
Yr.	1.70	-38%	2.75	NM	2.72	23%

Next earnings report expected: mid October

Bear Stearns

Business Summary - 25-AUG-95

This company owns Bear Stearns & Co., a leading investment banking and brokerage concern that serves U.S. and foreign corporations, governments, and institutional and individual investors. Revenue contributions in recent fiscal years were:

	1995	1994
Commissions	26%	20%
Principal transactions	42%	47%
Investment banking	17%	20%
Interest & dividends, net	14%	12%
Other	1%	1%

The company provides brokerage services primarily to institutional and high net worth clients. Its registered representatives generate average gross commissions of over $556,000 a year. It manages and participates in public offerings of debt and equity securities for a broad range of corporate clients, governments and agencies. BSC also provides advice and execution to clients on a wide range of financial matters.

BSC is one of the largest dealers making markets in corporate debt and equity securities, as well as mortgage-related and municipal securities. It owns Bear Stearns Securities Corp., one of the securities industry's largest clearing firms. At March 31, 1995, regulatory net capital of $1.32 billion exceeded the minimum requirement by $1.31 billion.

Important Developments

Aug. '95—Bear Stearns said results in the fiscal 1995 fourth quarter reflected a much improved business environment, as well as higher fee income from mergers and acquisitions and advisory assignments.

Capitalization

Long Term Debt: $3,499,914,000 (3/95).
Preferred Stock: $437,500,000.

Per Share Data ($) (Year Ended Jun. 30)

	1995	1994	1993	1992	1991	1990
Tangible Bk. Val.	NA	14.79	12.82	10.47	7.71	7.07
Cash Flow	NA	NA	NA	NA	NA	NA
Earnings	1.70	2.75	2.72	2.22	1.02	0.78
Dividends	0.60	0.54	0.51	0.50	0.40	0.34
Payout Ratio	35%	20%	19%	22%	39%	44%
Prices - High	$23\frac{3}{8}$	$22\frac{1}{2}$	$16\frac{1}{4}$	$16\frac{1}{4}$	$13\frac{7}{8}$	$9\frac{3}{4}$
- Low	$14\frac{1}{2}$	$15\frac{1}{4}$	$11\frac{5}{8}$	$11\frac{5}{8}$	$6\frac{3}{4}$	$5\frac{3}{8}$
P/E Ratio - High	14	8	6	7	12	13
- Low	9	6	4	5	6	7

Income Statement Analysis (Million $)

	1994	%Chg	1993	%Chg	1992	%Chg	1991
Commissions	483	15%	421	12%	375	11%	339
Int. Inc.	1,304	45%	902	-10%	997	-22%	1,279
Total Revs.	3,441	20%	2,857	7%	2,677	12%	2,380
Int. Exp.	1,020	44%	710	-15%	835	-27%	1,141
Pretax Inc.	643	5%	614	21%	508	121%	230
Eff. Tax Rate	40%	—	41%	—	42%	—	38%
Net Inc.	387	7%	362	23%	295	106%	143

Balance Sheet & Other Fin. Data (Million $)

	1994	1993	1992	1991	1990	1989
Total Assets	67,392	57,440	45,768	39,285	31,574	36,410
Cash Items	3,285	2,610	2,280	2,331	2,640	1,614
Receivables	49,014	38,840	30,292	27,317	19,504	24,325
Secs. Owned	14,444	15,215	12,162	8,792	8,746	9,733
Sec. Borrowed	34,847	28,743	24,630	24,077	13,439	17,254
Due Brokers & Cust.	17,098	14,634	11,338	9,011	11,864	8,875
Other Liabs.	9,722	10,404	7,483	4,443	4,812	8,831
Capitalization:						
Debt	3,408	1,883	1,040	682	384	385
Equity	1,729	1,439	1,127	1,001	1,001	964
Total	5,725	3,660	2,167	1,754	1,460	1,451

Ratio Analysis

	1994	1993	1992	1991	1990	1989
% Ret. on Revs.	11.2	12.7	11.0	6.0	5.0	7.3
% Ret. on Assets	0.6	0.7	0.7	0.4	0.4	0.5
% Ret. on Equity	22.9	27.7	28.1	13.9	11.8	18.0

Dividend Data —Dividends were initiated in 1986.

Amt. of Div. $	Date Decl.	Ex-Div. Date	Stock of Record	Payment Date
0.150	Oct. 25	Nov. 04	Nov. 11	Nov. 25 '94
0.150	Jan. 19	Feb. 06	Feb. 10	Feb. 24 '95
5%	Apr. 19	May. 08	May. 12	May. 26 '95
0.150	Apr. 19	May. 08	May. 12	May. 26 '95
0.150	Aug. 01	Aug. 09	Aug. 24	Aug. 25 '95

Data as orig. reptd.; bef. results of disc opers. and/or spec. items. Per share data adj. for stk. divs. as of ex-div. date. E-Estimated. NA-Not Available. NM-Not Meaningful. NR-Not Ranked.

Office—245 Park Ave., New York, NY 10167. **Tel**—(212) 272-2000. **Chrmn**—A. C. Greenberg. **Pres & CEO**—J. E. Cayne. **Secy**—K. L. Edlow. **Treas**—M. Minikes. **SVP-Fin**—S. L. Molinaro, Jr. **Investor Contact**—Hannah Burns (212-272-2395). **Dirs**—E. G. Bewkes III, D. A. Bovin, J. E. Cayne, P. Cherasia, S. M. Cunningham, P. M. Drittel, K. J. Finnerty, G. J. Fippinger, C. D. Glickman, T. R. Green, A. C. Greenberg, D. J. Harrington, R. Harriton, N. E. Havens-Hasty, J. Ilany, D. L. Keating, J. W. Kluge, D. A. Liebowitz, B. M. Lisman, M.J. Mancuso, V. J. Mattone, M. Minikes, W. J. Montgoris, D. R. Mullen, F. T. Nickell, C. M. Overlander, S. E. Raphael, J. P. Reich, R. B. Roberts, E. J. Rosenwald, Jr., F. V. Salerno, A. D. Schwartz, J. C. Sites Jr., W. J. Spector, R. M. Steinberg, M. L. Tarnopol, V. Tese, F. Wilpon, U. Zucker. **Transfer Agent & Registrar**—Chemical Bank, NYC. **Incorporated** in Delaware in 1985. **Empl**-7,600. **S&P Analyst:** Paul L. Huberman, CFA

Beckman Instruments

NYSE Symbol **BEC**
In S&P MidCap 400

06-OCT-95 **Industry:** Medical equipment/ supply

Summary: This company develops and manufactures automated systems and supplies used for biological analysis in laboratories for R&D and clinical diagnostics.

Quantitative Evaluations
Outlook (1 Lowest—5 Highest)
• **4-**
Fair Value
• **32⅝**
Risk
• **Low**
Earn./Div. Rank
• **NR**

Technical Eval.
• **Bullish** since 5/95
Rel. Strength Rank (1 Lowest—99 Highest)
• **79**
Insider Activity
• **Neutral**

Recent Price • 30¼
52 Wk Range • 31½-26
Yield • 1.4%
12-Mo. P/E • 17.7

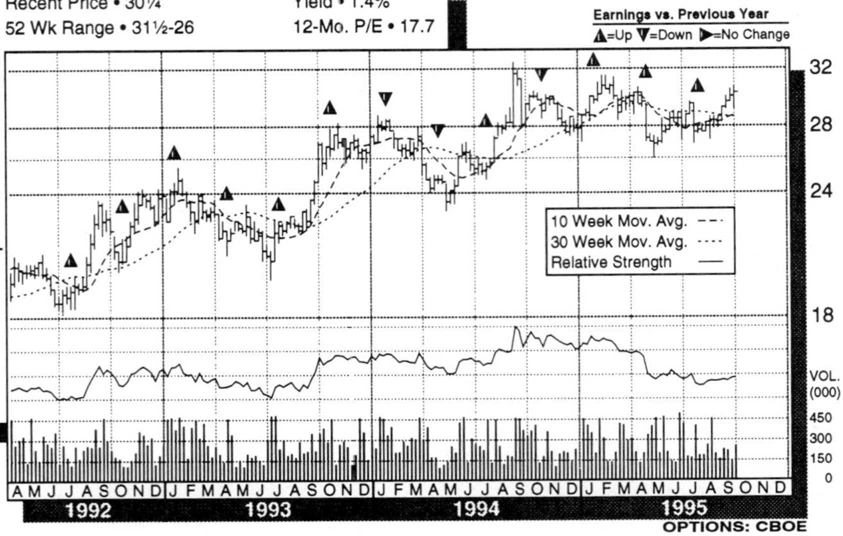

OPTIONS: CBOE

Business Profile - 06-OCT-95

A worldwide focus on health care related cost containment is restricting growth in the bioresearch and clinical diagostic markets. Despite this environment, Beckman has been able to realize market share gains through the introduction of several productivity enhancing products. The company operates in more than 120 countries.

Operational Review - 06-OCT-95

Excluding the effect of currency exchange rate gains, revenues for the first half of 1995 were unchanged, year to year. Reduced investment in new equipment throughout the global research and diagnostic markets has restricted top-line growth. Restucturing efforts have benefited operating results. Beckman's focus on developing productivity enhancing equipment could help jump-start revenue growth in future periods.

Stock Performance - 29-SEP-95

In the past 30 trading days, BEC's shares have increased 7%, compared to a 5% rise in the S&P 500. Average trading volume for the past five days was 50,260 shares, compared with the 40-day moving average of 49,664 shares.

Key Stock Statistics

Dividend Rate/Share	0.44	Shareholders	10,100
Shs. outstg. (M)	29.0	Market cap. (B)	$0.892
Avg. daily vol. (M)	0.053	Inst. holdings	64%
Tang. Bk. Value/Share	11.87	Insider holdings	NA
Beta	0.71		

Value of $10,000 invested 5 years ago: $ 18,542

Fiscal Year Ending Dec. 31

	1995	% Change	1994	% Change	1993	% Change
Revenues (Million $)						
1Q	205.0	3%	198.6	-2%	201.7	-5%
2Q	230.6	4%	222.2	NM	221.8	-1%
3Q	—	—	217.8	1%	215.6	-2%
4Q	—	—	250.0	6%	236.6	-5%
Yr.	—	—	888.6	1%	875.7	-4%
Income (Million $)						
1Q	10.30	5%	9.80	-4%	10.20	10%
2Q	13.80	6%	13.00	11%	11.70	9%
3Q	—	—	11.30	-2%	11.50	NM
4Q	—	—	13.20	NM	-67.00	NM
Yr.	—	—	47.30	NM	-33.60	NM
Earnings Per Share ($)						
1Q	0.36	3%	0.35	-3%	0.36	13%
2Q	0.48	4%	0.46	10%	0.42	14%
3Q	—	—	0.40	-5%	0.42	5%
4Q	—	—	0.47	NM	-2.41	NM
Yr.	—	—	1.68	NM	-1.21	NM

Next earnings report expected: late October

Beckman Instruments

Business Summary - 06-OCT-95

Beckman Instruments designs, manufactures, markets and services a broad range of laboratory instrument systems, reagents and related products, which customers typically use to conduct basic scientific research, new product research and development, or diagnostic analysis of patient samples.

In 1994, about 60% of total sales were for diagnostic applications, principally in hospital laboratories, while about 40% were for life sciences applications in universities, medical schools and research institutes or new product research and development in pharmaceutical and biotechnology companies.

Synthesis and sample preparation/handling products (less than 10% of sales in 1994) include DNA synthesizers and robotic workstations.

Separation process products (28%) include centrifuges, high performance liquid chromatographs, protein sequencers and electrophoresis systems.

Detection and measurement products (less than 10%) include spectrophotometer systems and nuclear counters.

Data processing (less than 10%) includes producing computer software programs to aid in the data processing functions of analytical laboratories.

Automated general chemistry systems for clinical diagnostics (40%) include the SYNCHRON systems.

Special chemistry applications for clinical diagnostic (20%) include immunochemistry systems, electrophoresis for clinical diagnostics and other products.

In 1994, foreign clients accounted for about 50% of sales.

Important Developments

Jul. '95—The company noted that beginning in the first quarter of 1995, it included the dilutive effect of unexercised stock options as common stock equivalents when calculating earnings per share (EPS). This change will lower 1995 reported EPS growth, compared with 1994, by 2%-3%. Without this change, EPS before nonrecurring charges for the second quarter and first half of 1995 would have grown 16%. Beckman noted that nonrecurring charges of $3.4 million ($0.08 per share) for the second quarter and $6.5 million ($0.15) for the first half were related to the company's restructuring program which is expected to be completed by the end of 1995.

Capitalization

Long Term Debt: $130,300,000 (6/95).

Per Share Data ($) (Year Ended Dec. 31)

	1994	1993	1992	1991	1990	1989
Tangible Bk. Val.	11.32	9.41	12.51	11.87	11.24	9.38
Cash Flow	4.18	1.03	3.76	3.23	2.92	2.85
Earnings	1.68	-1.21	1.53	1.32	1.26	1.47
Dividends	0.40	0.36	0.30	0.28	0.28	0.28
Payout Ratio	24%	NM	20%	21%	22%	19%
Prices - High	32½	28¼	24¼	20⅝	19	22¾
- Low	23	19⅝	17⅝	13⅞	11⅞	17⅛
P/E Ratio - High	19	NM	16	16	15	15
- Low	14	NM	12	11	9	12

Income Statement Analysis (Million $)

	1994	%Chg	1993	%Chg	1992	%Chg	1991
Revs.	889	1%	876	-4%	909	6%	858
Oper. Inc.	169	14%	148	-2%	151	16%	130
Depr.	70.1	13%	62.3	-3%	63.9	15%	55.5
Int. Exp.	13.2	4%	12.7	-2%	13.0	-15%	15.3
Pretax Inc.	74.9	NM	-53.9	NM	70.7	11%	63.8
Eff. Tax Rate	37%	—	NM	—	38%	—	40%
Net Inc.	47.3	NM	-33.6	NM	43.8	15%	38.1

Balance Sheet & Other Fin. Data (Million $)

	1994	1993	1992	1991	1990	1989
Cash	44.9	46.1	46.0	33.9	27.7	17.8
Curr. Assets	512	545	509	492	465	412
Total Assets	829	820	738	712	681	607
Curr. Liab.	269	323	281	264	247	225
LT Debt	117	114	59.5	59.0	64.6	75.9
Common Eqty.	317	276	357	343	326	269
Total Cap.	434	389	430	409	395	350
Cap. Exp.	97.4	92.8	91.4	69.7	67.3	56.6
Cash Flow	117	29.0	108	94.0	84.0	81.0

Ratio Analysis

	1994	1993	1992	1991	1990	1989
Curr. Ratio	1.9	1.7	1.8	1.9	1.9	1.8
% LT Debt of Cap.	26.9	29.2	13.8	14.4	16.4	21.7
% Net Inc.of Revs.	5.3	NM	4.8	4.4	4.4	5.3
% Ret. on Assets	5.7	NM	6.1	5.5	5.6	7.1
% Ret. on Equity	11.9	NM	12.6	11.4	12.1	16.7

Dividend Data —Dividends were initiated in 1989. A "poison pill" stock purchase rights plan was adopted in 1989.

Amt. of Div. $	Date Decl.	Ex-Div. Date	Stock of Record	Payment Date
0.100	Oct. 04	Nov. 04	Nov. 11	Dec. 01 '94
0.110	Feb. 03	Feb. 06	Feb. 10	Mar. 02 '95
0.110	Apr. 07	May. 08	May. 12	Jun. 01 '95
0.110	Aug. 04	Aug. 09	Aug. 11	Aug. 31 '95

Data as orig. reptd.; bef. results of disc. opers. and/or spec. items. Per share data adj. for stk. divs. as of ex-div. date. E-Estimated. NA-Not Available. NM-Not Meaningful. NR-Not Ranked.

Office—2500 Harbor Blvd., Fullerton, CA 92634. **Tel**—(714) 871-4848. **Chrmn & CEO**—L. T. Rosso. **Pres & COO**—J. P. Wareham. **VP-Fin & CFO**—D. K. Wilson. **VP & Secy**—W. H. May **Investor Contact**—Jay Steffenhagen (714) 773-7764. **Dirs**—E. H. Clark Jr., C. K. Davis. D. C. Fill, G. S. Herbert, W. N. Kelley, F. P. Lucier, C. R. O'Neil, L. T. Rosso, D. S. Tappan Jr., J. P. Wareham, H. Wendt, B. Woods. **Transfer Agent & Registrar**—First Chicago Trust Co. of New York, Jersey City, NJ. **Incorporated** in California in 1934; reincorporated in Delaware in 1988. **Empl**-5,900. **S&P Analyst:** SAJ

STANDARD & POOR'S

STOCK REPORTS

Belo (A. H.) Corp.

NYSE Symbol **BLC**
In S&P MidCap 400

02-AUG-95 **Industry:** Publishing

Summary: This media company publishes The Dallas Morning News and several community newspapers. Broadcasting properties include seven TV stations and a TV programming company.

S&P Opinion: Accumulate (★★★★)

Recent Price • 30½
52 Wk Range • 32⅝-23
Yield • 1.0%
12-Mo. P/E • 17.0

Quantitative Evaluations

Outlook
(1 Lowest—5 Highest)
• **5⁻**

Fair Value
• **34¼**

Risk
• **Low**

Earn./Div. Rank
• **B+**

Technical Eval.
• **Bullish** since 7/94

Rel. Strength Rank
(1 Lowest—99 Highest)
• **59**

Insider Activity
• **Neutral**

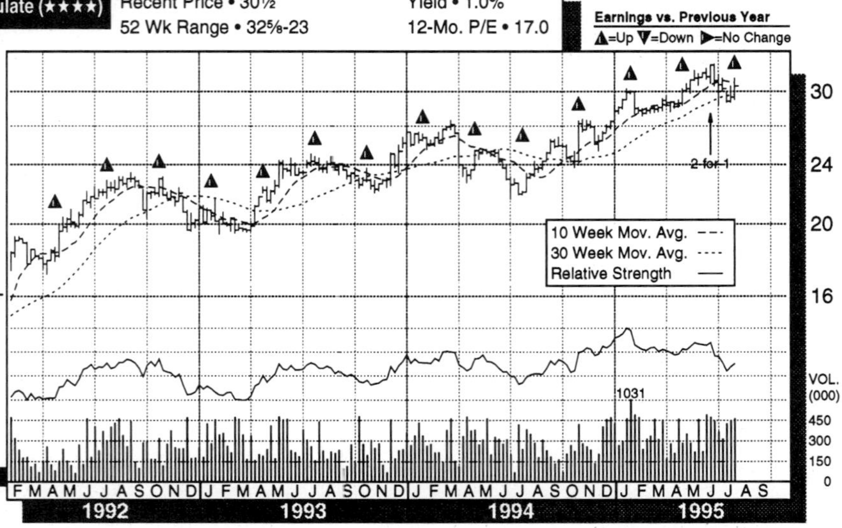

Overview - 02-AUG-95

A 10% to 12% rise in newspaper revenues is anticipated for 1995, aided largely by continued improvement in advertising linage, and price increases. Television advertising will be lack 1994's strong political advertising, but healthy double-digit growth in revenues should still be seen, boosted by the full-year inclusion of WWL and the acquisition of KIRO. Margins are expected to widen, despite the likelihood of rising newsprint prices over the course of the year, but a faster rise in noncash charges will restrict the gain in operating earnings. Interest expense will be substantially higher. The operating outlook for print and broadcast operations remains favorable for 1996.

Valuation - 02-AUG-95

The stock's near- and long-term prospects are good, and it should be a relatively strong market performer in coming months. Although the shares appear reasonably valued, currently trading at about 16X estimated 1995 EPS, they do not yet reflect strong earnings prospects that we anticipate for 1996. In addition, the location of Belo's media properties in markets with above-average growth potential, and its strong market position in each market, promise faster EPS growth over time. The acquisition of two television stations over the past year enhances the company's attractiveness as a media concern.

Key Stock Statistics

S&P EPS Est. 1995	1.95	Tang. Bk. Value/Share	NM
P/E on S&P Est. 1995	15.6	Beta	0.74
S&P EPS Est. 1996	2.40	Shareholders	1,300
Dividend Rate/Share	0.32	Market cap. (B)	$ 1.2
Shs. outstg. (M)	39.5	Inst. holdings	50%
Avg. daily vol. (M)	0.091	Insider holdings	NA

Value of $10,000 invested 5 years ago: $ 17,264

Fiscal Year Ending Dec. 31

	1995	% Change	1994	% Change	1993	% Change
Revenues (Million $)						
1Q	163.0	23%	132.1	7%	122.8	7%
2Q	189.8	22%	154.9	8%	143.8	7%
3Q	—	—	159.6	20%	132.5	4%
4Q	—	—	181.6	25%	145.6	5%
Yr.	—	—	628.1	15%	544.8	6%
Income (Million $)						
1Q	11.44	14%	10.04	38%	7.27	13%
2Q	21.20	9%	19.51	21%	16.14	30%
3Q	—	—	15.75	99%	7.93	11%
4Q	—	—	23.57	80%	13.13	18%
Yr.	—	—	68.87	55%	44.48	20%
Earnings Per Share ($)						
1Q	0.29	16%	0.24	32%	0.19	12%
2Q	0.53	10%	0.48	20%	0.40	27%
3Q	E0.46	—	0.39	103%	0.19	8%
4Q	E0.72	—	0.59	84%	0.32	14%
Yr.	E1.95	—	1.70	55%	1.10	16%

Next earnings report expected: late October

Belo (A. H.) Corp.

Business Summary - 02-AUG-95

A. H. Belo's principal businesses are newspaper publishing and television broadcasting. Segment contributions in 1994 were:

	Revs.	Profits
Newspaper publishing	59%	45%
TV broadcasting	41%	55%

Belo's major newspaper property is The Dallas Morning News, the only major newspaper in Dallas since the closing of a rival in December 1991. Average paid circulation in the six months ended September 30, 1994, was 524,567 daily and 797,206 Sunday, down 0.5% and 2.1%, respectively, from the year-earlier level. The company also publishes eight community newspapers, issued three times a week, serving suburban communities in the Dallas-Fort Worth metropolitan area.

The company owns seven television stations: WFAA-TV (an ABC affiliate), Dallas-Fort Worth; KHOU-TV (CBS), Houston; KXTV (CBS), Sacramento, Calif.; KOTV (CBS), Tulsa, Okla.; WVEC-TV (ABC), Hampton-Norfolk, Va.; WWL (CBS), New Orleans (acquired in June 1994); and KIRO-TV (UPN), Seattle (January 1995).

Important Developments

Jul. '95—The company said 1995 second quarter EPS included a gain of $0.04 from the sale of its investment in Stauffer Communications, Inc. Profits in the broadcast division were affected by acquisition and transition expenses associated with KIRO-TV, startup costs for Maxam Entertainment, and a slowdown in the rate of broadcast revenue growth in June.
Jan. '95—Belo acquired KIRO-TV (Seattle, Wash.) for $162.5 million in cash. KIRO is a UPN affiliate.
Jun. '94—The company acquired WWL-TV, a CBS affiliate in New Orleans, for $110 million in cash. WWL, which reaches about 50% of Louisiana's population, is the state's leading station.

Capitalization

Long Term Debt: $499,400,000 (6/95).
Class A Common Stk.: 15,064,924 shs. ($1.67 par).
Class B Common Stk.: 4,709,794 shs. ($1.67 par); 10 votes per sh.; limited transferability; conv. sh.-for-sh. into Cl. A.
About 24% of Cl. A and Cl. B stock closely held. Institutions hold about 50% of both classes.
Shareholders of record: 723.

Per Share Data ($) (Year Ended Dec. 31)

	1994	1993	1992	1991	1990	1989
Tangible Bk. Val.	-1.00	-0.20	-2.22	-3.39	-3.86	-3.78
Cash Flow	2.85	2.03	1.87	1.21	1.67	1.40
Earnings	1.70	1.10	0.95	0.32	0.77	0.58
Dividends	0.30	0.28	0.27	0.26	0.24	0.22
Payout Ratio	18%	25%	28%	79%	30%	37%
Prices - High	28⅝	26½	23½	16⅞	19⅜	20½
- Low	21⅝	19⅜	15⅜	12⅛	14⅛	11½
P/E Ratio - High	17	24	25	52	25	35
- Low	13	18	16	37	18	20

Income Statement Analysis (Million $)

	1994	%Chg	1993	%Chg	1992	%Chg	1991
Revs.	628	15%	545	6%	516	19%	432
Oper. Inc.	177	33%	133	13%	118	33%	89.0
Depr.	46.4	23%	37.7	5%	36.0	6%	34.1
Int. Exp.	16.3	-4%	17.0	-31%	24.6	1%	24.3
Pretax Inc.	108	43%	75.6	23%	61.6	NM	18.6
Eff. Tax Rate	36%	—	41%	—	40%	—	33%
Net Inc.	68.9	55%	44.5	20%	37.2	NM	12.4

Balance Sheet & Other Fin. Data (Million $)

	1994	1993	1992	1991	1990	1989
Cash	9.3	8.9	3.0	1.0	3.0	3.0
Curr. Assets	130	117	102	101	91.0	91.0
Total Assets	914	796	759	746	694	701
Curr. Liab.	83.7	59.7	69.7	75.7	61.7	66.4
LT Debt	330	277	302	337	280	291
Common Eqty.	383	346	281	230	224	233
Total Cap.	823	731	685	668	622	632
Cap. Exp.	47.4	62.1	55.9	19.7	26.3	21.8
Cash Flow	115	82.1	73.2	46.5	63.9	56.9

Ratio Analysis

	1994	1993	1992	1991	1990	1989
Curr. Ratio	1.6	2.0	1.5	1.3	1.5	1.4
% LT Debt of Cap.	40.1	38.0	44.1	50.5	45.1	46.0
% Net Inc.of Revs.	11.0	8.2	7.2	2.9	6.7	5.6
% Ret. on Assets	8.1	5.6	4.8	1.7	4.3	3.3
% Ret. on Equity	19.1	14.0	14.3	5.4	13.2	10.1

Dividend Data (Dividends have been paid since 1939. Payments are identical on the Class A and Class B shares. A poison pill stock purchase rights plan was adopted in 1986.)

Amt. of Div. $	Date Decl.	Ex-Div. Date	Stock of Record	Payment Date
0.150	Jul. 27	Aug. 08	Aug. 12	Sep. 09 '94
0.150	Sep. 28	Nov. 04	Nov. 11	Dec. 09 '94
0.150	Dec. 14	Feb. 13	Feb. 17	Mar. 10 '95
0.080	Feb. 22	May. 15	May. 19	Jun. 09 '95
2-for-1	Feb. 22	Jun. 12	May. 19	Jun. 09 '95
0.080	Jul. 26	Aug. 09	Aug. 11	Sep. 08 '95

Data as orig. reptd.; bef. results of disc. opers. and/or spec. items. Per share data adj. for stk. divs. as of ex-div. date. E-Estimated. NA-Not Available. NM-Not Meaningful. NR-Not Ranked.

Office—400 South Record St., Dallas, TX 75202. **Tel**—(214) 977-6600. **Chrmn, Pres & CEO**—R. W. Decherd. **Vice Chrmn**—W. L. Huey, Jr. **SVP & CFO**—M. D. Perry. **SVP & Secy**—M. J. McCarthy. **Investor Contact**—Harold Gaar (214-977-7650). **Dirs**—J. W. Bassett, Jr., J. L. Craven, J. M. Dealey, R. W. Decherd, D. D. Herndon, W. L. Huey, Jr., L. A. Levy, A. Madrid, J. M. Moroney, Jr., B. Osborne, H. G. Robinson, W. H. Seay, W. T. Solomon, T. B. Walker, Jr., J. M. Williams. **Transfer Agent & Registrar**—Chemical Bank, NYC. **Incorporated** in Texas in 1926; reincorporated in Delaware in 1987. **Empl**-3,082. **S&P Analyst:** William H. Donald

Bergen Brunswig

NYSE Symbol **BBC**
In S&P MidCap 400

18-SEP-95

Industry:
Drugs-Generic and OTC

Summary: This company is the largest U.S. supplier of pharmaceuticals to hospitals and a leading supplier of pharmaceuticals and healthcare products to pharmacies.

Quantitative Evaluations

Outlook
(1 Lowest—5 Highest)
• **4-**

Fair Value
• **22¾**

Risk
• **Average**

Earn./Div. Rank
• **A-**

Technical Eval.
• **Bearish** since 12/94

Rel. Strength Rank
(1 Lowest—99 Highest)
• **35**

Insider Activity
• **Unfavorable**

Recent Price • 21⅞
52 Wk Range • 29⅛-13⅝
Yield • 2.2%
12-Mo. P/E • 13.3

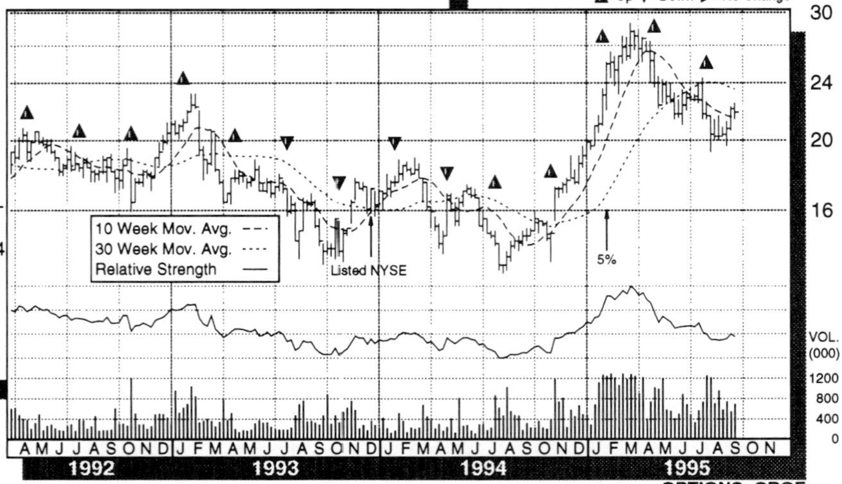

OPTIONS: CBOE

Business Profile - 18-SEP-95

Bergen Brunswig is experiencing strong growth as it receives large new distribution contracts and consolidates several acquisitions. However, the company must contend with a demanding healthcare environment, which is encouraging price competition and putting downward pressure on margins. Bergen Brunswig's strategy is to emphasize the more profitable elements of the business and focus on cost efficiency. The company is also investing heavily in information systems and distribution technology.

Operational Review - 18-SEP-95

Revenues in recent periods climbed steadily, as the company received new distribution contracts and completed several acquisitions. Gross margins narrowed due to price competition, which was partly offset by faster sales growth of higher-margin medicial-surgical supplies. However, distribution and SG&A expenses declined as a percentage of sales, reflecting operating efficiencies and the consolidation of distribution branches into larger regional distribution centers. Earnings continued to rise.

Stock Performance - 15-SEP-95

In the past 30 trading days, BBC's shares have increased 7%, compared to a 4% rise in the S&P 500. Average trading volume for the past five days was 136,060 shares, compared with the 40-day moving average of 182,879 shares.

Key Stock Statistics

Dividend Rate/Share	0.48	Shareholders	3,600
Shs. outstg. (M)	39.8	Market cap. (B)	$0.871
Avg. daily vol. (M)	0.132	Inst. holdings	61%
Tang. Bk. Value/Share	3.57	Insider holdings	NA
Beta	0.82		

Value of $10,000 invested 5 years ago: $ 13,169

Fiscal Year Ending Sep. 30

	1995	% Change	1994	% Change	1993	% Change
Revenues (Million $)						
1Q	1,984	8%	1,835	15%	1,600	39%
2Q	2,084	13%	1,845	9%	1,700	39%
3Q	2,157	15%	1,879	6%	1,765	32%
4Q	—	—	1,925	10%	1,756	31%
Yr.	—	—	7,484	10%	6,824	35%
Income (Million $)						
1Q	13.55	31%	10.33	-13%	11.93	80%
2Q	17.86	23%	14.53	-5%	15.36	NM
3Q	16.88	12%	15.03	4%	14.45	-10%
4Q	—	—	16.23	NM	-13.13	NM
Yr.	—	—	56.12	96%	28.61	-46%
Earnings Per Share ($)						
1Q	0.35	31%	0.27	-15%	0.31	106%
2Q	0.45	18%	0.38	-5%	0.40	2%
3Q	0.42	8%	0.39	2%	0.38	-7%
4Q	—	—	0.41	NM	-0.34	NM
Yr.	—	—	1.45	93%	0.75	-44%

Next earnings report expected: early November

Bergen Brunswig

Business Summary - 18-SEP-95

Bergen Brunswig Corporation is the largest U.S. supplier of pharmaceuticals to hospitals and managed-care facilities and a leading supplier of pharmaceuticals and healthcare products to chain and independent pharmacies.

The company's 33 drug distribution facilities in 23 states provide a full line of products, including pharmaceuticals, proprietary medicines, cosmetics, toiletries, personal health products, sundries and home healthcare supplies and equipment. These products are sold to a large number of hospital pharmacies, health maintenance organizations (HMOs), independent retail pharmacies, pharmacy chains, supermarkets, food-drug combination stores and other retailers in more than 44 states, Guam and Mexico. Bergen's 20 medical-surgical supply distribution facilities supply products to some 33,000 hospital, clinic, nursing home, veterinary clinic and physician accounts in 39 states.

Bergen Brunswig has been an innovator in the development and utilization of computer-based retailer order entry systems and electronic data interchange systems, including computer-to-computer ordering systems with suppliers. Substantially all orders received from customers are received via electronic order entry systems. Bergen is expanding its electronic interface with its suppliers and now electronically processes most of its purchase orders, invoices and payments.

The company consolidated six of its drug distribution facilities in fiscal 1994 and three the year before into more productive distribution centers. It recorded a net charge of $33 million related to the restructuring in the fourth quarter of fiscal 1993. The consolidations have reduced annual operating expenses by more than $18 million.

Important Developments

Aug. '95—Bergen Brunswig completed the acquisition of Colonial Healthcare Supply Co., a medical and surgical products distributor with 1994 reveneus of $180 million.

May '95—The company entered into an underwriting agreement to issue $100 million of 7.25% senior notes due 2005. Bergen intends to use the proceeds for the repayment of loans outstanding under its bank credit facility.

Jan. '95—BBC completed the acquisition of Biddle & Crowther Co., a privately held, Seattle-based medical-surgical supply distributor with 1994 revenues of $48 million. Separately, the company was selected as one of three authorized distribution agents for VHA Inc., the largest U.S. healthcare network. Additionally, Bergen said that it signed a five-year pharmaceutical distribution agreement with Safeway Inc., which is expected to generate over $1 billion in revenues.

Capitalization

Long Term Debt: $425,576,000 (3/95).

Per Share Data ($)

(Year Ended Sep. 30)

	1994	1993	1992	1991	1990	1989
Tangible Bk. Val.	3.26	2.08	8.78	8.90	8.29	7.19
Cash Flow	2.21	1.44	1.72	1.76	1.68	1.77
Earnings	1.45	0.75	1.34	1.43	1.39	1.41
Dividends	0.44	0.38	0.38	0.32	0.27	0.21
Payout Ratio	30%	51%	28%	22%	20%	19%
Prices - High	18⅞	23¼	21¼	25	22⅝	20¾
- Low	13⅛	13½	15⅞	15¼	15⅝	13¾
P/E Ratio - High	13	31	16	18	16	15
- Low	9	18	12	11	11	10

Income Statement Analysis (Million $)

	1994	%Chg	1993	%Chg	1992	%Chg	1991
Revs.	7,484	10%	6,824	35%	5,048	4%	4,838
Oper. Inc.	147	11%	132	26%	105	-20%	132
Depr.	29.5	5%	28.1	87%	15.0	1%	14.8
Int. Exp.	23.0	1%	22.7	NM	6.9	-52%	14.5
Pretax Inc.	98.0	104%	48.0	-42%	83.0	-19%	102
Eff. Tax Rate	43%	—	41%	—	37%	—	36%
Net Inc.	56.1	96%	28.6	-46%	53.0	-17%	64.1

Balance Sheet & Other Fin. Data (Million $)

	1994	1993	1992	1991	1990	1989
Cash	5.0	55.0	308	304	295	130
Curr. Assets	1,445	1,231	1,192	1,119	1,048	818
Total Assets	1,995	1,772	1,412	1,322	1,238	986
Curr. Liab.	1,191	1,045	771	610	550	509
LT Debt	321	286	224	211	199	48.0
Common Eqty.	462	418	395	455	446	391
Total Cap.	786	716	631	698	673	465
Cap. Exp.	24.9	33.9	18.9	22.4	30.1	17.8
Cash Flow	85.6	56.7	68.1	79.0	75.5	60.0

Ratio Analysis

	1994	1993	1992	1991	1990	1989
Curr. Ratio	1.2	1.2	1.5	1.8	1.9	1.6
% LT Debt of Cap.	40.8	39.9	35.5	30.2	29.5	10.3
% Net Inc.of Revs.	0.7	0.4	1.1	1.3	1.4	1.2
% Ret. on Assets	2.9	1.8	4.1	5.1	5.6	4.2
% Ret. on Equity	12.6	7.0	13.4	14.5	14.9	13.3

Dividend Data —Cash dividends have been paid since 1978. A "poison pill" stock purchase rights plan was adopted in 1994.

Amt. of Div. $	Date Decl.	Ex-Div. Date	Stock of Record	Payment Date
0.120	Oct. 21	Oct. 26	Nov. 01	Dec. 01 '94
0.120	Jan. 26	Jan. 31	Feb. 06	Mar. 01 '95
5%	Jan. 26	Jan. 31	Feb. 06	Mar. 01 '95
0.120	Apr. 27	May. 02	May. 08	Jun. 01 '95
0.120	Jul. 28	Aug. 03	Aug. 07	Sep. 01 '95

Data as orig. reptd.; bef. results of disc. opers. and/or spec. items. Per share data adj. for stk. divs. as of ex-div. date. E-Estimated. NA-Not Available. NM-Not Meaningful. NR-Not Ranked.

Office—4000 Metropolitan Dr., Orange, CA 92668-3510. **Tel**—(714) 385-4000. **Chrmn, Pres, CEO & COO**—R. E. Martini. **Exec VP & CFO**—N. F. Dimick. **Exec VP & Secy**—M. A. Sawdei. **Investor Contact**—Lisa Riordan (800) 840-5131. **Dirs**—J. E. Blanco, R. H. Brady, J. Calasibetta, N. F. Dimick, C. C. Edwards, C. J. Lee, G. R. Liddle, R. E. Martini, J. R. Mellor, G. E. Reinhardt Jr., F. G. Rodgers, D. A. Steffensen. **Transfer Agent & Registrar**—Chemical Trust Co. of California, Los Angeles. **Incorporated** in New Jersey in 1956. **Empl**-4,250. **S&P Analyst:** Philip J. Birbara

STANDARD & POOR'S

STOCK REPORTS

Best Buy

NYSE Symbol **BBY**

In S&P MidCap 400

17-OCT-95 **Industry:** Retail Stores

Summary: BBY sells consumer electronic products, home office and computer equipment and home appliances through more than 230 discount retail stores in 27 central U.S. states.

S&P Opinion: Hold (★★★)

Recent Price • 24¾ | Yield • Nil

52 Wk Range • 45¼-19⅞ | 12-Mo. P/E • 19.0

Quantitative Evaluations

Outlook (1 Lowest—5 Highest)
• **5-**

Fair Value
• **34⅜**

Risk
• **High**

Earn./Div. Rank
• **B**

Technical Eval.
• **Bearish** since 10/95

Rel. Strength Rank (1 Lowest—99 Highest)
• **30**

Insider Activity
• **NA**

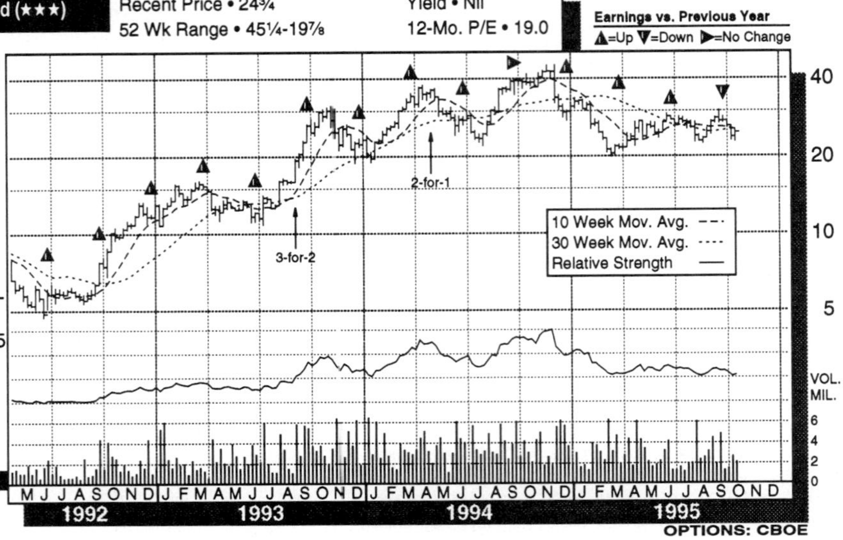

OPTIONS: CBOE

Overview - 13-OCT-95

We expect this fast-growing consumer electronics retailer to continue to post double-digit sales gains for the remainder of 1995-96, fueled by an aggressive store opening program in which about 47 new stores should be added. Same-store sales growth will most likely remain in the mid-single digits. Gross margins will continue to be squeezed by the increased percentage of lower margin personal computers in the sales mix, increasing price competition and costs associated with new store openings. Interest costs are also likely to be higher, reflecting increased borrowings to support higher inventory levels. Operating expense as a percentage of sales should stabilize, as economies of scale and well controlled costs offset higher preopening expense and greater advertising outlays.

Valuation - 13-OCT-95

The shares have been extremely volatile in recent years, reflecting differing views of earnings prospects. After reaching a record high in December 1994, the shares fell over 55%, and have recently stalled in the mid-20s. The long-term growth outlook remains favorable; we project annual EPS gains of 15% to 20% over the next several years. Although the stock is selling at a P/E lower than our estimated growth rate, there is considerable risk in owning the unpredictable shares.

Key Stock Statistics

S&P EPS Est. 1996	1.45	Tang. Bk. Value/Share	9.19
P/E on S&P Est. 1996	17.1	Beta	-1.69
S&P EPS Est. 1997	1.80	Shareholders	2,100
Dividend Rate/Share	Nil	Market cap. (B)	$ 1.1
Shs. outstg. (M)	42.7	Inst. holdings	52%
Avg. daily vol. (M)	0.359	Insider holdings	NA

Value of $10,000 invested 5 years ago: $ 123,750

Fiscal Year Ending Feb. 28

	1996	% Change	1995	% Change	1994	% Change
Revenues (Million $)						
1Q	1,275	50%	849.0	92%	441.9	79%
2Q	1,438	54%	933.2	66%	563.0	97%
3Q	—	—	1,350	67%	808.5	70%
4Q	—	—	1,947	63%	1,193	94%
Yr.	—	—	5,080	69%	3,007	86%
Income (Million $)						
1Q	4.67	10%	4.24	179%	1.52	23%
2Q	5.71	-25%	7.60	NM	7.59	190%
3Q	—	—	17.70	59%	11.16	114%
4Q	—	—	28.11	31%	21.44	99%
Yr.	—	—	57.65	38%	41.71	110%
Earnings Per Share ($)						
1Q	0.11	10%	0.10	130%	0.04	18%
2Q	0.13	-28%	0.18	NM	0.18	135%
3Q	E0.45	10%	0.41	58%	0.26	73%
4Q	E0.76	21%	0.63	26%	0.50	63%
Yr.	E1.45	9%	1.33	32%	1.01	77%

Next earnings report expected: mid December

Best Buy

Business Summary - 13-OCT-95

Best Buy is a discount retailer of brand name consumer electronics, personal computers and other home office products, major appliances and entertainment software. At October 5, 1995, it was operating 231 stores in 27 states, primarily in the central U.S. The number of stores in operation at the end of recent years was:

	1995	1994	1993	1992	1991
Stores	201	151	111	73	56

Revenue by product category in recent fiscal years were distributed as follows:

	1995	1994	1993
Video	20%	22%	26%
Audio	14%	16%	20%
Home office	37%	35%	27%
Appliances	8%	9%	11%
Entertainment software	14%	12%	9%
Other	7%	6%	7%

Most stores average 36,000 to 45,000 sq. ft. of sales space and contain self-demonstrating displays and answer centers staffed by salaried product specialists that allow the customer to control the purchase. The company believes that the use of commissioned sales staffs is inefficient. Concept II stores provide a warehouse style format geared toward self-service, with fewer employees.

In 1994, BBY introduced a new store format, Concept III, featuring increased product selection and extended use of interactive technology to provide customer assistance.

The company's marketing strategy is to provide a wide selection of brand name products, open product displays in bright spacious stores, low prices, sales personnel offering a high level of service, and installation, warranty and repair services.

BBY opened 53 new stores in 1994-5, and remodeled or relocated 28 units. A fourth distribution facility was opened in 1994, to service entry into the Los Angeles market. The company expects to open an additional 47 stores in 1995-6, including an entry into Miami with seven stores.

Important Developments

Oct. '95—Total sales in the five weeks ended September 30, 1995, climbed 40% year to year to $612 million; comparable-store sales were up 5%. The company opened seven stores in September: three in Los Angeles, three in the Baltimore/Washington D.C. area, and one in Chicago.

Capitalization

Long Term Debt: $212,143,000 (8/95).
6 1/2% Conv. Pfd. Stock: 4,600,000 shs. ($1 par). $50 liq. pref.; ea. conv. into 1.111 com.

Per Share Data ($) (Year Ended Feb. 28)

	1995	1994	1993	1992	1991	1990
Tangible Bk. Val.	8.91	7.46	5.29	4.68	2.28	2.66
Cash Flow	2.21	1.55	1.00	0.68	0.50	0.45
Earnings	1.33	1.01	0.57	0.33	0.18	0.23
Dividends	Nil	Nil	Nil	Nil	Nil	Nil
Payout Ratio	Nil	Nil	Nil	Nil	Nil	Nil
Cal. Yrs.	1994	1993	1992	1991	1990	1989
Prices - High	45¼	31⅜	13⅜	11¾	4¼	3⅞
- Low	19	10¾	4¾	1$^{13}/_{16}$	1½	1⅞
P/E Ratio - High	34	31	23	35	23	17
- Low	14	11	8	5	8	8

Income Statement Analysis (Million $)

	1995	%Chg	1994	%Chg	1993	%Chg	1992
Revs.	5,080	69%	3,007	86%	1,620	74%	930
Oper. Inc.	160	61%	100	96%	50.7	76%	28.8
Depr.	38.6	72%	22.4	51%	14.8	48%	10.0
Int. Exp.	27.9	NM	8.8	127%	3.9	13%	3.4
Pretax Inc.	94.1	38%	68.4	114%	32.0	108%	15.4
Eff. Tax Rate	39%	—	39%	—	38%	—	38%
Net Inc.	57.7	38%	41.7	110%	19.9	107%	9.6

Balance Sheet & Other Fin. Data (Million $)

	1995	1994	1993	1992	1991	1990
Cash	145	60.0	7.0	113	27.0	24.0
Curr. Assets	1,241	765	305	273	140	128
Total Assets	1,507	952	439	337	186	157
Curr. Liab.	632	402	187	146	75.0	50.0
LT Debt	227	211	48.1	14.9	35.4	35.1
Common Eqty.	376	311	182	158	57.0	66.0
Total Cap.	833	522	230	172	92.0	101
Cap. Exp.	118	114	83.6	25.3	20.3	9.7
Cash Flow	96.2	64.1	34.7	19.6	12.3	11.2

Ratio Analysis

	1995	1994	1993	1992	1991	1990
Curr. Ratio	2.0	1.9	1.6	1.9	1.9	2.6
% LT Debt of Cap.	27.3	40.4	20.9	8.6	38.4	34.7
% Net Inc.of Revs.	1.1	1.4	1.2	1.0	0.7	1.1
% Ret. on Assets	4.7	5.6	5.1	3.3	2.7	3.8
% Ret. on Equity	16.7	15.7	11.6	8.2	7.4	9.0

Dividend Data —No cash dividends have been paid.

Data as orig. reptd.; bef. results of disc. opers. and/or spec. items. Per share data adj. for stk. divs. as of ex-div. date. E-Estimated. NA-Not Available. NM-Not Meaningful. NR-Not Ranked.

Office—7075 Flying Cloud Drive, Eden Prairie, MN 55344. **Tel**—(612) 947-2000. **Chrmn & CEO**—R. M. Schulze. **Pres & COO**—B. H. Anderson. **EVP, CFO & Investor Contact**—Allen U. Lenzmeier. **Dirs**—B. H. Anderson, C. Davis, Jr., E. S. Kaplan, R. M. Schulze, D. Stanley, F. D. Trestman, J. Wetherbe. **Transfer Agent & Registrar**—Harris Trust & Savings Bank, Chicago. **Incorporated** in Minnesota in 1966. **Empl**-25,300. **S&P Analyst:** Maureen C. Carini

STANDARD & POOR'S

STOCK REPORTS

Betz Laboratories

NYSE Symbol **BTL**

In S&P MidCap 400

03-OCT-95 **Industry:** Chemicals

Summary: Betz is a leading supplier of specialty chemicals and programs for the treatment of water, wastewater and process systems for use in industrial and commercial applications.

S&P Opinion: Hold (★★★)

Recent Price • 40⅞
52 Wk Range • 50-40¾

Yield • 3.6%
12-Mo. P/E • 16.5

Quantitative Evaluations

Outlook (1 Lowest—5 Highest)
• **3-**

Fair Value
• **40⅜**

Risk
• **Low**

Earn./Div. Rank
• **A**

Technical Eval.
• **Bearish** since 7/95

Rel. Strength Rank (1 Lowest—99 Highest)
• **18**

Insider Activity
• **Neutral**

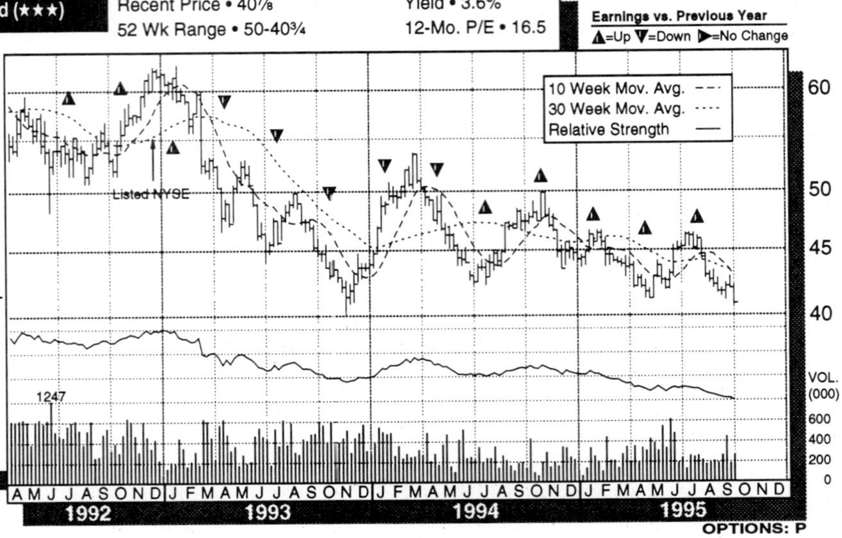

OPTIONS: P

Overview - 03-OCT-95

We expect sales to continue to rise at modest rates for the rest of 1995 and 1996, mainly due to continued strong gains in international markets (about 25% of total sales), aided by acquisitions. Domestic sales of processing chemicals are expected to continue to grow at good rates to the paper and metal treatment markets. However, sales of water treatment chemicals in the U.S. (about 50% of total sales) may continue to grow only at modest rates, limited by intense price pressures and difficult conditions in the petroleum refining industry. The purchase of W.R. Grace's Dearborn division, a leading competitor with annual sales of about $400 million, would greatly expand BTL's foreign and paper processing businesses.

Valuation - 03-OCT-95

This specialty chemicals producer's stock in recent years has been trading well below its all time high set in 1992. Sales growth has been sluggish over the past few years as a result of the general maturing of the U.S. water treatment market and difficult conditions in the petroleum processing industry. However, international expansion is expected to remain more robust due to strong growth in industrial activity. We are neutral on the stock in view of its historical record and premium multiple to the overall market. The dividend has been increased every year since 1965 and provides an above average yield.

Key Stock Statistics

S&P EPS Est. 1995	2.60	Tang. Bk. Value/Share	11.50
P/E on S&P Est. 1995	15.7	Beta	1.11
S&P EPS Est. 1996	2.85	Shareholders	3,800
Dividend Rate/Share	1.48	Market cap. (B)	$ 1.1
Shs. outstg. (M)	27.7	Inst. holdings	74%
Avg. daily vol. (M)	0.060	Insider holdings	NA

Value of $10,000 invested 5 years ago: $ 16,013

Fiscal Year Ending Dec. 31

	1995	% Change	1994	% Change	1993	% Change
Revenues (Million $)						
1Q	177.9	3%	172.9	3%	168.5	-4%
2Q	188.9	5%	179.7	5%	171.5	-3%
3Q	—	—	180.4	2%	176.5	-3%
4Q	—	—	175.3	4%	168.4	-2%
Yr.	—	—	708.3	3%	684.9	-3%
Income (Million $)						
1Q	18.74	1%	18.52	-3%	19.19	-5%
2Q	19.95	6%	18.90	NM	18.80	-8%
3Q	—	—	19.37	10%	17.64	-18%
4Q	—	—	16.39	111%	7.75	-61%
Yr.	—	—	73.17	15%	63.38	-23%
Earnings Per Share ($)						
1Q	0.63	3%	0.61	-2%	0.62	-6%
2Q	0.67	5%	0.64	5%	0.61	-9%
3Q	E0.67	3%	0.65	12%	0.58	-18%
4Q	E0.63	19%	0.53	121%	0.24	-64%
Yr.	E2.60	7%	2.43	19%	2.05	-24%

Next earnings report expected: early November

Betz Laboratories

03-OCT-95

Business Summary - 22-SEP-95

Betz Laboratories primarily produces specialty chemicals and related products for treatment of industrial and commercial water systems, industrial processes using water, and associated wastewater. The company also provides chemicals for use in a variety of process systems, and offers technical and laboratory services needed to employ its products effectively. Revenues from sales and services in recent years were divided as follows:

	1994	1993
Betz Industrial & Betz MetChem sales to basic industries	43%	43%
Betz PaperChem	15%	15%
Betz Entec commer. & light industrial markets	10%	10%
Betz Process Chemicals & Betz Energy Chemicals	8%	10%
International operations	19%	17%
Canadian operations	5%	5%

Foreign operations accounted for 19% of operating profits in 1994.

Specialty chemicals include products to control corrosion, scale, deposit formation and micro-organism growth, conserve energy, reduce waste generation, and improve process efficiency in boiler systems, cooling systems, heat exchangers, process systems, and both influent and effluent systems. The company also formulates laboratory reagents and chemical test kits for analyzing industrial water, and it markets feeding, monitoring and control treatment systems for applying its chemicals. Customers are primarily in such industries as chemicals, petrochemicals, petroleum, pulp and paper, steel, automobile, food processing, electronics, and electric utility, as well as institutional and government markets. A technical sales force of about 1,465 provides continuing guidance for effective use of Betz products. Betz also trains customer operating personnel.

Important Developments

Jul. '95—BTL said that second quarter results reflected a strong performance by its non-U.S. operations which reported a 21% gain in sales. Double digit gains were recorded in Canada, Southeast Asia, Korea, Australia, and Europe. Domestic sales rose 2% due to gains of process treatment chemicals, while U.S. sales of water treatment chemicals were sluggish.

May '95—Betz acquired Taiwan Peitz Co., a water, paper process and refinery process treatment business, with 1995 sales projected at over $12 million. The purchase strengthed Betz's presence in the Asia-Pacific region.

Capitalization

Long Term Debt (ESOP): $95,500,000 (6/95).
ESOP Preferred Stock: 491,184 shs.; conv. into 2,757,000 com. shs.

Per Share Data ($) (Year Ended Dec. 31)

	1994	1993	1992	1991	1990	1989
Tangible Bk. Val.	11.19	10.30	10.13	8.80	7.46	6.07
Cash Flow	3.93	3.40	3.95	3.55	3.17	5.20
Earnings	2.43	2.05	2.71	2.47	2.12	1.77
Dividends	1.42	1.38	1.30	1.16	1.01	0.89
Payout Ratio	58%	70%	50%	49%	48%	50%
Prices - High	53⅝	62⅞	66¼	62	43¼	31¼
- Low	42¼	40	48¼	38¾	27¾	23⅝
P/E Ratio - High	37	31	24	25	20	18
- Low	30	20	18	16	13	13

Income Statement Analysis (Million $)

	1994	%Chg	1993	%Chg	1992	%Chg	1991
Revs.	708	3%	685	-3%	707	6%	666
Oper. Inc.	163	3%	159	-6%	170	11%	153
Depr.	45.1	8%	41.8	9%	38.5	14%	33.8
Int. Exp.	1.3	-5%	1.3	-4%	1.4	-10%	1.5
Pretax Inc.	121	16%	104	-22%	134	8%	124
Eff. Tax Rate	40%	—	39%	—	39%	—	39%
Net Inc.	73.2	15%	63.4	-23%	82.0	9%	75.5

Balance Sheet & Other Fin. Data (Million $)

	1994	1993	1992	1991	1990	1989
Cash	43.9	43.9	46.4	59.0	39.8	29.3
Curr. Assets	230	209	202	201	176	145
Total Assets	555	521	511	476	427	369
Curr. Liab.	99	92.0	84.1	88.0	77.4	56.8
LT Debt	96.5	97.5	98.0	99	99	100
Common Eqty.	318	294	294	256	219	183
Total Cap.	441	419	423	385	348	310
Cap. Exp.	55.0	63.2	74.3	58.4	57.5	53.0
Cash Flow	110	97.0	113	101	87.0	77.0

Ratio Analysis

	1994	1993	1992	1991	1990	1989
Curr. Ratio	2.3	2.3	2.4	2.3	2.3	2.6
% LT Debt of Cap.	21.9	23.3	23.2	25.6	28.5	32.1
% Net Inc.of Revs.	10.3	9.3	11.6	11.3	11.0	10.8
% Ret. on Assets	13.7	12.4	16.6	16.7	16.4	16.2
% Ret. on Equity	21.4	19.0	26.9	28.4	28.4	26.2

Dividend Data —Dividends have been paid since 1958. A shareholder rights plan was adopted in 1988.

Amt. of Div. $	Date Decl.	Ex-Div. Date	Stock of Record	Payment Date
0.360	Aug. 11	Oct. 21	Oct. 27	Nov. 10 '94
0.360	Dec. 08	Jan. 20	Jan. 26	Feb. 09 '95
0.360	Apr. 13	Apr. 21	Apr. 27	May. 11 '95
0.370	Jun. 08	Jul. 25	Jul. 27	Aug. 10 '95

Data as orig. reptd.; bef. results of disc. opers. and/or spec. items. Per share data adj. for stk. divs. as of ex-div. date. E-Estimated. NA-Not Available. NM-Not Meaningful. NR-Not Ranked.

Office—4636 Somerton Rd., Trevose, PA 19053-6783. **Tel**—(215) 355-3300. **Chrmn**—J. F. McCaughan. **Pres & CEO**—W. R. Cook. **Secy**—W. C. Brafford. **VP-Fin, Treas & CFO**—G. L. James, III. **Investor Contact**—R. Dale Voncanon. **Dirs**—J. W. Boyer, Jr., P. F. Brennan, C. S. Burger, G. A. Butler, W. R. Cook, A. R. Hirsig, J. F. McCaughan, J. A. Miller, T. B. Palmer III, J. R. Quarles, Jr., J. A. H. Shober, G. Stengel, Jr., R. L. Yohe. **Transfer Agent & Registrar**—American Stock Transfer & Trust Co., NYC. **Incorporated** in Pennsylvania in 1957. **Empl**-3,980. **S&P Analyst:** Richard O'Reilly, CFA

STANDARD & POOR'S

STOCK REPORTS

Biogen, Inc.

NASDAQ Symbol **BGEN**
In S&P MidCap 400

05-SEP-95

Industry: Drugs-Generic and OTC

Summary: This biotechnology company derives its revenues principally from royalties paid by licensees that sell products based on Biogen technology.

S&P Opinion: Accumulate (★★★★) Recent Price • 54¾ 52 Wk Range • 58-32 Yield • Nil 12-Mo. P/E • NM

Quantitative Evaluations

Outlook
(1 Lowest—5 Highest)
• 1

Fair Value
• 35⅛

Risk
• Average

Earn./Div. Rank
• B-

Technical Eval.
• **Bullish** since 7/95

Rel. Strength Rank
(1 Lowest—99 Highest)
• 87

Insider Activity
• NA

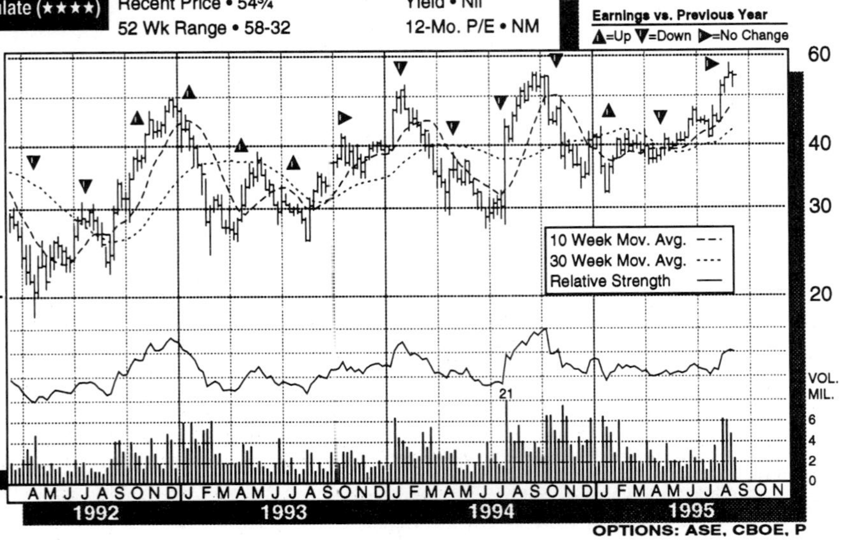

OPTIONS: ASE, CBOE, P

Overview - 03-SEP-95

Total revenues are expected to rise in 1996. Royalties from alpha interferon should benefit from anticipated expansion in that product's label to include malignant melanoma, while royalties from hepatitis B vaccines should be augmented by new governmental vaccination programs in Europe. Assuming regulatory approvals are obtained by mid-year, Biogen's new Avonex beta interferon treatment for multiple sclerosis should also make an important contribution to sales and earnings. Share profits for 1996 are estimated at $1.10, up from the $0.06 indicated for 1995 (which reflects heavy costs associated with building the infrastructure necessary to commercialize Avonex).

Valuation - 04-SEP-95

As has been typical of many biotechnology companies, Biogen's shares have been highly volatile over the past year, with clinical developments on its experimental biotech drugs triggering wide stock price swings. After holding fairly steady through much of the first half, the stock shot up in recent months, buoyed by investor enthusiasim over prospects for the company's new Avonex multiple sclerosis drug. Regulatory approvals for Avonex were filed in Europe and the U.S. in May, and an FDA advisory committee is likely to make a recommendation on the drug by year end. Avonex is expected to become a lead therapeutic for MS (a disease that afflicts more than 500,000 people worldwide). The shares have speculative appeal for long-term appreciation.

Key Stock Statistics

S&P EPS Est. 1995	0.06	Tang. Bk. Value/Share	9.85
P/E on S&P Est. 1995	NM	Beta	2.39
S&P EPS Est. 1996	1.10	Shareholders	3,200
Dividend Rate/Share	Nil	Market cap. (B)	$ 1.8
Shs. outstg. (M)	33.3	Inst. holdings	74%
Avg. daily vol. (M)	1.026	Insider holdings	NA

Value of $10,000 invested 5 years ago: $ 32,686

Fiscal Year Ending Dec. 31

	1995	% Change	1994	% Change	1993	% Change
Revenues (Million $)						
1Q	35.97	-20%	44.78	26%	35.42	85%
2Q	36.90	NM	36.78	-3%	37.85	81%
3Q	—	—	31.81	-15%	37.31	-8%
4Q	—	—	42.97	11%	38.71	-29%
Yr.	—	—	156.3	5%	149.3	10%
Income (Million $)						
1Q	2.83	-75%	11.23	NM	11.26	NM
2Q	0.71	16%	0.61	-89%	5.64	NM
3Q	—	—	-26.42	NM	11.28	1%
4Q	—	—	9.68	128%	4.24	-83%
Yr.	—	—	-4.90	NM	32.42	-15%
Earnings Per Share ($)						
1Q	0.08	-74%	0.31	-3%	0.32	NM
2Q	0.02	NM	0.02	-88%	0.17	NM
3Q	E-0.01	NM	-0.80	NM	0.33	NM
4Q	E-0.03	NM	0.27	145%	0.11	-85%
Yr.	E0.06	NM	-0.15	NM	0.93	-17%

Next earnings report expected: early November

Biogen, Inc.

Business Summary - 04-SEP-95

Biogen Inc. is a leading biotechnology company whose revenues are currently derived from products that are being sold by licensees or affiliates in various countries. During 1994, licensees generated total sales of $1.7 billion from these products, up from $1.5 billion in 1993. In the future, the company expects to derive additional revenues from the sale of proprietary products. Europe accounted for 41% of 1994 royalties and product sales, the U.S. for 31%, Japan 19%, and other 9%

	1994	1993	1992
Royalties & product sales	90%	91%	90%
R&D fees	Nil	Nil	2%
Interest	10%	9%	8%

Royalties are derived primarily from licensee sales of hepatitis B vaccines, alpha interferon and diagnostics. The company holds several important patents related to hepatitis B antigens produced by genetic engineering techniques. These antigens are used in recombinant hepatitis B vaccines sold primarily by licensees SmithKline Beecham and Merck. Hepatitis B vaccine sales by licensees exceeded $1 billion in 1994 ($750 million in 1993).

Biogen has also licensed rights to its recombinant alpha interferon (a naturally occurring protein produced by normal white blood cells) to Schering-Plough, which sells the product worldwide under the name Intron-A to treat hairy cell leukemia, hepatitis B & C, genital warts, and Kaposi's sarcoma. Sales of Intron A totaled $426 million in 1994 ($572 million in 1993). The company has also licensed Abbott Laboratories and others to market hepatitis B diagnostic kits.

Phase III clinical trials on the company's new Avonex beta interferon treatment for multiple sclerosis were completed in 1994, and Biogen has filed for regulatory approval. The research pipeline also includes therapeutics for respiratory and inflammatory diseases, certain cancers, AIDS and other ailments.

Important Developments

Aug. '95—Biogen signed a major collaborative research agreement for the development of human gene therapy treatments with Genovo, a gene therapy R&D concern. Under the agreement, BGEN will invest over $35 million in Genovo over five years, based on milestone achievements. The initial focus of the research will be on diseases such as cystic fibrosis and familial hypercholesterolemia. In July, Biogen filed for regulatory approval in Canada for its new Avonex treatment for multiple sclerosis. Filings were made in the U.S. and Europe in May.

Capitalization

Long Term Debt: $23,333,000 (6/95).
Warrants: To buy 1,800,000 com. shs. at $17 ea.

Per Share Data ($) (Year Ended Dec. 31)

	1994	1993	1992	1991	1990	1989
Tangible Bk. Val.	9.71	9.85	8.77	7.53	3.06	2.91
Cash Flow	0.10	1.13	1.33	0.32	0.22	0.15
Earnings	-0.15	0.93	1.12	0.15	0.07	0.01
Dividends	Nil	Nil	Nil	Nil	Nil	Nil
Payout Ratio	Nil	Nil	Nil	Nil	Nil	Nil
Prices - High	55¾	47¾	49¾	49	29⅜	18¼
- Low	27¼	24¼	18¼	24¼	14⅜	7⅛
P/E Ratio - High	NM	51	44	NM	NM	NM
- Low	NM	26	16	NM	NA	NA

Income Statement Analysis (Million $)

	1994	%Chg	1993	%Chg	1992	%Chg	1991
Revs.	140	3%	136	10%	124	102%	61.4
Oper. Inc.	22.6	-34%	34.4	-22%	44.1	NM	3.9
Depr.	8.1	21%	6.7	-7%	7.1	41%	5.1
Int. Exp.	Nil	—	Nil	—	Nil	—	Nil
Pretax Inc.	-1.9	NM	34.6	-13%	39.9	NM	7.4
Eff. Tax Rate	NM	—	6.40%	—	4.10%	—	3.50%
Net Inc.	-4.9	NM	32.4	-15%	38.3	NM	7.2

Balance Sheet & Other Fin. Data (Million $)

	1994	1993	1992	1991	1990	1989
Cash	268	270	228	186	104	110
Curr. Assets	295	309	268	209	121	120
Total Assets	378	357	311	253	158	145
Curr. Liab.	47.9	31.8	26.2	14.1	12.7	6.0
LT Debt	Nil	Nil	Nil	Nil	Nil	Nil
Common Eqty.	330	325	285	239	76.0	70.0
Total Cap.	330	325	285	239	146	139
Cap. Exp.	40.5	10.8	9.4	8.4	11.1	3.1
Cash Flow	3.2	39.1	45.5	9.6	5.6	3.6

Ratio Analysis

	1994	1993	1992	1991	1990	1989
Curr. Ratio	6.2	9.7	10.2	14.9	9.5	19.9
% LT Debt of Cap.	Nil	Nil	Nil	Nil	Nil	Nil
% Net Inc.of Revs.	NM	23.8	31.0	11.7	15.4	11.3
% Ret. on Assets	NM	9.6	13.4	3.1	5.0	2.8
% Ret. on Equity	NM	10.5	14.4	2.6	2.5	0.3

Dividend Data —No cash dividends have been paid on the common shares.

Data as orig. reptd.; bef. results of disc. opers. and/or spec. items. Per share data adj. for stk. divs. as of ex-div. date. E-Estimated. NA-Not Available. NM-Not Meaningful. NR-Not Ranked.

Office—14 Cambridge Center, Cambridge, MA 02142. **Tel**—(617) 252-9200. **Chrmn & CEO**—J. L. Vincent. **Pres**—J. R. Tobin. **VP-Fin, CFO & Treas**—T. M. Kish. **VP & Secy**—M. J. Astrue. **Investor Contact**—R. E. N. Lundberg (617-679-2822). **Dirs**—A. G. Bearn, A. Belzer, H. W. Buirkle, R. H. Morley, K. Murray, P. A. Sharp, J. W. Stevens, J. R. Tobin, J. L. Vincent. **Transfer Agent & Registrar**—State Street Bank & Trust Co., Boston. **Incorporated** in Massachusetts in 1988; predecessor company incorporated in Netherlands Antilles in 1979. **Empl**-331. **S&P Analyst:** H. B. Saftlas

STANDARD & POOR'S

STOCK REPORTS

Black Hills Corp.

NYSE Symbol **BKH**

In S&P MidCap 400

29-SEP-95 **Industry:** Utilities-Electric

Summary: This energy services company operates Black Hills Power and Light Co., and is engaged in the mining and sale of sub-bituminous coal, and oil and gas exploration and production.

Quantitative Evaluations

Outlook (1 Lowest—5 Highest) • **1+**

Fair Value • **20¾**

Risk • **Average**

Earn./Div. Rank • **A**

Technical Eval. • **Bullish** since 7/95

Rel. Strength Rank (1 Lowest—99 Highest) • **59**

Insider Activity • **NA**

Recent Price • 24½ | 52 Wk Range • 25⅞-17¾ | Yield • 5.5% | 12-Mo. P/E • 13.9

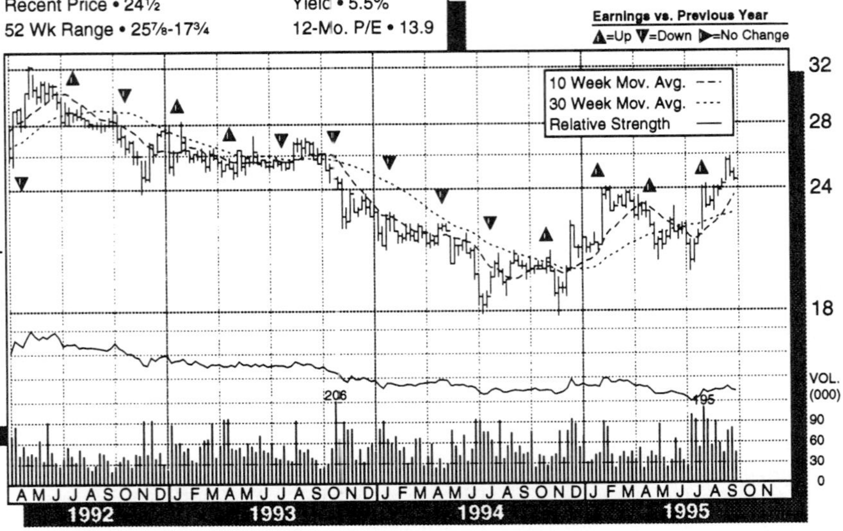

Business Profile - 28-SEP-95

BKH recently began operating its new, low cost, 80 mw plant in Wyoming, ahead of schedule and under budget. Regulators granted the company a 6.76% rate increase (two-thirds of the requested increase) for service to South Dakota customers, who constitute 85% of its total market. The new rate will also apply to a long term wholesale contract with nearby Montana-Dakota Utilities beginning in 1997. BKH's electric power costs are among the lowest in the U.S. due its use of coal for power generation.

Operational Review - 27-SEP-95

Year to year revenue growth in the 1995 first half was only fractional due to mild winter weather. Although operating margins were hurt by a sharp spike in administrative and general costs and an 8.6% increase in depreciation, depletion and amortization expense, strong profit gains in the coal mining segment combined with cost recoveries through the allowance for funds used during construction helped generate a 14% gain in net income.

Stock Performance - 22-SEP-95

In the past 30 trading days, BKH's shares have increased 5%, compared to a 5% rise in the S&P 500. Average trading volume for the past five days was 8,840 shares, compared with the 40-day moving average of 14,259 shares.

Key Stock Statistics

Dividend Rate/Share	1.34	Shareholders	7,100
Shs. outstg. (M)	14.4	Market cap. (B)	$0.353
Avg. daily vol. (M)	0.014	Inst. holdings	23%
Tang. Bk. Value/Share	12.34	Insider holdings	NA
Beta	0.83		

Value of $10,000 invested 5 years ago: $ 17,213

Fiscal Year Ending Dec. 31

	1995	% Change	1994	% Change	1993	% Change
Revenues (Million $)						
1Q	35.94	NM	35.66	4%	34.38	6%
2Q	34.60	NM	34.49	5%	32.92	2%
3Q	—	—	38.59	6%	36.30	3%
4Q	—	—	36.66	2%	35.77	1%
Yr.	—	—	145.4	4%	139.4	3%
Income (Million $)						
1Q	6.00	3%	5.80	-5%	6.10	9%
2Q	5.64	29%	4.38	-4%	4.58	-18%
3Q	—	—	6.98	16%	6.01	-4%
4Q	—	—	6.64	6%	6.26	1%
Yr.	—	—	23.81	4%	22.95	-3%
Earnings Per Share ($)						
1Q	0.42	2%	0.41	-9%	0.45	10%
2Q	0.39	26%	0.31	-6%	0.33	-20%
3Q	—	—	0.49	11%	0.44	-4%
4Q	—	—	0.45	2%	0.44	-2%
Yr.	—	—	1.66	NM	1.66	-4%

Next earnings report expected: late October

Black Hills Corp.

Business Summary - 29-SEP-95

Black Hills Corp. provides electricity (72% of 1994 revenues, 54% of net income) to 53,959 customers in a 9,300-square-mile area of western South Dakota, northeastern Wyoming and southeastern Montana. Its South Dakota area, which includes Rapid City, accounts for 85% of total electric sales. Principal industries served are tourism; cattle and sheep raising, farming and meat packing; and lumbering, mining and light manufacturing. BKH also engages in coal mining (20%; 41%) and oil and gas production (8%; 5%). Electric revenues in recent years were divided:

	1994	1993	1992	1991
Residential	28%	29%	28%	29%
General/commercial	35%	34%	33%	33%
Industrial	27%	28%	30%	29%
Other	10%	9%	9%	9%

Electric utility plant capacity is rated at 283 mw; coal is the dominant (99%) fuel BKH uses in electric generation. Peak demand for electricity in 1994 was 279 mw, with a forecasted 10-year, compound annual growth rate of about 2.1% for summer and 2.4% for winter. The utility also has 75 mw of additonal base load power available under a 40-year purchased power agreement with PacifiCorp's Pacific Power & Light subsidiary. The new 80-megawatt coal-fired plant, Neil Simpson Unit #2, near Gillette, Wy. was put into service in August 1995, increasing the rate base 55% and net plant roughly 3.7 mw.

Between September 1994 and July 1995, BKH issued a total of $90 million of bonds with interest ranging from 8.06% to 6.5% and maturities from 15 to 7 years to finance the $121 million Neil Simpson Unit #2 facility. Borrowings under its $41 million bank lines were $3.3 million at June 30, 1995.

The Wyodak Resources Development Corp. unit is a coal mining business with estimated reserves of 186 million tons, 30 million of which are committed for sale to the Wyodak plant. BKH's Western Production Co. is an oil production, exploration and operating company with interests in the Rocky Mountain region and Texas.

Important Developments

Aug. '95—The company received a 6.76% rate increase for its South Dakota customers as of August 1, 1995, in a rate case settlement that specified that BKH will not file for any increase in rates or invoke a fuel or purchased power automatic tariff to take effect during a rate freeze period ending January 1, 2000. The rate freeze excludes certain specified events such as material tax increases, forced outages at both its plants and certain other similar extreme events.

Capitalization

Long Term Debt: $158,362,000 (6/95).

Per Share Data ($)

(Year Ended Dec. 31)

	1994	1993	1992	1991	1990	1989
Tangible Bk. Val.	12.19	11.78	10.89	10.38	9.69	9.31
Earnings	1.66	1.66	1.73	1.66	1.68	1.60
Dividends	1.32	1.28	1.24	1.17	1.09	1.01
Payout Ratio	80%	77%	72%	71%	65%	63%
Prices - High	$22\frac{3}{4}$	$28\frac{1}{4}$	$32\frac{1}{4}$	$28\frac{5}{8}$	$20\frac{3}{4}$	20
- Low	$17\frac{3}{4}$	$21\frac{7}{8}$	$23\frac{3}{4}$	$19\frac{3}{8}$	17	$16\frac{5}{8}$
P/E Ratio - High	14	17	19	17	12	12
- Low	11	13	14	12	10	10

Income Statement Analysis (Million $)

	1994	%Chg	1993	%Chg	1992	%Chg	1991
Revs.	145	4%	139	3%	135	2%	133
Depr.	17.7	10%	16.1	16%	13.9	16%	12.0
Maint.	NA	—	6.9	6%	6.5	-3%	6.7
Fxd. Chgs. Cov.	4.3	-13%	4.9	4%	4.7	-5%	5.0
Constr. Credits	4.0	NM	0.7	92%	0.4	111%	0.2
Eff. Tax Rate	30%	—	28%	—	27%	—	27%
Net Inc.	23.8	4%	22.9	-3%	23.6	4%	22.7

Balance Sheet & Other Fin. Data (Million $)

	1994	1993	1992	1991	1990	1989
Gross Prop.	520	433	413	391	355	331
Cap. Exp.	28.7	27.3	25.6	25.6	22.2	10.1
Net Prop.	364	289	280	268	244	230
Capitalization:						
LT Debt	129	85.3	88.8	88.8	79.0	78.9
% LT Debt	42	34	37	40	37	38
Pfd.	Nil	Nil	Nil	Nil	Nil	Nil
% Pfd.	Nil	Nil	Nil	Nil	Nil	Nil
Common	175	168	149	142	135	127
% Common	58	66	63	60	63	62
Total Cap.	350	296	282	276	256	247

Ratio Analysis

	1994	1993	1992	1991	1990	1989
Oper. Ratio	80.5	79.3	79.4	79.8	83.7	83.9
% Earn. on Net Prop.	8.7	10.1	10.2	10.5	8.7	8.8
% Ret. on Revs.	16.4	16.5	17.5	17.0	18.0	18.3
% Ret. On Invest.Cap	10.5	10.7	11.6	11.5	11.0	10.7
% Return On Com.Eqty	13.6	13.7	15.8	16.0	16.9	16.6

Dividend Data —Dividends have been paid since 1942. A dividend reinvestment plan is available.

Amt. of Div. $	Date Decl.	Ex-Div. Date	Stock of Record	Payment Date
0.330	Oct. 26	Nov. 04	Nov. 10	Dec. 01 '94
0.335	Jan. 30	Feb. 06	Feb. 10	Mar. 01 '95
0.335	Apr. 27	May. 08	May. 12	Jun. 01 '95
0.335	Jul. 25	Aug. 09	Aug. 11	Sep. 01 '95

Data as orig. reptd.; bef. results of disc opers. and/or spec. items. Per share data adj. for stk. divs. as of ex-div. date. E-Estimated. NA-Not Available. NM-Not Meaningful. NR-Not Ranked.

Office—625 Ninth St., Rapid City, SD 57709. **Tel**—(605) 348-1700. **Chrmn & Pres**—D. P. Landguth. **SVP-Fin, CFO & Investor Contact**—Dale E. Clement. **Secy-Treas**—R. R. Basham. **Dirs**—G. C. Barber, B. B. Brundage, D. E. Clement, K. E. Dean, M. B. Enzi, J. R. Howard, E. E. Hoyt, K. S. Jorgensen, D. P. Landguth. **Transfer Agent & Registrar**—Chemical Bank, NYC. **Incorporated** in South Dakota in 1941. **Empl**-452. **S&P Analyst:** Jane Collin

STANDARD & POOR'S

STOCK REPORTS

Bob Evans Farms

NASDAQ Symbol **BOBE**

In S&P MidCap 400

31-AUG-95 **Industry:** Food serving

Summary: This company operates a chain of about 355 family-style restaurants in 19 states, and produces and distributes a variety of pork sausage products.

Quantitative Evaluations

Outlook
(1 Lowest—5 Highest)
• **4-**

Fair Value
• **18¾**

Risk
• **Low**

Earn./Div. Rank
• **A**

Technical Eval.
• **Bearish** since 7/95

Rel. Strength Rank
(1 Lowest—99 Highest)
• **10**

Insider Activity
• **NA**

Recent Price • 18⅝
52 Wk Range • 22⅝-18½

Yield • 1.7%
12-Mo. P/E • 14.3

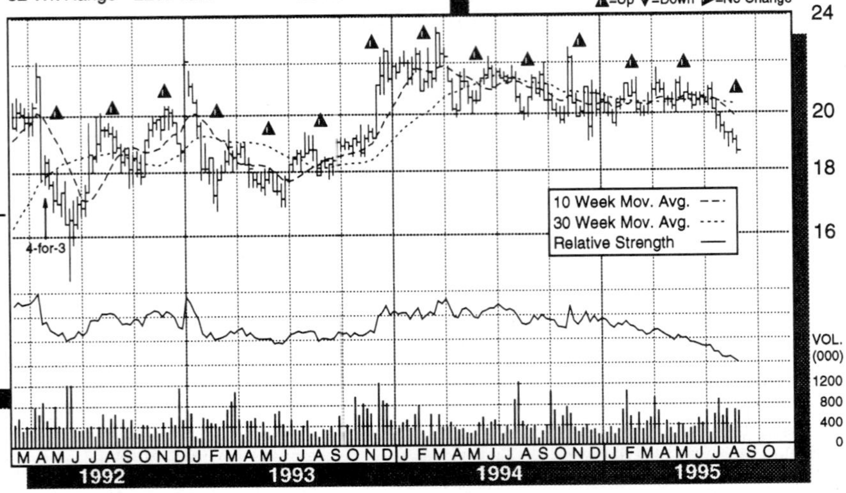

Business Profile - 31-AUG-95

Bob Evans Farms plans to expand through the addition of new restaurants; the expansion into new territories; the introduction of new high-quality products; acquisitions in both the restaurant and food products segments; and an effort to become known for its dinner menu as well as its popular breakfast offerings. Except for a decline in 1989-90, earnings have been in a long-term uptrend, and analysts are projecting double-digit EPS growth in 1995-6 (April).

Operational Review - 31-AUG-95

Net sales in the 13 weeks ended July 28, 1995, rose slightly, year to year, reflecting additional restaurants in operation and increased pounds of sausage products sold, partly offset by lower same-store sales and lower contributions from charcoal and salad products. Benefiting from wider sausage margins due to lower live hog costs, net income advanced. The company plans to open 13 restaurants in the second quarter of 1995-96, and 35 to 40 units in the full fiscal year.

Stock Performance - 25-AUG-95

In the past 30 trading days, BOBE's shares have declined 7%, compared to a 0.04% rise in the S&P 500. Average trading volume for the past five days was 128,160 shares, compared with the 40-day moving average of 116,592 shares.

Key Stock Statistics

Dividend Rate/Share	0.32	Shareholders	29,500
Shs. outstg. (M)	42.6	Market cap. (B)	$0.781
Avg. daily vol. (M)	0.107	Inst. holdings	41%
Tang. Bk. Value/Share	7.97	Insider holdings	NA
Beta	0.89		

Value of $10,000 invested 5 years ago: $ 19,144

Fiscal Year Ending Apr. 30

	1996	% Change	1995	% Change	1994	% Change
Revenues (Million $)						
1Q	205.9	4%	197.9	11%	178.4	12%
2Q	—	—	194.4	10%	177.0	8%
3Q	—	—	185.6	11%	166.6	-2%
4Q	—	—	189.0	7%	176.9	10%
Yr.	—	—	767.0	10%	699.0	7%
Income (Million $)						
1Q	14.40	9%	13.18	12%	11.82	14%
2Q	—	—	14.16	14%	12.41	12%
3Q	—	—	13.90	14%	12.20	7%
4Q	—	—	12.26	4%	11.75	15%
Yr.	—	—	53.51	11%	48.18	12%
Earnings Per Share ($)						
1Q	0.34	10%	0.31	11%	0.28	12%
2Q	—	—	0.34	13%	0.30	15%
3Q	—	—	0.33	14%	0.29	7%
4Q	—	—	0.29	4%	0.28	12%
Yr.	—	—	1.27	10%	1.15	12%

Next earnings report expected: early December

Bob Evans Farms

Business Summary - 31-AUG-95

Bob Evans Farms, Inc. operates family restaurants and produces a wide variety of pork sausage products. As a result of a general decline in the consumption of pork sausage, the company plans to continue to develop new food products to meet changes in consumer demand. In 1994-95, contributions to sales and pretax income by business segment were:

	Sales	Income
Restaurants	72%	69%
Food products	28%	31%

At August 14, 1995, BOBE was operating 366 family-style restaurants in 19 states, with the largest number of restaurants located in Ohio; other areas of concentration include Indiana, Michigan, Florida and Pennsylvania. The restaurants are typically open from 6 a.m. to 10 p.m. Sunday through Thursday, with extended hours on Friday and Saturday. Restaurants feature sausage products, with emphasis on breakfast entrees served all day.

New restaurant concepts continue to be developed. During 1990-91, the company opened its first Bob Evans General Store and Restaurant, combining a gift shop, bakery and 200 seat restaurant under one roof; several more General Stores have since been opened. The opening of the first Cantina del Rio in April 1992 was part of a planned chain of Mexican style restaurants located in Columbus, Ohio. A "small town" Bob Evans restaurant, designed to reduce building and operating costs, was developed in 1992-93. In 1994-95, the company opened 44 new restaurants; 35 to 40 new restaurants are planned for 1995-96.

The food products segment produces and distributes about 30 varieties of fresh, smoked and fully cooked pork sausage and ham products under the brand names Bob Evans Farms and Owens Country Sausage. In recent years, the company has begun to emphasize both new product development and sale of pork sausage and ham products to institutional and foodservice customers. In addition, BOBE is exploring the expansion of the products offered in its food products segment through the acquisition of companies producing food and food related products that complement the company's traditional sausage products.

Mrs. Giles Country Kitchens produces several lines of refrigerated delicatessen salads under the Mrs. Giles and Bob Evans Farms brand names. Hickory Specialties produces premium quality charcoal, wood smoking chips, natural smoke flavorings, gas grill ceramic briquets and grilling systems.

Important Developments

Sep. '95—The dividend was raised more than 10%, with the September 1995 payment. In July, directors authorized the repurchase of up to 500,000 shares.

Capitalization

Long Term Debt: $2,250,000 (4/28/95).

Per Share Data ($)

(Year Ended Apr. 30)

	1995	1994	1993	1992	1991	1990
Tangible Bk. Val.	9.00	7.97	7.04	6.23	5.72	5.11
Cash Flow	1.88	1.70	1.52	1.37	1.22	1.05
Earnings	1.27	1.15	1.03	0.94	0.80	0.65
Dividends	0.29	0.26	0.24	0.21	0.19	0.19
Payout Ratio	22%	23%	23%	22%	24%	30%
Cal. Yrs.	1994	1993	1992	1991	1990	1989
Prices - High	23½	22⅝	22⅜	20	11⅜	12⅛
- Low	19	16¾	14¾	10¼	8½	9¾
P/E Ratio - High	19	20	22	21	14	19
- Low	15	15	14	11	11	15

Income Statement Analysis (Million $)

	1995	%Chg	1994	%Chg	1993	%Chg	1992
Revs.	767	10%	699	7%	653	17%	556
Oper. Inc.	113	13%	100	10%	90.7	17%	77.7
Depr.	25.8	12%	23.1	11%	20.8	18%	17.7
Int. Exp.	0.6	NM	0.1	-11%	0.1	-59%	0.2
Pretax Inc.	86.9	14%	76.5	12%	68.5	10%	62.4
Eff. Tax Rate	38%	—	37%	—	37%	—	37%
Net Inc.	53.5	11%	48.2	12%	43.1	10%	39.3

Balance Sheet & Other Fin. Data (Million $)

	1995	1994	1993	1992	1991	1990
Cash	10.5	8.1	10.2	10.6	25.2	15.4
Curr. Assets	52.4	47.4	42.9	41.4	46.2	31.1
Total Assets	488	414	361	326	287	261
Curr. Liab.	85.6	59.6	44.8	45.0	38.5	33.5
LT Debt	2.3	Nil	Nil	1.2	1.6	2.0
Common Eqty.	394	349	309	274	242	219
Total Cap.	403	354	316	281	249	227
Cap. Exp.	94.8	72.9	53.6	45.0	28.6	32.8
Cash Flow	79.3	71.3	79.3	57.0	51.0	44.8

Ratio Analysis

	1995	1994	1993	1992	1991	1990
Curr. Ratio	0.6	0.8	1.0	0.9	1.2	0.9
% LT Debt of Cap.	0.6	Nil	Nil	0.4	0.6	0.9
% Net Inc.of Revs.	7.0	6.9	6.6	7.1	6.7	6.1
% Ret. on Assets	11.8	12.4	12.5	12.8	12.4	11.1
% Ret. on Equity	14.4	14.6	14.7	15.2	14.7	13.1

Dividend Data —Cash has been paid in each year since 1964. A dividend reinvestment plan is available.

Amt. of Div. $	Date Decl.	Ex-Div. Date	Stock of Record	Payment Date
0.073	Aug. 08	Aug. 15	Aug. 19	Sep. 01 '94
0.073	Oct. 28	Nov. 14	Nov. 18	Dec. 01 '94
0.073	Jan. 27	Feb. 13	Feb. 17	Mar. 01 '95
0.073	Apr. 28	May. 15	May. 19	Jun. 01 '95
0.080	Aug. 15	Aug. 22	Aug. 24	Sep. 01 '95

Data as orig. reptd.; bef. results of disc. opers. and/or spec. items. Per share data adj. for stk. divs. as of ex-div. date. E-Estimated. NA-Not Available. NM-Not Meaningful. NR-Not Ranked.

Office—3776 S. High St., Box 07863, Station G, Columbus, OH 43207-0863. **Tel**—(614) 491-2225. **Chrmn, CEO & Secy**—D. E. Evans. **EVP & COO**—S. K. Owens. **CFO & Treas**—D. J. Radkoski. **Dirs**—L. C. Corbin, D. E. Evans, J. T. Evans, D. A. Fronk, C. L. Krueger, G. R. Lucas II, S. K. Owens, R. E. H. Rabold, R. S. Wood. **Transfer Agent & Registrar**—Co. itself. **Incorporated** in Ohio in 1957; reincorporated in Delaware in 1985. **Empl**-28,300. **S&P Analyst:** Efraim Levy

STANDARD & POOR'S

STOCK REPORTS

Borland International

NASDAQ Symbol **BORL**

In S&P MidCap 400

05-AUG-95 **Industry:** Data Processing

Summary: Borland is primarily engaged in the sale of software tools and database software for personal computers.

S&P Opinion: Hold (★★★)	Recent Price • 11¼	Yield • Nil
	52 Wk Range • 14⅜-6	12-Mo. P/E • NM

Quantitative Evaluations

Outlook (1 Lowest—5 Highest)
• **1**

Fair Value
• **8⅝**

Risk
• **High**

Earn./Div. Rank
• **C**

Technical Eval.
• **Bullish** since 5/95

Rel. Strength Rank (1 Lowest—99 Highest)
• **17**

Insider Activity
• **NA**

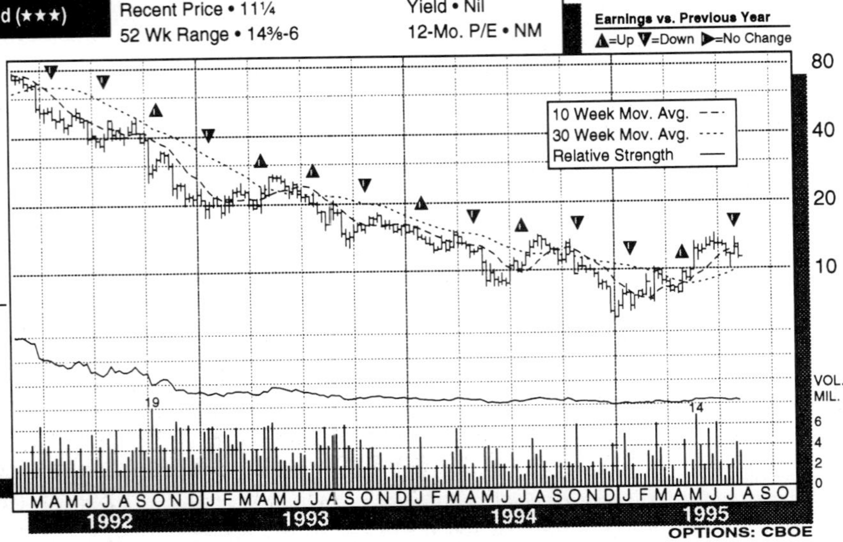

Overview - 03-AUG-95

While first quarter revenues were penalized by the absence of a non-recurring $24.5 million sale of Paradox licenses to Novell, revenues in fiscal 1995-96 are expected to advance modestly, reflecting acceptance of new tools products, including Delphi, the well reviewed application development tool; database segment revenues should advance in the second half of the fiscal year on new product upgrades. The company returned to profitability in the first quarter, primarily on expense reduction actions including workforce cuts and the consolidation of certain operations. Profitability should be maintained through fiscal 1995-96 year-end, on contributions from new products and the lower cost structure.

Valuation - 03-AUG-95

The shares, in a downtrend since 1992, have worked their way higher since the beginning of 1995, reflecting expectations of improving operating performance as well as the build-in of a takeover premium. Revenue growth from new products, namely Delphi, combined with several significant restructuring and expense reduction programs returned the company to profitability in the first quarter of fiscal 1995-96. This improved operating performance, combined with the favorable resolution of certain legal issues regarding huge copyright infringement damages, makes Borland an attractive acquisition candidate. However, uncertainties remain including risks associated with the continued acceptance of new products. We believe the shares will track the market in the months ahead.

Key Stock Statistics

S&P EPS Est. 1996	0.40	Tang. Bk. Value/Share	4.45
P/E on S&P Est. 1996	28.1	Beta	1.89
Dividend Rate/Share	Nil	Shareholders	3,900
Shs. outstg. (M)	27.8	Market cap. (B)	$0.313
Avg. daily vol. (M)	0.589	Inst. holdings	29%
		Insider holdings	NA

Value of $10,000 invested 5 years ago: $ 11,392

Fiscal Year Ending Mar. 31

	1996	% Change	1995	% Change	1994	% Change
Revenues (Million $)						
1Q	53.77	-22%	69.14	-44%	123.4	7%
2Q	—	—	81.29	-24%	107.4	-16%
3Q	—	—	48.14	-57%	111.7	7%
4Q	—	—	55.50	9%	51.05	-56%
Yr.	—	—	254.1	-35%	393.5	-15%
Income (Million $)						
1Q	2.81	-95%	61.37	NM	6.19	NM
2Q	—	—	0.35	-88%	2.83	-47%
3Q	—	—	-22.92	NM	-2.88	-95%
4Q	—	—	-50.98	NM	-76.02	NM
Yr.	—	—	-12.18	NM	-69.89	NM
Earnings Per Share ($)						
1Q	0.10	-95%	1.88	NM	0.22	NM
2Q	E0.10	—	0.01	-91%	0.11	-45%
3Q	E0.10	—	-0.80	NM	-0.11	NM
4Q	E0.10	—	-1.86	NM	-2.84	NM
Yr.	E0.40	—	-0.43	NM	-2.62	NM

Next earnings report expected: late October

STANDARD & POOR'S
STOCK REPORTS

Borland International

05-AUG-95

Business Summary - 03-AUG-95

Borland International designs and markets computer software products both for businesses and for software developers. Its key products run on personal computers that operate under the MS-DOS operating system and MS-Windows operating environment, although certain versions of the products also run under other operating systems including various UNIX-based operating systems. The company uses object-oriented programming, which increases the functionality of its applications and simplifies the software development process.

The company has two principal product families: language and database products. BORL is a leader in the design and marketing of computer language compilers and other software development tools. Such products assist users in developing new programs in certain computer languages and in translating them into machine language (instructions capable of being read and executed by a computer). Products include Borland C++, Turbo C++, Turbo Pascal and Delphi.

Database products include dBASE IV (acquired with Ashton-Tate in October 1991), a relational database management system that features the dBASE programming language; Paradox, a relational database management system known for its ease of use; and Interbase, a relational database management system that operates on minicomputers and workstations.

Other offerings include SideKick, a utility program that performs simple tasks, such as calendar, calculator and notebook functions, and ReportSmith, a database report writer. In June 1994, the company sold its Quattro Pro electronic spreadsheet to Novell for $110 million.

Products are sold worldwide, primarily through independent distributors, dealers and original equipment manufacturers (OEMs) and also directly to corporate, governmental and educational customers and to individual end-users.

Important Developments

Apr. '95—In the fourth quarter of fiscal 1994-5, the company recorded a $50 million restructuring charge ($1.49 a share after tax), primarily to reflect costs associated with further workforce reductions, outsourcing its manufacturing operations, and closing several international operations, as well as asset write-downs and certain other non-cash charges.

Oct. '94—In the first half of 1994-5, BORL recorded a $16.2 million ($0.48 a share) write-off of in-process R&D associated with its acquisition of ReportSmith. It also recorded a $99.9 million pretax gain ($2.58 after tax) on the sale of its Quattro Pro spreadsheet product line to Novell, as well as $24.5 million in revenue from the related sale to Novell of 1,000,000 licenses for the Paradox database.

Capitalization

Long Term Debt: $18,116,000 (6/95).

Per Share Data ($) (Year Ended Mar. 31)

	1995	1994	1993	1992	1991	1990
Tangible Bk. Val.	4.45	4.41	7.01	8.68	5.88	4.03
Cash Flow	0.37	-1.72	-1.01	-3.09	2.16	1.19
Earnings	-0.43	-2.62	-1.87	-4.29	1.81	0.90
Dividends	Nil	Nil	Nil	Nil	Nil	Nil
Payout Ratio	Nil	Nil	Nil	Nil	Nil	Nil
Cal. Yrs.	1994	1993	1992	1991	1990	1989
Prices - High	16	27¼	86¾	83½	32	10½
- Low	6	12¾	19¾	27⅞	9⅞	9⅝
P/E Ratio - High	NM	NM	NM	NM	18	12
- Low	NM	NM	NM	NM	5	10

Income Statement Analysis (Million $)

	1995	%Chg	1994	%Chg	1993	%Chg	1992
Revs.	254	-36%	394	-15%	464	-4%	483
Oper. Inc.	-37.3	NM	-18.8	NM	3.3	-93%	46.5
Depr.	22.5	-6%	24.0	5%	22.8	-26%	31.0
Int. Exp.	2.0	25%	1.6	47%	1.1	-19%	1.3
Pretax Inc.	-9.0	NM	-63.0	NM	-41.0	NM	-124
Eff. Tax Rate	NM	—	NM	—	NM	—	NM
Net Inc.	-12.0	NM	-70.0	NM	-49.0	NM	-109

Balance Sheet & Other Fin. Data (Million $)

	1995	1994	1993	1992	1991	1990
Cash	70.0	68.0	75.0	110	42.0	43.0
Curr. Assets	104	116	175	240	83.0	66.0
Total Assets	245	298	342	365	136	87.0
Curr. Liab.	101	158	130	107	40.0	22.0
LT Debt	10.1	11.3	9.8	9.8	10.0	10.2
Common Eqty.	123	120	188	228	85.0	54.0
Total Cap.	133	132	198	238	95.0	64.0
Cap. Exp.	7.0	52.2	73.7	59.4	29.0	2.9
Cash Flow	10.3	-45.9	-26.5	-79.5	32.0	15.7

Ratio Analysis

	1995	1994	1993	1992	1991	1990
Curr. Ratio	1.0	0.7	1.3	2.3	2.1	2.9
% LT Debt of Cap.	7.6	8.6	4.9	4.1	10.5	15.8
% Net Inc.of Revs.	NM	NM	NM	NM	11.8	10.4
% Ret. on Assets	NM	NM	NM	NM	23.7	16.0
% Ret. on Equity	NM	NM	NM	NM	38.0	27.1

Dividend Data (No cash dividends have been paid.)

Data as orig. reptd.; bef. results of disc. opers. and/or spec. items. Per share data adj. for stk. divs. as of ex-div. date. E-Estimated. NA-Not Available. NM-Not Meaningful. NR-Not Ranked.

Office—1800 Green Hills Rd., Scotts Valley, CA 95066. **Tel**—(408) 438-8400. **Chrmn, Pres & CEO**—P. Kahn. **SVP-Fin, CFO & Investor Contact**—Gary A. Wetsel. **VP & Secy**—R. H. Kohn. **Dirs**—D. C. Chance, S. M. Dow, G. Hara, D. Heller, P. R. Kahn, D. Little. **Transfer Agents & Registrars**—Chemical Trust Co. of California, SF; Ravensbourne Registration Services Ltd., Beckenham, Kent, England. **Incorporated** in Delaware in 1989. **Empl-** 1,650. **S&P Analyst:** Peter C. Wood, CFA

STANDARD & POOR'S

STOCK REPORTS

Bowater Inc.

NYSE Symbol **BOW**
In S&P MidCap 400

31-AUG-95 **Industry:** Paper/Products

Summary: This leading newsprint manufacturer also makes coated paper, directory and uncoated specialties, market pulp and lumber. BOW plans to divest its communications paper operations.

S&P Opinion: Accumulate (★★★★)

Recent Price • 47⅞ | Yield • 1.3%
52 Wk Range • 54⅜-23⅜ | 12-Mo. P/E • 16.1

Quantitative Evaluations

Outlook
(1 Lowest—5 Highest)
• **2+**

Fair Value
• **44⅛**

Risk
• **Average**

Earn./Div. Rank
• **B-**

Technical Eval.
• **Bearish** since 8/95

Rel. Strength Rank
(1 Lowest—99 Highest)
• **59**

Insider Activity
• **Unfavorable**

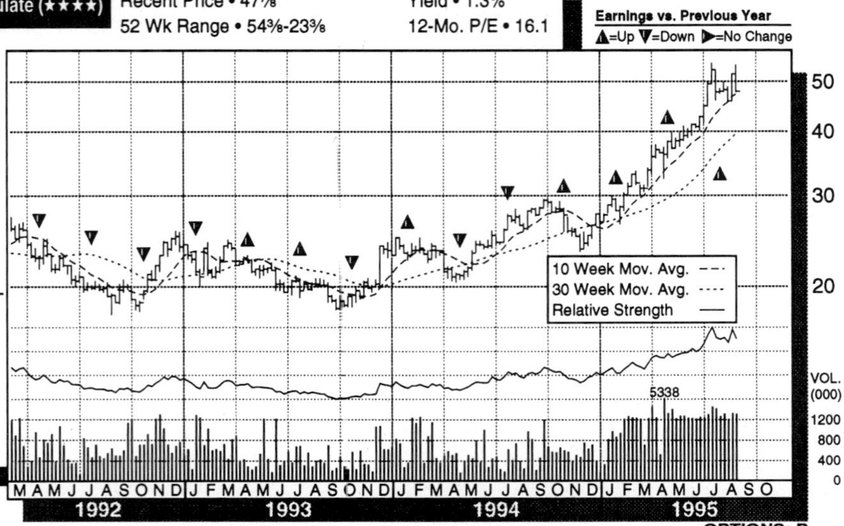

OPTIONS: P

Overview - 31-AUG-95

Sales should be strongly higher in 1995, as relatively healthy global economies are likely to generate continued solid demand for newsprint, pulp and coated paper products. Despite efforts of newspapers and publishers to cut back on their paper consumption, tight supply conditions should allow steep prices to remain in effect. Margins are expected to widen significantly on the favorable pricing conditions, along with aggressive cost reduction programs implemented in recent years. BOW's cost trimming continued in the second quarter of 1995, when it announced an additional 20% reduction of its salaried workforce. Margins should also be helped by Bowater's current focus on reducing debt, but nonrecurring items are likely to be less favorable, as a $24 million pretax charge was recognized for the workforce reductions.

Valuation - 31-AUG-95

Bowater's shares have surged since late 1994, as significantly improved market conditions for the company's products stimulated a vast turnaround in its operating performance. Although moderating U.S. economic conditions could jeopardize the uptrend, tight supply conditions should allow industry strength to extend into 1996. A further spark might also be provided by the recent downturn in long-term interest rates. Despite their sharp appreciation, BOW's shares appear undervalued in their recent trading range of six to seven times our EPS forecast for 1996.

Key Stock Statistics

S&P EPS Est. 1995	6.40	Tang. Bk. Value/Share	19.26
P/E on S&P Est. 1995	7.5	Beta	1.54
S&P EPS Est. 1996	8.00	Shareholders	6,600
Dividend Rate/Share	0.60	Market cap. (B)	$ 1.9
Shs. outstg. (M)	38.8	Inst. holdings	99%
Avg. daily vol. (M)	0.383	Insider holdings	NA

Value of $10,000 invested 5 years ago: $ 21,675

Fiscal Year Ending Dec. 31

	1995	% Change	1994	% Change	1993	% Change
Revenues (Million $)						
1Q	449.5	46%	308.9	-11%	348.9	-6%
2Q	486.8	52%	320.1	-3%	328.7	-8%
3Q	—	—	348.1	4%	335.7	-8%
4Q	—	—	381.9	12%	340.4	-15%
Yr.	—	—	1,359	NM	1,354	-9%
Income (Million $)						
1Q	45.05	NM	-21.44	NM	-22.95	NM
2Q	59.83	NM	-14.88	NM	-15.61	NM
3Q	—	—	10.53	NM	-30.83	NM
4Q	—	—	20.97	NM	4.89	NM
Yr.	—	—	-4.82	NM	-64.50	NM
Earnings Per Share ($)						
1Q	1.02	NM	-0.67	NM	-0.65	NM
2Q	1.35	NM	-0.53	NM	-0.45	NM
3Q	E1.93	NM	0.16	NM	-0.86	NM
4Q	E2.10	NM	0.44	NM	0.12	NM
Yr.	E6.40	NM	-0.59	NM	-1.84	NM

Next earnings report expected: mid October

Bowater Inc.

Business Summary - 31-AUG-95

Bowater Inc. is the largest producer of newsprint in the U.S., and the second largest in North America (newsprint operations accounted for 41% of revenues in 1995). Its annual newsprint capacity represents about 8% of the North American total. The company also produces coated paper (20% of revenues), directory and uncoated specialties (11%), market pulp (9%), communications papers (13%) and lumber and other products (6%).

Exports accounted for 13% of net sales in 1994.

The company manufactures pulp and paper products at fully integrated facilities in Tennessee, South Carolina, Maine and Nova Scotia. Operations are supported by some 3.7 million acres of owned and leased timberlands. A significant portion of BOW's newsprint tonnage is produced through joint ventures with major publishers, including Calhoun Newsprint Co. (49%-owned by Advance Publications, Inc.) and Bowater Mersey Paper Co. (49%-owned by The Washington Post).

Coated paper produced by BOW is used in special interest magazines, mail order catalogs, advertising pieces, textbooks and coupons. Bowater Communication Papers (which BOW has slated for sale) makes continuous stock computer forms at eight plants in the U.S. BOW also operates three sawmills.

In addition to furnishing its own pulp requirements, Bowater shipped 256,404 tons of bleached kraft market pulp in 1994 to manufacturers of fine papers, tissues and other paper products; BOW's timberland holdings provided 48% of its wood requirements in 1994.

Important Developments

Jul. '95—Bowater recorded pretax charges of $24 million in the second quarter of 1995 for the implementation of a program to reduce its salaried workforce by another 20%.
Jul. '95—The company repurchased $117 million of 8.25% notes, due October 1999, for which it would record a special charge of $5.3 million ($0.12 a share) in the third quarter of 1995. The transaction was part of BOW's effort to reduce its debt to capital ratio to 30% by 1996, and followed the retirement of $182 million of debt in 1995's first quarter (for which a special charge of $6.1 million or $0.14 a share was recorded).
May '95—The company announced that it planned to sell its Bowater Communication Papers Inc. unit, which had $190 million of sales in 1994. Bowater retained CS First Boston to advise on the sale.

Capitalization

Long Term Debt: $934,104,000 (6/95).
Minority Interests: $135,587,000.
LIBOR Preferred Stock: 1,500,000 shs. ($1 par).
7% Series B Conv. Pfd.: 1,223,404 shs. ($1 par).
8.4% Series C. Cum Pfd.: 850,000 shs. ($1 par).

Per Share Data ($) (Year Ended Dec. 31)

	1994	1993	1992	1991	1990	1989
Tangible Bk. Val.	19.08	18.53	20.90	24.48	24.42	23.49
Cash Flow	4.01	2.65	1.84	4.84	5.61	6.83
Earnings	-0.59	-1.84	-2.64	1.15	2.30	3.86
Dividends	0.60	0.60	1.20	1.20	1.20	1.14
Payout Ratio	NM	NM	NM	104%	52%	29%
Prices - High	29 5/8	24 5/8	27 1/4	30 3/8	28 1/2	34 1/8
- Low	20 3/8	18	17 5/8	18 5/8	16 1/8	25 3/4
P/E Ratio - High	NM	NM	NM	26	12	9
- Low	NM	NM	NM	16	7	7

Income Statement Analysis (Million $)

	1994	%Chg	1993	%Chg	1992	%Chg	1991
Revs.	1,359	NM	1,354	-9%	1,494	16%	1,289
Oper. Inc.	210	75%	120	29%	93.0	-61%	236
Depr.	168	3%	163	NM	162	23%	132
Int. Exp.	99	-2%	101	27%	79.7	75%	45.6
Pretax Inc.	-7.0	NM	-108	NM	-171	NM	69.0
Eff. Tax Rate	NM	—	NM	—	NM	—	37%
Net Inc.	-5.0	NM	-64.0	NM	-93.0	NM	46.0

Balance Sheet & Other Fin. Data (Million $)

	1994	1993	1992	1991	1990	1989
Cash	155	82.0	166	28.0	18.0	92.0
Curr. Assets	514	419	459	386	283	357
Total Assets	2,851	2,726	2,882	2,780	2,298	2,284
Curr. Liab.	211	239	266	282	223	246
LT Debt	1,117	1,118	1,120	840	488	504
Common Eqty.	755	732	818	943	935	907
Total Cap.	2,483	2,342	2,472	2,428	2,068	2,030
Cap. Exp.	216	79.0	139	131	150	389
Cash Flow	147	96.0	67.0	174	200	245

Ratio Analysis

	1994	1993	1992	1991	1990	1989
Curr. Ratio	2.4	1.8	1.7	1.4	1.3	1.5
% LT Debt of Cap.	45.0	47.8	45.3	34.6	23.6	24.8
% Net Inc.of Revs.	NM	NM	NM	3.5	6.3	10.0
% Ret. on Assets	NM	NM	NM	1.8	3.8	7.0
% Ret. on Equity	NM	NM	NM	4.4	8.9	16.0

Dividend Data —Quarterly dividends were initiated in 1984. A dividend reinvestment plan is available. A "poison pill" stock purchase rights plan was adopted in 1986.

Amt. of Div. $	Date Decl.	Ex-Div. Date	Stock of Record	Payment Date
0.150	Aug. 24	Sep. 02	Sep. 10	Oct. 03 '94
0.150	Nov. 16	Dec. 06	Dec. 12	Jan. 02 '95
0.150	Feb. 22	Mar. 06	Mar. 10	Apr. 03 '95
0.150	May. 24	Jun. 08	Jun. 12	Jul. 03 '95
0.150	Aug. 23	Sep. 07	Sep. 11	Oct. 02 '95

Data as orig. reptd.; bef. results of disc. opers. and/or spec. items. Per share data adj. for stk. divs. as of ex-div. date. E-Estimated. NA-Not Available. NM-Not Meaningful. NR-Not Ranked.

Office—55 East Camperdown Way, P. O. Box 1028, Greenville, SC 29602. **Tel**—(803) 271-7733. **Chrmn**—A. P. Gammie. **Pres & CEO**—A. M. Nemirow. **SVP-CFO**—R. C. Lancaster. **Secy**—W. C. Shiba. **Investor Contact**—Don D'Antuono (803) 282-9370. **Dirs**—F. J. Aguilar, H. D. Aycock, R. Barth, K. M. Curtis, A. P. Gammie, H. G. MacNeill, D. R. Melville, A. M. Nemirow, J. A. Rolls. **Transfer Agent & Registrar**—Bank of New York, NYC. **Incorporated** in Delaware in 1964. **Empl**-6,000. **S&P Analyst:** Michael W. Jaffe

STANDARD & POOR'S

Brinker International

STOCK REPORTS

NYSE Symbol **EAT**
In S&P MidCap 400

17-OCT-95 **Industry:** Food serving

Summary: This rapidly growing company operates or franchises about 420 Chili's restaurants, plus more than 130 other restaurants which are part of other chains.

S&P Opinion: Avoid (★★)

Recent Price • 13⅝
52 Wk Range • 23⅞-13⅛
Yield • Nil
12-Mo. P/E • 13.9

Quantitative Evaluations
Outlook
(1 Lowest—5 Highest)
• **5-**
Fair Value
• **21⅜**
Risk
• **Average**
Earn./Div. Rank
• **B+**

Technical Eval.
• **Bearish** since 8/95
Rel. Strength Rank
(1 Lowest—99 Highest)
• **11**
Insider Activity
• **Neutral**

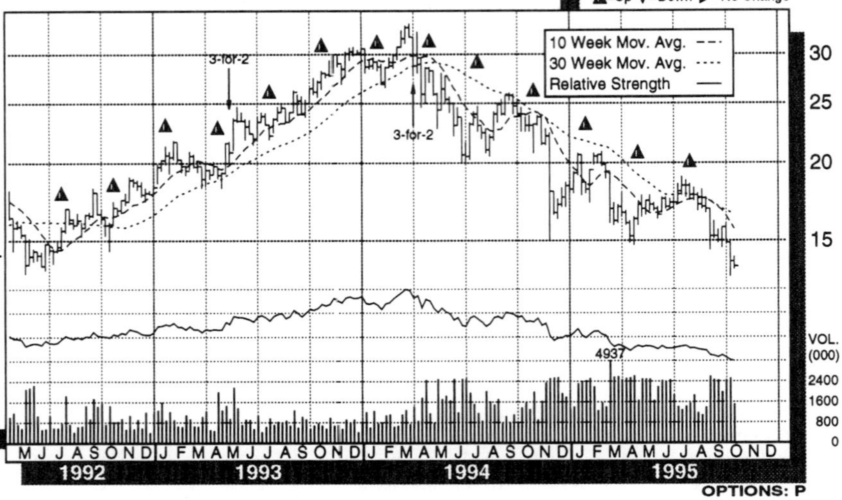

OPTIONS: P

Overview - 17-OCT-95

In fiscal 1996, we expect revenue growth for this restaurant operator to largely come from additional restaurants being open. We look for EAT's comparable-unit sales to be no better than flat with the year-ago level. Also, efforts to improve customer's dining experience is likely to cause at least some near-term margin pressure. Overall, we view fiscal 1996 as a transition year for EAT, in which the company implements some changes in its expansion strategy for various chains. There could be some charges related to restaurant closings. Also, we expect EAT's recent acquisition of the Maggiano's Little Italy and Corner Bakery businesses to be mildly dilutive to fiscal 1996 earnings.

Valuation - 17-OCT-95

We view the stock of this restaurant company as an attractive holding for capital gains. Although the profit outlook for fiscal 1996 is disappointing, we expect that efforts to improve customer's dining experience, and revised plans for allocation of expansion capital, will bear more fruit in subsequent years. Starting in fiscal 1997, we look for EAT to generate annual earnings growth of about 15%. In the U.S., EAT's portfolio of restaurant chains should provide future opportunities to cluster several units at attractive sites, and offer other ways to cross-promote sales. Overall, we see the stock of this company as a means of participating in the expected long-term movement of U.S. consumers toward casual dining restaurants.

Key Stock Statistics

S&P EPS Est. 1996	1.00	Tang. Bk. Value/Share	6.89
P/E on S&P Est. 1996	13.6	Beta	1.64
Dividend Rate/Share	Nil	Shareholders	2,400
Shs. outstg. (M)	76.6	Market cap. (B)	$ 1.1
Avg. daily vol. (M)	0.478	Inst. holdings	66%
		Insider holdings	NA

Value of $10,000 invested 5 years ago: $ 20,980

Fiscal Year Ending Jun. 30

	1995	% Change	1994	% Change	1993	% Change
Revenues (Million $)						
1Q	247.1	20%	205.4	36%	151.2	22%
2Q	246.6	16%	212.2	40%	151.9	25%
3Q	268.5	20%	224.5	36%	164.7	25%
4Q	280.0	18%	236.4	28%	185.1	31%
Yr.	1,042	19%	878.5	35%	652.9	26%
Income (Million $)						
1Q	18.55	26%	14.76	36%	10.84	29%
2Q	16.07	24%	13.00	22%	10.63	41%
3Q	18.24	14%	16.00	25%	12.82	38%
4Q	19.88	11%	17.89	22%	14.65	40%
Yr.	72.74	18%	61.61	26%	48.93	37%
Earnings Per Share ($)						
1Q	0.25	25%	0.20	29%	0.16	30%
2Q	0.22	29%	0.17	13%	0.15	42%
3Q	0.25	19%	0.21	17%	0.18	35%
4Q	0.27	12%	0.24	20%	0.20	32%
Yr.	0.98	18%	0.83	20%	0.69	36%

Next earnings report expected: mid October

Brinker International

Business Summary - 17-OCT-95

Brinker International (formerly Chili's, Inc.) is a large operator and franchisor of casual dining restaurants. In fiscal 1995, systemwide sales for all its restaurant concepts totaled $1.3 billion.

In EAT's largest restaurant chain, Chili's Grill & Bar, there were 424 units in operation as of June 1995. Of these, 316 were operated by EAT, and 108 were franchise units. The full-service, casual-atmosphere restaurants have a limited menu, including hamburgers, fajitas, chicken, seafood entrees, sandwiches, barbecued ribs, salads, appetizers and desserts. Entree prices range from about $3.85 to $9.95. Also, there is full bar service. Including alcoholic beverages, the average per-person revenue per meal has been about $8.45. In fiscal 1995, the Chili's chain grew by about 64 units.

Also, EAT operates the Romano's Macaroni Grill chain, which is an upscale Italian-theme concept. As of June 1995, this chain included about 51 (nearly all company-operated). There were 16 Macaroni Grill openings in fiscal 1995. Average per-person revenue per meal has been about $13.50. EAT's Spageddies chain is a moderately priced Italian-food concept. The first such unit opened in July 1992, and as of June 1995, there were about 16 Spageddies open (at least 10 company operated). Also, EAT operates more than 40 Grady's American Grill restaurants, which are casual, upscale dinnerhouses. Average per-person revenue per meal has been about $10.75.

In May 1994, EAT acquired the On the Border chain, which offers a casual Tex-Mex theme. As of June 1995, this chain included about 16 company-operated and five franchise units. Also, EAT is developing the Cozymel chain of casual, upscale Mexican-type restaurants. As of June 1995, there were three units open.

Important Developments

Aug. '95—EAT indicated that fiscal 1996's per share earnings could be relatively flat, year to year. Also, EAT expects 95-to-100 company restaurants, and 30-to-35 franchise units to open in fiscal 1996. More than one-third of the new company-operated restaurants, and most of the franchise units would be in the Chili's chain. Among EAT's other businesses, development of the Macaroni Grill and On-the-Border chains is likely to be faster than previously expected. However, the number of unit openings expected has been reduced for the Grady's and Spageddies chains. Also, EAT has formed a strategic alliance with Lettuce Entertain You Enterprises of Chicago. In the first step, EAT has acquired Lettuce's three-unit Maggiano's Little Italy and five-unit Corner Bakery food-service concepts for four million shares of EAT common stock.

Capitalization

Long Term Debt: $103,086,000 (6/95).

Per Share Data ($)

(Year Ended Jun. 30)

	1995	1994	1993	1992	1991	1990
Tangible Bk. Val.	6.89	5.78	4.88	3.91	3.24	2.30
Cash Flow	1.77	1.38	1.12	0.83	0.65	0.64
Earnings	0.98	0.83	0.69	0.51	0.41	0.33
Dividends	Nil	Nil	Nil	Nil	Nil	Nil
Payout Ratio	Nil	Nil	Nil	Nil	Nil	Nil
Prices - High	20⅞	33⅝	30⅞	18⅜	16⅞	7⅞
- Low	14¾	15	18¼	13¼	6	5
P/E Ratio - High	21	41	45	36	41	24
- Low	15	18	27	26	15	15

Income Statement Analysis (Million $)

	1995	%Chg	1994	%Chg	1993	%Chg	1992
Revs.	1,042	19%	878	34%	653	26%	519
Oper. Inc.	167	23%	136	32%	103	40%	73.5
Depr.	58.6	41%	41.6	33%	31.3	41%	22.2
Int. Exp.	2.9	163%	1.1	40%	0.8	-38%	1.3
Pretax Inc.	111	17%	95.4	26%	75.8	39%	54.5
Eff. Tax Rate	35%	—	35%	—	36%	—	35%
Net Inc.	72.7	18%	61.6	26%	48.9	37%	35.7

Balance Sheet & Other Fin. Data (Million $)

	1995	1994	1993	1992	1991	1990
Cash	38.8	3.6	5.5	10.1	23.9	7.1
Curr. Assets	94.0	47.2	30.9	30.9	42.3	23.2
Total Assets	733	559	435	337	266	198
Curr. Liab.	96.4	103	74.9	62.2	40.1	41.6
LT Debt	103	5.7	3.8	4.2	4.8	12.2
Common Eqty.	497	417	335	254	207	132
Total Cap.	613	435	347	270	221	152
Cap. Exp.	184	115	121	91.0	'112	57.0
Cash Flow	131	103	80.2	57.9	43.3	32.4

Ratio Analysis

	1995	1994	1993	1992	1991	1990
Curr. Ratio	1.0	0.5	0.4	0.5	1.1	0.6
% LT Debt of Cap.	16.8	1.3	1.1	1.5	2.2	8.0
% Net Inc.of Revs.	7.0	7.0	7.5	6.9	6.1	5.2
% Ret. on Assets	11.3	12.2	12.4	11.7	10.7	9.6
% Ret. on Equity	15.9	16.1	16.2	15.4	14.7	16.2

Dividend Data —No cash has been paid. Stock splits of 3-for-2 each were effected in March 1994, May 1993, November and March 1991, and June 1989.

Data as orig. reptd.; bef. results of disc. opers. and/or spec. items. Per share data adj. for stk. divs. as of ex-div. date. E-Estimated. NA-Not Available. NM-Not Meaningful. NR-Not Ranked.

Office—6820 LBJ Freeway, Dallas, TX 75240. **Tel**—(214) 980-9917. **Chrmn**—N. E. Brinker. **Pres & CEO**—R. A. McDougall. **COO**—C. L. Ford, III. **EVP-CFO & Investor Contact**—Debra L. Smithart. **EVP-Secy**—R. F. Thomson. **Dirs**—N. E. Brinker, F. L. Cardwell Jr., J. W. Evans, R. F. Evans, C. L. Ford III, J. M. Haggar Jr., J. I. Harris, F. B. Humphries, R. L. Hunt, R. A. McDougall, J. E. Oesterreicher, W. F. Regas, D. Smithart, R. T. Staubach, R. F. Thomson. **Transfer Agent & Registrar**—Chemical Mellon Shareholder Services, Dallas. **Incorporated** in Delaware in 1983. **Empl**-37,500. **S&P Analyst:** Tom Graves, CFA

STANDARD & POOR'S

STOCK REPORTS

Brooklyn Union Gas

NYSE Symbol **BU**
In S&P MidCap 400

16-OCT-95 **Industry:** Utilities-Gas

Summary: BU distributes natural gas in three New York City boroughs, has operations in gas exploration and production and invests in gas cogeneration and pipeline/storage projects.

S&P Opinion: Hold (★★★) | Recent Price • 25½ | 52 Wk Range • 26⅜-21½ | Yield • 5.5% | 12-Mo. P/E • 13.7

Quantitative Evaluations

Outlook
(1 Lowest—5 Highest)
• 2+

Fair Value
• 23⅛

Risk
• Low

Earn./Div. Rank
• A-

Technical Eval.
• **Bullish** since 8/95

Rel. Strength Rank
(1 Lowest—99 Highest)
• 62

Insider Activity
• NA

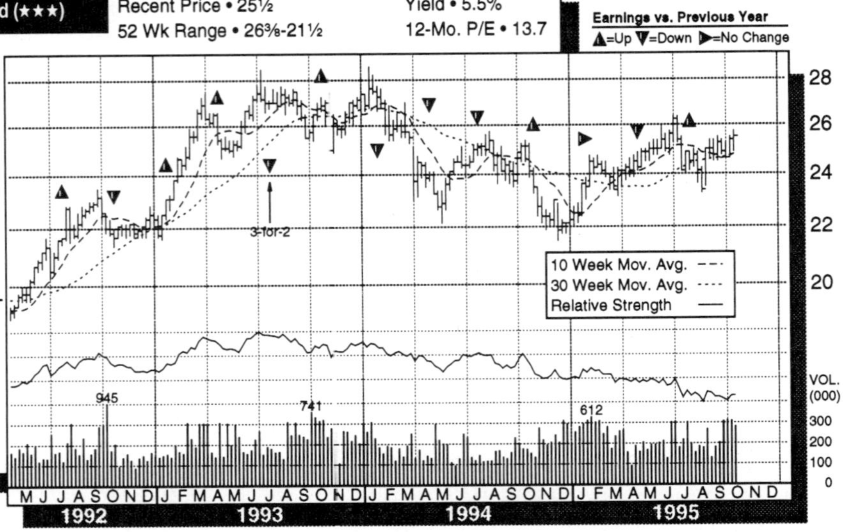

Overview - 16-OCT-95

Utility profits in fiscal 1995 should move slightly higher on increased gas sales to new, large customers, including multifamily dwelling complexes, schools and two cogeneration plants. While we believe weather-normalized gas sales will rise only 3% annually to the end of the decade as BU's mature single-family-home gas market generates only marginal growth, we expect margins will widen over the next three years due to regulatory approval of a rate plan helps the company lower its cost structure. Expansion of non-utility businesses in the U.S. and Canada, particularly those involved in gas exploration, production, marketing, pipeline transportation and storage, combined with the use of derivatives and hedging to offset low effective wellhead prices are helping boost earnings in fiscal 1995 .

Valuation - 16-OCT-95

Although BU shares have moved up a substantial 14.6% in the current year to date period, the rate of appreciation has not kept pace with broader market averages. Still, BU's customers and shareholders should eventually benefit nonetheless from performance-based incentives designed to boost earnings under a three-year rate plan approved in late 1994. Reported share earnings are flat through the 1995 nine months, but cash generated from operating activities remains strong and should continue to support BU's dividend yield, which compares favorably with the average for the gas industry, as does BU's P/E ratio.

Key Stock Statistics

S&P EPS Est. 1995	1.90	Tang. Bk. Value/Share	16.27
P/E on S&P Est. 1995	13.4	Beta	0.41
S&P EPS Est. 1996	1.95	Shareholders	35,200
Dividend Rate/Share	1.39	Market cap. (B)	$ 1.2
Shs. outstg. (M)	48.5	Inst. holdings	28%
Avg. daily vol. (M)	0.071	Insider holdings	NA

Value of $10,000 invested 5 years ago: $ 16,670

Fiscal Year Ending Sep. 30

	1995	% Change	1994	% Change	1993	% Change
Revenues (Million $)						
1Q	358.4	-4%	371.5	7%	347.3	12%
2Q	481.6	-12%	549.0	12%	489.0	13%
3Q	217.7	-10%	240.7	15%	208.5	14%
4Q	—	—	177.5	11%	160.3	8%
Yr.	—	—	1,339	11%	1,206	12%
Income (Million $)						
1Q	42.84	2%	42.16	4%	40.53	10%
2Q	73.64	NM	73.55	2%	71.83	23%
3Q	-6.10	NM	-7.60	NM	-6.65	NM
4Q	—	—	-20.73	NM	-29.14	NM
Yr.	—	—	87.38	14%	76.56	28%
Earnings Per Share ($)						
1Q	0.90	NM	0.90	-3%	0.93	9%
2Q	1.53	-3%	1.57	-4%	1.63	21%
3Q	-0.13	NM	-0.16	NM	-0.15	NM
4Q	E-0.40	NM	-0.44	NM	-0.66	NM
Yr.	E1.90	3%	1.85	7%	1.73	28%

Next earnings report expected: late October

Brooklyn Union Gas

Business Summary - 13-OCT-95

The Brooklyn Union Gas Company distributes natural gas in a service area of about 187 square miles in New York City, including the boroughs of Brooklyn and Staten Island and part of Queens, with an estimated population of four million. Firm volume sales in fiscal 1994 totaled 133.5 Bcf, up from 129.0 Bcf in fiscal 1993, as the number of heating degree days rose to 4,974 (normal is 4,824), from 4,802. Weather-normalization adjustment in rates largely offsets variations in revenues due to abnormal weather during the heating season.

Subsidiaries include Gas Energy Inc. and Gas Energy Cogeneration Inc., which participate in cogeneration projects; BRING Gas Services Corp., which sells gas produced by affiliates and others and arranges transportation services; North East Transmission Co., which has an 11% interest in the Iroquois Gas Transmission System, a 375-mile pipeline that supplies more than 650 MMcf of Canadian gas daily to 25 northeastern local distribution companies and power generators; and Fuel Resources Inc., which engages in gas exploration, development, production and marketing. At September 30, 1994, proved gas reserves totaled 110,225 MMcf. Non-regulated energy-related investments provided earnings of $0.22 a share in fiscal 1994.

The company obtains most of its gas supply through long-term contracts with natural gas sellers, including Amerada Hess and Mobil. In fiscal 1994, 64% of its gas supply came from long-term domestic contracts. Other sources of supply include stored and Canadian gas and a liquefied natural gas plant.

The New York Public Service Commission approved a three-year rate plan in October 1994 that allows BU to retain 75 out of the first 100 basis points of earnings above the allowed rate of return on utility common equity, and 50% thereafter based on improvements in operating efficiencies, off-system sales and increased customer satisfaction.

Important Developments

Aug. '95—BU filed a plan with the New York State Public Service Commission to reorganize gas distribution operations into a holding company that it expects will allow it to take advantage of business opportunities and compete more agressively in the open market. In February, BU formed a gas-marketing joint venture with Pennzoil, PennUnion Energy Services, L.L.C., to sell competitively priced natural gas to varied markets including electric generators, natural gas producers, local distribution companies and market cooperatives or other aggregations designed to manage gas price fluctuations.

Capitalization

Long Term Debt: $724,429,000 (6/95).
Red. Cum. Preferred Stock: $6,900,000.

Per Share Data ($)

(Year Ended Sep. 30)

	1994	1993	1992	1991	1990	1989
Tangible Bk. Val.	16.27	15.55	14.55	14.37	13.69	13.36
Earnings	1.85	1.73	1.35	1.45	1.43	1.68
Dividends	1.35	1.32	1.29	1.26	1.22	1.18
Payout Ratio	73%	76%	96%	86%	85%	70%
Prices - High	28$\frac{5}{8}$	28$\frac{1}{2}$	23$\frac{1}{2}$	20$\frac{7}{8}$	21$\frac{1}{2}$	21$\frac{1}{2}$
- Low	21$\frac{1}{2}$	21$\frac{5}{8}$	18$\frac{5}{8}$	18	16$\frac{5}{8}$	15$\frac{3}{8}$
P/E Ratio - High	15	16	17	14	15	13
- Low	12	12	14	12	12	9

Income Statement Analysis (Million $)

	1994	%Chg	1993	%Chg	1992	%Chg	1991
Revs.	1,339	11%	1,206	12%	1,075	8%	991
Depr.	70.0	8%	65.0	20%	54.2	27%	42.7
Maint.	54.0	-2%	55.0	4%	53.0	2%	51.8
Fxd. Chgs. Cov.	3.4	NM	3.4	12%	3.0	3%	2.9
Constr. Credits	NA	—	NA	—	NA	—	NA
Eff. Tax Rate	32%	—	35%	—	33%	—	28%
Net Inc.	87.4	14%	76.6	28%	59.9	-3%	61.8

Balance Sheet & Other Fin. Data (Million $)

	1994	1993	1992	1991	1990	1989
Gross Prop.	1,876	1,729	1,615	1,504	1,381	1,282
Cap. Exp.	277	205	173	148	134	158
Net Prop.	1,405	1,306	1,229	1,151	1,063	989
Capitalization:						
LT Debt	701	689	682	685	534	553
% LT Debt	47	49	52	51	49	51
Pfd.	7.2	7.5	7.8	44.5	45.4	46.3
% Pfd.	0.50	0.50	0.60	3.30	4.20	4.30
Common	774	721	632	608	510	485
% Common	52	51	48	45	47	45
Total Cap.	1,735	1,580	1,478	1,483	1,223	1,214

Ratio Analysis

	1994	1993	1992	1991	1990	1989
Oper. Ratio	90.0	88.8	90.8	90.4	90.6	89.9
% Earn. on Net Prop.	9.9	9.7	8.3	8.6	9.1	10.4
% Ret. on Revs.	6.5	6.4	5.6	6.2	5.7	6.6
% Ret. On Invest.Cap	8.4	8.2	6.9	7.6	8.3	9.3
% Return On Com.Eqty	11.6	10.8	8.7	9.6	9.8	12.1

Dividend Data —Dividends have been paid since 1949. A dividend reinvestment plan is available.

Amt. of Div. $	Date Decl.	Ex-Div. Date	Stock of Record	Payment Date
0.338	Sep. 29	Oct. 04	Oct. 11	Nov. 01 '94
0.348	Dec. 21	Dec. 27	Jan. 03	Feb. 01 '95
0.348	Mar. 22	Mar. 29	Apr. 04	May. 01 '95
0.348	Jun. 28	Jul. 07	Jul. 11	Aug. 01 '95
0.348	Sep. 27	Oct. 05	Oct. 10	Nov. 01 '95

Data as orig. reptd.; bef. results of disc opers. and/or spec. items. Per share data adj. for stk. divs. as of ex-div. date. E-Estimated. NA-Not Available. NM-Not Meaningful. NR-Not Ranked.

Office—One MetroTech Center, Brooklyn, NY 11201-3851. **Tel**—(718) 403-2000. **Pres & CEO**—R. B. Catell. **Sr VP & CFO**—V. D. Enright. **VP & Secy**—H. E. H. Knight Jr. **Investor Contact**—Jan C. Childress. **Dirs**— R. B. Catell, K. I. Chenault, A. S. Christensen, D. H. Elliott, A. H. Fishman, E. D. Miller, R. Pratt Jr., J. Q. Riordan. **Transfer Agent & Registrar**—First Chicago Trust Co. of New York, Jersey City, N.J. **Incorporated** in New York in 1895. **Empl**-3,506. **S&P Analyst:** Jane Collin

STANDARD & POOR'S

STOCK REPORTS

Brush Wellman

NYSE Symbol **BW**
In S&P MidCap 400

06-SEP-95 **Industry:** Metal

Summary: This company is a worldwide supplier of beryllium alloy products.

S&P Opinion: Hold (★★★)

Recent Price • 20⅝
52 Wk Range • 23⅝-14⅜
Yield • 1.9%
12-Mo. P/E • 16.5

Quantitative Evaluations

Outlook
(1 Lowest—5 Highest)
• **3+**

Fair Value
• **20**

Risk
• **Average**

Earn./Div. Rank
• **B-**

Technical Eval.
• **Bearish** since 8/95

Rel. Strength Rank
(1 Lowest—99 Highest)
• **23**

Insider Activity
• **NA**

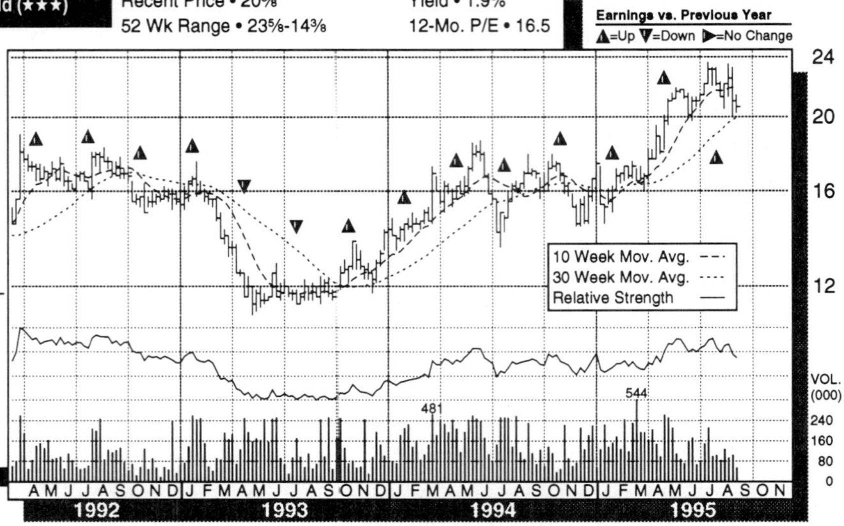

Overview - 06-SEP-95

BW operates in a volatile and very competitive business environment. Foreign exchange fluctuations and commodity prices directly affect gross margin results. Customers in BW's larger target markets continually change production processes, sometimes rendering certain supply parts obsolete. To remain competitive, BW must continually develop new products and lower production costs, which sometimes requires large increases in capital expenditures and research and development costs. About 50% of BW's total revenues are from sales of beryllium alloy products. BW's Alloy 174 is BW's fastest growing beryllium alloy offering, and is targeted to the automotive electronics market. BW plans to make a large capital commitment to expand 174 capacity to meet higher anticipated demand. Margins for 174 are lower than other beryllium alloys.

Valuation - 05-SEP-95

After record earnings results in 1994, profits, though increasing, are growing at a decreasing rate. The rebounding U.S. dollar should put pressure on BW's international sales for the balance of 1995. Shares of BW are currently trading at a P/E of 15 (based on estimated 1995 EPS of $1.35), which is 75% of BW's 10-year average P/E of 20. The light metals industry is trading at an average P/E of 11. Due to the stronger dollar, continued higher copper prices and expected flattening of 1996 car sales, BW shares should be held only by nimble traders.

Key Stock Statistics

S&P EPS Est. 1995	1.35	Tang. Bk. Value/Share	11.92
P/E on S&P Est. 1995	15.3	Beta	1.27
S&P EPS Est. 1996	1.55	Shareholders	2,600
Dividend Rate/Share	0.40	Market cap. (B)	$0.341
Shs. outstg. (M)	16.1	Inst. holdings	65%
Avg. daily vol. (M)	0.018	Insider holdings	NA

Value of $10,000 invested 5 years ago: $ 11,614

Fiscal Year Ending Dec. 31

	1995	% Change	1994	% Change	1993	% Change
Revenues (Million $)						
1Q	98.91	17%	84.79	22%	69.38	2%
2Q	97.28	12%	86.56	22%	70.85	5%
3Q	—	—	86.73	13%	76.82	22%
4Q	—	—	87.79	12%	78.43	17%
Yr.	—	—	345.9	17%	295.5	12%
Income (Million $)						
1Q	6.79	21%	5.59	NM	1.15	-73%
2Q	6.68	13%	5.89	NM	0.16	-95%
3Q	—	—	2.43	46%	1.66	47%
4Q	—	—	4.63	33%	3.48	67%
Yr.	—	—	18.55	187%	6.46	-38%
Earnings Per Share ($)						
1Q	0.42	20%	0.35	NM	0.07	-73%
2Q	0.40	11%	0.36	NM	0.01	-95%
3Q	E0.27	80%	0.15	50%	0.10	43%
4Q	E0.26	-7%	0.28	27%	0.22	69%
Yr.	E1.35	18%	1.14	185%	0.40	-38%

Next earnings report expected: late October

Brush Wellman

Business Summary - 06-SEP-95

Brush Wellman is the world's only fully integrated producer of products containing beryllium, and also supplies specialty metal systems and precious metal products. International sales, principally to western Europe and Asia, comprised 33% and 29% of total sales in 1994 and 1993, respectively.

Beryllium-containing products include beryllium alloys (principally beryllium copper), metallic beryllium and beryllia ceramic, which have high thermal and electrical conductivity, strength and hardness, excellent corrosion, wear and fatigue resistance, and good formability. Beryllium alloys are used in computer components and other electronic devices; as well as by the automobile electronics, telecommunications, energy development, and other consumer and industrial markets, including in molds used by the plastics industry. Alloy 174 is BW's fastest growing Beryllium alloy product. Alloy 174's selling price is one-half of BW's flagship Beryllium copper alloy products. BW anticipates significantly increased demand for Alloy 174, especially from the automoble electronics market. BW is expected to make a large capital commitment to increase Alloy 174 capacity.

Beryllium metal is the preferred material for many aerospace and defense components such as those used in guidance systems, satellite structures, optical platforms, mirrors and telescopes. Beryllia ceramic is an effective electrical insulator used in automotive and power electronic systems, cellular telephones, thermoelectric cooling systems and lasers.

Specialty clad metals produced by Technical Materials, Inc. are used for the high-speed production of complex electronic and electrical components. Williams Advanced Materials makes precious metal products for a variety of high reliability applications in electrical and electronic interconnection, packaging and processing markets. In October 1994, Williams acquired Hydrostatics, Inc., a manufacturer of fine, precious metal wire for semiconductor microelectronic packaging applications.

Important Developments

Aug. '95—The company said that it has found a new commercial application for its vapor deposition process in BW's precious metal products unit. BW anticipates that 1996 revenues from its vapor deposition process will more than offset $24 million of lost frame lid assemblies sales to semiconductor manufacturers.

Capitalization

Long Term Debt: $18,397,000 (6/95).

Per Share Data ($)

(Year Ended Dec. 31)

	1994	1993	1992	1991	1990	1989
Tangible Bk. Val.	11.59	10.70	10.49	10.10	13.43	13.10
Cash Flow	2.35	1.75	1.90	-0.30	2.58	2.35
Earnings	1.14	0.40	0.65	-1.72	1.09	1.10
Dividends	0.26	0.20	0.26	0.59	0.71	0.67
Payout Ratio	23%	50%	40%	NM	65%	58%
Prices - High	18⅝	17½	19	20	25¼	30¼
- Low	13⅜	11	12¼	9½	11½	20¼
P/E Ratio - High	16	44	29	NM	23	28
- Low	12	28	19	NM	11	18

Income Statement Analysis (Million $)

	1994	%Chg	1993	%Chg	1992	%Chg	1991
Revs.	346	17%	295	11%	265	NM	267
Oper. Inc.	47.3	37%	34.6	-10%	38.4	-14%	44.8
Depr.	19.6	-10%	21.7	7%	20.2	-42%	34.9
Int. Exp.	2.4	-24%	3.2	-17%	3.8	-13%	4.4
Pretax Inc.	23.0	199%	7.7	-44%	13.7	NM	-36.2
Eff. Tax Rate	19%	—	16%	—	24%	—	NM
Net Inc.	18.6	186%	6.5	-38%	10.5	NM	-27.5

Balance Sheet & Other Fin. Data (Million $)

	1994	1993	1992	1991	1990	1989
Cash	20.4	7.7	4.2	1.7	1.9	5.2
Curr. Assets	181	156	148	145	152	150
Total Assets	317	293	310	307	339	338
Curr. Liab.	65.9	51.0	59.9	64.7	62.8	71.6
LT Debt	18.5	24.0	33.8	34.9	26.7	21.1
Common Eqty.	187	172	169	162	216	212
Total Cap.	209	202	210	205	267	258
Cap. Exp.	17.8	12.7	14.5	20.0	21.9	20.1
Cash Flow	38.2	28.2	30.7	-4.8	41.6	39.7

Ratio Analysis

	1994	1993	1992	1991	1990	1989
Curr. Ratio	2.7	3.1	2.5	2.2	2.4	2.1
% LT Debt of Cap.	8.9	11.9	16.1	17.1	10.0	8.2
% Net Inc.of Revs.	5.4	2.2	4.0	NM	5.9	5.8
% Ret. on Assets	6.1	2.1	3.4	NM	5.2	5.5
% Ret. on Equity	10.3	3.8	6.3	NM	8.2	8.6

Dividend Data —Dividends have been paid since 1972. A dividend reinvestment plan is available. A "poison pill" stock purchase right was amended in 1989.

Amt. of Div. $	Date Decl.	Ex-Div. Date	Stock of Record	Payment Date
0.080	Aug. 02	Sep. 12	Sep. 16	Sep. 30 '94
0.080	Dec. 06	Dec. 14	Dec. 20	Jan. 03 '95
0.080	Mar. 07	Mar. 13	Mar. 17	Mar. 31 '95
0.080	Jun. 06	Jun. 14	Jun. 16	Jun. 30 '95
0.100	Aug. 01	Sep. 13	Sep. 15	Sep. 29 '95

Data as orig. reptd.; bef. results of disc. opers. and/or spec. items. Per share data adj. for stk. divs. as of ex-div. date. E-Estimated. NA-Not Available. NM-Not Meaningful. NR-Not Ranked.

Office—17876 St. Clair Ave., Cleveland, OH 44110. **Tel**—(216) 486-4200. **Chrmn & Pres**—G. D. Harnett. **VP & CFO**—C. Cramer. **Treas & Secy**—M. C. Hasychak. **VP-Investor Contact**—Timothy J. Reid. **Dirs**—A. C. Bersticker, C. F. Brush III, F. B. Carr, G. D. Harnett, W. P. Madar, G. C. McDonough, R. M. McInnes, H. G. Piper, J. Sherwin, Jr., C. G. Waite. **Transfer Agent & Registrar**—Society National Bank, Cleveland. **Incorporated** in Ohio in 1931. **Empl**-1,833. **S&P Analyst:** Robert E. Friedman

STANDARD & POOR'S

STOCK REPORTS

Buffets, Inc.

NASDAQ Symbol **BOCB**

In S&P MidCap 400

17-AUG-95 **Industry:** Food serving

Summary: This company operates a rapidly expanding chain of more than 215 Old Country Buffet restaurants.

S&P Opinion: Hold (★★★)

Recent Price • 13¼ | Yield • Nil
52 Wk Range • 20¼-7⅞ | 12-Mo. P/E • 17.5

Quantitative Evaluations

Outlook (1 Lowest—5 Highest)
• **5⁻**

Fair Value
• **17¾**

Risk
• **High**

Earn./Div. Rank
• **B+**

Technical Eval.
• **Bearish** since 7/95

Rel. Strength Rank (1 Lowest—99 Highest)
• **14**

Insider Activity
• **Neutral**

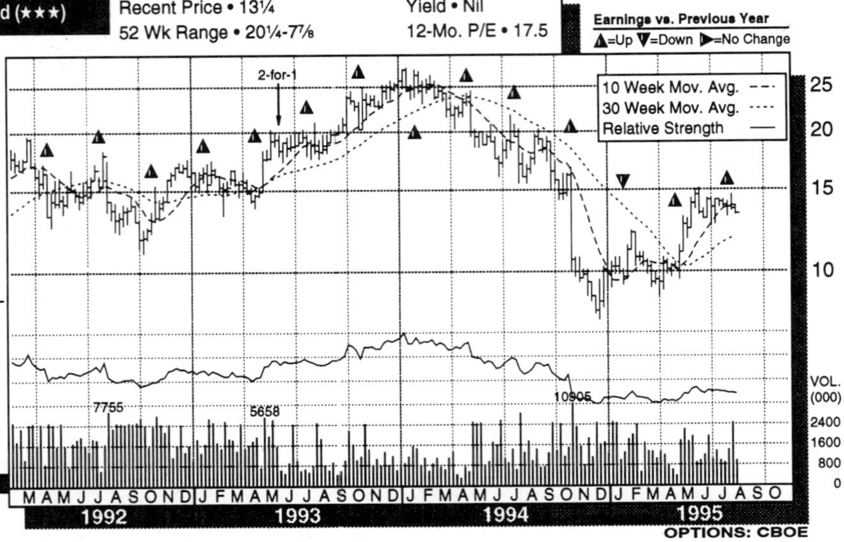

OPTIONS: CBOE

Overview - 17-AUG-95

We expect Buffet's sales to rise more than 20% in 1995, largely due to more restaurants being open. However, BOCB is likely to receive a smaller sales boost in 1995 than it has in past years from converting older units to a new "scatter system" format. Just about all of BOCB's restaurants are now using this system, in which BOCB's buffet product is offered to customers at up to eight food islands in the restaurant. Also, we expect BOCB's profit margins to narrow in 1995, as the company makes investments in labor and products in an effort to bolster customer traffic. If it's successful, we look for higher volumes to permit at least some margin recovery in 1996. Other factors that could help future results include the rollout of a new menu, and the potential widespread addition of more dessert offerings.

Valuation - 17-AUG-95

The stock price of this restaurant company has bounced back sharply from its recent lows, helped by the resumption of double-digit profit growth in early 1995. However, we don't expect the stock price to approach its peak levels of 1993-94 any time soon. Sales comparisons were disappointing in 1995's second quarter, and the company is sounding cautious about the upcoming third quarter earnings comparison. At the current share price, we would not be a buyer of the shares, but can see speculative appeal in holding the stock for capital gains.

Key Stock Statistics

S&P EPS Est. 1995	0.80	Tang. Bk. Value/Share	4.66
P/E on S&P Est. 1995	16.6	Beta	2.46
S&P EPS Est. 1996	0.90	Shareholders	11,300
Dividend Rate/Share	Nil	Market cap. (B)	$0.394
Shs. outstg. (M)	31.0	Inst. holdings	70%
Avg. daily vol. (M)	0.298	Insider holdings	NA

Value of $10,000 invested 5 years ago: $ 24,203

Fiscal Year Ending Dec. 31

	1995	% Change	1994	% Change	1993	% Change
Revenues (Million $)						
1Q	142.1	26%	112.5	27%	88.43	25%
2Q	119.3	21%	98.92	27%	77.69	35%
3Q	—	—	100.5	18%	84.99	41%
4Q	—	—	97.82	17%	83.79	43%
Yr.	—	—	409.7	22%	334.9	35%
Income (Million $)						
1Q	6.81	13%	6.02	32%	4.56	19%
2Q	7.57	9%	6.94	35%	5.14	29%
3Q	—	—	6.10	8%	5.65	35%
4Q	—	—	3.41	-31%	4.95	53%
Yr.	—	—	22.48	11%	20.30	33%
Earnings Per Share ($)						
1Q	0.22	16%	0.19	27%	0.15	15%
2Q	0.24	9%	0.22	29%	0.17	31%
3Q	E0.20	5%	0.19	6%	0.18	29%
4Q	E0.15	36%	0.11	-31%	0.16	45%
Yr.	E0.80	13%	0.71	8%	0.66	29%

Next earnings report expected: late October

Buffets, Inc.

Business Summary - 14-AUG-95

Buffets, Inc., was established in October 1983 to develop and operate a chain of buffet-style restaurants. Its first restaurant opened in March 1984. The number of company-owned and franchised restaurants at the end of recent years was as follows:

	Owned	Franchised
1994	208	6
1993	174	6
1992	134	6
1991	108	6
1990	88	6
1989	69	8
1988	47	9
1987	30	6
1986	18	5
1985	12	2

The restaurants, generally operating under the name Old Country Buffet, offer a wide variety of food items, including soups, salads, entrees, vegetables, nonalcoholic beverages and desserts for one fixed all-inclusive price. Most restaurants are in strip or neighborhood shopping centers. Lunches typically cost about $4.99 to $5.79, while dinners are priced at about $6.49 to $7.59. Limited breakfast service is available. Customers pay prior to entering a buffet line and selecting the items and portions of their choice. In units opened after March 1990, a new concept called the scatter system has been used, in which food is presented utilizing up to eight food islands scattered throughout the restaurant, thus reducing long lines that occurred under an earlier format. Most of the older units have been converted to the scatter concept. Most restaurants range in size from 8,000 sq. ft. to 13,850 sq. ft., with seating for 260 to 390 people. Buffets has not been actively seeking to grant additional franchises.

Important Developments

Aug. '95—In 1995's second quarter, BOCB's average weekly sales were down 3.7%, year to year, following a 1.1% rise in the first quarter. With the company making additional investments in food and labor, BOCB's restaurant operating margin narrowed to 15.1%, from a year-ago's 19.0%. However, BOCB's SG&A expense was down 22%, as the company spent much less on advertising. To increase sales, BOCB has started a sizable marketing campaign in the third quarter. This may put pressure on earnings in the current quarter, followed by a fuller benefit in the fourth quarter. Meanwhile, BOCB opened five new restaurants in the second quarter, bringing the number of company-operated units to 230 at July 12. Also, BOCB is rolling out a new menu, and is testing the addition of expanded dessert offerings.

Capitalization

Long Term Debt: $12,000,000 (4/19/95).
Minority Interest: $582,000 (4/19/95).

Per Share Data ($) (Year Ended Dec. 31)

	1994	1993	1992	1991	1990	1989
Tangible Bk. Val.	4.43	3.63	2.22	1.64	1.20	0.93
Cash Flow	1.33	1.16	0.88	0.66	0.50	0.36
Earnings	0.71	0.66	0.51	0.38	0.28	0.19
Dividends	Nil	Nil	Nil	Nil	Nil	Nil
Payout Ratio	Nil	Nil	Nil	Nil	Nil	Nil
Prices - High	27½	26¼	19⅝	16	8⅝	6⅛
- Low	7⅞	13¼	11	5⅝	4⅝	3⅛
P/E Ratio - High	39	40	38	42	31	31
- Low	11	20	22	15	17	16

Income Statement Analysis (Million $)

	1994	%Chg	1993	%Chg	1992	%Chg	1991
Revs.	410	22%	335	36%	247	26%	196
Oper. Inc.	55.7	14%	48.7	36%	35.8	35%	26.5
Depr.	19.7	29%	15.3	42%	10.8	30%	8.3
Int. Exp.	0.0	-94%	0.2	NM	0.0	-56%	0.1
Pretax Inc.	36.9	9%	33.8	34%	25.2	37%	18.4
Eff. Tax Rate	39%	—	40%	—	40%	—	40%
Net Inc.	22.5	11%	20.3	34%	15.2	37%	11.1

Balance Sheet & Other Fin. Data (Million $)

	1994	1993	1992	1991	1990	1989
Cash	6.8	12.2	4.9	2.0	3.3	4.8
Curr. Assets	20.5	24.3	13.1	7.7	7.2	7.4
Total Assets	209	160	113	78.3	60.5	48.7
Curr. Liab.	48.7	34.2	24.5	17.8	15.0	12.3
LT Debt	7.0	Nil	12.0	5.0	4.0	4.0
Common Eqty.	142	116	69.1	50.9	37.6	28.6
Total Cap.	160	126	88.2	60.5	45.5	36.4
Cap. Exp.	79.1	52.2	39.2	26.0	17.9	17.3
Cash Flow	42.1	35.6	26.1	19.4	14.3	10.2

Ratio Analysis

	1994	1993	1992	1991	1990	1989
Curr. Ratio	0.4	0.7	0.5	0.4	0.5	0.6
% LT Debt of Cap.	4.4	Nil	13.6	8.3	8.8	11.0
% Net Inc.of Revs.	5.5	6.1	6.2	5.7	5.5	4.8
% Ret. on Assets	12.2	14.6	15.9	15.9	14.5	13.9
% Ret. on Equity	17.4	21.5	25.3	25.0	23.9	22.5

Dividend Data —BOCB has not paid any cash dividends on its common stock and, pursuant to its credit agreement, is restricted from doing so without lender approval. Earnings are expected to be retained for the foreseeable future for use in expanding the company's business. A three-for-two stock split was effected in December 1991, and a two-for-one split was effected in June 1993.

Amt. of Div. $	Date Decl.	Ex-Div. Date	Stock of Record	Payment Date
2-for-1	Apr. 30	Jun. 01	May. 17	May. 28 '93

Data as orig. reptd.; bef. results of disc. opers. and/or spec. items. Per share data adj. for stk. divs. as of ex-div. date. E-Estimated. NA-Not Available. NM-Not Meaningful. NR-Not Ranked.

Office—10260 Viking Drive, Eden Prairie, MN 55344. **Tel**—(612) 942-9760. **Chrmn & CEO**—R. H. Hatlen. **EVP-Fin, Treas & Investor Contact**—Clark C. Grant. **Secy**—D. M. Hasbargen. **Dirs**—K. H. Erickson, R. H. Hatlen, R. A. Lipkin, A. S. McDowell, D. M. Winton. **Transfer Agent & Registrar**—American Stock Transfer & Trust Co., NYC. **Incorporated** in Minnesota in 1983. **Empl**-15,915. **S&P Analyst:** Tom Graves, CFA

STANDARD & POOR'S

STOCK REPORTS

Burlington Industries

NYSE Symbol **BUR**

In S&P MidCap 400

24-AUG-95 **Industry:** Textiles

Summary: Burlington Industries is a leading developer of fabrics and other textile products used in apparel and interior furnishings.

S&P Opinion: Hold (★★★)

Recent Price • 13⅝ | 52 Wk Range • 13⅞-9¼ | Yield • Nil | 12-Mo. P/E • 13.4

Quantitative Evaluations

Outlook (1 Lowest—5 Highest)
• **NA**

Fair Value
• **NA**

Risk
• **Average**

Earn./Div. Rank
• **NR**

Technical Eval.
• **Bearish** since 7/95

Rel. Strength Rank (1 Lowest—99 Highest)
• **62**

Insider Activity
• **NA**

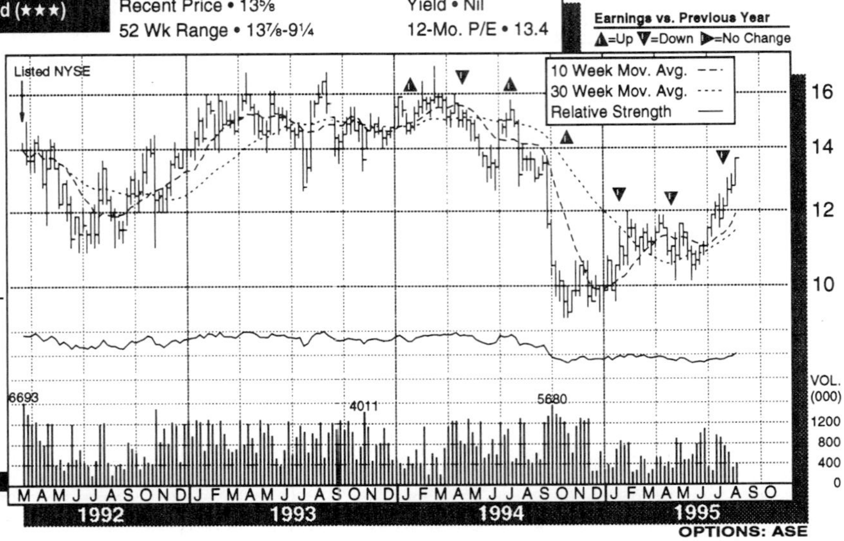

OPTIONS: ASE

Overview - 24-AUG-95

Sales gains in fiscal 1996 should accelerate from fiscal 1995's mediocre growth, aided by stronger volume for both apparel fabrics and home textiles. Apparel fabric sales should benefit from greater overall demand for apparel, and from new product introductions. Sales of home textile products should continue in an uptrend, boosted by higher demand for upholstery fabrics and cotton rugs, partly reflecting a stronger housing market. Margins should widen, as selling price hikes offset raw material price increases over the past few years. Results will also benefit from higher volume and efforts to contain costs. EPS comparisons will be aided by fewer shares outstanding, reflecting a 3.5 million share buyback program.

Valuation - 24-AUG-95

Shares of this leading textile manufacturer have been under pressure since mid-1994, reflecting contracting margins resulting from higher raw material prices, particularly in the apparel fabrics area. The company has not been able to fully pass on increased costs to customers. Pressure on apparel fabric sales also appears to be hurting margins. Earnings will remain under pressure through fiscal 1995, but could improve in fiscal 1996, when BUR expects to be able to fully pass on higher raw material prices. Although the shares appear undervalued at their current price, we are retaining a neutral stance until earnings growth resumes.

Key Stock Statistics

S&P EPS Est. 1995	1.15	Tang. Bk. Value/Share	NM
P/E on S&P Est. 1995	11.8	Beta	NA
S&P EPS Est. 1996	1.30	Shareholders	1,200
Dividend Rate/Share	Nil	Market cap. (B)	$0.820
Shs. outstg. (M)	64.9	Inst. holdings	71%
Avg. daily vol. (M)	0.099	Insider holdings	NA

Value of $10,000 invested 5 years ago: NA

Fiscal Year Ending Sep. 30

	1995	% Change	1994	% Change	1993	% Change
Revenues (Million $)						
1Q	514.8	9%	471.9	3%	459.0	-3%
2Q	583.4	11%	525.0	-2%	534.0	3%
3Q	582.0	NM	583.4	5%	554.0	3%
4Q	—	—	546.7	7%	511.1	-6%
Yr.	—	—	2,127	3%	2,058	NM
Income (Million $)						
1Q	12.85	-32%	18.98	58%	12.00	NM
2Q	22.18	-16%	26.52	-12%	30.12	NM
3Q	19.50	-53%	41.38	32%	31.38	-21%
4Q	—	—	12.43	38%	9.04	-72%
Yr.	—	—	99.3	22%	81.58	NM
Earnings Per Share ($)						
1Q	0.19	-32%	0.28	56%	0.18	—
2Q	0.34	-13%	0.39	-11%	0.44	—
3Q	0.30	-51%	0.61	33%	0.46	—
4Q	E0.32	78%	0.18	38%	0.13	—
Yr.	E1.15	-21%	1.46	23%	1.19	NM

Next earnings report expected: early November

Burlington Industries

Business Summary - 24-AUG-95

Burlington Industries, Inc. is one of the world's largest and most diversified textile products manufacturers. It is the successor to a company with the same name that was taken private in a leveraged buyout in 1987. Contributions by business segment in recent fiscal years were:

	1994	1993	1992
Apparel products	63%	64%	64%
Home furnishings	37%	36%	36%

Products for apparel markets are developed, made and sold by five divisions, each of which offers a distinct product line in terms of fabric and end-uses. The menswear division produces woven wool worsted and worsted blend fabrics supplied to manufacturers of men's and women's tailored apparel. The Klopman fabrics division makes woven synthetic fabrics that are used in a wide variety of apparel, interior furnishings and industrial products. The denim division is the leading U.S. maker of specialty denim fabrics. It provides more than 60 styles of denim to all major jeans manufacturers and to makers of other casual apparel. The knitted fabrics division produces all cotton knits for use in sport shirts, turtlenecks and other apparel. The Burlington Madison Yarn Co. division is the only U.S. manufacturer of both filament and spun synthetic yarns; it supplies more than 300 customers, as well as other Burlington divisions.

Products for interior furnishings markets are developed, manufactured and sold by three divisions. The Burlington House division produces ready-made and made-to-measure draperies, window coverings and coordinated bedroom ensembles, mattress ticking, upholstery fabrics, comforters, vertical blinds and other fabrics. Burlington House is the world's largest producer of jacquard fabrics. The carpet division produces tufted synthetic carpet and carpet tiles for commercial uses sold under the Lees brand name and tufted synthetic carpet fashion area rugs for residential use sold under the Lees brand name. The Burlington House Area Rugs division produces tufted area and bath rugs for home use.

Important Developments

Aug. '95—BUR attributed a substantial drop in its fiscal 1995 quarter earnings to decreased sales of apparel fabrics resulting from increased inventories in the pipeline. Operating income at the division fell 41%, reflecting weaker volume, as well as the inability to pass on higher raw material price increases. Sales increased slightly at the home textiles division, but margins contracted 4.5%, pressured by higher raw material prices.

Capitalization

Long Term Debt: $886,096,000 (7/1/95).

Per Share Data ($) (Year Ended Sep. 30)

	1994	1993	1992	1991	1990	1989
Tangible Bk. Val.	8.51	8.22	6.96	-1.41	NA	NA
Cash Flow	2.65	2.35	-0.52	1.70	NA	NA
Earnings	1.46	1.19	-2.42	0.38	NA	NA
Dividends	Nil	Nil	Nil	NA	NA	NA
Payout Ratio	Nil	Nil	Nil	NA	NA	NA
Prices - High	17⅞	16⅞	15	NA	NA	NA
- Low	9¼	12⅝	10⅞	NA	NA	NA
P/E Ratio - High	12	14	NM	NA	NA	NA
- Low	6	11	NM	NA	NA	NA

Income Statement Analysis (Million $)

	1994	%Chg	1993	%Chg	1992	%Chg	1991
Revs.	2,127	3%	2,058	NM	2,066	7%	1,926
Oper. Inc.	292	-11%	327	4%	314	27%	248
Depr.	81.0	3%	79.0	8%	73.0	-20%	91.0
Int. Exp.	50.0	-45%	91.0	-43%	160	30%	123
Pretax Inc.	169	17%	144	NM	-89.0	NM	26.0
Eff. Tax Rate	41%	—	43%	—	NM	—	Nil
Net Inc.	99	22%	81.6	NM	-88.9	NM	26.1

Balance Sheet & Other Fin. Data (Million $)

	1994	1993	1992	1991	1990	1989
Cash	41.0	21.0	30.0	35.0	NA	NA
Curr. Assets	734	665	472	411	NA	NA
Total Assets	1,907	1,813	1,676	1,639	NA	NA
Curr. Liab.	315	304	284	267	NA	NA
LT Debt	858	892	862	868	NA	NA
Common Eqty.	574	561	475	447	NA	NA
Total Cap.	1,534	1,454	1,337	1,315	NA	NA
Cap. Exp.	99	89.0	62.0	NA	NA	NA
Cash Flow	180	160	-20.0	117	NA	NA

Ratio Analysis

	1994	1993	1992	1991	1990	1989
Curr. Ratio	2.3	2.2	1.7	1.5	NA	NA
% LT Debt of Cap.	55.9	61.4	64.5	66.0	NA	NA
% Net Inc.of Revs.	4.7	4.0	NM	1.4	NA	NA
% Ret. on Assets	5.4	4.7	NM	NA	NA	NA
% Ret. on Equity	17.6	15.7	NM	NA	NA	NA

Dividend Data —The company does not currently intend to pay any cash dividends on the common stock and the non-voting common stock.

Data as orig. reptd.; bef. results of disc. opers. and/or spec. items. Per share data adj. for stk. divs. as of ex-div. date. E-Estimated. NA-Not Available. NM-Not Meaningful. NR-Not Ranked.

Office—3330 West Friendly Ave., Greensboro, NC 27410. **Tel**—(910) 379-2000. **Chrmn**—F. S. Greenberg. **Pres & CEO**—G. W. Henderson III. **Vice Chrmn**—B. A. Leventhal. **CFO**—J. D. Englar. **VP & Secy**—B. Eisenberg. **Treas**—Park R. Davidson. **Investor Contact**—Jim Clippard. **Dirs**—J. F. Abely, Jr., J. D. Englar, F. S. Greenberg, G. W. Henderson III, B. A. Leventhal, D. I. Margolis, J.G. Medlin, Jr., A. B. Stenberg. **Transfer Agent & Registrar**—Wachovia Bank of North Carolina, Winston-Salem, NC. **Incorporated** in North Carolina in 1923; reincorporated in Delaware. **Empl**-23,800. **S&P Analyst:** Elizabeth Vandeventer

STANDARD & POOR'S

STOCK REPORTS

CBI Industries

NYSE Symbol **CBI**
In S&P MidCap 400

27-SEP-95 **Industry:** Chemicals

Summary: Besides providing a variety of project management and other contracting services, this company is the world's largest supplier of carbon dioxide, through its Liquid Carbonic unit.

S&P Opinion: Hold (★★★)

Recent Price • 24¼
52 Wk Range • 27¾-20
Yield • 2.1%
12-Mo. P/E • 20.4

Quantitative Evaluations

Outlook (1 Lowest—5 Highest)
• **3⁻**

Fair Value
• **24⅛**

Risk
• **Average**

Earn./Div. Rank
• **B**

Technical Eval.
• **Bearish** since 4/95

Rel. Strength Rank (1 Lowest—99 Highest)
• **12**

Insider Activity
• **NA**

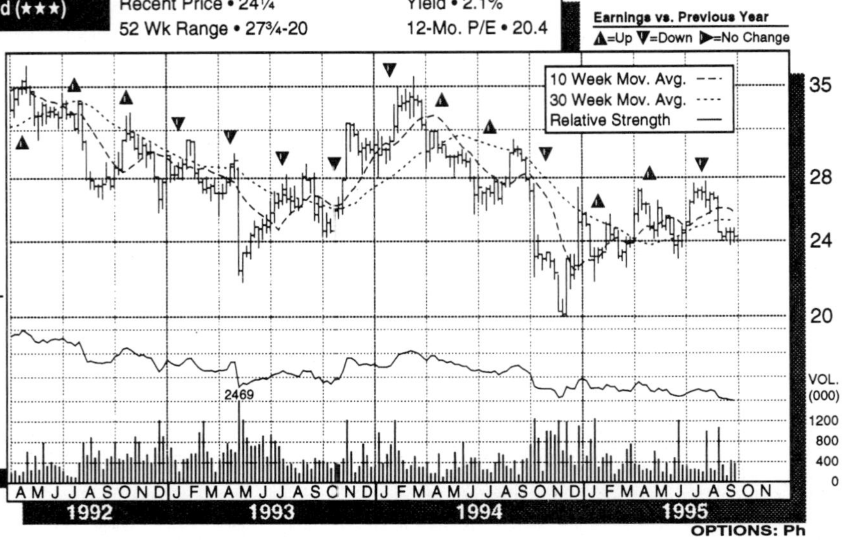

OPTIONS: Ph

Overview - 27-SEP-95

Revenues should continue to increase moderately in 1996, reflecting an improving economy and continued positive contributions from Liquid Carbonic Industries, aided by strong carbon dioxide sales, and from Statia Terminals, which should benefit from growing demand for hydrocarbon energy. Several international orders are in the pipeline for Contracting Services, but real growth is contingent upon stronger North American markets. We expect earnings to improve from recent restructuring efforts, which included workforce realignments and rationalization of operations to reflect the company's outlook on market opportunities for the future. The restructuring charge was mostly related to positioning Liquid Carbonic as a producer rather than a mass distributor.

Valuation - 27-SEP-95

Since bottoming in late 1994, CBI shares have rebounded over the past few months, spurred by the unsolicited offer for Liquid Carbonic Industries made by Airgas, Inc. in December 1994. The abandoned offer served to alert investors to the true value of Liquid Carbonic, which we believe is not currently reflected in the share price. However, the ongoing weakness in contracting services continues to depress the shares, and we thus view them as fairly valued at current levels, with further gains unlikely until a recovery takes place in that segment.

Key Stock Statistics

S&P EPS Est. 1995	1.55	Tang. Bk. Value/Share	16.04
P/E on S&P Est. 1995	15.6	Beta	0.91
S&P EPS Est. 1996	1.70	Shareholders	8,000
Dividend Rate/Share	0.48	Market cap. (B)	$0.893
Shs. outstg. (M)	38.2	Inst. holdings	71%
Avg. daily vol. (M)	0.059	Insider holdings	NA

Value of $10,000 invested 5 years ago: $ 12,334

Fiscal Year Ending Dec. 31

	1995	% Change	1994	% Change	1993	% Change
Revenues (Million $)						
1Q	463.3	15%	401.9	NM	397.9	NM
2Q	473.8	NM	470.0	10%	427.8	3%
3Q	—	—	489.2	20%	408.4	-5%
4Q	—	—	529.8	21%	437.6	1%
Yr.	—	—	1,891	13%	1,672	NM
Income (Million $)						
1Q	10.19	5%	9.67	73%	5.58	-77%
2Q	14.02	3%	13.57	61%	8.42	-58%
3Q	—	—	9.39	-9%	10.30	-48%
4Q	—	—	18.85	NM	-58.31	NM
Yr.	—	—	51.48	NM	-34.01	NM
Earnings Per Share ($)						
1Q	0.23	5%	0.22	100%	0.11	-68%
2Q	0.30	-6%	0.32	68%	0.19	-62%
3Q	E0.40	100%	0.20	-17%	0.24	-53%
4Q	E0.56	22%	0.46	NM	-1.61	NM
Yr.	E1.55	29%	1.20	NM	-1.07	NM

Next earnings report expected: mid October

CBI Industries

Business Summary - 27-SEP-95

CBI Industries, Inc. and its subsidiaries operate in three areas: contracting services, industrial gases and investments. Business outside the U.S. accounted for about 53% of total revenues in 1994. Segment contributions in 1994 were:

	Revs.	Profits
Contracting services	44%	13%
Industrial gases	48%	71%
Investments	8%	16%

The contracting services segment is organized under Chicago Bridge & Iron Co. as a global construction group that provides, through subsidiaries, services including design, engineering, fabrication, project management, general contracting and specialty construction services, including nondestructive and post-weld heat treatment associated mainly with metal plate vessels, as well as water and wastewater treatment structures. In 1993, CBI acquired Ershigs Inc., a leading maker of custom fiberglass-reinforced plastic products.

The industrial gases segment is organized under Liquid Carbonic Industries Corp. (LC), which is the world's largest supplier of carbon dioxide in various forms and makes and markets other gases for industrial, medical and specialty applications, including oxygen, nitrogen, argon, hydrogen, acetylene, carbon monoxide, nitrous oxide and liquefied natural gas. LC also assembles and sells industrial gas-related equipment.

Investments include Statia Terminals, which provides transshipment, storage, bunkering and blending services for hydrocarbon products at the island of St. Eustatius in the Caribbean and in Nova Scotia, Canada.

In December 1994, directors unanimously rejected an unsolicited offer from Airgas, Inc. for the acquisition of Liquid Carbonic Industries. CBI said a separation of LC from its other businesses would be inconsistent with its strategy, focus, business plan and capital investment program. In January 1995, Airgas decided not to proceed with the offer.

Important Developments

Aug. '95—CBI said Liquid Carbonic's 1995 first-half revenues increased 18%, year to year, with most of the growth occurring outside the U.S., particularly in Brazil, reflecting volume increases and favorable exchange rates.

Capitalization

Long Term Debt: $677,063,000 (6/95).
Minority Interest: $67,558,000.
Series C $2.27 Conv. Voting Preferred Stock: 3,514,696 shs. ($1 par); held by ESOP.
Series D 7.48% Cum. Preferred Stock: 550,000 shs.

Per Share Data ($) (Year Ended Dec. 31)

	1994	1993	1992	1991	1990	1989
Tangible Bk. Val.	15.72	15.06	18.55	14.93	11.89	8.93
Cash Flow	4.03	1.64	4.29	3.92	4.14	3.48
Earnings	1.20	-1.07	1.79	1.54	1.58	0.94
Dividends	0.48	0.48	0.48	0.44	0.40	0.40
Payout Ratio	40%	NM	27%	30%	27%	43%
Prices - High	35⅞	32	37½	37⅛	29⅝	22⅝
- Low	20	21¾	25¾	23⅝	20½	16⅞
P/E Ratio - High	30	NM	21	24	19	24
- Low	17	NM	14	15	13	18

Income Statement Analysis (Million $)

	1994	%Chg	1993	%Chg	1992	%Chg	1991
Revs.	1,891	13%	1,670	NM	1,666	4%	1,608
Oper. Inc.	268	24%	217	-14%	251	3%	243
Depr.	107	6%	101	10%	91.6	11%	82.6
Int. Exp.	45.7	33%	34.3	65%	20.8	-32%	30.6
Pretax Inc.	119	NM	-2.0	NM	146	7%	137
Eff. Tax Rate	47%	—	NM	—	43%	—	44%
Net Inc.	51.5	NM	-34.0	NM	71.1	16%	61.1

Balance Sheet & Other Fin. Data (Million $)

	1994	1993	1992	1991	1990	1989
Cash	51.0	23.2	38.0	41.0	47.0	62.0
Curr. Assets	518	471	434	457	451	429
Total Assets	2,009	1,870	1,685	1,479	1,432	1,359
Curr. Liab.	379	345	325	338	318	291
LT Debt	667	608	411	260	395	466
Common Eqty.	678	644	681	542	386	256
Total Cap.	1,487	1,395	1,255	1,085	1,052	1,015
Cap. Exp.	239	316	271	165	139	119
Cash Flow	153	61.0	157	136	125	100

Ratio Analysis

	1994	1993	1992	1991	1990	1989
Curr. Ratio	1.4	1.4	1.3	1.4	1.4	1.5
% LT Debt of Cap.	44.8	43.6	32.8	23.9	37.5	45.9
% Net Inc.of Revs.	2.7	NM	4.3	3.8	3.5	2.3
% Ret. on Assets	2.6	NM	4.5	4.0	3.7	2.5
% Ret. on Equity	6.8	NM	9.8	11.0	14.1	11.0

Dividend Data —Dividends have been paid since 1953. A dividend reinvestment plan is available. A "poison pill" stock purchase right was issued in 1986.

Amt. of Div. $	Date Decl.	Ex-Div. Date	Stock of Record	Payment Date
0.120	Oct. 12	Nov. 17	Nov. 23	Dec. 16 '94
0.120	Jan. 11	Feb. 09	Feb. 15	Mar. 10 '95
0.120	Mar. 08	May. 18	May. 24	Jun. 16 '95
0.120	May. 11	Aug. 21	Aug. 23	Sep. 15 '95

Data as orig. reptd.; bef. results of disc. opers. and/or spec. items. Per share data adj. for stk. divs. as of ex-div. date. E-Estimated. NA-Not Available. NM-Not Meaningful. NR-Not Ranked.

Office—800 Jorie Blvd., Oak Brook, IL 60521-2268. **Tel**—(708) 572-7000. **Chrmn, CEO & Pres**—J. E. Jones. **VP, CFO & Investor Contact**—Alan J. Schneider. **Secy**—C. C. Toerber. **Dirs**—L. E. Akin, W. N. Caldwell, E. H. Clark Jr., R. J. Daniels, R. J. Day, J. T. Horton, J. E. Jones, G. E. MacDougal, S. P. Marshall, E. J. Mooney Jr., J. F. Riordan, R. T. Stewart, R. G. Wallace, C. E. Willoughby **Transfer Agent & Registrar**—Co. itself. **Incorporated** in Illinois in 1889. **Empl**-14,440. **S&P Analyst:** Robert E. Friedman

STANDARD & POOR'S
STOCK REPORTS

CML Group

NYSE Symbol **CML**
In S&P MidCap 400

20-OCT-95 **Industry:** Retail Stores

Summary: This specialty retailer sells NordicTrack physical fitness and exercise equipment and nature-related merchandise.

Quantitative Evaluations
Outlook
(1 Lowest—5 Highest)
• **5⁻**
Fair Value
• **9**
Risk
• **Average**
Earn./Div. Rank
• **B**

Technical Eval.
• **Bearish** since 1/94
Rel. Strength Rank
(1 Lowest—99 Highest)
• **3**
Insider Activity
• **NA**

Recent Price • 6⅜
52 Wk Range • 11⅜-5⅝
Yield • 1.7%
12-Mo. P/E • NM

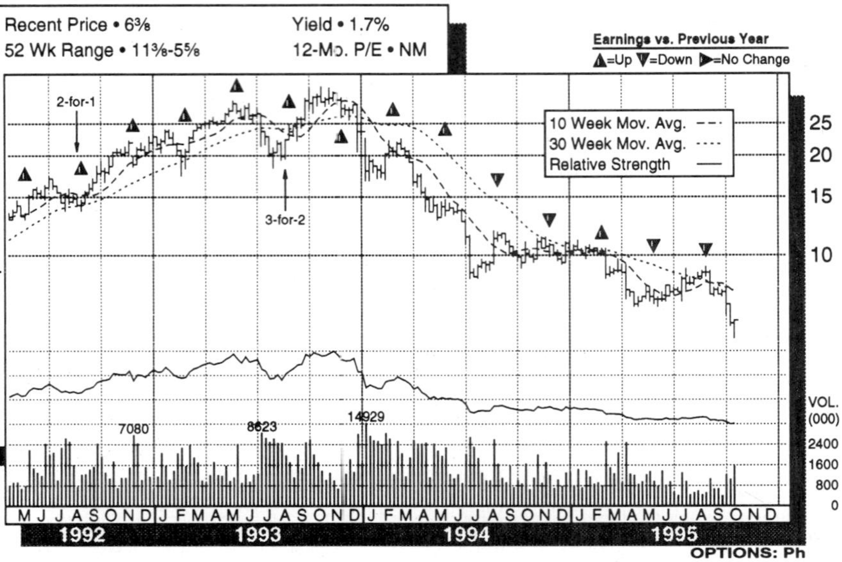

OPTIONS: Ph

Business Profile - 19-OCT-95

As a result of a weak performance in fiscal 1995, the company is currently realigning the organizations and product lines at its NordicTrack and The Nature Company units. This transition will likely continue through fiscal 1996's first half. Despite fiscal 1995's disappointing results, CML's balance sheet remains strong, and it invested about $36 million in stores and capital improvements during the year. It also repurchased over $20 million of its outstanding securities.

Operational Review - 19-OCT-95

Net sales in the fiscal year ended July 31, 1995, advanced 8.7% from the prior year's restated level, reflecting an 11% gain at NordicTrack and a 4% increase for The Nature Company. Profitability was penalized by reduced manufacturing and advertising efficiencies, costs related to the redesign of NordicTrack's low-end treadmill, and charges related to management changes at both NordicTrack and The Nature Company. Income from continuing operations fell 69% to $0.32 a share from $0.98.

Stock Performance - 13-OCT-95

In the past 30 trading days, CML's shares have declined 16%, compared to a 4% rise in the S&P 500. Average trading volume for the past five days was 303,500 shares, compared with the 40-day moving average of 177,090 shares.

Key Stock Statistics

Dividend Rate/Share	0.10	Shareholders	3,400
Shs. outstg. (M)	49.2	Market cap. (B)	$0.283
Avg. daily vol. (M)	0.214	Inst. holdings	60%
Tang. Bk. Value/Share	4.04	Insider holdings	NA
Beta	1.66		

Value of $10,000 invested 5 years ago: $ 19,182

Fiscal Year Ending Jul. 31

	1995	% Change	1994	% Change	1993	% Change
Revenues (Million $)						
1Q	129.2	-6%	137.2	28%	107.2	26%
2Q	279.0	-4%	292.0	24%	236.4	38%
3Q	179.5	-9%	198.1	17%	169.4	22%
4Q	124.9	-14%	145.1	9%	132.6	34%
Yr.	712.6	-8%	772.4	20%	645.5	31%
Income (Million $)						
1Q	1.53	-79%	7.14	24%	5.74	32%
2Q	36.90	-4%	38.30	18%	32.54	49%
3Q	-0.68	NM	17.06	14%	15.02	97%
4Q	-21.85	NM	-10.79	NM	4.64	54%
Yr.	15.91	-69%	51.72	-11%	57.93	57%
Earnings Per Share ($)						
1Q	0.03	-79%	0.14	24%	0.11	21%
2Q	0.73	1%	0.72	15%	0.63	47%
3Q	-0.01	NM	0.33	15%	0.29	95%
4Q	-0.44	NM	-0.21	NM	0.09	50%
Yr.	0.32	-68%	1.00	-10%	1.11	52%

Next earnings report expected: late November

CML Group

Business Summary - 19-OCT-95

CML Group, Inc. is a specialty retailing company that operates chains of stores under various trade names and also conducts mail-order operations. At fiscal 1994 year end, CML was operating 318 retail stores and 20 mall kiosks and had proprietary mail -order customer lists containing about 3.0 million names. In fiscal 1994, retail stores and mall kiosks accounted for 57.3% of total revenues, and direct response and mail order for 42.7%. Sales and operating income in fiscal 1994:

	Sales	Income
NordicTrack	59%	93%
The Nature Company	26%	4%
Britches for Men	15%	3%

NordicTrack designs, makes and markets high-quality aerobic and anaerobic exercise equipment to customers through direct-response advertising in print and on TV and through its NordicAdvantage subsidiary, which operates specialty retail stores and kiosks. Products include several models of cross country ski exercisers, which range in price from $300 to $1,500, and two models of NordicFlex Gold at $1,000 and $1,300. In November 1993, NordicTrack introduced a nonmotorized treadmill selling for approximately $600. At April 29, 1995, NordicAdvantage was operating 114 stores, up from 88 at fiscal 1994 year-end.

The Nature Company sells nature-related merchandise, including books, gifts, children's educational toys, music, clothing, accessories, backyard and garden items, minerals, sculpture, posters, optics, paper products, instruments, nature tapes and limited-edition prints. Smith & Hawken, acquired in February 1993, is a leading marketer of gardening tools, plants and accessories. Two early-stage retail concepts--Hear Music and Scientific Revolution--sell music and science-related merchandise, respectively. The segment had 146 stores in operation at April 29, 1995, compared with 133 at the end of fiscal 1994.

In May 1995, CML announced its intention to sell its Britches division, which sells men's apparel through 14 Britches of Georgetowne stores at July 31, 1994, and 83 Britches Great Outdoors outlets.

Important Developments

Sep. '95—The company said it expected to improve its results in fiscal 1996 under the new management at both NordicTrack and The Nature Company. CML noted that the transition at the two units, which includes the realignment of the organizations and their product lines, would continue through fiscal 1996's first half, with benefits to be realized in the second half of the year.

Capitalization

Long Term Debt: $41,772,000 (4/95), incl. $41,593,000 of 5.5% debs. due 2003, conv. into com. at $25.917 a sh.

Per Share Data ($) (Year Ended Jul. 31)

	1995	1994	1993	1992	1991	1990
Tangible Bk. Val.	NA	3.69	2.97	2.11	0.50	-0.13
Cash Flow	NA	1.43	1.45	0.97	0.74	0.55
Earnings	0.32	1.00	1.11	0.73	0.51	0.35
Dividends	0.08	0.08	0.05	0.02	Nil	Nil
Payout Ratio	27%	8%	5%	3%	Nil	Nil
Prices - High	11⅛	22⅝	32⅜	22⅞	11½	3¾
- Low	7	8½	17⅜	11⅛	2¾	2⅛
P/E Ratio - High	35	23	30	31	23	11
- Low	22	9	16	15	5	6

Income Statement Analysis (Million $)

	1994	%Chg	1993	%Chg	1992	%Chg	1991
Revs.	772	20%	645	31%	494	46%	339
Oper. Inc.	106	-8%	115	27%	90.4	73%	52.4
Depr.	22.2	26%	17.6	45%	12.1	30%	9.3
Int. Exp.	2.5	38%	1.8	34%	1.4	-83%	7.7
Pretax Inc.	81.2	-16%	96.6	52%	63.7	80%	35.4
Eff. Tax Rate	36%	—	40%	—	42%	—	42%
Net Inc.	51.7	-11%	57.9	57%	36.8	78%	20.7

Balance Sheet & Other Fin. Data (Million $)

	1994	1993	1992	1991	1990	1989
Cash	28.9	64.0	3.5	2.0	1.4	1.0
Curr. Assets	185	176	89.8	58.5	69.3	65.0
Total Assets	385	340	219	164	172	221
Curr. Liab.	81.1	75.2	63.4	41.6	30.3	72.3
LT Debt	59.0	59.0	5.0	59.0	108	108
Common Eqty.	219	184	130	50.0	25.0	37.0
Total Cap.	278	243	135	108	133	145
Cap. Exp.	61.1	44.4	43.3	19.7	12.8	10.5
Cash Flow	73.9	75.5	48.9	30.0	21.5	4.6

Ratio Analysis

	1994	1993	1992	1991	1990	1989
Curr. Ratio	2.3	2.3	1.4	1.4	2.3	0.9
% LT Debt of Cap.	21.1	24.3	4.0	54.1	81.0	74.5
% Net Inc.of Revs.	6.7	9.0	7.4	6.1	5.0	NM
% Ret. on Assets	14.4	20.3	17.7	12.2	7.0	NM
% Ret. on Equity	25.8	36.1	38.7	54.8	44.2	NM

Dividend Data —Cash dividends were initiated in 1991. A dividend reinvestment plan is available.

Amt. of Div. $	Date Decl.	Ex-Div. Date	Stock of Record	Payment Date
0.020	Oct. 04	Nov. 22	Nov. 29	Dec. 15 '94
0.020	Dec. 02	Feb. 23	Mar. 01	Mar. 16 '95
0.025	Mar. 02	May. 23	May. 30	Jun. 16 '95
0.025	Jun. 29	Aug. 31	Sep. 05	Sep. 20 '95
0.025	Oct. 03	Nov. 24	Nov. 28	Dec. 14 '95

Data as orig. reptd.; bef. results of disc. opers. and/or spec. items. Per share data adj. for stk. divs. as of ex-div. date. E-Estimated. NA-Not Available. NM-Not Meaningful. NR-Not Ranked.

Office—524 Main St., Acton, MA 01720. **Tel**—(508) 264-4155. **Chrmn & CEO**—C. M. Leighton. **Pres**—G. R. Tod. **SVP-Fin**—R. J. Samuelson. **Secy**—P. P. Brountas. **VP & Investor Contact**—Nancy Wang. **Dirs**—H. H. Callaway, C. M. Leighton, T. H. Lenagh, H. L. Luther Jr., R. W. Menninger, A. Taunton-Rigby, G. R. Tod, R. F. Verni. **Transfer Agent & Registrar**—First National Bank of Boston. **Incorporated** in 1969. **Empl**-5,613. **S&P Analyst:** Michael V. Pizzi

STANDARD & POOR'S

STOCK REPORTS

CMS Energy

NYSE Symbol **CMS**
In S&P MidCap 400

13-OCT-95 **Industry:** Util.-Diversified

Summary: This Michigan-based holding company's principal subsidiary is Consumers Power Co., Michigan's largest utility and the nation's fourth largest gas and electric utility.

S&P Opinion: Hold (★★★)

Recent Price • 27 | 52 Wk Range • 27-20⅞ | Yield • 3.6% | 12-Mo. P/E • 12.4

Quantitative Evaluations

Outlook
(1 Lowest—5 Highest)
• 1-

Fair Value
• 19⅛

Risk
• Low

Earn./Div. Rank
• B

Technical Eval.
• Bullish since 7/95

Rel. Strength Rank
(1 Lowest—99 Highest)
• 80

Insider Activity
• Neutral

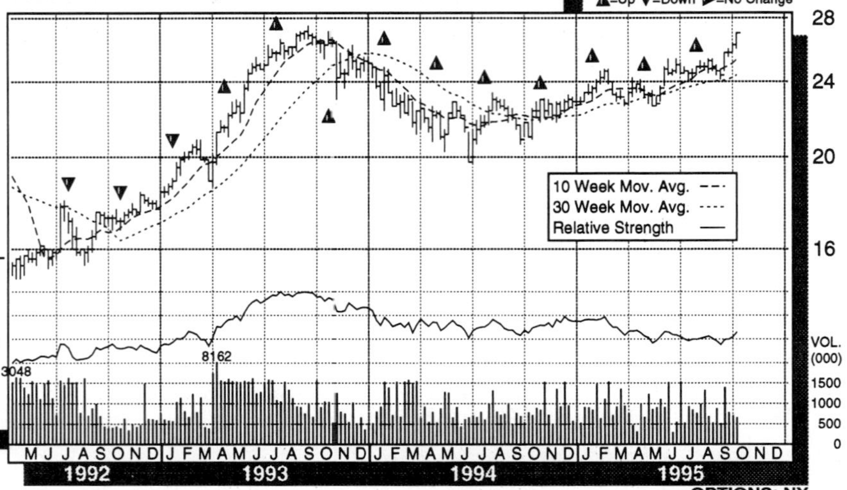

OPTIONS: NY

Overview - 13-OCT-95

Share earnings for 1995 should reflect modest increases in sales of both gas and electricity, despite a likely switch by industrial customers to cogeneration. Positive factors include the impact of a full year of rate hikes granted in mid-1994, and well-controlled operating and maintenance expenses. Results should further benefit from rapidly rising profits from non-utility operations, such as scale economies to be achieved at its northeastern U.S. independent power production facilities following the acquisition of HYDRA-CO Enterprises, Inc. from Niagara Mohawk Power Co. Aggressive growth in CMS's gas business is another strengthening factor as the company faces an increasingly competitive market for electric power.

Valuation - 13-OCT-95

As for most utilities, the shares of this substantial midwestern utility holding company will be driven more by changes in interest rates than by its ability to produce above average profit and dividend growth, at least over the near term. Longer term, we think CMS's diversification into international infrastructure development and operations--oil and gas exploration, power generation, and pipeline--adds another level of risk to earnings and, ultimately, share price volatility well above the average utility. Still, plans to raise the common dividend at a pace greater than the average utility could help CMS maintain an above average total return.

Key Stock Statistics

S&P EPS Est. 1995	2.25	Tang. Bk. Value/Share	12.40
P/E on S&P Est. 1995	12.0	Beta	0.21
S&P EPS Est. 1996	2.40	Shareholders	63,600
Dividend Rate/Share	0.96	Market cap. (B)	$ 2.4
Shs. outstg. (M)	88.2	Inst. holdings	57%
Avg. daily vol. (M)	0.158	Insider holdings	NA

Value of $10,000 invested 5 years ago: $ 8,237

Fiscal Year Ending Dec. 31

	1995	% Change	1994	% Change	1993	% Change
Revenues (Million $)						
1Q	1,119	-2%	1,142	9%	1,046	8%
2Q	837.0	5%	796.0	7%	742.0	12%
3Q	—	—	767.0	1%	758.0	27%
4Q	—	—	914.0	-2%	936.0	11%
Yr.	—	—	3,619	4%	3,482	13%
Income (Million $)						
1Q	86.00	10%	78.00	8%	71.92	41%
2Q	33.00	10%	30.00	25%	24.00	71%
3Q	—	—	40.00	25%	32.00	NM
4Q	—	—	31.00	15%	27.00	NM
Yr.	—	—	179.0	15%	155.0	NM
Earnings Per Share ($)						
1Q	0.99	8%	0.92	2%	0.90	41%
2Q	0.37	6%	0.35	17%	0.30	76%
3Q	E0.50	9%	0.46	15%	0.40	NM
4Q	E0.38	6%	0.36	20%	0.30	NM
Yr.	E2.25	8%	2.09	10%	1.90	NM

Next earnings report expected: late October

CMS Energy

Business Summary - 13-OCT-95

CMS Energy is the holding company for Consumers Power Co., an electric and gas utility serving Michigan's lower peninsula, and CMS Enterprises. Electricity comprised 61% of revenues in 1994, gas 36%, and oil and gas exploration and production, independent power production, gas marketing and natural gas processing 3%. Electricity sales by customer were:

	1994	1993	1992	1991
Residential	35%	35%	35%	36%
Commercial	29%	30%	30%	30%
Industrial	31%	31%	30%	29%
Other	5%	4%	5%	5%

Sources of generation in 1994 were coal 47%, nuclear 13%, hydro 1%, oil/gas 1%, and purchased and interchange power 38%. Peak demand in 1994 was 6,502 mw; capability was 7,406 mw, for a capacity margin of 12%. Gas sales and deliveries were 409 Bcf in 1994, up from 389 Bcf in 1993.

CMS estimates its capital budget for construction and improvements to electric and gas transmission and distribution systems over the next three years at $1.2 billion. It has earmarked funds for investments in unconsolidated subsidiaries, demand side management and new lease commitments. The company expects to fund most of its capital projects and also mandatory redemption or retirement of $190 million of debt internally. In 1994 capital outlays were $637 million, including $456 million for utility projects and $115 million for oil and gas exploration and production. CMS anticipates growth in demand for electricity will average 1.6% and for gas 2.3% a year over the next five years.

Important Developments

Sep. '95—Hearings on a final settlement agreement for a base rate increase of $49.9 million and on future annual base rate increases, a $35 million reduction in a residential rate subsidy, recovery of fuel and purchased power costs, and also recovery of costs on a cogeneration plant along with depreciation and special competitive service rates, were postponed until late October. In June the Michigan Public Service Commission ruled to allow CMS to establish a retail wheeling (sale of electric power to non-utility customers) program.

Jul. '95—CMS completed an initial public offering of a tracking stock, trading under the symbol CPG, tied to the financial performance of its regulated gas utility business. Some 7.5 million shares, or 23.5% of the 32 million outstanding, are held by the public; remaining shares represent CMS's retained interest. CMS used proceeds to repay debt.

Capitalization

Long Term Debt: $2,748,000,000 (6/95).
Subsid. Preferred Stock: $356,000,000.

Per Share Data ($) (Year Ended Dec. 31)

	1994	1993	1992	1991	1990	1989
Tangible Bk. Val.	12.40	10.39	7.73	13.23	17.28	23.86
Earnings	2.09	1.90	-3.72	-3.26	-6.07	3.80
Dividends	0.78	0.60	0.48	0.48	0.42	0.10
Payout Ratio	37%	32%	NM	NM	NM	3%
Prices - High	25	27½	22¾	33	38½	39⅝
- Low	19⅝	18⅛	14⅞	16⅝	24⅞	22½
P/E Ratio - High	12	14	NM	NM	NM	10
- Low	9	10	NM	NM	NM	6

Income Statement Analysis (Million $)

	1994	%Chg	1993	%Chg	1992	%Chg	1991
Revs.	3,619	4%	3,482	13%	3,073	4%	2,941
Depr.	379	4%	365	5%	348	23%	283
Maint.	192	-7%	206	1%	203	18%	172
Fxd. Chgs. Cov.	2.1	9%	2.0	—	NM	—	NM
Constr. Credits	6.0	20%	5.0	67%	3.0	-40%	5.0
Eff. Tax Rate	31%	—	31%	—	NM	—	NM
Net Inc.	179	15%	155	NM	-296	NM	-261

Balance Sheet & Other Fin. Data (Million $)

	1994	1993	1992	1991	1990	1989
Gross Prop.	9,125	8,605	8,101	7,618	7,310	6,819
Cap. Exp.	575	548	484	348	387	312
Net Prop.	4,826	4,583	4,326	4,121	4,033	3,839
Capitalization:						
LT Debt	2,817	2,520	2,823	2,009	3,389	3,289
% LT Debt	66	69	76	62	69	61
Pfd.	356	163	163	163	156	176
% Pfd.	8.30	4.40	4.40	5.00	3.20	3.30
Common	1,107	966	727	1,060	1,402	1,960
% Common	26	27	20	33	28	36
Total Cap.	5,043	4,349	4,263	3,902	5,928	6,744

Ratio Analysis

	1994	1993	1992	1991	1990	1989
Oper. Ratio	88.9	90.0	93.0	91.8	86.3	84.8
% Earn. on Net Prop.	8.5	7.8	5.1	5.9	10.4	11.8
% Ret. on Revs.	4.9	4.5	NM	NM	NM	10.5
% Ret. On Invest.Cap	8.7	8.7	NM	1.7	NM	7.6
% Return On Com.Eqty	17.3	18.3	NM	NM	NM	17.2

Dividend Data —CMS pays approximately 80% of its consolidated income as a continuing dividend policy. Dividends were omitted in 1984 and resumed in late 1989.

Amt. of Div. $	Date Decl.	Ex-Div. Date	Stock of Record	Payment Date
0.210	Oct. 28	Nov. 01	Nov. 07	Nov. 22 '94
0.210	Jan. 30	Feb. 02	Feb. 08	Feb. 22 '95
0.210	Apr. 28	May. 02	May. 08	May. 22 '95
0.240	Jul. 28	Aug. 04	Aug. 08	Aug. 22 '95

Data as orig. reptd.; bef. results of disc opers. and/or spec. items. Per share data adj. for stk. divs. as of ex-div. date. E-Estimated. NA-Not Available. NM-Not Meaningful. NR-Not Ranked.

Office—Fairlane Plaza South, Suite 1100, 330 Town Center Drive, Dearborn, MI 48126. **Tel**—(313) 436-9261. **Chrmn & CEO**—W. T. McCormick, Jr. **Vice-Chrmn**—S. K. Smith, Jr. **Pres**—V. J. Fryling. **VP & CFO**—A. M. Wright. **Secy & Treas**—T. A. McNish. **Investor Contact**—Laura L. Mountcastle (517-788-2590). **Dirs**—J. M. Duderstadt, K. R. Flaherty, V. J. Fryling, E. D. Holton, L. A. Lund, W. T. McCormick, Jr., F. H. Merlotti, W. U. Parfet, P. A. Pierre, S. K. Smith, Jr., K. Whipple, J. B. Yasinsky. **Transfer Agent & Registrar**—Co.'s office, Jackson, MI. **Incorporated** in Maine in 1910; reincorporated in Michigan in 1968. **Empl**-10,318. **S&P Analyst:** Jane Collin

STANDARD & POOR'S

STOCK REPORTS

CPI Corp.

NYSE Symbol **CPY**

In S&P MidCap 400

17-OCT-95

Industry: Leisure/Amusement

Summary: This company operates photographic studios as a licensee of Sears and also has one-hour photofinishing labs, high-tech copy stores and a chain of print, poster and framing stores.

Quantitative Evaluations

Recent Price • 20¼ | Yield • 2.7%

52 Wk Range • 22⅛-13¾ | 12-Mo. P/E • 16.6

Outlook (1 Lowest—5 Highest)
• **3+**

Fair Value
• **21¼**

Risk
• **Average**

Earn./Div. Rank
• **B+**

Technical Eval.
• **Bullish** since 9/95

Rel. Strength Rank (1 Lowest—99 Highest)
• **56**

Insider Activity
• **NA**

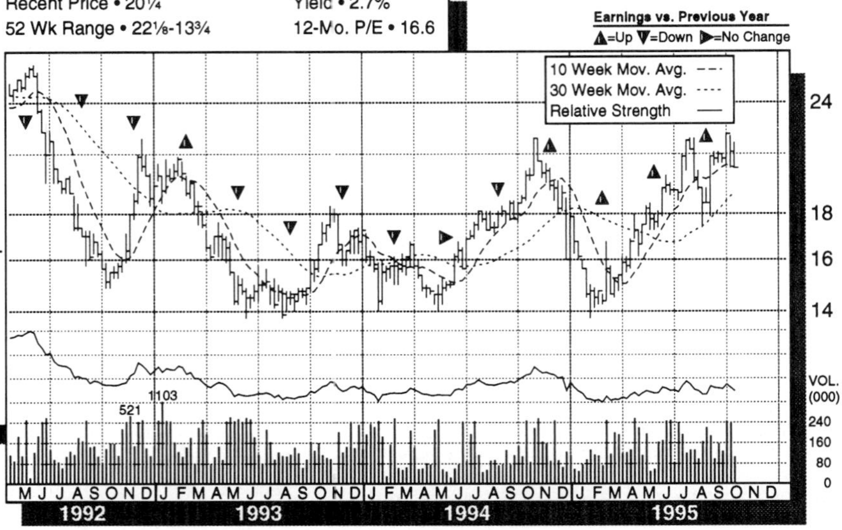

Business Profile - 13-OCT-95

This company derives most of its income from the operation of portrait photography studios as a licensee of Sears, Roebuck and Co., operating more than 1,000 studios as of late August 1995. It also operates 642 one-hour photofinishing labs, some 45 high-tech copy stores and a chain of about 135 print, poster and framing stores. The company said it is optimistic about 1995-6 as a result of new programs and plans for further business development.

Operational Review - 13-OCT-95

Sales for the first half of 1995-6 rose 6.6%, year to year, reflecting increased sales in the portrait studio and wall decor segments. Net income of $1.6 million ($0.11 a share) contrasted with a $0.9 million ($0.06) loss. The company believes the installation of new digital imaging technology has contributed significantly to sales growth. CPI noted that customers are also responding favorably to the Custom Portraits by Sears program.

Stock Performance - 13-OCT-95

In the past 30 trading days, CPY's shares have declined 3%, compared to a 4% rise in the S&P 500. Average trading volume for the past five days was 20,600 shares, compared with the 40-day moving average of 35,256 shares.

Key Stock Statistics

Dividend Rate/Share	0.56	Shareholders	2,300
Shs. outstg. (M)	13.9	Market cap. (B)	$0.284
Avg. daily vol. (M)	0.037	Inst. holdings	79%
Tang. Bk. Value/Share	7.88	Insider holdings	NA
Beta	0.86		

Value of $10,000 invested 5 years ago: $ 7,015

Fiscal Year Ending Jan. 31

	1996	% Change	1995	% Change	1994	% Change
Revenues (Million $)						
1Q	107.4	7%	100.1	13%	88.79	-4%
2Q	110.8	6%	104.7	10%	95.39	3%
3Q	—	—	175.4	21%	145.3	15%
4Q	—	—	153.0	5%	146.0	6%
Yr.	—	—	533.2	12%	475.5	6%
Income (Million $)						
1Q	-0.67	NM	-2.49	NM	2.54	17%
2Q	2.25	38%	1.63	-21%	2.07	-43%
3Q	—	—	3.83	14%	3.35	-46%
4Q	—	—	11.85	44%	8.24	-22%
Yr.	—	—	14.82	33%	11.12	-51%
Earnings Per Share ($)						
1Q	-0.05	NM	-0.17	NM	-0.17	NM
2Q	0.16	45%	0.11	-21%	0.14	-44%
3Q	—	—	0.28	22%	0.23	-45%
4Q	—	—	0.86	54%	0.56	-22%
Yr.	—	—	1.05	38%	0.76	-51%

Next earnings report expected: NA

CPI Corp.

Business Summary - 13-OCT-95

CPI Corp. derives the largest portion of its revenues from the operation of photographic studios in Sears, Roebuck and Co. department stores. It also operates one-hour photofinishing laboratories and conducts an electronic publishing business with retail stores. In 1993, CPI acquired the Prints Plus chain of print, poster and framing stores. Contributions to sales and operating profits (millions) in 1994-5 were:

	Sales	Profits
Portrait studios	52%	$39.1
One-hour photofinishing	36%	4.5
Wall decor	9%	5.5
Other products & services	3%	-3.5

As of early June 1995, the company was operating 1,015 portrait studios in the U.S., Puerto Rico and Canada as a licensee of Sears. The company is the only operator of Sears Portrait Studios in the U.S. and believes it is the largest participant in the over $1 billion preschool portrait market. Under the license agreement, CPI pays a fee of 15% of net sales per fixed location studio and 7.5% of sales for freestanding studios in retail malls that operate under the Sears name. CPI also provides all studio furniture, equipment and fixtures and conducts advertising at its expense.

CPI is the largest U.S. owner/operator of one-hour photofinishing minilabs, operating 645 stores throughout the U.S. as of early June 1995. The stores, operating under the CPI, Fox Photo and Proex names, are in major regional malls, strip shopping centers and freestanding buildings.

The company was operating a total of 40 high-tech copy stores as of early June 1995 in California, Dallas, Atlanta and the Midwest. At that time, CPI was also operating 133 Prints Plus stores in malls throughout the U.S.

Important Developments

Aug. '95—CPI said customer response in the portrait studios continues to be very positive with the rollout of the enhanced Custom Portraits by Sears program. The company noted that, over the past five quarters, U.S. portrait studio operating earnings averaged more than 50% year-to-year growth. Losses in the Canadian portrait studio market, which resulted from competition and a sluggish economy, are expected to be enhanced by a new marketing program similar to that of the U.S. studios. CPI does not see a significant uptrend in the photofinishing segment's operating earnings, but is hopeful that marketing tests could reach maturity in 1995-6.

Capitalization

Long Term Obligations: $59,777,818 (7/95).

Per Share Data ($)

(Year Ended Jan. 31)

	1995	1994	1993	1992	1991	1990
Tangible Bk. Val.	7.93	7.84	7.33	7.09	9.66	8.17
Cash Flow	3.63	2.95	3.42	3.46	3.66	3.32
Earnings	1.05	0.76	1.54	1.80	2.19	1.97
Dividends	0.56	0.56	0.56	0.56	0.50	0.42
Payout Ratio	53%	74%	36%	30%	22%	21%
Cal. Yrs.	1994	1993	1992	1991	1990	1989
Prices - High	21⅞	20⅞	27⅛	34¾	34⅜	33⅞
- Low	14	13¾	14⅞	21¾	23½	19¾
P/E Ratio - High	21	27	18	19	16	17
- Low	13	18	10	12	11	10

Income Statement Analysis (Million $)

	1995	%Chg	1994	%Chg	1993	%Chg	1992
Revs.	533	12%	476	6%	449	8%	415
Oper. Inc.	63.8	25%	50.9	-18%	62.4	-3%	64.4
Depr.	36.4	13%	32.1	17%	27.5	4%	26.5
Int. Exp.	5.3	165%	2.0	NM	0.2	13%	0.2
Pretax Inc.	23.5	27%	18.5	-49%	36.5	-16%	43.3
Eff. Tax Rate	37%	—	40%	—	38%	—	37%
Net Inc.	14.8	33%	11.1	-51%	22.6	-17%	27.1

Balance Sheet & Other Fin. Data (Million $)

	1995	1994	1993	1992	1991	1990
Cash	14.4	66.4	21.0	31.2	88.3	70.0
Curr. Assets	82.0	128	73.0	84.0	130	106
Total Assets	300	306	238	239	219	196
Curr. Liab.	69.8	65.2	56.8	67.1	51.4	47.8
LT Debt	59.7	59.8	0.3	0.6	0.5	0.3
Common Eqty.	166	176	172	160	152	133
Total Cap.	226	236	175	165	159	141
Cap. Exp.	77.1	45.4	13.3	40.6	20.3	25.6
Cash Flow	51.2	43.3	50.1	53.6	56.2	52.2

Ratio Analysis

	1995	1994	1993	1992	1991	1990
Curr. Ratio	1.2	2.0	1.3	1.2	2.5	2.2
% LT Debt of Cap.	26.4	25.4	0.2	0.3	0.3	0.2
% Net Inc.of Revs.	2.8	2.3	5.0	6.5	9.0	8.8
% Ret. on Assets	5.0	4.1	9.5	12.0	16.4	16.2
% Ret. on Equity	8.9	6.4	13.6	17.6	23.8	23.6

Dividend Data —Dividends were initiated in 1985. A "poison pill" stock purchase rights plan was adopted in 1989.

Amt. of Div. $	Date Decl.	Ex-Div. Date	Stock of Record	Payment Date
0.140	Nov. 03	Nov. 07	Nov. 14	Nov. 28 '94
0.140	Feb. 02	Feb. 07	Feb. 13	Feb. 27 '95
0.140	May. 04	May. 09	May. 15	May. 30 '95
0.140	Aug. 03	Aug. 10	Aug. 14	Aug. 28 '95

Data as orig. reptd.; bef. results of disc. opers. and/or spec. items. Per share data adj. for stk. divs. as of ex-div. date. E-Estimated. NA-Not Available. NM-Not Meaningful. NR-Not Ranked.

Office—1706 Washington Ave., St. Louis, MO 63103-1790. **Tel**—(314) 231-1575. **Chrmn & CEO**—A. V. Essman. **Pres**—R. Isaak. **Exec VP & CFO**—B. Arthur. **Secy**—J. E. Nelson. **Dirs**—M. Bohm, A. V. Essman, R. Isaak, M. A. Krey, L. M. Liberman, N. L. Reding, M. Sneider, R. L. Virgil. **Transfer Agent & Registrar**—Continental Stock Transfer & Trust Co., NYC. **Incorporated** in Delaware in 1982. **Empl**-12,400. **S&P Analyst:** Philip D. Wohl

STANDARD & POOR'S

STOCK REPORTS

Cabot Corp.

NYSE Symbol **CBT**
In S&P MidCap 400

10-OCT-95 **Industry:** Chemicals

Summary: Cabot has interests in specialty chemicals and materials (including carbon black and fumed silica) and energy (liquefied natural gas importing and coal handling).

S&P Opinion: Accumulate (★★★★) Recent Price • 50⅝ 52 Wk Range • 58¾-25½ Yield • 1.5% 12-Mo. P/E • 13.8

Quantitative Evaluations
Outlook (1 Lowest—5 Highest) • **4+**
Fair Value • **57⅞**
Risk • **Average**
Earn./Div. Rank • **B**

Technical Eval. • **Bearish** since 8/95
Rel. Strength Rank (1 Lowest—99 Highest) • **33**
Insider Activity • **Unfavorable**

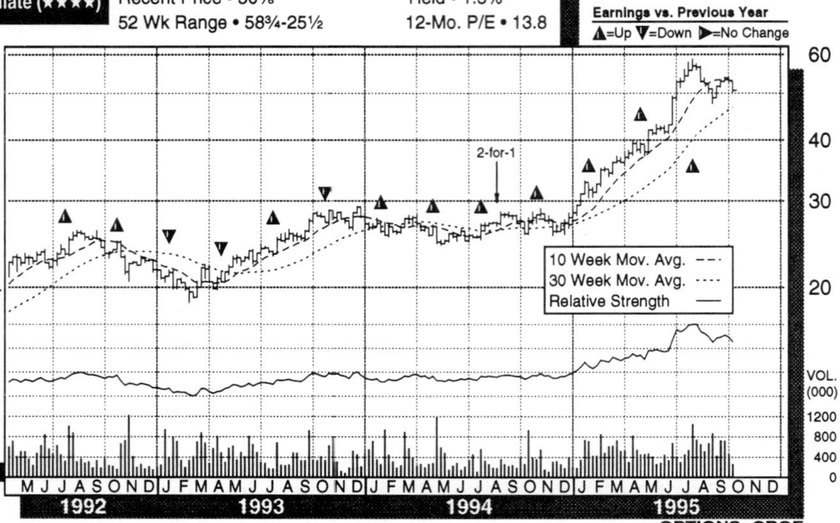

OPTIONS: CBOE

Overview - 10-OCT-95

We see profits for the specialty chemicals business rising in fiscal 1996, on greater demand and wider margins for carbon black and other products in most areas of the world. Price increases for carbon black achieved since late 1994 will continue to boost profits. The new supply agreements with certain U.S. tire customers will help to reduce margin volatility. The LNG business will likely continue to be restricted by reduced supplies from Algeria. The pending sale of the coal handling business and the recent divestiture of a majority interest in Cabot Safety will reduce reported annual sales by about $450 million. Reduced interest expense and stock repurchases will offset much of the loss of earnings generated by these two businesses.

Valuation - 10-OCT-95

The stock has been a strong performer in 1995, rising about 85%, year to date. Growing worldwide demand and very high industry operating rates have led to rising selling prices and margins for carbon black. The recently announced carbon black supply and margin agreements with several U.S. tire companies enhance the longer-term prospects for this material by reducing volatility of prices and earnings. CBT is making several attractive capital investments. The stock buyback program should also be positive. Despite the runup this year, the stock remains attractive in view of CBT's positive earnings outlook and reasonable P/E multiple.

Key Stock Statistics

S&P EPS Est. 1995	4.20	Tang. Bk. Value/Share	10.98
P/E on S&P Est. 1995	12.1	Beta	0.97
S&P EPS Est. 1996	4.75	Shareholders	2,100
Dividend Rate/Share	0.72	Market cap. (B)	$ 1.9
Shs. outstg. (M)	37.9	Inst. holdings	60%
Avg. daily vol. (M)	0.094	Insider holdings	NA

Value of $10,000 invested 5 years ago: NA

Fiscal Year Ending Sep. 30

	1995	% Change	1994	% Change	1993	% Change
Revenues (Million $)						
1Q	428.0	7%	398.5	NM	396.0	3%
2Q	481.3	11%	434.9	7%	407.6	-2%
3Q	497.0	16%	428.8	2%	418.8	13%
4Q	—	—	417.7	7%	391.9	2%
Yr.	—	—	1,680	4%	1,614	4%
Income (Million $)						
1Q	33.91	112%	15.96	34%	11.93	-28%
2Q	46.40	108%	22.35	60%	13.96	-37%
3Q	47.03	114%	22.00	19%	18.45	13%
4Q	—	—	18.40	NM	-6.90	NM
Yr.	—	—	78.69	110%	37.41	-40%
Earnings Per Share ($)						
1Q	0.85	115%	0.39	34%	0.29	-31%
2Q	1.17	109%	0.56	60%	0.35	-39%
3Q	1.18	113%	0.55	18%	0.47	12%
4Q	E1.00	122%	0.45	NM	-0.21	NM
Yr.	E4.20	114%	1.96	118%	0.90	-43%

Next earnings report expected: early November

Cabot Corp.

Business Summary - 10-OCT-95

Cabot Corporation has operations in specialty chemicals and materials and in energy. Segment contributions in fiscal 1994 were:

	Sales	Profits
Specialty chemicals & materials	74%	90%
Energy	26%	10%

International operations accounted for 39% of sales and 31% of profits in fiscal 1994.

CBT is the world's largest producer of carbon black, an essential reinforcing agent used in tires and rubber products and as a pigment in inks, coatings and plastics, with about one-fourth of the worldwide production capacity. It is also the world's second largest producer of fumed silica (used as a reinforcing and thickening agent in a variety of products), a major producer of electronic materials and refractory metals (primarily tantalum for electrolytic capacitors), and a leading European producer of plastic concentrates and compounds.

Cabot LNG is an importer and distributor of liquefied natural gas in the U.S. Northeast, and TUCO is a coal handling and distribution business. A 15% interest is held in KN Energy, Inc., a gas transmission company.

In July 1995, CBT sold a majority interest in Cabot Safety, a producer of safety eyewear, hearing protection and industrial noise control products.

Important Developments

Sep. '95—CBT began a new stock repurchase program for up to 3,000,000 common shares, with about 323,000 shares already acquired. CBT repurchased 908,000 shares since October 1994 under a previous program.

Jul. '95—CBT sold a 57.5% interest in its Cabot Safety unit in a transaction valued at $205 million. CBT received about $128 million after taxes. The unit has annual sales of more than $200 million. CBT also agreed to sell its TUCO, Inc. coal handling business for $77 million. Proceeds will be used to reinvest in CBT's core chemicals business. CBT plans to invest $50 million for a fumed silica plant and $30 million to expand its South American carbon black capacity.

Jun. '95—CBT signed long-term carbon black supply agreements with certain North American tire customers, allowing CBT to provide a secure supply and reduce the volatility of prices and earnings. CBT plans to increase its annual carbon black capacity by 200 million pounds.

Capitalization

Long Term Debt: $313,903,000 (6/95).
ESOP 7.75% Preferred Stock: $70,720,000; conv. into approx. 1.6 million com. shs.

Per Share Data ($) (Year Ended Sep. 30)

	1994	1993	1992	1991	1990	1989
Tangible Bk. Val.	12.65	9.53	9.01	6.97	8.00	8.05
Cash Flow	4.22	2.98	3.88	2.73	3.01	1.69
Earnings	1.96	0.90	1.59	0.85	1.36	-0.20
Dividends	0.92	0.52	0.52	0.52	0.52	0.51
Payout Ratio	47%	58%	33%	52%	38%	NM
Prices - High	29¼	29¼	26¼	18	19	22⅝
- Low	24⅜	18½	15⅞	13⅜	11½	16½
P/E Ratio - High	15	33	16	21	14	NM
- Low	12	21	10	16	8	NM

Income Statement Analysis (Million $)

	1994	%Chg	1993	%Chg	1992	%Chg	1991
Revs.	1,680	4%	1,614	4%	1,557	5%	1,482
Oper. Inc.	261	13%	230	-5%	242	29%	188
Depr.	86.0	10%	78.0	-7%	84.0	5%	80.0
Int. Exp.	41.7	-5%	44.0	-4%	45.7	-4%	47.4
Pretax Inc.	124	82%	68.0	-42%	117	65%	71.0
Eff. Tax Rate	36%	—	45%	—	47%	—	44%
Net Inc.	78.7	110%	37.4	-40%	62.2	56%	39.8

Balance Sheet & Other Fin. Data (Million $)

	1994	1993	1992	1991	1990	1989
Cash	81.0	40.0	31.0	39.0	48.0	16.0
Curr. Assets	606	544	555	494	579	487
Total Assets	1,617	1,489	1,555	1,462	1,732	1,417
Curr. Liab.	475	354	361	501	444	360
LT Debt	308	459	480	370	481	386
Common Eqty.	555	436	418	352	495	414
Total Cap.	995	988	1,103	870	1,184	975
Cap. Exp.	74.0	65.0	78.0	198	174	214
Cash Flow	161	112	143	116	148	87.0

Ratio Analysis

	1994	1993	1992	1991	1990	1989
Curr. Ratio	1.3	1.5	1.5	1.0	1.3	1.4
% LT Debt of Cap.	30.9	46.5	43.5	42.5	40.6	39.6
% Net Inc.of Revs.	4.7	2.3	4.0	2.7	4.2	NM
% Ret. on Assets	5.0	2.4	4.1	2.9	4.5	NM
% Ret. on Equity	15.1	7.2	15.2	10.0	14.8	NM

Dividend Data —Dividends have been paid since 1931. A dividend reinvestment plan is available. A "poison pill" stock purchase rights plan was adopted in 1986.

Amt. of Div. $	Date Decl.	Ex-Div. Date	Stock of Record	Payment Date
0.140	Nov. 11	Nov. 18	Nov. 25	Dec. 09 '94
0.140	Feb. 10	Feb. 17	Feb. 24	Mar. 10 '95
0.140	May. 12	May. 22	May. 26	Jun. 09 '95
0.180	Jul. 14	Aug. 23	Aug. 25	Sep. 08 '95

Data as orig. reptd.; bef. results of disc. opers. and/or spec. items. Per share data adj. for stk. divs. as of ex-div. date. E-Estimated. NA-Not Available. NM-Not Meaningful. NR-Not Ranked.

Office—75 State St., Boston, MA 02109-1806. **Tel**—(617) 345-0100. **Chrmn & CEO**—S. W. Bodman. **Pres**—K. F. Burns. **CFO**—K. C. Gilson. **Secy**—C. D. Gerlinger. **Investor Contact**—Kathryn D. Cadigan. **Dirs**—D. Ames, S. W. Bodman, J. C. Bradley, K. F. Burnes, J. G. L. Cabot, R. A. Charpie, J. D. Curtin Jr., R. P Henderson, A. C. Hiatt, G. Jeelof, J. H. McArthur, J. F. O'Brien, D. V. Ragone, C. P. Siess Jr., M. Tanenbaum, L. W. Thomas. **Transfer Agent & Registrar**—First National Bank of Boston. **Incorporated** in Delaware in 1960. **Empl**-5,400. **S&P Analyst:** Richard O'Reilly, CFA

STANDARD & POOR'S
STOCK REPORTS

Cadence Design Systems

NYSE Symbol **CDN**
In S&P MidCap 400

23-SEP-95 **Industry:** Data Processing

Summary: This company is a leading producer of electronic design automation software.

S&P Opinion: Accumulate (★★★★) Recent Price • 39⅜ 52 Wk Range • 41¾-16⅞ Yield • Nil 12-Mo. P/E • 27.5

Quantitative Evaluations
Outlook (1 Lowest—5 Highest)
• **2+**
Fair Value
• **37¼**
Risk
• **Average**
Earn./Div. Rank
• **B**

Technical Eval.
• **Bullish** since 2/94
Rel. Strength Rank (1 Lowest—99 Highest)
• **75**
Insider Activity
• **Neutral**

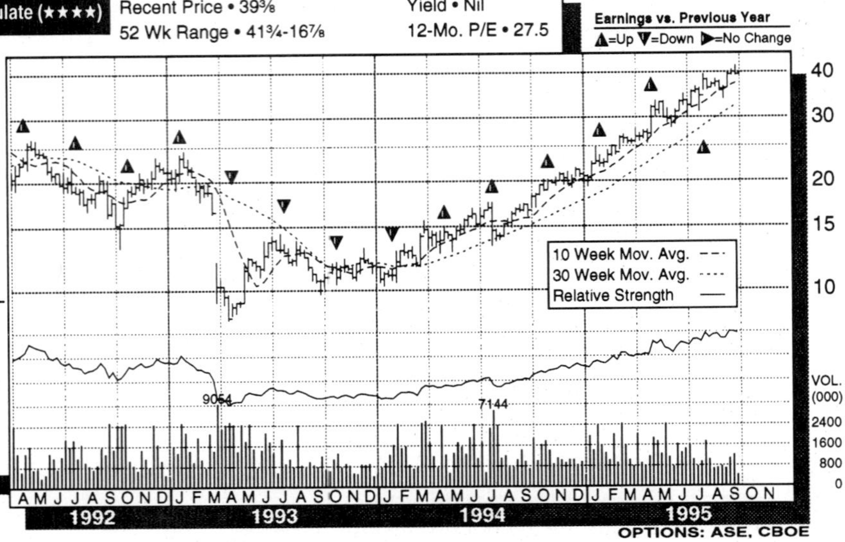

OPTIONS: ASE, CBOE

Overview - 22-SEP-95

Revenues should achieve double-digit growth in 1996, fueled by improved systems business sales and greater contributions from consulting business. In addition, strong conditions in the semiconductor industry will exert a very positive influence. International sales will also continue to play an important role. Japanese sales rose strongly in recent periods and are expected to continue to grow at an accelerated pace. A focus on reducing the cost structure aided earnings gains in recent periods. However, future gains may be limited, as results of cost-cutting efforts have peaked. Long-term results should benefit from a plan to review all product lines. EPS will be boosted by an aggressive stock repurchase program.

Valuation - 22-SEP-95

The shares, which are near their 52-week high, still have room to rise. The company is close to completion of a cost-reduction phase and has begun to concentrate on revenue growth. Product sales should continue to increase, aided by stronger sales in Europe and Japan. In addition, services and maintenance revenues, which carry a higher gross margin than product sales, form an increasing component of revenues. A recent outsourcing agreement with Unysis gives Cadence accesss to a highly regarded ASIC engineering team, which could pay big dividends in the future. Results will also be aided by a stock repurchase program. We continue to recommend the stock for capital appreciation.

Key Stock Statistics

S&P EPS Est. 1995	1.60	Tang. Bk. Value/Share	3.27
P/E on S&P Est. 1995	24.6	Beta	1.80
S&P EPS Est. 1996	2.00	Shareholders	2,100
Dividend Rate/Share	Nil	Market cap. (B)	$ 1.4
Shs. outstg. (M)	36.4	Inst. holdings	73%
Avg. daily vol. (M)	0.172	Insider holdings	NA

Value of $10,000 invested 5 years ago: $ 18,529

Fiscal Year Ending Dec. 31

	1995	% Change	1994	% Change	1993	% Change
Revenues (Million $)						
1Q	116.0	20%	96.78	27%	76.12	-25%
2Q	128.5	27%	101.0	14%	88.81	-16%
3Q	—	—	109.6	12%	97.62	-8%
4Q	—	—	121.7	15%	106.1	-12%
Yr.	—	—	429.1	16%	368.6	-15%
Income (Million $)						
1Q	13.55	NM	-3.85	NM	-15.84	NM
2Q	16.97	68%	10.08	NM	1.91	-85%
3Q	—	—	9.48	87%	5.07	-60%
4Q	—	—	20.93	154%	8.25	-59%
Yr.	—	—	36.65	NM	-0.61	NM
Earnings Per Share ($)						
1Q	0.32	NM	-0.09	NM	-0.36	NM
2Q	0.41	78%	0.23	NM	0.04	-86%
3Q	E0.41	86%	0.22	100%	0.11	-61%
4Q	E0.46	-6%	0.49	172%	0.18	-59%
Yr.	E1.60	90%	0.84	NM	-0.02	NM

Next earnings report expected: mid October

Cadence Design Systems

Business Summary - 22-SEP-95

Cadence Design Systems, Inc. develops, markets and supports computer software products that automate and accelerate the design and verification of integrated circuits (ICs) and electronic systems. It is the largest supplier of electronic design automation (EDA) software and a market leader in the integrated circuit design automation (ICDA) segment of EDA.

EDA uses computers and engineering software to design electronic circuits and systems. Virtually all complex computer, telecommunication, aerospace and semiconductor projects depend on EDA to handle large amounts of data.

Cadence's full line of integrated EDA software has been developed to support engineering with specific design needs and on larger projects. A commitment to industry-standard hardware platforms, operating systems and network protocols lets users configure an open design environment for their specific needs.

The company offers a full line of integrated EDA solutions for three basic design areas: IC design for digital, analog and mixed signal devices; system design for both analog and digital systems; and application-specific integrated circuit (ASIC) design, particularly for high-performance sub-micron ASICs.

Cadence continues to invest in new areas of EDA. With the formation of the Alta Group, it can provide a higher level of design automation for applications areas that include wireless communications, networking and multimedia.

The company's 55%-owned Integrated Measurement Systems, Inc. subsidiary manufacturers and markets engineering test stations and related test software.

International revenues represented 52% and 50% of the total in 1994 and 1993, respectively.

Important Developments

Aug. '95—CDN's directors authorized the repurchase of up to an additional 2.5 million common shares. During the first half, the company repurchased 3.2 million of its shares.

Jul. '95—The company said its second-quarter revenue growth was led by a gain in service revenues that reflected acceptance of its new business model that combines leading-edge technology with professional service at its Spectrum Services organization. It added that new bookings during the second quarter exceeded revenues and that it was continuing its previously announced share repurchase program. Separately, the company sold 2.6 million shares of its Integrated Measurement Systems subsidiary through a public offering that reduced CDN's ownership interest to 55%.

Capitalization

Long Term Debt: $9,168,000, incl. $7,387,000 of lease obligs. (7/95).

Per Share Data ($)

(Year Ended Dec. 31)

	1994	1993	1992	1991	1990	1989
Tangible Bk. Val.	4.64	5.01	5.67	4.48	5.30	3.76
Cash Flow	1.52	0.58	1.73	0.06	1.64	1.24
Earnings	0.84	-0.02	1.20	-0.56	1.19	0.93
Dividends	Nil	Nil	Nil	Nil	Nil	Nil
Payout Ratio	Nil	Nil	Nil	Nil	Nil	Nil
Prices - High	21¾	24⅜	29⅞	34⅝	28⅞	22
- Low	10¼	8¼	13⅛	14½	13¼	11⅛
P/E Ratio - High	26	NM	25	NM	24	24
- Low	12	NM	11	NM	11	12

Income Statement Analysis (Million $)

	1994	%Chg	1993	%Chg	1992	%Chg	1991
Revs.	429	16%	369	-15%	435	11%	392
Oper. Inc.	88.8	141%	36.9	-59%	89.9	46%	61.5
Depr.	30.1	17%	25.7	6%	24.2	-5%	25.6
Int. Exp.	1.0	46%	0.7	-23%	0.9	-66%	2.7
Pretax Inc.	49.3	NM	-0.5	NM	68.5	NM	-11.8
Eff. Tax Rate	25%	—	NM	—	19%	—	NM
Net Inc.	36.6	NM	-0.6	NM	55.4	NM	-21.7

Balance Sheet & Other Fin. Data (Million $)

	1994	1993	1992	1991	1990	1989
Cash	97.0	93.0	92.0	111	91.2	62.7
Curr. Assets	192	218	249	246	166	109
Total Assets	361	339	370	350	234	159
Curr. Liab.	164	113	95.0	123	58.1	40.7
LT Debt	2.1	4.0	6.0	4.1	7.9	9.4
Common Eqty.	176	206	249	189	158	104
Total Cap.	180	213	263	212	174	118
Cap. Exp.	15.2	19.3	31.4	29.6	22.2	6.2
Cash Flow	66.7	25.1	79.0	2.6	52.5	37.3

Ratio Analysis

	1994	1993	1992	1991	1990	1989
Curr. Ratio	1.2	1.9	2.6	2.0	2.9	2.7
% LT Debt of Cap.	1.2	1.9	2.3	1.9	4.6	7.9
% Net Inc.of Revs.	8.5	NM	12.7	NM	16.4	19.4
% Ret. on Assets	10.9	NM	15.1	NM	18.7	21.8
% Ret. on Equity	20.0	NM	24.6	NM	28.1	32.8

Dividend Data —Cadence has never paid cash dividends.

Data as orig. reptd.; bef. results of disc. opers. and/or spec. items. Per share data adj. for stk. divs. as of ex-div. date. E-Estimated. NA-Not Available. NM-Not Meaningful. NR-Not Ranked.

Office—555 River Oaks Parkway, San Jose, CA 95134. **Tel**—(408) 943-1234. **Chrmn**—D. L. Lucas. **Pres & CEO**—J. B. Costello. **Exec VP, CFO & Secy**—H. R. Bingham. **Investor Contact**—Douglas J. McCutcheon. **Dirs**—C. Bartz, J. B. Costello, H. E. Johnston, R. J. Lane, L. Y. W. Liu, D. L. Lucas, A. Sangiovanni-Vincentelli, G. M. Scalise, J. R. Shoven, J. E. Solomon. **Transfer Agent**—Harris Trust & Savings Bank, Chicago. **Incorporated** in Delaware in 1987. **Empl-** 2,449. **S&P Analyst:** Paul H. Valentine, CFA

STANDARD & POOR'S

STOCK REPORTS

Calgon Carbon

NYSE Symbol **CCC**
In S&P MidCap 400

04-OCT-95 **Industry:** Pollution Control

Summary: This company, the world's largest manufacturer of activated carbon products, also provides related equipment and services that employ activated carbon technology.

Quantitative Evaluations

Recent Price • 11¾ | 52 Wk Range • 13¾-9⅞ | Yield • 2.6% | 12-Mo. P/E • NM

Outlook
(1 Lowest—5 Highest)
• **2-**
Fair Value
• **10½**
Risk
• **Average**
Earn./Div. Rank
• **NR**

Technical Eval.
• **Bullish** since 8/95
Rel. Strength Rank
(1 Lowest—99 Highest)
• **33**
Insider Activity
• **Unfavorable**

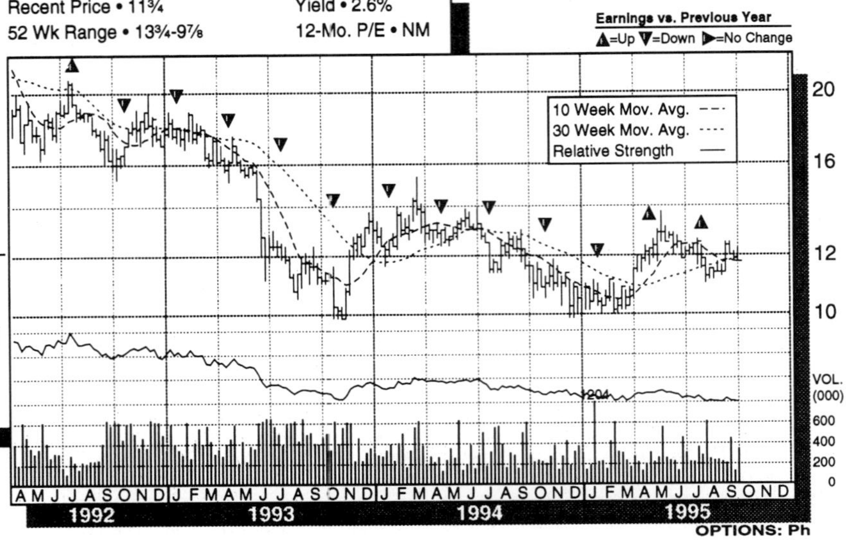

OPTIONS: Ph

Business Profile - 04-OCT-95

Following several years of depressed results, sales and earnings in 1995 have benefited from improved economic conditions in Europe, which should continue to help in the second half of the year as well. New products introduced in the first half have also aided results. As part of a strategic plan announced in late 1994, the company in mid-1995 formed partnerships with Safety-Kleen Corp. and Solarchem Environmental Systems, Inc., which will allow it to expand its range of services.

Operational Review - 04-OCT-95

Net sales for the six months ended June 30, 1995, rose 10%, year to year, reflecting increases in the chemical/pharmaceutical and original equipment manufacturer areas, and in the European energy category. Margins widened on the higher volume, aided by a decline in R&D expenditures; operating income was up 15%. Following lower depreciation charges and greater interest income, net income advanced 32%, to $9,970,000 ($0.25 a share) from $7,566,000 ($0.19).

Stock Performance - 29-SEP-95

In the past 30 trading days, CCC's shares have increased 3%, compared to a 5% rise in the S&P 500. Average trading volume for the past five days was 67,500 shares, compared with the 40-day moving average of 51,987 shares.

Key Stock Statistics

Dividend Rate/Share	0.30	Shareholders	1,300
Shs. outstg. (M)	40.4	Market cap. (B)	$0.470
Avg. daily vol. (M)	0.057	Inst. holdings	45%
Tang. Bk. Value/Share	5.30	Insider holdings	NA
Beta	1.09		

Value of $10,000 invested 5 years ago: $ 5,986

Fiscal Year Ending Dec. 31

	1995	% Change	1994	% Change	1993	% Change
Revenues (Million $)						
1Q	68.81	10%	62.50	-2%	63.73	-9%
2Q	75.97	10%	69.16	-5%	72.69	-8%
3Q	—	—	69.35	5%	65.97	-15%
4Q	—	—	73.23	9%	67.04	-6%
Yr.	—	—	274.2	2%	269.4	-10%
Income (Million $)						
1Q	3.92	68%	2.34	-55%	5.17	-23%
2Q	6.05	16%	5.22	-9%	5.72	-40%
3Q	—	—	3.72	-10%	4.12	-48%
4Q	—	—	-19.89	NM	4.15	-6%
Yr.	—	—	-8.61	NM	19.15	-33%
Earnings Per Share ($)						
1Q	0.10	67%	0.06	-54%	0.13	-19%
2Q	0.15	15%	0.13	-7%	0.14	-42%
3Q	—	—	0.09	-10%	0.10	-47%
4Q	—	—	-0.49	NM	0.10	-9%
Yr.	—	—	-0.21	NM	0.47	-33%

Next earnings report expected: mid October

Calgon Carbon

Business Summary - 04-OCT-95

Calgon Carbon is the world's largest manufacturer and supplier of granular activated carbon products. It also provides related adsorption equipment and services that utilize activated carbon technology. Manufacturing facilities are located in the U.S., Germany, Belgium and the U.K. Operations at a plant in Brilon Wald, Germany, were ceased in June 1995. Business segment contributions to sales in recent years were:

	1994	1993
Activated carbon	58%	59%
Services	25%	25%
Equipment	10%	9%
Charcoal/liquids	7%	7%

Sales to international customers, principally in Europe, accounted for 44% and 47% of the total in 1994 and 1993, respectively.

CCC's activated carbons consist of a broad range of untreated, impregnated or acid-washed carbons, in either powder, granular or pellet form. The company also provides carbon reactivation, handling and transportation services, as well as on-site purification, filtration and extraction services. In addition, CCC designs, assembles and sells activated carbon purification, filtration and extraction systems, and distillation systems. Charcoal is sold to retail consumers in Europe, principally Germany, for outdoor barbecue grilling. CCC's total annual activated carbon production capacity exceeds 200 million pounds, and approximately 90% of total production is granular, which can be reactivated and used over again by its customers.

Principal markets served include environmental (48% of sales in 1994); chemical and pharmaceutical (14%); food (12%); and original equipment manufacturers (9%). Products can be used to purify sweeteners, chemicals and pharmaceuticals; to decaffeinate coffee; to remove impurities from natural gas; and for gold recovery. Activated carbon can also be incorporated into products, such as water filters, cigarette filters, industrial and military respirators, and evaporative emissions control canisters in automobiles. CCC's activated carbon, services and equipment are used by municipalities to purify drinking water and to control sewage odor and by other companies to control air pollution and wastewater discharges.

Important Developments

Aug. '95—CCC and Solarchem Environmental Systems, Inc. were awarded a $700,000 contract to provide an activated carbon groundwater remediation system for the Fort Ord Army Base in Monterey, Calif. This is the first joint project for CCC and Solarchem since the two companies formed a partnership in July to pursue applications in the water treatment area.

Capitalization

Long Term Debt: $5,744,000 (6/95).

Per Share Data ($)

(Year Ended Dec. 31)

	1994	1993	1992	1991	1990	1989
Tangible Bk. Val.	5.62	6.03	5.84	5.67	4.92	3.99
Cash Flow	0.26	0.91	1.10	1.24	1.23	1.07
Earnings	-0.21	0.47	0.70	0.94	0.97	0.87
Dividends	0.16	0.16	0.16	0.16	0.15	0.11
Payout Ratio	NM	34%	23%	17%	15%	13%
Prices - High	15⅜	18⅞	26¾	30¾	25⅛	23¾
- Low	9⅞	9⅞	15¼	17½	14⅝	12⅛
P/E Ratio - High	NM	40	38	33	26	27
- Low	NM	21	22	19	15	14

Income Statement Analysis (Million $)

	1994	%Chg	1993	%Chg	1992	%Chg	1991
Revs.	274	2%	269	-10%	298	-3%	308
Oper. Inc.	44.1	-17%	52.9	-22%	68.0	-8%	73.7
Depr.	19.0	4%	18.2	13%	16.1	29%	12.5
Int. Exp.	0.8	-23%	1.0	-27%	1.4	30%	1.0
Pretax Inc.	-18.6	NM	30.8	-30%	44.0	-28%	60.7
Eff. Tax Rate	NM	—	38%	—	35%	—	37%
Net Inc.	-8.6	NM	19.2	-33%	28.6	-25%	38.1

Balance Sheet & Other Fin. Data (Million $)

	1994	1993	1992	1991	1990	1989
Cash	45.4	21.8	8.2	8.2	22.0	44.2
Curr. Assets	149	133	120	124	129	129
Total Assets	343	337	335	336	285	234
Curr. Liab.	65.8	38.3	45.1	46.5	46.9	38.6
LT Debt	6.4	6.5	6.8	27.7	11.2	17.7
Common Eqty.	227	247	239	231	200	162
Total Cap.	268	289	280	279	227	188
Cap. Exp.	7.1	15.1	24.0	70.6	47.6	24.3
Cash Flow	10.4	37.3	44.8	50.6	49.9	43.4

Ratio Analysis

	1994	1993	1992	1991	1990	1989
Curr. Ratio	2.3	3.5	2.7	2.7	2.8	3.3
% LT Debt of Cap.	2.4	2.2	2.4	9.9	5.0	9.4
% Net Inc.of Revs.	NM	7.1	9.6	12.4	13.9	13.9
% Ret. on Assets	NM	5.7	8.5	12.3	15.2	16.3
% Ret. on Equity	NM	7.9	12.2	17.7	21.9	24.8

Dividend Data —Dividends have been paid since 1987. A stockholder rights plan was adopted in February 1995.

Amt. of Div. $	Date Decl.	Ex-Div. Date	Stock of Record	Payment Date
0.040	Oct. 18	Dec. 07	Dec. 13	Jan. 03 '95
.50 Spl	Jan. 18	Jan. 26	Feb. 01	Feb. 14 '95
0.075	Jan. 18	Mar. 08	Mar. 14	Apr. 04 '95
0.075	Apr. 18	Jun. 08	Jun. 12	Jul. 03 '95
0.075	Aug. 15	Sep. 07	Sep. 11	Oct. 02 '95

Data as orig. reptd.; bef. results of disc. opers. and/or spec. items. Per share data adj. for stk. divs. as of ex-div. date. Book value incl. intangibles. E-Estimated. NA-Not Available. NM-Not Meaningful. NR-Not Ranked.

Office—400 Calgon Carbon Drive, Pittsburgh, PA 15205. **Tel**—(412) 787-6700. **Chrmn**—T. A. McConomy. **Pres & CEO**—C. Bailey. **SVP & CFO**—S. Keefer. **SVP & Secy**—J. A. Fischette. **Investor Contact**—Gail A. Gerono (412-787-6795). **Dirs**—C. Bailey, R. W. Cruickshank, A. L. Goeschel, T. A. McConomy, N. H. Prater, R. R. Tisch, H. H. Weil, R. H. Zanitsch. **Transfer Agent**—First Chicago Trust Co. of New York, NYC. **Incorporated** in Delaware in 1967. **Empl**-1,267. **S&P Analyst:** M.V.P.

California Energy

NYSE Symbol **CE**
In S&P MidCap 400

16-AUG-95 **Industry:** Machinery

Summary: This company primarily explores for and develops geothermal resources and converts them into electrical power and steam for sale to electric utilities.

Quantitative Evaluations
Outlook (1 Lowest—5 Highest) • **4**
Fair Value • **19½**
Risk • **Low**
Earn./Div. Rank • **B-**

Technical Eval. • **Bullish** since 7/95
Rel. Strength Rank (1 Lowest—99 Highest) • **73**
Insider Activity • **Favorable**

Recent Price • 18⅝
52 Wk Range • 19⅛-15¼
Yield • Nil
12-Mo. P/E • 18.1

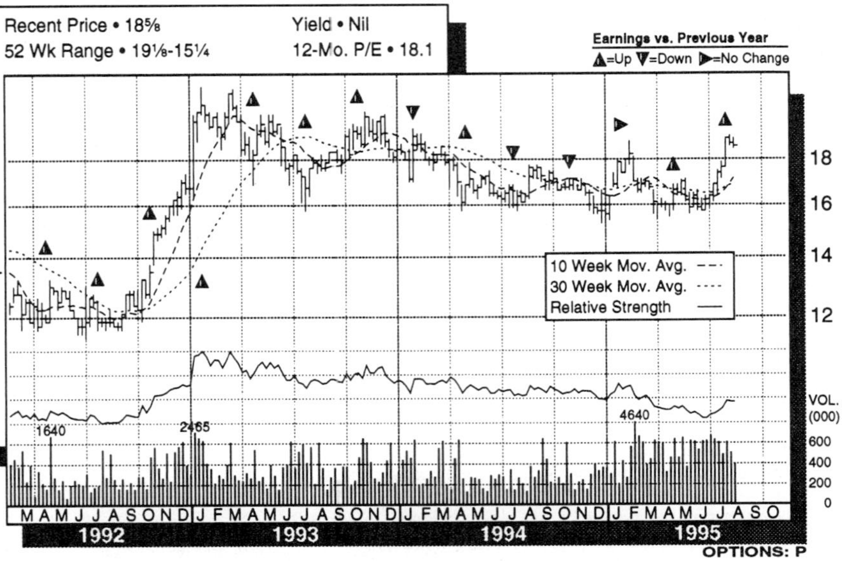

OPTIONS: P

Business Profile - 16-AUG-95

CE believes that it can achieve significant cost savings from its early 1995 acquisition of Magma Power Co., based in part on CE's experience in restructuring its operations since 1991. Through the implementation of existing organizational structure and cost controls, CE expects the cost of duplicate functions will be eliminated, and that the productivity of its combined operating and administrative staff will be increased. The Magma acquisition doubled CE's revenue base.

Operational Review - 16-AUG-95

Revenues for the first half of 1995 more than doubled, year to year, reflecting the acquisition of Magma Power and record kilowatt hour production from the Coso project. Profitability benefited from the increased volume, and net income rose sharply. Results include a nonrecurring charge of $0.06 a share in the 1994 period for the defeasance of senior debt. CE said that the results for the second quarter demonstrate that it has begun to recognize significant anticipated cost savings.

Stock Performance - 11-AUG-95

In the past 30 trading days, CE's shares have increased 14%, compared to a 2% rise in the S&P 500. Average trading volume for the past five days was 79,100 shares, compared with the 40-day moving average of 155,556 shares.

Key Stock Statistics

Dividend Rate/Share	Nil	Shareholders	1,400
Shs. outstg. (M)	49.9	Market cap. (B)	$0.936
Avg. daily vol. (M)	0.092	Inst. holdings	54%
Tang. Bk. Value/Share	3.61	Insider holdings	NA
Beta	1.27		

Value of $10,000 invested 5 years ago: $ 15,496

Fiscal Year Ending Dec. 31

	1995	% Change	1994	% Change	1993	% Change
Revenues (Million $)						
1Q	86.69	145%	35.41	14%	31.16	29%
2Q	97.10	115%	45.25	26%	35.92	28%
3Q	—	—	58.52	27%	46.26	22%
4Q	—	—	46.67	30%	35.91	33%
Yr.	—	—	185.9	25%	149.3	27%
Income (Million $)						
1Q	9.61	12%	8.61	15%	7.48	29%
2Q	13.89	66%	8.38	-21%	10.65	16%
3Q	—	—	14.41	-14%	16.68	6%
4Q	—	—	7.44	-10%	8.26	NM
Yr.	—	—	38.83	-10%	43.07	11%
Earnings Per Share ($)						
1Q	0.21	5%	0.20	25%	0.16	23%
2Q	0.27	35%	0.20	-20%	0.25	14%
3Q	—	—	0.38	-7%	0.41	5%
4Q	—	—	0.18	NM	0.18	-5%
Yr.	—	—	0.95	-5%	1.00	9%

Next earnings report expected: late October

STANDARD & POOR'S

STOCK REPORTS

California Energy

16-AUG-95

Business Summary - 16-AUG-95

California Energy Company explores and develops geothermal resources, which it converts into electrical power for sale to public utilities.

At the end of 1994, the company had substantial interests in, and operated, four geothermal facilities. Three of the facilities (the Coso Project) are located at the Naval Air Weapons Station at China Lake, Calif.; each is owned by a separate partnership.

The Coso project's three geothermal power production facilities--the Navy I Project, the BLM Project and the Navy II Project--have capacities of 88,000 gross kw each. Under three long-term power sales contracts (the PURPA Contracts) that expire in 2011, 2019 and 2010, respectively, Southern California Edison is required to purchase electricity produced by these facilities.

The Coso facilities operated at the following average net capacity in recent years:

	1994	1993	1992
Navy I	114.0%	111.2%	99.8%
BLM	99.5%	98.1%	87.2%
Navy II	105.9%	102.6%	98.1%

The Coso project continues to constitute the company's primary source of electrical generation capacity. CE owns and operates a 10,000 kw Desert Peak, Nev., geothermal plant that sells power to Sierra Pacific Power Co., and holds a 70% interest in a geothermal steam field at Roosevelt Hot Springs, Utah, supplying a 25,000-kw. power plant owned by Utah Power & Light Co. Under a pilot program, CE is developing a 30,000 MW geothermal project at Newberry, Ore., expected to start operating in 1997.

Although CE currently produces power solely from geothermal resources, it intends to pursue the acquisition of power generating projects outside of the geothermal area. It also intends to pursue opportunities in developing nations.

Important Developments

Feb. '95—CE completed the acquisition of Magma Power Co., a company that operates seven geothermal power plants in southern California for cash and CE common stock valued at a total of about $950 million. CE said the combined companies have projected annual revenues in excess of $400 million, its facilities will produce in excess of 545 mw of power and will have an additional 530 mw of power under construction.

Capitalization

Debt: $1,107,729 (3/95), incl. $100 million of sub. debs. due 2000, conv. into com. at $22.50 a sh.
Options: To buy 9,601,000 shs. at $3.00 to $19.00 ea. (12/94).

Per Share Data ($)

(Year Ended Dec. 31)

	1994	1993	1992	1991	1990	1989
Tangible Bk. Val.	6.42	5.99	4.79	4.38	2.37	1.85
Cash Flow	1.54	1.46	1.37	1.17	0.93	0.63
Earnings	0.95	1.00	0.92	0.75	0.44	0.38
Dividends	Nil	Nil	Nil	Nil	Nil	Nil
Payout Ratio	Nil	Nil	Nil	Nil	Nil	Nil
Prices - High	19½	21¾	17⅞	16⅝	14½	15⅞
- Low	15¼	15¾	11⅜	7	6½	7
P/E Ratio - High	21	22	19	22	33	41
- Low	16	16	12	9	15	18

Income Statement Analysis (Million $)

	1994	%Chg	1993	%Chg	1992	%Chg	1991
Revs.	186	25%	149	16%	128	12%	114
Oper. Inc.	130	27%	102	24%	82.3	14%	72.2
Depr.	21.2	19%	17.8	6%	16.8	14%	14.8
Int. Exp.	62.8	108%	30.2	47%	20.5	-27%	28.0
Pretax Inc.	55.8	-9%	61.3	21%	50.7	45%	34.9
Eff. Tax Rate	30%	—	30%	—	24%	—	24%
Net Inc.	38.8	-10%	43.1	11%	38.8	46%	26.6

Balance Sheet & Other Fin. Data (Million $)

	1994	1993	1992	1991	1990	1989
Cash	490	191	126	84.0	26.0	12.1
Curr. Assets	NA	NA	NA	NA	NA	NA
Total Assets	1,131	716	581	518	394	349
Curr. Liab.	NA	NA	NA	NA	NA	NA
LT Debt	751	355	283	236	271	260
Common Eqty.	180	212	169	143	55.0	42.0
Total Cap.	1,021	644	521	445	336	305
Cap. Exp.	117	87.0	32.0	68.0	32.0	130
Cash Flow	55.0	56.3	51.3	41.3	25.4	16.9

Ratio Analysis

	1994	1993	1992	1991	1990	1989
Curr. Ratio	NA	NA	NA	NA	NA	NA
% LT Debt of Cap.	73.5	55.2	54.3	53.0	80.5	85.3
% Net Inc.of Revs.	20.9	28.9	30.4	23.4	12.6	21.5
% Ret. on Assets	4.6	6.6	6.8	5.0	3.2	3.6
% Ret. on Equity	19.4	20.2	21.4	24.1	24.6	28.9

Dividend Data —No cash dividends have been paid. Annual stock dividends of 4% were paid in 1988-90.

Data as orig. reptd.; bef. results of disc. opers. and/or spec. items. Per share data adj. for stk. divs. as of ex-div. date. E-Estimated. NA-Not Available. NM-Not Meaningful. NR-Not Ranked.

Office—10831 Old Mill Rd., Omaha, NE 68154. **Tel**—(402) 330-8900. **Chrmn & CEO**—D. L. Sokol. **Pres & COO**—T. R. Mason. **VP, CFO, Treas & Investor Contact**—John Sylvia. **SVP & Secy**—S. A. McArthur. **Dirs**—E. D. Aronson, J. E. Ayres, J. Q. Crowe, R. K. Davidson, B. Holt, R. R. Jaros, E. B. Laybourne, H. L. Oakes, Jr., W. Scott, Jr., B. W. Shackelford, D. L. Sokol, D. E. Wit. **Transfer Agent & Registrar**—Chemical Trust Co. of California, SF. **Incorporated** in Delaware in 1971. **Empl**-530. **S&P Analyst:** S.S.

Callaway Golf

NYSE Symbol **ELY**
In S&P MidCap 400

20-SEP-95 **Industry:** Leisure/Amusement

Summary: This company designs, makes and markets premium, innovative golf clubs primarily under the "Big Bertha" brand name.

Quantitative Evaluations

Outlook (1 Lowest—5 Highest)
• **5**

Fair Value
• **23½**

Risk
• **Average**

Earn./Div. Rank
• **NR**

Technical Eval.
• **Bullish** since 9/95

Rel. Strength Rank (1 Lowest—99 Highest)
• **62**

Insider Activity
• **Neutral**

Recent Price • 16⅜
52 Wk Range • 20⅛-11¼

Yield • 1.3%
12-Mo. P/E • 13.2

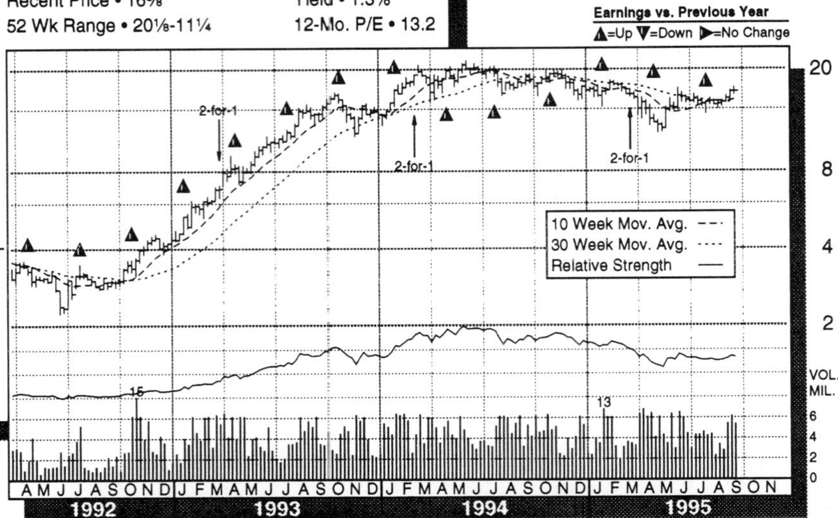

OPTIONS: ASE, CBOE, NY

Business Profile - 20-SEP-95

Callaway makes premium, innovative golf clubs incorporating an unique design concept. Sales and earnings have grown rapidly since the January 1991 introduction of Big Bertha metal woods. More recent growth has been fueled by contributions from Big Bertha irons, which began shipping in April 1994. Despite analysts' expectations of continued strong growth over the next few years, the shares are selling below their 1994 peak. ELY repurchased about 3.2 million shares in 1995's first half.

Operational Review - 20-SEP-95

Net sales for the first half of 1995 rose 36%, year to year, reflecting strong demand for new Big Bertha metal irons and woods. Margins narrowed, and net income was up 33%. For the second quarter alone, sales included $86.2 million of Big Bertha War Bird Metal Woods, $43.0 million of Big Bertha Irons, and $17.3 million of Great Big Bertha Drivers. Since their April 1994 introduction, ELY has sold over $160 million of Big Bertha Irons, consisting of over 1.85 million units.

Stock Performance - 15-SEP-95

In the past 30 trading days, ELY's shares have increased 9%, compared to a 4% rise in the S&P 500. Average trading volume for the past five days was 1,064,160 shares, compared with the 40-day moving average of 892,971 shares.

Key Stock Statistics

Dividend Rate/Share	0.20	Shareholders	NA
Shs. outstg. (M)	67.9	Market cap. (B)	$ 1.1
Avg. daily vol. (M)	1.055	Inst. holdings	31%
Tang. Bk. Value/Share	2.88	Insider holdings	NA
Beta	NA		

Value of $10,000 invested 5 years ago: NA

Fiscal Year Ending Dec. 31

	1995	% Change	1994	% Change	1993	% Change
Revenues (Million $)						
1Q	119.0	56%	76.07	58%	48.07	110%
2Q	155.7	23%	126.3	90%	66.57	82%
3Q	—	—	131.2	83%	71.76	100%
4Q	—	—	115.2	69%	68.25	86%
Yr.	—	—	448.7	76%	254.6	93%
Income (Million $)						
1Q	16.90	53%	11.04	64%	6.75	139%
2Q	27.33	24%	22.10	94%	11.39	91%
3Q	—	—	25.35	99%	12.74	138%
4Q	—	—	19.53	89%	10.33	101%
Yr.	—	—	78.02	89%	41.20	114%
Earnings Per Share ($)						
1Q	0.23	53%	0.15	43%	0.10	100%
2Q	0.39	30%	0.30	88%	0.16	64%
3Q	—	—	0.35	92%	0.18	106%
4Q	—	—	0.26	83%	0.15	76%
Yr.	—	—	1.07	81%	0.59	84%

Next earnings report expected: mid October

Business Summary - 20-SEP-95

Callaway Golf Company designs, develops, manufactures and markets high-quality, innovative golf clubs, which are sold at premium prices to both average and skilled golfers. Contributions to sales in recent years were:

	1994	1993	1992	1991
Metal woods	73%	82%	78%	68%
Irons	22%	12%	16%	25%
Putters, wedges & other	5%	6%	6%	7%

ELY believes that its Big Bertha metal drivers (introduced in January 1991) were the first oversized stainless steel drivers to be produced and merchandised in large quantities. The company also offers a line of Big Bertha fairway woods. All Big Bertha metal woods incorporate the company's S2H2 design concept, which involves significantly reducing or eliminating a club's hosel (neck), extending the shaft through the entire clubhead and moving the saved weight into more effective regions of the clubhead. ELY believes that by incorporating the S2H2 concept into an oversized stainless steel metal wood clubhead, it has developed a perimeter-weighted clubhead with a larger "sweet spot" and an increased resistance to deflection on off-center hits. Big Bertha metal woods accounted for nearly all sales growth from mid-1991 through the first half of 1994, at which time shipments of Big Bertha irons began.

In January 1994, the company introduced Big Bertha War Bird drivers and fairway woods (shipments were initiated in the first quarter), all of which incorporate the War Bird soleplate, which features a deep dish on either side of the central ridge running from clubface to trailing edge. The redistribution of mass allowed by the heavily contoured sole and internal design refinements permit a stronger flight pattern.

Big Bertha irons (shipments initiated in 1994's second quarter) combine a larger hitting area with the S2H2 concept and a unique patented 360-degree undercut channel. The design allows weight to be moved away from the face, creating the maximum amount of perimeter weighting.

ELY also offers conventional-size S2H2 metal woods, S2H2 and Bobby Jones irons, a line of putters (Big Bertha Blade putter introduced in 1995), and other golf-related equipment.

Important Developments

Jul. '95—In reporting 1995's second quarter results, Callaway said it had reduced its net inventories at the end of the period to its objective of $63.5 million, down 19% from the end of the first quarter.

Capitalization

Long Term Liabs.: $745,000 (6/95).

Per Share Data ($) (Year Ended Dec. 31)

	1994	1993	1992	1991	1990	1989
Tangible Bk. Val.	2.74	1.73	0.87	1.18	0.63	NA
Cash Flow	1.15	0.64	0.34	0.13	0.04	0.01
Earnings	1.07	0.60	0.32	0.12	0.04	0.01
Dividends	0.10	0.03	Nil	NA	NA	NA
Payout Ratio	9%	4%	Nil	NA	NA	NA
Prices - High	21¾	16⅜	4⅝	NA	NA	NA
- Low	12⅛	4¼	2¼	NA	NA	NA
P/E Ratio - High	20	27	14	NA	NA	NA
- Low	11	7	7	NA	NA	NA

Income Statement Analysis (Million $)

	1994	%Chg	1993	%Chg	1992	%Chg	1991
Revs.	449	76%	255	93%	132	140%	55.0
Oper. Inc.	133	86%	71.4	110%	34.0	198%	11.4
Depr.	6.2	105%	3.0	136%	1.3	106%	0.6
Int. Exp.	NA	—	NM	—	NM	—	0.2
Pretax Inc.	129	85%	69.6	110%	33.2	NM	10.8
Eff. Tax Rate	40%	—	41%	—	42%	—	40%
Net Inc.	78.0	89%	41.2	113%	19.3	NM	6.4

Balance Sheet & Other Fin. Data (Million $)

	1994	1993	1992	1991	1990	1989
Cash	54.4	49.0	20.0	5.2	1.3	NA
Curr. Assets	187	112	55.2	25.4	12.6	NA
Total Assets	244	144	68.9	28.8	14.7	NA
Curr. Liab.	56.6	27.8	15.8	9.2	3.9	NA
LT Debt	Nil	Nil	3.4	4.4	2.1	Nil
Common Eqty.	186	117	49.8	15.2	8.7	6.4
Total Cap.	186	117	53.1	19.7	10.8	6.4
Cap. Exp.	26.1	20.9	11.4	1.5	1.3	0.4
Cash Flow	84.2	44.2	20.6	7.0	2.1	0.5

Ratio Analysis

	1994	1993	1992	1991	1990	1989
Curr. Ratio	3.3	4.0	3.5	2.8	3.2	NA
% LT Debt of Cap.	Nil	Nil	6.3	22.6	19.3	Nil
% Net Inc.of Revs.	17.4	16.2	14.6	11.7	8.6	3.2
% Ret. on Assets	40.1	36.3	20.3	29.5	16.2	4.6
% Ret. on Equity	51.4	46.8	48.3	53.7	24.3	5.5

Dividend Data —Dividends were initiated in early 1993. A shareholder rights plan was adopted in 1995.

Amt. of Div. $	Date Decl.	Ex-Div. Date	Stock of Record	Payment Date
0.050	Oct. 20	Oct. 25	Oct. 31	Nov. 21 '94
0.100	Jan. 31	Feb. 06	Feb. 10	Mar. 10 '95
2-for-1	Jan. 31	Mar. 13	Feb. 10	Mar. 10 '95
0.050	Apr. 21	May. 04	May. 10	May. 31 '95
0.050	Jul. 20	Jul. 28	Aug. 01	Aug. 22 '95

Data as orig. reptd.; bef. results of disc. opers. and/or spec. items. Per share data adj. for stk. divs. as of ex-div. date. E-Estimated. NA-Not Available. NM-Not Meaningful. NR-Not Ranked.

Office—2285 Rutherford Rd., Carlsbad, CA 92008-8815. **Tel**—(619) 931-1771. **Chrmn & CEO**—Ely Callaway. **Pres & COO**—D. H. Dye. **VP & CFO**—D. Rane. **VP & Secy**—S. McCracken. **Investor Contact**—Krista Mallory. **Dirs**—W. C. Baker, E. Callaway, D. H. Dye, R. Rosenfield, W. A. Schreyer, M. Sherwin, E. Ward, Jr. **Transfer Agent & Registrar**—Chemical Trust of California, L.A. **Incorporated** in California in 1982. **Empl**-2,225. **S&P Analyst:** Michael V. Pizzi

STANDARD & POOR'S

STOCK REPORTS

CalMat Co.

NYSE Symbol **CZM**

In S&P MidCap 400

10-AUG-95 **Industry:** Building

Summary: CalMat is a major producer of aggregates, asphalt and ready-mixed concrete in California and neighboring states. It also has real estate operations.

Quantitative Evaluations

Outlook (1 Lowest—5 Highest)
• **1+**

Fair Value
• **16**

Risk
• **Low**

Earn./Div. Rank
• **B**

Technical Eval.
• **Bearish** since 5/95

Rel. Strength Rank (1 Lowest—99 Highest)
• **27**

Insider Activity
• **Neutral**

Recent Price • 19¼

52 Wk Range • 21⅜-16⅞

Yield • 2.1%

12-Mo. P/E • 31.6

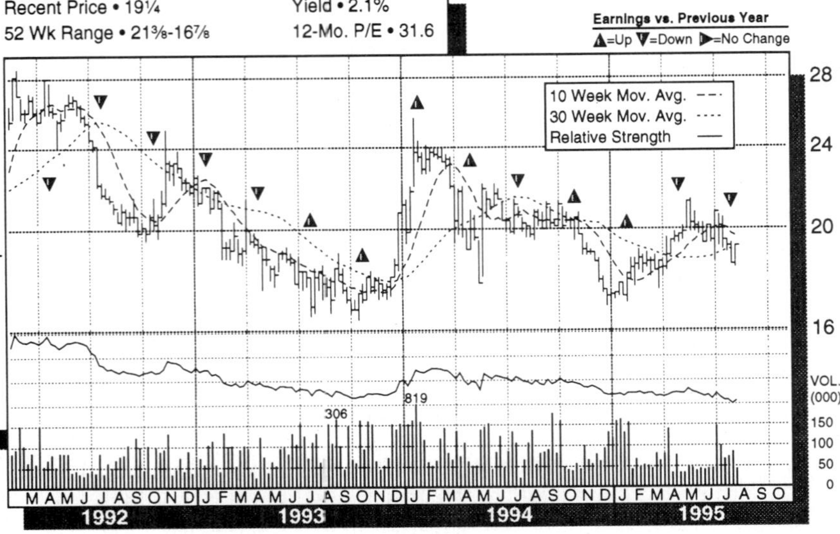

Business Profile - 10-AUG-95

CalMat primarily manufactures construction materials such as aggregates, ready mix concrete and hot mix asphalt. Operations are focused on major urban areas in California, Arizona and New Mexico. CalMat also has real estate operations, with activities in the areas of industrial and office buildings and undeveloped real property. CZM is vulnerable to the cyclicality of the construction industry, particularly in the area of infrastructure spending, as well as weather-related difficulties.

Operational Review - 10-AUG-95

Earnings in the first half of 1995 fell 68% on a year over year basis on flat sales. The difficulties were mostly related to record rainfall and associated flooding in California in the first quarter, and comparisons with a 1994 period that benefited from business activity related to the Los Angeles earthquake. The largest earnings declines were recorded in the areas of aggregates and asphalt. Results were also hurt by a one-time charge of $1.2 million (net) from management consolidations.

Stock Performance - 04-AUG-95

In the past 30 trading days, CZM's shares have declined 1%, compared to a 2% rise in the S&P 500. Average trading volume for the past five days was 8,400 shares, compared with the 40-day moving average of 15,213 shares.

Key Stock Statistics

Dividend Rate/Share	0.40	Shareholders	1,300
Shs. outstg. (M)	23.1	Market cap. (B)	$0.445
Avg. daily vol. (M)	0.012	Inst. holdings	51%
Tang. Bk. Value/Share	13.11	Insider holdings	NA
Beta	1.35		

Value of $10,000 invested 5 years ago: $ 7,443

Fiscal Year Ending Dec. 31

	1995	% Change	1994	% Change	1993	% Change
Revenues (Million $)						
1Q	69.95	-12%	79.52	28%	62.00	-5%
2Q	103.1	10%	93.65	-3%	96.44	NM
3Q	—	—	101.9	1%	100.4	-1%
4Q	—	—	101.8	8%	94.59	16%
Yr.	—	—	376.8	8%	348.4	1%
Income (Million $)						
1Q	-1.98	NM	1.45	NM	-3.42	41%
2Q	4.11	-21%	5.19	-8%	5.62	24%
3Q	—	—	6.30	39%	4.52	NM
4Q	—	—	5.78	NM	1.58	NM
Yr.	—	—	18.73	126%	8.30	NM
Earnings Per Share ($)						
1Q	-0.09	NM	0.06	NM	-0.15	NM
2Q	0.18	-18%	0.22	-8%	0.24	26%
3Q	—	—	0.27	35%	0.20	NM
4Q	—	—	0.25	NM	0.07	NM
Yr.	—	—	0.81	125%	0.36	NM

Next earnings report expected: late October

Business Summary - 09-AUG-95

CalMat is a major producer and supplier to the construction industry of aggregates, asphalt and ready-mixed concrete in California, Arizona and New Mexico. The company also has real estate operations. Segment contributions in 1994:

	Revs.	Profits
Concrete & aggregates	53%	27%
Asphalt	39%	31%
Properties	8%	42%

The concrete and aggregates division operates aggregates processing plants at 31 locations in the major markets of California and in Phoenix and Tucson, Arizona, and Albuquerque, New Mexico. Ready-mixed concrete batch plants are operated at 28 locations in these markets except for the Los Angeles and San Francisco Bay areas. CZM produces and sells construction aggregates and supplies ready-mixed concrete for use in commercial and residential construction, public construction projects and projects to build and repair roads and highways.

The asphalt division is the third largest supplier of hot mix asphalt to the construction industry nationwide, and the largest supplier in California. CZM locates its plants near aggregates sites, as well as near major metropolitan regions. At December 31, 1994, it was operating 34 asphalt plants in metropolitan Los Angeles, San Diego, Orange County and the San Francisco Bay and San Joaquin Valley areas in California, and in Phoenix, Tucson and Albuquerque. CZM also manufactures a specialty coating material called Guardtop, which is used for sealing asphalt paving to prevent water damage and erosion, and is the exclusive distributor in Los Angeles of a polypropylene reinforcing fabric used in resurfacing pavements.

The properties division is involved in the management of CZM's real estate portfolio, with activity in permitting, reclamation, acquisitions, sales and leasing.

Important Developments

Jul. '95—The company's union employees went on strike throughout Southern California, with a total of 220 CZM employees striking at 21 asphalt and 12 aggregates plants.

Jul. '95—CZM recorded a net charge of $1.2 million ($0.05 a share) for severance and other costs related to its decision to consolidate the management of its concrete and aggregates division and its asphalt division in the state of California. The management consolidation was expected to reduce future personnel costs by $2.5 million ($1.5 million net) annually. CalMat's construction materials operations in Arizona and New Mexico were previously consolidated in a similar manner.

Capitalization

Long Term Debt: $57,428,000 (3/95).

Per Share Data ($) (Year Ended Dec. 31)

	1994	1993	1992	1991	1990	1989
Tangible Bk. Val.	13.28	12.79	12.70	14.50	14.41	15.81
Cash Flow	2.10	1.74	0.75	1.93	2.44	3.86
Earnings	0.81	0.36	-0.45	0.81	1.08	2.52
Dividends	0.40	0.40	0.64	0.64	0.74	0.56
Payout Ratio	49%	111%	NM	79%	57%	22%
Prices - High	$25\frac{5}{8}$	$22\frac{5}{8}$	$28\frac{5}{8}$	$27\frac{1}{8}$	$36\frac{3}{8}$	$30\frac{5}{8}$
- Low	$16\frac{7}{8}$	$16\frac{3}{8}$	$19\frac{1}{2}$	18	$17\frac{3}{4}$	$24\frac{3}{4}$
P/E Ratio - High	32	63	NM	33	34	12
- Low	21	45	NM	22	16	10

Income Statement Analysis (Million $)

	1994	%Chg	1993	%Chg	1992	%Chg	1991
Revs.	373	7%	350	2%	342	-7%	369
Oper. Inc.	64.0	21%	53.0	39%	38.0	-38%	61.0
Depr.	29.9	-7%	32.0	15%	27.9	6%	26.2
Int. Exp.	4.5	-30%	6.5	85%	3.5	-5%	3.7
Pretax Inc.	30.0	100%	15.0	NM	-18.0	NM	31.0
Eff. Tax Rate	37%	—	44%	—	NM	—	40%
Net Inc.	18.7	125%	8.3	NM	-10.5	NM	18.9

Balance Sheet & Other Fin. Data (Million $)

	1994	1993	1992	1991	1990	1989
Cash	2.1	10.6	4.1	12.1	3.3	13.3
Curr. Assets	84.0	96.0	85.0	92.0	95.0	181
Total Assets	573	605	585	540	548	809
Curr. Liab.	49.5	56.3	51.6	51.0	59.7	87.5
LT Debt	69.0	110	116	37.7	40.0	82.7
Common Eqty.	361	351	351	384	387	527
Total Cap.	502	531	522	421	427	609
Cap. Exp.	25.8	12.1	32.1	32.4	76.6	46.8
Cash Flow	49.0	40.0	17.0	45.0	69.0	119

Ratio Analysis

	1994	1993	1992	1991	1990	1989
Curr. Ratio	1.7	1.7	1.6	1.8	1.6	2.1
% LT Debt of Cap.	13.7	20.7	22.2	9.0	9.4	13.6
% Net Inc.of Revs.	5.0	2.4	NM	5.1	7.2	11.5
% Ret. on Assets	3.2	1.4	NM	3.5	5.2	10.0
% Ret. on Equity	5.3	2.4	NM	4.9	7.7	15.6

Dividend Data (A "poison pill" stock purchase rights plan was adopted in 1987.)

Amt. of Div. $	Date Decl.	Ex-Div. Date	Stock of Record	Payment Date
0.100	Aug. 23	Sep. 01	Sep. 08	Oct. 05 '94
0.100	Nov. 22	Dec. 02	Dec. 08	Jan. 04 '95
0.100	Feb. 28	Mar. 09	Mar. 15	Apr. 04 '95
0.100	May. 23	Jun. 02	Jun. 08	Jul. 06 '95

Data as orig. reptd.; bef. results of disc. opers. and/or spec. items. Per share data adj. for stk. divs. as of ex-div. date. E-Estimated. NA-Not Available. NM-Not Meaningful. NR-Not Ranked.

Office—3200 San Fernando Rd., Los Angeles, CA 90065. **Tel**—(213) 258-2777. **Chrmn & Pres**—A. F. Gerstell. **EVP-CFO & Investor Contact**—H. J. Gallagher. **EVP-Secy**—P. Stanford. **Dirs**—J. C. Argue, A. Brown, H. M. Conger, R. S. Dezember, A. F. Gerstell, R. A. Grant Jr., G. R. Heyler, W. T. Huston, W. Jenkins, E. A. Landry, T. L. Lee, T. M. Linden, S. T. Peeler. **Transfer Agent & Registrar**—First Chicago Trust Co. of N.Y., NYC. **Incorporated** in Delaware in 1984. **Empl**-1,655. **S&P Analyst:** Michael W. Jaffe

STANDARD & POOR'S

STOCK REPORTS

Cardinal Health

NYSE Symbol **CAH**
In S&P MidCap 400

03-SEP-95

Industry: Drugs-Generic and OTC

Summary: Cardinal is a wholesale distributor of pharmaceuticals, medical/surgical supplies and related health products.

Quantitative Evaluations

Outlook (1 Lowest—5 Highest)
• **4+**

Fair Value
• **55½**

Risk
• **Low**

Earn./Div. Rank
• **A-**

Technical Eval.
• **Neutral** since 8/95

Rel. Strength Rank (1 Lowest—99 Highest)
• **69**

Insider Activity
• **Neutral**

Recent Price • 53¼
52 Wk Range • 55¼-38¼
Yield • 0.2%
12-Mo. P/E • 26.5

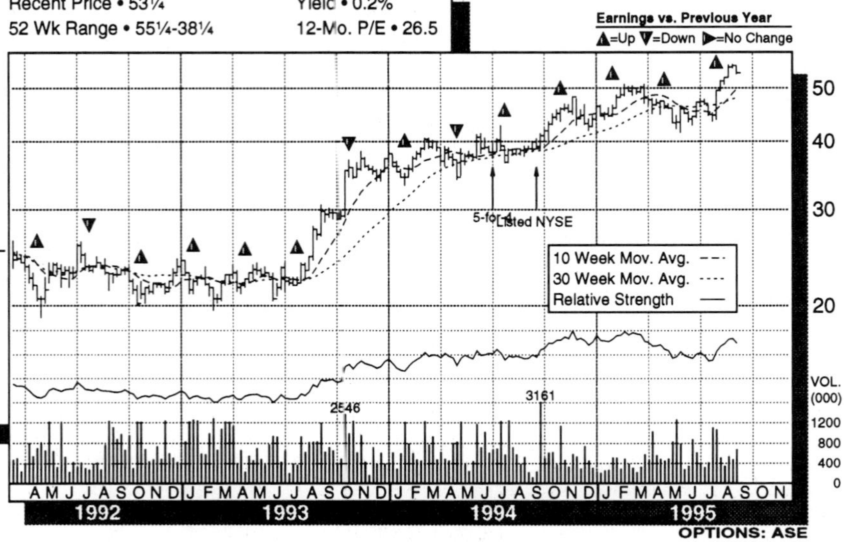

Business Profile - 01-SEP-95

Cardinal Health is experiencing rapid growth as it consolidates several acquisitions and realizes benefits from its national distribution capability, which attracts customers with a national presence. Despite competition, which is squeezing gross margins, the company is improving profitability through greater efficiency. CAH is investing heavily in advanced information systems, automation of distribution facilities, and a comprehensive training program for its sales force.

Operational Review - 01-SEP-95

Net sales in recent periods have advanced sharply, reflecting internal growth and several acquisitions. Margins widened as the company shifted its customer base from one comprised predominantly of retail independent pharmacies to one that is a more balanced mix of retail independent, retail chain and hospital/managed care pharmacies. The shift resulted in lower gross margins, which have been more than offset by improved productivity. Fiscal 1994 results include a $35.9 million merger charge.

Stock Performance - 01-SEP-95

In the past 30 trading days, CAH's shares have increased 19%, compared to a 2% rise in the S&P 500. Average trading volume for the past five days was 134,360 shares, compared with the 40-day moving average of 126,585 shares.

Key Stock Statistics

Dividend Rate/Share	0.12	Shareholders	900
Shs. outstg. (M)	41.9	Market cap. (B)	$ 2.2
Avg. daily vol. (M)	0.100	Inst. holdings	70%
Tang. Bk. Value/Share	12.53	Insider holdings	NA
Beta	0.95		

Value of $10,000 invested 5 years ago: $ 43,052

Fiscal Year Ending Jun. 30

	1995	% Change	1994	% Change	1993	% Change
Revenues (Million $)						
1Q	1,818	41%	1,291	168%	482.0	32%
2Q	1,986	42%	1,398	173%	512.0	13%
3Q	1,988	32%	1,511	NM	499.0	3%
4Q	2,033	28%	1,590	189%	550.0	16%
Yr.	7,825	35%	5,790	—	--	—
Income (Million $)						
1Q	16.03	—	—	—	—	—
2Q	20.88	—	—	—	—	—
3Q	25.90	—	—	—	—	—
4Q	22.16	—	—	—	—	—
Yr.	84.97	142%	35.14	-17%	42.17	25%
Earnings Per Share ($)						
1Q	0.39	30%	0.30	-21%	0.38	73%
2Q	0.49	32%	0.37	9%	0.34	21%
3Q	0.61	NM	-0.23	NM	0.44	22%
4Q	0.52	24%	0.42	27%	0.33	27%
Yr.	2.01	134%	0.86	—	--	—

Next earnings report expected: late October

Cardinal Health

Business Summary - 01-SEP-95

Cardinal Health, Inc. (formerly Cardinal Distribution, Inc.) is a full-service wholesaler distributing a broad line of pharmaceuticals, surgical and hospital supplies, health and beauty care products, and other items typically sold by retail drug stores, hospitals and other health care providers.

The company distributes products to drug stores, hospitals, alternate care centers, and the pharmacy departments of supermarkets and mass merchandisers located throught the continental U.S. Cardinal purchases products in quantities, enabling it to obtain favorable prices, and sells them at prices reflecting these savings. An important component of the company's distribution activities is the broad range of customer support services, designed to assist customers in maintaining and improving their market positions. Independent drug stores and chains accounted for 44% of fiscal 1994 sales volume, with hospitals providing 50%.

Cardinal provides a wide range of custom-tailored support services designed to assist its customers, such as order entry and confirmation, customer inventory control, automatic monitoring and implementation of pricing strategies and financial reporting systems and controls. An in-pharmacy computer system is designed to provide pharmacists with prescription pricing information, patient profiles, accounts receivable and third-party billing services, financial management, and other data.

The company's five largest suppliers accounted for 29% of sales in fiscal 1994. The loss of certain suppliers could adversely affect Cardinal's business, since many suppliers are its sole source of various pharmaceutical and medical/surgical products.

Important Developments

Aug. '95—Cardinal signed an agreement to acquire Medicine Shoppe International Inc., the largest franchiser of independent retail pharmacies in the U.S., for about $348 million in stock. Under the terms of the agreement, Cardinal will issue about 5.99 million to 6.755 million shares as long as the price of CAH stock is between $51.58 and $58.17. The transaction is expected to be completed in late 1995.
Mar. '95—Cardinal acquired the remaining 49% interest in Renlar Systems, Inc. that it did not already own. Renlar designs, installs, and services interactive pharmacy systems.

Capitalization

Long Term Debt: $209,250,000 (6/95).
Class A Common Stock: 41,717,532 shs. (no par).
Officers and directors own 12%
Institutions hold 68%.
Shareholders: About 1,150 of record (8/94).

Per Share Data ($) (Year Ended Jun. 30)

	1995	1994	1993	1992	1991	1990
Tangible Bk. Val.	NA	7.79	10.70	8.32	7.36	5.43
Cash Flow	NA	1.29	1.72	1.31	1.06	1.03
Earnings	2.01	0.86	1.42	1.07	0.84	0.66
Dividends	0.12	0.10	0.07	0.06	0.05	0.04
Payout Ratio	6%	11%	5%	6%	7%	6%
Prices - High	50⅞	42¾	27¼	31	18⅝	12⅝
- Low	41½	33¼	19	16	10⅛	6⅝
P/E Ratio - High	25	50	20	29	22	19
- Low	21	39	14	15	12	10

Income Statement Analysis (Million $)

	1994	%Chg	1993	%Chg	1992	%Chg	1991
Revs.	5,790	194%	1,967	19%	1,648	39%	1,184
Oper. Inc.	139	110%	66.3	25%	53.0	35%	39.3
Depr.	17.0	136%	7.2	27%	5.7	23%	4.6
Int. Exp.	18.1	35%	13.4	14%	11.8	11%	10.6
Pretax Inc.	70.8	31%	54.1	32%	41.0	44%	28.5
Eff. Tax Rate	50%	—	38%	—	39%	—	39%
Net Inc.	35.1	4%	33.6	33%	25.2	45%	17.4

Balance Sheet & Other Fin. Data (Million $)

	1994	1993	1992	1991	1990	1989
Cash	55.0	104	4.7	78.3	11.3	9.3
Curr. Assets	1,287	579	503	385	213	199
Total Assets	1,396	656	577	446	251	233
Curr. Liab.	816	214	168	163	121	115
LT Debt	210	185	188	90.0	5.0	50.0
Common Eqty.	368	256	219	193	125	68.0
Total Cap.	579	442	408	283	130	118
Cap. Exp.	11.2	5.3	8.9	10.9	3.8	8.1
Cash Flow	50.9	40.8	30.8	22.0	15.9	11.3

Ratio Analysis

	1994	1993	1992	1991	1990	1989
Curr. Ratio	1.6	2.7	3.0	2.4	1.8	1.7
% LT Debt of Cap.	36.3	41.9	46.1	31.6	3.6	42.3
% Net Inc.of Revs.	0.6	1.7	1.5	1.5	1.5	1.2
% Ret. on Assets	NA	5.4	4.9	4.8	4.2	4.0
% Ret. on Equity	NA	14.1	12.2	10.4	11.2	13.9

Dividend Data —Cash has been paid each year since 1983.

Amt. of Div. $	Date Decl.	Ex-Div. Date	Stock of Record	Payment Date
0.030	Sep. 09	Sep. 26	Oct. 01	Oct. 15 '94
0.030	Dec. 15	Dec. 23	Jan. 01	Jan. 15 '95
0.030	Feb. 15	Mar. 27	Apr. 01	Apr. 15 '95
0.030	May. 16	Jun. 28	Jul. 01	Jul. 15 '95
0.030	Aug. 15	Sep. 28	Oct. 02	Oct. 16 '95

Data as orig. reptd.; bef. results of disc. opers. and/or spec. items. Per share data adj. for stk. divs. as of ex-div. date. E-Estimated. NA-Not Available. NM-Not Meaningful. NR-Not Ranked.

Office—655 Metro Place S., Suite 925, Dublin, OH 43017. **Tel**—(614) 761-8700. **Chrmn & CEO**—R. D. Walter. **Pres & COO**—J. C. Kane. **EVP, CFO & Investor Contact**—David Bearman. **Secy**—G. H. Bennett, Jr. **Dirs**—J. F. Finn, R. L. Gerbig, J. F. Havens, R. E. Herzlinger, J. C. Kane, G. R. Manser, J. B. McCoy, M. E. Moritz, J. E. Robertson, L. J. Van Fossen, R. D. Walter, M. G. Whitmire. **Transfer Agent**—Bank One, Indianapolis. **Incorporated** in Ohio in 1971; reincorporated in 1982. **Empl**-3,500. **S&P Analyst:** Philip J. Birbara

Carlisle Companies

NYSE Symbol **CSL**
In S&P MidCap 400

13-SEP-95 **Industry:** Rubber

Summary: Carlisle is a diversified manufacturer of rubber, plastics and friction materials for construction, transportation and general industry markets.

Quantitative Evaluations
Outlook (1 Lowest—5 Highest) • **NA**
Fair Value • **NA**
Risk • **Low**
Earn./Div. Rank • **B+**
Technical Eval. • **Bullish** since 9/91
Rel. Strength Rank (1 Lowest—99 Highest) • **48**
Insider Activity • **Favorable**

Recent Price • 41½
52 Wk Range • 42-31¼
Yield • 2.1%
12-Mo. P/E • 16.3

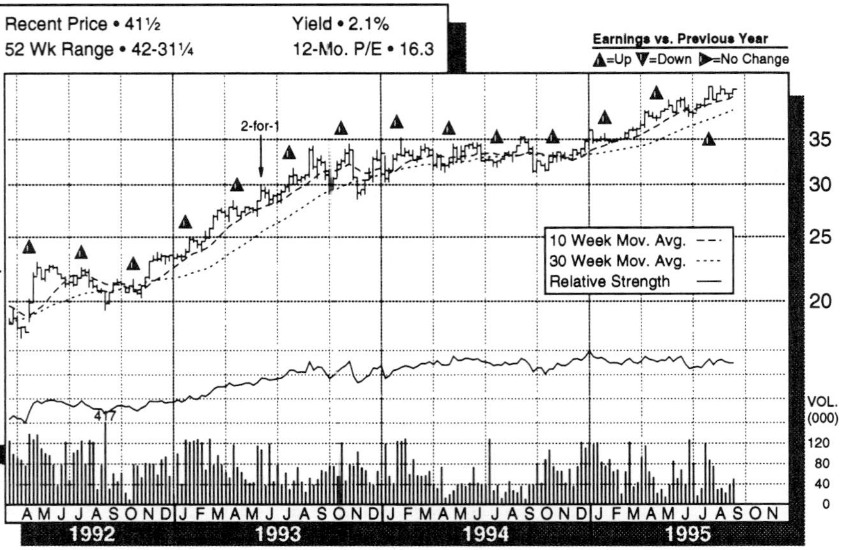

Business Profile - 13-SEP-95

CSL has been acquiring companies that provide a good fit with its core operations. The company recently increased its dividend 10%, marking the 19th consecutive year in which the payout has been raised. Earnings growth has continued for the past three years, and record earnings are expected for 1995, as the company continues to focus on competitive costs and balanced growth. Cash and cash equivalents decreased $29.3 million at June 30, 1995, year to year, reflecting acquisitions.

Operational Review - 13-SEP-95

Sales advanced 15%, year to year, in the first half of 1995, reflecting increases in all three business segments. Results benefited from strong growth in the general industry and transportation segments, and the company's cost-reduction programs, and net income rose sharply. The company expects record earnings for 1995, primarily on continued growth in the transportation and general industry segments.

Stock Performance - 08-SEP-95

In the past 30 trading days, CSL's shares have declined 0.90%, compared to a 2% rise in the S&P 500. Average trading volume for the past five days was 12,200 shares, compared with the 40-day moving average of 11,372 shares.

Key Stock Statistics

Dividend Rate/Share	0.88	Shareholders	2,400
Shs. outstg. (M)	15.4	Market cap. (B)	$0.640
Avg. daily vol. (M)	0.007	Inst. holdings	60%
Tang. Bk. Value/Share	14.86	Insider holdings	NA
Beta	1.06		

Value of $10,000 invested 5 years ago: $ 29,374

Fiscal Year Ending Dec. 31

	1995	% Change	1994	% Change	1993	% Change
Revenues (Million $)						
1Q	188.0	22%	154.7	12%	138.4	4%
2Q	200.8	9%	183.8	14%	160.8	13%
3Q	—	—	184.1	15%	160.6	20%
4Q	—	—	170.0	12%	151.4	27%
Yr.	—	—	692.7	13%	611.3	16%
Income (Million $)						
1Q	8.60	27%	6.76	15%	5.90	10%
2Q	12.42	23%	10.11	35%	7.48	15%
3Q	—	—	10.24	27%	8.06	22%
4Q	—	—	8.47	22%	6.93	20%
Yr.	—	—	35.57	25%	28.38	17%
Earnings Per Share ($)						
1Q	0.55	25%	0.44	16%	0.38	9%
2Q	0.79	22%	0.65	35%	0.48	13%
3Q	—	—	0.66	27%	0.52	21%
4Q	—	—	0.55	22%	0.45	20%
Yr.	—	—	2.30	26%	1.83	16%

Next earnings report expected: mid October

Carlisle Companies

Business Summary - 13-SEP-95

Carlisle Companies (formerly Carlisle Corp.) derived its sales and profits from the following markets in 1994:

	Sales	Profits
Construction materials	41.7%	50.1%
Transportation products	28.9%	19.3%
General industry	29.4%	30.6%

The construction materials segment includes Carlisle SynTec Systems, which makes elastomeric membranes (EPDM), adhesives and related items for roofing systems and water barrier applications. It is the largest U.S. producer in the single-ply roofing market. The business was expanded in 1993 with the acquisition of Goodyear Tire & Rubbber's roofing business (now Versico Inc.) and ECI Inc. (now Carlisle Engineered Metals), a manufacturer of architectural metal roofing. Re-roofing demand represents about two-thirds of the market for nonresidential roofing materials. CSL's joint venture to produce EPDM roofing in Russia continues to struggle.

Transportation products include brake linings for heavy-duty trucks, trailers and off-road vehicles; dry disc brakes and actuation systems for construction equipment; custom rubber and plastic components for use in passenger cars, appliances and other purposes; specialty industrial friction products, and high-performance insulated wire for aviation, aerospace and military markets.

General industry products include molded plastic foodservice products and melamine dinnerware; small pneumatic tires and stamped and roll-formed wheels used by most major lawn and garden equipment manufacturers, as well as custom molded plastic and rubber parts for the lawn and garden, automotive, power equipment and golf cart markets.

Important Developments

Sep. '95—Carlisle's recently acquired Trail King unit acquired Ti-Brook Inc., a privately held manufacturer and distributor of aluminum and steel dump bodies and trailers used in the transportation of coal, sludge, palletized loads, refuse and other products. Terms were not disclosed. Trail King Industries ($60 million in sales) manufactures heavy specialized lowbed trailers used in the transportation of construction equipment.

Aug. '95—CSL agreed to acquire Walker Stainless Equipment Co., a designer and maker of stainless steel components and equipment.

Mar. '95—The company's Geauga division acquired Thunderline Corp., a producer of precision rubber products for transportation markets with sales of between $15 million and $20 million annually. Terms of the acquisition were not disclosed.

Capitalization

Long Term Debt: $70,114,000 (6/95).

Per Share Data ($) (Year Ended Dec. 31)

	1994	1993	1992	1991	1990	1989
Tangible Bk. Val.	14.89	13.42	13.35	12.46	13.65	12.93
Cash Flow	3.48	3.00	2.70	1.58	2.61	2.77
Earnings	2.30	1.83	1.58	0.43	1.43	1.67
Dividends	0.76	0.70	0.66	0.63	0.61	0.59
Payout Ratio	33%	38%	42%	147%	41%	35%
Prices - High	36⅛	34½	23¾	20⅜	18⅛	22¼
- Low	30¼	23⅛	17⅝	14⅞	13⅜	16
P/E Ratio - High	16	19	15	47	13	13
- Low	13	13	11	34	9	10

Income Statement Analysis (Million $)

	1994	%Chg	1993	%Chg	1992	%Chg	1991
Revs.	693	13%	611	16%	528	5%	501
Oper. Inc.	79.8	19%	67.0	15%	58.4	15%	50.9
Depr.	18.3	1%	18.1	5%	17.2	-2%	17.5
Int. Exp.	4.7	8%	4.3	-17%	5.2	18%	4.4
Pretax Inc.	58.8	25%	46.9	18%	39.7	NM	10.6
Eff. Tax Rate	40%	—	40%	—	39%	—	38%
Net Inc.	35.6	25%	28.4	17%	24.2	NM	6.6

Balance Sheet & Other Fin. Data (Million $)

	1994	1993	1992	1991	1990	1989
Cash	71.0	51.8	90.6	14.4	17.6	24.1
Curr. Assets	273	237	237	197	213	203
Total Assets	485	420	384	356	374	338
Curr. Liab.	109	92.2	75.1	82.1	92.0	86.7
LT Debt	67.5	59.5	69.1	48.6	44.5	17.4
Common Eqty.	248	221	204	190	207	209
Total Cap.	315	280	273	239	252	226
Cap. Exp.	31.1	28.5	19.9	19.7	21.0	19.6
Cash Flow	53.9	46.5	41.4	24.1	41.6	44.7

Ratio Analysis

	1994	1993	1992	1991	1990	1989
Curr. Ratio	2.5	2.6	3.2	2.4	2.3	2.3
% LT Debt of Cap.	21.4	21.3	25.3	20.4	17.7	7.7
% Net Inc.of Revs.	5.1	4.6	4.6	1.3	3.7	4.9
% Ret. on Assets	7.8	7.1	6.5	1.8	6.6	8.1
% Ret. on Equity	15.1	13.4	12.3	3.3	11.2	13.5

Dividend Data —Dividends have been paid since 1950.

Amt. of Div. $	Date Decl.	Ex-Div. Date	Stock of Record	Payment Date
0.200	Nov. 02	Nov. 10	Nov. 17	Dec. 01 '94
0.200	Feb. 01	Feb. 14	Feb. 21	Mar. 01 '95
0.200	May. 03	May. 12	May. 18	Jun. 01 '95
0.220	Aug. 02	Aug. 16	Aug. 18	Sep. 01 '95

Data as orig. reptd.; bef. results of disc. opers. and/or spec. items. Per share data adj. for stk. divs. as of ex-div. date. E-Estimated. NA-Not Available. NM-Not Meaningful. NR-Not Ranked.

Office—250 South Clinton Street, Suite 201, Syracuse, NY 13202. **Tel**—(315) 474-2500. **Chrmn & CEO**—S. P. Munn. **Pres, CFO & Investor Contact**—Dennis J. Hall. **Secy**—S. C. Selbach. **Dirs**— M. O. Bryant, D. G. Calder, P. J. Choquette Jr., H. J. Forrest, D. J. Hall, P. Krogh, S. P. Munn, G. L. Ohrstrom, E. R. Scocimara, D. G. Thomas, E. N. White Jr. **Transfer Agent & Registrar**—Harris Trust and Savings Bank, Chicago. **Incorporated** in Delaware in 1917. **Empl**-4,800. **S&P Analyst:** Stewart Scharf

Carpenter Technology

NYSE Symbol **CRS**
In S&P MidCap 400

03-AUG-95 **Industry:** Steel-Iron

Summary: Carpenter Technology produces stainless and tool steels, high temperature and electronic alloys, and other special purpose metals for a variety of end-use markets.

S&P Opinion: Hold (★★★)

Recent Price • 73¾
52 Wk Range • 74½-53⅛
Yield • 3.3%
12-Mo. P/E • 13.1

Quantitative Evaluations
Outlook
(1 Lowest—5 Highest)
• **1**
Fair Value
• **59½**
Risk
• **Low**
Earn./Div. Rank
• **B+**

Technical Eval.
• **Bearish** since 8/94
Rel. Strength Rank
(1 Lowest—99 Highest)
• **77**
Insider Activity
• **Neutral**

Earnings vs. Previous Year
▲=Up ▼=Down ▶=No Change

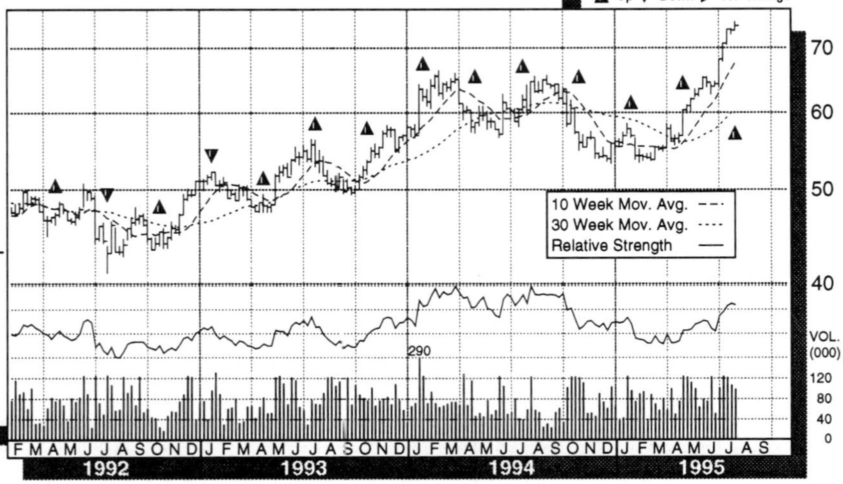

Overview - 03-AUG-95

We anticipate a sales increase of at least 7.0% in fiscal 1996, reflecting gains in both unit volume and pricing. The gain will trail fiscal 1995's large increase because of the probable absence of raw material surcharges which had the effect of inflating fiscal 1995's sales number. Our sales forecast assumes an upturn in demand from the aerospace industry and steady demand from automakers. Gross margins will widen on higher volume, increased pricing and stable raw material costs. Assuming a much smaller loss from equity affiliates and flat interest expense, earnings should increase again in fiscal 1996. Greater contributions from overseas affiliates, a more lucrative product mix, diversification into specialty metals along with acquisitions and joint ventures will boost long-term sales and profit growth.

Valuation - 03-AUG-95

Although the shares are reasonably priced on our 1996 earnings estimate and have an attractive dividend yield, we are maintaining our hold rating on CRS's stock. Through early August 1995 the stock has risen 34%, versus a 24% increase in the S&P 500. While it is possible that the shares may continue to rise near-term, we believe that the risk/reward for accumulating or buying the shares at current levels is poor. Longer-term we are enthusiastic about CRS based on its expansion overseas along with its entrance into the market for ceramics and its increasingly dominant position in the domestic market for stainless long products.

Key Stock Statistics

S&P EPS Est. 1996	6.75	Tang. Bk. Value/Share	30.70
P/E on S&P Est. 1996	10.9	Beta	0.73
Dividend Rate/Share	2.40	Shareholders	6,000
Shs. outstg. (M)	8.1	Market cap. (B)	$0.609
Avg. daily vol. (M)	0.027	Inst. holdings	70%
		Insider holdings	NA

Value of $10,000 invested 5 years ago: $ 19,817

Fiscal Year Ending Jun. 30

	1995	% Change	1994	% Change	1993	% Change
Revenues (Million $)						
1Q	156.1	21%	129.4	-7%	139.4	10%
2Q	172.4	17%	147.1	20%	123.0	-8%
3Q	211.6	21%	174.4	12%	155.4	-5%
4Q	217.4	22%	177.9	12%	158.5	8%
Yr.	757.5	20%	628.8	9%	576.3	1%
Income (Million $)						
1Q	4.93	78%	2.77	5%	2.65	21%
2Q	9.83	34%	7.36	NM	1.91	-69%
3Q	15.36	20%	12.83	26%	10.20	41%
4Q	17.37	13%	15.33	30%	11.77	NM
Yr	47.49	24%	38.29	44%	26.53	78%
Earnings Per Share ($)						
1Q	0.55	83%	0.30	7%	0.28	17%
2Q	1.16	35%	0.86	NM	0.19	-73%
3Q	1.82	18%	1.54	26%	1.22	47%
4Q	2.09	13%	1.85	30%	1.42	NM
Yr.	5.62	24%	4.55	46%	3.11	91%

Next earnings report expected: mid October

Carpenter Technology

Business Summary - 03-AUG-95

CRS is a leading manufacturer, fabricator, and international marketer of specialty steels and metals in a broad range of types, forms, and sizes for a variety of end-use markets. Revenues by product line in recent fiscal years were:

	1994	1993	1992	1991
Stainless steel	60%	60%	57%	58%
Special alloys	29%	33%	36%	36%
Tool steel	8%	7%	7%	6%
Other	3%	Nil	Nil	Nil

In fiscal 1994, aerospace accounted for 12% of sales, the transportation equipment market for 14% of sales, metal producing and distribution 14%, electrical/electronic equipment 12%, general industrial equipment 11%, chemical and petroleum processing 5%, power generation and distribution 8%, metalworking equipment 7%, consumer durables 5%, instruments and controls 4%, housing and construction 3%, and miscellaneous 5%.

Stainless steels include a broad range of corrosion resistant alloys, including conventional stainless steels and many proprietary grades for special applications.

Special alloys include those other than stainless steels that are used in critical components such as bearings and fasteners; heat resistant alloys such as those with a complex nickel or cobalt base; alloys for electronic/electrical applications; and zirconium base alloys for nuclear reactors.

Tool steels include extremely hard alloys used for tooling and other wear-resisting components in stamping, extrusion, and machining operations.

Important Developments

Jul. '95—CRS reported share earnings of $2.09 on a 22% rise in sales in fiscal 1995's fourth quarter, versus earnings of $1.85 a year earlier. Earnings in fiscal 1994's fourth quarter included LIFO gains of $0.37 a share while earnings for all of fiscal 1994 included LIFO gains of $1.50. The company attributed the improvement in earnings for the quarter and year ended June 30, 1995, to higher shipments and increased selling prices. Unit volumes rose 4.0% in the fourth quarter and 8.0% for fiscal 1995 due to increased demand for automotive and equipment applications and a strong recovery in the aerospace market. The company stated that incoming business remained strong, particularly in the auto, aerospace and power generation markets.

Capitalization

Long Term Debt: $167,155,000 (3/95).
8.25% Conv. Preferred Stock: $29,002,000; conv. into 459,300 com. shs. Held by ESOP.

Per Share Data ($) (Year Ended Jun. 30)

	1995	1994	1993	1992	1991	1990
Tangible Bk. Val.	NA	29.23	27.14	32.56	37.44	36.43
Cash Flow	NA	8.14	6.47	4.70	6.34	7.64
Earnings	5.62	4.55	3.11	1.63	3.52	5.05
Dividends	2.40	2.40	2.40	2.40	2.40	2.33
Payout Ratio	43%	53%	77%	145%	68%	44%
Prices - High	74½	66⅜	58¼	51⅛	54⅞	57
- Low	53¼	56½	47⅜	41	43¼	36½
P/E Ratio - High	13	15	19	31	16	11
- Low	9	12	15	25	12	7

Income Statement Analysis (Million $)

	1994	%Chg	1993	%Chg	1992	%Chg	1991
Revs.	629	9%	576	1%	570	1%	562
Oper. Inc.	107	26%	85.0	13%	75.0	-23%	97.0
Depr.	29.0	8%	26.9	5%	25.7	7%	24.1
Int. Exp.	19.6	-10%	21.8	6%	20.6	2%	20.1
Pretax Inc.	62.7	46%	42.8	88%	22.8	-51%	46.7
Eff. Tax Rate	39%	—	38%	—	35%	—	36%
Net Inc.	38.3	45%	26.5	78%	14.9	-50%	30.1

Balance Sheet & Other Fin. Data (Million $)

	1994	1993	1992	1991	1990	1989
Cash	5.4	45.8	9.3	4.7	3.7	3.7
Curr. Assets	171	217	234	263	258	249
Total Assets	730	700	715	717	695	674
Curr. Liab.	99	73.0	80.0	137	127	110
LT Debt	158	190	197	123	127	130
Common Eqty.	237	217	267	320	314	319
Total Cap.	472	475	626	573	565	558
Cap. Exp.	33.2	20.6	35.0	31.3	22.6	36.2
Cash Flow	65.7	51.9	39.2	54.2	68.1	51.3

Ratio Analysis

	1994	1993	1992	1991	1990	1989
Curr. Ratio	1.7	3.0	2.9	1.9	2.0	2.3
% LT Debt of Cap.	33.5	40.0	31.4	21.4	22.4	23.3
% Net Inc.of Revs.	6.1	4.6	2.6	5.3	7.7	4.6
% Ret. on Assets	5.3	3.8	2.1	4.3	6.8	4.4
% Ret. on Equity	16.1	9.9	4.7	9.5	14.7	9.2

Dividend Data (Dividends have been paid since 1907. A dividend reinvestment plan is available. A "poison pill" stock purchase right was adopted in 1986.)

Amt. of Div. $	Date Decl.	Ex-Div. Date	Stock of Record	Payment Date
0.600	Aug. 11	Aug. 17	Aug. 23	Sep. 01 '94
0.600	Oct. 24	Oct. 28	Nov. 03	Dec. 01 '94
0.600	Jan. 23	Jan. 27	Feb. 02	Mar. 02 '95
0.600	Apr. 25	May. 01	May. 05	Jun. 01 '95

Data as orig. reptd.; bef. results of disc. opers. and/or spec. items. Per share data adj. for stk. divs. as of ex-div. date. E-Estimated. NA-Not Available. NM-Not Meaningful. NR-Not Ranked.

Office—101 West Bern St., Reading, PA 19612-4662. **Tel**—(610) 208-2000. **Chrmn, Pres & CEO**—R. W. Cardy. **SVP-CFO**—G. W. Cottrell. **Secy**—J. R. Welty. **Treas & Investor Contact**—John A. Schuler. **Dirs**—M. C. Bennett, R. W. Cardy, D. M. Draeger, C. McC. Evarts, C. R. Garr, W. J. Hudson Jr., A. E. Humphrey, E. W. Kay, F. C. Langenberg, M. B. Mangum, M. Miller Jr., P. R. Roedel, K. C. Turner, K. L. Wolfe. **Transfer Agent & Registrar**—First Chicago Trust Co. of New York., NYC. **Incorporated** in New Jersey in 1904; reincorporated in Delaware in 1968. **Empl**-4,200. **S&P Analyst:** Leo Larkin

STANDARD & POOR'S

STOCK REPORTS

Carter-Wallace

NYSE Symbol **CAR**
In S&P MidCap 400

02-OCT-95 **Industry:** Cosmetics-Toiletries-Drugs

Summary: This company markets toiletries, proprietary drugs, pharmaceuticals, diagnostic specialties and pet products.

S&P Opinion: Hold (★★★)

Recent Price • 12½
52 Wk Range • 15⅜-10⅛
Yield • 1.3%
12-Mo. P/E • NM

Quantitative Evaluations

Outlook
(1 Lowest—5 Highest)
• **4-**

Fair Value
• **13¼**

Risk
• **Average**

Earn./Div. Rank
• **B**

Technical Eval.
• **Bullish** since 9/95

Rel. Strength Rank
(1 Lowest—99 Highest)
• **46**

Insider Activity
• **NA**

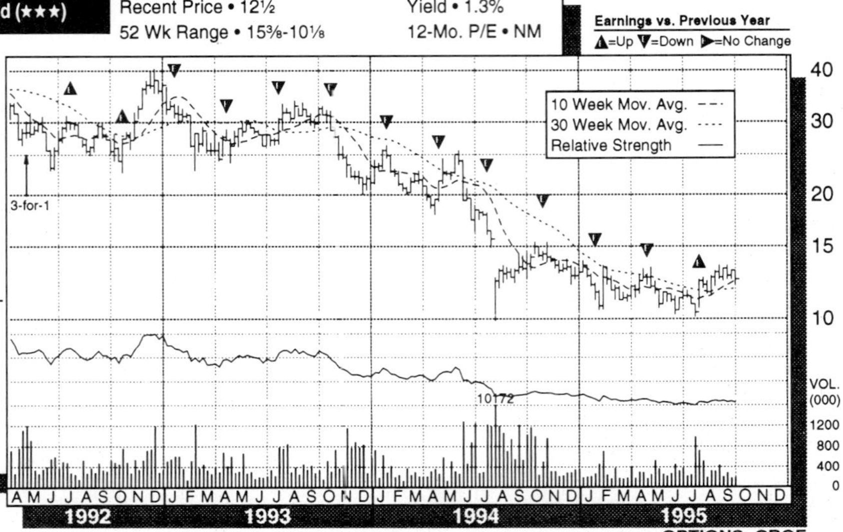

OPTIONS: CBOE

Overview - 02-OCT-95

Sales for 1995-96 should decline, on lower sales of Felbatol (felbamate). Sales of the company's line of consumer products are likely to be flat, reflecting increased competition. Margins should improve somewhat on the company's restructuring efforts. However, any improvement will be partially offset by a less profitable product mix, reflecting decreased emphasis on the profitable health care area. Ongoing pricing pressures in the consumer products area could also hurt profitability. However, the company should report profits in the absence of a one-time $129.3 million charge ($1.75 a share) related to a corporate restructuring and writeoffs of the Organidin and Felbatol drugs. Earnings will be hurt slightly by one-time charges of up to $0.30 in relation to closing a condom factory in Trenton, N.J.

Valuation - 02-OCT-95

The shares are down substantially since reaching a high of 45 3/4 early in 1992. We attribute this poor performance to a history of disappointing earnings. In recent years, the stock price and earnings have been hurt by the discontinuance of Organidin, and reduced distribution of Felbatol as a result of an FDA ruling by the Food and Drug Administration. While earnings could improve in 1995-96 before a one-time $0.30 a share charge, from 1994-95's level before a one-time $1.75 charge, we feel the estimate carries a high degree of uncertainty. Consequently, we are retaining a neutral opinion on this stock.

Key Stock Statistics

S&P EPS Est. 1996	0.65	Tang. Bk. Value/Share	4.33
P/E on S&P Est. 1996	19.2	Beta	1.45
S&P EPS Est. 1997	1.10	Shareholders	5,200
Dividend Rate/Share	0.16	Market cap. (B)	$0.576
Shs. outstg. (M)	46.1	Inst. holdings	31%
Avg. daily vol. (M)	0.042	Insider holdings	NA

Value of $10,000 invested 5 years ago: $ 7,072

Fiscal Year Ending Mar. 31

	1996	% Change	1995	% Change	1994	% Change
Revenues (Million $)						
1Q	177.0	-3%	183.3	13%	162.8	4%
2Q	—	—	168.1	12%	150.3	-10%
3Q	—	—	156.6	-11%	176.5	11%
4Q	—	—	155.6	-11%	175.3	4%
Yr.	—	—	663.6	NM	664.8	2%
Income (Million $)						
1Q	0.86	95%	0.44	-92%	5.84	-64%
2Q	—	—	-47.24	NM	1.38	-86%
3Q	—	—	-4.66	NM	12.89	-3%
4Q	—	—	-4.81	NM	6.51	-17%
Yr	—	—	-56.27	NM	26.61	-44%
Earnings Per Share ($)						
1Q	0.02	100%	0.01	-92%	0.13	-63%
2Q	E0.17	NM	-1.03	NM	0.03	-86%
3Q	E0.29	NM	-0.10	NM	0.28	-3%
4Q	E0.17	NM	-0.10	NM	0.14	-18%
Yr.	E0.65	NM	-1.22	NM	0.58	-44%

Next earnings report expected: early November

Carter-Wallace

Business Summary - 02-OCT-95

Business segment contributions (profits in millions) in fiscal 1994-95 were:

	Sales	Profits
Health care	40%	-$51.2
Antiperspirants & deodorants	18%	-10.8
Other consumer	42%	31.5

Operations outside the U.S. accounted for about 27% of sales and $13.3 million of operating profits in 1994-95. R&D equaled 6.2% of sales in 1994-95, slightly less than 1993-94's 7.9%.

Health care products include antiepileptic drugs, expectorants/antitussives, xanthine bronchodilators, cough/cold products, muscle relaxants, sedative hypnotics, rheumatoid arthritis drugs, xanthine bronchodilators, laxatives, topical antibacterial and anti-fungal agents, topical analgesics, analgesic/antipyretics, medicated throat lozenges, antidiarrheals, antacids, antinauseants, toothbrushes, vitamins, antiflatulents, and nasal decongestants. Also produced are tests for pregnancy, group A streptococcus, chlamydia, micro-organisms in the blood, mononucleosis, rheumatoid, blood hematocrit levels, streptococcal antibodies, and autoimmune, viral and bacterial diseases.

The consumer products segment is heavily dependent upon the Arrid line of antiperspirants and deodorants, which are available in sprays, roll-ons and creams. Other consumer products include Trojan condoms (which have over half of the U.S. retail market) and Pearl Drops tooth polish. Also produced are laxatives, depilatories, pregnancy tests and ovulation kits, lubricating jellies, skin care products, oral hygiene products, tapes and bandages, men's grooming products, denture adhesives, hair lotions, non-prescription eyeglasses and pet care items.

Important Developments

Jul. '95—CAR said that it will close its condom factory in Trenton, N.J., and transfer production from that factory to a newly acquired facility in Colonial Heights, Va. As a result of this decision, CAR incurred a one-time charge of $20.1 million (pretax), or $0.26 a share, in the first quarter of 1995-96. The company said that additional charges of $2 million (pretax) could be incurred in 1995-96 related to the closing of this facility.

Capitalization

Long Term Debt: $23,115,000 (3/95).
Class B Common Stk.: 12,512,858 shs. ($1 par); 10 votes per sh.; transfer restricted; conv. sh.-for-sh. into com.
The Hoyt family owns 94% of the Class B and 35% of the common stock.

Per Share Data ($)

(Year Ended Mar. 31)

	1995	1994	1993	1992	1991	1990
Tangible Bk. Val.	4.27	6.15	6.84	6.32	5.67	6.12
Cash Flow	-0.62	1.18	1.60	1.53	1.57	1.42
Earnings	-1.22	0.58	1.03	1.00	1.12	1.10
Dividends	0.29	0.33	0.33	0.33	0.30	0.26
Payout Ratio	NM	57%	32%	33%	26%	24%
Cal. Yrs.	1994	1993	1992	1991	1990	1989
Prices - High	26⅜	36⅝	45¾	41⅞	19½	20⅛
- Low	9⅞	20⅛	22⅝	17½	15	13
P/E Ratio - High	NM	63	45	42	17	18
- Low	NM	35	22	18	13	12

Income Statement Analysis (Million $)

	1995	%Chg	1994	%Chg	1993	%Chg	1992
Revs.	666	NM	668	2%	656	-3%	673
Oper. Inc.	79.0	11%	71.0	-22%	91.0	-16%	108
Depr.	27.8	1%	27.4	6%	25.8	5%	24.5
Int. Exp.	2.5	27%	2.0	11%	1.8	-47%	3.4
Pretax Inc.	-87.0	NM	37.4	-45%	68.4	2%	67.3
Eff. Tax Rate	NM	—	29%	—	31%	—	32%
Net Inc.	-56.3	NM	26.6	-44%	47.2	3%	45.7

Balance Sheet & Other Fin. Data (Million $)

	1995	1994	1993	1992	1991	1990
Cash	58.0	56.0	36.0	39.0	30.0	108
Curr. Assets	303	315	316	305	290	316
Total Assets	680	629	601	582	562	516
Curr. Liab.	203	130	132	134	138	131
LT Debt	23.2	9.5	13.4	15.2	17.0	21.3
Common Eqty.	327	394	431	409	383	345
Total Cap.	350	403	444	424	400	367
Cap. Exp.	18.9	24.3	25.5	22.3	18.7	34.9
Cash Flow	-28.4	54.1	73.0	70.2	72.2	64.9

Ratio Analysis

	1995	1994	1993	1992	1991	1990
Curr. Ratio	1.5	2.4	2.4	2.3	2.1	2.4
% LT Debt of Cap.	6.6	2.3	3.0	3.6	4.2	5.8
% Net Inc.of Revs.	NM	4.0	7.2	6.8	8.2	9.1
% Ret. on Assets	NM	4.3	8.0	8.0	9.6	10.2
% Ret. on Equity	NM	6.4	11.2	11.6	14.2	15.5

Dividend Data —Dividends have been paid since 1883.

Amt. of Div. $	Date Decl.	Ex-Div. Date	Stock of Record	Payment Date
0.083	Oct. 20	Nov. 01	Nov. 07	Nov. 29 '94
0.040	Jan. 19	Feb. 06	Feb. 10	Mar. 06 '95
0.040	Apr. 20	May. 04	May. 10	Jun. 06 '95
0.040	Jul. 19	Aug. 03	Aug. 07	Sep. 01 '95

Data as orig. reptd.; bef. results of disc. opers. and/or spec. items. Per share data adj. for stk. divs. as of ex-div. date. E-Estimated. NA-Not Available. NM-Not Meaningful. NR-Not Ranked.

Office—1345 Ave. of the Americas, New York, NY 10105. **Tel**—(212) 339-5000. **Chrmn & CEO**—H. H. Hoyt Jr. **Pres**—D. J. Black. **VP-Secy & Investor Contact**—Ralph Levine. **VP-Treas**—J. L. Wagar. **Dirs**—D. M. Baldwin, D. J. Black, R. L. Cruess, H. H. Hoyt Jr., S. C. Hoyt, R. Levine, H. M. Rinaldi, P. A. Veteri. **Transfer Agent & Registrar**—Bank of New York, NYC. **Incorporated** in Maryland in 1937; reincorporated in Delaware in 1968. **Empl**-3,670. **S&P Analyst:** E.A. Vandeventer

Centocor, Inc.

NASDAQ Symbol **CNTO**
In S&P MidCap 400

18-SEP-95

Industry: Drugs-Generic and OTC

Summary: This biotechnology company is developing therapeutic and diagnostic products for cardiovascular, inflammatory and infectious diseases.

S&P Opinion: Avoid (★★)

Recent Price • 11¼
52 Wk Range • 21-10⅞
Yield • Nil
12-Mo. P/E • NM

Quantitative Evaluations

Outlook (1 Lowest—5 Highest)
• **1**

Fair Value
• **5⅞**

Risk
• **High**

Earn./Div. Rank
• **C**

Technical Eval.
• **Bullish** since 4/95

Rel. Strength Rank (1 Lowest—99 Highest)
• **3**

Insider Activity
• **NA**

Earnings vs. Previous Year
▲=Up ▼=Down ▶=No Change

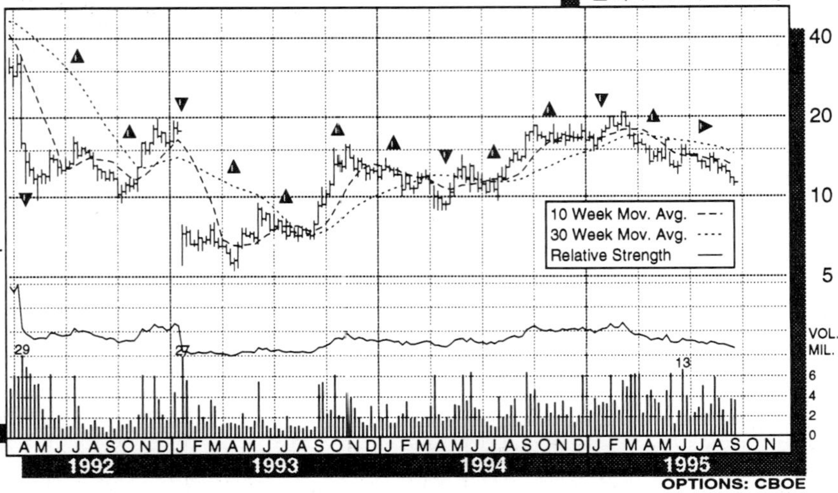

OPTIONS: CBOE

Overview - 18-SEP-95

Profitability eludes Centocor despite commercial availability of its first drug ReoPro, which is used in high risk coronary angioplasty procedures. Sluggish ReoPro sales have disappointed investors as hospital formularies find the drug price a little steep. Marketing partner Eli Lilly already has enough ReoPro inventory for 1995's second half. High operating costs continue to outpace diagnostic and drug sales. Ongoing studies include further applications for ReoPro and CenTNF in Crohn's disease and rheumatoid arthritis. Upcoming events include Phase III results for ReoPro in unstable angina (2Q, 1996), and Phase II data for CenTNF in Crohn's disease (early 1996). A corporate alliance with a major pharmaceutical firm for CenTNF is expected in the third or fourth quarter.

Valuation - 18-SEP-95

Although market acceptance of ReoPro is growing, hospitals are still reluctant to use it as often as the labeling indicates. Second quarter 1995 results were much worse than the median consensus estimate of -$0.11. Our estimate for 1995 is being revised to -$0.77 from -$0.45. Going forward, investors will be looking toward trial results for ReoPro and Phase II data of CenTNF in 1996. Even with favorable results in both trials, we don't anticipate profitability until at least 1997. We recommend avoiding purchase of the shares.

Key Stock Statistics

S&P EPS Est. 1995	-0.77	Tang. Bk. Value/Share	NM
P/E on S&P Est. 1995	NM	Beta	0.80
Dividend Rate/Share	Nil	Shareholders	5,000
Shs. outstg. (M)	58.3	Market cap. (B)	$0.656
Avg. daily vol. (M)	0.585	Inst. holdings	56%
		Insider holdings	NA

Value of $10,000 invested 5 years ago: $ 9,000

Fiscal Year Ending Dec. 31

	1995	% Change	1994	% Change	1993	% Change
Revenues (Million $)						
1Q	24.00	57%	15.27	2%	15.00	-31%
2Q	20.75	27%	16.38	19%	13.80	-33%
3Q	—	—	12.93	-23%	16.73	-67%
4Q	—	—	22.64	-26%	30.47	-9%
Yr.	—	—	67.23	-11%	75.93	-40%
Income (Million $)						
1Q	-8.24	NM	-50.64	NM	-25.53	NM
2Q	-17.31	NM	-15.42	NM	-26.02	NM
3Q	—	—	-17.58	NM	-15.80	NM
4Q	—	—	-43.02	NM	-7.02	NM
Yr.	—	—	-126.7	NM	-74.38	NM
Earnings Per Share ($)						
1Q	-0.14	NM	-1.13	NM	-0.62	NM
2Q	-0.30	NM	-0.30	NM	-0.63	NM
3Q	E-0.15	NM	-0.34	NM	-0.38	NM
4Q	E-0.18	NM	-0.83	NM	-0.17	NM
Yr.	E-0.77	NM	-2.55	NM	-1.79	NM

Next earnings report expected: early November

Centocor, Inc.

Business Summary - 13-SEP-95

Centocor, Inc. is a biopharmaceutical company that develops and commercializes monoclonal antibody-based products for human healthcare. The company focuses on four major disease areas: infectious, cardiovascular, autoimmune and cancer. The company's in-vitro diagnostic products generate the bulk of its revenues.

In December 1994, the company obtained a product license for ReoPro, a monoclonal antibody designed to inhibit clotting in the blood during and after high-risk coronary angioplasty. Commercial sales commenced in January 1995. The product has been shown to reduce the incidence of blood clot-related complications associated with coronary angioplasty. Eli Lilly (which holds global marketing rights) began selling ReoPro at a net wholesale price of $1,350 per course-of-therapy. Further studies of ReoPro are continuing in patients with unstable angina (Phase III) and restenosis (Phase III).

In February 1995, Centocor launched Panorex, used in the treatment of post-operative colorectal cancer, for sale in Germany. Long term Phase III trials are proceeding in the U.S. and Europe. Glaxo-Wellcome holds marketing rights. In the area of autoimmune disease therapy, CenTNF is in Phase II trials for the treatment of rheumatoid arthritis and inflammatory bowel diseases.

Centocor's in-vivo diagnostic, Myoscint, a cardiac imaging agent, has been approved in several European countries, although efforts to obtain U.S. marketing approval are still continuing.

In-vitro cancer blood tests include Ovarian Cancer Test CA 125, for clinical use in the U.S., Europe and Japan; Pancreatic Cancer Test CA 19-9, Breast Cancer Test CA 15-3 and Gastric Cancer Test CA 72-4, all sold for clinical use in Europe and Japan; Multidrug Resistance Test P-glycoCHEK, sold for investigational use in Europe and Japan; and Non-Small Cell Lung Cancer Test CYFRA 21-1, available for clinical use Europe and investigational use in Japan. In 1995, Centocor received U.S. clearance to market CAPTIA Syphilis G, a serology test performed in blood bank testing laboratories.

Important Developments

Aug. '95—The company posted a loss of $0.30 for the second quarter of 1995 which includes a special litigation charge of $0.07. The company said that discussions with potential marketing partners for CenTNF are progressing.

Capitalization

Long Term Debt: $259,979,000 (6/95).

Per Share Data ($) (Year Ended Dec. 31)

	1994	1993	1992	1991	1990	1989
Tangible Bk. Val.	-0.08	-0.65	0.31	3.67	5.78	5.31
Cash Flow	-2.19	-1.42	-4.48	-5.36	-4.47	0.24
Earnings	-2.55	-1.79	-4.90	-5.72	-5.10	0.01
Dividends	Nil	Nil	Nil	Nil	Nil	Nil
Payout Ratio	Nil	Nil	Nil	Nil	Nil	Nil
Prices - High	18¾	19½	60¼	56¼	24⅛	13½
- Low	8⅞	5¼	9½	19⅜	11⅞	7½
P/E Ratio - High	NM	NM	NM	NM	NM	NM
- Low	NM	NM	NM	NM	NM	NM

Income Statement Analysis (Million $)

	1994	%Chg	1993	%Chg	1992	%Chg	1991
Revs.	67.2	-11%	75.9	NM	76.2	43%	53.2
Oper. Inc.	-26.0	NM	-31.0	NM	-122	NM	-110
Depr.	18.2	17%	15.6	-7%	16.7	35%	12.4
Int. Exp.	19.8	-1%	20.1	2%	19.8	74%	11.4
Pretax Inc.	-126	NM	-74.0	NM	-193	NM	-195
Eff. Tax Rate	NM	—	NM	—	NM	—	NM
Net Inc.	-126	NM	-74.0	NM	-193	NM	-195

Balance Sheet & Other Fin. Data (Million $)

	1994	1993	1992	1991	1990	1989
Cash	182	123	150	181	96.0	64.0
Curr. Assets	215	153	187	284	158	88.0
Total Assets	306	281	349	473	273	180
Curr. Liab.	67.2	59.6	77.1	63.6	43.6	17.9
LT Debt	232	238	238	259	42.0	23.0
Common Eqty.	5.0	-19.0	31.0	144	169	133
Total Cap.	237	219	269	405	215	160
Cap. Exp.	4.6	2.0	23.3	32.5	47.8	15.4
Cash Flow	-107	-59.0	-176	-182	-115	5.0

Ratio Analysis

	1994	1993	1992	1991	1990	1989
Curr. Ratio	3.2	2.6	2.4	4.5	3.6	4.9
% LT Debt of Cap.	92.6	108.5	88.4	64.0	19.6	14.0
% Net Inc.of Revs.	NM	NM	NM	NM	NM	0.2
% Ret. on Assets	NM	NM	NM	NM	NM	0.1
% Ret. on Equity	NM	NM	NM	NM	NM	0.1

Dividend Data —No cash has been paid.

Data as orig. reptd.; bef. results of disc. opers. and/or spec. items. Per share data adj. for stk. divs. as of ex-div. date. E-Estimated. NA-Not Available. NM-Not Meaningful. NR-Not Ranked.

Office—200 Great Valley Parkway, Malvern, PA 19355. **Tel**—(610) 651-6000. **Chrmn**—H.J.P. Schoemaker. **Pres & CEO**—D.P. Holveck. **VP-Fin & CFO**—D.J. Caruso. **VP-Secy**—G. D. Hobbs. **Dirs**—A. B. Evnin, W. F. Hamilton, D. P. Holveck, A. T. Knoppers, R. A. Matricaria, H. J. P. Schoemaker, R. D. Spizzirri, L. Steinman. J.C. Tempel. **Transfer Agent & Registrar**—First National Bank of Boston, Canton. **Incorporated** in Pennsylvania in 1979. **Empl**-550. **S&P Analyst:** Thomas Tirney

Central Fidelity Banks

NASDAQ Symbol **CFBS**
In S&P MidCap 400

19-OCT-95 **Industry:** Banking

Summary: This Virginia bank holding company, with assets of $10.7 billion, has more than 240 branches throughout the state.

Quantitative Evaluations
Outlook
(1 Lowest—5 Highest)
• **3+**
Fair Value
• **33⅛**
Risk
• **Low**
Earn./Div. Rank
• **A**

Technical Eval.
• **Bullish** since 6/95
Rel. Strength Rank
(1 Lowest—99 Highest)
• **63**
Insider Activity
• **Neutral**

Recent Price • 33
52 Wk Range • 33½-23¾
Yield • 3.7%
12-Mo. P/E • 16.8

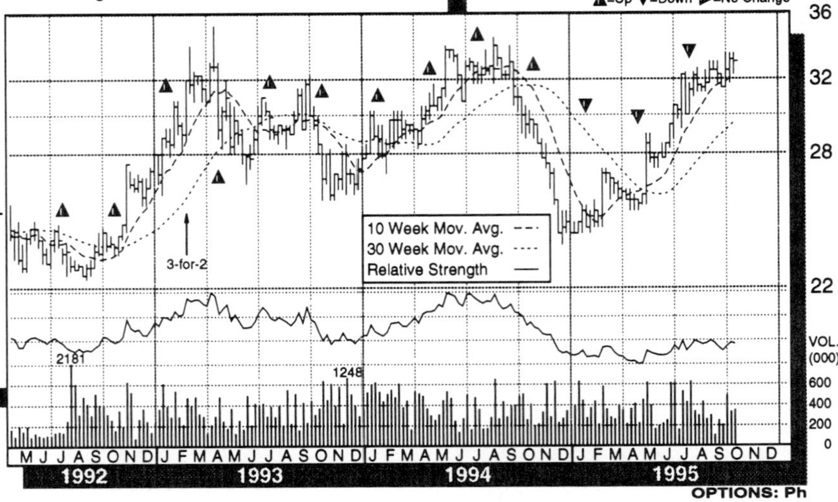

Business Profile - 19-OCT-95

This bank holding company, one of Virginia's largest banking organizations, maintains its core operating philosophy of remaining a Virginia-only independent bank. The June 1995 acquisition of the Virginia branches and deposits of Household Bank will enhance Central Fidelity's position in northern Virginia. As the bank has no presence in a number of key Virginia markets, acquisitions will continue to play a major role in its future growth.

Operational Review - 19-OCT-95

Net interest income in the nine months ended September 30, 1995, was flat, year to year; narrower net interest rate margins (3.59%, versus 3.88%) outweighed a 14% increase in average loans outstanding. The loan loss provision rose 6.3%, to $17,352,000. With a 17% decline in noninterest income and fractionally lower noninterest expense, pretax income dropped 9.1%. After taxes at 31.7%, versus 32.5%, net income was down 8.1%, to $79,296,000 ($2.00 a share), from $86,273,000 ($2.21).

Stock Performance - 13-OCT-95

In the past 30 trading days, CFBS's shares have increased 2%, compared to a 4% rise in the S&P 500. Average trading volume for the past five days was 68,140 shares, compared with the 40-day moving average of 57,359 shares.

Key Stock Statistics

Dividend Rate/Share	1.20	Shareholders	16,000
Shs. outstg. (M)	39.9	Market cap. (B)	$ 1.3
Avg. daily vol. (M)	0.068	Inst. holdings	34%
Tang. Bk. Value/Share	19.20	Insider holdings	NA
Beta	0.85		

Value of $10,000 invested 5 years ago: $ 29,962

Fiscal Year Ending Dec. 31

	1995	% Change	1994	% Change	1993	% Change
Revenues (Million $)						
1Q	203.6	7%	190.2	9%	175.2	13%
2Q	210.6	17%	180.5	4%	174.1	-2%
3Q	217.5	17%	186.7	-15%	218.7	14%
4Q	—	—	166.8	-3%	171.8	NM
Yr.	—	—	724.2	-2%	739.8	6%
Income (Million $)						
1Q	25.70	-12%	29.29	21%	24.13	53%
2Q	26.02	-12%	29.58	12%	26.32	33%
3Q	27.55	NM	27.39	2%	26.74	29%
4Q	—	—	-1.40	NM	25.73	16%
Yr.	—	—	84.86	-18%	102.9	31%
Earnings Per Share ($)						
1Q	0.65	-13%	0.75	19%	0.63	31%
2Q	0.66	-13%	0.76	12%	0.68	13%
3Q	0.69	-1%	0.70	1%	0.69	19%
4Q	—	—	-0.04	NM	0.66	14%
Yr.	—	—	2.17	-18%	2.66	18%

Next earnings report expected: mid January

Central Fidelity Banks

Business Summary - 19-OCT-95

Central Fidelity Banks, Inc. is a bank holding company headquartered in Richmond, Va. At December 31, 1994, it operated 230 branch offices throughout the state.

Loans outstanding totaled $5.77 bilion at 1994 year-end and were divided:

Commercial & commercial real estate	33%
Residential real estate	27%
Installment	15%
Bank card	10%
Consumer second mortgage	10%
Construction	5%

The allowance for loan losses at December 31, 1994, totaled $110,000,000 (1.91% of loans outstanding), versus $105,000,000 (2.18%) a year earlier. Net chargeoffs in 1994 amounted to $19,359,000 ($76,309,000 in 1993), equal to 0.36% (1.80%) of average loans. At December 31, 1994, nonperforming assets amounted to $90.3 million (1.56% of total assets), up from $132.1 million (1.37%) a year earlier.

Consolidated deposits of $7.23 billion at 1994 year-end were apportioned: 13% demand, 9% interest checking, 11% regular savings, 50% consumer certificates, 14% money-market accounts and 3% certificates of deposit $100,000 and over.

Total income in 1994 was derived: 59% from interest and fees on loans, 29% from securities available for sale, 1% from money market and trading account securities, 5% from deposit fees and charges, 2% from trust income, and 5% from other income.

On a taxable-equivalent basis, the average yield on interest-earning assets in 1994 was 7.47% (7.43% in 1993), while the average rate paid on interest-bearing liabilities was 4.21% (3.92%), for a net spread of 3.26% (3.51%).

Important Developments

Oct. '95—Nonperforming assets at September 30, 1995, totaled $67,502,000 (0.63% of total assets), down from $96,571,000 (0.97%) a year earlier. Net loan chargeoffs in the 1995 third quarter came to $8,704,000 (0.58% of average loans on an annualized basis), versus $3,900,000 (0.28%) in the 1994 period.

Oct. '95—Central Fidelity said return on assets was 1.06% in the third quarter, versus 1.14% in the 1994 period. Return on average shareholders' equity was 14.28%, down from 16.50%.

Capitalization

Long Term Debt: $158,283,000 (9/95), incl. $7,886,000 of cap. lease obligs.

Per Share Data ($) (Year Ended Dec. 31)

	1994	1993	1992	1991	1990	1989
Tangible Bk. Val.	15.84	18.61	15.71	13.13	11.83	10.90
Earnings	2.17	2.66	2.25	1.87	1.65	1.57
Dividends	1.12	1.00	0.81	0.73	0.62	0.54
Payout Ratio	52%	38%	36%	39%	37%	35%
Prices - High	34½	35¼	28⅜	26⅛	14½	15⅝
- Low	23¾	25¾	22⅜	8⅞	8	11⅞
P/E Ratio - High	16	13	13	14	9	10
- Low	11	10	10	5	5	8

Income Statement Analysis (Million $)

	1994	%Chg	1993	%Chg	1992	%Chg	1991
Net Int. Inc.	335	3%	324	10%	294	22%	241
Tax Equiv. Adj.	7.9	-18%	9.6	-12%	10.9	-17%	13.2
Non Int. Inc.	83.7	18%	70.9	8%	65.6	7%	61.2
Loan Loss Prov.	24.4	-69%	79.5	-20%	100	100%	49.9
% Exp/Op Revs.	57%	—	55%	—	54%	—	61%
Pretax Inc.	124	-16%	147	35%	109	38%	79.0
Eff. Tax Rate	32%	—	30%	—	28%	—	24%
Net Inc.	84.9	-18%	103	31%	78.5	30%	60.4
% Net Int. Marg.	3.80%	—	3.98%	—	4.40%	—	4.48%

Balance Sheet & Other Fin. Data (Million $)

	1994	1993	1992	1991	1990	1989
Earning Assets:						
Money Mkt.	198	195	283	213	382	237
Inv. Securities	3,486	4,100	3,903	2,480	1,592	1,124
Com'l Loans	1,880	1,711	1,577	1,538	1,583	1,634
Other Loans	3,893	3,101	2,377	2,082	1,994	1,899
Total Assets	10,054	9,662	8,712	6,806	6,173	5,335
Demand Deposits	954	927	823	672	602	610
Time Deposits	6,274	5,729	5,849	4,506	3,931	3,532
LT Debt	957	160	168	23.0	27.0	31.0
Common Eqty.	623	726	604	429	382	378

Ratio Analysis

	1994	1993	1992	1991	1990	1989
% Ret. on Assets	0.9	1.2	1.1	1.0	1.0	1.1
% Ret. on Equity	11.9	14.9	15.5	14.9	14.5	15.0
% Loan Loss Resv.	1.9	2.2	2.6	1.7	1.7	1.0
% Loans/Deposits	79.9	72.3	59.3	69.9	78.9	85.2
% Equity to Assets	7.5	7.7	6.8	6.7	7.1	7.6

Dividend Data —Central Fidelity or its predecessors paid dividends every year since 1911. A dividend reinvestment plan is available.

Amt. of Div. $	Date Decl.	Ex-Div. Date	Stock of Record	Payment Date
0.280	Nov. 10	Dec. 12	Dec. 16	Jan. 03 '95
0.280	Jan. 11	Mar. 13	Mar. 17	Apr. 01 '95
0.300	May. 10	Jun. 14	Jun. 16	Jul. 01 '95
0.300	Jul. 12	Sep. 13	Sep. 15	Oct. 02 '95

Data as orig. reptd.; bef. results of disc opers. and/or spec. items. Per share data adj. for stk. divs. as of ex-div. date. E-Estimated. NA-Not Available. NM-Not Meaningful. NR-Not Ranked.

Offices—1021 E. Cary St., P.O. Box 27602, Richmond, VA 23261-7602. **Tel**—(804) 782-4000. **Chrmn & CEO**—L. N. Miller, Jr. **Treas, CFO & Investor Contact**—Charles W. Tysinger. **Secy**—W. N. Stoyko. **Dirs**—J. F. Betts, A. R. Clements, P. L. Cothran, P. A. Ellison, J. H. Ferguson, R. L. Freeman, T. R. Glass, M. B. Lane, G. R. Lewis, G. B. Miller, L. N. Miller, Jr., T. J. Moore, Jr., R. L. Morrill, L. U. Noland, III, W. G. Reynolds, Jr., K. S. White. **Transfer Agent**—Central Fidelity National Bank, Richmond. **Incorporated** in Virginia in 1978. **Empl**-3,500. **S&P Analyst:** Brad Ohlmuller

STANDARD & POOR'S

Central Louisiana Electric

STOCK REPORTS

NYSE Symbol **CNL**

In S&P MidCap 400

06-OCT-95 **Industry:** Utilities-Electric

Summary: This electric utility serves 218,000 customers in west-central and southeastern Louisiana.

Quantitative Evaluations

Recent Price • 25⅝

52 Wk Range • 25⅝-20⅞

Yield • 5.8%

12-Mo. P/E • 13.1

Outlook (1 Lowest—5 Highest)
• **3+**

Fair Value
• **25¼**

Risk
• **Low**

Earn./Div. Rank
• **A-**

Technical Eval.
• **Bullish** since 8/95

Rel. Strength Rank (1 Lowest—99 Highest)
• **83**

Insider Activity
• **NA**

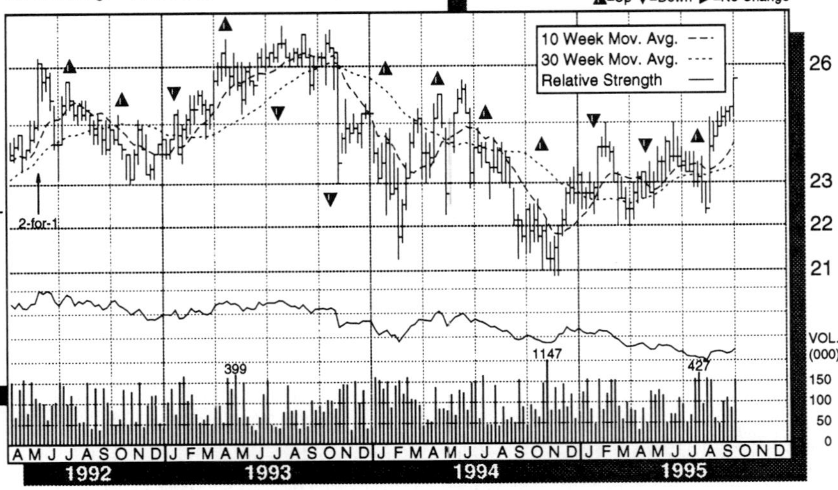

Business Profile - 06-OCT-95

Central Louisiana Electric serves approximately 218,000 customers in a 14,000-square-mile region of Louisiana that includes mostly small communities and rural areas. Generating units are fueled by coal, Louisiana lignite and natural gas. CNL does not expect the need for any rate increases in the forseeable future. The company raised its quarterly dividend 2.7%, with the April 1995 declaration.

Operational Review - 06-OCT-95

Revenues fell 2.5%, year to year, in 1995's first half, reflecting a decrease in fuel cost recovery revenues and warmer-than-normal weather. Changes in fuel costs are recovered through an adjustment mechanism that passes changes in fuel costs through to the customer. Benefiting from a 10.7% increase in kilowatt-hout sales in the June quarter, net income for the six months was up 3.5%, to $22,092,000 ($0.94 a share, after preferred dividends), from $21,350,000 ($0.91).

Stock Performance - 29-SEP-95

In the past 30 trading days, CNL's shares have increased 7%, compared to a 5% rise in the S&P 500. Average trading volume for the past five days was 33,600 shares, compared with the 40-day moving average of 23,726 shares.

Key Stock Statistics

Dividend Rate/Share	1.50	Shareholders	12,700
Shs. outstg. (M)	22.4	Market cap. (B)	$0.583
Avg. daily vol. (M)	0.024	Inst. holdings	36%
Tang. Bk. Value/Share	16.43	Insider holdings	NA
Beta	0.49		

Value of $10,000 invested 5 years ago: $ 19,886

Fiscal Year Ending Dec. 31

	1995	% Change	1994	% Change	1993	% Change
Revenues (Million $)						
1Q	79.87	-5%	84.15	12%	75.45	NM
2Q	100.6	NM	100.9	10%	92.07	7%
3Q	—	—	112.6	-11%	126.1	19%
4Q	—	—	81.88	-8%	88.81	5%
Yr.	—	—	379.6	NM	382.4	9%
Income (Million $)						
1Q	8.09	-6%	8.58	14%	7.52	6%
2Q	13.49	6%	12.77	6%	12.04	-3%
3Q	—	—	17.61	24%	14.15	-26%
4Q	—	—	6.09	-25%	8.09	20%
Yr.	—	—	45.04	8%	41.81	-8%
Earnings Per Share ($)						
1Q	0.34	-6%	0.36	16%	0.31	7%
2Q	0.60	9%	0.55	6%	0.52	-2%
3Q	—	—	0.76	25%	0.61	-27%
4Q	—	—	0.25	-26%	0.34	21%
Yr.	—	—	1.92	8%	1.78	-8%

Next earnings report expected: late October

Central Louisiana Electric

Business Summary - 06-OCT-95

Central Louisiana Electric Company, Inc. provides electric service to some 218,000 customers in 63 communities and contiguous rural ares in a 14,000-square-mile region in the State of Louisiana. Contributions to electric revenues by class of customer in recent years were:

	1994	1993	1992	1991
Residential	44%	44%	44%	45%
Commercial	19%	18%	19%	19%
Industrial	22%	22%	23%	23%
Other	15%	16%	14%	13%

CNL operates and either owns or has an ownership interest in four steam electric generating stations. The company is the sole owner of Coughlin Power Station, Teche Power Station and Rodemacher Power Station Unit 1. Also, CNL owns a 50% interest in Dolet Hills Power Station Unit 1 and a 30% interest in Rodemacher Power Station Unit 2. Peak demand in 1994 was 1,310 mw, and generating capability totaled 1,706 mw, for a capacity margin of 30.2%. During 1994, CNL sold 6,613 million kwh of electricity, up from 6,488 million kwh in 1993.

Construction expenditures, excluding AFUDC, for 1995 are estimated to be $57 million and for the five-year period ending 1999 are expected to total $284 million. Expenditures for the five-year period include a distribution resource management system, enhancements to the information technology infrastructure and, scheduled to begin in 1999, initial costs associated with the refurbishement of a retired natural gas unit.

Important Developments

Feb. '95—CNL announced a formal proposal for the acquisition of Washington-St. Tammany Electric Cooperative, Inc. (WST). The company first announced interest in the purchase of WST in December 1994. Any acquistion of WST would require approval of several regulatory agencies and WST's member/owners and would be subject to certain other conditions. Separately, the company and Teche Electric Cooperative, Inc. executed a purchase and sale agreement regarding the purchase by CNL of all of the assets of Teche for about $22.4 million. The acquisiton is subject to a number of conditions, including regulatory approval.

Capitalization

Long Term Debt: $336,063,000 (3/95).
Red. Preferred Stock: $6,920,000.
Cum. Preferred Stock: $30,519,000.

Per Share Data ($)

(Year Ended Dec. 31)

	1994	1993	1992	1991	1990	1989
Tangible Bk. Val.	16.19	15.73	15.35	14.81	14.31	13.74
Earnings	1.92	1.78	1.93	1.92	1.85	1.78
Dividends	1.45	1.41	1.37	1.33	1.27	1.20
Payout Ratio	76%	79%	71%	69%	68%	68%
Prices - High	25⅝	27⅛	26¼	24½	18¼	18
- Low	20⅞	23	22¾	17¼	15¾	15⅝
P/E Ratio - High	13	15	14	13	10	10
- Low	11	13	12	9	9	9

Income Statement Analysis (Million $)

	1994	%Chg	1993	%Chg	1992	%Chg	1991
Revs.	380	NM	382	9%	352	4%	337
Depr.	40.0	7%	37.3	7%	34.8	2%	34.0
Maint.	25.0	NM	25.0	-5%	26.2	2%	25.8
Fxd. Chgs. Cov.	3.2	7%	3.0	3%	2.9	NM	2.9
Constr. Credits	2.3	-23%	3.0	50%	2.0	100%	1.0
Eff. Tax Rate	31%	—	32%	—	29%	—	30%
Net Inc.	45.0	8%	41.8	-8%	45.2	NM	44.9

Balance Sheet & Other Fin. Data (Million $)

	1994	1993	1992	1991	1990	1989
Gross Prop.	1,323	1,275	1,236	1,178	1,129	1,088
Cap. Exp.	55.0	52.0	64.0	55.0	49.0	50.0
Net Prop.	912	895	879	851	828	814
Capitalization:						
LT Debt	337	351	311	387	315	256
% LT Debt	47	49	47	53	48	44
Pfd.	13.3	12.1	10.1	14.9	14.8	15.4
% Pfd.	1.90	1.70	1.50	2.00	2.30	2.70
Common	363	353	343	330	322	309
% Common	51	49	52	45	49	53
Total Cap.	977	977	819	883	798	720

Ratio Analysis

	1994	1993	1992	1991	1990	1989
Oper. Ratio	81.4	83.1	80.0	78.3	78.0	76.8
% Earn. on Net Prop.	7.8	7.3	8.1	8.7	9.0	9.1
% Ret. on Revs.	11.9	10.9	12.9	13.3	12.7	13.1
% Ret. On Invest.Cap	7.3	7.5	8.6	9.0	9.8	10.0
% Return On Com.Eqty	12.0	11.5	12.8	13.2	13.2	13.2

Dividend Data —Dividends have been paid since 1935. A dividend reinvestment plan is available.

Amt. of Div. $	Date Decl.	Ex-Div. Date	Stock of Record	Payment Date
0.365	Oct. 21	Oct. 25	Oct. 31	Nov. 15 '94
0.365	Jan. 27	Jan. 31	Feb. 06	Feb. 15 '95
0.375	Apr. 21	Apr. 25	May. 01	May. 15 '95
0.375	Jul. 21	Jul. 27	Jul. 31	Aug. 15 '95

Data as orig. reptd.; bef. results of disc opers. and/or spec. items. Per share data adj. for stk. divs. as of ex-div. date. E-Estimated. NA-Not Available. NM-Not Meaningful. NR-Not Ranked.

Office—2030 Donahue Ferry Rd., Pineville, LA 71360-5226. **Tel**—(318) 484-7400. **Pres & CEO**—G. L. Nesbitt. **VP-Fin & Investor Contact**—David K. Warner (800) 253-2652; in La. (800) 331-4132. **Secy & Treas**—M. P. Prudhomme. **Dirs**—S. G. Cadoria, J. P. Garrett, F. B. James Jr., H. J. Kelly, W. A. Lockwood, A. D. Martin Jr., G. L. Nesbitt, R. T. Ratcliff, E. M. Simmons, E. L. Williamson. **Transfer Agent & Registrar**—First Chicago Trust Co. of New York, Jersey City, N.J. **Incorporated** in Louisiana in 1934. **Empl**-1,220. **S&P Analyst:** S.R.V.

STANDARD & POOR'S

STOCK REPORTS

Central Maine Power

NYSE Symbol **CTP**

In S&P MidCap 400

20-SEP-95

Industry: Utilities-Electric

Summary: Central Maine Power provides electricity to a service area covering about 77% of Maine's population and the bulk of the state's industrial centers.

Quantitative Evaluations

Outlook (1 Lowest—5 Highest) • **4-**

Fair Value • **12¾**

Risk • **Low**

Earn./Div. Rank • **B**

Technical Eval. • **Bullish** since 9/95

Rel. Strength Rank (1 Lowest—99 Highest) • **66**

Insider Activity • **Neutral**

Recent Price • 12⅝ | 52 Wk Range • 14⅛-10¼ | Yield • 7.2% | 12-Mo. P/E • NM

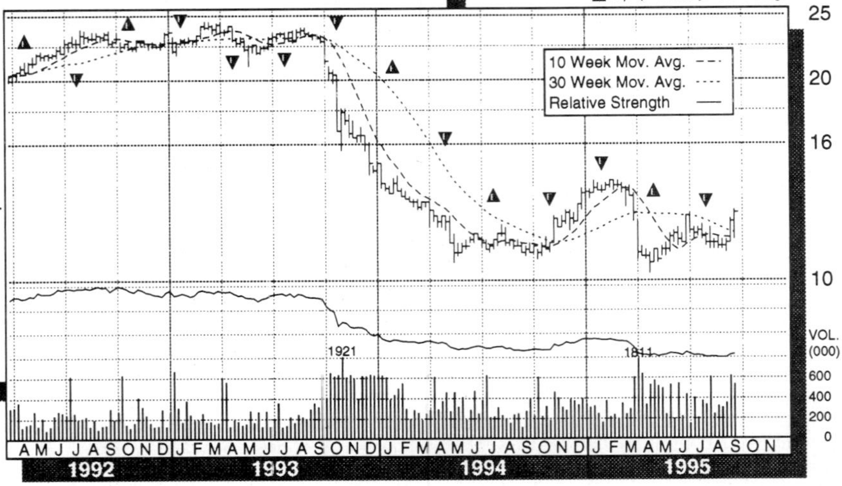

Business Profile - 20-SEP-95

After approval of a new rate plan effective January 1995 that provides more flexibility to negotiate prices, CTP focused on securing its customer base. Five-year contracts have been negotiated with 20 of its largest customers. However, under the rate plan, fuel expense is no longer subject to specific rate recovery. Due to this change, higher costs to obtain alternative power during the current outage of the Maine Yankee nuclear plant will adversely affect CTP's earnings in 1995.

Operational Review - 20-SEP-95

Revenues for the 12 months ended June 30, 1995, rose 0.6% from those of the preceding 12 months. Following an $11.7 million charge for repairs under way at the Maine Yankee plant and for costs associated with an early retirement program and a $100.4 million pretax charge related to the implementation of a new rate structure plan, there was a net loss of $32,231,000, versus net income of $52,750,000.

Stock Performance - 15-SEP-95

In the past 30 trading days, CTP's shares have increased 11%, compared to a 4% rise in the S&P 500. Average trading volume for the past five days was 106,220 shares, compared with the 40-day moving average of 87,731 shares.

Key Stock Statistics

Dividend Rate/Share	0.90	Shareholders	32,800
Shs. outstg. (M)	32.4	Market cap. (B)	$0.406
Avg. daily vol. (M)	0.099	Inst. holdings	29%
Tang. Bk. Value/Share	15.14	Insider holdings	NA
Beta	0.38		

Value of $10,000 invested 5 years ago: $ 9,385

Fiscal Year Ending Dec. 31

	1995	% Change	1994	% Change	1993	% Change
Revenues (Million $)						
1Q	263.3	9%	241.0	2%	236.0	-4%
2Q	202.6	-5%	212.3	7%	198.9	-2%
3Q	—	—	233.5	3%	227.4	10%
4Q	—	—	218.0	-6%	231.2	5%
Yr.	—	—	904.9	1%	893.6	2%
Income (Million $)						
1Q	26.38	131%	11.42	-47%	21.57	NM
2Q	-8.62	NM	15.31	12%	13.70	-9%
3Q	—	—	14.08	4%	13.56	-11%
4Q	—	—	-64.07	NM	12.47	6%
Yr.	—	—	-23.27	NM	61.30	-4%
Earnings Per Share ($)						
1Q	0.73	170%	0.27	-56%	0.62	-7%
2Q	-0.34	NM	0.39	5%	0.37	-18%
3Q	—	—	0.35	-3%	0.36	-18%
4Q	—	—	-2.06	NM	0.31	3%
Yr.	—	—	-1.04	NM	1.65	-11%

Next earnings report expected: late October

Central Maine Power

Business Summary - 20-SEP-95

Central Maine Power Company supplies electricity in central and southern Maine in an 11,000-sq.-mi. area with a population of about 936,000 (roughly 77% of the state's population). Revenue contributions by class of customer in recent years were:

	1994	1993	1992	1991
Residential	40%	40%	41%	40%
Industrial	28%	31%	30%	31%
Commercial	30%	27%	27%	27%
Other	2%	2%	2%	2%

The generation mix in 1994 was 29% nuclear, 37% non-utility generators, 12% oil, 13% hydro and 9% Canadian power. Peak demand in 1994 was 1,351 mw, and capability at time of peak was 1,977 mw, for a capacity margin of 46%. At 1994 year-end, CTP had 507,238 customers, up from 501,866 a year earlier.

CTP's territory covers most of Maine's industrial centers, including Portland, the state's largest city. CTP's industrial and commercial customers include producers of pulp and paper products, chemicals, plastics, electronic components, processed food and footwear and shipbuilders.

In January 1995, CTP began operating under a five-year trial of indexed price caps pursuant to a utilities commission rate order. The Alternative Rate Plan allows only a once-a-year adjustment of a cap that includes fuel costs for each customer class and permits flexibility to negotiate rates below the cap. Price increases are expected to be below the inflation rate. CTP took a pretax charge of $100.4 million in 1994's fourth quarter related to the new rate plan.

In conjunction with the new rate plan, CTP negotiated five-year agreements with 20 of its largest customers under which the companies agreed not to switch fuels, install self-generation equipment or seek other power sources. In return, rates were reduced 15% for these customers as of January 1, 1995, and further reductions of 3% will result by 1999. CTP expects to sign more of these agreements. In addition, electric rates were cut for all residential users by $5.6 million.

CTP's construction program for 1995-99 is estimated at $309 million, with $56 million budgeted for 1995. CTP expects most of the program to be financed internally. CTP also will incur costs of $10 million to $15 million for repairs to the Maine Yankee Nuclear Plant and excess replacement power fuel costs of $3.5 million to $4.5 million a month until the plant's outage ends, which is expected by the close of 1995.

Important Developments

Jul. '95—The second-quarter loss reflected a charge of $11.7 million to eliminate 200 employees, or 10% of the workforce, through early retirement.

Capitalization

Long Term Debt: $658,000,000 (6/95).
Red. Cum. Preferred Stock: $80,000,000.
Cum. Preferred Stock: $65,571,000.

Per Share Data ($) (Year Ended Dec. 31)

	1994	1993	1992	1991	1990	1989
Tangible Bk. Val.	15.14	17.09	16.68	12.42	12.17	11.67
Earnings	-1.04	1.65	1.85	1.82	1.68	1.92
Dividends	0.90	1.56	1.56	1.56	1.56	1.52
Payout Ratio	NM	95%	84%	86%	93%	79%
Prices - High	15	24½	23⅞	23	20⅝	20⅜
- Low	10⅝	14⅜	19⅞	16⅝	16⅛	16⅞
P/E Ratio - High	NM	15	13	13	12	11
- Low	NM	9	11	9	10	9

Income Statement Analysis (Million $)

	1994	%Chg	1993	%Chg	1992	%Chg	1991
Revs.	905	1%	894	2%	878	1%	867
Depr.	56.0	5%	53.1	5%	50.4	5%	47.9
Maint.	32.8	-2%	33.3	-18%	40.7	9%	37.4
Fxd. Chgs. Cov.	1.2	-48%	2.3	4%	2.2	NM	2.2
Constr. Credits	1.3	-46%	2.4	-14%	2.8	75%	1.6
Eff. Tax Rate	NA	—	24%	—	20%	—	23%
Net Inc.	-23.3	NM	61.3	-4%	63.6	8%	59.1

Balance Sheet & Other Fin. Data (Million $)

	1994	1993	1992	1991	1990	1989
Gross Prop.	1,593	1,585	1,553	1,500	1,445	1,350
Cap. Exp.	42.0	54.0	72.0	76.0	105	117
Net Prop.	1,074	1,083	1,079	1,053	1,017	951
Capitalization:						
LT Debt	639	582	499	519	496	431
% LT Debt	50	45	43	48	48	48
Pfd.	146	146	151	79.0	80.0	47.0
% Pfd.	11	11	13	7.30	7.70	5.30
Common	491	553	520	490	464	415
% Common	39	43	45	45	45	47
Total Cap.	1,658	1,659	1,347	1,254	1,200	1,038

Ratio Analysis

	1994	1993	1992	1991	1990	1989
Oper. Ratio	90.6	88.8	87.7	87.8	88.5	87.5
% Earn. on Net Prop.	8.4	9.8	10.1	11.0	9.7	10.5
% Ret. on Revs.	NM	6.9	7.2	6.8	6.4	6.9
% Ret. On Invest.Cap	1.7	7.3	9.0	9.4	9.1	9.6
% Return On Com.Eqty	NM	9.8	11.3	11.3	10.3	11.8

Dividend Data —Dividends have been paid since 1943. A dividend reinvestment plan is available. In 1995, CTP terminated a "poison pill" rights plan.

Amt. of Div. $	Date Decl.	Ex-Div. Date	Stock of Record	Payment Date
0.225	Sep. 21	Oct. 03	Oct. 10	Oct. 31 '94
0.225	Dec. 21	Jan. 04	Jan. 10	Jan. 31 '95
0.225	Mar. 15	Apr. 04	Apr. 10	Apr. 28 '95
0.225	Jun. 21	Jul. 06	Jul. 10	Jul. 31 '95

Data as orig. reptd.; bef. results of disc opers. and/or spec. items. Per share data adj. for stk. divs. as of ex-div. date. E-Estimated. NA-Not Available. NM-Not Meaningful. NR-Not Ranked.

Office—83 Edison Dr., Augusta, ME 04336. **Tel**—(207) 623-3521. **Chrmn**—C. D. Reed Jr. **Pres & CEO**—D. T. Flanagan. **VP & CFO**—D. E. Marsh. **Secy**—W. M. Finn. **Treas & Investor Contact**—Douglas Stevenson. **Dirs**—C. H. Abbott, C. M. Chase, E. J. Dufour, D. T. Flanagan, R. H. Gardiner, D. M. Jagger, P. J. Moynihan, C. E. Monty, C. D. Reed Jr., R. H. Reny, K. M. Weare. **Transfer Agent**—Chemical Bank, NYC or company. **Registrar**—Chemical Bank, NYC. **Incorporated** in Maine in 1905. **Empl**-1,800. **S&P Analyst:** J.M.H.

STANDARD & POOR'S **STOCK REPORTS**

Century Telephone Enterprises

NYSE Symbol **CTL**
In S&P MidCap 400

06-SEP-95

Industry: Telecommunications

Summary: This holding company provides local telephone services in designated areas of 14 states, with operations concentrated in Wisconsin, Louisiana, Michigan and Ohio.

S&P Opinion: Accumulate (★★★★)

Recent Price • 28
52 Wk Range • 33⅛-27
Yield • 1.2%
12-Mo. P/E • 13.7

Quantitative Evaluations
Outlook
(1 Lowest—5 Highest)
• **4-**
Fair Value
• **29⅜**
Risk
• **Low**
Earn./Div. Rank
• **A**

Technical Eval.
• **Bearish** since 8/94
Rel. Strength Rank
(1 Lowest—99 Highest)
• **27**
Insider Activity
• **NA**

Earnings vs. Previous Year
▲=Up ▼=Down ▶=No Change

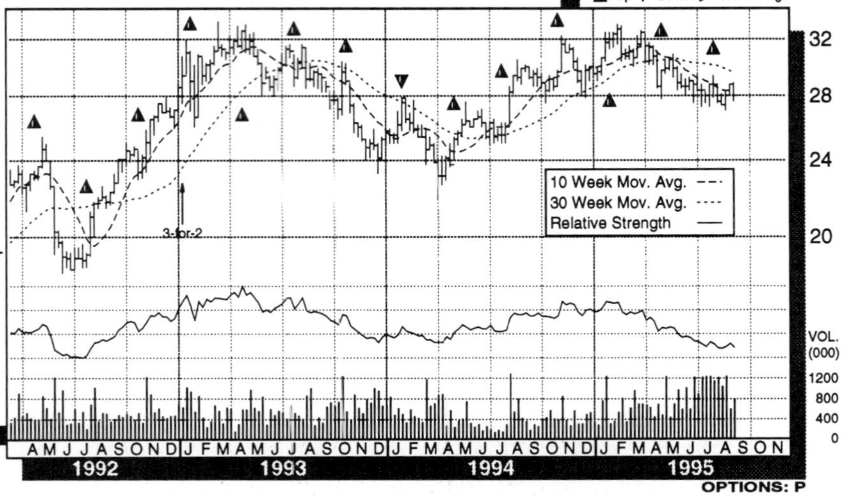

OPTIONS: P

Overview - 06-SEP-95

Although we still see growth from telephone operations continuing at a rate above the industry average, the revenue growth rate is expected to slow from the strong pace of recent years, reflecting a less aggressive acquisition forecast and some pricing pressures; however, enhanced service offerings should continue to add to revenues. Margins will benefit from operating efficiencies. Meanwhile, mobile operations will fuel continued strong earnings gains as CTL benefits from its expanding coverage area and efficiency gains from its clustering strategy. Results should further benefit from strong cash flows from the core telephone business and continued strong growth in the mobile unit.

Valuation - 06-SEP-95

While the shares have fallen about 10% since May 1995, we believe CTL remains attractive for long term capital appreciation. The rural or suburban nature of much of the company's operating territory make it somewhat more difficult for new competitors to enter the market. An added benefit is that the company has been upgrading its network with new technology. The continued solid performance of the core telephone operations combined with continued strong growth of the mobile unit should bolster future results.

Key Stock Statistics

S&P EPS Est. 1995	1.90	Tang. Bk. Value/Share	3.90
P/E on S&P Est. 1995	14.7	Beta	1.13
S&P EPS Est. 1996	2.18	Shareholders	7,000
Dividend Rate/Share	0.33	Market cap. (B)	$ 1.6
Shs. outstg. (M)	58.4	Inst. holdings	75%
Avg. daily vol. (M)	0.187	Insider holdings	NA

Value of $10,000 invested 5 years ago: $ 12,500

Fiscal Year Ending Dec. 31

	1995	% Change	1994	% Change	1993	% Change
Revenues (Million $)						
1Q	142.4	18%	121.0	25%	96.80	28%
2Q	149.7	13%	132.9	24%	107.3	21%
3Q	--	—	141.5	25%	112.8	22%
4Q	--	—	144.9	25%	116.3	16%
Yr.	--	—	540.2	25%	433.2	21%
Income (Million $)						
1Q	27.00	41%	19.20	22%	15.74	40%
2Q	26.17	22%	21.49	30%	16.52	31%
3Q	—	—	24.61	40%	17.60	16%
4Q	—	—	34.94	82%	19.15	-9%
Yr.	—	—	100.2	45%	69.00	15%
Earnings Per Share ($)						
1Q	0.48	33%	0.36	13%	0.32	33%
2Q	0.45	13%	0.40	25%	0.32	23%
3Q	E0.48	4%	0.46	35%	0.34	6%
4Q	E0.49	-26%	0.66	78%	0.37	-16%
Yr.	E1.90	1%	1.88	39%	1.35	8%

Next earnings report expected: early November

Century Telephone Enterprises

Business Summary - 01-SEP-95

Century Telephone Enterprises' telephone subsidiaries serve parts of 14 states. The company also provides cellular mobile telephone service through Century Cellunet. Century's paging operations were sold in October 1994. Business segment contributions in 1994 were:

	Revs.	Profits
Telephone	72%	81%
Mobile	28%	19%

CTL provides local telephone service in 14 states, the most important being Wisconsin, Louisiana, Michigan and Ohio. At December 31, 1994, CTL's telephone subsidiaries served about 454,963 access lines. The territories served are largely rural and suburban.

As of December 31, 1994, cellular mobile telephone service was being provided to more than 211,000 subscribers. CTL's cellular operations are in franchised areas with a total of 7.1 million POPs (population of the service area, adjusted for percentage ownership), with operations concentrated in the Michigan and Louisiana/Texas/Arkansas clusters. Approximately 300,000 of the 7.1 million POPS were either sold during the first quarter of 1995 or are subject to sale pursuant to definitive agreements.

Important Developments

Aug. '95—CTL completed its acquisition of closely held Mississippi-6 Cellular Corporation, a provider of cellular telephone service in the Jackson, Mississippi area. Terms were not disclosed.

Jul. '95—Restor Industries Inc. signed a repair service agreement with Century Telephone. Restor agreed to become the primary provider of repair and replacement services for all of Century's electronic or mechanical telecommunications equipment. Separately, CTL signed a definitive agreement with R&D Cellular Inc. to acquire its Mississippi-2 rural service area nonwireline cellular operation. Mississippi-2 includes nine counties and is based in Tupelo, Miss.

Jun. '95—Century sees its access revenues reduced by about $500,000 this year and by as much as $4.2 million annually upon completion of a two-year phase-in of a Louisiana Public Service Commission plan. Management does not expect the revenue reductions to be material to the company's consolidated operations and that the reduced access rates will make by-pass of Century's local exchange networks in Louisiana by long-distance carriers less likely.

Capitalization

Long Term Debt: $427,022,000 (3/95).
Cum. Preferred Stock: $2,268,000.

Per Share Data ($) (Year Ended Dec. 31)

	1994	1993	1992	1991	1990	1989
Tangible Bk. Val.	3.90	4.22	3.42	4.36	3.69	3.21
Cash Flow	3.65	2.84	2.56	1.92	1.70	NA
Earnings	1.88	1.35	1.25	0.80	0.67	0.49
Dividends	0.32	0.31	0.29	0.29	0.28	0.27
Payout Ratio	17%	23%	23%	36%	42%	55%
Prices - High	$32\frac{1}{4}$	$33\frac{3}{8}$	$28\frac{7}{8}$	$21\frac{5}{8}$	$24\frac{3}{8}$	24
- Low	$21\frac{7}{8}$	$23\frac{1}{4}$	$18\frac{3}{8}$	$15\frac{7}{8}$	$14\frac{5}{8}$	$13\frac{3}{8}$
P/E Ratio - High	17	25	23	27	36	49
- Low	12	18	15	20	22	27

Income Statement Analysis (Million $)

	1994	%Chg	1993	%Chg	1992	%Chg	1991
Revs.	540	25%	433	21%	357	27%	281
Depr.	94.4	23%	76.5	22%	62.9	20%	52.2
Maint.	NA	—	NA	—	52.8	21%	43.6
Constr. Credits	NA	—	NA	—	NA	—	NA
Eff. Tax Rate	38%	—	35%	—	35%	—	35%
Net Inc.	100	45%	69.0	15%	60.0	60%	37.4

Balance Sheet & Other Fin. Data (Million $)

	1994	1993	1992	1991	1990	1989
Gross Prop.	1,311	1,170	1,004	796	735	696
Net Prop.	947	828	676	535	491	474
Cap. Exp.	201	204	140	96.0	65.0	62.0
Total Cap.	1,169	1,045	828	676	612	615
Fxd. Chgs. Cov.	4.4	4.2	4.1	3.5	NA	NA
Capitalization:						
LT Debt	519	461	392	255	231	258
Pfd.	2.3	0.5	0.5	0.5	0.5	2.1
Common	648	514	385	320	280	256

Ratio Analysis

	1994	1993	1992	1991	1990	1989
% Ret. on Revs.	18.6	15.9	16.8	13.3	12.5	10.4
% Ret. On Invest.Cap	12.9	10.6	11.6	9.3	9.0	NA
% Return On Com.Eqty	17.2	15.4	17.0	12.5	11.6	10.8
% Earn. on Net Prop.	12.2	11.7	12.7	10.7	9.1	NA
% LT Debt of Cap.	44.4	47.3	50.4	44.3	45.1	50.0
Capital. % Pfd.	0.2	0.1	0.1	0.1	0.1	0.4
Capital. % Common	55.4	52.6	49.5	55.6	54.8	49.6

Dividend Data —Dividends have been paid since 1974. A dividend reinvestment plan is available. A "poison pill" stock purchase right was adopted in 1986.

Amt. of Div. $	Date Decl.	Ex-Div. Date	Stock of Record	Payment Date
0.080	Aug. 23	Aug. 29	Sep. 02	Sep. 16 '94
0.080	Nov. 17	Nov. 28	Dec. 02	Dec. 16 '94
0.083	Feb. 21	Feb. 27	Mar. 03	Mar. 17 '95
0.083	May. 23	May. 26	Jun. 02	Jun. 16 '95
0.083	Aug. 22	Aug. 30	Sep. 01	Sep. 15 '95

Office—100 Century Park Drive, P.O. Box 4065, Monroe, LA 71211-4065. **Tels**—(318) 388-9500; (800) 833-1188. **Chrmn**—C. M. Williams. **Vice Chmn, Pres & CEO**—G. F. Post III. **Sr VP-CFO**—R. S. Ewing Jr. **Secy**—H. P. Perry. **Investor Contact**—Robert E. Fudickar. **Dirs**—W. R. Boles Jr., V. Boulet, E. Butler Jr., C. Czeschin, J. B. Gardner, W. B. Hanks, R. L. Hargrove Jr., J. Hebert, F. E. Hogan, C. G. Melville Jr., H. P. Perry, G. F. Post III, J. D. Reppond, C. M. Williams. **Transfer Agent**—Society National Bank, Dallas. **Incorporated** in Louisiana in 1968. **Empl**-3,000. **S&P Analyst:** Kevin J. Gooley

STANDARD & POOR'S

STOCK REPORTS

Chesapeake Corp.

NYSE Symbol **CSK**

In S&P MidCap 400

28-SEP-95

Industry: Paper/Products

Summary: The primary businesses of this integrated forest products company are packaging, kraft and tissue products. In recent years, it has shifted its emphasis to value-added products.

S&P Opinion: Accumulate (★★★★)

Recent Price • 37

52 Wk Range • 39-28¼

Yield • 2.2%

12-Mo. P/E • 12.7

Quantitative Evaluations

Outlook (1 Lowest—5 Highest) • **4+**

Fair Value • **38⅛**

Risk • **Average**

Earn./Div. Rank • **B-**

Technical Eval. • **Bearish** since 8/95

Rel. Strength Rank (1 Lowest—99 Highest) • **55**

Insider Activity • **Neutral**

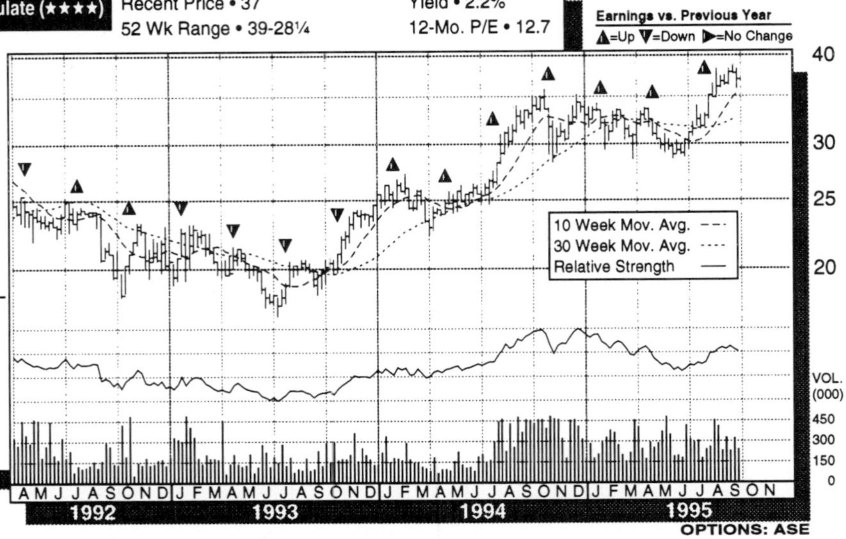

OPTIONS: ASE

Overview - 28-SEP-95

Strong sales gains are expected in 1995, as stable global economies should continue to generate solid demand for CSK's paper and packaging products, and allow steep price hikes of the past year to remain in effect (although further increases will likely be much more limited). Price increases for tissue products should also boost sales. Margins should widen on the favorable pricing trends, increased emphasis on value-added products, and efforts to control costs and increase productivity. Those factors should far outweigh higher raw materials costs, particularly for recycled fiber used in commercial tissue and kraft products operations; raw materials pricing should also have much less of a negative impact on second half earnings, given the sharp reversal of recycled fiber costs in the past few months.

Valuation - 28-SEP-95

Following a lackluster performance during much of 1995's first half, CSK's shares have risen strongly since mid-1995, as a drop in interest rates led investors to anticipate prolonged economic and industry upturns. The arrival of much stronger pricing trends in tissue markets also helped investor sentiment. While economic moderation causes worries, limited capacity expansion in recent years should allow industry strength to extend into 1996. The tissue segment's uptrend is also likely to continue for some time, as the sector was late to join the party. Given our forecast of earnings gains through 1996, CSK's shares should outperform the broader market over the next year.

Key Stock Statistics

S&P EPS Est. 1995	3.85	Tang. Bk. Value/Share	14.62
P/E on S&P Est. 1995	9.6	Beta	0.82
S&P EPS Est. 1996	4.55	Shareholders	7,500
Dividend Rate/Share	0.80	Market cap. (B)	$0.860
Shs. outstg. (M)	23.8	Inst. holdings	60%
Avg. daily vol. (M)	0.059	Insider holdings	NA

Value of $10,000 invested 5 years ago: $ 22,410

Fiscal Year Ending Dec. 31

	1995	% Change	1994	% Change	1993	% Change
Revenues (Million $)						
1Q	291.1	37%	212.0	1%	209.0	NM
2Q	315.1	33%	236.9	NM	236.4	3%
3Q	—	—	266.9	12%	238.3	NM
4Q	—	—	274.7	37%	201.0	-6%
Yr.	—	—	990.5	12%	885.0	NM
Income (Million $)						
1Q	20.80	NM	2.00	NM	-0.75	NM
2Q	18.50	NM	4.90	NM	1.27	-70%
3Q	—	—	14.40	NM	2.58	-60%
4Q	—	—	16.30	123%	7.30	NM
Yr.	—	—	37.60	NM	10.40	-28%
Earnings Per Share ($)						
1Q	0.87	NM	0.09	NM	-0.03	NM
2Q	0.77	NM	0.21	NM	0.05	-74%
3Q	E1.05	75%	0.60	NM	0.11	-61%
4Q	E1.15	69%	0.68	119%	0.31	NM
Yr.	E3.85	144%	1.58	NM	0.44	-30%

Next earnings report expected: mid October

Chesapeake Corp.

Business Summary - 26-SEP-95

Chesapeake Corp. is an integrated forest products company. In recent years, CSK shifted its emphasis from commodity products to more profitable, value-added products for niche markets. Segment contributions in 1994:

	Sales	Profits
Kraft products	34%	36%
Tissue	31%	40%
Packaging	35%	24%

CSK's kraft products segment manufactures white top and kraft paperboard, kraft paper, corrugating medium and bleached hardwood pulp at its mill in West Point, Va. Paperboard and corrugating medium are sold to independent and company-owned container and packaging plants. Kraft paper is sold to paper converters to make bags and wrappings. Bleached hardwood pulp is sold to manufacturers of printing and writing paper. Shipments from the West Point mill totaled 850,000 tons in 1994 (798,000 tons in 1993).

The kraft segment also includes CSK's wood products business, which operates four sawmills in Virginia and Maryland, manufacturing pine and hardwood lumber using materials from both company-owned timberlands and other landowners.

Wisconsin Tissue Mills produces napkins, tablecovers, towels, placemats, wipers and facial and bathroom tissue for commercial and industrial markets; the products are made from 100% recycled fiber. CSK also sells napkins, plates, cups, tablecovers and accessories to consumer markets throughout the U.S.

Packaging operations serve the point-of-sale display and specialty packaging requirements of national consumer products companies, providing creative design capabilities to customers. The company's Color-Box facility supplies consumer graphic packaging to customers requiring full litho-laminated point-of-sale packaging. Fifteen corrugated container plants produce corrugated boxes and specialty packaging.

Important Developments

Aug. '95—CSK purchased property in Bellmont, Ariz., where its Wisconsin Tissue Mills (WTM) unit plans to construct a 272,000 sq. ft. converting facility for away-from-home tissue products. WTM also purchased a mill in nearby Flagstaff, in May 1995, which would add 30,000 tons per year of tissuemaking capacity, and signed a letter of intent in July 1995, to acquire the Alsip, Ill., mill of Chicago Tissue Co., L.P. (50,000 tons per year of tissue capacity). Chesapeake also announced in July 1995, that it decided against the construction of a major tissue mill in Alabama; while in June 1995, CSK reported that it would attempt to sell the consumer products portion of its tissue operations.

Capitalization

Long Term Debt: $359,100,000 (6/95).

Per Share Data ($)

(Year Ended Dec. 31)

	1994	1993	1992	1991	1990	1989
Tangible Bk. Val.	14.65	14.36	14.51	13.80	13.63	13.45
Cash Flow	4.66	3.53	3.66	3.92	3.68	4.78
Earnings	1.58	0.44	0.63	0.75	0.81	2.31
Dividends	0.72	0.72	0.72	0.72	0.72	0.68
Payout Ratio	46%	164%	117%	96%	88%	29%
Prices - High	$35\frac{7}{8}$	$25\frac{3}{4}$	$29\frac{1}{8}$	24	$21\frac{1}{2}$	$24\frac{1}{8}$
- Low	$22\frac{1}{4}$	$17\frac{1}{8}$	$18\frac{1}{4}$	$13\frac{1}{4}$	$12\frac{5}{8}$	$17\frac{7}{8}$
P/E Ratio - High	23	59	46	32	27	10
- Low	14	39	29	18	16	8

Income Statement Analysis (Million $)

	1994	%Chg	1993	%Chg	1992	%Chg	1991
Revs.	991	12%	885	NM	888	6%	841
Oper. Inc.	154	33%	116	-4%	121	-2%	124
Depr.	73.3	1%	72.4	6%	68.6	5%	65.2
Int. Exp.	31.6	-2%	32.4	-8%	35.1	-7%	37.9
Pretax Inc.	58.2	181%	20.7	-8%	22.5	-14%	26.1
Eff. Tax Rate	35%	—	50%	—	36%	—	41%
Net Inc.	37.6	NM	10.4	-28%	14.4	-6%	15.4

Balance Sheet & Other Fin. Data (Million $)

	1994	1993	1992	1991	1990	1989
Cash	33.2	0.7	0.7	1.0	0.8	0.5
Curr. Assets	272	186	212	196	185	184
Total Assets	1,013	919	959	916	876	790
Curr. Liab.	127	99	89.7	94.7	92.2	85.3
LT Debt	364	333	383	416	381	301
Common Eqty.	393	368	370	318	314	314
Total Cap.	863	800	850	821	784	704
Cap. Exp.	54.0	64.0	85.0	92.0	125	148
Cash Flow	111	82.8	83.0	80.6	75.7	98.4

Ratio Analysis

	1994	1993	1992	1991	1990	1989
Curr. Ratio	2.1	1.9	2.4	2.1	2.0	2.2
% LT Debt of Cap.	42.2	41.7	45.1	50.7	48.6	42.7
% Net Inc.of Revs.	3.8	1.2	1.6	1.8	2.0	5.9
% Ret. on Assets	3.9	1.1	1.4	1.7	2.0	6.5
% Ret. on Equity	9.8	2.8	3.9	4.8	5.3	16.0

Dividend Data —Dividends have been paid since 1933. A dividend reinvestment plan is available. A "poison pill" stock purchase rights plan was adopted in 1988.

Amt. of Div. $	Date Decl.	Ex-Div. Date	Stock of Record	Payment Date
0.180	Aug. 08	Oct. 11	Oct. 17	Nov. 15 '94
0.180	Dec. 13	Jan. 09	Jan. 13	Feb. 15 '95
0.180	Feb. 14	Apr. 10	Apr. 17	May. 15 '95
0.200	Jun. 13	Jul. 13	Jul. 17	Aug. 15 '95
0.200	Aug. 08	Oct. 12	Oct. 16	Nov. 15 '95

Data as orig. reptd.; bef. results of disc. opers. and/or spec. items. Per share data adj. for stk. divs. as of ex-div. date. E-Estimated. NA-Not Available. NM-Not Meaningful. NR-Not Ranked.

Office—1021 East Cary St., Box 2350, Richmond, VA 23218-2350. **Tel**—(804) 697-1000. **Chrmn & CEO**—J. C. Fox. **Pres**—P. A. Dresser Jr. **VP, CFO & Investor Contact**—Andrew J. Kohut. **SVP & Secy**—J. P. Causey Jr. **Dirs**—P. A. Dresser Jr., M. K. Dwyer, J. C. Fox, R. L. Hintz, W. D. McCoy, C. E. Olsson, J. W. Rosenblum, F. S. Royal, W. Stettinius, J. H. Stookey, R. G. Tilghman, J.P. Viviano, H. H. Warner. **Transfer Agent & Registrar**—Harris Trust & Savings Bank, Chicago. **Incorporated** in Virginia in 1918. **Empl**-5,209. **S&P Analyst:** Michael W. Jaffe

STANDARD & POOR'S

STOCK REPORTS

Chiron Corp.

NASDAQ Symbol **CHIR**
In S&P MidCap 400

31-AUG-95 **Industry:** Drugs-Generic and OTC

Summary: This leading biotechnology concern is engaged in diagnostics, therapeutics, vaccines and ophthalmic products. Ciba-Geigy owns 49.9% of the stock.

S&P Opinion: Accumulate (★★★★) Recent Price • 87¾ 52 Wk Range • 93¼-47¾ Yield • Nil 12-Mo. P/E • NM

Quantitative Evaluations

Outlook (1 Lowest—5 Highest)
• **1−**

Fair Value
• **68**

Risk
• **High**

Earn./Div. Rank
• **C**

Technical Eval.
• **Bearish** since 12/94

Rel. Strength Rank (1 Lowest—99 Highest)
• **94**

Insider Activity
• **Neutral**

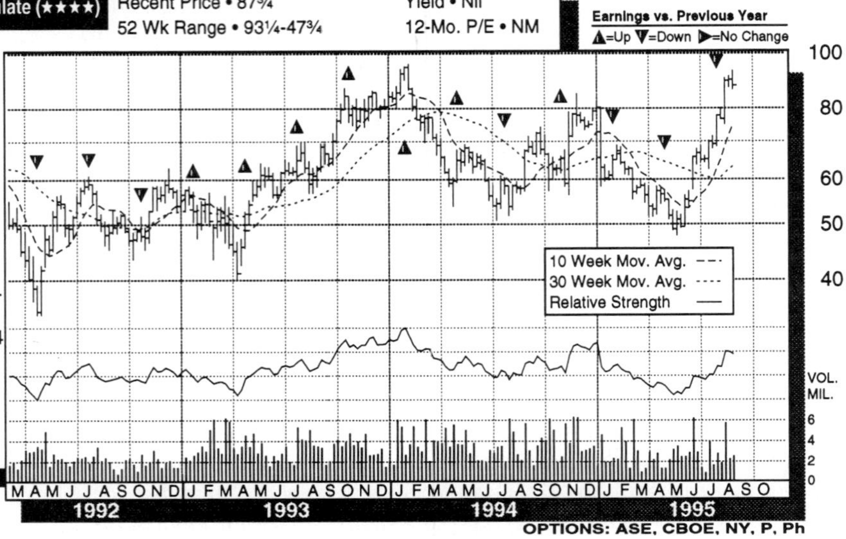

OPTIONS: ASE, CBOE, NY, P, Ph

Overview - 31-AUG-95

Total revenues are expected to grow further in 1996. Diagnostics and vaccine revenues should benefit from gains at Ciba Corning Diagnostics and Biocine (these units were acquired from Ciba-Geigy in January 1995), while ophthalmic sales should be augmented by full-year contributions from IOLAB and Domilens (acquired during the first half of 1995). Gains are also indicated for the oncology and DNA probe product lines. Sales of Betaseron multiple sclerosis drug may also increase, although gains may be limited by new rival MS drugs. Earnings in 1996 should benefit from productivity improvements, and comparisons will benefit from the absence of restructuring charges that are expected to result in a large net loss in 1995.

Valuation - 31-AUG-95

The shares have been outstanding performers in recent months, reflecting investor enthusiasm over positive clinical developments on several experimental products. The strength replaced first quarter weakness that followed the expiration of Ciba-Geigy's tender offer (Ciba purchased 11.9 million common shares at $117 each in January). Despite recent writeoffs, the Ciba alliance should provide important future benefits in R&D funding, production and marketing. Chiron has leading positions in the emerging biotechnology fields of gene therapy, combinatorial chemistry and DNA proteins. The shares have speculative appeal for long-term appreciation.

Key Stock Statistics

S&P EPS Est. 1995	-9.50	Tang. Bk. Value/Share	12.40
P/E on S&P Est. 1995	NM	Beta	1.45
S&P EPS Est. 1996	1.35	Shareholders	12,900
Dividend Rate/Share	Nil	Market cap. (B)	$ 3.6
Shs. outstg. (M)	40.2	Inst. holdings	39%
Avg. daily vol. (M)	0.646	Insider holdings	NA

Value of $10,000 invested 5 years ago: $ 30,789

Fiscal Year Ending Dec. 31

	1995	% Change	1994	% Change	1993	% Change
Revenues (Million $)						
1Q	218.3	139%	91.38	32%	69.05	22%
2Q	281.8	181%	100.1	30%	76.77	12%
3Q	—	—	128.2	64%	78.39	28%
4Q	—	—	134.3	44%	93.33	52%
Yr.	—	—	454.0	43%	317.5	28%
Income (Million $)						
1Q	-385.8	NM	4.82	91%	2.52	NM
2Q	0.83	-84%	5.11	-5%	5.38	NM
3Q	—	—	12.57	154%	4.95	NM
4Q	—	—	-4.17	NM	5.54	NM
Yr.	—	—	18.32	NM	18.38	NM
Earnings Per Share ($)						
1Q	-9.64	NM	0.14	75%	0.08	NM
2Q	0.02	-87%	0.15	-6%	0.16	NM
3Q	—	—	0.37	147%	0.15	NM
4Q	—	—	-0.13	NM	0.16	NM
Yr.	E-9.50	NM	0.53	-4%	0.55	NM

Next earnings report expected: early November

Chiron Corp.

Business Summary - 31-AUG-95

Chiron is a leading biotechnology company that focuses on the development of products in diagnostics, vaccines, therapeutics and ophthalmics. Swiss-based Ciba-Geigy, a leading global drug and chemical producer, increased its stake in the company to 49.9% in early 1995. Total revenues in recent years were derived as follows:

	1994	1993	1992
Product sales	61%	47%	45%
Equity in unconsol. units	18%	24%	30%
Collaborative research	15%	22%	16%
Other	6%	7%	9%

Foreign operations accounted for 16% of revenues in 1994. The principal customer, Johnson & Johnson, provided 22% of total 1994 revenues. R&D spending equaled 37% of 1994 revenues.

Product sales include ophthalmic surgical products used in cataract, corneal, refractive and other surgeries (23% of revenues in 1994); Betaseron (22%), a treatment for relapsing/remitting multiple sclerosis which Chiron manufactures for sale by Berlex Laboratories; oncology products such as Proleukin treatment for kidney cancer; and diagnostic products such Ciba Corning's critical blood analyte systems, immunodiagnostic systems and DNA probes.

Equity in unconsolidated joint businesses consists chiefly of a share of the earnings of a joint venture with Johnson & Johnson that produces diagnostic tests for hepatitis. Equity interests are also held in concerns that produce vaccines, generic drugs and other products. Collaborative research revenues consist of funds provided by other firms to research various drugs and vaacines in exchange for licenses to market resulting products. Other revenues include royalties, sales fees and government R&D grants.

Important Developments

Aug. '95—The company said it expected to acquire Viagene in September 1995, for about $125 million in cash and stock. Viagene, a development stage biotechnology company, has an important stake in the field of gene therapy. Separately, Chiron signed an agreement with Univax Biologics to jointly develop a new family of human immunotherapeutic products based on Chiron Biocine vaccines. The company also recently reported favorable clinical results for Depocyt, an anticancer therapeutic being developed jointly with Depotech; and for Mytropin, a drug for amyotrophic lateral sclerosis (ALS), which is being developed in conjunction with Cephalon.

Capitalization

Long Term Debt: $406,548,000 (6/95), incl. $305.5 million of conv. debs.

Per Share Data ($) (Year Ended Dec. 31)

	1994	1993	1992	1991	1990	1989
Tangible Bk. Val.	17.16	15.98	15.54	17.87	7.39	6.82
Cash Flow	1.98	1.29	-2.36	-21.68	0.57	-1.17
Earnings	0.53	0.55	-3.18	-22.12	0.24	-1.51
Dividends	Nil	Nil	Nil	Nil	Nil	Nil
Payout Ratio	Nil	Nil	Nil	Nil	Nil	Nil
Prices - High	96	86⅞	74½	79	44¾	34½
- Low	50¾	40	34¾	37¼	23½	13
P/E Ratio - High	NM	NM	NM	NM	NM	NM
- Low	NM	NM	NM	NA	NA	NA

Income Statement Analysis (Million $)

	1994	%Chg	1993	%Chg	1992	%Chg	1991
Revs.	372	55%	240	38%	174	154%	68.6
Oper. Inc.	9.0	NM	-44.0	NM	-108	NM	-54.1
Depr.	49.4	98%	25.0	1%	24.7	196%	8.3
Int. Exp.	20.2	66%	12.2	-29%	17.3	84%	9.4
Pretax Inc.	32.0	39%	23.0	NM	-92.0	NM	-423
Eff. Tax Rate	43%	—	20%	—	NM	—	NM
Net Inc.	18.0	NM	18.0	NM	-96.0	NM	-424

Balance Sheet & Other Fin. Data (Million $)

	1994	1993	1992	1991	1990	1989
Cash	222	238	257	558	154	89.0
Curr. Assets	434	362	349	617	174	101
Total Assets	1,050	969	712	895	265	124
Curr. Liab.	120	106	105	125	21.0	12.0
LT Debt	338	333	107	239	122	Nil
Common Eqty.	573	522	493	524	120	109
Total Cap.	911	855	600	763	242	109
Cap. Exp.	106	115	24.7	14.3	9.4	5.5
Cash Flow	68.0	43.0	-71.0	-416	10.0	-17.0

Ratio Analysis

	1994	1993	1992	1991	1990	1989
Curr. Ratio	3.6	3.4	3.3	5.0	8.3	8.2
% LT Debt of Cap.	37.1	38.9	17.9	31.3	50.3	NM
% Net Inc.of Revs.	4.9	7.7	NM	NM	7.7	NM
% Ret. on Assets	1.8	2.2	NM	NM	2.1	NM
% Ret. on Equity	3.3	3.6	NM	NM	3.5	NM

Dividend Data —No cash dividends have been paid.

Data as orig. reptd.; bef. results of disc. opers. and/or spec. items. Per share data adj. for stk. divs. as of ex-div. date. E-Estimated. NA-Not Available. NM-Not Meaningful. NR-Not Ranked.

Office—4560 Horton St., Emeryville, CA 94608. **Tel**—(510) 655-8730. **Chrmn**—W. J. Rutter. **Pres & CEO**—E. E. Penhoet. **SVP-Fin & CFO**—D. L. Winger. **SVP & Secy**—W. G. Green. **Investor Contact**—Larry Kurtz. **Dirs**—G. F. Amelio, L. W. Coleman, P. Douaze, D. A. Glaser, A. Krauer, F. L'Eplattenier, E. E. Penhoet, W. J. Rutter, H. Schramek, J. W. Schuler, P. J. Strijkert. **Transfer Agent & Registrar**—Continental Stock Transfer & Trust Co., NYC. **Reincorporated** in Delaware in 1987. **Empl**-2,668. **S&P Analyst:** Herman Saftlas

Chris-Craft Industries

NYSE Symbol **CCN**
In S&P MidCap 400

17-OCT-95 **Industry:** Broadcasting

Summary: Chris-Craft owns 73% of ASE-listed BHC Communications. In January 1995, in a joint venture with Paramount, it launched the United Paramount Network, a fifth television network.

S&P Opinion: Hold (★★★)

Recent Price • 42⅝ | Yield • Nil
52 Wk Range • 46¼-32⅛ | 12-Mo. P/E • 29.6

Quantitative Evaluations

Outlook (1 Lowest—5 Highest) • **NA**

Fair Value • **NA**

Risk • **Average**

Earn./Div. Rank • **B-**

Technical Eval. • **Bearish** since 9/94

Rel. Strength Rank (1 Lowest—99 Highest) • **67**

Insider Activity • **Unfavorable**

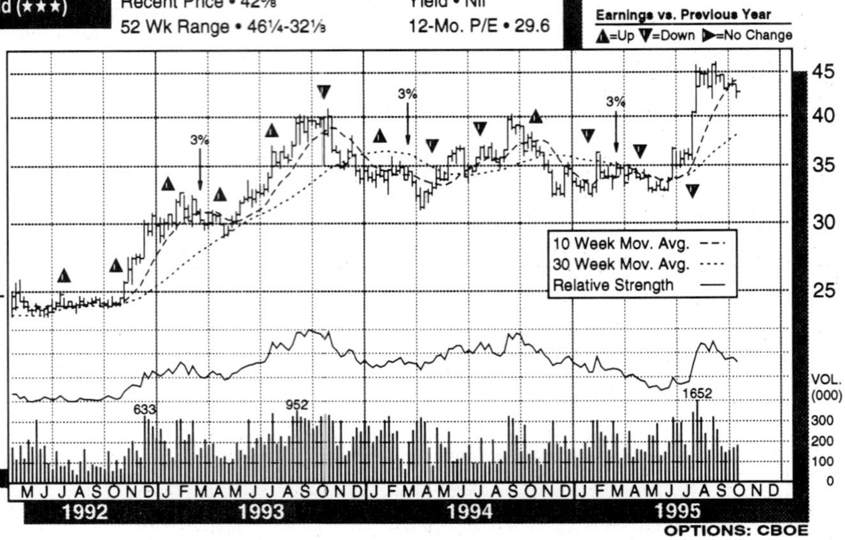

Overview - 16-OCT-95

Television advertising revenues should rise through 1996, bolstered by the Olympics and presidential election spending, though gains will be limited somewhat by ongoing sluggishness anticipated in the California economy. Cost-containment measures at BHC will provide an underlying boost to profitability. However, higher programming costs related to the startup of the United Paramount Network will severely hurt profitability. Investment earnings will benefit from moderately higher interest rates on average. CCN expects UPN operating losses and expenditures to significantly exceed the $150 million that it has committed through 1996. Such losses and expenses are expected to remain substantial thereafter.

Valuation - 14-OCT-95

The shares, which dropped sharply through the fourth quarter of 1994 and early 1995, have since recovered and moved to a new high. The market appears to a large degree to be discounting the sizeable startup costs related to the UPN joint venture. The market may also be assuming that Paramount Communications will exercise its option to acquire 50% of UPN by yearend 1996. The long term outlook for BHC's television operations is good, and asset values are further enhanced by pending legislation that would lift broadcast ownership restrictions. With no outstanding debt, and some $1.5 billion in cash, CCN is well situated. However, sizeable losses anticipated for UPN will restrict earnings momentum for the forseeable future.

Key Stock Statistics

S&P EPS Est. 1995	0.80	Tang. Bk. Value/Share	30.93
P/E on S&P Est. 1995	53.3	Beta	0.81
S&P EPS Est. 1996	0.70	Shareholders	5,000
Dividend Rate/Share	Nil	Market cap. (B)	$ 1.3
Shs. outstg. (M)	29.0	Inst. holdings	42%
Avg. daily vol. (M)	0.033	Insider holdings	NA

Value of $10,000 invested 5 years ago: $ 13,988

Fiscal Year Ending Dec. 31

	1995	% Change	1994	% Change	1993	% Change
Revenues (Million $)						
1Q	108.7	7%	101.8	6%	96.29	58%
2Q	125.2	NM	126.1	5%	120.3	59%
3Q	—	—	112.8	6%	106.7	27%
4Q	—	—	140.7	21%	116.5	5%
Yr.	—	—	481.4	9%	439.7	33%
Income (Million $)						
1Q	0.31	-97%	11.18	-77%	49.50	NM
2Q	6.36	-63%	17.12	-73%	62.47	NM
3Q	—	—	22.42	72%	13.01	-33%
4Q	—	—	14.02	-42%	24.08	36%
Yr.	—	—	64.74	-57%	149.1	129%
Earnings Per Share ($)						
1Q	0.01	-97%	0.38	-78%	1.71	NM
2Q	0.21	-63%	0.57	-74%	2.16	NM
3Q	E0.28	-63%	0.75	69%	0.44	-34%
4Q	E0.30	-36%	0.47	-41%	0.79	29%
Yr.	E0.80	-63%	2.17	-58%	5.11	127%

Next earnings report expected: mid October

Chris-Craft Industries

Business Summary - 16-OCT-95

Chris-Craft Industries is engaged primarily in television broadcasting. It also produces plastics. Industry segment contributions in 1994 were:

	Sales	Profits
Television	94%	93%
Industrial	6%	7%

BHC Communications Inc. (73% owned) operates VHF television stations in Los Angeles (KCOP), New York (WWOR-TV), and Portland, Ore. (KPTV). United Television (UTV), which is 56%-owned by BHC, owns and operates three VHF and two UHF television stations: KMSP Minneapolis, KTVX Salt Lake City, KMOL San Antonio, KBHK San Francisco and KUTP Phoenix. CCN is the eighth largest TV station group owner in the U.S., with coverage of about 18% of TV households. In partnership with Paramount Communications, BHC launched the United Paramount Network, a fifth broadcast TV network, in January 1995.

The industrial division makes plastic flexible films, water-disposable hospital laundry bags, nonwoven sound control and insulation padding, and fiber carpet underlay.

Important Developments

Jul. '95—CCN said that second-quarter operating results included start-up losses of $28.7 million at its United Paramount Network (UPN). UPN-related losses in the first half totaled $67.1 million. On January 16, 1995, in partnership with Viacom's Paramount Communications unit, BHC launched UPN, a new broadcast television network with two nights of limited prime-time programming, including the Star Trek Voyager series. Under terms of the partnership agreement, BHC will provide funding for UPN until Paramount exercises an option to acquire an equity interest equal to that of BHC. The option expires in January 1997. UPN will incur significant start-up losses for several years, and BHC has agreed to spend at least $150 million on behalf of the network through 1996.

Capitalization

Long Term Debt: None (6/95).
Minority Interest: $569,113,000.
$1 Cum. Prior Pfd. Stk.: 73,399 shs. (no par).
$1.40 Conv. Pfd. Stk.: 281,366 shs. (no par); red. at $40; conv. into 8,965,260 com. and/or B shs.
Class B Common Stock: 7,676,355 shs. ($0.50 par); 10 votes per sh.; limited transferability; conv. sh.-for-sh. into com.
Officers and directors hold 45%, and institutions hold 44% of com. and Cl. B.
Shareholders of record: 3,495 (2,378 Cl. B).

Per Share Data ($) (Year Ended Dec. 31)

	1994	1993	1992	1991	1990	1989
Tangible Bk. Val.	32.94	31.63	24.07	35.47	32.16	23.43
Cash Flow	2.87	5.83	3.82	2.27	10.25	16.43
Earnings	2.11	5.11	2.25	1.99	9.97	16.15
Dividends	Nil	Nil	Nil	Nil	Nil	Nil
Payout Ratio	Nil	Nil	Nil	Nil	Nil	Nil
Prices - High	40¼	40⅞	30⅞	28¼	30⅝	37
- Low	31⅛	28½	22	19¾	21	17
P/E Ratio - High	19	8	14	14	3	2
- Low	15	6	10	10	2	1

Income Statement Analysis (Million $)

	1994	%Chg	1993	%Chg	1992	%Chg	1991
Revs.	481	9%	440	33%	332	17%	284
Oper. Inc.	129	34%	96.3	NM	30.2	NM	4.3
Depr.	20.9	NM	21.0	57%	13.4	65%	8.1
Int. Exp.	Nil	—	Nil	—	2.3	-4%	2.4
Pretax Inc.	164	-57%	385	166%	145	9%	133
Eff. Tax Rate	35%	—	38%	—	26%	—	26%
Net Inc.	65.0	-56%	149	129%	65.0	12%	58.0

Balance Sheet & Other Fin. Data (Million $)

	1994	1993	1992	1991	1990	1989
Cash	1,520	1,536	984	962	870	1,057
Curr. Assets	1,769	1,791	1,229	1,168	1,088	1,260
Total Assets	2,232	2,283	2,161	2,050	1,939	1,613
Curr. Liab.	244	295	330	229	242	245
LT Debt	Nil	Nil	Nil	16.0	18.0	19.0
Common Eqty.	1,298	1,250	1,103	1,044	965	721
Total Cap.	1,890	1,874	1,677	1,698	1,597	1,265
Cap. Exp.	10.7	11.2	11.1	11.6	8.4	4.8
Cash Flow	85.0	170	78.0	66.0	300	481

Ratio Analysis

	1994	1993	1992	1991	1990	1989
Curr. Ratio	7.3	6.1	3.7	5.1	4.5	5.2
% LT Debt of Cap.	Nil	Nil	Nil	0.9	1.1	1.5
% Net Inc.of Revs.	13.4	33.9	19.7	20.5	98.0	176.9
% Ret. on Assets	2.8	6.7	3.1	2.9	16.4	37.4
% Ret. on Equity	5.0	12.5	6.0	5.8	34.5	115.5

Dividend Data —No cash dividends have been paid on the common since 1969. Stock dividends have been paid regularly.

Amt. of Div. $	Date Decl.	Ex-Div. Date	Stock of Record	Payment Date
3%	Feb. 09	Mar. 16	Mar. 22	Apr. 04 '95

Data as orig. reptd.; bef. results of disc. opers. and/or spec. items. Per share data adj. for stk. divs. as of ex-div. date. E-Estimated. NA-Not Available. NM-Not Meaningful. NR-Not Ranked.

Office—767 Fifth Ave., New York, NY 10153. **Tel**—(212) 421-0200. **Chrmn & Pres**—H. J. Siegel. **Secy**—B. C. Kelly. **VP & Treas**—Joelen K. Merkel. **Dirs**—H. Arvey, L. R. Barnett, T. C. Hardwick III, J. J. Kirkpatrick. D. F. Linowes, N. Perlmutter, J. J. Rochlis, A. R. Rozelle, H. J. Siegel, J. C. Siegel, W. D. Siegel, E. C. Thompson. **Transfer Agent**—First Chicago Trust Co. of New York, NYC. **Incorporated** in Delaware in 1928. **Empl**-941. **S&P Analyst:** William H. Donald

STANDARD & POOR'S

STOCK REPORTS

Church & Dwight

NYSE Symbol **CHD**
In S&P MidCap 400

01-AUG-95 **Industry:** Household Products

Summary: Church & Dwight sells baking soda and sodium bicarbonate-based products under the Arm & Hammer label to consumer and industrial markets.

S&P Opinion: Avoid (★★) | Recent Price • 20½ | 52 Wk Range • 26-16⅝ | Yield • 2.1% | 12-Mo. P/E • 93.2

Quantitative Evaluations
Outlook
(1 Lowest—5 Highest)
• 1
Fair Value
• 12¾
Risk
• Average
Earn./Div. Rank
• A

Technical Eval.
• Bearish since 6/95
Rel. Strength Rank
(1 Lowest—99 Highest)
• 42
Insider Activity
• NA

Earnings vs. Previous Year
▲=Up ▼=Down ▶=No Change

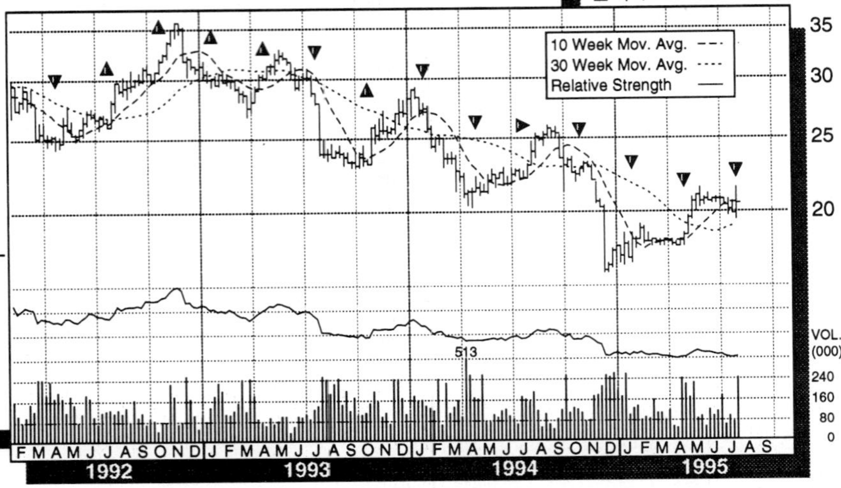

Overview - 01-AUG-95

Although quarterly earnings comparisons were down in the first six months of 1995, results improved significantly from the weak second half of 1994. Further improvement is expected in second half of 1995. Continued strong sales of dental care and deodorant products should help maintain the recent positive trend. Higher raw material and packaging costs could continue to pressure gross margins. Weak powder detergent sales could also be a problem. Earnings in 1996 are expected to benefit from increased capacity for liquid detergent. Our third quarter earnings estimate in 1995 excludes a $0.10 a share restructuring charge related to a reduction in the company's workforce.

Valuation - 01-AUG-95

CHD's shares have rebounded from their lows following last year's disappointing earnings, but still remain well below their high price of 1992. Even at the current depressed levels, we do not believe the shares are attractive. At recent prices, the company is selling at over 17 times our earnings estimate for 1996. The stock appears to be have discounted an earnings recovery, which limits upside potential. Furthermore, while management is pleased with the recent operating improvements, they are cautious about the future. If our earnings estimates prove to be overly optimistic, the shares could come under renewed selling pressure.

Key Stock Statistics

S&P EPS Est. 1995	1.00	Tang. Bk. Value/Share	7.66
P/E on S&P Est. 1995	20.5	Beta	1.09
S&P EPS Est. 1996	1.20	Shareholders	10,700
Dividend Rate/Share	0.44	Market cap. (B)	$0.406
Shs. outstg. (M)	19.5	Inst. holdings	47%
Avg. daily vol. (M)	0.027	Insider holdings	NA

Value of $10,000 invested 5 years ago: $ 12,024

Fiscal Year Ending Dec. 31

	1995	% Change	1994	% Change	1993	% Change
Revenues (Million $)						
1Q	118.0	6%	111.5	-10%	123.9	7%
2Q	129.0	-1%	130.7	NM	130.3	1%
3Q	—	—	132.6	3%	129.2	-3%
4Q	—	—	116.3	-6%	124.3	-11%
Yr.	—	—	491.0	-3%	507.6	-2%
Income (Million $)						
1Q	1.14	-53%	2.42	-61%	6.13	39%
2Q	5.64	-12%	6.39	NM	6.44	-13%
3Q	—	—	-0.26	NM	9.69	3%
4Q	—	—	-2.43	NM	7.22	-13%
Yr.	—	—	6.12	-79%	29.49	NM
Earnings Per Share ($)						
1Q	0.06	-50%	0.12	-60%	0.30	36%
2Q	0.29	-9%	0.32	NM	0.32	-11%
3Q	E0.35	—	-0.01	NM	0.48	4%
4Q	E0.30	—	-0.12	NM	0.36	-12%
Yr.	E1.00	—	0.31	-79%	1.46	NM

Next earnings report expected: late October

Church & Dwight

Business Summary - 01-AUG-95

Church & Dwight Co., Inc. (founded in 1846) is the world's leading producer of sodium bicarbonate, or baking soda. It specializes in sodium bicarbonate and sodium bicarbonate-based products, as well as other products that use the same raw materials or technology or are sold in the same markets. Consumer and specialty products accounted for 80% and 20% of 1994 sales, respectively. The company does 95% of its business in the U.S. and Canada.

Consumer products sold under the Arm & Hammer name include baking soda, dental care products, carpet and room deodorizer, deodorizer spray, laundry detergent powder, laundry detergent liquid, and deodorant anti-perspirant. Arm & Hammer baking soda performs a wide variety of uses in the home, including refrigerator and freezer deodorizer, scratchless cleaner and deodorizer for kitchen surfaces and cooking appliances, bath additive, dentifrice, cat litter deodorizer and swimming pool pH stabilizer. The company's largest consumer business is in the laundry detergent market, where it makes products for use in various stages of the laundry cycle.

The specialty products business consists primarily of the manufacture and sale of sodium bicarbonate in a range of grades and granulations for use in industrial markets and animal feed. In industrial markets, sodium bicarbonate is used as a leavening agent for commercial baked goods, an antacid in pharmaceuticals, a carbon dioxide release agent in fire extinguishers and an alkaline agent in swimming pool chemicals, detergents and various textile and tanning applications. A special grade of sodium bicarbonate is sold to the animal feed market for use as a buffer, or antacid, for dairy cattle. MEGALAC Rumen Bypass Fat is a nutritional supplement that allows cows to maintain energy levels during high milk-prodution periods. CHD is the sole U.S. producer of ammonium bicarbonate, used principally as a leavening agent in the food industry, and produces other chemicals related to sodium bicarbonate.

Important Developments

Jul. '95—While reporting second quarter earnings, the company announced it was restructuring its work force, laying off 51 employees. CHD will take a $0.10 a share charge in the third quarter for the restructuring.

Capitalization

Long Term Debt: $7,500,000 (6/95).

Per Share Data ($) (Year Ended Dec. 31)

	1994	1993	1992	1991	1990	1989
Tangible Bk. Val.	7.70	8.26	7.82	6.66	5.67	5.18
Cash Flow	0.88	1.94	1.92	1.79	1.54	0.83
Earnings	0.31	1.46	1.45	1.34	1.13	0.42
Dividends	0.44	0.42	0.38	0.34	0.30	0.26
Payout Ratio	142%	29%	26%	26%	26%	62%
Prices - High	29¼	32⅞	35¾	32½	20⅞	18⅞
- Low	16⅝	22⅞	24¼	16¼	13¾	9¾
P/E Ratio - High	94	23	25	24	18	45
- Low	54	16	17	12	12	23

Income Statement Analysis (Million $)

	1994	%Chg	1993	%Chg	1992	%Chg	1991
Revs.	491	-3%	508	-2%	517	6%	487
Oper. Inc.	19.6	-59%	48.3	-12%	55.0	9%	50.5
Depr.	11.2	14%	9.8	2%	9.6	6%	9.1
Int. Exp.	1.3	NM	0.4	-3%	0.4	-76%	1.7
Pretax Inc.	9.7	-80%	47.8	1%	47.2	12%	42.0
Eff. Tax Rate	37%	—	38%	—	37%	—	37%
Net Inc.	6.1	-79%	29.5	NM	29.5	11%	26.5

Balance Sheet & Other Fin. Data (Million $)

	1994	1993	1992	1991	1990	1989
Cash	7.6	9.6	25.6	8.7	45.7	43.3
Curr. Assets	124	123	124	117	133	130
Total Assets	296	282	262	245	253	245
Curr. Liab.	100	68.8	76.6	78.7	84.0	59.8
LT Debt	7.5	7.6	7.5	7.8	29.6	52.2
Common Eqty.	154	169	159	139	119	112
Total Cap.	181	200	184	164	167	184
Cap. Exp.	28.4	29.0	17.5	20.5	10.6	11.6
Cash Flow	17.3	39.3	39.1	35.5	31.5	17.1

Ratio Analysis

	1994	1993	1992	1991	1990	1989
Curr. Ratio	1.2	1.8	1.6	1.5	1.6	2.2
% LT Debt of Cap.	4.1	3.8	4.1	4.8	17.8	28.3
% Net Inc.of Revs.	1.2	5.8	5.7	5.4	5.4	2.2
% Ret. on Assets	2.1	10.9	11.6	10.6	9.4	3.6
% Ret. on Equity	3.8	18.1	19.8	20.5	20.4	7.8

Dividend Data (Cash has been paid each year by the company or its predecessor since 1901. A "poison pill" stock purchase right was adopted in 1989.)

Amt. of Div. $	Date Decl.	Ex-Div. Date	Stock of Record	Payment Date
0.110	Jul. 28	Aug. 11	Aug. 17	Sep. 01 '94
0.110	Oct. 27	Nov. 07	Nov. 14	Dec. 01 '94
0.110	Jan. 26	Feb. 06	Feb. 10	Mar. 01 '95
0.110	Apr. 27	May. 10	May. 16	Jun. 01 '95
0.110	Jul. 27	Aug. 15	Aug. 17	Sep. 01 '95

Data as orig. reptd.; bef. results of disc. opers. and/or spec. items. Per share data adj. for stk. divs. as of ex-div. date. E-Estimated. NA-Not Available. NM-Not Meaningful. NR-Not Ranked.

Office—469 North Harrison St., Princeton, NJ 08543-5297. **Tel**—(609) 683-5900. **Chrmn, Pres & CEO**—D. C. Minton. **VP-Fin, CFO & Investor Contact**—Anthony P. Deasey (609-683-7069). **VP & Secy**—M. A. Bilawsky. **Dirs**—C. C. Baldwin, Jr., W. R. Becklean, R. H. Beeby, R. B. Dixon, J. R. Leaman, Jr., J. D. Leggett III, R. A. McCabe, D. C. Minton, D. P. Phypers, J. J. Slade, J. O. Whitney. **Transfer Agent & Registrar**—Chemical Bank, NYC. **Incorporated** in Delaware in 1925 as the successor to a business founded in 1846. **Empl**-1,028. **S&P Analyst:** Stephen Madonna, CFA

STANDARD & POOR'S

STOCK REPORTS

Cintas Corporation

NASDAQ Symbol **CTAS**

In S&P MidCap 400

31-JUL-95 **Industry:** Services

Summary: Through 100 uniform rental facilities in 34 states, Cintas is a U.S. leader in designing, planning and implementing corporate identity uniform programs.

S&P Opinion: Hold (★★★)

Recent Price • 37⅝
52 Wk Range • 40¼-30½

Yield • 0.5%
12-Mo. P/E • 28.1

Quantitative Evaluations

Outlook
(1 Lowest—5 Highest)
• 3

Fair Value
• 37⅜

Risk
• Low

Earn./Div. Rank
• A+

Technical Eval.
• **Bullish** since 6/95

Rel. Strength Rank
(1 Lowest—99 Highest)
• 35

Insider Activity
• NA

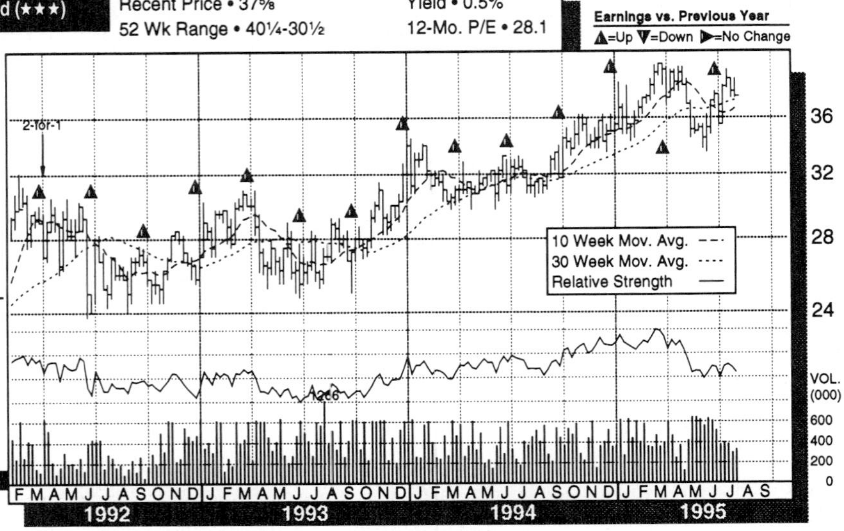

Overview - 31-JUL-95

Cintas has achieved record sales and earnings for 26 consecutive years, and is likely to do so again in 1995-6. Growth should come from geographic expansion, new products and services, increased market share, and acquisitions. Margins have been restricted by rising selling expenses, including additional salespeople and other costs related to entry into the St. Louis and Minneapolis markets. Capital spending in 1995-6 should range from $45 to $50 million, including investments in state-of-the-art wash room equipment that should improve operating efficiencies. Revenues from customers under contract should be a stabilizing factor in future recessions.

Valuation - 31-JUL-95

Cintas shares have recently rebounded, after minor selling pressure. Fears of an economic slowdown, which would limit employment growth and reduce demand for uniforms, have been a factor in the stock's underperformance. Recent reports of renewed economic strenth may change this. The shares, trading at about 24X estimated EPS for 1995-6, are near the low end of the P/E range over the past three years. Nevertheless, we believe that the shares are fairly valued, and expect them only to perform in line with the broader market.

Key Stock Statistics

S&P EPS Est. 1996	1.60	Tang. Bk. Value/Share	6.62
P/E on S&P Est. 1996	23.5	Beta	1.17
Dividend Rate/Share	0.20	Shareholders	900
Shs. outstg. (M)	47.0	Market cap. (B)	$ 1.8
Avg. daily vol. (M)	0.073	Inst. holdings	42%
		Insider holdings	NA

Value of $10,000 invested 5 years ago: $ 25,900

Fiscal Year Ending May 31

	1995	% Change	1994	% Change	1993	% Change
Revenues (Million $)						
1Q	142.0	16%	122.2	16%	105.0	12%
2Q	151.6	17%	129.8	17%	111.0	7%
3Q	151.2	17%	129.4	15%	112.8	14%
4Q	170.3	20%	141.8	14%	124.3	20%
Yr.	615.1	18%	523.2	16%	452.7	13%
Income (Million $)						
1Q	13.76	31%	10.54	—	—	—
2Q	15.76	16%	13.58	17%	11.65	20%
3Q	15.32	17%	13.06	19%	11.01	18%
4Q	17.91	19%	14.99	18%	12.65	16%
Yr.	62.74	20%	52.17	16%	44.87	23%
Earnings Per Share ($)						
1Q	0.29	26%	0.23	10%	0.21	50%
2Q	0.34	17%	0.29	16%	0.25	19%
3Q	0.33	18%	0.28	17%	0.24	20%
4Q	0.38	19%	0.32	19%	0.27	12%
Yr.	1.34	20%	1.12	15%	0.97	23%

Next earnings report expected: late September

Cintas Corporation

31-JUL-95

Business Summary - 31-JUL-95

Cintas Corporation is a leader in the uniform rental and sales business, with special expertise in designing, planning and implementing corporate-identity uniform programs. It concentrates on uniform rental services and custom uniform sales. Total revenues in recent fiscal years were derived as follows:

	1993-4	1992-3	1991-2
Uniform rentals	67%	68%	68%
Non-uniform rentals	21%	20%	19%
Uniform sales	11%	11%	12%
Other	1%	1%	1%

Cintas helps customers determine fabrics, color combinations, embroidered insignia and uniform designs that best meet their specific needs. Complete uniform service programs are offered, generally including the maintenance of appropriate inventories, periodic cleaning, replacement of worn items, adjustment of the program to match the customer's employment level and the redesign or modernization of uniform styles. The company provides service either on a rental basis or by selling uniforms to the customer. It also offers ancillary products, which include the rental or sale of walk-off mats, fender covers, towels, mops and linen products. Rental contracts generally provide for 36- to 60-month terms.

A substantial part of the company's standard uniform needs is met at four Kentucky facilities (additional needs are obtained from outside suppliers), with products sold to customers nationwide through distribution centers in Cincinnati and Los Angeles.

Geographic expansion has been one of the highest priorities. Cintas believes that it is one of the few uniform rental companies with a national presence and infrastructure that can provide service to large national corporations. As of late December 1994, it occupied 100 facilities in 33 states and in Ontario. In 1993-4, 1992-3 and 1991-2, it acquired three (including its entry into the tailored uniform market), 17 and eight uniform businesses, respectively; two additional purchases were made in the second quarter of 1994-5.

Important Developments

Jul. '95—Cintas said record sales and earnings were achieved in fiscal 1995, extending its uptrend to 26 consecutive years. Sales increased 18%, while net income and EPS advanced 20%.

Capitalization

Long Term Debt: $121,736,000 (2/95).

Per Share Data ($)

(Year Ended May 31)

	1995	1994	1993	1992	1991	1990
Tangible Bk. Val.	NA	6.62	5.69	4.88	4.28	3.71
Cash Flow	NA	1.74	1.56	1.21	1.12	0.92
Earnings	1.34	1.12	0.97	0.79	0.74	0.63
Dividends	0.20	0.17	0.14	0.11	0.09	0.08
Payout Ratio	15%	15%	15%	14%	13%	12%
Cal. Yrs.	1994	1993	1992	1991	1990	1989
Prices - High	36¼	34	32⅛	26⅜	17⅝	15
- Low	29¾	24¾	23¾	15⅜	12⅞	10¾
P/E Ratio - High	27	30	33	33	24	24
- Low	22	22	24	20	17	17

Income Statement Analysis (Million $)

	1994	%Chg	1993	%Chg	1992	%Chg	1991
Revs.	523	15%	453	13%	402	25%	322
Oper. Inc.	120	14%	105	27%	82.6	24%	66.5
Depr.	29.2	6%	27.5	42%	19.4	18%	16.4
Int. Exp.	7.1	-5%	7.5	34%	5.6	-1%	5.7
Pretax Inc.	85.5	20%	71.3	23%	58.2	19%	48.8
Eff. Tax Rate	39%	—	37%	—	37%	—	36%
Net Inc.	52.2	16%	44.9	23%	36.5	16%	31.4

Balance Sheet & Other Fin. Data (Million $)

	1994	1993	1992	1991	1990	1989
Cash	60.8	55.0	22.9	18.4	30.4	30.1
Curr. Assets	221	187	139	118	115	105
Total Assets	502	454	363	306	254	214
Curr. Liab.	91.5	65.2	51.9	53.4	46.8	37.9
LT Debt	84.2	104	67.8	58.9	43.6	36.9
Common Eqty.	310	265	226	186	157	134
Total Cap.	410	389	309	252	207	176
Cap. Exp.	37.3	31.5	31.6	57.9	42.3	29.0
Cash Flow	81.4	72.3	55.9	47.8	38.9	32.1

Ratio Analysis

	1994	1993	1992	1991	1990	1989
Curr. Ratio	2.4	2.9	2.7	2.2	2.5	2.8
% LT Debt of Cap.	20.5	26.6	21.9	23.3	21.0	21.0
% Net Inc.of Revs.	10.0	9.9	9.1	9.7	9.4	9.1
% Ret. on Assets	10.9	11.0	10.9	11.1	11.4	10.9
% Ret. on Equity	18.1	18.2	17.7	18.1	18.2	18.8

Dividend Data (Annual cash dividends were initiated in 1984.)

Amt. of Div. $	Date Decl.	Ex-Div. Date	Stock of Record	Payment Date
0.200	Feb. 15	Mar. 06	Mar. 10	Apr. 03 '95

Data as orig. reptd.; bef. results of disc. opers. and/or spec. items. Per share data adj. for stk. divs. as of ex-div. date. E-Estimated. NA-Not Available. NM-Not Meaningful. NR-Not Ranked.

Office—6800 Cintas Blvd., P.O. Box 625737, Cincinnati, OH 45262-5737. **Tel**—(513) 459-1200. **Chrmn & CEO**—R. T. Farmer. **Pres**—R. J. Kohlhepp. **SVP & Secy**—D. T. Jeanmougin. **VP Fin & CFO**—W. C. Gale. **Treas & Investor Contact**—Karen L. Carnahan. **Dirs**—G. V. Dirvin, R. T. Farmer, S. D. Farmer, J. J. Gardner, R. L. Howe, D. P. Klekamp, R. J. Kohlhepp, J. S. Lillard. **Transfer Agent**—Fifth Third Bank, Cincinnati. **Incorporated** in Ohio in 1968; reincorporated in Washington in 1986. **Empl**-8,581. **S&P Analyst:** Stephen Madonna, CFA

STANDARD & POOR'S

STOCK REPORTS

Circus Circus Enterprises

NYSE Symbol **CIR**

In S&P MidCap 400

19-OCT-95

Industry: Leisure/Amusement

Summary: This major casino company owns and operates 13 gaming facilities (12 in Nevada), and has joint venture interests in other gaming facilities.

S&P Opinion: Buy (★★★★★)

Recent Price • 27⅛

52 Wk Range • 36⅛-19¾

Yield • Nil

12-Mo. P/E • 20.9

Quantitative Evaluations

Outlook (1 Lowest—5 Highest)
• **5−**

Fair Value
• **32**

Risk
• **Average**

Earn./Div. Rank
• **B+**

Technical Eval.
• **Bearish** since 7/95

Rel. Strength Rank (1 Lowest—99 Highest)
• **22**

Insider Activity
• **Neutral**

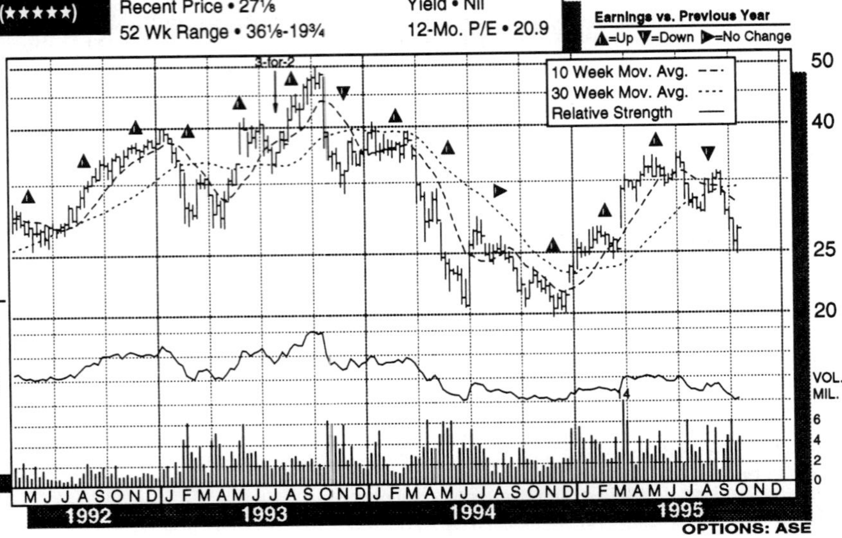

OPTIONS: ASE

Overview - 19-OCT-95

CIR's earnings in fiscal 1995-96 have already been hurt by $0.38-a-share in one-time charges, including a writedown related to a Louisiana casino boat project which has been discontinued. Also, in fiscal 1996-97, we expect that there will be some disruption from expansion and improvement projects at the Luxor and Excalibur casino/hotels. However, we look for CIR's longer-term profits to be helped by the additional investments in these facilities. Also, in the year ahead, we expect CIR to either repurchase a sizable amount of its stock, or make an acquisition which expands its geographic scope. Between now and the year 2000, we look for CIR to be involved in more casino development at the southern end of the Las Vegas Strip. Also, CIR may enter the Atlantic City market.

Valuation - 19-OCT-95

We recommend that aggressive investors buy this stock. Investor confidence should be bolstered by a recent strengthening of CIR's management ranks, and the stock may receive support in the year ahead from a recent authorization to repurchase up to 15% of the common shares. We look for long-term earnings to be helped by various improvement and expansion projects at both existing and new casino/hotels. Also, with development of gaming in new geographic regions having slowed, CIR's emphasis on Nevada operations is looking better.

Key Stock Statistics

S&P EPS Est. 1996	1.37	Tang. Bk. Value/Share	7.16
P/E on S&P Est. 1996	19.8	Beta	1.66
S&P EPS Est. 1997	1.80	Shareholders	5,100
Dividend Rate/Share	Nil	Market cap. (B)	$ 2.9
Shs. outstg. (M)	102.8	Inst. holdings	73%
Avg. daily vol. (M)	0.943	Insider holdings	NA

Value of $10,000 invested 5 years ago: $ 14,530

Fiscal Year Ending Jan. 31

	1996	% Change	1995	% Change	1994	% Change
Revenues (Million $)						
1Q	295.0	4%	284.9	36%	209.8	2%
2Q	326.8	9%	299.9	31%	228.5	3%
3Q	—	—	306.6	25%	244.6	9%
4Q	—	—	278.8	2%	272.1	42%
Yr.	—	—	1,170	23%	954.9	13%
Income (Million $)						
1Q	39.40	22%	32.29	-1%	32.78	11%
2Q	7.28	-80%	36.55	-2%	37.36	6%
3Q	—	—	36.60	78%	20.52	-43%
4Q	—	—	30.85	21%	25.53	28%
Yr.	—	—	136.3	17%	116.2	-4%
Earnings Per Share ($)						
1Q	0.46	21%	0.38	2%	0.37	8%
2Q	0.08	-81%	0.43	NM	0.43	4%
3Q	E0.45	5%	0.43	79%	0.24	-43%
4Q	E0.38	6%	0.36	20%	0.30	29%
Yr.	E1.37	-14%	1.59	19%	1.34	-5%

Next earnings report expected: late November

Circus Circus Enterprises

Business Summary - 12-OCT-95

CIR owns 13 gaming properties (12 in Nevada) which have more than 16,000 hotel rooms, and about 735,000 sq. ft. of casino space. Also, CIR is a joint venture partner various casino projects. CIR typically attracts business by providing reasonably priced hotel rooms, food and alternative entertainment in combination with gaming activity. Free circus acts are offered at several casino/hotels, and other facilities also have themes.

In Las Vegas, operations include the pyramid-shaped Luxor casino/hotel, the castle-themed Excalibur, and the older Circus Circus-Las Vegas facility. Also, CIR operates two smaller casinos in Las Vegas, and acquired the Hacienda Hotel in September 1995. Other CIR facilities in Nevada include Circus Circus-Reno, and a nearby joint venture casino/hotel called the Silver Legacy, which opened in July 1995. In Laughlin, CIR owns the riverboat-themed Colorado Belle, and the adjacent Edgewater Hotel and Casino. Also, CIR's June 1995 acquisition of Gold Strike Resorts included three casino/hotels in Jean and Henderson, Nev., a one-half interest in a riverboat casino project in Elgin, Ill., and a joint venture casino/hotel project which is under construction in Las Vegas. In Tunica County, Miss., CIR operates a casino which opened in August 1994, while in Windsor, Ontario, CIR is part of a joint-venture casino project which debuted in May 1994. In 1994-95, revenue and operating profit contributions were:

	Revenue	Profit
Luxor	24%	23%
Excalibur	25%	26%
CIR-Las Vegas	19%	18%
Reno	10%	9%
Laughlin	16%	15%
Other	6%	9%

Important Developments

Sep. '95—CIR's directors have authorized the repurchase of up to 15% of CIR's common stock. Also, CIR's long-term plans are likely to include sizable development at the southern end of the Las Vegas Strip. In 1995, CIR has spent about $153 million to acquire 73 undeveloped acres, plus the Hacienda Hotel, which are located south of CIR's Luxor property. Other long-term development may include a CIR casino/hotel in Atlantic City. Also, within the next two years, we expect CIR to open a joint venture casino/hotel in Las Vegas, to do a major expansion at the Luxor, and to improve facilities at the nearby Excalibur. In June 1995, CIR acquired Gold Strike Resorts, whose partners included several former CIR executives. The acquisition included the issuance of about 17 million common shares, and assumption of debt.

Capitalization

Long Term Debt: $731,485,000 (7/95).

Per Share Data ($)

(Year Ended Jan. 31)

	1995	1994	1993	1992	1991	1990
Tangible Bk. Val.	7.88	6.38	5.49	3.71	2.11	1.74
Cash Flow	2.55	2.01	1.97	1.81	1.44	1.24
Earnings	1.59	1.34	1.41	1.23	0.93	0.87
Dividends	Nil	Nil	Nil	Nil	Nil	Nil
Payout Ratio	Nil	Nil	Nil	Nil	Nil	Nil
Cal. Yrs.	1994	1993	1992	1991	1990	1989
Prices - High	40¾	49¾	38½	27⅞	23⅝	19
- Low	19¾	27¾	23⅜	16	11⅞	9⅝
P/E Ratio - High	26	37	27	22	25	22
- Low	12	21	17	13	13	11

Income Statement Analysis (Million $)

	1995	%Chg	1994	%Chg	1993	%Chg	1992
Revs.	1,170	23%	955	13%	843	5%	806
Oper. Inc.	342	23%	277	9%	254	2%	249
Depr.	82.8	40%	59.0	22%	48.2	-1%	48.9
Int. Exp.	46.9	29%	36.3	17%	31.0	-31%	44.8
Pretax Inc.	214	17%	183	NM	183	17%	157
Eff. Tax Rate	37%	—	36%	—	34%	—	24%
Net Inc.	136	17%	116	-4%	121	17%	103

Balance Sheet & Other Fin. Data (Million $)

	1995	1994	1993	1992	1991	1990
Cash	54.0	39.0	43.0	34.0	18.0	19.0
Curr. Assets	105	88.0	78.0	68.0	54.0	41.0
Total Assets	1,507	1,298	950	783	792	675
Curr. Liab.	82.0	92.1	87.5	59.5	61.5	62.1
LT Debt	633	567	308	338	497	408
Common Eqty.	686	560	490	326	185	161
Total Cap.	1,424	1,204	862	723	730	612
Cap. Exp.	143	392	209	27.0	149	197
Cash Flow	219	175	169	152	119	107

Ratio Analysis

	1995	1994	1993	1992	1991	1990
Curr. Ratio	1.3	1.0	0.9	1.1	0.9	0.7
% LT Debt of Cap.	44.4	47.1	35.7	46.7	68.1	66.8
% Net Inc.of Revs.	11.6	12.2	14.4	12.8	11.0	14.4
% Ret. on Assets	9.7	10.4	13.8	12.9	10.6	12.8
% Ret. on Equity	21.9	22.3	29.3	40.0	44.9	50.4

Dividend Data —No cash dividends have been paid and none are contemplated for the foreseeable future. The shares were split 3-for-2 in 1993. A "poison pill" stock purchase rights plan was adopted in 1994.

Data as orig. reptd.; bef. results of disc. opers. and/or spec. items. Per share data adj. for stk. divs. as of ex-div. date. E-Estimated. NA-Not Available. NM-Not Meaningful. NR-Not Ranked.

Office—2880 Las Vegas Blvd. South, Las Vegas, NV 89109-1120. **Tel**—(702) 734-0410. **Chrmn & CEO**—C. T. Turner. **Pres & CFO**—G. W. Schaeffer. **EVP, CFO, Treas, & Investor Contact**—Daniel N. Copp. **VP-Secy**—M. Sloan. **Dirs**—T. Coelho, C. F. Dodge, W. N. Pennington, A. M. Smith Jr., F. W. Smith, K. Sullivan, C. T. Turner. **Transfer Agent & Registrar**—First Chicago Trust Co. of New York, Jersey City, NJ. **Incorporated** in Nevada in 1974. **Empl**-18,000. **S&P Analyst:** Tom Graves, CFA

STANDARD & POOR'S

STOCK REPORTS

Cirrus Logic

NASDAQ Symbol **CRUS**

In S&P MidCap 400

18-SEP-95

Industry: Electronics/Electric

Summary: Cirrus develops architectures for analog and digital system functions, and translates them into advanced integrated circuits for various applications.

S&P Opinion: Accumulate (★★★★)

Recent Price • 55¼

52 Wk Range • 60⅜-10½

Yield • Nil

12-Mo. P/E • 52.1

Quantitative Evaluations

Outlook (1 Lowest—5 Highest)

• **3+**

Fair Value

• **58⅞**

Risk

• **High**

Earn./Div. Rank

• **B-**

Technical Eval.

• **Bullish** since 1/95

Rel. Strength Rank (1 Lowest—99 Highest)

• **93**

Insider Activity

• **Neutral**

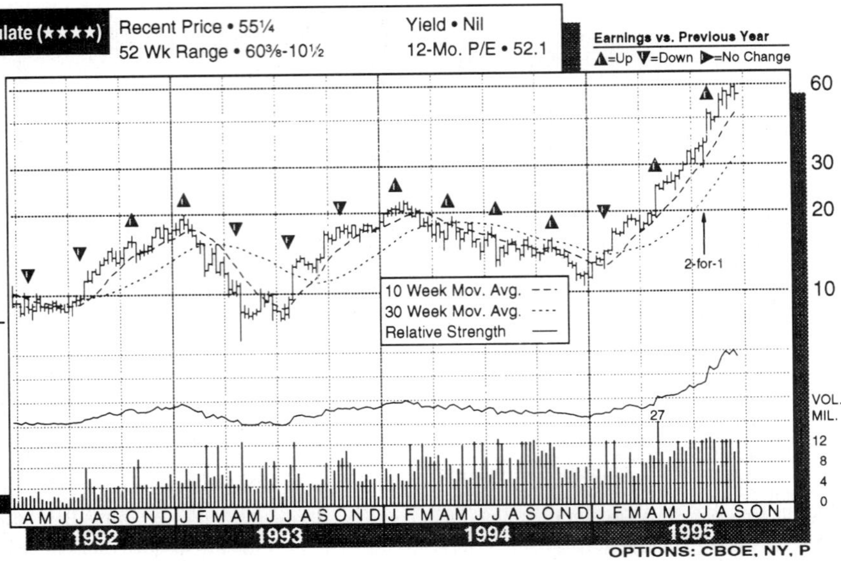

OPTIONS: CBOE, NY, P

Overview - 14-SEP-95

Revenues should continue to climb in fiscal 1996, driven by strong demand for the company's sole-sourced products. Capacity expansion, a major concern for the company as it has not been able to meet demand, should be significantly improved with the ramping up of the MiCRUS joint venture. MiCRUS is also expected to widen margins by reducing dependence on outside manufacturers and decreasing the number of inefficient special orders needed to meet client needs. With higher production rates and improving margins, we are raising our FY 1996 estimate to $1.80 a share, and expect $2.70 in FY 1997.

Valuation - 18-SEP-95

The shares have enjoyed a dramatic run this year, and are near their record high. Demand for integrated circuits should continue unabated, as the PC, telecommunications, and electronics markets all remain strong. Management believes that increased wafer production from the MiCRUS joint venture, and the expected margin improvement will be the driving forces behind the superb results expected in fiscal 1996 and 1997. Although the shares are now fully valued at about 31 times estimated 1996 earnings, CRUS's excellent long-term outlook makes the shares attractive for accumulation.

Key Stock Statistics

S&P EPS Est. 1996	1.80	Tang. Bk. Value/Share	6.92
P/E on S&P Est. 1996	30.7	Beta	2.66
S&P EPS Est. 1997	2.70	Shareholders	1,400
Dividend Rate/Share	Nil	Market cap. (B)	$ 3.4
Shs. outstg. (M)	62.1	Inst. holdings	87%
Avg. daily vol. (M)	2.850	Insider holdings	NA

Value of $10,000 invested 5 years ago: $ 105,238

Fiscal Year Ending Mar. 31

	1996	% Change	1995	% Change	1994	% Change
Revenues (Million $)						
1Q	300.3	71%	176.0	77%	99.2	47%
2Q	—	—	202.2	62%	124.8	50%
3Q	—	—	228.6	53%	149.9	51%
4Q	—	—	273.2	61%	170.2	63%
Yr.	—	—	889.0	63%	544.1	53%
Income (Million $)						
1Q	22.74	51%	15.01	NM	-3.71	NM
2Q	—	—	12.44	95%	6.38	-14%
3Q	—	—	14.49	-27%	19.81	83%
4Q	—	—	18.91	29%	14.61	NM
Yr.	—	—	61.40	66%	37.08	80%
Earnings Per Share ($)						
1Q	0.34	36%	0.25	NM	-0.08	NM
2Q	E0.42	115%	0.19	56%	0.13	-14%
3Q	E0.49	113%	0.23	-38%	0.37	164%
4Q	E0.55	86%	0.29	18%	0.25	NM
Yr.	E1.80	87%	0.96	39%	0.70	72%

Next earnings report expected: late October

Cirrus Logic

Business Summary - 18-SEP-95

Cirrus Logic is a leading producer of advanced integrated circuits for the desktop and portable computing, telecommunications, and consumer electronics market. The company offers a wide variety of products, including integrated chips, software, evaluation boards, manufacturing kits, subsystem modules, and telecommunications systems equipment.

CRUS's multimedia products include a line of PC graphics controllers for desktop and portable computers. Through its Crystal Semiconductor and Pixel Semiconductor subsidiaries, the company also offers a wide choice of audio and video products. Comprised of highly integrated circuits and software, these products bring CD-quality audio and cinema-quality video to multimedia applications for PCs, workstations, videoconferencing systems and consumer electronics.

Cirrus supplies chips that perform the key electronic functions contained in advanced disk drives. Since 1986, it has helped facilitate the development of higher-capacity 3.5-inch disk drives for desktop computers. In 1995, Cirrus began shipments of read channel products, and in 1993-94 the company added both read/write and motion control chips to its product line.

For wireline communications, the company introduced the industry's first two-chip intelligent fax/data/voice modem in 1992. More recently, it introduced a three-chip, high-performance version with enhanced error correction and data compression. In wireless communications, the company's Pacific Communication Sciences, Inc. unit has emerged as the technology leader for Cellular Digital Packet Data, which allows packets of digital data to be transmitted over existing Advanced Mobile Phone Service analog cellular networks.

In August 1994, Cirrus acquired PicoPower Technology Inc., a provider of system power management, in exchange for about 1.7 million common shares. Pico's products are used with microprocessors and other components to construct the system and internal bus functions of the PC, while greatly reducing overall power consumption.

In September 1994, the company formed a joint venture with IBM, called MiCRUS, to manufacture semiconductor wafers for both companies. Prior to this, Cirrus used outside manufacturers to make all of its wafers.

Important Developments

Jul. '95—The company noted that the first quarter of fiscal 1996 was the first in which the MiCRUS joint venture contributed significantly to wafer production. Management believes that margins will improve as MiCRUS ramps up production.

Capitalization

Long Term Obligs.: $29,572,000 (7/95).

Per Share Data ($) (Year Ended Mar. 31)

	1995	1994	1993	1992	1991	1990
Tangible Bk. Val.	6.92	5.96	2.97	2.62	2.42	1.76
Cash Flow	1.51	1.20	0.70	0.63	0.75	0.64
Earnings	0.96	0.70	0.40	0.41	0.59	0.51
Dividends	Nil	Nil	Nil	Nil	Nil	Nil
Payout Ratio	Nil	Nil	Nil	Nil	Nil	Nil
Cal. Yrs.	1994	1993	1992	1991	1990	1989
Prices - High	22 3/8	20	18 1/2	12 1/4	10 3/4	7 7/8
- Low	10 1/2	6 5/8	8	6 1/8	4	4 1/2
P/E Ratio - High	23	29	46	30	18	15
- Low	11	10	20	15	7	9

Income Statement Analysis (Million $)

	1995	%Chg	1994	%Chg	1993	%Chg	1992
Revs.	889	63%	544	53%	355	106%	172
Oper. Inc.	119	80%	66.0	33%	49.8	56%	32.0
Depr.	34.3	28%	26.9	77%	15.2	81%	8.4
Int. Exp.	2.4	13%	2.2	34%	1.6	94%	0.8
Pretax Inc.	89.6	64%	54.8	67%	32.9	43%	23.0
Eff. Tax Rate	32%	—	32%	—	37%	—	32%
Net Inc.	61.4	65%	37.1	80%	20.6	32%	15.6

Balance Sheet & Other Fin. Data (Million $)

	1995	1994	1993	1992	1991	1990
Cash	187	237	72.7	48.3	54.9	40.8
Curr. Assets	480	413	194	99	91.0	67.0
Total Assets	674	502	256	141	109	78.0
Curr. Liab.	228	145	95.8	32.9	25.9	21.7
LT Debt	26.2	19.1	18.1	11.9	9.3	3.1
Common Eqty.	419	338	143	96.0	74.0	52.0
Total Cap.	445	357	161	107	83.0	55.0
Cap. Exp.	47.3	34.9	26.7	5.5	10.9	7.3
Cash Flow	95.7	63.9	35.7	24.0	23.9	19.2

Ratio Analysis

	1995	1994	1993	1992	1991	1990
Curr. Ratio	2.1	2.8	2.0	3.0	3.5	3.1
% LT Debt of Cap.	5.9	5.4	11.3	11.1	11.2	5.6
% Net Inc.of Revs.	6.9	6.8	5.8	9.1	13.3	18.6
% Ret. on Assets	10.1	9.2	9.4	11.5	20.0	31.2
% Ret. on Equity	15.7	14.7	16.0	17.0	30.0	48.0

Dividend Data —No cash dividends have been paid.

Amt. of Div. $	Date Decl.	Ex-Div. Date	Stock of Record	Payment Date
2-for-1	Jun. 02	Jul. 18	Jun. 19	Jul. 17 '95

Data as orig. reptd.; bef. results of disc. opers. and/or spec. items. Per share data adj. for stk. divs. as of ex-div. date. E-Estimated. NA-Not Available. NM-Not Meaningful. NR-Not Ranked.

Office—3100 West Warren Ave., Fremont, CA 94538. **Tel**—(510) 623-8300. **Chrmn & EVP**—S. S. Patil. **Pres & CEO**—M. L. Hackworth. **SVP-Fin, CFO, Treas & Secy**—S. S. Srinivasan. **Investor Contact**—Mark Singer. **Dirs**—C. G. Bell, D. J. Guzy, M. L. Hackworth, D. L. Lyon, S. S. Patil, C. W. Rea Jr., W. C. Rhines, R. H. Smith. **Transfer Agent & Registrar**—First National Bank of Boston. **Incorporated** in California in 1984. **Empl**-2,331. **S&P Analyst:** Mike Cavanaugh

STANDARD & POOR'S

STOCK REPORTS

City National Corp.

NYSE Symbol **CYN**
In S&P MidCap 400

01-OCT-95 **Industry:** Banking

Summary: This holding company owns City National Bank, a commercial bank with 16 branches in Southern California, primarily in Los Angeles, Orange and San Diego counties.

S&P Opinion: Hold (★★★)

Recent Price • 13¼
52 Wk Range • 15⅜-8¼
Yield • 2.1%
12-Mo. P/E • 14.4

Quantitative Evaluations
Outlook
(1 Lowest—5 Highest)
• **NA**
Fair Value
• **NA**
Risk
• **Average**
Earn./Div. Rank
• **C**

Technical Eval.
• **Bearish** since 8/95
Rel. Strength Rank
(1 Lowest—99 Highest)
• **37**
Insider Activity
• **NA**

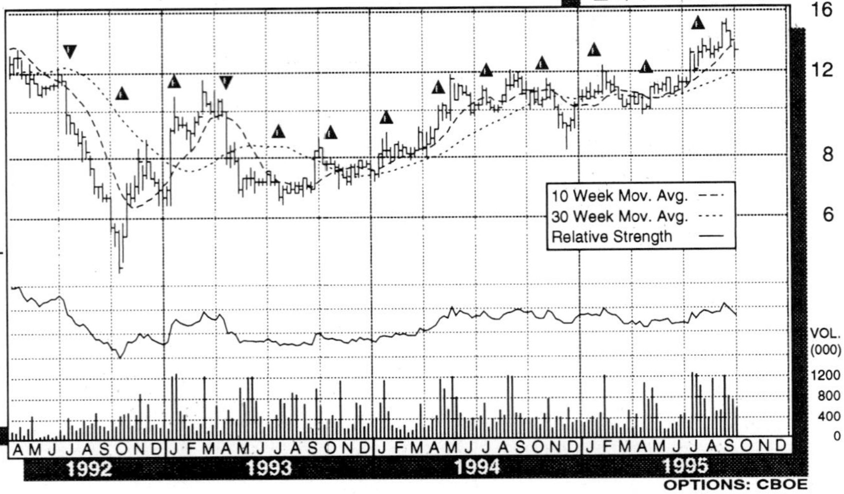

Overview - 01-OCT-95

In the three years prior to 1994, City National experienced losses associated with the recession that caused real estate values in Southern California to plummet. Earnings rebounded in 1994, and the favorable trend continued through the first half of 1995. In the six months ended June 30, 1995, net income was up 31%, year to year, as net interest income rose 17%, the provision for loan losses declined from $6.0 million to zero, and noninterest expenses were flat. By June 30, 1995, loans had risen 13% from their level a year earlier, fueled by construction and residential lending. Loans should continue growing at a 10%-to-13% annual rate through 1996. Asset quality has improved substantially, with the ratio of nonperforming assets to total assets at 1.67%, compared to 2.52%. The allowance for credit losses increased to 257.1% of nonaccrual loans, from 154.2%.

Valuation - 01-OCT-95

The shares thus far in 1995 have lagged both the bank indices and the broader market. Currently trading at about 13 times our 1996 earnings estimate, and 1.8 times tangible book value, the stock is fully valued, but warrants accumulating on improving fundamentals, including widening net interest margins and higher asset quality. Earnings should benefit from the continued improvement of the California real estate market.

Key Stock Statistics

S&P EPS Est. 1995	0.97	Tang. Bk. Value/Share	7.76
P/E on S&P Est. 1995	13.7	Beta	1.45
S&P EPS Est. 1996	1.05	Shareholders	2,600
Dividend Rate/Share	0.28	Market cap. (B)	$0.600
Shs. outstg. (M)	45.3	Inst. holdings	39%
Avg. daily vol. (M)	0.169	Insider holdings	NA

Value of $10,000 invested 5 years ago: $ 6,227

Fiscal Year Ending Dec. 31

	1995	% Change	1994	% Change	1993	% Change
Revenues (Million $)						
1Q	57.94	13%	51.06	-9%	56.25	-27%
2Q	61.83	15%	53.74	-3%	55.26	-24%
3Q	—	—	55.18	-8%	59.91	-11%
4Q	—	—	54.64	3%	53.19	-15%
Yr.	—	—	214.6	NM	215.6	-23%
Income (Million $)						
1Q	10.62	23%	8.66	NM	-25.85	NM
2Q	11.56	40%	8.23	119%	3.76	NM
3Q	—	—	10.41	199%	3.48	NM
4Q	—	—	9.86	115%	4.58	NM
Yr.	—	—	37.16	NM	-14.03	NM
Earnings Per Share ($)						
1Q	0.23	21%	0.19	NM	-0.80	NM
2Q	0.25	39%	0.18	64%	0.11	NM
3Q	E0.24	4%	0.23	188%	0.08	NM
4Q	E0.25	19%	0.21	110%	0.10	NM
Yr.	E0.97	20%	0.81	NM	-0.35	NM

Next earnings report expected: mid October

City National Corp.

Business Summary - 01-OCT-95

City National Corp. is the holding company for City National Bank ($2.8 billion in assets at June 30, 1995), a federally chartered commercial bank that conducts business in Southern California. Since its founding in 1954, the bank has served a well-defined niche market comprised of small to mid-size businesses, professionals, high-net-worth individuals and the entertainment industry. Headquartered in Beverly Hills, City National has 16 branches located in Los Angeles, Orange and San Diego counties. Emphasis in recent years has been directed to the commercial rather than the retail sector. Total loans of $1.6 billion at 1994 year end were divided:

	1994	1993
Commercial	55%	58%
Real estate - mortgage	41%	38%
Instalment	2%	3%
Real estate - construction	2%	1%

The reserve for loan losses at December 31, 1994, was $105.3 million (6.88% of average loans outstanding), down from $110.5 million (6.36%) a year earlier. Net chargeoffs in 1994 totaled $11.2 million (0.73% of average loans), versus $54.1 million (3.12%) in 1993. Nonaccrual loans and foreclosed real estate assets at December 31, 1994, were $61.2 million (2.03% of total assets), down from $76.6 million (2.47%) a year earlier.

Average core deposits during 1994 were apportioned: demand deposits 46%, money market accounts 32%, interest-bearing checking 14%, savings 4%, and time deposits under $100,000 4%. On a tax-equivalent basis, the average yield on interest-earning assets in 1994 was 7.07% (6.59% in 1993), while the average rate paid on interest-bearing liabilities was 2.45% (2.40%), for a net spread of 4.62% (4.19%).

Important Developments

Aug. '95—City National Bank agreed to acquire First Los Angeles Bank from San Paolo Bank Holding S.A. of Turin, Italy. First L.A. is based in Century City, California, and has 10 banking offices located in Southern California. As of June 30, 1995, it had approximately $882 million in assets, deposits of $762 million, and equity of $77 million. Terms of the transaction, which is subject to regulatory approvals, call for City National to pay $85 million in cash for First L.A; the merger should be completed in early 1996.

May '95—Directors authorized the purchase of up to 5%, or 2.28 million shares, of CYN common stock.

Capitalization

Long-term debt: None (6/95).

Per Share Data ($) (Year Ended Dec. 31)

	1994	1993	1992	1991	1990	1989
Tangible Bk. Val.	7.32	6.62	7.07	8.91	9.89	9.06
Earnings	0.81	-0.35	-1.84	-0.66	1.35	1.86
Dividends	0.05	Nil	Nil	0.32	0.64	0.58
Payout Ratio	6%	Nil	NM	NM	47%	31%
Prices - High	12⅛	11⅝	16	15¾	24¾	28
- Low	7⅛	6⅜	4⅝	8⅝	11	18
P/E Ratio - High	15	NM	NM	NM	18	15
- Low	9	NM	NM	NM	8	10

Income Statement Analysis (Million $)

	1994	%Chg	1993	%Chg	1992	%Chg	1991
Net Int. Inc.	143	12%	128	-14%	149	-18%	181
Tax Equiv. Adj.	1.1	-12%	1.3	-69%	4.2	-32%	6.2
Non Int. Inc.	32.8	-28%	45.8	NM	45.4	-40%	75.7
Loan Loss Prov.	6.0	-80%	30.0	-74%	115	-3%	118
% Exp/Op Revs.	66%	—	95%	—	88%	—	69%
Pretax Inc.	52.7	NM	-23.3	NM	-92.6	NM	-42.7
Eff. Tax Rate	29%	—	NM	—	NM	—	NM
Net Inc.	37.2	NM	-14.0	NM	-60.1	NM	-21.2
% Net Int. Marg.	5.59%	—	4.97%	—	4.41%	—	4.48%

Balance Sheet & Other Fin. Data (Million $)

	1994	1993	1992	1991	1990	1989
Earning Assets:						
Money Mkt.	297	266	494	617	874	918
Inv. Securities	659	902	444	731	622	555
Com'l Loans	904	940	1,192	1,501	1,766	1,574
Other Loans	734	681	897	1,129	1,312	1,148
Total Assets	3,013	3,101	3,514	4,565	4,956	4,699
Demand Deposits	1,152	1,088	1,260	1,238	1,196	1,169
Time Deposits	1,266	1,438	1,652	2,426	2,906	2,685
LT Debt	Nil	26.3	Nil	Nil	0.4	0.5
Common Eqty.	331	298	228	287	318	281

Ratio Analysis

	1994	1993	1992	1991	1990	1989
% Ret. on Assets	1.3	NM	NM	NM	1.0	1.4
% Ret. on Equity	11.9	NM	NM	NM	14.1	22.7
% Loan Loss Resv.	6.4	6.8	6.5	4.8	2.0	1.3
% Loans/Deposits	67.8	64.1	71.8	71.8	75.0	70.6
% Equity to Assets	11.1	8.8	6.6	6.9	6.8	6.3

Dividend Data —Cash dividends, paid each year since 1963, were omitted in August 1991 and reinstated in late 1994.

Amt. of Div. $	Date Decl.	Ex-Div. Date	Stock of Record	Payment Date
0.050	Oct. 27	Nov. 02	Nov. 08	Nov. 18 '94
0.050	Jan. 26	Jan. 31	Feb. 06	Feb. 16 '95
0.070	Apr. 18	Apr. 24	Apr. 28	May. 09 '95
0.070	Jul. 27	Aug. 04	Aug. 08	Aug. 18 '95

Data as orig. reptd.; bef. results of disc opers. and/or spec. items. Per share data adj. for stk. divs. as of ex-div. date. E-Estimated. NA-Not Available. NM-Not Meaningful. NR-Not Ranked.

Office—400 North Roxbury Drive, Beverly Hills, CA 90210. **Tel**—(310) 888-6000. **Chrmn & CEO**—B. Goldsmith. **Pres**—G. H. Benter, Jr. **Vice Chrmn**—S. D. Broidy. **SVP & Secy**—R. H. Sheehan. **EVP, CFO & Investor Contact**—F. P. Pekny. **Dirs**—G. H. Benter, Jr., R. L. Bloch, M. P. Bowers, S. D. Broidy, S. D. Buchalter, B. Goldsmith, R. D. Goldsmith, B. S. Horwitch, C. E. Rickershauser, Jr., E. Sanders, A. L. Van de Kamp, K. Ziffren. **Transfer Agent**—City National Bank. **Incorporated** in Delaware in 1968. **Empl**-1,200. **S&P Analyst:** Thomas C. Ferguson

STANDARD & POOR'S
STOCK REPORTS

Claire's Stores

NYSE Symbol **CLE**
In S&P MidCap 400

23-SEP-95 **Industry:** Retail Stores

Summary: This company operates the largest chain of specialty retail stores in the U.S. devoted solely to the sale of inexpensive fashion accessories.

Quantitative Evaluations

Recent Price • 21⅛ | Yield • 0.6%
52 Wk Range • 23-10¼ | 12-Mo. P/E • 17.3

Outlook
(1 Lowest—5 Highest)
• **5+**

Fair Value
• **28⅞**

Risk
• **Average**

Earn./Div. Rank
• **A-**

Technical Eval.
• **Bullish** since 7/95

Rel. Strength Rank
(1 Lowest—99 Highest)
• **62**

Insider Activity
• **NA**

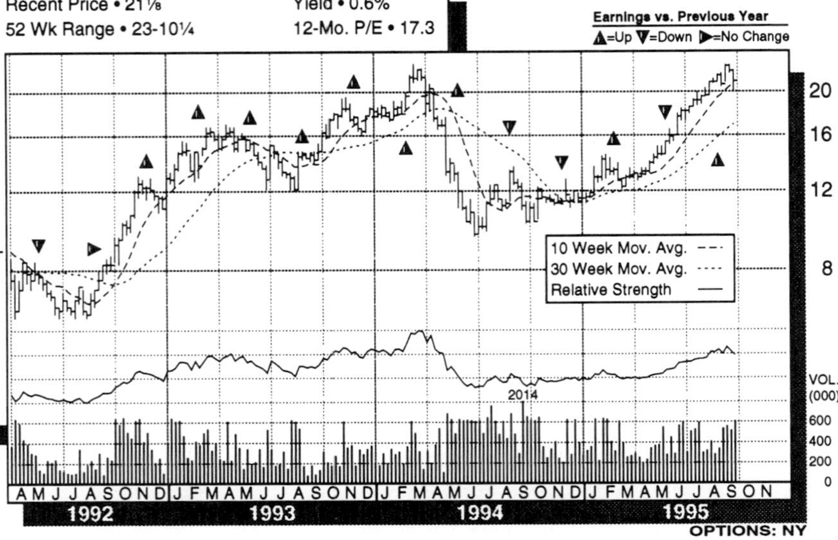

Business Profile - 22-SEP-95

Claire's Stores operates a chain of more than 1,260 specialty retail stores in the U.S. devoted solely to the sale of inexpensive fashion accessories. Costume jewelry accounts for about two-thirds of total sales. CLE plans to add some 150 new stores in 1995-6, including 20 stores in Japan and 30-40 stores in Canada. Expansion is expected to continue over the next five years, with approximately 130 new store openings annually. The balance sheet is strong, with no long-term debt.

Operational Review - 22-SEP-95

Sales for the six months ended July 29, 1995, rose 13%, year to year, aided by contributions from 128 more stores in operation and a 2.0% gain in same-store sales. Profitability benefited from the higher volume and, following an 11% increase in interest income, net earnings grew 32%. The company said that it was pleased with the improving results during the second quarter and believed that it could set new sales and earnings records for the year.

Stock Performance - 22-SEP-95

In the past 30 trading days, CLE's shares have increased 0.60%, compared to a 5% rise in the S&P 500. Average trading volume for the past five days was 124,900 shares, compared with the 40-day moving average of 91,059 shares.

Key Stock Statistics

Dividend Rate/Share	0.12	Shareholders	3,300
Shs. outstg. (M)	20.9	Market cap. (B)	$0.441
Avg. daily vol. (M)	0.114	Inst. holdings	55%
Tang. Bk. Value/Share	5.96	Insider holdings	NA
Beta	2.15		

Value of $10,000 invested 5 years ago: $ 16,284

Fiscal Year Ending Jan. 31

	1996	% Change	1995	% Change	1994	% Change
Revenues (Million $)						
1Q	68.05	7%	63.66	10%	58.05	13%
2Q	77.28	19%	64.93	5%	61.78	15%
3Q	—	—	69.46	6%	65.24	13%
4Q	—	—	103.3	7%	96.62	13%
Yr.	—	—	301.4	7%	281.7	14%
Income (Million $)						
1Q	2.04	-23%	2.65	32%	2.01	NM
2Q	4.15	104%	2.03	-24%	2.66	NM
3Q	—	—	2.90	-17%	3.48	113%
4Q	—	—	16.28	5%	15.49	33%
Yr.	—	—	23.86	NM	23.63	62%
Earnings Per Share ($)						
1Q	0.10	-23%	0.13	30%	0.10	NM
2Q	0.20	100%	0.10	-23%	0.13	NM
3Q	—	—	0.14	-18%	0.17	113%
4Q	—	—	0.78	4%	0.75	32%
Yr.	—	—	1.15	NM	1.15	62%

Next earnings report expected: early November

Claire's Stores

Business Summary - 22-SEP-95

Claire's Stores, Inc. is a leading mall-based retailer of women's popular-priced fashion accessories. As of March 31, 1995, CLE was operating 1,214 stores in 48 states, Canada, the Caribbean and Japan, consisting of 1,032 Claire's Boutiques stores, 130 Topkapi stores, 27 Dara Michelle stores and 15 L'ccessory stores (collectively the fashion accessory stores). The company also operates 10 Arcadia, Art Explosion or E. 57th stores (the trend gift stores, which are being converted or closed). Total stores in operation at the end of recent fiscal years were:

1995	1,203
1994	1,087
1993	1,038
1992	995
1991	916

In 1994-5, costume jewelry (including hair ornaments, pierced earrings and fees for piercing ears) accounted for 65% of sales, other fashion accessories for 31%, totebags for 2% and trend gifts for 2%.

The fashion accessory stores average about 889 sq. ft. and carry merchandise designed to appeal to females aged 13 to 40. The average product is priced around $4. The Dara Michelle, Topkapi and L'ccessory stores are similar in size and format to the Claire's Boutiques stores and give CLE the ability to add a second store in the malls that have a successful Claire's Boutiques store. The trend gift stores sell T-shirts, unframed posters, calendars, stationery products and seasonal items. Most sales are in the $5 to $10 range.

Merchandise, which is purchased from approximately 300 suppliers, is primarily either imported directly or purchased from importers. All merchandise is shipped to the company's distribution center in Wood Dale, Ill., a suburb of Chicago. After inspection, merchandise is shipped via common carrier to the individual stores. Stores receive three to five shipments a week.

In 1994-5, CLE entered into a joint-venture agreement with JUSCO Co., Ltd. of Tokyo to open and operate Claire's Boutiques stores in Japan. In addition, the company expanded its international store base with the opening of 45 stores in Canada.

Important Developments

Sep. '95—Claire's acquired an option to purchase Bow Bangles Holdings Ltd. of Birmingham, England, a 71-store retail chain of women's accessories in England, Scotland and Wales. The option may be exercised any time before July 1, 1997.

Capitalization

Long Term Debt: None (7/95).
Class A Common Stock: 1,282,415 shs. ($0.05 par); 10 votes per sh.; conv. into com. sh. for sh.; max. div. 50% of com. div.; limited transferability.
About 77% is controlled by the Schaefer family.

Per Share Data ($) (Year Ended Jan. 31)

	1995	1994	1993	1992	1991	1990
Tangible Bk. Val.	5.80	4.82	3.75	3.12	3.62	2.69
Cash Flow	1.82	1.77	1.34	0.88	1.60	1.40
Earnings	1.15	1.15	0.71	0.26	1.01	0.97
Dividends	0.12	0.10	0.10	0.10	0.10	0.10
Payout Ratio	10%	9%	14%	39%	10%	10%
Cal. Yrs.	1994	1993	1992	1991	1990	1989
Prices - High	23⅛	19½	13	17⅛	23⅞	14⅜
- Low	9½	12	6¼	6⅛	8½	4⅝
P/E Ratio - High	20	17	18	66	24	15
- Low	8	10	9	24	8	5

Income Statement Analysis (Million $)

	1995	%Chg	1994	%Chg	1993	%Chg	1992
Revs.	301	7%	282	14%	248	6%	234
Oper. Inc.	51.5	1%	50.8	33%	38.2	59%	24.0
Depr.	13.9	7%	13.0	NM	13.0	2%	12.8
Int. Exp.	NA	—	0.3	-81%	1.7	-39%	2.8
Pretax Inc.	38.5	3%	37.5	60%	23.5	180%	8.4
Eff. Tax Rate	38%	—	37%	—	38%	—	38%
Net Inc.	23.9	1%	23.6	62%	14.6	181%	5.2

Balance Sheet & Other Fin. Data (Million $)

	1995	1994	1993	1992	1991	1990
Cash	48.5	41.1	39.0	14.5	1.9	2.4
Curr. Assets	78.7	69.3	64.0	40.4	46.3	35.3
Total Assets	159	135	129	112	134	103
Curr. Liab.	30.0	27.1	40.8	19.8	26.0	35.1
LT Debt	3.0	6.0	10.0	25.0	28.9	5.8
Common Eqty.	122	100	76.8	64.0	73.6	54.6
Total Cap.	125	106	88.0	92.0	108	68.0
Cap. Exp.	24.8	12.8	8.2	14.2	32.9	28.3
Cash Flow	37.7	36.6	27.6	18.0	32.6	27.9

Ratio Analysis

	1995	1994	1993	1992	1991	1990
Curr. Ratio	2.6	2.6	1.6	2.0	1.8	1.0
% LT Debt of Cap.	2.4	5.7	11.4	27.2	26.7	8.7
% Net Inc.of Revs.	7.9	8.4	5.9	2.2	8.0	10.2
% Ret. on Assets	16.2	17.8	12.1	4.2	17.2	23.3
% Ret. on Equity	21.5	26.6	20.7	7.6	31.8	43.9

Dividend Data —Dividends were initiated in 1984.

Amt. of Div. $	Date Decl.	Ex-Div. Date	Stock of Record	Payment Date
0.030	Oct. 17	Oct. 27	Nov. 02	Nov. 16 '94
0.030	Jan. 17	Jan. 26	Feb. 01	Feb. 15 '95
0.030	Apr. 04	Apr. 27	May. 03	May. 17 '95
0.030	Jul. 20	Jul. 31	Aug. 02	Aug. 16 '95

Data as orig. reptd.; bef. results of disc. opers. and/or spec. items. Per share data adj. for stk. divs. as of ex-div. date. E-Estimated. NA-Not Available. NM-Not Meaningful. NR-Not Ranked.

Office—3 S.W. 129th Ave., Pembroke Pines, FL 33027. **Tel**—(305) 433-3900. **Chrmn & Pres**—R. Schaefer. **Secy**—H. E. Berritt. **CFO & Treas**—I. Kaplan. **Investor Contact**—H. Glenn Canary. **Dirs**—H. E. Berritt, F. D. Hirt, B. G. Miller, M. L. Schaefer, R. Schaefer, S. Schaefer, J. J. Silver. **Transfer Agent & Registrar**—First Union National Bank, Charlotte, N.C. **Incorporated** in Delaware in 1961. **Empl-** 5,500. **S&P Analyst:** Maureen C. Carini

STANDARD & POOR'S

STOCK REPORTS

Clayton Homes

NYSE Symbol **CMH**
In S&P MidCap 400

09-AUG-95 **Industry:** Mobile/Modular Homes

Summary: This producer and retailer of low- to medium-priced manufactured homes also provides related financing and insurance services, and manages communities of manufactured housing.

S&P Opinion: Buy (★★★★★)

Recent Price • 20
52 Wk Range • 20½-12¼
Yield • 0.4%
12-Mo. P/E • 17.4

Quantitative Evaluations
Outlook
(1 Lowest—5 Highest)
• **3+**
Fair Value
• **19⅝**
Risk
• **Average**
Earn./Div. Rank
• **B+**

Technical Eval.
• **Bullish** since 2/95
Rel. Strength Rank
(1 Lowest—99 Highest)
• **91**
Insider Activity
• **NA**

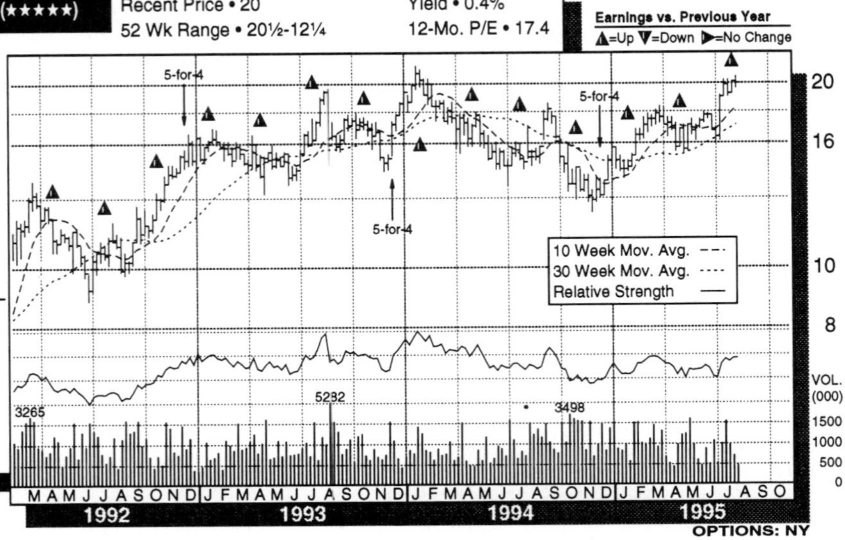

OPTIONS: NY

Overview - 09-AUG-95

Ongoing solid sales growth is likely through fiscal 1996, as this well managed company should continue to gain market share and surpass the 5% to 10% industry growth anticipated in the coming year. CMH should be aided by strong customer regard for the Clayton name, the opening of additional company-owned sales centers and the addition of new independent dealers. Growing sales of manufactured homes should also result in greater financial services income, while CMH's increased investment in manufactured housing communities should lead to higher rental income. Margins are expected to remain relatively stable, as cost control efforts offset the impact of growing competition.

Valuation - 09-AUG-95

Clayton's shares fell sharply from the time of the first Fed tightening in early 1994 through the latter part of the year, but have since staged a recovery on a decline in interest rates and continued earnings gains. While the market treats Clayton as a cyclical company, its strong operating strategy and diversity of operations have enabled it to record solid growth during both good times and bad. We would expect the shares to continue their uptrend on what we believe will be ongoing earnings gains and a continued environment of low interest rates.

Key Stock Statistics

S&P EPS Est. 1996	1.35	Tang. Bk. Value/Share	6.85
P/E on S&P Est. 1996	14.8	Beta	1.39
Dividend Rate/Share	0.08	Shareholders	1,600
Shs. outstg. (M)	75.5	Market cap. (B)	$ 1.6
Avg. daily vol. (M)	0.191	Inst. holdings	71%
		Insider holdings	NA

Value of $10,000 invested 5 years ago: $ 69,963

Fiscal Year Ending Jun. 30

	1995	% Change	1994	% Change	1993	% Change
Revenues (Million $)						
1Q	168.4	24%	136.0	24%	109.8	22%
2Q	177.5	22%	145.9	38%	106.0	28%
3Q	179.7	20%	150.2	34%	112.2	32%
4Q	232.5	19%	196.1	32%	148.2	30%
Yr.	758.1	21%	628.2	32%	476.2	28%
Income (Million $)						
1Q	18.23	23%	14.83	33%	11.16	39%
2Q	18.17	23%	14.83	42%	10.41	47%
3Q	22.31	27%	17.52	27%	13.80	45%
4Q	28.30	28%	22.10	20%	18.38	25%
Yr.	87.00	26%	69.30	29%	53.76	37%
Earnings Per Share ($)						
1Q	0.24	17%	0.20	28%	0.16	32%
2Q	0.24	15%	0.21	48%	0.14	29%
3Q	0.29	25%	0.23	21%	0.19	36%
4Q	0.38	28%	0.30	13%	0.26	24%
Yr.	1.15	22%	0.94	24%	0.76	31%

Next earnings report expected: mid October

Clayton Homes

Business Summary - 07-AUG-95

Clayton Homes is a vertically integrated producer and retailer of low- to medium-priced manufactured homes. It provides complete financing and insurance services to its retail customers, and develops communities for manufactured housing. Contributions to revenues in recent fiscal years:

	1995	1994	1993
Retail sales	53%	54%	56%
Wholesale sales	29%	27%	25%
Financial services and other	18%	19%	19%

A manufactured home is a factory-built, completely furnished dwelling, constructed to be transported by trucks, and designed as a permanent, primary residence when sited and attached to utilities. At June 30, 1995, Clayton's 16 plants (three opened during fiscal 1995) supplied homes to 192 company-owned dealers and 421 independent dealers. In addition to selling homes built by Clayton, nearly all of the company's retail centers sell homes made by others and previously owned manufactured homes.

The company makes more than 150 models of single- and multi-section homes. Retail prices range from $13,000 to $75,000, with sizes from 675 to 2,100 sq. ft. (all as of fiscal 1994 year-end). In fiscal 1995, Clayton sold 18,942 manufactured homes (58% to independent dealers), up from 16,337 (57%) in fiscal 1994; including non-Clayton homes sold by company-owned stores and homes sold in CMH's manufactured housing communities, Clayton sold a total of 26,123 homes in fiscal 1995, versus 22,791 in the prior year.

CMH offers retail customers a variety of home purchase finance programs through conventional lenders and directly through its finance subsidiary, Vanderbilt Mortgage and Finance, Inc. In fiscal 1994 (latest available), 74% of retail home sales were financed through Vanderbilt. At June 30, 1994, Vanderbilt was servicing about 88,000 contracts with an aggregate dollar amount of $1.3 billion.

In fiscal 1995, the company acquired about 2,500 sites in nine manufactured housing communities, bringing total sites owned at June 30, 1995, to 15,541 (in 55 communities). Occupancy at the sites at the end of fiscal 1995 was 68%, versus 64% a year earlier. The company attributes its low overall occupancy rate to its strategy of acquiring weaker, underperforming communities.

Important Developments

Aug. '95—The company reported that its opening of three new manufacturing plants in fiscal 1995 (16 now in operation) had dramatically increased overall capacity, and that it had started construction of its 17th plant, which would be operational near the end of fiscal 1996.

Capitalization

Long Term Liabilities: $54,488,000 (3/95).

Per Share Data ($)

(Year Ended Jun. 30)

	1995	1994	1993	1992	1991	1990
Tangible Bk. Val.	NA	6.14	4.98	4.20	3.12	2.22
Cash Flow	NA	1.03	0.82	0.63	0.56	0.45
Earnings	1.15	0.94	0.76	0.58	0.52	0.40
Dividends	0.06	Nil	Nil	Nil	Nil	Nil
Payout Ratio	5%	Nil	Nil	Nil	Nil	Nil
Prices - High	$20\frac{1}{2}$	$21\frac{3}{8}$	$19\frac{5}{8}$	$16\frac{5}{8}$	$9\frac{1}{2}$	$5\frac{5}{8}$
- Low	14	$13\frac{5}{8}$	$13\frac{1}{4}$	7	5	$2\frac{1}{2}$
P/E Ratio - High	18	23	26	27	18	14
- Low	12	14	17	12	10	6

Income Statement Analysis (Million $)

	1994	%Chg	1993	%Chg	1992	%Chg	1991
Revs.	628	32%	476	28%	371	16%	321
Oper. Inc.	115	30%	88.4	10%	80.5	21%	66.8
Depr.	6.7	36%	4.9	42%	3.4	24%	2.8
Int. Exp.	0.4	-75%	1.4	-93%	20.2	-7%	21.7
Pretax Inc.	108	30%	83.4	39%	60.1	35%	44.6
Eff. Tax Rate	36%	—	36%	—	35%	—	36%
Net Inc.	69.3	29%	53.8	37%	39.3	37%	28.6

Balance Sheet & Other Fin. Data (Million $)

	1994	1993	1992	1991	1990	1989
Cash	38.9	28.7	63.4	57.5	60.8	37.7
Curr. Assets	NA	NA	NA	NA	NA	NA
Total Assets	701	587	555	489	339	295
Curr. Liab.	NA	NA	NA	NA	NA	NA
LT Debt	71.0	112	163	227	177	163
Common Eqty.	462	349	293	201	108	87.0
Total Cap.	540	468	462	435	296	265
Cap. Exp.	35.6	22.7	19.1	4.9	4.3	3.0
Cash Flow	75.9	58.7	42.8	31.4	22.3	18.5

Ratio Analysis

	1994	1993	1992	1991	1990	1989
Curr. Ratio	NA	NA	NA	NA	NA	NA
% LT Debt of Cap.	13.1	23.9	35.4	52.3	59.9	61.7
% Net Inc.of Revs.	11.0	11.3	10.6	8.9	7.6	6.7
% Ret. on Assets	10.7	9.4	7.3	6.1	6.2	7.0
% Ret. on Equity	17.0	16.7	15.4	16.6	20.2	20.5

Dividend Data (Cash dividends were initiated with the January 1995 payment. The shares were split five-for-four in December of each of the past five years.)

Amt. of Div. $	Date Decl.	Ex-Div. Date	Stock of Record	Payment Date
5-for-4	Nov. 10	Dec. 09	Nov. 24	Dec. 10 '93
5-for-4	Nov. 09	Dec. 06	Nov. 21	Dec. 05 '94
0.020	Nov. 09	Dec. 15	Dec. 21	Jan. 04 '95
0.020	Feb. 09	Mar. 23	Mar. 29	Apr. 19 '95
0.020	May. 22	Jun. 26	Jun. 28	Jul. 19 '95

Data as orig. reptd.; bef. results of disc. opers. and/or spec. items. Per share data adj. for stk. divs. as of ex-div. date. E-Estimated. NA-Not Available. NM-Not Meaningful. NR-Not Ranked.

Office—623 Market St. (P.O. Box 15169), Knoxville, TN 37902. **Tel**—(615) 970-7200. **Chrmn & CEO**—J. L. Clayton. **Pres**—J. H. Stegmayer. **Secy**—K. T. Clayton. **Dirs**—B. J. Clayton, J. L. Clayton, J. D. Cockman, W. Doud, D. W. Evins, W. Jordan, C. W. Neel, J. H. Stegmayer. **Transfer Agent & Registrar**—Trust Co. Bank, Atlanta. **Incorporated** in Tennessee in 1968. **Empl**-3,955. **S&P Analyst:** Michael W. Jaffe

STANDARD & POOR'S

STOCK REPORTS

Cleveland-Cliffs

NYSE Symbol **CLF**
In S&P MidCap 400

19-OCT-95 **Industry:** Steel-Iron

Summary: Cleveland-Cliffs is the largest independent manager, processor and lessor of iron ore reserves in North America.

Quantitative Evaluations
Outlook
(1 Lowest—5 Highest)
• **4**
Fair Value
• **42¼**
Risk
• **Low**
Earn./Div. Rank
• **B**

Technical Eval.
• **Bearish** since 9/95
Rel. Strength Rank
(1 Lowest—99 Highest)
• **29**
Insider Activity
• **Unfavorable**

Recent Price • 39¼
52 Wk Range • 46¾-34
Yield • 3.2%
12-Mo. P/E • 8.4

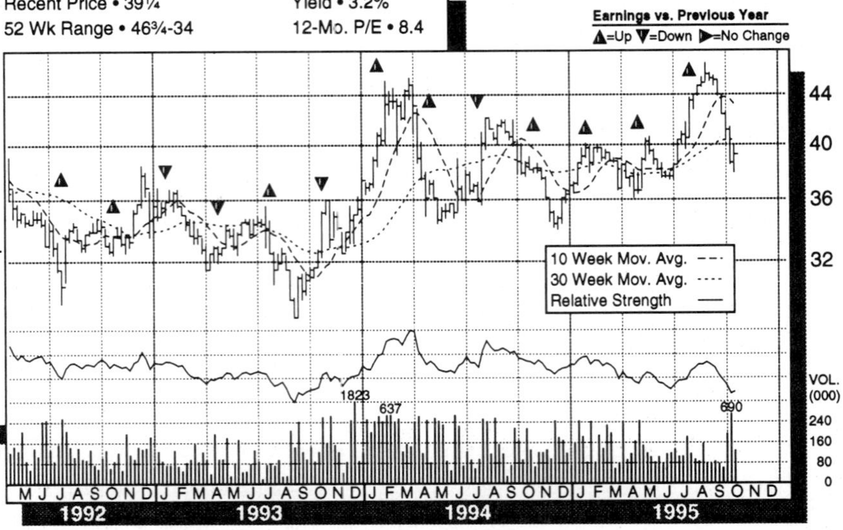

Business Profile - 19-OCT-95

CLF is engaged in the production and sale of iron ore pellets. The company expects iron ore production at its managed mines to total 40 million tons for 1995; pellet sales for the full year are expected to be about 10 million tons. CLF seeks to improve results by entering the scrap substitutes market and instituting a cost cutting program. Through July 31, 1995, the company had repurchased 214,300 shares of its common stock under a program calling for the repurchase of up to 600,000 shares.

Operational Review - 19-OCT-95

Total revenues in the six months ended June 30, 1995, rose 36%, reflecting higher iron ore production levels at the company's managed mines (resulting from the acquisition of Northshore Mining Company in September 1994) and increased pellet sales. Significantly higher other expenses limited the gain in pretax income to 11%. However, with a tax benefit of $7.1 million contrasting with taxes at 25.9%, net income more than doubled, to $25.9 million ($2.16 a share) from $12.6 million ($1.04).

Stock Performance - 13-OCT-95

In the past 30 trading days, CLF's shares have declined 13%, compared to a 4% rise in the S&P 500. Average trading volume for the past five days was 25,060 shares, compared with the 40-day moving average of 35,213 shares.

Key Stock Statistics

Dividend Rate/Share	1.30	Shareholders	3,700
Shs. outstg. (M)	11.9	Market cap. (B)	$0.477
Avg. daily vol. (M)	0.054	Inst. holdings	98%
Tang. Bk. Value/Share	26.95	Insider holdings	NA
Beta	0.32		

Value of $10,000 invested 5 years ago: $ 18,380

Fiscal Year Ending Dec. 31

	1995	% Change	1994	% Change	1993	% Change
Revenues (Million $)						
1Q	63.60	28%	49.50	14%	43.30	-19%
2Q	118.9	40%	85.00	-30%	121.7	30%
3Q	—	—	111.0	27%	87.60	-19%
4Q	—	—	143.4	39%	103.3	43%
Yr.	—	—	388.9	9%	355.9	9%
Income (Million $)						
1Q	5.00	127%	2.20	NM	-0.01	NM
2Q	20.90	101%	10.40	-69%	33.50	186%
3Q	—	—	14.80	106%	7.20	-50%
4Q	—	—	15.40	10%	14.00	NM
Yr.	—	—	42.80	-22%	54.60	77%
Earnings Per Share ($)						
1Q	0.41	128%	0.18	NM	-0.01	NM
2Q	1.75	103%	0.86	-69%	2.79	185%
3Q	—	—	1.23	105%	0.60	-50%
4Q	—	—	1.27	9%	1.17	NM
Yr.	—	—	3.54	-22%	4.55	77%

Next earnings report expected: mid October

Cleveland-Cliffs

Business Summary - 19-OCT-95

Cleveland-Cliffs is the largest independent manager and lessor of iron ore reserves in North America. Its principal business is the production and sale of iron ore pellets.

Through subsidiaries, CLF manages the development, construction and operation of six iron ore mines, including five in North America and one in Australia, and the concentrating and pelletizing plants to produce iron ore pellets for steelmakers. The subsidiaries are reimbursed by the participants of the various mining ventures for substantially all expenses directly and indirectly incurred in operating the respective mines. Additionally, they are paid a management fee based on the number of tons of iron ore produced, which is subject to quarterly adjustment.

Iron ore pellet production from the six mines managed by CLF totaled 36.7 million tons in 1994, versus 33.8 million tons in 1993. Sales from CLF's own mines were 9.7 million in 1994, versus 7.8 million in 1993. CLF's six mines and pellet plants in North America and Australia had 41.1 million tons of annual production capacity following the acquisition of Northshore Mining in September 1994.

CLF intends to discontinue its Australian operation in 1997's first quarter. Mine closure costs have been provided for in the company's capacity rationalization reserve.

In 1994, McLouth Steel Products, WCI and Weirton Steel Co. directly and indirectly accounted for 14.0%, 14.0% and 12.0% of total revenues.

Some 80% of the company's production is committed to multi-year sales contracts with pre-determined price escalation provisions.

Through joint ventures, CLF is engaged in refining technology to produce iron carbide, a form of reduced iron that does not have to be pelletized or briquetted before being charged into a steelmaking furnace.

Important Developments

Oct. '95—CLF announced that McLouth Steel Products Company, a major customer, has filed for Chapter 11 bankruptcy protection. McLouth intends to continue operations under its existing purchase arrangements, and CLF is currently continuing to ship to McLouth. Another significant customer, WCI Steel, Inc., has informed CLF that it is temporarily suspending operations due to a labor strike. Combined, McLouth and WCI represent approximately 23% of CLF's estimated 1995 products and services revenue.

Capitalization

Long Term Debt: $57,900,000 (6/95).

Per Share Data ($) (Year Ended Dec. 31)

	1994	1993	1992	1991	1990	1989
Tangible Bk. Val.	25.74	23.27	22.49	24.40	24.88	19.36
Cash Flow	3.84	4.77	2.80	4.80	6.50	5.58
Earnings	3.54	4.55	2.57	4.55	6.31	5.37
Dividends	1.23	2.20	1.17	5.03	0.80	0.40
Payout Ratio	35%	48%	46%	111%	13%	7%
Prices - High	45½	37½	40⅜	36½	35	34
- Low	34	28¾	29½	25	19⅝	25¾
P/E Ratio - High	13	8	16	8	6	6
- Low	10	6	11	5	3	5

Income Statement Analysis (Million $)

	1994	%Chg	1993	%Chg	1992	%Chg	1991
Revs.	380	23%	308	NM	311	-2%	317
Oper. Inc.	67.4	59%	42.4	11%	38.3	-15%	45.2
Depr.	3.7	42%	2.6	-7%	2.8	NM	2.8
Int. Exp.	6.6	NM	6.6	32%	5.0	32%	3.8
Pretax Inc.	58.0	-24%	76.0	85%	41.0	-41%	70.0
Eff. Tax Rate	26%	—	28%	—	26%	—	23%
Net Inc.	42.8	-22%	54.6	77%	30.8	-43%	53.8

Balance Sheet & Other Fin. Data (Million $)

	1994	1993	1992	1991	1990	1989
Cash	141	161	129	96.0	98.0	96.0
Curr. Assets	269	250	249	206	266	178
Total Assets	617	545	537	473	508	411
Curr. Liab.	100	64.0	60.0	66.0	941	79.0
LT Debt	70.0	75.0	75.0	29.0	41.0	53.0
Common Eqty.	311	281	270	291	291	226
Total Cap.	381	356	345	358	366	313
Cap. Exp.	6.9	2.8	2.9	2.9	2.5	2.9
Cash Flow	46.5	57.2	33.6	56.6	76.1	64.7

Ratio Analysis

	1994	1993	1992	1991	1990	1989
Curr. Ratio	2.7	3.9	4.1	3.1	2.8	2.3
% LT Debt of Cap.	18.4	21.1	21.8	8.2	11.3	16.9
% Net Inc.of Revs.	11.3	17.7	9.9	17.0	23.8	17.8
% Ret. on Assets	7.4	10.1	6.1	10.9	16.1	15.6
% Ret. on Equity	14.4	19.8	11.0	18.3	28.5	31.6

Dividend Data —Dividends were resumed in 1989 after having been omitted in 1986. A dividend reinvestment plan is available. A revised "poison pill" stock purchase rights plan was adopted in 1991.

Amt. of Div. $	Date Decl.	Ex-Div. Date	Stock of Record	Payment Date
0.325	Nov. 08	Dec. 06	Dec. 12	Dec. 27 '94
0.325	Jan. 10	Feb. 13	Feb. 20	Mar. 03 '95
0.325	May. 09	May. 17	May. 23	Jun. 07 '95
0.325	Jul. 11	Aug. 16	Aug. 18	Sep. 08 '95

Data as orig. reptd.; bef. results of disc. opers. and/or spec. items. Per share data adj. for stk. divs. as of ex-div. date. E-Estimated. NA-Not Available. NM-Not Meaningful. NR-Not Ranked.

Office—1100 Superior Ave., 18th Floor, Cleveland, OH 44114-2589. **Tel**—(216) 694-5700. **Chrmn & CEO**—M. T. Moore. **Secy**—J. E. Lenhard. **EVP-CFO**—J. S. Brinzo. **Investor Contact**—F. Rice. **Dirs**—R. S. Colman, J. D. Ireland III, G. F. Joklik, E. B. Jones, L. L. Kanuk, M. T. Moore, J. C. Morley, S. B. Oresman, A. Schwartz, S. K. Scovil, J. H. Wade, A. W. Whitehouse Jr. **Transfer Agent & Registrar**—Society National Bank, Cleveland. **Incorporated** in Ohio in 1947; reincorporated in Ohio in 1985. **Empl**-6,309. **S&P Analyst:** N. Rosenberg

STANDARD & POOR'S

STOCK REPORTS

Coca-Cola Enterprises

NYSE Symbol **CCE**

In S&P MidCap 400

20-OCT-95 **Industry:** Beverages

Summary: This company is the world's largest bottler of Coca-Cola beverage products, distributing to about 55% of the population of the U.S. Coca-Cola Co. holds 44% of CCE's common stock.

S&P Opinion: Buy (★★★★★)

Recent Price • 25⅝	Yield • 0.2%
52 Wk Range • 25⅝-16⅜	12-Mo. P/E • 35.1

Quantitative Evaluations

Outlook (1 Lowest—5 Highest)
• **1+**

Fair Value
• **19¾**

Risk
• **Low**

Earn./Div. Rank
• **B-**

Technical Eval.
• **Bullish** since 2/93

Rel. Strength Rank (1 Lowest—99 Highest)
• **92**

Insider Activity
• **NA**

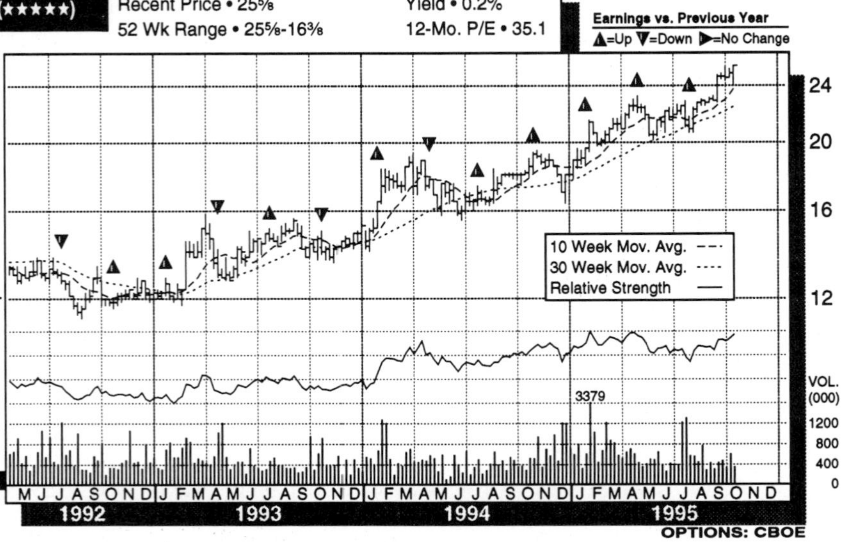

OPTIONS: CBOE

Overview - 19-OCT-95

Net operating revenues are expected to climb at a 10% to 15% annual rate through 1996, driven primarily by increased case volumes, higher net selling prices, and acquisition contributions. Near-term operating profit margins should be maintained, as growth in net operating revenue per case largely offsets higher material costs. This should be achieved by higher net selling prices, an improving product mix that increasingly emphasizes noncarbonated beverage offerings, and by a growing presence in the more-profitable cold drink distribution channel. Cash operating profits (operating income plus depreciation and amortization charges) are seen climbing 9% to 10% in 1995, and about 8% to 10% annually thereafter.

Valuation - 19-OCT-95

Given our bullish forecast for both cash operating profit and earnings per share growth through 1996, the shares are attractive at current levels. This equity has been a strong performer over the past two years, driven by an improved, more stable reported net earnings stream. We expect the shares to continue their upward climb near-term, boosted by steadily rising earnings per share. Longer-term prospects are also bright, reflecting CCE's aggressive acquisition policy, and substantial economies of scale advantages over competitors. Finances are sound despite a high debt load, due to a steady cash inflow, and to CCE's close relationship with deep-pocketed Coca-Cola Co.

Key Stock Statistics

S&P EPS Est. 1995	0.74	Tang. Bk. Value/Share	10.67
P/E on S&P Est. 1995	34.6	Beta	1.15
S&P EPS Est. 1996	0.85	Shareholders	8,900
Dividend Rate/Share	0.05	Market cap. (B)	$ 3.5
Shs. outstg. (M)	129.7	Inst. holdings	42%
Avg. daily vol. (M)	0.119	Insider holdings	NA

Value of $10,000 invested 5 years ago: $ 16,320

Fiscal Year Ending Dec. 31

	1995	% Change	1994	% Change	1993	% Change
Revenues (Million $)						
1Q	1,462	11%	1,320	9%	1,208	9%
2Q	1,827	13%	1,610	11%	1,448	5%
3Q	1,841	15%	1,595	7%	1,487	10%
4Q	—	—	1,486	12%	1,322	3%
Yr.	—	—	6,011	10%	5,465	7%
Income (Million $)						
1Q	3.00	NM	-6.00	NM	-5.00	NM
2Q	46.00	21%	38.00	138%	16.00	NM
3Q	36.00	38%	26.00	NM	-30.00	NM
4Q	—	—	11.00	175%	4.00	NM
Yr.	—	—	69.00	NM	-15.00	NM
Earnings Per Share ($)						
1Q	0.02	NM	-0.06	NM	-0.04	NM
2Q	0.35	21%	0.29	123%	0.13	NM
3Q	0.27	42%	0.19	NM	-0.23	NM
4Q	E0.10	11%	0.09	NM	0.03	NM
Yr.	E0.74	42%	0.52	NM	-0.11	NM

Next earnings report expected: late January

Coca-Cola Enterprises

Business Summary - 19-OCT-95

Coca-Cola Enterprises is the world's largest bottler of Coca-Cola beverage products, distributing approximately 55% of all bottle/can volume of carbonated soft-drink products of The Coca-Cola Co. (KO) in the United States.

CCE's bottling territories in the U.S. include portions of 38 states, the District of Columbia, the U.S. Virgin Islands, and the islands of Tortola and Grand Cayman. These territories contain approximately 139 million people, and represent about 54% of the population of the U.S. CCE also serves the Netherlands, whose population is about 15 million. In 1994, about 70% of CCE's equivalent-case sales represented products bearing the "Coca-Cola" or "Coke" trademarks, approximately 19% were of other soft drinks of KO and about 11% represented products of other soft-drink firms.

The company conducts its business primarily under bottle contracts with KO, whereby CCE receives the exclusive right to produce and market Coca-Cola soft drinks in authorized containers in specified territories and provide KO with the ability, in its sole discretion, to set prices for concentrates and syrups. CCE operates 45 soft-drink production facilities, 17 of which are solely production facilities, and 28 of which are combination production/distribution facilities. It also operates 223 facilities that are solely distribution facilities.

Important Developments

Oct. '95—On a comparable basis (adjusted for acquisitions), cash operating profit (operating income plus depreciation and amortization charges) in 1995's first half rose 9%, year to year, driven by higher (constant territory) case bottle/can volume (4%) and fountain gallon volume (7.5%). Although bottle and can cost of sales per case in 1995's first nine months rose 10.5%, year to year, these cost pressures were moderated by a 7% increase in net operating revenue per case during the same period. This was achieved primarily by higher net selling prices, and to a lesser extent, from favorable trends in product, package and channel mix. Separately, the effective tax rate during 1995's first nine months period eased to 43.3%, from 47.3%.

Capitalization

Long Term Debt: $4,331,000,000 (6/95).
Preferred Stock: 1,000,000 shs. ($35 stated value); conv. sh.-for-sh. into com.

Per Share Data ($) (Year Ended Dec. 31)

	1994	1993	1992	1991	1990	1989
Tangible Bk. Val.	10.14	9.53	9.70	-21.41	-14.55	-11.77
Cash Flow	4.06	3.13	2.90	1.38	2.62	2.18
Earnings	0.52	-0.11	-0.11	-0.79	0.65	0.41
Dividends	0.05	0.05	0.05	0.05	0.05	0.05
Payout Ratio	10%	NM	NM	NM	7%	11%
Prices - High	19½	15⅞	16¼	20⅜	16⅞	18¾
- Low	14	11¾	11¼	11¾	12¼	14¾
P/E Ratio - High	37	NM	NM	NM	26	46
- Low	27	NM	NM	NM	19	36

Income Statement Analysis (Million $)

	1994	%Chg	1993	%Chg	1992	%Chg	1991
Revs.	6,011	10%	5,465	7%	5,127	27%	4,051
Oper. Inc.	901	12%	804	16%	695	29%	538
Depr.	461	10%	419	8%	389	55%	251
Int. Exp.	310	-5%	328	5%	312	45%	215
Pretax Inc.	127	131%	55.0	NM	-12.0	NM	-91.0
Eff. Tax Rate	46%	—	127%	—	NM	—	NM
Net Inc.	69.0	NM	-15.0	NM	-15.0	NM	-82.0

Balance Sheet & Other Fin. Data (Million $)

	1994	1993	1992	1991	1990	1989
Cash	22.0	11.0	6.0	64.1	0.5	9.7
Curr. Assets	810	746	701	706	495	493
Total Assets	8,738	8,682	8,805	6,677	5,021	4,732
Curr. Liab.	1,089	1,007	1,304	1,385	1,055	996
LT Debt	3,896	4,083	3,509	3,407	1,960	1,756
Common Eqty.	1,310	1,231	1,254	1,443	1,376	1,430
Total Cap.	7,119	7,174	6,330	5,141	3,922	3,702
Cap. Exp.	366	353	291	238	259	273
Cash Flow	528	404	374	160	313	283

Ratio Analysis

	1994	1993	1992	1991	1990	1989
Curr. Ratio	0.7	0.7	0.5	0.5	0.5	0.5
% LT Debt of Cap.	54.7	56.9	55.4	66.3	50.0	47.4
% Net Inc.of Revs.	1.1	NM	NM	NM	2.3	1.8
% Ret. on Assets	0.8	NM	NM	NM	2.0	1.6
% Ret. on Equity	5.3	NM	NM	NM	5.7	3.7

Dividend Data —Dividends were initiated in 1987. A dividend reinvestment plan is available.

Amt. of Div. $	Date Decl.	Ex-Div. Date	Stock of Record	Payment Date
0.013	Oct. 18	Dec. 13	Dec. 19	Dec. 29 '94
0.013	Feb. 15	Mar. 20	Mar. 24	Apr. 03 '95
0.013	Apr. 17	Jun. 21	Jun. 23	Jul. 03 '95
0.013	Jul. 18	Sep. 20	Sep. 22	Oct. 02 '95
0.013	Oct. 17	Dec. 14	Dec. 18	Dec. 28 '95

Data as orig. reptd.; bef. results of disc. opers. and/or spec. items. Per share data adj. for stk. divs. as of ex-div. date. E-Estimated. NA-Not Available. NM-Not Meaningful. NR-Not Ranked.

Office—One Coca-Cola Plaza, N.W., Atlanta, GA 30313. **Tel**—(404) 676-2100. **Chrmn**—M. D. Ivester. **Vice Chrmn & CEO**—S. K. Johnston Jr. **Pres**—H. A. Schimberg. **Sr VP-CFO**—J. R. Alm. **Secy**—J. G. Beatty Jr. **Investor Contact**—Margaret Carton. **Dirs**—H. Buffett, J. L. Clendenin, J. B. Cole, T. M. Hahn Jr., C. M. Halle, L. P. Humann, E. N. Isdell, M. D. Ivester, J. E. Jacob, S. K. Johnston Jr., R. A. Keller, W. D. Looney, S. L. Probasco Jr., H. A. Schimberg, F. A. Tarkenton. **Transfer Agent & Registrar**—First Chicago Trust Co. of New York, NYC. **Incorporated** in Delaware in 1944. **Empl**-30,000. **S&P Analyst:** Kenneth A. Shea

STANDARD & POOR'S

STOCK REPORTS

Comdisco, Inc.

NYSE Symbol **CDO**
In S&P MidCap 400

09-SEP-95

Industry:
Data Processing

Summary: Comdisco is primarily involved in buying, selling and leasing new and used computer and high-technology equipment. It also provides disaster recovery services for computer users.

S&P Opinion: Buy (★★★★★)

Recent Price • 30½
52 Wk Range • 32½-19⅜
Yield • 1.2%
12-Mo. P/E • 21.5

Quantitative Evaluations

Outlook
(1 Lowest—5 Highest)
• **3+**

Fair Value
• **30¼**

Risk
• **Low**

Earn./Div. Rank
• **B-**

Technical Eval.
• **Neutral** since 8/95

Rel. Strength Rank
(1 Lowest—99 Highest)
• **26**

Insider Activity
• **Neutral**

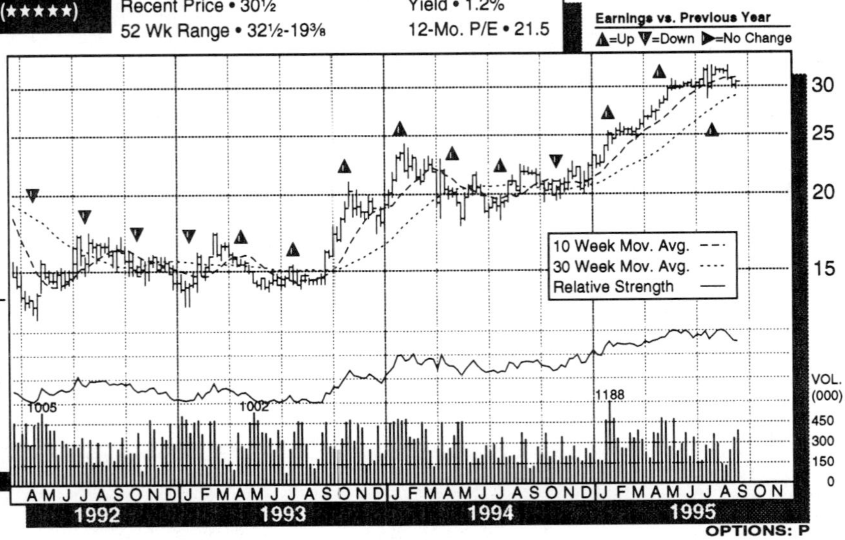

OPTIONS: P

Overview - 06-SEP-95

Earnings per share should achieve double-digit growth in fiscal 1996, as the leasing of non-IBM products and the remarketing of older equipment, both having higher margins, account for a greater percentage of total revenues. The Electronics Group, started in 1993, will begin to remarket its equipment in mid-1996. The electronics portfolio is CDO's most profitable portfolio sector. Contributions from the disaster recovery group should rise, fueled by internal growth and productivity improvements. The newly formed systems integration (SI) business, which is performing better than expected, should break even in fiscal 1996. The primary benefit of the SI entry is the additional leasing business that CDO would not otherwise book. The company hopes to continue its policy of using 50% of its earnings to repurchase stock (directors have authorized a $25 million program).

Valuation - 06-SEP-95

Trading at approximately 10x estimated 1996 per share earnings, these shares are undervalued. Fundamentals remain strong as revenue diversification has increased in the past year. In recent periods, an increasing percentage of revenues was attributed to higher-margin, non-IBM equipment, a trend that is expected to continue. Promodata S.A. (France) has already started to contribute to CDO's bottom line. Continued cost-cutting and higher margins from re-leasing equipment will boost future earnings.

Key Stock Statistics

S&P EPS Est. 1995	2.61	Tang. Bk. Value/Share	19.11
P/E on S&P Est. 1995	11.7	Beta	1.40
S&P EPS Est. 1996	2.95	Shareholders	2,200
Dividend Rate/Share	0.36	Market cap. (B)	$ 1.1
Shs. outstg. (M)	35.0	Inst. holdings	50%
Avg. daily vol. (M)	0.054	Insider holdings	NA

Value of $10,000 invested 5 years ago: $ 14,109

Fiscal Year Ending Sep. 30

	1995	% Change	1994	% Change	1993	% Change
Revenues (Million $)						
1Q	524.0	-2%	536.0	-6%	571.0	3%
2Q	593.0	12%	529.0	NM	530.0	NM
3Q	539.0	5%	514.0	NM	513.0	-9%
4Q	—	—	519.0	-4%	539.0	-3%
Yr.	—	—	2,098	-3%	2,153	-2%
Income (Million $)						
1Q	25.00	19%	21.00	5%	20.00	NM
2Q	26.00	18%	22.00	5%	21.00	NM
3Q	26.00	18%	22.00	-4%	23.00	35%
4Q	—	—	21.00	-9%	23.00	28%
Yr.	—	—	95.00	79%	53.00	165%
Earnings Per Share ($)						
1Q	0.62	15%	0.54	17%	0.46	-8%
2Q	0.64	16%	0.55	15%	0.48	NM
3Q	0.66	16%	0.57	14%	0.50	22%
4Q	E0.69	NM	-0.53	NM	0.53	20%
Yr.	E2.61	125%	1.16	-41%	1.97	NM

Next earnings report expected: late October

Comdisco, Inc.

Business Summary - 07-SEP-95

Comdisco is primarily involved in buying, selling and leasing new and used computer and other high-technology equipment and in providing disaster recovery services. The company also provides asset management and technical planning services. Revenue sources in recent fiscal years were:

	1994	1993	1992
Leasing	73%	74%	75%
Sales	13%	14%	14%
Disaster recovery	12%	10%	9%
Other	2%	2%	2%

The company buys or leases, and in turn sells, leases or subleases, IBM computer equipment, as well as computer equipment manufactured by others. Sales and lease transactions include mainframe central processing units and/or various peripherals, such as printers, tape and disk drives and other equipment used with a mainframe. The focus of activities with respect to particular models of computer equipment changes periodically as a result of changes in market conditions and advances in computer technology.

Comdisco leases other high-technology equipment, primarily telecommunications and other office and communications products, including PCs, workstations, point-of-sale devices, bridges and routers. Through subsidiaries, it leases and refurbishes medical equipment.

The company also provides disaster recovery services to support a customer's data processing needs in the event of fire, flood, power outage or other disaster. Services include emergency data processing backup, voice recovery and consulting services.

Important Developments

Jul. '95—The company was authorized to repurchase an aggregate of $25 million of CDO common and/or preferred stock. Comdisco also noted that during fiscal 1995's third quarter, its European operations reported record results. Additionally, the company noted that during the period, remarketing activity was strong and that its lease base continued to grow as the cost of equipment placed on lease exceeded $500 million for the third successive quarter. Management expects to report record earnings per share for the fiscal year.

Capitalization

Total Debt: $2,235,000,000 (6/95).
Discounted Lease Rentals: $1,254,000,000.
8.75% Cum. Pfd. Stock, Ser. A.: 3,000,000 shs. ($25 liq. preference).
8.75% Cum. Pfd. Stock, Ser. B.: 1,000,000 shs. ($25 liq. preference).

Per Share Data ($) (Year Ended Sep. 30)

	1994	1993	1992	1991	1990	1989
Tangible Bk. Val.	17.47	16.55	15.38	15.63	14.38	12.56
Cash Flow	26.91	21.91	20.88	20.99	17.40	13.58
Earnings	1.16	1.97	0.49	2.03	1.99	2.45
Dividends	0.35	0.29	0.27	0.27	0.26	0.23
Payout Ratio	30%	15%	56%	13%	12%	9%
Prices - High	24¼	21	21	27	27⅛	32⅜
- Low	17¾	13⅛	12½	17¼	14	19⅞
P/E Ratio - High	21	11	47	13	14	13
- Low	15	7	26	9	7	8

Income Statement Analysis (Million $)

	1994	%Chg	1993	%Chg	1992	%Chg	1991
Revs.	2,098	-3%	2,153	-2%	2,205	1%	2,174
Oper. Inc.	1,424	15%	1,236	-5%	1,297	1%	1,278
Depr.	992	24%	801	-4%	833	7%	776
Int. Exp.	263	-10%	291	-17%	350	-4%	366
Pretax Inc.	89.0	-38%	144	NM	34.0	-75%	136
Eff. Tax Rate	40%	—	30%	—	41%	—	39%
Net Inc.	53.0	-39%	87.0	NM	20.0	-76%	83.0

Balance Sheet & Other Fin. Data (Million $)

	1994	1993	1992	1991	1990	1989
Cash	88.0	118	142	141	75.0	21.0
Curr. Assets	NA	NA	NA	NA	NA	NA
Total Assets	4,807	4,960	5,236	5,006	4,785	4,045
Curr. Liab.	NA	NA	NA	NA	NA	NA
LT Debt	1,759	1,829	2,048	2,199	2,070	1,629
Common Eqty.	641	639	624	634	589	548
Total Cap.	2,729	2,766	2,966	3,057	2,832	2,335
Cap. Exp.	1,451	1,044	1,294	1,604	1,268	1,108
Cash Flow	1,036	881	853	859	742	598

Ratio Analysis

	1994	1993	1992	1991	1990	1989
Curr. Ratio	NA	NA	NA	NA	NA	NA
% LT Debt of Cap.	64.5	66.1	69.0	71.9	73.1	69.8
% Net Inc.of Revs.	2.5	4.0	0.9	3.8	4.4	6.4
% Ret. on Assets	1.1	1.8	0.4	1.7	2.0	2.9
% Ret. on Equity	7.0	13.0	3.2	13.6	15.4	21.6

Dividend Data —Dividends were initiated in 1977.

Amt. of Div. $	Date Decl.	Ex-Div. Date	Stock of Record	Payment Date
0.090	Jul. 20	Aug. 02	Aug. 08	Sep. 06 '94
0.090	Nov. 08	Nov. 14	Nov. 18	Dec. 05 '94
0.090	Jan. 24	Feb. 06	Feb. 10	Mar. 13 '95
0.090	Apr. 25	May. 22	May. 26	Jun. 19 '95
0.090	Jul. 25	Aug. 02	Aug. 04	Sep. 04 '95

Data as orig. reptd.; bef. results of disc. opers. and/or spec. items. Per share data adj. for stk. divs. as of ex-div. date. E-Estimated. NA-Not Available. NM-Not Meaningful. NR-Not Ranked.

Office—6111 North River Rd., Rosemont, IL 60018. **Tel**—(708) 698-3000. **Pres & CEO**—J. F. Slevin. **SVP & Secy**—P. A. Hewes **EVP & CFO**—J. J. Vosicky. **VP & Investor Contact**—James J. Hyland. **Dirs**—A. J. Andreini, R. A. Bardagy, E. H. Fiedler, Jr., C. K. Hartley, P. A. Hewes, R. Kash, T. H. Patrick, N. K. Pontikes, W. N. Pontikes, J. F. Slevin, B. R. Twist, Jr., J. J. Vosicky. **Registrar & Principal Transfer Agent**—Chemical Bank, NYC. **Incorporated** in Delaware in 1971. **Empl-** 2,000. **S&P Analyst:** Steven A. Jaworski

STANDARD & POOR'S

STOCK REPORTS

Comerica Inc.

NYSE Symbol **CMA**
In S&P MidCap 400

11-SEP-95 **Industry:** Banking

Summary: This Detroit-based bank holding company operates banking affiliates in Michigan, Texas, California, Illinois and Florida.

S&P Opinion: Hold (★★★)

Recent Price • 36¼ | 52 Wk Range • 36¾-24⅛ | Yield • 3.9% | 12-Mo. P/E • 10.8

Quantitative Evaluations
Outlook (1 Lowest—5 Highest) • 3+
Fair Value • 35⅞
Risk • Low
Earn./Div. Rank • A-

Technical Eval. • **Bullish** since 2/95
Rel. Strength Rank (1 Lowest—99 Highest) • 65
Insider Activity • **Unfavorable**

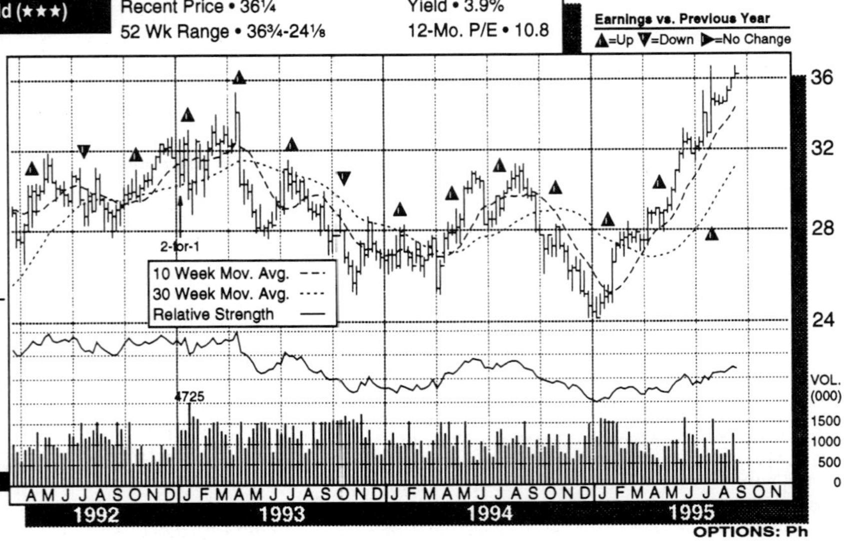

Overview - 11-SEP-95

Loan growth is expected to slow to the 8% - 12% range in the second half of 1995, from the 18% recorded for the first half of 1995, on reduced economic activity in the company's service territory. The net interest margin, penalized thus far this year on higher funding costs, is expected to level off slightly below the current level of 4.15% given projections of sluggish deposit growth, leading to an increase in net interest income of about 4%. Much of the expected earnings growth in the year ahead will likely come from a modest gain in noninterest income, mostly in the revolving credit fee area, and good control of operating expenses. The allowance for loan losses stood at 171% of nonperforming loans at June 30, 1995, and the provision for loan loss is not expected to be a drag on earnings.

Valuation - 11-SEP-95

The shares have risen strongly thus far in 1995, despite only modestly improved earnings, as investors continue to value the bank as a potential takeover target. However, with the shares trading above the price to earnings multiple of other regional banks and at about 1.7 times the company's book value, a large takeover premium from the current price is not likely. Fundamentally, with the expectation of slowing loan growth in the year ahead, the shares are ranked a hold for their above-average yield and the company's reasonably strong credit quality.

Key Stock Statistics

S&P EPS Est. 1995	3.50	Tang. Bk. Value/Share	22.02
P/E on S&P Est. 1995	10.4	Beta	1.44
S&P EPS Est. 1996	3.75	Shareholders	16,500
Dividend Rate/Share	1.40	Market cap. (B)	$ 4.1
Shs. outstg. (M)	112.8	Inst. holdings	62%
Avg. daily vol. (M)	0.173	Insider holdings	NA

Value of $10,000 invested 5 years ago: $ 28,757

Fiscal Year Ending Dec. 31

	1995	% Change	1994	% Change	1993	% Change
Revenues (Million $)						
1Q	741.1	33%	557.3	2%	543.9	-9%
2Q	781.9	24%	629.5	13%	557.5	-3%
3Q	—	—	657.6	20%	548.1	-1%
4Q	—	—	704.2	18%	595.8	10%
Yr.	—	—	2,559	14%	2,245	-1%
Income (Million $)						
1Q	100.0	10%	90.86	13%	80.67	9%
2Q	101.5	2%	99.2	18%	83.73	NM
3Q	—	—	100.6	20%	83.70	NM
4Q	—	—	96.60	7%	90.09	7%
Yr.	—	—	387.2	14%	340.6	51%
Earnings Per Share ($)						
1Q	0.85	8%	0.79	14%	0.69	9%
2Q	0.86	4%	0.83	19%	0.70	NM
3Q	E0.89	6%	0.84	20%	0.70	-1%
4Q	E0.90	10%	0.82	8%	0.76	6%
Yr.	E3.50	7%	3.28	15%	2.85	48%

Next earnings report expected: mid October

Comerica Inc.

Business Summary - 11-SEP-95

Comerica Inc. is the parent of Comerica Bank in Michigan, the second largest in the state, as well as Comerica Banks in Illinois, Texas, California and Florida. The company's five core businesses include corporate banking, consumer banking, private banking, institutional trust and investment management, and international finance and trade services.

Total loans at December 31, 1994, amounted to $22.2 billion, versus $19.12 billion a year earlier, and were divided:

	1994	1993
Commercial	48%	48%
Consumer	19%	19%
Comm'l. mortgage	14%	14%
Res. mortgages	11%	10%
International	5%	6%
Other	3%	3%

Nonperforming assets at year-end 1994 totaled $204 million (0.92% of loans and other real estate), down from $209 million (1.09%) a year earlier. The allowance for loan losses at December 31, 1994, was $326 million (1.47% of loans), up from $299 million (1.56%) at year-end 1993. Net chargeoffs during 1994 totaled $48 million (0.24% of average loans), down from $78 million (0.43%) in 1993.

Total deposits of $22.4 billion at year-end 1994 consisted of noninterest-bearing demand 23%, domestic interest-bearing deposits 66%, and foreign deposits 11%.

On a tax-equivalent basis, the average yield on interest-earning assets in 1994 was 7.28% (7.25% a year earlier), while the average rate paid on interest-bearing liabilities was 3.57% (3.18%), for a net interest spread of 3.71% (4.07%).

Important Developments

Jun. '95—The company reached a definitive agreement to acquire QuestStar Bank for $25 million in cash. QuestStar is a bank lender of small business administration loans that operates through three branch offices and four grocery store branches in the Houston, Texas, area.

May '95—CMA entered into an agreement to acquire Los Angeles-based Metrobank (assets of $1.3 billion) for about 4.2 million common shares valued at $120 million.

Mar. '95—The company acquired University Bank & Trust, Palo Alto, Calif. (assets of $490 million), for about 2.5 million common shares valued at $69 million.

Capitalization

Long Term Debt: $4,411,281,000 (6/95).

Per Share Data ($)

(Year Ended Dec. 31)

	1994	1993	1992	1991	1990	1989
Tangible Bk. Val.	18.31	18.99	15.46	13.51	12.77	11.32
Earnings	3.28	2.85	1.92	2.52	2.52	1.55
Dividends	1.24	1.07	0.96	0.92	0.87	0.77
Payout Ratio	38%	38%	50%	37%	34%	49%
Prices - High	31¼	35¼	32¾	26⅞	16⅜	19⅝
- Low	24⅛	25⅛	26¼	14	10¾	15⅛
P/E Ratio - High	10	12	17	11	6	13
- Low	7	9	14	6	4	10

Income Statement Analysis (Million $)

	1994	%Chg	1993	%Chg	1992	%Chg	1991
Net Int. Inc.	1,230	8%	1,134	4%	1,086	83%	595
Tax Equiv. Adj.	24.1	-20%	30.0	-20%	37.3	78%	21.0
Non Int. Inc.	463	NM	463	17%	395	117%	182
Loan Loss Prov.	56.0	-19%	69.0	-39%	113	95%	58.0
% Exp/Op Revs.	62%	—	64%	—	70%	—	63%
Pretax Inc.	582	19%	489	56%	313	44%	217
Eff. Tax Rate	33%	—	30%	—	28%	—	29%
Net Inc.	387	14%	341	51%	226	48%	153
% Net Int. Marg.	4.32%	—	4.65%	—	4.75%	—	4.87%

Balance Sheet & Other Fin. Data (Million $)

	1994	1993	1992	1991	1990	1989
Earning Assets:						
Money Mkt.	429	2,122	1,481	722	706	666
Inv. Securities	7,876	6,300	4,749	3,115	3,145	2,519
Com'l Loans	10,892	9,296	8,184	4,049	4,638	4,349
Other Loans	11,408	9,804	9,859	5,464	3,833	3,721
Total Assets	33,430	30,295	26,587	14,451	13,300	12,150
Demand Deposits	5,257	4,939	4,366	1,920	1,806	1,742
Time Deposits	17,175	16,011	16,029	9,521	8,949	8,141
LT Debt	1,742	1,461	737	239	264	274
Common Eqty.	2,392	2,182	1,988	1,010	749	663

Ratio Analysis

	1994	1993	1992	1991	1990	1989
% Ret. on Assets	1.2	1.3	0.9	1.1	1.1	0.7
% Ret. on Equity	16.7	15.9	12.0	16.6	17.8	12.0
% Loan Loss Resv.	1.5	1.6	1.6	1.3	1.3	2.5
% Loans/Deposits	99.4	91.2	88.5	81.9	77.6	80.4
% Equity to Assets	7.3	7.8	7.3	6.6	5.8	5.5

Dividend Data —Dividends have been paid since 1936. A dividend reinvestment plan is available. A "poison pill" stock purchase rights plan was adopted in 1988.

Amt. of Div. $	Date Decl.	Ex-Div. Date	Stock of Record	Payment Date
0.320	Jul. 19	Sep. 09	Sep. 15	Oct. 03 '94
0.320	Nov. 18	Dec. 09	Dec. 15	Jan. 02 '95
0.320	Jan. 20	Mar. 09	Mar. 15	Apr. 01 '95
0.350	May. 19	Jun. 13	Jun. 15	Jul. 01 '95
0.350	Jul. 21	Sep. 13	Sep. 15	Oct. 01 '95

Data as orig. reptd.; bef. results of disc opers. and/or spec. items. Per share data adj. for stk. divs. as of ex-div. date. E-Estimated. NA-Not Available. NM-Not Meaningful. NR-Not Ranked.

Office—Comerica Tower at Detroit Center, Detroit, MI 48226. **Tel**—(313) 222-3300. **Chrmn & CEO**—E. A. Miller. **Vice Chrmn**—J. D. Lewis. **Pres**—M. T. Monahan. **EVP & CFO**—P. H. Martzowka. **Investor Contact**—Allison Cione. **Dirs**—E. P. Casey, J. F. Cordes, J. P. DiNapoli, M. M. Fisher, J. D. Lewis, P. Shontz Longe, W. B. Lyon, G. V. MacDonald, E. A. Miller, M. T. Monahan, A. A. Piergallini, A. E. Schwartz, H. F. Sims. **Transfer Agent & Registrar**—Norwest Bank Minnesota, N.A., South St. Paul. **Incorporated** in Delaware in 1972. **Empl**-13,187. **S&P Analyst:** Stephen R. Biggar

Compuware Corp.

NASDAQ Symbol CPWR (Incl. in Nat'l Market) In S&P MidCap 400

Price	Range	P-E Ratio	Dividend	Yield	S&P Ranking	Beta
Oct. 16'95	1995					
18	43–17¾	11	None	None	NR	NA

Summary

This company provides software products and professional services designed to increase the productivity of the information systems departments of large enterprises deploying data processing technology.

Business Summary

Compuware Corp. develops, markets and supports an integrated line of software products focusing on programmer productivity. It also provides professional services to plan, develop and maintain computer systems for large corporations and public sector clients. Revenues in recent fiscal years were derived as follows:

	1995	1994
Software license fees	42%	42%
Maintenance fees	29%	29%
Professional service fees.....	29%	29%

The company's software products and professional services are designed to increase the productivity of the information systems departments of its target market, the largest 15,000 enterprises worldwide deploying data processing technology. Compuware's current products include an integrated line of mainframe run-time software products that improve programmer productivity in testing, debugging and maintaining large-scale application software, and client/server systems management and application development products that assist software developers in creating, deploying, managing and maintaining client/server applications.

Mainframe run-time software products are focused on improving the productivity of programmers and analysts in application testing, test data preparation, error analysis and maintenance of systems running on IBM and IBM-compatible mainframes. Products include file and data management tools such as the File-AID and XPERT series products, which provide a consistent, familiar and secure method for IS professionals to access data across all strategic environments; fault diagnosis products such as the Abend-AID, which assists programmers in more quickly and accurately analyzing and diagnosing software errors occurring during real time; interactive analysis and debugging products such as XPEDITER, which enables programmers to identify and resolve errors in complex software; and automatic testing products such as PLAYBACK, which simulates the on-line systems environment.

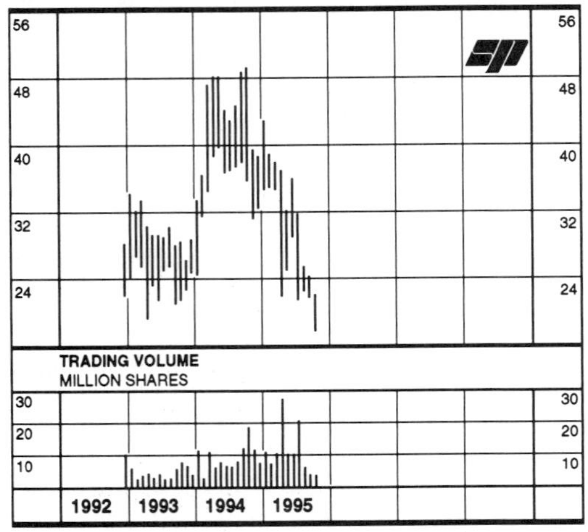

Client/server products include a family of applications testing products that provide testing of individual applications as well as load simulation of multiple terminals, transactions and users; systems management products that provide access to and control over entire systems of computers networks and applications; and application development tools such as UNIFACE, which is designed to assist software developers in the creation, deployment and maintenance of complex client/server applications.

The company's broad range of data processing professional services includes business systems analysis, design and programming, software conversion and systems planning and consulting.

Important Developments

Oct. '95— The company said it signed an agreement to acquire Los Altos, Calif.-based CoroNet Systems, which provides client/server networked applications performance management tools, for an undisclosed amount.

Per Share Data ($)

Yr. End Mar. 31	[1]1995	[1]1994	1993	[2]1992
Tangible Bk. Val.	**7.30**	6.31	4.62	d0.55
Cash Flow	**1.49**	1.70	1.19	d0.64
Earnings	**1.30**	1.52	1.03	d0.79
Dividends	**Nil**	Nil	Nil	Nil
Payout Ratio	**Nil**	Nil	Nil	Nil
Calendar Years	**1994**	1993	1992	1991
Prices—High	**49¼**	34¼	28¼	NA
Low	**24½**	19¼	24	NA
P/E Ratio—	**38–19**	23–13	27–23	NA

Data as orig. reptd. Adj. for stk. div. of 500% Dec. 1992. **1.** Refl. merger or acquisition. **2.** Refl. merger or acquisition and accounting change. NA-Not Available. d-Deficit.

Income Data (Million $)

Year Ended Mar. 31	Revs.	Oper. Inc.	% Oper. Inc. of Revs.	Cap. Exp.	Depr.	Int. Exp.	Net Bef. Taxes	Eff. Tax Rate	Net Inc.	% Net Inc. of Revs.	Cash Flow
[1]1995	**534**	**129**	**24.2**	**33.5**	**8.86**	**0.38**	**95.2**	**34.8%**	**62.1**	**11.6**	**71.0**
[1]1994	330	91	27.6	7.4	6.76	0.53	87.7	32.6%	59.1	17.9	65.9
1993	235	62	26.4	5.3	5.34	0.87	50.8	30.7%	35.2	15.0	40.2
[2]1992	175	29	16.3	4.0	4.89	2.09	d28.9	NM	d23.8	NM	d19.6

Balance Sheet Data (Million $)

Mar. 31	Cash	Curr. Assets	Curr. Liab.	Curr. Ratio	Total Assets	% Ret. on Assets	Long Term Debt	Common Equity	Total Cap.	% LT Debt of Cap.	% Ret. on Equity
1995	**165**	**370**	**180**	**2.1**	**524**	**12.8**	**Nil**	**336**	**344**	**NM**	**19.8**
1994	122	263	120	2.2	366	18.3	Nil	240	246	NM	28.2
1993	113	207	89	2.3	262	15.2	Nil	168	173	NM	NM
1992	5	85	101	0.8	135	NA	2.35	d9	35	6.7	NA

Data as orig. reptd. **1.** Refl. merger or acquisition. **2.** Refl. merger or acquisitionn and accounting change. NA-Not Available. NM-Not Meaingful. d-Deficit.

Revenues (Million $)

Quarter:	1995–96	1994–95
Jun.	126.2	109.6
Sep.		124.1
Dec.		147.5
Mar.		152.7
		533.9

Total revenues for the first quarter of fiscal 1996 advanced 15%, year to year, as higher maintenance and professional service fees offset a drop in license fees. Operating expenses rose only 0.9%, aided by the absence of restructuring and merger-related costs and purchased research and development, and net income of $7,788,000 ($0.17 a share, on 6.1% more shares) contrasted with a net loss of $4,691,000 ($0.11).

Common Share Earnings ($)

Quarter:	1995–96	1994–95
Jun.	0.17	d0.11
Sep.		0.37
Dec.		0.57
Mar.		0.46
		1.30

Dividend Data

No cash dividends have been paid. The company intends to retain its earnings for use in its business.

Finances

In May 1995, directors authorized the repurchase of up to $100 million of the company's common stock from time to time in the open market or private transactions. Through July 31, 1995, the company repurchased 955,000 shares at a total cost of $24.3 million.

At March 31, 1995, the company had no borrowings outstanding under a $30 million line of credit.

The company had about $23.7 million in net operating loss carryforwards available for income tax purposes at March 31, 1995.

In May 1994, Compuware issued 6,959,910 of its common shares to acquire Uniface Holding B.V., a supplier of client/server development tools for enterprise applications. In fiscal 1995, the company recognized $10.5 million of special charges related to the merger, restructuring and integration of Uniface. It also recorded an additional $8.5 million of merger costs related to claims made under a share escrow agreement entered into at the time of the merger.

Capitalization

Long Term Debt: None (6/95).

Common Stock: 43,987,261 shs. ($0.01 par). Institutions hold about 80%. Shareholders of record: 401 (6/95).

Options: To purchase 3,644,411 shs. at $0.37 to $41.75 ea. (3/95).

d-Deficit.

Office—31440 Northwestern Highway, Farmington Hills, MI 48334-2564. **Tel**—(810) 737-7300. **Chrmn & CEO**—P. Karmanos, Jr. **Pres & COO**—J. A. Nathan. **SVP, CFO & Treas**—R. A. Caponigro. **Dirs**—S. A. Denning, B. C. M. Douque, B. Goldsmith, W. O. Grabe, P. Karmanos, Jr., M. Lobsinger, J. A. Nathan, W. J. Prowse, T. Thewes. **Transfer Agent & Registrar**—NBD Bank, Boston. **Incorporated** in Michigan in 1973. **Empl**—4,105.

 Stephen R. Biggar

STANDARD & POOR'S

STOCK REPORTS

COMSAT Corp.

NYSE Symbol **CQ**
In S&P MidCap 400

18-OCT-95 **Industry:** Telecommunications

Summary: CQ has operations in international communications, mobile communications, entertainment and technology services.

S&P Opinion: Hold (★★★)

Recent Price • 21⅝
52 Wk Range • 24⅝-17½
Yield • 3.6%
12-Mo. P/E • 14.2

Quantitative Evaluations
Outlook
(1 Lowest—5 Highest)
• **1-**
Fair Value
• **16¾**
Risk
• **Average**
Earn./Div. Rank
• **B**

Technical Eval.
• **Bullish** since 7/95
Rel. Strength Rank
(1 Lowest—99 Highest)
• **25**
Insider Activity
• **Neutral**

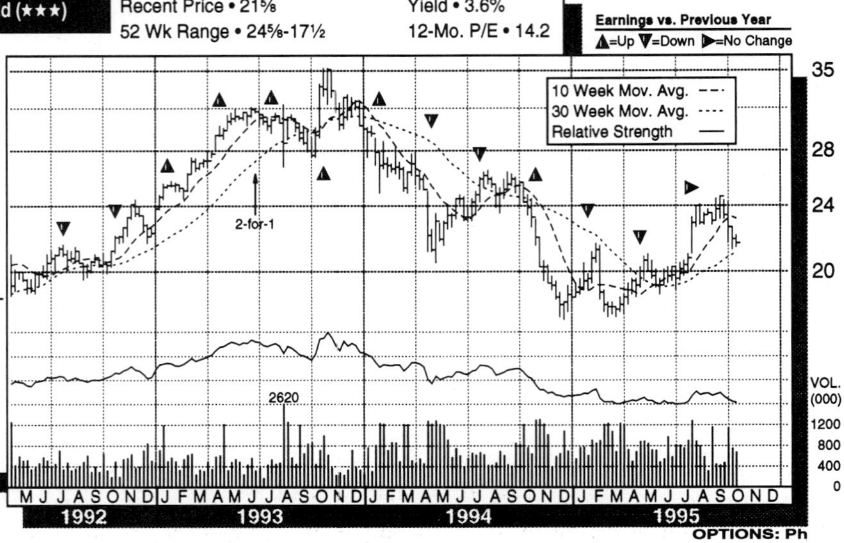

Overview - 18-OCT-95

The company recently announced that it expected its third quarter operating results to decline from those of the second quarter due to several factors. These include narrower margins in the RSI equipment and services unit, seasonal slowness in the sports business and higher borrowing costs. COMSAT also announced plans to restructure its operations in order to reduce costs. Core telecom operations should benefit from volume growth related to traffic commitments under long-term contracts with AT&T, MCI and Sprint, and from strong growth in its Latin American telecommunications operations. Positive trends in the mobile segment are also expected to continue. The company's portable wireless terminals allow users to communicate from virtually anywhere in the world, providing access in areas where cellular networks do not exist.

Valuation - 12-OCT-95

The shares fell sharply on news of the expected lower third quarter earnings. However, we believe the factors causing the lower results are temporary. Long-term results should benefit from the growing demand for wireless services, from rapid growth in the company's entertainment business and from the lower cost structure. The company is also well positioned to take advantage of the opening of global telecommunications markets. COMSAT expects to record a charge for the restructuring, which we have excluded from our third quarter and full year 1995 estimates. With favorable long-term prospects and a healthy dividend yield, the shares offer adequate total return prospects.

Key Stock Statistics

S&P EPS Est. 1995	1.65	Tang. Bk. Value/Share	15.87
P/E on S&P Est. 1995	13.1	Beta	0.68
S&P EPS Est. 1996	1.75	Shareholders	36,000
Dividend Rate/Share	0.78	Market cap. (B)	$ 1.0
Shs. outstg. (M)	47.3	Inst. holdings	72%
Avg. daily vol. (M)	0.155	Insider holdings	NA

Value of $10,000 invested 5 years ago: $ 14,952

Fiscal Year Ending Dec. 31

	1995	% Change	1994	% Change	1993	% Change
Revenues (Million $)						
1Q	207.9	4%	200.5	21%	166.3	30%
2Q	210.8	1%	207.9	35%	154.1	16%
3Q	—	—	200.8	32%	152.5	4%
4Q	—	—	217.8	30%	167.5	7%
Yr.	—	—	826.9	29%	640.4	14%
Income (Million $)						
1Q	14.60	-28%	20.18	10%	18.30	18%
2Q	22.02	2%	21.62	7%	20.15	19%
3Q	—	—	21.40	23%	17.40	NM
4Q	—	—	14.45	-20%	18.10	7%
Yr.	—	—	77.64	5%	74.04	73%
Earnings Per Share ($)						
1Q	0.31	-28%	0.43	-5%	0.46	14%
2Q	0.46	NM	0.46	-8%	0.50	16%
3Q	E0.39	-13%	0.45	5%	0.43	NM
4Q	E0.49	63%	0.30	-32%	0.44	4%
Yr.	E1.65	NM	1.64	-10%	1.82	67%

Next earnings report expected: late October

COMSAT Corp.

Business Summary - 18-OCT-95

COMSAT Corp. (formerly Communications Satellite) provides satellite communications services and information services. Business segment contributions (profits in million $) in 1994 were:

	Revs.	Profits
International	32%	$88.5
Mobile Communications	23%	47.9
Entertainment	19%	10.5
Technology Services	26%	15.5

The international segment provides telephone, data, video and audio communications services to U.S. communications carriers, U.S. and foreign broadcasters, and others using the INTELSAT (19.1% owned as of March 1995) satellite system. The segment also includes COMSAT International Ventures, which forms non-U.S. ventures with public telecommunications authorities and private concerns to provide international and domestic digital communications services.

The mobile communications segment provides maritime, aeronautical, and land mobile applications using the Inmarsat (24.1% owned) satellite system and COMSAT's land earth stations in Connecticut, California, Malaysia and Turkey.

Entertainment operations include COMSAT Video Enterprises (wholly-owned) and On Command Video (79.7% owned), which provide in-room entertainment and information services to hotels throughout the United States, Canada and the Carribean. CQ also owns the Denver Nuggets of the National Basketball Association. In December 1994, the company acquired Beacon Communications Corp., a film and television production company. Beacon's assets include a multipicture development, production and domestic distribution agreement with SONY Pictures Entertainment.

The technology services segment provides systems integration, voice and data communications products for emerging markets and specialized technical consulting. Through COMSAT Laboratories, the unit also conducts research and development activities for the telecommunications industry.

Important Developments

Sep. '95—News Corp. and its partner Globo Organization agreed to lease $100 million of satellite capacity from COMSAT over five years. Separately, CQ and MCI expanded their multimillion dollar agreement for transoceanic satellite capacity.

May '95—The company agreed to buy the Quebec Nordiques of the National Hockey Leaque for about $75 million. CQ will move the team to Denver, Colo., where it plans to build, in partnership with Anschutz Corp., a new $132 million arena.

Capitalization

Long Term Debt: $590,000,000 (6/95).
Minority Interest: $29,000,000.

Per Share Data ($) (Year Ended Dec. 31)

	1994	1993	1992	1991	1990	1989
Tangible Bk. Val.	15.84	15.05	14.13	15.35	16.29	16.79
Cash Flow	5.18	5.22	4.27	4.77	2.47	4.01
Earnings	1.64	1.82	1.09	1.88	-0.43	1.67
Dividends	0.76	0.74	0.70	0.67	0.66	0.66
Payout Ratio	46%	41%	64%	36%	NM	36%
Prices - High	30	35¼	24½	19	19¼	20⅝
- Low	17½	23¾	17⅛	11½	10¼	13
P/E Ratio - High	18	19	22	10	NM	12
- Low	11	13	16	6	NM	8

Income Statement Analysis (Million $)

	1994	%Chg	1993	%Chg	1992	%Chg	1991
Revs.	827	29%	640	13%	564	8%	523
Oper. Inc.	325	18%	276	10%	252	6%	238
Depr.	168	22%	138	10%	125	14%	110
Int. Exp.	48.9	8%	45.1	-2%	46.2	-1%	46.9
Pretax Inc.	127	2%	124	85%	67.0	-35%	103
Eff. Tax Rate	39%	—	41%	—	36%	—	31%
Net Inc.	77.6	5%	74.0	72%	42.9	-40%	71.4

Balance Sheet & Other Fin. Data (Million $)

	1994	1993	1992	1991	1990	1989
Cash	19.0	9.0	4.0	7.0	2.0	6.0
Curr. Assets	298	178	165	159	161	170
Total Assets	1,976	1,653	1,543	1,393	1,229	1,261
Curr. Liab.	317	278	170	214	142	129
LT Debt	516	402	486	383	375	368
Common Eqty.	827	679	621	585	558	595
Total Cap.	1,495	1,205	1,210	1,055	1,020	1,063
Cap. Exp.	275	230	233	282	203	227
Cash Flow	245	212	168	182	92.0	150

Ratio Analysis

	1994	1993	1992	1991	1990	1989
Curr. Ratio	0.9	0.6	1.0	0.7	1.1	1.3
% LT Debt of Cap.	34.5	33.4	40.2	36.3	36.8	34.6
% Net Inc.of Revs.	9.4	11.6	7.6	13.7	NM	15.2
% Ret. on Assets	4.0	4.6	2.9	5.4	NM	5.1
% Ret. on Equity	9.6	11.3	7.0	12.4	NM	10.8

Dividend Data —Dividends were initiated in 1970. A dividend reinvestment plan is available.

Amt. of Div. $	Date Decl.	Ex-Div. Date	Stock of Record	Payment Date
0.195	Oct. 25	Nov. 04	Nov. 11	Dec. 12 '94
0.195	Jan. 20	Feb. 06	Feb. 10	Mar. 13 '95
0.195	Apr. 21	May. 08	May. 12	Jun. 12 '95
0.195	Jul. 24	Aug. 09	Aug. 11	Sep. 11 '95

Data as orig. reptd.; bef. results of disc. opers. and/or spec. items. Per share data adj. for stk. divs. as of ex-div. date. E-Estimated. NA-Not Available. NM-Not Meaningful. NR-Not Ranked.

Office—6560 Rock Spring Dr., Bethesda, MD 20817. **Tel**—(301) 214-3000. **Chrmn**—M. R. Laird. **Pres & CEO**—B. L. Crockett. **Acting CFO**—A. Flowers. **VP & Secy**—W. Y. Zeger. **Investor Contact**—Mike Troiano. **Dirs**—L. W. Benson, R. E. Boschwitz, E. I. Colodny, B. L. Crockett, L. S. Eagleburger, N. B. Freeman, B. M. Goldwater, A. Hauspurg, P. S. Knight, M. R. Laird, P. W. Likins, H. M. Love, C. T. Manatt, R. G. Schwartz, C. J. Silas, D. D. Wharton. **Transfer Agent & Registrar**—The Bank of New York, NYC. **Incorporated** in Washington, D.C. in 1963. **Empl**-2,894. **S&P Analyst:** Kevin J. Gooley

STANDARD & POOR'S

STOCK REPORTS

Conner Peripherals

NYSE Symbol **CNR**

In S&P MidCap 400

28-SEP-95

Industry:
Data Processing

Summary: CNR is a leading designer and builder of information storage products, including disk drives, tape drives, storage management software and storage systems.

S&P Opinion: Hold (★★★)

Recent Price • 17¾

52 Wk Range • 19¼-9

Yield • Nil

12-Mo. P/E • 13.1

Quantitative Evaluations

Outlook
(1 Lowest—5 Highest)
• 2+

Fair Value
• 16⅞

Risk
• High

Earn./Div. Rank
• NR

Technical Eval.
• Bearish since 7/95

Rel. Strength Rank
(1 Lowest—99 Highest)
• 92

Insider Activity
• NA

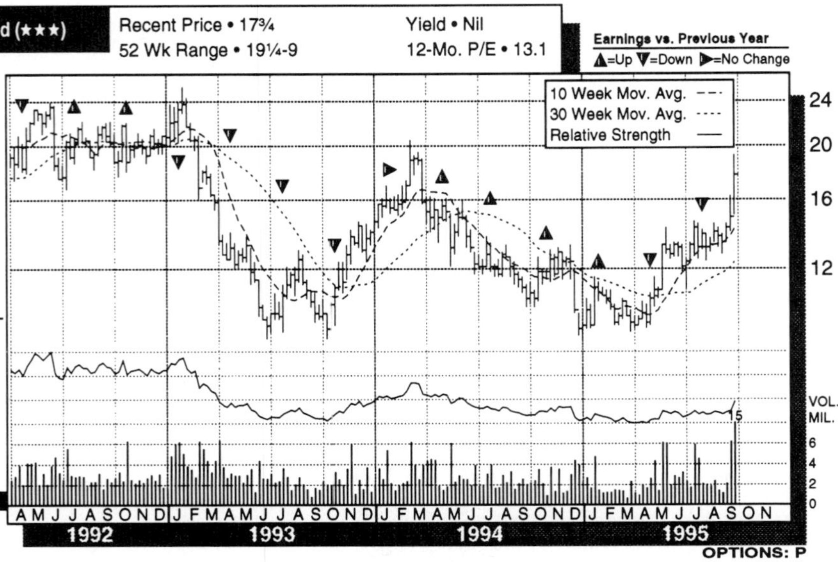

Overview - 28-SEP-95

Sales of the company as currently constituted, should rise through 1996, reflecting higher unit shipments of disk and tape drives, and increased demand for software offerings; all segments should be aided by new product introductions. Operating margins are expected to widen on a more favorable product mix and a lower cost structure. However, in the absence of particularly large net nonrecurring gains, earnings should decline in 1995. Earnings are expected to be solidly higher in 1996.

Valuation - 27-SEP-95

The shares of this major vendor of data storage solutions, which had been in a downtrend since March 1994, rebounded somewhat in May 1995 on an improved operating performance, and shot higher still in September on news of merger negotiations with Seagate Technology. The shares remain near their highs for this year. The company has resolved certain technical issues concerning its storage products and has rejuvenated its product line with a solid set of competitive storage offerings. Inventory levels are being brought down and expenses remain under tight control. However, underlying market conditions remain competitive and selected component shortages exist, which complicates manufacturing efficiency. We expect the shares to perform in line with the market in coming months.

Key Stock Statistics

S&P EPS Est. 1995	1.00	Tang. Bk. Value/Share	6.22
P/E on S&P Est. 1995	17.8	Beta	1.84
S&P EPS Est. 1996	1.30	Shareholders	1,300
Dividend Rate/Share	Nil	Market cap. (B)	$0.867
Shs. outstg. (M)	53.4	Inst. holdings	52%
Avg. daily vol. (M)	1.386	Insider holdings	NA

Value of $10,000 invested 5 years ago: $ 13,523

Fiscal Year Ending Dec. 31

	1995	% Change	1994	% Change	1993	% Change
Revenues (Million $)						
1Q	610.4	8%	564.0	1%	558.3	27%
2Q	642.3	-1%	650.1	33%	490.6	-11%
3Q	—	—	559.5	6%	528.4	-15%
4Q	—	—	591.6	3%	574.5	-7%
Yr.	—	—	2,365	10%	2,152	-4%
Income (Million $)						
1Q	0.08	-100%	23.80	NM	-22.54	NM
2Q	16.74	-47%	31.47	NM	-58.83	NM
3Q	—	—	10.23	NM	-372.4	NM
4Q	—	—	44.18	NM	8.46	NM
Yr.	—	—	109.7	NM	-445.3	NM
Earnings Per Share ($)						
1Q	Nil	—	0.46	NM	-0.46	NM
2Q	0.31	-48%	0.60	NM	-1.19	NM
3Q	E0.24	20%	0.20	NM	-7.54	NM
4Q	E0.45	-46%	0.84	NM	0.17	NM
Yr.	E1.00	-52%	2.10	NM	-9.03	NM

Next earnings report expected: mid October

Conner Peripherals

Business Summary - 27-SEP-95

Conner Peripherals designs, builds and sells information storage products, including a broad selection of hard disk drives, tape drives, software and integrated systems, for a wide range of computer applications.

The company's disk drive products address the requirements of high-performance microcomputers and workstations for greater storage capacity, faster access time, lower power consumption and smaller size. The product line consists of 2.5 inch and 3.5-inch drives offering storage capacities ranging from 270 megabytes (MBs) to over 1 gigabyte (GB) of formatted storage capacity.

Tape drives are peripheral hardware devices, primarily used for back-up storage applications, that permit low cost storage or data protection of large volumes of data through the use of digital tape stored on small cartridges used singly or in multiple autoloader applications.

Through its Arcada Holdings, Inc. subsidiary, CNR offers a variety of data protection and storage management software products that operate across multiple desktop and client-server environments.

The Storage Systems division integrates hardware and software to deliver turn-key data storage solutions.

The company's disk, tape and software products are marketed mainly through a direct sales force to original equipment manufacturers (OEMs) and also through distributors. Sales to Compaq Computer accounted for 13% of sales in each of 1994 and 1993.

International sales represented 48% and 54% of total sales in 1994 and 1993, respectively.

Important Developments

Sep. '95—The company agreed in principle to be acquired by Seagate Technology (SEG). Terms of the transaction, which is subject to, among other things, a definitive agreement and approvals of the Boards of Directors of both companies, call for each CNR share to be converted into 0.442 share of SEG common stock.

Jul. '95—Earnings for the first half of 1995 exclude a $6.2 million ($0.11 a share) special credit from the repurchase of debt securities.

Jan. '95—In the 1994 fourth quarter, CNR recorded a net gain of $55.3 million ($43.2 million, or $0.82 a share, after taxes), comprised of a $38.0 million reduction in restructuring reserves established in the third quarter of 1993, and a $22.3 million gain on the sale of 1.3 million Read-Rite common shares, partly offset by a $5 million charge to write off purchased R&D from the acquisition of Quest Development.

Capitalization

Long Term Debt: $527,896,000 (6/95).
Minority Interest: $3,122,000.

Per Share Data ($) (Year Ended Dec. 31)

	1994	1993	1992	1991	1990	1989
Tangible Bk. Val.	5.67	3.28	7.48	12.27	10.64	5.04
Cash Flow	3.85	-6.90	3.46	2.42	3.17	1.50
Earnings	2.10	-9.03	2.19	1.57	2.51	1.09
Dividends	Nil	Nil	Nil	Nil	Nil	Nil
Payout Ratio	Nil	Nil	Nil	Nil	Nil	Nil
Prices - High	20½	25½	23⅞	29¾	31¼	15½
- Low	9	9	15⅝	12½	12¼	6½
P/E Ratio - High	10	NM	11	19	12	14
- Low	4	NM	7	8	5	6

Income Statement Analysis (Million $)

	1994	%Chg	1993	%Chg	1992	%Chg	1991
Revs.	2,365	10%	2,152	-4%	2,238	40%	1,599
Oper. Inc.	225	NM	37.0	-87%	281	59%	177
Depr.	92.0	-12%	105	49%	70.3	40%	50.1
Int. Exp.	47.2	-8%	51.2	9%	46.9	101%	23.3
Pretax Inc.	152	NM	-471	NM	162	27%	128
Eff. Tax Rate	29%	—	NM	—	21%	—	26%
Net Inc.	110	NM	-444	NM	121	32%	92.0

Balance Sheet & Other Fin. Data (Million $)

	1994	1993	1992	1991	1990	1989
Cash	443	518	615	570	237	104
Curr. Assets	1,170	1,167	1,388	1,124	721	366
Total Assets	1,461	1,464	1,905	1,335	880	468
Curr. Liab.	365	490	436	169	183	124
LT Debt	627	661	705	368	37.0	123
Common Eqty.	337	209	626	713	604	201
Total Cap.	1,095	970	1,463	1,162	693	341
Cap. Exp.	95.0	102	116	87.7	95.9	80.7
Cash Flow	201	-340	191	143	164	57.0

Ratio Analysis

	1994	1993	1992	1991	1990	1989
Curr. Ratio	3.2	2.4	3.2	6.7	3.9	3.0
% LT Debt of Cap.	57.3	68.1	48.2	31.7	5.3	36.0
% Net Inc.of Revs.	416.0	NM	5.4	5.8	9.7	5.9
% Ret. on Assets	7.4	NM	8.0	8.3	16.8	11.9
% Ret. on Equity	39.6	NM	19.9	13.9	29.2	25.6

Dividend Data —No dividends have been paid. A shareholder rights plan was adopted in November 1994.

Data as orig. reptd.; bef. results of disc. opers. and/or spec. items. Per share data adj. for stk. divs. as of ex-div. date. E-Estimated. NA-Not Available. NM-Not Meaningful. NR-Not Ranked.

Office—3081 Zanker Rd., San Jose, CA 95134. **Tel**—(408) 456-4500. **Chrmn, Pres & CEO**—F. F. Conner. **EVP-Fin & CFO**—P. J. Bell. **VP & Treas**—J. A. Taylor. **SVP & Investor Contact**—Regina Gindin. **Dirs**—W. S. Anderson, L. P. Bremer, F. F. Conner, L. W. Hart, W. H. Lester, R. S. Penske, M. S. Rossi, W. J. Schroeder, J. P. Squires, R. E. White. **Transfer Agent & Registrar**—First National Bank of Boston. **Incorporated** in California in 1985; reincorporated in Delaware 1992. **Empl**-9,097. **S&P Analyst:** Peter C. Wood, CFA

STANDARD & POOR'S

STOCK REPORTS

Consolidated Papers

NYSE Symbol **CDP**
In S&P MidCap 400

26-SEP-95 **Industry:** Paper/Products

Summary: CDP derives the majority of revenues from the production of enamel papers for the print communications industry, and also makes coated specialty packaging and other paper products.

S&P Opinion: Hold (★★★)

Recent Price • 57
52 Wk Range • 64⅞-41⅞
Yield • 2.6%
12-Mo. P/E • 18.4

Quantitative Evaluations

Outlook
(1 Lowest—5 Highest)
• 4+

Fair Value
• 60⅝

Risk
• Low

Earn./Div. Rank
• B+

Technical Eval.
• **Bearish** since 9/95

Rel. Strength Rank
(1 Lowest—99 Highest)
• 15

Insider Activity
• **Neutral**

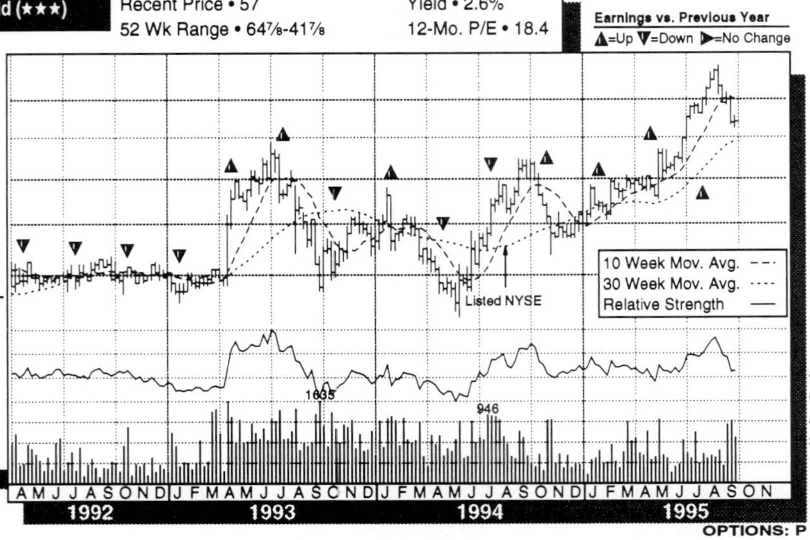

OPTIONS: P

Overview - 26-SEP-95

Sales should be strongly higher in 1995, as stable worldwide economies and a healthy printing and publishing industry should lead to continued solid demand and favorable prices for coated printing paper. Pricing should also continue to be supported by tight supply conditions, with little coated paper capacity added in recent years and only a modest level planned in upcoming periods. The top line will also be boosted substantially by the inclusion of acquisitions completed in mid-1995. Margins should widen sharply on the favorable pricing situation, and should also be helped by manufacturing efficiencies. Although high pulp costs will impact margins to an extent, CDP supplies about 75% of its own needs. Despite financing costs, CDP's recent acqusitions should boost profits considerably.

Valuation - 26-SEP-95

Despite a recent correction, the company's shares have risen sharply since late 1994, as CDP has benefited from favorable conditions in the print communications industry and reduced European import competition. Investor excitement over CDP's recent acquisitions (agreements announced in May 1995) also boosted its stock price. Although worries exist about the state of the U.S. economy, and publishers and printers are trying to reduce paper usage, a restricted level of capacity expansion should enable industry trends to remain strong through 1996. However, much of CDP's favorable prospects have been factored into its stock price, and the shares seem fairly valued in their recent trading range.

Key Stock Statistics

S&P EPS Est. 1995	4.90	Tang. Bk. Value/Share	23.50
P/E on S&P Est. 1995	11.6	Beta	0.32
S&P EPS Est. 1996	6.00	Shareholders	7,100
Dividend Rate/Share	1.48	Market cap. (B)	$ 2.5
Shs. outstg. (M)	44.5	Inst. holdings	27%
Avg. daily vol. (M)	0.070	Insider holdings	NA

Value of $10,000 invested 5 years ago: $ 15,410

Fiscal Year Ending Dec. 31

	1995	% Change	1994	% Change	1993	% Change
Revenues (Million $)						
1Q	308.9	33%	232.2	-4%	241.6	11%
2Q	336.6	44%	233.9	-10%	260.3	17%
3Q	—	—	272.9	19%	228.8	-2%
4Q	—	—	288.6	33%	216.7	-7%
Yr.	—	—	1,028	8%	947.3	5%
Income (Million $)						
1Q	40.61	166%	15.29	-12%	17.47	13%
2Q	48.56	108%	23.31	-9%	25.55	69%
3Q	—	—	19.46	167%	7.28	-34%
4Q	—	—	28.67	106%	13.89	42%
Yr.	—	—	86.73	35%	64.20	27%
Earnings Per Share ($)						
1Q	0.92	163%	0.35	-13%	0.40	21%
2Q	1.09	106%	0.53	-9%	0.58	66%
3Q	E1.44	NM	0.44	159%	0.17	-32%
4Q	E1.45	123%	0.65	110%	0.31	41%
Yr.	E4.90	149%	1.97	35%	1.46	27%

Next earnings report expected: mid October

Consolidated Papers

Business Summary - 26-SEP-95

Consolidated Papers is a leading producer of enamel printing papers (also known as coated printing papers) for the print communications industry and of coated specialty papers used largely in the packaging and labeling of food and consumer products. It also manufactures corrugated displays and containers and paperboard products. Company shipments (in tons) in recent years were:

	1994	1993
Enamel papers	968,313	875,715
Specialty papers	111,944	101,324
Paperboard	5,803	5,899
Paperboard products	27,921	31,789
Corrugated products	36,918	33,709

The company's coated printing papers, which accounted for 80% of revenues in the past two years, are used in magazines, books, brochures, advertising and corporate annual reports. These papers are sold directly to magazine publishers (accounting for 52% of coated paper sales in 1994) and through paper merchants to publishers and commercial printers (48%). The company's shipments of coated printing papers represented about 12% of the U.S. market for the product in 1994.

At 1994 year-end, CDP was operating eight manufacturing plants in five Wisconsin municipalities. Capacity utilization for coated papers in 1994 was 92.5% (87.8% in the prior year).

The company owns and manages 673,104 acres of timberland in Wisconsin, Michigan and Ontario. Its lands provided 17% of wood used in CDP's pulp mills in 1994. Consolidated produced 76% of the pulp used in its paper manufacturing operations in 1994, with the remainder purchased from outside sources.

Important Developments

Jun. '95—The company completed the acquisitions of Niagara of Wisconsin Paper Corp. and Lake Superior Paper Industries (effective July 1), for a total of $227 million in cash and the extinguishment of $52 million of debt. Niagara was purchased from Pentair, Inc., while Lake Superior was obtained from Pentair and Minnesota Power & Light Co., which had joint ownership of the unit. Niagara produces coated groundwood papers; while Lake Superior makes supercalendered paper used in magazines, catalogs and newspaper ad supplements, and operates Superior Recycled Fiber Industries, a producer of high-quality pulp from post-consumer wastepaper. The acquired firms had sales totaling more than $360 million in 1994.

Jun. '95—CDP broke ground for a new $166 million paper machine, which will have the capacity to produce 64,000 tpy of lightweight coated specialty papers. Completion was scheduled for April 1997.

Capitalization

Long Term Debt: $300,000,000 (6/95).

Per Share Data ($) (Year Ended Dec. 31)

	1994	1993	1992	1991	1990	1989
Tangible Bk. Val.	22.08	21.34	21.03	21.97	21.10	19.07
Cash Flow	3.75	3.73	3.20	3.58	4.56	5.02
Earnings	1.97	1.46	1.15	2.10	3.27	3.85
Dividends	1.28	1.26	1.28	1.28	1.26	1.15
Payout Ratio	65%	86%	111%	61%	39%	30%
Prices - High	52⅜	54¼	44¾	42	45¾	44
- Low	36¼	37½	36	32	30¼	34
P/E Ratio - High	27	37	39	20	14	11
- Low	18	26	31	15	9	9

Income Statement Analysis (Million $)

	1994	%Chg	1993	%Chg	1992	%Chg	1991
Revs.	1,028	9%	947	5%	904	4%	872
Oper. Inc.	215	NM	213	22%	175	-13%	202
Depr.	78.6	-21%	100	11%	89.5	38%	64.9
Int. Exp.	6.2	-30%	8.9	NM	8.9	27%	7.0
Pretax Inc.	143	30%	110	36%	81.0	-45%	146
Eff. Tax Rate	39%	—	42%	—	38%	—	37%
Net Inc.	87.0	36%	64.0	28%	50.0	-45%	91.0

Balance Sheet & Other Fin. Data (Million $)

	1994	1993	1992	1991	1990	1989
Cash	8.0	2.0	2.0	7.0	12.0	195
Curr. Assets	199	182	185	162	163	336
Total Assets	1,500	1,467	1,487	1,411	1,192	1,086
Curr. Liab.	157	146	158	83.0	91.0	91.0
LT Debt	68.0	121	171	178	Nil	Nil
Common Eqty.	976	939	922	960	920	832
Total Cap.	1,226	1,218	1,226	1,321	1,095	990
Cap. Exp.	98.0	83.0	137	280	331	150
Cash Flow	165	164	140	156	199	219

Ratio Analysis

	1994	1993	1992	1991	1990	1989
Curr. Ratio	1.3	1.2	1.2	2.0	1.8	3.7
% LT Debt of Cap.	5.5	9.9	13.9	13.5	Nil	Nil
% Net Inc.of Revs.	8.4	6.8	5.6	10.5	15.0	17.6
% Ret. on Assets	5.8	4.3	3.5	7.0	12.5	16.6
% Ret. on Equity	9.0	6.9	5.4	9.7	16.3	21.7

Dividend Data —Cash dividends have been paid in all years save two since 1906.

Amt. of Div. $	Date Decl.	Ex-Div. Date	Stock of Record	Payment Date
0.320	Oct. 18	Oct. 31	Nov. 04	Nov. 18 '94
0.320	Feb. 09	Feb. 13	Feb. 20	Mar. 03 '95
0.370	Apr. 24	May. 01	May. 05	May. 19 '95
0.370	Jul. 24	Aug. 02	Aug. 04	Aug. 18 '95

Data as orig. reptd.; bef. results of disc. opers. and/or spec. items. Per share data adj. for stk. divs. as of ex-div. date. E-Estimated. NA-Not Available. NM-Not Meaningful. NR-Not Ranked.

Office—P.O. Box 8050, Wisconsin Rapids, WI 54495-8050. **Tel**—(715) 422-3111. **Chrmn**—G. W. Mead. **Pres & CEO**—P. F. Brennan. **VP-Fin**—R. J. Kenney. **Secy**—C. H. Wartman. **Dirs**—R. B. Barker, J. R. Bostic, P. F. Brennan, W. N. Caldwell, S. M. Hands, B. S. Kubale, D. R. Mead, Jr., G. D. Mead, G. W. Mead, L. R. Nash, G. N. Rupp. **Transfer Agent**—Harris Trust & Savings Bank, Chicago. **Incorporated** in Wisconsin in 1894. **Empl**-5,815. **S&P Analyst:** Michael W. Jaffe

STANDARD & POOR'S

STOCK REPORTS

Convex Computer

NYSE Symbol **CNX**
In S&P MidCap 400

11-OCT-95

Industry: Data Processing

Summary: This producer and servicer of supercomputers for use in engineering, scientific and technical applications has agreed to be acquired by Hewlett-Packard.

S&P Opinion: Avoid (★★)

Recent Price • 4½
52 Wk Range • 8⅞-3⅝

Yield • Nil
12-Mo. P/E • NM

Quantitative Evaluations

Outlook
(1 Lowest—5 Highest)
• NA

Fair Value
• NA

Risk
• High

Earn./Div. Rank
• C

Technical Eval.
• Bearish since 9/94

Rel. Strength Rank
(1 Lowest—99 Highest)
• 26

Insider Activity
• NA

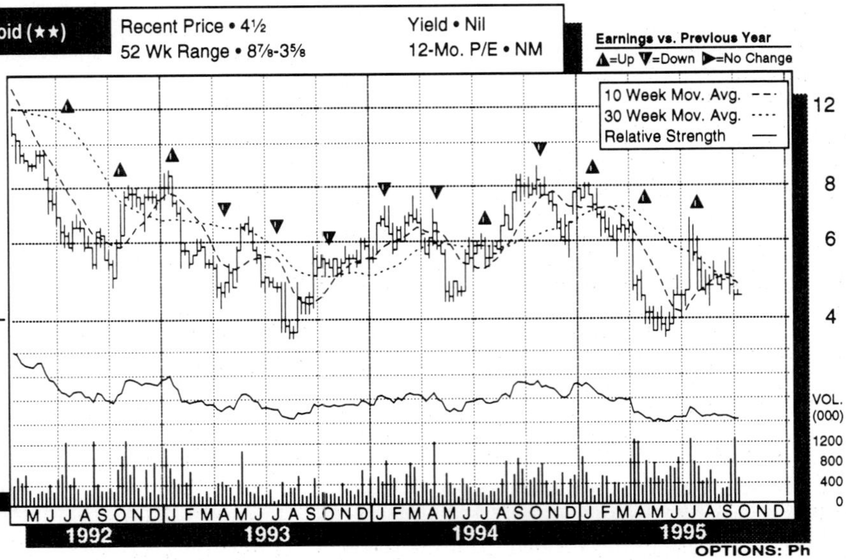

OPTIONS: Ph

Overview - 11-OCT-95

For Convex as a separate entity, revenues should grow significantly in 1996, as the company's aggressive efforts to bolster its product line begin to bear fruit. Specifically, the introduction of the SPP1200 and the planned launch of the SPP2000 should make the company's product line increasingly competitive. Continued tight control of operating expenses should allow the higher sales to return the company to profitability in 1996. However, a possible financing could result in higher interest expense or more common shares outstanding, which would restrain per share earnings. The long-term outlook remains clouded by the rapid technological advances required to keep its products competitive and the highly competitive nature of the markets that the company serves.

Valuation - 11-OCT-95

Convex Computer's shares are trading at a modest discount to the $4.83 a share acquisition offer that has been made by Hewlett-Packard. While a definitive agreement has been signed by the two companies, which work closely together, and Hewlett-Packard holds a 5% stake in the company, the shares appear fairly valued. In addition to customary conditions, including the approval of CNX's stockholders and required government approvals, CNX's operating losses still pose a hurdle to the transaction being completed on its current terms. The share are ranked as an "avoid."

Key Stock Statistics

S&P EPS Est. 1995	-0.80	Tang. Bk. Value/Share	1.69
P/E on S&P Est. 1995	NM	Beta	1.23
S&P EPS Est. 1996	0.25	Shareholders	1,900
Dividend Rate/Share	Nil	Market cap. (B)	$0.120
Shs. outstg. (M)	26.8	Inst. holdings	38%
Avg. daily vol. (M)	0.205	Insider holdings	NA

Value of $10,000 invested 5 years ago: $ 2,926

Fiscal Year Ending Dec. 31

	1995	% Change	1994	% Change	1993	% Change
Revenues (Million $)						
1Q	35.16	24%	28.42	-52%	59.08	8%
2Q	35.07	NM	35.03	-22%	45.09	-22%
3Q	—	—	36.44	-15%	42.99	-26%
4Q	—	—	44.29	-4%	45.96	-26%
Yr.	—	—	144.2	-25%	193.1	-17%
Income (Million $)						
1Q	-7.98	NM	-15.83	NM	0.05	-88%
2Q	-7.31	NM	-31.84	NM	-41.82	NM
3Q	—	—	-8.79	NM	-6.28	NM
4Q	—	—	-4.56	NM	-15.75	NM
Yr.	—	—	-61.02	NM	-63.80	NM
Earnings Per Share ($)						
1Q	-0.30	NM	-0.62	—	Nil	—
2Q	-0.27	NM	-1.23	NM	-1.67	NM
3Q	E-0.20	NM	-0.33	NM	-0.25	NM
4Q	E-0.03	NM	-0.17	NM	-0.62	NM
Yr.	E-0.80	NM	-2.35	NM	-2.53	NM

Next earnings report expected: late October

Convex Computer

Business Summary - 11-OCT-95

Convex Computer manufactures and services a family of supercomputers for engineering, scientific and technical users. As of December 31, 1994, 1,397 systems were installed at almost 680 customer sites. International revenues, mostly in Europe, accounted for 55% of the total in 1994.

CNX offers a single-processor scalar/vector machine to a high-end, eight-processor, tightly-coupled, parallel supercomputer. The systems integrate the three forms of processing common in scientific and engineering applications: scalar, in which operations are performed on one element at a time; vector, in which simultaneous operations occur on arrays of data; and parallel, in which two or more processors simultaneously operate on different parts of a program.

The Convex C3 Series supercomputers comprise three families of products: the high-end C3800 family, including the entry-level C3800/ES, which provides a growth path to high-end supercomputing; the departmental C3400 family; and the low-cost C3200 family. In June 1994, CNX unveiled the C4 family of high-end supercomputers, capable of exceeding one billion floating point operations per second. The C4 family is fully compatible with all previous supercomputer systems. The price of C series systems range from under $130,000 to more than $10 million.

In March 1994, the company introduced its Exemplar family of SPP (scalable parallel processing) systems, which are based on Hewlett-Packard's PA-RISC microprocessor technology. The systems feature a hardware and operating system achitecture that is different from CNX's previous product lines and are planned to scale from 2 to 128 processors.

Important Developments

Sep. '95—The company signed a definitive agreement for it to be acquired by Hewlett-Packard Co. (HWP). Under terms of the agreement, CNX shareholders will receive shares of HWP common shock with a value of $4.83 for each share of CNX common stock owned. HWP has a technology agreement with the company and holds a 5% stake in it. The acquisition agreement requires CNX to pay a termination fee if it accepts a higher offer, although CNX noted that no other discussions in this regard were currently taking place. Completion of the transaction is subject to customary conditions, including approval of CNX's stockholders and government approvals. The acquisition is expected to close by the end of calendar 1995.

Capitalization

Long Term Debt: $59,850,000 (6/95), incl. $53.5 million of 6% sub. debs. conv. into com. at $21.75 a sh.
Options: To buy 4,838,282 shs. at $4.00 to $11.25 ea. (12/94).

Per Share Data ($) (Year Ended Dec. 31)

	1994	1993	1992	1991	1990	1989
Tangible Bk. Val.	2.19	4.40	7.03	6.48	6.67	4.36
Cash Flow	-1.55	-1.75	0.67	0.31	1.54	1.22
Earnings	-2.35	-2.53	0.11	-0.31	0.88	0.60
Dividends	Nil	Nil	Nil	Nil	Nil	Nil
Payout Ratio	Nil	Nil	Nil	Nil	Nil	Nil
Prices - High	8⅞	8¾	16⅜	19¾	20⅞	16
- Low	4⅜	3⅝	4¾	8⅞	8⅜	9⅜
P/E Ratio - High	NM	NM	NM	NM	24	27
- Low	NM	NM	NM	NM	10	16

Income Statement Analysis (Million $)

	1994	%Chg	1993	%Chg	1992	%Chg	1991
Revs.	144	-25%	193	-17%	232	17%	198
Oper. Inc.	-19.6	NM	-5.1	NM	20.0	NM	4.7
Depr.	20.8	5%	19.8	43%	13.8	NM	13.7
Int. Exp.	4.9	-22%	6.3	-21%	7.9	16%	6.8
Pretax Inc.	-60.5	NM	-63.0	NM	4.1	NM	-9.1
Eff. Tax Rate	NM	—	NM	—	32%	—	NM
Net Inc.	-61.0	NM	-63.8	NM	2.8	NM	-6.9

Balance Sheet & Other Fin. Data (Million $)

	1994	1993	1992	1991	1990	1989
Cash	40.0	57.0	78.0	74.0	108	48.0
Curr. Assets	129	179	219	207	211	137
Total Assets	186	254	312	273	267	173
Curr. Liab.	64.9	74.3	67.4	63.0	59.8	31.5
LT Debt	63.2	67.6	71.1	63.8	64.0	61.3
Common Eqty.	58.0	112	174	146	143	80.0
Total Cap.	121	180	245	210	207	141
Cap. Exp.	13.5	10.6	17.7	16.2	25.1	15.3
Cash Flow	-40.2	-44.0	16.6	6.8	32.2	23.2

Ratio Analysis

	1994	1993	1992	1991	1990	1989
Curr. Ratio	2.0	2.4	3.2	3.3	3.5	4.3
% LT Debt of Cap.	52.1	37.6	29.0	30.4	31.0	43.5
% Net Inc.of Revs.	NM	NM	1.2	NM	8.8	7.2
% Ret. on Assets	NM	NM	0.9	NM	7.8	6.7
% Ret. on Equity	NM	NM	1.7	NM	15.6	15.7

Dividend Data —No cash dividends have been paid.

Data as orig. reptd.; bef. results of disc. opers. and/or spec. items. Per share data adj. for stk. divs. as of ex-div. date. E-Estimated. NA-Not Available. NM-Not Meaningful. NR-Not Ranked.

Office—3000 Waterview Parkway, Richardson, TX 75080. **Tel**—(214) 497-4000. **Chrmn & CEO**—R. J. Paluck. **Pres**—T. L. Rock. **VP & Secy**—P. N. Cardman. **VP-Fin & CFO**—D. W. Craig. **Dirs**—E. Bloch, H. B. Cash, M. D. Hopper, R. J. Paluck, S. K. Smith, S. J. Wallach, H. D. Wolfe. **Transfer Agent & Registrar**—Bank of Boston. **Incorporated** in Delaware in 1982. **Empl**-817. **S&P Analyst:** Paul H. Valentine, CFA

Coram Healthcare

NYSE Symbol **CRH**
In S&P MidCap 400

29-AUG-95

Industry: Health Care Centers

Summary: Coram is the largest provider of alternate-site infusion therapy in the U.S. Other services include lithotripsy, nonintravenous infusion products and physician support services.

Quantitative Evaluations

Outlook (1 Lowest—5 Highest)
• **5**

Fair Value
• **13½**

Risk
• **High**

Earn./Div. Rank
• **NR**

Technical Eval.
• **Bearish** since 8/95

Rel. Strength Rank (1 Lowest—99 Highest)
• **NA**

Insider Activity
• **NA**

Recent Price • 5⅞
52 Wk Range • 26¾-4⅞

Yield • Nil
12-Mo. P/E • NM

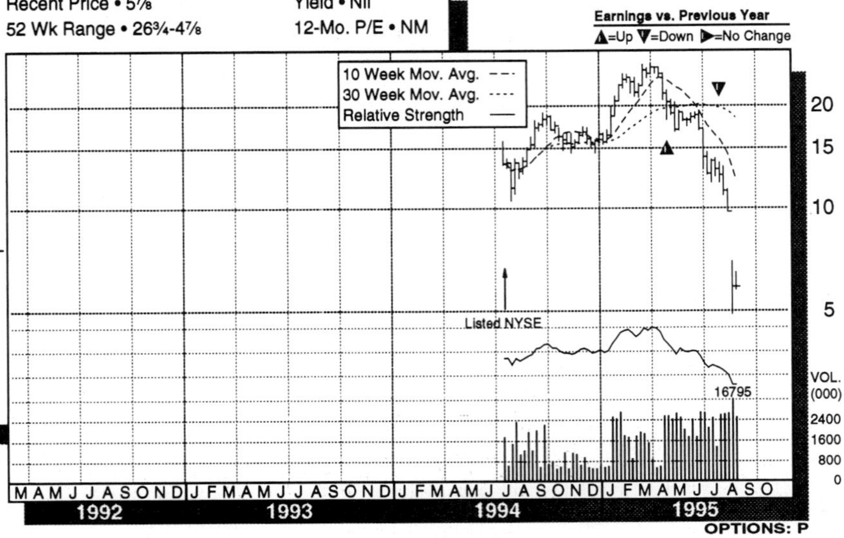

OPTIONS: P

Business Profile - 29-AUG-95

This company is facing greater-than-expected challenges integrating the six companies that were merged since mid-1994. With much worse-than-expected results during the second quarter of 1995, which reflected poor performance from the existing businesses and a significant underperformance by the business acquired from Caremark in 1995, the shares fell sharply. The company has implemented a program to immediately address the issues of revenue generation and cost reduction.

Operational Review - 29-AUG-95

Revenues advanced 25%, year to year, in the first half of 1995, reflecting the acquisition of Caremark's infusion business, which was partly offset by the termination of physician relationships inherited from predecessor companies and a substantial underperformance by the business acquired from Caremark. Second-quarter results included special pretax charges of $38.6 million for the cost of integrating the Caremark business and for expenses related to the terminated merger with Lincare Holding.

Stock Performance - 25-AUG-95

In the past 30 trading days, CRH's shares have declined 57%, compared to a 0.04% rise in the S&P 500. Average trading volume for the past five days was 717,840 shares, compared with the 40-day moving average of 1,091,236 shares.

Key Stock Statistics

Dividend Rate/Share	Nil	Shareholders	NA
Shs. outstg. (M)	39.7	Market cap. (B)	$0.223
Avg. daily vol. (M)	1.528	Inst. holdings	68%
Tang. Bk. Value/Share	NM	Insider holdings	NA
Beta	NA		

Value of $10,000 invested 5 years ago: NA

Fiscal Year Ending Dec. 31

	1995	% Change	1994	% Change	1993	% Change
Revenues (Million $)						
1Q	104.8	-7%	113.1	NM	113.0	—
2Q	179.3	57%	114.0	-3%	118.0	—
3Q	—	—	110.2	—	--	—
4Q	—	—	113.6	-54%	245.0	—
Yr.	—	—	450.5	-5%	476.0	19%
Income (Million $)						
1Q	4.59	43%	3.21	—	—	—
2Q	-62.90	NM	-9.00	—	—	—
3Q	—	—	-121.2	—	—	—
4Q	—	—	-1.10	—	—	—
Yr.	—	—	-128.1	NM	33.91	-49%
Earnings Per Share ($)						
1Q	0.11	38%	0.08	—	--	—
2Q	-1.53	NM	-0.23	—	--	—
3Q	—	—	-3.14	—	--	—
4Q	—	—	-0.03	—	--	—
Yr.	—	—	-3.33	NM	0.89	-52%

Next earnings report expected: mid November

Coram Healthcare

29-AUG-95

Business Summary - 29-AUG-95

Coram Healthcare Corporation is the largest provider of alternate-site infusion therapy and related services in the U.S. Other services offered by the company include lithotripsy, nonintravenous infusion products and physician support services. The company was formed in July 1994 through the merger of four home infusion therapy firms--T2 Medical, Curaflex Health Services, HealthInfusion and Medisys. The company acquired Caremark International's home infusion therapy business in April 1995.

Infusion therapy involves the intravenous administration of anti-infective, chemotherapy, pain management, nutrition and other therapies. Patient revenues in 1994 were derived as follows:

Anti-infective	40%
Parenteral & enteral nutrition	27%
Chemotherapy	11%
Pain management	10%
Other therapies	12%

Anti-infective therapy is the infusion of antibacterial, antiviral or antifungal medications into the patient's bloodstream for the treatment of a variety of infectious diseases. Parenteral nutrition involves the intravenous feeding of life-sustaining nutrients to patients with impaired or altered digestive tracts due to gastrointestinal illness or condition. Enteral nutrition therapy is administered to patients who cannot eat as a result of an obstruction to the upper gastrointestinal tract or other medical condition. Chemotherapy is the administration of cytotoxic drugs to patients suffering from various types of cancer. Pain management therapy is the administration of analgesic drugs to patients suffering from acute or chronic pain.

Lithotripsy is a noninvasive technique that uses shock waves to disintegrate kidney stones. As of March 1995, the company had a controlling interest in 15 lithotripsy partnerships, as well as a wholly owned lithotripter maintenance company.

The company is also implementing a physician practice management business that will provide a variety of consulting and administrative services to small and medium-size physician groups.

Important Developments

Jul. '95—Coram and Lincare Holding, Inc., the second largest provider of home respiratory therapy services, terminated their merger agreement. The companies agreed to cooperatively offer their services in targeted metropolitan areas.

Apr. '95—Coram acquired Caremark International's home infusion therapy business for $209 million in cash, $75 million in 7% convertible subordinated notes and $25 million in 12% subordinated notes.

Capitalization

Long Term Debt: $449,800,000 (6/95).
Minority Interest: $4,729,000 (3/95).

Per Share Data ($)

(Year Ended Dec. 31)

	1994	1993	1992	1991	1990	1989
Tangible Bk. Val.	-0.28	3.62	NA	NA	NA	NA
Cash Flow	-2.72	NA	NA	NA	NA	NA
Earnings	-3.33	0.89	1.85	1.39	NA	NA
Dividends	Nil	NA	NA	NA	NA	NA
Payout Ratio	Nil	NA	NA	NA	NA	NA
Prices - High	19⅛	NA	NA	NA	NA	NA
- Low	10½	NA	NA	NA	NA	NA
P/E Ratio - High	NM	NA	NA	NA	NA	NA
- Low	NM	NA	NA	NA	NA	NA

Income Statement Analysis (Million $)

	1994	%Chg	1993	%Chg	1992	%Chg	1991
Revs.	450	-5%	476	19%	399	45%	275
Oper. Inc.	49.8	—	NA	—	NA	—	NA
Depr.	22.9	—	NA	—	NA	—	NA
Int. Exp.	7.4	62%	4.6	45%	3.2	-23%	4.1
Pretax Inc.	-141	NM	66.2	-39%	109	52%	71.5
Eff. Tax Rate	NM	—	49%	—	39%	—	39%
Net Inc.	-127	NM	33.9	-49%	66.6	53%	43.4

Balance Sheet & Other Fin. Data (Million $)

	1994	1993	1992	1991	1990	1989
Cash	36.6	26.7	NA	NA	NA	NA
Curr. Assets	208	198	NA	NA	NA	NA
Total Assets	576	563	NA	NA	NA	NA
Curr. Liab.	124	103	NA	NA	NA	NA
LT Debt	121	16.1	NA	NA	NA	NA
Common Eqty.	322	434	NA	NA	NA	NA
Total Cap.	451	459	NA	NA	NA	NA
Cap. Exp.	8.9	NA	NA	NA	NA	NA
Cash Flow	-104	NA	NA	NA	NA	NA

Ratio Analysis

	1994	1993	1992	1991	1990	1989
Curr. Ratio	1.7	1.9	NA	NA	NA	NA
% LT Debt of Cap.	26.8	3.5	NA	NA	NA	NA
% Net Inc.of Revs.	NM	7.1	16.7	15.8	NA	NA
% Ret. on Assets	NA	NA	NA	NA	NA	NA
% Ret. on Equity	NA	NA	NA	NA	NA	NA

Dividend Data —No dividends have been paid.

Data as orig. reptd.; bef. results of disc. opers. and/or spec. items. Per share data adj. for stk. divs. as of ex-div. date. E-Estimated. NA-Not Available. NM-Not Meaningful. NR-Not Ranked.

Office—1125 17th St., Suite 1500, Denver, CO 80202. **Tel**—(303) 292-4973. **Chrmn, Pres & CEO**—J. M. Sweeney. **Vice Chrmn**—T. H. Carter. **CFO**—G. R. Wolford. **Dirs**—T. H. Carter, R. A. Fink, C. A. Laverty, S. G. Pagliuca, L. P. Smith, J. M. Sweeney, G. R. Wilensky. **Transfer Agent**—Bank of Boston. **Incorporated** in Delaware in 1994. **Empl**-2,400. **S&P Analyst:** Philip J. Birbara

STANDARD & POOR'S

STOCK REPORTS

Cordis Corp.

NASDAQ Symbol **CORD**

In S&P MidCap 400

23-OCT-95

Industry: Medical equipment/ supply

Summary: In mid-October, Johnson & Johnson began a cash tender offer of $100 a share for all shares of this maker of angiographic products and other medical devices.

S&P Opinion: Hold (★★★)

Recent Price • 109⅝ | 52 Wk Range • 109¾-55½ | Yield • Nil | 12-Mo. P/E • 34.4

Quantitative Evaluations

Outlook (1 Lowest—5 Highest) • **4+**

Fair Value • **87⅞**

Risk • **Average**

Earn./Div. Rank • **B-**

Technical Eval. • **Neutral** since 9/95

Rel. Strength Rank (1 Lowest—99 Highest) • **99**

Insider Activity • **Unfavorable**

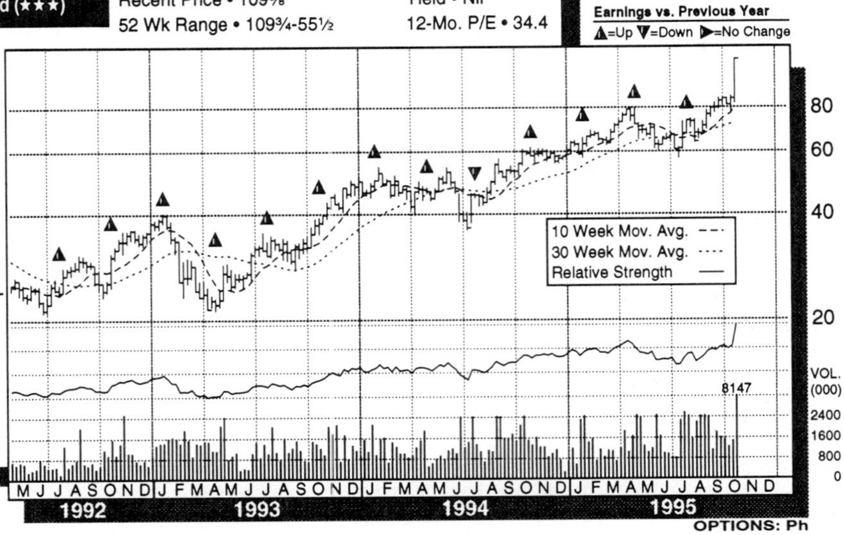

OPTIONS: Ph

Overview - 23-OCT-95

For the company as an independent entity, the core business should grow again in fiscal 1996, with EPS rising to $3.90, from fiscal 1995's $3.00. Greater international penetration and expected improvement in the U.S. hospital sector should boost demand for an expanding line of angiographic products. Robust gains are indicated in the Webster Laboratories electrophysiology catheter business. Sales of neuroscience products should also advance. Despite continued pricing pressures, mainly from the growing influence of managed care, Cordis should be able to maintain good control over its cost structure and continue to fund R&D at about 8% of revenues.

Valuation - 23-OCT-95

The shares soared 25% on October 19, following the start of J&J's cash tender offer of $100 a share for all shares. J&J said it would prefer to offer $105 a share in stock in a tax-free, negotiated transaction, representing a multiple of 31X trailing 12-month EPS. Cordis, a leading producer of coronary angioplasty products and diagnostic angiographic equipment, has been rumored as a takeover candidate for some time. The shares have recently traded above the J&J bid, as investors anticipate either a sweetened offer from J&J or a competing bid from a third party. We recommend that holders retain their shares for an eventual buyout.

Key Stock Statistics

S&P EPS Est. 1996	3.90	Tang. Bk. Value/Share	17.23
P/E on S&P Est. 1996	28.1	Beta	1.38
Dividend Rate/Share	Nil	Shareholders	1,000
Shs. outstg. (M)	16.4	Market cap. (B)	$ 1.8
Avg. daily vol. (M)	0.618	Inst. holdings	76%
		Insider holdings	NA

Value of $10,000 invested 5 years ago: $ 70,725

Fiscal Year Ending Jun. 30

	1996	% Change	1995	% Change	1994	% Change
Revenues (Million $)						
1Q	123.4	26%	98.11	42%	69.15	11%
2Q	—	—	105.3	32%	79.45	28%
3Q	—	—	118.0	33%	88.94	38%
4Q	—	—	121.8	28%	95.00	42%
Yr.	—	—	443.2	32%	336.5	32%
Income (Million $)						
1Q	15.09	30%	11.63	33%	8.72	—
2Q	—	—	12.98	42%	9.13	32%
3Q	—	—	13.78	31%	10.54	36%
4Q	—	—	11.81	30%	9.09	9%
Yr.	—	—	50.21	34%	37.49	29%
Earnings Per Share ($)						
1Q	0.89	27%	0.70	32%	0.53	26%
2Q	E0.96	23%	0.78	42%	0.55	17%
3Q	E1.00	22%	0.82	30%	0.63	19%
4Q	E1.05	50%	0.70	27%	0.55	-5%
Yr.	E3.90	30%	3.00	32%	2.27	14%

Next earnings report expected: late October

Cordis Corp.

Business Summary - 23-OCT-95

Cordis Corporation designs, manufactures and sells medical products and devices, primarily angiographic catheters, neuroscience devices and other related medical instrumentation. Net sales by major product class in recent fiscal years were as follows:

	1995	1994	1993	1992
Angiographic products	96%	95%	93%	92%
Neuroscience products	4%	5%	7%	8%

Cordis produces a wide range of angiographic devices for the diagnosis and treatment of cardiovascular diseases. Diagnostic devices include catheters and related equipment inserted into a patient's circulatory system to allow introduction of contrast media that enable a physician to study the heart, blood vessels and other soft-tissue organs to determine the proper treatment of patients exhibiting disorders of such tissues. Other diagnostic devices include electrophysiology catheters that are used to diagnose the patient's electrical system to identify and locate electrical conduction abnormalities (cardiac arrhythmias). Interventional devices include balloon dilatation catheters, guiding catheters, steerable guidewires and accessory products.

The company's neuroscience products include implantable cerebrospinal fluid (CSF) shunt systems for the treatment of hydrocephalus (an excess accumulation of CSF in the ventricles of the brain), and disposable intracranial pressure monitoring and drainage systems.

Products are sold worldwide to hospitals and other medical institutions and physicians. In fiscal 1995, foreign operations contributed 54% of net sales and 55% of pretax profits.

R&D spending in fiscal 1995 totaled $35.3 million (8.0% of revenues), up from $26.0 million (7.7%) in fiscal 1994.

Important Developments

Oct. '95—Johnson & Johnson began a cash tender offer of $100 a share for all Cordis common shares. J&J said it would prefer to effect the transaction through an exchange of $105 of stock for each share, but had resorted to a hostile bid after the company refused to discuss a negotiated transaction. Cordis said directors would evaluate the offer and communicate their position to shareholders no later than November 2, 1995. Cordis urged shareholders not to make a decision regarding the offer until they have are advised by the directors.

Capitalization

Long Term Debt: $1,484,000 (6/95).

Per Share Data ($)

(Year Ended Jun. 30)

	1995	1994	1993	1992	1991	1990
Tangible Bk. Val.	17.23	12.64	9.85	8.29	5.74	5.15
Cash Flow	3.95	2.92	2.65	2.28	1.96	1.31
Earnings	3.00	2.27	2.00	1.67	1.38	0.75
Dividends	Nil	Nil	Nil	Nil	Nil	Nil
Payout Ratio	Nil	Nil	Nil	Nil	Nil	Nil
Prices - High	80	61¾	50½	38	41	24¾
- Low	57¼	36	21¼	21	20½	12
P/E Ratio - High	27	27	25	23	30	33
- Low	19	16	11	13	15	16

Income Statement Analysis (Million $)

	1995	%Chg	1994	%Chg	1993	%Chg	1992
Revs.	443	31%	337	32%	255	14%	223
Oper. Inc.	101	41%	71.6	33%	53.7	29%	41.5
Depr.	15.8	46%	10.8	13%	9.5	10%	8.7
Int. Exp.	1.4	-22%	1.7	6%	1.6	-49%	3.2
Pretax Inc.	79.9	37%	58.4	51%	38.7	20%	32.3
Eff. Tax Rate	37%	—	36%	—	25%	—	26%
Net Inc.	50.2	34%	37.5	29%	29.1	21%	24.0

Balance Sheet & Other Fin. Data (Million $)

	1995	1994	1993	1992	1991	1990
Cash	101	55.6	38.4	13.1	11.6	9.2
Curr. Assets	288	203	143	107	84.0	84.0
Total Assets	395	288	204	168	142	146
Curr. Liab.	94.0	76.2	55.6	42.2	32.4	39.3
LT Debt	1.5	1.9	1.1	2.2	15.6	31.6
Common Eqty.	282	203	141	116	80.0	70.0
Total Cap.	283	205	142	119	97.0	103
Cap. Exp.	27.7	22.8	14.1	10.8	9.1	6.1
Cash Flow	66.0	48.3	38.6	32.7	27.4	17.7

Ratio Analysis

	1995	1994	1993	1992	1991	1990
Curr. Ratio	3.1	2.7	2.6	2.5	2.6	2.1
% LT Debt of Cap.	0.5	0.9	0.8	1.8	16.2	30.7
% Net Inc.of Revs.	11.3	11.1	11.4	10.8	9.7	6.2
% Ret. on Assets	14.7	14.5	15.5	15.4	13.3	7.3
% Ret. on Equity	20.7	20.8	22.4	24.4	25.6	16.6

Dividend Data —No cash has been paid.

Data as orig. reptd.; bef. results of disc. opers. and/or spec. items. Per share data adj. for stk. divs. as of ex-div. date. E-Estimated. NA-Not Available. NM-Not Meaningful. NR-Not Ranked.

Office—14201 N. W. 60th Ave., Miami Lakes, FL 33014. **Tel**—(305) 824-2000. **Chrmn, Pres & CEO**—R. C. Strauss. **VP & CFO**—A. J. Novak. **VP & Secy**—D. G. Hall. **VP & Investor Contact**—Chick McDowell. **Dirs**—C. M. Burzik, D. R. Challoner, R. W. Foxen, D. F. Malin, Jr., W. J. Razzouk, J. L. de Ruyter van Steveninck, R. C. Strauss, W. W. Webster, Jr., P. K. Woolf. **Transfer Agent & Registrar**—Chemical Bank, NYC. **Incorporated** in Florida in 1959. **Empl**-3,370. **S&P Analyst:** Herman Saftlas

STANDARD & POOR'S

STOCK REPORTS

Cracker Barrel Old Country

NASDAQ Symbol **CBRL**

In S&P MidCap 400

17-JUL-95 **Industry:** Food serving

Summary: This company operates more than 200 "country store" restaurants, primarily in the southeastern U.S.

S&P Opinion: Hold (★★★) | Recent Price • 21⅞ | 52 Wk Range • 27¼-17½ | Yield • 0.1% | 12-Mo. P/E • 20.6

Quantitative Evaluations

Outlook (1 Lowest—5 Highest)
• **5-**

Fair Value
• **29½**

Risk
• **Average**

Earn./Div. Rank
• **A**

Technical Eval.
• **Bearish** since 6/95

Rel. Strength Rank (1 Lowest—99 Highest)
• **21**

Insider Activity
• **Neutral**

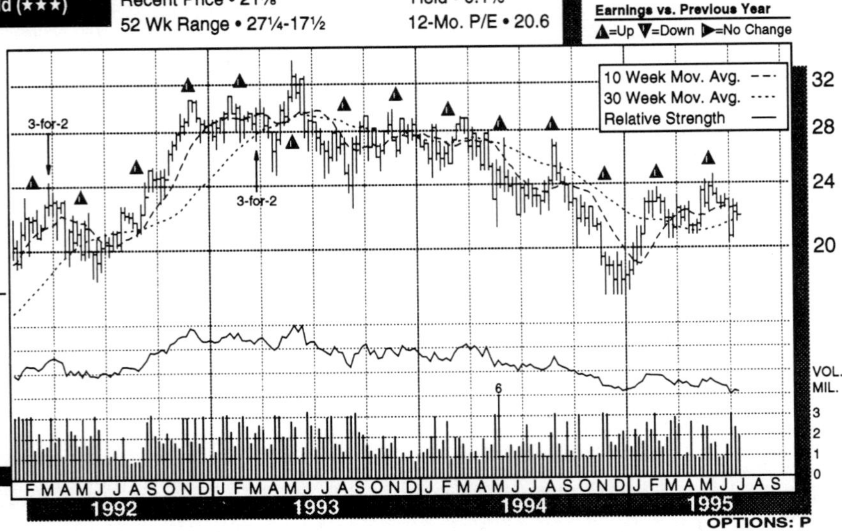

OPTIONS: P

Overview - 17-JUL-95

We expect sales increases for CBRL in fiscal 1996 to be fueled largely by more stores being in operation. During the year, the number of traditional units opened should increase by about 20%, following a similar rise the year before. By the end of fiscal 1996, we expect about 260 traditional units to be open. Also, we look for price-adjusted comparable sales of existing units to increase slightly in the year ahead, but profit margins may narrow somewhat. CBRL's long-term growth prospects include the development of a related food concept that is expected to place more emphasis on take-out service. This concept, called Corner Market, is now being tested. At the end of fiscal 1995, we expect CBRL to have four such units open, and several more Corner Markets may open in fiscal 1996.

Valuation - 17-JUL-95

This well-managed company continues to expand aggressively. In the year ahead, we look for earnings growth of close to 20%, with higher menu prices helping to offset pressure from labor costs. CBRL's fiscal year ends in July, but on a calendar-year basis, we expect 1995 per-share earnings to approach $1.25. Based on the company's growth prospects, the stock merits the premium valuation that it is currently given. However, we view the shares as adequately priced at a P/E that approximates its growth rate, based on expected year-ahead profits.

Key Stock Statistics

S&P EPS Est. 1995	1.10	Tang. Bk. Value/Share	7.88
P/E on S&P Est. 1995	19.9	Beta	1.55
S&P EPS Est. 1996	1.35	Shareholders	13,900
Dividend Rate/Share	0.02	Market cap. (B)	$ 1.3
Shs. outstg. (M)	60.0	Inst. holdings	35%
Avg. daily vol. (M)	0.453	Insider holdings	NA

Value of $10,000 invested 5 years ago: $ 39,068

Fiscal Year Ending Jul. 31

	1995	% Change	1994	% Change	1993	% Change
Revenues (Million $)						
1Q	184.9	21%	152.5	24%	123.0	34%
2Q	188.6	25%	150.8	26%	120.0	35%
3Q	188.3	21%	155.4	24%	125.2	25%
4Q	—	—	182.2	22%	149.9	25%
Yr.	—	—	640.9	24%	517.6	29%
Income (Million $)						
1Q	15.60	17%	13.37	32%	10.13	37%
2Q	12.32	24%	9.91	30%	7.65	52%
3Q	15.06	20%	12.60	25%	10.07	28%
4Q	—	—	21.08	18%	17.80	31%
Yr.	—	—	56.96	25%	45.65	35%
Earnings Per Share ($)						
1Q	0.26	18%	0.22	22%	0.18	38%
2Q	0.20	25%	0.16	23%	0.13	44%
3Q	0.25	19%	0.21	24%	0.17	21%
4Q	E0.39	—	0.35	21%	0.29	21%
Yr.	E1.10	—	0.94	21%	0.78	28%

Next earnings report expected: early September

Cracker Barrel Old Country

17-JUL-95

Business Summary - 17-JUL-95

Cracker Barrel Old Country Store, Inc. owns and operates a chain of full-service "country store" restaurants with gift shops, located largely in the southeastern and midwestern sections of the U.S., near interstate highways. As of May 1995, the company was operating 212 such restaurants. Also, CBRL is testing a related concept that is expected to place more of an emphasis on offering prepared food for take-out.

The restaurant portion of the units generates about 78% of total CBRL sales. CBRL typically serves breakfast, lunch and dinner, between 6:00 a.m. and 10:00 p.m. The restaurants feature home-style country cooking prepared on the premises from the company's own recipes. The moderately priced menu items include country ham, chicken, fish, barbecue pork ribs, roast beef, beans, turnip greens, vegetable plates, sandwiches, pancakes and eggs. The restaurants do not serve alcoholic beverages.

CBRL's gift shops (about 22% of total sales) offer a wide variety of items, consisting primarily of reproductions of early American and rural-style glassware, wrought-iron products, toys, soaps, woodcrafts and candles, as well as various candies, preserves, cheeses and other foodstuffs.

Cracker Barrel units are typically freestanding. Store interiors are subdivided into a dining area consisting of about 25% of the total interior space and a gift shop area consisting of about 22% of the space. The balance of the space consists primarily of kitchen and storage areas. The average cost for a new store is about $2.4 million, including land, building and equipment.

Comparable-store restaurant sales rose 3.7% in fiscal 1994, including a real sales increase of 0.6%. Same-store gift shop sales increased 7.0%.

Important Developments

May '95—In fiscal 1995's third quarter, CBRL's same-store restaurant sales were up 3.6%, year to year (0.1% when adjusted for menu price increases). Same-store gift shop sales increased 2.3%. These comparisons were weaker than those reported for fiscal 1995's second quarter. CBRL's third-quarter operating profit (including general and administrative expense) increased 17%, with overall sales up 21%. Ten new Cracker Barrel restaurants opened during the quarter, bringing the total operating to 211. In all of fiscal 1995, about 36 such new units are expected to open, followed by the debut of approximately 43 in fiscal 1996. Also, CBRL is testing a Corner Store concept, which is expected to place more of an emphasis on offering prepared food for take-out.

Capitalization

Long Term Debt: $19,500,000 (4/95).

Per Share Data ($) (Year Ended Jul. 31)

	1994	1993	1992	1991	1990	1989
Tangible Bk. Val.	7.18	6.16	4.05	3.35	2.10	1.79
Cash Flow	1.28	1.05	0.83	0.63	0.45	0.38
Earnings	0.94	0.78	0.61	0.45	0.31	0.25
Dividends	0.02	0.02	0.02	0.02	0.01	0.01
Payout Ratio	2%	2%	3%	3%	4%	6%
Prices - High	29⅛	34¼	30⅝	21⅝	8⅞	5⅞
- Low	21¼	22½	18⅜	7⅛	4⅝	3⅜
P/E Ratio - High	31	44	51	49	28	24
- Low	23	29	30	16	15	13

Income Statement Analysis (Million $)

	1994	%Chg	1993	%Chg	1992	%Chg	1991
Revs.	641	24%	518	29%	401	34%	300
Oper. Inc.	110	24%	89.0	31%	67.7	44%	47.0
Depr.	20.4	29%	15.8	26%	12.5	34%	9.3
Int. Exp.	2.1	-26%	2.9	-14%	3.4	19%	2.8
Pretax Inc.	90.6	24%	72.9	35%	54.2	48%	36.6
Eff. Tax Rate	37%	—	37%	—	37%	—	37%
Net Inc.	57.0	25%	45.7	35%	33.9	48%	22.9

Balance Sheet & Other Fin. Data (Million $)

	1994	1993	1992	1991	1990	1989
Cash	79.0	104	50.6	67.4	5.4	19.9
Curr. Assets	128	135	76.1	85.3	18.9	30.4
Total Assets	530	469	313	265	145	125
Curr. Liab.	67.2	59.2	43.5	35.0	24.7	18.6
LT Debt	25.2	38.4	43.3	44.5	16.0	17.3
Common Eqty.	430	367	222	180	100	85.0
Total Cap.	463	410	270	230	120	107
Cap. Exp.	102	85.0	71.5	64.0	38.4	25.9
Cash Flow	77.4	61.5	46.4	32.2	21.9	16.6

Ratio Analysis

	1994	1993	1992	1991	1990	1989
Curr. Ratio	1.9	2.3	1.7	2.4	0.8	1.6
% LT Debt of Cap.	5.4	9.4	16.1	19.4	13.2	15.2
% Net Inc.of Revs.	8.9	8.8	8.5	7.6	6.8	6.4
% Ret. on Assets	11.4	11.3	11.7	10.7	11.3	9.8
% Ret. on Equity	14.3	15.0	16.7	15.6	16.5	15.2

Dividend Data (Cash has been paid each year since 1972.)

Amt. of Div. $	Date Decl.	Ex-Div. Date	Stock of Record	Payment Date
0.005	Aug. 26	Sep. 06	Sep. 12	Sep. 23 '94
0.005	Nov. 22	Dec. 12	Dec. 16	Jan. 03 '95
0.005	Feb. 24	Mar. 13	Mar. 17	Mar. 31 '95
0.005	May. 25	Jun. 14	Jun. 16	Jun. 30 '95

Data as orig. reptd.; bef. results of disc. opers. and/or spec. items. Per share data adj. for stk. divs. as of ex-div. date. E-Estimated. NA-Not Available. NM-Not Meaningful. NR-Not Ranked.

Office—Hartmann Dr., P.O. Box 787, Lebanon, TN 37088-0787. **Tel**—(615) 444-5533. **Chrmn & CEO**—D. W. Evins. **Pres & COO**—R. N. Magruder. **Sr VP-Fin, CFO & Investor Contact**—Jimmie D. White. **Secy**—Evalena C. Bennett. **Dirs**—J. C. Bradshaw, R. V. Dale, D. W. Evins, E. W. Evins, W. D. Heydel, R. C. Hilton, C. E. Jones Jr., C. T. Lowe Jr., B. F. Lowery, G. L. Miller, M. M. Mitchell, J. H. Stewart, J. D. White. **Transfer Agent**—Trust Company Bank, Atlanta. **Incorporated** in Tennessee in 1969. **Empl**-21,796. **S&P Analyst:** Tom Graves, CFA

STANDARD & POOR'S

STOCK REPORTS

Crestar Financial Corp.

NYSE Symbol **CF**

In S&P MidCap 400

18-OCT-95 **Industry:** Banking

Summary: Crestar Financial Corp. is one of the largest bank holding companies in the Virginia/Maryland/Washington, D.C. area.

S&P Opinion: Accumulate (★★★★)

Recent Price • 57¾
52 Wk Range • 58⅜-36⅛
Yield • 3.1%
12-Mo. P/E • 11.9

Quantitative Evaluations

Outlook
(1 Lowest—5 Highest)
• **3+**

Fair Value
• **56½**

Risk
• **Low**

Earn./Div. Rank
• **B+**

Technical Eval.
• **Bullish** since 7/95

Rel. Strength Rank
(1 Lowest—99 Highest)
• **84**

Insider Activity
• **Neutral**

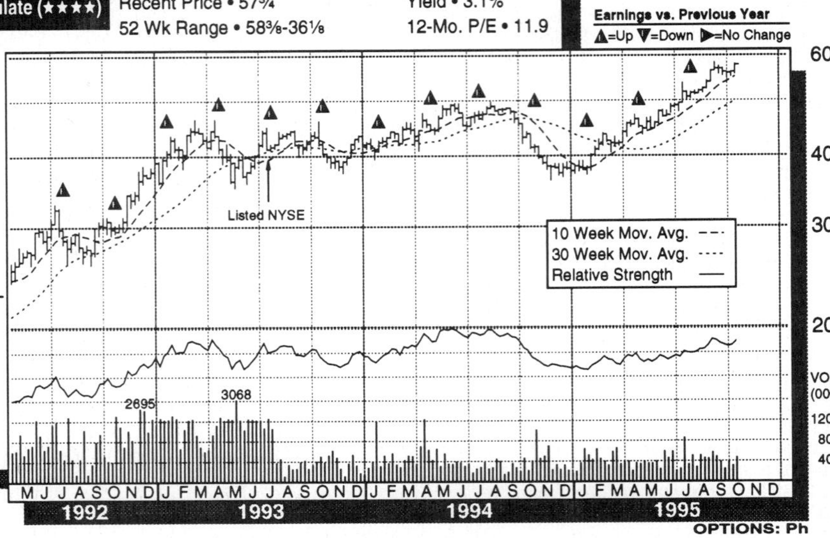

OPTIONS: Ph

Overview - 13-OCT-95

Earnings in the first nine months of 1995 benefited from a relatively stable net interest margin, solid loan growth, consistent fee income, and well contained noninterest expenses. Further earnings gains into 1996 are expected from continued improvement in (already excellent) credit quality, acquisitions, a healthy service territory, and control of noninterest expenses. As the interest rate environment stabilizes, the mortgage and trust businesses, which lagged in 1994 and the first half of 1995, have picked up. Despite CF's acquisition program (seven in 1994, and four thus far in 1995), nonperforming assets as a percent of total assets are trending down (0.51% at September 30, 1995, versus 0.60% last year). The company is continuing a strategy of aggressive expansion within its existing service territories.

Valuation - 13-OCT-95

With banking consolidation in the news and takeover speculation in the market, the shares are currently up about 60% from year-end 1994. With over 330 branches in the Virginia/Maryland/Washington, D.C. area, Crestar might make an inviting target, given its strong and growing retail and commercial customer base, excellent (and improving) asset quality, and the potential to earn significant noninterest income in a stable interest rate environment. Trading at about 10 times our 1996 earnings estimate of $5.35 a share, we recommend accumulation for conservative growth investors.

Key Stock Statistics

S&P EPS Est. 1995	5.00	Tang. Bk. Value/Share	28.32
P/E on S&P Est. 1995	11.6	Beta	0.87
S&P EPS Est. 1996	5.35	Shareholders	12,700
Dividend Rate/Share	1.80	Market cap. (B)	$ 2.2
Shs. outstg. (M)	37.7	Inst. holdings	47%
Avg. daily vol. (M)	0.066	Insider holdings	NA

Value of $10,000 invested 5 years ago: $ 26,151

Fiscal Year Ending Dec. 31

	1995	% Change	1994	% Change	1993	% Change
Revenues (Million $)						
1Q	318.9	14%	280.5	7%	262.5	-6%
2Q	331.8	12%	296.5	11%	267.8	-1%
3Q	NA	—	304.9	11%	274.5	3%
4Q	—	—	298.4	8%	276.1	4%
Yr.	—	—	1,180	9%	1,081	NM
Income (Million $)						
1Q	45.09	11%	40.48	31%	30.89	126%
2Q	47.38	11%	42.60	26%	33.70	101%
3Q	48.40	11%	43.60	17%	37.15	73%
4Q	—	—	42.39	10%	38.70	39%
Yr.	—	—	169.1	20%	140.5	76%
Earnings Per Share ($)						
1Q	1.20	12%	1.07	29%	0.83	108%
2Q	1.24	11%	1.12	27%	0.88	76%
3Q	1.27	10%	1.15	20%	0.96	50%
4Q	E1.29	14%	1.13	12%	1.01	29%
Yr.	E5.00	12%	4.47	21%	3.68	59%

Next earnings report expected: mid January

Crestar Financial Corp.

Business Summary - 13-OCT-95

Crestar Financial Corporation owns Crestar Bank of Virginia (one of the largest banks in that state), Crestar Bank, N.A. of Washington, D.C., and Crestar Bank of Maryland. At December 31, 1994, the company had 336 banking branches, with the large majority in Virginia. Other subsidiaries provide insurance, discount brokerage, mortgage banking and investment advisory services.

Total loans (net of unearned income) amounted to $9.29 billion at year-end 1994 and were divided:

Commercial	31%
Tax-exempt	2%
Instalment	20%
Bank card	16%
Real estate--mortgage	29%
Real estate--construction	2%

At the end of 1994, the allowance for loan losses totaled $219,189,000 (2.36% of loans outstanding), versus $210,958,000 (2.89) a year earlier. Net charge-offs were $37,138,000 in 1994 ($64,834,000 in 1993), equal to 0.45% (0.95%) of average loans. As of December 31, 1994, nonperforming assets amounted to $94,913,000 (1.02% of loans outstanding plus foreclosed properties), down from $96,765,000 (1.32%) a year earlier.

Deposits totaling $10.9 billion at December 31, 1994, were apportioned: demand 20%, interest-bearing demand 18%, money-market deposits 21%, regular savings 13%, time deposits 23%, and money-market certificates 5%.

On a tax-equivalent basis, the net interest margin was 4.83% in 1994, versus 4.78% in 1993.

Important Developments

Jun. '95—The company said it will purchase all the deposits ($450 million) and customer accounts, plus selected loans, of six branches of Chase Manhattan Bank of Maryland. The transaction is expected to be completed during the fourth quarter of 1995.

May '95—Crestar signed a definitive agreement to acquire Loyola Capital Corporation (NASDAQ: LOYC), the Baltimore-based holding company for Loyola Federal Savings Bank (assets of $2.5 billion and 35 branches) for about 5.6 million Crestar shares. The acquisition is expected to be completed around year-end 1995.

Mar. '95—CF completed the acquisition of TideMark Bank for Savings (deposits of $248 million) in a cash and stock transaction valued at $38 million.

Capitalization

Long Term Debt: $384,577,000 (6/95).

Per Share Data ($) (Year Ended Dec. 31)

	1994	1993	1992	1991	1990	1989
Tangible Bk. Val.	26.87	25.76	25.24	20.52	20.21	19.83
Earnings	4.47	3.68	2.32	0.98	1.87	3.28
Dividends	1.53	1.14	0.80	1.19	1.29	1.18
Payout Ratio	34%	31%	34%	121%	69%	36%
Prices - High	49¾	46½	39¾	25	29⅝	34⅛
- Low	36⅛	35⅛	17¼	11¼	12⅛	23½
P/E Ratio - High	11	13	17	26	16	10
- Low	8	10	7	11	6	7

Income Statement Analysis (Million $)

	1994	%Chg	1993	%Chg	1992	%Chg	1991
Net Int. Inc.	582	10%	527	9%	482	14%	421
Tax Equiv. Adj.	10.9	-13%	12.6	-21%	16.0	-28%	22.1
Non Int. Inc.	254	3%	246	14%	215	16%	186
Loan Loss Prov.	29.7	-39%	48.8	-51%	99	-53%	210
% Exp/Op Revs.	65%	—	67%	—	70%	—	65%
Pretax Inc.	255	25%	204	105%	100	149%	40.0
Eff. Tax Rate	34%	—	31%	—	20%	—	15%
Net Inc.	169	20%	141	76%	79.8	135%	34.0
% Net Int. Marg.	4.83%	—	4.78%	—	4.67%	—	4.29%

Balance Sheet & Other Fin. Data (Million $)

	1994	1993	1992	1991	1990	1989
Earning Assets:						
Money Mkt.	453	651	790	978	271	62.0
Inv. Securities	2,529	3,522	3,620	2,043	2,184	1,962
Com'l Loans	3,093	2,839	2,924	3,388	3,842	4,032
Other Loans	6,193	4,448	4,025	3,840	3,963	3,867
Total Assets	14,010	13,287	12,675	11,828	11,881	11,361
Demand Deposits	2,283	2,235	1,997	1,753	1,675	1,701
Time Deposits	8,630	7,931	7,584	7,137	6,831	6,766
LT Debt	367	191	210	162	168	170
Common Eqty.	1,126	1,062	914	750	726	705

Ratio Analysis

	1994	1993	1992	1991	1990	1989
% Ret. on Assets	1.2	1.1	0.7	0.3	0.5	1.0
% Ret. on Equity	15.4	14.2	10.3	4.5	8.5	16.3
% Loan Loss Resv.	2.4	2.9	3.0	2.9	1.9	1.2
% Loans/Deposits	85.1	71.7	72.5	81.3	91.8	93.3
% Equity to Assets	8.1	7.6	6.3	6.1	5.9	5.8

Dividend Data —Dividends have been paid by the company and its predecessors since 1870. A dividend reinvestment plan is available.

Amt. of Div. $	Date Decl.	Ex-Div. Date	Stock of Record	Payment Date
0.400	Oct. 24	Nov. 01	Nov. 07	Nov. 21 '94
0.400	Jan. 27	Jan. 31	Feb. 06	Feb. 21 '95
0.450	Apr. 28	May. 02	May. 08	May. 19 '95
0.450	Jul. 28	Aug. 03	Aug. 07	Aug. 21 '95

Data as orig. reptd.; bef. results of disc opers. and/or spec. items. Per share data adj. for stk. divs. as of ex-div. date. E-Estimated. NA-Not Available. NM-Not Meaningful. NR-Not Ranked.

Office—919 E. Main St., Richmond, VA 23261-6665. **Tel**—(804) 782-5000. **Chrmn & CEO**—R. G. Tilghman. **Pres**—J. M. Wells III. **EVP & CFO**—R. F. Katchuk. **EVP, Contr & Treas**—J. D. Barr. **SVP & Secy**—J. C. Clark III. **SVP-Investor Contact**—Eugene S. Putnam, Jr. **Dirs**—R. M. Bagley, J. C. Fox, B. G. Hill, G. A. James, H. G. Leggett, Jr., C. R. Longsworth, P. J. Maher, F. E. McCarthy, G. G. Minor III, G. F. Rainey, Jr., F. S. Royal, R. G. Tilghman, E. P. Trani, L. D. Walker, J. M. Wells III, K. H. Williams. **Transfer Agent**—Mellon Bank, Pittsburgh. **Incorporated** in Virginia in 1963. **Empl**-6,747. **S&P Analyst:** Robert Schpoont

Crompton & Knowles

NYSE Symbol **CNK**
In S&P MidCap 400

23-SEP-95 **Industry:** Chemicals

Summary: This company is a leading international producer and marketer of dyes, and of specialty process equipment and controls. It also makes specialty food and pharmaceutical ingredients.

S&P Opinion: Avoid (★★)

Recent Price • 15½ | Yield • 3.5%
52 Wk Range • 20-13⅝ | 12-Mo. P/E • 16.1

Quantitative Evaluations
Outlook
(1 Lowest—5 Highest)
• **2−**
Fair Value
• **14⅜**
Risk
• **Average**
Earn./Div. Rank
• **A+**

Technical Eval.
• **Bearish** since 1/95
Rel. Strength Rank
(1 Lowest—99 Highest)
• **49**
Insider Activity
• **NA**

Earnings vs. Previous Year
▲=Up ▼=Down ▶=No Change

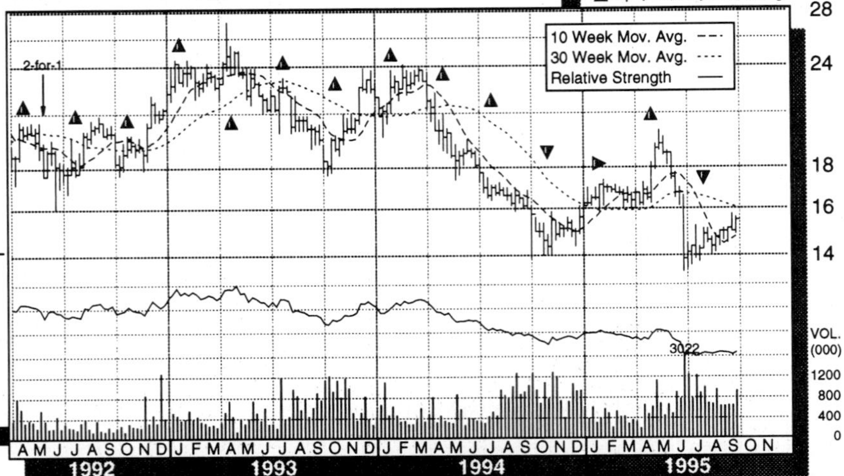

OPTIONS: P

Overview - 22-SEP-95

Earnings will remain essentially flat in 1995, as strong domestic and international demand for specialty process equipment (41% of total sales in the first half of 1995) will be offset by a decline in domestic dyes (29%), which have been hurt by the ongoing weakness in the apparel market. While the drop in domestic dyes has appeared to stabilize, we see operating margins for international dyes (15%) being severely eroded by intense pricing pressures. The ingredients segment (15%) will continue to show modest improvement, aided by new products for the food industry. Higher interest expense arising from acquisitions and stock repurchases (about 3 million common shares were acquired in 1994) will be another limiting factor, although share earnings will continue to benefit from the repurchases.

Valuation - 22-SEP-95

Although the stock has rebounded from CNK's June announcement that earnings for the second quarter (normally the strongest) would be about 20% below the year-earlier period, we would continue to avoid the shares until we see some more encouraging signs in the domestic dyes market. Earnings are expected to remain flat for the third consecutive year, and, while the stock seems fairly valued (based on our initial estimate of $1.15 for 1996), it remains, for the near term, a speculation on a dyes turnaround.

Key Stock Statistics

S&P EPS Est. 1995	1.00	Tang. Bk. Value/Share	3.77
P/E on S&P Est. 1995	15.5	Beta	0.92
S&P EPS Est. 1996	1.15	Shareholders	4,800
Dividend Rate/Share	0.54	Market cap. (B)	$0.745
Shs. outstg. (M)	48.0	Inst. holdings	54%
Avg. daily vol. (M)	0.149	Insider holdings	NA

Value of $10,000 invested 5 years ago: $ 22,675

Fiscal Year Ending Dec. 31

	1995	% Change	1994	% Change	1993	% Change
Revenues (Million $)						
1Q	168.2	26%	133.6	NM	134.0	18%
2Q	175.6	14%	154.4	5%	147.7	9%
3Q	—	—	142.8	7%	134.0	2%
4Q	—	—	158.9	11%	142.9	4%
Yr.	—	—	589.8	6%	558.3	8%
Income (Million $)						
1Q	13.20	3%	12.76	4%	12.30	25%
2Q	12.06	-25%	16.11	3%	15.65	22%
3Q	—	—	10.22	-11%	11.51	14%
4Q	—	—	11.83	-5%	12.50	20%
Yr.	—	—	50.92	-2%	51.96	20%
Earnings Per Share ($)						
1Q	0.27	8%	0.25	4%	0.24	20%
2Q	0.25	-19%	0.31	3%	0.30	15%
3Q	E0.22	10%	0.20	-9%	0.22	10%
4Q	E0.26	8%	0.24	NM	0.24	14%
Yr.	E1.00	NM	1.00	NM	1.00	15%

Next earnings report expected: mid October

Crompton & Knowles

23-SEP-95

Business Summary - 22-SEP-95

Crompton & Knowles produces dyes, specialty foods and pharmaceutical ingredients, and manufactures specialty extrusion equipment and control systems. Business segment contributions in 1994 were:

	Sales	Profits
Specialty chemicals	67%	66%
Specialty process equipment & controls	33%	34%

Foreign operations contributed 17% of sales and 14% of profits in 1994.

The specialty chemicals segment manufactures and sells dyes (75% of division sales) used on synthetic and natural fibers for knit and woven garments, home furnishings (carpets, draperies and upholstery) and automotive furnishings. Industrial dyes and chemicals are marketed to the paper, leather and ink industries for use on stationery, tissue, towels and other products. A line of chemical auxiliaries (leveling agents, dye fixatives and scouring agents) is also marketed to the textile industry. The company also makes and sells reaction and compounded flavor ingredients for the food processing, bakery, beverage and pharmaceutical industries, as well as food colorings and fragrance formulations. It is also a leading supplier of specialty sweeteners, seasonings and seasoning blends.

Specialty process equipment and controls include plastic and rubber extrusion equipment and industrial blow molding equipment. Extrusion systems are used to process plastic and rubber into various products such as plastic sheet used in appliances, automobiles, home construction, sports equipment and furniture; blown film used to package many consumer products; and extruded shapes used as house siding, furniture trim and substitutes for wood molding. Extrusion systems are also used to recycle and reclaim plastics and to apply insulation to cables and wires. The industrial blow molding equipment produced by CNK is sold to manufacturers of non-disposable plastic parts such as tool cases and beverage coolers.

Important Developments

Jul. '95—In its review of the second quarter of 1995, CNK noted that specialty chemical sales (58% of the total) were down 3.9%, with operating profits down 30%, and that specialty equipment sales (42%) were up 52%, with operating profits up 31%. CNK also said it did not see an imminent turnaround in the domestic dyes market.

Mar. '95—The company completed the acquisition of Killion Extruders, a producer of precision laboratory and small scale extrusion systems with annual sales of approximately $10 million.

Capitalization

Long Term Debt: $54,000,000 (7/95).

Per Share Data ($) (Year Ended Dec. 31)

	1994	1993	1992	1991	1990	1989
Tangible Bk. Val.	3.71	4.03	3.46	2.26	1.83	1.50
Cash Flow	1.26	1.23	1.10	0.94	0.77	0.64
Earnings	1.00	1.00	0.87	0.73	0.61	0.50
Dividends	0.46	0.38	0.31	0.25	0.20	0.15
Payout Ratio	44%	38%	36%	33%	31%	29%
Prices - High	24⅛	27¼	23⅞	21⅝	11⅝	7⅞
- Low	13⅞	17⅝	16	8½	6¾	3¾
P/E Ratio - High	24	27	27	30	19	16
- Low	14	18	18	12	11	7

Income Statement Analysis (Million $)

	1994	%Chg	1993	%Chg	1992	%Chg	1991
Revs.	590	6%	558	8%	518	15%	450
Oper. Inc.	94.4	NM	94.4	12%	84.4	18%	71.7
Depr.	13.3	10%	12.1	4%	11.6	16%	10.0
Int. Exp.	2.2	99%	1.1	-84%	7.0	-6%	7.4
Pretax Inc.	80.0	-3%	82.5	21%	68.3	21%	56.6
Eff. Tax Rate	36%	—	37%	—	37%	—	37%
Net Inc.	50.9	-2%	52.0	20%	43.3	21%	35.9

Balance Sheet & Other Fin. Data (Million $)

	1994	1993	1992	1991	1990	1989
Cash	1.8	9.3	2.4	8.5	11.3	4.9
Curr. Assets	261	220	207	185	164	127
Total Assets	432	363	351	309	283	218
Curr. Liab.	139	95.0	103	86.0	88.0	71.0
LT Debt	54.0	14.0	24.0	76.1	70.3	41.2
Common Eqty.	224	240	211	141	118	99
Total Cap.	285	259	239	223	194	147
Cap. Exp.	21.7	14.3	12.8	13.1	16.4	13.4
Cash Flow	64.2	64.0	54.9	46.0	38.0	31.0

Ratio Analysis

	1994	1993	1992	1991	1990	1989
Curr. Ratio	1.9	2.3	2.0	2.2	1.9	1.8
% LT Debt of Cap.	19.0	5.4	10.0	34.2	36.2	28.1
% Net Inc.of Revs.	8.6	9.3	8.4	8.0	7.7	6.9
% Ret. on Assets	13.1	14.5	12.7	12.1	12.0	11.5
% Ret. on Equity	22.6	23.0	23.9	27.7	27.7	26.9

Dividend Data —Dividends have been paid since 1933. A dividend reinvestment plan is available. A "poison pill" stock purchase rights plan was adopted in 1988.

Amt. of Div. $	Date Decl.	Ex-Div. Date	Stock of Record	Payment Date
0.120	Oct. 19	Oct. 31	Nov. 04	Nov. 25 '94
0.120	Feb. 06	Feb. 08	Feb. 10	Feb. 24 '95
0.135	Apr. 11	May. 01	May. 05	May. 26 '95
0.135	Jul. 19	Aug. 02	Aug. 04	Aug. 25 '95

Data as orig. reptd.; bef. results of disc. opers. and/or spec. items. Per share data adj. for stk. divs. as of ex-div. date. E-Estimated. NA-Not Available. NM-Not Meaningful. NR-Not Ranked.

Office—One Station Place, Metro Center, Stamford, CT 06902. **Tel**—(203) 353-5400. **Chrmn, Pres & CEO**—V. A. Calarco. **VP-Fin & CFO**—C. J. Marsden. **Secy**—J. T. Ferguson II. **Investor Contact**—Yanis Bibelnieks (212-949-2295). **Dirs**—J. A. Bitonti, V. A. Calarco, R. A. Fox, R. L. Headrick, L. I. Higdon, M. W. Huber, W. A. Law, C. J. Marsden, C.A. Piccolo, P. K. Woolf. **Transfer Agent & Registrar**—Mellon Securities Transfer Services, Pittsburgh, Pa. **Incorporated** in Massachusetts in 1900. **Empl-** 2,652. **S&P Analyst:** Justin McCann

STANDARD & POOR'S
STOCK REPORTS

Cross (A.T.) Co.

ASE Symbol **ATX.A**
In S&P MidCap 400

22-JUL-95 **Industry:** Office Equipment

Summary: This leading maker of fine writing instruments also markets leather products and other gift items.

S&P Opinion: Hold (★★★)

Recent Price • 15⅝
52 Wk Range • 17½-12½
Yield • 4.1%
12-Mo. P/E • 22.6

Quantitative Evaluations

Outlook
(1 Lowest—5 Highest)
• **NA**

Fair Value
• **NA**

Risk
• **NA**

Earn./Div. Rank
• **B**

Technical Eval.
• **Bearish** since 5/95

Rel. Strength Rank
(1 Lowest—99 Highest)
• **44**

Insider Activity
• **NA**

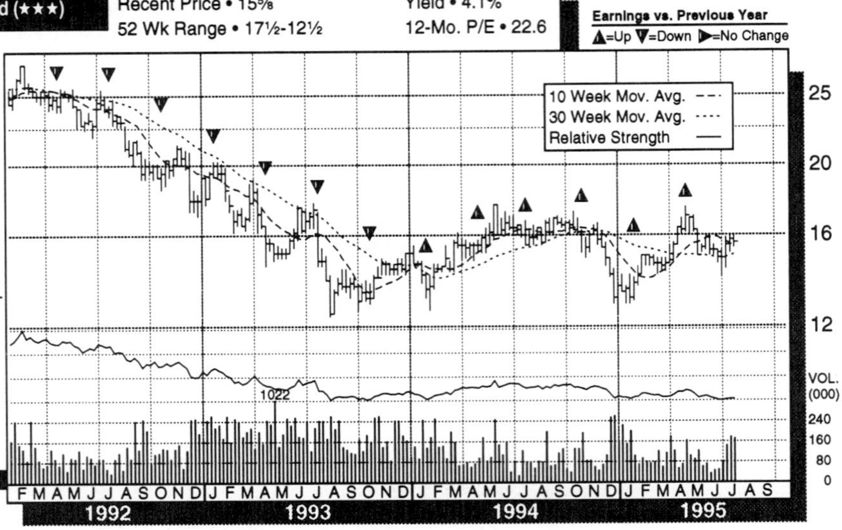

Overview - 21-JUL-95

Operational performance in 1995 will depend on consumer acceptance of the new Solo series of writing instruments. Solo was introduced in late May, and the company said it had a positive impact on second quarter sales. ATX's last new series, the Townsend line, has been successful, although the previously introduced Signature line was disappointing. It will be hard to measure Solo's success until the Christmas shopping season is completed. Solo is lower in price than other company products, which may enhance demand. Strong sales of the wider-girth Townsend and wider gross margins led to a strong second quarter. We anticipate further earnings gains in 1995, on continuing success of the Townsend line, strong foreign sales, and the potential of Solo. Higher interest income should also help earnings.

Valuation - 21-JUL-95

Although the share price has trended upward in 1995, it remains well below the 1992 high. A simple comparison of current and historical stock prices is not meaningful, since ATX is a different company after restructuring in 1993. The shares, trading at about 20X estimated 1995 EPS, appear expensive. However, the stock should receive support from its high dividend yield. In addition, the company has no long term debt, and has over $3.50 a share in cash, which will facilitate a share repurchase program.

Key Stock Statistics

S&P EPS Est. 1995	0.80	Tang. Bk. Value/Share	7.79
P/E on S&P Est. 1995	19.5	Beta	0.55
S&P EPS Est. 1996	0.90	Shareholders	2,200
Dividend Rate/Share	0.64	Market cap. (B)	$0.258
Shs. outstg. (M)	16.5	Inst. holdings	62%
Avg. daily vol. (M)	0.029	Insider holdings	NA

Value of $10,000 invested 5 years ago: $ 5,827

Fiscal Year Ending Dec. 31

	1995	% Change	1994	% Change	1993	% Change
Revenues (Million $)						
1Q	35.41	NM	35.19	-10%	39.10	-14%
2Q	44.88	10%	40.62	9%	37.29	-20%
3Q	—	—	45.93	15%	40.10	-12%
4Q	—	—	55.40	9%	50.74	-19%
Yr.	—	—	177.1	8%	164.6	-18%
Income (Million $)						
1Q	1.55	14%	1.36	43%	0.95	-56%
2Q	1.65	139%	0.69	NM	-6.79	NM
3Q	—	—	2.67	13%	2.36	-6%
4Q	—	—	5.81	45%	4.00	24%
Yr.	—	—	10.53	NM	0.52	-95%
Earnings Per Share ($)						
1Q	0.09	13%	0.08	NM	0.01	-92%
2Q	0.10	150%	0.04	NM	-0.35	NM
3Q	E0.19	—	0.16	14%	0.14	-7%
4Q	E0.42	—	0.34	42%	0.24	26%
Yr.	E0.80	—	0.62	NM	0.03	-95%

Next earnings report expected: mid October

Cross (A.T.) Co.

Business Summary - 16-MAY-95

A. T. Cross is a major international manufacturer of fine writing instruments and distributor of quality leather products and other gift items. Following the sale of substantially all of the assets of its Mark Cross, Inc. unit in June 1993, and the discontinuation of the company's retail business, A.T. Cross operates mainly in the writing instruments business. Approximately 39% of sales in 1994 were to foreign markets.

Writing instruments include ball-point pens, mechanical pencils, rolling/porous-point pens, and fountain pens. The limited introduction of the new Cross Townsend series in 1993 enabled the company to enter the popular wider-girth writing instrument segment. Townsend was fully launched in 1994 and the company had a limited introduction of its new Solo writing instrument line. The full launch of Solo is scheduled in the spring of 1995. The company also introduced in 1994 a gift package which included a Victorinox Swiss Army Knife and a pen and offered for the first time impulse packaging for its Century line products.

Cross sells its products through 37 manufacturers representatives. The company had about 7,500 active and wholesale accounts at the end of 1994. Retail demand for the company's products is highest during Christmas and other gift-giving occasions.

The company's Manetti-Farrow subsidiary distributes the Fendi brand of leather products and fashion accessories in the U.S. and Canada.

During 1993, Cross recorded restructuring charges totaling $11 million in connection with the consolidation of production and distribution facilities and reduction of excess manufacturing capacity; worldwide work force reductions; and the discontinuation of certain product lines.

Important Developments

Apr. '95—A. T. Cross Company reported that sales in the writing instrument division in the first quarter rose 2.8%; leather goods sales were down 15.5%. It noted that sales in the high-end Townsend line remain strong in all major markets.

Capitalization

Long Term Debt: None (12/94).
Class B Common Stock: 1,804,800 shs. ($1 par); conv. into Cl. A sh.-for-sh.; elects two-thirds of directors; entirely owned by the Boss family.
Class A Common Stock: 14,725,302 shs. ($1 par). Officers and directors (primarily the Boss family) hold 17%.

Per Share Data ($) (Year Ended Dec. 31)

	1994	1993	1992	1991	1990	1989
Tangible Bk. Val.	7.79	7.72	8.64	9.33	9.60	9.20
Cash Flow	1.00	0.40	0.98	1.58	1.93	2.64
Earnings	0.62	0.03	0.64	1.26	1.62	2.15
Dividends	0.64	0.96	1.28	1.28	1.25	1.18
Payout Ratio	103%	NM	200%	102%	77%	55%
Prices - High	17⅝	20¼	27⅝	28⅛	36	41
- Low	12½	12⅜	17	21½	20	32
P/E Ratio - High	28	NM	43	22	22	19
- Low	20	NM	27	17	12	15

Income Statement Analysis (Million $)

	1994	%Chg	1993	%Chg	1992	%Chg	1991
Revs.	177	7%	165	-18%	200	-8%	217
Oper. Inc.	21.4	31%	16.3	-21%	20.7	-31%	29.9
Depr.	6.3	3%	6.2	8%	5.7	5%	5.5
Int. Exp.	Nil	—	Nil	—	Nil	—	Nil
Pretax Inc.	19.0	NM	1.6	-90%	16.0	-46%	29.6
Eff. Tax Rate	45%	—	68%	—	32%	—	29%
Net Inc.	10.5	NM	0.5	-95%	10.8	-49%	21.2

Balance Sheet & Other Fin. Data (Million $)

	1994	1993	1992	1991	1990	1989
Cash	72.0	71.1	65.2	65.9	70.4	64.5
Curr. Assets	131	130	144	157	158	149
Total Assets	180	179	194	208	207	196
Curr. Liab.	46.8	40.2	39.8	42.7	41.5	38.4
LT Debt	Nil	Nil	Nil	Nil	Nil	Nil
Common Eqty.	129	134	151	162	162	154
Total Cap.	129	134	151	162	162	154
Cap. Exp.	7.7	8.5	5.4	8.4	5.9	9.8
Cash Flow	16.9	6.7	16.6	26.7	32.4	41.2

Ratio Analysis

	1994	1993	1992	1991	1990	1989
Curr. Ratio	2.8	3.2	3.6	3.7	3.8	3.9
% LT Debt of Cap.	Nil	Nil	Nil	Nil	Nil	Nil
% Net Inc.of Revs.	5.9	0.3	5.4	9.8	12.2	14.6
% Ret. on Assets	5.9	0.3	5.4	10.2	13.5	19.3
% Ret. on Equity	8.1	0.4	6.9	13.1	17.2	24.7

Dividend Data (Cash dividends were increased each year from 1968 to 1990. Class A and B common share equally in all disbursements.)

Amt. of Div. $	Date Decl.	Ex-Div. Date	Stock of Record	Payment Date
0.160	Jul. 21	Jul. 29	Aug. 04	Aug. 18 '94
0.160	Oct. 20	Oct. 28	Nov. 03	Nov. 17 '94
0.160	Dec. 06	Jan. 20	Jan. 26	Feb. 09 '95
0.160	Apr. 27	May. 03	May. 09	May. 23 '95
0.160	Jul. 19	Aug. 01	Aug. 03	Aug. 17 '95

Data as orig. reptd.; bef. results of disc. opers. and/or spec. items. Per share data adj. for stk. divs. as of ex-div. date. E-Estimated. NA-Not Available. NM-Not Meaningful. NR-Not Ranked.

Office—One Albion Rd., Lincoln, RI 02865. **Tel**—(401) 333-1200. **Chrmn**—B. R. Boss. **Pres & CEO**—R. A. Boss. **EVP & COO**—J. E. Buckley. **VP-Fin, Treas & CFO**—M. El-Hillow. **Secy**—T. C. Benik. **Dirs**—B. R. Boss, R. A. Boss, J. E. Buckley, B. V. Buonanno, Jr., H. F. Krimendahl II, T. C. McDermott, J. T. Murray, J. C. Tappan, E. M. Watson. **Transfer Agents**—Fleet National Bank of Rhode Island, Providence; Mellon Financial Securities, NYC. **Registrar**—Citizens Trust Co., Providence. **Incorporated** in Rhode Island in 1916. **Empl-** 1,200. **S&P Analyst:** Stephen Madonna, CFA

STANDARD & POOR'S
STOCK REPORTS

Cypress Semiconductor

NYSE Symbol **CY**
In S&P MidCap 400

07-SEP-95 **Industry:** Electronics/Electric

Summary: Cypress manufactures a broad line of high-performance integrated circuits.

S&P Opinion: Hold (★★★) Recent Price • 45¾ 52 Wk Range • 55½-15 Yield • Nil 12-Mo. P/E • 30.5

Quantitative Evaluations
Outlook (1 Lowest—5 Highest)
• **3+**
Fair Value
• **45**
Risk
• **High**
Earn./Div. Rank
• **B**

Technical Eval.
• **Bullish** since 7/95
Rel. Strength Rank (1 Lowest—99 Highest)
• **76**
Insider Activity
• **Neutral**

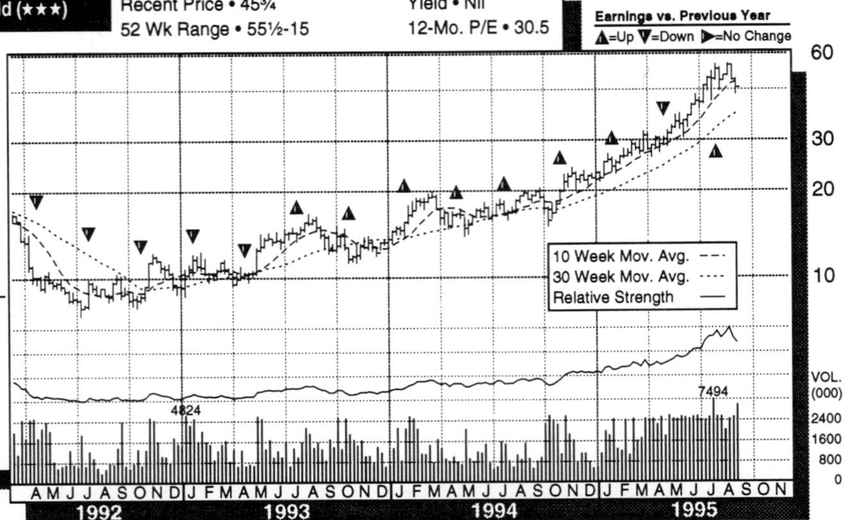

OPTIONS: CBOE

Overview - 07-SEP-95

Revenue growth for the second half of 1995 is projected to accelerate over the mid-30% rate realized in the first half. CY entered the third quarter with strong order momentum, a large backlog position and growing manufacturing capacity. The second quarter book-to-bill ratio was an impressive 1.49-to-1. This strong demand was fueled by increased PC unit volume and the resultant gain in sales static random access memories (SRAMs). SRAM accounted for 60% of CY's sales during the quarter and should continue to enjoy strong growth as Windows 95 has begun shipping. Gross margins should narrow in the third quarter due to the added capacity, but they are expected to rebound in the fourth quarter as efficiencies are realized. Operating costs should be well controlled, leading to substantial EPS leverage. Our $2.15 estimate ($1.95 fully diluted) for 1995 includes a $0.26 nonrecurring charge.

Valuation - 07-SEP-95

We have upgraded the shares to market performer from avoid, as semiconductor fundamentals remain strong. CY is well positioned for strong sales and earnings gains over the next 12 to 18 months, as the August 24 release of Windows 95 should fuel continued strong PC demand and corresponding sales of SRAM, of which CY is a leader. The shares currently trade at a premium to the market multiple, but we view this valuation as reasonable when compared to the company's two-to-three year estimated growth rate of 25%-30%.

Key Stock Statistics

S&P EPS Est. 1995	2.15	Tang. Bk. Value/Share	9.91
P/E on S&P Est. 1995	21.3	Beta	2.30
S&P EPS Est. 1996	3.05	Shareholders	2,700
Dividend Rate/Share	Nil	Market cap. (B)	$ 2.1
Shs. outstg. (M)	41.4	Inst. holdings	95%
Avg. daily vol. (M)	0.823	Insider holdings	NA

Value of $10,000 invested 5 years ago: $ 46,329

Fiscal Year Ending Dec. 31

	1995	% Change	1994	% Change	1993	% Change
Revenues (Million $)						
1Q	123.4	36%	90.96	31%	69.70	-6%
2Q	134.3	34%	100.2	34%	74.75	14%
3Q	—	—	104.0	35%	77.04	18%
4Q	—	—	111.2	34%	83.01	23%
Yr.	—	—	406.4	33%	304.5	12%
Income (Million $)						
1Q	9.11	-4%	9.53	NM	2.45	-38%
2Q	25.60	121%	11.57	NM	3.61	NM
3Q	—	—	13.61	124%	6.08	NM
4Q	—	—	15.77	NM	-4.09	NM
Yr.	—	—	50.47	NM	8.04	NM
Earnings Per Share ($)						
1Q	0.21	-13%	0.24	NM	0.07	-30%
2Q	0.57	97%	0.29	190%	0.10	NM
3Q	E0.65	97%	0.33	106%	0.16	NM
4Q	E0.75	103%	0.37	NM	-0.11	NM
Yr.	E2.15	75%	1.23	NM	0.21	NM

Next earnings report expected: mid October

Cypress Semiconductor

Business Summary - 07-SEP-95

Cypress Semiconductor designs, develops, manufactures and sells high-performance digital integrated circuits for a range of markets including computers, telecommunications, instrumentation and military systems. At the end of 1994, Cypress was shipping 295 products from its four divisions. International sales accounted for 32% of total sales in 1994.

The static memory division produces Static RAMs (Static Random Access Memories) and multichip modules. SRAMs are used for storage and retrieval of data in computers and other electronic systems. Multichip modules combine multiple chips into high-performance standard and custom memory subsystems.

The programmable products division makes EPROMs (Erasable Programmable Read-Only Memories), PLDs (Programmable Logic Devices), field programmable gate arrays (FPGAs) and FCT (Fast CMOS Technology) Logic Devices. EPROMs are used in computers and telecommunications systems to store fixed data that is not altered during machine operation. PLDs perform non-memory functions, such as floating-point mathematics. FCT Logic Devices are used for implementing bus interface and standard logic functions in high-speed systems.

The data communications division produces a range of products from the physical connection layer to system-level solutions.

The computation products division manufactures timing technology devices used in personal computers, including programmable clock oscillators, clock synthesizers and programmable metal can oscillators. This division also provides PC compatible systems logic through a recent acquisition. The company's goal is to provide all the silicon on a PC motherboard, except the CPU and DRAM.

Important Developments

Aug. '95—Directors declared a 2-for-1 stock split payable October 31 to shareholders of record on October 19. Separately, a judge reversed a $17 million judgement against CY in a patent infringement case against Texas Instruments.

Jul. '95—CY opened its new Fab 4 plant in Bloomington, Minn., which produces 8-inch silicon wafers and extends its production capacity by $200 million to $750 million. In addition, the company said its capacity will exceed $1 billion when new equipment is installed in the adjoining Fab 4B facility. Separately, the company introduced the hyperCache Chipset for Pentium-powered personal computers. CY believes that it is the first PC core logic chip set with integrated second level cache, which it expects will improve systems performance while offering savings in cost, board space and power usage.

Capitalization

Long Term Debt: $94,750,000 of debs. due 2001 & conv. into com. at $23.25 per sh. (7/3/95).

Per Share Data ($) (Year Ended Dec. 31)

	1994	1993	1992	1991	1990	1989
Tangible Bk. Val.	9.07	7.51	7.27	7.89	6.77	5.95
Cash Flow	2.32	1.20	0.71	1.78	1.67	1.44
Earnings	1.23	0.21	-0.56	0.85	0.87	0.80
Dividends	Nil	Nil	Nil	Nil	Nil	Nil
Payout Ratio	Nil	Nil	Nil	Nil	Nil	Nil
Prices - High	24⅛	16¾	18⅜	24½	15⅝	14½
- Low	13⅛	8⅝	7⅜	10⅞	8⅛	9¼
P/E Ratio - High	20	80	NM	29	18	18
- Low	11	41	NM	13	9	12

Income Statement Analysis (Million $)

	1994	%Chg	1993	%Chg	1992	%Chg	1991
Revs.	406	33%	305	12%	272	-5%	287
Oper. Inc.	123	86%	66.1	28%	51.7	-37%	82.3
Depr.	45.0	20%	37.5	-21%	47.6	27%	37.6
Int. Exp.	4.0	NM	0.3	-34%	0.4	-56%	1.0
Pretax Inc.	80.1	NM	12.6	NM	-32.9	NM	51.8
Eff. Tax Rate	37%	—	36%	—	NM	—	34%
Net Inc.	50.5	NM	8.0	NM	-21.0	NM	34.2

Balance Sheet & Other Fin. Data (Million $)

	1994	1993	1992	1991	1990	1989
Cash	193	81.0	82.0	104	92.0	97.0
Curr. Assets	317	186	184	212	192	179
Total Assets	556	341	321	375	309	286
Curr. Liab.	91.2	61.2	50.0	61.6	52.8	50.3
LT Debt	93.7	Nil	1.6	3.3	5.4	9.3
Common Eqty.	353	272	262	299	242	219
Total Cap.	461	279	271	313	257	235
Cap. Exp.	112	60.1	31.9	79.5	36.6	32.9
Cash Flow	95.5	45.6	26.6	71.7	63.8	55.2

Ratio Analysis

	1994	1993	1992	1991	1990	1989
Curr. Ratio	3.5	3.0	3.7	3.4	3.6	3.6
% LT Debt of Cap.	20.3	Nil	0.6	1.1	2.1	3.9
% Net Inc.of Revs.	12.4	2.6	NM	11.9	14.8	15.4
% Ret. on Assets	11.0	2.4	NM	9.7	11.3	11.5
% Ret. on Equity	15.6	3.0	NM	12.3	14.6	15.1

Dividend Data —No cash dividends have ever been paid. A 2-for-1 stock split was declared on August 31, 1995, and is payable on October 31.

Amt. of Div. $	Date Decl.	Ex-Div. Date	Stock of Record	Payment Date
2-for-1	Aug. 31	Nov. 01	Oct. 19	Oct. 31 '95

Data as orig. reptd.; bef. results of disc. opers. and/or spec. items. Per share data adj. for stk. divs. as of ex-div. date. E-Estimated. NA-Not Available. NM-Not Meaningful. NR-Not Ranked.

Office—3901 North First St., San Jose, CA 95134-1599. **Tel**—(408) 943-2600. **Pres & CEO**—T. J. Rodgers. **CFO, Secy & Investor Contact**—Emmanuel Hernandez. **Dirs**— P. R. Lamond (Chrmn), E. Benhamou, F. B. Bialek, J. C. Lewis, T. J. Rodgers. **Transfer Agent & Registrar**—First National Bank of Boston. **Incorporated** in California in 1982; reincorporated in Delaware in 1987. **Empl**-1,423. **S&P Analyst:** John D. Coyle, CFA

STANDARD & POOR'S

STOCK REPORTS

Danaher Corp.

NYSE Symbol **DHR**
In S&P MidCap 400

07-SEP-95 **Industry:** Building

Summary: Danaher produces tools, including all Sears Craftsman hand tools, transportation products, and process/environmental controls. In addition, it recently acquired Joslyn Corp.

S&P Opinion: Hold (★★★)

Recent Price • 33¼
52 Wk Range • 34-21⅝
Yield • 0.2%
12-Mo. P/E • 20.3

Quantitative Evaluations

Outlook
(1 Lowest—5 Highest)
• **2+**

Fair Value
• **30**

Risk
• **Low**

Earn./Div. Rank
• **B**

Technical Eval.
• **Bullish** since 10/92

Rel. Strength Rank
(1 Lowest—99 Highest)
• **66**

Insider Activity
• **NA**

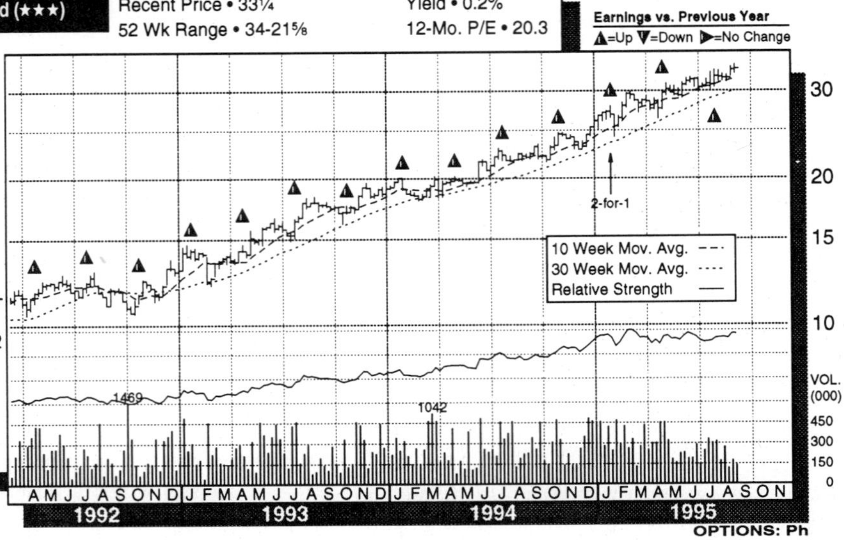

Overview - 07-SEP-95

Sales should rise strongly in 1995 and 1996, largely driven by acquisitions. Danaher Tools should benefit from increased sales to Sears, Roebuck, and process and environmental controls should continue growing. A steady flow of new and enhanced products should aid comparisons, as should greater sales of traditional tool lines. Recent acquisitions, including Armstrong Brothers Tool Co. and Hengstler GmbH will contribute some $220 million of profitable sales in 1995, and Joslyn Corp. will add $220 million on an annualized basis. Margins should widen over time as DHR consolidates the acquisitions and benefits from higher capacity utilization and productivity gains, including continued improvement in inventory management.

Valuation - 07-SEP-95

We rank the shares as hold, due to an above-average earnings multiple, despite DHR's relatively mature core markets. At 20X trailing 12-month, 19X projected 1995 and 17X expected 1996 EPS, the shares are not cheap. DHR's strategy is predicated on a steady stream of acquisitions to supplement modest internal growth. We expect the shares to be only average performers over the balance of 1995, particularly due to the acquisition of Joslyn Corp. which could result in a large addition of debt and which may take some time to consolidate. Although DHR is a sound long-term holding, we do not recommend adding to positions at this time.

Key Stock Statistics

S&P EPS Est. 1995	1.80	Tang. Bk. Value/Share	1.61
P/E on S&P Est. 1995	18.5	Beta	0.97
S&P EPS Est. 1996	2.00	Shareholders	5,200
Dividend Rate/Share	0.08	Market cap. (B)	$ 2.0
Shs. outstg. (M)	58.5	Inst. holdings	69%
Avg. daily vol. (M)	0.034	Insider holdings	NA

Value of $10,000 invested 5 years ago: $ 43,888

Fiscal Year Ending Dec. 31

	1995	% Change	1994	% Change	1993	% Change
Revenues (Million $)						
1Q	376.5	30%	289.1	16%	248.4	17%
2Q	391.5	23%	318.1	23%	258.9	9%
3Q	—	—	326.4	16%	281.0	14%
4Q	—	—	355.1	24%	287.2	10%
Yr.	—	—	1,289	20%	1,076	13%
Income (Million $)						
1Q	21.85	50%	14.53	44%	10.09	96%
2Q	27.22	41%	19.27	51%	12.80	59%
3Q	—	—	23.10	60%	14.47	49%
4Q	—	—	24.76	51%	16.40	89%
Yr.	—	—	81.65	52%	53.75	70%
Earnings Per Share ($)						
1Q	0.37	48%	0.25	43%	0.17	94%
2Q	0.45	36%	0.33	50%	0.22	57%
3Q	E0.48	22%	0.39	58%	0.25	47%
4Q	E0.50	19%	0.42	47%	0.29	90%
Yr.	E1.80	29%	1.40	51%	0.93	69%

Next earnings report expected: late October

Danaher Corp.

Business Summary - 07-SEP-95

Danaher Corp. is a leading manufacturer of hand tools, automotive and transportation products, and of process and environmental controls. Segment contributions (profits in million $) in 1994 were:

	Sales	Profits
Tools	45%	$58.9
Transportation	31%	44.0
Process/environmental controls	24%	56.6

Danaher Tools makes hand tools, tool holders, storage containers, fasteners and components for consumer, industrial and professional markets. The group consists of Iseli, Jacobs Chuck, Matco Tools, Special Markets and Professional Tools, and Delta Consolidated Industries (acquired in 1994). Products are sold under the Sears Craftsman, NAPA, Allen, Jacobs, Matco, Delta, Armstrong, K-D and Holo-Krome names. The company is the sole supplier of Sears Craftsman mechanics' hand tools, which accounted for 17% of sales in 1994 (18% in each of 1993 and 1992). Matco professional mechanics' tools are distributed by 1,100 independent mobile distributors.

Transportation includes Fayette Tubular (original equipment automobile air conditioning components), Hennessy Industries (Coats and Ammco tire changers, wheel aligners and balancers, brake lathes and lifts) and Jacobs Vehicle Equipment Co. (Jake Brake diesel engine retarders).

Process/Environmental Controls produces monitoring, sensing, controlling, measuring and counting products. Operating companies are Danaher Controls, Gulton Graphic Instruments, Hengstler GmbH, A. L. Hyde, Partlow/Anderson, Qualitrol, Veeder-Root, and West Instruments. A major growth area is environmental products, including inventory control and leak detection systems for underground petroleum storage tanks and fuel lines.

Foreign sales (8.5% of sales, $8.8 million of operating profit) should represent a larger part of DHR following its 1994 acquisition of Hengstler GmbH and four controls and instrument businesses from Mark IV Industries. These units should serve as a base for further expansion overseas.

Important Developments

Sep. '95—DHR completed a tender offer for Joslyn Corp. (JOSL) at $34 per share. After the tender offer DHR controlled some 75% of JOSL's 7.2 million shares. DHR said that it would proceed with conversion of the remaining JOSL shares into the right to receive $34 in cash. The total purchase price will be about $245 million. JOSL is a producer of electrical equipment, components and controls for electric utility, industrial and telecommunications markets with $220 million in annual sales.

Capitalization

Long Term Debt: $116,547,000 (6/95).

Per Share Data ($) (Year Ended Dec. 31)

	1994	1993	1992	1991	1990	1989
Tangible Bk. Val.	0.57	0.46	0.49	0.22	-0.01	-0.26
Cash Flow	2.16	1.64	1.04	0.82	1.15	1.39
Earnings	1.40	0.93	0.55	0.24	0.67	0.99
Dividends	0.06	0.06	Nil	Nil	Nil	Nil
Payout Ratio	5%	6%	Nil	Nil	Nil	Nil
Prices - High	26⅝	19⅝	13¾	11¾	11⅞	9¼
- Low	18	12⅛	9⅞	7⅞	6¾	6½
P/E Ratio - High	19	21	25	50	18	9
- Low	13	13	18	34	10	7

Income Statement Analysis (Million $)

	1994	%Chg	1993	%Chg	1992	%Chg	1991
Revs.	1,289	20%	1,074	13%	954	14%	836
Oper. Inc.	190	36%	140	43%	98.0	34%	73.0
Depr.	44.6	9%	40.9	46%	28.1	-15%	33.2
Int. Exp.	9.3	-10%	10.3	-6%	10.9	-25%	14.5
Pretax Inc.	137	50%	91.1	61%	56.7	116%	26.3
Eff. Tax Rate	40%	—	41%	—	44%	—	49%
Net Inc.	81.7	52%	53.7	70%	31.6	138%	13.3

Balance Sheet & Other Fin. Data (Million $)

	1994	1993	1992	1991	1990	1989
Cash	2.0	6.8	1.7	Nil	0.6	4.8
Curr. Assets	389	278	230	216	237	169
Total Assets	1,135	872	770	735	745	507
Curr. Liab.	396	235	212	174	181	144
LT Debt	117	131	137	182	186	143
Common Eqty.	476	364	348	319	305	192
Total Cap.	593	495	486	501	527	335
Cap. Exp.	54.5	40.3	33.9	41.8	33.0	22.9
Cash Flow	126	94.6	59.7	46.5	61.3	66.3

Ratio Analysis

	1994	1993	1992	1991	1990	1989
Curr. Ratio	1.0	1.2	1.1	1.2	1.3	1.2
% LT Debt of Cap.	19.7	26.5	28.3	36.3	35.3	42.7
% Net Inc.of Revs.	6.3	5.0	3.3	1.6	4.2	6.2
% Ret. on Assets	8.0	6.5	4.2	1.8	5.2	9.0
% Ret. on Equity	19.2	15.1	9.4	4.3	13.3	27.8

Dividend Data —Dividends, omitted in 1974, were resumed in March 1993.

Amt. of Div. $	Date Decl.	Ex-Div. Date	Stock of Record	Payment Date
0.030	Sep. 14	Sep. 20	Sep. 26	Oct. 28 '94
0.040	Dec. 07	Dec. 12	Dec. 16	Jan. 20 '95
2-for-1	Dec. 07	Jan. 23	Dec. 16	Jan. 20 '95
0.020	Mar. 17	Mar. 21	Mar. 27	Apr. 28 '95
0.020	Jun. 13	Jun. 28	Jun. 30	Jul. 28 '95

Data as orig. reptd.; bef. results of disc. opers. and/or spec. items. Per share data adj. for stk. divs. as of ex-div. date. E-Estimated. NA-Not Available. NM-Not Meaningful. NR-Not Ranked.

Office—1250 24th St., N.W., Washington, DC 20037. **Tel**—(202) 828-0850. **Chrmn**—S. M. Rales. **Pres & CEO**—G. M. Sherman. **SVP, CFO & Secy**—P. W. Allender. **VP, Contr & Investor Contact**—C. Scott Brannan. **Dirs**—M. M. Caplin, D. J. Ehrlich, W. G. Lohr, Jr., M. P. Rales, S. M. Rales, G. M. Sherman, A. E. Stephenson, Jr. **Transfer Agent**—Mellon Securities Trust Co., Pittsburgh. **Organized** in Massachusetts in 1969; reincorporated in Delaware in 1986. **Empl**-9,960. **S&P Analyst:** Joshua M. Harari, CFA

STANDARD & POOR'S

STOCK REPORTS

Datascope

NASDAQ Symbol **DSCP**

In S&P MidCap 400

20-SEP-95

Industry: Medical equipment/ supply

Summary: This company makes products for clinical health care markets in interventional cardiology, anesthesiology, critical care and cardiovascular and vascular surgery.

Quantitative Evaluations

Outlook (1 Lowest—5 Highest)
• **5+**

Fair Value
• **24⅝**

Risk
• **Average**

Earn./Div. Rank
• **B**

Technical Eval.
• **Bearish** since 4/95

Rel. Strength Rank (1 Lowest—99 Highest)
• **71**

Insider Activity
• **NA**

Recent Price • 21¼
52 Wk Range • 23-14½
Yield • Nil
12-Mo. P/E • 19.9

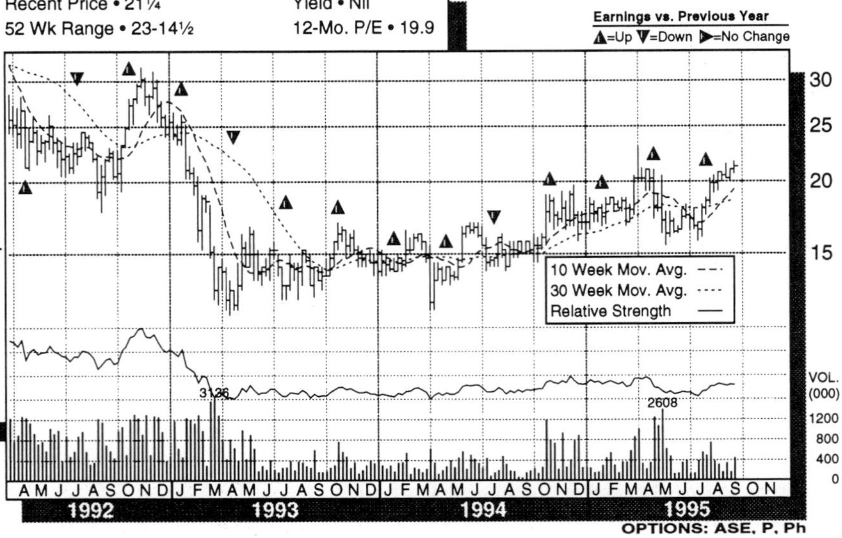

OPTIONS: ASE, P, Ph

Business Profile - 20-SEP-95

This company is experiencing growth as a result of strong demand for its innovative products. Positive trends should continue with the market acceptance of existing products. Additionally, growth will come from stronger international sales and new products. FDA approval of the company's VasoSeal product, as well as the re-introduction of the Point of View monitor, should contribute to future results.

Operational Review - 20-SEP-95

Net sales in recent periods have risen steadily, reflecting increased sales in the Cardiac Assist division, primarily due to strong global demand for intra-aortic balloon catheters and the new System 97 intra-aortic balloon pump and higher sales at the InterVascular division, which produces vascular grafts. Margins widened, and share earnings continued to advance.

Stock Performance - 15-SEP-95

In the past 30 trading days, DSCP's shares have increased 7%, compared to a 4% rise in the S&P 500. Average trading volume for the past five days was 86,360 shares, compared with the 40-day moving average of 75,185 shares.

Key Stock Statistics

Dividend Rate/Share	Nil	Shareholders	1,100
Shs. outstg. (M)	16.1	Market cap. (B)	$0.338
Avg. daily vol. (M)	0.058	Inst. holdings	38%
Tang. Bk. Value/Share	9.81	Insider holdings	NA
Beta	1.47		

Value of $10,000 invested 5 years ago: $ 19,173

Fiscal Year Ending Jun. 30

	1995	% Change	1994	% Change	1993	% Change
Revenues (Million $)						
1Q	41.60	9%	38.10	6%	36.00	14%
2Q	48.40	7%	45.20	-73%	166.0	NM
3Q	50.50	7%	47.30	13%	41.90	2%
4Q	55.20	6%	52.20	15%	45.40	NM
Yr.	195.7	7%	182.8	10%	166.0	6%
Income (Million $)						
1Q	2.76	13%	2.44	—	—	—
2Q	4.36	13%	3.87	13%	3.42	29%
3Q	4.52	8%	4.19	29%	3.26	-6%
4Q	5.70	10%	5.16	-26%	6.94	NM
Yr.	17.34	11%	15.67	NM	15.74	104%
Earnings Per Share ($)						
1Q	0.17	13%	0.15	15%	0.13	44%
2Q	0.27	12%	0.24	14%	0.21	31%
3Q	0.28	8%	0.26	30%	0.20	-5%
4Q	0.35	9%	0.32	-26%	0.43	NM
Yr.	1.07	10%	0.97	NM	0.97	106%

Next earnings report expected: early November

Datascope

Business Summary - 20-SEP-95

Datascope Corp. manufactures proprietary products for clinical healthcare markets in interventional cardiology, anesthesiology, cardiovascular and vascular surgery and for use in emergency rooms and intensive care units.

In the area of cardiac assist products (45% of fiscal 1994 sales), DSCP manufactures intra-aortic balloon pumping (IABP) systems. IABP therapy is used to stabilize heart function in instances of cardiac shock, before and after open heart surgery and in the management of heart failure. It is also used in acute angioplasty intervention, to relieve unstable angina, and to correct certain instances of medically resistant cardiac arrhythmias. Datascope also provides disposable intra-aortic balloon (IAB) catheters.

Datascope makes a broad line of multifunction patient safety monitor products (47% of fiscal 1994 sales) which are capable of continuous and simultaneous measurement of multiple parameters in various hospital settings. Its PASSPORT units measure EKG, blood pressure, temperature and respiration, pulse oximetry and carbon dioxide. A central station monitor, VISA, can be connected to up to eight PASSPORT transportable monitors. The top-of-the-line operating room monitor is the 3000A, a product that measures invasive and noninvasive blood pressure, blood oxygen saturation, heart rate, EKG and temperature. In the market for advanced patient monitoring in operating rooms and post-anesthesia care units, DSCP sells the "point of view" critical care monitoring system.

The Collagen Products unit produces and sells VasoSeal, a product used to rapidly seal femoral artery punctures after catheterization procedures (approved for sale in Japan, Canada, Australia and Italy); and hemostatic products used during surgery. This division also sells a collagen hemostatic pad and a fibrillar collagen hemostat which are used to control bleeding during surgery.

The InterVascular subsidiary makes a proprietary line of knitted and woven dacron vascular grafts and patches for reconstructive surgery.

Important Developments

Jun. '95—The company received a letter from the FDA informing it that the Pre-Market Approval (PMA) for VasoSeal was approvable for use in both coronary angiography and coronary angioplasty procedures. Final approval is subject to receipt by FDA of satisfactory information concerning the products labeling and packaging validation.

Oct. '94—The company suspended shipments of its point of view monitor after an audit disclosed certain regulatory issues. DSCP met with the FDA in November 1994, but product shipments will not resume until the agency's satisfactory review of data supporting the company's 510(k) filing.

Capitalization

Long Term Debt: None (3/95).

Per Share Data ($) (Year Ended Jun. 30)

	1995	1994	1993	1992	1991	1990
Tangible Bk. Val.	NA	8.98	7.97	7.01	6.46	5.99
Cash Flow	NA	1.36	1.31	0.76	0.82	0.98
Earnings	1.07	0.97	0.97	0.47	0.55	0.60
Dividends	Nil	Nil	Nil	Nil	Nil	Nil
Payout Ratio	Nil	Nil	Nil	Nil	Nil	Nil
Prices - High	23	19¾	26½	41¾	39⅛	11¼
- Low	15½	12	11¾	17¾	9½	6¼
P/E Ratio - High	21	20	27	89	71	19
- Low	14	12	12	38	17	10

Income Statement Analysis (Million $)

	1994	%Chg	1993	%Chg	1992	%Chg	1991
Revs.	183	10%	166	6%	157	16%	135
Oper. Inc.	27.1	15%	23.6	13%	20.9	54%	13.6
Depr.	6.3	13%	5.5	16%	4.8	11%	4.3
Int. Exp.	0.0	NM	0.0	-89%	0.2	NM	0.2
Pretax Inc.	22.1	NM	22.1	108%	10.6	-15%	12.5
Eff. Tax Rate	29%	—	29%	—	28%	—	31%
Net Inc.	15.7	NM	15.7	104%	7.7	-10%	8.6

Balance Sheet & Other Fin. Data (Million $)

	1994	1993	1992	1991	1990	1989
Cash	45.4	45.2	32.1	28.7	19.3	13.1
Curr. Assets	138	122	110	98.0	92.0	79.0
Total Assets	185	158	141	128	124	104
Curr. Liab.	33.3	23.2	25.5	23.9	27.0	17.7
LT Debt	Nil	Nil	Nil	Nil	0.1	0.4
Common Eqty.	144	128	110	100	92.0	82.0
Total Cap.	144	128	110	100	93.0	83.0
Cap. Exp.	19.0	11.2	5.3	4.2	9.4	8.5
Cash Flow	21.9	21.3	12.5	12.9	15.2	14.3

Ratio Analysis

	1994	1993	1992	1991	1990	1989
Curr. Ratio	4.2	5.2	4.3	4.1	3.4	4.5
% LT Debt of Cap.	Nil	Nil	Nil	Nil	0.1	0.5
% Net Inc.of Revs.	8.6	9.5	4.9	6.4	7.7	9.3
% Ret. on Assets	9.1	10.4	5.7	6.8	8.2	9.7
% Ret. on Equity	11.5	13.1	7.3	8.9	10.7	14.6

Dividend Data —No cash has been paid.

Data as orig. reptd.; bef. results of disc. opers. and/or spec. items. Per share data adj. for stk. divs. as of ex-div. date. E-Estimated. NA-Not Available. NM-Not Meaningful. NR-Not Ranked.

Office—14 Philips Pkwy., Montvale, NJ 07645-9998. **Tel**—(201) 391-8100. **Chrmn, Pres & CEO**—L. Saper. **SVP-Fin, Secy, CFO & Investor Contact**—Murray Pitkowsky (201-307-5504). **Dirs**—D. Altschiller, W. L. Asmundson, J. Grayzel, G. Heller, A. J. Patricof, L. Saper, N. M. Schneider. **Transfer Agent**—Continental Stock Transfer & Trust Co., NYC. **Incorporated** in New York in 1964. **Empl**-1,100. **S&P Analyst:** Philip J. Birbara

Dauphin Deposit Corp.

NASDAQ Symbol DAPN (Incl. in Nat'l Market) In S&P MidCap 400

Price	Range	P–E Ratio	Dividend	Yield	S&P Ranking	Beta
Aug. 21'95	1995					
27¼	28–23	14	1.00	3.7%	A	0.66

Summary

Headquartered in Harrisburg, this holding company owns Dauphin Deposit Bank & Trust Co., which includes the Bank of Pennsylvania division, Farmers Bank and Trust Co. of Hanover and Valley Bancorp. The banks operate over 100 branch offices in Pennsylvania. Share earnings have risen steadily for 23 consecutive years. Earnings fell 13% in the first half of 1995, penalized by a narrower net interest margin and higher noninterest expenses. Cash dividends, raised 8.7% in October 1994, have been increased for 18 consecutive years.

Business Summary

Dauphin Deposit Corporation is a bank holding company headquartered in Harrisburg, Pa. Its principal subsidiary is Dauphin Deposit Bank and Trust Co. The bank, which includes the Bank of Pennsylvania division, the Valleybank division (acquired January 1994) and Farmers Bank and Trust Co. of Hanover, operates over 100 offices in the counties of Adams, Berks, Chester, Cumberland, Dauphin, Franklin, Lancaster, Lebanon, Lehigh, Montgomery, Northampton and York. Nonbank subsidiaries include Eastern Mortgage Services Inc. (acquired in July 1994), Dauphin Life Insurance Co., Dauphin Investment Co., Financial Realty, Inc. and Hopper Soliday & Co.

Loans outstanding (net of unearned income) amounted to $2.86 billion at 1994 year end, divided as follows:

Commercial, financial & agricultural..	41%
Real estate–residential	32%
Real estate–construction	6%
Consumer	17%
Lease financing	4%

The allowance for loan losses totaled $40,216,000 at the end of 1994 (compared with $39,182,000 a year earlier) and was equal to 1.41% (1.52%) of year-end loans. Net chargeoffs were $6,359,000 in 1994 ($7,186,000 in 1993), or 0.24% (0.29%) of average loans. As of December 31, 1994, nonperforming loans aggregated $18,224,000 (0.53% of outstanding loans), compared with $27,783,000 (0.96%) a year earlier.

Deposits amounted to $3.51 billion at the end of 1994 and were apportioned: 13% noninterest-bearing demand, 15% NOW accounts, 14% savings, 15% money-market accounts, 35% time, and 8% time deposits of $100,000 or more.

Interest and fees on loans contributed 53% of total income in 1994, interest and dividends on investment securities 31%, other interest income 1%, income from fiduciary activities 4%, service charges on deposit accounts 3%, and other noninterest income 8%.

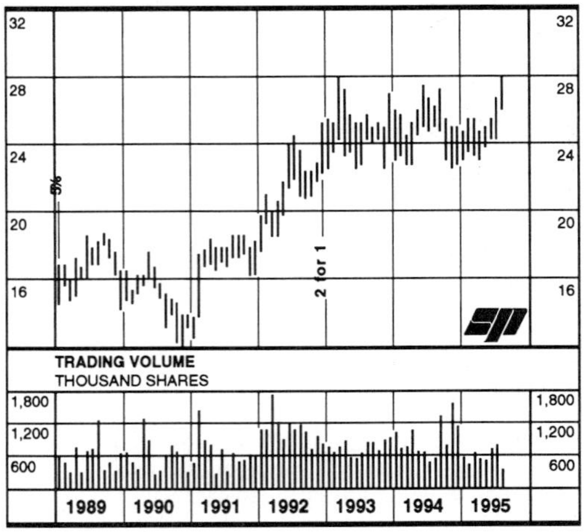

On a tax-equivalent basis, the average yield on total interest-earning assets was 7.01% in 1994 (7.04% in 1993), while the average rate paid on interest-bearing liabilities was 3.85% (3.80%), for an interest rate spread of 3.61% (3.67%).

Important Developments

Jul. '95— DAPN, which has engaged a national consulting firm to help reposition its community banking services, said it is focusing on improving competitiveness and efficiency. Also in July, the company reported that Eastern Mortgage Services, Inc. had posted its first quarter of profitability since its acquisition in July 1994. Earlier, in February 1995, DAPN authorized the repurchase of up to 1,500,000 shares of its common stock.

Next earnings report expected in mid-October.

Per Share Data ($)

Yr. End Dec. 31	1994	1993	[1]1992	1991	1990	1989	[1,2]1988	[1]1987	1986	1985
Tangible Bk. Val.	**15.08**	15.80	14.47	13.40	12.25	11.39	10.37	9.30	8.68	7.71
Earnings	**2.18**	2.15	1.93	1.84	1.78	1.71	1.57	1.49	1.38	1.22
Dividends	**0.940**	0.800	0.770	0.745	0.718	0.688	0.619	0.582	0.529	0.479
Payout Ratio	**43%**	37%	40%	41%	40%	40%	39%	39%	38%	39%
Prices—High	**27½**	28	25¼	18⅝	17⅝	18¾	16 5/16	17	18 11/16	13 9/16
Low	**22½**	22½	17⅝	12½	12	14 3/16	13 9/16	12¼	13 7/16	7⅞
P/E Ratio—	**13–10**	13–10	13–9	10–7	10–7	11–8	10–9	11–8	14–10	11–6

Data as orig. reptd. Adj. for stk. divs. of 100% Dec. 1992, 5% Jan. 1989, 100% Aug. 1985. **1.** Refl. merger or acq. **2.** Refl. acctg. change.

Income Data (Million $)

Year Ended Dec. 31	Net Int. Inc.	Tax Equiv. Adj.	Non Int. Inc.	Loan Loss Prov.	% Exp./ Op. Revs.	Net Bef. Taxes	Eff. Tax Rate	Net Inc.	% Net Int. Margin	—% Return On— Assets	Equity
1994	**178**	**15.1**	**57.6**	**7.49**	**55.4**	**92.8**	**24.5%**	**70.0**	**4.17**	**1.40**	**14.4**
1993	162	14.4	55.0	9.37	54.4	84.9	24.1%	64.5	4.16	1.43	14.3
[1]1992	153	14.2	50.0	10.90	56.1	74.4	23.1%	57.2	4.11	1.31	14.1
1991	118	12.9	37.8	7.90	55.5	57.0	19.8%	45.7	4.01	1.30	14.4
1990	110	11.4	34.5	6.45	52.9	57.8	21.5%	45.4	3.98	1.37	15.2
1989	109	8.6	31.7	6.18	51.3	60.1	26.1%	44.4	3.96	1.39	15.9
[1,2]1988	105	8.0	25.2	6.79	51.2	54.9	26.0%	40.7	3.92	1.31	16.0
[1]1987	96	10.1	20.0	4.29	51.5	49.3	29.4%	34.9	4.08	1.24	16.1
1986	84	14.5	16.4	4.75	50.0	40.1	26.7%	29.4	4.17	1.15	15.7
1985	75	12.5	14.3	3.70	53.0	32.8	25.7%	24.3	3.99	1.02	15.4

Balance Sheet Data (Million $)

Dec. 31	Total Assets	—Earning Assets— Mon. Mkt. Assets	Inv. Secs.	Com'l Loans	Other Loans	% Loan Loss Resv.	—Deposits— Demand	Time	% Loans/ Deposits	Long Term Debt	Common Equity	% Equity To Assets
1994	**5,070**	**15.04**	**1,784**	**1,284**	**1,581**	**1.41**	**465**	**3,050**	**81.4**	**92.0**	**467**	**9.74**
1993	4,596	8.49	1,960	1,077	1,294	1.53	394	2,907	71.7	92.5	473	9.98
1992	4,573	92.00	1,961	1,027	1,168	1.53	420	2,981	64.5	92.9	431	9.34
1991	3,612	23.00	1,506	899	917	1.22	354	2,469	64.2	36.1	334	9.00
1990	3,489	80.00	1,363	865	893	1.21	329	2,401	64.3	40.3	304	9.00
1989	3,259	186.00	1,129	792	883	1.20	331	2,283	63.9	47.3	296	8.70
1988	3,336	207.00	1,270	772	826	1.11	356	2,189	62.5	47.9	269	8.20
1987	2,905	168.00	1,034	700	781	1.13	352	1,987	63.3	48.5	229	7.80
1986	2,654	149.00	939	626	705	1.15	322	1,840	61.6	48.8	197	7.30
1985	2,598	308.00	911	576	601	1.15	280	1,820	56.1	20.4	179	6.70

Data as orig. reptd. **1.** Refl. merger or acq. **2.** Refl. acctg. change.

Review of Operations

Net interest income fell 1.7%, year to year, in the six months ended June 30, 1995, as a narrower net interest margin outweighed growth in interest earning assets. The provision for loan losses shrank 17%, to $3.1 million, and, following a 23% increase in noninterest income and 17% higher noninterest expense, pretax income declined 12%. After taxes at 25.0%, versus 24.5%, net income was down 13%, to $31,296,000 ($1.01 a share, on 4.4% fewer shares), from $35,868,000 ($1.11).

Common Share Earnings ($)

Quarter:	1995	1994	1993	1992
Mar.	0.49	0.55	0.56	0.49
Jun.	0.52	0.56	0.55	0.49
Sep.		0.54	0.54	0.47
Dec.		0.53	0.50	0.48
		2.18	2.15	1.93

Finances

In July 1994, Dauphin acquired Eastern Mortgage Services, Inc. of Trevose, Pa., a closely held mortgage banking company, for $20.5 million in cash. Eastern Mortgage, which primarily serves the eastern Pennsylvania and New Jersey markets, originated $917 million of first mortgages in 1993.

In January 1994, the company acquired Valley Bancorp., Inc., Chambersburg, Pa., for 2,600,643 common shares. The acquisition, which added $324 million in assets and 13 banking offices, extended the company's presence to Franklin County, Pa.

In January and October 1994, directors authorized the repurchase of up to 1,000,000 of the company's common shares on the open market or in privately negotiated transactions.

Dividend Data

Cash has been paid each year by the company or its predecessor banks since 1910. A dividend reinvestment plan is available.

Amt. of Divd. $	Date Decl.	Ex-divd. Date	Stock of Record	Payment Date
0.23	Jul. 25	Sep. 19	Sep. 23	Oct. 14'94
0.25	Oct. 24	Dec. 19	Dec. 23	Jan. 13'95
0.25	Jan. 23	Mar. 20	Mar. 24	Apr. 14'95
0.25	Apr. 17	Jun. 29	Jul. 3	Jul. 14'95
0.25	Aug. 21	Sep. 20	Sep. 22	Oct. 13'95

Capitalization

Long Term Debt: $40,809,000 (6/95).

Common Stock: 30,948,885 shs. ($5 par).
Institutions hold about 22%.
Shareholders: 11,689 of record (12/94).

Office—213 Market St., Harrisburg, PA 17105. **Tel**—(717) 255-2121. **Chrmn & CEO**—C. R. Jennings. **Pres & COO**—R. L. Fryer Jr. **EVP & CFO**—D. L. Dinger. **SVP & Treas**—J. T. Lysczek Jr. **SVP & Secy**—Claire D. Flemming. **VP & Investor Contact**—N. Bruce Pinto. **Dirs**—R. L. Fryer Jr., J. O. Green, D. C. Hathaway, A. G. Hemmerich, L. H. Javitch, C. R. Jennings, W. J. King, W. T. Kirchoff, L. J. LaMaina Jr., A. Maier II, J. E. Marley, R. F. Nation, E. E. Naugle, W. F. Raab, P. C. Raub, H. W. Rhoads, J. D. Seibert, R. C. Sheridan Jr. **Transfer Agent**—Dauphin Deposit Bank & Trust Co., Harrisburg. **Formed** in Pennsylvania in 1974. **Empl**—2,300.

 Robert Schpoont

STANDARD & POOR'S

STOCK REPORTS

Dean Foods

NYSE Symbol **DF**
In S&P MidCap 400

10-OCT-95 **Industry:** Food

Summary: This major producer of dairy goods also processes canned and frozen vegetables and other food items. Acquisitions have contributed significantly to growth in recent years.

S&P Opinion: Avoid (★★)

Recent Price • 28½
52 Wk Range • 31¾-26¼
Yield • 2.5%
12-Mo. P/E • 14.8

Quantitative Evaluations

Outlook (1 Lowest—5 Highest)
• **3+**

Fair Value
• **28½**

Risk
• **Low**

Earn./Div. Rank
• **A**

Technical Eval.
• **Bearish** since 8/94

Rel. Strength Rank (1 Lowest—99 Highest)
• **58**

Insider Activity
• **Neutral**

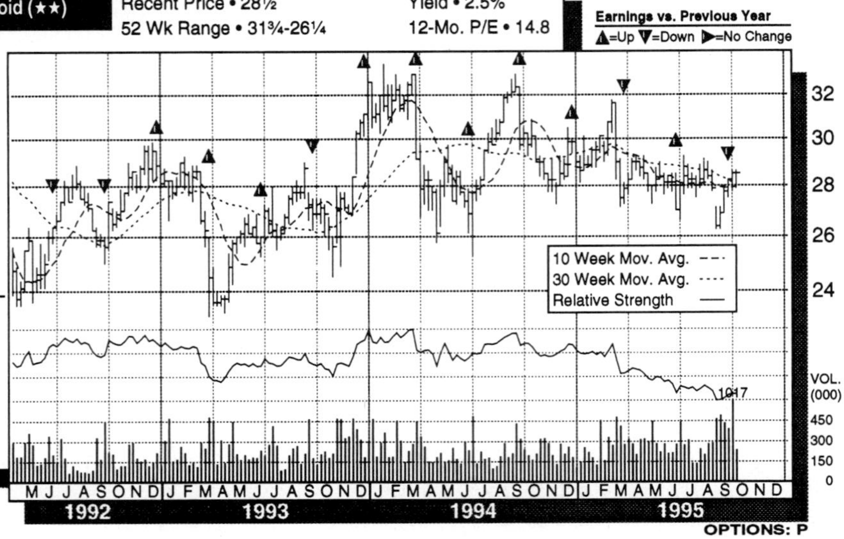

OPTIONS: P

Overview - 10-OCT-95

Sales in fiscal 1995-96 are projected to advance by approximately 5%, as internal growth and acquisition contributions help offset vegetable product selling pricing pressures. Dairy profits should benefit over the near term from stable raw milk costs and greater volumes, offset somewhat by current difficult competitive conditions in the ice cream sector. Specialty Food profits over the near term should benefit from a further favorable product mix shift toward value-added, frozen products (Bird's Eye), offset somewhat by a difficult pricing environment for canned vegetable products. The integration of acquisitions, combined with increased efforts to leverage DF's growing array of branded products, should allow earnings to extend their long, albiet modest, upward trend over the next few years.

Valuation - 10-OCT-95

Given our outlook of only modest earnings growth in fiscal 1995-96, we view the shares as unattractive at current levels. Although the shares currently trade at the low end of the company's historical P/E range, we believe that expansion in the multiple will be limited until improved earnings trends become evident. The current downsizing of Borden's dairy assets by its new owners, Kohlberg Kravis Roberts, may present a near-term opportunity for Dean to acquire some of that concern's facilities. However, given the company's uninspiring near-term earnings outlook, we recommend avoiding the stock.

Key Stock Statistics

S&P EPS Est. 1996	2.10	Tang. Bk. Value/Share	12.14
P/E on S&P Est. 1996	13.6	Beta	0.80
Dividend Rate/Share	0.72	Shareholders	9,900
Shs. outstg. (M)	40.1	Market cap. (B)	$ 1.1
Avg. daily vol. (M)	0.098	Inst. holdings	43%
		Insider holdings	NA

Value of $10,000 invested 5 years ago: $ 14,457

Fiscal Year Ending May 31

	1996	% Change	1995	% Change	1994	% Change
Revenues (Million $)						
1Q	651.5	6%	614.3	10%	559.7	3%
2Q	—	—	662.8	15%	577.1	NM
3Q	—	—	665.9	7%	622.9	10%
4Q	—	—	687.2	2%	671.5	13%
Yr.	—	—	2,630	8%	2,431	7%
Income (Million $)						
1Q	13.66	-19%	16.96	60%	10.59	-31%
2Q	—	—	20.03	15%	17.46	2%
3Q	—	—	17.18	-7%	18.44	15%
4Q	—	—	25.90	7%	24.28	22%
Yr.	—	—	80.06	13%	70.76	3%
Earnings Per Share ($)						
1Q	0.34	-21%	0.43	59%	0.27	-31%
2Q	E0.50	NM	0.50	14%	0.44	2%
3Q	E0.52	21%	0.43	-7%	0.46	12%
4Q	E0.74	14%	0.65	7%	0.61	22%
Yr.	E2.10	4%	2.01	13%	1.78	3%

Next earnings report expected: late December

Dean Foods

Business Summary - 10-OCT-95

Dean Foods produces and distributes dairy and specialty food products. Contributions to sales and profits (in millions) by business segment in 1994-95 were:

	Sales	Profits
Dairy products	58%	$77.2
Specialty foods	41%	97.8
Corporate & other	1%	-38.6

Fluid milk and specialty dairy products account for 86% of total dairy product sales. Products include homogenized, low-fat and skim milk, regular and low-fat cottage cheese, yogurt, half and half, buttermilk, chocolate milk, sour cream and egg nog. Ice cream products, which include ice milk, fruit sherbets, frozen dessert novelties, yogurt and a non-fat frozen dairy dessert, account for the remainder of dairy product sales. The Baskin Robbins franchise was sold in 1989, but the company continues to supply product to the franchise.

Specialty foods include canned and frozen vegetables (20% of sales), pickles, relishes and salad dressings (14%), which are sold in the Midwest, South and Southwest. Other categories include puddings, dips and sauces (3%) and powdered products (4%), mainly non-dairy coffee creamers.

Corporate and other sales reflect DF's transportation subsidiary (DFC Transportation Co.) and sales of canned meats processed under bid contracts with the federal government.

Important Developments

Sep. '95—During fiscal 1996's first quarter, Dairy segment profits rose 3.9%, on a 5.1% sales increase, year to year. Specialty foods segment profits fell 30% on a 7.8% sales increase, reflecting lower vegetable selling prices, and higher promotional costs related to higher industry-wide inventory levels and intense competitive activity. Additionally, 1995 weather conditions in the Midwest vegetable growing areas resulted in increased processing costs due to a lower pack. First quarter pickle operations earnings were adversely affected by the spring and early summer weather-related conditions in the Southeast growing areas. Management said that its outlook for DF's vegetable operations remained positive, and it anticipated that selling prices will improve as the year progresses as a result of the lower 1995 crop intake.

Capitalization

Long Term Obligations: $226,873,000 (8/95).

Per Share Data ($)

(Year Ended May 31)

	1995	1994	1993	1992	1991	1990
Tangible Bk. Val.	12.14	10.64	11.11	10.00	9.36	8.15
Cash Flow	3.64	3.25	3.03	2.72	2.88	2.41
Earnings	2.01	1.78	1.73	1.53	1.79	1.53
Dividends	0.68	0.64	0.60	0.56	0.49	0.44
Payout Ratio	34%	36%	35%	36%	28%	29%
Cal. Yrs.	1994	1993	1992	1991	1990	1989
Prices - High	33½	32⅞	31½	33½	27¼	25¼
- Low	25¼	23⅛	22¾	24⅞	20⅛	19¼
P/E Ratio - High	17	18	18	22	15	17
- Low	13	13	13	16	11	13

Income Statement Analysis (Million $)

	1995	%Chg	1994	%Chg	1993	%Chg	1992
Revs.	2,630	8%	2,431	7%	2,274	NM	2,289
Oper. Inc.	223	17%	191	7%	178	2%	175
Depr.	65.1	11%	58.5	13%	51.8	7%	48.3
Int. Exp.	22.4	45%	15.5	4%	14.9	-4%	15.6
Pretax Inc.	136	15%	118	3%	115	8%	106
Eff. Tax Rate	41%	—	40%	—	40%	—	41%
Net Inc.	80.1	13%	70.8	4%	68.4	10%	62.0

Balance Sheet & Other Fin. Data (Million $)

	1995	1994	1993	1992	1991	1990
Cash	4.8	11.0	41.6	34.0	44.1	43.5
Curr. Assets	519	460	406	397	399	372
Total Assets	1,202	1,109	893	857	817	745
Curr. Liab.	304	367	208	213	201	190
LT Debt	225	136	151	155	150	147
Common Eqty.	585	525	476	430	417	363
Total Cap.	819	724	674	627	599	539
Cap. Exp.	83.0	148	75.0	78.0	94.0	122
Cash Flow	145	129	120	110	117	97.0

Ratio Analysis

	1995	1994	1993	1992	1991	1990
Curr. Ratio	1.7	1.3	2.0	1.9	2.0	2.0
% LT Debt of Cap.	25.6	18.8	22.4	24.8	25.0	27.2
% Net Inc.of Revs.	3.0	2.9	3.0	2.7	3.4	3.1
% Ret. on Assets	6.9	7.1	7.8	7.5	9.3	9.1
% Ret. on Equity	14.4	14.1	15.1	14.8	18.6	18.4

Dividend Data —Dividends have been paid since 1941. A dividend reinvestment plan is available. A "poison pill" stock purchase rights plan was adopted in 1988 and amended in 1989.

Amt. of Div. $	Date Decl.	Ex-Div. Date	Stock of Record	Payment Date
0.170	Oct. 05	Nov. 14	Nov. 18	Dec. 15 '94
0.170	Jan. 30	Feb. 13	Feb. 17	Mar. 15 '95
0.170	Mar. 28	May. 15	May. 19	Jun. 15 '95
0.180	Jul. 28	Aug. 16	Aug. 18	Sep. 15 '95
0.180	Oct. 06	Nov. 15	Nov. 17	Dec. 15 '95

Data as orig. reptd.; bef. results of disc. opers. and/or spec. items. Per share data adj. for stk. divs. as of ex-div. date. E-Estimated. NA-Not Available. NM-Not Meaningful. NR-Not Ranked.

Office—3600 North River Rd., Franklin Park, IL 60131. **Tel**—(708) 678-1680. **Chrmn & CEO**—H. M. Dean. **Pres**—T. L. Rose. **VP & Secy**—E. A. Blanchard. **Dirs**—L. M. Collens, P. H. Crown, H. M. Dean, W. D. Fischer, J. P. Frazee, B. A. Getz, J. S. Llewellyn, Jr., A. J. McKenna, T. A. Ravencroft, T. L. Rose, A. J. Vogl. **Transfer Agent & Registrar**—Harris Trust & Savings Bank, Chicago. **Incorporated** in Illinois in 1929; reincorporated in Delaware in 1968. **Empl**-11,800. **S&P Analyst:** Kenneth A. Shea

STANDARD & POOR'S

STOCK REPORTS

Dell Computer

NASDAQ Symbol **DELL**

In S&P MidCap 400

14-OCT-95 **Industry:** Data Processing

Summary: Dell is the leading direct marketer and one of the world's top 10 manufacturers of personal computers compatible with industry standards established by IBM.

S&P Opinion: Accumulate (★★★★) | Recent Price • 83 | 52 Wk Range • 93⅞-36¾ | Yield • Nil | 12-Mo. P/E • 17.5

Quantitative Evaluations
Outlook (1 Lowest—5 Highest) • **4+**
Fair Value • **90⅞**
Risk • **Average**
Earn./Div. Rank • **B**

Technical Eval. • **Bullish** since 5/94
Rel. Strength Rank (1 Lowest—99 Highest) • **86**
Insider Activity • **Neutral**

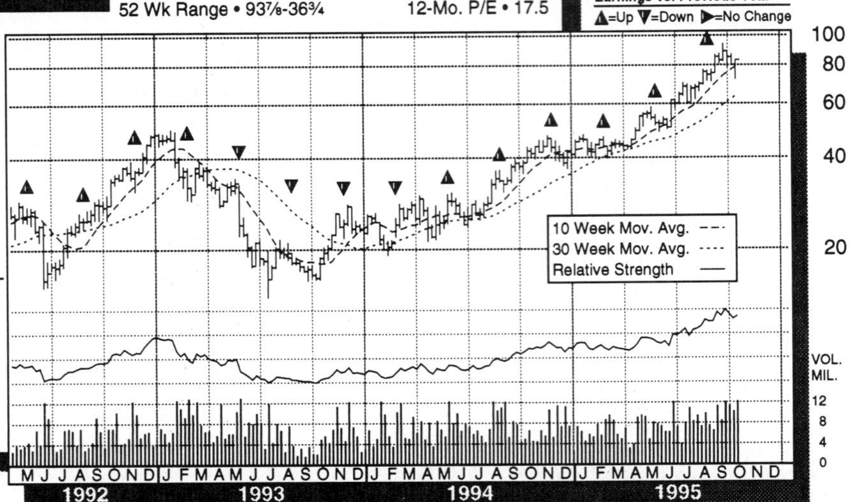

OPTIONS: Ph

Overview - 13-OCT-95

Dell is poised for strong growth for the balance of 1995-96, as the Windows 95 introduction and the ongoing transition to the Pentium processor is expected to fuel a powerful upgrade cycle through the holiday season. Worldwide demand for PCs could grow some 25% to 30% in 1995 and 15% to 20% over the next several years. Dell is well positioned for this growth, as its direct selling model offers unmatched flexibility in delivering the latest system features at aggressive price points. We are forecasting revenue growth in excess of 40% over the next two quarters, against reasonably tough comparisons. Margins could narrow slightly, reflecting ongoing pricing pressures and a less favorable product mix. Nevertheless, net income growth will remain robust, although the EPS increase will be less, due to the sharp increase in shares outstanding.

Valuation - 13-OCT-95

Despite the surge in recent periods, the shares remain attractive, due to the sales and earnings momentum expected through 1996-97. Dell remains a strong play on the PC upgrade cycle that is expected to occur over the next 6 to 18 months. Dell's direct selling approach offers certain comparative advantages over key competitors, particularly in the critical areas of inventory management and pricing. Because of these favorable fundamentals and because Dell trades at a low multiple to earnings based on our 1996-97 estimate, we continue to recommended the shares for their above average capital gains potential.

Key Stock Statistics

S&P EPS Est. 1996	5.45	Tang. Bk. Value/Share	15.83
P/E on S&P Est. 1996	15.2	Beta	1.22
S&P EPS Est. 1997	6.60	Shareholders	3,200
Dividend Rate/Share	Nil	Market cap. (B)	$ 3.8
Shs. outstg. (M)	45.9	Inst. holdings	67%
Avg. daily vol. (M)	2.298	Insider holdings	NA

Value of $10,000 invested 5 years ago: $ 226,343

Fiscal Year Ending Jan. 31

	1996	% Change	1995	% Change	1994	% Change
Revenues (Million $)						
1Q	1,136	48%	767.0	14%	672.4	84%
2Q	1,206	52%	791.5	13%	700.6	53%
3Q	—	—	884.5	17%	757.3	33%
4Q	—	—	1,033	39%	743.0	20%
Yr.	—	—	3,475	21%	2,873	43%
Income (Million $)						
1Q	61.70	NM	18.97	86%	10.19	-49%
2Q	65.07	128%	28.56	NM	-75.71	NM
3Q	—	—	41.35	NM	11.98	-58%
4Q	—	—	60.29	NM	17.71	-43%
Yr.	—	—	149.2	NM	-35.83	NM
Earnings Per Share ($)						
1Q	1.11	164%	0.42	68%	0.25	-52%
2Q	1.32	103%	0.65	NM	-2.03	NM
3Q	E1.40	51%	0.93	NM	0.26	-64%
4Q	E1.60	18%	1.36	NM	0.39	-49%
Yr.	E5.45	61%	3.38	NM	-1.06	NM

Next earnings report expected: mid November

Dell Computer

14-OCT-95

Business Summary - 12-SEP-95

Dell Computer Corporation is a direct marketer of personal computers, including desktops, notebooks and servers. International sales accounted for 31% of the total in 1994-5, up from 30% in 1993-4.

At January 29, 1995, the company had a total of 64 personal computer systems available under seven brand names. Dell's line of servers are sold under the PowerEdge name and are used in a networked environment to distribute files, database information, applications and communication products. Desktop PCs include the OmniPlex line, which is targeted at corporate users with high-performance needs; OptiPlex, which is for corporations seeking advanced features and performance; Dell Dimension XPS, a line targeted at technologically sophisticated business and individual users; and Dell Dimension, which is targeted at small-to-medium-sized businesses and individual users. During 1994, Dell introduced the Latitude and Latitude XP notebook lines.

In addition to its own branded products, Dell offers more than 7,000 popular software packages and peripheral products through its DellWare program. The company also offers a number of specialized services, including custom hardware and software integration and network installation and support.

Manufacturing operations are conducted at facilities in Austin, Tex., and Limerick, Ireland. In January 1995, the company announced plans to purchase a nine-acre site in Penang, Malaysia, for construction of a new 125,000 sq. ft. manufacturing facility to serve the Asia-Pacific region.

In July 1994, Dell discontinued retail channel sales to focus exclusively on its direct business.

Important Developments

Aug. '95—DELL introduced the OptiPlex G family of systems, which feature Pentium processors and a network interface card from 3Com Corp. The systems are targeted at price-sensitive corporate and government customers.

Jun. '95—The company unveiled the PowerEdge EL, a ready-to-run server package for small-to-medium-sized networks. The package combines Dell's PowerEdge servers with factory installation of Novell's NetWare 4.1 network operating system software and a 3Com network interface card.

May '95—Dell introduced a new generation of Latitude Notebooks, including systems based on Intel's 90 Mhz mobile Pentium processor.

Capitalization

Long Term Debt: $113,359,000 (7/30/95).

7% Conv. Series A Pfd. Stk.: 60,000 shs. ($100 liquid. pref.); conv. into 4.21 com.; red. after August 1996.

Options: To buy 5,591,523 shs. at $0.01 to $46.63 ea.

Per Share Data ($)

(Year Ended Jan. 31)

	1995	1994	1993	1992	1991	1990
Tangible Bk. Val.	13.27	9.08	10.02	7.66	3.86	2.83
Cash Flow	4.18	-0.24	3.09	1.78	1.17	0.37
Earnings	3.38	-1.06	2.59	1.40	0.91	0.18
Dividends	Nil	Nil	Nil	Nil	Nil	Nil
Payout Ratio	Nil	Nil	Nil	Nil	Nil	Nil
Cal. Yrs.	1994	1993	1992	1991	1990	1989
Prices - High	47⅜	49⅞	48	24⅛	12⅝	7⅛
- Low	19⅛	13⅞	15	10½	3⅛	3⅜
P/E Ratio - High	14	NM	19	17	14	39
- Low	6	NM	6	8	3	19

Income Statement Analysis (Million $)

	1995	%Chg	1994	%Chg	1993	%Chg	1992
Revs.	3,475	21%	2,873	43%	2,014	126%	890
Oper. Inc.	282	NM	83.0	-48%	159	93%	82.5
Depr.	33.1	8%	30.6	56%	19.6	42%	13.8
Int. Exp.	12.2	46%	8.4	6%	7.9	NM	1.8
Pretax Inc.	213	NM	-39.0	NM	143	95%	73.4
Eff. Tax Rate	30%	—	NM	—	29%	—	31%
Net Inc.	149	NM	-36.0	NM	102	100%	50.9

Balance Sheet & Other Fin. Data (Million $)

	1995	1994	1993	1992	1991	1990
Cash	527	337	95.0	155	37.0	Nil
Curr. Assets	1,470	1,048	853	512	236	143
Total Assets	1,594	1,140	927	560	264	172
Curr. Liab.	751	538	494	230	141	85.0
LT Debt	113	100	48.4	41.5	4.2	6.0
Common Eqty.	527	344	369	274	112	80.0
Total Cap.	765	571	418	316	116	86.0
Cap. Exp.	63.7	48.1	47.3	32.6	9.5	13.6
Cash Flow	174	-9.0	121	64.7	35.1	10.6

Ratio Analysis

	1995	1994	1993	1992	1991	1990
Curr. Ratio	2.0	1.9	1.7	2.2	1.7	1.7
% LT Debt of Cap.	14.8	17.5	11.6	13.1	3.6	7.0
% Net Inc.of Revs.	4.3	NM	5.0	5.7	5.0	1.3
% Ret. on Assets	10.9	NM	13.5	11.5	12.3	3.0
% Ret. on Equity	32.2	NM	31.2	24.7	28.1	6.6

Dividend Data —No cash dividends have been paid. A three-for-two stock split was effected in April 1992.

Amt. of Div. $	Date Decl.	Ex-Div. Date	Stock of Record	Payment Date
2-for-1	Oct. 09	Oct. 30	Oct. 20	Oct. 27 '95

Data as orig. reptd.; bef. results of disc. opers. and/or spec. items. Per share data adj. for stk. divs. as of ex-div. date. E-Estimated. NA-Not Available. NM-Not Meaningful. NR-Not Ranked.

Office—9505 Arboretum Blvd., Austin, TX 78759-7299. **Tel**—(512) 338-4400. **Chrmn & CEO**—M. S. Dell. **Vice-Chrmn**—M. L. Topher. **CFO**—T. J. Meredith. **Secy**—T. B. Green. **Dirs**—D. J. Carty, M. S. Dell, P. O. Hirschbiel, Jr., M. H. Jordan, G. Kozmetsky, T. W. Luce III, K. Luft, C. B. Malone, M. A. Miles. **Transfer Agent & Registrar**—American Stock Transfer & Trust Co., NYC. **Incorporated** in Delaware in 1987. **Empl-** 5,980. **S&P Analyst:** John D. Coyle, CFA

STANDARD & POOR'S

STOCK REPORTS

Delmarva Power & Light

NYSE Symbol **DEW**

In S&P MidCap 400

05-OCT-95 **Industry:** Util.-Diversified

Summary: This medium-sized electric and gas utility serves a population of one million on the Delmarva Peninsula.

Quantitative Evaluations

Outlook (1 Lowest—5 Highest) • **1+**

Fair Value • **18½**

Risk • **Low**

Earn./Div. Rank • **B+**

Technical Eval. • **Bearish** since 7/95

Rel. Strength Rank (1 Lowest—99 Highest) • **84**

Insider Activity • **NA**

Recent Price • 22⅞

52 Wk Range • 23-17⅝

Yield • 6.7%

12-Mo. P/E • 14.7

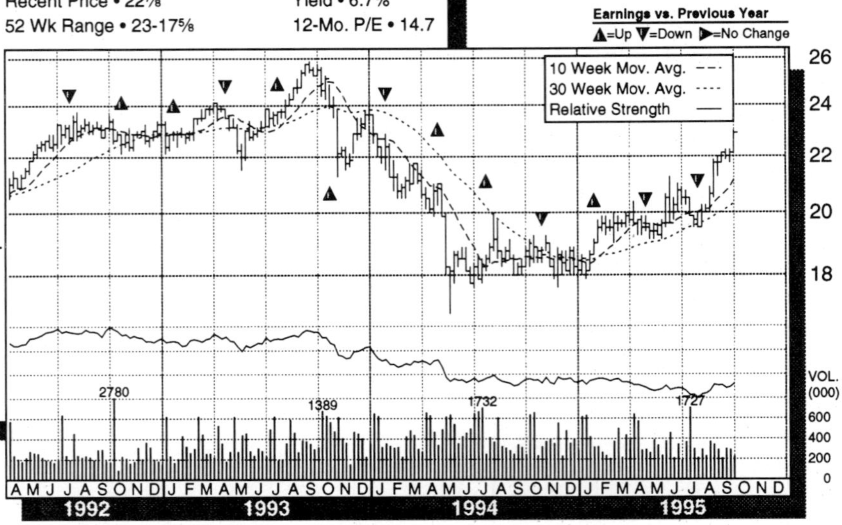

Business Profile - 05-OCT-95

Delmarva is pursuing a strategy that includes three initiatives designed to help the company maintain its current dividend level, grow earnings, and earn a return on equity of at least 11.5%, while keeping prices competitive. The three initiatives are: reduce costs by $15 to $20 million; increase revenues by $10 to $20 million through short-term energy sales to regional utilities and additional retail sales; and increase revenues through $10 to $15 million of targeted price increases.

Operational Review - 05-OCT-95

Earnings fell in 1995's first half, primarily reflecting lower electric sales due to moderate weather conditions, and decreased net electric revenues related to a resale customer's purchase of about 50% of its power from another utility. The revenue decline was partially offset by cost reduction efforts and modest price increases. EPS for non-utility subsidiaries rose due to higher recoveries of previously written-off joint venture assets and a gain on the sale of a leveraged lease interest.

Stock Performance - 29-SEP-95

In the past 30 trading days, DEW's shares have increased 11%, compared to a 5% rise in the S&P 500. Average trading volume for the past five days was 43,080 shares, compared with the 40-day moving average of 56,449 shares.

Key Stock Statistics

Dividend Rate/Share	1.54	Shareholders	58,100
Shs. outstg. (M)	60.4	Market cap. (B)	$ 1.4
Avg. daily vol. (M)	0.060	Inst. holdings	23%
Tang. Bk. Value/Share	14.20	Insider holdings	NA
Beta	0.22		

Value of $10,000 invested 5 years ago: $ 16,768

Fiscal Year Ending Dec. 31

	1995	% Change	1994	% Change	1993	% Change
Revenues (Million $)						
1Q	257.6	-12%	292.4	18%	248.0	10%
2Q	213.2	-2%	218.5	2%	214.6	11%
3Q	—	—	260.6	-5%	275.4	16%
4Q	—	—	219.6	-6%	232.6	12%
Yr.	—	—	991.0	2%	970.6	12%
Income (Million $)						
1Q	35.41	-11%	39.64	15%	34.41	-1%
2Q	19.44	-6%	20.78	11%	18.76	32%
3Q	—	—	29.37	-34%	44.28	30%
4Q	—	—	18.53	36%	13.63	-12%
Yr.	—	—	108.3	-2%	111.1	13%
Earnings Per Share ($)						
1Q	0.55	-13%	0.63	9%	0.58	-6%
2Q	0.28	-10%	0.31	15%	0.27	12%
3Q	—	—	0.46	-36%	0.72	22%
4Q	—	—	0.27	42%	0.19	-21%
Yr.	—	—	1.67	-5%	1.76	4%

Next earnings report expected: late October

Delmarva Power & Light

05-OCT-95

Business Summary - 05-OCT-95

Delmarva Power & Light provides electric service to the Delmarva Peninsula in an area consisting of about 5,700 square miles with a population of approximately 1.0 million. DEW's service area includes all of Delaware and parts of Maryland and Virginia. The company also provides gas service in an area consisting of about 275 square miles in northern Delaware. Some 89% of operating revenues and 94% of operating income in 1994 were derived from electric sales. Contributions to electric business by class:

	1994	1993	1992	1991
Residential	38%	38%	37%	37%
Commercial	30%	29%	30%	29%
Industrial	18%	19%	19%	19%
Other	14%	14%	14%	15%

The fuel mix in 1994 was 42% coal, 16% nuclear, 30% oil and gas, and 12% purchases and net interchange. DEW has a 7.51% interest in the Peach Bottom Nuclear Station and a 7.41% interest in the Salem Nuclear Power Station. Peak load in 1994 was 2,551 mw and system capability was 2,806 mw, for a capacity margin of 9.1%. Electricity sales in 1994 were 12,505,082 mwh, up 1.8% from 12,280,230 in 1993.

Total gas sales in 1994 were 18.08 million Mcf, up slightly from 18.07 million Mcf in 1993.

DEW has estimated its capital requirements for 1995-96 at $448 million, including $150 million for the purchase of Conowingo Power Co. (COPCO) and $263 million for utility construction, excluding AFUDC. Projects include $50 million of capital expenditures related to plans for environmental compliance. DEW anticipates that about $267 million will be generated internally. During 1995-96, long-term external financings are estimated at $221 million, including $170 million of long-term debt and $51 million of common stock.

In March 1995, DEW filed an application requesting approval to make fundamental changes to the structure of its natural gas business, services, and pricing. The proposal includes redesigning natural gas rates and modifying the gas cost adjustment mechanism. A ruling is expected in 1996.

Important Developments

Jul. '95—Salem units 1 and 2 were taken out of service in May and June 1995, respectively, due to operational problems and maintenance concerns. The units are expected to return to service in the first and second quarters of 1996, respectively. DEW has estimated that its share of additional costs related to the outage will be about $3 million and replacement power costs for 1995 are estimated to range from $7 million to $12 million.

Capitalization

Long Term Debt: $897,039,000 (6/95), incl. $17,516,000 capital lease obligations.
Cum. Preferred Stock: $168,085,000.

Per Share Data ($)

(Year Ended Dec. 31)

	1994	1993	1992	1991	1990	1989
Tangible Bk. Val.	14.20	13.96	13.14	13.22	12.63	13.49
Earnings	1.67	1.76	1.69	1.44	0.60	1.80
Dividends	1.54	1.54	1.54	1.54	1.54	1.50
Payout Ratio	92%	87%	91%	107%	257%	83%
Prices - High	23⅝	25⅞	23¾	21⅝	21⅜	21¼
- Low	16⅞	21¼	20	16⅝	17	17
P/E Ratio - High	14	15	14	15	36	12
- Low	10	12	12	12	28	9

Income Statement Analysis (Million $)

	1994	%Chg	1993	%Chg	1992	%Chg	1991
Revs.	991	2%	971	12%	864	2%	845
Depr.	110	9%	101	6%	95.3	7%	88.7
Maint.	NA	—	NA	—	NA	—	NA
Fxd. Chgs. Cov.	3.4	7%	3.2	13%	2.8	9%	2.6
Constr. Credits	6.8	-22%	8.7	-10%	9.7	24%	7.8
Eff. Tax Rate	38%	—	38%	—	36%	—	35%
Net Inc.	108	-3%	111	13%	99	22%	80.5

Balance Sheet & Other Fin. Data (Million $)

	1994	1993	1992	1991	1990	1989
Gross Prop.	3,110	2,985	2,862	2,667	2,533	2,204
Cap. Exp.	154	160	207	182	188	176
Net Prop.	2,047	1,995	1,932	1,817	1,721	1,588
Capitalization:						
LT Debt	794	760	813	799	773	663
% LT Debt	43	42	47	49	51	46
Pfd.	168	168	176	136	136	136
% Pfd.	9.10	9.40	10	8.30	9.00	9.50
Common	884	862	746	707	615	643
% Common	48	48	43	43	40	45
Total Cap.	2,399	2,337	2,140	2,038	1,912	1,828

Ratio Analysis

	1994	1993	1992	1991	1990	1989
Oper. Ratio	83.5	83.1	83.4	83.6	82.0	82.3
% Earn. on Net Prop.	8.1	8.4	7.7	7.8	8.8	9.0
% Ret. on Revs.	10.9	11.4	11.4	9.5	4.5	11.6
% Ret. On Invest.Cap	7.1	7.7	7.8	7.5	5.4	8.5
% Return On Com.Eqty	11.3	12.6	12.4	11.0	4.5	13.4

Dividend Data —Dividends have been paid since 1921. A dividend reinvestment plan is available.

Amt. of Div. $	Date Decl.	Ex-Div. Date	Stock of Record	Payment Date
0.385	Sep. 29	Oct. 07	Oct. 14	Oct. 31 '94
0.385	Dec. 21	Jan. 09	Jan. 13	Jan. 31 '95
0.385	Mar. 30	Apr. 07	Apr. 13	Apr. 29 '95
0.385	Jun. 29	Jul. 11	Jul. 13	Jul. 31 '95
0.385	Sep. 28	Oct. 11	Oct. 13	Oct. 31 '95

Data as orig. reptd.; bef. results of disc opers. and/or spec. items. Per share data adj. for stk. divs. as of ex-div. date. E-Estimated. NA-Not Available. NM-Not Meaningful. NR-Not Ranked.

Office—800 King St. (P.O. Box 231), Wilmington, DE 19899. **Tel**—(302) 429-3011. **Chrmn, Pres & CEO**—H. E. Cosgrove. **VP-Treas & CFO**—Barbara S. Graham. **Secy**—D. P. Connelly. **Investor Contact**—Carol C. Conrad (800-365-6495). **Dirs**—M. G. Abercrombie, R. D. Burris, H. E. Cosgrove, A. K. Doberstein, M. B. Emery, J. H. Gilliam, Jr., S. I. Gore, J. C. Johnson III, H. R. Landon, J. T. McKinstry. **Transfer Agents & Registrars**—Wilmington Trust Co., Wilmington; Chemical Bank, NYC. **Incorporated** in Delaware in 1909 and in Virginia in 1979. **Empl**-2,487. **S&P Analyst:** Ronald J. Gross

DENTSPLY International

NASDAQ Symbol XRAY Options on CBOE (Incl. in Nat'l Market) In S&P MidCap 400

Price	Range	P-E Ratio	Dividend	Yield	S&P Ranking	Beta
Oct. 18'95	1995					
34⅞	40¼–31¼	17	0.30	0.9%	B+	1.36

Summary

This company designs, develops, manufactures and markets dental consumable and laboratory products and dental equipment, which it distributes worldwide.

Business Summary

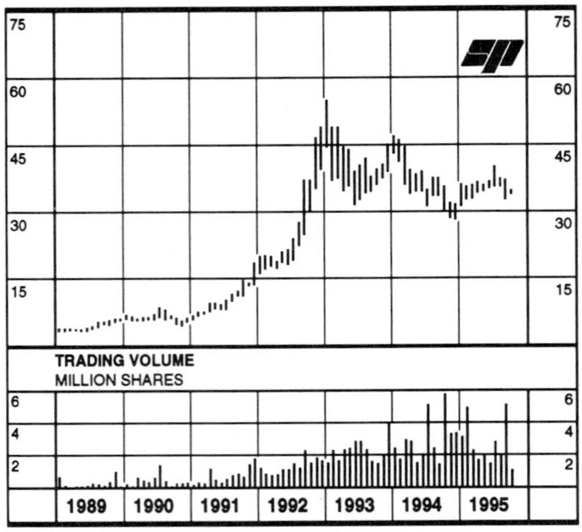

DENTSPLY International Inc. designs, develops, manufactures and markets dental consumable and laboratory products and dental equipment. Its products are produced in the U.S. and internationally and distributed worldwide. In late 1994, the company decided to exit the medical business, which manufactured medical x-ray tubes and systems and orthopedic bone cement.

Consumable and laboratory products consist of dental sundries used in dental offices in the treatment of patients and in dental laboratories in the preparation of dental appliances such as crowns and bridges. Products include resin-based and porcelain artificial teeth used to replace teeth lost through deterioration, disease or injury; impression materials used to make molds of teeth for fitting crowns, bridges and implants; and restorative materials used in sealing, lining and filling excavated tooth cavities and repairing broken or damaged teeth such as amalgams, bonding agents, light-cured composites and glass ionomer materials for aesthetic restorations.

The company also makes crown and bridge porcelains and ceramics used by dental laboratories in making crowns and inlays for restorative dental procedures to provide functional biting and chewing surfaces that appear and feel natural; dental implant systems such as endosseous root form dental implants and abutments designed to accommodate the anatomical zones found in the human jaw; and protective supplies designed to ameliorate possible sources of patient cross-contamination of infectious disease. Other consumable and laboratory products include scaling gels that aid in softening hardened tooth calculus, prophylaxis paste used in cleaning and polishing teeth, and endodontic products used in root canal treatment of severely damaged or decaying teeth.

Dental equipment product lines include x-ray systems and related support equipment and accessories, high and low speed handpieces, intraoral lighting systems, dental cutting instruments and ultrasonic scalers and polishers. The company offers a full line of dental x-ray equipment for intraoral, panoramic and cephalometric procedures, and x-ray support equipment such as x-ray film mounts, film holders and related equipment and accessories. DENTSPLY also supplies specialty chemical binders, refractory particles, investment mold materials and related products for the precision investment casting industry.

Foreign sales are made in over 100 countries and accounted for 45% and 42% of net sales in 1994 and 1993, respectively.

Important Developments

Sep. '95— DENSTPLY signed a letter of intent to purchase the dental manufacturing and distribution operations of Tulsa Dental Instruments LLC for $75 million in cash.

Jun. '95— The company acquired about 96% of Maillefer Instruments S.A., a manufacturer and distributor of endodontic instruments, for $65.8 million in cash.

Next earnings report expected in late October.

Per Share Data ($)

Yr. End Dec. 31[1]	1994	[2]1993	[2]1992	[2]1991	[2]1990	1989	1988	[2]1987	1986
Tangible Bk. Val.	**4.42**	1.61	3.32	1.78	0.09	1.31	1.76	1.46	0.53
Cash Flow	**2.67**	1.94	1.80	0.92	0.72	0.60	0.39	0.34	0.26
Earnings[3]	**1.95**	1.14	1.40	0.59	0.40	0.41	0.30	0.25	[4]0.16
Dividends	**0.150**	Nil	Nil	Nil	Nil	Nil	Nil	Nil	Nil
Payout Ratio	**8%**	Nil	Nil	Nil	Nil	Nil	Nil	Nil	Nil
Prices—High	**47**	55	49	18⅝	8⅝	6⅛	4⅞	4⅝	NA
Low	**28¼**	31½	16	5¾	4⅜	3⅛	3¼	2¾	NA
P/E Ratio—	**24–14**	48–28	35–11	32–10	22–11	15–8	17–11	19–11	NA

Data as orig. reptd. Adj. for stk. div. of 100% Aug. 1992. **1.** Prior to 1993 yrs. ended Mar. of fol. cal. yr. **2.** Refl. merger or acquisition. **3.** Bef. results of disc. opers. of +0.28 in 1994, and spec. items of -0.57 in 1993, +0.03 in 1986. **4.** Ful. dil.: 0.15 in 1986. NA-Not Available.

Income Data (Million $)

Year Ended Dec. 31[1]	Revs.	Oper. Inc.	% Oper. Inc. of Revs.	Cap. Exp.	Depr.	Int. Exp.	Net Bef. Taxes	Eff. Tax Rate	[5]Net Inc.	% Net Inc. of Revs.	Cash Flow
[2]1994	**525**	**117**	**22.4**	**13.8**	**20.0**	**8.0**	**91.7**	**40.9%**	**54.1**	**10.3**	**74.2**
[3]1993	553	94	17.1	10.8	19.8	[4]20.8	55.8	49.7%	28.1	5.1	47.8
[3]1992	156	32	20.2	5.8	4.2	2.2	25.1	41.7%	14.6	9.4	18.8
[3]1991	85	16	18.5	1.3	3.1	3.1	9.2	41.8%	5.3	6.3	8.4
[3]1990	55	10	18.8	0.9	2.4	3.0	5.0	41.5%	2.9	5.3	5.3
1989	29	6	20.0	0.3	1.2	0.8	3.9	39.3%	2.4	8.1	3.5
1988	19	3	17.5	0.2	0.5	0.1	2.8	37.6%	1.7	9.3	2.3
[3]1987	16	3	17.8	0.2	0.5	0.2	2.3	40.9%	1.3	8.2	1.8
1986	13	2	14.1	0.4	0.4	0.4	1.0	34.3%	0.7	5.1	1.0

Balance Sheet Data (Million $)

Dec. 31	Cash	Curr. Assets	Curr. Liab.	Curr. Ratio	Total Assets	% Ret. on Assets	Long Term Debt	Common Equity	Total Cap.	% LT Debt of Cap.	% Ret. on Equity
1994	**7.3**	**197**	**97**	**2.0**	**475**	**11.0**	**12.8**	**299**	**337**	**3.8**	**20.2**
1993	18.0	208	113	1.8	505	6.5	95.4	236	354	26.9	12.8
1992	0.3	63	39	1.6	129	13.1	7.9	74	86	9.2	22.4
1991	6.4	39	20	1.9	93	5.7	10.1	57	68	14.7	11.7
1990	Nil	29	21	1.4	77	5.3	22.0	29	53	41.3	12.5
1989	0.1	13	4	3.1	23	12.8	5.7	13	19	29.4	20.4
1988	2.7	11	2	4.4	14	13.2	NM	10	11	NM	18.1
1987	2.1	10	3	3.4	13	11.2	NM	9	9	NM	22.5
1986	Nil	6	2	2.5	9	NA	3.6	2	6	57.9	NA

Data as orig. reptd. **1.** Prior to 1993 yrs. ended Mar. of fol. cal. yr. **2.** Excl. disc. opers. **3.** Refl. merger or acquisition. **4.** Net of int. inc. **5.** Bef. results of disc. opers. and spec. items. NA-Not Available. NM-Not Meaningful.

Sales (Million $)

Quarter:	1995	1994
Mar.	133.1	126.8
Jun.	139.9	128.0
Sep.		129.9
Dec.		140.0
		524.7

Net sales for the first half of 1995 rose 7.1%, year to year. Gross margins widened on an improved product mix and manufacturing efficiencies, but with higher expenses related to several new product launches, the gain in operating income was held to 7.2%. Following other expenses, versus income, mostly related to a one-time charge for the closing and consolidation of certain operations, net income was up 4.2%. Earnings rose to $0.97 a share from $0.91, excluding a $0.04 special credit in 1994.

Common Share Earnings ($)

Quarter:	1995	1994
Mar.	0.48	0.42
Jun.	0.49	0.49
Sep.		0.50
Dec.		0.55
		1.95

Dividend Data

Cash dividends were initiated in 1994.

Amt. of Divd. $	Date Decl.	Ex-divd. Date	Stock of Record	Payment Date
0.075	Dec. 15	Dec. 22	Dec. 29	Jan. 10'95
0.075	Mar. 13	Mar. 27	Mar. 31	Apr. 12'95
0.075	May 24	Jun. 28	Jun. 30	Jul. 14'95
0.075	Sep. 28	Oct. 2	Oct. 4	Oct. 12'95

Finances

In March 1995, DENTSPLY acquired KV33 Corp., which makes disposable articulators (used to replicate human jaw movement during restorative procedures) for the dental laboratory market, for $11.5 million.

During 1995, the company repurchased 1.1 million shares of common stock for $38.4 million. In December 1994, directors authorized the repurchase of up to 2.8 million common shares.

Capitalization

Long Term Debt: $93,942,000 (6/95).

Minority Interest: $3,934,000.

Common Stock: 27,062,669 shs. ($0.01 par). Institutions hold about 76%. Shareholders of record: 750 (12/94).

Office—570 W. College Ave., P.O. Box 872, York, PA 17405-0872. **Tel**—(717) 845-7511. **Chrmn & CEO**—B. C. Borgely. **Pres & COO**—J. C. Miles II. **SVP & CFO**—E. D. Yates. **VP & Secy**—J. P. Clark. **Treas**—M. K. Duron III. **Dirs**—B. C. Borgely, D. K. Chapman, M. J. Coleman, A. A. Dugon, W. S. Green, A. L. Herbert, L. A. Jones, J. J. McDounough, J. C. Miles II, W. K. Smith. **Transfer Agent & Registrar**—Harris Trust & Savings Bank, Chicago. **Incorporated** in Delaware in 1983. **Empl**—4,450.

 Stephen R. Biggar

Dexter Corp.

NYSE Symbol **DEX**
In S&P MidCap 400

16-OCT-95 **Industry:** Chemicals

Summary: Dexter produces specialty materials used in the medical, food packaging, electronics, automotive and aerospace markets. It also has a 55% interest in Life Technologies.

Quantitative Evaluations
Outlook
(1 Lowest—5 Highest)
• **2+**
Fair Value
• **23⅜**
Risk
• **Low**
Earn./Div. Rank
• **B+**

Technical Eval.
• **Bearish** since 5/95
Rel. Strength Rank
(1 Lowest—99 Highest)
• **35**
Insider Activity
• **Neutral**

Recent Price • 24
52 Wk Range • 25⅞-19⅞
Yield • 3.7%
12-Mo. P/E • 14.2

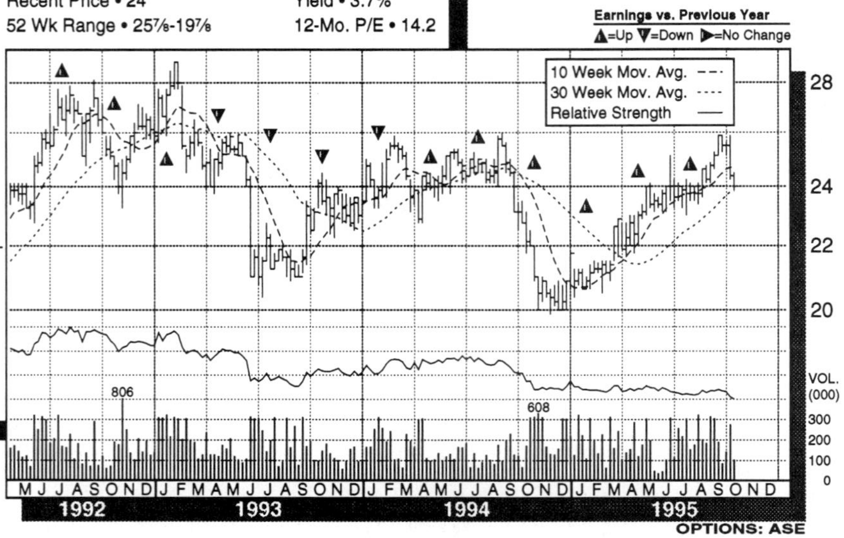

Business Profile - 16-OCT-95

Dexter is a leading supplier of specialty materials, with about 50% of profits derived from products sold outside the U.S. DEX completed a restructuring program in 1993 which included acquisitions and joint ventures that focused on strategic global markets, while divesting unprofitable or unrelated businesses. DEX expects to maintain its recent earnings growth despite the ongoing negative impact of higher raw material costs. The stock has turned in a poor performance over the past five years.

Operational Review - 16-OCT-95

Sales for the nine months ended September 30, 1995 rose 13%, year to year, reflecting an 8% volume increase, a 4% increase due to favorable translation rates, and 1% higher prices. Margins were adversely impacted by higher raw material costs of $0.33 a share, partly offset by the volume growth, productivity improvements, and cost containment. After taxes at 35.5%, against 36.0%, net income was up 11%, to $1.31 a share from $1.18.

Stock Performance - 13-OCT-95

In the past 30 trading days, DEX's shares have declined 3%, compared to a 4% rise in the S&P 500. Average trading volume for the past five days was 19,940 shares, compared with the 40-day moving average of 44,582 shares.

Key Stock Statistics

Dividend Rate/Share	0.88	Shareholders	3,600
Shs. outstg. (M)	24.5	Market cap. (B)	$0.588
Avg. daily vol. (M)	0.030	Inst. holdings	78%
Tang. Bk. Value/Share	11.96	Insider holdings	NA
Beta	0.77		

Value of $10,000 invested 5 years ago: $ 13,764

Fiscal Year Ending Dec. 31

	1995	% Change	1994	% Change	1993	% Change
Revenues (Million $)						
1Q	266.8	14%	233.5	8%	217.0	-11%
2Q	283.0	15%	247.1	8%	228.6	-10%
3Q	270.7	11%	243.3	10%	220.1	-5%
4Q	—	—	250.8	13%	221.2	-2%
Yr.	—	—	974.7	10%	887.1	-7%
Income (Million $)						
1Q	10.46	12%	9.30	20%	7.72	-14%
2Q	11.96	9%	10.98	12%	9.79	-15%
3Q	9.40	12%	8.41	2%	8.25	-9%
4Q	—	—	9.20	11%	8.30	-4%
Yr.	—	—	37.90	11%	34.05	-11%
Earnings Per Share ($)						
1Q	0.43	13%	0.38	19%	0.32	-14%
2Q	0.49	9%	0.45	13%	0.40	-17%
3Q	0.39	11%	0.35	3%	0.34	-8%
4Q	—	—	0.38	12%	0.34	-6%
Yr.	—	—	1.56	11%	1.40	-11%

Next earnings report expected: early February

Dexter Corp.

Business Summary - 12-OCT-95

Dexter produces specialty materials and chemicals and life science products. Contributions by market group in 1994:

	Sales	Profits
Medical	32%	35%
Food packaging	27%	32%
Electronics	16%	15%
Automotive	6%	3%
Aerospace	5%	-1%
Other	14%	16%

Operations outside North America accounted for 39% of sales and 49% of profits in 1994.

Medical products include nonwoven wraps, drapes, garments and absorbent products. Life Technologies (55% owned) produces cell culture and molecular biology research products. Products for food packaging consist of coatings for food and beverage cans, container sealants, coatings and adhesives for flexible and microwaveable packaging, and nonwoven materials for tea bags, filters and meat casings. Electronics materials include encapsulation compounds, printed wiring board materials (inks, masks, solder and etchants) and magnetic components. Automotive materials consist of polypropylene-based products, acoustical sealants, foam gasketing, adhesives, mold releases and liquid and powder coatings. Aerospace products include adhesives and structural materials (adhesives, primers, composite surfacing films and mold release agents) and coatings (external finishes, coatings and logos).

Other operations include the industrial coatings and wallcover businesses. In 1992, DEX sold its water treatment chemicals, composites and plastisols businesses.

DEX acquired two automotive coatings businesses in early 1994; the purchases positioned DEX as one of the top U.S. suppliers of interior auto coatings. In 1993, DEX exchanged its coil coatings business for Akzo's U.S. aerospace coatings business, and acquired Vernicolor A.G., Switzerland, a can coatings producer with annual sales of $20 million.

Important Developments

Oct. '95—Third quarter 1995 share earnings rose 11%, year to year, despite higher raw material costs which reduced earnings by $0.10 a share. Earnings benefited from 6% higher volumes, price increases, productivity improvements and cost containment. Products with strong sales included electronic encapsulation materials, magnetic materials, can coatings, nonwoven products, and Life Technologies. Sales of coatings for the aerospace and automotive markets were lower.

Capitalization

Long Term Debt: $224,017,000 (9/95).
Minority Interest: $73,186,000.

Per Share Data ($)

(Year Ended Dec. 31)

	1994	1993	1992	1991	1990	1989
Tangible Bk. Val.	14.11	9.86	10.69	10.36	11.53	9.78
Cash Flow	2.99	2.72	2.88	0.95	2.98	2.71
Earnings	1.56	1.40	1.58	-0.29	1.74	1.73
Dividends	0.88	0.88	0.88	0.88	0.88	0.82
Payout Ratio	56%	63%	56%	NM	50%	47%
Prices - High	26	28⅞	28⅛	26⅛	24½	34¾
- Low	19⅞	20⅜	20⅞	18½	18	20⅛
P/E Ratio - High	17	21	18	NM	14	20
- Low	13	15	13	NM	10	12

Income Statement Analysis (Million $)

	1994	%Chg	1993	%Chg	1992	%Chg	1991
Revs.	975	10%	887	-7%	951	1%	938
Oper. Inc.	116	9%	106	-8%	115	16%	99
Depr.	34.9	9%	32.0	2%	31.5	5%	30.0
Int. Exp.	20.5	9%	18.8	NM	18.8	12%	16.8
Pretax Inc.	73.6	11%	66.4	-9%	73.1	NM	11.2
Eff. Tax Rate	36%	—	37%	—	38%	—	110%
Net Inc.	37.9	11%	34.1	-11%	38.2	NM	-7.1

Balance Sheet & Other Fin. Data (Million $)

	1994	1993	1992	1991	1990	1989
Cash	55.0	52.7	65.0	39.7	81.0	77.5
Curr. Assets	393	356	361	362	363	336
Total Assets	881	821	782	784	762	694
Curr. Liab.	184	157	154	169	148	147
LT Debt	225	227	179	189	160	131
Common Eqty.	344	313	316	314	344	325
Total Cap.	657	615	584	586	591	535
Cap. Exp.	45.8	60.4	52.1	65.0	70.3	95.0
Cash Flow	72.8	66.1	69.7	22.9	72.4	67.3

Ratio Analysis

	1994	1993	1992	1991	1990	1989
Curr. Ratio	2.1	2.3	2.3	2.2	2.5	2.3
% LT Debt of Cap.	34.3	37.0	30.6	32.2	27.1	24.5
% Net Inc.of Revs.	3.9	3.8	4.0	NM	4.6	5.1
% Ret. on Assets	4.5	4.2	4.9	NM	5.9	6.5
% Ret. on Equity	11.5	10.8	12.1	NM	12.8	13.6

Dividend Data —Dividends have been paid since 1957. A dividend reinvestment plan is available. A "poison pill" stock purchase rights plan was adopted in 1986.

Amt. of Div. $	Date Decl.	Ex-Div. Date	Stock of Record	Payment Date
0.220	Oct. 28	Dec. 09	Dec. 15	Jan. 10 '95
0.220	Feb. 24	Mar. 09	Mar. 15	Apr. 10 '95
0.220	Apr. 27	Jun. 13	Jun. 15	Jul. 10 '95
0.220	Aug. 25	Sep. 13	Sep. 15	Oct. 10 '95

Data as orig. reptd.; bef. results of disc. opers. and/or spec. items. Per share data adj. for stk. divs. as of ex-div. date. E-Estimated. NA-Not Available. NM-Not Meaningful. NR-Not Ranked.

Office—One Elm St., Windsor Locks, CT 06096-2334. **Tel**—(203) 627-9051. **Chrmn, Pres & CEO**—K. G. Walker. **CFO**—Kathleen Burdett. **Secy**—B. H. Beatt. **Treas**—D. J. Ribaudo. **SVP & Investor Contact**—John D. Thompson. **Dirs**—C. H. Curl, B. M. Fox, R. M. Furek, M. C. Goss, P. G. Kelly, Jean-Francois Saglio, G. L. Urban, K. G. Walker, G. M. Whitesides. **Transfer Agents**—Mellon Securities Trust Co., East Hartford; Mellon Securities Transfer Services, NYC. **Registrar**—Mellon Securities Trust Co., East Hartford. **Incorporated** in Connecticut in 1914. **Empl**-4,700. **S&P Analyst:** Richard O'Reilly, CFA

STANDARD & POOR'S

STOCK REPORTS

Diagnostic Products

NYSE Symbol **DP**
In S&P MidCap 400

29-SEP-95

Industry: Medical equipment/ supply

Summary: This company is the world's leading independent producer of immunodiagnostic test kits and related instrumentation.

Quantitative Evaluations

Outlook (1 Lowest—5 Highest)
• **NA**

Fair Value
• **NA**

Risk
• **Average**

Earn./Div. Rank
• **B+**

Technical Eval.
• **Bearish** since 7/95

Rel. Strength Rank (1 Lowest—99 Highest)
• **44**

Insider Activity
• **Neutral**

Recent Price • 39⅛
52 Wk Range • 44⅞-20⅜

Yield • 1.2%
12-Mo. P/E • 25.2

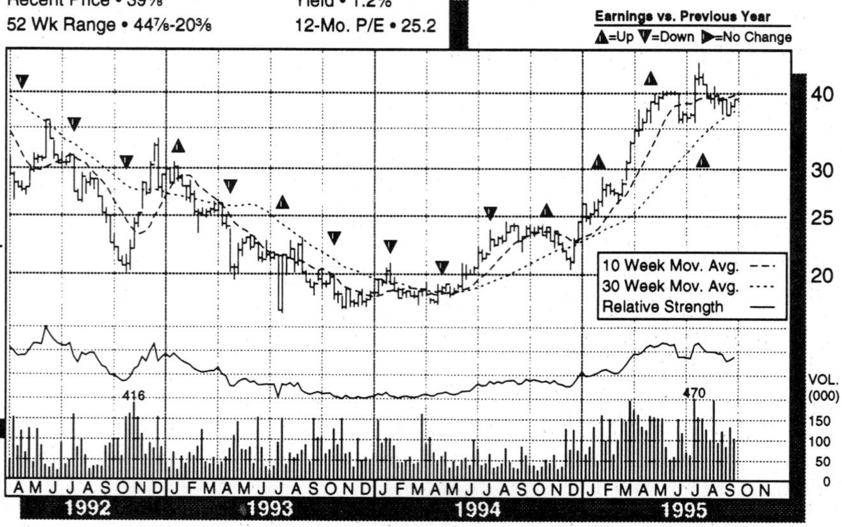

Business Profile - 29-SEP-95

This company is experiencing rapid growth, due to sales of its IMMULITE system. DP expects the system to account for the greatest amount of growth of all of its product lines for the foreseeable future. Although RIA kits continue to generate the majority of sales, this product line has matured and on a worldwide basis is experiencing a slow decline. Demand for IMMULITE systems should accelerate as laboratories seek easy-to-use technologies and improve productivity.

Operational Review - 29-SEP-95

Sales advanced considerably in recent periods reflecting continuing increased worldwide acceptance of the IMMULITE system and a weaker U.S. dollar. Margins widened on increased utilization of manufacturing facilities, and smaller increases in SG&A and R&D expenditures. Net income rose sharply.

Stock Performance - 22-SEP-95

In the past 30 trading days, DP's shares have declined 0.32%, compared to a 5% rise in the S&P 500. Average trading volume for the past five days was 20,820 shares, compared with the 40-day moving average of 31,087 shares.

Key Stock Statistics

Dividend Rate/Share	0.48	Shareholders	700
Shs. outstg. (M)	13.1	Market cap. (B)	$0.511
Avg. daily vol. (M)	0.021	Inst. holdings	28%
Tang. Bk. Value/Share	10.40	Insider holdings	NA
Beta	0.47		

Value of $10,000 invested 5 years ago: $ 12,451

Fiscal Year Ending Dec. 31

	1995	% Change	1994	% Change	1993	% Change
Revenues (Million $)						
1Q	39.20	41%	27.77	3%	27.03	9%
2Q	38.53	28%	30.13	14%	26.40	4%
3Q	—	—	30.64	15%	26.59	-2%
4Q	—	—	37.91	42%	26.77	3%
Yr.	—	—	126.4	18%	106.8	3%
Income (Million $)						
1Q	5.81	67%	3.47	-15%	4.07	-13%
2Q	6.11	57%	3.90	-12%	4.45	31%
3Q	—	—	4.32	65%	2.62	-40%
4Q	—	—	5.01	66%	3.02	-37%
Yr.	—	—	16.70	18%	14.17	-18%
Earnings Per Share ($)						
1Q	0.42	62%	0.26	-13%	0.30	-12%
2Q	0.44	52%	0.29	-12%	0.33	32%
3Q	—	—	0.32	68%	0.19	-41%
4Q	—	—	0.37	68%	0.22	-37%
Yr.	—	—	1.24	19%	1.04	-17%

Next earnings report expected: late October

Diagnostic Products

Business Summary - 25-SEP-95

Diagnostic Products develops, produces and sells medical immunodiagnostic test kits and related instrumentation that use state-of-the-art technology derived from immunology and molecular biology.

DP's kits are used by hospitals, clinical, veterinary and forensic laboratories, and doctors' offices to obtain precise and rapid identification and measurement of hormones, drugs, viruses, bacteria and other substances present in body fluids and tissues at infinitesimal concentrations.

The principal clinical applications of the company's more than 300 assays relate to diagnosis of thyroid conditions and anemia; testing for pregnancy, fertility and fetal well-being; management of diabetes and certain types of cancer; drug abuse testing; rapid diagnosis of infectious diseases (including sexually transmitted diseases); allergy testing; and diagnosis of disorders due to hormone and steroid imbalances. DP believes that it is the market leader in fertility testing. Its kits are used for in-vitro (outside the body) testing, and it is also developing products for in-vivo applications, such as imaging agents for certain tumors.

The kits utilize various techniques to detect and measure substances in a patient's body fluids and tissues. DP has historically concentrated on radioimmunoassay (RIA), the core technology of immunodiagnostics, which utilizes radioisotopes to achieve high levels of test specificity and sensitivity.

The May 1992 acquisition of Cirrus Diagnostics Inc. allowed the company to enter the market for fully automated, nonisotopic diagnostic instumentation systems, the fastest growing segment of the immunoassay market. The IMMULITE system, developed by Cirrus, is a fully automated, random-access instrument which performs immunoassays utilizing chemiluminescent technology. In 1994, DP developed 22 assays for the IMMULITE system, bringing the total number of IMMULITE assays to 47; 24 have been approved for U.S. marketing. DP currently offers the most complete panel of assays available in the areas of thyroid, fertility, and cancer testing.

Important Developments

Sep. '95—DP said that it received clearance from the FDA to market its radioimmunoassay kit to monitor prostate cancer.

Aug. '95—The company said that it received clearance from the FDA to market a new test to detect allergy to latex and latex-containing products. Separately, it acquired a 56% interest in DPC Medlab Produtos Medico Hospitalares LTDA, DP's Brazilian distributor.

Capitalization

Long Term Debt: None (6/95).

Per Share Data ($) (Year Ended Dec. 31)

	1994	1993	1992	1991	1990	1989
Tangible Bk. Val.	9.36	8.30	7.92	7.38	6.51	5.40
Cash Flow	1.67	1.35	1.60	1.79	1.64	1.42
Earnings	1.24	1.04	1.26	1.49	1.35	1.20
Dividends	0.40	0.30	0.32	0.32	0.24	0.20
Payout Ratio	32%	29%	24%	20%	17%	16%
Prices - High	26⅝	30¾	44	53¾	44	38
- Low	17¾	17⅛	20⅛	28¼	22¼	19¼
P/E Ratio - High	21	30	35	36	33	32
- Low	14	16	16	19	16	16

Income Statement Analysis (Million $)

	1994	%Chg	1993	%Chg	1992	%Chg	1991
Revs.	126	18%	107	4%	103	14%	90.1
Oper. Inc.	26.3	18%	22.3	-16%	26.6	2%	26.2
Depr.	5.9	39%	4.2	-10%	4.7	18%	4.0
Int. Exp.	Nil	—	Nil	—	Nil	—	Nil
Pretax Inc.	22.6	14%	19.9	-16%	23.7	-15%	27.9
Eff. Tax Rate	26%	—	29%	—	27%	—	31%
Net Inc.	16.7	18%	14.2	-18%	17.3	-10%	19.3

Balance Sheet & Other Fin. Data (Million $)

	1994	1993	1992	1991	1990	1989
Cash	14.8	12.9	22.7	30.2	24.3	20.3
Curr. Assets	78.3	68.9	70.3	76.3	64.3	53.4
Total Assets	153	137	134	131	102	84.0
Curr. Liab.	17.6	13.9	14.8	23.9	15.4	12.4
LT Debt	Nil	Nil	Nil	Nil	Nil	Nil
Common Eqty.	135	123	120	107	87.0	71.2
Total Cap.	135	123	120	107	87.0	71.2
Cap. Exp.	8.5	7.7	15.1	9.5	6.0	6.0
Cash Flow	22.6	18.4	22.0	23.3	21.1	17.9

Ratio Analysis

	1994	1993	1992	1991	1990	1989
Curr. Ratio	4.4	5.0	4.8	3.2	4.2	4.3
% LT Debt of Cap.	Nil	Nil	Nil	Nil	Nil	Nil
% Net Inc.of Revs.	13.2	13.3	16.7	21.5	22.8	25.2
% Ret. on Assets	11.6	10.5	12.6	16.5	18.5	20.3
% Ret. on Equity	13.0	11.7	14.8	19.8	21.7	23.5

Dividend Data —Dividends were initiated in 1988.

Amt. of Div. $	Date Decl.	Ex-Div. Date	Stock of Record	Payment Date
0.100	Oct. 03	Oct. 27	Nov. 02	Nov. 16 '94
0.100	Jan. 05	Jan. 26	Feb. 01	Feb. 15 '95
0.120	Apr. 03	Apr. 27	May. 03	May. 17 '95
0.120	Jul. 05	Jul. 31	Aug. 02	Aug. 16 '95

Data as orig. reptd.; bef. results of disc. opers. and/or spec. items. Per share data adj. for stk. divs. as of ex-div. date. E-Estimated. NA-Not Available. NM-Not Meaningful. NR-Not Ranked.

Office—5700 W. 96th St., Los Angeles, CA 90045. **Tel**—(213) 776-0180. **Chrmn & CEO**—S. Ziering. **Pres & COO**—M. Ziering. **VP-Fin, CFO & Investor Contact**—Julian R. Bockserman. **Secy**—Marilyn Ziering. **Dirs**—S. A. Aroesty, J. Kleiman, M. H. Salter, J. D. Watson, Marilyn Ziering, Michael Ziering, S. Ziering. **Transfer Agent & Registrar**—First Interstate Bank of California, LA. **Incorporated** in California in 1971. **Empl**-1000. **S&P Analyst:** Philip J. Birbara

STANDARD & POOR'S

STOCK REPORTS

Diamond Shamrock, Inc.

NYSE Symbol **DRM**

In S&P MidCap 400

03-SEP-95

Industry: Oil and Gas

Summary: This large Southwest regional refiner and marketer of petroleum products owns two Texas refineries, pipelines and terminals, and about 2,000 branded stores in eight states.

Quantitative Evaluations

Recent Price • 26⅞ | Yield • 2.1%

52 Wk Range • 29⅛-23⅛ | 12-Mo. P/E • 12.0

Outlook (1 Lowest—5 Highest)
• **3−**

Fair Value
• **26⅛**

Risk
• **Low**

Earn./Div. Rank
• **NR**

Technical Eval.
• **Bullish** since 7/95

Rel. Strength Rank (1 Lowest—99 Highest)
• **43**

Insider Activity
• **NA**

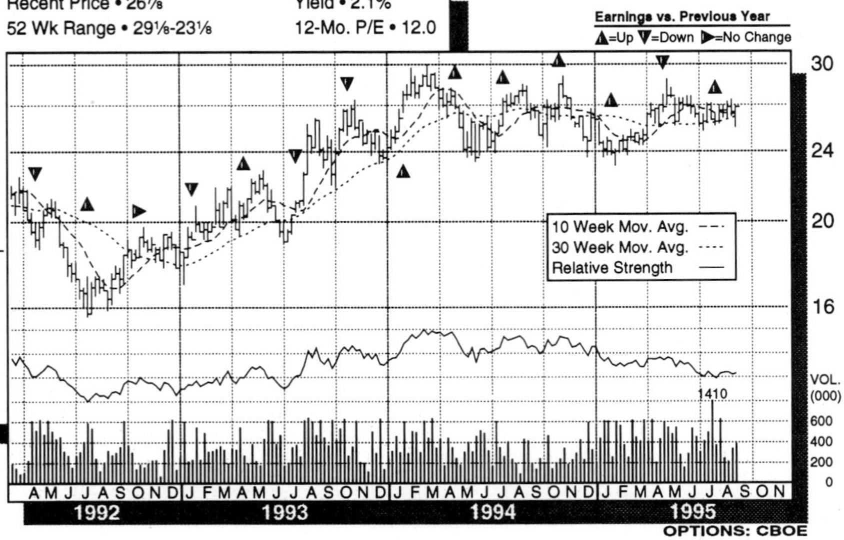

Business Profile - 31-AUG-95

This large Southwest regional refiner and marketer of petroleum products owns two Texas refineries, pipelines and terminals, and about 2,000 branded stores in eight states. Activities include crude oil refining, wholesale and retail marketing of refined products, manufacturing and marketing petrochemicals, and storage and marketing of natural gas liquids. Results may benefit from the recent completion of an expansion at the Three Rivers refinery and a diesel desulfurizer at the McKee refinery.

Operational Review - 01-SEP-95

Revenues advanced 19%, year to year, in 1995's first half, as the company's retail stores and allied businesses turned in a strong performance, and petroleum product prices rose. However, industry refining margins were the weakest since 1987 during the first quarter, and although margins improved in the second quarter, retail fuel margins were depressed for most of the quarter, only strengthening toward the end. Net income fell 16%, to $33.4 million ($1.08 a share), from $39.7 million ($1.29).

Stock Performance - 01-SEP-95

In the past 30 trading days, DRM's shares have increased 3%, compared to a 2% rise in the S&P 500. Average trading volume for the past five days was 76,240 shares, compared with the 40-day moving average of 107,177 shares.

Key Stock Statistics

Dividend Rate/Share	0.56	Shareholders	23,300
Shs. outstg. (M)	29.0	Market cap. (B)	$0.780
Avg. daily vol. (M)	0.058	Inst. holdings	85%
Tang. Bk. Value/Share	23.37	Insider holdings	NA
Beta	0.60		

Value of $10,000 invested 5 years ago: $ 12,321

Fiscal Year Ending Dec. 31

	1995	% Change	1994	% Change	1993	% Change
Revenues (Million $)						
1Q	680.9	17%	583.8	-6%	620.8	6%
2Q	789.7	22%	646.5	-2%	656.9	1%
3Q	—	—	700.4	8%	650.5	-7%
4Q	—	—	675.6	8%	627.2	-6%
Yr.	—	—	2,606	2%	2,555	-2%
Income (Million $)						
1Q	5.40	-56%	12.20	144%	5.00	NM
2Q	28.00	2%	27.50	67%	16.50	-30%
3Q	—	—	20.60	122%	9.30	-47%
4Q	—	—	15.50	NM	1.80	NM
Yr.	—	—	75.80	133%	32.60	23%
Earnings Per Share ($)						
1Q	0.15	-61%	0.38	124%	0.17	NM
2Q	0.93	2%	0.91	63%	0.56	-32%
3Q	—	—	0.67	139%	0.28	-54%
4Q	—	—	0.49	NM	0.02	NM
Yr.	—	—	2.45	136%	1.04	13%

Next earnings report expected: late October

Diamond Shamrock, Inc.

03-SEP-95

Business Summary - 01-SEP-95

Diamond Shamrock, Inc. is engaged in crude oil refining and wholesale marketing of refined petroleum products; retail marketing of refined petroleum products and other merchandise through more than 2,000 high-volume gasoline/convenience outlets; manufacturing and marketing of petrochemicals; and storage, distribution and marketing of natural gas liquids. Revenue and operating profit contributions in 1994 were:

	Revs.	Profits
Refining & wholesale	51%	63%
Retail marketing	37%	25%
Allied businesses	12%	12%

The company owns and operates two modern refineries. Total processing capacity is about 205,000 bbl. of crude oil daily: 135,000 bbl. at the McKee, Tex., refinery and 70,000 bbl. at the Three Rivers, Tex., refinery. Crude throughput was 195,663 bbl. a day in 1994 (180,229 in 1993). Wholesale refined product sales came to 225,697 bbl. daily. About 94% of refinery output is in high value products such as gasoline, diesel and liquid petroleum gases.

The company transports crude oil to its refineries through owned or leased pipelines. Refined products are distributed through its 2,484 mi. of pipelines connected to 16 terminals. DRM markets gasoline, diesel, and convenience merchandise through 840 company-operated Corner Store retail outlets in Texas, Colorado, Louisiana and New Mexico. An additional 2,016 Diamond Shamrock branded stations are supplied with gasoline and diesel by 135 jobbers. DRM's competitive position is supported by its own credit card program, with 562,000 active accounts.

Allied businesses encompass fields in which DRM has technical, operating or management expertise. The company markets natural gas liquids and ammonia fertilizer, and offers underground strorage tank services, as well as specialized telephone services for correctional facilities. Through a joint venture, it explores for, produces and refines oil and gas in South America. At its Mont Belvieu operations, DRM owns and operates the world's largest commercial underground natural liquids storage facility, with 77 million bbl. of storage.

Important Developments

Aug. '95—DRM announced the successful completion of an exploratory well in southern Bolivia, resulting in a major gas discovery for the joint venture company, Diamond Shamrock Boliviana, Ltd. The well, Nupuco-X101, is located in Gran Chaco Province; a 45 km. pipeline is to be built connecting Nupuco to a gas processing plant in the Porvenir Field.

Capitalization

Long Term Debt: $532,100,000 (3/95).
5% Conv. Preferred Stock: 1,725,000 shs.; conv. into com. at $26.50 a sh.

Per Share Data ($)

(Year Ended Dec. 31)

	1994	1993	1992	1991	1990	1989
Tangible Bk. Val.	20.31	18.14	15.18	15.26	13.84	11.11
Cash Flow	4.89	3.27	2.90	3.34	4.96	3.91
Earnings	2.45	1.04	0.92	1.39	3.04	2.20
Dividends	0.53	0.52	0.52	0.52	0.49	0.44
Payout Ratio	22%	50%	57%	40%	16%	20%
Prices - High	30	27³/₈	23⁵/₈	26⁵/₈	27³/₄	28¹/₂
- Low	23³/₈	17	15⁵/₈	18¹/₈	17¹/₄	14⁷/₈
P/E Ratio - High	12	26	26	19	9	13
- Low	10	16	17	13	6	7

Income Statement Analysis (Million $)

	1994	%Chg	1993	%Chg	1992	%Chg	1991
Revs.	2,606	2%	2,555	-2%	2,603	1%	2,576
Oper. Inc.	225	48%	152	15%	132	-2%	135
Depr. & Depl.	70.9	10%	64.3	13%	56.8	9%	52.3
Int. Exp.	45.6	-2%	46.7	NM	46.6	16%	40.2
Pretax Inc.	126	117%	58.0	32%	44.0	-24%	58.0
Eff. Tax Rate	40%	—	43%	—	40%	—	36%
Net Inc.	75.8	133%	32.6	23%	26.4	-29%	37.1

Balance Sheet & Other Fin. Data (Million $)

	1994	1993	1992	1991	1990	1989
Cash	27.4	12.8	17.5	15.7	23.3	26.8
Curr. Assets	540	356	359	410	449	375
Total Assets	1,621	1,349	1,298	1,222	1,134	1,027
Curr. Liab.	374	220	217	253	329	224
LT Debt	509	486	534	442	369	348
Common Eqty.	589	528	436	438	338	271
Total Cap.	1,180	1,063	1,031	945	760	744
Cap. Exp.	162	132	171	180	86.0	129
Cash Flow	142	95.0	83.0	89.0	122	96.0

Ratio Analysis

	1994	1993	1992	1991	1990	1989
Curr. Ratio	1.4	1.6	1.7	1.6	1.4	1.7
% LT Debt of Cap.	43.2	45.8	51.8	46.8	48.5	46.8
% Ret. on Assets	5.1	2.5	2.1	2.9	7.2	6.4
% Ret. on Equity	12.8	6.2	6.0	8.9	24.5	19.5

Dividend Data —Dividends were initiated in 1987. A revised "poison pill" stock purchase rights plan was adopted in 1990.

Amt. of Div. $	Date Decl.	Ex-Div. Date	Stock of Record	Payment Date
0.130	Aug. 02	Aug. 15	Aug. 19	Sep. 07 '94
0.140	Nov. 01	Nov. 14	Nov. 18	Dec. 07 '94
0.140	Feb. 07	Feb. 13	Feb. 20	Mar. 07 '95
0.140	May. 02	May. 15	May. 19	Jun. 07 '95
0.140	Aug. 01	Aug. 16	Aug. 18	Sep. 07 '95

Data as orig. reptd.; bef. results of disc opers. and/or spec. items. Per share data adj. for stk. divs. as of ex-div. date. E-Estimated. NA-Not Available. NM-Not Meaningful. NR-Not Ranked.

Office—9830 Colonnade Blvd., San Antonio, TX 78230; P.O. Box 696000, San Antonio, TX 78269-6000. **Tel**—(210) 641-6800. **Chrmn, Pres & CEO**—R. R. Hemminghaus. **VP & Treas**—R. C. Becker. **Secy**—J. D. King. **Investor Contact**—Bill Strain. **Dirs**—B. C. Ames, E. G. Biggs, W. E. Bradford, L. F. Cavazos, W. H. Clark, W. L. Fisher, R. R. Hemminghaus, B. Marbut, K. D. Ortega. **Transfer Agent**—Society National Bank, Cleveland. **Incorporated** in Delaware in 1987. **Empl**-6,400. **S&P Analyst:** Michael C. Barr

STANDARD & POOR'S

STOCK REPORTS

Diebold, Inc.

NYSE Symbol **DBD**
In S&P MidCap 400

18-SEP-95

Industry:
Data Processing

Summary: Diebold is a leading manufacturer and servicer of ATMs and electronic and physical security equipment. The dividend has been raised for 42 consecutive years.

S&P Opinion: Hold (★★★)

Recent Price • 48⅛
52 Wk Range • 48¼-33
Yield • 2.0%
12-Mo. P/E • 21.3

Quantitative Evaluations
Outlook
(1 Lowest—5 Highest)
• **2+**
Fair Value
• **42¾**
Risk
• **Low**
Earn./Div. Rank
• **A-**

Technical Eval.
• **Bearish** since 8/95
Rel. Strength Rank
(1 Lowest—99 Highest)
• **61**
Insider Activity
• **Neutral**

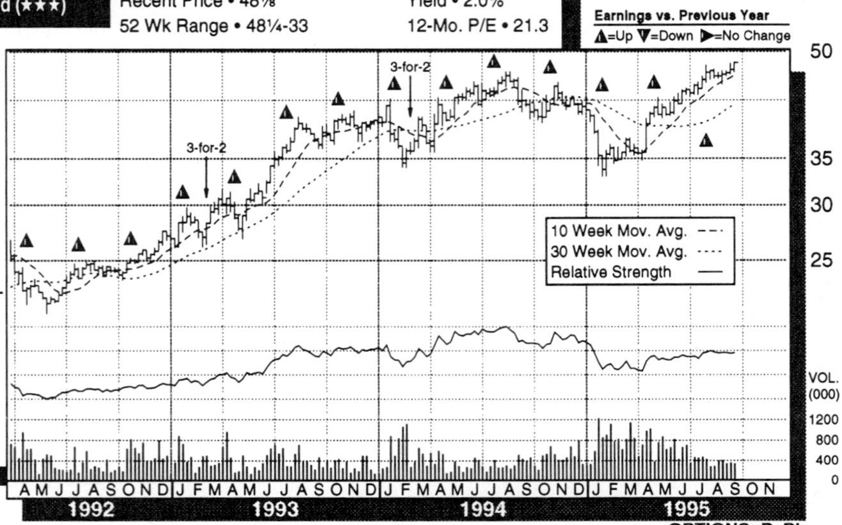

OPTIONS: P, Ph

Overview - 15-SEP-95

Revenues and earnings should continue to increase through 1995. Although revenues were up only 10% in the first half of the year, the order rate increased about 22% in the second quarter, giving the company a good start on the second half. International comparisons will likely be tougher over the next few quarters, reflecting ongoing execution problems in Europe and continued economic uncertainty in Mexico. Domestically, DBD should benefit from the trend toward greater ATM and smart card usage, particulary at non-banking premises. Overall, total revenues are projected to rise approximately 13% in 1995. Margins are expected to continue to improve on a better product mix, well controlled operating expenses, and some price increases.

Valuation - 15-SEP-95

The shares, which fell in early 1994 in response to a slowing order rate, subsequently recovered to new record levels as orders rebounded. Increased orders, along with improving margins, should maintain the upward momentum through the second half of the year. However, the shares now seem to be fairly valued at about 20 times the 1995 estimate of $2.40. Long term, the shares are attractive based on the company's excellent growth record, steady dividend and solid balance sheet.

Key Stock Statistics

S&P EPS Est. 1995	2.40	Tang. Bk. Value/Share	15.70
P/E on S&P Est. 1995	20.1	Beta	0.69
S&P EPS Est. 1996	2.75	Shareholders	3,400
Dividend Rate/Share	0.96	Market cap. (B)	$ 1.5
Shs. outstg. (M)	30.5	Inst. holdings	74%
Avg. daily vol. (M)	0.072	Insider holdings	NA

Value of $10,000 invested 5 years ago: $ 32,930

Fiscal Year Ending Dec. 31

	1995	% Change	1994	% Change	1993	% Change
Revenues (Million $)						
1Q	197.1	11%	176.8	31%	134.5	11%
2Q	206.9	10%	188.1	25%	150.1	11%
3Q	—	—	188.2	16%	162.3	22%
4Q	—	—	207.1	17%	176.4	14%
Yr.	—	—	760.2	22%	623.3	15%
Income (Million $)						
1Q	15.19	20%	12.71	47%	8.62	35%
2Q	18.94	17%	16.17	37%	11.80	36%
3Q	—	—	16.71	31%	12.71	16%
4Q	—	—	17.92	18%	15.24	NM
Yr.	—	—	63.51	31%	48.37	18%
Earnings Per Share ($)						
1Q	0.50	19%	0.42	46%	0.29	34%
2Q	0.62	17%	0.53	37%	0.39	35%
3Q	E0.60	9%	0.55	31%	0.42	15%
4Q	E0.70	19%	0.59	16%	0.51	1%
Yr.	E2.40	15%	2.09	31%	1.60	17%

Next earnings report expected: mid October

Diebold, Inc.

Business Summary - 15-SEP-95

Diebold, Incorporated manufactures a broad line of ATM and self-service systems, security products and software. Revenue contributions in recent years:

	1994	1993	1992
Products	63.1%	58.9%	56.5%
Services	36.9%	41.1%	43.5%

International sales contributed 20% of revenues in 1994, up from 18% in 1993.

DBD owns 70% of InterBold, a joint venture with IBM that provides automated teller machines and financial self-service systems worldwide. The company is the leading provider of ATMs in the U.S. and the second largest in the world. NCR, a unit of AT&T, is InterBold's largest competitor. During 1994, InterBold introduced the ix Performance Package, a modular ATM solution that protects the customer's investment in existing i Series ATMs by allowing for an easy upgrade whenever new features need to be added.

Electronic security systems include IBM and Tandem host-based and microprocessor-based monitoring systems. Other products include access control systems, video surveillance systems, film cameras, data line security, alarms and intrusion detection systems. Physical security products include a line of modular vault systems, vault doors, safe deposit boxes, security lockers, data safes, burglar- and fire-resistive safes and bullet-resistive barriers.

The company's Integrated Campus Access Management (ICAM) system allows students, faculty, staff and others in a campus-like environment to use identification cards to perform a variety of tasks, including paying fees, buying meals and gaining entry to events.

In November 1994, DBD acquired Central Security Systems, a Honolulu-based provider of alarm monitoring services, as well as sales and services of electronic security products. In January 1994, DBD purchased a 50% stake in OLTP ATM Systems, C.A., Caracas, Venezuela. The company also acquired the remaining 20% it did not already own in Hidromex, S.A. de C.V., based in Mexico City.

Important Developments

Apr. '95—DBD purchased Applied Network Technologies, Inc., the software provider for its Integrated Campus Access Management system. Separately, the company formed a strategic alliance with Optical Data Systems, Inc. (ODS), under which the companies will provide complete networking solutions to targeted markets. ODS will provide networking hardware, software and support under the agreement.

Capitalization

Long Term Debt: None (6/95).
Pensions & Postretirement Benefits: $36,636,000.
Minority Interest: $14,887,000.

Per Share Data ($) (Year Ended Dec. 31)

	1994	1993	1992	1991	1990	1989
Tangible Bk. Val.	15.08	14.11	13.27	13.25	12.70	12.78
Cash Flow	2.56	2.05	1.79	1.63	1.33	1.62
Earnings	2.09	1.60	1.37	1.20	0.91	1.22
Dividends	0.88	0.80	0.75	0.71	0.67	0.62
Payout Ratio	42%	50%	55%	60%	73%	51%
Prices - High	46¾	41⅛	27⅝	23½	20⅞	21¼
- Low	33⅞	26	20¾	14¾	13⅜	16⅛
P/E Ratio - High	22	26	20	20	23	17
- Low	16	16	15	12	15	13

Income Statement Analysis (Million $)

	1994	%Chg	1993	%Chg	1992	%Chg	1991
Revs.	760	22%	623	15%	544	8%	506
Oper. Inc.	105	27%	83.0	26%	66.0	16%	57.0
Depr.	14.2	4%	13.6	9%	12.5	-2%	12.8
Int. Exp.	Nil	—	NA	—	0.4	5%	0.4
Pretax Inc.	95.9	28%	75.0	32%	57.0	10%	52.0
Eff. Tax Rate	32%	—	30%	—	24%	—	26%
Net Inc.	63.5	31%	48.4	17%	41.3	16%	35.7

Balance Sheet & Other Fin. Data (Million $)

	1994	1993	1992	1991	1990	1989
Cash	56.0	72.0	56.0	68.0	85.0	80.0
Curr. Assets	326	313	292	321	313	289
Total Assets	662	609	559	536	520	490
Curr. Liab.	155	139	118	116	116	90.0
LT Debt	Nil	Nil	Nil	2.0	3.3	4.5
Common Eqty.	459	427	400	397	378	380
Total Cap.	474	441	412	414	399	397
Cap. Exp.	22.6	18.3	12.0	9.1	22.2	9.9
Cash Flow	77.8	62.0	53.6	48.6	39.7	48.1

Ratio Analysis

	1994	1993	1992	1991	1990	1989
Curr. Ratio	2.1	2.3	2.5	2.8	2.7	3.2
% LT Debt of Cap.	Nil	Nil	Nil	0.5	0.8	1.1
% Net Inc.of Revs.	8.4	7.8	7.6	7.1	5.7	7.7
% Ret. on Assets	10.0	8.3	7.5	6.8	5.4	7.7
% Ret. on Equity	14.3	11.7	10.3	9.2	7.1	9.8

Dividend Data —Dividends have been paid since 1954. The quarterly dividend was boosted 9.1% in January 1995. A dividend reinvestment plan is available.

Amt. of Div. $	Date Decl.	Ex-Div. Date	Stock of Record	Payment Date
0.220	Oct. 18	Nov. 10	Nov. 17	Dec. 08 '94
0.240	Jan. 31	Feb. 13	Feb. 17	Mar. 10 '95
0.240	Apr. 05	May. 15	May. 19	Jun. 09 '95
0.240	Jul. 14	Aug. 16	Aug. 18	Sep. 08 '95

Data as orig. reptd.; bef. results of disc. opers. and/or spec. items. Per share data adj. for stk. divs. as of ex-div. date. E-Estimated. NA-Not Available. NM-Not Meaningful. NR-Not Ranked.

Office—P.O. Box 8230, Canton, OH 44711-8230. **Tel**—(216) 489-4000. **Chrmn Pres & CEO**—R. W. Mahoney. **Exec VP & CFO**—G. F. Morris. **VP & Secy**—C. Francis-Vogelsang. **VP & Investor Contact**—Donald E. Eagon Jr. **Dirs**—L. V. Bockius III, D. T. Carroll, D. R. Gant, L. Lindsey Halstead, P. B. Lassiter, J. N. Lauer, R. W. Mahoney, W. F. Massy, W. R. Timken Jr. **Transfer Agent & Registrar**—KeyCorp Shareholder Services, Inc., Cleveland. **Incorporated** in Ohio in 1876. **Empl**-4,731. **S&P Analyst:** Michael T. Cavanaugh

Dole Food

NYSE Symbol **DOL**
In S&P MidCap 400

19-AUG-95 **Industry:** Food

Summary: This company is the largest worldwide producer and marketer of fresh fruits and vegetables, and sells a growing line of packaged foods.

S&P Opinion: Accumulate (★★★★) | Recent Price • 32⅞ | 52 Wk Range • 33¼-22½ | Yield • 1.2% | 12-Mo. P/E • 18.8

Quantitative Evaluations
Outlook (1 Lowest—5 Highest)
• **4+**
Fair Value
• **34½**
Risk
• **Low**
Earn./Div. Rank
• **B**

Technical Eval.
• **Bearish** since 4/95
Rel. Strength Rank (1 Lowest—99 Highest)
• **71**
Insider Activity
• **Neutral**

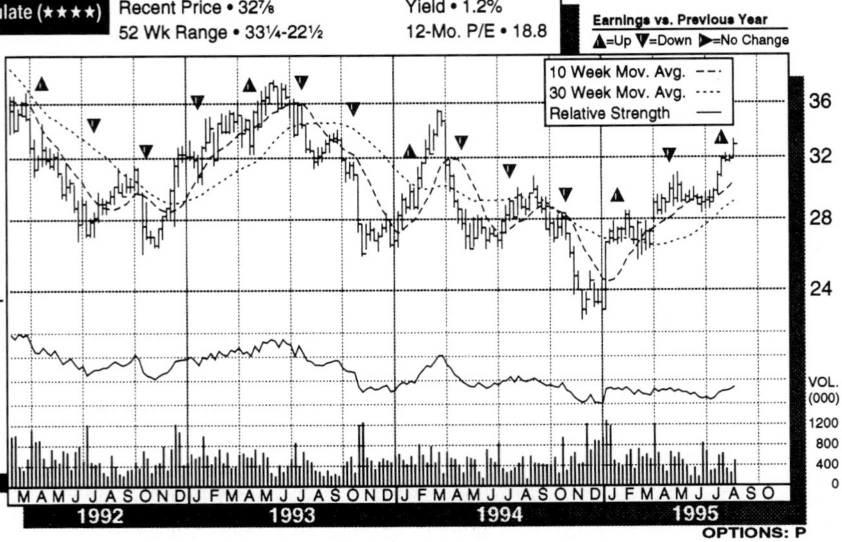

Overview - 18-AUG-95

Reduced revenues from food operations stemming from the sale of the company's worldwide juice business is expected to be partially offset by increased sales of bananas, increased penetration of the European market, and new product introductions. Real estate sales should benefit from the acquisition of the remainder of Castle & Cooke Homes. Food pricing pressure should be somewhat offset by cost-cutting efforts, increased commercial profits and the elimination of certain lower-margined agricultural operations. Continuation of these trends, along with improved contributions from Lana'i operations, should generate operating earnings growth in 1995 and 1996, although near-term profitability will be restricted by weakness in the Hawaiian real estate market.

Valuation - 18-AUG-95

The shares have recovered sharply from their seven-year low in late 1994, as profitability has rebounded. The company is reviewing its businesses and plans to sell or distribute lower margined operating segments. Because of the nature of its commodity-related businesses, earnings can fluctuate significantly. At about 15x our 1996 estimate of $2.15 a share, the price-to-earnings ratio is near the low end of its historical range. DOL's efforts to improve margins and reduce volatility should allow for some expansion of its PE multiple; we believe the stock can outperform the general market in the next six to 12 months.

Key Stock Statistics

S&P EPS Est. 1995	2.55	Tang. Bk. Value/Share	18.17
P/E on S&P Est. 1995	12.9	Beta	1.03
S&P EPS Est. 1996	2.15	Shareholders	15,500
Dividend Rate/Share	0.40	Market cap. (B)	$ 2.0
Shs. outstg. (M)	59.5	Inst. holdings	59%
Avg. daily vol. (M)	0.083	Insider holdings	0%

Value of $10,000 invested 5 years ago: $ 10,119

Fiscal Year Ending Dec. 31

	1995	% Change	1994	% Change	1993	% Change
Revenues (Million $)						
1Q	925.3	13%	818.8	7%	766.0	2%
2Q	1,152	17%	987.0	14%	863.7	-4%
3Q	—	—	1,081	8%	1,006	5%
4Q	—	—	954.5	20%	794.6	4%
Yr.	—	—	3,842	12%	3,431	2%
Income (Million $)						
1Q	23.62	-21%	29.75	-44%	53.26	100%
2Q	78.66	121%	35.65	-10%	39.66	NM
3Q	—	—	1.29	-75%	5.10	-76%
4Q	—	—	1.20	NM	-20.13	NM
Yr.	—	—	67.88	-13%	77.89	19%
Earnings Per Share ($)						
1Q	0.40	-20%	0.50	-44%	0.89	98%
2Q	1.32	120%	0.60	-9%	0.66	-1%
3Q	E0.41	NM	0.02	-78%	0.09	-75%
4Q	E0.42	NM	0.02	NM	-0.34	NM
Yr.	E2.55	124%	1.14	-12%	1.30	19%

Next earnings report expected: late October

Dole Food

Business Summary - 18-AUG-95

Dole Food is a leading worldwide producer, packer and marketer of fresh produce and packaged foods. It also develops real estate. Industry segment contributions in 1994 (profits in millions):

	Revs.	Profits
Food products:		
North America	48%	-$39
Latin America	6%	131
Far East	17%	16
Europe	20%	13
Real estate	8%	73
Resorts	2%	-37

The Dole Food unit is a major worldwide producer and marketer of branded food products, including fresh fruits, such as pineapples, bananas, table grapes and apples under the Dole label; approximately 25 types of fresh vegetables, including lettuce, celery, cauliflower and broccoli under the Dole and related brand labels; and processed foods, including canned pineapple, tropical fruit salad, and mandarin oranges, juice drinks and DOLEWHIP soft-serve, non-dairy dessert under the Dole and other company-owned brand names.

Real estate activities, including residential, resort, commercial and industrial projects in Hawaii, California, Arizona, North Carolina, Georgia and Mississippi are conducted under the Castle & Cooke name through the company's real estate group. In November 1994, Dole completed a tender offer for the 82% of Castle & Cooke that was publicly traded. The company's resort operations are located on the Hawaiian Island of Lana'i and include two luxury resorts: the Lodge at Koele and The Manele Bay Hotel.

Important Developments

Jun. '95—Dole said it discontinued negotiations to sell its California-based dried fruit business to Sun Diamond Growers of California for approximately $100 million. In May, it sold most of its worldwide juice business ($320 million in sales) to Seagram Co. for approximately $240 million cash. Separately, it agreed to sell the license rights to its juice brand in Japan to its joint venture partner, Snow Brand Milk Products Inc., for $30 million.

Nov. '94—The company completed its tender offer for the 17.2% of its Castle & Cooke Homes Inc. real estate development subsidiary that it did not already own. Shareholders tendered 5,019,947 shares under the offer at $15.75 cash per share, or about $81 million. The few remaining shares were converted to cash at the same price.

Capitalization

Long Term Debt: $1,108,711,000 (6/95).
Minority Interest: $26,769,000.

Per Share Data ($)

(Year Ended Dec. 31)

	1994	1993	1992	1991	1990	1989
Tangible Bk. Val.	17.97	17.54	16.80	17.53	15.67	14.11
Cash Flow	3.39	3.33	2.88	3.63	3.22	2.54
Earnings	1.14	1.30	1.09	2.24	2.03	1.60
Dividends	0.40	0.40	0.40	0.40	0.10	Nil
Payout Ratio	35%	31%	36%	18%	5%	Nil
Prices - High	35½	37⅞	40	48	38⅝	45¼
- Low	22½	25⅞	26	28	26¼	25⅜
P/E Ratio - High	31	29	37	21	19	28
- Low	20	20	24	13	13	16

Income Statement Analysis (Million $)

	1994	%Chg	1993	%Chg	1992	%Chg	1991
Revs.	3,842	12%	3,431	2%	3,375	5%	3,216
Oper. Inc.	308	NM	306	5%	291	-5%	307
Depr.	134	11%	121	13%	107	29%	83.0
Int. Exp.	95.9	26%	76.1	-3%	78.2	6%	73.5
Pretax Inc.	88.0	-10%	98.0	36%	72.0	-57%	169
Eff. Tax Rate	23%	—	21%	—	8.90%	—	21%
Net Inc.	68.0	-13%	78.0	20%	65.0	-51%	134

Balance Sheet & Other Fin. Data (Million $)

	1994	1993	1992	1991	1990	1989
Cash	47.0	37.0	57.0	42.0	27.0	44.0
Curr. Assets	1,346	1,142	981	977	875	922
Total Assets	3,849	3,388	3,095	2,793	2,423	2,270
Curr. Liab.	705	660	646	565	616	850
LT Debt	1,555	1,158	988	813	543	245
Common Eqty.	1,081	1,052	1,001	1,041	929	836
Total Cap.	3,000	2,596	2,303	1,881	1,495	1,121
Cap. Exp.	240	219	205	325	247	304
Cash Flow	202	199	172	217	191	151

Ratio Analysis

	1994	1993	1992	1991	1990	1989
Curr. Ratio	1.9	1.7	1.5	1.7	1.4	1.1
% LT Debt of Cap.	51.8	44.6	42.9	43.2	36.3	21.9
% Net Inc.of Revs.	1.8	2.3	1.9	4.2	4.0	3.5
% Ret. on Assets	1.9	2.4	2.2	5.1	5.1	4.5
% Ret. on Equity	6.4	7.6	6.4	13.6	13.6	12.0

Dividend Data —Dividends were resumed in December 1990 after having been omitted since 1982.

Amt. of Div. $	Date Decl.	Ex-Div. Date	Stock of Record	Payment Date
0.100	Jul. 14	Aug. 19	Aug. 25	Sep. 29 '94
0.100	Oct. 10	Nov. 04	Nov. 10	Dec. 15 '94
0.100	Dec. 16	Feb. 16	Feb. 23	Mar. 23 '95
0.100	Mar. 24	May. 05	May. 11	Jun. 15 '95
0.100	Jul. 13	Aug. 29	Aug. 31	Oct. 05 '95

Data as orig. reptd.; bef. results of disc. opers. and/or spec. items. Per share data adj. for stk. divs. as of ex-div. date. E-Estimated. NA-Not Available. NM-Not Meaningful. NR-Not Ranked.

Office—31355 Oak Crest Drive, Westlake Village, CA 91361. **Tel**—(818) 879-6600. **Chrmn & CEO**—D. H. Murdock. **EVP**—A. B. Sellers. **CFO**—M. S. Karsner **Dirs**—E. L. Chao, M. Curb, D. A. DeLorenzo, R. M. Ferry, J. F. Gary, F. J. Hata, D. H. Murdock. **Transfer Agent**—First National Bank of Boston. **Incorporated** in Hawaii in 1894. **Empl-** 46,000. **S&P Analyst:** Efraim Levy

STANDARD & POOR'S STOCK REPORTS

Dollar General

NYSE Symbol **DG**
In S&P MidCap 400

07-SEP-95

Industry: Retail Stores

Summary: This retailer specializes in merchandising inexpensive soft and hard goods to low-, middle- and fixed-income families through nearly 2,260 stores in small communities in 24 states.

S&P Opinion: Buy (★★★★★)

Recent Price • 26¾
52 Wk Range • 34-18⅜
Yield • 0.8%
12-Mo. P/E • 23.3

Quantitative Evaluations

Outlook
(1 Lowest—5 Highest)
• **5+**

Fair Value
• **34¼**

Risk
• **Average**

Earn./Div. Rank
• **A-**

Technical Eval.
• **Bullish** since 8/94

Rel. Strength Rank
(1 Lowest—99 Highest)
• **7**

Insider Activity
• **Unfavorable**

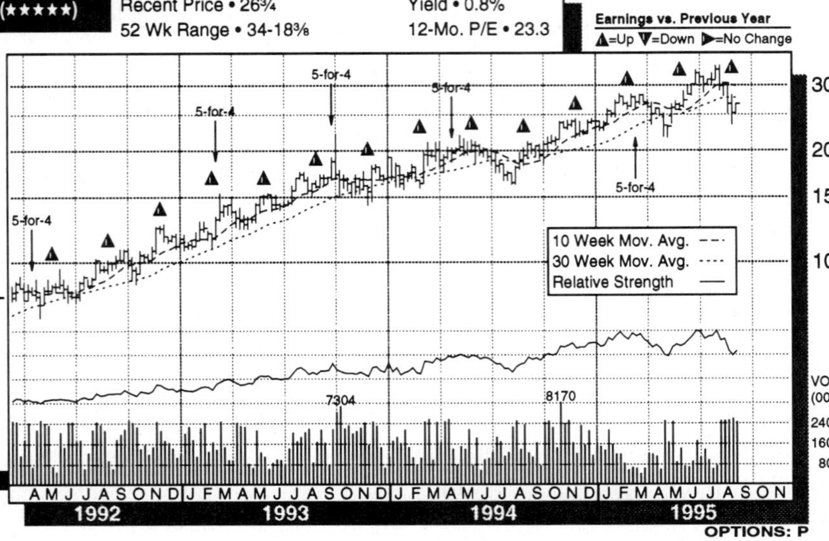

OPTIONS: P

Overview - 06-SEP-95

We project total sales gains for the balance of 1995-96 to be driven by an accelerated store opening program, which is expected to add up to 300 new stores by the end of the year. Same-store sales growth should remain in the mid-to-upper-single digit levels. Gross margins will benefit from higher beginning inventory markups and greater lower markdowns. This improvement should more than offset costs associated with the start-up of the Ardmore distribution center. Emphasis on cost controls and increasing efficiencies should further enhance earnings comparisons.

Valuation - 07-SEP-95

After soaring to an all time high in July, the shares of this leading discount retailer have recently fallen over 20% from that level. The decline reflects investors' concerns about the rate of same-store sales growth, and the impact of costs associated with the opening of the company's new distribution center. However, the customers' favorable response to better merchandise selection and to the company's commitment to everyday low pricing, accelerated new store development, aggressive overhead cost control and increased use of cost-effective information technology should fuel continued 20%-plus annual earnings growth for the foreseeable future. Based on this above-average earnings potential, we believe that DG shares have appeal for superior long-term appreciation.

Key Stock Statistics

S&P EPS Est. 1996	1.32	Tang. Bk. Value/Share	5.73
P/E on S&P Est. 1996	20.3	Beta	1.01
S&P EPS Est. 1997	1.65	Shareholders	3,200
Dividend Rate/Share	0.20	Market cap. (B)	$ 1.8
Shs. outstg. (M)	67.9	Inst. holdings	66%
Avg. daily vol. (M)	0.657	Insider holdings	NA

Value of $10,000 invested 5 years ago: $ 91,541

Fiscal Year Ending Jan. 31

	1996	% Change	1995	% Change	1994	% Change
Revenues (Million $)						
1Q	343.4	20%	287.0	29%	221.8	17%
2Q	408.2	29%	317.3	24%	255.6	18%
3Q	—	—	359.4	32%	272.6	22%
4Q	—	—	484.8	27%	383.1	31%
Yr.	—	—	1,449	28%	1,133	23%
Income (Million $)						
1Q	11.58	22%	9.51	61%	5.92	53%
2Q	17.69	27%	13.96	45%	9.62	43%
3Q	—	—	17.29	58%	10.97	33%
4Q	—	—	32.87	49%	22.04	32%
Yr.	—	—	73.63	52%	48.56	37%
Earnings Per Share ($)						
1Q	0.17	25%	0.14	56%	0.09	55%
2Q	0.25	25%	0.20	39%	0.14	40%
3Q	E0.32	29%	0.25	55%	0.16	30%
4Q	E0.58	23%	0.47	44%	0.33	30%
Yr.	E1.32	23%	1.07	49%	0.72	34%

Next earnings report expected: early November

Dollar General

Business Summary - 07-SEP-95

Dollar General Corporation operates a chain of nearly 2,260 small, self-service discount stores. The stores feature, at greatly reduced prices, a focused assortment of both brand name and irregular soft and hard goods.

Contributions to sales in recent fiscal years were:

	1994-95	1993-94
Soft goods (mainly apparel)	34%	35%
Hard goods	66%	65%

The company's strategy is to provide a focused assortment of basic quality merchandise at everyday low prices to low-, middle- and fixed-income families. The majority of the products in Dollar General stores are priced at $10 or less, with the most expensive item generally priced at $35. In recent years, the company has shifted its merchandise mix focus to hard goods, reflecting an increased commitment to be in-stock on basics, a greater emphasis on private-label products, and an expanded selection of brand name merchandise.

Irregular, overrun and closeout merchandise accounted for 5% of soft goods sales and 8% of hard goods sales in 1994-95, while brand name merchandise provided 20% and 40%, respectively.

In the fiscal year ended January 31, 1995, 302 new stores were opened and 43 stores were closed, with a total of 2,059 in operation at year-end. The stores were located in 24 states, with the greatest concentrations in Tennessee (167 stores), Texas (160), Florida (152), Kentucky (150), Missouri (138), Illinois (120) and Indiana (120). The typical store is relatively small (6,200 sq. ft. average size) and is located in a community of fewer than 25,000 people. About 65% of stores are located in strip shopping centers, with the remainder in freestanding and downtown buildings. The average store generated annual sales of $754,000 in 1994-95, versus $663,000 in 1993-94.

Merchandise is shipped from warehouses in Scottsville, Ky., and Homerville, Ga., or directly from suppliers. A new 500,000-sq.-ft. distribution center near Ardmore, Okla., is expected to be fully operational by the second quarter of 1995-96.

Important Developments

Aug. '95—Sales for the four weeks ended August 25, 1995, totaled $137.5 million, up 17.7% from $116.8 million in the 1994 period. Same-store sales edged up 0.4%. For the year-to-date, total sales increased 23%, on a 6.7% gain in same-store sales.

Aug. '95— In the second quarter of 1995-96, DG opened 107 new stores and closed nine, ending the period with 2,260 stores in operation.

Capitalization

Long Term Obligs.: $3,598,000 (7/95).
Series A Conv. Jr. Pfd. Stk.: 1,715,742 shs. (no par). 6.25 votes ea.; held by C. Turner Jr.

Per Share Data ($) (Year Ended Jan. 31)

	1995	1994	1993	1992	1991	1990
Tangible Bk. Val.	5.72	3.65	2.97	2.42	2.14	1.96
Cash Flow	1.31	0.90	0.66	0.44	0.34	0.30
Earnings	1.07	0.72	0.54	0.33	0.24	0.20
Dividends	0.15	0.11	0.08	0.06	0.06	0.06
Payout Ratio	14%	14%	14%	19%	25%	30%
Cal. Yrs.	1994	1993	1992	1991	1990	1989
Prices - High	$24\frac{3}{8}$	$21\frac{3}{4}$	$12\frac{5}{8}$	$8\frac{1}{8}$	$3\frac{1}{2}$	$3\frac{3}{4}$
- Low	$15\frac{5}{8}$	$10\frac{3}{4}$	7	$2\frac{1}{4}$	$2\frac{3}{16}$	$2\frac{1}{2}$
P/E Ratio - High	23	31	24	24	14	19
- Low	15	15	13	7	9	13

Income Statement Analysis (Million $)

	1995	%Chg	1994	%Chg	1993	%Chg	1992
Revs.	1,449	28%	1,133	23%	921	22%	754
Oper. Inc.	138	50%	91.9	33%	69.1	55%	44.5
Depr.	17.3	48%	11.7	42%	8.2	23%	6.7
Int. Exp.	2.8	28%	2.2	-17%	2.7	-15%	3.1
Pretax Inc.	118	57%	75.0	29%	58.2	68%	34.7
Eff. Tax Rate	38%	—	38%	—	39%	—	38%
Net Inc.	73.6	51%	48.6	37%	35.6	66%	21.5

Balance Sheet & Other Fin. Data (Million $)

	1995	1994	1993	1992	1991	1990
Cash	33.0	35.4	25.0	7.9	3.9	6.5
Curr. Assets	410	315	256	192	168	155
Total Assets	541	397	316	237	208	194
Curr. Liab.	209	148	117	62.4	55.1	45.1
LT Debt	4.8	5.7	7.0	21.2	19.1	26.8
Common Eqty.	323	241	190	151	132	121
Total Cap.	332	249	199	175	153	149
Cap. Exp.	65.8	35.0	24.7	12.8	8.9	17.0
Cash Flow	90.1	60.3	43.8	28.2	21.3	18.4

Ratio Analysis

	1995	1994	1993	1992	1991	1990
Curr. Ratio	2.0	2.1	2.2	3.1	3.1	3.4
% LT Debt of Cap.	1.4	2.3	3.5	12.1	12.5	18.0
% Net Inc.of Revs.	5.1	4.3	3.9	2.9	2.2	2.0
% Ret. on Assets	16.7	13.4	12.7	9.6	7.3	6.1
% Ret. on Equity	27.5	22.3	20.6	15.1	11.6	10.6

Dividend Data —Cash dividends were initiated in 1975.

Amt. of Div. $	Date Decl.	Ex-Div. Date	Stock of Record	Payment Date
0.050	Aug. 22	Nov. 21	Nov. 28	Dec. 16 '94
0.050	Dec. 12	Feb. 15	Feb. 22	Mar. 10 '95
5-for-4	Feb. 07	Mar. 07	Feb. 23	Mar. 06 '95
0.050	Feb. 07	May. 16	May. 22	Jun. 09 '95
0.050	Jun. 06	Aug. 24	Aug. 28	Sep. 15 '95

Data as orig. reptd.; bef. results of disc. opers. and/or spec. items. Per share data adj. for stk. divs. as of ex-div. date. Bk. val. figs. in Per Share Data tbl. incl. intangibles. E-Estimated. NA-Not Available. NM-Not Meaningful. NR-Not Ranked.

Office—104 Woodmont Blvd., Suite 500, Nashville, TN 37205. **Tel**—(615) 783-2000. **Chrmn, Pres & CEO**—C. Turner, Jr. **CFO**—T. W. Stoltz. **VP & Secy**—B. R. Carpenter. **Investor Contact**—Kiley Fleming. **Dirs**—J. L. Clayton, J. D. Cockman, R. D. Dickson, J. B. Holland, W. N. Rasmussen, C. Turner, C. Turner Jr., D. M. Wilds, W. S. Wire II. **Transfer Agent**—Trust Co. Bank, Atlanta. **Incorporated** in Kentucky in 1955. **Empl**-18,000. **S&P Analyst:** Maureen C. Carini

STANDARD & POOR'S

STOCK REPORTS

Donaldson Co.

NYSE Symbol **DCI**
In S&P MidCap 400

07-SEP-95

Industry:
Auto parts/equipment

Summary: Donaldson Co. produces air cleaners, filters and mufflers for internal combustion engines and industrial dust collectors and related products.

S&P Opinion: Hold (★★★)

Recent Price • 25¼
52 Wk Range • 28-20¾

Yield • 1.1%
12-Mo. P/E • 18.3

Quantitative Evaluations

Outlook
(1 Lowest—5 Highest)
• **2+**

Fair Value
• **23⅜**

Risk
• **Low**

Earn./Div. Rank
• **A**

Technical Eval.
• **Bullish** since 1/95

Rel. Strength Rank
(1 Lowest—99 Highest)
• **27**

Insider Activity
• **NA**

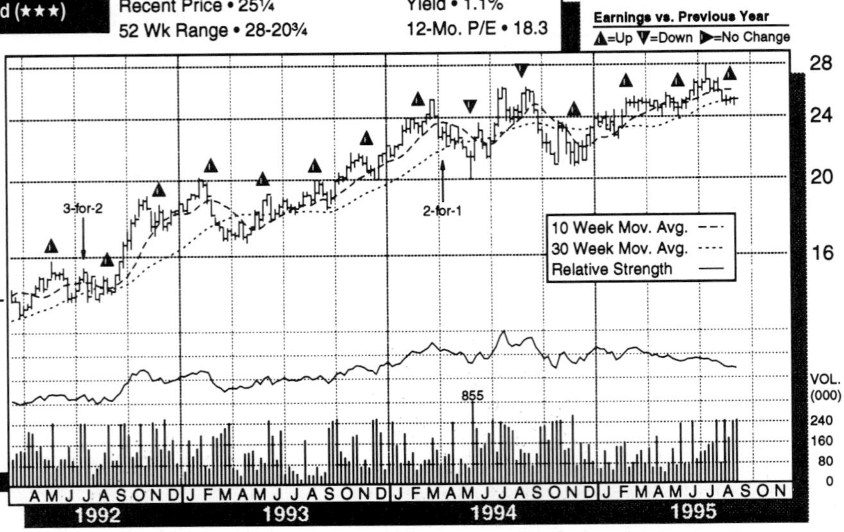

Overview - 07-SEP-95

Sales should rise in fiscal 1996, as the company's backlogs continued to expand in recent quarters reaching $205 million by April 30, 1995, up 35% from a year earlier. Engine products should remain the strongest segment aided by a vigorous heavy duty truck market and strong demand from construction equipment customers. Defense product sales are stabilizing after declining for several years. Industrial segment sales continued to rise with growth in all three product categories. Margins should benefit from plant capacity utilization increases, continued tight control of selling expenses, and modest price hikes to offset higher raw material prices. Net income should rise and share earnings should be augmented by an active share repurchase program.

Valuation - 07-SEP-95

This leader in the filtration business has a high degree of exposure to cyclical original equipment businesses. Combined with rather stable demand for replacement parts which account for 42% of sales, sales growth should average 10% a year for the next few years and earnings growth of 10% to 15% a year is possible. We believe that based on this modest outlook for earnings growth, the stock is fairly valued at 16 times expected fiscal 1996 earnings. With a strong balance sheet and little debt, excess cash is being directed to steady dividend increases and stock repurchases.

Key Stock Statistics

S&P EPS Est. 1995	1.45	Tang. Bk. Value/Share	7.16
P/E on S&P Est. 1995	17.4	Beta	0.75
S&P EPS Est. 1996	1.60	Shareholders	1,400
Dividend Rate/Share	0.28	Market cap. (B)	$0.666
Shs. outstg. (M)	26.3	Inst. holdings	60%
Avg. daily vol. (M)	0.047	Insider holdings	NA

Value of $10,000 invested 5 years ago: $ 36,366

Fiscal Year Ending Jul. 31

	1995	% Change	1994	% Change	1993	% Change
Revenues (Million $)						
1Q	164.2	15%	142.5	13%	126.0	12%
2Q	168.9	25%	135.6	8%	125.0	10%
3Q	186.8	21%	153.9	15%	133.4	5%
4Q	—	—	161.5	8%	149.2	17%
Yr.	—	—	593.5	11%	533.3	11%
Income (Million $)						
1Q	9.51	26%	7.56	20%	6.30	3%
2Q	7.69	23%	6.24	20%	5.22	6%
3Q	11.46	18%	9.71	26%	7.68	5%
4Q	—	—	8.44	-6%	9.01	22%
Yr.	—	—	31.95	13%	28.21	9%
Earnings Per Share ($)						
1Q	0.35	30%	0.27	20%	0.22	5%
2Q	0.29	26%	0.23	24%	0.19	6%
3Q	0.43	72%	0.25	-9%	0.28	6%
4Q	E0.38	23%	0.31	-6%	0.33	25%
Yr.	E1.45	24%	1.17	16%	1.01	10%

Next earnings report expected: late September

Donaldson Co.

Business Summary - 06-SEP-95

Donaldson Co. manufactures air cleaners, liquid filtration devices and exhaust products for engines, compressors, mobile equipment, gas turbine systems and industrial applications. The current focus is on increasing replacement lube filter element market share. Sales and profits by geographic area in fiscal 1994 were:

	Sales	Profits
United States	66%	50%
Europe	15%	22%
Japan	12%	16%
Other countries	7%	12%

DCI is a major factor in air cleaners and exhaust products for mobile heavy-duty internal combustion engines in the U.S. Related products include hydraulic filters, dust control devices for underground mining and special filters for varied purposes including in-plant air cleaning systems, computer disk drives, clean rooms and respirators. Liquid filtration devices are produced for hydraulic, lube, fuel, coolant and transmission applications. DCI is doubling the size of its Stevens Point, WI liquid filtration production facility in order to accommodate rising demand.

DCI also makes devices that remove particulate matter from streams of air, gas or liquid, and pulverizing and classifying systems. Lengthy research and development work on particulate trap oxidizers for diesel engines was abandoned in 1993. However, a product called catalytic mufflers was derived from the particulate trap research and is being manufactured for use in heavy duty trucks.

In fiscal 1994, Caterpillar (CAT) accounted for 11.6% of DCI's sales, primarily through a joint venture with DCI called AFSI, which manufactures lube, oil and hydraulic filters exclusively for CAT.

Important Developments

May '95—Fiscal 1995 third quarter sales reflected strong gains across all markets, particularly in Europe. Gross margins improved to 28.8% in the quarter, reflecting in part the absence of a charge in the 1994 quarter related to DCI's Brazilian operation. Total backlogs were $205 million at the end of the period, up 35% from a year earlier and 5% from the end of the second quarter. Hard order backlogs, those scheduled for delivery in 90 days, totaled $123.1 million, up 21% from a year earlier and unchanged from the second quarter.

Capitalization

Long Term Debt: $12,519,000 (4/30/95).

Per Share Data ($) (Year Ended Jul. 31)

	1994	1993	1992	1991	1990	1989
Tangible Bk. Val.	7.16	6.38	5.81	5.01	4.46	3.74
Cash Flow	1.75	1.55	1.42	1.26	1.08	0.90
Earnings	1.17	1.02	0.92	0.84	0.73	0.54
Dividends	0.25	0.21	0.19	0.15	0.13	0.13
Payout Ratio	21%	20%	20%	18%	18%	24%
Prices - High	26¼	22⅛	19⅛	13¾	11¾	8⅛
- Low	20	16⅝	12¼	10¼	7⅛	5½
P/E Ratio - High	22	22	21	16	16	15
- Low	17	17	13	12	10	10

Income Statement Analysis (Million $)

	1994	%Chg	1993	%Chg	1992	%Chg	1991
Revs.	594	11%	533	11%	482	5%	458
Oper. Inc.	68.0	13%	60.0	8%	55.3	4%	53.0
Depr.	15.9	7%	14.8	6%	14.0	20%	11.7
Int. Exp.	3.4	24%	2.7	1%	2.7	-24%	3.5
Pretax Inc.	50.2	12%	44.7	7%	41.7	6%	39.4
Eff. Tax Rate	36%	—	37%	—	38%	—	39%
Net Inc.	31.9	13%	28.2	9%	25.8	7%	24.0

Balance Sheet & Other Fin. Data (Million $)

	1994	1993	1992	1991	1990	1989
Cash	22.9	32.1	31.1	35.1	38.4	6.2
Curr. Assets	220	196	187	169	169	131
Total Assets	337	300	286	253	246	205
Curr. Liab.	116	93.7	90.0	77.5	79.9	58.0
LT Debt	16.0	18.9	23.5	25.7	28.3	30.8
Common Eqty.	190	174	160	139	129	108
Total Cap.	208	195	185	165	157	138
Cap. Exp.	26.8	15.0	15.5	17.1	16.4	12.1
Cash Flow	47.8	43.0	39.8	36.2	31.4	25.6

Ratio Analysis

	1994	1993	1992	1991	1990	1989
Curr. Ratio	1.9	2.1	2.1	2.2	2.1	2.3
% LT Debt of Cap.	7.7	9.7	12.7	15.6	18.0	22.2
% Net Inc.of Revs.	5.4	5.3	5.3	5.3	5.0	3.9
% Ret. on Assets	10.2	9.7	9.6	9.8	9.3	7.7
% Ret. on Equity	17.8	17.0	17.3	18.3	17.7	15.1

Dividend Data —Dividends have been paid since 1956. A dividend reinvestment plan is available. A "poison pill" stock purchase rights plan was adopted in 1986.

Amt. of Div. $	Date Decl.	Ex-Div. Date	Stock of Record	Payment Date
0.070	Jul. 29	Aug. 22	Aug. 26	Sep. 12 '94
0.070	Nov. 18	Nov. 29	Dec. 05	Dec. 13 '94
0.070	Jan. 20	Feb. 22	Feb. 28	Mar. 13 '95
0.070	May. 19	May. 30	Jun. 05	Jun. 13 '95
0.070	Jul. 28	Aug. 24	Aug. 28	Sep. 13 '95

Data as orig. reptd.; bef. results of disc. opers. and/or spec. items. Per share data adj. for stk. divs. as of ex-div. date. E-Estimated. NA-Not Available. NM-Not Meaningful. NR-Not Ranked.

Office—1400 West 94th St., P.O. Box 1299, Minneapolis, MN 55440. **Tel**—(612) 887-3131. **Chrmn & CEO**— W. A. Hodder. **Pres**—W. G. Van Dyke. **VP-CFO & Investor Contact**—James R. Giertz. **VP-Secy**—R. F. Vodovnik. **Dirs**—A. G. Ames, M. R. Bonsignore, J. W. Eugster, W. A. Hodder, K. B. Melrose, S. W. Richey, S. W. Sanger, W. G. Van Dyke, C. A. Wurtele. **Transfer Agent & Registrar**—Norwest Bank Minnesota, South St. Paul. **Incorporated** in Delaware in 1936. **Empl**-4,417. **S&P Analyst:** Joshua M. Harari, CFA

STANDARD & POOR'S

STOCK REPORTS

Dreyer's Grand Ice Cream

NASDAQ Symbol **DRYR**

In S&P MidCap 400

23-SEP-95

Industry: Food

Summary: Dreyer's principally manufactures and distributes premium-quality ice cream and other dairy dessert products.

S&P Opinion: Hold (★★★)

Recent Price • 38¼ | 52 Wk Range • 40-24¼ | Yield • 0.6% | 12-Mo. P/E • NM

Quantitative Evaluations

Outlook (1 Lowest—5 Highest)
• **2⁻**

Fair Value
• **37¾**

Risk
• **Low**

Earn./Div. Rank
• **B**

Technical Eval.
• **Bearish** since 10/93

Rel. Strength Rank (1 Lowest—99 Highest)
• **51**

Insider Activity
• **Neutral**

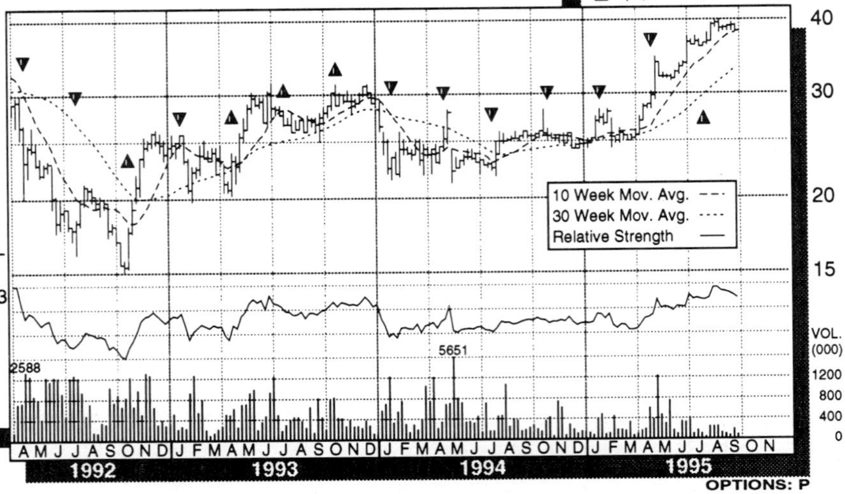

OPTIONS: P

Overview - 22-SEP-95

Sales should rise at least 20% in 1995, on further penetration in the eastern U.S., the start of distribution of Nestle Ice Cream Co.'s frozen novelty and ice cream products, increased sales of third party brands, and the introduction of new products. Margins will be restricted by a less favorable product mix and higher marketing spending aimed at boosting market share. However, net income should rebound from the depressed level of 1994. Share earnings will benefit from a reduction in common shares outstanding to 12.9 million (from 14.2 million at the end of 1994), following completion of the repurchase of 5 million shares. Profitability should advance sharply in 1996, as sales rise and annual advertising and consumer promotion expense levels off at $50 million.

Valuation - 22-SEP-95

We believe that the company's heavy marketing spending to increase market share is likely to succeed. However, increased advertising and promotion expense will continue to restrict growth in 1995. Based on several valuation measures, including the ratio of price to book value (48X) and P/E (24X our 1996 EPS estimate of $1.60), the shares seem fully valued. We expect the stock of this premium ice cream maker to be only a market performer over the next six to 12 months, as the relatively high P/E already reflects expectations of accelerated earnings growth.

Key Stock Statistics

S&P EPS Est. 1995	0.46	Tang. Bk. Value/Share	0.81
P/E on S&P Est. 1995	83.2	Beta	1.15
S&P EPS Est. 1996	1.60	Shareholders	3,700
Dividend Rate/Share	0.24	Market cap. (B)	$0.492
Shs. outstg. (M)	12.9	Inst. holdings	46%
Avg. daily vol. (M)	0.023	Insider holdings	NA

Value of $10,000 invested 5 years ago: $ 28,851

Fiscal Year Ending Dec. 31

	1995	% Change	1994	% Change	1993	% Change
Revenues (Million $)						
1Q	141.2	26%	112.0	9%	102.3	21%
2Q	188.1	27%	147.7	20%	123.5	13%
3Q	—	—	168.7	20%	140.1	16%
4Q	—	—	135.9	30%	104.8	13%
Yr.	—	—	564.4	20%	470.7	16%
Income (Million $)						
1Q	0.32	-80%	1.58	-25%	2.12	NM
2Q	3.66	NM	-1.44	NM	6.88	19%
3Q	—	—	2.26	-66%	6.61	7%
4Q	—	—	-1.41	NM	1.19	-29%
Yr.	—	—	1.00	-94%	16.79	20%
Earnings Per Share ($)						
1Q	0.02	-82%	0.11	-27%	0.15	NM
2Q	0.27	NM	-0.10	NM	0.47	24%
3Q	E0.24	60%	0.15	-67%	0.45	5%
4Q	E0.01	NM	-0.09	NM	0.08	-33%
Yr.	E0.46	NM	0.07	-94%	1.15	22%

Next earnings report expected: late October

Dreyer's Grand Ice Cream

Business Summary - 22-SEP-95

Dreyer's Grand Ice Cream makes and distributes premium-quality ice cream and other dairy dessert products. Its ice cream is the leading premium packaged ice cream product in most areas of the western U.S. In addition, its products are sold in certain markets in the Midwest, Mid-Atlantic and Southeast, and in the New York metropolitan area under the Edy's Grand Ice Cream label (because of an agreement regarding use of the Dreyer's name). Dreyer's products are also available in Japan, Hong Kong and certain other Far Eastern markets. The company's marketing strategy for packaged ice creams is based on maintaining quality, even if ingredients cost more. Dreyer's also distributes third party brands.

The company has responded to a growing customer preference for lower-fat and lower-cholesterol products by introducing several new products in recent years. Grand Light (introduced in 1987 and sold under the Dreyer's and Edy's brand names) is a premium light ice cream that is 93% fat-free and contains as few as 100 calories per serving. Dreyer's and Edy's Frozen Yogurt Inspirations (1989) are premium frozen yogurts. Dreyer's Low Fat (1992) has 3% total fat, and Dreyer's Fat Free (reintroduced under its current name in 1992) has no fat and no cholesterol. Grand Delights (1992) is a line of low-calorie ice cream snacks. Dreyer's and Edy's Lactose Reduced Ice Cream and Dreyer's and Edy's Grand Cones were introduced in 1994.

Dreyer's uses a direct-store delivery system consisting of company-owned and independent distribution operations. To leverage this system, it also distributes selected branded frozen dessert products manufactured by others, principally Nestle's Ice Cream Co.'s frozen novelty and ice cream products, Ben & Jerry's Homemade Ice Cream products, Dove-brand premium ice cream novelties and Mocha Mix (made by Dreyer's for Presto Food Products).

In May 1994, the company announced a five-year plan to accelerate the sale of branded products by greatly increasing consumer marketing efforts and expanding its distribution system to additional markets. Annual advertising and consumer promotion spending is projected at $50 million for 1995-8, (up from $40 million in 1994 and $12 million in 1993.)

In June 1994, Dreyer's sold to Nestle USA 3,000,000 common shares at $32 each, plus warrants to buy an additional 2,000,000 shares at $32 each (for $5 a warrant).

Important Developments

Aug. '95—Net income in the second quarter of 1995 replaced a loss in the 1994 period, as results benefited from higher comparative sales and lower SG&A expense.

Capitalization

Long Term Debt: $216,252,000 (7/1/95), incl. $100.75 million of 6.25% debs. conv. into 2,900,000 com. shs. (held by GE Capital).

Per Share Data ($) (Year Ended Dec. 31)

	1994	1993	1992	1991	1990	1989
Tangible Bk. Val.	3.42	3.41	2.58	7.36	6.24	3.34
Cash Flow	1.36	2.08	1.69	1.59	1.42	1.22
Earnings	0.07	1.15	0.94	1.05	0.88	0.69
Dividends	0.24	0.24	0.24	0.20	0.17	Nil
Payout Ratio	NM	21%	25%	19%	19%	Nil
Prices - High	29⅛	31½	36¼	36¾	24¼	17
- Low	21¼	19¾	15	17¼	12⅝	9
P/E Ratio - High	NM	27	39	35	28	25
- Low	NM	17	16	16	14	13

Income Statement Analysis (Million $)

	1994	%Chg	1993	%Chg	1992	%Chg	1991
Revs.	564	20%	471	16%	407	15%	355
Oper. Inc.	27.6	-43%	48.3	27%	38.0	3%	37.0
Depr.	19.0	40%	13.6	21%	11.2	36%	8.3
Int. Exp.	11.0	21%	9.1	55%	5.8	15%	5.1
Pretax Inc.	1.6	-94%	28.0	24%	22.5	-14%	26.1
Eff. Tax Rate	39%	—	40%	—	38%	—	39%
Net Inc.	1.0	-94%	16.8	20%	14.0	-12%	15.9

Balance Sheet & Other Fin. Data (Million $)

	1994	1993	1992	1991	1990	1989
Cash	6.3	2.5	0.6	3.0	7.6	7.1
Curr. Assets	99	90.2	82.3	74.0	68.8	51.3
Total Assets	362	322	289	224	180	139
Curr. Liab.	50.4	32.8	56.5	54.6	54.9	22.0
LT Debt	147	140	102	44.3	21.3	69.1
Common Eqty.	136	123	108	113	94.0	41.0
Total Cap.	312	289	232	169	124	117
Cap. Exp.	31.6	34.0	29.4	41.6	23.1	12.4
Cash Flow	20.0	30.4	25.2	24.1	19.1	15.0

Ratio Analysis

	1994	1993	1992	1991	1990	1989
Curr. Ratio	2.0	2.7	1.5	1.4	1.3	2.3
% LT Debt of Cap.	47.1	48.3	44.0	26.2	17.1	59.1
% Net Inc.of Revs.	0.2	3.6	3.4	4.5	3.8	3.7
% Ret. on Assets	0.3	5.5	5.6	7.8	6.7	6.5
% Ret. on Equity	0.8	14.5	13.0	15.2	16.4	24.0

Dividend Data —Cash payments were initiated in 1990, and quarterly dividends began in 1991.

Amt. of Div. $	Date Decl.	Ex-Div. Date	Stock of Record	Payment Date
0.060	Sep. 08	Sep. 19	Sep. 23	Oct. 04 '94
0.060	Nov. 30	Dec. 23	Dec. 30	Jan. 10 '95
0.060	Mar. 07	Mar. 28	Mar. 31	Apr. 11 '95
0.060	May. 10	Jun. 28	Jun. 30	Jul. 11 '95
0.060	Sep. 07	Sep. 27	Sep. 29	Oct. 10 '95

Data as orig. reptd.; bef. results of disc. opers. and/or spec. items. Per share data adj. for stk. divs. as of ex-div. date. E-Estimated. NA-Not Available. NM-Not Meaningful. NR-Not Ranked.

Office—5929 College Ave., Oakland, CA 94618. **Tel**—(510) 652-8187. **Chrmn & CEO**—T. G. Rogers. **Pres**—W. F. Cronk III. **VP & CFO**—P. R. Woodland. **Secy**—E. R. Manwell. **Treas & Investor Contact**—William C. Collett. **Dirs**—W. F. Cronk III, T. F. Crull, M. M. Halpern, J. L. Katz, J. W. Larson, E. R. Manwell, A. J. Martin, J. O. Peiffer, T. G. Rogers. **Transfer Agent & Registrar**—First Interstate Bank, SF. **Reincorporated** in Delaware in 1985. **Empl-** 2,062. **S&P Analyst:** Efraim Levy

STANDARD & POOR'S

STOCK REPORTS

Duriron Co.

NASDAQ Symbol **DURI**
In S&P MidCap 400

26-SEP-95 **Industry:** Machinery

Summary: Duriron manufactures fluid handling equipment, mainly pumps and valves, for industries that utilize corrosive fluids in manufacturing processes.

S&P Opinion: Hold (★★★)

Recent Price • 28¾ | 52 Wk Range • 30¼-15½ | Yield • 1.6% | 12-Mo. P/E • 26.1

Quantitative Evaluations

Outlook (1 Lowest—5 Highest)
• **1+**

Fair Value
• **21¼**

Risk
• **Low**

Earn./Div. Rank
• **B+**

Technical Eval.
• **Neutral** since 9/95

Rel. Strength Rank (1 Lowest—99 Highest)
• **86**

Insider Activity
• **Favorable**

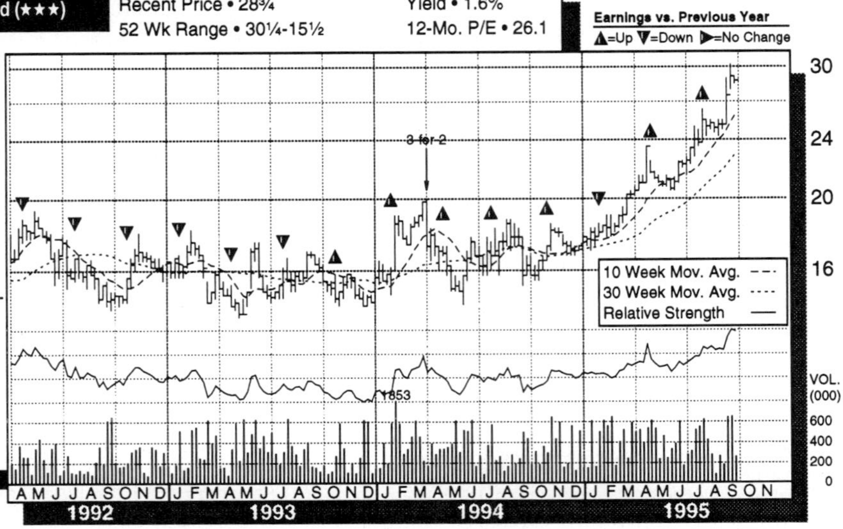

Overview - 26-SEP-95

We expect sales to increase for the balance of 1995 and full year 1996, reflecting higher volume from recent acquisitions and greater activity in the chemical industry, which will more than offset a potential slowing of overseas sales from a stronger U.S. dollar. Higher prices and utilization rates should offset rising raw material costs and permit margin expansion. With decreased costs for integrating acquisitions and only a small rise in interest expense, earnings should advance again in 1995. Assuming a continuation of growth in the global economy and a sustained upturn in process industries, earnings should continue to grow in 1996. New products, further acquisitions and consolidation in the pump and valve industries should boost long-term sales and earnings.

Valuation - 26-SEP-95

Although Duriron's shares represent a good way to play the later stages of an economic expansion, we currently rate the stock a hold, based on its high valuation and low dividend yield relative to the shares of other companies that serve the same markets. As the shares have climbed more than 70% since the beginning of 1995, we think that upside potential from the current level is not great. We find the risk/reward ratio to be unattractive and would not add to holdings, but could change our opinion in the event of a market pullback, if our sales and earnings projections remain unchanged.

Key Stock Statistics

S&P EPS Est. 1995	1.15	Tang. Bk. Value/Share	5.97
P/E on S&P Est. 1995	25.0	Beta	0.89
S&P EPS Est. 1996	1.40	Shareholders	2,100
Dividend Rate/Share	0.46	Market cap. (B)	$0.542
Shs. outstg. (M)	19.0	Inst. holdings	71%
Avg. daily vol. (M)	0.135	Insider holdings	NA

Value of $10,000 invested 5 years ago: $ 28,814

Fiscal Year Ending Dec. 31

	1995	% Change	1994	% Change	1993	% Change
Revenues (Million $)						
1Q	91.45	17%	77.96	5%	74.40	NM
2Q	99.2	16%	85.75	10%	78.31	8%
3Q	—	—	91.79	20%	76.69	4%
4Q	—	—	89.89	6%	84.66	6%
Yr.	—	—	345.4	10%	313.9	5%
Income (Million $)						
1Q	5.21	38%	3.77	31%	2.87	-37%
2Q	6.53	63%	4.01	11%	3.61	-23%
3Q	—	—	4.61	18%	3.91	-1%
4Q	—	—	4.77	-22%	6.10	NM
Yr.	—	—	17.16	4%	16.49	25%
Earnings Per Share ($)						
1Q	0.27	35%	0.20	30%	0.15	-36%
2Q	0.34	62%	0.21	12%	0.19	-20%
3Q	E0.30	25%	0.24	20%	0.20	3%
4Q	E0.29	16%	0.25	-22%	0.32	NM
Yr.	E1.15	28%	0.90	5%	0.86	25%

Next earnings report expected: mid October

Duriron Co.

Business Summary - 26-SEP-95

The Duriron Company, Inc. is engaged primarily in the design and production of fluid-handling equipment, mainly pumps and valves, for industries that utilize difficult-to-handle and often corrosive fluids in manufacturing processes. The company specializes in the development of precision-engineered equipment that can withstand the severely deteriorating effects associated with the flow of acids, chemical solutions, slurries and gases. Based upon its analysis of trade association data and other market information, Duriron considers itself a leading supplier of such equipment to the basic chemical industry.

Sales and operating profits (in millions) for 1994 were derived as follows:

	Sales	Profits
U.S.	70%	$29.2
Europe	21%	4.4
Canada	5%	0.8
Other	4%	-0.4

Duriron's main products--pumps, valves and related equipment--are manufactured under the Durco, Valtek, Atomac, Automax, Accord, Kammer, Mecair and Sereg tradenames.

Under the Durco tradename, the company makes several lines of centrifugal pumps, used mainly to move liquids during processing activities, as well as in auxiliary services such as waste removal, water treatment and pollution control.

Under the Valtek, Kammer and Sereg names, Duriron manufactures automatic control valves, valve actuators and related components. Control valves regulate the amount and rate of fluids moving in a manufacturing production system. The company also makes filtration products and related spare parts.

Important Developments

Sep. '95—Duriron reached a definitive agreement to acquire privately held, Michigan-based Durametallic Corp. (DC) in a $150 million tax-free exchange of common stock. Under the merger agreement, between 5.1 million and 6.5 million DURI shares will be issued. In 1994, DC reported sales and net income of $116.6 million and $7.2 million, respectively. DC makes a complete line of industrial pump seals, 80% of which are sold to the replacement market, with the 20% balance sold to original equipment makers. DURI said that DC sells about 60% of its products in North America and 40% overseas. DURI further noted that DC has very strong gross margins. The company expects the merger to be accretive to 1996 earnings. DC will be operated by current management as a wholly owned subsidiary of DURI. DURI expects to complete the transaction by December 31, 1995.

Capitalization

Long Term Debt: $43,528,000 (6/95).

Per Share Data ($)

(Year Ended Dec. 31)

	1994	1993	1992	1991	1990	1989
Tangible Bk. Val.	5.97	8.28	5.15	7.26	6.23	5.33
Cash Flow	1.63	2.18	1.31	1.55	1.59	1.44
Earnings	0.90	0.86	0.69	1.03	1.11	1.05
Dividends	0.42	0.40	0.40	0.37	0.33	0.31
Payout Ratio	47%	47%	57%	36%	30%	29%
Prices - High	20	18⅛	19⅜	18½	13¾	13⅝
- Low	14⅜	13⅞	14⅛	11⅞	9½	8⅜
P/E Ratio - High	22	21	28	18	12	13
- Low	16	16	20	11	9	8

Income Statement Analysis (Million $)

	1994	%Chg	1993	%Chg	1992	%Chg	1991
Revs.	345	10%	314	5%	300	1%	297
Oper. Inc.	47.2	15%	41.2	-2%	41.9	-5%	44.0
Depr.	14.0	25%	11.2	-5%	11.8	20%	9.9
Int. Exp.	4.3	13%	3.8	32%	2.9	-1%	3.0
Pretax Inc.	26.9	2%	26.4	28%	20.7	-33%	31.1
Eff. Tax Rate	36%	—	38%	—	36%	—	37%
Net Inc.	17.2	4%	16.5	25%	13.2	-33%	19.6

Balance Sheet & Other Fin. Data (Million $)

	1994	1993	1992	1991	1990	1989
Cash	16.3	22.6	17.3	21.6	17.0	25.2
Curr. Assets	150	139	135	133	132	129
Total Assets	274	248	251	213	206	194
Curr. Liab.	53.8	45.5	50.9	46.3	46.6	46.4
LT Debt	39.0	34.9	42.0	21.1	26.8	31.4
Common Eqty.	139	128	120	137	124	107
Total Cap.	178	162	162	167	158	144
Cap. Exp.	9.9	8.9	15.3	15.4	16.6	13.4
Cash Flow	31.2	27.7	25.0	29.5	29.8	27.0

Ratio Analysis

	1994	1993	1992	1991	1990	1989
Curr. Ratio	2.8	3.1	2.7	2.9	2.8	2.8
% LT Debt of Cap.	21.9	21.5	25.9	12.6	17.0	21.8
% Net Inc.of Revs.	5.0	5.3	4.4	6.6	7.0	7.0
% Ret. on Assets	6.6	6.6	5.7	9.3	10.4	10.4
% Ret. on Equity	12.9	13.3	10.3	15.1	18.1	19.5

Dividend Data —Cash has been paid in every year since 1935. A dividend reinvestment plan is available.

Amt. of Div. $	Date Decl.	Ex-Div. Date	Stock of Record	Payment Date
0.105	Oct. 20	Oct. 31	Nov. 04	Dec. 02 '94
0.115	Feb. 10	Feb. 17	Feb. 24	Mar. 10 '95
0.115	Apr. 21	May. 01	May. 05	Jun. 02 '95
0.115	Jul. 21	Aug. 02	Aug. 04	Sep. 01 '95

Data as orig. reptd.; bef. results of disc. opers. and/or spec. items. Per share data adj. for stk. divs. as of ex-div. date. E-Estimated. NA-Not Available. NM-Not Meaningful. NR-Not Ranked.

Office—3100 Research Blvd., Dayton, OH 45420. **Tel**—(513) 476-6100. **Chrmn**—J. S. Haddick. **Pres & CEO**—W. M. Jordan. **Sr VP & Investor Contact**—Bruce E. Hines. **VP & Secy**—R. F. Shuff. **Treas**—G. L. Smith. **Dirs**— H. K. Coble, R. E. Frazer, E. Green, J. S. Haddick, D. C. Harris, W. M. Jordan, R. L. Molen, J. F. Schorr, K. E. Sheehan. R. E. White. **Transfer Agent**—Bank One, Indianapolis. **Incorporated** in New York in 1912. **Empl**-2,575. **S&P Analyst:** Robert E. Friedman

STANDARD & POOR'S

STOCK REPORTS

Duty Free International

NYSE Symbol **DFI**

In S&P MidCap 400

12-SEP-95 **Industry:** Retail Stores

Summary: Through its four operating divisions, this company serves travelers at duty free shops and retail operations in locations throughout the U.S. and the Caribbean.

Quantitative Evaluations

Outlook (1 Lowest—5 Highest)
• 3+

Fair Value
• 11⅜

Risk
• **Average**

Earn./Div. Rank
• **B+**

Technical Eval.
• **Bullish** since 8/95

Rel. Strength Rank (1 Lowest—99 Highest)
• **92**

Insider Activity
• **NA**

Recent Price • 11½
52 Wk Range • 13⅝-7

Yield • 1.7%
12-Mo. P/E • NM

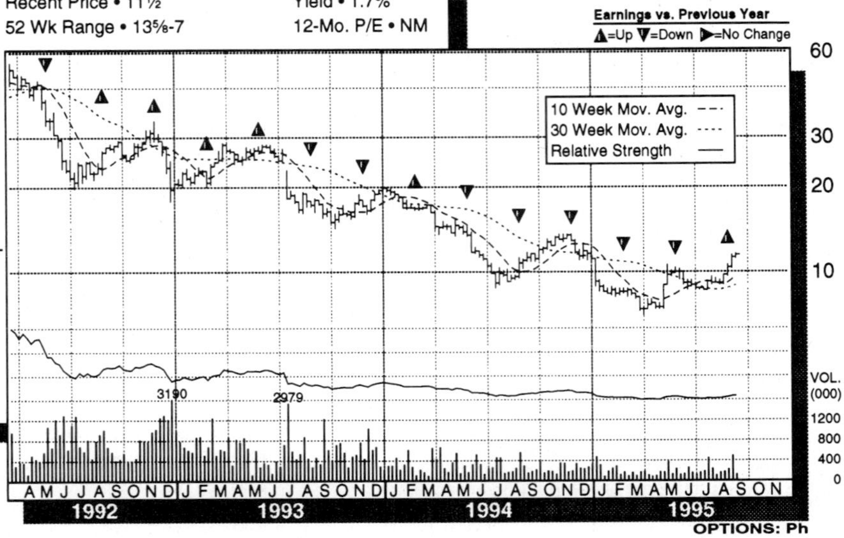

OPTIONS: Ph

Business Profile - 12-SEP-95

In late 1994, DFI undertook a series of management initiatives that should help to offset regional and divisional weaknesses. Moves included continued expansion in the Airport division, the addition of the Inflight division, a de-emphasis of the wholesale side of the Diplomatic and Wholesale division, and a comprehensive restructuring that included store and business closures and work force reductions.

Operational Review - 12-SEP-95

Sales rose modestly in the first half of 1995, reflecting the May 1994 acquisition of Inflight Services Group. Although the Airport division also posted double digit growth, sales fell at the Diplomatic and Wholesale division, and the devaluation of the Mexican peso hurt results at the Southern Border division. Gross margins widened, but SG&A costs rose as a percentage of sales. After sharply higher net interest and other expense, net earnings per share slid 4.3%.

Stock Performance - 08-SEP-95

In the past 30 trading days, DFI's shares have increased 26%, compared to a 2% rise in the S&P 500. Average trading volume for the past five days was 28,650 shares, compared with the 40-day moving average of 48,277 shares.

Key Stock Statistics

Dividend Rate/Share	0.20	Shareholders	400
Shs. outstg. (M)	27.2	Market cap. (B)	$0.320
Avg. daily vol. (M)	0.050	Inst. holdings	37%
Tang. Bk. Value/Share	4.13	Insider holdings	NA
Beta	1.58		

Value of $10,000 invested 5 years ago: $ 8,834

Fiscal Year Ending Jan. 31

	1996	% Change	1995	% Change	1994	% Change
Revenues (Million $)						
1Q	109.3	31%	83.20	7%	77.91	NM
2Q	130.4	-5%	137.2	38%	99.3	4%
3Q	—	—	144.9	38%	104.6	1%
4Q	—	—	136.4	44%	94.67	10%
Yr.	—	—	501.8	33%	376.4	4%
Income (Million $)						
1Q	1.47	-32%	2.17	-57%	5.08	178%
2Q	4.52	12%	4.05	-49%	7.96	-20%
3Q	—	—	-34.54	NM	8.10	-36%
4Q	—	—	3.51	-44%	6.26	4%
Yr.	—	—	-24.80	NM	27.39	-10%
Earnings Per Share ($)						
1Q	0.05	-38%	0.08	-58%	0.19	NM
2Q	0.17	13%	0.15	-48%	0.29	-17%
3Q	—	—	-1.27	NM	0.30	-33%
4Q	—	—	0.13	-43%	0.23	5%
Yr.	—	—	-0.91	NM	1.01	-6%

Next earnings report expected: late November

Duty Free International

Business Summary - 11-SEP-95

Duty Free International is the leading operator of duty-free stores along the U.S./Canada and U.S./Mexico borders, operates duty-free and retail stores at U.S. international airports, is a prime concessionaire and supplier of merchandise to international airlines' inflight duty free shops, and is the largest supplier of duty-free merchandise to foreign diplomats in the U.S. and to ships engaged in international travel in the northeastern U.S. Sales contributions by division in recent fiscal years were:

	1994-95	1993-94
Northern border	15%	25%
Southern border	29%	34%
Airport	18%	20%
Diplomatic/wholesale	14%	21%
Inflight	24%	NA

At January 31, 1995, the Border division was operating 80 duty-free and retail gift stores (which are not duty- or tax-free) along the Canadian (50 stores) and Mexican (30) borders. Products generally consisting of luxury items such as perfumes and cosmetics, premium-brand liquor, beer, wine and tobacco products and gift merchandise such as scarves and leather goods, are sold at prices generally 20% to 60% below retail prices in the countries of destination.

The Airport division operates 80 duty-free and retail gift stores at 14 international airports, and in the Caribbean and South Florida markets. It includes duty-free shops as well as specialty stores. standard news and gift shops and bookstores. Through a number of equity partnerships and strategic alliances, the division also participates in duty free and retail concessions in a number of international airports.

The Diplomatic and Wholesale division is the largest supplier of duty-free merchandise to foreign diplomats in the U.S. and also supplies duty-free merchandise to merchant and passenger ships departing ports in the northeastern U.S. and Miami.

The Inflight division is a leading concessionaire, operator and supplier of on-board duty free merchandise to international airlines through on-board concessions and a wholesale program, and is a major supplier of international airlines' first class and premium class amenity kits.

Important Developments

Aug. '95—During the first half of 1995-96, the Airport division opened 12 stores in the new Denver International Airport, two new shops in Boston's Logan International Airport, and one in San Juan International Airport, Puerto Rico. A third store is expected to open at Logan by the end of the third quarter. In addition, the Northern Border division acquired two duty free stores in Port Huron and Sault St. Marie, Mich.

Capitalization

Long Term Debt: $118,462,000 (7/95).

Per Share Data ($) (Year Ended Jan. 31)

	1995	1994	1993	1992	1991	1990
Tangible Bk. Val.	NA	5.89	5.66	5.09	3.89	3.37
Cash Flow	NA	1.39	1.38	1.36	0.78	0.67
Earnings	-0.91	1.01	1.08	1.08	0.67	0.56
Dividends	0.20	0.20	0.15	Nil	Nil	Nil
Payout Ratio	NM	20%	13%	Nil	Nil	Nil
Cal. Yrs.	1994	1993	1992	1991	1990	1989
Prices - High	20	29	56¼	49⅝	16¾	16¼
- Low	8¾	14¼	17¾	12⅜	7⅞	5⅛
P/E Ratio - High	NM	29	52	46	25	29
- Low	NM	14	16	11	12	9

Income Statement Analysis (Million $)

	1994	%Chg	1993	%Chg	1992	%Chg	1991
Revs.	382	4%	366	93%	190	78%	107
Oper. Inc.	50.0	-14%	58.2	36%	42.7	110%	20.3
Depr.	10.5	23%	8.5	38%	6.2	158%	2.4
Int. Exp.	1.5	44%	1.0	-78%	4.8	NM	0.9
Pretax Inc.	43.1	-13%	49.8	31%	37.9	66%	22.8
Eff. Tax Rate	36%	—	39%	—	37%	—	36%
Net Inc.	27.4	-10%	30.4	28%	23.8	63%	14.6

Balance Sheet & Other Fin. Data (Million $)

	1994	1993	1992	1991	1990	1989
Cash	132	38.2	59.9	55.2	64.2	3.0
Curr. Assets	238	129	96.0	82.8	80.4	13.7
Total Assets	388	256	199	125	105	29.0
Curr. Liab.	33.9	38.8	17.9	12.3	7.9	4.7
LT Debt	118	6.3	8.8	11.0	10.0	5.8
Common Eqty.	232	207	171	100	85.0	19.0
Total Cap.	350	214	180	100	96.0	24.0
Cap. Exp.	13.4	20.3	5.4	12.0	3.4	5.5
Cash Flow	37.8	38.9	30.0	17.0	12.1	6.5

Ratio Analysis

	1994	1993	1992	1991	1990	1989
Curr. Ratio	7.0	3.3	5.4	6.7	10.2	2.9
% LT Debt of Cap.	33.8	2.9	4.9	9.9	10.5	24.0
% Net Inc.of Revs.	7.2	8.3	12.5	13.7	11.5	8.5
% Ret. on Assets	8.5	12.7	14.2	12.7	13.4	18.1
% Ret. on Equity	12.4	15.2	17.0	15.7	17.6	29.6

Dividend Data —Quarterly dividends were initiated in July 1992.

Amt. of Div. $	Date Decl.	Ex-Div. Date	Stock of Record	Payment Date
0.050	Oct. 21	Oct. 25	Oct. 31	Nov. 15 '94
0.050	Jan. 18	Jan. 24	Jan. 30	Feb. 14 '95
0.050	Apr. 17	Apr. 25	May. 01	May. 15 '95
0.050	Jul. 28	Aug. 04	Aug. 08	Aug. 22 '95

Data as orig. reptd.; bef. results of disc. opers. and/or spec. items. Per share data adj. for stk. divs. as of ex-div. date. E-Estimated. NA-Not Available. NM-Not Meaningful. NR-Not Ranked.

Office—63 Copps Hill Rd., Ridgefield, CT 06877. **Tel**—(203) 431-6057. **Fax**—(203) 438-1356. **Pres & CEO**—A. Carfora. **VP-Fin, Treas, CFO & Secy**—G. F. Egan. **Investor Contact**—Dyan C. Cutro (212-754-5900). **Dirs**—J. Africk, D. H. Bernstein, A. Carfora, J. A. Couri, H. Diehl, C. Reimerdes, S. H. Stackhouse. **Transfer Agent & Registrar**—First National Bank of Maryland, Baltimore. **Incorporated** in Maryland in 1983. **Empl**-2,000. **S&P Analyst:** Maureen C. Carini

STANDARD & POOR'S

STOCK REPORTS

EMC Corp.

NYSE Symbol **EMC**
In S&P MidCap 400

17-AUG-95 **Industry:** Data Processing

Summary: This company makes high performance, high reliability storage systems for selected mainframe and midrange computer markets, as well as for the open systems storage market.

S&P Opinion: Accumulate (★★★★) | Recent Price • 19⅞ | 52 Wk Range • 27⅜-14¾ | Yield • Nil | 12-Mo. P/E • 14.3

Quantitative Evaluations
Outlook (1 Lowest—5 Highest) • **5**
Fair Value • **27⅝**
Risk • **High**
Earn./Div. Rank • **B**

Technical Eval. • **Bearish** since 7/95
Rel. Strength Rank (1 Lowest—99 Highest) • **26**
Insider Activity • **Neutral**

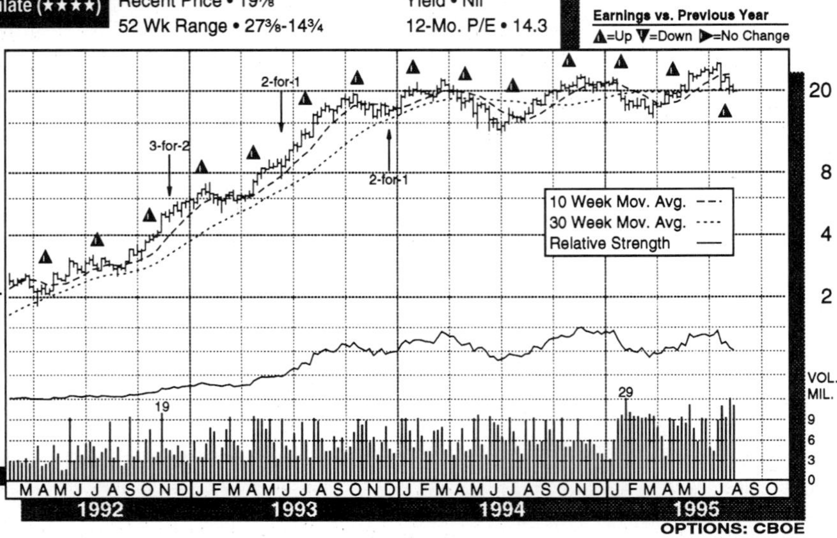

Overview - 17-AUG-95

Revenues are expected to continue to advance sharply through 1996, reflecting strong demand for Symmetrix storage systems for the mainframe environment, where the company continues to gain market share. Contributions from the Harmonix storage subsystem for the midrange market and Centriplex storage subsystem for computer networks should also aid results. The Asia/Pacific market should be particularly strong. Margins are expected to be maintained as volume efficiencies and well controlled costs are offset by modest price erosion. Earnings should benefit from the higher revenues and steady margins.

Valuation - 17-AUG-95

The shares of this leading supplier of storage solutions have climbed sharply over the last three years. Strong revenue and earnings gains have spurred the stock's advance. Growth is expected to continue. Earnings are projected to rise 20% in 1996 over the level estimated for 1995. EMC's storage subsystems offer very attractive price/performance features. The company continues to gain share in the core mainframe storage market, and has extended its product line to serve the midrange and networked markets as well. The shares, selling at a modest P/E multiple, are positioned to outperform the market over the next six to 12 months.

Key Stock Statistics

S&P EPS Est. 1995	1.50	Tang. Bk. Value/Share	3.65
P/E on S&P Est. 1995	13.3	Beta	1.00
S&P EPS Est. 1996	1.80	Shareholders	3,900
Dividend Rate/Share	Nil	Market cap. (B)	$ 4.7
Shs. outstg. (M)	213.3	Inst. holdings	66%
Avg. daily vol. (M)	3.945	Insider holdings	NA

Value of $10,000 invested 5 years ago: $ 366,697

Fiscal Year Ending Dec. 31

	1995	% Change	1994	% Change	1993	% Change
Revenues (Million $)						
1Q	420.6	57%	267.1	92%	138.8	111%
2Q	435.3	41%	308.1	72%	179.5	125%
3Q	—	—	371.6	72%	215.8	129%
4Q	—	—	430.7	73%	248.6	128%
Yr.	—	—	1,377	76%	782.6	124%
Income (Million $)						
1Q	77.98	60%	48.84	NM	14.90	188%
2Q	79.80	46%	54.57	102%	27.05	NM
3Q	—	—	69.40	80%	38.49	NM
4Q	—	—	77.86	66%	46.83	NM
Yr.	—	—	250.7	97%	127.1	NM
Earnings Per Share ($)						
1Q	0.36	57%	0.23	188%	0.08	146%
2Q	0.35	35%	0.26	86%	0.14	NM
3Q	E0.38	19%	0.32	68%	0.19	NM
4Q	E0.41	14%	0.36	57%	0.23	NM
Yr.	E1.50	27%	1.18	82%	0.65	NM

Next earnings report expected: mid October

EMC Corp.

Business Summary - 07-AUG-95

EMC Corp. designs, manufactures, markets and supports high performance storage products and provides related services for selected mainframe and midrange computer systems.

The company's principal products are based on Integrated Cached Disk Array (ICDA) technology, which combines high speed semiconductor cache memory with an array of industry standard disk drives. ICDA-based products represented 93% of revenues in 1994, 91% in 1993 and 74% in 1992.

Products include the Symmetrix series of high-speed ICDA-based storage system for IBM and IBM-compatible, Unisys and Bull mainframe computer markets. The Symmetrix product line includes the Model 5500, which features storage capacities of up to 360 gigabytes, hardware and channel redundancy, full system battery backup, nondisruptive component upgrade and replacement, and remote diagnostic features. An expanded version of the Model 5500, which extends its capacity to over 1 terabyte of storage, was introduced in May 1994. EMC also makes plug compatible main memory products and plug-in storage modules for IBM and compatible mainframes. Product sales to the mainframe storage market represented 88%, 82% and 70% of 1994, 1993 and 1992 product revenues, respectively.

The Harmonix series of high-speed ICDA-based storage systems serves IBM's AS/400 midrange computer market. The company also offers the Champion line of 8mm tape backup subsystems and provides main memory upgrades for selected AS/400 CPU models. Midrange revenues accounted for 10%, 15% and 28% of total revenues in 1994, 1993 and 1992, respectively.

In November 1994, EMC introduced the Centriplex family of ICDA products for the open systems storage market.

Products are marketed through multiple distribution channels, including a direct sales force, selected distributors and OEMs.

The company's ability to compete successfully depends upon the timely development and introduction of technologically advanced products. R&D costs totaled $117,922,000 (8.8% of net sales) in 1994, versus $58,977,000 (7.5%) in 1993.

Important Developments

Jul. '95—During the second quarter of 1995, the company introduced eight new software features and two new hardware platforms to its Symmetrix storage offering for the mainframe environment. The company also introduced the Symmetrix 3000 series of Integrated Cached Disk Arrays for the open systems market.

Capitalization

Long Term Debt: $246,814,000 (3/95), incl. $229,598,000 conv. sub. notes and debs., and $17,216,000 of capital lease obligs.

Per Share Data ($) (Year Ended Dec. 31)

	1994	1993	1992	1991	1990	1989
Tangible Bk. Val.	3.57	2.24	0.99	0.79	0.74	0.69
Cash Flow	1.30	0.76	0.29	0.14	0.11	-0.09
Earnings	1.18	0.65	0.18	0.08	0.06	-0.13
Dividends	Nil	Nil	Nil	Nil	Nil	Nil
Payout Ratio	Nil	Nil	Nil	Nil	Nil	Nil
Prices - High	24	$19\frac{1}{2}$	$6\frac{1}{8}$	$2\frac{3}{16}$	$1\frac{5}{8}$	1
- Low	$12\frac{1}{2}$	$5\frac{1}{8}$	$1\frac{13}{16}$	$\frac{13}{16}$	$\frac{9}{16}$	$\frac{7}{16}$
P/E Ratio - High	20	30	34	26	27	NM
- Low	11	8	11	10	9	NM

Income Statement Analysis (Million $)

	1994	%Chg	1993	%Chg	1992	%Chg	1991
Revs.	1,377	76%	783	124%	349	50%	232
Oper. Inc.	383	90%	202	NM	63.9	112%	30.1
Depr.	32.7	51%	21.7	25%	17.4	88%	9.3
Int. Exp.	15.3	153%	6.0	26%	4.8	149%	1.9
Pretax Inc.	355	97%	180	NM	42.3	110%	20.1
Eff. Tax Rate	30%	—	29%	—	32%	—	35%
Net Inc.	251	98%	127	NM	28.7	121%	13.0

Balance Sheet & Other Fin. Data (Million $)

	1994	1993	1992	1991	1990	1989
Cash	241	345	55.1	16.8	35.5	17.8
Curr. Assets	902	650	217	112	104	88.0
Total Assets	1,318	830	321	190	157	137
Curr. Liab.	301	133	76.3	44.1	28.2	14.0
LT Debt	286	274	75.7	15.7	15.8	15.4
Common Eqty.	728	419	158	126	108	98.0
Total Cap.	1,014	693	239	146	128	117
Cap. Exp.	109	51.3	28.5	19.6	16.2	9.0
Cash Flow	283	149	46.1	22.3	16.3	-13.5

Ratio Analysis

	1994	1993	1992	1991	1990	1989
Curr. Ratio	3.0	4.9	2.8	2.5	3.7	6.3
% LT Debt of Cap.	28.2	39.5	31.7	10.8	12.3	13.2
% Net Inc.of Revs.	18.2	16.2	8.2	5.6	5.2	NM
% Ret. on Assets	22.8	20.9	11.2	7.4	6.0	NM
% Ret. on Equity	42.7	41.6	20.0	11.0	8.5	NM

Dividend Data —No cash dividends have been paid.

Amt. of Div. $	Date Decl.	Ex-Div. Date	Stock of Record	Payment Date
2-for-1	May. 12	Jun. 08	May. 24	Jun. 08 '93
2-for-1	Oct. 25	Dec. 13	Nov. 26	Dec. 10 '93

Data as orig. reptd.; bef. results of disc. opers. and/or spec. items. Per share data adj. for stk. divs. as of ex-div. date. E-Estimated. NA-Not Available. NM-Not Meaningful. NR-Not Ranked.

Office—171 South St, Hopkinton, MA 01748-9103. **Tel**—(508) 435-1000. **Chrmn**—R. J. Egan. **Pres & CEO**—M. C. Ruettgers. **VP & CFO**—C. G. Patterson **Dirs**—M. J. Cronin, J. F. Cunningham, J. R. Egan, M. E. Egan, R. J. Egan, W. P. Fitzgerald, J. Oliveri, M. C. Ruettgers. **Transfer Agent & Registrar**—State Street Bank & Trust Co., Boston. **Incorporated** in Massachusetts in 1979. **Empl**-2,452. **S&P Analyst:** Peter C. Wood, CFA

STANDARD & POOR'S

STOCK REPORTS

Edison Bros. Stores

NYSE Symbol **EBS**

In S&P MidCap 400

17-OCT-95 **Industry:** Retail Stores

Summary: This leading specialty retailer of fashion apparel and footwear operates more than 2,730 stores in all 50 states, Puerto Rico, the Virgin Island, Mexico and Canada.

Quantitative Evaluations

Outlook (1 Lowest—5 Highest)
• **NA**

Fair Value
• **NA**

Risk
• **High**

Earn./Div. Rank
• **B+**

Technical Eval.
• **Bearish** since 3/94

Rel. Strength Rank (1 Lowest—99 Highest)
• **1**

Insider Activity
• **Neutral**

Recent Price • 5⅛ 52 Wk Range • 24⅝-2⅞

Yield • Nil 12-Mo. P/E • NM

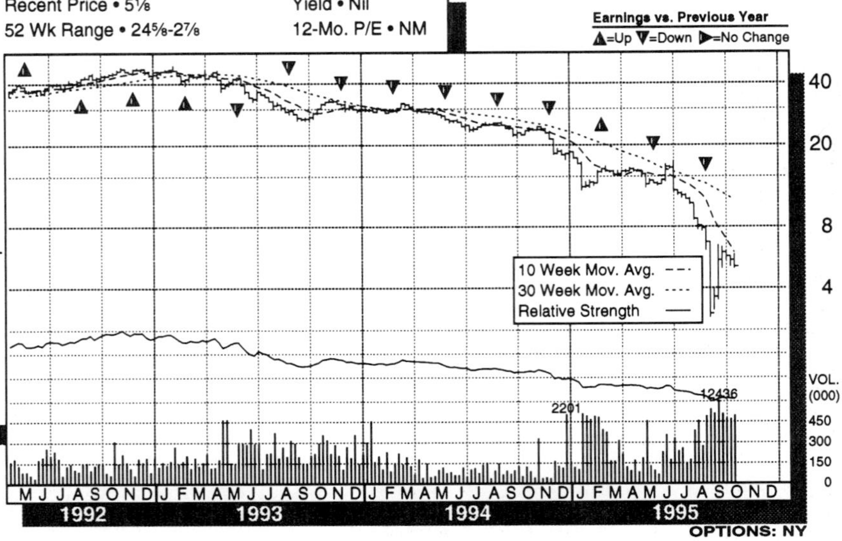

Business Profile - 13-OCT-95

Edison Brothers Stores is primarily a retailer of apparel and women's footwear, and also operates entertainment centers in shopping malls. Inconsistent consumer spending and pressures on margins have led to losses in recent periods. In 1995-96's second quarter, EBS implemented a program to eliminate some 250 underperforming apparel stores, about one-half of which are expected to close by year-end. A related $20.9 million pretax charge was taken in the second quarter.

Operational Review - 13-OCT-95

Net sales for the 26 weeks ended July 30, 1995 declined 3.7% year to year as 3.4% lower apparel same-store sales were only partly offset by 0.1% higher same-store sales of footwear. Profitability was hurt by greater markdowns taken in the highly promotional and competitive environment. With a 31% increase in interest expense and a $20.9 million charge to close up to 250 unprofitable stores, EBS reported a loss of $32.1 million ($1.46 per share) versus income of $2.7 million ($0.12).

Stock Performance - 13-OCT-95

In the past 30 trading days, EBS's shares have increased 71%, compared to a 4% rise in the S&P 500. Average trading volume for the past five days was 281,040 shares, compared with the 40-day moving average of 704,474 shares.

Key Stock Statistics

Dividend Rate/Share	Nil	Shareholders	4,900
Shs. outstg. (M)	22.1	Market cap. (B)	$0.110
Avg. daily vol. (M)	0.200	Inst. holdings	45%
Tang. Bk. Value/Share	9.83	Insider holdings	NA
Beta	1.56		

Value of $10,000 invested 5 years ago: NA

Fiscal Year Ending Jan. 31

	1996	% Change	1995	% Change	1994	% Change
Revenues (Million $)						
1Q	318.1	-3%	327.0	NM	329.2	NM
2Q	334.7	-5%	351.0	4%	338.0	-3%
3Q	—	—	353.6	3%	343.9	-5%
4Q	—	—	445.1	-1%	451.8	-4%
Yr.	—	—	1,476	NM	1,463	-3%
Income (Million $)						
1Q	-6.40	NM	1.90	-72%	6.90	-28%
2Q	-25.70	NM	0.80	-75%	3.20	-75%
3Q	—	—	0.60	-73%	2.20	-83%
4Q	—	—	17.20	76%	9.80	-72%
Yr.	—	—	20.50	-7%	22.10	-69%
Earnings Per Share ($)						
1Q	-0.29	NM	0.09	-71%	0.31	-30%
2Q	-1.17	NM	0.03	-80%	0.15	-75%
3Q	—	—	0.03	-70%	0.10	-84%
4Q	—	—	0.78	73%	0.45	-72%
Yr.	—	—	0.93	-8%	1.01	-69%

Next earnings report expected: early December

Edison Bros. Stores

Business Summary - 13-OCT-95

Edison Brothers Stores is engaged primarily in the retail sale of apparel and shoes through the operation of numerous chains of stores. A total of 2,761 stores were in operation at fiscal 1994-95 year-end, consisting of 1,941 apparel stores, 681 footwear stores and departments, and 139 entertainment centers. Business segment contributions in fiscal 1994-95:

	Sales	Profits
Apparel	71%	21%
Footwear	29%	79%

Number of stores in operation at fiscal year-end January 31:

1995	2,761
1994	2,866
1993	2,787
1992	2,781

The apparel division includes the following chains: JW/Jeans West (current fashion for young men), Coda (current fashion for young men), Oaktree (leading-edge fashion for young men), J. Riggings (traditional apparel for more conservative males), Zeidler & Zeidler/Webster (upscale contemporary for men), Repp Ltd. (big/tall/athletic for men), 5-7-9 Shops (for small-size teen girls) and Spirale (sizes 7 to 14 for preteen girls). Phoenix Big and Tall, a catalog operation that markets sportswear and clothing to big and tall men, was acquired by Repp in January 1994.

The footwear division includes the following shoe store chains: Bakers/Leeds, Precis and Wild Pair.

The entertainment division (acquired in fiscal 1990-91) consists of Time-Out, Space Port, Party Zone and Exhilarama centers (family amusement), and Horizon (exclusive distributor for virtual reality entertainment technology). Dave & Busters (restaurant/entertainment complexes) was spun off in June 1995.

Important Developments

Oct. '95—EBS said that sales for the five weeks ended September 30, 1995, totaled $116.7 million, a 10% decline year to year. Same-store sales were down 5.8%.

Sep. '95—Edison Bros. obtained a new $75 million secured revolving line of credit with BankAmerica Business Credit, Inc. The company expects that this new financing, which extends through February 29, 1996, will fully meet its working capital needs through the Christmas selling season. EBS also reached a standstill agreement with its existing lenders through February 1996. The agreement covers existing financial covenant violations, provides for modifications of third and fourth quarter financial covenants to conform to EBS's current business plan, and defers principal repayments.

Capitalization

Long Term Debt: None (7/95).

Per Share Data ($) (Year Ended Jan. 31)

	1995	1994	1993	1992	1991	1990
Tangible Bk. Val.	13.21	14.07	15.41	14.26	11.81	9.57
Cash Flow	4.09	4.05	6.17	5.60	5.04	4.68
Earnings	0.93	1.01	3.27	2.83	2.78	3.04
Dividends	1.24	1.24	1.15	1.06	1.04	0.93
Payout Ratio	133%	123%	36%	38%	38%	31%
Cal. Yrs.	1994	1993	1992	1991	1990	1989
Prices - High	32⅛	49⅛	48¼	44⅞	48⅞	35⅛
- Low	16⅞	26	31⅜	21¾	17½	16
P/E Ratio - High	35	49	15	16	18	12
- Low	18	26	10	8	6	5

Income Statement Analysis (Million $)

	1995	%Chg	1994	%Chg	1993	%Chg	1992
Revs.	1,476	NM	1,463	-3%	1,509	9%	1,385
Oper. Inc.	99	-19%	122	-37%	195	11%	175
Depr.	69.6	4%	67.1	7%	63.0	6%	59.5
Int. Exp.	20.6	NM	20.4	3%	19.9	NM	20.0
Pretax Inc.	32.0	-9%	35.0	-69%	113	17%	96.5
Eff. Tax Rate	37%	—	37%	—	37%	—	37%
Net Inc.	20.5	-7%	22.1	-69%	71.1	17%	60.8

Balance Sheet & Other Fin. Data (Million $)

	1995	1994	1993	1992	1991	1990
Cash	27.0	33.0	23.0	26.0	49.0	20.0
Curr. Assets	397	367	404	352	332	250
Total Assets	894	873	859	769	734	533
Curr. Liab.	256	221	172	214	189	191
LT Debt	174	159	194	120	145	52.0
Common Eqty.	387	412	418	385	343	244
Total Cap.	564	581	620	530	517	317
Cap. Exp.	61.7	78.4	92.9	76.7	83.7	51.8
Cash Flow	90.0	89.0	134	120	107	94.0

Ratio Analysis

	1995	1994	1993	1992	1991	1990
Curr. Ratio	1.6	1.7	2.4	1.6	1.8	1.3
% LT Debt of Cap.	30.7	27.4	31.4	22.5	28.0	16.3
% Net Inc.of Revs.	1.4	1.5	4.7	4.4	4.7	5.7
% Ret. on Assets	2.3	2.6	8.7	8.1	9.1	11.6
% Ret. on Equity	5.1	5.3	17.5	16.6	19.7	26.7

Dividend Data —Dividends, which had been paid since 1934, were suspended in mid-1995. A "poison pill" stock purchase right was adopted in 1988.

Amt. of Div. $	Date Decl.	Ex-Div. Date	Stock of Record	Payment Date
0.310	Nov. 15	Dec. 15	Dec. 21	Jan. 10 '95
0.310	Feb. 21	Feb. 28	Mar. 06	Mar. 14 '95
0.110	May. 10	May. 22	May. 26	Jun. 09 '95
Stk.	—	Jun. 30	Jun. 19	Jun. 29 '95

Data as orig. reptd.; bef. results of disc. opers. and/or spec. items. Per share data adj. for stk. divs. as of ex-div. date. E-Estimated. NA-Not Available. NM-Not Meaningful. NR-Not Ranked.

Office—501 North Broadway, St. Louis, MO 63102. **Tel**—(314) 331-6000. **Chrmn, Pres & CEO**—A. D. Miller. **EVP-Secy**—A. A. Sachs. **EVP-CFO**—D. B. Cooper Jr. **Dirs**—D. B. Cooper, Jr., J. I. Edison, P. A. Edison, J. Evans, M. H. Freund, K. W. Michner, A. D. Miller, A. E. Newman, E. P. Newman, A. A. Sachs, C. D. Schnuck, M. Sneider. **Transfer Agent & Registrar**—Boatmen's Trust Co., St. Louis. **Incorporated** in Delaware in 1929. **Empl**-23,400. **S&P Analyst:** Maureen C. Carini

STANDARD & POOR'S

STOCK REPORTS

Edwards (A. G.), Inc.

NYSE Symbol **AGE**

In S&P MidCap 400

20-OCT-95 **Industry:** Securities

Summary: A. G. Edwards owns the securities industry's fourth largest branch office network, with more than 500 locations coast to coast.

S&P Opinion: No Opinion

Recent Price • 26⅞ | 52 Wk Range • 26⅞-16½ | Yield • 2.2% | 12-Mo. P/E • 12.1

Quantitative Evaluations

Outlook
(1 Lowest—5 Highest)
• **3+**

Fair Value
• **26⅝**

Risk
• **Low**

Earn./Div. Rank
• **A**

Technical Eval.
• **Bullish** since 7/95

Rel. Strength Rank
(1 Lowest—99 Highest)
• **58**

Insider Activity
• **Neutral**

Earnings vs. Previous Year
▲=Up ▼=Down ▶=No Change

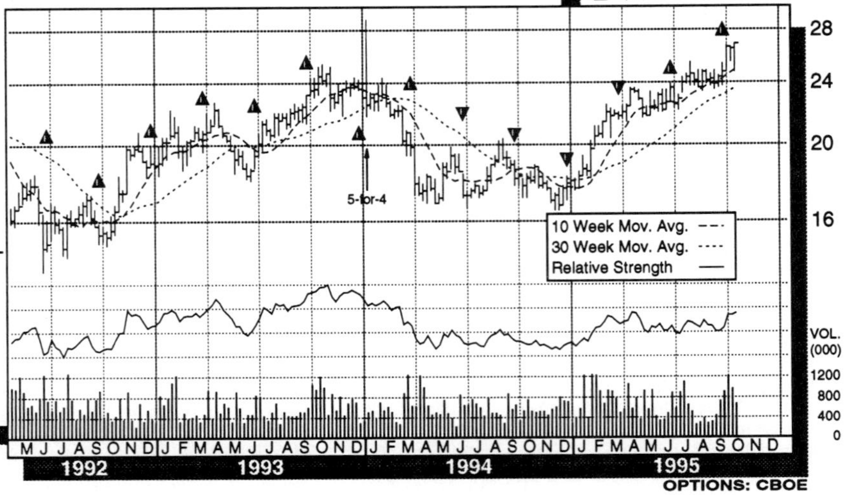

Overview - 19-OCT-95

Profits should recover in 1995-6 from last year's depressed level, which was impaired by the effect of higher interest rates on retail investor activity and a poor investment banking climate. One important positive is the stock market's record level as of October 1995, which implies a greater level of individual investors' equity market participation. Further, a projected decline in short-term interest rates through mid-1996 should stimulate investor activity by increasing the attractiveness of stocks relative to bonds. Improved investment banking revenues are expected with lower interest rates. Longer term, participation by individual investors in the financial markets should increase, aided by favorable demographics, rising income levels and an increased need to save for retirement.

Valuation - 19-OCT-95

A. G. Edwards is one of the lowest-risk situations in the volatile brokerage industry because of its extremely strong capital position, solid earnings record and above-average dividend yield. The firm has avoided the troubles currently afflicting other brokers because investment banking and trading comprise a much smaller part of its total business. The shares are trading at about a 70% premium to book value, above the average of the past several years. The stock, along with other brokerage issues, has rallied sharply off its 1994 low in response to the recent sharp drop in market interest rates and a number of favorable earnings reports.

Key Stock Statistics

S&P EPS Est. 1996	2.60	Tang. Bk. Value/Share	15.78
P/E on S&P Est. 1996	10.3	Beta	2.16
S&P EPS Est. 1997	2.90	Shareholders	22,800
Dividend Rate/Share	0.56	Market cap. (B)	$ 1.6
Shs. outstg. (M)	62.4	Inst. holdings	46%
Avg. daily vol. (M)	0.177	Insider holdings	NA

Value of $10,000 invested 5 years ago: $ 31,791

Fiscal Year Ending Feb. 28

	1996	% Change	1995	% Change	1994	% Change
Revenues (Million $)						
1Q	325.3	8%	302.0	-4%	314.9	24%
2Q	362.0	23%	295.5	-6%	314.4	22%
3Q	—	—	289.1	-12%	327.3	26%
4Q	—	—	292.1	-9%	322.1	5%
Yr.	—	—	1,178	-8%	1,279	19%
Income (Million $)						
1Q	35.37	16%	30.55	-20%	38.09	39%
2Q	43.26	37%	31.60	-11%	35.61	32%
3Q	—	—	29.86	-27%	41.11	43%
4Q	—	—	32.11	-20%	40.10	10%
Yr.	—	—	124.1	-20%	154.9	30%
Earnings Per Share ($)						
1Q	0.56	12%	0.50	-22%	0.64	33%
2Q	0.67	31%	0.51	-15%	0.60	27%
3Q	E0.67	40%	0.48	-29%	0.67	38%
4Q	E0.70	37%	0.51	-23%	0.66	6%
Yr.	E2.60	30%	2.00	-22%	2.57	25%

Next earnings report expected: late December

STANDARD & POOR'S

STOCK REPORTS

Edwards (A. G.), Inc.

20-OCT-95

Business Summary - 19-OCT-95

A. G. Edwards' primary subsidiary is A. G. Edwards & Sons, a securities broker-dealer based in St. Louis, Mo. The company provides securities and commodities brokerage for individual, corporate and institutional clients. AGE also offers asset management, real estate, insurance and investment banking services. Contributions to revenues in recent fiscal years were:

	1994-5	1993-4
Commissions	54%	60%
Interest (net)	9%	6%
Principal transactions	20%	15%
Investment banking	8%	11%
Other	9%	8%

At February 28, 1995, AGE's 5,483 investment brokers were providing financial products and services to individual, corporate and institutional clients from 516 offices. AGE has the fourth largest branch network in the U. S., based on number of branches. As opportunities arise, management expects to continue expanding the company's distribution system by adding new offices and hiring additional investment brokers in existing offices.

AGE acts as principal and agent in transactions with customers in the over-the-counter markets. The company also acts as broker in the purchase and sale of options. Investment banking activities include the underwriting of corporate and municipal securities, as well as corporate and municipal unit trusts. AGE also advises clients in mergers and acquisitions, acts as agent in private placements and as consultant. Through AGE Asset Management Inc., the company provides investment advisory services. Many factors affect the company's revenues, including changes in economic conditions, investor sentiment, the level and volatility of interest rates, inflation, political events and competition.

At August 31, 1995, the A. G. Edwards & Sons subsidiary had net capital (as defined) of $649.1 million, which was $623.1 million in excess of the minimum required.

Important Developments

Oct. '95—Management said that the six months ended August 31, 1995 saw an upturn of retail investor activity from the level experienced during last fiscal year. The number of investment brokers increased to 5,620, up from 5,483 at February 28, 1995.

Capitalization

Long Term Debt: None (8/95).

Per Share Data ($)

(Year Ended Feb. 28)

	1995	1994	1993	1992	1991	1990
Tangible Bk. Val.	14.76	13.08	10.66	8.85	7.20	6.46
Cash Flow	NA	NA	NA	NA	NA	NA
Earnings	2.00	2.57	2.06	1.88	1.10	1.10
Dividends	0.56	0.46	0.42	0.34	0.29	0.28
Payout Ratio	28%	18%	20%	18%	26%	25%
Cal. Yrs.	1994	1993	1992	1991	1990	1989
Prices - High	28⅞	25⅜	25¾	24½	11¾	12⅛
- Low	16½	18	13¾	8¼	6½	7¼
P/E Ratio - High	14	10	13	13	11	11
- Low	8	7	7	4	6	7

Income Statement Analysis (Million $)

	1995	%Chg	1994	%Chg	1993	%Chg	1992
Commissions	635	-18%	773	29%	601	15%	523
Int. Inc.	106	41%	74.6	15%	64.7	1%	63.9
Total Revs.	1,178	-8%	1,279	19%	1,074	14%	939
Int. Exp.	6.8	NM	1.1	-41%	1.9	59%	1.2
Pretax Inc.	199	-18%	244	28%	190	13%	168
Eff. Tax Rate	38%	—	36%	—	37%	—	37%
Net Inc.	124	-20%	155	30%	119	12%	106

Balance Sheet & Other Fin. Data (Million $)

	1995	1994	1993	1992	1991	1990
Total Assets	2,224	2,237	2,111	1,577	1,403	1,126
Cash Items	85.0	236	314	255	176	52.0
Receivables	1,711	1,594	1,426	966	907	772
Secs. Owned	152	168	150	161	139	144
Sec. Borrowed	Nil	Nil	Nil	Nil	1.0	33.0
Due Brokers & Cust.	985	1,090	1,192	831	856	608
Other Liabs.	320	356	304	254	160	141
Capitalization:						
Debt	Nil	Nil	Nil	Nil	Nil	Nil
Equity	919	790	615	492	386	344
Total	919	790	615	492	386	344

Ratio Analysis

	1995	1994	1993	1992	1991	1990
% Ret. on Revs.	10.5	12.1	11.1	11.2	8.8	9.7
% Ret. on Assets	5.6	7.1	6.4	7.1	4.7	5.4
% Ret. on Equity	14.5	22.0	21.6	24.0	16.2	18.3

Dividend Data —Dividends have been paid since 1971. A "poison pill" stock purchase rights plan was adopted in 1988.

Amt. of Div. $	Date Decl.	Ex-Div. Date	Stock of Record	Payment Date
0.140	Nov. 18	Nov. 28	Dec. 02	Jan. 03 '95
0.140	Feb. 24	Mar. 06	Mar. 10	Apr. 03 '95
0.140	May. 26	Jun. 06	Jun. 09	Jul. 03 '95
0.140	Aug. 25	Sep. 06	Sep. 08	Oct. 02 '95

Data as orig. reptd.; bef. results of disc opers. and/or spec. items. Per share data adj. for stk. divs. as of ex-div. date. E-Estimated. NA-Not Available. NM-Not Meaningful. NR-Not Ranked.

Office—One North Jefferson Ave., St. Louis, MO 63103. **Tel**—(314) 289-3000. **Chrmn & Pres**—B. F. Edwards III. **VP-Treas & Investor Contact**—David W. Mesker (314) 289-3510. **VP-Secy**—D. L. Kelly. **Dirs**—R. G. Avis, E. E. Carter, R. C. Dissett, B. F. Edwards III, L. Fernandez, S. Hutchinson, D. W. Mesker, D. M. Sisler, D. C. E. Williamson. **Transfer Agent & Registrar**—Boatmen's Trust Co., St. Louis. **Incorporated** in Delaware in 1967; predecessor founded in 1887. **Empl**-10,741. **S&P Analyst:** Paul L. Huberman, CFA

STANDARD & POOR'S

STOCK REPORTS

El Paso Natural Gas

NYSE Symbol **EPG**

In S&P MidCap 400

29-SEP-95

Industry: Utilities-Gas

Summary: This company operates a 17,000-mile natural gas pipeline system from the major producing basins of the Southwest to California and other states.

S&P Opinion: Hold (★★★)

Recent Price • 28¾ | 52 Wk Range • 34¾-24¾ | Yield • 4.7% | 12-Mo. P/E • 11.8

Quantitative Evaluations

Outlook (1 Lowest—5 Highest) • **2**

Fair Value • **26**

Risk • **Low**

Earn./Div. Rank • **NR**

Technical Eval. • **Bullish** since 9/95

Rel. Strength Rank (1 Lowest—99 Highest) • **37**

Insider Activity • **NA**

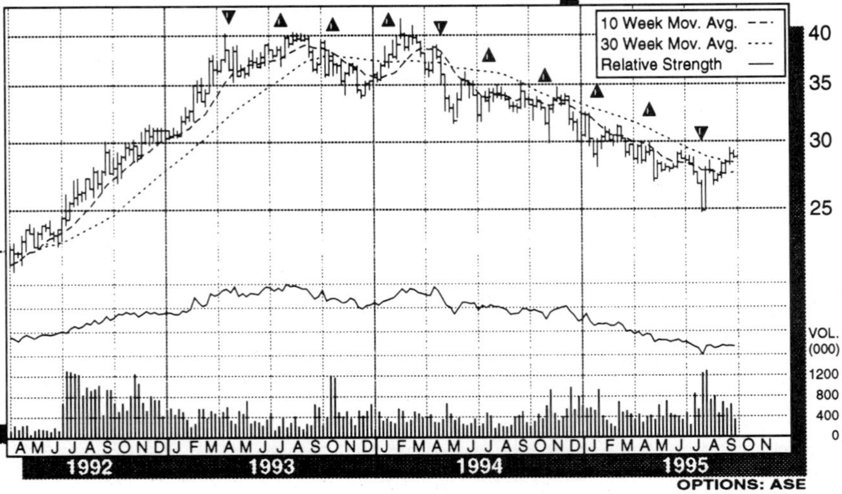

Overview - 29-SEP-95

The company will benefit in 1995 from the absence of a special charge related to litigation in 1994. However, increased availability of hydroelectric power in northern California will result in lessened demand for gas deliveries in that market. Overall deliveries, nevertheless, will rise, albeit modestly. Field service operations should benefit from higher throughput. System expansion into the northern portions of Mexico and California and out of the San Juan Basin is projected to be in service in 1996, relieving mainline constraints. Despite excess pipeline capacity in California, EPG should be able to boost its market share slightly, as its low cost structure allows it to compete effectively. Although all gas companies have been adversely affected by the drop in prices since the highs of 1993, prices have recovered somewhat and further gains are anticipated in the coming months.

Valuation - 29-SEP-95

The price of the company's shares has risen slightly as the weak market for natural gas has improved somewhat. The abnormally warm weather conditions of the previous winter served as a damper on demand and prices, but a price rise followed the drawing down of supplies in the late first quarter of 1995, which was then cut short. However, prices rallied again in September. Nevertheless, the shares remain near the bottom of their trading range of the past year, although further appreciation in price can be anticipated, as they are selling at a discount to the average for other pipeline companies.

Key Stock Statistics

S&P EPS Est. 1995	2.50	Tang. Bk. Value/Share	20.18
P/E on S&P Est. 1995	11.5	Beta	NA
S&P EPS Est. 1996	2.60	Shareholders	22,000
Dividend Rate/Share	1.32	Market cap. (B)	$0.955
Shs. outstg. (M)	34.1	Inst. holdings	63%
Avg. daily vol. (M)	0.106	Insider holdings	NA

Value of $10,000 invested 5 years ago: NA

Fiscal Year Ending Dec. 31

	1995	% Change	1994	% Change	1993	% Change
Revenues (Million $)						
1Q	204.1	-8%	221.9	5%	210.9	21%
2Q	185.1	-12%	210.8	-4%	220.6	17%
3Q	—	—	209.4	-15%	245.1	13%
4Q	—	—	227.7	-2%	232.4	4%
Yr.	—	—	869.9	-4%	908.9	13%
Income (Million $)						
1Q	21.97	4%	21.12	-32%	30.84	9%
2Q	20.20	-16%	24.01	16%	20.68	20%
3Q	—	—	21.10	15%	18.37	31%
4Q	—	—	23.39	7%	21.79	36%
Yr.	—	—	89.61	-2%	91.67	20%
Earnings Per Share ($)						
1Q	0.62	9%	0.57	-31%	0.83	-5%
2Q	0.58	-11%	0.65	18%	0.55	20%
3Q	E0.62	7%	0.58	18%	0.49	29%
4Q	E0.68	5%	0.65	10%	0.59	31%
Yr.	E2.50	2%	2.45	NM	2.46	16%

Next earnings report expected: mid October

El Paso Natural Gas

Business Summary - 22-SEP-95

El Paso Natural Gas owns and operates one of the nation's largest mainline natural gas transmission and gathering systems, connecting natural gas supply regions in New Mexico, Texas, Oklahoma and Colorado to markets in California, Nevada, Arizona, New Mexico, Texas and northern Mexico. At December 31, 1991, EPG was a wholly owned subsidiary of Burlington Resources Inc. ("BR"), but in March and June of 1992 BR's interests were distributed to the public.

The company owns and operates a 17,000-mile natural gas transmission system with 78 mainline compressor stations with a delivery capacity of 4,600,000 Mcf per day. EPG is directly connected to three of the nation's most prolific gas producing areas--the San Juan, Permian and Anadarko Basins. Since the late 1980's, in response to changing market conditions, EPG has been delivering substantial quantities of gas from the San Juan Basin to interconnecting pipelines for ultimate delivery to the Gulf Coast and the Midwest. EPG provides 48% of the total interstate pipeline capacity serving California, and, in 1994, the company delivered approximately 40% of all the natural gas consumed in the state. Natural gas deliveries in recent years were divided as follows:

	1994	1993	1992	1991
California	62%	64%	69%	72%
East-of-California	17%	17%	16%	14%
Off-system	21%	19%	15%	14%

Through wholly owned Mojave Pipeline Co., EPG transports gas principally for the production of steam for the enhanced oil recovery market of California. EPG is a member, with a 20% ownership interest, of a consortium that plans to build the proposed Samalayuca II Power Plant near Ciudad Juarez, Mexico.

In January 1994, EPG filed with the FERC for the deregulation of the company's gathering and processing services, and for permission to transfer those assets to a new subsidiary, El Paso Field Services Co. After receipt of regulatory approval, transfer would be effective on January 1, 1996.

El Paso Gas Marketing Co. conducts all of the company's gas marketing operations, including managing EPG's certificated sales arrangements with utilities and municipalities and remaining long-term gas purchase agreements.

Important Developments

Sep. '95—EPG completed the merger of Eastex Energy Inc. into a subsidiary of EPG. Earlier, in June, PG & E notified EPG that it would terminate its contract for firm capacity in 1997, although renewal is possible; 1994 revenues were approximately $129 million.

Capitalization

Long Term Debt: $775,494,000 (6/95).

Per Share Data ($) (Year Ended Dec. 31)

	1994	1993	1992	1991	1990	1989
Tangible Bk. Val.	19.96	19.19	18.02	17.38	NA	NA
Cash Flow	4.22	3.92	4.15	3.66	NA	NA
Earnings	2.45	2.46	2.12	1.97	NA	NA
Dividends	1.21	1.10	0.75	NA	NA	NA
Payout Ratio	49%	44%	35%	NA	NA	NA
Prices - High	41⅞	40⅜	31½	NA	NA	NA
- Low	29⅝	30¼	19	NA	NA	NA
P/E Ratio - High	17	16	15	NA	NA	NA
- Low	12	12	9	NA	NA	NA

Income Statement Analysis (Million $)

	1994	%Chg	1993	%Chg	1992	%Chg	1991
Revs.	870	-4%	909	13%	803	10%	730
Oper. Inc.	287	1%	283	10%	258	7%	241
Depr.	65.0	20%	54.0	-26%	73.0	19%	61.3
Int. Exp.	79.0	5%	75.0	10%	68.0	-34%	103
Pretax Inc.	148	-2%	151	23%	123	8%	114
Eff. Tax Rate	40%	—	39%	—	38%	—	37%
Net Inc.	90.0	-2%	92.0	21%	76.0	6%	71.9

Balance Sheet & Other Fin. Data (Million $)

	1994	1993	1992	1991	1990	1989
Cash	28.0	Nil	49.0	170	NA	NA
Curr. Assets	299	304	364	606	NA	NA
Total Assets	2,332	2,270	2,051	2,094	NA	NA
Curr. Liab.	452	356	373	469	NA	NA
LT Debt	779	796	637	639	NA	NA
Common Eqty.	710	708	669	633	NA	NA
Total Cap.	1,794	1,801	1,508	1,493	NA	NA
Cap. Exp.	173	164	246	NA	NA	NA
Cash Flow	155	146	150	133	NA	NA

Ratio Analysis

	1994	1993	1992	1991	1990	1989
Curr. Ratio	0.7	0.9	1.0	1.3	NA	NA
% LT Debt of Cap.	43.4	44.2	42.2	42.8	NA	NA
% Net Inc.of Revs.	10.3	10.1	9.5	9.9	NA	NA
% Ret. on Assets	4.0	4.3	3.2	NA	NA	NA
% Ret. on Equity	12.9	13.4	9.4	NA	NA	NA

Dividend Data —Dividend payments began in 1992. A "poison pill" stock purchase rights plan was adopted in 1992.

Amt. of Div. $	Date Decl.	Ex-Div. Date	Stock of Record	Payment Date
0.302	Jul. 15	Sep. 02	Sep. 09	Oct. 03 '94
0.302	Oct. 13	Dec. 05	Dec. 09	Jan. 03 '95
0.330	Jan. 13	Mar. 06	Mar. 10	Apr. 03 '95
0.330	Apr. 13	Jun. 06	Jun. 09	Jul. 03 '95
0.330	Jul. 21	Sep. 06	Sep. 08	Oct. 02 '95

Data as orig. reptd.; bef. results of disc. opers. and/or spec. items. Per share data adj. for stk. divs. as of ex-div. date. E-Estimated. NA-Not Available. NM-Not Meaningful. NR-Not Ranked.

Office—One Paul Kayser Center, 100 No. Stanton St., El Paso, TX 79901. **Tel**—(915) 541-2600. **Chrmn, Pres & CEO**—W. A. Wise. **Vice Chrmn**—L. Dell'Osso, Jr. **SVP & CFO**—H. B. Austin. **Secy**—S. J. James. **Investor Contact**—Norma F. Dunn. **Dirs**—B. Allumbaugh, J. F. Gibbons, E. G. Laguera, B. F. Love, L. Dell'Osso, Jr., K. L. Smalley, M. Wallop, W. A. Wise. **Transfer Agent & Registrar**—Bank of Boston. **Incorporated** in Delaware in 1928. **Empl**-2,403. **S&P Analyst:** Michael C. Barr

STANDARD & POOR'S

STOCK REPORTS

Electronic Arts

NASDAQ Symbol **ERTS**

In S&P MidCap 400

25-OCT-95 **Industry:** Data Processing

Summary: Electronic Arts produces entertainment software for CD-ROM-based platforms, including IBM PCs and compatibles, as well as Sega Genesis and Super Nintendo Entertainment systems.

S&P Opinion: Accumulate (★★★★)

Recent Price • 37 | Yield • Nil

52 Wk Range • 42¼-15⅝ | 12-Mo. P/E • 47.4

Quantitative Evaluations

Outlook (1 Lowest—5 Highest)
• **2**

Fair Value
• **35⅜**

Risk
• **High**

Earn./Div. Rank
• **B+**

Technical Eval.
• **Bullish** since 2/95

Rel. Strength Rank (1 Lowest—99 Highest)
• **77**

Insider Activity
• **Unfavorable**

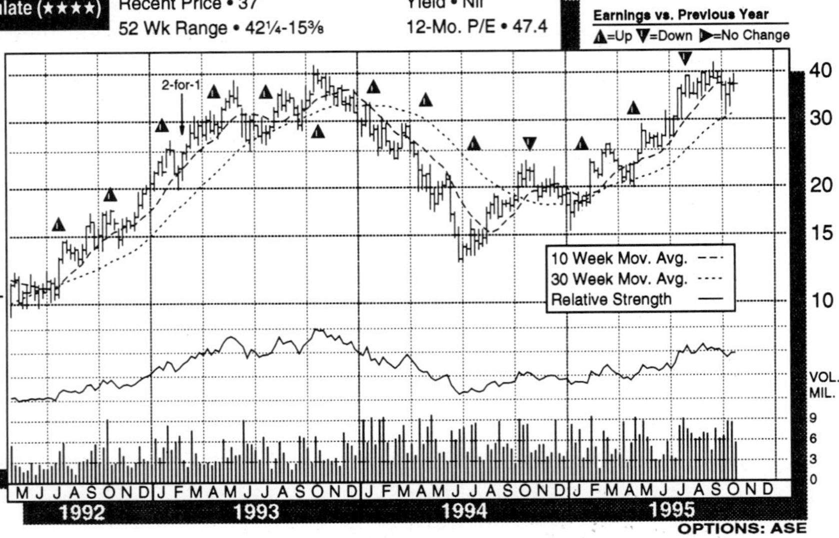

OPTIONS: ASE

Overview - 19-OCT-95

Revenues should rise in the second half of 1995-6 and in 1996-7, as strong sales of CD-based products, spurred by increased numbers of PCs in the home, and demand for software tailored for the new 32-bit entertainment systems outweigh sluggish sales of products for the Sega Genesis and Super Nintendo Entertainment systems. The life cycle of entertainment software is short, with lifespans of six to 18 months; with about 75% of annual revenues derived from the sale of new products, the continued introduction of new software offerings is encouraging. Margins should widen on the higher volume, a more favorable product mix and well-controlled expense levels. Earnings are expected to benefit from the increased revenues and wider margins.

Valuation - 19-OCT-95

Following a rapid rise, the stock declined sharply in the first half of 1994, reflecting a slowdown in the company's core 16-bit entertainment software markets. However, the shares have trended higher since then, reflecting the success of new products developed for CD-ROM-based hardware platforms, including IBM PCs and compatibles. The shares now trade at a premium to the market, reflecting expectations of strong operating earnings gains stemming from continued success in the PC-CD segment and hopes for growth associated with the upcoming generation of entertainment systems. In light of the earnings growth we project, the shares are expected to outperform the market over the next 12 months.

Key Stock Statistics

S&P EPS Est. 1996	1.05	Tang. Bk. Value/Share	4.74
P/E on S&P Est. 1996	35.2	Beta	2.42
S&P EPS Est. 1997	1.30	Shareholders	2,500
Dividend Rate/Share	Nil	Market cap. (B)	$ 1.9
Shs. outstg. (M)	51.3	Inst. holdings	80%
Avg. daily vol. (M)	1.493	Insider holdings	NA

Value of $10,000 invested 5 years ago: $ 162,209

Fiscal Year Ending Mar. 31

	1996	% Change	1995	% Change	1994	% Change
Revenues (Million $)						
1Q	80.03	8%	74.24	-7%	79.50	59%
2Q	93.66	9%	86.29	5%	82.09	50%
3Q	—	—	216.6	45%	149.5	40%
4Q	—	—	108.1	NM	107.2	24%
Yr.	—	—	493.4	18%	418.3	40%
Income (Million $)						
1Q	0.84	-93%	11.77	61%	7.32	54%
2Q	3.03	-55%	6.74	-16%	8.04	54%
3Q	—	—	23.84	32%	18.11	47%
4Q	—	—	12.58	12%	11.28	31%
Yr.	—	—	55.72	25%	44.74	45%
Earnings Per Share ($)						
1Q	0.02	-92%	0.24	60%	0.15	43%
2Q	0.06	-57%	0.14	-13%	0.16	45%
3Q	E0.59	23%	0.48	33%	0.36	44%
4Q	E0.38	58%	0.24	4%	0.23	35%
Yr.	E1.05	-2%	1.07	19%	0.90	38%

Next earnings report expected: mid January

Electronic Arts

Business Summary - 24-OCT-95

Electronic Arts Inc. creates, markets and distributes interactive entertainment software for a variety of platforms, including the Sega Genesis and Super Nintendo Entertainment systems, CD-ROM-based systems, mostly IBM PCs and compatibles, and floppy-disk-based PCs. Revenues by hardware type in recent fiscal years were:

	1994-5	1993-4
Sega Genesis	43%	53%
Super Nintendo	14%	21%
CD-ROM	21%	3%
Floppy-disk-based PCs	5%	12%
Other	16%	10%

At March 31, 1995, the company marketed approximately 120 titles it had created and distributed about 135 titles developed by other software publishers under its Affiliated Label program. Products are distributed through a direct sales force in the U.S., and primarily through third-party distributors in Europe and Asia, to more than 50,000 retail locations worldwide.

In 1994-5, international markets accounted for 32% of revenue, versus 25% in 1993-4.

Through year-end 1994-5, each of more than 60 titles developed by ERTS had generated net revenues exceeding $5,000,000. Popular games include "Madden Football," "NBA Live," "FIFA Soccer," "Shaq-Fu," "PGA Tour Golf," "NHL Hockey," "Urban Strike," "Bill Walsh College Football," "Road Rash" and "Wing Commander."

The company has established a CD Group to develop new products based on emerging CD technology.

Important Developments

Oct. '95—During the second quarter of 1995-6, CD-ROM products accounted for approximately 38% of revenues; 16-bit video game cartridges contributed about 39% of total revenues.

Jan. '95—In the third quarter of 1994-5, ERTS and Capital Cities/ABC, Inc. formed a joint venture to develop and publish interactive software for personal computers and video game machines; each company holds a 50% interest in the venture. In the first quarter of 1994-5, ERTS recorded a $10,000,000 payment from Broderbund Software ($8,600,000, net of costs incurred; $0.12 a share, after taxes) in connection with the termination of a merger agreement between the company and Broderbund.

Capitalization

Long Term Debt: None (9/95).
Minority Interest: $685,000.

Per Share Data ($)

(Year Ended Mar. 31)

	1995	1994	1993	1992	1991	1990
Tangible Bk. Val.	4.66	3.61	2.37	1.55	1.14	0.86
Cash Flow	1.27	1.05	0.73	0.40	0.26	0.20
Earnings	1.07	0.90	0.65	0.36	0.23	0.17
Dividends	Nil	Nil	Nil	Nil	Nil	Nil
Payout Ratio	Nil	Nil	Nil	Nil	Nil	Nil
Cal. Yrs.	1994	1993	1992	1991	1990	1989
Prices - High	33½	42	21¾	9⅝	4¼	2⅜
- Low	12¾	19¾	9⅛	2¼	1⁹⁄₁₆	1¾
P/E Ratio - High	31	47	33	26	19	14
- Low	12	22	14	6	7	10

Income Statement Analysis (Million $)

	1995	%Chg	1994	%Chg	1993	%Chg	1992
Revs.	493	18%	418	40%	298	84%	162
Oper. Inc.	74.2	8%	68.4	51%	45.2	84%	24.6
Depr.	9.3	19%	7.9	97%	4.0	129%	1.7
Int. Exp.	0.1	NM	0.1	-29%	0.1	-56%	0.2
Pretax Inc.	78.1	21%	64.3	47%	43.7	80%	24.3
Eff. Tax Rate	32%	—	30%	—	31%	—	36%
Net Inc.	55.7	25%	44.7	45%	30.9	97%	15.7

Balance Sheet & Other Fin. Data (Million $)

	1995	1994	1993	1992	1991	1990
Cash	185	142	98.0	56.9	27.6	22.0
Curr. Assets	272	234	153	91.2	53.7	39.8
Total Assets	341	274	181	101	63.0	47.0
Curr. Liab.	103	98.0	67.7	35.9	19.1	14.0
LT Debt	Nil	Nil	Nil	Nil	Nil	Nil
Common Eqty.	237	172	111	65.2	43.8	32.6
Total Cap.	238	176	114	65.2	43.9	32.7
Cap. Exp.	16.5	14.0	17.8	3.2	1.6	0.8
Cash Flow	65.1	52.6	34.9	17.4	10.6	7.2

Ratio Analysis

	1995	1994	1993	1992	1991	1990
Curr. Ratio	2.6	2.4	2.3	2.5	2.8	2.8
% LT Debt of Cap.	Nil	Nil	Nil	Nil	Nil	Nil
% Net Inc.of Revs.	11.3	10.7	10.3	9.7	9.0	8.3
% Ret. on Assets	17.6	19.4	21.1	18.4	16.5	16.6
% Ret. on Equity	26.5	31.3	33.8	27.7	23.7	24.8

Dividend Data —No cash dividends have been paid. Two-for-one stock splits were effected in 1992 and 1993.

Data as orig. reptd.; bef. results of disc. opers. and/or spec. items. Per share data adj. for stk. divs. as of ex-div. date. E-Estimated. NA-Not Available. NM-Not Meaningful. NR-Not Ranked.

Office—1450 Fashion Island Blvd., San Mateo, CA 94404. **Tel**—(415) 571-7171. **Chrmn, Pres & CEO**—L. F. Probst III. **Sr VP & CFO**—E. S. McKee Jr. **Secy**—G. K. Davidson. **Dirs**—R. M. Asher, W. J. Byron, D. H. Case III, R. Cohn, T. Mott, L. F. Probst III. **Transfer Agent & Registrar**—First Interstate Bank, San Francisco. **Incorporated** in California in 1982; reincorporated in Delaware in 1991. **Empl**-1,077. **S&P Analyst:** Peter C. Wood, CFA

STANDARD & POOR'S

STOCK REPORTS

Ennis Business Forms

NYSE Symbol **EBF**

In S&P MidCap 400

13-OCT-95 **Industry:** Office Equipment

Summary: This company is a leading producer of business forms, most of which are manufactured on a custom or semi-custom basis.

Quantitative Evaluations

Outlook (1 Lowest—5 Highest)
• **4⁻**

Fair Value
• **13⅞**

Risk
• **Low**

Earn./Div. Rank
• **A**

Technical Eval.
• **Bullish** since 10/93

Rel. Strength Rank (1 Lowest—99 Highest)
• **75**

Insider Activity
• **NA**

Recent Price • 13⅛ Yield • 4.4%

52 Wk Range • 14-11⅝ 12-Mo. P/E • 11.1

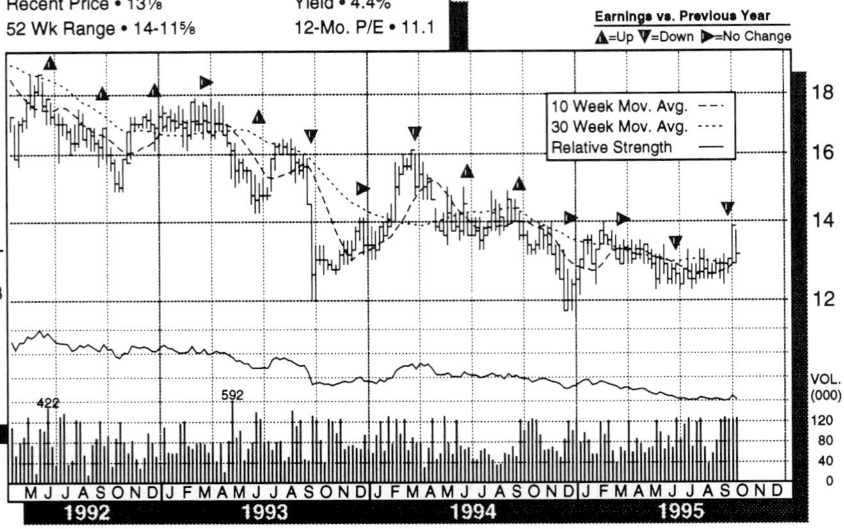

Business Profile - 13-OCT-95

The company does not expect any reversal in the long-term decline of many of its products. Moreover, EBF is not involved in any significant effort to develop new products. Ennis will attempt to grow through acquisitions, by improving customer service and by increasing marketing efforts. During 1993, the company ceased a longstanding practice of purchasing its stock on the open market, in order to conserve cash for acquisitions.

Operational Review - 13-OCT-95

Reflecting the long-term decline of the business forms industry, sales growth has been minimal in the past several years. Results in the first half of 1995-6 were hurt by competitive market conditions and rising material costs. Due to these conditions, selling price increases have lagged behind cost increases. The company's financial position is strong, with minimal long-term debt and more than $30 million in cash and temporary investments.

Stock Performance - 06-OCT-95

In the past 30 trading days, EBF's shares have increased 4%, compared to a 4% rise in the S&P 500. Average trading volume for the past five days was 35,980 shares, compared with the 40-day moving average of 25,421 shares.

Key Stock Statistics

Dividend Rate/Share	0.60	Shareholders	2,200
Shs. outstg. (M)	16.4	Market cap. (B)	$0.222
Avg. daily vol. (M)	0.032	Inst. holdings	50%
Tang. Bk. Value/Share	4.22	Insider holdings	NA
Beta	0.90		

Value of $10,000 invested 5 years ago: $ 9,619

Fiscal Year Ending Feb. 28

	1996	% Change	1995	% Change	1994	% Change
Revenues (Million $)						
1Q	35.11	3%	34.00	9%	31.27	NM
2Q	35.71	3%	34.59	2%	33.81	2%
3Q	—	—	35.25	2%	34.58	2%
4Q	—	—	36.21	9%	33.28	7%
Yr.	—	—	140.1	5%	132.9	3%
Income (Million $)						
1Q	4.49	-10%	4.98	8%	4.60	NM
2Q	4.64	-5%	4.89	9%	4.49	-15%
3Q	—	—	4.78	-2%	4.89	-1%
4Q	—	—	5.36	-2%	5.48	-7%
Yr.	—	—	20.02	3%	19.46	-6%
Earnings Per Share ($)						
1Q	0.27	-10%	0.30	11%	0.27	8%
2Q	0.29	-3%	0.30	11%	0.27	-10%
3Q	—	—	0.29	NM	0.29	NM
4Q	—	—	0.33	NM	0.33	-3%
Yr.	—	—	1.22	5%	1.16	-2%

Next earnings report expected: mid December

Ennis Business Forms

Business Summary - 13-OCT-95

Ennis Business Forms, Inc. prints and constructs a broad line of business forms for national distribution. Presentation folders were added to the company's product line through the 1991 acquisition of Admore Inc., and award ribbons were added through the 1992 acquisition of Lone Star Ribbon Co. Ennis also manufactures (through its Connolly Tool and Machine Co. subsidiary) tools, dies and special machinery, all to customers' specifications, for clients primarily in the Southwest.

Sales contributions in recent fiscal years were:

	1994-5	1993-4
Business products	95%	95%
Other	5%	5%

About 92% of the business forms manufactured by Ennis are custom or semi-custom, constructed in a wide variety of sizes, colors, number of parts and quantities on an individual-job basis, depending on customers' specifications.

Distribution of business forms throughout the U.S. is primarily through independent dealers, including business forms distributors, stationers and printers. Distribution of tools, dies and special machinery is on a contract basis with individual customers. No single customer accounts for as much as 10% of consolidated sales.

During the second quarter of 1992-3, the company completed the sale of substantially all the assets of American Business Equipment Inc., which sold copying machine supplies and sold and serviced copying machines.

The company is continually searching for acquisitions, but none were made in 1994-5. Ennis did, however, establish a 70%-owned business forms manufacturing operation in Mexico with a Mexican partner.

In its 1994-5 annual report, the company noted that the business forms industry is mature, with little or no growth in recent years. The market for many of its products is in a long-term decline, and this trend is not expected to reverse. Ennis plans to improve customer service and increase sales and marketing efforts in order to obtain growth from those products that have growth potential.

Important Developments

Sep. '95—The company attributed the decline in earnings for the first half of 1995-6 to higher raw material costs and increased selling, general and administrative expenses.

Capitalization

Long Term Debt: $360,000 (8/95).

Per Share Data ($) (Year Ended Feb. 28)

	1995	1994	1993	1992	1991	1990
Tangible Bk. Val.	3.95	3.31	3.28	3.41	3.05	3.10
Cash Flow	1.43	1.41	1.43	1.38	1.31	1.23
Earnings	1.22	1.16	1.18	1.14	1.12	1.05
Dividends	0.57	0.55	0.53	0.51	0.47	0.41
Payout Ratio	47%	48%	45%	45%	40%	38%
Cal. Yrs.	1994	1993	1992	1991	1990	1989
Prices - High	21 1/8	17 7/8	21 1/8	21 3/8	17 1/8	18 3/8
- Low	14 7/8	12	14 7/8	10 7/8	10 5/8	11 7/8
P/E Ratio - High	18	15	18	19	15	17
- Low	12	10	12	10	10	11

Income Statement Analysis (Million $)

	1995	%Chg	1994	%Chg	1993	%Chg	1992
Revs.	140	5%	133	3%	129	-2%	132
Oper. Inc.	34.2	-2%	34.8	-4%	36.4	NM	36.1
Depr.	3.5	-15%	4.1	-6%	4.4	NM	4.4
Int. Exp.	0.1	-25%	0.1	-52%	0.3	-26%	0.3
Pretax Inc.	32.0	3%	31.0	-4%	32.3	NM	32.3
Eff. Tax Rate	38%	—	37%	—	36%	—	36%
Net Inc.	20.0	3%	19.5	-6%	20.7	NM	20.8

Balance Sheet & Other Fin. Data (Million $)

	1995	1994	1993	1992	1991	1990
Cash	28.1	21.6	22.6	25.1	25.5	26.4
Curr. Assets	59.3	48.5	48.9	51.0	50.9	55.5
Total Assets	85.0	74.5	75.9	81.2	73.2	79.2
Curr. Liab.	13.0	12.5	12.1	9.6	10.2	10.1
LT Debt	0.4	0.4	0.5	2.4	3.2	4.2
Common Eqty.	69.3	58.9	60.6	66.5	55.8	60.7
Total Cap.	71.7	61.8	63.8	68.9	59.0	64.9
Cap. Exp.	4.0	2.2	1.3	2.5	3.7	3.6
Cash Flow	23.5	23.6	25.1	25.1	24.8	24.5

Ratio Analysis

	1995	1994	1993	1992	1991	1990
Curr. Ratio	4.6	3.9	4.0	5.3	5.0	5.5
% LT Debt of Cap.	0.5	0.7	0.8	3.5	5.4	6.4
% Net Inc.of Revs.	14.3	14.6	16.0	15.8	16.7	16.2
% Ret. on Assets	25.1	26.5	27.1	26.9	28.7	27.7
% Ret. on Equity	31.2	33.3	33.6	34.0	37.5	37.2

Dividend Data —Dividends have been paid since 1973.

Amt. of Div. $	Date Decl.	Ex-Div. Date	Stock of Record	Payment Date
0.145	Sep. 14	Oct. 07	Oct. 14	Nov. 01 '94
0.145	Dec. 14	Jan. 09	Jan. 16	Feb. 01 '95
0.145	Apr. 04	Apr. 07	Apr. 14	May. 01 '95
0.150	Jun. 15	Jul. 12	Jul. 14	Aug. 01 '95
0.150	Sep. 28	Oct. 12	Oct. 16	Nov. 01 '95

Data as orig. reptd.; bef. results of disc. opers. and/or spec. items. Per share data adj. for stk. divs. as of ex-div. date. E-Estimated. NA-Not Available. NM-Not Meaningful. NR-Not Ranked.

Office—107 N. Sherman St., Ennis, TX 75119. **Tel**—(214) 875-6581. **Chrmn, CEO & Investor Contact**—Kenneth A. McCrady. **Pres**—C. F. Ray. **VP-Fin & Secy**—H. Cathey. **Dirs**—H. M. Cornell Jr., J. B. Gardner, H. W. Hartley, K. A. McCrady, R. L. Mitchell, T. R. Price, C. F. Ray, P. G. Sorrells, E. L. Tankersley. **Transfer Agent & Registrar**—Ameritrust Corp., Dallas. **Incorporated** in Texas in 1909. **Empl**-1,368. **S&P Analyst:** Stephen Madonna, CFA

STANDARD & POOR'S

STOCK REPORTS

Equifax Inc.

NYSE Symbol **EFX**
In S&P MidCap 400

31-AUG-95 **Industry:** Services

Summary: This company provides businesses with information for insurance claims and credit evaluations and also provides market research and payment services.

Quantitative Evaluations
Outlook (1 Lowest—5 Highest)
• **4+**
Fair Value
• **38⅜**
Risk
• **Low**
Earn./Div. Rank
• **A-**

Technical Eval.
• **Bearish** since 2/95
Rel. Strength Rank (1 Lowest—99 Highest)
• **74**
Insider Activity
• **Neutral**

Recent Price • 38
52 Wk Range • 39⅞-24
Yield • 1.6%
12-Mo. P/E • 21.6

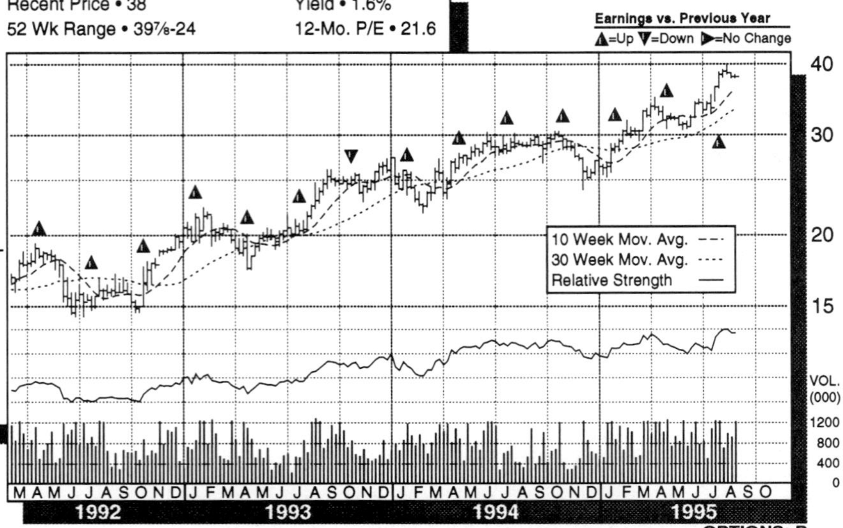

OPTIONS: P

Business Profile - 31-AUG-95

This company provides information services and automated systems that help customers grant credit, insure lives and property, select new employees, and market products and services. EFX has made four acquisitions thus far in 1995, following the 14 acquisitions it made in 1994. In July 1995, directors authorized an additional $50 million open market share repurchase program, doubling the amount authorized.

Operational Review - 31-AUG-95

Earnings advanced, on a year-to-year basis, in 1995's first half, reflecting higher revenues and wider gross margins. More than half the revenue increase was from acquisitions. Operating income increased as a result of revenue growth in higher-margin business units and continuing expense controls. Results were penalized by lower operating income in both the international operations and general information segments. Share earnings were restrained by 3.5% more shares outstanding.

Stock Performance - 25-AUG-95

In the past 30 trading days, EFX's shares have increased 13%, compared to a 0.04% rise in the S&P 500. Average trading volume for the past five days was 261,980 shares, compared with the 40-day moving average of 217,254 shares.

Key Stock Statistics

Dividend Rate/Share	0.62	Shareholders	8,800
Shs. outstg. (M)	79.7	Market cap. (B)	$ 3.1
Avg. daily vol. (M)	0.200	Inst. holdings	58%
Tang. Bk. Value/Share	1.02	Insider holdings	NA
Beta	0.82		

Value of $10,000 invested 5 years ago: $ 27,355

Fiscal Year Ending Dec. 31

	1995	% Change	1994	% Change	1993	% Change
Revenues (Million $)						
1Q	384.2	20%	319.4	16%	276.0	NM
2Q	407.4	19%	342.7	15%	298.0	8%
3Q	—	—	359.3	15%	312.0	12%
4Q	—	—	400.7	21%	331.0	9%
Yr.	—	—	1,422	17%	1,217	7%
Income (Million $)						
1Q	29.47	21%	24.30	34%	18.12	16%
2Q	35.81	25%	28.72	24%	23.25	8%
3Q	—	—	30.96	NM	-6.46	NM
4Q	—	—	36.37	27%	28.61	10%
Yr.	—	—	120.3	89%	63.52	-26%
Earnings Per Share ($)						
1Q	0.39	18%	0.33	38%	0.24	26%
2Q	0.47	21%	0.39	26%	0.31	19%
3Q	—	—	0.42	NM	-0.09	NM
4Q	—	—	0.48	26%	0.38	19%
Yr.	—	—	1.62	91%	0.85	-18%

Next earnings report expected: mid October

Equifax Inc.

Business Summary - 31-AUG-95

Equifax provides a broad range of information-based administrative services to business, industry and government. Contributions in 1994 were:

	Revs.	Profits
Credit information services	31%	60%
Payment services	17%	24%
Insurance information services	32%	8%
International operations	10%	7
General information services	10%	1%

The credit information segment primarily provides consumer and commercial credit services, including mortgage information services, risk management, collection services, fraud detection and prevention, and credit card marketing programs.

The payment segment includes check guarantee and check verification functions, as well as credit and debit card processing services for merchants and financial institutions that include on-line authorization of checks and flexible credit card marketing programs.

The international segment, which operates in Canada, the U.K., Spain, Argentina and Chile, primarily provides consumer credit services, but also offers financial services such as accounts receivable and collection, check guarantee services, life and health underwriting reports, motor vehicle records, and commercial property inspections.

The insurance information segment provides all major life and health insurance companies with information services to help determine the classification of applicants as risks for life and health insurance, and for assistance in settling claims. In addition, health data is provided for use in underwriting the health aspects of risks. The segment also offers similar informational services to major property and casualty underwriters. Osborn Labs tests blood and urine for life and health insurance applicants.

The general information segment provides informational and administrative services to the health care industry, as well as business in general, including market research and analysis, customer opinion surveys and PC-based marketing systems.

Important Developments

Aug. '95—EFX formed a new company, Equifax Business Geo-Metrics, and unveiled ProphetPoint, the new subsidiary's software/data package that will provide information on current and future economic activities.

Jul. '95—EFX acquired The Infocheck Group, the leading U.K. provider of on-line commercial information, for an undisclosed amount. Separately, Equifax Europe Ltd. signed a business collaboration agreement between ASNEF-Equifax in Spain and Portugal's Association of Financial Companies to provide the first automated credit reporting services in Portugal.

Capitalization

Long Term Debt: $243,196,000 (6/95).

Per Share Data ($)

(Year Ended Dec. 31)

	1994	1993	1992	1991	1990	1989
Tangible Bk. Val.	0.40	1.77	1.93	2.97	3.25	2.98
Cash Flow	2.51	1.58	1.70	1.34	1.23	1.33
Earnings	1.62	0.85	1.04	0.66	0.79	0.73
Dividends	0.60	0.56	0.52	0.52	0.48	0.43
Payout Ratio	37%	66%	50%	79%	61%	59%
Prices - High	30½	27⅞	20⅝	21⅛	22⅞	20
- Low	21⅞	17⅞	14⅞	13⅜	13½	13
P/E Ratio - High	19	32	20	32	28	27
- Low	14	20	14	20	17	18

Income Statement Analysis (Million $)

	1994	%Chg	1993	%Chg	1992	%Chg	1991
Revs.	1,422	17%	1,217	7%	1,134	4%	1,094
Oper. Inc.	281	27%	222	14%	195	8%	181
Depr.	66.5	21%	54.9	2%	53.8	-4%	55.9
Int. Exp.	15.6	43%	10.9	173%	4.0	-45%	7.3
Pretax Inc.	207	85%	112	-23%	145	54%	94.0
Eff. Tax Rate	42%	—	43%	—	41%	—	42%
Net Inc.	120	89%	63.5	-26%	85.3	58%	54.1

Balance Sheet & Other Fin. Data (Million $)

	1994	1993	1992	1991	1990	1989
Cash	79.0	86.0	87.0	105	115	14.0
Curr. Assets	376	303	279	304	324	178
Total Assets	1,021	731	709	716	754	551
Curr. Liab.	300	154	129	153	154	137
LT Debt	212	200	192	77.0	143	89.0
Common Eqty.	362	254	258	350	373	247
Total Cap.	581	461	464	447	570	384
Cap. Exp.	20.2	39.8	34.6	23.6	45.9	55.7
Cash Flow	187	118	139	110	100	65.0

Ratio Analysis

	1994	1993	1992	1991	1990	1989
Curr. Ratio	1.3	2.0	2.2	2.0	2.1	1.3
% LT Debt of Cap.	36.5	43.4	41.3	17.2	25.1	23.1
% Net Inc.of Revs.	8.5	5.2	7.5	4.9	5.9	4.2
% Ret. on Assets	13.7	8.9	12.5	7.3	7.7	7.3
% Ret. on Equity	38.8	25.0	29.4	14.9	16.4	15.1

Dividend Data —Dividends have been paid since 1913. A dividend reinvestment plan is available.

Amt. of Div. $	Date Decl.	Ex-Div. Date	Stock of Record	Payment Date
0.155	Jul. 27	Aug. 19	Aug. 25	Sep. 15 '94
0.155	Oct. 26	Nov. 17	Nov. 23	Dec. 15 '94
0.155	Jan. 25	Feb. 15	Feb. 22	Mar. 15 '95
0.155	Apr. 26	May. 19	May. 25	Jun. 15 '95
0.155	Jul. 26	Aug. 23	Aug. 25	Sep. 15 '95

Data as orig. reptd.; bef. results of disc. opers. and/or spec. items. Per share data adj. for stk. divs. as of ex-div. date. E-Estimated. NA-Not Available. NM-Not Meaningful. NR-Not Ranked.

Office—1600 Peachtree St., N.W., P.O. Box 4081, Atlanta, GA 30302 **Tel**—(404) 885-8000. **Chrmn & CEO**—C. B. Rogers, Jr. **Pres & COO**—D. W. McGlaughlin. **SVP & CFO**—D. U. Hallman. **VP & Secy**—T. H. Magis. **VP & Investor Contact**—Marietta E. Zakas. **Dirs**—L. A. Ault III, R. D. Barbaro, T. F. Chapman, J. C. Chartrand, J. L. Clendenin, A. W. Dahlberg, L. P. Humann, T. H. Irvin, D. W. McGlaughlin, L. L. Prince, D. R. Riddle, C. B. Rogers, Jr., B. L. Siegel, L. W. Sullivan. **Transfer Agent & Registrar**—Trust Co. Bank, Atlanta. **Incorporated** in Georgia in 1913. **Empl**-14,200. **S&P Analyst:** Ronald J. Gross

STANDARD & POOR'S STOCK REPORTS

Ethyl Corp.

NYSE Symbol **EY**
In S&P MidCap 400

03-OCT-95 **Industry:** Chemicals

Summary: This company is a major producer of fuel and lubricant additives, including lead antiknocks.

S&P Opinion: Hold (★★★)

Recent Price • 11⅛ | Yield • 4.5%
52 Wk Range • 12⅜-9½ | 12-Mo. P/E • 16.1

Quantitative Evaluations

Outlook (1 Lowest—5 Highest)
• **3⁻**

Fair Value
• **11⅛**

Risk
• **Low**

Earn./Div. Rank
• **NR**

Technical Eval.
• **Bearish** since 6/95

Rel. Strength Rank (1 Lowest—99 Highest)
• **46**

Insider Activity
• **NA**

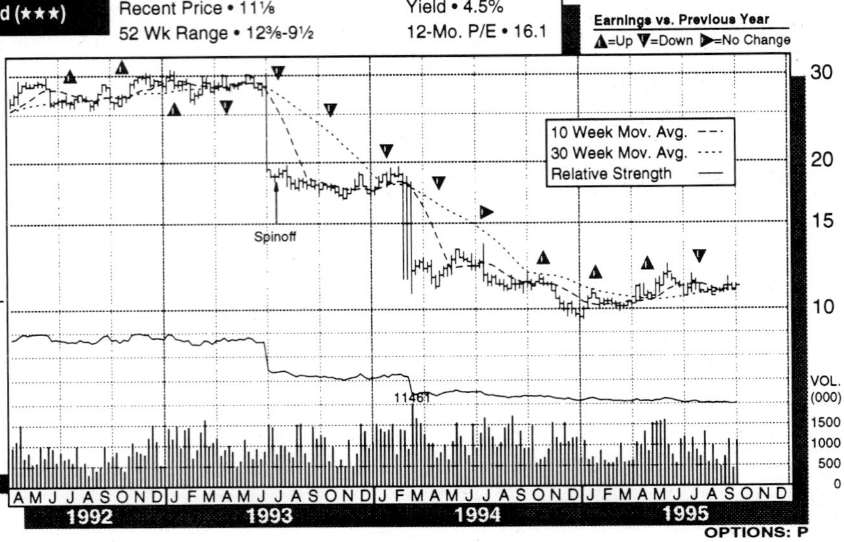

OPTIONS: P

Overview - 03-OCT-95

Sales and profits of the petroleum additives business should improve in late 1995 and in 1996, reflecting higher selling prices and modest volume gains for lubricant and certain fuel additives. High startup costs for new manufacturing and R&D facilities will begin to ease in the second half of 1995. The pending purchase of Texaco's lubricant additive business (annual sales of about $350 million) will greatly expand EY's business and should contribute to earnings in 1996 due to cost savings. We believe that profits for lead antiknocks should remain steady through 1996, as higher prices offset a continuing modest volume decline; however, 1995's second half volumes and profits will be higher than in the 1994 period due to normal fluctuations of shipments. Initial sales of HiTech 3000 (MMT) fuel additive in the U.S. will likely not occur until 1996.

Valuation - 03-OCT-95

Since the early 1994 spinoff of Albemarle Corp., the stock of this specialty chemical company has been a lackluster performer, despite a positive longer term outlook for lubricant additives. The proposed acquisition of Texaco's lubricant additive business will increase EY's market share and provide good cost savings. Lead antiknocks, the major portion of EY's earnings, is a declining business and limits the investment appeal of the stock. We recommend maintaining current holdings, in view of the P/E multiple and attractive yield.

Key Stock Statistics

S&P EPS Est. 1995	0.75	Tang. Bk. Value/Share	3.27
P/E on S&P Est. 1995	14.8	Beta	1.71
S&P EPS Est. 1996	0.95	Shareholders	12,600
Dividend Rate/Share	0.50	Market cap. (B)	$ 1.3
Shs. outstg. (M)	118.4	Inst. holdings	48%
Avg. daily vol. (M)	0.177	Insider holdings	NA

Value of $10,000 invested 5 years ago: NA

Fiscal Year Ending Dec. 31

	1995	% Change	1994	% Change	1993	% Change
Revenues (Million $)						
1Q	234.3	-40%	389.1	-17%	469.8	-31%
2Q	224.5	-19%	276.1	-44%	495.0	-25%
3Q	—	—	244.9	-50%	486.9	-39%
4Q	—	—	264.0	-46%	486.6	-42%
Yr.	—	—	1,174	-39%	1,938	-35%
Income (Million $)						
1Q	21.49	6%	20.26	-23%	26.33	-58%
2Q	13.01	-57%	30.38	-1%	30.83	-41%
3Q	—	—	22.49	13%	19.97	-72%
4Q	—	—	24.62	91%	12.90	-85%
Yr.	—	—	97.76	9%	90.02	-67%
Earnings Per Share ($)						
1Q	0.18	6%	0.17	-23%	0.22	-58%
2Q	0.11	-58%	0.26	NM	0.26	-41%
3Q	E0.19	NM	0.19	12%	0.17	-72%
4Q	E0.27	29%	0.21	91%	0.11	-84%
Yr.	E0.75	-10%	0.83	9%	0.76	-67%

Next earnings report expected: late October

Ethyl Corp.

Business Summary - 26-SEP-95

Ethyl Corp. is a producer of fuel and lubricant additives. On February 28, 1994, it spun off its specialty chemicals businesses as Albemarle Corp. The remaining 80% interest in First Colony Corp. insurance unit was spun off in July 1993 (First Colony was treated as a discontinued operation in 1993). Segment contributions in 1994 (excluding Albemarle) were:

	Sales	Profits
Petroleum additives	95%	100%
Whitby pharmaceuticals	5%	Nil

Foreign operations (including Albemarle) accounted for 33% of sales and 23% of profits in 1994.

Petroleum additives consist of fuel additives (lead and manganese antiknock compounds, cetane improvers, antioxidants, detergents, corrosion inhibitors, dyes) for gasoline, diesel fuels, and heating oils; and lubricant additive packages and components (antioxidants, detergents, dispersants, corrosion inhibitors, viscosity improvers) for engine oils, automatic transmission fluids, gear oils, hydraulic fluids and industrial oils. Lead antiknocks accounted for 60% of operating profits in 1994 (excluding Albemarle).

In September, 1994, the company sold Whitby, Inc., which markets ethical and OTC pharmaceuticals.

Albemarle Corp., spun off in early 1994, had sales of $903 million and net income of $15.8 million in 1993 (included in EY's financial statements), derived from olefins and derivatives; bromine chemicals; and specialty chemicals.

Important Developments

Sep. '95—EY agreed to purchase the worldwide lubricant additive business of Texaco Inc. Terms were not disclosed. The business had sales of about $350 million in 1994.

Jul. '95—The EPA granted a waiver for the use of EY's HiTEC 3000 manganese-based fuel additive. In April, 1994, a Federal appeals court ordered the EPA to grant the waiver. The company cannot begin selling the product until a decision favorable to EY is reached in a lawsuit challenging the EPA determination that EY must complete additional manganese health testing.

Jul. '95—The reduction in second quarter 1995 earnings from 1994 reflected expected lower lead antiknock sales and earnings compared to 1994's unusually high levels. Profits from lubricant and certain other fuel additives were also below 1994 results. Lower second quarter sales also reflected the absence of the pharmaceuticals business sold in September 1994.

Capitalization

Long Term Debt: $332,869,000 (6/95).

Per Share Data ($)

(Year Ended Dec. 31)

	1994	1993	1992	1991	1990	1989
Tangible Bk. Val.	3.12	5.40	10.70	9.29	8.00	6.48
Cash Flow	1.28	1.84	3.21	2.57	2.69	2.47
Earnings	0.83	0.76	2.27	2.55	2.74	1.83
Dividends	0.50	0.60	0.60	0.60	0.60	2.01
Payout Ratio	60%	79%	26%	34%	31%	109%
Prices - High	19⅝	30⅞	30½	33	33	29
- Low	9½	16¾	23¾	22¼	20½	21
P/E Ratio - High	24	41	13	19	17	16
- Low	11	22	10	13	11	11

Income Statement Analysis (Million $)

	1994	%Chg	1993	%Chg	1992	%Chg	1991
Revs.	1,174	-39%	1,938	-35%	2,975	16%	2,575
Oper. Inc.	224	-32%	331	-38%	533	16%	458
Depr.	54.0	-57%	127	14%	111	17%	95.0
Int. Exp.	33.4	-34%	50.9	-28%	70.7	4%	68.1
Pretax Inc.	141	5%	134	-70%	444	51%	295
Eff. Tax Rate	31%	—	33%	—	39%	—	30%
Net Inc.	98.0	9%	90.0	-67%	269	30%	207

Balance Sheet & Other Fin. Data (Million $)

	1994	1993	1992	1991	1990	1989
Cash	31.0	48.0	176	41.0	39.0	80.0
Curr. Assets	431	734	NA	NA	NA	NA
Total Assets	1,030	2,009	9,204	7,905	6,690	5,632
Curr. Liab.	183	327	NA	NA	NA	NA
LT Debt	350	687	702	811	684	497
Common Eqty.	391	753	1,401	1,219	1,048	898
Total Cap.	769	1,583	2,628	2,457	2,120	1,740
Cap. Exp.	147	205	164	180	166	127
Cash Flow	152	217	380	302	327	296

Ratio Analysis

	1994	1993	1992	1991	1990	1989
Curr. Ratio	2.4	2.2	NA	NA	NA	NA
% LT Debt of Cap.	45.5	43.4	26.7	33.0	32.3	28.6
% Net Inc.of Revs.	8.3	4.6	9.1	8.0	9.2	9.0
% Ret. on Assets	6.4	1.6	3.1	2.8	3.8	4.1
% Ret. on Equity	17.1	8.4	20.6	18.2	24.0	21.8

Dividend Data —Dividends have been paid since 1957. A "poison pill" stock purchase rights plan was adopted in 1987.

Amt. of Div. $	Date Decl.	Ex-Div. Date	Stock of Record	Payment Date
0.125	Jul. 28	Sep. 09	Sep. 15	Oct. 01 '94
0.125	Nov. 22	Dec. 09	Dec. 15	Jan. 01 '95
0.125	Feb. 23	Mar. 09	Mar. 15	Apr. 01 '95
0.125	Apr. 13	Jun. 13	Jun. 15	Jul. 01 '95
0.125	Jul. 27	Sep. 13	Sep. 15	Oct. 01 '95

Data as orig. reptd.; bef. results of disc. opers. and/or spec. items. Per share data adj. for stk. divs. as of ex-div. date. E-Estimated. NA-Not Available. NM-Not Meaningful. NR-Not Ranked.

Office—330 South Fourth St. Richmond, VA 23217. **Tel**—(804) 788-5000. **Chrmn & CEO**—B. C. Gottwald. **Pres**—T. E. Gottwald. **Vice Chrmn & CFO**—C. B. Walker. **VP & Secy**—E. W. Elmore. **Investor Contact**—John S. Patton. **Dirs**—L. B. Andrew. W. W. Berry, P. L. Cothran, A. C. Goolsby, B. C. Gottwald, B. C. Gottwald, Jr., F. D. Gottwald, Jr., T. E. Gottwald, W. M. Gottwald, G. M. Grosvenor, A. B. Lacy, E. J. Rice, S. B. Scott, C. B. Walker. **Transfer Agent & Registrar**—Harris Trust & Savings Bank, Chicago. **Incorporated** in Virginia in 1887. **Empl**-1,500. **S&P Analyst:** Richard O'Reilly, CFA

STANDARD & POOR'S
STOCK REPORTS

Exabyte Corp.

NASDAQ Symbol **EXBT**
In S&P MidCap 400

28-SEP-95

Industry: Data Processing

Summary: Exabyte designs, develops, manufactures and markets high-capacity 8mm cartridge and other tape subsystems for cost-effective data storage solutions.

S&P Opinion: Hold (★★★)	Recent Price • 13⅝	Yield • Nil
	52 Wk Range • 24-11¾	12-Mo. P/E • 11.0

Quantitative Evaluations

Outlook (1 Lowest—5 Highest)
• **5-**

Fair Value
• **18¼**

Risk
• **High**

Earn./Div. Rank
• **NR**

Technical Eval.
• **Bearish** since 12/94

Rel. Strength Rank (1 Lowest—99 Highest)
• **3**

Insider Activity
• **Neutral**

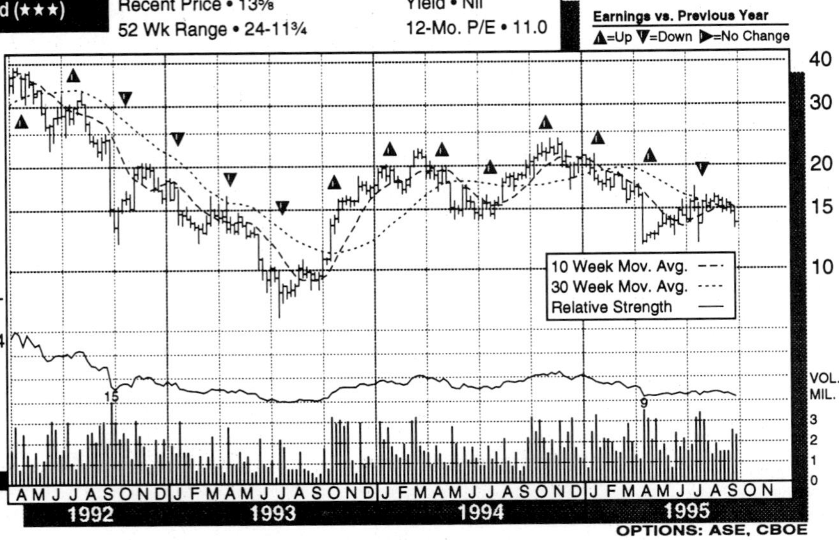

OPTIONS: ASE, CBOE

Overview - 28-SEP-95

Sales are expected to decline in the second half of 1995, owing to weakness in the domestic VAR channel and slower sales to certain OEM customers. However, sales are expected to advance in 1996, spurred by continued gains in 8mm half-height cartridge tape subsystems, a strong library business, growing international markets and the introduction of new products including Mammoth, the company's upcoming high-end tape drive. Margins are expected to remain under pressure through 1995 year end, but widen in 1996, aided by a more favorable product mix, and continued cost controls. Nonrecurring charges will penalize 1995 results.

Valuation - 28-SEP-95

The shares have declined sharply since the beginning of 1995, reflecting sluggish revenues and a higher than normal accumulation of inventory, which began in the first quarter. The pricing environment remains stable and costs are under control. While the company commands a leading position in the backup tape application market, weakness in the domestic value added reseller (VAR) channel and slower sales to certain original equipment manufacturers (OEM) makes next year's sales and earnings estimates less certain. We expect the shares to move in line with the market in the coming months.

Key Stock Statistics

S&P EPS Est. 1995	-0.50	Tang. Bk. Value/Share	9.52
P/E on S&P Est. 1995	NM	Beta	2.14
S&P EPS Est. 1996	1.20	Shareholders	800
Dividend Rate/Share	Nil	Market cap. (B)	$0.269
Shs. outstg. (M)	21.8	Inst. holdings	49%
Avg. daily vol. (M)	0.490	Insider holdings	NA

Value of $10,000 invested 5 years ago: $ 11,978

Fiscal Year Ending Dec. 31

	1995	% Change	1994	% Change	1993	% Change
Revenues (Million $)						
1Q	96.19	11%	86.89	14%	76.21	NM
2Q	96.98	5%	92.68	22%	75.76	-1%
3Q	—	—	99.0	32%	75.14	17%
4Q	—	—	103.3	24%	83.19	18%
Yr.	—	—	381.8	23%	310.3	8%
Income (Million $)						
1Q	7.47	6%	7.02	17%	6.01	-49%
2Q	1.69	-77%	7.44	NM	1.61	-86%
3Q	—	—	8.79	NM	2.62	NM
4Q	—	—	9.17	54%	5.94	12%
Yr.	—	—	32.41	100%	16.18	-21%
Earnings Per Share ($)						
1Q	0.34	6%	0.32	14%	0.28	-48%
2Q	0.08	-76%	0.34	NM	0.08	-85%
3Q	E-1.15	NM	0.40	NM	0.12	NM
4Q	E0.23	-44%	0.41	46%	0.28	12%
Yr.	E-0.50	NM	1.48	95%	0.76	-20%

Next earnings report expected: mid October

Exabyte Corp.

Business Summary - 28-SEP-95

Exabyte Corp. designs, makes and markets tape subsystems for data storage applications. The company's primary offerings include cartridge tape subsystems based on 8mm helical scan, 4mm helical scan and quarter-inch technologies. Its products are used in a broad spectrum of computer systems ranging from personal computers to supercomputers. A large majority of its units are used with workstations, network file servers and midrange systems. The capacity of these subsystems allows users to back up multiple disk drives and, in many cases, an entire computer system, on a single, standard tape cartridge.

The main products are 8mm tape drive subsystems, available in both full height and half-height configurations. The 8mm products accounted for 72%, 77% and 84% of sales in 1994, 1993 and 1992, respectively.

The company offers high-end 8mm automated tape library subsystems, which automates the storage and retrieval of substantial amounts of data. Libraries accounted for 11%, 7% and 4% of sales in 1994, 1993 and 1992, respectively.

EXBT's 4mm cartridge tape subsystems accounted for 5% and 2% of sales in 1994 and 1993, respectively. Quarter-inch tape drive subsystem products accounted for about 1% of revenues in both 1994 and 1993.

The product line also includes recording media, cleaning cartridges, data cartridge holders and other consumables, which accounted for approximately 8% of sales over the past three years. Repair and other services accounted for 4%, 4% and 3% of sales in 1994, 1993 and 1992.

Sales to OEMs represented 40% and 41% of the total in 1994 and 1993, respectively. Sales to VARs and system integrators accounted for 25% and 35% of sales in 1994 and 1993. Sales to distributors provided 35% and 24% in 1994 and 1993, respectively.

International sales came to 24% and 18% of revenues in 1994 and 1993.

Important Developments

Sep. '95—Exabyte said it expected revenues in the third quarter of 1995 to be lower than expected - between $82 million and $85 million, owing to softness in the domestic VAR channel, slower sales to certain OEM customers, as well as traditional seasonal summer softness in Europe. For the third quarter of 1995, the company also projected a per share loss of between $1.05 and $1.15, including $0.90 to $1.00 for the write-down of 4mm, quarter-inch and 8mm full-high inventories, the establishment of certain reserves and goodwill write-offs.

Capitalization

Long Term Debt: $873,000 of lease obligs. (7/1/95).

Per Share Data ($) (Year Ended Dec. 31)

	1994	1993	1992	1991	1990	1989
Tangible Bk. Val.	9.10	7.49	6.70	5.51	3.80	2.38
Cash Flow	2.07	1.36	1.36	1.78	1.47	0.73
Earnings	1.48	0.76	0.95	1.51	1.32	0.65
Dividends	Nil	Nil	Nil	Nil	Nil	Nil
Payout Ratio	Nil	Nil	Nil	Nil	Nil	Nil
Prices - High	24	18¾	40⅝	31⅝	25⅜	13⅛
- Low	14	7¼	12	13⅛	6⅝	10
P/E Ratio - High	16	25	43	21	19	20
- Low	9	10	13	9	5	15

Income Statement Analysis (Million $)

	1994	%Chg	1993	%Chg	1992	%Chg	1991
Revs.	382	23%	310	8%	287	23%	234
Oper. Inc.	61.3	74%	35.3	-41%	59.4	10%	54.2
Depr.	13.0	NM	12.9	44%	9.0	57%	5.7
Int. Exp.	0.2	NM	0.2	14%	0.1	8%	0.1
Pretax Inc.	47.8	100%	23.9	-39%	38.9	-23%	50.2
Eff. Tax Rate	32%	—	32%	—	47%	—	36%
Net Inc.	32.4	100%	16.2	-21%	20.5	-36%	32.2

Balance Sheet & Other Fin. Data (Million $)

	1994	1993	1992	1991	1990	1989
Cash	80.3	66.0	51.2	55.6	28.8	30.1
Curr. Assets	204	168	155	135	89.0	58.0
Total Assets	243	197	183	150	101	62.0
Curr. Liab.	45.6	38.3	42.3	37.7	25.5	16.5
LT Debt	0.2	0.4	0.5	0.1	0.2	0.2
Common Eqty.	197	159	140	112	75.0	46.0
Total Cap.	197	159	141	112	75.0	46.0
Cap. Exp.	13.6	8.0	17.8	6.8	9.3	2.8
Cash Flow	45.4	29.0	29.5	37.9	30.8	13.7

Ratio Analysis

	1994	1993	1992	1991	1990	1989
Curr. Ratio	4.5	4.4	3.7	3.6	3.5	3.5
% LT Debt of Cap.	0.1	0.3	0.4	0.1	0.3	0.4
% Net Inc.of Revs.	8.5	5.2	7.1	13.8	16.2	13.9
% Ret. on Assets	14.6	8.5	12.1	25.4	33.4	30.9
% Ret. on Equity	18.1	10.8	16.0	34.0	45.2	43.9

Dividend Data —The company has never paid cash dividends on its common stock. A shareholder rights plan was adopted in 1991.

Data as orig. reptd.; bef. results of disc. opers. and/or spec. items. Per share data adj. for stk. divs. as of ex-div. date. E-Estimated. NA-Not Available. NM-Not Meaningful. NR-Not Ranked.

Office—1685 38th St., Boulder, CO 80301-9803. **Tel**—(303) 442-4333. **Chrmn, Pres & CEO**—P. D. Behrendt. **EVP & COO**—D. L. Riegel. **EVP-Fin, CFO & Treas**—W. L. Marriner. **Investor Contact**—Susan Merriman (303-447-7434). **Dirs**—P. D. Behrendt, B. M. Holland, J. M. McCoy, T. E. Pardun, M. W. Perry, R. Z. Sorenson, T. G. Washing. **Transfer Agent & Registrar**—First National Bank of Boston. **Incorporated** in Delaware in 1985. **Empl**-1,042. **S&P Analyst:** Peter C. Wood, CFA

STANDARD & POOR'S

STOCK REPORTS

FHP International Corp.

NASDAQ Symbol **FHPC**

In S&P MidCap 400

11-SEP-95 **Industry:** Health Care Centers

Summary: This company operates staff, network and IPA model HMOs that serve nearly 1.8 million members in 11 states and Guam.

S&P Opinion: Avoid (★★)

Recent Price • 23½

52 Wk Range • 31-19½

Yield • Nil

12-Mo. P/E • 81.0

Earnings vs. Previous Year
▲=Up ▼=Down ▶=No Change

Quantitative Evaluations

Outlook
(1 Lowest—5 Highest)
• **2⁻**

Fair Value
• **22⅝**

Risk
• **Average**

Earn./Div. Rank
• **NR**

Technical Eval.
• **Bullish** since 5/95

Rel. Strength Rank
(1 Lowest—99 Highest)
• **15**

Insider Activity
• **Neutral**

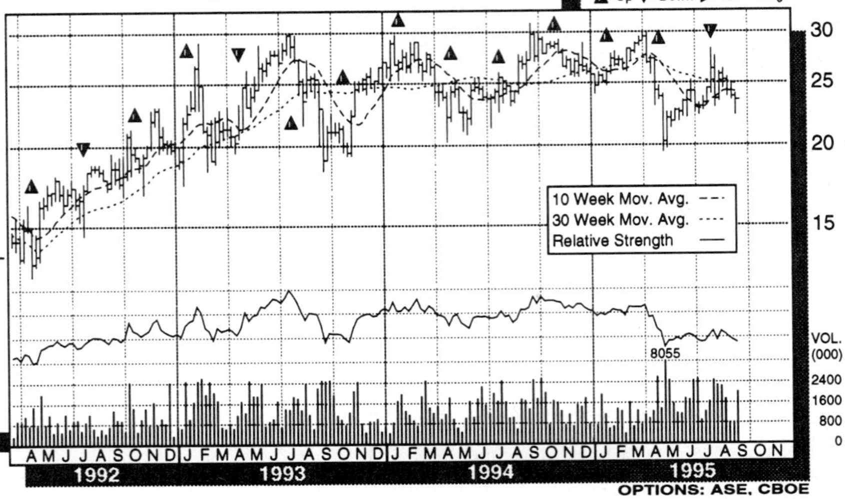

OPTIONS: ASE, CBOE

Overview - 11-SEP-95

Depressed earnings in fiscal 1995 reflected several negative developments in the California market, where commercial enrollment growth of only 2.9%, attributed to rising competition and a slow process of integrating the operations of recent acquisitions, was coupled with high health care costs in certain owned facilities, downward pressure on premium rates, some accounts receivables writeoffs and higher advertising and administrative costs. In August, management allerted analysts that these trends would hurt earnings in the fourth quarter, however core per-share profits (before restructuring charges) of $0.17, versus $0.57, fell below the revised estimates. Full year core EPS of $1.43 a share represented a 16% decline from fiscal 1994.

Valuation - 11-SEP-95

The prospect of eroding market share in California, combined with several trends likely to put downward margin pressure on the entire HMO group (particulary in California), suggest that FHP's shares will underperform both the S&P 500 Index and the shares of its HMO peers over the next six to twelve months. The creation of a physician practice management division could help results in the future, but earnings from the core HMO operations have shown little signs of improvement. As such, we remain concerned that core EPS (before additional restructuring charges) in fiscal 1996 will remain soft, and would continue to avoid the stock.

Key Stock Statistics

S&P EPS Est. 1996	1.30	Tang. Bk. Value/Share	NM
P/E on S&P Est. 1996	18.1	Beta	1.38
Dividend Rate/Share	Nil	Shareholders	400
Shs. outstg. (M)	40.2	Market cap. (B)	$0.945
Avg. daily vol. (M)	0.294	Inst. holdings	84%
		Insider holdings	NA

Value of $10,000 invested 5 years ago: $ 12,457

Fiscal Year Ending Jun. 30

	1995	% Change	1994	% Change	1993	% Change
Revenues (Million $)						
1Q	954.3	66%	576.4	30%	444.0	22%
2Q	954.4	61%	591.1	27%	464.5	24%
3Q	1,001	61%	622.5	16%	535.8	28%
4Q	1,000	46%	683.0	22%	561.4	31%
Yr.	3,909	58%	2,473	23%	2,006	26%
Income (Million $)						
1Q	20.72	84%	11.25	—	—	—
2Q	21.33	108%	10.25	67%	6.15	49%
3Q	28.41	69%	16.81	16%	14.45	-3%
4Q	-33.17	NM	21.00	23%	17.12	115%
Yr.	37.29	-37%	59.31	34%	44.17	34%
Earnings Per Share ($)						
1Q	0.37	12%	0.33	65%	0.20	11%
2Q	0.36	16%	0.31	63%	0.19	46%
3Q	0.53	6%	0.50	16%	0.43	-4%
4Q	-0.97	NM	0.57	12%	0.51	112%
Yr.	0.29	-83%	1.71	29%	1.33	33%

Next earnings report expected: early November

FHP International Corp.

11-SEP-95

Business Summary - 11-SEP-95

FHP International Corporation operates a federally qualified multi-state licensed health maintenance organization (HMO) serving nearly 1.8 million individuals in 11 states and Guam.

The company offers a full range of managed health-care products, including HMO, preferred provider network (PPO), point-of-service plans, third party administration plans and indemnity medical, group life and workers' compensation insurance. FHP provides services to commercial and government employees and Medicare beneficiaries.

FHP operates through two different HMO delivery models. In its staff model HMO, the company delivers health care through an employed staff of physicians and other health care providers at company operated facilities. As of June 30, 1994, it employed about 800 primary care physicians and physician specialists, 200 dentists and 600 other health care professionals. It also operated 59 medical and dental care centers, three acute care hospitals, and two sub-acute skilled nursing facilities. In the IPA model, the company contracts with independent medical and dental providers in facilities not operated by FHP. At June 30, 1994, it had contracts with more than 41,000 independent providers and more than 500 hospitals.

Through insurance subsidiaries, the company provided group term life insurance coverage for 63,000 individuals and group health and accident indemnity coverage for 48,000 individuals.

Important Developments

Aug. '95—FHP was selected by an American subsidiary of Nippon Life Insurance Company to provide health care benefits to California-based Japanese companies with operations in the U.S. The company's HMO products will be added to Nippon's current product portfolio in order to provide more comprehensive employee benefit choices for Japanese-affiliated companies in California.

Jun. '95—The company announced a restructuring under which its 57 medical centers will be organized into a new physician management company, Comprecare Medical Group, that will contract with unaffiliated HMOs and other health care payers. Comprecare will assume all of FHP's staff model operations in California, Utah, Arizona, New Mexico, Nevada and Guam, including the employment of over 500 physicians and 95 dentists. As part of the restructuring, FHP will sell its four hospitals and reduce its workforce by about 500 persons.

Capitalization

Long Term Obligations: $337,817,000 (6/95).
5% Ser. A Conv. Pfd. Stk.: 21,031,733 shs. ($25 stated value).
Ser. B Adj. Rate Pfd. Stk.: 61,757 shs.

Per Share Data ($) (Year Ended Jun. 30)

	1995	1994	1993	1992	1991	1990
Tangible Bk. Val.	NA	-12.36	10.92	9.61	8.38	5.12
Cash Flow	NA	3.04	2.21	1.70	2.01	1.52
Earnings	0.29	1.71	1.33	1.00	1.37	1.00
Dividends	Nil	Nil	Nil	Nil	Nil	Nil
Payout Ratio	Nil	Nil	Nil	Nil	Nil	Nil
Prices - High	30	31	30	23	29¾	20½
- Low	19½	20¼	17⅞	12½	9⅞	8⅞
P/E Ratio - High	NM	18	23	23	22	20
- Low	NM	12	13	13	7	9

Income Statement Analysis (Million $)

	1994	%Chg	1993	%Chg	1992	%Chg	1991
Revs.	2,473	23%	2,006	26%	1,586	22%	1,297
Oper. Inc.	128	52%	84.3	65%	51.0	-26%	68.6
Depr.	45.3	55%	29.2	26%	23.2	23%	18.8
Int. Exp.	6.6	134%	2.8	-26%	3.8	-11%	4.3
Pretax Inc.	96.8	39%	69.8	36%	51.5	-22%	65.7
Eff. Tax Rate	39%	—	37%	—	36%	—	39%
Net Inc.	59.3	34%	44.2	34%	32.9	-18%	40.1

Balance Sheet & Other Fin. Data (Million $)

	1994	1993	1992	1991	1990	1989
Cash	247	177	239	265	225	158
Curr. Assets	446	267	308	312	259	181
Total Assets	2,169	746	616	529	432	319
Curr. Liab.	588	296	254	207	240	163
LT Debt	378	20.8	23.3	29.8	32.8	34.4
Common Eqty.	585	364	311	270	142	110
Total Cap.	1,491	385	335	300	175	146
Cap. Exp.	86.0	91.0	111	61.0	49.0	34.0
Cash Flow	104	73.4	56.1	58.9	43.7	33.0

Ratio Analysis

	1994	1993	1992	1991	1990	1989
Curr. Ratio	0.8	0.9	1.2	1.5	1.1	1.1
% LT Debt of Cap.	25.3	5.4	7.0	10.0	18.8	23.5
% Net Inc.of Revs.	2.4	2.2	2.1	3.1	2.9	3.2
% Ret. on Assets	4.1	6.4	5.7	7.8	7.6	8.1
% Ret. on Equity	12.3	13.0	11.3	18.4	22.7	28.7

Dividend Data —No cash dividends have been paid on the common stock. A 10% stock dividend was paid in 1991, and a two-for-one stock split was effected in 1989.

Data as orig. reptd.; bef. results of disc. opers. and/or spec. items. Per share data adj. for stk. divs. as of ex-div. date. E-Estimated. NA-Not Available. NM-Not Meaningful. NR-Not Ranked.

Office—9900 Talbert Ave., Fountain Valley, CA 92708. **Tel**—(714) 963-7233. **Chrmn**—J. R. Anderson. **Vice Chrmn & CEO**—W. W. Price III. **EVP & COO**—J. Massimino. **SVP & CFO**—K. Ord. **SVP & Secy**—M. J. Weinstock. **Investor Contact**—Anna Marie Dunlap (714-378-5585). **Dirs**—J. R. Anderson, R. M. Burdge, B. F. Gumbiner, W. Heineman, R. W. Jamplis, R. C. Maxson, J. F. Prevratil, W. W. Price III. **Transfer Agent & Registrar**—American Stock Transfer & Trust Co., NYC. **Incorporated** in Delaware in 1984. **Empl**-14,000. **S&P Analyst:** Robert M. Gold

STANDARD & POOR'S

STOCK REPORTS

Family Dollar Stores

NYSE Symbol **FDO**
In S&P MidCap 400

19-AUG-95 **Industry:** Retail Stores

Summary: Family Dollar operates a chain of more than 2,400 retail discount stores in 37 states, located mostly in communities with populations under 50,000.

S&P Opinion: Avoid (★★)

Recent Price • 18 5/8
52 Wk Range • 19 3/4-9 7/8
Yield • 2.1%
12-Mo. P/E • 18.6

Quantitative Evaluations
Outlook
(1 Lowest—5 Highest)
• **4-**
Fair Value
• **18 7/8**
Risk
• **Average**
Earn./Div. Rank
• **A-**

Technical Eval.
• **Bullish** since 5/95
Rel. Strength Rank
(1 Lowest—99 Highest)
• **89**
Insider Activity
• **Unfavorable**

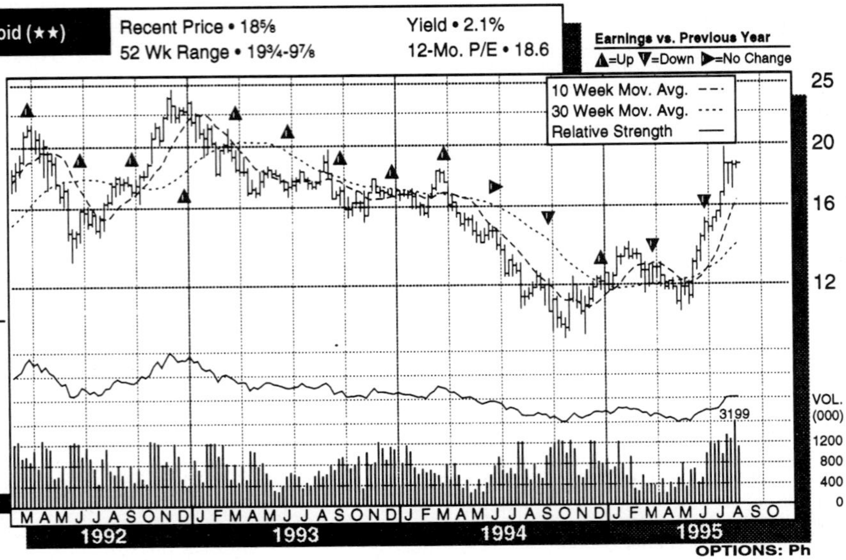

Overview - 18-AUG-95

We expect total sales to grow modestly during the remainder of fiscal 1995, spurred by the continuing addition of new stores. Sales at existing stores should advance in the low-single-digits, reflecting consumers' growing acceptance of the company's move toward an everyday low pricing strategy. Gross margins have been negatively affected by the lower prices and by soft apparel sales, necessitating higher promotional clearance markdowns. Family Dollar hopes to offset some of the negative effects of the gross margin erosion by lowering operating costs. Howver, earnings are likely to remain under pressure for the next several quarters.

Valuation - 18-AUG-95

The shares of this discount retailer recently rose more than 60%, to a 52-week high, aided by positive same-store sales comparisons in June and July. We expect top-line growth to benefit from the company's aggressive expansion program, expected to add at least 200 new stores in fiscal 1995. However, gross margins will continue to be adversely affected by the price reduction program. Unless the company is able to lower its expense structure, future earnings are likely to be disappointing. We believe the recent run-up in FDO's share price is premature and, until any success of the new merchandising strategy is evident, we see significant risk in owning the stock.

Key Stock Statistics

S&P EPS Est. 1995	0.99	Tang. Bk. Value/Share	7.12
P/E on S&P Est. 1995	18.8	Beta	1.47
S&P EPS Est. 1996	1.10	Shareholders	3,200
Dividend Rate/Share	0.40	Market cap. (B)	$ 1.1
Shs. outstg. (M)	56.7	Inst. holdings	56%
Avg. daily vol. (M)	0.429	Insider holdings	0%

Value of $10,000 invested 5 years ago: $ 39,502

Fiscal Year Ending Aug. 31

	1995	% Change	1994	% Change	1993	% Change
Revenues (Million $)						
1Q	356.3	6%	335.1	10%	305.0	16%
2Q	420.9	6%	398.8	12%	356.5	12%
3Q	379.8	9%	349.2	13%	310.1	11%
4Q	—	—	345.4	6%	326.3	10%
Yr.	—	—	1,428	10%	1,297	12%
Income (Million $)						
1Q	15.59	4%	14.95	8%	13.79	19%
2Q	17.04	-23%	22.02	6%	20.79	15%
3Q	16.40	-7%	17.57	NM	17.45	15%
4Q	—	—	7.42	-40%	12.40	13%
Yr.	—	—	61.96	-4%	64.43	16%
Earnings Per Share ($)						
1Q	0.28	4%	0.27	8%	0.25	19%
2Q	0.30	-23%	0.39	5%	0.37	16%
3Q	0.29	-6%	0.31	NM	0.31	15%
4Q	E0.12	-8%	0.13	-41%	0.22	10%
Yr.	E0.99	-10%	1.10	-4%	1.15	15%

Next earnings report expected: mid October

Family Dollar Stores

Business Summary - 18-AUG-95

This company operates a chain of self-service retail discount stores under the Family Dollar name. As of August 3, 1995, there were 2,402 stores operating in 37 states, ranging as far northwest as Minnesota, northeast to New Hampshire, southeast to Florida and southwest to New Mexico. States with significant concentrations of stores include North Carolina, Georgia, South Carolina, Virginia, Tennessee, Alabama, Florida, Kentucky, Louisiana, Ohio and Texas.

The number of stores in operation at the end of recent fiscal years were:

1994	2,215
1993	2,035
1992	1,885
1991	1,759
1990	1,680
1989	1,580
1988	1,429
1987	1,272
1986	1,107

Each Family Dollar store sells a wide variety of mostly first-quality merchandise, with 42% of sales in fiscal 1994 derived from soft goods, such as apparel, shoes, linen, blankets, bedspreads and curtains; the stores also carry hard goods, including automotive supplies, paints, toys, housewares, school supplies, candy and health and beauty aids.

Merchandise, the majority of which is priced at $17.99 or less, is purchased from about 1,400 suppliers. About 60% of the items carried are manufactured in the U.S.

Stores are located in both rural and urban areas, but most are in communities with populations under 50,000. The units are freestanding or located in shopping centers, with the typical store averaging 6,000 to 8,000 sq. ft. of total area. Most of the stores are leased.

Important Developments

Aug. '95—FDO reported that total sales in July 1995 advanced 13%, year to year; same-store sales were up 3.8%. Sales of hardlines continued to be stronger than sales of apparel. For the eleven months ended July 31, 1995, total sales rose 8.1%, despite a 1.0% decline in same-store sales.

Jul. '95—During 1994-95's third quarter, the company opened 49 new stores and closed two locations. It expected to open a net addition of at least 200 new stores for the full year.

Capitalization

Long Term Debt: None (5/95).

Per Share Data ($)

(Year Ended Aug. 31)

	1994	1993	1992	1991	1990	1989
Tangible Bk. Val.	6.54	5.74	4.85	4.08	3.55	3.23
Cash Flow	1.44	1.45	1.26	0.96	0.75	0.61
Earnings	1.10	1.15	1.00	0.72	22.00	0.39
Dividends	0.32	0.28	0.24	0.21	0.19	0.17
Payout Ratio	29%	24%	24%	29%	37%	44%
Prices - High	18 3/8	23 5/8	24 5/8	17 1/8	7 5/8	7 1/8
- Low	10 1/8	15 1/8	13 1/8	5 3/4	4 1/2	4 7/8
P/E Ratio - High	17	21	25	23	15	18
- Low	9	13	13	8	9	13

Income Statement Analysis (Million $)

	1994	%Chg	1993	%Chg	1992	%Chg	1991
Revs.	1,428	10%	1,297	12%	1,159	17%	989
Oper. Inc.	120	NM	120	17%	103	36%	76.0
Depr.	19.5	13%	17.2	17%	14.7	12%	13.1
Int. Exp.	0.4	105%	0.2	—	Nil	—	0.4
Pretax Inc.	100	-3%	103	16%	88.9	40%	63.7
Eff. Tax Rate	38%	—	37%	—	37%	—	37%
Net Inc.	62.0	-4%	64.4	16%	55.7	39%	40.2

Balance Sheet & Other Fin. Data (Million $)

	1994	1993	1992	1991	1990	1989
Cash	9.9	5.7	1.7	25.0	4.6	0.7
Curr. Assets	436	402	359	294	252	219
Total Assets	593	537	478	399	355	324
Curr. Liab.	206	197	188	158	144	132
LT Debt	Nil	Nil	Nil	Nil	Nil	Nil
Common Eqty.	370	323	272	227	197	179
Total Cap.	387	339	287	242	211	192
Cap. Exp.	42.6	32.5	30.1	14.8	12.5	18.3
Cash Flow	81.4	81.6	70.4	53.3	41.4	33.5

Ratio Analysis

	1994	1993	1992	1991	1990	1989
Curr. Ratio	2.1	2.0	1.9	1.9	1.8	1.7
% LT Debt of Cap.	Nil	Nil	Nil	Nil	Nil	Nil
% Net Inc.of Revs.	4.5	5.0	4.8	4.1	3.3	2.8
% Ret. on Assets	10.9	12.7	12.7	10.6	8.5	7.0
% Ret. on Equity	17.8	21.6	22.3	18.9	15.3	12.4

Dividend Data —Dividends were initiated in 1976.

Amt. of Div. $	Date Decl.	Ex-Div. Date	Stock of Record	Payment Date
0.085	Aug. 16	Sep. 09	Sep. 15	Oct. 14 '94
0.085	Nov. 10	Dec. 09	Dec. 15	Jan. 16 '95
0.100	Jan. 19	Mar. 09	Mar. 15	Apr. 14 '95
0.100	May. 15	Jun. 13	Jun. 15	Jul. 14 '95
0.100	Aug. 15	Sep. 13	Sep. 15	Oct. 16 '95

Data as orig. reptd.; bef. results of disc. opers. and/or spec. items. Per share data adj. for stk. divs. as of ex-div. date. E-Estimated. NA-Not Available. NM-Not Meaningful. NR-Not Ranked.

Office—10401 Old Monroe Rd., Matthews, NC 28105. **Tel**—(704) 847-6961. **Chrmn, CEO & Treas**—L. Levine. **Pres & COO**—J. D. Reier. **Exec VP-Secy & Investor Contact**—George R. Mahoney Jr. **Sr VP-Fin**—C. M. Sowers. **Dirs**—M. R. Bernstein, L. Levine, G. R. Mahoney Jr., T. R. Payne, J. D. Reier. **Transfer Agent & Registrar**—Chemical Bank, NYC. **Incorporated** in Delaware in 1969. **Empl-** 16,500. **S&P Analyst:** Maureen C. Carini

STANDARD & POOR'S

STOCK REPORTS

Federal-Mogul

NYSE Symbol **FMO**
In S&P MidCap 400

29-AUG-95 **Industry:** Auto parts/equipment

Summary: Federal-Mogul produces automotive bearings, oil seals, fuel systems and lighting for original equipment and replacement markets, and operates 79 retail stores in foreign markets.

S&P Opinion: Hold (★★★)

Recent Price • 22¼
52 Wk Range • 29⅝-16¾
Yield • 2.2%
12-Mo. P/E • 16.5

Quantitative Evaluations

Outlook
(1 Lowest—5 Highest)
• **3⁻**

Fair Value
• **22¾**

Risk
• **Average**

Earn./Div. Rank
• **B-**

Technical Eval.
• **Bullish** since 7/95

Rel. Strength Rank
(1 Lowest—99 Highest)
• **76**

Insider Activity
• **Neutral**

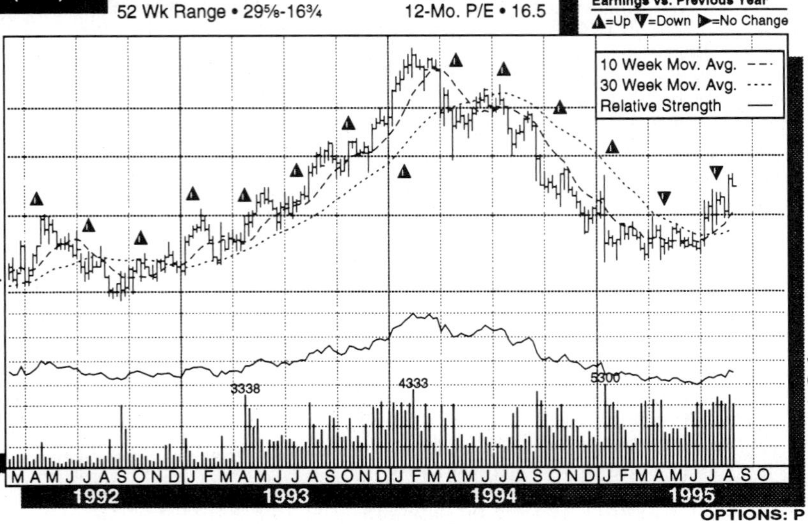

OPTIONS: P

Overview - 29-AUG-95

Sales should advance in 1995, on increased international revenues. Efforts to improve manufacturing efficiency should be aided by greater capacity utilization in Europe, which has emerged from recession, and by economies of scale resulting from the consolidation of the replacement parts distribution businesses of TRW and SPX Corp. However, hurt by losses in Mexico, an unexpected drop in aftermarket demand in the U.S., and a restructuring charge, earnings should decline in 1995. Clouding the longer-term outlook is an aggressive and risky plan to expand its small foreign retail auto parts store operation (assembled in 1993 and 1994) from 65 stores in South Africa, South America and Australia at the end of 1994, to 500 stores by 2000.

Valuation - 29-AUG-95

We continue to have reservations about FMO's operations. Problems range from lower U.S. aftermarket demand to the ongoing losses in Mexico. Also, the original equipment cycle is maturing, and may turn down in 1996. We remain troubled by FMO's venture in foreign retailing, not an area of company expertise. However, FMO's poor stock price performance over the past two years has not gone unnoticed and takeover rumors have begun to crop up. While we are not predicting that FMO will be acquired, we think pressure may increase and FMO's directors may be forced to take action to improve shareholder value. We have upgraded the stock to hold.

Key Stock Statistics

S&P EPS Est. 1995	1.35	Tang. Bk. Value/Share	7.36
P/E on S&P Est. 1995	16.5	Beta	1.26
S&P EPS Est. 1996	1.55	Shareholders	12,800
Dividend Rate/Share	0.48	Market cap. (B)	$0.774
Shs. outstg. (M)	35.0	Inst. holdings	68%
Avg. daily vol. (M)	0.358	Insider holdings	NA

Value of $10,000 invested 5 years ago: $ 13,098

Fiscal Year Ending Dec. 31

	1995	% Change	1994	% Change	1993	% Change
Revenues (Million $)						
1Q	524.3	14%	460.3	12%	410.5	38%
2Q	506.3	7%	474.8	18%	401.8	29%
3Q	—	—	445.3	20%	370.0	24%
4Q	—	—	515.5	31%	393.2	10%
Yr.	—	—	1,896	20%	1,576	25%
Income (Million $)						
1Q	14.20	-5%	15.00	100%	7.50	NM
2Q	14.20	-30%	20.40	33%	15.30	168%
3Q	—	—	16.10	61%	10.00	138%
4Q	—	—	11.80	62%	7.30	NM
Yr.	—	—	63.30	58%	40.10	NM
Earnings Per Share ($)						
1Q	0.34	-13%	0.39	70%	0.23	NM
2Q	0.35	-30%	0.50	6%	0.47	194%
3Q	E0.40	5%	0.38	46%	0.26	160%
4Q	E0.26	-4%	0.27	59%	0.17	NM
Yr.	E1.35	-13%	1.55	37%	1.13	NM

Next earnings report expected: mid October

Federal-Mogul

Business Summary - 29-AUG-95

Federal-Mogul, a leading producer of engine bearings, oil seals and anti-friction bearings for motor vehicles, also produces and distributes other precision parts to the original equipment and replacement motor vehicle parts markets worldwide, and operates retail stores in foreign markets. Sales by market segment in recent years were:

	1994	1993
Aftermarket	64%	63%
Auto & light truck components	22%	22%
Heavy truck, farm & construction equipment components	8%	8%
General industry	6%	7%

Foreign activities accounted for 31% of sales and 15% of operating profits in 1994.

Engine and transmission products accounted for 41% of sales in 1994, ball and roller bearings for 14%, sealing devices 14%, steering and suspension parts 11%, lighting, electrical and fuel systems 13%, and all other 7%.

Major brands include Federal-Mogul and Glyco engine bearings, Bruss, National and Mather oil seals, BCA ball bearings, Carter fuel systems, Sterling pistons, and Signal-Stat and Switches electrical components. The company produces all of its original equipment parts. It buys certain parts for aftermarket distribution from other manufacturers, including TRW Inc. and SPX Corp., both of which sold their aftermarket distribution businesses to FMO in recent years. TRW supplies primarily steering and suspension parts, while SPX Corp. provides engine and chassis parts.

At the end of 1994, FMO had a total of 65 retail parts stores located in South Africa (36 stores), Venezuela (12), Panama (7), Australia (6) and Chile (4). In 1995, plans call for adding a total of 26 stores in South Africa (14), Venezuela (7), Ecuador (3) and Chile (2). By 2000, the company expects to have 500 stores, all outside the U.S.

Important Developments

Jul. '95—Second quarter 1995 sales were hurt by a 9.7% drop in original equipment shipments and a 4.0% decline in replacement sales in North America. International replacement and original equipment sales rose sharply, due primarily to acquisitions. Second quarter earnings reflect a $7.8 million restructuring charge for termination of 223 employees, closing of an operation in Bahrain, lease terminations and asset writedowns.

Capitalization

Long Term Debt: $421,400,000 (6/95), including $39.0 million in ESOP obligs.

Series D Conv. Preferred Stock: $76,600,000. Conv. into 4,255,556 com. shs.

7.5% ESOP Conv. Preferred Stock: $59,000,000. Conv. into 1,888,032 com. shs.

Per Share Data ($)

(Year Ended Dec. 31)

	1994	1993	1992	1991	1990	1989
Tangible Bk. Val.	7.25	2.58	1.76	7.11	7.74	9.73
Cash Flow	3.09	2.93	1.87	1.03	2.14	3.03
Earnings	1.55	1.13	-0.01	-1.08	0.20	1.26
Dividends	0.48	0.48	0.48	0.92	0.92	0.90
Payout Ratio	31%	42%	NM	NM	461%	69%
Prices - High	37⅝	30	20⅛	19⅛	22½	29½
- Low	18⅝	16	14½	12¼	10¼	18⅝
P/E Ratio - High	24	27	NM	NM	NM	23
- Low	12	14	NM	NM	NM	15

Income Statement Analysis (Million $)

	1994	%Chg	1993	%Chg	1992	%Chg	1991
Revs.	1,896	20%	1,576	25%	1,264	15%	1,099
Oper. Inc.	178	39%	128	52%	84.0	11%	76.0
Depr.	55.7	10%	50.7	16%	43.7	-10%	48.7
Int. Exp.	21.2	-18%	25.9	-5%	27.2	-3%	27.9
Pretax Inc.	102	76%	58.0	NM	9.0	NM	-18.0
Eff. Tax Rate	38%	—	30%	—	51%	—	NM
Net Inc.	63.3	58%	40.1	NM	4.4	NM	-21.0

Balance Sheet & Other Fin. Data (Million $)

	1994	1993	1992	1991	1990	1989
Cash	25.0	24.0	19.0	45.0	27.0	10.0
Curr. Assets	704	574	488	399	507	411
Total Assets	1,496	1,292	1,100	884	1,084	810
Curr. Liab.	336	283	265	204	231	231
LT Debt	319	383	351	304	418	178
Common Eqty.	498	276	142	194	228	237
Total Cap.	926	767	614	602	769	536
Cap. Exp.	75.0	59.0	40.0	50.0	180	54.0
Cash Flow	108	80.1	41.8	22.9	47.7	70.0

Ratio Analysis

	1994	1993	1992	1991	1990	1989
Curr. Ratio	2.1	2.0	1.8	2.0	2.2	1.8
% LT Debt of Cap.	34.5	49.9	57.1	50.5	54.3	33.1
% Net Inc.of Revs.	3.3	2.5	0.3	NM	0.8	3.1
% Ret. on Assets	4.2	2.9	0.4	NM	1.0	4.4
% Ret. on Equity	12.8	12.7	NM	NM	1.9	10.4

Dividend Data —Dividends have been paid since 1936. A dividend reinvestment plan is available. A new poison pill stock purchase rights plan was adopted in 1988.

Amt. of Div. $	Date Decl.	Ex-Div. Date	Stock of Record	Payment Date
0.120	Jul. 20	Aug. 25	Aug. 31	Sep. 12 '94
0.120	Nov. 02	Nov. 23	Nov. 30	Dec. 12 '94
0.120	Feb. 08	Feb. 21	Feb. 27	Mar. 10 '95
0.120	Apr. 26	May. 23	May. 30	Jun. 12 '95
0.120	Jul. 19	Aug. 28	Aug. 30	Sep. 11 '95

Data as orig. reptd.; bef. results of disc. opers. and/or spec. items. Per share data adj. for stk. divs. as of ex-div. date. E-Estimated. NA-Not Available. NM-Not Meaningful. NR-Not Ranked.

Office—26555 Northwestern Highway, Southfield, MI 48034. **Tel**—(810) 354-7700. **Chrmn & Pres**—D. J. Gormley. **VP & Treas**—Michael J. Viola. **Investor Contact**—Bonnie J. Price (800-521-8607). **Dirs**—J. J. Fannon, D. J. Gormley, R. M. Hills, A. Madero, R. S. Miller, Jr., J. C. Pope, H. M. Sekyra. **Transfer Agent & Registrar**—Bank of New York, NYC. **Incorporated** in Michigan in 1924. **Empl**-15,600. **S&P Analyst:** Joshua M. Harari, CFA

STANDARD & POOR'S

STOCK REPORTS

Federal Signal

NYSE Symbol **FSS**
In S&P MidCap 400

03-AUG-95 **Industry:** Auto/Truck mfrs.

Summary: FSS makes fire trucks, street sweepers, ambulances and other special purpose vehicles, public safety and signaling equipment, parking gates, electronic signs and perishable tools.

S&P Opinion: Hold (★★★)

Recent Price • 23⅜
52 Wk Range • 24⅛-17¾
Yield • 2.1%
12-Mo. P/E • 20.9

Quantitative Evaluations
Outlook
(1 Lowest—5 Highest)
• **2**
Fair Value
• **21⅝**
Risk
• **Low**
Earn./Div. Rank
• **A+**

Technical Eval.
• **Bullish** since 11/94
Rel. Strength Rank
(1 Lowest—99 Highest)
• **59**
Insider Activity
• **Neutral**

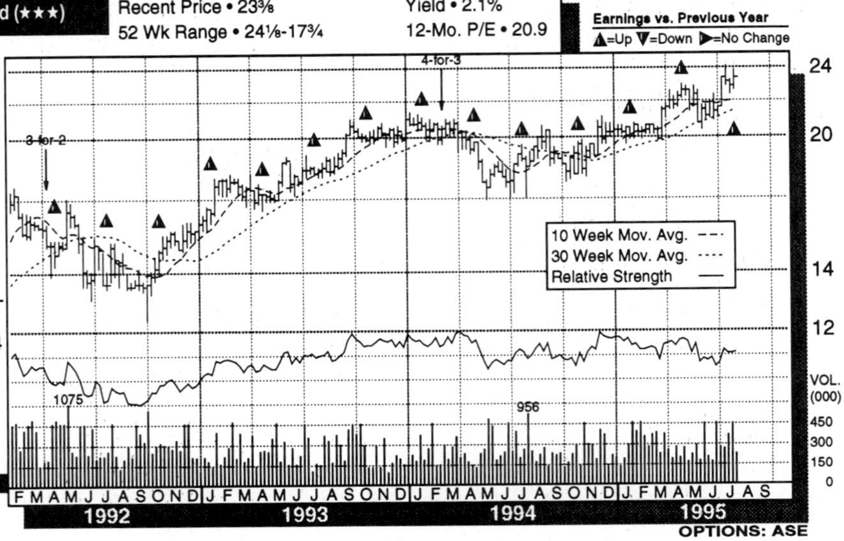

OPTIONS: ASE

Overview - 03-AUG-95

Strong sales growth in Vehicles is likely in 1995 as domestic demand for Emergency-One fire apparatus is up and bidding activity on municipal street sweepers is increasing, implying growth in orders and sales over the next few quarters. Safety Products (formerly Signal) sales will rise, sparked by increased manufacturing activity in the U.S. and Europe, and recent acquisitions. While the Sign division will remain the company's weakest unit, profit improvement is expected following the first profit in several years in 1994. Despite a decline in margins at the Tool unit, overall results wil be aided by improved operating efficiencies and expense controls, as well as prospective acquisitions in complementary domestic businesses and current business lines in Europe.

Valuation - 03-AUG-95

This company's steady growth in earnings in recent years reflects a combination of internally generated growth and the addition of businesses complementary to the four core operating segments in which it competes. Most of the company's businesses are dominant players within their respective market niches and, while this market leadership should be accorded an above average market multiple, we believe that the company is fairly valued at about 19 times our 1995 earnings projection, compared with an average multiple of about 17 for stocks in the Mid-Cap 400 Index.

Key Stock Statistics

S&P EPS Est. 1995	1.20	Tang. Bk. Value/Share	2.41
P/E on S&P Est. 1995	19.5	Beta	0.48
S&P EPS Est. 1996	1.35	Shareholders	10,000
Dividend Rate/Share	0.50	Market cap. (B)	$ 1.0
Shs. outstg. (M)	45.3	Inst. holdings	55%
Avg. daily vol. (M)	0.068	Insider holdings	NA

Value of $10,000 invested 5 years ago: $ 36,679

Fiscal Year Ending Dec. 31

	1995	% Change	1994	% Change	1993	% Change
Revenues (Million $)						
1Q	187.1	35%	138.1	8%	127.4	6%
2Q	199.4	22%	164.0	12%	146.5	11%
3Q	—	—	181.3	27%	142.7	5%
4Q	—	—	193.8	31%	148.5	13%
Yr.	—	—	677.2	20%	565.2	9%
Income (Million $)						
1Q	10.79	32%	8.16	14%	7.15	16%
2Q	14.48	17%	12.40	17%	10.60	14%
3Q	—	—	12.44	17%	10.66	15%
4Q	—	—	13.78	21%	11.37	18%
Yr.	—	—	46.77	18%	39.78	16%
Earnings Per Share ($)						
1Q	0.24	33%	0.18	14%	0.16	17%
2Q	0.32	19%	0.27	16%	0.23	15%
3Q	E0.31	—	0.27	16%	0.23	15%
4Q	E0.33	—	0.30	20%	0.25	19%
Yr.	E1.20	—	1.02	19%	0.86	32%

Next earnings report expected: mid October

Federal Signal

Business Summary - 02-AUG-95

Contributions (profits in millions) the four operating segments in 1994 were:

	Sales	Profits
Vehicle	52%	$33.5
Tool	18%	23.5
Safety (formerly Signal)	20%	23.3
Sign	10%	4.0

Sales by market in 1994 were divided 29% industrial and other, 28% municipal, 19% foreign, 12% commercial, 9% volunteer fire departments and 3% U.S. government. Foreign sales have increased steadily in recent years from 13% in 1990.

The Vehicle group includes Elgin Sweeper, Emergency One, Ravo International, Vactor Manufacturing, Superior Emergency Vehicles and Guzzler Manufacturing. They manufacture chassis, fire trucks including Class A pumpers, mini-pumpers and tankers, rescue vehicles and aerial ladder trucks, street cleaners, vacuum waste removal, sewer and catch basin cleaning vehicles, ambulances and mobile communication vehicles.

Tool products include die components for metal stamping; precision metal products for non-stamping needs; carbide, polycrystalline diamond and cubic boran nitride cutting tools; and industrial-grade, high-speed steel and carbide twist drills.

Safety Products (formerly Signal) includes visual and audible warning and signaling devices for private industry and governmental agencies; communications equipment for government, industrial and transportation-related uses; and paging, local signaling and building security. Federal APD offers parking, revenue and access control systems. Aplicaciones Tecnologicas Vama S.L. makes emergency vehicle signals in Spain, and Justrite makes hazardous materials storage containers.

The Sign group includes illuminated, non-illuminated and electronic advertising sign displays. Contractual maintenance services are provided for Federal's signs and signs made by others.

Important Developments

Jun. '95—FSS's Emergency One subsidiary announced entry to the Australian fire truck market. Emergency One received a 26 unit order for its Titan HPR, the latest generation aircraft rescue and fire fighting vehicle, for the Royal Australian Air Force and Royal Army Engineers. The new Titan HPR is a variation of the P-23 vehicle purchased by the U.S. Air Force, which unlike the P-23 is air transportable in a Hercules C-130.

Capitalization

Total Debt: $180,667,000 (3/95).

Per Share Data ($)

(Year Ended Dec. 31)

	1994	1993	1992	1991	1990	1989
Tangible Bk. Val.	2.31	2.92	2.73	2.63	2.57	2.35
Cash Flow	1.24	1.06	0.94	0.85	0.78	0.68
Earnings	1.02	0.86	0.75	0.68	0.61	0.50
Dividends	0.39	0.36	0.24	0.27	0.22	0.19
Payout Ratio	38%	56%	42%	40%	36%	37%
Prices - High	21⅜	21	17⅝	15¼	10¾	7⅛
- Low	16⅞	15⅝	12⅜	9¼	6¼	4¼
P/E Ratio - High	21	24	24	23	18	14
- Low	17	18	17	14	10	9

Income Statement Analysis (Million $)

	1994	%Chg	1993	%Chg	1992	%Chg	1991
Revs.	677	20%	565	9%	518	11%	467
Oper. Inc.	88.6	21%	73.1	14%	63.9	9%	58.8
Depr.	10.3	12%	9.2	6%	8.7	6%	8.2
Int. Exp.	8.5	38%	6.1	-5%	6.5	15%	5.7
Pretax Inc.	70.2	19%	58.8	18%	49.9	9%	45.6
Eff. Tax Rate	33%	—	32%	—	31%	—	32%
Net Inc.	46.8	18%	39.8	16%	34.4	11%	31.0

Balance Sheet & Other Fin. Data (Million $)

	1994	1993	1992	1991	1990	1989
Cash	4.6	2.6	2.2	0.1	1.5	2.5
Curr. Assets	NA	NA	NA	NA	NA	NA
Total Assets	522	406	364	341	296	271
Curr. Liab.	253	174	159	150	123	115
LT Debt	34.9	21.1	16.2	15.6	15.8	16.8
Common Eqty.	220	199	179	165	146	130
Total Cap.	269	231	205	191	173	157
Cap. Exp.	11.1	10.1	8.8	12.0	8.3	9.5
Cash Flow	57.1	49.0	43.2	39.3	35.9	31.1

Ratio Analysis

	1994	1993	1992	1991	1990	1989
Curr. Ratio	NA	NA	NA	NA	NA	NA
% LT Debt of Cap.	13.0	9.1	7.9	8.2	9.2	10.7
% Net Inc.of Revs.	6.9	7.0	6.6	6.6	6.4	5.6
% Ret. on Assets	10.1	10.3	9.8	9.7	10.0	8.8
% Ret. on Equity	22.4	21.0	20.0	19.9	20.4	18.7

Dividend Data (Dividends have been paid since 1948. A dividend reinvestment plan is available. A "poison pill" stock purchase right was adopted in 1988.)

Amt. of Div. $	Date Decl.	Ex-Div. Date	Stock of Record	Payment Date
0.105	Oct. 13	Dec. 05	Dec. 09	Jan. 04 '95
0.125	Feb. 02	Feb. 08	Feb. 14	Mar. 01 '95
0.125	Apr. 19	May. 01	May. 05	Jun. 01 '95
0.125	Jul. 14	Aug. 09	Aug. 11	Sep. 06 '95

Data as orig. reptd.; bef. results of disc. opers. and/or spec. items. Per share data adj. for stk. divs. as of ex-div. date. E-Estimated. NA-Not Available. NM-Not Meaningful. NR-Not Ranked.

Office—1415 West 22nd St., Oak Brook, IL 60521-9945. **Tel**—(708) 954-2000. **Chrmn, Pres & CEO**—J. J. Ross. **SVP, CFO & Investor Contact**—Henry L. Dykema. **VP & Secy**—K. A. Wehrenberg. **VP & Treas**—R. W. Racic. **Dirs**—J. P. Lannan, Jr., J. A. Lovell Jr., T. N. McGowen, Jr., W. R. Peirson, J. J. Ross, R. R. Thomas. **Transfer Agent & Registrar**—Harris Trust & Savings Bank, Chicago. **Incorporated** in Illinois in 1901; reincorporated in Delaware in 1969. **Empl**-5,243. **S&P Analyst:** Joshua M. Harari, CFA

STANDARD & POOR'S

STOCK REPORTS

Ferro Corp.

NYSE Symbol **FOE**

In S&P MidCap 400

04-OCT-95 **Industry:** Chemicals

Summary: Ferro producers specialty materials, including coatings, colors, plastics, chemicals and ceramics, for the building, appliance, furnishings, industrial and transportation markets.

S&P Opinion: Hold (★★★)

Recent Price • 24⅞

52 Wk Range • 30⅝-22¾

Yield • 2.2%

12-Mo. P/E • 14.5

Quantitative Evaluations

Outlook (1 Lowest—5 Highest)
• **4+**

Fair Value
• **25**

Risk
• **Low**

Earn./Div. Rank
• **B+**

Technical Eval.
• **Bearish** since 11/91

Rel. Strength Rank (1 Lowest—99 Highest)
• **15**

Insider Activity
• **NA**

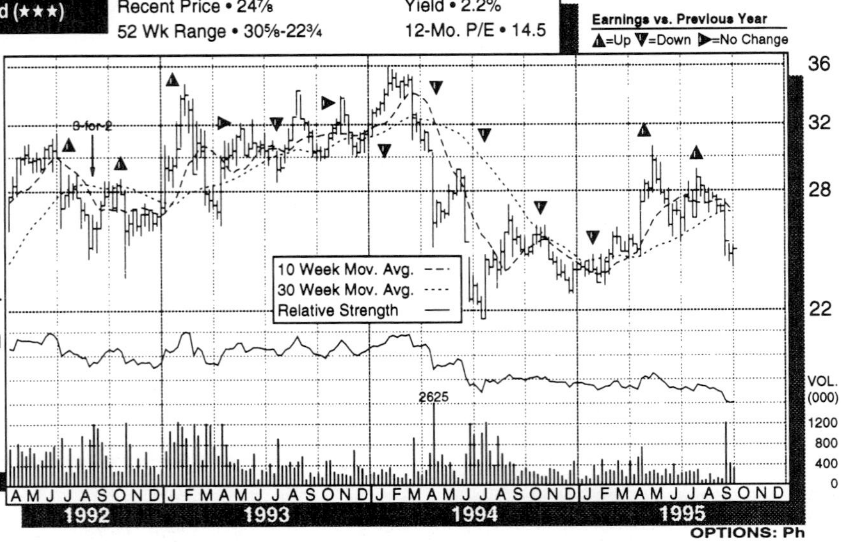

OPTIONS: Ph

Overview - 04-OCT-95

Revenues should increase modestly in 1995, restrained by a second half slowdown in key domestic markets, and a sharp drop in Latin American sales. European sales will benefit from improved economic conditions, and we see ongoing growth in the Asia/Pacific operations. Although growth in U.S. sales may slow, the recent agreement to acquire Synpro should increase revenues more than 8% and strengthen Ferro's position in polymer additives. Profitability will gain from the consolidation of the powder coatings business acquired in 1993, while price increases implemented to offset higher raw materials costs will help margins recover in plastics. Earnings growth in 1995 will be around 12%, with results hurt by the more than 50% drop in Latin American operating profits (14% of the 1994 total). We do, however, see the potential for greater than 20% growth in 1996.

Valuation - 04-OCT-95

The shares have declined sharply from their 1995 high (after the better-than-expected first quarter report), reflecting renewed concerns over the outlook for Latin American results, and, more recently, the announcement that third quarter results would fall well below expectations. Although we remain concerned over these negatives, we believe the positive potential for 1996 justifies the maintaining of current positions in the stock.

Key Stock Statistics

S&P EPS Est. 1995	1.70	Tang. Bk. Value/Share	10.36
P/E on S&P Est. 1995	14.6	Beta	1.29
S&P EPS Est. 1996	2.10	Shareholders	3,200
Dividend Rate/Share	0.54	Market cap. (B)	$0.679
Shs. outstg. (M)	27.9	Inst. holdings	69%
Avg. daily vol. (M)	0.109	Insider holdings	NA

Value of $10,000 invested 5 years ago: $ 16,378

Fiscal Year Ending Dec. 31

	1995	% Change	1994	% Change	1993	% Change
Revenues (Million $)						
1Q	343.0	21%	283.3	10%	257.0	-6%
2Q	334.0	11%	300.2	7%	279.7	-4%
3Q	—	—	296.8	13%	263.7	-3%
4Q	—	—	313.9	18%	265.3	2%
Yr.	—	—	1,194	12%	1,066	-3%
Income (Million $)						
1Q	13.10	16%	11.32	-14%	13.12	1%
2Q	14.66	22%	11.97	-12%	13.60	-8%
3Q	—	—	11.63	-22%	14.99	1%
4Q	—	—	12.47	-21%	15.80	-3%
Yr.	—	—	47.40	-18%	57.51	-2%
Earnings Per Share ($)						
1Q	0.44	26%	0.35	-17%	0.42	NM
2Q	0.49	29%	0.38	-12%	0.43	-9%
3Q	E0.34	-11%	0.38	-21%	0.48	NM
4Q	E0.43	5%	0.41	-20%	0.51	-4%
Yr.	E1.70	12%	1.52	-17%	1.83	-4%

Next earnings report expected: late October

Ferro Corp.

Business Summary - 04-OCT-95

Ferro is a worldwide producer of specialty materials. Contributions by business segment in 1994:

	Sales	Profits
Coatings, colors & ceramics	60%	85%
Plastics	22%	8%
Chemicals	18%	7%

International operations accounted for 50% of sales and 60% of profits in 1994.

Specialty coatings include porcelain enamel frit for appliances, architectural panels and other uses; ceramic glaze frit; and organic powder coatings for appliances, automotive parts and furniture. Specialty colors consists of inorganic color pigments for porcelain enamel and ceramic glaze coatings, plastics and paint; forehearth glass colorants; and enamels for glass and ceramic decorating. Electronic materials include electronic ceramics, thick-film pastes and sealing glasses and ceramic coated substrates. Specialty ceramics include kiln furniture, abrasion-resistant linings, radiants, refractories, grinding media, and porous ceramics. Ceramic polishing powders are also produced.

Plastics include filled and reinforced plastics (polypropylene compounds, polyolefin alloys, engineering thermoplastics), color and additive concentrates for plastics, gel coats for fiberglass-reinforced plastic products, and color dispersions for thermoset plastics.

Specialty chemicals include polymer additives (heat and light stabilizers, antimicrobials, antioxidants, plasticizers and flame retardants); lubricants; engine oil and fuel additives; and solvents, catalysts and intermediate chemicals.

Important Developments

Sep. '95—Ferro said third quarter 1995 earnings could decline approximately 10%, due to weakening demand in its domestic automotive and major appliance markets.

Aug. '95—FOE agreed to acquire Synthetic Products Company (Synpro), a Cleveland-based subsidiary of Cookson Group plc. Synpro, a producer of chemical additives used in the plastics and rubber industries, had sales in excess of $100 million during the past year.

Jul. '95—The company said that all segments increased operating profits in the second quarter of 1995, despite a softening in the domestic economy and a substantial decline in its Latin American operations.

Capitalization

Long Term Debt: $130,638,000 (6/95), excl. ESOP loan guarantee of $33,970,000.

ESOP 7% Conv. Preferred Stock: $70,500,000.

Per Share Data ($)

(Year Ended Dec. 31)

	1994	1993	1992	1991	1990	1989
Tangible Bk. Val.	10.36	9.70	10.49	8.07	7.81	7.30
Cash Flow	2.81	2.98	3.04	1.19	1.60	2.39
Earnings	1.52	1.83	1.90	0.05	0.55	1.50
Dividends	0.54	0.51	0.56	0.43	0.43	0.40
Payout Ratio	36%	28%	24%	NM	75%	25%
Prices - High	35⅞	34¾	31½	25¾	19⅝	27⅝
- Low	21⅝	26⅛	23½	10¼	11½	15
P/E Ratio - High	24	19	17	NM	35	18
- Low	14	14	12	NM	21	10

Income Statement Analysis (Million $)

	1994	%Chg	1993	%Chg	1992	%Chg	1991
Revs.	1,194	12%	1,066	-3%	1,098	4%	1,057
Oper. Inc.	123	-6%	131	-4%	137	29%	106
Depr.	37.1	10%	33.8	NM	33.5	2%	32.7
Int. Exp.	12.0	7%	11.2	12%	10.0	-14%	11.6
Pretax Inc.	74.3	-17%	89.3	-9%	97.7	NM	21.5
Eff. Tax Rate	36%	—	36%	—	40%	—	72%
Net Inc.	47.4	-17%	57.2	-3%	58.8	NM	4.8

Balance Sheet & Other Fin. Data (Million $)

	1994	1993	1992	1991	1990	1989
Cash	20.0	63.0	109	78.5	21.2	58.2
Curr. Assets	415	411	415	406	387	409
Total Assets	801	768	697	672	686	669
Curr. Liab.	228	199	205	213	221	210
LT Debt	115	123	104	55.7	58.0	60.8
Common Eqty.	339	337	328	235	235	227
Total Cap.	482	497	460	370	385	378
Cap. Exp.	59.7	43.7	44.8	39.0	61.4	53.5
Cash Flow	80.9	87.8	89.1	34.3	46.6	73.9

Ratio Analysis

	1994	1993	1992	1991	1990	1989
Curr. Ratio	1.8	2.1	2.0	1.9	1.7	1.9
% LT Debt of Cap.	23.9	24.8	22.6	15.0	15.1	16.1
% Net Inc.of Revs.	4.0	5.4	5.4	0.5	1.7	4.6
% Ret. on Assets	6.2	7.8	8.5	0.7	2.9	8.1
% Ret. on Equity	13.3	16.2	17.8	0.7	7.1	18.4

Dividend Data —Dividends have been paid since 1939. A dividend reinvestment plan is available. An amended "poison pill" stock purchase right was adopted in 1989.

Amt. of Div. $	Date Decl.	Ex-Div. Date	Stock of Record	Payment Date
0.135	Oct. 28	Nov. 08	Nov. 15	Dec. 10 '94
0.135	Jan. 27	Feb. 09	Feb. 15	Mar. 10 '95
0.135	Apr. 28	May. 09	May. 15	Jun. 10 '95
0.135	Jul. 28	Aug. 11	Aug. 15	Sep. 10 '95

Data as orig. reptd.; bef. results of disc. opers. and/or spec. items. Per share data adj. for stk. divs. as of ex-div. date. E-Estimated. NA-Not Available. NM-Not Meaningful. NR-Not Ranked.

Office—1000 Lakeside Ave., Cleveland, OH 44114-1183. **Tel**—(216) 641-8580..**Pres & CEO**—A. C. Bersticker. **EVP-Fin**—H. R. Ortino. **Secy**—M. A. Cusick. **Investor Contact**—Patrick Cavanagh. **Dirs**—S. H. Austin, A. C. Bersticker, P. S. Brentlinger, G. R. Brown, W. F. Bush, W. E. Butler, P. B. Campbell, A. J. Freeman, J. C. Morley, K. O'Donnell, H. R. Ortino, A. Posnick, R. A. Sebastian, D. W. Sullivan. **Transfer Agent & Registrar**—National City Bank, Cleveland. **Incorporated** in Ohio in 1919. **Empl**-6,817. **S&P Analyst:** Justin McCann

STANDARD & POOR'S
STOCK REPORTS

Fifth Third Bancorp

NASDAQ Symbol **FITB**
In S&P MidCap 400

26-SEP-95 **Industry:** Banking

Summary: This regional bank holding company, with about $16.9 billion in assets, operates more than 370 offices in Ohio, Indiana, Kentucky and Naples, Fla.

S&P Opinion: Accumulate (★★★★) Recent Price • 58 52 Wk Range • 58¼-46½ Yield • 2.4% 12-Mo. P/E • 14.3

Quantitative Evaluations
Outlook (1 Lowest—5 Highest) **• 2⁻**
Fair Value **• 55½**
Risk **• Low**
Earn./Div. Rank **• A+**

Technical Eval. **• Bullish** since 5/95
Rel. Strength Rank (1 Lowest—99 Highest) **• 60**
Insider Activity **• Neutral**

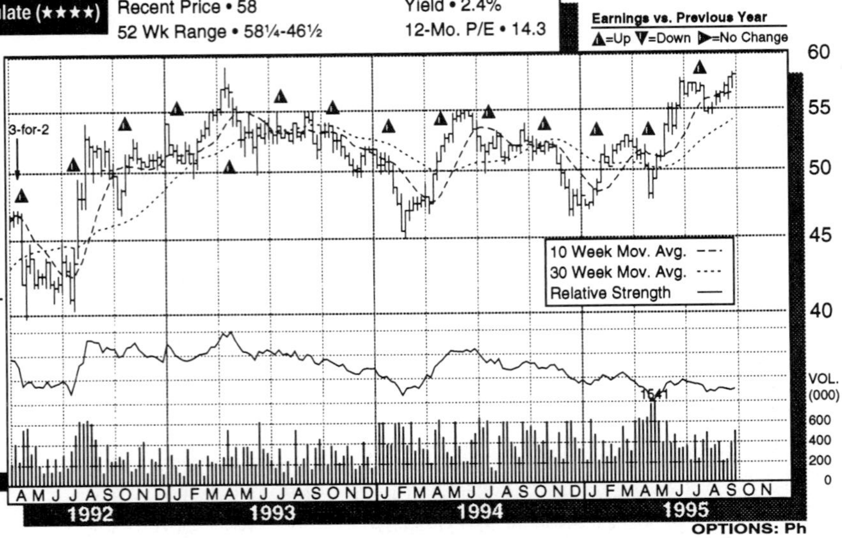

Overview - 26-SEP-95

Total loans and leases were up 7.1%, year to year, at June 30, 1995, driven by growth in the commercial loan portfolio. Excluding residential mortgage loans, consumer loans and leases were up 18% over 1994. The net interest margin narrowed 27 basis points, to 3.88%, due primarily to rising interest rates over the past year, which caused the cost of funds to rise faster than the yield on earning assets. FITB's credit quality remains at the top of the industry, with nonperforming assets as a percentage of loans, leases and other real estate owned at 0.26% as of June 30, 1995. FITB continues to distinguish itself with its diligent approach to limiting expense growth, lowering its efficiency ratio to 44.9%, compared to 47.4% a year earlier. We expect the company to continue to pursue its aggressive acquisition program.

Valuation - 26-SEP-95

The shares, which are up approximately 23% so far in 1995, have underperformed the overall market and those of other regional banks. Although the stock currently trades at a premium multiple of 12 times our earnings estimate for 1996, we continue to believe that the stock represents good value. With earnings expected to rise 12% in 1996, due to healthy loan growth, continued emphasis on limiting expense growth and potential acquisitions, the stock is expected to be an above-average performer over the next six to 12 months.

Key Stock Statistics

S&P EPS Est. 1995	4.30	Tang. Bk. Value/Share	23.55
P/E on S&P Est. 1995	13.5	Beta	0.93
S&P EPS Est. 1996	4.80	Shareholders	13,800
Dividend Rate/Share	1.40	Market cap. (B)	$ 3.8
Shs. outstg. (M)	65.2	Inst. holdings	33%
Avg. daily vol. (M)	0.067	Insider holdings	NA

Value of $10,000 invested 5 years ago: $ 26,723

Fiscal Year Ending Dec. 31

	1995	% Change	1994	% Change	1993	% Change
Revenues (Million $)						
1Q	339.5	24%	273.4	18%	231.4	8%
2Q	360.5	29%	280.2	18%	237.6	6%
3Q	—	—	290.4	20%	241.5	8%
4Q	—	—	334.2	37%	243.4	5%
Yr.	—	—	1,178	24%	953.9	7%
Income (Million $)						
1Q	66.12	21%	54.80	23%	44.64	23%
2Q	68.51	19%	57.38	20%	47.91	18%
3Q	—	—	62.84	22%	51.58	19%
4Q	—	—	64.65	24%	52.32	18%
Yr.	—	—	244.5	24%	196.4	20%
Earnings Per Share ($)						
1Q	1.02	15%	0.89	19%	0.75	23%
2Q	1.05	13%	0.93	16%	0.80	18%
3Q	E1.08	10%	0.98	14%	0.86	19%
4Q	E1.15	15%	1.00	15%	0.87	18%
Yr.	E4.30	13%	3.80	16%	3.28	19%

Next earnings report expected: mid October

Fifth Third Bancorp

Business Summary - 26-SEP-95

Fifth Third Bancorp is a regional bank holding company operating through affiliate banks in Ohio, Kentucky, Indiana and Naples, Fla. The company also owns subsidiaries engaged in payment services, discount brokerage, travel and leasing. At 1994 year-end, the company had 353 banking offices, including 81 grocery store locations.

Fifth Third has pursued an active acquisition policy. Acquisitions in 1992 included Pinnacle Bancorp Inc. of Middletown, Ohio ($215 million) and First Federal S&L of Lima, Ohio ($140 million). In 1993, the company made strategic deposit and branch purchases of Cincinnati's largest thrift, TriState Bancorp. In 1994, FITB acquired Cumberland Federal Bancorp. ($1.1 billion).

Gross loans and leases outstanding, which amounted to $10.29 billion at the end of 1994, versus $9.57 billion a year earlier, were divided:

	1994	1993
Commercial	29.5%	28.0%
Consumer installment	20.7%	19.7%
Consumer mortgage	22.8%	28.5%
Commercial mortgage	7.1%	7.3%
Other consumer	12.5%	9.7%
Other commercial	7.4%	6.8%

Underperforming assets at 1994 year-end amounted to $40.6 million (0.39% of loans, leases and other real estate owned), down from $50.3 million (0.52%) a year earlier. The reserve for loan losses at the end of 1994 was $155.9 million (1.52% of loans and leases outstanding), compared with $144.5 million (1.51%) a year earlier. Net chargeoffs in 1994 totaled $17.5 million (0.18% of average loans and leases), versus $27.1 million (0.31%) in 1993.

Sources of funds totaled $10.63 billion in 1994 and were divided: demand deposits 16%, interest checking 14%, savings 6%, money market 16%, other time 36%, CDs over $100,000 2% and foreign office 10%.

Important Developments

Aug. '95—Fifth Third Bancorp agreed to acquire Kentucky Enterprise Bancorp. The acquisition, which will be structured as an exchange of stock at a fixed exchange rate of 0.3823 of an FITB share for each share of Kentucky Enterprise common stock, is expected to be completed in early 1996. Based on the closing price of Fifth Third common on August 28, 1995, the transaction would have an aggregate value of $64.3 million. As of June 30, 1995, Kentucky Enterprise Bancorp had $280 million in assets and $227 million in deposits.

Capitalization

Long Term Debt: $169,000,000 (6/95), incl. conv. sub. notes of $144,000,000.

Per Share Data ($) (Year Ended Dec. 31)

	1994	1993	1992	1991	1990	1989
Tangible Bk. Val.	21.15	19.50	15.85	14.21	13.25	11.80
Earnings	3.80	3.28	2.75	2.33	2.05	1.86
Dividends	1.20	1.02	0.90	0.78	0.68	0.60
Payout Ratio	32%	31%	33%	33%	33%	32%
Prices - High	55	59	54	45½	24⅝	26½
- Low	45	49½	39¾	19⅝	15½	19¾
P/E Ratio - High	14	18	20	20	12	14
- Low	12	15	14	8	8	11

Income Statement Analysis (Million $)

	1994	%Chg	1993	%Chg	1992	%Chg	1991
Net Int. Inc.	517	19%	436	11%	394	19%	332
Tax Equiv. Adj.	24.6	21%	20.4	19%	17.2	-10%	19.1
Non Int. Inc.	256	13%	227	14%	199	18%	168
Loan Loss Prov.	35.8	-20%	44.5	-32%	65.3	17%	55.7
% Exp/Op Revs.	47%	—	48%	—	47%	—	48%
Pretax Inc.	365	24%	295	23%	240	21%	199
Eff. Tax Rate	33%	—	33%	—	32%	—	30%
Net Inc.	244	24%	196	20%	164	19%	138
% Net Int. Marg.	4.16%	—	4.51%	—	4.73%	—	4.58%

Balance Sheet & Other Fin. Data (Million $)

	1994	1993	1992	1991	1990	1989
Earning Assets:						
Money Mkt.	1,129	3.0	1.0	192	336	274
Inv. Securities	2,531	1,487	1,933	2,064	1,355	1,059
Com'l Loans	4,345	3,933	3,223	2,684	2,696	2,547
Other Loans	5,586	4,878	4,371	3,228	2,912	2,736
Total Assets	14,957	11,966	10,213	8,826	7,956	7,143
Demand Deposits	1,680	1,463	1,307	1,151	989	961
Time Deposits	8,951	7,165	6,225	5,536	5,396	4,822
LT Debt	179	283	254	13.0	14.0	13.0
Common Eqty.	1,399	1,198	1,005	879	783	699

Ratio Analysis

	1994	1993	1992	1991	1990	1989
% Ret. on Assets	1.8	1.8	1.7	1.7	1.6	1.6
% Ret. on Equity	18.6	18.2	17.3	16.6	16.2	16.5
% Loan Loss Resv.	1.5	1.5	1.5	1.6	1.5	1.5
% Loans/Deposits	95.3	100.5	99.2	86.8	86.1	89.3
% Equity to Assets	9.5	9.9	10.1	10.1	10.1	9.8

Dividend Data —Cash has been paid each year since 1952. A dividend reinvestment plan is available.

Amt. of Div. $	Date Decl.	Ex-Div. Date	Stock of Record	Payment Date
0.310	Sep. 20	Sep. 26	Sep. 30	Oct. 14 '94
0.310	Dec. 20	Dec. 23	Dec. 30	Jan. 13 '95
0.350	Mar. 21	Mar. 27	Mar. 31	Apr. 14 '95
0.350	Jun. 20	Jun. 28	Jun. 30	Jul. 14 '95
0.350	Sep. 20	Sep. 27	Sep. 29	Oct. 13 '95

Data as orig. reptd.; bef. results of disc opers. and/or spec. items. Per share data adj. for stk. divs. as of ex-div. date. E-Estimated. NA-Not Available. NM-Not Meaningful. NR-Not Ranked.

Office—38 Fountain Square Plaza, Cincinnati, OH 45263. **Tel**—(513) 579-5300. **Pres, CEO & COO**—G. A. Schaefer Jr. **Sr VP, CFO & Investor Contact**—P. Michael Brumm (513) 579-4216. **Sr VP & Secy**—M. K. Keating. **Treas**—N. E. Arnold. **Dirs**—J. F. Barrett, M. C. Boesel Jr., C. L. Buenger, N. W. Carson, G. V. Dirvin, T. B. Donnell, R. T. Farmer, J. D. Geary, I. W. Gorr, J. H. Head Jr., J. R. Herschede, W. G. Kagler, W. J. Keating, J. D. Kiggen, R. B. Morgan, M. H. Norris, B. H. Rowe, G. A. Schaefer Jr., J. J. Schiff Jr., D. J. Sullivan Jr., D. S. Taft. **Transfer Agent & Registrar**—Fifth Third Bank. **Incorporated** in Ohio in 1975. **Empl**-5,644. **S&P Analyst:** Brad Ohlmuller

STANDARD & POOR'S

STOCK REPORTS

Fingerhut Companies

NYSE Symbol **FHT**
In S&P MidCap 400

04-AUG-95 **Industry:** Retail Stores

Summary: A leading direct-mail marketer of consumer products, this company sells general merchandise through catalogs, television and other media.

Quantitative Evaluations
Outlook
(1 Lowest—5 Highest)
• **2**
Fair Value
• **14⅞**
Risk
• **Average**
Earn./Div. Rank
• **NR**

Technical Eval.
• **Bearish** since 9/94
Rel. Strength Rank
(1 Lowest—99 Highest)
• **84**
Insider Activity
• **Neutral**

Recent Price • 17¼
52 Wk Range • 29½-10⅞
Yield • 0.9%
12-Mo. P/E • 27.0

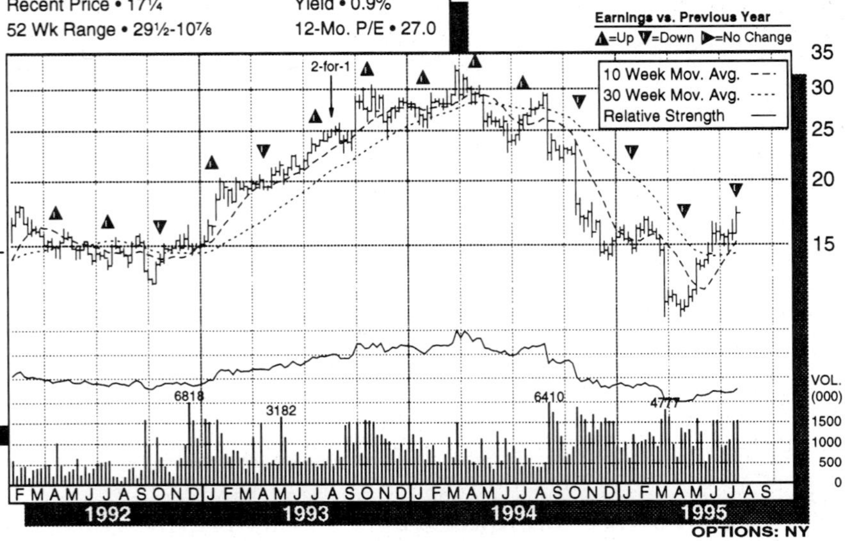

Business Profile - 04-AUG-95

In an effort to offset the negative effects of a postal rate hike, higher paper prices and rising interest rates, this multimedia direct marketing company initiated a $50 million cost reduction program in early 1995. It included several reengineering programs, the elimination of some 200 managerial positions and the closing or scaling back of less profitable product segments. In 1995, FHT expects to focus on improving operating efficiencies and growing its strong core business.

Operational Review - 04-AUG-95

Higher sales from the company's existing customer list and contributions from new customer acquisition programs fueled revenue growth in the first half of 1995. However, a higher average order size was partially offset by a lower response rate. Despite a slight improvement in gross margins, net earnings were restricted by the lower response rates, higher paper and postage prices, and solicitation and operating expenses associated with the startup of Direct Merchants Bank's MasterCard products.

Stock Performance - 28-JUL-95

In the past 30 trading days, FHT's shares have increased 10%, compared to a 4% rise in the S&P 500. Average trading volume for the past five days was 346,120 shares, compared with the 40-day moving average of 268,769 shares.

Key Stock Statistics

Dividend Rate/Share	0.16	Shareholders	700
Shs. outstg. (M)	45.8	Market cap. (B)	$0.756
Avg. daily vol. (M)	0.299	Inst. holdings	87%
Tang. Bk. Value/Share	9.81	Insider holdings	NA
Beta	1.47		

Value of $10,000 invested 5 years ago: NA

Fiscal Year Ending Dec. 31

	1995	% Change	1994	% Change	1993	% Change
Revenues (Million $)						
1Q	409.0	13%	362.1	-3%	371.8	20%
2Q	474.4	6%	446.0	6%	420.8	17%
3Q	—	—	429.5	13%	379.3	7%
4Q	—	—	696.8	10%	636.0	9%
Yr.	—	—	1,934	7%	1,808	13%
Income (Million $)						
1Q	6.18	-38%	9.97	28%	7.76	-19%
2Q	5.79	-64%	16.19	25%	12.98	15%
3Q	—	—	7.09	-48%	13.76	145%
4Q	—	—	12.67	-69%	40.83	15%
Yr.	—	—	45.93	-39%	75.33	22%
Earnings Per Share ($)						
1Q	0.13	-35%	0.20	29%	0.15	-16%
2Q	0.12	-63%	0.32	23%	0.26	21%
3Q	—	—	0.14	-48%	0.27	145%
4Q	—	—	0.26	-68%	0.81	18%
Yr.	—	—	0.91	-39%	1.50	26%

Next earnings report expected: mid October

Fingerhut Companies

Business Summary - 04-AUG-95

Fingerhut Companies, Inc. is a multimedia direct marketer of a broad range of consumer products and services using catalogs, television and other media to sell general merchandise to an active base of about seven million repeat customers. Merchandise includes a broad mix of quality brandname and private-label products, many of which are specially manufactured or packaged to appeal to Fingerhut's customers. Much of its merchandise is acquired through opportunistic purchases of product inventories.

The principal subsidiary, Fingerhut, markets general merchandise--including electronics (20% of the subsidiary's sales in 1994), housewares (17%), home textiles (18%), apparel (9%), jewelry (8%), furniture/home accessories (11%), leisure (8%), tools/automotive/lawn and garden products (6%) and financial service products and other (3%)--using catalogs and other direct-mail solicitations. In 1994, FHT mailed about 558 million catalogs and other promotions.

Figi's is a mail-order retailer of specialty foods (such as quality cheeses, smoked meats, candies and baked goods) and other gifts. Fingerhut had signed a letter of intent to sell Figi's, but in 1994's fourth quarter, the purchaser could not complete its financing.

USA Direct Inc. markets specially selected products through 30-minute direct respose television "infomercials." Its advertisements are distributed through cable networks and broadcast television stations.

Montgomery Ward Direct (MWD), a joint venture formed in 1991 and equally owned by FHT and Montgomery Ward & Co., produces specialty catalogs under the Montgomery Ward name. FHT provides order processing, shipping and computer facilities.

FHT derives additional revenues from manufacturing plastic products, wholesaling excess merchandise and list rental and package inserts.

Since 1993, the company has sold certain of its subsidiaries that did not fit into its long-term strategic direction, including COMB, which used catalogs and membership mailings to sell general merchandise acquired primarily through opportunistic purchases of product inventories, and FDC, Inc. a subsidiary of Figi's Inc. In November 1994, the company canceled the launch of S The Shopping Network, its proposed 24-hour cable television shopping channel. A related aftertax charge of $19.4 million was taken in 1994's fourth quarter.

Important Developments

Jun. '95—In order to finance the growth of its credit card business in a cost-effective manner, FHT formed "Fingerhut Financial Services Master Trust." The trust will issue series of certificates backed by receivables arising from MasterCard accounts owned by Direct Merchants Credit Card Bank, a wholly owned susidiary of FHT.

Capitalization

Long Term Debt: $246,460,000 (6/95).

Per Share Data ($) (Year Ended Dec. 31)

	1994	1993	1992	1991	1990	1989
Tangible Bk. Val.	9.74	9.07	7.35	6.68	5.43	4.66
Cash Flow	1.66	2.10	1.52	1.40	1.27	1.06
Earnings	0.91	1.50	1.19	1.07	0.98	0.79
Dividends	0.16	0.16	0.16	0.16	0.08	Nil
Payout Ratio	18%	11%	12%	15%	8%	Nil
Prices - High	33¼	30⅝	18	15⅝	13¼	NA
- Low	14	15	12⅝	7¼	6⅛	NA
P/E Ratio - High	37	20	15	15	13	NA
- Low	15	10	11	7	6	NA

Income Statement Analysis (Million $)

	1994	%Chg	1993	%Chg	1992	%Chg	1991
Revs.	1,934	7%	1,808	13%	1,606	12%	1,428
Oper. Inc.	163	-7%	176	22%	144	18%	122
Depr.	37.7	27%	29.7	77%	16.8	2%	16.5
Int. Exp.	25.7	-26%	34.9	4%	33.5	38%	24.3
Pretax Inc.	71.0	-37%	112	19%	93.9	15%	81.4
Eff. Tax Rate	35%	—	33%	—	34%	—	34%
Net Inc.	45.9	-39%	75.3	22%	61.8	15%	53.6

Balance Sheet & Other Fin. Data (Million $)

	1994	1993	1992	1991	1990	1989
Cash	85.4	66.6	86.7	9.2	4.3	1.8
Curr. Assets	792	682	682	591	489	351
Total Assets	1,098	972	926	802	651	498
Curr. Liab.	324	233	269	293	318	178
LT Debt	247	247	247	119	15.0	22.0
Common Eqty.	501	472	400	384	319	296
Total Cap.	769	735	653	505	334	319
Cap. Exp.	69.6	51.8	50.9	71.5	21.1	22.5
Cash Flow	84.0	105	78.6	70.0	62.0	51.3

Ratio Analysis

	1994	1993	1992	1991	1990	1989
Curr. Ratio	2.4	2.9	2.5	2.0	1.5	2.0
% LT Debt of Cap.	32.0	33.6	37.9	23.6	4.5	6.8
% Net Inc.of Revs.	2.4	4.2	3.8	3.7	3.8	3.6
% Ret. on Assets	4.5	7.9	7.3	7.3	8.5	NA
% Ret. on Equity	9.5	17.2	16.1	15.0	15.9	NA

Dividend Data (Dividends were initiated in 1990. A two-for-one stock split was effected in August 1993.)

Amt. of Div. $	Date Decl.	Ex-Div. Date	Stock of Record	Payment Date
0.040	Jul. 21	Jul. 29	Aug. 04	Aug. 25 '94
0.040	Oct. 20	Oct. 28	Nov. 03	Nov. 24 '94
0.040	Jan. 24	Feb. 01	Feb. 07	Feb. 23 '95
0.040	Apr. 20	Apr. 28	May. 04	May. 25 '95
0.040	Jul. 20	Aug. 01	Aug. 03	Aug. 24 '95

Data as orig. reptd.; bef. results of disc. opers. and/or spec. items. Per share data adj. for stk. divs. as of ex-div. date. E-Estimated. NA-Not Available. NM-Not Meaningful. NR-Not Ranked.

Office—4400 Baker Rd., Minnetonka, MN 55343. **Tel**—(612) 932-3100. **Chrmn & Pres**—T. Deikel. **Vice Chrmn**—R. K. Kaul. **Sr VP & CFO**—P. G. Michielutti. **Sr VP & Secy**—J. K. Ellingboe. **VP & Treas**—R. W. Oberrender. **Investor Contact**—M. N. Albrecht. **Dirs**—W. R. Anderson, T. Deikel, E. Gage, S. S. Hubbard, R. K. Kaul, R. M. Kovacevich, D. C. Mecum. **Transfer Agent & Registrar**—Norwest Bank Minnesota, Minneapolis. **Incorporated** in Minnesota in 1978; predecessor firm formed in 1948. **Empl**-9,000. **S&P Analyst:** Maureen C. Carini

STANDARD & POOR'S

STOCK REPORTS

First of America Bank

NYSE Symbol **FOA**

In S&P MidCap 400

17-OCT-95 **Industry:** Banking

Summary: The affiliate banks of this growing multibank holding company, headquartered in Kalamazoo, Mich., operate 630 offices in Michigan, Indiana, Illinois and Florida.

S&P Opinion: Accumulate (★★★★)

Recent Price • 45¼ | Yield • 3.9%
52 Wk Range • 45¾-29½ | 12-Mo. P/E • 12.7

Quantitative Evaluations

Outlook (1 Lowest—5 Highest)
• **2⁻**

Fair Value
• **43¾**

Risk
• **Low**

Earn./Div. Rank
• **A-**

Technical Eval.
• **Bearish** since 1/93

Rel. Strength Rank (1 Lowest—99 Highest)
• **82**

Insider Activity
• **Favorable**

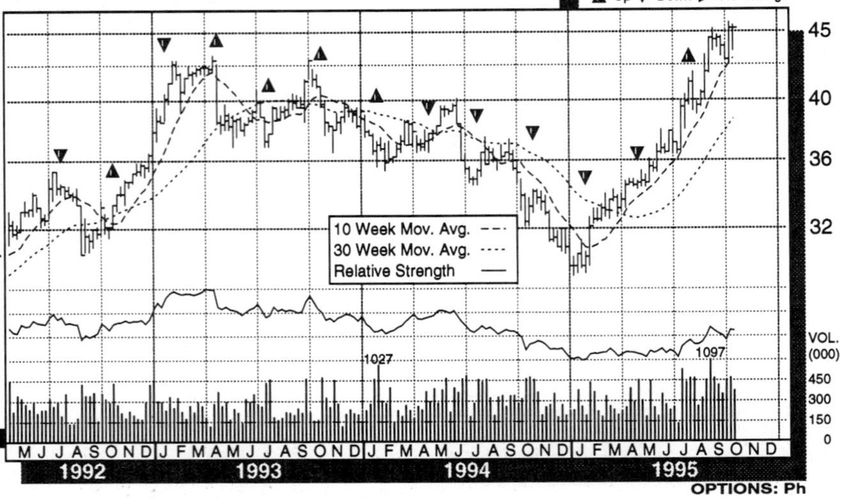

OPTIONS: Ph

Overview - 17-OCT-95

Earnings should pick up in 1996, as the bank benefits from restructuring initiatives. FOA reached its goal of a 60% efficiency ratio in the September 1995 quarter. The bank decreased staff, and is consolidating its bank affiliates and certain backroom functions into one bank in each state of operation. On the revenue side, the net interest margin has stabilized at about 40 basis points below last year's level, earning assets are growing through acquisitions, and noninterest income has been steadily rising. Long-term prospects remain favorable, given the bank's cost controls, excellent credit quality, and acquisitions that will continue to expand the asset base.

Valuation - 17-OCT-95

Investors have shown renewed interest in regional bank stocks in 1995, primarily due to increased merger activity in the banking sector along with a more stable interest rate outlook. Results were hampered in 1994 and the first nine months of 1995 on a narrowing net interest margin, acquisition costs and severance charges. The outlook should brighten into 1996, with modest asset growth and reduced sensitivity to interest rate volatility. Also, FOA is starting to benefit from greater fee income, and improved efficiency from streamlining efforts. Sporting a 3.9% dividend yield, and trading at 11X our 1996 EPS estimate, the shares are recommended for conservative growth investors.

Key Stock Statistics

S&P EPS Est. 1995	3.80	Tang. Bk. Value/Share	26.13
P/E on S&P Est. 1995	11.9	Beta	0.73
S&P EPS Est. 1996	4.20	Shareholders	28,400
Dividend Rate/Share	1.76	Market cap. (B)	$ 2.9
Shs. outstg. (M)	63.2	Inst. holdings	36%
Avg. daily vol. (M)	0.090	Insider holdings	NA

Value of $10,000 invested 5 years ago: $ 24,805

Fiscal Year Ending Dec. 31

	1995	% Change	1994	% Change	1993	% Change
Revenues (Million $)						
1Q	526.0	20%	439.0	-2%	448.9	30%
2Q	544.1	19%	457.5	1%	451.7	-2%
3Q	534.2	9%	488.2	8%	450.4	13%
4Q	—	—	500.5	11%	452.2	-2%
Yr.	—	—	1,885	5%	1,803	-3%
Income (Million $)						
1Q	47.39	-19%	58.30	NM	58.60	22%
2Q	56.59	6%	53.20	-11%	59.62	110%
3Q	66.70	18%	56.41	-11%	63.37	10%
4Q	—	—	52.57	-20%	65.79	81%
Yr.	—	—	220.5	-11%	247.4	46%
Earnings Per Share ($)						
1Q	0.75	-23%	0.98	-1%	0.99	21%
2Q	0.89	1%	0.88	-13%	1.01	124%
3Q	1.05	9%	0.96	-10%	1.07	8%
4Q	E1.11	28%	0.87	-23%	1.13	85%
Yr.	E3.80	3%	3.69	-12%	4.20	47%

Next earnings report expected: mid January

First of America Bank

Business Summary - 13-OCT-95

First of America Bank Corp. is a multibank holding company headquartered in Kalamazoo, Mich., whose affiliate banks operate 630 offices in Michigan, Indiana, Illinois and Florida. Nonbanking subsidiaries provide mortgage, trust, data processing, pension consulting, revolving credit, securities brokerage and investment advisory services.

Total loans at December 31, 1994, amounted to $16.83 billion, up from $14.39 billion a year earlier, and were divided:

	1994	1993
Real estate-mortgage	31%	48%
Consumer	35%	35%
Commercial, financial & agricultural	14%	15%
Real estate-construction	20%	2%

In 1994, loans outstanding accounted for 73% of average earning assets, investment securities for 25%, and other for 2%. Average sources of funds in 1994 were time deposits 39%, money market and checking accounts 18%, savings and NOW accounts 15%, demand deposits 12%, common shareholders' equity 7%, borrowings 8%, and other liabilities 1%.

The allowance for loan losses at 1994 year end was $228.1 million ($188.7 million a year earlier), or 1.36% (1.31%) of loans outstanding. Net chargeoffs in 1994 were $58.5 million ($72.9 million), or 0.39% (0.53%) of average loans outstanding. Nonperfoming assets at 1994 year end totaled $140.3 million (0.83% of loans outstanding), against $182.7 million (1.27%) a year earlier.

On a tax-equivalent basis, the average yield on interest-earning assets in 1994 was 7.75% (8.06% in 1993), while the average rate paid on interest-bearing liabilities was 3.65 (3.70%), for a net spread of 4.10% (4.36%).

Important Developments

Oct. '95—FOA reported that its internal restructuring, begun in August 1994, has progressed as expected, and that no charges related to the streamlining process were incurred in the third quarter.

Sep. '95—FOA said that a proposed one-time Savings Association Insurance Fund (SAIF) assessment of up to $0.85 per $100 of deposits would result in a pretax expense of about $38 million ($0.37 a share).

Jan. '95—FOA acquired F&C Bancshares, Inc., a Florida-based savings and loan holding company (assets of $400 million), in a stock transaction valued at about $65 million. Also in January, FOA acquired New England Trust Co. of Providence, R.I., which manages more than $600 million in assets. Earlier, in April 1994, FOA acquired $446 million of deposits of Goldome Federal Savings Bank located in Florida.

Capitalization

Long Term Debt: $490,403,000 (9/95).

Per Share Data ($) (Year Ended Dec. 31)

	1994	1993	1992	1991	1990	1989
Tangible Bk. Val.	21.10	23.27	19.94	20.84	18.75	17.72
Earnings	3.69	4.20	2.86	3.32	3.26	2.94
Dividends	1.62	1.55	1.34	1.24	1.15	1.08
Payout Ratio	44%	36%	47%	37%	35%	37%
Prices - High	40⅛	43¼	37⅞	31¾	26	28
- Low	29¾	36½	29	18¼	15⅝	19⅛
P/E Ratio - High	11	10	13	10	8	10
- Low	8	9	10	5	5	7

Income Statement Analysis (Million $)

	1994	%Chg	1993	%Chg	1992	%Chg	1991
Net Int. Inc.	939	4%	902	3%	875	44%	606
Tax Equiv. Adj.	17.0	-26%	23.1	-8%	25.1	-3%	25.9
Non Int. Inc.	279	1%	275	12%	246	45%	170
Loan Loss Prov.	86.6	2%	84.7	7%	78.8	73%	45.6
% Exp/Op Revs.	66%	—	64%	—	70%	—	68%
Pretax Inc.	323	-7%	346	33%	261	39%	188
Eff. Tax Rate	32%	—	29%	—	35%	—	28%
Net Inc.	221	-11%	247	46%	169	25%	135
% Net Int. Marg.	4.58%	—	4.86%	—	4.98%	—	4.92%

Balance Sheet & Other Fin. Data (Million $)

	1994	1993	1992	1991	1990	1989
Earning Assets:						
Money Mkt.	55.3	74.9	175	170	42.0	290
Inv. Securities	5,701	5,118	4,627	3,567	3,045	2,857
Com'l Loans	2,345	2,149	2,171	2,078	2,220	2,254
Other Loans	14,490	12,245	11,585	9,394	7,281	6,092
Total Assets	24,569	21,230	20,147	16,755	14,039	12,793
Demand Deposits	2,810	2,683	2,572	2,039	1,927	1,993
Time Deposits	17,390	15,561	15,463	12,982	10,614	9,373
LT Debt	467	254	254	221	137	137
Common Eqty.	1,579	1,523	1,261	908	828	754

Ratio Analysis

	1994	1993	1992	1991	1990	1989
% Ret. on Assets	1.0	1.2	0.9	1.0	1.0	1.0
% Ret. on Equity	14.4	17.8	15.2	17.1	19.2	19.7
% Loan Loss Resv.	1.4	1.3	1.3	1.3	1.2	1.3
% Loans/Deposits	83.3	78.9	76.3	76.4	75.8	73.4
% Equity to Assets	6.8	6.7	5.3	5.0	4.6	4.3

Dividend Data —Dividends have been paid since 1864. A dividend reinvestment plan is available. A "poison pill" stock purchase rights plan was adopted in 1990.

Amt. of Div. $	Date Decl.	Ex-Div. Date	Stock of Record	Payment Date
0.420	Aug. 17	Oct. 03	Oct. 07	Oct. 28 '94
0.420	Nov. 16	Jan. 03	Jan. 09	Jan. 30 '95
0.420	Feb. 17	Apr. 03	Apr. 07	Apr. 28 '95
0.420	May. 17	Jul. 05	Jul. 07	Jul. 28 '95
0.440	Aug. 16	Oct. 04	Oct. 09	Oct. 30 '95

Data as orig. reptd.; bef. results of disc opers. and/or spec. items. Per share data adj. for stk. divs. as of ex-div. date. E-Estimated. NA-Not Available. NM-Not Meaningful. NR-Not Ranked.

Office—211 S. Rose St., Kalamazoo, MI 49007-5264. **Tel**—(616) 376-9000. **Chrmn & CEO**—D. R. Smith. **Pres & COO**—R. F. Chormann. **EVP & Secy**—D. B. Wirt. **EVP & CFO**—T. W. Lambert. **Investor Contact**—Jennifer D. Cox (616-376-7115). **Dirs**—J. E. Barfield, J. W. Brown, R. F. Chormann, J. J. Fitzsimmons, J. N. Goldberg, C. L. Greenwalt, R. L. Hetzler, D. A. Johnson, M. M. Mertz, F. K. Neumann, G. C. Smith, J. S. Ware, J. W. Wogsland, W. J. Wolpin, J. L. Zabriskie. **Transfer Agent**—Stock Transfer and Trust Co., South St. Paul, Minn. **Incorporated** in Michigan in 1971. **Empl**-13,490. **S&P Analyst:** Robert Schpoont

STANDARD & POOR'S
STOCK REPORTS

First Brands

NYSE Symbol **FBR**
In S&P MidCap 400

16-AUG-95 **Industry:** Housewares

Summary: This company makes branded and private-label consumer products for the home and automotive markets.

Quantitative Evaluations

Recent Price • 42
52 Wk Range • 43⅝-31½
Yield • 0.9%
12-Mo. P/E • 16.1

Outlook
(1 Lowest—5 Highest)
• **5+**
Fair Value
• **52½**
Risk
• **Low**
Earn./Div. Rank
• **NR**

Technical Eval.
• **Bearish** since 1/95
Rel. Strength Rank
(1 Lowest—99 Highest)
• **60**
Insider Activity
• **Unfavorable**

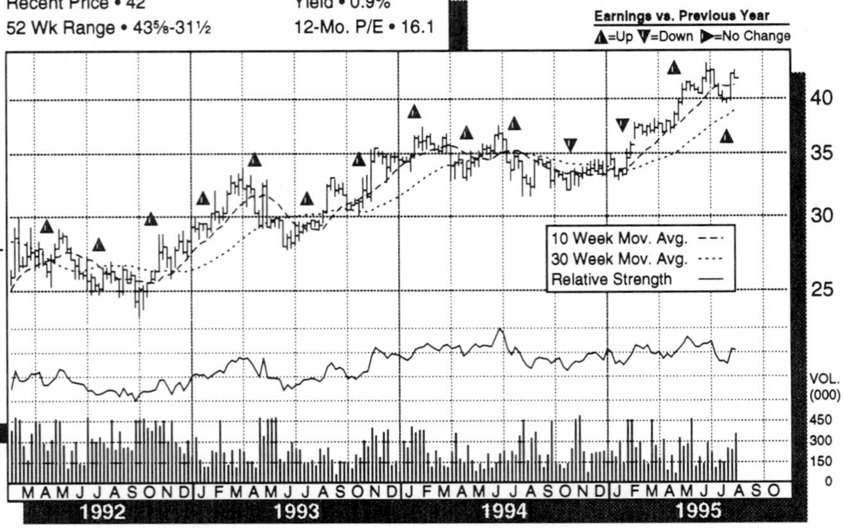

Business Profile - 16-AUG-95

FBR's well-known brand names include Glad plastic bags, STP and Simoniz automotive products, and Jonny Cat, Ever Clean, and Scoop Away kitty litters. FBR sold its Prestone Anti-Freeze business in August 1994. FBR plans extensive promotion of its new Glad Quick-Tie trash bag, which eliminates the need for twist ties. Additional production capacity for Glad-Lock bags is expected to come on line in the fall. FBR has repurchased 1.3 million shares under a 1.5 million-share authorization.

Operational Review - 16-AUG-95

Pro forma to exclude the Prestone business (sold in August 1994) and related items, sales for fiscal 1995 climbed 12%. Sales increased for all major product lines, and were given an added lift by the July 1994 acquisition of Jonny Cat. Operating income rose only 8.7%, as margins declined. Lower depreciation expense, a decline in FBR's tax rate and a reduction in average shares outstanding allowed EPS before extraordinary items to increase 18%.

Stock Performance - 11-AUG-95

In the past 30 trading days, FBR's shares have declined 2%, compared to a 2% rise in the S&P 500. Average trading volume for the past five days was 70,280 shares, compared with the 40-day moving average of 44,374 shares.

Key Stock Statistics

Dividend Rate/Share	0.40	Shareholders	600
Shs. outstg. (M)	20.9	Market cap. (B)	$0.892
Avg. daily vol. (M)	0.052	Inst. holdings	90%
Tang. Bk. Value/Share	5.82	Insider holdings	NA
Beta	1.29		

Value of $10,000 invested 5 years ago: $ 23,079

Fiscal Year Ending Jun. 30

	1995	% Change	1994	% Change	1993	% Change
Revenues (Million $)						
1Q	264.2	-6%	279.8	4%	269.0	3%
2Q	233.0	-14%	270.4	NM	268.0	10%
3Q	247.9	1%	244.4	11%	219.5	NM
4Q	291.4	NM	291.8	2%	285.4	8%
Yr.	1,005	-8%	1,086	4%	1,042	5%
Income (Million $)						
1Q	15.07	-8%	16.37	9%	15.00	11%
2Q	11.84	-28%	16.39	10%	14.89	31%
3Q	14.25	25%	11.39	28%	8.93	44%
4Q	15.49	-3%	16.02	15%	13.91	30%
Yr.	56.10	-7%	60.17	14%	52.73	27%
Earnings Per Share ($)						
1Q	0.68	-8%	0.74	12%	0.66	6%
2Q	0.55	-26%	0.74	9%	0.68	31%
3Q	0.67	31%	0.51	24%	0.41	46%
4Q	0.73	1%	0.72	14%	0.63	29%
Yr.	2.61	-4%	2.71	12%	2.41	26%

Next earnings report expected: early November

First Brands

Business Summary - 16-AUG-95

First Brands Corporation makes and sells branded and private-label consumer products for the home and automotive markets. Its businesses belonged to Union Carbide Corp. prior to their acquisition in July 1986. In August 1994, FBR sold its Prestone antifreeze business. Sales by class of products in recent fiscal years were:

	1995	1994	1993
Plastic wrap, bags & related products	62%	57%	58%
Antifreeze/coolant	3%	17%	16%
Automotive products	23%	19%	21%
Pet products	12%	7%	5%

Home products include the most complete line of branded plastic wrap, bags and drinking straws in the U.S. and Canada, sold under the Glad (and related Glad-lock) brand name. Plastic bags are also sold in Canada under the Surtec brand name. Sales to food outlets account for 70% of domestic sales of plastic wrap and bags and related products. Fabricante de Productos Plasticos SA de CV (acquired December 1993), distributes consumer products (including FBR's automotive products) in Mexico to mass marketers.

FBR's automotive products business manufactures branded oil and fuel additives, vinyl protectants, automotive specialty performance products and cleaners, polishes and waxes. Automotive products include specialty performance products sold under the STP brand name and cleaners, polishes and waxes sold under the Simoniz brand name.

Through Himolene, Inc. (acquired 1988), the company is the leading U.S. producer of high-molecular-weight, high-density polyethylene plastic trash can liners for institutional and industrial markets.

A&M Pet Products, Inc. manufactures Scoop Away and Ever Clean, the leading brands of cat litter in the U.S. In July 1994, A&M acquired the Jonny Cat brand of cat care products for about $45 million.

The company's products are sold directly to retailers and wholesalers. The largest 25 customers account for 48% of total sales, and sales to its largest customer (Wal-Mart Stores and Sams Wholesale Club) are 14% of total sales. In fiscal 1994, international sales were 9.2% of total sales.

Important Developments

Aug. '95—FBR said it was planning extensive promotion of its new Glad Quick-Tie trash bag, which has built-in flaps which close the bags securely and eliminate the need for twist-ties. The company also plans to introduce new automotive products, and add production capacity for Glad-Lock bags, both in the fall of 1995.

Capitalization

Long Term Debt: $184,554,000 (3/95).

Per Share Data ($)

(Year Ended Jun. 30)

	1995	1994	1993	1992	1991	1990
Tangible Bk. Val.	NA	5.82	13.99	11.88	10.85	8.74
Cash Flow	NA	4.59	3.38	3.18	3.82	2.62
Earnings	2.61	2.71	2.41	1.91	2.21	2.40
Dividends	0.46	0.30	0.19	0.04	0.04	0.02
Payout Ratio	18%	11%	8%	2%	2%	1%
Prices - High	43⅝	37½	35½	29⅞	35	29⅜
- Low	32¾	31½	27⅝	23½	19⅜	14½
P/E Ratio - High	17	14	15	16	16	12
- Low	13	12	11	12	9	6

Income Statement Analysis (Million $)

	1994	%Chg	1993	%Chg	1992	%Chg	1991
Revs.	1,086	4%	1,042	5%	989	-8%	1,073
Oper. Inc.	172	25%	138	-5%	145	-12%	164
Depr.	41.7	96%	21.3	-24%	27.9	-20%	34.9
Int. Exp.	23.5	-4%	24.5	-37%	38.7	-18%	47.0
Pretax Inc.	104	17%	89.0	17%	76.0	-10%	84.0
Eff. Tax Rate	42%	—	41%	—	46%	—	43%
Net Inc.	60.2	14%	52.7	26%	41.7	-13%	48.0

Balance Sheet & Other Fin. Data (Million $)

	1994	1993	1992	1991	1990	1989
Cash	13.4	11.7	12.5	13.4	15.3	2.5
Curr. Assets	291	280	316	391	401	395
Total Assets	814	807	836	816	836	830
Curr. Liab.	238	244	244	213	241	239
LT Debt	153	226	282	318	371	432
Common Eqty.	361	305	258	235	189	44.0
Total Cap.	558	541	567	573	566	554
Cap. Exp.	40.0	42.0	97.0	48.0	40.0	39.0
Cash Flow	102	74.0	69.6	82.9	55.0	67.2

Ratio Analysis

	1994	1993	1992	1991	1990	1989
Curr. Ratio	1.2	1.1	1.3	1.8	1.7	1.7
% LT Debt of Cap.	27.5	41.8	49.8	55.5	65.5	78.0
% Net Inc.of Revs.	5.5	5.1	4.2	4.5	4.6	4.7
% Ret. on Assets	7.4	6.4	5.0	5.8	1.2	6.7
% Ret. on Equity	18.0	18.7	16.9	22.6	16.0	356.7

Dividend Data —Dividends were initiated in 1990.

Amt. of Div. $	Date Decl.	Ex-Div. Date	Stock of Record	Payment Date
0.080	Aug. 09	Sep. 23	Sep. 29	Oct. 20 '94
0.100	Oct. 28	Dec. 23	Dec. 30	Jan. 20 '95
0.100	Mar. 17	Mar. 24	Mar. 30	Apr. 20 '95
0.100	May. 23	Jun. 27	Jun. 29	Jul. 20 '95
0.100	Aug. 09	Sep. 27	Sep. 29	Oct. 20 '95

Data as orig. reptd.; bef. results of disc. opers. and/or spec. items. Per share data adj. for stk. divs. as of ex-div. date. Full-yr. FY 1995 Revs., Inc. and EPS figs. are pro forma. Prior to FY 1994, bk. val. incl. intangibles. E-Estimated. NA-Not Available. NM-Not Meaningful. NR-Not Ranked.

Office—83 Wooster Heights Rd., Danbury, CT 06813-1911. **Tel**—(203) 731-2300. **Chrmn**—A. E. Dudley. **Pres & CEO**—W. V. Stephenson. **SVP-CFO, Treas & Investor Contact**—Donald A. DeSantis (203) 731-2306. **VP & Secy**—D. Raymond. **Dirs**—A. E. Dudley, A. C. Egler, G. E. Gardner, J. R. Maher, J. R. McManus, D. C. Minton, D. Newman, E. R. Shames, W. V. Stephenson, R. G. Tobin. **Transfer Agent & Registrar**—Contintental Stock Transfer & Trust Co., NYC. **Incorporated** in Delaware in 1986. **Empl**-3,000. **S&P Analyst:** Stephen Madonna, CFA

STANDARD & POOR'S

First Financial Management

STOCK REPORTS

NYSE Symbol **FFM**
In S&P MidCap 400

22-SEP-95 **Industry:** Data Processing

Summary: This leading provider of information services offers has agreed to merger with NYSE-listed First Data Crop.

S&P Opinion: Hold (★★★)

Recent Price • 94⅞
52 Wk Range • 95¾-53¾
Yield • 0.1%
12-Mo. P/E • 34.0

Quantitative Evaluations

Outlook (1 Lowest—5 Highest) • **1+**

Fair Value • **77¼**

Risk • **Low**

Earn./Div. Rank • **B+**

Technical Eval. • **Bullish** since 5/92

Rel. Strength Rank (1 Lowest—99 Highest) • **78**

Insider Activity • **NA**

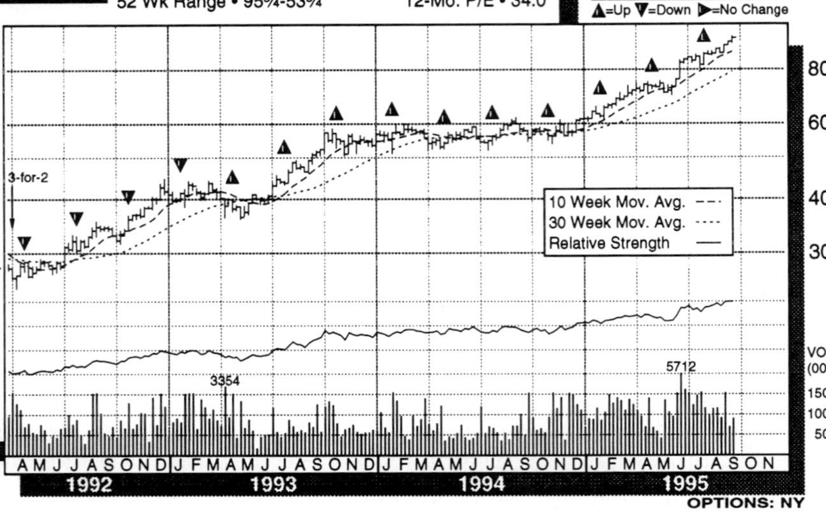

Overview - 22-SEP-95

The company's planned merger with First Data Corp. is expected to completed by the end of October. Earnings growth in 1995 (for FFM alone) is expected to exceed 20%, fueled by double digit revenue gains at merchant services, data imaging and health care services. FFM continues to penetrate regional markets for merchant credit card authorization, processing and settlement services. The consolidation of the health care services group will boost margins. Including of Western Union Financial Services (which may have to be divested following the merger), nine acquisitions (with aggregate annual revenues of $700 million) were completed in 1994.

Valuation - 22-SEP-95

The shares were downgraded to hold following the announcement of FFM's planned merger with First Data Corp. Regulatory approval has been received, and following meetings of shareholders of each company, the merger is expected to be completed by the end of October. FFM's fundamentals remain strong: revenues in the first half of 1995 soared 50%, year to year, and the company was able to maintain operating margins despite many recent acquisitions. Moreover, revenues should benefit from expanding market presence.

Key Stock Statistics

S&P EPS Est. 1995	3.05	Tang. Bk. Value/Share	NM
P/E on S&P Est. 1995	31.1	Beta	0.94
S&P EPS Est. 1996	3.70	Shareholders	1,800
Dividend Rate/Share	0.10	Market cap. (B)	$ 6.1
Shs. outstg. (M)	63.9	Inst. holdings	81%
Avg. daily vol. (M)	0.209	Insider holdings	NA

Value of $10,000 invested 5 years ago: $ 44,704

Fiscal Year Ending Dec. 31

	1995	% Change	1994	% Change	1993	% Change
Revenues (Million $)						
1Q	684.3	50%	455.1	32%	343.5	26%
2Q	782.0	53%	511.4	32%	387.4	18%
3Q	—	—	536.5	28%	418.0	14%
4Q	—	—	704.5	39%	506.9	16%
Yr.	—	—	2,208	32%	1,670	19%
Income (Million $)						
1Q	35.40	20%	29.50	43%	20.62	54%
2Q	44.50	30%	34.20	27%	26.84	49%
3Q	—	—	40.60	24%	32.68	56%
4Q	—	—	55.90	23%	45.60	NM
Yr.	—	—	160.2	26%	127.6	NM
Earnings Per Share ($)						
1Q	0.56	19%	0.47	34%	0.35	46%
2Q	0.69	25%	0.55	22%	0.45	45%
3Q	E0.79	22%	0.65	20%	0.54	50%
4Q	E1.01	13%	0.89	19%	0.75	NM
Yr.	E3.05	19%	2.56	22%	2.10	NM

Next earnings report expected: mid October

First Financial Management

Business Summary - 22-SEP-95

First Financial Management provides information services to a diverse customer base. It offers services to capture, manipulate and distribute data for many types of financial transactions. Revenues by business segment in recent years were:

	1994	1993
Merchant Services	71%	66%
Health Care Services	18%	21%
Data Imaging Services	11%	13%

Merchant services consist of NaBANCO, the largest U.S. merchant credit card processor; TeleCheck, a leader in check guarantee and verification services; Nationwide Credit, a leading provider of debt collection and accounts receivable management services; and Internatiional Banking Technologies, a leader in developing in-store branch banking programs for supermarkets. Western Union, the world's largest nonbank immediate money transfer business, was acquired in December 1994, for $893 million in cash, plus assumption of an underfunded pension fund (valued at about $300 million).

Health care services are provided by FIRST HEALTH Services, FIRST HEALTH Strategies and GENEX services. FIRST HEALTH provides Medicaid claims processing, pharmaceutical claims processing, third party administration, psychiatric and chemical dependency managed care, utilization review, provider networks, and data analysis. In 1994, over 50,000 health care claims were processed daily by systems operated or developed and supported by FIRST HEALTH. GENEX Services, Inc. is a leading provider of workers' compensation programs.

First Image Management Co. offers a wide array of total data imaging services including computer output micrographics, database management, customized printing and mailing of reports and statements, and other documents.

Important Developments

Sep. '95—The company said it had received regulatory clearance for a merger with NYSE-listed First Data Corp. (FDC). FFM shareholders would receive 1.5859 FDC common shares (recent price about $61) for every FFM common share. The transaction, subject to approval by shareholders of each company, is expected to be completed in late October.

Sep. '95—FFM said that, subject to approval by shareholders of Employee Benefits, Inc. (EBP), a provider of integrated health care services, it would acquire EBP for a total of about $173 million of common stock.

Capitalization

Long Term Debt: $202,500,000 (6/95).

Per Share Data ($)

(Year Ended Dec. 31)

	1994	1993	1992	1991	1990	1989
Tangible Bk. Val.	-5.05	10.03	8.50	8.10	1.98	1.94
Cash Flow	4.10	3.35	1.70	3.50	2.74	2.35
Earnings	2.56	2.10	0.27	1.92	1.79	1.53
Dividends	0.10	0.10	0.10	0.07	0.07	0.07
Payout Ratio	4%	5%	37%	3%	4%	4%
Prices - High	63½	58½	44⅝	31⅞	22½	26
- Low	51⅛	36	24¾	13½	9⅜	15½
P/E Ratio - High	25	28	NM	17	13	17
- Low	20	17	NM	7	5	10

Income Statement Analysis (Million $)

	1994	%Chg	1993	%Chg	1992	%Chg	1991
Revs.	2,204	33%	1,660	20%	1,388	-8%	1,502
Oper. Inc.	362	28%	282	30%	217	-37%	345
Depr.	97.7	29%	75.9	-8%	82.4	12%	73.6
Int. Exp.	NA	—	NA	—	9.0	-93%	128
Pretax Inc.	268	24%	216	NM	62.0	-58%	149
Eff. Tax Rate	40%	—	41%	—	75%	—	40%
Net Inc.	160	25%	128	NM	15.8	-82%	89.0

Balance Sheet & Other Fin. Data (Million $)

	1994	1993	1992	1991	1990	1989
Cash	326	186	16.0	386	417	526
Curr. Assets	903	597	539	NA	NA	NA
Total Assets	3,136	1,626	1,546	5,497	5,479	4,941
Curr. Liab.	694	295	377	NA	NA	NA
LT Debt	500	8.0	8.0	934	823	1,074
Common Eqty.	1,430	1,248	1,118	993	601	501
Total Cap.	1,930	1,320	1,166	1,927	1,424	1,574
Cap. Exp.	27.3	35.4	32.3	31.3	28.3	5.9
Cash Flow	258	204	98.0	163	112	87.3

Ratio Analysis

	1994	1993	1992	1991	1990	1989
Curr. Ratio	1.3	2.0	1.4	NA	NA	NA
% LT Debt of Cap.	25.9	0.6	0.7	48.5	57.8	68.2
% Net Inc.of Revs.	7.3	7.7	1.1	5.9	5.8	6.6
% Ret. on Assets	6.7	8.0	0.4	1.4	1.4	1.9
% Ret. on Equity	11.8	10.7	1.5	9.9	12.9	12.5

Dividend Data —Semiannual cash dividends were initiated in mid-1989. Payments in the past 12 months were:

Amt. of Div. $	Date Decl.	Ex-Div. Date	Stock of Record	Payment Date
0.050	Oct. 27	Nov. 25	Dec. 01	Jan. 03 '95
0.050	Apr. 27	May. 25	Jun. 01	Jul. 03 '95

Data as orig. reptd.; bef. results of disc. opers. and/or spec. items. Per share data adj. for stk. divs. as of ex-div. date. E-Estimated. NA-Not Available. NM-Not Meaningful. NR-Not Ranked.

Office—Suite 1400, 5660 New Northside Drive, Atlanta, GA 30328. **Tel**—(770) 857-0001. **Chrmn, Pres & CEO**—P.H. Thomas. **Vice Chrmn, CFO & Treas**—M. T. Pittard. **Vice Chrmn & Secy**—S. D. Kane. **Investor Contact**—Donald Y. Sharp (404-321-2118). **Dirs**—G. L. Cohen, R. E. Coleman, J. R. Kelly, Jr., H. A. Leslie, M. T. Pittard, C. B. Presley, P. H. Thomas, V. R. Williams. **Transfer Agent & Registrar**—Wachovia Bank of North Carolina, Winston-Salem. **Incorporated** in Georgia in 1971. **Empl**-15,000. **S&P Analyst:** Mike Cavanaugh

STANDARD & POOR'S

STOCK REPORTS

First Security Corp. (Utah)

NASDAQ Symbol **FSCO**

In S&P MidCap 400

22-AUG-95 **Industry:** Banking

Summary: This holding company owns six banks with assets of $12.2 billion and more than 250 offices in Utah, Idaho, Wyoming, Oregon, New Mexico and Nevada.

S&P Opinion: Accumulate (★★★★) Recent Price • 30¼ Yield • 3.7%
52 Wk Range • 32¾-21½ 12-Mo. P/E • 10.6

Quantitative Evaluations

Outlook
(1 Lowest—5 Highest)
• **3-**

Fair Value
• **29½**

Risk
• **Low**

Earn./Div. Rank
• **A**

Technical Eval.
• **Bullish** since 8/95

Rel. Strength Rank
(1 Lowest—99 Highest)
• **75**

Insider Activity
• **NA**

Earnings vs. Previous Year
▲=Up ▼=Down ▶=No Change

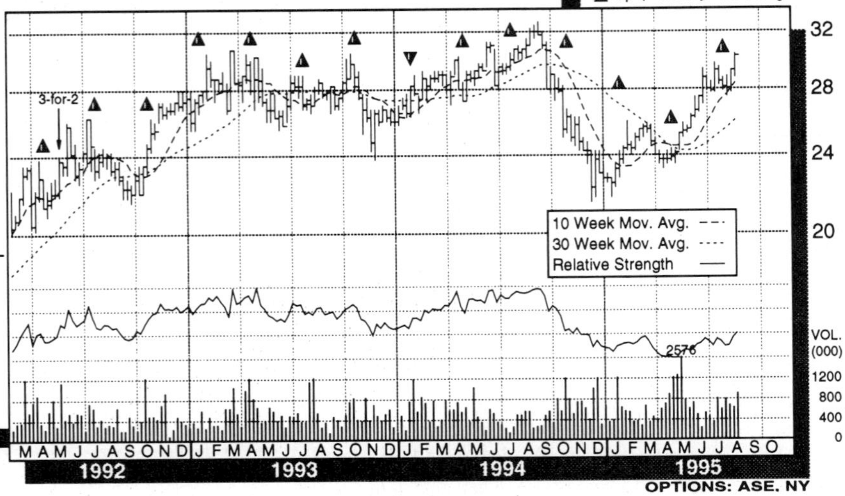

OPTIONS: ASE. NY

Overview - 17-AUG-95

Results into 1996 should continue to benefit from growth in interest-earning assets due to acquisitions, a nominal loan loss provision, and an improving efficiency ratio. The company has made substantial progress in boosting credit quality; nonperforming assets at June 30, 1995, totaled $23.0 million (0.19% of total assets), down 30% from $33.0 million (0.28%) a year earlier. Given FSCO's aggressive growth, conservative balance sheet and excellent credit quality, as well as a healthy regional economy, earnings momentum should continue.

Valuation - 22-AUG-95

As interest rates stabilize, there has been renewed interest in regional bank stocks. FSCO's results should continue to benefit from relatively strong demand for consumer loans in its six-state service territory. Recent acquisitions increased earning assets, and credit quality has continued to improve. The shares, currently near the high of their 1995 range, are trading at about 10X times our 1996 EPS estimate. With a solid 3.7% dividend yield providing downside protection, superior asset quality, and plans for expansion, the shares are recommended for investors seeking conservative growth.

Key Stock Statistics

S&P EPS Est. 1995	3.05	Tang. Bk. Value/Share	16.78
P/E on S&P Est. 1995	9.9	Beta	0.70
S&P EPS Est. 1996	3.10	Shareholders	8,700
Dividend Rate/Share	1.12	Market cap. (B)	$ 1.5
Shs. outstg. (M)	49.9	Inst. holdings	57%
Avg. daily vol. (M)	0.149	Insider holdings	0%

Value of $10,000 invested 5 years ago: $ 26,066

Fiscal Year Ending Dec. 31

	1995	% Change	1994	% Change	1993	% Change
Revenues (Million $)						
1Q	291.4	8%	270.3	38%	196.4	15%
2Q	295.3	14%	259.3	32%	196.8	15%
3Q	—	—	237.3	15%	206.3	20%
4Q	—	—	213.3	NM	212.3	27%
Yr.	—	—	980.1	21%	811.9	19%
Income (Million $)						
1Q	35.60	7%	33.16	8%	30.71	66%
2Q	36.23	3%	35.22	19%	29.69	43%
3Q	—	—	36.78	13%	32.59	35%
4Q	—	—	34.97	66%	21.06	-9%
Yr.	—	—	140.1	23%	114.1	32%
Earnings Per Share ($)						
1Q	0.70	4%	0.67	3%	0.65	35%
2Q	0.72	1%	0.71	15%	0.62	17%
3Q	E0.80	10%	0.73	7%	0.68	10%
4Q	E0.83	20%	0.69	60%	0.43	-27%
Yr.	E3.05	9%	2.81	18%	2.38	7%

Next earnings report expected: mid October

First Security Corp. (Utah)

Business Summary - 22-AUG-95

First Security Corporation owns six banking affiliates that operate more than 260 offices in Utah, Idaho, Wyoming, Oregon, New Mexico and Nevada. Its lead bank, First Security Bank of Utah, Salt Lake City, had deposits of $3.71 billion at the end of 1994.

Consolidated gross loans and leases at December 31, 1994, totaled $8.18 billion, divided as follows: residential real estate 26%, commercial real estate 13%, commercial, industrial and agricultural 22%, consumer auto 26%, other consumer 9%, and direct lease financing 4%.

The reserve for possible loan losses was $133,855,000 at the end of 1994 ($134,848,000 a year earlier), equal to 1.64% (2.06%) of loans outstanding. Net loan chargeoffs in 1994 were $7,092,000 (0.17% of average loans), versus $11,865,000 (0.30%) in 1993. Nonperforming assets at 1994 year end were $27,220,000 (0.22% of total assets), compared with $52,819,000 (0.52%) a year earlier.

Interest and fees on loans contributed 63% of total income in 1994, interest and dividends on investment securities 12%, other interest income 4%, service charges on deposit accounts 6%, and other noninterest income 15%.

Consolidated deposits of $8.05 billion at 1994 year end were divided: noninterest-bearing 21%, savings & NOW 30%, money market 14%, time certificates less than $100,000 28%, and time certificates $100,000 and greater 7%.

On a tax-equivalent basis, the average yield on interest-earning assets was 7.78% in 1994 (7.84% in 1993), while the average rate paid on interest-bearing liabilities was 3.73% (3.51%), for a net spread of 4.05% (4.33%).

Important Developments

Jul. '95—The company reported that while economic growth in the Intermountain West generally remains above the national average, the pace of expansion has moderated in several western states relative to last year; commercial construction remains strong.
Jul. '95—FSCO engaged a consulting firm to assist it in a five-month effort to enhance customer service and boost operating efficiency; the program will focus on increasing revenue and improving operating processes as well as cutting costs.
Oct. '94—FSCO and two subsidiaries issued $245 million of bank and senior notes for general funding purposes.

Capitalization

Long Term Debt: $682,382,000 (6/95).
$3.15 Preferred Stock Series A: 11,000 shs. (no par); ea. conv. into about 12 com. shs.

Per Share Data ($) (Year Ended Dec. 31)

	1994	1993	1992	1991	1990	1989
Tangible Bk. Val.	14.57	17.60	16.53	15.53	14.81	14.87
Earnings	2.81	2.38	2.22	1.76	1.41	1.55
Dividends	1.04	0.88	0.68	0.60	0.57	0.55
Payout Ratio	37%	37%	31%	34%	40%	36%
Prices - High	32¾	30¾	28	19⅜	14¾	15¼
- Low	21½	23¾	18⅛	9⅞	8	11
P/E Ratio - High	12	13	13	11	10	10
- Low	8	10	8	6	6	7

Income Statement Analysis (Million $)

	1994	%Chg	1993	%Chg	1992	%Chg	1991
Net Int. Inc.	458	13%	404	22%	330	20%	274
Tax Equiv. Adj.	7.9	4%	7.6	-4%	7.9	3%	7.7
Non Int. Inc.	208	25%	167	52%	110	7%	103
Loan Loss Prov.	1.0	-92%	12.0	-60%	30.0	-33%	45.0
% Exp/Op Revs.	66%	—	67%	—	62%	—	64%
Pretax Inc.	221	28%	173	31%	132	48%	89.0
Eff. Tax Rate	37%	—	34%	—	35%	—	33%
Net Inc.	140	23%	114	32%	86.6	45%	59.6
% Net Int. Marg.	4.64%	—	4.95%	—	5.19%	—	4.63%

Balance Sheet & Other Fin. Data (Million $)

	1994	1993	1992	1991	1990	1989
Earning Assets:						
Money Mkt.	599	1,005	564	394	253	237
Inv. Securities	2,246	1,763	1,349	1,185	1,020	969
Com'l Loans	2,177	1,849	1,535	1,558	1,484	1,426
Other Loans	5,996	4,724	3,470	3,196	3,106	2,646
Total Assets	12,149	10,212	7,608	7,015	6,493	5,795
Demand Deposits	1,719	1,698	1,149	968	882	752
Time Deposits	6,334	5,806	4,536	4,366	4,118	3,398
LT Debt	685	225	127	88.0	97.0	141
Common Eqty.	889	835	642	568	478	415

Ratio Analysis

	1994	1993	1992	1991	1990	1989
% Ret. on Assets	1.3	1.2	1.2	0.9	0.7	0.8
% Ret. on Equity	16.2	14.5	14.2	11.6	9.8	10.8
% Loan Loss Resv.	1.6	2.0	2.0	1.9	1.8	1.6
% Loans/Deposits	101.5	87.6	87.8	88.8	91.4	97.7
% Equity to Assets	7.8	8.5	8.5	7.6	7.3	7.4

Dividend Data —Cash has been paid each year since 1935. A dividend reinvestment plan is available.

Amt. of Div. $	Date Decl.	Ex-Div. Date	Stock of Record	Payment Date
0.260	Aug. 01	Aug. 17	Aug. 23	Sep. 06 '94
0.260	Nov. 01	Nov. 14	Nov. 18	Dec. 05 '94
0.280	Jan. 24	Feb. 13	Feb. 17	Mar. 06 '95
0.280	Apr. 25	May. 15	May. 19	Jun. 05 '95
0.280	Aug. 01	Aug. 16	Aug. 18	Sep. 04 '95

Data as orig. reptd.; bef. results of disc opers. and/or spec. items. Per share data adj. for stk. divs. as of ex-div. date. E-Estimated. NA-Not Available. NM-Not Meaningful. NR-Not Ranked.

Office—79 S. Main St., Salt Lake City, UT 84130-0006. **Tel**—(801) 246-5706. **Chrmn & CEO**—S. F. Eccles. **Pres & COO**—M. J. Evans. **EVP, CFO & Investor Contact**—Scott C. Ulbrich (801-246-5706). **Treas**—J. S. Bachman. **Secy**—A. W. Watson, Jr. **Dirs**—J. C. Beardall, R. H. Brady, J. E. Bruce, T. D. Dee II, S. F. Eccles, M. J. Evans, D. P. Gardner, R. H. Garff, U. E. Garrison, D. B. Haight, J. D. Harris, R. T. Heiner, K. H. Huntsman, G. F. Joklik, B. Z. Kastler, J. G. Maloof, S. S. Parker, A. K. Smith, J. L. Sorenson, H. J. Steele. **Transfer Agent & Registrar**—First Security Bank of Utah, N.A., Salt Lake City. **Incorporated** in Delaware in 1959. **Empl**-7,755. **S&P Analyst:** Robert Schpoont

STANDARD & POOR'S

STOCK REPORTS

First Tennessee National

NASDAQ Symbol **FTEN**

In S&P MidCap 400

10-OCT-95 **Industry:** Banking

Summary: This holding company, whose principal subsidiary is First Tennessee Bank, operates more than 220 offices and is the state's largest banking organization.

S&P Opinion: Accumulate (★★★★)

Recent Price • 55½ | Yield • 3.4%

52 Wk Range • 55¾-39¼ | 12-Mo. P/E • 12.2

Quantitative Evaluations

Outlook (1 Lowest—5 Highest)
• 3+

Fair Value
• 55¼

Risk
• Low

Earn./Div. Rank
• A-

Technical Eval.
• Bearish since 7/95

Rel. Strength Rank (1 Lowest—99 Highest)
• 82

Insider Activity
• Neutral

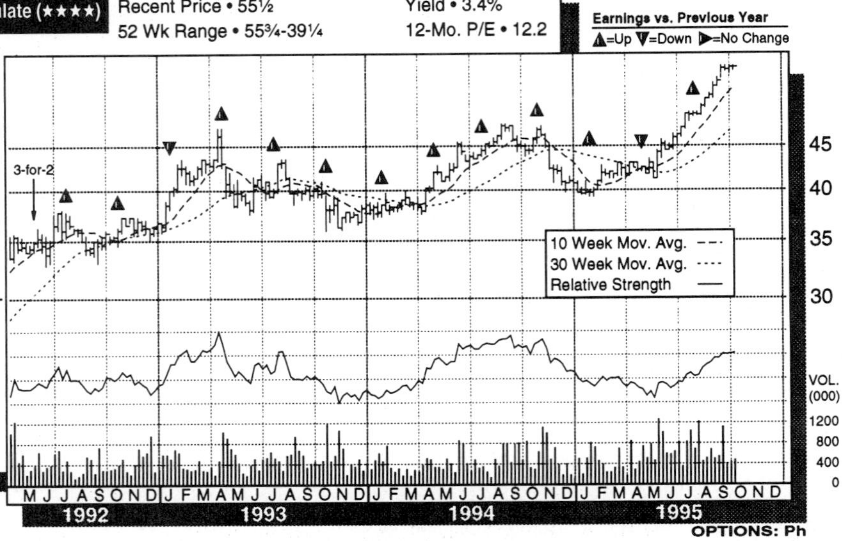

OPTIONS: Ph

Overview - 10-OCT-95

Earnings growth should continue into 1996, reflecting increased interest-earning assets, improvement in asset quality and a stabilized net interest rate margin. Strength in the company's service territory has led to a higher level of consumer lending and increases in commercial lending in recent periods. Acquisitions in late 1993 and early 1994 substantially expanded FTEN's mortgage origination operations and mortgage servicing and fee income. In the past year, rising interest rates held the bond division's income gains in check, but second-quarter results suggest a turnaround in that division. Also, other specialty lines of business (deposit transactions, cash management, bank card and trust services) are starting to pick up.

Valuation - 10-OCT-95

The shares of this service-oriented regional bank holding company are up 40% from their 1995 low, aided by a stable interest-rate environment and investor interest in bank stocks servicing strong regional economies such as Tennessee. FTEN's recent acquisitions, 10%+ loan growth and improving asset quality should continue to fuel earnings growth. FTEN is currently trading near its calendar-year high, but we expect the market eventually to value FTEN with a premium P/E multiple for deriving about half its income from fee-producing, specialty lines of business. Trading at about 10 times our 1996 earnings estimate, the shares are poised for further gains. We recommend accumulation of FTEN for investors seeking conservative growth.

Key Stock Statistics

S&P EPS Est. 1995	4.75	Tang. Bk. Value/Share	21.40
P/E on S&P Est. 1995	11.7	Beta	0.73
S&P EPS Est. 1996	5.30	Shareholders	7,800
Dividend Rate/Share	1.88	Market cap. (B)	$ 1.9
Shs. outstg. (M)	33.7	Inst. holdings	39%
Avg. daily vol. (M)	0.118	Insider holdings	NA

Value of $10,000 invested 5 years ago: $ 42,998

Fiscal Year Ending Dec. 31

	1995	% Change	1994	% Change	1993	% Change
Revenues (Million $)						
1Q	300.6	12%	269.6	30%	206.9	NM
2Q	317.5	24%	256.9	26%	204.5	-3%
3Q	—	—	261.7	24%	210.7	3%
4Q	—	—	267.5	14%	234.8	17%
Yr.	—	—	1,056	23%	857.0	4%
Income (Million $)						
1Q	31.61	-14%	36.63	21%	30.24	22%
2Q	40.75	14%	35.59	17%	30.34	16%
3Q	—	—	36.76	25%	29.45	11%
4Q	—	—	37.10	21%	30.63	160%
Yr.	—	—	146.4	21%	120.7	35%
Earnings Per Share ($)						
1Q	0.93	-19%	1.15	7%	1.07	20%
2Q	1.20	7%	1.12	4%	1.08	16%
3Q	E1.31	15%	1.14	9%	1.05	11%
4Q	E1.31	13%	1.16	9%	1.06	152%
Yr.	E4.75	4%	4.56	7%	4.26	34%

Next earnings report expected: mid October

STANDARD & POOR'S

STOCK REPORTS

First Tennessee National

10-OCT-95

Business Summary - 10-OCT-95

First Tennessee National Corporation, which owns First Tennessee Bank, N.A., is the largest bank holding company in that state, operating more than 220 locations in Tennessee's major metropolitan areas.

Consolidated gross loans totaling $6.35 billion at the end of 1994 were divided:

Commercial	46%
Consumer	35%
Permanent mortgage	9%
Credit card receivables	7%
Other	3%

The allowance for loan losses at December 31, 1994, was $106,989,000 (1.59% of loans, net of unearned income), compared with $107,723,000 (1.65%) a year earlier. Net chargeoffs in 1994 were $17,467,000 (0.27% of average loans, net), versus $28,772,000 (0.54%) in 1993. Nonperforming assets at 1994 year-end amounted to $36,741,000 (0.55% of total loans--net, plus foreclosed real estate and other assets), compared with $59,495,000 (0.91%) at the end of 1993.

Interest and fees on loans contributed 49% of total income in 1994, interest on investment securities 12%, other interest income 2%, mortgage banking 11%, deposit transactions and cash management 6% and other noninterest income 20%.

Consolidated deposits of $7.69 billion at year-end 1994 were divided: demand 22%, checking/interest 6%, savings 8%, money market 23%, certificates of deposit (CDs) of $100,000 or more 6% and other CDs and time 35%.

On a tax-equivalent basis, the average yield on total earning assets in 1994 was 7.49% (7.33% in 1993), while the average rate paid on interest-bearing liabilities was 3.87% (3.65%), for a net spread of 3.62% (3.68%).

Important Developments

Jul. '95—FTEN acquired certain assets of HomeBanc Mortgage Corp., Atlanta's leading residential first mortgage lender since 1992.

Apr. '95—The company acquired Peoples Commercial Services Corp., parent of Peoples Bank (deposits of $86.4 million), based in Senatobia, Miss., for about 421,000 shares.

Feb. '95—FTEN acquired Community Bancshares, parent of Community First Bank (deposits of $192 million), based in Germantown, Tenn., for about 1.42 million common shares. Also in February, FTEN agreed to acquire Financial Investment Corp., parent of First National Bank of Springdale (deposits of $295 million), of Springdale, Ark., for $70 million in stock.

Capitalization

Long Term Debt: $202,320,000 (6/95).

Per Share Data ($)

(Year Ended Dec. 31)

	1994	1993	1992	1991	1990	1989
Tangible Bk. Val.	18.42	19.34	21.25	15.64	15.83	14.64
Earnings	4.56	4.26	3.19	2.69	2.01	1.21
Dividends	1.73	1.50	1.26	1.14	1.08	0.97
Payout Ratio	38%	35%	39%	42%	54%	80%
Prices - High	47¾	47¼	38	27⅝	18⅛	19⅞
- Low	37	35¾	26¼	14⅜	11⅞	15⅝
P/E Ratio - High	10	11	12	10	9	16
- Low	8	8	8	5	6	13

Income Statement Analysis (Million $)

	1994	%Chg	1993	%Chg	1992	%Chg	1991
Net Int. Inc.	381	10%	347	7%	323	22%	265
Tax Equiv. Adj.	4.9	-9%	5.3	-31%	7.7	-22%	9.8
Non Int. Inc.	369	36%	270	19%	227	28%	177
Loan Loss Prov.	16.7	-52%	34.5	-20%	43.2	-20%	53.7
% Exp/Op Revs.	72%	—	64%	—	65%	—	67%
Pretax Inc.	207	13%	184	28%	144	70%	84.6
Eff. Tax Rate	29%	—	35%	—	38%	—	25%
Net Inc.	146	21%	121	35%	89.2	40%	63.8
% Net Int. Marg.	4.28%	—	4.35%	—	4.37%	—	4.43%

Balance Sheet & Other Fin. Data (Million $)

	1994	1993	1992	1991	1990	1989
Earning Assets:						
Money Mkt.	440	324	475	586	710	526
Inv. Securities	2,094	2,170	2,912	2,241	1,417	1,342
Com'l Loans	2,889	2,519	2,200	2,231	2,107	2,031
Other Loans	3,829	3,480	2,342	1,739	1,787	1,707
Total Assets	10,522	9,609	8,926	7,904	6,708	6,398
Demand Deposits	1,702	1,888	1,468	1,403	1,117	1,051
Time Deposits	5,987	5,258	5,449	4,638	4,227	3,899
LT Debt	92.4	90.0	127	127	127	128
Common Eqty.	749	679	598	438	398	381

Ratio Analysis

	1994	1993	1992	1991	1990	1989
% Ret. on Assets	1.5	1.4	1.1	0.9	0.7	0.5
% Ret. on Equity	20.0	19.0	15.4	15.3	12.3	7.7
% Loan Loss Resv.	1.6	1.7	2.1	2.2	2.2	1.7
% Loans/Deposits	87.4	83.8	65.4	65.2	71.7	74.0
% Equity to Assets	7.2	7.1	7.0	6.1	6.0	6.1

Dividend Data —Except for 1878 and 1895, dividends have been paid each year since organization in 1864. A dividend reinvestment plan is available.

Amt. of Div. $	Date Decl.	Ex-Div. Date	Stock of Record	Payment Date
0.470	Oct. 18	Dec. 12	Dec. 16	Jan. 01 '95
0.470	Jan. 17	Mar. 13	Mar. 17	Apr. 01 '95
0.470	Apr. 18	Jun. 14	Jun. 16	Jul. 01 '95
0.470	Jul. 18	Sep. 13	Sep. 15	Oct. 01 '95

Data as orig. reptd.; bef. results of disc opers. and/or spec. items. Per share data adj. for stk. divs. as of ex-div. date. E-Estimated. NA-Not Available. NM-Not Meaningful. NR-Not Ranked.

Office—165 Madison Ave., Memphis, TN 38103. **Tel**—(901) 523-4027. **Chrmn**—R. Terry. **Pres, CEO & COO**—R. Horn. **Exec VP & CFO**—E. L. Thomas Jr. **VP, Treas & Investor Contact**—Terry A. Fehrman. **Dirs**—J. A. Belz, R. C. Blattberg, R. Horn, J. R. Hyde III, R. B. Martin, J. Orgill III, R. E. Ray, V. G. Roman, M. D. Rose, W. B. Sansom, G. P. Street Jr., R. Terry. **Transfer Agent**—Norwest Bank Minnesota, South St. Paul. **Incorporated** in Tennessee in 1968; bank chartered in 1864. **Empl**-6,468. **S&P Analyst:** Robert Schpoont

STANDARD & POOR'S

STOCK REPORTS

First Virginia Banks

NYSE Symbol **FVB**

In S&P MidCap 400

24-AUG-95 **Industry:** Banking

Summary: This multibank holding company, with $7.9 billion in assets, is the fourth largest banking organization headquartered in Virginia, with operations also in Maryland and Tennessee.

S&P Opinion: Hold (★★★)

Recent Price • 39¾ | Yield • 3.5%
52 Wk Range • 40½-31⅝ | 12-Mo. P/E • 11.9

Quantitative Evaluations

Outlook
(1 Lowest—5 Highest)
• 1⁻

Fair Value
• 32¼

Risk
• Low

Earn./Div. Rank
• A

Technical Eval.
• Bullish since 5/95

Rel. Strength Rank
(1 Lowest—99 Highest)
• 55

Insider Activity
• Neutral

Earnings vs. Previous Year
▲=Up ▼=Down ▶=No Change

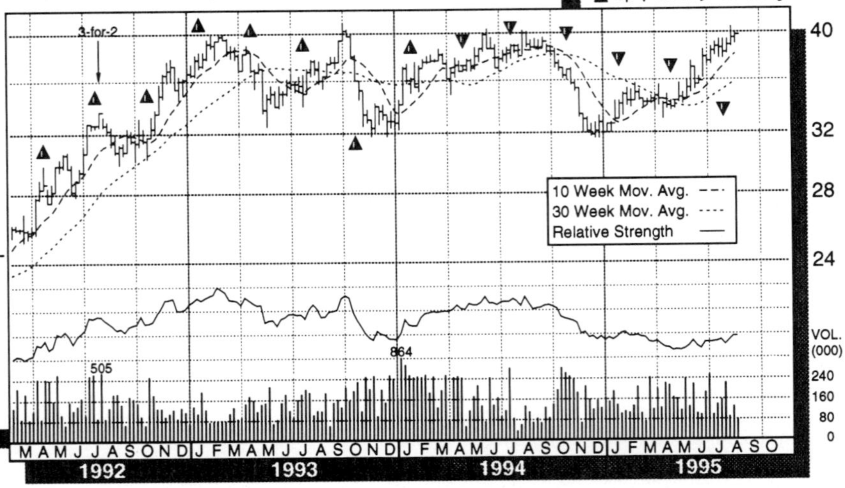

Overview - 22-AUG-95

Loans grew 14% in the second quarter of 1995, year to year, due to strong commercial loan demand and renewed interest in indirect automobile loans. Although average loans declined slightly compared to the first quarter, we expect 7% to 8% growth for the remainder of the year. With the help of an accomodating Federal Reserve, loans should continue to grow in the 7% to 8% range in 1996. There was a slight compression in the net interest margin in the second quarter, primarily due to rising interest rates over the past year which caused the cost of funds to rise faster than the yield on assets. With the recent drop in rates, the cost of funds should stabilize and then decline in the 3rd and 4th quarters. The bank expects the efficiency ratio to begin to decline in the fourth quarter, as a result of the recent conversion of Farmers National Bancorp (acq. 12/94) to First Virginia systems.

Valuation - 22-AUG-95

Following a rebound from the selloff in late 1994 on fears over rising interest rates and the direction of the economy, the shares appear to be fairly valued at present. With a 25% rise thus far in 1995, the stock currently trades at a valuation of about 11 times our earnings estimate for 1996, which is slightly higher than the multiple on the average regional bank. But, we believe that the bank's strong capital position, high level of asset quality, and above average dividend yield make the shares a worthwhile hold over the longer term.

Key Stock Statistics

S&P EPS Est. 1995	3.35	Tang. Bk. Value/Share	22.19
P/E on S&P Est. 1995	11.9	Beta	1.18
S&P EPS Est. 1996	3.60	Shareholders	18,900
Dividend Rate/Share	1.36	Market cap. (B)	$ 1.3
Shs. outstg. (M)	33.9	Inst. holdings	29%
Avg. daily vol. (M)	0.020	Insider holdings	NA

Value of $10,000 invested 5 years ago: $ 24,588

Fiscal Year Ending Dec. 31

	1995	% Change	1994	% Change	1993	% Change
Revenues (Million $)						
1Q	158.8	10%	143.9	-1%	145.7	-2%
2Q	167.2	13%	148.5	1%	146.5	-4%
3Q	—	—	147.6	NM	147.5	-2%
4Q	—	—	148.2	-3%	153.0	2%
Yr.	—	—	588.3	NM	587.3	-2%
Income (Million $)						
1Q	27.20	-6%	28.82	-1%	29.12	35%
2Q	27.57	-5%	29.03	NM	29.16	23%
3Q	—	—	27.59	-3%	28.52	11%
4Q	—	—	27.79	-4%	28.90	9%
Yr.	—	—	113.2	-2%	116.0	19%
Earnings Per Share ($)						
1Q	0.80	-10%	0.89	-1%	0.90	34%
2Q	0.81	-9%	0.89	-1%	0.90	22%
3Q	E0.85	NM	0.85	-3%	0.88	11%
4Q	E0.89	1%	0.88	-1%	0.89	9%
Yr.	E3.35	-5%	3.51	-2%	3.57	18%

Next earnings report expected: mid October

First Virginia Banks

Business Summary - 24-AUG-95

First Virginia Banks (formerly First Virginia Bankshares) is a bank holding company controlling 23 member banks with combined assets of approximately $7.9 billion at December 31, 1994. FVB conducts its operations through some 269 offices in Virginia, plus 57 offices in Maryland and 23 in Tennessee. The greatest concentration of offices is in the suburbs of Washington, D.C. Other subsidiaries are engaged in mortgage banking and insurance.

Gross loans outstanding were $5.35 billion at year-end 1994, compared with $4.35 billion a year earlier. Loans were divided as follows:

	1994	1993
Consumer:		
Automobile installment	35%	36%
Home equity	26%	29%
Revolving credit	4%	4%
Other	5%	4%
Real estate:		
Construction	2%	2%
Commercial mortgage	9%	7%
Residential mortgage	9%	10%
Other	1%	1%
Commercial	9%	7%

At December 31, 1994, loans accounted for 66% of average earning assets, investment securities for 30%, and federal funds sold and resale agreements for 3%.

Consolidated deposits of $6.82 billion at 1994 year-end were apportioned: noninterest-bearing 18%, interest-bearing transaction 20%, money market accounts 11%, savings deposits 21%, and certificates of deposit 30%.

The allowance for loan losses at December 31, 1994, totaled $58,860,000 (1.18% of loans outstanding), compared with $50,927,000 (1.27%) a year earlier. Net charge-offs in 1994 amounted to $4,942,000 (0.11% of average loans), down from $5,122,000 (0.13%) in the year-earlier period. At December 31, 1994, nonperforming assets (consisting of nonaccruing and restructured loans and foreclosed real estate) were $26.2 million (0.52% of total loans and foreclosed real estate), versus $27.6 million (0.68%) on December 31, 1993.

Important Developments

May '95—First Virginia announced that one of its member banks, First Virginia-Colonial, has agreed to purchase approximately $200 million in deposits and certain assets of four Virginia-based branches from Citizens Federal Savings Bank. The transaction, terms of which were not disclosed, is expected to be completed in 1995's third quarter.

Capitalization

Long Term Debt: $3,228,000, including $816,000 of mortgage notes payable (6/95).
Conv. Preferred Stock: $709,000.

Per Share Data ($)

(Year Ended Dec. 31)

	1994	1993	1992	1991	1990	1989
Tangible Bk. Val.	21.18	21.19	18.49	16.40	15.11	13.91
Earnings	3.51	3.57	3.02	2.17	2.03	2.13
Dividends	1.28	1.13	0.99	0.91	0.85	0.80
Payout Ratio	36%	32%	33%	42%	42%	38%
Prices - High	$40\frac{3}{8}$	41	$37\frac{7}{8}$	24	$20\frac{3}{8}$	$23\frac{3}{4}$
- Low	$31\frac{5}{8}$	$31\frac{3}{4}$	$23\frac{3}{8}$	$14\frac{1}{8}$	$11\frac{1}{4}$	$15\frac{7}{8}$
P/E Ratio - High	12	11	13	11	10	11
- Low	9	9	8	7	6	7

Income Statement Analysis (Million $)

	1994	%Chg	1993	%Chg	1992	%Chg	1991
Net Int. Inc.	342	NM	340	6%	320	25%	256
Tax Equiv. Adj.	7.5	-7%	8.1	-7%	8.7	-2%	8.9
Non Int. Inc.	83.7	2%	81.8	6%	77.3	7%	72.3
Loan Loss Prov.	6.5	NM	6.5	-63%	17.4	24%	14.0
% Exp/Op Revs.	58%	—	57%	—	59%	—	65%
Pretax Inc.	168	-1%	170	20%	141	48%	95.6
Eff. Tax Rate	33%	—	32%	—	31%	—	27%
Net Inc.	113	-3%	116	19%	97.5	40%	69.6
% Net Int. Marg.	5.28%	—	5.46%	—	5.46%	—	5.03%

Balance Sheet & Other Fin. Data (Million $)

	1994	1993	1992	1991	1990	1989
Earning Assets:						
Money Mkt.	NA	NA	NA	NA	NA	NA
Inv. Securities	2,086	2,176	2,165	1,813	1,287	1,069
Com'l Loans	473	385	382	406	434	493
Other Loans	4,879	4,030	3,812	3,487	3,409	3,231
Total Assets	7,865	7,037	6,841	6,119	5,384	5,124
Demand Deposits	1,234	1,040	1,012	835	785	794
Time Deposits	5,582	5,096	5,001	4,515	3,931	3,633
LT Debt	1.0	1.0	5.2	11.5	11.8	37.5
Common Eqty.	807	691	607	539	497	453

Ratio Analysis

	1994	1993	1992	1991	1990	1989
% Ret. on Assets	1.6	1.7	1.5	1.2	1.3	1.4
% Ret. on Equity	15.8	17.8	17.1	13.5	13.6	15.6
% Loan Loss Resv.	1.2	1.3	1.3	1.3	1.3	1.2
% Loans/Deposits	70.8	66.6	63.9	65.7	72.8	75.4
% Equity to Assets	10.0	9.4	8.8	9.1	9.2	8.9

Dividend Data —Dividends have been paid since 1960. A dividend reinvestment plan is available. A "poison pill" stock purchase right was adopted in 1988.

Amt. of Div. $	Date Decl.	Ex-Div. Date	Stock of Record	Payment Date
0.320	Aug. 24	Sep. 26	Sep. 30	Oct. 17 '94
0.330	Nov. 16	Dec. 23	Dec. 30	Jan. 09 '95
0.330	Feb. 22	Mar. 27	Mar. 31	Apr. 17 '95
0.340	May. 24	Jun. 28	Jun. 30	Jul. 17 '95
0.340	Aug. 23	Sep. 27	Sep. 30	Oct. 16 '95

Data as orig. reptd.; bef. results of disc opers. and/or spec. items. Per share data adj. for stk. divs. as of ex-div. date. E-Estimated. NA-Not Available. NM-Not Meaningful. NR-Not Ranked.

Office—6400 Arlington Blvd., Falls Church, VA 22042-2336. **Tel**—(703) 241-4000. **Chrmn & CEO**—R. H. Zalokar. **Pres**—P. H. Geithner Jr. **VP-Secy**—T. P. Jennings. **VP-Treas & Investor Contact**—Richard F. Bowman (703) 241-3685. **Dirs**—E. C. Brand, E. L. Breeden III, P. H. Geithner Jr., L. H. Ginn III, G. R. Giordano, T. K. Greer, E. C. Gruver, E. M. Holland, E. C. Kendrick, T. K. Malone Jr., W. L. Phillips Jr., J. P. Rowe III, R. T. Selden, R. H. Zalokar, A. F. Zettlemoyer. **Transfer Agent & Registrar**—Registrar & Transfer Co., Cranford, N.J. **Incorporated** in Virginia in 1949. **Empl**-5,575. **S&P Analyst:** Brad Ohlmuller

STANDARD & POOR'S

STOCK REPORTS

Flserv, Inc.

NASDAQ Symbol **FISV**
In S&P MidCap 400

10-AUG-95 **Industry:** Data Processing

Summary: Flserv is a leading full-service provider of computerized account processing and integrated information management systems for financial institutions.

Quantitative Evaluations

Outlook (1 Lowest—5 Highest) • **2-**

Fair Value • **25⅝**

Risk • **Average**

Earn./Div. Rank • **B+**

Technical Eval. • **Bullish** since 12/94

Rel. Strength Rank (1 Lowest—99 Highest) • **21**

Insider Activity • **Unfavorable**

Recent Price • 27⅛
52 Wk Range • 30¼-18¾
Yield • Nil
12-Mo. P/E • 26.1

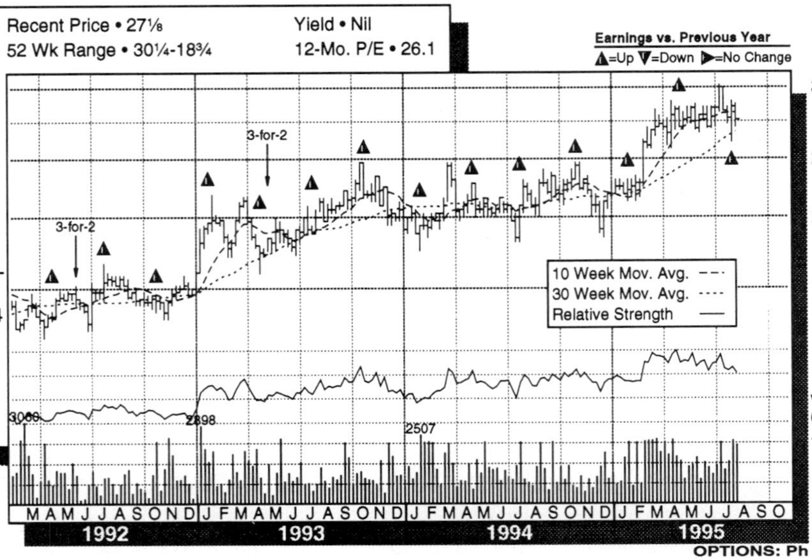

OPTIONS: Ph

Business Profile - 10-AUG-95

Flserv has capitalized on the desire of financial institutions to meet the growing needs of their customers. Consolidation within the financial processing industry continues as smaller, local and regional third-party data processors combine with larger providers. Additionally, an increasing number of financial institutions that previously maintained their own data processing ability are outsourcing their data processing requirements.

Operational Review - 10-AUG-95

Revenues in recent periods have shown steady growth, primarily attributable to acquisitions of complementary companies. Margins have improved due to a more favorable product mix. Partially offsetting these gains are the amortization of goodwill expense associated with acquisitions, and the increasing number of outstanding shares. Future results should benefit from cost cutting efforts and industry consolidation.

Stock Performance - 04-AUG-95

In the past 30 trading days, FISV's shares have declined 4%, compared to a 2% rise in the S&P 500. Average trading volume for the past five days was 230,120 shares, compared with the 40-day moving average of 193,351 shares.

Key Stock Statistics

Dividend Rate/Share	Nil	Shareholders	12,000
Shs. outstg. (M)	44.8	Market cap. (B)	$ 1.2
Avg. daily vol. (M)	0.209	Inst. holdings	75%
Tang. Bk. Value/Share	NM	Insider holdings	NA
Beta	1.09		

Value of $10,000 invested 5 years ago: $ 42,093

Fiscal Year Ending Dec. 31

	1995	% Change	1994	% Change	1993	% Change
Revenues (Million $)						
1Q	152.6	12%	136.0	36%	100.0	23%
2Q	173.5	28%	136.0	23%	111.0	35%
3Q	—	—	139.0	20%	116.0	38%
4Q	—	—	152.5	20%	127.0	49%
Yr.	—	—	563.6	24%	455.0	37%
Income (Million $)						
1Q	10.45	20%	8.69	28%	6.79	24%
2Q	11.98	28%	9.37	22%	7.66	35%
3Q	—	—	9.54	20%	7.94	35%
4Q	—	—	10.07	21%	8.30	39%
Yr.	—	—	37.66	23%	30.69	33%
Earnings Per Share ($)						
1Q	0.26	18%	0.22	16%	0.19	19%
2Q	0.28	17%	0.24	20%	0.20	18%
3Q	—	—	0.24	20%	0.20	18%
4Q	—	—	0.25	19%	0.21	24%
Yr.	—	—	0.95	19%	0.80	19%

Next earnings report expected: late October

Flserv, Inc.

Business Summary - 10-AUG-95

Flserv, Inc. is an independent provider of data processing outsourcing capabilities and related products and services for financial institutions. The company's system applications are designed to increase the operating efficiency, customer service and marketing capability of banks, credit unions, mortgage banks and other financial intermediaries.

Since its formation in 1984, the company has grown by developing highly specialized services and products, adding new clients and acquiring firms providing complementary services. Flserv operates full-service data centers, software system development centers, item processing and support centers in 62 cities, including international offices in London and Singapore. These centers design, develop, enhance and support integrated data processing systems for more than 2,500 financial institutions.

Flserv provides multiple, integrated solutions for financial institutions, including data center service bureau systems and support; disaster recovery; electronic funds transfer services, including cards and card management; in-house software systems development and support; item processing; marketing design and production of forms and graphics; mortgage banking processing systems; rate risk management systems and performance analysis; self-directed retirement plan processing; and strategic industry alliances.

The company's system solutions include dedicated service bureau capabilities on multiple hardware platforms, giving clients the flexibility of online systems compatible with their equipment or hardware.

Flserv has the largest U.S. check processing client base, processing about 1.75 billion items per year through a network of 30 regional item processing sites. The EFT division offers transaction authorization, ATM driving, ATM and point-of-sale network gateway access and card management services. The Sendero Corp. subsidiary is a leading provider of asset/liability management software products, profitability measurement systems and interest rate risk analysis services.

Important Developments

May '95—Flserv completed its acquisition of Information Technology (ITI), a privately held company involved in the design, development, delivery, installation and support of the ITI Premier banking software. ITI had revenues in excess of $100 million for 1994. The purchase price of $373 million consisted of approximately $250 million in cash and nearly 4.6 million common shares of Flserv stock.

Capitalization

Long Term Debt: $391,761,000 (6/95).

Per Share Data ($) (Year Ended Dec. 31)

	1994	1993	1992	1991	1990	1989
Tangible Bk. Val.	8.96	7.93	5.70	5.00	3.45	2.97
Cash Flow	1.70	1.35	1.14	0.99	0.83	0.73
Earnings	0.95	0.80	0.67	0.56	0.47	0.39
Dividends	Nil	Nil	Nil	Nil	Nil	Nil
Payout Ratio	Nil	Nil	Nil	Nil	Nil	Nil
Prices - High	23¾	23¾	17⅝	16⅞	9¼	7⅜
- Low	18	16¾	13⅝	8	5¾	5¼
P/E Ratio - High	25	30	26	30	19	19
- Low	19	21	21	14	12	13

Income Statement Analysis (Million $)

	1994	%Chg	1993	%Chg	1992	%Chg	1991
Revs.	564	24%	455	37%	332	18%	281
Oper. Inc.	99	32%	75.3	36%	55.3	21%	45.8
Depr.	30.0	40%	21.5	34%	16.1	8%	14.9
Int. Exp.	8.7	52%	5.7	14%	5.0	67%	3.0
Pretax Inc.	62.8	26%	50.0	35%	37.1	29%	28.7
Eff. Tax Rate	40%	—	39%	—	38%	—	36%
Net Inc.	37.7	23%	30.7	33%	23.0	26%	18.3

Balance Sheet & Other Fin. Data (Million $)

	1994	1993	1992	1991	1990	1989
Cash	28.0	36.0	302	389	346	223
Curr. Assets	NA	NA	NA	NA	NA	NA
Total Assets	1,418	1,182	898	740	565	443
Curr. Liab.	NA	NA	NA	NA	NA	NA
LT Debt	132	106	51.0	52.0	34.0	26.0
Common Eqty.	351	308	192	167	100	84.0
Total Cap.	505	429	260	230	143	116
Cap. Exp.	52.8	28.5	19.1	14.3	5.1	14.4
Cash Flow	67.7	52.2	39.1	32.5	24.1	20.9

Ratio Analysis

	1994	1993	1992	1991	1990	1989
Curr. Ratio	NA	NA	NA	NA	NA	NA
% LT Debt of Cap.	26.0	24.6	19.5	22.4	23.9	22.3
% Net Inc.of Revs.	6.7	6.8	6.9	6.5	7.5	6.9
% Ret. on Assets	2.9	2.8	2.8	1.3	2.7	3.9
% Ret. on Equity	11.4	11.6	12.7	6.5	14.8	14.5

Dividend Data (No cash dividends have been paid on the public shares, and the company intends to retain earnings to support future business opportunities. Three-for-two stock splits were effected in July 1991, June 1992 and May 1993.)

Data as orig. reptd.; bef. results of disc. opers. and/or spec. items. Per share data adj. for stk. divs. as of ex-div. date. Bk. val. figs. in Per Share Data tbl. incl. intangibles. E-Estimated. NA-Not Available. NM-Not Meaningful. NR-Not Ranked.

Office—255 Flserv Dr., Brookfield, WI 53045. **Tel**—(414) 879-5000. **Investor Relations Tel**—(800) 872-7882. **Chrmn & CEO**—G. D. Dalton. **Pres & COO**—L. M. Muma. **SEVP, CFO & Treas**—K. R. Jensen. **Dirs**—B. K. Anderson, G. D. Dalton, K. R. Jensen, G. J. Levy, L. M. Muma, L. W. Seidman, R. D. Sullivan, T. Shackelford. **Transfer Agent & Registrar**—First Bank, Milwaukee. **Incorporated** in Delaware in 1984; reincorporated in Wisconsin in 1992. **Empl**-6,195. **S&P Analyst:** Steven A. Jaworski

STANDARD & POOR'S

STOCK REPORTS

FlightSafety Int'l

NYSE Symbol **FSI**
In S&P MidCap 400

24-AUG-95 **Industry:** Education

Summary: FlightSafety provides training for aircraft pilots and operators of large ocean-going vessels, and manufactures sophisticated training equipment.

S&P Opinion: Hold (★★★)

Recent Price • 45¼
52 Wk Range • 49½-36¼

Yield • 1.1%
12-Mo. P/E • 17.6

Quantitative Evaluations

Outlook (1 Lowest—5 Highest)
• **4+**

Fair Value
• **47⅞**

Risk
• **Low**

Earn./Div. Rank
• **A**

Technical Eval.
• **Bearish** since 2/94

Rel. Strength Rank (1 Lowest—99 Highest)
• **15**

Insider Activity
• **NA**

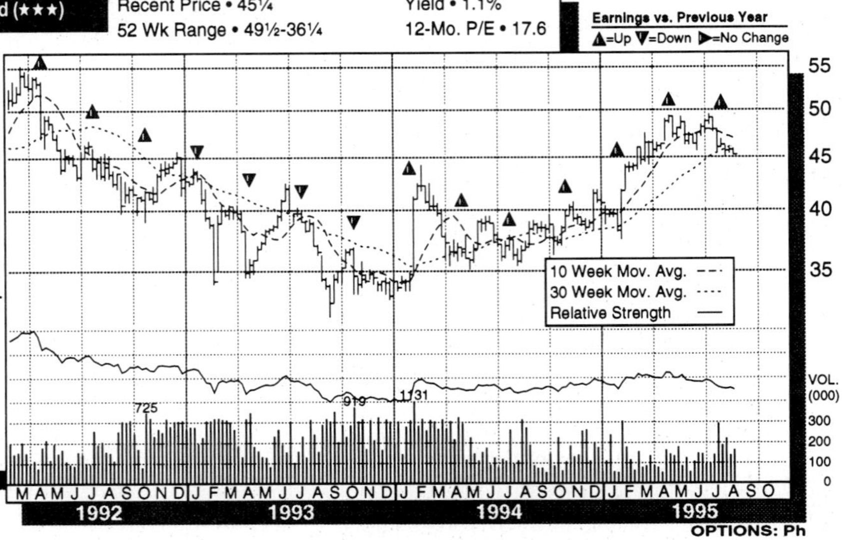

OPTIONS: Ph

Overview - 22-AUG-95

Revenues in 1995 are expected to rise nearly 10%, reflecting double-digit gains in training revenues, bolstered by rapid growth in Latin America and in the Asia-Pacific region. Profitability will continue to benefit from cost-containment measures. Ongoing stock repurchases will provide an added boost to share earnings. Barring major economic slumps, demand for training services should continue to expand at a healthy pace in 1996 and beyond, bolstered by the fact that aviation safety and training standards are under heavy national scrutiny. Product sales may not bounce back anytime soon. Depressed by lower demand and customer orders since mid-1993, they accounted for only 7% of total revenues in the 1995 first half, down from 16% in 1993.

Valuation - 24-AUG-95

FSI is the only major independent pilot training organization in the U.S., and its competitive position is also enhanced by the fact that airlines and governments are increasingly finding it more economical to turn to FSI for their pilot training needs. Developing Asian nations are a rapidly growing source of demand for training. FSI consistently provides high-caliber training using the most advanced technologies available in its training centers. With the rate of earnings growth expected to average in the mid-teens through 1996, the shares appear to be reasonably valued. The current $0.48 annual dividend provides a modest cushion under the stock.

Key Stock Statistics

S&P EPS Est. 1995	2.70	Tang. Bk. Value/Share	17.67
P/E on S&P Est. 1995	16.8	Beta	0.99
S&P EPS Est. 1996	3.10	Shareholders	10,800
Dividend Rate/Share	0.48	Market cap. (B)	$ 1.4
Shs. outstg. (M)	31.3	Inst. holdings	51%
Avg. daily vol. (M)	0.031	Insider holdings	NA

Value of $10,000 invested 5 years ago: $ 9,894

Fiscal Year Ending Dec. 31

	1995	% Change	1994	% Change	1993	% Change
Revenues (Million $)						
1Q	77.83	6%	73.25	NM	73.76	6%
2Q	79.39	7%	74.01	-6%	78.66	11%
3Q	—	—	70.49	4%	67.85	-2%
4Q	—	—	83.56	9%	76.82	12%
Yr.	—	—	301.3	1%	297.1	7%
Income (Million $)						
1Q	20.16	24%	16.20	-6%	17.24	-8%
2Q	20.91	13%	18.54	NM	18.51	-7%
3Q	—	—	16.24	47%	11.04	-57%
4Q	—	—	23.50	20%	19.64	9%
Yr.	—	—	74.48	12%	66.41	-19%
Earnings Per Share ($)						
1Q	0.64	25%	0.51	2%	0.50	-7%
2Q	0.67	16%	0.58	4%	0.56	-3%
3Q	E0.64	25%	0.51	50%	0.34	-55%
4Q	E0.75	NM	0.75	23%	0.61	17%
Yr.	E2.70	15%	2.35	17%	2.01	-16%

Next earnings report expected: mid October

FlightSafety Int'l

Business Summary - 24-AUG-95

FlightSafety International provides high-technology training programs for private, commercial, military and other government agency aircraft pilots. It also provides training for operators of large ocean-going vessels and manufactures training equipment. FSI operates 38 learning centers with more than 150 simulators in the U.S., Canada and Europe.

The most important aspect of the training program is the use of simulators, which reproduce sights and sounds, control responses and generate the total environment experienced by operators of a particular aircraft. As the authorized training organization for 23 aircraft makers, FSI trains over 40,000 pilots and maintenance technicians a year. More than 3,000 corporations train their crews with FSI.

The MarineSafety International subsidiary trains crews of ocean-going vessels in ship, cargo handling and engine room procedures. Customers include the U.S. Navy and Coast Guard.

FSI makes training devices and products (including flight simulators) and develops audiovisual programs and training manuals.

Training revenues were 90% of operating revenues in 1994 and 95% of operating earnings, while sales of manufactured products by the Simulation Systems division to unaffiliated customers were 10% and 5%, respectively. FSI sold its interest in PowerSafety International, a provider of training and equipment to the power and utility industry, in December 1994.

Important Developments

Jul. '95—In commenting on first-half operating results, FSI stated that training revenues were higher in all areas with particular strength in business aviation. Product sales continued to reflect reduced commercial orders for new training equipment produced by the Simulation Systems Division. Such sales declined 27%, to $11,076,000 in the 1995 first half from $15,179,000 in the year-earlier period. For all of 1994, product sales fell 44%.
Feb. '95—FSI said it expects to spend over $55 million for additional equipment and facilities in 1995. Capital expenditures in 1994 were $64 million.
Jan. '95—FSI signed a joint venture agreement to establish a training center in China.

Capitalization

Long Term Debt: $38,638,000 (3/95).

Per Share Data ($) (Year Ended Dec. 31)

	1994	1993	1992	1991	1990	1989
Tangible Bk. Val.	17.90	16.45	16.38	14.27	12.36	9.88
Cash Flow	3.82	3.35	3.53	3.13	3.12	2.66
Earnings	2.35	2.01	2.39	2.11	2.22	1.93
Dividends	0.42	0.37	0.30	0.25	0.21	0.17
Payout Ratio	18%	18%	13%	12%	9%	9%
Prices - High	44¼	44	55¼	57	65¼	51
- Low	33½	31⅝	39	37¾	35½	24⅛
P/E Ratio - High	19	22	23	27	29	26
- Low	14	16	16	18	16	13

Income Statement Analysis (Million $)

	1994	%Chg	1993	%Chg	1992	%Chg	1991
Revs.	301	1%	297	7%	278	4%	268
Oper. Inc.	154	5%	146	NM	145	7%	135
Depr.	46.7	5%	44.3	13%	39.1	12%	35.0
Int. Exp.	3.8	2%	3.7	-29%	5.2	3%	5.1
Pretax Inc.	116	5%	110	-14%	128	15%	111
Eff. Tax Rate	36%	—	39%	—	36%	—	35%
Net Inc.	74.5	12%	66.4	-19%	82.3	14%	72.4

Balance Sheet & Other Fin. Data (Million $)

	1994	1993	1992	1991	1990	1989
Cash	197	181	279	205	159	108
Curr. Assets	281	253	338	260	204	146
Total Assets	793	754	814	691	621	525
Curr. Liab.	79.0	75.0	107	75.4	77.6	60.3
LT Debt	39.8	41.6	44.6	29.7	35.1	33.8
Common Eqty.	560	526	564	490	423	337
Total Cap.	709	672	701	609	537	457
Cap. Exp.	64.4	64.0	68.3	49.5	78.9	68.4
Cash Flow	121	111	121	107	105	91.0

Ratio Analysis

	1994	1993	1992	1991	1990	1989
Curr. Ratio	3.6	3.4	3.2	3.4	2.6	2.4
% LT Debt of Cap.	5.6	6.2	6.4	4.9	6.5	7.4
% Net Inc.of Revs.	24.7	22.4	29.6	27.1	27.7	29.5
% Ret. on Assets	9.7	8.8	10.9	11.0	13.2	13.4
% Ret. on Equity	13.9	12.6	15.6	15.8	19.9	21.4

Dividend Data —Dividends have been paid since 1976.

Amt. of Div. $	Date Decl.	Ex-Div. Date	Stock of Record	Payment Date
0.120	Sep. 13	Oct. 06	Oct. 13	Nov. 03 '94
0.120	Dec. 02	Jan. 06	Jan. 12	Feb. 02 '95
0.120	Mar. 13	Apr. 10	Apr. 17	May. 09 '95
0.120	Jun. 21	Jul. 20	Jul. 24	Aug. 15 '95

Data as orig. reptd.; bef. results of disc. opers. and/or spec. items. Per share data adj. for stk. divs. as of ex-div. date. E-Estimated. NA-Not Available. NM-Not Meaningful. NR-Not Ranked.

Office—Marine Air Terminal, La Guardia Airport, Flushing, NY 11371. **Tel**—(718) 565-4100. **Chrmn & Pres**—A. L. Ueltschi. **Secy**—P. P. Mullen. **VP-Treas**—K. W. Motschwiller. **Investor Contact**—B. McDonald. **Dirs**—G. B. Beitzel, E. E. Hood Jr., C. R. Longsworth, J. A. Morgan, A. L. Ueltschi, B. N. Whitman. **Transfer Agent & Registrar**—American Stock Transfer & Trust Co., NYC. **Incorporated** in New York in 1951. **Empl**-2,500. **S&P Analyst:** William H. Donald

STANDARD & POOR'S

STOCK REPORTS

Florida Progress

NYSE Symbol **FPC**

In S&P MidCap 400

13-SEP-95 **Industry:** Utilities-Electric

Summary: Florida Progress is the holding company for Florida Power, which provides electric utility services to central, northern and Gulf Coast Florida.

S&P Opinion: Accumulate (★★★★)

Recent Price • 30¼
52 Wk Range • 32⅝-27⅜
Yield • 6.7%
12-Mo. P/E • 12.9

Quantitative Evaluations

Outlook
(1 Lowest—5 Highest)
• **2+**

Fair Value
• **27⅞**

Risk
• **Low**

Earn./Div. Rank
• **A-**

Technical Eval.
• **Bullish** since 11/94

Rel. Strength Rank
(1 Lowest—99 Highest)
• **22**

Insider Activity
• **NA**

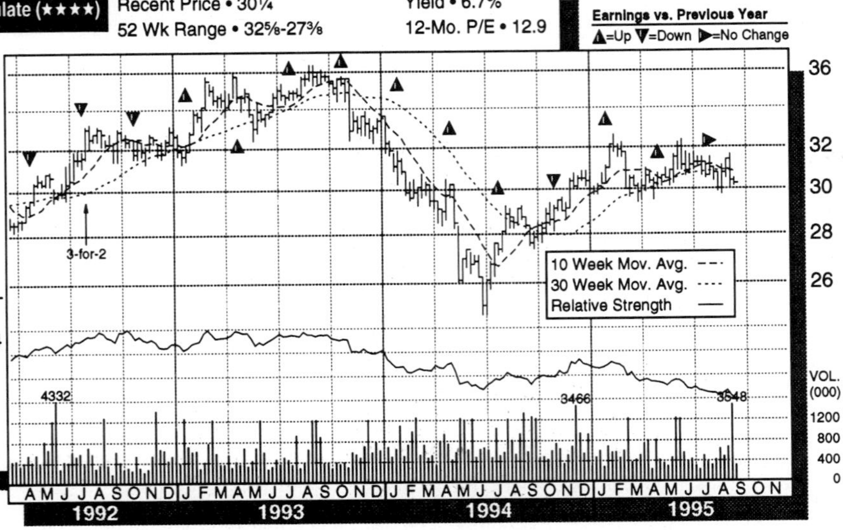

Overview - 12-SEP-95

Share earnings in 1995 and beyond should benefit from retail and wholesale rate increases, customer growth and a strengthening local economy. Results should also be aided by cost savings from a voluntary early retirement program, work force reductions, and the closing of two older plants. Contributions from diversified operations should advance, paced by growth in the energy and transportation unit, improved marine operations, the 1994 acquisitions of Steel Processing Services, Inc. and FM Industries, Inc., and greater coal sales. Long-term prospects should be enhanced by an expanding service territory and customer growth.

Valuation - 12-SEP-95

Reflecting the impact of rising interest rates and increased competition, FPC's shares fell substantially in 1994, although they finished the year with a rebound. The stock has moved up fractionally since the beginning of 1995. The shares were recently yielding 6.7%, slightly higher than the average yield for the industry. Dividend hikes of about 2.0% should continue in coming years. The shares were recently trading at 11 to 12 times estimated 1996 EPS of $2.55. Although this level is consistent with that of its industry, FPC's strong diversified operations should allow the shares to command a premium to the industry P/E. Therefore, based on the near-term prospects for earnings and dividend growth, the stock should be accumulated for both growth and income.

Key Stock Statistics

S&P EPS Est. 1995	2.45	Tang. Bk. Value/Share	20.90
P/E on S&P Est. 1995	12.3	Beta	0.35
S&P EPS Est. 1996	2.55	Shareholders	44,300
Dividend Rate/Share	2.02	Market cap. (B)	$ 2.9
Shs. outstg. (M)	95.5	Inst. holdings	37%
Avg. daily vol. (M)	0.256	Insider holdings	NA

Value of $10,000 invested 5 years ago: $ 16,107

Fiscal Year Ending Dec. 31

	1995	% Change	1994	% Change	1993	% Change
Revenues (Million $)						
1Q	703.2	10%	639.2	30%	493.0	6%
2Q	742.9	7%	693.2	25%	553.3	8%
3Q	—	—	756.2	-2%	768.9	23%
4Q	—	—	682.9	8%	633.5	28%
Yr.	—	—	2,772	13%	2,449	17%
Income (Million $)						
1Q	46.60	28%	36.50	9%	33.60	12%
2Q	55.20	3%	53.70	25%	43.00	23%
3Q	—	—	75.80	-8%	82.00	10%
4Q	—	—	46.00	24%	37.20	3%
Yr.	—	—	212.0	8%	195.8	11%
Earnings Per Share ($)						
1Q	0.49	20%	0.41	8%	0.38	6%
2Q	0.58	NM	0.58	18%	0.49	20%
3Q	E0.90	13%	0.80	-14%	0.93	8%
4Q	E0.48	-2%	0.49	17%	0.42	2%
Yr.	E2.45	7%	2.28	3%	2.22	8%

Next earnings report expected: late October

Florida Progress

Business Summary - 13-SEP-95

This holding company owns Florida Power Corp., which provides electric service to more than 1.2 million customers in 32 of Florida's 67 counties. In 1994, Florida Power accounted for 75% of total revenues and 90% of earnings. Nonutility businesses include coal mining and transportation and life insurance, but FPC wants to divest its leveraged leasing and real estate operations. Electric sales in recent years were derived as follows:

	1994	1993	1992	1991
Residential	46%	47%	47%	46%
Commercial	28%	28%	28%	27%
Industrial	12%	12%	12%	12%
Other	14%	13%	13%	15%

The fuel mix in 1994 was 45% coal, 16% oil, 17% nuclear, 21% purchased power, and 1% gas. Peak load in 1994 (winter) was 6,955 mw, and system capability (including purchased power sources) was 7,295 mw, for a 4.8% capacity margin. Retail electric kwh sales increased an average of 4.8% annually during the past 10-year period. FPC customers grew 2.4% in 1994.

In late 1994, Electric Fuels Corp., the company's energy and transportation unit, continued to expand with the acquisition of FM Industries, Inc., a Texas-based manufacturer and reconditioner of cushioning units for rail cars. In 1993, Electric Fuels acquired Steel Processing Services, Inc., which added $80 million to FPC revenues in 1993.

Important Developments

Jul. '95—FPC said Florida Power's retail kilowatt-hour sales increased by 4.6% in 1995's second quarter, compared with the prior-year quarter. Customer growth of about 2% and a stronger economy contributed to the improved energy sales. Also, earnings in the 1995 second quarter benefited from cost control initiatives. However, increased expenses for purchased power capacity costs, nuclear decommissioning, depreciation, and property taxes partially offset these positive factors.

Jan. '95—The company began a three-year test of revenue decoupling for residential customers, in effect separating revenues from energy sales. As a result, abnormal weather-related sales fluctuations will not affect residential sales earnings, because decoupling is designed to reconcile revenues to an authorized target level.

Capitalization

Long Term Debt: $1,811,200,000 (6/95).
Subsid. Cum. Pfd. Stk.: $143,500,000.

Per Share Data ($) (Year Ended Dec. 31)

	1994	1993	1992	1991	1990	1989
Tangible Bk. Val.	20.85	20.40	19.83	19.15	18.37	17.92
Earnings	2.28	2.22	2.06	2.16	2.33	2.45
Dividends	1.99	1.95	1.90	1.84	1.78	1.72
Payout Ratio	87%	88%	92%	88%	77%	70%
Prices - High	33⅝	36⅜	33¼	31½	27	26⅞
- Low	24¾	31¼	27⅞	24½	22⅜	22¼
P/E Ratio - High	15	16	16	15	12	11
- Low	11	14	14	11	10	9

Income Statement Analysis (Million $)

	1994	%Chg	1993	%Chg	1992	%Chg	1991
Revs.	2,081	6%	1,958	10%	1,774	3%	1,719
Depr.	262	9%	240	14%	210	2%	206
Maint.	123	-10%	137	-2%	140	4%	135
Fxd. Chgs. Cov.	3.2	NM	3.2	7%	3.0	9%	2.7
Constr. Credits	10.9	-30%	15.6	-17%	18.7	99%	9.4
Eff. Tax Rate	33%	—	35%	—	32%	—	33%
Net Inc.	212	8%	196	11%	176	NM	175

Balance Sheet & Other Fin. Data (Million $)

	1994	1993	1992	1991	1990	1989
Gross Prop.	5,878	5,674	5,252	4,851	4,581	4,382
Cap. Exp.	368	462	494	360	277	261
Net Prop.	3,669	3,641	3,442	3,193	3,077	2,998
Capitalization:						
LT Debt	1,860	1,867	1,656	1,581	1,326	1,127
% LT Debt	47	49	46	47	45	41
Pfd.	144	149	216	231	234	234
% Pfd.	3.60	3.90	6.00	6.80	7.80	8.60
Common	1,984	1,821	1,738	1,588	1,424	1,372
% Common	50	48	48	47	48	50
Total Cap.	4,842	4,712	4,556	4,367	3,955	3,690

Ratio Analysis

	1994	1993	1992	1991	1990	1989
Oper. Ratio	59.9	63.9	67.2	65.5	66.2	66.5
% Earn. on Net Prop.	13.0	12.5	12.2	13.3	14.3	NA
% Ret. on Revs.	10.1	10.0	9.9	10.2	10.5	11.5
% Ret. On Invest.Cap	10.0	7.1	6.8	7.9	8.8	9.1
% Return On Com.Eqty	11.1	11.0	10.6	11.6	12.9	13.9

Dividend Data —Dividends have been paid since 1937. A dividend reinvestment plan is available. A poison pill stock purchase rights plan was adopted in 1991.

Amt. of Div. $	Date Decl.	Ex-Div. Date	Stock of Record	Payment Date
0.495	Aug. 18	Aug. 30	Sep. 06	Sep. 20 '94
0.505	Nov. 17	Nov. 29	Dec. 05	Dec. 20 '94
0.505	Feb. 09	Feb. 28	Mar. 06	Mar. 20 '95
0.505	May. 18	May. 30	Jun. 05	Jun. 20 '95
0.505	Aug. 17	Aug. 31	Sep. 05	Sep. 20 '95

Data as orig. reptd.; bef. results of disc opers. and/or spec. items. Per share data adj. for stk. divs. as of ex-div. date. E-Estimated. NA-Not Available. NM-Not Meaningful. NR-Not Ranked.

Office—Barnett Tower, One Progress Plaza, St. Petersburg, FL 33701 (Mail: Box 33028, St. Petersburg, FL 33733). **Tel**—(813) 824-6400. **Chrmn & CEO**—J. R. Critchfield. **Pres & COO**—R. Korpan. **SVP & CFO**—J. R. Heinicka. **Secy**—K E. Armstrong. **Investor Contact**—Richard R. Champion (813-824-6428). **Dirs**—J. B. Critchfield, W. D. Frederick, M. P. Graney, A. J. Keesler, Jr., R. Korpan, C. V. McKee, V. J. Naimoli, R. A. Nunis, C. B. Reed, J. D. Ruffier, R. T. Stuart, Jr., J. G. Wittner. **Transfer Agent & Registrar**—Chemical Bank, NYC. **Incorporated** in Florida in 1899; reincorporated in Florida in 1982. **Empl**-7,394. **S&P Analyst:** Ronald J. Gross

STANDARD & POOR'S

STOCK REPORTS

Flowers Industries

NYSE Symbol **FLO**

In S&P MidCap 400

24-AUG-95 **Industry:** Food

Summary: This company is a major producer of baked goods, snack products and convenience foods for grocery, food service, restaurant and fast food customers.

S&P Opinion: Hold (★★★)

Recent Price • 21⅜

52 Wk Range • 21⅜-16½

Yield • 4.1%

12-Mo. P/E • 19.1

Quantitative Evaluations

Outlook (1 Lowest—5 Highest)
• **4+**

Fair Value
• **21½**

Risk
• **Low**

Earn./Div. Rank
• **B+**

Technical Eval.
• **Bearish** since 7/95

Rel. Strength Rank (1 Lowest—99 Highest)
• **72**

Insider Activity
• **Neutral**

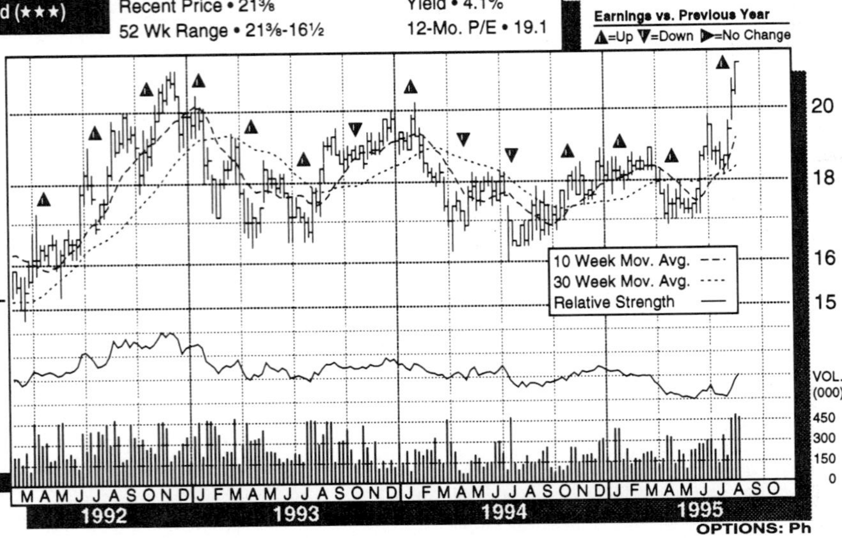

OPTIONS: Ph

Overview - 23-AUG-95

Sales for fiscal 1996 are projected to rise about 10%, driven by a combination of internal growth, contributions from acquisitions, selling price increases, and product line improvements. Recent progress at increasing manufacturing and distribution efficiencies should help support gross margins, while a somewhat easier competitive environment and a more profitable business mix should allow operating margins to widen. Significantly greater net interest expense may be a restraining factor to earnings, but solid earnings per share growth seems achievable in fiscal 1996.

Valuation - 23-AUG-95

Despite our forecast of low double-digit earnings per share growth in fiscal 1996 and FLO's generous 4% dividend yield, we are neutral on the shares. Earnings growth has been quite volatile over the years, due largely to FLO's high sensitivity to cyclical raw material cost increases (principally flour). Exacerbating this factor in recent years has been a softened consumer demand for sweet snack products, and a high level of competition, which has restricted the company's pricing flexibility. These factors are at least partly responsible for the steady consolidation of the U.S. baking industry, a long-term plus for FLO's prospects. However, given FLO's volatile earnings record and below-average return on capital, we expect only average total returns ahead.

Key Stock Statistics

S&P EPS Est. 1996	1.25	Tang. Bk. Value/Share	8.85
P/E on S&P Est. 1996	17.1	Beta	0.98
Dividend Rate/Share	0.84	Shareholders	4,000
Shs. outstg. (M)	39.4	Market cap. (B)	$0.813
Avg. daily vol. (M)	0.110	Inst. holdings	46%
		Insider holdings	NA

Value of $10,000 invested 5 years ago: $ 14,173

Fiscal Year Ending Jun. 30

	1995	% Change	1994	% Change	1993	% Change
Revenues (Million $)						
1Q	236.1	9%	217.4	3%	210.7	10%
2Q	270.0	15%	234.2	6%	220.0	7%
3Q	256.5	16%	221.7	5%	211.3	5%
4Q	369.2	17%	316.5	-1%	320.2	14%
Yr.	1,129	14%	989.8	3%	962.1	9%
Income (Million $)						
1Q	6.24	34%	4.67	-27%	6.44	75%
2Q	10.63	30%	8.19	10%	7.46	37%
3Q	9.10	23%	7.38	-4%	7.69	19%
4Q	16.34	76%	9.26	-47%	17.56	12%
Yr.	42.30	43%	29.50	-25%	39.16	24%
Earnings Per Share ($)						
1Q	0.17	31%	0.13	-28%	0.18	64%
2Q	0.28	27%	0.22	10%	0.20	25%
3Q	0.24	20%	0.20	-5%	0.21	5%
4Q	0.43	72%	0.25	-47%	0.47	7%
Yr.	1.12	40%	0.80	-25%	1.07	16%

Next earnings report expected: late October

Flowers Industries

Business Summary - 23-AUG-95

Flowers Industries produces and distributes baked foods, snack products and convenience foods for grocery, food service, restaurant and fast food markets in the Southeast, Central and Western U.S. It operates 35 production facilities. Products are distributed through 2,300 company-owned and independent distributor routes, and sold by distributors, salesmen and food brokers. FLO also operates a number of thrift outlets for the sale of surplus product. Sales to Winn-Dixie Stores, Inc. accounted for more than 10% of consolidated sales during fiscal 1994.

Baked foods include a variety of breads, rolls and buns under the company's own brand names (including Flowers, Nature's Own, Breads International, Cobblestone Mill, Rich Grain, Evangeline Maid, Buttermaid, Betsy Ross, Dandee, Purity, Ideal, Holsum) and franchised trademarks (Sunbeam, Bunny).

Snack food operations include the manufacture of sweet goods, snack cakes, baked and fried pies, doughnuts and potato chips sold under the Beebo, BlueBird and other house brands.

Convenience products include frozen vegetables, batter-dipped and breaded vegetables, fruits, baked goods, pie shells and food ingredient products, sold primarily under the Stilwell brand name.

Important Developments

Aug. '95—FLO attributed the 14% gain in sales for fiscal 1995 to a combination of internal growth, acquisitions, product mix changes, and pricing. Management also said it sees a continuation of strong revenue and profit growth in fiscal 1996, noting that the company was well positioned within its industry to take advantage of opportunities to produce significant internal growth as well as growth through acquisitions. Separately, FLO declared its 64th consecutive quarterly dividend increase, payable on September 1, 1995.

May '95—FLO sold its Rio Grande Foods, Inc. subsidiary to Dean Foods Co., for an undisclosed amount. Rio Grande Foods is a processor and distributor of non-breaded southern vegetables with annual sales of about $40 million.

Capitalization

Long Term Debt: $120,944,000 (6/95).

Per Share Data ($)

(Year Ended Jun. 30)

	1995	1994	1993	1992	1991	1990
Tangible Bk. Val.	NA	7.35	7.43	6.36	6.14	6.27
Cash Flow	NA	1.72	1.98	1.90	1.62	1.59
Earnings	1.12	0.80	1.07	0.92	0.71	0.98
Dividends	0.82	0.77	0.74	0.70	0.65	0.59
Payout Ratio	73%	97%	69%	76%	92%	60%
Prices - High	21¾	20¼	20½	21¼	17¼	20⅞
- Low	16⅞	16	16⅜	14¾	12¾	11⅞
P/E Ratio - High	19	25	19	23	24	21
- Low	15	20	15	16	18	12

Income Statement Analysis (Million $)

	1994	%Chg	1993	%Chg	1992	%Chg	1991
Revs.	990	3%	962	9%	879	7%	825
Oper. Inc.	75.7	-13%	87.2	7%	81.3	10%	73.9
Depr.	34.1	3%	33.1	NM	33.4	8%	31.0
Int. Exp.	4.3	8%	4.0	-51%	8.2	-13%	9.4
Pretax Inc.	47.2	-21%	60.0	22%	49.2	24%	39.8
Eff. Tax Rate	38%	—	35%	—	36%	—	40%
Net Inc.	29.5	-25%	39.2	24%	31.7	32%	24.0

Balance Sheet & Other Fin. Data (Million $)

	1994	1993	1992	1991	1990	1989
Cash	19.8	17.2	14.3	11.0	17.4	26.0
Curr. Assets	176	151	143	124	125	137
Total Assets	561	491	462	435	439	448
Curr. Liab.	122	120	99	86.7	77.0	88.1
LT Debt	93.0	36.0	95.0	92.0	92.0	102
Common Eqty.	276	280	218	206	216	208
Total Cap.	405	349	344	330	340	340
Cap. Exp.	64.0	52.0	33.0	63.0	103	103
Cash Flow	63.6	72.3	65.1	55.1	55.3	65.6

Ratio Analysis

	1994	1993	1992	1991	1990	1989
Curr. Ratio	1.4	1.3	1.4	1.4	1.6	1.5
% LT Debt of Cap.	22.9	10.3	27.7	28.0	26.9	29.9
% Net Inc.of Revs.	3.0	4.1	3.6	2.9	4.1	3.8
% Ret. on Assets	5.6	7.8	7.0	5.6	7.7	6.7
% Ret. on Equity	10.6	15.1	14.8	11.5	16.2	14.5

Dividend Data —Dividends have been paid quarterly since 1971. A dividend reinvestment plan is available. A "poison pill" stock purchase rights plan was adopted in 1989.

Amt. of Div. $	Date Decl.	Ex-Div. Date	Stock of Record	Payment Date
0.200	Aug. 05	Aug. 15	Aug. 19	Sep. 02 '94
0.202	Oct. 21	Oct. 31	Nov. 04	Nov. 18 '94
0.205	Jan. 13	Jan. 23	Jan. 27	Feb. 10 '95
0.208	Apr. 05	Apr. 17	Apr. 21	May. 05 '95
0.210	Aug. 04	Aug. 16	Aug. 18	Sep. 01 '95

Data as orig. reptd.; bef. results of disc. opers. and/or spec. items. Per share data adj. for stk. divs. as of ex-div. date. E-Estimated. NA-Not Available. NM-Not Meaningful. NR-Not Ranked.

Office—U.S. Highway 19 (PO Box 1338), Thomasville, GA 31799. **Tel**—(912) 226-9110. **Chrmn & CEO**—A. R. McMullian. **Pres**—H. Varnedoe III. **Secy**—G. A. Campbell. **VP-CFO & Investor Contact**—C. Martin Wood III. **Dirs**—E. L. Baker, F. L. Burke, G. A. Campbell, R. P. Crozer, J. B. Ellis, L. S. Flowers, W. H. Flowers Jr., R. M. Fryar, J. L. Lanier Jr., A. R. McMullian, J. V. Shields, H. Varnedoe III, C. M. Wood III. **Transfer Agent & Registrar**—Wachovia Bank of North Carolina, Winston-Salem. **Incorporated** in Delaware in 1968; reincorporated in Georgia in 1987. **Empl**-7,900. **S&P Analyst:** Kenneth A. Shea

STANDARD & POOR'S

STOCK REPORTS

Forest Laboratories

ASE Symbol **FRX**
In S&P MidCap 400

05-SEP-95 **Industry:** Drugs-Generic and OTC

Summary: This company develops and makes branded and generic ethical drug products, sold primarily in the U.S., Puerto Rico, and Western and Eastern Europe.

S&P Opinion: Hold (★★★) | Recent Price • 44¾ | 52 Wk Range • 52¼-41 | Yield • Nil | 12-Mo. P/E • 20.0

Quantitative Evaluations

Outlook (1 Lowest—5 Highest) • 5-

Fair Value • 55⅝

Risk • Low

Earn./Div. Rank • B+

Technical Eval. • **Bullish** since 5/95

Rel. Strength Rank (1 Lowest—99 Highest) • 41

Insider Activity • NA

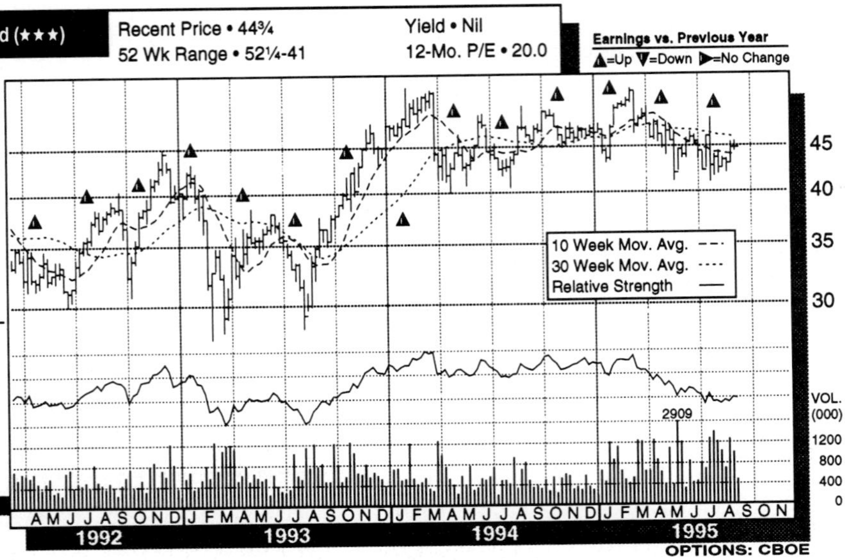

Overview - 05-SEP-95

This maker of small niche-oriented branded and generic drugs should maintain its strong sales and earnings growth record in 1995-6, with sales projected to rise 17%, to $470 million, and earnings expected to increase 19%, to $2.55 a share. Despite a projected decline in sales of generic propranolol, robust gains are seen for Aerobid asthma medication, Lorcet analgesic and Flumadine influenza A treatment. New products such as Cervidil, a product used to help cervical dilation and labor induction, and new marketing alliances should also bolster sales. Forest recently signed drug co-promotion agreements with Muro Pharmaceutical and Bock Pharmacal. Margins should benefit from better volume and cost efficiencies.

Valuation - 05-SEP-95

The shares have been in a modest downtrend in recent months, reflecting several disappointing announcements. In May, the FDA refused to accept Forest's New Drug Application (NDA) for Infasurf respiratory drug. In July, an FDA advisory committee voted against recommending approval for the company's Monorul broad spectrum antibiotic. However, after the submission of new data, the FDA said it would accept the Infasurf NDA, and Forest also remains optimistic about obtaining approval for Monurol. Long-term prospects are enhanced by several new niche-oriented drugs, an efficient marketing organization, and a strong balance sheet. The shares merit retention.

Key Stock Statistics

S&P EPS Est. 1996	2.55	Tang. Bk. Value/Share	11.47
P/E on S&P Est. 1996	17.5	Beta	1.04
S&P EPS Est. 1997	2.95	Shareholders	3,100
Dividend Rate/Share	Nil	Market cap. (B)	$ 2.0
Shs. outstg. (M)	45.2	Inst. holdings	77%
Avg. daily vol. (M)	0.200	Insider holdings	NA

Value of $10,000 invested 5 years ago: $ 21,372

Fiscal Year Ending Mar. 31

	1996	% Change	1995	% Change	1994	% Change
Revenues (Million $)						
1Q	110.7	20%	92.55	17%	79.25	16%
2Q	—	—	95.78	16%	82.81	14%
3Q	—	—	107.3	11%	97.00	24%
4Q	—	—	97.75	6%	92.58	20%
Yr.	—	—	393.4	12%	351.6	19%
Income (Million $)						
1Q	26.56	20%	22.14	26%	17.54	26%
2Q	—	—	24.57	26%	19.55	24%
3Q	—	—	25.72	24%	20.81	24%
4Q	—	—	27.72	24%	22.30	25%
Yr.	—	—	100.2	25%	80.20	25%
Earnings Per Share ($)						
1Q	0.57	19%	0.48	23%	0.39	26%
2Q	E0.63	19%	0.53	23%	0.43	23%
3Q	E0.65	18%	0.55	22%	0.45	22%
4Q	E0.70	19%	0.59	23%	0.48	23%
Yr.	E2.55	19%	2.15	23%	1.75	23%

Next earnings report expected: late October

Forest Laboratories

Business Summary - 05-SEP-95

Forest Laboratories develops, produces and sells branded and generic forms of prescription and over-the-counter drugs. Principal products include Aerobid, a metered dose inhaled steroid used to treat asthma (24% of 1994-5 sales); the Lorcet line of potent analgesics (17%); and Tessalon, a solid dose non-narcotic cough suppressant (5%, including sales of a generic formulation). Other products include Aerochamber, a spacer device used to improve the delivery of aerosol products; the ESGIC line of analgesics; Levothroid, a thyroid product; Flumadine, an antiviral used to treat and prevent Influenza A; and Cervidil, a product used to aid in cervical dilation and labor induction.

The generic product line, marketed in the U.S. by the Inwood Laboratories subsidiary, specializes in controlled-release pharmaceuticals. Three important controlled-release products are Propranolol E.R., a beta blocker used to treat hypertension (16% of 1994-5 sales); Indomethacin E.R., a non-steroidal anti-inflammatory drug used to treat arthritis; and Theochron, a theophylline tablet used in the treatment of asthma.

Key products sold by Forest's U.K. and Ireland subsidiaries include Sudocrem, a topical preparation for the treatment of diaper rash; Colomycin, an antibiotic used in the treatment of cystic fibrosis; and Suscard and Sustac, sustained action nitroglycerin tablets to treat angina. Sales in the U.K. and Ireland represented 10% of the 1994-5 total, and 6.2% of operating profits.

Products in development include Monurol, a single dose antibiotic used to treat uncomplicated urinary tract infections; Infasurf, a treatment for respiratory distress syndrome in premature infants; Synapton, a treatment for Alzheimer's disease; and Methoxatone, an anti-inflammatory. R&D spending in 1994-5 totaled $32,010,000 (equal to 7.9% of net revenues), versus $27,998,000 (7.7%) in 1993-4.

Important Developments

Aug. '95—The company and Procter & Gamble agreed to co-promote Forest's Lorcet 10/650 pain reliever to dental professionals. Earlier, in July, an FDA advisory committee voted against recommending approval for the company's Monurol antibiotic. However, Forest said it planned to submit new data to the FDA, and remained optimistic about prospects for obtaining FDA marketing approval for Monurol. In May, the company launched Cervidil, a product used to aid cervical dilation and labor induction.

Capitalization

Long Term Debt: None (6/95).
Options: To buy 4,745,277 shs. at $8.50 to $48.19 ea. (3/95).

Per Share Data ($) (Year Ended Mar. 31)

	1995	1994	1993	1992	1991	1990
Tangible Bk. Val.	11.47	9.51	7.80	5.67	3.13	4.19
Cash Flow	2.45	1.98	1.65	1.36	1.08	0.87
Earnings	2.15	1.75	1.42	1.13	0.90	0.72
Dividends	Nil	Nil	Nil	Nil	Nil	Nil
Payout Ratio	Nil	Nil	Nil	Nil	Nil	Nil
Cal. Yrs.	1994	1993	1992	1991	1990	1989
Prices - High	52½	47⅞	44⅞	43⅝	25⅜	22¼
- Low	40	27½	30	22¼	16¾	12⅛
P/E Ratio - High	24	27	32	39	28	31
- Low	19	16	21	20	19	17

Income Statement Analysis (Million $)

	1995	%Chg	1994	%Chg	1993	%Chg	1992
Revs.	393	12%	352	24%	285	19%	240
Oper. Inc.	159	26%	126	24%	102	22%	83.5
Depr.	14.1	32%	10.7	2%	10.5	2%	10.3
Int. Exp.	Nil	—	Nil	—	2.0	-47%	3.7
Pretax Inc.	156	25%	125	24%	101	30%	77.5
Eff. Tax Rate	36%	—	36%	—	36%	—	36%
Net Inc.	100	25%	80.2	25%	64.3	30%	49.6

Balance Sheet & Other Fin. Data (Million $)

	1995	1994	1993	1992	1991	1990
Cash	142	181	172	133	60.0	79.0
Curr. Assets	349	348	315	244	138	133
Total Assets	757	619	521	431	331	239
Curr. Liab.	57.6	52.2	41.1	55.9	42.0	14.2
LT Debt	Nil	Nil	Nil	Nil	23.1	Nil
Common Eqty.	699	567	479	373	264	223
Total Cap.	700	700	479	375	289	225
Cap. Exp.	22.2	27.1	6.3	3.6	8.9	4.3
Cash Flow	114	90.9	74.8	59.9	45.3	35.6

Ratio Analysis

	1995	1994	1993	1992	1991	1990
Curr. Ratio	6.1	6.7	7.6	4.4	3.3	9.4
% LT Debt of Cap.	Nil	Nil	Nil	Nil	8.0	Nil
% Net Inc.of Revs.	25.5	22.8	22.5	20.6	21.5	20.8
% Ret. on Assets	14.3	14.0	13.3	12.6	13.3	13.1
% Ret. on Equity	15.6	15.2	14.9	15.1	15.5	14.0

Dividend Data —No cash dividends have been paid. A shareholder rights plan, adopted in 1988, was revised in September 1994.

Data as orig. reptd.; bef. results of disc. opers. and/or spec. items. Per share data adj. for stk. divs. as of ex-div. date. E-Estimated. NA-Not Available. NM-Not Meaningful. NR-Not Ranked.

Office—150 E. 58th Street, New York, NY 10155-0015. **Tel**—(212) 421-7850. **Pres & CEO**—H. Solomon. **VP-Fin & Investor Contact**—Kenneth E. Goodman. **Secy**—W. J. Candee III. **Dirs**—W. J. Candee III, G. S. Cohan, D. L. Goldwasser, J. M. Schor, H. Solomon. **Transfer Agent**—Chemical Bank, NYC. **Incorporated** in Delaware in 1956. **Empl**-1,319. **S&P Analyst:** H. B. Saftlas

STANDARD & POOR'S

STOCK REPORTS

Foundation Health

NYSE Symbol **FH**

In S&P MidCap 400

31-JUL-95

Industry: Health Care Centers

Summary: This California-based company provides group, individual, Medicare and Medicaid health care coverage through an HMO and PPO network in several states.

S&P Opinion: Buy (★★★★★)	Recent Price • 33¾	Yield • Nil
	52 Wk Range • 39¼-26⅜	12-Mo. P/E • 37.5

Quantitative Evaluations

Outlook (1 Lowest—5 Highest)
• **5-**

Fair Value
• **33**

Risk
• **Average**

Earn./Div. Rank
• **NR**

Technical Eval.
• **Bullish** since 8/94

Rel. Strength Rank (1 Lowest—99 Highest)
• **85**

Insider Activity
• **Neutral**

Earnings vs. Previous Year
▲=Up ▼=Down ▶=No Change

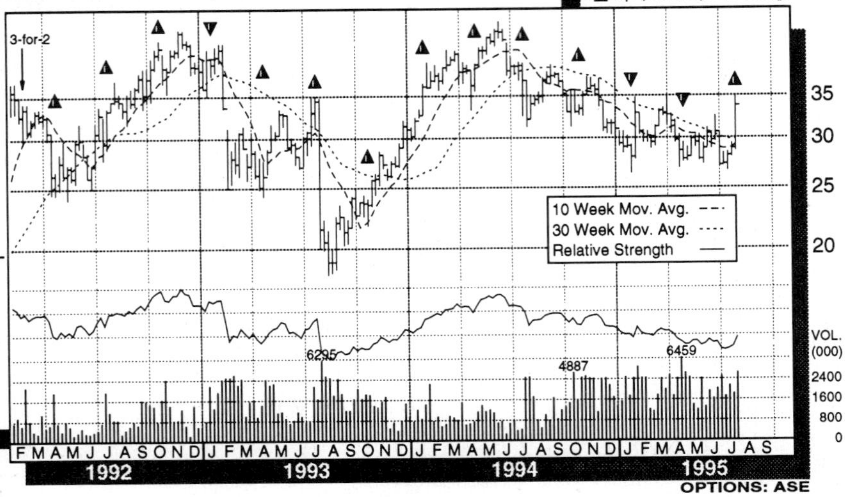

Overview - 31-JUL-95

Results for fiscal 1995 (June) met expectations, as substantial revenue growth (attributable to solid commercial enrollment gains) was coupled with a declining medical loss ratio and a lower tax rate. Per-share earnings of $0.90 included second quarter charges of $1.45 for restructuring and acquisition costs. Concerns regarding a tough premium environment in California, as well as margins in the workers' compensation business line, were somewhat alleviated in the fourth quarter. We would expect that expansion into new markets, increased commercial membership and benefits from recent acquisitions will lead to further earnings gains in fiscal 1996.

Valuation - 31-JUL-95

Based on our fiscal 1996 EPS estimate of $3.05, Foundation Health appears significantly undervalued at recent levels, both in terms of anticipated growth and compared with the company's HMO peers. The company has generated impressive commercial membership growth, while hospital utilization in the group and individual products has shown a downward trend. In the fourth quarter of fiscal 1995, the commercial medical loss ratio fell to 75.8% from 79.7% in the year-earlier period. Enrollment in fiscal 1996 will benefit from the addition of about 590,000 eligible beneficiaries of the Government's CHAMPUS program.

Key Stock Statistics

S&P EPS Est. 1996	3.05	Tang. Bk. Value/Share	5.25
P/E on S&P Est. 1996	11.1	Beta	NA
Dividend Rate/Share	Nil	Shareholders	18,000
Shs. outstg. (M)	57.1	Market cap. (B)	$ 1.9
Avg. daily vol. (M)	0.549	Inst. holdings	77%
		Insider holdings	NA

Value of $10,000 invested 5 years ago: NA

Fiscal Year Ending Jun. 30

	1995	% Change	1994	% Change	1993	% Change
Revenues (Million $)						
1Q	405.9	-16%	481.3	38%	349.0	32%
2Q	598.5	22%	490.3	47%	334.1	21%
3Q	615.6	53%	403.6	5%	383.1	42%
4Q	651.4	90%	342.6	-24%	451.0	36%
Yr.	2,460	43%	1,718	13%	1,517	33%
Income (Million $)						
1Q	19.94	4%	19.21	—	—	—
2Q	-49.27	NM	24.33	153%	9.60	-11%
3Q	36.29	85%	19.59	5%	18.65	53%
4Q	38.80	104%	19.03	NM	18.91	45%
Yr.	49.45	-40%	82.15	33%	61.91	35%
Earnings Per Share ($)						
1Q	0.68	3%	0.66	35%	0.49	7%
2Q	-0.90	NM	0.85	166%	0.32	-36%
3Q	0.63	-7%	0.68	10%	0.62	19%
4Q	0.68	3%	0.66	5%	0.63	17%
Yr.	0.90	-68%	2.84	39%	2.05	1%

Next earnings report expected: late October

Foundation Health

Business Summary - 31-JUL-95

Foundation Health administers the delivery of managed health care services to more than 2.9 million eligible individuals (as of June 1994) through its health maintenance organization (HMO), government contracting and specialty services managed care subsidiaries. Contributions to revenues in recent fiscal years were:

	1994	1993
HMO premiums	42%	41%
Government contracts	32%	49%
Specialty services & other	26%	10%

A company HMO operating throughout most of California arranges for the delivery of specified health care services to its enrollees for periodic, prepaid premiums that do not vary with the extent of medical services actually provided. FH manages medical and hospital costs through contractual arrangements with independent providers of health care services and through control of unnecessary utilization and the appropriate use of managed care. During fiscal 1994, the company filed applications to become licensed as an HMO in Texas, Louisiana, Florida, Alabama and Oklahoma and recently became licensed in Louisiana, Texas and Florida.

FH's government contracts subsidiary administers managed care programs for CHAMPUS and Medicaid, while its specialized managed care subsidiaries offer dental, vision, behavioral health, workers' compensation administration, pharmaceutical and ancillary products and services.

Important Developments

Jul. '95—Foundation signed a letter of intent to enter into comprehensive, multi-year agreements under which medical group and outpatient affiliates of Sutter Health in 16 Northern California counties will serve individuals covered by the company's managed care affiliates. The agreements, many of which take effect August 1, 1995, will cover most FH products including HMO, PPO, Point-of-Service, Medicare, Medi-Cal, workers' compensation and CHAMPUS.

May '95—The company was awarded a five-year contract, valued at up to $1.8 billion, to operate a comprehensive managed care program for about 590,000 eligible beneficiaries of the Civilian Health and Medical Program of the Uniform Services (CHAMPUS) in Oklahoma, most of Arkansas, Louisiana and Texas. Delivery of health care services is scheduled to begin in November 1995.

Capitalization

Long Term Obligations: $180,054,000 (6/95) of notes payable and capital lease obligations.

Per Share Data ($)

(Year Ended Jun. 30)

	1995	1994	1993	1992	1991	1990
Tangible Bk. Val.	NA	10.09	7.51	5.91	4.53	-8.84
Cash Flow	NA	3.60	2.52	2.33	1.65	1.90
Earnings	0.90	2.84	2.05	2.02	1.33	0.92
Dividends	Nil	Nil	Nil	Nil	Nil	Nil
Payout Ratio	Nil	Nil	Nil	Nil	Nil	Nil
Prices - High	34⅞	46	42½	44¾	23¾	10
- Low	26⅜	29¾	18⅛	22⅜	7⅛	6⅝
P/E Ratio - High	39	16	22	22	18	11
- Low	29	10	9	11	5	7

Income Statement Analysis (Million $)

	1994	%Chg	1993	%Chg	1992	%Chg	1991
Revs.	1,718	13%	1,517	33%	1,143	19%	963
Oper. Inc.	160	21%	132	67%	79.1	77%	44.6
Depr.	21.9	53%	14.3	99%	7.2	33%	5.4
Int. Exp.	10.2	NM	2.2	175%	0.8	-85%	5.3
Pretax Inc.	128	25%	103	45%	71.2	109%	34.0
Eff. Tax Rate	36%	—	40%	—	35%	—	27%
Net Inc.	82.2	33%	61.9	35%	45.9	84%	24.9

Balance Sheet & Other Fin. Data (Million $)

	1994	1993	1992	1991	1990	1989
Cash	621	355	189	93.0	48.0	46.0
Curr. Assets	NA	543	285	177	145	90.0
Total Assets	1,231	692	381	245	218	165
Curr. Liab.	NA	261	174	156	172	116
LT Debt	135	134	5.1	1.6	73.9	88.3
Common Eqty.	360	290	198	85.0	-47.0	-57.0
Total Cap.	495	431	207	89.0	46.0	49.0
Cap. Exp.	39.0	19.3	7.9	5.7	4.1	3.0
Cash Flow	104	76.2	53.1	28.6	20.6	NA

Ratio Analysis

	1994	1993	1992	1991	1990	1989
Curr. Ratio	NA	2.1	1.6	1.1	0.8	0.8
% LT Debt of Cap.	27.3	31.2	2.5	1.8	160.1	179.7
% Net Inc.of Revs.	4.8	4.1	4.0	2.6	1.2	NM
% Ret. on Assets	8.5	10.6	13.4	4.9	4.9	NM
% Ret. on Equity	25.3	23.1	30.3	NM	NM	NM

Dividend Data (The company has never paid cash dividends on its common stock, and currently intends to retain its earnings for the development of its business. A "poison pill" stock purchase rights plan was adopted in 1991.)

Data as orig. reptd.; bef. results of disc. opers. and/or spec. items. Per share data adj. for stk. divs. as of ex-div. date. E-Estimated. NA-Not Available. NM-Not Meaningful. NR-Not Ranked.

Office—3400 Data Drive, Rancho Cordova, CA 95670. **Tel**—(916) 631-5000. **Chrmn & Pres**—D. D. Crowley. **SVP & CFO**—J. L. Elder. **SVP & Secy**—A. J. Marabito. **Investor Contact**—Kurt D. Davis (916-631-5288). **Dirs**—R. Anderson, D. A. Boggs, D. D. Crowley, J. L. Elder, E. B. Fowler, R. W. Hanselman, R. D. Henderson, F. A. Olson, R. W. Stegemeier, S. D. Tough, R. S. Troubh. **Transfer Agent & Registrar**—Chemical Trust Co. of California, SF. **Incorporated** in Delaware in 1984. **Empl**-4,978. **S&P Analyst:** Robert M. Gold

Franklin Resources

NYSE Symbol **BEN**
In S&P MidCap 400

08-AUG-95 **Industry:** Securities

Summary: Franklin Resources is one of the world's largest publicly traded independent asset managers, with almost $126 billion of assets under management at June 30, 1995.

S&P Opinion: Hold (★★★)

Recent Price • 49⅛
52 Wk Range • 50⅞-33
Yield • 0.8%
12-Mo. P/E • 15.7

Quantitative Evaluations
Outlook
(1 Lowest—5 Highest)
• **4-**
Fair Value
• **55⅛**
Risk
• **Average**
Earn./Div. Rank
• **A**

Technical Eval.
• **Bullish** since 3/95
Rel. Strength Rank
(1 Lowest—99 Highest)
• **79**
Insider Activity
• **Unfavorable**

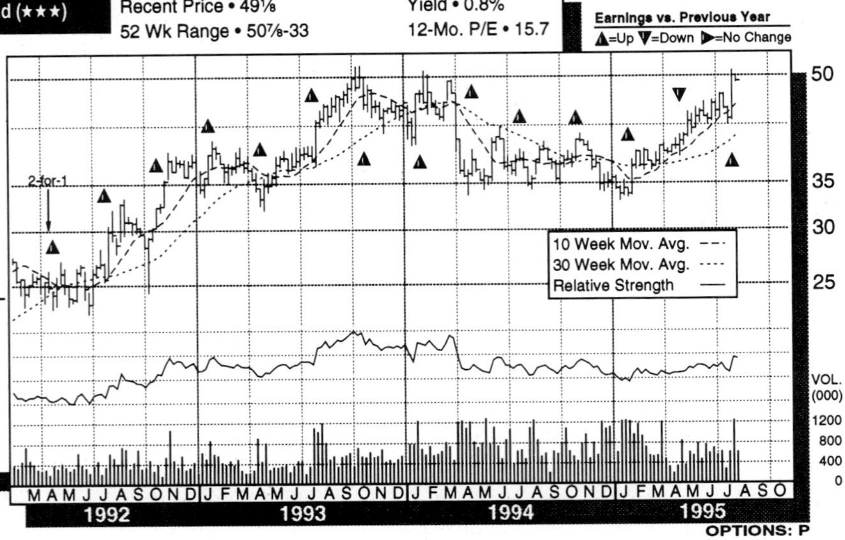

Overview - 08-AUG-95

Modest earnings per share growth of some 8-11% a year is anticipated for the foreseeable future, subject to market conditions. Market conditions, which determine the value of assets under management and thus fees, are not predictable. Long term growth factors include: the ongoing reinvestment of dividends and interest, anticipated legislation to encourage savings, favorable demographics, and an increasing awareness of international investing. Assets under management in the near term could be restricted by pressure on municipal bonds (which comprise a large percentage of total assets) due to the flat tax proposal, among other factors. One considerable strength is Franklin's extremely wide pretax margins (45.0% in the fiscal 1995 third quarter).

Valuation - 08-AUG-95

Although the shares possess attributes that would interest a value investor, valuation levels indicate a rating of "average performer." After the recent run up, Franklin trades at a P/E ratio of about 14 times projected fiscal 1996 earnings per share, close to the market's multiple. The stock is also near its all-time high, and on a historical note, the company is not likely to grow nearly as rapidly as it did in the early 1980s, the golden years of the mutual fund industry. Nothwithstanding these concerns, Franklin enjoys a modestly positive growth outlook, is well diversified by types of funds offered, and consistently generates high returns on shareholder's equity.

Key Stock Statistics

S&P EPS Est. 1995	3.20	Tang. Bk. Value/Share	4.47
P/E on S&P Est. 1995	15.4	Beta	1.75
S&P EPS Est. 1996	3.45	Shareholders	1,500
Dividend Rate/Share	0.40	Market cap. (B)	$ 3.9
Shs. outstg. (M)	80.9	Inst. holdings	38%
Avg. daily vol. (M)	0.151	Insider holdings	NA

Value of $10,000 invested 5 years ago: $ 36,126

Fiscal Year Ending Sep. 30

	1995	% Change	1994	% Change	1993	% Change
Revenues (Million $)						
1Q	215.6	9%	198.5	56%	126.9	42%
2Q	209.3	-2%	213.6	39%	153.6	60%
3Q	224.5	10%	204.9	26%	162.7	68%
4Q	--	—	209.9	6%	197.5	92%
Yr.	--	—	826.9	29%	640.7	66%
Income (Million $)						
1Q	63.30	7%	59.00	70%	34.80	21%
2Q	63.04	-8%	68.60	63%	42.20	36%
3Q	69.03	15%	60.02	34%	44.80	44%
4Q	—	—	63.68	19%	53.70	63%
Yr.	—	—	251.3	43%	175.5	41%
Earnings Per Share ($)						
1Q	0.76	9%	0.70	63%	0.43	16%
2Q	0.76	-7%	0.82	61%	0.51	28%
3Q	0.84	17%	0.72	33%	0.54	35%
4Q	E0.84	—	0.76	19%	0.64	52%
Yr.	E3.20	—	3.00	42%	2.12	33%

Next earnings report expected: late October

Franklin Resources

08-AUG-95

Business Summary - 08-AUG-95

Franklin Resources is one of the world's largest publicly traded independent asset managers. Operations were significantly expanded with the October 1992 acquisition of Templeton, Galbraith & Hansberger Ltd., a global investment management organization. Assets under management of $118.2 billion at September 30, 1994, and $107.5 billion a year earlier, were divided as follows:

	9/94	9/93
Fixed Income:		
Tax-Free Income	33%	38%
U. S. government fixed income	13%	17%
Money Fund	2%	2%
Global/Intl. fixed income	2%	2%
Equity and Income:		
U. Global/Intl. equity	24%	18%
U. S. Equity/income	15%	15%
Institutional	11%	8%

The four largest funds represented 38% of assets under management in the Franklin Templeton Group. Changes in net assets under management are the primary factor affecting the company's revenues. As of September 30, 1994 there were approximately 4.3 million shareholder accounts in the Franklin Templeton funds.

Fund shares are sold primarily through a large network of independent participating securities dealers. As of September 30, 1994, about 3,500 local, regional and national securities brokerage firms offered shares of the Franklin Templeton funds for sale to the investing public. The company has about 42 "wholesalers" who interface with the broker/dealer community. Generally, the funds pay advisory companies a fee payable monthly based upon a fund's net assets. Annual rates under the various investment management agreements range from 0.25% to a maximum of 1.75% and are generally reduced as average net assets exceed various threshold levels.

Franklin Bank (assets of $209 million) together with BEN's finance operations posted operating income of $5.4 million in fiscal 1994. Real estate and other operations had an operating loss of $1.1 million in fiscal 1994.

Important Developments

Jul. '95—The company said that assets under management rose to $125.9 billion from $113.0 billion this time last year and $118.8 billion at the end of the preceding quarter.

Capitalization

Long Term Debt: $382,399,000 (3/95).

Per Share Data ($)

(Year Ended Sep. 30)

	1994	1993	1992	1991	1990	1989
Tangible Bk. Val.	3.09	0.29	5.99	4.66	3.69	2.77
Cash Flow	NA	NA	NA	NA	NA	NA
Earnings	3.00	2.12	1.59	1.26	1.14	1.00
Dividends	0.32	0.28	0.26	0.23	0.20	0.15
Payout Ratio	11%	13%	16%	18%	18%	15%
Prices - High	51	51⅞	39	28¼	18	15⅛
- Low	33⅝	32	22¾	14¾	11¼	7½
P/E Ratio - High	17	24	25	23	16	15
- Low	11	15	14	12	10	8

Income Statement Analysis (Million $)

	1994	%Chg	1993	%Chg	1992	%Chg	1991
Commissions	96.6	11%	87.1	187%	30.3	24%	24.4
Int. Inc.	NA	—	NA	—	NA	—	NA
Total Revs.	827	29%	641	66%	385	21%	318
Int. Exp.	9.4	NM	9.4	-26%	12.7	9%	11.6
Pretax Inc.	363	32%	274	34%	205	26%	163
Eff. Tax Rate	31%	—	36%	—	39%	—	40%
Net Inc.	251	44%	175	41%	124	26%	98.2

Balance Sheet & Other Fin. Data (Million $)

	1994	1993	1992	1991	1990	1989
Total Assets	1,738	1,582	834	579	479	394
Cash Items	210	303	2.8	3.9	1.7	1.1
Receivables	51.7	248	171	119	83.0	85.0
Secs. Owned	189	217	598	408	351	277
Sec. Borrowed	Nil	Nil	Nil	Nil	Nil	Nil
Due Brokers & Cust.	127	91.7	34.6	35.9	32.0	28.4
Other Liabs.	297	355	177	174	154	143
Capitalization:						
Debt	384	455	156	5.6	4.2	6.1
Equity	931	720	467	363	289	217
Total	1,314	1,175	623	369	293	223

Ratio Analysis

	1994	1993	1992	1991	1990	1989
% Ret. on Revs.	30.4	27.4	32.2	30.9	31.1	31.0
% Ret. on Assets	15.1	14.5	17.6	18.6	20.5	21.9
% Ret. on Equity	30.4	29.6	29.9	30.1	35.4	42.9

Dividend Data (Dividends were initiated in 1981.)

Amt. of Div. $	Date Decl.	Ex-Div. Date	Stock of Record	Payment Date
0.080	Sep. 16	Sep. 26	Sep. 30	Oct. 15 '94
0.100	Dec. 12	Dec. 23	Dec. 31	Jan. 15 '95
0.100	Mar. 23	Mar. 28	Apr. 03	Apr. 17 '95
0.100	Jun. 22	Jun. 28	Jun. 30	Jul. 14 '95

Data as orig. reptd.; bef. results of disc opers. and/or spec. items. Per share data adj. for stk. divs. as of ex-div. date. E-Estimated. NA-Not Available. NM-Not Meaningful. NR-Not Ranked.

Office—777 Mariners Island Blvd., San Mateo, CA 94404. **Tel**—(415) 312-2000. **Pres & CEO**—C. B. Johnson. **EVP & Secy**—H. E. Burns. **SVP, Treas & CFO**—M. L. Flanagan. **SVP & Investor Contact**—Charles E. Johnson (415-312-3058). **Dirs**—H. E. Burns, J. R. Grosvenor, F. W. Hellman, C. B. Johnson, C. E. Johnson, R. H. Johnson, Jr., H. O. Kline, P. M. Sacerdote, L. E. Woodworth. **Transfer Agent & Registrar**—Bank of New York, NYC. **Incorporated** in Delaware in 1969. **Empl**-4,100. **S&P Analyst:** Paul L. Huberman, CFA

STANDARD & POOR'S

STOCK REPORTS

Frontier Corp.

NYSE Symbol **FRO**
In S&P MidCap 400

23-SEP-95 **Industry:** Telecommunications

Summary: The planned acquisition of ALC Communications Corp. would make this company the fifth largest U.S. long-distance carrier.

S&P Opinion: Hold (★★★)

Recent Price • 27⅜
52 Wk Range • 28⅝-19¼
Yield • 3.0%
12-Mo. P/E • 18.3

Quantitative Evaluations

Outlook
(1 Lowest—5 Highest)
• **2+**

Fair Value
• **27**

Risk
• **Average**

Earn./Div. Rank
• **B+**

Technical Eval.
• **Neutral** since 6/95

Rel. Strength Rank
(1 Lowest—99 Highest)
• **58**

Insider Activity
• **Neutral**

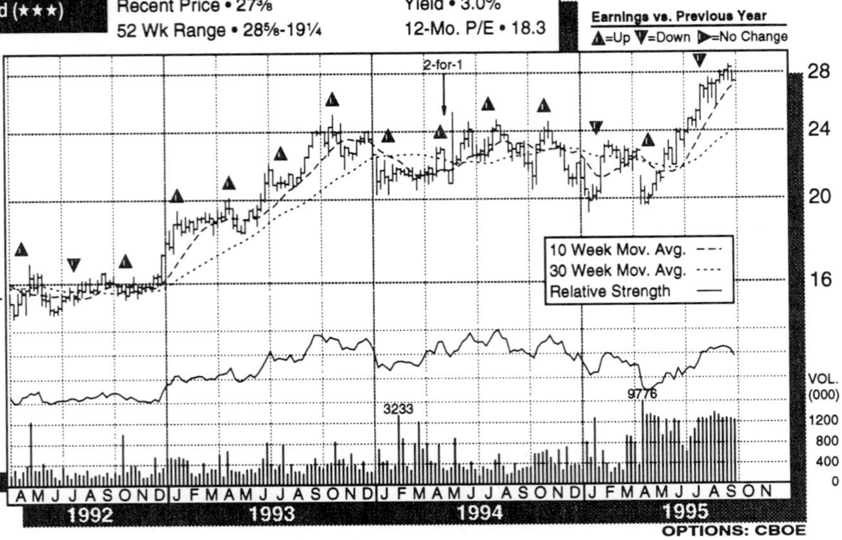

Overview - 22-SEP-95

This company has positioned itself for the anticipated opening of local telephone markets to competition by pushing its own pro-competitive plan through the regulatory process. Although near-term revenues and earnings from telephone operations may be hurt by rate cuts and loss of market share as competitors enter its market, in the long-term, Frontier's strategy should lead to earnings growth. Wireless operations should benefit from an association with NYNEX as the wireless market becomes more competitive, and growing long-distance operations should benefit from economies of scale. The recent acquisition of ALC Communications Corp. makes the company the fifth largest U.S. long-distance carrier, with revenues of nearly $2 billion.

Valuation - 22-SEP-95

Frontier's shares had risen 27% through August 31, 1995, versus 21% for the S&P local telephone companies index, as investors focus on the company's strong long term growth prospects. Near term results will be impacted by new competition resulting from a recently implemented regulatory plan, and by expected earnings dilution in 1995 and 1996 resulting from the acquisition of ALC. However, long-term results are expected to benefit from increased pricing flexibility and expanded long-distance operations; the stock offers adequate total return prospects.

Key Stock Statistics

S&P EPS Est. 1995	1.45	Tang. Bk. Value/Share	NM
P/E on S&P Est. 1995	18.9	Beta	0.32
S&P EPS Est. 1996	1.73	Shareholders	18,800
Dividend Rate/Share	0.83	Market cap. (B)	$ 4.4
Shs. outstg. (M)	161.2	Inst. holdings	25%
Avg. daily vol. (M)	0.382	Insider holdings	NA

Value of $10,000 invested 5 years ago: $ 17,160

Fiscal Year Ending Dec. 31

	1995	% Change	1994	% Change	1993	% Change
Revenues (Million $)						
1Q	283.4	17%	241.8	15%	211.0	9%
2Q	311.8	24%	251.8	13%	222.9	12%
3Q	—	—	243.1	5%	230.5	14%
4Q	—	—	248.8	3%	242.1	15%
Yr.	—	—	985.5	9%	906.5	13%
Income (Million $)						
1Q	31.68	41%	22.40	24%	18.02	18%
2Q	32.85	-6%	34.90	76%	19.83	20%
3Q	—	—	26.20	36%	19.24	4%
4Q	—	—	26.44	3%	25.64	27%
Yr.	—	—	109.9	33%	82.72	17%
Earnings Per Share ($)						
1Q	0.38	21%	0.32	19%	0.26	18%
2Q	0.40	-15%	0.47	62%	0.29	18%
3Q	E0.36	3%	0.35	25%	0.28	4%
4Q	E0.31	-14%	0.36	-4%	0.38	25%
Yr.	E1.45	-3%	1.50	24%	1.21	16%

Next earnings report expected: mid October

Frontier Corp.

Business Summary - 22-SEP-95

Frontier Corp. (formerly Rochester Telephone) is a diversified telecommunications company providing local, long-distance and wireless services. Segment contributions in 1994 were:

	Revs.	Profits
Telephone operations	62%	82%
Telecommunication services	38%	18%

The company provides telephone service in Rochester, N.Y., and adjacent areas, and also owns 36 small telephone companies operating in 13 states.

In January 1995, the Rochester telephone market was opened to full competition. The local telephone company was split into two companies, a wholesaler of telephone services (Rochester Telephone) and a retailer (Frontier Communications of Rochester). Rochester Telephone remains fully regulated, while Frontier will compete with providers of residential and business services.

Network services and systems include long-distance operations serving parts of the Northeast, MidAtlantic and Midwest; and Frontier Network Systems (formerly Rotelcom), which sells and maintains business communications equipment and systems.

Frontier provides cellular telephone and paging services in New York. After forming an equally owned joint venture with NYNEX Mobile Communications in July 1994, the company manages cellular operations covering 4.4 million POPs (adjusted for ownership).

Important Developments

Aug. '95—Shareholders of FRO and long-distance carrier ALC Communications approved the merger of the two companies in an exchange of stock valued at about $1.8 billion. Separately, FRO completed the purchase of Schneider Communications and its 81% stake in LinkUSA, for $127 million. Schneider offers long-distance services in the upper Midwest; LinkUSA provides wholesale enhanced services to the long-distance industry. In an unrelated transaction, MCI Communications will provide cellular services in upstate New York by reselling Frontier Cellular's network services.

Jul. '95—The company completed the purchase of Enhanced Telemanagement Inc., an integrator and reseller of local and long-distance services, for about $29 million. Separately, the founder of WCT Communications filed suit against Frontier, claiming the company deprived him of the benefits of their mutual agreement. Frontier recently acquired WCT.

Jan. '95—Concurrent with the opening of the Rochester telephone market to competition, the company completed a restructuring and changed its name to Frontier Corp.

Capitalization

Long Term Debt: $553,898,000 (6/95).
Minority Interests: $617,000.
Preferred Stock: $22,769,000.

Per Share Data ($) (Year Ended Dec. 31)

	1994	1993	1992	1991	1990	1989
Tangible Bk. Val.	9.03	7.10	6.90	6.53	6.73	7.78
Cash Flow	NA	NA	NA	NA	NA	NA
Earnings	1.50	1.21	1.04	1.18	0.86	1.00
Dividends	0.81	0.79	0.77	0.75	0.73	0.71
Payout Ratio	54%	65%	74%	64%	85%	71%
Prices - High	25¼	25⅛	17⅞	17	20¾	22⅞
- Low	20¼	17⅜	14⅝	13	12⅜	12⅞
P/E Ratio - High	17	21	17	14	24	23
- Low	13	14	14	11	14	13

Income Statement Analysis (Million $)

	1994	%Chg	1993	%Chg	1992	%Chg	1991
Revs.	985	9%	906	13%	804	14%	703
Depr.	117	2%	115	NM	114	18%	97.0
Maint.	NA	—	NA	—	NA	—	NA
Constr. Credits	1.1	-17%	1.3	2%	1.3	-17%	1.6
Eff. Tax Rate	34%	—	35%	—	34%	—	35%
Net Inc.	110	33%	82.7	17%	70.5	-4%	73.3

Balance Sheet & Other Fin. Data (Million $)

	1994	1993	1992	1991	1990	1989
Gross Prop.	1,591	1,594	1,615	1,514	1,190	1,025
Net Prop.	877	942	957	928	767	685
Cap. Exp.	87.0	102	124	106	106	105
Total Cap.	1,514	1,288	1,269	1,290	981	898
Fxd. Chgs. Cov.	3.8	2.7	3.1	3.5	3.2	3.7
Capitalization:						
LT Debt	579	493	526	591	363	338
Pfd.	22.8	22.8	22.8	22.8	22.8	22.8
Common	800	652	599	564	449	395

Ratio Analysis

	1994	1993	1992	1991	1990	1989
% Ret. on Revs.	11.2	9.1	8.8	10.4	8.3	9.2
% Ret. On Invest.Cap	15.6	10.1	9.3	10.4	8.7	9.4
% Return On Com.Eqty	14.0	13.0	11.6	15.0	11.2	18.9
% Earn. on Net Prop.	17.5	15.3	14.1	11.7	11.7	12.5
% LT Debt of Cap.	40.6	42.2	45.8	50.2	43.5	44.8
Capital. % Pfd.	1.6	2.0	2.0	1.9	2.7	3.0
Capital. % Common	57.8	55.9	52.2	47.9	53.8	52.2

Dividend Data —Dividends have been paid since 1926. A dividend reinvestment plan is available.

Amt. of Div. $	Date Decl.	Ex-Div. Date	Stock of Record	Payment Date
0.202	Sep. 19	Oct. 07	Oct. 14	Nov. 01 '94
0.208	Dec. 19	Jan. 09	Jan. 13	Feb. 01 '95
0.208	Mar. 30	Apr. 07	Apr. 14	May. 01 '95
0.208	Jul. 06	Jul. 12	Jul. 14	Aug. 01 '95
0.208	Sep. 22	Oct. 11	Oct. 13	Nov. 01 '95

Office—180 South Clinton Ave., Rochester, NY 14646-0700. **Tel**—(716) 777-1000. **Chmn, Pres & CEO**—R. L. Bittner. **Treas**—J. Enis. **Secy**—J. S. Trubek. **Investor Contact**—Philip Yawman. **Dirs**—P. C. Barron, R. L. Bittner, J. R. Block, B. Evans Edgerton, J. A. Estrada, R. Holland Jr., D. E. Gill, A. C. Hasselwander, D. H. McCorkindale, L. J. Thomas. **Transfer Agent & Registrar**—Bank of Boston. **Incorporated** in New York in 1920. **Empl-** 4,240. **S&P Analyst:** Kevin J. Gooley

Fuller (H.B.) Co.

NASDAQ Symbol **FULL**
In S&P MidCap 400

06-OCT-95 **Industry:** Chemicals

Summary: This company is an international manufacturer of adhesives, sealants, coatings, paints, specialty waxes and sanitation chemicals.

S&P Opinion: Hold (★★★)
Recent Price • 31½
52 Wk Range • 39¾-27¾
Yield • 2.0%
12-Mo. P/E • 13.2

Quantitative Evaluations
Outlook
(1 Lowest—5 Highest)
• **3-**
Fair Value
• **31¼**
Risk
• **Average**
Earn./Div. Rank
• **B+**

Technical Eval.
• **Bearish** since 7/95
Rel. Strength Rank
(1 Lowest—99 Highest)
• **16**
Insider Activity
• **NA**

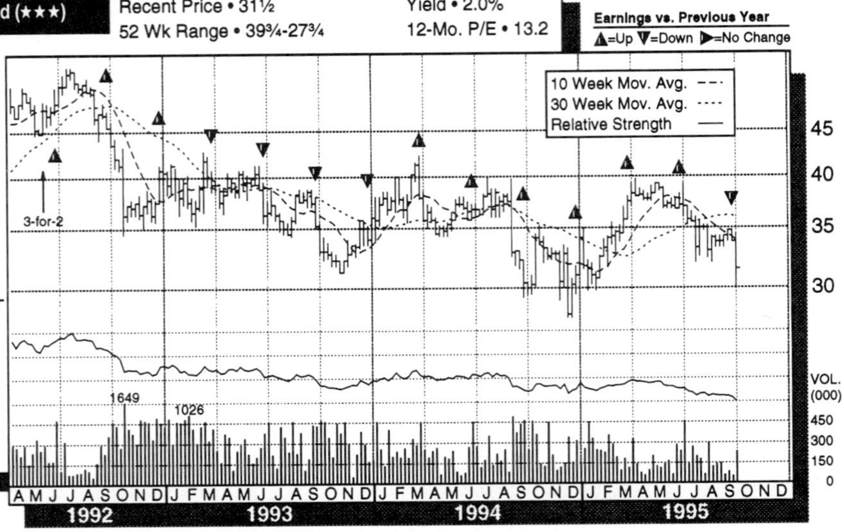

Overview - 06-OCT-95

S&P expects that sales will continue to advance about 10% in fiscal 1996, reflecting ongoing gains in most regions of the world. North American sales should advance, assuming that the important auto and construction related markets rebound. Sales growth in Europe may lag as the German economy has slowed and the U.S. dollar has strengthened in recent months. Price increases implemented since 1994 to offset higher raw material costs will also boost revenues. Raw material costs should stabilize. Profitability will benefit from a greater focus on cost controls, including personnel. The Asian region may return to profitability with the easing of the heavy investment spending of the past few years.

Valuation - 06-OCT-95

The stock in late September again declined on disappointing EPS for the second consecutive quarter and has now given up most of the appreciation achieved since late 1994. The stock has been a lackluster performer for the past three years due to investor concerns regarding weakening profit margins and high investment spending. We consider the stock to be a sound long-term holding for conservative investors, because of the company's good long-term growth prospects, based on continuing global expansion. The dividend, raised each year since 1968, has grown at a compound annual rate of 11% over the past 10 years.

Key Stock Statistics

S&P EPS Est. 1995	2.37	Tang. Bk. Value/Share	15.50
P/E on S&P Est. 1995	13.3	Beta	1.19
S&P EPS Est. 1996	2.70	Shareholders	5,300
Dividend Rate/Share	0.64	Market cap. (B)	$0.440
Shs. outstg. (M)	14.0	Inst. holdings	50%
Avg. daily vol. (M)	0.028	Insider holdings	NA

Value of $10,000 invested 5 years ago: $ 23,149

Fiscal Year Ending Nov. 30

	1995	% Change	1994	% Change	1993	% Change
Revenues (Million $)						
1Q	295.6	22%	242.5	6%	228.1	4%
2Q	322.4	18%	272.4	10%	247.3	5%
3Q	312.6	9%	286.8	14%	252.2	6%
4Q	—	—	295.7	19%	247.8	2%
Yr.	—	—	1,097	13%	975.3	4%
Income (Million $)						
1Q	6.03	49%	4.04	37%	2.95	-51%
2Q	10.07	8%	9.30	5%	8.87	-13%
3Q	8.76	-2%	8.93	2%	8.76	-15%
4Q	—	—	8.60	NM	1.58	-83%
Yr.	—	—	30.86	42%	21.70	-39%
Earnings Per Share ($)						
1Q	0.43	48%	0.29	53%	0.19	-56%
2Q	0.72	9%	0.66	5%	0.63	-14%
3Q	0.62	-3%	0.64	3%	0.62	-15%
4Q	E0.60	-2%	0.61	NM	0.11	-83%
Yr.	E2.37	8%	2.20	42%	1.55	-39%

Next earnings report expected: early January

Fuller (H.B.) Co.

Business Summary - 06-OCT-95

H.B. Fuller Company manufactures specialty chemical products, including the formulation, compounding and marketing of adhesives, sealants, coatings, paints, specialty waxes, sanitizing chemicals and other chemical products in the U.S., Canada, Latin America, Europe and the Pacific.

Sales in recent fiscal years were derived from:

	1994	1993
Adhesives, sealants & coatings	86%	84%
Paints	7%	8%
Sanitation chemicals	3%	3%
Specialty waxes	2%	2%
Other	2%	3%

By geographical area, the breakdown of fiscal 1994 results was: U.S. 58% of sales and 57% of operating profits, Europe 21% and 16%, Latin America 15% and 27% and Asia/Pacific 6% and Nil.

The company formulates and markets adhesives, sealants and coatings for the packaging, paper converting, woodworking, automotive, aerospace, graphic arts, appliances, filtration, windows, sporting goods, nonwovens, shoes and ceramic tile markets. Fuller also provides powder coatings to metal finishing industries; commercial and industrial paints in Latin American markets; specialty waxes in European markets; mastics and coatings for thermal insulation, indoor air quality and asbestors abatement applications; and cleaning and sanitizing chemicals for the dairy, beverage and food processing industries in the U.S. At year end 1994, Fuller had plants in 32 countries outside the U.S.

Important Developments

Sep. '95—Fuller said that although the third quarter results were disappointing, the year to date results were good considering the negative impact of weak global economies and escalating raw material costs. North American sales in the third quarter rose 2.4% as higher prices outweighed a volume decline. European sales were up 23%, with a positive currency impact of 17%. Profits rose less than expected due to raw material cost increases and the slow economy. Sales in Asia/Pacific rose 18%, but profits fell substantially, because of a slowdown in Japan and costs to expand operations. Fuller said that it would continued to control costs and investments as it expands sales globally and focus on improving operating results. The company indicated that fourth quarter share earnings were not expected to be below the 1994 level.

Capitalization

Long Term Debt: $155,607,000 (8/95).
$0.50 Cum. Preferred Stock: 45,900 shs. ($10 par); all owned by E.L. Andersen.

Per Share Data ($) (Year Ended Nov. 30)

	1994	1993	1992	1991	1990	1989
Tangible Bk. Val.	19.70	17.92	18.43	15.96	14.56	13.27
Cash Flow	5.09	3.36	4.37	3.57	3.01	2.25
Earnings	2.20	1.55	2.55	2.00	1.53	1.09
Dividends	0.57	0.54	0.46	0.41	0.40	0.38
Payout Ratio	26%	35%	18%	21%	26%	34%
Prices - High	42¼	42¾	53¼	42⅞	20⅞	22⅞
- Low	27¾	31¼	34½	19½	13¾	13⅞
P/E Ratio - High	19	28	21	21	14	21
- Low	13	20	14	10	9	13

Income Statement Analysis (Million $)

	1994	%Chg	1993	%Chg	1992	%Chg	1991
Revs.	1,097	13%	975	4%	934	9%	853
Oper. Inc.	107	26%	84.8	-12%	96.9	19%	81.6
Depr.	40.6	60%	25.4	NM	25.5	17%	21.8
Int. Exp.	12.9	13%	11.4	-10%	12.6	-18%	15.4
Pretax Inc.	51.0	25%	40.9	-33%	60.9	28%	47.4
Eff. Tax Rate	39%	—	47%	—	41%	—	40%
Net Inc.	30.9	42%	21.7	-39%	35.6	29%	27.7

Balance Sheet & Other Fin. Data (Million $)

	1994	1993	1992	1991	1990	1989
Cash	9.8	17.4	29.1	15.2	14.0	10.4
Curr. Assets	361	296	299	260	242	216
Total Assets	743	565	561	509	490	455
Curr. Liab.	232	176	168	151	146	120
LT Debt	130	60.0	53.0	72.0	88.0	101
Common Eqty.	274	249	255	219	197	186
Total Cap.	418	317	333	313	303	306
Cap. Exp.	101	44.0	36.0	30.0	31.5	40.9
Cash Flow	71.5	47.0	61.1	49.5	41.5	32.2

Ratio Analysis

	1994	1993	1992	1991	1990	1989
Curr. Ratio	1.6	1.7	1.8	1.7	1.7	1.8
% LT Debt of Cap.	31.1	19.0	16.0	22.9	29.1	32.9
% Net Inc.of Revs.	2.8	2.2	3.8	3.2	2.7	2.1
% Ret. on Assets	4.7	3.8	6.6	5.5	4.6	3.5
% Ret. on Equity	11.8	8.6	15.0	13.2	11.2	8.6

Dividend Data —Cash has been paid each year since 1953. A dividend reinvestment plan is available.

Amt. of Div. $	Date Decl.	Ex-Div. Date	Stock of Record	Payment Date
0.145	Oct. 20	Oct. 25	Oct. 31	Nov. 10 '94
0.145	Dec. 03	Jan. 20	Jan. 26	Feb. 10 '95
0.160	Apr. 20	Apr. 25	May. 01	May. 11 '95
0.160	Jul. 20	Jul. 28	Aug. 01	Aug. 10 '95

Data as orig. reptd.; bef. results of disc. opers. and/or spec. items. Per share data adj. for stk. divs. as of ex-div. date. E-Estimated. NA-Not Available. NM-Not Meaningful. NR-Not Ranked.

Office—2400 Energy Park Drive, St. Paul, MN 55108-1591. **Tel**—(612) 645-3401. **Chrmn**—A. L. Andersen. **Pres & CEO**—W. Kissling. **VP, Treas & CFO**—J. W. Bolanos. **Secy**—L. R. Mitau. **Investor Contact**—Richard Edwards (612-481-3650). **Dirs**—A. L. Andersen, N. R. Berg, E. L. Bronstien, Jr., R. J. Carlson, F. A. Ford, G. Fosler, R. C. King, W. Kissling, J. J. Mauriel, Jr., R. B. Schubert, L. C. Webster. **Transfer Agent & Registrar**—Norwest Bank Minnesota, So. St. Paul. **Incorporated** in Minnesota in 1915. **Empl-**6,400. **S&P Analyst:** Richard O'Reilly, CFA

GATX Corp.

NYSE Symbol GMT In S&P MidCap 400

Price	Range	P–E Ratio	Dividend	Yield	S&P Ranking	Beta
Aug. 8'95	1995					
51⅛	51½–40⅜	11	1.60	3.1%	A–	1.53

Summary

GATX is the largest U.S. lessor of rail tank cars, the world's largest independent tank terminal operator, the largest U.S. warehouser, a leading lessor of commercial aircraft and the largest Great Lakes shipping carrier. GATX should extend its profit gains in 1995, reflecting expansion of its railcar lease fleet, increased throughput and acquisitions of new terminal facilities and rising contributions from an expanding equipment lease portfolio.

Current Outlook

Earnings for 1995 are estimated at $4.50 a share, up from the $3.88 reported for 1994.

Dividends were lifted 6.7% in January 1995 to $0.40 a share quarterly, from $0.37½.

Railcar lease profits in 1995 will benefit from an expanded fleet and higher utilization thanks to strong demand for chemicals. Rates should increase moderately. Margins will benefit from an improved performance at General American's repair shops and lower environmental expense. Tank terminals will benefit from recent acquisitions, increased contributions from pipelines and moderate rate increases. Profits for GATX Capital should rise, reflecting increased fee and residual income. Disposition gains will be higher. Shipping profits should rise reflecting increased movements of iron ore and lower maintenance costs. An emphasis on longer-term contracts should help logistics boost profit margins.

Gross Income (Million $)

Quarter:	1995	1994	1993	1992
Mar.	288	261	237	232
Jun.	314	284	289	259
Sep.	---	299	280	273
Dec.	---	311	281	255
	---	1,155	1,089	1,019

Gross income for 1995's first half rose 11%, year to year. Net income was up 35%, to $2.42 a share, from $1.71.

Common Share Earnings ($)

Quarter:	1995	1994	1993	1992
Mar.	1.11	0.84	0.77	0.64
Jun.	1.31	0.87	1.15	0.68
Sep.	E1.10	1.09	0.42	d0.96
Dec.	E0.98	1.08	0.64	0.46
	E4.50	3.88	2.99	0.82

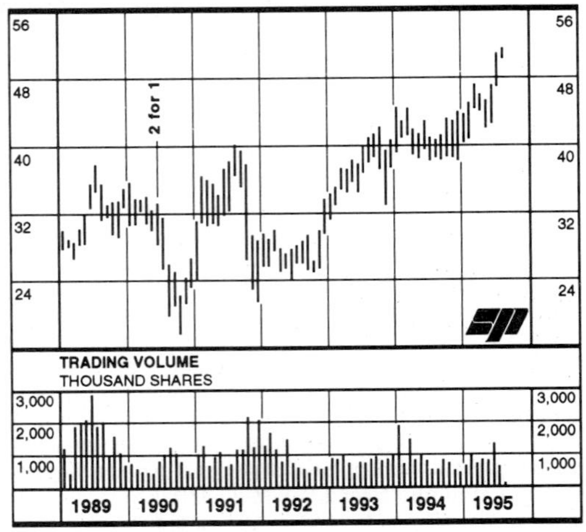

Important Developments

Jul. '95— GMT reported that throughput at GATX Terminals for 1995's first half fell 7.6%, year to year due to warm weather and disruptions at a facility in Texas due to flooding and the temporary shutdown of its New Orleans facility.

Dec. '94— GATX Terminals acquired a 925,000-bbl. petroleum products terminal in Seattle, Wash., and a 1.2 million-bbl. facility in Portland, Ore., from Shell Oil Co. for an undisclosed sum. In June, GMT acquired a 655,000-bbl. storage facility in Port Everglades, Fla., from British Petroleum.

Dec. '94— Terminales Portuarias, S.A. (TEPSA), a joint venture between GATX Terminals and Petrofrance Chimie, completed the construction of a 313,000-bbl. liquid chemical and petroleum products storage facility in Bilbao, Spain.

Next earnings report expected in late October.

Per Share Data ($)

Yr. End Dec. 31	1994	1993	1992	1991	1990	[1]1989	[1]1988	[1]1987	1986	1985
Book Value	**17.91**	14.25	12.58	15.38	13.83	[2]17.23	14.43	12.37	11.11	12.73
Cash Flow	**12.07**	10.57	7.92	10.10	9.60	8.23	7.15	6.12	4.43	3.20
Earnings[3]	**3.88**	2.99	0.82	3.56	3.61	3.18	2.52	1.82	1.10	d0.04
Dividends	**1.525**	1.400	1.300	1.200	1.100	1.000	0.900	0.750	0.675	0.600
Payout Ratio	**39%**	47%	159%	34%	30%	32%	34%	38%	49%	NM
Prices—High	**44⅝**	42	33¾	40¼	35¾	37⅞	28¼	25⅜	21	18¾
Low	**38¼**	31⅜	24¼	21½	17⅝	26¾	18½	16⅝	15	13⅞
P/E Ratio—	**12–10**	14–10	41–30	11–6	10–5	12–8	11–7	14–9	19–14	NM

Data as orig. reptd. Adj. for stk. div. of 100% Jun. 1990. **1.** Refl. merger or acq. **2.** Incl. intangibles. **3.** Bef. results of disc. ops. of +0.11 in 1986, -1.87 in 1985 & spec. item of -2.36 in 1992. E-Estimated. d-Deficit. NM-Not Meaningful.

Income Data (Million $)

Year Ended Dec. 31	[1]Revs.	Oper. Inc.	% Oper. Inc. of Revs.	Cap. Exp.	Depr.	Int. Exp.	Net Bef. Taxes	Eff. Tax Rate	[4]Net Inc.	% Net Inc. of Revs.	Cash Flow
1994	**1,155**	**431**	**37.3**	**596**	**165**	**151**	**140**	**34.8%**	**91.5**	**7.9**	**243**
1993	1,068	388	36.3	413	151	155	124	41.4%	72.7	6.8	210
1992	1,019	389	38.2	216	138	180	39	24.7%	29.3	2.9	154
1991	989	402	40.6	241	128	187	116	28.9%	82.7	8.4	197
1990	870	389	44.7	310	115	182	118	29.9%	82.9	9.5	185
[2]1989	702	349	49.7	257	98	167	101	35.1%	65.7	9.4	158
[2]1988	564	281	49.8	281	90	144	74	36.2%	47.0	8.2	136
[2]1987	521	250	48.0	104	86	136	56	38.5%	34.7	6.6	120
[3]1986	512	250	48.8	57	81	141	24	NM	26.2	5.1	106
[3]1985	694	260	37.5	56	84	136	1	NM	3.1	0.4	83

Balance Sheet Data (Million $)

Dec. 31	Cash	Curr. Assets	Curr. Liab.	Curr. Ratio	Total Assets	% Ret. on Assets	[5]Long Term Debt	Common Equity	Total Inv. Capital	% LT Debt of Cap.	% Ret. on Equity
1994	**27.3**	**NA**	**NA**	**NA**	**3,651**	**2.6**	**1,805**	**490**	**2,725**	**66.2**	**17.2**
1993	26.2	NA	NA	NA	3,392	2.1	1,714	417	2,552	67.2	14.7
1992	22.9	NA	NA	NA	3,426	0.8	1,725	385	2,516	68.5	3.9
1991	25.1	NA	NA	NA	3,514	2.4	1,799	441	2,716	66.2	16.7
1990	76.0	NA	NA	NA	3,310	2.6	1,715	384	2,603	65.9	19.5
1989	20.1	NA	NA	NA	3,060	2.2	1,456	328	2,320	62.8	20.0
1988	21.9	NA	NA	NA	2,605	1.9	1,306	256	1,926	67.8	19.6
1987	20.6	NA	NA	NA	2,200	1.6	1,221	218	1,796	68.0	16.7
1986	84.3	NA	NA	NA	2,234	1.3	1,233	201	1,784	69.1	10.8
1985	51.2	NA	NA	NA	2,392	0.1	1,153	328	1,873	61.6	NM

Data as orig. reptd. **1.** Incl. other inc. after 1988. **2.** Refl. merger or acq. **3.** Excl. disc. ops. **4.** Bef. spec. item in 1992. **5.** Incl. curr. portion. NM-Not Meaningful. NA-Not Available.

Business Summary

GATX provides a variety of transportation and distribution-related services. Business segment contributions (in millions) to net income before corporate charges in recent years were:

	1994	1993	1992	1991
Railcar leasing.......	$55.1	$47.6	$49.4	$55.2
Tank terminals.......	31.9	26.5	23.4	19.0
Financial services...	24.9	21.5	–16.7	28.5
Shipping..............	5.6	6.8	6.2	6.3
Warehousing.........	–0.5	0.1	0.9	–0.7

General American Transportation Corp. is the largest U.S. lessor of rail tank cars, with a fleet of 50,700 units at 1994 year-end. GMT also provides full-service leases for 9,100 specialty railcars. The chemical industry generated 54% of 1994 railcar lease revenues.

GATX Terminals Corp. is one of the world's largest independent bulk liquids storage company, primarily serving the petroleum and chemical industries. At 1994 year-end, GMT operated 46 facilities worldwide, with 76 million bbl. of capacity, plus pipeline systems in the U.S and the U.K.

GATX Capital Corp. provides asset-based financing primarily for transportation and industrial equipment. Its $1.3 billion lease portfolio at 1994 year-end consisted of commercial aircraft (46%), rail equipment (17%), warehouse and production equipment (8%), marine equipment (8%) golf courses (6%) and other (15%).

GATX Logistics is the largest U.S. full-service provider of warehousing, distribution and logistics support services, operating some 23 million sq. ft. of space at 113 facilities. American Steamship Co., with 11 self-unloading vessels on the Great Lakes, transported 26.3 million tons of coal, iron ore, limestone and aggregates in 1994.

Dividend Data

Dividends have been paid since 1919. A dividend reinvestment plan is available.

Amt of Divd. $	Date Decl.	Ex-divd. Date	Stock of Record	Payment Date
0.37½	Oct. 28	Dec. 9	Dec. 15	Dec. 31'94
0.40	Jan. 27	Mar. 6	Mar. 10	Mar. 31'95
0.40	Apr. 28	Jun. 13	Jun. 15	Jun. 30'95
0.40	Jul. 28	Sep. 13	Sep. 15	Sep. 30'95

Capitalization

Long Term Debt: $1,915,500,000 (6/95), incl. $247.4 million of lease obligs.

$2.50 Conv. Pfd. Stock: 42,050 shs. ($1 par).

$3.875 Conv. Pfd. Stock: 3,395,000 shs. ($1 par).

Common Stock: 19,935,798 shs. ($0.625 par). Institutions hold about 89%.
Shareholders of record: 3,503 (2/95).

Office—500 West Monroe, Chicago, IL 60661-3676. **Tel**—(312) 621-6200. **Chrmn & CEO**—J. J. Glasser. **Pres**—R. H. Zech. **VP-Fin**—D. M. Edwards. **VP-Secy**—D. B. Anderson. **Investor Contact**—George S. Lowman (312) 621-6599. **Dirs**—F. A. Cole, J. W. Cozad, J. M. Denny, W. C. Foote, D. M. Fretz, R. A. Giesen, J. J. Glasser, M. L. Marsh, C. Marshall, M. E. Murphy, R. H. Zech. **Transfer Agent & Registrar**—Chemical Bank, NYC. **Incorporated** in New York in 1916. **Empl**—5,800.

 Stephen R. Klein

STANDARD & POOR'S
STOCK REPORTS

GenCorp Inc.

NYSE Symbol **GY**
In S&P MidCap 400

25-SEP-95 **Industry:** Aerospace

Summary: GenCorp manufactures defense systems, automotive products and polymer products. After a long search, the company was unable to divest its defense business.

S&P Opinion: Avoid (★★)

Recent Price • 10⅞ | Yield • 5.5%
52 Wk Range • 14⅛-9⅞ | 12-Mo. P/E • 10.9

Quantitative Evaluations
Outlook (1 Lowest—5 Highest) • **3-**
Fair Value • **10⅝**
Risk • **Average**
Earn./Div. Rank • **B**

Technical Eval. • **Bullish** since 12/93
Rel. Strength Rank (1 Lowest—99 Highest) • **12**
Insider Activity • **Neutral**

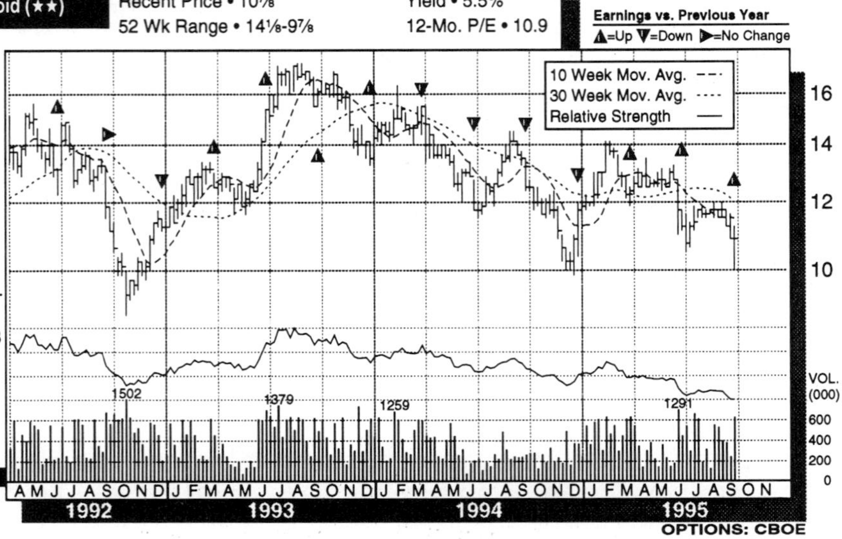

OPTIONS: CBOE

Overview - 25-SEP-95

Overall, GenCorp remains hampered by a number of structural problems which have plagued it in recent years, including weak sales trends, environmental liabilities and a highly leveraged balance sheet. Fiscal 1996 sales could benefit from slightly higher automotive sales, despite lower motor vehicle build rates, and from higher sales of commercial wallcovering and latex products. However, the continued weak performance of Aerojet is a cause for concern and GY was unable to sell the unit. Hurt by continued losses at HENNIGES, weak profits from Aerojet, costs to start up the automotive occupant sensor business and high interest expense, earnings could decline in fiscal 1996.

Valuation - 25-SEP-95

Although GY should remain profitable in fiscal 1995 in the absence of further restructuring charges, it remains challenged by Aerojet's problems, and by slow progress in growing its commercial businesses. We think the stock will continue to underperform. Furthermore, little progress has been made reducing debt despite pledges to improve the highly leveraged balance sheet. With capital expenditures below depreciation charges, GY should be able to continue its dividend payment, but it is questionable whether this policy is sound or sustainable in a downturn. GY has lagged its respective industries and we think it should be avoided. Income investors can find more attractive and secure alternatives.

Key Stock Statistics

S&P EPS Est. 1995	1.00	Tang. Bk. Value/Share	NM
P/E on S&P Est. 1995	10.9	Beta	1.38
S&P EPS Est. 1996	0.95	Shareholders	15,100
Dividend Rate/Share	0.60	Market cap. (B)	$0.357
Shs. outstg. (M)	32.8	Inst. holdings	57%
Avg. daily vol. (M)	0.108	Insider holdings	NA

Value of $10,000 invested 5 years ago: $ 12,752

Fiscal Year Ending Nov. 30

	1995	% Change	1994	% Change	1993	% Change
Revenues (Million $)						
1Q	428.1	7%	401.7	NM	401.5	-13%
2Q	461.9	-1%	467.7	-5%	492.3	-2%
3Q	431.4	15%	374.4	-22%	482.1	7%
4Q	—	—	495.7	-6%	529.2	NM
Yr.	—	—	1,740	-9%	1,905	-2%
Income (Million $)						
1Q	7.00	NM	-3.20	NM	6.10	177%
2Q	16.30	15%	14.20	-20%	17.80	31%
3Q	8.00	25%	6.40	-17%	7.70	57%
4Q	—	—	-30.40	NM	11.20	NM
Yr.	—	—	-13.00	NM	42.80	94%
Earnings Per Share ($)						
1Q	0.22	NM	-0.10	NM	0.19	171%
2Q	0.50	11%	0.45	-20%	0.56	30%
3Q	0.24	20%	0.20	-20%	0.25	67%
4Q	E0.04	NM	-0.95	NM	0.35	NM
Yr.	E1.00	NM	-0.41	NM	1.35	93%

Next earnings report expected: early November

GenCorp Inc.

Business Summary - 25-SEP-95

GenCorp Inc. manufactures space and defense systems, auto parts and polymer products. Sales and operating profits in fiscal 1994 were derived as follows (profits in million $):

	Sales	Profits
Aerospace & defense	34%	$25.0
Polymer products	33%	50.9
Automotive	33%	31.7
Unusual charges	--	-80.1

Aerojet General is in the aerospace and defense business, selling primarily to the U.S. government and its prime contractors. Aerojet has a mix of propulsion and defense electronics products. At the end of fiscal 1994, Aerojet's contract backlog was about $1.1 billion, down from $1.4 billion a year earlier. Funded backlog declined to $600 million in 1994, from $700 million in 1993. Several important programs have been canceled in recent years, and the ordnance division was sold to Olin Corp. in 1994. In June 1995, GY said that it was unable to obtain a sufficient price for Aerojet and would for the time being retain it instead.

GenCorp Automotive is a supplier of sealing systems, suspension components, reinforced plastic panels for vehicle bodies and other fiber-reinforced plastic components. The segment supplies products to all three of the domestic automakers for a variety of vehicles. General Motors accounted for 16% of sales in fiscal 1994. In 1994, GY acquired the remaining 75.5% equity interest in HENNIGES Elastomer-und Kunststofftechnik GmbH & Co. it did not already own. HENNIGES is a German molded and extruded rubber products supplier.

Polymer-based product lines include vinyl coated fabrics, gaskets, seals trim and magnetic rolls for appliances, automotive and office equipment industries, commercial roofing materials, vinyl woodgrain laminates and clear vinyl films. The specialty polymers unit produces latex used as coating for paper, binding agents for carpets and nonwoven fabrics, and tire cord adhesives. Other polymer products include wallcovering, tennis balls and racquetballs.

Important Developments

Sep. '95—GY said that third quarter automotive profits were hurt by start-up costs to fund its Automotive Occupant Sensor business which aims to participate in a new generation of airbags that would have variable deployment features.

May '95—GY discontinued efforts to divest Aerojet and instead decided to try to increase its value by improving its performance. GY divested the Westward Look Resort in Tucson, AZ, the last major asset remaining from GY's discontinued RKO operations.

Capitalization

Long Term Debt: $420,300,000 (8/95), incl. $115 million of 8% debs. conv. into com. at $16.065 a sh.

Per Share Data ($) (Year Ended Nov. 30)

	1994	1993	1992	1991	1990	1989
Tangible Bk. Val.	-0.22	7.41	6.71	6.71	6.30	4.88
Cash Flow	1.89	3.69	3.18	3.44	3.94	2.46
Earnings	-0.41	1.35	0.70	1.00	1.60	0.25
Dividends	0.60	0.60	0.60	0.60	0.60	0.60
Payout Ratio	NM	44%	86%	59%	37%	238%
Prices - High	16⅜	17⅞	15⅝	12¾	12⅞	19⅛
- Low	9⅞	11¼	8⅞	5⅝	5	10⅞
P/E Ratio - High	NM	13	22	13	8	77
- Low	NM	8	13	6	3	44

Income Statement Analysis (Million $)

	1994	%Chg	1993	%Chg	1992	%Chg	1991
Revs.	1,740	-9%	1,905	-2%	1,937	-3%	1,993
Oper. Inc.	170	-3%	175	-7%	188	12%	168
Depr.	73.0	-1%	74.0	-6%	79.0	3%	77.0
Int. Exp.	32.0	-11%	36.0	-22%	46.0	-12%	52.0
Pretax Inc.	-22.0	NM	70.0	89%	37.0	-24%	49.0
Eff. Tax Rate	NM	—	39%	—	41%	—	35%
Net Inc.	-13.0	NM	43.0	95%	22.0	-31%	32.0

Balance Sheet & Other Fin. Data (Million $)

	1994	1993	1992	1991	1990	1989
Cash	30.0	23.0	34.0	41.0	31.0	45.0
Curr. Assets	421	430	437	436	415	584
Total Assets	1,455	1,164	1,131	1,113	1,078	1,270
Curr. Liab.	367	341	408	379	365	448
LT Debt	378	416	344	355	345	496
Common Eqty.	-7.0	235	213	213	200	155
Total Cap.	371	651	557	582	559	652
Cap. Exp.	63.0	67.0	96.0	93.0	79.0	111
Cash Flow	60.0	117	101	109	125	78.0

Ratio Analysis

	1994	1993	1992	1991	1990	1989
Curr. Ratio	1.1	1.3	1.1	1.2	1.1	1.3
% LT Debt of Cap.	101.9	63.9	61.8	61.0	61.7	76.1
% Net Inc.of Revs.	NM	2.3	1.1	1.6	2.9	0.4
% Ret. on Assets	NM	3.7	2.0	2.9	4.3	0.6
% Ret. on Equity	NM	19.2	10.3	15.5	28.7	13.4

Dividend Data —Dividends have been paid since 1937. A dividend reinvestment plan is available. A "poison pill" stock purchase rights plan was adopted in 1987.

Amt. of Div. $	Date Decl.	Ex-Div. Date	Stock of Record	Payment Date
0.150	Sep. 09	Oct. 26	Nov. 01	Nov. 30 '94
0.150	Jan. 25	Jan. 31	Feb. 06	Feb. 28 '95
0.150	Mar. 29	Apr. 25	May. 01	May. 31 '95
0.150	Jul. 14	Jul. 28	Aug. 01	Aug. 31 '95
0.150	Sep. 08	Oct. 30	Nov. 01	Nov. 30 '95

Data as orig. reptd.; bef. results of disc. opers. and/or spec. items. Per share data adj. for stk. divs. as of ex-div. date. E-Estimated. NA-Not Available. NM-Not Meaningful. NR-Not Ranked.

Office—175 Ghent Rd., Fairlawn, OH 44333-3300. **Tel**—(216) 869-4200. **Chrmn, Pres & CEO**—J. B. Yasinsky. **Secy**—E. R. Dye. **VP & CFO**—D. M. Steuert. **Treas & Investor Contact**— Mike Hicks. **Dirs**—C. A. Corry, W. K. Hall, R. K. Jaedicke, P. X. Kelley, R. D. Kunisch, D. E. McGarry, J. M. Osterhoff, P. J. Phoenix, R. B. Pipes, J. R. Stover, J. B. Yasinsky. **Transfer Agents**—First Chicago Trust Co., NYC; Co.'s office. **Registrars**—First Chicago Trust Co., NYC; First National Bank of Ohio, Akron. **Incorporated** in Ohio in 1915. **Empl**-12,970. **S&P Analyst:** Joshua M. Harari, CFA

STANDARD & POOR'S

Genzyme Corp.-Gen'l Division

STOCK REPORTS

NASDAQ Symbol **GENZ**

In S&P MidCap 400

16-OCT-95

Industry: Drugs-Generic and OTC

Summary: This company (formerly Genzyme Corp.) makes therapeutic and diagnostic products, and offers genetic diagnostic services. Its lead product is Ceredase, a drug for Gaucher disease.

S&P Opinion: Accumulate (★★★★)

Recent Price • 52⅝
52 Wk Range • 64¼-26¼

Yield • Nil
12-Mo. P/E • 39.3

Quantitative Evaluations

Outlook
(1 Lowest—5 Highest)
• **3+**

Fair Value
• **50⅞**

Risk
• **Average**

Earn./Div. Rank
• **C**

Technical Eval.
• **Bearish** since 2/95

Rel. Strength Rank
(1 Lowest—99 Highest)
• **37**

Insider Activity
• **Unfavorable**

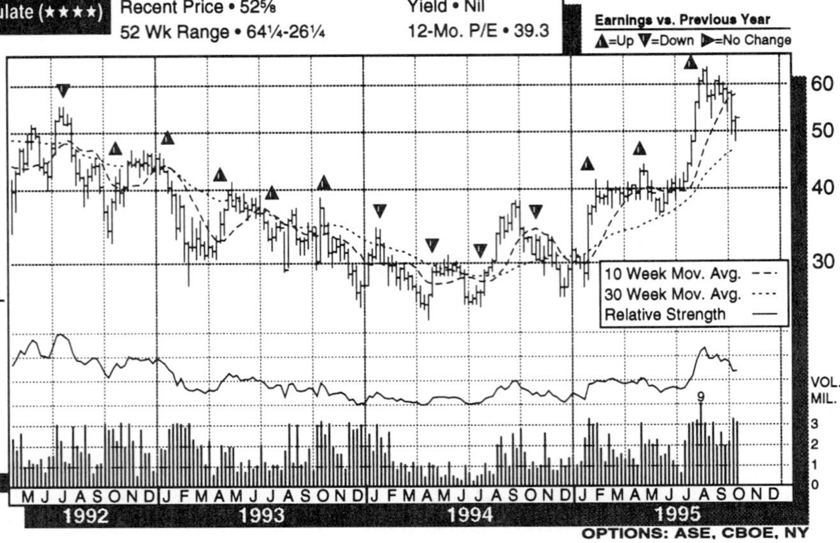

Overview - 16-OCT-95

Total revenues for 1996 should post another good advance. Product sales are expected to be augmented by further gains in Ceredase and Cerezyme treatments for Gaucher disease, higher sales of diagnostic products and the planned launch of Sepracoat and Seprafilm anti-adhesion products in the U.S. and Europe. Recent clinical trials have shown Sepracoat and Seprafilm effective in reducing the incidence of adhesions (fibrous scar tissue) occurring during surgeries. Revenues from contract research and development work done for other firms should also rise. Margins are expected to widen on the higher revenues and productivity enhancements, although a projected rise in average shares would restrict the EPS gain.

Valuation - 16-OCT-95

After trading in a relatively narrow range for several months, the stock ratcheted up during the summer on investor enthusiasm over GENZ's new Sepracoat and Seprafilm anti-adhesion products. These innovative products are aimed at a potential $1 billion worldwide market. Substantial future sales growth in those lines should more than compensate for expected flat or declining sales of Ceredase and Cerezyme (possible development of competing drugs resulted in some recent selling in the stock). The company's impressive R&D pipeline also includes promising treatments for thyroid cancer, burns, cystic fibrosis and other ailments. We recommend accumulation of the stock.

Key Stock Statistics

S&P EPS Est. 1995	1.85	Tang. Bk. Value/Share	13.91
P/E on S&P Est. 1995	28.4	Beta	2.91
S&P EPS Est. 1996	2.30	Shareholders	2,900
Dividend Rate/Share	Nil	Market cap. (B)	$ 1.5
Shs. outstg. (M)	27.9	Inst. holdings	83%
Avg. daily vol. (M)	0.710	Insider holdings	NA

Value of $10,000 invested 5 years ago: $ 36,293

Fiscal Year Ending Dec. 31

	1995	% Change	1994	% Change	1993	% Change
Revenues (Million $)						
1Q	88.19	20%	73.28	18%	62.29	37%
2Q	92.36	23%	75.38	10%	68.56	21%
3Q	—	—	79.18	9%	72.40	27%
4Q	—	—	82.89	23%	67.13	12%
Yr.	—	—	310.7	15%	270.4	23%
Income (Million $)						
1Q	10.37	2%	10.14	-7%	10.89	40%
2Q	12.97	32%	9.82	-15%	11.58	NM
3Q	—	—	9.86	-27%	13.52	42%
4Q	—	—	2.24	NM	-42.08	NM
Yr.	—	—	32.05	NM	-6.10	NM
Earnings Per Share ($)						
1Q	0.43	10%	0.39	-7%	0.42	35%
2Q	0.46	21%	0.38	-14%	0.44	NM
3Q	E0.47	27%	0.37	-29%	0.52	41%
4Q	E0.49	NM	0.09	NM	-1.74	NM
Yr.	E1.85	52%	1.22	NM	-0.25	NM

Next earnings report expected: late October

Genzyme Corp.-Gen'l Division

Business Summary - 13-OCT-95

Genzyme Corp.-General Division (formerly Genzyme Corp.) is a leading biotechnology company engaged in the development and marketing of therapeutic and diagnostic products, and genetic diagnostic services. Revenues in recent years were derived:

	1994	1993	1992
Product sales	77%	69%	64%
Service revs.	16%	19%	19%
R&D contracts	7%	12%	17%

Foreign operations accounted for 22% of product and service revenues in 1994. R&D costs equaled 16.6% of revenues in 1994 and 17.1% in 1993.

The company's lead products, Ceredase and Cerezyme (a recombinant version of Ceredase), are enzymes used to treat Gaucher disease, a debilitating disorder caused by defective genes for the enzyme glucocerebrosidase. Sales of these products totaled $173 million in 1994. Products in human clinical development include Thyrogen hormone for diagnosis and therapy of thyroid cancer; Vianain debriding agent for treatment of burns; biomaterial products based on hyaluronic acid to limit the formation of postoperative adhesions; and products to treat cystic fibrosis.

The diagnostic services division offers cytogenetic and biochemical testing services to physicians, hospitals, clinical laboratories, genetic centers and HMOs in the U.S. through IG Laboratories Inc. (69% owned) and Vivigen Inc. (100%). A fetal cell separation product is being developed for use by laboratories that conduct prenatal genetic testing. GENZ is also the leading independent U.S. supplier of diagnostic enzymes and substrates for reagents and clinical diagnostic kits. A line of immunobiologicals is also sold.

GENZ also sells fine chemicals, bulk pharmaceutical intermediaries, active drug substances, fine chemicals and related items to health care customers. Genzyme Transgenics Corp. (49.8%-owned) uses transgenic technology to develop and make recombinant proteins for therapy and diagnosis.

Important Developments

Oct. '95—GENZ completed a public offering of 2.5 million common shares at $51.25 a share. Proceeds were slated for general corporate purposes, including possible acquisitions. GENZ plans to file applications with the FDA for approval to market its Sepracoat and Seprafilm products to reduce the incidence of postoperative adhesions. GENZ also said that recent R&D on possible drugs from a genetically-engineered tobacco plant are unlikely to affect GENZ's Gaucher disease drugs.

Capitalization

Long Term Liabs.: $128,321,000 (6/95).
Warrants: To buy 5,934,381 shs. at $16.01 to $38.25 ea. (12/94).

Per Share Data ($)

(Year Ended Dec. 31)

	1994	1993	1992	1991	1990	1989
Tangible Bk. Val.	11.11	12.56	11.54	11.90	5.63	6.19
Cash Flow	1.00	0.20	-1.02	0.75	-1.37	-1.04
Earnings	1.22	-0.25	-1.41	0.50	-1.70	-1.32
Dividends	Nil	Nil	Nil	Nil	Nil	Nil
Payout Ratio	Nil	NM	NM	Nil	Nil	Nil
Prices - High	38¼	46¼	66⅜	58¾	28⅝	15½
- Low	24	25¼	32⅜	23⅜	12½	7½
P/E Ratio - High	31	NM	NM	NM	NM	NM
- Low	20	NM	NM	NM	NA	NA

Income Statement Analysis (Million $)

	1994	%Chg	1993	%Chg	1992	%Chg	1991
Revs.	311	15%	270	23%	219	101%	109
Oper. Inc.	58.8	7%	54.9	15%	47.9	NM	11.6
Depr.	13.5	24%	10.9	36%	8.0	43%	5.6
Int. Exp.	10.6	48%	7.2	-7%	7.8	NM	1.8
Pretax Inc.	29.1	NM	-22.4	NM	-13.2	NM	20.6
Eff. Tax Rate	50%	—	NM	—	NM	—	57%
Net Inc.	16.3	NM	-6.1	NM	-30.8	NM	11.2

Balance Sheet & Other Fin. Data (Million $)

	1994	1993	1992	1991	1990	1989
Cash	77.0	58.0	116	107	43.0	53.0
Curr. Assets	207	156	203	159	69.0	71.0
Total Assets	6.6	542	481	391	118	109
Curr. Liab.	103	56.8	36.6	23.3	10.4	9.9
LT Debt	127	145	105	101	2.0	5.0
Common Eqty.	419	334	323	260	96.0	91.0
Total Cap.	548	485	440	366	106	96.0
Cap. Exp.	102	119	61.0	8.0	9.0	6.2
Cash Flow	29.8	4.8	-22.8	16.8	-21.9	-10.2

Ratio Analysis

	1994	1993	1992	1991	1990	1989
Curr. Ratio	2.0	2.8	5.5	6.8	6.6	7.2
% LT Debt of Cap.	23.1	29.8	23.9	27.6	1.9	5.3
% Net Inc.of Revs.	5.2	NM	NM	10.2	NM	NM
% Ret. on Assets	2.3	NM	NM	4.1	NM	NM
% Ret. on Equity	3.6	NM	NM	5.9	NM	NM

Dividend Data —No cash dividends have been paid. In December 1994, the company spun off its Tissue Repair division to GENZ shareholders.

Amt. of Div. $	Date Decl.	Ex-Div. Date	Stock of Record	Payment Date
Stk.	—	Dec. 27	Dec. 16	Dec. 23 '94

Data as orig. reptd.; bef. results of disc. opers. and/or spec. items. Per share data adj. for stk. divs. as of ex-div. date. E-Estimated. NA-Not Available. NM-Not Meaningful. NR-Not Ranked.

Office—One Kendall Sq., Cambridge, MA 02139. **Tel**—(617) 252-7500. **Chrmn, Pres & CEO**—H.A. Termeer. **SVP-Fin & CFO**—D.J. McLachlan. **Investor Contact**—Steven Push (703-757-2226). **Dirs**—C. E. Anagnostopoulos, D. A. Berthiaume, H. E. Blair, R. J. Carpenter, C. L. Cooney, H. R. Lewis, H. A. Termeer. **Transfer Agent & Registrar**—American Stock Transfer & Trust Co., NYC. **Incorporated** in Delaware in 1981; reincorp. in Mass. in 1991. **Empl**-2,021. **S&P Analyst:** Herman Saftlas

STANDARD & POOR'S

STOCK REPORTS

Georgia Gulf

NYSE Symbol **GGC**
In S&P MidCap 400

09-AUG-95 **Industry:** Chemicals

Summary: This company is a major producer of several highly integrated lines of commodity chemicals and polymers, including aromatic, natural gas and electrochemical products.

S&P Opinion: Buy (★★★★★) | Recent Price • 34½ | Yield • 0.9%
52 Wk Range • 43¼-26⅝ | 12-Mo. P/E • 7.1

Quantitative Evaluations

Outlook
(1 Lowest—5 Highest)
• **5-**

Fair Value
• **54½**

Risk
• **Average**

Earn./Div. Rank
• **NR**

Technical Eval.
• **Bullish** since 7/95

Rel. Strength Rank
(1 Lowest—99 Highest)
• **55**

Insider Activity
• **NA**

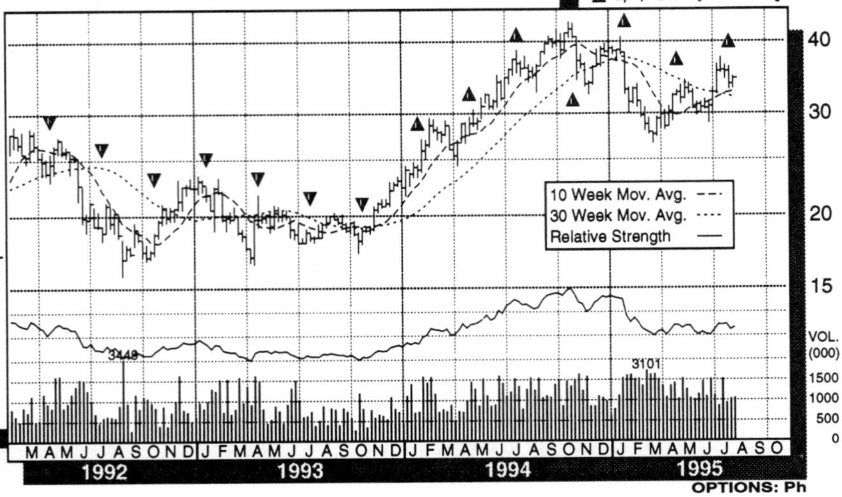

OPTIONS: Ph

Overview - 09-AUG-95

Sales and profits are expected to rise again in 1995 and 1996, in large part due to a surge in selling prices for caustic soda, phenol and PVC resins since early 1994. A recent decline in methanol prices will restrict earnings gains for the remainder of 1995. Demand for most products should remain strong, as we expect a pick-up in the U.S. economy from its current soft conditions. The addition of production capacity for PVC and methanol in 1994 and for compounds and cumene in 1996 will aid results. Interest expense will decline, largely due to the refinancing of the company's 15% notes in April 1995 with lower cost short-term borrowings. The repurchase of more than 10% of the common stock will boost share earnings. Capital spending will be about $90 million a year in 1995 and 1996, reflecting four expansion projects.

Valuation - 04-AUG-95

The shares of this commodity chemical producer are attractive as a cyclical play in the chemical industry. The shares have climbed from their first quarter low, as investors begin to realize that the outlook for GGC is positive, despite a drop in methanol prices and a slowdown in economic growth. Several important product lines are achieving upward price momentum, on strong demand and high industry operating rates, and conditions are expected to remain very favorable into 1996. The stock could respond to further news of tightening supply-demand conditions in the industry.

Key Stock Statistics

S&P EPS Est. 1995	5.25	Tang. Bk. Value/Share	0.24
P/E on S&P Est. 1995	6.6	Beta	2.04
S&P EPS Est. 1996	6.00	Shareholders	1,500
Dividend Rate/Share	0.32	Market cap. (B)	$ 1.3
Shs. outstg. (M)	38.0	Inst. holdings	67%
Avg. daily vol. (M)	0.190	Insider holdings	NA

Value of $10,000 invested 5 years ago: $ 29,803

Fiscal Year Ending Dec. 31

	1995	% Change	1994	% Change	1993	% Change
Revenues (Million $)						
1Q	314.0	63%	192.9	6%	181.9	-4%
2Q	275.8	32%	208.2	7%	195.2	1%
3Q	—	—	249.0	25%	199.6	NM
4Q	—	—	305.2	59%	192.2	-2%
Yr.	—	—	955.3	24%	768.9	-1%
Income (Million $)						
1Q	60.16	NM	12.73	26%	10.12	-22%
2Q	50.79	155%	19.95	74%	11.48	-15%
3Q	—	—	31.83	NM	10.15	-7%
4Q	—	—	57.65	NM	10.49	17%
Yr.	—	—	122.2	189%	42.23	-9%
Earnings Per Share ($)						
1Q	1.44	NM	0.30	25%	0.24	-35%
2Q	1.30	177%	0.47	68%	0.28	-20%
3Q	E1.20	—	0.75	NM	0.24	-8%
4Q	E1.31	—	1.35	NM	0.25	14%
Yr.	E5.25	—	2.88	185%	1.01	-14%

Next earnings report expected: mid October

Georgia Gulf

Business Summary - 09-AUG-95

Georgia Gulf is a leading producer of commodity chemicals and plastics, including highly integrated lines comprised of electrochemicals, aromatic chemical products, and natural gas products. Some commodity chemicals produced by the company are used as chemical intermediates for its product lines.

Electrochemicals, including chlorine (452,000 tons of annual capacity), caustic soda (501,000) and sodium chlorate (27,000), are used in the pulp, paper, aluminum and plastics industries. Chlorine is used to produce vinyl chloride monomer (1.26 billion lbs.), which is used to produce polyvinyl chloride resins (1.12 billion lbs.) and compounds (290 million lbs.). PVC resins and compounds find uses in construction and housing components, packaging, household goods, and molded machine casings. Aromatic chemicals consist of cumene (1,420 million lbs.), the feedstock for phenol (600 million) and acetone (370 million), which are used for adhesives, plastics, coatings and solvents. Natural gas products consist of methanol (160 million gallons), used in adhesives, polymers and gasoline additives. These products are manufactured at 12 plants in five locations, including six at a complex in Plaquemine, La.

GGC has a contract to supply, subject to certain limitations, a substantial percentage of Georgia-Pacific Corp.'s requirements for caustic soda, chlorine, methanol, phenol and sodium chlorate. Sales to Georgia-Pacific accounted for 15% of the total in 1994; international sales accounted for 13%.

Important Developments

May '95—GGC completed the repurchase of 10% of its common stock, authorized in December 1994, buying 4.17 million shares for $128.3 million. Directors authorized the acquisition of another 3.8 million shares (10% of the remaining shares). Separately, the company announced plans for a 60 million lb. expansion of its phenol unit in Plaquemine, La., bringing its annual capacity to 500 million lbs. The project is to be completed in 1997, at a cost of $23 million. GGC will modernize its cumene facility by the end of 1996, at a cost of about $20 million. It also plans to modernize and expand its vinyl chloride monomer (VCM) unit by the end of 1996, at a cost of about $85 million. The project will boost annual VCM capacity to 1.6 billion lbs., and enable the company to produce 400 million lbs. annually of ethylene dichloride (EDC), a precursor to VCM. A 240 million lb. vinyl resin expansion was completed near the end of 1994.
Apr. '95—The company redeemed $191 million of 15% subordinated notes due 2000.

Capitalization

Long Term Debt: $322,000,000 (6/95).

Per Share Data ($)

(Year Ended Dec. 31)

	1994	1993	1992	1991	1990	1989
Tangible Bk. Val.	0.74	-2.70	-4.00	-10.61	-12.63	12.80
Cash Flow	3.53	1.66	1.78	2.34	3.59	8.37
Earnings	2.88	1.01	1.18	1.75	3.07	7.58
Dividends	Nil	Nil	Nil	Nil	38.50	1.00
Payout Ratio	Nil	Nil	Nil	Nil	NM	13%
Prices - High	43¼	23¾	28⅝	24¾	45⅝	59⅞
- Low	21⅝	16½	15¾	8⅞	4⅞	36
P/E Ratio - High	15	24	24	14	15	8
- Low	8	16	13	5	2	5

Income Statement Analysis (Million $)

	1994	%Chg	1993	%Chg	1992	%Chg	1991
Revs.	955	24%	769	-1%	779	-7%	838
Oper. Inc.	258	87%	138	-9%	152	-20%	191
Depr.	27.8	3%	27.1	15%	23.6	13%	20.8
Int. Exp.	37.6	-16%	44.8	-27%	61.2	-24%	80.8
Pretax Inc.	193	192%	66.0	-3%	68.0	-24%	90.0
Eff. Tax Rate	37%	—	36%	—	32%	—	32%
Net Inc.	122	190%	42.0	-9%	46.0	-25%	61.0

Balance Sheet & Other Fin. Data (Million $)

	1994	1993	1992	1991	1990	1989
Cash	1.2	3.1	2.9	2.5	5.5	46.2
Curr. Assets	250	178	193	176	218	244
Total Assets	508	405	419	416	457	473
Curr. Liab.	123	110	130	149	161	106
LT Debt	314	365	409	588	683	1.0
Common Eqty.	31.0	-110	-160	-357	-423	330
Total Cap.	385	295	290	267	295	367
Cap. Exp.	59.1	29.6	14.3	27.5	61.9	54.2
Cash Flow	150	69.0	70.0	82.0	112	208

Ratio Analysis

	1994	1993	1992	1991	1990	1989
Curr. Ratio	2.0	1.6	1.5	1.2	1.3	2.3
% LT Debt of Cap.	81.5	123.6	141.3	220.5	231.5	0.2
% Net Inc.of Revs.	12.8	5.5	5.9	7.3	10.2	17.4
% Ret. on Assets	26.4	10.2	10.1	14.1	17.2	41.3
% Ret. on Equity	NM	NM	NM	NM	NM	65.6

Dividend Data (Dividends, initiated in 1987 and omitted in 1990, were resumed in February 1995.)

Amt. of Div. $	Date Decl.	Ex-Div. Date	Stock of Record	Payment Date
0.080	Feb. 07	Mar. 13	Mar. 17	Apr. 07 '95
0.080	May. 17	Jun. 14	Jun. 16	Jul. 07 '94

Data as orig. reptd.; bef. results of disc. opers. and/or spec. items. Per share data adj. for stk. divs. as of ex-div. date. E-Estimated. NA-Not Available. NM-Not Meaningful. NR-Not Ranked.

Office—400 Perimeter Center Terrace, Suite 595, Atlanta, GA 30346. **Tel**—(404) 395-4500. **Chrmn**—J. R. Kuse. **Pres & CEO**—J. R. Satrum. **VP, CFO & Treas**—R. B. Marchese. **VP & Secy**—J. I. Beerman. **Investor Contact**—John. F. Walker. **Dirs**—J. D. Bryan, D. M. Chorba, A. C. Eckert III, R. E. Flowerree, H. T. Green Jr., J. R. Kuse, J. R. Satrum, E. S. Smith. **Transfer Agent & Registrar**—Wachovia Bank, Winston-Salem, NC. **Incorporated** in Delaware in 1984. **Empl**-1,146. **S&P Analyst:** Richard O'Reilly, CFA

Gibson Greetings

NASDAQ Symbol GIBG (Incl. in Nat'l Market) Options on Phila In S&P MidCap 400

Price	Range	P-E Ratio	Dividend	Yield	S&P Ranking	Beta
Oct. 13'95	1995					
15⁵⁄₁₆	15¾–8	NM	3---	3---	B+	1.51

Summary

This leading U.S. producer of greeting cards and gift wrap also owns The Paper Factory, which operates more than 100 paper goods stores. Gibson said in July that it was exploring the sale of the entire company, not just its Cleo unit.

Current Outlook

A net loss of $2.40 a share is anticipated for 1995, versus 1994's loss of $1.77. Earnings of $1.20 are projected for 1996.

Quarterly dividends were omitted in early 1995.

Net sales and earnings in 1996 will continue to be hurt by competitive pricing and other factors. However, margins will benefit from efficiency measures. Gibson's return to profitability will reflect the absence of a third-quarter 1995 net charge of roughly $55 million, or $3.30 a share, from the sale of Cleo, Inc. Profitability will also benefit from sharply reduced lending levels.

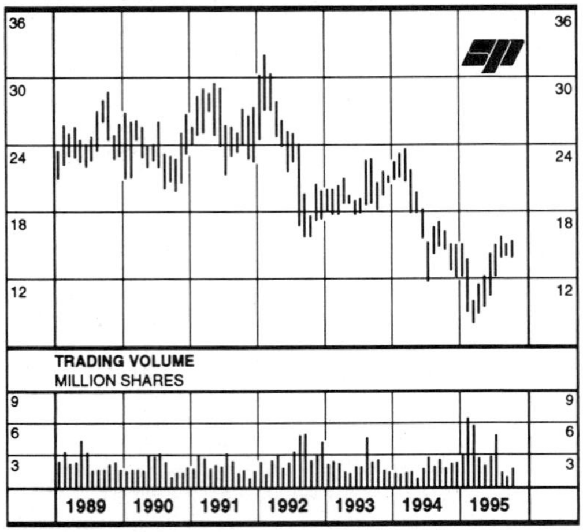

Revenues (Million $)

Quarter:	1995	1994	1993
Mar.	100.3	93.4	84.9
Jun.	97.5	90.7	84.0
Sep.	---	153.0	142.3
Dec.	---	211.5	235.8
	---	548.8	546.9

Revenues in 1995's first half rose 7.4%, year to year. In the absence of losses of $15.5 million from interest rate derivative transactions, net income of $912,000 ($0.06 a share) replaced a restated net loss of $27.8 million ($1.72).

Common Share Earnings ($)

Quarter:	1995	1994	1993
Mar.	0.02	d1.13	0.11
Jun.	0.04	d0.85	0.08
Sep.	Ed3.00	0.02	0.26
Dec.	E0.54	0.39	1.16
	Ed2.40	d1.77	1.61

Important Developments

Oct. '95— Gibson agreed to sell Cleo, Inc. to CSS Industries for $128.5 million. The consideration includes $96.5 million in cash, a 75-day $20 million note and $12 million to be held in escrow for post-closing adjustments. In addition, Gibson will be released from about $14 million in third-party debt.

Jul. '95— Gibson said it was exploring the sale of the entire company, rather than just its Cleo unit as announced earlier. Subsequently, American Greetings expressed interest in acquiring the company, but Gibson said it would not consider such a transaction, because of overwhelming antitrust considerations. The company feared that a lengthy battle with the Justice Department would seriously hurt Gibson. American has said that it is still interested in purchasing the company.

Next earnings report expected in mid-November.

Per Share Data ($)

Yr. End Dec. 31	1994	1993	1992	1991	1990	1989	1988	1987	1986	1985
Tangible Bk. Val.	[1]**17.24**	[1]20.15	[1]18.92	[1]18.86	[1]16.58	14.15	11.99	10.04	8.81	7.60
Cash Flow	**NA**	NA	NA	3.76	3.46	3.54	3.03	2.23	2.01	2.23
Earnings[2]	**d1.77**	1.61	0.50	2.61	2.51	2.68	2.25	1.53	1.43	1.81
Dividends	**0.400**	0.400	0.390	0.355	0.340	0.330	0.288	0.250	0.250	0.240
Payout Ratio	**NM**	25%	78%	14%	13%	12%	13%	16%	17%	13%
Prices—High	**23⅝**	22¾	32	29½	26⅞	28¾	23⅜	20¼	29⅜	24⅜
Low	**11¾**	17¾	15¹⁹⁄₃₂	21⅜	19⅞	21	12½	10⅜	14¼	16
P/E Ratio—	**NM**	14–11	64–32	11–8	11–8	11–8	10–6	13–7	21–10	13–9

Data as orig. reptd. Adj. for stk. div. of 50% Mar. 1985. **1.** Incl. intangibles. **2.** Bef. spec. items of -0.09 in 1992, +0.18 in 1985. **3.** See Dividend Data. d-Deficit. E-Estimated. NM-Not Meaningful. NA-Not Available.

Income Data (Million $)

Year Ended Dec. 31	Revs.	Oper. Inc.	% Oper. Inc. of Revs.	Cap. Exp.	Depr.	Int. Exp.	Net Bef. Taxes	Eff. Tax Rate	[2]Net Inc.	% Net Inc. of Revs.	Cash Flow
1994	**549**	**NA**	**NA**	**35.4**	**NA**	**10.6**	**d45.6**	**NM**	**d28.6**	**NM**	**NA**
1993	547	NA	NA	31.0	NA	7.7	44.0	41.2%	25.9	4.7	NA
1992	502	NA	NA	31.0	NA	7.9	13.1	38.9%	8.0	1.6	NA
1991	524	95.7	18.3	31.7	18.5	10.6	68.2	38.6%	41.9	8.0	60.4
1990	513	86.7	16.9	42.7	15.0	10.2	63.9	37.7%	39.8	7.8	54.8
1989	465	80.8	17.4	32.0	13.6	3.9	65.7	35.5%	42.4	9.1	55.9
1988	404	74.4	18.4	17.8	12.2	6.9	56.7	38.3%	35.0	8.7	47.3
1987	360	59.9	16.7	[1]13.7	11.0	6.4	43.4	44.5%	24.1	6.7	35.1
1986	323	55.1	17.0	17.9	9.3	6.1	40.2	43.7%	[3]22.6	7.0	31.9
1985	330	65.6	19.9	18.1	6.5	11.1	51.6	44.4%	28.7	8.7	35.2

Balance Sheet Data (Million $)

Dec. 31	Cash	Curr. Assets	Curr. Liab.	Curr. Ratio	Total Assets	% Ret. on Assets	Long Term Debt	Common Equity	Total Cap.	% LT Debt of Cap.	% Ret. on Equity
1994	**2.0**	**382**	**231**	**1.7**	**612**	**NM**	**63.2**	**278**	**341**	**18.6**	**NM**
1993	9.5	377	163	2.3	580	4.8	74.4	324	397	18.7	8.2
1992	9.5	334	110	3.0	501	1.5	70.2	303	376	18.7	2.6
1991	9.8	368	153	2.4	544	7.6	71.1	301	383	18.5	14.8
1990	25.0	379	250	1.5	553	8.0	21.8	261	295	7.4	16.3
1989	5.5	311	164	1.9	439	11.0	30.4	226	265	11.5	20.5
1988	15.4	269	108	2.5	326	11.3	18.6	186	214	8.7	20.5
1987	6.9	236	99	2.4	289	8.6	23.3	154	185	12.6	16.7
1986	16.2	216	93	2.3	275	8.4	28.0	138	175	16.0	17.6
1985	5.5	211	94	2.3	261	11.4	32.7	119	159	20.6	27.3

Data as orig. reptd. **1.** Net. **2.** Bef. spec. items. **3.** Refl. acctg. change. d-Deficit. NA-Not Available. NM-Not Meaningful.

Business Summary

Gibson Greetings, Inc., whose predecessors date from 1850, is the third largest U.S. manufacturer of greeting cards and gift wrapping paper. The Paper Factory, which operates 106 paper goods stores in the Midwest, South and West, was acquired in June 1993.

Net sales in recent years were derived as follows:

	1994	1993
Greeting cards	44%	49%
Gift wrap	37%	35%
Related products	19%	16%

Of Gibson's greeting card sales in 1994, everyday lines represented 61% and seasonal lines 39%. Principal tradenames are Gibson and Cleo. A Mexican subsidiary, formed in 1992, purchased the net assets of a Mexican manufacturer and marketer of greeting cards, to market company products primarily in Mexico. During 1991, a subsidiary was formed to market products in Europe. About 3% of 1994 revenues were derived from international sources. In 1994, the largest customer, Wal-Mart Stores, accounted for 10% of total revenues. The five largest customers accounted for 35%. Gibson's products are sold through 50,000 retail outlets worldwide, primarily deep discounters, supermarkets, mass merchandisers, drug stores and variety stores.

Other products include boxes, bags, boxed greeting cards, party goods, holiday decorations, candles, calendars and gift wrapping accessories. Gibson's products often incorporate well-known persons or characters. Net sales associated with licensed properties accounted for 17% of 1994 net sales.

Dividend Data

Dividends, paid since 1983, were omitted in February 1995. The most recent payment was:

Amt. of Divd. $	Date Decl.	Ex-divd. Date	Stock of Record	Payment Date
0.10	Nov. 18	Nov. 23	Nov. 30	Dec. 15'94

Capitalization

Long Term Debt: $52,474,000 (6/95).

Common Stock: 16,579,930 shs. ($0.01 par).
Institutions hold about 82%.
Shareholders: About 9,400 (2/95)

Office—2100 Section Rd., Cincinnati, OH 45237. **Tel**—(513) 841-6600. **Chrmn, Pres & CEO**—B. J. Sottile. **Secy**—H. L. Caldwell. **VP-Fin & CFO**—W. L. Flaherty. **VP & Treas**—A. L. Forcellini. **Dirs**—T. M. Cooney, J. Koppelman, C. D. Lindberg, R. J. Olson, C. St. Martin, A. R. Pezzillo, T. J. Smith, B. J. Sottile, B. B. Staniar, F. Stanton, R. T. Staubach, C. A. Wainwright, H. N. Walters. **Transfer Agent & Registrar**—Bank of New York, NYC. **Incorporated** in Delaware in 1982. **Empl**—4,500.

STANDARD & POOR'S

STOCK REPORTS

Glatfelter (P. H.) Co.

ASE Symbol **GLT**
In S&P MidCap 400

28-JUL-95 **Industry:** Paper/Products

Summary: This company makes printing, writing and specialty papers at three mills in Pennsylvania, Wisconsin and North Carolina.

S&P Opinion: Accumulate (★★★★) Recent Price • 20¾ | 52 Wk Range • 21¼-14⅝ | Yield • 3.3% | 12-Mo. P/E • NM

Quantitative Evaluations
Outlook (1 Lowest—5 Highest) • **2+**
Fair Value • **19⅝**
Risk • **Low**
Earn./Div. Rank • **B**

Technical Eval. • **Bearish** since 4/95
Rel. Strength Rank (1 Lowest—99 Highest) • **70**
Insider Activity • **NA**

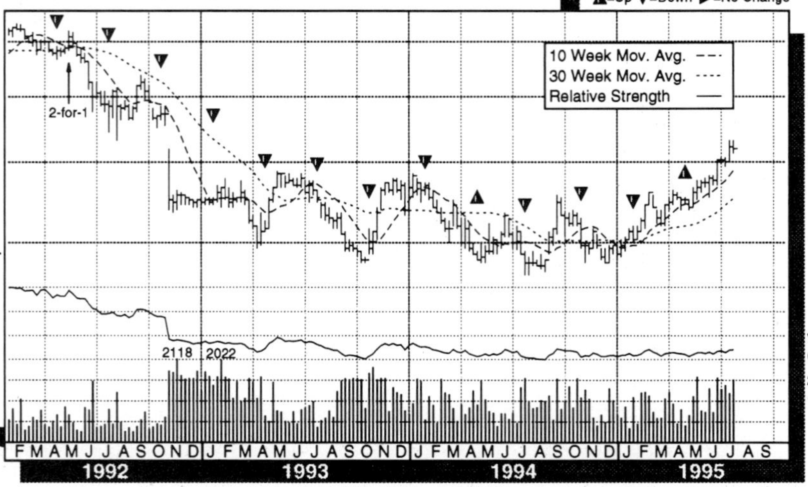

Overview - 28-JUL-95

Net sales are expected to continue to improve through 1996, reflecting strong demand for the company's products and additional price increases during the second half of the current year, and probably into 1996. Profitability should benefit from higher prices, greater unit volume of tobacco and other specialty papers, and improved operating efficiencies, which will outweigh increased raw material costs, especially for market pulp and wastepaper. Furthermore, minimal papermaking capacity increases are expected for the next two years. With lower depreciation charges following the Ecusta division asset writedown adding about $0.19 a share to earnings in both 1995 and 1996, improved economic conditions and better productivity, earnings should continue to grow.

Valuation - 28-JUL-95

The shares of this maker of printing, writing and specialty papers have traded in a relatively narrow range for the past two years, but have climbed more than 30% during 1995, reflecting strong volume and increased prices. Results had been hurt in 1994 by a sluggish paper market, but a strong uptrend in the industry has led to a significant earnings improvement, which is expected to continue at least through 1996. The company has been repurchasing shares, and with the stock trading at 13X our recently boosted 1995 EPS estimate of $1.55 (a discount to projected multiples for the MidCap 400), and only 11X our $1.85 projection for 1996, the opportunity exists for further capital appreciation.

Key Stock Statistics

S&P EPS Est. 1995	1.55	Tang. Bk. Value/Share	6.82
P/E on S&P Est. 1995	13.4	Beta	0.78
S&P EPS Est. 1996	1.85	Shareholders	5,100
Dividend Rate/Share	0.70	Market cap. (B)	$0.934
Shs. outstg. (M)	44.2	Inst. holdings	73%
Avg. daily vol. (M)	0.043	Insider holdings	NA

Value of $10,000 invested 5 years ago: $ 11,471

Fiscal Year Ending Dec. 31

	1995	% Change	1994	% Change	1993	% Change
Revenues (Million $)						
1Q	155.0	40%	110.8	-10%	123.0	-12%
2Q	166.9	45%	115.3	-6%	122.3	-12%
3Q	—	—	120.3	3%	116.3	-13%
4Q	—	—	131.9	17%	112.4	-13%
Yr.	—	—	478.3	1%	473.5	-12%
Income (Million $)						
1Q	12.51	NM	2.03	NM	-0.20	NM
2Q	19.03	NM	2.21	-76%	9.34	-40%
3Q	—	—	-1.50	NM	2.88	-76%
4Q	—	—	-121.0	NM	8.39	-41%
Yr.	—	—	-118.3	NM	20.41	-64%
Earnings Per Share ($)						
1Q	0.28	NM	0.05	—	Nil	—
2Q	0.43	NM	0.05	-76%	0.21	-40%
3Q	E0.40	—	-0.03	NM	0.07	-74%
4Q	E0.44	—	-2.73	NM	0.19	-41%
Yr.	E1.55	—	-2.67	NM	0.46	-64%

Next earnings report expected: mid October

Glatfelter (P. H.) Co.

Business Summary - 27-JUL-95

P. H. Glatfelter Co., formed in 1864, manufactures printing, writing and technical specialty papers at three paper mills in Pennsylvania, Wisconsin and North Carolina. Contributions to revenues in recent years were:

	1994	1993
Printing papers	70%	72%
Tobacco and other specialty papers	30%	28%

The Pennsylvania facility, in Spring Grove, manufactures printing and writing paper. The Wisconsin mill, in Neenah, employs recycled wastepaper as raw material, while the major raw materials used at the North Carolina mill, in Pisgah Forest, are purchased wood pulp and processed flax straw. Annual production capacity of the three mills is 533,000 tons.

The Ecusta division, acquired in 1987, is a leading maker of high quality light weight opaque specialty papers for use in the tobacco industry, the financial printing paper market, and in religious and other book applications where very lightweight opaque papers are required. The company recorded a $2.89 a share writedown of the division's assets in the fourth quarter of 1994. Subsequently, the company solicited offers to sell the division, but rejected all offers because they were below its valuation of assets.

Wholly owned Glatfelter Pulp Wood Co. is responsible for the management of 110,000 acres of woodlands in Pennsylvania, Delaware, Virginia and Maryland.

A major modernization of the pulp mill and wood handling operations at Spring Grove, begun in 1990, was completed in the third quarter of 1994, at a total cost of about $170 million.

In 1994, paper merchant National-Gottesman Inc. accounted for 13% of sales.

Important Developments

Jul. '95—GLT's board authorized the repurchase of an additional 1,000,000 common shares. Under a 10 million share buyback program, the company has repurchased 9,233,630 shares.

Capitalization

Long Term Debt: $150,000,000 of notes (3/95).

Per Share Data ($) (Year Ended Dec. 31)

	1994	1993	1992	1991	1990	1989
Tangible Bk. Val.	6.69	10.03	10.37	10.02	9.14	8.13
Cash Flow	-1.70	1.32	1.98	2.34	2.52	2.49
Earnings	-2.67	0.46	1.27	1.67	1.88	1.93
Dividends	0.70	0.70	0.68	0.60	0.55	0.50
Payout Ratio	NM	152%	53%	35%	28%	25%
Prices - High	19⅜	19½	29½	29⅞	23⅛	24½
- Low	14⅝	15⅛	17⅜	20⅜	16⅛	18½
P/E Ratio - High	NM	42	23	18	12	13
- Low	NM	33	14	12	9	10

Income Statement Analysis (Million $)

	1994	%Chg	1993	%Chg	1992	%Chg	1991
Revs.	478	NM	474	-12%	540	-5%	568
Oper. Inc.	56.0	-31%	81.0	-30%	115	-21%	145
Depr.	42.9	13%	38.1	19%	31.9	4%	30.7
Int. Exp.	9.4	34%	7.0	NM	0.1	—	Nil
Pretax Inc.	-192	NM	35.0	-62%	91.0	-26%	123
Eff. Tax Rate	NM	—	42%	—	38%	—	38%
Net Inc.	-117	NM	20.4	-64%	56.5	-26%	76.0

Balance Sheet & Other Fin. Data (Million $)

	1994	1993	1992	1991	1990	1989
Cash	3.2	46.4	3.1	44.8	28.5	2.8
Curr. Assets	135	181	131	177	165	125
Total Assets	651	842	648	630	599	550
Curr. Liab.	104	81.0	97.0	97.0	104	98.0
LT Debt	150	150	Nil	Nil	Nil	Nil
Common Eqty.	296	441	457	447	413	382
Total Cap.	506	722	546	527	489	448
Cap. Exp.	83.0	113	90.0	47.0	35.0	57.0
Cash Flow	-75.0	59.0	88.0	474	118	120

Ratio Analysis

	1994	1993	1992	1991	1990	1989
Curr. Ratio	1.3	2.2	1.3	1.8	1.6	1.3
% LT Debt of Cap.	29.6	20.8	Nil	Nil	Nil	Nil
% Net Inc.of Revs.	NM	4.3	10.5	13.4	14.1	15.5
% Ret. on Assets	NM	2.7	8.9	12.4	15.7	15.5
% Ret. on Equity	NM	4.5	12.6	17.8	22.6	26.2

Dividend Data (Cash has been paid each year since 1946.)

Amt. of Div. $	Date Decl.	Ex-Div. Date	Stock of Record	Payment Date
0.175	Sep. 28	Oct. 07	Oct. 14	Nov. 01 '94
0.175	Dec. 21	Jan. 09	Jan. 13	Feb. 01 '95
0.175	Mar. 16	Apr. 07	Apr. 14	May. 01 '95
0.175	Jun. 28	Jul. 12	Jul. 14	Aug. 01 '95

Data as orig. reptd.; bef. results of disc. opers. and/or spec. items. Per share data adj. for stk. divs. as of ex-div. date. E-Estimated. NA-Not Available. NM-Not Meaningful. NR-Not Ranked.

Office—228 S. Main St., Spring Grove, PA 17362. **Tel**—(717) 225-4711. **Chrmn, Pres & CEO**—T. C. Norris. **VP, Treas & Investor Contact**—R. P. Newcomer. **Secy**—R. S. Wood. **Dirs**—G. Baldwin, Jr., R. E. Chappell, G. H. Glatfelter, G. H. Glatfelter II, P. H. Glatfelter III, R. S. Hillas, M. A. Johnson II, J. W. Kennedy, T. C. Norris, P. R. Roedel, J. M. Sanzo, R. L. Smoot. **Transfer Agent & Registrar**—Wachovia Bank of North Carolina, Winston-Salem. **Incorporated** in Pennsylvania in 1905. **Empl**-2,851. **S&P Analyst:** Stewart Scharf

Global Marine

NYSE Symbol **GLM**
In S&P MidCap 400

07-AUG-95 **Industry:** Oil and Gas

Summary: This international offshore drilling contractor serves the oil and gas industry with a fleet of 27 premium rigs, and provides offshore drilling management services.

S&P Opinion: Buy (★★★★★)
Recent Price • 5½
52 Wk Range • 6⅛-3⅜
Yield • Nil
12-Mo. P/E • 25.0

Quantitative Evaluations
Outlook (1 Lowest—5 Highest) • **3+**
Fair Value • **5½**
Risk • **Average**
Earn./Div. Rank • **NR**

Technical Eval. • **Bearish** since 6/95
Rel. Strength Rank (1 Lowest—99 Highest) • **53**
Insider Activity • **NA**

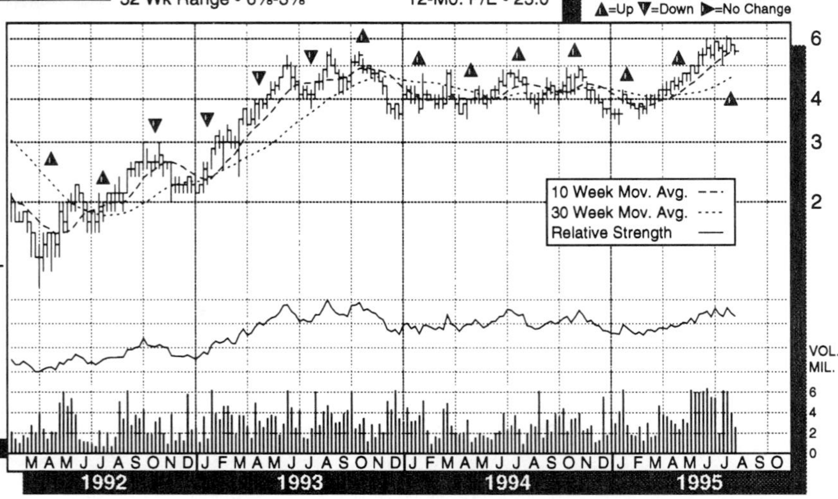

Overview - 07-AUG-95

Share earnings and cash flow for 1995 and 1996 should benefit from strength in the day rate business, growth in turnkey operations, and well controlled exploration, drilling and field development costs. We believe that within the next four to five years, balance will be achieved in the offshore rig market, since the number of excess rigs should continue to drop, leading to sharply higher day rates. Long-term prospects appear favorable, since GLM is well-positioned to take advantage of the rise in drilling activity that is being fueled by increased demand for natural gas by electric utilities. We expect rig utilization and offshore rig counts to remain stable in coming months, though it is a seasonally weak period. In the turnkey business, where returns are predictably in excess of 12%, the company will continue to benefit from its expertise as a contract driller.

Valuation - 07-AUG-95

The shares have been moving up in recent months on strengthening fundamentals for offshore rig markets. Day rates and rig utilization have been climbing and the trend should continue for the remainder of 1995 and into 1996, as stable commodity prices and a lack of suitable offshore rigs provide the underlying fundamentals for the healthy share price gains we anticipate. The shares trade at a modest premium to the group on a cash flow basis, as warranted by Global Marine's industry-leading rig fleet.

Key Stock Statistics

S&P EPS Est. 1995	0.30	Tang. Bk. Value/Share	1.32
P/E on S&P Est. 1995	18.3	Beta	0.80
S&P EPS Est. 1996	0.60	Shareholders	10,900
Dividend Rate/Share	Nil	Market cap. (B)	$0.907
Shs. outstg. (M)	164.9	Inst. holdings	70%
Avg. daily vol. (M)	0.989	Insider holdings	NA

Value of $10,000 invested 5 years ago: $ 15,172

Fiscal Year Ending Dec. 31

	1995	% Change	1994	% Change	1993	% Change
Revenues (Million $)						
1Q	116.1	71%	68.00	11%	61.00	-11%
2Q	102.4	34%	76.30	40%	54.50	-22%
3Q	—	—	91.40	36%	67.40	17%
4Q	—	—	123.3	43%	86.10	33%
Yr.	—	—	359.0	33%	269.0	3%
Income (Million $)						
1Q	4.50	NM	-1.70	NM	-9.30	NM
2Q	24.20	NM	-0.80	NM	-11.90	NM
3Q	—	—	1.10	NM	-6.80	-35%
4Q	—	—	6.20	NM	1.50	NM
Yr.	—	—	4.80	NM	-26.50	NM
Earnings Per Share ($)						
1Q	0.03	NM	-0.01	NM	-0.06	NM
2Q	0.14	—	Nil	—	-0.08	NM
3Q	E0.07	—	0.01	NM	-0.04	NM
4Q	E0.06	—	0.04	NM	0.01	NM
Yr.	E0.30	—	0.03	NM	-0.17	NM

Next earnings report expected: early October

Global Marine

Business Summary - 07-AUG-95

Global Marine is primarily a contractor engaged in the operation of offshore oil and gas drilling rigs. It also participates in oil and gas development and production, and provides offshore drilling management services on a turnkey basis. The company emerged from three years of Chapter 11 bankruptcy proceedings in February 1989. Revenue and operating income contributions in 1994:

	Revs.	Profits
Marine drilling	97%	92%
Oil, gas & other	3%	8%

In 1994, marine drilling revenues derived outside the U.S. represented 47% of total revenues (44% in 1993).

As of July 14, 1995, GLM's fleet consisted of 27 rigs, including 24 premium jacks, two third-generation semisubmersibles, a deep-water drillship, and a concrete island drilling system for use in the Arctic. Total fleet rig utilization averaged 90% in 1994, versus 87% in 1993 and 78% in 1992.

Challenger Minerals Inc. and Global Marine Oil and Gas Co. develop and produce oil and gas and participate in various drilling ventures offshore Texas and Louisiana in the Gulf of Mexico and onshore in Louisiana, Oklahoma and Texas. At December 31, 1994, proved reserves totaled 655,000 bbl. of oil and 11.8 Bcf of gas (368,000 bbl. and 10.6 Bcf at 1993 year-end). The estimated present value of future net cash flow from GLM's reserves (discounted at 10%) was $16.9 million at December 31, 1994, versus $16.3 million a year earlier.

In late 1992, a recapitalization was completed, including the sale of 26 million common shares at $2.125 each and a concurrent sale of $225 million of 12 3/4% senior secured notes due 1999.

Important Developments

Jul. '95—Second quarter earnings amounted to $24.2 million ($0.14 a share), versus a loss of $800,000 (less than one cent) the prior year. Results for the 1995 interim included a $14.7 million gain (pretax) from the sale of an offshore rig. Revenues from the dayrate business reached $59 million, up from $45 million the prior year. In the turnkey business, the 10 turnkey wells it operated generated $40 million in revenues, versus $29 million from 13 wells the prior year. GLM said that during June 1995, continuing weakness in Southeast Asia offset small improvements in the North Sea and Southeast Asia. There was no change in the company's worldwide Summary of Current Offshore Rig Economics (SCORE) compared to May. SCORE, at 40.5% as of June 1995, reflects current rig dayrates as a percent of the estimated rate required to justify building new rigs.

Capitalization

Long Term Debt: $225,000,000 (3/95).

Per Share Data ($) (Year Ended Dec. 31)

	1994	1993	1992	1991	1990	1989
Tangible Bk. Val.	1.29	1.26	1.10	0.39	0.01	0.13
Cash Flow	0.26	0.06	0.64	0.44	0.06	-0.22
Earnings	0.03	-0.17	0.24	0.01	-0.35	-0.61
Dividends	Nil	Nil	Nil	Nil	Nil	Nil
Payout Ratio	Nil	Nil	Nil	Nil	Nil	Nil
Prices - High	5	5⅝	3	5¼	6⅝	3¾
- Low	3½	2⅛	1⅛	1⅝	3	¼
P/E Ratio - High	NM	NM	13	NM	NM	NM
- Low	NM	NM	5	NM	NM	NM

Income Statement Analysis (Million $)

	1994	%Chg	1993	%Chg	1992	%Chg	1991
Revs.	359	33%	269	3%	260	-17%	315
Oper. Inc.	63.5	62%	39.1	-25%	52.0	-46%	96.0
Depr.	37.4	4%	35.9	-24%	47.1	1%	46.6
Int. Exp.	30.0	-6%	32.0	-27%	44.0	-12%	50.0
Pretax Inc.	5.0	NM	-26.0	NM	31.0	NM	4.0
Eff. Tax Rate	11%	—	NM	—	10%	—	71%
Net Inc.	5.0	NM	-27.0	NM	28.0	NM	1.0

Balance Sheet & Other Fin. Data (Million $)

	1994	1993	1992	1991	1990	1989
Cash	58.0	66.0	35.0	58.0	68.0	74.0
Curr. Assets	150	144	91.0	128	114	117
Total Assets	512	493	480	524	544	573
Curr. Liab.	56.0	37.0	61.0	40.0	43.0	50.0
LT Debt	225	225	225	386	437	443
Common Eqty.	212	205	155	45.0	1.0	13.0
Total Cap.	437	430	380	434	441	460
Cap. Exp.	75.9	64.0	21.0	23.0	19.0	10.0
Cash Flow	42.0	9.0	75.0	48.0	6.0	-22.0

Ratio Analysis

	1994	1993	1992	1991	1990	1989
Curr. Ratio	2.7	3.9	1.5	3.2	2.7	2.4
% LT Debt of Cap.	51.5	52.3	59.3	89.0	99.0	96.4
% Net Inc.of Revs.	1.3	NM	10.6	0.3	NM	NM
% Ret. on Assets	1.0	NM	4.9	0.2	NM	NM
% Ret. on Equity	2.3	NM	26.2	4.4	NM	NM

Dividend Data (No dividends have been paid since the 1989 reorganization. Dividends on the old common stock were omitted in 1985.)

Data as orig. reptd.; bef. results of disc. opers. and/or spec. items. Per share data adj. for stk. divs. as of ex-div. date. E-Estimated. NA-Not Available. NM-Not Meaningful. NR-Not Ranked.

Office—777 North Eldridge Rd., Houston, TX 77079. **Tel**—(713) 596-5100. **Chrmn, Pres & CEO**—C. R. Luigs. **SVP & CFO**—J. C. Martin. **Investor Contact**—David A. Herasimchuk. **Dirs**—P. M. Ahern, D. B. Brown, E. J. Campbell, P. T. Flawn, J. M. Galvin, L. L. Leigh, C. R. Luigs, J. C. Martin, S. A. Shuman, W. R. Thomas, W. C. Walker. **Transfer Agent & Registrar**—Harris Trust & Savings Bank, Chicago. **Incorporated** in Delaware in 1964. **Empl-** 1,500. **S&P Analyst:** Raymond J. Deacon

STANDARD & POOR'S

STOCK REPORTS

Goulds Pumps

NASDAQ Symbol **GULD**
In S&P MidCap 400

16-OCT-95 **Industry:** Machinery

Summary: Goulds is a leading manufacturer of pumps, motors and accessories for industrial, agricultural, commercial and consumer markets.

S&P Opinion: Accumulate (★★★★)

Recent Price • 23½
52 Wk Range • 25½-19⅛
Yield • 3.4%
12-Mo. P/E • 22.0

Quantitative Evaluations

Outlook (1 Lowest—5 Highest)
• **2-**

Fair Value
• **21**

Risk
• **Low**

Earn./Div. Rank
• **B+**

Technical Eval.
• **Bullish** since 7/95

Rel. Strength Rank (1 Lowest—99 Highest)
• **74**

Insider Activity
• **Neutral**

Earnings vs. Previous Year
▲=Up ▼=Down ▶=No Change

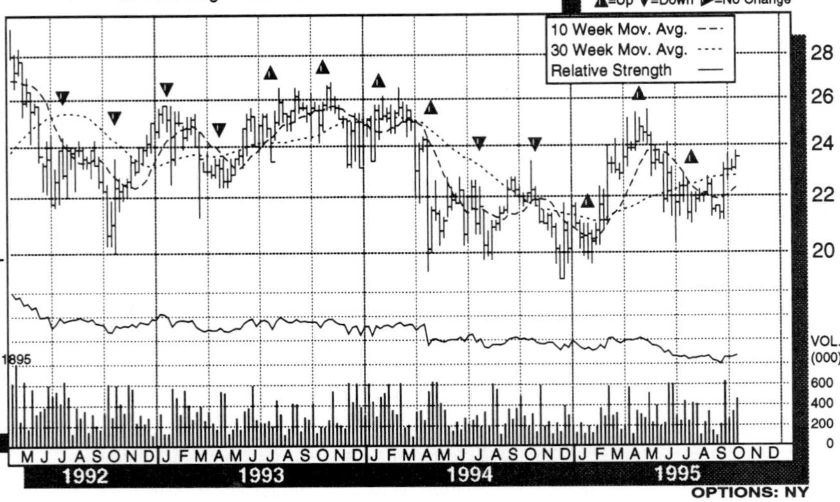

Overview - 13-OCT-95

We anticipate an 18% increase in sales for 1995, reflecting a 7.7% gain in orders and the acquisition of Vogel. Greater demand from the chemical, pulp and paper industries should boost sales in the industrial unit while water technologies will benefit from new product introductions. Better pricing, restructuring implemented in 1994 and only moderate increases in raw material costs should boost margins and lead to an increase in earnings from 1994's depressed levels. Assuming 2.6% GDP growth in 1996, sales and earnings should continue their uptrend. New products, acquisitions, the implementation of new management information systems, stronger economic activity in Europe and increased activity in the chemical, petroleum and pulp and paper industries will lift long-term sales and profits.

Valuation - 13-OCT-95

Through mid-October Gould has underperformed the S&P 500, rising 6.4% versus a 26% rise in the S&P 500. It has underperformed its peer companies by a narrower margin. However, we are maintaining our accumulate rating on Gould based upon our expectation for a substantial earnings improvement in 1995 and 1996 together with its attractive dividend yield. The stock has been depressed over the last two years by a combination of disappointing earnings and some other negative surprises. However, we believe the worst is over and the shares should begin to trend up.

Key Stock Statistics

S&P EPS Est. 1995	1.30	Tang. Bk. Value/Share	7.70
P/E on S&P Est. 1995	18.1	Beta	1.39
S&P EPS Est. 1996	1.50	Shareholders	5,300
Dividend Rate/Share	0.80	Market cap. (B)	$0.499
Shs. outstg. (M)	21.2	Inst. holdings	69%
Avg. daily vol. (M)	0.095	Insider holdings	NA

Value of $10,000 invested 5 years ago: $ 16,157

Fiscal Year Ending Dec. 31

	1995	% Change	1994	% Change	1993	% Change
Revenues (Million $)						
1Q	160.1	17%	136.6	10%	124.0	-8%
2Q	180.7	20%	150.1	-2%	152.4	3%
3Q	—	—	154.9	3%	149.9	2%
4Q	—	—	143.9	12%	129.0	NM
Yr.	—	—	585.5	5%	555.7	NM
Income (Million $)						
1Q	5.43	42%	3.82	12%	3.41	-51%
2Q	8.27	50%	5.50	-33%	8.21	8%
3Q	—	—	5.14	-40%	8.59	13%
4Q	—	—	3.75	11%	3.37	NM
Yr.	—	—	18.20	-23%	23.57	8%
Earnings Per Share ($)						
1Q	0.26	44%	0.18	13%	0.16	-53%
2Q	0.39	50%	0.26	-33%	0.39	8%
3Q	E0.44	83%	0.24	-41%	0.41	14%
4Q	E0.21	17%	0.18	13%	0.16	NM
Yr.	E1.30	51%	0.86	-23%	1.12	8%

Next earnings report expected: late October

Goulds Pumps

Business Summary - 13-OCT-95

Goulds Pumps designs, manufactures and services pumps, motors and accessories for industrial, agricultural, commercial and consumer markets.

Contributions by segment in 1994 were:

	Sales	Profits
Industrial	55%	47%
Water technologies	45%	53%

The Industrial Products group manufactures end-suction, double-suction, multistage, axial flow, vertical turbine, sump and slurry pumps for industrial and municipal markets. The segment's long-term plan is to focus on four key markets: chemical, pulp and paper, minerals and energy. Products are sold to U.S. customers through some 60 sales engineers in branch sales offices and 35 distributors.

The Water Technologies group makes water pump systems, which include pumps, motors, pressure tanks and related accessories used to supply water for farms, single- and multiple-family residences, office buildings, restaurants and other commercial uses and municipal water supply and sewage treatment facilities. The home water systems market accounts for 52% of segment sales. Demand from the home water market is tied to general economic conditions and the weather. Products are marketed through some 50 water system sales representatives who call on about 500 distributors.

In 1994, the U.S. accounted for 73% of total sales and $36.2 million of operating profit, Europe for 17% and $5.4 million in operating profit and other foreign for 10% and a $2.5 million operating loss.

The company operates at its lowest level during the first and fourth quarter of each calendar year due primarily to the Water Technologies Group market decline in winter months.

Important Developments

Sep. '95—GULD said that the U. S. District Court for the Western District of New York dismissed an action brought against the company and its former chief executive which alleged that false statements made by the company caused injury to the plaintiff.

Jul. '95—GULD announced that members of the UnitedSteelworkers of America ratified a four year labor pact which provided for wage increases of 3% in each of the first three years of the contract and 3.5% in the final year. It also provided for increased pension benefits and a no layoff provision for employees with six or more years of service.

Capitalization

Long Term Debt: $90,634,000 (6/95).

Per Share Data ($)

(Year Ended Dec. 31)

	1994	1993	1992	1991	1990	1989
Tangible Bk. Val.	8.90	8.50	9.08	10.45	9.94	8.80
Cash Flow	2.04	2.29	2.17	2.60	2.48	2.38
Earnings	0.86	1.12	1.04	1.51	1.49	1.41
Dividends	0.80	0.80	0.80	0.80	0.76	0.76
Payout Ratio	93%	71%	77%	53%	51%	54%
Prices - High	26½	26¾	29⅜	26	28½	24⅝
- Low	19⅛	21¼	20	18	15⅛	16½
P/E Ratio - High	31	24	20	17	19	17
- Low	22	19	19	12	10	12

Income Statement Analysis (Million $)

	1994	%Chg	1993	%Chg	1992	%Chg	1991
Revs.	585	5%	556	NM	558	-2%	567
Oper. Inc.	65.4	11%	58.8	-14%	68.5	-11%	76.9
Depr.	24.9	NM	24.8	4%	23.8	4%	22.8
Int. Exp.	6.6	22%	5.4	8%	5.0	-22%	6.4
Pretax Inc.	29.6	-14%	34.4	-4%	35.8	-30%	51.3
Eff. Tax Rate	39%	—	32%	—	39%	—	39%
Net Inc.	18.2	-23%	23.6	8%	21.9	-30%	31.3

Balance Sheet & Other Fin. Data (Million $)

	1994	1993	1992	1991	1990	1989
Cash	7.4	7.2	13.7	17.3	37.9	28.3
Curr. Assets	256	248	237	224	256	237
Total Assets	457	439	419	396	425	394
Curr. Liab.	139	138	115	102	129	110
LT Debt	53.8	38.9	40.9	44.4	55.3	70.2
Common Eqty.	191	187	193	219	207	182
Total Cap.	245	230	234	264	262	252
Cap. Exp.	28.1	24.7	40.0	38.8	28.0	21.3
Cash Flow	43.1	48.4	45.7	54.1	51.0	48.6

Ratio Analysis

	1994	1993	1992	1991	1990	1989
Curr. Ratio	1.8	1.8	2.1	2.2	2.0	2.2
% LT Debt of Cap.	21.9	16.9	17.5	16.8	21.1	27.9
% Net Inc.of Revs.	3.1	4.2	3.9	5.5	5.5	5.7
% Ret. on Assets	4.1	5.5	5.3	7.6	7.4	7.5
% Ret. on Equity	9.6	12.4	10.5	14.6	15.7	15.1

Dividend Data —Cash has been paid each year since 1948. A dividend reinvestment plan is available. A "poison pill" rights plan was adopted in 1988.

Amt. of Div. $	Date Decl.	Ex-Div. Date	Stock of Record	Payment Date
0.200	Sep. 20	Sep. 29	Oct. 05	Oct. 14 '94
0.200	Dec. 15	Dec. 29	Jan. 05	Jan. 13 '95
0.200	Mar. 21	Mar. 30	Apr. 05	Apr. 14 '95
0.200	Jun. 23	Jun. 30	Jul. 05	Jul. 14 '95
0.200	Sep. 18	Oct. 03	Oct. 05	Oct. 13 '95

Data as orig. reptd.; bef. results of disc. opers. and/or spec. items. Per share data adj. for stk. divs. as of ex-div. date. E-Estimated. NA-Not Available. NM-Not Meaningful. NR-Not Ranked.

Tel—(716) 387-6600. **Chrmn, Pres & CEO**—T. C. McDermott. **VP & Secy**—E. B. Bradshaw. **Treas**—Linda L. Polcaro. **VP, CFO & Investor Contact**—Sean P. Murphy. **Dirs**— W. W. Goessel, M. Howard, B. B. Lucas, T. C. McDermott, J. C. Miller III, P. Oddleifson, A. M. Richardson. **Transfer Agent & Registrar**—American Stock Transfer & Trust Co., New York, NY. **Incorporated** in New York in 1864; reincorporated in Delaware in 1984. **Empl**-4,200. **S&P Analyst:** Leo Larkin

Granite Construction

NASDAQ Symbol GCCO (Incl. in Nat'l Market) In S&P MidCap 400

Price	Range	P-E Ratio	Dividend	Yield	S&P Ranking	Beta
Aug. 4'95	1995					
25⅝	25¾–18	11	0.30	1.2%	B	0.76

Summary

This heavy-construction contractor primarily serves the public sector (building highways, dams, airports, etc.), as well as the private sector (site preparation for buildings and plants). It also makes asphalt, concrete base rock and other construction materials. Following earnings gains in 1994, further improvment was seen in the first half of 1995

Business Summary

Granite Construction is one of the largest U.S. heavy-construction contractors. It operates throughout the U.S., focusing primarily on the West and Southwest, and serves both public and private-sector clients. Revenues in recent years were derived as follows:

	1994	1993	1992
Private sector	12.6%	16.5%	19.4%
Federal agencies	8.3%	7.4%	11.3%
State agencies	35.4%	31.3%	33.5%
Local public agencies	35.3%	34.1%	25.4%
Construction material	8.4%	10.7%	10.4%

In 1994, contracts with the California Department of Transportation accounted for 13% of revenues.

The Branch division (74% of 1994 revenues) has both public and private-sector clients. Public activities include both new construction and improvement of streets, roads, highways and bridges. In the private sector, major contracts include site preparation for housing, including excavation, grading and street paving, and installation of curbs, gutters, sidewalks and underground utilities. Many of GCCO's 11 branch offices mine aggregates and operate plants that process aggregates into construction materials for internal use and for sale to others.

The Heavy Construction division (26%) undertakes projects that are usually larger and more complex than those performed by the Branch division. Heavy-construction projects generally have a contract amount averaging over $15 million, with average duration of more than two years. Large infrastructure projects are undertaken, including construction of major highways, large dams, mass transit facilities, bridges, pipelines, canals, tunnels, waterway locks and dams, and airport runways. Activities also include contract mine stripping and reclamation and large site preparation, demolition, clearing, excavation, dewatering, drainage, embankment fill, structural concrete, concrete and asphalt paving, and tunneling.

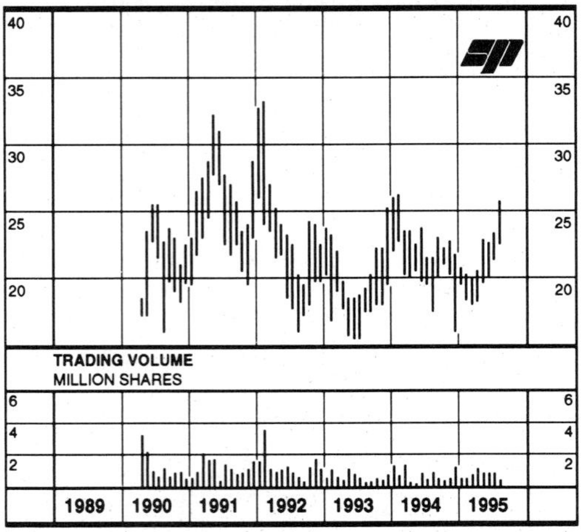

GCCO owns and leases substantial aggregate reserves, and owns 76 construction materials processing plants and one of the largest U.S. heavy-construction contractor equipment fleets.

Important Developments

May '95— GCCO said a bankruptcy court judge approved a settlement agreement for the Orange County Investment Pool that gave the Transportation Corridor Agency (TCA) a higher settlement than the company expected. GCCO added that the increased settlement gave it greater assurance that the San Joaquin Hills Toll Road project would be completed on schedule.

May '95— The company said it had acquired Gibbons Co., for about $42 million of cash and debt. Salt Lake City-based Gibbons, a contractor and construction materials producer with $90 million in annual revenues, conducts business mostly in Utah and surrounding states.

Next earnings report expected in early November.

Per Share Data ($)

Yr. End Dec. 31	1994	1993	[2]1992	1991	1990	1989	1988	1987	1986	1985
Tangible Bk. Val.	**[3]15.55**	[3]14.06	[3]13.83	13.44	11.62	8.91	7.16	5.33	4.22	2.71
Cash Flow	**3.84**	2.36	2.50	3.68	3.75	3.36	3.23	2.40	NA	NA
Earnings[1]	**1.66**	0.30	0.34	1.51	1.70	1.42	1.50	0.85	1.14	0.89
Dividends	**0.20**	0.20	0.20	0.20	0.15	Nil	Nil	Nil	Nil	Nil
Payout Ratio	**12%**	67%	59%	13%	9%	Nil	Nil	Nil	Nil	Nil
Prices—High	**26¼**	25¼	33¼	32¼	25½	NA	NA	NA	NA	NA
Low	**16**	15½	16	19½	16	NA	NA	NA	NA	NA
P/E Ratio—	**16–10**	84–52	98–47	21–13	15–9	NA	NA	NA	NA	NA

Data as orig. reptd. **1.** Bef. spec. item(s) of +0.09 in 1993. **2.** Refl. merger or acq. **3.** Incl. intangibles. NA-Not Available.

Income Data (Million $)

Year Ended Dec. 31	Revs.	Oper. Inc.	% Oper. Inc. of Revs.	Cap. Exp.	Depr.	Int. Exp.	Net Bef. Taxes	Eff. Tax Rate	Net Inc.	% Net Inc. of Revs.	Cash Flow
1994	**693**	**52.9**	**7.6**	**39.1**	**25.7**	**2.53**	**30.5**	**36.0%**	**[2]19.5**	**2.8**	**45.2**
1993	570	27.7	4.9	17.9	24.1	2.31	5.2	33.0%	[2]3.5	0.6	27.6
[1]1992	518	28.9	5.6	45.4	25.3	2.20	5.5	29.3%	[2]3.9	0.8	29.2
1991	564	48.2	8.5	39.9	25.2	2.08	27.0	34.7%	[2]17.6	3.1	42.9
1990	558	48.9	8.8	29.9	22.8	3.12	29.1	35.2%	[2]18.8	3.4	41.6
1989	504	38.3	7.6	36.6	19.4	4.51	22.0	35.5%	[2]14.2	2.8	33.6
1988	437	39.2	9.0	21.9	17.3	5.63	23.7	36.6%	15.0	3.4	32.3
1987	381	29.6	7.8	15.9	15.4	5.45	13.8	37.6%	8.6	2.3	24.0
1986	374	NA	NA	NA	NA	6.26	20.8	44.7%	11.5	3.1	NA
1985	336	NA	NA	NA	NA	7.12	13.5	33.4%	9.0	2.7	NA

Balance Sheet Data (Million $)

Dec. 31	Cash	Curr. Assets	Curr. Liab.	Curr. Ratio	Total Assets	% Ret. on Assets	Long Term Debt	Common Equity	Total Cap.	% LT Debt of Cap.	% Ret. on Equity
1994	**48.6**	**199**	**133**	**1.5**	**349**	**5.8**	**17.2**	**183**	**216**	**8.0**	**11.2**
1993	48.8	176	111	1.6	319	1.1	28.6	164	208	13.7	2.1
1992	54.1	162	109	1.5	308	1.3	38.6	161	200	19.3	2.5
1991	55.0	162	104	1.6	275	6.6	14.8	156	171	8.7	12.1
1990	50.5	160	105	1.5	258	7.0	19.1	134	153	12.5	15.9
1989	46.3	152	115	1.3	243	6.4	39.7	89	129	30.8	17.7
1988	19.5	130	87	1.5	203	7.9	44.3	72	116	38.2	24.0
1987	19.8	NA	NA	NA	176	5.0	49.5	53	103	48.2	18.0
1986	16.8	NA	NA	NA	166	7.1	50.2	42	92	54.3	33.2
1985	24.5	NA	NA	NA	155	NA	61.6	27	89	69.4	NA

Data as orig. reptd. **1.** Refl. merger or acquisition. **2.** Bef. spec. item(s). NA-Not Available.

Operating Revenues (Million $)

Quarter:	1995	1994	1993	1992
Mar.	105	107	78	68
Jun.	227	174	143	130
Sep.		240	184	187
Dec.		173	166	136
		693	570	518

Revenues in the six months ended June 30, 1995, increased 18%, year to year, aided by the inclusion of Gibbons Co. Margins benefited from more work; net income surged to $9,560,000 ($0.81 a share), from $2,530,000 ($0.22).

Common Share Earnings ($)

Quarter:	1995	1994	1993	1992
Mar.	0.10	d0.18	d0.45	d0.33
Jun.	0.70	0.39	Nil	0.24
Sep.		1.16	0.49	0.37
Dec.		0.28	0.25	0.06
		1.66	0.30	0.34

Dividend Data

Cash dividends were initiated in 1990.

Amt. of Divd. $	Date Decl.	Ex–divd. Date	Stock of Record	Payment Date
0.05	Aug. 25	Sep. 26	Sep. 30	Oct. 21'94
0.05	Dec. 16	Dec. 23	Dec. 30	Jan. 20'95
0.05	Mar. 13	Mar. 27	Mar. 31	Apr. 21'95
0.07½	Jun. 1	Jun. 28	Jun. 30	Jul. 21'95
0.15 Spl.	Jun. 1	Jun. 28	Jun. 30	Jul. 21'95

Finances

Backlog at June 30, 1995, totaled $720.6 million, up 13% from the level a year earlier. In the 1995 first quarter, GCCO received an award for a $108 million freeway reconstruction project in Dallas, Tex.

Capitalization

Long Term Debt: $16,715,000 (3/95).

Common Stock: 11,859,248 shs. ($0.01 par).
ESOP holds 36%.
Institutions hold 49%.
Shareholders: 380 (3/95).

d-Deficit.

Office—585 W. Beach St., Watsonville, CA 95076. **Tel**—(408) 724-1011. **Chrmn**—R. C. Solari. **Pres & CEO**—D. H. Watts. **VP & CFO**—W. E. Barton. **VP & Secy**—R. L. Reddy. **Investor Contact**—Michael Lawson (408) 761-4717. **Dirs**—J. J. Barclay, R. M. Brooks, A. S. Ferrante, R. A. McDonald, D. K. McNear, R. E. Miles, R. H. Roberts, R. C. Solari, D. H. Watts. **Transfer Agent & Registrar**—First Interstate Bank of California, SF. **Incorporated** in Delaware in 1990. **Empl**—3,048.

 Leo Larkin

STANDARD & POOR'S

STOCK REPORTS

Green Tree Financial

NYSE Symbol **GNT**
In S&P MidCap 400

06-SEP-95 **Industry:** Finance

Summary: This company primarily originates, pools, sells and services conditional sales contracts for manufactured homes, home improvements, consumer products and commercial products.

S&P Opinion: Buy (★★★★★)

Recent Price • 58
52 Wk Range • 58¾-24¼
Yield • 0.7%
12-Mo. P/E • 19.1

Quantitative Evaluations

Outlook
(1 Lowest—5 Highest)
• **2+**

Fair Value
• **55⅝**

Risk
• **Average**

Earn./Div. Rank
• **B+**

Technical Eval.
• **Bullish** since 12/94

Rel. Strength Rank
(1 Lowest—99 Highest)
• **82**

Insider Activity
• **NA**

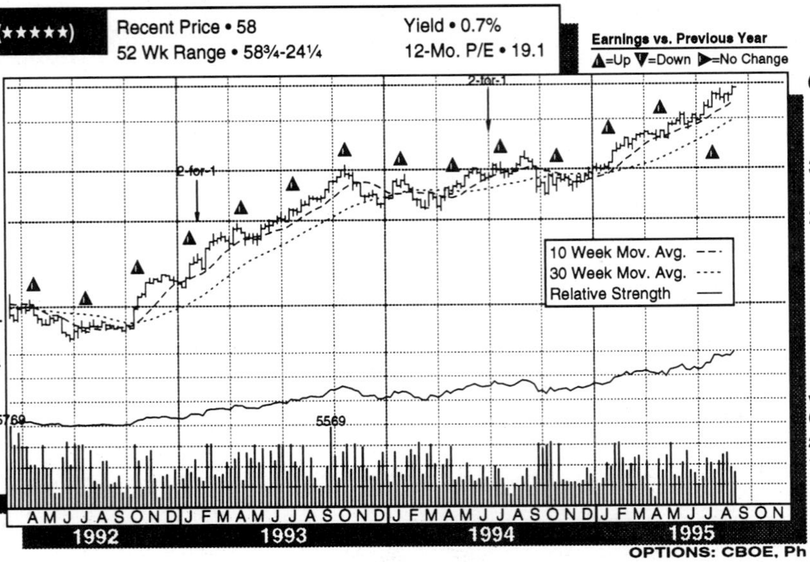

OPTIONS: CBOE, Ph

Overview - 06-SEP-95

Manufactured housing loan originations are expected to continue at a strong pace in 1995, aided by gains in market share, growth in the average contract size due to a shift to higher-priced units and price increases by manufacturers. A growing network of financing relationships with contractors, remodelers and dealers should also lead to an increased contribution from the home improvement segment. In addition, a rapid expansion of the consumer and commercial products segments will substantially boost originations. Servicing income should advance along with a greater volume of loans sold. A commensurate increase in general and administrative expenses to support expanded operations is anticipated. GNT's high margins and return on equity reflect its focus on a geographically diverse niche business, favorable pricing and efficient operations.

Valuation - 06-SEP-95

The shares were upgraded in mid-July following the release of extremely favorable second quarter earnings. GNT's growth rate has accelerated in recent periods, led by strong volume of core manufactured housing originations and a rapid expansion of product type financings to include sports vehicles and commercial items such as aircraft and trucks. The company entered the third quarter of 1995 with a record origination backlog. Trading at 14 times estimated 1996 earnings of $4.05 a share and with a projected earnings growth rate of 17%, the shares are attractive for superior appreciation potential.

Key Stock Statistics

S&P EPS Est. 1995	3.45	Tang. Bk. Value/Share	12.34
P/E on S&P Est. 1995	16.8	Beta	2.67
S&P EPS Est. 1996	4.05	Shareholders	400
Dividend Rate/Share	0.38	Market cap. (B)	$ 3.9
Shs. outstg. (M)	68.5	Inst. holdings	84%
Avg. daily vol. (M)	0.336	Insider holdings	NA

Value of $10,000 invested 5 years ago: $ 177,027

Fiscal Year Ending Dec. 31

	1995	% Change	1994	% Change	1993	% Change
Revenues (Million $)						
1Q	128.2	22%	104.8	57%	66.65	—
2Q	153.3	36%	112.3	60%	70.12	—
3Q	—	—	126.1	27%	98.93	—
4Q	—	—	154.3	30%	118.5	75%
Yr.	—	—	497.4	36%	366.7	49%
Income (Million $)						
1Q	50.73	32%	38.49	74%	22.06	74%
2Q	61.71	40%	44.23	52%	29.19	48%
3Q	—	—	52.07	61%	32.32	40%
4Q	—	—	46.50	42%	32.86	94%
Yr.	—	—	181.3	56%	116.4	61%
Earnings Per Share ($)						
1Q	0.73	30%	0.56	58%	0.36	65%
2Q	0.88	38%	0.64	38%	0.46	43%
3Q	E0.91	21%	0.75	47%	0.51	34%
4Q	E0.93	39%	0.67	41%	0.47	73%
Yr.	E3.45	32%	2.61	44%	1.81	50%

Next earnings report expected: mid October

Green Tree Financial

Business Summary - 06-SEP-95

Green Tree Financial originates conditional sales contracts for manufactured homes, home improvements, consumer products and commecial products, and provides floor plan financing to manufactured housing dealers. It also markets physical damage and term mortgage life insurance relating to the contracts it services, and acts as a servicer for manufactured housing contracts originated by other lenders. GNT operates through regional service centers located throughout the U.S.

GNT finances both new and previsouly owned manufactured homes, and originates conventional contracts as well as contracts insured by the FHA. Consumer products are financed using instalment sales contracts. Over the past two years, GNT has expanded the product types it finances to include sports vehicles, trailers for recreational activities and certain musical instruments. In November 1994, it began financing contracts for commercial products including general aviation aircraft and over-the-road tractor trailers. The floor plan lending division makes loans to manufactured housing dealers for purposes of financing new and previously owned manufactured home inventory.

During 1994, the company originated a total of 168,450 contracts (120,021 a year earlier), with an average size of $22,340 ($22,213) and a weighted average interest rate of 11.2% (10.3%).

The company securitizes substantially all of the contracts it originates, retaining the servicing on the contracts. Conventional manufactured housing contracts are pooled and structured into asset-backed securities that are then sold in the public securities market. GNT's FHA-insured and VA-guaranteed manufactured home contracts are converted into GNMA certificates and sold in the secondary market. At year-end 1994, GNT's servicing portfolio totaled $9.65 billion (up from $7.19 billion at year-end 1993).

The company records income at the time of the sale of its loan contracts, taking the present value of future cash flows into income.

Important Developments

Jul. '95—The company reported that contract originations in the second quarter of 1995 rose by 39%, to $1.4 billion, reflecting increases of 27% for manufactured housing, 46% for home improvements and 343% for consumer products. For the six months, contract originations increased 34%, to $2.3 billion.

Feb. '95—Directors authorized the repurchase of up to 3.5 million GNT common shares, or about 5% of those outstanding, in the open market.

Capitalization

Long Term Debt: $289,667,000 (6/95).

Per Share Data ($) (Year Ended Dec. 31)

	1994	1993	1992	1991	1990	1989
Tangible Bk. Val.	10.69	8.16	4.92	1.95	0.99	0.52
Earnings	2.61	1.81	1.20	1.00	0.59	0.43
Dividends	0.23	0.17	0.15	0.15	0.15	0.15
Payout Ratio	9%	9%	13%	15%	26%	34%
Prices - High	34⅞	31¼	13	11⅞	4⅝	4⅝
- Low	21½	11⅝	7⅝	2¼	2 1/16	1 7/16
P/E Ratio - High	13	17	11	12	8	9
- Low	8	6	6	2	4	3

Income Statement Analysis (Million $)

	1994	%Chg	1993	%Chg	1992	%Chg	1991
Total Revs.	497	35%	367	49%	247	15%	215
Int. Exp.	41.6	-19%	51.2	14%	44.9	-8%	49.0
% Exp/Op Revs.	39%	—	45%	—	52%	—	57%
Pretax Inc.	302	50%	201	69%	119	29%	92.2
Eff. Tax Rate	40%	—	42%	—	39%	—	39%
Net Inc.	181	56%	116	60%	72.5	28%	56.7

Balance Sheet & Other Fin. Data (Million $)

	1994	1993	1992	1991	1990	1989
Cash & Secs.	623	315	239	181	113	39.0
Loans	700	843	532	438	420	349
Total Assets	1,772	1,740	1,034	876	789	711
ST Debt	NA	NA	NA	NA	NA	NA
Capitalization:						
Debt	309	515	376	361	279	283
Equity	726	549	299	94.0	49.0	28.0
Total	1,035	1,064	675	599	471	454
Price Times Book HI	3.3	3.8	2.6	6.1	4.6	8.9
Price Times Book LO	2.0	1.4	1.5	1.2	2.1	2.7

Ratio Analysis

	1994	1993	1992	1991	1990	1989
% Ret. on Revs.	36.4	31.8	29.4	26.4	20.8	20.4
% Ret. on Assets	1.0	8.0	7.0	7.0	4.9	4.3
% Ret. on Equity	28.4	27.3	33.6	66.2	70.9	95.1
Loans/Equity	1.2	1.8	1.8	1.9	2.1	1.9

Dividend Data —Cash dividends were initiated in 1986. A "poison pill" stock purchase rights plan was adopted in 1985.

Amt. of Div. $	Date Decl.	Ex-Div. Date	Stock of Record	Payment Date
0.063	Aug. 31	Sep. 09	Sep. 15	Sep. 30 '94
0.063	Oct. 18	Dec. 09	Dec. 15	Dec. 31 '94
0.094	Feb. 06	Mar. 09	Mar. 15	Mar. 31 '95
0.094	Apr. 17	Jun. 13	Jun. 15	Jun. 30 '95
0.094	Jul. 20	Sep. 13	Sep. 15	Sep. 30 '95

Data as orig. reptd.; bef. results of disc opers. and/or spec. items. Per share data adj. for stk. divs. as of ex-div. date. E-Estimated. NA-Not Available. NM-Not Meaningful. NR-Not Ranked.

Office—1100 Landmark Towers, 345 Saint Peter St., Saint Paul, MN 55102-1639. **Tel**—(612) 293-3400. **Fax**—(612) 293-5746. **Chrmn & CEO**—L. M. Coss. **Pres & COO**—R. D. Potts. **Exec VP, CFO, Treas & Investor Contact**—John W. Brink. **Exec VP & Secy**—R. G. Evans. **Dirs**—L. M. Coss, R. G. Evans, W. M. McGee, T. A. Modic, R. S. Nickoloff, R. D. Potts. **Transfer Agent & Registrar**—Firstar Trust Co., Milwaukee. **Incorporated** in Minnesota in 1975. **Empl**-2,158. **S&P Analyst:** Stephen R. Biggar

STANDARD & POOR'S

STOCK REPORTS

Hancock Fabrics

NYSE Symbol **HKF**
In S&P MidCap 400

12-SEP-95 **Industry:** Retail Stores

Summary: This company, which sells fabrics and related items primarily at retail to the home sewing market, operates about 500 stores in 33 states.

S&P Opinion: Hold (★★★)

Recent Price • 10½
52 Wk Range • 11¾-6½
Yield • 3.0%
12-Mo. P/E • 21.4

Quantitative Evaluations

Outlook (1 Lowest—5 Highest)
• **2-**

Fair Value
• **10**

Risk
• **Average**

Earn./Div. Rank
• **NR**

Technical Eval.
• **Bullish** since 7/95

Rel. Strength Rank (1 Lowest—99 Highest)
• **59**

Insider Activity
• **NA**

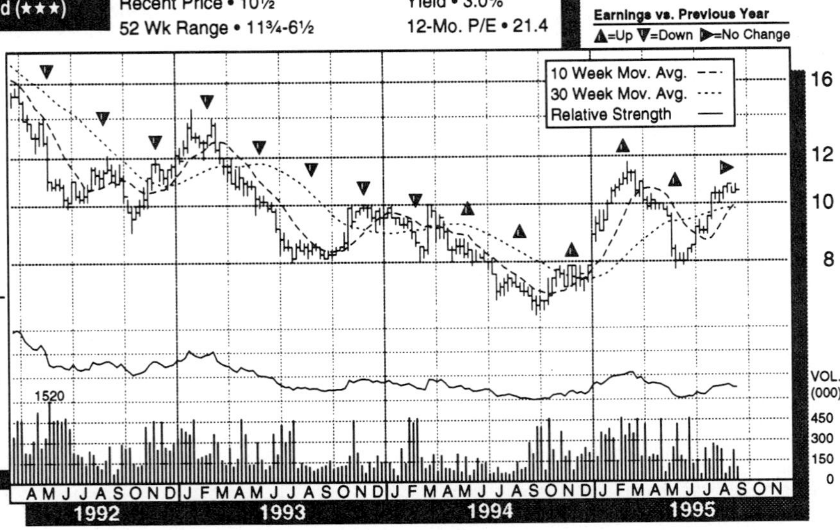

Overview - 12-SEP-95

Recent results were hurt by a slower than expected industry shakeout, leading to continued impact from the liquidation of competing stores; by a lack of fresh apparel products in Hancock's own stores; and by above-average temperatures. The industry consolidation is expected to eliminate most excess store capacity by early 1996. The company should benefit from reduced competition, and results will also be aided by cost controls. Hancock should be one of the industry survivors, but needs to tighten fundamentals in the interim.

Valuation - 12-SEP-95

The shares, which rose strongly on investor hopes that an industry shakeout would lead to better business conditions, have flattened, as the industry consolidation is progressing slowly. The shares were recently trading at about 21X projected 1995-6 EPS. A lack of upward movement in the stock price reflects industry fundamentals: customers currently seem more oriented to price than loyal to a given store. However, completion of the industry consolidation by the beginning of 1996 could boost the shares.

Key Stock Statistics

S&P EPS Est. 1996	0.50	Tang. Bk. Value/Share	5.41
P/E on S&P Est. 1996	21.0	Beta	0.99
S&P EPS Est. 1997	0.60	Shareholders	12,300
Dividend Rate/Share	0.32	Market cap. (B)	$0.226
Shs. outstg. (M)	21.5	Inst. holdings	70%
Avg. daily vol. (M)	0.023	Insider holdings	NA

Value of $10,000 invested 5 years ago: $ 7,218

Fiscal Year Ending Jan. 31

	1996	% Change	1995	% Change	1994	% Change
Revenues (Million $)						
1Q	90.07	-3%	92.90	NM	92.80	-3%
2Q	81.55	NM	81.81	-2%	83.58	-4%
3Q	—	—	96.51	-3%	99.0	-2%
4Q	—	—	95.60	4%	92.32	-4%
Yr.	—	—	366.8	NM	367.8	-3%
Income (Million $)						
1Q	1.30	27%	1.02	26%	0.81	-76%
2Q	0.84	-3%	0.87	NM	0.10	-95%
3Q	—	—	3.91	19%	3.29	-18%
4Q	—	—	4.33	NM	1.23	-52%
Yr.	—	—	10.14	86%	5.44	-55%
Earnings Per Share ($)						
1Q	0.06	20%	0.05	25%	0.04	-73%
2Q	0.04	NM	0.04	—	Nil	—
3Q	E0.20	11%	0.18	13%	0.16	-16%
4Q	E0.20	-5%	0.21	NM	0.06	-50%
Yr.	E0.50	4%	0.48	85%	0.26	-54%

Next earnings report expected: mid November

Hancock Fabrics

Business Summary - 12-SEP-95

Hancock Fabrics sells fabrics and related items at retail to the home sewing and home decorating markets. It also has wholesale operations, which account for a relatively small portion of total business. At August 15, 1995, the company was operating 501 fabric stores in 33 states under the names Hancock Fabrics, Minnesota Fabrics, Fabric Warehouse and Fabric Market.

Stores added or closed in recent years and the number of units in operation at year-end (January 31) were:

	1994-5	1993-4	1992-3	1991-2
Opened/acquired	16	29	37	31
Closed/relocated	16	11	14	9
In operation	500	500	482	459

Retail stores, located primarily in neighborhood shopping centers, are generally open seven days a week. They offer a wide selection of clothing fabrics, notions (including zippers, buttons, threads and ornamentation), patterns, quilting materials and supplies, decorative fabrics (including drapery and upholstery fabrics), craft items, and related supplies. Each store maintains an inventory of cotton, wool and synthetic staple fabrics such as broadcloth, poplin, gabardine, unbleached muslin and corduroy, as well as seasonal and current fashion fabrics.

Hancock mainly serves the home sewing and home decorating markets, which consist largely of value-conscious women who sew clothing for themselves and their families and decorations for their homes, or who hire professional home seamstresses to sew for them. Sales are seasonally highest in the fall and pre-Easter weeks.

Wholesale operations involve the sale of fabrics to about 200 independent retailers in locations in which the company has elected not to open its own stores. These operations have generally accounted for less than 5% of sales.

Beginning in early 1995, almost 10 million U.S. households began receiving the weekly half-hour sewing project show Sew Perfect, sponsored by Hancock, on the new Home and Garden Television Network. In the fall of 1995, the company's magazine entitled "Home Expressions" will be on sale at newsstands and in its stores.

Important Developments

Aug. '95—Same-store sales in the 13 weeks ended July 30, 1995, edged up only 0.5%, year to year. Results were restricted by a high level of promotional activity in the retail home sewing market. Hancock said that the fabric industry continues to consolidate and shake out excess capacity.

Capitalization

Long Term Debt: $36,000,000 (4/30/95).

Per Share Data ($) (Year Ended Jan. 31)

	1995	1994	1993	1992	1991	1990
Tangible Bk. Val.	4.54	4.37	4.44	4.41	4.18	3.71
Cash Flow	0.68	0.46	0.77	1.21	1.40	1.20
Earnings	0.48	0.26	0.57	1.03	1.23	1.06
Dividends	0.32	0.32	0.32	0.32	0.28	0.24
Payout Ratio	67%	123%	56%	31%	22%	21%
Cal. Yrs.	1994	1993	1992	1991	1990	1989
Prices - High	10	14½	19	27¾	20⅝	17⅛
- Low	6½	8	9	14¼	15½	9
P/E Ratio - High	21	56	33	27	17	16
- Low	14	31	16	14	13	9

Income Statement Analysis (Million $)

	1995	%Chg	1994	%Chg	1993	%Chg	1992
Revs.	367	NM	368	-3%	380	-2%	388
Oper. Inc.	23.2	55%	15.0	-42%	25.8	-39%	42.6
Depr.	4.2	-1%	4.2	NM	4.3	8%	4.0
Int. Exp.	2.4	6%	2.3	-13%	2.6	-5%	2.8
Pretax Inc.	16.8	93%	8.7	-54%	19.1	-48%	36.6
Eff. Tax Rate	40%	—	37%	—	37%	—	37%
Net Inc.	10.1	87%	5.4	-55%	12.1	-47%	23.0

Balance Sheet & Other Fin. Data (Million $)

	1995	1994	1993	1992	1991	1990
Cash	3.9	4.3	9.0	4.1	8.8	7.0
Curr. Assets	180	180	185	189	173	154
Total Assets	209	209	214	218	196	176
Curr. Liab.	56.0	53.3	47.4	58.5	64.4	51.6
LT Debt	37.0	45.0	58.0	50.3	35.5	35.8
Common Eqty.	97.0	94.0	95.0	97.0	93.0	86.0
Total Cap.	131	139	153	148	131	124
Cap. Exp.	4.0	2.8	4.2	6.3	4.9	5.0
Cash Flow	14.3	9.7	16.4	26.9	31.9	29.6

Ratio Analysis

	1995	1994	1993	1992	1991	1990
Curr. Ratio	3.2	3.4	3.9	3.2	2.7	3.0
% LT Debt of Cap.	27.0	32.5	38.0	34.1	27.1	29.0
% Net Inc.of Revs.	2.8	1.5	3.2	5.9	7.3	7.5
% Ret. on Assets	4.9	2.6	5.7	11.2	15.4	15.8
% Ret. on Equity	10.6	5.8	12.9	24.3	31.9	28.6

Dividend Data —Dividends were initiated in 1987. A poison pill stock purchase rights plan was adopted in 1987.

Amt. of Div. $	Date Decl.	Ex-Div. Date	Stock of Record	Payment Date
0.080	Sep. 08	Sep. 26	Oct. 01	Oct. 15 '94
0.080	Dec. 07	Dec. 23	Jan. 01	Jan. 15 '95
0.080	Mar. 09	Mar. 27	Apr. 01	Apr. 15 '95
0.080	Jun. 08	Jun. 28	Jul. 01	Jul. 15 '95
0.080	Sep. 07	Sep. 27	Oct. 01	Oct. 15 '95

Data as orig. reptd.; bef. results of disc. opers. and/or spec. items. Per share data adj. for stk. divs. as of ex-div. date. E-Estimated. NA-Not Available. NM-Not Meaningful. NR-Not Ranked.

Office—3406 West Main St., Tupelo, MS 38803. **Tel**—(601) 842-2834. **Chrmn & CEO**—M. O. Jarvis. **Pres, CFO & Investor Contact**—Larry G. Kirk. **EVP & COO**—J. W. Busby, Jr. **Secy**—L. D. Fair. **Dirs**—R. R. Devening, D. L. Fruge, M. O. Jarvis, L. G. Kirk, I. Owen, D. L. Weaver. **Transfer Agent & Registrar**—Continental Stock Transfer & Trust Co., NYC. **Incorporated** in Delaware in 1987; predecessor businesses incorporated at various times through 1971. **Empl**-7,100. **S&P Analyst:** Philip D. Wohl

STANDARD & POOR'S

STOCK REPORTS

Hanna (M. A.)

NYSE Symbol **MAH**
In S&P MidCap 400

09-AUG-95 **Industry:** Plastic/Products

Summary: This specialty chemical company's primary businesses are plastics and rubber compounding, color and additive concentrates, resin distribution and polymer products.

S&P Opinion: Accumulate (★★★★) | Recent Price • 27⅜ | 52 Wk Range • 30-21⅝ | Yield • 1.9% | 12-Mo. P/E • 8.2

Quantitative Evaluations

Outlook (1 Lowest—5 Highest)
• **4+**

Fair Value
• **28⅛**

Risk
• **Low**

Earn./Div. Rank
• **B**

Technical Eval.
• **Bearish** since 5/95

Rel. Strength Rank (1 Lowest—99 Highest)
• **59**

Insider Activity
• **NA**

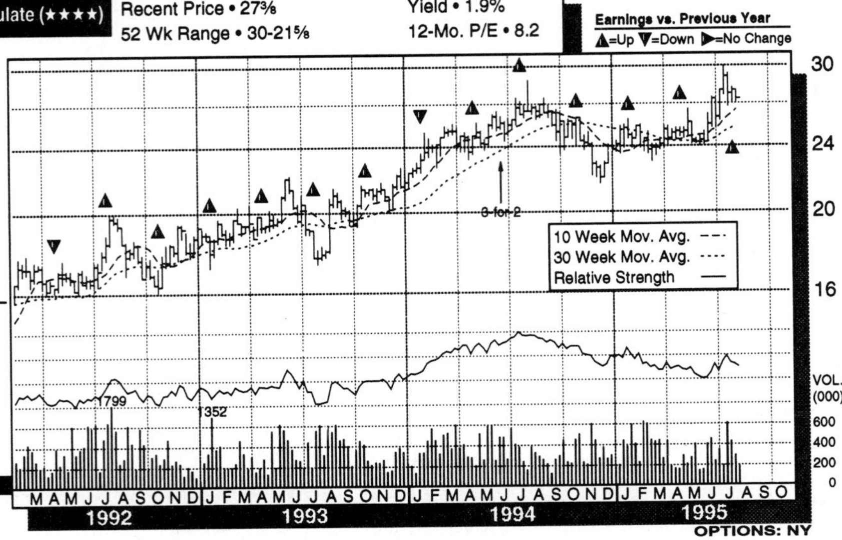

Overview - 09-AUG-95

Revenue growth is expected to slow from the 20% achieved in the first half of 1995 (aided by the July 1994 acquisition of Bergman) to a 5% to 7% range in the second half. With volume remaining flat, all of the growth will result from price increases. Margins should widen slightly, as raw material costs stabilize, and the higher pricing outweighs a less favorable product mix (with a greater percentage of lower-margin resin distribution sales). Proceeds from the sale of Day International and MAH's 8% interest in the Iron Ore Company of Canada (IOC) were used to reduce debt by $56 million (to 32% of total capital), with the remainder raising the cash level to more than $140 million. MAH would still like to establish a presence in Asia, and expects to increase its international business to one-fifth of total sales by 1996.

Valuation - 09-AUG-95

Although the shares have pulled back from their recent high, MAH has still gained more than 12% since our upgrading of the stock in late April. We continue to recommend the accumulation of the shares based on our 1995 estimate of $1.70 from continuing operations and 1996 estimate of $2.00 per share; the $1.88 stated estimate includes the $0.18 from the sale of MAH's 8% interest in IOC.

Key Stock Statistics

S&P EPS Est. 1995	1.88	Tang. Bk. Value/Share	2.51
P/E on S&P Est. 1995	14.6	Beta	1.19
S&P EPS Est. 1996	2.00	Shareholders	3,900
Dividend Rate/Share	0.54	Market cap. (B)	$0.990
Shs. outstg. (M)	35.5	Inst. holdings	68%
Avg. daily vol. (M)	0.075	Insider holdings	NA

Value of $10,000 invested 5 years ago: $ 17,479

Fiscal Year Ending Dec. 31

	1995	% Change	1994	% Change	1993	% Change
Revenues (Million $)						
1Q	492.8	27%	388.5	7%	362.0	22%
2Q	483.3	14%	422.5	10%	385.0	16%
3Q	—	—	448.6	16%	388.0	9%
4Q	—	—	459.7	20%	384.5	10%
Yr.	—	—	1,719	13%	1,520	14%
Income (Million $)						
1Q	12.01	93%	6.21	42%	4.36	83%
2Q	19.36	107%	9.37	12%	8.34	30%
3Q	—	—	11.27	27%	8.86	28%
4Q	—	—	10.16	15%	8.85	-16%
Yr.	—	—	37.00	23%	30.05	15%
Earnings Per Share ($)						
1Q	0.39	95%	0.20	36%	0.15	83%
2Q	0.62	107%	0.30	15%	0.26	18%
3Q	E0.45	—	0.36	29%	0.28	20%
4Q	E0.42	—	0.33	15%	0.29	-19%
Yr.	E1.88	—	1.20	23%	0.97	7%

Next earnings report expected: mid October

Hanna (M. A.)

Business Summary - 02-AUG-95

M.A. Hanna Co. is one of North America's largest independent producers of plastic and rubber compounds and a leading producer of color and additive concentrates for plastics. It is also an international distributor of engineered plastic shapes and resins, and manufactured polymer products. Contributions by segment in 1994 were:

	Sales	Profits
Processing	54%	72%
Distribution	44%	20%
Other	2%	8%

The processing segment is engaged in the custom compounding of plastic and rubber materials--mixing plastic resins or rubber with additives to achieve a desired physical and/or aesthetic quality--for customers throughout the U.S., Canada and Europe. It also makes custom formulated colorants for plastics. In March 1994, the company acquired North Coast Compounders (now called M. A. Hanna Thermoplastic Elastomers).

The company's resin distribution group links the major thermoplastics producers with thousands of processors and manufacturers, while Cadillac Plastic engages in worldwide distribution of plastic shapes, including sheet, rod, tube and film. Colonial Rubber Works manufactures molded sponge automotive parts.

Foreign operations provided 14% of sales and profits in 1994. In July 1994, MAH acquired Theodor Bergmann GmbH & Co. Kunststoffwerk KG, one of Germany's largest producers of specialty and reinforced thermoplastic compounds.

Other segments include MAH's diversified polymer products business, its marine and insurance operations, and management of an iron ore mine. In 1991, the company divested its natural resources businesses and, in April 1995, announced an agreement to sell Day International, a manufacturer of highly engineered printing blankets.

Important Developments

Jul. '95—M.A. Hanna said price increases accounted for 10% of its 14% revenue growth in the second quarter. The July 1994 Bergman acquisition accounted for 4%, with a 1% decline in volume offset by a 1% gain in foreign exchange.

Jun. '95—The company sold Day International, its printing and textile products business (with 1994 annual sales of more than $100 million), to American Industrial Partners Capital Fund. Although the terms were not disclosed, MAH said the sale was within its $175-$200 million target range. Earlier, Hanna sold its 8% equity interest in the Iron Ore Company of Canada (IOC) to IOC.

Capitalization

Long Term Debt: $232,462,000 (6/95).

Per Share Data ($) (Year Ended Dec. 31)

	1994	1993	1992	1991	1990	1989
Tangible Bk. Val.	2.36	-0.49	-0.07	-0.20	4.15	3.20
Cash Flow	2.56	2.53	2.59	0.72	2.36	3.27
Earnings	1.20	0.97	0.91	-0.50	1.35	2.23
Dividends	0.51	0.47	0.44	0.42	0.37	0.30
Payout Ratio	43%	49%	59%	NM	26%	15%
Prices - High	28⅞	22⅝	20	17¼	18⅛	19⅞
- Low	21⅜	17⅛	13⅛	11⅞	9⅞	12⅞
P/E Ratio - High	24	23	19	NM	13	9
- Low	18	18	12	NM	7	6

Income Statement Analysis (Million $)

	1994	%Chg	1993	%Chg	1992	%Chg	1991
Revs.	1,719	13%	1,515	14%	1,330	16%	1,146
Oper. Inc.	142	6%	134	11%	121	13%	107
Depr.	41.9	-13%	48.1	NM	47.9	11%	43.2
Int. Exp.	28.5	-12%	32.3	NM	32.5	40%	23.2
Pretax Inc.	66.0	25%	53.0	26%	42.0	NM	-1.0
Eff. Tax Rate	44%	—	44%	—	37%	—	NM
Net Inc.	37.0	23%	30.0	15%	26.0	NM	-17.0

Balance Sheet & Other Fin. Data (Million $)

	1994	1993	1992	1991	1990	1989
Cash	23.1	42.7	80.0	24.5	25.5	18.3
Curr. Assets	566	420	439	296	292	280
Total Assets	1,215	1,141	1,178	1,033	1,065	1,036
Curr. Liab.	337	274	252	202	197	182
LT Debt	289	322	351	331	138	135
Common Eqty.	415	365	398	380	568	543
Total Cap.	704	688	749	711	705	677
Cap. Exp.	47.0	23.4	19.2	26.8	28.3	25.6
Cash Flow	79.0	78.0	74.0	25.0	98.0	124

Ratio Analysis

	1994	1993	1992	1991	1990	1989
Curr. Ratio	1.7	1.5	1.7	1.5	1.5	1.5
% LT Debt of Cap.	41.0	46.8	46.9	46.5	19.5	19.9
% Net Inc.of Revs.	2.2	2.0	2.0	NM	5.0	7.8
% Ret. on Assets	3.1	2.6	2.3	NM	5.4	7.6
% Ret. on Equity	9.5	7.8	6.7	NM	10.3	16.7

Dividend Data (Dividends have been paid since 1944.)

Amt. of Div. $	Date Decl.	Ex-Div. Date	Stock of Record	Payment Date
0.125	Aug. 03	Aug. 11	Aug. 17	Sep. 12 '94
0.135	Nov. 02	Nov. 17	Nov. 23	Dec. 12 '94
0.135	Feb. 01	Feb. 13	Feb. 17	Mar. 13 '95
0.135	May. 03	May. 17	May. 23	Jun. 12 '95
0.135	Aug. 02	Aug. 15	Aug. 17	Sep. 12 '95

Data as orig. reptd.; bef. results of disc. opers. and/or spec. items. Per share data adj. for stk. divs. as of ex-div. date. E-Estimated. NA-Not Available. NM-Not Meaningful. NR-Not Ranked.

Office—200 Public Square, Suite 36-5000, Cleveland, OH 44114-2304. **Tel**—(216) 589-4000. **Chrmn & CEO**—M. D. Walker. **Pres & COO**—D. J. McGregor. **VP, CFO & Treas**—M. S. Duffey. **VP & Secy**—J. S. Pyke, Jr. **Investor Contact**—Barbara Gould (800-688-4259). **Dirs**—B. C. Ames, C. A. Cartwright, W. R. Embry, J. T. Eyton, G. D. Kirkham, M. L. Mann, D. J. McGregor, R. W. Pogue, M. D. Walker. **Transfer Agent & Registrar**—Society National Bank, Cleveland. **Incorporated** in Delaware in 1927. **Empl**-6,599. **S&P Analyst:** Justin McCann

STANDARD & POOR'S

STOCK REPORTS

Hannaford Bros.

NYSE Symbol **HRD**
In S&P MidCap 400

11-AUG-95 **Industry:** Retail Stores

Summary: This company is the largest food retailer in northern New England, with some 120 supermarkets located throughout Maine and New Hampshire and parts of five other eastern states.

Quantitative Evaluations

Outlook (1 Lowest—5 Highest)
• **3−**

Fair Value
• **26**

Risk
• **Low**

Earn./Div. Rank
• **A+**

Technical Eval.
• **Bearish** since 6/95

Rel. Strength Rank (1 Lowest—99 Highest)
• **16**

Insider Activity
• **NA**

Recent Price • 26½ | Yield • 1.6%
52 Wk Range • 29-21¾ | 12-Mo. P/E • 16.0

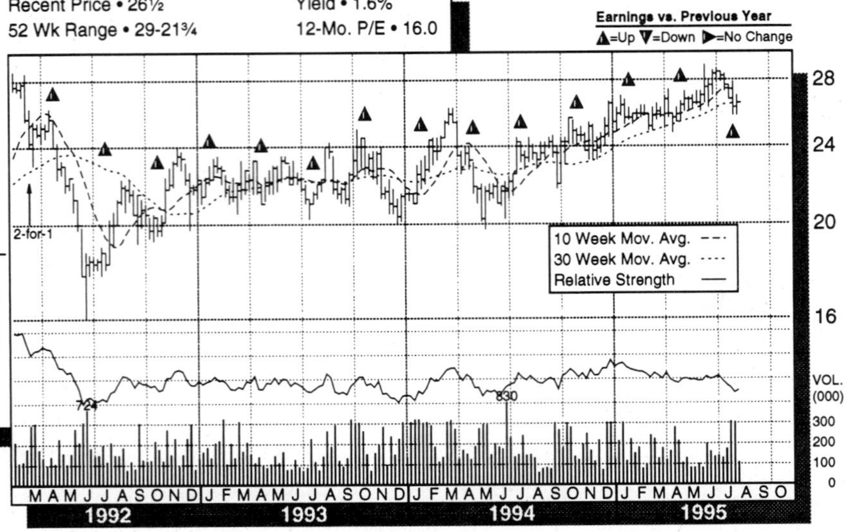

Business Profile - 11-AUG-95

Hannaford is the largest food retailer in northern New England, with some 120 supermarkets located throughout Maine and New Hampshire, and in parts of Vermont, New York, Massachusetts, North Carolina and South Carolina. Earnings have advanced to record levels in recent periods, aided by contributions from the August 1994 acquisition of Wilson's Supermarkets, a North Carolina-based chain of 20 supermarkets. HRD recently agreed to purchased eight supermarket sites in the Richmond, Va. market.

Operational Review - 11-AUG-95

Net sales in the six months ended July 1, 1995, advanced 17%, year to year, primarily reflecting contributions from the Wilson's Supermarkets acquisition; same-store sales edged up 1.5%. Lower gross margins were more than offset by well controlled SG&A expenses. Following a 3.4% increase in net interest expense, pretax profits rose 27%. After taxes at 40.4%, versus 40.5%, net income was also up about 27%, to $33,589,000 ($0.80 a share, based on 1.4% more shares), from $26,468,000 ($0.64).

Stock Performance - 04-AUG-95

In the past 30 trading days, HRD's shares have declined 7%, compared to a 2% rise in the S&P 500. Average trading volume for the past five days was 21,180 shares, compared with the 40-day moving average of 38,646 shares.

Key Stock Statistics

Dividend Rate/Share	0.42	Shareholders	11,900
Shs. outstg. (M)	42.0	Market cap. (B)	$ 1.1
Avg. daily vol. (M)	0.045	Inst. holdings	37%
Tang. Bk. Value/Share	9.01	Insider holdings	NA
Beta	0.76		

Value of $10,000 invested 5 years ago: $ 17,317

Fiscal Year Ending Dec. 31

	1995	% Change	1994	% Change	1993	% Change
Revenues (Million $)						
1Q	598.8	15%	519.1	6%	490.6	NM
2Q	634.8	18%	538.2	4%	518.0	1%
3Q	—	—	622.5	17%	530.1	NM
4Q	—	—	611.9	19%	516.3	-4%
Yr.	—	—	2,292	12%	2,055	NM
Income (Million $)						
1Q	14.56	32%	11.06	13%	9.77	11%
2Q	19.02	23%	15.41	6%	14.49	15%
3Q	—	—	19.10	19%	16.00	11%
4Q	—	—	16.72	17%	14.35	7%
Yr.	—	—	62.29	14%	54.61	11%
Earnings Per Share ($)						
1Q	0.35	30%	0.27	12%	0.24	9%
2Q	0.45	22%	0.37	6%	0.35	13%
3Q	—	—	0.46	18%	0.39	11%
4Q	—	—	0.40	14%	0.35	6%
Yr.	—	—	1.50	13%	1.33	10%

Next earnings report expected: late October

Hannaford Bros.

Business Summary - 11-AUG-95

Hannaford Bros. Co. was operating 118 supermarkets as of December 31, 1994, and is also engaged in wholesaling to supermarkets. Its drug store operation was phased out in 1994.

Retail outlets at the end of recent years were:

	1994	1993	1992	1991
Supermarkets	118	93	93	88
Drug stores	0	3	6	42
Total	118	96	99	130

The company is the largest food retailer in northern New England. Its supermarkets, which are located throughout Maine and New Hampshire, and in parts of Vermont, New York, Massachusetts, North Carolina and South Carolina, are primarily operated under the names Shop 'n Save, Sun Foods and Wilson's. HRD also sells on a wholesale basis to 18 supermarkets in which it has no ownership interest. In addition, 57 of the company's supermarkets or combination stores contain pharmacies.

The average number of square feet of selling area per store in recent years was:

	1994	1993	1992	1991
Supermarkets	30,100	29,800	28,200	26,700
Drug stores	---	5,000	4,900	6,000

More than 75% of HRD's 97 supermarkets in the Northeast have been expanded or relocated in the past 10 years. Since 1983, 62 combination stores ranging in size from 22,300 sq. ft. to 61,700 sq. ft. have been opened or acquired. The new stores also include four super warehouse stores of 36,000 to 46,600 sq. ft., operated under the name Sun Foods.

Through the August 1994 acquisition of Wilson's Supermarkets, the company added 20 conventional supermarkets in North and South Carolina, and five additional store sites (one new store was opened in September 1994 and two are under construction). The stores range in size from 16,300 to 28,000 sq. ft. of selling area.

In 1994, HRD also opened seven new food stores with selling areas ranging from 28,800 to 47,500 sq. ft., and relocated three existing stores to new, larger facilities. During 1995, the company plans to open 14 stores, three of which will be located in the Northeast, and seven in new market areas of North Carolina and Virginia. Four northeastern stores will be relocated.

Important Developments

Jul. '95—The company agreed to purchase eight supermarket locations from Farm Fresh Inc., a privately held supermarket company, with stores in the Richmond and Tidewater areas of Virginia, for $25 million.

Capitalization

Long Term Debt: $220,883,000 (4/95), incl. $69,220,000 of lease obligs.

Per Share Data ($)

(Year Ended Dec. 31)

	1994	1993	1992	1991	1990	1989
Tangible Bk. Val.	10.88	9.63	8.48	7.42	6.46	5.48
Cash Flow	2.93	2.51	2.56	2.15	1.88	1.61
Earnings	1.50	1.33	1.21	1.08	1.07	0.96
Dividends	0.38	0.34	0.30	0.26	0.22	0.18
Payout Ratio	25%	26%	25%	24%	21%	19%
Prices - High	26⅝	25	28⅝	22¾	20¼	20⅜
- Low	19¾	20	16	16⅜	14⅞	10½
P/E Ratio - High	18	19	24	21	19	21
- Low	13	15	13	15	14	11

Income Statement Analysis (Million $)

	1994	%Chg	1993	%Chg	1992	%Chg	1991
Revs.	2,292	12%	2,055	NM	2,066	3%	2,008
Oper. Inc.	185	16%	160	2%	157	15%	137
Depr.	59.7	22%	48.8	-11%	54.9	28%	42.9
Int. Exp.	25.1	2%	24.5	NM	24.5	10%	22.2
Pretax Inc.	104	13%	92.2	13%	81.7	13%	72.6
Eff. Tax Rate	40%	—	41%	—	40%	—	40%
Net Inc.	62.2	14%	54.4	11%	48.9	13%	43.1

Balance Sheet & Other Fin. Data (Million $)

	1994	1993	1992	1991	1990	1989
Cash	41.0	97.4	100	33.2	Nil	6.7
Curr. Assets	201	256	250	206	170	133
Total Assets	878	795	769	706	629	470
Curr. Liab.	159	137	145	137	115	96.0
LT Debt	223	216	227	215	209	124
Common Eqty.	454	397	346	298	256	214
Total Cap.	700	638	601	540	489	361
Cap. Exp.	84.0	71.0	73.0	81.0	107	81.0
Cash Flow	122	103	104	86.0	74.0	62.8

Ratio Analysis

	1994	1993	1992	1991	1990	1989
Curr. Ratio	1.3	1.9	1.7	1.5	1.5	1.4
% LT Debt of Cap.	31.9	33.8	37.7	39.8	42.7	34.4
% Net Inc.of Revs.	2.7	2.6	2.4	2.1	2.5	2.4
% Ret. on Assets	7.4	6.9	6.8	6.4	7.6	8.5
% Ret. on Equity	14.5	14.6	15.5	15.5	17.7	19.2

Dividend Data (Dividends have been paid since 1948. A dividend reinvestment plan is available. A "poison pill" stock purchase rights plan was adopted in 1988.)

Amt. of Div. $	Date Decl.	Ex-Div. Date	Stock of Record	Payment Date
0.095	Aug. 11	Sep. 02	Sep. 09	Sep. 22 '94
0.095	Oct. 19	Dec. 05	Dec. 09	Dec. 22 '94
0.105	Feb. 07	Mar. 06	Mar. 10	Mar. 23 '95
0.105	May. 24	Jun. 06	Jun. 09	Jun. 22 '95
0.105	Aug. 08	Sep. 06	Sep. 08	Sep. 21 '95

Data as orig. reptd.; bef. results of disc. opers. and/or spec. items. Per share data adj. for stk. divs. as of ex-div. date. E-Estimated. NA-Not Available. NM-Not Meaningful. NR-Not Ranked.

Office—145 Pleasant Hill Rd., Scarborough, ME 04074. **Tel**—(207) 883-2911. **Chrmn**—J. L. Moody Jr. **Pres & CEO**—H. G. Farrington. **SVP & CFO**—N. E. Brackett. **VP & Secy**—A. P. Geoghegan. **Asst Secy & Investor Contact**—Charles H. Crockett. **Dirs**—B. G. Albright, W. A. Andres, R. D. Bolinder, L. Cutler, W. T. End, H. G. Farrington, J. W. Gogan, R. K. Lochridge, C. B. Malone, J. L. Moody Jr., W. J. Salmon, D. F. Sobey, R. L. Strickland. **Transfer Agent & Registrar**—Continental Stock Transfer & Trust Co. **Incorporated** in Maine in 1902. **Empl**-16,500. **S&P Analyst:** Maureen C. Carini

Harley-Davidson

NYSE Symbol **HDI**
In S&P MidCap 400

22-JUL-95 **Industry:** Auto/Truck mfrs.

Summary: The world's leading producer of heavyweight motorcycles and the only U.S. motorcycle maker, Harley-Davidson also produces recreational and commercial vehicles.

S&P Opinion: Buy (★★★★★)

Recent Price • 25
52 Wk Range • 29⅞-22
Yield • 0.6%
12-Mo. P/E • 17.9

Quantitative Evaluations
Outlook (1 Lowest—5 Highest) • **1⁻**
Fair Value • **23**
Risk • **Low**
Earn./Div. Rank • **B+**

Technical Eval. • **Bullish** since 7/95
Rel. Strength Rank (1 Lowest—99 Highest) • **42**
Insider Activity • **Neutral**

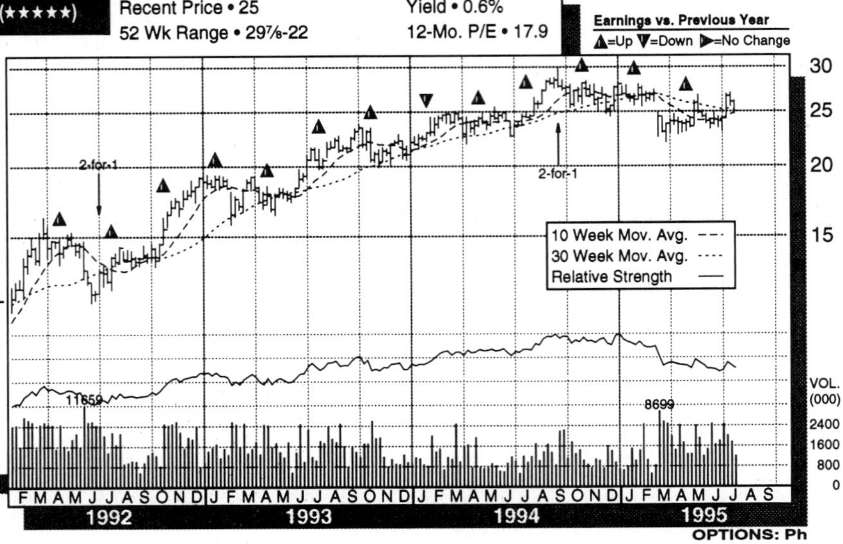

OPTIONS: Ph

Overview - 20-JUL-95

Motorcycle production should rise to 103,000 units in 1995. Production rates were boosted twice in the second quarter, to 430 units a day, from 395. HDI has raised its capacity goal to 115,000 by the end of 1996; long-term plans are being prepared. Although costs to redesign work processes are restricting margins in 1995, lower production costs and improved first-run quality should be seen in subsequent years. Plans call for eventual operation of up to four assembly lines at the York, Pa., plant, with each line dedicated to a single model. Engine production at the Milwaukee plant was split into two lines in 1994. Parts manufacturing is being optimized by breaking bottlenecks. With modest price hikes, rapid growth in parts and accessories, and despite a stalled turnaround at Holiday Rambler, strong earnings growth should continue.

Valuation - 20-JUL-95

Following a stiff decline in the first half of 1995, we upgraded the stock to a strong buy. The company has more than doubled production since 1987, yet dealers continue to report little if any inventory of HDI motorcycles. Clearly, market conditions permit substantial production hikes from current levels. We believe that the absence of any fear of market saturation and the healthy outlook we foresee for profits should give the stock an above-average multiple. Trading at 15X expected 1996 EPS, the shares are undervalued, and should be aggressively purchased for capital gains.

Key Stock Statistics

S&P EPS Est. 1995	1.50	Tang. Bk. Value/Share	5.68
P/E on S&P Est. 1995	16.7	Beta	1.70
S&P EPS Est. 1996	1.75	Shareholders	28,100
Dividend Rate/Share	0.16	Market cap. (B)	$ 1.9
Shs. outstg. (M)	74.7	Inst. holdings	63%
Avg. daily vol. (M)	0.407	Insider holdings	NA

Value of $10,000 invested 5 years ago: $ 51,524

Fiscal Year Ending Dec. 31

	1995	% Change	1994	% Change	1993	% Change
Revenues (Million $)						
1Q	389.7	13%	343.7	27%	269.6	9%
2Q	486.5	21%	401.4	20%	334.4	22%
3Q	—	—	384.0	35%	284.4	5%
4Q	—	—	412.7	25%	329.1	5%
Yr.	—	—	1,542	27%	1,217	10%
Income (Million $)						
1Q	23.64	14%	20.80	38%	15.10	73%
2Q	33.40	-3%	34.60	45%	23.80	34%
3Q	—	—	23.77	45%	16.40	24%
4Q	—	—	25.10	NM	-36.90	NM
Yr.	—	—	104.3	NM	18.44	-66%
Earnings Per Share ($)						
1Q	0.31	13%	0.28	38%	0.20	67%
2Q	0.45	-1%	0.46	44%	0.32	29%
3Q	E0.36	—	0.31	44%	0.22	19%
4Q	E0.38	—	0.33	NM	-0.49	NM
Yr.	E1.50	—	1.37	NM	0.24	-68%

Next earnings report expected: mid October

Harley-Davidson

Business Summary - 21-JUL-95

Harley-Davidson is the leading producer of heavyweight motorcycles and also makes recreational vehicles and specialized commercial vehicles. Segment contributions in 1994 (profits in millions $) were:

	Sales	Profits
Motorcycles & related products	75%	$163.5
Transportation vehicles	25%	6.7

The company, which is only U.S. motorcycle manufacturer, competes exclusively in the superheavyweight (850cc engines or larger) market segment. HDI shipped 95,811 superheavyweight touring and custom motorcycles in 1994, versus 81,696 in 1993, 76,495 in 1992 and 68,626 in 1991. Its share of the U.S. superheavyweight market exceeded 55% in each of 1994, 1993, 1992 and 1991. The company sells 20 models, with retail prices ranging from $5,000 to $17,500, through 600 independent U.S. dealers, 75% of whose new motorcycle sales are exclusively Harley Davidsons. Motorcycles are based on five chassis designs and are powered by one of three air-cooled, twin cylinder, "V" configuration engines with displacements of 883cc, 1200cc and 1340cc. The use of advanced manufacturing techniques, including quality circles, just-in-time inventory and statistical process control, has significantly improved productivity and quality. The company exports 30% of its motorcycles. Related products, including parts and merchandising of the Harley Davidson name and trademarks, rose 29%, to over $250 million in 1994 (including $100 million of Motorclothes sales), from $199 million in 1993.

Holiday Rambler (HR) produces recreational and specialized commercial vehicles. HR is implementing a number of manufacturing and marketing strategies designed to turn around its operations, which have been only marginally profitable in recent years. After 1993's $59.5 million operating loss, which reflected a $57 million charge to write down goodwill associated with HR's acquisition in the mid-1980s, a $6.7 million profit was reported for 1994, aided by a small rise in recreational vehicle market share.

Important Developments

Jul. '95—HDI said motorcycle production was raised to 430 units a day in the 1995 second quarter, and would continue at that rate for the third and fourth quarters. Production had been boosted to 420 units a at the start of the second quarter, from the level of 395 units a day established in October 1994.

Capitalization

Total Debt: $ 9,410,000 (12/94).

Per Share Data ($) (Year Ended Dec. 31)

	1994	1993	1992	1991	1990	1989
Tangible Bk. Val.	5.58	4.24	3.68	2.51	1.91	1.30
Cash Flow	1.85	0.68	1.17	0.84	0.85	0.68
Earnings	1.37	0.24	0.76	0.52	0.54	0.47
Dividends	0.24	0.06	Nil	Nil	Nil	Nil
Payout Ratio	18%	24%	Nil	Nil	Nil	Nil
Prices - High	29⅞	23¾	19⅜	15¼	8⅝	5⅜
- Low	21⅝	15¾	10⅞	4½	3⅜	3⅛
P/E Ratio - High	22	97	26	29	16	11
- Low	16	64	14	9	6	6

Income Statement Analysis (Million $)

	1994	%Chg	1993	%Chg	1992	%Chg	1991
Revs.	1,542	27%	1,217	10%	1,105	18%	940
Oper. Inc.	197	23%	160	26%	127	40%	91.0
Depr.	36.9	12%	33.0	12%	29.4	30%	22.6
Int. Exp.	2.4	20%	2.0	-66%	5.9	-37%	9.4
Pretax Inc.	162	144%	66.5	-25%	88.8	53%	58.1
Eff. Tax Rate	36%	—	72%	—	39%	—	36%
Net Inc.	104	NM	18.4	-66%	54.2	46%	37.0

Balance Sheet & Other Fin. Data (Million $)

	1994	1993	1992	1991	1990	1989
Cash	59.3	77.7	44.1	30.9	14.0	39.1
Total Assets	406	583	522	474	407	379
LT Debt	15.7	Nil	2.0	47.0	48.0	75.0
Total Debt	Nil	21.4	19.3	88.0	72.2	102
Common Eqty.	433	325	335	238	199	156
Cap. Exp.	94.7	55.2	47.2	48.2	38.5	24.4
Cash Flow	141	51.4	83.6	59.6	60.7	46.8

Ratio Analysis

	1994	1993	1992	1991	1990	1989
% Ret. on Assets	739.0	3.3	10.6	8.4	9.6	8.3
% Ret. on Equity	27.5	5.6	18.4	16.9	21.4	23.4
% LT Debt of Cap.	Nil	Nil	0.7	16.1	19.2	31.5

Dividend Data (Dividends were initiated in 1993. A dividend reinvestment plan is available. A new poison pill stock purchase rights plan was adopted in 1990.)

Amt. of Div. $	Date Decl.	Ex-Div. Date	Stock of Record	Payment Date
0.080	Aug. 17	Aug. 23	Aug. 29	Sep. 12 '94
2-for-1	Aug. 17	Sep. 13	Aug. 29	Sep. 12 '94
0.040	Nov. 17	Nov. 21	Nov. 28	Dec. 12 '94
0.040	Feb. 02	Feb. 13	Feb. 17	Mar. 05 '95
0.040	May. 08	May. 18	May. 24	Jun. 05 '95

Data as orig. reptd.; bef. results of disc. opers. and/or spec. items. Per share data adj. for stk. divs. as of ex-div. date. E-Estimate. NA-Not Available. NM-Not Meaningful. NR-Not Ranked.

Office—3700 West Juneau Ave., Milwaukee, WI 53208. **Tel**—(414) 342-4680. **Chrmn**—V. L. Beals Jr. **Pres & CEO**—R. F. Teerlink. **VP, CFO & Investor Contact**—James L. Ziemer. **VP-Secy**—T. K. Hoelter. **Dirs**—B. K. Allen, W. F. Andrews, V. L. Beals, Jr., R. Hermon-Taylor, D. A. James, R. G. LeFauve, J. A. Norling, W. B. Potter, R. F. Teerlink. **Transfer Agent & Registrar**—Firstar Trust Co., Milwaukee. **Incorporated** in Delaware in 1981; reincorporated in Wisconsin in 1991. **Empl-** 6,700. **S&P Analyst:** Joshua M. Harari, CFA

STANDARD & POOR'S
STOCK REPORTS

Harsco Corp.

NYSE Symbol **HSC**
In S&P MidCap 400

31-JUL-95

Industry: Conglomerate/diversified

Summary: Harsco provides a variety of products and services primarily for industrial, commercial and construction applications.

S&P Opinion: Accumulate (★★★★)

Recent Price • 55¼ | Yield • 2.7%
52 Wk Range • 55⅝-38⅜ | 12-Mo. P/E • 13.8

Quantitative Evaluations

Outlook (1 Lowest—5 Highest)
• 2

Fair Value
• 51⅜

Risk
• Low

Earn./Div. Rank
• B+

Technical Eval.
• **Bearish** since 6/95

Rel. Strength Rank (1 Lowest—99 Highest)
• 67

Insider Activity
• Neutral

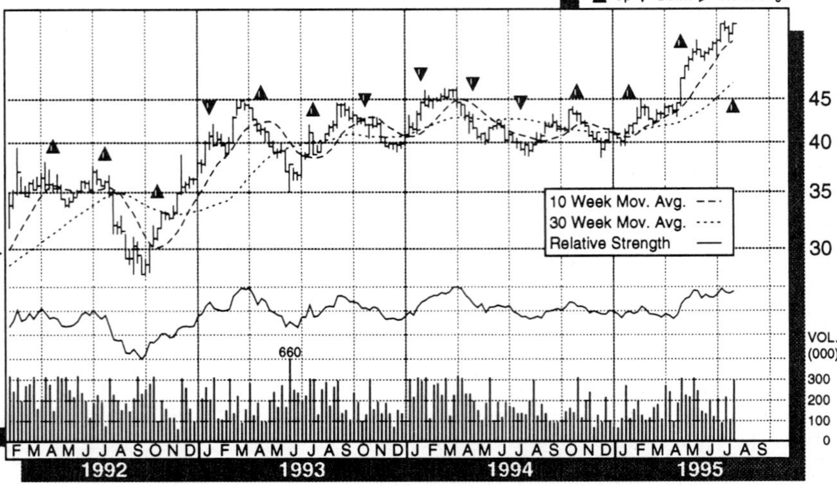

Overview - 28-JUL-95

We anticipate an 8.0% rise in sales for 1995, reflecting gains at all three segments. Metal reclamation should post a solid increase, on higher global steel production and commencement of work at a new mill. Continued economic growth will lift sales in the infrastructure and construction and process industry units. Margins should widen on 1994's cost cutting in metals reclamation, the absence of startup costs at Heckett, and discontinuation of the bus operations. The gain in operating profit, along with lower interest expense, should outweigh a decline in equity income and lead to a rise in earnings in 1995 from 1994's $3.03 from continuing operations. Acquisitions and an expected upturn in equity income in 1996 and 1997 will boost long-term sales and earnings growth.

Valuation - 31-JUL-95

Although the shares are up some 24% since we raised our opinion to accumulate, we are maintaining our positive view on the shares. Relative to other multi-industry companies we follow, HSC is still attractively priced at some 14X estimated 1995 earnings, versus multiples ranging from 15X to 18X for other diversified companies. HSC has not gained the all the recognition it deserves for streamlining MultiServ and joint venturing its defense business. The shares should trend higher as investors begin to examine HSC more carefully and conclude that HSC deserves a higher multiple. Also, we think the company could achieve a positive upside earnings surprise in 1995.

Key Stock Statistics

S&P EPS Est. 1995	3.90	Tang. Bk. Value/Share	15.23
P/E on S&P Est. 1995	14.2	Beta	0.67
S&P EPS Est. 1996	4.30	Shareholders	7,700
Dividend Rate/Share	1.48	Market cap. (B)	$ 1.4
Shs. outstg. (M)	25.2	Inst. holdings	56%
Avg. daily vol. (M)	0.037	Insider holdings	NA

Value of $10,000 invested 5 years ago: $ 26,632

Fiscal Year Ending Dec. 31

	1995	% Change	1994	% Change	1993	% Change
Revenues (Million $)						
1Q	375.9	18%	318.7	-8%	345.8	-15%
2Q	386.7	14%	338.1	-5%	354.6	-8%
3Q	—	—	348.1	11%	314.9	-24%
4Q	—	—	352.9	-13%	407.0	-2%
Yr.	—	—	1,357	-5%	1,422	-12%
Income (Million $)						
1Q	25.46	37%	18.63	-23%	24.16	16%
2Q	24.56	40%	17.55	-21%	22.28	19%
3Q	—	—	22.34	22%	18.26	-32%
4Q	—	—	28.04	74%	16.12	-36%
Yr.	—	—	86.55	7%	80.82	-12%
Earnings Per Share ($)						
1Q	1.01	36%	0.74	-22%	0.95	20%
2Q	0.97	39%	0.70	-21%	0.89	24%
3Q	E0.97	—	0.89	20%	0.74	-28%
4Q	E0.95	—	1.12	72%	0.65	-34%
Yr.	E3.90	—	3.45	7%	3.23	-8%

Next earnings report expected: late October

Harsco Corp.

Business Summary - 28-JUL-95

Harsco provides a variety of products and services for industrial, commercial and construction markets. Segment contributions in 1994 were:

	Sales	Profits
Metal & mill services	38%	45%
Infrastructure/construction	29%	12%
Process industry products	33%	43%

The Heckett MultiServ division provides specialized services to steel producers and other nonferrous metallurgical industries worldwide. Services include metal reclamation, scrap handling, cleaning of slag pits, handling of raw material and molten slag, full and grading of specified areas and rental of various types of plant equipment.

Infrastructure/Construction includes the production of railway maintenance equipment, 8% of sales; scaffolding, shoring and concrete forming equipment, 8%; industrial grating products, 7%; wheeled vehicles, 3% (discontinued in 1995); roofing granules, slag abrasives and miscellaneous, 3%.

Process industry products makes gas containment and control products, which include propane tanks, cryogenic equipment, high pressure cyclinders and composite products, while gas control products include valves and regulators,15% of sales; pipe fittings,7%; process equipment,7%, structural composites, metal fabrication and wear products, 4%.

Construction-related operations accounted for 11% of total sales in 1994, versus 9% in 1993.

In January 1994, the company formed a joint venture, United Defense L.P., combining its BMY Combat Systems division with FMC Corp.'s defense systems unit. Harsco owns 40% of the venture and FMC 60%. United Defense L.P. and other joint ventures provided equity income of $64 million in 1994. As a result of the formation of the joint venture, sales to U.S. government agencies declined to 1% of the total in 1994 versus 21%, 35% and 44% of the total in 1993, 1992 and 1991, respectively.

Important Developments

Jun. '95— HSC began providing steel mill services at Gallatin Steel's new thin-cast facility in Ghent, Kentucky. HSC's contract with Gallatin Steel was expected to generate revenues of some $50 million over the next ten years.

May '95—HSC said that it received two contracts to provide mill and scrap management services at Ispco Steel's Montpelier, Iowa flat rolled steel plant. Work was expected to begin in 1996's second quarter. HSC said that the pacts were expected to generate $100 million in revenues over the next ten years.

Capitalization

Long Term Debt: $227,605,000 (6/95).

Per Share Data ($) (Year Ended Dec. 31)

	1994	1993	1992	1991	1990	1989
Tangible Bk. Val.	14.56	12.05	18.82	17.55	16.03	14.43
Cash Flow	7.04	6.01	5.72	5.11	4.92	2.57
Earnings	3.45	3.23	3.52	2.91	2.77	0.43
Dividends	1.40	1.40	1.32	1.20	1.20	1.20
Payout Ratio	41%	43%	38%	41%	43%	277%
Prices - High	46⅞	45	39½	30⅜	28¾	31⅛
- Low	38⅜	35	27¾	22¾	17¾	22½
P/E Ratio - High	13	14	11	10	10	72
- Low	11	11	8	8	6	52

Income Statement Analysis (Million $)

	1994	%Chg	1993	%Chg	1992	%Chg	1991
Revs.	1,358	-5%	1,422	-12%	1,625	-16%	1,943
Oper. Inc.	182	-9%	199	-3%	205	13%	181
Depr.	90.2	30%	69.6	22%	57.1	-1%	57.7
Int. Exp.	34.4	72%	20.0	4%	19.2	2%	18.9
Pretax Inc.	149	9%	137	-3%	141	17%	120
Eff. Tax Rate	40%	—	41%	—	35%	—	36%
Net Inc.	86.6	7%	80.8	-12%	91.5	20%	76.5

Balance Sheet & Other Fin. Data (Million $)

	1994	1993	1992	1991	1990	1989
Cash	44.0	59.0	50.0	120	10.0	11.0
Curr. Assets	537	600	598	662	593	599
Total Assets	1,315	1,428	991	1,060	991	978
Curr. Liab.	282	417	281	377	367	387
LT Debt	340	365	120	120	123	127
Common Eqty.	581	523	495	480	437	394
Total Cap.	951	921	632	624	582	538
Cap. Exp.	91.0	83.4	60.3	56.8	83.9	67.6
Cash Flow	177	150	149	134	130	68.0

Ratio Analysis

	1994	1993	1992	1991	1990	1989
Curr. Ratio	1.9	1.4	2.1	1.8	1.6	1.5
% LT Debt of Cap.	35.8	39.6	19.0	19.3	21.1	23.7
% Net Inc.of Revs.	6.4	5.7	5.6	3.9	4.1	0.8
% Ret. on Assets	6.3	6.7	9.1	7.5	7.4	1.2
% Ret. on Equity	15.6	16.0	19.1	16.7	17.4	2.8

Dividend Data (Dividends have been paid since 1939. A dividend reinvestment plan is available. A "poison pill" stock purchase right was issued in 1987.)

Amt. of Div. $	Date Decl.	Ex-Div. Date	Stock of Record	Payment Date
0.350	Sep. 27	Oct. 07	Oct. 14	Nov. 15 '94
0.370	Nov. 15	Jan. 09	Jan. 13	Feb. 15 '95
0.370	Mar. 16	Apr. 07	Apr. 14	May. 15 '95
0.370	Jun. 27	Jul. 12	Jul. 14	Aug. 15 '95

Data as orig. reptd.; bef. results of disc. opers. and/or spec. items. Per share data adj. for stk. divs. as of ex-div. date. E-Estimated. NA-Not Available. NM-Not Meaningful. NR-Not Ranked.

Office—350 Poplar Church Rd., Camp Hill, PA 17011-8888. **Tel**—(717) 763-7064. **Chrmn, Pres & CEO**—D. C. Hathaway. **SVP & CFO**—L. A. Campanaro. **SVP & Secy**—P. C. Coppock. **VP & Treas**—B. M. Sullivan. **Investor Contact**—Gene Truett. **Dirs**—J. J. Burdge, D. C. Hathaway, R. L. Kirk, J. E. Marley, R. F. Nation, N. H. Prater, J. I. Scheiner, R. C. Smith, A. J. Sordoni III, R. C. Wilburn. **Transfer Agent & Registrar**—Mellon Securities Trust, Ridgefield Park, NJ. **Incorporated** in Pennsylvania in 1899; reincorporated in Delaware in 1956. **Empl**-13,000. **S&P Analyst:** Leo Larkin

STANDARD & POOR'S
STOCK REPORTS

Hartford Steam Boiler

NYSE Symbol **HSB**
In S&P MidCap 400

05-OCT-95 **Industry:** Insurance

Summary: This company is the largest underwriter of boiler and machinery insurance in North America, and also provides other specialized engineering and consulting services.

S&P Opinion: Hold (★★★)	Recent Price • 48⅜	Yield • 4.7%
	52 Wk Range • 49⅜-35⅞	12-Mo. P/E • 17.9

Quantitative Evaluations

Outlook
(1 Lowest—5 Highest)
• **3+**

Fair Value
• **46⅞**

Risk
• **Low**

Earn./Div. Rank
• **B+**

Technical Eval.
• **Bearish** since 9/95

Rel. Strength Rank
(1 Lowest—99 Highest)
• **73**

Insider Activity
• **NA**

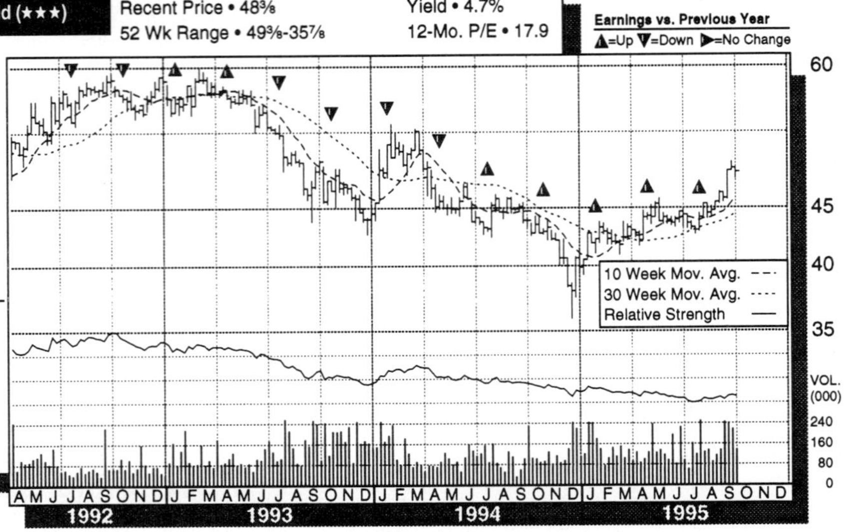

Overview - 05-OCT-95

Earnings growth in 1995 will be aided by the acquisition of General Re's 50% interest in the Engineering Insurance Group joint venture, and by improved underwriting trends that began to emerge in mid-1994. The absence of $2.9 million of pretax charges for Proposition 103 rebates will also aid comparisons in 1995. Further profit gains are predicated on HSB's ability to garner adequate price increases in its existing book of business. Tighter underwriting standards may drive away some business, but HSB's dominant market position within this highly focused niche should afford it a greater degree of pricing control. Also, slower growth in the U.S. will be offset to a degree by an increased international presence. Cost cuts and a shift to a higher-margin business mix will aid engineering profits.

Valuation - 05-OCT-95

After falling during most of 1994 amid the negative effects of higher interest rates and concerns over its eroding premium base as it restructures its operations, HSB shares have regained most of their lost ground. Because of the highly specialized nature of its business, HSB shares tend to trade at a higher P/E multiple than those of a standard lines insurer. Nevertheless, we believe the stock is fairly valued, near term, at about 16 times our 1995 operating earnings estimate of $3.00 a share (before realized investment gains or losses). But, with a yield approaching 5%, the shares are worth holding. A pullback of 10%-15% from current levels would likely lead us to review our opinion.

Key Stock Statistics

S&P EPS Est. 1995	3.00	Tang. Bk. Value/Share	15.86
P/E on S&P Est. 1995	16.1	Beta	0.96
S&P EPS Est. 1996	3.25	Shareholders	5,800
Dividend Rate/Share	2.28	Market cap. (B)	$0.983
Shs. outstg. (M)	20.4	Inst. holdings	52%
Avg. daily vol. (M)	0.042	Insider holdings	NA

Value of $10,000 invested 5 years ago: $ 11,538

Fiscal Year Ending Dec. 31

	1995	% Change	1994	% Change	1993	% Change
Revenues (Million $)						
1Q	161.6	6%	152.7	-9%	168.6	—
2Q	169.9	13%	150.0	-10%	165.9	—
3Q	—	—	151.3	-5%	159.4	—
4Q	—	—	152.7	-2%	155.5	-11%
Yr.	—	—	603.6	-5%	636.1	-7%
Income (Million $)						
1Q	14.00	18%	11.90	-33%	17.80	NM
2Q	15.70	10%	14.30	160%	5.50	-71%
3Q	—	—	12.30	NM	-22.60	NM
4Q	—	—	13.40	8%	12.40	-28%
Yr.	—	—	51.90	NM	13.10	-77%
Earnings Per Share ($)						
1Q	0.69	19%	0.58	-33%	0.86	1%
2Q	0.77	10%	0.70	169%	0.26	-71%
3Q	—	—	0.60	NM	-1.09	NM
4Q	—	—	0.66	10%	0.60	-28%
Yr.	E3.00	18%	2.54	NM	0.63	-77%

Next earnings report expected: late October

Hartford Steam Boiler

05-OCT-95

Business Summary - 05-OCT-95

The Hartford Steam Boiler Inspection and Insurance Co. underwrites boiler and machinery insurance and provides engineering services. Contributions to revenues in recent years were as follows:

	1994	1993
Premiums earned	56%	55%
Engineering services	38%	36%
Investment income/gains	6%	9%

Boiler and machinery insurance provides for the indemnification of the policyholder for financial loss resulting from destruction or damage to an insured boiler, pressure vessel or other machine caused by an accident. This financial loss can include the cost to repair or replace the damaged equipment, the cost of product spoilage, and lost profits arising from business interruption stemming from an accident. HSB provides a high level of loss prevention services with its insurance products. This tends to increase underwriting and inspection expenses, while reducing loss and loss adjustment expenses.

Though boiler and machinery coverage accounts for most of its business, HSB has expanded its product line to include, among other things, coverage for air conditioning and computer software systems. HSB also provides coverage to the commercial clients of over 100 multi-line insurers.

Radian Corp., which provides an array of environmental engineering services, accounts for about 75% of Engineering Services revenues. Other subsidiaries provide specialized consulting and inspection services related to the design and applications of boilers, pressure vessels and other types of equipment.

Important Developments

Jul. '95—The 15% growth in HSB's premiums during 1995's first half mainly reflected the December 1994 acquisition of General Reinsurance Corp.'s 50% interest in Engineering Insurance Group, a U.K. joint venture, for $20 million in preferred stock.

Mar. '95—HSB's improved profitability in 1994 reflected the impact of a 1993 restructuring. In the third quarter of 1993, HSB took pretax charges of $20 million to cover staff cutbacks and office consolidations, and a $19 million reserve boost to cover the adverse development of prior years' loss reserves. HSB said the fractional decline in insurance premiums was an anticipated result of its efforts at tightening underwriting standards. Partly offsetting these gains was a $2.9 million pretax third quarter 1994 charge to cover rebates under California's Proposition 103.

Capitalization

Long Term Debt: $53,400,000 (6/95), incl. $27.8 million of capital lease obligations.

Per Share Data ($) (Year Ended Dec. 31)

	1994	1993	1992	1991	1990	1989
Tangible Bk. Val.	14.67	15.84	18.08	19.47	17.05	16.29
Oper. Earnings	2.26	-0.19	1.73	NA	NA	NA
Earnings	2.54	0.63	2.71	3.53	3.80	3.78
Dividends	2.14	2.12	2.03	1.85	1.70	1.50
Payout Ratio	84%	336%	75%	52%	45%	40%
Prices - High	53$\frac{3}{8}$	59$\frac{7}{8}$	59$\frac{1}{4}$	63$\frac{3}{4}$	62$\frac{1}{8}$	59$\frac{1}{4}$
- Low	35$\frac{7}{8}$	42$\frac{5}{8}$	45$\frac{1}{8}$	46$\frac{1}{8}$	43$\frac{1}{2}$	34$\frac{3}{4}$
P/E Ratio - High	21	95	22	18	16	16
- Low	14	68	17	13	11	9

Income Statement Analysis (Million $)

	1994	%Chg	1993	%Chg	1992	%Chg	1991
Premium Income	337	-3%	349	NM	350	8%	323
Net Invest. Inc.	26.2	-11%	29.3	-20%	36.5	-12%	41.4
Oth. Revs.	241	-7%	258	-13%	296	11%	266
Total Revs.	604	-5%	636	-7%	682	8%	630
Pretax Inc.	74.0	NM	17.0	-77%	73.0	-28%	101
Net Oper. Inc.	46.2	NM	-3.9	—	NA	—	NA
Net Inc.	51.9	NM	13.1	-77%	56.3	-24%	73.9

Balance Sheet & Other Fin. Data (Million $)

	1994	1993	1992	1991	1990	1989
Cash & Equiv.	12.1	7.3	8.7	6.0	11.6	5.6
Premiums Due	83.1	68.5	64.8	61.3	61.1	55.2
Inv Assets Bonds	273	209	198	197	244	250
Inv. Assets Stock	205	290	310	333	251	302
Inv. Assets Loans	Nil	Nil	Nil	Nil	Nil	Nil
Inv. Assets Total	490	506	508	530	495	552
Deferred Policy Cost	35.5	30.0	30.6	28.4	27.8	26.4
Total Assets	906	878	888	889	827	795
Debt	28.4	28.4	61.9	68.4	73.9	39.5
Common Eqty.	300	325	374	409	355	335

Ratio Analysis

	1994	1993	1992	1991	1990	1989
Prop&Cas Loss	42.5	57.1	50.7	43.8	37.2	33.3
Prop&Cas Expense	50.5	50.5	49.9	50.1	50.8	50.6
Prop&Cas Comb.	93.0	107.6	100.6	93.9	88.0	83.9
% Ret. on Revs.	8.6	2.1	8.3	11.7	14.0	16.0
% Return on Equity	16.9	3.7	14.5	19.3	22.8	25.8

Dividend Data —Dividends have been paid since 1873. A dividend reinvestment plan is available. A "poison pill" stock purchase rights plan was adopted in 1988.

Amt. of Div. $	Date Decl.	Ex-Div. Date	Stock of Record	Payment Date
0.550	Sep. 26	Oct. 03	Oct. 10	Oct. 27 '94
0.550	Nov. 28	Jan. 04	Jan. 10	Jan. 26 '95
0.550	Mar. 27	Apr. 04	Apr. 10	Apr. 27 '95
0.550	Jun. 26	Jul. 06	Jul. 10	Jul. 27 '95
0.570	Jul. 24	Oct. 05	Oct. 10	Oct. 26 '95

Data as orig. reptd.; bef. results of disc. opers. and/or spec. items. Per share data adj. for stk. divs. as of ex-div. date. E-Estimated. NA-Not Available. NM-Not Meaningful. NR-Not Ranked.

Office—One State St., Hartford, CT 06102. **Tel**—(203) 722-1866. **Pres & CEO**—G. W. Kreh. **SVP-Secy**—R. K. Price. **SVP-Treas & CFO**—S. A. Basch. **VP-Investor Contact**—James C. Rowan Jr. (203) 722-5180. **Dirs**—J. B. Alvord, C. G. Campbell, D. M. Carlton, R. G. Dooley, W. B. Ellis, E. J. Ferland, G. W. Kreh, J. A. Powers, L. D. Rice, P. A. Vatter, J. M. Washburn Jr., W. Wilde. **Transfer Agent & Registrar**—First National Bank of Boston. **Incorporated** in Connecticut in 1866. **Empl**-4,036. **S&P Analyst:** Catherine A. Seifert

STANDARD & POOR'S

Hawaiian Electric Industries

STOCK REPORTS

NYSE Symbol **HE**
In S&P MidCap 400

10-AUG-95 **Industry:** Utilities-Electric

Summary: This holding company owns Hawaiian Electric Co., a public utility that provides electric service to 95% of Hawaii's population, and various non-utility subsidiaries.

Quantitative Evaluations

Outlook (1 Lowest—5 Highest)
• **2+**

Fair Value
• **32⅞**

Risk
• **Low**

Earn./Div. Rank
• **A-**

Technical Eval.
• **Bullish** since 12/92

Rel. Strength Rank (1 Lowest—99 Highest)
• **22**

Insider Activity
• **NA**

Recent Price • 35⅝
52 Wk Range • 36¾-29⅞

Yield • 6.8%
12-Mo. P/E • 12.6

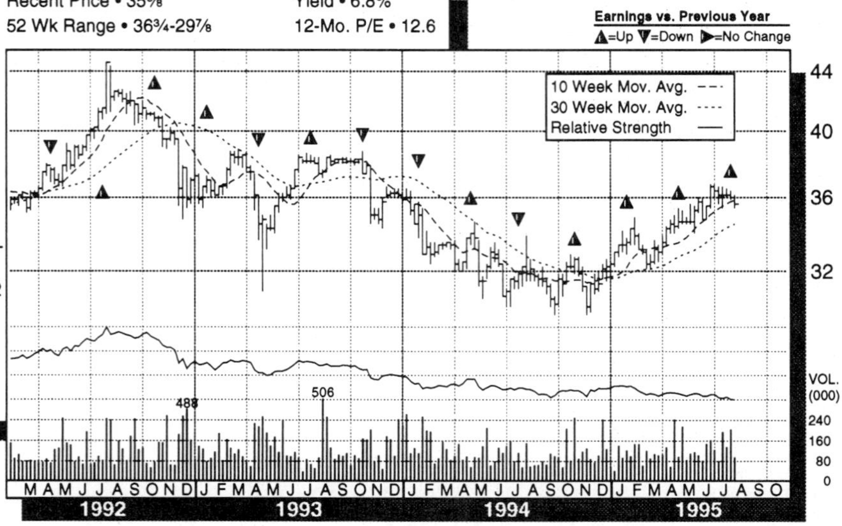

Business Profile - 09-AUG-95

HE is one of the more diversified electric utilty holding companies, based on the contribution of non-utility operations to net income. The company's utility subsidiaries provide electric service for 95% of the Hawaiian population. HE also owns one of the largest S&Ls on the islands. In response to limited growth prospects for utilites, the company plans to form a new subsidiary to pursue independent power projects in Asia.

Operational Review - 09-AUG-95

Revenues in the first half of 1995 climbed 14%, year to year, reflecting increases at the electric utility and savings bank units. Operating earnings were up 27% at electric utilities, but were down slightly at the savings bank on a narrower interest rate spread. HE's other operations reported mixed results, as advances at maritime freight transportation and passive investment subsidiaries were offset by a weakening real estate market. After moderately improved margins, net income rose 25%.

Stock Performance - 04-AUG-95

In the past 30 trading days, HE's shares have declined 3%, compared to a 2% rise in the S&P 500. Average trading volume for the past five days was 18,340 shares, compared with the 40-day moving average of 28,818 shares.

Key Stock Statistics

Dividend Rate/Share	2.36	Shareholders	40,700
Shs. outstg. (M)	29.0	Market cap. (B)	$ 1.0
Avg. daily vol. (M)	0.028	Inst. holdings	33%
Tang. Bk. Value/Share	28.57	Insider holdings	NA
Beta	0.63		

Value of $10,000 invested 5 years ago: $ 12,727

Fiscal Year Ending Dec. 31

	1995	% Change	1994	% Change	1993	% Change
Revenues (Million $)						
1Q	306.3	16%	265.0	-5%	279.0	18%
2Q	319.9	12%	285.0	1%	282.0	17%
3Q	--	—	319.0	7%	299.0	10%
4Q	--	—	319.8	13%	282.0	NM
Yr.	--	—	1,189	4%	1,142	11%
Income (Million $)						
1Q	17.85	51%	11.79	27%	9.29	-30%
2Q	18.88	7%	17.63	-7%	18.98	22%
3Q	—	—	22.69	41%	16.09	-3%
4Q	—	—	20.92	21%	17.33	5%
Yr.	—	—	73.03	18%	61.68	NM
Earnings Per Share ($)						
1Q	0.62	48%	0.42	11%	0.38	-31%
2Q	0.65	3%	0.63	-17%	0.76	19%
3Q	—	—	0.80	31%	0.61	-10%
4Q	—	—	0.73	16%	0.63	-6%
Yr.	—	—	2.60	9%	2.38	-6%

Next earnings report expected: mid October

Hawaiian Electric Industries

Business Summary - 09-AUG-95

Hawaiian Electric Industries is the holding company for Hawaiian Electric, Maui Electric and Hawaii Electric Light companies, which provide electric service on the islands of Oahu, Hawaii, Maui, Lanai and Molokai. About 95% of the state's population is supplied. Electric sales accounted for 77% of revenues and 78% of operating income in 1994. About 10% of electric revenues in each of 1994, 1993 and 1992 came from federal government agencies. Contributions to electric revenues by customer class in recent years were:

	1994	1993	1992	1991
Residential	33%	33%	32%	32%
Commercial	31%	30%	31%	30%
Industrial	35%	36%	36%	37%
Other	1%	1%	1%	1%

Fuel used for generation is primarily oil. Peak load in 1994 was 1,527 mw and system capability was 2,102 mw, for a capacity margin of 27%. To meet increases in demand, HE has entered into long-term power purchase agreements with independent suppliers for 465 mw of firm capacity.

The company has estimated net electric utility capital spending for 1995-9 at $747 million, including $170 million for 1995.

In 1993 and 1994, HE's electric utility subsidiaries successfully filed various rate increase requests with the Hawaii Public Utilities Commission. In January 1995, Hawaiian Electric received an interim increase of $13.2 million for a 1995 test year rate case.

Nonutility subsidiaries contributed 22% of operating income in 1994. American Savings Bank F.S.B., with 46 branch offices at year-end 1994, and total assets of over $3.1 billion. Hawaiian Tug & Barge Corp. and Young Brothers Ltd. are the principal movers of maritime cargo within the state, operating a fleet of 11 tugs and 10 barges. Consolidated assets totaled $55 million at year-end 1994. Malama Pacific Corp. is developing five residential projects involving nearly 600 homes and lots on Oahu, Maui and Hawaii. Consolidated assets at year-end 1994 totaled $52 million.

In response to reduced growth prospects for utilities, HE is forming a new subsidiary to pursue independent power projects in Asia.

Important Developments

Jul. '95—HE said its savings bank subsidiary is performing "about as well as can be expected" in light of interest rate pressures and Hawaii's current slow economy. The bank's interest rate spread dropped to 2.98% in 1995's first half from 3.79% in the 1994 period.

Capitalization

Long Term Debt: $742,677,000 (3/95).
Subsidiary Red. Preferred Stock: $43,440,000.
Subsidiary Preferred Stock: $48,293,000.

Per Share Data ($) (Year Ended Dec. 31)

	1994	1993	1992	1991	1990	1989
Tangible Bk. Val.	28.38	21.39	20.06	21.89	20.33	19.93
Earnings	2.60	2.38	2.54	2.40	2.02	3.06
Dividends	2.33	2.29	2.25	2.21	2.17	2.07
Payout Ratio	90%	96%	90%	96%	109%	69%
Prices - High	36½	38⅞	44⅝	37⅞	40	40¼
- Low	29⅞	31	34¾	29⅜	27¼	29⅜
P/E Ratio - High	14	16	18	16	20	13
- Low	11	13	14	12	13	10

Income Statement Analysis (Million $)

	1994	%Chg	1993	%Chg	1992	%Chg	1991
Revs.	1,189	4%	1,142	11%	1,031	-5%	1,084
Depr.	72.3	12%	64.3	4%	61.9	6%	58.3
Maint.	46.4	5%	44.3	NM	44.7	13%	39.5
Fxd. Chgs. Cov.	3.1	-4%	3.2	7%	3.0	13%	2.7
Constr. Credits	13.1	21%	10.8	21%	8.9	—	NA
Eff. Tax Rate	42%	—	41%	—	32%	—	35%
Net Inc.	73.0	18%	61.7	NM	61.7	13%	54.8

Balance Sheet & Other Fin. Data (Million $)

	1994	1993	1992	1991	1990	1989
Gross Prop.	2,425	2,221	2,003	1,858	1,707	NA
Cap. Exp.	201	214	191	158	137	NA
Net Prop.	1,678	1,542	1,388	1,285	1,190	NA
Capitalization:						
LT Debt	1,335	988	777	799	683	NA
% LT Debt	63	57	55	54	53	NA
Pfd.	93.1	95.0	85.2	87.0	88.5	NA
% Pfd.	4.40	5.50	6.00	5.90	6.90	NA
Common	682	643	548	581	511	NA
% Common	32	37	39	40	40	NA
Total Cap.	2,329	1,938	1,609	1,683	1,493	1,311

Ratio Analysis

	1994	1993	1992	1991	1990	1989
Oper. Ratio	89.8	90.3	89.7	90.7	91.4	NA
% Earn. on Net Prop.	10.8	10.8	10.3	10.6	10.1	NA
% Ret. on Revs.	6.1	5.4	6.0	5.1	4.3	NA
% Ret. On Invest.Cap	8.2	8.9	8.3	8.5	7.3	NA
% Return On Com.Eqty	11.0	10.4	10.9	10.0	8.7	NA

Dividend Data (Dividends, paid since 1901, have increased each year for 30 consecutive years. A dividend reinvestment plan is available.)

Amt. of Div. $	Date Decl.	Ex-Div. Date	Stock of Record	Payment Date
0.590	Oct. 18	Nov. 04	Nov. 10	Dec. 12 '94
0.590	Jan. 17	Feb. 09	Feb. 15	Mar. 10 '95
0.590	Apr. 26	May. 04	May. 10	Jun. 13 '95
0.590	Jul. 19	Aug. 08	Aug. 10	Sep. 11 '95

Data as orig. reptd.; bef. results of disc opers. and/or spec. items. Per share data adj. for stk. divs. as of ex-div. date. E-Estimated. NA-Not Available. NM-Not Meaningful. NR-Not Ranked.

Office—900 Richards St., Honolulu, HI 96813. **Tel**—(808) 543-5662. **Pres & CEO**—R. F. Clarke. **VP-Fin & CFO**—R. F. Mougeot. **Treas & Investor Contact**—Constance H. Lau (808-543-7384). **Secy**—Betty Ann M. Splinter. **Dirs**—E. L. Carter, R. F. Clarke, J. D. Field, R. Henderson, B. F. Kaito, V. H. Li, B. D. Mills, A. M. Myers, R. M. Ono, D. J. Plotts, J. K. Scott, O. K. Stender, K. H. Taketa, J. N. Watanabe, H. D. Williamson. **Transfer Agents**—Continental Stock Transfer & Trust Co., NYC; Co.'s office. **Incorporated** in Hawaii in 1891; reincorporated in Hawaii in 1983. **Empl**-3,386. **S&P Analyst:** Michael C. Barr

STANDARD & POOR'S

STOCK REPORTS

Health Care & Retirement

NYSE Symbol **HCR**
In S&P MidCap 400

03-OCT-95

Industry: Health Care Centers

Summary: This leading provider of long term healthcare services operates 127 care centers in 16 states with some 16,400 beds, as well as 16 outpatient rehabilitation therapy facilities.

S&P Opinion: Hold (★★★)

Recent Price • 32⅛
52 Wk Range • 34¼-25
Yield • Nil
12-Mo. P/E • 22.9

Quantitative Evaluations

Outlook (1 Lowest—5 Highest)
• **NA**

Fair Value
• **NA**

Risk
• **Average**

Earn./Div. Rank
• **NR**

Technical Eval.
• **Bullish** since 7/95

Rel. Strength Rank (1 Lowest—99 Highest)
• **54**

Insider Activity
• **NA**

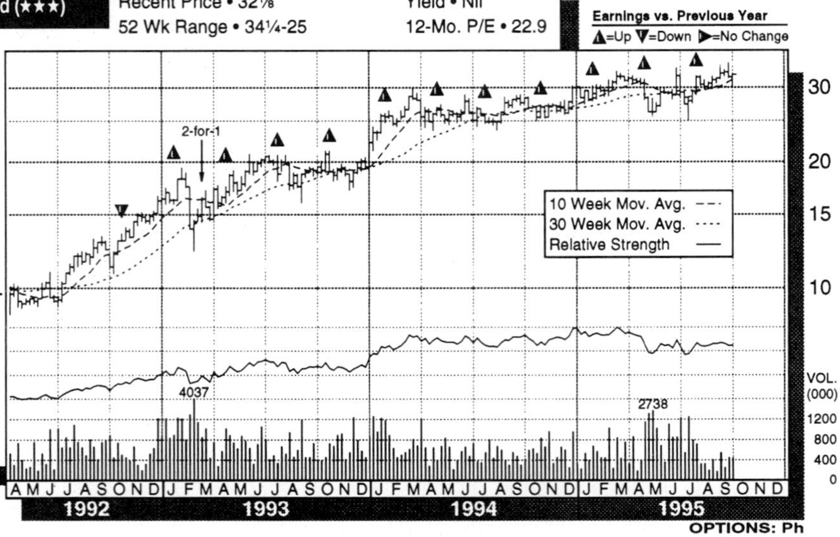

Overview - 03-OCT-95

The company's strategic acquisition program, along with improved demand from existing sites, led to solid revenue and earnings gains in the first half of 1995. Demand for subacute and specialty care, along with contributions from the expanding home health business, should lead to continued improvements in the second half of the year and into 1996. Operating margins are expected to improve on a more favorable business mix, and net profits will benefit from a lower effective tax rate, due in part to benefits derived from the creation of a partnership structure in the pharmaceuticals business. During the second quarter of 1995, the company's net margin expansion was aided by an improved quality mix, the percentage of non-Medicaid revenues to total revenues, to 67% from 62%.

Valuation - 03-OCT-95

Although the fundamental outlook for Health Care & Retirement is positive, the shares appear to be fairly valued with a recent P/E multiple of about 21x our 1995 EPS estimate and 18x our 1996 estimate. As such, we would be hesitant to add to positions at the recent price. HCR generated top-line growth of 15% in the first half of 1995, and continued demand for specialty, home care and subacute segments, along with contributions from acquisitions, is expected to fuel revenues in the second half of the year. Along with improved operating margins and a lower tax rate, EPS should expand by approximately 16% in 1996.

Key Stock Statistics

S&P EPS Est. 1995	1.55	Tang. Bk. Value/Share	11.33
P/E on S&P Est. 1995	20.7	Beta	NA
S&P EPS Est. 1996	1.80	Shareholders	300
Dividend Rate/Share	Nil	Market cap. (B)	$0.985
Shs. outstg. (M)	31.0	Inst. holdings	80%
Avg. daily vol. (M)	0.084	Insider holdings	NA

Value of $10,000 invested 5 years ago: NA

Fiscal Year Ending Dec. 31

	1995	% Change	1994	% Change	1993	% Change
Revenues (Million $)						
1Q	171.3	14%	150.3	14%	132.2	12%
2Q	176.9	17%	151.7	9%	139.2	14%
3Q	—	—	155.5	9%	143.3	13%
4Q	—	—	157.6	9%	144.7	11%
Yr.	—	—	615.1	10%	559.3	13%
Income (Million $)						
1Q	11.99	24%	9.64	26%	7.67	39%
2Q	12.45	19%	10.47	20%	8.72	30%
3Q	—	—	10.84	27%	8.51	21%
4Q	—	—	11.09	21%	9.17	26%
Yr.	—	—	42.03	23%	34.07	28%
Earnings Per Share ($)						
1Q	0.36	24%	0.29	26%	0.23	35%
2Q	0.38	23%	0.31	19%	0.26	24%
3Q	E0.40	25%	0.32	23%	0.26	18%
4Q	E0.42	27%	0.33	18%	0.28	27%
Yr.	E1.55	23%	1.26	22%	1.03	26%

Next earnings report expected: late October

Business Summary - 26-SEP-95

Health Care and Retirement Corp. is a leading provider of long-term care, subacute care and rehabilitative services. At 1994 year-end, HCR operated 129 long-term care centers (119 owned) with over 16,600 beds, located in 16 states including Ohio (31), Florida (26) and Michigan (22). The company also offers subacute care programs, rehabilitation programs and Alzheimer's disease care programs. At the end of 1994, HCR operated 50 medical specialty units with more than 1,500 beds.

In 1994, about 38% of revenues were derived from the Medicaid program, 24% from Medicare and 38% from private pay/other sources.

Most of the company's long-term care centers provide healthcare services emphasizing skilled nursing care. Nurses provide services prescribed by the patient's attending physician, including the administration of medication and injections, on a 24-hour basis. Licensed therapists provide physical, speech, occupational and respiratory therapy for patients in many of the centers that are recovering from strokes, heart attacks, orthopedic conditions or other illnesses, injuries or disabilities. The centers also provide daily dietary services, social services, therapeutic recreational activities, housekeeping and laundry services. Dentistry, podiatry, psychological counseling and laboratory, pharmacy and X-ray services are also available.

Assisted living or personal care services are offered at a number of HCR's centers. Three centers are dedicated to providing residential services to those with less demanding health needs.

Some of the company's centers provide specialized nursing or rehabilitative care for patients whose medical problems are more acute or require more sophisticated treatment. These services include subacute care, high-intensity rehabilitation care and Alzheimer's disease care.

Heartland Rehabilitation Services provides rehabilitative services in eight outpatient clinics, as well as in hospitals and long-term care facilities. HCR owns a 50% stake in Heartland Healthcare Services, which provides pharmaceuticals, related clinical services and infusion therapy to long-term care centers.

Important Developments

May '95—HCR purchased a skilled-nursing facility in Ohio. The company plans to expand the facility to include a subacute rehabilitation unit with 21 beds for patients recovering from stroke, orthopedic disabilities and surgery. In February, HCR acquired an Ohio-based operator of three outpatient rehabilitation clinics, and a provider of home health and rehabilitation care with offices in 28 communities in Ohio, Michigan and Illinois.

Capitalization

Long Term Debt: $145,839,000 (6/95).

Per Share Data ($) (Year Ended Dec. 31)

	1994	1993	1992	1991	1990	1989
Tangible Bk. Val.	10.90	9.86	8.53	7.83	7.69	NA
Cash Flow	1.90	1.57	1.30	NA	0.86	NA
Earnings	1.26	1.03	0.82	0.55	0.37	NA
Dividends	Nil	Nil	Nil	Nil	NA	NA
Payout Ratio	Nil	Nil	Nil	Nil	NA	NA
Prices - High	30¼	22¼	16⅝	11½	NA	NA
- Low	21¼	12½	8½	8½	NA	NA
P/E Ratio - High	24	22	20	22	NA	NA
- Low	17	12	11	16	NA	NA

Income Statement Analysis (Million $)

	1994	%Chg	1993	%Chg	1992	%Chg	1991
Revs.	615	10%	559	12%	497	14%	437
Oper. Inc.	92.2	15%	80.5	14%	70.8	—	NA
Depr.	21.3	17%	18.2	17%	15.6	—	NA
Int. Exp.	9.4	-5%	9.9	-23%	12.9	—	NA
Pretax Inc.	62.3	18%	52.8	24%	42.5	—	NA
Eff. Tax Rate	33%	—	36%	—	38%	—	NA
Net Inc.	42.0	23%	34.1	29%	26.5	48%	17.9

Balance Sheet & Other Fin. Data (Million $)

	1994	1993	1992	1991	1990	1989
Cash	29.9	11.3	4.3	3.4	0.2	NA
Curr. Assets	133	113	97.0	82.0	75.0	NA
Total Assets	671	636	554	523	523	NA
Curr. Liab.	113	103	83.0	64.0	63.5	NA
LT Debt	149	156	177	199	213	NA
Common Eqty.	345	317	287	259	247	NA
Total Cap.	553	531	471	459	460	NA
Cap. Exp.	26.2	24.6	30.7	NA	NA	NA
Cash Flow	63.3	52.3	42.2	NA	27.1	NA

Ratio Analysis

	1994	1993	1992	1991	1990	1989
Curr. Ratio	1.2	1.1	1.2	1.3	1.2	NA
% LT Debt of Cap.	26.9	29.3	37.5	43.3	46.3	NA
% Net Inc.of Revs.	6.8	6.1	5.3	4.1	3.1	NA
% Ret. on Assets	6.5	5.8	4.9	2.9	NA	NA
% Ret. on Equity	12.8	11.3	9.7	5.9	NA	NA

Dividend Data —No cash dividends have been paid. A shareholder rights plan was adopted in May 1995.

Data as orig. reptd.; bef. results of disc. opers. and/or spec. items. Per share data adj. for stk. divs. as of ex-div. date. E-Estimated. NA-Not Available. NM-Not Meaningful. NR-Not Ranked.

Office—One SeaGate, Toledo, OH 43604-2616. **Tel**—(419) 252-5500. **Chrmn, Pres & CEO**—P.A. Ormond. **Sr Exec VP & COO**—M. K. Weikel. **Exec VP, CFO, Treas & Investor Contact**—Geoffrey G. Meyers. **VP & Secy**—R. J. Bixler. **Dirs**—J. J. Clair Jr., J. H. Lemieux, G. G. Meyers, P. A. Ormond, R. G. Siefers, M. K. Weikel, T. L. Young. **Transfer Agent & Registrar**—Harris Trust & Savings Bank, Chicago. **Incorporated** in Delaware in 1991. **Empl**-16,500. **S&P Analyst:** Robert M. Gold

STANDARD & POOR'S

STOCK REPORTS

HealthCare COMPARE

NASDAQ Symbol **HCCC**
In S&P MidCap 400

11-SEP-95

Industry:
Health Care Centers

Summary: This company provides a broad array of medical cost management services to corporate, government and other health care payer groups.

S&P Opinion: Hold (★★★)

Recent Price • 40⅛
52 Wk Range • 40⅜-24⅜

Yield • Nil
12-Mo. P/E • 23.9

Quantitative Evaluations

Outlook
(1 Lowest—5 Highest)
• **5+**

Fair Value
• **51½**

Risk
• **Average**

Earn./Div. Rank
• **B**

Technical Eval.
• **Bullish** since 8/95

Rel. Strength Rank
(1 Lowest—99 Highest)
• **88**

Insider Activity
• **Neutral**

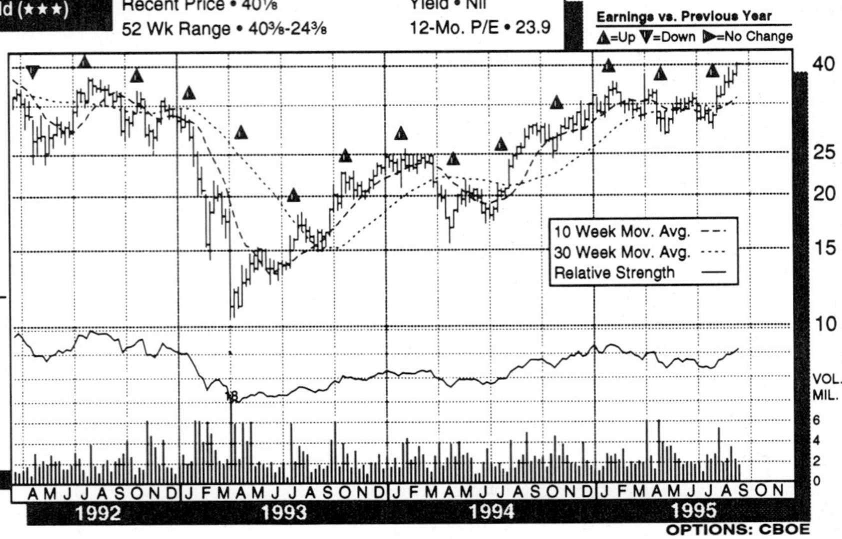

Overview - 08-SEP-95

HealthCare COMPARE should continue to benefit from cost-containment efforts in the health care industry, as demand for its services is driven by the desire of corporate, government and other payers to reduce their medical costs. One of the fastest-growing areas in the managed care sector is currently the Preferred Provider Organization (PPO), an area which generates about 75% of HCCC's revenues. As such, we would expect continued top-line momentum through 1996, while well-controlled operating costs allow for solid EPS growth. In addition, per-share earnings will benefit from an ongoing common share repurchase program.

Valuation - 08-SEP-95

Based on our 1995 EPS estimate of $1.88, we continue to advise investors to hold the shares of HealthCare COMPARE, as they appear to be fairly valued at recent levels. The company is expected to generate good earnings growth in 1995 and 1996, aided by continued penetration of the PPO market, and the likelihood of an increased presence in the group health and workers' compensation markets. However, the shares are trading at a substantial premium to the S&P 500, and any earnings shortfall could trigger a selloff. Nevertheless, HCCC shares remain a solid long term holding in the managed care industry.

Key Stock Statistics

S&P EPS Est. 1995	1.88	Tang. Bk. Value/Share	6.87
P/E on S&P Est. 1995	21.3	Beta	1.90
S&P EPS Est. 1996	2.25	Shareholders	1,500
Dividend Rate/Share	Nil	Market cap. (B)	$ 1.4
Shs. outstg. (M)	34.3	Inst. holdings	68%
Avg. daily vol. (M)	0.485	Insider holdings	NA

Value of $10,000 invested 5 years ago: $ 149,274

Fiscal Year Ending Dec. 31

	1995	% Change	1994	% Change	1993	% Change
Revenues (Million $)						
1Q	51.38	20%	42.99	15%	37.41	19%
2Q	53.06	15%	46.04	18%	38.86	20%
3Q	—	—	48.13	21%	39.72	18%
4Q	—	—	49.44	19%	41.66	16%
Yr.	—	—	186.6	18%	157.6	18%
Income (Million $)						
1Q	14.77	33%	11.08	24%	8.93	NM
2Q	16.46	34%	12.26	32%	9.28	31%
3Q	—	—	13.39	35%	9.92	26%
4Q	—	—	13.94	35%	10.35	21%
Yr.	—	—	50.67	32%	38.47	112%
Earnings Per Share ($)						
1Q	0.42	35%	0.31	24%	0.25	NM
2Q	0.47	34%	0.35	35%	0.26	30%
3Q	E0.49	26%	0.39	39%	0.28	27%
4Q	E0.50	25%	0.40	38%	0.29	21%
Yr.	E1.88	30%	1.45	34%	1.08	112%

Next earnings report expected: early November

HealthCare COMPARE

Business Summary - 08-SEP-95

HealthCare COMPARE Corp. develops and manages preferred provider organizations (PPOs), and provides medical cost management services to clients including insurance carriers, managed care entities, third party administrators, corporate employers and government employee groups. Revenues in recent years were derived as follows:

	1994	1993	1992
PPO & fee schedule services	83%	79%	78%
Utilization review	14%	17%	18%
Govt. contract services	3%	4%	4%

HealthCare COMPARE assists clients with medical cost management through an array of programs designed to manage specific cost elements. Its medical review programs help clients manage the number of units of medical services (volume), while its PPO products help manage the cost of units of service (price). Through its OUCH Systems capabilities, the company provides workers' compensation bill review services nationally. These services are coupled with the company's review programs and PPO networks to provide a comprehensive product offering in the workers' compensation arenas where medical costs have been rising faster than in the group health arenas.

The company's PPO services are offered through its AFFORDABLE Health Care Concepts subsidiary. AFFORDABLE develops and manages payor-based PPO networks throughout the U.S. The AFFORDABLE PPO networks contain about 1,900 hospitals in 47 states. In each case, rates are negotiated for the full range of hospital services, including inpatient and outpatient services. AFFORDABLE has also established outpatient care networks comprising physicians, clinical laboratories, surgery centers, radiology facilities and other providers in 49 states and the District of Columbia.

HealthCare COMPARE offers several utilization review and cost management programs from which clients may select. Most clients subscribe to the Medical/Surgical Hospital Review program, which serves as a base to which other programs may be added. About 90% of clients subscribe to at least one additional program. Other cost management programs include case management, surgical opinion, psychiatric and substance abuse review and disability management, all of which are also offered on a stand-alone basis.

Important Developments

Jul. '95—HealthCare COMPARE said that strong earnings generated in the first six months of 1995 reflected continued demand for the company's unique managed care offerings. The company expects that future performance will benefit from increased penetration in the group health and workers' compensation markets.

Capitalization

Long Term Debt: None (6/95).

Per Share Data ($)

(Year Ended Dec. 31)

	1994	1993	1992	1991	1990	1989
Tangible Bk. Val.	5.86	4.87	3.75	2.58	1.86	1.62
Cash Flow	1.76	1.31	0.70	0.64	0.34	0.22
Earnings	1.45	1.08	0.51	0.50	0.23	0.12
Dividends	Nil	Nil	Nil	Nil	Nil	Nil
Payout Ratio	Nil	Nil	Nil	Nil	Nil	Nil
Prices - High	34 3/8	31 7/8	44	40 3/4	9 3/8	4 1/8
- Low	15 1/2	10 1/2	23 3/4	7 1/8	2 5/8	2 1/4
P/E Ratio - High	24	30	86	82	40	36
- Low	11	10	47	14	11	20

Income Statement Analysis (Million $)

	1994	%Chg	1993	%Chg	1992	%Chg	1991
Revs.	187	18%	158	18%	134	89%	70.9
Oper. Inc.	91.0	35%	67.3	28%	52.5	148%	21.2
Depr.	11.0	38%	8.0	21%	6.6	94%	3.4
Int. Exp.	0.1	NM	0.1	-62%	0.1	—	Nil
Pretax Inc.	85.0	34%	63.4	96%	32.3	59%	20.3
Eff. Tax Rate	40%	—	39%	—	44%	—	37%
Net Inc.	50.7	32%	38.5	113%	18.1	41%	12.8

Balance Sheet & Other Fin. Data (Million $)

	1994	1993	1992	1991	1990	1989
Cash	66.5	50.6	73.1	25.9	34.8	25.0
Curr. Assets	94.0	76.0	100	40.0	41.6	40.5
Total Assets	215	187	146	69.3	52.1	50.1
Curr. Liab.	15.4	16.7	15.6	7.8	7.4	10.8
LT Debt	Nil	Nil	Nil	Nil	0.1	0.2
Common Eqty.	200	171	130	61.4	43.1	37.4
Total Cap.	200	171	130	61.4	43.2	37.6
Cap. Exp.	8.4	11.1	10.2	22.6	3.6	4.2
Cash Flow	61.7	46.5	24.7	16.2	8.2	4.9

Ratio Analysis

	1994	1993	1992	1991	1990	1989
Curr. Ratio	6.1	4.5	6.4	5.2	5.6	3.7
% LT Debt of Cap.	Nil	Nil	Nil	Nil	0.2	0.6
% Net Inc.of Revs.	27.2	24.4	13.6	18.0	13.1	8.4
% Ret. on Assets	25.5	23.0	14.7	20.8	10.8	5.9
% Ret. on Equity	27.7	25.5	16.5	24.1	13.7	7.3

Dividend Data —No cash dividends have been paid.

Data as orig. reptd.; bef. results of disc. opers. and/or spec. items. Per share data adj. for stk. divs. as of ex-div. date. Bk. val. in 1992 incl. intangibles. E-Estimated. NA-Not Available. NM-Not Meaningful. NR-Not Ranked.

Office—3200 Highland Ave., Downers Grove, IL 60515. **Tel**—(708) 241-7900. **Chrmn**—T. J. Pritzker. **Pres & CEO**—J. C. Smith. **VP-Fin, CFO & Investor Contact**—Joseph E. Whitters. **EVP & Secy**—R. H. Galowich. **Dirs**—R. J. Becker, M. J. Boskin, D. S. Brunner, R. S. Colman, J. P. Foley, R. H. Galowich, B. W. Kanter, T. J. Pritzker, D. E. Simon, J. C. Smith. **Transfer Agent & Registrar**—LaSalle National Bank of Chicago. **Incorporated** in Delaware in 1982. **Empl**-1,600. **S&P Analyst:** Robert M. Gold

STANDARD & POOR'S

STOCK REPORTS

Healthsource, Inc.

NYSE Symbol **HS**
In S&P MidCap 400

08-SEP-95 **Industry:** Health Care Centers

Summary: Healthsource provides managed-healthcare services and owns health maintenance organizations in nine states.

S&P Opinion: Hold (★★★)

Recent Price • 40 | Yield • Nil
52 Wk Range • 47¾-29½ | 12-Mo. P/E • 28.2

Quantitative Evaluations

Outlook
(1 Lowest—5 Highest)
• NA

Fair Value
• NA

Risk
• High

Earn./Div. Rank
• B

Technical Eval.
• Bullish since 8/95

Rel. Strength Rank
(1 Lowest—99 Highest)
• 75

Insider Activity
• Neutral

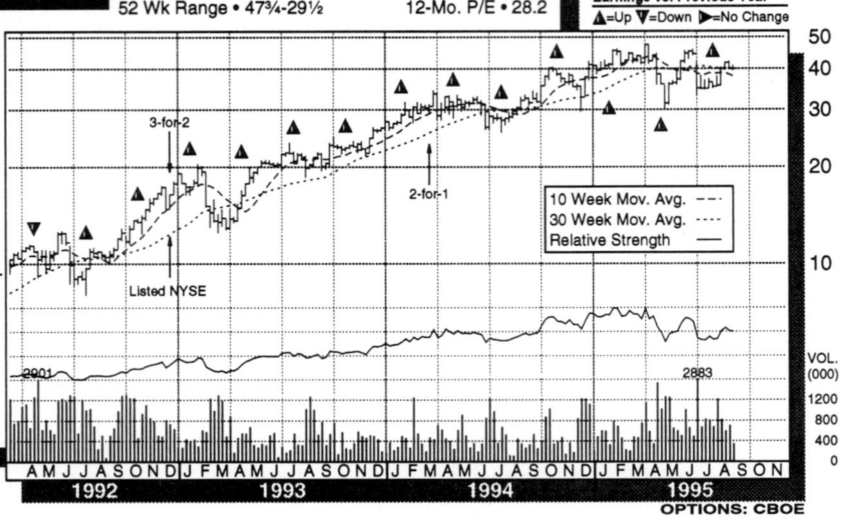

OPTIONS: CBOE

Overview - 08-SEP-95

Healthsource should continue to generate substantial membership growth for the balance of 1995 and through 1996, aided by the benefits accruing from its dominant regional presence and the anticipated conversion of many Provident Life and Accident Insurance Co. members to managed care plans from traditional fee-for-service plans. Margins going forward may be restricted by an increasingly competitive HMO environment, and by an inability to raise premium rates in many markets. However, the company's ability to control its medical costs will help sustain operating profits, and HS should benefit from expansion into new, underpenetrated markets, where price competition is less severe.

Valuation - 08-SEP-95

Although the company has generated impressive earnings in recent quarters, we remain concerned regarding margins in the HMO segment. In addition, the prospect of flat-to-lower premium rates in many markets has made earnings far less visible, and has resulted in an uncertain climate for most HMO-related stocks. In such an environment, any earnings shortfall could result in a rapid decline in the company's stock price. HS has shown an ability to grow despite the poor premium environment, but at a recent multiple of about 21 times our 1996 EPS estimate, we would not aggressively accumulate the stock.

Key Stock Statistics

S&P EPS Est. 1995	1.65	Tang. Bk. Value/Share	0.26
P/E on S&P Est. 1995	24.2	Beta	1.72
S&P EPS Est. 1996	2.15	Shareholders	900
Dividend Rate/Share	Nil	Market cap. (B)	$ 1.4
Shs. outstg. (M)	31.3	Inst. holdings	92%
Avg. daily vol. (M)	0.117	Insider holdings	NA

Value of $10,000 invested 5 years ago: $ 84,210

Fiscal Year Ending Dec. 31

	1995	% Change	1994	% Change	1993	% Change
Revenues (Million $)						
1Q	208.4	91%	109.3	86%	58.89	85%
2Q	286.7	89%	151.8	108%	72.95	70%
3Q	—	—	155.6	100%	77.78	53%
4Q	—	—	167.6	106%	81.22	56%
Yr.	—	—	584.2	101%	290.8	64%
Income (Million $)						
1Q	11.77	40%	8.41	53%	5.49	33%
2Q	13.62	44%	9.49	58%	6.01	61%
3Q	—	—	10.14	50%	6.76	52%
4Q	—	—	11.00	41%	7.81	67%
Yr.	—	—	39.04	50%	26.06	53%
Earnings Per Share ($)						
1Q	0.37	32%	0.28	27%	0.22	29%
2Q	0.39	30%	0.30	30%	0.23	48%
3Q	E0.43	34%	0.32	33%	0.24	33%
4Q	E0.46	35%	0.34	31%	0.26	37%
Yr.	E1.65	33%	1.24	29%	0.96	39%

Next earnings report expected: early November

Healthsource, Inc.

Business Summary - 07-SEP-95

Healthsource is a healthcare management company that has interests in or manages individual practice association (IPA) model health maintenance organizations (HMOs) that market and provide prepaid healthcare services to about 560,000 members in nine states. The company also offers point-of-service plans, utilization review services, pharmacy benefit management services and workers' compensation managed-care services and provides managed-care services to other healthcare payors.

HMOs operated by the company include Healthsource New Hampshire (100% owned; 101,600 members as of June 30, 1995), Healthsource South Carolina (100%; 90,700); Healthsource Indiana (97%; 65,000), Healthsource Tennessee (100%; 42,900); Healthsource Maine (100%; 58,300), Healthsource Arkansas (70%; 21,000), Physicians Health Plan, in North Carolina (100%; 122,400), Patients' Choice, in Syracuse, N.Y. (40%; 23,400), and Healthsource Georgia (100%; 6,000). Healthsource has also received HMO licenses in Dayton, Ohio, and Louisville, Ky., and is seeking to enter markets in Connecticut and Texas. To supplement Healthsource New Hampshire's HMO services, the company offers traditional indemnity insurance coverage to employers through Healthsource Insurance Group, Inc.

HS has formed a joint venture with ChubbLife Insurance Co. of America to operate ChubbHealth, an HMO that began serving New York City and surrounding areas in April 1994, and at June 30, 1995 had 28,400 members. ChubbLife has more than 250,000 members insured in its greater New York City indemnity health plans; the joint venture will seek to enable these members to convert to HMO coverage. Healthsource has an initial 15% interest in the venture, with an option to increase its ownership to 50%.

Important Developments

Jun. '95—The company acquired the group health, HMO and third-party administrative business of Provident Life and Accident Insurance Co. for $231 million in cash and securities. The acquired business administers or insures about 2.4 million lives.

Apr. '95—The company agreed to acquire Central Massachusetts Health Plan, a not-for-profit HMO serving Worcester, Mass., with 84,000 members, for approximately $62.5 million. Separately, the company received an HMO license in Kentucky.

Capitalization

Long Term Debt: None (6/95).
Minority Interest: $3,674,000.

Per Share Data ($)

(Year Ended Dec. 31)

	1994	1993	1992	1991	1990	1989
Tangible Bk. Val.	7.86	6.91	4.06	3.57	1.74	1.71
Cash Flow	1.60	1.18	0.85	0.60	0.51	0.46
Earnings	1.24	0.96	0.70	0.57	0.47	0.43
Dividends	Nil	Nil	Nil	Nil	Nil	Nil
Payout Ratio	Nil	Nil	Nil	Nil	Nil	Nil
Prices - High	42¼	28¼	19⅞	11⅞	5½	5
- Low	25½	12½	8	4¼	2⅞	4⅜
P/E Ratio - High	34	29	28	20	12	12
- Low	21	13	12	8	6	10

Income Statement Analysis (Million $)

	1994	%Chg	1993	%Chg	1992	%Chg	1991
Revs.	584	101%	291	63%	178	103%	87.5
Oper. Inc.	53.4	65%	32.3	62%	19.9	62%	12.3
Depr.	11.3	87%	6.0	54%	3.9	NM	0.9
Int. Exp.	Nil	—	NA	—	0.0	-71%	0.1
Pretax Inc.	56.4	55%	36.4	54%	23.7	35%	17.5
Eff. Tax Rate	32%	—	29%	—	28%	—	27%
Net Inc.	39.0	49%	26.1	54%	17.0	34%	12.7

Balance Sheet & Other Fin. Data (Million $)

	1994	1993	1992	1991	1990	1989
Cash	162	155	67.1	63.1	22.5	35.0
Curr. Assets	196	176	77.3	69.9	26.3	36.6
Total Assets	424	295	147	115	51.0	40.0
Curr. Liab.	96.0	48.5	25.5	13.3	8.3	7.9
LT Debt	Nil	Nil	NA	0.3	1.9	4.4
Common Eqty.	322	242	119	101	40.0	28.0
Total Cap.	326	244	121	102	42.0	32.0
Cap. Exp.	23.3	11.3	5.6	2.6	0.6	0.3
Cash Flow	50.3	32.1	20.9	13.6	8.9	5.7

Ratio Analysis

	1994	1993	1992	1991	1990	1989
Curr. Ratio	2.0	3.6	3.0	5.2	3.2	4.6
% LT Debt of Cap.	Nil	Nil	Nil	0.3	4.4	13.6
% Net Inc.of Revs.	6.7	9.0	9.6	14.5	13.5	10.9
% Ret. on Assets	10.6	11.0	12.9	14.1	17.0	NA
% Ret. on Equity	13.5	13.4	15.3	16.6	22.9	NA

Dividend Data —No cash dividends have been paid on the public shares.

Data as orig. reptd.; bef. results of disc. opers. and/or spec. items. Per share data adj. for stk. divs. as of ex-div. date. E-Estimated. NA-Not Available. NM-Not Meaningful. NR-Not Ranked.

Office—2 College Park Dr., Hooksett, NH 03106. **Tel**—(603) 268-7000. **Chrmn**—M. Bagan. **Pres & CEO**—N. C. Payson. **COO**—Sally W. Crawford. **CFO**—T. M. Congoran. **Investor Contact**—Tracey Turner. **Dirs**—M. Bagan, P. D. Baron, R. H. Bilbro, R. S. Cathcart, J. H. Chandler, D. F. Eubank, R. A. Leipold, F. G. Middleton, N. C. Payson, D. W. Schall. **Transfer Agent**—First National Bank of Boston, Canton, Mass. **Incorporated** in New Hampshire in 1985. **Empl**-1,800. **S&P Analyst:** Robert M. Gold

STANDARD & POOR'S

STOCK REPORTS

HEALTHSOUTH Corp.

NYSE Symbol **HRC**

In S&P MidCap 400

12-OCT-95

Industry: Health Care Centers

Summary: This company is the largest U.S. provider of outpatient and rehabilitative healthcare services, with about 500 locations in 38 states.

S&P Opinion: Accumulate (★★★★)

Recent Price • 25

52 Wk Range • 25¾-16⅛

Yield • Nil

12-Mo. P/E • 45.5

Quantitative Evaluations

Outlook
(1 Lowest—5 Highest)
• **4+**

Fair Value
• **26⅛**

Risk
• **Average**

Earn./Div. Rank
• **B**

Technical Eval.
• **Bearish** since 7/95

Rel. Strength Rank
(1 Lowest—99 Highest)
• **86**

Insider Activity
• **Neutral**

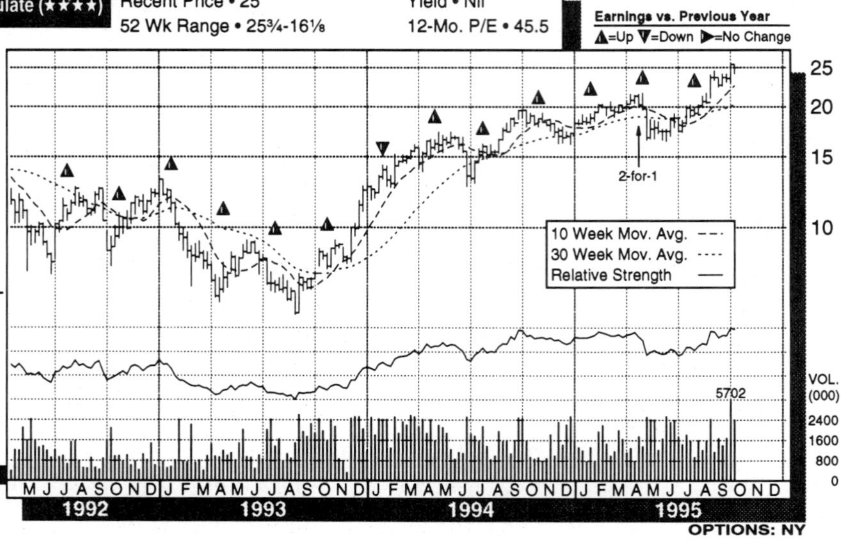

Overview - 11-OCT-95

The fundamentals underlying the physical rehabilitation sector are positive, and the company's broad geographic range allows for substantial future growth. In addition, the proposed acquisition of Surgical Care Affiliates (SCA) will be additive to 1996 EPS, reflecting the potential for enormous cost savings and the probability that many of SCA's patients will use HRC's rehabilitation centers following their surgical procedures. HEALTHSOUTH's inpatient and outpatient facilities should experience strong demand from payers seeking to move patients out of costly acute care hospitals. Following HRC's May 1995 transaction with NovaCare Inc., it now operates about 40% of the rehabilitation hospitals in the U.S.

Valuation - 11-OCT-95

Based on our recently revised EPS estimates of $1.00 and $1.15, respectively, for 1995 and 1996, we continue to view the shares of HEALTHSOUTH Corp. as attractive at current levels. Our revisions were made following the sale of 13 million HRC shares in September 1995. The 1996 forecast does not yet factor in the benefits of the Surgical Care acquisition, which will boost net income by at least 3% in 1996. HRC has established itself as a dominant player in the rapidly-consolidating rehabilitation sector, and the SCA transaction will help create the largest domestic operator of outpatient surgery centers.

Key Stock Statistics

S&P EPS Est. 1995	1.00	Tang. Bk. Value/Share	1.53
P/E on S&P Est. 1995	25.0	Beta	1.98
S&P EPS Est. 1996	1.15	Shareholders	1,300
Dividend Rate/Share	Nil	Market cap. (B)	$ 2.3
Shs. outstg. (M)	93.5	Inst. holdings	62%
Avg. daily vol. (M)	0.746	Insider holdings	NA

Value of $10,000 invested 5 years ago: $ 43,478

Fiscal Year Ending Dec. 31

	1995	% Change	1994	% Change	1993	% Change
Revenues (Million $)						
1Q	307.0	33%	231.3	99%	116.2	24%
2Q	378.9	53%	247.4	107%	119.6	17%
3Q	—	—	261.1	115%	121.3	19%
4Q	—	—	301.6	141%	125.3	15%
Yr.	—	—	1,127	134%	482.3	19%
Income (Million $)						
1Q	19.13	58%	12.12	37%	8.82	88%
2Q	23.00	73%	13.31	39%	9.58	22%
3Q	—	—	14.52	51%	9.59	17%
4Q	—	—	6.83	NM	-21.30	NM
Yr.	—	—	53.23	NM	6.69	-78%
Earnings Per Share ($)						
1Q	0.24	26%	0.19	27%	0.15	88%
2Q	0.26	27%	0.21	24%	0.17	22%
3Q	E0.23	5%	0.22	33%	0.17	18%
4Q	E0.27	NM	0.09	NM	-0.35	NM
Yr.	E1.00	43%	0.70	NM	0.11	-78%

Next earnings report expected: mid October

HEALTHSOUTH Corp.

Business Summary - 12-OCT-95

HEALTHSOUTH Corp. (formerly HEALTHSOUTH Rehabilitation Corp.) is the largest U.S. provider of rehabilitative healthcare services. At June 30, 1995, it had nearly 500 locations in 35 states, the District of Columbia and Ontario, including 288 outpatient rehabilitation facilities, 66 inpatient sites, five medical centers and 42 locations providing other services. The company believes that demand for rehabilitative healthcare services will continue to be driven by advances in medical technology, an aging population, and a recognition on the part of payers (insurers, self-insured companies, managed care organizations, and government entities) that properly administered rehabilitative services can improve quality of life and lower overall healthcare costs.

Through its outpatient and inpatient rehabilitation facilities, HEALTHSOUTH has established interdisciplinary programs for the rehabilitation of patients experiencing disability resulting from physical conditions such as stroke, head injury, orthopaedic problems, neuromuscular disease and sports-related injuries. Its rehabilitation services include physical therapy, sports medicine, work hardening, neurorehabilitation, occupational therapy, respiratory therapy, speech-language pathology and rehabilitation nursing. In addition, company medical centers provide general and specialty medical and surgical healthcare services including home healthcare, diagnostic services, physician services and contract management of hospital-based rehabilitative healthcare services.

In 1994, revenues generated from patients under Medicare and Medicaid plans, respectively, accounted for 41.0% (versus 30.6% in 1993) and 3.2% (1.0%), of total revenues.

Important Developments

Oct. '95—HRC agreed to acquire Surgical Care Affiliates (NYSE: SCA), an operator of 67 outpatient surgery centers located in 24 states, for HRC common stock valued at $1.2 billion (subject to adjustments). The acquisition is expected to close by early 1996. Assuming completion of its previously announced agreement to purchase Sutter Surgery Centers Inc. (Sacramento, California), an independent operator of 12 outpatient surgery centers located throughout California, Utah and Arizona, HEALTHSOUTH will be the largest domestic operator of outpatient surgery centers with a total of 122 facilities.

Sep. '95—HRC completed the public sale of 13,000,000 common shares at $23.25 each (excluding overallotment options to buy 1,950,000 shares) through underwriters led by Smith Barney Inc., Merrill Lynch & Co. and Morgan Stanley & Co. Inc. Funds will be used to reduce bank debt.

Capitalization

Long Term Debt: $964,233,000 (3/95).
Minority Interest: $3,911,000.

Per Share Data ($) (Year Ended Dec. 31)

	1994	1993	1992	1991	1990	1989
Tangible Bk. Val.	6.24	5.09	5.04	4.98	3.35	2.14
Cash Flow	1.70	0.73	0.82	0.63	0.57	0.40
Earnings	0.70	0.11	0.50	0.43	0.36	0.25
Dividends	Nil	Nil	Nil	Nil	Nil	Nil
Payout Ratio	Nil	Nil	Nil	Nil	Nil	Nil
Prices - High	19¾	13¼	18⅝	17⅝	8⅝	6⅜
- Low	11¾	6⅛	7⅝	7⅜	4⅝	3⅛
P/E Ratio - High	28	NM	37	41	24	25
- Low	17	NM	15	17	13	12

Income Statement Analysis (Million $)

	1994	%Chg	1993	%Chg	1992	%Chg	1991
Revs.	1,127	134%	482	18%	407	81%	225
Oper. Inc.	234	119%	107	42%	75.6	50%	50.3
Depr.	75.6	107%	36.5	93%	18.9	80%	10.5
Int. Exp.	59.0	NM	15.1	18%	12.8	8%	11.9
Pretax Inc.	87.3	NM	10.9	-77%	46.5	31%	35.4
Eff. Tax Rate	39%	—	37%	—	33%	—	33%
Net Inc.	53.2	NM	6.7	-77%	29.7	33%	22.4

Balance Sheet & Other Fin. Data (Million $)

	1994	1993	1992	1991	1990	1989
Cash	83.0	62.0	86.0	107	71.0	32.0
Curr. Assets	396	262	213	185	128	87.0
Total Assets	1,552	1,168	642	472	301	219
Curr. Liab.	177	90.1	42.4	19.9	17.2	14.9
LT Debt	930	780	300	164	150	133
Common Eqty.	426	295	290	279	128	66.0
Total Cap.	1,362	1,078	599	444	279	200
Cap. Exp.	124	111	133	104	39.0	43.0
Cash Flow	129	43.2	48.7	32.8	20.9	13.0

Ratio Analysis

	1994	1993	1992	1991	1990	1989
Curr. Ratio	2.2	2.9	5.0	9.3	7.4	5.8
% LT Debt of Cap.	68.3	72.3	50.0	37.0	53.7	66.3
% Net Inc.of Revs.	4.7	1.4	7.3	9.9	7.2	7.1
% Ret. on Assets	3.6	0.7	5.3	4.9	4.5	4.6
% Ret. on Equity	13.8	2.3	10.3	9.6	12.3	13.1

Dividend Data —No cash dividends have been paid. A two-for-one stock split was effected April 17, 1995.

Amt. of Div. $	Date Decl.	Ex-Div. Date	Stock of Record	Payment Date
2-for-1	Mar. 23	Apr. 18	Apr. 03	Apr. 17 '95

Data as orig. reptd.; bef. results of disc. opers. and/or spec. items. Per share data adj. for stk. divs. as of ex-div. date. E-Estimated. NA-Not Available. NM-Not Meaningful. NR-Not Ranked.

Office—Two Perimeter Park South, Birmingham, AL 35243. **Tel**—(205) 967-7116. **Chrmn, Pres & CEO**—R. M. Scrushy. **EVP, CFO & Investor Contact**—Aaron Beam, Jr. **EVP & Secy**—A. J. Tanner. **Dirs**—A. Beam, Jr., J. P. Bennett, P. D. Brown, J. S. Chamberlin, R. F. Celeste, C. S. Givens, L. R. House, C. W. Newhall III, R. M. Scrushy, G. H. Strong, A. J. Tanner, P. C. Watkins. **Transfer Agent & Registrar**—Chemical Bank, NYC. **Incorporated** in Delaware in 1984. **Empl**-18,423. **S&P Analyst:** Robert M. Gold

STANDARD & POOR'S

STOCK REPORTS

Heilig-Meyers Co.

NYSE Symbol **HMY**
In S&P MidCap 400

11-OCT-95 **Industry:** Retail Stores

Summary: This Richmond-based home furnishings retailer operates more than 690 stores located mostly in small towns in 26 states and Puerto Rico.

S&P Opinion: Accumulate (★★★★)

Recent Price • 22¼ | 52 Wk Range • 30⅝-19¼ | Yield • 1.3% | 12-Mo. P/E • 17.4

Quantitative Evaluations

Outlook (1 Lowest—5 Highest)
• **5-**

Fair Value
• **29⅝**

Risk
• **Average**

Earn./Div. Rank
• **A+**

Technical Eval.
• **Bearish** since 9/95

Rel. Strength Rank (1 Lowest—99 Highest)
• **22**

Insider Activity
• **Neutral**

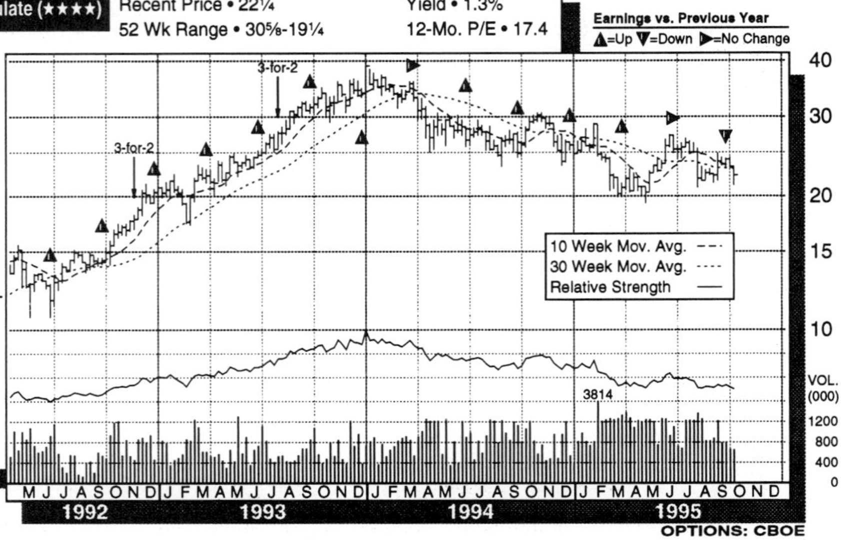

Overview - 11-OCT-95

Sales should grow at about 20% during 1995-96 on new store openings and a low single-digit increase in same-store sales. The company, which had previously committed to improving margins, recently moved to counteract an extremely slow pace of store traffic. HMY attempted to stimulate sales by increasing advertising expenditures and lowering prices on many items, causing operating margins to decline. We do not see consumer spending climbing significantly throughout the second half of 1995-96, and expect that HMY's operating margins will continue to be squeezed at the expense of maintaining customer traffic.

Valuation - 11-OCT-95

A lack of earnings momentum and a general wariness of retail stocks by investors have caused the shares to tumble recently. HMY is trading at 17x our 1995-96 earnings estimate of $1.30 a share, and 15x our 1996-96 estimate of $1.45 a share. These estimates have been scaled down from $1.40 and $1.60, respectively, as consumer reluctance to spend money on big-ticket items such as furniture dims the outlook for retailers like HMY. The company's margins will suffer until consumers decide to return to the stores, but we do not look for any significant movement on that front until calendar 1996. Nevertheless, when such an upturn does occur, HMY's shares stand to benefit more than those of its peers, based on the company's underlying strength.

Key Stock Statistics

S&P EPS Est. 1996	1.30	Tang. Bk. Value/Share	7.15
P/E on S&P Est. 1996	17.1	Beta	1.56
S&P EPS Est. 1997	1.45	Shareholders	1,700
Dividend Rate/Share	0.28	Market cap. (B)	$ 1.0
Shs. outstg. (M)	48.6	Inst. holdings	76%
Avg. daily vol. (M)	0.139	Insider holdings	NA

Value of $10,000 invested 5 years ago: $ 38,699

Fiscal Year Ending Feb. 28

	1996	% Change	1995	% Change	1994	% Change
Revenues (Million $)						
1Q	319.0	19%	269.0	44%	186.8	24%
2Q	324.9	21%	269.1	31%	204.7	34%
3Q	—	—	315.1	37%	230.4	34%
4Q	—	—	299.1	24%	241.9	33%
Yr.	—	—	1,152	33%	863.8	31%
Income (Million $)						
1Q	18.47	NM	18.31	36%	13.46	28%
2Q	11.32	-24%	14.82	30%	11.42	44%
3Q	—	—	18.77	18%	15.86	60%
4Q	—	—	14.92	5%	14.26	49%
Yr.	—	—	66.81	21%	55.00	45%
Earnings Per Share ($)						
1Q	0.37	NM	0.37	26%	0.29	26%
2Q	0.23	-23%	0.30	30%	0.23	33%
3Q	E0.37	-3%	0.38	19%	0.32	45%
4Q	E0.33	10%	0.30	7%	0.28	NM
Yr.	E1.30	-3%	1.34	20%	1.12	33%

Next earnings report expected: mid December

Heilig-Meyers Co.

Business Summary - 11-OCT-95

Heilig-Meyers is engaged primarily in the retail sale of home furnishings. As of September 30, 1995, the company was operating 692 stores in 26 states in the Southeast, Midwest, West, Southwest and Puerto Rico. Stores in operation at fiscal year end were:

1995	647
1994	570
1993	425
1992	374
1991	322
1990	304
1989	277
1988	258
1987	220
1986	214

Some 79% of all stores are in towns with populations of less than 50,000 and at least 25 miles from a major population center. The stores generally range in size from 10,000 to 35,000 sq. ft.

In 1994-95, 59% of HMY's revenues were from furniture and accessories (59% the year before), 11% from consumer electronics (12%), 8% from major appliances (8%), 10% from bedding (10%), and 12% from other items, including jewelry, small appliances and seasonal goods (11%).

The vast majority of merchandise is distributed to stores through HMY's seven distribution centers, which typically are located within 250 miles of a store. The company's seventh center, located in Fontana, Calif., was opened in 1994-95's second quarter, and is being used to support HMY's recent expansion into the West and Southwest.

Historically, over 80% of sales have been made on credit, principally under instalment sales.

Important Developments

Sep. '95—The company said that during the first half of 1995-96, it opened 42 stores, including one in Oklahoma and five in Louisiana, its first stores in those states. HMY noted that it selected Athens, Texas as the site for its eighth distribution center. The 340,000 square-foot facility will be designed to serve approximately 150 stores in a 250-mile radius. The center, scheduled to open in the fall of 1996, will support planned expansion in Texas, Louisiana and Oklahoma.

Capitalization

Long Term Debt: $359,084,000 (8/95).

Per Share Data ($)

(Year Ended Feb. 28)

	1995	1994	1993	1992	1991	1990
Tangible Bk. Val.	7.30	7.01	5.98	5.29	4.45	4.24
Cash Flow	1.82	1.54	1.18	0.97	0.89	0.84
Earnings	1.34	1.12	0.84	0.65	0.59	0.52
Dividends	0.23	0.20	0.16	0.14	0.13	0.12
Payout Ratio	17%	17%	19%	23%	22%	23%
Cal. Yrs.	1994	1993	1992	1991	1990	1989
Prices - High	38⅜	39	21⅜	12⅜	8¾	7¾
- Low	23¼	17¼	10⅝	6⅛	4¾	4¾
P/E Ratio - High	29	35	25	19	15	15
- Low	17	15	13	9	8	9

Income Statement Analysis (Million $)

	1995	%Chg	1994	%Chg	1993	%Chg	1992
Revs.	1,152	33%	864	31%	658	27%	520
Oper. Inc.	163	23%	132	35%	98.1	29%	76.0
Depr.	23.9	16%	20.6	32%	15.6	17%	13.3
Int. Exp.	34.6	39%	24.9	6%	23.5	8%	21.8
Pretax Inc.	106	22%	87.2	47%	59.4	44%	41.2
Eff. Tax Rate	37%	—	37%	—	36%	—	35%
Net Inc.	66.8	21%	55.0	45%	38.0	41%	27.0

Balance Sheet & Other Fin. Data (Million $)

	1995	1994	1993	1992	1991	1990
Cash	10.4	6.3	3.9	2.8	2.2	2.4
Curr. Assets	853	765	567	470	380	376
Total Assets	1,209	1,040	741	618	507	502
Curr. Liab.	299	312	252	120	149	169
LT Debt	370	249	176	226	164	148
Common Eqty.	490	433	306	264	185	171
Total Cap.	910	728	489	497	358	334
Cap. Exp.	49.1	36.3	27.4	24.0	12.5	18.4
Cash Flow	90.7	75.6	53.6	40.3	31.9	29.9

Ratio Analysis

	1995	1994	1993	1992	1991	1990
Curr. Ratio	2.9	2.5	2.3	3.9	2.5	2.2
% LT Debt of Cap.	40.7	34.2	36.1	45.5	45.9	44.5
% Net Inc.of Revs.	5.8	6.4	5.8	5.2	4.7	4.7
% Ret. on Assets	5.9	6.0	5.5	4.4	4.1	3.7
% Ret. on Equity	14.5	14.4	13.2	11.0	11.7	11.3

Dividend Data —Dividends have been paid since 1975. A "poison pill" stock purchase rights plan was adopted in 1988.

Amt. of Div. $	Date Decl.	Ex-Div. Date	Stock of Record	Payment Date
0.060	Oct. 19	Nov. 03	Nov. 09	Nov. 26 '94
0.060	Dec. 15	Jan. 11	Jan. 18	Feb. 18 '95
0.070	Apr. 06	Apr. 21	Apr. 28	May. 21 '95
0.070	Jun. 21	Jul. 17	Jul. 19	Aug. 26 '95

Data as orig. reptd.; bef. results of disc. opers. and/or spec. items. Per share data adj. for stk. divs. as of ex-div. date. E-Estimated. NA-Not Available. NM-Not Meaningful. NR-Not Ranked.

Office—2235 Staples Mill Rd., Richmond, VA 23230. **Tel**—(804) 359-9171. **Chrmn & CEO**—W. C. DeRusha. **Pres & COO**—T. A. Peery, Jr. **EVP-CFO**—J. R. Jenkins. **VP-Secy & Treas**—R. B. Goodman. **Dirs**—A. Alexander, R. L. Burrus Jr., A. D. Charpentier, W. C. DeRusha, B. F. Edwards III, A. G. Fleischer, N. Krumbein, H. Meyers, S. S. Meyers, T. A. Peery Jr., L. N. Smith, G. A. Thornton III. **Transfer Agent & Registrar**—Wachovia Bank of North Carolina, Winston-Salem. **Incorporated** in 1972 as successor to a partnership founded in 1913. **Empl**-12,510. **S&P Analyst:** Philip D. Wohl

Hibernia Corp.

NYSE Symbol **HIB**
In S&P MidCap 400

02-OCT-95 **Industry:** Banking

Summary: Hibernia Corp. is the holding company for Hibernia National Bank, Louisiana's largest statewide bank, with assets of $6.7 billion.

S&P Opinion: Hold (★★★)

Recent Price • 10⅛
52 Wk Range • 10¾-6⅞
Yield • 2.4%
12-Mo. P/E • 11.5

Quantitative Evaluations
Outlook (1 Lowest—5 Highest) • **1-**
Fair Value • **8**
Risk • **Low**
Earn./Div. Rank • **B-**

Technical Eval. • **Bullish** since 4/95
Rel. Strength Rank (1 Lowest—99 Highest) • **58**
Insider Activity • **Unfavorable**

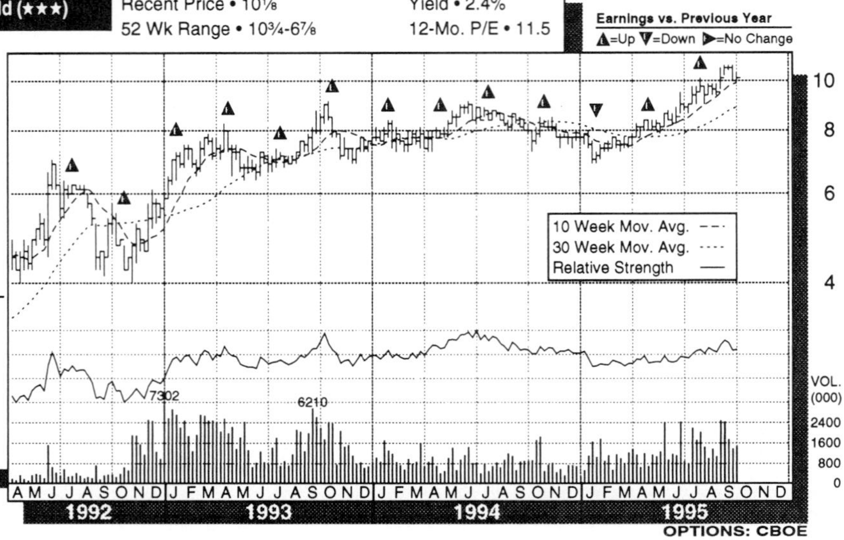

Overview - 02-OCT-95

Hibernia's market reach encompasses 70% of Louisiana's population. Growth has been fueled by an aggressive acquisiton program combined with an operating focus on businesses in which HIB enjoys competitive advantages. In the six months ended June 30, 1995, net income rose 26%, year to year. Results were enhanced by the recognition of deferred tax benefits, gains on sales of the student loan portfolio and the municipal bond administration business, and lower noninterest expenses. At June 30, 1995, loans, led by the commercial and consumer segments, were 19% higher than a year earlier, while nonperforming assets were 55% lower. Future earnings will be driven by above average loan growth as the local economy gathers momentum in the wake of a shakeout in the gaming industry.

Valuation - 02-OCT-95

Following a flat 1994, shares of HIB rebounded in the first half of 1995, but continued to lag the bank indices and the broader market. While earnings growth was strong in the first half of 1995, we expect a decline in 1996 as the bank consolidates its recent mergers. Currently trading at almost 12 times our 1996 estimate, and 1.8 times book value, the shares appear fairly valued. Given HIB's improving fundamentals and its market penetration, the company is well positioned for the longer term.

Key Stock Statistics

S&P EPS Est. 1995	1.03	Tang. Bk. Value/Share	5.51
P/E on S&P Est. 1995	9.8	Beta	0.90
S&P EPS Est. 1996	0.85	Shareholders	12,800
Dividend Rate/Share	0.24	Market cap. (B)	$ 1.2
Shs. outstg. (M)	119.3	Inst. holdings	28%
Avg. daily vol. (M)	0.367	Insider holdings	NA

Value of $10,000 invested 5 years ago: $ 5,770

Fiscal Year Ending Dec. 31

	1995	% Change	1994	% Change	1993	% Change
Revenues (Million $)						
1Q	140.9	18%	119.1	29%	92.27	-33%
2Q	148.9	21%	122.6	31%	93.44	-24%
3Q	—	—	126.8	40%	90.31	-1%
4Q	—	—	127.7	40%	90.93	NM
Yr.	—	—	496.2	35%	367.0	-17%
Income (Million $)						
1Q	26.36	16%	22.78	122%	10.28	NM
2Q	28.81	46%	19.68	71%	11.52	NM
3Q	—	—	25.72	111%	12.21	NM
4Q	—	—	16.48	18%	13.94	NM
Yr.	—	—	84.65	77%	47.95	NM
Earnings Per Share ($)						
1Q	0.24	14%	0.21	75%	0.12	NM
2Q	0.26	44%	0.18	29%	0.14	NM
3Q	E0.26	8%	0.24	60%	0.15	NM
4Q	E0.27	80%	0.15	-12%	0.17	NM
Yr.	E1.03	32%	0.78	34%	0.58	NM

Next earnings report expected: mid October

Hibernia Corp.

Business Summary - 01-OCT-95

Hibernia Corp. is the holding company for Hibernia National Bank, Louisiana's largest statewide bank. At September 7, 1995, Hibernia National had 160 banking locations serving 25 parishes and 60 cities, representing more than 70% of the state's population. In terms of deposit market share, Hibernia National is one of the top three banks in 19 of the parishes it serves. Gross loans outstanding of $3.37 billion at December 31, 1994, and $2.94 billion at December 31, 1993, were divided as follows:

	1994	1993
Consumer	26.1%	22.3%
Residential mortgage	18.1%	19.0%
Commercial and industrial	18.0%	18.6%
Commercial real estate	14.1%	14.7%
Services	8.5%	9.0%
Health care	6.3%	7.3%
Transportation, utilities and communications	3.3%	3.8%
Other commercial	2.9%	3.0%
Energy-related	2.7%	2.3%

At 1994 year end, the reserve for possible loan losses was $148.6 million (4.40% of gross loans), compared with $172.5 million (5.86%) a year earlier. Net loan chargeoffs during 1994 were $6.7 million (0.22% of average loans), versus $23.6 million (0.83%) the year before. Nonperforming assets totaled $34.9 million at 1994 year end (1.03% of loans and foreclosed assets), down from $103.9 million (3.49%) at 1993 year end.

Average deposits of $5.38 billion in 1994 were divided: 18% demand, 11% NOW, 20% money market, 6% savings, 30% time, 12% public fund time, and 3% time over $100,000. The average yield on interest-earning assets in 1994 was 7.20% (7.14% in 1993), while the average rate paid on interest-bearing liabilities was 3.37% (3.11%), for a net spread of 3.83% (4.03%).

Important Developments

Sep. '95—HIB agreed to acquire Bunkie Bancshares, Inc., parent of Bunkie Bank & Trust Co. Bunkie has $109 million in assets and three offices. The transaction, which should close by year end, will be paid for by HIB through the issuance of 1,874,760 of its common shares to Bunkie shareholders.

Jun. '95—The company agreed to acquire FNB Bancshares, Inc., parent of First National Bank of Lake Providence in northeast Louisiana. FNB has $54 million in assets and two offices. As payment for the transaction, HIB will issue 889,640 shares of common stock to FNB shareholders. The transaction is expected to be completed by year end.

Capitalization

Long Term Debt: $4,700,000 (6/95).

Per Share Data ($)

(Year Ended Dec. 31)

	1994	1993	1992	1991	1990	1989
Tangible Bk. Val.	4.88	4.65	3.86	5.09	13.16	12.12
Earnings	0.78	0.58	-0.27	-5.12	-0.40	2.30
Dividends	0.19	0.03	Nil	0.15	0.90	0.91
Payout Ratio	24%	5%	Nil	NM	NM	39%
Prices - High	9⅛	9⅛	7	8¼	22⅞	26
- Low	7¼	5⅞	2½	2	5⅞	17⅜
P/E Ratio - High	12	16	NM	NM	NM	11
- Low	9	10	NM	NM	NM	8

Income Statement Analysis (Million $)

	1994	%Chg	1993	%Chg	1992	%Chg	1991
Net Int. Inc.	260	33%	196	NM	197	-16%	235
Tax Equiv. Adj.	4.6	14%	4.0	-33%	6.0	-50%	12.0
Non Int. Inc.	85.7	28%	67.0	-3%	69.0	-24%	91.0
Loan Loss Prov.	-17.2	NM	6.0	-91%	66.0	-63%	178
% Exp/Op Revs.	77%	—	82%	—	83%	—	91%
Pretax Inc.	88.0	77%	49.6	NM	-8.0	NM	-142
Eff. Tax Rate	3.76%	—	3.40%	—	Nil	—	NM
Net Inc.	84.7	76%	48.0	NM	-8.0	NM	-143
% Net Int. Marg.	4.55%	—	4.60%	—	4.38%	—	3.99%

Balance Sheet & Other Fin. Data (Million $)

	1994	1993	1992	1991	1990	1989
Earning Assets:						
Money Mkt.	186	220	578	290	122	15.0
Inv. Securities	2,274	1,921	1,450	1,225	1,299	1,263
Com'l Loans	NA	532	685	1,028	1,302	1,542
Other Loans	3,376	1,633	1,675	2,774	3,909	3,213
Total Assets	6,336	4,796	4,734	6,018	7,358	6,699
Demand Deposits	1,063	813	760	829	1,060	869
Time Deposits	4,443	3,273	3,277	4,473	5,430	5,001
LT Debt	5.7	Nil	8.0	8.0	104	55.0
Common Eqty.	557	429	369	199	367	393

Ratio Analysis

	1994	1993	1992	1991	1990	1989
% Ret. on Assets	1.4	1.0	NM	NM	NM	1.0
% Ret. on Equity	15.6	11.0	NM	NM	NM	17.0
% Loan Loss Resv.	4.4	6.8	7.8	5.6	3.0	1.4
% Loans/Deposits	61.3	57.0	58.5	70.6	79.6	80.9
% Equity to Assets	8.7	8.4	4.2	4.1	5.2	5.8

Dividend Data —Dividends were initiated in 1935, omitted in 1991 and resumed in 1993. A dividend reinvestment plan is available.

Amt. of Div. $	Date Decl.	Ex-Div. Date	Stock of Record	Payment Date
0.060	Oct. 25	Oct. 31	Nov. 04	Nov. 22 '94
0.060	Jan. 24	Jan. 30	Feb. 03	Feb. 22 '95
0.060	Apr. 18	Apr. 24	Apr. 28	May. 23 '95
0.060	Jul. 18	Jul. 26	Jul. 28	Aug. 22 '95

Data as orig. reptd.; bef. results of disc opers. and/or spec. items. Per share data adj. for stk. divs. as of ex-div. date. E-Estimated. NA-Not Available. NM-Not Meaningful. NR-Not Ranked.

Office—313 Carondelet St., New Orleans. LA 70130. **Tel**—(504) 533-5333. **Chrmn**—R. H. Boh. **Pres & CEO**—S. A. Hansel. **EVP-Treas**—R. W. Close. **Secy**—P. C. Meringer. **Investor Contact**—Linda M. Meche (800-245-4388). **Dirs**—W. J. Amoss Jr., R. H. Boh, J. H. Boydstun, J. T. Brown, E. R. Campbell, B. H. Duncan, R. W. Freeman Jr., R. L. Goodwin, S. A. Hensel, D. H. Hearin, R. T. Holleman, E. R. King, H. J. Kelly, J. P. Laborde, S. W. Lassen, D. J. Nalty, R. T. Ratcliff, D. Shackelford, J. H. Stone, V. E. Weinmann, E. L. Williamson, R. E. Zetzmann. **Transfer Agent & Registrar**—Chemical Bank, NYC. **Incorporated** in Louisiana in 1972; bank chartered under National Banking Act in 1933. **Empl**-3,261. **S&P Analyst:** Thomas C. Ferguson

STANDARD & POOR'S

STOCK REPORTS

Home Shopping Network

NYSE Symbol **HSN**
In S&P MidCap 400

18-JUL-95 **Industry:** Retail Stores

Summary: Home Shopping Network sells consumer products over televised programs. Liberty Media Corp. has a 71% voting stake in HSN.

S&P Opinion: Hold (★★★) Recent Price • 8⅞ 52 Wk Range • 13-6½ Yield • Nil 12-Mo. P/E • NM

Quantitative Evaluations
Outlook
(1 Lowest—5 Highest)
• **5+**
Fair Value
• **9⅞**
Risk
• **Average**
Earn./Div. Rank
• **B-**

Technical Eval.
• **Bullish** since 5/94
Rel. Strength Rank
(1 Lowest—99 Highest)
• **71**
Insider Activity
• **Neutral**

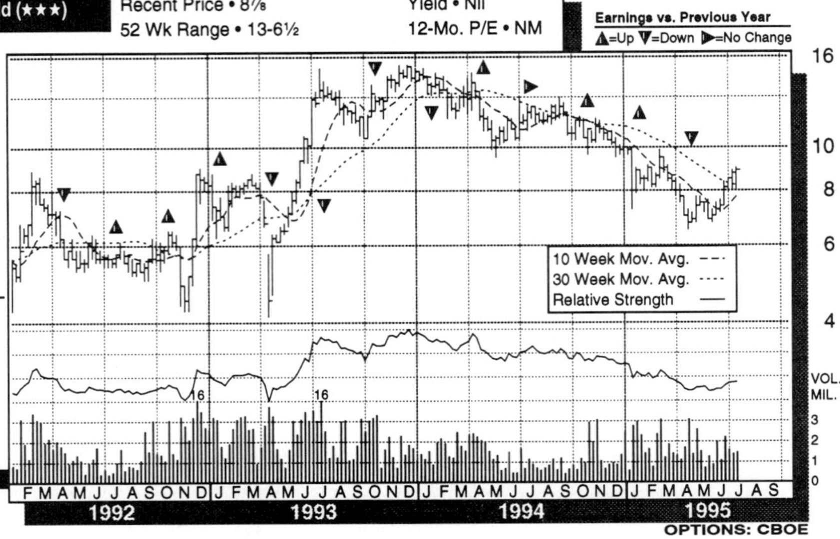

OPTIONS: CBOE

Overview - 18-JUL-95

Sales for 1995 should remain about level with the preceding year, reflecting weaker consumer spending. Gross margins will narrow as the company shifts to a new merchandise strategy; heavy markdowns will be taken on older merchandise to be replaced by higher quality, branded goods. Selling and marketing expense will rise as a percentage of sales, reflecting weak sales and expenses related to new programming and marketing strategies. HSN has formed two joint ventures. One will produce and air infomercials worldwide, while the other will test a new shopping program in conjunction with another cable programmer. The company is repurchasing its shares under an authorization to buy up to $75 million of common stock. A merger with another company remains possible.

Valuation - 18-JUL-95

Despite large losses in the first half of 1995, the shares remain well above their 1995 low. We believe that the possibility of a buyout in the consolidating home shopping industry is buoying the shares. HSN's new management is attempting to upgrade the company's merchandise and programing to improve its image with television viewers. Although we anticipate a return to profitability, with consumer spending for apparel weak and the country vastly overstored, HSN may have difficulty in putting earnings on a growth track.

Key Stock Statistics

S&P EPS Est. 1995	0.05	Tang. Bk. Value/Share	1.94
P/E on S&P Est. 1995	NM	Beta	1.45
S&P EPS Est. 1996	0.25	Shareholders	8,700
Dividend Rate/Share	Nil	Market cap. (B)	$0.804
Shs. outstg. (M)	90.6	Inst. holdings	44%
Avg. daily vol. (M)	0.338	Insider holdings	NA

Value of $10,000 invested 5 years ago: $ 12,241

Fiscal Year Ending Dec. 31

	1995	% Change	1994	% Change	1993	% Change
Revenues (Million $)						
1Q	243.6	-11%	274.0	15%	239.0	-13%
2Q	246.7	-10%	274.0	10%	250.0	-3%
3Q	—	—	276.6	6%	260.0	NM
4Q	—	—	301.7	2%	296.0	8%
Yr.	—	—	1,127	8%	1,047	-2%
Income (Million $)						
1Q	-8.80	NM	6.65	NM	-16.58	NM
2Q	-9.74	NM	1.91	-5%	2.00	-75%
3Q	—	—	7.35	NM	1.12	-88%
4Q	—	—	1.79	NM	-1.68	NM
Yr.	—	—	17.70	NM	-15.54	NM
Earnings Per Share ($)						
1Q	-0.10	NM	0.07	NM	-0.19	NM
2Q	-0.11	NM	0.02	NM	0.02	-71%
3Q	E0.05	—	0.08	NM	0.01	-88%
4Q	E0.11	—	0.02	NM	-0.02	NM
Yr.	E0.05	—	0.19	NM	-0.18	—

Next earnings report expected: mid October

Home Shopping Network

Business Summary - 18-JUL-95

Home Shopping Network (HSN) is a holding company whose subsidiaries are involved in direct marketing activities that include electronic retail sales, and catalog and mail order sales.

The principal operating subsidiary, Home Shopping Club Inc. (HSC), sells consumer products by means of live, customer-interactive, televised sales programs (primarily Home Shopping Club). The sales programs use the spontaneity of live television, viewer participation, club membership and quality products at bargain prices to attract viewers and promote sales. HSC produces three separate retail sales programming networks: HSN 1, which is carried by cable systems throughout the U.S.; HSN 2, carried primarily by TV broadcast stations owned by or affiliated with HSC as well as by cable systems that retransmit the broadcast TV signal of one of the stations carrying HSN 2; and HSN Spree, which is carried by both cable systems and broadcast TV systems on either a full- or part-time basis and provides system operators and broadcasters with income-producing programming during portions of the day when programming may otherwise not be scheduled. As of December 31, 1994, 24.8 million U.S. homes were able to receive HSN 1, 23.1 million could view HSN 2, and HSN Spree was being carried by 116 TV broadcast stations.

The company spun off its Silver King Communications subsidiary to shareholders in December 1992. Silver King owns 12 UHF television stations that primarily broadcast HSN programming.

Important Developments

Jul. '95—HSN said it made significant progress in the past quarter in strengthening its merchandise, programming and internal structure. The company's new merchandising strategy includes offering greater product quality and variety, stronger private label lines, more branded goods, improved product sourcing, and better programming, with regularly scheduled themed shows and better on-air presentations. HSN has been investing in long-term carriage agreements and new marketing and merchandising strategies that, while putting pressure on short-term earnings, should have significant positive impact in the future.

Capitalization

Long Term Debt: $77,365,000 (6/95).
Cl. B Common Stock: 20,000,000 shs. ($0.01 par); 10 votes ea.; conv. sh.-for-sh. into com.; 100% owned by Liberty Media Corp.
Options: To buy 4,843,000 com. shs. at $3.25 to $14.75 each.

Per Share Data ($) (Year Ended Dec. 31)

	1994	1993	1992	1991	1990	1989
Tangible Bk. Val.	2.22	2.07	1.94	0.63	0.60	0.08
Cash Flow	0.49	0.07	0.78	0.22	0.63	0.02
Earnings	0.19	-0.18	0.42	-0.11	0.35	-0.25
Dividends	Nil	Nil	Nil	Nil	Nil	Nil
Payout Ratio	Nil	Nil	Nil	Nil	Nil	Nil
Prices - High	15⅛	15⅜	9	7⅝	9¼	7⅝
- Low	9½	4⅛	4¼	3½	2⅞	3
P/E Ratio - High	80	NM	21	10	26	NM
- Low	50	NM	10	10	8	NM

Income Statement Analysis (Million $)

	1994	%Chg	1993	%Chg	1992	%Chg	1991
Revs.	1,127	8%	1,047	-5%	1,098	2%	1,079
Oper. Inc.	56.0	NM	15.0	-87%	115	22%	94.0
Depr.	29.1	33%	21.9	-33%	32.7	12%	29.1
Int. Exp.	5.5	-50%	10.9	-52%	22.6	-5%	23.8
Pretax Inc.	30.5	NM	-19.6	NM	64.5	NM	6.1
Eff. Tax Rate	42%	—	NM	—	42%	—	257%
Net Inc.	17.7	NM	-15.5	NM	37.4	NM	-9.6

Balance Sheet & Other Fin. Data (Million $)

	1994	1993	1992	1991	1990	1989
Cash	33.6	35.6	53.5	61.6	58.6	67.6
Curr. Assets	229	217	202	229	230	210
Total Assets	446	501	520	565	556	534
Curr. Liab.	206	209	155	176	132	94.0
LT Debt	27.0	87.0	173	205	225	285
Common Eqty.	206	197	170	162	177	140
Total Cap.	241	292	365	389	424	440
Cap. Exp.	19.0	18.0	36.0	53.0	35.0	30.0
Cash Flow	46.8	6.4	70.1	19.5	60.5	1.6

Ratio Analysis

	1994	1993	1992	1991	1990	1989
Curr. Ratio	1.1	1.0	1.3	1.3	1.7	2.2
% LT Debt of Cap.	11.4	29.8	47.4	52.7	53.1	64.8
% Net Inc.of Revs.	1.6	NM	3.4	NM	3.2	NM
% Ret. on Assets	3.7	NM	6.9	NM	6.0	NM
% Ret. on Equity	8.8	NM	22.4	NM	20.5	NM

Dividend Data (No cash dividends have been paid, and HSN does not expect to pay dividends for the foreseeable future.)

Data as orig. reptd.; bef. results of disc. opers. and/or spec. items. Per share data adj. for stk. divs. as of ex-div. date. E-Estimated. NA-Not Available. NM-Not Meaningful. NR-Not Ranked.

Office—2501 118th Ave. North, St. Petersburg, FL 33716-1900. **Tel**—(813) 572-8585. **Pres & CEO**—G. Hogan. **COO**—D. F. Dyer. **SVP & Treas**—K. J. McKeon. **Dirs**—R. R. Bennett, J.M. Draper, D. F. Dyer, J. A. Forstmann, L. J. Hindery, G. F. Hogan, G. C. McNamee. **Transfer Agent & Registrar**—Bank of New York, NYC. **Incorporated** in Florida in 1985; reincorporated in Delaware in 1986. **Empl**-4,383. **S&P Analyst:** Karen J. Sack, CFA

STANDARD & POOR'S

STOCK REPORTS

HON INDUSTRIES

NASDAQ Symbol **HONI**
In S&P MidCap 400

24-JUL-95

Industry: Office Equipment

Summary: This major manufacturer of wood and metal office furniture also makes fireplaces, woodburning stoves and accessories.

Quantitative Evaluations

Outlook
(1 Lowest—5 Highest)
• **2+**

Fair Value
• **25⅝**

Risk
• **Average**

Earn./Div. Rank
• **A-**

Technical Eval.
• **Bearish** since 3/95

Rel. Strength Rank
(1 Lowest—99 Highest)
• **11**

Insider Activity
• **NA**

Recent Price • 25¾
52 Wk Range • 30½-23
Yield • 1.9%
12-Mo. P/E • 14.9

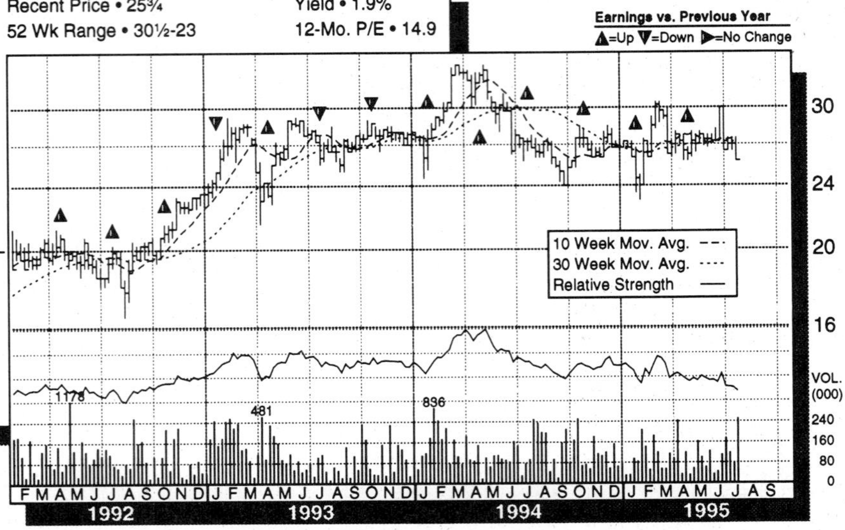

Business Profile - 20-JUL-95

HON's strategy is to accelerate growth via acquisitions in one or more of its three basic market segments for office furniture, including higher-priced furniture for larger customers, lower-priced offerings for retailers, and the middle market catering to small to midsize businesses. Management's long-term strategy of doubling earnings every five years requires a 15% average annual growth rate. The company has repurchased over 14.8 million shares of its common stock over the past 10 years.

Operational Review - 20-JUL-95

The company attributed the decline in its 1995 second quarter results to an aggressive marketing strategy and one-time inventory adjustments by a few major customers during the period. HON believes that despite the disappointing second quarter, it remains on course to meet its financial goals for 1995. The company also said it has nearly 250,000 square feet of manufacturing, warehousing, and distribution space under construction to accommodate anticipated continued sales growth.

Stock Performance - 21-JUL-95

In the past 30 trading days, HONI's shares have declined 6%, compared to a 5% rise in the S&P 500. Average trading volume for the past five days was 66,300 shares, compared with the 40-day moving average of 26,287 shares.

Key Stock Statistics

Dividend Rate/Share	0.48	Shareholders	5,600
Shs. outstg. (M)	30.7	Market cap. (B)	$0.789
Avg. daily vol. (M)	0.038	Inst. holdings	28%
Tang. Bk. Value/Share	6.62	Insider holdings	NA
Beta	0.39		

Value of $10,000 invested 5 years ago: $ 14,993

Fiscal Year Ending Dec. 31

	1995	% Change	1994	% Change	1993	% Change
Revenues (Million $)						
1Q	216.5	8%	200.7	8%	186.1	17%
2Q	206.6	7%	193.1	9%	177.5	8%
3Q	—	—	222.1	9%	203.1	4%
4Q	—	—	230.1	8%	213.6	14%
Yr.	—	—	846.0	8%	780.3	10%
Income (Million $)						
1Q	12.58	8%	11.63	43%	8.13	13%
2Q	7.73	-16%	9.22	12%	8.22	-6%
3Q	—	—	15.54	34%	11.61	-5%
4Q	—	—	18.00	8%	16.68	59%
Yr.	—	—	54.39	22%	44.64	15%
Earnings Per Share ($)						
1Q	0.41	11%	0.37	48%	0.25	14%
2Q	0.25	-17%	0.30	20%	0.25	-4%
3Q	—	—	0.49	36%	0.36	-5%
4Q	—	—	0.58	9%	0.53	66%
Yr.	—	—	1.74	25%	1.39	18%

Next earnings report expected: mid October

HON INDUSTRIES

Business Summary - 24-JUL-95

The principal business of HON INDUSTRIES Inc. is the production of office furniture and products. The company also manufactures prefabricated fireplaces, woodburning stoves and accessories.

In the area of office furniture and products, the company manufactures, through its HON Co. division and its BPI Inc., Holga Inc., Gunlocke Co. and Chandler Attwood Ltd. subsidiaries, a broad line of metal and wood office furniture. Products include file cabinets, desks, chairs, storage cabinets, combination cabinets, tables, bookcases, machine stands, credenzas, reception area furniture, freestanding office partitions, panel systems, wall systems, office coordinates and stools. These products are available in both contemporary and conventional styles and are priced to sell in all price ranges. HON Co. also makes commercial file cabinets and a limited line of file cabinets designed principally for the home market. Also included in this product area is Ring King Visibles, which manufactures personal computer and workstation accessories, and also markets a line of rubber bands and general office products under the Plymouth brand name. During 1993, HON formed a new operation to manufacture new assembly hardware and casegoods furniture for the growing used systems furniture market.

Heatilator Inc. makes factory-built fireplaces, fireplace inserts, freestanding stoves and accessories serving the homebuilding products industry. Heatilator was expanded in late 1993 through the $1.2 million acquisition of the Dovre brand of cast-iron fireplaces and wood stoves (for North and South America) from Dovre Industries, NV. Heatilator's products accounted for less than 10% of total revenues in the past three years.

HON Export Ltd. markets selected products from all company operating units. Its selling efforts are conducted outside of the U.S. and Canada.

Office furniture is marketed throughout the U.S. through more than 5,000 stationery and office furniture retailers and 30 wholesalers/distributors. HON also makes products for sale by mass-market retailers and office product specialists, and several operating companies sell directly to the U.S. government. Fireplace and stove products are sold through 1,600 dealers and 200 distributors. HON Export Ltd. sales are made through more than 90 office furniture dealers and 200 distributors.

The largest customer in 1994 was United Stationers, accounting for 10% of revenues (13% in 1993).

Important Developments

Jul. '95—HON attributed the decline in 1995's second quarter results to an aggressive marketing strategy and inventory adjustments by a few major customers.

Capitalization

Long Term Liabs.: $54,810,000 (4/1/95), incl. $8,454,000 of lease obligs.

Per Share Data ($) (Year Ended Dec. 31)

	1994	1993	1992	1991	1990	1989
Tangible Bk. Val.	6.35	5.67	5.04	4.64	4.06	3.76
Cash Flow	2.35	1.89	1.62	1.43	1.69	1.14
Earnings	1.74	1.39	1.18	1.02	1.30	0.79
Dividends	0.44	0.40	0.37	0.36	0.30	0.24
Payout Ratio	25%	29%	31%	35%	23%	30%
Prices - High	34	29¼	23½	20½	23	19⅞
- Low	24	21½	16½	13¼	13½	8¾
P/E Ratio - High	20	21	20	20	18	25
- Low	14	15	14	13	10	11

Income Statement Analysis (Million $)

	1994	%Chg	1993	%Chg	1992	%Chg	1991
Revs.	846	8%	780	10%	707	16%	608
Oper. Inc.	106	21%	87.3	14%	76.8	13%	67.8
Depr.	19.0	19%	15.9	10%	14.5	9%	13.3
Int. Exp.	3.3	4%	3.1	-9%	3.4	-3%	3.5
Pretax Inc.	86.3	22%	70.9	15%	61.9	17%	52.7
Eff. Tax Rate	37%	—	37%	—	38%	—	38%
Net Inc.	54.4	22%	44.6	15%	38.7	18%	32.9

Balance Sheet & Other Fin. Data (Million $)

	1994	1993	1992	1991	1990	1989
Cash	30.7	44.4	45.9	34.6	32.4	37.0
Curr. Assets	189	188	171	151	147	163
Total Assets	373	352	323	281	277	284
Curr. Liab.	111	111	92.0	82.0	93.0	106
LT Debt	54.7	51.1	54.2	35.7	39.6	38.3
Common Eqty.	195	180	163	150	132	128
Total Cap.	261	242	231	199	184	178
Cap. Exp.	35.0	28.9	36.1	15.2	25.6	32.2
Cash Flow	73.4	60.5	53.2	46.2	55.9	39.6

Ratio Analysis

	1994	1993	1992	1991	1990	1989
Curr. Ratio	1.7	1.7	1.9	1.8	1.6	1.5
% LT Debt of Cap.	20.9	21.2	23.5	18.0	21.6	21.5
% Net Inc.of Revs.	6.4	5.7	5.5	5.4	6.5	4.6
% Ret. on Assets	15.2	13.4	12.8	11.8	15.8	10.2
% Ret. on Equity	29.5	26.3	24.7	23.5	34.1	20.9

Dividend Data (Cash has been paid each year since 1955.)

Amt. of Div. $	Date Decl.	Ex-Div. Date	Stock of Record	Payment Date
0.110	Aug. 08	Aug. 12	Aug. 18	Sep. 01 '94
0.110	Nov. 15	Nov. 18	Nov. 25	Dec. 01 '94
0.120	Feb. 13	Feb. 16	Feb. 23	Mar. 01 '95
0.120	May. 08	May. 12	May. 18	Jun. 01 '95

Data as orig. reptd.; bef. results of disc. opers. and/or spec. items. Per share data adj. for stk. divs. as of ex-div. date. E-Estimated. NA-Not Available. NM-Not Meaningful. NR-Not Ranked.

Office—414 East Third St., P.O. Box 1109, Muscatine, IA 52761-7109. **Tel**—(319) 264-7400. **Chrmn**—S. M. Howe. **Vice Chrmn**—R. H. Stanley. **Pres & CEO**—J. D. Michaels. **VP & CFO**—D. C. Stuebe. **Treas**—W. F. Snydacker. **VP & Secy**—A. M. Harvey, Jr. **Dirs**—R. C. Cox, W. J. Farrell, S. M. Howe, L. Liu, J. D. Michaels, C. C. Michalski, M. S. Plunkett, H. J. Schmidt, R. H. Stanley, J. K. Ver Hagen, L. R. Waxlax. **Transfer Agent**—Co.'s office. **Incorporated** in Iowa in 1944. **Empl-**6,131. **S&P Analyst:** Philip D. Wohl

Horizon/CMS Healthcare

NYSE Symbol HHC Options on ASE, CBOE (Jan-Apr-Jul-Oct) In S&P MidCap 400

Price	Range	P-E Ratio	Dividend	Yield	S&P Ranking	Beta
Oct. 2'95	1995					
22	28¼–16⅝	NM	None	None	B	1.16

Summary

This company (formerly Horizon Healthcare) operates long-term care centers and provides a broad range of health care services, including nursing, rehabilitation and other therapies, institutional pharmacy services, specialty care to Alzheimer's patients, and subacute care. The mid-1995 acquisition of Continental Medical Systems should fuel revenue growth and margin expansion.

Current Outlook

Share earnings for 1995-6 are estimated at $1.60 (before charges of $0.92), with a gain to $1.95 seen for 1996-7.

The initiation of cash dividends is unlikely.

The acquisition of Continental Medical Systems (CMS), which is expected to be accretive to earnings in 1995-6, its first full year, is a sound strategic acquisition for the company, and should help it solidify its position as the leading U.S. provider of post-acute healthcare. HHC offers a full array of cost-effective long-term care and specialized ancillary services, which should prove valuable as the company increases its presence in the managed care market. Margin expansion should be fueled by marketing specialty services in rehabilitation clinics, and will allow the company to translate top-line growth into strong earnings gains.

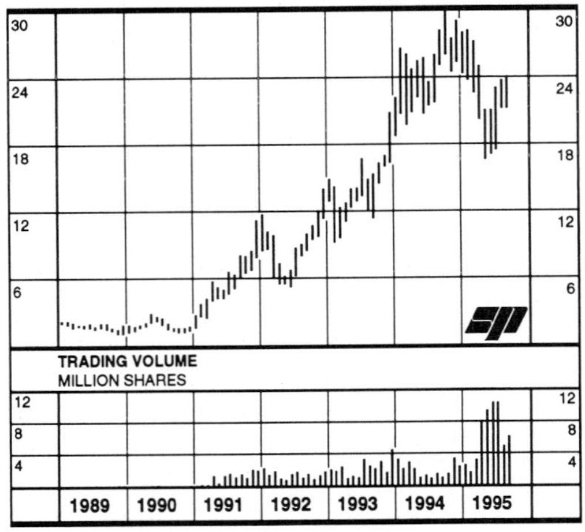

Operating Revenues (Million $)

Quarter:	1995–96	1994–95	1993–94	1992–93
Aug.	431.4	137.7	75.0	46.7
Nov.		155.2	78.9	52.7
Feb.		166.5	88.6	60.9
May		179.6	132.6	71.9
		639.1	375.1	232.2

Revenues in the first quarter of 1995-6 rose 13%, year to year. Operating margins widened, but results were penalized by charges of $63.5 million ($0.92 a share) related to the CMS acquisition and restructuring; a net loss of $28.9 million ($0.56 a share) replaced net income of $12.1 million ($0.27).

Common Share Earnings ($)

Quarter:	1995–96	1994–95	1993–94	1992–93
Aug.	d0.56	0.28	0.24	0.13
Nov.	E0.38	0.29	0.26	0.16
Feb.	E0.42	0.31	0.24	0.17
May	E0.44	0.28	0.25	0.20
	E0.68	1.16	d0.66	0.66

Important Developments

Aug. '95— The company was notified by the SEC that its planned disposition of eight long-term care facilities did not qualify for treatment as discontinued operations. As a result, a net charge of $7.1 million was recorded in the first quarter of 1995-6 for expected loss on the sale, and any operating profits or losses from the facilities will be included in earnings from continuing operations. In addition, EPS for 1994-5 were revised to $1.16, from $1.40.

Jul. '95— HHC acquired Continental Medical Systems Inc. (CMS), one of the largest U.S. providers of inpatient and outpatient medical rehabilitative services, in exchange for 21 million common shares valued at about $394 million. At June 30, 1995, CMS operated 37 freestanding comprehensive medical rehabilitation hospitals in 15 states, with a total of 2,016 licensed acute rehabilitation beds.

Next earnings report expected in late December.

Per Share Data ($)

Yr. End May 31	1995	[1]1994	1993	[1]1992	1991	1990	1989	1988
Tangible Bk. Val.	**11.33**	[3]10.23	[3]4.27	[3]3.60	[3]2.75	1.99	1.62	1.58
Cash Flow	**1.84**	1.35	0.89	0.63	0.44	0.32	d0.13	0.32
Earnings[2]	**1.16**	0.99	0.66	0.44	0.24	0.10	d0.28	0.13
Dividends	**Nil**	Nil	Nil	Nil	Nil	Nil	Nil	Nil
Payout Ratio	**Nil**	Nil	Nil	Nil	Nil	Nil	Nil	Nil
Calendar Years	**1994**	1993	1992	1991	1990	1989	1988	1987
Prices—High	**30**	20⅞	14	11¼	2⅞	2¼	3½	8
Low	**18¾**	9¼	5¼	1⅝	1¼	1⅛	2	2½
P/E Ratio—	**26–16**	21–9	21–8	26–4	12–5	23–11	NM	62–19

Data as orig. reptd. **1.** Refl. merger or acq. **2.** Bef. results of disc. ops. of -0.02 in 1988 & spec. items of +0.01 in 1991, +0.06 in 1990, +0.06 in 1988. **3.** Incl. intangibles. d-Deficit. E-Estimated. NM-Not Meaningful.

Income Data (Million $)

Year Ended May 31	Revs.	Oper. Inc.	% Oper. Inc. of Revs.	Cap. Exp.	Depr.	Int. Exp.	Net Bef. Taxes	Eff. Tax Rate	[2]Net Inc.	% Net Inc. of Revs.	Cash Flow
1995	**639**	**88.1**	**13.8**	**38.0**	**18.50**	**18.50**	**[4]51.20**	**39.0%**	**31.20**	**4.9**	**49.70**
[3]1994	375	39.0	10.4	124.0	5.99	6.24	[4]26.70	37.9%	16.60	4.4	22.60
[3]1993	232	18.8	8.1	51.1	2.67	4.25	11.80	34.3%	7.78	3.4	10.50
[3]1992	159	11.0	6.9	10.3	2.16	2.21	6.66	24.5%	5.03	3.2	7.18
1991	111	6.2	5.6	1.6	1.47	2.57	2.13	18.2%	1.74	1.6	3.21
1990	106	5.7	5.4	2.3	1.44	2.85	1.01	38.0%	0.63	0.6	2.07
1989	110	2.3	2.1	2.6	1.13	2.59	d1.67	NM	d1.67	NM	d0.54
[1]1988	82	5.0	6.0	58.9	1.15	2.56	1.26	37.5%	0.79	1.0	1.94

Balance Sheet Data (Million $)

May 31	Cash	Curr. Assets	Curr. Liab.	Curr. Ratio	Total Assets	% Ret. on Assets	Long Term Debt	Common Equity	Total Cap.	% LT Debt of Cap.	% Ret. on Equity
1995	**20.4**	**200.0**	**47.4**	**4.22**	**724**	**5.5**	**232.0**	**420.0**	**662.0**	**35.0**	**9.6**
1994	11.0	112.0	49.1	2.30	406	4.7	108.0	229.0	337.0	31.9	10.2
1993	5.9	44.0	24.7	1.80	150	6.1	75.5	48.3	124.0	60.6	17.5
1992	29.5	46.5	14.9	3.10	104	5.3	48.5	39.8	88.3	54.9	14.3
1991	1.2	15.9	11.4	1.40	56	3.0	23.8	20.0	43.8	54.3	8.8
1990	0.1	16.2	14.3	1.10	53	1.2	20.8	17.2	38.0	54.8	3.9
1989	0.1	18.8	18.3	1.00	58	NM	23.4	16.0	39.4	59.4	NM
1988	0.1	11.9	11.0	1.10	55	2.0	24.5	16.2	40.6	60.2	5.1

Data as orig. reptd. **1.** Excl. disc. ops. **2.** Bef. spec. items. **3.** Refl. merger or acq. **4.** Incl. equity in earns. of nonconsol. subs. d-Deficit. NM-Not Meaningful.

Business Summary

Horizon/CMS Healthcare (formerly Horizon Healthcare) is a leading provider of specialty health care services and long-term care, principally in the Midwest, Southwest and Northeast. It seeks to use its long-term or geriatric care and subacute facilities as platforms to provide a continuum of post-acute care more typically delivered in the acute care hospital setting. In 1994-5, long-term care services accounted for 53% of the total, specialty health care services for 45%, and other (management fees, interest income, rental income and other miscellaneous services) for 2%.

Following its July 1995 acquisition of Continental Medical Systems Inc. (CMS), the company was operating 37 acute rehabilitation hospitals and 125 long-term care centers with a total of 18,972 beds; provided subacute care through 25 specialty hospitals and specialty subacute care units; and offered outpatient rehabilitation services at over 130 locations. In addition, HHC provides contract therapy services in 31 states and institutional pharmacy services in 16 states.

Basic patient services provided in long-term care facilities include daily dietary services, recreational activities, social services, housekeeping and laundry services, pharmaceutical and medical supplies, and 24-hour-a-day access to registered nurses, licensed practical nurses and related services prescribed by the patient's physician. The company also provides specialty services and programs for patients with more complex health care needs, including rehabilitation therapies (occupational, speech and physical), Alzheimer's care, institutional pharmacy services, subacute care, medical laboratory services and non-invasive medical diagnostic testing services.

In 1994-5, 41% of revenues came from Medicaid patients, 20% from Medicare patients, and 39% from private pay and other sources.

Dividend Data

Cash dividends have never been paid.

Finances

In August 1995, the company began tender offers for all outstanding CMS 10.875% senior subordinated notes due 2002, at $1,090 per $1,000 principal amount, plus accrued interest; and all outstanding CMS 10.375% senior subordinated notes due 2003, at $1,092.50 per $1,000 principal amount, plus accrued interest. As a result, $127.1 million of the 10.875% notes (87.1%) and $107.6 million of the 10.375% notes (90.6%) were tendered.

In July 1995, HHC increased its available bank credit line to $485 million, from $250 million.

Capitalization

Long Term Debt: $205,290,000 (5/95), incl. $47,557,000 of cap. lease obligs.

Common Stock: 50,480,302 shs. ($0.001 par).

Shareholders: 2,658 of record (8/95).

Office—6001 Indian School Rd., N.E., Suite 530, Albuquerque, NM 87110. **Tel**—(505) 881-4961. **Chrmn, Pres & CEO**—N. M. Elliott. **SVP & CFO**—E. A. Schofield. **Dirs**—K.L. Belt, Jr., R.L. Carson, B.C. Cressey, N.M. Elliott, C.H. Gonzales, M.A. Jeffries, G.M. Martin, F.M. McCord, R. Noveck, Rocco A. Ortenzio, Robert A. Ortenzio, B.M. Portnoy, L.S. Zimmerman. **Transfer Agent & Registrar**—Chemical Mellon Shareholder Services, LA. **Incorporated** in Delaware in 1986. **Empl**—15,500.

 Robert M. Gold

STANDARD & POOR'S **Hospitality Franchise Systems**

STOCK REPORTS

NYSE Symbol **HFS**
In S&P MidCap 400

31-JUL-95 **Industry:** Hotels/Motels/Inns

Summary: HFS, the largest hotel franchisor in the world, licenses six brand names, including Days Inn, Ramada, Howard Johnson and Super 8, to independent hotel operators.

Quantitative Evaluations
Outlook (1 Lowest—5 Highest) • **NA**
Fair Value • **NA**
Risk • **High**
Earn./Div. Rank • **NR**

Technical Eval. • **Bullish** since 1/95
Rel. Strength Rank (1 Lowest—99 Highest) • **93**
Insider Activity • **NA**

Recent Price • 43⅜
52 Wk Range • 44⅛-20¾
Yield • Nil
12-Mo. P/E • 36.5

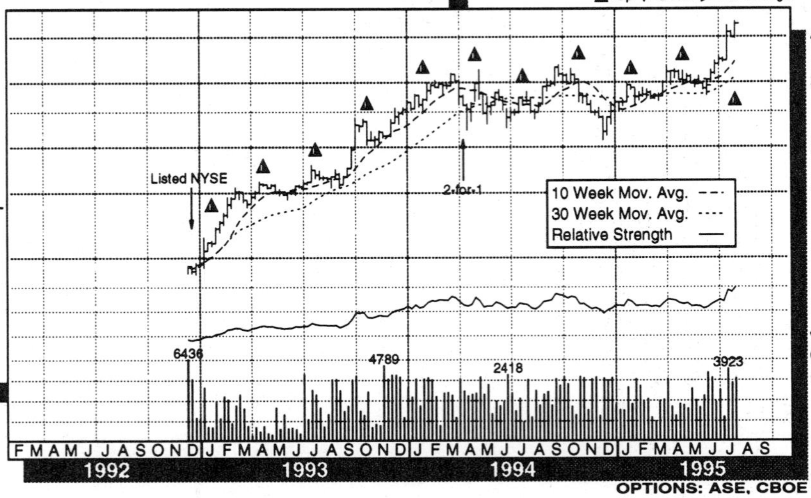

OPTIONS: ASE, CBOE

Business Profile - 31-JUL-95

This company's fixed cost structure provides for substantial operating leverage. Record revenues and earnings have been achieved for 11 consecutive quarters, and results should continue to benefit from new property openings and improving industry conditions. HFS recently agreed to purchase Century 21 Real Estate Corp. from Metropolitan Life Insurance Co., for about $200 million, plus up to $30 million in contingent payments.

Operational Review - 31-JUL-95

Higher revenues in the first half of 1995 reflected net room additions, higher occupancy rates, and increased average daily room rates. Expenses rose less rapidly, and earnings climbed strongly. Future results should benefit from continued favorable market conditions, room expansion, joint ventures, and preferred vendor arrangements.

Stock Performance - 28-JUL-95

In the past 30 trading days, HFS's shares have increased 37%, compared to a 4% rise in the S&P 500. Average trading volume for the past five days was 305,200 shares, compared with the 40-day moving average of 342,874 shares.

Key Stock Statistics

Dividend Rate/Share	Nil	Shareholders	NA
Shs. outstg. (M)	47.5	Market cap. (B)	$ 2.1
Avg. daily vol. (M)	0.363	Inst. holdings	94%
Tang. Bk. Value/Share	NM	Insider holdings	NA
Beta	NA		

Value of $10,000 invested 5 years ago: NA

Fiscal Year Ending Dec. 31

	1995	% Change	1994	% Change	1993	% Change
Revenues (Million $)						
1Q	74.15	15%	64.29	34%	47.94	24%
2Q	96.33	19%	81.04	23%	65.87	17%
3Q	—	—	95.02	16%	82.07	33%
4Q	—	—	72.21	18%	61.19	32%
Yr.	—	—	312.5	22%	257.1	26%
Income (Million $)						
1Q	12.06	22%	9.92	125%	4.41	104%
2Q	20.18	43%	14.10	45%	9.71	2%
3Q	—	—	18.60	43%	13.04	NM
4Q	—	—	10.87	52%	7.16	73%
Yr.	—	—	53.49	56%	34.32	73%
Earnings Per Share ($)						
1Q	0.24	20%	0.20	122%	0.09	NM
2Q	0.38	36%	0.28	40%	0.20	33%
3Q	—	—	0.37	42%	0.26	24%
4Q	—	—	0.22	57%	0.14	155%
Yr.	—	—	1.06	54%	0.69	50%

Next earnings report expected: late October

Hospitality Franchise Systems

Business Summary - 31-JUL-95

Hospitality Franchise Systems is the world's largest hotel franchisor, as measured by number of hotel rooms, with four nationally recognized brand names: Days Inn, Ramada (in the U.S.), Howard Johnson and Super 8. It also franchises Park Inn International hotels and Villager Lodge. The company licenses hotel operators to use its brand names, but does not itself own or operate hotels. Its system at the end of recent years (pro forma to reflect ownership of Super 8 in all periods) consisted of:

	1994	1993	1992
Days Inn:			
Hotels	1,586	1,441	1,330
Rooms	153,581	145,079	139,522
Ramada:			
Hotels	775	676	593
Rooms	116,472	106,896	96,878
Howard Johnson:			
Hotels	582	566	543
Rooms	63,283	62,558	60,173
Super 8:			
Hotels	1,220	1061	942
Rooms	74,344	64,715	57,638

At the end of 1994, the HFS franchise system consisted of 4,229 properties containing 416,285 rooms (3,783 properties and 383,931 rooms a year earlier). In 1994, the occupany rate was 58.3% and the average daily room rate was $43.99.

Based on number of rooms, Days Inn is the third largest individual lodging brand in the U.S.; it operates in the economy segment (average nightly room rates of less than $46). Ramada is the fourth largest lodging brand in the U.S., operating in the middle market segment (rates generally $46 to $70 per night). Howard Johnson, the ninth largest U.S. lodging brand, is a middle market hotel focusing on the leisure travel market. The Super 8 chain operates economy/limited service motels.

Important Developments

Jun. '95—The company agreed to purchase Century 21 Real Estate Corp. from Metropolitan Life Insurance Co., for about $200 million, plus up to $30 million in contingent payments. Irvine, Calif.-based Century 21, with more than 4,800 offices across the U.S., has revenues of about $130 million. Earlier, in May, HFS acquired Casino & Credit Services Inc., a provider of gambling patron information to the casino industry, in exchange for about 1.2 million common shares.

Capitalization

Long Term Debt: $352,000,000 (3/95).
Options: To purchase 7,893,951 shares at $5.74 to $26.81 ea.

Per Share Data ($)

(Year Ended Dec. 31)

	1994	1993	1992	1991	1990	1989
Tangible Bk. Val.	-7.86	-7.56	-4.60	-5.96	NA	NA
Cash Flow	1.53	1.08	0.77	0.15	NA	NA
Earnings	1.06	0.68	0.44	-0.19	NA	NA
Dividends	Nil	Nil	Nil	NA	NA	NA
Payout Ratio	Nil	Nil	Nil	NA	NA	NA
Prices - High	33½	26⅞	10⅛	NA	NA	NA
- Low	20¾	9⅜	8	NA	NA	NA
P/E Ratio - High	32	39	23	NA	NA	NA
- Low	20	14	18	NA	NA	NA

Income Statement Analysis (Million $)

	1994	%Chg	1993	%Chg	1992	%Chg	1991
Revs.	292	14%	257	27%	203	3%	197
Oper. Inc.	112	26%	88.6	38%	64.1	78%	36.0
Depr.	23.7	23%	19.2	29%	14.9	NM	14.8
Int. Exp.	18.7	-7%	20.2	-20%	25.1	-25%	33.5
Pretax Inc.	90.6	49%	60.7	111%	28.7	NM	-8.0
Eff. Tax Rate	41%	—	43%	—	31%	—	NM
Net Inc.	53.5	56%	34.3	72%	19.9	NM	-8.5

Balance Sheet & Other Fin. Data (Million $)

	1994	1993	1992	1991	1990	1989
Cash	6.0	16.9	25.1	NA	NA	NA
Curr. Assets	76.4	79.5	80.2	NA	NA	NA
Total Assets	774	736	545	530	NA	NA
Curr. Liab.	70.0	49.9	69.6	NA	NA	NA
LT Debt	347	348	236	245	NA	NA
Common Eqty.	281	267	227	211	NA	NA
Total Cap.	700	680	470	NA	NA	NA
Cap. Exp.	11.4	8.3	6.4	NA	NA	NA
Cash Flow	77.2	53.5	32.5	6.3	NA	NA

Ratio Analysis

	1994	1993	1992	1991	1990	1989
Curr. Ratio	1.1	1.6	1.2	NA	NA	NA
% LT Debt of Cap.	49.6	51.1	50.3	NA	NA	NA
% Net Inc.of Revs.	18.3	14.0	10.0	NM	NA	NA
% Ret. on Assets	6.9	5.3	4.2	NA	NA	NA
% Ret. on Equity	19.1	13.7	8.7	NA	NA	NA

Dividend Data (HFS plans to retain any earnings for development and expansion of its business and repayment of debt, and does not expect to pay cash dividends on the common stock for the foreseeable future. A two-for-one stock split was effected in April 1994. Shareholders of record November 14, 1994, received one common share of National Gaming Corp., a corporation formed to hold the company's casino development business, for every 10 HFS shares held.)

Amt. of Div. $	Date Decl.	Ex-Div. Date	Stock of Record	Payment Date
Stk	—	Nov. 29	Nov. 14	Nov. 28 '94

Data as orig. reptd.; bef. results of disc. opers. and/or spec. items. Per share data adj. for stk. divs. as of ex-div. date. E-Estimated. NA-Not Available. NM-Not Meaningful. NR-Not Ranked.

Office—339 Jefferson Rd., Parsippany, NJ 07054. **Tel**—(201) 428-9700. **Chrmn & CEO**—H. R. Silverman. **Pres & COO**—J. D. Snodgrass. **EVP & CFO**—S. P. Holmes. **Secy**—J. M. Murphy. **Investor Contact**—Michael Wargotz (201-952-8444). **Dirs**— J. E. Buckman, M. L. Edelman, S. P. Holmes, R. W. Pittman, L. Schutzman, H. R. Silverman, R. F. Smith, J. D. Snodgrass, R. J. Stone, Jr. **Transfer Agent & Registrar**—Mellon Securities Trust Co., Ridgefield Park, NJ. **Incorporated** in Delaware in 1990. **Empl**-2,100. **S&P Analyst:** Efraim Levy

Houghton Mifflin

NYSE Symbol **HTN**
In S&P MidCap 400

03-OCT-95 **Industry:** Publishing

Summary: This company, which derives the bulk of its revenues from the sale of elementary and secondary school textbooks, is also a major publisher of college, general and reference books.

S&P Opinion: Hold (★★★) | Recent Price • 46½ | 52 Wk Range • 54¾-39¾ | Yield • 2.1% | 12-Mo. P/E • 38.1

Quantitative Evaluations

Outlook
(1 Lowest—5 Highest)
• **5⁻**

Fair Value
• 55¾

Risk
• **Low**

Earn./Div. Rank
• A-

Technical Eval.
• **Bullish** since 8/95

Rel. Strength Rank
(1 Lowest—99 Highest)
• **14**

Insider Activity
• **NA**

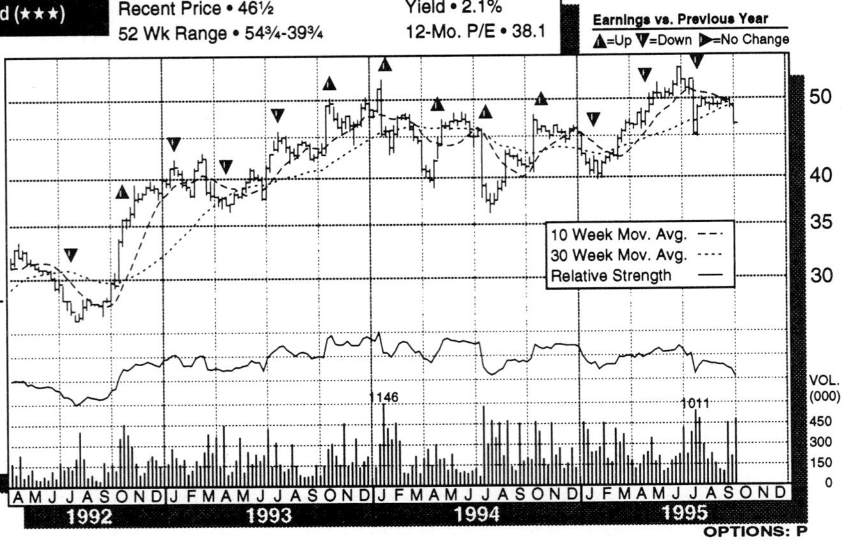

OPTIONS: P

Overview - 03-OCT-95

Revenues in 1996 will be boosted by the D. C. Heath acquisition, as well as a cyclical peak in school adoptions, and by gains in market share achieved by several new integrated multimedia programs. Aided by a slower increase in paper costs, improved efficiencies and the stronger sales, operating margins should improve. Heath's operating profits and cost savings will be more than countered by interest and amortization charges. Higher earnings are expected at INSO Corp., but HTN's equity ownership has been reduced to about 35.9%, from 40%. HTN has set an ambitious goal to become a $1 billion company by the year 2000, through acquisitions, introduction of new products and services, entry into new markets and leveraging of current franchises through line extensions and technology.

Valuation - 03-OCT-95

The shares were buffeted during the last week of September on news that HTN would acquire D. C. Heath and incur substantial fourth-quarter charges, aggregating roughly $3.35 a share. HTN's market performance is likely to improve in 1996 in reflection of accelerating earnings gains, even though Heath will not become a net contributor to profits until 1997. Long-term earnings and stock performance should reflect the company's strengthening position in secondary school publishing, which coincides with a cyclical upturn in secondary school enrollment, as well as favorable growth prospects stemming from new multimedia opportunities.

Key Stock Statistics

S&P EPS Est. 1995	-0.80	Tang. Bk. Value/Share	6.55
P/E on S&P Est. 1995	NM	Beta	0.90
S&P EPS Est. 1996	3.30	Shareholders	4,500
Dividend Rate/Share	0.96	Market cap. (B)	$0.662
Shs. outstg. (M)	14.5	Inst. holdings	74%
Avg. daily vol. (M)	0.082	Insider holdings	NA

Value of $10,000 invested 5 years ago: $ 17,057

Fiscal Year Ending Dec. 31

	1995	% Change	1994	% Change	1993	% Change
Revenues (Million $)						
1Q	50.51	2%	49.39	NM	49.72	-5%
2Q	104.7	-11%	117.1	-3%	121.2	-4%
3Q	—	—	230.3	10%	208.5	5%
4Q	—	—	86.24	3%	83.53	7%
Yr.	—	—	483.1	4%	463.0	2%
Income (Million $)						
1Q	-18.53	NM	3.21	NM	-14.93	NM
2Q	-5.10	NM	8.70	94%	4.48	-62%
3Q	—	—	47.57	15%	41.54	22%
4Q	—	—	-7.05	NM	0.28	NM
Yr.	—	—	52.43	67%	31.37	64%
Earnings Per Share ($)						
1Q	-1.34	NM	0.23	NM	-1.08	NM
2Q	-0.37	NM	0.63	97%	0.32	-61%
3Q	E4.20	22%	3.45	15%	3.00	22%
4Q	E-3.29	NM	-0.51	NM	0.02	NM
Yr.	E-0.80	NM	3.79	67%	2.27	68%

Next earnings report expected: mid October

Houghton Mifflin

Business Summary - 03-OCT-95

Houghton Mifflin Company is a leading publisher. Contributions to sales in recent years were:

	1994	1993
Textbooks & other educational materials	63%	58%
College publishing	17%	19%
General & reference publishing	20%	23%

Elementary and high-school texts are sold to school systems, generally on a contract basis for a period of three to six years, with the bulk of deliveries made in the first few years. The company's major textbook representation is in reading and mathematics. Social studies and foreign language texts are also important. The school division is actively developing integrated multimedia programs in all of its subject areas. The March 1994 purchase of McDougal, Littell & Co. strengthened HTN's presence in secondary-school publishing, particularly in economics and literature. The acquisition also provided a strong sales force for the secondary market. College books are sold through school or private book stores. Riverside Publishing Co. provides educational and psychological test and measurement materials to schools and colleges, in addition to providing guidance information and products.

The trade and reference division publishes all types of books for the general reading public. Reference materials are published for six markets: trade, international, college, school, office products and electronic. The software division was spun off into a publicly owned company, INSO Corporation, in March 1994, with HTN retaining a 40% interest. Software language-aid products are licensed to word processing equipment vendors worldwide.

Important Developments

Sep. '95—HTN agreed to purchase D. C. Heath & Co., a textbook publisher, from Raytheon Co. for $455 million in cash. A leading publisher of modern language, science, language arts, social studies and mathematics textbooks, Heath had revenues of $180 million in 1994. As a result of the transaction, which is expected to close in the fourth quarter, HTN will take a one-time charge of about $70 million for acquisition and integration-related costs and changes in accouting policies. HTN expects dilution to be minimal in 1996, with moderate accretion in 1997 and substantial gains accruing from the purchase in 1998 and beyond.

Apr. '95—HTN said it is holding serious talks with three software publishers to form a joint venture to enter the home learning market this year. HTN expects to become a leading player in educational software for the home, a market it expects to grow 30% per year through 2000.

Capitalization

Long Term Debt: $99,475,000 (6/95).

Per Share Data ($)

(Year Ended Dec. 31)

	1994	1993	1992	1991	1990	1989
Tangible Bk. Val.	8.32	14.07	12.34	14.91	13.90	12.82
Cash Flow	7.01	5.08	4.33	4.56	3.67	3.91
Earnings	3.79	2.27	1.35	1.75	1.27	1.62
Dividends	0.87	0.83	0.79	0.77	0.71	0.67
Payout Ratio	24%	37%	59%	43%	56%	41%
Prices - High	53	50⅝	39⅞	30⅝	34⅜	50¼
- Low	36⅛	36⅜	26⅝	22¼	18⅜	28⅛
P/E Ratio - High	14	22	30	17	27	31
- Low	10	16	20	13	14	17

Income Statement Analysis (Million $)

	1994	%Chg	1993	%Chg	1992	%Chg	1991
Revs.	483	4%	463	2%	455	-3%	467
Oper. Inc.	104	3%	101	17%	86.0	-2%	87.7
Depr.	44.4	14%	38.8	-7%	41.7	3%	40.3
Int. Exp.	6.5	83%	3.5	-20%	4.4	-27%	6.1
Pretax Inc.	85.1	74%	49.0	73%	28.4	-30%	40.4
Eff. Tax Rate	38%	—	36%	—	33%	—	38%
Net Inc.	52.4	67%	31.4	64%	19.1	-24%	25.1

Balance Sheet & Other Fin. Data (Million $)

	1994	1993	1992	1991	1990	1989
Cash	47.2	85.3	68.6	92.8	77.4	37.3
Curr. Assets	250	268	234	268	251	210
Total Assets	497	398	371	382	366	321
Curr. Liab.	105	111	83.9	92.1	92.6	81.9
LT Debt	99	26.4	52.6	53.0	53.0	29.0
Common Eqty.	244	224	200	223	210	200
Total Cap.	344	251	253	278	262	229
Cap. Exp.	33.7	36.5	38.2	41.0	40.2	39.9
Cash Flow	96.8	70.2	60.8	65.3	52.3	55.6

Ratio Analysis

	1994	1993	1992	1991	1990	1989
Curr. Ratio	2.4	2.4	2.8	2.9	2.7	2.6
% LT Debt of Cap.	28.9	10.5	20.8	19.0	20.2	12.7
% Net Inc.of Revs.	10.9	6.8	4.2	5.4	4.3	5.7
% Ret. on Assets	11.7	8.1	5.0	6.7	5.2	7.9
% Ret. on Equity	22.5	14.7	9.0	11.6	8.8	11.9

Dividend Data —Dividends have been paid since 1908. A dividend reinvestment plan is available. A "poison pill" stock purchase rights plan was adopted in 1988.

Amt. of Div. $	Date Decl.	Ex-Div. Date	Stock of Record	Payment Date
0.225	Oct. 26	Nov. 03	Nov. 09	Nov. 23 '94
0.225	Jan. 25	Feb. 02	Feb. 08	Feb. 22 '95
0.225	Apr. 26	May. 04	May. 10	May. 24 '95
0.240	Jul. 25	Aug. 07	Aug. 09	Aug. 23 '95

Data as orig. reptd.; bef. results of disc. opers. and/or spec. items. Per share data adj. for stk. divs. as of ex-div. date. E-Estimated. NA-Not Available. NM-Not Meaningful. NR-Not Ranked.

Office—222 Berkeley St., Boston, MA 02116-3764. **Tel**—(617) 351-5000. **Chrmn, Pres & CEO**—N. F. Darehshori. **Exec VP & CFO**—J. F. Stack. **Sr VP & Secy**—P. D. Weaver. **VP & Investor Contact**—Susan E. Hardy (617) 351-5114. **Dirs**—J. A. Baute, N. F. Darehshori, G. Deegan, J. O. Freedman, S. O. Jaeger, M. H. Lindsay, C. R. Longsworth, J. F. Magee, C. B. Malone, A. L. McDougal, G. Putnam, R. Z. Sorenson, D. C. Thomas. **Transfer Agent & Registrar**—Bank of Boston. **Incorporated** in Massachusetts in 1908. **Empl**-2,023. **S&P Analyst:** William H. Donald

STANDARD & POOR'S

STOCK REPORTS

Hubbell Inc.

NYSE Symbol **HUB.B**
In S&P MidCap 400

28-SEP-95 **Industry:** Electronics/Electric

Summary: Hubbell produces a broad range of electrical and electronic products for commercial, industrial, telecommunications and utility applications.

Quantitative Evaluations

Outlook (1 Lowest—5 Highest) • **NA**

Fair Value • **NA**

Risk • **NA**

Earn./Div. Rank • **A**

Technical Eval. • **Bearish** since 11/94

Rel. Strength Rank (1 Lowest—99 Highest) • **44**

Insider Activity • **NA**

Recent Price • 58¾
52 Wk Range • 60¼-49⅝
Yield • 3.2%
12-Mo. P/E • 17.1

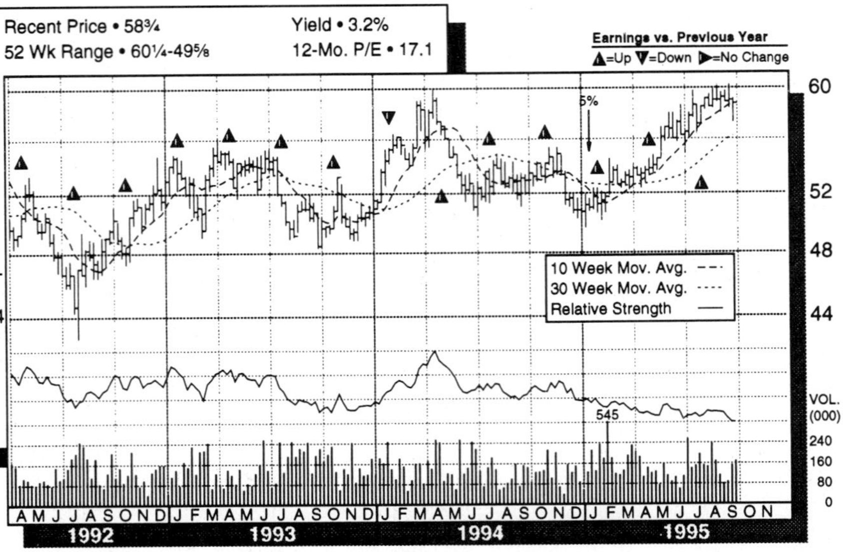

Business Profile - 28-SEP-95

Hubbell manufactures electrical and electronic products in the U.S., Canada, Puerto Rico, Mexico, Singapore and the U.K. and participates in joint ventures in Germany and Taiwan. Earnings have increased consistently since 1961, with the exception of 1993 (when profits were penalized by a restructuring charge). HUB reported record sales and net income for 1994, and results continued to improve in 1995's first half. Hubbell family trusts hold nearly 40% of the supervoting Class A shares.

Operational Review - 28-SEP-95

For the first half of 1995, net sales rose 22%, year to year, reflecting improved economic conditions in the U.S. and Canadian markets and the inclusion of A.B. Chance. Margins narrowed on a less favorable product mix; operating income was up 18%. Following higher interest charges stemming from greater borrowings and costs related to the expansion of the life insurance program to include the operations of A.B. Chance, the gain in net income was limited to 15%.

Stock Performance - 22-SEP-95

In the past 30 trading days, HUB.B's shares have increased 0.43%, compared to a 5% rise in the S&P 500. Average trading volume for the past five days was 33,280 shares, compared with the 40-day moving average of 29,210 shares.

Key Stock Statistics

Dividend Rate/Share	1.88	Shareholders	5,400
Shs. outstg. (M)	32.9	Market cap. (B)	$ 1.9
Avg. daily vol. (M)	0.026	Inst. holdings	55%
Tang. Bk. Value/Share	15.14	Insider holdings	NA
Beta	0.97		

Value of $10,000 invested 5 years ago: $ 18,602

Fiscal Year Ending Dec. 31

	1995	% Change	1994	% Change	1993	% Change
Revenues (Million $)						
1Q	278.4	34%	207.0	5%	198.0	5%
2Q	295.0	13%	261.9	24%	211.3	8%
3Q	—	—	267.5	27%	211.5	5%
4Q	—	—	277.2	31%	211.7	5%
Yr.	—	—	1,014	22%	832.4	6%
Income (Million $)						
1Q	28.41	17%	24.33	1%	24.03	2%
2Q	30.08	14%	26.46	6%	25.01	3%
3Q	—	—	27.29	17%	23.39	3%
4Q	—	—	28.46	NM	-6.12	NM
Yr.	—	—	106.5	61%	66.31	-30%
Earnings Per Share ($)						
1Q	0.85	16%	0.73	1%	0.72	3%
2Q	0.90	14%	0.79	5%	0.75	3%
3Q	—	—	0.82	16%	0.70	3%
4Q	—	—	0.86	NM	-0.18	NM
Yr.	—	—	3.20	60%	2.00	-29%

Next earnings report expected: mid October

Hubbell Inc.

Business Summary - 28-SEP-95

Hubbell Incorporated manufactures a wide variety of electrical products used in low-voltage applications (wiring devices, industrial controls and lighting products) and high-voltage applications (insulated electric wire and cable and power distribution equipment). Other products include outlet boxes and fittings, a line of telecommunications equipment and holding devices. Industry segment contributions in 1994 were:

	Sales	Profits
Low voltage	45%	58%
High voltage	20%	14%
Other	35%	28%

International sales accounted for about 5.5% of total sales in 1994 and exports for 6.2%.

Low-voltage products (600 volts and less) are made by the Wiring Device division, which specializes in the manufacture and sale of highly durable and reliable wiring devices primarily for industrial and commercial customers; the Lighting subsidiary, which sells lighting fixtures for both outdoor and indoor applications; the Industrial Controls subsidiary, which makes and sells a variety of heavy-duty electrical control products with broad application in the control of industrial equipment and processes; and the Killark Electric subsidiary, which manufactures and sells weatherproof and hazardous-location products for explosion-proof and other hostile-area applications.

In the high-voltage area (over 600 volts), the Kerite unit makes and sells high-performance insulated electric power cable for application in vital circuits of electric utilities and major industries; and Ohio Brass makes polymer insulators and surge arrestors used in electrical transmission and distribution lines and substations. A.B. Chance Industries (acquired in April 1994) makes electrical distribution switches, cutouts, sectionalizers, fuses and insulators. Hipotronics, Inc. makes high-voltage test and measurement systems.

Other products include outlet boxes and fittings; fabricated steel enclosures such as rainproof and dust-tight panels, consoles and cabinets; voice and data signal processing equipment; and holding devices (grips) and cord connectors.

Important Developments

Aug. '95—Hubbell filed a shelf registration for up to $200 million in senior debt securities. Proceeds were earmarked for general corporate purposes, including capital expenditures, the financing of possible acquisitions and the repayment of debt.

Capitalization

Long Term Debt: $2,700,000 (6/95).
Class A Stock: 5,799,000 shs. ($0.01 par); 20 votes per share.
Class B Stock: 27,120,000 shs. ($0.01 par).
Options: To buy 2,005,882 Cl. A and Cl. B shs. at $19.07 to $53.99 ea. (12/94).

Per Share Data ($) (Year Ended Dec. 31)

	1994	1993	1992	1991	1990	1989
Tangible Bk. Val.	14.19	14.96	14.70	14.81	13.95	12.85
Cash Flow	4.23	2.78	3.64	3.34	3.11	2.88
Earnings	3.20	2.00	2.83	2.73	2.61	2.40
Dividends	1.62	1.55	1.51	1.40	1.25	1.07
Payout Ratio	51%	78%	53%	50%	47%	44%
Prices - High	59⅞	56⅛	57⅛	51¼	43	39¾
- Low	50	48⅜	42¾	38¼	30⅜	27⅞
P/E Ratio - High	19	28	20	19	16	17
- Low	16	24	15	14	12	11

Income Statement Analysis (Million $)

	1994	%Chg	1993	%Chg	1992	%Chg	1991
Revs.	1,014	22%	832	6%	786	4%	756
Oper. Inc.	175	20%	146	NM	145	4%	139
Depr.	34.0	31%	25.9	-3%	26.8	33%	20.2
Int. Exp.	6.1	79%	3.4	NM	0.7	11%	0.6
Pretax Inc.	146	80%	81.0	-38%	131	2%	129
Eff. Tax Rate	27%	—	19%	—	28%	—	30%
Net Inc.	107	61%	66.3	-30%	94.1	4%	90.6

Balance Sheet & Other Fin. Data (Million $)

	1994	1993	1992	1991	1990	1989
Cash	39.0	44.0	28.0	92.0	103	101
Curr. Assets	445	362	330	344	354	341
Total Assets	1,042	874	807	685	625	576
Curr. Liab.	332	230	200	111	105	101
LT Debt	2.7	2.7	2.7	8.1	8.1	8.1
Common Eqty.	609	558	541	519	469	428
Total Cap.	625	565	559	556	505	463
Cap. Exp.	53.2	25.1	22.9	38.9	40.9	21.5
Cash Flow	141	92.0	121	111	103	95.0

Ratio Analysis

	1994	1993	1992	1991	1990	1989
Curr. Ratio	1.3	1.6	1.6	3.1	3.4	3.4
% LT Debt of Cap.	0.4	0.5	0.5	1.5	1.6	1.8
% Net Inc.of Revs.	10.5	8.0	12.0	12.0	12.0	11.9
% Ret. on Assets	11.1	7.9	12.6	13.8	14.3	14.5
% Ret. on Equity	18.2	12.1	17.7	18.3	19.2	19.4

Dividend Data —Dividends have been paid since 1934. Payments on the Class A and Class B shares are identical. A dividend reinvestment plan is available. A "poison pill" stock purchase rights plan is in effect.

Amt. of Div. $	Date Decl.	Ex-Div. Date	Stock of Record	Payment Date
0.430	Dec. 14	Dec. 19	Dec. 26	Jan. 11 '95
5%	Dec. 14	Jan. 09	Jan. 13	Feb. 03 '95
0.430	Mar. 14	Mar. 21	Mar. 27	Apr. 11 '95
0.470	Jun. 14	Jun. 22	Jun. 26	Jul. 11 '95
0.470	Sep. 14	Sep. 21	Sep. 25	Oct. 11 '95

Data as orig. reptd.; bef. results of disc. opers. and/or spec. items. Per share data adj. for stk. divs. as of ex-div. date. E-Estimated. NA-Not Available. NM-Not Meaningful. NR-Not Ranked.

Office—584 Derby Milford Rd., Orange, CT 06477. **Tel**—(203) 799-4100. **Chrmn & Pres**—G. J. Ratcliffe. **Treas**—J. H. Biggart Jr. **Secy**—R. W. Davies. **Dirs**—E. R. Brooks, G. W. Edwards Jr., J. S. Hoffman, H. G. McDonell, A. McNally IV, D. J. Meyer, G. J. Ratcliffe, J. A. Urquhart, M. Wallop. **Transfer Agent & Registrar**—Chemical Bank, NYC. **Incorporated** in Connecticut in 1905. **Empl**-7,405. **S&P Analyst:** J.C.

STANDARD & POOR'S
Hunt (J.B.) Transport Services

STOCK REPORTS

NASDAQ Symbol **JBHT**

In S&P MidCap 400

05-SEP-95 **Industry:** Trucking

Summary: This company is a leading truckload carrier, provides flatbed and special commodities transportation services, and derives some 35% of revenues from intermodal services.

S&P Opinion: Avoid (★★)

Recent Price • 15⅝
52 Wk Range • 20⅛-15

Yield • 1.3%
12-Mo. P/E • 23.3

Quantitative Evaluations

Outlook (1 Lowest—5 Highest)
• **1-**

Fair Value
• **11⅞**

Risk
• **Average**

Earn./Div. Rank
• **B+**

Technical Eval.
• **Bearish** since 7/95

Rel. Strength Rank (1 Lowest—99 Highest)
• **6**

Insider Activity
• **Neutral**

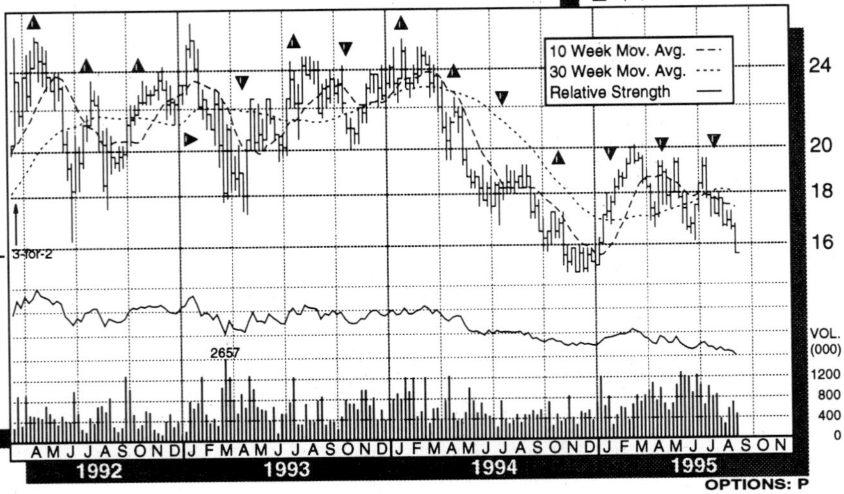

OPTIONS: P

Overview - 05-SEP-95

Lower profits are projected for 1995, partly reflecting costs to evolve from a truckload carrier to a full-service transportation firm. While intermodal volumes should grow moderately, the economic lull evident since the second quarter has left JBHT with excess capacity. Strong gains are still anticipated for logistics, dedicated carriage and the special commodities divisions. Recently launched catalog distribution and auto hauling also will boost revenue growth. Hurting margins will be higher purchased transportation costs, higher driver pay and recruitment costs. JBHT's dry van business is being plagued by reduced revenues per mile as competitive pressures force it to accept less profitable shipments, and a higher percentage of empty miles. Also hurting profits are reduced equipment gains and increased interest costs.

Valuation - 05-SEP-95

In August shares of this trucker revisited their 1994 lows after posting a poor profit performance in 1995's second quarter. JBHT has invested heavily recently to reposition it to handle more intermodal volumes and provide a broad array of transportation activities. Investors have been frustrated by the slow payback evident so far. In fact, the first half performance of JBHT's intermodal division proved that there are limits to its growth and a large cyclical element as well. Assuming stronger economic activity in 1995's second half and 1996, JBHT appears already to more amply discount the expected rebound in profits.

Key Stock Statistics

S&P EPS Est. 1995	0.65	Tang. Bk. Value/Share	9.81
P/E on S&P Est. 1995	24.1	Beta	1.26
S&P EPS Est. 1996	1.10	Shareholders	2,000
Dividend Rate/Share	0.20	Market cap. (B)	$0.603
Shs. outstg. (M)	38.6	Inst. holdings	34%
Avg. daily vol. (M)	0.098	Insider holdings	NA

Value of $10,000 invested 5 years ago: $ 12,643

Fiscal Year Ending Dec. 31

	1995	% Change	1994	% Change	1993	% Change
Revenues (Million $)						
1Q	309.4	17%	264.7	7%	247.2	23%
2Q	329.2	11%	297.7	14%	260.4	16%
3Q	—	—	313.9	24%	253.6	5%
4Q	—	—	331.3	28%	259.8	6%
Yr.	—	—	1,208	18%	1,021	12%
Income (Million $)						
1Q	4.89	-15%	5.73	15%	4.98	-21%
2Q	-2.14	NM	11.58	-14%	13.50	33%
3Q	—	—	12.26	40%	8.78	-18%
4Q	—	—	10.83	-1%	10.96	12%
Yr.	—	—	40.39	6%	38.22	3%
Earnings Per Share ($)						
1Q	0.13	-13%	0.15	15%	0.13	-28%
2Q	-0.06	NM	0.30	-14%	0.35	21%
3Q	E0.25	-22%	0.32	39%	0.23	-23%
4Q	E0.33	18%	0.28	-3%	0.29	12%
Yr.	E0.65	-38%	1.05	5%	1.00	-3%

Next earnings report expected: mid October

Hunt (J.B.) Transport Services

Business Summary - 05-SEP-95

J.B. Hunt Transport Services provides a variety of motor transport services throughout the U.S. mainland and to points in Canada and Mexico.

JBHT is the nation's second largest dry van truckload motor carrier. In 1994 dry van operations accounted for some 45% of total revenues. In 1994, the company moved 1,187,815 loads, versus 1,081,013 loads in 1993. Total tractor-miles in 1994 were 740.6 million, compared with 718.8 million in 1993. Contributions to revenues by traffic group in recent years were:

	1994	1993
Food	28%	29%
Paper	21%	24%
Transportation equipment	17%	15%
Stone, clay & glass	6%	6%
Electrical equipment	4%	4%
Chemicals	3%	3%
Primary metals	2%	3%
Rubber & plastic	3%	3%
Petroleum & coal	1%	1%
Other	15%	12%

J.B. Hunt Transport, Inc. derives some 35% of total revenues from the movement of intermodal freight (trailers and containers on rail flatcars) through arrangements with 12 U.S. and Canadian railroads. JBHT is in the process of converting its dry van trailer fleet to containers in order to obtain cost savings by harnessing low-cost rail doublestack service for its line-haul movements.

JBHT also offers regional truckload services; performs flatbed hauling (the movement of raw materials and finished goods on platform trailers); provides dedicated contract carriage and offers a parcel management service for direct marketers. JBHT's special commodities unit transports hazardous wastes and materials. J.B. Hunt Logistics, Inc. offers a variety of transportation and logistics management services.

Important Developments

Jul. '95—JBHT reported that it had completed the conversion of more than 80% of its dry van fleet to containers from trailers. Consequently, capital outlays for 1995 were expected to be lower than the $219 million spent in 1994. Through June 30, 1995, JBHT had spent $97.9 million for property additions, compared with $126.2 million in 1994's first half. At June 30, 1995, JBHT's total equipment fleet consisted of 16,302 containers and 7,771 trailers. By employing containers, JBHT can achieve a cost advantage through the use of lower-rated rail doublestack service for long-haul intermodal freight.

Capitalization

Long Term Debt: $292,506,000 (6/95).

Per Share Data ($)

(Year Ended Dec. 31)

	1994	1993	1992	1991	1990	1989
Tangible Bk. Val.	9.81	8.95	8.10	6.19	5.52	4.95
Cash Flow	NM	3.70	3.66	2.99	2.57	2.36
Earnings	1.05	1.00	1.03	0.85	0.85	0.87
Dividends	0.20	0.20	0.20	0.19	0.16	0.16
Payout Ratio	19%	20%	19%	22%	18%	19%
Prices - High	25¾	26¾	26	20½	15½	17⅞
- Low	15	17¼	16¼	11⅜	9⅝	11⅞
P/E Ratio - High	25	27	25	24	18	20
- Low	14	17	16	13	11	13

Income Statement Analysis (Million $)

	1994	%Chg	1993	%Chg	1992	%Chg	1991
Revs.	1,208	18%	1,021	12%	912	24%	733
Oper. Inc.	NA	—	182	12%	163	22%	134
Depr.	NA	—	103	10%	94.0	27%	74.3
Int. Exp.	19.7	43%	13.8	27%	10.9	2%	10.7
Pretax Inc.	65.1	NM	64.8	11%	58.2	20%	48.7
Eff. Tax Rate	38%	—	41%	—	37%	—	40%
Net Inc.	40.4	6%	38.2	4%	36.9	25%	29.5

Balance Sheet & Other Fin. Data (Million $)

	1994	1993	1992	1991	1990	1989
Cash	2.1	3.4	1.8	2.5	8.4	1.8
Curr. Assets	181	168	142	135	115	89.0
Total Assets	994	862	716	520	453	385
Curr. Liab.	178	95.7	80.7	57.2	61.8	51.6
LT Debt	299	303	216	157	138	105
Common Eqty.	378	344	309	216	191	176
Total Cap.	799	755	615	445	391	333
Cap. Exp.	283	286	289	152	122	136
Cash Flow	NM	142	131	104	91.0	84.0

Ratio Analysis

	1994	1993	1992	1991	1990	1989
Curr. Ratio	1.0	1.8	1.8	2.4	1.9	1.7
% LT Debt of Cap.	37.5	40.2	35.2	35.3	35.2	31.5
% Net Inc.of Revs.	3.3	3.7	4.0	4.0	5.2	6.0
% Ret. on Assets	4.3	4.8	5.8	6.0	7.3	8.9
% Ret. on Equity	11.2	11.7	13.6	14.4	16.6	18.8

Dividend Data —Cash has been paid each year since 1985.

Amt. of Div. $	Date Decl.	Ex-Div. Date	Stock of Record	Payment Date
0.050	Oct. 13	Oct. 31	Nov. 04	Nov. 22 '94
0.050	Jan. 27	Jan. 30	Feb. 02	Feb. 17 '95
0.050	Apr. 13	Apr. 27	May. 03	May. 19 '95
0.050	Jul. 20	Jul. 31	Aug. 02	Aug. 18 '95

Data as orig. reptd.; bef. results of disc. opers. and/or spec. items. Per share data adj. for stk. divs. as of ex-div. date. E-Estimated. NA-Not Available. NM-Not Meaningful. NR-Not Ranked.

Office—615 J.B. Hunt Corporate Dr., Lowell, AR 72745. **Tel**—(501) 820-0000. **Chrmn**—W. Garrison. **Pres, CEO & Investor Contact**—Kirk Thompson. **EVP-CFO**—J. W. Walton. **Secy**—J. D. Hunt. **Dirs**—J. A. Cooper Jr., F. K. Darragh Jr., W. Garrison, G. George, T. L. Hardeman, J. B. Hunt, J. B. Hunt Jr., J. D. Hunt, L. E. Peterson, K. Thompson. **Transfer Agent & Registrar**—First Chicago Trust Co. of New York, Jersey City, N.J. **Incorporated** in Arkansas in 1961. **Empl**-11,837. **S&P Analyst:** Stephen R. Klein

STANDARD & POOR'S

STOCK REPORTS

IBP, inc.

NYSE Symbol **IBP**
In S&P MidCap 400

09-AUG-95 **Industry:** Food

Summary: IBP is the world's largest producer of both fresh and boxed beef and pork products and of edible and inedible allied products.

S&P Opinion: Buy (★★★★★)

Recent Price • 48⅜ | Yield • 0.4%
52 Wk Range • 50⅝-28¾ | 12-Mo. P/E • 8.8

Quantitative Evaluations

Outlook (1 Lowest—5 Highest) • **5+**

Fair Value • **53⅞**

Risk • **Low**

Earn./Div. Rank • **NR**

Technical Eval. • **Bullish** since 1/95

Rel. Strength Rank (1 Lowest—99 Highest) • **90**

Insider Activity • **Neutral**

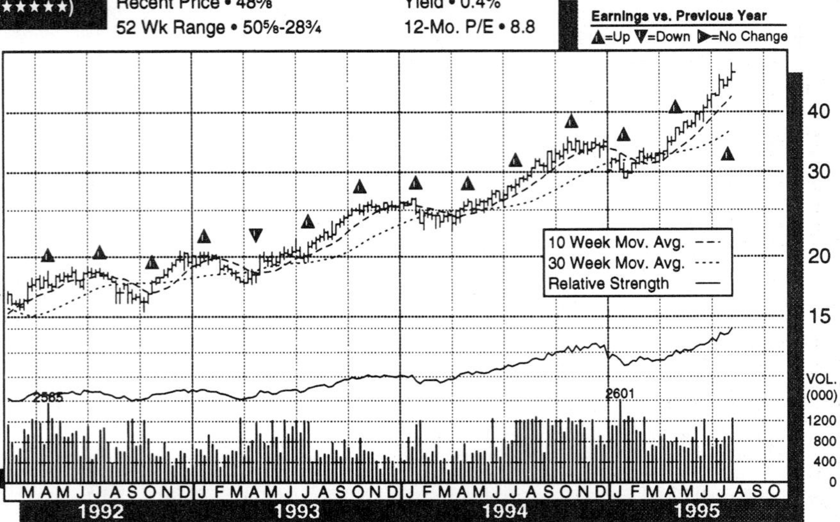

OPTIONS: ASE, Ph

Overview - 09-AUG-95

Sales are projected to rise at a middle single-digit annual pace through 1996, as tonnage volume growth and contributions from acquisitions help to outweigh stable or lower average prices for both beef and pork products. Our projection of generally favorable near-term cattle and hog market supply conditions, combined with a high level of company production efficiency, should help to sustain operating profit margins over the next few quarters. In addition, easing net interest costs are likely to drive 1995 net earnings sharply above record 1994 levels. Investors should note that earnings volatility for this company is much higher than for most other food companies, due to IBP's relatively thin profit margins and close ties to the constantly changing livestock commodity markets.

Valuation - 09-AUG-95

Based on our expectations of continued strong earnings momentum over at least the next few quarters, we view the shares as very attractive at current levels. Although the stock has been a strong performer since late 1992, we believe further above-average gains are in store as investors increasingly become more confident in IBP's ability to sustain its recent strong earnings growth. An improving balance sheet and an increased emphasis on more-profitable value-added meat products should allow for a more stable earnings stream. The stock's P/E multiple, at a substantial discount to the S&P 500, also makes IBP an attractive defensive play in a slow economy.

Key Stock Statistics

S&P EPS Est. 1995	5.45	Tang. Bk. Value/Share	12.95
P/E on S&P Est. 1995	8.9	Beta	0.62
S&P EPS Est. 1996	5.25	Shareholders	7,500
Dividend Rate/Share	0.20	Market cap. (B)	$ 2.4
Shs. outstg. (M)	47.4	Inst. holdings	95%
Avg. daily vol. (M)	0.238	Insider holdings	NA

Value of $10,000 invested 5 years ago: $ 35,004

Fiscal Year Ending Dec. 31

	1995	% Change	1994	% Change	1993	% Change
Revenues (Million $)						
1Q	3,007	7%	2,819	3%	2,745	4%
2Q	3,209	6%	3,040	NM	3,043	8%
3Q	—	—	2,982	-2%	3,054	6%
4Q	—	—	3,234	14%	2,829	2%
Yr.	—	—	12,075	3%	11,671	5%
Income (Million $)						
1Q	51.82	149%	20.85	69%	12.31	-37%
2Q	85.84	149%	34.47	68%	20.50	64%
3Q	—	—	49.16	121%	22.25	67%
4Q	—	—	77.82	NM	22.40	22%
Yr.	—	—	182.3	135%	77.46	22%
Earnings Per Share ($)						
1Q	1.08	151%	0.43	65%	0.26	-37%
2Q	1.78	147%	0.72	67%	0.43	65%
3Q	E1.30	—	1.02	122%	0.46	64%
4Q	E1.29	—	1.61	NM	0.47	24%
Yr.	E5.45	—	3.79	134%	1.62	21%

Next earnings report expected: mid October

IBP, inc.

09-AUG-95

Business Summary - 09-AUG-95

IBP, inc. is the world's largest producer of fresh and boxed beef and pork products and of edible and inedible allied products. Segment contributions in recent years were:

	1994	1993
Boxed beef products	66%	67%
Beef carcasses	4%	4%
Pork products	17%	18%
Beef & pork allied products	13%	11%

The company operates 12 beef slaughtering plants, seven of which have adjoining facilities to reduce carcasses into primal cuts, such as loins, ribs, rounds and chucks, and sub-primal cuts, including sirloins, strips and tenderloins. IBP's carcass and beef processing facilities operated in 1994 at nearly 89% of their production capacities.

Eight of IBP's beef plants include hide treatment facilities. Substantially all hides from its other four beef plants are transported to these facilities, which include brine curing operations and, in four locations, chrome hide tanneries.

The company operates six pork facilities in Iowa and Nebraska. The facilities include both carcass production and processing of fresh pork products, employing a production process similar to that employed in beef operations. In 1993, IBP purchased a seventh pork facility in Indiana, which is currently being renovated. In 1994, IBP's pork plants operated at 88% of production capacity.

Sales to international customers are made through the IBP International, Inc. subsidiary, which has sales offices in London and Tokyo. In 1994, export sales accounted for 13% of total net sales.

Important Developments

Aug. '95—IBP attributed its strong year-to-year earnings gain in 1995's first half primarily to continued production efficiency, increased export sales, and, to a lesser extent, recent acquisition contributions. Newly-acquired operations, including the early 1995 purchase of cow processing facilities; and the 1994 acquisition of Lakeside Farm Industries Ltd., a diversified Canadian agribusiness, were positive contributors to earnings. Separately, a new four-year labor agreement was ratified by employees of IBP's Dakota City beef production complex. During the second quarter, IBP implemented organizational changes which included the establishment of four separate divisions, to be named Fresh Meats, Consumer Products, Allied Group, and Corporate Development.

Capitalization

Long Term Debt: $361,320,000 (6/95), incl. lease obligs.

Per Share Data ($) (Year Ended Dec. 31)

	1994	1993	1992	1991	1990	1989
Tangible Bk. Val.	11.88	8.21	6.61	5.39	5.83	5.37
Cash Flow	5.11	2.84	2.64	1.38	2.22	1.83
Earnings	3.79	1.62	1.34	0.03	1.01	0.74
Dividends	0.20	0.20	0.30	0.60	0.60	0.60
Payout Ratio	5%	12%	22%	NM	59%	80%
Prices - High	35½	26¼	20⅝	26¼	21¾	17¾
- Low	22⅝	17½	14½	12⅞	14¾	13½
P/E Ratio - High	9	16	15	NM	22	24
- Low	6	11	11	NM	15	18

Income Statement Analysis (Million $)

	1994	%Chg	1993	%Chg	1992	%Chg	1991
Revs.	12,075	3%	11,671	5%	11,128	7%	10,388
Oper. Inc.	411	76%	233	5%	222	76%	126
Depr.	63.4	8%	58.8	-5%	62.0	-4%	64.6
Int. Exp.	45.1	-2%	45.8	-16%	54.7	-11%	61.3
Pretax Inc.	309	136%	131	20%	109	NM	2.0
Eff. Tax Rate	41%	—	41%	—	41%	—	40%
Net Inc.	182	135%	77.5	22%	63.6	NM	1.4

Balance Sheet & Other Fin. Data (Million $)

	1994	1993	1992	1991	1990	1989
Cash	161	25.2	25.0	22.6	15.4	19.0
Curr. Assets	974	703	702	626	677	565
Total Assets	1,865	1,539	1,499	1,450	1,533	1,353
Curr. Liab.	615	367	372	388	443	382
LT Debt	362	461	511	510	507	416
Common Eqty.	780	613	534	483	511	497
Total Cap.	1,224	1,153	1,111	1,049	1,079	961
Cap. Exp.	84.0	60.0	36.0	25.0	126	112
Cash Flow	246	136	126	66.0	106	87.0

Ratio Analysis

	1994	1993	1992	1991	1990	1989
Curr. Ratio	1.6	1.9	1.9	1.6	1.5	1.5
% LT Debt of Cap.	29.6	40.0	46.0	48.6	47.0	43.3
% Net Inc.of Revs.	1.5	0.7	0.6	NM	0.5	0.4
% Ret. on Assets	10.7	5.1	4.3	0.1	3.3	2.6
% Ret. on Equity	26.2	13.5	12.5	0.3	9.6	7.2

Dividend Data (Dividends were initiated in 1987.)

Amt. of Div. $	Date Decl.	Ex-Div. Date	Stock of Record	Payment Date
0.050	Aug. 25	Sep. 02	Sep. 09	Oct. 14 '94
0.050	Oct. 19	Dec. 05	Dec. 09	Jan. 13 '95
0.050	Jan. 19	Mar. 06	Mar. 10	Apr. 14 '95
0.050	Apr. 19	Jun. 06	Jun. 09	Jul. 14 '95
0.050	Jul. 20	Sep. 06	Sep. 08	Oct. 13 '95

Data as orig. reptd.; bef. results of disc. opers. and/or spec. items. Per share data adj. for stk. divs. as of ex-div. date. E-Estimated. NA-Not Available. NM-Not Meaningful. NR-Not Ranked.

Office—IBP Ave., P.O. Box 515, Dakota City, NE 68731. **Tel**—(402) 494-2061. **Chrmn, Pres & CEO**—R. L. Peterson. **Exec VP-Fin**—L. O. Grigsby. **VP, Treas & Investor Contact**—John N. Borgh. **Dirs**—J. S. Chalsty, A. P. Courtelis, W. L. Gramm, E. D. Leman, R. L. Peterson, J. D. Smith, D. C. Tinstman. **Transfer Agent & Registrar**—Chemical Mellon Shareholders Services, Pittsburgh. **Incorporated** in Delaware in 1961. **Empl**-32,000. **S&P Analyst:** Kenneth A. Shea

STANDARD & POOR'S

IMC Global Inc.

STOCK REPORTS

NYSE Symbol **IGL**
In S&P MidCap 400

13-OCT-95 **Industry:** Chemicals

Summary: This company is one of the world's largest producers of crop nutrients. It mines potash in North America and is a partner in the world's largest producer of phosphate nutrients.

S&P Opinion: Hold (★★★)

Recent Price • 64⅝ | 52 Wk Range • 66⅝-36¼ | Yield • 0.6% | 12-Mo. P/E • 15.0

Quantitative Evaluations

Outlook (1 Lowest—5 Highest) • **2+**

Fair Value • **60¼**

Risk • **Average**

Earn./Div. Rank • **NR**

Technical Eval. • **Bullish** since 9/94

Rel. Strength Rank (1 Lowest—99 Highest) • **94**

Insider Activity • **NA**

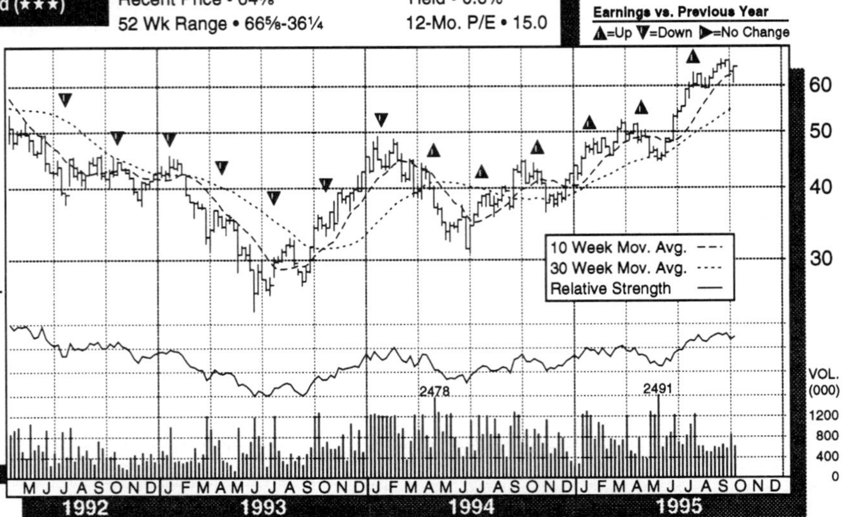

OPTIONS: NY, P

Overview - 13-OCT-95

We expect that sales and earnings for this major fertilizer producer will continue to advance in fiscal 1996. We see domestic corn acreage and fertilizer usage increasing about 10% in 1996, largely as a result of the projected sharp drop in 1995's crop production caused by adverse weather in the Midwest. Foreign shipments are projected to remain strong, especially phosphates to China during the first half. Selling prices for both phosphate and potash should remain near 1995's robust levels. In addition, the IMC-Agrico venture is expected to achieve its annual cost reduction goal of about $135 million. Interest expense will also decline as IGL continues to reduce debt.

Valuation - 13-OCT-95

The shares of this major fertilizer producer have climbed about 45% this year to their highest levels in almost four years due on the favorable near-term sales and earnings outlook. Worldwide fertilizer demand and selling prices are projected to remain strong for the rest of 1995 and into 1996. Longer term, the company should continue to benefit from its strategy of more closely balancing output with customers' needs to ease the adverse financial impact of market fluctuations. It also intends to increase its international and non-agricultural businesses. We recommend holding current positions.

Key Stock Statistics

S&P EPS Est. 1996	5.00	Tang. Bk. Value/Share	25.84
P/E on S&P Est. 1996	12.9	Beta	0.39
Dividend Rate/Share	0.40	Shareholders	300
Shs. outstg. (M)	29.5	Market cap. (B)	$ 2.1
Avg. daily vol. (M)	0.151	Inst. holdings	87%
		Insider holdings	NA

Value of $10,000 invested 5 years ago: $ 20,877

Fiscal Year Ending Jun. 30

	1995	% Change	1994	% Change	1993	% Change
Revenues (Million $)						
1Q	420.8	58%	266.4	21%	221.0	-15%
2Q	451.8	37%	329.0	66%	198.0	-22%
3Q	550.0	34%	410.5	84%	222.8	-17%
4Q	501.4	15%	435.6	70%	255.9	-9%
Yr.	1,924	33%	1,442	61%	897.1	-15%
Income (Million $)						
1Q	21.80	NM	-22.50	NM	19.70	-7%
2Q	27.90	NM	-3.60	NM	3.90	-83%
3Q	45.70	NM	5.40	NM	-113.7	NM
4Q	31.70	85%	17.10	NM	-22.80	NM
Yr.	127.1	NM	-3.60	NM	-120.0	NM
Earnings Per Share ($)						
1Q	0.74	NM	-1.02	NM	0.84	-13%
2Q	0.94	NM	-0.14	NM	0.13	-88%
3Q	1.54	NM	0.21	NM	-5.20	NM
4Q	1.07	75%	0.61	NM	-1.21	NM
Yr.	4.30	NM	-0.14	NM	-5.44	NM

Next earnings report expected: mid October

IMC Global Inc.

Business Summary - 13-OCT-95

IMC Global (formerly IMC Fertilizer Group) is one of the world's leading producers of crop nutrients. Sales contributions in recent fiscal years:

	1995	1994
Phosphate chemicals	65%	61%
Potash	13%	14%
Phosphate rock	12%	13%
Mixed fertilizers	6%	7%
Uranium	1%	1%
Other	3%	4%

Exports accounted for 41% of sales in fiscal 1995.

On July 1, 1993, the company and Freeport McMoRan Resource Partners (FRP) formed IMC-Agrico Co., a joint venture combining their respective phosphate fertilizer businesses, including phosphate rock and uranium. Distributions from the venture will reflect each partner's contribution and an equal share of anticipated savings of more than $95 million a year. IMC-Agrico has 31.5 million tons of annual phosphate rock capacity, accounting for about 48% of U.S. phosphate rock capacity and 19% of world capacity. Shipments in fiscal 1995 were 24.8 million tons. IMC-Agrico has annual phosphate chemicals production capacity of 3.9 million tons, accounting for 32% of U.S. capacity and 11% of world capacity. It also produces uranium oxide, which is extracted during the process that produces phosphate chemicals and is sold for upgrading into nuclear power plant fuel.

IGL has 5.35 million tons of annual potash capacity, accounting for 19% of North American capacity, and 7% of world potash capacity. The company's potash reserves, which exceed 1.6 billion tons, are among the largest in the world. A 25% interest is held in a 69-million-ton sulphur deposit and oil and natural gas reserve in the Gulf of Mexico. Sulphur production was 2.3 million tons in fiscal 1995.

Important Developments

Aug. '95—IMC-Agrico announced that it resumed production at its Taft, La. phosphate plant which had been idled since early May. The company cited the stregthening tone of the markets, coupled with declining inventories for the restart. In May, IGL announced that the Phosphate Chemicals Export Association reached a new sales agreement with China for the second half of calendar 1995. The contract's total volume could equal the committed tonnage to China during the first half of 1995.

Capitalization

Long Term Debt: $515,500,000 (6/95).
Minority Interest: $479,900,000.

Per Share Data ($)

(Year Ended Jun. 30)

	1995	1994	1993	1992	1991	1990
Tangible Bk. Val.	25.84	22.23	19.36	27.78	32.10	31.13
Cash Flow	8.82	4.70	-2.65	7.89	7.47	6.64
Earnings	4.30	-0.14	-5.44	4.12	3.85	3.13
Dividends	0.30	Nil	0.81	1.08	1.08	1.08
Payout Ratio	7%	Nil	NM	26%	28%	34%
Prices - High	63¼	49¼	47¼	68	60	38⅝
- Low	41¼	30¾	24⅜	37¼	33	30⅜
P/E Ratio - High	15	NM	NM	17	16	12
- Low	10	NM	NM	9	9	10

Income Statement Analysis (Million $)

	1995	%Chg	1994	%Chg	1993	%Chg	1992
Revs.	1,924	33%	1,442	61%	897	-15%	1,059
Oper. Inc.	508	92%	264	110%	126	-49%	248
Depr.	134	9%	122	99%	61.5	-26%	83.3
Int. Exp.	52.4	-36%	81.7	27%	64.2	NM	63.7
Pretax Inc.	336	NM	63.0	NM	-176	NM	141
Eff. Tax Rate	24%	—	18%	—	NM	—	36%
Net Inc.	127	NM	-3.6	NM	-119	NM	91.0

Balance Sheet & Other Fin. Data (Million $)

	1995	1994	1993	1992	1991	1990
Cash	196	169	112	33.0	39.0	30.0
Curr. Assets	504	534	433	266	296	246
Total Assets	2,693	2,778	2,056	1,778	1,739	1,585
Curr. Liab.	252	209	238	186	248	212
LT Debt	516	688	893	631	608	385
Common Eqty.	763	655	430	615	699	820
Total Cap.	2,158	2,294	1,641	1,459	1,349	1,234
Cap. Exp.	64.2	41.0	106	178	169	94.0
Cash Flow	261	119	-59.0	174	186	175

Ratio Analysis

	1995	1994	1993	1992	1991	1990
Curr. Ratio	2.0	2.6	1.8	1.4	1.2	1.2
% LT Debt of Cap.	23.9	30.0	54.4	43.2	45.0	31.2
% Net Inc.of Revs.	6.6	NM	NM	8.6	8.5	7.5
% Ret. on Assets	4.6	NM	NM	5.1	6.3	5.1
% Ret. on Equity	17.9	NM	NM	13.7	14.0	10.4

Dividend Data —Dividends, omitted in April 1993 after having been paid since 1988, were resumed in January 1995. A "poison pill" stock purchase rights plan was adopted in 1989.

Amt. of Div. $	Date Decl.	Ex-Div. Date	Stock of Record	Payment Date
0.100	Dec. 15	Dec. 29	Jan. 05	Jan. 17 '95
0.100	Feb. 16	Mar. 13	Mar. 17	Mar. 31 '95
0.100	Jun. 15	Jun. 22	Jun. 26	Jun. 30 '95
0.100	Aug. 17	Sep. 13	Sep. 15	Sep. 30 '95

Data as orig. reptd.; bef. results of disc. opers. and/or spec. items. Per share data adj. for stk. divs. as of ex-div. date. E-Estimated. NA-Not Available. NM-Not Meaningful. NR-Not Ranked.

Office—2100 Sanders Rd., Northbrook, IL 60062-6146. **Tel**—(708) 272-9200. **Chrmn & CEO**—W. F. Bueche. **Pres & COO**—J. D. Speir. **EVP-CFO**—R. C. Brauneker. **SVP & Secy**—M. I. Smith. **VP, Treas & Investor Contact**—Peter Hong (708-205-4820). **Dirs**—W. F. Bueche, R. F. Bentele, F. W. Considine, J. M. Davidson, R. A. Lenon, D. B. Mathis, T. H. Roberts Jr., J. D. Speir, B. B. Turner. **Transfer Agent & Registrar**—American Stock Transfer & Trust Co., NYC. **Incorporated** in Delaware in 1987. **Empl**-6,800. **S&P Analyst:** Richard O'Reilly, CFA

IVAX Corp.

ASE Symbol **IVX**
In S&P MidCap 400

27-SEP-95

Industry:
Drugs-Generic and OTC

Summary: IVAX is a leading developer and marketer of generic drugs. Subsidiaries also sell personal care products, chemicals, medical diagnostics and intravenous products and services.

S&P Opinion: Accumulate (★★★★)

Recent Price • 31½
52 Wk Range • 31⅝-17½
Yield • 0.3%
12-Mo. P/E • 40.9

Quantitative Evaluations

Outlook
(1 Lowest—5 Highest)
• **4−**

Fair Value
• **33⅝**

Risk
• **Average**

Earn./Div. Rank
• **B-**

Technical Eval.
• **Bullish** since 9/95

Rel. Strength Rank
(1 Lowest—99 Highest)
• **90**

Insider Activity
• **Neutral**

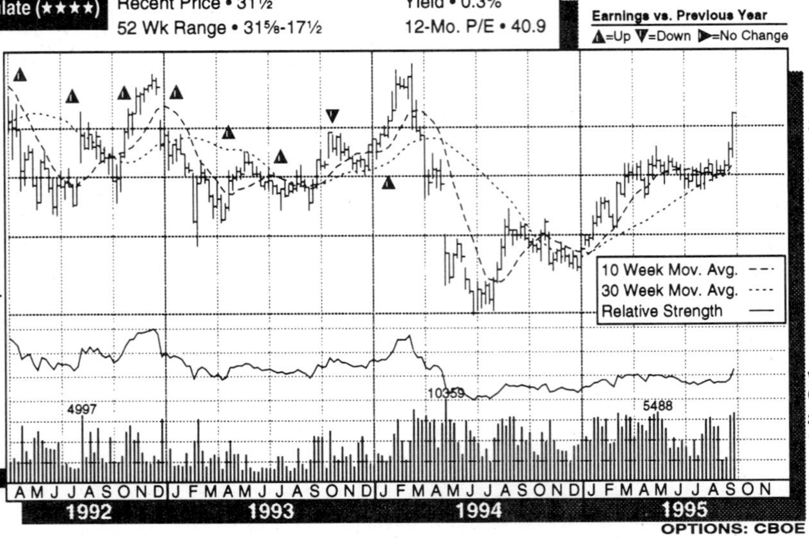

Overview - 27-SEP-95

Revenues are expected to show further growth in 1996. Pharmaceutical sales should be bolstered by recently launched new drugs such as generic equivalents of Ceclor antibiotic and Glucotrol diabetes treatment, and by anticipated approval of a generic form of Albuterol anti-asthma and other drugs now under FDA review. Growth is also indicated for intravenous products, but sales in most remaining businesses will probably be fairly flat. Margins should benefit from the better volume, a more favorable product mix (as the proportion of higher-margin manufactured products rises), and cost synergies as IVAX continues to integrate Zenith Laboratories.

Valuation - 27-SEP-95

The shares have chalked up a creditable performance thus far in 1995, with recent strength attributable to takeover rumors. Large European drugmakers such as Astra AB, Bayer AG and BASF have been mentioned as possible suitors. Speculation was sparked by BASF's recent announcement that it plans to acquire a 4.9% interest in IVAX once FTC clearance is obtained. Earlier in 1995, BASF and the company formed a generic joint venture in Europe. Prospects are enhanced by a projected steady stream of new generic approvals, expanded international operations, synergies from recent acquisitions, and contributions from several promising proprietary drugs. The shares are recommended for above-average long-term appreciation.

Key Stock Statistics

S&P EPS Est. 1995	1.10	Tang. Bk. Value/Share	4.37
P/E on S&P Est. 1995	28.6	Beta	1.97
S&P EPS Est. 1996	1.40	Shareholders	6,900
Dividend Rate/Share	0.08	Market cap. (B)	$ 3.5
Shs. outstg. (M)	115.4	Inst. holdings	29%
Avg. daily vol. (M)	0.672	Insider holdings	NA

Value of $10,000 invested 5 years ago: $ 60,029

Fiscal Year Ending Dec. 31

	1995	% Change	1994	% Change	1993	% Change
Revenues (Million $)						
1Q	281.1	19%	236.5	71%	138.6	33%
2Q	306.7	NM	97.60	-37%	154.8	59%
3Q	—	—	266.4	54%	173.1	43%
4Q	—	—	296.1	66%	178.8	39%
Yr.	—	—	1,135	76%	645.3	43%
Income (Million $)						
1Q	23.30	6%	21.93	22%	17.99	NM
2Q	28.13	20%	23.47	25%	18.72	NM
3Q	—	—	23.32	3%	22.56	4%
4Q	—	—	11.96	-53%	25.45	94%
Yr.	—	—	89.87	6%	84.72	90%
Earnings Per Share ($)						
1Q	0.20	—	--	—	0.25	NM
2Q	0.24	—	--	—	0.26	NM
3Q	E0.30	-55%	0.67	116%	0.31	-54%
4Q	E0.36	NM	0.10	-71%	0.34	79%
Yr.	E1.10	43%	0.77	-34%	1.17	80%

Next earnings report expected: late October

IVAX Corp.

27-SEP-95

Business Summary - 27-SEP-95

IVAX Corp. is a holding company with subsidiaries engaged in pharmaceuticals, intravenous solutions, specialty chemicals, personal care products and diagnostics. Pharmaceutical operations were significantly expanded by the December 1994 acquisition of Zenith Laboratories in exchange for 27.2 million common shares. Revenues and operating profits in 1994 were derived as follows:

	Revenues	Profits
Pharmaceuticals	57%	69%
Intravenous products	30%	27%
Specialty chemicals	6%	-2%
Personal care items	5%	4%
Diagnostics	2%	2%

Foreign operations (substantially all in Europe) accounted for 19% of revenues and 27% of profits in 1994.

Pharmaceuticals include a wide range of generic and OTC products and vitamin supplements, which together accounted for 49% of 1994 sales. About 80 generic and OTC drugs are made and sold in the U.S., with an additional 750 distributed. Through its Norton Healthcare unit, IVAX sells 135 generic and OTC products in the U.K, Ireland and other countries under the Norton name. A line of branded drugs is also made and marketed under the Baker Norton name. DVM Pharmaceuticals distributes veterinary products in the U.S.

Intravenous products are manufactured by McGaw, a leading producer of I.V. solutions, sets, pumps and related infusion supplies and equipment. Personal care items consist of more than 250 hair care and cosmetic products, primarily for African-American consumers. Specialty chemicals include vacuum pump fluids, textile chemicals and industrial maintenance products. Diagnostic items consist of tests for infectious diseases and autoimmune disorders.

Important Developments

Sep. '95—IVAX received FDA marketing approval for a generic equivalent of Pfizer's Glucotrol drug to control hyperglycemia in diabetes patients. Earlier in 1995, FDA approval was received for generic forms of Ansaid anti-inflammatory, Tagamet antiulcer, Ceclor antibiotic, Bumex diuretic, Dyazide heart drug, and six other drugs. Also in September, leading German drug and chemicals conglomerate BASF announced plans to acquire a 4.9% interest in the company. In March, IVAX and BASF formed a joint venture to market generic pharmaceuticals in Europe.

Capitalization

Long Term Debt: $281,468,000 (6/95).

Per Share Data ($) (Year Ended Dec. 31)

	1994	1993	1992	1991	1990	1989
Tangible Bk. Val.	3.90	3.02	1.71	1.22	0.67	0.59
Cash Flow	1.16	1.43	0.87	0.27	0.07	-0.15
Earnings	0.77	1.17	0.65	0.19	-0.01	-0.21
Dividends	0.06	0.04	Nil	Nil	Nil	Nil
Payout Ratio	8%	3%	Nil	Nil	Nil	Nil
Prices - High	38⅛	29¾	40⅞	41⅜	6⅛	6½
- Low	14⅞	19¼	21⅝	5⅛	4	4½
P/E Ratio - High	50	25	63	NM	NM	NM
- Low	19	16	33	NM	NM	NM

Income Statement Analysis (Million $)

	1994	%Chg	1993	%Chg	1992	%Chg	1991
Revs.	1,135	76%	645	43%	451	148%	182
Oper. Inc.	199	24%	160	128%	70.1	NM	18.6
Depr.	45.5	139%	19.0	26%	15.1	185%	5.3
Int. Exp.	21.5	176%	7.8	-29%	11.0	NM	3.5
Pretax Inc.	122	-11%	137	153%	54.2	NM	13.6
Eff. Tax Rate	25%	—	38%	—	18%	—	19%
Net Inc.	89.9	6%	84.7	90%	44.6	NM	11.1

Balance Sheet & Other Fin. Data (Million $)

	1994	1993	1992	1991	1990	1989
Cash	37.0	73.0	49.0	118	5.2	5.0
Curr. Assets	524	342	253	267	64.6	29.7
Total Assets	1,107	658	504	449	117	76.0
Curr. Liab.	192	112	106	111	39.4	13.6
LT Debt	254	129	133	135	16.2	7.8
Common Eqty.	634	411	259	201	58.7	50.9
Total Cap.	899	540	392	336	74.9	58.7
Cap. Exp.	93.9	29.5	20.8	13.2	6.3	2.2
Cash Flow	135	104	59.7	16.4	3.6	-6.1

Ratio Analysis

	1994	1993	1992	1991	1990	1989
Curr. Ratio	2.7	3.1	2.4	2.4	1.6	2.2
% LT Debt of Cap.	28.2	23.9	33.9	40.2	21.6	13.3
% Net Inc.of Revs.	1.9	13.1	9.9	6.1	NM	NM
% Ret. on Assets	8.1	14.2	9.0	3.8	NM	NM
% Ret. on Equity	14.0	24.7	18.7	8.2	NM	NM

Dividend Data —Semi-annual cash payments were initiated in April 1993. Recent payments were:

Amt. of Div. $	Date Decl.	Ex-Div. Date	Stock of Record	Payment Date
0.030	Oct. 31	Nov. 08	Nov. 15	Dec. 01 '94
0.040	May. 01	May. 08	May. 12	Jun. 01 '95

Data as orig. reptd.; bef. results of disc. opers. and/or spec. items. Per share data adj. for stk. divs. as of ex-div. date. EPS for 1994 third quarter represents nine mos. data. E-Estimated. NA-Not Available. NM-Not Meaningful. NR-Not Ranked.

Office—8800 N.W. 36th St., Miami, FL 33178. **Tel**—(305) 590-2200. **Chrmn, CEO & Pres**—P. Frost. **Deputy CEO**—I. Kaye. **Vice Chrmn**—J. Fishman. **SVP & CFO**—M. W. Fipps. **Dirs**—M. Andrews, L. Bentsen, E. Biekert, L. B. Daniels, D. B. Fascell, J. Fishman, P. Frost, H. S. Geneen, P. M. Gottsegen, C. Hsaio, L. Kasprick, I. Kaye, H. M. Krueger, J. H. Moxley III, M. L. Pearce, M. Weintraub. **Transfer Agent & Registrar**—Southeast Bank, Miami. **Reincorporated** in Florida in 1993. **Empl**-8,185. **S&P Analyst:** Herman Saftlas

Idaho Power

NYSE Symbol **IDA**
In S&P MidCap 400

29-SEP-95 **Industry:** Utilities-Electric

Summary: This utility provides electric service to a 20,000-square-mile area in southern Idaho, eastern Oregon and northern Nevada.

Quantitative Evaluations

Outlook (1 Lowest—5 Highest) • **1+**

Fair Value • **22¾**

Risk • **Low**

Earn./Div. Rank • **B**

Technical Eval. • **Bearish** since 7/95

Rel. Strength Rank (1 Lowest—99 Highest) • **75**

Insider Activity • **NA**

Recent Price • 26⅞ Yield • 6.7%
52 Wk Range • 27-22 12-Mo. P/E • 14.4

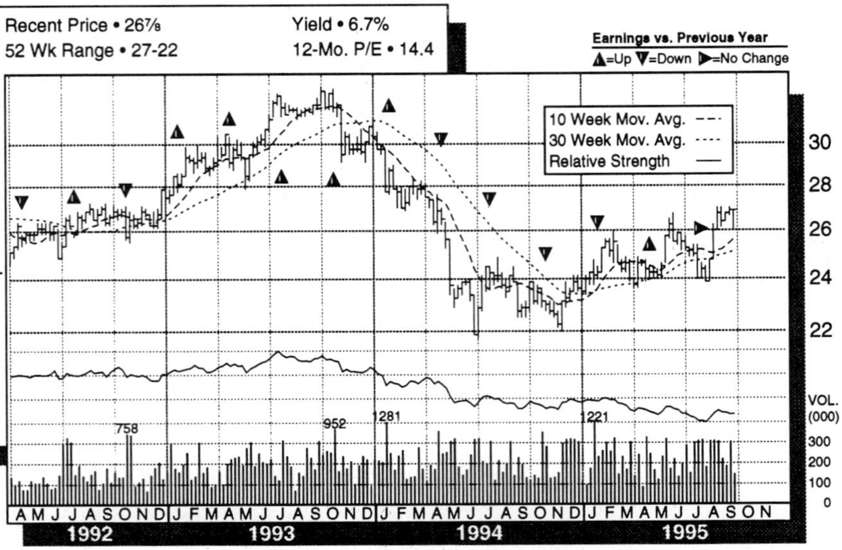

Business Profile - 29-SEP-95

IDA provides electric service in Idaho and, to a much lesser extent, in eastern Oregon and northern Nevada. In a normal year, about 60% of power generation is hydroelectric; most of the remainder is coal. In January 1995, IDA received $17.2 million in general rate relief, substantially below the $37.1 million requested. IDA is evaluating all options available to move toward financial recovery, including substantial reductions in expenditures and a review of customer programs and service levels.

Operational Review - 29-SEP-95

Earnings advanced, year to year, in 1995's first half, reflecting rate relief and an increase in customers, partially offset by milder winter and spring weather that reduced residential loads for heating and cooling. Operating expenses fell 8.5%, due to improved hydroelectric generation conditions, and operating income advanced 19%. However, following a 4.9% increase in interest charges, a higher effective tax rate and 12% higher preferred dividends, share earnings were up only 7.1%.

Stock Performance - 22-SEP-95

In the past 30 trading days, IDA's shares have increased 9%, compared to a 5% rise in the S&P 500. Average trading volume for the past five days was 28,840 shares, compared with the 40-day moving average of 56,272 shares.

Key Stock Statistics

Dividend Rate/Share	1.86	Shareholders	26,200
Shs. outstg. (M)	37.6	Market cap. (B)	$ 1.0
Avg. daily vol. (M)	0.046	Inst. holdings	19%
Tang. Bk. Value/Share	17.89	Insider holdings	NA
Beta	0.49		

Value of $10,000 invested 5 years ago: $ 13,654

Fiscal Year Ending Dec. 31

	1995	% Change	1994	% Change	1993	% Change
Revenues (Million $)						
1Q	131.3	2%	128.8	-9%	140.8	22%
2Q	130.3	1%	128.5	NM	129.5	4%
3Q	—	—	151.0	12%	134.6	4%
4Q	—	—	135.3	NM	135.6	4%
Yr.	—	—	543.7	NM	540.4	9%
Income (Million $)						
1Q	20.73	14%	18.26	-14%	21.35	60%
2Q	17.59	3%	17.03	-8%	18.52	49%
3Q	—	—	16.29	NM	16.43	9%
4Q	—	—	23.35	-17%	28.17	47%
Yr.	—	—	74.93	-11%	84.46	41%
Earnings Per Share ($)						
1Q	0.50	14%	0.44	-20%	0.55	57%
2Q	0.41	NM	0.41	-13%	0.47	47%
3Q	—	—	0.38	-5%	0.40	5%
4Q	—	—	0.57	-20%	0.71	45%
Yr.	—	—	1.80	-16%	2.14	38%

Next earnings report expected: late October

Idaho Power

29-SEP-95

Business Summary - 29-SEP-95

Idaho Power Company supplies electricity in an area of 20,000 square miles (Snake River Valley) in southern Idaho (serving all or a portion of 28 counties), eastern Oregon (three) and northern Nevada (one) with a population of about 695,000. As of December 31, 1994, the company supplied electric energy to about 330,300 general business customers. IDA is a combination hydro-thermal utility, with 17 hydro power plants and part ownership in three coal-fired generating plants. Contributions to revenues by class of customer:

	1994	1993	1992	1991
Commercial-industrial	38%	36%	39%	38%
Residential	34%	34%	34%	35%
Irrigation	12%	14%	19%	16%
Public utilities	11%	16%	8%	11%
Other	5%	---	---	---

The fuel mix in 1994 was 40% hydro, 46% coal and 14% purchased power. IDA is a dual-peaking system, with the larger energy peak generally occurring in the summer. Peak load in 1994 was 2,392 mw, up 11% from 1993. IDA estimated its customer energy demand growth at 1.1% per year for the next 20 years. Electricity sales for 1995 are projected at about 15.3 million mw.

In October 1992, IDA completed the Milner hydroelectric facility, and work to double capacity at the Swan Falls plant was completed in 1994. A fivefold capacity expansion project at the Twin Falls facility was completed in July 1995.

Important Developments

Aug. '95—The Idaho Public Utilities Commission (IPUC) authorized Idaho Power to increase its annual Idaho retail rates by $3.8 million, or 0.9%. This interim increase was granted subject to refund pending a review of legal briefs. The company originally applied for a $6.3 million (1.5%) increase. Separately, Idaho Power filed an application with the IPUC for an accounting order to defer and amortize the extraordinary costs associated with IDA's ongoing reorganization. Idaho Power has asked that these costs be spread over a 10-year period beginning in October 1995, with no change in rates. The company also asked the IPUC to approve a plan to modify the way it amortizes its accumulated deferred investment tax credits.

Capitalization

Long Term Debt: $673,055,000 (6/95).
Preferred Stock: $132,325,000.

Per Share Data ($) (Year Ended Dec. 31)

	1994	1993	1992	1991	1990	1989
Tangible Bk. Val.	17.91	17.86	17.28	17.06	17.38	16.69
Earnings	1.80	2.14	1.55	1.56	1.91	2.37
Dividends	1.86	1.86	1.86	1.86	1.86	1.83
Payout Ratio	103%	87%	120%	119%	97%	77%
Prices - High	30⅝	33	28¾	28¾	29⅜	30
- Low	21¾	27¼	24⅜	24¼	22¾	22
P/E Ratio - High	17	15	19	18	15	13
- Low	12	13	16	16	12	9

Income Statement Analysis (Million $)

	1994	%Chg	1993	%Chg	1992	%Chg	1991
Revs.	544	NM	540	8%	498	3%	483
Depr.	60.2	3%	58.7	-2%	59.8	4%	57.6
Maint.	43.5	NM	43.1	20%	35.9	-19%	44.4
Fxd. Chgs. Cov.	2.6	-6%	2.8	26%	2.2	NM	2.2
Constr. Credits	3.5	-36%	5.5	12%	4.9	23%	4.0
Eff. Tax Rate	31%	—	30%	—	28%	—	27%
Net Inc.	74.9	-11%	84.5	41%	60.0	3%	58.0

Balance Sheet & Other Fin. Data (Million $)

	1994	1993	1992	1991	1990	1989
Gross Prop.	2,432	2,345	2,269	2,169	2,044	1,976
Cap. Exp.	111	97.0	119	136	80.0	62.0
Net Prop.	1,657	1,616	1,585	1,529	1,452	1,457
Capitalization:						
LT Debt	693	694	702	630	562	543
% LT Debt	46	47	49	48	46	46
Pfd.	132	133	108	108	59.0	59.0
% Pfd.	8.80	8.90	7.50	8.20	4.80	4.90
Common	674	662	625	580	591	589
% Common	45	45	44	44	49	50
Total Cap.	1,952	1,919	1,719	1,596	1,487	1,459

Ratio Analysis

	1994	1993	1992	1991	1990	1989
Oper. Ratio	78.8	76.8	79.6	78.2	76.3	74.3
% Earn. on Net Prop.	7.1	7.8	6.5	7.1	7.7	9.0
% Ret. on Revs.	13.8	15.6	12.0	12.0	14.9	17.1
% Ret. On Invest.Cap	6.6	7.6	6.8	7.4	8.3	9.4
% Return On Com.Eqty	10.1	12.2	9.0	9.0	11.0	13.9

Dividend Data —Dividends have been paid since 1917. A poison pill stock purchase right was adopted in 1990. A dividend reinvestment plan is available.

Amt. of Div. $	Date Decl.	Ex-Div. Date	Stock of Record	Payment Date
0.465	Sep. 08	Oct. 19	Oct. 25	Nov. 21 '94
0.465	Jan. 12	Jan. 19	Jan. 25	Feb. 21 '95
0.465	Mar. 09	Apr. 19	Apr. 25	May. 19 '95
0.465	Jul. 13	Jul. 21	Jul. 25	Aug. 21 '95
0.465	Sep. 14	Oct. 23	Oct. 25	Nov. 20 '95

Data as orig. reptd.; bef. results of disc opers. and/or spec. items. Per share data adj. for stk. divs. as of ex-div. date. E-Estimated. NA-Not Available. NM-Not Meaningful. NR-Not Ranked.

Office—1221 W. Idaho St., Boise, ID 83702-5627. **Tel**—(208) 388-2200. **Chrmn & CEO**—J. W. Marshall. **Pres & COO**—L. R. Gunnoe. **VP & CFO**—J. L. Keen. **VP & Treas**—D. K. Bowers. **Investor Contact**—Lawrence F. Spencer. **Dirs**—R. D. Bolinder, R. L. Breezley, J. B. Carley, L. R. Gunnoe, P. T. Johnson, J. K. Lemley, E. Loveless, J. W. Marshall, J. H. Miller, P. S. O'Neill, G. C. Rose, P. Soulen. **Transfer Agents**—Co.'s office; Bank of New York, NYC. **Registrars**—First Security Bank of Idaho, Boise; Bank of New York, NYC. **Incorporated** in Maine in 1915; reincorporated in Idaho in 1989. **Empl**-1,609. **S&P Analyst:** Ronald J. Gross

Illinois Central

NYSE Symbol **IC**
In S&P MidCap 400

25-SEP-95

Industry: Railroads

Summary: IC operates a 2,700-mile railroad serving six Midwestern and Southern states between Chicago and the Gulf of Mexico. Chemical traffic generates about 25% of freight revenues.

S&P Opinion: Accumulate (★★★★)

Recent Price • 40¾ | Yield • 2.5%
52 Wk Range • 42-28⅝ | 12-Mo. P/E • 13.8

Quantitative Evaluations

Outlook (1 Lowest—5 Highest)
• **5+**

Fair Value
• **51⅛**

Risk
• **Low**

Earn./Div. Rank
• **NR**

Technical Eval.
• **Bullish** since 12/94

Rel. Strength Rank (1 Lowest—99 Highest)
• **62**

Insider Activity
• **Neutral**

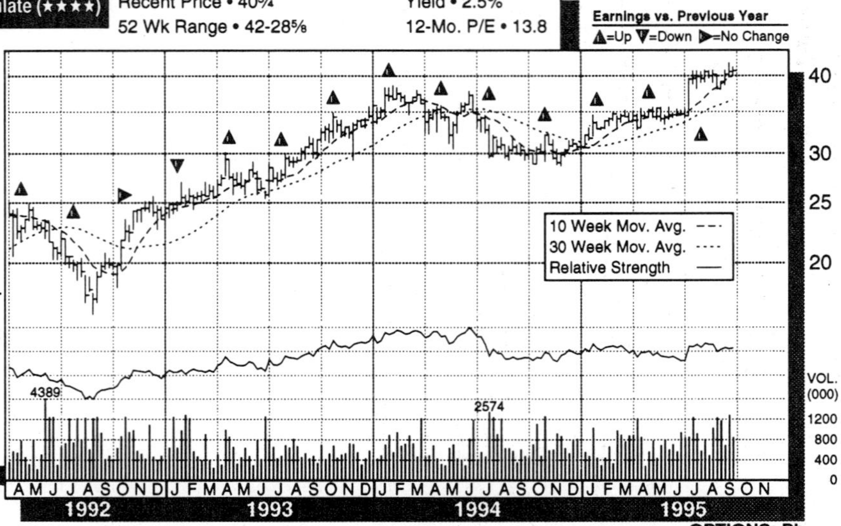

OPTIONS: Ph

Overview - 25-SEP-95

Intermodal traffic in 1995 will benefit from a new pact with Southern Pacific plus increased container volumes from shipping lines. Chemical shipments will benefit from economic growth, a new bulk transfer facility and the absence of disruptions at two major petrochemical plants in 1994. Grain traffic will benefit from increased movements to poultry producers, stronger export markets and a diversion of volume from barge operators. Coal volumes are expected to fall, reflecting the loss of the Georgia Power contract and reduced demand from domestic utilities stemming from a mild winter. Increased shipments of paper and motor vehicles are anticipated. Margins should widen as fuel costs decline, equipment lease expense is pared and personal injury claims are checked.

Valuation - 25-SEP-95

The shares of this Midwestern railroad reached all-time highs in September as investors once again embraced cyclical issues. IC also has attracted speculators seeking the next rail acquisition target in a year that has seen two rail mergers completed and a third proposed. IC's second quarter profit performance was exceptional in view of the sluggish economic backdrop. While IC now is no longer undervalued, we believe the shares can continue to outperform the market as it is assigned a higher earnings multiple. We think IC deserves a premium to other rail issues for consistently posting the industry's highest return on investment.

Key Stock Statistics

S&P EPS Est. 1995	3.10	Tang. Bk. Value/Share	10.96
P/E on S&P Est. 1995	13.1	Beta	1.62
S&P EPS Est. 1996	3.45	Shareholders	15,000
Dividend Rate/Share	1.00	Market cap. (B)	$ 1.7
Shs. outstg. (M)	41.8	Inst. holdings	88%
Avg. daily vol. (M)	0.235	Insider holdings	NA

Value of $10,000 invested 5 years ago: NA

Fiscal Year Ending Dec. 31

	1995	% Change	1994	% Change	1993	% Change
Revenues (Million $)						
1Q	167.5	14%	147.5	3%	142.7	3%
2Q	156.2	8%	145.2	10%	132.1	2%
3Q	—	—	146.7	NM	147.4	12%
4Q	—	—	154.5	8%	142.5	-3%
Yr.	—	—	593.9	5%	564.7	3%
Income (Million $)						
1Q	34.30	24%	27.70	15%	24.00	14%
2Q	29.60	19%	24.80	25%	19.90	18%
3Q	—	—	25.90	20%	21.50	22%
4Q	—	—	35.50	35%	26.30	56%
Yr.	—	—	113.9	24%	91.70	26%
Earnings Per Share ($)						
1Q	0.81	25%	0.65	16%	0.56	12%
2Q	0.71	22%	0.58	23%	0.47	17%
3Q	E0.70	15%	0.61	22%	0.50	22%
4Q	E0.88	6%	0.83	36%	0.61	56%
Yr.	E3.10	16%	2.67	25%	2.14	26%

Next earnings report expected: late October

Illinois Central

Business Summary - 22-SEP-95

Illinois Central Corp. is the parent company of Illinois Central Railroad Co., which traces its origins to 1851. A plan to merge with Kansas City Southern Railway was abandoned in October 1994.

The Illinois Central Railroad operates the nation's 10th largest rail network. Its system includes 2,700 miles of main lines (including 190 miles of trackage rights), 1,700 miles of passing, yard and switching track and 200 miles of secondary main lines. IC serves shippers in Illinois, Kentucky, Tennessee, Alabama, Mississippi and Louisiana. The northern terminus is at Chicago, while the southernmost point is the Gulf of Mexico.

Contributions to freight revenues in recent years:

	1994	1993	1992
Chemicals	24.8%	25.0%	24.3%
Coal	15.2%	12.8%	15.3%
Grain	10.2%	14.0%	12.2%
Paper	12.2%	12.4%	12.1%
Mill/food products	8.5%	9.8%	8.8%
Intermodal	6.6%	5.4%	5.4%
All other	22.5%	20.6%	21.9%

Some 74% of the railroad's traffic originates on its system (of which 28% is forwarded to other railroads), 17% is received from other carriers and terminated by IC and 9% is represented by bridge or through traffic. The average haul in 1994 was 286 miles, compared with 293 miles in 1993. In 1994, IC transported 21.2 billion ton-miles of freight generating average revenue of 2.7 cents per ton-mile, compared with 20.3 billion ton-miles in 1993 earning 2.7 cents. The operating ratio in 1994 was 66.3%, compared with 68.2% in 1993.

IC's equipment fleet at 1994 year end consisted of 417 locomotives (of which 274 are owned), 16,498 freight cars (10,060 owned) and 625 pieces of work equipment and 898 highway trailers and tractors.

Important Developments

Jul. '95—IC signed a new labor agreement, covering wages and work rule issues through 1999 year-end, with the Brotherhood of Electrical Workers. Since 1994, IC has reached labor settlements with eight unions representing some 42% of its union workforce.
Jul. '95—IC made an $11.4 million extraordinary charge ($0.27 a share) reflecting costs associated with the prepayment of $160 million face amount of notes due between 1998 and 2001.
Jun. '95—Through the end of 1995's first quarter IC has repurchased 828,100 (or 2.0%) of its common shares for $28.0 million (or $33.81 a share) under a $60 million program authorized in November 1994.

Capitalization

Long Term Debt: $352,100,000 (6/95).

Per Share Data ($) (Year Ended Dec. 31)

	1994	1993	1992	1991	1990	1989
Tangible Bk. Val.	10.66	8.86	7.94	6.15	3.61	-0.04
Cash Flow	3.31	2.69	2.20	2.14	1.99	0.66
Earnings	2.67	2.14	1.70	1.64	1.31	0.09
Dividends	0.88	0.70	0.50	Nil	Nil	Nil
Payout Ratio	33%	33%	29%	Nil	Nil	Nil
Prices - High	38⅝	36	25⅝	23⅜	11⅞	NA
- Low	28⅝	23⅝	16½	7⅞	5⅝	NA
P/E Ratio - High	14	17	15	14	9	NA
- Low	11	11	10	4	4	NA

Income Statement Analysis (Million $)

	1994	%Chg	1993	%Chg	1992	%Chg	1991
Revs.	594	5%	565	3%	547	NM	550
Oper. Inc.	228	12%	203	12%	182	10%	166
Depr.	27.4	19%	23.0	7%	21.4	7%	20.0
Int. Exp.	31.2	-11%	35.2	-24%	46.2	-23%	59.7
Pretax Inc.	173	17%	148	35%	110	14%	96.2
Eff. Tax Rate	34%	—	38%	—	34%	—	32%
Net Inc.	114	24%	91.7	26%	72.5	11%	65.4

Balance Sheet & Other Fin. Data (Million $)

	1994	1993	1992	1991	1990	1989
Cash	24.2	10.7	34.6	32.7	13.5	27.3
Curr. Assets	108	147	165	180	174	236
Total Assets	1,309	1,259	1,206	1,184	1,152	1,165
Curr. Liab.	173	179	168	183	218	309
LT Debt	329	360	367	414	486	538
Common Eqty.	454	377	339	260	128	-1.0
Total Cap.	1,001	940	877	846	774	773
Cap. Exp.	90.0	96.0	51.0	50.0	89.0	991
Cash Flow	141	115	93.9	85.4	62.7	18.7

Ratio Analysis

	1994	1993	1992	1991	1990	1989
Curr. Ratio	0.6	0.8	1.0	1.0	0.8	0.8
% LT Debt of Cap.	32.8	38.3	41.9	48.9	62.8	69.6
% Net Inc.of Revs.	19.2	16.2	13.2	11.9	8.5	2.5
% Ret. on Assets	8.9	7.4	6.0	5.1	3.5	NA
% Ret. on Equity	27.4	25.6	24.1	31.7	NM	NA

Dividend Data —Dividends were initiated in 1992. A dividend reinvestment plan is available.

Amt. of Div. $	Date Decl.	Ex-Div. Date	Stock of Record	Payment Date
0.210	Sep. 08	Sep. 16	Sep. 22	Oct. 06 '94
0.250	Nov. 22	Dec. 09	Dec. 15	Jan. 05 '95
0.250	Mar. 02	Mar. 17	Mar. 23	Apr. 06 '95
0.250	Jun. 01	Jun. 20	Jun. 22	Jul. 06 '95
0.250	Sep. 07	Sep. 19	Sep. 21	Oct. 05 '95

Data as orig. reptd.; bef. results of disc. opers. and/or spec. items. Per share data adj. for stk. divs. as of ex-div. date. E-Estimated. NA-Not Available. NM-Not Meaningful. NR-Not Ranked.

Office—455 N. Cityfront Plaza Drive, Chicago, IL 60611-5504. **Tel**—(312) 755-7500. **Chrmn**—G. H. Lamphere. **Pres & CEO**—E. H. Harrison. **VP-Secy**—R. A. Lane. **VP-CFO**—D. W. Phillips. **Investor Contact**—Ann G. Thoma (312-755-7591). **Dirs**—T. A. Barron, G. D. Gould, E. H. Harrison, W. B. Johnson, G. H. Lamphere, A. P. Lynch, S. F. Prior IV, F. J. Taylor, J. V. Tunney, A. H. Washkowitz. **Transfer Agent & Registrar**—First National Bank of Boston. **Incorporated** in Delaware in 1989. **Empl**-3,250. **S&P Analyst:** Stephen R. Klein

STANDARD & POOR'S

STOCK REPORTS

Illinova Corp.

NYSE Symbol **ILN**
In S&P MidCap 400

06-SEP-95 **Industry:** Utilities-Electric

Summary: This holding company, formed in May 1994, owns Illinois Power, an electric and gas utility that serves a 15,000 sq. mi. area in northern, central and southern Illinois.

S&P Opinion: Hold (★★★)

Recent Price • 25¼ | Yield • 4.0%
52 Wk Range • 26-18⅛ | 12-Mo. P/E • 11.9

Quantitative Evaluations

Outlook (1 Lowest—5 Highest)
• **1+**
Fair Value
• **20⅞**
Risk
• **Low**
Earn./Div. Rank
• **B**

Technical Eval.
• **Bullish** since 12/94
Rel. Strength Rank (1 Lowest—99 Highest)
• **45**
Insider Activity
• **NA**

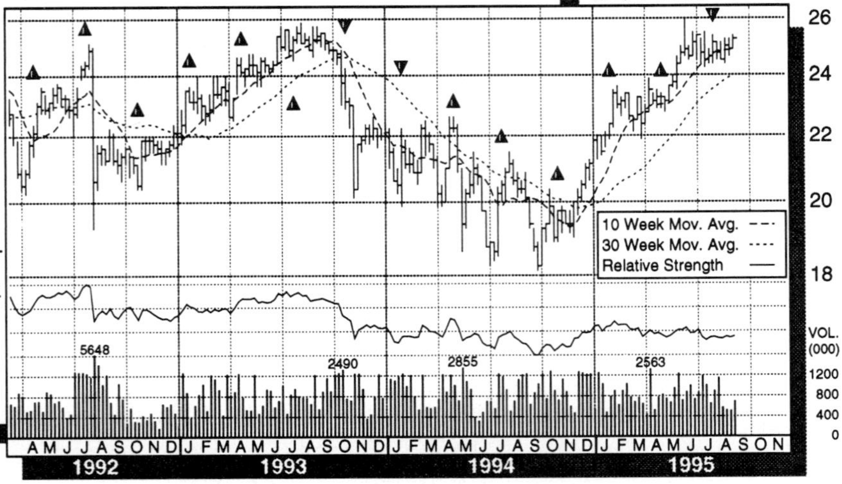

Overview - 06-SEP-95

Share earnings in 1995 should benefit from the remainder of the April 1994 gas rate increase, and industrial and commercial sales growth (reflecting an improving regional economy). Successful cost management efforts will be partially offest by costs associated with the recently completed outage at the Clinton Power Station and the costs of implementing an early retirement program (scheduled for the fourth quarter). Results in 1996 and beyond should benefit from annual savings of about $35 million related to the work force reduction.

Valuation - 05-SEP-95

ILN's shares, like those of many in its industry, fell substantially in 1994. However, the shares made a partial rebound at the end of the year, and have risen about 15% since the beginning of 1995. The dividend was boosted 25% with the February 1995 payment, and the shares are currently yielding 4.0%. The payout ratio is well below the industry average, and future dividend hikes should continue in line with earnings growth. The shares are currently trading at about 11X estimated 1996 EPS of $2.30. Although this is slightly below the average multiple of the industry, the discount is justified by risks inherent in owning the Clinton nuclear station, which represents 52% of total assets. However, with a 4.0% yield, and the likely prospect for growing dividends, the shares are an attractive holding for total return.

Key Stock Statistics

S&P EPS Est. 1995	2.15	Tang. Bk. Value/Share	19.48
P/E on S&P Est. 1995	11.7	Beta	0.84
S&P EPS Est. 1996	2.30	Shareholders	38,800
Dividend Rate/Share	1.00	Market cap. (B)	$ 1.9
Shs. outstg. (M)	75.6	Inst. holdings	73%
Avg. daily vol. (M)	0.119	Insider holdings	NA

Value of $10,000 invested 5 years ago: $ 15,713

Fiscal Year Ending Dec. 31

	1995	% Change	1994	% Change	1993	% Change
Revenues (Million $)						
1Q	425.5	-4%	442.9	12%	395.0	3%
2Q	344.3	-2%	349.6	NM	350.5	4%
3Q	—	—	428.9	-5%	452.4	15%
4Q	—	—	368.1	-4%	383.2	5%
Yr.	—	—	1,590	NM	1,581	7%
Income (Million $)						
1Q	32.40	19%	27.30	-2%	27.90	87%
2Q	26.30	-11%	29.50	NM	29.30	43%
3Q	—	—	71.80	NM	-123.9	NM
4Q	—	—	23.20	113%	10.90	-48%
Yr.	—	—	151.8	NM	-55.80	NM
Earnings Per Share ($)						
1Q	0.43	19%	0.36	29%	0.28	180%
2Q	0.35	-10%	0.39	30%	0.30	67%
3Q	E1.00	5%	0.95	NM	-1.72	NM
4Q	E0.37	-5%	0.39	NM	0.06	-67%
Yr.	E2.15	3%	2.09	NM	-1.08	NM

Next earnings report expected: early October

Illinova Corp.

Business Summary - 06-SEP-95

Illinova is the holding company for Illinois Power Co. (IPC), an electric and gas utility that supplies electricity and natural gas to 555,000 customers in a 15,000 sq. mi. area of Illinois. Electric operations provided 81% of revenues and 94% of operating income in 1994, and gas activities provided 19% and 6%, respectively. Revenues by type of customer in 1994 were:

	Electric	Gas
Residential	37%	64%
Commercial	23%	22%
Industrial	29%	10%
Other	11%	4%

The fuel mix in 1994 was 66% coal, 33% nuclear and 1% oil and gas. Peak demand in 1994 was 3,395 mw, and system capacity was 4,121 mw, for a capacity margin of 17.6%. Gas sales in 1994 were 584 million therms, versus 597 million in 1993.

The cost of construction and capital requirements for 1995-9 is estimated at $1.25 billion. With operation of the 950,000 kw Clinton nuclear unit starting in November 1987, IPC does not expect additional generating capacity to be required until after 2000.

Wholly owned Illinova Generating Co. (IGC) invests in energy supply projects worldwide, and competes in the independent power market. In August 1994, IGC purchased 50% of the North American Energy Services Co., a supplier of operations, maintenance and support services to the independent power generation industry. In July 1994, ILN formed Illinova Power Marketing, Inc., which plans to become active in brokering and marketing electric power and gas to various customers.

Important Developments

Aug. '95—ILN agreed in principle to buy certain Soyland Power Cooperative assets, including Soyland's 13% interest in Clinton Power Station and two diesel units, and its 21 power supply contracts for central Illinois electric cooperatives. Financial terms were not disclosed. The agreement is subject to regulatory approval.

Feb. '95—ILN said that if it meets its reduced employment levels primarily through an early retirement program, and assuming that its bargaining unit employees negotiate a program similar to one offered to salaried employees, it will incur a pretax charge of about $42 million in the 1995 fourth quarter. The reductions are expected to save about $35 million annually in operating and maintenance expenses, beginning in 1996. The company added that it expects double-digit earnings and dividend growth in 1995, as a result of cost management efforts and improved service.

Capitalization

Long Term Debt: $1,937,400,000 (6/95).
Cum. Pfd. & Pref. Stock: $318,500,000.

Per Share Data ($)

(Year Ended Dec. 31)

	1994	1993	1992	1991	1990	1989
Tangible Bk. Val.	19.17	17.26	17.65	18.27	17.97	19.77
Earnings	2.09	-1.08	1.23	1.04	-1.53	-4.34
Dividends	0.80	0.80	0.80	0.20	Nil	1.32
Payout Ratio	38%	NM	65%	19%	Nil	NM
Prices - High	22⅝	25⅞	25⅛	24⅛	19⅜	21¾
- Low	18⅛	20⅛	19¼	15⅜	12¾	13⅜
P/E Ratio - High	11	NM	20	23	NM	NM
- Low	9	NM	16	15	NM	NM

Income Statement Analysis (Million $)

	1994	%Chg	1993	%Chg	1992	%Chg	1991
Revs.	1,590	NM	1,581	7%	1,480	NM	1,475
Depr.	176	4%	169	5%	161	-9%	177
Maint.	90.0	-11%	101	NM	102	17%	87.0
Fxd. Chgs. Cov.	2.7	135%	1.1	-41%	1.9	12%	1.7
Constr. Credits	9.3	29%	7.2	44%	5.0	67%	3.0
Eff. Tax Rate	42%	—	NM	—	39%	—	40%
Net Inc.	152	NM	-55.8	NM	122	12%	109

Balance Sheet & Other Fin. Data (Million $)

	1994	1993	1992	1991	1990	1989
Gross Prop.	6,747	6,614	6,239	6,056	5,945	6,014
Cap. Exp.	194	278	244	141	131	97.0
Net Prop.	4,644	4,640	4,429	4,371	4,412	4,624
Capitalization:						
LT Debt	1,946	1,926	2,017	2,153	2,204	2,352
% LT Debt	52	54	53	54	54	54
Pfd.	358	352	403	413	449	475
% Pfd.	9.50	9.80	11	10	11	11
Common	1,450	1,321	1,423	1,456	1,415	1,554
% Common	39	40	37	36	35	36
Total Cap.	4,964	4,736	4,753	4,877	4,877	5,179

Ratio Analysis

	1994	1993	1992	1991	1990	1989
Oper. Ratio	79.8	80.7	80.7	80.2	81.8	81.3
% Earn. on Net Prop.	6.9	6.7	6.5	6.6	5.6	5.0
% Ret. on Revs.	9.6	NM	8.3	7.4	NM	NM
% Ret. On Invest.Cap	6.5	2.2	6.0	5.9	2.4	NM
% Return On Com.Eqty	11.4	NM	6.5	5.5	NM	NM

Dividend Data —Except for 1990, common dividends have been paid each year since 1947.

Amt. of Div. $	Date Decl.	Ex-Div. Date	Stock of Record	Payment Date
0.200	Aug. 10	Oct. 03	Oct. 10	Nov. 01 '94
0.250	Oct. 12	Jan. 01	Jan. 10	Feb. 01 '95
0.250	Feb. 08	Apr. 04	Apr. 10	May. 01 '95
0.250	Jun. 15	Jul. 06	Jul. 10	Aug. 01 '95
0.250	Aug. 09	Oct. 05	Oct. 10	Nov. 01 '95

Data as orig. reptd.; bef. results of disc opers. and/or spec. items. Per share data adj. for stk. divs. as of ex-div. date. E-Estimated. NA-Not Available. NM-Not Meaningful. NR-Not Ranked.

Office—500 South 27th St., Decatur, IL 62525. **Tel**—(217) 424-6600. **Chrmn, Pres & CEO**—L. D. Haab. **SVP & CFO**—L. F. Altenbaumer. **VP & Secy**—Leah M. Stetzner. **Investor Contact**—Russel J. Naylor (217-424-8715). **Dirs**—R. R. Berry, L. D. Haab, D. E. Lasater, D. S. Perkins, R. M. Powers, W. D. Scott, R. L. Thompson, W. M. Vannoy, M. von Ferstel, C. W. Wells, J. D. Zeglis, V. K. Zimmerman. **Transfer Agent & Registrar**—Co. itself. **Incorporated** in Illinois in 1994. **Empl**-4,350. **S&P Analyst:** Ronald J. Gross

STANDARD & POOR'S

STOCK REPORTS

Indiana Energy

NYSE Symbol **IEI**
In S&P MidCap 400

29-SEP-95 **Industry:** Utilities-Gas

Summary: This holding company has subsidiaries that are primarily engaged in providing natural gas distribution and related services.

Quantitative Evaluations

Outlook (1 Lowest—5 Highest)
• **1+**

Fair Value
• **17¾**

Risk
• **Average**

Earn./Div. Rank
• **B+**

Technical Eval.
• **Bearish** since 6/95

Rel. Strength Rank (1 Lowest—99 Highest)
• **67**

Insider Activity
• **Neutral**

Recent Price • 21⅛
52 Wk Range • 22-17½
Yield • 5.2%
12-Mo. P/E • 14.8

Earnings vs. Previous Year
▲=Up ▼=Down ▶=No Change

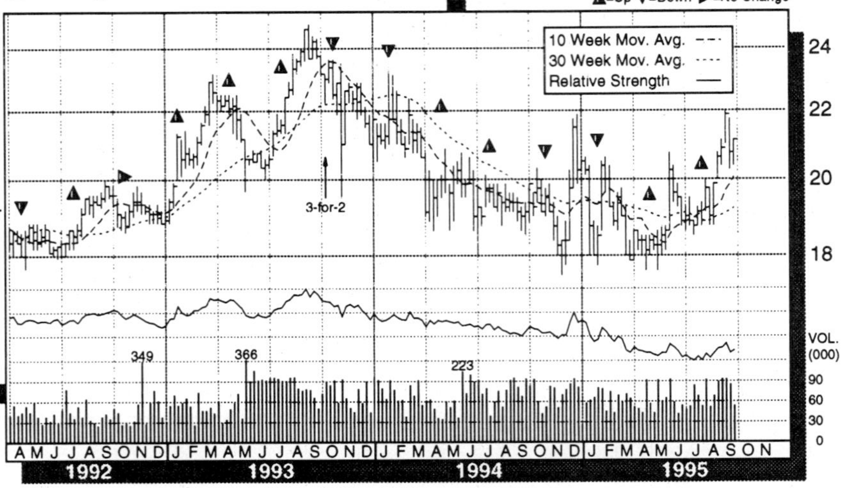

Business Profile - 21-SEP-95

Through its main subsidiary, Indiana Gas, this holding company distributes natural gas to more than 450,000 customers in central, north central and southern Indiana. The company does not serve Indianapolis, where it is headquartered. Residential customers provided about 60% of revenues in fiscal 1994. IEI Investments Inc. was formed to control nonregulated investments, including IGC Energy, Inc. and Energy Realty, Inc.

Operational Review - 29-SEP-95

Utility operating revenues fell nearly 19%, year to year, in the first nine months of fiscal 1995, reflecting weather that was 16% warmer than the same period last year and 14% warmer than normal, partially offset by additional residential and commercial customers. Gas costs fell even faster, and with operating expenses down 7.2% and a 60% decrease in other expense, share earnings fell just 5.2%.

Stock Performance - 22-SEP-95

In the past 30 trading days, IEI's shares have increased 11%, compared to a 5% rise in the S&P 500. Average trading volume for the past five days was 10,600 shares, compared with the 40-day moving average of 17,182 shares.

Key Stock Statistics

Dividend Rate/Share	1.10	Shareholders	11,400
Shs. outstg. (M)	22.6	Market cap. (B)	$0.477
Avg. daily vol. (M)	0.017	Inst. holdings	19%
Tang. Bk. Value/Share	12.57	Insider holdings	NA
Beta	0.19		

Value of $10,000 invested 5 years ago: $ 19,725

Fiscal Year Ending Sep. 30

	1995	% Change	1994	% Change	1993	% Change
Revenues (Million $)						
1Q	113.1	-26%	151.9	-2%	155.5	16%
2Q	150.5	-23%	195.7	10%	178.3	20%
3Q	83.08	7%	77.83	-23%	101.3	41%
4Q	—	—	49.91	-51%	101.2	80%
Yr.	—	—	475.3	-5%	499.3	21%
Income (Million $)						
1Q	10.87	-28%	15.20	-27%	20.69	87%
2Q	22.08	2%	21.67	23%	17.56	16%
3Q	4.22	73%	2.44	NM	0.65	NM
4Q	—	—	-4.87	NM	-4.31	NM
Yr.	—	—	—	—	34.58	44%
Earnings Per Share ($)						
1Q	0.48	-28%	0.67	-33%	1.00	88%
2Q	0.98	2%	0.96	14%	0.84	15%
3Q	0.19	73%	0.11	NM	0.03	NM
4Q	—	—	-0.21	NM	-0.20	NM
Yr.	—	—	1.53	-6%	1.62	40%

Next earnings report expected: late October

Indiana Energy

Business Summary - 29-SEP-95

Indiana Energy is a holding company whose main subsidiary, Indiana Gas, distributes natural gas in the lower two-thirds of that state. IEI Investments Inc. controls the company's nonregulated investments. Revenues by customer class were:

	1994	1993	1992
Residential	59%	53%	56%
Commercial	25%	22%	23%
Industrial-interruptible	6%	12%	11%
Industrial-firm	9%	7%	8%
Other	1%	6%	3%

Gas volumes sold and transported in fiscal 1994 amounted to 116.3 Bcf (111.4 Bcf in fiscal 1993), including residential sales of 46.7 Bcf (44.7 Bcf), commercial sales of 22.9 Bcf (23.0 Bcf), interruptible industrial sales of 7.1 Bcf (21.9 Bcf), firm industrial sales of 9.4 Bcf (9.5 Bcf), and gas transported 30.1 Bcf (12.3 Bcf).

Customers served at September 30, 1994, totaled 441,765, up from 431,334 a year earlier. The service area contains diversified manufacturing and agriculture-related enterprises, including automotive parts, feed, flour and grain processing, and metal castings. Degree days in fiscal 1994 were 102% of normal, versus 99% in fiscal 1993.

Indiana Gas (IG) purchases all of its natural gas from producers, brokers and marketers under short and medium-term contracts. IG also has contracts with pipelines for storage and transportation of natural gas.

IEI Investments has two subsidiaries--IGC Energy, Inc. and Energy Realty, Inc. In November 1994, IGC Energy formed Indiana Energy Services, Inc., which will provide natural gas services to large volume industrial and commercial customers, as well as to small local distribution companies in Indiana. IGC Energy also has an investment in Loggins, Inc., a distributor of flexible gas pipe and of products for distributing and using natural gas. In fiscal 1994, nonutility operations recorded a $0.2 million loss, versus income of $6.3 million in fiscal 1993.

In October 1994, the Indiana Utility Regulatory Commission raised Indiana Gas's authorized net operating income to $51.1 million, from $47.1 million.

Important Developments

Jul. '95—Directors authorized the company to repurchase up to 700,000 shares of its outstanding common stock.

May '95— The Indiana Utility Regulatory Commission determined that the costs incurred by Indiana Gas Co. to investigate and clean up former manufactured gas plant sites are not recoverable as operating expenses from its customers.

Capitalization

Long Term Debt: $175,538,000 (6/95).

Per Share Data ($) (Year Ended Sep. 30)

	1994	1993	1992	1991	1990	1989
Tangible Bk. Val.	1.72	11.22	9.90	8.51	8.55	8.33
Earnings	1.53	1.62	1.16	1.11	1.27	1.28
Dividends	1.03	0.99	0.96	0.92	0.87	0.83
Payout Ratio	67%	61%	82%	82%	68%	65%
Prices - High	23⅜	24¾	20	20½	16½	14⅝
- Low	17½	18¾	17½	14	12½	10⅝
P/E Ratio - High	15	15	17	18	13	11
- Low	11	12	15	13	10	8

Income Statement Analysis (Million $)

	1994	%Chg	1993	%Chg	1992	%Chg	1991
Revs.	47.3	-91%	499	21%	411	5%	390
Depr.	0.3	-99%	26.8	7%	25.1	6%	23.6
Maint.	NA	—	NA	—	NA	—	NA
Fxd. Chgs. Cov.	4.2	17%	3.6	8%	3.3	8%	3.1
Constr. Credits	NA	—	NA	—	NA	—	NA
Eff. Tax Rate	40%	—	37%	—	33%	—	36%
Net Inc.	2.8	-92%	34.6	44%	24.0	4%	23.1

Balance Sheet & Other Fin. Data (Million $)

	1994	1993	1992	1991	1990	1989
Gross Prop.	825	773	725	639	598	518
Cap. Exp.	57.1	56.9	59.1	47.9	43.0	38.9
Net Prop.	533	506	477	418	391	337
Capitalization:						
LT Debt	159	165	150	161	103	121
% LT Debt	37	39	39	42	32	43
Pfd.	Nil	Nil	21.1	21.5	21.2	20.0
% Pfd.	Nil	Nil	5.50	5.50	6.50	7.10
Common	271	259	212	206	201	140
% Common	63	61	55	53	62	50
Total Cap.	12.2	494	453	456	392	343

Ratio Analysis

	1994	1993	1992	1991	1990	1989
Oper. Ratio	89.9	91.1	90.7	90.9	91.1	90.5
% Earn. on Net Prop.	9.2	9.0	8.3	8.8	8.7	10.0
% Ret. on Revs.	7.3	4.9	5.8	5.9	6.2	6.1
% Ret. On Invest.Cap	NA	NA	NA	NA	NA	10.3
% Return On Com.Eqty	12.6	14.4	11.3	11.1	13.5	15.0

Dividend Data —Dividends have been paid since 1946. A dividend reinvestment plan is available. A "poison pill" stock purchase rights plan was adopted in 1986.

Amt. of Div. $	Date Decl.	Ex-Div. Date	Stock of Record	Payment Date
0.265	Oct. 31	Nov. 08	Nov. 15	Dec. 01 '94
0.265	Jan. 09	Feb. 09	Feb. 15	Mar. 01 '95
0.265	Apr. 28	May. 09	May. 15	Jun. 01 '95
0.275	Jul. 31	Aug. 11	Aug. 15	Sep. 01 '95

Data as orig. reptd.; bef. results of disc opers. and/or spec. items. Per share data adj. for stk. divs. as of ex-div. date. E-Estimated. NA-Not Available. NM-Not Meaningful. NR-Not Ranked.

Office—1630 N. Meridian St., Indianapolis, IN 46202. **Tel**—(317) 926-3351. **Chrmn**—D. M. Amundson. **Pres & CEO**—L. A. Ferger. **VP, Treas & CFO**—N. C. Ellerbrook. **Secy**—R. E. Christian. **VP & Investor Contact**—Anthony L. Brown (317-321-0512). **Dirs**—D. M. Amudson, P. T. Baker, G. L. Bepko, H. J. Cofield, N. C. Ellerbrook, L. K. Evans, L. A. Ferger, O. N. Frenzel III, A. H. George, D. E. Marsh, R. P. Rechter, J. C. Shook. **Transfer Agent & Registrar**—First Chicago Trust Co. of New York, Jersey City, N.J. **Incorporated** in Indiana in 1945. **Empl**-1,129. **S&P Analyst:** Ronald J. Gross

STANDARD & POOR'S

Information Resources

STOCK REPORTS

NASDAQ Symbol **IRIC**

In S&P MidCap 400

16-OCT-95

Industry:
Data Processing

Summary: IRI provides information services to the consumer packaged goods industry in the U.S. and software services to a wide range of industries worldwide.

Quantitative Evaluations

Outlook
(1 Lowest—5 Highest)
• **1-**

Fair Value
• **9⅝**

Risk
• **High**

Earn./Div. Rank
• **B-**

Technical Eval.
• **Bearish** since 6/95

Rel. Strength Rank
(1 Lowest—99 Highest)
• **24**

Insider Activity
• **Neutral**

Recent Price • 12⅝
52 Wk Range • 18⅝-11½

Yield • Nil
12-Mo. P/E • NM

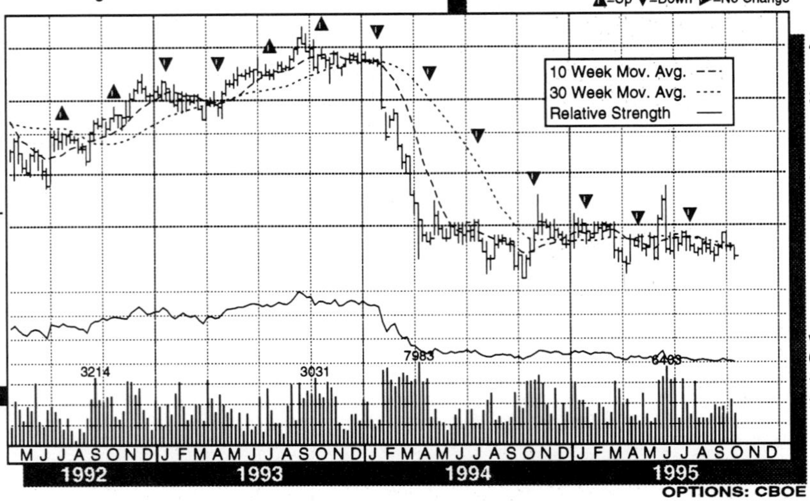

OPTIONS: CBOE

Business Profile - 16-OCT-95

Information Resources develops and maintains computerized proprietary databases, decision support software and analytical models to assist clients, primarily in the consumer packaged goods industry, in testing, monitoring, evaluating and executing their sales and marketing plans. The company's software products, with applications for executive information systems, planning, marketing, sales, finance and operations, are licensed across a wide variety of industries and governmental agencies.

Operational Review - 16-OCT-95

The net loss widened in 1995's first half, despite increased revenues and the absence of a $5 million litigation expense. Revenues advanced due to growth in business intelligence software and the expansion of international data and analysis services. Operating expenses rose sharply as a result of an expansion of the international information business, higher compensation expense, greater amortization, and increases in computer operations and client service staff.

Stock Performance - 13-OCT-95

In the past 30 trading days, IRIC's shares have declined 2%, compared to a 4% rise in the S&P 500. Average trading volume for the past five days was 146,040 shares, compared with the 40-day moving average of 168,492 shares.

Key Stock Statistics

Dividend Rate/Share	Nil	Shareholders	600
Shs. outstg. (M)	26.9	Market cap. (B)	$0.339
Avg. daily vol. (M)	0.171	Inst. holdings	69%
Tang. Bk. Value/Share	8.46	Insider holdings	NA
Beta	2.08		

Value of $10,000 invested 5 years ago: $ 9,805

Fiscal Year Ending Dec. 31

	1995	% Change	1994	% Change	1993	% Change
Revenues (Million $)						
1Q	104.8	20%	87.68	16%	75.70	23%
2Q	109.3	19%	92.18	12%	82.11	24%
3Q	—	—	92.92	6%	87.78	22%
4Q	—	—	103.8	17%	89.00	16%
Yr.	—	—	376.6	13%	334.5	21%
Income (Million $)						
1Q	-3.29	NM	-1.29	NM	3.93	-3%
2Q	-3.61	NM	0.01	-100%	6.46	35%
3Q	—	—	-3.10	NM	7.36	26%
4Q	—	—	-4.54	NM	4.47	-3%
Yr.	—	—	-8.92	NM	22.22	15%
Earnings Per Share ($)						
1Q	-0.12	NM	-0.05	NM	0.15	-12%
2Q	-0.13	—	Nil	—	0.24	20%
3Q	—	—	-0.12	NM	0.27	12%
4Q	—	—	-0.17	NM	0.16	-11%
Yr.	—	—	-0.34	NM	0.82	5%

Next earnings report expected: late October

Information Resources

Business Summary - 10-OCT-95

Information Resources, Inc. (IRI) provides a variety of information services and business intelligence software products to its customers. The company is a leading provider of information services to the consumer packaged goods industry and believes that its proprietary data bases, analytical models and business intelligence software enable consumer packaged goods manufacturers and retailers to make better, more cost effective decisions in marketing and selling their products. The company's business intelligence software products are also used across a wide range of industries and governmental agencies worldwide. Revenues in recent years were derived as follows:

	1994	1993	1992	1991
Information services	68%	68%	70%	68%
Software support services	32%	32%	30%	32%

IRI's InfosScan, InfoScan Panel and InfoScan Census are tracking and evaluation services for the consumer packaged goods industry. Using the scanning code printed on products, and scanners installed in retail outlets, InfoScan tracks consumer purchasing of products sold in a representative national, projectable sample of stores. In 1994, IRI introduced InfoScan Census, a service for manufacturers that tracks consumer purchasing in all stores within participating retail chains rather than just stores within projectable samples.

IRI's BehaviorScan system permits clients to measure the effects of different marketing variables on consumer purchasing. It uses a patented electronic system to target television advertising to individual households and electronic scanner data to measure consumer purchase behavior in an unobtrusive manner as part of normal televison programming.

In May 1992, the company acquired Towne-Oller & Associates, Inc. in exchange for about 690,000 common shares. Towne-Oller tracks deliveries of health and beauty care products from retailer and wholesaler warehouses to 30,000 individual drug stores and 30,000 individual grocery stores.

Important Developments

Sep. '95—IRI and Tokyo-based Mitsui & Co. Ltd., announced the completion of a joint venture, Information Resources Japan Ltd., to provide retail support services, on-line analytical processing software products, value-added consulting and information services for the Japanese market.

Jul. '95—IRI completed the sale of a portion of its software business to Oracle Corp. for about $100 million. Proceeds from the sale were used to retire existing bank debt, pay transaction fees and for general corporate purposes.

Capitalization

Long Term Debt: None (7/95).

Per Share Data ($)

(Year Ended Dec. 31)

	1994	1993	1992	1991	1990	1989
Tangible Bk. Val.	8.05	8.36	7.35	5.12	2.78	2.88
Cash Flow	0.44	1.63	1.54	1.31	0.82	0.69
Earnings	-0.34	0.82	0.79	0.63	0.25	-0.17
Dividends	Nil	Nil	Nil	Nil	Nil	Nil
Payout Ratio	Nil	Nil	Nil	Nil	Nil	Nil
Prices - High	39¾	44¾	36¼	29¼	16⅝	15⅜
- Low	11¼	27	18½	9⅛	7¾	8⅞
P/E Ratio - High	NM	55	46	46	67	NM
- Low	NM	33	23	14	31	NM

Income Statement Analysis (Million $)

	1994	%Chg	1993	%Chg	1992	%Chg	1991
Revs.	377	13%	335	21%	276	33%	208
Oper. Inc.	27.0	-57%	62.4	11%	56.2	47%	38.2
Depr.	20.3	-5%	21.4	16%	18.5	20%	15.4
Int. Exp.	2.4	127%	1.0	-59%	2.5	-4%	2.6
Pretax Inc.	-13.7	NM	36.0	12%	32.2	45%	22.2
Eff. Tax Rate	NM	—	43%	—	40%	—	36%
Net Inc.	-8.9	NM	22.2	16%	19.2	35%	14.2

Balance Sheet & Other Fin. Data (Million $)

	1994	1993	1992	1991	1990	1989
Cash	11.8	19.4	53.6	24.9	8.8	1.8
Curr. Assets	143	149	142	105	62.0	51.0
Total Assets	355	328	264	189	133	135
Curr. Liab.	73.6	57.5	53.6	52.6	38.8	47.4
LT Debt	31.5	3.1	4.7	6.6	23.5	29.4
Common Eqty.	227	229	187	117	60.0	51.0
Total Cap.	275	264	204	130	88.0	87.0
Cap. Exp.	22.8	25.9	20.0	11.6	9.2	7.6
Cash Flow	11.4	43.6	37.8	29.6	15.5	11.8

Ratio Analysis

	1994	1993	1992	1991	1990	1989
Curr. Ratio	1.9	2.6	2.6	2.0	1.6	1.1
% LT Debt of Cap.	11.4	1.2	2.3	5.1	26.8	33.9
% Net Inc.of Revs.	NM	6.6	7.0	6.9	2.9	NM
% Ret. on Assets	NM	7.4	8.0	8.3	3.4	NM
% Ret. on Equity	NM	10.5	12.0	15.3	8.4	NM

Dividend Data —No cash has been paid. In October 1990, the company distributed to shareholders one VideOcart, Inc. common share for every two IRI shares held. VideOcart's products provide point-of-purchase advertising and promotion messages.

Data as orig. reptd.; bef. results of disc. opers. and/or spec. items. Per share data adj. for stk. divs. as of ex-div. date. E-Estimated. NA-Not Available. NM-Not Meaningful. NR-Not Ranked.

Office—150 N. Clinton St., Chicago, IL 60661. **Tel**—(312) 726-1221. **Chrmn**—T. W. Wilson, Jr. **Co-CEO**—G. M. Fulgoni. **EVP & CFO**—G. M. Hill. **Vice Chrmn**—G. Eskin. **Secy**—E. S. Berger. **Dirs**—J. G. Andress, G. Eskin, E. E. Epstein, J. D. C. Little, L. M. Lodish, E. E. Lucente, E. W. Martin, G. G. Montgomery, Jr., J. P. Stamen, G. L. Urban, T. W. Wilson, Jr. **Transfer Agent & Registrar**—Harris Trust & Savings Bank, Chicago. **Incorporated** in Delaware in 1982. **Empl**-6,360. **S&P Analyst:** Ronald J. Gross

STANDARD & POOR'S

STOCK REPORTS

Informix Corp.

NASDAQ Symbol **IFMX**
In S&P MidCap 400

31-JUL-95

Industry: Data Processing

Summary: This company develops and markets high-performance relational database management and applications development software.

S&P Opinion: Accumulate (★★★★)

Recent Price • 30⅞	Yield • Nil
52 Wk Range • 32⅜-9⅝	12-Mo. P/E • 51.5

Quantitative Evaluations

Outlook (1 Lowest—5 Highest) • **NA**

Fair Value • **NA**

Risk • **High**

Earn./Div. Rank • **B**

Technical Eval. • **Bullish** since 8/94

Rel. Strength Rank (1 Lowest—99 Highest) • **93**

Insider Activity • **Neutral**

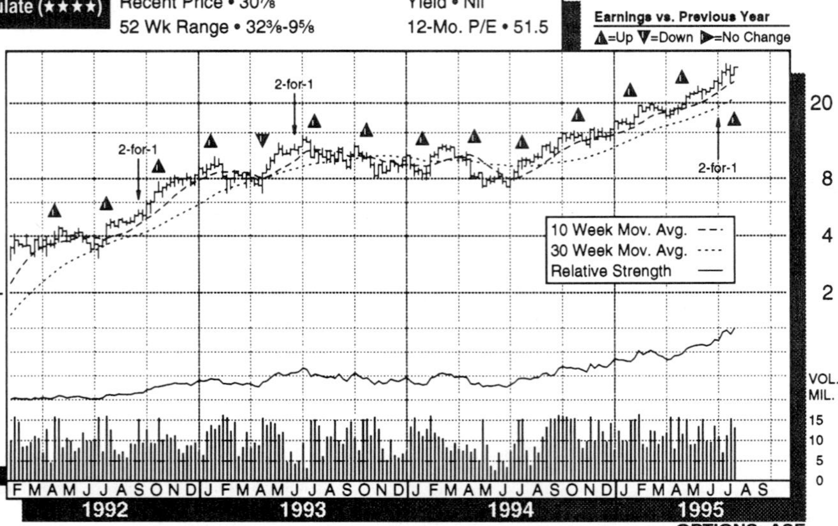

OPTIONS: ASE

Overview - 31-JUL-95

Revenues are expected to advance strongly through 1996, driven by continued robust worldwide demand for UNIX relational database management system software, tools and related services. All geographic markets are expected to be strong. New products, including the company's new generation of development tools, have begun to boost revenues. Margins are expected to be maintained, as volume efficiencies offset a less favorable revenue mix of services, continued large investments in marketing, and increases in the international sales force. Earnings should benefit from the higher sales and steady margins. Continued repurchases of the company's common stock would aid per-share results.

Valuation - 31-JUL-95

In mid-1994, the stock broke out strongly to the upside from its erratic trading range of the prior two years, driven by an acceleration of sales and earnings growth. The relational database software market is growing rapidly, as organizations cope with managing and manipulating the massive amounts of data stored on their computer systems. Informix is growing at least as fast as the market, as its new database and tools products are being well received. The sales and earnings gains we project should continue to help the stock outperform the market over the coming months.

Key Stock Statistics

S&P EPS Est. 1995	0.70	Tang. Bk. Value/Share	2.10
P/E on S&P Est. 1995	44.1	Beta	1.66
S&P EPS Est. 1996	0.93	Shareholders	1,600
Dividend Rate/Share	Nil	Market cap. (B)	$ 4.1
Shs. outstg. (M)	131.9	Inst. holdings	91%
Avg. daily vol. (M)	2.533	Insider holdings	NA

Value of $10,000 invested 5 years ago: $ 160,639

Fiscal Year Ending Dec. 31

	1995	% Change	1994	% Change	1993	% Change
Revenues (Million $)						
1Q	147.8	54%	96.10	25%	77.09	30%
2Q	163.6	55%	105.7	25%	84.33	40%
3Q	—	—	116.8	30%	90.07	32%
4Q	—	—	150.1	48%	101.4	6%
Yr.	—	—	468.7	33%	352.9	24%
Income (Million $)						
1Q	19.10	53%	12.52	9%	11.51	NM
2Q	22.12	67%	13.25	10%	12.03	33%
3Q	—	—	16.59	14%	14.52	21%
4Q	—	—	23.84	32%	18.05	-19%
Yr.	—	—	66.20	18%	56.12	3%
Earnings Per Share ($)						
1Q	0.14	47%	0.09	12%	0.08	-8%
2Q	0.16	60%	0.10	11%	0.09	29%
3Q	E0.18	—	0.13	19%	0.10	17%
4Q	E0.22	—	0.17	30%	0.13	15%
Yr.	E0.70	—	0.49	18%	0.42	11%

Next earnings report expected: late October

Informix Corp.

Business Summary - 31-JUL-95

Informix Corporation engages primarily in design, development, marketing and support of relational database management system (RDMS) software products, and also provides related training, consulting and maintenance services. Its database products are based on Structured Query Language (SQL), an industry standard created by IBM. At 1994 year end, the company's RDMS software was being run on over 100 models of computers from more than 25 manufacturers.

The company's INFORMIX-OnLine Dynamic Server, INFORMIX-OnLine and INFORMIX-SE relational database management software products are used primarily on midrange computers running on the UNIX, Windows, NetWare and Windows/NT operating systems. The company believes it has the largest installed base of RDMS software for computers running the UNIX operating system.

Various database development tools allow users to build and maintain applications. The company's newest generation of application development tools is INFORMIX-NewEra, an object-oriented, client/server development environment. INFORMIX-NewEra allows customers to create new graphical applications; it also enables existing character-based programs built with its INFORMIX-4GL character-based developing environment to be transformed into the graphical format.

Connectivity products allow data from various databases to be accessed and manipulated across a network.

The company provides maintenance services to its database customers on an optional basis for fees ranging from 10% to 18% of the license fees paid by the customer. Service revenues, which include maintenance, consulting and training fees, represented 22% and 19% of total revenues in 1994 and 1993, respectively.

Net sales from international customers accounted for 54% of net revenues in 1994 (58% in 1993).

Important Developments

Jul. '95—For the second quarter of 1995, database server revenues increased 56%, database tools rose 33%, and services revenues climbed 78%, year to year.

Jul. '95—IFMX said that during the second quarter of 1995, new customer wins included Wells Fargo Bank, Time Inc., and Tele-charge Systems.

Jul. '95—The company formally launched INFORMIX-OnLine Extended Parallel Server for massively parallel and loosely coupled systems. The product, which is scheduled to be available in the fourth quarter of 1995, is capable of managing very large, complex databases, while improving overall system performance and scalability.

Capitalization

Long Term Debt: None (6/95).

Per Share Data ($) (Year Ended Dec. 31)

	1994	1993	1992	1991	1990	1989
Tangible Bk. Val.	2.10	1.60	1.05	0.48	0.36	0.75
Cash Flow	0.61	0.50	0.45	0.19	-0.15	0.13
Earnings	0.49	0.42	0.38	0.10	-0.23	0.06
Dividends	Nil	Nil	Nil	Nil	Nil	Nil
Payout Ratio	Nil	Nil	Nil	Nil	Nil	Nil
Prices - High	16⅛	13⅝	9½	2	2$\frac{3}{16}$	1$\frac{15}{16}$
- Low	7⅛	6¾	1$\frac{11}{16}$	$\frac{5}{16}$	$\frac{7}{16}$	$\frac{15}{16}$
P/E Ratio - High	33	33	25	20	NM	31
- Low	15	16	4	3	NM	15

Income Statement Analysis (Million $)

	1994	%Chg	1993	%Chg	1992	%Chg	1991
Revs.	469	33%	353	24%	284	58%	180
Oper. Inc.	119	23%	96.8	18%	81.9	NM	24.3
Depr.	16.2	42%	11.4	15%	9.9	12%	8.8
Int. Exp.	0.4	3%	0.4	-84%	2.3	-20%	2.8
Pretax Inc.	103	17%	87.7	42%	61.7	NM	13.9
Eff. Tax Rate	36%	—	36%	—	23%	—	12%
Net Inc.	66.2	18%	56.1	17%	47.8	NM	12.2

Balance Sheet & Other Fin. Data (Million $)

	1994	1993	1992	1991	1990	1989
Cash	192	144	119	41.9	20.5	25.2
Curr. Assets	348	269	196	97.0	69.0	107
Total Assets	444	327	231	133	110	143
Curr. Liab.	154	113	97.0	53.4	41.4	36.5
LT Debt	0.3	0.5	1.3	25.4	29.8	30.3
Common Eqty.	276	207	133	54.2	38.1	74.0
Total Cap.	291	213	134	80.0	68.0	106
Cap. Exp.	25.2	22.1	9.7	4.2	6.6	6.3
Cash Flow	82.4	67.5	57.7	21.0	-15.6	12.7

Ratio Analysis

	1994	1993	1992	1991	1990	1989
Curr. Ratio	2.3	2.4	2.0	1.8	1.7	2.9
% LT Debt of Cap.	0.1	0.2	0.9	31.9	43.9	28.5
% Net Inc.of Revs.	14.1	15.9	16.8	6.8	NM	4.4
% Ret. on Assets	17.1	19.9	25.1	9.9	NM	4.9
% Ret. on Equity	27.3	32.6	49.4	26.0	NM	9.0

Dividend Data (No cash dividends have been paid.)

Amt. of Div. $	Date Decl.	Ex-Div. Date	Stock of Record	Payment Date
2-for-1	May. 19	Jun. 26	Jun. 09	Jun. 23 '95

Data as orig. reptd.; bef. results of disc. opers. and/or spec. items. Per share data adj. for stk. divs. as of ex-div. date. E-Estimated. NA-Not Available. NM-Not Meaningful. NR-Not Ranked.

Office—4100 Bohannon Dr., Menlo Park, CA 94025. **Tel**—(415) 926-6300. **Chrmn, Pres & CEO**—P. E. White. **SVP-Fin & CFO**—H. H. Graham. **VP, Treas & Investor Contact**—Margaret Reilly. **VP & Secy**—D. H. Stanley. **Dirs**—A. F. Knorp, Jr., J. L. Koch, T. A. McDonnell, P. E. White, C. J. Yansouni. **Transfer Agent & Registrar**—First National Bank of Boston. **Incorporated** in Delaware in 1986. **Empl**-2,123. **S&P Analyst:** Peter C. Wood, CFA

STANDARD & POOR'S

Integrated Device Technology

STOCK REPORTS

NASDAQ Symbol **IDTI**
In S&P MidCap 400

23-OCT-95

Industry: Electronics/Electric

Summary: This company designs and manufactures high-performance integrated circuits using CMOS and BiCMOS process technology.

S&P Opinion: Hold (★★★)

Recent Price • 20⅛
52 Wk Range • 33½-12⅛
Yield • Nil
12-Mo. P/E • 15.0

Quantitative Evaluations

Outlook
(1 Lowest—5 Highest)
• **4+**

Fair Value
• **21⅝**

Risk
• **High**

Earn./Div. Rank
• **B-**

Technical Eval.
• **Bearish** since 9/95

Rel. Strength Rank
(1 Lowest—99 Highest)
• **4**

Insider Activity
• **Unfavorable**

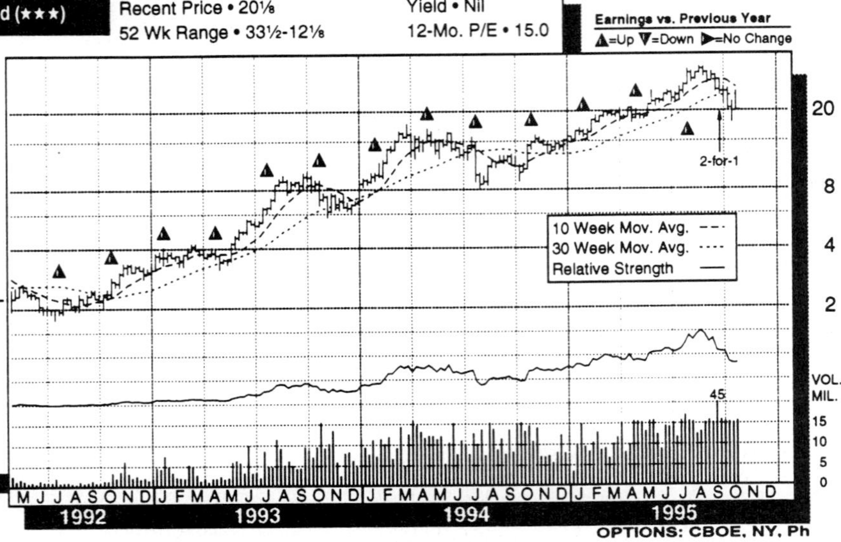

OPTIONS: CBOE, NY, Ph

Overview - 23-OCT-95

Sales for fiscal 1995-96 are projected to advance as much as 50%, assuming a continuation of the extremely strong conditions that currently exist in the semiconductor industry. The gain should be led by sharply higher shipments of static random access memories (SRAMs). The company is benefiting from strong demand for its fast SRAMs, as well as stable pricing. Other products should also experience strong sales. Margins are likely to narrow somewhat, due to an estimated $18 million-$20 million in startup costs on a new plant in Oregon. In addition, the tax rate should rise to 32%, from 25%.

Valuation - 23-OCT-95

The shares of this semiconductor company moved sharply higher in the past 12 months as industry conditions strengthened well beyond initial estimates and earnings exceeded expectations. While the company's strong sales and earnings are being led by aggressive demand and stable pricing for SRAMs, some investors believe that these memory chips have over time displayed commodity characteristics, including periods of aggressive price competition. We believe that as long as (financial) market participants maintain the belief that SRAMs could be hurt by pricing pressures, share appreciation will be restrained.

Key Stock Statistics

S&P EPS Est. 1996	1.35	Tang. Bk. Value/Share	5.82
P/E on S&P Est. 1996	14.9	Beta	2.07
Dividend Rate/Share	Nil	Shareholders	1,100
Shs. outstg. (M)	76.8	Market cap. (B)	$ 1.5
Avg. daily vol. (M)	3.708	Inst. holdings	42%
		Insider holdings	NA

Value of $10,000 invested 5 years ago: $ 49,538

Fiscal Year Ending Mar. 31

	1996	% Change	1995	% Change	1994	% Change
Revenues (Million $)						
1Q	152.2	60%	95.04	31%	72.77	35%
2Q	178.5	87%	95.59	19%	80.30	40%
3Q	—	—	105.8	24%	85.33	41%
4Q	—	—	125.8	37%	92.07	43%
Yr.	—	—	422.2	28%	330.5	40%
Income (Million $)						
1Q	28.79	71%	16.88	NM	4.63	NM
2Q	34.34	102%	17.01	120%	7.73	NM
3Q	—	—	19.80	70%	11.63	NM
4Q	—	—	24.62	52%	16.18	NM
Yr.	—	—	78.30	95%	40.17	NM
Earnings Per Share ($)						
1Q	0.36	51%	0.24	NM	0.08	NM
2Q	0.42	79%	0.24	96%	0.12	NM
3Q	E0.35	30%	0.27	54%	0.17	NM
4Q	E0.36	18%	0.31	36%	0.22	NM
Yr.	E1.35	30%	1.04	72%	0.60	NM

Next earnings report expected: late October

Integrated Device Technology

Business Summary - 23-OCT-95

Integrated Device Technology, Inc. (IDT) designs, makes and sells high-performance proprietary and industry-standard integrated circuits. The company offers more than 3,000 products in four areas: static random access memories (SRAMs), specialty memory products (SMPs), logic circuits and reduced instruction set computing (RISC) microprocessor components and subsystems.

The SRAMs sold by the company are memory circuits used for storage and retrieval of data during a computer system's operation in 16K, 64K, 256K and 1 meg densities. SRAMs maintain their contents without requiring electrical reinforcement to ensure data integrity.

IDT's SMPs offer differentiated features that enhance system performance beyond the capability of standard memory products. They include FIFOs (first in/first out memory circuits), multi-ported memory products and memory modules.

Logic circuits process data communications between elements of electronic systems, such as between a microprocessor and a memory circuit.

The company currently makes MIPS's 32-bit and 64-bit standard microprocessors and also offers RISC subsystem products, including modules, development and production tools and software.

International sales are made through subsidiaries in France, Germany, Hong Kong, Italy, Japan, Sweden and the U.K. Sales to customers in Japan and the Pacific Rim accounted for 14% of 1993-4 sales; sales to Europe accounted for 18%.

Important Developments

Oct. '95—In releasing fiscal 1995-96 first-quarter earnings, IDT said that demand for its products was robust for a summer quarter across all product and geographic segments. The company had record output both from its wafer fabrication plants and its Malaysian assembly operations. Backlog at the end of the quarter was a record. Going forward, IDT expects gross margins to widen as it continues to gain productivity improvements through the transition to smaller die sizes.

May '95—The company announced the completion of its new assembly and test facility in Penang, Malaysia. The plant increased capabilities for shipping by 21%, back-end finish operations by 77% and stocking by 50%.

Capitalization

Long Term Liabilities: $34,551,000 (10/95).

Per Share Data ($) (Year Ended Mar. 31)

	1995	1994	1993	1992	1991	1990
Tangible Bk. Val.	5.44	3.36	2.08	2.18	2.60	2.58
Cash Flow	1.57	1.14	0.70	0.36	0.57	0.85
Earnings	1.05	0.60	0.09	-0.41	0.03	0.33
Dividends	Nil	Nil	Nil	Nil	Nil	Nil
Payout Ratio	Nil	Nil	Nil	Nil	Nil	Nil
Cal. Yrs.	1994	1993	1992	1991	1990	1989
Prices - High	17¼	9⅞	3⅞	4⅞	4	6⅜
- Low	8	3⅛	1¾	1 9/16	1⅝	3⅝
P/E Ratio - High	16	16	43	NM	NM	19
- Low	8	5	19	NM	NM	11

Income Statement Analysis (Million $)

	1995	%Chg	1994	%Chg	1993	%Chg	1992
Revs.	422	28%	330	40%	236	16%	203
Oper. Inc.	138	57%	87.7	91%	46.0	19%	38.5
Depr.	38.8	10%	35.4	-2%	36.0	-11%	40.4
Int. Exp.	3.3	-36%	5.2	-12%	5.9	-17%	7.1
Pretax Inc.	104	107%	50.2	NM	6.3	NM	-34.8
Eff. Tax Rate	25%	—	20%	—	15%	—	NM
Net Inc.	78.3	95%	40.2	NM	5.3	NM	-21.6

Balance Sheet & Other Fin. Data (Million $)

	1995	1994	1993	1992	1991	1990
Cash	232	122	24.4	21.1	21.9	36.0
Curr. Assets	375	222	113	114	117	126
Total Assets	562	350	240	242	261	263
Curr. Liab.	103	79.2	62.0	65.2	53.6	62.9
LT Debt	14.4	30.0	35.8	44.5	56.8	62.8
Common Eqty.	415	224	118	116	135	131
Total Cap.	437	263	171	175	208	200
Cap. Exp.	94.7	38.1	28.2	25.7	36.1	77.8
Cash Flow	117	75.6	41.3	18.8	30.0	43.8

Ratio Analysis

	1995	1994	1993	1992	1991	1990
Curr. Ratio	3.6	2.8	1.8	1.7	2.2	2.0
% LT Debt of Cap.	3.3	11.4	20.9	25.5	27.3	31.4
% Net Inc.of Revs.	18.5	12.2	2.3	NM	0.6	8.1
% Ret. on Assets	16.3	12.7	2.1	NM	0.5	7.3
% Ret. on Equity	23.4	22.1	4.4	NM	0.9	14.0

Dividend Data —No cash has been paid. A three-for-two stock split was effected in 1987.

Amt. of Div. $	Date Decl.	Ex-Div. Date	Stock of Record	Payment Date
2-for-1	Aug. 02	Sep. 18	Aug. 25	Sep. 15 '95

Data as orig. reptd.; bef. results of disc. opers. and/or spec. items. Per share data adj. for stk. divs. as of ex-div. date. E-Estimated. NA-Not Available. NM-Not Meaningful. NR-Not Ranked.

Office—2975 Stender Way, Santa Clara, CA 95054. **Tel**—(408) 727-6116. **Chrmn**—D. J. Carey. **Pres & CEO**—L. C. Perham. **VP-Fin & CFO**—W. D. Snyder. **VP & Secy**—J. Menache. **Dirs**—C. E. Berg, J. C. Bolger, D. J. Carey, F. Faggin, L. C. Perham. **Transfer Agent & Registrar**—First National Bank of Boston. **Incorporated** in California in 1980; reincorporated in Delaware in 1987. **Empl**-2,960. **S&P Analyst:** Steven A. Jaworski

STANDARD & POOR'S
STOCK REPORTS

Intelligent Electronics

NASDAQ Symbol **INEL**
In S&P MidCap 400

16-OCT-95 **Industry:** Data Processing

Summary: INEL is a leading provider of information technology products, services and solutions for business, government and other customers using technology to create efficiency.

S&P Opinion: Avoid (★★)

Recent Price • 8
52 Wk Range • 17-7¼
Yield • 5.0%
12-Mo. P/E • NM

Quantitative Evaluations
Outlook (1 Lowest—5 Highest) • **4-**
Fair Value • **8⅞**
Risk • **High**
Earn./Div. Rank • **NR**

Technical Eval. • **Bearish** since 8/95
Rel. Strength Rank (1 Lowest—99 Highest) • **3**
Insider Activity • **NA**

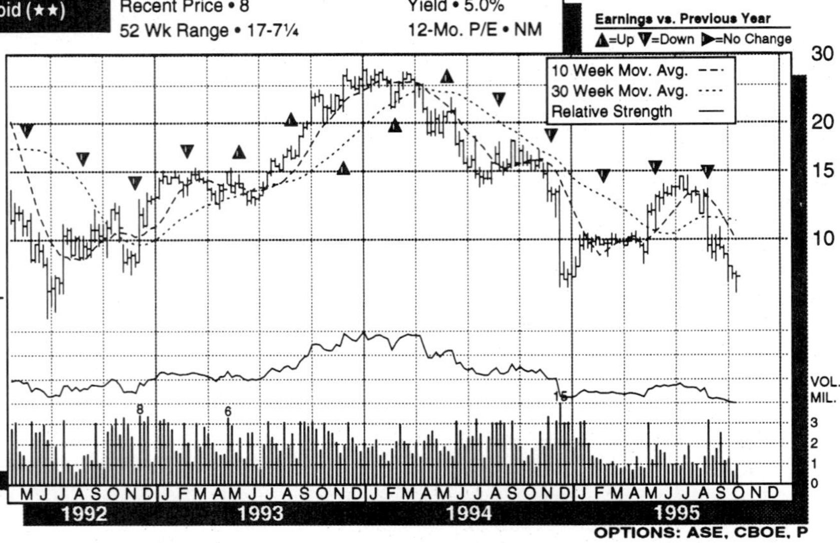

OPTIONS: ASE, CBOE, P

Overview - 16-OCT-95

Revenues are likely to grow in the upper-single to low double-digit range for the remainder of fiscal 1995, fueled by increasing acceptance of advanced technology products, strong demand for computers and peripherals, and sales to new customers. Operating efficiencies should result from a recent reengineering effort that is expected to reduce annual expenses by some $20 million. As part of its business transformation, INEL has converted to a new financial accounting system, upgraded core operating systems, consolidated warehouses, and improved service levels. The company expects to initiate similar actions at the newly acquired FNOW. Results for the next few quarters are likely to be hurt by additional charges associated with these actions and further core consolidations.

Valuation - 13-OCT-95

Following weaker than expected second quarter results, which included special charges related to the company's reengineering effort and its acquisition of The Future Now, INEL shares fell over 30% and were recently trading near a 52-week low. Future results should benefit from increased demand, enhanced capacity and production, and growth of the reseller network. Sales should also benefit from the August 1995 launch of Windows '95. However, due to the uncertain magnitude of future costs associated with the company's continued restructuring and its integration of FNOW, we see considerable risk in owning INEL shares.

Key Stock Statistics

S&P EPS Est. 1996	0.02	Tang. Bk. Value/Share	2.44
P/E on S&P Est. 1996	NM	Beta	2.35
Dividend Rate/Share	0.40	Shareholders	900
Shs. outstg. (M)	35.7	Market cap. (B)	$0.286
Avg. daily vol. (M)	0.196	Inst. holdings	50%
		Insider holdings	NA

Value of $10,000 invested 5 years ago: $ 13,487

Fiscal Year Ending Jan. 31

	1996	% Change	1995	% Change	1994	% Change
Revenues (Million $)						
1Q	827.4	9%	762.0	24%	617.0	24%
2Q	881.6	11%	793.3	29%	613.3	31%
3Q	—	—	831.1	23%	675.9	40%
4Q	—	—	821.4	11%	740.0	30%
Yr.	—	—	3,208	21%	2,646	31%
Income (Million $)						
1Q	4.89	-62%	12.79	54%	8.32	5%
2Q	-5.93	NM	2.70	-71%	9.19	NM
3Q	—	—	-3.02	NM	10.85	92%
4Q	—	—	-4.41	NM	12.75	90%
Yr.	—	—	8.06	-80%	41.12	86%
Earnings Per Share ($)						
1Q	0.16	-56%	0.36	57%	0.23	10%
2Q	-0.19	NM	0.08	-69%	0.26	NM
3Q	E-0.05	NM	-0.09	NM	0.30	30%
4Q	E0.10	NM	-0.14	NM	0.35	94%
Yr.	E0.02	-91%	0.23	-80%	1.13	95%

Next earnings report expected: mid December

STANDARD & POOR'S

STOCK REPORTS

Intelligent Electronics

16-OCT-95

Business Summary - 13-OCT-95

Intelligent Electronics, Inc. is a leading wholesale distributor of office productivity solutions, including personal computers and related equipment. It sells primarily to small and medium-size businesses, through a network of more than 2,500 franchised and affiliated customers.

INEL's Reseller Network division provides wholesale distribution of microcomputers to the Intelligent (IE) Network, which in turn offers value-added systems solutions to end-users. The Reseller Network also provides product selection, technical support, cost-efficient marketing programs and promotions, configuration and identification of marketing opportunities for the Intelligent Network. Centers in the IE Network purchase products from the company on a cost-plus basis, generally at a lower price than could be obtained independently.

The franchise agreements provide for the operation of a business center and the sale of microcomputer systems and related products and services, as well as other advanced technology products under the company's proprietary trademarks, "Todays Computers Business Centers" (TCBC), "Entre Computer Centers," or "Connecting Point of America" (CPA).

Programs designed for specific members of the Network include the Intelligent Systems Group, which targets end-users with a regional or national presence and focuses primarily on high-end or technically advanced products, the ISG National Service Network, the Minority Technical Alliance and the Business Technology Centers program.

INEL's InteLogistics division was formed to provide logistics services to unaffiliated third parties. Services being developed and marketed include warehousing, freight consolidation, transportation management, inventory management, invoicing, credit and collection services, returns processing and customized information systems.

In 1994-95, sales of COMPAQ, Hewlett-Packard, Apple and IBM products accounted for 25%, 24%, 12% and 15% of total revenues, respectively. The company currently distributes products of about 100 vendors.

Important Developments

Aug. '95—INEL completed the acquisition of the remaining 69% of The Future Now, Inc. for approximately three million shares of INEL common stock. FNOW, one of the largest computer sales and consulting companies in the U.S., accounted for approximately 16% of the company's revenues in 1994-95.

Aug. '95—Through July 29, 1995, INEL had repurchased 8.3 million shares under buyback plans calling for the repurchase of up to 13.6 million shares.

Capitalization

Long Term Debt: None (7/95).

Per Share Data ($) (Year Ended Jan. 31)

	1995	1994	1993	1992	1991	1990
Tangible Bk. Val.	3.07	4.19	5.64	1.35	0.89	0.24
Cash Flow	0.52	1.39	0.81	1.47	1.28	0.68
Earnings	0.23	1.13	0.58	1.11	1.05	0.51
Dividends	0.36	2.16	Nil	Nil	Nil	Nil
Payout Ratio	157%	191%	Nil	Nil	Nil	Nil
Cal. Yrs.	1994	1993	1992	1991	1990	1989
Prices - High	27⅝	28	30⅜	18¾	11⅞	8⅞
- Low	7½	12	6¼	8¾	4⅞	2⅞
P/E Ratio - High	NM	25	52	17	11	17
- Low	NM	6	11	8	5	6

Income Statement Analysis (Million $)

	1995	%Chg	1994	%Chg	1993	%Chg	1992
Revs.	3,208	21%	2,646	31%	2,017	—	NA
Oper. Inc.	59.9	-13%	68.9	28%	53.9	—	NA
Depr.	10.1	9%	9.3	8%	8.6	—	NA
Int. Exp.	1.2	38%	0.9	-88%	7.4	—	NA
Pretax Inc.	21.9	-67%	66.5	69%	39.4	—	NA
Eff. Tax Rate	63%	—	38%	—	44%	—	NA
Net Inc.	8.1	-80%	41.1	86%	22.1	—	NA

Balance Sheet & Other Fin. Data (Million $)

	1995	1994	1993	1992	1991	1990
Cash	77.0	183	52.0	NA	93.0	121
Curr. Assets	535	471	526	NA	439	338
Total Assets	671	577	630	NA	707	442
Curr. Liab.	503	355	348	NA	402	293
LT Debt	Nil	Nil	Nil	NA	29.8	29.5
Common Eqty.	167	219	281	NA	274	120
Total Cap.	167	219	281	NA	304	149
Cap. Exp.	28.0	7.4	4.6	NA	15.4	3.6
Cash Flow	18.2	50.4	30.7	NA	50.8	35.6

Ratio Analysis

	1995	1994	1993	1992	1991	1990
Curr. Ratio	1.1	1.3	1.5	NA	1.1	1.2
% LT Debt of Cap.	Nil	Nil	Nil	NA	9.8	19.8
% Net Inc.of Revs.	0.3	1.6	1.1	NA	2.0	2.0
% Ret. on Assets	1.4	7.9	3.3	NA	5.8	7.6
% Ret. on Equity	4.5	16.8	8.0	NA	17.4	28.5

Dividend Data —INEL paid a special dividend of $2.00 a share on June 1, 1993. Quarterly dividends were initiated in July 1993.

Amt. of Div. $	Date Decl.	Ex-Div. Date	Stock of Record	Payment Date
0.100	Oct. 31	Nov. 08	Nov. 15	Dec. 01 '94
0.100	Jan. 27	Feb. 09	Feb. 15	Mar. 01 '95
0.100	Apr. 27	May. 09	May. 15	Jun. 01 '95
0.100	Jul. 27	Aug. 11	Aug. 15	Sep. 01 '95

Data as orig. reptd.; bef. results of disc. opers. and/or spec. items. Per share data adj. for stk. divs. as of ex-div. date. E-Estimated. NA-Not Available. NM-Not Meaningful. NR-Not Ranked.

Incorporated—in Pennsylvania in 1982. **Office**—411 Eagleview Blvd., Exton, PA 19341. **Tel**—(610) 458-5500. **Chrmn & CEO**—R. D. Sanford. **Pres & COO**—G. A. Pratt. **VP & CFO**—E. A. Meltzer. **Corporate Counsel**—S. M. Kawalick. **VP, Secy & Treas**—S. D. Cohen. **VP & Investor Contact**—Kathleen Mayo. **Dirs**—B. M. Abelson, J. M. Ciccarelli, C. T. G. Fish, R. J. Fritz, A. S. Hoffman, G. A. Pratt, J. Porter, W. L. Rulon-Miller, R. D. Sanford, M. R. Shabazian, A. Wilson. **Transfer Agent**—Mellon Financial Services, Ridgefield Park, N.J. **Empl**-1,162. **S&P Analyst:** Maureen C. Carini

STANDARD & POOR'S

STOCK REPORTS

Int'l Dairy Queen

NASDAQ Symbol **INDQA**

In S&P MidCap 400

26-JUL-95 **Industry:** Food serving

Summary: This company develops, franchises and services the Dairy Queen, Orange Julius, Karmelkorn Shoppe and Golden Skillet foodservice concepts.

S&P Opinion: Accumulate (★★★★) | Recent Price • 21⅝ | 52 Wk Range • 21¾-15¾ | Yield • Nil | 12-Mo. P/E • 15.9

Quantitative Evaluations

Outlook (1 Lowest—5 Highest)
• **2+**

Fair Value
• **20⅜**

Risk
• **Low**

Earn./Div. Rank
• **B+**

Technical Eval.
• **Bearish** since 4/95

Rel. Strength Rank (1 Lowest—99 Highest)
• **66**

Insider Activity
• **NA**

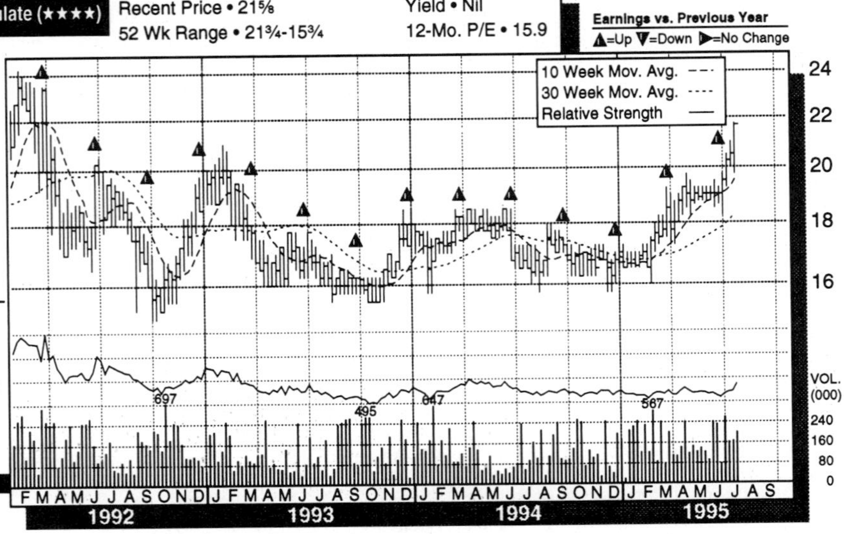

Overview - 26-JUL-95

In the year ahead, we expect revenues of this franchise food-service company to be helped by a modest improvement in the U.S. economy, and by the installation of new menu boards at thousands of Dairy Queen franchise outlets. We look for a moderate rise in INDQA's per share earnings, including benefits from repurchase of common shares. Long-term growth opportunities for INDQA include boosting service fees through acquisition of territorial franchising rights, overseas expansion and a gradual upgrading to higher-volume franchise outlets, which may include stronger locations, larger units and adding more menu items at some of the more limited-menu outlets.

Valuation - 26-JUL-95

We view this stock as being attractive for value-oriented investors. We expect the company's long string of earnings per share increases to continue in the forseeable future. Also, we look for the stock to get support from further share repurchases by the company. At the end of fiscal 1995's second quarter, INDQA had cash equivalents and marketable securities totaling $31 million, compared to $25 million of long-term debt. With the stock having the potential for a wide bid/ask spread, prospective buyers should place orders carefully.

Key Stock Statistics

S&P EPS Est. 1995	1.40	Tang. Bk. Value/Share	5.53
P/E on S&P Est. 1995	15.5	Beta	1.01
S&P EPS Est. 1996	1.55	Shareholders	1,500
Dividend Rate/Share	Nil	Market cap. (B)	$0.473
Shs. outstg. (M)	22.8	Inst. holdings	42%
Avg. daily vol. (M)	0.051	Insider holdings	NA

Value of $10,000 invested 5 years ago: $ 14,703

Fiscal Year Ending Nov. 30

	1995	% Change	1994	% Change	1993	% Change
Revenues (Million $)						
1Q	67.53	10%	61.18	5%	58.38	3%
2Q	106.2	10%	96.68	11%	87.33	NM
3Q	—	—	107.5	9%	98.77	7%
4Q	—	—	75.52	13%	66.61	7%
Yr.	—	—	340.8	10%	311.1	5%
Income (Million $)						
1Q	4.91	7%	4.61	1%	4.55	3%
2Q	9.85	6%	9.26	6%	8.73	NM
3Q	—	—	11.16	4%	10.68	1%
4Q	—	—	6.38	7%	5.94	8%
Yr.	—	—	31.42	5%	29.89	3%
Earnings Per Share ($)						
1Q	0.21	11%	0.19	6%	0.18	6%
2Q	0.42	11%	0.38	9%	0.35	6%
3Q	E0.49	—	0.46	7%	0.43	5%
4Q	E0.29	—	0.27	12%	0.24	14%
Yr.	E1.40	—	1.30	9%	1.19	6%

Next earnings report expected: early October

STANDARD & POOR'S
STOCK REPORTS

Int'l Dairy Queen

26-JUL-95

Business Summary - 22-JUL-95

INDQA is engaged in developing, licensing and servicing various foodservice concepts, including Dairy Queen, Orange Julius and Karmelkorn Shoppe. In addition to separate outlets, INDQA has a Treat Center concept, which combines Dairy Queen menu items with products from the Orange Julius and/or Karmelkorn menus at shopping malls. INDQA is also a franchisor of Golden Skillets in foreign markets.

Nearly all of INDQA's outlets are franchised. A sizable portion of revenue comes from sales of supplies to independently owned warehouses, which in turn sell them to franchisees, and from sales of equipment to franchisees. At recent fiscal year-ends, the number of units open (excluding Golden Skillets in the U.S.), by concept, was:

	11/94	11/93
Dairy Queens	5,418	5,360
Treat Centers	124	111
Orange Julius	454	480
Karmelkorn Shoppes	82	95
Golden Skillets	21	17
Total	6,099	6,063

Most Dairy Queen units are located in smaller towns and suburbs of larger cities. Some franchised units serve only soft-serve dairy products, and others offer some or all of a limited-food menu known as the Brazier product line. The Dairy Queen chain is franchised either directly by INDQA or indirectly through agreements with territorial operators. The level of franchise fees to the company within the system varies.

The Orange Julius chain features blended drinks made from orange and other fruit flavors, and the Karmelkorn concept sells popcorn, candy and other treat items. Also, INDQA has a 60% interest in Firstaff, Inc., which is involved in the placement of permanent and temporary office support personnel.

Important Developments

Jun. '95—In fiscal 1995's first half, INDQA's 12% rise in net sales included an $8.6 million increase in product sales to authorized warehouses (for resale to franchisees), plus a $2.1 million rise in equipment sales (helped by a higher level of new store development), a $2.0 million increase in promotional items sold to Dairy Queen stores, and a $1.7 million rise in fees for the 60%-owned Firstaff business. Also, INDQA's service fees from franchisees rose 5.0%. In the six-month period, INDQA repurchased 724,889 common shares.

Capitalization

Long Term Debt: $25,014,000 (5/95).
Class A Common Stock: 14,501,927 shs. ($0.01 par) (3/95); limited voting rights. Officers & directors own about 20%.
Class B Common Stock: 8,642,483 shs. ($0.01 par) (3/95). Officers & directors own about 45%.

Per Share Data ($) (Year Ended Nov. 30)

	1994	1993	1992	1991	1990	1989
Tangible Bk. Val.	5.53	5.13	4.40	3.69	3.09	2.70
Cash Flow	1.47	1.35	1.27	1.20	1.13	0.97
Earnings	1.30	1.19	1.12	1.05	0.97	0.83
Dividends	Nil	Nil	Nil	Nil	Nil	Nil
Payout Ratio	Nil	Nil	Nil	Nil	Nil	Nil
Prices - High	18½	21	24¼	25¾	20¾	15¾
- Low	15¾	15½	15	14¼	14⅝	11⅜
P/E Ratio - High	14	18	22	25	21	19
- Low	12	13	13	14	15	14

Income Statement Analysis (Million $)

	1994	%Chg	1993	%Chg	1992	%Chg	1991
Revs.	340	10%	310	5%	296	3%	287
Oper. Inc.	53.5	5%	50.8	NM	50.3	6%	47.4
Depr.	4.3	5%	4.1	NM	4.1	6%	3.9
Int. Exp.	1.9	-14%	2.2	-43%	3.9	2%	3.8
Pretax Inc.	51.9	5%	49.4	4%	47.3	4%	45.4
Eff. Tax Rate	40%	—	40%	—	39%	—	39%
Net Inc.	31.4	5%	29.9	3%	29.1	4%	27.9

Balance Sheet & Other Fin. Data (Million $)

	1994	1993	1992	1991	1990	1989
Cash	38.7	31.2	38.3	32.7	28.8	21.9
Curr. Assets	80.3	64.8	72.1	64.6	61.4	47.5
Total Assets	196	184	179	175	161	129
Curr. Liab.	26.4	28.5	36.5	27.9	32.2	27.6
LT Debt	23.3	23.9	25.8	46.0	41.8	21.7
Common Eqty.	131	127	112	96.8	83.2	75.7
Total Cap.	170	155	143	146	129	101
Cap. Exp.	1.9	8.5	0.9	1.6	1.3	2.3
Cash Flow	35.7	34.0	33.2	31.8	30.9	27.2

Ratio Analysis

	1994	1993	1992	1991	1990	1989
Curr. Ratio	3.0	2.3	2.0	2.3	1.9	1.7
% LT Debt of Cap.	13.8	15.4	18.1	31.4	32.5	21.5
% Net Inc.of Revs.	9.3	9.6	9.8	9.7	9.4	9.2
% Ret. on Assets	16.8	16.7	16.6	16.8	18.6	19.2
% Ret. on Equity	24.8	25.4	28.1	31.4	34.0	35.1

Dividend Data (No cash dividends have been paid.)

Data as orig. reptd.; bef. results of disc. opers. and/or spec. items. Per share data adj. for stk. divs. as of ex-div. date. E-Estimated. NA-Not Available. NM-Not Meaningful. NR-Not Ranked.

Office—7505 Metro Boulevard, Minneapolis, MN, 55439. **Tel**—(612) 830-0200. **Chrmn**—J. W. Mooty. **Pres & CEO**—M. P. Sullivan. **Secy**—D. M. Bond. **CFO, VP, Treas & Investor Contact**—Chuck Mooty. **Dirs**—E. F. Dorn, R. I. Giertsen, F. L. Heit, R. Luther, R. Mithun, J. N. Mooty, J. W. Mooty, R. C. Schweigert, M. P. Sullivan. **Transfer Agent & Registrar**—Norwest Bank Minnesota, South St. Paul. **Incorporated** in Delaware in 1962. **Empl**-564. **S&P Analyst:** Tom Graves, CFA

STANDARD & POOR'S

STOCK REPORTS

International Game Technology

NYSE Symbol **IGT**
In S&P MidCap 400

24-JUL-95

Industry: Leisure/Amusement

Summary: This company is a leading maker of gaming machines and proprietary software systems for gaming machine networks.

S&P Opinion: Avoid (★★)

Recent Price • 13⅝
52 Wk Range • 24¾-12⅜
Yield • 0.9%
12-Mo. P/E • 16.0

Quantitative Evaluations

Outlook
(1 Lowest—5 Highest)
• **5−**

Fair Value
• **17¾**

Risk
• **Average**

Earn./Div. Rank
• **B**

Technical Eval.
• **Bearish** since 11/93

Rel. Strength Rank
(1 Lowest—99 Highest)
• **8**

Insider Activity
• **Neutral**

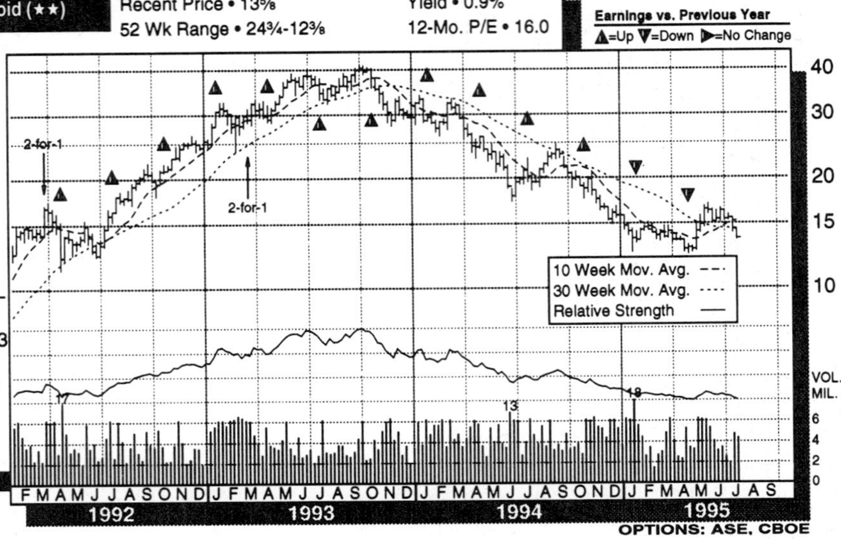

OPTIONS: ASE, CBOE

Overview - 24-JUL-95

In fiscal 1996, we expect IGT's revenues and profits to recover, helped by the strength of IGT's progressive systems business (linked gaming machines with potentially large jackpots). However, in IGT's larger product sales business, shipments of gaming machines have been restrained by the relatively slow development of new gaming markets. We can see machine sales rebounding somewhat in fiscal 1996, helped by demand from new casinos in Indiana and the larger international sales. However, the total number of machines sold is not likely to reach fiscal 1994's peak level. In the U.S., the availability of a bill-acceptor feature has likely accelerated the replacement cycle for older U.S. gaming machines. Long term, we expect international markets to make a growing contribution to IGT's revenues and profits.

Valuation - 24-JUL-95

This stock can be viewed as a proxy for growth of the overall gaming industry, since IGT is the largest supplier of coin-operated machines to casinos. During the past year, the stock has been hurt by snags in the development of new U.S. gaming markets. The share price is down more than 60% from its 1993 high. Also, IGT's pace of development or penetration in international markets is disappointing. Although we are looking for profit growth to resume in fiscal 1996, we do not view IGT's earnings prospects as robust enough to enthuse about the stock. Also, there has been speculation that IGT will be acquired by a Japanese consumer electronics company, but we are skeptical that this will occur.

Key Stock Statistics

S&P EPS Est. 1995	0.75	Tang. Bk. Value/Share	3.94
P/E on S&P Est. 1995	18.2	Beta	2.33
S&P EPS Est. 1996	1.00	Shareholders	8,800
Dividend Rate/Share	0.12	Market cap. (B)	$ 1.8
Shs. outstg. (M)	129.9	Inst. holdings	41%
Avg. daily vol. (M)	0.745	Insider holdings	NA

Value of $10,000 invested 5 years ago: $ 85,537

Fiscal Year Ending Sep. 30

	1995	% Change	1994	% Change	1993	% Change
Revenues (Million $)						
1Q	159.2	6%	149.8	72%	87.30	19%
2Q	150.0	-9%	164.5	67%	98.70	31%
3Q	150.8	-20%	187.7	42%	132.0	7%
4Q	—	—	172.5	8%	160.1	26%
Yr.	—	—	674.5	41%	478.0	20%
Income (Million $)						
1Q	25.63	-16%	30.39	43%	21.18	101%
2Q	23.06	-27%	31.41	66%	18.88	72%
3Q	25.36	-36%	39.91	35%	29.65	48%
4Q	—	—	38.74	8%	35.87	54%
Yr.	—	—	140.4	33%	105.6	63%
Earnings Per Share ($)						
1Q	0.19	-17%	0.23	28%	0.18	100%
2Q	0.18	-25%	0.24	60%	0.15	67%
3Q	0.20	-33%	0.30	25%	0.24	45%
4Q	E0.19	—	0.29	4%	0.28	44%
Yr.	E0.75	—	1.07	26%	0.85	57%

Next earnings report expected: early November

International Game Technology

Business Summary - 24-JUL-95

IGT is likely the world's largest manufacturer of coin-operated casino products, such as slot and video machines. It has also developed and has interests in various multi-location progressive slot machine systems, including operations in Nevada, Atlantic City, Macau, Mississippi and Deadwood, S.D. In these systems, which link machines at various sites, large jackpots can be won by gamblers. The company also makes specialized video gaming terminals (VGTs), for lotteries and other applications, and sells proprietary systems that monitor VGTs.

Revenue contributions from continuing operations by business segment in recent fiscal years (progressive systems and lease operations included in gaming operations) were:

	1994	1993
Product sales	76%	70%
Gaming operations	24%	30%

Legalization and use of coin-operated gaming machines is growing both in the U.S. and overseas. In fiscal 1994, IGT sold about 95,000 machines, up from 68,900 in fiscal 1993. IGT's markets include casinos in Nevada and Atlantic City, plus riverboat casinos and Indian gaming facilities in various states. International markets include Canada, Australia, Europe and Japan. The gaming operations segment also includes progressive systems and leased slot machines.

In September 1994, IGT completed a $100 million private placement of 7.84% senior notes. The use of proceeds is expected to include the financing of a new manufacturing and headquarters facility. At June 30, 1995, IGT had cash and short-term investments totaling $216.7 million.

IGT has divested other assets, including its interest in a riverboat gaming business and a relatively small casino business.

Important Developments

Jul. '95—In fiscal 1995's third quarter, IGT sold approximately 18,100 gaming machines, down about 33% from the year-earlier period. A 38% decline in gross profit from product sales more than offset a 16% rise from gaming operations, which largely consist of IGT's systems on linked machines that offer progressive jackpots. IGT's machine sales have suffered from a slowdown in the development of new gaming markets. However, casinos are expected to debut in Indiana later in 1995, and future sales should get a boost from another building boom in Las Vegas, and the likely expansion of gaming in South Africa. Meanwhile, since June 1994, IGT has repurchased 6.4 million shares of its common stock; however, none was bought back in fiscal 1995's third quarter.

Capitalization

Long Term Debt: $111,846,000 (6/95).

Per Share Data ($) (Year Ended Sep. 30)

	1994	1993	1992	1991	1990	1989
Tangible Bk. Val.	3.94	3.03	1.83	1.10	0.82	0.7[illegible]
Cash Flow	1.22	1.02	0.70	0.36	0.25	0.17
Earnings	1.07	0.85	0.54	0.26	0.17	0.11
Dividends	0.12	0.06	Nil	Nil	Nil	Nil
Payout Ratio	11%	7%	Nil	Nil	Nil	Nil
Prices - High	34	41⅜	26⅜	12	2½	2[illegible]
- Low	14⅞	23¾	10⅞	1⅞	1⅛	1
P/E Ratio - High	32	49	49	46	15	1[illegible]
- Low	14	28	20	7	7	11

Income Statement Analysis (Million $)

	1994	%Chg	1993	%Chg	1992	%Chg	1991
Revs.	674	41%	478	20%	399	68%	237
Oper. Inc.	218	28%	170	37%	124	118%	57.0
Depr.	20.1	NM	20.2	6%	19.0	58%	12.0
Int. Exp.	11.8	-7%	12.7	-8%	13.8	50%	9.2
Pretax Inc.	215	24%	174	61%	108	125%	48.0
Eff. Tax Rate	35%	—	39%	—	39%	—	39%
Net Inc.	140	32%	106	64%	64.8	115%	30.2

Balance Sheet & Other Fin. Data (Million $)

	1994	1993	1992	1991	1990	1989
Cash	203	217	149	126	22.0	16.0
Curr. Assets	559	460	323	227	125	108
Total Assets	868	647	490	346	209	170
Curr. Liab.	78.4	83.7	66.1	42.6	44.2	39.6
LT Debt	111	61.0	114	113	28.0	24.0
Common Eqty.	521	379	214	124	93.0	82.0
Total Cap.	643	456	351	254	135	115
Cap. Exp.	73.2	46.1	33.7	22.8	14.9	16.6
Cash Flow	161	126	83.7	42.2	29.4	19.8

Ratio Analysis

	1994	1993	1992	1991	1990	1989
Curr. Ratio	7.1	5.5	4.9	5.3	2.8	2.7
% LT Debt of Cap.	17.3	13.3	32.5	44.6	20.5	20.8
% Net Inc.of Revs.	20.8	22.1	16.2	12.7	9.5	8.7
% Ret. on Assets	18.1	18.0	15.3	10.9	10.7	8.8
% Ret. on Equity	30.5	34.8	37.8	28.0	23.3	17.6

Dividend Data (Quarterly dividends were initiated following a two-for-one stock split in 1993.)

Amt. of Div. $	Date Decl.	Ex-Div. Date	Stock of Record	Payment Date
0.030	Jul. 20	Jul. 26	Aug. 01	Sep. 01 '94
0.030	Oct. 20	Oct. 26	Nov. 01	Dec. 01 '94
0.030	Jan. 04	Jan. 26	Feb. 01	Mar. 01 '95
0.030	Apr. 20	Apr. 25	May. 01	Jun. 01 '95

Data as orig. reptd.; bef. results of disc. opers. and/or spec. items. Per share data adj. for stk. divs. as of ex-div. date. E-Estimated. NA-Not Available. NM-Not Meaningful. NR-Not Ranked.

Office—520 South Rock Blvd., Reno, NV 89502. **Tel**—(702) 688-0100. **Chrmn**—C. N. Mathewson. **CEO**—J. J. Russell. **Pres & COO**—D. P. Hanlon. **Secy**—B. McKay. **Dirs**—A. J. Crosson, W. K. Keating, C. N. Mathewson, W. L. Nelson, F. B. Rentschler, J. J. Russell, R. A. Schnabel, C. B. Williams. **Transfer Agent & Registrar**—Continental Stock Transfer & Trust Co., NYC. **Incorporated** in Nevada in 1980. **Empl**-2,100. **S&P Analyst:** Tom Graves, CFA

STANDARD & POOR'S

STOCK REPORTS

International Multifoods

NYSE Symbol **IMC**
In S&P MidCap 400

29-SEP-95 **Industry:** Food

Summary: This leading U.S. food service company also produces bakery products in both North America and Venezuela.

S&P Opinion: Accumulate (★★★★) Recent Price • 22⅝ 52 Wk Range • 23-15¾ Yield • 3.6% 12-Mo. P/E • 12.0

Quantitative Evaluations
Outlook (1 Lowest—5 Highest) • **4-**
Fair Value • **24⅜**
Risk • **Low**
Earn./Div. Rank • **B+**

Technical Eval. • **Bearish** since 7/95
Rel. Strength Rank (1 Lowest—99 Highest) • **38**
Insider Activity • **NA**

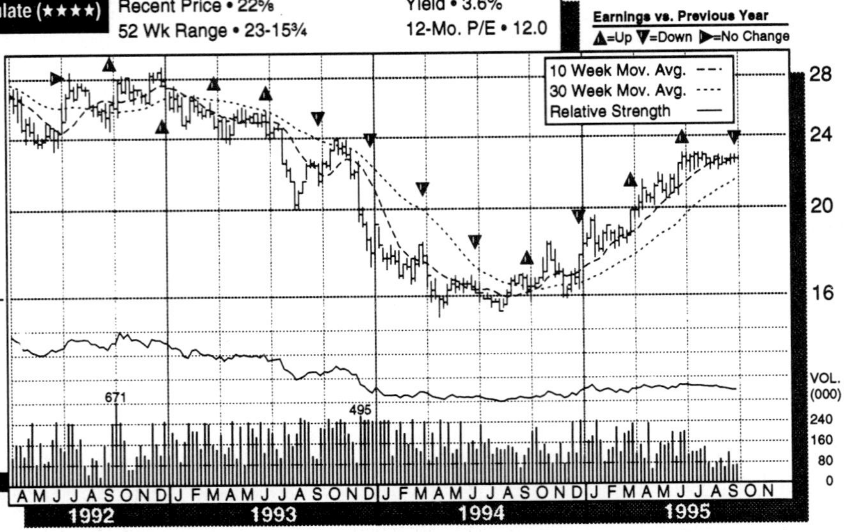

Overview - 29-SEP-95

Broad-based profit growth is expected from the company's continuing operations through fiscal 1996-97. Foodservice Distribution profits should trend upward, driven by growth in existing operations and the ongoing acquisition of complementary businesses. Also, the implemenation of a business information system should help give vending distribution margins and earnings a lift in coming quarters. Bakery profits should extend their upward trend, helped by favorable frozen bakery product market conditions, and continued benefits from recent restructuring actions. Venezuelan segment profits should benefit from core business growth, but the risk of a potentially disruptive currency devaluation near-term is high.

Valuation - 28-SEP-95

Based on our expectations of continued, albiet modest, earnings growth from continuing operations through fiscal 1996-97, we view the shares as attractive at current levels. Over the past two years, management has effectively repositioned the company for sustainable long-term profit growth by shedding unrelated businesses, acquiring businesses that fit well with its important Foodservice Distribution operations, and by cutting costs. We expect IMC to steadily reap the benefits from these actions through 1996-97. The stock, at a significant discount to other S&P MidCap 400 stocks, and yielding about 3.5%, appears to be an above-average total return play over the next 12 months. Investors should note, though, that the risk of a currency devaluation in Venezuela is high, which could penalize reported earnings.

Key Stock Statistics

S&P EPS Est. 1996	1.75	Tang. Bk. Value/Share	10.16
P/E on S&P Est. 1996	12.9	Beta	0.95
S&P EPS Est. 1997	1.90	Shareholders	5,100
Dividend Rate/Share	0.80	Market cap. (B)	$0.401
Shs. outstg. (M)	18.0	Inst. holdings	55%
Avg. daily vol. (M)	0.018	Insider holdings	NA

Value of $10,000 invested 5 years ago: $ 14,255

Fiscal Year Ending Feb. 28

	1996	% Change	1995	% Change	1994	% Change
Revenues (Million $)						
1Q	634.6	16%	548.0	-1%	555.8	1%
2Q	621.3	31%	476.0	-9%	521.5	-4%
3Q	—	—	653.0	12%	585.6	-2%
4Q	—	—	617.5	10%	561.8	5%
Yr.	—	—	2,295	3%	2,225	NM
Income (Million $)						
1Q	4.56	50%	3.04	-53%	6.40	7%
2Q	7.00	-78%	31.36	NM	-27.20	NM
3Q	—	—	10.91	-12%	12.45	-19%
4Q	—	—	11.70	NM	-5.10	NM
Yr.	—	—	57.02	NM	-13.44	NM
Earnings Per Share ($)						
1Q	0.25	47%	0.17	-48%	0.33	6%
2Q	0.38	-78%	1.74	NM	-1.41	NM
3Q	E0.62	2%	0.61	-8%	0.66	-18%
4Q	E0.50	-23%	0.65	NM	-0.28	NM
Yr.	E1.75	-45%	3.16	NM	-0.72	NM

Next earnings report expected: late December

International Multifoods

Business Summary - 29-SEP-95

International Multifoods operates in three businesses: foodservice distribution in the United States; bakery products in the United States and Canada; and bakery and agricultural products in Venezuela. Contributions by business segment in fiscal 1994-95 (excluding divested businesses and special items) were:

	Sales	Profits
Foodservice Distribution	64%	29%
Bakery	21%	38%
Venezuela Foods	15%	33%

The Foodservice Distribution segment includes the company's vending distribution unit (VSA); the limited-menu distribution unit, which comprises the newly acquired foodservice distribution business of Leprino Foods Co. and the former Pueringer specialty foodservice distribution unit; and the food exporting business.

The Bakery segment comprises consumer products in Canada, which include primarily home baking products and condiments; as well as U.S. and Canadian bakery products for foodservice, retail bakery, in-store bakery and wholesale bakery customers.

Venezuela Foods consists of consumer products for home baking; bakery products for commercial food processors and retail bakeries; and products for the agricultural sector.

Important Developments

Sep. '95—During fiscal 1995-96's first half, Foodservice Distribution segment profits (before unusual items) rose 19%, year to year, as improved earnings from the limited-menu distribution business offset lower vending distribution profits. Bakery profits rose 11%, led by improved volumes and 1993-94 restructuring actions. Venezuela Foods profits more than doubled, due primarily to strong volume growth, price increases in most product categories, and the effect of government-imposed exchange controls as compared to the year ago period (offset somewhat by IMC's use of a free-market exchange rate effective August 31, 1995). Separately, fiscal 1995-96 second quarter results include a $6.2 million pretax restructuring charge, which was partially offset by a $500,000 net gain from the sale of IMC's surimi seafood business and the favorable impact of a tax settlement.

Capitalization

Long Term Debt: $164,100,000 (8/95).
Red. Preferred Stock: $3,700,000.

Per Share Data ($) (Year Ended Feb. 28)

	1995	1994	1993	1992	1991	1990
Tangible Bk. Val.	16.16	13.63	16.64	16.19	10.50	9.08
Cash Flow	4.67	0.60	3.62	3.66	3.49	2.94
Earnings	3.16	-0.72	2.13	2.00	1.81	1.30
Dividends	0.80	0.80	0.80	0.79	0.79	0.79
Payout Ratio	25%	NM	38%	40%	44%	61%
Cal. Yrs.	1994	1993	1992	1991	1990	1989
Prices - High	19⅛	27½	29¼	31½	25	22¼
- Low	15⅛	2	23¼	22	16⅛	18¼
P/E Ratio - High	6	NM	14	16	14	17
- Low	5	6	11	11	9	14

Income Statement Analysis (Million $)

	1995	%Chg	1994	%Chg	1993	%Chg	1992
Revs.	2,295	3%	2,225	NM	2,224	-2%	2,281
Oper. Inc.	87.0	-6%	93.0	-11%	105	-11%	118
Depr.	27.0	-10%	29.9	4%	28.8	-11%	32.4
Int. Exp.	16.3	23%	13.2	-10%	14.6	-32%	21.6
Pretax Inc.	71.7	NM	-24.9	NM	66.1	-2%	67.4
Eff. Tax Rate	21%	—	NM	—	38%	—	42%
Net Inc.	57.0	NM	-13.4	NM	41.2	5%	39.1

Balance Sheet & Other Fin. Data (Million $)

	1995	1994	1993	1992	1991	1990
Cash	10.8	10.5	11.0	4.2	6.0	17.7
Curr. Assets	472	439	416	413	428	474
Total Assets	847	815	803	768	806	844
Curr. Liab.	316	302	243	285	312	348
LT Debt	183	195	167	104	115	135
Common Eqty.	291	250	322	313	321	303
Total Cap.	494	471	512	436	474	476
Cap. Exp.	30.8	51.9	45.7	51.2	57.3	69.6
Cash Flow	83.9	11.3	69.8	71.3	67.7	56.7

Ratio Analysis

	1995	1994	1993	1992	1991	1990
Curr. Ratio	1.5	1.5	1.7	1.4	1.4	1.4
% LT Debt of Cap.	37.1	41.4	32.6	23.8	24.3	28.3
% Net Inc.of Revs.	2.5	NM	1.9	1.7	1.6	1.2
% Ret. on Assets	6.9	NM	5.2	5.0	4.2	3.2
% Ret. on Equity	21.2	NM	12.9	12.3	11.2	8.4

Dividend Data —Dividends have been paid since 1923. A dividend reinvestment plan is available. A poison pill stock purchase rights plan was adopted in 1986.

Amt. of Div. $	Date Decl.	Ex-Div. Date	Stock of Record	Payment Date
0.200	Sep. 16	Sep. 22	Sep. 28	Oct. 17 '94
0.200	Dec. 16	Dec. 21	Dec. 28	Jan. 16 '95
0.200	Mar. 17	Mar. 22	Mar. 28	Apr. 17 '95
0.200	Jun. 16	Jun. 26	Jun. 28	Jul. 17 '95
0.200	Sep. 15	Sep. 26	Sep. 28	Oct. 16 '95

Data as orig. reptd.; bef. results of disc. opers. and/or spec. items. Per share data adj. for stk. divs. as of ex-div. date. E-Estimated. NA-Not Available. NM-Not Meaningful. NR-Not Ranked.

Office—33 South Sixth St., P.O. Box 2942, Minneapolis, MN 55402-0942. **Tel**—(612) 340-3300. **Chrmn & Pres**—A. Luiso. **VP-CFO**—D. H. Cocroft. **VP-Secy**—F. W. Bonvino. **Investor Contact**—Tony Brausen (612-340-3621). **Dirs**—W. A. Andres, J. G. Fifield, A. Luiso, R. M. Price, N. L. Reding, J. D. Rehm, L. D. Rice, P. S. Willmott. **Transfer Agent & Registrar**—Norwest Bank Minnesota, South St. Paul. **Incorporated** in Delaware in 1969; business established in 1892. **Empl-** 8,390. **S&P Analyst:** Kenneth A. Shea

IPALCO Enterprises

NYSE Symbol **IPL**
In S&P MidCap 400

16-OCT-95 **Industry:** Utilities-Electric

Summary: This utility holding company owns Indianapolis Power & Light, which serves a diversified regional economy. Its Mid-America Capital Resources operates IPL's unregulated businesses.

S&P Opinion: Hold (★★★)

Recent Price • 37
52 Wk Range • 37¼-28½
Yield • 5.8%
12-Mo. P/E • 15.5

Quantitative Evaluations

Outlook (1 Lowest—5 Highest)
• **2+**

Fair Value
• **34½**

Risk
• **Low**

Earn./Div. Rank
• **B+**

Technical Eval.
• **Bullish** since 1/95

Rel. Strength Rank (1 Lowest—99 Highest)
• **80**

Insider Activity
• **Favorable**

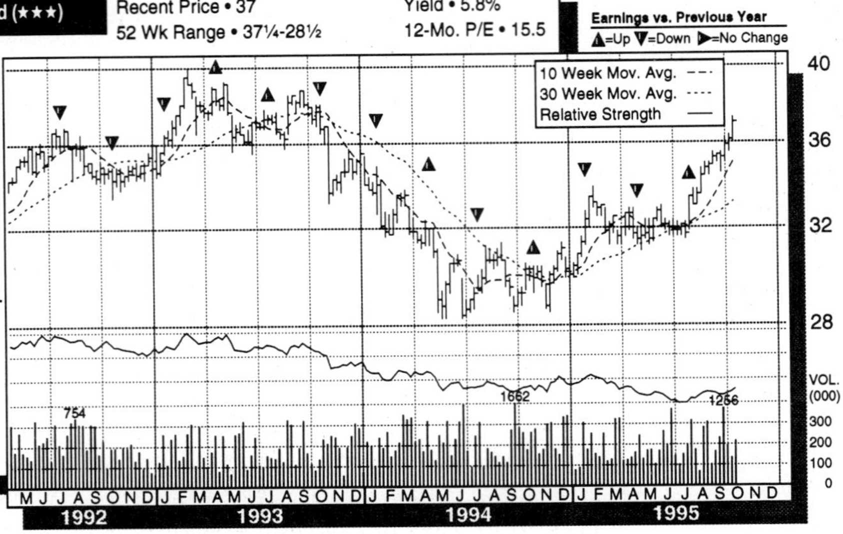

Overview - 16-OCT-95

This comparatively small utility has relatively low production costs, competitive rates, a healthy service area economy and a favorable regulatory environment. We expect earnings growth for 1995, however, to be restrained by first quarter weakness that resulted from the impact of a mild winter on kwh sales, despite a strong third quarter due to an abnormally hot summer. On the plus side, management is active in economic development in the region, and IPL is one of the faster growing utilities within its region. With a strong focus on cost control, a nominal obligation to wholesale customers, and rate increases this September and in mid-1996, we expect a moderate expansion of earnings growth. Another plus would be an improved performance of nonregulated businesses.

Valuation - 16-OCT-95

IPL's common shares have moved up 24% in 1995, about in line with the S&P Electric Company Index, as investors gain confidence in the company's ability to withstand an increasingly competitive industry. Although the recent rate settlement should help IPL keep its debt to capital ratio below the industry average, the ban on further base load construction leaves it dependent on costly, long-term purchased power contracts that could stunt earnings and dividend growth. Still, speculation regarding further Federal Reserve Board easing and takeover speculation should keep the shares of this well-managed company buoyant.

Key Stock Statistics

S&P EPS Est. 1995	2.55	Tang. Bk. Value/Share	20.65
P/E on S&P Est. 1995	14.5	Beta	0.43
S&P EPS Est. 1996	2.68	Shareholders	25,700
Dividend Rate/Share	2.16	Market cap. (B)	$ 1.4
Shs. outstg. (M)	37.8	Inst. holdings	42%
Avg. daily vol. (M)	0.090	Insider holdings	NA

Value of $10,000 invested 5 years ago: $ 19,919

Fiscal Year Ending Dec. 31

	1995	% Change	1994	% Change	1993	% Change
Revenues (Million $)						
1Q	175.5	-3%	181.2	7%	169.0	6%
2Q	159.6	NM	161.1	5%	153.1	2%
3Q	—	—	183.7	NM	183.3	10%
4Q	—	—	160.1	NM	158.9	1%
Yr.	—	—	686.1	3%	664.3	5%
Income (Million $)						
1Q	25.90	-15%	30.37	2%	29.87	10%
2Q	17.88	11%	16.14	-2%	16.52	22%
3Q	—	—	28.90	163%	10.99	-60%
4Q	—	—	17.59	-3%	18.05	-10%
Yr.	—	—	92.99	23%	75.42	-15%
Earnings Per Share ($)						
1Q	0.69	-15%	0.81	3%	0.79	8%
2Q	0.47	9%	0.43	-2%	0.44	22%
3Q	E0.85	10%	0.77	166%	0.29	-60%
4Q	E0.55	17%	0.47	-2%	0.48	-9%
Yr.	E2.55	4%	2.46	23%	2.00	-15%

Next earnings report expected: late October

IPALCO Enterprises

Business Summary - 15-OCT-95

IPALCO Enterprises is the holding company for Indianapolis Power & Light, which supplies electricity (95% of 1994 revenues) and steam (5%) to nearly 403,000 customers. IPALCO also owns Mid-America Capital Resources, Inc., a holding company for its nonregulated businesses, most of which are energy-related research and development operations. Nonutility businesses reported modest losses in 1994 and 1993. Electric revenues are derived:

	1994	1993	1992	1991
Residential	36%	36%	36%	36%
Small comm'l & ind'l	20%	20%	21%	22%
Large comm'l & ind'l	41%	41%	41%	39%
Other	3%	3%	2%	3%

IPL generates nearly all of its kilowatt hours sold from coal, which it buys under contract from in-state suppppliers. Peak load in 1994 was 2,640 mw, and system summer capability totaled 3,157 mw, for a capacity margin of 16%. For the five-year period 1994-8, IPL has projected that retail kwh sales will increase at a compound annual rate of some 2.0%. To maintain adequate summer capacity margin in the near term, IPL has a five-year firm power purchase agreement with Indiana Michigan Power Co.through March 1997.

The company forecasts a rise in annual peak demand from 1994 to 1999 of 1.3% and in retail kwh of 1.8%. It estimates construction costs for 1995 through 1997 of $609 million, with $214 million budgeted for 1995. Of the total, $253 million is earmarked to extend, add or improve transmission and distribution lines, substations, regulating equipment, and other distribution facilities. Costs to comply with environmental regulation are roughly $168 million. IPL also projects it will need some 600 mw of additional capacity by the year 2000, which it will obtain from demand-side management, power purchases and new peaking turbines. It plans to fund its five-year construction program with long-term debt, internally generated funds and short-term borrowings.

Important Developments

Sep. '95—Indianapolis Power & Light implemented a $35 million rate increase granted in July by the Indiana Regulatory Commission. The commission also ordered a $25 million hike June 30, 1996, after IPL installs two pollution control scrubbers at the Petersburg generating plant. The rate order reflects IPL's need to recover costs to comply with Clean Air Act regulations, two new peaking units, a purchased power agreement and certain accounting expenses. IPL, which last received a rate order in 1986, agreed not to file another rate request prior to 1997 or add any large base-load generating capacity before the year 2000.

Capitalization

Long Term Debt: $654,585,000 (6/95).
Subsid. Cum. Pfd. Stock: $51,898,000.

Per Share Data ($)

(Year Ended Dec. 31)

	1994	1993	1992	1991	1990	1989
Tangible Bk. Val.	20.50	20.20	20.26	19.98	19.26	18.46
Earnings	2.46	2.00	2.35	2.72	2.58	2.54
Dividends	2.12	2.04	1.96	1.88	1.80	1.72
Payout Ratio	86%	102%	83%	69%	70%	68%
Prices - High	35 3/8	40	36 7/8	33 3/8	27 1/2	26 5/8
- Low	28 1/4	33 1/8	31 1/2	25 1/2	23 1/8	21 3/4
P/E Ratio - High	14	20	16	12	11	10
- Low	11	17	13	9	9	9

Income Statement Analysis (Million $)

	1994	%Chg	1993	%Chg	1992	%Chg	1991
Revs.	686	7%	644	2%	633	-2%	648
Depr.	87.0	11%	78.4	NM	78.6	NM	78.6
Maint.	68.6	2%	67.3	8%	62.4	3%	60.5
Fxd. Chgs. Cov.	4.0	-2%	4.1	-2%	4.2	1%	4.1
Constr. Credits	9.4	70%	5.5	8%	5.1	96%	2.6
Eff. Tax Rate	29%	—	32%	—	32%	—	31%
Net Inc.	93.0	23%	75.4	-14%	88.0	-14%	102

Balance Sheet & Other Fin. Data (Million $)

	1994	1993	1992	1991	1990	1989
Gross Prop.	2,629	2,485	2,357	2,245	2,167	2,087
Cap. Exp.	178	146	118	95.0	90.0	90.0
Net Prop.	1,712	1,609	1,538	1,489	1,464	1,439
Capitalization:						
LT Debt	666	542	550	547	537	539
% LT Debt	44	39	40	40	40	41
Pfd.	51.9	51.9	52.0	52.0	52.0	72.0
% Pfd.	3.40	3.80	3.70	3.80	3.90	5.50
Common	802	787	788	770	738	709
% Common	53	57	57	56	56	54
Total Cap.	1,854	1,707	1,735	1,709	1,662	1,652

Ratio Analysis

	1994	1993	1992	1991	1990	1989
Oper. Ratio	79.1	78.6	78.8	76.9	76.5	76.1
% Earn. on Net Prop.	8.6	9.0	8.9	10.2	9.9	10.0
% Ret. on Revs.	13.6	11.4	14.0	15.7	15.9	16.1
% Ret. On Invest.Cap	7.9	7.1	7.7	9.1	9.1	9.3
% Return On Com.Eqty	11.7	9.6	11.3	13.5	13.4	13.8

Dividend Data —Dividends have been paid since 1934. A dividend reinvestment plan is available. A "poison pill" stock purchase rights plan was adopted in 1990.

Amt. of Div. $	Date Decl.	Ex-Div. Date	Stock of Record	Payment Date
0.530	Aug. 30	Sep. 19	Sep. 23	Oct. 15 '94
0.530	Nov. 29	Dec. 19	Dec. 23	Jan. 15 '95
0.540	Feb. 28	Mar. 20	Mar. 24	Apr. 15 '95
0.540	May. 30	Jun. 21	Jun. 23	Jul. 15 '95
0.540	Aug. 29	Sep. 20	Sep. 22	Oct. 15 '95

Data as orig. reptd.; bef. results of disc opers. and/or spec. items. Per share data adj. for stk. divs. as of ex-div. date. E-Estimated. NA-Not Available. NM-Not Meaningful. NR-Not Ranked.

Office—25 Monument Circle, P.O. Box 1595, Indianapolis, IN 46206-1595. **Tel**—(317) 261-8261. **Chrmn & Pres**—J. R. Hodowal. **Secy**—M. E. Woods. **VP-Treas & Investor Contact**—John R. Brehm. **Dir**—J. D. Barnette Jr., R. A. Borns, M. E. Daniels Jr., R. C. Early, O. N. Frenzel III, M. L. Gibson, E. J. Goss, E. B. Herr Jr., J. R. Hodowal, R. L. Humke, S. H. Jones, A. B. Lacy, L. B. Lytle, M. S. Maurer, T. M. Miller, S. W. Rowland, T. H. Sams, Z. G. Todd. **Transfer Agents & Registrars**—Indianapolis Power & Light Shareholder Services, Indianapolis; Chemical Bank, NYC. **Incorporated** in Indiana in 1926. **Empl**-2,363. **S&P Analyst:** Jane Collin

STANDARD & POOR'S

Jacobs Engineering Group

STOCK REPORTS

NYSE Symbol **JEC**
In S&P MidCap 400

11-AUG-95 **Industry:** Building

Summary: This company provides engineering, construction and maintenance services to both private industry and federal government agencies on a worldwide basis.

S&P Opinion: Accumulate (★★★★) Recent Price • 23 | 52 Wk Range • 24¾-16⅞ | Yield • Nil | 12-Mo. P/E • 28.8

Quantitative Evaluations
Outlook (1 Lowest—5 Highest) • **5-**
Fair Value • **27⅛**
Risk • **Average**
Earn./Div. Rank • **B**

Technical Eval. • **Bearish** since 5/95
Rel. Strength Rank (1 Lowest—99 Highest) • **62**
Insider Activity • **NA**

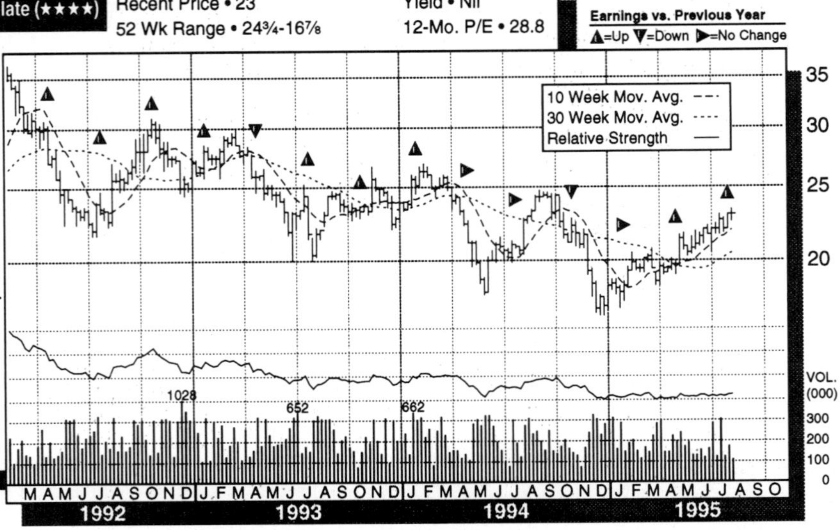

Overview - 11-AUG-95

We expect revenues to increase by about 12% in fiscal 1996, reflecting backlog growth and an increase in work performed. Aided by an expected increase in engineering revenues as a percent of total revenues, gross margins should expand. Benefiting further from well controlled SG&A, lower costs for integrating acquisitions and minimal interest expense, earnings should increase again in fiscal 1996. JEC's longer term revenue and earnings growth will be aided by the present upturn in the chemical and pulp and paper industries, increased spending for environmental remediation, additional acquisitions and an eventual recovery in spending by pharmaceutical companies and acquisitions.

Valuation - 11-AUG-95

While shares of JEC are not cheap based on our projected earnings for fiscal 1996, we intend to maintain our accumulate rating on the shares for now. We view the shares as a special situation earnings turnaround. Through acquisitions, the company is positioning itself to regain the 15% to 20% annual earnings growth of the late 1980s and early 1990s. JEC has risen 24% through early August 1995, versus a 22% gain in the S&P 500. Currently trading at slighlty lower multiple than two of its peer companies and with a very solid balance sheet, we believe that shares are worth accumulating in anticipation of a positive turn in profitability.

Key Stock Statistics

S&P EPS Est. 1995	1.25	Tang. Bk. Value/Share	7.13
P/E on S&P Est. 1995	18.4	Beta	1.60
S&P EPS Est. 1996	1.45	Shareholders	2,600
Dividend Rate/Share	Nil	Market cap. (B)	$0.581
Shs. outstg. (M)	25.3	Inst. holdings	49%
Avg. daily vol. (M)	0.026	Insider holdings	NA

Value of $10,000 invested 5 years ago: $ 33,758

Fiscal Year Ending Sep. 30

	1995	% Change	1994	% Change	1993	% Change
Revenues (Million $)						
1Q	412.4	58%	260.6	-13%	298.6	18%
2Q	396.8	46%	272.6	-5%	286.3	6%
3Q	444.6	69%	263.8	-4%	273.9	-3%
4Q	—	—	368.7	30%	284.1	-5%
Yr.	—	—	1,166	2%	1,143	3%
Income (Million $)						
1Q	7.30	NM	7.28	5%	6.92	21%
2Q	7.55	3%	7.30	1%	7.22	-11%
3Q	8.40	15%	7.28	NM	7.26	16%
4Q	—	—	-3.09	NM	7.27	12%
Yr.	—	—	18.77	-35%	28.67	8%
Earnings Per Share ($)						
1Q	0.29	NM	0.29	4%	0.28	17%
2Q	0.30	3%	0.29	NM	0.29	-15%
3Q	0.33	14%	0.29	NM	0.29	12%
4Q	E0.33	—	-0.12	NM	0.29	7%
Yr.	E1.25	—	0.75	-35%	1.15	4%

Next earnings report expected: early November

Jacobs Engineering Group

Business Summary - 11-AUG-95

Jacobs Engineering Group provides engineering, construction and plant maintenance services to both private industry and federal government agencies worldwide. Contributions to revenues by industry in recent fiscal years:

	1994	1993
Chemical and pharmaceutical	36%	34%
Facilities systems	15%	14%
Refining	32%	35%
Environmental	15%	14%
Minerals and fertilizers	2%	3%

Jacobs provides three categories of basic services.

Engineering services (41% of fiscal 1994 revenues) include the engineering and design of modern process plants and high technology facilities, as well as remedial engineering and design preparation for major environmental and hazardous waste programs. JEC billed 8.9 million professional service hours to contracts in 1994, versus 8.5 million in 1993 and 7.8 million hours in 1992.

Construction services (39%) includes the construction of process plants for industries such as petroleum refining, chemicals and pharmaceuticals; and facility projects, including high technology or special purpose buildings.

Maintenance services (20%) include all tasks required to keep a process plant in day-to-day operations.

In fiscal 1994, some 83% of contracts were cost plus, versus 90% in 1993, 87% in 1992 and 79% in 1991; 8% were guaranteed maximum, versus 3% in 1993, 4% in 1992 and 2% in 1991; and 9% were fixed price, against 7% in 1993, 9% in 1992 and 19% in 1991.

About 15.4% of total revenues were derived from Federal government agencies in fiscal 1994, versus 14.1% in 1993, 9.4% in 1992 and 6.3% in 1991.

Revenues from outside North America were 5.6% in 1994, versus 10.8% in fiscal 1993, versus 16.3% in fiscal 1992 and 8.4% in 1991.

Important Developments

Jul. '95— JEC reported share earnings of $0.33 on a 69% increase in revenues for fiscal 1995's third quarter, versus $0.29 in the year earlier period. The revenue growth was mainly attributable to the acquisition of CRS Sirrine Engineers and CRSS Constructors. Earnings lagged the gain in revenues due to a less favorable business mix compared with 1994's third fiscal quarter. Backlog at June 30, 1995, totaled $2.56 billion, versus $2.56 billion at March 31, 1995, and $1.97 billion at June 30, 1994.

Capitalization

Long Term Debt: $10,000,000 (3/95).

Per Share Data ($) (Year Ended Sep. 30)

	1994	1993	1992	1991	1990	1989
Tangible Bk. Val.	6.44	6.42	5.33	4.18	3.24	2.46
Cash Flow	1.22	1.50	1.43	1.15	0.89	0.67
Earnings	0.75	1.15	1.11	0.86	0.64	0.48
Dividends	Nil	Nil	Nil	Nil	Nil	Nil
Payout Ratio	Nil	Nil	Nil	Nil	Nil	Nil
Prices - High	26⅞	29⅞	36½	28⅞	13⅝	7¼
- Low	16⅞	20	21⅝	10⅛	6¾	5⅝
P/E Ratio - High	36	26	33	34	21	15
- Low	23	17	19	12	10	12

Income Statement Analysis (Million $)

	1994	%Chg	1993	%Chg	1992	%Chg	1991
Revs.	1,166	2%	1,143	3%	1,106	7%	1,036
Oper. Inc.	43.8	-20%	54.9	19%	46.2	18%	39.2
Depr.	12.0	36%	8.8	14%	7.7	12%	6.9
Int. Exp.	0.8	-7%	0.9	150%	0.3	-38%	0.6
Pretax Inc.	31.4	-36%	49.3	7%	45.9	31%	35.1
Eff. Tax Rate	40%	—	42%	—	42%	—	42%
Net Inc.	18.8	-34%	28.7	8%	26.6	30%	20.4

Balance Sheet & Other Fin. Data (Million $)

	1994	1993	1992	1991	1990	1989
Cash	48.5	40.6	35.1	34.1	22.5	25.5
Curr. Assets	367	265	258	207	202	172
Total Assets	504	351	317	260	254	213
Curr. Liab.	261	164	171	146	163	140
LT Debt	25.0	Nil	Nil	Nil	Nil	6.3
Common Eqty.	200	174	140	107	83.0	59.0
Total Cap.	225	174	141	109	84.0	66.0
Cap. Exp.	24.3	9.9	12.1	8.5	5.6	6.7
Cash Flow	30.7	37.5	34.3	27.3	19.9	14.3

Ratio Analysis

	1994	1993	1992	1991	1990	1989
Curr. Ratio	1.4	1.6	1.5	1.4	1.2	1.2
% LT Debt of Cap.	11.1	Nil	Nil	Nil	Nil	9.6
% Net Inc.of Revs.	1.6	2.5	2.4	2.0	1.6	1.3
% Ret. on Assets	4.4	8.4	9.2	7.8	6.0	4.9
% Ret. on Equity	10.0	17.9	21.4	21.1	19.9	20.2

Dividend Data (Cash dividends were omitted in 1984. The shares were split 2-for-1 in May 1991, 2-for-1 in April 1990, and 3-for-2 in March 1981; a 10% stock dividend was paid in February 1988. A "poison pill" stock purchase rights plan was adopted in 1990.)

Data as orig. reptd.; bef. results of disc. opers. and/or spec. items. Per share data adj. for stk. divs. as of ex-div. date. E-Estimated. NA-Not Available. NM-Not Meaningful. NR-Not Ranked.

Office—251 South Lake Ave., Pasadena, CA 91101. **Tel**—(818) 449-2171. **Chrmn**—J. J. Jacobs. **Pres & CEO**—N. G. Watson. **Secy**—R. M. Barton. **SVP-Fin, Treas & Investor Contact**—John W. Prosser, Jr. **Dirs**—J. F. Alibrandi, R. M. Barton, P. H. Dailey, R. B. Gwyn, J. J. Jacobs, L. K. Jacobs, J. C. LaForce, D. R. Laurance, D. M. Petrone, J. Rainey Jr., N. G. Watson. **Transfer Agent & Registrar**—First Interstate Bank of California, Los Angeles. **Incorporated** in California in 1957; reincorporated in Delaware in 1987. **Empl**-6,940. **S&P Analyst:** Leo Larkin

STANDARD & POOR'S

STOCK REPORTS

Jones Apparel Group

NYSE Symbol **JNY**
In S&P MidCap 400

07-AUG-95 **Industry:** Textiles

Summary: JNY is a leader in the women's sportswear, suit and dress businesses and sells under its flagship brands Jones New York, Rena Rowan for Saville, and Evan-Picone.

Quantitative Evaluations

Outlook (1 Lowest—5 Highest) • **NA**

Fair Value • **NA**

Risk • **Average**

Earn./Div. Rank • **NR**

Technical Eval. • **Bullish** since 3/95

Rel. Strength Rank (1 Lowest—99 Highest) • **81**

Insider Activity • **Neutral**

Recent Price • 34⅛
52 Wk Range • 34¾-22
Yield • Nil
12-Mo. P/E • 15.4

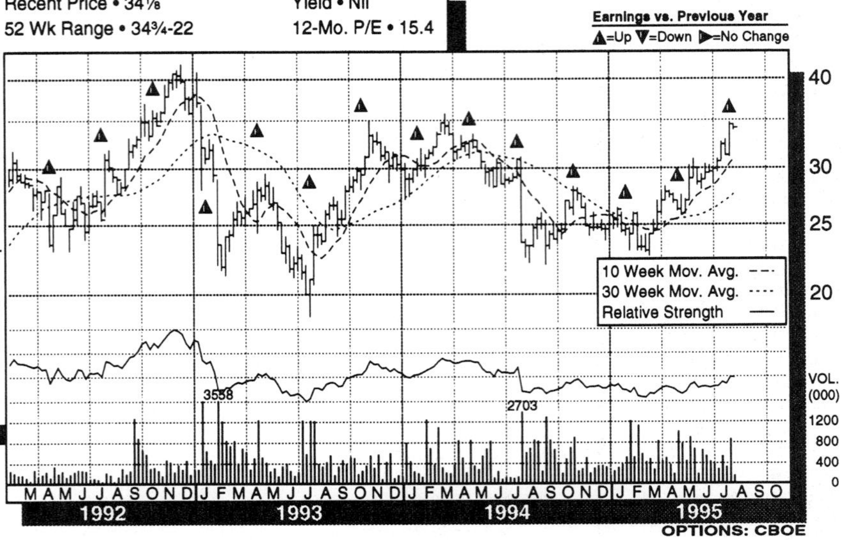

Business Profile - 07-AUG-95

This designer of women's suits and sportswear reported record results for 1994, and is expected to grow further in 1995, armed with a sound balance sheet and popular product offerings. The consensus Wall Street earnings estimate calls for 14% growth in 1995 to $2.37 a share. JNY has responded well to the growing trend of moderately-priced, comfortable apparel. Quality merchandise, name recognition, and timely fashion should translate into double-digit earnings growth for the foreseeable future.

Operational Review - 07-AUG-95

Net sales for the first half of 1995 rose 17%, year to year, reflecting increases in all product lines. With sharply higher interest expense, the gain in net income was held to 13%. Future earnings should benefit substantially from higher Jones New York Sport and Jones & Co. division shipments, and the growth momentum and market share gains experienced in this category. Margins have been squeezed by the aggressive expansion of JNY's retail outlet division.

Stock Performance - 04-AUG-95

In the past 30 trading days, JNY's shares have increased 15%, compared to a 2% rise in the S&P 500. Average trading volume for the past five days was 27,880 shares, compared with the 40-day moving average of 87,400 shares.

Key Stock Statistics

Dividend Rate/Share	Nil	Shareholders	100
Shs. outstg. (M)	25.9	Market cap. (B)	$0.885
Avg. daily vol. (M)	0.091	Inst. holdings	65%
Tang. Bk. Value/Share	9.17	Insider holdings	NA
Beta	NA		

Value of $10,000 invested 5 years ago: NA

Fiscal Year Ending Dec. 31

	1995	% Change	1994	% Change	1993	% Change
Revenues (Million $)						
1Q	192.0	19%	161.7	11%	145.1	37%
2Q	156.3	15%	135.7	12%	121.6	23%
3Q	—	—	193.7	17%	165.7	19%
4Q	—	—	142.1	31%	108.7	18%
Yr.	—	—	633.3	17%	541.2	24%
Income (Million $)						
1Q	16.73	13%	14.78	15%	12.87	25%
2Q	10.72	13%	9.47	12%	8.49	17%
3Q	—	—	20.69	5%	19.63	13%
4Q	—	—	9.98	35%	7.38	16%
Yr.	—	—	54.92	14%	48.36	17%
Earnings Per Share ($)						
1Q	0.64	14%	0.56	12%	0.50	25%
2Q	0.41	14%	0.36	13%	0.32	14%
3Q	—	—	0.79	5%	0.75	12%
4Q	—	—	0.38	36%	0.28	17%
Yr.	—	—	2.08	12%	1.85	16%

Next earnings report expected: late October

Jones Apparel Group

Business Summary - 07-AUG-95

Jones Apparel Group designs, contracts for the manufacture of, and markets a broad range of primarily better and upper moderate priced women's sportswear, suits and dresses. Sales by product category in recent years:

	1994	1993	1992	1991
Career sportswear	65%	67%	73%	76%
Casual sportswear	17%	14%	11%	7%
Suits, dresses, other	18%	19%	16%	17%

In the career sportswear area, the company's flagship label is Jones New York, under which it offers an extensive range of sportswear garments primarily for the career woman's working needs. The Jones New York products are sold in petite, misses, and women's sizes, and marketed under the Jones New York, Jones New York Petites, and Jones New York Woman labels. The Rena Rowan for Saville label was introduced for the spring 1991 season, while shipments of the Jones*Wear career sportswear line began in 1992. The Evan Picone Career Sportswear line was launched for the spring 1994 season; Jones acquired worldwide rights to the Evan-Picone trademark in November 1993 for $30.5 million.

Casual sportswear under the Jones New York Sport label, which is offered in misses, petite and women's sizes, includes a collection of weekend and leisure sportswear. Products offered in this line are intended for a less formal working environment as well as for casual wear. To complement the Jones New York Sport line JNY introduced the Jones & Co. casual sportswear line of washed and relaxed woven products. JNY also introduced the Saville Sport for Rena Rowan line of casual clothing (targeted at traditional buyers of Rena Rowan products, which are priced below Jones New York products).

Suits are designed to sell in four price ranges under the brand names Christian Dior (a "bridge" brand that relies on a collaborative design effort between JNY and Christian Dior Paris; the Christian Dior name is used by JNY under a licensing agreement), Jones New York (a better priced brand), Saville (upper moderate priced) and Ellen Kaye (a moderate priced brand).

In June 1992, JNY initiated shipments of career dresses under the Jones New York brand name. The Rena Rowan for Saville dress line was introduced for the fall 1994 season.

Important Developments

Jul. '95—Jones said that all of its product lines have performed well through the first half of 1995. Sales in the casual divisions Jones Sport and Jones & Co. more than doubled over the first half of 1994.

Capitalization

Long Term Debt: $7,030,000 (4/95), incl. $6,943,000 of cap. lease obligs.

Per Share Data ($) (Year Ended Dec. 31)

	1994	1993	1992	1991	1990	1989
Tangible Bk. Val.	8.51	6.21	5.34	3.47	1.80	1.02
Cash Flow	2.23	1.98	1.69	1.47	0.94	0.59
Earnings	2.08	1.85	1.59	1.25	0.86	0.50
Dividends	Nil	Nil	Nil	Nil	Nil	Nil
Payout Ratio	Nil	Nil	Nil	Nil	Nil	Nil
Prices - High	35¾	41	42	29⅞	NA	NA
- Low	22	18⅝	23	13⅝	NA	NA
P/E Ratio - High	17	22	26	24	NA	NA
- Low	11	10	14	11	NA	NA

Income Statement Analysis (Million $)

	1994	%Chg	1993	%Chg	1992	%Chg	1991
Revs.	642	19%	541	24%	437	31%	334
Oper. Inc.	92.1	12%	82.5	18%	70.2	28%	54.9
Depr.	4.2	17%	3.6	35%	2.7	27%	2.1
Int. Exp.	1.2	68%	0.7	-38%	1.2	-60%	2.9
Pretax Inc.	87.3	11%	79.0	19%	66.6	33%	50.1
Eff. Tax Rate	37%	—	39%	—	38%	—	32%
Net Inc.	54.9	13%	48.4	17%	41.3	21%	34.1

Balance Sheet & Other Fin. Data (Million $)

	1994	1993	1992	1991	1990	1989
Cash	21.1	27.0	33.0	17.0	1.4	1.6
Curr. Assets	261	212	167	117	80.0	60.0
Total Assets	318	267	185	129	88.0	68.0
Curr. Liab.	54.4	52.8	45.1	37.7	47.9	42.2
LT Debt	8.0	9.6	4.8	5.2	4.6	5.0
Common Eqty.	249	189	135	85.8	35.9	20.5
Total Cap.	257	199	140	91.0	40.6	25.5
Cap. Exp.	9.5	11.6	7.1	2.5	2.0	0.6
Cash Flow	59.1	51.9	44.0	36.2	20.4	12.7

Ratio Analysis

	1994	1993	1992	1991	1990	1989
Curr. Ratio	4.8	4.0	3.7	3.1	1.7	1.4
% LT Debt of Cap.	3.1	4.8	3.4	5.8	11.4	19.6
% Net Inc.of Revs.	8.6	8.9	9.5	10.2	6.5	5.1
% Ret. on Assets	18.7	21.3	26.1	28.6	NM	NM
% Ret. on Equity	24.9	29.7	37.1	52.4	NM	NM

Dividend Data (No dividends have been paid.)

Data as orig. reptd.; bef. results of disc. opers. and/or spec. items. Per share data adj. for stk. divs. as of ex-div. date. E-Estimated. NA-Not Available. NM-Not Meaningful. NR-Not Ranked.

Offices—250 Rittenhouse Circle, Keystone Park, Bristol, PA 19007. **Tel**—(215) 785-4000. **Chrmn**—S. Kimmel. **Vice Chrmn & Secy**—H. J. Goodfriend. **CFO & Investor Contact**—Wesley R. Card. **Dirs**—H. Gittis, H. J. Goodfriend, S. Kimmel, I. Samelman, G. Stutz. **Transfer Agent & Registrar**—Mellon Securities Transfer Services, Ridgefield Park, NJ. **Incorporated** in Pennsylvania in 1975. **Empl**-2,325. **S&P Analyst:** Maureen C. Carini

STANDARD & POOR'S

STOCK REPORTS

Kansas City Power & Light

NYSE Symbol **KLT**
In S&P MidCap 400

23-AUG-95 **Industry:** Utilities-Electric

Summary: This midsize electric utility serves over 429,000 customers in 23 counties in western Missouri and eastern Kansas. It derives 95% of its business from metropolitan Kansas City, Mo.

S&P Opinion: Hold (★★★)

Recent Price • 22¾ | Yield • 6.9%
52 Wk Range • 24½-20⅛ | 12-Mo. P/E • 13.1

Quantitative Evaluations
Outlook (1 Lowest—5 Highest) • **2⁻**
Fair Value • **21⅝**
Risk • **Low**
Earn./Div. Rank • **B+**

Technical Eval. • **Bullish** since 7/95
Rel. Strength Rank (1 Lowest—99 Highest) • **39**
Insider Activity • **Neutral**

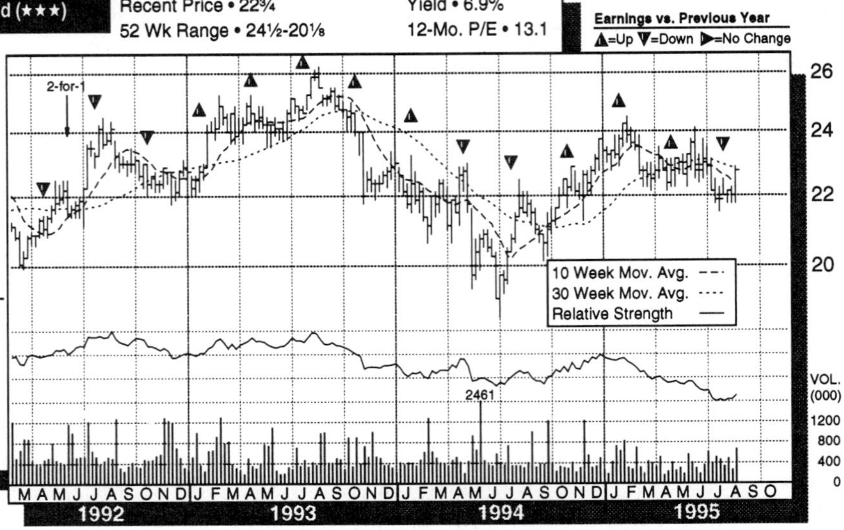

Overview - 23-AUG-95

Share earnings have been helped in 1995 by gains on the sale of railcars and lower preferred dividends, but profitability has weakened due to milder weather, costs to repair storm damage, and continuing charges for the Wolf Creek early retirement program. KLT should benefit from savings from a lower headcount in 1996. Its fuel costs are two-thirds of the regional average and, given a strengthening regional economy and the absence of one-time charges, KLT is well positioned for growing competition in wholesale markets due to its low cost power, and in industrial markets where price cutting is common. Less than 18% of KLT's retail sales are from industrial customers, versus 35% for the industry.

Valuation - 16-AUG-95

KLT's shares have fallen 5.4% since the beginning of the year, primarily due to investor concerns about the company's vulnerability to competition under proposed Federal Energy Regulatory Commission rules to deregulate the industry. Competitive pricing in wholesale and industrial markets could reduce this comparatively small utility's business in its service area. However, the stock is less vulnerable to market fluctuations than most of its peers and, although its dividend payout ratio is comparatively high, cash flows remain strong, and the dividend is secure. With a yield of 7%, the shares are a worthwhile investment for income.

Key Stock Statistics

S&P EPS Est. 1995	1.80	Tang. Bk. Value/Share	14.01
P/E on S&P Est. 1995	12.6	Beta	0.38
S&P EPS Est. 1996	1.96	Shareholders	31,600
Dividend Rate/Share	1.56	Market cap. (B)	$ 1.4
Shs. outstg. (M)	61.9	Inst. holdings	28%
Avg. daily vol. (M)	0.088	Insider holdings	0%

Value of $10,000 invested 5 years ago: $ 18,735

Fiscal Year Ending Dec. 31

	1995	% Change	1994	% Change	1993	% Change
Revenues (Million $)						
1Q	198.9	NM	199.3	4%	191.4	6%
2Q	205.3	-8%	223.1	7%	208.3	6%
3Q	—	—	253.8	-1%	256.9	12%
4Q	—	—	192.1	-4%	200.8	2%
Yr.	—	—	868.3	1%	857.5	7%
Income (Million $)						
1Q	22.89	131%	9.89	-37%	15.80	90%
2Q	18.70	-25%	24.78	-4%	25.73	21%
3Q	—	—	50.10	12%	44.92	18%
4Q	—	—	20.01	4%	19.32	4%
Yr.	—	—	104.8	NM	105.7	22%
Earnings Per Share ($)						
1Q	0.35	133%	0.15	-38%	0.24	100%
2Q	0.29	-24%	0.38	-5%	0.40	21%
3Q	E0.83	4%	0.80	11%	0.72	20%
4Q	E0.33	6%	0.31	3%	0.30	3%
Yr.	E1.80	10%	1.64	-1%	1.66	23%

Next earnings report expected: mid October

Kansas City Power & Light

Business Summary - 23-AUG-95

Kansas City Power & Light supplies electricity to over 429,000 customers in a 4,700-square-mile area located in 23 counties in western Missouri and eastern Kansas. Some 95% of the company's business is derived from metropolitan Kansas City, Mo. Revenues by customer class in recent years were:

	1994	1993	1992	1991
Residential	33%	34%	32%	35%
Commercial	42%	42%	44%	43%
Industrial	13%	14%	15%	14%
Other	12%	10%	9%	8%

The fuel mix in 1994 was 75% coal, 24% nuclear, and 1% other. Peak load in 1994 was 2,714 mw and system capacity was 3,098 mw, for a capacity margin of 12%. The Wolf Creek nuclear station (47% owned), completed in 1985, provides roughly 25% of annual kilowatt hour generation.

The company has estimated construction expenditures (excluding AFUDC) for the 1995-1999 period at $752 million. The plan includes $146 million to build three new 136 megawatt gas-fired combustion turbines. It also includes outlays for distribution and general facilities. KLT believes it will be able to meet a significant portion of these expenditures with funds generated internally.

The company also plans to prepay $208 million of debt maturing through 1999 with funds from operations, refinancing or short term debt. In November 1994, KLT filed a shelf registration for $125 million secured medium term notes. Proceeds will be used to repay debt and for general purposes.

The company's KLT Inc. unit pursues opportunities in unregulated, energy-related businesses.

Important Developments

Jul. '95—The company reported that revenues for the six months ended June 30, 1995 fell 4.3% from the year earlier period due to milder than normal weather, a sharp decline in sales to other utilities and lower prices for industrial customers. Fuel and other costs were also lower, operating income increased 6.6%, and other income was up sharply. Net income after preferred dividends rose 20% to $0.64 a share from $0.53. Results included a gain of $0.08 on the sale of rail cars in 1995 and $0.24 in charges in 1994 for the effect of the early retirement program at Wolf Creek.

Capitalization

Long Term Debt: $837,564,000 (6/95).
Red. Preferred Stock: $1,436,000.
Cum. Preferred Stock: $89,000,000.

Per Share Data ($)

(Year Ended Dec. 31)

	1994	1993	1992	1991	1990	1989
Tangible Bk. Val.	14.13	13.99	13.79	13.89	13.74	13.49
Earnings	1.64	1.66	1.35	1.58	1.56	1.66
Dividends	1.50	1.46	1.43	1.37	1.31	1.25
Payout Ratio	91%	88%	106%	87%	84%	76%
Prices - High	23⅞	26¼	24½	23¾	18	18⅛
- Low	18⅝	21¾	20	17⅛	14⅝	14⅛
P/E Ratio - High	15	16	18	15	12	11
- Low	11	13	15	11	9	8

Income Statement Analysis (Million $)

	1994	%Chg	1993	%Chg	1992	%Chg	1991
Revs.	868	1%	857	7%	803	-3%	825
Depr.	94.4	4%	91.1	3%	88.8	2%	86.8
Maint.	72.5	-8%	78.6	-3%	81.2	NM	80.9
Fxd. Chgs. Cov.	4.3	7%	4.1	23%	3.3	3%	3.2
Constr. Credits	3.9	-21%	5.0	67%	3.0	NM	3.0
Eff. Tax Rate	39%	—	39%	—	38%	—	37%
Net Inc.	105	NM	106	23%	86.0	-17%	104

Balance Sheet & Other Fin. Data (Million $)

	1994	1993	1992	1991	1990	1989
Gross Prop.	3,429	3,338	3,233	3,145	3,051	2,999
Cap. Exp.	125	129	130	122	93.0	103
Net Prop.	2,336	2,318	2,285	2,253	2,221	2,222
Capitalization:						
LT Debt	798	734	788	823	750	879
% LT Debt	45	43	46	48	44	49
Pfd.	90.6	90.8	90.9	41.1	94.2	94.4
% Pfd.	5.10	5.40	5.20	2.40	5.60	5.20
Common	875	866	854	860	851	836
% Common	50	51	49	50	50	46
Total Cap.	2,491	2,406	2,401	2,373	2,322	2,414

Ratio Analysis

	1994	1993	1992	1991	1990	1989
Oper. Ratio	82.8	81.8	82.5	79.5	76.1	74.5
% Earn. on Net Prop.	6.4	6.8	6.2	7.6	8.2	8.4
% Ret. on Revs.	12.1	12.3	10.8	12.6	13.5	14.8
% Ret. On Invest.Cap	6.2	6.6	6.0	7.3	7.5	8.0
% Return On Com.Eqty	11.6	11.9	9.7	11.4	11.4	12.4

Dividend Data —Dividends have been paid since 1921.

Amt. of Div. $	Date Decl.	Ex-Div. Date	Stock of Record	Payment Date
0.380	Aug. 02	Aug. 23	Aug. 29	Sep. 20 '94
0.380	Nov. 01	Nov. 22	Nov. 29	Dec. 20 '94
0.380	Feb. 07	Feb. 22	Feb. 28	Mar. 20 '95
0.380	May. 02	May. 23	May. 30	Jun. 20 '95
0.390	Aug. 01	Aug. 25	Aug. 29	Sep. 20 '95

Data as orig. reptd.; bef. results of disc opers. and/or spec. items. Per share data adj. for stk. divs. as of ex-div. date. E-Estimated. NA-Not Available. NM-Not Meaningful. NR-Not Ranked.

Office—1201 Walnut, Kansas City, MO 64106. **Tel**—(816) 556-2200. **Chrmn & Pres**—Drue Jennings. **VP-Fin, Treas and CFO**—J. J. DeStefano. **Secy**—J. S. Latz. **Investor Contact**—Robert Levesque (816-556-2312). **Dirs**—D. L. Bodde, W. H. Clark, R. J. Dineen, A. J. Doyle, W. T. Grant II, D. Jennings, G. E. Nettels, Jr., L. H. Talbott, R. H. West. **Transfer Agent & Registrar**—UMB Bank, Kansas City, MO. **Incorporated** in Missouri in 1922. **Empl**-2,335. **S&P Analyst:** Jane Collin

Kansas City Southern Industries

NYSE Symbol KSU Options on Pacific In S&P MidCap 400

Price	Range	P-E Ratio	Dividend	Yield	S&P Ranking	Beta
Aug. 11'95	1995					
39⅛	41¼–31	22	0.30	0.8%	B	1.01

Summary

In April 1995, this rail and financial services company said that it would make an initial public offering during 1995's fourth quarter of 51% of its DST Systems unit (37% of total revenues). Concurrently, a 6,000,000 share repurchase plan (13.8% of KSU's total shares) was authorized. In late 1994 KSU expanded its assets under management by some 15% through the acquisition of a controlling stake in Berger Associates Inc. Profits in 1995 are being hurt by some $0.44 in unusual costs.

Current Outlook

Earnings for 1995 (including 100% of DST) are projected at $2.25 a share (including $0.44 of unusual costs), versus the $2.32 (after $0.28 of net charges) reported for 1994.

Dividends at $0.07½ quarterly are not expected to be lifted during 1995.

Rail comparisons in 1995 will be penalized a charge to cover employee separation costs, asset writedowns, and reserve additions. Operating income will benefit from increased shipments of chemicals and petroleum products and a rebound in grain exports. Intermodal shipments will benefit from coordinated service with Norfolk Southern. Coal traffic will rebound as a major plant in Texas comes back on line. Mutual funds' profits will rise moderately, as heavier marketing costs are offset by the absence of 1994's charge and contributions from Berger Associates. Contributions from DST will benefit from steady expansion of shareowner accounts. Equity income will fall reflecting the sale of KSU's stake in Investors Fiduciary Trust Co.

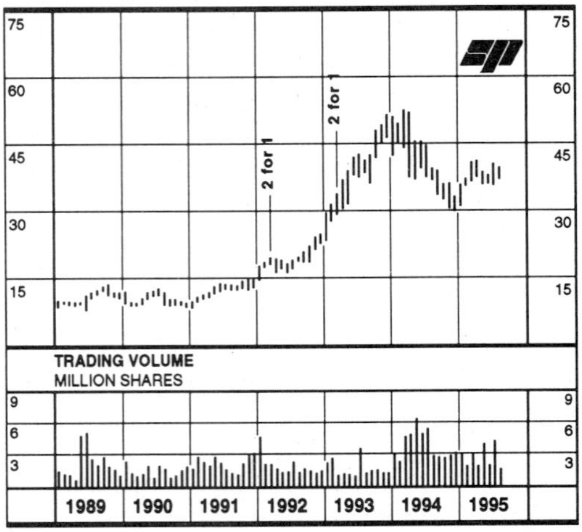

Gross Revenues (Million $)

Quarter:	1995	1994	1993	1992
Mar.	302.2	265.1	214.6	175.1
Jun.	308.7	267.2	231.7	177.8
Sep.		273.4	253.3	189.5
Dec.		292.2	261.5	199.0
		1,097.9	961.1	741.4

Revenues for 1995's first half rose 15%, year to year. Net income fell 40%, to $0.80 a share from $1.31.

Common Share Earnings ($)

Quarter:	1995	1994	1993	1992
Mar.	0.61	0.61	0.49	0.33
Jun.	0.19	0.70	0.48	0.35
Sep.	E0.70	0.64	0.52	0.36
Dec.	E0.75	0.37	0.67	0.39
	E2.25	2.32	2.16	1.43

Important Developments

Jul. '95— KSU said profits for 1995's second quarter were reduced by $17.8 million ($0.39 a share; $0.44 for the first half), primarily reflecting unusual costs at its rail operations.

Apr. '95— KSU's directors approved a public offering of 51% of the firm's DST Systems unit. KSU said it plans to transfer its 80% stake in Berger Associates to DST prior to the offering, which is planned for 1995's fourth quarter. KSU expects the offering to enhance shareholder value by drawing attention to DST's performance. In 1994 DST had net income of $32 million on revenues of $404 million. Proceeds from the offering would be used partly to fund a 6,000,000-share repurchase program (13.8% of KSU's total shares) authorized in April.

Next earnings report expected in late October.

Per Share Data ($)

Yr. End Dec. 31	1994	[3]1993	1992	1991	[1]1990	1989	1988	1987	1986	1985
Tangible Bk. Val.	**10.46**	9.17	9.56	7.99	7.25	7.45	6.26	8.63	8.51	10.13
Cash Flow	**4.97**	4.04	2.84	2.45	2.24	2.21	0.25	2.32	1.02	2.57
Earnings[2]	**2.32**	2.16	1.43	1.08	0.99	0.89	d1.13	0.83	d0.65	1.23
Dividends	**0.313**	0.300	0.300	0.270	0.270	0.270	0.270	0.270	0.270	0.260
Payout Ratio	**13%**	14%	20%	25%	27%	31%	NM	33%	NM	21%
Prices—High	**52⅝**	51½	24⅞	15	12 11/16	13 11/16	14 13/16	19 15/16	16¼	14⅝
Low	**29⅞**	23 7/16	14⅝	8⅜	8⅝	7⅞	8⅛	8¾	11⅝	11 5/16
P/E Ratio—	**23–13**	24–11	17–10	14–8	13–9	15–9	NM	24–11	NM	12–9

Data as orig. reptd. Adj. for stk. div(s). of 100% Mar. 1993, 100% Mar. 1992. **1.** Reflects acctg. change. **2.** Bef. results of disc. opers. of +0.26 in 1989, -0.35 in 1987, -0.43 in 1986, bef. spec. item(s) of -0.15 in 1993, -0.09 in 1991, +0.36 in 1988, -0.03 in 1987. **3.** Refl. merger or acquis. E-Estimated. d-Deficit. NM-Not Meaningful.

Income Data (Million $)

Year Ended Dec. 31	Revs.	Oper. Inc.	% Oper. Inc. of Revs.	Cap. Exp.	Depr.	Int. Exp.	[3]Net Bef. Taxes	Eff. Tax Rate	[4]Net Inc.	% Net Inc. of Revs.	Cash Flow
1994	**[6]1,098**	**322**	**29.3**	**288**	**119.0**	**53.6**	**174**	**36.6%**	**105.0**	**9.6**	**224**
[5]1993	961	296	30.8	526	83.9	51.2	175	39.4%	97.0	10.1	181
1992	741	188	25.4	174	62.4	33.1	104	33.9%	63.8	8.6	126
1991	610	156	25.5	124	57.5	32.1	74	35.2%	45.7	7.5	103
[1]1990	528	137	26.0	109	49.7	31.4	62	30.4%	41.4	7.8	91
[2]1989	497	137	27.5	101	55.0	30.4	58	34.0%	37.1	7.5	92
1988	507	116	22.9	78	56.6	41.7	d69	NM	d46.3	NM	10
[2]1987	508	144	28.4	87	57.2	25.4	62	43.6%	31.9	6.3	89
[2]1986	479	110	23.0	144	65.7	37.7	d68	NM	d25.3	NM	40
1985	475	120	25.2	155	53.8	22.6	69	21.8%	49.9	10.5	103

Balance Sheet Data (Million $)

Dec. 31	Cash	Curr. Assets	Curr. Liab.	Ratio	Total Assets	% Ret. on Assets	Long Term Debt	Common Equity	Total Cap.	% LT Debt of Cap.	% Ret. on Equity
1994	**30**	**380**	**340**	**1.1**	**2,231**	**5.0**	**929**	**660**	**1,811**	**51.3**	**17.1**
1993	26	336	288	1.2	1,917	6.1	776	556	1,530	50.7	18.9
1992	24	246	219	1.1	1,248	5.5	387	456	952	40.7	14.8
1991	44	232	201	1.2	1,092	4.3	317	405	829	38.3	11.7
1990	87	239	172	1.4	1,034	4.1	345	369	801	43.1	11.7
1989	106	252	200	1.3	965	3.8	283	332	708	40.0	11.9
1988	109	266	258	1.0	979	NM	300	285	664	45.2	NM
1987	87	229	183	1.3	927	3.3	225	354	712	31.6	9.0
1986	74	214	196	1.1	1,006	NM	320	348	790	40.6	NM
1985	93	216	147	1.5	1,066	5.2	302	431	891	33.9	12.0

Data as orig. reptd. **1.** Reflects accounting change. **2.** Excl. disc. oper. **3.** Incl. equity in earns. of nonconsol. subs. **4.** Bef. results of disc. opers. and spec. item(s). **5.** Refl. merger or acquis., revs. incl. other inc. **6.** Incl. other inc. d-Deficit. NM-Not Meaningful.

Business Summary

Business segment contributions to operating profits (in million $) in recent years:

	1994	1993	1992
Transportation	$124.9	$116.7	$75.3
DST Systems	34.7	31.2	17.8
Janus Capital	53.1	80.0	45.7

Kansas City Southern Railway operates a 2,880-mile rail system (including 174 miles of leased or trackage rights) spanning nine southern and midwestern states. The railway operates the most direct route between Kansas City and the Gulf of Mexico and serves the ports of Beaumont and Port Arthur in Texas and New Orleans and Baton Rouge in Louisiana. Some 22% of the combined rail system's traffic is generated from coal; chemicals generated 13% of traffic while intermodal and lumber each accounted for 12% of carloads. The equipment fleet at 1994 year-end consisted of 382 locomotives and 15,698 freight cars.

DST Systems Inc. primarily provides on-line accounting and recordkeeping services for 32 million shareholder accounts at mutual funds, financial services and insurance companies. An initial public offering of 51% of DST is planned for late 1995. DST also has equity interests in firms that perform securities transfer services, portfolio accounting and pharmaceutical claims processing. Janus Capital Corp. (83%-owned) manages $22.9 billion of funds for 2.0 million shareowners through the Janus and IDEX mutual funds and for private accounts. KSU also owns 80% of Berger Associates, which managed $3.0 billion of funds.

Dividend Data

A "poison pill" stock purchase right was redeemed in 1994.

Amt. of Divd. $	Date Decl.	Ex–divd. Date	Stock of Record	Payment Date
0.07½	Aug. 15	Aug. 22	Aug. 26	Sep. 20'94
0.07½	Nov. 17	Nov. 28	Dec. 2	Dec. 30'94
0.07½	Jan. 20	Feb. 17	Feb. 24	Mar. 21'95
0.07½	May 3	May 22	May 26	Jun. 20'95

Capitalization

Long Term Debt: $1,031,700,000 (6/95).

Minority Interest: $7,400,000.

$1 Non-Cum. Pfd. Stock: 649,736 shs. ($25 par).

Series B Pfd. Stk.: 1,000,000 shs. ($200 liq. val.) ea. conv. into four com. shs.; held by ESOP.

Common Stock: 42,796,066 shs. ($0.01). Employees hold 12% through an ESOP. Institutions hold about 70%. Shareholders of record: 5,611 (12/94).

Office—114 West 11th St., Kansas City, MO 64105-1804. **Tel**—(816) 556-0303. **Chrmn**—P. H. Henson. **Pres & CEO**—L. H. Rowland. **VP-Secy**—R. P. Bruening. **VP-Treas**—A. P. McCarthy. **VP-CFO & Investor Contact**—Joseph D. Monello. **Dirs**—A.E. Allinson, P. F. Balser, J. E. Barnes, T. S. Carter, M. G. Fitt, M. R. Haverty, P. H. Henson, T. A. McDonnell, L. H. Rowland, M. I. Sosland. **Transfer Agents**—United Missouri Bank of Kansas City; Company's office. **Registrar**—United Missouri Bank of Kansas City. **Incorporated** in Del. in 1962. **Empl**—8,217.

 Stephen R. Klein

STANDARD & POOR'S

STOCK REPORTS

Kaydon Corp.

NYSE Symbol **KDN**
In S&P MidCap 400

13-SEP-95 **Industry:** Machinery

Summary: This company designs, makes and sells anti-friction bearings, bearing systems and components, filters, filter housings and other custom-engineered products.

Quantitative Evaluations
Outlook
(1 Lowest—5 Highest)
• 1+
Fair Value
• 25½
Risk
• Low
Earn./Div. Rank
• A-

Technical Eval.
• **Bearish** since 10/94
Rel. Strength Rank
(1 Lowest—99 Highest)
• 64
Insider Activity
• NA

Recent Price • 31⅜
52 Wk Range • 31⅝-20¾
Yield • 1.4%
12-Mo. P/E • 15.1

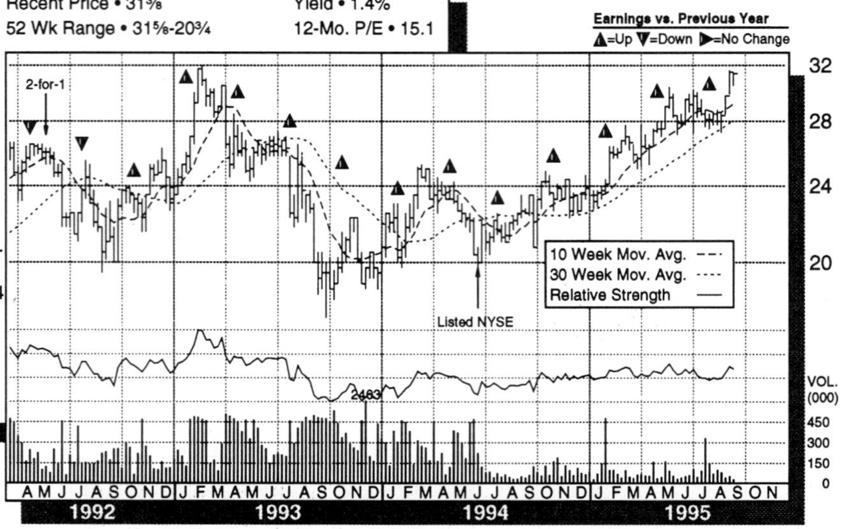

Business Profile - 13-SEP-95

In third quarter 1995, KDN acquired an Iowa-based hydraulic cylinder manufacturer. Kaydon continues to evaluate acquisitions, for which it can use an $85 million revolving credit facility and $56 million of cash and securities. In May 1995, directors authorized the repurchase of up to one million common shares, in addition to an earlier program to buy one million shares, under which 833,600 shares had been purchased by the end of 1994. The dividend has been boosted for 10 consecutive years.

Operational Review - 13-SEP-95

Net revenues in 1995's first six months rose 11%, year to year, due to the favorable sales results in virtually all operating divisions. Margins widened, reflecting the greater volume and increased productivity; operating income expanded 19%. After a 10-fold increase in interest income, net income climbed 23%. Backlog increased to $91.7 million at July 31, 1995, from $90.1 million at April 1, 1995.

Stock Performance - 08-SEP-95

In the past 30 trading days, KDN's shares have increased 12%, compared to a 2% rise in the S&P 500. Average trading volume for the past five days was 5,950 shares, compared with the 40-day moving average of 20,895 shares.

Key Stock Statistics

Dividend Rate/Share	0.44	Shareholders	1,700
Shs. outstg. (M)	16.7	Market cap. (B)	$0.517
Avg. daily vol. (M)	0.009	Inst. holdings	78%
Tang. Bk. Value/Share	8.27	Insider holdings	NA
Beta	1.08		

Value of $10,000 invested 5 years ago: $ 21,480

Fiscal Year Ending Dec. 31

	1995	% Change	1994	% Change	1993	% Change
Revenues (Million $)						
1Q	55.47	11%	50.13	4%	48.04	5%
2Q	57.56	11%	52.03	10%	47.20	-3%
3Q	—	—	50.28	14%	44.02	1%
4Q	—	—	52.26	17%	44.80	-3%
Yr.	—	—	204.7	11%	184.1	NM
Income (Million $)						
1Q	9.04	26%	7.19	6%	6.77	20%
2Q	9.72	21%	8.02	14%	7.01	2%
3Q	—	—	7.71	13%	6.81	12%
4Q	—	—	8.30	17%	7.10	-3%
Yr.	—	—	31.23	13%	27.70	8%
Earnings Per Share ($)						
1Q	0.54	26%	0.43	10%	0.39	22%
2Q	0.58	21%	0.48	20%	0.40	3%
3Q	—	—	0.46	18%	0.39	11%
4Q	—	—	0.54	29%	0.42	2%
Yr.	—	—	1.87	17%	1.60	9%

Next earnings report expected: mid October

Kaydon Corp.

Business Summary - 13-SEP-95

Kaydon Corporation, which was spun off from Bairnco Corp. in 1984, designs, makes and sells custom-engineered products for a broad and diverse customer base. Its principal products include anti-friction bearings, bearing systems, filters, filter housings, high-performance rings, sealing rings, specialty retaining rings and balls, shaft seals and slip-rings. These products are used in medical, instrumentation, material handling, machine tool positioning, aerospace, defense, construction and other industrial areas. Operations have been expanded considerably through acquisitions since 1985. Sales in recent years were derived as follows:

	1994	1993
Replacement parts & exports	38%	38%
Special industrial machinery	30%	28%
Aerospace & military equipment	19%	22%
Heavy industrial equipment	13%	12%

The company sells a range of custom-engineered products, working closely with customers to engineer required solutions to design problems. Designs may be for a protracted time period and in large numbers, or for a single use. Kaydon sells products to more than 1,000 companies worldwide.

Kaydon's anti-friction bearing products incorporate various rolling elements. Its ball, tapered roller, cylindrical roller and needle roller bearings are made in sizes ranging from needle bearings with a 1/2-in. outside diameter to heavy-duty ball bearings with an outside diameter of 180 in.

In December 1991, Prizerandom Ltd., the holding company for Cooper Bearings Ltd., was acquired. Cooper units make or distribute complete bearings and related component parts. In December 1993, Kaydon acquired Kenyon Power Transmission Ltd., which makes pulleys and drive components that complement Cooper's products.

In January 1994, Dexter, Mich.-based Industrial Tectonics (ITI) was acquired for $7.3 million. ITI makes balls of alloyed steel, plastic, tungsten carbide, glass and other materials, for use in gauges, floats, measuring instruments, ball point pens and anti-friction bearings.

The company's 16 facilities are located in the U.S., Mexico, Germany and England.

Important Developments

Aug. '95—KDN acquired Iowa-based Seabee Corp. for $22 million, including assumed debt. Seabee, with estimated 1995 sales of $20 million, makes large, custom-ordered hydraulic cylinders for construction and safety equipment companies, and supplies alloy steel castings to a broad spectrum of industries.

Capitalization

Long Term Debt: $8,000,000 (7/1/95).

Per Share Data ($)

(Year Ended Dec. 31)

	1994	1993	1992	1991	1990	1989
Tangible Bk. Val.	10.01	8.62	7.83	7.94	6.63	4.27
Cash Flow	2.50	2.19	2.04	1.98	1.98	1.74
Earnings	1.87	1.60	1.47	1.47	1.51	1.33
Dividends	0.41	0.36	0.32	0.26	0.21	0.16
Payout Ratio	22%	23%	21%	18%	14%	12%
Prices - High	25¼	32	26⅝	23⅞	18⅞	19¼
- Low	19¾	17½	19½	16	13⅝	13½
P/E Ratio - High	14	20	18	16	13	14
- Low	11	11	13	11	9	10

Income Statement Analysis (Million $)

	1994	%Chg	1993	%Chg	1992	%Chg	1991
Revs.	205	11%	184	NM	184	14%	161
Oper. Inc.	60.4	11%	54.6	4%	52.5	8%	48.7
Depr.	10.6	3%	10.3	3%	10.0	13%	8.9
Int. Exp.	0.3	11%	0.3	-85%	1.8	14%	1.6
Pretax Inc.	50.4	13%	44.5	9%	40.8	4%	39.4
Eff. Tax Rate	38%	—	38%	—	37%	—	36%
Net Inc.	31.2	13%	27.7	8%	25.6	NM	25.5

Balance Sheet & Other Fin. Data (Million $)

	1994	1993	1992	1991	1990	1989
Cash	39.7	24.5	13.7	7.9	17.7	1.0
Curr. Assets	12.7	107	97.5	96.3	93.1	70.0
Total Assets	244	217	211	217	176	154
Curr. Liab.	40.9	34.7	40.8	37.1	30.3	27.0
LT Debt	8.0	13.7	8.0	33.7	22.6	27.2
Common Eqty.	167	144	136	138	114	91.0
Total Cap.	175	158	144	180	146	127
Cap. Exp.	6.7	5.1	6.1	15.4	6.5	22.4
Cash Flow	41.9	38.0	35.6	34.3	34.1	29.9

Ratio Analysis

	1994	1993	1992	1991	1990	1989
Curr. Ratio	3.1	3.1	2.4	2.6	3.1	2.6
% LT Debt of Cap.	4.6	8.7	5.6	18.7	15.5	21.4
% Net Inc.of Revs.	15.3	15.0	13.9	15.8	15.3	15.1
% Ret. on Assets	13.6	13.2	11.9	12.9	15.7	16.5
% Ret. on Equity	20.1	20.2	18.7	20.2	25.4	28.4

Dividend Data —Kaydon changed to quarterly payments, from semiannual distributions, in 1987. A "poison pill" stock purchase rights plan was adopted in July 1995.

Amt. of Div. $	Date Decl.	Ex-Div. Date	Stock of Record	Payment Date
0.100	Jun. 22	Sep. 13	Sep. 19	Oct. 03 '94
0.110	Oct. 25	Dec. 13	Dec. 19	Jan. 02 '95
0.110	Jan. 25	Mar. 14	Mar. 20	Apr. 03 '95
0.110	Apr. 26	Jun. 15	Jun. 19	Jul. 03 '95
0.110	Jun. 21	Sep. 14	Sep. 18	Oct. 02 '95

Data as orig. reptd.; bef. results of disc. opers. and/or spec. items. Per share data adj. for stk. divs. as of ex-div. date. E-Estimated. NA-Not Available. NM-Not Meaningful. NR-Not Ranked.

Office—19345 U.S. 19 North, Clearwater, FL 34624. **Tel**—(813) 531-1101. **Fax**—(813) 530-9247. **Chrmn & CEO**—L. J. Cawley. **Pres & COO**—S. K. Clough. **Contr**—T. C. Sorrells III. **VP & Secy**—J. F. Brocci. **Investor Contact**—Shelley Schwemley. **Dirs**—G. W. Bailey, G. J. Breen, L. J. Cawley, S. K. Clough, J. H. F. Haskell, Jr., N. Stevens. **Transfer Agent & Registrar**—Continental Stock Transfer & Trust Co., NYC. **Incorporated** in Delaware in 1983. **Empl**-1,682. **S&P Analyst:** Robert E. Friedman

STANDARD & POOR'S
STOCK REPORTS

Kelly Services

NASDAQ Symbol **KELYA**
In S&P MidCap 400

01-AUG-95 **Industry:** Services

Summary: This leading supplier of temporary personnel serves a diversified group of customers, domestically and abroad. It also provides staff leasing and in-home health care services.

S&P Opinion: Accumulate (★★★★)

Recent Price • 27½
52 Wk Range • 37-24
Yield • 2.9%
12-Mo. P/E • 15.7

Quantitative Evaluations

Outlook
(1 Lowest—5 Highest)
• **3-**

Fair Value
• **28⅝**

Risk
• **Low**

Earn./Div. Rank
• **A**

Technical Eval.
• **Bullish** since 7/95

Rel. Strength Rank
(1 Lowest—99 Highest)
• **13**

Insider Activity
• **NA**

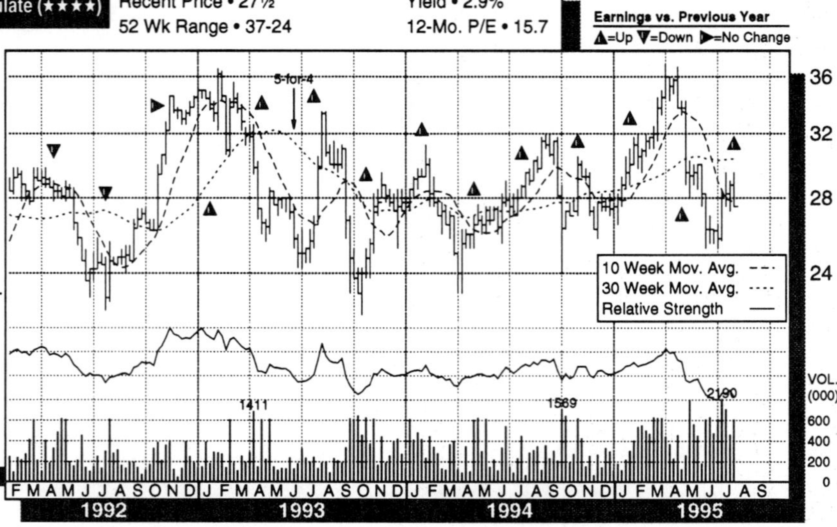

Overview - 01-AUG-95

Sales should advance about 15% through the remainder of 1995, on strong demand for temporary services and recent acquisitions. Margins should remain stable for the rest of the year; a more favorable revenue mix will be offset by rising general and administrative expenses. The recent acquisition of Wallace Law Registry gives Kelly a presence in the growing market for temporary legal workers. Strong cash flow should facilitate future acquisitions, enhancing long-term growth prospects. The company is subject to cyclical risks, as indicated by results in 1991, when earnings were penalized in part by the recession. However, provided that the economy remains sound, earnings should continue to advance in 1996.

Valuation - 01-AUG-95

The shares have fluctuated within a trading range from the low 20s to the mid-30s over the past several years. Concerns about a recession pushed the shares toward the lower end of their range in the second quarter. Earnings were depressed in 1991 to 1993 by the effects of recession and competitive pressures. A recovery began in 1994, and 1995 EPS are expected to equal 1990's record $1.90. The shares were recently trading at less than 15X projected 1995 EPS. The stock is attractively valued at this P/E, in light of its growth potential.

Key Stock Statistics

S&P EPS Est. 1995	1.90	Tang. Bk. Value/Share	10.46
P/E on S&P Est. 1995	14.5	Beta	1.41
Dividend Rate/Share	0.80	Shareholders	2,000
Shs. outstg. (M)	38.0	Market cap. (B)	$ 1.0
Avg. daily vol. (M)	0.245	Inst. holdings	42%
		Insider holdings	NA

Value of $10,000 invested 5 years ago: $ 9,879

Fiscal Year Ending Dec. 31

	1995	% Change	1994	% Change	1993	% Change
Revenues (Million $)						
1Q	620.7	17%	530.2	18%	450.6	20%
2Q	652.4	14%	570.8	18%	482.0	16%
3Q	—	—	630.2	22%	517.6	15%
4Q	—	—	631.4	25%	504.3	6%
Yr.	—	—	2,363	21%	1,955	13%
Income (Million $)						
1Q	12.26	33%	9.23	34%	6.88	11%
2Q	16.66	16%	14.42	44%	10.01	18%
3Q	—	—	19.29	37%	14.03	23%
4Q	—	—	18.12	33%	13.64	4%
Yr.	—	—	61.06	37%	44.56	14%
Earnings Per Share ($)						
1Q	0.32	33%	0.24	30%	0.18	10%
2Q	0.44	16%	0.38	41%	0.27	21%
3Q	E0.59	—	0.51	38%	0.37	22%
4Q	E0.55	—	0.48	33%	0.36	5%
Yr.	E1.90	—	1.61	36%	1.18	13%

Next earnings report expected: late October

Kelly Services

Business Summary - 01-AUG-95

Kelly Services, Inc. is one of the largest U.S. suppliers of temporary personnel. The company provides office clerical, marketing, technical, light industrial, home care services, managed services, testing and training and other business services to a diversified group of customers. In recent years, more than 200,000 customers, including the largest U.S. industrial corporations, have used Kelly's services.

The company operates through about 1,000 offices in all 50 states, the District of Columbia, Puerto Rico, Mexico, Canada, France, England, Ireland, the Netherlands, Switzerland, Australia, New Zealand, Denmark, Norway, Scotland and Wales. All offices are directly operated by Kelly; the last five licensed branches were converted to directly operated branches in February 1995.

The Kelly Temporary Services division provides temporary office help to accommodate customer needs caused by absences for vacations, illness, inventories, special projects, and unexpected work volume increases. It also supplies marketing support services, semi-skilled light industrial services and technical services. Kelly Assisted Living Services assists clients who need help with daily living needs. Staff leasing services are provided in California through Your Staff.

The company uses testing programs to determine a temporary employee's capabilities, particularly in evaluation of office automation skills. New training programs are continually developed to ensure that employees have specific skills that customers require.

During 1994, Kelly employed 665,000 people for temporary periods. As the employer, the company is responsible for Social Security taxes, workers' compensation, liability insurance and similar costs.

Important Developments

Jun. '95—Kelly unveiled Pin-Point, an interactive CD-ROM software program designed to tutor temporary workers on Microsoft Office and Lotus Smart-Suite programs. Pin-Point allows the user to work in the program while learning to use it. Although Pin-Point will initially be used internally, the company is discussing the possibility of marketing the software.

Capitalization

Long Term Debt: None (4/2/95).

Per Share Data ($)

(Year Ended Dec. 31)

	1994	1993	1992	1991	1990	1989
Tangible Bk. Val.	10.46	9.76	9.42	9.10	8.70	7.42
Cash Flow	2.06	1.62	1.42	1.29	2.13	2.10
Earnings	1.61	1.18	1.04	1.02	1.90	1.89
Dividends	0.70	0.63	0.58	0.58	0.53	0.46
Payout Ratio	43%	54%	56%	56%	28%	24%
Prices - High	32	36⅝	35	33⅜	32¼	33⅝
- Low	23	22	22¼	21⅝	21⅝	21⅜
P/E Ratio - High	20	31	34	33	17	18
- Low	14	19	21	21	11	11

Income Statement Analysis (Million $)

	1994	%Chg	1993	%Chg	1992	%Chg	1991
Revs.	2,363	21%	1,955	13%	1,723	20%	1,438
Oper. Inc.	109	35%	81.0	8%	75.0	7%	70.0
Depr.	17.3	4%	16.6	19%	14.0	43%	9.8
Int. Exp.	Nil	—	Nil	—	Nil	—	Nil
Pretax Inc.	98.0	38%	71.0	16%	61.0	2%	60.0
Eff. Tax Rate	38%	—	37%	—	36%	—	36%
Net Inc.	61.1	37%	44.6	14%	39.2	2%	38.6

Balance Sheet & Other Fin. Data (Million $)

	1994	1993	1992	1991	1990	1989
Cash	192	181	184	227	217	189
Curr. Assets	526	447	409	411	393	354
Total Assets	642	542	496	479	444	394
Curr. Liab.	211	156	129	124	106	111
LT Debt	Nil	Nil	Nil	Nil	Nil	Nil
Common Eqty.	432	386	367	355	338	284
Total Cap.	432	386	367	355	338	284
Cap. Exp.	18.4	16.1	32.4	23.5	12.0	11.2
Cash Flow	78.4	61.2	53.2	48.4	80.0	78.7

Ratio Analysis

	1994	1993	1992	1991	1990	1989
Curr. Ratio	2.5	2.9	3.2	3.3	3.7	3.2
% LT Debt of Cap.	Nil	Nil	Nil	Nil	Nil	Nil
% Net Inc.of Revs.	2.6	2.3	2.3	2.7	4.8	5.1
% Ret. on Assets	10.3	8.6	8.0	8.4	17.0	19.6
% Ret. on Equity	14.9	11.8	10.9	11.1	22.9	27.6

Dividend Data (Cash has been paid each year since 1962. Recent dividends on Class A stock were:)

Amt. of Div. $	Date Decl.	Ex-Div. Date	Stock of Record	Payment Date
0.180	Aug. 17	Aug. 23	Aug. 29	Sep. 12 '94
0.180	Nov. 16	Nov. 21	Nov. 28	Dec. 12 '94
0.180	Feb. 15	Feb. 21	Feb. 27	Mar. 13 '95
0.200	May. 17	May. 23	May. 30	Jun. 13 '95

Data as orig. reptd.; bef. results of disc. opers. and/or spec. items. Per share data adj. for stk. divs. as of ex-div. date. E-Estimated. NA-Not Available. NM-Not Meaningful. NR-Not Ranked.

Office—999 W. Big Beaver Rd., Troy, MI 48084. **Tel**—(810) 362-4444. **Chrmn**—W. R. Kelly. **Pres & CEO**—T. E. Adderley. **SVP & CFO**—P. K. Geiger. **EVP-Oper**—R. G. Barranco. **Dirs**—T. E. Adderley, C. V. Fricke, H. E. Guenther, V. G. Istock, W. R. Kelly, B. J. White. **Transfer Agent & Registrar**—NBD Bank, Boston. **Incorporated** in Delaware in 1952. **Empl**-4,800. **S&P Analyst:** Stephen Madonna, CFA

Kemper Corp.

NYSE Symbol KEM Options on Phila (Jan-Apr-Jul-Oct) In S&P MidCap 400

Price	Range	P-E Ratio	Dividend	Yield	S&P Ranking	Beta
Aug. 9'95	1995					
47⅞	48¼–38	61	0.92	1.9%	B	1.45

Summary

This major financial services company is primarily engaged in life insurance, asset management and investment services. On May 16, 1995 KEM agreed definitively to be acquired for $49.50 a share in cash by an investor group comprised of Zurich Insurance Group and Insurance Partners. Prior to closing, expected in late 1995, KEM would complete its previously announced plan to spin off 44% of its securities brokerage unit to shareholders after selling 55% to the unit's employees.

Current Outlook

Operating earnings for 1995 could rise to $4.00 a share (before realized capital gains and losses), up from the $3.34 reported for 1994. Operating earnings of $4.50 a share are expected for 1996.

The $0.23 quarterly dividend is the minimum expected.

Continued robust demand for savings vehicles (such as annuities), favorable mortality trends, and lower operating expenses should aid life insurance margins in 1995. However, a shift in product mix and disruptive effects of KEM's uncertain ownership structure may hurt policy sales. The disruptive effects of KEM's pending takeover by Zurich Insurance Group has also hurt asset management results. The drag on investment income from underperforming real estate assets will be reduced from 1994 levels, but is still a factor. At March 31, 1995, real estate and mortgage loans equaled 19% of invested assets. During 1994 the real estate segment was able to trim its operating losses through more aggressive sales, refinancings and restructurings. This trend will likely continue.

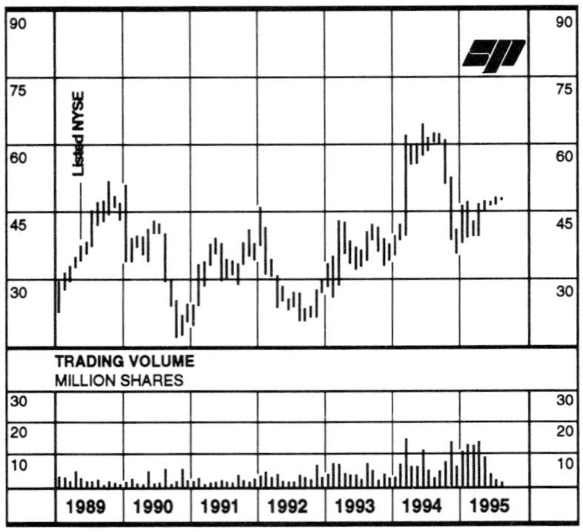

Review of Operations

Revenues for the six months ended June 30, 1995, declined 5.9%, year to year. Margins were impaired by $33.5 million of investment losses, versus gains of $16.0 million, and net income from continuing operations declined 46%, to $40.4 million from $75.0 million. Primary share earnings were $0.82 ($1.78 of operating income), compared with $1.86 ($1.39). Share results exclude a loss of $1.97 from discontinued operations, versus income of $0.07.

Common Share Earnings ($)

Quarter:	1995	1994	1993	1992
Mar.	1.14	1.43	d0.14	0.40
Jun.	d0.32	0.43	d0.59	d0.22
Sep.		0.24	d3.24	d0.11
Dec.		d0.27	1.60	d4.32
		1.80	d2.52	d4.28

Important Developments

May. '95— KEM agreed definitively to be acquired by Zurich Insurance Group and Insurance Partners for $49.50 a share in cash (revised from $47.50 in cash and $2 in preferred stock) in a transaction set to close late in 1995. Prior to the closing, KEM would complete its previously announced plan to sell a 55% interest in its securities brokerage unit to an employee stock ownership plan and spin off 44% to KEM shareholders of record July 27, 1995 in a transaction valued at approximately $1.50 per KEM share. Before negotiations broke down in November 1994, Conseco, Inc. (CNC) was set to acquire KEM for $60 a share ($56 cash and $4 common stock). KEM put itself up for sale in May 1994 following a $60 a share takeover bid from General Electric Corp. GE originally made an unsolicited $55 a share bid in March, but was rebuffed by KEM.

Next earnings report expected in late October.

Per Share Data ($)

Yr. End Dec. 31	1994	1993	1992	1991	1990	1989	1988	1987	1986	1985
Tangible Bk. Val.	**26.06**	38.24	33.77	37.92	34.20	35.25	29.97	26.50	23.48	19.18
Oper. Earnings[1]	**3.34**	2.09	0.32	4.20	d0.15	4.17	3.37	3.19	2.51	1.54
Earnings[1,2]	**1.80**	d2.52	d4.28	4.25	0.25	4.44	3.64	4.12	3.40	1.89
Dividends	**0.92**	0.92	0.92	0.92	0.92	0.81	0.72	0.60	0.60	0.60
Payout Ratio	**51%**	NM	NM	22%	NM	18%	20%	15%	18%	32%
Prices—High	**64⅝**	43	46⅛	41	51	51⅞	27½	38¾	35½	24⅜
Low	**35⅝**	26⅛	20¾	19¾	17⅛	22¾	20¾	19¼	23	14¾
P/E Ratio—	**36–20**	[3]NM	[3]NM	[3]10–5	[3]23–8	[3]12–5	[3]8–6	[3]12–6	[3]14–9	[3]16–10

Data as orig. reptd. Adj. for stk. div. of 200% in 1986. **1.** Bef. results of disc. opers. of +0.17 in 1994, +7.52 in 1993, +0.45 in 1992, +1.52 in 1989, +0.17 in 1988 & spec. item(s) of +0.06 in 1993, -0.33 in 1992. **2.** Aft. gains/losses on securities trans. **3.** Based on oper. earns. prior to 1989. d-Deficit. NM-Not Meaningful.

Income Data (Million $)

Year Ended Dec. 31	Life Ins. In Force	Premium Income [4]Life	A & H	Other	Net Invest. Inc.	Total Revs.	Net Bef. Taxes	[1]Net Oper. Inc.	[1]Net Inc.	% Return On [2]Revs.	Assets	[2,3]Equity
1994	**96,491**	**152**	**Nil**	**Nil**	**485**	**1,602**	**121**	**NA**	**85.7**	**5.4**	**[2]0.6**	**5.8**
1993	91,300	158	Nil	Nil	427	1,549	d109	NA	d89.0	NM	NM	NM
1992	84,200	678	Nil	Nil	541	2,201	d290	16	d209.0	NM	NM	NM
1991	73,429	1,147	Nil	Nil	750	3,131	292	202	205.0	6.5	1.4	11.8
1990	59,000	Nil	NA	Nil	765	2,929	40	d8	12.0	0.4	0.1	0.7
1989	49,100	NA	NA	NA	713	2,774	312	216	230.0	8.3	NA	13.3
1988	39,966	NA	NA	NA	595	3,488	269	198	952.0	5.7	NA	12.4
1987	NA	NA	NA	NA	542	3,369	243	195	619.0	5.3	NA	12.8
1986	NA	NA	NA	NA	487	3,330	212	148	777.0	4.4	NA	11.8
1985	NA	NA	NA	NA	421	2,882	77	76	600.0	2.6	NA	8.4

Balance Sheet Data (Million $)

Dec. 31	Cash & Equiv.	Premiums Due	Investment Assets Bonds	Stocks	[7]Loans	Total	Invest. Yield	Deferred Policy Costs	Total Assets	Debt	Common Equity
1994	**231**	**[8]633**	**5,201**	**25**	**1,478**	**7,390**	**6.3**	**697**	**13,154**	**[5]761**	**897**
1993	253	[8]617	[6]6,047	99	1,654	8,072	5.6	623	14,038	[5]789	1,258
1992	334	[8]1,175	[6]6,119	287	2,070	8,989	5.9	649	14,791	659	1,665
1991	254	[8]1,544	[6]5,961	405	2,429	9,336	8.2	590	14,697	558	1,838
1990	197	205	[6]6,275	432	2,313	9,020	9.0	510	13,588	523	1,625
1989	245	158	[6]5,837	499	1,626	7,963	NA	439	12,696	696	1,722
1988	255	345	[6]5,860	487	1,311	7,657	NA	363	12,078	679	1,737
1987	186	321	[6]5,193	452	1,029	6,675	NA	332	10,742	554	1,543
1986	163	293	[6]4,666	303	792	5,761	NA	307	9,735	502	1,417
1985	166	237	[6]4,177	293	407	4,877	NA	295	9,264	542	994

Data as orig. reptd. **1.** Bef. results of disc. opers. and bef. spec. items. **2.** Based on oper. earns. prior to 1989. **3.** Common. **4.** Incl. reinsurance prior to 1993. **5.** Total debt. **6.** Incl. short-term invest. **7.** Incl. other invest. **8.** Notes receiv. and accts. receiv. excl. brokerage firms and customers. d-Deficit. NA-Not Available. NM-Not Meaningful.

Business Summary

This diversified financial services holding company is exiting the securities brokerage business to better focus on its life insurance and asset management operations. Contributions to pretax earnings (in million $) from continuing operations in recent years:

	1994	1993
Life insurance	$142.9	$128.7
Securities brokerage	−12.8	−1.5
Asset management	72.6	131.5
Real estate	−28.1	−346.2
Corporate & other	−54.0	−21.7

Life insurance operations, conducted by Federal Kemper Life Assurance Co. and Kemper Investors Life Insurance Co., offer an array of term and interest sensitive life insurance, and fixed and variable rate annuities. At year end 1994, life insurance in force equaled $97.5 billion.

The Kemper Securities Group, Inc. is the holding company for five regional securities firms that provide retail and insitiutional securities brokerage and investment banking services through 1,330 brokers in 163 offices throughout the U.S. As of March 31, 1995 these operations have been classified as discontinued, pending a sale/spinoff.

Asset management activities are conducted by Kemper Financial Services, Inc. and its 96%-owned INVEST Financial Corp. and Kemper Service Co. At December 31, 1994 58 open and closed end mutual funds were being offered. At year end 1994, assets under management totaled $62.7 billion.

Real estate activities are conducted by Kemper Portfolio Corp. and its subsidiaries.

Dividend Data

Dividends have been paid since 1968. A dividend reinvestment plan is available. A "poison pill" stock purchase right was adopted in July 1990.

Amt. of Divd. $	Date Decl.	Ex-divd. Date	Stock of Record	Payment Date
0.23	Oct. 25	Nov. 3	Nov. 9	Nov. 30'94
0.23	Jan. 10	Feb. 1	Feb. 7	Feb. 28'95
0.23	Apr. 18	May 4	May 10	May 31'95
0.23	Jul. 18	Aug. 8	Aug. 10	Aug. 31'95

Capitalization

Long Term Debt: $388,326,000 (3/95).

Preferred Stock: $360,363,000.

Common Stock: 34,587,050 shs. ($5 par).
Institutions hold some 48%.
Shareholders of record: 12,200 (3/95).

Office—One Kemper Dr., Long Grove, IL 60049. **Tel**—(708) 320-4700. **Chrmn & CEO**—D. B. Mathis. **Pres**—S. B. Timbers. **VP-CFO**—J. H. Fitzpatrick. **Secy**—K. A. Gallichio. **Treas**—J. W. Burns. **Investor Contact**—John A. Effrein (708-320-3435). **Dirs**—J. T. Chain, Jr., J. R. Coleman, R. F. Farley, J. H. Fitzpatrick, P. B. Hamilton, G. D. Kennedy, D. B. Mathis, R. D. Nordman, K. A. Randall, S. B. Timbers, D. R. Toll. **Transfer Agent**—Harris Trust and Savings Bank, Chicago. **Incorporated** in Delaware in 1967. **Empl**—6,059.

 Catherine A. Seifert

STANDARD & POOR'S

STOCK REPORTS

Kennametal Inc.

NYSE Symbol **KMT**
In S&P MidCap 400

08-OCT-95 **Industry:** Metal

Summary: Kennametal manufactures tools made of cemented carbide, ceramics and other materials, distributes tooling products, and provides supplies and services to the metalworking industry.

S&P Opinion: Accumulate (★★★★)

Recent Price • 34½ | Yield • 1.7%
52 Wk Range • 41⅛-23 | 12-Mo. P/E • 13.4

Quantitative Evaluations

Outlook
(1 Lowest—5 Highest)
• **3+**

Fair Value
• **36⅛**

Risk
• **Average**

Earn./Div. Rank
• **B+**

Technical Eval.
• **Bearish** since 9/95

Rel. Strength Rank
(1 Lowest—99 Highest)
• **18**

Insider Activity
• **Neutral**

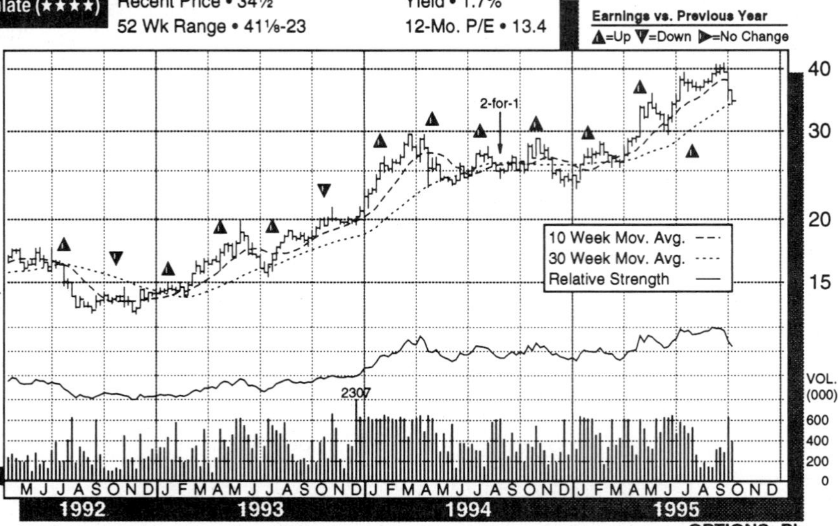

OPTIONS: Ph

Overview - 08-OCT-95

Sales should advance by about 15%-20% in fiscal 1996 on continued strength in U.S. markets, contributions from Hertel operations, and improving European and other foreign economies. Gains anticipated for metalworking product sales include benefits from KMT's full-service supply programs, the expansion of catalog sales and from a rebound in cyclical markets, such as automotive. Construction and mining tools sales should also continue to reflect higher demand tied to the improving U.S. economy. Internationally, once the Hertel integration is completed, margins are likely to widen on efficiency gains from increased capacity utilization and elimination of redundant operations. We expect KMT's greater global presence, especially in Asia-Pacific countries such as China, Korea and Singapore, to increase market share and add to the long-term outlook.

Valuation - 08-OCT-95

The shares of this metalworking instrument manufacturer have had a strong move upwards, over 60% since early January. Earnings have risen sharply in recent periods as the company benefits from strong sales gains in the U.S., excellent results from a quickly improving European economy, growing contributions from Asia-Pacific, and operating efficiency gains; this trend is expected to continue for some time. Despite the recent impressive price gains, we still consider the shares attractive at slightly more than 12x our fiscal 1996 estimate.

Key Stock Statistics

S&P EPS Est. 1996	3.00	Tang. Bk. Value/Share	13.53
P/E on S&P Est. 1996	11.5	Beta	0.84
Dividend Rate/Share	0.60	Shareholders	2,800
Shs. outstg. (M)	26.6	Market cap. (B)	$0.917
Avg. daily vol. (M)	0.094	Inst. holdings	76%
		Insider holdings	NA

Value of $10,000 invested 5 years ago: $ 56,904

Fiscal Year Ending Jun. 30

	1995	% Change	1994	% Change	1993	% Change
Revenues (Million $)						
1Q	218.8	25%	175.7	18%	148.8	NM
2Q	230.3	18%	195.2	39%	140.7	NM
3Q	268.1	27%	211.8	38%	153.7	NM
4Q	266.6	21%	219.9	42%	155.3	3%
Yr.	983.9	23%	802.5	34%	598.5	NM
Income (Million $)						
1Q	10.67	NM	-18.06	NM	3.03	-18%
2Q	11.87	190%	4.09	97%	2.08	86%
3Q	22.15	100%	11.09	51%	7.33	36%
4Q	23.60	71%	13.79	80%	7.66	186%
Yr.	68.29	NM	10.92	-46%	20.09	56%
Earnings Per Share ($)						
1Q	0.40	NM	-0.82	NM	0.14	-20%
2Q	0.45	150%	0.18	89%	0.09	90%
3Q	0.84	95%	0.43	26%	0.34	36%
4Q	0.89	68%	0.53	51%	0.35	180%
Yr.	2.58	NM	0.45	-51%	0.92	53%

Next earnings report expected: late October

Kennametal Inc.

Business Summary - 08-OCT-95

Kennametal makes a broad line of cemented carbide and other hard metal products, as well as tools and accessories, and provides comprehensive solutions to manufacturing problems of metalworking industry customers. Sales by product line in recent fiscal years were:

	1994	1993	1992	1991
Metalworking	84%	80%	81%	83%
Mining & construction	13%	17%	15%	14%
Metallurgical & other	3%	3%	4%	3%

International sales (primarily to Canada and Western Europe, but also increasingly to Asia) accounted for 35% of the total in fiscal 1994, up from 27% in fiscal 1993.

The metalworking segment serves the automotive, aerospace, machine tool, farm machinery, fabricated metals, construction machinery and oil and gas drilling industries. KMT makes a broad line of coated and uncoated carbide, cermet (titanium alloy) and other tools for most metalcutting and metalforming applications. It also manufactures a line of toolholders and toolholding systems.

Through GIS and J&L America (acquired in 1990), the company provides a complete line of industrial tools and supplies to the metalworking industry. J&L is one of the largest U.S. mail-order distributors of industrial products, and GIS is one of the leading regional distributors.

Mining and construction products include cemented carbide tools for mining coal and a line of road construction and maintenance tools. In August 1993, KMT acquired an 81% interest in Hertel AG, a manufacturer and marketer of cemented carbide tools and tooling systems.

Metallurgical products consist of proprietary metallurgical powders and related materials, including intermediate carbide powders, hardfacing materials and matrix powders.

Important Developments

Jul. '95—In reporting results for fiscal 1995, KMT said earnings continued to benefit from strong demand for metalworking products in North American and Europe. In addition, earnings increased from the successful turnaround and integration of Hertel AG (acquired in 1994), and the expansion of catalog sales at J&L Industrial Supply. Sales of mining and construction tools increased 6%, which also contributed to growth. International sales gained 35%, fueled by strong demand for metalworking products in Europe and Canada. The company expects worldwide growth for its metalworking products to continue in fiscal 1996.

Capitalization

Long Term Debt: $78,700,000 (6/95).
Minority Interest: $13,209,000.

Per Share Data ($) (Year Ended Jun. 30)

	1995	1994	1993	1992	1991	1990
Tangible Bk. Val.	13.53	11.03	10.27	10.09	9.78	9.18
Cash Flow	4.08	2.23	2.35	2.06	2.55	2.98
Earnings	2.58	0.45	0.93	0.60	1.00	1.54
Dividends	0.75	0.58	0.58	0.58	0.58	0.58
Payout Ratio	29%	129%	62%	97%	59%	38%
Prices - High	39⅜	29⅝	23	17⅝	19¾	18½
- Low	23	21⅛	14	13	13¼	12⅛
P/E Ratio - High	15	66	25	29	20	12
- Low	9	47	15	22	13	8

Income Statement Analysis (Million $)

	1995	%Chg	1994	%Chg	1993	%Chg	1992
Revs.	984	23%	803	34%	598	NM	595
Oper. Inc.	166	57%	106	46%	72.3	16%	62.4
Depr.	39.3	-9%	43.2	40%	30.9	-1%	31.3
Int. Exp.	12.8	-7%	13.8	45%	9.5	-6%	10.1
Pretax Inc.	11.3	-57%	26.0	-24%	34.1	62%	21.0
Eff. Tax Rate	40%	—	60%	—	41%	—	39%
Net Inc.	68.2	NM	10.9	-46%	20.1	56%	12.9

Balance Sheet & Other Fin. Data (Million $)

	1995	1994	1993	1992	1991	1990
Cash	10.8	17.2	4.1	9.0	11.3	10.3
Curr. Assets	409	333	209	218	228	220
Total Assets	782	698	448	472	476	451
Curr. Liab.	225	202	88.0	110	139	111
LT Debt	78.7	90.2	87.9	95.3	73.1	81.3
Common Eqty.	392	323	255	252	244	232
Total Cap.	492	432	354	355	328	313
Cap. Exp.	43.4	27.3	23.1	36.6	55.3	36.0
Cash Flow	108	54.1	51.0	44.2	53.8	62.3

Ratio Analysis

	1995	1994	1993	1992	1991	1990
Curr. Ratio	1.8	1.6	2.4	2.0	1.6	2.0
% LT Debt of Cap.	16.0	20.9	24.8	26.9	22.3	26.0
% Net Inc.of Revs.	6.9	1.4	3.4	2.2	3.4	5.5
% Ret. on Assets	9.2	1.9	4.3	2.7	4.5	7.7
% Ret. on Equity	19.0	3.8	7.9	5.2	8.8	14.7

Dividend Data —Dividends have been paid since 1944. A dividend reinvestment plan is available. A "poison pill" stock purchase right was adopted in 1990. A two-for-one stock split was effected in August 1994.

Amt. of Div. $	Date Decl.	Ex-Div. Date	Stock of Record	Payment Date
0.150	Oct. 31	Nov. 04	Nov. 10	Nov. 25 '94
0.150	Jan. 30	Feb. 06	Feb. 10	Feb. 24 '95
0.150	May. 02	May. 04	May. 10	May. 25 '95
0.150	Jul. 31	Aug. 08	Aug. 10	Aug. 25 '95

Data as orig. reptd.; bef. results of disc. opers. and/or spec. items. Per share data adj. for stk. divs. as of ex-div. date. E-Estimated. NA-Not Available. NM-Not Meaningful. NR-Not Ranked.

Office—Route 981 at Westmoreland County Airport, P.O. Box 231, Latrobe, PA 15650. **Tel**—(412) 539-5000. **Chrmn**—Q. C. McKenna. **Pres & CEO**—R. L. McGeehan. **VP & CFO**—R. J. Orwig. **VP & Secy**—D. T. Cofer. **Investor Contact**—Michael J. Mussog. **Dirs**—R. C. Alberding, P. B. Bartlett, A. P. Held, R. N. Eslyn, W. H. Hollinshead, R. L. McGeehan, Q. C. McKenna, A. T. McLaughlin, Jr., W. R. Newlin, L. Yost. **Transfer Agent & Registrar**—Mellon Bank, Pittsburgh. **Incorporated** in Pennsylvania in 1943. **Empl**-6,600. **S&P Analyst:** Robert E. Friedman

STANDARD & POOR'S

STOCK REPORTS

Keystone International

NYSE Symbol **KII**
In S&P MidCap 400

05-OCT-95 **Industry:** Machinery

Summary: This company manufactures and distributes worldwide valves and other flow control products for use in a broad range of industries.

S&P Opinion: Accumulate (★★★★)

Recent Price • 21½
52 Wk Range • 22¾-16¾
Yield • 3.4%
12-Mo. P/E • 25.0

Quantitative Evaluations

Outlook (1 Lowest—5 Highest)
• **3+**

Fair Value
• **21⅜**

Risk
• **Low**

Earn./Div. Rank
• **B+**

Technical Eval.
• **Bearish** since 2/95

Rel. Strength Rank (1 Lowest—99 Highest)
• **65**

Insider Activity
• **Favorable**

Earnings vs. Previous Year
▲=Up ▼=Down ▶=No Change

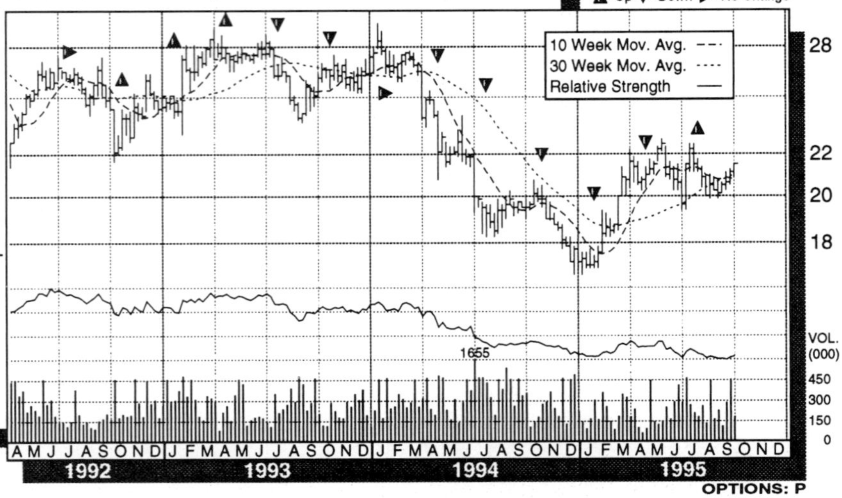

OPTIONS: P

Overview - 05-OCT-95

Based on our forecast of 2.6% GDP growth and continued recovery in Europe, we anticipate a 9% sales gain for 1996 excluding possible acquisitions. Aided by continued high operating rates, stable pricing in North American markets for butterfly valves and actuators, cost savings from restructuring and lower SG&A expense, margins should widen and operating income should increase. Assuming no change in the tax rate, earnings should rise again in 1996. Acquisitions, industry consolidation, aggressive pursuit of markets in Asia, and continued strength in capital spending in the chemical, petrochemical, petroleum, pulp and paper and power industries will lift long-term sales and earnings.

Valuation - 05-OCT-95

KII's shares are up 22% thus far in 1995 (though early October), with most of this gain occurring in the first half. Through most of the third quarter, the shares have moved sideways. While the shares have underperformed the S&P 500, the stock has performed in line with its peers. As there is little near-term impetus to drive the stock higher, we are maintaining our accumulate rating, based on an attractive dividend yield and KII's appeal as a late cycle and earnings turnaround play. Following several restructurings, and with expected upturn in late cycle industries such as chemicals and pulp and paper, sales and earnings should continue to trend up in 1996. Utlimately, the share price should follow the rise in sales and profits.

Key Stock Statistics

S&P EPS Est. 1995	1.00	Tang. Bk. Value/Share	7.36
P/E on S&P Est. 1995	21.5	Beta	1.38
S&P EPS Est. 1996	1.35	Shareholders	3,500
Dividend Rate/Share	0.74	Market cap. (B)	$0.761
Shs. outstg. (M)	35.4	Inst. holdings	58%
Avg. daily vol. (M)	0.054	Insider holdings	NA

Value of $10,000 invested 5 years ago: $ 12,021

Fiscal Year Ending Dec. 31

	1995	% Change	1994	% Change	1993	% Change
Revenues (Million $)						
1Q	138.2	14%	121.7	-5%	128.0	NM
2Q	152.1	14%	133.1	2%	130.8	-3%
3Q	—	—	135.9	8%	126.4	-6%
4Q	—	—	144.4	10%	131.0	NM
Yr.	—	—	535.1	4%	516.1	-2%
Income (Million $)						
1Q	4.04	-44%	7.23	-26%	9.72	4%
2Q	9.76	6%	9.21	-12%	10.45	-13%
3Q	—	—	7.42	-22%	9.46	-19%
4Q	—	—	9.11	-4%	9.50	NM
Yr.	—	—	32.97	-16%	39.14	-8%
Earnings Per Share ($)						
1Q	0.11	-48%	0.21	-25%	0.28	4%
2Q	0.28	8%	0.26	-13%	0.30	-12%
3Q	E0.30	43%	0.21	-22%	0.27	-21%
4Q	E0.31	19%	0.26	-4%	0.27	NM
Yr.	E1.00	6%	0.94	-16%	1.12	-8%

Next earnings report expected: late October

Keystone International

05-OCT-95

Business Summary - 05-OCT-95

Keystone International manufactures and distributes valves and other specialized industrial products to control the flow of liquids, gases, and fibrous and slurry materials for use in a wide variety of industries. Sales and operating profits by geographic area in 1994 were:

	Sales	Profits
U.S.	43%	30%
Europe, Middle East & Africa	27%	34%
Asia-Pacific	23%	30%
Canada & South America	7%	6%

In 1994, sales by unit were: industrial valves 40%, safety and environmental products 23%, Keystone controls 19%, specialty valve products 12%, and Keystone Vanessa 6%.

Flow control products include butterfly valves, actuators, electronic controls, and other devices to regulate the movement of liquids, gases and solid materials.

Anderson, Greenwood & Co. designs, engineers, manufactures and markets special-purpose and conventional precision valves for use by the petroleum, chemical, natural gas, pulp and paper, power and other process industries. Yarway Corp. designs, produces and sells specially engineered products and services used in the power generation and process industries.

In 1994, the chemical industry accounted for 14% of total sales, OEMs/industrial plants for 17%, power 10%, food and beverage 10%, marine and government 5%, commercial construction 6%, water treatment 7%, mining and metals 6%, petroleum refining 7%, oil and gas pipeline 6%, petroleum production 8%, pulp and paper 3%, and other 1%.

Important Developments

Aug. '95—KII announced that it had signed an agreement to buy some 80% of the shares of Gachot SA and all of the stock of Chemat GmbH for a total of $21 million. Paris-based Gachot, and Chemat, which is based in Renchen, Germany, are affiliated companies. Both manufacture ball valves primarily for the European market and had combined sales of $34 million in 1994. The transaction was expected to close in late 1995.

Jul. '95—KII reported earnings of $0.28 on a 14% increase in sales for 1995's second quarter, versus $0.26 a year earlier. Earnings for 1995's second quarter included a $0.03-a-share charge for plant closure costs. Orders at quarter end totaled $152.2 million, up from $142.3 million at June 30, 1994.

Capitalization

Long Term Debt: $61,437,000 (6/95).

Per Share Data ($) (Year Ended Dec. 31)

	1994	1993	1992	1991	1990	1989
Tangible Bk. Val.	7.36	6.90	6.47	6.12	6.02	5.00
Cash Flow	1.50	1.63	1.77	1.17	1.75	1.49
Earnings	0.94	1.12	1.22	0.66	1.31	1.10
Dividends	0.74	0.71	0.67	0.63	0.59	0.53
Payout Ratio	78%	63%	55%	96%	45%	48%
Prices - High	29½	29⅛	30⅜	35⅜	29¾	21¼
- Low	16¾	23	21⅜	23½	18⅞	14½
P/E Ratio - High	31	26	25	54	23	19
- Low	18	21	18	36	14	13

Income Statement Analysis (Million $)

	1994	%Chg	1993	%Chg	1992	%Chg	1991
Revs.	535	4%	516	-2%	528	2%	520
Oper. Inc.	81.2	-9%	88.8	-11%	100	6%	94.3
Depr.	19.9	10%	18.1	-6%	19.3	9%	17.7
Int. Exp.	5.6	-6%	5.9	-17%	7.1	-7%	7.6
Pretax Inc.	52.3	-16%	62.1	-11%	69.9	62%	43.1
Eff. Tax Rate	37%	—	37%	—	39%	—	47%
Net Inc.	33.0	-16%	39.1	-8%	42.5	86%	22.8

Balance Sheet & Other Fin. Data (Million $)

	1994	1993	1992	1991	1990	1989
Cash	18.7	19.9	29.4	12.5	32.3	29.7
Curr. Assets	313	280	278	290	270	234
Total Assets	496	457	438	459	417	366
Curr. Liab.	127	108	157	147	120	103
LT Debt	60.0	62.0	14.0	58.0	48.0	51.0
Common Eqty.	286	271	253	239	231	199
Total Cap.	353	333	267	298	291	259
Cap. Exp.	35.1	33.6	19.5	35.6	32.5	21.8
Cash Flow	52.8	57.3	61.9	40.5	58.8	49.8

Ratio Analysis

	1994	1993	1992	1991	1990	1989
Curr. Ratio	2.5	2.6	1.8	2.0	2.2	2.3
% LT Debt of Cap.	17.1	18.7	5.4	19.6	16.6	19.9
% Net Inc.of Revs.	6.2	7.6	8.1	4.4	9.9	9.8
% Ret. on Assets	6.9	8.7	9.4	5.1	11.2	10.4
% Ret. on Equity	11.8	14.9	17.2	9.6	20.3	19.3

Dividend Data —Dividends have been paid since 1972. A poison pill stock purchase rights plan was adopted in 1990.

Amt. of Div. $	Date Decl.	Ex-Div. Date	Stock of Record	Payment Date
0.185	Sep. 21	Oct. 27	Nov. 02	Nov. 16 '94
0.185	Dec. 14	Jan. 26	Feb. 01	Feb. 15 '95
0.185	Mar. 15	Apr. 27	May. 03	May. 17 '95
0.185	Jun. 21	Jul. 31	Aug. 02	Aug. 16 '95
0.185	Sep. 20	Oct. 30	Nov. 01	Nov. 15 '95

Data as orig. reptd.; bef. results of disc. opers. and/or spec. items. Per share data adj. for stk. divs. as of ex-div. date. E-Estimated. NA-Not Available. NM-Not Meaningful. NR-Not Ranked.

Office—9600 West Gulf Bank Drive (P.O. Box 40010), Houston, TX 77040. **Tel**—(713) 466-1176. **Chrmn, Pres & CEO**—N. Teshoian. **VP, CFO & Investor Contact**—Mark E. Baldwin. **Secy**—Donna D. Moore. **Dirs**—F. A. Cailloux, A. L. French, B. G. Gower, F. O'Neil Griffin, M. E. Hamilton, F. G. Huber, Jr., D. P. Jones, W. W. Patterson, A. F. Rhodes, N. Teshoian, W. S. Wilson. **Transfer Agent**—Continental Stock Transfer & Trust Co., NYC. **Incorporated** in Texas in 1947. **Empl**-4,000. **S&P Analyst:** Leo Larkin

STANDARD & POOR'S

STOCK REPORTS

Kohl's Corp.

NYSE Symbol **KSS**
In S&P MidCap 400

13-OCT-95 **Industry:** Retail Stores

Summary: This company operates 117 specialty department stores, primarily in the Midwest. The stores feature moderately priced apparel, shoes, accessories and products for the home.

S&P Opinion: Hold (★★★) | Recent Price • 50 | 52 Wk Range • 54⅝-38 | Yield • Nil | 12-Mo. P/E • 26.0

Quantitative Evaluations

Outlook (1 Lowest—5 Highest)
• **NA**

Fair Value
• **NA**

Risk
• **Average**

Earn./Div. Rank
• **NR**

Technical Eval.
• **Bullish** since 8/95

Rel. Strength Rank (1 Lowest—99 Highest)
• **66**

Insider Activity
• **NA**

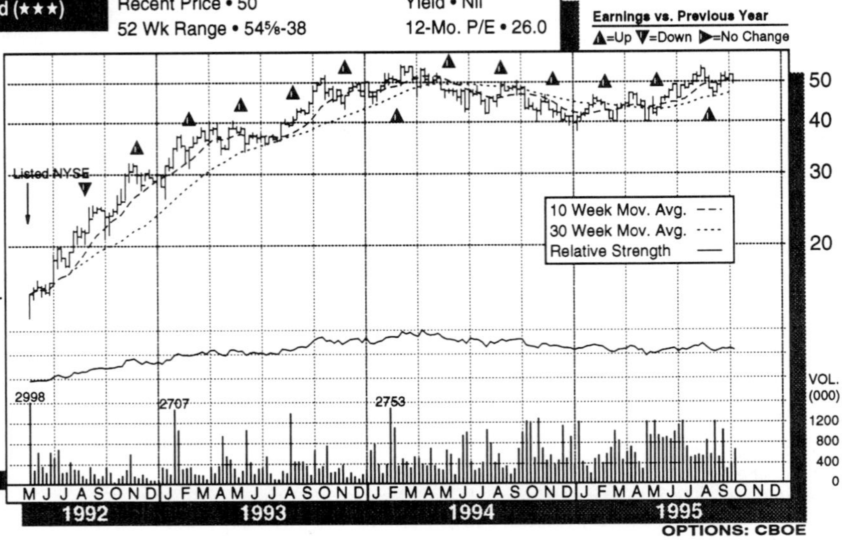

OPTIONS: CBOE

Overview - 13-OCT-95

Sales should increase some 26% in 1995-96, boosted by strong same-store sales growth of about 6% to 7% and about 20 new stores. Gross margins should narrow as pricing remains competitive. Selling, general and adminstrative expenses should decrease as a percentage of sales, reflecting the leveraging of store, advertising and headquarters expenses as a result of increased sales. Operating income should increase 21%. Interest expense will be higher on increased debt to fund capital expenditures of $100 million to $110 million. The company's bringing the management of its credit card receiveables in-house in the third quarter of 1995-96 should boost earnings by $0.10 a share beginning in 1996-97. This also should improve sales as KSS aggressively markets its credit card and targets customers for promotions and special events. Earnings gains should reach 20% annually in the next few years.

Valuation - 12-OCT-95

The shares of this well-managed regional retailer appear fully valued at current levels. With overall apparel sales weak, Kohl's has continued to gain marketshare and outperform most other apparel retailers by a wide margin. This good news is already reflected in the shares. The company's aggressive store opening program, low cost structure and conservative balance sheet bode well for earnings gains over the next two years. The shares remain a worthwhile holding.

Key Stock Statistics

S&P EPS Est. 1996	2.20	Tang. Bk. Value/Share	7.21
P/E on S&P Est. 1996	22.7	Beta	NA
S&P EPS Est. 1997	2.65	Shareholders	3,300
Dividend Rate/Share	Nil	Market cap. (B)	$ 1.9
Shs. outstg. (M)	36.8	Inst. holdings	77%
Avg. daily vol. (M)	0.081	Insider holdings	NA

Value of $10,000 invested 5 years ago: NA

Fiscal Year Ending Jan. 31

	1996	% Change	1995	% Change	1994	% Change
Revenues (Million $)						
1Q	368.4	20%	308.0	23%	250.3	18%
2Q	363.5	24%	292.4	14%	257.4	18%
3Q	—	—	389.5	14%	341.0	20%
4Q	—	—	564.3	23%	457.1	20%
Yr.	—	—	1,554	19%	1,306	19%
Income (Million $)						
1Q	11.80	4%	11.33	51%	7.50	—
2Q	11.14	18%	9.48	38%	6.89	—
3Q	—	—	13.84	5%	13.15	30%
4Q	—	—	33.87	20%	28.12	25%
Yr.	—	—	68.51	23%	55.66	94%
Earnings Per Share ($)						
1Q	0.32	3%	0.31	55%	0.20	82%
2Q	0.30	15%	0.26	37%	0.19	NM
3Q	E0.43	13%	0.38	6%	0.36	24%
4Q	E1.15	25%	0.92	19%	0.77	20%
Yr.	E2.20	18%	1.87	23%	1.52	73%

Next earnings report expected: mid November

Kohl's Corp.

Business Summary - 13-OCT-95

Kohl's operates 117 family oriented, specialty department stores, primarily in the Midwest. The stores feature quality, moderately priced national brand merchandise, including apparel, shoes, accessories, soft home products and housewares. Sales by merchandise category in recent fiscal years were:

	1994-95	1993-94
Apparel	57.0%	56.2%
Accessories/shoes	19.3%	19.5%
Soft home/housewares	12.7%	12.1%
Hardlines	11.0%	12.2%

At January 28, 1995, the company had 108 stores, located in Wisconsin (28), Illinois (29), Michigan (14), Indiana (11), Minnesota (9), Ohio (11), Iowa (3), Kentucky (1), North Dakota (1) and South Dakota (1). Stores are designed to help customers shop without assistance, and feature simple layouts and in-store signs. The company owned 42 stores and leased the other 66.

As a complement to its national brands, KSS offers private label merchandise under several names. It plans to increase private label sales, which accounted for 14% of the total in 1993-94, to about 20%.

The company plans to open about 20 new stores in 1995-96 and 20 to 25 the following year. Capital expenditures for 1995-96 are projected at $100 million to $110 million. Emphasis is placed on existing markets where it can leverage advertising, purchasing, transportation and other regional expenses; contiguous markets where it can extend regional facilities; and on new markets.

Important Developments

Oct. '95—KSS said that same-store sales increased 14.2% in September; total sales rose 39.3%. During the first half of 1995-96, sales rose 21.9% and operating income increased 16.3% over the same period a year ago. The company converted its credit card file to an in-house operation. In conjunction with this, Kohl's will incur a $7 to $8 million one-time aftertax charge in the third quarter of 1995-96. The company expects to benefit by about $0.10 a share annually from servicing its accounts receivable in-house. In September, the company entered the Kansas City market with three stores and opened one in Topeka, Kansas. Four stores were slated to open in October in Cleveland, Ohio; stores in Canton and Youngstown, Ohio and Maple Grove, Minnesota were also set to debut.

Capitalization

Long Term Debt: $177,844,000 (7/95).

Per Share Data ($) (Year Ended Jan. 31)

	1995	1994	1993	1992	1991	1990
Tangible Bk. Val.	7.21	5.77	4.11	2.16	0.79	NA
Cash Flow	2.61	2.15	1.39	1.25	NA	NA
Earnings	1.87	1.52	0.88	0.60	0.66	NA
Dividends	Nil	Nil	Nil	Nil	NA	NA
Payout Ratio	Nil	Nil	Nil	Nil	NA	NA
Cal. Yrs.	1994	1993	1992	1991	1990	1989
Prices - High	55¼	52⅛	32	NA	NA	NA
- Low	39⅛	26⅛	13¼	NA	NA	NA
P/E Ratio - High	30	34	36	NA	NA	NA
- Low	21	17	15	NA	NA	NA

Income Statement Analysis (Million $)

	1995	%Chg	1994	%Chg	1993	%Chg	1992
Revs.	1,554	19%	1,306	19%	1,097	9%	1,006
Oper. Inc.	151	20%	126	27%	99	34%	73.9
Depr.	27.4	18%	23.2	39%	16.7	-11%	18.7
Int. Exp.	7.4	10%	6.7	-54%	14.7	-27%	20.2
Pretax Inc.	117	21%	96.7	93%	50.1	58%	31.7
Eff. Tax Rate	42%	—	42%	—	43%	—	45%
Net Inc.	68.5	23%	55.7	94%	28.7	64%	17.5

Balance Sheet & Other Fin. Data (Million $)

	1995	1994	1993	1992	1991	1990
Cash	30.4	8.5	4.2	0.9	NA	NA
Curr. Assets	286	202	211	179	NA	NA
Total Assets	659	469	445	398	NA	NA
Curr. Liab.	172	115	106	139	NA	NA
LT Debt	109	52.0	95.0	89.0	108	NA
Common Eqty.	334	263	207	134	121	NA
Total Cap.	463	329	314	232	NA	NA
Cap. Exp.	108	58.8	46.3	27.5	11.3	NA
Cash Flow	95.9	78.9	45.4	36.2	41.6	NA

Ratio Analysis

	1995	1994	1993	1992	1991	1990
Curr. Ratio	1.7	1.8	2.0	1.3	NA	NA
% LT Debt of Cap.	23.5	15.7	30.3	38.5	NA	NA
% Net Inc.of Revs.	4.4	4.3	2.6	1.7	2.6	NA
% Ret. on Assets	12.1	12.2	6.1	4.0	NA	NA
% Ret. on Equity	22.9	23.7	26.5	24.6	NA	NA

Dividend Data —No cash dividends have been paid. The company has no current plans to pay dividends on its common stock and intends to retain all earnings for investment in its business.

Data as orig. reptd.; bef. results of disc. opers. and/or spec. items. Per share data adj. for stk. divs. as of ex-div. date. E-Estimated. NA-Not Available. NM-Not Meaningful. NR-Not Ranked.

Office—N54 W13600 Woodale Drive, Menomonee Falls, WI 53051. **Tel**—(414) 783-5800. **Chrmn & CEO**—W. S. Kellogg. **Pres**—J. H. Baker. **VP, CFO & Investor Contact**—Arlene Meier (414 783-1646). **VP & Secy**—J. F. Herma. **Dirs**—J. H. Baker, J. F. Herma, W. S. Kellogg, L. Montgomery, F. V. Sica, H. Simon, P. M. Sommerhauser, R. E. White. **Transfer Agent & Registrar**—Bank of New York, NYC. **Incorporated** in Delaware in 1988, reincorporated in Wisconsin in 1993. **Empl**-17,600. **S&P Analyst:** Karen J. Sack, CFA

STANDARD & POOR'S STOCK REPORTS

LG&E Energy

NYSE Symbol **LGE**
In S&P MidCap 400

16-OCT-95

Industry: Util.-Diversified

Summary: LG&E is an electric and gas utility holding company serving Louisville and adjacent areas of Kentucky.

Quantitative Evaluations

Recent Price • 40⅞ | Yield • 5.4%
52 Wk Range • 41⅛-36¼ | 12-Mo. P/E • 12.9

Outlook
(1 Lowest—5 Highest)
• **2+**

Fair Value
• **37**

Risk
• **Low**

Earn./Div. Rank
• **B+**

Technical Eval.
• **Bullish** since 1/95

Rel. Strength Rank
(1 Lowest—99 Highest)
• **70**

Insider Activity
• **NA**

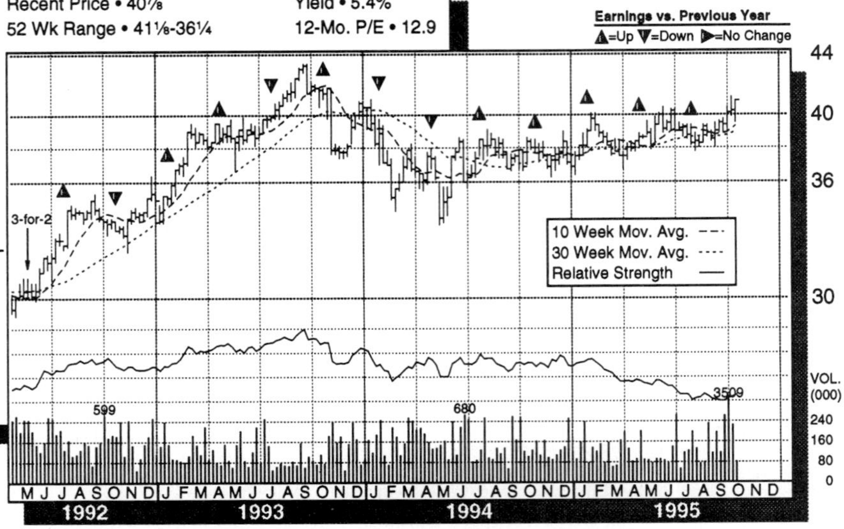

Business Profile - 13-OCT-95

LG&E Energy is an energy services holding company that owns and operates diversified energy services businesses. Effective January 1, 1994, the company realigned into two primary business units: LG&E Energy Services, a group that concentrates on generation, development and wholesale power marketing, and Louisville Gas and Electric Company, a regulated public utility that concentrates its efforts on the retail distribution of electric and gas services.

Operational Review - 13-OCT-95

Net income from continuing operations for 1995's first half reflected the absence of nonrecurring charges of $0.91 a share and a charitable expense of $0.27. The inclusion of Hadson outweighed reduced gas sales resulting from warmer weather. Results benefited from higher retail electric industrial sales and higher equity earnings. Share earnings from continuing operations were $1.34, versus $0.06. There was a gain on sale of discontinued operations of $1.57 a share in the 1994 period.

Stock Performance - 13-OCT-95

In the past 30 trading days, LGE's shares have increased 6%, compared to a 4% rise in the S&P 500. Average trading volume for the past five days was 15,900 shares, compared with the 40-day moving average of 126,551 shares.

Key Stock Statistics

Dividend Rate/Share	2.22	Shareholders	31,700
Shs. outstg. (M)	33.1	Market cap. (B)	$ 1.4
Avg. daily vol. (M)	0.214	Inst. holdings	28%
Tang. Bk. Value/Share	21.81	Insider holdings	NA
Beta	0.43		

Value of $10,000 invested 5 years ago: $ 20,808

Fiscal Year Ending Dec. 31

	1995	% Change	1994	% Change	1993	% Change
Revenues (Million $)						
1Q	208.1	-15%	244.5	3%	238.4	16%
2Q	249.1	29%	192.4	-4%	200.4	6%
3Q	—	—	202.6	-8%	220.9	5%
4Q	—	—	190.3	-21%	240.3	4%
Yr.	—	—	829.7	-8%	900.0	8%
Income (Million $)						
1Q	21.31	NM	-19.96	NM	18.57	41%
2Q	26.28	19%	22.09	44%	15.38	-10%
3Q	—	—	37.08	11%	33.26	13%
4Q	—	—	17.62	29%	13.62	-14%
Yr.	—	—	56.83	-30%	80.83	7%
Earnings Per Share ($)						
1Q	0.60	NM	-0.61	NM	0.57	39%
2Q	0.75	12%	0.67	43%	0.47	-11%
3Q	—	—	1.12	10%	1.02	12%
4Q	—	—	0.54	32%	0.41	-16%
Yr.	—	—	1.72	-30%	2.47	6%

Next earnings report expected: late October

LG&E Energy

Business Summary - 13-OCT-95

LG&E Energy Corp. is the holding company for Louisville Gas & Electric Co., a public utility that supplies natural gas to approximately 270,000 customers and electricity to about 345,000 customers in a 700-square-mile area that includes Louisville, Ky. The LG&E Energy Systems unit was formed in 1991 to conduct nonutility operations. In December 1991, LG&E Energy Systems acquired Hadson Power Systems (renamed LG&E Power Systems, Inc.), which develops independent power projects. In January 1994, it sold its 36.5% interest in Natural Gas Clearinghouse, a leading gas marketing company. In 1994, electric service accounted for 74% of revenues and 92% of operating profits and gas for 26% and 8%. Electric revenues by class of customer in recent years were:

	1994	1993	1992
Residential	35%	34%	33%
Large industrial	19%	18%	20%
Large commercial	15%	15%	15%
Small commercial & industrial	13%	12%	13%
Other	18%	21%	19%

LGE's electric generating capacity is 90% coal-fired, with the remainder consisting of a hydroelectric plant and combustion turbine peaking units fueled by natural gas and oil. Peak load in 1994 was 2,219 mw, and system capability totaled 2,613 mw, for a capacity margin of 17.8%. Gas sold or transported totaled 50,012,000 Mcf (51,219,000 Mcf in 1993).

In May 1995, LGE acquired Hadson Corp., a natural gas marketing, gathering, processing, storage and transportation company, for $143 million.

In November 1994, LGE formed a joint venture that will build and operate a $54 million natural-gas-fired power plant in north central Argentina. Investment in the 114-megawatt facility will be made through the company's LG&E International Inc. subsidiary. The project was expected to be built and operational before the end of 1995.

Important Developments

Apr. '95—The Public Service Commission of Kentucky approved an environmental cost recovery surcharge that will increase LG&E's electric revenues by about $3.4 million in 1995 and $7.2 million in 1996. Separately, LG&E International formed a joint venture that will build and operate a wind-power plant in Tarifa, Spain.

Capitalization

Long Term Debt: $646,854,000 (6/95).
Subsid. Preferred Stock: $116,716,000.

Per Share Data ($) (Year Ended Dec. 31)

	1994	1993	1992	1991	1990	1989
Tangible Bk. Val.	22.86	21.39	20.67	20.41	19.71	18.75
Earnings	1.72	2.47	2.34	2.57	2.30	2.13
Dividends	2.11	2.04	1.98	1.92	1.87	1.83
Payout Ratio	123%	83%	85%	75%	81%	86%
Prices - High	41	43⅜	36⅜	32	28	27⅞
- Low	33⅝	33¾	29⅛	25⅜	23½	21⅜
P/E Ratio - High	24	18	16	12	12	13
- Low	20	14	12	10	10	10

Income Statement Analysis (Million $)

	1994	%Chg	1993	%Chg	1992	%Chg	1991
Revs.	830	-8%	900	8%	835	17%	715
Depr.	84.2	5%	79.9	NM	79.9	4%	76.7
Maint.	NA	—	NA	—	NA	—	49.6
Fxd. Chgs. Cov.	2.8	-18%	3.5	11%	3.1	-1%	3.2
Constr. Credits	NA	—	NA	—	NA	—	NA
Eff. Tax Rate	35%	—	38%	—	36%	—	37%
Net Inc.	56.8	-30%	80.8	7%	75.6	-9%	83.0

Balance Sheet & Other Fin. Data (Million $)

	1994	1993	1992	1991	1990	1989
Gross Prop.	2,538	2,464	2,373	2,285	2,215	2,277
Cap. Exp.	96.0	100	102	88.0	118	174
Net Prop.	1,656	1,641	1,619	1,592	1,584	1,695
Capitalization:						
LT Debt	663	663	686	687	687	613
% LT Debt	663	44	46	47	47	46
Pfd.	117	117	117	117	117	118
% Pfd.	7.60	7.70	7.90	7.90	8.00	8.90
Common	763	730	685	675	649	602
% Common	49	48	46	46	45	45
Total Cap.	1,901	1,946	1,890	1,851	1,816	1,678

Ratio Analysis

	1994	1993	1992	1991	1990	1989
Oper. Ratio	88.7	85.3	85.8	80.8	80.4	81.2
% Earn. on Net Prop.	NA	8.6	7.4	8.7	8.4	7.7
% Ret. on Revs.	6.8	9.0	9.1	11.6	10.5	11.2
% Ret. On Invest.Cap	5.6	7.0	7.2	7.9	7.8	7.8
% Return On Com.Eqty	7.6	11.4	11.1	12.5	11.7	11.3

Dividend Data —Dividends have been paid since 1913. A dividend reinvestment plan is available. A "poison pill" stock purchase right was adopted in 1990.

Amt. of Div. $	Date Decl.	Ex-Div. Date	Stock of Record	Payment Date
0.538	Sep. 01	Sep. 26	Sep. 30	Oct. 15 '94
0.538	Dec. 08	Dec. 23	Dec. 30	Jan. 17 '95
0.538	Mar. 01	Mar. 27	Mar. 31	Apr. 15 '95
0.538	Jun. 07	Jun. 28	Jun. 30	Jul. 15 '95
0.555	Sep. 06	Sep. 27	Sep. 29	Oct. 16 '95

Data as orig. reptd.; bef. results of disc opers. and/or spec. items. Per share data adj. for stk. divs. as of ex-div. date. E-Estimated. NA-Not Available. NM-Not Meaningful. NR-Not Ranked.

Office—220 West Main St., Louisville, KY 40232. **Tel**—(502) 627-2000. **Chrmn, Pres & CEO**—R. W. Hale. **VP-Fin & Treas**—C. A. Markel. **VP & Secy**—J. R. McCall. **Investor Contact**—Martha Dunbar Hall (502) 627-3998. **Dirs**—W. C. Ballard Jr., O. Brown II, S. G. Dabney, G. P. Gardner, J. D. Grissom, R. W. Hale, D. B. Lewis, A. H. McNamara, T. B. Morton Jr., D. C. Swain. **Transfer Agents**—Co.'s office; Continental Stock Transfer & Trust Co., NYC. **Incorporated** in Kentucky in 1913; reincorporated in Kentucky in 1990. **Empl**-2,971. **S&P Analyst:** R.J.G.

STANDARD & POOR'S

STOCK REPORTS

LSI Logic

NYSE Symbol **LSI**
In S&P MidCap 400

08-AUG-95 **Industry:** Electronics/Electric

Summary: This company is a leading supplier of custom performance semiconductors.

S&P Opinion: Buy (★★★★★)

Recent Price • 44½ | 52 Wk Range • 49⅞-13⅞ | Yield • Nil | 12-Mo. P/E • 31.8

Quantitative Evaluations
Outlook (1 Lowest—5 Highest) • **1+**
Fair Value • **34⅛**
Risk • **Average**
Earn./Div. Rank • **B-**

Technical Eval. • **Bullish** since 6/95
Rel. Strength Rank (1 Lowest—99 Highest) • **79**
Insider Activity • **Neutral**

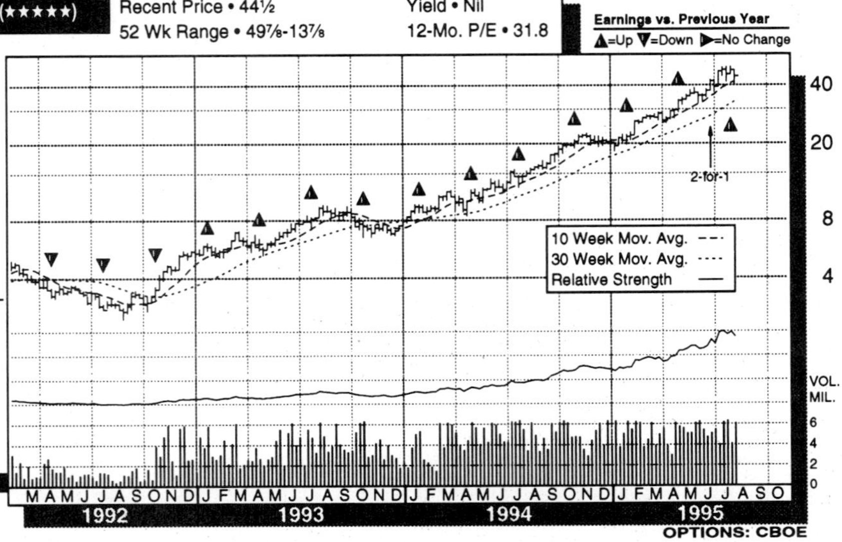

OPTIONS: CBOE

Overview - 07-AUG-95

Sales are expected to grow about 40% in 1995. Results should benefit from strong demand from the computer, communications and consumer electronics sectors. LSI's ability to reduce a customer's time to market has allowed the company to choose well-known customers in dynamic sectors that it feels will aid it in the long run. Recent successes include shipment to Sony of a chip for the world's first 32-bit, CD-based home video game system, PlayStation, as well as design wins with Hewlett-Packard for set-top boxes used in cable TV reception. LSI continues to add wafer capacity, and plans to open a new fabrication facility in early 1997. Margins should widen on higher volume and firmer prices.

Valuation - 07-AUG-95

LSI should continue to generate above-average earnings growth in the foreseeable future, as consumer and communications markets overtake the surging computer sector. Gross margins should widen, as the product mix shifts to more profitable CoreWare products. LSI's proven ability to reduce a client's time to market, a major concern for end-product users, lets the company selectively choose its clients. A shift from 1.0 micron to sub-0.5 micron will further strengthen LSI's position, from both chip design and wafer yield aspects. The company is currently not capacity-constrained. We regard the share as undervalued at 18X estimated 1996 EPS of $2.50.

Key Stock Statistics

S&P EPS Est. 1995	1.80	Tang. Bk. Value/Share	6.52
P/E on S&P Est. 1995	24.7	Beta	1.85
S&P EPS Est. 1996	2.50	Shareholders	1,700
Dividend Rate/Share	Nil	Market cap. (B)	$ 5.8
Shs. outstg. (M)	126.4	Inst. holdings	93%
Avg. daily vol. (M)	1.330	Insider holdings	NA

Value of $10,000 invested 5 years ago: $ 124,912

Fiscal Year Ending Dec. 31

	1995	% Change	1994	% Change	1993	% Change
Revenues (Million $)						
1Q	280.2	45%	193.8	15%	168.9	12%
2Q	307.1	45%	212.1	20%	177.1	17%
3Q	—	—	240.2	31%	183.8	19%
4Q	—	—	255.7	35%	189.0	17%
Yr.	—	—	901.8	25%	718.8	16%
Income (Million $)						
1Q	45.26	134%	19.36	82%	10.61	NM
2Q	55.75	138%	23.44	79%	13.07	NM
3Q	—	—	29.47	105%	14.38	NM
4Q	—	—	36.48	133%	15.69	134%
Yr.	—	—	108.7	102%	53.75	NM
Earnings Per Share ($)						
1Q	0.38	103%	0.19	68%	0.11	NM
2Q	0.44	100%	0.22	63%	0.13	NM
3Q	E0.47	—	0.26	79%	0.15	NM
4Q	E0.52	—	0.31	100%	0.15	107%
Yr.	E1.80	—	0.99	82%	0.54	NM

Next earnings report expected: late October

LSI Logic

Business Summary - 07-AUG-95

LSI Logic designs, develops, makes and markets application-specific integrated circuits (ASICs). Standard products are also produced. Revenue contributions in recent years were:

	1994	1993	1992
Components	89%	87%	83%
Design & services	11%	13%	17%

LSI provides computer-aided engineering design and technology services and software design tools using proprietary technologies for design and development of ASICs by the company and its customers. Its ASIC technologies and engineering design services let customers reduce component design costs, improve product performance, retain control over proprietary logic, and shorten product development cycle.

A key factor in the company's approach to the ASIC market is its CoreWare product library, comprised of predefined and characterized cells of industry standard functions, protocols and interfaces. By allowing the customer to add custom features alongside the core products, it is possible to rapidly develop a sub-micron system on a chip, optimized for customer application, as opposed to using a general-purpose standard chip designed to perform a wide range of tasks. The CoreWare methodology is applicable to any market.

By combining its sub-micron process technology, a library of industry standard core elements, a set of design tools to stitch the cores together, and high-volume factories, LSI moved from from a low-volume manufacturer of gate-arrays to a high-volume provider of high-end ASICs and CoreWare based systems on a chip.

The company focuses on trendsetting customers in fast growing segments in consumer electronics, communications and computer markets.

Important Developments

Jul. '95—LSI said it expects to begin shipping 0.35 micron product protypes in the fourth quarter, with volume shipments scheduled for the 1996 first quarter. Separately, it solid publicly 5 million common shares at $44.50 each. Proceeds were earmarked for capacity expansion at current wafer fabrication facilities and for construction of a new eight-inch wafer manufacturing facility, to open in 1997, in Gresham, Ore. Cost of the first phase of construction is estimated at $600 to $800 million; total cost (over 15 years) could reach $4 billion.

Capitalization

Long Term Liabilities: $299,100,000 (6/95), incl. $143,800.000 of notes conv. into com. at $24.50 a sh.
Minority Interest: $28,900,000.

Per Share Data ($) (Year Ended Dec. 31)

	1994	1993	1992	1991	1990	1989
Tangible Bk. Val.	4.72	2.94	2.17	3.35	3.28	3.62
Cash Flow	1.93	1.21	-0.08	1.01	0.80	0.76
Earnings	0.99	0.54	-1.24	0.09	-0.40	-0.30
Dividends	Nil	Nil	Nil	Nil	Nil	Nil
Payout Ratio	Nil	Nil	Nil	Nil	Nil	Nil
Prices - High	22¾	9⅝	5⅝	6¼	6½	6¼
- Low	7¾	5⅛	2 7/16	2¾	2⅝	3⅛
P/E Ratio - High	23	18	NM	66	NM	NM
- Low	8	9	NM	28	NM	NM

Income Statement Analysis (Million $)

	1994	%Chg	1993	%Chg	1992	%Chg	1991
Revs.	902	25%	719	17%	617	-12%	698
Oper. Inc.	261	74%	150	44%	104	3%	101
Depr.	104	58%	66.0	-36%	103	30%	79.0
Int. Exp.	18.5	20%	15.4	5%	14.7	-24%	19.4
Pretax Inc.	156	93%	80.7	NM	-99	NM	12.3
Eff. Tax Rate	28%	—	30%	—	NM	—	50%
Net Inc.	109	102%	54.0	NM	-109	NM	8.3

Balance Sheet & Other Fin. Data (Million $)

	1994	1993	1992	1991	1990	1989
Cash	429	202	153	157	159	153
Curr. Assets	731	426	350	386	439	392
Total Assets	1,270	853	736	748	784	765
Curr. Liab.	308	189	211	161	193	151
LT Debt	263	220	192	166	190	204
Common Eqty.	545	292	198	293	276	297
Total Cap.	937	638	525	587	591	614
Cap. Exp.	166	90.0	142	78.0	71.0	121
Cash Flow	212	120	-7.3	87.1	67.4	62.9

Ratio Analysis

	1994	1993	1992	1991	1990	1989
Curr. Ratio	2.4	2.3	1.7	2.4	2.3	2.6
% LT Debt of Cap.	28.0	34.5	36.5	28.3	32.1	33.3
% Net Inc.of Revs.	12.1	7.5	NM	1.2	NM	NM
% Ret. on Assets	9.7	6.5	NM	1.1	NM	NM
% Ret. on Equity	24.7	21.1	NM	2.9	NM	NM

Dividend Data (LSI has never paid cash dividends. A three-for-two stock split was effected in 1986. A poison pill stock purchase rights plan was adopted in 1988.)

Amt. of Div. $	Date Decl.	Ex-Div. Date	Stock of Record	Payment Date
2-for-1	May. 12	Jun. 22	May. 23	Jun. 21 '95

Data as orig. reptd.; bef. results of disc. opers. and/or spec. items. Per share data adj. for stk. divs. as of ex-div. date. E-Estimated. NA-Not Available. NM-Not Meaningful. NR-Not Ranked.

Office—1551 McCarthy Blvd., Milpitas, CA 95035. **Tel**—(408) 433-8000. **Chrmn & CEO**—W. J. Corrigan. **SVP & CFO**—A. A. Pimentel. **VP & Secy**—D. E. Sanders. **VP & Investor Contact**—Bruce L. Entin. **Dirs**—T. Z. Chu, W. J. Corrigan, M. R. Currie, J. H. Keyes, R. D. Norby. **Transfer Agent & Registrar**—Bank of Boston. **Incorporated** in California in 1980; reincorporated in Delaware in 1986. **Empl**-3,750. **S&P Analyst:** Steven A. Jaworski

Laboratory Corp. of America

NYSE Symbol LH In S&P MidCap 400

Price	Range	P-E Ratio	Dividend	Yield	S&P Ranking	Beta
Aug. 15'95	1995					
13⅜	15½–11¾	NA	None	None	NR	1.07

Summary

Laboratory Corporation of America Holdings was formed by the merger of National Health Laboratories Inc. and Hoffmann-La Roche Inc.'s Roche Biomedical Laboratories unit. The shares began trading on the New York Stock Exchange on May 1, 1995. The company is a national clinical laboratory orginization, offering more than 1,700 clinical assays through 40 primary testing facilities nationwide. The company reported revenues of $611 million and net income of $28 million, excluding a special restructuring charge and an extraordinary loss, through the first six months of 1995.

Business Summary

Laboratory Corp. of America Holdings was formed by the merger of National Health Laboratories Inc. (NHL), a publicly traded company losted on the New York Stock Exchange, and Roche Biomedical Laboratories, (RBL) a unit of Hoffman-La Roche Inc. In the transaction, each NHL share was exhanged for 0.72 common shares of the new concern and $5.60 in cash. NHL shareholders received a 50.1% interest in the new company and about $475 million in cash. NHL also declared a dividend of 0.163 warrant for each NHL common share held. The warrants, exercisable after five years, entitle holders to buy shares of Laboratory Corp. of America at $22 a share. NHL shareholders approved the merger on April 28, 1995 and the new company began trading on the NYSE on May 1, 1995.

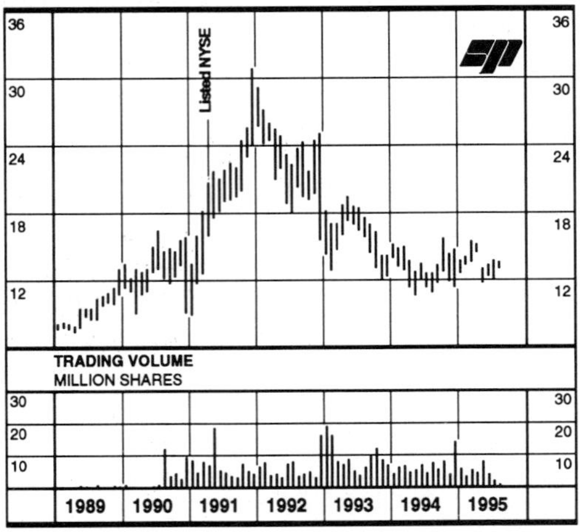

NHL, together with its Allied Clinical Laboratory subsidiary, was the third largest clinical laboratory in the country. NHL offered a broad range of testing services used by the medical profession to diagnose, monitor and treat diseases and other clincal states. Office based physicans constituted most of NHL's clients.

At the time of the merger, NHL had 23 laboratories and 950 service sites consisting of sales ports, patient service centers and STAT laboratories serving customers in 45 states.

At the time of the merger, RBL was the fourth largest clincial laboratory in the United States. RBL provided clinical testing services to hospitals, laboratories and physicians. RBL offered 1,600 tests and procedures, with the majority performed in RBL's 17 major testing centers. For the year ended December 31, 1994, the company derived 58% of its revenues from physicians, 11% from hospitals, and 31% from other clinical laboratories and clients.

Important Developments

Aug. '95— In reporting earnings for the second quarter, the company said results were in line with expectations and the company was finished with significant restructuring charges. Furthermore, management believes the company is ahead of its schedule in realizing operating synergies and may be able to generate more than the previously estimated $90 million in cost savings over the next two years.

Next earnings report expected in late October.

[1]Per Share Data ($)

Yr. End Dec. 31	1994	1993	1992	1991	1990	1989	1988	1987
Tangible Bk. Val.	**d4.55**	d1.66	0.27	1.39	0.65	[2]3.33	[2]2.68	0.95
Cash Flow	**0.88**	1.62	0.71	1.27	1.02	0.79	0.60	NA
Earnings	**0.36**	1.26	0.43	1.05	0.83	0.65	0.50	[3]0.36
Dividends[4]	**0.08**	0.32	0.31	0.27	1.58	Nil	Nil	Nil
Payout Ratio	**22%**	25%	72%	26%	189%	Nil	Nil	Nil
Prices—High	**15¾**	19½	29¼	30⅞	16½	13	10	NA
Low	**10⅝**	12	15⅝	8⅞	9	7⅜	7⅝	NA
P/E Ratio—	**44–30**	15–10	68–36	29–8	20–11	20–11	20–15	NA

Data as orig. reptd. **1.** Data for National Health Laboratories only. **2.** Incl. intangibles. **3.** Pro forma. **4.** Divs. decl. d-Deficit. NA-Not Available.

[1]Income Data (Million $)

Year Ended Dec. 31	Revs.	Oper. Inc.	% Oper. Inc. of Revs.	Cap. Exp.	Depr.	Int. Exp.	Net Bef. Taxes	Eff. Tax Rate	Net Inc.	% Net Inc. of Revs.	Cash Flow
1994	**873**	**158**	**18.1**	**48.9**	**44.4**	**34.5**	**55**	**45.7%**	**30**	**3.4**	**75**
1993	761	218	28.6	33.6	32.2	10.9	191	41.0%	113	14.8	145
1992	721	227	31.5	34.9	26.9	4.2	62	34.6%	41	5.6	68
1991	604	188	31.1	25.4	22.0	Nil	169	38.6%	104	17.2	126
1990	502	152	30.2	14.9	18.4	NA	137	39.8%	83	16.5	101
1989	402	120	29.9	23.7	13.3	NA	108	40.0%	65	16.1	78
1988	314	93	29.6	11.3	10.7	NA	84	41.7%	49	15.6	60
1987	271	81	30.2	21.2	8.9	NA	69	49.0%	35	13.1	NA
1986	205	61	29.6	11.2	6.6	NA	51	54.3%	23	11.4	NA
1985	170	45	26.3	6.3	2.1	NA	43	48.9%	22	13.0	NA

[1]Balance Sheet Data (Million $)

Dec. 31	Cash	Curr. Assets	Curr. Liab.	Curr. Ratio	Total Assets	% Ret. on Assets	Long Term Debt	Common Equity	Total Cap.	% LT Debt of Cap.	% Ret. on Equity
1994	**26.8**	**293**	**203.0**	**1.4**	**1,013**	**3.8**	**564.00**	**166**	**750**	**75.1**	**19.6**
1993	12.3	183	121.0	1.5	586	22.2	288.00	141	432	66.7	67.9
1992	33.4	180	147.6	1.2	477	9.6	84.60	213	297	28.5	15.9
1991	51.3	135	71.1	1.9	411	26.4	Nil	331	337	Nil	35.4
1990	45.8	124	94.5	1.3	374	22.2	22.00	257	279	7.9	28.1
1989	32.0	114	31.8	3.6	368	18.9	Nil	330	330	Nil	21.7
1988	12.6	84	47.0	1.8	315	15.4	Nil	265	265	Nil	17.5
1987	0.2	59	25.4	2.3	322	11.8	1.12	296	297	0.4	12.7
1986	3.6	46	15.2	3.0	276	12.9	0.53	260	261	0.2	14.1
1985	NA	NA	NA	NA	85	28.0	0.70	70	71	1.0	34.3

Data as orig. reptd. 1. Data for National Health Laboratories only. NA-Not Available.

[1]Net Sales (Million $)

Quarter:	1995	1994	1993	1992
Mar.	244	185	200	176
Jun.	367	204	197	181
Sep.		249	195	184
Dec.		235	169	180
		873	761	721

Net sales in the first six months of 1995 were $611.1 million. Pre-tax income was $51.2 million; after taxes at 45.3%, net income was $28 million. ($0.29 a share). These results are prior to a $75 million charge related to restructuring and other provisions, and an extraordinary loss of $8.3 million related to the early extinguishment of debt. Furthermore, results reflect the April 28, 1995 merger of NHL and RBL, and are not comparable to prior periods. After the special change the loss in the period before extraordinary items was $18.8 million ($0.20).

[1]Common Share Earnings ($)

Quarter:	1995	1994	1993	1992
Mar.	0.15	0.10	0.36	0.31
Jun.	0.14	0.16	0.37	0.33
Sep.		Nil	0.43	0.32
Dec.		0.10	0.10	d0.53
		0.36	1.26	0.43

Dividend Data

In conjunction with the merger, a dividend of 0.16308 warrant per each outstanding share of NHL stock was paid April 28, 1995, to holders of record April 21.

Finances

Total funds of $474,700,000 were paid to the shareholders of National Health Laboratories in connection with the merger. This amount was paid through a cash contribution of $288,000,000 from National Health Laboratories, a $135,651,000 contribution from a unit of Hoffman-LaRoche Inc., and $51,048,900 from warrants purchased by Hoffman-LaRoche.

In connnection with the merger, NHL expected to obtain bank financing consisting of not more than $800,000,000 of a six year amortizing senior term loan facility, and not more than $450,000,000 as a senior five year revolving credit facility.

Capitalization

Long Term Debt: $900,000,000 apx. (6/95).

Common Stock: 122,900,000 shs. ($0.01 par).

1. Pr. to 1995, data for National Health Laboratories only. d-Deficit.

Office—358 South Main Street, Burlington, NC 27215. **Tel**—(800) 222-7566. **Chrmn**—J. R. Maher. **Pres & CEO**—J. B. Powell. **Exec VP & CFO**—H. D. Cochrane. **VP-Secy**—B. Smith. **Dirs**—J. L. Belingard, J. R. Maher, T. P. McMahon, J. B. Powell, L. G. Robinson. **Transfer Agent & Registrar**—American Stock Transfer & Trust Co., NYC. **Incorporated** in Delaware in 1971.

STANDARD & POOR'S

STOCK REPORTS

Lancaster Colony

NASDAQ Symbol **LANC**

In S&P MidCap 400

24-SEP-95 **Industry:** Food

Summary: This company produces specialty foods, aftermarket and original equipment automotive products, and glassware and candle products.

Quantitative Evaluations

Outlook (1 Lowest—5 Highest)
• **2+**

Fair Value
• **32⅝**

Risk
• **Low**

Earn./Div. Rank
• **A**

Technical Eval.
• **Bullish** since 3/95

Rel. Strength Rank (1 Lowest—99 Highest)
• **33**

Insider Activity
• **Unfavorable**

Recent Price • 35¾
52 Wk Range • 37¾-28¼
Yield • 1.7%
12-Mo. P/E • 15.2

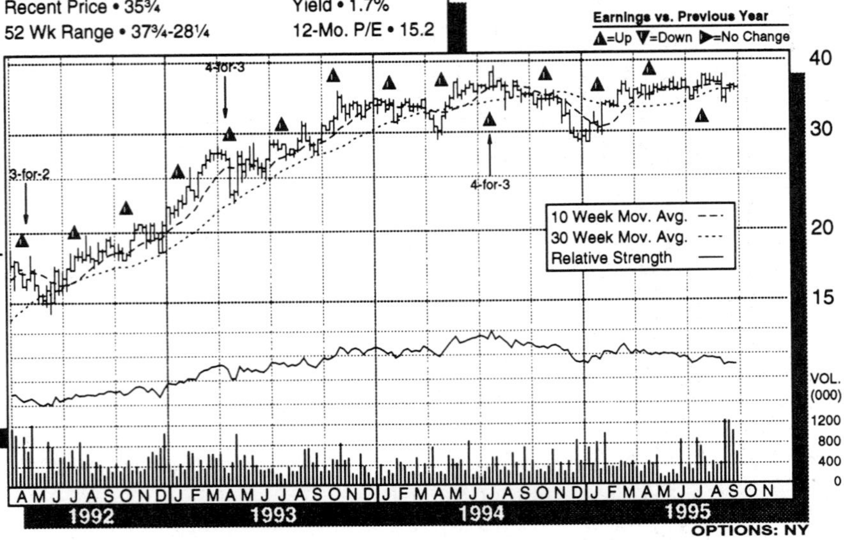

OPTIONS: NY

Business Profile - 24-SEP-95

The impact of increased raw material costs has been pronounced within the automotive segment, with aluminum, rubber and resin-based plastic materials prices climbing in excess of the company's ability to boost related sales prices. Increased costs for soybean oil, a major ingredient of the specialty foods segment, also hurt results. However, the company expects declining raw material costs to aid earnings growth in fiscal 1996.

Operational Review - 24-SEP-95

Net sales advanced 10% in the fiscal year ended June 30, 1995. Results were aided by strength in the glassware and candles group. Net income rose 18% despite large raw material cost increases throughout the year. However, by year end, there were signs that raw material costs were easing. Lancaster recently raised its quarterly dividend for the 33rd consecutive year.

Stock Performance - 22-SEP-95

In the past 30 trading days, LANC's shares have declined 2%, compared to a 5% rise in the S&P 500. Average trading volume for the past five days was 122,280 shares, compared with the 40-day moving average of 151,718 shares.

Key Stock Statistics

Dividend Rate/Share	0.60	Shareholders	15,000
Shs. outstg. (M)	29.8	Market cap. (B)	$ 1.1
Avg. daily vol. (M)	0.227	Inst. holdings	52%
Tang. Bk. Value/Share	6.96	Insider holdings	NA
Beta	1.55		

Value of $10,000 invested 5 years ago: $ 43,168

Fiscal Year Ending Jun. 30

	1995	% Change	1994	% Change	1993	% Change
Revenues (Million $)						
1Q	189.1	9%	172.8	14%	152.0	15%
2Q	225.3	17%	192.8	13%	171.0	16%
3Q	192.0	12%	171.5	15%	149.0	14%
4Q	188.8	2%	184.7	16%	158.8	9%
Yr.	795.1	10%	721.7	14%	630.6	13%
Income (Million $)						
1Q	15.32	18%	13.02	24%	10.54	40%
2Q	19.98	29%	15.52	29%	12.04	54%
3Q	16.41	24%	13.24	37%	9.63	52%
4Q	18.81	4%	18.08	29%	14.02	32%
Yr.	70.52	18%	59.86	29%	46.23	43%
Earnings Per Share ($)						
1Q	0.51	19%	0.43	24%	0.35	39%
2Q	0.66	29%	0.51	28%	0.40	51%
3Q	0.55	28%	0.43	37%	0.32	50%
4Q	0.63	5%	0.60	31%	0.46	30%
Yr.	2.35	19%	1.97	30%	1.52	42%

Next earnings report expected: early November

Lancaster Colony

Business Summary - 22-SEP-95

Lancaster Colony Corporation makes specialty foods, automotive products, and glassware and candles. Contributions in fiscal 1994 were:

	Sales	Profits
Specialty foods	40%	40%
Automotive	33%	30%
Glassware & candles	27%	30%

Specialty food products made and sold by Lancaster include salad dressings and sauces marketed under the Marzetti, Pfeiffer and Girard's brand names; Mountain Top and Reames frozen unbaked pies; hearth-baked frozen breads marketed under the New York Frozen Foods name; refrigerated chip and produce dips, dairy snacks and desserts sold under the Oak Lake Farms, Allen and Marzetti names; Inn Maid and Amish Kitchen premium dry egg noodles; Reames frozen noodles, pastas and breaded specialty items; and caviar under the Romanoff brand name.

The company produces and markets rubber, vinyl and carpeted car mats for both original equipment manufacturers and the auto aftermarket; pickup truck bed mats, running boards, bed liners and other accessories for pickup trucks and vans; truck and trailer splash guards and quarter fenders; accessories such as tissue holders, litter caddies and oil drain pans; and new car components. Auto aftermarket products are sold primarily through mass merchandisers and automotive outlets under the name Rubber Queen. Ford Motor Co. and General Motors Corp. have been significant purchasers of this segment's products.

Glass products include a broad range of machine pressed and machine blown consumer glassware and technical glass products such as cathode ray tubes, lighting components, lenses and silvered reflectors. The company's consumer glassware products include a diverse line of decorative and ornamental items such as tumblers, bowls, pitchers, jars and barware, for which the most important trademarks are Indiana Glass, Tiara, Colony and Fostoria. It also sells glass vases and containers under the Brody name, as well as under private labels. In addition, the segment offers candles in all popular sizes, shapes and scents, under the Candle-lite name.

Important Developments

Aug. '95—Management noted that top and bottom line growth for fiscal 1995 was generated primarily from the company's glassware and candles group. Lancaster expects sales and earnings to continue to grow during fiscal 1996, aided by an anticipated drop in raw material costs.

Capitalization

Long Term Debt: $32,082,000 (3/95).

Per Share Data ($) (Year Ended Jun. 30)

	1995	1994	1993	1992	1991	1990
Tangible Bk. Val.	NA	7.52	6.34	5.25	4.55	4.18
Cash Flow	NA	2.71	2.15	1.68	1.25	1.05
Earnings	2.35	1.97	1.52	1.07	0.69	0.51
Dividends	0.71	0.44	0.37	0.32	0.30	0.28
Payout Ratio	30%	22%	25%	30%	43%	55%
Prices - High	37¾	39¼	35⅝	22	15¼	9½
- Low	28¾	28¼	20⅝	13¾	5¾	4⅞
P/E Ratio - High	16	20	24	21	22	19
- Low	12	14	14	13	8	10

Income Statement Analysis (Million $)

	1994	%Chg	1993	%Chg	1992	%Chg	1991
Revs.	722	14%	631	13%	556	11%	500
Oper. Inc.	121	24%	97.5	24%	78.5	26%	62.5
Depr.	20.1	3%	19.5	4%	18.8	7%	17.5
Int. Exp.	2.8	-21%	3.6	-35%	5.6	-36%	8.7
Pretax Inc.	98.1	32%	74.3	38%	53.9	59%	33.8
Eff. Tax Rate	39%	—	38%	—	40%	—	37%
Net Inc.	59.9	30%	46.2	43%	32.4	53%	21.2

Balance Sheet & Other Fin. Data (Million $)

	1994	1993	1992	1991	1990	1989
Cash	30.4	16.5	7.4	5.3	0.7	3.2
Curr. Assets	238	188	172	168	183	172
Total Assets	355	302	290	287	309	290
Curr. Liab.	74.0	62.0	75.0	75.0	107	93.0
LT Debt	32.9	34.6	40.0	57.2	60.2	45.3
Common Eqty.	237	192	159	139	129	138
Total Cap.	273	232	206	204	202	197
Cap. Exp.	23.5	18.9	17.0	13.5	21.2	18.1
Cash Flow	82.3	65.7	51.2	38.7	33.3	38.6

Ratio Analysis

	1994	1993	1992	1991	1990	1989
Curr. Ratio	3.2	3.1	2.3	2.3	1.7	1.9
% LT Debt of Cap.	12.1	14.9	19.4	28.0	29.8	23.0
% Net Inc.of Revs.	8.3	7.3	5.8	4.2	3.2	4.5
% Ret. on Assets	18.2	15.6	11.3	7.2	5.4	7.8
% Ret. on Equity	27.9	26.3	21.7	15.9	12.2	16.5

Dividend Data —Cash has been paid in each year since 1963.

Amt. of Div. $	Date Decl.	Ex-Div. Date	Stock of Record	Payment Date
0.120	Aug. 25	Sep. 02	Sep. 09	Sep. 30 '94
0.140	Nov. 21	Dec. 05	Dec. 09	Dec. 30 '94
0.140	Feb. 23	Mar. 06	Mar. 10	Mar. 31 '95
0.150	May. 25	Jun. 06	Jun. 09	Jun. 30 '95
0.150	Aug. 31	Sep. 07	Sep. 11	Sep. 29 '95

Data as orig. reptd.; bef. results of disc. opers. and/or spec. items. Per share data adj. for stk. divs. as of ex-div. date. E-Estimated. NA-Not Available. NM-Not Meaningful. NR-Not Ranked.

Office—37 W. Broad St., Columbus, OH 43215. **Tel**—(614) 224-7141. **Chrmn & CEO**—J. B. Gerlach. **Pres, COO & Secy**—J. B. Gerlach, Jr. **Treas**—J. L. Boylan. **Dirs**—F. W. Batsch, R. L. Fox, J. B. Gerlach, J. B. Gerlach, Jr., M. S. Halpern, R. S. Hamilton, E. H. Jennings, R. R. Murphey Jr., H. M. O'Neill Jr., D. J. Zuver. **Transfer Agent & Registrar**—American Stock Transfer & Trust Co., Brooklyn, N.Y. **Incorporated** in Delaware in 1961; reincorporated in Ohio in 1992. **Empl**-5,600. **S&P Analyst:** Philip D. Wohl

STANDARD & POOR'S

STOCK REPORTS

Lance, Inc.

NASDAQ Symbol **LNCE**

In S&P MidCap 400

14-OCT-95 **Industry:** Food

Summary: This manufacturer of snack foods and bakery products has customers located in 36 states and the District of Columbia.

S&P Opinion: Avoid (★★)

Recent Price • 17¼ | Yield • 5.6%

52 Wk Range • 20-16¼ | 12-Mo. P/E • 23.6

Quantitative Evaluations

Outlook
(1 Lowest—5 Highest)
• **2+**

Fair Value
• **15⅞**

Risk
• **Low**

Earn./Div. Rank
• **B+**

Technical Eval.
• **Bearish** since 5/95

Rel. Strength Rank
(1 Lowest—99 Highest)
• **30**

Insider Activity
• **NA**

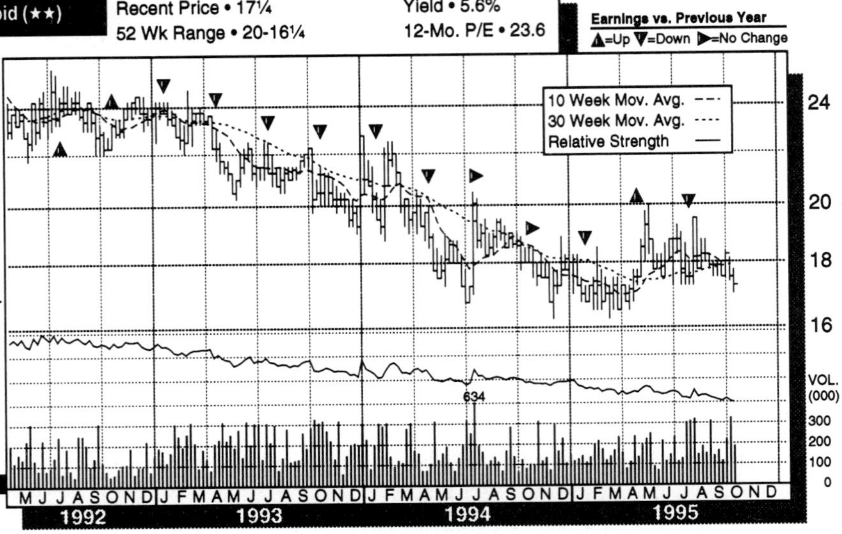

Overview - 13-OCT-95

A rebound in unit volume at the Vista Bakery operations, expanded supermarket distribution and increased penetration of the West Coast market are expected to contribute to low single-digit sales increases in coming periods. Margins have been weak in recent quarters and are likely to continue to be pressured by an unfavorable product mix shift and high production and insurance costs. However, improved operating efficiencies and better pricing will contribute to a modest rebound in earnings in 1996. Long-term profitability should benefit from consolidation in the baking industry. Despite quarterly dividends that have exceeded per share earnings (but not cash flow), we believe the controlling family is unlikely to allow the above-average dividend to be cut.

Valuation - 13-OCT-95

The shares of this manufacturer of snack foods and bakery products have declined more than 35% from a high of $28.25 in 1991, as annual earnings have declined more than 30% from their record levels of 1990. In light of continued unfavorable competitive conditions, we do not believe the shares' recent level of approximately 22X our 1996 EPS estimate of $0.80 is justified. Although the hefty dividend and a one million share repurchase authorization (about 3% of shares outstanding) may continue to support the shares, we believe the stock will continue to underperform the market.

Key Stock Statistics

S&P EPS Est. 1995	0.74	Tang. Bk. Value/Share	7.57
P/E on S&P Est. 1995	23.3	Beta	0.18
S&P EPS Est. 1996	0.80	Shareholders	5,400
Dividend Rate/Share	0.96	Market cap. (B)	$0.525
Shs. outstg. (M)	30.4	Inst. holdings	36%
Avg. daily vol. (M)	0.053	Insider holdings	NA

Value of $10,000 invested 5 years ago: $ 9,353

Fiscal Year Ending Dec. 31

	1995	% Change	1994	% Change	1993	% Change
Revenues (Million $)						
1Q	112.7	4%	108.1	2%	106.4	1%
2Q	114.3	-3%	117.5	4%	113.2	3%
3Q	107.2	NM	107.6	1%	106.1	1%
4Q	—	—	154.7	5%	147.0	4%
Yr.	—	—	488.0	3%	472.8	3%
Income (Million $)						
1Q	5.98	3%	5.79	-22%	7.44	-25%
2Q	4.86	-42%	8.45	NM	8.44	-16%
3Q	4.13	-24%	5.43	-4%	5.64	-36%
4Q	—	—	7.31	-24%	9.66	-7%
Yr.	—	—	26.98	-13%	31.18	-20%
Earnings Per Share ($)						
1Q	0.20	5%	0.19	-21%	0.24	-25%
2Q	0.16	-41%	0.27	NM	0.27	-16%
3Q	0.14	-22%	0.18	NM	0.18	-36%
4Q	E0.23	-4%	0.24	-23%	0.31	-6%
Yr.	E0.74	-16%	0.88	-12%	1.00	-20%

Next earnings report expected: late February

Lance, Inc.

Business Summary - 13-OCT-95

Lance, Inc. manufactures and distributes a variety of snacks and bread-basket items.

Principal snack products include cracker sandwiches, cookie sandwiches, peanuts, potato chips, corn chips, popcorn, cakes, cookies, candies, chewing gum, beef snacks and sausages. New products introduced in 1994 included Swiss Roll, Fat Free Apple Bar and Reduced Fat Toastee. Principal bread-basket items are wafers, crackers and breadsticks, individually packed and sold to restaurants and similar institutions.

Net sales and other operating revenue in recent years were derived as follows:

	1994	1993	1992
Snack items	89%	88%	88%
Bread-basket items	8%	9%	9%
Other	3%	3%	3%

Snack foods are sold through Lance's own sales force to convenience stores, independent and chain supermarkets, discount stores, military commissaries, restaurants, schools, hospitals and other customers in 36 states and the District of Columbia, principally east of the Mississippi River and in the midwestern and southwestern U.S.

About 79% of 1994 revenues were derived from company-packaged products, with the balance purchased from others and resold by Lance. A significant portion of output is sold through vending machines, which are made available to customers on a rental, sale or commission basis. Restaurants and similar institutions are the main customers for the bread-basket items.

Midwest Biscuit Co. manufactures cookies and crackers for both private label and its own Vista label. Sales are made primarily to wholesale grocers, supermarket chains and distributors throughout the U.S., with the majority of business in the Midwest.

Wholly owned Caronuts, Inc. is a 12-million-pound peanut-buying station in Boykins, Va.

Important Developments

Oct. '95—Lance said lower unit volume at the Vista Bakery plants, reflecting intense competition, was the primary cause of the year to year reduction in third quarter revenues. Higher insurance, raw material and packaging costs, and the lower sales contributed to the decline in net income.

Feb. '95—Directors authorized the repurchase of up to one million of the company's common shares. Under a prior authorization, 869,500 shares had been repurchased.

Capitalization

Long Term Debt: None (6/95).

Per Share Data ($)

(Year Ended Dec. 31)

	1994	1993	1992	1991	1990	1989
Tangible Bk. Val.	7.67	7.97	8.06	7.75	7.42	6.97
Cash Flow	1.67	1.79	1.99	1.90	2.10	2.01
Earnings	0.88	1.00	1.25	1.21	1.46	1.42
Dividends	0.96	0.96	0.92	0.88	0.82	0.72
Payout Ratio	109%	96%	74%	73%	58%	51%
Prices - High	22¾	24¾	27¼	28¼	27¼	25
- Low	16¼	19	21¼	20	19¼	17¼
P/E Ratio - High	26	25	22	23	19	18
- Low	18	19	17	17	13	12

Income Statement Analysis (Million $)

	1994	%Chg	1993	%Chg	1992	%Chg	1991
Revs.	488	3%	473	3%	461	2%	450
Oper. Inc.	64.5	-8%	69.9	-10%	77.6	7%	72.8
Depr.	24.5	NM	24.7	6%	23.2	6%	21.8
Int. Exp.	Nil	—	Nil	—	Nil	—	Nil
Pretax Inc.	44.3	-13%	50.7	-16%	60.2	3%	58.7
Eff. Tax Rate	39%	—	39%	—	35%	—	36%
Net Inc.	27.0	-13%	31.2	-20%	39.1	4%	37.7

Balance Sheet & Other Fin. Data (Million $)

	1994	1993	1992	1991	1990	1989
Cash	45.9	39.6	59.0	75.9	60.7	64.4
Curr. Assets	123	110	128	139	126	130
Total Assets	297	308	313	300	289	276
Curr. Liab.	32.9	31.5	32.2	29.5	28.6	28.7
LT Debt	Nil	Nil	Nil	Nil	Nil	Nil
Common Eqty.	233	247	252	242	232	220
Total Cap.	253	267	278	268	257	245
Cap. Exp.	17.9	22.4	51.0	21.4	47.6	30.2
Cash Flow	51.5	55.9	62.4	59.5	65.9	63.5

Ratio Analysis

	1994	1993	1992	1991	1990	1989
Curr. Ratio	3.8	3.5	4.0	4.7	4.4	4.5
% LT Debt of Cap.	Nil	Nil	Nil	Nil	Nil	Nil
% Net Inc.of Revs.	5.5	6.6	8.5	8.4	10.3	10.4
% Ret. on Assets	9.0	10.1	12.8	12.8	16.3	16.9
% Ret. on Equity	11.3	12.5	15.8	15.9	20.3	21.4

Dividend Data —Except in 1944, cash has been paid each year since 1935. A dividend reinvestment plan is available.

Amt. of Div. $	Date Decl.	Ex-Div. Date	Stock of Record	Payment Date
0.240	Oct. 04	Oct. 26	Nov. 01	Nov. 15 '94
0.240	Jan. 17	Jan. 26	Feb. 01	Feb. 15 '95
0.240	Apr. 21	Apr. 25	May. 01	May. 15 '95
0.240	Jul. 18	Jul. 28	Aug. 01	Aug. 15 '95
0.240	Oct. 10	Oct. 30	Nov. 01	Nov. 15 '95

Data as orig. reptd.; bef. results of disc. opers. and/or spec. items. Per share data adj. for stk. divs. as of ex-div. date. E-Estimated. NA-Not Available. NM-Not Meaningful. NR-Not Ranked.

Office—8600 South Boulevard, P.O. Box 32368, Charlotte, NC 28232. **Tel**—(704) 554-1421. **Pres & CEO**—P. A. Stroup III. **Treas**—E. D. Leake. **Secy, Treas & Investor Contact**—James W. Helms Jr. **Dirs**—A. T. Dickson, J. W. Disher, J. H. Hance, Jr., W. R. Holland, T. B. Horack, S.C. Lea, E. D. Leake, W. B. Meacham, G. R. Melvin, L. Robinson, R. V. Sisk, A. F. Sloan, G. K. Smith, V. S. Sutton, R. G. Swain, I. Tidwell, N. Van Every McLaurin, — S. H. Van Every Jr., S. L. Van Every, R. A. Zimmerman. **Transfer Agent**—Wachovia Bank & Trust Co., Winston-Salem, N.C. **Incorporated** in North Carolina in 1926. **Empl-** 5,818. **S&P Analyst:** Efraim Levy

STANDARD & POOR'S
STOCK REPORTS

Lands' End

NYSE Symbol **LE**
In S&P MidCap 400

13-OCT-95 **Industry:** Retail Stores

Summary: Lands' End is a specialty mail order retailer of traditionally styled recreational and informal clothing, accessories, shoes and soft luggage.

S&P Opinion: Avoid (★★)

Recent Price • 15
52 Wk Range • 19½-13
Yield • Nil
12-Mo. P/E • 16.9

Quantitative Evaluations
Outlook (1 Lowest—5 Highest)
• **3-**
Fair Value
• **15⅛**
Risk
• **Average**
Earn./Div. Rank
• **B+**

Technical Eval.
• **Bearish** since 10/95
Rel. Strength Rank (1 Lowest—99 Highest)
• **24**
Insider Activity
• **NA**

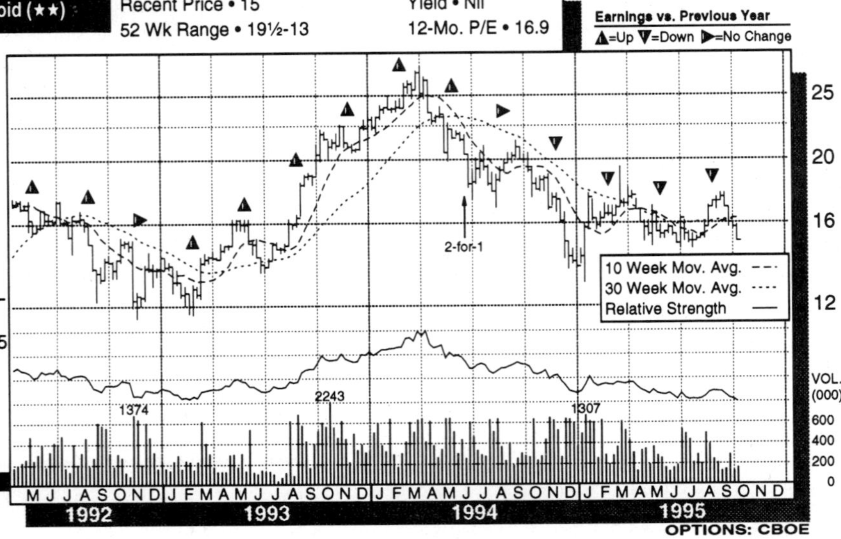

OPTIONS: CBOE

Overview - 13-OCT-95

Sales should increase only moderately in fiscal 1995-96, reflecting competitive pricing by other retailers. But improved merchandise offerings and newer specialty catalogs will boost customer orders. Gross margins should widen due to growth in higher margin businesses and lower merchandise costs, primarily as a result of improvements in sourcing and better inventory management. Expense ratios should continue to rise due to increased catalog mailing expenses - postage and paper - and startup costs of overseas operations and new ventures. Earnings per share should reflect fewer shares outstanding. As of June 1995, 6.4 million common shares had been repurchased under a 1989 authorization to repurchase a total of 8.2 million shares.

Valuation - 13-OCT-95

Disappointing apparel sales has resulted in downward revisions of earnings estimates for 1995-96 to about level with last year. A value conscious consumer and sharp pricing competition from other apparel retailers to gain market share has created a highly competitive environment. Although we anticipate improved sales in the second half of this year, expenses will grow faster than sales reflecting both the lack of pricing power and the investment in new businesses for long-term growth. As a result, we believe that the shares will underperform the market in the near-term.

Key Stock Statistics

S&P EPS Est. 1996	0.95	Tang. Bk. Value/Share	5.31
P/E on S&P Est. 1996	15.8	Beta	0.88
S&P EPS Est. 1997	1.20	Shareholders	3,100
Dividend Rate/Share	Nil	Market cap. (B)	$0.513
Shs. outstg. (M)	33.9	Inst. holdings	23%
Avg. daily vol. (M)	0.042	Insider holdings	NA

Value of $10,000 invested 5 years ago: $ 15,519

Fiscal Year Ending Jan. 31

	1996	% Change	1995	% Change	1994	% Change
Revenues (Million $)						
1Q	207.1	11%	187.0	20%	156.3	11%
2Q	189.1	5%	179.8	19%	151.1	9%
3Q	—	—	246.2	14%	215.1	23%
4Q	—	—	379.0	9%	347.5	24%
Yr.	—	—	992.1	14%	870.0	19%
Income (Million $)						
1Q	1.31	-73%	4.88	15%	4.24	NM
2Q	1.69	-50%	3.41	-4%	3.55	42%
3Q	—	—	3.83	-52%	7.98	44%
4Q	—	—	23.97	-10%	26.66	26%
Yr.	—	—	36.10	-15%	42.43	27%
Earnings Per Share ($)						
1Q	0.04	-71%	0.14	17%	0.12	4%
2Q	0.05	-50%	0.10	NM	0.10	43%
3Q	E0.08	-27%	0.11	-50%	0.22	42%
4Q	E0.78	13%	0.69	-7%	0.74	25%
Yr.	E0.95	-8%	1.03	-13%	1.18	28%

Next earnings report expected: early November

Lands' End

Business Summary - 13-OCT-95

Lands' End is a specialty mail order retailer; merchandise is offered through regular mailings of its catalog. The company's products include traditionally styled recreational and informal clothing mostly for men and women, accessories, shoes and soft luggage. Target mailings of the company's specialty catalogs are made, including a children's catalog, a dress shirt and tie catalog, and a specialty catalog focusing on bed and bath products. Lands' End is also pursuing opportunities in the U.K., Canada and Japan. In March 1993, the company purchased a majority interest in The Territory Ahead, a California-based upscale casual clothing catalog for men and women.

The growth of the specialty mail order catalog industry can be attributed to more widespread use of credit cards, the use of toll-free telephone lines, the increase in the number of working women, and new applications of computer technology. Customers may purchase merchandise by using a toll-free number 24 hours a day, seven days a week (except Christmas). About 80% of current catalog orders are placed by telephone.

Efforts undertaken to improve sales have included new products, improving product quality, increasing the number of catalogs mailed, and utilizing computer applications to refine the customer list. The company's mailing list consisted of 20.4 million people at the end of 1994-95.

During 1994-95, LE mailed 12 issues of its regular catalog with an average of 167 pages per issue and mailed 191 million catalogs, including specialty catalogs and abridged issues.

All goods are purchased from independent manufacturers (except for soft luggage), mostly in the U.S. LE determines product specifications, including fabrics and styling. Overstocks and end-of-season closeouts are sold at reduced prices through catalogs and 15 outlet stores.

Important Developments

Aug. '95—Net sales in the second quarter of 1995-96 rose 5.1%, year-to-year, reflecting continued growth in international and new businessess. Gross margin widened to 43.8% of sales due to strong growth in higher margin businesses and lower merchandise costs. Liquidations of excess inventory were about 9% of net sales, down from 10% a year earlier. SG&A expenses increased to 42.6% of sales from 39.8% a year ago, as a result of higher paper prices and postal rates and lower sales per catalog mailed in the U.S. International and new businesses experienced stronger growth rates, but operating costs are higher than the company's other businesses. Second quarter ending inventory was about $200 million, compared with almost $195 million a year ago.

Capitalization

Long Term Debt: None (7/95).

Per Share Data ($) (Year Ended Jan. 31)

	1995	1994	1993	1992	1991	1990
Tangible Bk. Val.	5.43	4.94	3.86	3.43	3.04	2.88
Cash Flow	1.32	1.41	1.14	0.96	0.55	0.85
Earnings	1.03	1.18	0.93	0.76	0.38	0.73
Dividends	Nil	0.10	0.10	0.10	0.10	0.10
Payout Ratio	Nil	8%	11%	13%	26%	14%
Cal. Yrs.	1994	1993	1992	1991	1990	1989
Prices - High	27¾	23¾	19	15¼	10½	17⅞
- Low	13⅝	11⅝	11½	6¾	4½	9½
P/E Ratio - High	27	20	20	20	27	25
- Low	13	10	12	9	12	13

Income Statement Analysis (Million $)

	1995	%Chg	1994	%Chg	1993	%Chg	1992
Revs.	992	14%	870	19%	734	7%	683
Oper. Inc.	73.6	-6%	78.6	24%	63.5	12%	56.6
Depr.	10.3	25%	8.2	4%	7.9	6%	7.4
Int. Exp.	1.8	NM	0.4	-73%	1.3	-14%	1.5
Pretax Inc.	59.7	-14%	69.6	29%	54.0	14%	47.5
Eff. Tax Rate	40%	—	39%	—	38%	—	40%
Net Inc.	36.1	-15%	42.4	27%	33.5	17%	28.7

Balance Sheet & Other Fin. Data (Million $)

	1995	1994	1993	1992	1991	1990
Cash	5.4	21.6	22.8	1.4	27.3	8.3
Curr. Assets	198	192	135	131	108	100
Total Assets	298	274	209	206	185	167
Curr. Liab.	103	91.0	67.3	74.5	60.8	43.9
LT Debt	Nil	Nil	Nil	1.7	3.3	5.0
Common Eqty.	189	177	139	127	117	115
Total Cap.	195	183	142	131	125	123
Cap. Exp.	NA	18.7	8.6	5.4	17.7	25.2
Cash Flow	46.4	50.7	41.4	36.2	21.8	34.3

Ratio Analysis

	1995	1994	1993	1992	1991	1990
Curr. Ratio	1.9	2.1	2.0	1.8	1.8	2.3
% LT Debt of Cap.	Nil	Nil	Nil	1.3	2.7	4.1
% Net Inc.of Revs.	3.6	4.9	4.6	4.2	2.4	5.3
% Ret. on Assets	12.8	17.6	16.3	15.0	8.5	18.3
% Ret. on Equity	20.0	26.8	25.5	24.1	13.0	28.2

Dividend Data —Prior to their elimination in May 1994, annual cash dividends had been paid since 1987. A 2-for-1 stock split was effected in June 1994.

Data as orig. reptd.; bef. results of disc. opers. and/or spec. items. Per share data adj. for stk. divs. as of ex-div. date. E-Estimated. NA-Not Available. NM-Not Meaningful. NR-Not Ranked.

Office—Lands' End Lane, Dodgeville, WI 53595. **Tel**—(608) 935-9341. **Chrmn**—G. C. Comer. **Vice Chrmn**—R. C. Anderson. **Pres & CEO**—M. Smith. **EVP, CFO & COO**—S. A. Orum. **VP & Investor Contact**—Charlotte LaComb. **Dirs**—R. C. Anderson, G. C. Comer, D. B. Heller, H. G. Krane, J. N. Latter, M. Smith. **Transfer Agent & Registrar**—Firstar Trust Co., Milwaukee. **Incorporated** in Delaware in 1986. **Empl**-5,400. **S&P Analyst:** Karen J. Sack, CFA

Lawson Products

NASDAQ Symbol **LAWS**
In S&P MidCap 400

25-SEP-95 **Industry:** Machinery

Summary: This company distributes replacement fasteners and other expendable parts and supplies used for the repair and maintenance of capital equipment, buildings and automobiles.

S&P Opinion: Hold (★★★)

Recent Price • 26¾ | 52 Wk Range • 28½-24¾ | Yield • 1.9% | 12-Mo. P/E • 15.6

Quantitative Evaluations

Outlook (1 Lowest—5 Highest)
• **1+**

Fair Value
• **21⅛**

Risk
• **Low**

Earn./Div. Rank
• **A-**

Technical Eval.
• **Bearish** since 10/94

Rel. Strength Rank (1 Lowest—99 Highest)
• **24**

Insider Activity
• **NA**

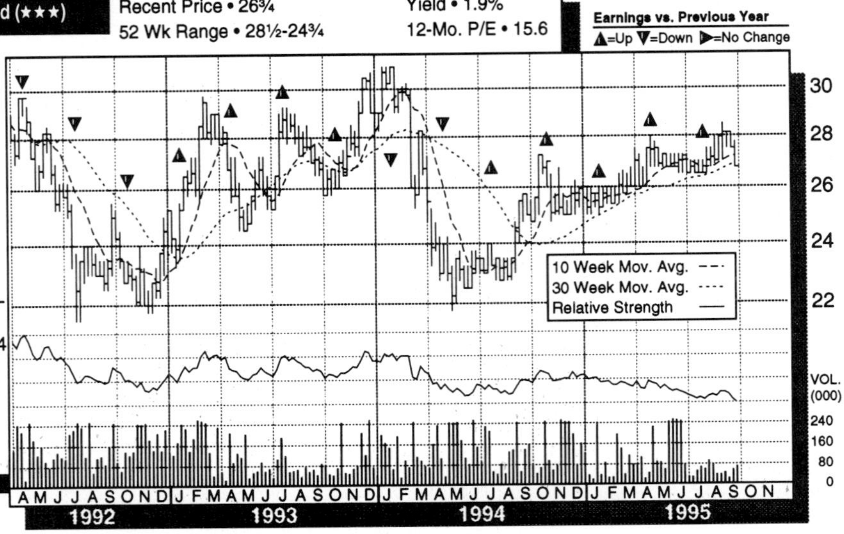

Overview - 25-SEP-95

Net sales should increase at a mid single-digit rate for the remainder of 1995 and for 1996, reflecting modest strength in all of the business segments. Revenues will be primarily lifted by double-digit growth in the specialty chemical and welding equipment and supply distribution subsidiaries, and by the improvement in the international group, led by the continuing recovery in the Canadian operation. Although the percentage increase in SG&A expenses will continue to exceed that of sales, margins should stay flat on the greater volume and the high degree of relatively fixed costs. The balance sheet remains strong, with cash flow being used to add to investment income and to enhance earnings per share growth through the ongoing stock repurchase program.

Valuation - 25-SEP-95

Although the stock has slipped from its recent high, the shares have rebounded more than 20% from the two-year low reached in the second quarter of 1994. However, the stock has been essentially trading well within its 1995 range of \$25 to \$28, roughly the same level as at the beginning of the year, which suggests that the market is expecting a slower rate of growth and has fully discounted the impact of the share repurchase program on projected earnings. Although LAWS has been trading towards the lower end of its five-year P/E range, the shares seem to be fairly valued given the company's current growth prospects.

Key Stock Statistics

S&P EPS Est. 1995	1.70	Tang. Bk. Value/Share	10.09
P/E on S&P Est. 1995	15.7	Beta	0.61
S&P EPS Est. 1996	1.90	Shareholders	1,400
Dividend Rate/Share	0.52	Market cap. (B)	$0.316
Shs. outstg. (M)	11.8	Inst. holdings	35%
Avg. daily vol. (M)	0.009	Insider holdings	NA

Value of $10,000 invested 5 years ago: $ 13,065

Fiscal Year Ending Dec. 31

	1995	% Change	1994	% Change	1993	% Change
Revenues (Million $)						
1Q	54.85	10%	49.77	6%	47.05	4%
2Q	56.10	4%	53.75	8%	49.59	4%
3Q	—	—	55.54	11%	49.84	4%
4Q	—	—	54.04	10%	49.25	7%
Yr.	—	—	213.1	9%	195.7	5%
Income (Million $)						
1Q	5.02	23%	4.07	-11%	4.59	40%
2Q	5.28	2%	5.16	7%	4.82	18%
3Q	—	—	5.25	13%	4.66	23%
4Q	—	—	6.05	64%	3.69	-12%
Yr.	—	—	20.52	15%	17.77	16%
Earnings Per Share ($)						
1Q	0.40	33%	0.30	-12%	0.34	42%
2Q	0.43	13%	0.38	6%	0.36	20%
3Q	E0.45	13%	0.40	18%	0.34	21%
4Q	E0.42	-11%	0.47	74%	0.27	-13%
Yr.	E1.70	10%	1.55	17%	1.32	17%

Next earnings report expected: late October

Lawson Products

Business Summary - 18-SEP-95

Lawson Products distributes expendable maintenance, repair and replacement products to approximately 200,000 customers. All products are manufactured by others to company specifications, with about 90% sold under the Lawson label.

Revenue contributions by product line were:

	1994	1993
Industrial supplies	53%	52%
Fasteners, fittings & related parts	41%	42%
Automotive & equipment maintenance parts	6%	6%

In 1994, Canadian operations accounted for less than 3% of total sales, while operations in the UK and Mexico each accounted for less than 1%.

Industrial supplies include hoses and hose fittings, lubricants, cleansers, adhesives and other chemicals, as well as files, drills, welding products and other shop supplies. Fasteners, fittings and related parts include screws, nuts, rivets and other fasteners. Auto and equipment maintenance parts include primary wiring, connectors and other electrical supplies and exhaust and other auto parts.

Sales breakdown by markets in recent years was:

	1994	1993
Heavy-duty equipment maintenance	45%	46%
In-plant & building maintenance	41%	40%
Passenger car maintenance	12%	12%

Heavy-duty equipment maintenance customers include operators of trucks, buses, agricultural implements, construction and road-building equipment, mining, and logging and drilling equipment. The in-plant and building maintenance market includes plants engaged in a broad range of manufacturing and processing activities, as well as institutions such as hospitals, universities, school districts and government agencies. Passenger car maintenance customers include auto service center chains, independent garages, auto dealers, and car rental agencies.

Important Developments

Jul. '95—Lawson said it had purchased 741,500 shares (of the 1,000,000 authorized) in the first half of 1995, at a cost of $19,541,000. The company said its nearly 24% year-to-year gain in earnings per share for the first half of 1995 was aided by insurance proceeds (approximately $0.03 a share) in the first quarter and its common stock repurchase program (8.8% fewer shares were outstanding). The 13% increase in second quarter EPS was aided by 9.3% fewer shares than the year-earlier period.

Capitalization

Long Term Debt: None (6/95).

Per Share Data ($)

(Year Ended Dec. 31)

	1994	1993	1992	1991	1990	1989
Tangible Bk. Val.	10.41	10.37	9.50	8.87	8.04	6.74
Cash Flow	1.78	1.55	1.35	1.41	1.82	1.76
Earnings	1.55	1.32	1.13	1.23	1.67	1.61
Dividends	0.48	0.44	0.40	0.40	0.37	0.33
Payout Ratio	31%	33%	35%	33%	22%	20%
Prices - High	31	30¾	31¾	35¼	30½	26
- Low	21¾	23¼	21½	22½	22¾	18½
P/E Ratio - High	20	23	28	29	18	16
- Low	14	18	19	18	14	11

Income Statement Analysis (Million $)

	1994	%Chg	1993	%Chg	1992	%Chg	1991
Revs.	213	9%	196	5%	187	3%	182
Oper. Inc.	35.4	27%	27.8	1%	27.5	3%	26.7
Depr.	3.1	-3%	3.2	7%	3.0	22%	2.4
Int. Exp.	0.1	150%	0.0	100%	0.0	-80%	0.1
Pretax Inc.	34.0	22%	27.8	9%	25.4	-4%	26.4
Eff. Tax Rate	40%	—	36%	—	40%	—	37%
Net Inc.	20.5	15%	17.8	16%	15.3	-8%	16.6

Balance Sheet & Other Fin. Data (Million $)

	1994	1993	1992	1991	1990	1989
Cash	31.7	71.9	59.6	61.3	52.3	39.1
Curr. Assets	92.0	127	112	110	102	86.0
Total Assets	168	171	158	150	138	119
Curr. Liab.	19.8	15.6	16.0	18.4	18.7	18.8
LT Debt	Nil	Nil	Nil	Nil	Nil	Nil
Common Eqty.	131	141	129	120	109	91.0
Total Cap.	131	141	129	120	109	92.0
Cap. Exp.	6.9	1.4	8.2	4.8	6.4	7.9
Cash Flow	23.6	21.0	18.3	19.1	24.7	23.9

Ratio Analysis

	1994	1993	1992	1991	1990	1989
Curr. Ratio	4.7	8.1	7.0	6.0	5.4	4.6
% LT Debt of Cap.	Nil	Nil	Nil	Nil	Nil	Nil
% Net Inc.of Revs.	9.6	9.1	8.2	9.2	12.2	12.3
% Ret. on Assets	12.5	10.8	10.0	11.6	17.6	19.7
% Ret. on Equity	15.7	13.2	12.3	14.5	22.5	25.6

Dividend Data —Cash payments began in 1973.

Amt. of Div. $	Date Decl.	Ex-Div. Date	Stock of Record	Payment Date
0.120	Aug. 16	Sep. 26	Sep. 30	Oct. 14 '94
0.120	Dec. 14	Dec. 27	Jan. 03	Jan. 17 '95
0.120	Feb. 14	Mar. 30	Apr. 05	Apr. 19 '95
0.130	May. 09	Jun. 30	Jul. 05	Jul. 19 '95
0.130	Aug. 08	Sep. 27	Sep. 27	Oct. 13 '95

Data as orig. reptd.; bef. results of disc. opers. and/or spec. items. Per share data adj. for stk. divs. as of ex-div. date. E-Estimated. NA-Not Available. NM-Not Meaningful. NR-Not Ranked.

Office—1666 E. Touhy Ave., Des Plaines, IL 60018. **Tel**—(708) 827-9666. **Chrmn & CEO**—B. Kalish. **Pres & COO**—P. G. Smith. **VP, Treas & CFO**—J. Shaffer. **Secy**—R. J. Washlow. **VP, Contr & Investor Contact**—Joseph L. Pawlick. **Dirs**—J. T. Brophy, L. L. Carrol, B. Kalish, R. B. Port, S. L. Port, R. G. Rettig, J. Shaffer, P. G. Smith. **Transfer Agent**—First National Bank of Chicago. **Incorporated** in Illinois in 1952; reincorporated in Delaware in 1982. **Empl**-763. **S&P Analyst:** Justin McCann

STANDARD & POOR'S

STOCK REPORTS

Lawter International

NYSE Symbol **LAW**

In S&P MidCap 400

09-AUG-95

Industry: Graphic Arts

Summary: This company makes printing ink vehicles, wax compounds and powders, synthetic and hydrocarbon resins, fluorescent pigments and coatings, and thermographic and rota-matic machines.

Quantitative Evaluations

Outlook (1 Lowest—5 Highest) • **4-**

Fair Value • **12¼**

Risk • **Low**

Earn./Div. Rank • **A-**

Technical Eval. • **Bullish** since 6/95

Rel. Strength Rank (1 Lowest—99 Highest) • **9**

Insider Activity • **NA**

Recent Price • 11⅛ | Yield • 3.6%

52 Wk Range • 14⅜-10⅞ | 12-Mo. P/E • 16.1

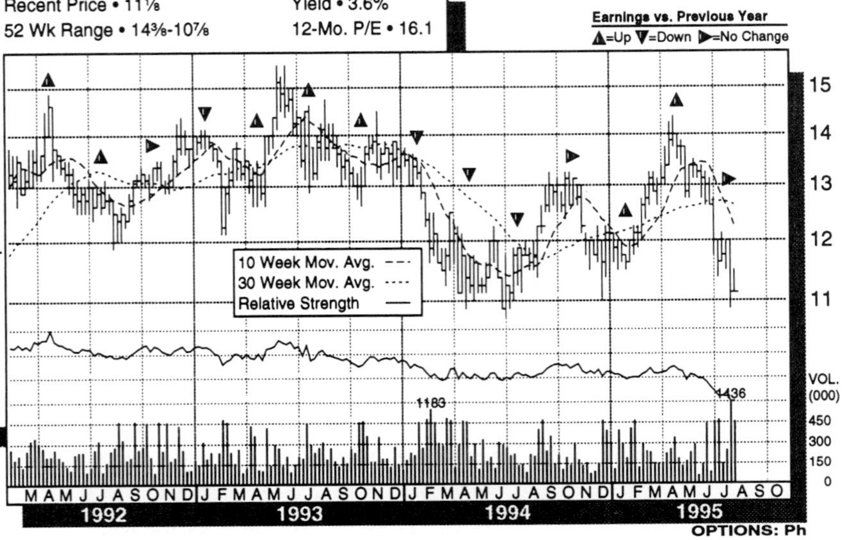

OPTIONS: Ph

Business Profile - 09-AUG-95

This international specialty chemical company manufactures products for the graphic arts and industrial coatings industries. Foreign operations account for almost 50% of sales. In 1994, results benefited from greater domestic and international demand, and from the acquisition of Cremona Resine, an Italian resins company. In 1995, margins have been pressured by the higher costs of raw materials. A new state-of-the-art plant in Antwerp, Belgium, is expected to start production in July 1996.

Operational Review - 09-AUG-95

Revenues advanced 18% in the first six months of 1995, reflecting higher prices, strength in Europe, the Cremona Resine acquisition, and favorable foreign exchange rates. However, profitability was restricted by startup costs at the new resin plant in Wisconsin and by higher raw material costs. Net income for the period grew 10% to $0.34 a share.

Stock Performance - 04-AUG-95

In the past 30 trading days, LAW's shares have declined 12%, compared to a 2% rise in the S&P 500. Average trading volume for the past five days was 91,620 shares, compared with the 40-day moving average of 99,713 shares.

Key Stock Statistics

Dividend Rate/Share	0.40	Shareholders	3,400
Shs. outstg. (M)	45.0	Market cap. (B)	$0.506
Avg. daily vol. (M)	0.120	Inst. holdings	45%
Tang. Bk. Value/Share	2.99	Insider holdings	NA
Beta	1.01		

Value of $10,000 invested 5 years ago: $ 18,307

Fiscal Year Ending Dec. 31

	1995	% Change	1994	% Change	1993	% Change
Revenues (Million $)						
1Q	52.49	23%	42.61	1%	42.07	2%
2Q	50.01	13%	44.42	6%	42.08	3%
3Q	—	—	48.84	12%	43.63	1%
4Q	—	—	55.18	24%	44.47	5%
Yr.	—	—	191.1	11%	172.3	3%
Income (Million $)						
1Q	8.09	20%	6.73	-11%	7.60	7%
2Q	7.05	NM	7.03	-8%	7.67	11%
3Q	—	—	7.66	3%	7.42	15%
4Q	—	—	8.00	NM	-21.68	NM
Yr.	—	—	29.41	NM	1.00	-96%
Earnings Per Share ($)						
1Q	0.18	20%	0.15	-12%	0.17	6%
2Q	0.16	NM	0.16	-6%	0.17	6%
3Q	—	—	0.17	NM	0.17	13%
4Q	—	—	0.18	NM	-0.49	NM
Yr.	—	—	0.66	NM	0.02	-97%

Next earnings report expected: late October

Lawter International

Business Summary - 09-AUG-95

Lawter International manufactures and markets printing ink vehicles, slip additives, synthetic and hydrocarbon resins, fluorescent pigments and coatings, thermographic compounds and thermographic and rota-matic machines. While the graphic arts industry is a major market, Lawter also serves the industrial coatings, adhesives and other industries. Sales by product group in recent years:

	1994	1993	1992
Printing ink & slip additives	47.5%	47.0%	49.4%
Synthetic/hydrocarbon resins	46.7%	46.7%	44.1%
Fluorescent & thermographic	5.8%	6.3%	6.5%

International operations contributed 48% of sales and 42% of pretax income in 1994.

Printing ink vehicles are fluid and gelled compositions that give printing inks the ability to carry color onto a variety of printing surfaces. Printing ink vehicles influence printing quality, gloss, drying speed, adhesion, rub resistance and press speed. Slip additives are used in printing inks to provide additional surface slip and rub resistance to the ink film. These products are sold to printing ink manufacturers.

Synthetic and hydrocarbon resins are used to produce adhesives, liquid printing inks and printing ink vehicles, rubber compounds, paints and various coatings to improve durability, chemical resistance, appearance, adhesion and speed of drying.

Fluorescent pigments and coatings are used in the manufacture of paints, printing inks, paper coatings, plastic products, rubber compounds, textile inks and other products where striking colors are desired. Fluorescent products are used for greater visibility in safety marking applications, in toys and bottles, and in display advertising.

Thermographic machines and compounds are used in the production of thermographic printing, a process that produces raised printing. Rota-matic machines are used to cut, score or perforate paper products. These machines are used in the manufacture of greeting cards, specialty printing, business cards, stationery and advertising material.

In June 1994, the company acquired Cremona Resine SpA, an Italian manufacturer and marketer of specialty chemicals, predominantly resins for the graphic arts industry.

Important Developments

Jul. '95—Lawter said it does not expect its Pleasant Prairie resin plant to be in full production until the end of 1995. Separately, LAW noted continuing customer resistance to increased selling prices engendered by higher raw material and other costs.

Capitalization

Long Term Obligations: $4,152,000 (3/95).

Per Share Data ($)

(Year Ended Dec. 31)

	1994	1993	1992	1991	1990	1989
Tangible Bk. Val.	2.84	2.47	2.83	2.68	2.44	2.04
Cash Flow	0.75	0.12	0.71	0.70	0.63	0.53
Earnings	0.66	0.02	0.62	0.61	0.55	0.46
Dividends	0.40	0.40	0.40	0.35	0.29	0.29
Payout Ratio	61%	NM	66%	57%	54%	65%
Prices - High	13¾	15½	14⅞	13¾	8⅝	7⅞
- Low	10¾	12⅛	11⅞	7⅞	6½	6½
P/E Ratio - High	21	NM	24	23	16	17
- Low	16	NM	19	13	12	14

Income Statement Analysis (Million $)

	1994	%Chg	1993	%Chg	1992	%Chg	1991
Revs.	191	11%	172	2%	168	10%	153
Oper. Inc.	39.5	36%	29.0	-18%	35.5	4%	34.0
Depr.	4.3	1%	4.3	3%	4.2	7%	3.9
Int. Exp.	NA	—	NA	—	NA	—	NA
Pretax Inc.	39.7	35%	29.5	-19%	36.6	NM	36.4
Eff. Tax Rate	26%	—	97%	—	26%	—	27%
Net Inc.	29.4	NM	1.0	-96%	27.0	2%	26.5

Balance Sheet & Other Fin. Data (Million $)

	1994	1993	1992	1991	1990	1989
Cash	71.3	83.1	73.3	64.7	57.2	43.9
Curr. Assets	150	142	130	124	108	94.0
Total Assets	232	209	187	178	154	134
Curr. Liab.	64.5	58.1	36.5	38.0	25.5	23.6
LT Debt	4.2	4.2	4.9	5.2	4.3	4.4
Common Eqty.	128	111	127	117	105	88.0
Total Cap.	167	151	151	140	127	110
Cap. Exp.	10.6	12.9	7.6	8.9	6.2	3.1
Cash Flow	33.7	5.3	31.2	30.4	26.9	23.0

Ratio Analysis

	1994	1993	1992	1991	1990	1989
Curr. Ratio	2.3	2.5	3.6	3.3	4.2	4.0
% LT Debt of Cap.	2.5	2.8	3.2	3.7	3.4	4.0
% Net Inc.of Revs.	15.4	0.6	16.1	17.3	15.6	14.4
% Ret. on Assets	13.3	0.5	14.6	15.9	16.3	15.0
% Ret. on Equity	24.6	0.8	21.9	23.8	24.2	23.3

Dividend Data (Dividends have been paid since 1959.)

Amt. of Div. $	Date Decl.	Ex-Div. Date	Stock of Record	Payment Date
0.100	Jul. 25	Aug. 11	Aug. 17	Sep. 01 '94
0.100	Oct. 19	Nov. 09	Nov. 16	Dec. 01 '94
0.100	Jan. 31	Feb. 09	Feb. 15	Mar. 01 '95
0.100	Apr. 24	May. 10	May. 16	Jun. 01 '95
0.100	Jul. 25	Aug. 15	Aug. 17	Sep. 01 '95

Data as orig. reptd.; bef. results of disc. opers. and/or spec. items. Per share data adj. for stk. divs. as of ex-div. date. E-Estimated. NA-Not Available. NM-Not Meaningful. NR-Not Ranked.

Office—990 Skokie Blvd., Northbrook, IL 60062. **Tel**—(708) 498-4700. **Chrmn & CEO**—D. J. Terra. **Pres, COO & Investor Contact**—Richard D. Nordman. **VP, Secy & Treas**—W. S. Russell. **Dirs**—W. P. Clark, A. A. Hartman, L. P. Judy, R. D. Nordman, F. G. Steingraber, D. J. Terra. **Transfer Agent & Registrar**—Harris Trust and Savings Bank, Chicago. **Incorporated** in Delaware in 1958. **Empl**-577. **S&P Analyst:** Justin McCann

STANDARD & POOR'S

STOCK REPORTS

Lee Enterprises

NYSE Symbol **LEE**
In S&P MidCap 400

26-JUL-95 **Industry:** Publishing

Summary: Lee is a diversified media company whose core products include newspapers, television stations, specialty publications, printing plates for newspapers, and media services.

Quantitative Evaluations
Outlook (1 Lowest—5 Highest) • **4+**
Fair Value • **37⅜**
Risk • **Low**
Earn./Div. Rank • **A-**

Technical Eval. • **Bearish** since 7/95
Rel. Strength Rank (1 Lowest—99 Highest) • **26**
Insider Activity • **NA**

Recent Price • 36¾
52 Wk Range • 39¾-31⅝
Yield • 2.4%
12-Mo. P/E • 14.8

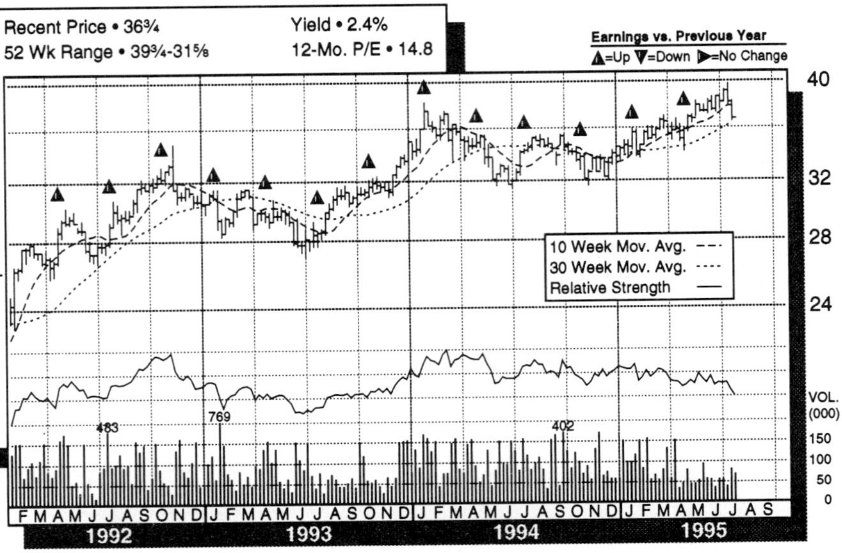

Business Profile - 25-JUL-95

Lee publishes 19 daily newspapers and numerous weekly newspapers in nine midwestern and western states. The company also operates eight televison stations and owns NAPP Systems (USA) Inc., a leading maker of graphic system products. Lee recently purchased two additional television stations in Kansas for $48.8 million. It also acquired the 50.25% of the outstanding stock of Journal-Star Printing it did not already own.

Operational Review - 25-JUL-95

The company continued to report favorable earnings comparisons in the third quarter of fiscal 1995. The largest percentage increase in operating income for the quarter came from the broadcasting segment, which benefited from increased compensation from networks. Rising newsprint costs, however, slowed net income growth from rates realized in the first two quarters of the year. Gains in earnings per share for the quarter were limited by an increase in the average number of outstanding shares.

Stock Performance - 21-JUL-95

In the past 30 trading days, LEE's shares have declined 4%, compared to a 5% rise in the S&P 500. Average trading volume for the past five days was 13,600 shares, compared with the 40-day moving average of 11,676 shares.

Key Stock Statistics

Dividend Rate/Share	0.88	Shareholders	8,100
Shs. outstg. (M)	23.2	Market cap. (B)	$0.857
Avg. daily vol. (M)	0.021	Inst. holdings	45%
Tang. Bk. Value/Share	0.47	Insider holdings	NA
Beta	0.98		

Value of $10,000 invested 5 years ago: $ 13,945

Fiscal Year Ending Sep. 30

	1995	% Change	1994	% Change	1993	% Change
Revenues (Million $)						
1Q	113.1	11%	102.1	6%	96.35	2%
2Q	98.64	4%	94.92	12%	84.91	NM
3Q	117.1	14%	103.0	6%	97.04	4%
4Q	—	—	102.5	8%	94.61	3%
Yr.	—	—	402.5	8%	372.9	2%
Income (Million $)						
1Q	16.83	26%	13.32	16%	11.50	19%
2Q	11.12	16%	9.56	47%	6.50	3%
3Q	16.44	14%	14.37	21%	11.85	NM
4Q	—	—	13.61	20%	11.38	6%
Yr.	—	—	50.85	23%	41.24	7%
Earnings Per Share ($)						
1Q	0.73	28%	0.57	16%	0.49	17%
2Q	0.49	20%	0.41	46%	0.28	4%
3Q	0.68	11%	0.61	20%	0.51	2%
4Q	—	—	0.58	18%	0.49	7%
Yr.	—	—	2.17	23%	1.76	7%

Next earnings report expected: early November

Lee Enterprises

Business Summary - 25-JUL-95

Lee Enterprises, Incorporated publishes daily and weekly newspapers and special industry publications, owns and operates television stations and manufactures graphic systems products. Segment contributions in fiscal 1994 were:

		Revs.	Profits
Newspapers		60%	70%
Advertising	33%		
Circulation	17%		
Other	10%		
Broadcasting		22%	20%
Media products & services		15%	10%
Equity earns.		3%	---

The company publishes, directly or through affiliates, 19 daily newspapers and numerous weekly newspapers, shoppers and special industry publications in nine states--Montana, Iowa, Minnesota, Wisconsin, Nebraska, North Dakota, South Dakota, Oregon and Illinois. In March 1995, Lee acquired all of the stock of Journal-Star Printing in Lincoln, Neb. The company also has a 50% interest in a newspaper publishing company in Madison, Wis.

Local run-of-press advertising, the company's largest source of newspaper revenue, is seasonal and tends to fluctuate with retail sales in markets served; historically, it is higher in the first and third quarters.

Eight network-affiliated television stations are owned and operated in Tucson, Ariz. (KGUN), Honolulu, Hawaii (KGMB), Omaha, Neb. (KMTV), Portland, Ore. (KOIN), Huntington/Charleston, W.Va. (WSAZ), Albuquerque, N.M. (KRQE), Roswell, N.M. (KBIM), and Las Cruces, N.M. (KZIA). KGMB also operates satellite stations in Hilo, Hawaii (KGMD), and Maui, Hawaii (KGMV). In March, 1995 Lee agreed to purchase KSNW in Wichita, Kan., and KSNT in Topeka, Kan.

NAPP Systems (USA) Inc., formerly a joint venture with Nippon Paint Co. of Osaka, Japan, manufactures and sells photosensitive polymer plastic printing plates and sells related plate processing equipment manufactured by others to newspaper publishers, preprint or telephone directory printing businesses throughout the world. Lee acquired the remaining 50% interest in NAPP in September 1990 for $100 million.

Important Developments

Jul. '95—In reporting results for the third quarter, the company noted that operating margins for the printing and advertising segment declined, due to higher newsprint prices.

Capitalization

Long Term Debt: $73,367,000 (3/95).

Per Share Data ($) (Year Ended Sep. 30)

	1994	1993	1992	1991	1990	1989
Tangible Bk. Val.	0.72	-0.81	-1.84	-3.17	-3.39	1.26
Cash Flow	3.17	2.81	2.67	2.38	2.54	2.30
Earnings	2.17	1.76	1.65	1.35	1.82	1.74
Dividends	0.84	0.80	0.77	0.76	0.72	0.68
Payout Ratio	39%	45%	47%	56%	38%	38%
Prices - High	38¼	35	34⅞	31⅞	31⅛	34¾
- Low	31½	27	23	20⅛	19¾	24¾
P/E Ratio - High	18	20	21	24	17	20
- Low	15	15	14	15	11	14

Income Statement Analysis (Million $)

	1994	%Chg	1993	%Chg	1992	%Chg	1991
Revs.	392	8%	363	2%	356	5%	340
Oper. Inc.	109	13%	96.4	NM	96.7	10%	87.6
Depr.	23.5	-5%	24.8	5%	23.7	NM	23.9
Int. Exp.	13.6	-11%	15.3	-9%	16.9	-10%	18.7
Pretax Inc.	84.9	25%	67.9	3%	66.0	24%	53.2
Eff. Tax Rate	40%	—	39%	—	42%	—	41%
Net Inc.	50.9	24%	41.2	7%	38.5	22%	31.5

Balance Sheet & Other Fin. Data (Million $)

	1994	1993	1992	1991	1990	1989
Cash	57.6	62.6	48.1	18.3	16.1	20.5
Curr. Assets	136	135	126	94.5	91.1	69.7
Total Assets	475	482	475	459	466	329
Curr. Liab.	100	91.7	86.0	76.9	85.3	50.8
LT Debt	99	127	153	166	178	76.0
Common Eqty.	242	223	204	183	173	176
Total Cap.	362	377	377	364	361	255
Cap. Exp.	17.6	10.0	4.0	6.4	15.2	24.3
Cash Flow	74.4	66.0	62.2	55.4	60.8	57.0

Ratio Analysis

	1994	1993	1992	1991	1990	1989
Curr. Ratio	1.4	1.5	1.5	1.2	1.1	1.4
% LT Debt of Cap.	27.3	33.8	40.6	45.7	49.3	30.0
% Net Inc.of Revs.	13.0	11.3	10.8	9.3	15.8	16.9
% Ret. on Assets	10.7	8.6	8.2	6.8	11.1	13.7
% Ret. on Equity	22.0	19.3	19.9	17.7	25.4	25.3

Dividend Data (Dividends have been paid since 1960.)

Amt. of Div. $	Date Decl.	Ex-Div. Date	Stock of Record	Payment Date
0.210	Jul. 22	Aug. 26	Sep. 01	Sep. 30 '94
0.220	Nov. 17	Dec. 05	Dec. 09	Jan. 02 '95
0.220	Feb. 03	Feb. 23	Mar. 01	Apr. 03 '95
0.220	Apr. 13	May. 25	Jun. 01	Jul. 03 '95
0.220	Jul. 21	Aug. 30	Sep. 01	Sep. 29 '95

Data as orig. reptd.; bef. results of disc. opers. and/or spec. items. Per share data adj. for stk. divs. as of ex-div. date. E-Estimated. NA-Not Available. NM-Not Meaningful. NR-Not Ranked.

Office—215 N. Main St., Davenport, IA 52801. **Tel**—(319) 383-2100. **Chrmn**—L. G. Schermer. **Pres & CEO**—R. D. Gottlieb. **VP-Treas & CFO**—L. Bloom. **Secy**—C. D. Waterman III. **Investor Contact**—R. Galligan. **Dirs**—R. E. Crain, H. A. Fischer Jr., R. D. Gottlieb, J. P. Guerin, A. E. Newman, C. E. Rickershauser Jr., R. L. Rickman, L. G. Schermer, P. Sewell, R. W. Sonnenfeldt, M. Vittert. **Transfer Agent & Registrar**—First Chicago Trust Co. **Incorporated** in Delaware in 1950. **Empl**-4,700. **S&P Analyst:** Stephen Madonna, CFA

Leggett & Platt

NYSE Symbol **LEG**
In S&P MidCap 400

05-SEP-95 **Industry:** Home Furnishings

Summary: This company makes components and related finished products for the home furnishings industry, as well as diversified products that utilize similar manufacturing technology.

S&P Opinion: Buy (★★★★★)

Recent Price • 48½
52 Wk Range • 49⅝-33⅜
Yield • 1.6%
12-Mo. P/E • 16.0

Quantitative Evaluations

Outlook
(1 Lowest—5 Highest)
• **4⁻**

Fair Value
• **49⅛**

Risk
• **Low**

Earn./Div. Rank
• **A**

Technical Eval.
• **Bearish** since 7/95

Rel. Strength Rank
(1 Lowest—99 Highest)
• **66**

Insider Activity
• **Neutral**

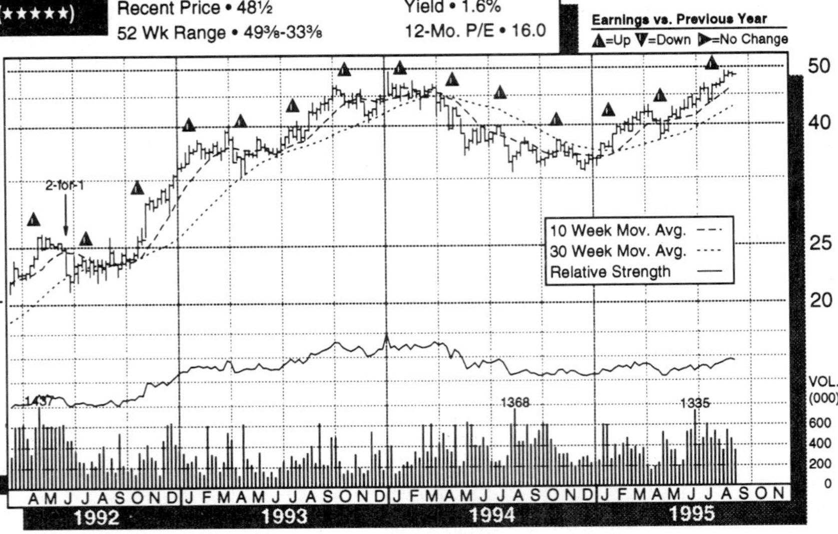

Overview - 05-SEP-95

Sales should be solidly higher through 1995, on improving conditions in the furnishings industry and contributions from recent acquisitions. Margins should continue to benefit from a strong emphasis on control of operating costs, but could be adversely affected to an extent by higher raw materials prices. The company has been adhering closely to an acquisition strategy that seeks to achieve synergies through the purchase of complementary businesses; LEG is looking to purchase additional operations that fit into existing technology or marketing parameters. Moderating interest rates combined with improving economic conditions will continue to be less restrictive on growth in LEG's key housing and home furnishings markets.

Valuation - 05-SEP-95

The share prices of many retail companies serving the housing and household furnishings markets took a beating in 1994 and continued to slide into 1995. However, interest rates have moderated and there is a strong belief that cyclical companies have already skimmed the bottom of the barrel. LEG was able to weather the difficult conditions and a possible slowdown in its markets, aided by high industry regard for its products and the fact that it derives about one-third of revenues from less-cyclical bedding components. The shares have risen strongly in 1995 and are still attractive at around 15 times estimated 1995 earnings.

Key Stock Statistics

S&P EPS Est. 1995	3.15	Tang. Bk. Value/Share	12.97
P/E on S&P Est. 1995	15.4	Beta	1.09
S&P EPS Est. 1996	3.50	Shareholders	17,700
Dividend Rate/Share	0.80	Market cap. (B)	$ 2.0
Shs. outstg. (M)	42.0	Inst. holdings	57%
Avg. daily vol. (M)	0.084	Insider holdings	NA

Value of $10,000 invested 5 years ago: $ 36,019

Fiscal Year Ending Dec. 31

	1995	% Change	1994	% Change	1993	% Change
Revenues (Million $)						
1Q	523.1	20%	434.6	20%	363.0	27%
2Q	517.7	15%	448.8	21%	371.7	31%
3Q	—	—	482.6	22%	395.5	30%
4Q	—	—	492.1	24%	396.6	33%
Yr.	—	—	1,858	22%	1,527	30%
Income (Million $)						
1Q	32.90	27%	26.00	33%	19.60	41%
2Q	33.00	17%	28.20	34%	21.00	42%
3Q	—	—	30.20	35%	22.30	25%
4Q	—	—	31.00	35%	23.03	44%
Yr.	—	—	115.4	34%	85.91	38%
Earnings Per Share ($)						
1Q	0.78	24%	0.63	31%	0.48	26%
2Q	0.78	15%	0.68	33%	0.51	31%
3Q	E0.80	10%	0.73	35%	0.54	17%
4Q	E0.80	8%	0.74	32%	0.56	37%
Yr.	E3.15	13%	2.78	33%	2.09	27%

Next earnings report expected: late October

Leggett & Platt

Business Summary - 05-SEP-95

Leggett & Platt manufactures components and related finished products for the home furnishings industry and also makes diversified products with technology similar to its home furnishings operations. Foreign sales are not significant. Business segment contributions in 1994 were:

	Sales	Profits
Home furnishing products	75%	78%
Diversified	25%	22%

The company's component customers manufacture furniture and bedding for homes, offices and institutions. These customers offer their products for sale to wholesalers, retailers, institutions and others. In 1994, bedding components accounted for 29% of sales, with furniture components providing 28%.

LEG also makes finished products for the home furnishings industry (19% of 1994 sales), including sleep-related finished furniture and carpet cushioning materials. Some finished furniture products are sold to bedding and furniture manufacturers, which resell the furniture under their own labels to wholesalers or retailers, while other finished furniture is sold directly to retailers. Carpet cushioning materials are sold primarily to floor covering distributors, with some direct contract sales.

Outside of the home furnishings area, the company produces a diversified line of components and other products for home, industrial and commercial uses.

During 1994, the company acquired Talbot Industries (annual sales of $40 million), a custom fabricator of a wide variety of specialized wire products, for 419,867 common shares. The acquisition followed a variety of other purchases, including Southeastern Manufacturing Company (sales of $11 million), a maker of an assortment of welded wire products, for 158,569 common shares (August 1994); Super Sagless Corp. (annual sales of about $70 million), a producer of furniture components, for $40 million in cash (July 1994); and three small companies in 1994's second quarter (adding $55 million to the annual revenue base), for a total of $33.8 million in cash (net of cash acquired). LEG also completed several purchases in 1993's third quarter, including Hanes Holding Co. (annual sales of $150 million) and VWR Textiles & Supplies ($70 million in sales).

Important Developments

Jul. '95—The company said that sales for the first half of 1995 were a record $1.04 billion, an 18% increase over 1994's first half; sales rose 5.0% excluding the effect of acquisitions. LEG recently effected a two-for-one stock split payable in mid-September to shareholders of record on August 25.

Capitalization

Long Term Debt: $224,300,000 (6/95).

Per Share Data ($) (Year Ended Dec. 31)

	1994	1993	1992	1991	1990	1989
Tangible Bk. Val.	11.60	9.84	9.59	7.75	7.13	7.41
Cash Flow	3.95	3.04	2.65	2.01	1.69	2.07
Earnings	2.78	2.09	1.64	1.11	0.84	1.33
Dividends	0.62	0.54	0.46	0.43	0.42	0.37
Payout Ratio	22%	26%	28%	39%	50%	28%
Prices - High	49½	50⅛	35¼	19⅛	19	17½
- Low	33¼	32¾	18¾	13	10	11⅞
P/E Ratio - High	18	24	21	17	23	13
- Low	12	16	11	12	12	9

Income Statement Analysis (Million $)

	1994	%Chg	1993	%Chg	1992	%Chg	1991
Revs.	1,858	22%	1,527	31%	1,170	8%	1,082
Oper. Inc.	251	26%	199	39%	143	35%	106
Depr.	48.8	25%	39.1	2%	38.2	20%	31.9
Int. Exp.	9.8	-4%	10.2	76%	5.8	-53%	12.3
Pretax Inc.	190	35%	141	41%	100	56%	63.9
Eff. Tax Rate	39%	—	39%	—	37%	—	38%
Net Inc.	115	34%	85.9	37%	62.5	59%	39.4

Balance Sheet & Other Fin. Data (Million $)

	1994	1993	1992	1991	1990	1989
Cash	2.7	0.4	4.0	5.3	3.3	2.9
Curr. Assets	545	436	340	322	342	293
Total Assets	1,120	902	678	656	676	568
Curr. Liab.	233	166	119	111	128	113
LT Debt	205	166	101	179	213	147
Common Eqty.	625	516	425	333	303	282
Total Cap.	872	725	553	539	540	449
Cap. Exp.	88.5	88.3	33.2	39.7	42.7	63.0
Cash Flow	164	125	101	71.3	59.6	71.6

Ratio Analysis

	1994	1993	1992	1991	1990	1989
Curr. Ratio	2.3	2.6	2.9	2.9	2.7	2.6
% LT Debt of Cap.	23.5	22.9	18.4	33.3	39.4	32.8
% Net Inc.of Revs.	6.2	5.6	5.3	3.6	2.7	4.6
% Ret. on Assets	11.3	10.6	9.0	5.9	4.7	8.7
% Ret. on Equity	19.9	17.8	15.9	12.3	10.0	17.3

Dividend Data —Dividends have been paid since 1939. A "poison pill" stock purchase right was adopted in 1989.

Amt. of Div. $	Date Decl.	Ex-Div. Date	Stock of Record	Payment Date
0.160	Nov. 09	Nov. 18	Nov. 25	Jan. 02 '95
0.180	Feb. 08	Feb. 17	Feb. 24	Mar. 15 '95
0.180	May. 10	May. 22	May. 26	Jun. 15 '95
0.200	Aug. 09	Aug. 23	Aug. 25	Sep. 15 '95
2-for-1	Aug. 09	Sep. 18	Aug. 25	Sep. 15 '95

Data as orig. reptd.; bef. results of disc. opers. and/or spec. items. Per share data adj. for stk. divs. as of ex-div. date. E-Estimated. NA-Not Available. NM-Not Meaningful. NR-Not Ranked.

Office—One Leggett Rd., Carthage, MO 64836. **Tel**—(417) 358-8131. **Chrmn & CEO**—H. M. Cornell Jr. **Pres & COO**—F. E. Wright. **Sr VP-Fin**—M. A. Glauber. **Treas**—S. S. Higdon. **VP & Investor Contact**—J. Richard Calhoon. **Dirs**—R. F. Bentele, H. M. Cornell Jr., R. T. Enloe III, R. T. Fisher, F. E. Ford Jr., R. A. Jefferies Jr., A. M. Levine, R. L. Pearsall, M. E. Purnell Jr., F. E. Wright. **Transfer Agent & Registrar**—Mellon Securities Trust Co. **Incorporated** in Missouri in 1901. **Empl**-16,000. **S&P Analyst:** Philip D. Wohl

STANDARD & POOR'S

STOCK REPORTS

Lincoln Telecommunications

NASDAQ Symbol **LTEC**
In S&P MidCap 400

22-AUG-95 **Industry:** Telecommunications

Summary: This diversified communications firm offers local, long-distance, and cellular phone services and products to businesses, consumers, government and other customers in Nebraska.

Quantitative Evaluations

Outlook
(1 Lowest—5 Highest)
• **4-**

Fair Value
• **17 3/8**

Risk
• **Average**

Earn./Div. Rank
• **A**

Technical Eval.
• **Bearish** since 7/95

Rel. Strength Rank
(1 Lowest—99 Highest)
• **67**

Insider Activity
• **Neutral**

Recent Price • 16 7/8
52 Wk Range • 17½-14
Yield • 3.2%
12-Mo. P/E • 15.5

Earnings vs. Previous Year
▲=Up ▼=Down ▶=No Change

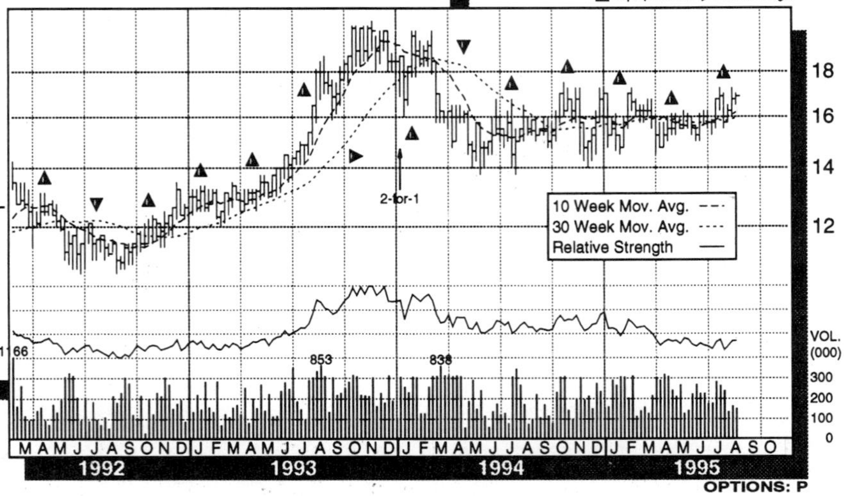

OPTIONS: P

Business Profile - 22-AUG-95

This holding company, through subsidiaries such as Lincoln Telephone and Telegraph Co., supplies local, cellular, and long distance services in Nebraska. In addition, LTEC offers related services and equipment. In July 1995, the company expanded its cellular operations with the acquisition of Nebraska Cellular Telecommunications Corp., for 4.3 million common shares and $61.6 million in cash. In the past 12 months, the company has increased the number of customer access landlines 4.1%.

Operational Review - 22-AUG-95

Total revenues for the six months ended June 30, 1995, rose 5.1%, year to year, due to growth in cellular operations, telephone network services, and business equipment sales. Margins benefited from the higher volume, and in the absence of a prior-year nonrecurring depreciation charge of $2.2 million, net income advanced 38%, to $0.59 a share from $0.43.

Stock Performance - 18-AUG-95

In the past 30 trading days, LTEC's shares have increased 7%, compared to a 0.51% rise in the S&P 500. Average trading volume for the past five days was 29,640 shares, compared with the 40-day moving average of 40,054 shares.

Key Stock Statistics

Dividend Rate/Share	0.56	Shareholders	7,700
Shs. outstg. (M)	36.7	Market cap. (B)	$0.633
Avg. daily vol. (M)	0.036	Inst. holdings	29%
Tang. Bk. Value/Share	6.23	Insider holdings	0%
Beta	0.63		

Value of $10,000 invested 5 years ago: $ 12,340

Fiscal Year Ending Dec. 31

	1995	% Change	1994	% Change	1993	% Change
Revenues (Million $)						
1Q	50.35	5%	48.00	7%	44.70	4%
2Q	51.31	5%	48.70	8%	45.30	4%
3Q	—	—	49.80	6%	47.00	6%
4Q	—	—	50.31	6%	47.30	4%
Yr.	—	—	196.8	7%	184.4	5%
Income (Million $)						
1Q	9.24	86%	4.98	-38%	8.07	31%
2Q	9.97	11%	8.97	13%	7.97	14%
3Q	—	—	9.70	17%	8.28	-3%
4Q	—	—	9.96	12%	8.87	12%
Yr.	—	—	33.61	1%	33.19	12%
Earnings Per Share ($)						
1Q	0.28	87%	0.15	-40%	0.25	32%
2Q	0.31	11%	0.28	12%	0.25	19%
3Q	—	—	0.30	15%	0.26	NM
4Q	—	—	0.31	15%	0.27	12%
Yr.	—	—	1.03	2%	1.01	12%

Next earnings report expected: late October

Lincoln Telecommunications

Business Summary - 22-AUG-95

Lincoln Telecommunications Company is a holding company, with Lincoln Telephone and Telegraph Co. (LT&T) its principal subsidiary. Through LT&T and its nonregulated telecommunications subsidiaries, LinTel Systems and Prairie Communications, the company provides local exchange and long distance service, paging and cellular service, and telephone equipment sales and service. Since 1988, telephone operations have provided almost 90% of total revenues, with the balance coming from diversified nonregulated operations.

LT&T operates a telephone system for both local and long-distance service in 22 counties in southeastern Nebraska. At the end of 1994, LT&T had 246,963 access lines in service, up from 238,142 a year earlier. More than 70% of the lines are for residential use, with the balance used by businesses. Lincoln, Neb., the largest city in the company's service area, is a regional retail, financial and insurance center; otherwise, the economies in LT&T's service area are chiefly agricultural.

Lincoln Telephone Cellular operates in the Lincoln-Lancaster County Metropolitan Statistical Area (MSA), which has a population of about 220,000. Cellular equipment is sold directly to customers and through sales agents. The unit also operates a wide area paging system covering 138 communities in Nebraska.

In January 1992, the company formed a partnership to hold Centel Corp.'s 55.2% interest in the Omaha Cellular Limited Partnership and assumed operating control of the franchise (subsequently renamed First Cellular Omaha). LTEC purchased a 50% interest in the new partnership for $11.9 million and holds a $23.8 million discount note, with proceeds from the note distributed to Centel; the company will have an option to purchase the remaining 50% over a two-year period beginning December 31, 1996.

LinTel Systems Inc. is a reseller of long distance services, primarily in Lincoln Telephone's service area, and provides this service by aggregating traffic to take advantage of volume discounts. It also sells and services a wide range of PBX, key systems, fax machines, and LANs to businesses in eastern Nebraska.

Expenditures for network improvements totaled $31.3 million in 1994, compared to $25.0 million in 1993. Over $42 million will be spent in 1995.

Important Developments

Jul. '95—LTEC acquired Nebraska Cellular Telephone Corp., for 4.3 million common shares and about $61.6 million in cash. Nebraska Cellular had revenues of $23.4 million in 1994.

Capitalization

Long Term Debt: $44,000,000 (6/95).

Per Share Data ($) (Year Ended Dec. 31)

	1994	1993	1992	1991	1990	1989
Tangible Bk. Val.	6.07	5.58	5.80	5.42	5.01	4.65
Cash Flow	2.02	1.89	1.80	1.70	1.60	1.59
Earnings	1.03	1.01	0.90	0.83	0.74	0.75
Dividends	0.53	0.49	0.43	0.40	0.37	0.38
Payout Ratio	51%	49%	48%	48%	50%	51%
Prices - High	20	20½	14¼	14⅝	16¾	17⅞
- Low	13¾	12	10⅝	10½	9¾	8⅝
P/E Ratio - High	19	20	16	18	23	23
- Low	13	12	12	13	13	11

Income Statement Analysis (Million $)

	1994	%Chg	1993	%Chg	1992	%Chg	1991
Revs.	197	7%	184	5%	176	NM	176
Depr.	31.9	12%	28.5	-3%	29.5	3%	28.6
Maint.	NA	—	20.0	-6%	21.2	—	NA
Constr. Credits	NA	—	NA	—	NA	—	NA
Eff. Tax Rate	39%	—	37%	—	35%	—	38%
Net Inc.	34.0	3%	33.0	13%	29.3	7%	27.4

Balance Sheet & Other Fin. Data (Million $)

	1994	1993	1992	1991	1990	1989
Gross Prop.	459	450	435	436	418	NA
Net Prop.	242	246	250	253	250	NA
Cap. Exp.	32.0	25.0	27.3	33.4	35.1	34.3
Total Cap.	269	260	308	306	300	261
Fxd. Chgs. Cov.	8.9	6.9	5.6	6.1	4.2	NA
Capitalization:						
LT Debt	44.0	44.0	73.6	80.3	85.8	55.1
Pfd.	4.5	4.5	4.4	7.2	7.7	NA
Common	196	184	189	178	165	153

Ratio Analysis

	1994	1993	1992	1991	1990	1989
% Ret. on Revs.	17.1	17.9	16.6	15.5	14.1	NA
% Ret. On Invest.Cap	15.2	14.7	12.7	11.7	NA	NA
% Return On Com.Eqty	17.5	17.7	15.9	16.0	15.2	16.7
% Earn. on Net Prop.	15.0	15.0	14.0	13.2	NA	NA
% LT Debt of Cap.	18.0	18.9	27.5	30.3	33.2	NA
Capital. % Pfd.	1.8	1.9	1.7	2.7	3.0	NA
Capital. % Common	80.2	79.2	70.8	67.0	63.8	NA

Dividend Data —Dividends on the common stock have been paid every year since 1937. A dividend reinvestment plan is available.

Amt. of Div. $	Date Decl.	Ex-Div. Date	Stock of Record	Payment Date
0.130	Sep. 21	Sep. 22	Sep. 27	Oct. 10 '94
0.140	Dec. 14	Dec. 20	Dec. 27	Jan. 10 '95
0.140	Mar. 15	Mar. 24	Mar. 30	Apr. 10 '95
0.140	Jun. 21	Jun. 28	Jun. 30	Jul. 10 '95

Data as orig. reptd.; bef. results of disc. opers. and/or spec. items. Per share data adj. for stk. divs. as of ex-div. date. E-Estimated. NA-Not Available. NM-Not Meaningful. NR-Not Ranked.

Office—1440 M Street, Lincoln, NE 68508. **Tel**—(402) 474-2211. **Chrmn**—T. C. Woods III. **Pres & CEO**—F. H. Hilsabeck. **SVP-CFO**—R. L. Tyler. **VP, Secy, Treas & Investor Contact**—Michael J. Tavlin. **Dirs**—D. W. Acklie, W. W. Cook, Jr., T. L. Fairfield, J. E. Geist, J. T. Greer, J. Haessler, C. R. Hermes, F. H. Hilsabeck, D. H. Pegler, Jr., P. C. Schorr III, W. C. Smith, J. W. Strand, C. N. Wheatley, T. C. Woods III, L. W. Zeigenbein. **Transfer Agent & Registrar**—Mellon Security Trust Co., Ridgefield Park, N.J. **Incorporated** in Delaware in 1928; holding co. incorporated in Nebraska in 1981. **Empl**-1,612. **S&P Analyst:** Mike Cavanaugh

STANDARD & POOR'S

Linear Technology Corp.

STOCK REPORTS

NASDAQ Symbol **LLTC**

In S&P MidCap 400

10-AUG-95 **Industry:** Electronics/Electric

Summary: This rapidly growing company manufactures high-performance linear integrated circuits.

S&P Opinion: Accumulate (★★★★)

Recent Price • 78⅝ | Yield • 0.4%
52 Wk Range • 80½-37½ | 12-Mo. P/E • 35.4

Quantitative Evaluations

Outlook (1 Lowest—5 Highest)
• **5+**

Fair Value
• **103⅞**

Risk
• **Average**

Earn./Div. Rank
• **B+**

Technical Eval.
• **Bullish** since 8/94

Rel. Strength Rank (1 Lowest—99 Highest)
• **87**

Insider Activity
• **NA**

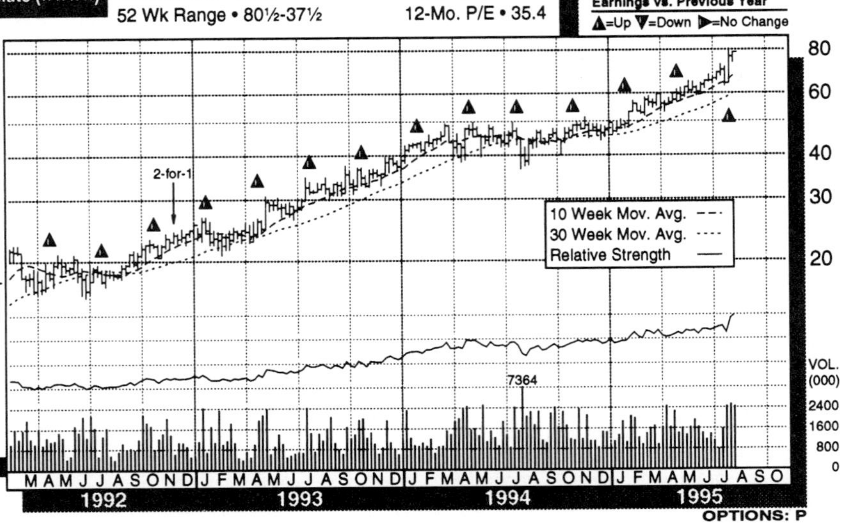

OPTIONS: P

Overview - 10-AUG-95

Sales are projected to advance about 30% in fiscal 1996. Results should benefit from continued rapid growth of the high-performance linear integrated circuit market, an aggressive new product introduction program, and participation in some of the fastest-growing segments of the semiconductor industry. The company's technological lead and continued sales growth should allow it to maintain its high gross margins (nearly 69% in fiscal 1995). LLTC is selective in its bookings, seeking to ensure that incoming orders contain a large percentage of proprietary technology. It is one of the few analog vendors not currently experiencing capacity constraints.

Valuation - 10-AUG-95

The shares have risen sharply since LLTC reported fiscal 1995 fourth quarter results that were better than expected. Continued strong demand from the industrial, telecommunications and computer sectors should spur future sales growth. Capacity expansion is still available at the Milipitas, Calif., facility, and completion of a new wafer fabrication facility in Camus, Wash., is scheduled for the second half of calendar 1996. Depreciation of the new facility will not begin until revenue-generating product shipments start, thereby minimizing the impact on earnings. Despite their recent gains, we believe that the shares remain a good long-term investment, despite possible near-term consolidation associated with the high-tech sector.

Key Stock Statistics

S&P EPS Est. 1996	3.00	Tang. Bk. Value/Share	7.66
P/E on S&P Est. 1996	26.2	Beta	1.74
Dividend Rate/Share	0.32	Shareholders	800
Shs. outstg. (M)	36.7	Market cap. (B)	$ 2.9
Avg. daily vol. (M)	0.518	Inst. holdings	92%
		Insider holdings	NA

Value of $10,000 invested 5 years ago: $ 153,872

Fiscal Year Ending Jun. 30

	1995	% Change	1994	% Change	1993	% Change
Revenues (Million $)						
1Q	58.08	29%	45.04	34%	33.60	23%
2Q	62.10	29%	48.03	35%	35.60	23%
3Q	68.14	32%	51.67	33%	38.81	27%
4Q	76.70	37%	55.80	30%	42.81	31%
Yr.	265.0	32%	200.5	33%	150.9	26%
Income (Million $)						
1Q	17.83	51%	11.81	55%	7.62	41%
2Q	19.24	47%	13.10	56%	8.40	46%
3Q	21.81	43%	15.22	59%	9.57	46%
4Q	25.82	55%	16.70	54%	10.84	49%
Yr.	84.70	49%	56.83	56%	36.44	46%
Earnings Per Share ($)						
1Q	0.47	47%	0.32	52%	0.21	40%
2Q	0.51	46%	0.35	52%	0.23	44%
3Q	0.57	43%	0.40	54%	0.26	44%
4Q	0.67	52%	0.44	52%	0.29	45%
Yr.	2.22	47%	1.51	53%	0.99	43%

Next earnings report expected: mid October

Linear Technology Corp.

Business Summary - 10-AUG-95

Linear Technology Corporation designs and makes a broad line of standard high-performance linear integrated circuits.

Linear (also called analog) circuits monitor, condition, amplify or transform continuous analog signals associated with such physical properties as temperature, pressure, weight, light, sound and speed, and they play an important role in bridging between real-world phenomena and a variety of electronic systems. Linear circuits also provide voltage regulation.

The company's product line includes operational, instrumentation and audio amplifiers; voltage regulators, references, comparators and converters; switched-capacitor filters; communications interface circuits; one-chip data acquisition systems; pulse-width modulators and sample-and-hold devices. About 3,800 finished part types are offered, of which more than 80% are proprietary. About 90% of net sales in fiscal 1995 were of proprietary products.

LLTC is targeting the high-performance segments of the linear circuit market, which is characterized by higher precision, both high power or micropower, higher speed, more subsystem integration on a single chip and many other special features. Applications for its products include laptop and desktop computers, computer peripherals, cellular telephones, electronic testers, industrial and medical electronic instruments, automotive controls, process controls, factory automation products and avionics.

The company's wafer fabrication and manufacturing facility is located at its headquarters in Milpitas, Calif. A new fabrication facility in Camus, Wash., currently under construction, is expected to start product level shipments in late 1996. During fiscal 1995, LLTC brought on line its first assembly plant, located in Peneng, Malaysia.

International sales accounted for 49% of the total in fiscal 1995, versus 45% in fiscal 1994.

R&D spending totaled $23.9 million (9.0% of net sales) in fiscal 1995, versus $18.4 million (9.2%) in fiscal 1994.

Important Developments

Jul. '95—LLTC said it experienced robust sales growth in the fiscal 1995 fourth quarter for all product lines and geographical areas. For the full year, international markets accounted for 49% of sales. The company expects international sales in future periods to provide a greater percentage of total sales, because two-thirds to three-quarters of the analog market is located outside the U.S.

Capitalization

Long Term Debt: None (7/95).

Per Share Data ($) (Year Ended Jun. 30)

	1995	1994	1993	1992	1991	1990
Tangible Bk. Val.	NA	6.15	4.56	3.53	2.66	2.10
Cash Flow	NA	1.68	1.14	0.82	0.59	0.46
Earnings	2.22	1.51	0.99	0.69	0.48	0.34
Dividends	0.27	0.23	0.15	Nil	Nil	Nil
Payout Ratio	12%	15%	15%	Nil	Nil	Nil
Prices - High	80½	49¾	39½	25½	16⅜	7¼
- Low	46	36½	20¾	15¾	6¼	4⅛
P/E Ratio - High	36	33	40	37	34	21
- Low	21	24	21	21	13	12

Income Statement Analysis (Million $)

	1994	%Chg	1993	%Chg	1992	%Chg	1991
Revs.	201	33%	151	27%	119	27%	94.0
Oper. Inc.	88.2	51%	58.6	46%	40.1	49%	26.9
Depr.	6.3	9%	5.8	28%	4.5	18%	3.8
Int. Exp.	0.1	-79%	0.5	-49%	1.0	-17%	1.3
Pretax Inc.	86.5	55%	55.7	45%	38.5	47%	26.2
Eff. Tax Rate	34%	—	35%	—	35%	—	35%
Net Inc.	56.8	56%	36.4	46%	25.0	48%	16.9

Balance Sheet & Other Fin. Data (Million $)

	1994	1993	1992	1991	1990	1989
Cash	177	128	95.3	69.2	53.4	46.5
Curr. Assets	231	169	134	100	80.0	70.0
Total Assets	268	196	160	121	96.0	85.0
Curr. Liab.	42.9	32.4	33.5	23.7	18.6	16.9
LT Debt	Nil	0.3	1.7	6.4	8.2	9.0
Common Eqty.	223	163	124	90.0	69.0	58.0
Total Cap.	225	164	126	97.0	78.0	68.0
Cap. Exp.	16.2	7.6	9.8	8.2	3.9	6.1
Cash Flow	63.2	42.2	29.6	20.8	15.3	12.2

Ratio Analysis

	1994	1993	1992	1991	1990	1989
Curr. Ratio	5.4	5.2	4.0	4.2	4.3	4.1
% LT Debt of Cap.	Nil	0.2	1.4	6.6	10.5	13.3
% Net Inc.of Revs.	28.3	24.2	20.9	18.0	14.9	13.8
% Ret. on Assets	24.3	20.3	17.5	15.4	12.5	11.6
% Ret. on Equity	29.2	25.3	23.1	21.1	17.8	16.7

Dividend Data (Cash dividends were initiated in October 1992.)

Amt. of Div. $	Date Decl.	Ex-Div. Date	Stock of Record	Payment Date
0.070	Oct. 17	Oct. 24	Oct. 28	Nov. 16 '94
0.070	Jan. 17	Jan. 23	Jan. 27	Feb. 15 '95
0.070	Apr. 18	Apr. 24	Apr. 28	May. 17 '95
0.080	Jul. 25	Aug. 02	Aug. 14	Aug. 23 '95
2-for-1	Jul. 25	Sep. 05	Aug. 11	Sep. 01 '95

Data as orig. reptd.; bef. results of disc. opers. and/or spec. items. Per share data adj. for stk. divs. as of ex-div. date. E-Estimated. NA-Not Available. NM-Not Meaningful. NR-Not Ranked.

Office—1630 McCarthy Blvd., Milpitas, CA 95035-7487. **Tel**—(408) 432-1900. **Pres & CEO**—R. H. Swanson, Jr. **VP & COO**—C. B. Davies. **VP-Fin, CFO & Investor Contact**—Paul Coghlan. **Secy**—A. F. Schneiderman. **Dirs**—D. S. Lee, G. M. Mueller, R. H. Swanson, Jr., T. S. Volpe. **Transfer Agent & Registrar**—First National Bank of Boston, Palo Alto, CA. **Incorporated** in California in 1981. **Empl**-1,000. **S&P Analyst:** Steven A. Jaworski

Litton Industries

NYSE Symbol **LIT**
In S&P MidCap 400

11-OCT-95

Industry: Conglomerate/diversified

Summary: Litton mainly provides advanced electronic and defense systems and marine engineering. The company also sells electronic interconnects. Oilfield services were spun-off in 1994.

S&P Opinion: Hold (★★★)

Recent Price • 41⅜
52 Wk Range • 44¼-32½
Yield • Nil
12-Mo. P/E • 14.6

Quantitative Evaluations
Outlook (1 Lowest—5 Highest) • **3+**
Fair Value • **40⅝**
Risk • **Low**
Earn./Div. Rank • **B**

Technical Eval. • **Bearish** since 7/95
Rel. Strength Rank (1 Lowest—99 Highest) • **77**
Insider Activity • **Unfavorable**

Earnings vs. Previous Year
▲=Up ▼=Down ▶=No Change

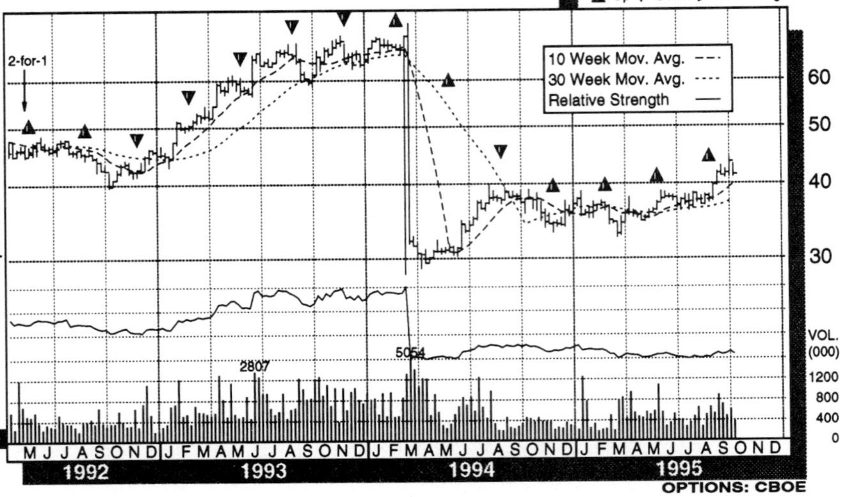

OPTIONS: CBOE

Overview - 11-OCT-95

Sales for the fiscal year ending July 31, 1996, are forecast to rise moderately from those of fiscal 1995, due to acquisitions. The advanced electronics division (including navigation and communications and electronic data systems) is expected to advance more than 10%. Robust growth is also projected to continue for interconnect products. Nevertheless, further cuts in defense spending and the completion of certain contracts should result in lower marine engineering sales. Margins are forecast to widen, reflecting the addition of higher-margin businesses and the effects of downsizing activities. Interest charges should remain about the same, as acquisitions will be financed predominantly through strong internal cash flow.

Valuation - 06-OCT-95

Primarily a subcontractor without any major contracts, the company is exceedingly susceptible to falling defense spending. Still, earnings may benefit from effective cost-reduction efforts and continued defense electronics acquisitions. The company has significant excess debt capacity for such purposes. Accordingly, the stock could move based on acquisition announcements made by Litton or by other defense/electronics companies. However, given the company's limited growth opportunities and minimal diversification efforts, we view the shares as fairly valued at about 14 times our EPS estimate of $3.05 for fiscal 1996.

Key Stock Statistics

S&P EPS Est. 1996	3.05	Tang. Bk. Value/Share	11.74
P/E on S&P Est. 1996	13.6	Beta	0.91
Dividend Rate/Share	Nil	Shareholders	36,900
Shs. outstg. (M)	46.1	Market cap. (B)	$ 1.9
Avg. daily vol. (M)	0.104	Inst. holdings	49%
		Insider holdings	NA

Value of $10,000 invested 5 years ago: NA

Fiscal Year Ending Jul. 31

	1995	% Change	1994	% Change	1993	% Change
Revenues (Million $)						
1Q	788.8	-6%	841.0	-4%	873.0	-36%
2Q	694.4	-14%	803.9	7%	754.0	-45%
3Q	861.4	-10%	957.1	6%	902.0	-41%
4Q	975.1	16%	843.9	-11%	945.0	-35%
Yr.	3,320	-4%	3,446	NM	3,474	-39%
Income (Million $)						
1Q	32.08	24%	25.93	7%	24.22	-42%
2Q	28.60	22%	23.40	27%	18.42	-57%
3Q	35.64	18%	30.25	26%	23.97	-46%
4Q	38.70	NM	-28.28	NM	20.74	-54%
Yr.	135.0	163%	51.31	-41%	87.34	-50%
Earnings Per Share ($)						
1Q	0.68	24%	0.55	-7%	0.59	-42%
2Q	0.60	18%	0.51	16%	0.44	-58%
3Q	0.75	17%	0.64	8%	0.59	-45%
4Q	0.81	NM	-0.62	NM	0.49	-55%
Yr.	2.84	158%	1.10	-48%	2.10	-50%

Next earnings report expected: early December

Litton Industries

Business Summary - 06-OCT-95

Litton Industries, Inc., following the March 1994 spinoff of Western Atlas, concentrates on electronics and shipbuilding operations. Contributions by segment (preliminary) in fiscal 1995 were:

	Sales	Profits
Advanced electronics	50%	45%
Marine engineering/production	41%	47%
Interconnect products	9%	8%

U.S. Government contracts or subcontracts accounted for 73% of total sales and service revenues in fiscal 1994 and also in fiscal 1993.

Advanced electronics include inertial navigation and guidance systems; command, control, communications and intelligence systems; electronic warfare systems; optical systems and night vision devices; laser systems; and other electronic instruments. At July 31, 1995, the segment backlog was $1.8 billion, compared with $1.7 billion a year earlier.

The marine engineering/production segment's Ingalls Shipbuilding subsidiary is a leading designer and builder of surface combat ships for the U.S. Navy. Current work includes Aegis destroyers, amphibious assault ships and corvette coastal warships. It is also a major provider of modernization, overhaul and repair work. As of July 31, 1995, the backlog was $3.3 billion, down from $3.7 billion a year earlier.

The company's interconnect products operations provide interconnection subsystems, electronic and electrical connectors, printed circuit boards, back panels, card cages and solder products.

The Resource Exploration division and the industrial automation division were spun off as Western Atlas Inc. in March 1994.

Important Developments

Sep. '95—Litton signed a letter of intent to purchase the Inertial Systems business unit of Hughes Electronics' Delco Systems. The navigation and guidance systems business has estimated 1995 sales of more than $70 million.

Jun. '95—The company acquired Imo Industries Inc.'s Electro-Optical Systems operations. The producer of laser and night vision equipment had 1994 sales of $110 million. In a separate transaction, Litton purchased the Electro-Optical Sensors division of Intevac Industries, which had annual sales of $15 million.

Jan. '95—LIT purchased Teledyne's Electronic Systems division. The airborne computers, radar, avionics and displays business had 1994 sales of $150 million.

Capitalization

Long Term Obligations: $103,631,000 (7/95).
$2 Cum. Series B Pfd. Stk.: 410,643 shs. ($5 par).

Per Share Data ($) (Year Ended Jul. 31)

	1995	1994	1993	1992	1991	1990
Tangible Bk. Val.	NA	10.10	33.35	21.30	16.90	19.08
Cash Flow	NA	3.26	4.55	9.96	6.51	8.01
Earnings	2.84	1.10	2.10	4.22	1.45	3.63
Dividends	Nil	Nil	Nil	Nil	Nil	Nil
Payout Ratio	Nil	Nil	Nil	Nil	Nil	Nil
Prices - High	38⅞	74¾	69⅜	49¾	46⅛	40¾
- Low	32½	28¼	42¾	39½	37	34½
P/E Ratio - High	14	68	33	12	32	11
- Low	11	26	20	9	26	9

Income Statement Analysis (Million $)

	1994	%Chg	1993	%Chg	1992	%Chg	1991
Revs.	3,446	NM	3,474	-39%	5,693	9%	5,219
Oper. Inc.	308	NM	311	-54%	670	12%	599
Depr.	98.0	-3%	101	-57%	236	7%	220
Int. Exp.	59.0	-29%	83.0	-46%	153	-10%	170
Pretax Inc.	91.0	-37%	144	-56%	330	79%	184
Eff. Tax Rate	43%	—	40%	—	40%	—	55%
Net Inc.	51.0	-41%	87.0	-50%	174	172%	64.0

Balance Sheet & Other Fin. Data (Million $)

	1994	1993	1992	1991	1990	1989
Cash	117	354	354	758	1,244	1,069
Curr. Assets	1,264	1,661	2,622	2,912	3,208	3,210
Total Assets	2,254	3,834	4,839	4,998	5,196	5,258
Curr. Liab.	1,227	1,225	1,835	1,680	1,613	1,774
LT Debt	106	498	928	1,289	1,452	1,454
Common Eqty.	602	1,656	1,356	1,149	1,292	1,259
Total Cap.	765	2,162	2,562	2,681	2,968	2,923
Cap. Exp.	81.0	74.0	389	255	200	249
Cash Flow	149	187	410	283	393	382

Ratio Analysis

	1994	1993	1992	1991	1990	1989
Curr. Ratio	1.0	1.4	1.4	1.7	2.0	1.8
% LT Debt of Cap.	13.8	23.1	36.2	48.1	48.9	49.7
% Net Inc.of Revs.	1.5	2.5	3.1	1.2	3.5	3.5
% Ret. on Assets	1.7	1.9	3.5	1.3	3.6	3.5
% Ret. on Equity	4.5	5.4	13.7	5.5	14.5	14.9

Dividend Data —Common dividends were discontinued following a payment of $0.25 a share (adjusted) in July 1985. In March 1994, one share of Western Atlas Inc. was distributed for each LIT common share held. A "poison pill" purchase right was distributed in August 1994. A two-for-one stock split was effected in May 1992.

Data as orig. reptd.; bef. results of disc. opers. and/or spec. items. Per share data adj. for stk. divs. as of ex-div. date. E-Estimated. NA-Not Available. NM-Not Meaningful. NR-Not Ranked.

Office—21240 Burbank Blvd., Woodland Hills, CA 91367-6675. **Tel**—(818) 598-5000. **Chrmn**—A. J. Brann. **Pres & CEO**—J. M. Leonis (Chrmn eff. Dec. '95). **EVP & COO**—M. R. Brown. **Sr VP & CFO**—R. E. Lang Jr. **Secy**—J. M. Thomas. **Investor Contact**—Kathleen Wailes (818) 598-2026. **Dirs**—A. J. Brann, M. R. Brown, J. T. Casey, C. B. Hallett, T. B. Hayward, O. L. Hoch, D. E. Jeremiah, R. E. Lang Jr., R. H. Lentz, J. M. Leonis, W. P. Sommers, C. B. Thornton Jr. **Transfer Agent & Registrar**—Bank of New York, NYC. **Incorporated** in Delaware in 1953. **Empl**-29,000. **S&P Analyst:** Joe Victor Shammas

STANDARD & POOR'S
STOCK REPORTS

Loctite Corp.

NYSE Symbol **LOC**
In S&P MidCap 400

29-SEP-95 **Industry:** Chemicals

Summary: This company manufactures and sells engineering adhesives, sealants, coatings, specialty chemicals and electroluminescent lighting systems for industrial and consumer applications.

S&P Opinion: Hold (★★★) | Recent Price • 48⅜ | 52 Wk Range • 50⅞-41⅝ | Yield • 2.1% | 12-Mo. P/E • 18.5

Quantitative Evaluations
Outlook (1 Lowest—5 Highest) • **2−**
Fair Value • **46⅝**
Risk • **Low**
Earn./Div. Rank • **A**
Technical Eval. • **Bullish** since 2/94
Rel. Strength Rank (1 Lowest—99 Highest) • **43**
Insider Activity • **Favorable**

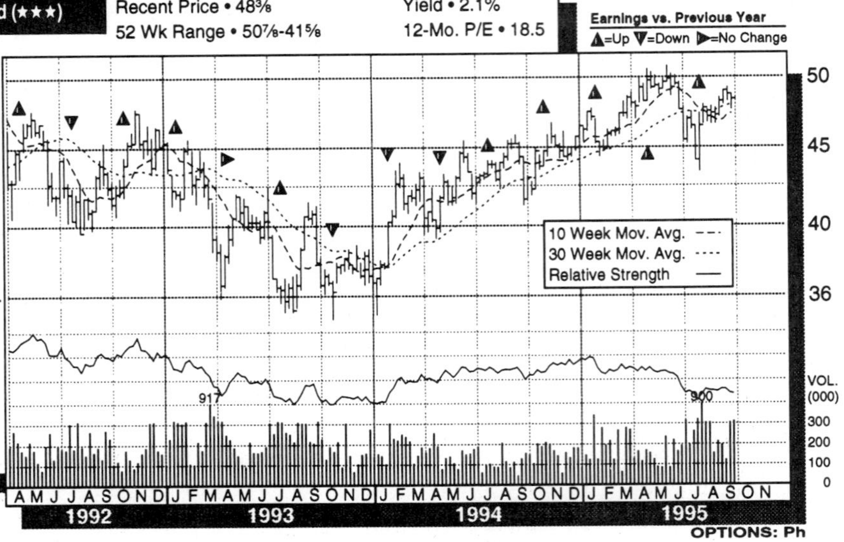

OPTIONS: Ph

Overview - 29-SEP-95

S&P expects that sales growth will slow in the second half of 1995 to about 8% from the 18% rate posted in the first half, due to sluggish North American markets and less favorable currency exchange rates. Sales growth will remain healthy in most other regions of the world, especially Latin American and Pacific areas, reflecting good economic growth. The introduction of two new consumer products in the U.S. should make a significant sales contribution. Margins may narrow slighlty on increased advertising costs, and LOC will take a nonrecurring charge of $0.12 share in the third quarter for the realignment of North American operations. Sales in 1996 could advance by 10% assuming a pickup in domestic markets and profitability will benefit from cost reductions. Share earnings comparisons will also be boosted by a stock repurchase program.

Valuation - 29-SEP-95

The shares of this specialty chemicals producer have been lackluster in 1995, performing well below the overall stock market, in part due to disappointing earnings growth since the second quarter. While selling at a modest premium earnings multiple versus the overall market, we consider the stock to be a sound, long term holding. The company's favorable long term growth prospects are based on its strategy of global expansion, market penetration, and a high pace of new product introductions. A recently announced aggressive stock repurchase program is an added positive factor.

Key Stock Statistics

S&P EPS Est. 1995	2.60	Tang. Bk. Value/Share	9.43
P/E on S&P Est. 1995	18.6	Beta	0.92
S&P EPS Est. 1996	3.10	Shareholders	3,700
Dividend Rate/Share	1.00	Market cap. (B)	$ 1.7
Shs. outstg. (M)	35.4	Inst. holdings	40%
Avg. daily vol. (M)	0.071	Insider holdings	NA

Value of $10,000 invested 5 years ago: $ 22,996

Fiscal Year Ending Dec. 31

	1995	% Change	1994	% Change	1993	% Change
Revenues (Million $)						
1Q	196.8	23%	159.9	7%	149.1	1%
2Q	201.2	13%	177.8	12%	158.1	3%
3Q	—	—	183.3	20%	153.4	-4%
4Q	—	—	182.6	20%	152.0	4%
Yr.	—	—	703.6	15%	612.6	NM
Income (Million $)						
1Q	24.64	35%	18.30	-7%	19.66	NM
2Q	24.11	19%	20.20	16%	17.44	50%
3Q	—	—	22.63	39%	16.31	-24%
4Q	—	—	21.26	43%	14.83	-24%
Yr.	—	—	82.40	21%	68.25	-6%
Earnings Per Share ($)						
1Q	0.70	35%	0.52	-4%	0.54	NM
2Q	0.68	19%	0.57	14%	0.50	56%
3Q	E0.55	-14%	0.64	39%	0.46	-22%
4Q	E0.67	12%	0.60	43%	0.42	-22%
Yr.	E2.60	12%	2.33	21%	1.92	-4%

Next earnings report expected: mid October

Loctite Corp.

Business Summary - 21-SEP-95

Loctite produces high performance adhesives, sealants, coatings, specialized chemicals, and electroluminescent lamps and lighting systems. Products are sold to the industrial and electronics manufacturing and repair, medical products, professional automotive maintenance, and home and car do-it-yourself repair markets.

Contributions by geographic segment in 1994 were:

	Sales	Profits
North America	42%	38%
Europe	37%	45%
Latin America	9%	10%
Asia/Pacific	10%	8%
Luminescent & other	2%	-1%

The company has three principal user markets: industrial (56% of 1994 sales), automotive aftermarket (17%) and consumer (27%). Product lines include thread locking sealants, structural adhesives, instant adhesives, gasketing compounds, automotive body repair materials, home care products, sealants for electronic components, lubricating and cleaning compounds, and other specialty chemicals. The principal products are anaerobic sealants and adhesives and cyanoacrylate adhesives. LOC also produces solid state surface electroluminescent lights and lighting systems.

Anaerobic sealants and adhesives remain liquid while exposed to air but harden when air is excluded, while cyanoacrylate adhesives harden quickly when applied in a thin film and exposed to moisture. Anaerobics are used primarily for locking, sealing and bonding machine elements while cyanoacrylates are used to form bonds between parts made of metal, plastic, wood and glass.

Important Developments

Sep. '95—LOC said that it will take a charge in the third quarter of $5.5 million for the realignment of its North American business. LOC anticipated an annual benefit in excess of $7.0 million, which will be invested in further growth opportunities and improving profitability. Separately, directors authorized the repurchase of up to 3.35 million common shares (9.5% of those outstanding).

Jul. '95—LOC said that sales growth of 8.5% in local currency in the 1995 second quarter enabled it to post an earnings increase of 19% despite additional promotion and advertising expenses. The industrial business was the largest contributor to growth, despite some slowing in North America. Sales of the retail business were up 11% with good growth in Europe, while the auto after-market was flat.

Capitalization

Long Term Debt: $2,717,000 (6/95).

Per Share Data ($)

(Year Ended Dec. 31)

	1994	1993	1992	1991	1990	1989
Tangible Bk. Val.	8.89	10.14	8.39	7.67	7.10	5.89
Cash Flow	3.00	2.41	2.45	2.38	2.02	1.78
Earnings	2.33	1.92	1.99	1.98	1.70	1.52
Dividends	0.82	0.79	0.74	0.68	0.57	0.45
Payout Ratio	35%	41%	37%	34%	34%	30%
Prices - High	46¾	45⅝	50⅞	50⅛	30¾	25½
- Low	35	34¾	39⅝	28	20⅝	16⅜
P/E Ratio - High	20	24	26	25	18	17
- Low	15	18	20	14	12	11

Income Statement Analysis (Million $)

	1994	%Chg	1993	%Chg	1992	%Chg	1991
Revs.	704	15%	613	NM	608	8%	561
Oper. Inc.	138	20%	115	-12%	130	14%	114
Depr.	23.8	36%	17.5	4%	16.8	14%	14.7
Int. Exp.	7.3	35%	5.4	-4%	5.6	2%	5.5
Pretax Inc.	110	21%	91.0	-4%	95.1	NM	95.9
Eff. Tax Rate	25%	—	25%	—	24%	—	25%
Net Inc.	82.4	21%	68.3	-6%	72.3	NM	71.9

Balance Sheet & Other Fin. Data (Million $)

	1994	1993	1992	1991	1990	1989
Cash	68.0	96.1	81.4	84.1	87.8	86.1
Curr. Assets	342	329	315	302	298	257
Total Assets	669	603	557	529	440	362
Curr. Liab.	218	216	137	128	106	89.0
LT Debt	4.9	3.0	14.1	25.3	35.8	36.8
Common Eqty.	423	358	383	361	286	229
Total Cap.	428	362	398	387	322	266
Cap. Exp.	59.1	45.7	40.2	33.5	26.9	16.0
Cash Flow	106	85.7	89.1	86.7	73.1	63.8

Ratio Analysis

	1994	1993	1992	1991	1990	1989
Curr. Ratio	1.6	1.5	2.3	2.4	2.8	2.9
% LT Debt of Cap.	1.1	0.8	3.6	6.6	11.1	13.8
% Net Inc.of Revs.	11.7	11.1	11.9	12.8	12.0	11.9
% Ret. on Assets	13.0	11.9	13.3	14.9	15.2	15.4
% Ret. on Equity	21.1	18.7	19.4	22.2	23.7	25.0

Dividend Data —Dividends have been paid since 1962. A dividend reinvestment plan is available. A "poison pill" stock purchase right was adopted in 1994.

Amt. of Div. $	Date Decl.	Ex-Div. Date	Stock of Record	Payment Date
0.210	Aug. 16	Sep. 02	Sep. 09	Oct. 03 '94
0.210	Nov. 15	Dec. 05	Dec. 09	Jan. 02 '95
0.210	Feb. 21	Mar. 06	Mar. 10	Apr. 03 '95
0.250	Apr. 26	Jun. 06	Jun. 09	Jul. 05 '95
0.250	Aug. 15	Sep. 06	Sep. 08	Oct. 02 '95

Data as orig. reptd.; bef. results of disc. opers. and/or spec. items. Per share data adj. for stk. divs. as of ex-div. date. E-Estimated. NA-Not Available. NM-Not Meaningful. NR-Not Ranked.

Office—10 Columbus Blvd., Hartford, CT 06106. **Tel**—(203) 520-5000. **Chrmn**—K. W. Butterworth. **Pres & CEO**—D. Freeman. **VP & Secy**—E. F. Miller. **SVP-Fin & CFO**—R. L. Aller. **Investor Contact**—Western A. Todd. **Dirs**— W. Barnes, P. C. Browning, K. W. Butterworth, R. Dohr, R. W. Fiondella, D. Freeman, C. Henkel, R. E. Ix, F. B. Krieble, J. Manchot, S. F. Page, S. J. Trachtenberg. **Transfer Agent & Registrar**—Bank of Boston. **Incorporated** in Connecticut in 1953; reincorporated in Delaware in 1987. **Empl-**4,242. **S&P Analyst:** Richard O'Reilly, CFA

STANDARD & POOR'S

STOCK REPORTS

Longview Fibre

NYSE Symbol **LFB**
In S&P MidCap 400

21-SEP-95 **Industry:** Paper/Products

Summary: This operator of tree farms in the Pacific Northwest produces logs, paper and paperboard and converted products.

Quantitative Evaluations

Outlook (1 Lowest—5 Highest)
• **5-**

Fair Value
• **18**

Risk
• **Average**

Earn./Div. Rank
• **B**

Technical Eval.
• **Bearish** since 7/95

Rel. Strength Rank (1 Lowest—99 Highest)
• **8**

Insider Activity
• **NA**

Recent Price • 15⅞
52 Wk Range • 19⅝-14¾

Yield • 3.6%
12-Mo. P/E • 12.1

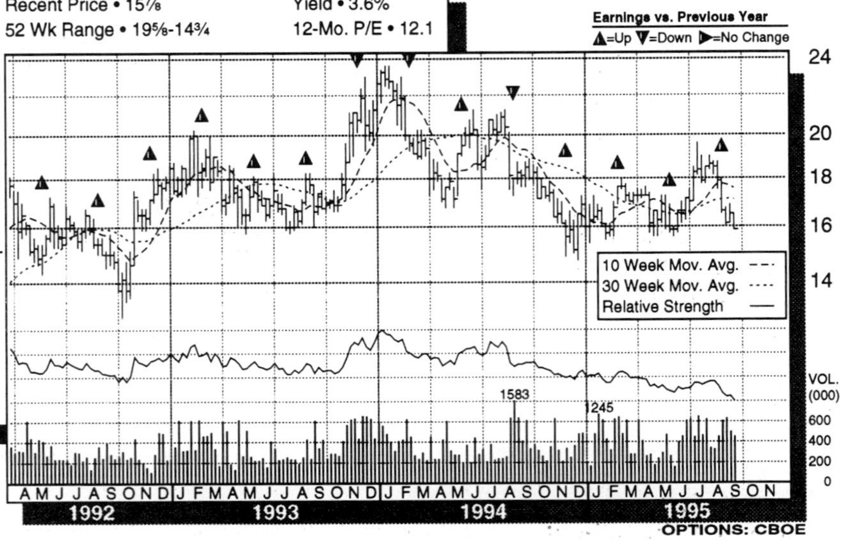

Business Profile - 21-SEP-95

Despite the return to profitability of the paper and converted products segments in recent quarters, margins have been restricted by high raw material costs. The company has embarked on major capital improvement programs at its mill and box plants to install equipment capable of making more specialized products. At June 30, 1995, the backlog of approved projects was $120 million.

Operational Review - 21-SEP-95

Sales climbed 27%, year to year, in the nine months ended July 31, 1995, as strong sales in the paper and paperboard and converted products segments outweighed continued weak timber results. Profitability benefited from increased prices, which offset a rise in raw material costs, and net income more than doubled. Near-term results should continue to improve on increased prices in the manufacturing segments.

Stock Performance - 15-SEP-95

In the past 30 trading days, LFB's shares have declined 15%, compared to a 4% rise in the S&P 500. Average trading volume for the past five days was 89,220 shares, compared with the 40-day moving average of 110,667 shares.

Key Stock Statistics

Dividend Rate/Share	0.56	Shareholders	13,000
Shs. outstg. (M)	51.8	Market cap. (B)	$0.815
Avg. daily vol. (M)	0.126	Inst. holdings	43%
Tang. Bk. Value/Share	8.50	Insider holdings	NA
Beta	1.07		

Value of $10,000 invested 5 years ago: $ 15,290

Fiscal Year Ending Oct. 31

	1995	% Change	1994	% Change	1993	% Change
Revenues (Million $)						
1Q	227.5	37%	166.1	7%	155.9	2%
2Q	234.2	24%	189.2	6%	179.1	3%
3Q	253.4	22%	207.3	18%	175.8	-1%
4Q	—	—	228.3	28%	178.8	-5%
Yr.	—	—	790.9	15%	689.5	NM
Income (Million $)						
1Q	16.55	NM	1.78	-65%	5.09	31%
2Q	22.54	61%	13.99	5%	13.36	38%
3Q	18.91	152%	7.49	-49%	14.63	68%
4Q	—	—	10.16	41%	7.21	-27%
Yr.	—	—	33.41	-17%	40.29	26%
Earnings Per Share ($)						
1Q	0.32	NM	0.03	-70%	0.10	25%
2Q	0.44	63%	0.27	4%	0.26	37%
3Q	0.37	164%	0.14	-50%	0.28	65%
4Q	—	—	0.20	43%	0.14	-26%
Yr.	—	—	0.64	-18%	0.78	26%

Next earnings report expected: early December

Longview Fibre

Business Summary - 21-SEP-95

Longview Fibre owns and operates tree farms in Oregon and Washington that produce logs for sale. At its mill in Longview, Wash., the company produces pulp that is manufactured into kraft paper and containerboard. Shipping containers and merchandise and grocery bags are produced at 15 converting plants in 10 states. Segment contributions (profits in millions) in fiscal 1994 were:

	Sales	Profits
Timber	25%	$111.9
Paper & paperboard	28%	-15.7
Converted products	47%	-19.4

Export sales, principally to Japan, Hong Kong and Southeast Asia, accounted for about 20% of sales in fiscal 1994.

Log sales in fiscal 1994 totaled 250 million board feet, up 18% from fiscal 1993. Most logs produced from the company's timberlands are sold to independent sawmills, plywood plants, U.S. exporters and foreign importers.

Paper sales in fiscal 1994 totaled 236,000 tons, compared with 226,000 the year before, and paperboard sales were 181,000 tons, up from 96,000 tons in fiscal 1993. Wrapping and converting paper is marketed through the company's sales force and paper merchants. Paper is sold mainly in the domestic market, with some grades sold in the export market, while containerboard is marketed in the export market and in the Pacific Coast states.

Converted product sales in fiscal 1994 totaled 549,000 tons, versus 506,000 tons the year before. The tonnage of paper and containerboard used in the converting plants equals about 64% of the Longview mill's production. Bags are sold directly or through paper merchants. Corrugated and solid-fibre boxes are marketed directly.

At October 31, 1994, the company owned in fee 545,193 acres of tree farms.

Important Developments

Aug. '95—The company attributed its improved operating results in the third quarter of 1995 to sharply higher prices for paper and paperboard, which were offset by increased raw material costs. To improve margins, LFB has undertaken major capital improvement programs at its mill and box plants to install equipment capable of making more specialized products.

Capitalization

Long Term Debt: $397,374,000 (7/95).

Per Share Data ($) (Year Ended Oct. 31)

	1994	1993	1992	1991	1990	1989
Tangible Bk. Val.	7.80	7.69	7.39	7.29	7.49	7.05
Cash Flow	2.05	2.11	1.85	1.44	2.03	1.98
Earnings	0.64	0.78	0.62	0.32	1.13	1.21
Dividends	0.52	0.52	0.52	0.52	0.52	0.48
Payout Ratio	81%	67%	84%	162%	44%	39%
Prices - High	23⅝	23	18¾	15⅝	13⅝	16½
- Low	14⅞	15¾	12⅞	9⅜	8¾	12⅜
P/E Ratio - High	37	29	30	49	12	14
- Low	23	20	21	29	8	10

Income Statement Analysis (Million $)

	1994	%Chg	1993	%Chg	1992	%Chg	1991
Revs.	791	15%	690	NM	691	7%	644
Oper. Inc.	149	-3%	154	15%	134	35%	99
Depr.	72.7	5%	69.0	9%	63.4	9%	58.0
Int. Exp.	24.4	7%	22.8	-7%	24.4	NM	24.2
Pretax Inc.	54.0	-14%	63.0	34%	47.0	104%	23.0
Eff. Tax Rate	39%	—	36%	—	32%	—	26%
Net Inc.	33.4	-17%	40.3	26%	32.1	93%	16.6

Balance Sheet & Other Fin. Data (Million $)

	1994	1993	1992	1991	1990	1989
Cash	Nil	Nil	Nil	Nil	0.9	1.9
Curr. Assets	175	148	149	137	132	126
Total Assets	1,022	944	951	927	874	739
Curr. Liab.	139	114	118	110	105	97.0
LT Debt	366	327	362	356	303	195
Common Eqty.	404	399	382	377	387	385
Total Cap.	874	824	828	813	764	642
Cap. Exp.	125	58.0	74.0	104	174	136
Cash Flow	106	109	95.0	75.0	110	109

Ratio Analysis

	1994	1993	1992	1991	1990	1989
Curr. Ratio	1.3	1.3	1.3	1.3	1.3	1.3
% LT Debt of Cap.	41.9	39.7	43.8	43.8	39.7	30.3
% Net Inc.of Revs.	4.2	5.8	4.6	2.6	8.9	9.5
% Ret. on Assets	3.4	4.2	3.4	1.8	7.8	9.7
% Ret. on Equity	8.3	10.3	8.5	4.4	16.3	18.1

Dividend Data —Cash has been paid since 1937. A "poison pill" stock purchase rights plan was adopted in 1989.

Amt. of Div. $	Date Decl.	Ex-Div. Date	Stock of Record	Payment Date
0.130	Dec. 06	Dec. 19	Dec. 23	Jan. 10 '95
0.140	Mar. 07	Mar. 20	Mar. 24	Apr. 10 '95
0.140	Jun. 07	Jun. 21	Jun. 23	Jul. 10 '95
0.050	Sep. 05	Sep. 21	Sep. 25	Oct. 10 '95
0.140	Sep. 05	Sep. 21	Sep. 25	Oct. 10 '95

Data as orig. reptd.; bef. results of disc. opers. and/or spec. items. Per share data adj. for stk. divs. as of ex-div. date. E-Estimated. NA-Not Available. NM-Not Meaningful. NR-Not Ranked.

Office—P.O. Box 639, Longview, WA 98632. **Tel**—(360) 425-1550. **Chrmn, Pres & CEO**—R. P. Wollenberg. **SVP-Fin, Treas, Secy & Investor Contact**—Lisa J. Holbrook. **Dirs**—R. B. Arkel, D. L. Bowden, M. A. Dow, L. J. Holbrook, C. H. Monroe, G. E. Schwartz, D. C. Stibich, J. E. Wertheimer, R. E. Wertheimer, D. A. Wollenberg, R. P. Wollenberg. **Transfer Agent**—Chemical Trust Co. of California, SF. **Incorporated** in Delaware in 1926; reincorporated in Washington in 1990. **Empl**-3,750. **S&P Analyst:** Stewart Scharf

STANDARD & POOR'S

Lubrizol Corp.

STOCK REPORTS

NYSE Symbol **LZ**
In S&P MidCap 400

05-OCT-95 **Industry:** Chemicals

Summary: Lubrizol is believed to be the largest supplier of chemical additives used in lubricants and fuels. It also develops and produces specialty vegetable oils and their derivatives.

S&P Opinion: Hold (★★★)

Recent Price • 32⅝
52 Wk Range • 37⅜-28½
Yield • 2.9%
12-Mo. P/E • 10.9

Quantitative Evaluations
Outlook (1 Lowest—5 Highest)
• **5-**
Fair Value
• **37¾**
Risk
• **Low**
Earn./Div. Rank
• **B+**

Technical Eval.
• **Bearish** since 8/95
Rel. Strength Rank (1 Lowest—99 Highest)
• **38**
Insider Activity
• **Neutral**

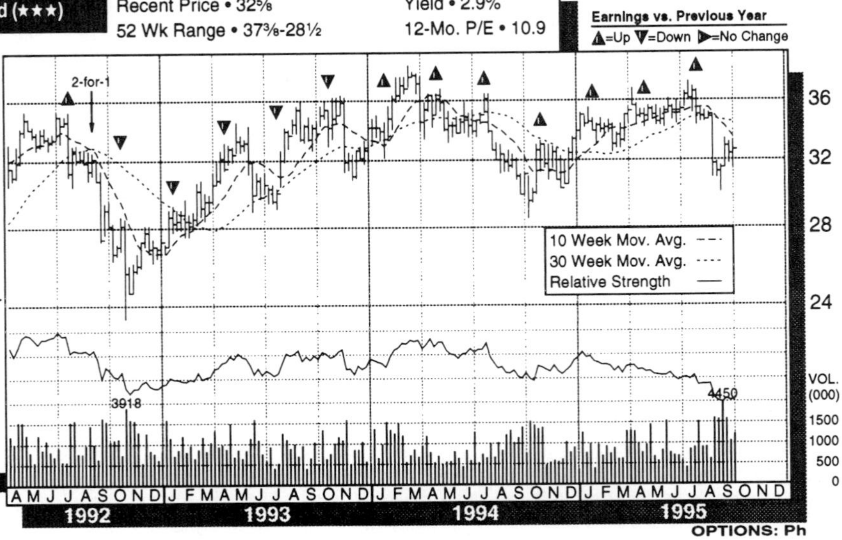

OPTIONS: Ph

Overview - 05-OCT-95

S&P sees revenues advancing close to 10% in 1995 on higher prices for specialty additives and favorable currency exchange rates. Volumes will remain soft through the second half due to a weak North American engine oil market. Profitability should also benefit from a more favorable product mix and manufacturing cost reductions, offsetting higher technology costs for a planned new automotive engine oil requirement. Raw material costs will likely remain unfavorable in the second half. The agribusiness should turn profitable on lower costs. LZ realized a gain of about $0.39 a share in the first half from the sale of its remaining interest in Genentech. A modest pace of stock buybacks will also boost EPS comparisons.

Valuation - 05-OCT-95

This stock has been a poor performer in 1995, virtually unchanged year to date. The stock dropped in late August on projections of disappointing third quarter EPS due to lower than expected volumes caused by weak North American lubricant markets. Long term industry volume growth for lubricant additives should be slow, reflecting increasing performance specifications. With heavy technology investment, the company is expected to exceed this growth rate, but only modestly. Also, the pace of stock buybacks will likely slow following the sale in the second quarter of the remaining interest in Genentech. Consequently, we feel that LZ shares are fairly valued at its current P/E. Dividends have been raised for 12 consecutive years.

Key Stock Statistics

S&P EPS Est. 1995	2.85	Tang. Bk. Value/Share	12.42
P/E on S&P Est. 1995	11.4	Beta	0.64
S&P EPS Est. 1996	2.65	Shareholders	6,500
Dividend Rate/Share	0.96	Market cap. (B)	$ 2.1
Shs. outstg. (M)	63.5	Inst. holdings	72%
Avg. daily vol. (M)	0.331	Insider holdings	NA

Value of $10,000 invested 5 years ago: $ 20,526

Fiscal Year Ending Dec. 31

	1995	% Change	1994	% Change	1993	% Change
Revenues (Million $)						
1Q	416.7	4%	399.7	9%	367.3	-12%
2Q	438.5	7%	408.5	4%	394.3	-5%
3Q	—	—	397.9	1%	392.8	8%
4Q	—	—	392.9	6%	371.1	4%
Yr.	—	—	1,599	5%	1,526	-2%
Income (Million $)						
1Q	49.10	13%	43.28	22%	35.43	-20%
2Q	61.25	25%	49.13	57%	31.34	-30%
3Q	—	—	47.93	NM	-15.91	NM
4Q	—	—	35.23	3%	34.11	104%
Yr.	—	—	175.6	107%	84.98	-32%
Earnings Per Share ($)						
1Q	0.76	17%	0.65	25%	0.52	-19%
2Q	0.96	30%	0.74	61%	0.46	-29%
3Q	E0.57	-22%	0.73	NM	-0.24	NM
4Q	E0.56	4%	0.54	6%	0.51	112%
Yr.	E2.85	7%	2.67	114%	1.25	-31%

Next earnings report expected: late October

Lubrizol Corp.

05-OCT-95

Business Summary - 05-OCT-95

Lubrizol is a specialty chemical company that serves the transportation, industrial and agricultural markets. Its principal products are chemical additives for lubricants and fuels. It also produces specialty vegetable oils. In December 1992, LZ transferred its Agrigenetics crop seed business to 25%-owned Mycogen Corp.

Contributions by geographic segment in 1994:

	Revs.	Profits
United States	44%	65%
Europe	32%	22%
Far East	14%	7%
Other	10%	6%

Specialty chemicals consist of chemical additives (including detergents, dispersants, oxidation and wear inhibitors, viscosity improvers, and pour depressants) for automotive and industrial lubricants, functional fluids and fuels. Additives are used primarily in engine oils, automotive transmission fluids, gear oils, hydraulic fluids, machine oils, metal working compounds, greases, and gasoline and diesel fuels for use in cars, trucks, buses, off-highway equipment, marine engines, and industrial applications. Additives for engine oil accounted for 51% of revenues in 1994. Other chemical products include specialty monomers, coatings additives, oil field chemicals, and refrigerant lubricants. About 60% of chemical sales are made to customers outside North America.

SVO Enterprises develops and sells specialty vegetable oils and products derived from oilseed crops, primarily sunflower and safflower, and operates an oilseed crushing and refining facility.

Important Developments

Sep. '95—The U.S. Court of Appeals overturned a jury verdict that LZ had infringed a patent. The ruling also overturned a $129 million judgment against LZ.

Jul. '95—LZ said second quarter 1995 earnings included a gain of $0.26 a share from the sale of its remaining stock in Genentech, versus $0.12 a share in the 1994 period. First half share earnings included a gain of $0.39 from the sale of its investment, versus $0.23. Excluding nonrecurring items, share earnings in the second quarter grew 13% on a 7% increase in revenues, reflecting higher prices and favorable exchange rates. Volumes declined 3% as a result of the absence of spot sales to certain international customers; ongoing shipments were up 2%. LZ repurchased 875,000 common shares in the second quarter. The company said that about 3.6 million shares remain available for repurchase under a 4 million share program authorized in April 1994.

Capitalization

Long Term Debt: $218,151,000 (6/95).

Per Share Data ($) (Year Ended Dec. 31)

	1994	1993	1992	1991	1990	1989
Tangible Bk. Val.	12.19	10.45	11.74	11.26	10.36	8.96
Cash Flow	3.60	2.14	2.65	2.58	3.43	2.21
Earnings	2.67	1.25	1.81	1.79	2.67	1.26
Dividends	0.89	0.85	0.81	0.77	0.73	0.69
Payout Ratio	33%	68%	44%	43%	27%	55%
Prices - High	38⅝	36⅜	35⅜	30	24⅞	22¾
- Low	28½	26⅝	23⅜	21¼	16¼	16⅞
P/E Ratio - High	14	29	20	17	9	18
- Low	11	21	13	12	6	13

Income Statement Analysis (Million $)

	1994	%Chg	1993	%Chg	1992	%Chg	1991
Revs.	1,599	5%	1,526	-2%	1,552	5%	1,476
Oper. Inc.	263	18%	223	1%	220	NM	222
Depr.	61.3	3%	59.6	2%	58.4	7%	54.6
Int. Exp.	3.2	-24%	4.2	15%	3.6	-53%	7.7
Pretax Inc.	251	109%	120	-32%	177	NM	178
Eff. Tax Rate	30%	—	29%	—	30%	—	31%
Net Inc.	176	107%	85.0	-32%	125	NM	124

Balance Sheet & Other Fin. Data (Million $)

	1994	1993	1992	1991	1990	1989
Cash	36.0	24.0	77.0	126	76.0	82.0
Curr. Assets	624	569	591	702	669	543
Total Assets	1,394	1,183	1,127	1,172	1,115	960
Curr. Liab.	254	224	206	262	248	181
LT Debt	114	55.3	23.3	35.0	54.0	53.2
Common Eqty.	832	732	819	794	736	663
Total Cap.	974	799	880	868	827	750
Cap. Exp.	161	128	95.8	82.0	77.0	65.0
Cash Flow	237	145	183	178	244	165

Ratio Analysis

	1994	1993	1992	1991	1990	1989
Curr. Ratio	2.5	2.5	2.9	2.7	2.7	3.0
% LT Debt of Cap.	11.7	6.9	2.6	4.0	6.5	7.1
% Net Inc.of Revs.	11.0	5.6	8.0	8.4	13.1	7.7
% Ret. on Assets	13.8	7.5	10.9	10.8	18.9	9.9
% Ret. on Equity	22.7	11.1	15.5	16.2	28.0	14.3

Dividend Data —Dividends have been paid since 1935. A dividend reinvestment plan is available. A "poison pill" stock purchase rights plan was adopted in 1991.

Amt. of Div. $	Date Decl.	Ex-Div. Date	Stock of Record	Payment Date
0.230	Oct. 24	Nov. 04	Nov. 10	Dec. 09 '94
0.230	Jan. 23	Feb. 06	Feb. 10	Mar. 10 '95
0.230	Apr. 24	May. 04	May. 10	Jun. 09 '95
0.230	Jul. 24	Aug. 08	Aug. 10	Sep. 08 '95
0.240	Sep. 25	Nov. 08	Nov. 10	Dec. 08 '95

Data as orig. reptd.; bef. results of disc. opers. and/or spec. items. Per share data adj. for stk. divs. as of ex-div. date. E-Estimated. NA-Not Available. NM-Not Meaningful. NR-Not Ranked.

Office—29400 Lakeland Blvd., Wickliffe, OH 44092. **Tel**—(216) 943-4200. **Chrmn & CEO**—L. E. Coleman. **Pres**—W. G. Bares. **Secy & Investor Contact**—K. H. Hopping. **Treas**—W. R. Jones. **Dirs**—W. G. Bares, E. F. Bell, L. E. Coleman, P. G. Elliott, G. D. Harnett, D. H. Hoag, T. C. MacAvoy, W. P. Madar, R. A. Miller, R. A. Mitsch. R. D. Thompson, K. E. Ware. **Transfer Agent & Registrar**— KeyCorp, Cleveland, Ohio. **Incorporated** in Ohio in 1928. **Empl**-4,520. **S&P Analyst:** Richard O'Reilly, CFA

Lukens Inc.

NYSE Symbol **LUC**
In S&P MidCap 400

22-SEP-95 **Industry:** Steel-Iron

Summary: Lukens is the third largest U.S. producer of carbon steel plate and the fourth largest producer of stainless steel.

S&P Opinion: Hold (★★★)

Recent Price • 30¾ | Yield • 3.3%
52 Wk Range • 36-25¾ | 12-Mo. P/E • 13.1

Quantitative Evaluations
Outlook (1 Lowest—5 Highest)
• 3+
Fair Value
• 30¾
Risk
• Average
Earn./Div. Rank
• B

Technical Eval.
• Bullish since 9/95
Rel. Strength Rank (1 Lowest—99 Highest)
• 17
Insider Activity
• NA

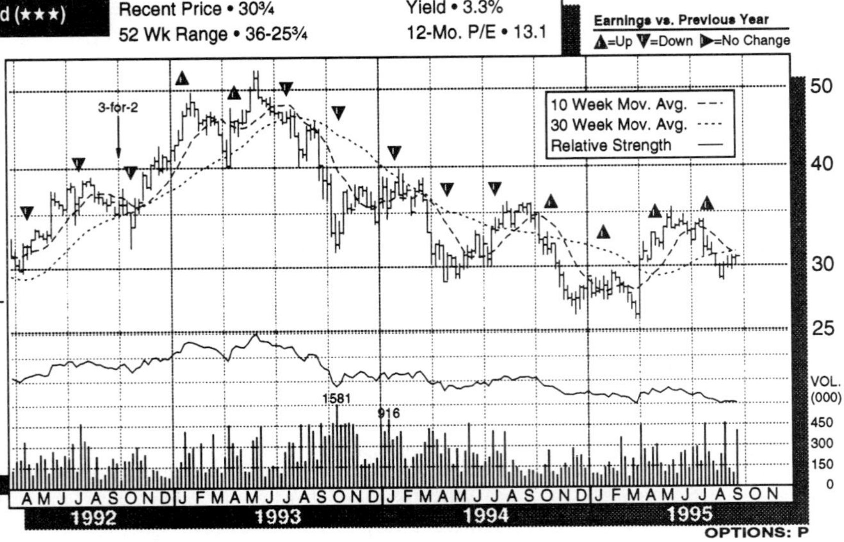

OPTIONS: P

Overview - 22-SEP-95

Assuming GDP growth of about 2.6% in 1996, we look for 10% sales growth in 1996, reflecting a recovery in volume in both the plate and stainless products segments. The volume of shipments was restricted in 1995 as a result of new equipment installations. This is not expected to occur in 1996. Volume will also be lifted by rebuilding of stainless products inventory by service centers. Aided by increased capacity utilization, rising prices for both plate and stainless and only moderate increases in scrap costs, margins and operating profit per ton should exceed 1995's levels. Assuming flat to slightly lower interest expense and an unchanged tax rate, earnings should advance again in 1996. Strong secular demand for stainless flat roll products, along with debt reduction, will bolster long-term sales and profit growth.

Valuation - 22-SEP-95

While LUC's stock offers good value at 11X our projected earnings for 1996 and has an attractive dividend yield, we are recommending a hold rating on the shares due to our concern that flat roll stainless has probably peaked near term. Also, the company is currently installing new equipment, and this process often involves risks to production and profits, with some potential for negative surprises. Through late September, LUC was up 3.0%, versus a 24% gain in the S&P 500, and it also lagged behind peers Allegheny Ludlum and J&L Specialty.

Key Stock Statistics

S&P EPS Est. 1995	2.10	Tang. Bk. Value/Share	14.69
P/E on S&P Est. 1995	14.6	Beta	0.96
S&P EPS Est. 1996	2.80	Shareholders	5,600
Dividend Rate/Share	1.00	Market cap. (B)	$0.439
Shs. outstg. (M)	14.7	Inst. holdings	73%
Avg. daily vol. (M)	0.040	Insider holdings	NA

Value of $10,000 invested 5 years ago: $ 14,442

Fiscal Year Ending Dec. 31

	1995	% Change	1994	% Change	1993	% Change
Revenues (Million $)						
1Q	260.0	18%	220.9	NM	221.1	58%
2Q	271.8	12%	242.2	7%	226.9	-6%
3Q	—	—	231.5	9%	211.4	-17%
4Q	—	—	252.4	25%	202.7	-17%
Yr.	—	—	947.0	10%	862.1	-2%
Income (Million $)						
1Q	9.10	NM	-2.50	NM	6.18	18%
2Q	9.55	45%	6.59	-18%	8.03	-21%
3Q	—	—	7.37	28%	5.77	-37%
4Q	—	—	10.71	NM	-6.85	NM
Yr.	—	—	22.18	69%	13.12	-60%
Earnings Per Share ($)						
1Q	0.58	NM	-0.21	NM	0.39	3%
2Q	0.61	49%	0.41	-20%	0.51	-33%
3Q	E0.40	-15%	0.47	31%	0.36	-42%
4Q	E0.51	-26%	0.69	NM	-0.51	NM
Yr.	E2.10	53%	1.37	80%	0.76	-67%

Next earnings report expected: mid October

Lukens Inc.

Business Summary - 22-SEP-95

Lukens is the third largest U.S. producer of steel plate and the fourth largest stainless steel maker. Non-steel units were discontinued in 1993. Contributions by business group in 1994 were:

	Sales	Profits
Lukens Steel	50%	39%
Washington Stainless	50%	61%

Lukens Steel produces a broad range of carbon, alloy and clad plates for service centers and a wide range of markets in the capital goods sector. LUC produces raw steel at its Coatesville, Pa., plant and performs rolling and fabrication at facilities in Coatesville and Conshohocken. All plants operated near capacity in 1994. Shipments in 1994 totaled 725,900 tons, versus 711,800 tons in 1993.

Shipments by market in 1994 were: service centers 40%, machinery and industrial equipment 32%, infrastructure 8%, transportation 12%, international 4%, environmental and energy 3% and military and defense 1%.

Washington Stainless manufactures light-gauge stainless steel sheet, strip, continuous mill plate, hot band and slabs. It is the fourth largest stainless producer in the U.S. and a leading maker of 304 and 316 series stainless. Shipments totaled 259,500 tons in 1994, versus 208,800 tons in 1993.

Shipments by market in 1994 were: service centers 37%, process industries 34%, foodservice equipment 10%, international 4%, architecture and construction 6%, transportation 3% and consumer durables 6%.

Melting operations for Washington Stainless are conducted in Houston, Pa., while finishing and rolling are performed at Washington, Pa., and Massilon, Ohio. Utilization of the finishing and rolling facilities ranged between 85% and 100% in 1994, while melting facilities operated at full capacity.

Backlog at 1994 year-end totaled $168.5 million, versus $101.6 million a year earlier.

Important Developments

Aug. '95—LUC said it expects 1995's third-quarter carbon steel shipments will trail 1994's third quarter by some 20,000 tons as a result of a commissioning program of its new Steckel Mill Advanced Rolling Technology (SMART) system at Conshohocken, Pa. It added that its fourth-quarter production of carbon plate was expected to exceed that of 1994's fourth quarter.

Capitalization

Long Term Debt: $229,028,000 (6/95).
8.0% Conv. Pfd. Stk: 506,300 shs. (liquid. pref. $60); ea. conv. into two com. shs.; held by ESOP.

Per Share Data ($)

(Year Ended Dec. 31)

	1994	1993	1992	1991	1990	1989
Tangible Bk. Val.	15.27	14.17	18.90	17.09	16.26	13.73
Cash Flow	4.31	3.79	5.20	3.63	5.35	4.97
Earnings	1.37	0.76	2.31	1.68	3.38	3.15
Dividends	1.00	1.00	0.99	0.99	0.95	0.73
Payout Ratio	73%	132%	43%	58%	28%	23%
Prices - High	39¾	52⅞	42⅝	34	30¼	26
- Low	26⅛	31¼	26½	23	18¾	16⅜
P/E Ratio - High	29	70	19	20	9	8
- Low	19	41	12	14	6	5

Income Statement Analysis (Million $)

	1994	%Chg	1993	%Chg	1992	%Chg	1991
Revs.	947	10%	862	-2%	881	40%	629
Oper. Inc.	94.0	1%	93.0	-12%	106	73%	61.1
Depr.	44.0	-3%	45.5	16%	39.2	58%	24.8
Int. Exp.	15.8	-4%	16.4	21%	13.6	NM	2.3
Pretax Inc.	36.4	79%	20.3	-62%	53.9	46%	36.9
Eff. Tax Rate	39%	—	35%	—	39%	—	38%
Net Inc.	22.2	69%	13.1	-60%	33.1	44%	23.0

Balance Sheet & Other Fin. Data (Million $)

	1994	1993	1992	1991	1990	1989
Cash	9.8	11.5	15.0	59.9	35.2	4.2
Curr. Assets	281	308	294	204	184	170
Total Assets	826	817	760	432	412	377
Curr. Liab.	175	162	152	99	87.5	82.3
LT Debt	201	221	219	46.6	54.6	57.4
Common Eqty.	269	260	325	215	203	170
Total Cap.	478	488	577	320	314	285
Cap. Exp.	120	67.4	36.0	34.7	35.0	25.5
Cash Flow	63.6	56.0	70.7	46.2	67.3	63.2

Ratio Analysis

	1994	1993	1992	1991	1990	1989
Curr. Ratio	1.6	1.9	1.9	2.1	2.1	2.1
% LT Debt of Cap.	42.1	45.3	37.9	14.6	17.4	20.1
% Net Inc.of Revs.	2.3	1.5	3.8	3.7	6.5	6.4
% Ret. on Assets	2.7	1.7	5.3	5.4	11.1	11.6
% Ret. on Equity	7.4	3.6	10.4	10.2	22.7	23.4

Dividend Data —Dividends have been paid since 1940. A dividend reinvestment plan is available. A new "poison pill" stock purchase right was adopted in 1990.

Amt. of Div. $	Date Decl.	Ex-Div. Date	Stock of Record	Payment Date
0.250	Oct. 26	Nov. 01	Nov. 07	Nov. 18 '94
0.250	Jan. 25	Jan. 31	Feb. 06	Feb. 17 '95
0.250	Apr. 26	May. 02	May. 08	May. 19 '95
0.250	Jul. 26	Aug. 03	Aug. 07	Aug. 18 '95

Data as orig. reptd.; bef. results of disc. opers. and/or spec. items. Per share data adj. for stk. divs. as of ex-div. date. E-Estimated. NA-Not Available. NM-Not Meaningful. NR-Not Ranked.

Office—50 South First Ave., Coatesville, PA 19320-0911. **Tel**—(610) 383-2000. **Chrmn & CEO**—R. W. Van Sant. **VP-Treas**—J. C. van Roden Jr. **VP-Secy**—W. D. Sprague. **Investor Contact**—Barbara L. Gasper. **Dirs**—M. O. Alexander, R. F. Dammeyer, T. K. Dunnigan, S. L. Helton, N. H. Hansen, W. H. Nelson III, S. J. Northrop, H. C. Stonecipher, J. L. Thomas, W. P. Tippett, R. W. Van Sant. **Transfer Agent & Registrar**—American Stock Transfer & Trust Co., NYC. **Incorporated** in Pennsylvania in 1917; reincorporated in Delaware in 1987. **Empl**-4,060. **S&P Analyst:** Leo Larkin

STANDARD & POOR'S

STOCK REPORTS

Lyondell Petrochemical

NYSE Symbol **LYO**

In S&P MidCap 400

03-SEP-95

Industry: Chemicals

Summary: This company is a leading producer of a wide variety of petrochemicals and has a 90% interest in Lyondell-CITGO Refining Co. (formed July 1993).

S&P Opinion: Accumulate (★★★★)

Recent Price • 27½ | 52 Wk Range • 33-21⅝ | Yield • 3.3% | 12-Mo. P/E • 5.1

Quantitative Evaluations

Outlook (1 Lowest—5 Highest)
• **2+**

Fair Value
• **24¾**

Risk
• **Average**

Earn./Div. Rank
• **NR**

Technical Eval.
• **Bearish** since 7/95

Rel. Strength Rank (1 Lowest—99 Highest)
• **44**

Insider Activity
• **NA**

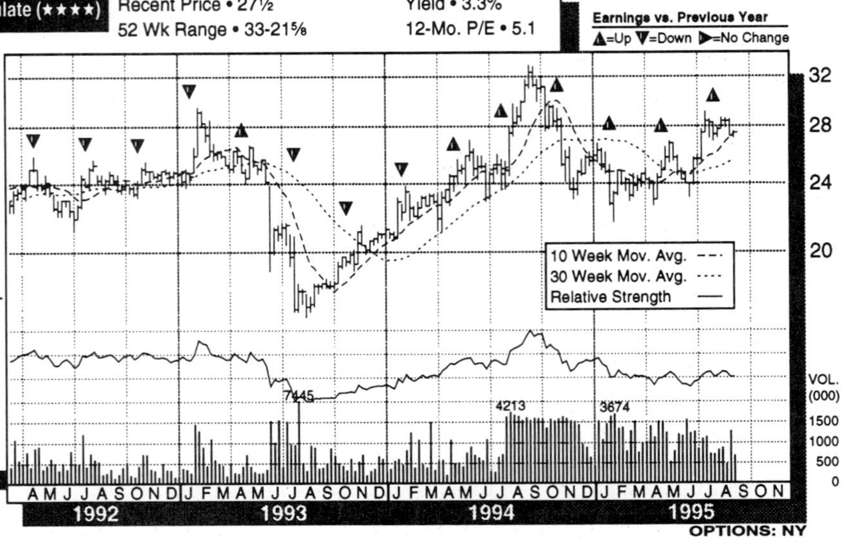

OPTIONS: NY

Overview - 01-SEP-95

We expect LYO's petrochemical profits to decline in the 1995 second half from the first half level, as selling prices for olefins and polymers have softened in recent months due to slower U.S. economic growth and increased industry capacity. Profit margins for chemicals should remain relatively healthy, and results will also benefit from planned capacity expansions. The fourth quarter will also be restricted by maintenance downtime at one olefin plant. Methanol prices have fallen since early 1995. The 90%-owned refining business will continue to realize operational benefits from an upgrade project performed late in 1994 as well as higher volumes of low-cost Venezuelan heavy crude oil, though lower industry refining margins and an unexpected outage will hurt the third quarter. Capital spending for 1995 is budgeted at $180 million.

Valuation - 01-SEP-95

The stock this year has remained below its September 1994 peak, reflecting concerns regarding the soft near-term profit outlook for petrochemicals. We feel that LYO's longer term outlook remains very positive, as further earnings growth is expected as a result of a refinery upgrade scheduled for completion in late 1996, the recent acquisition of a major polyethylene business, and several planned capacity expansions. The shares, yielding 3.3% on a secure dividend of $0.90 a year, are attractive at their current P/E multiple.

Key Stock Statistics

S&P EPS Est. 1995	5.50	Tang. Bk. Value/Share	0.79
P/E on S&P Est. 1995	5.0	Beta	1.21
S&P EPS Est. 1996	5.00	Shareholders	2,300
Dividend Rate/Share	0.90	Market cap. (B)	$ 2.2
Shs. outstg. (M)	80.0	Inst. holdings	55%
Avg. daily vol. (M)	0.162	Insider holdings	NA

Value of $10,000 invested 5 years ago: $ 21,347

Fiscal Year Ending Dec. 31

	1995	% Change	1994	% Change	1993	% Change
Revenues (Million $)						
1Q	1,174	42%	824.0	-23%	1,064	4%
2Q	1,370	52%	900.0	-17%	1,080	-11%
3Q	—	—	1,037	17%	885.0	-34%
4Q	—	—	1,096	34%	820.0	-33%
Yr.	—	—	3,857	NM	3,850	-20%
Income (Million $)						
1Q	127.0	NM	22.00	NM	-8.00	NM
2Q	135.0	NM	32.00	NM	-11.00	NM
3Q	—	—	66.00	NM	-9.00	NM
4Q	—	—	103.0	NM	14.00	-22%
Yr.	—	—	223.0	NM	4.00	-85%
Earnings Per Share ($)						
1Q	1.59	NM	0.27	NM	-0.09	NM
2Q	1.68	NM	0.40	NM	-0.14	NM
3Q	E1.12	35%	0.83	NM	0.12	-20%
4Q	E1.11	-13%	1.28	NM	0.17	-23%
Yr.	E5.50	98%	2.78	NM	0.06	-81%

Next earnings report expected: late October

Lyondell Petrochemical

03-SEP-95

Business Summary - 01-SEP-95

Lyondell Petrochemical is an integrated petrochemical and petroleum processor and marketer. Contributions by segment in 1994 were:

	Sales	Profits
Petrochemicals	46%	88%
Refined products	54%	12%

The petrochemical complex in Channelview, Tex., consists of two large olefins plants, a methanol plant, a product flexibility unit, and other processing and recovery units. Olefins consist of ethylene (annual capacity of 3.6 billion lbs.), propylene (2.1 billion lbs.) and butadiene (615 million lbs.), which are used to make plastics, rubbers, fibers, anti-freeze and detergents. LYO is one of the largest domestic merchant marketers of ethylene and propylene. Methanol (233 million gallons) is used for adhesives, polyester fibers, and as an octane enhancer. The Channelview complex also includes two MTBE units (167 million gallons).

The company produces low-density polyethylene (annual capacity 140 million lbs.) and polypropylene (300 million lbs.) in Bayport, Texas. In May 1995, LYO acquired a high-density polyethylene business with an annual capacity of 1.5 billion pounds.

Lyondell-CITGO Refining Co. (90% owned; formed in July 1993) has a Houston refinery, with operable crude capacity of 265,000 bbl. per day, that produces gasoline, diesel fuel, heating oil, jet fuels, lubricant oils, chemical feedstocks, aromatics and industrial products. It will expand the refinery's heavy crude oil processing capacity by 1997 to 200,000 bbl. daily, from the current 130,000 bbl., at a total cost of $980 million. Aromatics (305 million gallons a year, including those produced at Channelview) include benzene (140 million gallons), paraxylene (400 million lbs.) and orthoxylene (270 million lbs.) for styrene, polyester fibers and films, and plasticizers.

Important Developments

Aug. '95—LYO and two other companies jointly announced plans for a new 1.5 billion pound per year olefins plant to be located at LYO's Channelview complex.

May '95—LYO acquired the high-density polyethylene business of Occidental Petroleum for $355 million plus $64 million for inventory. LYO used $185 million of cash and $240 million of debt for the acquisition. The business consists of two plants in Texas with total annual capacity of 1.5 billion pounds, making LYO the nation's third largest producer. The company noted that the purchase provides additional downstream integration for its petrochemical business.

Capitalization

Long Term Debt: $588,000,000 (6/95).
Minority Interest: $421,000,000.

Per Share Data ($) (Year Ended Dec. 31)

	1994	1993	1992	1991	1990	1989
Tangible Bk. Val.	0.79	-1.10	-0.08	1.53	0.48	0.11
Cash Flow	3.60	0.60	0.83	3.29	4.86	4.94
Earnings	2.78	0.06	0.32	2.78	4.45	4.67
Dividends	0.90	1.35	1.80	1.75	4.10	1.20
Payout Ratio	32%	225%	554%	63%	92%	26%
Prices - High	33	29½	25⅞	26⅛	21½	33½
- Low	20⅝	16¾	21⅛	14⅝	13⅛	16¾
P/E Ratio - High	12	NM	81	9	5	7
- Low	7	NM	66	5	3	4

Income Statement Analysis (Million $)

	1994	%Chg	1993	%Chg	1992	%Chg	1991
Revs.	3,857	NM	3,850	-20%	4,805	-16%	5,729
Oper. Inc.	489	NM	137	13%	121	-71%	413
Depr.	65.0	48%	44.0	10%	40.0	-2%	41.0
Int. Exp.	74.0	NM	74.0	-6%	79.0	7%	74.0
Pretax Inc.	355	NM	21.0	-40%	35.0	-90%	340
Eff. Tax Rate	36%	—	57%	—	26%	—	35%
Net Inc.	223	NM	4.0	-85%	26.0	-88%	222

Balance Sheet & Other Fin. Data (Million $)

	1994	1993	1992	1991	1990	1989
Cash	94.0	119	121	307	127	245
Curr. Assets	697	523	568	889	788	801
Total Assets	1,663	1,231	1,215	1,479	1,372	1,267
Curr. Liab.	433	299	345	514	550	434
LT Debt	707	717	725	710	658	714
Common Eqty.	63.0	-88.0	-6.0	122	38.0	9.0
Total Cap.	1,147	854	798	927	773	790
Cap. Exp.	252	85.0	97.0	43.0	145	176
Cash Flow	288	48.0	66.0	263	389	395

Ratio Analysis

	1994	1993	1992	1991	1990	1989
Curr. Ratio	1.6	1.7	1.6	1.7	1.4	1.8
% LT Debt of Cap.	61.6	84.0	90.9	76.6	85.1	90.4
% Net Inc.of Revs.	5.8	0.1	0.5	3.9	5.5	7.0
% Ret. on Assets	15.4	0.3	1.9	15.6	27.0	34.3
% Ret. on Equity	NM	NM	NM	277.5	NM	302.8

Dividend Data —Quarterly dividends were initiated in 1989. A dividend reinvestment plan is available.

Amt. of Div. $	Date Decl.	Ex-Div. Date	Stock of Record	Payment Date
0.225	Jul. 22	Aug. 08	Aug. 12	Sep. 15 '94
0.225	Oct. 25	Nov. 18	Nov. 25	Dec. 15 '94
0.225	Jan. 23	Feb. 17	Feb. 24	Mar. 15 '95
0.225	Apr. 24	May. 19	May. 25	Jun. 15 '95
0.225	Jul. 24	Aug. 23	Aug. 25	Sep. 15 '95

Data as orig. reptd.; bef. results of disc. opers. and/or spec. items. Per share data adj. for stk. divs. as of ex-div. date. E-Estimated. NA-Not Available. NM-Not Meaningful. NR-Not Ranked.

Office—1221 McKinney Ave., Suite 1600, Houston, TX 77010. **Tel**—(713) 652-7200. **Chrmn & CEO**—B. G. Gower. **Pres**—D. F. Smith. **SVP, CFO & Treas**—R. S. Young. **SVP & Secy**—J. R. Pendergraft. **Investor Contact**—David M. Balderston. **Dirs**— W. T. Butler, C. J. Crawford, D. T. Engen, B. G. Gower, S. F. Hinchliffe, Jr., D. C. Mecum II, D. F. Smith, P. R. Staley. **Transfer Agent & Registrar**—Bank of New York, NYC. **Incorporated** In Delaware in 1985. **Empl**-2,263. **S&P Analyst:** Richard O'Reilly, CFA

MCN Corp.

NYSE Symbol **MCN**
In S&P MidCap 400

25-SEP-95 **Industry:** Utilities-Gas

Summary: This holding company's Michigan Consolidated Gas subsidiary distributes gas to more than one million customers in the Detroit metropolitan area and various Michigan communities.

S&P Opinion: Accumulate (★★★★) | Recent Price • 19¾ | 52 Wk Range • 20-16⅜ | Yield • 4.5% | 12-Mo. P/E • 17.6

Quantitative Evaluations

Outlook (1 Lowest—5 Highest)
• 1+

Fair Value
• 15⅞

Risk
• Low

Earn./Div. Rank
• NR

Technical Eval.
• **Bullish** since 7/95

Rel. Strength Rank (1 Lowest—99 Highest)
• 60

Insider Activity
• NA

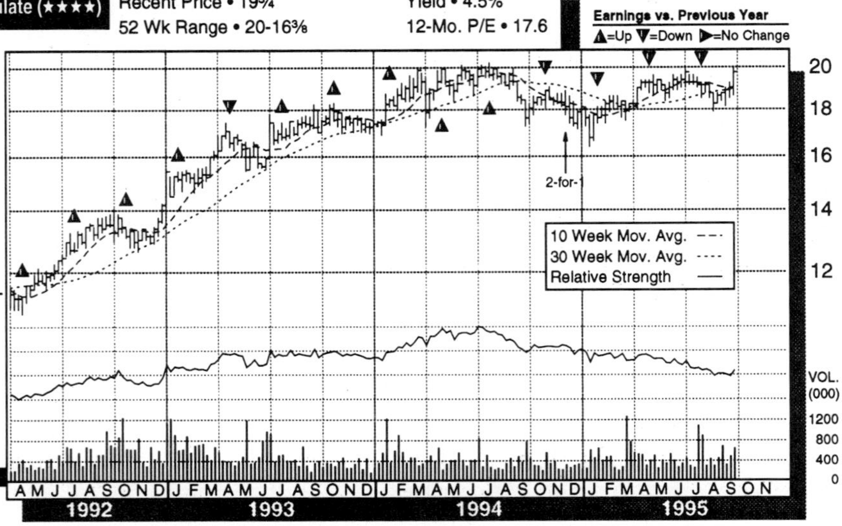

Overview - 22-SEP-95

Share earnings should improve in 1995, primarily reflecting strong growth in the diversified services group. Higher gas production from exploration and production activities should continue to add to the bottom line. Also, improved margins from gas marketing operations and higher gas sales will bolster earnings. Assuming normal weather, utility profits in 1995 are expected to rise as a result of customer growth and higher deliveries. However, weather in 1995's first half, which was significantly warmer than comparable periods in 1994, will negatively affect full-year results. Furthermore, 7% more common shares outstanding will restrain share earnings. Results in 1996 should benefit from large planned expenditures in the areas of gas distribution and exploration and production.

Valuation - 22-SEP-95

Following an industrywide decline in stock prices in 1994, MCN's shares have appreciated since the beginning of 1995. The shares are currently trading at about 11 to 12 times our 1996 earnings estimate of $1.60 a share and have a dividend yield of some 4.7%. Dividend hikes of approximately 2.5% should continue in the coming years. Based on MCN's potential for significant earnings growth, its strong nonregulated activities and the likelihood of increasing dividends, the shares should outperform the market over the next six to 12 months and should be accumulated for both growth and income.

Key Stock Statistics

S&P EPS Est. 1995	1.45	Tang. Bk. Value/Share	8.56
P/E on S&P Est. 1995	13.6	Beta	0.18
S&P EPS Est. 1996	1.60	Shareholders	24,700
Dividend Rate/Share	0.89	Market cap. (B)	$ 1.3
Shs. outstg. (M)	66.0	Inst. holdings	46%
Avg. daily vol. (M)	0.110	Insider holdings	NA

Value of $10,000 invested 5 years ago: $ 23,187

Fiscal Year Ending Dec. 31

	1995	% Change	1994	% Change	1993	% Change
Revenues (Million $)						
1Q	548.0	-17%	657.0	18%	557.0	4%
2Q	283.1	4%	272.6	-5%	288.0	7%
3Q	—	—	204.4	13%	181.0	-2%
4Q	—	—	412.1	-7%	445.0	-1%
Yr.	—	—	1,546	5%	1,470	2%
Income (Million $)						
1Q	61.59	-11%	69.12	28%	54.04	-5%
2Q	2.31	-34%	3.48	79%	1.94	27%
3Q	—	—	-15.57	NM	-11.22	NM
4Q	—	—	20.74	-26%	28.03	104%
Yr.	—	—	77.77	7%	72.79	27%
Earnings Per Share ($)						
1Q	1.02	-13%	1.17	26%	0.93	-14%
2Q	0.04	-33%	0.06	71%	0.03	17%
3Q	E-0.20	NM	-0.26	NM	-0.19	NM
4Q	E0.59	69%	0.35	-26%	0.47	98%
Yr.	E1.45	11%	1.31	6%	1.24	18%

Next earnings report expected: mid October

MCN Corp.

Business Summary - 19-SEP-95

MCN Corp. is the holding company (formed in 1989) for Michigan Consolidated Gas (MichCon), which distributes natural gas to customers in the Detroit, Grand Rapids, Ann Arbor, Traverse City, Muskegon and Adrian metropolitan areas and other Michigan communities. Nonutility operations, conducted through MCN Investment, provide gas services, gas storage, gas technology and computer operations services. Contributions (profits in millions) in 1994 were:

	Revs.	Profits
Utility	72%	$128.7
Gas services	23%	27.0
Computer operations services	5%	6.6
Other	---	-7.9

Gas sales and transportation volume in 1994 totaled 648.0 Bcf (615.1 Bcf in 1993). In 1994, utility customers averaged 1,141,491 (1,129,752). Degree days in 1994 amounted to 6,489 (4.2% warmer than normal), versus 6,675 (2.2% warmer than normal) in 1993. In 1994, the average utility cost of gas purchased per Mcf was $2.66 ($2.92).

Nonutility gas actvities include the purchasing and sale of natural gas to large-volume gas users throughout the eastern U.S. and Canada; development of cogeneration facilities throughout the U.S. and Canada; providing gas gathering and processing services; natural gas exploration, development and production; providing gas storage services to other gas utilities, pipeline companies and large-volume gas users. Computer processing services are provided through Genix Group. Other activities involve developing storage technologies and combustion applications for natural gas, and residential and commercial community development partnerships.

In March 1995, MCN sold 5,750,000 shares of new common stock in a public offering, generating net proceeds of about $99 million.

Important Developments

Sep. '95—MCN's CoEnergy Offshore Pipeline & Processing subsidiary signed an agreement with the Blue Dolphin Energy Co. of Houston to purchase a one-third interest in a natural gas, oil and condensate gathering system in the Gulf of Mexico for $10 million. The system includes a pipeline about 40 miles offshore from Freeport, Texas, a separation facility, and a barge loading terminal.

Jun. '95—The Genix Group subsidiary signed a five-year agreement to provide computer operations management and electronic printing services to Handleman Co., North America's largest distributor of recorded music, video products, books and computer software. The contract is valued at about $25 million.

Capitalization

Long Term Debt: $706,225,000 (6/95).
Subsid. Red. Cum. Preferred Sec.: $100,000,000.

Per Share Data ($)

(Year Ended Dec. 31)

	1994	1993	1992	1991	1990	1989
Tangible Bk. Val.	8.56	7.68	7.44	6.33	6.00	6.43
Earnings	1.31	1.24	1.05	0.71	0.69	1.10
Dividends	0.87	0.85	0.82	0.82	0.80	0.79
Payout Ratio	66%	68%	78%	115%	115%	72%
Prices - High	20¼	18⅜	15½	12¼	11⅞	12
- Low	16⅞	14½	10⅞	9¾	9⅛	8½
P/E Ratio - High	15	15	15	17	17	11
- Low	13	12	10	14	13	8

Income Statement Analysis (Million $)

	1994	%Chg	1993	%Chg	1992	%Chg	1991
Revs.	1,546	5%	1,470	2%	1,438	13%	1,276
Depr.	104	27%	81.6	7%	76.4	3%	74.1
Maint.	NA	—	NA	—	328	2%	323
Fxd. Chgs. Cov.	3.1	-17%	3.8	19%	3.2	36%	2.3
Constr. Credits	NA	—	NA	—	1.6	123%	0.7
Eff. Tax Rate	27%	—	32%	—	33%	—	34%
Net Inc.	77.8	7%	72.8	27%	57.1	63%	35.1

Balance Sheet & Other Fin. Data (Million $)

	1994	1993	1992	1991	1990	1989
Gross Prop.	2,605	2,285	2,098	1,942	1,822	1,684
Cap. Exp.	356	209	171	127	145	78.0
Net Prop.	1,492	1,237	1,115	1,023	965	874
Capitalization:						
LT Debt	686	495	380	328	321	307
% LT Debt	53	51	46	48	50	49
Pfd.	103	5.6	9.0	12.0	15.0	18.0
% Pfd.	7.90	0.60	1.10	1.80	2.30	2.90
Common	511	470	434	349	302	299
% Common	39	48	53	51	47	48
Total Cap.	1,524	1,183	997	846	779	776

Ratio Analysis

	1994	1993	1992	1991	1990	1989
Oper. Ratio	91.9	92.7	93.3	93.8	94.4	94.2
% Earn. on Net Prop.	9.1	9.2	9.0	8.0	7.4	8.7
% Ret. on Revs.	5.0	5.0	4.0	2.7	2.7	3.8
% Ret. On Invest.Cap	9.7	10.3	10.5	9.4	9.1	10.7
% Return On Com.Eqty	15.8	16.1	14.6	10.8	10.8	18.2

Dividend Data —Dividends were initiated in 1988. A dividend reinvestment plan is available. A "poison pill" stock purchase right was adopted in 1989.

Amt. of Div. $	Date Decl.	Ex-Div. Date	Stock of Record	Payment Date
0.445	Oct. 27	Nov. 04	Nov. 10	Nov. 25 '94
2-for-1	Oct. 27	Nov. 29	Nov. 10	Nov. 28 '94
0.222	Jan. 26	Feb. 06	Feb. 10	Feb. 24 '95
0.222	Apr. 27	May. 05	May. 11	May. 25 '95
0.222	Jul. 27	Aug. 09	Aug. 11	Aug. 25 '95

Data as orig. reptd.; bef. results of disc opers. and/or spec. items. Per share data adj. for stk. divs. as of ex-div. date. E-Estimated. NA-Not Available. NM-Not Meaningful. NR-Not Ranked.

Office—500 Griswold St., Detroit, MI 48226. **Tel**—(313) 256-5500. **Chrmn, Pres & CEO**—A. R. Glancy III. **Vice Chrmn & CFO**—W. K. McCrackin. **VP & Secy**—D. L. Schiffer. **VP, Treas & Investor Contact**—Sebastian Coppola. **Dirs**—S. E. Ewing, R. Fridholm, A. R. Glancy III, F. M. Hennessey, T. H. Jeffs II, A. L. Johnson, D. A. Johnson, W. K. McCrackin, H. O. Petrauskas, H. F. Sims. **Transfer Agent & Registrar**—Securities Transfer Services, Boston. **Incorporated** in Michigan in 1898. **Empl**-3,889. **S&P Analyst:** Ronald J. Gross

STANDARD & POOR'S

STOCK REPORTS

Mac Frugal's Bargains

NYSE Symbol **MFI**
In S&P MidCap 400

19-OCT-95 **Industry:** Retail Stores

Summary: This discount retailer operates over 300 stores in 16 states, primarily in California and Texas. The stores specialize in selling new close-out merchandise.

S&P Opinion: Accumulate (★★★★) Recent Price • 13¾ 52 Wk Range • 21¼-12⅞ Yield • Nil 12-Mo. P/E • 10.3

Quantitative Evaluations
Outlook (1 Lowest—5 Highest)
• **5⁻**
Fair Value
• **16⅛**
Risk
• **Average**
Earn./Div. Rank
• **B**

Technical Eval.
• **Bearish** since 9/95
Rel. Strength Rank (1 Lowest—99 Highest)
• **5**
Insider Activity
• **NA**

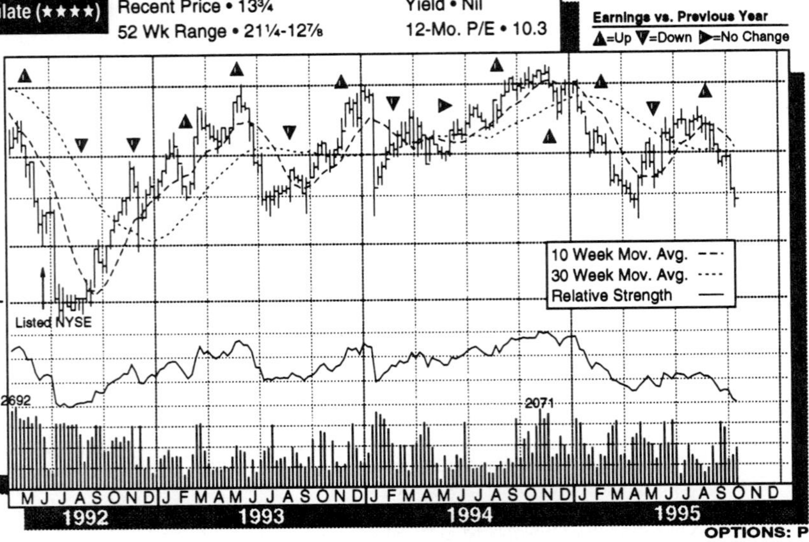

OPTIONS: P

Overview - 19-OCT-95

Sales should continue to increase at a rate in the upper single digits over the next several quarters, aided by contributions from new stores. The cannibalization of sales by newer stores in existing markets, combined with a temporary shortfall of new merchandise, led to lower same-store sales in recent months. However, this trend should reverse, benefiting from new close-out purchases, more merchandise variety in stores, and continued price sensitivity on the part of consumers. Gross margins are expected to firm on higher initial markups, but the benefit is likely to be offset by sharply higher interest expense. The continuing economic weakness in California, where about 63% of the company's sales are generated, is likely to temper earnings growth for the balance of 1995-96.

Valuation - 19-OCT-95

MFI shares have fallen over 35% in 1995 to date, to a 52-week low, primarily reflecting a declining same-store sales trend. The company has recently changed its product assortment to deemphasize apparel and increase its exposure to more attractive hardline items. Sales comparisons should also improve as the company penetrates new markets and becomes less dependent on California stores. Improved margins, together with well controlled operating costs, should allow for an expansion of the P/E multiple. A $10 million share buyback program now in progress should further boost earnings comparisons. The shares, trading at a P/E multiple below our estimated growth level, are seen as undervalued.

Key Stock Statistics

S&P EPS Est. 1996	1.55	Tang. Bk. Value/Share	8.62
P/E on S&P Est. 1996	8.9	Beta	0.95
S&P EPS Est. 1997	1.75	Shareholders	1,000
Dividend Rate/Share	Nil	Market cap. (B)	$0.329
Shs. outstg. (M)	25.5	Inst. holdings	88%
Avg. daily vol. (M)	0.062	Insider holdings	NA

Value of $10,000 investe rs ago: $ 10,487

Fiscal Year Ending Jan. 31

	1996	% Change	1995	% Change	1994	% Change
Revenues (Million $)						
1Q	154.3	9%	142.0	12%	126.7	11%
2Q	146.8	10%	134.0	15%	116.1	6%
3Q	—	—	158.5	13%	140.6	17%
4Q	—	—	247.8	2%	243.7	24%
Yr.	—	—	682.1	9%	627.1	16%
Income (Million $)						
1Q	3.32	-44%	5.91	NM	5.89	9%
2Q	3.29	30%	2.53	23%	2.05	-24%
3Q	—	—	5.23	45%	3.60	NM
4Q	—	—	25.21	24%	20.40	-12%
Yr.	—	—	38.88	22%	31.94	181%
Earnings Per Share ($)						
1Q	0.13	-35%	0.20	NM	0.20	11%
2Q	0.13	44%	0.09	29%	0.07	-22%
3Q	E0.23	21%	0.19	58%	0.12	NM
4Q	E1.06	10%	0.96	41%	0.68	-13%
Yr.	E1.55	13%	1.37	28%	1.07	189%

Next earnings report expected: late November

Mac Frugal's Bargains

Business Summary - 19-OCT-95

Mac Frugal's Bargains Close-outs Inc. (formerly Pic 'N' Save Corp.) operates a chain of self-service, cash-and-carry retail stores under the names Pic 'N' Save and Mac Frugal's Bargains Close-outs. The stores specialize in the sale of new "close-out" merchandise. At January 29, 1995, the company was operating 278 stores in 12 states, principally in California (157), Texas (37), Arizona (20) and Florida (16).

Close-out merchandise is first-quality merchandise--much of it carrying nationally recognized brand names--that becomes available at prices below initial wholesale cost for reason such as the inability of suppliers to sell products through normal distribution channels, the discontinuance of merchandise due to a change in style, color, shape or packaging, or the termination of a business by a manufacturer or wholesaler.

The stores offer, on a self-service basis, a wide selection of merchandise, including apparel and accessories, notions, novelties, toys, games, stationery, greeting cards, books, candles, luggage, artificial flowers, beauty aids, candy, snacks, beverages, housewares, domestics, Christmas theme items and giftware. Merchandise is typically sold at 40% to 70% below regular retail prices.

MFI purchases from more than 2,000 suppliers who can distribute close-out merchandise through the company's stores without conflict with their normal channels of distribution.

MFI opened a net 41 stores in 1994-95, with more than half located in California. Expansion plans for 1995-96 call for the addition of 30 new stores, including at least 10 in new markets.

During 1994-95, the company repurchased 4,258,100 common shares at an average price of $19.08 per share, pursuant to an authorization in 1993-94's fourth quarter to buy up to 1,500,000 shares and an additional 3,000,000 million repurchase program authorized in 1994-95.

Important Developments

Oct. '95—Sales in the five weeks ended October 1, 1995, totaled $57.1 million, a 3.7% decline from the prior year. Same-store sales were down 11.8%. For the 35 weeks year-to-date, total sales advanced 6.4% despite 5.5% lower same-store sales.

Aug. '95—In response to the continuing weakness in apparel sales, the company said that it will reduce the amount of selling space dedicated to apparel merchandise in its stores. MFI will use the extra space to introduce greeting cards into its merchandise assortment.

Aug. '95—During the first half of fiscal 1995, MFI opened six stores in Illinois, marking its entry into the Midwest.

Capitalization

Long Term Debt: $119,972,000 (7/95).

Per Share Data ($) (Year Ended Jan. 31)

	1995	1994	1993	1992	1991	1990
Tangible Bk. Val.	8.49	8.67	7.58	7.38	6.24	6.14
Cash Flow	1.94	1.58	0.95	1.61	0.92	1.20
Earnings	1.37	1.07	0.37	1.12	0.52	0.87
Dividends	Nil	Nil	Nil	Nil	Nil	Nil
Payout Ratio	Nil	Nil	Nil	Nil	Nil	Nil
Cal. Yrs.	1994	1993	1992	1991	1990	1989
Prices - High	21¼	20⅛	23⅜	23¼	14⅜	18⅞
- Low	13⅛	13⅛	9⅜	8½	5¾	11¼
P/E Ratio - High	16	19	63	21	28	22
- Low	10	12	25	8	11	13

Income Statement Analysis (Million $)

	1995	%Chg	1994	%Chg	1993	%Chg	1992
Revs.	682	9%	627	16%	540	NM	543
Oper. Inc.	86.6	14%	76.1	-3%	78.2	NM	78.4
Depr.	16.0	4%	15.4	NM	15.4	1%	15.2
Int. Exp.	7.0	30%	5.4	-33%	8.1	-31%	11.7
Pretax Inc.	64.3	22%	52.9	NM	17.4	-68%	54.9
Eff. Tax Rate	40%	—	40%	—	35%	—	38%
Net Inc.	38.9	22%	31.9	182%	11.3	-67%	34.2

Balance Sheet & Other Fin. Data (Million $)

	1995	1994	1993	1992	1991	1990
Cash	6.7	1.0	21.8	41.5	18.3	6.5
Curr. Assets	204	198	188	183	130	124
Total Assets	386	358	372	397	344	306
Curr. Liab.	160	89.6	81.7	78.3	75.7	60.9
LT Debt	4.5	3.9	54.5	81.6	67.5	13.5
Common Eqty.	217	257	224	226	190	221
Total Cap.	227	269	290	319	268	244
Cap. Exp.	40.8	28.4	15.3	9.1	51.8	62.8
Cash Flow	54.9	47.3	28.6	49.4	30.8	42.8

Ratio Analysis

	1995	1994	1993	1992	1991	1990
Curr. Ratio	1.3	2.2	2.3	2.3	1.7	2.0
% LT Debt of Cap.	2.0	1.4	18.8	25.6	25.2	5.5
% Net Inc.of Revs.	5.7	5.1	2.1	6.3	3.3	6.5
% Ret. on Assets	11.2	8.7	3.0	9.2	5.7	10.9
% Ret. on Equity	17.7	13.2	5.1	16.4	9.1	15.0

Dividend Data —No cash dividends have been paid. Poison pill stock purchase rights, issued in March 1988, were redeemed in August 1990.

Data as orig. reptd.; bef. results of disc. opers. and/or spec. items. Per share data adj. for stk. divs. as of ex-div. date. E-Estimated. NA-Not Available. NM-Not Meaningful. NR-Not Ranked.

Office—2430 East Del Amo Blvd., Dominguez, CA 90220-6306. **Tel**—(310) 537-9220. **Chrmn**—P. S. Willmott. **Pres, CEO & Investor Contact**—P. L. Carter. **Dirs**—D. H. Batchelder, P. L. Carter, A. Luiso, B. E. Karatz, M. J. Miller, R. P. Spogli. B. M. Thomas, P. S. Willmot, J. J. Zehentbauer. **Transfer Agent & Registrar**—Bank of New York, NYC. **Incorporated** in Delaware in 1971. **Empl**-8,177. **S&P Analyst:** Maureen C. Carini

STANDARD & POOR'S
STOCK REPORTS

MagneTek, Inc.

NYSE Symbol **MAG**
In S&P MidCap 400

30-AUG-95 **Industry:** Electronics/Electric

Summary: MagneTek manufactures electric motors, drives, generators, transformers, power supplies and lighting equipment.

Quantitative Evaluations

Recent Price • 12⅝ | 52 Wk Range • 16½-12⅜ | Yield • Nil | 12-Mo. P/E • 45.1

Outlook (1 Lowest—5 Highest)
• **5⁻**
Fair Value
• **21½**
Risk
• **Low**
Earn./Div. Rank
• **B-**

Technical Eval.
• **Bullish** since 7/95
Rel. Strength Rank (1 Lowest—99 Highest)
• **15**
Insider Activity
• **Neutral**

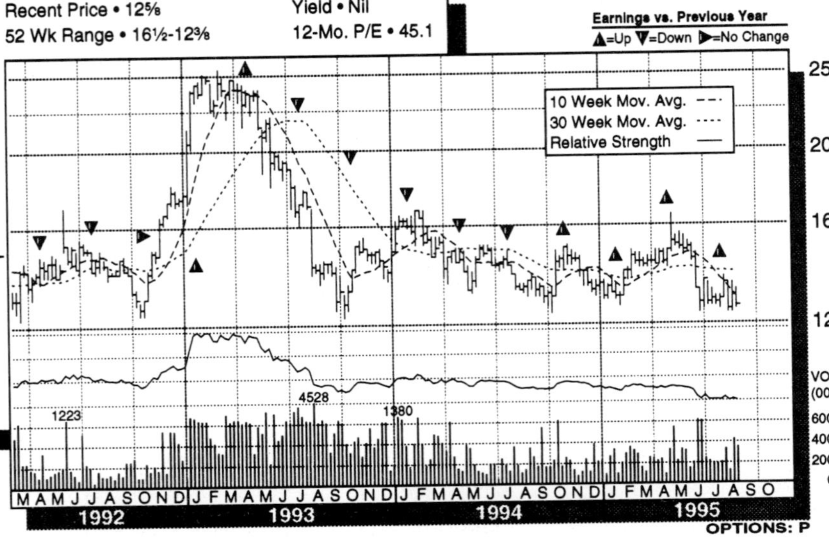

Business Profile - 30-AUG-95

MagneTek has been able to capitalize on the growing interest in energy saving lighting products and higher demand for electrical equipment stemming from upticks in the North American and European economies. Nearing completion of a major restructuring program, the company has sold off non-core assets and used the proceeds to pay down some $160 million of debt (of a total $200 million in planned reductions).

Operational Review - 30-AUG-95

Higher revenues and wider gross margins have played a big role in returning the company to profitability. The current restructuring plan has also paid dividends in the form of lower SG&A costs and one-time gains from the sale of non-core businesses. The recent substitution of lower interest financing for high cost debt will aid future results.

Stock Performance - 25-AUG-95

In the past 30 trading days, MAG's shares have declined 2%, compared to a 0.04% rise in the S&P 500. Average trading volume for the past five days was 70,100 shares, compared with the 40-day moving average of 51,774 shares.

Key Stock Statistics

Dividend Rate/Share	Nil	Shareholders	400
Shs. outstg. (M)	24.6	Market cap. (B)	$0.311
Avg. daily vol. (M)	0.059	Inst. holdings	74%
Tang. Bk. Value/Share	3.21	Insider holdings	NA
Beta	1.29		

Value of $10,000 invested 5 years ago: $ 15,303

Fiscal Year Ending Jun. 30

	1995	% Change	1994	% Change	1993	% Change
Revenues (Million $)						
1Q	274.8	-2%	280.6	-16%	336.0	14%
2Q	290.6	12%	259.3	-30%	372.0	31%
3Q	318.6	11%	287.1	-26%	385.7	25%
4Q	318.5	4%	306.4	-27%	418.6	22%
Yr.	1,203	6%	1,133	-25%	1,512	23%
Income (Million $)						
1Q	2.66	89%	1.41	-79%	6.75	2%
2Q	4.48	NM	-42.50	NM	8.24	23%
3Q	6.90	NM	1.68	-81%	8.93	36%
4Q	-10.04	NM	0.23	-93%	3.10	85%
Yr.	7.10	NM	-16.94	NM	27.03	-8%
Earnings Per Share ($)						
1Q	0.11	83%	0.06	-79%	0.28	NM
2Q	0.18	NM	-0.88	NM	0.34	21%
3Q	0.28	133%	0.12	-66%	0.35	30%
4Q	0.30	NM	0.01	-92%	0.12	-68%
Yr.	0.87	NM	-0.69	NM	0.87	-29%

Next earnings report expected: late October

MagneTek, Inc.

Business Summary - 30-AUG-95

MagneTek Inc. designs, manufactures and markets a broad range of electrical, electronic and industrial components and products. International sales accounted for 18% of total sales in fiscal 1994.

The ballast and transformer segment accounted for 58% of total revenues and 30% of profits in fiscal 1994. This unit includes a broad range of equipment in two general product groups: lighting products and transformer products. Lighting products consist of fluorescent ballasts, high intensity discharge (HID) ballasts and specialty lines. Transformer products are comprised of electronic power supplies that are custom designed for business machines and industrial equipment. MagneTek is an industry leader in magnetic fluorescent and HID ballasts. Ballasts are transformers that serve to regulate or alter electrical current for use in a wide range of fluorescent and other lighting applications.

The motors and controls segment manufactures motors and generators, including fractional, integral and medium voltage generators, and electronic adjustable speed and other drives and drive systems. Generators manufactured by the company range in size from 50 to 2,250 kilowatts. Over 90% of generator sales are to Caterpillar, Inc. This segment accounted for 42% of the company's total revenues and 70% of its profits in fiscal 1994.

As part of the company's restructuring plan that called for the divestiture of non-core businesses, MagneTek sold substantially all the assets of its Columbus, Ohio, utility equipment service business in March 1995. In July 1994, substantially all of the assets of the company's industrial controls business had been sold to a group led by First Atlantic Capital, Ltd. and the current management of the business.

Important Developments

Jul. '95— The company sold its medium power transformer business. Proceeds were used to pay down a $75 million term loan, cutting MagneTek's total debt to approximately $380 million from $457 million on March 30, 1995.

Apr. '95—The company entered into new bank agreements that include a $225 million revolving line of credit and a $75 million term facility. Both are LIBOR based, variable-rate facilities with current interest rates of approximately 8%. MagneTek drew upon the facilities to redeem $112.5 million in 11.45% notes. The redemption involved an early payment penalty of $5 million ($0.20) net of taxes, which was recorded as a special charge in the third quarter of fiscal 1995.

Capitalization

Long Term Debt: $395,266,000 (3/95); incl. $75 million of 8% sub. notes due 2001 (listed NYSE), conv. into com. at $16 a sh.

Per Share Data ($) (Year Ended Jun. 30)

	1995	1994	1993	1992	1991	1990
Tangible Bk. Val.	NA	3.21	6.76	8.24	6.89	5.77
Cash Flow	NA	0.79	2.84	2.92	2.98	2.72
Earnings	0.87	-0.69	1.09	1.22	1.47	1.40
Dividends	Nil	Nil	Nil	Nil	Nil	Nil
Payout Ratio	Nil	Nil	Nil	Nil	Nil	Nil
Prices - High	16½	16¾	25½	17	16¼	12½
- Low	12⅜	13	12¼	12¼	10	6¾
P/E Ratio - High	19	NM	23	14	11	9
- Low	14	NM	12	10	7	5

Income Statement Analysis (Million $)

	1994	%Chg	1993	%Chg	1992	%Chg	1991
Revs.	1,133	-25%	1,512	23%	1,230	8%	1,134
Oper. Inc.	46.3	-67%	142	1%	140	-3%	145
Depr.	36.4	-17%	43.7	7%	40.7	14%	35.7
Int. Exp.	32.0	-36%	50.0	11%	44.9	3%	43.8
Pretax Inc.	-24.4	NM	45.6	-13%	52.4	-15%	61.8
Eff. Tax Rate	NM	—	41%	—	44%	—	44%
Net Inc.	-16.9	NM	27.0	-8%	29.3	-15%	34.6

Balance Sheet & Other Fin. Data (Million $)

	1994	1993	1992	1991	1990	1989
Cash	7.0	7.8	2.0	7.5	1.7	5.5
Curr. Assets	454	632	509	422	391	375
Total Assets	931	1,053	917	785	712	647
Curr. Liab.	248	287	276	244	184	154
LT Debt	474	516	433	365	379	366
Common Eqty.	113	163	196	159	132	99
Total Cap.	606	697	641	541	528	492
Cap. Exp.	43.3	67.8	35.1	28.8	33.3	25.6
Cash Flow	19.5	70.8	70.0	70.3	63.9	47.2

Ratio Analysis

	1994	1993	1992	1991	1990	1989
Curr. Ratio	1.8	2.2	1.8	1.7	2.1	2.4
% LT Debt of Cap.	78.2	74.0	67.6	67.4	71.8	74.4
% Net Inc.of Revs.	NM	1.8	2.4	3.1	3.1	2.2
% Ret. on Assets	NM	2.7	3.4	4.6	4.9	3.0
% Ret. on Equity	NM	14.9	16.2	23.8	28.4	26.4

Dividend Data —Dividends have never been paid.

Data as orig. reptd.; bef. results of disc. opers. and/or spec. items. Per share data adj. for stk. divs. as of ex-div. date. E-Estimated. NA-Not Available. NM-Not Meaningful. NR-Not Ranked.

Office—26 Century Blvd., POB 20159, Nashville, TN 37229. **Tel**—(615) 316-5100. **Fax**—(615) 316-5188. **Chrmn & CEO**—A. G. Galef. **EVP & CFO**—D. P. Reiland. **VP & Secy**—S. A. Miley. **VP & Investor Contact**—Robert W. Murray. **Dirs**—D. K. Cross, C. H. Dean, Jr., A. G. Galef, P. K. Kofmehl, A. C. Kotchian, C. Nevin, K. A. Ruck. **Transfer Agent & Registrar**—Bank of New York, NYC. **Incorporated** in Delaware in 1984. **Empl**-12,000. **S&P Analyst:** Steven A. Jaworski

STANDARD & POOR'S

STOCK REPORTS

Manpower Inc.

NYSE Symbol **MAN**
In S&P MidCap 400

11-SEP-95 **Industry:** Services

Summary: MAN is the world's largest nongovernmental temporary employment services organization, providing employment to more than one and a half million people each year in 40 countries.

S&P Opinion: Accumulate (★★★★)
Recent Price • 32
52 Wk Range • 34¼-24¼
Yield • 0.4%
12-Mo. P/E • 22.5

Quantitative Evaluations
Outlook
(1 Lowest—5 Highest)
• 5
Fair Value
• 40½
Risk
• Average
Earn./Div. Rank
• NR

Technical Eval.
• Bullish since 8/95
Rel. Strength Rank
(1 Lowest—99 Highest)
• 81
Insider Activity
• NA

Earnings vs. Previous Year
▲=Up ▼=Down ▶=No Change

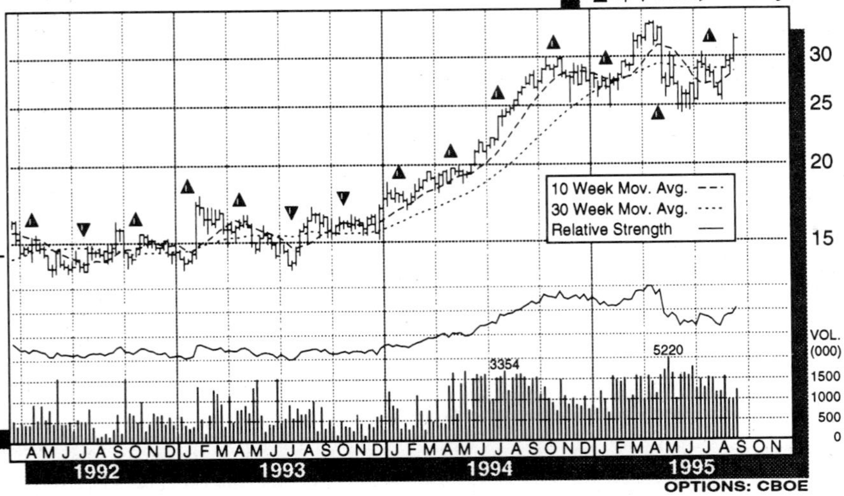

OPTIONS: CBOE

Overview - 11-SEP-95

The very strong growth realized by Manpower in 1995 reflects increased demand for staffing services and the continuing economic recovery in Europe. Manpower has been effective in establishing contractual relationship with major clients. Under these agreements, Manpower takes sole responsibility for the client's staffing needs, and at times will establish its own office at the client's location. This gives Manpower a competitive edge in an industry with limited barriers to entry. A potential negative factor in near-term earnings comparisons is the recent strength of the dollar, as Manpower generates a majority of its revenues outside the U.S. Nevertheless, given a sound economy in the company's major markets, we believe EPS will increase to $1.65 in 1995 and $2.00 in 1996.

Valuation - 11-SEP-95

Manpower's shares, which performed well in 1994 despite difficult market conditions, sold off in the second quarter of 1995 due to recession fears. The stock has since rebounded, and we believe the shares will outperform the market over the next 12 months. The threat of a recession in the U.S. appears to be fading. In addition, the impact of a recession in a particular country or region should be lessened by the company's global diversity. Contract business with large clients should also give stability to results. Trading at around 20 times our estimated 1995 earnings, the shares are reasonably priced for investors seeking long-term capital gains.

Key Stock Statistics

S&P EPS Est. 1995	1.65	Tang. Bk. Value/Share	3.66
P/E on S&P Est. 1995	19.4	Beta	0.85
S&P EPS Est. 1996	2.00	Shareholders	NA
Dividend Rate/Share	0.12	Market cap. (B)	$ 2.4
Shs. outstg. (M)	75.2	Inst. holdings	97%
Avg. daily vol. (M)	0.272	Insider holdings	NA

Value of $10,000 invested 5 years ago: NA

Fiscal Year Ending Dec. 31

	1995	% Change	1994	% Change	1993	% Change
Revenues (Million $)						
1Q	2,000	146%	811.5	16%	700.5	1%
2Q	1,371	39%	988.0	27%	778.2	1%
3Q	—	—	1,241	42%	875.3	-7%
4Q	—	—	1,256	52%	826.3	5%
Yr.	—	—	4,296	35%	3,180	NM
Income (Million $)						
1Q	18.19	190%	6.27	NM	-17.29	NM
2Q	28.25	65%	17.15	NM	-12.56	NM
3Q	—	—	33.62	NM	-23.33	NM
4Q	—	—	26.90	NM	4.24	NM
Yr.	—	—	83.93	NM	-48.94	NM
Earnings Per Share ($)						
1Q	0.24	NM	0.08	NM	-0.23	NM
2Q	0.37	61%	0.23	NM	-0.17	NM
3Q	E0.56	24%	0.45	NM	-0.32	NM
4Q	E0.48	33%	0.36	NM	0.06	NM
Yr.	E1.65	47%	1.12	NM	-0.66	NM

Next earnings report expected: late October

Manpower Inc.

Business Summary - 11-SEP-95

Manpower Inc. (formerly Manpower PLC and, prior to that, Blue Arrow), now a U.S. holding company, is the largest nongovernmental temporary employment services organization in the world. At the beginning of 1995, there were more than 2,100 offices in 40 countries. Contributions by area in 1994 were:

	Sales	Profits
Europe	62%	50%
U.S.	31%	46%
Other	7%	4%

MAN's principal operating subsidiary, Manpower International (MI), has offices in Continental Europe, the U.S., the U.K. and elsewhere. MI's principal business is to provide temporary employment services, but permanent placement services (limited principally to the U.K.) and training of customers' permanent staff are also provided. MI assigned more than 1.5 million workers throughout the world in 1994.

MI's operations in Continental Europe constitute the largest nongovernmental temporary employment services firm in the European Economic Community, with its largest operations located in France. U.S. operations, which primarily provide temporary employment services, are conducted through branch offices and franchised offices. U.K. operations provide temporary employment services (permanent placement is provided on a limited basis) in the office, industrial, technical, computer and transport markets. Additional operations are in Japan, Canada, Israel, Mexico, Australia, and seven countries in South America. Manpower supplies temporary workers to the industrial, general office, and technical markets in these countries.

Brook Street Bureau, a subsidiary with operations solely in the U.K., provides temporary placement services in the office, industrial and catering markets. Its permanent placement business consists of recruitment for office workers and provides placement services for executive and accountancy positions and is engaged in psychometric testing.

Important Developments

Aug. '95—The company announced that it will redeem all $100 million of its 6 1/4% convertible subordinated debentures due 2002. The last day to convert the debentures is October 13.

Capitalization

Long Term Debt: $122,847,000 (6/95).
Options: To buy 3,351,925 shs. at $10.68 to $29.75 ea. (12/94)

Per Share Data ($) (Year Ended Dec. 31)

	1994	1993	1992	1991	1990	1989
Tangible Bk. Val.	2.69	1.29	1.06	0.84	NA	NA
Cash Flow	1.49	0.65	0.84	0.66	NA	NA
Earnings	1.12	-0.66	-0.54	-0.73	NA	NA
Dividends	0.11	Nil	Nil	Nil	NA	NA
Payout Ratio	10%	Nil	Nil	Nil	NA	NA
Prices - High	29⅞	17⅞	17⅛	15⅛	NA	NA
- Low	16⅞	13½	13¼	11⅛	NA	NA
P/E Ratio - High	27	NM	NM	NM	NA	NA
- Low	15	NM	NM	NA	NA	NA

Income Statement Analysis (Million $)

	1994	%Chg	1993	%Chg	1992	%Chg	1991
Revs.	4,296	35%	3,180	NM	3,187	14%	2,800
Oper. Inc.	179	75%	102	NM	102	10%	93.0
Depr.	28.0	-71%	97.0	-4%	101	NM	101
Int. Exp.	12.3	-15%	14.4	-26%	19.5	-24%	25.7
Pretax Inc.	136	NM	-28.0	NM	-13.0	NM	-34.0
Eff. Tax Rate	39%	—	NM	—	NM	—	NM
Net Inc.	83.9	NM	-48.9	NM	-39.7	NM	-53.3

Balance Sheet & Other Fin. Data (Million $)

	1994	1993	1992	1991	1990	1989
Cash	82.0	63.3	50.6	44.7	38.1	43.1
Curr. Assets	1,007	651	671	646	643	676
Total Assets	1,204	833	922	981	1,080	815
Curr. Liab.	668	471	458	454	490	528
LT Debt	131	130	203	210	221	226
Common Eqty.	204	103	160	222	274	4.0
Total Cap.	334	233	363	471	536	248
Cap. Exp.	26.6	17.6	22.2	26.7	41.4	44.6
Cash Flow	112	48.0	62.0	48.0	32.0	87.0

Ratio Analysis

	1994	1993	1992	1991	1990	1989
Curr. Ratio	1.5	1.4	1.5	1.4	1.3	1.3
% LT Debt of Cap.	39.1	55.9	56.0	44.6	41.3	91.2
% Net Inc.of Revs.	2.0	NM	NM	NM	NM	2.4
% Ret. on Assets	8.2	NM	NM	NM	NM	7.8
% Ret. on Equity	54.7	NM	NM	NM	NM	236.0

Dividend Data —Semiannual cash dividends were initiated in 1994.

Amt. of Div. $	Date Decl.	Ex-Div. Date	Stock of Record	Payment Date
0.060	Nov. 08	Nov. 18	Nov. 25	Dec. 14 '94
0.060	May. 05	May. 22	May. 26	Jun. 14 '95

Data as orig. reptd.; bef. results of disc. opers. and/or spec. items. Per share data adj. for stk. divs. as of ex-div. date. E-Estimated. NA-Not Available. NM-Not Meaningful. NR-Not Ranked.

Office—5301 N. Ironwood Rd., Box 2053, Milwaukee, WI 53201. **Tel**—(414) 961-1000. **Chrmn, CEO & Pres**—M. S. Fromstein. **EVP, CFO & Secy**—J. F. Chait. **Treas**—M. Van Handel. **Dirs**—J. F. Chait, A. Freedman, M. S. Fromstein, D. J. Godfrey Jr., M. B. Goodman, J. I. Harris, N. N. Minow, G. Palay, D. Stevenson. **Transfer Agent & Registrar**—First National Bank of Chicago. **Reincorporated** in Wisconsin in 1990; predecessor firm incorporated in England in 1982; predecessor firm organized in 1948. **Empl-7,400. S&P Analyst:** Stephen Madonna, CFA

STANDARD & POOR'S

STOCK REPORTS

MAPCO Inc.

NYSE Symbol **MDA**
In S&P MidCap 400

24-SEP-95

Industry: Utilities-Gas

Summary: This company engages in oil refining, gas liquids transmission, coal production, propane distribution, and the operation of retail gasoline outlets.

Quantitative Evaluations

Recent Price • 53⅝
52 Wk Range • 59¼-49¾
Yield • 1.9%
12-Mo. P/E • 14.3

Outlook
(1 Lowest—5 Highest)
• **5**
Fair Value
• **67½**
Risk
• **Low**
Earn./Div. Rank
• **A-**

Technical Eval.
• **Bearish** since 7/95
Rel. Strength Rank
(1 Lowest—99 Highest)
• **21**
Insider Activity
• **NA**

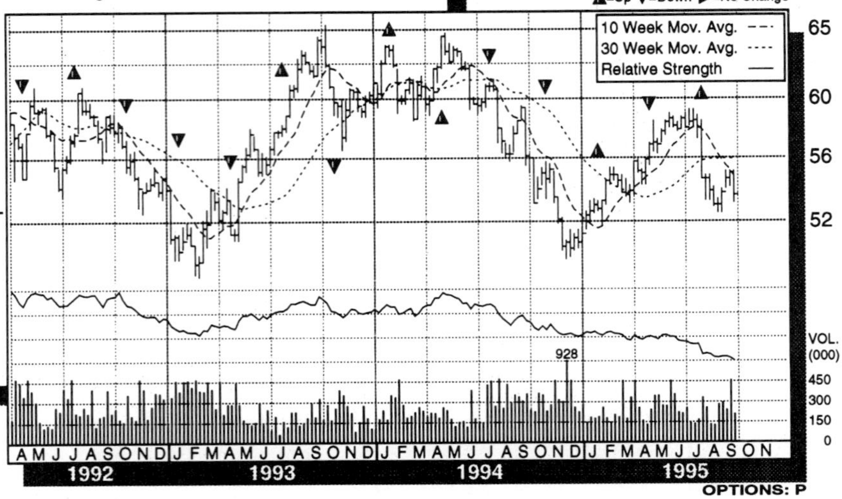

OPTIONS: P

Business Profile - 21-SEP-95

MDA recorded a $68.7 million charge in 1994 in connection with a royalty oil settlement with the State of Alaska. By the end of 1995, MDA expects to complete an $87 million expansion of its Rocky Mountain line, which will lift capacity by 37%. The company's natural gas liquids unit expects to benefit further from its interest in a joint venture for the transportation of gas liquids to Mexico.

Operational Review - 21-SEP-95

Revenues advanced 19%, year to year, in the first half of 1995, primarily reflecting higher transportation revenues and retail propane sales, and improved petroleum sales due to a change in trading strategies implemented during 1994. Profitability benefited from the increased revenues and well controlled operating costs and expenses, and in the absence of a $68.7 million charge related to a royalty settlement with Alaska, net income almost tripled.

Stock Performance - 22-SEP-95

In the past 30 trading days, MDA's shares have declined 0.46%, compared to a 5% rise in the S&P 500. Average trading volume for the past five days was 40,960 shares, compared with the 40-day moving average of 51,326 shares.

Key Stock Statistics

Dividend Rate/Share	1.00	Shareholders	5,900
Shs. outstg. (M)	29.8	Market cap. (B)	$ 1.6
Avg. daily vol. (M)	0.066	Inst. holdings	75%
Tang. Bk. Value/Share	18.01	Insider holdings	NA
Beta	0.40		

Value of $10,000 invested 5 years ago: $ 14,928

Fiscal Year Ending Dec. 31

	1995	% Change	1994	% Change	1993	% Change
Revenues (Million $)						
1Q	777.2	12%	692.1	NM	691.7	3%
2Q	927.6	26%	738.1	11%	663.3	-2%
3Q	—	—	805.3	21%	665.6	-5%
4Q	—	—	823.8	19%	694.7	-6%
Yr.	—	—	3,059	13%	2,715	-3%
Income (Million $)						
1Q	29.00	-30%	41.40	22%	33.90	-2%
2Q	21.20	NM	-24.60	NM	31.30	35%
3Q	—	—	24.70	-8%	26.90	-13%
4Q	—	—	37.60	8%	34.90	191%
Yr.	—	—	79.10	-38%	127.0	26%
Earnings Per Share ($)						
1Q	0.97	-30%	1.38	22%	1.13	-3%
2Q	0.71	NM	-0.82	NM	1.04	33%
3Q	—	—	0.83	-8%	0.90	-13%
4Q	—	—	1.25	7%	1.17	193%
Yr.	—	—	2.64	-38%	4.24	26%

Next earnings report expected: late October

MAPCO Inc.

Business Summary - 21-SEP-95

MAPCO is a diversified energy concern. Segment contributions to operating profits in recent years were:

	1994	1993	1992
Gas liquids	68%	43%	51%
Petroleum	14%	40%	33%
Coal	18%	17%	16%

The gas liquids segment includes the Mid-America Pipeline, a 7,204-mile natural gas liquids system extending from Wyoming to Texas with branches to markets in the upper Midwest. A 1,093-mile line moves anhydrous ammonia from Texas to the upper Midwest. Seminole Pipeline (80%-owned) operates a 1,311-mile gas liquids line within Texas. Total pipeline movements in 1994 were 273 million bbl., versus 245 million. MDA also processes natural gas liquids from 234,000 acres in Texas and has a 50% stake in a 107,000 bbl./day gas liquids fractionator. MDA is the fourth largest distributor of propane in the U.S., distributing propane under the Thermogas and Fuel Gas names at 192 outlets in 15 states. MDA also distributes liquid fertilizers at 43 outlets.

MDA operates a 130,000 bbl./day refinery near Fairbanks, Alaska. In Alaska, it markets petroleum products for both wholesale and retail markets including 22 MAPCO Express convenience outlets in Alaska. MDA's Mid-South system includes a 90,000 bbl./day refinery in Memphis that supplies wholesale markets, and 182 gasoline/convenience outlets under the MAPCO Express and Shell brands in nine southern states. The company also processes, sells and trades crude oil and gas liquids.

MDA operates six underground and one surface coal mine in Kentucky, Maryland, Illinois and Virginia. It sold 14.5 milion tons of coal in 1994, versus 14.4 million in 1993. Coal reserves at 1994 year end aggregated 343 million tons.

Important Developments

Sep. '95—MAPCO's Mettiki Coal unit was in talks for a 10-year, 2.25-million-ton-per-year supply contract with Dominion Resources Inc.'s Virginia Electric & Power Co. unit. Mettiki produces about 2.5 million tons of coal a year.

Mar. '95—MDA revealed an $87 million expansion plan for its Rocky Mountain line. Construction of the new 400-mile gas liquids line, which will lift capacity by 37%, is expected to be completed by 1995 year end.

Mar. '95—MDA acquired 27 gasoline/convenience outlets in the Nashville area for $10.3 million.

Capitalization

Long Term Debt: $742,100,000 (6/95).
Minority Interest: $25,700,000.

Per Share Data ($)

(Year Ended Dec. 31)

	1994	1993	1992	1991	1990	1989
Tangible Bk. Val.	20.82	19.21	15.97	13.76	10.93	11.78
Cash Flow	6.07	7.32	6.41	7.08	6.61	4.97
Earnings	2.64	4.24	3.37	4.20	4.13	3.04
Dividends	1.00	1.00	1.00	1.00	1.00	0.88
Payout Ratio	38%	24%	30%	24%	23%	26%
Prices - High	64¾	65⅜	62⅛	63¾	46⅞	42¾
- Low	49¾	48¾	52½	38½	36⅝	27⅛
P/E Ratio - High	25	15	18	15	11	14
- Low	19	11	16	9	9	9

Income Statement Analysis (Million $)

	1994	%Chg	1993	%Chg	1992	%Chg	1991
Revs.	2,902	13%	2,567	-3%	2,640	NM	2,643
Oper. Inc.	342	4%	330	6%	311	-2%	317
Depr.	103	11%	92.5	2%	91.0	5%	86.4
Int. Exp.	53.2	8%	49.3	-13%	56.4	-3%	58.3
Pretax Inc.	117	-42%	203	40%	145	-21%	183
Eff. Tax Rate	308%	—	37%	—	31%	—	30%
Net Inc.	79.0	-38%	127	26%	101	-20%	126

Balance Sheet & Other Fin. Data (Million $)

	1994	1993	1992	1991	1990	1989
Cash	31.0	70.0	56.0	52.0	78.0	72.0
Curr. Assets	479	456	458	375	412	349
Total Assets	2,166	1,941	1,912	1,702	1,700	1,481
Curr. Liab.	426	383	393	308	373	325
LT Debt	721	586	669	639	654	504
Common Eqty.	623	574	478	413	330	408
Total Cap.	1,662	1,456	1,428	1,345	1,282	1,131
Cap. Exp.	NA	144	215	136	315	152
Cash Flow	182	220	192	212	208	190

Ratio Analysis

	1994	1993	1992	1991	1990	1989
Curr. Ratio	1.1	1.2	1.2	1.2	1.1	1.1
% LT Debt of Cap.	43.4	40.2	46.9	47.5	51.0	44.6
% Net Inc.of Revs.	2.7	4.9	3.8	4.8	4.8	5.8
% Ret. on Assets	3.9	6.6	5.6	7.4	8.7	8.7
% Ret. on Equity	13.2	24.1	22.7	34.0	37.9	24.8

Dividend Data —Dividends have been paid since 1965. A dividend reinvestment plan is available.

Amt. of Div. $	Date Decl.	Ex-Div. Date	Stock of Record	Payment Date
0.250	Dec. 02	Dec. 06	Dec. 12	Dec. 27 '94
0.250	Jan. 25	Feb. 21	Feb. 27	Mar. 10 '95
0.250	May. 26	Jun. 01	Jun. 07	Jun. 23 '95
0.250	Jul. 31	Aug. 16	Aug. 18	Sep. 15 '95

Data as orig. reptd.; bef. results of disc. opers. and/or spec. items. Per share data adj. for stk. divs. as of ex-div. date. E-Estimated. NA-Not Available. NM-Not Meaningful. NR-Not Ranked.

Office—1800 South Baltimore Ave., Tulsa, OK 74119. **Tel**—(918) 581-1800. **Chrmn, CEO & COO**—J. E. Barnes. **SVP, CFO & Treas**—P. W. Baxter. **SVP & Secy**—D. W. Bowman. **SVP-Investor Contact**—David S. Leslie. **Dirs**—J. E. Barnes, H. A. Fischer, Jr., W. K. Goettsche, D. P. Hodel, M. T. Hopkins, P. C. Lauinger, Jr., D. L. Mellish, R. L. Parker, H. J. Schmidt, S. F. Segnar. **Transfer Agent**—Harris Trust Co., NYC. **Incorporated** in Delaware in 1958. **Empl**-6,051. **S&P Analyst:** Stewart Scharf

Mark IV Industries

NYSE Symbol **IV**
In S&P MidCap 400

16-SEP-95

Industry: Auto parts/equipment

Summary: Mark IV manufactures automotive products primarily under the Dayco and Purolator brandnames, as well as mass transit, traffic control, and professional audio products.

S&P Opinion: Hold (★★★)

Recent Price • 23⅜
52 Wk Range • 23¾-16⅝
Yield • 0.5%
12-Mo. P/E • 17.4

Quantitative Evaluations

Outlook
(1 Lowest—5 Highest)
• **4**

Fair Value
• **23¼**

Risk
• **Average**

Earn./Div. Rank
• **B+**

Technical Eval.
• **Bullish** since 7/95

Rel. Strength Rank
(1 Lowest—99 Highest)
• **64**

Insider Activity
• **Unfavorable**

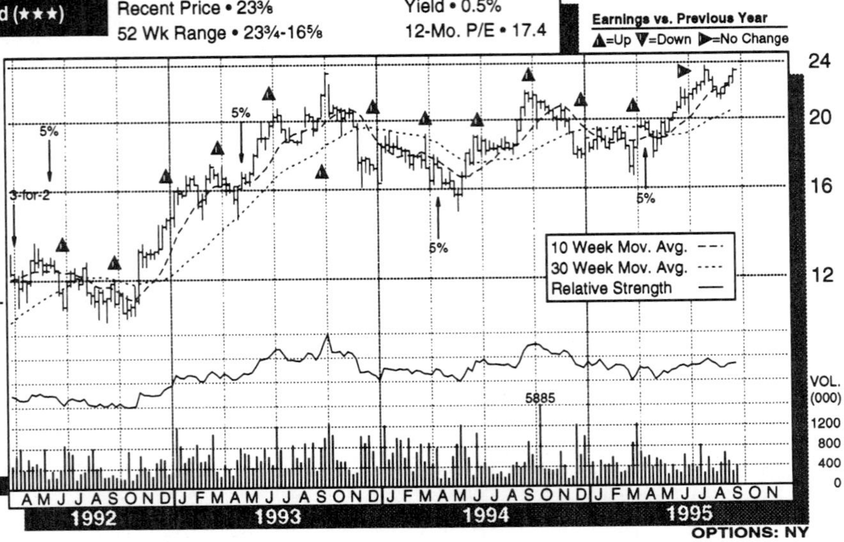

OPTIONS: NY

Overview - 15-SEP-95

With the acquisition of Purolator Products, IV is now largely an automotive products company with smaller interests in mass transit systems and professional audio. The automotive business is diversified between original equipment and aftermarket items and has a sizable foreign component. The company's focus in fiscal 1995-96 will be on consolidating the Dayco belts and hoses segment with the lower margin Purolator filters business in order to streamline overhead costs and distribution operations. This should permit modest improvement of margins over time. Longer term goals include raising return on sales to over 5.0%, maintaining a better than 15% return on equity, increasing earnings per share by 15% a year, and increasing foreign sales to 50% of sales by 2001.

Valuation - 15-SEP-95

Despite a share offering and a forced debt conversion, the balance sheet is still leveraged following the PFIL acquisition. This is not cause for concern, because of the stability of IV's businesses and several additional years of growth expected in the economic cycle, allowing time to further reduce debt. However, we are troubled by aggressive earnings projections for PFIL, which we believe will make only a modest contribution in 1995-96. Once debt is further reduced and distribution systems are rationalized, PFIL should yield good returns, but at 15 times our projected 1995-96 EPS projection of $1.55, the shares are fairly valued.

Key Stock Statistics

S&P EPS Est. 1996	1.55	Tang. Bk. Value/Share	4.44
P/E on S&P Est. 1996	15.1	Beta	1.22
S&P EPS Est. 1997	1.80	Shareholders	2,600
Dividend Rate/Share	0.12	Market cap. (B)	$ 1.4
Shs. outstg. (M)	60.2	Inst. holdings	63%
Avg. daily vol. (M)	0.091	Insider holdings	NA

Value of $10,000 invested 5 years ago: $ 34,709

Fiscal Year Ending Feb. 28

	1996	% Change	1995	% Change	1994	% Change
Revenues (Million $)						
1Q	518.5	42%	364.0	26%	287.9	-7%
2Q	509.5	43%	357.2	13%	316.6	4%
3Q	—	—	397.3	24%	320.0	6%
4Q	—	—	485.0	52%	319.8	5%
Yr.	—	—	1,603	29%	1,244	2%
Income (Million $)						
1Q	24.60	44%	17.10	26%	13.60	10%
2Q	24.10	44%	16.70	27%	13.10	9%
3Q	—	—	16.50	29%	12.82	7%
4Q	—	—	17.60	52%	11.60	21%
Yr.	—	—	67.90	33%	51.10	11%
Earnings Per Share ($)						
1Q	0.41	NM	0.41	33%	0.31	19%
2Q	0.40	8%	0.37	24%	0.30	19%
3Q	E0.38	11%	0.34	22%	0.28	12%
4Q	E0.36	15%	0.31	22%	0.26	19%
Yr.	E1.55	11%	1.40	22%	1.14	9%

Next earnings report expected: mid December

Mark IV Industries

16-SEP-95

Business Summary - 15-SEP-95

Mark IV Industries manufactures products primarily for the automotive, mass transit and professional audio markets. Segment contributions in 1994-5 were:

	Sales	Profits
Power and fluid transfer	88%	88%
Professional audio	12%	12%

Foreign operations contributed 30% of sales and profits in 1994-5. IV's goal is to derive 50% of sales from foreign markets by 2001.

Power and fluid transfer includes the former automotive and transportation segments. Products for both the automotive aftermarket and original equipment include filters, belts, hoses, couplings, accessory drives, and fluid transfer assemblies, industrial belts and hydraulic hose, gasoline vapor recovery hose and fittings, temperature controls and protective closures, and garden hose. In 1993, IV acquired Pirelli Transmissioni Industriali, a European maker of belts and hydraulic hose (annual sales of $165 million). In November 1994, Purolator Products Co., a leading producer of automotive filters with sales of $450 million, was acquired.

Transportation products include door systems, information displays, interior lighting and air diffuser systems for buses, rail vehicles and aircraft, and traffic controls such as vehicle identification and control systems, traffic signs and signals, automated toll collection devices and other products.

Professional audio produces professional-quality microphones, speakers, mixers and amplifiers, high-fidelity public address musical instrument loudspeaker systems, signal processors and other sound and audio equipment.

The instrumentation products segment was discontinued in 1993-4, and the businesses were sold in 1994 to Danaher Corp.

Important Developments

Sep. '95—IV said that on a pro forma basis to reflect the acquisition of Purolator Products, sales, operating income, net income and fully diluted earnings per share for the first half of fiscal 1995-6 were up 8%, 11%, 20% and 14%, respectively. For the second quarter alone pro forma results for the same items mentioned above were up 8%, 10%, 18% and 11%, respectively. The process of merging Purolator with Dayco was continuing. Earlier in 1995, the Dayco Automotive Aftermarket Division was formed, combining Purolator's and Dayco's domestic aftermarket businesses. As part of streamlining and cost reduction efforts, Dayco's corporate office in Dayton, Ohio will be merged with IV's Amherst, New York corporate office.

Capitalization

Long Term Debt: $629,300,000 (5/95).

Per Share Data ($)

(Year Ended Feb. 28)

	1995	1994	1993	1992	1991	1990
Tangible Bk. Val.	4.66	3.33	4.69	3.90	3.04	3.72
Cash Flow	2.46	2.02	1.78	1.62	1.71	1.47
Earnings	1.40	1.14	1.04	0.89	0.94	0.92
Dividends	0.10	0.09	0.08	0.06	0.04	Nil
Payout Ratio	7%	8%	7%	9%	4%	Nil
Cal. Yrs.	1994	1993	1992	1991	1990	1989
Prices - High	22	23½	14⅝	10½	7⅜	7⅞
- Low	14⅞	14¼	9⅝	4¼	3⅝	3⅝
P/E Ratio - High	16	21	14	12	8	9
- Low	11	12	9	5	4	4

Income Statement Analysis (Million $)

	1995	%Chg	1994	%Chg	1993	%Chg	1992
Revs.	1,603	29%	1,244	2%	1,222	7%	1,146
Oper. Inc.	216	26%	171	8%	159	9%	146
Depr.	51.5	32%	38.9	20%	32.5	27%	25.5
Int. Exp.	53.9	7%	50.5	-11%	56.9	-21%	71.8
Pretax Inc.	110	35%	81.7	17%	70.1	49%	47.1
Eff. Tax Rate	39%	—	38%	—	35%	—	35%
Net Inc.	67.9	33%	51.1	11%	45.9	49%	30.9

Balance Sheet & Other Fin. Data (Million $)

	1995	1994	1993	1992	1991	1990
Cash	1.0	1.0	3.0	5.0	6.0	7.0
Curr. Assets	805	583	501	505	518	399
Total Assets	1,846	1,282	1,095	1,090	1,077	849
Curr. Liab.	425	270	209	207	161	120
LT Debt	611	567	497	525	718	544
Common Eqty.	636	345	359	322	178	165
Total Cap.	1,246	913	856	847	895	709
Cap. Exp.	50.0	119	35.0	34.0	109	23.0
Cash Flow	119	90.0	78.4	56.4	49.3	43.4

Ratio Analysis

	1995	1994	1993	1992	1991	1990
Curr. Ratio	1.9	2.2	2.4	2.4	3.2	3.3
% LT Debt of Cap.	49.0	62.2	58.1	62.0	80.1	76.7
% Net Inc.of Revs.	4.2	4.1	3.8	2.7	2.7	3.3
% Ret. on Assets	3.8	4.3	4.2	2.1	2.7	3.0
% Ret. on Equity	12.4	14.4	13.4	9.9	15.1	20.5

Dividend Data —Dividends have been paid since 1990. A "poison pill" stock purchase right was issued in May 1995.

Amt. of Div. $	Date Decl.	Ex-Div. Date	Stock of Record	Payment Date
0.028	Dec. 05	Dec. 14	Dec. 20	Jan. 03 '95
0.030	Mar. 01	Mar. 13	Mar. 17	Apr. 03 '95
5%	Mar. 29	Apr. 10	Apr. 17	Apr. 28 '95
0.030	Jun. 01	Jun. 14	Jun. 16	Jul. 05 '95
0.030	Aug. 31	Sep. 13	Sep. 15	Oct. 02 '95

Data as orig. reptd.; bef. results of disc. opers. and/or spec. items. Per share data adj. for stk. divs. as of ex-div. date. E-Estimated. NA-Not Available. NM-Not Meaningful. NR-Not Ranked.

Office—501 John James Audubon Parkway, P.O. Box 810, Amherst, NY 14226-0810. **Tel**—(716) 689-4972. **Chrmn**—S. H. Alfiero. **Pres**—C. R. Arrison. **EVP & CFO**—W. P. Montague. **Secy**—G. S. Lippes. **Investor Contact**—Sharlene Vogler. **Dirs**—S. H. Alfiero, C. R. Arrison, J. G. Donohoo, G. S. Lippes, H. Roth, Jr. **Transfer Agent**—American Stock Transfer & Trust Co., NYC. **Incorporated** in Delaware in 1970. **Empl-** 16,200. **S&P Analyst:** Joshua M. Harari, CFA

STANDARD & POOR'S

STOCK REPORTS

Marshall & Ilsley Corp.

NASDAQ Symbol **MRIS**

In S&P MidCap 400

17-OCT-95 **Industry:** Banking

Summary: Marshall & Ilsley Corp., with $13.0 billion in assets, operates 29 affiliate banks in Wisconsin with more than 225 offices and a bank in Phoenix, Arizona, with 12 offices.

S&P Opinion: Avoid (★★)

Recent Price • 25¼
52 Wk Range • 26½-17¾
Yield • 2.6%
12-Mo. P/E • 22.0

Quantitative Evaluations

Outlook (1 Lowest—5 Highest)
• **3-**

Fair Value
• **24⅞**

Risk
• **Low**

Earn./Div. Rank
• **A-**

Technical Eval.
• **Bullish** since 2/95

Rel. Strength Rank (1 Lowest—99 Highest)
• **65**

Insider Activity
• **Neutral**

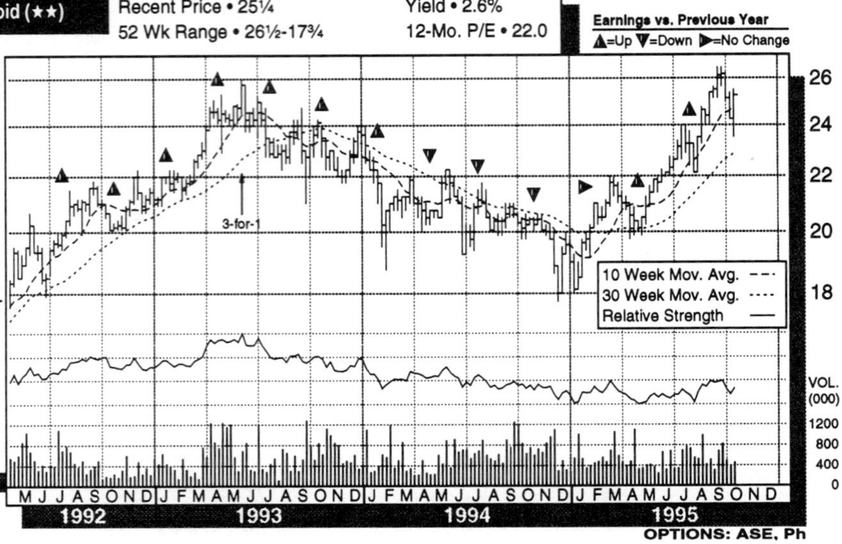

OPTIONS: ASE, Ph

Overview - 17-OCT-95

Earnings in 1994 were depressed by a $76.6 million merger related charge incurred during the second quarter to assimilate the operations of Valley Bancorporation. Much of MRIS's growth in recent years has been fueled by acquisitions, leading to the company's status as the largest bank holding company in Wisconsin. Marshall & Ilsley is a well diversified financial institution, with sizeable revenues and growth deriving from its data processing operations. In the nine months ended September 30, 1995, net income rose to $141.0 million, from $47.5 million, year to year. Earnings per share were $1.43, versus $0.47. Total loans at September 30, 1995, grew to $9.1 billion, from $8.9 billion a year earlier. Return on average assets was 1.49% and return on average equity was 15.96% for the 1995 third quarter, versus 1.42% and 16.50%, respectively, in the comparable 1994 quarter.

Valuation - 17-OCT-95

Shares of Marshall & Ilsley Corp. have risen over 30% thus far in 1995, slightly underperforming the regional bank indices, but outperforming the broader market. We anticipate continued slow loan growth, the absence of material net margin expansion, and possible dilution resulting from ongoing acquisitions. Given a current price that is 2.4 times tangible book value, and 12.0 times our 1996 per share earnings estimate, we view shares of MRIS as overvalued.

Key Stock Statistics

S&P EPS Est. 1995	1.94	Tang. Bk. Value/Share	10.40
P/E on S&P Est. 1995	13.0	Beta	0.81
S&P EPS Est. 1996	2.10	Shareholders	18,900
Dividend Rate/Share	0.66	Market cap. (B)	$ 2.4
Shs. outstg. (M)	94.0	Inst. holdings	33%
Avg. daily vol. (M)	0.099	Insider holdings	NA

Value of $10,000 invested 5 years ago: $ 25,705

Fiscal Year Ending Dec. 31

	1995	% Change	1994	% Change	1993	% Change
Revenues (Million $)						
1Q	319.4	12%	285.0	47%	193.4	-3%
2Q	333.0	18%	282.1	45%	194.8	-2%
3Q	—	—	301.8	53%	197.0	NM
4Q	—	—	309.8	53%	202.3	NM
Yr.	—	—	1,179	50%	787.4	-1%
Income (Million $)						
1Q	46.14	20%	38.51	24%	31.04	11%
2Q	46.24	NM	-37.06	NM	31.93	11%
3Q	48.58	8%	44.89	45%	30.95	8%
4Q	—	—	48.05	52%	31.57	NM
Yr.	—	—	94.40	-25%	125.5	8%
Earnings Per Share ($)						
1Q	0.47	21%	0.39	-15%	0.46	12%
2Q	0.47	NM	-0.39	NM	0.47	9%
3Q	0.49	9%	0.45	-2%	0.46	10%
4Q	E0.50	2%	0.49	NM	0.49	7%
Yr.	E1.94	104%	0.95	-49%	1.87	8%

Next earnings report expected: mid January

Marshall & Ilsley Corp.

Business Summary - 17-OCT-95

Marshall & Ilsley Corp. owns 29 banks with more than 225 offices in Wisconsin, a savings association in Wisconsin, one bank with 12 offices in the Phoenix, Ariz., area, and 10 financial services affiliates, including a data processing subsidiary, which contributed 14% of total revenues in 1994. Total assets exceed $12 billion. In April 1994, Marshall & Ilsley completed its acquisition of Valley Bancorporation, an Appleton, Wisc.-based bank holding company with $4.6 billion in assets and 160 branches. Consolidated gross loans of $8.79 billion at 1994 year end and $8.62 billion a year earlier were divided:

	1994	1993
Commercial, financial & agricultural	30%	30%
Real estate--residential	26%	26%
Real estate--commercial	24%	23%
Instalment	13%	14%
Real estate--construction	4%	4%
Leasing & other	3%	3%

The allowance for possible loan losses at 1994 year end was $154.0 million (1.75% of gross loans), up from $133.6 million (1.55%) a year earlier. Net charge-offs during 1994 were $4.5 million (0.05% of average loans), versus $9.4 million (0.11%) during 1993. As of December 31, 1994, nonperforming assets totaled $70.1 million (0.80% of total loans and other real estate owned), up from $69.3 million (0.80%) a year earlier.

Average deposits totaled $9.67 billion in 1994, and were divided: noninterest-bearing demand 21%, money market savings 16%, savings and NOW 25%, time deposits 33%, and CDs greater than $100,000 5%. On a tax-equivalent basis, the average yield on interest-earning assets in 1994 was 7.27% (7.33% in 1993), while the average rate paid on interest-bearing liabilities was 3.61% (3.60%), for a net spread of 3.66% (3.73%).

Important Developments

Jul. '95—Marshall & Ilsley acquired Citizens Bank of Delavan, Wis. and Sharon State Bank of Sharon, Wis., with total assets of about $95.2 million and $19.4 million, respectively. The banks have respective rates of return on assets of 2.79% and 2.58%, which are substantially higher than the industry average. Terms were not disclosed.

Capitalization

Long Term Debt: $642,413,000 (6/95).

Per Share Data ($)

(Year Ended Dec. 31)

	1994	1993	1992	1991	1990	1989
Tangible Bk. Val.	10.40	12.37	11.19	10.00	8.84	8.13
Earnings	0.95	1.87	1.73	1.50	1.08	1.28
Dividends	Nil	0.54	0.48	0.43	0.39	0.35
Payout Ratio	Nil	29%	28%	29%	36%	27%
Prices - High	24	26	22¼	18⅝	11⅞	12⅝
- Low	17¾	20⅞	16⅞	9	7¾	9⅜
P/E Ratio - High	25	14	13	12	11	10
- Low	19	11	10	6	7	7

Income Statement Analysis (Million $)

	1994	%Chg	1993	%Chg	1992	%Chg	1991
Net Int. Inc.	491	59%	309	NM	308	7%	289
Tax Equiv. Adj.	9.6	26%	7.6	-30%	10.8	-23%	14.1
Non Int. Inc.	367	22%	300	16%	258	16%	223
Loan Loss Prov.	24.9	174%	9.1	-40%	15.2	-26%	20.6
% Exp/Op Revs.	76%	—	66%	—	67%	—	66%
Pretax Inc.	168	-15%	197	13%	174	19%	146
Eff. Tax Rate	44%	—	36%	—	33%	—	32%
Net Inc.	94.4	-24%	125	7%	117	17%	99
% Net Int. Marg.	NA	—	4.53%	—	4.68%	—	4.57%

Balance Sheet & Other Fin. Data (Million $)

	1994	1993	1992	1991	1990	1989
Earning Assets:						
Money Mkt.	254	147	138	321	153	55.0
Inv. Securities	2,295	1,674	1,882	1,561	1,561	1,544
Com'l Loans	2,933	2,053	1,947	2,003	1,941	1,995
Other Loans	5,859	2,982	2,932	2,812	2,866	2,665
Total Assets	12,613	7,970	7,850	7,628	7,460	7,151
Demand Deposits	2,199	1,724	1,636	1,496	1,446	1,311
Time Deposits	7,300	4,472	4,576	4,637	4,533	4,274
LT Debt	654	203	130	182	178	149
Common Eqty.	1,026	750	742	656	581	546

Ratio Analysis

	1994	1993	1992	1991	1990	1989
% Ret. on Assets	0.9	1.6	1.6	1.4	1.0	1.2
% Ret. on Equity	NA	16.1	16.2	15.9	12.4	16.5
% Loan Loss Resv.	1.8	1.7	1.8	1.5	1.4	1.2
% Loans/Deposits	92.6	83.9	78.5	77.8	79.7	82.8
% Equity to Assets	NA	10.1	9.3	8.5	8.0	7.6

Dividend Data —Cash has been paid each year since 1938. A dividend reinvestment plan is available.

Amt. of Div. $	Date Decl.	Ex-Div. Date	Stock of Record	Payment Date
0.150	Oct. 13	Nov. 23	Nov. 30	Dec. 14 '94
0.150	Feb. 16	Feb. 23	Feb. 28	Mar. 14 '95
0.156	Feb. 16	Feb. 23	Feb. 28	Mar. 14 '95
0.165	Apr. 25	May. 24	May. 31	Jun. 14 '95
0.165	Aug. 10	Aug. 29	Aug. 31	Sep. 14 '95

Data as orig. reptd.; bef. results of disc opers. and/or spec. items. Per share data adj. for stk. divs. as of ex-div. date. E-Estimated. NA-Not Available. NM-Not Meaningful. NR-Not Ranked.

Office—770 North Water St., Milwaukee, WI 53202. **Tel**—(414) 765-7801. **Chrmn & CEO**—J. B. Wigdale. **Pres**—D. J. Kuester. **EVP-CFO**—G. H. Gunnlaugsson. **SVP-Secy, Treas & Investor Contact**—Michael A. Hatfield. **Dirs**—R. A. Abdoo, J. P. Bolduc, O. C. Boldt, W. F. Bueche, J. F. Chait, G. A. Francke, G. H. Gunnlaugsson, B. E. Jacobs, J. F. Kellner, J. F. Kress, D. J. Kuester, E. L. Meyer, Jr., D. R. O'Hare, S. W. Orr, Jr., P. M. Platten, III, J. A. Puelicher, S. W. Tisdale, J. B. Wigdale, J. O. Wright, J. O. Zuehlke. **Transfer Agent & Registrar**—First National Bank of Boston. **Incorporated** in Wisconsin in 1959. **Empl**-8,600. **S&P Analyst:** Thomas C. Ferguson

STANDARD & POOR'S

STOCK REPORTS

MAXXAM Inc.

ASE Symbol **MXM**
In S&P MidCap 400

24-SEP-95 **Industry:** Aluminum

Summary: This company, through its majority-owned Kaiser Aluminum Corp., primarily processes aluminum. MXM also has interests in forest products and real estate operations.

Quantitative Evaluations

Outlook
(1 Lowest—5 Highest)
• **NA**

Fair Value
• **NA**

Risk
• **Average**

Earn./Div. Rank
• **C**

Technical Eval.
• **Bearish** since 9/95

Rel. Strength Rank
(1 Lowest—99 Highest)
• **8**

Insider Activity
• **NA**

Recent Price • 48¼
52 Wk Range • 67⅝-27¼
Yield • Nil
12-Mo. P/E • NM

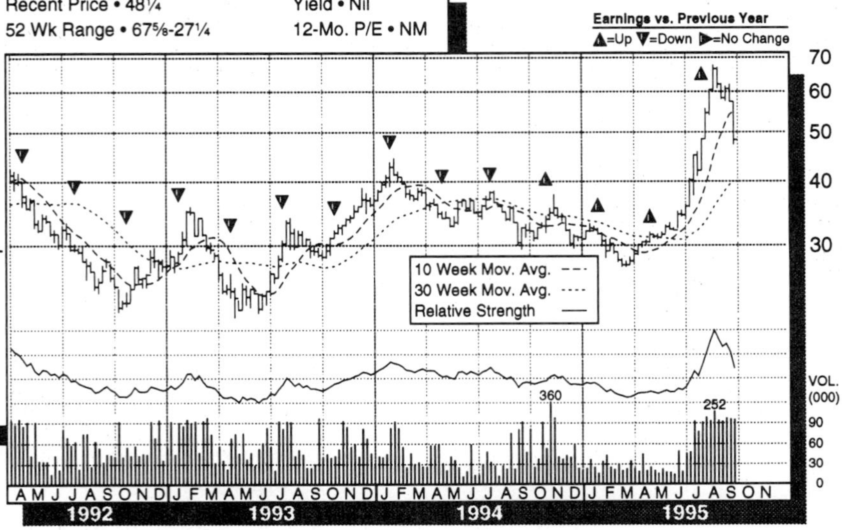

Business Profile - 22-SEP-95

Maxxam, through its majority-owned Kaiser unit, primarily processes aluminum. Kaiser's operating results are sensitive to aluminum prices, as well as to volume, product mix, and commodity and currency hedging strategies. Losses, incurred since late 1992, were replaced by gains in 1995's first half, mostly reflecting a strong recovery in aluminum prices. In 1994, MXM's highly seasonal forest products segment contributed 12% of total revenues.

Operational Review - 22-SEP-95

Revenues in 1995's first half climbed 21%, year to year, mostly due to a sharp rise in aluminum prices in the Kaiser segment. Margins greatly widened, on the higher prices and controlled operating expenses at Kaiser, which more than offset costs from two strikes and an alumina production malfunction; operating income increased sharply. Results were further aided by the absence of a large litigation settlement and net income of $24.4 million replaced a net loss of $77.7 million.

Stock Performance - 22-SEP-95

In the past 30 trading days, MXM's shares have declined 20%, compared to a 5% rise in the S&P 500. Average trading volume for the past five days was 28,800 shares, compared with the 40-day moving average of 32,351 shares.

Key Stock Statistics

Dividend Rate/Share	Nil	Shareholders	6,100
Shs. outstg. (M)	8.7	Market cap. (B)	$0.420
Avg. daily vol. (M)	0.029	Inst. holdings	24%
Tang. Bk. Value/Share	NM	Insider holdings	NA
Beta	0.98		

Value of $10,000 invested 5 years ago: $ 10,265

Fiscal Year Ending Dec. 31

	1995	% Change	1994	% Change	1993	% Change
Revenues (Million $)						
1Q	581.3	19%	489.0	-5%	513.7	-3%
2Q	673.3	24%	543.8	7%	507.9	-10%
3Q	—	—	544.9	8%	506.5	-5%
4Q	—	—	538.0	7%	503.0	-13%
Yr.	—	—	2,116	4%	2,031	-8%
Income (Million $)						
1Q	-1.00	NM	-34.50	NM	-25.90	NM
2Q	25.40	NM	-43.20	NM	-15.80	NM
3Q	—	—	-14.90	NM	-26.80	NM
4Q	—	—	-24.10	NM	-63.40	NM
Yr.	—	—	-116.7	NM	-131.9	NM
Earnings Per Share ($)						
1Q	-0.11	NM	-3.65	NM	-2.74	NM
2Q	2.69	NM	-4.57	NM	-1.67	NM
3Q	—	—	-1.58	NM	-2.83	NM
4Q	—	—	-2.55	NM	-6.71	NM
Yr.	—	—	-12.35	NM	-13.95	NM

Next earnings report expected: late October

MAXXAM Inc.

Business Summary - 22-SEP-95

MAXXAM (formerly MCO Holdings) is a holding company with subsidiaries engaged in aluminum production, forest products operations, and real estate management and development. Segment results in 1994 (profits in millions) were:

	Sales	Profits
Aluminum processing	64%	-$55.9
Bauxite and alumina	20%	5.6
Forest products	12%	79.1
Real estate	4%	-10.0

International sales were 26% of the total in 1994.

Kaiser Aluminum Corp. (62% owned), a fully integrated aluminum producer, is one of the world's leading producers of alumina, primary aluminum and fabricated aluminum products, and is a major domestic and international supplier of alumina and primary aluminum. Its products are used in automotive and truck products, beverage cans, and aerospace products. Kaiser has five business units: alumina, primary products, flat-rolled products, extruded products/rod-bar-wire, and forgings.

Forest products operations are conducted primarily through Pacific Lumber Co., a major producer of redwood and Douglas fir lumber, with operations supported by 189,000 acres of commercial timberlands located in Humboldt County in northern California. Redwood lumber is Pacific Lumber's largest product category, constituting 77% of its total lumber revenues and 63% of total revenues in 1994. It also sells logs and wood chips to surrounding mills and various other third parties.

Real estate operations, principally MAXXAM Property Co., hold assets including single- and multi-family communities, large landholdings, and resorts. In 1993, the company became the largest owner of Sam Houston Race Park in the Houston, Tex., area

Important Developments

Sep. '95—MXM announced that it elected to defer its proposed private placement of $75,000,000 of Exch. Sr. Secured Bonds, due 2005. MXM has not made a determination when or if it will proceed with such offering. Also, MAXXAM's 62%-owned Kaiser Aluminum Corp. unit appointed an independent committee to explore a recapitalization, in which voting or non-voting stock might be issued.

Aug. '95—MXM's Kaiser unit announced that, effective September 5, 1995, it will raise prices between 5%-8% on all heat-treatable coil, sheet and plate alloys sold to distributors and OEM markets.

Capitalization

Long Term Debt: $1,617,500,000 (6/95).
Minority Interest: $350,400,000.
$0.05 Class A Pfd. Stock: 669,957 shs. ($0.50 par); 10 votes ea.; conv. sh.-for-sh. into com.

Per Share Data ($)

(Year Ended Dec. 31)

	1994	1993	1992	1991	1990	1989
Tangible Bk. Val.	-31.65	-23.11	49.14	51.90	45.82	27.02
Cash Flow	0.47	-1.47	10.37	16.40	25.71	23.13
Earnings	-12.35	-13.95	-0.77	6.08	15.19	12.97
Dividends	Nil	Nil	Nil	Nil	Nil	Nil
Payout Ratio	Nil	Nil	Nil	Nil	Nil	Nil
Prices - High	44½	38⅞	43½	54¾	67½	51
- Low	29½	21¾	22¼	26	26⅜	23⅜
P/E Ratio - High	NM	NM	NM	9	4	4
- Low	NM	NM	NM	4	2	2

Income Statement Analysis (Million $)

	1994	%Chg	1993	%Chg	1992	%Chg	1991
Revs.	2,116	4%	2,031	-8%	2,203	-2%	2,255
Oper. Inc.	128	121%	58.0	-78%	265	-20%	333
Depr.	121	3%	118	12%	105	7%	98.0
Int. Exp.	180	-5%	190	-5%	201	-7%	216
Pretax Inc.	-171	NM	-210	NM	-13.0	NM	67.0
Eff. Tax Rate	NM	—	NM	—	NM	—	3.00%
Net Inc.	-116	NM	-131	NM	-7.0	NM	58.0

Balance Sheet & Other Fin. Data (Million $)

	1994	1993	1992	1991	1990	1989
Cash	125	129	153	159	88.0	289
Curr. Assets	1,091	992	1,033	1,093	1,028	1,271
Total Assets	3,691	3,572	3,125	3,215	3,028	3,183
Curr. Liab.	678	577	561	669	657	844
LT Debt	1,583	1,568	1,593	1,552	1,446	1,551
Common Eqty.	-275	-167	444	459	395	233
Total Cap.	1,652	1,624	2,213	2,191	1,964	1,919
Cap. Exp.	89.0	82.0	128	130	131	130
Cash Flow	4.0	-14.0	98.0	155	247	208

Ratio Analysis

	1994	1993	1992	1991	1990	1989
Curr. Ratio	1.6	1.7	1.8	1.6	1.6	1.5
% LT Debt of Cap.	95.8	96.5	72.0	70.8	73.6	80.8
% Net Inc.of Revs.	NM	NM	NM	2.6	6.1	4.8
% Ret. on Assets	NM	NM	NM	1.8	4.6	3.2
% Ret. on Equity	NM	NM	NM	13.4	46.0	66.7

Dividend Data —Cash dividends have never been paid.

Data as orig. reptd.; bef. results of disc. opers. and/or spec. items. Per share data adj. for stk. divs. as of ex-div. date. E-Estimated. NA-Not Available. NM-Not Meaningful. NR-Not Ranked.

Office—5847 San Felipe, Suite 2600, Houston, TX 77057. **Tel**—(713) 975-7600. **Chrmn, Pres & CEO**—C. E. Hurwitz. **SVP, Treas. & Investor Contact**—John T. La Duc. **EVP & CFO**—P. N. Schwartz. **VP & Secy**—B. L. Wade. **Dirs**—R. J. Cruikshank, C. E. Hurwitz, E. G. Levin, S. D. Rosenberg. **Transfer Agent & Registrar**—Bank of New York, NYC. **Incorporated** in Delaware in 1955. **Empl-** 12,000. **S&P Analyst:** Robert E. Friedman

STANDARD & POOR'S

STOCK REPORTS

McCormick & Co.

NASDAQ Symbol **MCCRK**

In S&P MidCap 400

24-SEP-95

Industry: Food

Summary: This company primarily produces spices, seasonings and flavorings for the retail food, foodservice and industrial markets. Trademarks include McCormick and Schilling.

S&P Opinion: Hold (★★★)

Recent Price • 22⅝ | 52 Wk Range • 23½-17¾ | Yield • 2.3% | 12-Mo. P/E • 35.4

Quantitative Evaluations

Outlook (1 Lowest—5 Highest)
• **3⁻**

Fair Value
• **21⅝**

Risk
• **Low**

Earn./Div. Rank
• **A**

Technical Eval.
• **Bullish** since 2/95

Rel. Strength Rank (1 Lowest—99 Highest)
• **49**

Insider Activity
• **NA**

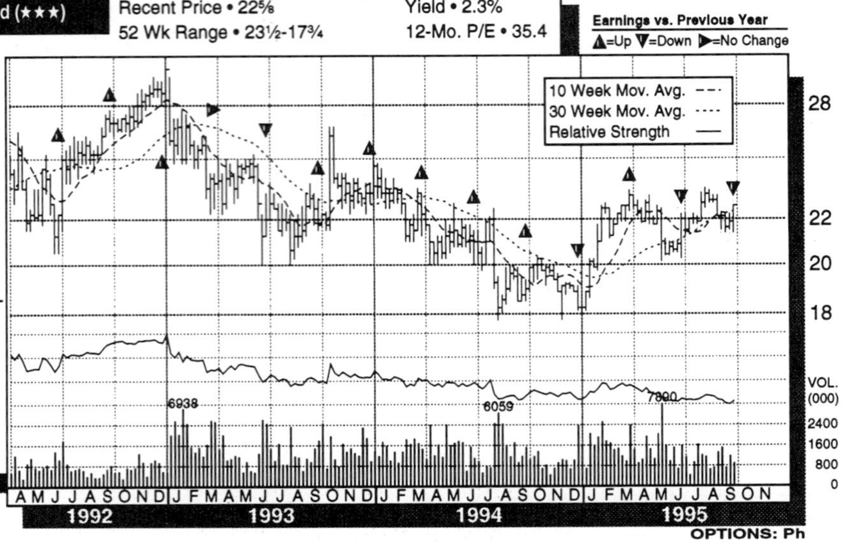

OPTIONS: Ph

Overview - 22-SEP-95

Sales are projected to grow at an approximate 10% annual rate through fiscal 1996, led by continued good growth in the company's industrial and foodservice businesses. However, near-term operating profit margins may continue to be restricted by the growing sales mix shift to low-margin industrial sales, highly competitive U.S. consumer products markets, and by elevated material costs. Such pressures on margins should be alleviated somewhat by late 1994's cost-cutting measures (workforce reduction, plant closings), but higher interest costs and extended troubles for unconsolidated Mexican operations could limit earnings progress over the near term.

Valuation - 22-SEP-95

Given the recent pressure on the company's earnings, we expect these shares to be market performers over the near term. Longer-term growth prospects are bright for this leading consumer spice company, but investors will likely remain cautious until there is evidence of an earnings upturn. In late 1994, management addressed the recent erosion in its operating margin by announcing a sweeping restructuring plan which included, among other things, employee cuts (nearly 7% of workforce), the closing of two plants, and the sale of a subsidiary. The stock, down about 20% from early 1993's level, is a worthwhile holding for long-term accounts. The company could be a potential takeover candidate upon any further weakness in the shares.

Key Stock Statistics

S&P EPS Est. 1995	1.30	Tang. Bk. Value/Share	3.59
P/E on S&P Est. 1995	17.4	Beta	1.26
S&P EPS Est. 1996	1.50	Shareholders	13,000
Dividend Rate/Share	0.52	Market cap. (B)	$ 1.8
Shs. outstg. (M)	81.2	Inst. holdings	43%
Avg. daily vol. (M)	0.226	Insider holdings	NA

Value of $10,000 invested 5 years ago: $ 19,560

Fiscal Year Ending Nov. 30

	1995	% Change	1994	% Change	1993	% Change
Revenues (Million $)						
1Q	425.4	16%	367.7	8%	339.6	5%
2Q	445.0	12%	396.3	10%	361.3	7%
3Q	432.0	2%	422.1	7%	394.9	10%
4Q	—	—	508.6	10%	460.8	2%
Yr.	—	—	1,695	9%	1,557	6%
Income (Million $)						
1Q	19.35	6%	18.31	6%	17.26	NM
2Q	16.04	-16%	19.13	9%	17.54	-7%
3Q	19.91	-25%	26.44	8%	24.37	2%
4Q	—	—	-2.72	NM	40.51	16%
Yr.	—	—	61.16	-39%	99.7	5%
Earnings Per Share ($)						
1Q	0.24	4%	0.23	10%	0.21	NM
2Q	0.20	-13%	0.23	10%	0.21	-9%
3Q	0.25	-22%	0.32	7%	0.30	3%
4Q	E0.61	NM	-0.03	NM	0.50	16%
Yr.	E1.30	73%	0.75	-39%	1.22	5%

Next earnings report expected: mid January

McCormick & Co.

Business Summary - 22-SEP-95

McCormick & Company produces spices, seasonings, flavorings and other specialty food products, which are sold worldwide to the retail food, foodservice and industrial markets under the McCormick and Schilling names. The company also makes plastic bottles and tubes for various industries. Sales in recent fiscal years were derived as follows:

	1994	1993	1992
Americas	42%	45%	46%
Europe	14%	13%	14%
Asia/Pacific	2%	2%	2%
Industrial	31%	29%	29%
Packaging	8%	8%	6%
Gilroy Energy	3%	3%	3%

The Americas segment includes the U.S. consumer products business, the Food Service Division, Golden West Foods, and wholly-owned subsidiaries in Canada, El Salvador, and Venezuela. New product development continues to be an important factor in generating sales growth for this division.

The European segment includes the company's operations in the United Kingdom, Switzerland and Finland. The Asia/Pacific segment operations participate in consumer, foodservice and industrial businesses.

The McCormick industrial division serves food processors and major restaurant chains with spices, seasonings and flavorings. International markets served include Mexico and India.

Plastic bottles and tubes are produced in the packaging division for the pharmaceutical, cosmetics and food industries. Gilroy Foods produces onion, garlic and capsicums.

Important Developments

Sep. '95—For the first nine months of fiscal 1995, income from consolidated operations declined 7%, year to year, to $54.9 million. Income from unconsolidated operations during the period fell 92% to $376,000, due primarily to economic problems in Mexico. Management said that the company's domestic sales during fiscal 1995's third quarter were adversely affected by timing differences of price increases versus the prior year. All other operations combined showed strong sales growth over the year ago period. During the quarter, strong earnings performance in the industrial group was somewhat offset by lower garlic crop yields at Gilroy Foods. Earnings were also again impacted in the quarter by weakness in the Mexican economy, higher raw material costs, and interest expense. Management said that it looked for a strong fourth quarter.

Capitalization

Long Term Debt: $362,952,000 (5/95).

Per Share Data ($) (Year Ended Nov. 30)

	1994	1993	1992	1991	1990	1989
Tangible Bk. Val.	3.62	4.15	4.36	4.00	3.61	3.48
Cash Flow	1.45	1.79	1.65	1.43	1.23	0.96
Earnings	0.75	1.22	1.16	0.98	0.83	0.60
Dividends	0.60	0.44	0.38	0.28	0.23	0.17
Payout Ratio	80%	36%	33%	28%	28%	27%
Prices - High	24¾	29¾	30¼	26½	13¼	13½
- Low	17¾	20	20½	12¼	9	6⅞
P/E Ratio - High	33	24	26	27	16	22
- Low	24	16	18	13	11	11

Income Statement Analysis (Million $)

	1994	%Chg	1993	%Chg	1992	%Chg	1991
Revs.	1,695	9%	1,557	6%	1,471	3%	1,428
Oper. Inc.	256	13%	227	10%	207	13%	183
Depr.	56.8	22%	46.7	17%	40.0	8%	37.0
Int. Exp.	38.7	24%	31.1	NM	30.9	12%	27.5
Pretax Inc.	95.0	-41%	160	8%	148	19%	124
Eff. Tax Rate	36%	—	38%	—	36%	—	35%
Net Inc.	61.2	-39%	100	5%	95.2	18%	80.9

Balance Sheet & Other Fin. Data (Million $)

	1994	1993	1992	1991	1990	1989
Cash	15.6	12.8	1.8	6.0	5.3	51.6
Curr. Assets	658	540	468	445	409	427
Total Assets	1,569	1,313	1,131	1,032	947	865
Curr. Liab.	601	393	420	360	306	245
LT Debt	374	346	201	208	211	211
Common Eqty.	490	467	438	389	364	346
Total Cap.	883	852	697	652	623	606
Cap. Exp.	87.7	97.0	92.0	75.9	60.6	56.6
Cash Flow	118	146	135	118	103	84.0

Ratio Analysis

	1994	1993	1992	1991	1990	1989
Curr. Ratio	1.1	1.4	1.1	1.2	1.3	1.7
% LT Debt of Cap.	42.4	40.6	28.8	31.8	34.0	34.7
% Net Inc.of Revs.	3.6	6.4	6.5	5.7	5.2	4.2
% Ret. on Assets	4.2	8.1	8.8	8.2	7.8	6.7
% Ret. on Equity	12.8	21.9	22.9	21.5	19.9	17.0

Dividend Data —Cash has been paid each year since 1925. A dividend reinvestment plan is available.

Amt. of Div. $	Date Decl.	Ex-Div. Date	Stock of Record	Payment Date
0.120	Sep. 20	Sep. 26	Sep. 30	Oct. 10 '94
0.130	Dec. 19	Dec. 23	Dec. 30	Jan. 20 '95
0.130	Mar. 15	Mar. 27	Mar. 31	Apr. 10 '95
0.130	Jun. 26	Jul. 03	Jul. 06	Jul. 14 '95
0.130	Sep. 19	Sep. 27	Sep. 29	Oct. 09 '95

Data as orig. reptd.; bef. results of disc. opers. and/or spec. items. Per share data adj. for stk. divs. as of ex-div. date. E-Estimated. NA-Not Available. NM-Not Meaningful. NR-Not Ranked.

Office—18 Loveton Circle, Sparks, MD 21152-6000. **Tel**—(410) 771-7301. **Chrmn**—C. P. McCormick Jr. **Pres & CEO**—H. E. Blattman. **VP & Secy**—R. W. Single Sr. **VP-CFO**—R. G. Davey. **VP-Treas & Investor Contact**—D. A. Palumbo. **Dirs**—J. J. Albrecht, H. E. Blattman, J. S. Cook, R. G. Davey, H. J. Handley, G. W. Koch, R. J. Lawless, C. P. McCormick Jr., G. V. McGowan, C. D. Nordhoff, R. W. Single Sr., W. E. Stevens, K. D. Weatherholtz. **Transfer Agent & Registrar**—Co. office. **Co-Transfer Agent**—Security Trust Co., Baltimore. **Incorporated** in Maryland in 1915. **Empl-** 8,900. **S&P Analyst:** Kenneth A. Shea

McKesson Corp.

NYSE Symbol MCK In S&P MidCap 400 Options on Pacific (Feb-May-Aug-Nov)

Price	Range	P–E Ratio	Dividend	Yield	S&P Ranking	Beta
Aug. 10'95	1995					
43¼	47⅝–31¼	NM	1.00	2.3%	B+	1.09

Summary

This company is the successor to McKesson Corp. (old) owning all of the businesses formerly owned by the predecessor except the PCS benefit management business, which was purchased by Eli Lilly & Co. in December 1994 for $4 billion. The company distributes drugs, health and beauty aids and general merchandise, and also owns 55% of Armor All Products Corp., a producer of car care products.

Current Outlook

Share earnings for the fiscal year ending March 31, 1996, are projected at $2.95, versus $2.52 (excluding one-time charges of $6.81) in fiscal 1994-95.

The $0.25 quarterly dividend is the minimum expected.

Revenues from continuing operations should increase moderately in fiscal 1995-96. Operating profits in the drug distribution segment should improve, reflecting higher drug price inflation, better inventory management and cost controls. Operating profit in the water distribution business should also benefit from increased efficiencies.

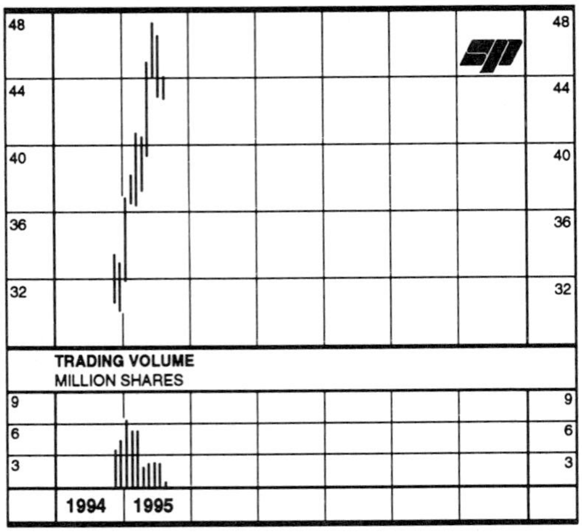

Revenues (Million $)

Quarter:	1995–96	1994–95	1993–94
Jun.	3,336	3,235	2,932
Sep.		3,256	2,989
Dec.		3,350	3,206
Mar.		3,348	3,124
		13,189	12,251

Revenues from continuing operations for the three months ended June 30, 1995, rose 3.1%, year to year, reflecting increases from Health Care Services and water products and additional interest income from the sale of PCS, partly offset by a decline at Armor All. Profitability was aided by the improved interest income, and income from continuing operations advanced 24% to $32.8 million ($0.70 a share) from $26.4 million ($0.60). Results in the fiscal 1994 period exclude income from discontined operations of $0.23.

Common Share Earnings ($)

Quarter:	1995–96	1994–95	1993–94
Jun.	0.70	0.60	1.16
Sep.	E0.65	0.36	0.51
Dec.	E0.70	d6.24	0.54
Mar.	E0.90	0.86	0.72
	E2.95	d4.51	2.93

Important Developments

Jun. '95— MCK acquired a minority interest in Multum Information Services, Inc., a provider of patient specific drug therapy information systems for physicians, pharmacists and hospitals, for $10 million. In addition, the two companies entered into a strategic alliance agreement under which they will jointly develop an array of information and service offerings for health care providers.

May '95— McKesson said that it would repurchase up to 3.5 million common shares from time to time in open market or private transactions.

Apr. '95— The company created a new unit, McKesson Health Systems, which will provide pharmaceutical products, information technology services and custom delivery services to hospitals, long-term care facilities, clinics and other health care providers.

Next earnings report expected in mid-October.

Per Share Data ($)

Yr. End Mar. 31	1995	[1]1994	1993	1992	1991	1990	[1]1989	1988	[1]1987	[1]1986
Tangible Bk. Val.	**18.01**	4.95	4.34	2.34	5.07	5.92	8.58	9.28	10.40	8.93
Cash Flow	**d2.91**	5.66	4.62	2.94	4.49	4.00	3.69	3.60	3.17	3.45
Earnings[2]	**d4.51**	3.68	2.69	0.84	2.46	2.23	2.22	2.23	2.17	1.98
Dividends	**1.51**	1.66	1.60	1.60	1.60	1.44	1.44	1.28	1.26	1.20
Payout Ratio	**NM**	45%	60%	65%	65%	63%	62%	56%	57%	64%
Calendar Years	**1994**	1993	1992	1991	1990	1989	1988	1987	1986	1985
Prices—High	**109¼**	57¼	44¼	40⅛	38⅜	39⅝	35¾	40⅛	35¼	26⅝
Low	**30⅛**	38½	30¼	30⅜	26¾	29½	25⅝	23¼	24⅝	18½
P/E Ratio—	**NM**	16–10	16–11	48–36	16–11	18–13	16–12	18–10	16–11	14–9

Data as orig. reptd.; prior to 1995, data as reported for predecessor co. (Old McKesson). Adj. for stk. div. of 100% Oct. 1986. **1.** Reflects merger of acquisition. **2.** Bef. results of disc. opers. of +13.72 in 1995, -0.19 in 1992, -0.12 in 1991, +0.16 in 1989, -0.10 in 1987, and spec. items of -0.51 in 1994, -2.85 in 1992. NM-Not Meaningful. d-Deficit. E-Estimated.

Income Data (Million $)

Year Ended Mar. 31	Revs.	Oper. Inc.	% Oper. Inc. of Revs.	Cap. Exp.	Depr.	Int. Exp.	[3]Net Bef. Taxes	Eff. Tax Rate	[4]Net Inc.	% Net Inc. of Revs.	Cash Flow
[1]1995	**13,171**	**305**	**2.3**	**82**	**69.8**	**46.0**	**d71**	**NM**	**d193**	**NM**	**d127**
[2]1994	12,428	360	2.9	100	80.7	41.4	275	39.7%	[5]157	1.3	231
1993	11,669	324	2.8	70	77.4	49.5	197	40.0%	115	1.0	185
[1]1992	10,313	304	2.9	73	81.5	57.7	82	48.8%	[5]40	0.4	114
[1]1991	8,421	303	3.6	82	78.2	55.8	169	37.0%	105	1.3	173
1990	7,791	292	3.7	74	71.7	53.3	167	38.1%	99	1.3	162
[1,2]1989	7,046	275	3.9	104	61.7	47.1	167	39.7%	94	1.3	155
1988	7,283	281	3.9	88	57.7	44.6	179	43.9%	95	1.3	152
[1,2]1987	6,672	247	3.7	66	43.1	44.4	173	44.2%	94	1.4	137
[2]1986	6,264	229	3.7	85	57.4	42.8	149	47.8%	[5]78	1.2	135

Balance Sheet Data (Million $)

Mar. 31	Cash	Curr. Assets	Curr. Liab.	Curr. Ratio	Total Assets	% Ret. on Assets	Long Term Debt	Common Equity	Total Cap.	% LT Debt of Cap.	% Ret. on Equity
1995	**693**	**2,699**	**1,738**	**1.6**	**3,479**	**NM**	**459**	**1,014**	**1,532**	**29.9**	**NM**
1994	96	2,186	1,784	1.2	3,193	5.2	463	553	1,193	38.8	28.7
1993	120	1,898	1,615	1.2	2,800	4.0	347	493	986	35.2	23.0
1992	161	1,814	1,493	1.2	2,757	1.5	490	426	1,061	46.2	6.6
1991	146	1,469	1,179	1.2	2,461	4.5	534	545	1,282	41.7	17.5
1990	157	1,403	1,134	1.2	2,323	4.5	427	553	1,189	35.9	14.7
1989	48	1,221	925	1.3	2,106	4.4	414	685	1,180	35.1	13.8
1988	56	1,415	1,007	1.4	2,255	4.3	438	695	1,248	35.1	13.2
1987	48	1,451	952	1.5	2,208	4.2	396	754	1,256	31.6	12.8
1986	46	1,364	897	1.5	2,176	4.0	490	686	1,279	38.3	11.8

Data as orig. reptd.; prior to 1995, data as reported for predecessor co. (Old McKesson). **1.** Excl. disc. opers. **2.** Refl. merger or acq. **3.** Incl. equity in earns. of nonconsol. subs. **4.** Bef. results of disc. opers. and spec. items. **5.** Refl. acctg. change. d-Deficit. NM-Not Meaningful.

Business Summary

McKesson Corp. (formerly Foremost-McKesson) is a leading distributor of drugs, health and beauty aids, and bottled water. Contributions by business segment in 1994-95:

	Revs.	Profits
Distribution services	96%	75%
Bottled water	2%	11%
Armor All	2%	14%

The distribution services core business is McKesson Drug Co., the largest U.S. distributor of ethical and proprietary drugs and health and beauty aids. Under the Valu-Rite name, the company provides independent pharmacies with a comprehensive set of programs, including private label products and computer systems. Service merchandising distributes health and beauty aids, general merchandise and foods to retail stores.

McKesson Water Products Co. processes bottled drinking water delivered to homes and businesses and packaged water sold through retail stores in California, Arizona, Nevada and Texas.

Armor All Products Corp. (55% owned) markets automotive appearance products.

On December 1, 1994, Eli Lilly & Co. (LLY) completed the merger with McKesson Corp. under which shareholders received $76 a share in cash and one share of common stock of a new corporation for each share of McKesson. McKesson Corp. (new) owns all the businesses formerly owned by MCK (old) other than PCS benefits management business, which became a subsidiary of Eli Lilly. The company's gain on the PCS sale amounted to $577 million; the gain was partially offset by special charges of $154 million related to the transaction. Until redeployed, the company has invested the cash proceeds from the sale of PCS in U.S. securities.

Dividend Data

Dividends have been paid on the shares of the company or its predecessor since 1962. A dividend reinvestment plan is available.

Amt of Divd. $	Date Decl.	Ex–divd. Date	Stock of Record	Payment Date
0.25	Nov. 30	Dec. 9	Dec. 15	Jan. 3'95
0.25	Jan. 25	Feb. 23	Mar. 1	Apr. 3'95
0.25	Apr. 26	May 25	Jun. 1	Jul. 3'95
0.25	Jul. 26	Aug. 30	Sep. 1	Sep. 22'95

Capitalization

Long Term Debt: $458,800,000 (3/95).

Minority Interest: $59,900,000.

Common Stock: 44,626,319 shs. ($2 par). Institutions hold some 52%.

Shareholders of record: 15,765 (3/95).

Office—One Post St., San Francisco, CA 94104. **Tel**—(415) 983-8300. **Chrmn & CEO**—A. Seelenfreund. **Pres**—D. E. McDowell. **VP-CFO**—K. B. Ferrell. **VP-Secy**—N. A. Miller. **Investor Contact**—Janet M. Bley (415-983-9357). **Dirs**—M. G. F. Bitterman, T. Friedman, J. R. Harvey, G. M. Keller, L. L. Luttgens, D. E. McDowell, J. M. Pietruski, A. Seelenfreund, J. E. Shaw, R. H. Waterman Jr. **Transfer Agent & Registrar**—First Chicago Trust Co. of New York, NYC. **Incorporated** in Delaware in 1994; predecessor originally incorporated in Maryland in 1928. **Empl**—12,200.

 Philip J. Birbara

STANDARD & POOR'S

STOCK REPORTS

Measurex Corp.

NYSE Symbol **MX**
In S&P MidCap 400

17-OCT-95 **Industry:** Electronics/Electric

Summary: This company makes and services computer integrated manufacturing systems that control continuous batch manufacturing processes, primarily for the pulp and paper industries.

Quantitative Evaluations
Outlook (1 Lowest—5 Highest)
• **3+**
Fair Value
• **33¾**
Risk
• **Average**
Earn./Div. Rank
• **B-**

Technical Eval.
• **Bullish** since 9/95
Rel. Strength Rank (1 Lowest—99 Highest)
• **85**
Insider Activity
• **Neutral**

Recent Price • 34¼
52 Wk Range • 35⅝-20

Yield • 1.3%
12-Mo. P/E • 35.7

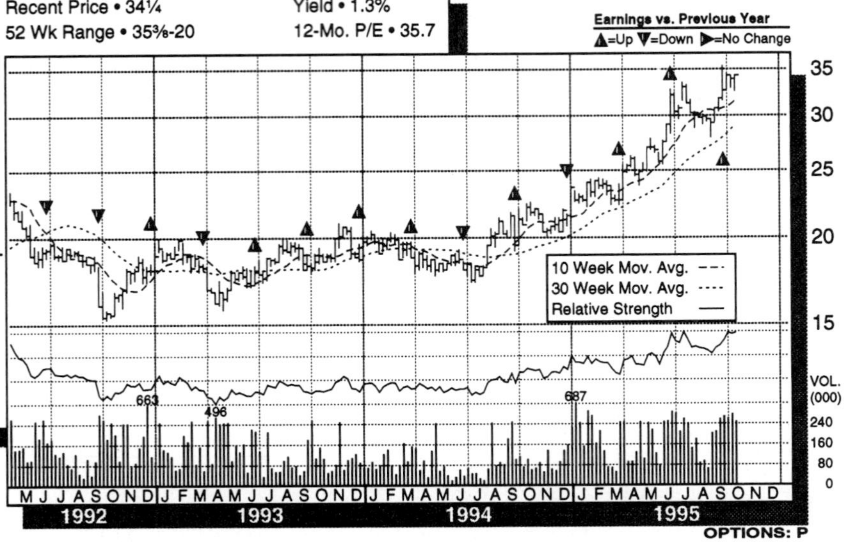

OPTIONS: P

Business Profile - 13-OCT-95

A downtrend in system orders reversed in the fiscal 1994 third quarter, reflecting an upturn in worldwide demand for the company's paper systems. In September 1994, MX announced a restructuring of operations, including the closing of several overseas facilities. Recent cost-cutting measures and growth in the paper industry should aid future profitability. A pending acquisition will allow Measurex to penetrate the steel industry.

Operational Review - 13-OCT-95

Worldwide orders for paper systems rose sharply in recent periods, reflecting continued improvement in the paper industry. Industrial systems business also showed improvement. Increased paper industry orders reflect upgrades and replacements from the installed customer base, as well as expanded product offerings resulting from acquisitions. Margins widened, aided by the greater volume and cost-containment measures.

Stock Performance - 13-OCT-95

In the past 30 trading days, MX's shares have increased 17%, compared to a 4% rise in the S&P 500. Average trading volume for the past five days was 61,380 shares, compared with the 40-day moving average of 69,321 shares.

Key Stock Statistics

Dividend Rate/Share	0.44	Shareholders	1,400
Shs. outstg. (M)	15.4	Market cap. (B)	$0.524
Avg. daily vol. (M)	0.093	Inst. holdings	83%
Tang. Bk. Value/Share	11.98	Insider holdings	NA
Beta	1.21		

Value of $10,000 invested 5 years ago: $ 15,451

Fiscal Year Ending Nov. 30

	1995	% Change	1994	% Change	1993	% Change
Revenues (Million $)						
1Q	73.44	19%	61.65	NM	61.80	NM
2Q	76.99	23%	62.58	-5%	66.14	5%
3Q	91.64	40%	65.65	2%	64.27	4%
4Q	—	—	70.10	14%	61.75	-6%
Yr.	—	—	260.0	2%	254.0	NM
Income (Million $)						
1Q	3.48	59%	2.19	26%	1.74	-52%
2Q	5.22	193%	1.78	-18%	2.17	3%
3Q	8.48	NM	2.54	9%	2.34	48%
4Q	—	—	-0.92	NM	1.96	NM
Yr.	—	—	5.58	-32%	8.22	NM
Earnings Per Share ($)						
1Q	0.20	67%	0.12	20%	0.10	-50%
2Q	0.30	NM	0.10	-17%	0.12	9%
3Q	0.51	NM	0.14	8%	0.13	44%
4Q	—	—	-0.05	NM	0.11	NM
Yr.	—	—	0.31	-33%	0.46	NM

Next earnings report expected: mid December

Measurex Corp.

Business Summary - 13-OCT-95

Measurex Corporation makes and services computer integrated manufacturing (CIM) systems. These sensor-based computerized systems, which control continuous, batch and discrete manufacturing processes and provide plantwide and millwide information, are designed to increase productivity, reduce raw material usage and energy consumption and improve product quality and uniformity. Principal industries served are pulp and paper, plastics, metals and rubber. The company supports its installed systems with a worldwide field service organization. MX offers customers a broad range of on-site and on-call services, including 24-hour-a-day and 365-days-a-year service contracts. To support its product line, the company has 44 regional sales offices and service centers, located in 30 countries throughout the world.

Revenue contributions in recent years were:

	1994	1993	1992
System sales to:			
Pulp & paper industries	51%	51%	46%
Industrial systems	9%	9%	13%
Service revenues	40%	40%	41%

International operations accounted for 57% and 63% of sales in fiscal 1994 and 1993, respectively.

Products and systems include MXOpen, an integrated information and control system that uses industry-standard computer and communication protocols; OptiVISION Full Spectrum Production and Quality Management Systems, which manage processes from long-term planning and order entry, through scheduling, product tracking, shipping and invoicing products. The company is also a leader in sensor technology for the process industries, currently offering more than 70 sensors that monitor various physical properties of products, including weight, moisture, gloss, opacity and spacing. In addition, MX is a leader in cross-direction profile controls, a technology that provides manufacturers with precise control over product characteristics during the manufacturing processs.

Through its 1993 acquisition of Roilbox Oy, MX offers a web inspection system (MXOpen web inspection system) that analyzes a moving paper web by measuring the intensity variations of light transmitted through, or reflected from, a sheet of paper.

Important Developments

Sep. '95—MX signed a definitive agreement to acquire Data Measurement Corp. (DMC) for approximately $30 million. DMC's revenues in the first half of 1995 were $15 million, a 32% year-to-year increase. The acquisition provides a significant entry for Measurex into the process control business for the steel industry.

Capitalization

Long Term Debt: $39,754,000 (9/95).

Per Share Data ($)

(Year Ended Nov. 30)

	1994	1993	1992	1991	1990	1989
Tangible Bk. Val.	11.98	11.87	12.12	12.82	13.33	12.51
Cash Flow	0.88	1.07	0.65	0.69	1.82	2.64
Earnings	0.31	0.46	0.04	0.02	1.26	2.17
Dividends	0.44	0.44	0.44	0.44	0.43	0.37
Payout Ratio	142%	96%	NM	NM	34%	17%
Prices - High	23⅝	21	25	24⅝	26	32
- Low	17¼	15¾	15¼	15¼	15⅛	23
P/E Ratio - High	76	46	NM	NM	21	15
- Low	56	34	NM	NM	12	11

Income Statement Analysis (Million $)

	1994	%Chg	1993	%Chg	1992	%Chg	1991
Revs.	260	2%	254	NM	253	NM	254
Oper. Inc.	21.6	16%	18.6	49%	12.5	-19%	15.4
Depr.	10.4	-6%	11.1	-2%	11.3	-7%	12.1
Int. Exp.	1.3	41%	0.9	17%	0.8	-2%	0.8
Pretax Inc.	9.2	-28%	12.7	NM	1.7	NM	0.5
Eff. Tax Rate	39%	—	35%	—	57%	—	25%
Net Inc.	5.6	-32%	8.2	NM	0.7	75%	0.4

Balance Sheet & Other Fin. Data (Million $)

	1994	1993	1992	1991	1990	1989
Cash	109	111	115	127	143	151
Curr. Assets	208	214	218	236	255	263
Total Assets	320	318	323	340	337	333
Curr. Liab.	84.0	76.0	84.8	80.8	69.6	76.2
LT Debt	12.2	16.8	0.8	4.7	4.8	5.0
Common Eqty.	217	212	218	232	239	230
Total Cap.	236	242	238	259	268	257
Cap. Exp.	6.7	8.3	7.8	NA	NA	NA
Cash Flow	16.0	19.3	12.0	12.5	32.7	49.5

Ratio Analysis

	1994	1993	1992	1991	1990	1989
Curr. Ratio	2.5	2.8	2.6	2.9	3.7	3.5
% LT Debt of Cap.	5.2	6.9	0.4	1.8	1.8	1.9
% Net Inc.of Revs.	2.1	3.2	0.3	0.2	8.5	14.3
% Ret. on Assets	1.7	2.6	0.2	0.1	6.8	12.8
% Ret. on Equity	2.6	3.8	0.3	0.2	9.7	18.8

Dividend Data —Dividends were initiated in 1977, omitted in 1982 and resumed in 1983.

Amt. of Div. $	Date Decl.	Ex-Div. Date	Stock of Record	Payment Date
0.110	Dec. 14	Dec. 27	Jan. 03	Jan. 11 '95
0.110	Mar. 22	Mar. 30	Apr. 05	Apr. 19 '95
0.110	Jun. 20	Jun. 30	Jul. 05	Jul. 19 '95
0.110	Sep. 20	Oct. 02	Oct. 04	Oct. 18 '95

Data as orig. reptd.; bef. results of disc. opers. and/or spec. items. Per share data adj. for stk. divs. as of ex-div. date. E-Estimated. NA-Not Available. NM-Not Meaningful. NR-Not Ranked.

Office—One Results Way, Cupertino, CA 95014-5991. **Tel**—(408) 255-1500. **Fax**—(408) 864-7570. **Chrmn & CEO**—D. A. Bossen. **Pres**—J. C. Gingerich. **Sr VP, CFO & Investor Contact**—Robert McAdams Jr. **Secy**—C. Van Orden. **Dirs**—P. Bancroft III, D. C. Baum, D. A. Bossen, J. C. Gingerich, J. T. Grade, O. L. Hoch, J. W. Larson, J. W. McKittrick, G. Tyson. **Transfer Agent & Registrar**—Bank of New York, NYC. **Incorporated** in California in 1968; reincorporated in Delaware in 1984. **Empl**-2,090. **S&P Analyst:** Steven A. Jaworski

Media General

ASE Symbol **MEG.A**
In S&P MidCap 400

18-OCT-95 **Industry:** Publishing

Summary: This major newspaper publisher and newsprint recycler also owns three TV stations and two cable television systems. Media properties are located in four southern states.

S&P Opinion: Hold (★★★)

Recent Price • 32⅛
52 Wk Range • 38⅜-27⅛
Yield • 1.5%
12-Mo. P/E • 18.1

Quantitative Evaluations

Outlook (1 Lowest—5 Highest)
• **NA**

Fair Value
• **NA**

Risk
• **NA**

Earn./Div. Rank
• **B**

Technical Eval.
• **Bearish** since 3/95

Rel. Strength Rank (1 Lowest—99 Highest)
• **19**

Insider Activity
• **Neutral**

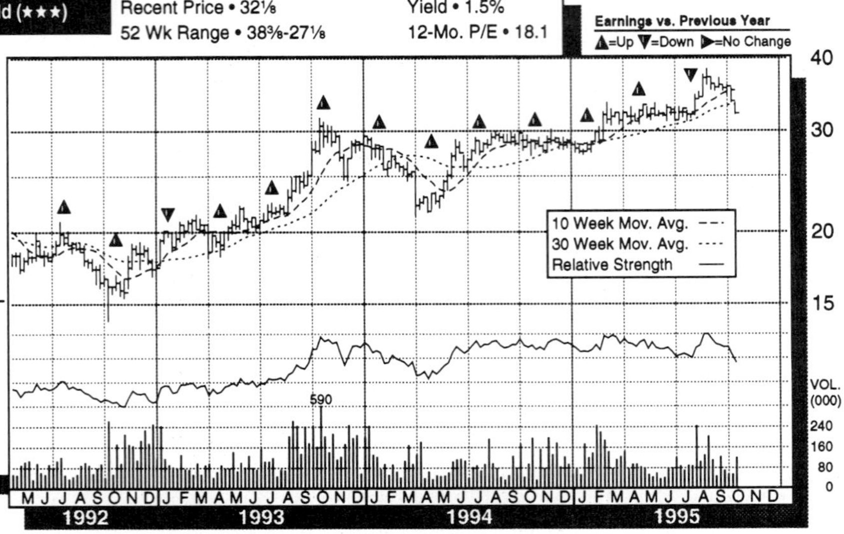

Overview - 18-OCT-95

Revenues are expected to rise sharply in 1996, boosted by a major newspaper acquisition. Pro forma revenues should rise moderately, largely reflecting continuing healthy broadcasting, newsprint and cable gains. Although price hikes should taper off in 1996, higher average newsprint prices will reduce profitability at the newspaper division. Overall corporate profitability will benefit from the higher average prices however, because the company produces more newsprint than it consumes. Newsprint margins are expected to be little changed, while broadcasting and cable profitability should improve. Debt levels and noncash charges will be sharply higher due to the acquisition of the Worrell newspapers.

Valuation - 18-OCT-95

Media General stock was a satisfactory market performer through the third quarter of 1995, gaining roughly in line with the market. The company's ownership of Garden State Paper Co., the very positive outlook for TV broadcasting, and the much-improved longer-term scenario for cable TV operations are currently viewed as positive factors bolstering the stock. But the market is relatively cool toward newspaper stocks, given the slow-growth scenario for newspaper advertising and margin pressure from higher newsprint prices. Media General derives over 50% of revenues from newspaper operations and that percentage will rise sharply with the pending acquisition of a group of Virginia newspapers.

Key Stock Statistics

S&P EPS Est. 1995	1.85	Tang. Bk. Value/Share	11.77
P/E on S&P Est. 1995	17.4	Beta	0.31
S&P EPS Est. 1996	2.20	Shareholders	2,700
Dividend Rate/Share	0.48	Market cap. (B)	$0.840
Shs. outstg. (M)	26.4	Inst. holdings	56%
Avg. daily vol. (M)	0.016	Insider holdings	NA

Value of $10,000 invested 5 years ago: $ 11,486

Fiscal Year Ending Dec. 31

	1995	% Change	1994	% Change	1993	% Change
Revenues (Million $)						
1Q	165.1	11%	149.4	4%	144.0	1%
2Q	173.5	12%	154.6	1%	153.0	4%
3Q	168.5	9%	155.2	5%	147.5	5%
4Q	—	—	167.1	7%	156.5	5%
Yr.	—	—	626.3	4%	600.8	4%
Income (Million $)						
1Q	12.68	NM	3.95	16%	3.41	29%
2Q	13.19	-86%	92.89	NM	8.14	30%
3Q	8.85	10%	8.02	57%	5.10	183%
4Q	—	—	12.15	34%	9.06	20%
Yr.	—	—	117.0	NM	25.71	40%
Earnings Per Share ($)						
1Q	0.48	NM	0.15	15%	0.13	30%
2Q	0.50	-86%	3.54	NM	0.31	29%
3Q	0.33	10%	0.30	50%	0.20	186%
4Q	E0.54	17%	0.46	35%	0.34	17%
Yr.	E1.85	-58%	4.45	NM	0.98	40%

Next earnings report expected: late January

Media General

Business Summary - 13-OCT-95

Media General is a major newspaper publisher, recycler of newsprint and owner of TV and cable systems. Contributions in 1994 were:

	Revs.	Profits
Newspapers	52%	47%
Broadcasting	30%	52%
Newsprint	16%	1%
Other	2%	Nil

Daily and Sunday newspapers are published in Richmond, Va., Tampa, Fla., and Winston-Salem, N.C., with combined circulation of roughly 570,000 daily and 724,000 Sunday. The company also publishes 14 weekly and semiweekly newspapers and shoppers in Florida.

Broadcast operations include one NBC affiliate in Tampa, two ABC affiliates in Charleston and Jacksonville and cable TV systems in Fairfax County and Fredericksburg, Va., that serve over 220,000 subscribers.

Garden State Paper Co. is a major recycler of newsprint. Its patented process is involved in the production of about 10% of U.S. newsprint. Other operations include products and services in publishing, printing, graphic arts and financial services.

Important Developments

Sep. '95—Media General agreed to acquire several Virginia newspapers from Worrell Enterprises, Inc. for $230 million. The properties include daily and Sunday newspapers in Charlottesville, Culpeper, Lynchburg and Suffolk with a combined circulation of over 81,000 daily and 85,000 Sunday. Also involved are weeklies and shoppers in Culpeper, Charlottesville, Suffolk and Richlands, and in Greene, Madison and Orange counties. The deal was expected to close in the fourth quarter.
Jun. '95—The Garden State Paper Co. subsidiary fully implemented its third price increase of the year and announced another increase later in 1995. The higher selling prices were partly offset by escalating costs for old newspapers, which climbed by more than 160%, year to year, in the second quarter

Capitalization

Long Term Debt: $136,000,000 (6/95).
Class A Common Stock: 25,729,694 shs. ($5 par).
Officers & directors control 15%.
Institutions hold about 58%, incl. 31% by a group led by Mario J. Gabelli.
Shareholders: 2,900 of record.
Class B Common Stock: 556,574 shs. ($5 par).
About 71% is closely held.
Cl. B shs. elect 75% of directors.

Per Share Data ($) (Year Ended Dec. 31)

	1994	1993	1992	1991	1990	1989
Tangible Bk. Val.	11.00	6.86	6.24	5.92	8.80	8.20
Cash Flow	6.56	3.16	2.80	-0.47	2.81	2.56
Earnings	4.45	0.98	0.70	-2.39	0.98	0.80
Dividends	0.44	0.44	0.44	0.44	0.44	0.42
Payout Ratio	10%	45%	63%	NM	45%	53%
Prices - High	30¼	31⅝	22⅞	23⅛	31¾	40½
- Low	21⅜	17½	14	16½	15¼	29⅞
P/E Ratio - High	7	32	33	NM	32	51
- Low	5	18	20	NM	16	37

Income Statement Analysis (Million $)

	1994	%Chg	1993	%Chg	1992	%Chg	1991
Revs.	626	4%	601	4%	578	-1%	586
Oper. Inc.	122	4%	117	21%	97.0	-1%	98.0
Depr.	55.5	-2%	56.8	4%	54.6	9%	49.9
Int. Exp.	17.7	-18%	21.6	-3%	22.3	NM	22.1
Pretax Inc.	143	NM	38.9	48%	26.3	NM	-52.7
Eff. Tax Rate	18%	—	34%	—	30%	—	NM
Net Inc.	117	NM	25.7	40%	18.3	NM	-62.1

Balance Sheet & Other Fin. Data (Million $)

	1994	1993	1992	1991	1990	1989
Cash	11.7	2.9	3.0	4.6	3.1	8.2
Curr. Assets	115	92.0	90.0	109	110	140
Total Assets	787	745	787	762	776	783
Curr. Liab.	100	83.0	80.0	105	89.0	78.0
LT Debt	164	261	321	276	234	276
Common Eqty.	333	225	210	202	274	259
Total Cap.	594	575	625	592	635	650
Cap. Exp.	57.0	33.0	92.0	115	74.0	69.0
Cash Flow	172	82.6	72.9	-12.1	73.0	66.4

Ratio Analysis

	1994	1993	1992	1991	1990	1989
Curr. Ratio	1.1	1.1	1.1	1.0	1.2	1.8
% LT Debt of Cap.	27.5	45.4	51.3	46.6	36.9	42.4
% Net Inc.of Revs.	18.7	4.3	3.2	NM	4.2	3.4
% Ret. on Assets	15.3	3.3	2.4	NM	3.3	22.5
% Ret. on Equity	41.9	11.8	8.9	NM	9.6	8.1

Dividend Data —Cash has been paid each year since 1923. A dividend reinvestment and stock purchase plan is available.

Amt. of Div. $	Date Decl.	Ex-Div. Date	Stock of Record	Payment Date
0.110	Sep. 16	Nov. 23	Nov. 30	Dec. 15 '94
0.120	Jan. 26	Feb. 22	Feb. 28	Mar. 15 '95
0.120	Mar. 16	May. 24	May. 31	Jun. 15 '95
0.120	Jul. 27	Aug. 29	Aug. 31	Sep. 15 '95
0.120	Sep. 14	Nov. 28	Nov. 30	Dec. 15 '95

Data as orig. reptd.; bef. results of disc. opers. and/or spec. items. Per share data adj. for stk. divs. as of ex-div. date. E-Estimated. NA-Not Available. NM-Not Meaningful. NR-Not Ranked.

Office—333 E. Grace St., Richmond, VA 23219 (P.O. Box C-32333, Richmond 23293). **Tel**—(804) 649-6000. **Chrmn, Pres & CEO**—J. S. Bryan III. **Vice Chrmn**—J. S. Evans. **Sr VP & CFO**—M. N. Morton. **Secy**—G. L. Mahoney. **Investor Contact**— Robert W. Pendergast. **Dirs**—R. P. Black, D. T. Bryan, J. S. Bryan III, C. A. Davis, A. S. Donnahoe, J. S. Evans, R. V. Hatcher, J. G. Medlin, H. L. Valentine II. **Transfer Agent & Registrar**—Wachovia Bank of North Carolina, Winston-Salem. **Incorporated** in Virginia in 1969. **Empl**-7,300. **S&P Analyst:** William H. Donald

STANDARD & POOR'S

STOCK REPORTS

Mentor Graphics

NASDAQ Symbol **MENT**

In S&P MidCap 400

17-OCT-95 **Industry:** Data Processing

Summary: Mentor is a worldwide leader in electronic design automation systems for the integrated circuit and systems design markets.

S&P Opinion: Accumulate (★★★★)

Recent Price • 19½ | Yield • Nil

52 Wk Range • 21⅜-10⅞ | 12-Mo. P/E • 28.3

Quantitative Evaluations

Outlook (1 Lowest—5 Highest)
• **1+**

Fair Value
• **17¼**

Risk
• **Average**

Earn./Div. Rank
• **C**

Technical Eval.
• **Bearish** since 11/94

Rel. Strength Rank (1 Lowest—99 Highest)
• **54**

Insider Activity
• **Neutral**

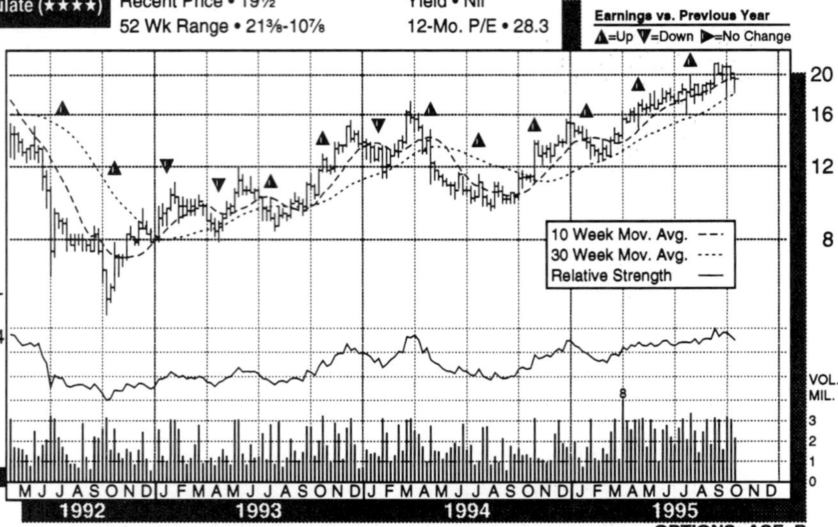

OPTIONS: ASE, P

Overview - 16-OCT-95

Revenues are expected to increase substantially in 1996, reflecting the pending acquisition of Microtec Research, which is expected to be completed by 1995 year-end. Mentor should continue to benefit not only from strong growth in the semiconductor industry, but also from favorable trends within the design automation industry. The company's products are geared to the mixed signal and analog segments of the semiconductor industry, which are experiencing especially rapid growth. New design tools and methodologies to support the growth of deep submicron technologies should continue to create a favorable operating environment for the company in the design automation industry. Margins should expand as pricing remains favorable and costs are well controlled.

Valuation - 16-OCT-95

Following several years of either losses or only modest profitability caused by challenging industry conditions, Mentor is now benefiting from a dramatic change in its competitive conditions. The combination of a boom in the semiconductor industry and a shift to deep submicron semiconductors has allowed for substantial growth and should lead to sharply higher earnings in 1995 and 1996. In addition, acquisitions, including the pending purchase of Microtec Research, Inc., should continue to provide incremental earnings. A continuation of these trends should allow the shares to continue to move higher.

Key Stock Statistics

S&P EPS Est. 1995	0.85	Tang. Bk. Value/Share	4.49
P/E on S&P Est. 1995	22.9	Beta	0.65
S&P EPS Est. 1996	1.05	Shareholders	1,800
Dividend Rate/Share	Nil	Market cap. (B)	$ 1.1
Shs. outstg. (M)	54.3	Inst. holdings	77%
Avg. daily vol. (M)	0.608	Insider holdings	NA

Value of $10,000 invested 5 years ago: $ 12,555

Fiscal Year Ending Dec. 31

	1995	% Change	1994	% Change	1993	% Change
Revenues (Million $)						
1Q	84.71	NM	85.30	3%	82.64	-17%
2Q	93.77	13%	82.67	-7%	88.42	NM
3Q	—	—	83.54	-2%	84.95	9%
4Q	—	—	96.78	16%	83.77	NM
Yr.	—	—	348.3	3%	339.8	-3%
Income (Million $)						
1Q	6.69	45%	4.61	NM	-4.30	NM
2Q	11.98	147%	4.85	NM	0.29	NM
3Q	—	—	5.07	NM	1.49	NM
4Q	—	—	13.01	NM	-29.56	NM
Yr.	—	—	27.54	NM	-32.07	NM
Earnings Per Share ($)						
1Q	0.13	44%	0.09	NM	-0.09	NM
2Q	0.22	144%	0.09	NM	0.01	NM
3Q	E0.23	130%	0.10	NM	0.03	NM
4Q	E0.27	8%	0.25	NM	-0.63	NM
Yr.	E0.85	60%	0.53	NM	-0.69	NM

Next earnings report expected: late October

Business Summary - 17-OCT-95

Mentor Graphics Corp. designs, manufactures, markets and services electronic design automation software for the integrated circuit (IC) and systems design markets. Its systems enable engineers and designers to analyze, design and test custom ICs, application-specific integrated circuits (ASICs), printed circuit boards, multichip modules, and other electronic systems and subsystems.

Mentor's Falcon Framework software provides a common foundation for its EDA software products and also allows for the integration of third party software tools developed by other commercial EDA vendors and by customers for their own internal use. The company's products help customers reduce development time in producing innovative hardware products of high quality. In addition to software products, Mentor's service division offers consulting, support and training to enhance customers' success in the design and manufacture of hardware products.

The company's software runs on workstations in a broad range of price and performance levels, including workstations made by Sun Microsystems, Digital Equipment Corp., Hewlett-Packard, NEC Corp. and IBM. Products are marketed through a worldwide network of sales and support offices. Customers are in the computer, aerospace, telecommunications, consumer electronics and semiconductor industries. Sales outside of North America represented 45% of revenues in 1994 (46% in 1993).

In May, 1995, the company completed the acquisition of Axiom Datorer Skandinavien AB, which is primarily enaged in developing, marketing and supporting software library tools used to model electronic components. In 1994 the company acquired Model Technology, a leading suppier of VHDL simulation and ANACAD Electrical Engineering Software GmbH, the Europena analog and mixed signal technology leader.

Important Developments

Oct. '95—The company announced that it was merging with Microtec Research, Inc. (Nasdaq: MTEC) to become the world leader in complete electronic handware and software design solutions. Under the terms of the agreement, each outstanding common share of MTEC will be converted into approximately 0.693 share of MENT common stock. The total value of the transaction is estimated to be approximately $130 million. The transaction, which is subject to various conditions, including approval by MTEC shareholders, is expected to close by the end of the year. For the fiscal year ended March 31, 1995, MTEC had revenues of $45.2 million.

Aug. '95—Directors approved a plan to repurchase up to $50 million of the company's common stock on the open market over the next eighteen months.

Capitalization

Long Term Debt: $53,449,000 (6/95).

Per Share Data ($)

(Year Ended Dec. 31)

	1994	1993	1992	1991	1990	1989
Tangible Bk. Val.	4.60	4.11	4.86	6.14	7.70	7.84
Cash Flow	1.00	-0.10	-0.56	-0.74	1.15	1.76
Earnings	0.53	-0.69	-1.13	-1.43	0.53	1.22
Dividends	Nil	0.18	0.24	0.24	0.22	0.15
Payout Ratio	Nil	NM	NM	NM	39%	12%
Prices - High	17¼	15½	22¼	19	26	22⅜
- Low	9⅜	7⅞	5¼	11½	9	13⅜
P/E Ratio - High	33	NM	NM	NM	49	18
- Low	18	NM	NM	NM	17	11

Income Statement Analysis (Million $)

	1994	%Chg	1993	%Chg	1992	%Chg	1991
Revs.	348	2%	340	-3%	351	-12%	400
Oper. Inc.	56.4	145%	23.0	NM	-2.1	NM	-3.7
Depr.	24.7	-11%	27.6	7%	25.8	-13%	29.7
Int. Exp.	2.7	-39%	4.4	-20%	5.5	-5%	5.8
Pretax Inc.	30.9	NM	-29.6	NM	-48.3	NM	-63.0
Eff. Tax Rate	11%	—	NM	—	NM	—	NM
Net Inc.	27.5	NM	-32.1	NM	-50.9	NM	-61.6

Balance Sheet & Other Fin. Data (Million $)

	1994	1993	1992	1991	1990	1989
Cash	138	110	109	144	162	145
Curr. Assets	238	198	208	294	331	273
Total Assets	394	354	379	446	504	362
Curr. Liab.	99	102	99	125	123	79.0
LT Debt	53.6	54.3	55.7	50.6	50.2	7.2
Common Eqty.	239	196	221	268	326	274
Total Cap.	293	250	277	318	377	281
Cap. Exp.	14.3	26.6	24.7	97.0	79.4	39.2
Cash Flow	52.2	-4.5	-25.1	-31.9	51.4	64.8

Ratio Analysis

	1994	1993	1992	1991	1990	1989
Curr. Ratio	2.4	1.9	2.1	2.4	2.7	3.4
% LT Debt of Cap.	18.3	21.7	20.1	15.9	13.3	2.6
% Net Inc.of Revs.	7.9	NM	NM	NM	5.4	11.8
% Ret. on Assets	7.1	NM	NM	NM	5.0	13.7
% Ret. on Equity	12.2	NM	NM	NM	7.2	17.8

Dividend Data —Prior to omission in October 1993, cash dividends had been paid since 1988.

Data as orig. reptd.; bef. results of disc. opers. and/or spec. items. Per share data adj. for stk. divs. as of ex-div. date. Bk. val. figs. for 1993-1989 incl. intangibles. E-Estimated. NA-Not Available. NM-Not Meaningful. NR-Not Ranked.

Office—8005 S.W. Boeckman Rd., Wilsonville, OR 97070-7777. **Tel**—(503) 685-7000. **Chrmn**—T. Bruggere. **Pres & CEO**—W. C. Rhines. **CFO**—R. D. Norby. **VP & Secy**—F. S. Delia. **Treas & Investor Contact**—Bob van Leyen. **Dirs**—T. H. Bruggere, M. B. Congdon, D. R. Hathaway, W. C. Rhines, F. K. Richardson, J. A. Shirley, D. N. Strohm. **Transfer Agent & Registrar**—First Interstate Bank of Oregon, Portland. **Incorporated** in Oregon in 1981. **Empl**-2,050. **S&P Analyst:** Paul H. Valentine, CFA

STANDARD & POOR'S

STOCK REPORTS

Mercantile Bancorp.

NYSE Symbol **MTL**
In S&P MidCap 400

27-JUL-95 **Industry:** Banking

Summary: This St. Louis-based holding company owns 52 banks throughout Missouri, Kansas, Illinois, Iowa and Arkansas.

S&P Opinion: Accumulate (★★★★) Recent Price • 45⅛ 52 Wk Range • 47-29½ Yield • 2.9% 12-Mo. P/E • 11.6

Quantitative Evaluations
Outlook (1 Lowest—5 Highest) • **2−**
Fair Value • **42⅞**
Risk • **Low**
Earn./Div. Rank • **B+**

Technical Eval. • **Bullish** since 2/95
Rel. Strength Rank (1 Lowest—99 Highest) • **70**
Insider Activity • **Neutral**

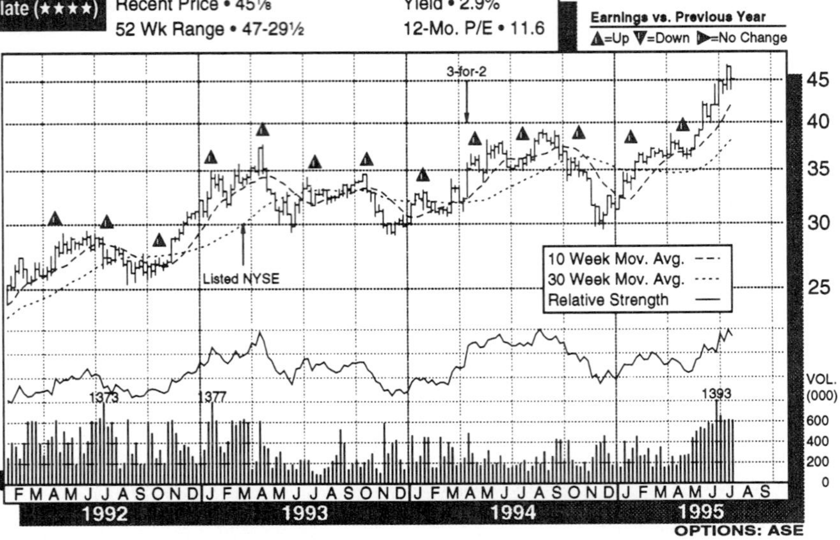

Overview - 26-JUL-95

Loans grew 13% in 1995's second quarter and should continue to advance in the low double digit range over the next few quarters, driven by strong growth in almost all loan categories. MTL expects residential real estate loans to trend downward as more customers switch from adjustable to fixed rate mortgages, which the bank does not hold on the balance sheet. Although the net interest margin narrowed 35 basis points in the second quarter, it is expected to remain relatively stable for the remainder of 1995. Noninterest income rose 13% in 1995's second quarter, and is expected to continue to register healthy gains on higher credit card fee income. Credit quality remains strong, with nonperforming loans at 0.42% of total loans at June 30, 1995. Earnings should continue to benefit from improved operating efficiencies gained through recent merger activity.

Valuation - 24-JUL-95

The shares, up approximately 45% so far this year, have significantly outpaced the broader market and those of other regional banks. The stock currently trades at around 11 times our earnings estimate for 1995, which is slightly higher that the multiple on the average major regional bank. But, due to above average loan growth, a stabilizing net interest margin, improving operating efficiencies and higher noninterest income, we believe the shares deserve the premium multiple and remain attractive at 10 times our 1996 estimate.

Key Stock Statistics

S&P EPS Est. 1995	4.00	Tang. Bk. Value/Share	24.93
P/E on S&P Est. 1995	11.3	Beta	1.15
S&P EPS Est. 1996	4.35	Shareholders	13,600
Dividend Rate/Share	1.32	Market cap. (B)	$ 2.4
Shs. outstg. (M)	52.7	Inst. holdings	39%
Avg. daily vol. (M)	0.143	Insider holdings	NA

Value of $10,000 invested 5 years ago: $ 32,552

Fiscal Year Ending Dec. 31

	1995	% Change	1994	% Change	1993	% Change
Revenues (Million $)						
1Q	295.8	19%	248.9	10%	225.6	18%
2Q	341.8	37%	249.5	11%	225.5	9%
3Q	—	—	257.9	17%	220.8	5%
4Q	—	—	267.0	21%	221.1	7%
Yr.	—	—	1,023	15%	892.9	9%
Income (Million $)						
1Q	44.06	13%	38.86	43%	27.18	41%
2Q	52.36	30%	40.20	43%	28.09	33%
3Q	—	—	41.04	36%	30.26	37%
4Q	—	—	40.93	30%	31.44	39%
Yr.	—	—	161.0	38%	117.0	38%
Earnings Per Share ($)						
1Q	0.97	7%	0.91	17%	0.78	13%
2Q	0.99	6%	0.93	16%	0.80	11%
3Q	E1.01	—	0.95	12%	0.85	16%
4Q	E1.03	—	0.95	7%	0.89	18%
Yr.	E4.00	—	3.74	13%	3.32	14%

Next earnings report expected: mid October

Mercantile Bancorp.

Business Summary - 24-JUL-95

Mercantile Bancorporation, a St. Louis-based bank holding company, owned 42 banks in Missouri, southern Illinois and eastern Kansas, at 1994 year-end, with total assets of $12.24 billion. Its largest subsidiary bank, Mercantile Bank of St. Louis, had assets totaling $6.4 billion at December 31, 1994.

Consolidated total loans outstanding were $8.11 billion at year end 1994, compared with $7.38 bilion a year earlier. Loans were divided as follows:

	1994	1993
Real estate	49%	51%
Commercial	26%	26%
Consumer, credit card & foreign	25%	23%

The reserve for loan losses was $170.9 million at December 31, 1994 ($168.7 million a year earlier), equal to 2.11% (2.28%) of loans outstanding. Net chargeoffs in 1994 were $31.2 million ($60.2 million in 1993), or 0.41% (0.81%) of average loans. As of 1994 year-end, nonperforming loans totaled $25.3 million (0.31% of total loans), versus $57.5 million (0.78%) a year earlier.

Total deposits of $9.05 billion at the end of 1994 consisted of 17% noninterest-bearing demand, 17% interest-bearing demand, 16% money-market accounts, 9% savings, 33% consumer time CDs under $100,000, 5% time CDs of $100,000 or more, and 3% other time and foreign.

On a tax-equivalent basis, the average yield on interest-earning assets in 1994 was 7.59% (7.55% in 1993), while the average rate paid on interest-bearing liabilities was 3.57% (3.59%), for a net interest spread of 4.02% (3.96%).

Subsidiaries include firms in brokerage services, asset-based lending, investment advisory services, credit card services, general insurance, and credit life insurance.

Important Developments

Jul. '95—Mercantile completed its previously announced acquisition of Plains Spirit Financial Corporation (PSFC), the holding company for First Federal Savings Bank of Iowa. Under terms of the transaction, PSFC shareholders were entitled to receive $31.25 a share in cash or 0.7634 of an MTL share for each PSFC share owned. First Federal Savings Bank of Iowa is the second largest thrift based in Iowa, with five offices and assets of $439 million.

May '95—Mercantile completed the acquisition of Central Mortgage Bancshares (CMBI), a $650 million-asset bank holding company headquartered in Kansas City. Under the terms of the transaction, each CMBI share was exchangeable for 0.5970 of an MTL share.

Capitalization

Long Term Debt: $279,958,000 (6/95).

Per Share Data ($) (Year Ended Dec. 31)

	1994	1993	1992	1991	1990	1989
Tangible Bk. Val.	23.29	14.54	20.57	18.18	16.44	15.56
Earnings	3.74	3.32	2.91	2.57	2.33	0.02
Dividends	1.12	0.99	0.93	0.93	0.93	0.93
Payout Ratio	30%	30%	32%	36%	40%	NM
Prices - High	39¼	37⅝	32⅛	25⅛	18⅜	19½
- Low	29½	29⅛	23⅛	12⅝	11⅝	16⅝
P/E Ratio - High	10	11	11	10	8	NM
- Low	8	9	8	5	5	NM

Income Statement Analysis (Million $)

	1994	%Chg	1993	%Chg	1992	%Chg	1991
Net Int. Inc.	511	14%	446	23%	364	25%	292
Tax Equiv. Adj.	9.1	17%	7.8	20%	6.5	NM	6.5
Non Int. Inc.	188	7%	175	23%	142	16%	122
Loan Loss Prov.	33.5	-34%	50.4	-17%	61.0	22%	50.0
% Exp/Op Revs.	58%	—	62%	—	63%	—	64%
Pretax Inc.	253	38%	184	48%	124	32%	93.9
Eff. Tax Rate	36%	—	36%	—	32%	—	29%
Net Inc.	161	38%	117	38%	85.0	28%	66.6
% Net Int. Marg.	4.67%	—	4.73%	—	4.51%	—	4.37%

Balance Sheet & Other Fin. Data (Million $)

	1994	1993	1992	1991	1990	1989
Earning Assets:						
Money Mkt.	113	344	265	406	224	150
Inv. Securities	3,019	2,922	2,423	1,553	1,117	1,111
Com'l Loans	2,120	1,886	1,741	1,697	1,892	1,888
Other Loans	5,995	4,401	4,159	3,693	3,531	3,018
Total Assets	12,242	10,513	9,476	8,089	7,617	6,942
Demand Deposits	1,529	1,562	1,244	1,147	1,267	1,187
Time Deposits	7,525	6,674	6,288	5,334	4,895	4,260
LT Debt	387	220	221	116	117	118
Common Eqty.	1,068	841	669	546	440	407

Ratio Analysis

	1994	1993	1992	1991	1990	1989
% Ret. on Assets	1.3	1.1	0.9	0.9	0.8	0.0
% Ret. on Equity	15.8	14.9	13.7	13.6	13.4	0.1
% Loan Loss Resv.	2.1	2.4	2.4	2.3	2.4	2.5
% Loans/Deposits	89.6	76.3	78.3	83.2	87.4	89.3
% Equity to Assets	8.4	7.4	6.8	6.5	6.1	6.5

Dividend Data (Dividends, including those of predecessors, have been paid in every year since 1909. A dividend reinvestment plan is available.)

Amt. of Div. $	Date Decl.	Ex-Div. Date	Stock of Record	Payment Date
0.280	Aug. 01	Sep. 02	Sep. 10	Oct. 03 '94
0.280	Oct. 14	Dec. 05	Dec. 09	Jan. 02 '95
0.330	Feb. 09	Mar. 06	Mar. 10	Apr. 03 '95
0.330	May. 22	Jun. 06	Jun. 10	Jul. 03 '95
0.330	Jul. 13	Sep. 07	Sep. 11	Oct. 02 '95

Data as orig. reptd.; bef. results of disc opers. and/or spec. items. Per share data adj. for stk. divs. as of ex-div. date. E-Estimated. NA-Not Available. NM-Not Meaningful. NR-Not Ranked.

Office—Mercantile Tower, P.O. Box 524, St. Louis, MO 63166-0524. **Tel**—(314) 425-2525. **Chrmn, Pres & CEO**—T. H. Jacobsen. **Vice Chrmn**—R. W. Babb, Jr. **Sr EVP & CFO**— W. R. Adams. **Secy**—J. W. Bilstrom. **Investor Contact**—Diana P. Yates (314) 425-2268. **Dirs**—R. P. Conerly, H. M. Cornell, Jr., E. K. Dille, J. C. Eason, B. A. Edison, W. A. Hall, T. A. Hays, W. G. Heckman, T. H. Jacobsen, C. H. Price II, H. Saligman, C. D. Schnuck, R. L. Stark, P. T. Stokes, F. A. Stroble, J. A. Wright. **Transfer Agent & Registrar**—KeyCorp Shareholder Services Inc., Cleveland. **Incorporated** in Missouri in 1970; bank founded in 1929. **Empl**-6,609. **S&P Analyst:** Brad Ohlmuller

STANDARD & POOR'S

STOCK REPORTS

Mercantile Bankshares

NASDAQ Symbol **MRBK**

In S&P MidCap 400

24-SEP-95

Industry: Banking

Summary: This Maryland bank holding company, with approximately $5.9 billion in assets, owned 20 affiliate banks and a mortgage banking company at December 31, 1994.

S&P Opinion: Hold (★★★)

Recent Price • 27⅜

52 Wk Range • 27¾-18⅜

Yield • 3.4%

12-Mo. P/E • 13.6

Quantitative Evaluations

Outlook
(1 Lowest—5 Highest)
• **2+**

Fair Value
• **25⅞**

Risk
• **Low**

Earn./Div. Rank
• **A**

Technical Eval.
• **Bearish** since 7/95

Rel. Strength Rank
(1 Lowest—99 Highest)
• **76**

Insider Activity
• **Neutral**

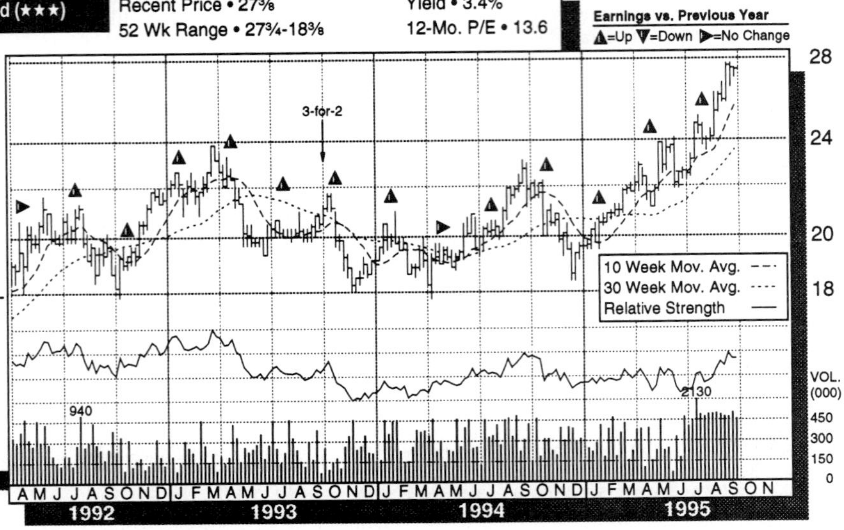

Overview - 24-SEP-95

Average loans advanced 9%, year to year, in the second quarter of 1995, driven by growth in the commercial loan portfolio. The net interest margin increased 9%, primarily due to higher yields on interest earning assets, which were partially offset by higher rates paid on interest bearing liabilities and a shift in the earning asset mix; net interest income was up 11%. Asset quality remained strong, as the ratio of total nonperforming assets to total assets was 0.50% at June 30, 1995. Noninterest income declined 4%, as MRBK experienced higher losses on investment securities and a 4% decline in trust fees. Earnings for the remainder of 1995 will be driven by healthy commercial loan demand, a stable net interest margin, and a continued focus on cost controls. In early 1995, directors authorized the repurchase of up to 2 million shares.

Valuation - 24-SEP-95

The shares of this Maryland bank holding company, up 38% so far in 1995, have outpaced the broader market and performed in line with those of other regional banks. The stock currently trades at a valuation of about 12 times our earning estimate for 1996, which is at the high end of its historical range and slightly above that of the average regional bank. However, we believe that healthy commercial loan demand, strong asset quality and an above-average dividend yield make the shares a worthwhile holding over the longer term.

Key Stock Statistics

S&P EPS Est. 1995	2.10	Tang. Bk. Value/Share	15.32
P/E on S&P Est. 1995	13.1	Beta	1.49
S&P EPS Est. 1996	2.30	Shareholders	8,500
Dividend Rate/Share	0.92	Market cap. (B)	$ 1.3
Shs. outstg. (M)	47.4	Inst. holdings	38%
Avg. daily vol. (M)	0.149	Insider holdings	NA

Value of $10,000 invested 5 years ago: $ 19,871

Fiscal Year Ending Dec. 31

	1995	% Change	1994	% Change	1993	% Change
Revenues (Million $)						
1Q	132.3	15%	114.6	3%	111.6	-7%
2Q	137.6	18%	117.0	3%	113.5	-6%
3Q	—	—	100.3	-12%	114.6	-21%
4Q	—	—	163.7	42%	115.3	NM
Yr.	—	—	—	—	454.9	-9%
Income (Million $)						
1Q	24.21	11%	21.82	6%	20.49	9%
2Q	26.11	19%	21.99	8%	20.41	9%
3Q	—	—	23.77	16%	20.58	8%
4Q	—	—	22.86	9%	20.93	7%
Yr.	—	—	90.44	10%	82.42	8%
Earnings Per Share ($)						
1Q	0.50	11%	0.45	NM	0.45	9%
2Q	0.55	20%	0.46	3%	0.45	8%
3Q	E0.53	8%	0.49	9%	0.45	7%
4Q	E0.52	8%	0.48	4%	0.46	8%
Yr.	E2.10	12%	1.88	4%	1.80	8%

Next earnings report expected: mid October

Mercantile Bankshares

Business Summary - 24-SEP-95

Mercantile Bankshares Corporation, headquartered in Baltimore, Md., owns 20 commercial banks and a mortgage banking company. The lead bank is Mercantile-Safe Deposit and Trust Co., which had total assets of $2.26 billion as of December 31, 1994. At that date, there were 155 retail banking offices.

Total loans outstanding were $3.94 billion at year end 1994, compared with $3.72 billion a year earlier. Loans were divided as follows:

	1994	1993
Commercial	33.3%	33.3%
Real estate-mortgage	46.5%	45.6%
Real estate-construction	8.1%	8.6%
Consumer	12.1%	12.5%

The allowance for loan losses at the end of 1994 was $91,257,000 ($92,567,000 a year earlier), equal to 2.4% (2.5%) of average loans outstanding. Net chargeoffs in 1994 were $8,366,000 ($11,466,000 in 1993), or 0.22% (0.31%) of average loans outstanding. As of December 31, 1994, nonperforming loans totaled $33,648,000 (0.85% of loans outstanding), compared with $66,063,000 (1.78%) a year earlier.

Average deposits of $4.69 billion in 1994 and $4.63 billion in 1993 were apportioned:

	1994	1993
Noninterest bearing	19%	18%
Savings and NOW accounts	34%	33%
Money market	18%	19%
CDs and other time less than $100,000	22%	23%
CDs $100,000 and over	7%	7%

Total income in 1994 was derived as follows: interest and fees on loans 64%, interest and dividends on investment securities 18%, trust division services 9%, and other noninterest income 10%.

On a tax-equivalent basis, the average yield on interest-earning assets was 7.50% in 1994 (7.30% in 1993), while the average rate paid on interest-earning liabilities was 3.40% (3.40%), for a net interest spread of 4.10% (3.90%).

Trust services are provided throughout Maryland by the trust division of Mercantile-Safe Deposit and Trust Co.

Important Developments

Aug. '95—MRBK reported that its net interest margin widened to 5.2% in the six months ended June 30, 1995, compared to 4.7% in the year ago period. Contributing to the increase were higher yields on earning assets, which were partially offset by higher rates paid on interest earning liabilities and a shift in the earning asset mix.

Capitalization

Long Term Debt: $26,011,000 (6/95).

Per Share Data ($)

(Year Ended Dec. 31)

	1994	1993	1992	1991	1990	1989
Tangible Bk. Val.	14.60	13.80	12.61	11.46	10.39	9.68
Earnings	1.88	1.80	1.67	1.56	1.55	1.60
Dividends	0.74	0.64	0.58	0.57	0.54	0.48
Payout Ratio	39%	36%	35%	37%	35%	30%
Prices - High	23 1/8	23 7/8	22 1/8	19	17 5/8	18 3/8
- Low	17 3/4	18	17	12 1/8	8 7/8	11 5/8
P/E Ratio - High	12	13	13	12	11	12
- Low	9	10	10	8	6	7

Income Statement Analysis (Million $)

	1994	%Chg	1993	%Chg	1992	%Chg	1991
Net Int. Inc.	263	11%	238	4%	229	10%	209
Tax Equiv. Adj.	3.5	2%	3.4	-10%	3.8	-28%	5.3
Non Int. Inc.	93.6	11%	84.3	4%	81.0	14%	71.3
Loan Loss Prov.	7.1	-44%	12.6	-72%	45.3	117%	20.9
% Exp/Op Revs.	56%	—	54%	—	53%	—	54%
Pretax Inc.	147	9%	135	10%	123	10%	112
Eff. Tax Rate	38%	—	39%	—	38%	—	37%
Net Inc.	90.4	10%	82.4	8%	76.3	8%	70.6
% Net Int. Marg.	4.86%	—	4.73%	—	4.70%	—	4.57%

Balance Sheet & Other Fin. Data (Million $)

	1994	1993	1992	1991	1990	1989
Earning Assets:						
Money Mkt.	0.1	1.1	122	142	279	76.0
Inv. Securities	1,606	1,684	1,505	1,345	941	707
Com'l Loans	1,311	1,229	1,126	1,100	1,142	1,034
Other Loans	2,627	2,348	2,363	2,275	2,170	1,863
Total Assets	5,938	5,554	5,460	5,183	4,886	4,018
Demand Deposits	954	915	896	802	771	749
Time Deposits	3,811	3,609	3,621	3,472	3,217	2,618
LT Debt	31.5	32.3	15.1	16.6	17.3	23.1
Common Eqty.	724	655	598	542	487	402

Ratio Analysis

	1994	1993	1992	1991	1990	1989
% Ret. on Assets	1.6	1.5	1.5	1.4	1.6	1.7
% Ret. on Equity	12.8	13.1	13.3	13.6	14.7	16.3
% Loan Loss Resv.	2.3	2.5	2.6	2.0	1.6	1.6
% Loans/Deposits	82.6	79.1	77.3	79.0	83.1	86.0
% Equity to Assets	12.1	11.7	10.9	10.5	10.6	10.2

Dividend Data —Cash dividends have been paid since 1909. A dividend reinvestment plan is available.

Amt. of Div. $	Date Decl.	Ex-Div. Date	Stock of Record	Payment Date
0.200	Sep. 13	Sep. 19	Sep. 23	Sep. 30 '94
0.200	Dec. 13	Dec. 19	Dec. 23	Dec. 31 '94
0.200	Mar. 14	Mar. 20	Mar. 24	Mar. 31 '95
0.200	Jun. 13	Jun. 21	Jun. 23	Jun. 30 '95
0.230	Sep. 12	Sep. 20	Sep. 22	Sep. 29 '95

Data as orig. reptd.; bef. results of disc opers. and/or spec. items. Per share data adj. for stk. divs. as of ex-div. date. E-Estimated. NA-Not Available. NM-Not Meaningful. NR-Not Ranked.

Office—2 Hopkins Plaza, P.O. Box 1477, Baltimore, MD 21203. **Tel**—(410) 237-5900. **Chrmn & CEO**—H. F. Baldwin. **Vice Chrmn**—D. W. Dodge. **Pres**—E. K. Dunn Jr. **Exec VP-Treas**—K. A. Bourne Jr. **Sr VP-Secy**—J. A. O'Connor Jr. **Investor Contact**—David Borowy (410) 347-8361. **Dirs**—H. F. Baldwin, T. M. Bancroft Jr., R. O. Berndt, J. A. Block, G. L. Bunting Jr., D. W. Dodge, E. K. Dunn Jr., B. L. Jenkins, R. D. Kunisch, W. J. McCarthy, M. W. Offit, C. H. Poindexter, W. C. Richardson, B. L. Robinson, D. J. Shepard, B. B. Topping, C. J. Zamoiski Jr. **Transfer Agent**—Mercantile-Safe Deposit & Trust Co., Baltimore. **Incorporated** in Maryland in 1969. **Empl**-2,845. **S&P Analyst:** Brad Ohlmuller

Meridian Bancorp

NASDAQ Symbol **MRDN**
In S&P MidCap 400

16-OCT-95 **Industry:** Banking

Summary: This $15.1 billion bank and financial services holding company recently signed a definitive agreement to be acquired by CoreStates Financial Corp.

S&P Opinion: Hold (★★★)

Recent Price • 45
52 Wk Range • 45¼-25½
Yield • 3.3%
12-Mo. P/E • 15.5

Quantitative Evaluations

Outlook
(1 Lowest—5 Highest)
• **2+**

Fair Value
• **35⅝**

Risk
• **Low**

Earn./Div. Rank
• **A-**

Technical Eval.
• **Bullish** since 2/95

Rel. Strength Rank
(1 Lowest—99 Highest)
• **96**

Insider Activity
• **Neutral**

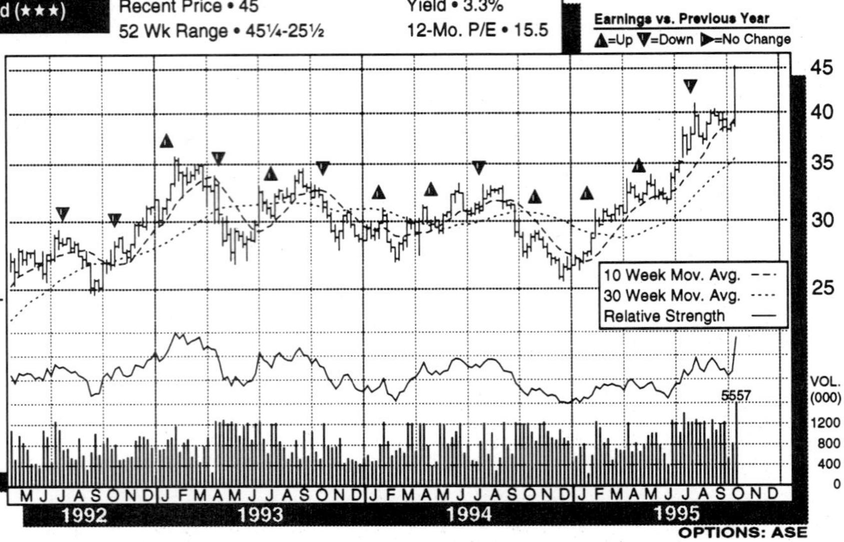

OPTIONS: ASE

Overview - 16-OCT-95

MRDN's primary market includes the prosperous Middle Atlantic region encompassing Delaware, eastern Pennsylvania and southern New Jersey. Its focus is providing retail banking services to individuals and small-to-medium sized businesses, as well as asset management, advisory and brokerage services to both individuals and institutions. In June 1995, MRDN restructured its marketing and delivery capabilities and underwent a general corporate downsizing. Although MRDN experienced a $0.37 per share, after tax, restructuring charge in that quarter, benefits were realized by 1995's third quarter, when the company attributed an $0.11 per share earnings increase on its cost reduction program. With the stated goal of improving MRDN's efficiency ratio to 59.6% by early 1996, management believes the reorganization will generate after-tax cost savings and revenue enhancements of about $0.78 a share.

Valuation - 16-OCT-95

MRDN shares rose sharply on news of its definitive agreement to be acquired by CoreStates Financial Corp. At 2.02 times tangible book value, and 13 times estimated 1996 earnings, MRDN currently trades at a premium, and should not outperform the overall market. Given a 6% discount to the acquisition price, which currently approximates $45.94 a share, MRDN is a worthwhile hold for modest capital gains until completion of the merger, expected in the second quarter of 1996. The transaction still faces regulatory and shareholder approval.

Key Stock Statistics

S&P EPS Est. 1995	3.05	Tang. Bk. Value/Share	21.56
P/E on S&P Est. 1995	14.8	Beta	1.47
S&P EPS Est. 1996	3.40	Shareholders	27,300
Dividend Rate/Share	1.48	Market cap. (B)	$ 2.6
Shs. outstg. (M)	57.3	Inst. holdings	37%
Avg. daily vol. (M)	0.416	Insider holdings	NA

Value of $10,000 invested 5 years ago: $ 31,969

Fiscal Year Ending Dec. 31

	1995	% Change	1994	% Change	1993	% Change
Revenues (Million $)						
1Q	331.5	17%	282.3	-3%	290.3	7%
2Q	349.5	17%	300.0	-5%	315.6	18%
3Q	—	—	318.0	-3%	326.9	25%
4Q	—	—	325.5	4%	314.2	11%
Yr.	—	—	1,226	-2%	1,247	15%
Income (Million $)						
1Q	41.24	2%	40.54	34%	30.31	12%
2Q	25.93	-36%	40.78	9%	37.25	27%
3Q	54.40	49%	36.62	6%	34.63	23%
4Q	—	—	44.15	5%	42.07	39%
Yr.	—	—	162.1	8%	150.5	31%
Earnings Per Share ($)						
1Q	0.73	4%	0.70	32%	0.53	-13%
2Q	0.46	-34%	0.70	-7%	0.75	15%
3Q	0.96	52%	0.63	5%	0.60	-5%
4Q	E0.90	17%	0.77	5%	0.73	11%
Yr.	E3.05	9%	2.80	7%	2.61	2%

Next earnings report expected: mid January

Meridian Bancorp

Business Summary - 11-OCT-95

Meridian Bancorp, Inc. is the fourth largest bank holding company based in Pennsylvania, with nearly $15 billion in total assets. Commercial banking operations are conducted through a network of 325 branches in Delaware, eastern Pennsylvania, and southern New Jersey; nonbanking subsidiaries offer financial and real estate services.

Total loans of $9.76 billion at year-end 1994 were divided:

	1994	1993
Commercial, financial & agricultural	41%	40%
Consumer	27%	28%
Real estate/commercial mortgage	17%	18%
Real estate/residential	12%	11%
Real estate/construction	3%	3%

At December 31, 1994, the reserve for possible loan losses was $169.4 million (1.74% of loans outstanding), down from $173.4 million (1.93%) a year earlier. Net loan chargeoffs in 1994 were $32.5 million (0.35% of average loans), compared with $51.3 million (0.59%) the year before. Nonperforming assets at the end of 1994 amounted to $121.7 million (0.81% of total assets), versus $178.8 million (1.27%) a year earlier.

Total deposits of $11.4 billion at the end of 1994 were divided: money-market 20%, demand 18%, NOW accounts 13%, savings deposits 16%, and time 33%. On a tax-equivalent basis, the average yield on interest-earning assets in 1994 was 7.53% (7.63% in 1993), while the average rate paid on interest-bearing liabilities was 3.29% (3.11%), for a net spread of 4.24% (4.52%).

Important Developments

Oct. '95—Meridian signed a definitive agreement to merge with CoreStates Financial Corp. (CFL), in a stock-for-stock exchange whereby MRDN shareholders will receive 1.225 shares of CFL common stock for each share of Meridian in a tax-free exchange. Based on the October 9, 1995 closing price of CFL common stock, the transaction has a value of $47.16 per share for a total of $3.2 billion. The new corporation will operate under the CoreStates name, and the transaction is expected to close in the second quarter of 1996.

Capitalization

Long Term Debt: $512,182,000 (6/95).

Per Share Data ($)

(Year Ended Dec. 31)

	1994	1993	1992	1991	1990	1989
Tangible Bk. Val.	18.79	19.10	19.00	17.12	16.00	16.33
Earnings	2.80	2.61	2.55	2.56	1.20	2.32
Dividends	1.34	1.26	1.20	1.20	1.20	1.13
Payout Ratio	48%	48%	47%	47%	100%	49%
Prices - High	33¼	35¾	32	24⅛	21⅛	26½
- Low	25½	26¾	22⅛	9¼	9½	17½
P/E Ratio - High	12	14	13	9	18	11
- Low	9	10	9	4	8	8

Income Statement Analysis (Million $)

	1994	%Chg	1993	%Chg	1992	%Chg	1991
Net Int. Inc.	612	NM	617	25%	495	15%	432
Tax Equiv. Adj.	17.7	-20%	22.1	26%	17.5	-24%	23.1
Non Int. Inc.	238	-9%	260	14%	228	-7%	244
Loan Loss Prov.	27.3	-51%	56.1	-6%	59.7	-40%	99
% Exp/Op Revs.	68%	—	71%	—	69%	—	62%
Pretax Inc.	233	11%	210	36%	154	7%	144
Eff. Tax Rate	30%	—	28%	—	26%	—	26%
Net Inc.	162	8%	150	31%	115	7%	107
% Net Int. Marg.	4.73%	—	4.96%	—	4.84%	—	4.48%

Balance Sheet & Other Fin. Data (Million $)

	1994	1993	1992	1991	1990	1989
Earning Assets:						
Money Mkt.	567	153	216	178	173	1,081
Inv. Securities	3,307	3,060	2,616	2,184	1,776	1,938
Com'l Loans	4,006	3,591	3,108	3,154	3,177	2,928
Other Loans	5,954	6,164	4,767	4,583	5,415	5,152
Total Assets	15,053	14,085	12,208	11,337	11,866	11,925
Demand Deposits	1,999	1,849	1,644	1,359	1,273	1,183
Time Deposits	9,381	9,497	8,529	8,094	7,990	8,419
LT Debt	372	421	206	122	145	116
Common Eqty.	1,215	1,186	904	807	689	713

Ratio Analysis

	1994	1993	1992	1991	1990	1989
% Ret. on Assets	1.1	1.1	1.0	1.0	0.4	0.9
% Ret. on Equity	13.5	13.5	13.4	14.6	6.8	13.4
% Loan Loss Resv.	1.7	1.8	2.0	2.1	1.7	1.1
% Loans/Deposits	86.5	85.0	77.4	81.4	92.5	83.9
% Equity to Assets	8.3	7.9	7.3	6.6	6.2	6.5

Dividend Data —Dividends have been paid since 1828. A dividend reinvestment plan is available.

Amt. of Div. $	Date Decl.	Ex-Div. Date	Stock of Record	Payment Date
0.340	Oct. 25	Nov. 08	Nov. 15	Dec. 01 '94
0.340	Jan. 24	Feb. 09	Feb. 15	Mar. 01 '95
0.370	Apr. 25	May. 09	May. 15	Jun. 01 '95
0.370	Jul. 25	Aug. 11	Aug. 15	Sep. 01 '95

Data as orig. reptd.; bef. results of disc opers. and/or spec. items. Per share data adj. for stk. divs. as of ex-div. date. E-Estimated. NA-Not Available. NM-Not Meaningful. NR-Not Ranked.

Office—35 N. Sixth St., P.O. Box 1102, Reading, PA 19603. **Tel**—(610) 655-2000. **Chrmn, Pres & CEO**—S. A. McCullough. **Vice Chrmn & CFO**—D. E. Sparks. **Secy**—W. L. Gaunt. **Investor Contact**—Michael J. Hughes. **Dirs**—D. E. Breidegam Jr., T. F. Burke Jr., R. W. Cardy, H. Corless, W. D. Davis, J. W. Erving, F. D. Hafer, J. H. Jones, L. C. Karlson, E. S. Ketchum, S. D. Kline Jr., G. W. Leighow, S. A. McCullough, J. F. Paquette Jr., D. H. Polett, L. R. Pugh, P. R. Roedel, W. R. Schultz, R. B. Seidel, D. E. Sparks, G. Strawbridge Jr., A. A. Summers, J. M. von Seldeneck, E. A. Wooton. **Transfer Agent & Registrar**—Co.'s office. **Incorporated** in Pennsylvania in 1983. **Empl**-6,939. **S&P Analyst:** Thomas C. Ferguson

STANDARD & POOR'S

STOCK REPORTS

Fred Meyer

NYSE Symbol **FMY**
In S&P MidCap 400

06-SEP-95

Industry: Retail Stores

Summary: This leading retailer, which operates mainly in the Pacific Northwest, offers a wide range of food, apparel and general merchandise through one-stop, multi-department stores.

Quantitative Evaluations

Outlook (1 Lowest—5 Highest)
• **4-**

Fair Value
• **25¾**

Risk
• **Average**

Earn./Div. Rank
• **B**

Technical Eval.
• **Bearish** since 8/94

Rel. Strength Rank (1 Lowest—99 Highest)
• **8**

Insider Activity
• **NA**

Recent Price • 23⅞
52 Wk Range • 35¾-23½

Yield • Nil
12-Mo. P/E • NM

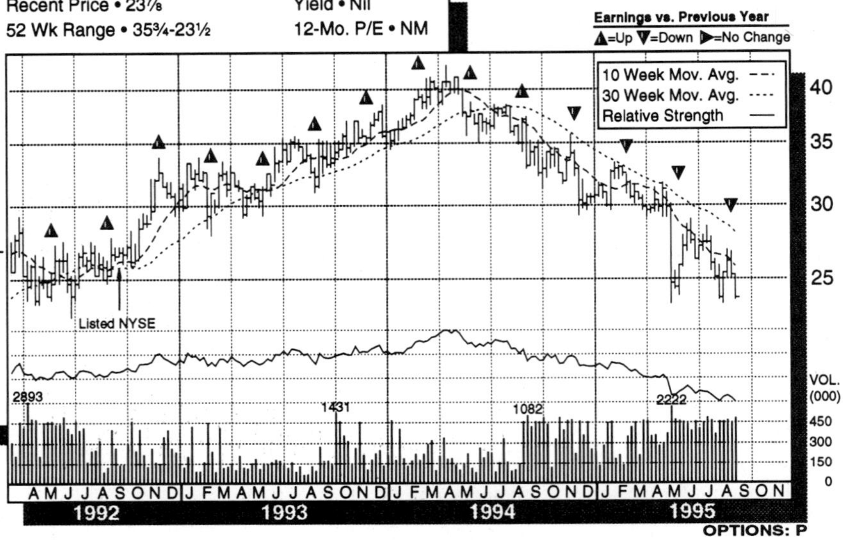

OPTIONS: P

Business Profile - 06-SEP-95

Earnings in 1994-95 were penalized by the impact of an 88-day strike in the Portland area (settled in November), estimated to have cost the company $60 million in aftertax earnings, and by a $16 million pretax charge related to a decision to exit the Northern California market. In 1995-96, FMY expects to lower its merchandise distribution costs, with the opening of a new food distribution center in Puyallup, Wash. during the second quarter. An affiliate of KKR controls 40% of the common shares.

Operational Review - 06-SEP-95

Revenues advanced 2.6%, year to year, for the 28 weeks ended August 12, 1995, as contributions from more stores in operation more than offset declines of 0.5% and 5.2%, respectively, in comparable food and non-food sales. Gross margins narrowed, primarily reflecting lower sales in higher margin seasonal categories and higher markdowns. Results were also hurt by residual effects of the 1994 strikes, startup costs associated with the new distribution center, and increased competition.

Stock Performance - 01-SEP-95

In the past 30 trading days, FMY's shares have declined 8%, compared to a 2% rise in the S&P 500. Average trading volume for the past five days was 158,460 shares, compared with the 40-day moving average of 116,603 shares.

Key Stock Statistics

Dividend Rate/Share	Nil	Shareholders	1,300
Shs. outstg. (M)	26.7	Market cap. (B)	$0.644
Avg. daily vol. (M)	0.122	Inst. holdings	53%
Tang. Bk. Value/Share	20.08	Insider holdings	NA
Beta	0.70		

Value of $10,000 invested 5 years ago: $ 12,905

Fiscal Year Ending Jan. 31

	1996	% Change	1995	% Change	1994	% Change
Revenues (Million $)						
1Q	936.7	NM	932.0	9%	852.1	3%
2Q	775.8	5%	737.3	9%	674.7	5%
3Q	—	—	626.8	-3%	644.5	2%
4Q	—	—	832.0	3%	807.8	7%
Yr.	—	—	3,128	5%	2,979	4%
Income (Million $)						
1Q	3.08	-81%	15.99	14%	14.01	21%
2Q	10.67	-44%	19.19	13%	16.96	14%
3Q	—	—	-36.58	NM	9.90	19%
4Q	—	—	8.57	-71%	30.03	16%
Yr.	—	—	7.17	-90%	70.90	17%
Earnings Per Share ($)						
1Q	0.11	-80%	0.56	12%	0.50	14%
2Q	0.38	-43%	0.67	12%	0.60	11%
3Q	—	—	-1.28	NM	0.35	17%
4Q	—	—	0.30	-71%	1.05	14%
Yr.	—	—	0.25	-90%	2.50	13%

Next earnings report expected: early December

Fred Meyer

Business Summary - 05-SEP-95

Fred Meyer, Inc. is a leading West Coast retailer, emphasizing large, one-stop-shopping stores that offer more than 225,000 food and nonfood products. As of August 1995, there were 133 stores in operation under the Fred Meyer name in Oregon, Washington, Utah, Alaska, Idaho, California and Montana. Most stores are located in or near well-populated residential areas.

The number of stores in operation at recent fiscal year-ends was:

1995	131
1994	127
1993	123
1992	122
1991	122

Of the 133 stores in operation at August 12, 1995, 99 were freestanding, multi-department units, averaging 140,814 sq. ft. of retail space and providing one-stop shopping for necessities and items of everyday use; of these, 90 contained food and nonfood departments and 9 contained nonfood departments only. These multi-department stores, accounting for 99% of total sales, contained up to seven departments, including food, home products, apparel, home electronics, fine jewelry, nutrition, health and beauty aids, pharmacy and either a restaurant or a snack bar. The 34 remaining stores included 29 fine jewelry stores located in regional malls.

Sales in recent fiscal years were distributed:

	1994-95	1993-94	1992-93
Nonfood products	61.7%	62.5%	63.3%
Food products	38.3%	37.5%	36.7%

The company operates centralized distribution facilities near Portland, Ore., containing 1,528,000 sq. ft., and in Salt Lake City, Utah, with approximately 122,000 sq. ft. Sales per sq. ft. of selling space were $304 in 1994-95 and $312 in 1993-94. Nearly all properties are leased.

Operations began in December 1981, following the acquisition of the Fred Meyer business for $200 million in a management leveraged buyout arranged by Kohlberg Kravis Roberts & Co.

Important Developments

Aug. '95—In 1995-96's second quarter, FMY remodeled two stores. The company said it expects to open four new stores during the third quarter, and close three stores. One additional new store is scheduled to open in the fourth quarter.

Capitalization

Long Term Debt: $594,108,000 (8/95), incl. $13,766,000 of lease obligs.

Options: To buy 1,566,441 shs. at $3.24 ea. (held by an affiliate of KKR) and 2,358,000 shs. at $12.13 to $41.25 ea. (1/95).

Per Share Data ($) (Year Ended Jan. 31)

	1995	1994	1993	1992	1991	1990
Tangible Bk. Val.	20.08	19.77	17.37	14.36	12.36	10.88
Cash Flow	3.38	4.99	4.66	3.96	3.06	1.26
Earnings	0.25	2.50	2.21	1.80	1.37	-0.28
Dividends	Nil	Nil	Nil	Nil	Nil	Nil
Payout Ratio	Nil	Nil	Nil	Nil	Nil	Nil
Cal. Yrs.	1994	1993	1992	1991	1990	1989
Prices - High	42½	38½	33⅞	26⅞	18¾	23
- Low	29¼	27⅞	22¾	11¼	10	15¾
P/E Ratio - High	NM	15	15	15	14	NM
- Low	NM	11	10	6	7	NM

Income Statement Analysis (Million $)

	1995	%Chg	1994	%Chg	1993	%Chg	1992
Revs.	3,128	5%	2,979	4%	2,854	6%	2,703
Oper. Inc.	145	-32%	213	22%	175	20%	146
Depr.	89.5	27%	70.7	5%	67.3	23%	54.5
Int. Exp.	31.8	32%	24.1	99%	12.1	-38%	19.4
Pretax Inc.	12.0	-90%	121	26%	96.2	35%	71.0
Eff. Tax Rate	38%	—	41%	—	37%	—	36%
Net Inc.	7.2	-90%	70.9	17%	60.6	34%	45.2

Balance Sheet & Other Fin. Data (Million $)

	1995	1994	1993	1992	1991	1990
Cash	34.9	34.1	31.9	30.0	29.0	24.9
Curr. Assets	642	592	530	487	465	452
Total Assets	1,563	1,319	1,079	973	906	797
Curr. Liab.	392	383	345	313	305	281
LT Debt	554	336	212	259	251	206
Common Eqty.	539	528	450	335	285	252
Total Cap.	1,115	882	679	611	550	467
Cap. Exp.	284	250	145	106	164	135
Cash Flow	97.0	142	128	100	74.9	31.3

Ratio Analysis

	1995	1994	1993	1992	1991	1990
Curr. Ratio	1.6	1.5	1.5	1.6	1.5	1.6
% LT Debt of Cap.	49.7	38.1	31.3	42.4	45.5	44.2
% Net Inc.of Revs.	0.2	2.4	2.1	1.7	1.4	NM
% Ret. on Assets	0.5	5.8	5.6	4.8	3.9	NM
% Ret. on Equity	1.3	14.3	14.7	14.5	12.5	NM

Dividend Data —No dividends have been paid.

Data as orig. reptd.; bef. results of disc. opers. and/or spec. items. Per share data adj. for stk. divs. as of ex-div. date. E-Estimated. NA-Not Available. NM-Not Meaningful. NR-Not Ranked.

Office—3800 S.E. 22nd Ave., Portland, OR 97202. **Tel**—(503) 232-8844. **Chrmn & CEO**—R. G. Miller. **Pres**—C. K. Green. **SVP-Fin & CFO & Investor Contact**—Kenneth Thrasher (503-797-7900). **SVP & Secy**—R. A. Cooke. **Dirs**—S. A. Fox, A. M. Gleason, J. Kohlberg, Jr., R. S. Meier, M. W. Michelson, R. G. Miller, P. E. Raether. **Transfer Agent & Registrar**—Chemical Trust Co. of California, SF. **Incorporated** in Delaware in 1981. **Empl**-27,000. **S&P Analyst:** Maureen C. Carini

STANDARD & POOR'S
STOCK REPORTS

Michael Foods

NASDAQ Symbol **MIKL**
In S&P MidCap 400

22-AUG-95 **Industry:** Food

Summary: This food processor and distributor has interests in eggs and egg products, refrigerated grocery products, frozen and refrigerated potato products and specialty dairy products.

S&P Opinion: Hold (★★★)

Recent Price • 14⅛
52 Wk Range • 14½-9

Yield • 1.4%
12-Mo. P/E • 16.8

Quantitative Evaluations

Outlook
(1 Lowest—5 Highest)
• **3-**

Fair Value
• **13⅞**

Risk
• **High**

Earn./Div. Rank
• **NR**

Technical Eval.
• **Bullish** since 7/95

Rel. Strength Rank
(1 Lowest—99 Highest)
• **80**

Insider Activity
• **NA**

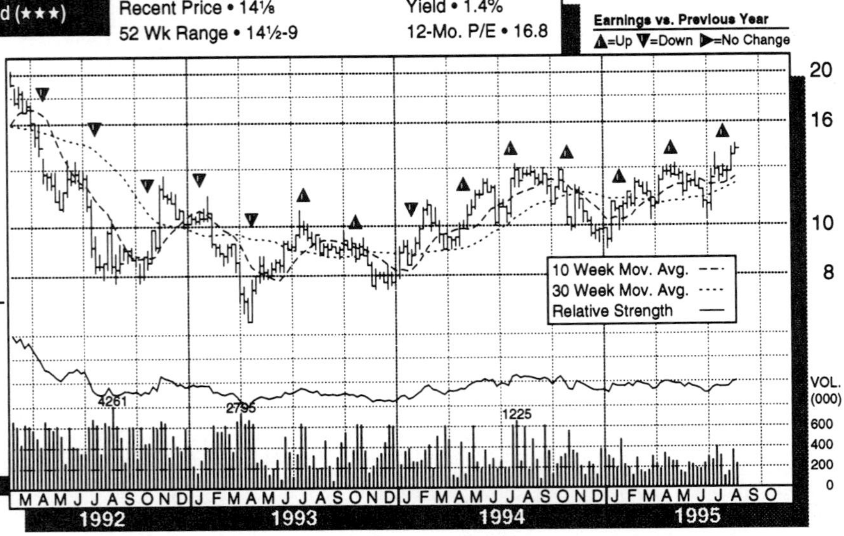

Overview - 22-AUG-95

Sales in coming periods should benefit from additional advertising spending and unit volume increases. MIKL should benefit from the continued national rollout of new value-added egg products, increased production at the Texas plant, higher penetration of chain stores, and the addition of new products and new accounts. Receipt of a product patent for extended shelf life liquid whole eggs would be very positive. Earnings should continue to improve in coming periods, on greater unit volume, an increased proportion of value-added products and a lower proportion of commodity products, favorable feed costs, and the absence of losses from Sunnyside Vegetable Packing. However, anticipated higher SG&A expense will restrict profit growth.

Valuation - 22-AUG-95

The shares of this food processor and distributor recently broke out of a two- year trading range reaching a new 52-week high. Sales have been growing at a single digit rate in recent years, as volume increases outweighed fluctuations in commodity prices. Revenues are expected to grow 4.0% to 5.0% in 1995. Earnings, which can be affected by sudden changes in commodity prices, have been good in recent periods, despite a poor environment. The shares, trading at about 14X projected 1996 EPS of $1.00, are in the middle of their historic range, and are yielding about 1.4%. We see the stock as a market performer.

Key Stock Statistics

S&P EPS Est. 1995	0.90	Tang. Bk. Value/Share	6.31
P/E on S&P Est. 1995	15.7	Beta	0.90
S&P EPS Est. 1996	1.00	Shareholders	700
Dividend Rate/Share	0.20	Market cap. (B)	$0.271
Shs. outstg. (M)	19.3	Inst. holdings	47%
Avg. daily vol. (M)	0.041	Insider holdings	0%

Value of $10,000 invested 5 years ago: $ 17,155

Fiscal Year Ending Dec. 31

	1995	% Change	1994	% Change	1993	% Change
Revenues (Million $)						
1Q	126.7	4%	121.6	16%	104.9	-2%
2Q	130.9	4%	125.5	5%	119.4	9%
3Q	—	—	127.9	6%	120.7	10%
4Q	—	—	130.9	NM	129.7	13%
Yr.	—	—	506.0	7%	474.8	7%
Income (Million $)						
1Q	3.69	15%	3.21	NM	0.51	-62%
2Q	4.22	14%	3.69	73%	2.13	NM
3Q	—	—	3.64	170%	1.35	85%
4Q	—	—	4.65	NM	-20.31	NM
Yr.	—	—	15.19	NM	-16.32	NM
Earnings Per Share ($)						
1Q	0.19	12%	0.17	NM	0.03	-57%
2Q	0.22	16%	0.19	73%	0.11	NM
3Q	E0.24	26%	0.19	171%	0.07	75%
4Q	E0.25	4%	0.24	NM	-1.05	NM
Yr.	E0.90	14%	0.79	NM	-0.84	NM

Next earnings report expected: mid October

Michael Foods

Business Summary - 10-AUG-95

Michael Foods, Inc. is a diversified producer and distributor of food products, operating in four basic areas: eggs and egg products, distribution of refrigerated grocery products, refrigerated and frozen potato products, and dairy products.

Through M. G. Waldbaum Co., the company produces, processes and distributes shell eggs and numerous egg products. Principal value-added egg products are ultrapasteurized Easy Eggs, salmonella-free liquid eggs. Products also include frozen and dried egg whites, yolks and whole eggs, frozen whole eggs, pre-cooked egg patties and omelets and frozen breakfast entrees.

Crystal Farms Refrigerated Distribution Co. manages MIKL's refrigerated distribution operations. Distributed products include cheese, bagels, butter, margarine, muffins, potato products, juice and ethnic foods. In 1991, Crystal Farms opened a cheese packaging facility in Lake Mills, Wis.; cheese now accounts for about 53% of Crystal's sales.

The potato products division processes and sells frozen potato products, primarily french fries and refrigerated potato products to both foodservice and retail markets. The refrigerated product line consists of extended shelf-life hash brown and mashed potatoes.

Kohler Mix Specialties, Inc. processes and sells soft serve mix, ice cream mix, frozen yogurt mix and milk and specialty dairy products, many of which are ultra-high temperature (UHT) pasteurized products. Kohler has about 600 customers, including branded ice cream manufacturers, distributors to fast food businesses and independent ice milk and ice cream retailers.

Sunnyside Vegetable Packing Inc., a unprofitable processor and distributor of refrigerated soups and salads for the foodservice and retail markets, was sold in December 1994.

Important Developments

Jul. '95—The U.S. Court of Appeals handed down a ruling that clears the way for the granting of a product patent for extended shelf-life liquid eggs manufactured by MIKL. The ruling reversed a July 1994 decision of the U.S. Patent Office to reject the application to have one of the four existing process patents governing the process of ultrapasteurized liquid eggs reissued as a product patent. In February, Michael Foods said competitors filed protests with the U.S. patent office challenging the validity of one or more claims under the patents.

Capitalization

Long Term Debt: $88,773,000 (3/95).

Per Share Data ($)

(Year Ended Dec. 31)

	1994	1993	1992	1991	1990	1989
Tangible Bk. Val.	6.14	5.50	6.22	6.13	3.49	4.47
Cash Flow	1.91	0.32	1.30	2.03	1.89	1.03
Earnings	0.79	-0.84	0.20	1.07	1.11	0.71
Dividends	0.20	0.20	0.20	0.20	0.22	0.13
Payout Ratio	25%	NM	100%	20%	19%	19%
Prices - High	13¼	11½	20½	23⅝	15⅛	14⅝
- Low	7⅞	6½	7¾	12½	8¼	8¼
P/E Ratio - High	17	NM	NM	22	14	21
- Low	10	NM	NM	12	7	12

Income Statement Analysis (Million $)

	1994	%Chg	1993	%Chg	1992	%Chg	1991
Revs.	506	7%	475	7%	443	-3%	455
Oper. Inc.	54.8	27%	43.1	16%	37.1	-36%	57.9
Depr.	21.6	-4%	22.4	4%	21.5	22%	17.6
Int. Exp.	8.8	-4%	9.2	-10%	10.2	-5%	10.7
Pretax Inc.	24.7	NM	-21.6	NM	6.0	-80%	30.7
Eff. Tax Rate	39%	—	NM	—	36%	—	36%
Net Inc.	15.2	NM	-16.3	NM	3.9	-80%	19.7

Balance Sheet & Other Fin. Data (Million $)

	1994	1993	1992	1991	1990	1989
Cash	1.6	0.2	6.1	4.6	4.0	7.8
Curr. Assets	94.0	83.7	93.3	99	86.2	58.1
Total Assets	337	329	370	357	304	187
Curr. Liab.	60.4	61.5	38.5	39.9	72.8	29.0
LT Debt	89.0	94.0	129	115	99	54.6
Common Eqty.	166	155	177	176	111	95.0
Total Cap.	276	268	332	317	231	158
Cap. Exp.	23.0	12.0	32.0	48.4	40.2	35.1
Cash Flow	36.8	6.1	25.3	37.3	31.6	17.5

Ratio Analysis

	1994	1993	1992	1991	1990	1989
Curr. Ratio	1.6	1.4	2.4	2.5	1.2	2.0
% LT Debt of Cap.	32.1	35.2	38.8	36.4	42.7	34.6
% Net Inc.of Revs.	3.0	NM	0.9	4.3	4.0	4.7
% Ret. on Assets	4.6	NM	1.1	5.5	7.6	7.8
% Ret. on Equity	9.5	NM	2.2	12.9	18.1	13.3

Dividend Data —Dividends were initiated in 1987.

Amt. of Div. $	Date Decl.	Ex-Div. Date	Stock of Record	Payment Date
0.050	Jul. 28	Aug. 02	Aug. 08	Aug. 22 '94
0.050	Oct. 27	Nov. 01	Nov. 07	Nov. 21 '94
0.050	Jan. 26	Jan. 31	Feb. 06	Feb. 21 '95
0.050	Apr. 28	May. 02	May. 08	May. 22 '95
0.050	Jul. 28	Aug. 03	Aug. 07	Aug. 21 '95

Data as orig. reptd.; bef. results of disc. opers. and/or spec. items. Per share data adj. for stk. divs. as of ex-div. date. E-Estimated. NA-Not Available. NM-Not Meaningful. NR-Not Ranked.

Office—5353 Wayzata Blvd., Minneapolis, MN 55416. **Tel**—(612) 546-1500. **Chrmn**—J. H. Michael. **Pres & CEO**—G. A. Ostrander. **VP-Fin, CFO & Treas**—J. D. Reedy. **EVP & Secy**—J. M. Shapiro. **Investor Contact**—Mark Witmer. **Dirs**—R. A. Coonrod, M. E. Efron, O. L. Freeman, A. C. Knudtson, J. D. Marshburn, J. H. Michael, J. J. Michael, R. G. Olson, G. A. Ostrander. **Transfer Agent & Registrar**—First National Bank of Boston. **Incorporated** in Delaware in 1987. **Empl**-2,700. **S&P Analyst:** Efraim Levy

Micro Warehouse

NASDAQ Symbol MWHS (Incl. in Nat'l Market) In S&P MidCap 400

Price	Range	P-E Ratio	Dividend	Yield	S&P Ranking	Beta
Oct. 18'95	1995					
48¼	56⅞–26¾	36	None	None	NR	NA

Summary

This specialty-catalog retailer of Macintosh and IBM-compatible personal computers, software, accessories and peripherals markets its products through mailings of its eight distinctive catalogs and through telemarketing which focuses on medium to large commercial, educational and governmental accounts. In October 1995, MWHS sold publicly 1.2 million common shares at $44.50 each.

Business Summary

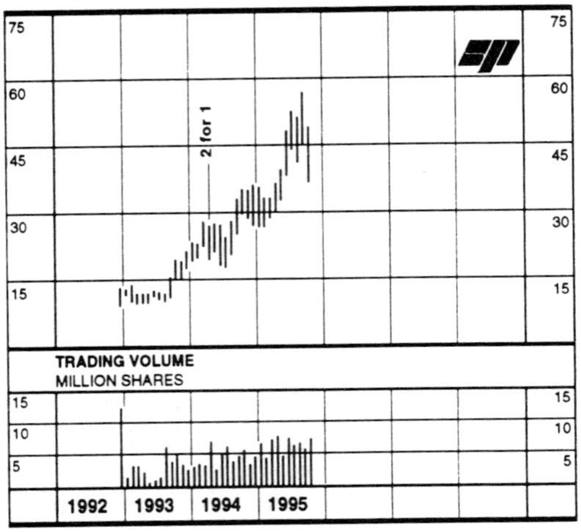

Micro Warehouse, Inc. is a leading direct marketer of microcomputer hardware and software products for users of Apple Macintosh and IBM-compatible personal computers. Through its catalogs, the company offers a broad selection of over 20,000 products at prices generally ranging from 30% to 60% below manufacturers' suggested retail prices. MWHS offers popular brand name hardware (including microcomputers, printers, modems, monitors, data storage devices, add-on circuit boards, mice, connectivity products and certain business machines), software and peripherals from leading vendors such as Adobe, Apple, Claris, Daystar, Farallon, Hayes, Hewlett-Packard, IBM, Lotus, Microsoft, Quark and Texas Instruments.

Software sales represented about 55% of 1994 net sales, hardware 46%, and supplies and accessories 14%. Domestic sales of products for Apple Macintosh computers represented about 55% of 1994 net sales.

As of December 31, 1994, the company produced eight distinctive catalogs. Its two core catalogs are MacWarehouse for the Macintosh market, and MicroWarehouse for the PC/Windows market and its five specialty catalogs: Data CommWarehouse, a catalog directed to the data communications and networking markets for use in micro and mainframe computers; CD-RomWarehouse, targeted to the interactive, education and entertainment CD-Rom market; Micro SuppliesWarehouse, directed at computer users' basic needs for supplies, such as floppy disks, data cartridges, stands, bases, etc.; Paper designWarehouse, published to fill the specialty needs of users of laser printers; and Micro SystemsWarehouse, featuring brand name microcomputer systems and peripherals. Home ComputerWarehouse is targeted to home computer users.

During 1994, the company mailed about 54 million catalogs and it had 1,333,000 active customers (those who made purchases during the past 12 months), up from 863,000 the year before; other customers totaled 1,092,000 in 1994, up from 660,000 in 1993. Active customers receive a catalog monthly and all customers receive a catalog with every order shipped. The catalogs are printed in 10 languages. Operations in Europe accounted for 16% of 1994 net sales and a $1.1 million loss from operations.

MWHS's telemarketing representatives assist customers in purchasing decisions, process product orders and respond to customer inquires on order status and product pricing and availability. Toll-free numbers are available to customers. The company's sales force targets mid-size to large commercial, governmental and educational accounts.

Important Developments

Oct. '95— MWHS attributed the higher sales for 1995's third quarter to increased hardware sales, which accounted for 70% of total sales versus 55% a year earlier. Catalog circulation increased 52% to 18 million during the quarter from 11.8 million a year earlier. The active customer base rose 33%, to nearly 1.7 million.

Next earnings report expected in late January.

Per Share Data ($)

Yr. End Dec. 31	[1]1994	[1]1993	1992	1991
Tangible Bk. Val.[2]	**8.11**	3.91	2.65	0.17
Cash Flow	**1.21**	0.74	0.12	0.30
Earnings	**1.01**	0.64	0.01	0.24
Dividends	**Nil**	Nil	Nil	Nil
Payout Ratio	**Nil**	Nil	Nil	Nil
Prices—High	**36¼**	21⅜	13¼	NA
Low	**17¾**	9⅝	10¾	NA
P/E Ratio—	**36–18**	34–15	NM	NA

Data as orig. reptd. Adj. for stk. div. of 100% Apr. 1994. **1.** Refl. merger or acq. **2.** Incl. intangibles. NM-Not Meaningful. NA-Not Available.

Income Data (Million $)

Year Ended Dec. 31	Revs.	Oper. Inc.	% Oper. Inc. of Revs.	Cap. Exp.	Depr.	Int. Exp.	Net Bef. Taxes	Eff. Tax Rate	Net Inc.	% Net Inc. of Revs.	Cash Flow
[1]**1994**	**776**	**50.7**	**6.5**	**13.6**	**5.31**	**NA**	**46.9**	**40.3%**	**28.0**	**3.6**	**33.3**
[1]1993	450	28.0	6.2	4.8	2.53	NA	26.0	42.2%	15.0	3.3	17.5
1992	270	15.5	5.7	3.6	1.94	1.26	3.5	94.0%	0.2	0.1	2.2
1991	164	8.4	5.1	1.4	1.12	0.73	4.3	1.6%	4.3	2.6	5.4

Balance Sheet Data (Million $)

Dec. 31	Cash	Curr. Assets	Curr. Liab.	Curr. Ratio	Total Assets	% Ret. on Assets	Long Term Debt	Common Equity	Total Cap.	% LT Debt of Cap.	% Ret. on Equity
1994	**74.5**	**249**	**53.8**	**4.6**	**294**	**12.1**	**0.65**	**240**	**240**	**0.3**	**15.8**
1993	30.6	128	44.1	2.9	141	13.3	Nil	97	97	Nil	18.4
1992	18.6	71	15.9	4.5	77	0.3	1.36	60	61	2.2	0.7
1991	1.7	29	22.2	1.3	32	NA	6.75	3	9	71.7	NA

Data as orig. reptd. **1.** Refl. merger or acq. NA-Not Available.

Net Sales (Million $)

Quarter:	1995	1994	1993
Mar.	277.5	156.8	98.8
Jun.	289.2	167.0	101.5
Sep.	337.3	201.3	109.4
Dec.		251.2	140.7
		776.3	450.4

Net sales for the nine months ended September 30, 1995, advanced 72%, year to year. The gain primarily reflected an increase in the circulation of both the MacWarehouse and MicroWarehouse catalogs. However, profitability was restricted by a shift toward hardware sales, which typically have lower margins than software. Net income was up 64%, to $31,365,000 from $19,068,000 in the year-earlier period. Earnings per share were equal to $1.04 based on 12% more average shares, compared with $0.71.

Common Share Earnings ($)

Quarter:	1995	1994	[1]1993
Mar.	0.33	0.23	0.12
Jun.	0.33	0.23	0.13
Sep.	0.37	0.25	0.16
Dec.		0.30	0.21
		1.01	0.64

Dividend Data

No cash dividends have been paid. The company has no present plans to pay any dividends. It intends to retain its earnings to finance the growth and development of its business.

Finances

In October 1995, the company sold publicly 1.2 million common shares at $44.50 each; certain shareholders also sold 1 million shares at the same price. Company proceeds were earmarked for working capital, including the financing of expected increases in inventories and accounts receivable, and other general purposes.

The company believes that its existing cash reserves, cash flow from operations and existing credit facilities will be sufficient to satisfy its operating cash needs for at least the next 12 months.

Capitalization

Long Term Debt: $519,000 of equipment obligs. (6/95).

Common Stock: 30,940,000 shs. ($0.01 par). Institutions hold about 78%. Shareholders: 128 of record (12/94).

1. Sum of quarters does not reconcile with full-year total because of change in shares outstanding.

Office—535 Connecticut Ave., Norwalk, CT 06854. **Tel**—(203) 899-4000. **Chrmn, Pres & CEO**—P. Godfrey. **VP-CFO & Treas**—S. Purcell. **Investor Contact**—Margarita T. DeLutri (203) 899-4672. **Dirs**—F. Dennis, F. H. Fruitman, P. Godfrey, M. Setler, J. M. Walsh. **Transfer Agent & Registrar**—State Street Bank & Trust Co., North Quincy, Mass. **Incorporated** in Connecticut in 1987; reincorporated in Delaware in 1992. **Empl**—2,300.

 J. J. Schemitsch

MidAmerican Energy

NYSE Symbol MEC In S&P MidCap 400

Price	Range	P-E Ratio	Dividend	Yield	S&P Ranking	Beta
Oct. 19'95	1995					
15⅞	16¼–13⅝	13	1.20	7.6%	NR	0.24

Summary

MidAmerican Energy, the largest utility company in Iowa, was formed through the July 1995 merger of Midwest Resources Inc. and Iowa-Illinois Gas & Electric Co. The combined company provides natural gas and electric service to a population of about 1.7 million in 545 Iowa communities; service is also provided in portions of Illinois, Nebraska and South Dakota. MEC's electricity production and gas supply costs are among the lowest in the industry.

Business Summary

MidAmerican Energy Co. was formed through the July 1995 pooling-of-interests merger of Midwest Resources Inc. and Iowa-Illinois Gas & Electric Co. In the merger, the company issued one MidAmerican common share for each Midwest Resources common share and 1.47 MidAmerican common shares for each Iowa-Illinois common share held. The merger was expected to result in cost savings for the combined entity estimated at more than $500 million over 10 years. Utility operations are conducted through two principal units: an electric business unit and a natural gas business unit. MEC also owns two subsidiaries engaged in various non-regulated activities.

The largest utility company in Iowa, MidAmerican serves about 628,000 electric customers and 592,000 natural gas customers in 545 communities throughout that state, as well as in portions of Illinois, Nebraska and South Dakota. In 1994, electric operations accounted for 67% of pro forma consolidated operating revenues (65% in 1993) and gas operations 33% (35%). Pro forma consolidated electric revenues by customer class in 1994:

	1994
Residential	39%
Commercial	25%
Industrial	20%
Other	16%

MidAmerican is a low-cost electricity producer, with unit production costs in 1994 of $0.0225 per kwh. MEC has five jointly and five wholly owned coal-fired electric generating plants, and a 25% interest in the Quad-Cities nuclear generating station. It also has a long-term contract to purchase 50% of the output of Cooper Nuclear Station. Sources of power in 1994 were coal (primarily low sulfur) 84% and nuclear 16%. Historic peak demand in 1994 was a combined 3,374 MW, and total capacity was 4,353 MW, for a capacity margin of 23%.

The company forecasts utility capital expenditures of $997 million for 1995 through 1999. During that period, MEC also expects to contribute $43 million to an external trust for Quad-Cities nuclear decommissioning. Some 90% of utility capital spending in the 1995-1999 period is expected to be financed with cash generated from utility operations.

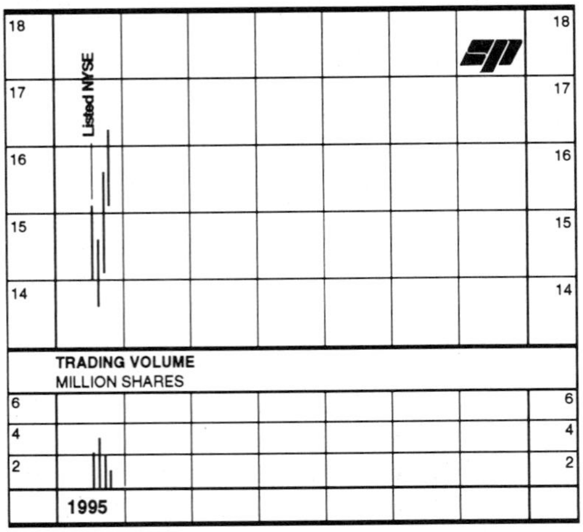

Non-regulated subsidiaries include InterCoast Energy Co., which conducts oil and gas, energy marketing, and financial management businesses; and Midwest Capital Group, a regional business development company. These subsidiaries contributed $15.2 million to net income in 1994.

Important Developments

Aug. '95— MEC recorded a charge of $0.04 a share in 1995's first half related to a restructuring plan expected to reduce its workforce by about 15% from July 1994 levels. Remaining merger-related restructuring costs would be recorded in 1995's second half.

Next earnings report expected in mid-November.

Per Share Data ($)

Yr. End Dec. 31	[1]1994	[1]1993	[1]1992	[1]1991	[1]1990	[1]1989
Tangible Bk. Val.	**12.08**	12.07	11.86	12.08	11.86	11.85
Earnings[2]	**1.28**	1.43	0.83	1.32	1.33	1.64
Dividends	**NA**	NA	NA	NA	NA	NA
Payout Ratio	**NA**	NA	NA	NA	NA	NA
Prices—High	**NA**	NA	NA	NA	NA	NA
Low	**NA**	NA	NA	NA	NA	NA
P/E Ratio—	**NA**	NA	NA	NA	NA	NA

Data as reptd. in SEC Form 8-K dated Jul. 1, 1995; prior to 1994, data as reptd. in joint proxy statement/prospectus dated Nov. 3, 1994. **1.** Pro forma combined. **2.** Bef. results of disc. opers. of -0.06 in 1994. NA-Not Available.

Income Data (Million $)

Year Ended Dec. 31	Revs.	Depr.	Maint.	Oper. Ratio	[1]Fxd. Chgs. Cover.	Constr. Credits	Eff. Tax Rate	[4]Net Inc.	% Return On Revs.	% Return On [2]Invest. Capital	% Return On Com. Equity
[3]1994	**1,514**	**154**	**101**	**86.9%**	**3.20**	**3.96**	**33.1%**	**141**	**9.3**	**NA**	**10.9**
[3]1993	1,542	151	102	86.8%	3.22	2.19	31.6%	148	9.6	NA	11.9
[3]1992	1,421	145	94	87.6%	2.20	3.38	31.5%	88	6.2	NA	6.9
[3]1991	1,442	135	92	85.2%	2.80	4.47	33.9%	128	8.9	NA	10.8
[3]1990	1,388	NA	NA	84.6%	NA	NA	NA	126	9.1	NA	11.2
[3]1989	1,426	NA	NA	84.5%	NA	NA	NA	155	10.9	NA	NA

Balance Sheet Data (Million $)

Dec. 31	Gross Prop.	Capital Expend.	Net Prop.	% Earn. on Net Prop.	Total Cap.	Capitalization LT Debt	% LT Debt	Pfd.	% Pfd.	Com.	% Com.
[3]1994	**4,530**	**NA**	**2,644**	**NA**	**3,569**	**1,398**	**51.0**	**140**	**5.1**	**1,204**	**43.9**
[3]1993	4,292	NA	2,491	NA	3,458	1,341	50.1	160	6.0	1,181	44.0
[3]1992	NA	NA	NA	NA	NA	1,369	51.6	123	4.7	1,160	43.7
[3]1991	NA	NA	NA	NA	NA	1,351	51.4	153	5.8	1,125	42.8
[3]1990	NA	NA	NA	NA	NA	1,225	51.0	114	4.8	1,061	44.2
[3]1989	NA	NA	NA	NA	NA	1,215	50.8	115	4.8	1,061	44.4

Data as reptd. in SEC Form 8-K dated Jul. 1, 1995; prior to 1994, data as reptd. in joint proxy statement/prospectus dated Nov. 3, 1994.
1. Times int. exp. & pfd. covered (pretax basis). **2.** Based on income bef. int. charges. **3.** Pro forma combined. **4.** Bef. results of disc. opers.
NA-Not Available.

Operating Revenues (Million $)

Quarter:	1995	[1]1994	[1]1993	[1]1992
Mar.	[1]419	472	458	---
Jun.	[1]338	327	327	---
Sep.		346	362	---
Dec.		368	395	---
		1,514	1,542	1,421

Operating revenues in the six months ended June 30, 1995, decreased 5.2%, year to year, reflecting an 18% drop in gas sales on warmer winter weather. After a charge of $6,000,000 ($0.04 after tax) from expenses recorded for workforce reduction programs, reduced contributions from non-utility subsidiaries, and greater interest costs, income from continuing operations fell 11%. After preferred dividends, share earnings were $0.59, versus $0.68, before $0.01 of income and $0.01 of losses from discontinued operations in the respective interims.

Common Share Earnings ($)

Quarter:	1995	[1]1994	[1]1993	[1]1992
Mar.	[1]0.36	0.46	0.46	---
Jun.	[1]0.24	0.23	0.24	---
Sep.		0.40	0.53	---
Dec.		0.19	0.19	---
		1.28	1.43	0.83

Dividend Data

Dividends on the common stock of MidAmerican Energy were initiated with the September 1, 1995, payment. A dividend reinvestment plan is available.

Amt. of Divd. $	Date Decl.	Ex-divd. Date	Stock of Record	Payment Date
0.30 Init.	Jul. 26	Aug. 4	Aug. 8	Sep. 1'95

Finances

At July 31, 1995, the company had available bank lines of credit totalling $250 million. Its InterCoast subsidiary had a $110 million revolving credit agreement, under which $36.5 million was outstanding at June 30, 1995.

Capitalization

Long Term Debt: $1,398,539,000 (6/95).

Red. Cum. Preference Stock: $50,000,000.

Cum. Preferred Stock: $89,955,000.

Common Stock: 100,751,877 shs. (no par).

1. Pro forma combined.

Office—666 Grand Ave. (P.O. Box 9244), Des Moines, IA 50306-9244. **Tel**—(515) 242-4300. **Chrmn**—R. E. Christiansen. **Pres**—S. J. Bright. **CFO**—L. E. Cooper. **Secy**—P. J. Leighton. **Investor Contact**—Sue Rozema (515) 281-2250. **Dirs**—J. W. Aalfs, B. T. Asher, S. J. Bright, R. A. Burnett, R. D. Christensen, R. E. Christiansen, J. W. Colloton, F. S. Cottrell, J. W. Eugster, W. C. Fletcher, M. Foster, Jr., N. Gentry, J. M. Hoak, Jr., R. L. Lawson, R. L. Peterson, R. A. Schneider, N. L. Seifert, W. S. Tinsman, L. L. Woodruff. **Transfer Agent & Registrar**—Co. itself. **Incorporated** in Iowa in 1994. **Empl**—3,750.

 William P. Andrews

STANDARD & POOR'S

STOCK REPORTS

Miller (Herman)

NASDAQ Symbol **MLHR**
In S&P MidCap 400

11-SEP-95 **Industry:** Office Equipment

Summary: This company is a leading international designer and manufacturer of office systems products and related products.

Quantitative Evaluations

Outlook
(1 Lowest—5 Highest)
• **4+**
Fair Value
• **26⅜**
Risk
• **Average**
Earn./Div. Rank
• **B**

Technical Eval.
• **Bullish** since 4/94
Rel. Strength Rank
(1 Lowest—99 Highest)
• **46**
Insider Activity
• **Neutral**

Recent Price • 25½
52 Wk Range • 26¾-19¼
Yield • 2.0%
12-Mo. P/E • NM

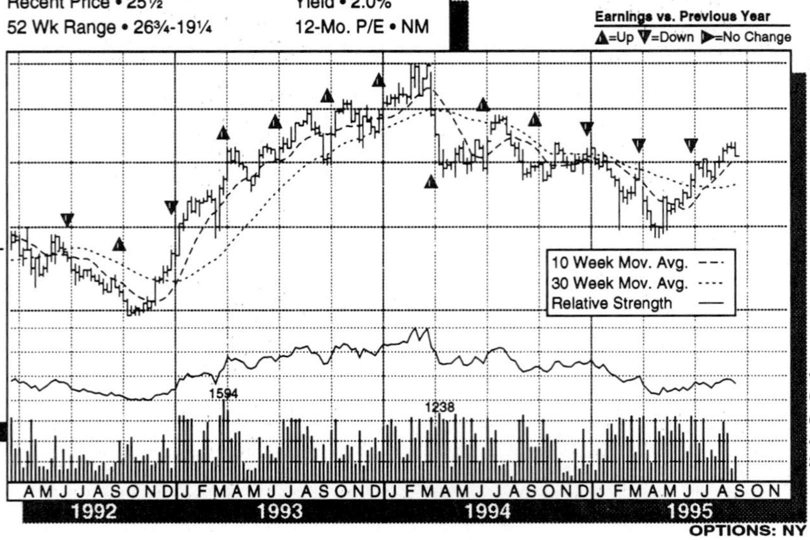

Business Profile - 11-SEP-95

This leading designer and manufacturer of office and institutional furniture sells its products throughout the U.S., as well as in Canada, Europe and elsewhere. A restructuring program is expected to produce annual cost savings of $20 million upon completion (scheduled for 1997-8), and to increase unit production capacity by 40%.

Operational Review - 11-SEP-95

Record net sales in the fiscal year ended June 3, 1995, reflected the success of the new Aeron seating line. New orders also reached record levels. However, earnings fell sharply, reflecting pretax restructuring charges totaling $31.9 million, as well a a pretax reserve of $12 million for anticipated patent litigation.

Stock Performance - 08-SEP-95

In the past 30 trading days, MLHR's shares have increased 7%, compared to a 2% rise in the S&P 500. Average trading volume for the past five days was 60,825 shares, compared with the 40-day moving average of 67,995 shares.

Key Stock Statistics

Dividend Rate/Share	0.52	Shareholders	11,000
Shs. outstg. (M)	24.8	Market cap. (B)	$0.633
Avg. daily vol. (M)	0.076	Inst. holdings	65%
Tang. Bk. Value/Share	11.55	Insider holdings	NA
Beta	0.80		

Value of $10,000 invested 5 years ago: $ 14,916

Fiscal Year Ending May 31

	1995	% Change	1994	% Change	1993	% Change
Revenues (Million $)						
1Q	252.8	14%	221.6	11%	200.0	8%
2Q	279.1	15%	241.8	18%	205.0	NM
3Q	260.0	7%	241.9	11%	217.5	9%
4Q	291.2	17%	247.9	6%	233.6	9%
Yr.	1,083	14%	953.2	11%	855.7	6%
Income (Million $)						
1Q	7.94	6%	7.47	—	—	—
2Q	1.44	-87%	11.18	NM	3.56	-33%
3Q	4.26	-62%	11.18	54%	7.24	86%
4Q	-9.30	NM	10.54	19%	8.85	NM
Yr.	4.34	-89%	40.37	83%	22.05	NM
Earnings Per Share ($)						
1Q	0.32	7%	0.30	NM	0.10	11%
2Q	0.06	-86%	0.44	NM	0.14	-33%
3Q	0.17	-61%	0.44	52%	0.29	81%
4Q	-0.37	NM	0.42	20%	0.35	NM
Yr.	0.18	-89%	1.60	82%	0.88	NM

Next earnings report expected: late September

Miller (Herman)

Business Summary - 11-SEP-95

Herman Miller, Inc. researches, designs, manufactures and sells modular space division, storage and materials handling furniture systems. In each of the past three fiscal years, sales for use in office/institution environments, including offices and related conference, lobby and lounge areas, and general public areas such as transportation terminals, accounted for over 95% of the total; most of the remainder went to hospitals, laboratories and other health/science environments. Foreign operations contributed 15% of sales in 1993-4, but resulted in a loss of $2.0 million.

Products and systems for the office/institution market consist of the "Action Office" and "Ethospace" systems and a wide selection of seating products, tables and desks. "Action Office" is a freestanding office partition and furnishing system (Miller offers three types of Action Office series), believed to be the first such system to be marketed nationally. The modular systems represent a major portion of sales. "Ethospace" is a system of movable full- and partial-height walls, with panels and individual wall segments that attach to wall framework. The company also offers a broad array of seating (including Equa and Ergon office chairs), storage (including Meridian filing products) and freestanding furniture products.

Health/science products consist of a number of furniture items and systems, including "Co-Struc," a unique, modular system for storing and manually handling materials and supplies within health care facilities and laboratories.

The company markets its products through its own sales staff. Some 84% of sales in 1993-4 were made to or through nonexclusive, independent dealers, and the balance directly to end-users. Foreign sales are made through subsidiaries and dealers. Herman Miller has redefined its foreign operations to focus on four major markets: Canada, Europe, Latin America and the Asia/Pacific region. In certain other foreign markets, the company licenses others to make its products.

Important Developments

Jul. '95—Miller said its sharply lower earnings in 1994-5 reflected $31.9 million of restructuring charges related to reducing its cost structure, as well as a reserve of $12 million for anticipated patent litigation.

Capitalization

Long Term Debt: $60,145,000 (6/3/95).

Per Share Data ($) (Year Ended May 31)

	1995	1994	1993	1992	1991	1990
Tangible Bk. Val.	NA	12.05	11.36	11.14	12.33	11.82
Cash Flow	NA	2.85	2.12	1.05	1.66	2.87
Earnings	0.18	1.60	0.88	-0.14	0.55	1.82
Dividends	0.65	0.52	0.52	0.52	0.52	0.52
Payout Ratio	NM	33%	59%	59%	95%	29%
Cal. Yrs.	1994	1993	1992	1991	1990	1989
Prices - High	35	31	21 1/8	22 1/2	24 3/8	23 1/8
- Low	23 3/8	18 1/8	14 3/4	15	16 3/8	17 3/4
P/E Ratio - High	NM	19	24	NM	44	13
- Low	NM	11	17	NM	30	10

Income Statement Analysis (Million $)

	1994	%Chg	1993	%Chg	1992	%Chg	1991
Revs.	953	11%	856	6%	805	-8%	879
Oper. Inc.	93.0	24%	75.0	32%	57.0	-42%	99
Depr.	31.5	2%	31.0	4%	29.9	4%	28.7
Int. Exp.	1.8	-14%	2.1	-70%	6.9	-33%	10.3
Pretax Inc.	63.5	50%	42.4	NM	-1.0	NM	33.2
Eff. Tax Rate	36%	—	48%	—	NM	—	58%
Net Inc.	40.4	83%	22.1	NM	-3.5	NM	14.1

Balance Sheet & Other Fin. Data (Million $)

	1994	1993	1992	1991	1990	1989
Cash	22.7	16.5	16.9	15.4	11.8	11.1
Curr. Assets	229	208	205	222	243	225
Total Assets	534	484	471	493	534	495
Curr. Liab.	178	145	139	108	116	122
LT Debt	20.6	21.1	29.4	54.7	89.0	86.1
Common Eqty.	296	284	280	315	314	270
Total Cap.	321	312	310	382	416	370
Cap. Exp.	43.2	43.2	32.8	32.6	35.0	57.9
Cash Flow	71.9	53.1	26.4	42.8	73.6	63.8

Ratio Analysis

	1994	1993	1992	1991	1990	1989
Curr. Ratio	1.3	1.4	1.5	2.1	2.1	1.8
% LT Debt of Cap.	6.4	6.8	9.5	14.3	21.4	23.3
% Net Inc.of Revs.	4.2	2.6	NM	1.6	5.4	5.2
% Ret. on Assets	8.0	4.6	NM	2.7	8.8	9.0
% Ret. on Equity	14.0	7.8	NM	4.5	15.5	16.1

Dividend Data —Cash has been paid each year since 1945.

Amt. of Div. $	Date Decl.	Ex-Div. Date	Stock of Record	Payment Date
0.130	Jul. 13	Aug. 29	Sep. 02	Oct. 15 '94
0.130	Oct. 06	Nov. 28	Dec. 02	Jan. 16 '95
0.130	Jan. 05	Feb. 27	Mar. 03	Apr. 15 '95
0.130	Apr. 04	May. 26	Jun. 02	Jul. 17 '95
0.130	Jul. 12	Aug. 30	Sep. 01	Oct. 16 '95

Data as orig. reptd.; bef. results of disc. opers. and/or spec. items. Per share data adj. for stk. divs. as of ex-div. date. E-Estimated. NA-Not Available. NM-Not Meaningful. NR-Not Ranked.

Office—855 E. Main Ave., Zeeland, MI 49464-0302. **Tel**—(616) 654-3000. **Chrmn**—R. Ruch. **Pres & CEO**—M. A. Volkema. **VP, CFO, Treas & Investor Contact**—James H. Bloem. **Dirs**—W. K. Brehm, E. D. Crockett, A. M. Fern, B. Griffiths, D. L. Nelson, C. W. Pollard, C. D. Ray, R. A. Reister, R. H. Ruch, M. A. Volkema. **Transfer Agent & Registrar**—First Chicago Trust Co. of New York, Jersey City, NJ. **Incorporated** in Michigan in 1905; reorganized in Delaware in 1970; reorganized in Michigan in 1981. **Empl**-6,453. **S&P Analyst:** Philip D. Wohl

STANDARD & POOR'S

STOCK REPORTS

Minnesota Power & Light

NYSE Symbol **MPL**

In S&P MidCap 400

24-AUG-95 **Industry:** Utilities-Electric

Summary: This moderate-sized electric utility serves much of Minnesota's mining industry and also operates a water utility and other, non-regulated subsidiaries.

Quantitative Evaluations

Recent Price • 27¾ | Yield • 7.4%
52 Wk Range • 28-24¼ | 12-Mo. P/E • 10.7

Outlook
(1 Lowest—5 Highest)
• **4-**

Fair Value
• **28**

Risk
• **Low**

Earn./Div. Rank
• **B+**

Technical Eval.
• **Bullish** since 6/95

Rel. Strength Rank
(1 Lowest—99 Highest)
• **46**

Insider Activity
• **NA**

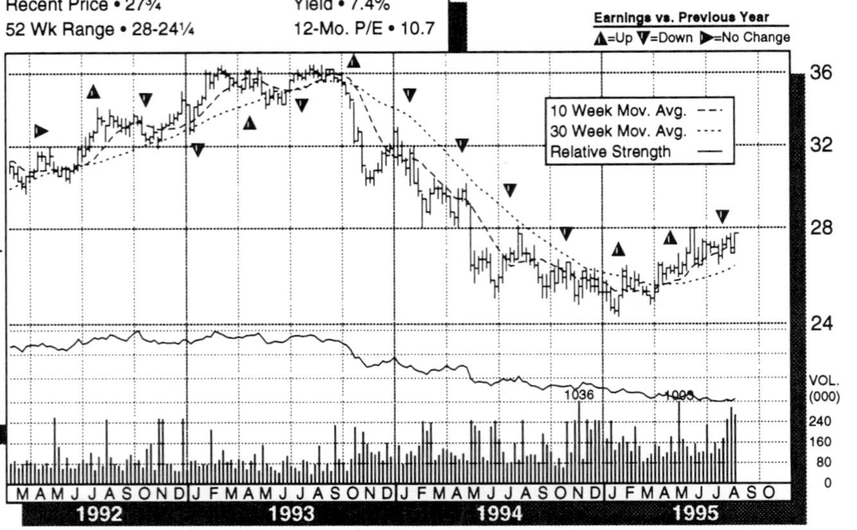

Business Profile - 24-AUG-95

Once exclusively an electric utility, MPL has in the past decade invested in a variety of non-electric businesses. MPL's goal was to lessen its dependence on its base of customers in taconite mining, which is tied to the cyclical steel industry. The company is also preparing for a more competitive future under FERC proposals. MPL's objective is that by the year 2000 each of its three core businesses -- electric, water and non-regulated investments -- will provide a third of its income.

Operational Review - 24-AUG-95

Total operating revenue and income rose 5.2% during the first six months of 1995, year to year, reflecting higher electric rates, tempered by increased maintenance and purchased power expenses. Prior to their sale, the company's paper and pulp businesses increased their contribution; securities investment income also advanced. Income from continuing operations soared 56% to $34,728,000, from $22,254,000.

Stock Performance - 18-AUG-95

In the past 30 trading days, MPL's shares have increased 2%, compared to a 0.51% rise in the S&P 500. Average trading volume for the past five days was 105,860 shares, compared with the 40-day moving average of 62,500 shares.

Key Stock Statistics

Dividend Rate/Share	2.04	Shareholders	27,000
Shs. outstg. (M)	31.3	Market cap. (B)	$0.860
Avg. daily vol. (M)	0.090	Inst. holdings	13%
Tang. Bk. Value/Share	21.20	Insider holdings	NA
Beta	0.60		

Value of $10,000 invested 5 years ago: $ 14,738

Fiscal Year Ending Dec. 31

	1995	% Change	1994	% Change	1993	% Change
Revenues (Million $)						
1Q	168.7	12%	150.6	18%	127.9	2%
2Q	147.3	-3%	152.3	21%	126.3	4%
3Q	—	—	155.8	24%	126.1	8%
4Q	—	—	179.1	43%	125.2	NM
Yr.	—	—	637.8	26%	505.5	3%
Income (Million $)						
1Q	25.46	172%	9.37	-47%	17.75	10%
2Q	10.92	-16%	12.97	-1%	13.12	-30%
3Q	—	—	15.20	-12%	17.35	23%
4Q	—	—	23.80	65%	14.41	-26%
Yr.	—	—	61.33	-2%	62.62	-9%
Earnings Per Share ($)						
1Q	0.87	190%	0.30	-53%	0.64	19%
2Q	0.36	-18%	0.44	-4%	0.46	-29%
3Q	—	—	0.51	-16%	0.61	33%
4Q	—	—	0.81	65%	0.49	-26%
Yr.	—	—	2.06	-6%	2.20	-5%

Next earnings report expected: late October

STANDARD & POOR'S
STOCK REPORTS

Minnesota Power & Light

24-AUG-95

Business Summary - 18-AUG-95

Minnesota Power & Light provides electric service in a 26,000 sq. mi. area of central and northeastern Minnesota. The service territory includes the wood-products industry and the Mesabi Iron Range, the major source of taconite pellets used in U.S. steelmaking. Through its Superior Water, Light & Power (SWL&P) subsidiary, MPL also provides electric, water and gas service in Superior, Wis., and adjacent areas.

Other major subsidiaries are engaged in coal mining, paper manufacturing and recycling, financial services, real estate and operation of water utility and wastewater treatment plants in Florida and the Carolinas. Electric utility operations contributed 62% of earnings in 1994, water operations 23%, and non-utility 15%.

As of December 31, 1994, the company was supplying retail electric service to 119,100 customers in 135 cities, towns and communities and outlying rural areas. It had power contracts that required MPL to have a certain amount of capacity available at all times with five large taconite and five paper producing customers, each requiring 10 mw or more.

The fuel mix in 1994 was 52% steam (mostly coal), 7% hydro and 41% purchased. Peak load in 1994 was 1,338 mw and system capability was 1,469 mw, for a capacity margin of 16%.

In November 1994, the Minnesota Public Utilities Commission issued an order granting the company an increase in annual electric operating revenue of $19 million, or 6.4%, with an 11.6% return on equity. Rates for large industrial customers will increase less than 4.0%, while the rate for small businesses will increase 6.5%. The rate increase for residential customers will be phased in over three years: 13.5% in 1995, and 3.75% each in 1996 and 1997. Negotiated savings on coal purchase and transportation costs are to be passed onto customers.

MPL's Southern States Utilities (SSU) subsidiary is the largest independent supplier of water and wastewater utility service in Florida. A subsidiary of SSU supplies sanitation service to Lehigh Acres in southwest Florida. Heater Utilites provides water and wastewater in the Carolinas.

Non-regulated activities include interests in Capital Re Corp., a financial guaranty reinsurance company; Lehigh Acquisition Corp., a southwest Florida real estate company; and Superior Recycled Fiber Industries, a Duluth recycled pulp production plant.

Important Developments

Jun. '95—MPL completed its merger with ADESA Corp. in a transaction valued at $167 million. MPL also sold its interests in Lake Superior Paper and Superior Fiber to Consolidated Papers for $118 million.

Capitalization

Long Term Debt: $568,725,000 (6/95).
Cum. Preferred Stock: $28,547,000.
Red. Ser. Preferred Stock: $20,000,000.

Per Share Data ($)

(Year Ended Dec. 31)

	1994	1993	1992	1991	1990	1989
Tangible Bk. Val.	20.76	21.14	19.89	19.26	19.16	20.30
Earnings	2.06	2.20	2.31	2.46	2.37	2.90
Dividends	2.02	1.98	1.94	1.90	1.86	1.78
Payout Ratio	98%	90%	84%	77%	78%	61%
Prices - High	33	36½	35	32½	27⅜	27⅝
- Low	24¾	30	29⅝	26	22¼	22⅞
P/E Ratio - High	16	17	15	13	12	10
- Low	12	14	13	11	9	8

Income Statement Analysis (Million $)

	1994	%Chg	1993	%Chg	1992	%Chg	1991
Revs.	638	26%	506	3%	489	1%	484
Depr.	50.2	15%	43.5	11%	39.1	5%	37.2
Maint.	NA	—	26.7	8%	24.8	-5%	26.1
Fxd. Chgs. Cov.	2.4	-14%	2.8	2%	2.8	NM	2.8
Constr. Credits	Nil	—	Nil	—	Nil	—	Nil
Eff. Tax Rate	26%	—	30%	—	27%	—	26%
Net Inc.	61.3	-2%	62.6	-9%	68.5	-9%	75.5

Balance Sheet & Other Fin. Data (Million $)

	1994	1993	1992	1991	1990	1989
Gross Prop.	1,666	1,602	1,553	1,489	1,415	1,424
Cap. Exp.	80.0	68.0	74.0	69.0	69.0	67.0
Net Prop.	1,080	1,066	1,048	1,016	977	999
Capitalization:						
LT Debt	601	596	542	534	520	517
% LT Debt	50	49	50	50	47	48
Pfd.	48.5	48.5	49.5	52.5	56.5	58.5
% Pfd.	4.00	4.00	4.60	5.00	5.20	5.40
Common	562	563	488	472	522	508
% Common	46	47	45	45	48	47
Total Cap.	1,491	1,492	1,447	1,426	1,441	1,417

Ratio Analysis

	1994	1993	1992	1991	1990	1989
Oper. Ratio	83.1	84.7	84.3	85.7	84.8	84.4
% Earn. on Net Prop.	10.1	7.3	7.4	7.0	7.3	7.4
% Ret. on Revs.	9.6	12.4	14.0	15.6	15.6	19.2
% Ret. On Invest.Cap	7.6	7.4	8.1	8.8	8.5	9.6
% Return On Com.Eqty	10.5	11.5	15.3	15.4	13.6	16.9

Dividend Data —Dividends have been paid since 1945. A dividend reinvestment plan is available.

Amt. of Div. $	Date Decl.	Ex-Div. Date	Stock of Record	Payment Date
0.505	Jul. 27	Aug. 09	Aug. 15	Sep. 01 '94
0.505	Oct. 26	Nov. 08	Nov. 15	Dec. 01 '94
0.510	Jan. 25	Feb. 09	Feb. 15	Mar. 01 '95
0.510	Apr. 26	May. 09	May. 15	Jun. 01 '95
0.510	Jul. 26	Aug. 11	Aug. 15	Sep. 01 '95

Data as orig. reptd.; bef. results of disc opers. and/or spec. items. Per share data adj. for stk. divs. as of ex-div. date. E-Estimated. NA-Not Available. NM-Not Meaningful. NR-Not Ranked.

Office—30 West Superior St., Duluth, MN 55802. **Tel**—(218) 722-2641. **Chrmn & CEO**—A. J. Sandbulte. **Pres**—E. L. Russell. **EVP & COO**—R. D. Edwards. **VP-Fin & CFO**—D. G. Gartzke. **Secy**—P. R. Halverson. **Investor Contact**—Timothy J. Thorp (218-723-3953). **Dirs**—M. K. Cragun, D. E. Evans, K. Hoffer, P. J. Johnson, P. F. McQueen, R. S. Nickoloff, J. I. Rajala, C. A. Russell, A. J. Sandbulte, N. Smith, B. W. Stender, D. C. Wegmiller. **Transfer Agents**—Co.'s office; Norwest Bank Minnesota. **Registrars**—First Bank, Duluth; Norwest Bank Minnesota. **Incorporated** in Minnesota in 1906. **Empl**-2,500. **S&P Analyst:** Michael C. Barr

STANDARD & POOR'S

STOCK REPORTS

Mirage Resorts

NYSE Symbol **MIR**
In S&P MidCap 400

28-JUL-95 **Industry:** Leisure/Amusement

Summary: This major gaming company, which owns four casino/hotels in Nevada, is pursuing growth possibilities both there, and in other existing or prospective markets.

S&P Opinion: Hold (★★★)

Recent Price • 28⅞
52 Wk Range • 33⅜-17½
Yield • Nil
12-Mo. P/E • 18.0

Quantitative Evaluations
Outlook
(1 Lowest—5 Highest)
• **3**
Fair Value
• **28¾**
Risk
• **Average**
Earn./Div. Rank
• **B-**

Technical Eval.
• **Bearish** since 4/95
Rel. Strength Rank
(1 Lowest—99 Highest)
• **52**
Insider Activity
• **NA**

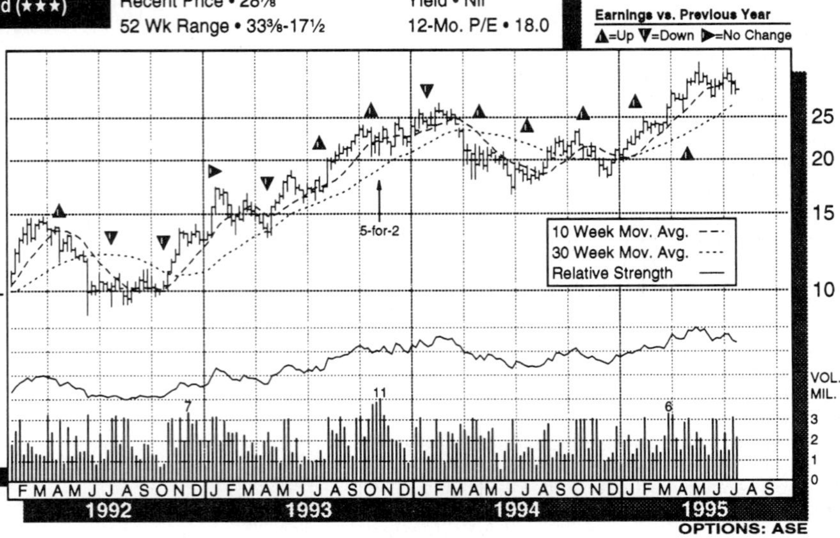

OPTIONS: ASE

Overview - 27-JUL-95

In 1995, we look for MIR's earnings to be helped by improved operating efficiencies from the Treasure Island casino/hotel, which opened in October 1993. However, earnings at MIR's flagship Mirage property have been restrained by a sizable refurbishing program which is scheduled to be completed in late August. Longer-term, two new MIR gaming projects (including a joint venture) are expected to open in Las Vegas in 1996-97. Other future expansion possibilities include a return by MIR to Atlantic City. Meanwhile, MIR has halted a proposal to spin-off ownership of its Golden Nugget properties (in downtown Las Vegas and Laughlin, Nev.) to shareholders.

Valuation - 27-JUL-95

In the year ahead, we expect MIR's stock to increasingly be valued based on earnings prospects for two new Las Vegas casino/hotels that are slated to debut in 1996-97. Also, the stock could benefit if MIR makes progress toward developing a large casino project in a new gaming market outside of Nevada. However, within the U.S., opportunities for such large-scale casinos look relatively slim. Since mid-1993, there has been little legislative movement toward legalization of non-Indian gaming in new states. Meanwhile, during the past several years, MIR's balance sheet has been strengthened, including repayment and refinancing of debt. We advise holding the speculative shares for capital gains.

Key Stock Statistics

S&P EPS Est. 1995	1.60	Tang. Bk. Value/Share	11.84
P/E on S&P Est. 1995	18.0	Beta	2.37
S&P EPS Est. 1996	1.75	Shareholders	12,500
Dividend Rate/Share	Nil	Market cap. (B)	$ 2.8
Shs. outstg. (M)	91.1	Inst. holdings	73%
Avg. daily vol. (M)	0.536	Insider holdings	NA

Value of $10,000 invested 5 years ago: $ 26,369

Fiscal Year Ending Dec. 31

	1995	% Change	1994	% Change	1993	% Change
Revenues (Million $)						
1Q	352.9	17%	300.5	40%	214.8	NM
2Q	299.1	-2%	306.4	33%	231.1	20%
3Q	—	—	336.4	47%	228.1	13%
4Q	—	—	311.0	11%	279.3	25%
Yr.	—	—	1,254	32%	953.3	14%
Income (Million $)						
1Q	51.66	121%	23.35	125%	10.40	-26%
2Q	28.62	-5%	30.16	68%	17.98	NM
3Q	—	—	39.51	129%	17.29	40%
4Q	—	—	31.72	NM	2.40	-78%
Yr.	—	—	124.7	159%	48.07	30%
Earnings Per Share ($)						
1Q	0.54	125%	0.24	82%	0.13	-41%
2Q	0.30	-6%	0.32	43%	0.22	—
3Q	E0.32	—	0.42	98%	0.21	26%
4Q	E0.44	—	0.34	NM	0.03	-79%
Yr.	E1.60	—	1.32	128%	0.58	9%

Next earnings report expected: mid October

Mirage Resorts

Business Summary - 26-JUL-95

This major gaming company (formerly Golden Nugget) operates three casino/hotels in Las Vegas and a casino/hotel in Laughlin, Nev.

In 1994, MIR's largest casino/hotel, The Mirage, accounted for the bulk of MIR's revenue and operating profit. This facility, which opened on the Las Vegas Strip in November 1989, has about 3,030 hotel rooms and suites and 95,500 sq. ft. of casino space. In October 1993, adjacent to The Mirage, MIR opened a pirate-theme casino/hotel, called Treasure Island, which has about 2,900 hotel rooms and about 75,000 sq. ft. of casino space. Also on the Las Vegas Strip, MIR plans to develop a large new casino/hotel project, called Bellagio, which would open in late 1997 or early 1998. In addition, MIR and joint venture partner Circus Circus Enterprises are planning to develop another casino/hotel, slated to open in 1996, near the Bellagio site.

In downtown Las Vegas, MIR's Golden Nugget casino/hotel has 1,907 hotel rooms and suites and about 38,000 sq. ft. of casino space. MIR also owns the Golden Nugget casino/hotel in Laughlin, Nev. The facility has about 300 hotel rooms and a 32,000 sq. ft. casino. In addition, MIR has been pursuing expansion opportunities outside of Nevada.

In April 1995, the amount available under MIR's revolving bank credit facility was increased to $1 billion. At May 12, 1995, there were borrowings of $115 million outstanding under the facility.

Important Developments

Jul. '95—MIR is proposing the development of a large casino/hotel project in Atlantic City's Marina area. The project, which would have about 2,000 hotel rooms, has an estimated cost of $500-to-$650 million. It could be open in 1998. MIR would be building on city land for which developers are being sought. Also, MIR has invited Circus Circus Enterprises (CIR) to develop an adjoining resort property. Previously, MIR owned and operated what is now known as The Grand casino/hotel in Atlantic City. That property was sold to Bally's Entertainment in 1987. Also, MIR has renamed a casino/hotel project planned for Las Vegas. Formerly known as Beau Rivage, it will now be called Bellagio, named after a village on Lake Como in Italy. This facility may open in 1997's second half. In addition, MIR and partner Circus Circus are planning another new Las Vegas casino/hotel resort nearby. This project, to be managed by CIR, would be targeted toward value-oriented vacationers, and would open in the summer of 1996.

Capitalization

Long Term Debt: $329,336,000 (3/95).
Exercisable Stock Options: To purchase 6.8 million shs. (12/93).

Per Share Data ($) (Year Ended Dec. 31)

	1994	1993	1992	1991	1990	1989
Tangible Bk. Val.	11.33	10.05	7.42	5.47	2.93	2.12
Cash Flow	2.30	1.50	1.46	1.92	1.80	0.10
Earnings	1.32	0.58	0.53	0.80	0.63	-0.51
Dividends	Nil	Nil	Nil	Nil	Nil	Nil
Payout Ratio	Nil	Nil	Nil	Nil	Nil	Nil
Prices - High	27	25	14⅞	12½	16½	13⅝
- Low	16⅝	13⅛	8¾	6½	5⅛	6½
P/E Ratio - High	20	43	28	16	26	NM
- Low	13	23	17	8	8	NM

Income Statement Analysis (Million $)

	1994	%Chg	1993	%Chg	1992	%Chg	1991
Revs.	1,254	32%	953	14%	833	1%	823
Oper. Inc.	331	39%	238	25%	191	-15%	225
Depr.	93.4	21%	77.0	19%	64.8	5%	61.8
Int. Exp.	52.0	-42%	89.0	-14%	103	-10%	114
Pretax Inc.	196	172%	72.0	57%	46.0	-32%	68.0
Eff. Tax Rate	36%	—	34%	—	19%	—	34%
Net Inc.	125	160%	48.0	30%	37.0	-18%	45.0

Balance Sheet & Other Fin. Data (Million $)

	1994	1993	1992	1991	1990	1989
Cash	47.0	57.0	143	194	134	93.0
Curr. Assets	180	197	260	278	243	171
Total Assets	1,641	1,705	1,580	1,316	1,315	1,159
Curr. Liab.	152	191	156	160	134	124
LT Debt	360	535	831	798	1,009	900
Common Eqty.	1,031	911	554	301	122	88.0
Total Cap.	1,481	1,506	1,416	1,150	1,175	1,032
Cap. Exp.	69.0	432	221	66.0	129	406
Cash Flow	218	125	102	106	85.0	4.0

Ratio Analysis

	1994	1993	1992	1991	1990	1989
Curr. Ratio	1.2	1.0	1.7	1.7	1.8	1.4
% LT Debt of Cap.	24.3	35.5	58.7	69.4	85.8	87.2
% Net Inc.of Revs.	9.9	5.0	4.4	5.4	3.3	NM
% Ret. on Assets	7.4	2.7	2.2	2.9	2.4	NM
% Ret. on Equity	12.8	6.1	7.7	19.3	28.3	NM

Dividend Data (The only cash dividend since 1972 was paid in 1978. The shares were split 5-for-2 in November 1993.)

Data as orig. reptd.; bef. results of disc. opers. and/or spec. items. Per share data adj. for stk. divs. as of ex-div. date. E-Estimated. NA-Not Available. NM-Not Meaningful. NR-Not Ranked.

Office—3400 Las Vegas Boulevard South, Las Vegas, NV 89109. **Tel**—(702) 791-7111. **Chrmn & Pres**—S. A. Wynn. **VP-Secy**—K. R. Wynn. **SVP-Fin, CFO, Treas, & Investor Contact**—Daniel R. Lee. **Dirs**—R. D. Bronson, G. S. Darman, G. J. Mason, R. M. Popeil, D. B. Wayson, M. B. Wolzinger, E. P. Wynn, K. R. Wynn, S. A. Wynn. **Transfer Agent & Registrar**—American Stock Transfer & Trust Co., NYC. **Incorporated** in Nevada in 1949. **Empl**-16,800. **S&P Analyst:** Tom Graves, CFA

STANDARD & POOR'S

STOCK REPORTS

Modine Manufacturing

NASDAQ Symbol **MODI**

In S&P MidCap 400

14-AUG-95 **Industry:** Auto parts/equipment

Summary: Modine makes heat-transfer products for original equipment manufacturers, the automotive aftermarket, and nonresidential building markets.

S&P Opinion: Hold (★★★)

Recent Price • 31½ | 52 Wk Range • 40½-25¼ | Yield • 1.9% | 12-Mo. P/E • 10.8

Quantitative Evaluations

Outlook (1 Lowest—5 Highest)
• **3+**

Fair Value
• **31⅞**

Risk
• **Average**

Earn./Div. Rank
• **A**

Technical Eval.
• **Bullish** since 7/94

Rel. Strength Rank (1 Lowest—99 Highest)
• **7**

Insider Activity
• **Unfavorable**

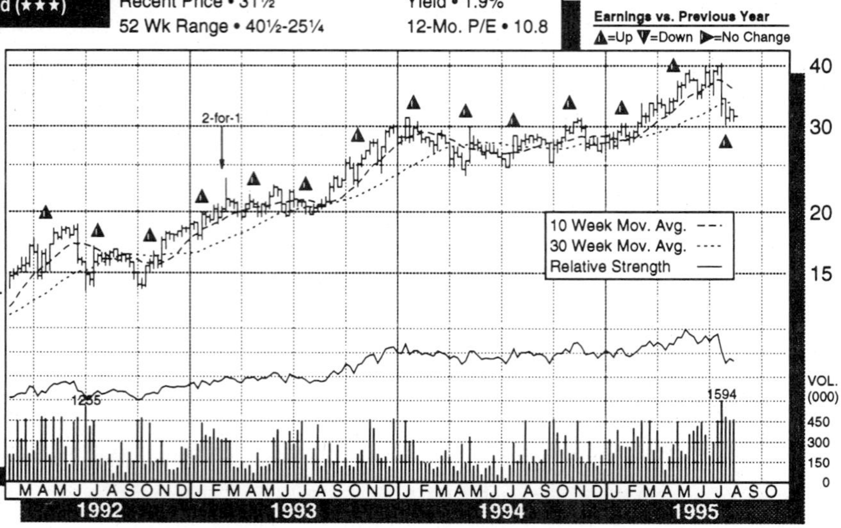

Overview - 14-AUG-95

Sales should rise 10% to 15% in 1995-96, on strong demand for original equipment and replacement radiators, oil coolers and air conditioning components in North America. Improving economic prospects in Europe should boost sales of recent acquisitions. Growth will be aided by market share gains and new customer programs as MODI continues to exploit its proprietary parallel-flow heat exchanger technology. Rapid growth areas for MODI's aluminum heat exchangers include applications in automotive air conditioning. Despite rapid consolidation and reduction of overhead costs, higher interest expense and rapid increases in raw materials costs will restrain the increase in earnings in 1995-96. Faster earnings growth should follow in 1996-97 as productivity increases and price adjustments are realized.

Valuation - 14-AUG-95

We continue the hold recommendation instituted on June 30 when the stock reached our target. A sharp drop followed in mid-July, due to a tempered EPS projection by MODI. MODI's fundamentals remain strong and we expect it to continue to exploit its proprietary technology. A recent patent extends the range of MODI's patents to air conditioning applications. However, we think the stock will be only an average performer near term. The stock should be held by long-term investors, as we expect MODI to resume its strong growth record as it obtains contracts for new applications and price adjustments on existing ones.

Key Stock Statistics

S&P EPS Est. 1996	2.40	Tang. Bk. Value/Share	9.23
P/E on S&P Est. 1996	13.1	Beta	0.56
S&P EPS Est. 1997	2.65	Shareholders	2,700
Dividend Rate/Share	0.60	Market cap. (B)	$0.936
Shs. outstg. (M)	29.7	Inst. holdings	39%
Avg. daily vol. (M)	0.174	Insider holdings	NA

Value of $10,000 invested 5 years ago: $ 38,097

Fiscal Year Ending Mar. 31

	1996	% Change	1995	% Change	1994	% Change
Revenues (Million $)						
1Q	239.2	15%	208.4	42%	147.2	10%
2Q	—	—	221.8	41%	157.0	9%
3Q	—	—	240.5	40%	172.4	17%
4Q	—	—	242.3	26%	193.1	32%
Yr.	—	—	913.0	36%	669.5	17%
Income (Million $)						
1Q	15.98	8%	14.83	50%	9.88	19%
2Q	—	—	16.80	44%	11.64	37%
3Q	—	—	17.41	64%	10.63	13%
4Q	—	—	19.40	77%	10.95	15%
Yr.	—	—	68.44	59%	43.09	28%
Earnings Per Share ($)						
1Q	0.52	6%	0.49	53%	0.32	14%
2Q	E0.58	—	0.55	41%	0.39	39%
3Q	E0.60	—	0.57	63%	0.35	40%
4Q	E0.70	—	0.63	80%	0.35	13%
Yr.	E2.40	—	2.24	59%	1.41	26%

Next earnings report expected: mid October

STANDARD & POOR'S

Stock Reports

Modine Manufacturing

14-AUG-95

Business Summary - 14-AUG-95

Modine Manufacturing Company is a maker of heat-transfer equipment, serving vehicular, industrial, commercial and building HVAC (heating, ventilating, air-conditioning) and refrigeration equipment markets. The company makes heat exchangers for various original equipment manufacturer applications and for sale to the automotive aftermarket (as replacement parts) and to a wide variety of building markets.

Sales in recent fiscal years were derived as follows:

	1994-95	1993-94
Radiators/radiator cores	42%	45%
Oil coolers	16%	15%
Vehicular condensers/evaporators	14%	12%
Charge air coolers	12%	11%
Building HVAC	9%	11%
Miscellaneous	7%	6%

Heat exchangers are supplied for cooling all types of engines, transmissions, auxiliary hydraulic equipment, air-conditioning components used in cars, trucks, farm and construction machinery and equipment, and heating and cooling equipment for residential and commercial building HVAC.

Shipment of replacement parts to automotive aftermarket customers is the largest single market, at 24% of sales, but original equipment shipments for cars and light trucks has grown in recent years and now accounts for 22% of sales. Export sales from the U.S. accounted for 14% of sales in the each of the last three years. In addition, foreign operations accounted for 27% of sales in fiscal 1994-95, up from 14% in 1993-94. Foreign operations should continue to grow faster than domestic shipments, due to greater growth opportunities overseas and modest acquisitions in foreign markets.

Important Developments

Jul. '95—MODI acquired the Signet Systems division of Equion Corp. With sales of $90 million, Signet supplies climate control systems and components to automotive, truck and off-highway vehicle markets in North America and Europe. Separately, MODI announced plans to build a new plant in South Carolina to manufacture parallel-flow oil coolers for vehicles. The plant will enter service in 1996.

May '95—MODI agreed to sell its copper tubing manufacturing business to National Tube Holding Co. Inc. Separately, MODI acquired its partner's 57% interest in Radinam which owns Mexpar, a Mexico City radiator manufacturer with 1994 sales of $17 million. MODI also acquired Radiadores Montana S.A., a Spanish manufacturer of aftermarket heat transfer equipment for on- and off-highway vehicles and industrial uses, with sales of $4.4 million.

Capitalization

Long Term Debt: $37,247,000 (6/26/95).

Per Share Data ($)

(Year Ended Mar. 31)

	1995	1994	1993	1992	1991	1990
Tangible Bk. Val.	9.23	7.42	7.31	7.05	6.64	6.05
Cash Flow	3.34	2.25	1.96	1.77	1.74	1.37
Earnings	2.24	1.41	1.12	0.94	1.02	0.84
Dividends	0.52	0.46	0.42	0.38	0.34	0.30
Payout Ratio	23%	33%	38%	40%	33%	35%
Cal. Yrs.	1994	1993	1992	1991	1990	1989
Prices - High	31¼	30¼	18⅞	14⅜	11½	11
- Low	23¾	17½	11¾	7⅞	8⅝	7¾
P/E Ratio - High	14	21	17	15	11	13
- Low	11	12	10	8	8	9

Income Statement Analysis (Million $)

	1995	%Chg	1994	%Chg	1993	%Chg	1992
Revs.	913	36%	670	17%	571	8%	527
Oper. Inc.	146	43%	102	23%	83.1	20%	69.2
Depr.	33.5	32%	25.4	NM	25.5	2%	25.1
Int. Exp.	6.4	6%	6.0	1%	5.9	-16%	7.1
Pretax Inc.	109	49%	73.0	35%	54.1	25%	43.4
Eff. Tax Rate	37%	—	41%	—	38%	—	36%
Net Inc.	68.4	59%	43.1	28%	33.7	20%	28.0

Balance Sheet & Other Fin. Data (Million $)

	1995	1994	1993	1992	1991	1990
Cash	32.7	38.5	33.6	18.8	27.0	27.0
Curr. Assets	340	272	221	202	212	189
Total Assets	590	510	405	383	398	328
Curr. Liab.	170	140	94.7	75.7	88.1	73.8
LT Debt	62.2	77.6	52.4	74.3	88.1	55.4
Common Eqty.	308	252	223	215	205	184
Total Cap.	383	339	287	308	310	254
Cap. Exp.	34.1	28.0	23.6	16.9	28.8	20.5
Cash Flow	102	68.5	59.2	53.1	51.8	41.2

Ratio Analysis

	1995	1994	1993	1992	1991	1990
Curr. Ratio	2.0	1.9	2.3	2.7	2.4	2.6
% LT Debt of Cap.	16.2	22.9	18.3	24.1	28.4	21.8
% Net Inc.of Revs.	7.5	6.4	5.9	5.3	6.3	5.8
% Ret. on Assets	12.4	9.4	8.5	7.2	8.4	8.2
% Ret. on Equity	24.4	18.1	15.3	13.4	15.7	14.3

Dividend Data (Cash has been paid in each year since 1959. A dividend reinvestment plan is available.)

Amt. of Div. $	Date Decl.	Ex-Div. Date	Stock of Record	Payment Date
0.130	Oct. 19	Nov. 21	Nov. 28	Dec. 08 '94
0.130	Jan. 18	Feb. 21	Feb. 27	Mar. 09 '95
0.150	May. 17	May. 23	May. 30	Jun. 08 '95
0.150	Jul. 19	Aug. 24	Aug. 28	Sep. 07 '95

Data as orig. reptd.; bef. results of disc. opers. and/or spec. items. Per share data adj. for stk. divs. as of ex-div. date. E-Estimated. NA-Not Available. NM-Not Meaningful. NR-Not Ranked.

Office—1500 DeKoven Ave., Racine, WI 53403-2552. **Tel**—(414) 636-1200. **Chrmn, Pres & CEO**—R. T. Savage. **SVP & Secy**—W. E. Pavlick. **VP-Fin & CFO**—A. D. Reid. **Treas**—R. M. Gunnerson. **Investor Contact**—Gerald J. Sweda. **Dirs**—R. J. Doyle, T. J. Guendel, F. W. Jones, D. J. Kuester. V. L. Martin, G. L. Neale, R. T. Savage, S. W. Tisdale, M. T. Yonker. **Transfer Agent & Registrar**—American Stock Transfer & Trust Co., NYC. **Incorporated** in Wisconsin in 1916. **Empl**-7,551. **S&P Analyst:** Joshua M. Harari, CFA

STANDARD & POOR'S

STOCK REPORTS

Molex Inc.

NASDAQ Symbol **MOLX**
In S&P MidCap 400

13-SEP-95

Industry: Electronics/Electric

Summary: Molex makes electrical and electronic devices which are sold primarily to OEMs in the computer, telecommunications, home appliance and home entertainment industries.

Quantitative Evaluations
Outlook
(1 Lowest—5 Highest)
• **4+**
Fair Value
• **45**
Risk
• **Low**
Earn./Div. Rank
• **A**

Technical Eval.
• **Bullish** since 5/94
Rel. Strength Rank
(1 Lowest—99 Highest)
• **53**
Insider Activity
• **NA**

Recent Price • 42
52 Wk Range • 44⅞-31

Yield • 0.2%
12-Mo. P/E • 27.1

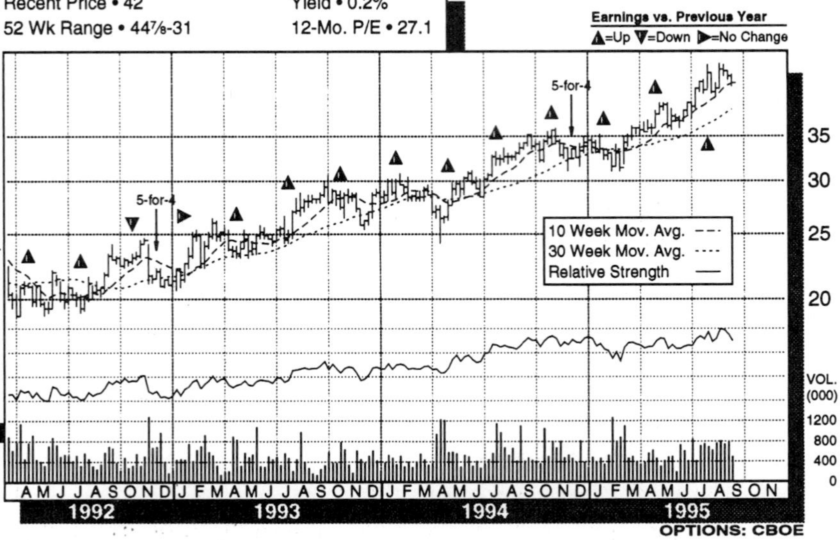

OPTIONS: CBOE

Business Profile - 12-SEP-95

The company has benefitted from the rising worldwide demand for electronic equipment. Products manufactured and sold outside the U.S. accounted for approximately 70% of sales in fiscal 1994 and fiscal 1993. Strong demand in Europe and the Far East have ignited sales growth in recent periods. Long-term, Molex should continue its successful strategy of expanding in both the fastest growing market segments and geographical regions. A 5-for-4 stock split is to be paid September 15.

Operational Review - 12-SEP-95

Revenue growth has been strong, aided by solid business conditions both in the U.S. and abroad. Gross margins continue to widen on the higher sales volume, a trend which should continue, reflecting not only a record backlog at the end of the fiscal 1995 but also the positive effects of the weaker dollar overseas. Earnings growth should continue at its robust pace as Molex expands through acquisitions and entrance into fast growing market segments.

Stock Performance - 08-SEP-95

In the past 30 trading days, MOLX's shares have declined 3%, compared to a 2% rise in the S&P 500. Average trading volume for the past five days was 121,350 shares, compared with the 40-day moving average of 143,115 shares.

Key Stock Statistics

Dividend Rate/Share	0.08	Shareholders	5,100
Shs. outstg. (M)	80.7	Market cap. (B)	$ 3.5
Avg. daily vol. (M)	0.147	Inst. holdings	23%
Tang. Bk. Value/Share	13.02	Insider holdings	NA
Beta	1.43		

Value of $10,000 invested 5 years ago: $ 33,954

Fiscal Year Ending Jun. 30

	1995	% Change	1994	% Change	1993	% Change
Revenues (Million $)						
1Q	268.9	15%	233.2	8%	215.0	15%
2Q	275.0	22%	224.9	11%	202.0	7%
3Q	305.8	28%	238.6	16%	206.0	7%
4Q	348.1	30%	267.4	14%	235.6	13%
Yr.	1,198	24%	964.1	12%	859.3	11%
Income (Million $)						
1Q	27.35	28%	21.38	—	—	—
2Q	27.91	30%	21.41	28%	16.71	2%
3Q	31.79	35%	23.60	34%	17.57	6%
4Q	36.98	30%	28.47	27%	22.44	14%
Yr.	124.0	31%	94.85	27%	74.66	11%
Earnings Per Share ($)						
1Q	0.34	26%	0.27	48%	0.18	-4%
2Q	0.35	29%	0.27	31%	0.21	NM
3Q	0.40	35%	0.30	32%	0.22	8%
4Q	0.46	28%	0.36	25%	0.29	16%
Yr.	1.55	29%	1.20	26%	0.95	10%

Next earnings report expected: mid October

Molex Inc.

Business Summary - 12-SEP-95

Molex Inc. designs, manufactures and distributes electrical and electronic devices such as terminals, connectors, planer cable, cable assemblies, interconnection systems, fiber-optic interconnection systems, backplanes and mechanical and electronic switches. With a market share of 4.7%, the company believes that it is the world's second largest connector maker.

Company products are sold primarily to OEMs and subcontractors and suppliers. In the U.S. and Canada, Molex sells through direct sales engineers, manufacturers' representatives and industrial distributors. Internationally, it sells primarily through distributors and its own sales organizations. Contributions by geographic area in fiscal 1994 were:

	Sales	Net Inc.
U.S.	30%	32%
Far East North	32%	42%
Far East South	18%	27%
Europe	17%	12%
Americas (non-U.S.)	3%	1%
Other	NM	-14%

The computer, business equipment and telecommunications markets account for about 47% of net revenue, with the balance coming from the home entertainment, home appliance automotive markets. Due to the volatile nature of these markets, Molex is uncertain as to what market groups will be its major customers in the future.

The company's products are typically used in computers, peripheral equipment, calculators, copiers, televisions, stereos, compact disc players, videotape recorders, camcorders, electronic games, microwave ovens, refrigerators, freezers, dishwashers, air conditioners, automobiles, farm equipment, electronic medical equipment, and security equipment.

Important Developments

Aug. '95—Directors renewed Molex's stock repurchase authorization for up to $50 million of common or Class A common shares through June 30, 1996.

Feb. '95—Molex acquired Mod-Tap W. Corp., a maker of interconnection products and systems for data and voice communications, in exchange for 974,988 shares of Class A common stock and $9.3 million in cash.

Capitalization

Long Term Debt: $8,914,000 (3/95).
Minority Interest: $1,890,000 (3/95).
Cl. A Common: 40,533,379 shs. ($0.05 par); nonvoting; conv. into com. stock under certain circumstances.
Cl. B Common: 94,255 shs. ($0.05 par).
The Krehbiel family controls 46% of com., 15% of Cl. A com., and 99.8% of Cl. B com.

Per Share Data ($) (Year Ended Jun. 30)

	1995	1994	1993	1992	1991	1990
Tangible Bk. Val.	NA	11.09	9.52	8.40	7.06	6.18
Cash Flow	NA	2.32	1.90	1.72	1.73	1.48
Earnings	1.55	1.20	0.95	0.86	0.83	0.79
Dividends	0.03	0.02	0.02	0.01	0.01	0.01
Payout Ratio	2%	2%	2%	1%	2%	2%
Prices - High	44⅞	33⅝	30⅝	25¼	23¼	16½
- Low	31	24¼	20⅝	18⅞	14⅛	10½
P/E Ratio - High	29	28	32	29	28	21
- Low	20	20	22	22	17	13

Income Statement Analysis (Million $)

	1994	%Chg	1993	%Chg	1992	%Chg	1991
Revs.	964	12%	859	11%	776	10%	708
Oper. Inc.	246	18%	208	16%	180	5%	171
Depr.	88.8	18%	75.0	11%	67.6	15%	58.7
Int. Exp.	Nil	—	Nil	—	NM	—	NM
Pretax Inc.	159	20%	133	14%	117	NM	118
Eff. Tax Rate	40%	—	44%	—	42%	—	45%
Net Inc.	94.9	27%	74.7	11%	67.5	4%	64.6

Balance Sheet & Other Fin. Data (Million $)

	1994	1993	1992	1991	1990	1989
Cash	229	186	157	150	144	124
Curr. Assets	587	500	436	395	355	316
Total Assets	1,139	962	850	710	607	541
Curr. Liab.	205	180	168	144	110	99
LT Debt	7.4	7.5	7.9	9.1	8.0	5.8
Common Eqty.	882	752	660	551	481	429
Total Cap.	905	772	678	563	493	439
Cap. Exp.	129	93.0	133	109	73.0	94.0
Cash Flow	184	150	135	135	116	109

Ratio Analysis

	1994	1993	1992	1991	1990	1989
Curr. Ratio	2.9	2.8	2.6	2.7	3.2	3.2
% LT Debt of Cap.	1.0	1.0	1.2	1.6	1.6	1.3
% Net Inc.of Revs.	9.8	8.7	8.7	9.1	10.4	10.1
% Ret. on Assets	9.0	8.2	8.6	9.8	10.9	11.1
% Ret. on Equity	11.6	10.6	11.1	12.5	13.7	14.1

Dividend Data —Cash dividends have been paid since 1976.

Amt. of Div. $	Date Decl.	Ex-Div. Date	Stock of Record	Payment Date
0.010	Oct. 22	Sep. 26	Sep. 30	Oct. 25 '94
5-for-4	Oct. 21	Mar. 27	Mar. 31	Apr. 25 '95
0.010	Oct. 21	Jun. 28	Jun. 30	Jul. 25 '95
5-for-4	Aug. 02	Sep. 18	Aug. 25	Sep. 15 '95
0.015	Aug. 02	Sep. 27	Sep. 29	Oct. 25 '95

Data as orig. reptd.; bef. results of disc. opers. and/or spec. items. Per share data adj. for stk. divs. as of ex-div. date. E-Estimated. NA-Not Available. NM-Not Meaningful. NR-Not Ranked.

Office—2222 Wellington Court, Lisle, IL 60532. **Tel**—(708) 969-4550. **Chrmn & CEO**—F. A. Krehbiel. **Pres**—J. H. Krehbiel, Jr. **VP, Treas & CFO**—J. C. Psaltis. **Secy**—L. A. Hecht. **Investor Contact**—Neil Lefort (708-527-4344). **Dirs**—M. J. Birck, R. H. Hayes, E. D. Jannotta, F. A. Krehbiel, F. L. Krehbiel, J. H. Krehbiel, Jr., D. G. Lubin, M. Naitoh, L. E. Platt, R. J. Potter. **Transfer Agent**—Harris Trust & Savings Bank of Chicago. **Reincorporated** in Delaware in 1972. **Empl**-8,100. **S&P Analyst:** Steven A. Jaworski

Montana Power

NYSE Symbol MTP In S&P MidCap 400

Price	Range	P–E Ratio	Dividend	Yield	S&P Ranking	Beta
Sep. 8'95	1995					
22¼	24⅛–21⅛	12	1.60	7.2%	B+	0.46

Summary

This company operates an electric and gas utility in Montana and derives a significant portion of its profits from coal, oil and gas and independent power projects. In August 1995, MTP said that it planned to seek up to a $38 million annual rate hike for its electric utility and $14 million for its gas utility. Profits in 1995's first quarter were reduced by about $0.05 a share, reflecting the settlement of a coal pricing dispute with Puget Sound Power & Light.

Current Outlook

Earnings for 1995 are estimated at $1.95 a share, up from the $2.00 reported for 1994.

The $0.40 quarterly dividend is not expected to be increased over the next 12 months.

Profits from electric utility operations should advance in 1995, reflecting higher rates and reduced power costs as MTP derives more electricity from hydrogeneration and wins a price concession at its Colstrip #1 and #2 power plants. Gas sales should increase, reflecting an expanding customer base and colder weather. Oil and gas profits may be flat, as output from recently acquired properties is offset by lower natural gas prices. Coal profits will be sharply lower, owing to the loss of a contract with Wisconsin Power & Light, price concession on a major contract and continued losses at Golden Eagle. Cogeneration profits will decline, as MTP obtains reduced project development fees.

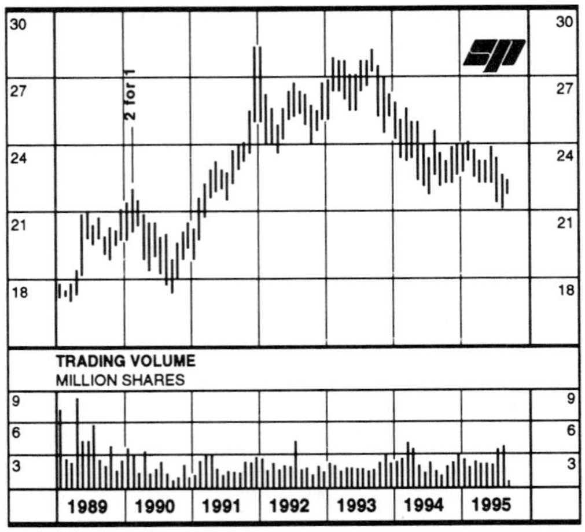

[1]Total Revenues (Million $)

Quarter:	1995	1994	1993	1992
Mar.	262	290	301	270
Jun.	206	217	220	201
Sep.	---	246	247	230
Dec.	---	303	307	296
	---	1,056	1,076	997

Revenues for 1995's first half fell 3.2%, year to year. Net income was down 16%. After preferred dividends, share earnings were $0.71, versus $0.88.

Common Share Earnings ($)

Quarter:	1995	1994	1993	1992
Mar.	0.61	0.70	0.76	0.80
Jun.	0.11	0.17	0.08	0.08
Sep.	E0.30	0.31	0.21	0.29
Dec.	E0.94	0.82	0.93	0.85
	E1.95	2.00	1.98	2.02

Important Developments

Aug. '95— MTP reported that it planned to file a general rate hike requesting up to $38 million in annual revenues for its electric utility (8.8%) and $14 million for its gas utility (13%).

Jun. '95— Construction was halted at the 248 mw Frederickson, Wash. power project after the Bonneville Power Administration (BPA) abrogated a contract to purchase the facility's power. Tenaska Washington Partners II (of which MTP has a 25.3% stake) have filed a 1.06 billion lawsuit against BPA.

Apr. '95— Profits for 1995's first quarter were reduced by some $0.05 a share related to the arbitrated settlement of a coal pricing dispute with Puget Sound Power & Light.

Next earnings report expected in late October.

Per Share Data ($)

Yr. End Dec. 31	1994	1993	1992	1991	1990	1989	1988	1987	1986	1985
Tangible Bk. Val.	**17.83**	17.36	16.82	16.40	15.78	16.12	16.00	15.87	15.89	15.26
Cash Flow	**2.91**	2.86	2.87	2.85	2.63	2.28	2.24	2.05	2.18	3.42
Earnings[2]	**2.00**	1.98	2.02	2.03	1.84	1.45	1.42	1.26	1.40	2.62
Dividends	**1.600**	1.580	1.540	1.480	1.420	1.380	1.350	1.340	1.255	1.000
Payout Ratio	**81%**	81%	77%	74%	78%	95%	95%	106%	90%	38%
Prices—High	**25⅞**	28¼	28⅜	28⅜	22	21⅛	18½	20⅞	21¾	17⅛
Low	**21¾**	24½	23⅝	18⅞	17⅜	17	15⅛	14¾	15¾	9½
P/E Ratio—	**13–11**	14–12	14–12	14–9	12–9	15–12	13–11	17–12	16–11	5–4

Data as orig. reptd. Adj. for stk. div. of 100% Feb. 1990. **1.** Incl. intersegment revs. prior to 1995. **2.** Bef. spec. item of +0.43 in 1986. E-Estimated.

Income Data (Million $)

Year Ended Dec. 31	[1]Revs.	Oper. Inc.	% Oper. Inc. of Revs.	Cap. Exp.	Depr.	Int. Exp.	Net Bef. Taxes	Eff. Tax Rate	[2]Net Inc.	% Net Inc. of Revs.	Cash Flow
1994	**541**	**176**	**32.5**	**137**	**48.1**	**46.2**	**168**	**32.2%**	**114**	**21.0**	**154**
1993	545	190	34.8	101	46.1	48.8	161	33.5%	107	19.7	149
1992	505	170	33.8	92	43.5	49.3	153	29.9%	107	21.2	147
1991	498	173	34.7	83	41.4	51.9	156	32.3%	106	21.2	143
1990	450	156	34.7	64	39.7	48.7	135	29.7%	95	21.1	131
1989	452	170	37.6	92	40.9	59.1	100	25.9%	74	16.5	112
1988	444	130	29.3	53	39.4	53.5	105	31.5%	72	16.2	107
1987	422	123	29.1	65	37.1	54.0	87	28.2%	62	14.8	96
1986	447	155	34.6	60	35.5	52.2	111	39.7%	67	15.0	99
1985	425	152	35.7	63	34.8	72.2	156	22.1%	122	28.6	149

Balance Sheet Data (Million $)

Dec. 31	Cash	Curr. Assets	Curr. Liab.	Curr. Ratio	Total Assets	% Ret. on Assets	Long Term Debt	Common Equity	Total Inv. Capital	% LT Debt of Cap.	% Ret. on Equity
1994	**21.6**	**295**	**313**	**0.9**	**2,513**	**4.6**	**589**	**956**	**2,017**	**29.2**	**11.3**
1993	11.6	257	313	0.8	2,386	4.5	572	911	1,945	29.4	11.5
1992	8.9	245	327	0.7	2,285	4.9	581	867	1,840	31.6	12.1
1991	4.7	237	288	0.8	2,085	5.2	603	831	1,686	35.8	12.5
1990	8.5	250	242	1.0	1,985	4.8	600	788	1,635	36.7	11.4
1989	8.7	236	216	1.1	1,946	3.8	563	794	1,606	35.0	8.9
1988	3.1	219	242	0.9	1,926	3.7	551	774	1,580	34.9	8.8
1987	4.5	192	226	0.9	1,863	3.3	562	748	1,555	36.1	7.8
1986	5.5	183	227	0.8	1,836	3.7	568	730	1,530	37.1	8.8
1985	29.4	168	235	0.7	1,743	6.8	581	677	1,435	40.5	17.7

Data as orig. reptd. **1.** Excl. nonutility opers. **2.** Bef. spec. item in 1986.

Business Summary

Contributions by segment to operating income (in million $) in recent years:

	1994	1993	1992
Electric utility	$98.1	$112.5	$104.6
Gas utility	29.6	30.9	22.3
Independent power	13.0	−1.3	4.5
Coal	45.6	43.1	48.2
Oil and gas	13.6	11.7	13.9
Other	1.2	0.5	0.1

MTP's electric utility serves 267,000 customers Montana. In 1994, 44% of the company's 1,601 mw of system capability was provided from coal, 27% from hydroelectric and 29% was purchased. Hydroelectric capability will increase 8.4% in late 1995 with the completion of the Thompson Falls project. Total firm sales in 1994 were 7.3 billion kilowatt hours (kwh), versus 7.1 billion kwh in 1993. An additional 3.0 billion kwh of power was sold to other utilities in 1994 (3.3 billion kwh). The average residential revenue per kwh in 1994 was 5.7 cents, versus 5.6 cents in 1993.

In 1994, MTP distributed 19.6 Bcf of natural gas to 131,000 customers, versus 24.1 Bcf in 1993. Gas transportation volumes in 1994 were 23.7 Bcf (18.3 Bcf). Average residential revenue per Mcf in 1994 was $4.64 ($4.35).

The independent power group has minority investments in six operating, non-regulated power porjects and two facilities under construction. MTP has a 50% stake in a firm that performs managerial and maintenance services for power plants.

In 1994 MTP produced 23.4 million tons of coal (20.7 million in 1993) from mines in Montana, Texas and Colorado. Some 83% of coal revenues in 1994 was derived from unaffiliated utilities. Proved coal reserves at 1994 year-end were 1.88 billion tons (substantially all held under lease). In 1994, MTP produced 4.93 million bbl. of oil and equivalents. Proved reserves at 1994 year-end were 232 Bcf of gas and 16 million bbl. of oil and gas liquids. MTP also provides telecommunications services to 10,278 customers in five western states.

Dividend Data

Dividends have been paid since 1935. A dividend reinvestment plan is available.

Amt of Divd. $	Date Decl.	Ex–divd. Date	Stock of Record	Payment Date
0.40	Sep. 27	Oct. 3	Oct. 10	Nov. 1'94
0.40	Dec. 13	Jan. 4	Jan. 10	Jan. 31'95
0.40	Mar. 29	Apr. 3	Apr. 7	Apr. 28'95
0.40	Jun. 27	Jul. 10	Jul. 12	Aug. 1'95

Capitalization

Long Term Debt: $608,359,000 (6/95).

Preferred Stock: $101,416,000.

Common Stock: 54,295,352 shs. (no par). Institutions hold about 31%. Shareholders of record: 40,956 (12/94).

Office—40 East Broadway, Butte, MT 59701-9989. **Tel**—(406) 723-5421. **Chrmn & CEO**—D. T. Berube. **VP & Secy**—P. K. Merrell. **VP-Fin & CFO**—J. P. Pederson. **Investor Contact**—Laure L. Riley. **Dirs**—T. H. Adams, D. T. Berube, A. F. Cain, R. D. Corette, K. Foster, R. P. Gannon, B. D. Harris, C. T. Hibbard, J. Jester, D. P. Lambros, C. Lehrkind III, J. P. Lucas, A. K. Neill, J. P. Pederson, G. H. Selover, N. E. Vosburg. **Transfer Agents**—Co.'s office; First Chicago Trust Co. of New York, NYC. **Registrars**—First Bank Montana, Butte; First Chicago Trust Co. of New York, NYC. **Incorporated** in Montana in 1961. **Empl**—3,686.

 Stephen R. Klein

STANDARD & POOR'S

STOCK REPORTS

Morrison Restaurants

NYSE Symbol **RI**
In S&P MidCap 400

22-SEP-95

Industry: Food serving

Summary: Operations of this diversified foodservice company include a rapidly expanding casual dining restaurant business, contract feeding operations, and a public cafeteria business.

S&P Opinion: Hold (★★★)

Recent Price • 19
52 Wk Range • 29¾-17⅝
Yield • 1.9%
12-Mo. P/E • 11.0

Quantitative Evaluations

Outlook (1 Lowest—5 Highest)
• **5⁻**

Fair Value
• **27½**

Risk
• **Average**

Earn./Div. Rank
• **A**

Technical Eval.
• **Neutral** since 8/95

Rel. Strength Rank (1 Lowest—99 Highest)
• **4**

Insider Activity
• **Neutral**

Earnings vs. Previous Year
▲=Up ▼=Down ▶=No Change

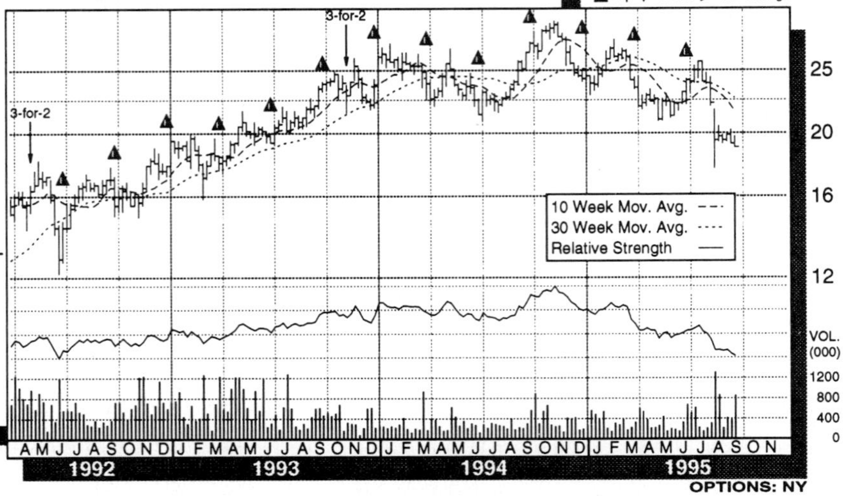

OPTIONS: NY

Overview - 22-SEP-95

In fiscal 1995-96, we expect RI's earnings to rise moderately from the $1.38 a share that would have been reported for 1994-95 if one-time items were excluded. We look for 1995-96 to have a relatively slow start, with soft summer sales restricting RI to a flattish profit comparison in the first quarter. During the full year, RI is likely to open at least 45 Ruby Tuesday units, plus about five restaurants in both the Mozzarella Grill and Tia's chains. Most of the Ruby Tuesday openings are likely to be in existing markets. This should allow for advertising efficiencies and other economies of scale, but there is a risk that new units will attract some sales from older restaurants.

Valuation - 22-SEP-95

Our enthusiasm for this stock is restrained by the prospect of relatively weak earnings comparisons for fiscal 1995-96's first quarter, and our skepticism about RI's ability to generate sustained 20% annual profit growth. However, based on the current valuation, we see some appeal to holding the stock. In the year ahead, we look for RI's large casual dining business to be facing difficult competitive conditions, including price discounting by fast-food chains. Also, with a number of RI units being located at or near malls or shopping centers, the general level of retail traffic is likely to have a bearing on sales. Both RI and other labor-intensive businesses may face some wage-cost pressure, as they seek to attract, train, and retain good employees.

Key Stock Statistics

S&P EPS Est. 1996	1.50	Tang. Bk. Value/Share	6.32
P/E on S&P Est. 1996	12.7	Beta	0.83
Dividend Rate/Share	0.35	Shareholders	6,900
Shs. outstg. (M)	34.5	Market cap. (B)	$0.630
Avg. daily vol. (M)	0.097	Inst. holdings	46%
		Insider holdings	NA

Value of $10,000 invested 5 years ago: $ 17,968

Fiscal Year Ending May 31

	1995	% Change	1994	% Change	1993	% Change
Revenues (Million $)						
1Q	241.3	-14%	282.2	14%	248.0	2%
2Q	252.5	-19%	310.4	10%	282.0	8%
3Q	272.0	-12%	310.0	9%	284.0	9%
4Q	269.4	-13%	310.9	9%	286.3	4%
Yr.	1,035	-15%	1,213	10%	1,100	6%
Income (Million $)						
1Q	24.51	NM	8.11	—	—	—
2Q	12.13	NM	12.04	16%	10.36	17%
3Q	13.14	7%	12.30	17%	10.55	15%
4Q	12.39	1%	12.24	19%	10.28	15%
Yr.	62.17	39%	44.68	17%	38.16	17%
Earnings Per Share ($)						
1Q	0.67	NM	0.22	18%	0.19	22%
2Q	0.34	6%	0.32	17%	0.27	14%
3Q	0.37	12%	0.33	21%	0.27	11%
4Q	0.35	6%	0.33	24%	0.27	14%
Yr.	1.73	44%	1.20	20%	1.00	15%

Next earnings report expected: late September

Morrison Restaurants

Business Summary - 22-SEP-95

Morrison Restaurants (formerly Morrison Inc.) is a diversified foodservice company with operations in more than 40 states. The company was founded in 1920 and had its first and only public stock offering in 1928. Currently, RI operates more than 330 casual dining restaurants, plus a large public cafeteria chain and various foodservice facilities.

Segment contributions in 1994-95, including some assets that have been divested or are being discontinued:

	Revs.	Profits
Casual dining restaurants	49.8%	51.7%
Public cafeterias, and contract feeding & management	50.2%	48.3%

As of June 3, 1995, RI's casual dining restaurants included 275 Ruby Tuesdays, whose menu includes fajitas, ribs, chicken, soups, and a salad bar. In 1994-95, RI added 57 Ruby Tuesday units and closed five. Also, RI had 44 Mozzarella Cafes, including restaurants that have been converted from the former Silver Spoon concept. In January 1995, RI acquired the Tia's Restaurants chain, which features Mexican and southwestern U.S. food. As of June 1995, there were 14 Tia's units open. Also, RI has been phasing out its L&N Seafood Grills concept, which previously had 41 units. L&N restaurants were to be converted into Ruby Tuesdays or Mozzarella Cafes, sold or closed.

RI is also a provider of contract food services, with an emphasis in the health care industry. In the summer of 1994, RI sold, for $100 million, certain contracts and assets related to education, business and industry accounts. Also, RI has a family dining business that included, as of June 1995, 151 public cafeterias, and 23 quick-service units.

Important Developments

Jun. '95—In fiscal 1994-95's fourth quarter, RI's pretax income was up 6.2%, year to year, despite lower comparable-unit sales weakness in the Ruby Tuesday, Mozzarella Grill, and family dining businesses. On a full-year basis, comparable-unit sales were up 0.9% at Ruby Tuesdays, and declined 1.9% and 1.1%, for Mozzarella Grill and family dining, respectively. Also, RI's first quarter profit included a net gain of $0.38 a share related to a gain on RI's sale of a portion of its contract food service business and a charge connected to the phasing out of its L&N restaurant business. However, excluding one-time items, we expect that the contract food-service divestiture was modestly dilutive to RI's overall earnings. Also, in January 1995, RI acquired the Tia's restaurant chain, which features Mexican and southwestern U.S. food.

Capitalization

Long Term Debt: $52,095,000 (6/3/95).

Per Share Data ($) (Year Ended May 31)

	1995	1994	1993	1992	1991	1990
Tangible Bk. Val.	6.32	6.26	6.01	5.51	4.91	4.60
Cash Flow	2.84	2.29	1.96	1.81	1.57	1.33
Earnings	1.73	1.20	1.00	0.87	0.71	0.59
Dividends	0.35	0.33	0.32	0.29	0.28	0.28
Payout Ratio	20%	28%	32%	34%	40%	47%
Cal. Yrs.	1994	1993	1992	1991	1990	1989
Prices - High	29¾	26¼	19⅞	13	12⅛	15⅛
- Low	20⅞	15⅞	11⅜	6	5⅜	10¼
P/E Ratio - High	17	22	20	15	17	26
- Low	12	13	11	7	8	17

Income Statement Analysis (Million $)

	1995	%Chg	1994	%Chg	1993	%Chg	1992
Revs.	1,033	-15%	1,210	10%	1,098	6%	1,039
Oper. Inc.	117	8%	108	12%	96.1	10%	87.5
Depr.	39.9	-2%	40.8	12%	36.5	4%	35.1
Int. Exp.	2.2	-3%	2.3	-19%	2.8	-33%	4.1
Pretax Inc.	105	47%	71.2	17%	60.9	18%	51.4
Eff. Tax Rate	41%	—	37%	—	37%	—	37%
Net Inc.	62.2	39%	44.7	17%	38.2	17%	32.7

Balance Sheet & Other Fin. Data (Million $)

	1995	1994	1993	1992	1991	1990
Cash	8.3	5.0	31.4	50.1	22.5	15.5
Curr. Assets	80.2	80.0	105	113	89.0	81.0
Total Assets	484	408	398	370	331	316
Curr. Liab.	125	123	103	90.4	76.8	70.2
LT Debt	52.1	9.5	13.1	35.9	38.0	35.7
Common Eqty.	245	221	220	204	181	176
Total Cap.	309	242	256	256	241	229
Cap. Exp.	131	90.3	63.0	37.8	43.9	55.9
Cash Flow	102	85.5	74.7	67.7	58.3	51.7

Ratio Analysis

	1995	1994	1993	1992	1991	1990
Curr. Ratio	0.6	0.6	1.0	1.3	1.2	1.1
% LT Debt of Cap.	16.9	3.9	5.1	14.0	15.8	15.6
% Net Inc.of Revs.	6.0	3.7	3.5	3.1	2.7	2.6
% Ret. on Assets	13.9	11.3	10.0	9.3	8.2	7.7
% Ret. on Equity	26.6	20.6	18.1	17.0	14.9	13.3

Dividend Data —Dividends have been paid since 1936. A dividend reinvestment plan is available.

Amt. of Div. $	Date Decl.	Ex-Div. Date	Stock of Record	Payment Date
0.087	Sep. 28	Oct. 07	Oct. 14	Oct. 31 '94
0.087	Jan. 04	Jan. 10	Jan. 17	Jan. 31 '95
0.087	Mar. 30	Apr. 07	Apr. 14	Apr. 28 '95
0.087	Jun. 30	Jul. 12	Jul. 14	Jul. 31 '95

Data as orig. reptd.; bef. results of disc. opers. and/or spec. items. Per share data adj. for stk. divs. as of ex-div. date. E-Estimated. NA-Not Available. NM-Not Meaningful. NR-Not Ranked.

Office—4721 Morrison Drive, Mobile, AL 36609. **Tel**—(205) 344-3000. **Chrmn**—E. E. Bishop. **Pres & CEO**—S. E. Beall III. **Vice Chrmn**—A. R. Outlaw. **SVP & Secy**—P. G. Hunt. **SVP-Fin & Investor Contact**—J. R. Mothershed. **Dirs**—C. L. Arnold, S. E. Beall III, E. E. Bishop, W. R. Bunn, J. B. McKinnon, A. R. Outlaw, B. F. Payton, D. Ratajczak, D. W. von Arx. **Transfer Agent & Registrar**—AmSouth Bank, N.A., Birmingham, Ala. **Incorporated** in Florida in 1954; reincorporated in Delaware in 1987. **Empl**-36,000. **S&P Analyst:** Tom Graves, CFA

STANDARD & POOR'S

STOCK REPORTS

Multimedia, Inc.

NASDAQ Symbol **MMEDC**

In S&P MidCap 400

17-OCT-95 **Industry:** Broadcasting

Summary: This diversified media company agreed in July 1995 to be acquired by Gannett Co., Inc. for $45.25 a share.

S&P Opinion: Hold (★★★)	Recent Price • 43⅞	Yield • Nil
	52 Wk Range • 44⅛-25¾	12-Mo. P/E • 18.9

Quantitative Evaluations

Outlook (1 Lowest—5 Highest)
• **1+**

Fair Value
• **30½**

Risk
• **Average**

Earn./Div. Rank
• **B+**

Technical Eval.
• **Bearish** since 9/95

Rel. Strength Rank (1 Lowest—99 Highest)
• **67**

Insider Activity
• **Neutral**

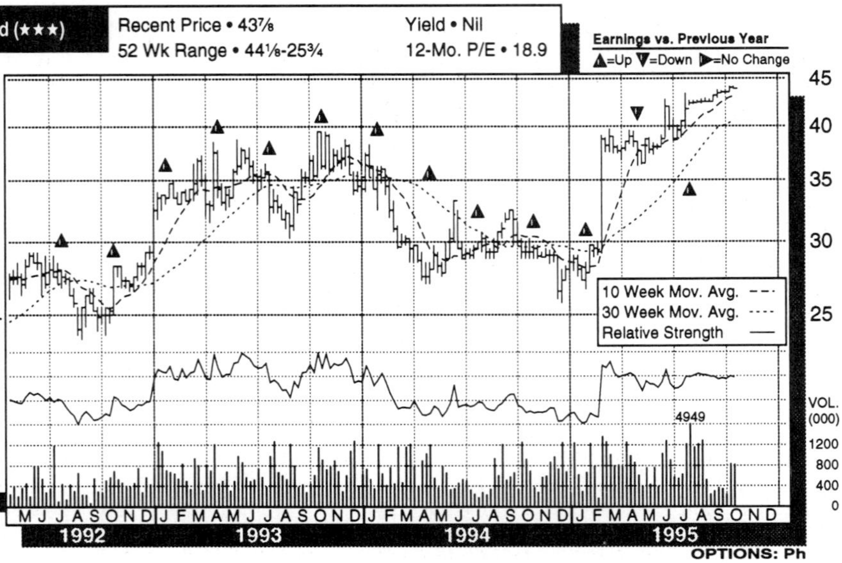

Overview - 14-OCT-95

We expect revenues to rise moderately through 1996, reflecting continued gains in newspaper, television and radio advertising, as well as growth in the cable and security businesses. Advertising will be boosted by Olympics and national election spending plus a generally healthy advertising market. Broadcast television in particular will benefit from four of the five stations' affiliation with the top-rated NBC network. Margins, overall, will be helped by cost efficiencies. But ongoing start-up losses related to NewsTalk Television, the new cable programming network, and the negative impact on revenues and profitability of heightened competition among talk shows will continue to hurt the entertainment division.

Valuation - 14-OCT-95

We recently downgraded our opinion on Multimedia to 'hold' inasmuch as the current stock price is within striking distance of the $45.25 per-share buyout bid that directors of Multimedia and Gannett Co. agreed to in July. A partnership comprised of Ellis Communications and Kelso Co. have not to date raised their initial $41 buyout offer made in June, nor have other suitors stepped forward. Thus, it appears likely that no competing bids will be forthcoming. Shareholders are expected to approve the Gannett offer at a meeting to be held in mid November. The companies expect to close the transaction as soon as possible following receipt of regulatory approvals.

Key Stock Statistics

S&P EPS Est. 1995	2.10	Tang. Bk. Value/Share	NM
P/E on S&P Est. 1995	20.9	Beta	1.23
S&P EPS Est. 1996	2.35	Shareholders	1,300
Dividend Rate/Share	Nil	Market cap. (B)	$ 1.7
Shs. outstg. (M)	37.9	Inst. holdings	75%
Avg. daily vol. (M)	0.113	Insider holdings	NA

Value of $10,000 invested 5 years ago: $ 13,965

Fiscal Year Ending Dec. 31

	1995	% Change	1994	% Change	1993	% Change
Revenues (Million $)						
1Q	156.4	7%	146.4	2%	144.1	14%
2Q	170.3	7%	159.2	-3%	163.5	15%
3Q	—	—	152.6	NM	153.3	9%
4Q	—	—	172.2	NM	173.7	4%
Yr.	—	—	630.5	NM	634.6	10%
Income (Million $)						
1Q	14.85	-14%	17.33	14%	15.20	47%
2Q	21.17	9%	19.44	6%	18.27	16%
3Q	—	—	30.47	NM	30.24	101%
4Q	—	—	22.78	4%	21.81	13%
Yr.	—	—	90.03	5%	85.52	41%
Earnings Per Share ($)						
1Q	0.39	-13%	0.45	13%	0.40	43%
2Q	0.54	6%	0.51	6%	0.48	14%
3Q	E0.52	-35%	0.80	1%	0.79	97%
4Q	E0.65	10%	0.59	5%	0.56	10%
Yr.	E2.10	-11%	2.35	5%	2.23	39%

Next earnings report expected: late October

Multimedia, Inc.

Business Summary - 14-OCT-95

Contributions by business segment in 1994 were:

	Revs.	Profit
Cable	26%	26%
Newspapers	24%	22%
Entertainment	23%	25%
Broadcasting	23%	25%
Security	4%	2%

The company owns five network-affiliated VHF TV stations, in Cincinnati, Ohio, St. Louis, Mo., Knoxville, Tenn., Cleveland, Ohio (51% owned), and Macon, Ga., and radio stations in Macon, Ga. and Spartanburg, S.C. During 1994, the company sold radio stations in Greenville, S.C., Shreveport, La., and Milwaukee, Wis.

A subsidiary produces and syndicates TV programs, including the Phil Donahue, Sally Jessy Raphael, Jerry Springer and Rush Limbaugh shows. The Susan Powter and Dennis Prager shows, as well as NewsTalk Television (NTT), a 24-hour cable service, premiered in the fall of 1994. Start-up costs in 1994 related to NTT in 1994 were $4.5 million (net), or $0.12 per share. The negative cash flow for 1995 is anticipated to be roughly $15.3 million. Positive cash flow is presumed by 1998.

The cable television division had over 450,000 subscribers at the end of June, 1995, in Kansas, Oklahoma, Indiana, Illinois and North Carolina. A five-year, $150-million system upgrade program was begun in 1993. The investment will allow the company to replace the coaxial wire in its cable systems with fiber and will include the integration of digital compression and the installation of interactive converter boxes in the homes of roughly 50% of Multimedia's cable subscribers. Multimedia Security Service monitors and services securities systems for over 76,000 customers, placing it among the 20 largest home security providers in the country.

Multimedia publishes the only daily and Sunday newspapers in 11 markets, and also publishes 49 nondaily publications.

Important Developments

Jul. '95—The company agreed to be acquired by Gannett Co., Inc. for over $1.71 billion cash (or $45.25 a share), plus the assumption of debt. A shareholder vote is scheduled for mid November. Closing is also subject to regulatory approvals.

Jan. '95—Multimedia's 1994 operating results included $27.6 million in gains from the sale of its wireless cable systems and three radio properties. A net loss of $1.8 million ($0.05) was recorded on the closing of its made-for-television production business.

Capitalization

Long Term Debt: $548,001,000 (6/95).
Minority Interest: $20,321,000.

Per Share Data ($)

(Year Ended Dec. 31)

	1994	1993	1992	1991	1990	1989
Tangible Bk. Val.	-8.48	-11.53	-15.21	-17.25	-19.05	-17.79
Cash Flow	3.75	3.54	2.75	2.33	2.14	1.83
Earnings	2.35	2.23	1.61	1.30	1.32	1.04
Dividends	Nil	Nil	Nil	Nil	Nil	Nil
Payout Ratio	Nil	Nil	Nil	Nil	Nil	Nil
Prices - High	38¼	39½	32⅜	30	32	36
- Low	25¾	30¼	22⅜	19⅜	17½	24⅝
P/E Ratio - High	16	18	20	23	24	35
- Low	11	14	14	15	13	24

Income Statement Analysis (Million $)

	1994	%Chg	1993	%Chg	1992	%Chg	1991
Revs.	630	NM	635	10%	577	10%	524
Oper. Inc.	243	3%	235	9%	216	11%	194
Depr.	53.4	6%	50.2	17%	43.0	12%	38.4
Int. Exp.	59.0	-5%	62.0	-14%	72.0	-9%	79.0
Pretax Inc.	156	26%	124	23%	101	31%	77.1
Eff. Tax Rate	42%	—	31%	—	41%	—	39%
Net Inc.	90.0	5%	85.5	41%	60.5	25%	48.4

Balance Sheet & Other Fin. Data (Million $)

	1994	1993	1992	1991	1990	1989
Cash	6.2	11.0	4.6	6.7	5.1	3.4
Curr. Assets	139	134	115	112	105	94.0
Total Assets	684	655	628	556	536	404
Curr. Liab.	143	104	91.0	101	89.0	76.0
LT Debt	542	665	744	743	789	746
Common Eqty.	-77.0	-177	-290	-374	-432	-486
Total Cap.	538	549	536	451	442	325
Cap. Exp.	83.0	47.4	37.5	32.2	28.5	25.5
Cash Flow	143	136	103	86.8	79.3	68.2

Ratio Analysis

	1994	1993	1992	1991	1990	1989
Curr. Ratio	1.0	1.3	1.3	1.1	1.2	1.2
% LT Debt of Cap.	100.8	121.1	138.0	164.9	178.6	229.5
% Net Inc.of Revs.	14.3	13.5	10.5	9.2	10.1	8.4
% Ret. on Assets	13.4	13.3	10.0	8.8	10.3	9.5
% Ret. on Equity	NM	NM	NM	NM	NM	NM

Dividend Data —Cash dividends were suspended in the fourth quarter of 1985. A shareholder rights plan was adopted in 1989. The shares were split three-for-one in April 1991.

Data as orig. reptd.; bef. results of disc. opers. and/or spec. items. Per share data adj. for stk. divs. as of ex-div. date. E-Estimated. NA-Not Available. NM-Not Meaningful. NR-Not Ranked.

Office—305 South Main St., P.O. Box 1688, Greenville, SC 29602. **Tel**—(803) 298-4373. **Chrmn & CEO**—D. Sbarra. **Pres & COO**—D. J. Greenlaw. **SVP-Fin & CFO**—R. E. Hamby, Jr. **Treas**—A. D. Austin. **Secy**—D. L. Freeman. **VP & Investor Contact**—Markeeta L. McNatt. **Dirs**—G. H. V. Cecil, R. T. Eskew, D. L. Freeman, D. J. Greenlaw, D. Hagy, R. E. Hamby, Jr., J. T. LaMacchia, L. G. McCraw, D. P. Ramsaur, D. S. Sbarra, E. P. Stall, W. C. Stutt. **Transfer Agent & Registrar**—Wachovia National Bank of North Carolina, Winston-Salem. **Incorporated** in South Carolina in 1968. **Empl**-3,700. **S&P Analyst:** William H. Donald

STANDARD & POOR'S STOCK REPORTS

Murphy Oil

NYSE Symbol **MUR**
In S&P MidCap 400

04-OCT-95 **Industry:** Oil and Gas

Summary: Murphy Oil is an integrated oil company, with exploration, production, refining and marketing interests in the U.S. and worldwide.

S&P Opinion: Hold (★★★)

Recent Price • 40
52 Wk Range • 49⅛-38⅜
Yield • 3.3%
12-Mo. P/E • 19.5

Quantitative Evaluations
Outlook
(1 Lowest—5 Highest)
• **1-**
Fair Value
• **31⅜**
Risk
• **Low**
Earn./Div. Rank
• **B**

Technical Eval.
• **Bullish** since 12/94
Rel. Strength Rank
(1 Lowest—99 Highest)
• **27**
Insider Activity
• **NA**

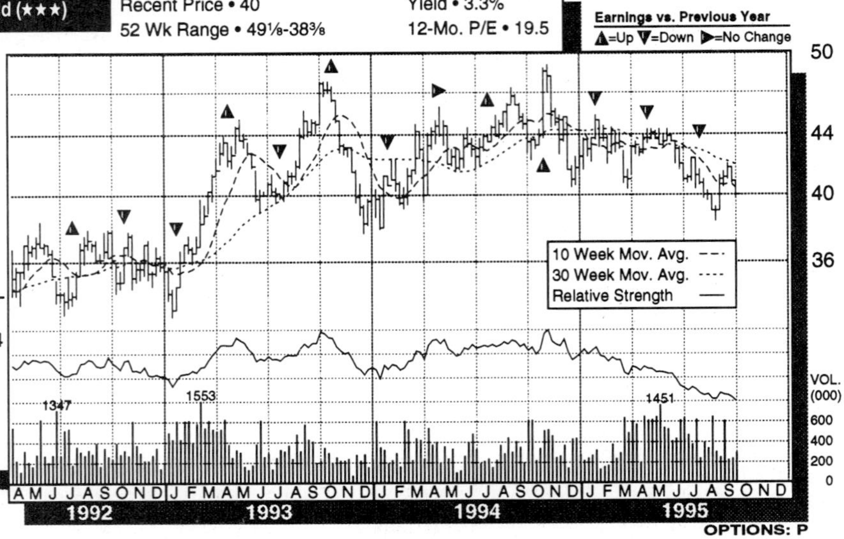

Overview - 04-OCT-95

Revenues should show modest improvement in the near-term, on increased commodity and refined product volumes. Near term results will be restrained by lower oil prices caused by fears that OPEC will soon increase production levels, however. Longer-term, MUR is well situated to capitalize upon growing U.S. and foreign natural gas markets. Yet, gas markets in the U.S. and Europe look oversupplied at the moment, and Murphy will likely curtail production for the remainder of the year, absent a pickup in product price realizations. Profitability should improve marginally over first quarter levels in 1995 when refining margins were abysmal. May saw a peak in refining margins which have turned down since then. We are forecasting that increased demand should lift refining and marketing results during 1996. A relatively low debt burden makes acquisitions likely.

Valuation - 04-OCT-95

The shares have trended lower over the past several weeks, coinciding with the deterioration in oil fundamentals. We expect flat to slightly lower gas prices to partially offset the earnings impact of a drop in oil prices in the near term. And with refining fundamentals improving, we believe the shares, which are fully valued on a P/E and cash flow basis, will continue to trade at current levels for the remainder of 1995. Looking forward to 1996, we are more optimistic, with a number of important projects expected to lead to higher oil and gas volumes.

Key Stock Statistics

S&P EPS Est. 1995	1.40	Tang. Bk. Value/Share	28.78
P/E on S&P Est. 1995	28.6	Beta	0.38
S&P EPS Est. 1996	2.00	Shareholders	4,800
Dividend Rate/Share	1.30	Market cap. (B)	$ 1.8
Shs. outstg. (M)	44.8	Inst. holdings	59%
Avg. daily vol. (M)	0.074	Insider holdings	NA

Value of $10,000 invested 5 years ago: $ 11,554

Fiscal Year Ending Dec. 31

	1995	% Change	1994	% Change	1993	% Change
Revenues (Million $)						
1Q	421.2	3%	409.5	3%	398.5	11%
2Q	449.0	3%	434.8	1%	430.3	5%
3Q	—	—	492.8	17%	420.0	1%
4Q	—	—	431.4	2%	422.4	-6%
Yr.	—	—	1,768	6%	1,671	2%
Income (Million $)						
1Q	16.03	-32%	23.69	NM	23.84	NM
2Q	20.56	-25%	27.52	21%	22.69	-17%
3Q	—	—	37.27	85%	20.18	37%
4Q	—	—	18.16	-10%	20.07	-7%
Yr.	—	—	106.6	23%	86.78	38%
Earnings Per Share ($)						
1Q	0.36	-32%	0.53	NM	0.53	NM
2Q	0.46	-25%	0.61	20%	0.51	-16%
3Q	E0.22	-73%	0.83	84%	0.45	36%
4Q	E0.36	-10%	0.40	-11%	0.45	-6%
Yr.	E1.40	-41%	2.37	22%	1.94	39%

Next earnings report expected: late October

Murphy Oil

Business Summary - 04-OCT-95

Murphy Oil is an integrated crude oil and natural gas company operating in the U.S. and overseas, and has interests in farming, timber and real estate. Profits and losses (million $) in recent years were derived as follows:

	1994	1993
U.S. exploration/production	$18.1	$32.7
Foreign exploration/production	33.5	18.6
U.S. refining/marketing	17.7	7.2
Foreign refining/marketing	12.5	20.3
Farm, real estate & timber	17.5	13.2
Corporate	7.4	-5.2

Exploration and production are conducted in the U.S., onshore and offshore, and throughout the world, most notably in the U.K. sector of the North Sea, Canada, Ecuador, Spain, Gabon, Peru, and China.

In 1994, crude oil and liquids production averaged 51,328 bbl. a day (34,311 b/d in 1993), of which 24% was from the U.S., with 26% coming from the U.K.; natural gas sales were 256,258 Mcf a day (274,908), of which 76% came from the U.S. MUR owns two U.S. refineries and a 30% share in a U.K. refinery. Crude capacity of refineries at December 31, 1994 was 167,400 b/d. Oil processed in 1994 amounted to 149,613 b/d (147,431), and petroleum product sales were 161,130 b/d (146,042). Principal wholesale and retail markets are the U.S., Western Europe and Canada.

Proved reserves at 1994 year-end were estimated at 220.3 million bbl. of crude oil (202.4 million a year earlier), and 643.6 million Mcf of natural gas (653.5 million).

Important Developments

Sep. '95—Murphy Oil Corporation announced several management changes. Woods W. Allen was made responsible for all worldwide exploration activities other than those in Canada. John C. Higgins was also made responsible for all U.S. exploration activities, both onshore and offshore, while Martin Whitely has been placed in charge of all exploration activities in the United Kingdom. Both Higgins and Whitely will report to Allen.

Aug. '95—The company announced third quarter results will be impacted by an unsuccessful attempt to complete a sidetrack well in Mobile Block 908. Costs related to the project of $13 million (after-tax) will be included in the third quarter's results.

Capitalization

Long Term Debt: $172,036,000 (6/95), incl. $150,348,000 nonrecourse debt of a subsidiary.

Per Share Data ($)

(Year Ended Dec. 31)

	1994	1993	1992	1991	1990	1989
Tangible Bk. Val.	28.31	27.28	26.76	26.71	25.76	22.71
Cash Flow	7.24	6.13	5.44	4.63	9.44	7.83
Earnings	2.37	1.94	1.40	-0.24	3.00	1.37
Dividends	1.30	1.25	1.20	1.20	1.00	1.00
Payout Ratio	55%	64%	86%	NM	33%	73%
Prices - High	49⅛	47⅞	38⅜	40¼	47½	44¼
- Low	37⅞	33	32⅜	31⅝	34	29⅝
P/E Ratio - High	21	25	27	NM	16	32
- Low	16	17	23	NM	11	22

Income Statement Analysis (Million $)

	1994	%Chg	1993	%Chg	1992	%Chg	1991
Revs.	1,738	6%	1,637	NM	1,631	2%	1,601
Oper. Inc.	347	20%	290	37%	212	-14%	247
Depr.	218	16%	188	3%	182	-5%	192
Int. Exp.	12.4	63%	7.6	-56%	17.1	-45%	31.0
Pretax Inc.	157	17%	134	94%	69.0	130%	30.0
Eff. Tax Rate	32%	—	35%	—	9.50%	—	124%
Net Inc.	107	23%	87.0	38%	63.0	NM	-10.0

Balance Sheet & Other Fin. Data (Million $)

	1994	1993	1992	1991	1990	1989
Cash	71.0	141	378	242	275	243
Curr. Assets	519	543	799	671	724	618
Total Assets	2,312	2,169	1,937	2,175	2,137	2,075
Curr. Liab.	440	413	427	515	627	482
LT Debt	172	109	25.0	193	208	330
Common Eqty.	1,271	1,222	1,200	1,201	873	770
Total Cap.	1,584	1,449	1,269	1,452	1,329	1,362
Cap. Exp.	414	570	191	185	187	165
Cash Flow	325	275	245	183	320	266

Ratio Analysis

	1994	1993	1992	1991	1990	1989
Curr. Ratio	1.2	1.3	1.9	1.3	1.2	1.3
% LT Debt of Cap.	10.9	7.5	2.0	13.3	15.6	24.3
% Net Inc.of Revs.	6.1	5.3	3.8	NM	5.1	2.8
% Ret. on Assets	4.8	4.2	3.1	NM	4.8	2.2
% Ret. on Equity	8.6	7.2	5.2	NM	12.4	6.1

Dividend Data —Dividends have been paid since 1961. A "poison pill" stock purchase right was issued in 1989.

Amt. of Div. $	Date Decl.	Ex-Div. Date	Stock of Record	Payment Date
0.325	Oct. 05	Nov. 08	Nov. 15	Dec. 01 '94
0.325	Feb. 01	Feb. 09	Feb. 15	Mar. 01 '95
0.325	Apr. 05	May. 09	May. 15	Jun. 01 '95
0.325	Aug. 02	Aug. 14	Aug. 16	Sep. 01 '95

Data as orig. reptd.; bef. results of disc. opers. and/or spec. items. Per share data adj. for stk. divs. as of ex-div. date. E-Estimated. NA-Not Available. NM-Not Meaningful. NR-Not Ranked.

Office—200 Peach St., El Dorado, AR 71731-7000. **Tel**—(501) 862-6411. **Fax**—(501) 862-9057. **Chrmn**—R. M. Murphy. **Pres & CEO**—C. P. Deming. **Treas.**—O. F. Vaughan. **Secy**—W. B. Rowe. **Contr & Investor Contact**—Ronald W. Herman. **Dirs**—B. R. R. Butler, C. P. Deming, H. R. Hart, V. T. Hughes, Jr., J. W. McNutt, C. H. Murphy, Jr., M. W. Murphy, R. M. Murphy, W. C. Nolan, Jr., C. G. Theus, L. C. Webster. **Transfer Agent & Registrar**—Harris Trust Co. of New York, NYC. **Incorporated** in Delaware in 1963. **Empl**-1,767. **S&P Analyst:** Raymond J. Deacon

STANDARD & POOR'S

STOCK REPORTS

Mylan Laboratories

NYSE Symbol **MYL**
In S&P MidCap 400

30-AUG-95 **Industry:** Drugs-Generic and OTC

Summary: This leading manufacturer of generic pharmaceuticals produces more than 80 generic drugs in varying strengths.

S&P Opinion: Accumulate (★★★★)
Recent Price • 22¼
52 Wk Range • 23¼-16
Yield • 0.6%
12-Mo. P/E • 20.8

Quantitative Evaluations
Outlook
(1 Lowest—5 Highest)
• **5+**
Fair Value
• **30⅜**
Risk
• **Average**
Earn./Div. Rank
• **A-**

Technical Eval.
• **Bullish** since 8/93
Rel. Strength Rank
(1 Lowest—99 Highest)
• **94**
Insider Activity
• **NA**

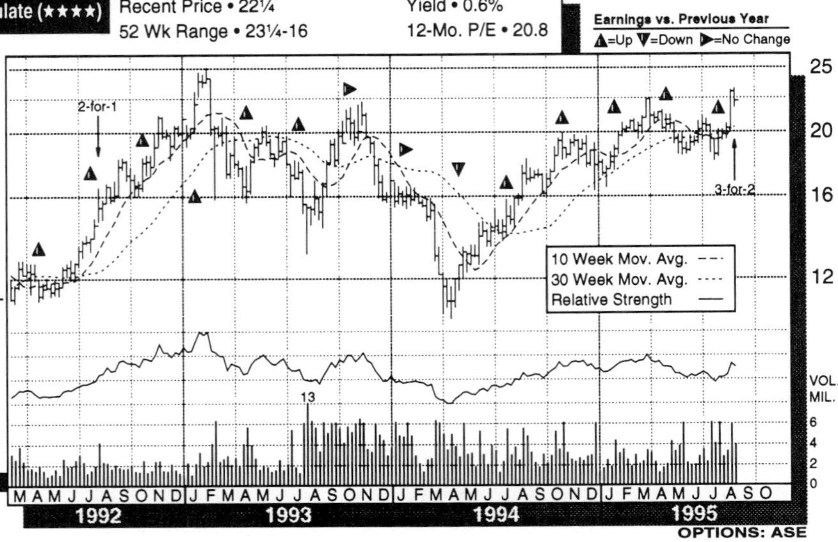

Overview - 30-AUG-95

Sales are expected to rise 20% to 25% in the fiscal year ending March 31, 1996. Despite price weakness in certain lines, volume should benefit from new drugs and expansion of the customer base. During the first quarter, Mylan launched a generic version of Sectral beta blocker; 11 new generic drugs were introduced in 1994-5. Several additional generic approvals are anticipated during 1995-6, including a generic form of Bristol-Myers Squibb's popular Capoten antihypertensive drug. Increased sales are also indicated for drugs sold under a marketing agreement with Eli Lilly & Co. Results should benefit from greater volume, productivity improvements, and higher other income.

Valuation - 30-AUG-95

The shares have traded in a narrow range in recent months, consolidating after a strong rise in 1994. Mylan has increased its share of the growing generic drug market by expanding its product portfolio, superior marketing, and a reputation for high quality products. Acquisitions in recent years diversified the company's business into managed care and transdermal drug delivery systems. Increasing emphasis on co-marketing arrangements with brand name drugmakers and continuing development of proprietary products enhance prospects. The stock's relatively rich P/E multiple appears justified in view of strong forward earnings momentum. The shares (which split three for two in August) merit accumulation.

Key Stock Statistics

S&P EPS Est. 1996	1.15	Tang. Bk. Value/Share	4.07
P/E on S&P Est. 1996	19.3	Beta	0.99
S&P EPS Est. 1997	1.35	Shareholders	85,200
Dividend Rate/Share	0.13	Market cap. (B)	$ 2.7
Shs. outstg. (M)	119.3	Inst. holdings	83%
Avg. daily vol. (M)	0.788	Insider holdings	NA

Value of $10,000 invested 5 years ago: $ 28,483

Fiscal Year Ending Mar. 31

	1996	% Change	1995	% Change	1994	% Change
Revenues (Million $)						
1Q	109.2	28%	85.15	46%	58.51	51%
2Q	—	—	96.01	66%	57.76	13%
3Q	—	—	104.3	57%	66.44	9%
4Q	—	—	110.7	60%	69.07	13%
Yr.	—	—	396.1	57%	251.8	19%
Income (Million $)						
1Q	33.17	22%	27.13	68%	16.11	42%
2Q	—	—	28.66	64%	17.44	4%
3Q	—	—	31.84	44%	22.12	4%
4Q	—	—	33.24	91%	17.39	-19%
Yr.	—	—	120.9	65%	73.07	3%
Earnings Per Share ($)						
1Q	0.28	24%	0.23	62%	0.14	40%
2Q	E0.27	12%	0.24	64%	0.15	NM
3Q	E0.29	9%	0.27	43%	0.19	NM
4Q	E0.31	11%	0.28	91%	0.15	-21%
Yr.	E1.15	14%	1.01	63%	0.62	1%

Next earnings report expected: late October

Mylan Laboratories

Business Summary - 30-AUG-95

Mylan Laboratories Inc. manufactures generic pharmaceutical products in finished tablet, capsule and powder dosage forms for resale by others. More than 70 generic drugs are produced in varying strengths. The company aims to become a fully integrated pharmaceutical concern, with proprietary as well as generic products.

Generic drugs are the chemical equivalents of branded drugs marketed after patent expirations on the primary products. Mylan's generic drugs encompass 22 different therapeutic classes, including analgesics, antianginals, antianxiety agents, antibiotics, antidepressants, antidiabetics, antidiarrheals, an antigout drug, an antihistamine, antihypertensives, anti-inflammatories, antipsychotics, anxiolytics, a bronchial dilator, diuretics, hypnotic agents, a muscle relaxant and a uricosuric. The company holds a patent on Maxzide, an antihypertensive drug that is marketed under an exclusive license by American Cyanamid (now a unit of American Home Products).

Eldepryl, a treatment for Parkinson's disease, is marketed by Somerset Pharmaceuticals, which is jointly owned by the company and Circa Pharmaceuticals (which is being acquired by Watson Pharmaceuticals). Eldepryl is also sold by Sandoz Pharmaceuticals under an agreement with Somerset. Mylan had equity of $0.28 a share in Somerset's earnings in 1994-5 ($0.27 in 1993-4).

Subsidiaries include Dow Hickam, a manufacturer and marketer of specialty pharmaceuticals and wound care products; and Bertek, a producer of transdermal drug delivery systems. R&D spending amounted to $30.5 million in 1994-5 (equal to 7.7% of sales), up from $21.6 million in 1993-4 (8.6%).

Important Developments

Aug. '95—Mylan said it had filed Investigational New Drug (IND) applications with the FDA for three new proprietary drugs: dotarazine, an anti-migraine agent; sertaconazole, an anti-fungal; and a gastrointestinal drug. Three additional INDs are expected to be filed, for a wound care product, a topical anesthetic and a burn treatment. As of late August, the company had 19 ANDAs (generic drug marketing applications) under review at the FDA, representing 12 different chemical entities. An additional four were planned to be submitted within a few weeks. Mylan is constructing a 150,000 sq. ft. Morgantown, Pa., R&D center, expected to be completed during 1995.

Capitalization

Long Term Obligations: $7,807,000 (6/95).

Per Share Data ($) (Year Ended Mar. 31)

	1996	1995	1994	1993	1992	1991
Tangible Bk. Val.	NA	3.81	2.92	2.20	1.67	1.41
Cash Flow	NA	1.12	0.71	0.65	0.39	0.33
Earnings	1.01	1.01	0.62	0.61	0.35	0.30
Dividends	0.03	0.22	0.10	0.08	0.07	0.07
Payout Ratio	3%	22%	16%	13%	19%	22%
Cal. Yrs.	1995	1994	1993	1992	1991	1990
Prices - High	22½	19⅞	25⅛	21¼	14⅛	8¼
- Low	16½	10⅜	13⅛	10½	5⅝	4⅝
P/E Ratio - High	22	20	40	35	41	28
- Low	16	10	21	17	16	15

Income Statement Analysis (Million $)

	1995	%Chg	1994	%Chg	1993	%Chg	1992
Revs.	396	57%	252	19%	212	61%	132
Oper. Inc.	151	117%	69.7	-10%	77.5	141%	32.1
Depr.	12.7	13%	11.2	120%	5.1	NM	5.1
Int. Exp.	NA	—	0.0	-50%	0.1	-83%	0.3
Pretax Inc.	171	96%	87.1	-10%	97.3	94%	50.1
Eff. Tax Rate	30%	—	16%	—	27%	—	20%
Net Inc.	121	66%	73.1	4%	70.6	76%	40.1

Balance Sheet & Other Fin. Data (Million $)

	1995	1994	1993	1992	1991	1990
Cash	180	88.5	98.2	60.3	37.5	21.9
Curr. Assets	331	210	180	120	83.0	63.0
Total Assets	546	403	351	227	170	138
Curr. Liab.	56.4	17.9	26.5	17.9	11.9	7.2
LT Debt	Nil	Nil	Nil	Nil	Nil	0.2
Common Eqty.	483	380	296	203	153	127
Total Cap.	483	381	298	205	156	129
Cap. Exp.	17.5	20.2	12.3	10.0	8.4	7.2
Cash Flow	134	84.2	75.7	45.2	35.6	28.7

Ratio Analysis

	1995	1994	1993	1992	1991	1990
Curr. Ratio	5.9	11.7	6.8	6.7	7.0	8.7
% LT Debt of Cap.	Nil	Nil	Nil	Nil	Nil	0.1
% Net Inc.of Revs.	30.5	29.0	33.3	30.4	35.9	27.5
% Ret. on Assets	25.4	19.3	24.3	19.7	21.3	20.9
% Ret. on Equity	28.0	21.5	28.1	21.9	23.3	22.6

Dividend Data —Dividends have been paid each year since 1983.

Amt. of Div. $	Date Decl.	Ex-Div. Date	Stock of Record	Payment Date
0.100	Dec. 14	Dec. 23	Dec. 30	Jan. 13 '95
0.050	Dec. 14	Dec. 23	Dec. 30	Jan. 13 '95
0.050	Mar. 17	Mar. 27	Mar. 21	Apr. 13 '95
0.050	Jun. 16	Jun. 29	Jul. 03	Jul. 14 '95
3-for-2	Jun. 28	Aug. 16	Jul. 31	Aug. 15 '95

Data as orig. reptd.; bef. results of disc. opers. and/or spec. items. Per share data adj. for stk. divs. as of ex-div. date. E-Estimated. NA-Not Available. NM-Not Meaningful. NR-Not Ranked.

Office—1030 Century Building, Pittsburgh, PA 15222. **Tel**—(412) 232-0100. **Chrmn, Pres & CEO**—M. Puskar. **Secy**—R. W. Smiley. **Investor Contact**—Patricia Sunseri. **Dirs**—D. G. Barnett, L. S. DeLynn, J. C. Gaisford, R. A. Graciano, M. Puskar, R. W. Smiley, C. B. Todd. **Transfer Agent & Registrar**—American Stock Transfer & Trust Co., NYC. **Incorporated** in Pennsylvania in 1970. **Empl**-1,240. **S&P Analyst:** H. B. Saftlas

STANDARD & POOR'S

STOCK REPORTS

NCH Corp.

NYSE Symbol **NCH**
In S&P MidCap 400

10-AUG-95 **Industry:** Chemicals

Summary: NCH is a worldwide distributor of maintenance products, including specialty chemicals, welding supplies, and electrical and plumbing parts.

Quantitative Evaluations

Outlook
(1 Lowest—5 Highest)
• **NA**

Fair Value
• **NA**

Risk
• **Low**

Earn./Div. Rank
• **B+**

Technical Eval.
• **Bearish** since 2/94

Rel. Strength Rank
(1 Lowest—99 Highest)
• **59**

Insider Activity
• **NA**

Recent Price • 58¾
52 Wk Range • 67-54⅜

Yield • 2.0%
12-Mo. P/E • 13.7

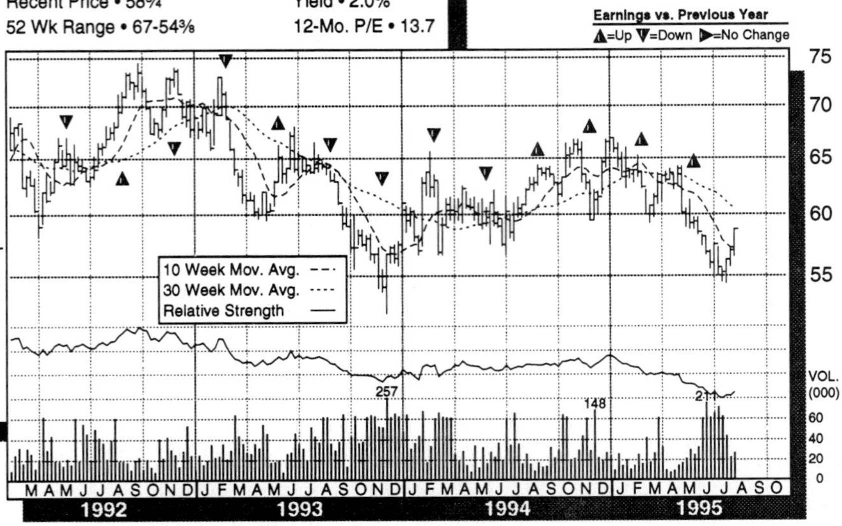

Business Profile - 10-AUG-95

As a worldwide distributor of maintenance products, NCH serves industrial and institutional markets in over 50 countries, including many large home centers in the U.S. Earnings have benefited from continued strength in domestic markets. The U.S. provides more than half of its sales, with Europe accounting for one-third. In 1994-95, international sales (with the exception of Latin America) were aided by significant currency translation gains. The Levy family owns more than 50% of the shares.

Operational Review - 10-AUG-95

Net sales increased 8.1% in the fiscal year ended April 30, 1995, reflecting strong domestic demand and currency translation gains on international sales. Margins widened, as improved international efficiencies outweighed higher domestic costs and marketing expenses. Aided by the absence of the prior fiscal year's $340,000 loss in foreign currency revaluation, earnings advanced 14% to $4.29 a share.

Stock Performance - 04-AUG-95

In the past 30 trading days, NCH's shares have increased 5%, compared to a 2% rise in the S&P 500. Average trading volume for the past five days was 5,300 shares, compared with the 40-day moving average of 19,097 shares.

Key Stock Statistics

Dividend Rate/Share	1.20	Shareholders	700
Shs. outstg. (M)	8.3	Market cap. (B)	$0.503
Avg. daily vol. (M)	0.005	Inst. holdings	43%
Tang. Bk. Value/Share	38.04	Insider holdings	NA
Beta	1.17		

Value of $10,000 invested 5 years ago: $ 11,334

Fiscal Year Ending Apr. 30

	1995	% Change	1994	% Change	1993	% Change
Revenues (Million $)						
1Q	178.7	5%	169.6	-3%	175.0	4%
2Q	184.6	13%	163.2	-4%	169.4	5%
3Q	186.6	9%	170.6	1%	168.7	-2%
4Q	185.2	5%	176.6	6%	166.7	NM
Yr.	735.1	8%	680.0	NM	679.9	1%
Income (Million $)						
1Q	7.83	4%	7.56	—	—	—
2Q	10.70	15%	9.27	—	—	—
3Q	7.04	23%	5.73	-25%	7.65	-25%
4Q	10.02	16%	8.65	-5%	9.10	17%
Yr.	35.58	14%	31.21	-17%	37.61	-5%
Earnings Per Share ($)						
1Q	0.95	4%	0.91	-32%	1.34	3%
2Q	1.29	15%	1.12	-5%	1.18	-9%
3Q	0.85	23%	0.69	-25%	0.92	-26%
4Q	1.21	15%	1.05	-4%	1.09	16%
Yr.	4.29	14%	3.77	-17%	4.53	-5%

Next earnings report expected: early September

NCH Corp.

Business Summary - 08-AUG-95

NCH (formerly National Chemsearch) markets in the U.S. and abroad a wide range of maintenance products, many of which are manufactured by the company. The product line includes specialty chemicals, fasteners, welding supplies, electronic and plumbing parts, and safety supplies. Customers include industry, institutions and government. Contributions by region (income in millions) in 1994-95:

	Sales	Income
United States	56%	$22.3
Europe	33%	13.4
Latin America/Canada	7%	-0.4
Asia/Pacific	4%	0.3

The original division of NCH, the maintenance chemical group, offers water treatments, fuel supplements, cleaners and degreasers, disinfectants and deodorizers, floor and carpet cleaners, cutting fluids, insecticides, specialty coatings, ground care products, lubricants, skin care products, and adhesives. X-Chem develops and markets oil field production chemicals such as corrosion controllers, emulsion breakers, water treatments, paraffin combatants, cleaners, and production-related products.

The plumbing group offers parts for plumbing and hardware maintenance. Resource Electronics supplies custom-built cable assemblies, data communication wire, cable and connectors, and devices for computer telecommunications hookups and networks. Safety and identification products include goggles, face shields, hard hats, and first aid kits and supplies.

The Partsmaster companies sell repair and maintenance items including fasteners, welding supplies and electrical products. Industrial and institutional supplies are marketed by Cornerstone Direct, primarily through mail and telemarketing.

The retail products group sells pet stain removal and deodorizing products through stores, veterinarians and carpet cleaning companies. The Bramton Company recently expanded its enzyme product group with other specialty pet products such as foam-cushioned pet beds, which are produced in a variety of shapes and fabrics and can be machine washed and dried.

Important Developments

Jun. '95—In its review of results for 1994-95, NCH noted that its 10% increase in international sales was aided by the decreased value of the U.S. dollar. Measured on a local currency basis, sales were up 7%; with Europe up 6% and the Pacific and Far East up 10%. Latin American sales, however, were negatively effected by the increased value of the U.S. dollar. The gain on revaluation of currencies was $41,000 in 1994-95, compared to losses of $340,000 in 1993-94 and $1,792,000 in 1992-93.

Capitalization

Long Term Debt: $4,761,000 (4/95).

Per Share Data ($) (Year Ended Apr. 30)

	1995	1994	1993	1992	1991	1990
Tangible Bk. Val.	36.13	35.41	34.40	33.06	30.10	25.36
Cash Flow	5.96	5.20	6.04	6.15	6.53	5.80
Earnings	4.29	3.77	4.53	4.77	5.19	4.69
Dividends	2.10	2.00	2.00	1.00	0.94	0.84
Payout Ratio	49%	53%	44%	21%	18%	18%
Cal. Yrs.	1994	1993	1992	1991	1990	1989
Prices - High	67	73	74½	78¼	66¾	60½
- Low	56⅝	52⅛	58⅛	54½	45	40½
P/E Ratio - High	16	19	16	16	13	13
- Low	13	14	13	11	9	9

Income Statement Analysis (Million $)

	1995	%Chg	1994	%Chg	1993	%Chg	1992
Revs.	735	8%	680	NM	680	1%	671
Oper. Inc.	70.8	14%	62.2	-15%	72.8	-8%	79.3
Depr.	13.9	17%	11.9	-5%	12.5	10%	11.4
Int. Exp.	5.7	12%	5.1	9%	4.7	-41%	8.0
Pretax Inc.	59.5	14%	52.1	-18%	63.5	-4%	66.1
Eff. Tax Rate	40%	—	40%	—	41%	—	40%
Net Inc.	35.6	14%	31.2	-17%	37.6	-5%	39.4

Balance Sheet & Other Fin. Data (Million $)

	1995	1994	1993	1992	1991	1990
Cash	128	125	123	119	89.0	66.0
Curr. Assets	404	364	335	342	314	281
Total Assets	529	485	467	471	438	394
Curr. Liab.	116	101	92.0	108	110	106
LT Debt	4.8	6.8	8.8	10.5	8.2	11.4
Common Eqty.	316	293	286	274	248	214
Total Cap.	321	300	295	284	256	225
Cap. Exp.	13.5	15.1	18.0	14.2	16.1	16.5
Cash Flow	49.4	43.1	50.1	50.8	54.2	49.2

Ratio Analysis

	1995	1994	1993	1992	1991	1990
Curr. Ratio	3.5	3.6	3.6	3.2	2.9	2.7
% LT Debt of Cap.	1.5	2.3	3.0	3.7	3.2	5.1
% Net Inc.of Revs.	4.8	4.6	5.5	5.9	6.4	6.3
% Ret. on Assets	7.0	6.6	8.0	8.7	10.5	10.6
% Ret. on Equity	11.7	10.8	13.4	15.1	18.9	19.6

Dividend Data (Dividends have been paid since 1965.)

Amt. of Div. $	Date Decl.	Ex-Div. Date	Stock of Record	Payment Date
0.250	Jul. 28	Aug. 26	Sep. 01	Sep. 15 '94
0.300	Sep. 14	Nov. 25	Dec. 01	Dec. 15 '94
1.00 Spl.	Sep. 14	Nov. 25	Dec. 01	Dec. 15 '94
0.300	Jan. 19	Feb. 23	Mar. 01	Mar. 15 '95
0.300	Apr. 12	May. 25	Jun. 01	Jun. 15 '95
0.300	Jul. 27	Aug. 30	Sep. 01	Sep. 15 '95

Data as orig. reptd.; bef. results of disc. opers. and/or spec. items. Per share data adj. for stk. divs. as of ex-div. date. E-Estimated. NA-Not Available. NM-Not Meaningful. NR-Not Ranked.

Office—2727 Chemsearch Blvd., Irving, TX 75015; P. O. Box 152170, Irving, TX 75015-2170. **Tel**—(214) 438-0211. **Chrmn**—L. A. Levy. **Pres**—I. L. Levy. **VP-Secy & Investor Contact**—Joe Cleveland. **VP-Fin**—T. Hetzer. **Dirs**—R. L. Blumenthal, R. Fulgham Jr., I. L. Levy, L. A. Levy, M. P. Levy Jr., J. M. Trim, T. B. Walker Jr. **Transfer Agent & Registrar**—Chemical Mellon Shareholder Services, Ridgefield Park, NJ. **Incorporated** in Delaware in 1965. **Empl**-10,569. **S&P Analyst:** Justin McCann

STANDARD & POOR'S

STOCK REPORTS

NIPSCO Industries

NYSE Symbol **NI**
In S&P MidCap 400

16-OCT-95 **Industry:** Util.-Diversified

Summary: This utility holding company provides gas and electric services in northern Indiana to a largely industrial base that includes the nearby steel industry.

S&P Opinion: Accumulate (★★★★)

Recent Price • 35⅞
52 Wk Range • 35⅞-27⅛
Yield • 4.3%
12-Mo. P/E • 14.2

Quantitative Evaluations

Outlook
(1 Lowest—5 Highest)
• **1+**

Fair Value
• **28⅛**

Risk
• **Low**

Earn./Div. Rank
• **B+**

Technical Eval.
• **Bullish** since 9/94

Rel. Strength Rank
(1 Lowest—99 Highest)
• **82**

Insider Activity
• **Neutral**

Earnings vs. Previous Year
▲=Up ▼=Down ▶=No Change

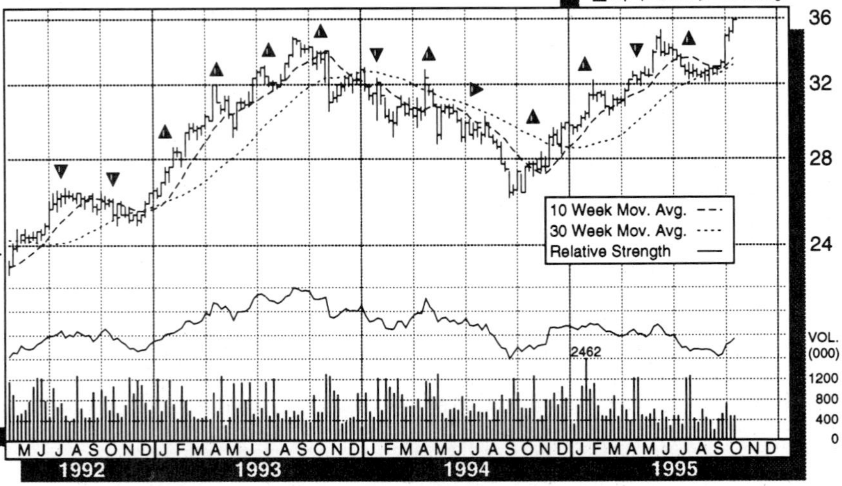

Overview - 16-OCT-95

NI owns the largest gas company and second largest electric utility in Indiana. Its commercial and residential base is growing and, although its heavily industrialized electric service territory is dependent on steelmaking, NI's highly efficient plants are likely to be more fully utilized in weak steel cycles. Gas services are low-cost, and rates competitive. Earnings gains in 1995 should reflect higher sales of electricity and gas and cost controls. EPS could receive a further boost from buybacks of some 1.7 million shares already authorized. A move into natural gas marketing and distribution and other downstream activities should accelerate earnings growth, while strong cash flow, modest debt requirements, and a favorable regulatory environment add to long-term prospects.

Valuation - 16-OCT-95

NI's shares are up nearly 21% in 1995 to date, primarily due to lower interest rates, and tracking in line with gains in the overall gas utility sector. Although the broad market's year-to-date climb eclipsed NI's performance, we believe that the stock could move up another 15% this year based on its potential for accelerating earnings growth due to diversification. Also, given prospects for 10% growth in earnings, the low dividend payout ratio should support above-average increases in the dividend in coming periods. The P/E ratio for the shares of this well-managed company exceeds that of the average utility, reflecting its natural gas component.

Key Stock Statistics

S&P EPS Est. 1995	2.60	Tang. Bk. Value/Share	17.28
P/E on S&P Est. 1995	13.8	Beta	0.41
S&P EPS Est. 1996	2.86	Shareholders	39,200
Dividend Rate/Share	1.56	Market cap. (B)	$ 2.3
Shs. outstg. (M)	63.0	Inst. holdings	52%
Avg. daily vol. (M)	0.108	Insider holdings	NA

Value of $10,000 invested 5 years ago: $ 24,319

Fiscal Year Ending Dec. 31

	1995	% Change	1994	% Change	1993	% Change
Revenues (Million $)						
1Q	522.5	-8%	565.5	8%	521.7	10%
2Q	360.5	4%	348.0	NM	348.8	6%
3Q	—	—	334.6	-2%	342.5	8%
4Q	—	—	428.2	-8%	464.9	NM
Yr.	—	—	1,676	NM	1,678	6%
Income (Million $)						
1Q	60.33	-7%	65.04	11%	58.56	21%
2Q	26.95	25%	21.48	NM	21.66	17%
3Q	—	—	28.54	5%	27.29	31%
4Q	—	—	48.93	NM	48.63	NM
Yr.	—	—	164.0	5%	156.1	14%
Earnings Per Share ($)						
1Q	0.92	-5%	0.97	11%	0.87	24%
2Q	0.41	32%	0.31	NM	0.31	19%
3Q	E0.48	12%	0.43	7%	0.40	33%
4Q	E0.79	5%	0.75	4%	0.72	-1%
Yr.	E2.60	5%	2.48	7%	2.31	16%

Next earnings report expected: late October

NIPSCO Industries

Business Summary - 15-OCT-95

NIPSCO Industries is a holding company formed in 1988 by Northern Indiana Public Service Co., which supplies electricity (59% of 1994 revenues, 81% of operating income) and gas (41%, 19%) to a population of about 2.2 million in the northern third of Indiana. The steel industry accounted for 26% of electric revenues and 3% of gas revenues in 1994. Distribution of electric revenues by customer class in recent years was:

	1994	1993	1992	1991
Residential	26%	27%	26%	28%
Commercial	24%	24%	25%	25%
Industrial	45%	43%	43%	40%
Other	5%	6%	6%	7%

The mix of fuel used for generation in 1994 was coal 85%, natural gas 4%, and purchased power 11%. Internal system peak demand in 1994 was 2,653 mw, and capability at peak totaled 3392 mw, for a capacity margin of 21.8%. NI abandoned a nuclear construction program in 1981. Gas sales in 1994 were 307,175,000 dth, up from 291,047,000 dth in 1993.

NI's electric system is interconnected with that of Indiana Michigan Power, Commonwealth Edison, Public Service Co. of Indiana, Consumers Power, and Central Illinois Public Service, among others. Electricity is purchased from, sold to, or exchanged with these utilities.

Outlays for utility construction in 1994 were $201 million, financed with internally generated funds. The company estimates construction spending over the next five years at $774 million, which it plans to fund internally. NI expects costs to comply with amendments to the 1990 sulfur dioxide regulations of the Clean Air Act will change electric rates less than 5% in the future.

Important Developments

Oct. '95—NI acquired a 50% partnership interest in Canada-based Fuelmaker, the world's only manufacturer of natural gas vehicle refueling appliances. To date, Fuelmaker has sold more than 6,000 compressed gas refueling systems, which are used with fleets of commercial and in-plant vehicles such as forklift and specialty vehicles. The companies see potential uses for the system in residential markets as well. In September, NI announced plans to build a $68 million, 161 megawatt cogeneration project for U.S. Steel (NYSE: USX). The project, to begin in early 1996, is the third cogeneration facility NI has built for steel companies since January 1995, freeing nearly 300 megawatts of capacity for NI to support demand growth in its service area.

Capitalization

Long Term Debt: $1,343,500,000 (6/95).
Subsid. Preferred Stock: $147,040,000.
Red. Preferred Stock: $35,000,000.

Per Share Data ($)

(Year Ended Dec. 31)

	1994	1993	1992	1991	1990	1989
Tangible Bk. Val.	17.28	15.74	15.04	14.46	13.95	13.19
Earnings	2.48	2.31	2.00	1.94	1.81	1.72
Dividends	1.44	1.32	1.24	1.16	1.04	0.84
Payout Ratio	58%	57%	62%	60%	57%	49%
Prices - High	33	34⅞	26⅝	27	19¼	19⅝
- Low	26⅛	26⅛	22½	18½	15¾	13⅛
P/E Ratio - High	13	15	13	14	11	11
- Low	11	11	11	10	9	8

Income Statement Analysis (Million $)

	1994	%Chg	1993	%Chg	1992	%Chg	1991
Revs.	1,676	NM	1,678	6%	1,582	3%	1,535
Depr.	194	4%	187	2%	183	4%	176
Maint.	80.2	-4%	83.5	-2%	85.5	-9%	93.5
Fxd. Chgs. Cov.	3.4	2%	3.3	16%	2.9	7%	2.7
Constr. Credits	4.4	NM	1.4	133%	0.6	-54%	1.3
Eff. Tax Rate	33%	—	37%	—	36%	—	34%
Net Inc.	164	5%	156	14%	137	3%	133

Balance Sheet & Other Fin. Data (Million $)

	1994	1993	1992	1991	1990	1989
Gross Prop.	5,433	5,283	5,054	4,829	4,672	4,547
Cap. Exp.	201	181	172	169	152	151
Net Prop.	3,231	3,231	3,177	3,135	3,145	3,161
Capitalization:						
LT Debt	1,180	1,193	1,026	1,069	1,166	1,262
% LT Debt	48	48	45	47	49	53
Pfd.	187	201	204	188	194	166
% Pfd.	7.60	8.00	9.00	8.30	8.20	6.90
Common	1,108	1,095	1,035	1,012	1,008	966
% Common	45	44	46	45	43	40
Total Cap.	3,174	3,064	2,987	2,988	3,092	3,097

Ratio Analysis

	1994	1993	1992	1991	1990	1989
Oper. Ratio	84.4	84.4	84.4	83.4	83.7	83.8
% Earn. on Net Prop.	8.1	8.2	7.8	8.1	7.9	8.0
% Ret. on Revs.	9.8	9.3	8.6	8.7	8.2	7.9
% Ret. On Invest.Cap	8.3	8.7	8.3	8.4	8.2	8.2
% Return On Com.Eqty	14.6	14.4	13.1	12.9	12.7	12.4

Dividend Data —Common dividends were resumed in August 1987 after having been omitted since December 1985. A dividend reinvestment is available. A poison pill stock purchase rights plan was adopted in 1990.

Amt. of Div. $	Date Decl.	Ex-Div. Date	Stock of Record	Payment Date
0.360	Sep. 27	Oct. 25	Oct. 31	Nov. 18 '94
0.390	Dec. 16	Jan. 25	Jan. 31	Feb. 17 '95
0.390	Mar. 28	Apr. 24	Apr. 28	May. 19 '95
0.390	Jun. 27	Jul. 27	Jul. 31	Aug. 18 '95
0.390	Sep. 26	Oct. 27	Oct. 31	Nov. 20 '95

Data as orig. reptd.; bef. results of disc opers. and/or spec. items. Per share data adj. for stk. divs. as of ex-div. date. E-Estimated. NA-Not Available. NM-Not Meaningful. NR-Not Ranked.

Office—5265 Hohman Ave., Hammond, IN 46320. **Tel**—(219) 853-5200. **Chrmn & Pres**—G. L. Neale. **EVP, CFO & Treas**—S. P. Adik. **Secy**—Nina M. Rausch. **Investor Contact**—Dennis E. Senchak. **Dirs**—S. C. Beering, A. J. Decio, G. L. Neale, E. M. Raclin, D. E. Ribordy, I. M. Rolland, E. A. Schroer, J. W. Thompson, R. J. Welsh, Jr. **Transfer Agent & Registrar**—Harris Trust and Savings Bank, Chicago. **Incorporated** in Indiana in 1912. **Empl**-4,441. **S&P Analyst:** Jane Collin

STANDARD & POOR'S

STOCK REPORTS

Nabors Industries

ASE Symbol **NBR**
In S&P MidCap 400

08-SEP-95 **Industry:** Oil and Gas

Summary: This company provides contract drilling and oilfield services worldwide. Strong growth in recent years has stemmed from acquisitions.

S&P Opinion: Buy (★★★★★)

Recent Price • 9½ | 52 Wk Range • 9⅝-5⅞ | Yield • Nil | 12-Mo. P/E • 19.0

Quantitative Evaluations
Outlook (1 Lowest—5 Highest) • **4-**
Fair Value • **10**
Risk • **Average**
Earn./Div. Rank • **B-**

Technical Eval. • **Bearish** since 11/94
Rel. Strength Rank (1 Lowest—99 Highest) • **72**
Insider Activity • **Neutral**

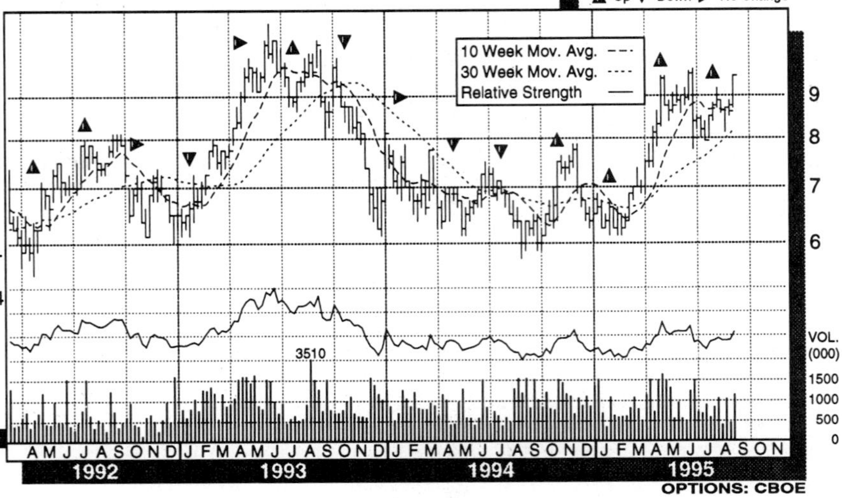

OPTIONS: CBOE

Overview - 01-SEP-95

World supply of oil rigs is finally coming into balance with demand after ten years of oversupply. Oil companies are looking to improve reserve replacement after many years of depleting their oil and gas asset bases. That should increase demand for NBR's services. Rig utilization and day rates are expected to rise steadily over the next two years. Oil companies are seeking longer term contracts with fewer contractors, benefitting a large, geographically diversified driller like NBR as rigs of several smaller competitors obsolesce. The improving industry outlook could lead to substantially higher earnings over the next several years.

Valuation - 06-SEP-95

The expected increase in NBR's earnings is unrelated to oil and gas prices, which have been relatively flat. Huge upside earnings potential exists, however, should oil and gas price increases outpace inflation. The full positive effects of the October, 1994 acquisition of Sundowner Offshore Services, Inc. have not yet been realized, and revenues and earnings should be positively impacted for the next several years. With the shares currently trading at roughly 17 times fiscal 1995 estimated earnings, and 15 times our fiscal 1996 earnings estimate, we believe these shares do not fully reflect the improving industry fundamentals, and therefore recommend them for purchase.

Key Stock Statistics

S&P EPS Est. 1995	0.55	Tang. Bk. Value/Share	3.30
P/E on S&P Est. 1995	17.3	Beta	1.13
S&P EPS Est. 1996	0.65	Shareholders	2,100
Dividend Rate/Share	Nil	Market cap. (B)	$0.794
Shs. outstg. (M)	84.1	Inst. holdings	61%
Avg. daily vol. (M)	0.184	Insider holdings	NA

Value of $10,000 invested 5 years ago: $ 27,142

Fiscal Year Ending Sep. 30

	1995	% Change	1994	% Change	1993	% Change
Revenues (Million $)						
1Q	126.0	7%	117.6	68%	69.88	2%
2Q	143.3	38%	103.5	31%	78.90	5%
3Q	152.7	58%	96.88	16%	83.27	21%
4Q	—	—	104.6	-13%	120.0	63%
Yr.	—	—	422.9	20%	352.0	23%
Income (Million $)						
1Q	11.07	30%	8.54	11%	7.71	-6%
2Q	12.28	75%	7.01	-19%	8.67	6%
3Q	13.05	NM	-24.14	NM	10.84	32%
4Q	—	—	9.25	31%	7.04	-23%
Yr.	—	—	0.65	-98%	34.26	1%
Earnings Per Share ($)						
1Q	0.13	8%	0.12	NM	0.12	-8%
2Q	0.14	40%	0.10	-23%	0.13	NM
3Q	0.15	NM	-0.33	NM	0.16	23%
4Q	E0.13	NM	0.13	30%	0.10	-29%
Yr.	E0.55	NM	0.01	-98%	0.50	-4%

Next earnings report expected: mid November

Business Summary - 08-SEP-95

Nabors Industries, Inc. (formerly Anglo Energy, Inc.) is the largest land drilling contractor in the world. The company has been engaged in oil, gas and geothermal land drilling operations in Alaska, the U.S. lower 48 states and Canada, and internationally in the Middle East, the Far East, the CIS, North and West Africa and South and Central America. Nabors also operates offshore platform rigs in the U.K. North Sea and the Gulf of Mexico, barge rigs in Venezuela and the U.S. Gulf Coast and a jackup rig in the Middle East. The U.S. and Canada accounted for 64% of fiscal 1994 revenues, up from 49% in fiscal 1993.

The company expanded its offshore business through the October 1994 acquisition of Sundowner Offshore Services, Inc. Nabors currently operates approximately 270 land rigs, and 19 platform, seven jackup and six barge rigs. The company also provides offshore well servicing and workover services, oilfield management, engineering, transportation, construction, maintenance and other support services in selected domestic and international markets.

The company emerged from bankruptcy proceedings in May 1988. Since new management was installed in 1987, NBR's primary business strategy has been to develop a group of profitable, synergistic and growth-oriented business units in geographically diversified areas, where the company can achieve profitability through critical mass and a sustainable competitive advantage. The strategy has been implemented through several acquisitions and internal growth.

The contract drilling, workover and well servicing industry is highly fragmented, intensively competitive and cyclical. Seasonality is not a significant factor. Each of the company's rigs is employed under an individual contract that extends either over a stated period of time or the time required to drill a number of wells. The contracts are generally obtained through competitive bidding and sometimes by negotiation, and are subject to cancellation by a customer on short notice.

Through 50%-owned Peak Oilfield Services, Nabors also provides, in Alaska, road, pad and pipeline construction and maintenance, general hauling, facilities maintenance, rig moving and warehousing.

Important Developments

Jul. '95—Nabors said it expects to show continuous improvement, with full-year operating income sharply higher than that of fiscal 1994, excluding one-time charges. Four additional rigs are to be deployed to South America in the fiscal 1995 fourth quarter, and equipment is being mobilized for Alaska. In addition, a newly built platform workover rig is to commence work in the next quarter.

Capitalization

Long Term Debt: $54,567,000 (3/95).

Options: To buy 7,708,000 shs. at $0.75 to $16.25 ea.

Per Share Data ($) (Year Ended Sep. 30)

	1994	1993	1992	1991	1990	1989
Tangible Bk. Val.	3.91	3.84	3.15	2.52	1.92	1.02
Cash Flow	0.28	0.77	0.74	0.58	0.35	0.19
Earnings	0.01	0.50	0.52	0.44	0.27	0.12
Dividends	Nil	Nil	Nil	Nil	Nil	Nil
Payout Ratio	Nil	Nil	Nil	Nil	Nil	Nil
Prices - High	7⅞	11	8⅛	8⅛	7¼	4
- Low	5¾	6⅛	5½	4	3¼	1½
P/E Ratio - High	NM	22	16	18	27	33
- Low	NM	12	11	9	12	13

Income Statement Analysis (Million $)

	1994	%Chg	1993	%Chg	1992	%Chg	1991
Revs.	423	20%	352	23%	286	19%	240
Oper. Inc.	55.7	11%	50.1	4%	48.4	37%	35.3
Depr.	19.6	6%	18.5	28%	14.4	69%	8.5
Int. Exp.	7.2	-10%	8.0	43%	5.6	8%	5.2
Pretax Inc.	4.2	-88%	36.4	3%	35.5	19%	29.8
Eff. Tax Rate	85%	—	6.00%	—	4.90%	—	9.30%
Net Inc.	0.7	-98%	34.3	1%	33.8	25%	27.1

Balance Sheet & Other Fin. Data (Million $)

	1994	1993	1992	1991	1990	1989
Cash	45.1	63.1	14.8	16.4	28.8	6.7
Curr. Assets	160	188	102	83.0	83.0	25.0
Total Assets	419	427	309	263	209	68.0
Curr. Liab.	76.1	80.3	65.7	67.8	51.9	16.4
LT Debt	57.5	68.9	47.0	37.0	38.0	6.0
Common Eqty.	277	268	185	141	103	45.0
Total Cap.	335	337	234	180	144	52.0
Cap. Exp.	37.4	62.3	54.4	80.0	68.5	18.3
Cash Flow	20.3	52.7	48.2	35.5	19.1	8.7

Ratio Analysis

	1994	1993	1992	1991	1990	1989
Curr. Ratio	2.1	2.3	1.5	1.2	1.6	1.5
% LT Debt of Cap.	17.2	20.5	20.0	20.7	26.3	11.3
% Net Inc.of Revs.	0.2	9.7	11.8	11.3	10.5	7.4
% Ret. on Assets	0.2	8.6	11.6	11.3	10.0	8.7
% Ret. on Equity	0.2	14.1	20.3	21.8	18.4	13.6

Dividend Data —Class A dividends were paid from 1973 until omission in July 1982.

Data as orig. reptd.; bef. results of disc. opers. and/or spec. items. Per share data adj. for stk. divs. as of ex-div. date. E-Estimated. NA-Not Available. NM-Not Meaningful. NR-Not Ranked.

Office—515 West Greens Rd., Suite 1200, Houston, TX 77067. **Tel**—(713) 874-0035. **Chrmn & CEO**—E. M. Isenberg. **Vice Chrmn**—R. A. Stratton. **Pres & COO**—A. G. Petrello. **VP & Secy**—D. McLachlin. **Contr**—B. P. Koch. **Investor Contact**—Dennis Smith. **Dirs**—G. T. Hurford, E. M. Isenberg, A. G. Petrello, H. W. Schmidt, M. M. Sheinfeld, R. A. Stratton, J. Wexler, M. J. Whitman. **Transfer Agent & Registrar**—First Chicago Trust of New York, NYC. **Incorporated** in Delaware in 1978. **Empl**-4,833. **S&P Analyst:** R.N., N.R.

National Fuel Gas

NYSE Symbol NFG In S&P MidCap 400

Price	Range	P-E Ratio	Dividend	Yield	S&P Ranking	Beta
Oct. 17'95	1995					
30⅞	29½–25	15	1.62	5.2%	B+	0.40

Summary

National Fuel Gas distributes natural gas in the Buffalo, N.Y., area and in extensive contiguous districts reaching into western Pennsylvania and eastern Ohio. The company is also engaged in exploration, development and purchasing of oil and natural gas reserves; pipeline construction; and the gathering, transmission, storage and marketing of natural gas. Following three consecutive years of gains, NFG expected an earnings decline for fiscal 1995, reflecting the impact of restructuring.

Business Summary

National Fuel Gas and its subsidiaries make up an integrated natural gas operation, consisting of operations which are regulated as to their rates and operations which are not regulated. Regulated operations fall within two business segments: utility operations; and pipeline and storage. Nonregulated operations consist of exploration and production; and other nonregulated businesses. Segment contributions in fiscal 1994:

	Revs.	Profits
Utility operations	76%	51%
Pipeline & storage	12%	35%
Exploration & production	6%	12%
Other nonregulated	6%	1%

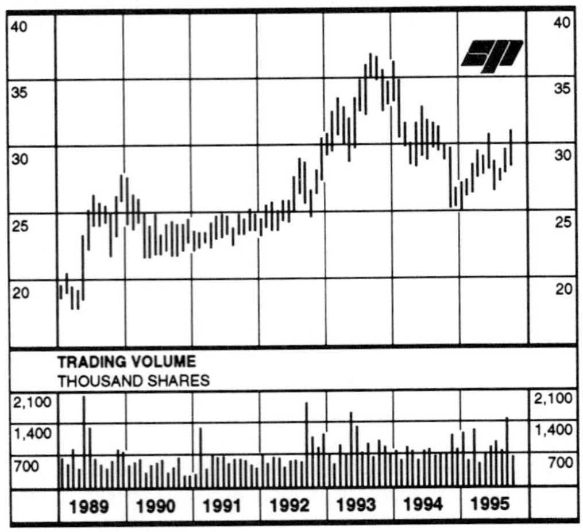

Utility operations, represented by the National Fuel Gas Distribution (NFGD) subsidiary, sell and transport natural gas in western New York and northwestern Pennsylvania. An average of 727,700 retail customers were served in fiscal 1994. Principal metropolitan areas served are: Buffalo, Niagara Falls and Jamestown, N.Y.; and Erie and Sharon, Pa.

Pipeline and storage consists of the National Fuel Gas Supply Corp. (NFGS) subsidiary which transports and stores natural gas for NFGD's local market as well as for utilities and pipeline companies in Northeastern U.S. markets. NFGS owns and operates both a 3,259-mile gas pipeline network (extending from southwestern Pennsylvania to the New York-Canadian border at Niagara Falls, N.Y.) and 30 underground natural gas storage fields, and is joint owner and operator of four additional storage fields. NFGS is regulated by the Federal Energy Regulatory Commission (FERC).

Exploration and production and other nonregulated activities are conducted through various subsidiaries including Seneca Resources (explores for, develops, and purchases oil and natural gas reserves in the Gulf Coast region of Texas and Louisiana, the Appalachian Region and in California), National Fuel Resources (markets and brokers natural gas for utilities and retail customers), Utility Constructors (constructs pipelines and other facilities for system companies and third parties), High Land & Minerals (operates a sawmill and kiln at Kane, Pa.), Leidy Hub (operates a market center where pipelines intersect, involving transportation, storage, purchase, sale, exchange, and lending of natural gas), and Data-Track Account Services (performs collection services for NFG subsidiaries).

Important Developments

Dec. '94— National Fuel Gas received a $4.8 million annual rate increase in Pennsylvania. In October 1994, NFG filed in New York for a $57 million rate hike. Also in October, NFG filed with the FERC for a $21 million rate increase. In July 1994, NFG was granted an $11 million rate increase in New York. Separately, In November, NFG said it expected an earnings decline for fiscal 1995, reflecting the impact of restructuring as requried by FERC Order 636.

Next earnings report expected in November.

Per Share Data ($)

Yr. End Sep. 30	1994	1993	1992	1991	1990	1989	1988	1987	1986	1985
Tangible Bk. Val.	**20.93**	19.30	18.68	17.53	16.97	16.44	15.66	15.21	14.14	13.53
Cash Flow	**4.24**	4.14	3.72	3.33	3.37	3.56	3.32	2.98	3.32	3.24
Earnings[1]	**2.23**	2.15	1.94	1.63	1.83	1.93	1.65	1.49	1.75	1.90
Dividends	**1.56**	1.51	1.48	1.44	1.38	1.30	1.23	1.17	1.09	0.99
Payout Ratio	**70%**	70%	76%	88%	75%	67%	75%	79%	62%	52%
Prices[2]—High	**36¼**	36⅞	30½	25¼	27⅝	27⅞	20¾	24	20⅞	15⅜
Low	**25¼**	28¾	23¼	22⅛	21⅝	17⅞	16½	16¼	14⅜	12½
P/E Ratio—	**16–11**	17–13	16–12	15–14	15–12	14–9	13–10	16–11	12–8	8–7

Data as orig. reptd. Adj. for stk. div. of 100% Jun. 1987. **1.** Bef. spec. item(s) of +0.09 in 1994, +0.27 in 1987. **2.** Cal. yr.

Income Data (Million $)

Year Ended Sep. 30	Revs.	Oper. Inc.	% Oper. Inc. of Revs.	Cap. Exp.	Depr.	Int. Exp.	Net Bef. Taxes	Eff. Tax Rate	[1]Net Inc.	% Net Inc. of Revs.	Cash Flow
1994	**1,141**	**248**	**21.8**	**135**	**74.8**	**47.1**	**130**	**36.4%**	**82.4**	**7.2**	**157**
1993	1,020	233	22.8	132	69.4	52.1	116	34.9%	75.2	7.4	145
1992	920	205	22.2	158	55.7	60.1	95	36.4%	60.3	6.6	116
1991	865	173	19.9	156	50.8	63.5	72	31.5%	49.0	5.7	100
1990	892	174	19.5	162	43.7	59.1	79	33.9%	52.0	5.8	96
1989	856	168	19.7	130	44.4	52.4	77	32.3%	52.4	6.1	97
1988	769	141	18.3	128	43.2	41.9	61	29.6%	42.6	5.5	86
1987	737	130	17.7	127	36.0	39.8	60	39.8%	35.9	4.9	72
1986	906	142	15.7	97	37.4	32.7	75	42.1%	43.4	4.8	79
1985	971	141	14.5	88	31.4	32.8	80	41.2%	46.9	4.8	76

Balance Sheet Data (Million $)

Sep. 30	Cash	Curr. Assets	Curr. Liab.	Curr. Ratio	Total Assets	% Ret. on Assets	Long Term Debt	Common Equity	Total Cap.	% LT Debt of Cap.	% Ret. on Equity
1994	**29.0**	**221**	**375**	**0.6**	**1,982**	**4.3**	**463**	**780**	**1,530**	**30.2**	**10.8**
1993	13.6	209	350	0.6	1,802	4.1	478	736	1,418	33.7	10.6
1992	76.3	248	424	0.6	1,761	3.5	480	632	1,310	36.6	9.8
1991	20.3	170	351	0.5	1,561	3.1	442	542	1,170	37.8	9.2
1990	16.6	150	387	0.4	1,437	3.8	397	484	1,035	38.4	10.9
1989	15.6	159	310	0.5	1,312	4.0	384	464	989	38.8	11.6
1988	15.7	123	325	0.4	1,177	3.7	297	406	841	35.3	10.6
1987	11.5	149	292	0.5	1,119	3.2	266	393	800	33.3	9.5
1986	10.6	138	248	0.6	1,011	4.5	274	337	745	36.8	12.7
1985	9.8	117	230	0.5	922	5.1	221	320	674	32.8	14.5

Data as orig. reptd. 1. Bef. spec. items.

Operating Revenues (Million $)

Quarter:	1994–95	1993–94	1992–93	1991–92
Dec.	272	310	294	272
Mar.	377	474	392	346
Jun.		216	186	177
Sep.		141	149	125
		1,141	1,020	920

Operating revenues for the nine months ended June 30, 1995 fell 16%, year to year. Profits were adversely affected by warmer weather and the absence of certain refunds related to joint storage sites; net income was down 7.1%, to $2.02 a share, from $2.21 (before a $0.10 special credit).

Common Share Earnings ($)

Quarter:	1994–95	1993–94	1992–93	1991–92
Dec.	0.69	0.76	0.77	0.87
Mar.	1.12	1.18	1.33	1.29
Jun.		0.26	0.09	0.06
Sep.		0.03	0.02	d0.28
		2.23	2.15	1.94

Finances

In July 1994, NFG sold $100 million of medium term notes. Net proceeds were used to retire outstanding short-term borrowings.

Dividend Data

Dividends have been paid since 1903. A dividend reinvestment plan is available.

Amt. of Divd. $	Date Decl.	Ex-divd. Date	Stock of Record	Payment Date
0.39½	Dec. 7	Dec. 23	Dec. 31	Jan. 15'95
0.39½	Mar. 15	Mar. 27	Mar. 31	Apr. 15'95
0.40½	Jun. 8	Jun. 28	Jun. 30	Jul. 15'95
0.40½	Sep. 20	Sep. 27	Sep. 29	Oct. 15'95

Capitalization

Long Term Debt: $504,000,000 (6/95).

Common Stock: 37,422,313 shs. ($1 par). Institutions hold about 30%. Shareholders: 22,465 (9/94).

d-Deficit.

Office—10 Lafayette Sq., Buffalo, NY 14203. **Tel**—(716) 857-6980. **Chrmn, Pres & CEO**—B. J. Kennedy. **Secy**—R. M. DiValerio. **Treas**—J. P. Pawlowski. **Investor Contact**—Paula K. Ciprich. **Dirs**—P. C. Ackerman, J. M. Brown, R. T. Brady, D. N. Campbell, L. F. Kahl, B. J. Kennedy, B. S. Lee, E. T. Mann, L. Rochwarger, G. H. Schofield. **Transfer Agent & Registrar**—Chemical Bank, NYC. **Incorporated** in New Jersey in 1902. **Empl**—3,148.

 N.J. DeVita

National Presto

NYSE Symbol **NPK**
In S&P MidCap 400

24-AUG-95 **Industry:** Electronics/Electric

Summary: This company makes small electrical appliances and housewares, including comfort appliances, pressure cookers and canners, and private-label and premium sales products.

Quantitative Evaluations

Outlook
(1 Lowest—5 Highest)
• **2⁻**

Fair Value
• **40⅜**

Risk
• **Low**

Earn./Div. Rank
• **B+**

Technical Eval.
• **Bullish** since 3/95

Rel. Strength Rank
(1 Lowest—99 Highest)
• **25**

Insider Activity
• **NA**

Recent Price • 45⅛
52 Wk Range • 48-39⅛

Yield • 4.4%
12-Mo. P/E • 15.0

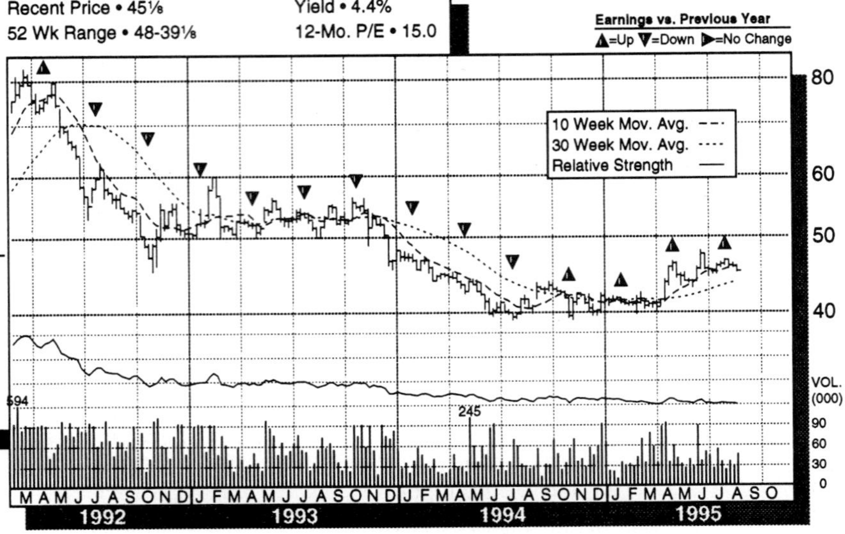

Business Profile - 24-AUG-95

National Presto continues to focus resources on the housewares industry, having dropped earlier modestly successful efforts in door-to-door selling, graphic arts, tool and die fabrication, and trucking. The company's operations have survived the Pentagon's decision to eliminate much of its armament support for conventional warfare (thus eliminating its defense products), as well as the loss of Kmart as a major customer. A spending consumer and successful new products are keys to future growth.

Operational Review - 24-AUG-95

Net sales for the six months ended July 2, 1995, rose 3.5%, year to year. The company said net sales declined in the second quarter due to sluggish consumer spending for houseware items, which was experienced on an industrywide basis. NPK added that it has been unable to raise prices to keep pace with the increased costs associated with commodity and intermediate components, and it expects this condition to continue through the remainder of 1995.

Stock Performance - 18-AUG-95

In the past 30 trading days, NPK's shares have declined 0.28%, compared to a 0.51% rise in the S&P 500. Average trading volume for the past five days was 9,240 shares, compared with the 40-day moving average of 7,497 shares.

Key Stock Statistics

Dividend Rate/Share	1.95	Shareholders	1,400
Shs. outstg. (M)	7.3	Market cap. (B)	$0.328
Avg. daily vol. (M)	0.007	Inst. holdings	47%
Tang. Bk. Value/Share	31.65	Insider holdings	NA
Beta	1.01		

Value of $10,000 invested 5 years ago: $ 16,130

Fiscal Year Ending Dec. 31

	1995	% Change	1994	% Change	1993	% Change
Revenues (Million $)						
1Q	17.96	11%	16.20	-28%	22.37	-10%
2Q	15.88	-4%	16.49	15%	14.28	-18%
3Q	—	—	35.49	44%	24.66	-8%
4Q	—	—	59.89	5%	57.27	-3%
Yr.	—	—	128.1	8%	118.6	-8%
Income (Million $)						
1Q	2.55	16%	2.19	-29%	3.10	-34%
2Q	2.50	13%	2.22	-16%	2.63	-34%
3Q	—	—	4.80	11%	4.34	-20%
4Q	—	—	12.24	42%	8.60	-27%
Yr.	—	—	21.46	15%	18.66	-28%
Earnings Per Share ($)						
1Q	0.35	13%	0.31	-28%	0.43	-34%
2Q	0.35	17%	0.30	-17%	0.36	-35%
3Q	—	—	0.66	10%	0.60	-19%
4Q	—	—	1.65	42%	1.16	-27%
Yr.	—	—	2.92	15%	2.55	-28%

Next earnings report expected: early November

National Presto

Business Summary - 24-AUG-95

National Presto Industries, Inc. produces and distributes electrical appliances and housewares, including comfort appliances, pressure cookers and canners, and private-label and premium sales products. In the past, the company also supplied defense products.

NPK's consumer products consist of pressure cookers and canners; the Presto Control Master single thermostatic control line of fry pans; griddles; combination griddle/warmers; multi-purpose cookers; deep fryers; food processors; can openers; slicer/shredders; curly cutters; potato chippers; ice cream makers; electric shoe polishers; electric heaters; corn poppers; coffeemakers; electric tea kettles; electric knives; electric knife sharpeners; bread slicers; and timers.

In 1994, approximately 43% of revenues (48% in 1993) were derived from cast products such as fry pans, griddles, deep fryers and electric cookers; 22% (26%) from motorized nonthermal appliances, consisting of can openers, slicer/shredders, curly cutters, ice cream makers, knife sharpeners, potato chippers, electric knives, bread slicing systems and shoe polishers; and 31% (20%) from noncast/thermal appliances, including stamped cookers and canners, stainless steel cookers, corn poppers (hot air and microwave), coffeemakers, tea kettles and heaters.

Sales to Wal-Mart Stores accounted for 35% of revenues in 1994 (34% in 1993).

In the area of defense products, the company has manufactured 105MM projectiles, as well as 8" projectiles, but NPK's standby contract with the U.S. Government was not renewed after its September 1992 expiration. The company received a storage-only contract, which expired in September 1993. At that time, the government decided to abandon its equipment, giving NPK an opportunity to derive revenues from the sale of the equipment, which it is currently in the process of completing.

Important Developments

Jul. '95—Management said the company's recent decline in sales reflected sluggish consumer spending for houseware items, which has been experienced by most of the participants in the industry. National Presto also said that it would make small shipments to Kmart, formerly a large customer, in the fall of 1995 for the Christmas season.

Capitalization

Long Term Debt: $5,103,000 (4/2/95) of 10% senior debs. due Jan. 1996 & conv. into com. at a price based on avg. daily stock prices.

Per Share Data ($) (Year Ended Dec. 31)

	1994	1993	1992	1991	1990	1989
Tangible Bk. Val.	33.11	32.08	29.53	29.79	27.48	27.66
Cash Flow	3.03	2.67	3.65	5.11	4.06	3.99
Earnings	2.92	2.55	3.53	4.98	3.94	3.89
Dividends	1.90	Nil	3.80	2.70	4.15	2.25
Payout Ratio	65%	Nil	108%	54%	104%	57%
Prices - High	48	60⅛	83	62¼	44½	40⅝
- Low	39⅛	45½	45¼	39⅝	33½	32½
P/E Ratio - High	16	24	24	13	11	10
- Low	13	18	13	8	9	8

Income Statement Analysis (Million $)

	1994	%Chg	1993	%Chg	1992	%Chg	1991
Revs.	128	8%	119	-7%	128	-21%	162
Oper. Inc.	25.4	17%	21.8	-29%	30.7	-30%	43.8
Depr.	1.2	2%	1.1	-8%	1.3	-2%	1.3
Int. Exp.	0.5	-28%	0.8	12%	0.7	20%	0.6
Pretax Inc.	30.5	16%	26.2	-29%	36.7	-30%	52.4
Eff. Tax Rate	30%	—	29%	—	30%	—	30%
Net Inc.	21.5	15%	18.7	-28%	25.9	-29%	36.7

Balance Sheet & Other Fin. Data (Million $)

	1994	1993	1992	1991	1990	1989
Cash	222	221	206	201	191	179
Curr. Assets	279	273	249	259	234	235
Total Assets	291	283	260	266	242	243
Curr. Liab.	43.0	42.6	38.2	43.0	35.4	34.1
LT Debt	5.1	5.1	5.1	5.1	5.1	6.1
Common Eqty.	243	235	217	218	201	203
Total Cap.	248	240	222	223	207	209
Cap. Exp.	1.7	1.0	1.5	0.8	1.2	1.5
Cash Flow	22.6	19.8	27.1	38.0	30.4	29.8

Ratio Analysis

	1994	1993	1992	1991	1990	1989
Curr. Ratio	6.5	6.4	6.5	6.0	6.6	6.9
% LT Debt of Cap.	2.1	2.1	2.3	2.3	2.5	2.9
% Net Inc.of Revs.	16.8	15.7	20.2	22.7	22.9	22.5
% Ret. on Assets	7.5	6.9	9.8	14.4	12.0	12.1
% Ret. on Equity	9.0	8.3	11.9	17.5	14.4	14.6

Dividend Data —Dividends have been paid since 1945. Since 1989, directors have been declaring one annual dividend rather than four quarterly payments. Extra dividend payments were made in each year from 1989 through 1993; after no extra payments in 1994, they were resumed in 1995.

Amt. of Div. $	Date Decl.	Ex-Div. Date	Stock of Record	Payment Date
0.200	Feb. 17	Feb. 22	Feb. 28	Mar. 10 '95
1.950	Feb. 17	Feb. 22	Feb. 28	Mar. 10 '95

Data as orig. reptd.; bef. results of disc. opers. and/or spec. items. Per share data adj. for stk. divs. as of ex-div. date. E-Estimated. NA-Not Available. NM-Not Meaningful. NR-Not Ranked.

Office—3925 North Hastings Way, Eau Claire, WI 54703-3703. **Tel**—(715) 839-2121. **Chrmn**—Melvin S. Cohen. **Vice Chrmn**—J. H. Berney. **Pres, CEO, CFO & Investor Contact**—Maryjo Cohen. **Secy**—J. F. Bartl. **Dirs**—J. H. Berney, Maryjo Cohen, Melvin S. Cohen, W. G. Ryberg, J. M. Sirianni, R. Strangis. **Transfer Agent & Registrar**—Harris Trust & Savings Bank, Chicago. **Incorporated** in Wisconsin in 1905. **Empl**-674. **S&P Analyst:** Philip D. Wohl

STANDARD & POOR'S

STOCK REPORTS

Nellcor Inc.

NASDAQ Symbol **NELL**
In S&P MidCap 400

15-AUG-95 **Industry:** Electronics/Electric

Summary: Nellcor makes and markets electronic patient monitoring instruments for use primarily in hospital critical care units.

S&P Opinion: Accumulate (★★★★) Recent Price • 54⅜ | 52 Wk Range • 54¾-26 | Yield • Nil | 12-Mo. P/E • 24.7

Quantitative Evaluations

Outlook (1 Lowest—5 Highest)
• **3+**

Fair Value
• **54¼**

Risk
• **Average**

Earn./Div. Rank
• **B**

Technical Eval.
• **Bullish** since 6/95

Rel. Strength Rank (1 Lowest—99 Highest)
• **85**

Insider Activity
• **NA**

Overview - 15-AUG-95

Net revenues from ongoing operations are expected to grow about 15% in fiscal 1996, reflecting continuing strength in the oximetry business, contributions from product line extensions and gains at EdenTec and Pierre Medical. Margins could flatten as Nellcor focuses on increasing marketshare by offering price concessions for long term, volume contracts. The FDA granted marketing approval for the N-3000 product line in May. Anticipated FDA approval for the fetal oximeter has been pushed back to fiscal 1997. Both of these products have been well received overseas. The proposed merger with Puritan-Bennett (PBEN) will aid long term growth as health providers shift to larger suppliers to meet needs. PBEN's current product line complements Nellcor's. PBEN's lower margins are likely to squeeze consolidated margins until cost saving measures take hold.

Valuation - 15-AUG-95

We have downgraded NELL from buy to accumulate on basis of price. Though fundamentals remain strong, a consolidation is possible after the recent runup. International sales continued to rise in the latest fiscal year, up over 40%, from the prior year. Non-U.S. revenues accounted for almost 23% of total sales during fiscal 1995, up from 18% in fiscal 1994. This trend should continue, aided by the acquistion of Pierre Medical and recent agreements with two new foreign OEMs. The proposed merger with Puritan-Bennett (PBEN) will benefit the company in the long term by expanded its presence in the home care sector; PBEN is seen adding $0.25 to fiscal 1996 EPS.

Key Stock Statistics

S&P EPS Est. 1996	2.70	Tang. Bk. Value/Share	11.35
P/E on S&P Est. 1996	20.1	Beta	1.22
Dividend Rate/Share	Nil	Shareholders	800
Shs. outstg. (M)	16.5	Market cap. (B)	$0.889
Avg. daily vol. (M)	0.210	Inst. holdings	85%
		Insider holdings	NA

Value of $10,000 invested 5 years ago: $ 29,000

Fiscal Year Ending Jun. 30

	1995	% Change	1994	% Change	1993	% Change
Revenues ()						
1Q	55.71	11%	50.15	3%	48.60	19%
2Q	64.02	10%	58.11	8%	54.00	12%
3Q	71.04	15%	61.65	10%	56.20	6%
4Q	73.27	13%	65.07	10%	59.39	10%
Yr.	264.0	12%	235.0	8%	218.2	11%
Income ()						
1Q	5.86	21%	4.86	NM	4.82	32%
2Q	8.48	24%	6.86	17%	5.87	24%
3Q	11.06	18%	9.35	36%	6.90	15%
4Q	11.77	NM	-0.51	NM	7.53	9%
Yr.	37.17	81%	20.56	-18%	25.12	18%
Earnings Per Share ()						
1Q	0.35	21%	0.29	NM	0.29	26%
2Q	0.50	22%	0.41	17%	0.35	21%
3Q	0.65	18%	0.55	34%	0.41	14%
4Q	0.69	NM	-0.03	NM	0.45	7%
Yr.	2.20	80%	1.22	-19%	1.50	15%

Next earnings report expected: mid October

Nellcor Inc.

Business Summary - 15-AUG-95

Nellcor makes electronic monitoring instruments and related sensors and airway adapters for patient safety and management wherever patients are treated. Europe accounted for 13% of total revenues in each of fiscal 1994 and 1993.

The company's N-200 and N-180 pulse oximeters provide continuous noninvasive measurement of a patient's arterial blood oxygen saturation. Such monitoring is needed because, left untreated, a severe lack of blood oxygen can cause permanent brain damage or death within minutes. The N-200 product line features Nellcor's proprietary C-LOCK ECG synchronization system, which improves monitor performance by distinguishing true arterial pulses from motion artifact and enhancing signal quality in patients with weak pulses. The OXINET pulse oximetry network permits remote monitoring of multiple patients from a central location.

In fiscal 1993, Nellcor began distributing the ULTRA CAP N-6000 monitor, which combines pulse oximetry with advanced capnography. During the second half of fiscal 1994, Nellcor began international sales of its N-3000 pulse oximeter and the N-3100 noninvasive blood pressure module. The N-3000 and N-3100 are the first two modules of a planned system to monitor patient vital signs on the hospital general care floor and in mobile environments. U.S. sales of both systems began in May 1995. Sales of the N-1000 malfunction monitor were discontinued in fiscal 1994.

The company also produces the N-10, N-20 and N-30 portable pulse oximeters, as well as a variety of disposable and reusable sensors and airway adapters used in conjunction with its monitors. Nellcor's oximetry sensors can also be used with instruments produced under license from the company, and with multiparameter monitors that incorporate Nellcor's OEM module.

The EdenTec Corp. subsidiary specializes in infant and adult apnea monitors and diagnostic systems for home and hospital markets.

Important Developments

Aug. '95—Shareholders of Nellcor and Puritan-Bennett Corp. (Nasdaq: PBEN) are to vote August 24 on a previously-announced agreement under which Nellcor will issue approximately 11.4 million of its common shares for all the outstanding shares of PBEN. The merger, which should close by the end of the year, will combine the worldwide leaders in two complementary areas, patient safety monitoring and respiratory therapy. The combined company, to be renamed Nellcor Puritan Bennett Inc., will have annual revenues of approximately $600 million.

Capitalization

Long Term Debt: None (7/2/95).

Per Share Data () (Year Ended Jun. 30)

	1995	1994	1993	1992	1991	1990
Tangible Bk. Val.	NA	12.75	11.03	8.98	7.79	6.47
Cash Flow	NA	1.85	2.04	1.79	1.62	1.40
Earnings	2.20	1.22	1.50	1.31	1.05	0.96
Dividends	Nil	Nil	Nil	Nil	Nil	Nil
Payout Ratio	Nil	Nil	Nil	Nil	Nil	Nil
Prices - High	53	29½	34½	35⅞	31¾	24⅜
- Low	31½	24¼	17½	22¾	12¾	8⅝
P/E Ratio - High	24	24	23	27	30	25
- Low	14	20	12	17	12	9

Income Statement Analysis ()

	1994	%Chg	1993	%Chg	1992	%Chg	1991
Revs.	235	8%	218	11%	196	23%	159
Oper. Inc.	54.0	15%	46.8	20%	38.9	19%	32.6
Depr.	10.6	18%	9.0	14%	7.9	-9%	8.7
Int. Exp.	Nil	—	Nil	—	Nil	—	Nil
Pretax Inc.	33.0	-19%	40.8	19%	34.3	33%	25.8
Eff. Tax Rate	38%	—	39%	—	38%	—	37%
Net Inc.	20.6	-18%	25.1	18%	21.3	31%	16.3

Balance Sheet & Other Fin. Data ()

	1994	1993	1992	1991	1990	1989
Cash	122	117	82.6	68.3	43.5	35.6
Curr. Assets	188	177	142	117	95.0	75.0
Total Assets	238	226	189	143	121	90.0
Curr. Liab.	33.6	33.1	33.6	20.6	22.3	14.8
LT Debt	Nil	Nil	Nil	Nil	0.7	Nil
Common Eqty.	204	192	154	121	98.0	76.0
Total Cap.	205	193	155	122	99	76.0
Cap. Exp.	14.1	14.8	12.6	7.4	11.5	8.7
Cash Flow	31.2	34.1	29.2	25.0	21.1	13.4

Ratio Analysis

	1994	1993	1992	1991	1990	1989
Curr. Ratio	5.6	5.3	4.2	5.7	4.3	5.0
% LT Debt of Cap.	Nil	Nil	Nil	Nil	0.7	Nil
% Net Inc.of Revs.	8.7	11.5	10.9	10.2	10.1	6.8
% Ret. on Assets	9.0	11.9	12.6	12.1	13.3	9.3
% Ret. on Equity	10.6	14.2	15.2	14.6	16.2	11.3

Dividend Data —No cash has been paid. A preferred stock purchase rights plan has been adopted by NELL.

Data as orig. reptd.; bef. results of disc. opers. and/or spec. items. Per share data adj. for stk. divs. as of ex-div. date. E-Estimated. NA-Not Available. NM-Not Meaningful. NR-Not Ranked.

Office—4280 Hacienda Dr., Pleasanton, CA 94588. **Tel**—(510) 463-4000. **Pres & CEO**—C. R. Larkin, Jr. **VP-Fin, CFO & Investor Contact**—Michael P. Downey. **Secy**—Laureen DeBuono. **Dirs**—R. J. Glaser, F. M. Grafton, D. L. Hammond, C. R. Larkin, Jr., W. J. McNerney, E. E. van Bronkhorst. **Transfer Agent & Registrar**—First National Bank of Boston. **Incorporated** in Delaware in 1986. **Empl**-1,797. **S&P Analyst:** Steven A. Jaworski

STANDARD & POOR'S

STOCK REPORTS

Nevada Power

NYSE Symbol **NVP**

In S&P MidCap 400

08-AUG-95 **Industry:** Utilities-Electric

Summary: This electric utility serves over 428,000 customers in the gaming and tourist economy of Las Vegas.

S&P Opinion: Hold (★★★)

Recent Price • 19⅜ | Yield • 8.3%

52 Wk Range • 21⅜-19⅛ | 12-Mo. P/E • 12.7

Quantitative Evaluations

Outlook (1 Lowest—5 Highest) • 1⁻

Fair Value • 15½

Risk • Low

Earn./Div. Rank • B+

Technical Eval. • **Bullish** since 6/94

Rel. Strength Rank (1 Lowest—99 Highest) • 17

Insider Activity • Neutral

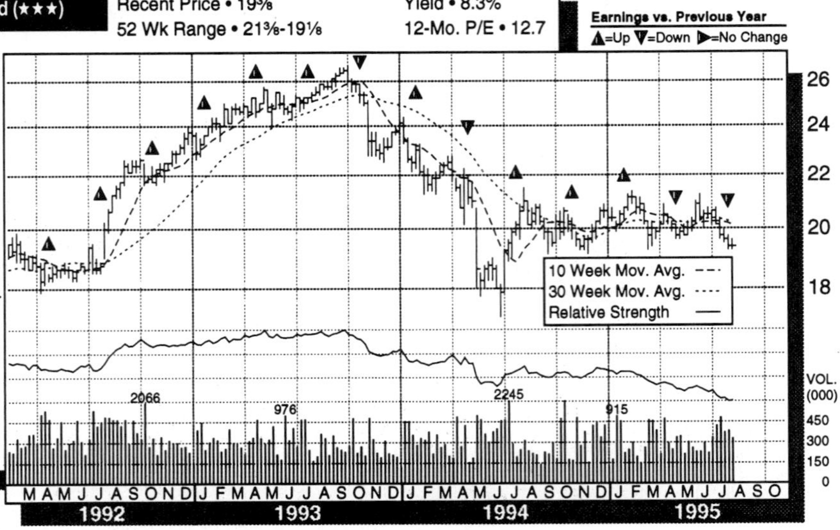

Overview - 01-AUG-95

NVP is continuing an extensive construction program designed to help meet continued growth in its service territory. To meet rising demand for electricity, the company plans to use short term purchased power from independent producers rather than build new plant to take advantage of highly competitive markets. Share earnings for 1995 should reflect modestly higher kwh sales despite mild weather in the second quarter compared to abnormally high temperatures a year earlier. However, the full year effect of a rate decrease effective October 1, 1994, and the absence of a partial reversal of a 1990 charge from a 1985 outage at the Mojave plant will depress earnings somewhat. Other negatives include a rise in interest expense and a greater number of common shares outstanding. For 1996, full recovery to the 1994 level appears unlikely.

Valuation - 07-AUG-95

NVP's share price has rebounded from the sharp decline in mid-1994 on an improving interest rate outlook, but its recovery is one of the weakest in the S&P Electric Utilities Index, due in large part to a decline in both actual and forecasted earnings. Also, despite strong growth in its service area, NVP has applied for a substantial rate reduction. If granted as proposed, it is likely to hinder earnings growth, and will be among the factors raising doubts about the company's ability to maintain the dividend at its current level. Overall, we believe the shares are adequately valued at 12 times trailing 12-month earnings.

Key Stock Statistics

S&P EPS Est. 1995	1.73	Tang. Bk. Value/Share	15.52
P/E on S&P Est. 1995	11.2	Beta	0.21
S&P EPS Est. 1996	1.79	Shareholders	50,600
Dividend Rate/Share	1.60	Market cap. (B)	$0.883
Shs. outstg. (M)	45.9	Inst. holdings	19%
Avg. daily vol. (M)	0.079	Insider holdings	NA

Value of $10,000 invested 5 years ago: $ 11,444

Fiscal Year Ending Dec. 31

	1995	% Change	1994	% Change	1993	% Change
Revenues (Million $)						
1Q	145.2	NM	144.7	9%	132.8	12%
2Q	173.4	-11%	195.8	38%	142.3	2%
3Q	—	—	268.4	16%	232.3	14%
4Q	—	—	155.4	8%	144.4	15%
Yr.	—	—	764.2	17%	651.8	11%
Income (Million $)						
1Q	4.55	-3%	4.69	-44%	8.38	NM
2Q	13.41	-42%	23.19	52%	15.24	49%
3Q	—	—	50.47	7%	47.11	10%
4Q	—	—	3.51	24%	2.82	84%
Yr.	—	—	81.87	11%	73.55	30%
Earnings Per Share ($)						
1Q	0.08	-11%	0.09	-55%	0.20	NM
2Q	0.27	-49%	0.53	43%	0.37	42%
3Q	E1.18	—	1.16	3%	1.13	-2%
4Q	E0.20	—	0.06	50%	0.04	NM
Yr.	E1.73	—	1.82	3%	1.76	20%

Next earnings report expected: late October

Nevada Power

Business Summary - 08-AUG-95

Nevada Power serves the city of Las Vegas and adjoining areas of Clark County, Nevada, with a population of some 999,000. Revenues by customer class in recent years:

	1994	1993	1992	1991
Residential	43%	41%	42%	40%
Commercial & industrial	50%	50%	52%	53%
Other	7%	9%	6%	7%

Peak demand in 1994 was 2,920 mw and capability totaled 3,462 mw, for a capacity margin of 16%. In 1994, some 51% of kwh sold was company generated, while 4% came from the Hoover Dam, and 45% from purchased power. Sources of company generation were coal 85% and natural gas 15%.

The Las Vegas economy is characterized by robust growth in the resort, gaming and convention industry. Also, the local economy has experienced a sharp increase in population. For the next five years, NVP estimates growth in its customer base at an average 5.4% and demand for electricity at 4.5%. The company built a 90 mw combined cycle unit in 1993, added another in 1994, and is building a 72 mw unit to be operating in the summer of 1995. But to meet rising base load needs through the late 1990s, it intends to purchase power on a short term basis through regional energy markets.

Construction expenditures for 1994 were $184 million; budgeted outlays for 1995 are $169 million and for 1996 $175 million, primarily to add transmission facilities. The company plans to meet capital expenditure needs with internal funds and proceeds from debt, equity and preferred stock offerings. In November 1994, NVP sold 2 million common shares; net proceeds of $37.7 million were used for construction and debt repayment.

Important Developments

Jul. '95—As a result of lower fuel prices and reduced purchased power costs -- despite increased costs from local independent power producers -- NVP filed a plan with the Public Service Commission of Nevada (PSCN) that would reduce its existing rates by $20 million. It would also guarantee no future rate increases until 1997. If approved, $2 million of the decrease would go to residential customers, another $2 million to small and medium customers and $16 million to several other customer classes. In mid-July 1994, NVP received a rate order to reduce non-residential rates $6.25 million as of October 1, 1994, while retaining its overall rate of return of 9.66%, which is based on a common equity return of 12.5% as previously authorized by the PSCN.

Capitalization

Long Term Debt: $717,000,000 (3/95).
Red. Cum. Preferred Stock: $4,064,000.
Auction Preferred Stock: $38,000,000.

Per Share Data ($) (Year Ended Dec. 31)

	1994	1993	1992	1991	1990	1989
Tangible Bk. Val.	15.52	14.87	13.65	13.58	13.60	13.87
Earnings	1.82	1.76	1.47	1.05	0.78	1.81
Dividends	1.60	1.60	1.60	1.60	1.58	1.54
Payout Ratio	88%	91%	109%	152%	203%	85%
Prices - High	24⅜	26¾	24	22½	25¾	25⅞
- Low	17⅛	22½	17⅞	16⅝	20	19¼
P/E Ratio - High	13	15	16	21	33	14
- Low	9	13	12	16	26	11

Income Statement Analysis (Million $)

	1994	%Chg	1993	%Chg	1992	%Chg	1991
Revs.	764	17%	652	11%	587	9%	539
Depr.	50.4	16%	43.4	10%	39.5	13%	35.1
Maint.	38.8	10%	35.4	-7%	37.9	-21%	47.9
Fxd. Chgs. Cov.	3.5	NM	3.5	24%	2.8	31%	2.1
Constr. Credits	11.0	-30%	15.7	26%	12.5	39%	9.0
Eff. Tax Rate	35%	—	35%	—	34%	—	30%
Net Inc.	81.9	11%	73.5	29%	56.8	61%	35.2

Balance Sheet & Other Fin. Data (Million $)

	1994	1993	1992	1991	1990	1989
Gross Prop.	2,080	1,901	1,740	1,562	1,345	1,188
Cap. Exp.	184	163	171	151	156	121
Net Prop.	1,584	1,450	1,329	1,187	997	866
Capitalization:						
LT Debt	713	717	715	579	521	460
% LT Debt	48	51	55	54	54	52
Pfd.	42.1	42.3	42.5	42.7	42.9	43.1
% Pfd.	2.80	3.00	3.30	3.90	4.40	4.90
Common	732	646	532	460	406	383
% Common	49	46	41	43	42	43
Total Cap.	1,655	1,566	1,411	1,187	1,071	983

Ratio Analysis

	1994	1993	1992	1991	1990	1989
Oper. Ratio	86.2	83.4	82.9	85.6	84.7	81.6
% Earn. on Net Prop.	7.5	7.8	7.9	7.1	7.9	9.4
% Ret. on Revs.	10.7	11.3	9.7	6.5	5.2	12.3
% Ret. On Invest.Cap	7.8	7.8	7.6	6.7	6.2	9.0
% Return On Com.Eqty	11.3	11.8	10.6	7.5	5.6	12.8

Dividend Data (Dividends have been paid since 1951. A dividend reinvestment plan is available.)

Amt. of Div. $	Date Decl.	Ex-Div. Date	Stock of Record	Payment Date
0.400	Oct. 03	Oct. 06	Oct. 13	Nov. 01 '94
0.400	Jan. 03	Jan. 09	Jan. 13	Feb. 01 '95
0.400	Apr. 03	Apr. 07	Apr. 13	May. 01 '95
0.400	Jul. 03	Jul. 11	Jul. 13	Aug. 01 '95

Data as orig. reptd.; bef. results of disc opers. and/or spec. items. Per share data adj. for stk. divs. as of ex-div. date. E-Estimated. NA-Not Available. NM-Not Meaningful. NR-Not Ranked.

Office—6226 West Sahara Ave., Las Vegas, NV 89102. **Tel**—(702) 367-5000. **Chrmn, CEO & COO**—C. A. Lenzie. **VP-Treas & CFO**—S. W. Rigazio. **VP-Secy**—R. L. Hinckley. **Investor Contact**—Ruth A. Urbantke. **Dirs**—M. L. Coleman, F. D. Gibson Jr., J. L. Goolsby, J. Herbst, C. A. Lenzie, C. L. Ryan, F. E. Scott, A. M. Smith, J. A. Tiberti. **Transfer Agents**—Company's office; Manufacturers Hanover Trust, NYC. **Registrars**—First Interstate Bank of Nevada, Las Vegas; Chemical Bank, NYC. **Incorporated** in Nevada in 1929. **Empl-** 1,759. **S&P Analyst:** Jane Collin

STANDARD & POOR'S

STOCK REPORTS

New England Electric System

NYSE Symbol **NES**

In S&P MidCap 400

18-JUL-95 **Industry:** Utilities-Electric

Summary: This utility holding company serves 1.3 million customers throughout Massachusetts, Rhode Island and New Hampshire. It is the second largest utility system in New England.

S&P Opinion: Hold (★★★)	Recent Price • 33¾	Yield • 7.0%
	52 Wk Range • 35¼-28⅞	12-Mo. P/E • 12.3

Quantitative Evaluations

Outlook (1 Lowest—5 Highest)
• **2−**

Fair Value
• **31½**

Risk
• **Low**

Earn./Div. Rank
• **A-**

Technical Eval.
• **Bearish** since 6/95

Rel. Strength Rank (1 Lowest—99 Highest)
• **32**

Insider Activity
• **NA**

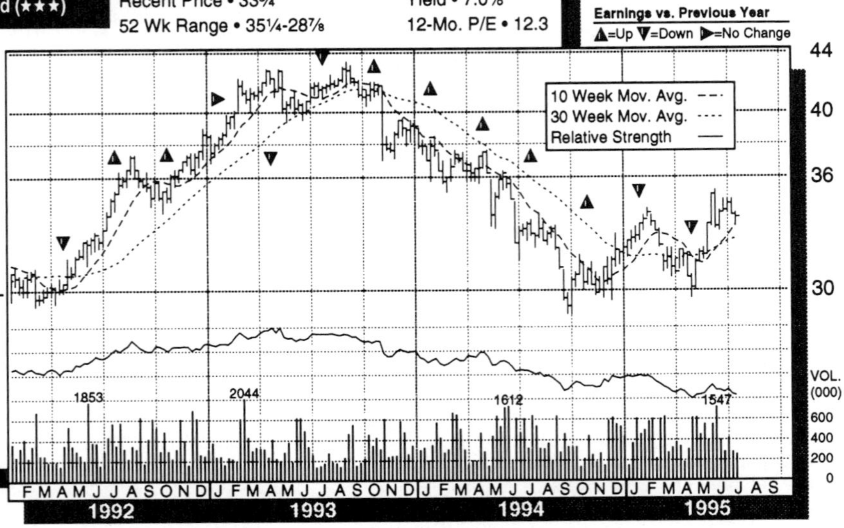

Overview - 18-JUL-95

Share earnings should benefit in 1995 from the Federal Energy Regulatory Commission's (FERC) ruling in February allowing recoveries for fuel plant investment and retiree benefits costs. Also, the absence of a rate decrease that was in effect through October 1994 under an October 1993 FERC agreement to resolve environmental cost issues, as well as a decline in depreciation charges and a rise in construction credits, should have a favorable impact on 1995 earnings. Somewhat offsetting will be higher operating and maintenance expenses from refueling at several nuclear plants and lower revenue recognition following the expiration of the October 1993 FERC agreement. Positive decisions with regard to the Rhode Island rate case due in November and a Massachussetts rate case in September could add to future results.

Valuation - 18-JUL-95

Over the past several months, the price of NES shares has risen nearly 20%, far more than most of its peers. Based on projected 1995 earnings, the stock is currently trading at a premium to the S&P electric utilities group, even after pulling back from its peak of 35 1/4 in May during the group's recent recovery. Absent additional momentum in the business cycle, the stock appears adequately valued. Cash flow is likely to increase, however, allowing a steady, above average 2.5% rate of growth in the dividend and enhancing the stock's appeal as a total return holding.

Key Stock Statistics

S&P EPS Est. 1995	3.15	Tang. Bk. Value/Share	24.17
P/E on S&P Est. 1995	10.7	Beta	0.62
S&P EPS Est. 1996	3.30	Shareholders	54,600
Dividend Rate/Share	2.36	Market cap. (B)	$ 2.2
Shs. outstg. (M)	65.0	Inst. holdings	32%
Avg. daily vol. (M)	0.062	Insider holdings	NA

Value of $10,000 invested 5 years ago: $ 16,958

Fiscal Year Ending Dec. 31

	1995	% Change	1994	% Change	1993	% Change
Revenues (Million $)						
1Q	558.3	-3%	577.0	NM	579.0	NM
2Q	—	—	517.0	NM	518.0	4%
3Q	—	—	592.0	3%	577.0	7%
4Q	—	—	557.4	NM	560.0	-1%
Yr.	—	—	2,243	NM	2,234	2%
Income (Million $)						
1Q	47.66	-31%	69.27	29%	53.59	-17%
2Q	—	—	33.59	75%	19.15	-37%
3Q	—	—	58.85	6%	55.53	15%
4Q	—	—	37.72	-39%	61.96	47%
Yr.	—	—	199.4	5%	190.2	3%
Earnings Per Share ($)						
1Q	0.73	-32%	1.07	30%	0.82	-17%
2Q	E0.53	—	0.51	70%	0.30	-36%
3Q	E0.95	—	0.91	7%	0.85	15%
4Q	E0.94	—	0.58	-40%	0.96	48%
Yr.	E3.15	—	3.07	5%	2.93	3%

Next earnings report expected: late July

New England Electric System

Business Summary - 18-JUL-95

New England Electric System is a utility holding company that provides electric service to 1.3 million customers in Massachusetts, Rhode Island and New Hampshire. The second largest electric utility in New England, NES generates, transmits, distributes and sells electric energy and provides related services. It also operates several related companies, including an oil and gas exploration company that has been unprofitable since 1986 but is additive to cash flow.

Sales to residential customers accounted for 43% of revenues from electric power in 1994 (41% in 1993); the remainder was to commercial and industrial customers, mostly small and medium sized companies. Roughly 80% of NES's large municipal, commercial and industrial customers have contracts providing a 5% discount in exchange for giving three to five years notice before changing suppliers. To meet increasing competition, in December 1994, NES agreed to hold rates it charges to municipal, commercial and industrial customers at their present level until at least 1997.

According to NES, its rates for electric service are the lowest in New England, largely due to a debt level and embedded or capital and plant operating costs, including payroll, that are below those of its peers. In 1994, fuel costs absorbed 24% of revenues. Coal comprised 37% of power generation, nuclear 19%, gas 16%, hydro 12%, oil 10%, and other 6%. Peak load in 1994 was 4,385 mw, and capability totaled 5,533 mw (including 1,148 mw of purchased power), for a capacity margin of 21%.

Utility plant expenditures, which totaled $466 million in 1994, are estimated at $325 million for 1995, of which 75% will be funded by internal resources. About one-half the 1995 outlays are for construction of generating and transmission facilities, and the remainder largely for distribution facilities.

Important Developments

Jul. '95—The governor of Rhode Island vetoed bills designed to allow certain customers in industrial parks to buy power in the open market. Both the Massachussetts and Narragansett Electric subsidiaries had earlier filed with their respective state commissions principles for restructuring that would widen retail customers' choice of suppliers while allowing utilities to cover the cost of their past commitments. The New Hampshire Public Utilities Commission (PUC) is studying retail wheeling and restructuring issues while the Massachussetts and Rhode Island PUCs are expected to issue separate decisions this summer.

Capitalization

Long Term Debt: $1,600,325,000 (3/95).
Minority Interest: $53,029,000.
Subsid. Red. Preferred Stock: $147,016,000.

Per Share Data ($) (Year Ended Dec. 31)

	1994	1993	1992	1991	1990	1989
Tangible Bk. Val.	24.17	23.46	22.88	22.05	21.30	19.09
Earnings	3.07	2.93	2.85	2.77	4.11	2.36
Dividends	2.28	2.22	2.14	2.07	2.04	2.04
Payout Ratio	74%	76%	75%	75%	50%	86%
Prices - High	39	43⅜	39	32⅝	28⅝	28⅞
- Low	28⅞	36⅞	29¼	24	22½	22¼
P/E Ratio - High	13	15	14	12	7	12
- Low	9	13	10	9	5	9

Income Statement Analysis (Million $)

	1994	%Chg	1993	%Chg	1992	%Chg	1991
Revs.	2,243	NM	2,234	2%	2,182	4%	2,094
Depr.	301	1%	297	-2%	302	9%	278
Maint.	161	10%	146	-10%	163	10%	148
Fxd. Chgs. Cov.	4.2	13%	3.7	9%	3.4	7%	3.2
Constr. Credits	18.0	172%	6.6	35%	4.9	14%	4.3
Eff. Tax Rate	39%	—	38%	—	37%	—	36%
Net Inc.	199	5%	190	3%	185	3%	180

Balance Sheet & Other Fin. Data (Million $)

	1994	1993	1992	1991	1990	1989
Gross Prop.	5,327	4,994	4,790	4,666	4,548	4,222
Cap. Exp.	438	305	242	193	218	532
Net Prop.	3,717	3,483	3,375	3,321	3,302	3,073
Capitalization:						
LT Debt	1,520	1,512	1,533	1,548	1,679	1,638
% LT Debt	46	47	47	48	51	53
Pfd.	202	203	223	226	225	217
% Pfd.	6.10	6.30	6.90	7.00	6.90	7.10
Common	1,581	1,530	1,486	1,440	1,380	1,212
% Common	48	47	46	45	42	40
Total Cap.	4,150	4,049	3,969	3,930	3,991	3,764

Ratio Analysis

	1994	1993	1992	1991	1990	1989
Oper. Ratio	86.8	86.4	86.0	86.1	86.3	85.3
% Earn. on Net Prop.	8.2	8.8	9.1	8.8	8.0	8.4
% Ret. on Revs.	8.9	8.5	8.5	8.6	14.1	8.4
% Ret. On Invest.Cap	7.6	7.9	8.2	7.8	9.8	7.1
% Return On Com.Eqty	12.7	12.6	12.6	12.6	20.5	12.6

Dividend Data (Dividends have been paid since 1947. A dividend reinvestment plan is available.)

Amt. of Div. $	Date Decl.	Ex-Div. Date	Stock of Record	Payment Date
0.575	Aug. 23	Sep. 02	Sep. 09	Oct. 01 '94
0.575	Nov. 22	Dec. 05	Dec. 09	Jan. 03 '95
0.575	Feb. 28	Mar. 06	Mar. 10	Apr. 01 '95
0.590	May. 23	Jun. 06	Jun. 09	Jul. 01 '95

Data as orig. reptd.; bef. results of disc opers. and/or spec. items. Per share data adj. for stk. divs. as of ex-div. date. E-Estimated. NA-Not Available. NM-Not Meaningful. NR-Not Ranked.

Office—25 Research Drive, Westborough, MA 01582. **Tel**—(508) 366-9011. **Chrmn**—J. T. Bok. **Pres & CEO**—J. W. Rowe. **VP & Secy**—F. E. Greenman. **VP & CFO**— A. D. Houston. **Investor Contact**—Robert G. Seega. **Dirs**—J. T. Bok, P. L. Joskow, J. M. Kucharski, E. H. Ladd, J. A. McClure, M. McLane, F. A. Mirando, Jr., J. W. Rowe, G. M. Sage, C. E. Soule, A. Wexler, J. Q. Wilson, J. R. Winoker. **Transfer Agent & Registrar**—Bank of Boston. **Organized** in Massachusetts in 1926. **Empl**-5,000. **S&P Analyst:** Jane Collin

STANDARD & POOR'S

STOCK REPORTS

N.Y. State Electric & Gas

NYSE Symbol **NGE**

In S&P MidCap 400

06-SEP-95 **Industry:** Util.-Diversified

Summary: This utility provides electricity to about 799,000 customers and gas to 231,000 customers in central, eastern and western New York.

S&P Opinion: Hold (★★★)

Recent Price • 24
52 Wk Range • 24⅞-17¾
Yield • 5.7%
12-Mo. P/E • 10.0

Quantitative Evaluations

Outlook
(1 Lowest—5 Highest)
• 3+

Fair Value
• 23⅞

Risk
• Low

Earn./Div. Rank
• B

Technical Eval.
• **Bullish** since 1/95

Rel. Strength Rank
(1 Lowest—99 Highest)
• 54

Insider Activity
• NA

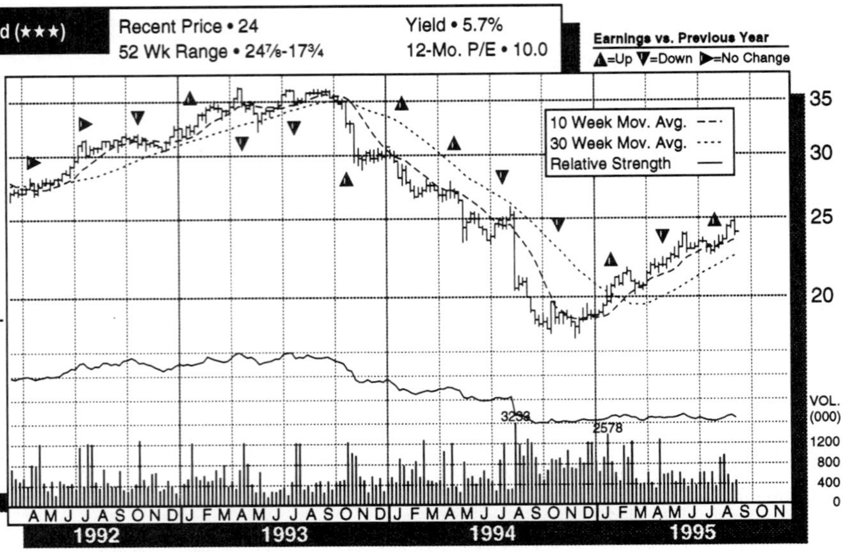

Overview - 06-SEP-95

Share earnings in 1995 and beyond should benefit from reduced operating and maintenance expenses, reflecting cost controls and a recent work force reduction. NGE's recently approved electric rate agreement will increase electric revenues by $45.1 million, $45.3 million, and $45.5 million, on August 1 of 1995, 1996 and 1997, respectively. However, the effects of unfavorable weather in 1995's first quarter, coupled with continued sluggish economic conditions in NGE's service territory, should partially offset these positive factors. Over the long term, the company's comprehensive strategic plan, combined with the late 1994 dividend cut, should better position it for deregulation and greater wholesale competition.

Valuation - 06-SEP-95

As a result of increased competition, rising interest rates and a lower dividend, the shares fell about 40% in 1994. However, they have appreciated about 25% since the beginning of 1995. In an effort to improve its competitive stance in preparation for further deregulation, NGE cut its dividend 36% in November 1994. The shares currently yield about 5.8%, on a payout ratio of 60% (based on 1994 earnings), and were recently trading at about 9.6X estimated 1996 EPS of $2.50. Based on the current industry environment and the company's near-term prospects, the stock is fairly valued. However, with a stable dividend, which is likely to rise, the shares are an attractive holding for total return.

Key Stock Statistics

S&P EPS Est. 1995	2.45	Tang. Bk. Value/Share	21.54
P/E on S&P Est. 1995	9.8	Beta	0.44
S&P EPS Est. 1996	2.50	Shareholders	56,300
Dividend Rate/Share	1.40	Market cap. (B)	$ 1.7
Shs. outstg. (M)	71.5	Inst. holdings	39%
Avg. daily vol. (M)	0.121	Insider holdings	NA

Value of $10,000 invested 5 years ago: $ 12,666

Fiscal Year Ending Dec. 31

	1995	% Change	1994	% Change	1993	% Change
Revenues (Million $)						
1Q	571.9	1%	565.2	8%	522.0	7%
2Q	439.9	13%	388.6	NM	389.0	-3%
3Q	—	—	432.5	9%	396.4	8%
4Q	—	—	512.6	4%	492.8	14%
Yr.	—	—	1,899	5%	1,800	6%
Income (Million $)						
1Q	75.58	-11%	84.69	14%	74.04	-3%
2Q	24.63	99%	12.40	-42%	21.50	-54%
3Q	—	—	30.95	-5%	32.54	22%
4Q	—	—	59.60	57%	37.95	11%
Yr.	—	—	187.6	13%	166.0	-10%
Earnings Per Share ($)						
1Q	0.99	-12%	1.13	14%	0.99	-10%
2Q	0.28	155%	0.11	-52%	0.23	-62%
3Q	E0.40	8%	0.37	-5%	0.39	26%
4Q	E0.78	1%	0.77	64%	0.47	12%
Yr.	E2.45	3%	2.37	14%	2.08	-13%

Next earnings report expected: mid October

N.Y. State Electric & Gas

Business Summary - 06-SEP-95

New York State Electric & Gas Corp. provides electricity to about 799,000 customers and gas to 231,000 customers in central, eastern and western New York. The upstate New York economy is composed of light industry, high technology businesses, agriculture, recreation facilities, and colleges and universities. In 1994, electric sales accounted for 84% of revenues and gas for 16%. Contributions to electric revenues by customer class in recent years were:

	1994	1993	1992	1991
Residential	42%	42%	41%	40%
Commercial	23%	22%	22%	21%
Industrial	15%	15%	16%	15%
Other	20%	21%	21%	24%

Power sources in 1994 were 67% coal, 7% nuclear, 2% hydro, and 14% purchased. The 1994-5 winter peak load was 2,558 mw, and current system capability totals 3,284 mw, for a capacity margin of 22%. Gas sales in 1994 came to 58.6 million dth, versus 58.0 million dth in 1993.

In September 1993, NGE's new rate-settlement agreement became effective. Under the agreement, allowed return on equity is 10.8% in the first year, and 11.4% in the second and third years. Additional annual electric revenues are $99.6 million (7.4%) in the first year, $109.5 million (7.6%) in the second, and $87.8 million (5.6%) in the third. Natural gas rate increases for the three years total about $22.9 million in extra revenues.

Through wholly owned NGE Enterprises, the company owns two unregulated subsidiaries: EnerSoft Corp., a computer software company that produces and markets software for natural gas utilities, marketers and pipeline operators; and XENERGY Inc., an energy services, information systems and energy-consulting company.

Important Developments

Aug. '95—The Public Service Commission (PSC) approved a three-year electric rate-settlement agreement for the period August 1, 1995, through July 31, 1998 (the first year superseding the third year of the existing agreement). The agreement increases NGE's average electric prices by 2.9% in the first year, 2.8% in the second, and 2.7% in the third. Allowed returns on common equity would be 11.1% in the first year and 11.2% in the second and third years. Separately, the PSC approved a 3.2% increase in natural gas base rates, effective August 1, 1995. An 11% return on common equity was also approved.

Capitalization

Long Term Debt: $1,618,534,000 (6/95).
Red. Preferred Stock: $125,000,000.
Cum. Preferred Stock: $140,500,000.

Per Share Data ($)

(Year Ended Dec. 31)

	1994	1993	1992	1991	1990	1989
Tangible Bk. Val.	21.54	21.15	21.29	20.59	20.35	19.08
Earnings	2.37	2.08	2.40	2.36	2.48	2.53
Dividends	2.00	2.18	2.14	2.10	2.06	2.02
Payout Ratio	84%	105%	89%	89%	83%	80%
Prices - High	30½	36½	32¾	29⅝	29¼	29
- Low	17¾	28¾	26⅛	24	21⅜	21⅞
P/E Ratio - High	13	18	14	13	12	11
- Low	7	14	11	10	9	9

Income Statement Analysis (Million $)

	1994	%Chg	1993	%Chg	1992	%Chg	1991
Revs.	1,899	6%	1,800	6%	1,692	9%	1,556
Depr.	178	8%	165	4%	159	5%	152
Maint.	107	-4%	112	9%	103	-6%	110
Fxd. Chgs. Cov.	2.8	17%	2.4	-4%	2.5	8%	2.4
Constr. Credits	4.0	NM	4.0	NM	4.0	-50%	8.0
Eff. Tax Rate	38%	—	34%	—	33%	—	33%
Net Inc.	188	13%	166	-10%	184	9%	169

Balance Sheet & Other Fin. Data (Million $)

	1994	1993	1992	1991	1990	1989
Gross Prop.	5,630	5,462	5,261	5,063	4,766	4,575
Cap. Exp.	247	265	265	244	211	191
Net Prop.	3,987	3,920	3,833	3,753	3,591	3,512
Capitalization:						
LT Debt	1,651	1,631	1,777	1,789	1,756	1,788
% LT Debt	46	46	49	52	53	56
Pfd.	266	266	267	269	171	172
% Pfd.	7.40	7.60	7.40	7.80	5.20	5.40
Common	1,665	1,616	1,586	1,405	1,364	1,225
% Common	47	46	44	41	41	39
Total Cap.	4,586	4,483	4,568	4,455	4,254	4,126

Ratio Analysis

	1994	1993	1992	1991	1990	1989
Oper. Ratio	83.0	83.3	80.9	80.0	78.9	78.1
% Earn. on Net Prop.	8.2	7.8	8.5	8.5	8.9	9.0
% Ret. on Revs.	9.9	9.2	10.9	10.8	10.6	11.1
% Ret. On Invest.Cap	71.0	6.8	7.4	7.5	7.8	8.2
% Return On Com.Eqty	10.3	9.1	10.6	10.7	11.4	11.5

Dividend Data —Dividends have been paid since 1910. A dividend reinvestment plan is available.

Amt. of Div. $	Date Decl.	Ex-Div. Date	Stock of Record	Payment Date
0.350	Oct. 14	Oct. 19	Oct. 25	Nov. 15 '94
0.350	Jan. 06	Jan. 19	Jan. 25	Feb. 15 '95
0.350	Apr. 07	Apr. 19	Apr. 25	May. 15 '95
0.350	Jul. 14	Jul. 21	Jul. 25	Aug. 15 '95

Data as orig. reptd.; bef. results of disc opers. and/or spec. items. Per share data adj. for stk. divs. as of ex-div. date. E-Estimated. NA-Not Available. NM-Not Meaningful. NR-Not Ranked.

Office—Ithaca-Dryden Rd. (P.O. Box 3287), Ithaca, NY 14851-3287. **Tel**—(607) 347-4131. **Chrmn, Pres & CEO**—J. A. Carrigg. **VP, Treas & CFO**—S. J. Rafferty. **VP & Secy**—D. W. Farley. **Investor Contact**—Robert D. Kump. **Dirs**—J. A. Carrigg, A. P. Casarett, E. A. Gilmour, P. L. Gioia, J. M. Keeler, A. E. Kintigh, B. E. Lynch, A. G. Marshall, D. R. Newcomb, R. A. Plane, C. W. Stuart. **Transfer Agent**—Chemical Bank, NYC. **Incorporated** in New York in 1852. **Empl**-4,192. **S&P Analyst:** Ronald J. Gross

NEXTEL Communications

NASDAQ Symbol CALL Options on CBOE (Incl. in Nat'l Market) In S&P MidCap 400

Price	Range	P–E Ratio	Dividend	Yield	S&P Ranking	Beta
Oct. 18'95	1995					
15¾	21¾–9⅜	NM	None	None	NR	NA

Summary

NEXTEL is the leading provider of specialized mobile radio communications services. Wireless pioneer Craig McCaw and certain members of his family have agreed to invest up to $1.1 billion in the company.

Current Outlook

A loss of $2.00 a share is projected for 1995, versus 1994's loss of $1.51. The loss is expected to expand to $2.05 in 1996.

Initiation of cash dividends is not expected.

Revenues should grow rapidly in 1995, reflecting acquisitions. However, margins will narrow, restricted by costs related to the construction of a digital mobile network. Results will also reflect higher depreciation charges and more shares outstanding. A planned $1.1 billion investment in the company by Craig McCaw and his family will provide needed capital to continue to build the digital network. CALL will also benefit from Mr. McCaw's wireless expertise. The company will now focus on providing enhanced dispatch services to its customers, instead of cellular-type services.

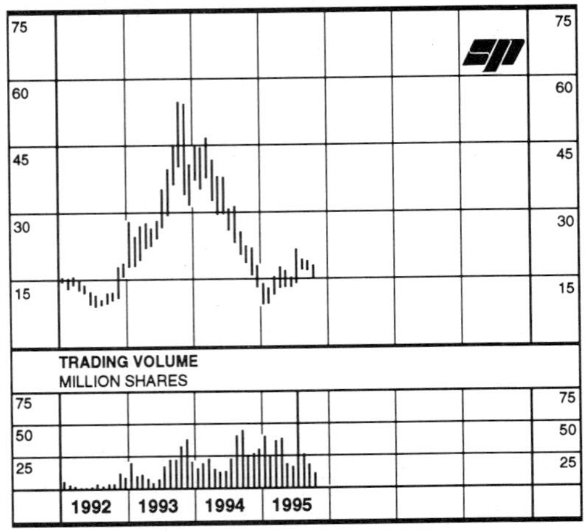

Revenues (Million $)

Quarter:	1996	1995	[1]1994	1993
Mar.	---	37.1	19.0	13.2
Jun.	---	42.9	21.5	12.8
Sep.	---	---	29.6	17.0
Dec.	---	---	32.6	19.1
	---	---	102.7	---

Revenues in the six months ended June 30, 1995, rose 98%, year to year, aided by recent acquisitions. Gross margins narrowed sharply, as substantially higher costs related to the digital mobile networks outweighed increased profitability of acquired businesses. With sharply higher SG&A and corporate expenses and increased interest, depreciation and amortization charges, the net loss widened to $110.2 million ($1.03 a share, on 16% more shares), from $57.4 million ($0.63).

Common Share Earnings ($)

Quarter:	1996	1995	[1]1994	1993
Mar.	---	d0.50	d0.27	d0.05
Jun.	---	d0.53	d0.35	d0.08
Sep.	---	Ed0.47	d0.41	d0.17
Dec.	---	Ed0.50	d0.48	d0.16
	Ed2.05	Ed2.00	d1.51	---

Important Developments

Sep. '95— The company activated its digital wireless service in the metropolitan area of Baltimore and Washington. In August, NEXTEL issued 4.2 million common shares to complete its acquisition of American Mobile Systems, a provider of specialized mobile radio (SMR) service in Florida.

Jul. '95— NEXTEL received stockholder and bondholder approval to complete pending transactions with Motorola, Craig McCaw and OneComm. In 1994, the company agreed to merge with OneComm, a provider of SMR services in the Rocky Mountain and Pacific Northwest regions. NEXTEL will be the surviving corporation.

Apr. '95— Craig McCaw and certain members of his family agreed to purchase up to $1.1 billion of company stock over the next six years through purchases from both NEXTEL and Motorola, a current shareholder. Mr. McCaw became a director, with control over a newly created operations committee.

Next earnings report expected in mid-November.

Per Share Data ($)

Yr. End Dec. 31[2]	1994	[4]1993	1992	1991	1990	1989	1988	1987
Tangible Bk. Val.	**d0.98**	d0.50	1.75	0.55	NA	NA	NA	NA
Cash Flow	**0.01**	0.02	0.28	0.30	0.76	0.26	0.09	0.02
Earnings[3]	**d1.51**	d0.73	d0.16	d0.65	d0.30	d0.36	d0.20	d0.03
Dividends	**Nil**	Nil	Nil	Nil	Nil	Nil	Nil	Nil
Payout Ratio	**Nil**	Nil	Nil	Nil	Nil	Nil	Nil	Nil
Prices[5]—High	**46¾**	54⅞	18¾	NA	NA	NA	NA	NA
Low	**13¼**	17⅞	9	NA	NA	NA	NA	NA
P/E Ratio—	**NM**	NM	NM	NM	NM	NM	NM	NM

Data as orig. reptd. **1.** Historical, reflects yr. end change. **2.** Yrs. ended Mar. 31 of the fol. cal. yr. prior to 1994. **3.** Bef. spec. items of -0.47 in 1992, -0.03 in 1991, -0.08 in 1990. **4.** Refl. merger or acquis. **5.** Cal. yrs. d-Deficit. E-Estimated. NM-Not Meaningful. NA-Not Available.

Income Data (Million $)

Year Ended Dec. 31[1]	Revs.	Oper. Inc.	% Oper. Inc. of Revs.	Cap. Exp.	Depr.	Int. Exp.	Net Bef. Taxes	Eff. Tax Rate	[3]Net Inc.	% Net Inc. of Revs.	Cash Flow
[5]1994	**194.1**	**d44.2**	**NM**	**NA**	**195.2**	**NA**	**d291.0**	**NM**	**d193.1**	**NM**	**2.1**
[4]1993	67.9	d1.8	NM	241.00	58.4	37.7	[2]d78.3	NM	d56.9	NM	1.5
1992	53.0	13.0	24.5	96.80	25.9	2.6	[2]d10.6	NM	d9.6	NM	16.3
1991	52.5	19.1	36.3	7.80	25.7	12.8	[2]d18.9	NM	d15.7	NM	8.2
1990	53.9	19.3	35.7	2.74	24.6	14.2	[2]d15.4	NM	d7.0	NM	17.7
1989	36.3	9.6	26.5	4.16	14.2	7.2	d13.5	NM	d8.2	NM	5.9
1988	17.3	4.7	27.4	3.25	5.9	3.6	d4.6	NM	d4.1	NM	1.8
1987	2.1	0.2	11.2	NA	0.4	0.2	d0.3	NM	d0.3	NM	0.1

Balance Sheet Data (Million $)

Dec. 31[1]	Cash	Curr. Assets	Curr. Liab.	Curr. Ratio	Total Assets	% Ret. on Assets	Long Term Debt	Common Equity	Total Cap.	% LT Debt of Cap.	% Ret. on Equity
1994	**473.9**	**504.2**	**NA**	**NA**	**2,889**	**NM**	**1,163.0**	**1,269**	**2,432**	**47.8**	**NM**
1993	910.0	922.0	103.0	8.9	2,197	NM	108.1	846	2,094	51.6	NM
1992	31.9	39.9	23.3	1.7	334	NM	55.0	255	310	17.7	NM
1991	13.4	20.2	17.5	1.2	211	NM	1.0	191	193	0.5	NM
1990	0.5	10.1	18.2	0.6	212	NM	106.0	24	161	66.0	NM
1989	3.2	17.9	15.8	1.1	207	NM	98.0	28	156	63.0	NM
1988	0.9	13.2	NA	NA	100	NM	47.0	12	78	60.8	NM
1987	0.5	10.1	NA	NA	38	NM	15.0	9	24	61.7	NM

Data as orig. reptd. **1.** Yrs. ended Mar. 31 of the fol. cal. yr. prior to 1994. **2.** Incl. equity in earns. of nonconsol. subs. **3.** Bef. spec. items. **4.** Refl. merger or acquis. **5.** Pro forma. d-Deficit. NM-Not Meaningful. NA-Not Available.

Business Summary

NEXTEL Communications, Inc. (formerly Fleet Call, Inc.) is a leading provider of specialized mobile radio (SMR) wireless communications services, providing service to 351,000 subscriber units in more than 25 states including 44 of the top 50 metropolitan areas in the U.S. The vast majority of subscribers are dispatch users utilizing the 800/900 megahertz bands of the radio spectrum. The FCC has authorized the company to replace most current SMR systems with advanced digital mobile networks that will be constructed using new digital technology developed by Motorola, Inc.

CALL believes that digital mobile networks will enable it to become a major provider of high-quality, enhanced mobile communications services, including two-way radio dispatch, paging, data, mobile telephone service and interconnection with the public switched telephone system. The company also expe cts the implementation of its digital network design and technology to significantly boost capacity of existing SMR channels. As of December 31, 1994, its new digital mobile networks were operating throughout much of California and in the greater metropolitan areas of New York and Chicago.

Dividend Data

No cash dividends have been paid.

Finances

In July 1995, Comcast Corp. said it would sell its 11,266 367 company common shares at $18.875 each. Comcast still holds options to buy 25 million shares, and may receive options to purchase an additional 10 million shares.

In April 1994, CALL formed an alliance with Nippon Telephone and Telegraph (NTT) under which NTT will provide the company with certain technical services and access to its R&D resources. NTT purchased about 1.53 million CALL shares at $48.925 each.

The company has entered into agreements with Motorola, regarding the purchase of infrastructure equipment and services related to the construction of the initial phase of the digital mobile networks, and with Northern Telecom, which will manufacture the switch equipment to be provided by Motorola under the purchase agreement; the agreements provide financing of up to $260 million and $40 million, respectively, for the purchase of such equipment. In addition, Motorola will assign substantially all of its 800 Mhz SMR licenses to CALL in exchange for 59.5 million common shares, subject to the company's planned merger with OneComm Corp.

Capitalization

Long Term Debt: $1,434,707,000 (6/95).

Class A Common Stock: 192,180,000 shs. ($0.001 par).
Institutions hold 23%.
Shareholders of record: 1,805 (12/94).

Office—201 Route 17 North, Rutherford, NJ 07070. **Tel**—(201) 438-1400. **Chrmn**—M. E. O'Brien. **Vice Chmn**—B. D. McAuley. **Acting CEO**—D. Weibling. **COO**—J. Jaschke. **Treas & Secy**—E. G. Long. **Investor Contact**—Paul Blalock. **Dirs**—K. Bane, R. Cooper, K. Hayashi, S. Jarvis, B. D. McAuley, C. O. McCaw, M. E. O'Brien, J. A. Schleicher, S. W. Schovee, M. Torimoto, D. Weibling. **Transfer Agent & Registrar**—First Chicago Trust Co. of New York, NYC. **Incorporated** in Delaware in 1987. **Empl**—1,600.

 Kevin J. Gooley

Nine West Group

NYSE Symbol NIN Options on Pacific (Mar-Jun-Sep-Dec) In S&P MidCap 400

Price	Range	P–E Ratio	Dividend	Yield	S&P Ranking	Beta
Oct. 19'95	1995					
44½	46⅛–26⅜	28	None	None	NR	NA

Summary

This company is a leading designer, developer and marketer of fashionable women's footwear, which it markets in the better, upper moderate and moderate price ranges. NIN markets the shoes on a wholesale basis to more than 2,000 department, specialty and independent stores, and operates its own retail outlets. The company recently acquired the footwear business of U.S. Shoe Corp.

Business Summary

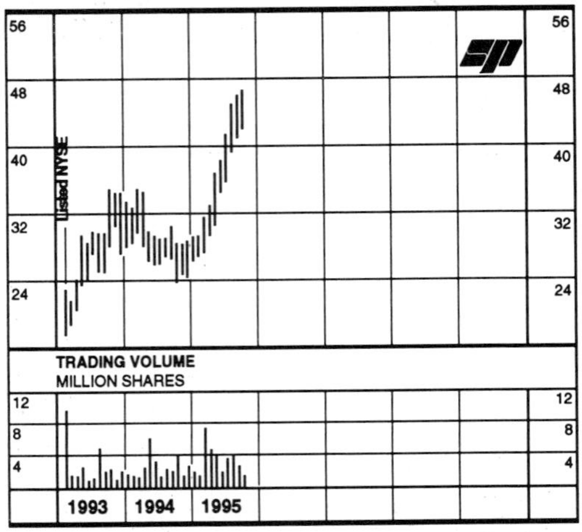

Nine West Group is a designer, developer and marketer of quality fashionable women's footwear. It markets a full collection of casual, career and dress footwear in the better, upper moderate and moderate price ranges. In addition to its flagship Nine West label, the company's nationally recognized brands include Enzo Angiolini, Calico, 9 & Co., and Westies. In 1994, 58% of sales were made through the wholesale division (63% in 1993), with the remaining 42% (37%) through NIN's own retail stores.

The company targets distinct market segments by creating a unique personality for each label at price points ranging from $25 to $80 for shoes and $35 to $140 for boots. NIN believes that its long-standing relationships with low-cost Brazilian manufacturers (which produce virtually all of its footwear products) have been instrumental in its ability to respond quickly to changing trends.

NIN's wholesale division markets its products to more than 2,000 department, specialty and independent stores encompassing more than 6,500 locations. The division sells both brand name and private label footwear in the U.S. and Canada, as well as private label footwear in the U.K.

The retail division markets footwear directly to consumers through a total of 419 stores (as of late April 1995) in 38 states, the District of Columbia and Puerto Rico, including 229 Nine West specialty stores, 100 Nine West Outlet stores, 43 9 & Co. stores, and 34 Enzo Angiolini stores. Nine West specialty stores sell the Nine West brand and, in certain locations, a selection of Enzo Angiolini shoes. Nine West Outlet stores sell selected prior seasons' styles from all of the company's brands, and serve as a distribution channel for residual inventory. The 9 & Co. concept offers value priced footwear in a full service environment. In January 1995, the company acquired the operations of L.J.S. Accessories Collections, Inc., which designs and markets quality handbags and small leather goods in NIN's accessories division. Enzo Angiolini stores (introduced in the 1993) are designed to service the better segment of the women's footwear market, offering the Enzo Angiolini line.

NIN opened 100 retail stores during 1994 and planned to open up to 100 additional stores in 1995.

Important Developments

May '95— Nine West completed the acquisition of the shoe business of U.S. Shoe Corp. (NYSE: USR) for $560 million in cash, plus warrants exercisable for a period of over eight years to purchase approximately 3.7 million shares of NIN common stock at $35.50 per share. The transaction created the largest company in the women's footwear industry, with combined revenues of approximately $1.4 billion and about 850 retail stores.

Next earnings report expected in late November.

Per Share Data ($)

Yr. End Dec. 31	1994	1993	1992	1991
Tangible Bk. Val.	[5]**6.78**	4.81	[1]3.07	NA
Cash Flow	**2.07**	1.63	NA	NA
Earnings[3]	**1.85**	[4]1.43	[2]1.26	[2]0.93
Dividends	**Nil**	Nil	NA	NA
Payout Ratio	**Nil**	Nil	NA	NA
Prices—High	**35**	35	NA	NA
Low	**23¾**	17½	NA	NA
P/E Ratio—	**19–13**	24–12	NA	NA

Data as orig. reptd., prior to 1993 data as reptd. in prospectus dated Feb. 2, 1993. **1.** As of Sep. 30, 1992, as reptd. by Co., pro forma. **2.** Supplemental pro forma. **3.** Bef. spec. item(s) of +0.35 in 1993. **4.** Pro forma. **5.** Incl. intangibles. NA-Not Available.

Income Data (Million $)

Year Ended Dec. 31	Revs.	Oper. Inc.	% Oper. Inc. of Revs.	Cap. Exp.	Depr.	Int. Exp.	Net Bef. Taxes	Eff. Tax Rate	Net Inc.	% Net Inc. of Revs.	Cash Flow
1994	**652**	**116.0**	**17.8**	**23.1**	**7.56**	**[3]2.20**	**107.0**	**40.2%**	**[2]63.9**	**9.8**	**71.4**
[1]1993	552	88.7	16.1	17.7	6.59	[3]3.26	80.6	40.6%	[2]47.8	8.7	54.4
[1]1992	462	NA	NA	NA	NA	NA	NA	40.0%	[2]38.2	8.3	NA
[1]1991	409	NA	NA	NA	NA	NA	NA	40.0%	28.1	6.9	NA

Balance Sheet Data (Million $)

Dec. 31	Cash	Curr. Assets	Curr. Liab.	Curr. Ratio	Total Assets	% Ret. on Assets	Long Term Debt	Common Equity	Total Cap.	% LT Debt of Cap.	% Ret. on Equity
1994	**5.49**	**231**	**61.3**	**3.8**	**303**	**21.3**	**2.4**	**235**	**237**	**1.0**	**31.8**
1993	8.70	240	68.7	3.5	297	19.3	51.0	165	216	23.5	43.5
[4]1992	NA	NA	NA	NA	214	NA	46.0	102	148	31.1	NA

Data as orig. reptd., prior to 1993 data as reptd. in prospectus dated Feb 2, 1993. **1.** Pro forma. **2.** Bef. spec. items. **3.** Net. **4.** As of Sep. 30, 1992, pro forma as adj. for offering. NA-Not Available.

[1]Revenues (Million $)

Quarter:	1995	1994	1993	[2]1992
Apr.	170.6	150.7	120.4	109.8
Jul.	345.7	152.8	125.3	100.1
Oct.		179.6	158.8	133.5
Jan.		169.1	147.6	118.3
		652.2	552.1	461.6

Effective in June 1995, Nine West changed its reporting period to a 52/53 week fiscal year ending on or near January 31, from a calendar year basis.

Based on a brief report, revenues for the 26 weeks ended July 29, 1995, climbed 71%, year to year, as restated for the fiscal year end change, primarily reflecting the May 1995 acquisition of U.S. Shoe Corp. Same-store sales advanced 0.9%. After purchase accounting adjustments associated with the acquisition, net income fell 29%, to $17,074,000 ($0.49 per share), from $24,009,000 ($0.69).

[1]Common Share Earnings ($)

Quarter:	1995–96	1994–95	[2]1993–94	[2]1992–93
Apr.	0.40	0.33	0.13	0.21
Jul.	0.09	0.40	0.34	0.26
Oct.		0.63	0.54	0.46
Jan.		0.50	0.40	0.33
		1.85	1.43	1.26

Dividend Data

No cash dividends have been paid, and the company does not intend to make any cash payments in the immediate future.

Finances

In January 1995, the company acquired the New York-based LJS Accessory Collections, Inc., a designer of handbags and other women's fashion accessories, for an undisclosed price. The new Nine West Accessories Division will design and develop a complete line of Nine West and Enzo Angiolini handbags as well as continue the LJS Accessory Collections label.

In December 1994, NIN said it opened four Nine West locations in Hong Kong with a freestanding specialty store in the Pacific Place Mall and concept shops in the Episode stores in Harbor City Mall, Hankow Road and Times Square Mall. The four stores are a joint venture with Jeffrey Fang, CEO of Toppy International, a large Pacific rim retailer.

In June 1994, the company entered into a new credit agreement that provides up to $75 million of borrowings on a revolving basis and through letters of credit. At October 28, 1994, $25.3 million was outstanding against the line.

Capitalization

Long Term Debt: $7,000,000 (3/95).

1. Prior to 1995-96, qtrs. ended Mar., Jun., Oct. Dec. **2.** Pro forma.

Office—9 West Broad St., Stamford, CT 06902. **Tel**—(314) 579-8812. **Chrmn**—J. Fisher. **CEO**—V. Camuto. **Pres & COO**—N. Hord. **EVP, CFO, Treas & Investor Contact**—Richard L. White. **Secy**—J. K. Bedol. **Dirs**—V. Camuto, J. Fisher, C. G. Goldsmith, H. W. Pascarella, S. M. Salibello. **Transfer Agent & Registrar**—Chemical Bank, NYC. **Empl**—3,900.

 Maureen C. Carini

STANDARD & POOR'S

STOCK REPORTS

Noble Affiliates

NYSE Symbol **NBL**
In S&P MidCap 400

10-OCT-95 **Industry:** Oil and Gas

Summary: This independent energy company explores for and develops crude oil and natural gas throughout the major basins in the U.S., as well as in Canada, Africa and Indonesia.

S&P Opinion: Hold (★★★)

Recent Price • 25¼
52 Wk Range • 30⅜-21¼

Yield • 0.6%
12-Mo. P/E • NM

Quantitative Evaluations

Outlook
(1 Lowest—5 Highest)
• 1-

Fair Value
• 18

Risk
• Average

Earn./Div. Rank
• B

Technical Eval.
• Bearish since 9/95

Rel. Strength Rank
(1 Lowest—99 Highest)
• 23

Insider Activity
• NA

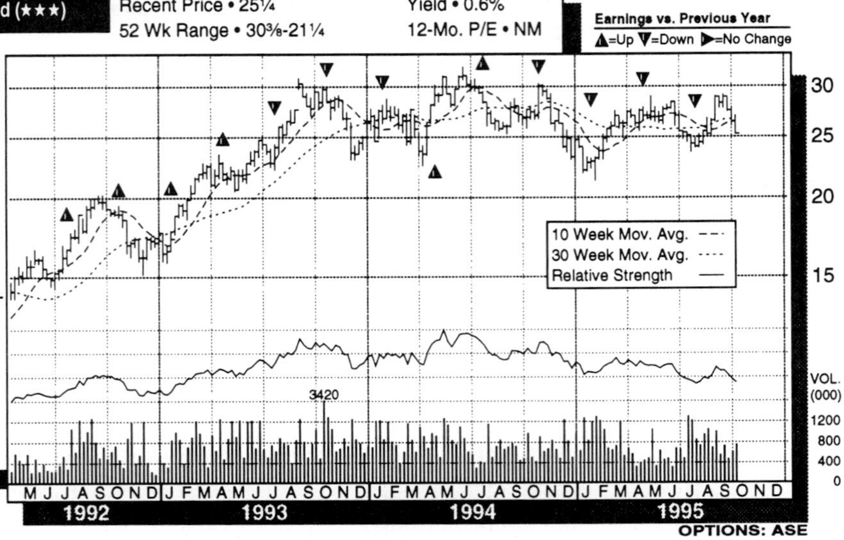

Overview - 10-OCT-95

Share earnings should increase in 1995 and beyond, reflecting higher oil and gas production levels. Also, contributions from NBL's newly formed natural gas marketing subsidiary should enhance results. However, although the long-term outlook for natural gas prices is favorable, relatively low natural gas prices are not expected to improve in the near term and will continue to depress earnings. Results should be bolstered by significantly lower depreciation, depletion and amortization charges per unit of production, decreased interest expense, and the absence of nonrecurring charges.

Valuation - 10-OCT-95

In light of the extreme weakness in wellhead natural gas prices in 1994, NBL's shares declined along with the rest of the industry. However, the shares have appreciated over 5.0% since the beginning of 1995. Part of the support behind the shares is NBL's potential earnings power, as recent acquisitions should lead to strong production growth. Although the cash flow and earnings should grow strongly, investors are likely to be somewhat hesitant to commit to the shares owing to a P/E multiple of about 29 times our 1996 estimate. However, with the long-term outlook for natural gas prices favorable, the above-average earnings growth is expected to make the stock an average performer.

Key Stock Statistics

S&P EPS Est. 1995	0.40	Tang. Bk. Value/Share	8.24
P/E on S&P Est. 1995	63.1	Beta	0.51
S&P EPS Est. 1996	0.90	Shareholders	1,900
Dividend Rate/Share	0.16	Market cap. (B)	$ 1.2
Shs. outstg. (M)	50.0	Inst. holdings	71%
Avg. daily vol. (M)	0.135	Insider holdings	NA

Value of $10,000 invested 5 years ago: $ 15,834

Fiscal Year Ending Dec. 31

	1995	% Change	1994	% Change	1993	% Change
Revenues (Million $)						
1Q	91.86	10%	83.54	20%	69.85	14%
2Q	107.1	16%	92.03	39%	66.33	-32%
3Q	—	—	97.64	52%	64.35	-6%
4Q	—	—	85.38	NM	86.06	12%
Yr.	—	—	358.4	25%	286.6	-6%
Income (Million $)						
1Q	0.44	-95%	8.42	88%	4.49	76%
2Q	3.36	-23%	4.38	10%	4.00	-83%
3Q	—	—	2.05	-52%	4.27	-35%
4Q	—	—	-11.68	NM	-0.13	NM
Yr.	—	—	3.17	-75%	12.63	-69%
Earnings Per Share ($)						
1Q	0.01	-94%	0.17	70%	0.10	67%
2Q	0.07	-22%	0.09	13%	0.08	-85%
3Q	E0.10	150%	0.04	-56%	0.09	-40%
4Q	E0.22	NM	-0.23	NM	-0.01	NM
Yr.	E0.40	NM	0.06	-77%	0.26	-72%

Next earnings report expected: late October

Noble Affiliates

Business Summary - 10-OCT-95

Noble Affiliates is an independent energy company with exploration and production operations conducted through its Samedan Oil Corp. subsidiary throughout major basins in the U.S., including the Gulf of Mexico, and in Canada, Africa and Indonesia.

Production in 1994 averaged 22,751 bbl. of oil a day (19,496 in 1993) and 247.6 MMcf of gas a day (211.1). Average price per bbl. of oil in 1994 was $14.90, versus $15.91 in 1993. Gas prices averaged $1.97 per Mcf in 1994, versus $2.10 in 1993. NBL's finding cost per bbl. of oil equivalents (BOE) in 1994 was $4.64, versus $5.14 in 1993. At December 31, 1994, estimated proved reserves amounted to 75,500,000 bbl. of oil and condensate (72,955,000 in 1993) and 779,000 MMcf of natural gas (691,530).

The company intends to be active drilling in the Gulf of Mexico, as well as selected onshore areas of the U.S. Internationally, NBL plans to focus on exploration and development in Canada and drilling operations in Tunisia.

The company's capital budget for 1995 is $206 million, up 8.0% from the $191 million budgeted in 1994.

Noble Gas Marketing, Inc. was formed in 1994 to seek opportunities to enhance the value of NBL's gas by marketing directly to end users. NBL expects the unit to also engage in the installation, purchase and operation of gas gathering lines.

In May 1992, the company sold its 32% interest in Natural Gas Clearinghouse, which provides energy services, including gas marketing, processing and crude oil trading.

Important Developments

Oct. '95—Noble purchased interests in three offshore Gulf of Mexico properties for $24.7 million. The properties are presently being developed and will require additional capital to install production facilities and pipelines, and for additional drilling and completion activities. NBL estimates it will incur about $15 million of development costs on these properties over the next nine months.

Jul. '95—Noble's Samedan Oil Corp. acquired two leases in the Gulf of Mexico from Union Pacific Resources Co. The company acquired the full working interest in West Cameron 599 and 600 for $5.3 million. Initial production from the field is projected for June 1996.

Capitalization

Long Term Debt: $376,974,000 (6/95).

Per Share Data ($) (Year Ended Dec. 31)

	1994	1993	1992	1991	1990	1989
Tangible Bk. Val.	8.24	8.32	6.83	5.99	5.69	5.15
Cash Flow	2.77	2.74	3.30	2.37	2.54	2.36
Earnings	0.06	0.26	0.93	0.44	0.65	0.52
Dividends	0.16	0.16	0.16	0.16	0.16	0.14
Payout Ratio	NM	62%	17%	37%	25%	27%
Prices - High	32¼	31	20¼	17¾	19⅛	17
- Low	22½	15¾	11⅝	12½	13⅝	10⅝
P/E Ratio - High	NM	NM	22	40	29	33
- Low	NM	NM	13	28	21	20

Income Statement Analysis (Million $)

	1994	%Chg	1993	%Chg	1992	%Chg	1991
Revs.	350	26%	278	7%	260	15%	226
Oper. Inc.	150	2%	147	4%	142	21%	117
Depr. Depl. & Amort.	135	13%	119	13%	105	24%	85.0
Int. Exp.	24.7	21%	20.4	NM	20.5	-2%	21.0
Pretax Inc.	5.0	-76%	21.0	-66%	61.0	110%	29.0
Eff. Tax Rate	39%	—	39%	—	33%	—	33%
Net Inc.	3.2	-75%	12.6	-69%	41.2	113%	19.3

Balance Sheet & Other Fin. Data (Million $)

	1994	1993	1992	1991	1990	1989
Cash	22.0	176	119	1.8	39.0	34.6
Curr. Assets	104	257	189	78.0	108	83.0
Total Assets	934	1,068	626	590	588	544
Curr. Liab.	72.0	147	55.7	56.7	64.0	48.0
LT Debt	377	454	225	225	225	225
Common Eqty.	412	415	305	265	251	226
Total Cap.	815	914	563	524	514	485
Cap. Exp.	166	510	66.0	123	97.0	97.0
Cash Flow	138	132	146	104	112	103

Ratio Analysis

	1994	1993	1992	1991	1990	1989
Curr. Ratio	1.4	1.8	3.4	1.4	1.7	1.7
% LT Debt of Cap.	44.3	49.6	39.9	42.9	43.7	46.3
% Ret. on Assets	0.3	1.4	6.8	3.3	5.0	4.2
% Ret. on Equity	0.8	3.3	14.4	7.5	11.9	10.6

Dividend Data —Dividends were initiated in 1975.

Amt. of Div. $	Date Decl.	Ex-Div. Date	Stock of Record	Payment Date
0.040	Oct. 26	Nov. 01	Nov. 07	Nov. 22 '94
0.040	Jan. 31	Feb. 07	Feb. 13	Feb. 27 '95
0.040	Apr. 24	May. 02	May. 08	May. 22 '95
0.040	Jul. 26	Aug. 07	Aug. 09	Aug. 23 '95

Data as orig. reptd.; bef. results of disc opers. and/or spec. items. Per share data adj. for stk. divs. as of ex-div. date. E-Estimated. NA-Not Available. NM-Not Meaningful. NR-Not Ranked.

Office—110 West Broadway, Ardmore, OK 73401. **Tel**—(405) 223-4110. **Chrmn, Pres & CEO**—R. Kelley. **VP-Fin, Treas & Investor Contact**—William D. Dickson. **Secy**—O. Walraven. **Dirs**—A. A. Baker, R. Butler, M. A. Cawley, E. F. Cox, J. C. Day, R. Kelley, H. F. Kleinman, G. J. McLeod, G. W. Nichols, J. F. Snodgrass. **Transfer Agent & Registrar**—Liberty National Bank & Trust Co. of Oklahoma City. **Incorporated** in Delaware in 1969. **Empl**-521. **S&P Analyst:** Ronald J. Gross

STANDARD & POOR'S

STOCK REPORTS

Nordson Corporation

NASDAQ Symbol **NDSN**

In S&P MidCap 400

26-AUG-95 **Industry:** Manufacturing/Distr

Summary: This company manufactures and markets systems that apply adhesives, sealants and coatings to consumer and industrial products during manufacturing processes.

Quantitative Evaluations

Outlook
(1 Lowest—5 Highest)
• **3-**

Fair Value
• **56⅛**

Risk
• **Low**

Earn./Div. Rank
• **A**

Technical Eval.
• **Bullish** since 12/94

Rel. Strength Rank
(1 Lowest—99 Highest)
• **51**

Insider Activity
• **Unfavorable**

Recent Price • 57½
52 Wk Range • 61-52

Yield • 1.1%
12-Mo. P/E • 20.9

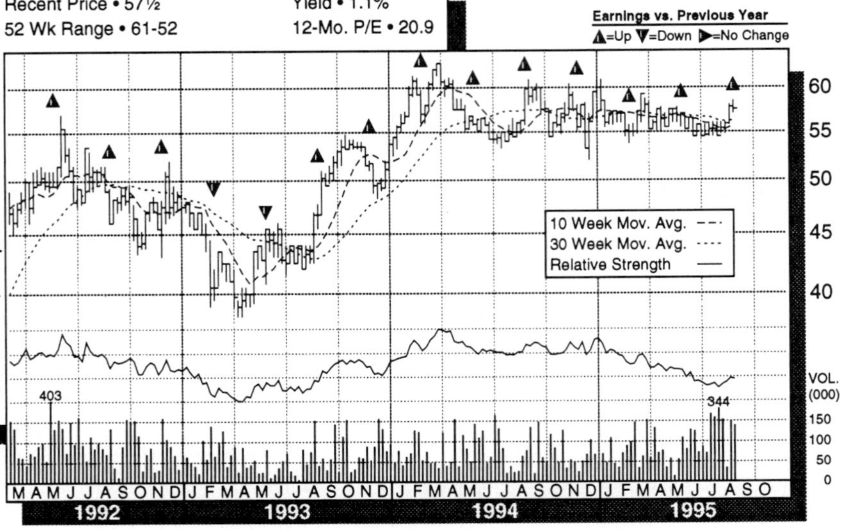

Business Profile - 24-AUG-95

Nordson's international sales have been growing. The company now derives over 50% of revenues from outside North America. Nordson markets its products worldwide through direct operations and a comprehensive distribution network. In 1994, it expanded its sales operations into China, Malaysia, Mexico and Poland. North American sales, however, remain the major contributor to earnings. Recent results benefited from currency translation gains. The dividend has been boosted for 31 consecutive years.

Operational Review - 25-AUG-95

Revenues grew 17% in the first nine months of fiscal 1995, reflecting strength in North America, the Pacific Rim and Latin America, and currency translation gains. Results were restricted by a less favorable product mix, and despite currency, the increase in operating income was held to 14%. With higher other income and slightly lower interest expense, EPS advanced 18% (on 2.4% fewer shares), to $1.16.

Stock Performance - 25-AUG-95

In the past 30 trading days, NDSN's shares have increased 4%, compared to a 0.04% rise in the S&P 500. Average trading volume for the past five days was 27,440 shares, compared with the 40-day moving average of 36,874 shares.

Key Stock Statistics

Dividend Rate/Share	0.64	Shareholders	3,000
Shs. outstg. (M)	18.2	Market cap. (B)	$ 1.0
Avg. daily vol. (M)	0.024	Inst. holdings	24%
Tang. Bk. Value/Share	10.21	Insider holdings	NA
Beta	0.77		

Value of $10,000 invested 5 years ago: $ 24,475

Fiscal Year Ending Oct. 31

	1995	% Change	1994	% Change	1993	% Change
Revenues (Million $)						
1Q	123.5	18%	104.7	4%	100.3	7%
2Q	143.1	18%	121.5	11%	109.3	3%
3Q	155.2	16%	133.4	8%	123.3	17%
4Q	—	—	147.1	14%	128.7	7%
Yr.	—	—	506.7	10%	461.6	8%
Income (Million $)						
1Q	8.94	15%	7.80	17%	6.68	-9%
2Q	12.69	18%	10.75	22%	8.79	-14%
3Q	14.85	13%	13.12	9%	12.08	17%
4Q	—	—	14.99	13%	13.23	14%
Yr.	—	—	46.65	14%	40.78	3%
Earnings Per Share ($)						
1Q	0.48	17%	0.41	17%	0.35	-8%
2Q	0.68	21%	0.56	22%	0.46	-12%
3Q	0.80	16%	0.69	10%	0.63	19%
4Q	—	—	0.79	14%	0.69	15%
Yr.	—	—	2.45	15%	2.13	5%

Next earnings report expected: early December

Nordson Corporation

Business Summary - 25-AUG-95

Nordson Corporation develops, manufactures and markets worldwide sophisticated systems that apply liquid and powder coatings, sealants and adhesives to consumer and industrial products during manufacturing processes.

Contributions by geographic area in fiscal 1994 were:

	Sales	Profits
North America	44%	77%
Europe	33%	14%
Japan	15%	6%
Pacific & Latin America	8%	3%

Markets for company equipment include packaging, product assembly, nonwoven products, converting, advanced gasketing, powder coatings, liquid finishings, automotive products, container coatings and electronic products.

Nordson markets its products through four international sales divisions, supported by a network of 32 direct operations.

Hot-melting equipment is used to apply adhesives, sealants, caulking and other thermoplastic materials. Thermoplastic material is applied in heated, liquid form, either by hand-held or automatic guns, to the various package or product surfaces to be closed or fastened.

The company's adhesive application equipment is used in the packaging market for the fastening of industrial and consumer products and in industrial production applications for the assembly of various items.

Nordson's powder product line consists of application, recovery and recycle equipment that applies both organic and inorganic coating materials to a wide variety of substrates.

The company also markets air driers, flame detectors, gun movers and programmable controllers, providing the capability to supply complete powder finishing systems to its customers.

Nordson emphasizes product development through its own research staff. In fiscal 1994, R&D sxpending totaled $24,434,000 (4.8% of sales), versus $20,521,000 (4.4%) in fiscal 1993 and $18,431,000 (4.3%) in fiscal 1992.

Important Developments

Aug. '95—Nordson said fiscal 1995 third quarter local sales grew 10% in North America and Europe, and 18% in Pacific/Latin American operations. Japanese sales were unchanged in local currency terms. The company added that improving results in Europe should help to mitigate any weakening in North American operations.

Capitalization

Long Term Debt: $17,864,000 (7/95).

Per Share Data ($) (Year Ended Oct. 31)

	1994	1993	1992	1991	1990	1989
Tangible Bk. Val.	9.92	9.03	7.79	6.87	5.99	4.98
Cash Flow	3.25	2.84	2.70	2.39	2.09	2.15
Earnings	2.45	2.13	2.03	1.77	1.53	1.77
Dividends	0.56	0.48	0.44	0.40	0.36	0.32
Payout Ratio	23%	23%	22%	22%	23%	18%
Prices - High	63	$54\frac{3}{4}$	57	46	$26\frac{1}{4}$	$29\frac{1}{2}$
- Low	52	$38\frac{1}{4}$	43	$22\frac{1}{8}$	$16\frac{7}{8}$	22
P/E Ratio - High	26	26	28	26	17	17
- Low	21	18	21	13	11	12

Income Statement Analysis (Million $)

	1994	%Chg	1993	%Chg	1992	%Chg	1991
Revs.	507	10%	462	8%	426	10%	388
Oper. Inc.	89.6	10%	81.2	1%	80.3	14%	70.2
Depr.	15.2	10%	13.8	6%	13.0	9%	11.9
Int. Exp.	4.4	-31%	6.4	-5%	6.8	-7%	7.3
Pretax Inc.	70.9	14%	62.2	2%	60.8	17%	52.0
Eff. Tax Rate	34%	—	35%	—	35%	—	35%
Net Inc.	46.7	14%	40.8	3%	39.5	17%	33.8

Balance Sheet & Other Fin. Data (Million $)

	1994	1993	1992	1991	1990	1989
Cash	11.1	23.4	13.0	10.5	8.8	5.8
Curr. Assets	250	242	232	194	174	156
Total Assets	381	358	346	297	270	236
Curr. Liab.	123	116	127	107	108	102
LT Debt	19.3	22.1	26.8	25.5	25.5	20.1
Common Eqty.	212	196	178	153	130	107
Total Cap.	232	219	207	180	158	130
Cap. Exp.	20.6	20.5	17.6	14.2	21.2	35.9
Cash Flow	61.9	54.6	52.5	45.7	40.3	41.6

Ratio Analysis

	1994	1993	1992	1991	1990	1989
Curr. Ratio	2.0	2.1	1.8	1.8	1.6	1.5
% LT Debt of Cap.	8.3	10.1	12.9	14.2	16.2	15.5
% Net Inc.of Revs.	9.2	8.8	9.3	8.7	8.5	12.1
% Ret. on Assets	12.7	11.6	12.3	11.9	11.6	17.3
% Ret. on Equity	23.0	21.8	23.9	23.9	24.7	35.1

Dividend Data —Dividends, paid each year since 1969, are targeted at 6% of shareholders' equity at the beginning of each fiscal year. A dividend reinvestment plan is available.

Amt. of Div. $	Date Decl.	Ex-Div. Date	Stock of Record	Payment Date
0.140	Aug. 17	Aug. 29	Sep. 02	Sep. 27 '94
0.160	Nov. 16	Nov. 28	Dec. 02	Jan. 03 '95
0.160	Feb. 15	Feb. 27	Mar. 03	Mar. 28 '95
0.160	May. 17	May. 26	Jun. 02	Jun. 27 '95
0.160	Aug. 16	Aug. 31	Sep. 05	Sep. 26 '95

Data as orig. reptd.; bef. results of disc. opers. and/or spec. items. Per share data adj. for stk. divs. as of ex-div. date. E-Estimated. NA-Not Available. NM-Not Meaningful. NR-Not Ranked.

Office—28601 Clemens Rd., Westlake, OH 44145. **Tel**—(216) 892-1580. **Chrmn**—E. T. Nord. **Pres & CEO**—W. P. Madar. **Secy**—W. D. Ginn. **VP-Fin, Treas & Investor Contact**—Nicholas D. Pellecchia. **Dirs**—G. R. Brown, W. W. Colville, W. D. Ginn, S. R. Hardis, A. O. Krueger, W. P. Madar, E. T. Nord, E. W. Nord, W. L. Robinson. **Transfer Agent & Registrar**—Society National Bank, Cleveland. **Incorporated** in Ohio in 1954. **Empl-** 3,281. **S&P Analyst:** Justin McCann

STANDARD & POOR'S

STOCK REPORTS

Northeast Utilities

NYSE Symbol **NU**

In S&P MidCap 400

13-OCT-95 **Industry:** Utilities-Electric

Summary: This utility holding company serves more than 1.7 million customers in Connecticut, western Massachusetts and New Hampshire, and is expanding wholesale marketing to New York State.

S&P Opinion: Hold (★★★)

Recent Price • 24½
52 Wk Range • 24½-21

Yield • 7.1%
12-Mo. P/E • 11.8

Quantitative Evaluations

Outlook
(1 Lowest—5 Highest)
• **1−**

Fair Value
• **21⅛**

Risk
• **Low**

Earn./Div. Rank
• **B**

Technical Eval.
• **Bearish** since 2/95

Rel. Strength Rank
(1 Lowest—99 Highest)
• **77**

Insider Activity
• **NA**

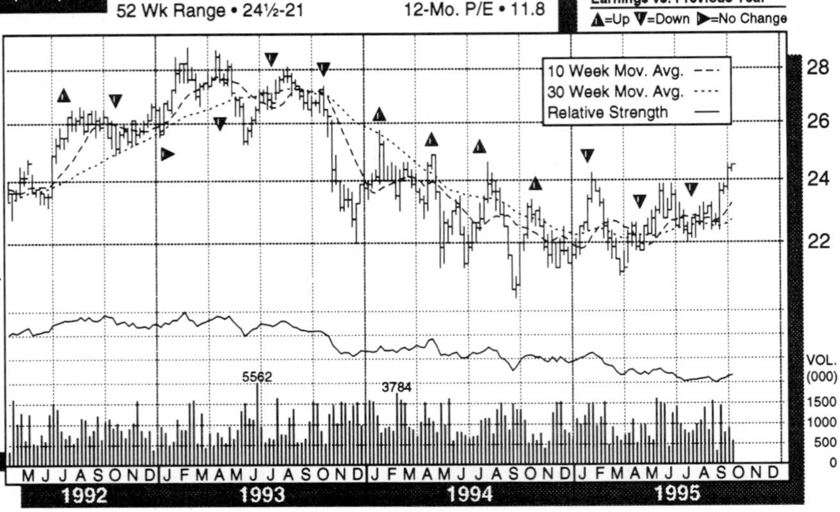

Overview - 13-OCT-95

NU's first half earnings are down in 1995, mostly because of a substantial 6.5% decline in kilowatt hour sales to residential customers, their largest customer group. Although a rise in demand from this sector in the third quarter may be somewhat offsetting, much lower operating and maintenance costs are important to a positive trend in earnings. A recent early retirement program, debt refinancing to lower Public Service of New Hampshire interest costs, and new, lower cost purchased power contracts will add to 1995 second half results. NU's focus on attracting new business and retaining old contracts through lower rates is a long-term positive, but near term, a weak economy in its largest service area, Connecticut and Massachusetts, is a barrier to growth.

Valuation - 13-OCT-95

Expectations of weak earnings comparisons in 1995 and 1996 have dampened investors' enthusiasm for these shares in recent periods; the stock has underperformed both the industry and the market average this year. Excess generating capacity limit NU's earnings growth, but with a low capital budget focused on repairs and plant efficiency, cash flow appears sufficient to protect NU's above average yield over the near term. A below average payout suggests a possible dividend increase, but none is likely until the company's aggressive marketing activities promote a more positive trend in earnings.

Key Stock Statistics

S&P EPS Est. 1995	2.20	Tang. Bk. Value/Share	18.38
P/E on S&P Est. 1995	11.1	Beta	0.47
S&P EPS Est. 1996	2.30	Shareholders	137,900
Dividend Rate/Share	1.76	Market cap. (B)	$ 3.1
Shs. outstg. (M)	126.3	Inst. holdings	31%
Avg. daily vol. (M)	0.144	Insider holdings	NA

Value of $10,000 invested 5 years ago: $ 16,617

Fiscal Year Ending Dec. 31

	1995	% Change	1994	% Change	1993	% Change
Revenues (Million $)						
1Q	944.7	-2%	966.2	NM	958.2	26%
2Q	840.3	-2%	854.6	NM	853.8	19%
3Q	—	—	923.7	NM	915.2	8%
4Q	—	—	898.2	NM	901.9	2%
Yr.	—	—	3,643	NM	3,629	13%
Income (Million $)						
1Q	86.28	-10%	95.89	49%	64.35	-14%
2Q	42.40	-31%	61.15	NM	18.28	-72%
3Q	—	—	65.03	31%	49.68	-19%
4Q	—	—	64.81	-2%	65.96	15%
Yr.	—	—	286.9	45%	198.3	-23%
Earnings Per Share ($)						
1Q	0.69	-10%	0.77	57%	0.49	-22%
2Q	0.34	-31%	0.49	NM	0.12	-76%
3Q	E0.56	8%	0.52	41%	0.37	-21%
4Q	E0.61	17%	0.52	-16%	0.62	44%
Yr.	E2.20	-4%	2.30	44%	1.60	-21%

Next earnings report expected: late October

Northeast Utilities

Business Summary - 13-OCT-95

Northeast Utilities, the largest utility in New England, is a holding company with four subsidiaries serving some 1.75 million customers in Connecticut and western Massachusetts, and, since the mid-1992 acquisition of the once bankrupt Public Service Co. of New Hampshire (PSNH), New Hampshire. NU's system interconnects with all the major utilities in New England and three of the largest electric utilities in New York. Electric revenues by customer class in recent years were:

	1994	1993	1992	1991
Residential	41%	39%	38%	37%
Commercial	34%	29%	30%	31%
Industrial	14%	18%	18%	16%
Other	11%	14%	16%	16%

In 1994, retail kilowatt hour (kwh) sales rose 2.9%, including a 3.2% advance for commercial customers. Retail kwh sales accounted for 77% of total sales. Wholesale kwh sales (or sales to other utilities or independent power generators) comprised 23% (9.2% of revenues), and rose 0.8% due to entry into new wholesale markets.

Power sources in 1994 were nuclear 54%, coal 8%, oil 7%, hydro 4%, gas 3%, purchased power 10%, and other 14%. Peak demand in 1994 was 6,339 mw, and capability at peak totaled 8,948 mw, for a capacity margin of 29%.

NU estimates construction program expenditures, including allowance for funds used during construction, at $1.2 billion for the next five years. It plans to generate funds for the program, which will focus on maintaining and upgrading the transmission and distribution system as well as nuclear and fossil-generating systems, with internally generated funds. The company does not anticipate a need for new, major generating facilities until 2009.

Important Developments

Jul. '95—NU reported a decline in earnings for the six months ended June 30, 1995 compared to the comparable 1994 period due to lower kilowatt hour sales stemming from mild weather in the first quarter, and to higher fuel and purchased power costs. Continued deferral of cogeneration expense and lower maintenance costs were partly offsetting. Also in July, the company announced an early retirement and layoff program that it expected would cost $10 to $12 million.

Capitalization

Long Term Debt: $3,693,416,000 (6/95).
Subsid. Preferred Stock: $475,950,000.

Per Share Data ($)

(Year Ended Dec. 31)

	1994	1993	1992	1991	1990	1989
Tangible Bk. Val.	18.21	17.52	15.87	15.55	16.15	15.94
Earnings	2.30	1.60	2.02	2.12	1.94	1.87
Dividends	1.76	1.76	1.76	1.76	1.76	1.76
Payout Ratio	77%	110%	87%	83%	91%	94%
Prices - High	25¾	28⅞	26¾	24⅜	22⅝	23
- Low	20⅜	22	22½	19	17⅞	18½
P/E Ratio - High	11	18	13	12	12	12
- Low	9	14	11	9	9	10

Income Statement Analysis (Million $)

	1994	%Chg	1993	%Chg	1992	%Chg	1991
Revs.	3,643	NM	3,629	13%	3,217	17%	2,754
Depr.	335	4%	321	13%	283	18%	239
Maint.	306	15%	266	-3%	274	19%	230
Fxd. Chgs. Cov.	2.8	27%	2.2	-14%	2.6	-8%	2.8
Constr. Credits	10.0	-29%	14.0	56%	9.0	NM	9.0
Eff. Tax Rate	49%	—	47%	—	41%	—	39%
Net Inc.	287	45%	198	-23%	256	8%	237

Balance Sheet & Other Fin. Data (Million $)

	1994	1993	1992	1991	1990	1989
Gross Prop.	9,897	9,692	9,468	7,440	7,299	7,093
Cap. Exp.	288	309	352	274	379	293
Net Prop.	6,603	6,670	6,719	5,258	5,265	5,314
Capitalization:						
LT Debt	4,108	4,216	4,505	2,830	2,713	2,772
% LT Debt	59	60	61	54	54	54
Pfd.	610	620	654	568	569	574
% Pfd.	8.70	8.80	8.90	11	11	11
Common	2,309	2,224	2,174	1,876	1,791	1,752
% Common	33	32	30	36	35	34
Total Cap.	9,183	9,174	8,116	6,055	5,745	5,736

Ratio Analysis

	1994	1993	1992	1991	1990	1989
Oper. Ratio	85.0	87.6	86.3	85.9	85.5	82.5
% Earn. on Net Prop.	8.2	6.7	7.4	7.4	7.2	7.2
% Ret. on Revs.	7.9	5.5	8.0	8.6	8.1	9.2
% Ret. On Invest.Cap	6.7	6.2	7.8	8.0	8.2	8.0
% Return On Com.Eqty	12.7	11.4	12.7	13.0	12.0	11.8

Dividend Data —Dividends have been paid since 1927. A dividend reinvestment plan is available.

Amt. of Div. $	Date Decl.	Ex-Div. Date	Stock of Record	Payment Date
0.440	Oct. 31	Nov. 25	Dec. 01	Dec. 30 '94
0.440	Jan. 24	Feb. 23	Mar. 01	Mar. 31 '95
0.440	May. 02	May. 25	Jun. 01	Jun. 30 '95
0.440	Aug. 01	Aug. 30	Sep. 01	Sep. 29 '95

Data as orig. reptd.; bef. results of disc opers. and/or spec. items. Per share data adj. for stk. divs. as of ex-div. date. E-Estimated. NA-Not Available. NM-Not Meaningful. NR-Not Ranked.

Office—P.O. Box 270, Hartford, CT 06141. **Tel**—(203) 665-5000. **Chrmn**—W. B. Ellis. **Pres & CEO**—B. M. Fox. **VP & CFO**—R. E. Busch. **VP & Secy**—J. B. Keane. **Investor Contact**—Jeff Kotkin. **Trustees**—A. F. Boschulte, C. M. Cleveland, G. David, D. J. Donahue, W. B. Ellis, B. M. Fox, G. N. Kelley, E. T. Kennan, D. C. Lunt, Jr., W. J. Pape II, R. E. Patricelli, J. F. Swope, J. F. Turner. **Transfer Agents & Registrars**—Northeast Utilities Service Co., Hartford, Conn.; State Street Bank & Trust Co., Boston. **Organized** in Massachusetts in 1927. **Empl**-9,395. **S&P Analyst:** Jane Collin

STANDARD & POOR'S
STOCK REPORTS

Northern Trust Corp.

NASDAQ Symbol **NTRS**
In S&P MidCap 400

28-SEP-95 **Industry:** Banking

Summary: This Chicago-based interstate bank holding company's lead subsidiary is Northern Trust Co., the fourth largest commercial bank in Illinois.

S&P Opinion: Accumulate (★★★★)

Recent Price • 45½ | Yield • 2.3%
52 Wk Range • 47⅝-31¾ | 12-Mo. P/E • 13.9

Quantitative Evaluations
- Outlook (1 Lowest—5 Highest) • **4+**
- Fair Value • **46¼**
- Risk • **Low**
- Earn./Div. Rank • **B+**

Technical Eval. • **Bullish since 4/95**
Rel. Strength Rank (1 Lowest—99 Highest) • **75**
Insider Activity • **Neutral**

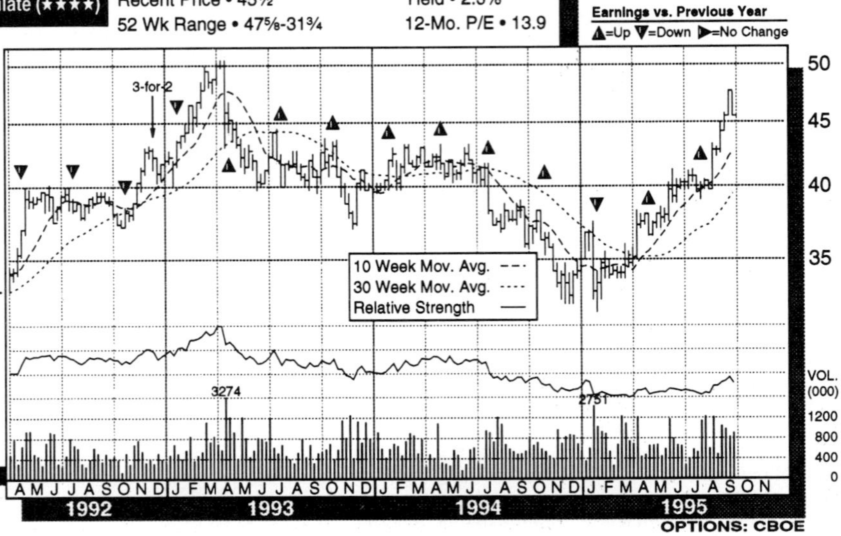

Overview - 28-SEP-95

Second quarter earnings advanced 9%, year to year, due primarily to increased trust fees, higher net interest income, and growth in foreign exchange trading profits. Noninterest income, which accounted for 63% of total revenue, rose 12% (excluding the effect of a $28.5 million pretax gain in the 1994 period), led by a 9% advance in trust fees. At June 30, 1995, the trust services division administered $549.3 billion ($91.1 billion in managed assets), up from $481.1 billion ($78.5 billion) a year earlier. Average loans grew 8.5%, led by double-digit growth in the residential mortgage and commercial loan portfolios. Credit quality in the lending segment remains strong, as evidenced by recent levels of nonperforming assets, which amounted to $34.5 million (0.18% of total assets) at June 30, 1995, down from $39.6 million at June 30, 1994 (0.21%).

Valuation - 28-SEP-95

As a leader in the corporate and personal trust business, NTRS is well positioned for the future. Recent expansion into the important Texas and Florida markets, through the acquisitions of Beach One Financial (Vero Beach, Fla.) and Tanglewood Bank (Houston, Tex.), should help propel trust fees higher. Although the stock is trading near its 52-week high and at around 11 to 12 times our earnings estimate for 1996, higher trust fees, strong loan growth, and the continued focus on cost control suggest the stock will be an above average performer over the next 6 to 12 months.

Key Stock Statistics

S&P EPS Est. 1995	3.65	Tang. Bk. Value/Share	21.84
P/E on S&P Est. 1995	12.5	Beta	1.02
S&P EPS Est. 1996	4.00	Shareholders	3,000
Dividend Rate/Share	1.04	Market cap. (B)	$ 2.5
Shs. outstg. (M)	55.9	Inst. holdings	67%
Avg. daily vol. (M)	0.166	Insider holdings	NA

Value of $10,000 invested 5 years ago: $ 25,003

Fiscal Year Ending Dec. 31

	1995	% Change	1994	% Change	1993	% Change
Revenues (Million $)						
1Q	422.8	27%	333.4	8%	308.3	NM
2Q	439.6	16%	378.2	21%	312.7	NM
3Q	—	—	373.4	17%	320.2	5%
4Q	—	—	393.5	24%	317.6	4%
Yr.	—	—	1,479	17%	1,259	2%
Income (Million $)						
1Q	49.30	9%	45.40	13%	40.20	12%
2Q	53.10	9%	48.70	17%	41.60	12%
3Q	—	—	48.00	12%	42.80	12%
4Q	—	—	40.10	-7%	43.30	12%
Yr.	—	—	182.2	9%	167.9	12%
Earnings Per Share ($)						
1Q	0.86	7%	0.80	13%	0.71	11%
2Q	0.90	6%	0.85	16%	0.73	12%
3Q	E0.94	13%	0.83	11%	0.75	12%
4Q	E0.95	38%	0.69	-9%	0.76	12%
Yr.	E3.65	15%	3.17	7%	2.96	12%

Next earnings report expected: mid October

Northern Trust Corp.

Business Summary - 28-SEP-95

Northern Trust Corporation is an interstate bank holding company whose lead bank is Northern Trust Co. of Chicago, the fourth largest bank in Illinois. It also owns a growing network of smaller banks and nonbanking subsidiaries in Illinois, Florida, Arizona, California, New York and Texas, providing banking, stock brokerage and other services. At December 31, 1994, total assets came to $18.6 billion, and trust assets under administration totaled $499 billion. Gross loans of $8.6 billion at December 31, 1994, were divided:

Real estate--residential	38%
Commercial	31%
Leasing & other	9%
Consumer	8%
Real estate--commercial	6%
International	5%
Brokerage	3%

The allowance for loan losses at 1994 year-end was $144.8 million (1.69% of gross loans and leases outstanding), down from $145.5 million (1.91%) a year earlier. Net chargeoffs during 1994 amounted to $6.7 million (equal to 0.08% of average loans), down from $19.5 million (0.27%) in 1993. Nonperforming assets at December 31, 1994, totaled $30.0 million (0.16% of total assets), versus $37.0 million (0.22%) at 1993 year-end.

Total deposits of $11.7 billion at year-end 1994 were divided: demand and other noninterest-bearing 22%, savings and money market 27%, savings certificates 13%, other time 3% and foreign 35%.

On a tax-equivalent basis, the average yield on interest-earning assets was 5.61% in 1994 (5.39% in 1993), while the average rate paid on interest-bearing liabilities was 3.87% (3.23%), for a net spread of 1.74% (2.16%).

Important Developments

Jun. '95—Northern Trust announced that its four banks in Illinois have reached an agreement with the Department of Justice ending an 18-month investigation into the banks' mortgage lending practices. As part of the agreement, the banks will create a $700,000 fund to compensate minority applicants who were denied loans in 1992 and 1993, but would have received loans or counteroffers if the banks' current standards were applied. NTRS expects payments to be made to less than 100 applicants and to average under $10,000.

Capitalization

Notes Payable: $558,100,000 (6/95).
Ser. C Auction Rate Cum. Pfd. Stk.: 600 shs.
Ser. D Flex. Auction Rate Cum. Pfd. Stk.: 600 shs.
Ser. E 6.25% Cum. Conv. Pfd. Stk.: 50,000 shs., ea. conv. into 1.2048 com. shs.

Per Share Data ($)

(Year Ended Dec. 31)

	1994	1993	1992	1991	1990	1989
Tangible Bk. Val.	20.53	17.02	14.37	12.82	11.04	9.68
Earnings	3.17	2.96	2.64	2.29	2.06	2.08
Dividends	0.92	0.77	0.66	0.58	0.52	0.44
Payout Ratio	29%	26%	25%	25%	25%	21%
Prices - High	43¼	50½	43⅛	35	22½	23¾
- Low	32¼	37	32⅝	18	13	14⅝
P/E Ratio - High	14	17	16	15	11	11
- Low	10	13	12	8	6	7

Income Statement Analysis (Million $)

	1994	%Chg	1993	%Chg	1992	%Chg	1991
Net Int. Inc.	338	3%	329	6%	311	10%	282
Tax Equiv. Adj.	33.4	-2%	34.1	5%	32.5	-10%	36.0
Non Int. Inc.	630	14%	551	9%	506	24%	409
Loan Loss Prov.	6.0	-70%	20.0	-33%	30.0	-3%	31.0
% Exp/Op Revs.	70%	—	69%	—	69%	—	69%
Pretax Inc.	262	12%	234	13%	207	26%	164
Eff. Tax Rate	30%	—	28%	—	28%	—	22%
Net Inc.	182	8%	168	12%	150	18%	127
% Net Int. Marg.	2.36%	—	2.65%	—	2.96%	—	3.00%

Balance Sheet & Other Fin. Data (Million $)

	1994	1993	1992	1991	1990	1989
Earning Assets:						
Money Mkt.	2,642	2,705	2,318	1,710	1,397	970
Inv. Securities	5,053	4,002	3,180	3,115	2,194	2,244
Com'l Loans	3,107	2,809	2,881	3,176	2,831	2,924
Other Loans	5,484	4,814	4,055	3,104	2,706	2,736
Total Assets	18,562	16,903	14,960	13,193	11,789	10,938
Demand Deposits	2,830	2,762	2,712	1,824	2,021	1,803
Time Deposits	8,904	7,572	7,159	6,737	6,088	5,236
LT Debt	792	1,144	545	266	172	241
Common Eqty.	1,111	982	841	701	589	531

Ratio Analysis

	1994	1993	1992	1991	1990	1989
% Ret. on Assets	1.0	1.1	1.1	1.0	1.0	1.1
% Ret. on Equity	16.7	17.9	18.3	19.0	19.8	22.8
% Loan Loss Resv.	1.7	1.9	2.1	2.3	2.7	2.7
% Loans/Deposits	73.2	73.8	70.3	73.4	68.3	80.4
% Equity to Assets	5.9	5.8	5.8	5.2	4.7	4.4

Dividend Data —Cash has been paid each year since 1896.

Amt. of Div. $	Date Decl.	Ex-Div. Date	Stock of Record	Payment Date
0.220	Aug. 16	Sep. 02	Sep. 09	Oct. 03 '94
0.260	Nov. 15	Dec. 05	Dec. 09	Jan. 03 '95
0.260	Feb. 21	Mar. 06	Mar. 10	Apr. 03 '95
0.260	May. 16	Jun. 06	Jun. 09	Jul. 03 '95
0.260	Aug. 15	Sep. 06	Sep. 08	Oct. 02 '95

Data as orig. reptd.; bef. results of disc opers. and/or spec. items. Per share data adj. for stk. divs. as of ex-div. date. E-Estimated. NA-Not Available. NM-Not Meaningful. NR-Not Ranked.

Office—50 S. LaSalle St., Chicago, IL 60675. **Tel**—(312) 630-6000. **Chrmn & CEO**—D. W. Fox. **Pres & COO**—W. A. Osborn. **Vice Chrmn**—B. G. Hastings. **SEVP & CFO**—P. R. Pero. **EVP & Secy**—P. L. Rossiter. **Investor Contact**—Laurie K. McMahon (312-444-7811). **Dirs**—W. H. Clark, D. E. Cross, D. W. Fox, R. S. Hamada, B. G. Hastings, R. A. Helman, A. L. Kelly, A. Krainik, R. D. Krebs, F. A. Krehbiel, W. G. Mitchell, W. A. Osborn, H. B. Smith, W. D. Smithburg, B. L. Thomas. **Transfer Agent & Registrar**—Harris Trust & Savings Bank, Chicago. **Incorporated** in Delaware in 1971; bank chartered in Illinois in 1889. **Empl**-6,608. **S&P Analyst:** Brad Ohlmuller

STANDARD & POOR'S

STOCK REPORTS

NovaCare

NYSE Symbol **NOV**
In S&P MidCap 400

17-SEP-95 **Industry:** Health Care Centers

Summary: NovaCare is the largest U.S. provider of contract rehabilitation therapy and orthotic and prosthetic patient care services.

S&P Opinion: Hold (★★★)

Recent Price • 7⅞
52 Wk Range • 16-7⅛
Yield • Nil
12-Mo. P/E • 8.3

Quantitative Evaluations

Outlook
(1 Lowest—5 Highest)
• 5-

Fair Value
• 9¾

Risk
• High

Earn./Div. Rank
• NR

Technical Eval.
• Neutral since 8/95

Rel. Strength Rank
(1 Lowest—99 Highest)
• 14

Insider Activity
• NA

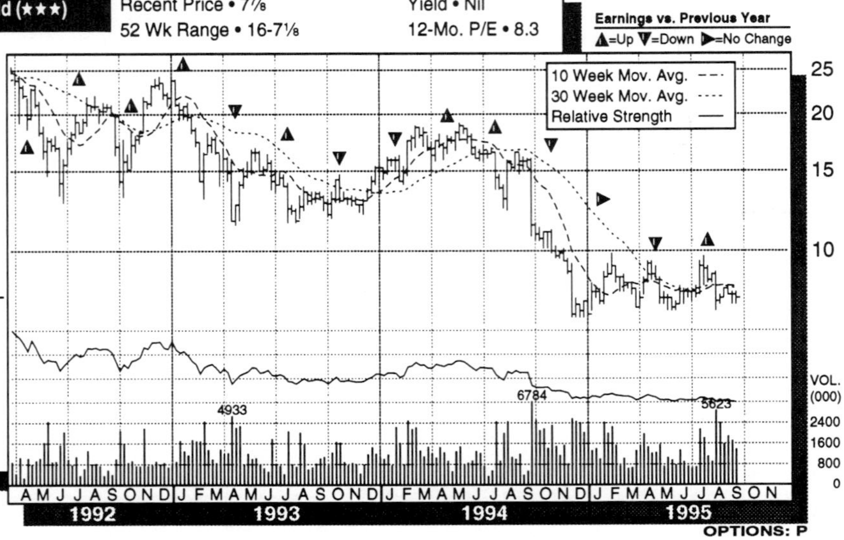

Overview - 15-SEP-95

Excluding nonrecurring gains of $0.34 a share, profits in fiscal 1995 were slightly below our estimate of $0.65 a share, reflecting high therapist turnover and low productivity, as well as certain acquisition-related costs. Fiscal 1996 results should benefit from a sharper focus on providing rehabilitation and subacute services to other healthcare companies, while the sale of the rehabilitation hospital division will allow the company to reduce fixed assets (hospitals) and improve operating flexibility. However, earnings are likely to be adversely affected by efforts to improve the contract services operations and by continued pricing pressures across business lines.

Valuation - 15-SEP-95

We remain cautious regarding any dramatic turnaround in the company's core operations, reflecting concerns over regulatory issues in the contract therapy division and downward pressure on reimbursement rates. These negative factors may offset any productivity or cost-containment gains. Comparisons versus fiscal 1995 will also suffer from the absence of results from the rehabilitation hospitals that were sold in May 1995. Additionally, efforts to improve therapist productivity have been hampered by rising customer turnover, which requires the reassignment of therapists to different facilities. We recently lowered our EPS estimate for fiscal 1996 to $0.77, from $0.85, and would not recommend adding to positions until signs of a turnaround are evident.

Key Stock Statistics

S&P EPS Est. 1996	0.77	Tang. Bk. Value/Share	0.44
P/E on S&P Est. 1996	10.2	Beta	2.87
Dividend Rate/Share	Nil	Shareholders	1,800
Shs. outstg. (M)	65.3	Market cap. (B)	$0.515
Avg. daily vol. (M)	0.344	Inst. holdings	40%
		Insider holdings	NA

Value of $10,000 invested 5 years ago: $ 9,545

Fiscal Year Ending Jun. 30

	1995	% Change	1994	% Change	1993	% Change
Revenues (Million $)						
1Q	230.8	31%	176.4	50%	117.3	38%
2Q	232.2	18%	196.1	51%	129.5	40%
3Q	240.9	18%	204.0	46%	139.3	40%
4Q	201.4	-6%	213.2	39%	152.9	41%
Yr.	905.4	15%	789.8	47%	539.1	40%
Income (Million $)						
1Q	11.05	-11%	12.44	—	—	—
2Q	8.89	-23%	11.54	-9%	12.70	103%
3Q	8.95	-44%	15.96	113%	7.50	-30%
4Q	33.04	72%	19.23	32%	14.52	26%
Yr.	61.92	6%	58.21	24%	46.78	25%
Earnings Per Share ($)						
1Q	0.17	-19%	0.21	-13%	0.24	33%
2Q	0.14	NM	0.14	-44%	0.25	92%
3Q	0.14	-44%	0.25	67%	0.15	-29%
4Q	0.51	70%	0.30	3%	0.29	26%
Yr.	0.95	6%	0.90	-3%	0.93	24%

Next earnings report expected: late October

NovaCare

Business Summary - 15-SEP-95

NovaCare, Inc. is a leading U.S. provider of comprehensive medical rehabilitation services. These services are provided: (1) on a contract basis, primarily to long-term healthcare institutions; (2) through inpatient rehabilitation hospitals and community integrated programs; and (3) through a national network of patient care centers providing orthotic and prosthetic rehabilitation services. The company provides multidisciplinary programs comprising speech-language pathology, occupational therapy and physical therapy to patients experiencing physical disability.

At March 31, 1995, the company provided rehabilitation services under 5,267 contracts in 2,090 facilities located in 40 states. Orthotic and prosthetic rehabilitation services are provided by orthotists and prosthetists, referred to as practitioners, through 130 patient care centers in 26 states. Orthotic rehabilitation is the fitting and fabrication of custom-made braces and support devices for treatment of musculoskeletal conditions. Prosthetic rehabilitation is the fitting and fabrication of custom-made artificial limbs. NovaCare provides outpatient physical and occupational therapy services at 365 clinics in 29 states. These services involve manual, aquatic and electrical modalities and controlled exercise strengthening programs to rehabilitate patients with musculoskeletal injuries or after surgery. The company also manages subacute programs for nursing facilities on a contract basis.

Customers include the largest nursing home chains in the U.S., with Beverly Enterprises Inc. accounting for 12% of net revenues in fiscal 1994 and in fiscal 1993.

NovaCare seeks to consolidate and integrate selected parts of the medical rehabilitation industry in order to offer a continuum of rehabilitation services and diversify patient caseload and payors. Its strategy is being implemented through a program of disciplined internal growth and acquisitions and is designed to capitalize on growing demand for rehabilitation services, particularly in lower-cost, post-acute settings; highly fragmented competition; and the lack of professional management, information systems and access to capital, which is characteristic of much of the industry.

Important Developments

May '95—NOV sold its rehabilitation hospital division (including 11 rehabilitation hospitals in seven states, 12 other rehabilitation facilities and two certificates of need) to HEALTHSOUTH Corp. for $215 million in cash, plus the assumption by HEALTHSOUTH of $20 million of liabilities. The unit accounted for 16% of revenues for the quarter ended March 31, 1995.

Capitalization

Long Term Debt: $345,662,000 (3/95).
Minority Interest: $1,820,000.

Per Share Data ($) (Year Ended Jun. 30)

	1995	1994	1993	1992	1991	1990
Tangible Bk. Val.	NA	1.13	3.26	2.84	2.67	1.25
Cash Flow	NA	1.25	1.10	0.89	0.70	0.49
Earnings	0.95	0.90	0.93	0.75	0.64	0.44
Dividends	Nil	Nil	Nil	Nil	Nil	Nil
Payout Ratio	Nil	Nil	Nil	Nil	Nil	Nil
Prices - High	9⅞	19⅛	23⅞	30¼	29⅞	11⅝
- Low	7⅜	7⅛	11⅜	12¾	9	6½
P/E Ratio - High	10	21	26	40	47	27
- Low	8	8	12	17	14	15

Income Statement Analysis (Million $)

	1994	%Chg	1993	%Chg	1992	%Chg	1991
Revs.	790	47%	539	40%	385	153%	152
Oper. Inc.	144	59%	90.5	34%	67.7	116%	31.4
Depr.	22.9	162%	8.8	17%	7.5	NM	1.9
Int. Exp.	17.1	175%	6.2	NM	2.0	NM	0.6
Pretax Inc.	96.4	30%	74.4	30%	57.3	87%	30.7
Eff. Tax Rate	39%	—	37%	—	34%	—	34%
Net Inc.	58.2	24%	46.8	25%	37.5	85%	20.3

Balance Sheet & Other Fin. Data (Million $)

	1994	1993	1992	1991	1990	1989
Cash	73.1	151	29.9	33.1	27.8	21.6
Curr. Assets	335	331	144	80.0	55.0	41.0
Total Assets	851	548	292	127	88.0	73.0
Curr. Liab.	141	72.7	46.5	13.2	13.8	8.2
LT Debt	283	186	14.3	0.4	10.9	14.5
Common Eqty.	416	284	224	114	63.0	50.0
Total Cap.	704	471	240	114	74.0	65.0
Cap. Exp.	17.7	11.0	9.9	1.4	1.2	0.6
Cash Flow	81.1	55.5	45.0	22.2	14.0	6.7

Ratio Analysis

	1994	1993	1992	1991	1990	1989
Curr. Ratio	2.4	4.6	3.1	6.1	4.0	5.1
% LT Debt of Cap.	40.0	39.5	6.0	0.4	14.7	22.3
% Net Inc.of Revs.	7.3	8.7	9.7	13.4	12.1	7.2
% Ret. on Assets	7.9	11.1	15.4	17.5	15.3	7.0
% Ret. on Equity	15.6	18.3	18.9	21.6	21.9	10.8

Dividend Data —No cash dividends have been paid. A shareholder rights plan was adopted in March 1995.

Data as orig. reptd.; bef. results of disc. opers. and/or spec. items. Per share data adj. for stk. divs. as of ex-div. date. E-Estimated. NA-Not Available. NM-Not Meaningful. NR-Not Ranked.

Office—1016 W. 9th Ave., King of Prussia, PA 19406. **Tel**—(215) 992-7200. **Chrmn & CEO**—J. H. Foster. **Pres & COO**—T. E. Foster. **Sr VP & CFO**—B. J. Colburn. **VP Comm. & Investor Contact**—Susan J. Campbell. **Dirs**—F. W. Cash, J. H. Foster, T. E. Foster, E. M. Gibson, S. S. Marshall, S. E. O'Neil, C. A. Renschler, G. W. Siguler, R. G. Stone Jr., D. C. Tosteson. **Transfer Agent & Registrar**—American Stock Transfer & Trust Co., NYC. **Incorporated** in Delaware in 1984. **Empl-** 11,512. **S&P Analyst:** Robert M. Gold

OEA, Inc.

NYSE Symbol **OEA**
In S&P MidCap 400

13-OCT-95

Industry: Auto parts/equipment

Summary: This company is the dominant producer of air bag initiators for automobiles. It also manufactures explosive-actuated devices used in space vehicles, aircraft and missiles.

S&P Opinion: Hold (★★★)

Recent Price • 27⅞
52 Wk Range • 33⅜-21⅞
Yield • 0.7%
12-Mo. P/E • 26.8

Quantitative Evaluations

Outlook (1 Lowest—5 Highest)
• **5+**

Fair Value
• **45⅝**

Risk
• **Average**

Earn./Div. Rank
• **B+**

Technical Eval.
• **Bearish** since 7/95

Rel. Strength Rank (1 Lowest—99 Highest)
• **18**

Insider Activity
• **NA**

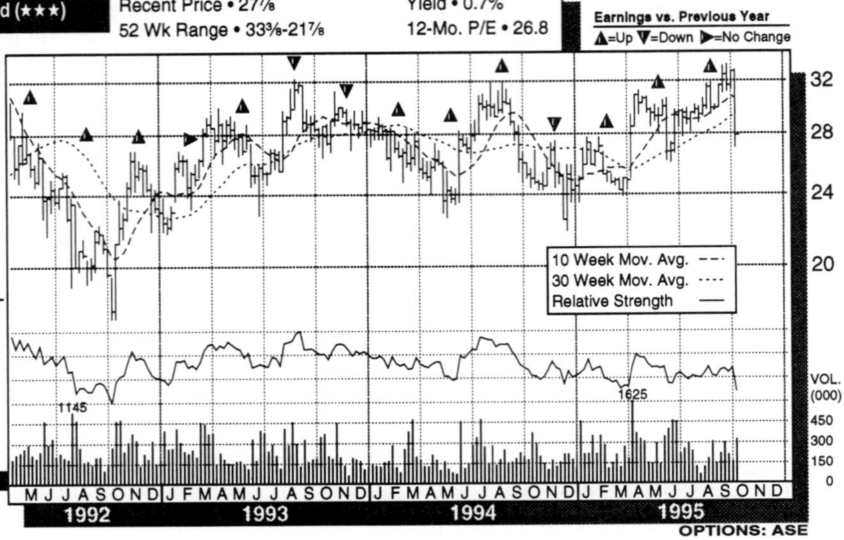

OPTIONS: ASE

Overview - 13-OCT-95

Revenues in the fiscal year ending July 31, 1996, are expected to grow strongly from those of fiscal 1995. Driving the sales gains will be the increasing installation of air bags in new cars in North America. Automotive revenues will also be aided by sales from the new European subsidiary. Nonautomotive sales are projected to end their multiyear decline. Margins are forecast to widen from cost reduction initiatives in the nonautomotive division. In addition, comparative results will benefit from the absence of inventory writedowns. Other income will likely suffer, despite the absence of a $2.25 million environmental charge, due to lower licensing fees.

Valuation - 13-OCT-95

Disappointing fiscal fourth quarter earnings have sparked concern that the pace of air bag sales growth may be slowing. Considering that penetration of driver's side air bags is almost at 90% (passenger side is now over 60%), and automobile production growth is forecast to be minimal in the coming year, we also remain cautious on the outlook for air bags. Expansion opportunities should shift to foreign markets. There also exists the possibility that side air bags will gain acceptance among auto manufacturers and consumers. Consequently, we view the stock's long-term potential as attractive, but at its current level of nearly 22 times our fiscal 1996 estimate of $1.30, the stock is expected to be an average performer.

Key Stock Statistics

S&P EPS Est. 1996	1.30	Tang. Bk. Value/Share	6.48
P/E on S&P Est. 1996	21.4	Beta	1.40
Dividend Rate/Share	0.20	Shareholders	1,500
Shs. outstg. (M)	20.5	Market cap. (B)	$0.574
Avg. daily vol. (M)	0.049	Inst. holdings	43%
		Insider holdings	NA

Value of $10,000 invested 5 years ago: $ 56,894

Fiscal Year Ending Jul. 31

	1996	% Change	1995	% Change	1994	% Change
Revenues (Million $)						
1Q	—	—	28.02	19%	23.62	5%
2Q	—	—	31.90	29%	24.82	12%
3Q	—	—	33.98	15%	29.59	35%
4Q	—	—	35.32	11%	31.87	16%
Yr.	—	—	129.2	18%	109.9	17%
Income (Million $)						
1Q	—	—	2.29	-28%	3.19	-11%
2Q	—	—	5.05	33%	3.79	10%
3Q	—	—	6.11	18%	5.17	53%
4Q	—	—	7.82	35%	5.81	40%
Yr.	—	—	21.28	19%	17.95	23%
Earnings Per Share ($)						
1Q	E0.28	155%	0.11	-31%	0.16	-11%
2Q	E0.31	24%	0.25	32%	0.19	12%
3Q	E0.33	10%	0.30	20%	0.25	47%
4Q	E0.38	NM	0.38	36%	0.28	40%
Yr.	E1.30	25%	1.04	18%	0.88	22%

Next earnings report expected: mid December

Business Summary - 13-OCT-95

OEA, Inc.'s products have applications mainly in the aerospace industry and in the manufacture of automotive air bags. Segment contributions in fiscal 1995 were:

	Sales	Profits
Automotive	70%	80%
Nonautomotive	30%	20%

Foreign sales accounted for 12% of total revenues in fiscal 1994, versus 13% the year before.

The automotive segment manufactures electric initiators for automobile air bags. OEA is the leader in this market. The company also makes hybrid gas generators and, in mid-1995, introduced a new smokeless hybrid inflator. Pyroindustrie was established in fiscal 1995 to supply the European air bag industry with initiators and inflators.

Nonautomotive products include propellant and explosive-actuated devices used in personnel escape systems for high-speed aircraft, in separation and release devices for space vehicles and aircraft and in the control, separation, ejection and jettison of missiles. The ET, Inc. subsidiary manufactures flexible linear-shaped charges and mild detonating cord systems. The principal customers for these products are the U.S. Government and major aircraft and aerospace companies holding prime government contracts. The major portion of the business comes from fixed-price subcontracts. Most military aircraft, missiles/launchers, satellites and the Space Shuttle use these products. Pyrospace, a 45%-owned joint venture, produces pyrotechnic devices in Europe.

Other company products and services include hot gas and explosive initiated valves, fluid control systems, inflatable systems, glass-to-metal sealing and neutron radiography inspection.

Sales to Morton International (air bag initiators) accounted for 52% of total sales in fiscal 1994, while prime contracts with the U.S. Government accounted for 10%.

Important Developments

Jun. '95—OEA said it granted Japan's Daicel Chemical Industries, Ltd. exclusive manufacturing and selling rights to the company's smokeless hybrid inflators in Asia.

Feb. '95—The company's 89%-owned Pyroindustrie subsidiary began manufacturing initiators for the European automotive market. Its facility has an annual capacity of four million units, which is expected to be expanded to 12 million units.

Capitalization

Long Term Debt: None (4/95).
Minority Interest: $466,899.

Per Share Data ($)

(Year Ended Jul. 31)

	1995	1994	1993	1992	1991	1990
Tangible Bk. Val.	NA	5.95	5.23	4.65	4.00	3.48
Cash Flow	NA	1.15	0.94	0.88	0.71	0.56
Earnings	1.04	0.88	0.72	0.75	0.60	0.47
Dividends	0.20	0.15	0.12	0.10	0.08	Nil
Payout Ratio	19%	17%	17%	13%	14%	Nil
Prices - High	33⅜	32	32¼	37	28	13⅝
- Low	23½	22⅝	21¾	17½	11⅝	4⅝
P/E Ratio - High	32	36	45	49	47	29
- Low	23	26	30	23	19	10

Income Statement Analysis (Million $)

	1994	%Chg	1993	%Chg	1992	%Chg	1991
Revs.	110	17%	94.2	7%	88.1	5%	83.7
Oper. Inc.	35.6	26%	28.3	35%	21.0	NM	21.0
Depr.	5.5	18%	4.7	82%	2.5	12%	2.3
Int. Exp.	0.1	10%	0.1	100%	0.1	25%	0.0
Pretax Inc.	29.5	24%	23.7	3%	23.1	20%	19.2
Eff. Tax Rate	39%	—	39%	—	34%	—	37%
Net Inc.	18.0	23%	14.6	-4%	15.2	26%	12.1

Balance Sheet & Other Fin. Data (Million $)

	1994	1993	1992	1991	1990	1989
Cash	4.8	1.3	2.2	6.0	8.9	0.3
Curr. Assets	62.4	60.9	57.0	61.2	56.6	53.3
Total Assets	135	123	106	92.0	80.0	74.0
Curr. Liab.	8.9	11.9	7.8	8.6	7.9	11.2
LT Debt	Nil	Nil	Nil	0.4	0.5	0.5
Common Eqty.	122	107	94.5	81.0	70.2	60.5
Total Cap.	125	110	97.0	82.6	72.0	62.3
Cap. Exp.	16.8	19.6	18.4	8.2	5.3	6.2
Cash Flow	23.4	19.2	17.8	14.4	11.3	8.9

Ratio Analysis

	1994	1993	1992	1991	1990	1989
Curr. Ratio	7.0	5.1	7.3	7.1	7.2	4.8
% LT Debt of Cap.	Nil	Nil	Nil	0.5	0.6	0.8
% Net Inc.of Revs.	16.3	15.5	17.3	14.5	12.3	11.7
% Ret. on Assets	13.9	12.7	15.4	14.1	12.2	10.5
% Ret. on Equity	15.7	14.5	17.3	16.0	14.4	12.8

Dividend Data —Annual cash dividends, omitted in fiscal 1983, were resumed in late 1990.

Amt. of Div. $	Date Decl.	Ex-Div. Date	Stock of Record	Payment Date
0.200	Nov. 07	Nov. 23	Nov. 30	Dec. 09 '94

Data as orig. reptd.; bef. results of disc. opers. and/or spec. items. Per share data adj. for stk. divs. as of ex-div. date. E-Estimated. NA-Not Available. NM-Not Meaningful. NR-Not Ranked.

Office—34501 East Quincy Ave., P.O. Box 100488, Denver, CO 80250. **Tel**—(303) 693-1248. **Chrmn & CEO**—A. D. Kafadar. **Pres**—C. B. Kafadar. **Secy**—J. E. Banko. **VP, Treas & Investor Contact**—Paul J. Martin. **Dirs**—G. S. Ansell, J. E. Banko, J. R. Burnett, H. P. Colhoun, P. E. Johnson, A. D. Kafadar, C. B. Kafadar, R. J. Schultz, L. W. Watson. **Transfer Agent & Registrar**—Chemical Trust Co. of California, San Francisco. **Incorporated** in Delaware in 1969. **Empl**-855. **S&P Analyst:** Joe Victor Shammas

Octel Communications

NASDAQ Symbol **OCTL**
In S&P MidCap 400

23-AUG-95 **Industry:** Telecommunications

Summary: This company is a leading supplier of voice information processing systems.

Quantitative Evaluations

Outlook
(1 Lowest—5 Highest)
• **5+**

Fair Value
• **43¾**

Risk
• **Average**

Earn./Div. Rank
• **B**

Technical Eval.
• **Bullish** since 7/95

Rel. Strength Rank
(1 Lowest—99 Highest)
• **85**

Insider Activity
• **Neutral**

Recent Price • 36⅞
52 Wk Range • 39¼-17¾
Yield • Nil
12-Mo. P/E • 29.3

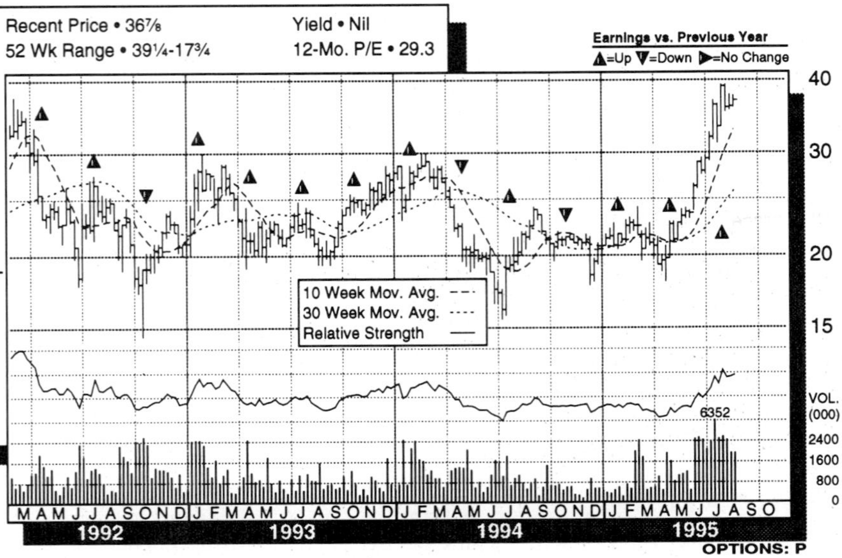

OPTIONS: P

Business Profile - 22-AUG-95

This company manufactures voice information systems and services which allow users to access and manage voice, data, and image information via telephone networks. The company's strategy is to simplify the access and delivery of many forms of data through worldwide communication systems. The strategy focuses on introducing the new OcteLink global network messaging system, and developing unified voice, data, and image communications into one electronic mail system.

Operational Review - 22-AUG-95

Based on a preliminary report, net revenues for the fiscal year ended June 30, 1995, rose 16% from those of the previous year, due to strong demand for the company's products. Margins widened on the higher volume and as a result of cost cutting efforts; net income surged to $1.26 a share from $0.54. The company has a solid balance sheet, with a 2.3 current ratio and very little long-term debt. The shares are currently trading at about 29 times fiscal 1995 earnings.

Stock Performance - 18-AUG-95

In the past 30 trading days, OCTL's shares have increased 16%, compared to a 0.51% rise in the S&P 500. Average trading volume for the past five days was 384,360 shares, compared with the 40-day moving average of 640,720 shares.

Key Stock Statistics

Dividend Rate/Share	Nil	Shareholders	2,700
Shs. outstg. (M)	23.6	Market cap. (B)	$0.860
Avg. daily vol. (M)	0.499	Inst. holdings	68%
Tang. Bk. Value/Share	10.97	Insider holdings	1%
Beta	2.07		

Value of $10,000 invested 5 years ago: $ 16,761

Fiscal Year Ending Jun. 30

	1995	% Change	1994	% Change	1993	% Change
Revenues (Million $)						
1Q	105.8	15%	91.62	89%	48.50	15%
2Q	116.2	15%	100.9	66%	60.70	34%
3Q	115.0	18%	97.20	52%	63.80	33%
4Q	135.6	16%	116.5	52%	76.45	43%
Yr.	472.6	16%	406.2	63%	249.6	32%
Income (Million $)						
1Q	3.81	-36%	5.96	91%	3.12	-15%
2Q	8.76	3%	8.47	49%	5.70	14%
3Q	6.09	NM	-11.60	NM	6.04	5%
4Q	12.47	16%	10.72	37%	7.81	13%
Yr.	31.13	130%	13.54	-40%	22.67	6%
Earnings Per Share ($)						
1Q	0.15	-38%	0.24	50%	0.16	-20%
2Q	0.36	6%	0.34	13%	0.30	11%
3Q	0.25	NM	-0.49	NM	0.31	3%
4Q	0.50	16%	0.43	5%	0.41	11%
Yr.	1.26	133%	0.54	-55%	1.19	4%

Next earnings report expected: mid October

Octel Communications

Business Summary - 22-AUG-95

Octel Communications Corporation designs, makes and markets voice information processing systems that allow users to access, manage and integrate multiple forms of information--voice, image and data--across the telephone network in a single call from any touch-tone telephone in the world. Users with a mailbox on a voice information processing system can send or retrieve voice messages, receive and forward faxes, send or retrieve data and receive notice of electronic mail (E-mail). In fiscal 1991, voice processing capabilities were added, as the company expanded its product line to incorporate data, fax and E-mail. Through Octel Network Services (ONS, formerly Tigon Corporation), the company also provides voice information processing-related services to telephone companies and large corporations.

The company was founded to develop and market voice processing products; its first system was introduced in 1984. Octel initially focused on serving large corporate customers, but has since expanded its markets to include telephone companies; cellular operators and service bureaus; small and medium-size businesses; federal, state and local governments; medical organizations; and universities and other nonprofit organizations. The product line now covers a range of system sizes and feature functionality.

During fiscal 1993, Octel changed to a divisional organization structure related to its two principal customer markets--customer premise equipment (CPE) customers and voice information services (VIS) providers--to increase global customer focus and to operate more effectively. VIS providers buy voice information processing systems and resell their services to customers, generally for a monthly service charge. The VIS market, which accounts for a majority of the company's total sales, has been growing more rapidly than the CPE market, primarily as a result of growth in international sales.

In March 1994, the company acquired VMX, Inc., a designer, manufacturer and marketer of integrated voice processing systems and software products that permit the creation of customer-specific communications solutions.

Export sales, primarily to Canada and Western Europe, represented 24% of revenues in both 1994 and 1993.

Important Developments

Jul. '95—The company announced that it had signed a memorandum of understanding with Stentor Resource Center Inc. (SRCI). SRCI is the marketing division of Stentor Alliance, a consortium of large Canadian telephone companies. Under this agreement, Stentor will bring Octel's new OcteLink electronic post office program into the Canadian market.

Capitalization

Long Term Debt: $602,000 (6/95).

Per Share Data ($)

(Year Ended Jun. 30)

	1995	1994	1993	1992	1991	1990
Tangible Bk. Val.	NA	10.46	10.12	9.72	8.31	7.25
Cash Flow	NA	1.26	2.14	1.75	1.52	1.40
Earnings	1.26	0.54	1.19	1.14	1.00	1.04
Dividends	Nil	Nil	Nil	Nil	Nil	Nil
Payout Ratio	Nil	Nil	Nil	Nil	Nil	Nil
Prices - High	39¼	30	30	37½	28½	27¾
- Low	18	15½	18	14½	10⅛	7½
P/E Ratio - High	31	56	25	33	29	27
- Low	14	29	15	13	10	7

Income Statement Analysis (Million $)

	1994	%Chg	1993	%Chg	1992	%Chg	1991
Revs.	406	62%	250	32%	189	18%	160
Oper. Inc.	56.2	17%	47.9	32%	36.2	16%	31.1
Depr.	18.0	-2%	18.3	58%	11.6	26%	9.2
Int. Exp.	0.3	NM	0.0	-70%	0.1	—	Nil
Pretax Inc.	17.3	-49%	33.6	10%	30.5	13%	27.1
Eff. Tax Rate	22%	—	33%	—	30%	—	35%
Net Inc.	13.5	-41%	22.7	6%	21.4	21%	17.7

Balance Sheet & Other Fin. Data (Million $)

	1994	1993	1992	1991	1990	1989
Cash	86.0	81.0	108	88.0	84.0	40.0
Curr. Assets	221	173	176	142	123	67.0
Total Assets	346	247	209	168	144	80.0
Curr. Liab.	88.5	54.4	37.2	25.5	22.8	17.5
LT Debt	1.4	1.3	Nil	Nil	0.1	0.0
Common Eqty.	256	192	172	143	121	62.0
Total Cap.	258	193	172	143	122	62.0
Cap. Exp.	61.2	27.8	12.1	8.7	11.5	8.7
Cash Flow	31.6	40.9	32.9	27.0	23.7	14.9

Ratio Analysis

	1994	1993	1992	1991	1990	1989
Curr. Ratio	2.5	3.2	4.7	5.6	5.4	3.8
% LT Debt of Cap.	0.5	0.7	Nil	Nil	0.1	0.1
% Net Inc.of Revs.	3.3	9.1	11.3	11.0	13.8	13.5
% Ret. on Assets	4.0	9.8	11.2	11.2	12.3	19.0
% Ret. on Equity	5.3	12.3	13.4	13.3	19.3	24.6

Dividend Data —No cash dividends have been paid.

Data as orig. reptd.; bef. results of disc. opers. and/or spec. items. Per share data adj. for stk. divs. as of ex-div. date. E-Estimated. NA-Not Available. NM-Not Meaningful. NR-Not Ranked.

Office—1001 Murphy Ranch Rd., Milpitas, CA 95035-7912. **Tel**—(408) 321-2000. **Chrmn, Pres & CEO**—R. Cohn. **EVP, CFO & Investor Contact**—G. A. Wetsel. **Secy**—D. S. Daley. **Dirs**—A. Beard, L. J. Chamberlain, R. Cohn, D. A. Coleman, J. Freidenrich, R. C. Hawk, N. de Rothschild, D. Tellefsen, W. M.West. **Transfer Agent & Registrar**—Chemical Trust Co. of California, SF. **Incorporated** in California in 1984; reincorporated in Delaware in 1989. **Empl-** 2,393. **S&P Analyst:** Mike Cavanaugh

STANDARD & POOR'S

STOCK REPORTS

Office Depot

NYSE Symbol **ODP**

In S&P MidCap 400

21-SEP-95

Industry: Retail Stores

Summary: This company operates the largest chain of office products warehouse stores in the U.S., with 454 stores in the U.S. and Canada, and 24 delivery and contract stationers in the U.S.

Quantitative Evaluations

Outlook (1 Lowest—5 Highest)
• **5-**

Fair Value
• **42¼**

Risk
• **Average**

Earn./Div. Rank
• **NR**

Technical Eval.
• **Bullish** since 6/95

Rel. Strength Rank (1 Lowest—99 Highest)
• **61**

Insider Activity
• **NA**

Recent Price • 31⅛

52 Wk Range • 32⅛-20⅞

Yield • Nil

12-Mo. P/E • 39.9

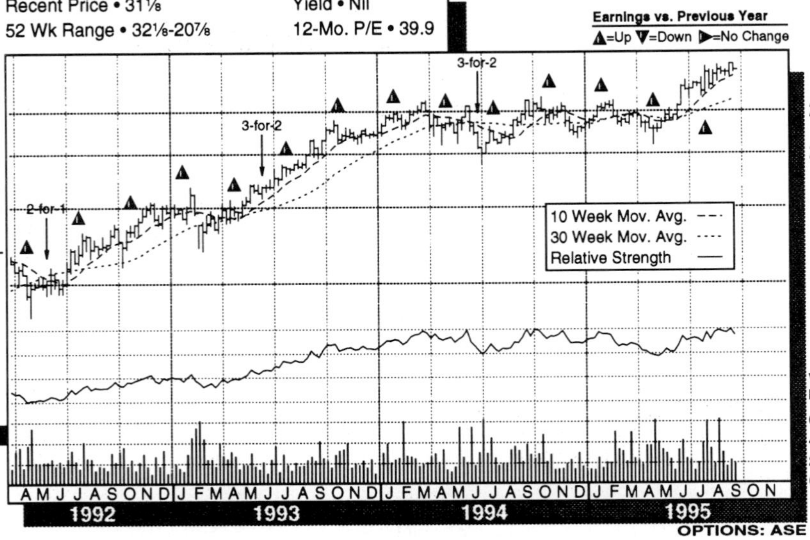

Business Profile - 19-SEP-95

ODP stores cater to small and mid-size businesses, the growing home office market, students, teachers and all business professionals. The company's significant investment in acquired contract stationers has allowed it to build a national delivery network servicing the office supply needs of large companies. The opening of 70 to 80 new stores in 1995 and about 80 stores in 1996, higher same-store sales, and wider margins should aid future earnings comparisons.

Operational Review - 19-SEP-95

Revenues in the first 26 weeks of 1995 soared 30%, year to year, paced by new stores in operation and a 19% gain for same-store sales. Although gross margins narrowed slightly, reflecting higher paper prices and a shift in the sales mix toward lower margin business machines, profitability was enhanced by the increased volume and well controlled costs; pretax income rose 32%. After taxes at 40.5%, versus 40.4%, net income also rose 32% to $59,892,000 ($0.39 a share) from $45,355,000 ($0.30).

Stock Performance - 15-SEP-95

In the past 30 trading days, ODP's shares have increased 8%, compared to a 4% rise in the S&P 500. Average trading volume for the past five days was 364,820 shares, compared with the 40-day moving average of 720,559 shares.

Key Stock Statistics

Dividend Rate/Share	Nil	Shareholders	3,800
Shs. outstg. (M)	154.6	Market cap. (B)	$ 4.8
Avg. daily vol. (M)	0.400	Inst. holdings	71%
Tang. Bk. Value/Share	3.93	Insider holdings	NA
Beta	1.71		

Value of $10,000 invested 5 years ago: $ 77,812

Fiscal Year Ending Dec. 31

	1995	% Change	1994	% Change	1993	% Change
Revenues (Million $)						
1Q	1,351	30%	1,041	79%	582.1	34%
2Q	1,200	30%	925.0	75%	527.9	36%
3Q	—	—	1,045	58%	659.9	52%
4Q	—	—	1,255	55%	809.6	69%
Yr.	—	—	4,266	65%	2,579	49%
Income (Million $)						
1Q	32.47	32%	24.55	74%	14.14	51%
2Q	27.42	32%	20.81	92%	10.86	68%
3Q	—	—	27.41	59%	17.21	76%
4Q	—	—	32.19	52%	21.21	73%
Yr.	—	—	105.0	65%	63.42	68%
Earnings Per Share ($)						
1Q	0.21	31%	0.16	60%	0.10	50%
2Q	0.18	29%	0.14	75%	0.08	64%
3Q	—	—	0.18	50%	0.12	69%
4Q	—	—	0.21	43%	0.15	65%
Yr.	—	—	0.69	53%	0.45	65%

Next earnings report expected: mid October

Office Depot

Business Summary - 19-SEP-95

Office Depot operates a chain of large volume office products warehouse stores that sell high quality, brand name office products primarily to small and medium-sized businesses. At August 21, 1995, there were 454 stores, including 430 in the U.S. and 24 in Canada, with the heaviest concentrations in California, Florida and Texas (together accounting for over 40% of the network).

The number of stores in operation at the end of recent years was:

1994	420
1993	344
1992	284
1991	228
1990	122

Stores average 25,000 sq. ft. in size and use a warehouse format. Each store offers about 5,600 brand name office products, including general office supplies, business machines, office furniture and computer hardware and software.

Sales in recent years were derived as follows:

	1994	1993	1992
General office supplies	48%	51%	53%
Business machines & supplies	39%	36%	34%
Office furniture	13%	13%	13%

ODP offers a wide selection of brand-name office products at everyday low prices. Substantially all inventory is purchased directly from manufacturers in large volumes. The company does not use a central warehouse, but maintains inventory on the sales floor of its no frills stores. ODP believes that its prices are significantly lower than those typically offered to small and medium-sized businesses by their traditional sources of supply.

The Business Services Division, formed in 1994, provides delivery services to small- and medium-size businesses and full-service contract stationer services to medium- and large-size businesses. At August 15, 1995, delivery services were provided through 24 customer service centers (delivery centers and contract stationer warehouses) and certain retail stores.

Important Developments

Aug. '95—ODP sold through underwriters 17,825,000 common shares, including 13,500,000 for Carrefour S.A., at $29.25 each. Net proceeds to the company of $122.2 million were earmarked for the repayment of debt and for general corporate purposes. As a result of the offering, Carrefour's interest in ODP was reduced to about 6% from 15%. Separately, ODP said it opened 29 new stores in 1995's first half, and plans to open between 40 to 50 additional stores in the remainder of 1995 and about 80 stores in 1996.

Capitalization

Long Term Debt: $519,691,000 (7/95; adjusted).

Per Share Data ($) (Year Ended Dec. 31)

	1994	1993	1992	1991	1990	1989
Tangible Bk. Val.	3.45	2.51	2.85	2.38	1.60	1.46
Cash Flow	1.01	0.65	0.42	0.25	0.23	0.13
Earnings	0.69	0.45	0.28	0.12	0.13	0.09
Dividends	Nil	Nil	Nil	Nil	Nil	Nil
Payout Ratio	Nil	Nil	Nil	Nil	Nil	Nil
Prices - High	27	23⅞	15½	12	4¾	6
- Low	18⅞	11⅞	8⅜	3⅛	2 7/16	2⅜
P/E Ratio - High	39	54	56	NM	36	68
- Low	27	27	30	NM	18	27

Income Statement Analysis (Million $)

	1994	%Chg	1993	%Chg	1992	%Chg	1991
Revs.	4,266	65%	2,579	49%	1,733	33%	1,301
Oper. Inc.	243	71%	142	72%	82.6	54%	53.5
Depr.	49.6	68%	29.6	45%	20.4	32%	15.4
Int. Exp.	19.7	86%	10.6	NM	1.5	-39%	2.4
Pretax Inc.	179	67%	107	72%	62.1	131%	26.9
Eff. Tax Rate	41%	—	41%	—	39%	—	47%
Net Inc.	105	66%	63.4	68%	37.8	163%	14.4

Balance Sheet & Other Fin. Data (Million $)

	1994	1993	1992	1991	1990	1989
Cash	32.0	138	130	40.2	8.1	28.4
Curr. Assets	1,274	978	664	423	207	144
Total Assets	1,904	1,464	848	559	275	182
Curr. Liab.	787	537	307	243	147	81.0
LT Debt	394	367	155	6.5	14.5	0.1
Common Eqty.	715	555	382	305	111	101
Total Cap.	1,109	921	537	312	126	101
Cap. Exp.	175	126	61.3	56.2	36.3	24.5
Cash Flow	155	93.1	58.2	29.8	16.3	8.8

Ratio Analysis

	1994	1993	1992	1991	1990	1989
Curr. Ratio	1.6	1.8	2.2	1.7	1.4	1.8
% LT Debt of Cap.	35.5	39.8	28.8	2.1	11.5	0.1
% Net Inc.of Revs.	2.5	2.5	2.2	1.1	1.5	1.9
% Ret. on Assets	6.7	5.4	5.3	2.7	4.2	4.4
% Ret. on Equity	16.1	13.3	10.8	5.6	9.1	8.5

Dividend Data —No cash dividends have been paid. A three-for-two stock split was effected June 17, 1994. The shares were also split three for two in June 1993, two for one in May 1992, and three for two in May 1989.

Data as orig. reptd.; bef. results of disc. opers. and/or spec. items. Per share data adj. for stk. divs. as of ex-div. date. E-Estimated. NA-Not Available. NM-Not Meaningful. NR-Not Ranked.

Office—2200 Old Germantown Rd., Delray Beach, FL 33445. **Tel**—(407) 278-4800. **Chrmn, Pres & CEO**—D. I. Fuente. **EVP, CFO & Secy**—B. J. Goldstein. **Investor Contacts**—Gary Schweikhart, Barry J. Goldstein. **Dirs**—M. D. Begelman, D. Defforey, D. I. Fuente, W. S. Hedrick, J. B. Mumford, M. J. Myers, P. J. Solomon, C. C. Turk, A. L. Wurtzel. **Transfer Agent**—Mellon Financial Services, Pittsburgh. **Incorporated** in Delaware in 1986. **Empl**-26,000. **S&P Analyst:** Michael V. Pizzi

STANDARD & POOR'S

Oklahoma Gas & Electric

STOCK REPORTS

NYSE Symbol **OGE**
In S&P MidCap 400

10-OCT-95 **Industry:** Utilities-Electric

Summary: This electric utility, known as OG&E Electric Services, serves a large part of Oklahoma and western Arkansas.

S&P Opinion: Hold (★★★)

Recent Price • 37½ | 52 Wk Range • 38½-32 | Yield • 7.1% | 12-Mo. P/E • 13.5

Quantitative Evaluations

Outlook (1 Lowest—5 Highest) • **1-**

Fair Value • **30½**

Risk • **Low**

Earn./Div. Rank • **A-**

Technical Eval. • **Bearish** since 7/93

Rel. Strength Rank (1 Lowest—99 Highest) • **78**

Insider Activity • **Neutral**

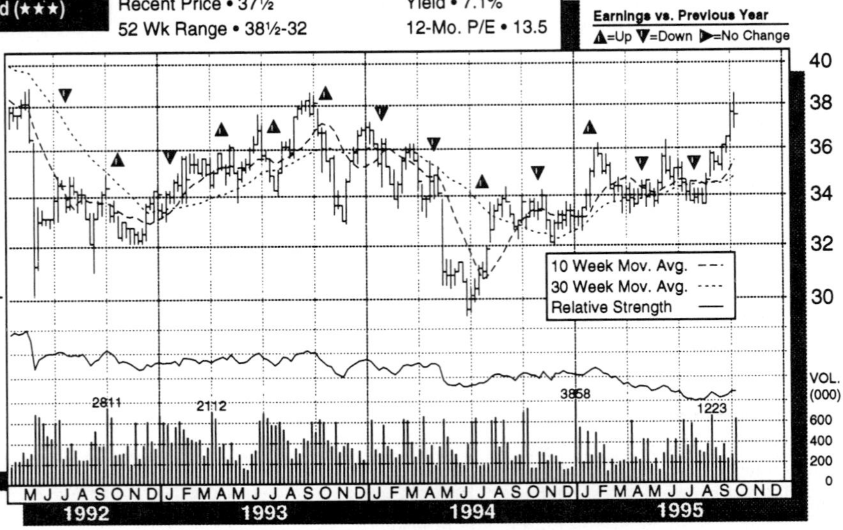

Overview - 05-OCT-95

Share earnings should grow modestly in 1995 and beyond, reflecting cost savings from a recent redesign of operations that resulted in a significant workforce reduction, combined with modest customer growth. Results should be bolstered further in 1996 by increased contributions from the Enogex subsidiary. However, these positive factors will be largely offset by an annual electric rate reduction of $15 million that became effective in January 1995. Residential customers will save about $2.4 million a year, with the remainder of the reduction directed toward making OGE a more competitive option for industrial and commercial customers. Long-term competitive positioning should improve as a result of reduced rates and a leaner cost structure.

Valuation - 05-OCT-95

As a result of increased competition and rising interest rates, in 1994 OGE's shares dropped to their lowest level since 1988. However, the stock managed to finish the year with a partial rebound. Continuing its struggle upward, the stock has appreciated about 13% since the beginning of 1995. The shares currently have a yield of 7.1%, which is well above the average yield of the industry. The shares are trading at about 12-times estimated 1996 earnings of $3.10 a share. Based on the current industry environment and OGE's near-term prospects, the shares are fairly valued. However, the company's above-average dividend yield makes the shares an attractive holding for total return.

Key Stock Statistics

S&P EPS Est. 1995	3.05	Tang. Bk. Value/Share	22.62
P/E on S&P Est. 1995	12.3	Beta	0.41
S&P EPS Est. 1996	3.10	Shareholders	44,500
Dividend Rate/Share	2.66	Market cap. (B)	$ 1.5
Shs. outstg. (M)	40.4	Inst. holdings	22%
Avg. daily vol. (M)	0.087	Insider holdings	NA

Value of $10,000 invested 5 years ago: $ 14,472

Fiscal Year Ending Dec. 31

	1995	% Change	1994	% Change	1993	% Change
Revenues (Million $)						
1Q	246.4	-13%	284.0	-6%	303.4	16%
2Q	304.1	-12%	346.6	1%	341.8	12%
3Q	—	—	443.2	-11%	500.6	13%
4Q	—	—	281.4	-7%	301.4	NM
Yr.	—	—	1,355	-6%	1,447	10%
Income (Million $)						
1Q	-0.86	NM	1.50	-78%	6.69	NM
2Q	24.26	-22%	31.08	52%	20.40	20%
3Q	—	—	86.25	-5%	90.81	19%
4Q	—	—	4.95	NM	-3.62	NM
Yr.	—	—	123.8	8%	114.3	15%
Earnings Per Share ($)						
1Q	-0.04	NM	0.02	-87%	0.15	NM
2Q	0.59	-22%	0.76	55%	0.49	20%
3Q	E2.25	6%	2.12	-5%	2.24	20%
4Q	E0.25	127%	0.11	NM	-0.10	NM
Yr.	E3.05	1%	3.01	8%	2.78	15%

Next earnings report expected: late October

Oklahoma Gas & Electric

Business Summary - 05-OCT-95

This electric utility, known as OG&E Electric Services, supplies electricity to a population of about 1,400,000 in a 30,000 square mile area in Oklahoma and western Arkansas. Approximately 91% of 1994 revenues were derived from Oklahoma. OG&E owns and operates an interconnected electric production, transmission and distribution system which includes eight active generating stations. The Enogex Inc. subsidiary owns and operates over 3,000 miles of natural gas transmission and gathering pipelines, has interests in four gas processing plants, markets natural gas and natural gas products, and invests in the exploration and production of natural gas. Contributions to revenues by class of customers in recent years were as follows:

	1994	1993	1992	1991
Residential	35%	34%	33%	35%
Commercial	22%	21%	21%	22%
Industrial	19%	19%	20%	20%
Other	24%	26%	26%	23%

The fuel mix in 1994 was 28% natural gas and 72% coal. The cost of fuel per million Btu was $3.58 for gas and $0.78 for coal. Peak load in 1994 was 5,060 mw and generating capability at time of peak was 5,637 mw. Total customers in 1994 were 669,705, up 1.7% from 1993.

The primary capital requirements for 1995 are estimated at $114 million, consisting of $89 million for construction expenditures, including AFUDC, and $25 million for maturities of long-term debt and sinking fund requirements. Approximately $7.4 million of OGE's 1995 construction expenditures are to comply with environmental laws and regulations.

Important Developments

Sep. '95—OG&E has proposed a corporate restructuring pursuant to which it will become a subsidiary of a newly-formed holding company, known as OGE Energy Corp., and OGE's common stock will be exchanged on a share-for-share basis for common stock of the holding company. Also, OG&E's subsidiary, Enogex Inc., will become a direct subsidiary of OGE Energy. The formation of the new company has been approved by OG&E's board but is still subject to regulatory and shareholder approval. OGE expects that the holding company may be created by the end of 1995.

Capitalization

Long Term Debt: $731,215,000 (6/95).
Cum. Preferred Stock: $49,973,260.

Per Share Data ($)

(Year Ended Dec. 31)

	1994	1993	1992	1991	1990	1989
Tangible Bk. Val.	22.62	22.25	22.12	22.36	21.68	21.14
Earnings	3.01	2.78	2.42	3.27	3.38	3.05
Dividends	2.66	2.66	2.66	2.58	2.48	2.38
Payout Ratio	88%	96%	110%	79%	73%	78%
Prices - High	37¼	38⅝	44	44	39¾	39
- Low	29⅜	32⅞	30⅛	36½	32⅞	32
P/E Ratio - High	12	14	18	13	12	13
- Low	10	12	12	11	10	10

Income Statement Analysis (Million $)

	1994	%Chg	1993	%Chg	1992	%Chg	1991
Revs.	1,355	-6%	1,447	10%	1,315	NM	1,315
Depr.	126	5%	120	8%	111	3%	108
Maint.	67.2	-15%	78.7	9%	72.4	NM	71.9
Fxd. Chgs. Cov.	3.2	NM	3.2	8%	3.0	-18%	3.7
Constr. Credits	1.1	149%	0.4	-47%	0.8	-65%	2.3
Eff. Tax Rate	37%	—	39%	—	37%	—	36%
Net Inc.	124	9%	114	14%	100	-25%	134

Balance Sheet & Other Fin. Data (Million $)

	1994	1993	1992	1991	1990	1989
Gross Prop.	3,814	3,690	3,508	3,402	3,302	3,206
Cap. Exp.	151	128	142	115	117	109
Net Prop.	2,327	2,320	2,241	2,223	2,215	2,205
Capitalization:						
LT Debt	731	839	839	854	854	854
% LT Debt	43	47	47	47	48	48
Pfd.	50.0	50.0	50.0	50.0	50.0	55.0
% Pfd.	2.90	2.80	2.80	2.80	2.80	3.10
Common	921	907	902	911	883	875
% Common	54	51	50	50	49	49
Total Cap.	2,287	2,373	2,273	2,302	2,283	2,279

Ratio Analysis

	1994	1993	1992	1991	1990	1989
Oper. Ratio	85.2	86.5	86.5	83.9	82.8	82.4
% Earn. on Net Prop.	8.6	8.6	7.9	9.5	9.6	9.1
% Ret. on Revs.	9.1	7.9	7.6	10.2	11.3	11.3
% Ret. On Invest.Cap	9.4	8.3	7.7	9.2	9.3	8.9
% Return On Com.Eqty	13.3	12.4	10.7	14.7	15.6	12.1

Dividend Data —Dividends have been paid since 1908. A dividend reinvestment plan is available. A "poison pill" stock purchase right was adopted in 1991.

Amt. of Div. $	Date Decl.	Ex-Div. Date	Stock of Record	Payment Date
0.665	Sep. 13	Oct. 03	Oct. 07	Oct. 28 '94
0.665	Nov. 08	Jan. 04	Jan. 10	Jan. 30 '95
0.665	Mar. 15	Apr. 04	Apr. 10	Apr. 28 '95
0.665	May. 18	Jul. 06	Jul. 10	Jul. 28 '95
0.665	Sep. 20	Oct. 05	Oct. 10	Oct. 30 '95

Data as orig. reptd.; bef. results of disc opers. and/or spec. items. Per share data adj. for stk. divs. as of ex-div. date. E-Estimated. NA-Not Available. NM-Not Meaningful. NR-Not Ranked.

Office—101 North Robinson, Oklahoma City, OK 73101-0321. **Tel**—(405) 553-3000. **Chrmn**—J. G. Harlow, Jr. **Vice Chrmn**—P. J. Ryan. **Pres & CEO**—S. E. Moore. **Secy**—Irma B. Elliott. **Treas**—J. R. Hatfield. **VP-Fin & Investor Contact**—Al M. Strecker (405-272-3216). **Dirs**—H. H. Champlin, W. E. Durrett, M. W. Griffin, J. G. Harlow, Jr., H. L. Hembree III, S. E. Moore, J. F. Snodgrass, B. Swisher, J. A. Taylor, R. H. White. **Transfer Agent & Registrar**—Liberty Bank & Trust Co. of Oklahoma City. **Incorporated** in Oklahoma in 1902. **Empl**-2,808. **S&P Analyst:** Ronald J. Gross

STANDARD & POOR'S

STOCK REPORTS

Olin Corp.

NYSE Symbol **OLN**
In S&P MidCap 400

07-SEP-95 **Industry:** Chemicals

Summary: This company is a diversified manufacturer of industrial, specialty and consumer chemicals, metal products, sporting and defense ammunition, and aerospace and defense products.

S&P Opinion: Accumulate (★★★★) | Recent Price • 64½ | 52 Wk Range • 65⅛-48⅜ | Yield • 3.6% | 12-Mo. P/E • 12.6

Quantitative Evaluations

Outlook (1 Lowest—5 Highest)
• **3+**

Fair Value
• **62⅝**

Risk
• **Low**

Earn./Div. Rank
• **B**

Technical Eval.
• **Bearish** since 7/94

Rel. Strength Rank (1 Lowest—99 Highest)
• **85**

Insider Activity
• **NA**

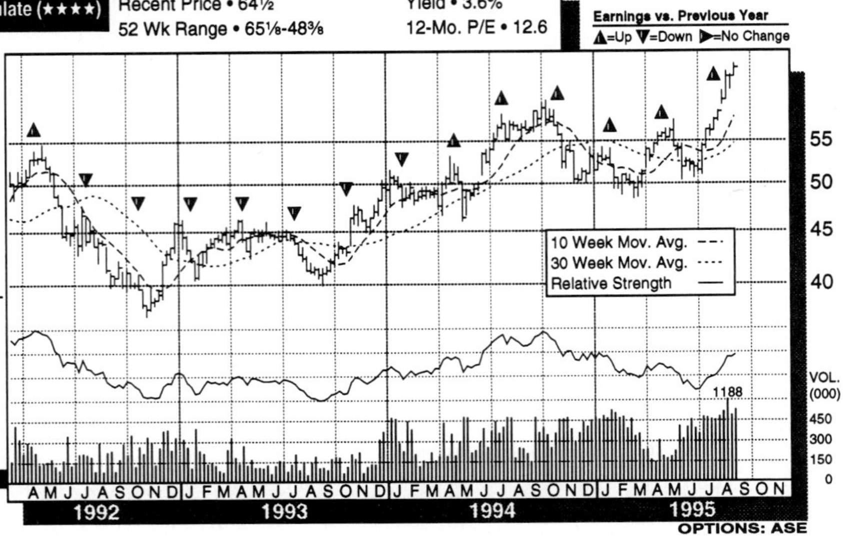

OPTIONS: ASE

Overview - 07-SEP-95

We see chemical profits again climbing in 1996, boosted by the expected contributions of a recently acquired business and a capacity expansion in electronic materials. Flexible urethanes will benefit from the start-up of new TDI capacity in mid-1995 and higher prices, while the specialty urethanes business could finally turn profitable on higher sales. Low retail inventories of pool chemicals, as a result of 1995's hot weather, bodes well for another very good year for this product line in 1996. Earnings of the metals segment should remain very healthy, aided by the expected rebound in markets for durable goods. Assuming the end of an inventory reduction by dealers, the Winchester ammunition business should advance in 1996, while the aerospace and ordnance units are expected to be relatively unchanged.

Valuation - 07-SEP-95

The stock has been very strong since July, reaching its highest level since 1989. Olin's profit outlook is positive as chlor-alkali prices should remain near their historical high levels, while the electronic chemicals business is expected to advance in 1996. The shares, attractive at only 12 times 1995 estimated EPS, could respond to further news of tightening of supply-demand conditions in the chemical industry. The dividend, which provides a yield well above the market average, may be raised in early 1996.

Key Stock Statistics

S&P EPS Est. 1995	5.60	Tang. Bk. Value/Share	26.86
P/E on S&P Est. 1995	11.5	Beta	0.78
S&P EPS Est. 1996	6.00	Shareholders	12,100
Dividend Rate/Share	2.40	Market cap. (B)	$ 1.6
Shs. outstg. (M)	24.3	Inst. holdings	70%
Avg. daily vol. (M)	0.194	Insider holdings	NA

Value of $10,000 invested 5 years ago: $ 14,059

Fiscal Year Ending Dec. 31

	1995	% Change	1994	% Change	1993	% Change
Revenues (Million $)						
1Q	766.1	27%	604.9	2%	591.9	-4%
2Q	803.7	14%	708.1	13%	625.5	-1%
3Q	—	—	666.9	10%	606.8	5%
4Q	—	—	678.2	13%	598.4	8%
Yr.	—	—	2,658	10%	2,423	2%
Income (Million $)						
1Q	38.40	151%	15.30	31%	11.70	-51%
2Q	43.60	58%	27.60	93%	14.30	-32%
3Q	—	—	22.10	NM	5.00	-15%
4Q	—	—	25.80	NM	-122.5	NM
Yr.	—	—	90.80	NM	-91.50	NM
Earnings Per Share ($)						
1Q	1.52	145%	0.62	38%	0.45	-57%
2Q	1.74	50%	1.16	104%	0.57	-35%
3Q	E1.10	28%	0.86	NM	0.15	-17%
4Q	E1.24	23%	1.01	NM	-5.69	NM
Yr.	E5.60	53%	3.65	NM	-4.52	NM

Next earnings report expected: mid October

Olin Corp.

Business Summary - 06-SEP-95

Olin Corp. is a diversified concern with interests in three major areas. Segment contributions in 1994:

	Sales	Profits
Chemicals	45%	37%
Metals	28%	35%
Defense & ammunition	27%	28%

Foreign operations accounted for 8% of sales and operating profits in 1994.

Chemicals include urethanes (TDI, polyols, urethane systems, isocyanates) used in flexible foams and coatings; chlor-alkalies (chlorine, caustic soda and reduction and bleaching chemicals) for pulp and paper, plastics, chemical processing and bleach; acids, surfactants, functional fluids, glycols, hydrazine solutions and propellants, biocides, pool sanitizers and water purification chemicals; and electronics materials (photoresists, acids and solvents, dopants, etchants, toners, developers, and metal packaging systems for integrated circuits).

The Metals group produces copper and copper alloy sheet, strip, foil, tube and fabricated products, and stainless steel strip for the appliance, automotive, electrical, electronics, plumbing, coinage and ammunition markets, and includes the A.J. Oster network of metals service centers.

Defense and ammunition includes Winchester sporting ammunition, military ammunition (small, medium and large caliber), propellants, and aerospace products (rocket engines, inflation systems, gas generators, power devices, electronic test equipment, anti-armor warheads, and pulsed power systems).

Important Developments

Aug. '95—OLN acquired Ciba-Geigy A.G.'s 50% share of OCG Micoelectronics Materials, a joint venture formed in 1990. OLN said that sales of its electronic materials business would now exceed $250 million a year.

Jul. '95—Olin reported that second quarter results were driven by record sales and profits in its chlor-alkali, electronic chemicals and metals businesses and improved performance in the urethanes business. The company said that the first phase of its 50% expansion of its semiconductor chemicals capacity will open in the third quarter. Separately, the FTC approved the sale of a dry sanitizer plant and a related packaging facility to Israel Chemicals Ltd. OLN also sold its SUN brand pool chemicals business to Aqua Clear Industries.

Capitalization

Long Term Debt: $425,700,000 (6/95).
ESOP $5.97 Pfd. Stk.: $83,700,000.

Per Share Data ($) (Year Ended Dec. 31)

	1994	1993	1992	1991	1990	1989
Tangible Bk. Val.	26.86	22.56	30.20	22.88	26.79	23.95
Cash Flow	9.18	1.37	7.45	5.58	10.44	12.10
Earnings	3.65	-4.52	2.17	-0.92	4.03	6.02
Dividends	2.20	2.20	2.20	2.20	2.15	1.95
Payout Ratio	60%	NM	NM	NM	54%	31%
Prices - High	60⅛	50½	54¾	54	60⅝	68¼
- Low	46	39⅞	37¼	33½	28⅛	49⅜
P/E Ratio - High	16	NM	25	NM	15	11
- Low	13	NM	17	NM	7	8

Income Statement Analysis (Million $)

	1994	%Chg	1993	%Chg	1992	%Chg	1991
Revs.	2,658	10%	2,423	2%	2,376	4%	2,275
Oper. Inc.	308	33%	231	-4%	240	-8%	262
Depr.	140	NM	139	13%	123	-3%	127
Int. Exp.	38.0	-5%	40.0	-7%	43.0	-10%	48.0
Pretax Inc.	141	NM	-149	NM	88.0	NM	-25.0
Eff. Tax Rate	36%	—	NM	—	38%	—	NM
Net Inc.	91.0	NM	-92.0	NM	55.0	NM	-13.0

Balance Sheet & Other Fin. Data (Million $)

	1994	1993	1992	1991	1990	1989
Cash	7.0	3.0	4.0	8.0	6.0	12.0
Curr. Assets	880	740	760	768	734	790
Total Assets	2,030	1,930	2,030	2,012	1,866	1,904
Curr. Liab.	618	604	581	683	522	585
LT Debt	418	449	477	520	466	501
Common Eqty.	687	545	702	567	615	565
Total Cap.	1,167	1,045	1,280	1,210	1,229	1,226
Cap. Exp.	149	135	173	201	187	142
Cash Flow	214	30.0	161	106	199	242

Ratio Analysis

	1994	1993	1992	1991	1990	1989
Curr. Ratio	1.4	1.2	1.3	1.1	1.4	1.4
% LT Debt of Cap.	35.8	43.0	37.3	43.0	37.9	40.9
% Net Inc.of Revs.	3.4	NM	2.3	NM	3.2	4.9
% Ret. on Assets	4.3	NM	2.7	NM	4.5	6.7
% Ret. on Equity	11.4	NM	5.6	NM	12.9	20.0

Dividend Data —Dividends have been paid since 1926. A dividend reinvestment plan is available. A "poison pill" stock purchase rights plan was adopted in 1986.

Amt. of Div. $	Date Decl.	Ex-Div. Date	Stock of Record	Payment Date
0.550	Jul. 28	Aug. 04	Aug. 10	Sep. 09 '94
0.550	Oct. 27	Nov. 04	Nov. 10	Dec. 09 '94
0.600	Jan. 26	Feb. 06	Feb. 10	Mar. 10 '95
0.600	Apr. 27	May. 04	May. 10	Jun. 09 '95
0.600	Jul. 28	Aug. 08	Aug. 10	Sep. 08 '95

Data as orig. reptd.; bef. results of disc. opers. and/or spec. items. Per share data adj. for stk. divs. as of ex-div. date. E-Estimated. NA-Not Available. NM-Not Meaningful. NR-Not Ranked.

Office—120 Long Ridge Rd., Stamford, CT 06904-1355. **Tel**—(203) 356-2000. **Chrmn & CEO**—J. W. Johnstone Jr. **Pres**—D. W. Griffin. **Secy**—J. M. Jackson Jr. **VP & Treas**—J. M. Pierpont. **Investor Contact**—Richard Koch. **Dirs**—W. J. Alley, R. R. Frederick, D. W. Griffin, W. W. Higgins, S. D. Jaffe, J. W. Johnstone Jr., J. D. Kuehler, H. W. Lichtenberger, G. J. Ratcliffe Jr., W. L. Read, J. P. Schaefer, I. Shain. **Transfer Agents & Registrars**—Chemical Bank, NYC. **Incorporated** in Virginia in 1892. **Empl**-12,800. **S&P Analyst:** Richard O'Reilly, CFA

STANDARD & POOR'S

STOCK REPORTS

Olsten Corp.

NYSE Symbol **OLS**

In S&P MidCap 400

06-SEP-95 **Industry:** Services

Summary: This company is North America's largest provider of home health care and related services, and is one of the world's leading providers of staffing services.

S&P Opinion: Buy (★★★★★)

Recent Price • 35¾ | Yield • 0.9%

52 Wk Range • 38⅞-28¼ | 12-Mo. P/E • 19.1

Quantitative Evaluations

Outlook (1 Lowest—5 Highest)
• **5-**

Fair Value
• **44⅛**

Risk
• **Average**

Earn./Div. Rank
• **B+**

Technical Eval.
• **Bullish** since 7/95

Rel. Strength Rank (1 Lowest—99 Highest)
• **56**

Insider Activity
• **NA**

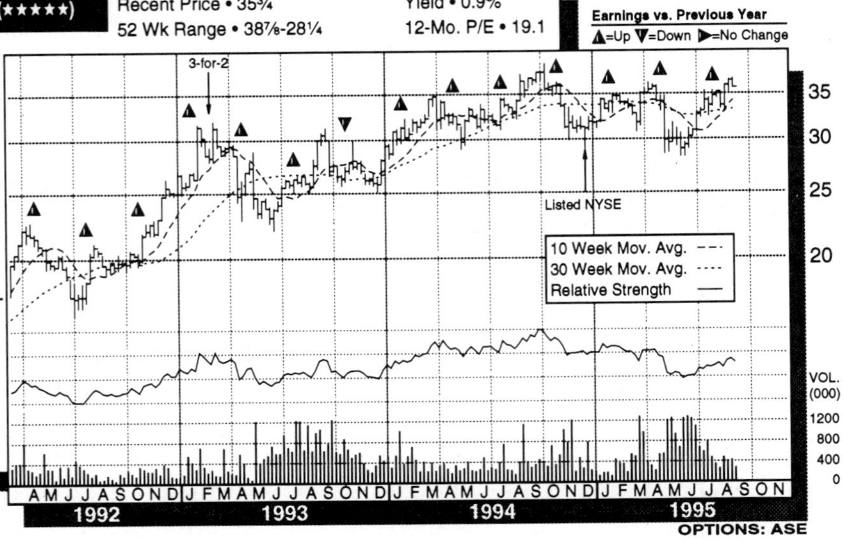

OPTIONS: ASE

Overview - 06-SEP-95

We are anticipating strong gains in earnings in the remainder of 1995 and in 1996. These gians will be fueled by the continued growth in the demand for temporary staffing services and the expansion of the company's home health care client base. The number of hospitals the company has under contract to provide home health care management services increased to 40 from 29 in the second quarter. Revenue growth in 1995 has been limited by the sale of certain home health care operations and the repositioning of Medicare business from a company owned to a company managed business under the hospital contract program. These changes should increase the profitability of the home health care segment. Despite a slowdown in the economy, staffing service revenues have increased 23% thus far in 1995.

Valuation - 06-SEP-95

OLS has not particiated in the bull market of 1995 despite its earnings growth this year. The shares sold off earlier in the year as investors feared that weak employment reports portended a recession and a decline in the demand for staffing services. While the shares have recovered due to strong second quarter earnings and an improving economy, they still sell below their highest levels of 1994. OLS is attractively valued at 18 times estimated 1995 earnings, considering the company's growth record and potential. We believe the shares should be purchased by aggressive investors seeking capital gains.

Key Stock Statistics

S&P EPS Est. 1995	2.05	Tang. Bk. Value/Share	4.95
P/E on S&P Est. 1995	17.4	Beta	1.10
S&P EPS Est. 1996	2.40	Shareholders	1,900
Dividend Rate/Share	0.32	Market cap. (B)	$ 1.5
Shs. outstg. (M)	41.7	Inst. holdings	70%
Avg. daily vol. (M)	0.078	Insider holdings	NA

Value of $10,000 invested 5 years ago: $ 33,955

Fiscal Year Ending Dec. 31

	1995	% Change	1994	% Change	1993	% Change
Revenues (Million $)						
1Q	575.5	7%	537.5	101%	267.0	22%
2Q	601.7	7%	562.9	97%	286.0	22%
3Q	—	—	578.3	4%	556.7	119%
4Q	—	—	581.6	6%	546.5	96%
Yr.	—	—	2,260	5%	2,158	119%
Income (Million $)						
1Q	18.70	30%	14.35	39%	10.35	189%
2Q	20.95	28%	16.40	52%	10.79	122%
3Q	—	—	18.18	NM	-46.20	NM
4Q	—	—	21.19	61%	13.13	95%
Yr.	—	—	70.12	NM	-11.94	NM
Earnings Per Share ($)						
1Q	0.44	26%	0.35	75%	0.20	33%
2Q	0.50	28%	0.39	50%	0.26	24%
3Q	E0.53	23%	0.43	NM	-1.14	NM
4Q	E0.58	16%	0.50	56%	0.32	23%
Yr.	E2.05	23%	1.67	NM	-0.30	NM

Next earnings report expected: late October

Olsten Corp.

Business Summary - 06-SEP-95

Olsten Corp., a major supplier of temporary personnel, operates principally under the trade names Olsten Kimberly QualityCare (formerly Olsten HealthCare) and Olsten Staffing Services (formerly Temporary Services). In July 1993, Lifetime Corp. was acquired. The company currently serves more than 500,000 client/patient accounts and employs more than 650,000 temporary employees.

Olsten conducts business through about 1,200 offices in 50 states, the District of Columbia, Puerto Rico, Mexico, eight Canadian provinces and the U.K. Of the offices, about 105 are owned by franchisees and 90 by licensed area representatives. U.K. and Canadian operations do not account for a significant portion of revenues or net income.

The HealthCare Services division provides licensed health care personnel (caregivers), such as registered nurses and licensed practical nurses, and unlicensed health care personnel, such as home health aides, homemakers, companions and nursing assistants, to individuals in the home and to hospitals and other health care facilities. Health Care Services accounted for 47% of revenues in 1994. About 38% of Health Care Services revenues were derived from Medicare.

The Staffing Services division provides temporary personnel (assignment employees), in the following broad service areas: office automation, general office services, accounting, production/assembly/distribution, technical, legal support, records management, marketing support and teleservices. Personnel specializing in accounting services are also provided under the trade name Olsten Professional Accounting Services. Sales of Staffing Services accounted for about 53% of revenues in 1994.

In July 1993, Lifetime Corp., the leading North American provider (through its Kimberly QualityCare subsidiary) of home health care services and supplemental staffing to medical institutions, was acquired for a total of $600 million in stock and the assumption of debt. In 1990, Upjohn HealthCare Services was purchased for $58 million.

Important Developments

Aug. '95—The company signed a new contract with United HealthCare Corp. to provide home nursing and infusion therapy services to the 3 million lives covered by United's health plans. Also, Olsten purchased P. J. Ward Associates, a Canadian information technology staffing company with revenues in U.S. dollars of $10.2 million. OLS also completed its previously announced acquisition of information technology staffing company IMI Systems Inc.

Capitalization

Long Term Debt: $125,000,000 (7/2/95), of 4 7/8% debs. conv. into common at $34.80 a sh.

Per Share Data ($)

(Year Ended Dec. 31)

	1994	1993	1992	1991	1990	1989
Tangible Bk. Val.	4.46	2.46	5.51	3.25	2.89	3.30
Cash Flow	2.23	0.35	1.18	0.93	0.78	1.01
Earnings	1.67	-0.30	0.87	0.62	0.53	0.78
Dividends	0.24	0.27	0.19	0.16	0.16	0.15
Payout Ratio	14%	NM	24%	26%	30%	18%
Prices - High	38⅞	32	26⅞	16⅝	11¾	15⅝
- Low	28⅛	22	15⅝	7⅛	5⅛	10⅝
P/E Ratio - High	23	NM	31	27	22	20
- Low	17	NM	18	12	10	14

Income Statement Analysis (Million $)

	1994	%Chg	1993	%Chg	1992	%Chg	1991
Revs.	2,260	5%	2,158	119%	987	17%	843
Oper. Inc.	150	18%	127	187%	44.2	30%	34.1
Depr.	23.5	-9%	25.7	NM	7.5	NM	7.4
Int. Exp.	8.1	-61%	20.6	NM	3.3	-23%	4.3
Pretax Inc.	121	NM	2.1	-94%	34.0	47%	23.1
Eff. Tax Rate	42%	—	680%	—	38%	—	37%
Net Inc.	70.1	NM	-11.9	NM	21.1	45%	14.6

Balance Sheet & Other Fin. Data (Million $)

	1994	1993	1992	1991	1990	1989
Cash	68.3	24.7	18.1	22.0	18.0	66.8
Curr. Assets	440	407	171	157	154	150
Total Assets	726	690	224	212	206	178
Curr. Liab.	165	166	41.8	39.1	39.3	32.0
LT Debt	125	176	Nil	60.0	65.5	54.5
Common Eqty.	386	304	182	113	101	92.0
Total Cap.	511	480	182	173	167	146
Cap. Exp.	42.1	30.1	4.0	2.7	2.5	2.9
Cash Flow	93.6	13.7	28.6	22.0	18.1	23.3

Ratio Analysis

	1994	1993	1992	1991	1990	1989
Curr. Ratio	2.7	2.5	4.1	4.0	3.9	4.7
% LT Debt of Cap.	24.5	36.6	Nil	34.7	39.3	37.3
% Net Inc.of Revs.	3.1	NM	2.1	1.7	2.0	3.1
% Ret. on Assets	9.8	NM	9.1	7.0	6.4	10.3
% Ret. on Equity	20.1	NM	13.6	13.6	12.8	21.4

Dividend Data —Cash has been paid in each year since 1976.

Amt. of Div. $	Date Decl.	Ex-Div. Date	Stock of Record	Payment Date
0.060	Nov. 08	Nov. 15	Nov. 21	Dec. 01 '94
0.080	Feb. 13	Feb. 16	Feb. 23	Mar. 03 '95
0.080	Apr. 28	May. 09	May. 15	Jun. 01 '95
0.080	Jul. 28	Aug. 11	Aug. 15	Sep. 01 '95

Data as orig. reptd.; bef. results of disc. opers. and/or spec. items. Per share data adj. for stk. divs. as of ex-div. date. E-Estimated. NA-Not Available. NM-Not Meaningful. NR-Not Ranked.

Office—175 Broad Hollow Rd., Melville, NY 11747-8905. **Tel**—(516) 844-7800. **Chrmn & CEO**—F. N. Liguori. **Vice Chrmn, Pres & COO**—S. Olsten. **SVP-Fin, Treas, CFO & Investor Contact**—Anthony J. Puglisi. **VP & Secy**—L. L. Laderoute, Jr. **Dirs**—A. N. Heine, S. R. Levine, F. N. Liguori, J. M. May, M. Olsten, S. Olsten, R. J. Sharoff, R. S. Troubh, J. S. Weston. **Transfer Agent & Registrar**—Mellon Securities Trust Co. **Incorporated** in Delaware in 1967. **Empl**-8,600. **S&P Analyst:** Stephen Madonna, CFA

STANDARD & POOR'S

STOCK REPORTS

Omnicom Group

NYSE Symbol **OMC**
In S&P MidCap 400

20-OCT-95

Industry:
Advertising/Communications

Summary: Omnicom owns DDB Needham Worldwide, BBDO Worldwide and TBWA, three leading full-service global advertising agency networks. OMC also heads a diversified agency services group.

S&P Opinion: Hold (★★★)

Recent Price • 66⅛
52 Wk Range • 66⅝-49
Yield • 2.1%
12-Mo. P/E • 19.4

Quantitative Evaluations

Outlook
(1 Lowest—5 Highest)
• **5+**

Fair Value
• **83⅞**

Risk
• **Low**

Earn./Div. Rank
• **A**

Technical Eval.
• **Bearish** since 7/95

Rel. Strength Rank
(1 Lowest—99 Highest)
• **66**

Insider Activity
• **Unfavorable**

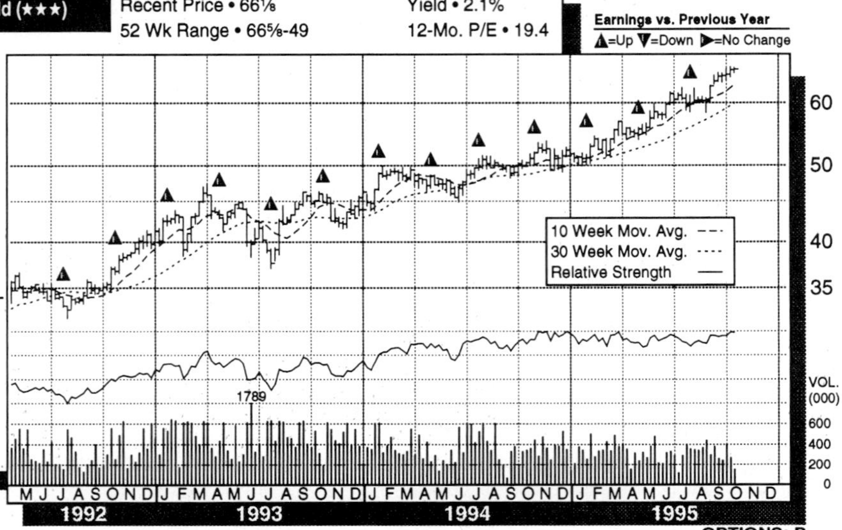

OPTIONS: P

Overview - 20-OCT-95

Commissions and fees are expected to advance more than 20% in 1995, reflecting a roughly 12% gain in underlying volume, bolstered in addition by several significant acquisitions, including Ross Roy, Chiat/Day, and Griffin Bacal. Currency translation gains will also play a significant part. A strong U.S. advertising market, and healthy gains in Latin America and the Pacific Rim are contributing factors. There should continue to be modest improvement in margins. The favorable advertising climate should extend through 1996. Longer term, the company should continue to grow faster than the underlying rate of growth in advertising demand worldwide, aided by acquisitions and gains in market share.

Valuation - 20-OCT-95

OMC performed well versus the market throughout the first nine months of 1995, reflecting strong double-digit growth in revenues and earnings, which have benefited from a healthy advertising market worldwide, as well as the positive impact from acquisitions and currency translations. Although national spot advertising appears to be slowing, advertising in general should remain strong through 1996. The outlook for OMC is bolstered as well by continued growth through acquisitions and new markets. Favorable earnings news going forward, combined with a generous dividend, should keep OMC ahead of the market. Shareholders are expected to approve a 2-for-1 stock split at a November 28, 1995 meeting.

Key Stock Statistics

S&P EPS Est. 1995	3.67	Tang. Bk. Value/Share	NM
P/E on S&P Est. 1995	18.0	Beta	1.01
S&P EPS Est. 1996	4.25	Shareholders	2,600
Dividend Rate/Share	1.40	Market cap. (B)	$ 2.4
Shs. outstg. (M)	36.3	Inst. holdings	77%
Avg. daily vol. (M)	0.051	Insider holdings	NA

Value of $10,000 invested 5 years ago: $ 30,596

Fiscal Year Ending Dec. 31

	1995	% Change	1994	% Change	1993	% Change
Revenues (Million $)						
1Q	459.9	22%	376.5	11%	339.0	10%
2Q	526.0	24%	425.2	11%	382.0	10%
3Q	—	—	422.3	24%	339.5	4%
4Q	—	—	532.2	17%	456.0	14%
Yr.	—	—	1,756	16%	1,516	9%
Income (Million $)						
1Q	24.14	28%	18.92	29%	14.68	64%
2Q	42.15	26%	33.50	23%	27.26	22%
3Q	—	—	18.15	41%	12.85	24%
4Q	—	—	37.57	22%	30.78	29%
Yr.	—	—	108.1	27%	85.35	30%
Earnings Per Share ($)						
1Q	0.68	17%	0.58	16%	0.50	56%
2Q	1.17	15%	1.02	13%	0.90	15%
3Q	E0.60	15%	0.52	21%	0.43	16%
4Q	E1.22	17%	1.04	9%	0.95	13%
Yr.	E3.67	17%	3.15	13%	2.79	21%

Next earnings report expected: late October

Omnicom Group

Business Summary - 19-OCT-95

Omnicom Group Inc. was formed in 1986 through the three-way merger of Doyle Dane Bernbach Group Inc., BBDO International Inc. and Needham Harper Worldwide Inc. The company was then reorganized into two major independent ad agency networks--the BBDO Worldwide network and the DDB Needham Worldwide network--plus the Diversified Agency Services group. Omnicom was the third largest advertising agency group worldwide at year-end 1994, based on combined worldwide billings. The company has grown rapidly in the past several years, bolstered by its acquisitions of TBWA International (1993), Griffin Bacal (1994) and Chiat/Day (1995). In 1994, OMC's 10 largest clients accounted for about 18% of billings, and no client represented more than 5%.

Operations cover the major regions of North America, the United Kingdom, Europe, the Middle East, Africa, Latin America, the Far East and Australia. In 1994, 51% of the company's commissions and fees and 47% of operating profit came from international operations.

The BBDO Worldwide network, the DDB Needham Worldwide network, and TBWA Chiat/Day, operate globally through subsidiaries and affiliates. Their primary business is to create marketing comunications for their clients' goods and services across the total spectrum of advertising and promotion media. Each of the agency networks has its own clients and competes with oeach other in the same markets.

The Diversified Agency Services group includes a wide range of general and industry-focused ad agencies and marketing services firms.

Commissions charged on media billings are the primary source of revenues for OMC. Commission rates are no longer uniform, having moved away from the standard 15%, and are negotiated with the client.

Important Developments

Sep. '95—OMC completed the acquisition of Ross Roy Communications, the 27th largest agency in the U.S., with 1994 billings of $508 million.

Aug. '95—OMC's TBWA International (with $1.3 billion in annual billings) and Chiat/Day Holdings Inc. (about $900 million) completed their previously announced merger into a new agency called TBWA Chiat/Day. The new agency has offices in the U.S., Canada and 32 other countries.

Jan. '95—OMC acquired a 20% minority interest in GPC International Holdings Inc., Canada's leading public affairs firm. GPC is the parent of GPC Government Policy Consultants Inc., GPC Consilium (Quebec) Inc., GPC Pacific Public Affairs (British Columbia), GPC Communications Inc. and Government Policy Consultants (Europe) Ltd.

Capitalization

Long Term Debt: $403,882,000 (3/95).

Per Share Data ($)

(Year Ended Dec. 31)

	1994	1993	1992	1991	1990	1989
Tangible Bk. Val.	-6.03	-6.07	-5.96	-2.85	-6.06	-5.27
Cash Flow	4.97	4.54	4.07	3.77	3.79	3.18
Earnings	3.15	2.79	2.31	2.08	2.01	1.81
Dividends	1.24	1.24	1.20	1.10	1.07	0.98
Payout Ratio	39%	44%	52%	55%	55%	55%
Prices - High	53¾	47½	41⅞	34	27½	25¾
- Low	43¾	37	31¼	21	16⅛	19⅜
P/E Ratio - High	17	17	18	16	14	14
- Low	14	13	14	10	8	11

Income Statement Analysis (Million $)

	1994	%Chg	1993	%Chg	1992	%Chg	1991
Revs.	1,756	16%	1,516	9%	1,385	12%	1,236
Oper. Inc.	267	20%	223	10%	203	12%	181
Depr.	62.8	17%	53.5	7%	49.8	8%	46.2
Int. Exp.	34.8	-16%	41.2	NM	40.9	-1%	41.4
Pretax Inc.	200	28%	156	18%	132	9%	121
Eff. Tax Rate	37%	—	38%	—	40%	—	41%
Net Inc.	108	27%	85.3	30%	65.5	15%	57.1

Balance Sheet & Other Fin. Data (Million $)

	1994	1993	1992	1991	1990	1989
Cash	257	213	131	157	123	126
Curr. Assets	1,602	1,274	1,137	1,111	1,027	937
Total Assets	2,852	2,290	1,952	1,886	1,749	1,548
Curr. Liab.	1,987	1,524	1,311	1,197	1,106	981
LT Debt	187	278	235	245	279	267
Common Eqty.	541	402	309	366	298	238
Total Cap.	770	709	589	657	617	543
Cap. Exp.	38.5	33.6	34.9	32.1	32.7	33.4
Cash Flow	171	139	115	103	98.0	82.0

Ratio Analysis

	1994	1993	1992	1991	1990	1989
Curr. Ratio	0.8	0.8	0.9	0.9	0.9	1.0
% LT Debt of Cap.	24.3	39.3	39.9	37.3	45.2	49.2
% Net Inc.of Revs.	6.2	5.6	4.7	4.6	4.4	4.6
% Ret. on Assets	4.0	3.7	3.4	3.0	3.1	3.4
% Ret. on Equity	22.1	32.4	19.4	16.6	19.3	20.5

Dividend Data —Prior to the business combination in 1986, BBDO had paid cash dividends in each year since 1938 and Doyle Dane Bernbach Group in each year since 1964. In November 1993, OMC changed its dividend policy from a payout of a majority of annual earnings to a payout of 30%-40% of annual earnings.

Amt. of Div. $	Date Decl.	Ex-Div. Date	Stock of Record	Payment Date
0.310	Nov. 28	Dec. 09	Dec. 15	Jan. 06 '95
0.310	Jan. 23	Mar. 14	Mar. 20	Apr. 04 '95
0.310	May. 22	Jun. 13	Jun. 15	Jul. 06 '95
0.350	Sep. 18	Sep. 27	Sep. 29	Oct. 12 '95

Data as orig. reptd.; bef. results of disc. opers. and/or spec. items. Per share data adj. for stk. divs. as of ex-div. date. E-Estimated. NA-Not Available. NM-Not Meaningful. NR-Not Ranked.

Office—437 Madison Ave., New York, NY 10022. **Tel**—(212) 415-3600. **Chrmn & CEO**—B. Crawford. **Pres**—J. D. Wren. **VP-CFO**—F. J. Meyer. **Secy**—R. McGovern. **Investor Contact**—Louis Tripodi. **Dirs**—B. Brochand, R. J. Callander, J. A. Cannon, L. S. Coleman Jr., B. Crawford, P. Jones, F. J. Meyer, J. R. Purcell, K. L. Reinhard, A. Rosenshine, G. L. Roubos, Q. I. Smith Jr., R. B. Smith, W. G. Tragos, J. D. Wren, E. P. S. Zehnder. **Transfer Agent & Registrar**—Chemical Bank, NYC. **Incorporated** in New York in 1986. **Empl**-16,100. **S&P Analyst:** William H. Donald

Oregon Steel Mills

NYSE Symbol OS Options on Phila (Feb-May-Aug-Nov) In S&P MidCap 400

Price	Range	P-E Ratio	Dividend	Yield	S&P Ranking	Beta
Jul. 26'95	1995					
17⅝	19¾–14⅞	28	0.56	3.2%	B	0.96

Summary

This company operates the only hot-rolled steel plate minimill in the 11 western states in the U.S. It also manufactures large diameter steel pipe. Despite higher sales, earnings declined in 1994, due to modernization costs for CF&I and higher scrap costs. Earnings increased slightly in 1995's first half, entirely reflecting nonrecurring insurance proceeds received in the second quarter.

Business Summary

Oregon Steel Mills produces steel products through its Oregon Steel and CF&I steel divisions.

Sales by product line in 1994: plate 25%; wire, rod, and bar 24%; welded pipe 27%; rail 14%; OCTG 7%; and other 3%. Total shipments increased to 1,686,300 tons in 1994 from 1,403,000 tons in 1993. Shipments of pipe products totaled 451,200 tons in 1994, versus 323,700 tons in 1993.

The Oregon Steel division consists of the Portland Steel Mill, the Napa large diameter pipe mill and the Camrose large diameter pipe and ERW mills. The Fontana plate mill was closed in December 1994. Shipments totaled 920,700 tons in 1994, versus 778,300 in 1993. The average selling price was $542 a ton in 1994, versus $533 per ton in 1993.

The Portland mill currently makes steel plate in dimensions up to 102 inches wide and 3/16 to 6 inches thick. The Combination Mill (expected to begin operation in 1996's third quarter) will enable OS to produce plate with widths from 48 inches to 136 inches, in thicknesses from 3/16 inches to 8 inches.

The Napa plant produces pipe with an outside diameter ranging from 16 to 42 inches, with wall thicknesses of up to 1-1/16 inches and in lengths up to 80 feet.

The Camrose facility produces large diameter pipe ranging from 20 to 42 inches in diameter, in lengths up to 80 feet. It also makes ERW pipe in sizes 4½ inches through 16 inches.

The CF&I division (acquired in 1993) makes long-length and standard steel rails, seamless oil country tubular goods (OCTG), wire rod and wire products and reinforcing bar. Shipments totaled 765,600 tons in 1994, versus 624,700 tons in 1993 and the average selling price was $443 a ton in 1994, versus $424 a ton in 1993.

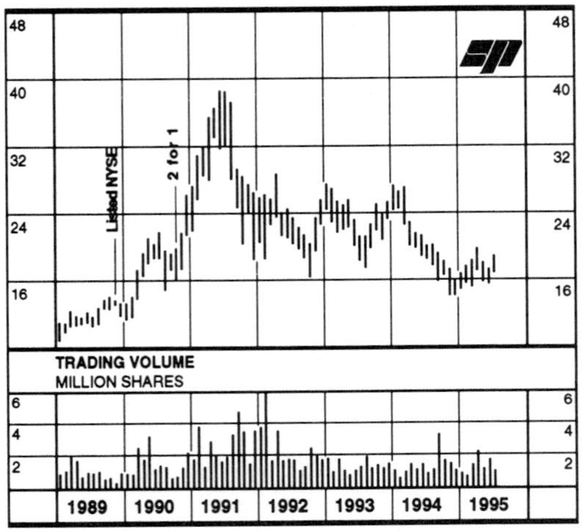

Important Developments

Apr. '95— OS reported share earnings of $0.10 on a 15% decline in sales for 1995's first quarter, versus $0.18 in the year-earlier quarter. Tonnage shipped in 1995's first quarter totaled 395,100 tons, versus 422,000 tons in the year-earlier period. The average selling price per ton declined to $473 a ton in 1995's first quarter from $519 in 1994. The average selling price fell, due to reduced pipe shipments in 1995 compared with 1994, and increased slab shipments from the Portland mill in 1995. Operating profit per ton decreased to $12.25 a ton from $17.78 a ton. OS stated that operating margins were hurt by costs for the closure of the Fontana mill and start-up of capital projects at CF&I. An explosion in 1994 delayed the CF&I start-up and caused a reduction in 1995's first quarter shipments at CF&I.

Next earnings report expected in late October.

Per Share Data ($)

Yr. End Dec. 31	1994	[2]1993	1992	1991	1990	1989	1988	1987	1986	1985
Tangible Bk. Val.	**12.04**	12.15	13.41	12.85	8.44	7.09	6.05	2.99	NA	NA
Cash Flow	**1.71**	1.79	1.89	2.63	2.33	1.70	1.76	0.48	NA	NA
Earnings[1]	**0.60**	0.75	1.04	1.97	1.78	1.33	1.43	0.32	d0.05	d0.01
Dividends	**0.56**	0.56	0.56	0.50	0.42	0.40	0.20	Nil	Nil	Nil
Payout Ratio	**93%**	75%	54%	26%	24%	30%	15%	Nil	Nil	Nil
Prices—High	**27⅜**	27½	28¾	38⅝	26¼	14⅛	13⅞	NA	NA	NA
Low	**14⅛**	17½	16⅜	18½	11⅜	8⅞	7¼	NA	NA	NA
P/E Ratio—	**46–24**	37–23	26–16	20–9	15–6	11–7	10–5	NA	NA	NA

Data as orig. reptd. Adj. for stk. div(s). of 100% Oct. 1990. **1.** Bef. spec. item(s) of +0.04 in 1988, +0.05 in 1986, -0.01 in 1985. **2.** Refl. merger or acquis. d-Deficit. NA-Not Available.

Income Data (Million $)

Year Ended Dec. 31	Revs.	Oper. Inc.	% Oper. Inc. of Revs.	Cap. Exp.	Depr.	Int. Exp.	Net Bef. Taxes	Eff. Tax Rate	[2]Net Inc.	% Net Inc. of Revs.	Cash Flow
1994	**838**	**45.8**	**5.5**	**128.0**	**22.0**	**11.30**	**[1]12.4**	**NM**	**12.1**	**1.4**	**34.1**
[4]1993	680	45.6	6.7	69.4	20.8	5.69	[1]24.2	30.5%	14.8	2.2	35.6
1992	398	53.7	13.5	34.3	16.3	0.32	[1]33.4	43.4%	[3]20.0	5.0	36.2
1991	489	69.5	14.2	38.5	12.4	1.40	[1]58.6	37.0%	36.9	7.5	49.4
1990	334	54.7	16.4	33.3	8.6	2.20	[1]45.9	38.0%	28.5	8.5	37.1
1989	231	36.6	15.8	36.6	5.9	1.91	[1]32.2	35.5%	20.8	9.0	26.6
1988	190	32.6	17.1	16.1	4.8	1.04	[1]30.7	33.4%	20.4	10.7	25.2
1987	127	17.8	14.0	20.8	4.3	1.03	[1]13.5	40.3%	8.0	6.3	12.4
1986	85	5.0	5.9	3.1	4.0	2.30	d2.4	NM	d1.2	NM	NA
1985	85	d2.9	NM	3.9	4.0	2.27	d2.3	NM	d0.3	NM	NA

Balance Sheet Data (Million $)

Dec. 31	Cash	Curr. Assets	Curr. Liab.	Curr. Ratio	Total Assets	% Ret. on Assets	Long Term Debt	Common Equity	Total Cap.	% LT Debt of Cap.	% Ret. on Equity
1994	**5.0**	**259**	**118.0**	**2.2**	**666**	**2.0**	**188.0**	**276**	**493**	**38.1**	**4.4**
1993	9.6	256	116.0	2.2	550	3.3	76.5	275	381	20.1	5.5
1992	5.2	155	55.7	2.8	356	5.8	NA	258	285	NA	7.9
1991	14.7	167	43.3	3.9	325	12.0	3.4	246	261	1.3	18.1
1990	2.5	124	86.0	1.4	246	13.8	5.2	137	154	3.4	22.8
1989	8.5	69	27.8	2.5	163	13.7	6.9	112	131	5.3	20.0
1988	31.7	75	18.6	4.0	138	15.9	8.6	95	111	7.8	28.5
1987	1.7	30	19.7	1.5	84	11.3	17.6	35	58	30.3	27.1
1986	0.8	24	15.0	1.6	59	NM	12.1	25	41	29.7	NM
1985	NA	26	15.5	1.7	63	NM	15.4	26	41	37.1	NM

Data as orig. reptd. **1.** Incl. equity in earnings of nonconsol. subs. **2.** Bef. spec. items. **3.** Reflects acctg. change. **4.** Refl. merger or acquis. d-Deficit. NM-Not Meaningful. NA-Not Available.

Net Sales (Million $)

Quarter:	1995	1994	1993	1992
Mar.	187.0	218.9	149.0	126.6
Jun.	151.4	234.8	204.1	125.1
Sep.		193.1	174.2	90.7
Dec.		191.5	152.5	55.4
		838.3	679.8	397.7

Based on a brief report, sales for the six months ended June 30, 1995, fell 25%, year to year. Including after-tax insurance proceeds of about $2.5 million ($0.12 a share) received in 1995's second quarter for business interruption caused by an explosion during construction of a mill, net income was up 7.4%, to $7,656,000 ($0.38 a share) from $7,126,000 ($0.36) in the year-earlier period.

Common Share Earnings ($)

Quarter:	1995	1994	1993	1992
Mar.	0.10	0.18	0.35	0.56
Jun.	0.29	0.17	0.46	0.55
Sep.		d0.02	Nil	0.18
Dec.		0.27	d0.06	d0.25
		0.60	0.75	1.04

Dividend Data

Dividends were initiated in 1988.

Amt. of Divd. $	Date Decl.	Ex-divd. Date	Stock of Record	Payment Date
0.14	Jul. 27	Aug. 8	Aug. 12	Aug. 31'94
0.14	Oct. 26	Nov. 4	Nov. 11	Nov. 30'94
0.14	Jan. 26	Feb. 6	Feb. 10	Feb. 28'95
0.14	Apr. 28	May 8	May 12	May 31'95

Finances

In August 1994, Nippon Steel Corp. of Japan acquired a 10% interest in New CF&I,Inc., which is the sole general partner of CF&I Steel, L. P. Additionally, Nippon agreed to license its proprietary technology for producing deep head hardened rail products to CF&I.

Capitalization

Long Term Debt: $195,013,000 (3/95).

Minority Interest: $19,174,000.

Common Stock: 19,421,643 shs. ($0.01 par). Employee stock ownership plan owns 12.6%. Institutions hold 74%. Shareholders of record: 846 (12/94).

d-Deficit.

Offices—1000 Broadway Building, Suite 2200, 1000 S. W. Broadway, Portland, OR 97205. **Tel**—(503) 223-9228. **Chrmn & CEO**—T. B. Boklund. **VP & CFO**—L. R. Adams. **Secy**—L. F. Lee. **Investor Contact**—Vicki A. Tagliafico. **Dirs**—T. B. Boklund, C. L. Emerson, V. N. Fulton, E. C. Gendron, R. W. Keener, R. G. Landis, J. A. Maggetti, J. A. Sproul, W. Swindells. **Transfer Agent & Registrar**—First Interstate Bank of Washington, Seattle. **Reincorporated** in Delaware in 1974. **Empl**—3,019.

 Leo Larkin

STANDARD & POOR'S

STOCK REPORTS

Outback Steakhouse

NASDAQ Symbol **OSSI**

In S&P MidCap 400

15-AUG-95 **Industry:** Food serving

Summary: This fast-growing company operates or franchises more than 200 Outback Steakhouse restaurants, most of which are at least 80% owned by OSSI.

S&P Opinion: Avoid (★★)

Recent Price • 33⅝
52 Wk Range • 35½-22⅝

Yield • Nil
12-Mo. P/E • 33.0

Quantitative Evaluations

Outlook
(1 Lowest—5 Highest)
• **5**

Fair Value
• **44**

Risk
• **Average**

Earn./Div. Rank
• **NR**

Technical Eval.
• **Bullish** since 5/95

Rel. Strength Rank
(1 Lowest—99 Highest)
• **74**

Insider Activity
• **Neutral**

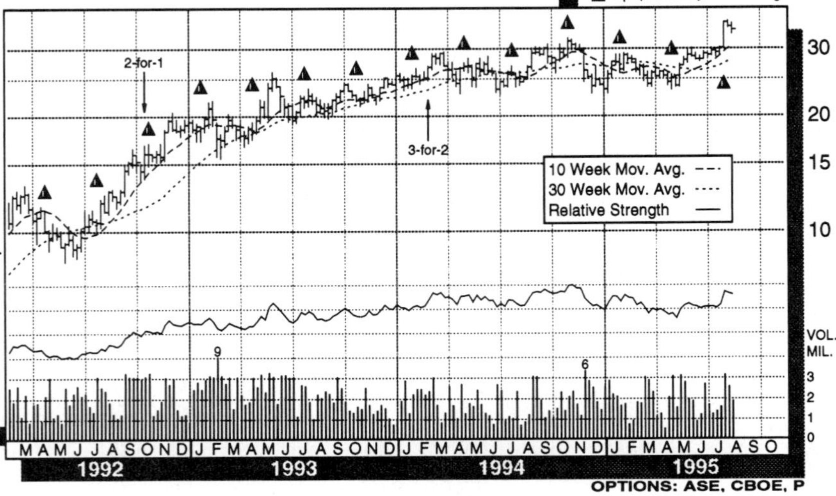

OPTIONS: ASE, CBOE, P

Overview - 15-AUG-95

In the year ahead, we expect OSSI's revenue growth to largely come from more restaurants being in operation. In calendar 1995, we look for OSSI to open more than 60 new company-operated Outback units, plus six-to-eight restaurants in the Carrabara chain. However, due to capacity constraints, comparable-unit sales growth is likely to be less than historic levels, and we expect Outback to be facing some margin pressure from labor costs. This could be at least partially offset by economies of scale, as certain relatively fixed costs are spread out over a larger revenue base. Longer-term, OSSI should continue to have sizable potential to develop its distinctive Outback concept in new markets and expand its presence in others.

Valuation - 15-AUG-95

With per share earnings expected to grow about 25% in 1996, the stock of this fast-growing company deserves a premium valuation. The Outback restaurant concept should still have considerable expansion potential, and development of the 50%-owned Carrabara Italian Grill chain gives OSSI another prospective long-term growth business. However, the P/E multiple on OSSI's estimated 1996 earnings is close to the profit growth rate we are projecting. With the stock price near its 52-week high, we would not be a purchaser of the shares at this time.

Key Stock Statistics

S&P EPS Est. 1995	1.15	Tang. Bk. Value/Share	4.29
P/E on S&P Est. 1995	29.2	Beta	NA
S&P EPS Est. 1996	1.45	Shareholders	2,800
Dividend Rate/Share	Nil	Market cap. (B)	$ 1.4
Shs. outstg. (M)	43.1	Inst. holdings	61%
Avg. daily vol. (M)	0.523	Insider holdings	NA

Value of $10,000 invested 5 years ago: NA

Fiscal Year Ending Dec. 31

	1995	% Change	1994	% Change	1993	% Change
Revenues ()						
1Q	140.7	39%	100.8	70%	59.18	139%
2Q	154.5	39%	110.9	66%	66.65	131%
3Q	—	—	115.8	67%	69.21	115%
4Q	—	—	124.3	63%	76.12	99%
Yr.	—	—	451.9	67%	271.2	119%
Income ()						
1Q	11.57	40%	8.25	68%	4.90	96%
2Q	12.86	33%	9.69	69%	5.74	102%
3Q	—	—	9.63	60%	6.02	92%
4Q	—	—	11.04	66%	6.66	65%
Yr.	—	—	38.61	63%	23.70	90%
Earnings Per Share ()						
1Q	0.26	37%	0.19	46%	0.13	63%
2Q	0.29	32%	0.22	57%	0.14	56%
3Q	E0.29	32%	0.22	50%	0.15	47%
4Q	E0.31	24%	0.25	56%	0.16	33%
Yr.	E1.15	31%	0.88	52%	0.58	71%

Next earnings report expected: late October

Outback Steakhouse

Business Summary - 14-AUG-95

The company's principal business is operation of the fast-growing Outback Steakhouse restaurant chain, which, as of December 31, 1994, had 214 units open, of which 164 were company owned and 50 were franchised or joint venture units. During 1994, OSSI acquired 20 Outback restaurants from franchisees. All of OSSI's company-owned restaurants are structured as partnerships in which OSSI is the general partner. OSSI's ownership interests in such units range from 81% to 90%, with minority interests owned by restaurant managers and joint venture partners. In addition to the Outback chain, OSSI has a 50% interest in the Carrabba's Italian Grill chain, which had about 12 restaurants open at year-end 1994.

The Outback restaurants serve dinner only. OSSI's efforts to differentiate the units include emphasizing consistently high-quality food and service, featuring generous portions at moderate prices, and providing a casual atmosphere suggestive of the Australian outback. The Outback Steakhouse menu includes several cuts of freshly prepared, specially seasoned and seared steaks, plus prime rib, barbecued ribs, pork chops, chicken, seafood and pasta. It also includes several specialty appetizers and desserts, together with full bar service featuring Australian beer and wine. Liquor service accounts for about 16% of revenues.

Systemwide sales (including franchises) for the Outback chain totaled $549 million in 1994, up 58% from the year before. Comparable-unit sales were up 3.5%. In 1994, 68 new Outback restaurants opened (including franchise units), following the debut of 61 in 1993.

Important Developments

Aug. '95—In 1995's second quarter, OSSI's systemwide sales from the Outback Steakhouse and Carraba's Italian Grill chains were up 53%, year to year, to $205 million. During the quarter, 20 new Outback restaurants and two Carrabba's units opened. As of late July, there were 263 Outbacks and 14 Carraba's operating in 34 states. Also, OSSI's comparable-unit sales in the second quarter were up 1.4%, but this was offset by unusually high produce costs. OSSI's operating profit in the second quarter increased 33%, but the operating margin narrowed to 15.8%, from a year-ago 16.6%. This was largely due to pressure from labor-related costs, which increased to 21.7% of revenues, from 20.4%. These costs include the February 1995 initiation of health insurance coverage for certain hourly employees. Overall, this additional coverage is expected to add about $3.5 million to 1995's full-year labor costs.

Capitalization

Long Term Debt: About $16,700,000 (3/95).
Minority Interest: $2,255,000 (12/94).

Per Share Data () (Year Ended Dec. 31)

	1994	1993	1992	1991	1990	1989
Tangible Bk. Val.	NA	3.06	2.45	0.85	0.27	0.12
Cash Flow	NA	0.70	0.39	0.26	0.13	0.07
Earnings	0.88	0.58	0.34	0.19	0.10	0.05
Dividends	Nil	Nil	Nil	Nil	Nil	Nil
Payout Ratio	Nil	Nil	Nil	Nil	Nil	Nil
Prices - High	32	26⅛	20½	10¼	NA	NA
- Low	22⅝	15½	8⅜	3⅜	NA	NA
P/E Ratio - High	36	46	60	53	NA	NA
- Low	26	27	25	17	NA	NA

Income Statement Analysis ()

	1993	%Chg	1992	%Chg	1991	%Chg	1990
Revs.	271	119%	124	125%	55.2	143%	22.7
Oper. Inc.	48.0	138%	20.2	80%	11.2	160%	4.3
Depr.	5.2	156%	2.0	-1%	2.1	197%	0.7
Int. Exp.	0.1	NM	0.0	-75%	0.2	60%	0.1
Pretax Inc.	44.5	100%	22.3	165%	8.4	171%	3.1
Eff. Tax Rate	31%	—	30%	—	31%	—	38%
Net Inc.	28.7	130%	12.5	116%	5.8	145%	2.4

Balance Sheet & Other Fin. Data ()

	1993	1992	1991	1990	1989	1988
Cash	29.4	57.9	16.2	2.6	1.3	0.3
Curr. Assets	36.9	61.5	17.8	3.0	1.5	0.4
Total Assets	141	109	34.7	10.2	4.0	1.0
Curr. Liab.	17.2	13.7	6.3	2.2	0.8	0.3
LT Debt	0.7	Nil	0.8	0.8	0.9	0.3
Common Eqty.	122	92.6	26.6	6.7	2.3	0.3
Total Cap.	124	94.8	28.4	7.9	3.3	0.7
Cap. Exp.	51.3	22.3	7.2	2.8	1.6	0.5
Cash Flow	28.9	14.6	7.9	3.1	1.3	0.1

Ratio Analysis

	1993	1992	1991	1990	1989	1988
Curr. Ratio	2.1	4.5	2.8	1.4	2.0	1.2
% LT Debt of Cap.	0.5	Nil	2.6	9.5	25.8	45.4
% Net Inc.of Revs.	8.7	10.1	10.5	10.4	8.1	2.0
% Ret. on Assets	18.3	16.7	23.7	33.2	39.0	NA
% Ret. on Equity	21.6	20.1	32.7	52.5	74.9	NA

Dividend Data —OSSI has never paid cash dividends on its common stock, and it intends to retain earnings to support operations and finance expansion. A three-for-two stock split was effected in February 1994, and a two-for-one stock split was effected in October 1992.

Amt. of Div. $	Date Decl.	Ex-Div. Date	Stock of Record	Payment Date
3-for-2	Jan. 13	Feb. 22	Feb. 04	Feb. 18 '94

Data as orig. reptd.; bef. results of disc. opers. and/or spec. items. Per share data adj. for stk. divs. as of ex-div. date. E-Estimated. NA-Not Available. NM-Not Meaningful. NR-Not Ranked.

Office—550 North Reo St., Suite 204, Tampa, FL 33609. **Tel**—(813) 282-1225. **Chrmn & CEO**—C. T. Sullivan. **Pres & COO**—R. D. Basham. **SVP-Fin, CFO, Treas, & Investor Contact**—Robert S. Merritt. **Dirs**—R. D. Basham, J. A. Brabson Jr., C. H. Bridges, W. R. Carey, E. L. Flom, J. T. Gannon, R. S. Merritt, L. R. Selmon, H. W. Smith, C. T. Sullivan. **Transfer Agent & Registrar**—Bank of New York, NYC. **Incorporated** in Florida in 1987; reincorporated in Delaware in 1991. **Empl-** **S&P Analyst:** Tom Graves, CFA

STANDARD & POOR'S

Overseas Shipholding Group

STOCK REPORTS

NYSE Symbol **OSG**
In S&P MidCap 400

18-OCT-95 **Industry:** Shipping/shipbuilding

Summary: This leading bulk shipping company operates under both U.S. and foreign flags. It also participates in the cruise business through a joint venture with Chandris Group.

S&P Opinion: Sell (★)

Recent Price • 19⅜
52 Wk Range • 24⅜-18½
Yield • 3.2%
12-Mo. P/E • NM

Quantitative Evaluations

Outlook
(1 Lowest—5 Highest)
• **NA**

Fair Value
• **NA**

Risk
• **Average**

Earn./Div. Rank
• **B+**

Technical Eval.
• **Bullish** since 8/95

Rel. Strength Rank
(1 Lowest—99 Highest)
• **13**

Insider Activity
• **NA**

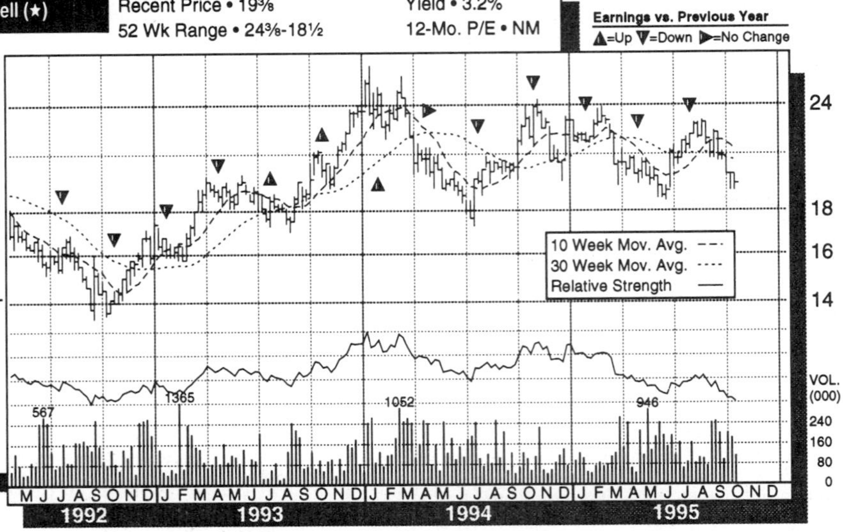

Overview - 18-OCT-95

Higher rates are anticipated in 1995 for certain tanker classes, as rising vessel scrappings cut excess industry capacity. While higher oil consumption is projected, demand is expected to be met with oil moved over less profitable short-haul North Sea and Latin American routes. U.S. tanker operations are expected to be unprofitable until late 1995 when two vessels commence charters for BP America. The outlook for 1996 is positive as oil exports from Alaska commence. Dry bulk volumes will benefit from increased demand for coal and iron ore in Europe and Asia and increased movements of grain to Japan and China. Bulk rates should increase despite some capacity expansion. Cruise line profits will may slip reflecting intensified competition from Caribbean resorts. Interest and depreciation charges will increase.

Valuation - 18-OCT-95

The shares of this shipping line moved down to the lower end of their two-year trading range reflecting some softness in tanker rates after vessel scrappings slowed. We believe investors have grown weary of OSG's dismal profit performance and may push prices to new lows. Though we see international tanker rates rising long-term as older vessels are scrapped, the process may be dragged out over a longer period of time than investors anticipate. While the pending repeal of the ban on exporting Alaskan oil is good news (and fully discounted), the unexpected slump in the North American cruise industry is worrisome.

Key Stock Statistics

S&P EPS Est. 1995	0.05	Tang. Bk. Value/Share	21.83
P/E on S&P Est. 1995	NM	Beta	1.23
S&P EPS Est. 1996	1.25	Shareholders	1,100
Dividend Rate/Share	0.60	Market cap. (B)	$0.675
Shs. outstg. (M)	36.2	Inst. holdings	41%
Avg. daily vol. (M)	0.031	Insider holdings	NA

Value of $10,000 invested 5 years ago: $ 10,239

Fiscal Year Ending Dec. 31

	1995	% Change	1994	% Change	1993	% Change
Revenues (Million $)						
1Q	106.9	6%	100.5	-1%	102.0	3%
2Q	92.52	15%	80.15	-15%	94.71	6%
3Q	—	—	88.60	-10%	98.45	12%
4Q	—	—	95.76	2%	94.22	NM
Yr.	—	—	364.1	-6%	389.4	5%
Income (Million $)						
1Q	-3.31	NM	5.02	3%	4.88	-53%
2Q	-5.98	NM	-4.60	NM	5.51	NM
3Q	—	—	-2.31	NM	4.52	NM
4Q	—	—	-4.30	NM	3.04	NM
Yr.	—	—	-6.20	NM	17.95	NM
Earnings Per Share ($)						
1Q	-0.09	NM	0.15	NM	0.15	-52%
2Q	-0.17	NM	-0.14	NM	0.17	NM
3Q	E0.05	NM	-0.06	NM	0.14	NM
4Q	E0.26	NM	-0.12	NM	0.09	NM
Yr.	E0.05	NM	-0.17	NM	0.55	—

Next earnings report expected: early November

Overseas Shipholding Group

Business Summary - 17-OCT-95

Overseas Shipholding Group is one of the world's largest shippers of liquid and dry cargos operating in international and U.S. waters. OSG also has a 49% interest in a cruise line venture. At February 21, 1995, OSG's shipping fleet consisted of 61 vessels aggregating 5,846,100 dwt. The two-year charter position of OSG's fleet at February 21, 1995, was as follows:

	1995	1996
Int'l fleet	27%	24%
U.S. fleet	2%	2%

OSG operates its fleet without fixed routes or schedules primarily under time or voyage charters where all personnel are supplied by OSG. Some 78% of shipping revenues in 1994 were generated from the movement of crude oil and petroleum products. BP Oil Company, USA, generated 18% of total voyage revenues in 1994. Other bulk commodities transported are coal, iron ore and grain.

The international fleet at February 21, 1995, consisted of 45 vessels aggregating 4,852,750 dwt, with 13 bulk carriers and 32 tankers or petroleum product carriers. OSG is scheduled to take delivery of two 295,250 dwt-tankers in 1995. OSG's U.S. fleet at February 21, 1995, consisted of 16 vessels aggregating 993,350 dwt. The U.S. fleet is engaged primarily in the transport of Alaskan oil. OSG also operates a 5,000-unit auto carrier.

Celebrity Cruise Lines Inc. (49%-owned) operates three premium cruise ships under the Celebrity trade name and two vessels under the Fantasy name for budget-conscious passengers. OSG, which operates a total of 5,377 berths, will add 5,500 berths by 1997 year end upon the delivery of three new vessels under construction.

Important Developments

Oct. '95—A joint House-Senate conference committee had substantially reconciled measures that would repeal the 22-year ban on exportation of Alaskan oil. The bill, which is expected to be signed by President Clinton by 1995 year-end, would require that Alaskan oil be carried solely in U.S.-flag vessels. In anticipation of passage of the legislation, BP America entered charters for two of OSG's 120,000 dwt. U.S.-flag tankers.

May '95—OSG reported that it had purchased during 1995's first quarter two 1994-built 94,000-dwt double-hulled tankers. Through 1997, OSG plans to take delivery of eight new vessels aggregating some 2.0 million dwt.

Capitalization

Long Term Debt: $1,063,690,000 (6/95), incl. $155.6 million of lease obligs.

Minority Interest: $3,093,000.

Per Share Data ($)

(Year Ended Dec. 31)

	1994	1993	1992	1991	1990	1989
Tangible Bk. Val.	22.36	23.50	23.33	23.05	21.40	20.09
Cash Flow	1.51	2.35	1.72	3.37	3.25	2.89
Earnings	-0.17	0.55	Nil	1.67	1.63	1.46
Dividends	0.60	0.60	0.60	0.55	0.50	0.50
Payout Ratio	NM	109%	NM	33%	30%	34%
Prices - High	26¾	24¼	21¼	22⅜	27⅜	25¾
- Low	17¼	15¾	13⅜	15½	12½	18
P/E Ratio - High	NM	44	NM	13	17	18
- Low	NM	29	NM	9	8	12

Income Statement Analysis (Million $)

	1994	%Chg	1993	%Chg	1992	%Chg	1991
Revs.	359	-5%	377	3%	367	-11%	411
Oper. Inc.	75.0	-13%	86.0	5%	82.0	-45%	150
Depr.	60.0	2%	58.7	4%	56.5	NM	56.2
Int. Exp.	71.1	40%	50.7	NM	50.7	-9%	56.0
Pretax Inc.	-10.2	NM	27.0	NM	-3.6	NM	79.8
Eff. Tax Rate	NM	—	33%	—	NM	—	31%
Net Inc.	-6.2	NM	17.9	NM	0.1	-100%	55.1

Balance Sheet & Other Fin. Data (Million $)

	1994	1993	1992	1991	1990	1989
Cash	100	110	86.0	114	98.0	66.0
Curr. Assets	161	163	160	163	147	137
Total Assets	1,905	1,824	1,715	1,546	1,498	1,541
Curr. Liab.	71.2	63.6	59.0	72.0	54.0	57.0
LT Debt	910	876	784	576	613	673
Common Eqty.	810	768	762	760	707	701
Total Cap.	1,826	1,749	1,645	1,456	1,428	1,469
Cap. Exp.	146	164	81.0	69.0	36.0	279
Cash Flow	54.0	77.0	57.0	111	111	103

Ratio Analysis

	1994	1993	1992	1991	1990	1989
Curr. Ratio	2.3	2.6	2.7	2.3	2.7	2.4
% LT Debt of Cap.	49.8	50.1	47.7	39.6	42.9	45.8
% Net Inc.of Revs.	NM	4.9	Nil	13.4	14.2	16.9
% Ret. on Assets	NM	1.0	Nil	3.6	3.8	3.7
% Ret. on Equity	NM	2.3	Nil	7.5	8.1	7.6

Dividend Data —Dividends were initiated in 1973.

Amt. of Div. $	Date Decl.	Ex-Div. Date	Stock of Record	Payment Date
0.150	Oct. 13	Oct. 26	Nov. 01	Nov. 23 '94
0.150	Feb. 02	Feb. 09	Feb. 15	Feb. 27 '95
0.150	May. 03	May. 09	May. 15	May. 31 '95
0.150	Jun. 06	Jul. 28	Aug. 01	Aug. 25 '95
0.150	Sep. 28	Oct. 30	Nov. 01	Nov. 28 '95

Data as orig. reptd.; bef. results of disc. opers. and/or spec. items. Per share data adj. for stk. divs. as of ex-div. date. E-Estimated. NA-Not Available. NM-Not Meaningful. NR-Not Ranked.

Office—1114 Ave. of the Americas, New York, NY 10036. **Tel**—(212) 869-1222. **Pres**—M. P. Hyman. **SVP-Secy**—R. N. Cowen. **SVP-CFO**—M. R. Itkin. **Investor Contact**—Catherine J. Mathis. **Dirs**—G. C. Blake, R. N. Cowen, T. H. Dean, M. Fribourg, W. L. Frost, R. Hettena, M. P. Hyman, S. Komaroff, S. N. Merkin, J. I. Picket, M. A. Recanati, R. Recanati. **Transfer Agent & Registrar**—Mellon Securities Trust Co., NYC. **Incorporated** in Delaware in 1969. **Empl**-2,000. **S&P Analyst:** Stephen R. Klein

STANDARD & POOR'S

STOCK REPORTS

PHH Corporation

NYSE Symbol **PHH**
In S&P MidCap 400

20-SEP-95 **Industry:** Services

Summary: PHH provides a range of integrated services, including vehicle management and relocation and real estate services, to corporate clients, and mortgage banking services to consumers.

Quantitative Evaluations

Outlook (1 Lowest—5 Highest)
• **4+**
Fair Value
• **48¼**
Risk
• **Low**
Earn./Div. Rank
• **A-**

Technical Eval.
• **Bullish** since 1/95
Rel. Strength Rank (1 Lowest—99 Highest)
• **30**
Insider Activity
• **Neutral**

Recent Price • 43⅝
52 Wk Range • 48-33½
Yield • 3.1%
12-Mo. P/E • 10.3

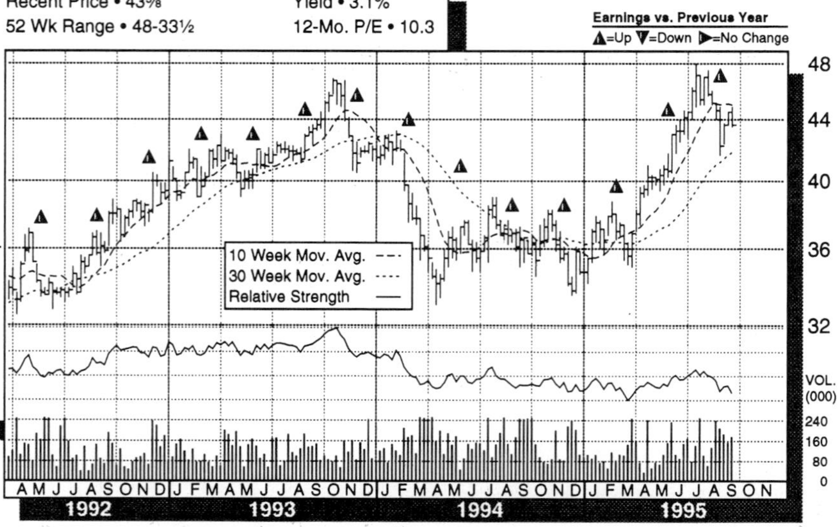

Business Profile - 19-SEP-95

PHH expects to derive an increasing share of future income from fee-based services (relocation and real estate services), versus capital-intensive asset-based services (auto leasing and mortgage banking). Significant growth markets targeted by PHH include associations and other affinity groups, financial institutions in need of asset management and resale, employee groups, and emerging businesses. In addition, PHH is looking to expand its vehicle management services in Europe from its U.K. base.

Operational Review - 19-SEP-95

The increase in first quarter earnings reflects favorable results in mortgage banking services. Operating income for this segment rose over 50%, due to the company's expanded relationships with affinity groups and credit unions. Profits for real estate services were flat, as higher global fee-based services and volume increases in the U.K. were offset by margin pressure in the U.S. and Canada. Vehicle management had a 13% decline in income, due to lower used vehicle marketing revenues.

Stock Performance - 15-SEP-95

In the past 30 trading days, PHH's shares have declined 5%, compared to a 4% rise in the S&P 500. Average trading volume for the past five days was 34,940 shares, compared with the 40-day moving average of 32,028 shares.

Key Stock Statistics

Dividend Rate/Share	1.36	Shareholders	2,500
Shs. outstg. (M)	16.9	Market cap. (B)	$0.741
Avg. daily vol. (M)	0.039	Inst. holdings	87%
Tang. Bk. Value/Share	31.97	Insider holdings	NA
Beta	1.41		

Value of $10,000 invested 5 years ago: $ 16,052

Fiscal Year Ending Apr. 30

	1996	% Change	1995	% Change	1994	% Change
Revenues (Million $)						
1Q	581.9	12%	520.3	-3%	538.6	5%
2Q	—	—	510.1	-6%	545.4	8%
3Q	—	—	494.1	-4%	516.8	6%
4Q	—	—	546.0	2%	533.9	4%
Yr.	—	—	2,071	-3%	2,135	6%
Income (Million $)						
1Q	18.30	11%	16.52	12%	14.79	17%
2Q	—	—	17.61	9%	16.20	27%
3Q	—	—	16.76	9%	15.41	7%
4Q	—	—	20.77	14%	18.16	9%
Yr.	—	—	71.66	11%	64.56	14%
Earnings Per Share ($)						
1Q	1.05	11%	0.95	13%	0.84	14%
2Q	—	—	1.01	12%	0.90	23%
3Q	—	—	0.98	13%	0.87	5%
4Q	—	—	1.21	17%	1.03	8%
Yr.	—	—	4.15	14%	3.64	12%

Next earnings report expected: late November

PHH Corporation

Business Summary - 19-SEP-95

PHH Corporation (formerly PHH Group), through subsidiaries, offers a broad range of vehicle management and relocation and real estate management services to more than 3,000 clients. It also provides mortgage banking services to consumers. Business segment contributions in fiscal 1994-95 were:

	Revs.	Income
Vehicle management	61%	46%
Real estate	33%	29%
Mortgage banking	6%	25%

European operations accounted for 9% of consolidated revenues and 6% of operating income in 1994-95.

Vehicle-related services consist of truck and auto fleet management, and leasing and vehicle cost-control services for corporations and governmental agencies in the U.S., Canada, U.K., Republic of Ireland, and Germany. Services include purchasing and arranging for delivery of new vehicles; fleet financing; registration, title, tax and insurance compliance; used vehicle sales; business travel expense-control programs; fuel purchasing and control programs; and centralized billing programs. The number of vehicles under management was 463,200 at April 30, 1995, up from 450,400 a year earlier.

Real estate services (U.S., Canada and Europe) consist of counseling transferred employees of corporate clients and the purchase, management and resale of their homes. Relocation subsidiaries also provide home marketing, moving services, rental management, spousal career counseling and consulting services for transferred employees. Other subsidiaries provides real estate services to financial institutions and governmental agencies. During 1994-95, the company sold 25,300 homes (28,900 in 1993-94) at an average price of $171,000 ($165,000) for U.S. homes.

The company provides U.S. residential mortgage banking services through PHH Mortgage Services Corporation. Services consist of the origination, sale and servicing of residential first mortgage loans nationwide.

Important Developments

Aug. '95—PHH and First Interstate Bancorp reached a joint venture agreement to market and originate residential mortgage loans through a newly formed enterprise called First Interstate Residential Mortgage, or FIRM. PHH will be the primary servicer of newly originated mortgages that are to be marketed across First Interstate's 13-state territory.

Capitalization

Total Debt: $3,815,515,000 (4/95).
Options: To buy 1,672,968 shs. at $19.88 to $42.00 ea. (4/95).

Per Share Data ($) (Year Ended Apr. 30)

	1995	1994	1993	1992	1991	1990
Tangible Bk. Val.	28.94	25.08	22.57	20.72	19.57	17.76
Cash Flow	56.63	51.28	45.89	39.36	39.20	40.00
Earnings	4.15	3.64	3.25	2.92	2.78	3.38
Dividends	1.28	1.20	1.20	1.20	1.20	1.16
Payout Ratio	31%	33%	37%	41%	43%	34%
Cal. Yrs.	1994	1993	1992	1991	1990	1989
Prices - High	43¼	46⅞	41½	36¾	37⅛	38⅞
- Low	33	38¾	32½	22½	17⅝	31⅝
P/E Ratio - High	10	13	13	13	13	12
- Low	8	11	10	8	6	9

Income Statement Analysis (Million $)

	1995	%Chg	1994	%Chg	1993	%Chg	1992
Revs.	2,071	-3%	2,135	6%	2,021	5%	1,931
Oper. Inc.	1,199	7%	1,116	9%	1,028	46%	706
Depr.	905	7%	844	14%	738	19%	620
Int. Exp.	173	7%	162	-16%	194	—	NA
Pretax Inc.	121	10%	110	17%	94.2	13%	83.1
Eff. Tax Rate	41%	—	41%	—	40%	—	40%
Net Inc.	71.7	11%	64.6	15%	56.4	13%	50.0

Balance Sheet & Other Fin. Data (Million $)

	1995	1994	1993	1992	1991	1990
Cash	3.4	Nil	1.0	1.0	Nil	1.0
Curr. Assets	NA	NA	NA	NA	NA	NA
Total Assets	5,040	4,767	4,613	4,365	4,199	4,464
Curr. Liab.	NA	NA	NA	NA	NA	NA
LT Debt	736	1,301	1,299	1,001	823	1,264
Common Eqty.	540	498	457	423	393	363
Total Cap.	1,400	1,892	1,848	1,521	1,315	1,773
Cap. Exp.	16.4	32.7	20.8	24.0	26.0	21.9
Cash Flow	977	908	794	670	663	678

Ratio Analysis

	1995	1994	1993	1992	1991	1990
Curr. Ratio	NA	NA	NA	NA	NA	NA
% LT Debt of Cap.	52.6	68.7	70.3	65.8	62.6	71.3
% Net Inc.of Revs.	3.4	3.0	2.8	2.6	2.3	3.0
% Ret. on Assets	1.5	1.4	1.2	1.2	1.1	1.3
% Ret. on Equity	13.8	13.5	12.7	12.2	12.5	16.1

Dividend Data —Dividends have been paid since 1959. A "poison pill" stock purchase right was adopted in 1986.

Amt. of Div. $	Date Decl.	Ex-Div. Date	Stock of Record	Payment Date
0.320	Sep. 19	Oct. 03	Oct. 07	Oct. 31 '94
0.320	Nov. 21	Dec. 30	Jan. 06	Jan. 31 '95
0.320	Mar. 07	Apr. 03	Apr. 07	Apr. 28 '95
0.340	Jun. 28	Jul. 05	Jul. 07	Jul. 31 '95
0.340	Aug. 25	Oct. 04	Oct. 06	Oct. 31 '95

Data as orig. reptd.; bef. results of disc. opers. and/or spec. items. Per share data adj. for stk. divs. as of ex-div. date. E-Estimated. NA-Not Available. NM-Not Meaningful. NR-Not Ranked.

Office—11333 McCormick Rd., Hunt Valley, MD 21031. **Tel**—(410) 771-3600. **Chrmn & CEO**—R. D. Kunisch. **SVP-CFO**—R. A. Meierhenry. **SVP-Secy**—E. A. Arbaugh. **Investor Contact**—Gene Truett (410-771-2463). **Dirs**—J. S. Beard, A. F. Brimmer, G. L. Bunting, Jr., A. Hoblitzell, P. X. Kelley, L. P. Kline, R. D. Kunisch, F. P. Lucier, K. C. Nelson, D. J. Shepard, A. M. Tatlock, A. B. Trowbridge. **Transfer Agent**—First Chicago Trust Co. of New York, NYC. **Registrar**—Co.'s office. **Incorporated** in Maryland in 1953. **Empl**-5,000. **S&P Analyst:** Stephen Madonna, CFA

STANDARD & POOR'S

STOCK REPORTS

PacifiCare Health Systems

NASDAQ Symbol **PHSYB**

In S&P MidCap 400

16-AUG-95

Industry: Health Care Centers

Summary: PacifiCare operates federally qualified HMOs serving over 1,500,000 commercial, Medicare and Medicaid members in California, Florida, Oregon, Washington, Oklahoma and Texas.

S&P Opinion: Accumulate (★★★★)

Recent Price • 54½ | Yield • Nil

52 Wk Range • 77-44 | 12-Mo. P/E • 15.9

Quantitative Evaluations

Outlook (1 Lowest—5 Highest)
• **5-**

Fair Value
• **78¼**

Risk
• **Average**

Earn./Div. Rank
• **B+**

Technical Eval.
• **Bullish** since 8/95

Rel. Strength Rank (1 Lowest—99 Highest)
• **9**

Insider Activity
• **NA**

OPTIONS: CBOE, P

Overview - 16-AUG-95

PacifiCare is one of the leading managed care providers in the U.S., and generates a substantial portion of its premiums from payments under the Medicare program. Acquisitions outside of the California market should also help spur revenue gains, although margins from these newer areas are typically below those in established markets. Although Medicaid is currently a small portion of the company's business, this segment is also growing rapidly. During the third quarter of fiscal 1995, total membership rose 34%, to 1,682,371 members (including about 100,000 members from acquisitions).

Valuation - 16-AUG-95

The company appears likely to meet its target of 20% EPS growth in fiscal 1995, making our $3.60 estimate quite reachable. Per-share profits in fiscal 1996 should advance 15% - 20%, based on the prospects for strong commercial membership gains, and increased Medicare enrollment. In addition, the recent approval of a 10% Medicare rate increase in 1996 could add up to $0.10 a share to the bottom line in fiscal 1996. We continue to recommend that investors accumulate the shares of PacifiCare, due to its favorable growth prospects and reasonable valuation. However, the company will need to reduce its medical costs in order to meet the upper end of EPS estimates.

Key Stock Statistics

S&P EPS Est. 1995	3.60	Tang. Bk. Value/Share	11.98
P/E on S&P Est. 1995	15.1	Beta	2.03
S&P EPS Est. 1996	4.25	Shareholders	NA
Dividend Rate/Share	Nil	Market cap. (B)	$ 1.7
Shs. outstg. (M)	30.7	Inst. holdings	53%
Avg. daily vol. (M)	0.392	Insider holdings	NA

Value of $10,000 invested 5 years ago: NA

Fiscal Year Ending Sep. 30

	1995	% Change	1994	% Change	1993	% Change
Revenues (Million $)						
1Q	821.6	27%	645.8	33%	484.8	35%
2Q	912.8	28%	714.4	29%	555.1	31%
3Q	981.2	30%	752.3	31%	575.7	29%
4Q	—	—	780.8	29%	605.5	33%
Yr.	—	—	2,893	30%	2,221	32%
Income (Million $)						
1Q	20.06	36%	14.74	—	—	—
2Q	27.36	31%	20.84	—	—	—
3Q	30.25	13%	26.80	36%	19.71	35%
4Q	—	—	22.21	30%	17.11	41%
Yr.	—	—	84.59	35%	62.70	NM
Earnings Per Share ($)						
1Q	0.71	34%	0.53	36%	0.39	34%
2Q	0.96	28%	0.75	39%	0.54	29%
3Q	0.97	2%	0.95	34%	0.71	18%
4Q	E0.96	22%	0.79	30%	0.61	30%
Yr.	E3.60	19%	3.02	34%	2.25	26%

Next earnings report expected: mid November

PacifiCare Health Systems

Business Summary - 16-AUG-95

PacifiCare Health Systems, Inc. is a regionally focused health care company with health maintenance organizations (HMOs) operating in California (68% of total membership at June 30, 1995), Florida (4%), Oklahoma (7%), Oregon (8%), Texas (7%) and Washington (6%).

PacifiCare primarily serves two types of HMO member groups--commercial members and Medicare beneficiaries. Commercial members join its programs primarily through employer groups, while the company provides health care services to individual Medicare beneficiaries through its Secure Horizons programs.

At June 30, 1995, the company's commercial membership had grown to 1,175,777 from 873,922 a year earlier. Through its HMOs, PacifiCare arranges for the delivery of a comprehensive range of health care services to members, including primary and specialty physician care, hospital care, laboratory and radiology services, prescription drugs, dental care, vision care, skilled nursing care, physical therapy, and psychological counseling. The company's Secure Horizons programs offer a comprehensive package of benefits extending beyond those to which most beneficiaries are entitled by Medicare. At June 30, 1995, the company's HMOs served 506,594 non-commercial enrollees (Medicare and Medicaid), up from 381,392 a year earlier.

In addition to its core HMO and Secure Horizons operations, PacifiCare offers certain specialty products and services to group purchasers and to other managed care organizations and their beneficiaries, including Medicare-risk management services, pharmacy benefit management, military health care management, coordination of managed care products for multi-region employers, health and life insurance, behavioral health, workers' compensation, dental and vision services, and health promotion.

Important Developments

Mar. '95—Underwriters completed a public offering of 5.2 million PacifiCare Class B common shares at $68 a share, including 3.0 million new financing and 2.2 million sold for UniHealth Inc. Net company proceeds, estimated at about $200 million, were earmarked to repay debt, increase working capital and for possible acquitions.

Capitalization

Long Term Debt: $12,287,000 (6/95).
Minority Interest: $413,000 (9/94).
Class A Common Stock: 12,258,233 ($0.01 par). UniHealth, Inc. owns 48%.
Shareholders: 286 of record (9/94).
Class B Common Stock: 18,291,879 shs. ($0.01 par). UniHealth, Inc. owns about 9%.
Shareholders: 237 of record (9/94).

Per Share Data ($) (Year Ended Sep. 30)

	1994	1993	1992	1991	1990	1989
Tangible Bk. Val.	8.95	8.79	4.52	4.00	2.95	2.00
Cash Flow	3.78	2.80	2.21	1.37	0.92	0.59
Earnings	3.02	2.25	1.78	1.10	0.74	0.48
Dividends	Nil	Nil	Nil	Nil	Nil	Nil
Payout Ratio	Nil	Nil	Nil	Nil	Nil	Nil
Prices - High	75	50	45	NA	NA	NA
- Low	37¼	20	22½	NA	NA	NA
P/E Ratio - High	25	22	25	NA	NA	NA
- Low	12	9	13	NA	NA	NA

Income Statement Analysis (Million $)

	1994	%Chg	1993	%Chg	1992	%Chg	1991
Revs.	2,922	30%	2,245	32%	1,704	37%	1,242
Oper. Inc.	171	36%	126	42%	88.9	147%	36.0
Depr.	21.4	39%	15.4	45%	10.6	68%	6.3
Int. Exp.	4.1	70%	2.4	-30%	3.4	NM	0.2
Pretax Inc.	145	34%	108	44%	74.9	68%	44.5
Eff. Tax Rate	42%	—	42%	—	42%	—	42%
Net Inc.	84.6	35%	62.7	44%	43.6	70%	25.7

Balance Sheet & Other Fin. Data (Million $)

	1994	1993	1992	1991	1990	1989
Cash	711	437	272	206	160	143
Curr. Assets	822	515	329	241	199	174
Total Assets	1,106	694	498	322	232	194
Curr. Liab.	591	352	280	219	156	147
LT Debt	101	21.8	18.5	2.3	0.3	2.3
Common Eqty.	413	319	199	100	75.0	44.0
Total Cap.	515	342	218	103	76.0	47.0
Cap. Exp.	25.0	19.6	10.5	46.1	10.1	6.0
Cash Flow	106	78.1	54.2	32.0	21.9	13.3

Ratio Analysis

	1994	1993	1992	1991	1990	1989
Curr. Ratio	1.4	1.5	1.2	1.1	1.3	1.2
% LT Debt of Cap.	19.6	6.4	8.5	2.2	0.4	4.9
% Net Inc.of Revs.	2.9	2.8	2.6	2.1	1.8	1.7
% Ret. on Assets	9.4	10.2	10.1	9.3	8.1	6.6
% Ret. on Equity	23.0	23.6	28.0	29.5	29.2	27.5

Dividend Data —The company has never paid cash dividends on its common stock. In June 1992, one new Class B common share was distributed for each common share (reclassified as Class A common), having the effect of a two-for-one stock split.

Data as orig. reptd.; bef. results of disc. opers. and/or spec. items. Per share data adj. for stk. divs. as of ex-div. date. E-Estimated. NA-Not Available. NM-Not Meaningful. NR-Not Ranked.

Office—5995 Plaza Dr., Cypress, CA 90630-5028. **Tel**—(714) 952-1121. **Chrmn**—T. O. Hartshorn. **Pres & CEO**—A. Hoops. **EVP & CFO**—W. Lowell. **Investor Contacts**—David Erickson & Laurie Little. **Secy**—J. S. Konowiecki. **Dirs**—D. R. Carpenter, T. O. Hartshorn, A. Hoops, G. L. Leary, W. E. Pinckert II, D. A. Reed, L. Ross, J. B. Smith. **Transfer Agent & Registrar**—First Interstate Bank of California, LA. **Incorporated** in Delaware in 1975. **Empl**-3,856. **S&P Analyst:** Robert M. Gold

PaineWebber Group

NYSE Symbol **PWJ**
In S&P MidCap 400

20-OCT-95 **Industry:** Securities

Summary: PWJ is one of the largest U.S. full-service securities and commodities concerns. GE holds a 25% stake (fully diluted).

S&P Opinion: No Opinion

Recent Price • 22⅜
52 Wk Range • 22⅝-12¾

Yield • 2.2%
12-Mo. P/E • NM

Quantitative Evaluations

Outlook
(1 Lowest—5 Highest)
• **1+**

Fair Value
• **19¼**

Risk
• **Average**

Earn./Div. Rank
• **B**

Technical Eval.
• **Bearish** since 5/95

Rel. Strength Rank
(1 Lowest—99 Highest)
• **89**

Insider Activity
• **Neutral**

Earnings vs. Previous Year
▲=Up ▼=Down ▶=No Change

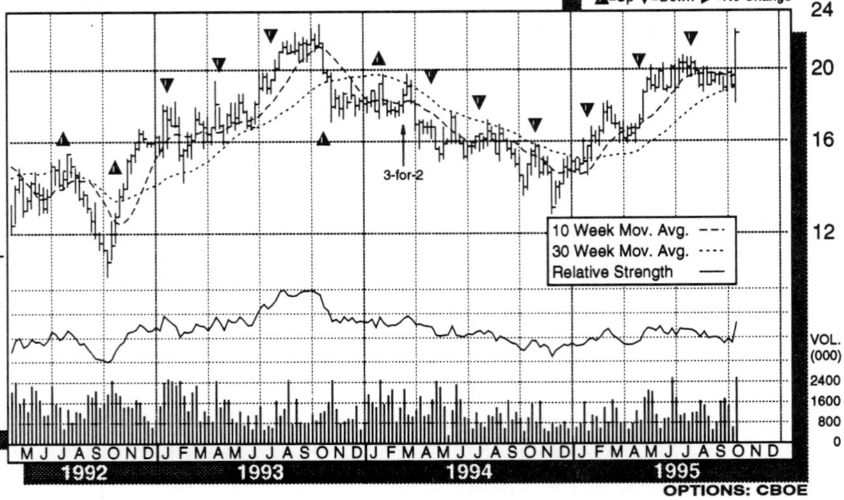

Overview - 20-OCT-95

Profits are expected to show a healthy increase in 1996 from 1995 levels (excluding the 1995 second quarter charge related to the sale of limited partnerships). Commissions should benefit from higher national savings rates, greater retail investor interest in stocks as opposed to bonds, and the contribution of Kidder's most productive brokers. Investment banking revenues should increase with lower interest rates stimulating debt offerings and a strong stock market fueling more equity deals. Asset management revenues have been in a long uptrend, which is expected to continue. Net interest income will benefit from greater trading activity and a positively sloped yield curve. Only modestly higher costs are anticipated.

Valuation - 20-OCT-95

Price to tangible book value is the preferred method to use in valuing brokerage stocks. Brokers have highly liquid balance sheets that can be readily marked to market. In addition, the traditional P/E ratio makes the stocks appear undervalued at market tops and overvalued at market lows. As of late October 1995, the shares were trading at about a 45% premium to book value, well above their average of the past several years, reflecting a 1995 rally in brokerage stocks. PWJ stock tends to trade at lower price to book value ratios than that of comparable brokers, in part because of the company's earnings volatility.

Key Stock Statistics

S&P EPS Est. 1995	0.65	Tang. Bk. Value/Share	14.52
P/E on S&P Est. 1995	34.4	Beta	2.43
S&P EPS Est. 1996	1.90	Shareholders	6,500
Dividend Rate/Share	0.48	Market cap. (B)	$ 2.2
Shs. outstg. (M)	99.0	Inst. holdings	41%
Avg. daily vol. (M)	0.393	Insider holdings	NA

Value of $10,000 invested 5 years ago: $ 34,346

Fiscal Year Ending Dec. 31

	1995	% Change	1994	% Change	1993	% Change
Revenues (Million $)						
1Q	1,234	14%	1,082	16%	930.7	6%
2Q	1,332	48%	902.3	-6%	954.9	17%
3Q	1,380	47%	940.0	-10%	1,043	25%
4Q	—	—	1,039	-3%	1,076	29%
Yr.	—	—	3,964	-1%	4,005	19%
Income (Million $)						
1Q	34.31	-38%	55.65	-21%	70.88	-5%
2Q	-90.55	NM	-25.06	NM	59.30	30%
3Q	78.19	NM	20.34	-66%	59.12	14%
4Q	—	—	-19.30	NM	56.88	37%
Yr.	—	—	31.63	-87%	246.2	15%
Earnings Per Share ($)						
1Q	0.27	-62%	0.71	-20%	0.89	-13%
2Q	-1.06	NM	-0.35	NM	0.74	-20%
3Q	0.71	163%	0.27	-64%	0.74	6%
4Q	E0.73	NM	-0.28	NM	0.74	45%
Yr.	E0.65	59%	0.41	-87%	3.11	10%

Next earnings report expected: late January

PaineWebber Group

Business Summary - 18-OCT-95

PaineWebber Group is the holding company for PaineWebber Inc. (PWI), one of the largest U.S. investment services concerns. In January 1995, operations were considerably expanded with the purchase of the Kidder, Peabody Group from General Electric for $603 million in common and preferred stock. Contributions to total revenues in recent years were:

	1994	1993
Commissions	38%	35%
Principal transactions	21%	27%
Interest income (net)	11%	9%
Investment banking	11%	14%
Asset mgmt. & other	19%	15%

PWJ's primary business is comprised of four major groups: retail sales; institutional sales and trading; asset management; and banking. Retail sales consists of a domestic branch office system that provides clients with investment products and services. Institutional sales and trading includes the institutional equity and fixed income divisions, and international operations. The banking group provides financial advice to, and raises capital for, a broad range of corporate clients.

At June 30, 1995, customer assets entrusted to PWJ's 6,125 investment executives amounted to $200 billion, up from $138 billion a year earlier.

At June 30 1995, net capital, as defined, totaled $446.8 million, in excess of the regulatory minimum requirement by $351.8 million.

Important Developments

Oct. '95—PWJ said that it would continue to aggressively manage its cost structure to further improve profitability now and in 1996. Management attributed a strong third quarter performance partly to the Kidder, Peabody acquisition.

Capitalization

Long Term Debt: $2,471,258,000 (6/95).
Preferred Stock: $286,362,000, incl. $100 million of 6% Pfd. conv. into 5,515,720 shs. at $18.13 each.

Per Share Data ($)

(Year Ended Dec. 31)

	1994	1993	1992	1991	1990	1989
Tangible Bk. Val.	15.41	15.51	13.51	11.23	10.05	11.59
Cash Flow	NA	NA	NA	NA	NA	NA
Earnings	0.41	3.11	2.83	2.10	-1.44	0.47
Dividends	0.48	0.38	0.31	0.24	0.23	0.23
Payout Ratio	117%	12%	11%	11%	NM	50%
Prices - High	$19\frac{3}{4}$	$23\frac{1}{8}$	$17\frac{7}{8}$	$16\frac{1}{2}$	$9\frac{1}{8}$	$10\frac{1}{2}$
- Low	$12\frac{3}{4}$	$14\frac{1}{8}$	$10\frac{1}{2}$	$4\frac{7}{8}$	$5\frac{1}{8}$	7
P/E Ratio - High	48	7	6	8	NM	23
- Low	31	5	4	2	NM	15

Income Statement Analysis (Million $)

	1994	%Chg	1993	%Chg	1992	%Chg	1991
Commissions	970	-3%	996	21%	822	14%	723
Int. Inc.	1,695	23%	1,377	26%	1,095	-10%	1,214
Total Revs.	3,964	-1%	4,005	19%	3,364	6%	3,166
Int. Exp.	1,429	26%	1,131	29%	879	-17%	1,056
Pretax Inc.	44.0	-89%	408	20%	339	50%	226
Eff. Tax Rate	29%	—	40%	—	37%	—	33%
Net Inc.	32.0	-87%	246	15%	213	41%	151

Balance Sheet & Other Fin. Data (Million $)

	1994	1993	1992	1991	1990	1989
Total Assets	35,856	37,027	26,509	22,622	18,151	22,096
Cash Items	629	568	760	788	1,098	700
Receivables	23,022	20,877	15,994	13,358	10,725	13,551
Secs. Owned	10,784	14,847	8,923	6,620	4,949	6,232
Sec. Borrowed	20,989	21,809	14,128	12,718	8,899	13,810
Due Brokers & Cust.	3,202	3,409	4,345	3,585	3,242	3,143
Other Liabs.	7,314	8,388	5,806	4,452	4,457	3,620
Capitalization:						
Debt	2,315	1,936	1,151	816	657	522
Equity	1,530	1,195	892	712	557	655
Total	4,132	3,131	2,231	1,866	1,553	1,523

Ratio Analysis

	1994	1993	1992	1991	1990	1989
% Ret. on Revs.	0.8	6.1	6.3	4.8	NM	1.8
% Ret. on Assets	0.1	0.8	0.9	0.7	NM	0.3
% Ret. on Equity	2.2	23.6	24.5	20.1	NM	4.2

Dividend Data —Dividends have been paid since 1975.

Amt. of Div. $	Date Decl.	Ex-Div. Date	Stock of Record	Payment Date
0.120	Oct. 21	Nov. 29	Dec. 05	Jan. 04 '95
0.120	Feb. 03	Feb. 24	Mar. 02	Apr. 05 '95
0.120	May. 04	May. 26	Jun. 02	Jul. 07 '95
0.120	Aug. 11	Aug. 31	Sep. 05	Oct. 04 '95

Data as orig. reptd.; bef. results of disc opers. and/or spec. items. Per share data adj. for stk. divs. as of ex-div. date. E-Estimated. NA-Not Available. NM-Not Meaningful. NR-Not Ranked.

Office—1285 Avenue of the Americas, New York, NY 10019. **Founded**—in 1879; incorporated in Delaware in 1973. **Tel**—(212) 713-2000. **Chrmn & CEO**—D. B. Marron. **VP & Secy**—T. A. Levine. **VP & Treas**—P. R. Smith. **Dirs**—T. S. Armour, E. G. Bewkes, Jr., R. Braun, J. A. Bult, F. P. Doyle, Y. Fujisawa, J. J. Grano, Jr., J. W. Kinnear, J. E. Kilgore, Jr., R. M. Loeffler, D. B. Marron, E. Randall III, H. Rosovsky, K. Sorimachi. **Transfer Agents & Registrars**—Mellon Financial Services, Ridgefield Park, NJ. **Empl**-16,025. **S&P Analyst:** Paul L. Huberman, CFA

STANDARD & POOR'S

STOCK REPORTS

Parametric Technology

NASDAQ Symbol **PMTC**
In S&P MidCap 400

24-OCT-95 **Industry:** Data Processing

Summary: This company is a leader in the mechanical design automation industry with its Pro/ENGINEER line of integrated software products.

S&P Opinion: Accumulate (★★★★) Recent Price • 64½ 52 Wk Range • 69-31¼ Yield • Nil 12-Mo. P/E • 53.8

Quantitative Evaluations
Outlook (1 Lowest—5 Highest) • 3+
Fair Value • 63⅜
Risk • **Average**
Earn./Div. Rank • **NR**

Technical Eval. • **Bullish** since 9/94
Rel. Strength Rank (1 Lowest—99 Highest) • **93**
Insider Activity • **Neutral**

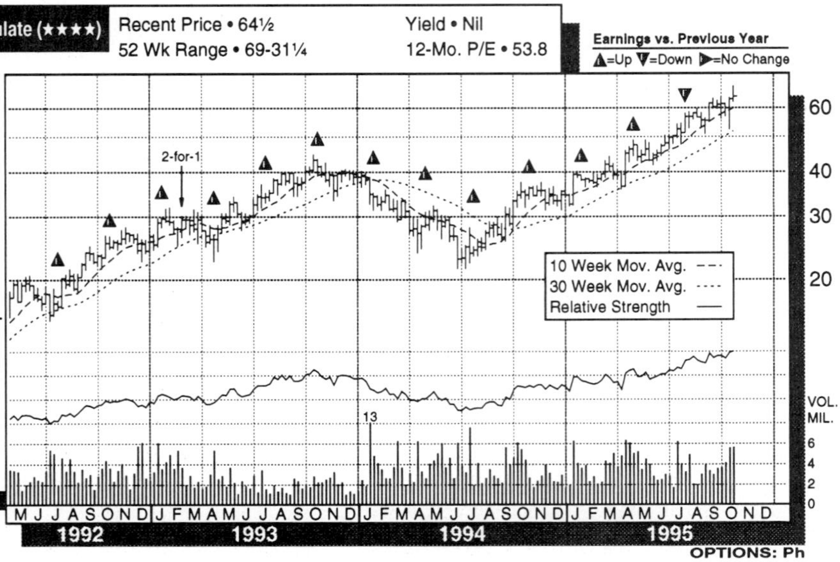

OPTIONS: Ph

Overview - 24-OCT-95

Revenues are expected to continue in a strong uptrend in fiscal 1996. The company obtains a high level of repeat business and continues to add new accounts, gaining market share at the expense of more established competitors. Margins are expected to narrow slightly, as volume efficiencies are outweighed by a less favorable revenue mix of services business and additions to the worldwide sales force. Earnings should benefit from the higher revenues we anticipate. Strengthening of the worldwide economies would further aid results.

Valuation - 24-OCT-95

The shares now are near their all-time high. The overall market for mechanical design automation software is growing slowly; however, Parametric itself has posted very rapid growth. Its Pro/ENGINEER product line is gaining market share, through the displacement of incumbent competitors in accounts, as well as through the addition of seats within its own list of customers. We expect continued market share gains as the company invests in enhancing Pro/ENGINEER with additional features and performance capabilities, and strengthens its worldwide sales organization. The stock's premium valuation is deserved. In light of projected earnings, the shares are expected to outperform the market in the coming months.

Key Stock Statistics

S&P EPS Est. 1996	2.20	Tang. Bk. Value/Share	5.63
P/E on S&P Est. 1996	29.3	Beta	2.01
Dividend Rate/Share	Nil	Shareholders	1,700
Shs. outstg. (M)	61.6	Market cap. (B)	$ 4.1
Avg. daily vol. (M)	0.977	Inst. holdings	93%
		Insider holdings	NA

Value of $10,000 invested 5 years ago: $ 184,285

Fiscal Year Ending Sep. 30

	1995	% Change	1994	% Change	1993	% Change
Revenues (Million $)						
1Q	72.02	35%	53.52	65%	32.50	97%
2Q	83.53	44%	58.02	53%	38.00	98%
3Q	97.02	52%	63.62	46%	43.52	85%
4Q	119.2	73%	69.09	41%	49.01	78%
Yr.	394.3	61%	244.3	50%	163.1	88%
Income (Million $)						
1Q	19.37	33%	14.60	77%	8.27	118%
2Q	22.27	40%	15.92	62%	9.81	109%
3Q	13.17	-26%	17.80	55%	11.45	101%
4Q	21.04	13%	18.60	39%	13.41	95%
Yr.	77.36	16%	66.92	56%	42.93	104%
Earnings Per Share ($)						
1Q	0.33	32%	0.25	67%	0.15	114%
2Q	0.37	37%	0.27	59%	0.17	113%
3Q	0.22	-27%	0.30	50%	0.20	100%
4Q	0.32	NM	0.32	39%	0.23	92%
Yr.	1.20	5%	1.14	52%	0.75	103%

Next earnings report expected: mid January

Parametric Technology

Business Summary - 24-OCT-95

Parametric Technology Corporation develops, markets and supports a family of fully integrated software products for the automation of the mechanical design-through-manufacturing process--a complex, iterative process encompassing a broad spectrum of distinct engineering disciplines that is essential to the development of virtually all manufactured products, from consumer items to jet aircraft.

The company's mechanical design automation (MDA) products enable end-users to reduce the time-to-market and manufacturing costs for their products and, through the easy evaluation of multiple design alternatives, to improve product quality.

As of September 30, 1994, Parametric's product line consisted of its core product, Pro/ENGINEER, and 30 released family modules. First shipped in January 1988, Pro/ENGINEER is a parametric, feature-driven solid modeling system used in the detailed design phase of the MDA cycle. Other modules include Pro/DESIGN, a conceptual design tool; Pro/DETAIL and Pro/DRAFT, which generate detailed manufacturing drawings; and Pro/ASSEMBLY, used to design and manage very complex assemblies. The company's practice has been to issue two major releases of its product line annually, with each generally including several new products. Parametric's ability to develop new products rapidly is facilitated by the modular structure of its software code. The company's products run on a wide range of workstations.

Marketing and sales efforts are focused primarily on electronic equipment, aerospace, automotive, consumer products and telecommunications companies, with sales made directly to strategic customers and indirectly through value-added resellers and original equipment manufacturers. Sales and support offices are located in 53 cities throughout the U.S. and in 50 cities in 21 foreign countries including Japan, France, Italy, Germany, the U.K., the Netherlands, Spain, Sweeden, Switzerland, Hong Kong, Korea, China and Singapore.

End-users of the company's products range from small companies to some of the world's largest manufacturing organizations.

Important Developments

Oct. '95—In the fourth quarter of fiscal 1995, the company shipped 4,700 seats (units) of software, added more than 730 new cuctomers, and derived 84% of license revenue from repeat customers.

Jul. '95—In the third quarter of fiscal 1995, the company recorded a $19.0 million ($0.19 a share) nonrecurring charge for purchased R&D in-process, related to its acquisition of the Conceptual Design and Rendering System software business from Evans & Sutherland Computer Corp.

Capitalization

Long Term Debt: None (9/30/95).

Per Share Data ($) (Year Ended Sep. 30)

	1995	1994	1993	1992	1991	1990
Tangible Bk. Val.	NA	4.25	2.69	1.51	0.85	0.60
Cash Flow	NA	1.22	0.79	0.40	0.20	0.12
Earnings	1.20	1.14	0.75	0.38	0.19	0.11
Dividends	Nil	Nil	Nil	Nil	Nil	Nil
Payout Ratio	Nil	Nil	Nil	Nil	Nil	Nil
Prices - High	69	40¼	44¾	28⅛	15⅜	5¼
- Low	32	21½	22½	12⅝	3¾	2½
P/E Ratio - High	57	35	60	76	81	48
- Low	27	19	30	34	20	23

Income Statement Analysis (Million $)

	1994	%Chg	1993	%Chg	1992	%Chg	1991
Revs.	244	50%	163	88%	86.7	94%	44.7
Oper. Inc.	107	56%	68.8	113%	32.3	114%	15.1
Depr.	4.6	72%	2.7	104%	1.3	88%	0.7
Int. Exp.	NA	—	NM	—	NM	—	0.1
Pretax Inc.	107	56%	68.5	106%	33.2	109%	15.9
Eff. Tax Rate	37%	—	37%	—	37%	—	35%
Net Inc.	66.9	56%	42.9	103%	21.1	105%	10.3

Balance Sheet & Other Fin. Data (Million $)

	1994	1993	1992	1991	1990	1989
Cash	207	123	73.5	34.5	24.6	3.3
Curr. Assets	271	165	99	48.7	33.1	6.8
Total Assets	287	177	107	51.0	35.0	8.0
Curr. Liab.	44.3	28.9	27.0	7.7	4.5	2.2
LT Debt	NA	NM	Nil	0.0	0.2	0.6
Common Eqty.	242	147	78.7	42.0	28.8	-0.9
Total Cap.	243	148	80.2	43.2	30.1	5.4
Cap. Exp.	9.1	7.4	3.6	0.8	0.5	0.1
Cash Flow	71.5	45.6	22.4	11.0	6.2	1.8

Ratio Analysis

	1994	1993	1992	1991	1990	1989
Curr. Ratio	6.1	5.7	3.7	6.3	7.3	3.1
% LT Debt of Cap.	NA	Nil	Nil	NM	0.7	10.3
% Net Inc.of Revs.	27.4	26.3	24.3	23.1	22.0	14.5
% Ret. on Assets	28.4	29.7	26.2	23.9	13.3	NA
% Ret. on Equity	33.8	37.5	34.3	28.8	NM	NA

Dividend Data —No cash dividends have been paid. The shares were split two-for-one in February 1993 and 1992.

Data as orig. reptd.; bef. results of disc. opers. and/or spec. items. Per share data adj. for stk. divs. as of ex-div. date. E-Estimated. NA-Not Available. NM-Not Meaningful. NR-Not Ranked.

Office—128 Technology Drive, Waltham, MA 02154. **Tel**—(617) 894-7111. **Fax**—(617) 891-1069. **Chrmn**—S. C. Walske. **Pres & COO**—C. R. Harrison. **CFO**—E. Gillis. **SVP, Treas**—M. J. Gallagher. **VP & Investor Contact**—Louis J. Volpe. **Dirs**—D. W. Feddersen, R. N. Goldman, D. K. Grierson, C. R. Harrison, N. G. Posternak, S. C. Walske. **Transfer Agent & Registrar**—American Stock Transfer & Trust Co., NYC. **Incorporated** in Massachusetts in 1985. **Empl**-1,281. **S&P Analyst:** Peter C. Wood, CFA

STANDARD & POOR'S

STOCK REPORTS

Parker & Parsley Petroleum

NYSE Symbol **PDP**
In S&P MidCap 400

17-AUG-95 **Industry:** Oil and Gas

Summary: This oil and gas company has producing properties primarily in the Permian Basin and other U.S. areas and in Australia, as well as interests in nine natural gas processing plants.

Quantitative Evaluations

Outlook (1 Lowest—5 Highest)
• **NA**
Fair Value
• **NA**
Risk
• **Average**
Earn./Div. Rank
• **B**

Technical Eval.
• **Bearish** since 10/94
Rel. Strength Rank (1 Lowest—99 Highest)
• **33**
Insider Activity
• **Neutral**

Recent Price • 19⅝
52 Wk Range • 27¼-16¼
Yield • 0.5%
12-Mo. P/E • NM

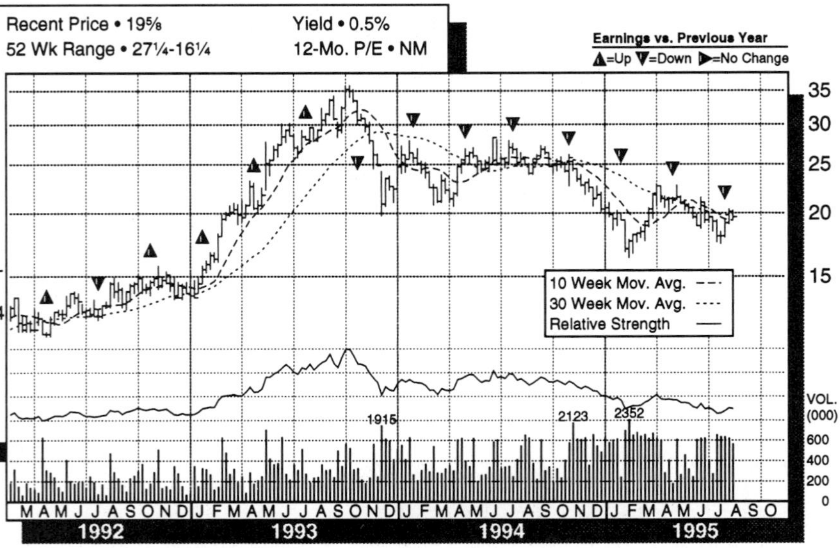

Business Profile - 17-AUG-95

PDP's focus is on the Permian Basin and the onshore Gulf Coast region. The company expanded its property base through acquisitions in 1994, some of which are near existing properties, with no material increase in general and administrative costs. This is in line with PDP's approach of concentrating on low-risk development activities, as opposed to exploration, within defined geographical areas. As the recent acquisitions are absorbed, revenues and income should be favorably affected.

Operational Review - 17-AUG-95

Revenues rose 41%, year to year, in the first half of 1995, reflecting substantially increased production of oil and gas and higher prices for oil, partially offset by lower gas prices. Expenses included more than $101 million for the impairment of oil and gas properties, and there was a net loss of $77.2 million ($2.19 a share, based on 25% more shares), versus income of $3.9 million ($0.14). Cash flow increased to $74.4 million, from $56.2 million.

Stock Performance - 11-AUG-95

In the past 30 trading days, PDP's shares were unchanged, compared to a 2% rise in the S&P 500. Average trading volume for the past five days was 111,700 shares, compared with the 40-day moving average of 153,244 shares.

Key Stock Statistics

Dividend Rate/Share	0.10	Shareholders	80,800
Shs. outstg. (M)	35.0	Market cap. (B)	$0.682
Avg. daily vol. (M)	0.152	Inst. holdings	76%
Tang. Bk. Value/Share	13.88	Insider holdings	NA
Beta	0.33		

Value of $10,000 invested 5 years ago: $ 28,038

Fiscal Year Ending Dec. 31

	1995	% Change	1994	% Change	1993	% Change
Revenues ()						
1Q	129.4	26%	102.9	82%	56.66	27%
2Q	158.6	57%	100.9	15%	87.78	83%
3Q	—	—	146.3	44%	101.8	83%
4Q	—	—	146.1	63%	89.86	49%
Yr.	—	—	496.2	51%	329.0	67%
Income ()						
1Q	-14.78	NM	0.39	-94%	6.02	69%
2Q	-62.40	NM	3.48	-79%	16.96	NM
3Q	—	—	-8.97	NM	7.37	-18%
4Q	—	—	-9.53	NM	1.05	-90%
Yr.	—	—	-13.99	NM	31.40	16%
Earnings Per Share ()						
1Q	-0.42	NM	0.01	-95%	0.22	29%
2Q	-1.77	NM	0.12	-80%	0.61	NM
3Q	—	—	-0.29	NM	0.26	-21%
4Q	—	—	-0.28	NM	0.04	-89%
Yr.	—	—	-0.47	NM	1.13	8%

Next earnings report expected: late October

Parker & Parsley Petroleum

Business Summary - 17-AUG-95

Parker & Parsley Petroleum Company is an independent energy company formed in 1990 through the conversion of Parker & Parsley Development Partners, L.P., a master oil and gas limited partnership formed in 1985, into a corporation, together with the acquisition of eight limited partnerships affiliated with Damson Oil Corp. In connection with the transactions, 21,187,546 PDP common shares were issued. Holders of limited partnership units received two common shares for each unit held. The company is now engaged in the oil and gas business, including production of oil and gas, exploration for and development of oil and gas reserves, and acquisition and operation of oil and gas properties and natural gas processing plants.

The company has producing oil and gas properties in the Permian Basin of West Texas, Gulf Coast, mid-Continent, Rocky Mountain and Appalachian regions and Australia. As of December 31, 1994, PDP owned interests in 8,179 producing oil wells (4,442 net) and 3,767 producing gas wells (1,722) and operated approximately 8,100. At December 31, 1994, total proved reserves were 144,500,000 bbl. of oil and condensate (94,000,000 bbl. at 1993 year-end) and 827,500,000 Mcf of natural gas (527,752,000 Mcf). The aggregate present value of estimated future net revenues at December 31, 1994, was $1.1 billion ($732 million a year earlier). In 1994, oil production totaled 12,147,000 bbl. (7,549,000 in 1993), sold at an average price of $15.40 per bbl. ($16.36). Gas production totaled 79,674,000 Mcf, sold at an average price of $1.89 per Mcf; production cost per BOE was $5.00 ($5.47); depletion cost per BOE was $5.18 ($4.39).

PDP owns interests in nine natural gas processing plants in Texas and Oklahoma, which account for 13.1 million bbl. of dedicated natural gas liquids. At December 31, 1994, the present value of estimated future net revenues from the 13.1 million bbl. of natural gas liquids was $44 million.

The company seeks to increase reserves, production and cash flow by developing existing reserves through low-risk development drilling or enhanced recovery projects, by acquiring properties with development and exploitation opportunities and significant cost reduction potential and by concentrating on focused geographic areas to achieve operating and technical efficiencies.

Important Developments

Aug. '95—PDP announced the public offering of $100 million of senior notes due 2007 through an underwriting syndicate comprised of Salomon Bros. and J.P. Morgan Securities. Separately, through the first six months of 1995, the company sold $178 million of nonstrategic assets and spudded over 260 of 550 wells budgeted for 1995, with an overall success rate of 97%.

Capitalization

Long Term Debt: $592,306,000 (6/95).

Per Share Data () (Year Ended Dec. 31)

	1994	1993	1992	1991	1990	1989
Tangible Bk. Val.	14.59	12.49	10.84	9.40	8.80	10.07
Cash Flow	4.37	3.88	2.95	2.34	2.26	3.14
Earnings	-0.47	1.13	1.05	0.77	0.83	1.01
Dividends	0.10	0.10	0.10	0.05	0.90	1.20
Payout Ratio	NM	9%	10%	7%	108%	113%
Prices - High	28¼	35⅞	15¾	14¼	10⅛	8¼
- Low	19⅛	13⅝	11⅜	6⅞	7	5¾
P/E Ratio - High	NM	32	15	19	12	8
- Low	NM	12	11	9	9	6

Income Statement Analysis ()

	1994	%Chg	1993	%Chg	1992	%Chg	1991
Revs.	480	53%	314	59%	197	38%	143
Oper. Inc.	163	30%	125	47%	85.2	52%	56.0
Depr. Depl. & Amort.	145	89%	76.9	57%	49.0	56%	31.5
Int. Exp.	50.6	117%	23.3	51%	15.4	57%	9.8
Pretax Inc.	-20.5	NM	48.4	61%	30.1	95%	15.4
Eff. Tax Rate	NM	—	35%	—	10%	—	Nil
Net Inc.	-14.0	NM	31.4	16%	27.1	76%	15.4

Balance Sheet & Other Fin. Data ()

	1994	1993	1992	1991	1990	1989
Cash	39.9	32.5	15.5	16.4	8.2	11.0
Curr. Assets	166	163	63.7	69.6	55.6	42.6
Total Assets	1,605	1,017	577	489	197	172
Curr. Liab.	122	124	55.8	53.9	38.8	27.7
LT Debt	709	521	205	212	51.0	34.0
Common Eqty.	510	349	295	197	108	111
Total Cap.	1,464	870	500	409	158	145
Cap. Exp.	NA	444	157	327	33.0	71.0
Cash Flow	131	108	76.1	46.8	28.1	35.8

Ratio Analysis

	1994	1993	1992	1991	1990	1989
Curr. Ratio	1.4	1.3	1.1	1.3	1.4	1.5
% LT Debt of Cap.	48.4	59.9	41.0	51.9	32.0	23.6
% Ret. on Assets	NM	3.9	4.5	3.5	3.5	7.3
% Ret. on Equity	NM	9.6	9.9	7.4	5.8	10.6

Dividend Data (The company and its predecessor have paid dividends since 1987. A "poison pill" stock purchase rights plan was adopted in 1991.)

Amt. of Div. $	Date Decl.	Ex-Div. Date	Stock of Record	Payment Date
0.050	Jan. 16	Jan. 25	Jan. 31	Mar. 15 '95
0.050	Jul. 14	Jul. 27	Jul. 31	Sep. 15 '95

Data as orig. reptd.; bef. results of disc opers. and/or spec. items. Per share data adj. for stk. divs. as of ex-div. date. E-Estimated. NA-Not Available. NM-Not Meaningful. NR-Not Ranked.

Office—303 West Wall, Suite 101, Midland, TX 79701. **Tel**—(915) 683-4768. **Chrmn, Pres & CEO**—S. D. Sheffield. **Sr VP, CFO & Treas**—T. M. Dunn. **Sr VP & Secy**—M. L. Withrow. **Investor Contact**—Lon C. Kile. **Dirs**—R. J. Castor, J. L. Houghton, J. P. Jones, J. D. Moring, C. E. Ramsey Jr., S. D. Sheffield, A. L. Smith, E. O. Vetter, M. D. Wortley. **Transfer Agent**—First National Bank of Boston. **Incorporated** in Delaware in 1990. **Empl**-1,004. **S&P Analyst:** Michael C. Barr

Parker Drilling

NYSE Symbol **PKD**
In S&P MidCap 400

19-SEP-95 **Industry:** Oil and Gas

Summary: Parker is an international land drilling contractor for the oil and gas industry, specializing in arctic, remote location, geothermal and deep, difficult drilling projects.

Quantitative Evaluations

Outlook (1 Lowest—5 Highest) • 1+

Fair Value • 4

Risk • Average

Earn./Div. Rank • C

Technical Eval. • Bearish since 5/95

Rel. Strength Rank (1 Lowest—99 Highest) • 62

Insider Activity • NA

Recent Price • 6⅛ | 52 Wk Range • 6⅜-4⅜ | Yield • Nil | 12-Mo. P/E • NM

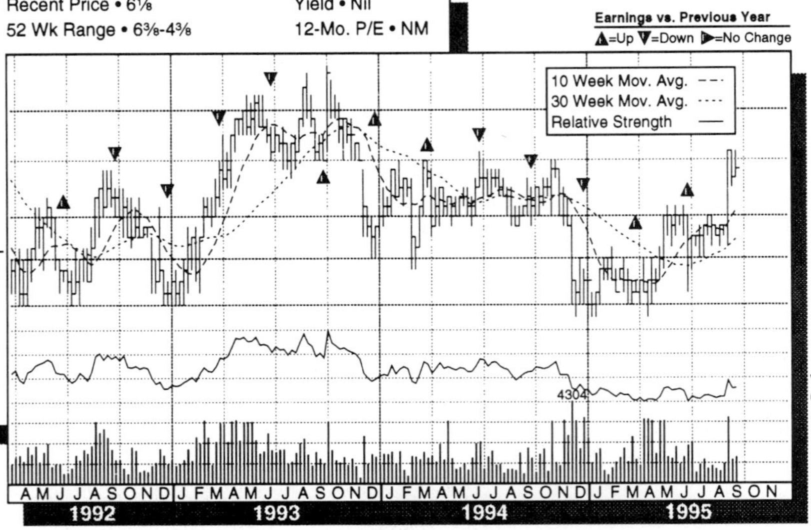

Business Profile - 19-SEP-95

This company conducts land contract drilling services on a worldwide basis for firms in the oil and gas industry. Results in fiscal 1995's third quarter benefited from improving margins and stronger drilling markets, particularly for international operations. Domestic and foreign rig utilization for the quarter was 55% and 20%, respectively, up from 53% and 16% a year earlier. In June 1995, Parker was awarded a three-year contract to drill production wells and provide other services in Russia.

Operational Review - 19-SEP-95

Revenues for the nine months ended May 31, 1995, were down 1.9%, year to year, due primarily to lower rig utilization, especially in international markets. Margins widened, reflecting improvement in international operations. Following a $4.5 million increase in other income, reflecting a gain on the reversal of a prior year's foreign currency accrual and higher gains on sales of fixed assets, net income was $1,026,000 ($0.02 a share), in contrast to a net loss of $1,933,000 ($0.04).

Stock Performance - 15-SEP-95

In the past 30 trading days, PKD's shares have increased 14%, compared to a 4% rise in the S&P 500. Average trading volume for the past five days was 100,140 shares, compared with the 40-day moving average of 118,297 shares.

Key Stock Statistics

Dividend Rate/Share	Nil	Shareholders	4,900
Shs. outstg. (M)	55.7	Market cap. (B)	$0.327
Avg. daily vol. (M)	0.176	Inst. holdings	66%
Tang. Bk. Value/Share	3.28	Insider holdings	NA
Beta	1.28		

Value of $10,000 invested 5 years ago: $ 6,125

Fiscal Year Ending Aug. 31

	1995	% Change	1994	% Change	1993	% Change
Revenues (Million $)						
1Q	33.28	-17%	40.04	67%	23.92	-10%
2Q	38.74	-5%	40.73	61%	25.31	-21%
3Q	43.26	18%	36.68	47%	25.03	-23%
4Q	—	—	34.97	32%	26.54	-18%
Yr.	—	—	152.4	51%	100.8	-18%
Income (Million $)						
1Q	-1.09	NM	1.61	NM	-2.53	NM
2Q	0.07	NM	-0.75	NM	-4.97	NM
3Q	2.05	NM	-2.79	NM	-2.11	NM
4Q	—	—	-26.87	NM	-1.08	NM
Yr.	—	—	-28.81	NM	-10.69	NM
Earnings Per Share ($)						
1Q	-0.02	NM	0.03	NM	-0.05	NM
2Q	Nil	—	-0.01	NM	-0.09	NM
3Q	0.04	NM	-0.05	NM	-0.04	NM
4Q	—	—	-0.49	NM	-0.02	NM
Yr.	—	—	-0.53	NM	-0.20	NM

Next earnings report expected: mid October

Parker Drilling

Business Summary - 19-SEP-95

Parker Drilling Company provides land contract drilling services on a worldwide basis to the oil and gas industry. Customers include major international oil companies, foreign national oil and gas companies, independent oil and gas companies and industrial users.

In fiscal 1994, about 80% of revenues were derived from foreign operations, and there was a domestic operating loss of $30.5 million and foreign operating income of $1.7 million. PKD operates in 16 countries outside the U.S. The markets the company believes hold the most potential include Colombia, the former Soviet Republic Kazakhstan, the U.S. (natural gas), Argentina and China.

During fiscal 1994, the company acquired six rigs in Argentina and one in Colombia, disposed of 16 domestic rigs and retired three international rigs, decreasing PKD's fleet of drilling rigs to 96 at August 31, 1994, from 108 at August 31, 1993. Some 44% of the rigs were in the U.S., with the remainder in South America, Africa, Asia Pacific, the Middle East and the Commonwealth of Independent States. Internationally, the company specializes in difficult wells and drilling in remote locations, utilizing equipment that is specially designed by PKD to be easily transported by helicopter or other vehicles into difficult access areas. Domestically, it specializes in arctic drilling and the drilling of deep gas wells (to 15,000 feet or deeper). PKD also engages in coring and geothermal operations.

In fiscal 1994, PKD's domestic and foreign rig utilization rates, excluding rigs that were disposed of or reclassified as assets held for sale in fiscal 1994, were 15% and 56%, respectively, versus 14% and 40% the year before.

Parker Technology, Inc. (Partech) designs and constructs specialized rigs and components. In the past three fiscal years, Partech accounted for less than 10% of PKD's revenues.

Parker Kinetic Designs, Inc. develops electric launch technology and other pulse power applications and equipment and provides specialized engineering services.

Parker has a $7,500,000 revolving credit facility, all of which was available at May 31, 1995.

Important Developments

Aug. '95—The company said it formed a joint venture with Environmental Safeguards, Inc., called OnSite Technology L.L.C., which will operate mobile units that remediate hydrocarbon-contaminated soil on location.
Jun. '95—Parker said it was awarded a three-year contract to provide drilling services in Russia.

Capitalization

Long Term Debt: $1,586,000 (5/95).

Per Share Data ($)

(Year Ended Aug. 31)

	1994	1993	1992	1991	1990	1989
Tangible Bk. Val.	3.28	3.78	3.89	4.17	4.06	3.46
Cash Flow	-0.13	0.18	0.29	0.38	-0.01	0.18
Earnings	-0.53	-0.20	-0.21	0.04	-0.37	-0.98
Dividends	Nil	Nil	Nil	Nil	Nil	Nil
Payout Ratio	Nil	Nil	Nil	Nil	Nil	Nil
Prices - High	6⅜	7⅞	6⅜	9¼	12⅞	10⅛
- Low	4⅞	4½	4⅜	5⅛	5¾	4⅜
P/E Ratio - High	NM	NM	NM	NM	NM	NM
- Low	NM	NM	NA	NA	NA	NA

Income Statement Analysis (Million $)

	1994	%Chg	1993	%Chg	1992	%Chg	1991
Revs.	152	50%	101	-18%	123	9%	113
Oper. Inc.	12.8	60%	8.0	-11%	9.0	-25%	12.0
Depr.	22.0	8%	20.4	-22%	26.1	47%	17.8
Int. Exp.	Nil	—	0.1	-75%	0.4	-56%	0.9
Pretax Inc.	-26.8	NM	-11.2	NM	-9.0	NM	3.0
Eff. Tax Rate	NM	—	NM	—	NM	—	61%
Net Inc.	-28.8	NM	-10.7	NM	-11.2	NM	2.0

Balance Sheet & Other Fin. Data (Million $)

	1994	1993	1992	1991	1990	1989
Cash	14.0	44.0	37.0	43.0	83.0	31.0
Curr. Assets	62.0	81.0	82.0	92.0	130	77.0
Total Assets	209	236	246	265	265	245
Curr. Liab.	21.6	21.0	23.0	29.0	26.0	31.0
LT Debt	Nil	Nil	Nil	2.0	7.0	32.0
Common Eqty.	181	208	210	219	210	155
Total Cap.	184	212	219	230	230	209
Cap. Exp.	34.8	18.7	28.0	59.0	13.0	20.0
Cash Flow	-6.9	9.7	15.0	20.0	Nil	8.0

Ratio Analysis

	1994	1993	1992	1991	1990	1989
Curr. Ratio	2.9	3.9	3.5	3.2	5.0	2.5
% LT Debt of Cap.	Nil	Nil	0.1	0.8	3.1	15.1
% Net Inc.of Revs.	NM	NM	NM	1.8	NM	NM
% Ret. on Assets	NM	NM	NM	0.7	NM	NM
% Ret. on Equity	NM	NM	NM	0.9	NM	NM

Dividend Data —Common dividends were omitted in 1987, after having been paid since 1976.

Data as orig. reptd.; bef. results of disc. opers. and/or spec. items. Per share data adj. for stk. divs. as of ex-div. date. E-Estimated. NA-Not Available. NM-Not Meaningful. NR-Not Ranked.

Office—Parker Building, Eight East Third St., Tulsa, OK 74103-3637. **Tel**—(918) 585-8221. **Chrmn**—R. L. Parker. **Pres & CEO**—R. L. Parker Jr. **VP-Fin & CFO**—J. J. Davis. **Secy**—K. J. Kucharski. **VP-Treas & Investor Contact**—Ed Hendrix Jr. **Dirs**—D. L. Fist, E. F. Gloyna, J. W. Linn, R. L. Parker, R. L. Parker Jr., R. R. Reinfrank. **Transfer Agent & Registrar**—Chemical Bank, NYC. **Incorporated** in Oklahoma in 1954; reincorporated in Delaware in 1976. **Empl**-2,106. **S&P Analyst:** G.A.S.

STANDARD & POOR'S

STOCK REPORTS

Paychex, Inc.

NASDAQ Symbol **PAYX**

In S&P MidCap 400

26-JUL-95

Industry: Data Processing

Summary: This company mainly provides computerized payroll accounting services to small and medium-size firms nationwide.

Quantitative Evaluations

Outlook (1 Lowest—5 Highest)
• **5+**

Fair Value
• **47¼**

Risk
• **Average**

Earn./Div. Rank
• **B+**

Technical Eval.
• **Bullish** since 9/94

Rel. Strength Rank (1 Lowest—99 Highest)
• **82**

Insider Activity
• **NA**

Recent Price • 39
52 Wk Range • 40-21

Yield • 0.6%
12-Mo. P/E • 44.8

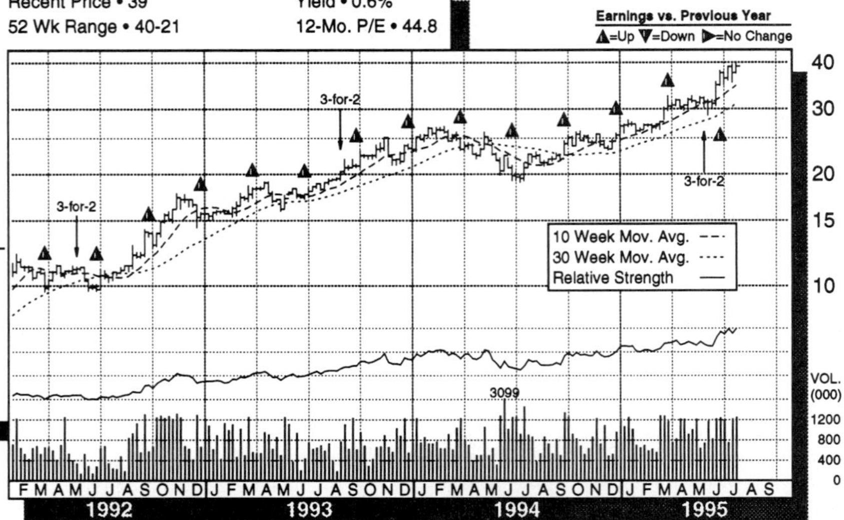

OPTIONS: Ph

Business Profile - 26-JUL-95

Paychex is a national payroll processing and payroll tax preparation company for small to medium-size businesses. Also, the company provides human resource products and services, including Section 125 Cafeteria Plans, an employee handbook service, insurance services, and employee evaluation tools. In June 1995, the company acquired Pay-Fone Systems, a small provider of payroll and tax preparation services, for about $10.5 million in stock.

Operational Review - 26-JUL-95

Revenues for fiscal 1994-95 (preliminary) advanced from those of 1993-94, aided by growth in payroll clients and increased use of the company's tax filing and salary deposit systems. Margins widened as operating costs were well controlled. After taxes at 28.2%, versus 28.0%, net income rose 39%. Share earnings were adjusted for the three-for-two stock split effected in May 1995 .

Stock Performance - 21-JUL-95

In the past 30 trading days, PAYX's shares have increased 26%, compared to a 5% rise in the S&P 500. Average trading volume for the past five days was 336,480 shares, compared with the 40-day moving average of 251,676 shares.

Key Stock Statistics

Dividend Rate/Share	0.24	Shareholders	2,200
Shs. outstg. (M)	45.0	Market cap. (B)	$ 1.7
Avg. daily vol. (M)	0.253	Inst. holdings	69%
Tang. Bk. Value/Share	2.42	Insider holdings	NA
Beta	1.27		

Value of $10,000 invested 5 years ago: $ 70,021

Fiscal Year Ending May 31

	1995	% Change	1994	% Change	1993	% Change
Revenues (Million $)						
1Q	62.92	18%	53.33	18%	45.30	19%
2Q	63.77	17%	54.31	19%	45.70	17%
3Q	68.64	19%	57.57	18%	48.60	17%
4Q	71.85	22%	58.84	17%	50.37	19%
Yr.	267.2	19%	224.1	18%	190.0	18%
Income (Million $)						
1Q	9.55	38%	6.92	36%	5.10	50%
2Q	9.64	36%	7.10	38%	5.16	36%
3Q	9.35	41%	6.65	51%	4.41	46%
4Q	10.50	42%	7.40	40%	5.29	52%
Yr.	39.04	39%	28.07	41%	19.96	46%
Earnings Per Share ($)						
1Q	0.21	39%	0.15	33%	0.12	53%
2Q	0.21	33%	0.16	39%	0.12	37%
3Q	0.21	41%	0.15	50%	0.10	47%
4Q	0.23	38%	0.17	39%	0.12	50%
Yr.	0.87	38%	0.63	41%	0.45	43%

Next earnings report expected: mid September

Paychex, Inc.

Business Summary - 21-JUL-95

Paychex, Inc. was formed in 1979 through the consolidation of 17 corporations providing computerized payroll accounting services nationwide. The company concentrates on small to medium-size firms. Its 70 branch operating centers were furnishing services to about 196,000 clients as of November 30, 1994, compared with 186,000 clients at 1993-94 year-end. Paychex believes it ranks as the second-largest payroll accounting services company in the U.S.

Services include preparation of paychecks, earnings statements and internal accounting records. Paychex supplies its clients with all required monthly, quarterly and annual payroll tax returns for federal, state and local governments. The market for such services has evolved primarily as a result of legal requirements that employers act as "tax collectors" for the various taxing authorities, making businesses responsible for complying with a wide variety of complex, changing regulations. The computerized Paychex system utilizes proprietary software that is regularly updated to accommodate regulatory changes.

Taxpay, an extension of the payroll service, became available nationwide during 1990-91. Paychex deposits payroll taxes and files returns for its Taxpay clients and assumes full responsibility for accurate and timely filings. Taxpay is utilized by over 43% of the company's clients nationwide.

Paychex does not have written contracts with its clients, but some 80% of the businesses served in 1991-92 and 1992-93 continued to be clients in 1993-94. Services are warranteed, with the company agreeing to reimburse clients for any penalties and interest incurred as a result of a Paychex error. Warranty expense was $400,000 in 1993-94 and $130,000 the year before.

In 1990-91, Paychex established a Human Resources Services division to consolidate its fringe benefit products and personnel management services. Products include group health and disability insurance, workers' compensation and group life, the preparation of employee handbooks and Section 125 Cafeteria Plans. The cafeteria plans allow employees to pay for certain fringe benefits with pretax dollars, with a resultant savings to the employer of Social Security taxes.

Important Developments

Jul. '95—The company said that new client additions were above plan for fiscal 1994-95 and clients utilizing the Taxpay tax filing and payment feature increased over 30% from 1993-94. Also, clients using the Electronic Salary Deposit service and Digital Check Signing increased 62% and 34%, respectively, during the past year.

Capitalization

Long Term Debt: $523,000 (5/95).

Per Share Data ($) (Year Ended May 31)

	1995	1994	1993	1992	1991	1990
Tangible Bk. Val.	NA	2.42	1.91	1.52	1.24	1.07
Cash Flow	NA	0.87	0.68	0.52	0.41	0.36
Earnings	0.87	0.63	0.45	0.31	0.22	0.20
Dividends	0.22	0.15	0.10	0.07	0.06	0.04
Payout Ratio	25%	23%	22%	22%	26%	23%
Cal. Yrs.	1994	1993	1992	1991	1990	1989
Prices - High	27⅛	25⅛	17¾	10⅜	6⅛	8⅛
- Low	19	15	9⅝	4¼	3½	5⅛
P/E Ratio - High	31	40	40	33	28	42
- Low	22	24	21	14	16	26

Income Statement Analysis (Million $)

	1994	%Chg	1993	%Chg	1992	%Chg	1991
Revs.	224	18%	190	18%	161	18%	137
Oper. Inc.	47.8	29%	37.1	31%	28.4	31%	21.7
Depr.	11.0	6%	10.4	9%	9.6	14%	8.4
Int. Exp.	0.1	-8%	0.1	-14%	0.1	-36%	0.2
Pretax Inc.	39.0	39%	28.0	44%	19.5	39%	14.0
Eff. Tax Rate	28%	—	29%	—	30%	—	32%
Net Inc.	28.1	41%	20.0	46%	13.7	42%	9.6

Balance Sheet & Other Fin. Data (Million $)

	1994	1993	1992	1991	1990	1989
Cash	55.6	38.1	20.0	11.0	15.8	19.4
Curr. Assets	87.0	64.2	41.6	29.7	31.4	32.5
Total Assets	130	107	86.2	70.4	62.1	54.8
Curr. Liab.	19.0	17.8	13.7	10.5	10.2	9.5
LT Debt	0.7	1.2	1.6	2.0	1.6	2.1
Common Eqty.	109	85.2	67.4	54.5	47.2	40.2
Total Cap.	110	87.8	70.7	58.3	50.6	44.4
Cap. Exp.	11.6	8.7	13.5	17.4	15.4	9.1
Cash Flow	39.1	30.4	23.3	18.0	15.9	15.4

Ratio Analysis

	1994	1993	1992	1991	1990	1989
Curr. Ratio	4.6	3.6	3.0	2.8	3.1	3.4
% LT Debt of Cap.	0.7	1.4	2.3	3.5	3.3	4.8
% Net Inc.of Revs.	12.5	10.5	8.5	7.0	7.1	9.3
% Ret. on Assets	23.7	20.6	17.4	14.5	14.6	19.4
% Ret. on Equity	28.9	26.1	22.4	18.9	19.6	26.3

Dividend Data (Cash dividends were initiated in 1988. Three-for-two stock splits were effected in 1986, 1987, 1992, 1993 and 1995.)

Amt. of Div. $	Date Decl.	Ex-Div. Date	Stock of Record	Payment Date
0.060	Jul. 14	Jul. 27	Aug. 02	Aug. 24 '94
0.090	Oct. 06	Oct. 24	Oct. 28	Nov. 22 '94
0.090	Jan. 12	Jan. 26	Feb. 01	Feb. 23 '95
0.090	Apr. 13	Apr. 21	Apr. 27	May. 18 '95
3-for-2	Apr. 13	May. 26	May. 02	May. 25 '95
0.060	Jul. 13	Jul. 31	Aug. 02	Aug. 24 '95

Data as orig. reptd.; bef. results of disc. opers. and/or spec. items. Per share data adj. for stk. divs. as of ex-div. date. E-Estimated. NA-Not Available. NM-Not Meaningful. NR-Not Ranked.

Office—911 Panorama Trail South, Rochester, NY 14625-0397. **Tel**—(716) 383-3406. **Chrmn, Pres & CEO**—B. T. Golisano. **CFO, Secy, Treas & Investor Contact**—G. Thomas Clark. **Dirs**—D. W. Brinckman, G. T. Clark, B. T. Golisano, P. Horsley, G. M. Inman, H. P. Messina Jr., J. R. Sebo. **Transfer Agent**—American Stock Transfer & Trust Co., NYC. **Incorporated** in Delaware in 1979. **Empl**-3,100. **S&P Analyst:** Ronald J. Gross

STANDARD & POOR'S

STOCK REPORTS

Pentair, Inc.

NASDAQ Symbol **PNTA**
In S&P MidCap 400

31-JUL-95

Industry: Conglomerate/diversified

Summary: This diversified manufacturer operates businesses that produce and market industrial products, sporting ammunition and specialty products, such as tools and pumps.

S&P Opinion: Accumulate (★★★★) | Recent Price • 45½ | Yield • 1.8%
52 Wk Range • 49-37¼ | 12-Mo. P/E • 12.2

Quantitative Evaluations

Outlook (1 Lowest—5 Highest) • **2**

Fair Value • **40¾**

Risk • **Low**

Earn./Div. Rank • **A-**

Technical Eval. • **Bullish** since 6/94

Rel. Strength Rank (1 Lowest—99 Highest) • **40**

Insider Activity • **NA**

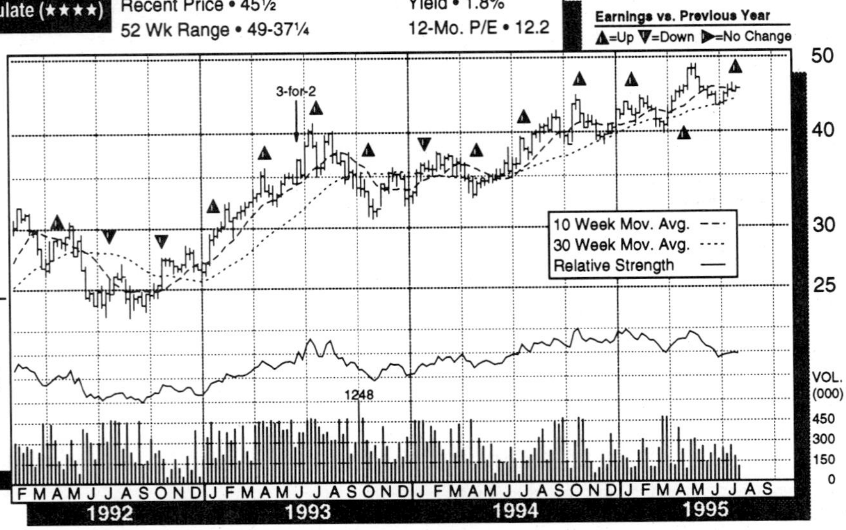

Overview - 31-JUL-95

Sales are expected to continue to rise through 1996, reflecting new products and a rebound in economic conditions overseas. Margins should benefit from continued strong results at Porter-Cable, Hoffman Engineering and the Schroff Group and improved productivity, which will outweigh increased raw material costs and competitive pricing pressures in the sporting ammunition area. Additionally, Pentair will continue to seek acquisitions in the industrial area, as it focuses its growth in those segments following the recent sale of its remaining paper businesses. Long-term prospects are seen benefiting from stronger demand in most segments, higher selling prices and cost-control efforts.

Valuation - 31-JUL-95

The shares should benefit from the company's focus on growing its industrial businesses through acquisitions and the resulting improvement in sales and operating income. The stock price, which has risen about 40% since early 1994, was recently about 16X our EPS projection of $2.80 (excluding the paper operations) for 1995, a small discount to the multiple for the MidCap 400. With the recent sale of the company's paper operations enabling Pentair to strengthen its core businesses, the prospects for long-term capital appreciation remain favorable.

Key Stock Statistics

S&P EPS Est. 1995	2.80	Tang. Bk. Value/Share	15.03
P/E on S&P Est. 1995	16.3	Beta	0.76
S&P EPS Est. 1996	3.20	Shareholders	3,100
Dividend Rate/Share	0.80	Market cap. (B)	$0.834
Shs. outstg. (M)	18.3	Inst. holdings	67%
Avg. daily vol. (M)	0.040	Insider holdings	NA

Value of $10,000 invested 5 years ago: $ 28,327

Fiscal Year Ending Dec. 31

	1995	% Change	1994	% Change	1993	% Change
Revenues (Million $)						
1Q	333.8	-14%	389.3	21%	321.8	10%
2Q	338.2	-14%	391.9	22%	320.3	8%
3Q	—	—	426.1	23%	345.5	5%
4Q	—	—	441.9	30%	340.6	6%
Yr.	—	—	1,649	24%	1,328	7%
Income (Million $)						
1Q	13.85	25%	11.10	17%	9.50	9%
2Q	13.35	13%	11.83	21%	9.78	20%
3Q	—	—	13.78	4%	13.30	15%
4Q	—	—	16.90	21%	14.02	-6%
Yr.	—	—	53.60	15%	46.60	9%
Earnings Per Share ($)						
1Q	0.68	28%	0.53	17%	0.45	15%
2Q	0.64	12%	0.57	24%	0.46	28%
3Q	E0.70	—	0.67	2%	0.66	11%
4Q	E0.78	—	0.85	23%	0.69	-14%
Yr.	E2.80	—	2.62	16%	2.26	5%

Next earnings report expected: mid October

Pentair, Inc.

Business Summary - 31-JUL-95

Pentair, Inc. is a diversified manufacturing company that until mid-1995 conducted operations through three industrial groups, which contributed as follows to sales and operating profits in 1994:

	Sales	Profits
Specialty products	28%	35%
General industrial	48%	54%
Paper products	24%	11%

The specialty products segment produces woodworking machinery, portable power tools, water pumps, sump and sewage pumps, grinders (for environmental engineering applications) and related systems.

The general industrial segment manufactures electrical enclosures and wireways, material-dispensing equipment, industrial lubrication systems and automotive service (lubricating and lifting) equipment and sporting ammunition.

In February 1994, the company acquired Schroff Group, a Germany-based enclosure manufacturer, for $153 million. Schroff, with $160 million in 1993 sales, makes cabinets, cases, subracks and accessories for the electronics industry.

Important Developments

Jun. '95—Pentair completed the sale of its remaining paper assets to Consolidated Papers, Inc., for $109 million, plus assumed debt and lease obligations. The assets included Niagara of Wisconsin Paper Corp., Pentair's 50% interest in the Lake Superior Paper Industries joint venture and its 12% share of Superior Recycled Fiber Industries. In April, PNTA sold its Cross Pointe Paper unit to Toronto-based Noranda Forest, Inc. for $200 million. Cross Pointe had sales of $237 million in 1994. Earlier, PNTA noted that it will seek acquisitions ($50 million to $200 million in sales) during 1995 at a faster pace than in other years.

Capitalization

Long Term Debt: $438,851,000 (3/95).
$7.50 Cum. Conv. Pfd. Stk.: 134,165 shs. ($0.10 par); redeemable; ea. conv. into 3.75 com. shs.
8% Cum. Voting Conv. Pfd. Stk.: 1,819,078 shs.; all held by co. ESOP; conv. into com. at $26.22 a sh.

Per Share Data ($) (Year Ended Dec. 31)

	1994	1993	1992	1991	1990	1989
Tangible Bk. Val.	11.34	13.11	10.25	11.25	9.73	8.75
Cash Flow	6.10	5.07	5.16	5.05	4.29	4.33
Earnings	2.62	2.26	2.15	2.20	1.69	1.99
Dividends	0.72	0.68	0.65	0.61	0.59	0.53
Payout Ratio	27%	30%	30%	28%	35%	27%
Prices - High	44¾	41¼	32	28⅞	21⅞	23⅜
- Low	32¼	26	22⅞	15⅞	14	17
P/E Ratio - High	17	18	15	13	13	12
- Low	12	12	11	7	8	9

Income Statement Analysis (Million $)

	1994	%Chg	1993	%Chg	1992	%Chg	1991
Revs.	1,649	24%	1,328	7%	1,239	6%	1,169
Oper. Inc.	182	21%	150	7%	140	6%	132
Depr.	64.2	28%	50.2	5%	48.0	1%	47.3
Int. Exp.	34.4	47%	23.4	NM	23.6	4%	22.7
Pretax Inc.	89.1	15%	77.4	6%	72.7	-2%	74.1
Eff. Tax Rate	40%	—	40%	—	41%	—	45%
Net Inc.	53.6	15%	46.6	9%	42.8	4%	41.1

Balance Sheet & Other Fin. Data (Million $)

	1994	1993	1992	1991	1990	1989
Cash	32.7	10.3	8.4	6.1	8.8	8.7
Curr. Assets	569	439	399	373	357	360
Total Assets	1,281	959	869	791	769	781
Curr. Liab.	286	218	209	185	172	168
LT Debt	409	239	212	198	225	251
Common Eqty.	391	337	260	276	195	241
Total Cap.	863	617	554	568	560	575
Cap. Exp.	93.0	73.0	67.0	49.0	61.0	83.0
Cash Flow	112	90.7	82.3	79.8	69.0	70.1

Ratio Analysis

	1994	1993	1992	1991	1990	1989
Curr. Ratio	2.0	2.0	1.9	2.0	2.1	2.1
% LT Debt of Cap.	47.3	38.7	38.2	34.9	40.1	43.7
% Net Inc.of Revs.	3.3	3.5	3.5	3.5	2.8	3.1
% Ret. on Assets	4.8	4.8	5.1	5.2	4.3	4.7
% Ret. on Equity	13.2	12.8	12.7	12.4	11.8	14.1

Dividend Data (Cash has been paid each year since 1976. A dividend reinvestment plan is available.)

Amt. of Div. $	Date Decl.	Ex-Div. Date	Stock of Record	Payment Date
0.180	Oct. 07	Oct. 17	Oct. 21	Nov. 11 '94
0.200	Jan. 18	Jan. 24	Jan. 30	Feb. 13 '95
0.200	Apr. 19	Apr. 25	May. 01	May. 15 '95
0.200	Jul. 07	Jul. 27	Jul. 31	Aug. 14 '95

Data as orig. reptd.; bef. results of disc. opers. and/or spec. items. Per share data adj. for stk. divs. as of ex-div. date. E-Estimated. NA-Not Available. NM-Not Meaningful. NR-Not Ranked.

Office—Waters Edge Plaza, 1500 County Rd. B2 West, St. Paul, MN 55113-3105. **Tel**—(612) 636-7920. **Chrmn, Pres & CEO**—W. H. Buxton. **Sr VP & CFO**—D. D. Harrison. **Sr VP & Investor Contact**—J. R. Collins. **VP, Treas & Secy**—R. T. Rueb. **Dirs**—G. N. Butzow, W. H. Buxton, C. A. Haggerty, H. V. Haverty, Q. J. Hietpas, W. Kissling, D. E. Nugent, R. M. Schulze, K. E. Welke. **Transfer Agent & Registrar**—Norwest Bank Minnesota, South St. Paul. **Incorporated** in Minnesota in 1966. **Empl**-8,700. **S&P Analyst:** Stewart Scharf

STANDARD & POOR'S

STOCK REPORTS

Perrigo Company

NASDAQ Symbol **PRGO**

In S&P MidCap 400

21-SEP-95

Industry: Drugs-Generic and OTC

Summary: This company is the largest U.S. manufacturer of OTC pharmaceuticals and personal care products for the retail private label market.

S&P Opinion: Hold (★★★)

Recent Price • 13¼

52 Wk Range • 16¾-10½

Yield • Nil

12-Mo. P/E • 22.8

Quantitative Evaluations

Outlook (1 Lowest—5 Highest) • **1**

Fair Value • **11⅝**

Risk • **Average**

Earn./Div. Rank • **NR**

Technical Eval. • **Bullish** since 8/95

Rel. Strength Rank (1 Lowest—99 Highest) • **46**

Insider Activity • **NA**

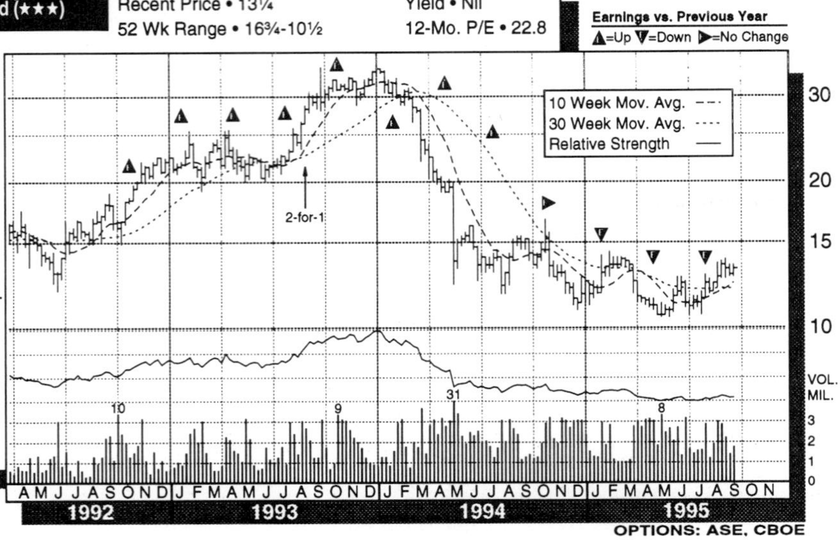

OPTIONS: ASE, CBOE

Overview - 21-SEP-95

Fiscal 1996 sales are expected to advance 13% from fiscal 1995's $717 million. Growth should be paced by further expansion in the private label market, new products, higher prices, strategic alliances with customers, and the inclusion for the full year of Vi-Jon Laboratories Inc. (acquired in January 1995). A return to a more normal cough and cold season (1994-5 was very mild) would also boost sales. A planned restructuring charge of about $0.04 a share should be largely offset by cost savings from job cuts. However, profits are expected to be reduced by $0.05 a share by legal costs (which may be covered by insurance). Fiscal 1996 EPS are estimated at $0.70, up from fiscal 1995's $0.58 (after nonrecurring costs of about $0.05).

Valuation - 21-SEP-95

Although still well below earlier highs, the shares have rebounded in recent months, buoyed by the overall market advance and expectations of improved earnings in fiscal 1996. In response to a customer survey and lower profits in fiscal 1995, Perrigo recently undertook a strategic review of operations, and decided on certain restructuring measures. These included the consolidation of many functions and the elimination of 180 jobs. Benefits from cost cutting and similar moves should enhance productivity and profitability in coming years. In addition, long-term prospects for the private label OTC and personal care products fields remain favorable. The depressed shares merit retention for recovery.

Key Stock Statistics

S&P EPS Est. 1996	0.70	Tang. Bk. Value/Share	3.80
P/E on S&P Est. 1996	18.9	Beta	NA
Dividend Rate/Share	Nil	Shareholders	NA
Shs. outstg. (M)	76.0	Market cap. (B)	$0.978
Avg. daily vol. (M)	0.394	Inst. holdings	46%
		Insider holdings	NA

Value of $10,000 invested 5 years ago: NA

Fiscal Year Ending Jun. 30

	1995	% Change	1994	% Change	1993	% Change
Revenues (Million $)						
1Q	182.7	6%	173.0	21%	143.0	64%
2Q	174.7	NM	174.0	23%	141.0	52%
3Q	185.3	14%	163.0	15%	142.0	17%
4Q	174.4	10%	158.2	9%	145.0	33%
Yr.	717.1	7%	669.3	17%	571.0	39%
Income (Million $)						
1Q	14.77	NM	14.65	41%	10.40	21%
2Q	12.85	-16%	15.29	30%	11.78	77%
3Q	11.42	-14%	13.27	18%	11.25	37%
4Q	5.39	-53%	11.55	3%	11.19	120%
Yr.	44.43	-19%	54.76	23%	44.62	56%
Earnings Per Share ($)						
1Q	0.19	NM	0.19	46%	0.13	30%
2Q	0.17	-15%	0.20	33%	0.15	36%
3Q	0.15	-12%	0.17	13%	0.15	36%
4Q	0.07	-53%	0.15	7%	0.14	40%
Yr.	0.58	-18%	0.71	22%	0.58	41%

Next earnings report expected: early November

Perrigo Company

Business Summary - 21-SEP-95

Perrigo Company is the largest U.S. manufacturer of over-the-counter (OTC) pharmaceuticals, personal care products and vitamins for the store brand market. Products are sold under a retailer's own label and compete with nationally advertised brand name products. Business segment contributions in recent fiscal years were:

	1994	1993	1992
OTC pharmaceuticals	65%	64%	63%
Personal care	26%	28%	28%
Vitamins	9%	8%	9%

OTC pharmaceuticals include analgesics such as ibuprofen tablets and caplets, acetaminophen, aspirin and effervescent pain relief; cough and cold remedies, including cough syrup, cold capsules, flu and cold medicine, nasal spray and nose drops; antacids; laxatives; anti-diarrheals; suppositories; feminine hygiene; and diet products. Personal care products include oral hygiene products such as toothpaste and mouthwash; skin care products; sun and hair care products; deodorants and antiperspirants; baby care products; and wets and drys, including rubbing alcohol, hydrogen peroxide, Epsom salt, mineral oil and related items.

Perrigo markets about 900 store brand products to 2,250 customers, including major retail drug, supermarket and mass merchandise chains and major wholesalers. Wal-Mart accounted for 15% of net sales in fiscal 1994.

The company also markets under its own brand names the Nature's Glo and Perrigo lines of natural vitamins, sun care products, skin and hair care items and other OTC drug and personal care products. Sales of brand name products account for 6% to 8% of the total. Perrigo also produces OTC drugs, vitamins and personal care products under contract for manufacturers of national brand products.

Important Developments

Aug. '95—Perrigo said fiscal 1995 financial results were hurt by weak sales of analgesics and cough and cold products (the company's two largest product categories) and pressures on gross margins. Softness in product demand reflected a relatively mild cough, cold and flu season in 1994-5. Analagesic sales were also down slightly in the fourth quarter of fiscal 1995. In addition, fiscal 1995 results included pretax restructuring costs totaling $4,904,000, and unusual litigation expense of $1,043,000.

Capitalization

Long Term Debt: $99,140,000 (6/95).

Per Share Data ($) (Year Ended Jun. 30)

	1995	1994	1993	1992	1991	1990
Tangible Bk. Val.	NA	NA	2.72	2.51	0.60	NA
Cash Flow	NA	NA	0.78	0.57	0.35	NA
Earnings	0.58	0.71	0.58	0.41	0.20	NA
Dividends	Nil	Nil	Nil	Nil	Nil	NA
Payout Ratio	Nil	Nil	Nil	Nil	Nil	NA
Prices - High	14⅜	34¼	34⅞	22⅝	15⅜	NA
- Low	10½	11¾	19⅛	12	8	NA
P/E Ratio - High	25	48	61	55	77	NA
- Low	18	17	33	29	40	NA

Income Statement Analysis (Million $)

	1993	%Chg	1992	%Chg	1991	%Chg	1990
Revs.	571	39%	410	46%	281	—	NA
Oper. Inc.	88.9	37%	64.7	56%	41.4	—	NA
Depr.	15.4	41%	10.9	20%	9.1	—	NA
Int. Exp.	3.3	-63%	8.8	-29%	12.4	—	NA
Pretax Inc.	70.1	55%	45.1	134%	19.3	—	NA
Eff. Tax Rate	36%	—	37%	—	37%	—	NA
Net Inc.	44.6	56%	28.6	134%	12.2	—	NA

Balance Sheet & Other Fin. Data (Million $)

	1993	1992	1991	1990	1989	1988
Cash	0.2	0.5	0.1	NA	NA	NA
Curr. Assets	208	164	94.0	NA	NA	NA
Total Assets	414	317	183	NA	NA	NA
Curr. Liab.	85.9	72.5	55.1	NA	NA	NA
LT Debt	75.2	46.0	82.1	NA	NA	NA
Common Eqty.	235	184	33.0	NA	NA	NA
Total Cap.	328	244	128	NA	NA	NA
Cap. Exp.	67.6	20.2	7.7	NA	NA	NA
Cash Flow	60.0	39.4	21.3	NA	NA	NA

Ratio Analysis

	1993	1992	1991	1990	1989	1988
Curr. Ratio	2.4	2.3	1.7	NA	NA	NA
% LT Debt of Cap.	22.9	18.8	64.3	NA	NA	NA
% Net Inc.of Revs.	7.8	7.0	4.3	NA	NA	NA
% Ret. on Assets	12.1	10.2	NA	NA	NA	NA
% Ret. on Equity	21.1	25.1	NA	NA	NA	NA

Dividend Data —No cash dividends have been paid.

Data as orig. reptd.; bef. results of disc. opers. and/or spec. items. Per share data adj. for stk. divs. as of ex-div. date. E-Estimated. NA-Not Available. NM-Not Meaningful. NR-Not Ranked.

Office—117 Water St., Allegan, MI 49010. **Tel**—(616) 673-8451. **Chrmn & CEO**—M. J. Jandernoa. **Pres, COO & Secy**—R. G. Hansen. **VP-Fin, CFO & Treas**—S. M. Neil. **Dirs**—F. F. Bell, P. R. Formanek, R. G. Hansen, L. R. Jalenak, Jr., M. J. Jandernoa, R. E. Klingemeyer, L. L. Smith, J. Spoelhof, W. C. Swaney, M. A. Taylor. **Transfer Agent**—State Street Bank & Trust Co., Boston. **Incorporated** in Michigan in 1988. **Empl**-3,879. **S&P Analyst:** Herman Saftlas

Pinnacle West Capital

STANDARD & POOR'S
STOCK REPORTS

NYSE Symbol **PNW**
In S&P MidCap 400

20-OCT-95 **Industry:** Utilities-Electric

Summary: This utility holding company is the parent of Arizona Public Service Co., Arizona's largest electric utility.

S&P Opinion: Accumulate (★★★★)

Recent Price • 27⅛ | Yield • 3.3%
52 Wk Range • 27⅛-18 | 12-Mo. P/E • 10.9

Quantitative Evaluations

Outlook (1 Lowest—5 Highest) • **1+**

Fair Value • **24¼**

Risk • **Low**

Earn./Div. Rank • **B**

Technical Eval. • **Bullish** since 5/94

Rel. Strength Rank (1 Lowest—99 Highest) • **83**

Insider Activity • **NA**

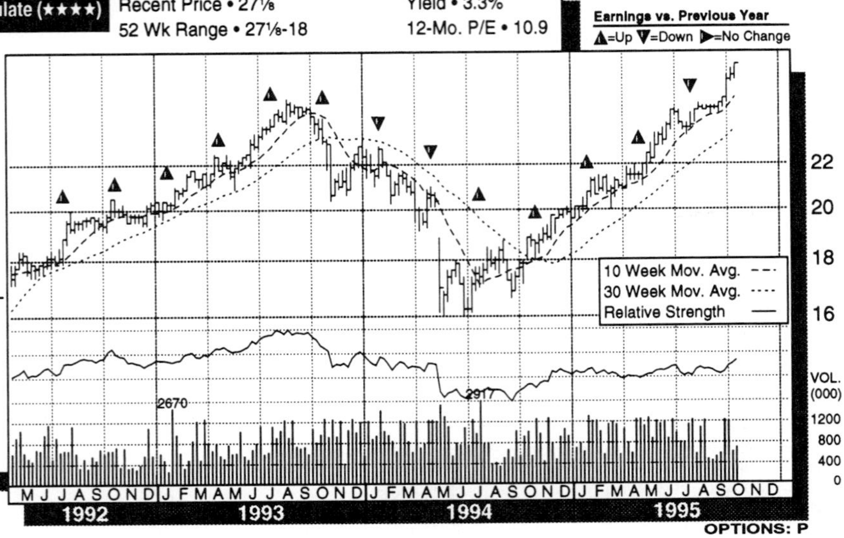

OPTIONS: P

Overview - 20-OCT-95

Earnings in 1995 should reflect an increase in kwh sales combined with a full year of cost savings from a 7% workforce reduction, lower income taxes, and a sharp fall in debt costs since management refinanced all of PNW's high-coupon senior securities at favorable interest rates. Also boosting profitability will be greater utilization of capacity at the Palo Verde station, the company's largest single asset, and reduced operating and maintenance costs. Given continued gains in customer growth--the rate was nearly four times the national average as of late 1995--and a buoyant Arizona economy, prospects for above-average profit growth in 1996 remain strong. The company benefits from fairly competitive cost of fuel compared to other utilities in its service region. Improving results at its non-utility subsidiaries will be important to earnings progress as well.

Valuation - 20-OCT-95

PNW's stock has performed well since the beginning of the year, having risen well in excess of the gain for the S&P Utilities Index. The shares have displayed a strongly positive price trend since late last fall, when directors raised the quarterly dividend 12.5%. Management, which has indicated its intent to maintain relatively level dividend growth on a percentage basis over the next several years, also raised the dividend 11% in mid-October this year. Its payout ratio remains well below the industry average; We believe dividend increases of 10% to 12% are sustainable in the foreseeable future.

Key Stock Statistics

S&P EPS Est. 1995	2.20	Tang. Bk. Value/Share	20.38
P/E on S&P Est. 1995	12.3	Beta	0.35
S&P EPS Est. 1996	2.30	Shareholders	55,400
Dividend Rate/Share	0.90	Market cap. (B)	$ 2.4
Shs. outstg. (M)	87.4	Inst. holdings	69%
Avg. daily vol. (M)	0.167	Insider holdings	NA

Value of $10,000 invested 5 years ago: $ 26,272

Fiscal Year Ending Dec. 31

	1995	% Change	1994	% Change	1993	% Change
Revenues (Million $)						
1Q	346.1	-3%	355.5	-4%	371.0	8%
2Q	393.2	-5%	412.6	1%	407.0	NM
3Q	558.8	NM	554.4	6%	525.0	2%
4Q	—	—	363.0	-5%	383.0	-4%
Yr.	—	—	1,685	NM	1,686	NM
Income (Million $)						
1Q	24.62	14%	21.62	-21%	27.47	NM
2Q	42.25	-13%	48.70	25%	38.90	NM
3Q	114.5	22%	93.99	8%	86.73	2%
4Q	—	—	36.31	115%	16.87	-10%
Yr.	—	—	200.6	18%	170.0	13%
Earnings Per Share ($)						
1Q	0.28	12%	0.25	-22%	0.32	NM
2Q	0.48	-14%	0.56	24%	0.45	2%
3Q	1.31	21%	1.08	9%	0.99	1%
4Q	E0.13	-68%	0.41	116%	0.19	-10%
Yr.	E2.20	-4%	2.30	18%	1.95	13%

Next earnings report expected: mid October

Pinnacle West Capital

Business Summary - 19-OCT-95

Pinnacle West Capital (formerly AZP Group) is a utility holding company whose main subsidiary, Arizona Public Service Co., provides electricity to nearly half the population of Arizona. Other operations include real estate development and venture capital units.

Sources of electric generation in 1994 were coal 58%, nuclear 30%, gas 5%, and purchased and other 7%. Peak demand in 1994 was 4,214 mw, and resources at peak totaled 4,514 mw, for a capacity margin of 8.1%. PNW has a 29.1% interest in the three-unit, 3,810 mw Palo Verde nuclear generating station, operated by El Paso Electric Co. El Paso currently is operating under Chapter 11 of the bankruptcy code; PNW does not anticipate any material adverse effect on its operations or financial position if El Paso does not merge with Central and South West Corp. as previously planned.

In a June 1994 rate settlement, the Arizona Corporation Commission (ACC) reduced PNW's net annual rate approximately $32.3 million ($19 million after tax), or 2.2% on average. As part of the rate settlement, APS reversed approximately $20 million of depreciation ($15 million after tax) related to a 1991 Palo Verde writeoff. The settlement also imposed a moratorium on filing for permanent rate changes prior to the end of 1996, and provided an incentive rewarding reduction in fuel and operating and maintenance cost per kilowatt hours below established targets.

Pinnacle West has planned construction outlays of approximately $300 million, $257 million and $236 million for 1995, 1996, and 1997--$793 million in total--primarily to expand transmission and distribution capabilities to meet customer growth and upgrade existing plant, and for environmental projects. The budget includes about $27 million each year for nuclear fuel expenditures. Construction costs from 1992 through 1994 totaled $728 million.

Important Developments

Oct. '95—Earnings in the 1995 third quarter shot up 20%, reflecting 3.8% customer growth, lower operating and maintenance expense, and the favorable impact of early debt repayment on interest costs. PNW expects to record a significant penalty to prepay up to $100 million of its $310 million parent-company debt in the fourth quarter.

Jun. '95—The Palo Verde nuclear generating station staff completed refueling Unit 1 after a 56-day outage nearly two weeks ahead of schedule. Palo Verde's previous refueling record was 67 days in May 1994. In 1994, Palo Verde generated 22 billion kw hours, nearly two billion more than the second largest producer in the U.S.

Capitalization

Long Term Debt: $2,541,422,000 (6/95).
Subsid. Red. Preferred Stock: $75,000,000.
Subsid. Cum. Preferred Stock: $193,561,000.

Per Share Data ($)

(Year Ended Dec. 31)

	1994	1993	1992	1991	1990	1989
Tangible Bk. Val.	20.32	18.87	17.00	15.23	17.40	16.31
Earnings	2.30	1.95	1.73	-3.91	0.81	1.44
Dividends	0.82	0.20	Nil	Nil	Nil	1.20
Payout Ratio	36%	10%	Nil	Nil	Nil	83%
Prices - High	22⅞	25¼	20½	17⅞	18⅝	16⅜
- Low	16	19⅝	16¾	9⅝	9⅜	5
P/E Ratio - High	10	13	12	NM	23	11
- Low	7	10	10	NM	12	3

Income Statement Analysis (Million $)

	1994	%Chg	1993	%Chg	1992	%Chg	1991
Revs.	1,685	-2%	1,719	2%	1,690	15%	1,475
Depr.	237	6%	224	2%	220	NM	219
Maint.	120	NM	119	NM	120	3%	116
Fxd. Chgs. Cov.	2.2	-6%	2.3	20%	1.9	—	NM
Constr. Credits	9.4	45%	6.5	-19%	8.0	-27%	11.0
Eff. Tax Rate	38%	—	43%	—	44%	—	NM
Net Inc.	201	18%	170	13%	150	NM	-339

Balance Sheet & Other Fin. Data (Million $)

	1994	1993	1992	1991	1990	1989
Gross Prop.	6,827	6,660	6,497	6,410	6,797	6,669
Cap. Exp.	255	275	224	179	255	294
Net Prop.	4,624	4,601	4,524	4,487	5,126	5,169
Capitalization:						
LT Debt	2,589	2,633	2,774	2,997	3,218	3,424
% LT Debt	56	56	60	64	63	66
Pfd.	269	391	394	396	361	373
% Pfd.	5.80	8.40	8.50	8.40	7.10	7.20
Common	1,776	1,650	1,482	1,325	1,512	1,414
% Common	38	35	32	28	30	27
Total Cap.	6,052	6,080	5,547	5,587	6,139	6,168

Ratio Analysis

	1994	1993	1992	1991	1990	1989
Oper. Ratio	75.6	77.6	76.0	101.5	76.1	75.9
% Earn. on Net Prop.	8.9	8.4	9.0	NM	7.4	7.1
% Ret. on Revs.	11.9	9.9	8.9	NM	4.4	8.3
% Ret. On Invest.Cap	7.7	7.5	7.6	0.3	7.3	7.0
% Return On Com.Eqty	11.7	12.1	10.7	NM	4.8	7.2

Dividend Data —Common dividends, omitted in 1989, were resumed in October 1993. A "poison pill" stock purchase right was adopted in 1989.

Amt. of Div. $	Date Decl.	Ex-Div. Date	Stock of Record	Payment Date
0.225	Oct. 20	Oct. 26	Nov. 01	Dec. 01 '94
0.225	Jan. 19	Jan. 26	Feb. 01	Mar. 01 '95
0.225	Apr. 19	Apr. 25	May. 01	Jun. 01 '95
0.225	Jul. 20	Jul. 28	Aug. 01	Sep. 01 '95

Data as orig. reptd.; bef. results of disc opers. and/or spec. items. Per share data adj. for stk. divs. as of ex-div. date. E-Estimated. NA-Not Available. NM-Not Meaningful. NR-Not Ranked.

Office—400 East Van Buren St., Phoenix, AZ 85004. **Tel**—(602) 379-2500. **Chrmn & Pres**—R. Snell. **VP & Secy**—F. Widenmann. **Investor Contact**—Rebecca L. Hickman. **Dirs**—M. DeMichele, P. Grant, R. A. Herberger, Jr., M. O. Hesse, B. Jamieson, Jr., H. S. Lopez, J. R. Norton III, H. B. Sargent, R. Snell, D. J. Wall. **Transfer Agents & Registrars**—Co.'s office; First National Bank of Boston. **Incorporated** in Arizona in 1920. **Empl**-7,440. **S&P Analyst:** Jane Collin

STANDARD & POOR'S

Policy Management Systems

STOCK REPORTS

NYSE Symbol **PMS**

In S&P MidCap 400

15-AUG-95 **Industry:** Data Processing

Summary: This company is a leading supplier of standardized software systems and related processing and support services to the insurance industry.

S&P Opinion: Hold (★★★)

Recent Price • 52¼
52 Wk Range • 53⅞-33½

Yield • Nil
12-Mo. P/E • NM

Quantitative Evaluations

Outlook
(1 Lowest—5 Highest)
• **4-**

Fair Value
• **54⅛**

Risk
• **Average**

Earn./Div. Rank
• **C**

Technical Eval.
• **Bullish** since 1/95

Rel. Strength Rank
(1 Lowest—99 Highest)
• **65**

Insider Activity
• **NA**

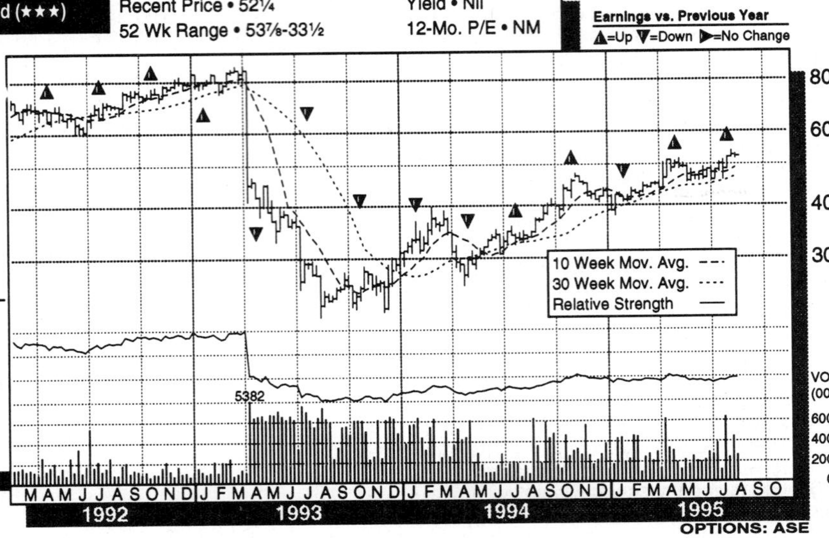

Overview - 15-AUG-95

Revenues are expected to continue rising through 1996 on continued strength in outsourcing and professional services and gains in software licences. The property and casualty business unit should continue to expand, despite weakness in the information services segment. The life insurance unit should also grow. Selective acquisitions should continue to aid revenues. International markets should be particularly strong. Operating profits are expected to benefit from the higher volume and well-controlled costs. The company remains the leading vendor of software and service solutions to the insurance industry.

Valuation - 15-AUG-95

The stock of this leading provider of software and services to the insurance industry has risen sharply from the lows recorded in 1993, reflecting the resolution of past accounting irregularities, a return to traditional levels of profitability and a resumption of the predictable growth the company was once known for. A major portion of Policy Management's business, however, is service-related, and while the company remains well positioned within its industry segment, the environment remains competitive. We expect the shares to track the market in the coming months.

Key Stock Statistics

S&P EPS Est. 1995	2.40	Tang. Bk. Value/Share	16.13
P/E on S&P Est. 1995	21.8	Beta	1.14
S&P EPS Est. 1996	2.90	Shareholders	1,600
Dividend Rate/Share	Nil	Market cap. (B)	$ 1.0
Shs. outstg. (M)	19.4	Inst. holdings	85%
Avg. daily vol. (M)	0.080	Insider holdings	NA

Value of $10,000 invested 5 years ago: $ 15,367

Fiscal Year Ending Dec. 31

	1995	% Change	1994	% Change	1993	% Change
Revenues ()						
1Q	133.4	15%	115.9	-4%	120.4	4%
2Q	133.5	7%	124.7	15%	108.3	-12%
3Q	—	—	127.0	17%	108.9	-14%
4Q	—	—	125.0	8%	115.5	-12%
Yr.	—	—	492.7	9%	453.1	-9%
Income ()						
1Q	11.32	103%	5.57	-43%	9.78	-29%
2Q	12.09	41%	8.60	NM	-70.12	NM
3Q	—	—	9.72	NM	0.35	-98%
4Q	—	—	-33.55	NM	3.95	-75%
Yr.	—	—	-9.66	NM	-56.13	NM
Earnings Per Share ()						
1Q	0.58	132%	0.25	-40%	0.42	-29%
2Q	0.62	55%	0.40	NM	-3.02	NM
3Q	E0.60	22%	0.49	NM	0.02	-97%
4Q	E0.60	NM	-1.73	NM	0.12	-83%
Yr.	E2.40	NM	-0.46	NM	-2.46	NM

Next earnings report expected: late October

Policy Management Systems

Business Summary - 14-AUG-95

Policy Management Systems Corporation is a leader in providing standardized insurance software systems and related automation, administration and information services to the insurance industry. Prior to 1985, the company primarily served property and casualty insurers. It has since broadened its product and service offerings through internal development and acquisitions and now also serves the life insurance industry. PMS offers more than 130 major products and services, including over 90 application software products.

The company's software products automate virtually every insurance processing function, including risk analysis, policy rating, premium calculation, policy issuance and claims management, as well as various accounting, financial reporting and cash management functions. Systems have been designed to permit ease of use and adaptability to a particular customer's requirements. PMS's primary software systems run on medium- and large-scale IBM and IBM-compatible computers utilizing most IBM operating systems. The company also provides software for use with intelligent workstations. Most PMS systems will operate on a stand-alone basis or in conjunction with each other. The company also offers to insurance companies certain processing services, information services and professional services such as business needs analysis, consulting, education and implementation support.

PMS's Series III client/server technologies serve as a platform for the company's systems.

Products are marketed to several thousand property and casualty insurance companies, life insurance companies and independent agents and adjusters in the U.S. and Canada. Software products and related automation support services are also offered in about 25 other countries. At December 31, 1994, the company was providing information services to more than 8,700 insurance companies, agents and adjusters.

Important Developments

Aug. '95—In the second quarter of 1995, PMS recorded a $8.1 million pretax gain from the sale of its Health Division. It also recorded a $7.9 million pretax charge for certain legal expenses. The net effect of the nonrecurring gain and charge was to increase earnings by $0.09 a share.

Feb. '95—The company recorded a net aftertax charge of $44.2 million ($2.27 a share) in the fourth quarter of 1994 as follows: a $21.3 million charge for settlement of a class action and associated litigation costs, net of insurance recovery; a $24.3 million charge for the writeoff of intangible assets and certain software; $4.6 million in charges related to the acquisition of Creative Group Holdings Ltd., an international insurance software and services company; and a $6.0 million benefit from the settlement of a tax audit.

Capitalization

Long Term Debt: None (6/95).

Per Share Data () (Year Ended Dec. 31)

	1994	1993	1992	1991	1990	1989
Tangible Bk. Val.	15.45	17.27	20.12	16.96	11.84	10.34
Cash Flow	1.33	-0.86	3.96	3.32	2.97	2.57
Earnings	-0.46	-2.46	2.55	2.21	1.92	1.60
Dividends	Nil	Nil	Nil	Nil	Nil	Nil
Payout Ratio	Nil	Nil	Nil	Nil	Nil	Nil
Prices - High	47¾	87¼	83½	66⅜	43½	37½
- Low	25¾	21⅝	59¾	39⅜	30	21¾
P/E Ratio - High	NM	NM	33	30	23	23
- Low	NM	NM	23	18	16	14

Income Statement Analysis ()

	1994	%Chg	1993	%Chg	1992	%Chg	1991
Revs.	493	9%	453	-9%	497	20%	415
Oper. Inc.	85.0	47%	58.0	-48%	112	27%	87.9
Depr.	37.4	2%	36.5	12%	32.6	35%	24.1
Int. Exp.	NA	—	NA	—	NA	—	NA
Pretax Inc.	-18.5	NM	-66.4	NM	91.4	26%	72.7
Eff. Tax Rate	NM	—	NM	—	35%	—	35%
Net Inc.	-9.7	NM	-56.1	NM	59.4	25%	47.6

Balance Sheet & Other Fin. Data ()

	1994	1993	1992	1991	1990	1989
Cash	29.0	157	239	197	153	144
Curr. Assets	168	288	345	306	246	238
Total Assets	524	660	684	592	508	461
Curr. Liab.	76.9	81.0	51.3	48.9	45.2	42.2
LT Debt	4.0	6.0	6.0	6.0	103	103
Common Eqty.	377	477	574	497	325	285
Total Cap.	436	557	625	535	454	411
Cap. Exp.	24.8	39.3	56.0	20.0	35.8	21.1
Cash Flow	27.7	-19.7	92.0	71.7	57.5	43.0

Ratio Analysis

	1994	1993	1992	1991	1990	1989
Curr. Ratio	2.2	3.6	6.7	6.2	5.4	5.6
% LT Debt of Cap.	1.0	1.0	1.0	1.1	22.6	25.1
% Net Inc.of Revs.	NM	NM	11.9	11.5	10.7	10.1
% Ret. on Assets	NM	NM	9.2	7.9	7.7	6.4
% Ret. on Equity	NM	NM	11.0	10.8	12.2	11.5

Dividend Data —No cash dividends have ever been paid.

Data as orig. reptd.; bef. results of disc. opers. and/or spec. items. Per share data adj. for stk. divs. as of ex-div. date. E-Estimated. NA-Not Available. NM-Not Meaningful. NR-Not Ranked.

Office—One PMS Center, Blythewood, SC 29016 (P.O. Box 10, Columbia, SC 29202). **Tel**—(803) 735-4000. **Chrmn & Pres**—G. L. Wilson. **Exec VP, CFO & Investor Contact**—Timothy V. Williams. **Dirs**—S. A. Denning, R. L. Faulks, J. M. Henson, F. B. Karl, J. M. Palms, J. D. Sargent, J. P. Seibels, R. G. Trub, G. L. Wilson. **Transfer Agent & Registrar**—American Stock Transfer & Trust Co., NYC. **Incorporated** in South Carolina in 1980. **Empl**-4,678. **S&P Analyst:** Peter C. Wood, CFA

STANDARD & POOR'S

STOCK REPORTS

Portland General

NYSE Symbol **PGN**
In S&P MidCap 400

02-AUG-95 **Industry:** Utilities-Electric

Summary: This holding company owns Portland General Electric, a utility providing electric service to a 3,170-square-mile area of Oregon.

S&P Opinion: Avoid (★★)

Recent Price • 23⅛ | Yield • 5.2%
52 Wk Range • 23¼-16½ | 12-Mo. P/E • 16.1

Quantitative Evaluations

Outlook
(1 Lowest—5 Highest)
• 1

Fair Value
• 17¼

Risk
• Low

Earn./Div. Rank
• B

Technical Eval.
• Bullish since 11/94

Rel. Strength Rank
(1 Lowest—99 Highest)
• 62

Insider Activity
• NA

Earnings vs. Previous Year
▲=Up ▼=Down ▶=No Change

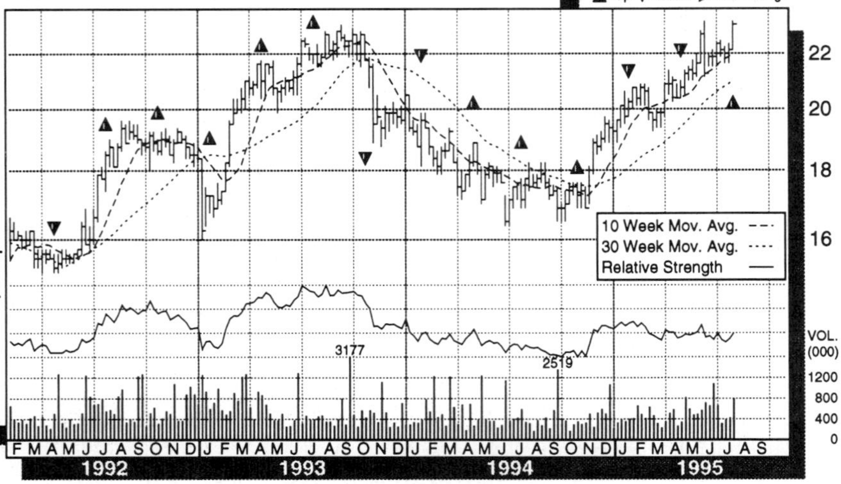

Overview - 01-AUG-95

Share earnings should increase in the second half of 1995, as results benefit from an aggressive wholesale marketing program, growing wholesale kilowatt hour sales, and retail customer growth. Costs are benefitting from ample rainfall in most of PGN's hydro-power areas, which has generated very competitive prices for purchased power. A one-time charge to write off disallowed nuclear decommissioning charges that will lower earnings $0.73 is currently the only factor depressing earnings this year. However, PGN has an added level of risk from its dependence on long term purchased power when prices are falling; it may also be restrained by the need to build and/or buy replacement power supplies. Longer-term prospects for both the industrial and retail bases should be boosted by a growing, high-energy-using high technology industry in its service area.

Valuation - 01-AUG-95

As a result of lower interest rates and an increasingly competitive environment, PGN's share price has advanced 21% in 1995. The sharp rise, however, has lowered the dividend yield below the average for electric utility stocks. In addition, its high P/E has restrained upside potential for now as good earnings growth, before one time charges in the first quarter, have been fully priced at 14 times estimated earnings in 1995. Given that good earnings growth in 1996 has been factored into PGN's valuation as well, most of the stock's upside potential has been exploited for now.

Key Stock Statistics

S&P EPS Est. 1995	1.65	Tang. Bk. Value/Share	16.70
P/E on S&P Est. 1995	14.0	Beta	0.80
S&P EPS Est. 1996	1.95	Shareholders	45,200
Dividend Rate/Share	1.20	Market cap. (B)	$ 1.2
Shs. outstg. (M)	50.7	Inst. holdings	41%
Avg. daily vol. (M)	0.105	Insider holdings	NA

Value of $10,000 invested 5 years ago: $ 15,385

Fiscal Year Ending Dec. 31

	1995	% Change	1994	% Change	1993	% Change
Revenues (Million $)						
1Q	259.2	-7%	278.0	NM	277.7	17%
2Q	219.9	9%	202.1	5%	192.2	-2%
3Q	—	—	214.2	2%	209.2	7%
4Q	—	—	265.1	-1%	268.6	6%
Yr.	—	—	959.4	1%	946.8	7%
Income (Million $)						
1Q	-1.95	NM	39.17	7%	36.56	38%
2Q	32.40	85%	17.49	31%	13.33	16%
3Q	—	—	11.89	87%	6.35	-49%
4Q	—	—	24.51	-25%	32.89	-16%
Yr.	—	—	93.06	4%	89.12	NM
Earnings Per Share ($)						
1Q	-0.04	NM	0.80	4%	0.77	35%
2Q	0.64	83%	0.35	25%	0.28	12%
3Q	E0.26	—	0.24	85%	0.13	-52%
4Q	E0.79	—	0.49	-29%	0.69	-18%
Yr.	E1.65	—	1.86	-1%	1.88	-3%

Next earnings report expected: late October

Portland General

Business Summary - 01-AUG-95

Portland General Corp. is the holding company for Portland General Electric (PGE), an Oregon electric utility supplying a 3,170-square-mile area containing 45% of the state's population and 60% of its economic base. PGN is in the process of phasing out its nonutility businesses. Utility revenues in recent years were derived as follows:

	1994	1993	1992	1991
Residential	38%	36%	35%	35%
Commercial	32%	32%	33%	32%
Industrial	15%	16%	16%	15%
Other	15%	16%	16%	18%

The fuel mix in 1994 was 10% hydro, 37% thermal (nuclear, coal, and gas), and 53% purchased power. Total kilowatt-hour sales rose 1.8% in 1994, to 19,503 million from 18,106 million in 1993.

Capital outlays in 1994 were $247 million, primarily for new generating resources and to expand and upgrade PGE's transmission and distribution system. Expenditures for 1995 are expected to be at similar levels. PGN plans to begin operating The Coyote Springs Generation Project, a 220 megawatt cogeneration facility under construction in Oregon, in late 1995. It also plans to obtain site permits for potential new generating resources, but does not anticipate new construction in the foreseeable future. PGE is in the process of decommissioning the Trojan Nuclear Plant, which was providing 23% of its energy needs when taken out of service in late 1992.

In February 1994, PGN raised $41 million from the sale of 2.3 million common shares; it used the proceeds to purchase outstanding PGE common stock. PGE will use the funds to reduce debt and finance an ongoing construction program.

Important Developments

Jul. '95—The company said that good hydro conditions from Canada to California, lower gas prices and an increasingly competitive wholesale market allowed PGE to reduce thermal plant generation some 31% to take advantage of an historically low price level for purchased power. On March 29, Oregon regulators issued an order on PGE's 1993 general rate request authorizing a 5% average rate increase and a return on equity of 11.6%, a decrease from the previously authorized 12.5%. PGE was also allowed to recover all of its estimated Trojan Nuclear decommissioning costs and 87% of its remaining investment in the plant. PGN recorded a first quarter after tax charge to income of roughly $0.73 a share for the remaining disallowed costs.

Capitalization

Long Term Debt: $835,360,000 (3/95).
Subsid. Red. Cum. Preferred Stock: $50,000,000.
Subsid. Cum. Preferred Stock: $69,704,000.

Per Share Data ($)

(Year Ended Dec. 31)

	1994	1993	1992	1991	1990	1989
Tangible Bk. Val.	17.00	15.21	15.87	14.03	16.10	15.94
Earnings	1.86	1.88	1.93	-0.43	2.17	-0.21
Dividends	1.20	1.20	1.20	1.20	1.20	1.96
Payout Ratio	65%	64%	62%	NM	55%	NM
Prices - High	20½	23⅛	19⅝	18⅞	22⅛	25½
- Low	16⅜	16	15	12¾	14⅞	20⅞
P/E Ratio - High	11	12	10	NM	10	12
- Low	9	9	8	NM	7	10

Income Statement Analysis (Million $)

	1994	%Chg	1993	%Chg	1992	%Chg	1991
Revs.	959	1%	947	7%	884	NM	890
Depr.	124	2%	122	23%	99	-12%	113
Maint.	47.4	-14%	55.3	-22%	70.5	-23%	91.3
Fxd. Chgs. Cov.	3.1	7%	2.9	1%	2.9	130%	1.3
Constr. Credits	4.3	NM	0.8	-71%	2.8	40%	2.0
Eff. Tax Rate	44%	—	45%	—	42%	—	46%
Net Inc.	93.0	4%	89.0	-1%	90.0	NM	-21.0

Balance Sheet & Other Fin. Data (Million $)

	1994	1993	1992	1991	1990	1989
Gross Prop.	2,575	2,384	2,277	2,790	2,669	2,584
Cap. Exp.	223	126	144	139	109	119
Net Prop.	1,617	1,490	1,451	1,801	1,779	1,778
Capitalization:						
LT Debt	836	843	874	927	763	817
% LT Debt	46	48	50	53	45	47
Pfd.	120	140	152	150	152	154
% Pfd.	6.60	8.00	8.70	8.50	9.00	8.90
Common	858	760	724	679	771	762
% Common	47	44	41	39	46	44
Total Cap.	2,558	2,463	2,227	2,208	2,126	2,100

Ratio Analysis

	1994	1993	1992	1991	1990	1989
Oper. Ratio	83.9	83.1	81.4	84.6	79.4	79.7
% Earn. on Net Prop.	9.9	10.9	8.8	7.6	9.9	9.1
% Ret. on Revs.	9.7	9.4	10.1	NM	11.7	NM
% Ret. On Invest.Cap	6.8	7.4	7.8	3.3	9.2	3.8
% Return On Com.Eqty	11.5	12.1	12.8	NM	13.0	NM

Dividend Data (Dividends have been paid since 1948. A dividend reinvestment plan is available.)

Amt. of Div. $	Date Decl.	Ex-Div. Date	Stock of Record	Payment Date
0.300	Aug. 02	Sep. 20	Sep. 26	Oct. 15 '94
0.300	Dec. 06	Dec. 21	Dec. 28	Jan. 15 '95
0.300	Feb. 07	Mar. 20	Mar. 24	Apr. 15 '95
0.300	May. 02	Jun. 22	Jun. 26	Jul. 15 '95

Data as orig. reptd.; bef. results of disc opers. and/or spec. items. Per share data adj. for stk. divs. as of ex-div. date. E-Estimated. NA-Not Available. NM-Not Meaningful. NR-Not Ranked.

Office—121 SW Salmon St., Portland, OR 97204. **Tel**—(503) 464-8820. **Chrmn & CEO**—K. L. Harrison. **VP-Fin, CFO & Treas**— J. M. Hirko. **SVP-Secy**—L. A. Girard. **Investor Contact**—M. Jo Smith (503-464-7120). **Dirs**—G. E. G. Booth, P. J. Brix, C. S. Chambers, J. W. Creighton Jr., K. L. Harrison, J. E. Hudson, W. E. McCain, J. J. Meyer, R. L. Miller, R. G. Reiten, B. G. Willison. **Transfer Agent & Registrar**—First Chicago Trust Co. of N.Y., Jersey City, NJ. **Incorporated** in Oregon in 1930. **Empl**-2,536. **S&P Analyst:** Jane Collin

STANDARD & POOR'S

STOCK REPORTS

Potomac Electric Power

NYSE Symbol **POM**

In S&P MidCap 400

23-AUG-95

Industry: Utilities-Electric

Summary: This electric utility provides service to 672,000 consumers in Washington D.C. and suburban Maryland and to the Federal Government and commercial users in the nation's capitol.

S&P Opinion: Hold (★★★)	Recent Price • 21¼	Yield • 7.9%
	52 Wk Range • 22½-18¼	12-Mo. P/E • 35.4

Quantitative Evaluations

Outlook (1 Lowest—5 Highest)
• **1⁻**

Fair Value
• **15⅝**

Risk
• **Low**

Earn./Div. Rank
• **B+**

Technical Eval.
• **Bullish** since 4/95

Rel. Strength Rank (1 Lowest—99 Highest)
• **45**

Insider Activity
• **Neutral**

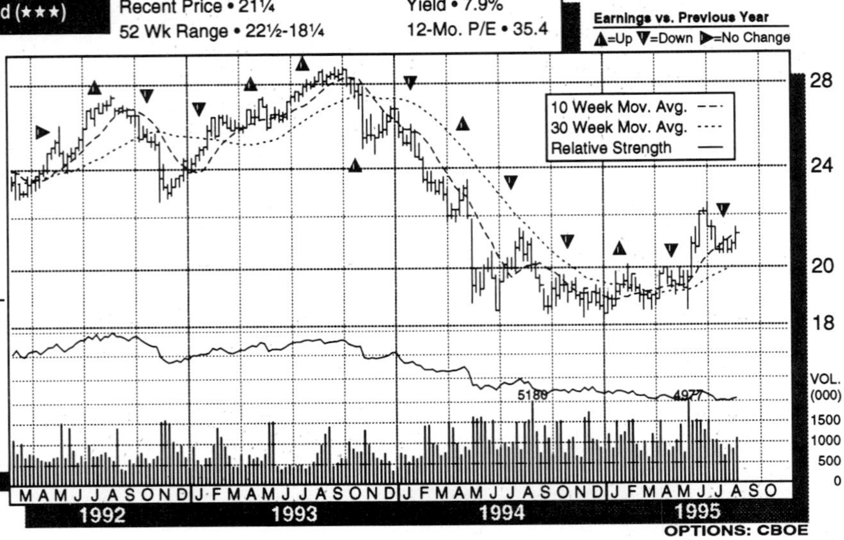

Overview - 23-AUG-95

Share earnings for 1995, before onetime noncash charges, should reflect slightly higher kwh sales, a 3.8% rate hike in the District of Columbia and efforts to control operating costs. However, these positive factors will be partially offset by higher depreciation and amortization expenses, and by a $1.01 a share charge to write down its nonutility subsidiary's investments in airplane leases. Absent further writeoffs as POM disposes of these leases, earnings for 1996 could increase to $1.82 a share from 1995's $1.65 before nonrecurring writeoffs.

Valuation - 23-AUG-95

POM's shares have risen more than 12% to date this year, well below the S&P 500's performance but about in line with its peers. As with most utility stocks, its price will move lower in a rising interest rate environment and rise when interest rates are moving down. In 1995, positive news from a regulatory rate hike as well as recovery of demand side management costs have augmented the favorable impact of lower interest rates. We expect very strong third quarter earnings growth to move the stock higher later this summer. However, given the risk of another writedown of aircraft leasing assets, which have become unprofitable over time, we see little further upside potential in these shares.

Key Stock Statistics

S&P EPS Est. 1995	0.65	Tang. Bk. Value/Share	16.27
P/E on S&P Est. 1995	32.7	Beta	0.60
S&P EPS Est. 1996	1.82	Shareholders	104,000
Dividend Rate/Share	1.66	Market cap. (B)	$ 2.5
Shs. outstg. (M)	118.3	Inst. holdings	19%
Avg. daily vol. (M)	0.179	Insider holdings	0%

Value of $10,000 invested 5 years ago: $ 13,276

Fiscal Year Ending Dec. 31

	1995	% Change	1994	% Change	1993	% Change
Revenues (Million $)						
1Q	364.9	-7%	393.0	16%	339.5	4%
2Q	445.4	-5%	467.5	11%	419.7	7%
3Q	—	—	607.5	-1%	614.3	11%
4Q	—	—	355.1	NM	351.8	6%
Yr.	—	—	1,823	6%	1,725	8%
Income (Million $)						
1Q	-3.97	NM	14.41	11%	13.04	62%
2Q	-56.84	NM	64.29	-17%	77.02	57%
3Q	—	—	134.7	-7%	144.7	18%
4Q	—	—	13.75	101%	6.84	-67%
Yr.	—	—	227.2	-6%	241.6	20%
Earnings Per Share ($)						
1Q	-0.07	NM	0.09	13%	0.08	100%
2Q	-0.52	NM	0.51	-19%	0.63	54%
3Q	E1.14	3%	1.11	-8%	1.21	14%
4Q	E0.10	25%	0.08	NM	0.02	-87%
Yr.	E0.65	-64%	1.79	-8%	1.95	17%

Next earnings report expected: early October

Potomac Electric Power

Business Summary - 23-AUG-95

Potomac Electric Power provides retail electric service in the Washington metropolitan area, including the District of Columbia (41% of revenues) and major portions of Montgomery and Prince Georges counties in Maryland (59%), with a population of some 1.9 million. Electricity is also sold at wholesale. POM's unique service territory, with virtually no heavy industry, benefits from economic stability and low unemployment. Electric revenues by customer class in recent years were:

	1994	1993	1992	1991
Residential	30%	30%	28%	29%
Commercial	47%	47%	48%	47%
Federal government	14%	14%	15%	15%
Other	9%	9%	9%	9%

Sources of electric generation in 1994 were coal 69%, oil and natural gas 18%, and purchases 13%. Peak demand in 1994 was 5,660 mw, and capability at peak totaled 6,723 mw, for a capacity margin of 16%.

POM expects annual growth in kwh sales to range between 1% and 2% from 1995 to 2004, and estimates that peak demand will grow at a compound annual rate of about 1% during the period 1994-2003. The company's ongoing strategies to meet increasing electric demand include conservation and energy use management programs designed to curtail growth in peak demand and defer construction of additional generating capacity. It also expects to rely more heavily on purchased power.

POM's non-utility unit, Potomac Capital Investment Co., primarily leases wide-body commercial aircraft and satellite communications equipment.

Important Developments

Jul. '95—The District of Columbia Public Service Commission authorized a $27.9 million increase in POM's base rate revenues. Return on the rate base allowed was 9.09%, including a return of 11.1% on utility common stock equity. The company had sought a $60.6 million (8.2%) increase in base rate revenue, a return of 9.92% on average rate base, and a 12.75% return on common equity. POM was also granted recovery of a 1993 conservation expenditure which will initially result in $15 million of additional revenue annually. Separately, the company filed with the SEC for a shelf offering for up to $250 million in debt securities, bringing the total shelf to $350 million, to reduce short term debt and fund its construction program. Also, the non-utility subsidiary, Potomac Capital Investment Corp., announced it will dispose of 13 aircraft as part of a plan to end its aircraft leasing business over the next 18 to 24 months.

Capitalization

Long Term Debt: $2,741,423,000 (6/95).
Red. Preferred Stock: $143,485,000.
Cum. Preferred Stock: $125,401,000.

Per Share Data ($) (Year Ended Dec. 31)

	1994	1993	1992	1991	1990	1989
Tangible Bk. Val.	16.27	16.33	15.68	15.31	14.26	14.11
Earnings	1.79	1.95	1.66	1.87	1.62	2.16
Dividends	1.66	1.64	1.60	1.56	1.52	1.46
Payout Ratio	93%	84%	96%	83%	94%	68%
Prices - High	26⅝	28⅞	27½	25⅛	24	24¼
- Low	18¼	23⅞	22⅝	19⅝	18	19¼
P/E Ratio - High	15	15	17	13	15	11
- Low	10	12	14	10	11	9

Income Statement Analysis (Million $)

	1994	%Chg	1993	%Chg	1992	%Chg	1991
Revs.	1,791	5%	1,702	9%	1,562	NM	1,552
Depr.	180	10%	163	9%	150	12%	134
Maint.	93.0	-1%	94.0	3%	91.0	1%	90.0
Fxd. Chgs. Cov.	3.1	5%	3.0	18%	2.5	-20%	3.1
Constr. Credits	19.0	-17%	23.0	-23%	29.7	-10%	32.9
Eff. Tax Rate	35%	—	31%	—	31%	—	28%
Net Inc.	227	-6%	242	20%	201	-4%	210

Balance Sheet & Other Fin. Data (Million $)

	1994	1993	1992	1991	1990	1989
Gross Prop.	5,938	5,665	5,368	5,048	4,659	4,271
Cap. Exp.	317	323	358	432	420	345
Net Prop.	4,298	4,131	3,931	3,707	3,398	3,098
Capitalization:						
LT Debt	3,001	2,617	2,468	2,483	2,117	1,639
% LT Debt	57	54	54	56	57	52
Pfd.	269	272	274	226	176	126
% Pfd.	5.10	5.60	6.00	5.10	4.70	4.00
Common	1,955	1,955	1,823	1,716	1,435	1,394
% Common	37	54	40	39	39	44
Total Cap.	6,005	5,698	5,164	4,982	4,270	3,691

Ratio Analysis

	1994	1993	1992	1991	1990	1989
Oper. Ratio	82.2	81.2	84.6	81.3	81.9	80.3
% Earn. on Net Prop.	7.7	8.1	6.3	8.2	7.9	9.2
% Ret. on Revs.	13.0	14.0	12.9	13.5	12.1	15.4
% Ret. On Invest.Cap	6.1	6.9	6.4	7.1	7.0	8.8
% Return On Com.Eqty	10.8	11.9	11.4	12.6	11.3	15.5

Dividend Data —Dividends have been paid since 1904. A dividend reinvestment plan is available.

Amt. of Div. $	Date Decl.	Ex-Div. Date	Stock of Record	Payment Date
0.415	Jul. 28	Aug. 24	Aug. 30	Sep. 30 '94
0.415	Oct. 27	Nov. 22	Nov. 29	Dec. 30 '94
0.415	Jan. 26	Feb. 21	Feb. 27	Mar. 31 '95
0.415	Apr. 26	May. 23	May. 30	Jun. 30 '95
0.415	Jul. 27	Aug. 28	Aug. 30	Sep. 29 '95

Data as orig. reptd.; bef. results of disc opers. and/or spec. items. Per share data adj. for stk. divs. as of ex-div. date. E-Estimated. NA-Not Available. NM-Not Meaningful. NR-Not Ranked.

Office—1900 Pennsylvania Ave, N.W., Washington, D.C. 20068. **Tel**—(202) 872-2456. **Chrmn & CEO**—E. F. Mitchell. **Pres**—J. M. Derrick, Jr. **Vice Chrmn & CFO**—H. L. Davis. **VP-Secy**—W. T. Torgerson. **Investor Contact**—Peyton G. Middleton, Jr. **Dirs**—R. R. Blunt Sr., A. J. Clark, H. L. Davis, J. M. Derrick, Jr., R. E. Marriott, D. O. Maxwell, F. D. McKenzie, A. D. McLaughlin, E. F. Mitchell, P. F. O'Malley, L. A. Simpson, A. T. Young. **Transfer Agents & Registrars**—Chemical Bank, NYC; The Bank of New York. **Incorporated** in District of Columbia in 1896. **Empl**-4,863. **S&P Analyst:** Jane Collin

STANDARD & POOR'S

STOCK REPORTS

Precision Castparts

NYSE Symbol **PCP**
In S&P MidCap 400

01-AUG-95

Industry:
Aircraft manufacturing/ components

Summary: This maker of components for the aerospace, industrial turbine, electronic, automotive and health care industries primarily sells complex structural aerospace investment castings.

S&P Opinion: Accumulate (★★★★)

Recent Price • 35½
52 Wk Range • 36⅛-18
Yield • 0.7%
12-Mo. P/E • 23.2

Quantitative Evaluations

Outlook
(1 Lowest—5 Highest)
• NA

Fair Value
• NA

Risk
• NA

Earn./Div. Rank
• A-

Technical Eval.
• NA

Rel. Strength Rank
(1 Lowest—99 Highest)
• 78

Insider Activity
• Neutral

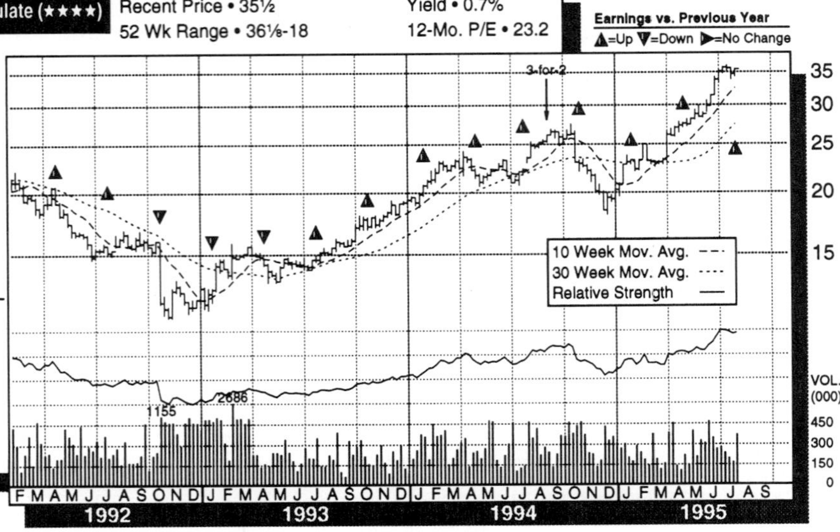

Overview - 01-AUG-95

Sales are likely to rise strongly in 1995-96, aided by the acquisition of Quamco in March 1995 and the onset of the long-awaited recovery in the aerospace industry. Margins should widen, as competitive pricing pressures should be outweighed by cost reduction efforts and productivity gains. Longer term, growth should come as demand recovers (dictated by engine replacements), airline profitability is restored, and new designs for jet aircraft engines that meet fuel efficiency and noise reduction requirements make greater use of PCP's type of structural investment castings. PCP's recent diversification moves into non-aerospace industries (such as the ACC Electronics acquisition in April 1994 and the Quamco acquisition) are already beginning to benefit earnings.

Valuation - 01-AUG-95

PCP's shares have appreciated significantly since the beginning of 1995, as the long-awaited recovery of the aerospace markets in which PCP participates appears to have finally materialized, and they now trade close to their 52-week high. The company has reported positive earnings surprises in its last two quarters, aided greatly by the recent Quamco acquisition, and we expect these excellent results to continue. Despite trading at a fairly high multiple to our estimate of fiscal 1996 earnings, the shares are attractively valued, long term. Near term, we would look for a pullback of 10%-15% from current levels before adding to positions.

Key Stock Statistics

S&P EPS Est. 1996	1.85	Tang. Bk. Value/Share	12.79
P/E on S&P Est. 1996	19.2	Beta	1.11
Dividend Rate/Share	0.24	Shareholders	2,300
Shs. outstg. (M)	20.3	Market cap. (B)	$0.722
Avg. daily vol. (M)	0.049	Inst. holdings	83%
		Insider holdings	NA

Value of $10,000 invested 5 years ago: $ 17,719

Fiscal Year Ending Mar. 31

	1996	% Change	1995	% Change	1994	% Change
Revenues (Million $)						
1Q	137.2	25%	110.2	9%	101.4	-17%
2Q	—	—	102.8	-5%	107.9	-10%
3Q	—	—	102.4	-1%	103.6	-4%
4Q	—	—	121.0	13%	107.5	-3%
Yr.	—	—	436.4	4%	420.4	-9%
Income (Million $)						
1Q	9.40	25%	7.50	7%	7.00	-20%
2Q	—	—	7.20	31%	5.50	-8%
3Q	—	—	6.40	7%	6.00	NM
4Q	—	—	7.90	20%	6.60	14%
Yr.	—	—	29.00	31%	22.20	NM
Earnings Per Share ($)						
1Q	0.46	21%	0.38	6%	0.36	10%
2Q	E0.44	—	0.36	29%	0.28	24%
3Q	E0.41	—	0.32	4%	0.31	NM
4Q	E0.53	—	0.39	15%	0.34	55%
Yr.	E1.85	—	1.45	12%	1.29	NM

Next earnings report expected: late October

Precision Castparts

Business Summary - 28-JUL-95

Precision Castparts is a leading supplier to the aerospace industry of large, complex structural investment castings, as well as other investment castings from stainless steel and alloys of nickel, cobalt and titanium. PCP also manufactures precision cast airfoils, consisting primarily of blades and vanes used as replacement parts and as original equipment in commercial and military aircraft jet engines. Airfoils are also sold for use in industrial and marine gas turbines.

Contributions to sales in recent fiscal years were:

	1994-95	1993-94	1992-93
Aerospace castings	79%	84%	87%
Other castings	21%	16%	13%

The company's Structurals division manufactures large, complex structural castings that are sold primarily as original equipment to aircraft jet engine manufacturers. PCP's strategy is to develop large castings required for new engine programs, promote the continued substitution of cast parts for fabricated parts, increase the use of castings made from titanium alloys and increase its participation in the market for smaller castings.

PCP's Airfoils division manufactures precision cast airfoils including the stationary vanes and rotating blades used in the turbine section of the aircraft jet engines. In addition, PCP casts parts for turbochargers used on diesel engines for trucks, buses, off-highway equipment and a variety of other parts for commercial and industrial use.

In March 1995, the company acquired Quamco Inc., a designer, manufacturer and marketer of premium metalworking tools and machines and specialty powdered metal parts and other specialty industrial components, which operates as the Specialty Products division. Quamco had net sales of $78.8 in 1993-94. PCP expects the acquisition to more than double its non-aerospace business by adding 15% to 20% to total sales.

In 1994-95, General Electric Co. and the Pratt & Whitney Aircraft division of United Technologies Corp. together accounted for 38% of sales.

Important Developments

Jul. '95—PCP noted that 80% of its sales increase in the first quarter of fiscal 1996 came from the addition of the new Specialty Products division, and most of the balance was due to increased aircraft engine spares requirements at Airfoils. Also, the higher gross margins were the result of internal growth and acquisitions which increased PCP's non-aerospace business.

Capitalization

Long Term Debt: $13,700,000 (4/2/95).

Per Share Data ($)

(Year Ended Mar. 31)

	1995	1994	1993	1992	1991	1990
Tangible Bk. Val.	12.79	11.34	9.81	11.94	10.21	8.81
Cash Flow	2.65	2.57	0.81	2.50	1.91	1.71
Earnings	1.45	1.29	0.07	1.78	1.28	1.13
Dividends	0.24	0.12	0.08	0.08	0.08	0.05
Payout Ratio	17%	9%	87%	5%	6%	5%
Cal. Yrs.	1994	1993	1992	1991	1990	1989
Prices - High	27½	48⅜	24	28⅝	23⅞	25⅞
- Low	18	33⅛	11⅛	17⅜	16⅝	17⅝
P/E Ratio - High	19	26	NM	16	19	23
- Low	12	18	NM	10	13	16

Income Statement Analysis (Million $)

	1995	%Chg	1994	%Chg	1993	%Chg	1992
Revs.	436	4%	420	-9%	461	-21%	583
Oper. Inc.	69.2	9%	63.6	13%	56.2	-26%	75.8
Depr.	23.9	-5%	25.1	26%	20.0	5%	19.1
Int. Exp.	NM	—	1.1	-42%	1.9	-14%	2.2
Pretax Inc.	46.8	25%	37.4	NM	-0.3	NM	53.0
Eff. Tax Rate	38%	—	33%	—	NM	—	11%
Net Inc.	29.0	16%	25.1	NM	1.8	-96%	47.3

Balance Sheet & Other Fin. Data (Million $)

	1995	1994	1993	1992	1991	1990
Cash	3.9	55.2	68.9	25.3	6.1	0.8
Curr. Assets	190	211	285	278	281	230
Total Assets	407	343	433	443	422	360
Curr. Liab.	100	85.0	150	93.0	113	90.0
LT Debt	13.7	10.8	14.7	18.6	27.4	30.7
Common Eqty.	258	223	203	319	270	229
Total Cap.	289	245	233	350	310	270
Cap. Exp.	10.9	7.4	15.5	28.8	28.8	23.0
Cash Flow	52.9	50.2	21.8	66.4	49.7	43.9

Ratio Analysis

	1995	1994	1993	1992	1991	1990
Curr. Ratio	1.9	2.5	1.9	3.0	2.5	2.6
% LT Debt of Cap.	4.8	4.4	6.3	5.3	8.9	11.4
% Net Inc.of Revs.	6.7	6.0	0.4	8.1	6.2	6.4
% Ret. on Assets	7.8	6.4	0.5	10.9	8.5	8.2
% Ret. on Equity	12.1	11.7	0.8	16.0	13.3	13.7

Dividend Data (Dividends have been paid since 1978.)

Amt. of Div. $	Date Decl.	Ex-Div. Date	Stock of Record	Payment Date
3-for-2	Aug. 03	Aug. 29	Aug. 15	Aug. 26 '94
0.060	Aug. 03	Sep. 02	Sep. 09	Oct. 03 '94
0.060	Nov. 22	Nov. 28	Dec. 02	Jan. 03 '95
0.060	Feb. 07	Feb. 27	Mar. 03	Apr. 03 '95
0.060	May. 22	May. 26	Jun. 02	Jul. 03 '95

Data as orig. reptd.; bef. results of disc. opers. and/or spec. items. Per share data adj. for stk. divs. as of ex-div. date. E-Estimated. NA-Not Available. NM-Not Meaningful. NR-Not Ranked.

Office—4600 S.E. Harney Drive, Portland, OR 97206-0898. **Tel**—(503) 777-3881. **Chrmn, Pres & CEO**—W. C. McCormick. **VP-CFO**—W. D. Larsson. **VP-Secy & Investor Contact**—Roy M. Marvin. **Dirs**—P. R. Bridenbaugh, E. H. Cooley, D. C. Frisbee, D. R. Graber, H. W. Hill, R. M. Marvin, W. C. McCormick, K. H. Pierce, S. G. Rothmeier, D. A. Sangrey. **Transfer Agent**—First Interstate Bank of Oregon. **Incorporated** in Oregon in 1956. **Empl**-5,166. **S&P Analyst:** Alan Aaron

STANDARD & POOR'S

STOCK REPORTS

Progressive Corp.

NYSE Symbol **PGR**

In S&P MidCap 400

12-OCT-95

Industry: Insurance

Summary: This leading underwriter of nonstandard auto and other specialty personal lines coverages is expanding its product line in an attempt to evolve into a full service auto insurer.

S&P Opinion: Hold (★★★)

Recent Price • 42¾

52 Wk Range • 48-32¼

Yield • 0.5%

12-Mo. P/E • 11.3

Quantitative Evaluations

Outlook
(1 Lowest—5 Highest)
• **4−**

Fair Value
• **45⅝**

Risk
• **Low**

Earn./Div. Rank
• **B+**

Technical Eval.
• **Bearish** since 9/95

Rel. Strength Rank
(1 Lowest—99 Highest)
• **39**

Insider Activity
• **Unfavorable**

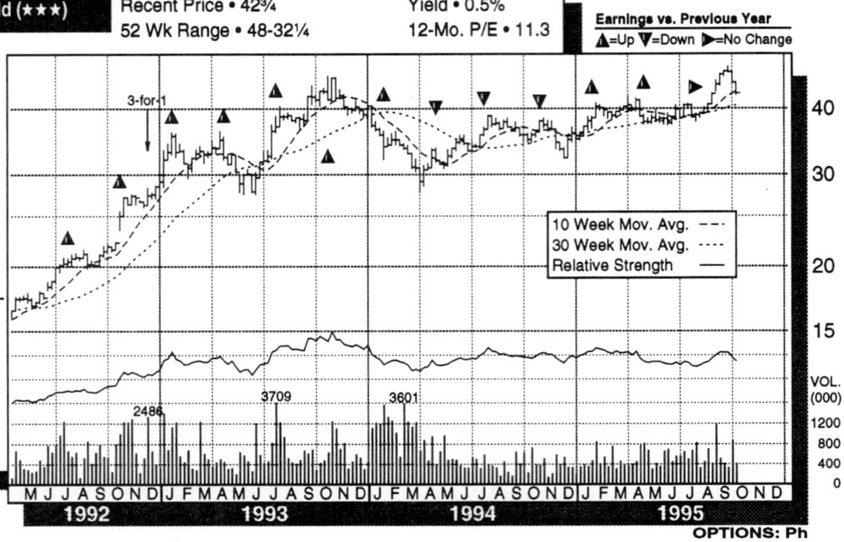

OPTIONS: Ph

Overview - 12-OCT-95

Though earned premium growth in 1995 will likely exceed 25%, operating earnings growth is not likely to grow as fast. This is due to PGR's recently implemented strategy to aggressively price its policies and shrink its margins to gain market share in an attempt to evolve into a full service auto insurer from a specialty underwriter of nonstandard coverage. PGR's attempt at expanding its share of the overall auto insurance market is also aided by the pullback of several large carriers from this market. The positive effects of PGR's aggressive cost-cutting will also aid this effort, since well controlled costs are key to profit growth in the price competitive standard auto insurance market. Long-term prospects are also aided by the exit from the unprofitable long-haul truck market, and by the settlement of Proposition 103 refunds.

Valuation - 12-OCT-95

The shares of this property-casualty insurer have trended upward along with the general market during most of 1995. Although PGR's decision to aggressively grow its share of the overall auto insurance market will lead to premium growth rates well above industry averages, evolving into a full service insurer versus a niche player will lead to a lower P/E multiple for its stock. (The market typically rewards niche players with higher multiples than full service carriers.) Consequently, the shares are fairly valued near term at almost 14 times our aggressive 1995 operating earnings estimate.

Key Stock Statistics

S&P EPS Est. 1995	3.10	Tang. Bk. Value/Share	17.14
P/E on S&P Est. 1995	13.8	Beta	0.91
S&P EPS Est. 1996	3.45	Shareholders	4,900
Dividend Rate/Share	0.22	Market cap. (B)	$ 3.0
Shs. outstg. (M)	71.9	Inst. holdings	63%
Avg. daily vol. (M)	0.106	Insider holdings	NA

Value of $10,000 invested 5 years ago: $ 35,469

Fiscal Year Ending Dec. 31

	1995	% Change	1994	% Change	1993	% Change
Revenues (Million $)						
1Q	693.8	33%	522.4	20%	435.1	—
2Q	759.5	28%	594.0	20%	494.4	—
3Q	—	—	634.1	23%	515.6	—
4Q	—	—	664.8	30%	509.7	18%
Yr.	—	—	2,415	24%	1,955	12%
Income (Million $)						
1Q	60.70	26%	48.10	-7%	51.60	136%
2Q	60.80	NM	60.50	-24%	79.70	99%
3Q	—	—	64.80	-22%	82.60	85%
4Q	—	—	100.9	89%	53.40	62%
Yr.	—	—	274.3	3%	267.3	91%
Earnings Per Share ($)						
1Q	0.79	27%	0.62	-13%	0.71	129%
2Q	0.79	NM	0.79	-29%	1.11	85%
3Q	—	—	0.85	-23%	1.10	77%
4Q	—	—	1.34	97%	0.68	28%
Yr.	E3.10	-14%	3.59	NM	3.59	72%

Next earnings report expected: mid October

Progressive Corp.

Business Summary - 11-OCT-95

Progressive Corp. is an insurance holding company with 60 operating subsidiaries and one mutual insurance company affiliate. The companies write personal automobile and other specialty property-casualty and credit-related insurance and provide related services throughout the U.S. and Canada. Contributions to written premiums by division in recent years were as follows:

	1994	1993
Core lines	95%	93%
Diversified lines	5%	7%

PGR's core business (accounting for 95% of 1994's $2.5 billion in net written premiums) consists of underwriting private passenger automobile and small commercial vehicle insurance. The bulk of PGR's core business consists of nonstandard insurance programs, which provide coverage for accounts rejected or canceled by other companies. PGR estimates that, based on its 1994 written premium volume, it was the fourth largest insurer serving this market.

As part of a strategy to expand its share of the personal automobile insurance market, the company is selectively underwriting standard and preferred risk automobile insurance coverage.

The company's other core personal lines products are dominated by motorcycle insurance, but also include recreational vehicle, motor home, mobile home and boat coverages.

PGR's diversified division mainly provides credit-related insurance and services to lending institutions and risk management services to trade and professional organizations. The transportation division, which provided insurance coverage and related services primarily to the trucking industry, was discontinued in 1992.

Important Developments

Jul. '95—PGR attributed the 22% rise in net written premiums during 1995's first half to growth in its core private passenger auto and small commercial and recreational vehicle lines. This growth was due to PGR's competitive rates. However, claim costs rose at a more rapid pace than premiums, and accounted for 72% of earned premiums in 1995's first six months, versus 65% in the year-earlier period. As a result, the combined ratio increased to 95.0% from 90.8%.

Capitalization

Total Debt: $675,000,000 (6/95).
9.375% Cum. Preferred Stock: 3,500,000 shs. ($25 liquid. pref.).

Per Share Data ($) (Year Ended Dec. 31)

	1994	1993	1992	1991	1990	1989
Tangible Bk. Val.	14.95	12.59	7.94	5.83	5.89	5.71
Oper. Earnings	2.76	2.62	1.94	NA	NA	NA
Earnings	3.59	3.59	2.09	0.41	1.28	0.98
Dividends	0.21	0.20	0.19	0.17	0.16	0.15
Payout Ratio	6%	6%	9%	43%	13%	15%
Prices - High	40½	46⅛	29⅜	20¾	18⅞	14½
- Low	27¾	27½	14¾	15⅛	11	7½
P/E Ratio - High	11	13	14	51	15	15
- Low	8	8	7	37	9	8

Income Statement Analysis (Million $)

	1994	%Chg	1993	%Chg	1992	%Chg	1991
Premium Income	2,191	31%	1,669	15%	1,451	13%	1,287
Net Invest. Inc.	159	18%	135	-12%	154	1%	152
Oth. Revs.	66.0	-57%	152	13%	134	148%	54.0
Total Revs.	2,415	24%	1,955	12%	1,739	16%	1,493
Pretax Inc.	380	2%	373	108%	179	NM	33.0
Net Oper. Inc.	NA	—	189	—	NA	—	NA
Net Inc.	274	3%	267	91%	140	NM	33.0

Balance Sheet & Other Fin. Data (Million $)

	1994	1993	1992	1991	1990	1989
Cash & Equiv.	56.8	42.4	50.0	48.3	52.7	54.5
Premiums Due	542	381	312	323	269	235
Inv Assets Bonds	2,704	2,333	1,988	1,955	1,908	1,885
Inv. Assets Stock	476	454	399	349	184	243
Inv. Assets Loans	Nil	Nil	Nil	Nil	Nil	Nil
Inv. Assets Total	3,180	2,785	2,386	2,304	2,093	2,128
Deferred Policy Cost	162	125	101	110	105	111
Total Assets	4,675	4,011	3,005	2,979	2,695	2,647
Debt	676	477	569	644	644	646
Common Eqty.	1,066	910	533	466	409	435

Ratio Analysis

	1994	1993	1992	1991	1990	1989
Prop&Cas Loss	NA	NA	68.3	65.7	62.1	67.9
Prop&Cas Expense	NA	NA	29.8	33.5	31.1	32.6
Prop&Cas Comb.	NA	NA	98.1	99.2	93.2	100.5
% Ret. on Revs.	11.3	13.7	8.0	2.2	6.8	5.6
% Return on Equity	NA	37.0	34.7	6.7	21.5	17.4

Dividend Data —Cash has been paid each year since 1965.

Amt. of Div. $	Date Decl.	Ex-Div. Date	Stock of Record	Payment Date
0.055	Oct. 21	Dec. 05	Dec. 09	Dec. 31 '94
0.055	Feb. 10	Mar. 06	Mar. 10	Mar. 31 '95
0.055	May. 01	Jun. 06	Jun. 09	Jun. 30 '95
0.055	Jul. 28	Sep. 06	Sep. 08	Sep. 30 '95

Data as orig. reptd.; bef. results of disc. opers. and/or spec. items. Per share data adj. for stk. divs. as of ex-div. date. E-Estimated. NA-Not Available. NM-Not Meaningful. NR-Not Ranked.

Office—6300 Wilson Mills Rd., Mayfield Village, OH 44143. **Tel**—(216) 461-5000. **Chrmn, Pres & CEO**—P. B. Lewis. **VP-CFO, Treas & Investor Contact**—Charles B. Chokel. **Secy**—D. M. Schneider. **Dirs**—M. N. Allen, B. C. Ames, S. R. Hardis, J. Hill, P. B. Lewis, N. S. Matthews, D. B. Shackelford, P. B. Sigler. **Transfer Agent & Registrar**—National City Bank, Cleveland. **Incorporated** in Ohio in 1965. **Empl**-7,544. **S&P Analyst:** Catherine A. Seifert

Promus Hotel Corp.

NYSE Symbol PRH In S&P MidCap 400

Price	Range	P–E Ratio	Dividend	Yield	S&P Ranking	Beta
Oct. 18'95	1995					
23½	26⅜–20⅜	29	Nil	Nil	NR	NA

Summary

This company, which was spun off from Promus Companies (now called Harrah's Entertainment) in June 1995, operates or franchises more than 650 hotels in the Embassy Suites, Hampton Inn, and Homewood Suites chains. In the company's various chains, there was a net addition of 72 hotels in 1995's first nine months.

Current Outlook

Earnings for 1996 are estimated at $1.00 a share, up from the $0.83 expected for 1995.

Initiation of cash dividends is not expected.

In the year ahead, we expect PRH's revenues and earnings to benefit from the addition of more properties to its lodging chains. Also, we look for results to be helped by a further cyclical upturn in the lodging industry. With a modestly growing U.S. economy, we expect PRH to have additional opportunities for increases in both average room rates and revenues per available room.

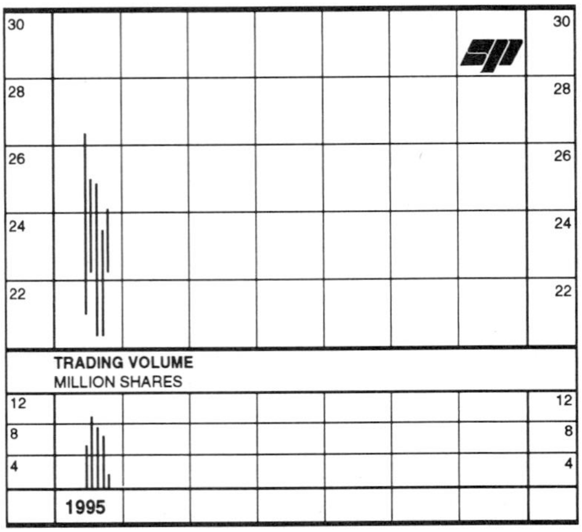

[1]Revenues (Million $)

Weeks:	1995	1994	1993
Mar.	63.2	55.6	---
Jun.	69.6	63.5	---
Sep.	72.0	65.5	---
Dec.	---	58.3	---
	---	242.7	231.2

Revenues for the nine months ended September 30, 1995, were up 11%, year to year. Including non-recurring items, operating profit increased 13%, which led to a 16% rise in pretax income. Net income was up 18%, to $35.3 million, from $29.9. Assuming about 51.6 million common shares in both periods, per share earnings increased to $0.70, from $0.58. This excludes a $0.03 extraordinary benefit in the 1995 period.

[1]Common Share Earnings ($)

Weeks:	1995	1994	1993
Mar.	0.19	0.12	---
Jun.	0.23	0.20	---
Sep.	0.27	0.26	---
Dec.	E0.15	0.12	---
	E0.83	0.70	0.33

Important Developments

Sep. '95— A subsidiary of PRH is expected to franchise and assume management of up to 18 Crown Sterling Suites hotels. This would occur after the properties are acquired and converted to Embassy Suites by FelCor Suites Hotels, Inc., of Irving, Tex. PRH would earn management fees and franchise royalties from operating the hotels as Embassy Suites under 20-year franchise license agreements and 10-year management agreements. Also, PRH (or a subsidiary) would purchase up $50 million of a new $300 million equity offering by FelCor, and would guarantee a $25 million third-party loan. These funds would go toward purchase of the hotels by FelCor and upgrading of the properties. Earlier in June 1995, ownership of PRH was spun off to shareholders of Promus Cos. (now known as Harrah's Entertainment).

Next earnings report expected in late January.

[1]Per Share Data ($)

Yr. End Dec. 31	1994
Tangible Bk. Val.	2.73
Cash Flow	1.11
Earnings	[2]0.65
Dividends	NA
Payout Ratio	NA
Prices—High	NA
Low	NA
P/E Ratio—	NA

Data as orig. reptd. prospectus dated April 25, 1995. 1. All data before 1995 as submitted by Promus Hotel Corp. on a historical pro forma basis. 2. Reflects additional pro forma adjustments. NA-Not Available.

Income Data (Million $)

Year Ended Dec. 31	Revs.	Oper. Inc.	% Oper. Inc. of Revs.	Cap. Exp.	Depr.	Int. Exp.	Net Bef. Taxes	Eff. Tax Rate	Net Inc.	% Net Inc. of Revs.	Cash Flow
[1]1994	245	113	45.9	NA	23.5	31.0	58.2	42.7%	33.3	13.6	56.8

Balance Sheet Data (Million $)

Dec. 31	Cash	Curr. Assets	Curr. Liab.	Curr. Ratio	Total Assets	% Ret. on Assets	Long Term Debt	Common Equity	Total Cap.	% LT Debt of Cap.	% Ret. on Equity
[1]1994	2.22	25.6	34.5	0.7	443	NA	215	140	380	56.7	NA

Data as orig. reptd. prospectus dated April 25, 1995. **1.** Reflects pro forma adjustments. NA-Not Available.

Business Summary

Promus Hotel Corp. is a major hotel company which franchises and operates the Embassy Suites, Hampton Inn, and Homewood Suites lodging chains. Ownership of PRH was spun off to shareholders of the former Promus Companies (now called Harrah's Entertainment) on June 30, 1995. As of that date, PRH's various hotel systems had a total of 620 hotels, with 82,889 rooms and suites. PRH's hotel brands included 32 owned and operated properties, 42 joint venture hotels (generally operated by PRH), 30 properties which PRH operated under management contracts, and 516 franshised hotels.

Embassy Suites hotels are located in about 33 U.S. states and the District of Columbia. Also, there are two hotels are in Canada, and some others were recently under construction in Thailand, Columbia and Mexico. Embassy Suites hotels typically range in size between 225 and 250 rooms- offering a separate living room and dining/ work area with a television, refrigerator and wet bar in addition to the traditional bedroom. Free cooked-to-order breakfasts and free cocktails in the evening are available. Embassy Suites is designed to appeal to travelers desiring greater space and more focused services than are available in traditional upscale hotels.

Hampton Inn hotels are located in about 45 U.S. states. Also, there the chain has a limited presence in Canada, Costa Rica, and Mexico. Hampton Inn hotels typically range in size between 80 and 150 rooms- offering standardized guest rooms with television, free in-room movies, and free local telephone calls. Free continental breakfast is available. Hampton Inn is designed to appeal to business and leisure travelers desiring affordable quality accomidations.

Homewood Suites are located in about 17 U.S. states. Homewood Suites hotels feature "residential-style" accomodations which consist of a living room area, separate bedroom, bath, and a fully-equipped kitchen. Homewood Suites hotels, which offer free breakfast and an evening social function with beverage and food, are designed to accommodate travelers staying five or more consecutive nights.

In December 1993, PRH announced a new brand- Hampton Inn & Suites- which is currently under development. Hampton Inn & Suites will offer the traditional hotel room features of Hampton Inn and the apartment-style suites of Homewood Suites within the same property.

The relative performance of the three established chains based on the number of hotels, revenue per available room and occupancy rate is illustrated as follows:

	1994	1993
Number of Hotels:		
Embassy Suites	107	107
Hampton Inn	437	372
Homewood Suites	26	24
Total	570	503
Revenue/Available Room:		
Embassy Suites	$72.86	$68.58
Hampton Inn	39.74	37.10
Homewood Suites	59.67	54.91
Occupancy Rate:		
Embassy Suites	74.9%	73.0%
Hampton Inn	74.3%	73.0%
Homewood Suites	78.1%	75.8%

Finances

In June 1995, Promus Companies (now Harrah's Entertainment, Inc.) distributed 51.6 million shares of common stock to Promus Companies shareholders on a one-for-two basis.

Dividend Data

No cash dividends have been paid, and the company has no plans to pay any in the foreseeable future.

Capitalization

Long Term Debt: $219,760,000 (6/95).

Common Stock: 51,570,000 shs. ($0.10 par).

Office—6800 Popular Ave, Suite 200, Memphis, TN 38138. **Tel**—(901) 758-3100. **Chrmn**—M.D. Rose. **Pres & CEO**—R.E. Schultz. **EVP & COO**—D.C. Sullivan. **SVP & CFO**—D.H. Dempsey. **Investor Contact**—Gregg Swearingen (901-680-7266). **Dirs**—B.C. Peternell, M.D. Rose, R.E. Schultz, D.C. Sullivan. **Transfer Agent & Registrar**—Continental Stock Transfer & Trust Co. **Incorporated** in Delaware in 1995. **Empl**—7,800.

 Tom Graves, CFA

Provident Life & Accident

NYSE Symbol PVB In S&P MidCap 400

Price	Range	P-E Ratio	Dividend	Yield	S&P Ranking	Beta
Oct. 16'95	1995					
27¼	27½–20½	13	0.72	2.6%	B	1.70

Summary

This leading provider of individual, non-cancelable disability insurance also offers group disability policies, life insurance and pension products. Its group medical business was sold in June 1995. Under a recapitalization plan to be completed in late 1995, Class A and Class B shares will be exchanged for new common stock, and PVB's name will be changed to Provident Companies, Inc.

Current Outlook

Excluding realized investment gains or losses, operating share earnings of $2.75 are seen for 1995, versus $3.20 in 1994. Operating earnings could rise to $3.25 in 1996.

The quarterly dividend was cut 31%, to $0.18, from $0.26, in March 1995.

An expected drop in 1995 operating earnings reflects a slowdown in new pension and individual disability sales, due to lingering adverse market reaction to a claims paying rating downgrade in late 1994. That move was sparked by eroding fundamentals in the individual disability line. A rebound in 1994 operating earnings was skewed by a charge of $275 million ($6.08 a share) in 1993, to cover adverse morbidity and interest rate trends in the individual disability line. Although aggressive reserving hurt near-term results, steps taken to tighten underwriting standards aid the long-term outlook. Recent steps such as restructuring around marketing channels, versus product lines, should aid cross-selling and cost-cutting opportunities. The sale of the group health unit is positive if proceeds are used to strengthen core lines.

Review of Operations

Revenues in the six months ended June 30, 1995, declined 1.5%, year to year, reflecting a 3.0% drop in premium income, pretax realized investment losses of $28.5 million versus $7.6 million, and 15% lower other income, partly offset by 2.0% higher investment income and a $21.8 million gain on the sale of a business unit. Margins narrowed, and net income was down 35%, to $0.90 a share ($1.31 of operating income), from $1.48 ($1.62).

Common Share Earnings ($)

Quarter:	1995	1994	1993	1992
Mar.	0.20	0.72	0.71	0.61
Jun.	0.70	0.76	1.26	0.63
Sep.		0.63	d5.41	0.68
Dec.		0.60	1.41	0.57
	E2.75	2.71	d2.03	2.49

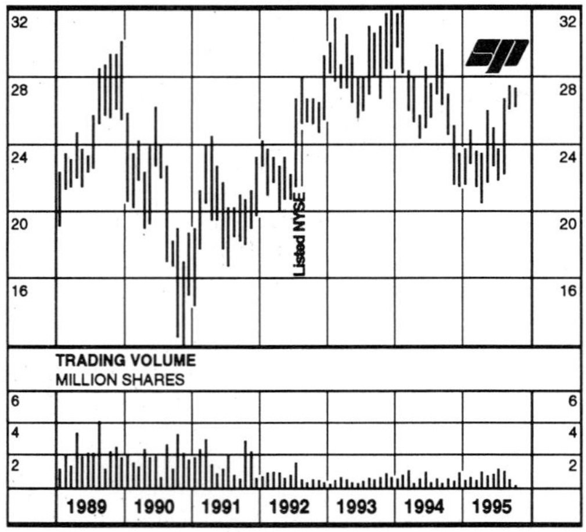

Important Developments

Aug. '95— The company's first half 1995 results included a $14.2 million ($0.31 a share) net gain from the sale of its medical services unit to NYSE listed Healthsource Inc. (HS) for $231 million (comprised of $131 million in cash and $100 million of HS preferred stock). Also, the company restated its first quarter 1995 results to reflect an error in premium income and expenses that was detected during the sale process. As a result, first quarter net income was reduced by $0.09, to $0.20. Separately, shareholders approved a restructuring into a new holding company, Provident Companies, Inc. All existing Class A and B common stock would be exchanged share-for-share for new common stock; all preferred shares would also be exchanged, share-for-share, for new preferred stock. The transaction is set to be completed by late 1995.

Next earnings report expected in early November.

Per Share Data ($)

Yr. End Dec. 31	1994	1993	1992	1991	1990	[2]1989	1988	1987	1986	1985
Tangible Bk. Val.	**NA**	27.52	[1]30.74	[1]29.99	[1]28.88	[1]25.88	[1]23.24	[1]21.96	[1]21.60	[1]19.21
Oper. Earnings	**3.20**	d2.66	2.94	NA	NA	NA	1.83	0.33	1.72	2.31
Earnings[3]	**2.71**	d2.03	2.49	2.53	3.85	3.17	1.95	2.01	3.14	2.67
Dividends	**1.040**	1.040	1.000	0.960	0.830	0.710	0.674	0.673	0.656	0.700
Payout Ratio	**38%**	NM	40%	38%	22%	22%	35%	33%	21%	26%
Prices—High	**31⅞**	31⅞	29¼	24½	26¼	30⅛	22⅞	23	26⅝	23
Low	**21½**	25⅝	20	14⅜	12	19⅛	12½	11⅜	18⅜	15⅜
P/E Ratio—[4]	**12–8**	NM	12–8	10–6	7–3	10–6	13–7	70–35	15–11	10–7

Data as orig. reptd. Adj. for stk. divs. of 25% (Class A stk.) Oct. 1988, 200% & 33⅓% May 1985. **1.** As reptd. by Co. **2.** Reflects acctg. change. **3.** Bef. spec. item of -0.68 in 1991; aft. gains/losses on security trans. **4.** Based on oper. earns. prior to 1989. d-Deficit. E-Estimated. NM-Not Meaningful. NA-Not Available.

Income Data (Million $)

Year Ended Dec. 31	Life Ins. In Force	Premium Income Life	Premium Income A & H	Premium Income Other	Net Invest. Inc.	Total Revs.	Net Bef. Taxes	Net Oper. Inc.	[2]Net Inc.	% Return On Revs.	% Return On Assets	% Return On Equity
1993	**NA**	**NA**	**[3]1,400**	**Nil**	**1,319**	**2,938**	**d140**	**NA**	**d81**	**NM**	**NM**	**NM**
1992	79,956	129	1,361	Nil	1,242	2,867	180	NA	113	3.9	0.7	8.3
1991	82,434	131	1,406	NA	1,195	2,846	169	NA	117	4.1	0.8	8.6
1990	82,432	136	1,420	NA	1,088	2,751	253	NA	179	6.5	1.4	14.1
[1]1989	80,048	112	1,453	NA	971	2,639	223	NA	148	5.6	1.3	12.0
1988	81,564	595	1,257	NA	889	2,827	128	85	91	3.0	0.8	8.1
1987	96,181	603	1,080	NA	743	2,515	21	15	94	0.9	0.3	2.1
1986	62,526	655	682	NA	613	2,018	125	80	147	4.0	1.2	8.4
1985	58,770	540	631	NA	456	1,688	164	108	125	6.4	2.1	12.8
1984	50,944	445	602	NA	295	1,384	153	130	129	9.4	3.5	17.7

Balance Sheet Data (Million $)

Dec. 31	Cash & Equiv.	Premiums Due	Investment Assets Bonds	Investment Assets Stocks	Investment Assets Loans	Investment Assets Total	Invest. Yield	Deferred Policy Costs	Total Assets	Debt	Common Equity
1993	**296**	**65**	**11,310**	**15**	**2,968**	**15,010**	**9.0**	**603**	**16,892**	**248**	**1,245**
1992	381	93	10,602	142	3,031	14,344	9.0	561	15,925	206	1,388
1991	326	102	9,439	167	3,179	13,324	9.4	514	14,787	207	1,371
1990	298	119	7,957	143	3,432	12,161	9.6	464	13,522	208	1,343
1989	280	127	6,509	103	3,605	10,539	9.7	424	11,852	215	1,208
1988	267	158	5,648	103	3,488	9,410	10.1	380	10,722	222	1,085
1987	237	164	4,916	115	3,085	8,220	10.0	351	9,455	219	1,025
1986	176	129	3,732	341	2,412	6,571	10.6	320	7,468	Nil	1,009
1985	150	142	2,824	336	1,756	4,991	10.7	295	5,812	Nil	898
1984	133	143	1,996	278	1,199	3,563	9.7	266	4,314	Nil	788

Data as orig. reptd. **1.** Reflects acctg. change. **2.** Bef. spec. item in 1991. **3.** Total premium income. d-Deficit. NA-Not Available. NM-Not Meaningful.

Business Summary

This company offers life, disability and select health insurance coverage on a group and individual basis throughout the U.S., Puerto Rico and parts of Canada. Segment contributions in 1994 (before investment gains or losses) were:

	Revenues	Pretax Profits
Individual life/disability	34%	23%
Other operations	32%	39%
Employee benefits	20%	31%
Medical services	14%	7%

The individual life/disability division offers term and universal life insurance and single premium deferred annuities. The company is also one of the largest underwriters of individual disability insurance in the U.S.

The employee benefits segment offers a group long term disability, group life insurance, medical stop-loss coverage and various other related products to associations and employee groups.

Other operations consist of guaranteed investment contracts (GICs) and single premium annuities that had been offered to pension accounts. In late 1994, PVB stopped marketing all but synthetic GICs, of which funds under management totaled $1.6 billion at year end 1994. The medical services unit, which offers group health benefits on a fee for services, administrative services only (ASO) and managed care basis, was sold in June 1995.

Dividend Data

Dividends have been paid since 1925. In 1988, the company distributed one-fourth of a Class A share for each Class B share held. Payments are identical on the Class A and B common.

Amt. of Divd. $	Date Decl.	Ex-divd. Date	Stock of Record	Payment Date
0.26	Oct. 12	Nov. 23	Nov. 30	Dec. 9'94
0.18	Dec. 20	Feb. 22	Feb. 28	Mar. 10'95
0.18	Mar. 22	May 24	May 31	Jun. 9'95
0.18	Aug. 2	Aug. 25	Aug. 29	Sep. 8'95

Capitalization

Long Term Debt: $200,300,000 (6/95).

Preferred Stock: $156,200,000.

Cl. A Common Stock: 8,592,888 shs. ($1 par). Has 0.05 vote per sh. Shareholders: 1,497 (2/95).

Cl. B Common Stock: 36,795,968 shs. ($1 par). Some 50% controlled by Maclellan family and related trusts. Shareholders: 1,375 (2/95).

Office—One Fountain Square, Chattanooga, TN 37402. **Tel**—(615) 755-1011. **Pres & CEO**—J. H. Chandler. **EVP & CFO**—T. R. Watjen. **Dirs**—W. L. Armstrong, J. H. Chandler, C. M. Heffner, H. B. Jacks, W. B. Johnson, H. O. Maclellan, Jr., A. S. Macmillan, C. W. Pollard, S. L. Probasco, Jr., S. S. Reinemund, B. E. Sorensen. **Transfer Agent & Registrar**—First Chicago Trust Co., NYC. **Incorporated** in Tennessee in 1887. **Empl**—4,200.

 Catherine A. Seifert

Public Service of Colorado

NYSE Symbol **PSR**
In S&P MidCap 400

17-OCT-95 **Industry:** Util.-Diversified

Summary: This electric and natural gas utility and Texas-based Southwestern Public Service Co. agreed in late August to merge through an exchange of shares in a new unnamed holding company.

S&P Opinion: Hold (★★★)

Recent Price • 34⅛
52 Wk Range • 35-26
Yield • 6.0%
12-Mo. P/E • 12.5

Quantitative Evaluations

Outlook
(1 Lowest—5 Highest)
• **3+**

Fair Value
• **34**

Risk
• **Low**

Earn./Div. Rank
• **B+**

Technical Eval.
• **Bearish** since 12/94

Rel. Strength Rank
(1 Lowest—99 Highest)
• **65**

Insider Activity
• **Favorable**

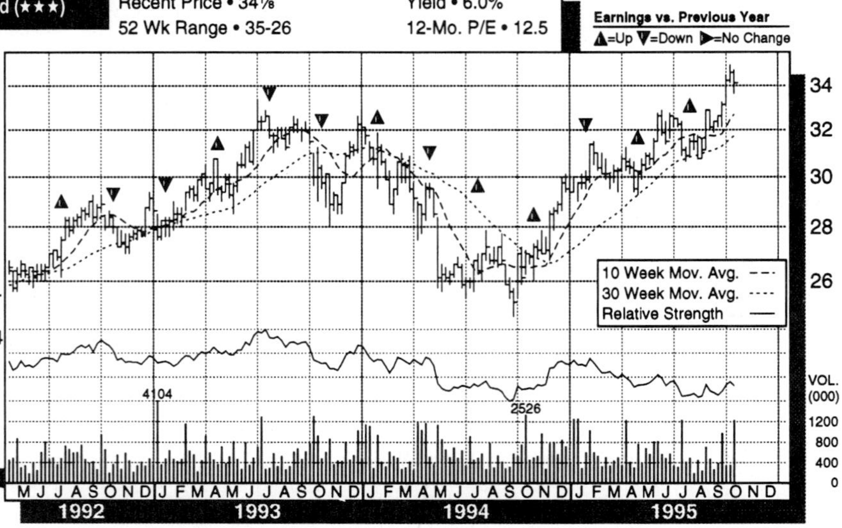

Overview - 13-OCT-95

PSR is currently more than 70% through the lengthy process of decommissioning its troubled Fort St. Vrain nuclear plant, which it plans to convert to two low-cost gas combustion turbine systems with two heat recovery steam plants. The repowering effort, to be completed in 1999, should add to PSR's longer-term competitive stance in relation to non-utility generators in Colorado. In 1995, share earnings should benefit from higher energy sales and a full year of cost savings from workforce reductions. However, these positive factors are likely to be more than offset by an absence of net one-time gains from asset sales of $0.14. We expect long term prospects will be enhanced by the merger proposed in August with Southwestern Public Service Co., another low cost producer, early in 1997, pending approvals.

Valuation - 13-OCT-95

As with most utility stocks, PSR's share price tends to rise in anticipation of a decline in interest rates and move down as interest rates increase. However, market volatility should by mitigated by the positive impact on earnings of efficient power generation coming on line, and comparatively good economic growth in the company's service area. Long-term prospects should benefit from the rising quality of earnings and the company's growing cash generating potential, which improves its ability to raise the dividend. The shares should be a worthwhile holding in a P/E range of 12 to 13.

Key Stock Statistics

S&P EPS Est. 1995	2.55	Tang. Bk. Value/Share	20.65
P/E on S&P Est. 1995	13.4	Beta	0.14
S&P EPS Est. 1996	2.60	Shareholders	64,400
Dividend Rate/Share	2.04	Market cap. (B)	$ 2.1
Shs. outstg. (M)	63.1	Inst. holdings	34%
Avg. daily vol. (M)	0.152	Insider holdings	NA

Value of $10,000 invested 5 years ago: $ 19,501

Fiscal Year Ending Dec. 31

	1995	% Change	1994	% Change	1993	% Change
Revenues (Million $)						
1Q	620.6	1%	612.4	NM	607.0	15%
2Q	498.7	4%	477.6	7%	448.0	6%
3Q	—	—	432.0	2%	422.4	4%
4Q	—	—	535.4	3%	520.9	3%
Yr.	—	—	2,057	3%	1,999	7%
Income (Million $)						
1Q	53.64	15%	46.53	-21%	58.69	27%
2Q	28.26	18%	23.88	17%	20.44	-29%
3Q	—	—	49.05	92%	25.53	-14%
4Q	—	—	50.81	-4%	52.71	67%
Yr.	—	—	170.3	8%	157.4	15%
Earnings Per Share ($)						
1Q	0.81	14%	0.71	-24%	0.94	24%
2Q	0.40	18%	0.34	17%	0.29	-36%
3Q	E0.51	-32%	0.75	97%	0.38	-17%
4Q	E0.83	8%	0.77	-6%	0.82	67%
Yr.	E2.55	NM	2.57	6%	2.43	13%

Next earnings report expected: late October

Public Service of Colorado

Business Summary - 03-OCT-95

Public Service of Colorado and its subsidiaries supply electric and natural gas service to a population of some 2.8 million throughout Colorado, including Denver. Other interests are primarily in energy-related operations and real estate holdings. Segment contributions in 1994 were:

	Revs.	Profits
Electric	68%	92%
Gas	30%	4%
Other	2%	4%

In 1994, coal represented 98.6% of PSR's generation, and natural gas/oil accounted for 1.4%. About 32% of the total electric system input was from purchased power. Peak load in 1994 was 3,972 mw and capability was 4,980 mw, for a capacity margin of 25%. Plant construction costs in 1994 totaled $320 million, 70% of which were for electric facilities. PSR estimates outlays for 1995 at $293 million, with 62% for electric facilities.

In July 1994, PSR was authorized to repower the Fort St. Vrain nuclear plant as a gas-fired combined-cycle steam plant with total generating capacity of 471 mw in three phases, the first of which is to be completed in 1996. The company had shut down the plant and removed it from the rate base in 1989, due to its history of limited operation. At 1994 year-end, PSR had decommissioned about 70% of the plant, and in March 1995, it estimated costs to decommission and defuel the plant at $290.6 million, with $71.2 million remaining to be spent. Recovery of $124.4 million in decommissioning costs from customers began in July 1993, at a rate of $13.9 million a year.

In PSR's 1994 financial statements, auditors noted uncertainties as to whether costs to decommission the plant as estimated can be accomplished and whether resolution of issues regarding storage and shipment of spent fuel is possible.

Important Developments

Aug. '23—PSR and Southwestern Public Service Co. (NYSE:SPS) signed a definitive agreement to combine as a "merger of equals" into a new holding company. Pending approvals, holders of PSR common will receive one share of the new company for each PSR share held for 61.9% of the new equity base. SPS holders will receive 0.95 shares for each share owned, for a 38.1% ownership position in one of the largest utility service areas in the U.S. Market capitalization of the new company would be $3.2 billion, annual revenues $3 billion and total assets $6 billion.

Capitalization

Long Term Debt: $1,081,746,000 (6/95).
Red. Cum. Preferred Stock: $42,665,000.
Cum. Preferred Stock: $140,008,000.

Per Share Data ($) (Year Ended Dec. 31)

	1994	1993	1992	1991	1990	1989
Tangible Bk. Val.	20.11	19.11	18.48	18.02	17.36	16.80
Earnings	2.57	2.43	2.16	2.48	2.49	2.59
Dividends	2.00	2.00	2.00	2.00	2.00	2.00
Payout Ratio	78%	82%	93%	81%	80%	77%
Prices - High	32⅛	33⅜	29⅜	27⅛	26½	27
- Low	24¾	27½	24½	20⅞	20	20
P/E Ratio - High	12	14	14	11	11	10
- Low	10	11	11	8	8	8

Income Statement Analysis (Million $)

	1994	%Chg	1993	%Chg	1992	%Chg	1991
Revs.	2,057	3%	1,999	7%	1,862	4%	1,795
Depr.	139	-1%	141	11%	127	13%	112
Maint.	67.1	-12%	76.2	5%	72.5	8%	67.2
Fxd. Chgs. Cov.	2.4	3%	2.3	NM	2.3	-17%	2.8
Constr. Credits	7.2	-43%	12.7	12%	11.3	20%	9.4
Eff. Tax Rate	22%	—	28%	—	28%	—	32%
Net Inc.	170	8%	157	15%	137	-9%	150

Balance Sheet & Other Fin. Data (Million $)

	1994	1993	1992	1991	1990	1989
Gross Prop.	5,152	5,010	4,814	4,274	4,039	3,825
Cap. Exp.	317	294	262	261	261	174
Net Prop.	3,291	3,193	3,078	2,746	2,609	2,468
Capitalization:						
LT Debt	1,155	1,135	1,197	900	883	904
% LT Debt	44	45	48	43	43	45
Pfd.	183	183	183	184	186	189
% Pfd.	7.00	7.30	7.40	8.70	9.20	9.50
Common	1,267	1,184	1,101	1,034	964	905
% Common	49	47	44	49	47	45
Total Cap.	3,210	3,072	2,886	2,505	2,398	2,333

Ratio Analysis

	1994	1993	1992	1991	1990	1989
Oper. Ratio	86.8	85.9	86.6	86.4	86.3	85.9
% Earn. on Net Prop.	8.4	9.0	8.6	9.1	9.4	10.1
% Ret. on Revs.	8.3	7.9	7.3	8.3	8.4	8.6
% Ret. On Invest.Cap	9.6	9.7	9.6	10.2	10.3	10.8
% Return On Com.Eqty	12.9	12.7	11.7	13.8	14.3	15.4

Dividend Data —Dividends have been paid since 1907. A dividend reinvestment plan is available.

Amt. of Div. $	Date Decl.	Ex-Div. Date	Stock of Record	Payment Date
0.500	Sep. 27	Oct. 07	Oct. 14	Nov. 01 '94
0.500	Dec. 20	Jan. 09	Jan. 13	Feb. 01 '95
0.510	Mar. 28	Apr. 07	Apr. 13	May. 01 '95
0.510	Jun. 27	Jul. 12	Jul. 14	Aug. 01 '95
0.510	Sep. 26	Oct. 11	Oct. 13	Nov. 01 '95

Data as orig. reptd.; bef. results of disc opers. and/or spec. items. Per share data adj. for stk. divs. as of ex-div. date. E-Estimated. NA-Not Available. NM-Not Meaningful. NR-Not Ranked.

Office—1225 17th St., Denver, CO 80202. **Tel**—(303) 571-7511. **Chrmn & CEO**—D. D. Hock. **Pres & COO**—W. H. Brunetti. **Secy**—W. W. Brown. **SVP & CFO**—R. C. Kelly. **Investor Contact**—Michael D. Pritchard. **Dirs**—W. H. Brunetti, C. P. Chandler, Jr., D. M. Drury, T. T. Farley, G. L. Greer, A. B. Hirschfeld, D. D. Hock, G. B. McKinley, W. F. Nicholson, Jr., J. M. Powers, T. E. Rodriguez, R. E. Slifer, W. T. Stephens, R. G. Tointon. **Transfer Agent & Registrar**—First Chicago Trust Co. of New York, Jersey City, N.J. **Incorporated** in Colorado in 1924 **Empl-**5,160. **S&P Analyst:** Jane Collin

STANDARD & POOR'S **Public Service of New Mexico**

STOCK REPORTS

NYSE Symbol **PNM**
In S&P MidCap 400

05-OCT-95 **Industry:** Utilities-Electric

Summary: This company operates electric, gas and water utilities in New Mexico.

Quantitative Evaluations

Outlook
(1 Lowest—5 Highest)
• **3+**

Fair Value
• **16 3/8**

Risk
• **Low**

Earn./Div. Rank
• **B**

Technical Eval.
• **Bearish** since 12/94

Rel. Strength Rank
(1 Lowest—99 Highest)
• **87**

Insider Activity
• **Neutral**

Recent Price • 16 3/8
52 Wk Range • 16 3/8-11 5/8
Yield • Nil
12-Mo. P/E • 9.5

Earnings vs. Previous Year
▲=Up ▼=Down ▶=No Change

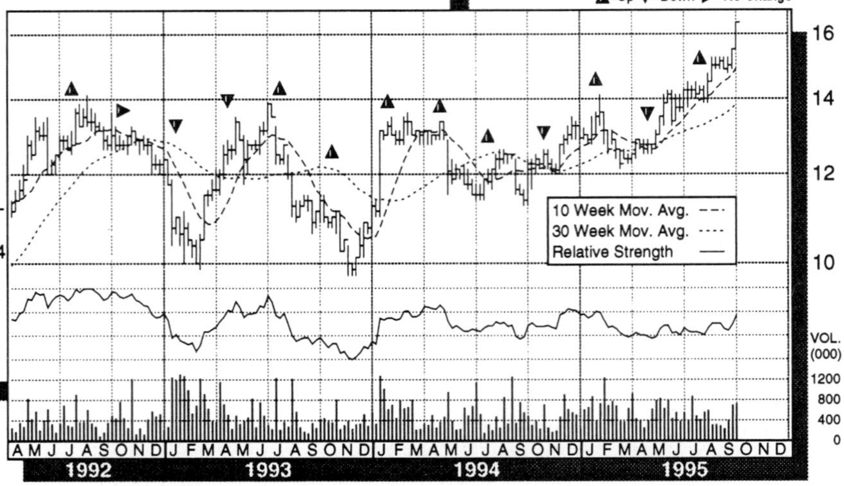

Business Profile - 05-OCT-95

PNM is following a strategic plan that includes reducing its debt, cutting operating expenses, and better meeting the needs of its customers. In 1994, PNM retired $45 million of first mortgage bonds and in August 1995, it retired three series of its cumulative preferred stock in the amount of $64 million. In November 1994, PNM received approval to reduce annual electric rates by $30 million. In August 1995, PNM Gas Services filed for a $13.3 million rate increase for its New Mexico customers.

Operational Review - 05-OCT-95

Earnings fell in 1995's first half, reflecting the 1994 electric retail rate reduction, the expiration of three off-system sales contracts and poor wholesale market conditions, and warmer than normal first quarter weather. Other income rose sharply due to a $0.31 a share gain on the sale of gas assets, and interest charges fell 15%, primarily as a result of the retirement of $130 million of long-term debt in March 1995, and the retirement of $45 million of first mortgage bonds in April 1994.

Stock Performance - 29-SEP-95

In the past 30 trading days, PNM's shares have increased 9%, compared to a 5% rise in the S&P 500. Average trading volume for the past five days was 141,980 shares, compared with the 40-day moving average of 88,203 shares.

Key Stock Statistics

Dividend Rate/Share	Nil	Shareholders	22,000
Shs. outstg. (M)	41.8	Market cap. (B)	$0.679
Avg. daily vol. (M)	0.115	Inst. holdings	62%
Tang. Bk. Value/Share	15.51	Insider holdings	NA
Beta	0.62		

Value of $10,000 invested 5 years ago: $ 11,196

Fiscal Year Ending Dec. 31

	1995	% Change	1994	% Change	1993	% Change
Revenues (Million $)						
1Q	230.2	-12%	260.8	5%	248.6	5%
2Q	191.5	-6%	204.3	7%	190.8	NM
3Q	—	—	218.7	7%	203.8	-1%
4Q	—	—	220.9	-4%	230.7	5%
Yr.	—	—	904.7	4%	873.9	3%
Income (Million $)						
1Q	18.18	-25%	24.10	102%	11.96	-26%
2Q	23.42	22%	19.25	NM	5.65	11%
3Q	—	—	21.79	-9%	23.95	182%
4Q	—	—	15.18	NM	-103.1	NM
Yr.	—	—	80.32	NM	-61.49	NM
Earnings Per Share ($)						
1Q	0.40	-26%	0.54	116%	0.25	-26%
2Q	0.52	24%	0.42	NM	0.09	13%
3Q	—	—	0.48	-9%	0.53	NM
4Q	—	—	0.33	NM	-2.51	NM
Yr.	—	—	1.77	NM	-1.64	NM

Next earnings report expected: late October

Public Service of New Mexico

Business Summary - 05-OCT-95

Public Service of New Mexico, which operates electric (68.7% of 1994 revenues), gas (29.8%), and water (1.5%) utilities, serves some 1.2 million people primarily in Albuquerque and throughout the state. Electric revenues in recent years:

	1994	1993	1992	1991
Residential	28%	28%	27%	27%
Commercial	37%	37%	35%	37%
Industrial	13%	13%	12%	12%
Wholesale	16%	17%	21%	19%
Other	6%	5%	5%	5%

Sources of generation in 1994 were coal 72% and nuclear 28%. Peak demand in 1994 was 1,189 mw, and system capability totaled 1,506 mw, for a capacity margin of 27%. Total customers in 1994 were 322,730, up 3.1% from 1993. For the years 1990 through 1994, retail kwh sales grew at a compound annual rate of about 4.2%.

The company distributes natural gas through its Gas Company of New Mexico (GCNM) division to most of the major communities in New Mexico, serving about 382,000 customers as of December 31, 1994. For 1994, GCNM had throughput of approximately 85.0 million decatherms, including sales of 41.9 million decatherms to sales-service customers. In June 1995, PNM completed the sale of substantially all of its gas gathering and processing assets to Williams Gas Processing-Blanco, Inc. for $154.1 million in cash. PNM recorded a $0.31 a share gain in 1995's second quarter. In July 1995, PNM sold its water division to the City of Santa Fe for $51.2 million. As a result, PNM will record a gain of $0.15 a share in 1995's third quarter.

In November 1994, the New Mexico Public Utility Commission approved PNM's rate proposal for a $30 million annual electric rate reduction.

The company currently estimates a total of $864 million for its capital requirements for the years 1995 through 1999. PNM expects that such cash requirements will be met primarily through internally generated cash.

Important Developments

Aug. '95—PNM Gas Services requested a $13.3 million increase in rates, primarily for its New Mexico residential customers. PNM expects the New Mexico Public Utility Commission to rule on the case within the next 10 months, allowing implementation of the new rates in July 1996. Separately, the company redeemed, at par, all of its 8.45% series, 8.80% series, and 8.75% series of cumulative preferred stock outstanding as of July 6, 1995.

Capitalization

Long Term Debt: $742,763,000 (6/95).
Cum. Preferred Stock: $13,000,000.

Per Share Data ($) (Year Ended Dec. 31)

	1994	1993	1992	1991	1990	1989
Tangible Bk. Val.	15.09	13.29	15.00	17.69	17.36	18.02
Earnings	1.77	-1.64	-2.67	0.32	-0.23	1.73
Dividends	Nil	Nil	Nil	Nil	Nil	0.38
Payout Ratio	Nil	Nil	Nil	Nil	Nil	22%
Prices - High	13⅝	13⅞	14⅛	11⅝	15½	15⅞
- Low	11	9¾	9⅜	7⅝	8	10¾
P/E Ratio - High	8	NM	NM	36	NM	9
- Low	6	NM	NM	24	NM	6

Income Statement Analysis (Million $)

	1994	%Chg	1993	%Chg	1992	%Chg	1991
Revs.	905	4%	874	3%	852	NM	857
Depr.	74.1	-4%	77.3	-3%	79.3	4%	76.1
Maint.	61.4	8%	56.8	5%	54.3	4%	52.2
Fxd. Chgs. Cov.	2.5	—	NM	—	NM	—	1.4
Constr. Credits	0.3	-36%	0.4	-65%	1.2	-59%	2.9
Eff. Tax Rate	36%	—	NM	—	NM	—	31%
Net Inc.	80.3	NM	-61.5	NM	-103	NM	23.0

Balance Sheet & Other Fin. Data (Million $)

	1994	1993	1992	1991	1990	1989
Gross Prop.	2,588	2,550	2,690	2,665	2,612	2,585
Cap. Exp.	119	101	95.0	80.0	81.0	74.0
Net Prop.	1,697	1,704	1,877	1,905	1,914	1,932
Capitalization:						
LT Debt	752	958	911	786	790	801
% LT Debt	52	60	56	49	49	48
Pfd.	77.0	83.4	84.7	86.0	105	108
% Pfd.	5.30	5.20	5.20	5.30	6.40	6.50
Common	631	555	626	739	725	753
% Common	43	35	39	46	45	45
Total Cap.	1,609	1,721	1,807	1,907	1,883	1,926

Ratio Analysis

	1994	1993	1992	1991	1990	1989
Oper. Ratio	83.3	84.7	86.7	88.7	89.2	83.3
% Earn. on Net Prop.	8.9	7.4	5.9	5.1	4.8	8.0
% Ret. on Revs.	8.9	NM	NM	2.7	0.1	9.0
% Ret. On Invest.Cap	9.1	1.4	NM	4.7	3.6	8.0
% Return On Com.Eqty	12.4	NM	NM	1.8	NM	9.5

Dividend Data —Common dividends were omitted in April 1989 after having been paid since 1942. Dividends on the preferred stock issues have been maintained.

Data as orig. reptd.; bef. results of disc opers. and/or spec. items. Per share data adj. for stk. divs. as of ex-div. date. E-Estimated. NA-Not Available. NM-Not Meaningful. NR-Not Ranked.

Office—Alvarado Square, Albuquerque, NM 87158. **Tel**—(505) 241-2700. **Chrmn**—J. T. Ackerman. **Pres & CEO**—B. F. Montoya. **VP-CFO**—M. H. Maerki. **Investor Contact**—Barbara Barsky. **Dirs**—J. T. Ackerman, R. G. Armstrong, J. A. Godwin, L. H. Lattman, M. Lujan, Jr., B. F. Montoya, R. U. Ortiz, R. M. Price, P. F. Roth. **Transfer Agent & Registrar**—Company's office. **Incorporated** in New Mexico in 1917. **Empl**-2,768. **S&P Analyst:** Ronald J. Gross

STANDARD & POOR'S

Puget Sound Power & Light

STOCK REPORTS

NYSE Symbol **PSD**

In S&P MidCap 400

17-SEP-95

Industry: Utilities-Electric

Summary: This moderate-size electric utility serves 823,000 customers in the Puget Sound region of Washington State.

S&P Opinion: Hold (★★★)

Recent Price • 22⅜ | 52 Wk Range • 23⅜-18⅝ | Yield • 8.2% | 12-Mo. P/E • 12.8

Quantitative Evaluations

Outlook (1 Lowest—5 Highest)
• **1⁻**

Fair Value
• **19⅜**

Risk
• **Low**

Earn./Div. Rank
• **B+**

Technical Eval.
• **Bullish** since 1/95

Rel. Strength Rank (1 Lowest—99 Highest)
• **39**

Insider Activity
• **NA**

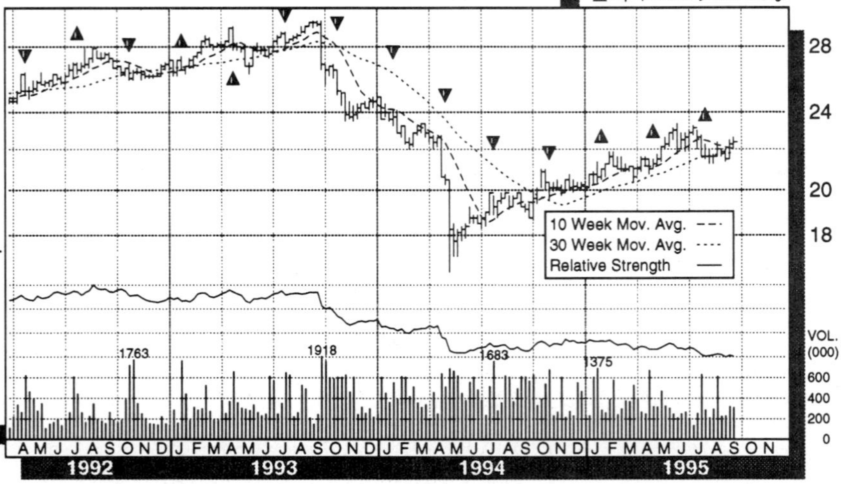

Overview - 15-SEP-95

Share earnings are projected to be flat in 1995, as compared to 1994 (before a $0.21 a share non-recurring charge), despite customer growth resulting from a strengthening local economy. Profitability should also be bolstered by estimated pretax cost savings of $16 million relating to 1994 work force reductions. In addition, cutbacks in planned capital spending should improve PSD's near-term results, as well as its long-term competitive standing. However, these positive factors will be largely offset by a 1993 rate order that reduced the allowed return on equity to 10.5%, from 12.8%. Furthermore, winter storm damage, which hurt first quarter results, will restrict full-year profitability. In June 1995, PSD strengthened its balance sheet through the sale of about $202 million of its investment in energy conservation measures.

Valuation - 15-SEP-95

As with the majority of electric utility equities, PSD's shares dropped significantly in 1994, as a result of rising interest rates and increased competition. However, the shares have rebounded somewhat in 1995, and are up over 10% since the end of 1994. The shares currently have a dividend yield of about 8.3%, well above the industry average. With an estimated 1995 payout approaching 100%, the dividend is secure, but near-term increases are unlikely. The shares are fully valued at approximately 11X estimated 1996 EPS of $1.95, but, with an above average yield, they are an attractive holding for total return.

Key Stock Statistics

S&P EPS Est. 1995	1.85	Tang. Bk. Value/Share	18.35
P/E on S&P Est. 1995	12.1	Beta	0.41
S&P EPS Est. 1996	1.95	Shareholders	62,400
Dividend Rate/Share	1.84	Market cap. (B)	$ 1.4
Shs. outstg. (M)	63.6	Inst. holdings	22%
Avg. daily vol. (M)	0.064	Insider holdings	NA

Value of $10,000 invested 5 years ago: $ 15,523

Fiscal Year Ending Dec. 31

	1995	% Change	1994	% Change	1993	% Change
Revenues (Million $)						
1Q	338.4	3%	329.2	2%	324.0	16%
2Q	261.6	NM	263.6	11%	237.6	-1%
3Q	—	—	264.3	15%	230.2	5%
4Q	—	—	336.9	5%	321.1	13%
Yr.	—	—	1,194	7%	1,113	9%
Income (Million $)						
1Q	48.75	5%	46.53	-15%	54.68	14%
2Q	22.86	29%	17.77	-32%	26.21	-11%
3Q	—	—	14.93	-17%	18.07	NM
4Q	—	—	40.83	4%	39.36	-2%
Yr.	—	—	120.1	-13%	138.3	2%
Earnings Per Share ($)						
1Q	0.70	4%	0.67	-22%	0.86	4%
2Q	0.30	36%	0.22	-41%	0.37	-21%
3Q	E0.25	47%	0.17	-26%	0.23	-8%
4Q	E0.60	3%	0.58	4%	0.56	-10%
Yr.	E1.85	13%	1.64	-18%	2.00	-7%

Next earnings report expected: mid October

Puget Sound Power & Light

Business Summary - 15-SEP-95

Puget Sound Power & Light provides electricity to about 823,000 customers located in a suburban and rural area of western Washington State. Contributions to revenues by customer class in recent years were:

	1994	1993	1992	1991
Residential	47%	45%	46%	50%
Commercial	33%	32%	34%	32%
Industrial	14%	13%	14%	13%
Other	6%	10%	6%	5%

The fuel mix in 1994 was 47% hydroelectric and 53% coal. Total energy sales in 1994 totaled 21,901 kwh, up 9.0% from 1993. Peak load in 1994 was 4,247 mw, and system capability was 5,366 mw, for a capacity margin of 20.9%.

PSD and other utilities are joint owners of four mine-mouth, coal-fired, steam-electric generating units at Colstrip, Montana. Puget owns a 50% interest (330,000 kw) in units 1 and 2, and a 25% interest (350,000 kw) in units 3 and 4. The company owns a 7.0% interest (91,900 kw) in a coal-fired, steam-electric generating plant near Centralia, Washington, with a net capability of 1,313,000 kw. PSD owns several other plants with an aggregate net generating capability of 1,012,300 kw.

Construction expenditures for 1995 and 1996 are expected to total $154.9 million and $198.1 million, respectively. The company expects to fund an average of 72% of its estimated construction expenditures in 1995 and 1996 from cash from operations, and to fund the balance through the sale of securities.

In a September 1993 general rate case order, PSD's allowed return on common equity was reduced from 12.8% to 10.5%.

Important Developments

Aug. '95—The Washington Utilities and Transportation Commission approved a $58.8 million increase in revenues for Puget Power, effective October 1, 1995, under the periodic rate adjustment mechanism.

Jul. '95—PSD and Duke/Louis Dreyfus signed a memorandum of understanding to jointly pursue bulk power supply and energy service opportunities in the Pacific Northwest. The alliance will identify opportunities to enhance Puget Power's wholesale power business and form a stand-alone energy services venture that will offer electric distribution engineering, multiple fuels capability and supply, and administrative and customer services.

Capitalization

Long Term Debt: $928,366,000 (6/95).
Red. Cum. Preferred Stock: $89,039,000.
Cum. Preferred Stock: $125,000,000.

Per Share Data ($)

(Year Ended Dec. 31)

	1994	1993	1992	1991	1990	1989
Tangible Bk. Val.	18.29	18.50	17.57	16.82	16.37	15.95
Earnings	1.64	2.00	2.16	2.21	2.16	1.88
Dividends	1.84	1.83	1.79	1.76	1.76	1.76
Payout Ratio	112%	91%	83%	80%	81%	94%
Prices - High	24⅞	29¾	27⅞	26⅞	22½	22½
- Low	16½	23½	23⅞	19⅛	18⅝	18
P/E Ratio - High	15	15	13	12	10	12
- Low	10	12	11	9	9	10

Income Statement Analysis (Million $)

	1994	%Chg	1993	%Chg	1992	%Chg	1991
Revs.	1,194	7%	1,113	9%	1,025	7%	957
Depr.	116	NM	116	-6%	123	6%	116
Maint.	51.3	-5%	53.9	-3%	55.7	NM	56.2
Fxd. Chgs. Cov.	2.8	-3%	2.9	8%	2.7	-6%	2.8
Constr. Credits	4.2	-16%	5.0	43%	3.5	-22%	4.5
Eff. Tax Rate	40%	—	38%	—	34%	—	29%
Net Inc.	120	-13%	138	1%	136	2%	133

Balance Sheet & Other Fin. Data (Million $)

	1994	1993	1992	1991	1990	1989
Gross Prop.	3,307	3,135	3,010	2,846	2,701	2,586
Cap. Exp.	214	156	186	154	132	130
Net Prop.	2,267	2,153	1,909	1,846	1,792	1,766
Capitalization:						
LT Debt	963	1,036	1,045	1,052	1,006	980
% LT Debt	41	43	45	49	48	48
Pfd.	216	208	259	160	169	175
% Pfd.	9.20	8.60	11	7.40	8.10	8.50
Common	1,173	1,186	1,040	942	918	859
% Common	50	49	44	44	44	44
Total Cap.	2,894	2,961	2,367	2,177	2,119	2,093

Ratio Analysis

	1994	1993	1992	1991	1990	1989
Oper. Ratio	83.8	81.0	79.1	77.7	77.0	78.7
% Earn. on Net Prop.	8.8	9.9	11.4	11.8	12.1	10.8
% Ret. on Revs.	10.1	12.4	13.2	13.9	14.2	13.3
% Ret. On Invest.Cap	7.0	8.1	10.2	10.2	10.3	9.6
% Return On Com.Eqty	8.8	11.0	12.6	13.2	13.3	11.7

Dividend Data —Dividends have been paid since 1943. A dividend reinvestment plan is available. A preferred stock rights plan was adopted in January 1991.

Amt. of Div. $	Date Decl.	Ex-Div. Date	Stock of Record	Payment Date
0.460	Oct. 10	Oct. 18	Oct. 24	Nov. 15 '94
0.460	Jan. 10	Jan. 17	Jan. 23	Feb. 15 '95
0.460	Apr. 11	Apr. 18	Apr. 24	May. 15 '95
0.460	Jul. 11	Jul. 20	Jul. 24	Aug. 15 '95

Data as orig. reptd.; bef. results of disc opers. and/or spec. items. Per share data adj. for stk. divs. as of ex-div. date. E-Estimated. NA-Not Available. NM-Not Meaningful. NR-Not Ranked.

Office—411 - 108th Ave. N.E., Bellevue, WA 98004-5515. **Tel**—(206) 454-6363. **Chrmn, Pres & CEO**—R. R. Sonstelie. **Secy**—J. Elredge. **CFO**—W. S. Weaver. **Treas**—D. E. Gaines. **Investor Contact**—U. Earl Dunn. **Dirs**—D. P. Beighle, C. W. Bingham, P. J. Campbell, J. D. Durbin, J. W. Ellis, D. J. Evans, N. L. Jacob, R. R. Sonstelie, W. S. Weaver, R. K. Wilson. **Transfer Agents & Registrars**—Bank of New York, NYC; Co.'s office. **Incorporated** in Washington in 1960. **Empl-** 2,221. **S&P Analyst:** Ronald J. Gross

Quaker State

NYSE Symbol **KSF**
In S&P MidCap 400

29-AUG-95 **Industry:** Oil and Gas

Summary: This leading producer of branded motor oils and lubricants also makes automotive products and vehicular lighting, and operates fast lube auto service centers.

S&P Opinion: Buy (★★★★★)

Recent Price • 14⅞
52 Wk Range • 16½-13
Yield • 2.7%
12-Mo. P/E • 42.5

Quantitative Evaluations
Outlook
(1 Lowest—5 Highest)
• **NA**
Fair Value
• **NA**
Risk
• **Low**
Earn./Div. Rank
• **B-**

Technical Eval.
• **Neutral** since 7/95
Rel. Strength Rank
(1 Lowest—99 Highest)
• **27**
Insider Activity
• **Neutral**

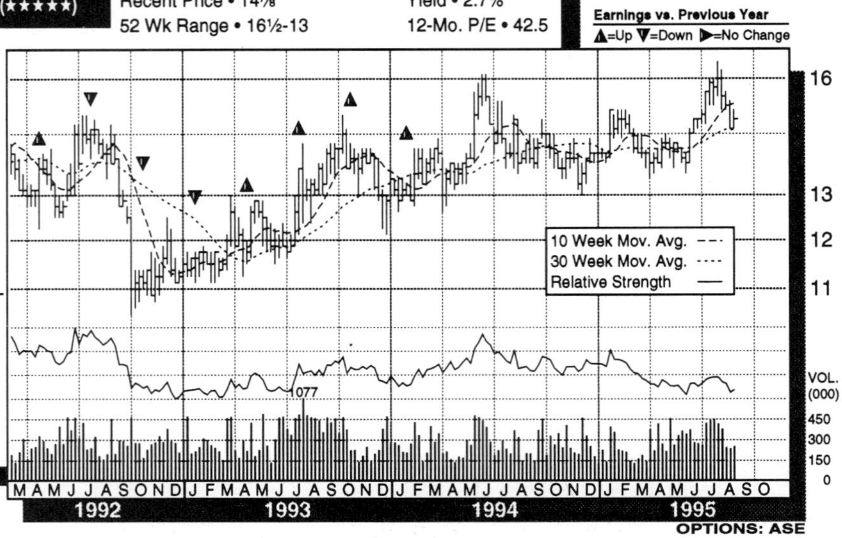

OPTIONS: ASE

Overview - 29-AUG-95

Revenues will rise in 1995, reflecting the acquisition of Specialty Oil and Slick 50, and increased motor oil sales volumes. Margin pressures should be offset by higher private label sales volumes, and earnings from continuing operations will improve sharply. Growth of the "do-it-for-me" market will remain stronger than that of the "do-it-yourself" market, and we expect Q-Lube to benefit from this. Product pull through at Q-Lube, the introduction of higher-margin products like Quaker State 4X4 motor oil, and further conversion of Minit Lubes into Q-Lube units will help the company to come closer to its goals for overall return on sales. Focus on core lubricants businesses and divestiture of peripheral businesses should aid future profit growth.

Valuation - 29-AUG-95

The shares have underperformed the broad market thus far in 1995; investors were deterred by low margins and restructuring costs. However, KSF's motor oil market share continues to increase, and is growing faster than that of any other company in this segment. We believe that motor oil segment margins will widen in the second half of 1995, as raw material costs stabilize. The biggest boost to the share price, however, should come from exposure to new markets. News of further high-margin product line acquisitions, which we believe will be made, should also help the stock.

Key Stock Statistics

S&P EPS Est. 1995	0.58	Tang. Bk. Value/Share	5.09
P/E on S&P Est. 1995	25.6	Beta	0.73
S&P EPS Est. 1996	1.00	Shareholders	11,800
Dividend Rate/Share	0.40	Market cap. (B)	$0.469
Shs. outstg. (M)	31.5	Inst. holdings	43%
Avg. daily vol. (M)	0.053	Insider holdings	NA

Value of $10,000 invested 5 years ago: $ 13,839

Fiscal Year Ending Dec. 31

	1995	% Change	1994	% Change	1993	% Change
Revenues (Million $)						
1Q	245.0	40%	175.5	-2%	179.8	4%
2Q	257.7	-25%	343.7	76%	195.1	3%
3Q	—	—	184.4	-4%	192.4	3%
4Q	—	—	227.2	18%	191.9	10%
Yr.	—	—	755.3	NM	759.2	5%
Income (Million $)						
1Q	5.60	47%	3.82	12%	3.40	198%
2Q	-4.53	NM	3.55	-19%	4.38	9%
3Q	—	—	3.92	-2%	3.98	55%
4Q	—	—	2.72	40%	1.94	16%
Yr.	—	—	14.01	2%	13.70	46%
Earnings Per Share ($)						
1Q	0.18	—	--	—	0.13	NM
2Q	-0.10	NM	0.27	69%	0.16	7%
3Q	E0.56	NM	0.14	NM	0.14	40%
4Q	E-0.06	NM	0.09	29%	0.07	17%
Yr.	E0.58	18%	0.49	-2%	0.50	43%

Next earnings report expected: mid October

Quaker State

Business Summary - 29-AUG-95

Quaker State makes and markets motor oils. Overall market share of 14.3% is second only to the Pennzoil brand. The company is seeking to expand market share, and is developing aggressive marketing strategies for additional sales of higher-margined products. KSF also sells refined products and products for the auto aftermarket, including filters, anti-freeze, brake and power-steering fluids, chemicals and coatings. The company operates a nationwide network of fast lube centers (458 stores, with 400 company-owned) that provide car care services, including oil changes, filter replacement, and maintenance of power steering, brake and transmission fluids. Fast lube centers are operated under the Quaker State Q Lube name. Profits (in million $) by segment in recent years were:

	1994	1993
Motor Oil	$16.4	$17.5
Natural gas E&P	5.4	3.1
Fast lube	5.7	3.0
Truck-Lite	11.8	5.7
Docks	1.8	1.1

The company makes and markets a synthetic motor oil, Quaker State 4X4, specifically designed and formulated for light trucks, sport/utility vehicles and minivans, the fastest growing segment of the automotive industry (accounting for nearly half of all U.S. passenger vehicles). In late 1994, KSF acquired the Speciality Oil Cos, providing a distribution network spanning the South and Southwest, and servicing both domestic and international customers. Specialty markets a wide range of branded and private-label lubricants and antifreeze for automotive use, as well as custom-formulated heavy-duty lubricants and greases for fleet, commercial and industrial customers. It unit also recycles used oil and other fluids.

Important Developments

Aug. '95—KSF said it was comfortable with analyst estimates of 1995 operating earnings from continuing operations of $0.52 to $0.58 a share ($0.33 in 1994). This excludes a restructuring charge of $0.30 associated with relocating the company's headquarters to Dallas.

Jul. '95—Operating income from continuing operations in the 1995 second quarter came to $0.15 a share, versus $0.05 in the 1994 period. The natural gas exploration and production division was classified as discontinued in the 1995 interim, reflecting a May 1995 agreement to sell the division.

Capitalization

Long Term Debt: $70,000,000 (3/95).

Per Share Data ($)

(Year Ended Dec. 31)

	1994	1993	1992	1991	1990	1989
Tangible Bk. Val.	5.09	6.93	7.04	11.34	11.18	11.32
Cash Flow	1.63	1.53	1.42	1.82	2.04	1.78
Earnings	0.49	0.50	0.35	0.58	0.72	0.44
Dividends	0.40	0.60	0.80	0.80	0.80	0.80
Payout Ratio	82%	120%	231%	140%	111%	183%
Prices - High	16⅛	15	15⅛	15¾	14¾	19⅜
- Low	12⅝	11⅛	10½	9¾	7⅞	13⅝
P/E Ratio - High	33	30	43	27	20	44
- Low	26	22	30	17	11	31

Income Statement Analysis (Million $)

	1994	%Chg	1993	%Chg	1992	%Chg	1991
Revs.	755	NM	759	5%	724	-11%	814
Oper. Inc.	49.0	20%	41.0	NM	41.0	-21%	52.0
Depr.	32.3	16%	27.9	-5%	29.3	-14%	33.9
Int. Exp.	5.1	-4%	5.3	10%	4.8	-28%	6.7
Pretax Inc.	21.0	31%	16.0	60%	10.0	-50%	20.0
Eff. Tax Rate	34%	—	15%	—	7.40%	—	22%
Net Inc.	14.0	2%	13.7	46%	9.4	-39%	15.5

Balance Sheet & Other Fin. Data (Million $)

	1994	1993	1992	1991	1990	1989
Cash	29.8	49.4	50.0	25.4	31.3	40.6
Curr. Assets	222	139	205	143	146	170
Total Assets	630	784	793	751	757	765
Curr. Liab.	121	104	130	100	105	93.0
LT Debt	70.0	51.0	74.0	84.0	67.0	97.0
Common Eqty.	252	189	191	308	303	307
Total Cap.	321	240	265	413	414	456
Cap. Exp.	36.4	29.8	25.7	32.0	40.2	37.9
Cash Flow	46.3	41.6	38.7	49.5	55.3	48.2

Ratio Analysis

	1994	1993	1992	1991	1990	1989
Curr. Ratio	1.8	1.3	1.6	1.4	1.4	1.8
% LT Debt of Cap.	21.6	21.3	27.8	20.4	16.3	21.4
% Net Inc.of Revs.	1.9	1.8	1.3	1.9	2.2	1.4
% Ret. on Assets	1.8	1.7	1.2	2.1	2.6	1.6
% Ret. on Equity	6.0	7.2	3.8	5.1	6.4	3.8

Dividend Data —Dividends have been paid since 1931. A dividend reinvestment plan is available.

Amt. of Div. $	Date Decl.	Ex-Div. Date	Stock of Record	Payment Date
0.100	Jul. 28	Aug. 09	Aug. 15	Sep. 15 '94
0.100	Oct. 27	Nov. 08	Nov. 15	Dec. 15 '94
0.100	Jan. 26	Feb. 09	Feb. 15	Mar. 15 '95
0.100	Apr. 28	May. 09	May. 15	Jun. 15 '95
0.100	Jul. 28	Aug. 11	Aug. 15	Sep. 15 '95

Data as orig. reptd.; bef. results of disc. opers. and/or spec. items. Per share data adj. for stk. divs. as of ex-div. date. E-Estimated. NA-Not Available. NM-Not Meaningful. NR-Not Ranked.

Office—255 Elm Street (P.O. Box 989), Oil City, PA 16301. **Tel**—(814) 676-7676. **Chrmn & CEO**—H. M. Baum. **Vice Chrmn & CFO**—C. A. Conrad. **V. Chrmn**—D. Myatt. **Pres & COO**—J. D. Barr. **VP & Secy**—P. E. Konney. **Investor Contact**—S. D. Blum. **Dirs**—H. M. Baum, L. M. Carroll, C. A. Conrad, L. Cutler, C. F. Fetterolf, T. A. Gardner, F. W. Grube, F. R. Haselton, D. J. McQuaide, D. Myatt, R. A. Ross Jr., L. R. Waxlax. **Transfer Agent & Registrar**—Mellon Securities Trust Co., NYC. **Incorporated** in Delaware in 1931. **Empl**-3,848. **S&P Analyst:** Raymond J. Deacon

Quantum Corp.

NASDAQ Symbol **QNTM**
In S&P MidCap 400

10-SEP-95

Industry:
Data Processing

Summary: This major vendor of hard disk drives for use in personal computers and workstations, expanded its operations with the late 1994 purchase of Digital Equipment's storage business.

S&P Opinion: Accumulate (★★★★)

Recent Price • 26
52 Wk Range • 28½-13¾
Yield • Nil
12-Mo. P/E • 35.6

Quantitative Evaluations

Outlook
(1 Lowest—5 Highest)
• **5-**

Fair Value
• **29¾**

Risk
• **Average**

Earn./Div. Rank
• **B-**

Technical Eval.
• **Bearish** since 6/95

Rel. Strength Rank
(1 Lowest—99 Highest)
• **68**

Insider Activity
• **NA**

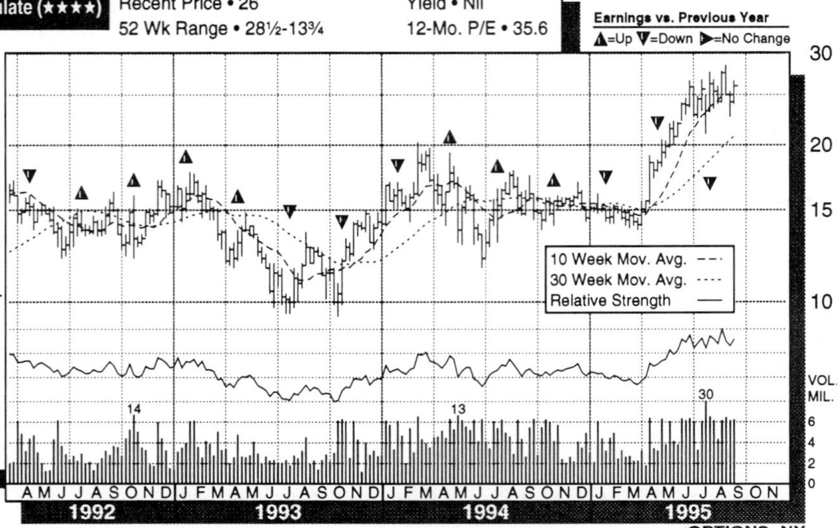

OPTIONS: NY

Overview - 14-AUG-95

Sales should continue to rise in 1995-96, on greater unit volume reflecting continued strong demand for personal computers and contributions from the storage business acquired from Digital Equipment (DEC) in December 1994. Margins narrowed in the first quarter of 1995-96, on lower than expected sales owing to component shortages and delays in high-end product qualifications, as well as costs of integrating DEC's storage unit. However, profitabillity should improve for the remainder of 1995-96 on improvements in component availability, the final qualification and subsequent shipment of major products, a favorable pricing environment, merger-related synergies and continued cost controls. Earnings comparisons for the full fiscal 1995-96 year should benefit from the higher revenues and the absence of nonrecurring charges.

Valuation - 14-AUG-95

The shares of this leading disk drive vendor broke out sharply to the upside in April 1995 on evidence of strong demand and indications of a less aggressive pricing environment. Despite a weak June 1995 quarter, stemming from issues related to major product transitions (since resolved), demand for disk drives remains strong and earnings for fiscal 1995-96 are expected to advance. Strong relationships with major OEMs, as well as the company's ability to manage product cycles, add a level of confidence that could boost the current low P/E multiple. Based on our projected EPS, the shares should outperform the market.

Key Stock Statistics

S&P EPS Est. 1996	2.20	Tang. Bk. Value/Share	9.84
P/E on S&P Est. 1996	11.8	Beta	1.59
Dividend Rate/Share	Nil	Shareholders	2,000
Shs. outstg. (M)	51.7	Market cap. (B)	$ 1.3
Avg. daily vol. (M)	1.670	Inst. holdings	79%
		Insider holdings	NA

Value of $10,000 invested 5 years ago: $ 35,862

Fiscal Year Ending Mar. 31

	1996	% Change	1995	% Change	1994	% Change
Revenues (Million $)						
1Q	941.3	30%	725.3	51%	479.1	30%
2Q	—	—	726.2	47%	494.0	36%
3Q	—	—	932.7	78%	523.0	14%
4Q	—	—	983.8	55%	635.0	25%
Yr.	—	—	3,368	58%	2,131	26%
Income (Million $)						
1Q	12.94	-78%	58.24	NM	3.37	-84%
2Q	—	—	48.60	NM	-45.34	NM
3Q	—	—	-48.31	NM	6.14	-78%
4Q	—	—	23.06	-40%	38.50	47%
Yr.	—	—	81.59	NM	2.67	-97%
Earnings Per Share ($)						
1Q	0.25	-80%	1.24	NM	0.08	-83%
2Q	E0.60	-42%	1.03	NM	-1.02	NM
3Q	E0.65	NM	-1.06	NM	0.14	-77%
4Q	E0.70	46%	0.48	-42%	0.83	43%
Yr.	E2.20	28%	1.72	NM	0.06	-97%

Next earnings report expected: late October

Quantum Corp.

Business Summary - 22-AUG-95

Quantum Corporation designs, manufactures and markets mass stoarge products, including 31/2-inch and 21/2-inch hard disk drives for use in desktop personal computers (PCs), workstations and notebook computers.

The company's primary product line consists of 3.5-inch hard disk drives designed for the desktop PC and workstation marketplace. Drive capacities range from 270 megabytes (MBs) to 4.3 gigabytes (GBs) and are available with imbedded Small Computer Systems Interface (SCSI) or AT-bus controllers.

Quantum's line of 2.5-inch hard disk drives are designed for the notebook and subnotebook computer markets. Capacities range from 256 to 514 MBs, and they also are available with imbedded SCSI or AT-bus controllers.

The company also makes solid state disks, tape drives and PCMCIA-based flash memory cards.

High-volume disk drives are made by the company's Japanese partner, Matsushita-Kotobuki Electronics, which manufactured products contributing about 80% of company sales in 1994-5, versus 90% in 1993-4. Higher-capacity, more technically complex products are made in Quantum's California manufacturing facility.

The company markets its products directly to original equipment manufacturers (OEMs) and distributors through a worldwide sales force.

In 1994-5, Compaq Computer accounted for 16% of sales (10% in fiscal 1993-4) and Apple Computer accounted for 12% of sales (22%). International sales provided 53% (53%) of the total.

Important Developments

Jul. '95—Revenue for the first quarter of fiscal 1995-6 was below expectations, reflecting delays in customer qualification of certain new high end disk drives, as well as component shortages which limited the number of drives able to be manufactured. The company said that it had finalized or was near final qualification of the high end products at several important OEM customers, and had taken steps that would lessen the impact of the component availability issues going forward.

Jul. '95—During the first quarter of fiscal 1995-6, the company shipped about 4.6 million disk drives.

Jan. '95—During the 1994-5 third quarter, QNTM recorded a charge of $72,945,000 ($1.21 a share) for in process R&D and certain other costs related to the acquisition of Digital Equipment Corp's storage business.

Capitalization

Long Term Debt: $339,056,000 (6/95), incl. 149,056,000 of 6.375% sub. debs. due 2002, conv. into com. at $18.15 a sh.

Per Share Data ($) (Year Ended Mar. 31)

	1995	1994	1993	1992	1991	1990
Tangible Bk. Val.	8.96	9.22	9.01	7.19	6.09	3.90
Cash Flow	2.85	0.71	2.64	1.68	2.00	1.27
Earnings	1.72	0.06	2.05	1.05	1.69	1.14
Dividends	Nil	Nil	Nil	Nil	Nil	Nil
Payout Ratio	Nil	Nil	Nil	Nil	Nil	Nil
Cal. Yrs.	1994	1993	1992	1991	1990	1989
Prices - High	20¼	17¾	18	18⅛	17⅛	11
- Low	11⅝	9⅜	11⅛	8⅞	5⅞	2⅞
P/E Ratio - High	12	NM	9	17	10	10
- Low	7	NM	5	8	3	2

Income Statement Analysis (Million $)

	1995	%Chg	1994	%Chg	1993	%Chg	1992
Revs.	3,368	58%	2,131	26%	1,697	50%	1,128
Oper. Inc.	214	NM	62.0	-65%	176	71%	103
Depr.	53.3	82%	29.3	9%	26.9	-4%	28.1
Int. Exp.	23.0	54%	14.9	3%	14.4	86%	7.8
Pretax Inc.	145	NM	4.0	-97%	147	99%	74.0
Eff. Tax Rate	44%	—	27%	—	36%	—	37%
Net Inc.	81.6	NM	2.7	-97%	93.8	100%	46.8

Balance Sheet & Other Fin. Data (Million $)

	1995	1994	1993	1992	1991	1990
Cash	188	330	289	145	115	79.0
Curr. Assets	1,090	896	830	453	396	185
Total Assets	1,481	997	927	547	489	243
Curr. Liab.	644	374	316	236	248	83.0
LT Debt	328	213	213	Nil	Nil	Nil
Common Eqty.	509	411	398	308	238	154
Total Cap.	837	624	611	311	242	160
Cap. Exp.	128	38.4	36.1	37.8	46.0	16.7
Cash Flow	135	32.0	121	75.0	87.1	52.5

Ratio Analysis

	1995	1994	1993	1992	1991	1990
Curr. Ratio	1.7	2.4	2.6	1.9	1.6	2.2
% LT Debt of Cap.	39.2	34.1	34.8	Nil	Nil	Nil
% Net Inc.of Revs.	2.4	0.1	5.5	4.2	8.4	10.6
% Ret. on Assets	6.6	0.3	12.7	8.7	19.8	23.2
% Ret. on Equity	17.7	0.7	26.4	16.5	36.9	36.6

Dividend Data —No cash has been paid on the common stock.

Data as orig. reptd.; bef. results of disc. opers. and/or spec. items. Per share data adj. for stk. divs. as of ex-div. date. E-Estimated. NA-Not Available. NM-Not Meaningful. NR-Not Ranked.

Office—500 McCarthy Blvd., Milpitas, CA 95035. **Tel**—(408) 894-4000. **Chrmn & CEO**—W. J. Miller. **EVP**—M. A. Brown. **EVP-Fin, CFO & Secy**—J. T. Rodgers. **Dirs**—S. M. Berkley, D. A. Brown, R. J. Casale, E. M. Esber, Jr., W. J. Miller, S. C. Wheelwright. **Transfer Agent**—Harris Trust Co. of California (c/o Harris Trust & Savings Bank, Chicago). **Incorporated** in California in 1980; reincorporated in Delaware in 1987. **Empl**-7,265. **S&P Analyst:** Peter C. Wood, CFA

STANDARD & POOR'S

STOCK REPORTS

Questar Corp.

NYSE Symbol **STR**
In S&P MidCap 400

27-SEP-95 **Industry:** Utilities-Gas

Summary: This integrated natural gas holding company is primarily engaged in gas and oil exploration, interstate gas gathering, transportation and storage, and retail gas distribution.

S&P Opinion: Hold (★★★)

Recent Price • 32¾ | Yield • 3.7%
52 Wk Range • 33-26⅛ | 12-Mo. P/E • 15.8

Quantitative Evaluations

Outlook (1 Lowest—5 Highest) • **2-**

Fair Value • **30¼**

Risk • **Low**

Earn./Div. Rank • **A-**

Technical Eval. • **Bullish** since 9/95

Rel. Strength Rank (1 Lowest—99 Highest) • **68**

Insider Activity • **Neutral**

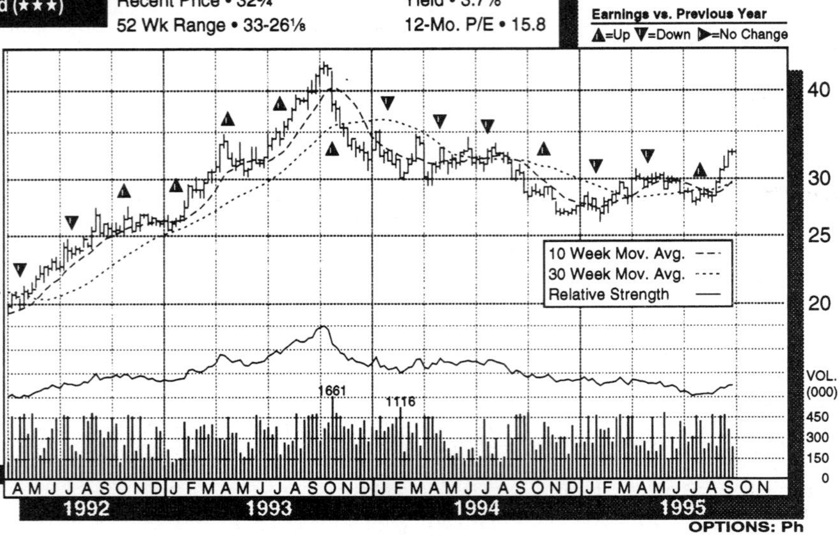

OPTIONS: Ph

Overview - 27-SEP-95

Share earnings are projected to decrease modestly in 1995 from $2.16 in 1994 (before a non-recurring gain and a writedown), as low wellhead gas prices continue to negatively impact results. However, earnings should rebound in 1996, reflecting rising gas prices and improved exploration and production operations, higher gathering volumes at Questar Pipeline, and increased volumes delivered to industrial customers by Mountain Fuel. A strong local economy, cost containment efforts, and an early retirement program should also contribute to increased profitability. In July 1995, Questar Pipeline filed a general rate case for an annual increase in revenue of $23.3 million.

Valuation - 27-SEP-95

STR shares plummeted about 22% in 1994, reflecting the impact of rising interest rates and depressed natural gas prices. However, the shares have rebounded about 18% since the beginning of 1995, and were recently trading at about 14X the 1996 EPS estimate of $2.30. The dividend was recently increased 3.5%, and the shares are currently yielding around 3.7%. Dividend hikes of 3% to 4% should continue in coming years. Although energy prices should rise in 1996, and long-term prospects appear bright, the shares are fairly valued, and should be only average market performers over the next 12 months.

Key Stock Statistics

S&P EPS Est. 1995	2.10	Tang. Bk. Value/Share	15.93
P/E on S&P Est. 1995	15.6	Beta	0.35
S&P EPS Est. 1996	2.30	Shareholders	11,500
Dividend Rate/Share	1.18	Market cap. (B)	$ 1.3
Shs. outstg. (M)	40.6	Inst. holdings	77%
Avg. daily vol. (M)	0.091	Insider holdings	NA

Value of $10,000 invested 5 years ago: $ 21,610

Fiscal Year Ending Dec. 31

	1995	% Change	1994	% Change	1993	% Change
Revenues (Million $)						
1Q	215.9	-3%	223.3	-9%	245.5	9%
2Q	138.6	2%	135.4	3%	131.7	20%
3Q	—	—	112.2	12%	100.2	11%
4Q	—	—	201.2	10%	183.0	2%
Yr.	—	—	670.3	1%	660.4	9%
Income (Million $)						
1Q	27.07	-13%	31.09	-14%	36.02	19%
2Q	14.56	5%	13.93	-13%	16.03	166%
3Q	—	—	9.03	30%	6.97	12%
4Q	—	—	-4.64	NM	25.44	-12%
Yr.	—	—	49.42	-41%	84.46	18%
Earnings Per Share ($)						
1Q	0.67	-13%	0.77	-14%	0.90	18%
2Q	0.35	3%	0.34	-15%	0.40	167%
3Q	E0.25	14%	0.22	29%	0.17	13%
4Q	E0.83	NM	-0.12	NM	0.64	-12%
Yr.	E2.10	74%	1.21	-42%	2.10	17%

Next earnings report expected: late October

Questar Corp.

Business Summary - 27-SEP-95

Questar is a holding company whose subsidiaries are engaged primarily in natural gas distribution and transmission, and in the exploration and production of natural gas and oil. It also provides data processing and microwave communication services and owns and manages real estate. Contributions by business segment in 1994 were:

	Revs.	Profits
Gas distribution	56%	26%
Expl. & prod.	38%	38%
Gas transmission	6%	34%
Other	Nil	2%

Natural gas distribution operations are conducted by Mountain Fuel Supply, which at 1994 year-end served 572,174 customers, with 96% in Utah and the remainder in southwestern Wyoming and southeastern Idaho. Gas deliveries in 1994 totaled 135 million decatherms, down from 139 million in 1993. The number of heating degree days in 1994 amounted to 5,290, versus 6,073 in 1993.

Oil and gas exploration and production operations are conducted through Celsius Energy Co. mainly in the Rocky Mountain region; Universal Resources Corp. in Midcontinent areas; and Wexpro Co., which develops gas reserves owned by Mountain Fuel Supply. Total proved reserves at year-end 1994 were estimated at 13.5 million bbl. of oil and 267.8 million Mcf of gas.

Questar Pipeline Co. owns and operates interstate pipeline systems in Utah, Wyoming and Colorado, and operates gas storage facilities in Utah and Wyoming. It also has an 18% interest in and operates the 88-mile Overthrust segment of the 800-mile Trailblazer Pipeline running between Wyoming and Nebraska.

Other units include Questar Development Corp. and Questar InfoComm, Inc. The Questar Telecom subsidiary was sold in August 1994.

Important Developments

Sep. '95—Questar Pipeline entered into an agreement to purchase Tenneco Gas' 50% interest in the Kern River gas pipeline for about $225 million in cash. The transaction is subject to a right to match by The Williams Cos., which owns 50% of Kern River.

Jul. '95—Questar Pipeline filed a general rate case with the FERC seeking a $23.3 million increase in annual revenues, effective January 1, 1996. The pipeline, currently earning about a 13% return on equity, asked for a 14.5% return on equity. Questar Pipeline concurrently filed a plan to "spin down" its gathering division by transferring about $60 million in net assets to Questar Gas Management Co., a wholly owned, non-regulated subsidiary.

Capitalization

Long Term Debt: $477,692,000 (6/95).
Cum. Red. Preferred Stock: $6,218,000.

Per Share Data ($)

(Year Ended Dec. 31)

	1994	1993	1992	1991	1990	1989
Tangible Bk. Val.	16.17	14.99	13.55	12.49	11.76	11.54
Cash Flow	3.52	4.37	3.80	3.45	3.16	2.91
Earnings	1.21	2.10	1.79	1.63	1.46	1.28
Dividends	1.13	1.09	1.04	1.01	0.97	0.95
Payout Ratio	93%	52%	59%	63%	66%	75%
Prices - High	35¼	44	27½	24¾	19⅞	19⅞
- Low	26⅝	25⅜	18½	16⅝	16⅜	15¾
P/E Ratio - High	29	21	15	15	14	16
- Low	22	12	10	10	11	12

Income Statement Analysis (Million $)

	1994	%Chg	1993	%Chg	1992	%Chg	1991
Revs.	670	2%	660	9%	605	-4%	632
Oper. Inc.	248	4%	239	12%	213	7%	200
Depr.	93.0	2%	91.2	15%	79.4	13%	70.3
Int. Exp.	41.6	17%	35.7	-3%	36.9	NM	37.1
Pretax Inc.	58.0	-51%	118	12%	105	4%	101
Eff. Tax Rate	15%	—	28%	—	32%	—	37%
Net Inc.	48.8	-42%	83.8	19%	70.5	12%	63.1

Balance Sheet & Other Fin. Data (Million $)

	1994	1993	1992	1991	1990	1989
Cash	7.5	6.4	7.3	6.0	11.1	22.5
Curr. Assets	193	187	177	165	165	163
Total Assets	1,586	1,418	1,324	1,220	1,151	1,075
Curr. Liab.	220	223	215	173	173	164
LT Debt	495	372	365	354	328	276
Common Eqty.	654	602	554	502	460	456
Total Cap.	1,319	1,149	1,095	1,033	965	898
Cap. Exp.	268	161	169	133	138	92.0
Cash Flow	142	175	150	133	123	113

Ratio Analysis

	1994	1993	1992	1991	1990	1989
Curr. Ratio	0.9	0.8	0.8	1.0	1.0	1.0
% LT Debt of Cap.	37.5	32.4	33.3	34.3	34.0	30.7
% Net Inc.of Revs.	7.3	12.7	11.7	10.0	10.5	9.7
% Ret. on Assets	3.2	6.1	5.5	5.3	5.1	4.6
% Ret. on Equity	7.8	14.4	13.3	13.0	12.5	10.7

Dividend Data —Dividends have been paid since 1935. A poison pill stock purchase rights plan was adopted in 1986.

Amt. of Div. $	Date Decl.	Ex-Div. Date	Stock of Record	Payment Date
0.285	Oct. 28	Nov. 14	Nov. 18	Dec. 12 '94
0.285	Feb. 14	Feb. 17	Feb. 24	Mar. 13 '95
0.285	May. 16	May. 22	May. 26	Jun. 19 '95
0.295	Aug. 08	Aug. 16	Aug. 18	Sep. 11 '95

Data as orig. reptd.; bef. results of disc. opers. and/or spec. items. Per share data adj. for stk. divs. as of ex-div. date. E-Estimated. NA-Not Available. NM-Not Meaningful. NR-Not Ranked.

Office—180 East First South St., Salt Lake City, UT 84147. **Tel**—(801) 534-5000. **Chrmn, Pres & CEO**—R. D. Cash. **SVP & CFO**—W. F. Edwards. **VP & Secy**—Connie C. Holbrook. **VP & Treas**—S. E. Parks. **Investor Contact**—R. Curtis Burnett. **Dirs**—R. D. Cash, P. J. Early, U. E. Garrison, J. A. Harmon, W. W. Hawkins, W. N. Jones, R. E. Kadlec, D. L. Leavitt, N. A. Maxwell, M. Mead, G. G. Michael, N. Rose, H. H. Simmons. **Transfer Agents**—First Chicago Trust Co. of New York, Jersey City, NJ; Co.'s office. **Registrars**—Mellon Bank, Pittsburgh; Zions First National Bank, Salt Lake City. **Incorporated** in Utah in 1935. **Empl**-2,624. **S&P Analyst:** Ronald J. Gross

STANDARD & POOR'S
STOCK REPORTS

RPM, Inc.

NASDAQ Symbol **RPOW**
In S&P MidCap 400

31-JUL-95

Industry: Coatings, paint, varnishes

Summary: RPM makes specialty coatings and products for the structural waterproofing and corrosion control markets, as well as products for the consumer, do-it-yourself and hobby markets.

S&P Opinion: Hold (★★★)

Recent Price • 20⅛
52 Wk Range • 20⅞-17¼
Yield • 2.8%
12-Mo. P/E • 18.8

Quantitative Evaluations
Outlook
(1 Lowest—5 Highest)
• 1-
Fair Value
• 15¾
Risk
• Low
Earn./Div. Rank
• A+

Technical Eval.
• Bullish since 7/95
Rel. Strength Rank
(1 Lowest—99 Highest)
• 38
Insider Activity
• NA

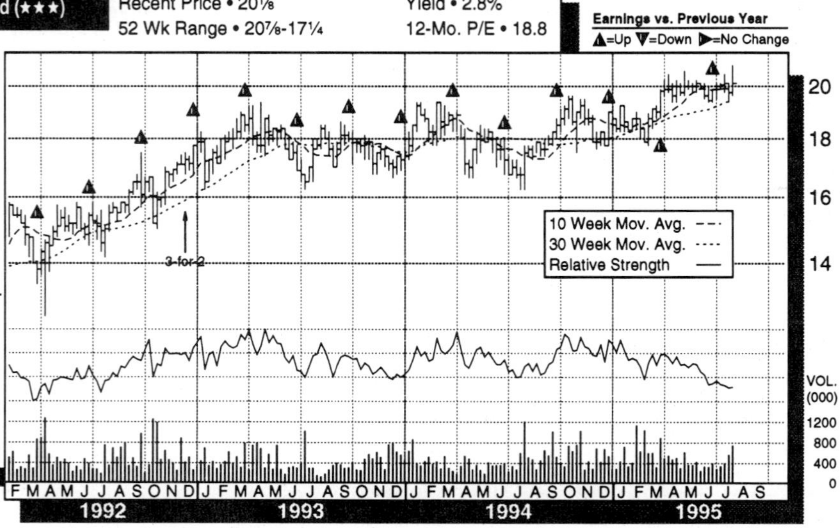

Overview - 31-JUL-95

Sales (which passed the $1 billion mark in 1994-5) and earnings are expected to show double digit growth in 1995-6, aided by the integration of Rust-Oleum. The planned acquisition of Dryvit Systems (expected to completed by the end of September) should further boost results. Internal growth should continue, with core industrial and consumer products expected to stay strong. Although the addition of Rust-Oleum will lead to higher SG&A expense, it will also result in wider gross and operating margins, as it shifts the revenue mix to the higher-margin consumer segment. Although the acquisition substantially increased interest expense, the balance sheet should remain strong.

Valuation - 31-JUL-95

The shares have gained more than 20% since the June 1994 acquisition of Rust-Oleum. The acquisition contributed significantly to 25% growth in sales in 1994-5, and should be a major factor in double-digit sales and earnings growth expected for 1995-6. In a year when the industry was hurt by a strong rise in the cost of raw materials, RPM's gross margins widened, as the strength of its branded consumer products enabled it to pass on cost increases. Nevertheless, the shares seem fairly valued at current levels.

Key Stock Statistics

S&P EPS Est. 1996	1.20	Tang. Bk. Value/Share	3.13
P/E on S&P Est. 1996	16.8	Beta	1.16
Dividend Rate/Share	0.56	Shareholders	19,200
Shs. outstg. (M)	56.9	Market cap. (B)	$ 1.1
Avg. daily vol. (M)	0.104	Inst. holdings	38%
		Insider holdings	NA

Value of $10,000 invested 5 years ago: $ 23,314

Fiscal Year Ending May 31

	1995	% Change	1994	% Change	1993	% Change
Revenues (Million $)						
1Q	253.5	21%	210.0	27%	166.0	28%
2Q	253.2	25%	202.2	32%	153.0	10%
3Q	229.8	23%	186.6	35%	138.6	10%
4Q	280.4	29%	217.0	30%	167.5	7%
Yr.	1,017	25%	815.6	30%	625.7	13%
Income (Million $)						
1Q	18.39	32%	13.92	—	—	—
2Q	15.27	10%	13.93	30%	10.74	7%
3Q	7.30	11%	6.57	39%	4.72	10%
4Q	20.10	—	—	—	11.95	21%
Yr.	61.10	16%	52.64	34%	39.38	13%
Earnings Per Share ($)						
1Q	0.32	19%	0.27	8%	0.25	19%
2Q	0.27	8%	0.25	9%	0.23	10%
3Q	0.13	8%	0.12	20%	0.10	11%
4Q	0.35	21%	0.29	16%	0.25	19%
Yr.	1.07	15%	0.93	12%	0.83	14%

Next earnings report expected: early October

RPM, Inc.

Business Summary - 31-JUL-95

RPM, Inc. is a worldwide producer of coatings, sealants and specialty chemicals for industrial and consumer markets.

The company participates in five broad market categories worldwide: industrial waterproofing and general maintenance; industrial corrosion-control; specialty chemicals; consumer do-it-yourself; and consumer hobby and leisure. It serves niche markets within these broader categories, providing a foundation for its strategy of growth through product line extensions.

Protective coating products manufactured by RPM are used primarily to provide waterproofing and corrosion control for existing goods or structures and are generally not affected by cyclical movements in the economy.

The company has pursued an aggressive acquisition policy. In June 1991, it purchased Rust-Oleum's European operations. In June 1994, Rust-Oleum's remaining worldwide operations were acquired.

In October 1991, Day-Glo Color Corp., an Ohio manufacturer and marketer of fluorescent pigments and colorants, was acquired. In March 1992, RPM purchased, through its wholly owned Belgian subsidiary Radiant Color N.V., Martin Mathys N.V., a Belgian manufacturer and seller of specialized protective coatings.

In May 1992, the company bought Sentry Polymers, a manufacturer of high performance concrete coatings. In June 1993, the company purchased Dynatron/Bondo Corp., a supplier of specialty automotive repair materials.

International operations currently account for about 12% of sales. RPM also receives license fees and royalty income from many license agreements and joint ventures in other countries.

The company markets its products in more than 110 countries, and operates more than 45 plants worldwide.

Important Developments

Jul. '95—RPM agreed to acquire Dryvit Systems, a leading maker and marketer of exterior insulation and finishing systems, with annual sales of about $70 million. The transaction is expected to close by September 30, 1995.

Capitalization

Long Term Debt: $406,375,000 (5/95).

Per Share Data ($) (Year Ended May 31)

	1995	1994	1993	1992	1991	1990
Tangible Bk. Val.	NA	3.13	2.12	1.68	2.43	1.43
Cash Flow	NA	1.38	1.28	1.15	0.99	0.95
Earnings	1.07	0.93	0.83	0.73	0.69	0.65
Dividends	0.55	0.51	0.47	0.44	0.40	0.35
Payout Ratio	51%	55%	57%	60%	58%	54%
Cal. Yrs.	1994	1993	1992	1991	1990	1989
Prices - High	19⅝	19⅜	18½	15½	12⅛	11
- Low	16¼	16¼	12⅝	10⅞	8¼	8⅛
P/E Ratio - High	18	21	22	21	18	16
- Low	15	17	15	15	12	13

Income Statement Analysis (Million $)

	1994	%Chg	1993	%Chg	1992	%Chg	1991
Revs.	816	30%	626	13%	552	10%	500
Oper. Inc.	127	26%	101	15%	88.1	25%	70.6
Depr.	25.9	21%	21.4	10%	19.4	35%	14.4
Int. Exp.	14.3	46%	9.8	-29%	13.9	43%	9.7
Pretax Inc.	88.1	33%	66.1	15%	57.3	11%	51.7
Eff. Tax Rate	40%	—	40%	—	40%	—	38%
Net Inc.	52.6	34%	39.4	13%	34.8	9%	31.8

Balance Sheet & Other Fin. Data (Million $)

	1994	1993	1992	1991	1990	1989
Cash	25.4	24.8	27.3	18.6	2.5	6.0
Curr. Assets	335	281	263	205	186	150
Total Assets	661	585	559	401	375	286
Curr. Liab.	108	118	90.1	75.7	63.2	56.8
LT Debt	233	221	239	114	145	77.0
Common Eqty.	314	239	222	206	161	147
Total Cap.	552	467	467	324	311	229
Cap. Exp.	25.7	18.4	17.1	16.4	10.7	8.9
Cash Flow	78.5	60.8	53.9	46.2	39.9	34.4

Ratio Analysis

	1994	1993	1992	1991	1990	1989
Curr. Ratio	3.1	2.4	2.9	2.7	2.9	2.6
% LT Debt of Cap.	42.2	47.3	51.1	35.3	46.7	33.6
% Net Inc.of Revs.	6.5	6.3	6.2	6.4	6.2	6.4
% Ret. on Assets	7.7	6.9	7.1	7.8	8.4	8.9
% Ret. on Equity	17.5	17.1	16.0	16.6	18.0	17.1

Dividend Data (Cash has been paid each year since 1969.)

Amt. of Div. $	Date Decl.	Ex-Div. Date	Stock of Record	Payment Date
0.140	Oct. 10	Oct. 17	Oct. 21	Oct. 31 '94
0.140	Jan. 09	Jan. 13	Jan. 20	Jan. 31 '95
0.140	Apr. 03	Apr. 07	Apr. 14	Apr. 28 '95
0.140	Jul. 06	Jul. 13	Jul. 17	Jul. 31 '95

Data as orig. reptd.; bef. results of disc. opers. and/or spec. items. Per share data adj. for stk. divs. as of ex-div. date. E-Estimated. NA-Not Available. NM-Not Meaningful. NR-Not Ranked.

Office—2628 Pearl Rd., P.O. Box 777, Medina, OH 44258. **Tel**—(216) 273-5090. **Fax**—(216) 225-8743. **Chrmn & CEO**—T. C. Sullivan. **Pres & COO**—J. A. Karman. **VP & CFO**—F. C. Sullivan. **VP & Secy**—P. A. Granzier. **VP & Treas**—R. E. Klar. **Investor Contact**—Kathy Rogers. **Dirs**—M.D. Amstutz, E. B. Brandon, L. Gustin, R. H. Holdt, E. B. Jones, J. A. Karman, D. K. Miller, J. H. Morris, Jr., K. O'Donnell, W. A. Papenbrock, S. Stranahan, T. C. Sullivan. **Registrar & Transfer Agent**—Society Corp., Cleveland. **Incorporated** in Ohio in 1947. **Empl**-4,500. **S&P Analyst:** Justin McCann

Ranger Oil

NYSE Symbol RGO Options on Toronto In S&P MidCap 400

Price	Range	P–E Ratio	Dividend	Yield	S&P Ranking	Beta
Oct. 8'95	1995					
5⅞	7½–5⅜	84	[1]0.08	[1]1.4%	B	0.22

Summary

This Canadian company explores for and produces crude oil and natural gas in the U.K., the Netherlands' sectors of the North Sea, North America, Africa and Peru. Earnings rose in 1995's first half, aided by increased oil and gas production and higher transportation and processing income.

Business Summary

Ranger Oil Limited explores for, develops and produces crude oil and natural gas in North America, including offshore the U.S. Gulf Coast, the U.K. and the Netherlands' sectors of the North Sea. In 1994, Ranger also conducted exploration activities in Angola, Namibia, Algeria and Peru. Other activities include a 50% interest in offshore drilling equipment used in the North Sea.

Northeastern British Columbia became Ranger's largest gas production area in North America in 1994, with east central Alberta becoming the second largest. In the U.S. Gulf Coast, gas production rates built up in 1994 and are expected to increase in 1995 as new wells are brought onstream.

Ranger's two main oil producing fields in the North Sea, Ninian and Columba, are located in the northern sector. Ninian has been producing since 1979 and Columba commenced production in 1994. In 1994, a 4.2% interest was acquired in the Claymore oil field, and Ranger increased its interests in the Ninian and Columba oil fields to 15.8% and 55%, respectively.

The Southern Gas Basin contains Ranger's two producing gas fields: Anglia (37.9% interest) and Markham (3.9% interest). In 1994, Ranger sold its 10% interest in Block 29/5b containing the Franklin and part of the Elgin gas and condensate fields for $42.5 million. Exploration efforts are being concentrated in the Faeroe-Shetland basin west of the Shetland Islands. Ranger has a 25% interest in Tranche 8, which is adjacent to two major discoveries made by British Petroleum.

Daily production in 1994 totaled 15,039 bbl. of crude oil and natural gas liquids (13,779 in 1993) and 106,200 Mcf of natural gas (112,900). Proved reserves at December 31, 1994, amounted to 51,516,000 bbl. of oil and natural gas liquids (36,931,000 bbl. a year earlier), of which 82% was in the North Sea and 18% was in North America, and 301.0 Bcf of natural gas (293.2 Bcf), with 33% in the North Sea and 67% in North America.

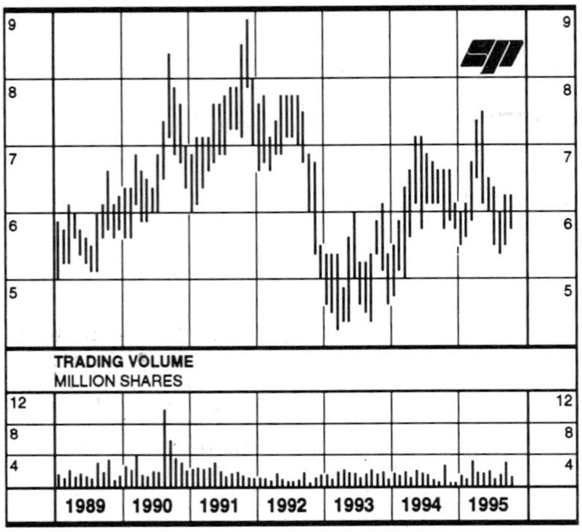

At 1994 year-end, the company had 610,182 gross (213,737 net) developed acres, mostly in Canada, and 6,548,485 gross (2,202,177 net) undeveloped acres, primarily in Africa and other foreign areas. During 1994, RGO spent $179 million on oil and gas property acquisition, exploration and development activities, up 50% from the 1993 level.

Important Developments

Aug. '95— Net capital expenditures in the first six months of 1995 were $48.1 million ($23.6 million in North America), compared with $55.0 million in 1994's first half. In the North Sea, outlays of $15.4 million were focused on developing the Harding, Columba and Claymore oil fields. Total international expenditures of $9.1 million were incurred primarily in Angola, Namibia and Peru. Ranger drilled 24 exploration and appraisal wells in 1995's first half, with a success rate of 63%.

Next earnings report expected in early November.

Per Share Data (U.S. $)

Yr. End Dec. 31	1994	1993	[6]1992	1991	1990	1989	1988	1987	[2]1986	1985
Tangible Bk. Val.	**4.65**	4.67	4.55	4.39	4.36	3.69	2.71	2.52	2.22	3.03
Cash Flow	**0.82**	0.90	0.93	0.53	1.11	0.84	0.68	0.66	0.72	0.42
Earnings[3]	**0.06**	0.21	0.24	0.06	[4]0.46	[4]0.27	0.12	0.20	0.06	d0.35
Dividends[5]	**0.08**	0.08	0.08	0.08	0.06	Nil	Nil	Nil	Nil	Nil
Payout Ratio	**133%**	38%	34%	146%	14%	Nil	Nil	Nil	Nil	Nil
Prices—High	**7⅛**	6⅛	7¾	8⅞	8⅜	6⅝	6½	6¾	5⅛	5½
Low	**4¾**	4¼	5	6	5⅝	5	4	3⅛	2⅝	2½
P/E Ratio—	**NM**	29–20	32–21	NM	18–12	25–19	54–33	34–16	85–44	NM

Data as orig. reptd. **1.** Annual divd. paid in Apr. 1995; in U.S. funds, bef. 15% Canadian tax to U.S. residents. **2.** Refl. merger or acq. & acctg. change. **3.** Bef. spec items of +0.36 in 1989, +0.07 in 1988, +0.10 in 1987, -0.95 in 1986, +0.02 in 1985. **4.** Ful dil.: 0.45 in 1990, 0.26 in 1989. **5.** Bef. 15% Canadian tax to U.S. residents. **6.** Refl. merger or acq. d-Deficit. NM-Not Meaningful.

Income Data (Million U.S. $)

Year Ended Dec. 31	[1]Revs.	Oper. Inc.	% Oper. Inc. of Revs.	Cap. Exp.	Depr.	Int. Exp.	[3]Net Bef. Taxes	Eff. Tax Rate	[4]Net Inc.	% Net Inc. of Revs.	Cash Flow
1994	**156**	**89.5**	**57.4**	**177**	**75.1**	**5.12**	**11.9**	**49.0%**	**6.1**	**3.9**	**81.2**
1993	144	86.4	60.0	120	68.9	2.00	24.2	16.5%	20.2	14.0	89.1
[6]1992	144	76.0	52.9	185	68.3	1.30	16.4	NM	23.5	16.3	91.8
1991	112	54.0	48.5	157	46.4	1.80	4.5	NM	5.8	5.2	51.8
1990	144	87.0	60.6	89	57.2	5.20	41.2	NM	[5]42.4	29.5	98.3
1989	118	69.0	58.6	110	45.1	6.30	32.6	28.7%	23.2	19.7	67.0
1988	85	55.0	64.4	100	42.0	9.50	13.0	21.6%	10.2	12.0	50.8
1987	80	51.0	64.3	28	34.6	7.80	25.6	35.7%	16.5	20.6	49.7
[2]1986	77	50.0	64.0	66	48.3	5.10	7.7	28.8%	5.5	7.1	52.3
1985	142	62.0	43.3	49	53.8	7.90	d26.6	NM	d23.9	NM	28.9

Balance Sheet Data (Million U.S. $)

Dec. 31	Cash	Curr. Assets	Curr. Liab.	Curr. Ratio	Total Assets	% Ret. on Assets	Long Term Debt	Common Equity	Total Cap.	% LT Debt of Cap.	% Ret. on Equity
1994	**46**	**77**	**104**	**0.7**	**752**	**0.8**	**50**	**459**	**599**	**8.3**	**1.3**
1993	21	54	36	1.5	680	3.1	50	460	594	8.4	4.4
1992	13	57	29	2.0	641	3.8	33	448	567	5.8	5.3
1991	58	93	44	2.1	590	1.0	3	432	506	0.6	1.3
1990	168	197	47	4.2	589	6.9	6	423	506	1.2	10.5
1989	156	184	48	3.8	565	4.3	82	312	485	16.9	8.1
1988	116	140	31	4.5	459	2.2	82	202	402	20.3	4.5
1987	186	208	45	4.6	471	3.7	87	188	405	21.6	8.5
1986	118	154	57	2.7	420	1.1	37	166	345	10.6	2.1
1985	90	136	43	3.2	504	NM	50	210	446	11.2	NM

Data as orig. reptd. **1.** Excl. other inc. **2.** Refl. merger or acq. & acctg. change. **3.** Incl. equity in earns. of nonconsol. subs. **4.** Bef. spec. items. **5.** Refl. acctg. change. **6.** Refl. merger or acq. d-Deficit. NM-Not Meaningful.

[1]Total Revenues (Million U.S. $)

Quarter:	1995	1994	1993	1992
Mar.	53.8	37.2	43.3	34.2
Jun.	51.0	32.9	38.0	38.0
Sep.		37.3	32.0	40.6
Dec.		51.2	39.3	41.0
		158.6	152.6	153.7

Revenues for the six months ended March 31, 1995, advanced 49%, year to year, primarily reflecting increased oil and gas production and higher transportation and processing income. Expenses rose 46%, and after taxes at 52.1%, versus 23.3%, net income was up 8.7%, to $4,652,000 ($0.05 a share), from $4,280,000 ($0.04).

Common Share Earnings (U.S. $)

Quarter:	1995	1994	1993	1992
Mar.	0.04	0.04	0.07	0.08
Jun.	0.01	Nil	0.05	0.08
Sep.		0.02	0.03	0.02
Dec.		Nil	0.06	0.07
		0.06	0.21	0.24

Finances

In September 1995, Ranger announced its intention to make a cash tender offer of C$1.30 a share for all of the common stock of Czar Resources Ltd. Czar has nearly 70 million common shares outstanding.

In March 1995, RGO said it had entered into an agreement with a third party to sell its interest in the Markham gas field, with the closing planned for the second half of 1995.

In September 1994, the company acquired the remaining 79% of Union Jack Oil plc. RGO now owns 4.2% of the Claymore oil field, and its interest in the Banff oil field rose to 25%.

Dividend Data

Annual dividends were initiated in 1990. A shareholder rights plan was adopted in January 1994.

Amt. of Divd. $	Date Decl.	Ex-divd. Date	Stock of Record	Payment Date
0.08	Mar. 2	Mar. 27	Mar. 31	Apr. 17'95

Capitalization

Long Term Debt: $50,000,000 (6/95).

Common Stock: 98,590,304 shs. (no par). Institutions hold about 33%. Shareholders of record: 7,906 (12/94).

1. Incl. other inc.

Office—Suite 1600, 321 Sixth Ave. S.W., Calgary, AB T2P 3H3, Canada. **Tel**—(403) 232-5200. **Chrmn**—S. S. Reisman. **Pres & CEO**—F. J. Dyment. **VP-Fin & CFO**—J. M. D'Aguiar. **VP & Secy**—J. E. Fletcher. **VP & Investor Contact**—John G. Faulds. **Dirs**—E. M. Bronfman, R. W. Campbell, C. M. Carr Jr., F. J. Dyment, W. A. Gatenby, P. D. Irwin, F. R. Matthews, J. A. Rae, S. S. Reisman. **Transfer Agents & Registrars**—R-M Trust Co., Montreal, Calgary, Vancouver, Toronto, London (U.K.); Mellon Securities Trust Co., NYC. **Incorporated** in Ontario in 1950. **Empl**—190.

STANDARD & POOR'S

STOCK REPORTS

Rayonier Inc.

NYSE Symbol **RYN**
In S&P MidCap 400

31-JUL-95 **Industry:** Building

Summary: RYN trades, merchandises and produces logs, timber and wood products and makes specialty pulps. It owns or controls 1.5 million acres of timberland in the U.S. and New Zealand.

S&P Opinion: Accumulate (★★★★) | Recent Price • 38¾ | 52 Wk Range • 39⅛-27 | Yield • 2.6% | 12-Mo. P/E • 13.5

Quantitative Evaluations
Outlook (1 Lowest—5 Highest) • **NA**
Fair Value • **NA**
Risk • **Low**
Earn./Div. Rank • **NR**

Technical Eval. • **Neutral** since 7/95
Rel. Strength Rank (1 Lowest—99 Highest) • **74**
Insider Activity • **Neutral**

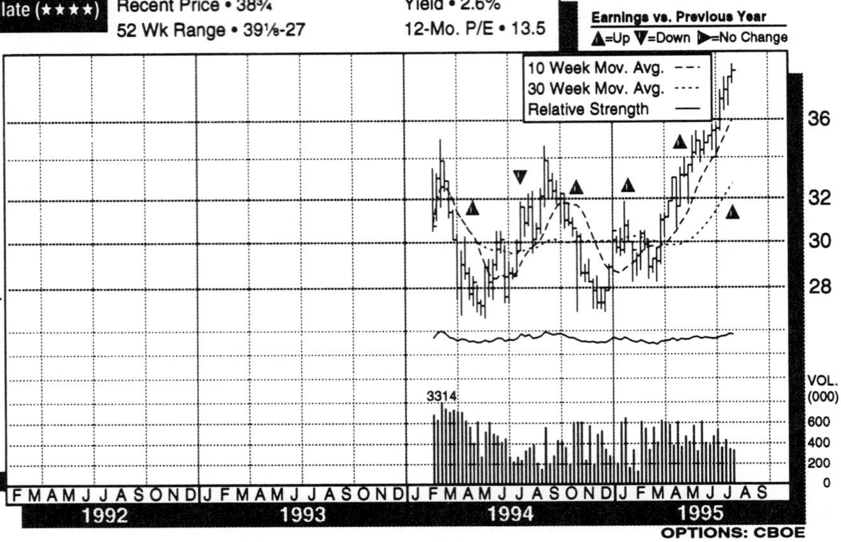

OPTIONS: CBOE

Overview - 31-JUL-95

Sales should be solidly higher in 1995, on continued strength in log trading and merchandising operations, along with the turnaround in pulp operations that ensued in the second half of 1994. Despite soft domestic lumber markets, RYN's timber sales should remain solid, on good demand from the uptrending pulp and paper industry and a tight supply situation brought on by federal environmental policies. RYN's specialty pulp sector is likely to continue to benefit from recovering global economies, which should allow for additional price hikes. Margins should widen on the solid sales conditions in RYN's two major industry sectors, much higher pulp prices and manufacturing cost reduction efforts. RYN's bottom line should also benefit from a gain of about $0.83 a share on the pending sale of a small portion of its New Zealand timber base.

Valuation - 31-JUL-95

RYN's shares have appreciated substantially since the latter part of 1994, on a turnaround in specialty pulp industry trends and continued strength in timber operations. We believe that conditions will remain favorable in both sectors for an extended period, with our forecasts for upcoming periods calling for strong gains in operating income; the limited EPS gain forecast for 1996 is related to the expected inclusion of a gain on the pending sale of a timber interest. Given our belief that Rayonier's earnings will continue strong in the foreseeable future, further appreciation of the company's shares is likely.

Key Stock Statistics

S&P EPS Est. 1995	4.40	Tang. Bk. Value/Share	22.75
P/E on S&P Est. 1995	8.8	Beta	NA
S&P EPS Est. 1996	4.50	Shareholders	35,500
Dividend Rate/Share	1.00	Market cap. (B)	$ 1.1
Shs. outstg. (M)	29.6	Inst. holdings	78%
Avg. daily vol. (M)	0.077	Insider holdings	NA

Value of $10,000 invested 5 years ago: NA

Fiscal Year Ending Dec. 31

	1995	% Change	1994	% Change	1993	% Change
Revenues (Million $)						
1Q	285.8	11%	257.7	19%	216.3	-7%
2Q	313.6	25%	250.8	-2%	256.6	9%
3Q	—	—	286.0	26%	226.4	-15%
4Q	—	—	275.0	16%	237.0	-1%
Yr.	—	—	1,070	14%	936.0	-4%
Income (Million $)						
1Q	25.15	16%	21.70	33%	16.32	—
2Q	26.30	86%	14.11	-43%	24.79	—
3Q	—	—	16.41	112%	7.73	—
4Q	—	—	17.80	NM	3.12	—
Yr.	—	—	70.00	33%	52.47	NM
Earnings Per Share ($)						
1Q	0.84	15%	0.73	28%	0.57	24%
2Q	0.88	83%	0.48	-43%	0.84	NM
3Q	E1.73	—	0.55	112%	0.26	-40%
4Q	E0.95	—	0.60	NM	0.10	NM
Yr.	E4.40	—	2.36	33%	1.77	NM

Next earnings report expected: mid October

Rayonier Inc.

Business Summary - 31-JUL-95

Spun off from ITT Corp. in February 1994, Rayonier is engaged primarily in trading, merchandising and manufacturing logs, timber and wood products and in producing and marketing value-added specialty pulps. Segment contributions in 1994 were:

	Revs.	Profits
Timber & wood products	54%	93%
Pulp products	46%	7%

More than 50% of 1994 sales were shipped to customers outside the U.S., with Asian customers accounting for 30% of sales and Western European customers 10%.

RYN owns, leases or controls about 1.5 million acres of timberland in the U.S. and New Zealand and operates three pulp mills and three lumber manufacturing facilities in the U.S. (the third was purchased in April 1995 from Pacific Crown Timber Products).

The timber and wood products segment owns, buys and harvests timber stumpage and purchases logs in North America and New Zealand for subsequent sale into export markets (principally Japan, Korea and China) and to domestic lumber and pulp mills. RYN also produces dimension and specialty lumber products for residential construction and industrial uses. Rayonier harvests logs from third-party parcels on which it has cutting rights, and to a lesser extent, from company owned parcels; it also purchases logs on the open market. RYN manages timber properties and sells cutting rights to the timber, and also manufactures lumber products for construction and other uses.

Rayonier is one of the world's largest makers of chemical cellulose, or dissolving pulp, which is used by customers in the production of textile, industrial and filtration fibers, plastics and other industrial products. The company also makes fluff pulps, which customers use to manufacture diapers and other sanitary products, and specialty paper pulps used to produce filters and decorative laminates. RYN makes more than 25 grades of pulp at three wood pulp mills having a total annual capacity of about 826,000 metric tons.

Important Developments

Jul. '95—RYN agreed to sell a 75% interest in a 23,000 acre portion of its timber holdings in New Zealand (total holdings in New Zealand 253,000 acres) to a timber investment fund advised by a division of UBS Asset Management (New York). Rayonier was to receive a $46 million payment for the interest, which is located on New Zealand's North Island (apart from most of the company's forests) and accounted for 7% of RYN's harvest volume in 1994. Rayonier would record an $0.83 a share gain on the transaction, which was expected to close in the third quarter of 1995.

Capitalization

Long Term Debt: $482,783,000 (3/95).
Minority Interest: $22,202,000.

Per Share Data ($) (Year Ended Dec. 31)

	1994	1993	1992	1991	1990	1989
Tangible Bk. Val.	22.15	20.51	22.85	NA	NA	NA
Cash Flow	5.40	4.42	-0.13	3.84	5.85	6.49
Earnings	2.36	1.77	-2.77	1.50	3.70	4.33
Dividends	0.72	NA	NA	NA	NA	NA
Payout Ratio	31%	NA	NA	NA	NA	NA
Prices - High	35	NA	NA	NA	NA	NA
- Low	26¾	NA	NA	NA	NA	NA
P/E Ratio - High	15	NA	NA	NA	NA	NA
- Low	11	NA	NA	NA	NA	NA

Income Statement Analysis (Million $)

	1994	%Chg	1993	%Chg	1992	%Chg	1991
Revs.	1,069	14%	936	-4%	974	NM	979
Oper. Inc.	254	22%	208	16%	180	8%	166
Depr.	90.2	15%	78.3	NM	77.9	12%	69.3
Int. Exp.	31.3	34%	23.4	10%	21.3	53%	13.9
Pretax Inc.	140	69%	83.0	NM	-131	NM	64.0
Eff. Tax Rate	27%	—	37%	—	NM	—	31%
Net Inc.	70.0	33%	52.5	NM	-81.5	NM	44.3

Balance Sheet & Other Fin. Data (Million $)

	1994	1993	1992	1991	1990	1989
Cash	9.2	6.0	10.7	NA	NA	NA
Curr. Assets	297	299	292	NA	NA	NA
Total Assets	1,511	1,475	1,476	NA	NA	NA
Curr. Liab.	179	338	285	NA	NA	NA
LT Debt	483	316	302	NA	NA	NA
Common Eqty.	655	606	676	NA	NA	NA
Total Cap.	1,288	1,085	1,101	NA	NA	NA
Cap. Exp.	101	72.0	96.0	132	99	80.0
Cash Flow	160	131	-3.6	114	173	192

Ratio Analysis

	1994	1993	1992	1991	1990	1989
Curr. Ratio	1.7	0.9	1.0	NA	NA	NA
% LT Debt of Cap.	37.5	29.1	27.4	NA	NA	NA
% Net Inc.of Revs.	6.5	5.6	NM	4.5	9.9	11.8
% Ret. on Assets	NM	3.6	NA	NA	NA	NA
% Ret. on Equity	NM	8.2	NA	NA	NA	NA

Dividend Data (Cash dividends were initiated in March 1994.)

Amt. of Div. $	Date Decl.	Ex-Div. Date	Stock of Record	Payment Date
0.180	Jul. 18	Sep. 02	Sep. 09	Sep. 30 '94
0.180	Oct. 18	Dec. 05	Dec. 09	Dec. 30 '94
0.250	Feb. 17	Mar. 06	Mar. 10	Mar. 31 '95
0.250	May. 19	Jun. 06	Jun. 09	Jun. 30 '95
0.250	Jul. 21	Sep. 06	Sep. 08	Sep. 29 '95

Data as orig. reptd.; bef. results of disc. opers. and/or spec. items. Per share data adj. for stk. divs. as of ex-div. date. E-Estimated. NA-Not Available. NM-Not Meaningful. NR-Not Ranked.

Office—1177 Summer St., Stamford, CT 06905-5529. **Tel**—(203) 348-7000. **Chrmn, Pres & CEO**—R. M. Gross. **Sr VP-CFO**—G. J. Pollack. **Investor Contact**—John A. Doumlele. **Dirs**—W. J. Alley, R. V. Araskog, D. W. Griffin, R. M. Gross, P. G. Kirk Jr., K. D. Ortega, B. R. Roberts, N. L. Trivisonno, G. I. Ulmer. **Transfer Agent & Registrar**—Bank of New York, NYC. **Incorporated** in North Carolina. **Empl**-2,700. **S&P Analyst:** Michael W. Jaffe

Regions Financial

NASDAQ Symbol **RGBK**
In S&P MidCap 400

17-OCT-95 **Industry:** Banking

Summary: Formerly First Alabama Banchares, Inc., this major southeastern bank holding company operates 286 offices in Alabama, Florida, Georgia, Louisiana and Tennessee.

S&P Opinion: Accumulate (★★★★) | Recent Price • 40½ | 52 Wk Range • 41⅜-29¾ | Yield • 3.3% | 12-Mo. P/E • 11.1

Quantitative Evaluations
Outlook (1 Lowest—5 Highest)
• **1-**
Fair Value
• **35⅛**
Risk
• **Low**
Earn./Div. Rank
• **A+**

Technical Eval.
• **Bullish** since 6/95
Rel. Strength Rank (1 Lowest—99 Highest)
• **58**
Insider Activity
• **Neutral**

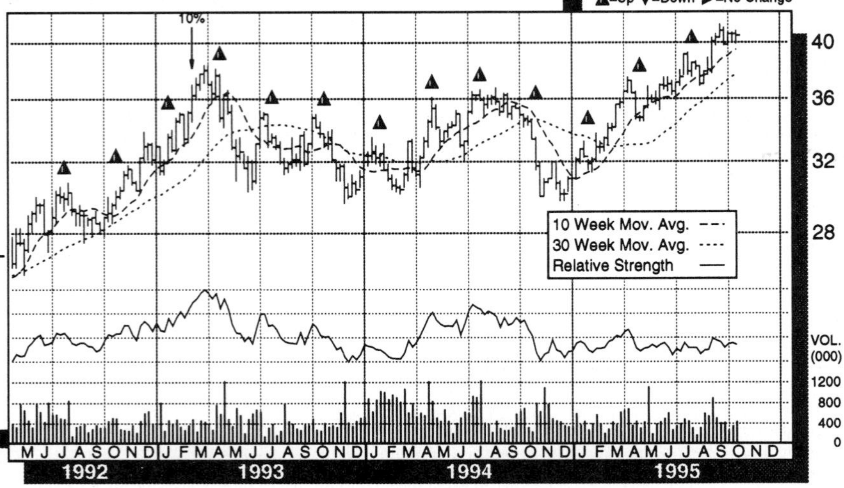

Overview - 17-OCT-95

Earnings into 1996 should continue to benefit from an aggressive acquisition program and strong loan growth, particularly in consumer and residential mortgages. Asset quality remains well above that of peer banks, with nonperforming assets at about 0.55% of loans and other real estate. Growth in noninterest income should also fuel earnings, aided by rising deposit service charges and trust fees. The acquisition program is continuing to expand the company's presence in the southeast. However, acquisitions are generally financed with stock and therefore may be dilutive in the near term. Overall, earnings are expected to rise about 11% in 1996.

Valuation - 17-OCT-95

With mega-bank mergers in the news and a less volatile interest rate environment, investors are showing renewed interest in regional bank stocks. Regions Financial, with 23 consecutive years of increased earnings, has a solid franchise and an appetite for expansion. The company's aggressive acquisition strategy (nine acquisitions in 1994, two already completed in 1995, and several others pending) should fuel earnings growth into 1996. Also, loan growth and noninterest income should benefit from the moderately strong southeastern economy. While RGBK is currently selling near its 52-week high, it is trading at only about 10 times our 1996 earnings estimate. We recommend accumulation of the shares for investors seeking conservative growth.

Key Stock Statistics

S&P EPS Est. 1995	3.71	Tang. Bk. Value/Share	23.76
P/E on S&P Est. 1995	10.9	Beta	0.81
S&P EPS Est. 1996	4.10	Shareholders	23,600
Dividend Rate/Share	1.32	Market cap. (B)	$ 1.8
Shs. outstg. (M)	45.4	Inst. holdings	30%
Avg. daily vol. (M)	0.070	Insider holdings	NA

Value of $10,000 invested 5 years ago: $ 31,551

Fiscal Year Ending Dec. 31

	1995	% Change	1994	% Change	1993	% Change
Revenues (Million $)						
1Q	271.0	25%	216.4	30%	166.4	2%
2Q	289.9	30%	223.3	31%	170.4	4%
3Q	NA	—	237.7	37%	173.7	6%
4Q	—	—	251.8	42%	177.2	7%
Yr.	—	—	929.2	35%	687.7	5%
Income (Million $)						
1Q	40.21	16%	34.67	42%	24.43	11%
2Q	40.92	12%	36.54	31%	27.94	21%
3Q	43.99	18%	37.43	31%	28.62	14%
4Q	—	—	37.25	20%	31.01	26%
Yr.	—	—	145.9	30%	112.1	18%
Earnings Per Share ($)						
1Q	0.90	13%	0.80	8%	0.74	21%
2Q	0.90	7%	0.84	12%	0.75	19%
3Q	0.96	9%	0.88	14%	0.77	12%
4Q	E0.95	8%	0.88	17%	0.75	12%
Yr.	E3.71	9%	3.40	13%	3.01	16%

Next earnings report expected: mid January

Regions Financial

Business Summary - 13-OCT-95

Regions Financial Corp. (formerly First Alabama Bancshares, Inc.) is a southeastern bank holding company that operates 282 offices in Alabama, Florida, Georgia, Louisiana and Tennessee. The lead bank, First Alabama Bank, operates through 176 full-service offices and had assets of $9.8 billion at 1994 year end.

Consolidated loans aggregated $9.01 billion at December 31, 1994, and were divided:

Commercial	21%
Consumer	25%
Real estate--construction	4%
Real estate--mortgage	50%

At December 31, 1994, the reserve for loan losses totaled $116,988,000 (1.30% of net loans outstanding), compared with $100,762,000 (1.47%) a year earlier. Net chargeoffs in 1994 were $12,732,000 (0.17% of average loans outstanding), versus $10,389,000 (0.19%) in 1993. Nonperforming assets at 1994 year end amounted to $52,742,000 (0.58% of loans and other real estate), against $70,436,000 (1.03%) a year earlier.

Deposits averaged $9.23 billion in 1994 ($6.88 billion in 1993) and were apportioned: 14% noninterest-bearing demand, 14% NOW, 15% money market, 9% savings, 9% certificates of $100,000 or more, and 39% other interest-bearing deposits.

Interest and fees on loans provided 65% of total income in 1994, interest on investment securities 17%, other interest income 2%, service charges on deposit accounts 5%, mortgage servicing and origination fees 5%, and other noninterest income 6%.

On a tax-equivalent basis, the average yield on total interest-earning assets in 1994 was 7.61% (7.74% in 1993), while the average rate paid on interest-bearing liabilities was 3.91% (3.49%), for a net spread of 3.70% (4.25%).

Important Developments

Oct. '95—RGBK agreed to acquire First Federal Bank of Northwest Georgia in Cedartown (deposits of $76 million) in a tax-free exchange of stock. Exact terms of the transaction were not disclosed.

Aug. '95—RGBK signed a definitive agreement to acquire Metro Financial Corp. (deposits of $180 million), of Atlanta, Ga., for stock valued at about $28 million; the transaction is expected to close in the first quarter of 1996. Also in August, RGBK reached an agreement in principle to acquire Enterprise National Bank of Atlanta ($44 million), of Dunwoody, Ga. Terms were not disclosed.

Jul. '95—RGBK agreed to acquire Prudential Savings Bank's Cartersville, Ga. operation for an undisclosed amount.

Capitalization

Long Term Borrowings: $585,991,000 (6/95).

Per Share Data ($)

(Year Ended Dec. 31)

	1994	1993	1992	1991	1990	1989
Tangible Bk. Val.	20.26	19.54	16.60	14.63	13.38	12.72
Earnings	3.40	3.01	2.60	2.16	1.91	1.73
Dividends	1.20	1.04	0.91	0.87	0.84	0.76
Payout Ratio	35%	35%	35%	40%	44%	44%
Prices - High	36¾	38⅜	33⅞	27⅛	16⅞	17⅝
- Low	29¾	29⅝	23¾	15⅞	13¼	13¾
P/E Ratio - High	11	13	13	13	9	10
- Low	9	10	9	7	7	8

Income Statement Analysis (Million $)

	1994	%Chg	1993	%Chg	1992	%Chg	1991
Net Int. Inc.	436	27%	342	9%	313	18%	265
Tax Equiv. Adj.	10.6	1%	10.5	-33%	15.6	27%	12.3
Non Int. Inc.	143	8%	132	11%	119	17%	102
Loan Loss Prov.	19.0	-12%	21.5	-21%	27.1	13%	24.0
% Exp/Op Revs.	58%	—	59%	—	59%	—	61%
Pretax Inc.	217	31%	166	19%	140	25%	112
Eff. Tax Rate	33%	—	32%	—	32%	—	30%
Net Inc.	146	30%	112	18%	95.0	21%	78.3
% Net Int. Marg.	4.26%	—	4.82%	—	4.98%	—	4.78%

Balance Sheet & Other Fin. Data (Million $)

	1994	1993	1992	1991	1990	1989
Earning Assets:						
Money Mkt.	70.6	138	85.0	156	75.0	155
Inv. Securities	2,609	2,368	1,670	1,576	1,489	1,133
Com'l Loans	1,871	1,498	1,437	1,328	1,376	1,169
Other Loans	7,277	5,658	3,964	3,158	2,925	2,607
Total Assets	12,839	10,476	7,881	6,745	6,344	5,550
Demand Deposits	1,450	1,197	1,042	875	852	836
Time Deposits	8,643	7,574	5,659	5,042	4,501	3,908
LT Debt	519	463	134	16.0	20.0	45.0
Common Eqty.	1,014	851	657	573	524	489

Ratio Analysis

	1994	1993	1992	1991	1990	1989
% Ret. on Assets	1.3	1.4	1.3	1.2	1.2	1.2
% Ret. on Equity	16.0	16.1	15.6	14.3	13.6	13.2
% Loan Loss Resv.	1.3	1.4	1.4	1.3	1.1	1.0
% Loans/Deposits	90.4	81.2	77.5	74.3	78.4	77.7
% Equity to Assets	8.1	8.7	8.6	8.6	9.0	9.1

Dividend Data —Cash has been paid each year since 1968. A dividend reinvestment plan is available.

Amt. of Div. $	Date Decl.	Ex-Div. Date	Stock of Record	Payment Date
0.300	Nov. 17	Dec. 12	Dec. 16	Jan. 03 '95
0.330	Jan. 18	Mar. 15	Mar. 17	Apr. 03 '95
0.330	May. 03	Jun. 14	Jun. 16	Jul. 03 '95
0.330	Jul. 19	Sep. 13	Sep. 15	Oct. 02 '95

Data as orig. reptd.; bef. results of disc opers. and/or spec. items. Per share data adj. for stk. divs. as of ex-div. date. E-Estimated. NA-Not Available. NM-Not Meaningful. NR-Not Ranked.

Office—417 North 20th St., Birmingham, AL 35202-0247. **Tel**—(334) 832-8450. **Chrmn & CEO**—J. S. Mackin. **Vice Chrmn**—R. D. Horsley. **Secy**—S. E. Upchurch, Jr. **EVP, CFO & Investor Contact**—Robert P. Houston. **Dirs**—S. S. Blair, W. R. Boles Sr., J. B. Boone Jr., A. P. Brewer, J. S. M. French, R. D. Horsley, C. Jones, O. B. King, J. S. Mackin, H. E. Simpson, R. E. Steiner III, L. J. Styslinger Jr. **Transfer Agent**—First Alabama Bank, Montgomery. **Incorporated** in Delaware in 1970. **Empl**-6,007. **S&P Analyst:** Robert Schpoont

STANDARD & POOR'S

STOCK REPORTS

Revco D.S.

NYSE Symbol **RXR**
In S&P MidCap 400

11-AUG-95

Industry: Retail Stores

Summary: One of the leading drug store chains in the U.S., this company operates over 2,100 high-quality, health-oriented neighborhood stores in nine eastern states.

Quantitative Evaluations

Outlook
(1 Lowest—5 Highest)
• NA

Fair Value
• NA

Risk
• Average

Earn./Div. Rank
• NR

Technical Eval.
• Bullish since 3/95

Rel. Strength Rank
(1 Lowest—99 Highest)
• 10

Insider Activity
• Neutral

Recent Price • 21
52 Wk Range • 25⅜-15⅞
Yield • Nil
12-Mo. P/E • 22.1

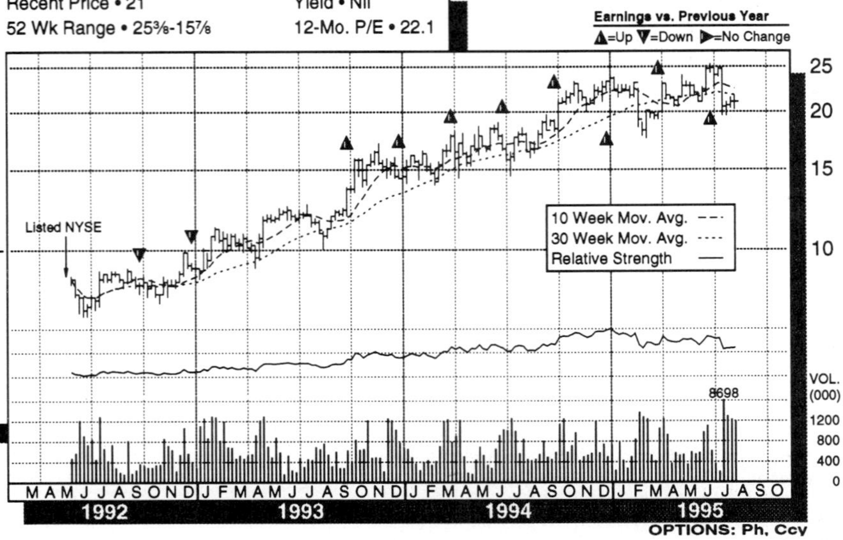

OPTIONS: Ph, Ccv

Business Profile - 10-AUG-95

In mid-1992, this leading drug store retailer emerged from nearly four years of bankruptcy protection, under a reorganization plan that cut debt and liabilities by $1 billion. A recapitalization completed in early 1993 reduced long-term debt by $150 million and boosted stockholders' equity by over $100 million. Recent results have benefited from higher same-store sales and well controlled operating expenses. The July 1994 acquisition of Hook-SupeRx, Inc. nearly doubled the company's size.

Operational Review - 10-AUG-95

Net sales soared in the fiscal year ended June 3, 1995 (53 weeks), mainly reflecting the acquisition of Hook-SupeRx and a 9.4% gain in same-store sales. Despite wider operating margins, the gain in earnings per share was somewhat restricted by sharply higher interest expense, and 15.5 million additional shares issued as part of the Hook acquisition. Future results should benefit from same-store sales growth, an ongoing expansion program, and a one million share repurchase program.

Stock Performance - 04-AUG-95

In the past 30 trading days, RXR's shares have declined 16%, compared to a 2% rise in the S&P 500. Average trading volume for the past five days was 236,560 shares, compared with the 40-day moving average of 406,628 shares.

Key Stock Statistics

Dividend Rate/Share	Nil	Shareholders	1,400
Shs. outstg. (M)	66.6	Market cap. (B)	$ 1.4
Avg. daily vol. (M)	0.310	Inst. holdings	66%
Tang. Bk. Value/Share	4.11	Insider holdings	NA
Beta	NA		

Value of $10,000 invested 5 years ago: NA

Fiscal Year Ending May 31

	1995	% Change	1994	% Change	1993	% Change
Revenues (Million $)						
1Q	694.4	33%	521.0	10%	473.0	8%
2Q	1,027	88%	546.3	13%	485.0	5%
3Q	1,133	82%	621.2	12%	552.4	6%
4Q	1,577	93%	815.5	11%	731.4	11%
Yr.	4,432	77%	2,504	12%	2,242	7%
Income (Million $)						
1Q	5.80	112%	2.73	—	—	—
2Q	5.00	52%	3.30	—	—	—
3Q	17.70	42%	12.50	193%	4.27	—
4Q	32.60	61%	20.20	69%	11.97	—
Yr.	61.10	58%	38.70	173%	14.20	NM
Earnings Per Share ($)						
1Q	0.10	100%	0.05	NM	-0.04	NM
2Q	0.08	14%	0.07	NM	-0.01	NM
3Q	0.27	8%	0.25	127%	0.11	—
4Q	0.49	22%	0.40	67%	0.24	—
Yr.	0.95	23%	0.77	120%	0.35	—

Next earnings report expected: late September

Revco D.S.

Business Summary - 11-AUG-95

Revco is a leading retail drug store chain. Following its July 1994 acquisition of Hook-SupeRx, which added approximately 800 drug stores, 35 home health care stores and a mail order operation to its base, the company was operating 2,086 drug stores and 34 home health care stores in 14 contiguous states at February 4, 1995. In June 1992, Revco emerged from Chapter 11 bankruptcy protection, which it had entered in July 1988.

The number of stores in operation at the end of recent fiscal years was as follows:

1994	1,248
1993	1,190
1992	1,143
1991	1,125
1990	1,853
1989	1,888

At May 28, 1994, Revco's stores were located in North Carolina (287), Ohio (224), South Carolina (178), Virginia (186), Georgia (160), Pennsylvania (77), Tennessee (70), Maryland (38) and West Virginia (28). The company services its stores through five distribution centers located in Knoxville, Tenn., Aiken County, S.C., Henderson, N.C., Somerset, Pa., and Glendale, Ariz.

The stores operate on a self-service, high volume, low overhead, cash and carry basis, and typically feature prescription and over-the-counter drugs, health and beauty aids, toiletries, vitamins, cosmetics and sundries, and a broad line of consumer products. Most stores are located in shopping centers, in leased premises ranging in size from 3,000 to 21,000 sq. ft., with a typical new store averaging 8,450 sq. ft.

In 1993-94, prescription drugs accounted for 53% of total sales, up from 50% in 1992-93.

The company strategy to enhance market share and improve profitability includes aggressive marketing efforts, new store openings and strategic acquisitions, continued utilization of management information systems, and the expanded provision of patient counseling for prescription drugs.

Important Developments

Jul. '95—Revco reported that it had opened 112 new stores in 1994-95, 37 of which were relocations, and closed 27 stores. It also added 21 stores by acquiring independent pharmacies, and purchased prescription files from another 182 stores. The company also successfully completed the conversion of all the Hook-SupeRx stores to encompass Revco's standard mix.

Capitalization

Long Term Debt: $646,500,000 (2/4/95).

Per Share Data ($) (Year Ended May 31)

	1995	1994	1993	1992	1991	1990
Tangible Bk. Val.	NA	9.48	8.61	NA	NA	NA
Cash Flow	NA	1.81	1.48	NA	NA	NA
Earnings	0.95	0.77	0.35	NA	NA	NA
Dividends	Nil	Nil	Nil	NA	NA	NA
Payout Ratio	Nil	Nil	Nil	NA	NA	NA
Cal. Yrs.	1994	1993	1992	1991	1990	1989
Prices - High	24½	17⅛	9⅞	NA	NA	NA
- Low	13⅞	8⅝	7⅛	NA	NA	NA
P/E Ratio - High	26	22	28	NA	NA	NA
- Low	15	11	20	NA	NA	NA

Income Statement Analysis (Million $)

	1994	%Chg	1993	%Chg	1992	%Chg	1991
Revs.	2,504	12%	2,242	7%	2,086	—	NA
Oper. Inc.	153	25%	122	155%	47.9	—	NA
Depr.	52.6	14%	46.3	15%	40.3	—	NA
Int. Exp.	24.0	-43%	42.0	-14%	49.0	—	NA
Pretax Inc.	77.0	120%	35.0	NM	7.7	—	NA
Eff. Tax Rate	50%	—	59%	—	130%	—	NA
Net Inc.	39.0	179%	14.0	NM	-2.3	—	NA

Balance Sheet & Other Fin. Data (Million $)

	1994	1993	1992	1991	1990	1989
Cash	24.0	18.0	79.2	NA	NA	NA
Curr. Assets	585	552	558	NA	NA	NA
Total Assets	1,061	1,045	1,056	NA	NA	NA
Curr. Liab.	341	330	301	NA	NA	NA
LT Debt	200	253	435	NA	NA	NA
Common Eqty.	500	454	320	NA	NA	NA
Total Cap.	720	716	755	NA	NA	NA
Cap. Exp.	36.0	22.9	NA	NA	NA	NA
Cash Flow	91.0	61.0	37.9	NA	NA	NA

Ratio Analysis

	1994	1993	1992	1991	1990	1989
Curr. Ratio	1.7	1.7	1.9	NA	NA	NA
% LT Debt of Cap.	27.8	35.4	57.6	NA	NA	NA
% Net Inc.of Revs.	1.5	0.6	NM	NA	NA	NA
% Ret. on Assets	3.7	1.1	NA	NA	NA	NA
% Ret. on Equity	8.1	3.1	NA	NA	NA	NA

Dividend Data (The company's working capital agreement and indentures for debt issued pursuant to its plan of reorganization prohibit the payment of cash dividends for a specified period of time from the effective date of the plan, and restrict payment of cash dividends thereafter.)

Data as orig. reptd.; bef. results of disc. opers. and/or spec. items. Per share data adj. for stk. divs. as of ex-div. date. E-Estimated. NA-Not Available. NM-Not Meaningful. NR-Not Ranked.

Office—1925 Enterprise Parkway, Twinsburg, OH 44087. **Tel**—(216) 425-9811. **Co-Chrmn**—T. R. Embry, S. Zell. **Pres & CEO**—D. D. Hoven. **EVP & COO**—C. A. Bellini. **EVP & CFO**—J. J. Hagen. **VP & Secy**—J. A. Staph. **VP & Treas**—W. H. Grove. **Investor Contact**—Carol McLeod. **Dirs**—C. A. Bellini, L. M. Borghese, R. F. Dammeyer, T. R. Embry, B. Evans, J. V. Guttag, D. D. Hoven, W. B. Reinhold, S. Z. Rosenberg, D. M. Shulte, T. O. Thorsen, S. Zell. **Transfer Agent**—Society National Bank, Cleveland. **Incorporated** in Delaware in 1986. **Empl**-18,000. **S&P Analyst:** Maureen C. Carini

STANDARD & POOR'S

STOCK REPORTS

Reynolds & Reynolds

NYSE Symbol **REY**

In S&P MidCap 400

01-OCT-95

Industry:
Office Equipment

Summary: This company is the leading provider of integrated information management systems. REY primarily serves the automotive, professional, medical and general business markets.

S&P Opinion: Buy (★★★★★)

Recent Price • 34⅜

52 Wk Range • 36⅝-22¼

Yield • 1.2%

12-Mo. P/E • 19.2

Quantitative Evaluations

Outlook
(1 Lowest—5 Highest)
• **4-**

Fair Value
• **35¾**

Risk
• **Average**

Earn./Div. Rank
• **B+**

Technical Eval.
• **Bullish** since 2/95

Rel. Strength Rank
(1 Lowest—99 Highest)
• **65**

Insider Activity
• **Neutral**

Earnings vs. Previous Year
▲=Up ▼=Down ▶=No Change

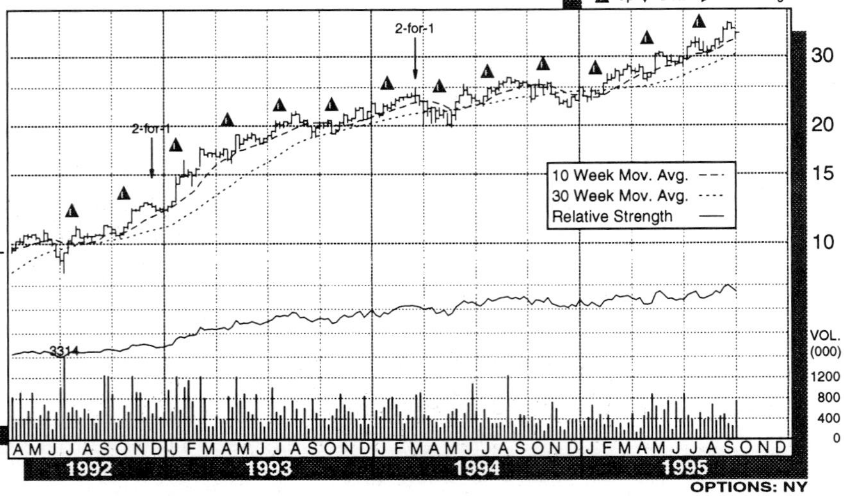

OPTIONS: NY

Overview - 29-SEP-95

The current healthy pace of revenue growth should continue through fiscal 1996, aided by acquisitions, healthy market conditions and other factors. REY's order backlogs remain strong across all businesses, and the company continues to broaden its portfolio of products and services. Profitability will benefit from the revenue gains, a shift toward higher-margin businesses, benefits from restructuring actions undertaken in fiscal 1994 and savings realized from the consolidation of acquired operations. Longer term, the ongoing consolidation of the healthcare industry into physician groups and integrated healthcare delivery networks will provide REY with additional opportunities to serve the industry's increasingly sophisticated and complex information management needs.

Valuation - 29-SEP-95

REY's stellar long-term market track record is directly attributable to its favorable revenue and earnings history. Profits advanced more than 25% in each of the past three reported fiscal years, and gains of over 20% are expected for fiscal 1995 and 1996. Nevertheless, REY's P/E continues to hover in the high teens, providing substantial room for appreciation of the shares once investors realize that REY's business is largely independent of the level of new car sales. The long-range outlook is enhanced by REY's strategy to rapidly grow the Healthcare Systems business, a market where management sees tremendous opportunities.

Key Stock Statistics

S&P EPS Est. 1995	1.87	Tang. Bk. Value/Share	4.57
P/E on S&P Est. 1995	18.4	Beta	1.48
S&P EPS Est. 1996	2.30	Shareholders	2,200
Dividend Rate/Share	0.40	Market cap. (B)	$ 1.4
Shs. outstg. (M)	41.2	Inst. holdings	68%
Avg. daily vol. (M)	0.093	Insider holdings	NA

Value of $10,000 invested 5 years ago: $ 64,569

Fiscal Year Ending Sep. 30

	1995	% Change	1994	% Change	1993	% Change
Revenues (Million $)						
1Q	208.7	8%	192.6	18%	163.5	8%
2Q	228.5	11%	205.5	20%	171.1	6%
3Q	231.2	14%	202.3	19%	169.8	6%
4Q	—	—	208.4	8%	192.5	12%
Yr.	—	—	808.8	16%	697.0	8%
Income (Million $)						
1Q	18.90	31%	14.41	20%	12.05	47%
2Q	19.30	25%	15.47	14%	13.62	45%
3Q	19.86	10%	18.10	32%	13.69	41%
4Q	—	—	18.23	30%	13.98	30%
Yr.	—	—	66.20	26%	52.52	38%
Earnings Per Share ($)						
1Q	0.44	33%	0.33	20%	0.28	57%
2Q	0.46	31%	0.35	13%	0.31	55%
3Q	0.47	15%	0.41	30%	0.32	54%
4Q	E0.50	19%	0.42	31%	0.32	39%
Yr.	E1.87	24%	1.51	26%	1.20	48%

Next earnings report expected: early November

Reynolds & Reynolds

01-OCT-95

Business Summary - 29-SEP-95

The Reynolds and Reynolds Company is the leading provider of integrated information management systems in the U.S. Segment contributions in fiscal 1994 were:

	Revs.	Profits
Business forms	53%	26%
Computer systems:		
Products & services	45%	61%
Financial services	2%	13%

The business forms segment manufactures standard, imprint and custom business forms for automobile dealers and related vehicle, parts and service businesses. The division also markets its forms to office products dealers, other small businesses, financial institutions, hospitals and large healthcare organizations. The company's Arnold Corp. unit produces continuous and snap-out custom forms, computer stock forms and entertainment, sporting event and lottery tickets. Arnold also markets forms management services to its general business customers.

The computer systems segment sells turnkey information management systems and professional services primarily to automobile dealers. Service and support functions are provided by more than 1,200 personnel located in nearly 175 offices in principal cities in North America. Reynolds and Reynolds Healthcare Systems provides an array of turnkey computer systems to medical practices.

Important Developments

Jul. '95—REY acquired the assets of The Nickelsen Group, a Cleveland-based general management consulting firm for the auto industry. In June, REY acquired the assets of Dealer Internet Services Corp. (DISC) of Lynnwood, Wash. Through DISC's DealerNet service, auto makers, dealers and other auto-related industries can market vehicles and services directly to consumers over the Internet. REY plans to expand DealerNet nationwide and will enhance DealerNet with services such as the vehicle locator and parts locator. Terms were not disclosed.

May '95—REY said that the just-completed acquisition of Salcris Systems of Birmingham, Ala., and the November 1994 purchase of PD Medical Systems of Portland, Ore., are evidence of its plans to rapidly become the leading provider of information management systems for physician groups and integrated healthcare delivery networks.

Capitalization

Long Term Debt: $41,741,000 (6/95), excl. notes payable.

Cl. A Common Stock: 41,245,972 shs. ($0.625 par).

Cl. B Common Stock: 10,000,000 shs. ($0.03125 par); ea. conv. into 0.05 of a Cl. A sh.

R. H. Grant III owns all Cl. B shs. & controls over 20% of the total voting power.

Per Share Data ($)

(Year Ended Sep. 30)

	1994	1993	1992	1991	1990	1989
Tangible Bk. Val.	5.03	4.19	4.22	4.20	3.71	3.22
Cash Flow	2.31	1.77	1.33	1.05	1.11	1.11
Earnings	1.51	1.20	0.81	0.54	0.57	0.63
Dividends	0.33	0.26	0.22	0.21	0.20	0.19
Payout Ratio	22%	19%	26%	39%	35%	30%
Prices - High	26⅝	23	12¾	9¼	6⅛	8½
- Low	19¾	12⅛	8⅜	4	2⅞	5¾
P/E Ratio - High	18	19	16	17	11	13
- Low	13	10	10	8	5	9

Income Statement Analysis (Million $)

	1994	%Chg	1993	%Chg	1992	%Chg	1991
Revs.	809	16%	697	8%	645	8%	599
Oper. Inc.	145	25%	116	26%	91.7	34%	68.5
Depr.	34.9	39%	25.1	3%	24.4	11%	22.0
Int. Exp.	3.8	3%	3.7	-27%	5.1	-39%	8.3
Pretax Inc.	97.3	9%	89.3	39%	64.4	67%	38.6
Eff. Tax Rate	32%	—	41%	—	41%	—	42%
Net Inc.	66.2	26%	52.5	38%	38.1	69%	22.5

Balance Sheet & Other Fin. Data (Million $)

	1994	1993	1992	1991	1990	1989
Cash	20.2	9.4	23.8	27.7	30.2	28.7
Curr. Assets	NA	NA	NA	NA	NA	NA
Total Assets	635	571	522	515	515	487
Curr. Liab.	NA	NA	NA	NA	NA	NA
LT Debt	114	103	69.0	82.0	103	114
Common Eqty.	293	263	257	248	235	221
Total Cap.	458	410	380	388	396	389
Cap. Exp.	27.9	18.9	17.4	15.6	19.6	18.2
Cash Flow	101	77.6	62.5	44.5	47.2	48.1

Ratio Analysis

	1994	1993	1992	1991	1990	1989
Curr. Ratio	NA	NA	NA	NA	NA	NA
% LT Debt of Cap.	24.8	25.1	18.0	21.2	26.0	29.3
% Net Inc.of Revs.	8.2	7.5	5.9	3.8	4.1	4.5
% Ret. on Assets	11.1	9.8	7.2	4.4	4.9	6.2
% Ret. on Equity	24.1	20.5	14.8	9.3	10.8	12.9

Dividend Data —Cash dividends have been paid each year since 1953. A "poison pill" stock purchase right was issued in 1991. A dividend reinvestment plan is available.

Amt. of Div. $	Date Decl.	Ex-Div. Date	Stock of Record	Payment Date
0.100	Nov. 15	Dec. 12	Dec. 16	Jan. 12 '95
0.100	Feb. 09	Mar. 21	Mar. 27	Apr. 13 '95
0.100	May. 01	May. 15	May. 19	Jun. 13 '95
0.100	Aug. 08	Aug. 23	Aug. 25	Sep. 13 '95

Data as orig. reptd.; bef. results of disc. opers. and/or spec. items. Per share data adj. for stk. divs. as of ex-div. date. E-Estimated. NA-Not Available. NM-Not Meaningful. NR-Not Ranked.

Office—115 South Ludlow St., P.O. Box 2608, Dayton, OH 45402. **Tel**—(513) 449-4210. **Chrmn & Pres**—D. R. Holmes. **VP, CFO & Investor Contact**—Dale L. Medford (513) 449-4099. **Secy**—A. M. Lutynski. **Dirs**—J. N. Bausman, D. E. Fry, R. H. Grant Jr., R. H. Grant III, D. R. Holmes, D. L. Medford, R. C. Nevin, G. B. Price Jr., K. W. Thiele, M. D. Walker. **Transfer Agent & Registrar**—Bank One, Indianapolis. **Incorporated** in Ohio in 1889. **Empl-** 5,478. **S&P Analyst:** William H. Donald

STANDARD & POOR'S

STOCK REPORTS

Rohr, Inc.

NYSE Symbol **RHR**
In S&P MidCap 400

12-JUL-95

Industry: Aerospace

Summary: This company is a leading supplier of jet engine nacelle assemblies. Results are closely correlated to deliveries of commercial jet transports.

Quantitative Evaluations

Outlook (1 Lowest—5 Highest) • 1+

Fair Value • 9½

Risk • **Average**

Earn./Div. Rank • **B-**

Technical Eval. • **Bullish** since 6/95

Rel. Strength Rank (1 Lowest—99 Highest) • **84**

Insider Activity • **Neutral**

Recent Price • 14⅜
52 Wk Range • 15⅝-8¼
Yield • Nil
12-Mo. P/E • 26.1

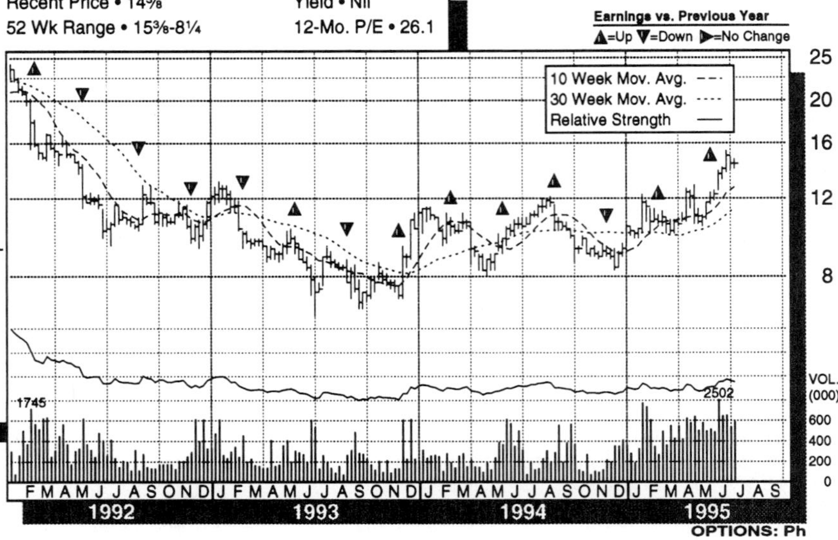

OPTIONS: Ph

Business Profile - 11-JUL-95

In April 1995, RHR said it expected a decline in sales for fiscal 1996, with the downturn in commercial aerospace seen continuing through calendar 1996. However, order activity for new aircraft, most of which will be delivered after fiscal 1996, has picked up, and RHR believes it is well-set to take advantage of this upturn. In addition to its firm backlog, RHR has an additional $3 billion in anticipated backlog which represents existing contracts with options that are expected to be exercised.

Operational Review - 11-JUL-95

Sales for the first nine months of fiscal 1995 decreased moderately from a year earlier, primarily as a result of declining commercial delivery rates and reduced sales on government programs. However, operating margins continued to improve, aided by a reduction in overhead and material costs and gains in manufacturing efficiencies, and net income soared. Backlog at April 30, 1995, was approximately $900 million, down from $1.2 billion at July 30, 1994.

Stock Performance - 07-JUL-95

In the past 30 trading days, RHR's shares have increased 20%, compared to a 6% rise in the S&P 500. Average trading volume for the past five days was 145,750 shares, compared with the 40-day moving average of 193,039 shares.

Key Stock Statistics

Dividend Rate/Share	Nil	Shareholders	4,500
Shs. outstg. (M)	18.1	Market cap. (B)	$0.266
Avg. daily vol. (M)	0.170	Inst. holdings	59%
Tang. Bk. Value/Share	8.60	Insider holdings	NA
Beta	1.49		

Value of $10,000 invested 5 years ago: $ 7,055

Fiscal Year Ending Jul. 31

	1995	% Change	1994	% Change	1993	% Change
Revenues (Million $)						
1Q	192.2	-19%	237.1	-17%	284.0	-13%
2Q	219.8	-6%	234.8	-31%	342.0	11%
3Q	210.8	-5%	221.7	-25%	296.8	NM
4Q	—	—	224.6	-11%	252.4	-28%
Yr.	—	—	918.1	-22%	1,175	-8%
Income (Million $)						
1Q	1.37	-76%	5.76	61%	3.58	-59%
2Q	3.25	143%	1.34	NM	-12.10	NM
3Q	2.57	NM	-2.95	NM	-22.20	-12%
4Q	—	—	0.52	NM	0.14	-98%
Yr.	—	—	4.67	NM	-30.58	NM
Earnings Per Share ($)						
1Q	0.08	-75%	0.32	60%	0.20	-60%
2Q	0.18	157%	0.07	NM	-0.68	NM
3Q	0.14	NM	-0.16	NM	-1.24	NM
4Q	—	—	0.03	NM	0.01	-98%
Yr.	—	—	0.26	NM	-1.71	NM

Next earnings report expected: mid September

Rohr, Inc.

Business Summary - 11-JUL-95

Rohr, Inc. (formerly Rohr Industries) is engaged primarily in the manufacture of systems for commercial and military aircraft and for space vehicles. The company's primary emphasis is on the market for commercial aircrafts which seat 100 or more passengers.

The manufacture of components for and the assembly of nacelles (pods that surround aircraft engines), pylons (which attach the propulsion system to the aircraft) and thrust reversers (which aid aircraft deceleration after landing) comprise the bulk of the company's sales. Complete nacelle systems, which usually include the cowling, nozzle systems and thrust reversers, are made for commercial, military and general aviation aircraft under contracts with major airframe and engine manufacturers. Other products include noise suppression systems, engine components and structures for high-temperature environments.

Sales by customer in recent years were:

	1994	1993
International Aero Engines	16%	9%
General Electric	15%	14%
Pratt & Whitney	14%	17%
Rolls-Royce	10%	8%
CFM International	9%	8%
Boeing	9%	11%
McDonnell Douglas	7%	11%
Other	20%	22%

Direct or indirect sales to the U.S. Government (including some overlap with the above) accounted for about 14% of the total (14%).

Space operations, which account for a small part of sales, consist primarily of the manufacture of solid rocket motor nozzles and insulated cases for the Titan Space Launch Vehicle.

Important Developments

Jun. '95—The company said it signed an agreement with Boeing to design and manufacture the inlet and fan cowls for the CFMI CFM56-7 powered 737-700. Delivery of production hardware is scheduled to start in August 1996, and the potential sales of the contract are estimated at more than $200 million.

Apr. '95—RHR announced that sales for fiscal 1996 are anticipated to be down approximately 8% from levels expected for fiscal 1995. The anticipated reduction in sales reflects the conclusion of certain space and military programs and continuing softness in commercial aircraft orders.

Capitalization

Long Term Debt: $562,439,000 (4/95), incl. $57.5 million of 7.75% sub. notes due 2004 & conv. into com. at $10.35 a sh.

Per Share Data ($) (Year Ended Jul. 31)

	1994	1993	1992	1991	1990	1989
Tangible Bk. Val.	8.14	10.13	25.17	25.23	23.42	23.34
Cash Flow	1.51	-0.28	1.66	3.32	1.52	3.30
Earnings	0.26	-1.71	0.08	1.74	Nil	1.90
Dividends	Nil	Nil	Nil	Nil	Nil	Nil
Payout Ratio	Nil	Nil	Nil	Nil	Nil	Nil
Prices - High	12⅛	13⅛	24¼	26	26¼	37⅞
- Low	8	6½	9¼	14⅞	11½	18⅞
P/E Ratio - High	47	NM	NM	15	NM	20
- Low	31	NM	NM	9	NM	10

Income Statement Analysis (Million $)

	1994	%Chg	1993	%Chg	1992	%Chg	1991
Revs.	918	-22%	1,175	-8%	1,280	-8%	1,385
Oper. Inc.	82.0	NM	24.0	-67%	73.0	-43%	128
Depr.	22.5	-12%	25.6	-8%	27.9	NM	27.7
Int. Exp.	46.8	-2%	47.9	-29%	67.0	22%	54.8
Pretax Inc.	4.6	NM	-49.6	NM	-17.8	NM	46.9
Eff. Tax Rate	NM	—	NM	—	NM	—	35%
Net Inc.	4.7	NM	-30.6	NM	1.5	-95%	30.5

Balance Sheet & Other Fin. Data (Million $)

	1994	1993	1992	1991	1990	1989
Cash	116	42.0	21.0	26.0	26.0	51.0
Curr. Assets	645	607	1,008	1,050	982	878
Total Assets	1,057	1,018	1,364	1,408	1,320	1,165
Curr. Liab.	184	256	308	337	346	323
LT Debt	574	481	525	542	484	361
Common Eqty.	147	182	449	441	414	412
Total Cap.	721	663	1,017	1,036	959	833
Cap. Exp.	5.8	27.5	62.9	32.4	28.9	39.0
Cash Flow	27.2	-5.0	29.3	58.2	27.1	58.3

Ratio Analysis

	1994	1993	1992	1991	1990	1989
Curr. Ratio	3.5	2.4	3.3	3.1	2.8	2.7
% LT Debt of Cap.	79.6	72.5	51.6	52.3	50.5	43.3
% Net Inc.of Revs.	1.0	NM	0.1	2.2	NM	3.2
% Ret. on Assets	0.5	NM	0.1	2.2	NA	3.3
% Ret. on Equity	2.8	NM	0.3	7.2	NA	8.5

Dividend Data (No dividends have been paid since 1975. A "poison pill" stock purchase right was issued in 1986.)

Data as orig. reptd.; bef. results of disc. opers. and/or spec. items. Per share data adj. for stk. divs. as of ex-div. date. E-Estimated. NA-Not Available. NM-Not Meaningful. NR-Not Ranked.

Office—850 Lagoon Drive, Chula Vista, CA 91910. **Tel**—(619) 691-4111. **Chrmn**—W. Barnes. **Pres & CEO**—R. H. Rau. **Sr VP & CFO**—L. A. Chapman. **VP & Secy**—R. W. Madsen. **VP & Treas**—R. Miller. **Dirs**—W. Barnes, E. E. Covert, W. M. Hoffman, S. F. Iacobellis, D. L. Moore, R. M. Price, R. H. Rau, W. P. Sommers, J. D. Steele, J. R. Wilson. **Transfer Agent & Registrar**—First Chicago Trust Co. of New York, Jersey City, NJ. **Incorporated** in California in 1949; reincorporated in Delaware in 1969. **Empl**-4,900. **S&P Analyst:** Alan Aaron

STANDARD & POOR'S

STOCK REPORTS

Rollins Environmental

NYSE Symbol **REN**
In S&P MidCap 400

08-OCT-95 **Industry:** Pollution Control

Summary: This hazardous waste management company operates six high-temperature incinerators and a rotary reactor that effectively destroy a variety of organic hazardous wastes.

S&P Opinion: Avoid (★★)

Recent Price • 4¼
52 Wk Range • 6⅛-3¾
Yield • Nil
12-Mo. P/E • NM

Quantitative Evaluations

Outlook (1 Lowest—5 Highest) • **1-**

Fair Value • **2⅝**

Risk • **Average**

Earn./Div. Rank • **B**

Technical Eval. • **Bearish** since 7/95

Rel. Strength Rank (1 Lowest—99 Highest) • **13**

Insider Activity • **Neutral**

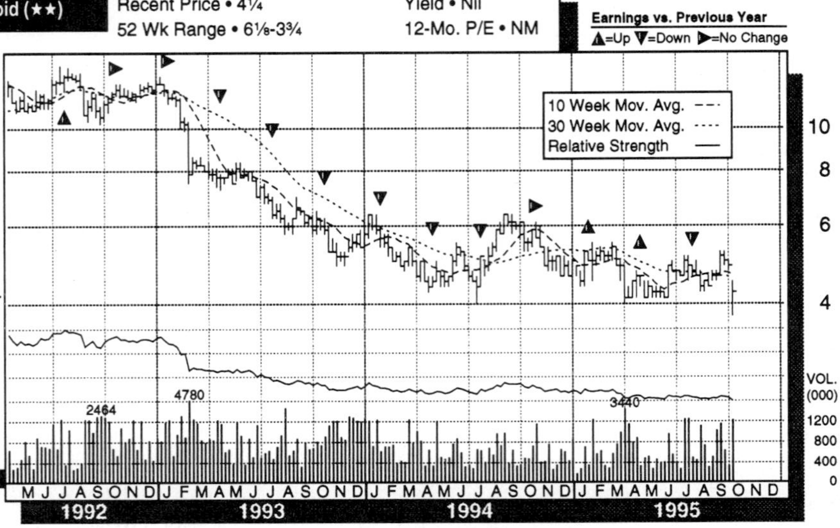

Overview - 06-OCT-95

Revenues are expected to climb more than 20% in fiscal 1996, primarily reflecting contributions from the acquisition of Aptus (March 1995) and improved pricing as Rollins has recently taken a price leadership position in the industry. Cement kilns, which are less costly to operate and have taken away large volumes from incinerators, have come under greater scrutiny by regulators, which should divert waste volumes to REN and help prices. Margins are expected to improve somewhat from ongoing streamlining efforts through the consolidation of acquisitions, and expense reductions, but with soft market conditions continuing, and higher interest expense resulting from debt related to the Aptus acquisition, losses are seen continuing through at least the first three quarters of fiscal 1996.

Valuation - 06-OCT-95

Rollins has aggressively expanded its operations by acquiring Aptus and Highway 36. However, overall weakness in the hazardous waste industry will probably continue into 1996. With additional incineration capacity in the industry, and an increased debt burden stemming from the Aptus acquisition, losses are likely to continue through much of fiscal 1996. The shares have dropped almost 70% since early 1993.
Long-term prospects have been dampened by excess capacity and by customer waste minimization efforts. We suggest avoiding purchase of the shares.

Key Stock Statistics

S&P EPS Est. 1995	-0.29	Tang. Bk. Value/Share	2.96
P/E on S&P Est. 1995	NM	Beta	1.22
Dividend Rate/Share	Nil	Shareholders	6,800
Shs. outstg. (M)	60.4	Market cap. (B)	$0.257
Avg. daily vol. (M)	0.177	Inst. holdings	51%
		Insider holdings	NA

Value of $10,000 invested 5 years ago: $ 3,156

Fiscal Year Ending Sep. 30

	1995	% Change	1994	% Change	1993	% Change
Revenues (Million $)						
1Q	49.91	5%	47.52	-19%	59.00	9%
2Q	43.35	5%	41.36	-24%	54.61	-14%
3Q	63.29	36%	46.70	-9%	51.56	-16%
4Q	—	—	45.90	-8%	49.68	-20%
Yr.	—	—	181.5	-16%	214.8	-11%
Income (Million $)						
1Q	1.22	NM	0.11	-98%	6.07	1%
2Q	-4.58	NM	-12.37	NM	2.88	-67%
3Q	-6.61	NM	1.57	-36%	2.46	-70%
4Q	—	—	0.22	-58%	0.52	-94%
Yr.	—	—	-10.48	NM	11.92	-63%
Earnings Per Share ($)						
1Q	0.02	—	Nil	—	0.10	NM
2Q	-0.08	NM	-0.20	NM	0.05	-64%
3Q	-0.11	NM	0.02	-50%	0.04	-71%
4Q	E-0.12	NM	0.01	NM	0.01	-93%
Yr.	E-0.29	NM	-0.17	NM	0.20	-62%

Next earnings report expected: late October

Rollins Environmental

Business Summary - 06-OCT-95

Rollins Environmental Services operates six high-temperature incinerators (2,000 degrees F plus) and a rotary reactor that effectively destroy organic hazardous wastes. It has a combined capacity greater than that of any other commercial operator. The company also disposes of aqueous wastes at a deep-injection well. Contributions to revenues in recent fiscal years were:

	1994	1993
Incineration	74.7%	79.2%
Transportation	8.8%	8.4%
CHEMPAK services	5.5%	4.7%
Other	11.0%	7.7%

REN's high-temperature incinerators are located in Deer Park, Tex. (two), Bridgeport, N.J., Baton Rouge, La., Aragonite, Utah, and Coffeyville, Kan. The incinerators eliminate organic wastes such as herbicides, plastics, halogenated solvents, pesticides, pharmaceuticals and refinery wastes, whether they are gases, liquids, sludges or solids. The rotary reactor, located in Deer Park, processes low-heat-content sludge wastes.

The company also transports wastes to its plants and other waste disposal facilities for treatment and disposal and operates landfills in Deer Trail, Colo., and at the Deer Park and Baton Rouge plants for disposal of hazardous wastes. Through its CHEMPAK unit, REN provides treatment and disposal services to generators of small quantities of hazardous wastes. In addition, the company treats, stores, recycles and repackages industrial chemical wastes for disposal at its plants or other facilities.

Important Developments

Sep. '95—Rollins said it expects to report a loss in fiscal 1995's fourth quarter comparable to or slightly larger than the $0.11 a share loss incurred in the third quarter, reflecting additional provisions for employee reductions, acquisition-related expenses and continued softness in the market.

Apr. '95—Rollins acquired Allworth of Tennessee, Inc., a waste processing facility, for $2.3 million in cash and the assumption of $6.4 million of debt.

Mar. '95—Rollins acquired Aptus, Inc. from Westinghouse Electric Corp. for $135 million in cash, debentures and the assumption of debt. Aptus, which has annual revenues of about $85 million, provides hazardous waste transportation, storage, laboratory analysis and incineration services from facilities in Utah, Kansas, Colorado, Texas and Minnesota.

Capitalization

Long Term Debt: $133,719,000 (6/95); incl. $66 million of 7.25% debs. due 2005, conv. into com. at $6.15 a sh.

Per Share Data ($) (Year Ended Sep. 30)

	1994	1993	1992	1991	1990	1989
Tangible Bk. Val.	3.36	3.53	3.43	2.99	2.65	2.26
Cash Flow	0.20	0.54	0.82	0.69	0.71	-0.03
Earnings	-0.17	0.20	0.53	0.43	0.46	-0.23
Dividends	Nil	0.10	0.09	0.09	0.08	0.08
Payout Ratio	Nil	51%	50%	21%	18%	NM
Prices - High	6⅜	13⅞	13⅞	12⅞	15¼	14⅛
- Low	4	4⅞	9¾	8⅜	7¼	9⅝
P/E Ratio - High	NM	69	26	30	33	NM
- Low	NM	24	18	19	16	NM

Income Statement Analysis (Million $)

	1994	%Chg	1993	%Chg	1992	%Chg	1991
Revs.	181	-16%	215	-10%	240	9%	221
Oper. Inc.	20.8	-48%	40.0	-41%	67.6	19%	56.6
Depr.	22.8	12%	20.4	15%	17.7	12%	15.8
Int. Exp.	0.4	-12%	0.4	-39%	0.7	-9%	0.8
Pretax Inc.	-16.9	NM	19.2	-61%	49.2	23%	40.0
Eff. Tax Rate	NM	—	38%	—	35%	—	35%
Net Inc.	-10.5	NM	11.9	-63%	32.0	24%	25.9

Balance Sheet & Other Fin. Data (Million $)

	1994	1993	1992	1991	1990	1989
Cash	54.8	47.5	55.1	48.8	42.8	23.7
Curr. Assets	100	89.0	105	97.0	85.0	75.0
Total Assets	273	279	283	258	234	216
Curr. Liab.	33.7	24.5	36.3	35.9	33.9	41.6
LT Debt	4.0	4.6	5.4	7.9	5.8	5.4
Common Eqty.	203	213	207	180	159	136
Total Cap.	221	233	227	201	174	148
Cap. Exp.	18.0	33.0	37.4	28.7	22.0	25.2
Cash Flow	12.3	32.3	49.7	41.7	42.8	-1.7

Ratio Analysis

	1994	1993	1992	1991	1990	1989
Curr. Ratio	3.0	3.6	2.9	2.7	2.5	1.8
% LT Debt of Cap.	1.8	2.0	2.4	4.0	3.3	3.7
% Net Inc.of Revs.	NM	5.6	13.3	11.7	13.9	NM
% Ret. on Assets	NM	4.2	11.8	10.5	12.4	NM
% Ret. on Equity	NM	5.7	16.6	15.3	18.9	NM

Dividend Data —Dividends were initiated in 1984 and omitted in October 1993. A "poison pill" stock purchase rights plan was adopted in 1989.

Data as orig. reptd.; bef. results of disc. opers. and/or spec. items. Per share data adj. for stk. divs. as of ex-div. date. E-Estimated. NA-Not Available. NM-Not Meaningful. NR-Not Ranked.

Office—One Rollins Plaza, Wilmington, DE 19803. **Tel**—(302) 426-3314. **Chrmn & CEO**—J. W. Rollins, Sr. **Vice Chrmn**—N. Pappas. **Pres & COO**—J. V. Flynn. **GVP-Fin & Treas**—F. H. Minner. **GVP & Investor Contact**—Jack Hornberger (302-426-2949). **Secy**—M. B. Kinnard. **Dirs**—P. J. Bagley, N. Pappas, W. B. Philipbar, Jr., J. W. Rollins, Sr., J. W. Rollins, Jr., H. B. Tippie. **Transfer Agent & Registrar**—Registrar & Transfer Co., Cranford, NJ. **Reincorporated** in Delaware in 1978. **Empl-** 1,295. **S&P Analyst:** Stewart Scharf

Rollins, Inc.

NYSE Symbol **ROL**
In S&P MidCap 400

26-JUL-95 **Industry:** Services

Summary: Rollins primarily offers termite and pest control services under the Orkin name. It also provides lawn care and landscaping services and sells electronic security systems.

S&P Opinion: Avoid (★★)

Recent Price • 23½
52 Wk Range • 28⅝-22
Yield • 2.4%
12-Mo. P/E • 16.5

Quantitative Evaluations
Outlook (1 Lowest—5 Highest) • **3-**
Fair Value • **22⅞**
Risk • **Low**
Earn./Div. Rank • **A-**

Technical Eval. • **Bullish** since 6/95
Rel. Strength Rank (1 Lowest—99 Highest) • **9**
Insider Activity • **NA**

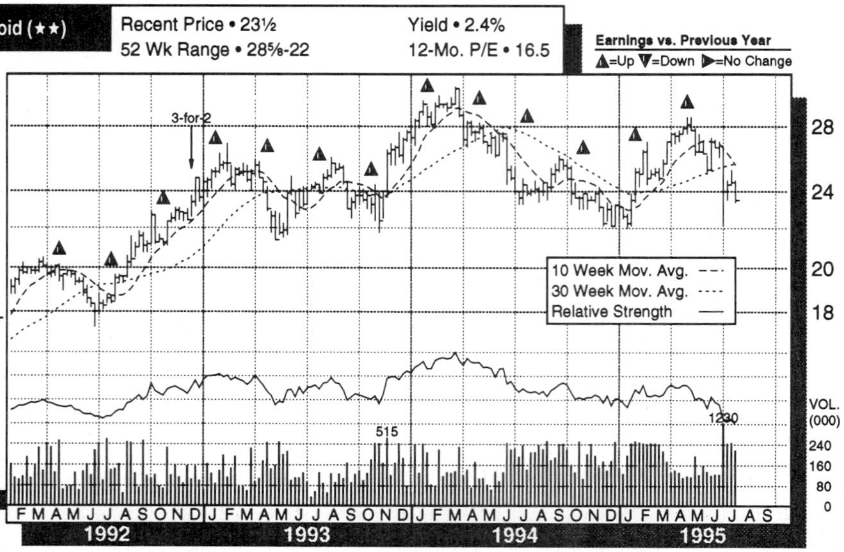

Overview - 26-JUL-95

Rollins reported unchanged earnings per share for the second quarter of 1995 and a very modest year-to-year increase in sales. The company said that cold and wet spring weather had an unfavorable effect on demand for termite services. Similar problems limited sales growth all last year, although cost controls enabled Rollins to realize an 11% gain in earnings. The unfavorable weather should again limit sales growth this year. Furthermore, operating margins began to narrow in 1995's second quarter. We therefore believe that earnings growth will be unimpressive in 1995 and project that earnings per share will increase about 4%, to $1.45.

Valuation - 26-JUL-95

Rollins shares sold off in late June when the company announced that second-quarter earnings would be flat to up slightly. Rollins had been selling at a premium to the market on a price-to-earnings basis, and the stock was vulnerable to disappointing news regarding earnings. The shares now sell at a more moderate 16 times estimated 1995 earnings, which is the low end of the company's P/E range over the past three years. Despite this more conservative valuation, we do not believe the shares will advance significantly until the outlook for earnings growth improves.

Key Stock Statistics

S&P EPS Est. 1995	1.45	Tang. Bk. Value/Share	4.33
P/E on S&P Est. 1995	16.2	Beta	1.00
S&P EPS Est. 1996	1.55	Shareholders	4,000
Dividend Rate/Share	0.56	Market cap. (B)	$0.851
Shs. outstg. (M)	35.8	Inst. holdings	37%
Avg. daily vol. (M)	0.102	Insider holdings	NA

Value of $10,000 invested 5 years ago: $ 25,272

Fiscal Year Ending Dec. 31

	1995	% Change	1994	% Change	1993	% Change
Revenues (Million $)						
1Q	142.6	5%	136.4	7%	127.3	8%
2Q	175.4	2%	171.9	5%	163.3	9%
3Q	—	—	158.0	4%	151.8	10%
4Q	—	—	139.0	4%	133.4	9%
Yr.	—	—	605.3	5%	575.8	9%
Income (Million $)						
1Q	7.81	13%	6.89	17%	5.87	15%
2Q	21.10	NM	21.07	10%	19.07	16%
3Q	—	—	13.01	11%	11.69	13%
4Q	—	—	8.60	10%	7.84	26%
Yr.	—	—	49.56	11%	44.47	17%
Earnings Per Share ($)						
1Q	0.22	16%	0.19	19%	0.16	14%
2Q	0.59	NM	0.59	9%	0.54	15%
3Q	E0.38	—	0.36	9%	0.33	18%
4Q	E0.26	—	0.25	14%	0.22	22%
Yr.	E1.45	—	1.39	11%	1.25	17%

Next earnings report expected: late October

Rollins, Inc.

Business Summary - 26-JUL-95

Rollins, Inc. provides termite and pest control, lawn care and plantscaping services under the Orkin name, as well as security-related products and services. Contributions by business segment in 1994 were:

	Revs.	Profits
Orkin	88%	89%
Rollins Protective	10%	7%
Other	2%	4%

Orkin Pest Control is one of the world's largest termite and pest control service concerns. Continuous protection against termites, insects and rodents through periodic preventive treatments is provided to homes and businesses, including hotel, foodservice and transportation companies. Operations are conducted from 367 company-owned branches serving customers in 49 states, the District of Columbia, Puerto Rico, the Bahamas and Mexico. The seasonal business is strongest in the spring and summer.

Orkin Lawn Care provides fertilization, weed and insect control, seeding, aeration of lawns and tree and shrub care through 22 branches serving customers in 10 states. The company sold 11 northern Orkin branches to Barefoot Grass Lawn Service Inc. effective December 31, 1994; the branches were sold to allow the company to focus on its lawn service business in the Sunbelt region.

Orkin Plantscaping was added in 1990 through acquisitions. From nine branches and one supply outlet, Plantscaping provides interior landscaping services in 17 states and the District of Columbia to commercial businesses such as hotels, shopping malls, restaurants and office buildings.

Rollins Protective Services offers a full range of protective services to residential and commercial clients. Operations are conducted from 48 company-owned branches serving customers in 35 states and the District of Columbia. In addition to designing and installing wireless and hardwired electronic security systems, the company provides guaranteed routine maintenance programs, as well as 24-hour emergency repair and 24-hour alarm monitoring services.

Important Developments

Jul. '95—The Rollins Protective Services subsidiary announced it completed the purchase of the Baltimore Central Station operations of Thorn Automated Systems, Inc., which services over 5,000 accounts, for an undisclosed consideration. Earlier, Rollins Protective acquired Family Home Security of Louisville, Ky., and Paradise Valley Alarms in Phoenix, Ariz.

Capitalization

Long Term Debt: None (3/95).

Per Share Data ($)

(Year Ended Dec. 31)

	1994	1993	1992	1991	1990	1989
Tangible Bk. Val.	4.23	3.32	2.46	1.79	1.27	0.90
Cash Flow	1.61	1.48	1.29	1.11	0.99	0.87
Earnings	1.39	1.25	1.07	0.89	0.77	0.67
Dividends	0.50	0.44	0.40	0.39	0.37	0.36
Payout Ratio	36%	35%	37%	44%	48%	54%
Prices - High	30¾	27¾	24¾	19⅛	14⅜	14
- Low	22⅛	21⅜	17⅞	12⅜	10⅝	11¼
P/E Ratio - High	22	22	23	22	19	21
- Low	16	17	16	14	14	17

Income Statement Analysis (Million $)

	1994	%Chg	1993	%Chg	1992	%Chg	1991
Revs.	605	5%	576	9%	528	11%	476
Oper. Inc.	85.7	9%	78.8	14%	68.9	19%	58.0
Depr.	8.1	-2%	8.3	4%	8.0	3%	7.8
Int. Exp.	Nil	—	Nil	—	Nil	—	Nil
Pretax Inc.	80.6	11%	72.9	16%	62.8	21%	52.1
Eff. Tax Rate	39%	—	39%	—	40%	—	40%
Net Inc.	49.6	11%	44.5	17%	38.0	21%	31.5

Balance Sheet & Other Fin. Data (Million $)

	1994	1993	1992	1991	1990	1989
Cash	83.7	69.1	50.7	41.2	31.8	26.0
Curr. Assets	215	185	152	121	95.0	84.0
Total Assets	295	267	236	205	178	160
Curr. Liab.	66.9	67.0	62.1	56.4	49.6	40.4
LT Debt	Nil	Nil	Nil	Nil	Nil	Nil
Common Eqty.	194	161	130	105	87.0	72.0
Total Cap.	206	173	151	126	105	97.0
Cap. Exp.	8.3	7.7	6.6	8.0	8.0	9.0
Cash Flow	57.7	52.8	46.0	39.3	34.9	31.0

Ratio Analysis

	1994	1993	1992	1991	1990	1989
Curr. Ratio	3.2	2.8	2.4	2.1	1.9	2.1
% LT Debt of Cap.	Nil	Nil	Nil	Nil	Nil	Nil
% Net Inc.of Revs.	8.2	7.7	7.2	6.6	6.3	5.8
% Ret. on Assets	17.6	17.6	17.2	16.5	16.2	15.3
% Ret. on Equity	27.9	30.6	32.3	32.8	34.5	35.3

Dividend Data (Dividends have been paid since 1961. A dividend reinvestment plan is available.)

Amt. of Div. $	Date Decl.	Ex-Div. Date	Stock of Record	Payment Date
0.125	Jul. 26	Aug. 04	Aug. 10	Sep. 09 '94
0.125	Oct. 25	Nov. 04	Nov. 10	Dec. 09 '94
0.140	Jan. 24	Feb. 06	Feb. 10	Mar. 10 '95
0.140	Apr. 25	May. 04	May. 10	Jun. 09 '95

Data as orig. reptd.; bef. results of disc. opers. and/or spec. items. Per share data adj. for stk. divs. as of ex-div. date. E-Estimated. NA-Not Available. NM-Not Meaningful. NR-Not Ranked.

Office—2170 Piedmont Rd., N.E., Atlanta, GA 30324. **Tel**—(404) 888-2000. **Chrmn & CEO**—R. R. Rollins. **Pres**—G. W. Rollins. **CFO, Secy, Treas & Investor Contact**—Gene L. Smith. **Dirs**—B. J. Dismuke, W. Looney, G. W. Rollins, J. W. Rollins, R. R. Rollins, H. B. Tippie, J. B. Williams. **Transfer Agent & Registrar**—Trust Co. Bank, Atlanta. **Incorporated** in Delaware in 1948. **Empl**-8,774. **S&P Analyst:** Stephen Madonna, CFA

STANDARD & POOR'S

STOCK REPORTS

Ruddick Corp.

NYSE Symbol **RDK**
In S&P MidCap 400

23-AUG-95 **Industry:** Retail Stores

Summary: This diversified holding company derives the bulk of its profits from supermarket operations. It also manufactures thread and yarn, and makes and distributes business forms.

Quantitative Evaluations
Outlook (1 Lowest—5 Highest) • **5+**
Fair Value • **28**
Risk • **Low**
Earn./Div. Rank • **A**
Technical Eval. • **Bullish** since 12/94
Rel. Strength Rank (1 Lowest—99 Highest) • **78**
Insider Activity • **NA**

Recent Price • 24½
52 Wk Range • 25¼-17
Yield • 2.6%
12-Mo. P/E • 14.8

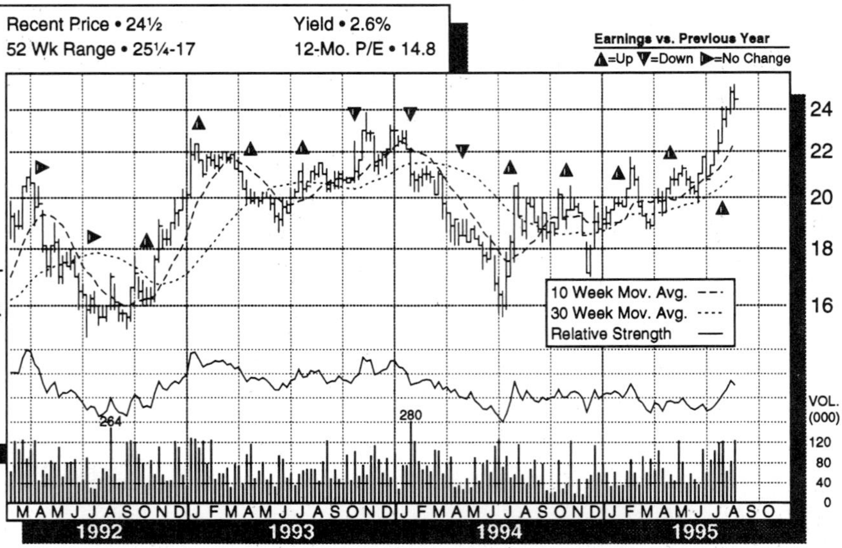

Business Profile - 23-AUG-95

This diversified holding company operates 142 supermarkets in five southeastern states under the Harris Teeter name, manufactures and distributes industrial sewing thread and yarn, produces and distributes business forms and labels, and operates a venture capital division. Sales and earnings gains in recent periods have benefited from continued strength at A&E and Harris Teeter, and improved performance at Jordan Graphics. A two-for-one stock split is scheduled to be paid on October 1, 1995.

Operational Review - 23-AUG-95

Net sales in the nine months ended July 2, 1995, advanced 9.0%, year to year, benefiting from gains of 11%, 8.2% and 19%, respectively, at American & Efird, Harris Teeter and Jordan Graphics. Gross margins widened, and total operating profits increased 27%. After 29% higher net interest expenses, and taxes at 34.8%, versus 36.5%, net income climbed 30%, to $29,875,000 ($1.28 a share, based on 1.6% fewer shares), from $22,960,000 ($0.97).

Stock Performance - 18-AUG-95

In the past 30 trading days, RDK's shares have increased 15%, compared to a 0.51% rise in the S&P 500. Average trading volume for the past five days was 30,100 shares, compared with the 40-day moving average of 20,369 shares.

Key Stock Statistics

Dividend Rate/Share	0.64	Shareholders	14,100
Shs. outstg. (M)	23.1	Market cap. (B)	$0.571
Avg. daily vol. (M)	0.020	Inst. holdings	61%
Tang. Bk. Value/Share	12.57	Insider holdings	NA
Beta	0.85		

Value of $10,000 invested 5 years ago: $ 19,430

Fiscal Year Ending Sep. 30

	1995	% Change	1994	% Change	1993	% Change
Revenues (Million $)						
1Q	508.3	9%	464.6	10%	422.4	9%
2Q	509.9	9%	465.9	12%	417.7	8%
3Q	526.0	8%	486.6	15%	424.4	6%
4Q	—	—	491.4	5%	468.0	19%
Yr.	—	—	1,908	10%	1,733	10%
Income (Million $)						
1Q	8.27	32%	6.27	-22%	8.01	4%
2Q	10.30	38%	7.44	-7%	8.01	10%
3Q	11.30	22%	9.25	6%	8.76	8%
4Q	—	—	8.85	70%	5.22	-32%
Yr.	—	—	31.81	6%	30.00	-3%
Earnings Per Share ($)						
1Q	0.35	35%	0.26	-24%	0.34	6%
2Q	0.45	41%	0.32	-3%	0.33	6%
3Q	0.48	23%	0.39	5%	0.37	9%
4Q	—	—	0.38	73%	0.22	-33%
Yr.	—	—	1.35	7%	1.26	-3%

Next earnings report expected: early November

Ruddick Corp.

Business Summary - 23-AUG-95

Ruddick Corporation is a diversified holding company whose subsidiaries operate supermarkets, manufacture yarn and thread and business forms, and make venture capital investments. Contributions by subsidiary (profits in millions) in fiscal 1994 were:

	Sales	Profits
Harris Teeter	83%	$26.9
American & Efird	14%	$38.8
Jordan Graphics	3%	-$1.4

The Harris Teeter (HT) subsidiary operates supermarkets, with a total of 139 stores in operation as of fiscal 1994 year end, in North Carolina (91), South Carolina (25), Virginia (19), Georgia (three) and Tennessee (one). The stores carry typical food items sold by supermarkets, as well as nonfood items such as health and beauty aids. Most HT stores feature a full-service deli, bakery, fresh seafood and meat counters, and wine and floral departments. HT's policy is have each store undergo a major remodel every eight years. Three stores were remodeled during fiscal 1994, and an additional six stores are expected to be remodeled in fiscal 1995.

The number of HT stores at recent fiscal year ends:

1994	139
1993	138
1992	135
1991	132
1990	130

American & Efird (A&E) makes industrial sewing thread from natural and synthetic fibers for use by clothing, automotive, upholstered furniture, home furnishings and footwear manufacturers. It also manufactures sales yarn used by the knitting and weaving industries and consumer sewing thread for the home.

Jordan Graphics (formerly Jordan Business Forms) produces and distributes a broad line of business forms, labels, envelopes, special items and laser printed products.

Ruddick Investment Co. is a wholly owned venture-capital concern, with capital gains as its principal objective.

Important Developments

Jul. '95—RDK noted that third quarter sales at American & Efird advanced 9.4%, year to year, reflecting improving market share; operating profit climbed 36%. Harris Teeter's sales rose 7.5%, aided by improved sales volume and product mix, and operating profits were up 14%. Despite an 18% sales gain, operating profit at Jordan Graphics fell 91% after a one-time charge associated with the sale of the Baltimore plant.

Capitalization

Long Term Debt: $133,737,000 (7/2/95).

Per Share Data ($) (Year Ended Sep. 30)

	1994	1993	1992	1991	1990	1989
Tangible Bk. Val.	12.57	11.89	11.03	10.10	9.30	8.37
Cash Flow	3.03	2.81	2.74	2.65	2.61	2.39
Earnings	1.35	1.26	1.30	1.24	1.19	1.04
Dividends	0.43	0.43	0.39	0.37	0.35	0.31
Payout Ratio	32%	34%	29%	32%	29%	29%
Prices - High	23	$23\frac{7}{8}$	$21\frac{1}{4}$	$17\frac{3}{8}$	$15\frac{1}{8}$	$14\frac{3}{4}$
- Low	$15\frac{5}{8}$	$18\frac{5}{8}$	$14\frac{7}{8}$	10	$9\frac{1}{2}$	$10\frac{3}{8}$
P/E Ratio - High	17	19	16	14	13	14
- Low	12	15	11	8	8	10

Income Statement Analysis (Million $)

	1994	%Chg	1993	%Chg	1992	%Chg	1991
Revs.	1,908	10%	1,733	10%	1,569	6%	1,478
Oper. Inc.	98.0	-2%	100	6%	93.9	8%	87.0
Depr.	39.7	8%	36.9	8%	34.3	12%	30.6
Int. Exp.	8.6	1%	8.5	-11%	9.5	-28%	13.2
Pretax Inc.	50.0	1%	49.5	-2%	50.4	16%	43.6
Eff. Tax Rate	37%	—	39%	—	38%	—	38%
Net Inc.	31.8	6%	30.0	-3%	30.8	15%	26.8

Balance Sheet & Other Fin. Data (Million $)

	1994	1993	1992	1991	1990	1989
Cash	14.5	12.4	20.4	10.8	11.4	10.5
Curr. Assets	277	258	242	216	199	183
Total Assets	641	587	542	498	468	439
Curr. Liab.	190	162	144	136	124	123
LT Debt	104	98.0	89.0	74.0	109	112
Common Eqty.	291	274	254	232	183	157
Total Cap.	431	406	386	351	333	307
Cap. Exp.	68.2	55.8	48.6	43.2	48.1	50.6
Cash Flow	71.5	66.8	65.0	57.3	52.6	46.8

Ratio Analysis

	1994	1993	1992	1991	1990	1989
Curr. Ratio	1.5	1.6	1.7	1.6	1.6	1.5
% LT Debt of Cap.	24.2	24.2	23.1	21.2	32.7	36.6
% Net Inc.of Revs.	1.7	1.7	2.0	1.8	1.7	1.6
% Ret. on Assets	5.2	5.3	5.9	5.1	5.2	4.8
% Ret. on Equity	11.2	11.4	12.6	12.0	13.8	13.4

Dividend Data —Dividends have been paid since 1976. A stock purchase rights plan was adopted in 1990. A 2-for-1 stock split was declared on August 17, 1995, with an ex-dividend date of September 13, 1995, a record date of September 15, 1995, and a payment date of October 1, 1995.

Amt. of Div. $	Date Decl.	Ex-Div. Date	Stock of Record	Payment Date
0.070	Nov. 17	Nov. 28	Dec. 02	Jan. 01 '95
0.070	Feb. 16	Mar. 06	Mar. 10	Apr. 01 '95
0.080	May. 18	Jun. 06	Jun. 09	Jul. 01 '95
.08 Ext.	Aug. 17	Sep. 13	Sep. 15	Oct. 01 '95
0.060	Aug. 17	Sep. 13	Sep. 15	Oct. 01 '95

Data as orig. reptd.; bef. results of disc. opers. and/or spec. items. Per share data adj. for stk. divs. as of ex-div. date. E-Estimated. NA-Not Available. NM-Not Meaningful. NR-Not Ranked.

Office—2000 Two First Union Center, Charlotte, NC 28282. **Tel**—(704) 372-5404. **Chrmn**—A. T. Dickson. **Pres**—J. W. Copeland. **VP-Fin & Investor Contact**—Richard N. Brigden. **Secy**—D. B. Williford. **Treas**—D. A. Stephenson. **Dirs**—T. M. Belk, E. B. Borden Jr., J. W. Copeland, A. T. Dickson, R. S. Dickson, B. F. Dolan, R. Dowd, J. E. S. Hynes, H. L. McColl Jr., E. C. Wall Jr. **Transfer Agent & Registrar**—Wachovia Bank of North Carolina, Winston-Salem. **Incorporated** in North Carolina in 1968. **Empl**-19,000. **S&P Analyst:** Maureen C. Carini

STANDARD & POOR'S

Savannah Foods & Industries

STOCK REPORTS

NYSE Symbol **SFI**

In S&P MidCap 400

12-OCT-95 **Industry:** Food

Summary: This company refines both beet and cane sugar for sale in a variety of forms to consumers and processors.

Quantitative Evaluations

Outlook
(1 Lowest—5 Highest)
• 1−

Fair Value
• 9½

Risk
• **Average**

Earn./Div. Rank
• **B**

Technical Eval.
• **Bullish** since 4/95

Rel. Strength Rank
(1 Lowest—99 Highest)
• **94**

Insider Activity
• **Neutral**

Recent Price • 13¼
52 Wk Range • 14¾-9
Yield • 0.7%
12-Mo. P/E • NM

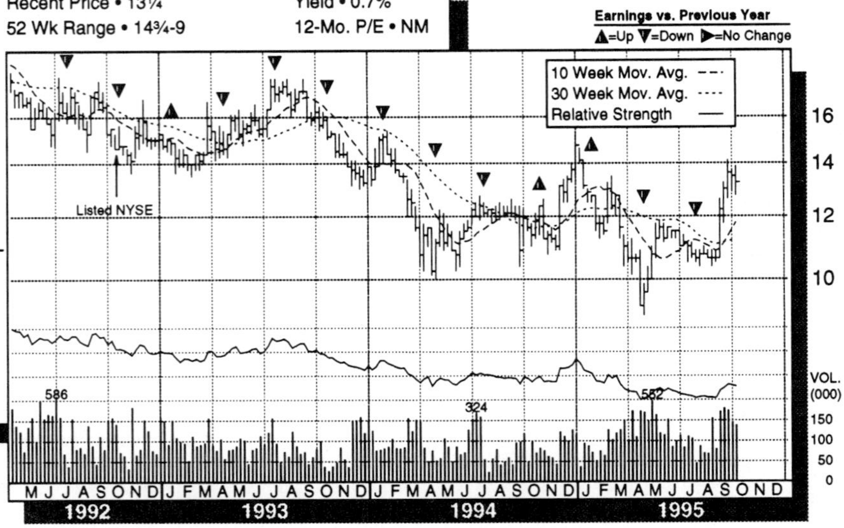

Business Profile - 06-OCT-95

The company's strategy is to expand outside of the United States and to sell non-sugar related products that fit with existing customer relationships and distribution channels. Savannah's future profitability will be affected by the 1995 Farm Bill being debated in Congress. SFI believes its low cost structure and efficient manufacturing operations will allow it benefit from any resultant industry changes. The dividend was cut 81% with the July 1995 payment.

Operational Review - 12-OCT-95

Sales in the 39 weeks ended July 2, 1995, edged up 1.4%, year to year, as sugar volume was flat and selling prices rose slightly. Margins narrowed on higher raw sugar costs, and increased operating costs at the beet molasses desugarization facility; selling, general and administrative expenses declined. Results were further penalized by increased net other expense. Despite a tax benefit, versus taxes at 33.1%, a net loss contrasted with income.

Stock Performance - 06-OCT-95

In the past 30 trading days, SFI's shares have increased 25%, compared to a 4% rise in the S&P 500. Average trading volume for the past five days was 27,400 shares, compared with the 40-day moving average of 45,033 shares.

Key Stock Statistics

Dividend Rate/Share	0.10	Shareholders	3,500
Shs. outstg. (M)	26.2	Market cap. (B)	$0.354
Avg. daily vol. (M)	0.044	Inst. holdings	31%
Tang. Bk. Value/Share	6.86	Insider holdings	NA
Beta	0.93		

Value of $10,000 invested 5 years ago: $ 5,696

Fiscal Year Ending Sep. 30

	1995	% Change	1994	% Change	1993	% Change
Revenues (Million $)						
1Q	282.5	NM	280.2	-8%	305.0	4%
2Q	253.4	3%	247.0	-3%	255.0	NM
3Q	275.5	NM	272.9	NM	271.0	-4%
4Q	—	—	274.3	-6%	292.0	-2%
Yr.	—	—	1,074	-4%	1,123	-1%
Income (Million $)						
1Q	3.62	2%	3.54	34%	2.65	-42%
2Q	-1.93	NM	-0.27	NM	1.49	-80%
3Q	-2.43	NM	0.23	-85%	1.49	-73%
4Q	—	—	2.24	157%	0.87	-91%
Yr.	—	—	5.74	-61%	14.63	-46%
Earnings Per Share ($)						
1Q	0.14	8%	0.13	-65%	0.37	6%
2Q	-0.07	NM	-0.01	NM	0.10	-41%
3Q	-0.10	NM	0.01	-83%	0.06	-79%
4Q	—	—	0.09	NM	0.03	-86%
Yr.	—	—	0.22	-61%	0.56	-45%

Next earnings report expected: early December

Savannah Foods & Industries

Business Summary - 06-OCT-95

Savannah Foods & Industries, Inc. is one of the largest refined cane and beet sugar producers in the U.S. Products are marketed primarily in the eastern half of the country. The company operates three cane sugar refineries, five sugar beet processing plants and a raw sugar mill.

The Savannah Sugar Refinery division refines and processes sugar and sugar products (including blends with corn syrups) and liquid animal feeds at a refinery near Savannah, Ga. Output is marketed mainly in the Southeast under the brand name Dixie Crystals, considered the leading brand of sugar marketed in the area. Packaged sugars are also distributed under other brand names and private labels.

Wholly owned Everglades Sugar Refinery produces bulk, liquid (including corn syrup blends) and a limited line of packaged sugars under the names Evercane and Dixie Crystals. Grocery sugars are marketed both directly and through brokers in Florida. Industrial sugars are marketed throughout the East and Midwest.

Colonial Sugars refines sugar and sugar products (including blends) and by-products of the sugar refining process. It markets a complete line of bulk, packaged and liquid sugars under the Colonial name.

Michigan Sugar Co. processes sugar beets into refined sugar and produces beet pulp and molasses. Products are sold under the Pioneer brand name, primarily in Michigan and, to a lesser extent, in the midwestern and eastern portions of the U.S.

A line of sugar envelopes and portion-control items, consisting of individual servings of salt, pepper, nondairy creamers, etc., is produced by Dixie Crystals Foodservice, Inc. and is sold under the names Dixie Crystals and Pioneer and various private labels. Saccharin- and aspartame-based sweeteners are marketed under the Sweet Thing and Sweet Thing II brand names, respectively.

Other subsidiaries include Phoenix Packaging, which packages powdered and brown sugars; Raceland Sugars, a producer of raw sugar and by-products; and Food Carrier Inc., an irregular-route transporter of sugar products and general commodities.

Important Developments

Oct. '95—The company said it and other industry particpants are lobbying the Department of Agriculture to allow foreign sugar to enter the U.S. for the next quota year. This would help reduce raw sugar prices. At recent levels, raw sugar costs and refined sugar prices were virtually the same, making cane sugar refining unprofitable throughout the industry.

Aug. '95—SFI attributed losses in the second and third quarters of fiscal 1995 to the sharp increase in raw sugar prices since October 1994.

Capitalization

Long Term Debt: $111,976,000 (7/2/95).

Per Share Data ($) (Year Ended Sep. 30)

	1994	1993	1992	1991	1990	1989
Tangible Bk. Val.	6.87	7.42	8.03	8.39	7.50	6.24
Cash Flow	1.32	1.97	1.88	2.15	2.41	2.08
Earnings	0.22	0.56	1.03	1.43	1.80	1.53
Dividends	0.54	0.54	0.52	0.49	0.39	0.29
Payout Ratio	NM	97%	50%	34%	22%	19%
Prices - High	15⅜	17⅞	20½	26½	33	28⅛
- Low	10	13	13⅝	15	19¼	9
P/E Ratio - High	70	32	20	19	18	18
- Low	45	23	13	10	11	6

Income Statement Analysis (Million $)

	1994	%Chg	1993	%Chg	1992	%Chg	1991
Revs.	1,074	-4%	1,123	-1%	1,138	-5%	1,200
Oper. Inc.	49.3	-28%	68.6	-4%	71.5	-17%	86.2
Depr.	29.0	-22%	37.1	66%	22.4	15%	19.4
Int. Exp.	13.4	2%	13.1	25%	10.5	7%	9.8
Pretax Inc.	8.6	-60%	21.4	-48%	41.0	-32%	60.1
Eff. Tax Rate	33%	—	32%	—	33%	—	36%
Net Inc.	5.7	-61%	14.6	-47%	27.3	-29%	38.3

Balance Sheet & Other Fin. Data (Million $)

	1994	1993	1992	1991	1990	1989
Cash	28.4	27.2	8.0	59.6	26.4	52.9
Curr. Assets	199	270	371	357	310	319
Total Assets	486	568	636	582	496	482
Curr. Liab.	85.0	155	234	223	179	201
LT Debt	140	142	126	94.4	77.4	76.4
Common Eqty.	188	195	211	224	201	170
Total Cap.	328	341	346	339	302	269
Cap. Exp.	24.0	69.9	45.3	55.7	41.6	34.5
Cash Flow	34.7	51.7	49.7	57.6	65.2	56.0

Ratio Analysis

	1994	1993	1992	1991	1990	1989
Curr. Ratio	2.3	1.7	1.6	1.6	1.7	1.6
% LT Debt of Cap.	42.7	41.7	36.6	27.8	25.6	28.4
% Net Inc.of Revs.	0.5	1.3	2.4	3.2	4.0	3.7
% Ret. on Assets	1.1	2.4	4.5	7.1	10.0	9.3
% Ret. on Equity	3.0	7.2	12.7	18.0	26.4	26.8

Dividend Data —Dividends have been paid since 1924. A dividend reinvestment plan is available.

Amt. of Div. $	Date Decl.	Ex-Div. Date	Stock of Record	Payment Date
0.135	Oct. 20	Dec. 05	Dec. 09	Dec. 29 '94
0.135	Feb. 16	Mar. 06	Mar. 10	Apr. 01 '95
0.025	Apr. 20	May. 31	Jun. 06	Jul. 01 '95
0.025	Aug. 17	Sep. 06	Sep. 08	Oct. 02 '95

Data as orig. reptd.; bef. results of disc. opers. and/or spec. items. Per share data adj. for stk. divs. as of ex-div. date. E-Estimated. NA-Not Available. NM-Not Meaningful. NR-Not Ranked.

Office—P.O. Box 339, Savannah, GA 31402. **Tel**—(912) 234-1261. **Pres, CEO & COO**—W. W. Sprague III. **SVP-Fin**—W. R. Steinhauer. **Secy**—J. M. Tatum. **Dirs**—W. W. Bradley, J. D. Carswell, R. E. Cartledge, D. C. Critz, L. B. Durham Jr., F. S. Exley, E. Flegenheimer, A. M. Gignilliat Jr., R. L. Harrison, R. S. Jepson Jr., W. W. Sprague III, H. M. Tarbutton, A. Tenenbaum. **Transfer Agent & Registrar**—Wachovia Bank of North Carolina, Winston-Salem. **Incorporated** in New York in 1916; reincorporated in Delaware in 1969. **Empl**-2,095. **S&P Analyst:** Efraim Levy

STANDARD & POOR'S

STOCK REPORTS

Sbarro, Inc.

NYSE Symbol **SBA**
In S&P MidCap 400

18-AUG-95 **Industry:** Food serving

Summary: This company operates and franchises a national chain of more than 700 cafeteria-style Italian restaurants under the Sbarro name.

S&P Opinion: Avoid (★★) | Recent Price • 22⅝ | 52 Wk Range • 27⅞-19⅞ | Yield • 3.4% | 12-Mo. P/E • 14.7

Quantitative Evaluations
Outlook
(1 Lowest—5 Highest)
• **5-**
Fair Value
• **30⅞**
Risk
• **Average**
Earn./Div. Rank
• **B+**

Technical Eval.
• **Bullish** since 7/95
Rel. Strength Rank
(1 Lowest—99 Highest)
• **13**
Insider Activity
• **NA**

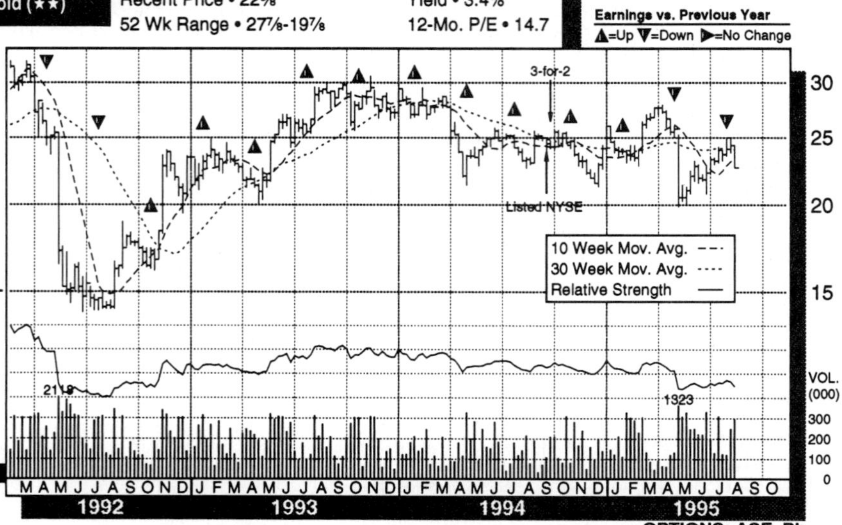

OPTIONS: ASE, Ph

Overview - 17-AUG-95

We expect SBA's revenue growth in 1995 to come largely from the operation of more company-owned units. During the year, we look for approximately 65 such units to open, plus about 45 franchises. However, with comparable-unit sales expected to be up only modestly from the year-earlier level, we look for 1995 profit margins to narrow from prior-year levels. We expect better earnings and margin comparisons in 1995's second half than there were in the year's disappointing first half. Following relatively flat full-year earnings per share in 1995, we look for earnings growth of about 13% in 1996. Also, SBA has a strong balance sheet; at the end of the first quarter, cash equivalents and marketable securities totaled $60 million, and SBA had no debt.

Valuation - 17-AUG-95

Based on expected earnings in 1996, the current valuation on this restaurant company stock seems modest. However, after a profit disappointment in early 1995, we feel that investors should be increasingly wary of accepting SBA as a predictable growth company. Looking farther out, we are skeptical of the company's ability to generate long-term annual profit growth that is much of above 10%. As a result, we advise avoiding the shares at this time.

Key Stock Statistics

S&P EPS Est. 1995	1.60	Tang. Bk. Value/Share	8.87
P/E on S&P Est. 1995	14.1	Beta	1.01
S&P EPS Est. 1996	1.75	Shareholders	500
Dividend Rate/Share	0.76	Market cap. (B)	$0.450
Shs. outstg. (M)	20.3	Inst. holdings	51%
Avg. daily vol. (M)	0.053	Insider holdings	0%

Value of $10,000 invested 5 years ago: $ 15,021

Fiscal Year Ending Dec. 31

	1995	% Change	1994	% Change	1993	% Change
Revenues (Million $)						
1Q	84.61	9%	77.41	12%	69.21	12%
2Q	68.76	9%	63.01	12%	56.25	16%
3Q	—	—	69.78	11%	62.59	13%
4Q	—	—	85.79	11%	77.56	8%
Yr.	—	—	296.0	11%	265.5	12%
Income (Million $)						
1Q	4.61	-25%	6.17	7%	5.77	53%
2Q	5.49	-6%	5.84	16%	5.04	45%
3Q	—	—	8.06	25%	6.46	5%
4Q	—	—	12.96	17%	11.09	4%
Yr.	—	—	33.03	17%	28.35	18%
Earnings Per Share ($)						
1Q	0.23	-25%	0.31	7%	0.29	54%
2Q	0.27	-6%	0.29	16%	0.25	42%
3Q	E0.41	3%	0.40	25%	0.32	7%
4Q	E0.69	10%	0.63	15%	0.55	4%
Yr.	E1.60	-2%	1.63	16%	1.40	19%

Next earnings report expected: mid November

Sbarro, Inc.

Business Summary - 17-AUG-95

Sbarro, Inc. operates and franchises a chain of family-style Italian restaurants, under the "Sbarro," "Sbarro the Italian Eatery" and "Cafe Sbarro" names. At July 16, 1995, there were 588 company-owned restaurants and 180 franchised restaurants in operation.

Most of SBA's restaurants are located in the U.S., including many that are in enclosed shopping malls. The restaurants are typically cafeteria-style units, featuring a menu of popular Italian food, including pizza with a variety of toppings, a selection of pasta dishes, other hot and cold Italian entrees, salads, sandwiches, cheesecake and other desserts. Pizza, which is sold largely by the slice, is believed to account for roughly 50% of restaurant sales.

In 1994, there was a net addition of 80 restaurants, including 52 company-owned units and 28 franchise outlets. Comparable-unit sales at company-owned restaurants were up 3.1% in 1994, following a 2.5% rise in 1993, and a slight decline in 1992. SBA is increasingly using a higher-volume self-serve buffet format, but this is in a relatively small percentage of company-owned units.

The company's basic franchise agreement generally requires a $35,000 initial license fee and royalty payments totaling 5% to 7% of gross revenues. SBA's business has some seasonality. In the past, the fourth quarter has accounted for 40% of annual earnings, reflecting higher sales in shopping malls during the holidays.

As of April 23, 1995, SBA had cash equivalents and marketable securities totaling $60.1 million.

Important Developments

Aug. '95—In 1995's second quarter, SBA's operating margin for company-operated units narrowed to 15.5% from 17.7% a year ago. All major expense categories were up as a percent of sales. However, the extent of margin deterioration was less than SBA experienced in 1995's first quarter, when the restaurant operating margin narrowed to 11.9%, from 15.1%. Also, as of July 16, 1995, SBA had 768 restaurants in operation, up 15% from the year-earlier level. This included 588 company-owned units (up 12%) and 180 franchise outlets (up 26%). In all of 1995, SBA is looking to open about 70 company-operated restaurants and 40 franchise units. Separately, SBA's common shares began trading on the New York Stock Exchange on September 23, 1994, with the same symbol (SBA) that was used when the shares were traded on the American Stock Exchange.

Capitalization

Long Term Debt: None (4/23/95).

Per Share Data ($) (Year Ended Dec. 31)

	1994	1993	1992	1991	1990	1989
Tangible Bk. Val.	8.83	7.83	6.91	5.72	4.64	3.61
Cash Flow	2.69	2.25	1.89	1.69	1.53	1.14
Earnings	1.63	1.40	1.19	1.07	1.01	0.72
Dividends	0.64	0.53	Nil	Nil	Nil	Nil
Payout Ratio	39%	38%	Nil	Nil	Nil	Nil
Prices - High	29½	30⅝	33⅞	32	23¼	16⅛
- Low	21¼	20⅛	14	20⅛	13¼	9¼
P/E Ratio - High	18	22	28	30	23	22
- Low	13	14	12	19	13	13

Income Statement Analysis (Million $)

	1994	%Chg	1993	%Chg	1992	%Chg	1991
Revs.	294	11%	264	12%	236	13%	208
Oper. Inc.	71.6	17%	61.3	21%	50.7	6%	47.7
Depr.	21.7	26%	17.2	19%	14.4	14%	12.6
Int. Exp.	Nil	—	Nil	—	Nil	—	0.0
Pretax Inc.	53.3	13%	47.0	21%	38.8	8%	36.0
Eff. Tax Rate	38%	—	40%	—	38%	—	39%
Net Inc.	33.0	17%	28.3	17%	24.1	11%	21.8

Balance Sheet & Other Fin. Data (Million $)

	1994	1993	1992	1991	1990	1989
Cash	69.4	70.6	61.9	51.0	35.9	20.3
Curr. Assets	76.5	75.8	66.6	55.3	40.2	25.3
Total Assets	232	208	183	159	133	108
Curr. Liab.	33.2	30.6	25.2	25.9	22.7	22.7
LT Debt	Nil	Nil	Nil	Nil	Nil	0.1
Common Eqty.	180	159	140	116	94.0	72.0
Total Cap.	199	177	158	133	110	85.0
Cap. Exp.	32.1	32.9	30.1	23.5	21.3	28.5
Cash Flow	54.7	45.5	38.5	34.4	30.9	23.0

Ratio Analysis

	1994	1993	1992	1991	1990	1989
Curr. Ratio	2.3	2.5	2.6	2.1	1.8	1.1
% LT Debt of Cap.	Nil	Nil	Nil	Nil	Nil	0.1
% Net Inc.of Revs.	11.2	10.7	10.2	10.5	10.8	9.8
% Ret. on Assets	15.0	14.5	14.1	15.0	17.0	14.8
% Ret. on Equity	19.5	18.9	18.8	20.8	24.6	22.3

Dividend Data —Quarterly dividends were initiated with the April 1993 payment.

Amt. of Div. $	Date Decl.	Ex-Div. Date	Stock of Record	Payment Date
3-for-2	Aug. 23	Sep. 23	Sep. 09	Sep. 22 '94
0.160	Aug. 23	Sep. 29	Oct. 05	Oct. 14 '94
0.160	Nov. 22	Dec. 16	Dec. 22	Jan. 06 '95
0.190	Feb. 23	Mar. 15	Mar. 21	Apr. 05 '95
0.190	May. 25	Jun. 19	Jun. 21	Jul. 06 '95

Data as orig. reptd.; bef. results of disc. opers. and/or spec. items. Per share data adj. for stk. divs. as of ex-div. date. E-Estimated. NA-Not Available. NM-Not Meaningful. NR-Not Ranked.

Office—763 Larkfield Rd., Commack, NY 11725. **Tel**—(516) 864-0200. **Fax**—(516) 462-9058. **Chrmn & CEO**—M. Sbarro. **Pres & Treas**—A. Sbarro. **Sr Exec VP & Secy**—J. Sbarro. **VP-Fin, CFO & Investor Contact**—Robert S. Koebele. **Dirs**—H. L. Kestenbaum, R. A. Mandell, T. J. Sandleitner, A. Sbarro, J. Sbarro, M. Sbarro, P. A. Vatter, T. Vince, B. Zimmerman. **Transfer Agent**—Chemical Bank, NYC. **Incorporated** in New York in 1977. **Empl**-8,200. **S&P Analyst:** Tom Graves, CFA

STANDARD & POOR'S
STOCK REPORTS

SCANA Corp.

NYSE Symbol **SCG**
In S&P MidCap 400

20-SEP-95 **Industry:** Util.-Diversified

Summary: This holding company is principally engaged, through subsidiaries, in electric and natural gas utility operations and other energy-related businesses.

S&P Opinion: Accumulate (★★★★)
Recent Price • 23 | 52 Wk Range • 23½-20½ | Yield • 6.3% | 12-Mo. P/E • 21.9

Quantitative Evaluations

Outlook (1 Lowest—5 Highest)
• **2+**

Fair Value
• **21⅜**

Risk
• **Low**

Earn./Div. Rank
• **A-**

Technical Eval.
• **Bearish** since 7/95

Rel. Strength Rank (1 Lowest—99 Highest)
• **51**

Insider Activity
• **Neutral**

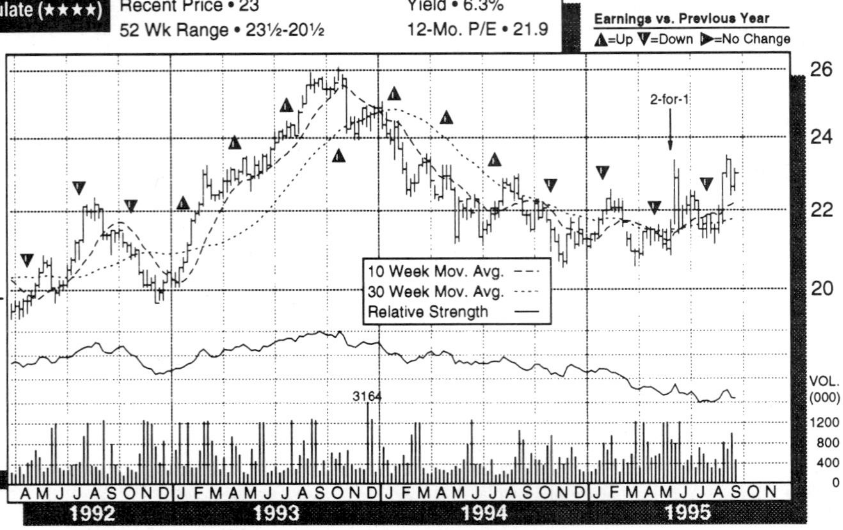

Overview - 20-SEP-95

Share earnings in 1995 should increase to $1.65 (including a non-cash reserve adjustment of $0.16), from 1994's $1.59 (including a charge of $0.13), benefiting from an improving regional economy and the second step of a two-step rate order for $18.5 million in additional annual revenues. Diversified operations should focus on an expanded oil and gas subsidiary, now that the company has sold its real estate unit. SCANA's competitive position will benefit from a leaner cost structure and employee reductions. Its service area continues to attract new and expanding industry. These positive factors will be partly offset by the negative impact of depressed natural gas prices on SCANA Petroleum Resources. Hearings on a recently filed application for a $76.7 million (8.35%) increase in electric rates are expected in November 1995.

Valuation - 20-SEP-95

The shares fell substantially in 1994, reflecting rising interest rates and increased competition. However, the stock finished the year with a partial rebound, and is up about 9% since the beginning of 1995. The dividend was recently raised 2.1%, and the shares are currently yielding 6.3%. Annual dividend hikes of 2.0% to 2.5% should continue in the coming years. The shares are currently trading at about 12X estimated 1996 EPS of $1.85. Based on SCANA's near-term potential and secure and rising dividend, the stock should be accumulated for both growth and income.

Key Stock Statistics

S&P EPS Est. 1995	1.65	Tang. Bk. Value/Share	14.50
P/E on S&P Est. 1995	13.9	Beta	0.48
S&P EPS Est. 1996	1.85	Shareholders	39,500
Dividend Rate/Share	1.44	Market cap. (B)	$ 2.2
Shs. outstg. (M)	97.6	Inst. holdings	45%
Avg. daily vol. (M)	0.152	Insider holdings	NA

Value of $10,000 invested 5 years ago: $ 18,603

Fiscal Year Ending Dec. 31

	1995	% Change	1994	% Change	1993	% Change
Revenues (Million $)						
1Q	344.8	NM	347.0	8%	322.0	8%
2Q	311.1	5%	296.0	6%	280.0	10%
3Q	--	—	361.3	NM	359.0	17%
4Q	--	—	317.4	5%	302.0	8%
Yr.	--	—	1,322	5%	1,264	11%
Income (Million $)						
1Q	46.98	-6%	50.12	11%	45.11	32%
2Q	15.59	-47%	29.17	8%	26.91	61%
3Q	—	—	49.69	-23%	64.43	63%
4Q	—	—	22.22	-30%	31.54	17%
Yr.	—	—	151.2	-10%	168.0	43%
Earnings Per Share ($)						
1Q	0.53	NM	0.54	5%	0.51	23%
2Q	0.16	-48%	0.31	2%	0.31	49%
3Q	E0.65	25%	0.52	-26%	0.71	47%
4Q	E0.31	35%	0.23	-32%	0.34	6%
Yr.	E1.65	4%	1.59	-15%	1.86	31%

Next earnings report expected: mid October

SCANA Corp.

Business Summary - 20-SEP-95

SCANA Corp. is the holding company for South Carolina Electric & Gas (SCE&G), a utility serving about 476,400 electric customers in a 15,000 sq. mi. territory in central, southern, and southwestern South Carolina. Natural gas service is provided to 238,600 customers in a 20,000 sq. mi. service territory. Urban bus service is provided in the metropolitan areas of Columbia and Charleston. Nonregulated diversified operations include Petroleum Resources, which owns and operates oil and gas producing properties, Suburban Propane, which purchases and sells propane, and MPX Systems, which is involved in telecommunications-related ventures. Business segment contributions (operating income in million $) in 1994 were:

	Revs.	Profit
Electric	73.8%	$232.2
Gas	25.9%	34.1
Transportation	0.3%	-6.8

The fuel mix in 1994 was 77% coal, 17% nuclear, and 6% hydro and other. Peak load in 1994 was 3,344 mw, and system capacity was 3,876 mw, for a capacity margin of 12.5%. Gas sales in 1994 totaled 778.1 million therms, up 8.6% from 1993.

In 1994, residential sales of electricity accounted for 42% of electric sales revenue; commercial sales 30%; industrial sales 21%; sales for resale 4%; and all other 3%.

In 1994, the company sold substantially all of the real estate assets of SCANA Development Corp. to Liberty Properties Group, Inc., for $49.6 million.

Important Developments

Sep. '95—The company filed with the SEC for a public offering of up to 5,175,000 common shares, through underwriters led by PaineWebber Inc. and The Robinson-Humphrey Co., Inc. Proceeds would be used to reduce short-term debt and for general corporate purposes.

Jul. '95—SCE&G filed an application with The Public Service Commission of South Carolina requesting a $76.7 million (8.35%) increase in retail electric base rates. The increase would be implemented in two phases over a two-year period beginning in January 1996. Public hearings on the application are expected to be held by November 1995.

Capitalization

Long Term Debt: $1,605,907,000 (3/95).
Subsidiary Red. Pfd. Stk.: $47,543,000.
Subsidiary Pfd. Stk.: $26,027,000.

Per Share Data ($)

(Year Ended Dec. 31)

	1994	1993	1992	1991	1990	1989
Tangible Bk. Val.	14.50	14.09	13.07	12.46	12.18	11.29
Earnings	1.60	1.86	1.42	1.68	2.22	1.52
Dividends	1.41	1.37	1.34	1.31	1.26	1.23
Payout Ratio	88%	74%	94%	78%	57%	81%
Prices - High	25⅛	26⅛	22⅜	22⅛	18	17⅞
- Low	20½	20⅛	19⅜	16¾	15⅛	14⅞
P/E Ratio - High	16	14	16	13	8	12
- Low	13	11	14	10	7	10

Income Statement Analysis (Million $)

	1994	%Chg	1993	%Chg	1992	%Chg	1991
Revs.	1,322	5%	1,264	11%	1,138	NM	1,148
Depr.	119	5%	113	5%	108	5%	103
Maint.	63.7	-6%	67.7	4%	65.4	6%	61.6
Fxd. Chgs. Cov.	3.2	-7%	3.4	25%	2.7	-14%	3.2
Constr. Credits	15.3	1%	15.1	54%	9.8	18%	8.3
Eff. Tax Rate	39%	—	35%	—	33%	—	35%
Net Inc.	151	-10%	168	42%	118	-13%	136

Balance Sheet & Other Fin. Data (Million $)

	1994	1993	1992	1991	1990	1989
Gross Prop.	4,627	4,264	4,003	3,789	3,587	3,400
Cap. Exp.	405	322	278	239	230	182
Net Prop.	3,294	3,004	2,810	2,665	2,550	2,444
Capitalization:						
LT Debt	1,538	1,424	1,205	1,122	939	1,004
% LT Debt	51	50	49	50	46	50
Pfd.	75.6	79.0	82.0	88.0	90.0	94.0
% Pfd.	2.50	2.80	3.40	3.90	4.40	4.70
Common	1,410	1,333	1,162	1,029	1,004	918
% Common	47	47	47	46	49	46
Total Cap.	3,704	3,499	3,087	2,874	2,647	2,615

Ratio Analysis

	1994	1993	1992	1991	1990	1989
Oper. Ratio	80.4	80.6	81.6	80.6	80.1	81.0
% Earn. on Net Prop.	8.2	8.4	7.7	8.5	9.0	8.8
% Ret. on Revs.	11.4	13.3	10.3	11.8	16.0	10.9
% Ret. On Invest.Cap	7.4	8.4	7.4	8.5	10.7	8.7
% Return On Com.Eqty	11.0	13.5	10.7	13.4	18.9	13.5

Dividend Data —Dividends have been paid since 1946. A dividend reinvestment plan is available.

Amt. of Div. $	Date Decl.	Ex-Div. Date	Stock of Record	Payment Date
0.705	Oct. 18	Dec. 05	Dec. 09	Jan. 01 '95
0.720	Feb. 14	Mar. 06	Mar. 10	Apr. 01 '95
2-for-1	Apr. 26	May. 26	May. 11	May. 25 '95
0.360	Apr. 26	Jun. 03	Jun. 09	Jul. 01 '95
0.360	Aug. 23	Sep. 06	Sep. 08	Oct. 01 '95

Data as orig. reptd.; bef. results of disc opers. and/or spec. items. Per share data adj. for stk. divs. as of ex-div. date. E-Estimated. NA-Not Available. NM-Not Meaningful. NR-Not Ranked.

Office—1426 Main Street, Columbia, SC 29201. **Tel**—(803) 748-3000. **Chrmn, Pres & CEO**—L. M. Gressette, Jr. **VP-Fin, Secy & Treas**—K. B. Marsh. **EVP & CFO**—W. B. Timmerman. **Investor Contact**—H. John Winn III (803-748-3240). **Dirs**—B. L. Amick, W. B. Bookhart, Jr., W. T. Cassels, Jr., H. M. Chapman, J. B. Edwards, E. T. Freeman, L. M. Gressette, Jr., B. A. Hagood, W. H. Hipp, B. D. Kenyon, F. C. McMaster, H. Ponder, J. B. Rhodes, W. B. Timmerman. E. C. Wall, Jr. **Transfer Agent & Registrar**—Co.'s offices. **Incorporated** in South Carolina in 1924. **Empl**-4,575. **S&P Analyst:** Ronald J. Gross

STANDARD & POOR'S

STOCK REPORTS

Scherer (R.P.)

NYSE Symbol **SHR**
In S&P MidCap 400

28-SEP-95

Industry:
Drugs-Generic and OTC

Summary: This company is the world's largest manufacturer of soft gelatin capsules (softgels). It also develops advanced drug delivery systems.

Quantitative Evaluations
Outlook
(1 Lowest—5 Highest)
• **NA**
Fair Value
• **NA**
Risk
• **Low**
Earn./Div. Rank
• **NR**

Technical Eval.
• **Bullish** since 6/95
Rel. Strength Rank
(1 Lowest—99 Highest)
• **29**
Insider Activity
• **NA**

Recent Price • 42¼
52 Wk Range • 50¼-37¼
Yield • Nil
12-Mo. P/E • 22.0

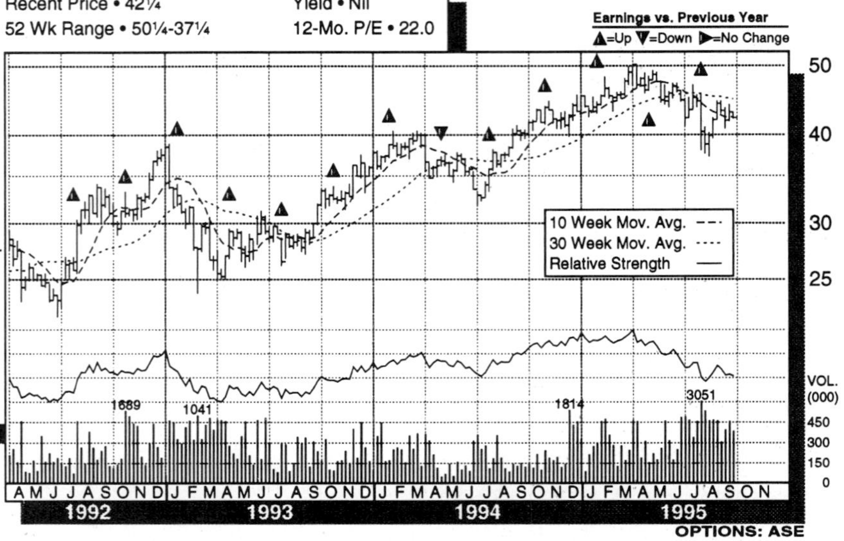

OPTIONS: ASE

Business Profile - 28-SEP-95

Earnings have been in a strong uptrend in recent years, with international soft-gel product sales providing strong growth. Recently, two large customers notified Scherer that orders over the near term would be reduced. As a result, the company expects second quarter fiscal 1995-96 net income to be well below the prior year's. However, SHR believes that third and fourth quarter earnings will be above year-earlier levels. Capital expenditures for 1995-96 are planned at $75 - $85 million.

Operational Review - 28-SEP-95

Sales for the three months ended June 30, 1995, increased 12%, year to year, aided by aided by gains in European markets and favorable exchange rates. Demand for nutritional soft-gel products was soft and partially offset the strong advances made in international markets. Margins narrowed slightly, and operating income was up 11%. After taxes at 32.0% versus 35.4%, and minority interest, net income was up 20%, to $13.7 million ($0.56 a share) from $11.4 million ($0.47).

Stock Performance - 22-SEP-95

In the past 30 trading days, SHR's shares have increased 6%, compared to a 5% rise in the S&P 500. Average trading volume for the past five days was 76,240 shares, compared with the 40-day moving average of 128,885 shares.

Key Stock Statistics

Dividend Rate/Share	Nil	Shareholders	100
Shs. outstg. (M)	23.3	Market cap. (B)	$0.980
Avg. daily vol. (M)	0.086	Inst. holdings	94%
Tang. Bk. Value/Share	4.38	Insider holdings	NA
Beta	NA		

Value of $10,000 invested 5 years ago: NA

Fiscal Year Ending Mar. 31

	1996	% Change	1995	% Change	1994	% Change
Revenues (Million $)						
1Q	148.4	12%	132.9	23%	108.4	5%
2Q	—	—	121.3	15%	105.2	8%
3Q	—	—	132.2	15%	114.8	17%
4Q	—	—	150.2	24%	120.8	22%
Yr.	—	—	536.7	19%	449.3	13%
Income (Million $)						
1Q	13.70	20%	11.43	33%	8.60	3%
2Q	—	—	9.14	39%	6.56	8%
3Q	—	—	11.61	30%	8.90	25%
4Q	—	—	12.68	85%	6.86	-7%
Yr.	—	—	44.86	45%	30.91	7%
Earnings Per Share ($)						
1Q	0.56	19%	0.47	31%	0.36	3%
2Q	—	—	0.37	37%	0.27	8%
3Q	—	—	0.47	27%	0.37	28%
4Q	—	—	0.51	82%	0.28	-10%
Yr.	—	—	1.83	44%	1.27	6%

Next earnings report expected: early November

Scherer (R.P.)

Business Summary - 28-SEP-95

R.P. Scherer Corporation is a leading international developer and manufacturer of oral drug delivery systems and the world's largest producer of soft gelatin capsules (softgels). It is also developing and selling advanced drug delivery systems that improve the efficacy of drugs by regulating their dosage, rate of absorption and place of release. Sherer has 19 manufacturing facilities in 11 countries.

The company produces and markets over 4,000 products in softgel form. Such products accounted for 90% of 1994-95 sales. Softgels are used for a wide range of drug, vitamin, cosmetic and recreational products and are especially effective in encapsulating oils, other liquids and solids in suspension in an oral dose. Because the therapeutically active ingredients of a drug are in a suspended or liquid state when encapsulated in softgels, in certain circumstances the rapid dissolution or disintegration characteristics of this dosage form can provide improved bioavailabilty (rate and extent of absorption into the body) and efficacy. In 1994-95, about 50% of SHR's softgel sales were derived from pharmaceutical products.

Using its expertise in softgel technology, the company developed its Scherersol systems to broaden the range of pharmaceuticals that may be encapsulated in softgel form. The systems, most of which are patented, often enable pharmaceutical companies to combine the advantages of drugs in liquid solution with the convenience and dosage accuracy of softgels. In addition, Scherersol technologies, by providing a unique, patented dosage delivery system, can protect a drug compound against generic competition throughout the life of the Scherersol patents.

The Scherer DDS division develops advanced drug delivery systems, including the Zydis and Pulsincap technologies. Zydis is an oral dosage form that dissolves instantaneously on the tongue and does not require water to aid swallowing. Pulsincap is an oral drug delivery device that releases a drug at a predetermined time or at a predetermined site in the gastrointestinal tract. SHR produces two Zydis products containing lorazepam and oxazepam tranquilizers for sale in Europe by Wyeth-Ayerst International.

The U.K.-based Advanced Therapeutics Products (ATP) Group was formed in September 1993 to manage the development and registration of pharmaceutical products using off-patent compounds and the company's drug delivery technologies.

Important Developments

Sep. '95—The company announced that its DDS affiliate signed an agreeement with Coordinated Drug Development Limited (CDD) under which Scherer would obtain exclusive rights to novel pulmonary delivery technology from CDD.

Capitalization

Long Term Debt: $188,447,000 (6/95).
Minority Interest: $33,794,000.

Per Share Data ($) (Year Ended Mar. 31)

	1995	1994	1993	1992	1991	1990
Tangible Bk. Val.	3.78	1.13	2.04	1.20	0.11	NA
Cash Flow	2.93	2.20	2.06	0.89	1.43	NA
Earnings	1.83	1.27	1.20	-0.50	0.55	NA
Dividends	Nil	Nil	Nil	Nil	NA	NA
Payout Ratio	Nil	Nil	Nil	Nil	NA	NA
Cal. Yrs.	1994	1993	1992	1991	1990	1989
Prices - High	45½	38⅞	38½	30¾	NA	NA
- Low	31¾	23⅞	22⅛	18	NA	NA
P/E Ratio - High	25	31	32	NM	NA	NA
- Low	17	19	18	NA	NA	NA

Income Statement Analysis (Million $)

	1995	%Chg	1994	%Chg	1993	%Chg	1992
Revs.	537	20%	449	13%	398	18%	338
Oper. Inc.	131	19%	110	NM	109	12%	97.5
Depr.	27.0	19%	22.6	8%	20.9	-1%	21.2
Int. Exp.	15.0	-36%	23.4	-8%	25.4	-33%	38.1
Pretax Inc.	91.6	47%	62.3	-6%	66.3	126%	29.3
Eff. Tax Rate	33%	—	30%	—	36%	—	76%
Net Inc.	44.9	45%	30.9	7%	29.0	NM	-1.2

Balance Sheet & Other Fin. Data (Million $)

	1995	1994	1993	1992	1991	1990
Cash	38.8	22.6	33.9	50.8	27.5	NA
Curr. Assets	224	183	167	177	153	NA
Total Assets	704	613	532	542	506	NA
Curr. Liab.	112	95.0	86.0	98.0	90.0	NA
LT Debt	183	188	141	192	205	NA
Common Eqty.	274	215	203	192	161	NA
Total Cap.	535	469	408	408	384	NA
Cap. Exp.	54.1	39.5	33.2	23.8	NA	NA
Cash Flow	71.8	53.6	49.8	13.6	32.3	NA

Ratio Analysis

	1995	1994	1993	1992	1991	1990
Curr. Ratio	2.0	1.9	2.0	1.8	1.7	NA
% LT Debt of Cap.	34.2	40.1	34.6	47.2	53.3	NA
% Net Inc.of Revs.	8.4	6.9	7.3	NM	4.1	NA
% Ret. on Assets	6.8	5.4	5.4	NM	NA	NA
% Ret. on Equity	18.4	14.8	14.6	NM	NA	NA

Dividend Data —The company has never paid cash dividends on its common stock, and is currently restricted from paying dividends under certain terms of long term debt agreements.

Data as orig. reptd.; bef. results of disc. opers. and/or spec. items. Per share data adj. for stk. divs. as of ex-div. date. E-Estimated. NA-Not Available. NM-Not Meaningful. NR-Not Ranked.

Office—2075 West Big Beaver Rd., Troy, MI 48084. **Tel**—(810) 649-0900. **Chrmn & Co-CEO**—J. P. Cashman. **Pres & Co-CEO**—A. Erdeljan. **EVP, CFO, Secy & Investor Contact**—Nicole S. Williams. **Dirs**—J. E. Avery, J. P. Cashman, A. Erdeljan, F. Frank, L. G. Koffman, L. Lasagna, R. H. Rock, J. A. Stern. **Transfer Agent & Registrar**—Society National Bank, Cleveland. **Incorporated** in Delaware in 1989. **Empl**-3,300. **S&P Analyst:** Thomas Tirney

STANDARD & POOR'S

STOCK REPORTS

Scholastic Corp.

NASDAQ Symbol **SCHL**

In S&P MidCap 400

28-AUG-95 **Industry:** Publishing

Summary: This company is a leading publisher and distributor of children's books, classroom and professional magazines and other educational materials.

S&P Opinion: Hold (★★★)

Recent Price • 60 | 52 Wk Range • 66¾-45 | Yield • Nil | 12-Mo. P/E • 25.2

Quantitative Evaluations

Outlook (1 Lowest—5 Highest)
• **NA**

Fair Value
• **NA**

Risk
• **Low**

Earn./Div. Rank
• **NR**

Technical Eval.
• **Bullish** since 7/95

Rel. Strength Rank (1 Lowest—99 Highest)
• **48**

Insider Activity
• **Unfavorable**

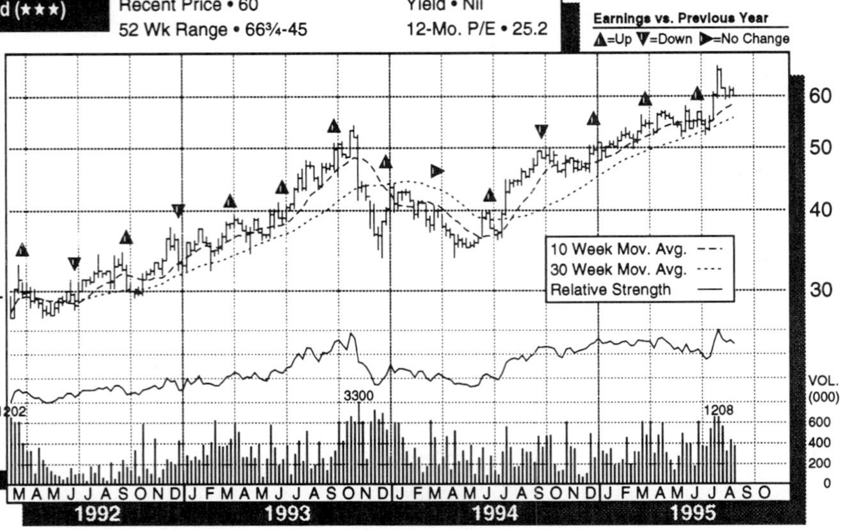

Overview - 28-AUG-95

Revenues are expected to rise another 20% or so in 1995-6, again largely bolstered by strong domestic book publishing gains. Revenues from international operations, magazine publishing and video and software should also continue to grow at a brisk pace. Although paper prices are up more than 30% from year-earlier levels, the company reprices books as it reprints them. Still, margins will be under some pressure due to the lag effect. Higher debt levels will also restrict the pace of earnings growth. No change in the effective tax rate is expected. Longer term, Scholastic should continue to experience strong revenue and profit growth, aided by expansion in markets and products.

Valuation - 28-AUG-95

The stock has a number of positive long-range factors in its favor, including the probability that the best-selling series "Goosebumps" will continue to be a strong seller. A new "Goosebumps" program (financed by FOX) that will debut in the fall on the FOX network should build demand for the series. A number of other measures, such as the planned expansion into Walmart and a licensing agreement with Microsoft, are also positive. The "Magic Schoolbus" and other titles are doing well. Although the market values Scholastic's stock at a premium to underlying earnings growth, SCHL should continue to perform at least as well as the market over the longer term.

Key Stock Statistics

S&P EPS Est. 1996	2.80	Tang. Bk. Value/Share	13.28
P/E on S&P Est. 1996	21.4	Beta	NA
Dividend Rate/Share	Nil	Shareholders	3,000
Shs. outstg. (M)	15.6	Market cap. (B)	$0.938
Avg. daily vol. (M)	0.084	Inst. holdings	70%
		Insider holdings	NA

Value of $10,000 invested 5 years ago: NA

Fiscal Year Ending May 31

	1995	% Change	1994	% Change	1993	% Change
Revenues (Million $)						
1Q	87.07	13%	77.22	19%	65.00	12%
2Q	254.1	19%	212.9	11%	192.0	13%
3Q	179.9	20%	150.3	14%	132.0	10%
4Q	228.8	20%	191.2	17%	163.8	15%
Yr.	749.9	19%	631.6	14%	552.3	13%
Income (Million $)						
1Q	-11.17	NM	-7.27	—	—	—
2Q	27.32	18%	23.07	9%	21.16	40%
3Q	7.97	24%	6.42	NM	6.43	75%
4Q	14.45	35%	10.72	3%	10.43	125%
Yr.	38.58	17%	32.93	17%	28.10	117%
Earnings Per Share ($)						
1Q	-0.72	NM	-0.47	NM	-0.87	NM
2Q	1.68	17%	1.43	6%	1.35	-5%
3Q	0.49	22%	0.40	NM	0.40	21%
4Q	0.89	35%	0.66	2%	0.65	117%
Yr.	2.38	17%	2.04	15%	1.77	64%

Next earnings report expected: late September

Scholastic Corp.

Business Summary - 28-AUG-95

Scholastic Corporation is a leading publisher and distributor of children's books, classroom and professional magazines and other educational materials, with operations in the U.S., Canada, the U.K., Australia, New Zealand, France and Mexico. The company also publishes educational computer software and produces family-oriented video and TV programming. For the most part, products are distributed directly to children and teachers in elementary and secondary schools.

The company's domestic book publishing business consists primarily of the publication and distribution of children's books in paperback editions through school book clubs, school book fairs and classroom and library sales, as well as through trade distribution in retail stores. In 1993-4, the company sold more than 160 million children's books in the U.S.

Scholastic's magazine publishing business involves primarily the publication of some 30 classroom magazines distributed to children in school classrooms, four professional magazines directed to teachers and other education professionals and one consumer magazine directed at the growing home office market. In 1993-4, the U.S. circulation of the company's classroom magazines was 7.9 million.

Other domestic operations include the publication and distribution of educational computer software, the production of children's and family-oriented video and television programming and, through a joint venture, the development and production of theatrical motion pictures. In 1993, SCHL and America Online Inc. launched an on-line education product that connects teachers and students in their classrooms and homes and allows them to conduct on-line data searches.

International business consists of four operating subsidiaries, each of which publishes and distributes children's books, magazines, supplementary test products and educational software. In 1993-4, about 70% of international revenues were derived from the sale of children's books.

Important Developments

Jul. '95—Scholastic said that it completed Literacy Place, its new basal reading program, and is confident that the investment in Literacy Place and its other basal programs will add to future revenues and profits.

Capitalization

Long Term Debt: $83,000,000 (2/95).

Per Share Data ($)

(Year Ended May 31)

	1995	1994	1993	1992	1991	1990
Tangible Bk. Val.	NA	13.28	9.98	9.39	7.91	NM
Cash Flow	NA	2.51	2.14	1.54	1.91	1.15
Earnings	2.38	2.04	1.77	1.08	1.29	0.23
Dividends	Nil	Nil	Nil	Nil	Nil	Nil
Payout Ratio	Nil	Nil	Nil	Nil	Nil	Nil
Cal. Yrs.	1994	1993	1992	1991	1990	1989
Prices - High	52½	54¼	37¾	NA	NA	NA
- Low	33¾	32¼	22½	NA	NA	NA
P/E Ratio - High	22	27	21	NA	NA	NA
- Low	14	16	13	NA	NA	NA

Income Statement Analysis (Million $)

	1994	%Chg	1993	%Chg	1992	%Chg	1991
Revs.	632	14%	552	13%	489	16%	423
Oper. Inc.	63.2	15%	54.9	13%	48.8	13%	43.0
Depr.	7.6	31%	5.8	5%	5.5	-19%	6.8
Int. Exp.	3.0	7%	2.8	-77%	12.0	-17%	14.4
Pretax Inc.	52.7	13%	46.8	117%	21.6	-4%	22.5
Eff. Tax Rate	38%	—	40%	—	40%	—	39%
Net Inc.	32.9	17%	28.1	116%	13.0	-6%	13.8

Balance Sheet & Other Fin. Data (Million $)

	1994	1993	1992	1991	1990	1989
Cash	4.1	4.1	17.1	12.7	16.5	NA
Curr. Assets	220	166	154	124	111	NA
Total Assets	390	263	226	188	168	144
Curr. Liab.	120	105	89.7	71.0	64.1	NA
LT Debt	40.0	3.0	23.0	109	109	100
Common Eqty.	206	153	112	6.0	-7.0	-16.0
Total Cap.	245	157	135	115	102	84.0
Cap. Exp.	41.5	16.0	7.4	4.0	8.3	4.5
Cash Flow	40.5	33.9	18.5	20.6	11.4	9.1

Ratio Analysis

	1994	1993	1992	1991	1990	1989
Curr. Ratio	1.8	1.6	1.7	1.7	1.7	NA
% LT Debt of Cap.	16.1	2.1	17.3	94.6	106.9	119.0
% Net Inc.of Revs.	5.2	5.1	2.6	3.3	0.7	NM
% Ret. on Assets	10.1	9.9	4.8	7.8	1.8	NM
% Ret. on Equity	18.3	16.4	21.2	NM	NM	NM

Dividend Data —No cash dividends have been paid. The company intends to retain earnings to finance the growth of its business.

Data as orig. reptd.; bef. results of disc. opers. and/or spec. items. Per share data adj. for stk. divs. as of ex-div. date. E-Estimated. NA-Not Available. NM-Not Meaningful. NR-Not Ranked.

Office—555 Broadway, New York, NY 10012. **Tel**—(212) 343-6100. **Chrmn, Pres & CEO**—R. Robinson. **Exec VP & CFO**—K. McEnery. **VP-Fin & Investor Contact**—Ray Marchuk. **VP & Secy**—Lynette E. Allison. **Treas**—V. M. Marzano. **Dirs**—H. V. Benham, J. Brademas, J. C. Burton, A. A. Crim, R. J. Denison, A. S. Hedden, M. C. Jemison, R. A. Krinsley, J. D. Manley, J. G. McDonald, R. Robinson, I. G. Seidenberg, R. M. Spaulding. **Transfer Agent & Registrar**—Chemical Bank, NYC. **Incorporated** in Delaware in 1986. **Empl**-3,143. **S&P Analyst:** William H. Donald

STANDARD & POOR'S

STOCK REPORTS

Schulman (A.), Inc.

NASDAQ Symbol **SHLM**

In S&P MidCap 400

14-AUG-95

Industry:
Plastic/Products

Summary: This company is a leading international supplier of high performance plastic compounds and resins. Schulman also produces specialty color concentrates and additive masterbatches.

S&P Opinion: Accumulate (★★★★)

Recent Price • 26
52 Wk Range • 32¾-24¼

Yield • 1.3%
12-Mo. P/E • 17.6

Quantitative Evaluations

Outlook
(1 Lowest—5 Highest)
• **3+**

Fair Value
• **27¼**

Risk
• **Low**

Earn./Div. Rank
• **A**

Technical Eval.
• **Bullish** since 7/95

Rel. Strength Rank
(1 Lowest—99 Highest)
• **7**

Insider Activity
• **Neutral**

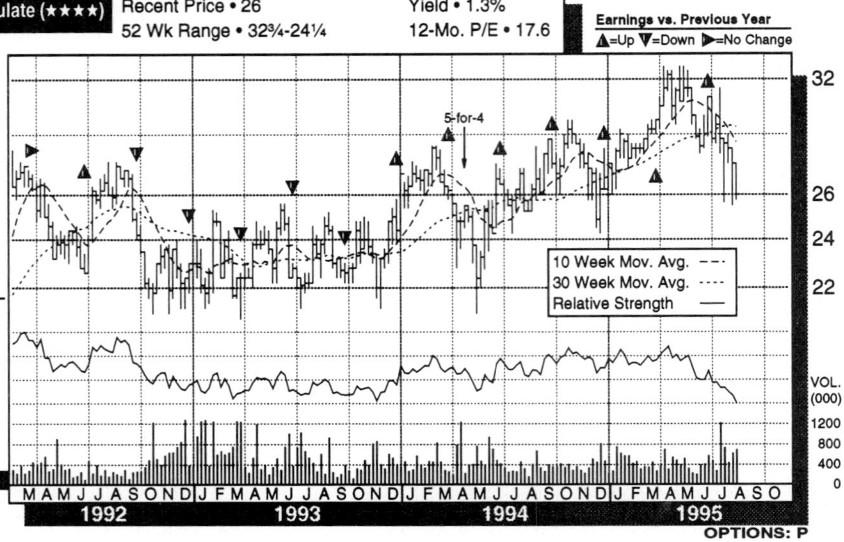

OPTIONS: P

Overview - 14-AUG-95

Despite a slowdown in the second half, net sales for fiscal 1995 are likely to exceed $1 billion. The sharp rise reflects higher first half selling prices, capacity expansions, and a significantly improved European market (aided by a weaker U.S. dollar). However, North Amerian operations declined 17% in the third quarter, hurt by intense price competition and higher interest expense. Domestic margins are expected to remain under pressure for the next couple of quarters, due to the difficulty of passing on the sharply higher costs of raw materials. International growth is expected to continue, although at a slower pace; with more than half of its earnings derived from European markets, the company will continue to benefit from translation gains.

Valuation - 14-AUG-95

Although the shares have declined from their recent high, we still believe they are an attractive investment value. Margins have narrowed, particularly in domestic operations, and while we share the concerns this has caused regarding near-term results, we think this has already been discounted in the current valuation of the stock, which is now trading at the lower end of its recent P/E range. With recent acquisitions and new facilities providing the expanded capacity necessary for continued growth, we would accumulate the shares.

Key Stock Statistics

S&P EPS Est. 1995	1.50	Tang. Bk. Value/Share	9.21
P/E on S&P Est. 1995	17.3	Beta	0.78
S&P EPS Est. 1996	1.75	Shareholders	1,400
Dividend Rate/Share	0.34	Market cap. (B)	$0.977
Shs. outstg. (M)	37.6	Inst. holdings	67%
Avg. daily vol. (M)	0.122	Insider holdings	NA

Value of $10,000 invested 5 years ago: $ 21,822

Fiscal Year Ending Aug. 31

	1995	% Change	1994	% Change	1993	% Change
Revenues ()						
1Q	253.0	49%	170.1	-8%	184.0	-2%
2Q	251.3	48%	169.9	5%	162.0	-7%
3Q	286.5	39%	205.6	10%	187.0	-3%
4Q	—	—	210.7	32%	160.0	-13%
Yr.	—	—	748.8	8%	693.0	-6%
Income ()						
1Q	13.24	35%	9.79	11%	8.82	-6%
2Q	13.08	46%	8.96	15%	7.80	-20%
3Q	15.24	26%	12.07	18%	10.26	-13%
4Q	—	—	13.76	14%	12.02	-93%
Yr.	—	—	44.57	15%	38.91	-11%
Earnings Per Share ()						
1Q	0.35	33%	0.26	10%	0.24	-6%
2Q	0.35	46%	0.24	11%	0.22	-18%
3Q	0.41	28%	0.32	18%	0.27	-15%
4Q	E0.39	5%	0.37	16%	0.32	-7%
Yr.	E1.50	26%	1.19	14%	1.04	-12%

Next earnings report expected: late October

Schulman (A.), Inc.

Business Summary - 14-AUG-95

A. Schulman, Inc. is a leading international supplier of high performance plastic compounds and resins in various forms for use as raw materials. Sales and income by segment in fiscal 1994 were:

	Sales	Income
Manufacturing	60%	68%
Merchant activities	20%	17%
Distribution	20%	15%

Foreign sales, primarily in Europe, accounted for 57% of revenues and 56% of operating income in fiscal 1994.

The company's principal product line consists of engineered plastic compounds, which are custom formulated to match customer product specifications. SHLM also produces specialty color concentrates and additive masterbatches, which are widely used in plastic products.

Schulman performs custom compounding (tolling), which involves the use of resins and formulas provided by customers. A minor portion of its business is the manufacture of rubber shims and tie pads for the automotive industry. These proprietary plastic compounds are formulated in the company's laboratories and manufactured in SHLM's nine plastics compounding plants in North America and Europe.

Acting as a merchant, Schulman buys plastic resins and resells these commodities, without further processing, to a variety of users. The company purchases prime resins as well as supplies of resins resulting from overruns, changes in customers' specifications and failure to meet rigid prime specifications.

The company also distributes products for several major resin producers, including Huels AG, BASF, Dow Chemical, Exxon Chemical and ATOCHEM. Distributing throughout North America and Europe, it is frequently granted exclusive distribution rights for a product in a particular area.

Important Developments

Jul. '95—The company said translation gains from the weaker dollar increased earnings $0.04 a share in the third quarter and $0.09 for the first nine months. Separately, in March 1995, Schulman entered into a new $75,000,000 revolving credit facility, replacing the prior $40,000,000 agreement. Earlier, the company acquired the assets of the Polymer Services division of J. M. Huber Corp. The division is a supplier of tolling services, custom compounding and various engineered plastic compounds with an annual capacity of about 140 million pounds.

Capitalization

Long Term Debt: $75,107,000 (5/95).
Minority Interest: $1,479,000.

Per Share Data () (Year Ended Aug. 31)

	1994	1993	1992	1991	1990	1989
Tangible Bk. Val.	9.21	7.84	8.26	6.26	5.91	4.39
Cash Flow	1.58	1.43	1.58	1.50	1.24	1.05
Earnings	1.19	1.04	1.18	1.14	0.95	0.82
Dividends	0.29	0.25	0.22	0.19	0.15	0.14
Payout Ratio	24%	24%	18%	16%	16%	17%
Prices - High	29¾	27	28¼	23¼	17¼	12⅞
- Low	21	20¾	21	15¼	11⅛	9⅜
P/E Ratio - High	25	26	24	20	18	16
- Low	18	20	18	13	12	12

Income Statement Analysis ()

	1994	%Chg	1993	%Chg	1992	%Chg	1991
Revs.	749	9%	685	-6%	732	NM	736
Oper. Inc.	79.4	13%	70.4	-14%	81.8	1%	80.7
Depr.	14.7	NM	14.7	NM	14.6	12%	13.0
Int. Exp.	1.2	3%	1.2	-14%	1.4	NM	1.4
Pretax Inc.	70.9	13%	62.7	-14%	73.2	5%	70.0
Eff. Tax Rate	37%	—	38%	—	40%	—	40%
Net Inc.	44.6	15%	38.9	-11%	43.8	4%	42.3

Balance Sheet & Other Fin. Data ()

	1994	1993	1992	1991	1990	1989
Cash	122	114	82.9	44.6	19.2	18.2
Curr. Assets	399	313	327	255	241	187
Total Assets	510	408	428	344	328	258
Curr. Liab.	108	74.8	83.6	81.5	76.5	64.8
LT Debt	23.1	10.1	10.1	9.0	7.0	10.0
Common Eqty.	345	293	307	231	223	166
Total Cap.	375	309	327	250	240	185
Cap. Exp.	25.3	18.2	15.8	18.0	17.7	26.0
Cash Flow	59.2	53.6	58.3	55.2	46.8	39.4

Ratio Analysis

	1994	1993	1992	1991	1990	1989
Curr. Ratio	3.7	4.2	3.9	3.1	3.2	2.9
% LT Debt of Cap.	6.2	3.3	3.1	3.6	2.9	5.4
% Net Inc.of Revs.	6.0	5.7	6.0	5.8	5.3	4.9
% Ret. on Assets	9.7	9.3	11.3	12.7	12.3	12.4
% Ret. on Equity	13.9	12.9	16.2	18.8	18.5	19.9

Dividend Data —Cash has been paid each year since 1968.

Amt. of Div. $	Date Decl.	Ex-Div. Date	Stock of Record	Payment Date
0.075	Jul. 12	Jul. 21	Jul. 27	Aug. 05 '94
0.075	Oct. 07	Oct. 18	Oct. 24	Nov. 02 '94
0.085	Jan. 12	Jan. 24	Jan. 30	Feb. 08 '95
0.085	Apr. 13	Apr. 24	Apr. 28	May. 08 '95
0.085	Jul. 12	Jul. 25	Jul. 27	Aug. 04 '95

Data as orig. reptd.; bef. results of disc. opers. and/or spec. items. Per share data adj. for stk. divs. as of ex-div. date. E-Estimated. NA-Not Available. NM-Not Meaningful. NR-Not Ranked.

Office—3550 W. Market St., P.O. Box 1710, Akron, OH 44333. **Tel**—(216) 666-3751. **Chrmn & CFO**—R. A. Stefanko. **Pres & CEO**—T. L. Haines. **Secy**—J. H. Berick. **Treas**—B. R. Colbow. **Dirs**—J. H. Berick, P. G. Elliott, T. L. Haines, G. E. Heffern, L. A. Kushkin, F. A. Loehr, A. L. Ockene, P. C. Roberts, R. C. Rombouts, R. A. Stefanko, R. G. Wallace. **Transfer Agent**—Society National Bank, Cleveland. **Incorporated** in Delaware in 1969. **Empl**-1,763. **S&P Analyst:** Justin McCann

STANDARD & POOR'S

STOCK REPORTS

Schwab (Charles)

NYSE Symbol **SCH**

In S&P MidCap 400

18-OCT-95 **Industry:** Securities

Summary: Charles Schwab & Co. is the largest discount brokerage firm in the U.S., serving 3.3 million active investor accounts through more than 200 branch offices.

S&P Opinion: No Opinion

Recent Price • 26¼
52 Wk Range • 29-9⅞
Yield • 0.6%
12-Mo. P/E • 28.5

Quantitative Evaluations

Outlook (1 Lowest—5 Highest)
• **1+**

Fair Value
• **23⅜**

Risk
• **Average**

Earn./Div. Rank
• **NR**

Technical Eval.
• **Bullish** since 8/94

Rel. Strength Rank (1 Lowest—99 Highest)
• **74**

Insider Activity
• **Unfavorable**

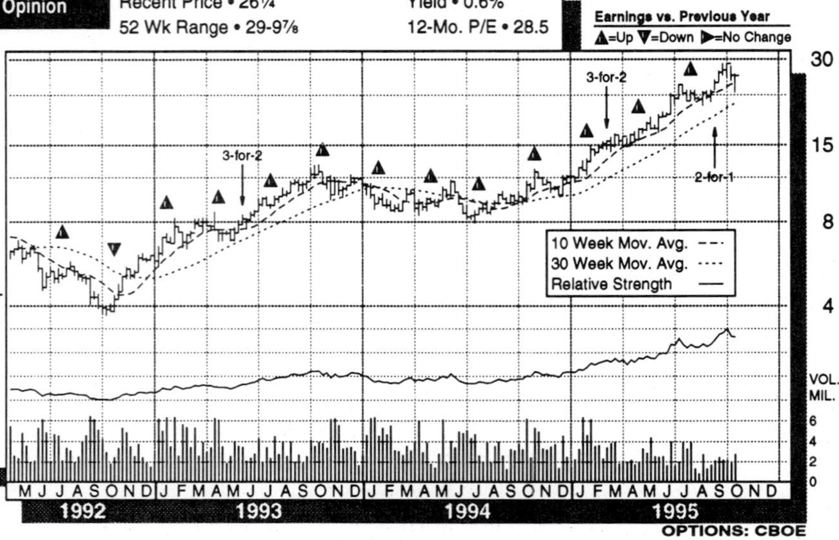

OPTIONS: CBOE

Overview - 01-AUG-95

Subject to market conditions, Schwab's revenues appear to be in a long-term uptrend. Commissions stand to benefit from increased trading volume on the major exchanges, the internationalization of markets, higher savings rates, new branches and the company's dominant market position. One caveat: trading by individuals can be volatile on a quarterly basis. Fees are increasing, aided by the growth of in-house mutual fund assets and the popularity of the Mutual Fund OneSource product, which allows investors to choose among a variety of mutual funds without transaction fees. Margins should be maintained, a result of SCH's high degree of automation and a central phone system. Stock buybacks could aid comparisons.

Valuation - 18-OCT-95

A host of factors should be considered in valuing this brokerage/special situation stock. On a price/earnings basis, the stock trades at about 22 times estimated 1996 earnings per share of $1.17. This is a rich P/E ratio compared to the market's P/E, SCH's historic P/E range and our projected earnings gain of 20% for 1996 compared to 1995. The shares, however, deserve a premium to the general brokerage group due to the company's growth record, leading market position, impressive returns on common equity, and high level of insider ownership.

Key Stock Statistics

S&P EPS Est. 1995	1.00	Tang. Bk. Value/Share	2.89
P/E on S&P Est. 1995	26.3	Beta	2.34
S&P EPS Est. 1996	1.20	Shareholders	1,900
Dividend Rate/Share	0.16	Market cap. (B)	$ 4.5
Shs. outstg. (M)	174.1	Inst. holdings	47%
Avg. daily vol. (M)	0.416	Insider holdings	NA

Value of $10,000 invested 5 years ago: $ 133,100

Fiscal Year Ending Dec. 31

	1996	% Change	1995	% Change	1994	% Change
Revenues (Million $)						
1Q	—	—	296.9	3%	287.9	22%
2Q	—	—	342.7	33%	258.2	11%
3Q	—	—	385.5	55%	248.1	4%
4Q	—	—	—	—	270.4	5%
Yr.	—	—	—	—	1,065	10%
Income (Million $)						
1Q	—	—	38.38	NM	38.19	8%
2Q	—	—	44.42	38%	32.16	2%
3Q	—	—	47.20	51%	31.20	8%
4Q	—	—	—	—	33.80	19%
Yr.	—	—	—	—	135.3	9%
Earnings Per Share ($)						
1Q	E0.28	27%	0.22	2%	0.22	7%
2Q	E0.31	24%	0.25	35%	0.19	5%
3Q	E0.33	27%	0.26	44%	0.18	13%
4Q	E0.28	4%	0.27	42%	0.19	19%
Yr.	E1.20	20%	E1.00	30%	0.77	11%

Next earnings report expected: mid January

Schwab (Charles)

Business Summary - 17-OCT-95

The Charles Schwab Corp. provides brokerage and investment services to more than 3.0 million active investor accounts, whose assets entrusted to the company totaled $122.6 billion at December 31, 1994. It serves some 42% of the discount brokerage market through a network of 208 branch offices in 46 states at year-end 1994. Mayer & Schweitzer Inc. is a market maker in over-the-counter securities. Operating revenues in recent years:

	1994	1993	1992
Commissions	51%	50%	49%
Interest	16%	23%	28%
Principal transactions	15%	15%	14%
Mutual fund service fees	15%	9%	7%
Other	3%	3%	2%

Schwab primarily serves investors who wish to conduct their own research and make their own investment decisions and do not wish to pay, through brokerage commissions, for research or portfolio management. To attract and accommodate investors who want such services, Schwab offers a variety of fee-based (primarily third-party) research and portfolio management products.

Commission revenues in 1994 were derived as follows: 51% listed securities (54% in 1993), 31% over-the-counter securities (31%), 11% mutual funds (8%), and 7% options (7%). Interest revenues in 1994 were derived 46% from investments and 54% from margin loans and other.

For a given number of new accounts, trading is at its highest initially, then declines over time. Advertising plays a crucial role in obtaining new customers. The company opened 736,000 new accounts in 1994, 706,000 in 1993, 562,000 in 1992, and 384,000 new accounts in 1991. Accounts opened during 1994, 1993, and 1992 generated about 14%, 16%, and 18% of total commission revenues during each of those years, respectively. At June 30, 1995, SCH's regulatory net capital was $342 million (11% of aggregate debit balances), which was $280 million in excess of the minimum required net capital.

Important Developments

Oct. '95—The company said that commissions and principal transaction revenues benefited from record trading volumes during 1995's third quarter.

Capitalization

Long Term Debt: $196,312,000 (6/95).

Per Share Data ($)

(Year Ended Dec. 31)

	1994	1993	1992	1991	1990	1989
Tangible Bk. Val.	2.58	1.97	1.23	0.78	0.42	0.36
Cash Flow	NA	NA	NA	NA	NA	NA
Earnings	0.77	0.70	0.46	0.28	0.09	0.10
Dividends	0.09	0.06	0.04	0.03	0.02	0.01
Payout Ratio	12%	9%	11%	10%	21%	13%
Prices - High	12 3/8	12 3/4	8 3/8	7 1/8	2 5/8	2 1/2
- Low	7 7/8	5 1/2	3 3/4	1 11/16	1 9/16	1
P/E Ratio - High	16	18	18	25	29	25
- Low	10	8	8	6	17	10

Income Statement Analysis (Million $)

	1994	%Chg	1993	%Chg	1992	%Chg	1991
Commissions	546	-1%	552	25%	441	26%	349
Int. Inc.	363	44%	252	NM	251	-17%	302
Total Revs.	1,065	10%	965	6%	909	14%	795
Int. Exp.	198	50%	132	-17%	159	-30%	226
Pretax Inc.	224	9%	206	41%	146	66%	88.1
Eff. Tax Rate	40%	—	40%	—	45%	—	44%
Net Inc.	135	9%	124	53%	81.2	64%	49.5

Balance Sheet & Other Fin. Data (Million $)

	1994	1993	1992	1991	1990	1989
Total Assets	7,918	6,897	5,905	5,026	4,188	3,480
Cash Items	4,587	3,956	3,714	3,467	3,141	2,335
Receivables	3,010	2,625	1,952	1,350	842	932
Secs. Owned	Nil	Nil	Nil	Nil	Nil	Nil
Sec. Borrowed	Nil	Nil	Nil	Nil	Nil	Nil
Due Brokers & Cust.	7,084	6,173	5,376	4,605	3,856	3,121
Other Liabs.	195	159	118	102	52.0	57.0
Capitalization:						
Debt	171	185	152	119	126	131
Equity	467	379	259	200	154	172
Total	638	565	410	319	280	302

Ratio Analysis

	1994	1993	1992	1991	1990	1989
% Ret. on Revs.	12.7	12.9	8.9	6.2	2.7	3.4
% Ret. on Assets	1.8	1.9	1.5	1.1	0.4	0.6
% Ret. on Equity	32.0	39.0	35.4	28.0	10.3	11.4

Dividend Data —Dividends were initiated in 1989. A dividend reinvestment plan is available.

Amt. of Div. $	Date Decl.	Ex-Div. Date	Stock of Record	Payment Date
3-for-2	Jan. 17	Mar. 02	Feb. 01	Mar. 01 '95
0.060	Apr. 18	Apr. 25	May. 01	May. 15 '95
0.080	Jul. 18	Jul. 28	Aug. 01	Aug. 15 '95
2-for-1	Jul. 18	Sep. 05	Aug. 01	Sep. 01 '95
0.040	Oct. 17	Oct. 30	Nov. 01	Nov. 15 '95

Data as orig. reptd.; bef. results of disc opers. and/or spec. items. Per share data adj. for stk. divs. as of ex-div. date. E-Estimated. NA-Not Available. NM-Not Meaningful. NR-Not Ranked.

Office—101 Montgomery St., San Francisco, CA 94104. **Tel**—(415) 627-7000. **Chrmn & CEO**—C. R. Schwab. **Pres**—D. S. Pottruck. **EVP-Fin & CFO**—A. J. Gambs. **Secy**—M. B. Templeton. **Investor Contact**—Mark Thompson (415) 627-7810. **Dirs**—N. H. Bechtle, C. P. Butcher, D. G. Fisher, A. M. Frank, J. R. Harvey, S. T. McLin, D. S. Pottruck, C. R. Schwab, L. J. Stupski, R. O. Walther. **Transfer Agent & Registrar**—Harris Trust Co., Chicago, IL. **Incorporated** in California in 1971. **Empl**-6,500. **S&P Analyst:** Paul L. Huberman, CFA

STANDARD & POOR'S

STOCK REPORTS

Seagate Technology

NYSE Symbol **SEG**

In S&P MidCap 400

28-SEP-95 **Industry:** Data Processing

Summary: Seagate is a leading maker of rigid magnetic disk drives for a wide range of computers from PCs to supercomputers. It also makes disk drive parts and other storage products.

S&P Opinion: Buy (★★★★★)

Recent Price • 44

52 Wk Range • 49⅜-21½

Yield • Nil

12-Mo. P/E • 12.5

Quantitative Evaluations

Outlook
(1 Lowest—5 Highest)
• **5+**

Fair Value
• **57⅞**

Risk
• **Average**

Earn./Div. Rank
• **B**

Technical Eval.
• **Bearish** since 7/95

Rel. Strength Rank
(1 Lowest—99 Highest)
• **24**

Insider Activity
• **Neutral**

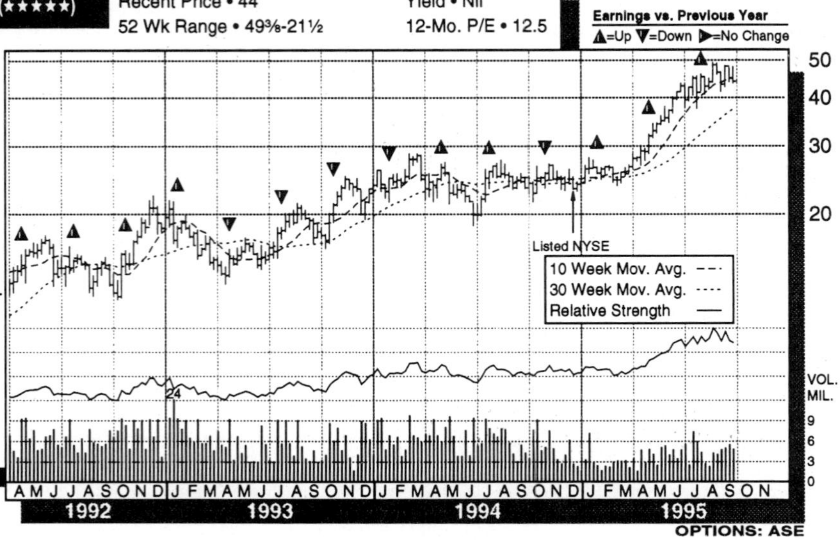

Overview - 28-SEP-95

Sales should rise sharply in fiscal 1996, reflecting a higher level of unit shipments. Strong demand for desktop and other small computers is spurring sales of disk drives and other PC components. Seagate is particularly well positioned at the high end of the disk drive market, and should benefit from an industrywide move to higher capacity drives, stemming from greater storage requirements of enhanced graphics, video, sound and computer networks. The acquisition of Conner Peripherals would further aid sales, and in general is viewed favorably. Margins are expected to widen, on volume efficiencies, further manufacturing cost reductions, and a more favorable product mix. Earnings should benefit from greater sales and wider margins.

Valuation - 28-SEP-95

The shares of this highly regarded disk drive vendor broke out sharply to the upside in April 1995, spurred by another quarter of solid financial results, underlying expansion of the storage market, and continued evidence that disk drive demand remains strong. SEG remains well positioned, particularly in the high capacity/high performance (and higher margin) segment of the market. The acquisition of Conner Peripherals would be viewed positively. Strong relationships with major OEMs, together with a proven ability to manage product cycles, should continue to help the shares outperform the market in coming months.

Key Stock Statistics

S&P EPS Est. 1996	5.00	Tang. Bk. Value/Share	18.79
P/E on S&P Est. 1996	8.8	Beta	2.13
Dividend Rate/Share	Nil	Shareholders	4,600
Shs. outstg. (M)	72.0	Market cap. (B)	$ 3.0
Avg. daily vol. (M)	1.007	Inst. holdings	90%
		Insider holdings	NA

Value of $10,000 invested 5 years ago: $ 29,333

Fiscal Year Ending Jun. 30

	1995	% Change	1994	% Change	1993	% Change
Revenues (Million $)						
1Q	933.2	21%	773.9	4%	742.6	20%
2Q	1,130	38%	815.9	5%	776.7	12%
3Q	1,185	30%	909.3	21%	754.1	-3%
4Q	1,292	29%	1,001	30%	770.2	-1%
Yr.	4,540	30%	3,500	15%	3,044	6%
Income (Million $)						
1Q	22.54	-38%	36.07	-40%	59.63	NM
2Q	79.27	85%	42.74	-32%	63.27	NM
3Q	70.27	5%	67.05	72%	39.02	-4%
4Q	88.01	11%	79.25	136%	33.51	-43%
Yr.	260.1	16%	225.1	15%	195.4	NM
Earnings Per Share ($)						
1Q	0.30	-41%	0.51	-41%	0.86	NM
2Q	1.07	81%	0.59	-35%	0.91	NM
3Q	0.97	7%	0.91	63%	0.56	-5%
4Q	1.19	11%	1.07	123%	0.48	-43%
Yr.	3.52	14%	3.08	10%	2.80	NM

Next earnings report expected: mid October

Seagate Technology

Business Summary - 27-SEP-95

Seagate Technology designs and manufactures a broad line of rigid magnetic disk drives and related storage products for use in a wide range of computer systems from notebook computers to workstations and supercomputers as well as in multimedia applications such as digital video and video-on-demand. Products are sold to original equipment manufacturers (OEMs) for inclusion in their computer systems or subsystems, to distributors, value-added resellers (VARs) and dealers that service the add-in and add-on computer market and to system integrators.

The company offers more than 100 disk drive models with form factors of 2.5, 3.5, and 5.25 inches, and capacities ranging from 130 megabytes (MBs) to 9 gigabytes (GBs). Products are differentiated by form factor and on a price/performance basis.

SEG pursues a strategy of vertical integration and is a major designer and manufacturer of disk drive components, including thin film heads, head stack assemblies and motors. Products are manufactured primarily in the Far East and the U.S.

In addition to its core disk drive business, the company is broadening its strategy to more fully address the markets for the storage, retrieval and management of data. It is investigating investment opportunities in the software arena, and sells flash memory products manufactured by SunDisk Corp., ranging from 1.8 to 41.9 MBs.

Important Developments

Sep. '95—The company announced that it had agreed in principle to acquire Conner Peripherals, a leading vendor of disk and tape drives and other storage solutions, for about 23 million SEG common shares valued at about $975 million. The merger is subject to, among other things, the execution of a definitive agreement and the approval of the Boards of Directors of both companies.

Jun. '95—In the fiscal 1995 fourth quarter, SEG recorded a $15 million ($0.21 a share) writeoff of in-process R&D in connection with the acquisitions of Creative Interaction Technologies and Frye Computer Systems, developers of network management software products.

Apr. '95—In the third quarter of fiscal 1995, the company recorded a $12,780,000 ($0.20 a share) charge associated with the acquisitions of Network Computing, Inc., and NetLabs, Inc., developers of network management software products.

Oct. '94—In the first quarter of fiscal 1995, a charge of $43,000,000 ($0.62 a share) was incurred related to the August 1994 acquisition of Palindrome Corp., a developer of data protection software.

Capitalization

Long Term Debt: $539,874,000 (6/95); incl. $266.8 million of 6.75% sub. debs. conv. into com. at $42.50 a sh., and $270.8 million of 5% sub. debs. conv. into com. at $26.25 a sh.

Per Share Data ($) (Year Ended Jun. 30)

	1995	1994	1993	1992	1991	1990
Tangible Bk. Val.	18.79	18.24	15.34	12.63	11.76	10.64
Cash Flow	6.05	4.97	5.02	3.37	3.04	3.84
Earnings	3.52	3.08	2.80	0.92	0.95	1.92
Dividends	Nil	Nil	Nil	Nil	Nil	Nil
Payout Ratio	Nil	Nil	Nil	Nil	Nil	Nil
Prices - High	45½	28¾	25⅛	22⅜	19⅞	19¾
- Low	23⅝	18⅝	13⅛	9	7⅛	5⅝
P/E Ratio - High	13	9	9	24	21	10
- Low	7	6	5	10	8	3

Income Statement Analysis (Million $)

	1995	%Chg	1994	%Chg	1993	%Chg	1992
Revs.	4,540	30%	3,500	15%	3,044	6%	2,875
Oper. Inc.	630	40%	449	2%	439	42%	309
Depr.	187	36%	138	-11%	155	-8%	169
Int. Exp.	33.0	25%	26.3	12%	23.5	-31%	34.0
Pretax Inc.	409	27%	322	19%	271	NM	85.0
Eff. Tax Rate	37%	—	30%	—	28%	—	26%
Net Inc.	260	16%	225	15%	195	NM	63.0

Balance Sheet & Other Fin. Data (Million $)

	1995	1994	1993	1992	1991	1990
Cash	1,247	1,334	629	504	252	263
Curr. Assets	2,445	2,246	1,471	1,259	1,184	1,139
Total Assets	3,361	2,878	2,031	1,817	1,880	1,851
Curr. Liab.	910	703	544	502	591	550
LT Debt	540	549	281	321	393	510
Common Eqty.	1,542	1,328	1,045	862	766	675
Total Cap.	2,326	2,097	1,450	1,280	1,254	1,269
Cap. Exp.	353	198	174	82.0	99	58.0
Cash Flow	447	363	350	232	201	235

Ratio Analysis

	1995	1994	1993	1992	1991	1990
Curr. Ratio	2.7	3.2	2.7	2.5	2.0	2.1
% LT Debt of Cap.	23.2	26.2	19.4	25.0	31.4	40.2
% Net Inc.of Revs.	5.7	6.4	6.4	2.2	2.3	4.9
% Ret. on Assets	8.4	8.9	10.2	3.3	3.3	7.3
% Ret. on Equity	18.2	18.4	20.5	7.6	8.6	19.0

Dividend Data —No cash has been paid.

Data as orig. reptd.; bef. results of disc. opers. and/or spec. items. Per share data adj. for stk. divs. as of ex-div. date. E-Estimated. NA-Not Available. NM-Not Meaningful. NR-Not Ranked.

Office—920 Disc Drive, Scotts Valley, CA 95066. **Tel**—(408) 438-6550. **Chrmn, Pres, CEO & COO**—A. F. Shugart. **SVP-Fin, CFO & Secy**—D. L. Waite. **Investor Contact**—Nancy E. Hamm. **Dirs**—G. B. Filler, K. E. Haughton, R. A. Kleist, L. Perlman, A. F. Shugart, T. P. Stafford, L. L. Wilkening. **Transfer Agent & Registrar**—Chemical Trust Co. of California, SF. **Incorporated** in California in 1978; reincorporated in Delaware in 1986. **Empl**-53,000. **S&P Analyst:** Peter C. Wood, CFA

STANDARD & POOR'S

STOCK REPORTS

Seagull Energy

NYSE Symbol **SGO**
In S&P MidCap 400

14-AUG-95 **Industry:** Oil and Gas

Summary: Seagull Energy is an independent energy company focused on natural gas. Operations are conducted through three major segments, most prominent being exploration and production.

S&P Opinion: Hold (★★★) | Recent Price • 18¼ | 52 Wk Range • 26-15¼ | Yield • Nil | 12-Mo. P/E • NM

Quantitative Evaluations
Outlook (1 Lowest—5 Highest)
• **1-**
Fair Value
• **12½**
Risk
• **Average**
Earn./Div. Rank
• **B-**

Technical Eval.
• **Bullish** since 4/95
Rel. Strength Rank (1 Lowest—99 Highest)
• **41**
Insider Activity
• **Neutral**

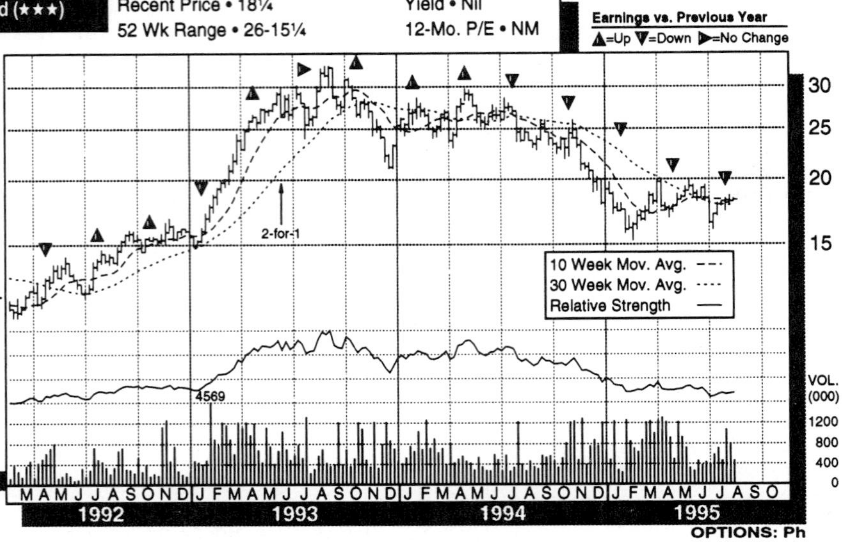

OPTIONS: Ph

Overview - 14-AUG-95

With the long-term outlook for natural gas prices positive, future earnings growth prospects have been enhanced by recent acquisitions. However, prices have been weak throughou: 1995 and production has been curtailed as a conseq.ence. The company can anticipate a loss for the ye .r due to both a non-cash charge related to the .mpairment of long-lived assets and the costs of an ir.mediate work force reduction. Planned exploration and production expenditures will be used to build the company's base of oil and gas reserves, but they are discretionary and will be adjusted downward to ensure debt reduction. The balance sheet should improve, even if SGO's plan to sell its Alaskan gas transmission and distribution unit remains on hold, as other assets sales are completed.

Valuation - 14-AUG-95

The company's stock recovered in the spring from the 52-week low reached early in the 1995 calendar year, as the shares advanced on news in April of a work force reduction and office closings at SGO. The shares faltered at the beginning of the summer, but have risen again on the announcement of a recent asset disposition. However, the fundamentals for the gas industry, while improving from the depressed levels of this past winter, will improve only gradually. Thus, significant upward movement in the price of the shares is not likely to occur anytime during the balance of this year. The stock is best held for its long-term growth prospects.

Key Stock Statistics

S&P EPS Est. 1995	-0.82	Tang. Bk. Value/Share	11.16
P/E on S&P Est. 1995	NM	Beta	0.55
S&P EPS Est. 1996	0.20	Shareholders	2,800
Dividend Rate/Share	Nil	Market cap. (B)	$0.659
Shs. outstg. (M)	36.1	Inst. holdings	84%
Avg. daily vol. (M)	0.138	Insider holdings	NA

Value of $10,000 invested 5 years ago: $ 16,043

Fiscal Year Ending Dec. 31

	1995	% Change	1994	% Change	1993	% Change
Revenues (Million $)						
1Q	94.85	-25%	127.1	23%	103.2	53%
2Q	81.49	-18%	99.6	14%	87.00	77%
3Q	--	—	81.00	NM	81.80	67%
4Q	--	—	100.4	-5%	105.2	44%
Yr.	--	—	408.1	8%	377.2	58%
Income (Million $)						
1Q	-38.55	NM	12.92	NM	3.85	NM
2Q	-7.13	NM	2.58	-29%	3.62	39%
3Q	—	—	-6.29	NM	7.27	NM
4Q	—	—	-5.96	NM	12.45	NM
Yr.	—	—	3.25	-88%	27.20	NM
Earnings Per Share ($)						
1Q	-1.07	NM	0.35	192%	0.12	NM
2Q	-0.20	NM	0.07	-30%	0.10	NM
3Q	E0.20	—	-0.17	NM	0.20	NM
4Q	E0.25	—	-0.16	NM	0.34	143%
Yr.	E-0.82	—	0.09	-88%	0.76	NM

Next earnings report expected: mid October

Seagull Energy

Business Summary - 14-AUG-95

Seagull Energy is an independent energy company focused on natural gas. Operations are conducted through three major segments, the most prominent of which involves natural gas exploration and production. Exploration and production operations in North America are conducted offshore Texas and Louisiana in shallow waters of the Gulf of Mexico and onshore in eastern Texas, northern Louisiana, eastern Oklahoma and western Arkansas; western Oklahoma and the Texas Panhandle; and western Canada. The company also is involved in exploration ventures in waters off the east and west coasts of Great Britain. Other activities include pipeline operations, principally in the Southwest, and gas transmission and distribution in Alaska. Segment contributions in 1994 were:

	Revs.	Profits
Exploration & production	64%	46%
Alaska transmission & distribution	26%	35%
Pipeline operations	10%	19%

At December 31, 1994, total net proved reserves came to 1,069 Bcf of gas (915 Bcf at 1993 year end) and 17.4 million bbl. of crude oil, condensate and natural gas liquids (14.8 million). Daily production in 1994 totaled 355.2 MMcf of gas (279.5 MMcf in 1993), 4,186 bbl. of oil and condensate (3,868 bbl.), and 877 bbl. of natural gas liquids (773 bbl.). In 1994, average sales prices for natural gas were $1.83 per Mcf ($1.99 in 1993), for oil and condensate $15.28 per bbl. ($16.72), and for natural gas liquids $9.03 per bbl. ($11.10).

ENSTAR Alaska engages in transmission and distribution of natural gas in south-central Alaska, including Anchorage. There were 90,100 customers served at 1994 year end, up from 88,200 a year earlier. Gas volumes delivered in 1994 totaled 44.1 MMcf, up from 40.2 MMcf in 1993. Degree days in 1994 totaled 10,291 versus 9,382 in 1993.

Pipeline operations transport natural gas, hydrocarbon products, and petrochemicals in Texas, Louisiana, and Mississippi. SGO is also involved in pipeline engineering, design, construction and operation, as well as natural gas processing, third-party natural gas marketing, and the marketing of all uncommitted natural gas and liquids production.

Important Developments

Jul. '95—As part of its efforts to streamline operations, SGO announced that it and units of Enron Corp., Panhandle Eastern Corp. and Amoco Corp. had agreed to sell their interests in 19 natural gas gathering systems and a gas processing plant to Tejas Power Corp. SGO's share of gross proceeds will be $100 million; net proceeds will be used to pay down bank debt.

Capitalization

Long Term Debt: $628,690,000 (6/95).

Per Share Data ($) (Year Ended Dec. 31)

	1994	1993	1992	1991	1990	1989
Tangible Bk. Val.	12.22	12.19	9.51	9.23	8.59	5.50
Cash Flow	4.01	4.02	2.65	2.56	2.72	2.12
Earnings	0.09	0.76	0.17	0.23	1.11	0.70
Dividends	Nil	Nil	Nil	Nil	Nil	Nil
Payout Ratio	Nil	Nil	Nil	Nil	Nil	Nil
Prices - High	29¾	32⅞	16⅞	15¾	16⅞	11½
- Low	17⅝	14⅞	10⅞	10½	9⅛	7⅜
P/E Ratio - High	NM	43	99	70	15	16
- Low	NM	20	64	47	8	11

Income Statement Analysis (Million $)

	1994	%Chg	1993	%Chg	1992	%Chg	1991
Revs.	408	8%	377	58%	239	-4%	249
Oper. Inc.	207	7%	193	107%	93.1	12%	83.1
Depr. Depl. & Amort.	145	24%	117	85%	63.2	19%	52.9
Int. Exp.	52.2	38%	37.7	104%	18.5	-6%	19.6
Pretax Inc.	0.9	-97%	33.3	NM	6.9	30%	5.3
Eff. Tax Rate	NM	—	18%	—	36%	—	3.80%
Net Inc.	3.2	-88%	27.2	NM	4.4	-14%	5.1

Balance Sheet & Other Fin. Data (Million $)

	1994	1993	1992	1991	1990	1989
Cash	6.4	5.6	3.9	6.2	5.2	14.1
Curr. Assets	119	115	99	90.9	85.7	90.9
Total Assets	1,300	1,118	1,103	619	386	331
Curr. Liab.	133	124	144	105	98.0	77.0
LT Debt	621	460	608	219	49.0	114
Common Eqty.	441	439	244	236	193	77.0
Total Cap.	1,109	927	878	485	271	236
Cap. Exp.	150	135	510	274	99	35.0
Cash Flow	148	144	67.6	58.0	50.7	28.6

Ratio Analysis

	1994	1993	1992	1991	1990	1989
Curr. Ratio	0.9	0.9	0.7	0.9	0.9	1.2
% LT Debt of Cap.	56.0	49.6	69.2	45.2	18.2	48.3
% Ret. on Assets	0.3	2.0	0.5	1.0	4.5	4.1
% Ret. on Equity	0.7	7.0	1.8	2.2	13.0	12.1

Dividend Data (No cash dividends have ever been paid on the common stock. A "poison pill" stock purchase rights plan was adopted in 1989.)

Data as orig. reptd.; bef. results of disc opers. and/or spec. items. Per share data adj. for stk. divs. as of ex-div. date. E-Estimated. NA-Not Available. NM-Not Meaningful. NR-Not Ranked.

Office—1001 Fannin Street, Suite 1700, Houston, TX 77002-6714. **Tel**—(713) 951-4700. **Chrmn, Pres & CEO**—B. J. Galt. **EVP & COO**—J. W. Elias. **EVP & CFO**—R. W. Shower. **VP & Treas**—R. M. King. **Investor Contact**—Alan Payne. **Dirs**—J. E. Attwell, J. W. Elias, P. J. Fluor, B. J. Galt, W. R. Grant, D. P. Guerin, R. M. Morrow, D. S. Osborne, S. F. Segnar, R. W. Shower, G. M. Sullivan. **Transfer Agent & Registrar**—Bank of Boston. **Incorporated** in Texas in 1973. **Empl**-759. **S&P Analyst:** Michael C. Barr

STANDARD & POOR'S

STOCK REPORTS

Sealed Air

NYSE Symbol **SEE**
In S&P MidCap 400

12-OCT-95 **Industry:** Plastic/Products

Summary: This company makes protective packaging materials and systems and selected food packaging products, including air cellular cushioning materials and foam-in-place packaging systems.

S&P Opinion: Accumulate (★★★★)

Recent Price • 26⅜
52 Wk Range • 28¼-15½
Yield • Nil
12-Mo. P/E • 23.9

Quantitative Evaluations
Outlook (1 Lowest—5 Highest)
• **5+**
Fair Value
• **31¾**
Risk
• **Low**
Earn./Div. Rank
• **A-**

Technical Eval.
• **Bullish** since 7/94
Rel. Strength Rank (1 Lowest—99 Highest)
• **30**
Insider Activity
• **NA**

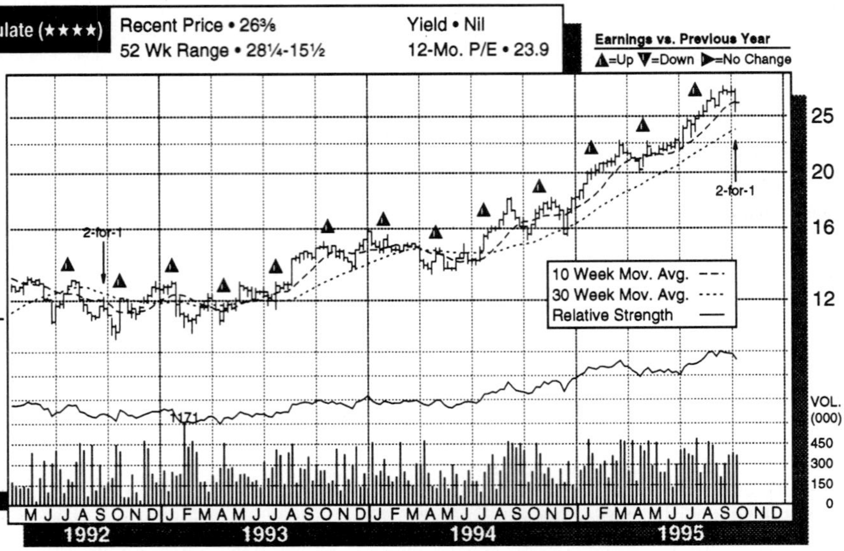

Overview - 12-OCT-95

Sales are expected to continue to improve through the balance of 1995 and into 1996, reflecting contributions from all major segments as economic conditions rebound overseas. Profitability should benefit from increased unit volume of Instapak products, polyethylene foams and other products, contributions from the Trigon Industries acquisition, additional acquisitions, new product development and marketing programs, well controlled operating costs and expenses, lower interest expense and a slightly lower effective tax rate. Long-term growth is seen benefiting from increased demand for the company's products, higher average selling prices and further expansion overseas.

Valuation - 12-OCT-95

The shares should continue to benefit from steady double-digit earnings growth reflecting strong demand for the company's products. Despite an 88% rise in the stock price since early 1994, further appreciation is expected as economic conditions rebound overseas and margins improve as a result of higher average selling prices and well controlled costs and expenses. Although the shares are trading at about 22 times our 1995 EPS estimate, a premium to the MidCap 400 P/E ratio, and 18 times our 1996 projection, we recommend accumulation of the stock as strong earnings growth continues.

Key Stock Statistics

S&P EPS Est. 1995	1.20	Tang. Bk. Value/Share	0.36
P/E on S&P Est. 1995	22.0	Beta	1.48
S&P EPS Est. 1996	1.45	Shareholders	1,200
Dividend Rate/Share	Nil	Market cap. (B)	$ 1.0
Shs. outstg. (M)	42.1	Inst. holdings	65%
Avg. daily vol. (M)	0.070	Insider holdings	NA

Value of $10,000 invested 5 years ago: $ 51,776

Fiscal Year Ending Dec. 31

	1995	% Change	1994	% Change	1993	% Change
Revenues (Million $)						
1Q	173.4	48%	117.5	8%	109.2	NM
2Q	182.1	44%	126.8	12%	113.7	1%
3Q	—	—	131.1	19%	110.2	NM
4Q	—	—	143.8	21%	118.7	4%
Yr.	—	—	519.2	15%	451.7	1%
Income (Million $)						
1Q	11.57	53%	7.55	25%	6.06	21%
2Q	12.62	46%	8.67	23%	7.03	23%
3Q	—	—	10.31	77%	5.83	25%
4Q	—	—	10.69	53%	7.00	30%
Yr.	—	—	37.22	44%	25.91	25%
Earnings Per Share ($)						
1Q	0.28	45%	0.19	23%	0.15	19%
2Q	0.30	40%	0.22	19%	0.18	20%
3Q	E0.30	15%	0.26	73%	0.15	25%
4Q	E0.32	20%	0.27	54%	0.17	25%
Yr.	E1.20	28%	0.93	42%	0.66	22%

Next earnings report expected: mid October

Sealed Air

Business Summary - 11-OCT-95

Sealed Air produces a wide variety of protective packaging materials and systems. In 1987, it significantly expanded its protective packaging operations with the acquisition of Jiffy Packaging Corp., a maker of padded shipping envelopes and other protective packaging products. Business segment contributions in recent years were:

	1994	1993	1992
Surface protection/cushioning products	47%	47%	46%
Engineered products	40%	40%	40%
Food packaging products	11%	11%	12%
Other products	2%	2%	2%

Foreign operations accounted for 29% of sales and 21% of operating profits in 1994.

The company's surface protection and other cushioning products include its air cellular packaging materials, which are plastic sheets containing encapsulated air bubbles that protect products from damage through shock or vibration during shipment. Also included in this group are thin polyethylene foams and automated packaging systems.

SEE's engineered products consist of its Instapak foam-in-place packaging systems, which provide protective packaging for a variety of products, including computer, electronic, office, medical and communications equipment, and void-fill packaging of office supplies, books, cosmetics and other small products for distribution. During 1993, the company began selling its VoidPak inflatable packaging system, which consists of a compact, portable inflator and self-sealing inflatable plastic bags.

Food Packaging products consist of absorbent pads and supermarket display case liners used in the display of meat, fish and poultry.

In July 1994, SEE redeemed the $170 million of its 12.625% senior subordinated notes due 1999, through a new $275 million bank credit facility and a public offering of senior subordinated debt. The refinancing resulted in a net charge of about $5.6 million primarily due to the call premium on the notes.

Important Developments

Aug. '95—Sealed Air authorized a 2,000,000 share (adjusted for 2-for-1 split in September 1995) repurchase program on the open market for use in its employee benefit programs.

Jan. '95—Sealed Air completed the acquisition of Trigon Industries, Ltd., a New Zealand-based manufacturer of flexible packaging materials sold primarily for food packaging, durable envelope products and specialty adhesive products, for 1,765,860 (adjusted) common shares and $25.5 million in cash. Trigon had sales of $77 million in its latest fiscal year.

Capitalization

Long Term Debt: $185,972,000 (6/95).

Per Share Data ($)

(Year Ended Dec. 31)

	1994	1993	1992	1991	1990	1989
Tangible Bk. Val.	0.28	-0.74	-1.73	-2.49	-3.75	-4.78
Cash Flow	1.30	1.04	0.90	0.77	0.65	0.52
Earnings	0.93	0.66	0.54	0.44	0.32	0.22
Dividends	Nil	Nil	Nil	Nil	Nil	10.04
Payout Ratio	Nil	Nil	Nil	Nil	Nil	NM
Prices - High	18⅛	16	14¼	11⅜	8	13½
- Low	13⅜	10½	10¼	5⅜	4⅝	2¾
P/E Ratio - High	19	24	26	26	25	61
- Low	14	16	19	12	14	12

Income Statement Analysis (Million $)

	1994	%Chg	1993	%Chg	1992	%Chg	1991
Revs.	519	15%	452	1%	446	3%	435
Oper. Inc.	99	11%	89.0	3%	86.3	6%	81.8
Depr.	14.9	NM	14.9	6%	14.1	15%	12.3
Int. Exp.	19.4	-33%	28.8	-7%	31.1	-12%	35.3
Pretax Inc.	61.2	35%	45.5	17%	38.8	23%	31.5
Eff. Tax Rate	39%	—	43%	—	47%	—	49%
Net Inc.	37.2	44%	25.9	25%	20.8	28%	16.2

Balance Sheet & Other Fin. Data (Million $)

	1994	1993	1992	1991	1990	1989
Cash	11.2	19.4	26.0	20.2	17.2	24.4
Curr. Assets	152	128	123	118	107	111
Total Assets	331	280	268	275	225	229
Curr. Liab.	136	94.3	93.4	100	84.5	77.0
LT Debt	155	190	225	254	259	302
Common Eqty.	11.0	-29.0	-66.0	-95.0	-131	-159
Total Cap.	184	176	159	159	128	141
Cap. Exp.	17.5	27.0	12.4	43.1	12.1	13.8
Cash Flow	52.1	40.8	34.8	28.5	22.4	17.4

Ratio Analysis

	1994	1993	1992	1991	1990	1989
Curr. Ratio	1.1	1.4	1.3	1.2	1.3	1.4
% LT Debt of Cap.	84.6	108.2	141.7	159.5	203.2	NM
% Net Inc.of Revs.	7.2	5.7	4.7	3.7	2.8	1.9
% Ret. on Assets	12.1	9.3	7.6	6.2	4.9	3.0
% Ret. on Equity	NM	NM	NM	NM	NM	242.5

Dividend Data —Dividends, initiated in 1975, were discontinued in May 1989. A two-for-one stock split was paid September 29, 1995, to holders of record September 15, 1995.

Amt. of Div. $	Date Decl.	Ex-Div. Date	Stock of Record	Payment Date
2-for-1	Aug. 17	Oct. 02	Sep. 15	Sep. 29 '95

Data as orig. reptd.; bef. results of disc. opers. and/or spec. items. Per share data adj. for stk. divs. as of ex-div. date. E-Estimated. NA-Not Available. NM-Not Meaningful. NR-Not Ranked.

Office—Park 80 Plaza East, Saddle Brook, NJ 07662-5291. **Tel**—(201) 791-7600. **Pres & CEO**—T. J. D. Dunphy. **EVP & CFO**—W. V. Hickey. **SVP-Fin**—W. H. McCandless. **Secy**—R. M. Grace, Jr. **VP & Investor Contact**—Mary A. Coventry. **Dirs**—J. K. Castle, L. R. Codey, T. J. D. Dunphy, C. F. Farrell, Jr., D. Freeman, S. A. Jackson, A. H. Miller, R. L. San Soucie. **Transfer Agent**—First Chicago Trust Co. of New York, NYC. **Incorporated** in New Jersey in 1960; reincorporated in Delaware in 1969. **Empl**-3,000. **S&P Analyst:** Stewart Scharf

STANDARD & POOR'S

STOCK REPORTS

Sensormatic Electronics

NYSE Symbol **SRM**
In S&P MidCap 400

31-AUG-95 **Industry:** Electronics/Electric

Summary: This company makes and services electronic and video surveillance equipment used to deter theft in retail stores and other environments.

S&P Opinion: Buy (★★★★★)

Recent Price • 25 | Yield • 0.9%
52 Wk Range • 38¼-21 | 12-Mo. P/E • 19.1

Quantitative Evaluations

Outlook
(1 Lowest—5 Highest)
• **2⁻**

Fair Value
• **24⅛**

Risk
• **High**

Earn./Div. Rank
• **B+**

Technical Eval.
• **Neutral** since 7/95

Rel. Strength Rank
(1 Lowest—99 Highest)
• **6**

Insider Activity
• **Neutral**

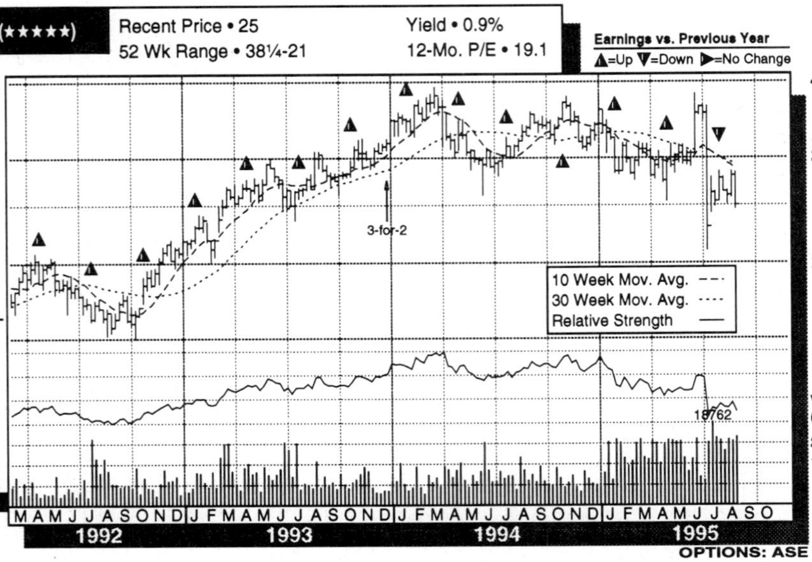

Overview - 31-AUG-95

The leading supplier of integrated electronic security systems, this company will continue to benefit from the increasing security concerns of businesses and institutions around the world. While the company's electronic article surveillance (EAS) products were initially used primarily by retailers, the fastest growing segment of Sensormatic's business is the huge industrial sector. This includes businesses, universities, casinos, hospitals and health clubs, where customers protect assets from unauthorized removal, as well as personnel. We believe revenues and earnings will continue to advance strongly in fiscal 1996 and 1997.

Valuation - 31-AUG-95

Despite strong revenue and earnings growth since 1989, the shares are currently depressed following disappointing results indicated for the fourth quarter of fiscal 1995. Although revenues were said to be in line with expectations, earnings came in well below consensus estimates because of revenue and margin shortfalls in European operations. Nevertheless, we have upgraded the stock on the strength of its still strong fundamentals: excellent revenue and earnings growth, a solid balance sheet, and a dominant market presence. The shares are currently valued well below the company's low-range PE of 22 over the past two years. Our price target is $32-34, based on a conservative PE of 20 times 1996 earnings.

Key Stock Statistics

S&P EPS Est. 1995	1.24	Tang. Bk. Value/Share	6.33
P/E on S&P Est. 1995	20.2	Beta	0.96
S&P EPS Est. 1996	1.60	Shareholders	4,600
Dividend Rate/Share	0.22	Market cap. (B)	$ 1.8
Shs. outstg. (M)	72.8	Inst. holdings	96%
Avg. daily vol. (M)	0.794	Insider holdings	NA

Value of $10,000 invested 5 years ago: $ 33,338

Fiscal Year Ending Jun. 30

	1995	% Change	1994	% Change	1993	% Change
Revenues (Million $)						
1Q	190.9	33%	143.3	20%	119.7	73%
2Q	217.8	36%	159.9	31%	122.1	56%
3Q	238.6	47%	162.2	42%	114.5	57%
4Q	--	—	190.7	46%	131.0	46%
Yr.	--	—	656.0	35%	487.3	57%
Income (Million $)						
1Q	20.09	36%	14.81	36%	10.89	62%
2Q	25.29	34%	18.82	38%	13.60	68%
3Q	24.12	47%	16.39	38%	11.87	95%
4Q	—	—	22.04	24%	17.72	66%
Yr.	—	—	72.07	33%	54.08	72%
Earnings Per Share ($)						
1Q	0.29	16%	0.25	19%	0.21	31%
2Q	0.36	16%	0.31	29%	0.24	29%
3Q	0.33	22%	0.27	29%	0.21	50%
4Q	E0.26	-24%	0.34	10%	0.31	26%
Yr.	E1.24	7%	1.16	21%	0.96	31%

Next earnings report expected: mid October

Sensormatic Electronics

31-AUG-95

Business Summary - 31-AUG-95

Sensormatic Electronics produces and services electronic article surveillance (EAS) and electronic asset protection (EAP) systems and closed-circuit television systems (CCTV) used to deter shoplifting and internal theft in retail stores, as well as in nonretail environments.

The standard EAS system, used primarily by clothing retailers, consists of sensitized tags and/or disposable labels that are attached to merchandise and then removed using a detaching or deactivator device when the item is purchased. If an item is taken through the controlled exit with the label attached, an alarm is activated. A similar EAS system is designed for various hard goods in drug stores, discount stores, record and video stores, supermarkets, and auto parts and hardware stores.

The company's industrial division markets EAS, CCTV and access control systems for the protection and control of assets and people in warehouses, hospitals, airports, office complexes and power plants.

SRM's point-of-sale exception monitoring systems consist of proprietary software interfaces that link retail cash registers with CCTV systems, which are programmed to record predetermined types of transactions. These systems allow store management to deter and detect internal theft.

In November 1994, the company acquired the international operations of Knogo Corp., which also produces EAP systems, for 3.1 million common shares. In January 1995, SRM acquired systems integrator Glen Industrial Communications. Earlier acquisitions included privately held systems integrator Security Specialists Inc. in March 1994, and Robot Research, a maker of closed circuit television products, in late 1993. In June 1993, the company had acquired the 70% of Security Tag Systems it did not already own for about $40 million of common stock.

Important Developments

Jun. '95—A group of major retailers, including K mart and Home Depot, introduced a program intended to advance the use of source tagging utilizing SRM's Ultra-Max technology. Source tagging involves the insertion of anti-theft tags into merchandise during the manufacturing or packaging processes.

May '95—Sensormatic announced that the Appellate Court in Amsterdam, Holland, recently overturned a lower court ruling against the company pertaining to the effect of Ultra-Max products on other systems. The sale of Ultra-Max SpeedStation bulk deactivators was halted after Esselte Meto charged that bulk-deactivated Ultra-Max labels caused false alarms in its magnetic EAS systems.

Capitalization

Long Term Debt: $377,487,000 (3/95).

Per Share Data ($)

(Year Ended Jun. 30)

	1994	1993	1992	1991	1990	1989
Tangible Bk. Val.	10.76	8.43	4.78	4.14	4.05	3.94
Cash Flow	1.70	1.47	1.07	0.89	0.71	0.62
Earnings	1.16	0.96	0.73	0.60	0.48	0.40
Dividends	0.21	0.20	0.20	0.20	0.08	0.03
Payout Ratio	18%	21%	27%	33%	17%	8%
Prices - High	39¼	35	20⅜	10⅞	9⅜	7¼
- Low	26	20	9¼	6¼	6⅜	4⅞
P/E Ratio - High	34	36	28	18	19	18
- Low	22	21	13	10	13	12

Income Statement Analysis (Million $)

	1994	%Chg	1993	%Chg	1992	%Chg	1991
Revs.	656	35%	487	57%	310	30%	239
Oper. Inc.	138	39%	99	71%	58.1	34%	43.3
Depr.	32.8	15%	28.4	96%	14.5	23%	11.8
Int. Exp.	22.7	21%	18.7	64%	11.4	NM	2.8
Pretax Inc.	96.0	33%	72.0	76%	41.0	31%	31.2
Eff. Tax Rate	25%	—	25%	—	23%	—	21%
Net Inc.	72.1	33%	54.1	72%	31.5	28%	24.7

Balance Sheet & Other Fin. Data (Million $)

	1994	1993	1992	1991	1990	1989
Cash	55.0	118	63.0	102	27.0	53.0
Curr. Assets	NA	NA	NA	NA	NA	NA
Total Assets	1,156	927	462	422	265	255
Curr. Liab.	NA	NA	NA	62.5	49.5	47.4
LT Debt	151	264	134	137	9.0	10.0
Common Eqty.	728	490	256	222	200	192
Total Cap.	878	754	390	359	216	208
Cap. Exp.	NA	NA	39.0	35.6	25.4	92.4
Cash Flow	105	82.5	46.1	36.5	29.4	25.9

Ratio Analysis

	1994	1993	1992	1991	1990	1989
Curr. Ratio	NA	NA	NA	NA	NA	NA
% LT Debt of Cap.	17.2	35.1	34.4	38.1	4.3	4.9
% Net Inc.of Revs.	11.0	11.1	10.2	10.3	10.5	11.1
% Ret. on Assets	6.5	NA	7.0	7.2	7.8	7.0
% Ret. on Equity	11.1	NA	13.0	11.6	10.4	9.0

Dividend Data —Dividends have been paid since 1978.

Amt. of Div. $	Date Decl.	Ex-Div. Date	Stock of Record	Payment Date
0.055	Oct. 18	Oct. 28	Nov. 03	Nov. 17 '94
0.055	Jan. 24	Jan. 30	Feb. 03	Feb. 17 '95
0.055	Apr. 21	Apr. 27	May. 03	May. 17 '95
0.055	Jul. 24	Aug. 02	Aug. 04	Aug. 18 '95

Data as orig. reptd.; bef. results of disc. opers. and/or spec. items. Per share data adj. for stk. divs. as of ex-div. date. E-Estimated. NA-Not Available. NM-Not Meaningful. NR-Not Ranked.

Office—500 N.W. 12th Ave, Deerfield Beach, FL 33442-1795. **Tel**—(305) 420-2000. **Chrmn, Pres & CEO**—R. G. Assaf. **EVP, COO & CFO**—Michael E. Pardue. **VP & Treas**—M. A. Flores. **Dirs**—R. G. Assaf, T. V. Buffet, T.P. Hartman, J. M. LeWine, J. E. Lineberger, A. G. Milnes, M. E. Pardue, J. T. Ray, Jr. **Transfer Agent & Registrar**—First National Bank of Boston. **Incorporated** in Delaware in 1968. **Empl**-6,500. **S&P Analyst:** Mike Cavanaugh

Sequa Corp.

NYSE Symbol SQA.A In S&P MidCap 400

Price	Range	P–E Ratio	Dividend	Yield	S&P Ranking	Beta
Aug. 22'95	1995					
26⅝	31¾–21⅞	NM	None	None	C	0.84

Summary

Following the discontinuation and sale of several units, Sequa is focusing on technology-oriented operations: aerospace, metals and machinery, and specialty chemicals. Sales have fallen for several years, reflecting further divestitures and a weak aviation industry. Quarterly losses have been posted for more than two years.

Business Summary

Sequa Corp. is a multi-industry company that provides a broad range of products and services. Contributions by segment (operating profits in million $) in 1994 were:

	Sales	Profits
Aerospace	60%	–12.8
Machinery & metal coatings	18%	28.6
Specialty chemicals	17%	43.3
Other	5%	6.1

European operations comprised 23% of sales in 1994; exports accounted for another 18%.

Aerospace includes the manufacture, repair and coating of blades, vanes and other components of gas turbine engines used for commercial and military jet aircraft. Through ARC Propulsion, it produces rocket propulsion systems. The segment also makes electro-optical and electronic devices for military weapons as well as avionic instruments and medical diagnostic equipment.

Machinery is comprised of the manufacture of equipment for the two-piece food and beverage can industry and the web offset printing industry. The company also coats metal coils for the building, container, truck trailer, and appliance industries.

Specialty chemicals makes a nonchlorine bleach additive used in the overseas laundry detergent industry. It also produces chemicals for the domestic textile and paper industries.

Other operations include the manufacture of automotive products, such as cigarette lighters and sensing devices, the production of easy-open steel lids for cans, and a real estate holding company.

During 1992, Sequa sold the Valley Line, Sabine Towing, its engineered services operations, its men's apparel unit, and part of its financial services operations. In early 1994, the professional services division was sold.

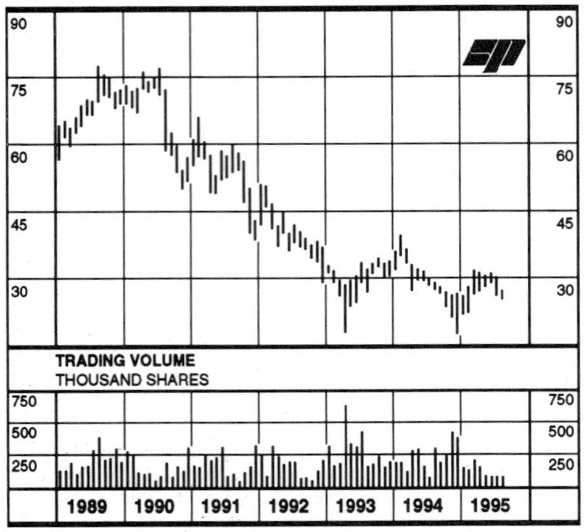

Important Developments

Jul. '95— The company purchased the coil coatings operations of Enamel Proucts and Plating Co. Management said that the two facilities acquired will extend Sequa's presence in the Northeast and Midwest and enhance the company's service capabilities.

Aug. '95— Sequa said 1995 second quarter aerospace division sales fell 11%, year to year. Machinery and metal coatings division sales climbed 19%, but specialty chemicals sales were flat, and other revenues declined 5.3%.

Next earnings report due in November.

Per Share Data ($)

Yr. End Dec. 31	1994	1993	1992	1991	1990	1989	[2]1988	[3]1987	[2]1986
Tangible Bk. Val.[1]	**21.63**	20.72	27.23	31.17	32.27	28.27	25.68	25.71	42.57
Cash Flow[1]	**7.83**	4.71	13.78	11.80	13.22	13.43	13.25	8.58	4.46
Earnings[1,4]	**d2.87**	d6.07	1.53	1.24	3.03	5.55	6.31	4.28	3.24
Dividends	**Nil**	0.30	0.60	0.60	0.60	0.60	0.60	0.60	0.48
Payout Ratio	**Nil**	NM	39%	48%	20%	10%	9%	14%	20%
Prices—High	**39¾**	34½	51	66⅛	77	77½	68¾	88⅝	84¾
Low	**17⅝**	17⅞	29	38¾	50	56⅝	49⅝	40¾	34¾
P/E Ratio—	**NM**	NM	33–19	53–31	25–17	14–10	11–8	21–10	13–12

Data as orig. reptd. **1.** Combined Class A and B. **2.** Reflects accounting change. **3.** Reflects merger or acquisition. **4.** Bef. results of disc. opers. of -2.26 in 1992, -2.27 in 1991, -0.45 in 1989, -0.17 in 1988, -0.33 in 1987, +16.66 in 1986 & spec. item(s) of -0.88 in 1993, - 0.76 in 1992. d-Deficit. NM-Not Meaningful.

Income Data (Million $)

Year Ended Dec. 31	Revs.	Oper. Inc.	% Oper. Inc. of Revs.	Cap. Exp.	Depr.	Int. Exp.	Net Bef. Taxes	Eff. Tax Rate	Net Inc.	% Net Inc. of Revs.	Cash Flow
1994	**1,420**	**144**	**10.1**	**59**	**104**	**59**	**[5]d28**	**NM**	**[6]d24.7**	**NM**	**76**
1993	1,697	146	8.6	98	104	67	d64	NM	[6]d55.5	NM	45
1992	1,868	242	13.0	93	118	73	44	59.1%	[6]17.9	1.0	133
[1]1991	1,879	218	11.6	124	101	83	36	53.2%	[6]15.0	0.8	112
1990	2,211	342	15.5	170	98	109	75	54.2%	32.7	1.5	127
[1]1989	1,959	303	15.4	121	80	88	[5]112	45.7%	60.5	3.1	137
[1,2]1988	1,713	265	15.5	99	74	76	[5]120	40.3%	71.5	4.2	142
[1,3]1987	1,133	169	14.9	101	47	34	[5]79	35.5%	50.9	4.5	94
[1,2]1986	371	41	11.1	17	10	20	[5]29	9.3%	26.1	7.0	36
1985	884	85	9.7	45	25	[4]20	[5]12	66.6%	4.1	0.5	29

Balance Sheet Data (Million $)

Dec. 31	Cash	Curr. Assets	Curr. Liab.	Curr. Ratio	Total Assets	% Ret. on Assets	Long Term Debt	Common Equity	Total Cap.	% LT Debt of Cap.	% Ret. on Equity
1994	**19**	**604**	**321**	**1.9**	**1,648**	**NM**	**587**	**540**	**1,163**	**50.5**	**NM**
1993	25	662	377	1.8	1,804	NM	624	549	1,227	50.9	NM
1992	15	679	350	1.9	1,912	0.9	690	625	1,383	49.9	2.3
1991	16	779	403	1.9	2,108	0.6	825	670	1,571	52.6	1.7
1990	51	941	449	2.1	2,517	1.4	1,101	690	1,896	58.0	4.3
1989	87	945	451	2.1	2,344	2.9	923	673	1,712	53.9	8.6
1988	69	786	424	1.9	1,959	4.0	631	667	1,382	45.6	10.5
1987	86	777	396	2.0	1,663	3.3	493	641	1,182	41.7	7.6
1986	489	870	413	2.1	1,395	2.2	273	598	922	29.7	6.0

Data as orig. reptd.; finance subs. consol. after 1987. **1.** Excludes disc. opers. **2.** Reflects accounting change. **3.** Reflects merger or acquisition. **4.** Net of interest income. **5.** Incl. equity in earns. of nonconsol. subs. **6.** Bef. spec. items. d-Deficit. NM-Not Meaningful.

Revenues (Million $)

Quarter:	1995	1994	1993	1992
Mar.	328	351	427	461
Jun.	357	361	412	474
Sep.		331	407	469
Dec.		377	450	464
		1,420	1,697	1,868

Revenues in the six months ended June 30, 1995, fell 3.8%, year to year, reflecting the disposition of several business units. Margins narrowed, but results benefited from gains from the sale of assets, and from the absence of year-earlier charges. After taxes of $1,100,000, versus tax credits of $3,950,000, losses widened to $7,962,000 ($0.97 a share), from $3,809,000 ($0.56; excluding an extraordinary charge of $0.11).

Common Share Earnings ($)

Quarter:	1995	1994	1993	1992
Mar.	d0.27	d0.23	d0.44	0.27
Jun.	d0.70	d0.33	d2.00	0.45
Sep.		d0.94	d2.48	0.48
Dec.		d1.35	d1.15	0.33
		d2.87	d6.07	1.53

Dividend Data

As a result of deficiencies under covenants of the company's senior notes, payments on Class A and B common shares and $5 cumulative preferred shares were suspended in August 1993. In November 1994, directors approved the payment of dividend arrearages on the preferred stock; Sequa declared and paid all dividends in arrears in 1994's fourth quarter.

Capitalization

Long Term Debt: $578,334,000 (3/95).

$5 Cum. Conv. Preferred Stock: 633,316 shs. ($1 par); ea. conv. into 1.3219 Cl. A com. shs.

Class A Common Stock: 6,535,881 shs. (no par). N.E. Alexander owns 31%.
Shareholders of record: 3,170 (3/95).

Class B Common Stock: 3,330,778 shs. (no par). Has 10 votes per sh.; conv. sh.-for-sh. into Cl. A. N.E. Alexander owns 57%.
Shareholders of record: 730 (3/95).

d-Deficit.

Office—200 Park Ave., New York, NY 10166. **Tel**—(212) 986-5500. **Chrmn & CEO**—N. E. Alexander. **Pres & COO**—J. J. Quicke. **VP & Secy**—I. A. Schreger. **VP & Treas**—K. A. Drucker. **Investor Contact**—Linda G. Kyriakou. **Dirs**—N. E. Alexander, A. Dworman, A. L. Fergenson, D. S. Gottesman, S. Z. Krinsly, D. D. Kummerfeld, R. S. LeFrak, J. J. Quicke, F. R. Sullivan, G. Tsai, Jr. **Transfer Agent & Registrar**—Continental Stock Transfer & Trust Co., NYC. **Incorporated** in Delaware in 1929. **Empl**—9,200.

 Joe Victor Shammas

STANDARD & POOR'S

Sequent Computer Systems

STOCK REPORTS

NASDAQ Symbol **SQNT**
In S&P MidCap 400

12-OCT-95 **Industry:** Data Processing

Summary: Sequent is a leading architect and provider of open client/server systems used mainly for on-line transaction processing, decision support and messaging applications.

S&P Opinion: Hold (★★★) | Recent Price • 19⅛ | 52 Wk Range • 25⅞-14⅛ | Yield • Nil | 12-Mo. P/E • 16.5

Quantitative Evaluations
Outlook
(1 Lowest—5 Highest)
• **5+**
Fair Value
• **22**
Risk
• **Average**
Earn./Div. Rank
• **B-**

Technical Eval.
• **Bearish** since 8/95
Rel. Strength Rank
(1 Lowest—99 Highest)
• **2**
Insider Activity
• **Unfavorable**

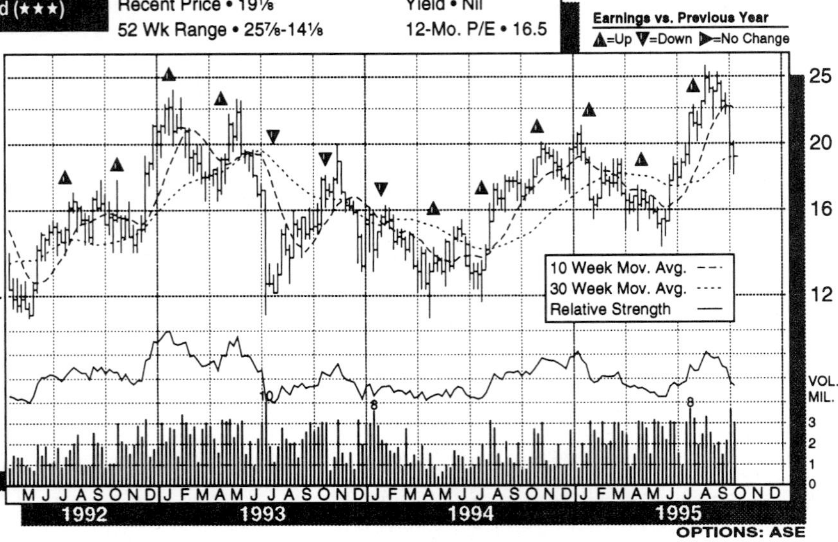

Overview - 12-OCT-95

Year to year sales growth in the third quarter is expected to approximate 10%, which is well off of first half growth rates, reflecting the slippage of several large deals into the fourth quarter. Sales growth should pick up in the fourth quarter as these deals are booked, resulting in some 20% growth for the year. We also believe that this level of growth could be sustained in 1996, reflecting the growing market acceptance of client/server technology and SQNT's expertise in these new platforms. Gross margins will remain volatile, reflecting quarterly changes in the sales mix, but expense-management efforts are expected to offset any weakness. Pretax income should grow more than 45% in 1995, but a sharp jump in the tax rate will limit EPS growth to about 17%.

Valuation - 12-OCT-95

After lowering our opinion on the shares to accumulate from strong buy on September 20 on concerns about the third quarter, we have since lowered our opinion to hold on SQNT's new guidance for lower than expected EPS. On September 26, SQNT said that third quarter results would be lower than expected, due to timing issues related to several large deals. On October 9, SQNT indicated that several other deals did not close and again guided expectations lower. We are clearly disappointed, particularly after such a strong first half and SQNT's initial optimism about third quarter prospects. As a result, we believe the shares will only be an average performer until SQNT proves it can generate consistent revenue and EPS growth.

Key Stock Statistics

S&P EPS Est. 1995	1.20	Tang. Bk. Value/Share	9.13
P/E on S&P Est. 1995	15.9	Beta	1.46
S&P EPS Est. 1996	1.40	Shareholders	1,300
Dividend Rate/Share	Nil	Market cap. (B)	$0.513
Shs. outstg. (M)	32.3	Inst. holdings	59%
Avg. daily vol. (M)	0.846	Insider holdings	NA

Value of $10,000 invested 5 years ago: $ 9,562

Fiscal Year Ending Dec. 31

	1995	% Change	1994	% Change	1993	% Change
Revenues (Million $)						
1Q	116.1	24%	93.87	21%	77.60	20%
2Q	139.2	28%	108.8	35%	80.79	12%
3Q	—	—	121.3	33%	91.14	11%
4Q	—	—	126.9	22%	104.3	18%
Yr.	—	—	450.8	27%	353.8	15%
Income (Million $)						
1Q	5.95	26%	4.72	38%	3.41	NM
2Q	11.01	54%	7.16	NM	0.26	-91%
3Q	—	—	8.87	125%	3.94	-6%
4Q	—	—	12.39	NM	-15.13	NM
Yr.	—	—	33.13	NM	-7.52	NM
Earnings Per Share ($)						
1Q	0.18	20%	0.15	25%	0.12	NM
2Q	0.33	43%	0.23	NM	0.01	-92%
3Q	E0.20	-29%	0.28	115%	0.13	-19%
4Q	E0.49	29%	0.38	NM	-0.50	NM
Yr.	E1.20	17%	1.03	NM	-0.26	NM

Next earnings report expected: late October

Sequent Computer Systems

Business Summary - 10-OCT-95

Sequent Computer Systems makes high-performance symmetric multiprocessing (SMP) computer systems and parallel-enabled software for the commercial open systems marketplace. SQNT also provides consulting and professional services to assist clients in their migration to open, client/server computing from host-based computing. Revenue contributions in recent years were:

	1994	1993	1992
End-user products	71%	72%	68%
OEM products	24%	7%	14%
Service & other	5%	21%	18%

International sales accounted for 48% of 1994 revenues (44% in 1993).

SQNT'S Symmetry 5000 systems incorporate up to 30 Intel Pentium microprocessors to provide superior price/performance and scalability for open systems on-line transaction processing (OLTP), relational database management software (RDBMS) and network and client server applications. These systems feature DYNIX/ptx, an enhanced version of the UNIX operating system, and support large numbers of concurrent users with high throughput, fast response times and a growing library of applications. System prices in 1994 ranged from $80,000 to over $2 million.

The company's family of WinServer SMP computer systems runs the Microsoft Windows NT operating system and supports multiple Pentium processors. These systems provide database and application services for workgroup, departmental and enterprise-level computing requirements, and range in price from under $20,000 to over $200,000.

In September 1994, SQNT entered into a new three-year OEM agreement with Unisys Corp., under which the latter will market symmetric multiprocessing (SMP) systems based on the company's Symmetry 5000 series of UNIX-based servers.

Important Developments

Oct. '95—The company said it expected to report net income of $0.20 to $0.25 a share in 1995's third quarter on revenue of $133 million. The company attributed the lower than expected results to the failure to close several large projects in the quarter.
Aug. '95—SQNT was awarded a $6.7 million contract for systems and services by United Kingdom's Employment Service. The contract includes six Symmetry 5000 SE70 systems with a total of 72 Intel Pentium chips and $800,000 worth of professional services.
Jul. '95—SQNT announced a $2.5 million contract with the Nasdaq Stock Market under which it will provide its Symmetry systems and related professional services and education to support Nasdaq's future market system for traders.

Capitalization

Long Term Debt: $10,184,000 (7/1/95), incl. cap. leases.

Per Share Data ($) (Year Ended Dec. 31)

	1994	1993	1992	1991	1990	1989
Tangible Bk. Val.	9.29	8.05	7.68	7.25	9.82	6.65
Cash Flow	2.12	0.64	1.49	-1.16	1.40	1.07
Earnings	1.03	-0.26	0.55	-2.10	0.81	0.70
Dividends	Nil	Nil	Nil	Nil	Nil	Nil
Payout Ratio	Nil	Nil	Nil	Nil	Nil	Nil
Prices - High	20⅝	24	22	19¾	34	21
- Low	11⅛	11¼	11⅛	7½	12½	9⅛
P/E Ratio - High	20	NM	40	NM	42	30
- Low	11	NM	20	NM	15	13

Income Statement Analysis (Million $)

	1994	%Chg	1993	%Chg	1992	%Chg	1991
Revs.	451	27%	354	15%	307	44%	213
Oper. Inc.	74.3	64%	45.4	-17%	54.4	NM	-6.1
Depr.	34.8	32%	26.4	7%	24.6	13%	21.8
Int. Exp.	4.7	35%	3.5	-29%	4.9	22%	4.0
Pretax Inc.	38.8	NM	-6.3	NM	15.9	NM	-52.4
Eff. Tax Rate	15%	—	NM	—	9.10%	—	NM
Net Inc.	33.1	NM	-7.5	NM	14.4	NM	-48.7

Balance Sheet & Other Fin. Data (Million $)

	1994	1993	1992	1991	1990	1989
Cash	106	80.3	44.4	36.0	37.0	28.1
Curr. Assets	301	253	168	153	164	103
Total Assets	436	375	279	246	251	147
Curr. Liab.	132	119	81.1	86.8	40.2	32.7
LT Debt	10.3	10.9	24.0	7.2	13.6	1.8
Common Eqty.	291	243	173	149	195	111
Total Cap.	302	254	197	157	209	113
Cap. Exp.	54.6	44.4	47.5	33.5	59.8	24.3
Cash Flow	67.9	18.9	39.0	-26.9	32.6	20.9

Ratio Analysis

	1994	1993	1992	1991	1990	1989
Curr. Ratio	2.3	2.1	2.1	1.8	4.1	3.2
% LT Debt of Cap.	3.4	4.3	12.2	4.6	6.5	1.6
% Net Inc.of Revs.	7.3	NM	4.7	NM	7.6	9.5
% Ret. on Assets	8.0	NM	5.5	NM	8.9	12.2
% Ret. on Equity	12.2	NM	9.0	NM	11.5	16.4

Dividend Data —No cash dividends have been paid. A two-for-one stock split was effected in 1989.

Data as orig. reptd.; bef. results of disc. opers. and/or spec. items. Per share data adj. for stk. divs. as of ex-div. date. E-Estimated. NA-Not Available. NM-Not Meaningful. NR-Not Ranked.

Office—15450 S.W. Koll Pkwy., Beaverton, OR 97006-6063. **Tel**—(503) 626-5700. **Chrmn & CEO**—K. C. Powell, Jr. **Pres & COO**—J. McAdam. **SVP-Fin, & CFO**—R. S. Gregg. **Dirs**—D. R. Hathaway, R. C. Mathis, M. S. S. Morton, R. C. Palermo, K. C. Powell, Jr., R. W. Wilmot. **Transfer Agent & Registrar**—Chemical Trust Co. of California, SF. **Incorporated** in Delaware in 1983. **Empl**-2,012. **S&P Analyst:** John D. Coyle, CFA

Service Merchandise

NYSE Symbol **SME**
In S&P MidCap 400

14-AUG-95 **Industry:** Retail Stores

Summary: This retailer conducts a general merchandise business on high-volume, low-margin principles through a chain of 405 catalog stores in 37 states.

Quantitative Evaluations
Outlook
(1 Lowest—5 Highest)
• **5−**
Fair Value
• **12⅝**
Risk
• **Average**
Earn./Div. Rank
• **B**

Technical Eval.
• **Bullish** since 6/95
Rel. Strength Rank
(1 Lowest—99 Highest)
• **92**
Insider Activity
• **Neutral**

Recent Price • 7
52 Wk Range • 7⅜-4⅛
Yield • Nil
12-Mo. P/E • 13.2

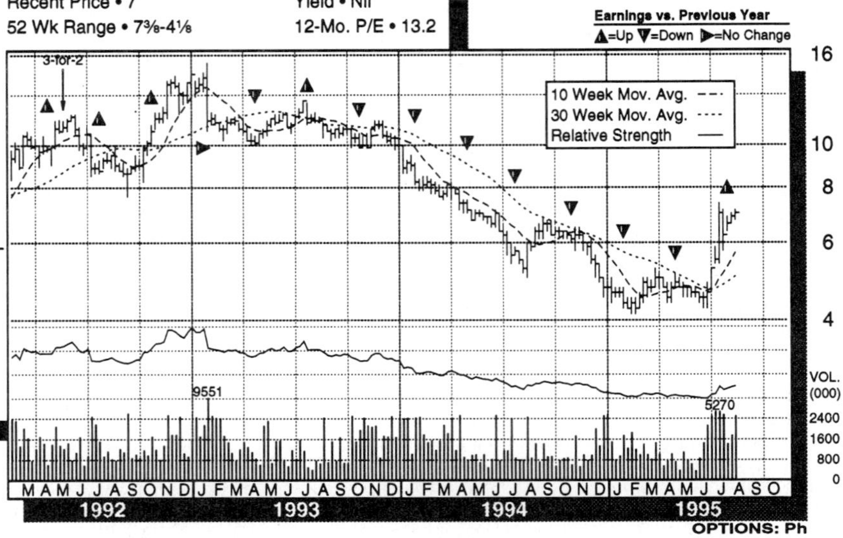

Business Profile - 10-AUG-95

SME conducts a general merchandise business on high-volume, low-margin principles via a chain of more than 400 retail catalog stores. Business is seasonal and SME historically incurs a net loss in the first nine months of each year. Objectives for 1995 include: completing the formation of the new senior management team, revitalizing marketing and merchandising activities, improving expense productivity, and focusing on the profitability of existing stores rather than on new store openings.

Operational Review - 10-AUG-95

Higher sales in 1995's first half primarily reflected the addition of 14 new stores. Same-store sales slid 1.7%. Gross margins widened on a shift in sales mix toward higher-margin jewelry. However, SG&A expenses rose as a percentage of sales, reflecting increased advertising costs for four additional publications, the addition of new stores, and higher costs for store personnel added to deliver better customer service. The seasonal net loss widened to $0.22 per share, from $0.14.

Stock Performance - 11-AUG-95

In the past 30 trading days, SME's shares have increased 33%, compared to a 2% rise in the S&P 500. Average trading volume for the past five days was 690,240 shares, compared with the 40-day moving average of 683,410 shares.

Key Stock Statistics

Dividend Rate/Share	Nil	Shareholders	7,300
Shs. outstg. (M)	99.7	Market cap. (B)	$0.698
Avg. daily vol. (M)	0.533	Inst. holdings	51%
Tang. Bk. Value/Share	3.14	Insider holdings	NA
Beta	1.38		

Value of $10,000 invested 5 years ago: $ 14,000

Fiscal Year Ending Dec. 31

	1995	% Change	1994	% Change	1993	% Change
Revenues (Million $)						
1Q	737.1	2%	724.2	8%	672.9	1%
2Q	864.9	2%	845.9	5%	803.1	3%
3Q	—	—	757.7	8%	704.1	NM
4Q	—	—	1,723	5%	1,635	4%
Yr.	—	—	4,050	6%	3,815	3%
Income (Million $)						
1Q	-23.01	NM	-12.82	NM	-10.86	16%
2Q	0.85	NM	-1.27	NM	8.42	39%
3Q	—	—	-10.33	NM	-4.30	150%
4Q	—	—	85.99	-3%	89.06	NM
Yr.	—	—	61.57	-25%	82.32	-3%
Earnings Per Share ($)						
1Q	-0.23	NM	-0.13	NM	-0.11	NM
2Q	0.01	NM	-0.01	NM	0.08	33%
3Q	—	—	-0.10	NM	-0.04	NM
4Q	—	—	0.85	-2%	0.87	-1%
Yr.	—	—	0.61	-24%	0.80	-4%

Next earnings report expected: mid October

Service Merchandise

Business Summary - 10-AUG-95

Service Merchandise is a catalog showroom merchandiser that was operating 405 catalog stores in 37 states as of July 11, 1995. The stores offer a wide variety of jewelry, diamonds, housewares, small appliances, giftware, silverware, cameras, luggage, radios, televisions, other home electronics, sporting goods, toys and patio, lawn and garden products. SME believes its prices are competitive with those of other retailers selling similar lines of merchandise and operating on high-volume, low-profit-margin principles.

The company's stores are divided into several departments. Only the jewelry and sight-and-sound departments require personnel for customer assistance. In those departments, the merchandise is displayed in showcases, and sales personnel deliver it to the customer and accept payment. In self-service sections, customers select the merchandise from a shelf and take it to a checkout counter to complete the purchase. In the remainder of the store, only a sample of the merchandise is displayed and order forms are available at various locations. After the customer orders the merchandise by filling out the form, a store cashier is paid and the merchandise is delivered to a pickup station. Management believes this merchandising technique reduces selling space requirements, handling and payroll costs and provides greater control over customer-related inventory shrinkage.

Customers may also phone in orders for mail delivery 24 hours a day, seven days a week, fax an order to the company's mail-order department or call a store to pick up an order.

Principal promotional efforts are made through an annual fall catalog of approximately 560 pages and a spring catalog of about 175 pages. SME also distributes a 160-page Christmas catalog, as well as seasonal flyers and newspaper inserts.

Most of the company's stores display and maintain an inventory of substantially all of the catalog items and some merchandise not described in the published catalogs in warehouse space contiguous to the sales area. Merchandise is purchased from about 2,150 suppliers. SME monitors inventory through an extensive on-line data processing network consisting of computerized terminals located in each store connected by satellite or phone lines to a central host computer.

Important Developments

Jul. '95—Service Merchandise said that in the second half of 1995 it would concentrate on improving the productivity of its cost structure and increasing the profitability of existing stores. It expected that the general selling environment would continue to be weak for the remainder of the year.

Capitalization

Long Term Debt: $621,464,000 (7/2/95), incl. $70,124,000 of capital lease obligations.

Per Share Data ($)

(Year Ended Dec. 31)

	1994	1993	1992	1991	1990	1989
Tangible Bk. Val.	3.37	2.81	1.96	1.06	0.26	-0.43
Cash Flow	1.22	1.41	1.41	1.31	1.17	1.29
Earnings	0.61	0.80	0.83	0.76	0.62	0.74
Dividends	Nil	Nil	Nil	Nil	Nil	5.35
Payout Ratio	Nil	Nil	Nil	Nil	Nil	NM
Prices - High	10	15⅜	14⅝	9	5¼	12
- Low	4¼	9¾	6½	2¾	2	4⅛
P/E Ratio - High	16	19	18	12	9	16
- Low	7	12	8	4	3	5

Income Statement Analysis (Million $)

	1994	%Chg	1993	%Chg	1992	%Chg	1991
Revs.	4,050	6%	3,815	3%	3,713	9%	3,400
Oper. Inc.	238	-14%	277	-3%	285	NM	285
Depr.	62.5	1%	61.8	5%	58.7	4%	56.2
Int. Exp.	75.0	3%	73.0	-22%	93.0	-15%	109
Pretax Inc.	101	-26%	137	-1%	139	11%	125
Eff. Tax Rate	39%	—	40%	—	39%	—	39%
Net Inc.	61.6	-25%	82.3	-3%	84.5	11%	76.1

Balance Sheet & Other Fin. Data (Million $)

	1994	1993	1992	1991	1990	1989
Cash	173	325	165	111	208	198
Curr. Assets	1,260	1,347	1,099	965	1,040	1,046
Total Assets	1,927	2,012	1,709	1,573	1,653	1,664
Curr. Liab.	967	1,033	809	744	787	754
LT Debt	618	699	697	715	827	930
Common Eqty.	336	280	194	104	25.0	-42.0
Total Cap.	959	979	900	829	866	910
Cap. Exp.	82.0	117	70.0	63.0	56.0	90.0
Cash Flow	124	144	143	132	115	126

Ratio Analysis

	1994	1993	1992	1991	1990	1989
Curr. Ratio	1.3	1.3	1.4	1.3	1.3	1.4
% LT Debt of Cap.	64.5	71.3	77.4	86.2	95.5	NM
% Net Inc.of Revs.	1.5	2.2	2.3	2.2	1.8	2.2
% Ret. on Assets	3.1	4.4	5.1	4.7	3.7	4.2
% Ret. on Equity	20.0	34.7	56.5	117.2	NM	40.3

Dividend Data —SME discontinued its quarterly dividend in conjunction with the payment in July 1989 of a special distribution of $5.33 a share (adjusted). Previously, dividends had been paid since 1977. The shares were split 3-for-2 in 1992.

Data as orig. reptd.; bef. results of disc. opers. and/or spec. items. Per share data adj. for stk. divs. as of ex-div. date. E-Estimated. NA-Not Available. NM-Not Meaningful. NR-Not Ranked.

Office—7100 Service Mechandise Drive, Brentwood, TN 37027. **Tel**—(615) 660-6000. **Chrmn & CEO**—R. Zimmerman. **Pres & COO**—G. M. Witkin. **VP-CFO & Investor Contact**—Sam Cusano. **VP-Treas**—M. E. Hogrefe. **VP-Secy**—G. A. Bodzy. **Dirs**—R. P. Crane Jr., R. M. Holt, C. V. Moore, J. E. Poole, H. Roitenberg, G. M. Witkin, R. Zimmerman. **Transfer Agent**—Harris Trust & Savings Bank, Chicago. **Incorporated** in Tennessee in 1970. **Empl**-28,836. **S&P Analyst:** Maureen C. Carini

STANDARD & POOR'S

STOCK REPORTS

Shaw Industries

NYSE Symbol **SHX**
In S&P MidCap 400

24-AUG-95 **Industry:** Home Furnishings

Summary: This company is the world's largest carpet manufacturer, producing tufted carpet for residential and commercial use.

S&P Opinion: Accumulate (★★★★) Recent Price • 15½ | 52 Wk Range • 17⅞-12 | Yield • 2.0% | 12-Mo. P/E • 25.4

Quantitative Evaluations

Outlook (1 Lowest—5 Highest) • **2⁻**

Fair Value • **14¼**

Risk • **Average**

Earn./Div. Rank • **A**

Technical Eval. • **Bullish** since 7/95

Rel. Strength Rank (1 Lowest—99 Highest) • **16**

Insider Activity • **NA**

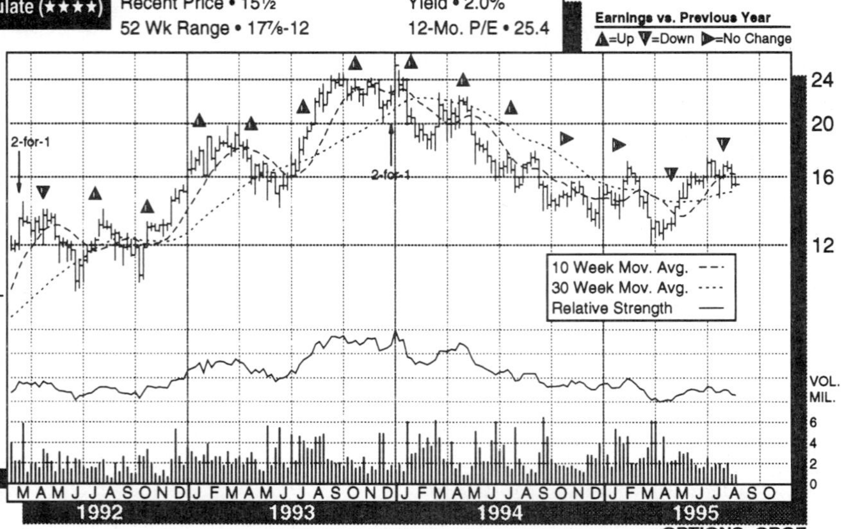

OPTIONS: CBOE

Overview - 24-AUG-95

Despite soft consumer demand for carpeting, sales should increase somewhat in 1995, reflecting acquisitions, greater market share (Shaw is aiming for a 40% share), and improvement in the housing market in the second half of the year. Trustmark, a new marketing program, should also boost sales. The program lets consumers retrieve information on fiber, twist, density, wearability and style via a fully interactive display. Typically, buying carpets has been a difficult process for the comsumer, with little product differentiation in the industry. Results may be hurt by rising raw material prices, a less favorable product mix, and a charge associated with plant downtime. Interest costs may be slightly higher. However, EPS should benefit from fewer shares outstanding.

Valuation - 24-AUG-95

The shares fell nearly 50% from their late 1993 high to their 1994 low. Although they recovered have somewhat in 1995, the stock remains under pressure, reflecting investor concerns over a weak housing industry and soft demand for carpet. However, the housing industry appears to be picking up, and we believe that SHX will be a major beneficiary by the second half of 1995. Although 1995 earnings are estimated to be substantially below those of 1994, because of the weak first half, we expect earnings growth to fully recover by 1995. As a result, we think this is a good time for investors to accumulate this stock.

Key Stock Statistics

S&P EPS Est. 1995	0.70	Tang. Bk. Value/Share	4.46
P/E on S&P Est. 1995	22.1	Beta	1.57
S&P EPS Est. 1996	0.95	Shareholders	4,400
Dividend Rate/Share	0.30	Market cap. (B)	$ 2.1
Shs. outstg. (M)	135.8	Inst. holdings	57%
Avg. daily vol. (M)	0.249	Insider holdings	NA

Value of $10,000 invested 5 years ago: $ 21,747

Fiscal Year Ending Dec. 31

	1995	% Change	1994	% Change	1993	% Change
Revenues (Million $)						
1Q	677.0	9%	620.0	19%	519.0	28%
2Q	738.3	2%	722.0	8%	669.0	34%
3Q	--	—	734.0	13%	650.0	19%
4Q	--	—	712.0	12%	638.0	9%
Yr.	--	—	2,789	—	--	—
Income (Million $)						
1Q	4.48	-82%	25.33	—	—	—
2Q	18.67	-57%	43.84	79%	24.54	96%
3Q	—	—	25.33	53%	16.60	87%
4Q	—	—	28.06	-26%	37.67	61%
Yr.	—	—	130.4	30%	100.6	73%
Earnings Per Share ($)						
1Q	0.03	-82%	0.17	42%	0.12	71%
2Q	0.14	-53%	0.30	15%	0.26	44%
3Q	E0.28	17%	0.24	NM	0.24	50%
4Q	E0.25	25%	0.20	NM	0.20	11%
Yr.	E0.70	-23%	0.91	—	--	—

Next earnings report expected: late October

Shaw Industries

Business Summary - 24-AUG-95

Shaw Industries is the world's largest carpet manufacturer. Much of its growth has been derived from acquisitions. Purchases included the carpet and rug division of West Point Pepperell (1987); the carpet division of Armstrong World Industries (1989); Salem Carpet Mills and Amoco Fabric and Fibers Co.'s polypropylene fiber manufacturing facilities (1992); and Kosset Carpets in Bradford, England, and Abingdon Carpets in Gwent, England (1993). In 1993, the company bought the remaining interest that it already did not own in Australia-based Capital Carpets Industries and Invicta Group Industries. In mid-1994, it entered into a joint venture to produce carpets with a Mexican manufacturer. In early 1995, SHX acquired the carpet division of Coats Viyella Plc, and its joint venture in Mexico acquired two carpet manufacturers in Mexico.

Products include 2,500 styles of tufted and woven residential and commerical carpet sold under the Philadelphia, Trustmark, Cabin Crafts, Shaw Commercial Carpets, Stratton, Networx, Shawmark, Evans Black, Salem, Sutton, Kosset, Crossley, Abingdon, Redbook, Minster, Invicta and Terza trade names and under certain private labels.

Carpet is sold in a broad range of prices, patterns, colors and textures, with the majority of sales in the medium to high price range. The company sells to retailers, distributors and commercial users throughout the U.S. and in certain foreign markets. Marketing is conducted through 1,050 salaried sales personnel.

In June 1994, a federal grand jury in Atlanta began investigating possible antitrust violations in the carpet industry in order to determine whether SHX and several other carpet manufacturers had engaged in price fixing. The company believes that the investigation, when completed, will not have a material adverse effect on its financial condition or operations.

Important Developments

Jul. '95—SHX said 1995 second quarter earnings fell significantly from those of the 1994 period, reflecting a minimal 2.2% sales increase, a pretax charge of $5.4 million for plant shutdown cost, and competitive pressures. The company added that it expects consumer demand for carpets to begin to improve, as a result of lower interest rates and a stronger housing market.

Capitalization

Long Term Debt: $661,300,000 (7/1/95).

Per Share Data ($) (Year Ended Dec. 31)

	1994	1993	1992	1991	1990	1989
Tangible Bk. Val.	4.42	5.08	4.68	3.30	1.91	1.98
Cash Flow	1.51	1.51	1.24	0.97	0.81	0.91
Earnings	0.91	0.91	0.72	0.46	0.29	0.53
Dividends	0.22	0.29	0.20	0.14	0.13	0.11
Payout Ratio	24%	32%	22%	31%	41%	21%
Prices - High	25	25	25½	17⅛	9⅝	8⅝
- Low	12⅞	12⅞	14⅛	8½	4⅞	3¾
P/E Ratio - High	NM	27	35	37	33	16
- Low	NM	14	20	18	17	7

Income Statement Analysis (Million $)

	1994	%Chg	1993	%Chg	1992	%Chg	1991
Revs.	2,789	6%	2,630	13%	2,321	33%	1,751
Oper. Inc.	320	NM	319	21%	263	44%	183
Depr.	84.9	-2%	86.5	18%	73.6	16%	63.2
Int. Exp.	30.4	17%	25.9	-5%	27.3	7%	25.5
Pretax Inc.	211	NM	212	30%	163	73%	94.0
Eff. Tax Rate	38%	—	37%	—	38%	—	38%
Net Inc.	130	-2%	133	32%	101	74%	58.0

Balance Sheet & Other Fin. Data (Million $)

	1994	1993	1992	1991	1990	1989
Cash	34.4	12.6	47.5	16.7	10.8	4.5
Curr. Assets	922	931	761	677	475	483
Total Assets	1,697	1,682	1,280	1,090	814	794
Curr. Liab.	305	526	327	286	219	225
LT Debt	612	382	248	316	357	304
Common Eqty.	713	710	670	456	205	237
Total Cap.	1,380	1,144	945	797	589	564
Cap. Exp.	159	164	157	51.0	78.0	168
Cash Flow	215	219	174	121	92.0	112

Ratio Analysis

	1994	1993	1992	1991	1990	1989
Curr. Ratio	3.0	1.8	2.3	2.4	2.2	2.1
% LT Debt of Cap.	44.3	33.4	26.3	39.6	60.7	53.9
% Net Inc.of Revs.	4.7	5.0	4.3	3.3	2.1	4.4
% Ret. on Assets	NA	8.9	8.2	5.6	4.3	9.8
% Ret. on Equity	NA	19.2	17.3	16.4	15.8	31.1

Dividend Data —Dividends have been paid in each year since 1972. Two quarterly payments were omitted in 1982. A poison pill stock purchase rights plan was adopted in 1989.

Amt. of Div. $	Date Decl.	Ex-Div. Date	Stock of Record	Payment Date
0.055	Oct. 31	Nov. 07	Nov. 14	Nov. 28 '94
0.075	Jan. 26	Feb. 06	Feb. 10	Feb. 24 '95
0.075	Apr. 27	May. 09	May. 15	May. 30 '95
0.075	Jul. 28	Aug. 11	Aug. 15	Aug. 29 '95

Data as orig. reptd.; bef. results of disc. opers. and/or spec. items. Per share data adj. for stk. divs. as of ex-div. date. E-Estimated. NA-Not Available. NM-Not Meaningful. NR-Not Ranked.

Office—616 East Walnut Ave., Dalton, GA 30720. **Tel**—(706) 278-3812. **Chrmn**—J. C. Shaw. **Pres & CEO**—R. E. Shaw. **SVP & Treas**—W. C. Lusk, Jr. **VP & Secy**—B. M. Laughter. **VP & Investor Contact**—W. M. Sims, Jr. **Dirs**—T. G. Cousins, S. T. Grigg, R. R. Harlin, C. M. Kirtland, Jr., J. H. Lanier, W. N. Little, W. C. Lusk, Jr., R. J. McCamy, J. C. Shaw, R. E. Shaw. **Transfer Agent & Registrar**—Wachovia Bank of North Carolina. **Incorporated** in Georgia in 1967. **Empl**-24,600. **S&P Analyst:** Elizabeth Vandeventer

STANDARD & POOR'S

STOCK REPORTS

Sizzler International

NYSE Symbol **SZ**
In S&P MidCap 400

18-OCT-95

Industry: Food serving

Summary: This large restaurant company (formerly Collins Foods) operates the Sizzler chain, and is also a franchisee of Kentucky Fried Chicken units in Australia.

S&P Opinion: Sell (★)

Recent Price • 5¼ | Yield • Nil
52 Wk Range • 7⅛-4¾ | 12-Mo. P/E • 32.8

Quantitative Evaluations

Outlook (1 Lowest—5 Highest)
• **2**

Fair Value
• **5⅛**

Risk
• **Average**

Earn./Div. Rank
• **NR**

Technical Eval.
• **Bearish** since 9/95

Rel. Strength Rank (1 Lowest—99 Highest)
• **8**

Insider Activity
• **Neutral**

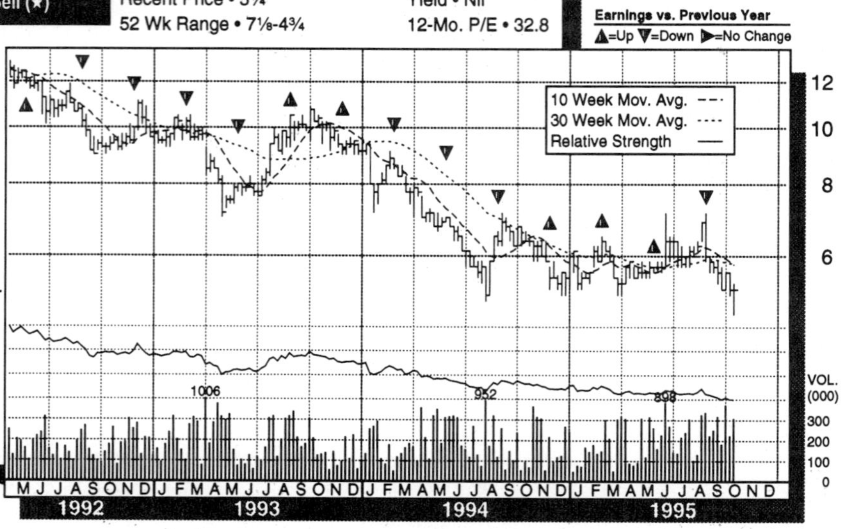

Overview - 18-OCT-95

In fiscal 1995-96, we expect a larger annual loss from SZ's U.S. operations, largely due to lower comparable-unit sales. However, during the next few years, we look for investments in restaurant remodeling, plus operational improvements, to help SZ's customer counts and profit in the U.S. An image revision of the Sizzler chain is starting to use the "Sizzler American Grill" name. From SZ's international business we expect 1995-96 earnings of about $19 million, but this would be down from the year-ago level. In the next several years, most of SZ's restaurants openings (including franchises) are likely be to be overseas. Also, we expect SZ's 1995-96 earnings to be limited by an unusually high tax rate due to an absence of profit from the U.S.

Valuation - 18-OCT-95

At the current share price, we advise investors to sell, or stay clear, of this restaurant stock. We are concerned about recent weak sales in the flagship Sizzler chain, and we expect the company's fiscal 1995-96 earnings to be far below 1991-92's recent peak. We view efforts to revitalize the U.S. restaurant business, and SZ's plan to open 125 Italian Oven restaurants in Australia as multi-year projects. On a brighter note, we do not view the recent suspension of SZ's $0.16-a-share cash dividend as an indication of dire financial straits. Even though SZ is likely to be a net borrower in 1995-96, the company's debt level is relatively modest, and SZ has close to $1.00-a- share of non-cash depreciation expense.

Key Stock Statistics

S&P EPS Est. 1996	0.05	Tang. Bk. Value/Share	6.07
P/E on S&P Est. 1996	NM	Beta	1.51
Dividend Rate/Share	Nil	Shareholders	3,100
Shs. outstg. (M)	27.8	Market cap. (B)	$0.135
Avg. daily vol. (M)	0.079	Inst. holdings	61%
		Insider holdings	NA

Value of $10,000 invested 5 years ago: NA

Fiscal Year Ending Apr. 30

	1996	% Change	1995	% Change	1994	% Change
Revenues (Million $)						
1Q	105.5	-6%	111.9	-5%	118.2	-4%
2Q	—	—	108.2	-5%	113.8	-4%
3Q	—	—	136.8	-4%	142.4	-4%
4Q	—	—	105.3	-7%	113.1	-2%
Yr.	—	—	462.1	-5%	487.5	-3%
Income (Million $)						
1Q	0.44	-84%	2.78	-30%	3.96	—
2Q	—	—	2.27	39%	1.63	—
3Q	—	—	0.27	NM	-2.04	NM
4Q	—	—	1.39	NM	-98.43	NM
Yr.	—	—	6.69	NM	-94.89	NM
Earnings Per Share ($)						
1Q	0.02	-80%	0.10	-29%	0.14	NM
2Q	E-0.01	NM	0.08	33%	0.06	20%
3Q	E-0.02	NM	0.01	NM	-0.07	NM
4Q	E0.06	20%	0.05	NM	-3.40	NM
Yr.	E0.05	-79%	0.24	NM	-3.26	NM

Next earnings report expected: late November

Sizzler International

Business Summary - 18-OCT-95

Sizzler International (SZ) was formed through a series of transactions that occurred in the first half of 1991. It was formerly known as Collins Foods Inc., a successor company to Collins Foods International.

As of April 30, 1995, the Sizzler restaurant business included 600 company-operated, joint-venture and franchised units (down from 648 at April 30, 1994). There were about 474 units in the U.S. and 126 were in other countries (mostly in Australia). Of the 600 systemwide restaurants, about 41% were company-operated.

Domestic Sizzler restaurants serve moderately priced meals from a menu that includes steak, chicken, seafood, sandwiches and a fruit and salad bar. A Family Program features a Just for Kids food bar. Many U.S. Sizzler restaurants are in California. SZ has also developed a new western-theme restaurant concept called Buffalo Ranch Steakhouses. The first such unit opened in December 1992 in Mission Viejo, Calif. As of April 1995, there were eight Buffalo Ranch units open. In 1994-95, SZ had total U.S. revenues of $274 million, down from $308 million the year before. Including franchises, systemwide sales in the U.S. totaled $607 million, down from $682 million.

SZ's international segment had 1994-95 revenues of $188 million, up from $179 million year before. Systemwide sales, including franchises amnd affiliates, totaled $331 million, up from $308 million. At April 30, 1995, in addition to about 126 international Sizzler restaurants (47 company, 77 franchise and two joint venture), SZ operated 88 Kentucky Fried Chicken units in Australia.

Fiscal 1993-94 included a restructuring charge of $3.42 a share related to such factors as expected unit closings, writeoff of intangible assets, and liquidation of surplus property.

Important Developments

Oct. '95—SZ suspended its annual dividend of $0.16-a-share. In the year ahead, we expect the $4.5 million dividend saving to reduce SZ's borrowing needs as the company makes various investments to reposition its flagship Sizzler restaurant business in the U.S. under the name of Sizzler American Grills. Changes are expected to include the remodeling of restaurants and a greater emphasis on grill food items. SZ said that early results from 11 repositioned Sacramento, Cal., restaurants have been encouraging. Meanwhile, in fiscal, 1995-96's first quarter, SZ's overall results were limited by lower comparable-unit sales, higher food produce costs, and a higher tax rate. Also, SZ has reached an agreement under which it would develop 125 Italian Oven franchise restaurants in Australia. Italian Oven is a full-service, Italian-oriented, family restaurant chain which has units in the U.S.

Capitalization

Long Term Debt: $15,895,000 (7/23/95).

Per Share Data ($) (Year Ended Apr. 30)

	1995	1994	1993	1992	1991	1990
Tangible Bk. Val.	6.08	5.91	9.60	10.21	9.69	NA
Cash Flow	1.24	-2.27	0.68	1.68	NA	NA
Earnings	0.24	-3.26	-0.33	0.75	0.85	1.06
Dividends	0.16	0.16	0.16	0.16	0.04	NM
Payout Ratio	67%	NM	NM	21%	NM	NM
Cal. Yrs.	1994	1993	1992	1991	1990	1989
Prices - High	9⅜	10⅞	15⅛	18⅞	NM	NM
- Low	5	7	9	9⅝	NM	NM
P/E Ratio - High	39	NM	NM	25	NM	NM
- Low	21	NM	NM	13	NM	NM

Income Statement Analysis (Million $)

	1995	%Chg	1994	%Chg	1993	%Chg	1992
Revs.	462	-5%	488	-3%	504	-7%	543
Oper. Inc.	39.6	10%	35.9	-7%	38.7	-41%	65.2
Depr.	28.3	-2%	29.0	NM	29.2	6%	27.5
Int. Exp.	1.5	7%	1.4	-18%	1.7	-41%	2.9
Pretax Inc.	11.1	NM	-13.1	NM	-16.4	NM	37.5
Eff. Tax Rate	40%	—	NM	—	NM	—	41%
Net Inc.	6.7	NM	-94.9	NM	-9.5	NM	22.1

Balance Sheet & Other Fin. Data (Million $)

	1995	1994	1993	1992	1991	1990
Cash	12.2	11.1	11.4	9.7	27.3	38.8
Curr. Assets	34.0	32.0	31.0	30.0	47.3	63.0
Total Assets	277	277	413	443	446	369
Curr. Liab.	39.4	38.1	55.1	63.1	72.5	50.4
LT Debt	17.0	21.0	21.0	16.8	24.3	25.6
Common Eqty.	177	180	280	298	288	198
Total Cap.	205	215	341	365	312	270
Cap. Exp.	13.8	17.0	29.0	55.0	NA	NA
Cash Flow	35.0	-65.9	19.7	49.6	NA	55.8

Ratio Analysis

	1995	1994	1993	1992	1991	1990
Curr. Ratio	0.9	0.9	0.6	0.5	0.7	1.2
% LT Debt of Cap.	8.4	9.7	6.0	4.6	7.8	9.5
% Net Inc.of Revs.	1.5	NM	NM	4.1	5.1	7.4
% Ret. on Assets	2.5	NM	NM	5.0	6.2	NA
% Ret. on Equity	3.8	NM	NM	7.6	10.4	NA

Dividend Data —Cash dividends, initiated in 1991, were suspended in October 1995.

Amt. of Div. $	Date Decl.	Ex-Div. Date	Stock of Record	Payment Date
0.040	Dec. 14	Dec. 19	Dec. 26	Jan. 17 '95
0.040	Feb. 15	Mar. 28	Apr. 03	Apr. 14 '95
0.040	Jun. 19	Jun. 29	Jul. 03	Jul. 17 '95
0.040	Aug. 24	Sep. 26	Sep. 28	Oct. 12 '95

Data as orig. reptd.; bef. results of disc. opers. and/or spec. items. Per share data adj. for stk. divs. as of ex-div. date. E-Estimated. NA-Not Available. NM-Not Meaningful. NR-Not Ranked.

Office—12655 West Jefferson Blvd., Los Angeles, CA 90066. **Tel**—(310) 827-2300. **Chrmn**—J. A. Collins. **Pres & CEO**—K. Perkins. **EVP-Fin & CFO**—C. R. Thomas. **Treas, Secy, & Investor Contact**—John Bayley (ext. 3326). **Dirs**—R. P. Bermingham, J. A. Collins, P. H. Dailey, T. L. Gregory, W. S. Hansen, W. G. Kees, H. W. Merryman, K. W. Perkins, C. A. Scott, D. L. Tilton. **Transfer Agent**—Bank of New York, NYC. **Incorporated** in Delaware in 1991. **Empl**-16,000. **S&P Analyst:** Tom Graves, CFA

STANDARD & POOR'S

STOCK REPORTS

Smith International

NYSE Symbol **SII**
In S&P MidCap 400

05-SEP-95 **Industry:** Oil and Gas

Summary: This company is an international supplier of drilling tools and services used mainly in the drilling of oil and gas wells.

S&P Opinion: Hold (★★★)

Recent Price • 17¾
52 Wk Range • 19⅜-11
Yield • Nil
12-Mo. P/E • 17.1

Quantitative Evaluations
Outlook (1 Lowest—5 Highest)
• 5+
Fair Value
• 21⅛
Risk
• Average
Earn./Div. Rank
• B-

Technical Eval.
• **Bearish** since 5/95
Rel. Strength Rank (1 Lowest—99 Highest)
• 72
Insider Activity
• Neutral

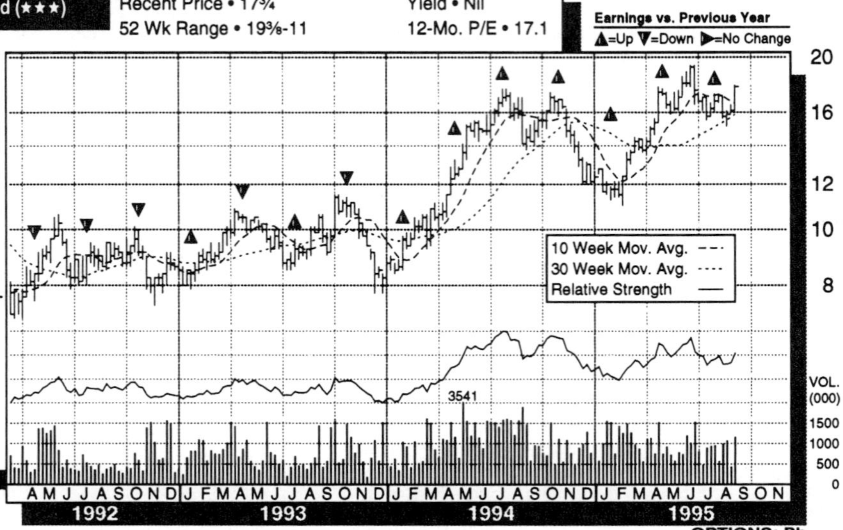

OPTIONS: Ph

Overview - 28-AUG-95

Smith International manufactures and markets a wide range of products and services used in the drilling of oil and gas wells. The worldwide decline in drilling that occurred in 1992 led SII to reassess its strategy from both a business portfolio and financial flexibility standpoint. This resulted in the sale of the company's directional drilling systems and services business for $248 million, with proceeds used to reduce debt burden and to pursue growth objectives. Product lines were acquired from A-Z/Grant and Lindsey Completion Systems, and a controlling interest was purchased in M-I Drilling Liquids. Sales to the international market are a key focus, generating over 50% of revenues. Except in Canada, continued sluggishness is anticipated for North American drilling in 1995; growth is expected in other producing areas of the world, where activity is less volatile.

Valuation - 28-AUG-95

The stock has retreated from its 52-week high, reflecting the ongoing general malaise affecting oil and gas, which will dampen earnings potential. However, growth will be enhanced by recent acquisitions, especially the interest in M-I Drilling, which has a strong niche. Also, the company's significant amount of international business will somewhat counter the sagging North American market. Overall prospects are for an improved, if not spectacular, future 6-12 months. At its current P/E ratio, the stock is attractively priced compared to many of its peers.

Key Stock Statistics

S&P EPS Est. 1995	1.08	Tang. Bk. Value/Share	5.96
P/E on S&P Est. 1995	16.4	Beta	0.65
S&P EPS Est. 1996	1.20	Shareholders	5,000
Dividend Rate/Share	Nil	Market cap. (B)	$0.695
Shs. outstg. (M)	39.1	Inst. holdings	88%
Avg. daily vol. (M)	0.180	Insider holdings	NA

Value of $10,000 invested 5 years ago: $ 14,200

Fiscal Year Ending Dec. 31

	1995	% Change	1994	% Change	1993	% Change
Revenues (Million $)						
1Q	199.6	98%	100.8	102%	50.00	-7%
2Q	206.0	19%	173.4	NM	52.74	6%
3Q	—	—	181.5	NM	59.04	11%
4Q	—	—	198.2	NM	58.98	10%
Yr.	—	—	653.9	196%	220.7	5%
Income (Million $)						
1Q	10.81	42%	7.59	NM	1.33	-35%
2Q	10.12	19%	8.47	NM	2.65	NM
3Q	—	—	9.35	NM	-14.16	NM
4Q	—	—	10.48	69%	6.19	NM
Yr.	—	—	35.88	NM	-4.00	NM
Earnings Per Share ($)						
1Q	0.28	40%	0.20	NM	0.03	-40%
2Q	0.26	18%	0.22	NM	0.06	NM
3Q	E0.26	8%	0.24	NM	-0.36	NM
4Q	E0.28	4%	0.27	69%	0.16	NM
Yr.	E1.08	17%	0.92	NM	-0.13	NM

Next earnings report expected: late October

Smith International

Business Summary - 28-AUG-95

Smith International is a leading worldwide supplier of products and services used in the drilling of oil and gas wells. The company sold its directional drilling and services business in March 1993. Smith produces and markets drilling fluids and systems, manufactures and markets technologically advanced drill bits, and manufactures and markets drilling and completion products and services. Substantially all of the company's products and services are used in the process of drilling oil and natural gas wells, with the remainder used in the mining industry. Revenues from continuing operations by product group in recent years:

	1994	1993	1992
Drilling fluids	59%	---	---
Drill bits	27%	73%	69%
Drilling and completion services	14%	27%	31%

International markets accounted for 57% of 1994's total revenues from continuing operations, versus 53% in 1993. About 52% of Smith's revenues are denominated in U.S. dollars.

Drilling fluid products and systems are used to cool and lubricate the bit during drilling operations, contain formation pressures, keep rock cuttings in suspension to remove them from the hole, and maintain the stability of the wellbore.

The company offers more than 900 drill bits, consisting mainly of three-cone drill bits for the petroleum and mining industries. It also makes drill bits featuring inserts made of polycrystalline diamond cutters or natural diamonds.

Smith provides a full line of downhole tools and remedial services. Downhole tools include tubular drill string components, stabilizers and reamers. Various remedial tools are manufactured for use in the drill string for specialized drilling and workover operations. Field service centers provide inspection and repair services for the drill string components, customer-owned tubular goods and the company's own rental tools.

Management believes that the company has available manufacturing facilities to accommodate a worldwide demand level equivalent to approximately 3,000 average active drilling rigs, which compares with approximately 1,700 average active drilling rigs estimated for 1995.

Important Developments

Jul. '95—Net income in the first six months of 1995 included the results from operations of M-I Drilling Fluids, Supradiamant and Baker Hughes Treatment Services -- acquisitions of the past year. With recovery in Canadian drilling and demand for new technologies, SII said it expects a strong second half.

Capitalization

Long Term Debt: $119,859,000 (6/95).
Minority Interest: $75,488,000.

Per Share Data ($)

(Year Ended Dec. 31)

	1994	1993	1992	1991	1990	1989
Tangible Bk. Val.	5.49	5.54	3.58	3.78	3.42	2.83
Cash Flow	1.48	0.08	0.61	0.46	0.88	0.58
Earnings	0.92	-0.13	-0.02	-0.38	0.21	-0.18
Dividends	Nil	Nil	Nil	Nil	Nil	Nil
Payout Ratio	Nil	Nil	Nil	Nil	Nil	Nil
Prices - High	17⅝	11½	10⅝	17⅛	18¾	14⅛
- Low	8⅜	7¾	6⅛	6¾	11	8½
P/E Ratio - High	19	NM	NM	NM	89	NM
- Low	9	NM	NM	NM	52	NM

Income Statement Analysis (Million $)

	1994	%Chg	1993	%Chg	1992	%Chg	1991
Revs.	654	196%	221	5%	211	-48%	403
Oper. Inc.	81.9	NM	26.0	-21%	33.0	-47%	62.0
Depr.	21.8	176%	7.9	-65%	22.7	-10%	25.2
Int. Exp.	10.0	67%	6.0	-43%	10.6	-50%	21.4
Pretax Inc.	52.0	NM	-4.0	—	NM	—	-4.0
Eff. Tax Rate	13%	—	NM	—	NM	—	NM
Net Inc.	36.0	NM	-4.0	NM	1.0	NM	-10.0

Balance Sheet & Other Fin. Data (Million $)

	1994	1993	1992	1991	1990	1989
Cash	8.0	102	16.0	18.0	30.0	17.0
Curr. Assets	422	256	296	240	257	211
Total Assets	620	348	370	397	396	325
Curr. Liab.	164	80.0	214	132	125	83.0
LT Debt	116	48.0	2.0	100	146	138
Common Eqty.	253	214	130	137	98.0	81.0
Total Cap.	439	219	156	263	267	242
Cap. Exp.	24.1	31.0	27.0	43.0	41.0	22.0
Cash Flow	58.0	3.0	22.0	14.0	27.0	17.0

Ratio Analysis

	1994	1993	1992	1991	1990	1989
Curr. Ratio	2.6	3.2	1.4	1.8	2.1	2.6
% LT Debt of Cap.	26.4	17.8	1.1	38.0	54.5	57.1
% Net Inc.of Revs.	55.0	NM	0.6	NM	2.1	NM
% Ret. on Assets	7.4	NM	0.3	NM	2.3	NM
% Ret. on Equity	15.3	NM	NM	NM	7.3	NM

Dividend Data —Common dividends were omitted in 1986 after having been paid since 1956. A "poison pill" stock purchase rights plan was adopted in 1990.

Data as orig. reptd.; bef. results of disc. opers. and/or spec. items. Per share data adj. for stk. divs. as of ex-div. date. E-Estimated. NA-Not Available. NM-Not Meaningful. NR-Not Ranked.

Office—16740 Hardy St., Houston, TX 77032. **Tel**—(713) 443-3370. **Chrmn, Pres & CEO**—D. L. Rock. **EVP & CFO**—L. K. Carroll. **VP & Secy**—N. S. Sutton. **Dirs**—B. J. Bailar, G. C. Buck, L. K. Carroll, J. R. Gibbs, J. W. Neely, D. L. Rock, H. M. Rollins. **Transfer Agent & Registrar**—First Chicago Trust Co. of New York, NYC. **Incorporated** in California in 1937; reincorporated in Delaware in 1983. **Empl**-4,100. **S&P Analyst:** Michael C. Barr

STANDARD & POOR'S

STOCK REPORTS

Smucker (J. M.)

NYSE Symbol **SJM.A**
In S&P MidCap 400

24-AUG-95 **Industry:** Food

Summary: This company is a leading producer of jellies, preserves and related food products. The Smucker family controls 27% of both the Class A (supervoting) and Class B common stock.

S&P Opinion: Avoid (★★)

Recent Price • 21½
52 Wk Range • 25-20⅜
Yield • 2.4%
12-Mo. P/E • 17.1

Quantitative Evaluations
Outlook (1 Lowest—5 Highest)
• **NA**
Fair Value
• **NA**
Risk
• **NA**
Earn./Div. Rank
• **A**

Technical Eval.
• **Bullish** since 4/95
Rel. Strength Rank (1 Lowest—99 Highest)
• **24**
Insider Activity
• **Neutral**

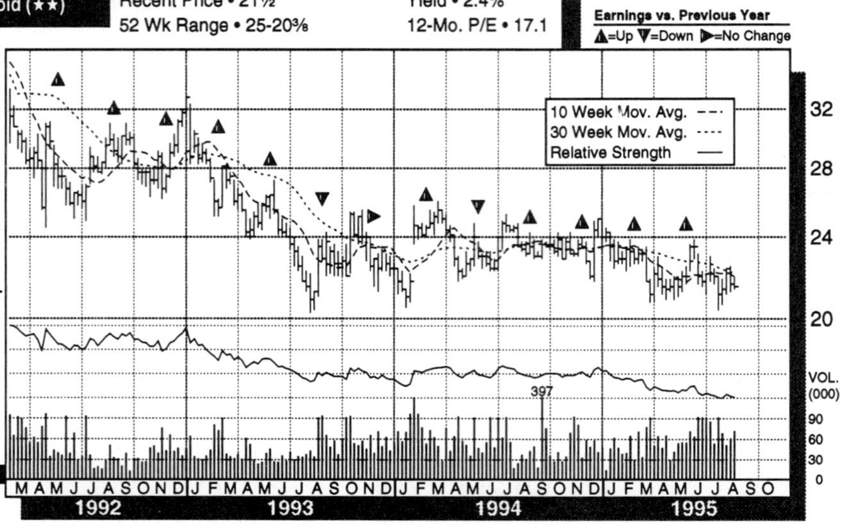

Overview - 24-AUG-95

Net sales for fiscal 1995-96 are expected to increase at a high single-digit pace, following the strong gain posted in 1994-95 which benefited from numerous acquisitions. Operating margins are expected to hold steady, as the inclusion of the less-profitable acquired businesses, combined with an increase in marketing spending behind new and existing products, may offset any potential synergistic benefits arising from the acquired businesses. Substantially greater acquisition-related net interest, depreciation and amortization expenses will also be a restraining factor to earnings. In all, we expect share earnings to advance to $1.35 in 1995-96, up 8% from 1994-95's $1.25.

Valuation - 24-AUG-95

Given our projection of high single-digit annual earnings per share growth for the foreseeable future, we view these shares as fully valued, and would avoid them for now. Earnings have risen steadily over the years, benefiting from increased demand for fruit spreads and related products. However, recently increased competition in the maturing fruit spread category has restricted the company's pricing flexibility and margins. As a result, the company has increasingly diversified into other, related businesses. Finances are sound, allowing additional future acquisitions. Although optimistic about long-term growth prospects, we anticipate the shares to be near-term laggards relative to the overall market.

Key Stock Statistics

S&P EPS Est. 1996	1.35	Tang. Bk. Value/Share	6.08
P/E on S&P Est. 1996	15.9	Beta	0.67
S&P EPS Est. 1997	1.45	Shareholders	12,000
Dividend Rate/Share	0.52	Market cap. (B)	$0.627
Shs. outstg. (M)	29.2	Inst. holdings	17%
Avg. daily vol. (M)	0.013	Insider holdings	NA

Value of $10,000 invested 5 years ago: $ 6,436

Fiscal Year Ending Apr. 30

	1996	% Change	1995	% Change	1994	% Change
Revenues (Million $)						
1Q	148.0	3%	144.4	22%	118.3	-5%
2Q	—	—	184.3	33%	138.4	3%
3Q	—	—	157.4	30%	120.6	10%
4Q	—	—	142.3	6%	134.2	10%
Yr.	—	—	628.3	23%	511.5	4%
Income (Million $)						
1Q	9.52	3%	9.22	3%	8.91	-6%
2Q	—	—	12.33	18%	10.42	2%
3Q	—	—	8.69	18%	7.39	1%
4Q	—	—	6.07	61%	3.78	-63%
Yr.	—	—	36.30	19%	30.50	-18%
Earnings Per Share ($)						
1Q	0.33	3%	0.32	3%	0.31	-3%
2Q	E0.42	NM	0.42	20%	0.35	NM
3Q	E0.32	7%	0.30	15%	0.26	4%
4Q	E0.28	33%	0.21	62%	0.13	-63%
Yr.	E1.35	8%	1.25	19%	1.05	-17%

Next earnings report expected: mid November

Smucker (J. M.)

Business Summary - 24-AUG-95

J. M. Smucker Co. manufactures and markets food products, principally fruit spreads, frozen pies, dessert toppings, syrups, peanut butter, industrial fruit products (such as bakery and yogurt fillings), fruit and vegetable juices, juice beverages, pie fillings, condiments, and gift packages. Principal company trademarks include: Smucker's, Mrs. Smith's, The R. W. Knudsen Family, After The Fall, Mary Ellen, Dickinson's, Lost Acres, IXL, Laura Scudder's, and Simply Fruit.

The company is structured around seven strategic business areas: Consumer, Mrs. Smith's, Beverage, International, Foodservice, Industrial and Specialty Foods. Within the domestic markets, the company's products are sold primarily through brokers to chain, wholesale, cooperative and independent grocery accounts and other consumer markets and to foodservice distributors and chains, including hotels, restaurants and institutions.

Industrial products such as bakery and fruit fillings are typically sold direct to other food manufacturers and marketers for inclusion in their products.

Smucker's distribution outside the U.S. is principally in Canada, Australia, the United Kingdom and Latin America, although products are exported to other countries. International sales represent approximately 11% of the company's total.

Important Developments

Aug. '95—Management said that during fiscal 1995-96's first quarter, sales rose, year to year, in the Consumer, Beverage, Foodservice, Industrial, and International areas. Consumer segment sales growth was led by increases in sales of Simply Fruit and Low Sugar fruit spreads, and Sundae Syrups ice cream toppings, plus the addition of the Laura Scudder's natural peanut butter business. Beverage segment sales growth reflected the inclusion of a full quarter's sales of After The Fall business. In the International segment, most of the increase came from higher sales of Smucker's branded products in Latin America and the Middle East. Sales of Mrs. Smith's products were down in the first quarter, primarily due to the discontinuation of the SmartStyle line, which was in national distribution last year.

Capitalization

Long Term Debt: \$67,100,000 (7/95).
Class A Common Stock: 14,384,839 shs. (no par); one vote per sh. (10 votes per sh. on shs. held for four yrs.).
Shareholders of record: 7,457.
Class B Common Stock: 14,778,839 shs. (no par); nonvoting; divd. at least equal to Cl. A divd.
The Smucker family controls 27% of both Cl. A and Cl. B com.
Shareholders of record: 4,991.

Per Share Data (\$) (Year Ended Apr. 30)

	1995	1994	1993	1992	1991	1990
Tangible Bk. Val.	6.08	5.99	6.76	6.47	5.68	4.87
Cash Flow	1.94	1.48	1.64	1.52	1.40	1.32
Earnings	1.25	1.05	1.27	1.16	1.08	1.03
Dividends	0.50	0.45	0.42	0.38	0.34	0.26
Payout Ratio	40%	43%	33%	33%	32%	25%
Cal. Yrs.	1994	1993	1992	1991	1990	1989
Prices - High	26	32 3/8	39	38 7/8	23 1/4	19 1/2
- Low	20 1/2	20 1/4	24 1/2	20	16 1/8	14 1/2
P/E Ratio - High	21	31	31	34	22	19
- Low	16	19	19	17	15	14

Income Statement Analysis (Million \$)

	1995	%Chg	1994	%Chg	1993	%Chg	1992
Revs.	628	23%	512	4%	491	2%	483
Oper. Inc.	82.7	30%	63.5	-10%	70.9	9%	65.2
Depr.	20.1	58%	12.7	14%	11.1	3%	10.8
Int. Exp.	4.5	NM	0.5	33%	0.4	-13%	0.4
Pretax Inc.	61.4	17%	52.7	-14%	61.5	10%	56.1
Eff. Tax Rate	41%	—	42%	—	39%	—	39%
Net Inc.	36.3	19%	30.5	-18%	37.4	10%	34.1

Balance Sheet & Other Fin. Data (Million \$)

	1995	1994	1993	1992	1991	1990
Cash	11.2	14.1	50.4	36.3	24.5	18.4
Curr. Assets	192	172	168	162	141	120
Total Assets	421	379	295	278	252	225
Curr. Liab.	79.8	83.2	56.5	53.6	50.0	45.7
LT Debt	67.1	48.6	Nil	3.8	4.3	4.3
Common Eqty.	258	234	220	212	190	167
Total Cap.	330	285	224	223	201	178
Cap. Exp.	19.0	18.7	21.0	17.4	17.3	18.1
Cash Flow	56.4	43.2	48.5	44.9	41.3	38.9

Ratio Analysis

	1995	1994	1993	1992	1991	1990
Curr. Ratio	2.4	2.1	3.0	3.0	2.8	2.6
% LT Debt of Cap.	20.3	17.0	Nil	1.7	2.1	2.4
% Net Inc.of Revs.	5.8	6.0	7.6	7.1	7.0	7.1
% Ret. on Assets	9.1	9.1	13.1	12.9	13.3	14.2
% Ret. on Equity	14.7	13.4	17.4	17.0	17.8	19.3

Dividend Data —Dividends have been paid since 1949. A dividend reinvestment plan is available.

Amt. of Div. \$	Date Decl.	Ex-Div. Date	Stock of Record	Payment Date
0.125	Jul. 19	Aug. 12	Aug. 18	Sep. 01 '94
0.125	Oct. 28	Nov. 10	Nov. 17	Dec. 01 '94
0.125	Jan. 20	Feb. 09	Feb. 15	Mar. 01 '95
0.130	Apr. 18	May. 12	May. 18	Jun. 01 '95
0.130	Jul. 14	Aug. 16	Aug. 18	Sep. 01 '95

Data as orig. reptd.; bef. results of disc. opers. and/or spec. items. Per share data adj. for stk. divs. as of ex-div. date. E-Estimated. NA-Not Available. NM-Not Meaningful. NR-Not Ranked.

Office—Strawberry Lane, Orrville, OH 44667-0280. **Tel**—(216) 682-3000. **Chrmn**—T. P. Smucker. **Chrmn Exec Comm**—P. H. Smucker. **Pres**—R. K. Smucker. **Treas**—P. P. Yuschak. **Secy & Investor Contact**—Steven J. Ellcessor. **Dirs**—L. C. Bailey, W. P. Boyle Jr., R. G. Mawby, C. S. Mechem Jr., R. R. Morrison, V. D. Netzly, P. H. Smucker, R. K. Smucker, T. P. Smucker, W. H. Steinbrink, B. B. Tregoe Jr., B. Trueman, W. Wrigley Jr. **Transfer Agent & Registrar**—KeyCorp Shareholder Services, Cleveland. **Incorporated** in Ohio in 1921. **Empl**-2,600. **S&P Analyst:** Kenneth A. Shea

STANDARD & POOR'S

STOCK REPORTS

Sonoco Products

NYSE Symbol **SON**
In S&P MidCap 400

13-SEP-95 **Industry:** Containers

Summary: This international maker of paper and plastic packaging products, which serves a variety of industries and markets worldwide, operates in more than 250 locations in 26 countries.

S&P Opinion: Hold (★★★)

Recent Price • 27⅜ | Yield • 2.1%
52 Wk Range • 27⅝-18¾ | 12-Mo. P/E • 17.7

Quantitative Evaluations

Outlook
(1 Lowest—5 Highest)
• **3+**

Fair Value
• **27⅛**

Risk
• **Low**

Earn./Div. Rank
• **A-**

Technical Eval.
• **Bearish** since 5/95

Rel. Strength Rank
(1 Lowest—99 Highest)
• **69**

Insider Activity
• **Neutral**

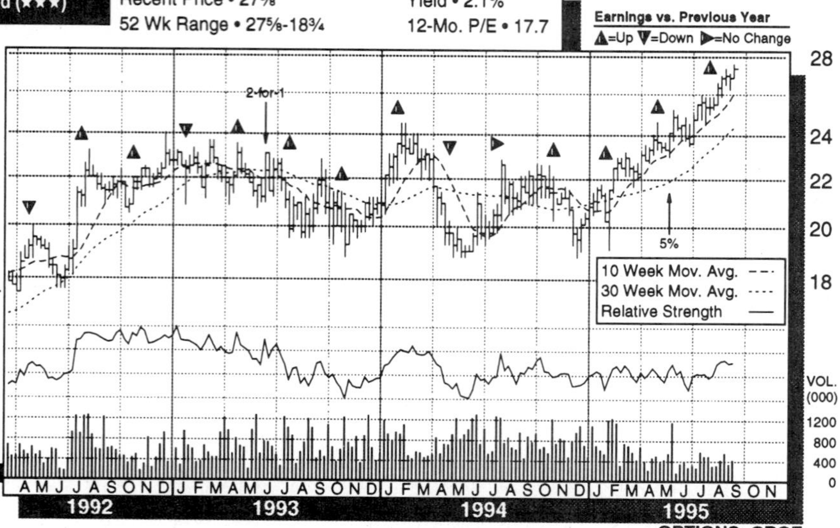

OPTIONS: CBOE

Overview - 13-SEP-95

Sales are expected to post a solid advance in 1995, on higher product prices, aggressive marketing of value-added products to niche markets, global expansion and continued focus on tactical acquisitions; corporate takeovers have added some $900 million in sales over the past decade. Margins should be aided by restructuring programs implemented in recent years, which addressed key issues of competitiveness in both domestic and international markets. Although Sonoco has been contending with sharply higher raw materials prices, the cost of recovered old corrugated containers, its major raw material, reversed course in the spring of 1995 after surging early in the year. While the U.S. economy has slowed in recent months, industry trends should benefit from the recent drop in long-term interest rates, which is likely to provide a further spark to the economy.

Valuation - 13-SEP-95

Sonoco's shares have sustained a solid advance to date in 1995, with the benefits of recovered global economies, higher product prices and restructuring programs generating expectations of record earnings in 1995. Although moderating economic trends cause worries about an approaching industry slowdown, our forecast believes the economy has enough kick left to enable SON's growth to continue into 1996. However, despite our optimism about Sonoco's upcoming prospects, the shares appear fairly valued in their recent trading range of about 14X our 1996 estimate.

Key Stock Statistics

S&P EPS Est. 1995	1.70	Tang. Bk. Value/Share	3.63
P/E on S&P Est. 1995	16.1	Beta	0.85
S&P EPS Est. 1996	1.90	Shareholders	34,000
Dividend Rate/Share	0.60	Market cap. (B)	$ 2.6
Shs. outstg. (M)	91.2	Inst. holdings	33%
Avg. daily vol. (M)	0.085	Insider holdings	NA

Value of $10,000 invested 5 years ago: $ 17,749

Fiscal Year Ending Dec. 31

	1995	% Change	1994	% Change	1993	% Change
Revenues (Million $)						
1Q	645.1	20%	537.4	15%	466.9	9%
2Q	691.7	23%	564.4	18%	478.5	4%
3Q	—	—	591.2	28%	462.1	NM
4Q	—	—	607.2	13%	539.5	11%
Yr.	—	—	2,300	18%	1,947	6%
Income (Million $)						
1Q	37.54	34%	28.10	4%	26.91	22%
2Q	44.11	34%	32.84	3%	31.81	10%
3Q	—	—	32.51	14%	28.50	5%
4Q	—	—	36.41	20%	30.35	NM
Yr.	—	—	129.9	9%	118.8	46%
Earnings Per Share ($)						
1Q	0.39	37%	0.29	-3%	0.30	22%
2Q	0.46	34%	0.34	NM	0.34	9%
3Q	E0.40	20%	0.33	6%	0.31	5%
4Q	E0.45	21%	0.37	11%	0.33	NM
Yr.	E1.70	28%	1.33	4%	1.29	45%

Next earnings report expected: mid October

Sonoco Products

Business Summary - 13-SEP-95

Sonoco Products Company is a major manufacturer of paper and plastic packaging products. It has expanded and diversified from its original product line of paper cones for the southern textile market to serve a large variety of industries and markets worldwide. As of July 1995, the company had more than 250 operations in 26 countries. Sales to unaffiliated customers and operating profits for 1994 were derived as follows:

	Sales	Profits
Converted products	76%	70%
Paper	5%	24%
International	19%	6%

The largest subsidiaries abroad are located in the U.K., Canada, France, Mexico, Australia and Germany.

The various divisions of the converted products segment manufacture paperboard tubes, cores and cones; fibre and plastic drums and intermediate bulk containers; wood, plywood and metal reels for the wire and cable industries; injection molded and extrusion plastics; fibre and specialty partitions; protective packaging products; composite canisters used to package a variety of food and other products; plastic bags for grocers and retailers and agricultural use; and pressure-sensitive labels and package inserts, paperboard cartons and flexible packaging.

SON's paper segment has an annual cylinder board capacity of around 1,000,000 tons, more than 80% of which is sold to Sonoco's paper converting operations. Its Paper Stock Dealers subsidiary purchases and processes recovered paper. The paper segment also produces corrugated medium sold under contract to Georgia-Pacific Corp.

Important Developments

Jul. '95—Sonoco recorded a 34% year-to-year earnings gain in the second quarter of 1995, on a 23% sales rise, with strong performances recorded in nearly all of the company's business units (both domestic and international). Sonoco said that it continued to anticipate record earnings in 1995.

Capitalization

Long Term Debt: $601,585,000 (7/2/95).
$2.25 Ser. A Preferred Stock: 3,450,000 shs. (liq. pref. $50); conv. into com at $24.1078 a sh..

Per Share Data ($) (Year Ended Dec. 31)

	1994	1993	1992	1991	1990	1989
Tangible Bk. Val.	3.27	2.97	10.99	5.52	5.05	4.79
Cash Flow	2.57	2.32	3.61	1.89	1.34	1.85
Earnings	1.33	1.29	0.90	1.05	0.55	1.12
Dividends	0.53	0.50	0.47	0.44	0.43	0.39
Payout Ratio	40%	39%	52%	42%	78%	34%
Prices - High	24½	23¾	24	18½	18¼	18⅝
- Low	18¾	18¾	16⅛	13⅝	12	15½
P/E Ratio - High	18	18	27	18	33	17
- Low	14	15	18	13	22	14

Income Statement Analysis (Million $)

	1994	%Chg	1993	%Chg	1992	%Chg	1991
Revs.	2,300	18%	1,947	6%	1,838	8%	1,697
Oper. Inc.	357	16%	308	10%	280	11%	252
Depr.	113	18%	95.7	14%	83.8	9%	76.6
Int. Exp.	35.9	15%	31.2	3%	30.4	8%	28.2
Pretax Inc.	212	9%	194	46%	133	-16%	158
Eff. Tax Rate	39%	—	39%	—	39%	—	40%
Net Inc.	130	9%	119	47%	81.0	-15%	95.0

Balance Sheet & Other Fin. Data (Million $)

	1994	1993	1992	1991	1990	1989
Cash	28.4	25.9	38.1	28.6	39.9	25.7
Curr. Assets	571	513	465	421	432	376
Total Assets	1,835	1,707	1,247	1,136	1,114	995
Curr. Liab.	349	303	312	257	248	183
LT Debt	488	455	241	228	279	226
Common Eqty.	660	616	562	562	513	512
Total Cap.	1,320	1,244	803	790	866	812
Cap. Exp.	127	116	109	91.0	118	109
Cash Flow	235	213	165	171	123	171

Ratio Analysis

	1994	1993	1992	1991	1990	1989
Curr. Ratio	1.6	1.7	1.5	1.6	1.7	2.1
% LT Debt of Cap.	37.0	36.6	30.0	28.8	32.2	27.9
% Net Inc.of Revs.	5.6	6.1	4.4	5.6	3.0	6.3
% Ret. on Assets	7.4	8.0	6.8	8.4	4.8	10.5
% Ret. on Equity	19.2	19.9	14.4	17.6	9.9	21.4

Dividend Data —Cash has been paid each year since 1925. A dividend reinvestment plan is available.

Amt. of Div. $	Date Decl.	Ex-Div. Date	Stock of Record	Payment Date
0.140	Oct. 19	Nov. 14	Nov. 18	Dec. 09 '94
0.140	Feb. 01	Feb. 13	Feb. 17	Mar. 10 '95
5%	Apr. 19	May. 15	May. 19	Jun. 09 '95
0.150	Apr. 19	May. 15	May. 19	Jun. 09 '95
0.150	Jul. 19	Aug. 16	Aug. 18	Sep. 08 '95

Data as orig. reptd.; bef. results of disc. opers. and/or spec. items. Per share data adj. for stk. divs. as of ex-div. date. E-Estimated. NA-Not Available. NM-Not Meaningful. NR-Not Ranked.

Office—North Second St., Hartsville, SC 29550-0161. **Tel**—(803) 383-7000. **Chrmn & Pres**—C. W. Coker. **VP-Fin & CFO**—F. T. Hill. **VP-Treas & Secy**—C. J. Hupfer. **Investor Contact**—Dick Puffer (803-383-7425). **Dirs**—L. Benatar, C. J. Bradshaw, R. J. Brown, P. C. Browning, C. W. Coker, F. L. H. Coker, J. L. Coker, T. C. Coxe III, A. T. Dickson, R. E. Elberson, J. C. Fort, P. Fulton, B. L. M. Kasriel, R. C. King Jr., E. H. Lawton Jr., H. L. McColl Jr.. E. C. Wall Jr. **Transfer Agent**—Wachovia Bank of North Carolina, Winston-Salem, N. C. **Registrar**—Co.'s office. **Incorporated** in South Carolina in 1899. **Empl**-17,200. **S&P Analyst:** Michael W. Jaffe

STANDARD & POOR'S

STOCK REPORTS

Sotheby's Holdings

NYSE Symbol **BID**
In S&P MidCap 400

30-AUG-95 **Industry:** Services

Summary: This company is the world's largest auctioneer of fine art, primarily paintings, and of jewelry and decorative art. It also has real estate and financial service operations.

Quantitative Evaluations

Outlook
(1 Lowest—5 Highest)
• **4+**

Fair Value
• **14¼**

Risk
• **Low**

Earn./Div. Rank
• **NR**

Technical Eval.
• **Bearish** since 5/95

Rel. Strength Rank
(1 Lowest—99 Highest)
• **63**

Insider Activity
• **Neutral**

Recent Price • 13¾
52 Wk Range • 14¾-10⅜
Yield • 1.7%
12-Mo. P/E • 33.5

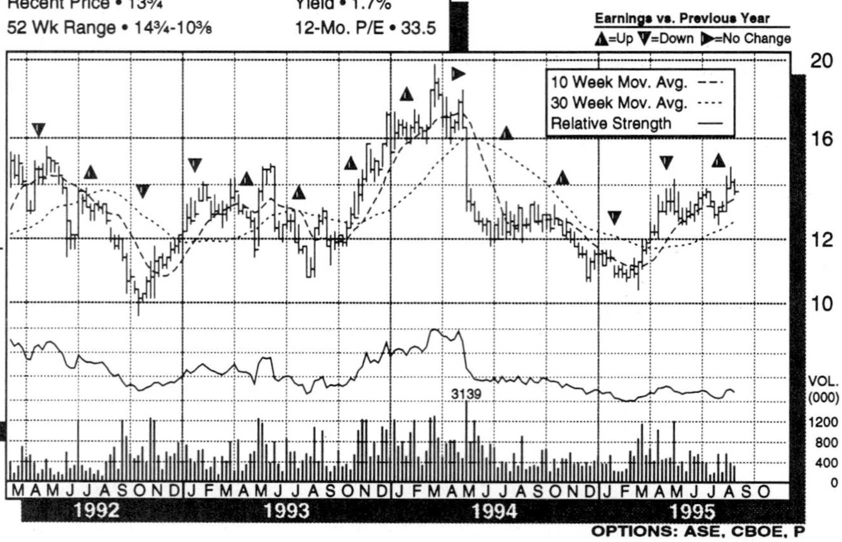

Business Profile - 29-AUG-95

Sotheby's has completed a successful spring auction season, with auction sales up 20% in the first half of 1995. The company has secured several important consignments for the fall season, and there will be a 15 day auction in Germany which Sotheby's believes will be the largest in several years. The company's commission structure may be affected by changes in the value-added tax in Europe, and by competitor Christie's new practice of charging commissions on a non-negotiable sliding scale basis.

Operational Review - 29-AUG-95

The favorable auction results helped the company report its highest six month earnings since 1990. Auctions sales were strong due to a strengthening art market and the availability of several estate collections. Operating margins rose, despite the fact that the company's revenues as a percentage of auction sales declined. Higher profits from the company's financial services operations also contributed to the increase in net income.

Stock Performance - 25-AUG-95

In the past 30 trading days, BID's shares have increased 3%, compared to a 0.04% rise in the S&P 500. Average trading volume for the past five days was 63,940 shares, compared with the 40-day moving average of 69,241 shares.

Key Stock Statistics

Dividend Rate/Share	0.24	Shareholders	1,500
Shs. outstg. (M)	55.9	Market cap. (B)	$0.782
Avg. daily vol. (M)	0.079	Inst. holdings	56%
Tang. Bk. Value/Share	3.48	Insider holdings	NA
Beta	1.15		

Value of $10,000 invested 5 years ago: $ 8,020

Fiscal Year Ending Dec. 31

	1995	% Change	1994	% Change	1993	% Change
Revenues (Million $)						
1Q	42.49	9%	38.95	5%	37.00	3%
2Q	108.4	16%	93.41	7%	87.40	12%
3Q	—	—	30.43	23%	24.68	-5%
4Q	—	—	96.78	-6%	103.0	22%
Yr.	—	—	259.6	3%	252.3	12%
Income (Million $)						
1Q	-6.95	NM	-5.09	NM	-5.20	NM
2Q	23.67	24%	19.07	15%	16.64	48%
3Q	—	—	-11.50	NM	-12.71	NM
4Q	—	—	17.78	-14%	20.56	76%
Yr.	—	—	20.26	5%	19.29	NM
Earnings Per Share ($)						
1Q	-0.12	NM	-0.09	NM	-0.09	NM
2Q	0.42	24%	0.34	13%	0.30	50%
3Q	—	—	-0.21	NM	-0.23	NM
4Q	—	—	0.31	-14%	0.36	71%
Yr.	—	—	0.36	3%	0.35	NM

Next earnings report expected: late October

Sotheby's Holdings

Business Summary - 29-AUG-95

Sotheby's Holdings, Inc. is the world's largest auctioneer of fine art, specializing in paintings, jewelry, decorative art and a wide range of other property. It is also engaged in art-related financing and the luxury real estate business. Revenue and pretax profit contributions by business segment in 1994 were:

	Revs.	Profits
Auction	92%	84%
Financial services	4%	9%
Real estate	4%	7%

Operations in North America accounted for 51% of revenues and operating income of $28.7 million in 1994, Europe 45% of revenues and operating income of $9.9 million and Asia 4% of revenues and a loss of $1.7 million.

Auction sales totaled $1.33 billion in 1994 (about the same as the year before), of which fine art accounted for 46%, decorative art 34% and jewelry, rare books and other property 20%. BID identifies, evaluates and authenticates works of art, uses marketing techniques to stimulate purchaser interest and matches sellers and buyers through the auction process.

Sotheby's normally functions as an agent accepting property on consignment from its selling clients. It bills and receives payments from buyers and remits the proceeds to the consignor. Buyers pay a premium to the company on auction purchases, which in most locations is 15% of the hammer price of items sold for up to $50,000 and 10% on the amount in excess of $50,000. In addition, the seller is charged a commission. Business is highly seasonal, with approximately 80% of revenues generally occurring in the second and fourth quarters.

Financial services primarily involve making loans secured by consigned art and loans to collectors or dealers secured by property not intended for sale. In January 1990, BID discontinued financing auction purchases.

Real estate operations involve acting as an exclusive marketing agent providing services to licensed real estate brokerage offices and operating its own real estate brokerage offices.

Important Developments

Aug. '95—Sotheby's said that they have secured several important cosignments for the fall season and are optimistic about their prospects for the second half of 1995 and for 1996.

Capitalization

Long Term Debt: $10,000,000 of commercial paper (6/95).

Per Share Data ($)

(Year Ended Dec. 31)

	1994	1993	1992	1991	1990	1989
Tangible Bk. Val.	3.26	2.97	3.03	4.21	4.90	4.34
Cash Flow	0.51	0.49	0.22	0.39	1.79	2.18
Earnings	0.36	0.35	0.07	0.25	1.66	1.96
Dividends	0.24	0.42	0.60	0.95	1.45	0.61
Payout Ratio	66%	121%	831%	373%	77%	31%
Prices - High	$19\frac{3}{4}$	$17\frac{1}{4}$	$15\frac{5}{8}$	$15\frac{1}{4}$	$26\frac{1}{2}$	37
- Low	$10\frac{5}{8}$	$10\frac{5}{8}$	$9\frac{5}{8}$	$9\frac{5}{8}$	$8\frac{7}{8}$	$9\frac{7}{8}$
P/E Ratio - High	55	49	NM	61	16	19
- Low	30	31	NM	39	5	5

Income Statement Analysis (Million $)

	1994	%Chg	1993	%Chg	1992	%Chg	1991
Revs.	260	3%	252	12%	225	1%	222
Oper. Inc.	40.0	NM	40.0	150%	16.0	-6%	17.0
Depr.	8.4	1%	8.3	1%	8.2	11%	7.4
Int. Exp.	4.0	-7%	4.3	-31%	6.2	-43%	10.8
Pretax Inc.	33.8	5%	32.2	NM	6.5	-69%	21.0
Eff. Tax Rate	40%	—	40%	—	39%	—	39%
Net Inc.	20.0	5%	19.0	NM	4.0	-69%	13.0

Balance Sheet & Other Fin. Data (Million $)

	1994	1993	1992	1991	1990	1989
Cash	35.0	91.8	85.7	43.3	66.4	31.1
Curr. Assets	405	472	488	553	702	908
Total Assets	557	578	595	665	811	1,000
Curr. Liab.	300	348	396	415	530	755
LT Debt	27.5	34.0	Nil	Nil	0.1	0.8
Common Eqty.	211	195	198	246	278	243
Total Cap.	257	230	199	249	281	246
Cap. Exp.	7.9	8.3	9.9	11.3	13.5	9.2
Cash Flow	28.0	28.0	12.0	21.0	102	125

Ratio Analysis

	1994	1993	1992	1991	1990	1989
Curr. Ratio	1.4	1.4	1.2	1.3	1.3	1.2
% LT Debt of Cap.	10.7	14.8	Nil	Nil	Nil	0.3
% Net Inc.of Revs.	7.8	7.6	1.8	5.9	25.0	25.3
% Ret. on Assets	3.6	3.3	0.6	1.8	10.4	14.1
% Ret. on Equity	10.0	9.8	1.7	4.9	36.2	55.1

Dividend Data —Cash has been paid each year since 1988.

Amt. of Div. $	Date Decl.	Ex-Div. Date	Stock of Record	Payment Date
0.060	Aug. 19	Sep. 12	Sep. 16	Oct. 06 '94
0.060	Oct. 27	Nov. 25	Dec. 01	Dec. 15 '94
0.060	Feb. 09	Mar. 03	Mar. 09	Mar. 20 '95
0.060	Apr. 25	May. 15	May. 19	Jun. 08 '95
0.060	Aug. 17	Sep. 01	Sep. 06	Sep. 26 '95

Data as orig. reptd.; bef. results of disc. opers. and/or spec. items. Per share data adj. for stk. divs. as of ex-div. date. E-Estimated. NA-Not Available. NM-Not Meaningful. NR-Not Ranked.

New York Office—1334 York Ave., New York, NY 10021. **Tel**—(212) 606-7507. **Chrmn**—A. A. Taubman. **Pres & CEO**—D. D. Brooks. **Sr VP & CFO**—K. A. Bousquette. **VP-Treas**—J. S. Brittain Jr. **Investor Contacts**—Jeffrey Pierne, Deborah Murray. **Dirs**—Viscount Blakenham, D. D. Brooks, Lord Camoys, W. J. P. Curley, M. M. Fisher, The Earl of Gowrie, The Marquess of Hartington, S. de Pury, A. A. Taubman, R. J. de la M. Thompson. **Transfer Agents**—Mellon Securities Trust Co., Ridgefield Park, N.J.; Royal Bank of Scotland, Bristol, England. **Incorporated** in Michigan in 1983; predecessor firm founded in 1744. **Empl**-1,558. **S&P Analyst:** Stephen Madonna, CFA

Southdown, Inc.

NYSE Symbol **SDW**
In S&P MidCap 400

13-SEP-95 **Industry:** Building

Summary: Southdown is one of the leading U.S. producers of cement and ready-mixed concrete.

Quantitative Evaluations

Outlook
(1 Lowest—5 Highest)
• **3+**

Fair Value
• **18⅝**

Risk
• **Average**

Earn./Div. Rank
• **C**

Technical Eval.
• **Bearish** since 8/95

Rel. Strength Rank
(1 Lowest—99 Highest)
• **18**

Insider Activity
• **NA**

Recent Price • 18¾
52 Wk Range • 21¾-11½

Yield • Nil
12-Mo. P/E • 89.3

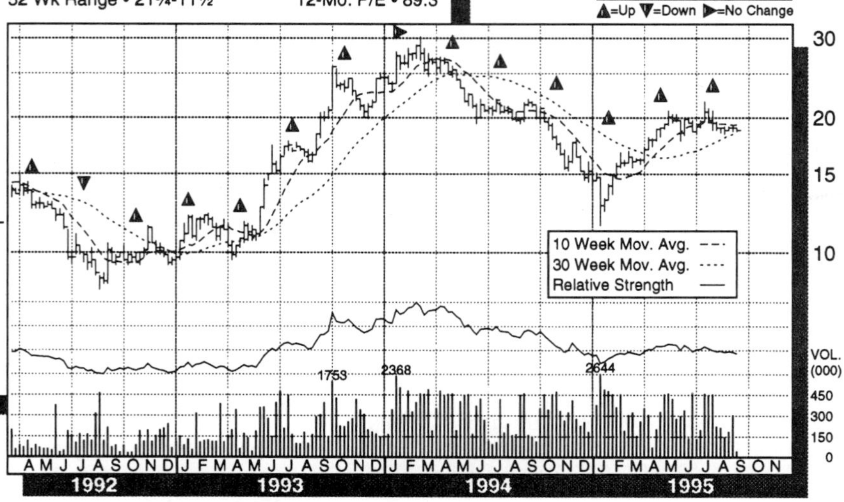

Business Profile - 11-SEP-95

Recent results benefited from higher prices in both the cement and concrete products segments. Demand for cement outstrips supply in almost all markets, and Southdown's plants are capacity constrained. In addition, concrete products have recovered significantly, on improved pricing, aided by a robust construction market in Florida and a return to profitability for California concrete and aggregate operations. Total debt, cut 32% in 1994, stands at its lowest level in more than five years.

Operational Review - 11-SEP-95

Revenues in 1995's first six months rose 5.1%, due to price increases, which more than offset volume decreases, in both the cement and concrete products segments. Margins widened, due to the higher prices, and from favorable operating results from the California unit of the concrete products segment; operating income climbed 24%. After a decline in net interest expense (from debt retirement), which more than offset a decrease in other income, income before taxes and special charges soared 83%.

Stock Performance - 08-SEP-95

In the past 30 trading days, SDW's shares have declined 4%, compared to a 2% rise in the S&P 500. Average trading volume for the past five days was 9,300 shares, compared with the 40-day moving average of 51,136 shares.

Key Stock Statistics

Dividend Rate/Share	Nil	Shareholders	1,800
Shs. outstg. (M)	17.3	Market cap. (B)	$0.322
Avg. daily vol. (M)	0.035	Inst. holdings	81%
Tang. Bk. Value/Share	10.73	Insider holdings	NA
Beta	0.71		

Value of $10,000 invested 5 years ago: $ 7,126

Fiscal Year Ending Dec. 31

	1995	% Change	1994	% Change	1993	% Change
Revenues (Million $)						
1Q	119.1	7%	111.8	5%	106.1	-2%
2Q	155.0	3%	149.8	4%	144.4	5%
3Q	—	—	158.5	2%	156.1	12%
4Q	—	—	141.8	3%	138.2	11%
Yr.	—	—	561.9	3%	544.8	7%
Income (Million $)						
1Q	6.10	NM	-1.30	NM	-4.40	NM
2Q	13.60	12%	12.10	NM	2.60	NM
3Q	—	—	8.60	NM	1.50	NM
4Q	—	—	10.70	NM	0.30	NM
Yr.	—	—	30.10	—	Nil	—
Earnings Per Share ($)						
1Q	0.21	NM	-0.20	NM	-0.34	NM
2Q	0.63	17%	0.54	NM	0.08	NM
3Q	—	—	0.35	NM	0.01	NM
4Q	—	—	0.48	NM	-0.05	NM
Yr.	—	—	1.20	NM	-0.30	NM

Next earnings report expected: early November

Southdown, Inc.

Business Summary - 13-SEP-95

Southdown is one of the leading U.S. cement and ready-mixed concrete producers. In November 1994, it decided to exit the hazardous waste business. Business segment contributions (operating profits in millions) in 1994 were:

	Sales	Profits
Cement	66%	$91.2
Concrete products	34%	9.3

The company operates eight quarrying and manufacturing facilities and a network of 17 terminals for production and distribution of portland and masonry cement, primarily in the Southwest, Southeast and Ohio Valley. The principal raw material used in the production of portland cement is calcium carbonate found in the form of limestone. The company's total estimated recoverable reserves of limestone are approximately 690 million tons located on about 19,000 acres, most of which are owned in fee. Cement sales are made generally within a radius of 300 miles of each plant, principally to ready-mixed concrete producers and manufacturers of concrete products such as blocks, roof tile, pipe and prefabricated building components.

SDW has vertically integrated its operations in the areas surrounding its two largest cement plants, in Southern California and Florida. The Transmix division is a major producer of ready-mixed concrete and a supplier of aggregates in Southern California. The Florida Mining & Materials division produces and supplies ready-mixed concrete and concrete products in Florida and southeastern Georgia. Concrete product operations consist of some 500 ready-mixed concrete trucks, 71 batch plants, two aggregate quarries and 12 concrete block plants.

SDW recorded a charge of $21.6 million in 1994's fourth quarter as a result of its decision to exit the hazardous waste business. In April 1995, it sold its remaining hazardous waste processing facilities for $11.8 million plus certain working capital items.

Important Developments

Jun. '95—SDW attributed second-quarter earnings growth in the cement segment to price increases, which more than offset volume decreases from inclement weather in Colorado and the Midwest. Excluding a gain from the sale of ready-mix trucks, concrete products earnings were flat.

Capitalization

Long Term Debt: $227,600,000 (6/95).
Minority Interest: $30,600,000.
$0.70 Series A Cum. Conv. Pfd. Stk.: 1,994,000 shs. ($10 stated val.); ea. conv. into 0.5 com.
$3.75 Series B Cum. Exch. Pfd. Stk.: 914,360 shs. ($50 stated val.); ea. conv. into 2.5 com.
$2.875 Series D Cum. Conv. Pfd. Stk.: 1,725,000 shs. ($50 stated val.); ea. conv. into 1.511 com.

Per Share Data ($) (Year Ended Dec. 31)

	1994	1993	1992	1991	1990	1989
Tangible Bk. Val.	6.17	7.03	10.17	11.48	14.69	15.70
Cash Flow	3.40	2.05	-0.07	-0.24	2.87	4.84
Earnings	1.20	-0.30	-2.74	-2.86	0.44	0.99
Dividends	Nil	Nil	Nil	0.13	0.50	0.50
Payout Ratio	Nil	NM	Nil	NM	111%	50%
Prices - High	30¼	25⅞	16	19⅞	31½	29¼
- Low	14¼	9⅝	8¼	11⅛	9½	19¼
P/E Ratio - High	25	NM	NM	NM	72	30
- Low	12	NM	NM	NM	22	19

Income Statement Analysis (Million $)

	1994	%Chg	1993	%Chg	1992	%Chg	1991
Revs.	562	3%	545	7%	507	NM	505
Oper. Inc.	111	22%	91.0	86%	49.0	48%	33.0
Depr.	39.4	-2%	40.2	-11%	45.3	2%	44.2
Int. Exp.	27.7	-30%	39.3	-13%	45.0	10%	41.0
Pretax Inc.	48.1	NM	2.6	NM	-59.0	NM	-70.6
Eff. Tax Rate	29%	—	NM	—	NM	—	NM
Net Inc.	30.1	—	Nil	—	-41.4	NM	-43.2

Balance Sheet & Other Fin. Data (Million $)

	1994	1993	1992	1991	1990	1989
Cash	7.0	7.0	13.0	15.0	18.0	108
Curr. Assets	178	167	171	194	199	280
Total Assets	881	907	911	986	1,040	1,064
Curr. Liab.	104	112	98.0	104	92.0	159
LT Debt	186	274	307	323	308	254
Common Eqty.	185	194	248	294	342	343
Total Cap.	675	693	785	852	909	858
Cap. Exp.	29.0	24.0	17.0	31.0	43.0	37.0
Cash Flow	60.1	35.2	-1.1	-4.1	49.1	81.6

Ratio Analysis

	1994	1993	1992	1991	1990	1989
Curr. Ratio	1.7	1.5	1.7	1.9	2.2	1.8
% LT Debt of Cap.	27.5	39.6	39.1	37.9	33.8	29.6
% Net Inc.of Revs.	5.4	Nil	NM	NM	2.4	3.9
% Ret. on Assets	3.3	Nil	NM	NM	1.3	2.0
% Ret. on Equity	10.8	NM	NM	NM	2.2	5.2

Dividend Data —Dividends on the common stock, resumed in 1975, were omitted again in 1991. A poison pill stock purchase rights plan was adopted in 1991.

Data as orig. reptd.; bef. results of disc. opers. and/or spec. items. Per share data adj. for stk. divs. as of ex-div. date. E-Estimated. NA-Not Available. NM-Not Meaningful. NR-Not Ranked.

Office—1200 Smith St., Suite 2400, Houston, TX 77002-4486. **Tel**—(713) 650-6200. **Chrmn**—F. J. Ryan. **Pres & CEO**—C. C. Comer. **EVP-Fin & Investor Contact**—James L. Persky. **Secy**—W. E. Phillips II. **Dirs**—F. Bracewell, C. C. Comer, W. J. Conway, K. L. Huger, Jr., G. W. Loewenbaum II, E. J. Marston III, M. A. Nicolais, F. J. Ryan, R. J. Slater, R. N. Tutor, V. H. Van Horn III, S. B. Wolitzer. **Transfer Agent & Registrar**—Chemical Bank, NYC. **Incorporated** in Louisiana in 1930. **Empl**-2,600. **S&P Analyst:** Robert E. Friedman

Southern New England Telecom.

NYSE Symbol SNG Options on NYSE In S&P MidCap 400

Price	Range	P-E Ratio	Dividend	Yield	S&P Ranking	Beta
Aug. 1'95	1995					
33½	35⅞–31¾	12	1.76	5.3%	A–	0.61

Summary

This holding company, which provides telephone service to virtually all of Connecticut, has moved into nonregulated telecommunications businesses. In May 1994, legislation was passed that opened Connecticut's telecommunications service markets to full competition.

Current Outlook

Earnings for 1995 are projected at $2.67 a share (including $0.12 net nonrecurring charges), versus the $2.77 reported for 1994.

The $0.44 quarterly dividend is expected to be maintained.

Following legislation passed in May 1994 that opened Connecticut's telephone markets to competition, SNG's revenues are likely to be adversely affected by loss of market share to new entrants. The company hopes to offset softness in core telephone operations through increased investment in nonregulated opportunities, such as wireless and long-distance operations, which offer higher growth potential. Meanwhile, the company is continuing to focus on rationalizing its cost structure for a more competitive environment.

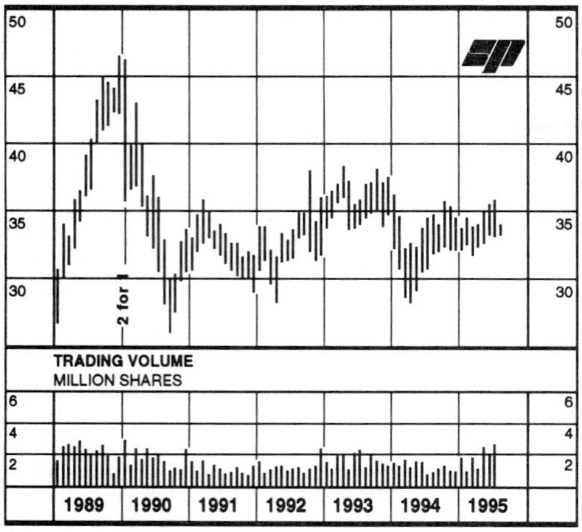

Revenues (Million $)

Quarter:	1995	1994	1993	1992
Mar.	443	423	402	398
Jun.	453	428	411	405
Sep.		430	414	405
Dec.		436	427	406
		1,717	1,654	1,614

Revenues for the six months ended June 30, 1995, increased 5.3%, year to year, aided by a sharp gain in cellular revenues and strong long distance revenues. However, results were penalized by after-tax charges of $6 million resulting from a court ruling on labor practices and other litigation and $4 million for state tax adjustments. These were partially offset by an after-tax gain of $2 million on the sale of real estate. Net income fell 2.3%, to $86.8 million ($1.34 a share), from $88.8 million ($1.39).

Common Share Earnings ($)

Quarter:	1995	1994	1993	1992
Mar.	0.72	0.68	0.58	0.63
Jun.	0.62	0.71	0.64	0.66
Sep.	E0.71	0.73	0.77	0.63
Dec.	E0.62	0.65	d2.66	0.64
	E2.67	2.77	d0.68	2.56

Important Developments

Jul. '95— The company completed the accquisition of certain cellular properties in Rhode Island and Massachusetts for $450 million in cash. The properties, which are within or adjacent to properties already operated by SNG, cover about 2.3 million pops. Following the acquisition, SNG serves a market of over 5.5 million pops. Separately, Paging Network completed its purchase of certain paging assets from SNG's paging unit. Terms were not disclosed.

Jun. '95— SNG signed a seven-year, $200 million contract to have Computer Sciences Corp. manage its data center operations. SNG expects the agreement will cut its data center costs by 20%. Separately, the company filed in Connecticut for price regulation instead of rate-of-return regulation.

Apr. '95— The company's video unit will ask the FCC for approval to provide services.

Next earnings report expected in late October.

Per Share Data ($)

Yr. End Dec. 31	1994	1993	1992	1991	1990	1989	1988	1987	1986	1985
Tangible Bk. Val.	**14.77**	13.38	19.79	18.78	18.19	19.56	18.48	17.44	16.52	15.62
Cash Flow	**7.88**	3.89	6.51	6.09	6.20	6.77	5.95	NA	NA	NA
Earnings[1]	**2.77**	d0.68	2.56	2.06	2.17	3.04	2.50	2.27	2.23	1.91
Dividends	**1.760**	1.760	1.760	1.760	1.760	1.640	1.515	1.455	1.410	1.370
Payout Ratio	**64%**	NM	69%	85%	81%	54%	61%	64%	63%	72%
Prices—High	**36¼**	38⅜	38	35⅞	46¼	46½	27¾	30	30¾	23½
Low	**28¼**	33⅝	28¼	29	26	26¾	22⅝	21½	21½	17½
P/E Ratio—	**13–10**	NM	15–11	17–14	21–12	15–9	11–9	13–9	14–10	12–9

Data as orig. reptd. Adj. for stk. divs of 100% Jan. 1990. **1.** Bef. results of disc. opers. of -0.16 in 1993, -0.08 in 1992, and spec. items of -4.15 in 1993, -0.04 in 1992. d-Deficit. E-Estimated. NM-Not Meaningful. NA-Not Available.

Southern New England Telecommunications Corporation

Income Data (Million $)

Year Ended Dec. 31	Revs.	Depr.	Maint.	Oper. Ratio	[2]Fxd. Chgs. Cover.	Constr. Credits	Eff. Tax Rate	[3]Net Inc.	% Return On Revs.	[4]Invest. Capital	[5]Com. Equity	Cash Flow
1994	**1,717**	**329**	**325**	**85.3%**	**5.00**	**NA**	**40.7%**	**178.0**	**10.3**	**11.1**	**19.4**	**506**
1993	[1]1,654	291	314	105.3%	0.04	NA	NM	d43.6	NM	NM	NM	248
1992	[1]1,614	250	308	84.1%	3.76	NA	40.9%	159.0	9.9	8.8	12.5	409
1991	[1]1,633	254	316	85.5%	2.92	NA	41.2%	126.0	7.7	8.3	10.8	380
1990	[1]1,619	253	322	85.5%	3.13	NA	39.3%	132.0	8.2	8.6	11.2	385
1989	[1]1,671	232	329	86.6%	5.39	2.9	43.1%	189.0	11.3	10.1	15.8	421
1988	[1]1,583	215	313	84.8%	3.98	3.9	28.5%	155.0	9.8	9.9	13.9	370
1987	[1]1,470	206	290	86.7%	4.75	7.1	33.6%	140.0	9.5	9.2	13.3	NA
1986	[1]1,433	197	253	87.3%	5.46	4.5	38.0%	139.0	9.7	9.1	13.8	NA
1985	[1]1,304	182	245	84.8%	4.35	2.6	37.5%	120.0	9.2	8.6	12.4	NA

Balance Sheet Data (Million $)

Dec. 31	Gross Prop.	Capital Expend.	Net Prop.	% Earn. on Net Prop.	Total Cap.	[6]LT Debt	% LT Debt	Capitalization Pfd.	% Pfd.	Com.	% Com.
1994	**4,251**	**282**	**2,712**	**9.2**	**2,323**	**952**	**50.0**	**Nil**	**Nil**	**953**	**50.0**
1993	4,200	267	2,770	NM	2,211	984	53.5	Nil	Nil	855	46.5
1992	4,069	290	2,767	9.4	2,954	1,048	45.5	Nil	Nil	1,254	54.5
1991	3,917	321	2,713	8.9	2,916	1,107	48.5	Nil	Nil	1,176	51.5
1990	3,762	393	2,644	9.1	2,785	1,022	47.5	Nil	Nil	1,128	52.5
1989	3,753	390	2,502	9.3	2,689	879	42.2	Nil	Nil	1,203	57.8
1988	3,486	328	2,312	10.7	2,569	855	42.6	Nil	Nil	1,155	57.4
1987	3,226	381	2,127	9.6	2,244	648	37.5	Nil	Nil	1,080	62.5
1986	2,968	289	1,942	9.6	2,159	646	39.0	Nil	Nil	1,011	61.0
1985	2,768	244	1,856	10.8	2,065	573	36.2	68.7	4.3	944	59.5

Data as orig. reptd. **1.** Aft. prov. for uncollectible accounts. **2.** Times int. exp. & pfd. divs. covered (pretax basis). **3.** Bef. results of disc. opers. and spec. items. **4.** Based on income bef. interest charges. **5.** As reptd. by Co. **6.** Incl. capital lease obligations. d-Deficit. NA-Not Available. NM-Not Meaningful.

Business Summary

Southern New England Telecommunications is the holding company for Southern New England Telephone (SNET), which provides local telephone service throughout most of Connecticut. At December 31, 1994, SNET served 2,009,000 customer access lines. Contributions to revenues by type of service in recent years were:

	1994	1993	1992
Local service	36%	34%	32%
Intrastate toll	17%	21%	22%
Network access	21%	21%	20%
Sales & other	16%	13%	14%
Publishing	10%	11%	12%

In addition to providing telephone service, SNET publishes and distributes telephone directories throughout Connecticut and certain adjacent communities.

The company also engages in various nonregulated telecommunications businesses, including: SNET Cellular, SNET MobileCom and SNET Paging, which provide wholesale and retail cellular mobile telephone and paging services; and SNET Diversified Group, which sells and leases communications equipment to residential and small business customers. During 1993, the company disbanded its SNET Systems unit, a distributor of telecommunications equipment; telecommunications equipment will continue as a product line, but the reorganization will change the focus to the telco's central office-based solutions.

Cellular operations had net income of $17.1 million in 1994 on revenues of $99.6 million, versus net income of $16.1 million on revenues of $70.1 million in 1993.

Dividend Data

Dividends have been paid since 1891. A dividend reinvestment plan is available. A "poison pill" stock purchase right was adopted in 1987.

Amt. of Divd. $	Date Decl.	Ex-divd. Date	Stock of Record	Payment Date
0.44	Sep. 14	Sep. 20	Sep. 26	Oct. 15'94
0.44	Dec. 14	Dec. 20	Dec. 27	Jan. 17'95
0.44	Mar. 8	Mar. 14	Mar. 20	Apr. 15'95
0.44	Jun. 14	Jun. 22	Jun. 26	Jul. 15'95

Capitalization

Long Term Debt: $944,000,000 (3/95).

Common Stock: 64,780,000 shs. ($1 par). Institutions hold about 38%. Shareholders of record: 55,485 (1/95).

Office—227 Church St., New Haven, CT 06510. **Tel**—(203) 771-5200. **Chmn & CEO**—D. J. Miglio. **Sr VP & CFO**—D. R. Shassian. **VP-Secy**—M. M. DeMatteo. **VP-Treas**—J. J. Miller. **Investor Contact**—James A. Magrone. **Dirs**—F. G. Adams, W. F. Andrews, R. H. Ayers, Z. Baird, R. L. Bennett, B. M. Bloom, F. J. Connor, W. F. Fenoglio, C. L. Gaudiani, J. R. Greenfield, B. G. Malkiel, D. J. Miglio, F. R. O'Keefe Jr. **Transfer Agent**—Company's office. **Registrar**—Union Trust Co., New Haven. **Incorporated** in Connecticut in 1882. **Empl**—9,797.

 Kevin J. Gooley

STANDARD & POOR'S

STOCK REPORTS

SouthTrust Corp.

NASDAQ Symbol **SOTR**
In S&P MidCap 400

06-OCT-95 **Industry:** Banking

Summary: This regional bank holding company, based in Birmingham, Ala., operates over 435 offices in Alabama, Florida, Georgia, Mississippi, North Carolina, South Carolina and Tennessee.

Quantitative Evaluations

Outlook (1 Lowest—5 Highest)
• **3-**

Fair Value
• **24⅞**

Risk
• **Low**

Earn./Div. Rank
• **A**

Technical Eval.
• **Bearish** since 7/95

Rel. Strength Rank (1 Lowest—99 Highest)
• **48**

Insider Activity
• **Favorable**

Recent Price • 25⅛
52 Wk Range • 27¼-17

Yield • 3.2%
12-Mo. P/E • 11.1

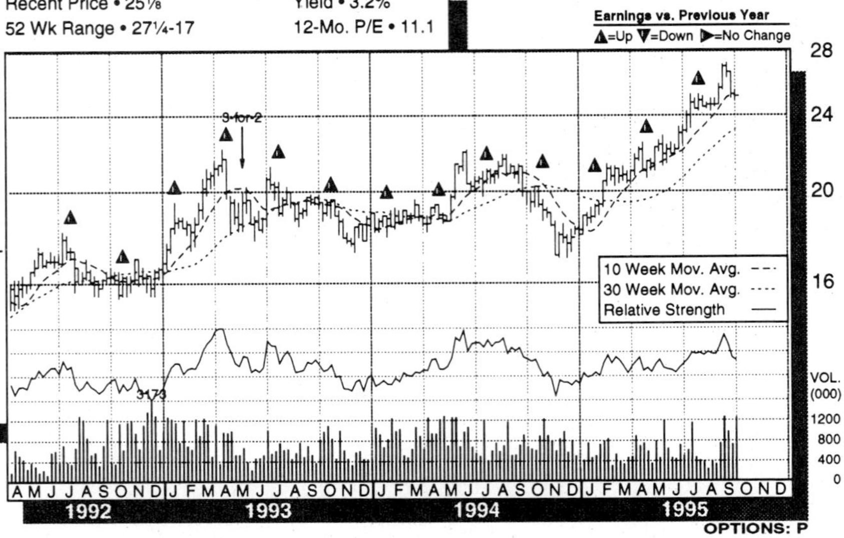

OPTIONS: P

Business Profile - 06-OCT-95

SouthTrust serves the financial needs of consumers and middle market commercial customers by delivering fundamental banking products at a low cost, while maintaining outstanding credit quality and operating efficiencies. SOTR continues to expand through internal growth and an aggressive acquisition policy (nine banks purchased in 1994, adding $709.3 million in assets) -- focusing on the highest growth areas of the Southeast. Loans increased 27% in the 12 months to June 30, 1995.

Operational Review - 06-OCT-95

Net interest income in the six months ended June 30, 1995, rose 14%, year to year, as higher earning assets, primarily from strong demand for loans in the Southeast, outweighed a lower net interest margin (4.11% versus 4.25%). Following a 19% increase in the provision for loan losses, higher non-interest income and non-interest expense, and after taxes of 34.1%, versus 33.5%, net income grew 14%, to $94,869,000 ($1.15 a share, based on 3.2% more shares), from $83,129,000 ($1.04).

Stock Performance - 29-SEP-95

In the past 30 trading days, SOTR's shares have increased 2%, compared to a 5% rise in the S&P 500. Average trading volume for the past five days was 323,040 shares, compared with the 40-day moving average of 175,026 shares.

Key Stock Statistics

Dividend Rate/Share	0.80	Shareholders	12,300
Shs. outstg. (M)	87.4	Market cap. (B)	$ 2.2
Avg. daily vol. (M)	0.212	Inst. holdings	38%
Tang. Bk. Value/Share	15.07	Insider holdings	NA
Beta	1.27		

Value of $10,000 invested 5 years ago: $ 30,831

Fiscal Year Ending Dec. 31

	1995	% Change	1994	% Change	1993	% Change
Revenues (Million $)						
1Q	387.5	36%	285.0	9%	262.4	14%
2Q	413.4	35%	306.4	12%	273.4	14%
3Q	—	—	338.6	14%	296.2	21%
4Q	—	—	367.3	36%	270.3	8%
Yr.	—	—	1,293	17%	1,102	14%
Income (Million $)						
1Q	46.84	15%	40.74	17%	34.84	35%
2Q	48.03	13%	42.39	14%	37.24	36%
3Q	—	—	44.50	14%	39.07	34%
4Q	—	—	45.37	15%	39.38	23%
Yr.	—	—	173.0	15%	150.5	32%
Earnings Per Share ($)						
1Q	0.57	12%	0.51	11%	0.46	18%
2Q	0.58	9%	0.53	10%	0.48	17%
3Q	—	—	0.55	10%	0.50	19%
4Q	—	—	0.56	12%	0.50	14%
Yr.	—	—	2.15	11%	1.94	17%

Next earnings report expected: mid October

SouthTrust Corp.

Business Summary - 06-OCT-95

SouthTrust Corporation is a regional multibank holding company headquartered in Birmingham, Ala. At December 31, 1994, the company had subsidiary banks in Alabama, Florida, Georgia, Mississippi, South Carolina, North Carolina and Tennessee, as well as seven bank-related affiliates. The lead bank is the $10-billion-asset SouthTrust Bank of Alabama. SouthTrust is pursuing an aggressive policy of expansion through acquisitions.

Loans outstanding increased to $12.22 billion at the end of 1994, from $9.53 billion a year earlier, and were divided as follows:

	1994	1993
Commercial, financial & agricultural	41%	30%
Real estate:		
Construction	6%	5%
Commercial mortgage	15%	27%
Residential mortgage	24%	24%
Consumer	14%	14%

The allowance for loan losses was $171,692,000 (1.42% of net loans outstanding) at the end of 1994, up from $135,233,000 (1.43%) a year earlier. Net loans charged off in 1994 were $19,776,000 (0.19% of average loans), down from $24,615,000 (0.29%) in 1993. At December 31, 1994, nonperforming assets (including nonaccrual and restructured loans and other real estate owned) amounted to $102.7 million (0.84% of loans, net of unearned income), down from $113.1 million (1.19%) a year earlier.

Average deposits of $11.9 billion in 1994 were apportioned: 66% time deposits, 16% noninterest-bearing demand, 12% interest-bearing demand, and 6% savings.

In 1994, interest and fees on loans accounted for 67% of total income, interest on investment securities for 19%, service charges on deposit accounts for 7%, and other noninterest income for 7%.

On a tax-equivalent basis, the average yield on total interest-earning assets was 7.62% in 1994 (7.52% in 1993), while the average rate paid on interest-bearing liabilities was 3.92% (3.64%), for a net spread of 3.70% (3.88%).

Important Developments

Aug. '95—The company filed a shelf registration statement with the Securities and Exchange Commission for the sale of up to $300 million in corporate debt and equity securities. Proceeds would be used for general corporate purposes.

Jan. '95—SouthTrust declared an 18% increase in its quarterly dividend, marking the 25th consecutive year of dividend increases. During that period, the cash dividend rose 1,459% (an 11.6% compounded annual rate).

Capitalization

Long Term Debt: $889,858,000 (6/95).

Per Share Data ($)

(Year Ended Dec. 31)

	1994	1993	1992	1991	1990	1989
Tangible Bk. Val.	13.94	13.25	11.55	10.06	8.98	8.31
Earnings	2.15	1.94	1.66	1.42	1.14	1.21
Dividends	0.68	0.60	0.52	0.48	0.46	0.43
Payout Ratio	32%	31%	31%	34%	40%	35%
Prices - High	22⅛	22⅛	18⅛	17¼	10⅜	11¼
- Low	17	16⅝	14⅛	6⅝	5¾	8⅞
P/E Ratio - High	10	11	11	12	9	9
- Low	8	9	9	5	5	7

Income Statement Analysis (Million $)

	1994	%Chg	1993	%Chg	1992	%Chg	1991
Net Int. Inc.	608	15%	530	18%	449	27%	353
Tax Equiv. Adj.	16.0	-10%	17.7	-10%	19.6	-13%	22.5
Non Int. Inc.	184	5%	175	33%	132	26%	105
Loan Loss Prov.	45.0	NM	45.0	4%	43.3	14%	38.0
% Exp/Op Revs.	60%	—	60%	—	62%	—	62%
Pretax Inc.	261	16%	225	36%	165	34%	123
Eff. Tax Rate	34%	—	33%	—	31%	—	27%
Net Inc.	173	15%	151	32%	114	27%	90.0
% Net Int. Marg.	4.23%	—	4.35%	—	4.65%	—	4.36%

Balance Sheet & Other Fin. Data (Million $)

	1994	1993	1992	1991	1990	1989
Earning Assets:						
Money Mkt.	37.0	60.0	103	164	145	259
Inv. Securities	3,953	3,733	3,756	3,104	2,449	2,068
Com'l Loans	5,058	2,814	2,378	1,911	1,900	1,716
Other Loans	7,322	6,713	5,442	4,127	3,707	3,048
Total Assets	17,632	14,708	12,714	10,158	9,006	7,763
Demand Deposits	2,040	1,783	1,598	1,106	1,053	929
Time Deposits	10,762	9,732	8,484	7,172	6,175	5,126
LT Debt	640	470	258	140	149	145
Common Eqty.	1,135	1,052	860	662	550	507

Ratio Analysis

	1994	1993	1992	1991	1990	1989
% Ret. on Assets	1.1	1.1	1.0	1.0	0.9	1.0
% Ret. on Equity	15.9	15.8	15.7	15.2	13.3	15.4
% Loan Loss Resv.	1.4	1.4	1.3	1.4	1.3	1.3
% Loans/Deposits	96.0	82.7	76.8	72.1	76.5	77.5
% Equity to Assets	6.8	7.0	6.6	6.3	6.4	6.7

Dividend Data —Cash dividends, paid since 1944, have been increased each year since 1971. A dividend reinvestment plan is available.

Amt. of Div. $	Date Decl.	Ex-Div. Date	Stock of Record	Payment Date
0.170	Oct. 19	Nov. 18	Nov. 25	Jan. 02 '95
0.200	Jan. 18	Feb. 17	Feb. 24	Apr. 01 '95
0.200	Apr. 19	May. 22	May. 26	Jul. 01 '95
0.200	Jul. 19	Aug. 23	Aug. 25	Oct. 02 '95

Data as orig. reptd.; bef. results of disc opers. and/or spec. items. Per share data adj. for stk. divs. as of ex-div. date. E-Estimated. NA-Not Available. NM-Not Meaningful. NR-Not Ranked.

Office—420 N. 20th St., Birmingham, AL 35203. **Tel**—(205) 254-6868. **Chrmn & CEO**—W. D. Malone Jr. **Secy, Treas & Contr**—A. D. Barnard. **Investor Contact**—Butch Crouch (208-254-6868). **Dirs**—J. M. Bradford, H. A. Franklin, B. L. Harbert, W. C. Hulsey, A. J. Keesler Jr., W. D. Malone Jr., T. W. Mitchell, H. Stockham, C. G. Taylor, W. K. Upchurch Jr. **Transfer Agent**—Mellon Securities Trust Co., NYC. **Incorporated** in Delaware in 1968. **Empl**-7,000. **S&P Analyst:** Robert Schpoont

STANDARD & POOR'S

STOCK REPORTS

Southwestern Public Service

NYSE Symbol **SPS**

In S&P MidCap 400

05-OCT-95

Industry: Utilities-Electric

Summary: This utility supplies electricity to a population of about one million in a 52,000-square-mile area of the Panhandle region of Texas and parts of New Mexico, Oklahoma and Kansas.

S&P Opinion: Avoid (★★)

Recent Price • 32⅝
52 Wk Range • 32⅞-25½

Yield • 6.7%
12-Mo. P/E • 13.3

Quantitative Evaluations

Outlook (1 Lowest—5 Highest)
• **2+**

Fair Value
• **29½**

Risk
• **Low**

Earn./Div. Rank
• **A-**

Technical Eval.
• **Bearish** since 9/95

Rel. Strength Rank (1 Lowest—99 Highest)
• **83**

Insider Activity
• **Neutral**

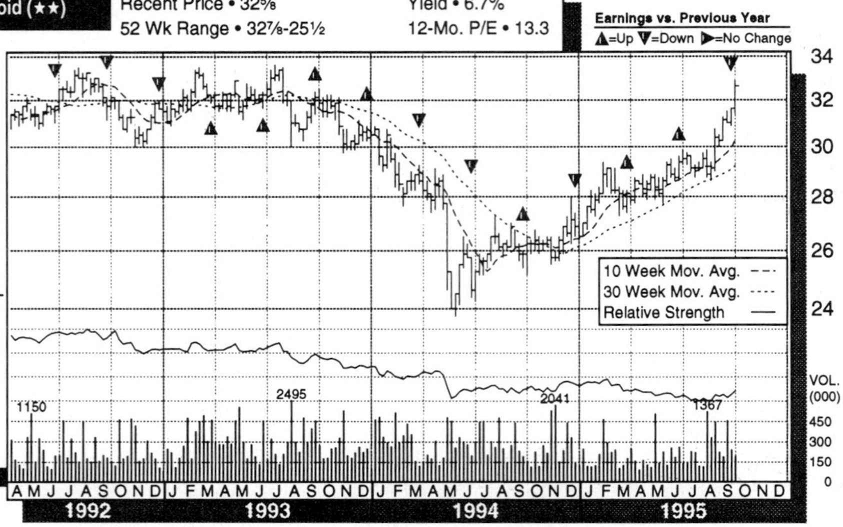

Overview - 05-OCT-95

As a stand-alone company, some 55% of SPS's revenues are currently derived from operations in Texas, but the company has been expanding through short-term sales to other utilities in 15 states from Mississippi to the Pacific Northwest. It recently doubled sales of power to Public Service Co. of New Mexico to 200 mw and has expanded into Missouri via a sizable contract with a rural electric company in Joplin. Power sales have also grown via a gradual upturn in new customers and in its service area economy. SPS's service rates and production expenses are among the lowest in the U.S. Although pricing is expected to trend still lower, further growth in customers and demand in 1996 should boost earnings modestly. The proposed combination with Public Service Co. of Colorado in early 1997 should allow signigicant cost savings longer term.

Valuation - 05-OCT-95

Given the negative effects of rate reductions and increasingly competitive markets for electricity, earnings are likely to have fallen modestly in fiscal 1995, despite SPS's growing customer base. The merger with Public Service of Colorado, assuming regulatory and other approvals, should help these two low-cost producers keep costs low, but, near term, we would not look for significant growth in the dividend and, with a P/E ratio somewhat higher than the industry average, believe the shares are fairly valued.

Key Stock Statistics

S&P EPS Est. 1995	2.35	Tang. Bk. Value/Share	16.89
P/E on S&P Est. 1995	13.9	Beta	0.31
S&P EPS Est. 1996	2.40	Shareholders	32,800
Dividend Rate/Share	2.20	Market cap. (B)	$ 1.3
Shs. outstg. (M)	40.9	Inst. holdings	28%
Avg. daily vol. (M)	0.060	Insider holdings	NA

Value of $10,000 invested 5 years ago: $ 16,206

Fiscal Year Ending Aug. 31

	1995	% Change	1994	% Change	1993	% Change
Revenues (Million $)						
1Q	187.2	-8%	203.1	6%	192.0	4%
2Q	181.9	-4%	189.4	5%	180.0	4%
3Q	205.2	5%	196.2	2%	193.3	10%
4Q	—	—	254.8	4%	244.5	13%
Yr.	—	—	843.5	4%	809.8	8%
Income (Million $)						
1Q	21.17	-19%	26.05	8%	24.21	-3%
2Q	18.68	8%	17.37	-21%	21.87	6%
3Q	26.43	34%	19.78	-11%	22.13	2%
4Q	—	—	38.97	5%	37.04	4%
Yr.	—	—	102.2	-3%	105.3	2%
Earnings Per Share ($)						
1Q	0.49	-20%	0.61	11%	0.55	-4%
2Q	0.43	10%	0.39	-22%	0.50	9%
3Q	0.62	38%	0.45	-12%	0.51	4%
4Q	E0.81	-13%	0.93	7%	0.87	6%
Yr.	E2.35	-1%	2.38	-2%	2.43	4%

Next earnings report expected: mid October

Southwestern Public Service

05-OCT-95

Business Summary - 05-OCT-95

Southwestern Public Service Company provides electricity to a population of some one million in the Panhandle and South Plains region of Texas (about 55% of revenues) and parts of Kansas, Oklahoma and New Mexico. Contributions to revenues by class of customer in recent fiscal years were:

	1994	1993	1992	1991
Residential	19%	20%	20%	20%
Commercial	17%	18%	18%	18%
Industrial	33%	33%	35%	34%
Other	31%	29%	27%	28%

Some 25% of fiscal 1994 kwh sales were derived from industrial customers engaged in oil and gas production and petroleum refining. Chemical, mineral and light manufacturing industries are also of prime importance in the area served.

The fuel mix in fiscal 1994 was 71.9% coal, 27.3% gas and 0.8% other. Peak load in fiscal 1994 was 3,682 mw, and system capability was 4,062 mw, for a capacity margin of 9.4%. Sales of electricity were 20,403 mw, up 5.9% from 19,269 mw the year before. The company does not expect it will need new base-load generating facilities before 2000.

The company's demand for capital is related primarily to construction of utility plant and equipment. In November 1994, it projected construction expenditures, excluding AFUDC, at $92 million for fiscal 1995 and $618 million for fiscal 1995-9. SPS anticipated providing 70% of its capital expenditures from internally generated funds in fiscal 1995.

Through subsidiaries, SPS also provides engineering, design and construction management services to various industries and is involved in a number of non-utility power generation projects.

Important Developments

Aug. '95—The company and Public Service Co. of Colorado (PSR) jointly announced the signing of a definitive merger agreement. PSR stockholders would receive one share of the new holding company (as yet unnamed) for each PSR share held, while SPS stockholders would receive 0.95 of a share for each SPS share held. PSR shareholders would own a 61.9% interest in the new holding company and SPS shareholders 38.1%. Combined market capitalization of the new company would be $3.2 billion. The companies expect to adopt Southwestern's dividend policy for the new dividend rate, which on a pro forma basis will be $2.32 annually.

Capitalization

Long Term Debt: $576,201,000 (6/95).
Cum. Preferred Stock: $72,680,000.

Per Share Data ($)

(Year Ended Aug. 31)

	1994	1993	1992	1991	1990	1989
Tangible Bk. Val.	17.01	16.84	16.57	16.47	16.04	15.51
Earnings	2.38	2.43	2.34	2.63	2.73	2.45
Dividends	2.20	2.20	2.20	2.20	2.20	2.20
Payout Ratio	92%	91%	94%	84%	81%	90%
Prices - High	30⅞	33⅝	34⅛	34⅜	30⅞	31⅜
- Low	23¾	29¾	30	27⅛	25⅛	25¼
P/E Ratio - High	13	14	15	13	11	13
- Low	10	12	13	10	9	10

Income Statement Analysis (Million $)

	1994	%Chg	1993	%Chg	1992	%Chg	1991
Revs.	843	4%	810	8%	749	3%	725
Depr.	60.6	-1%	61.3	4%	59.1	4%	57.1
Maint.	28.3	3%	27.4	6%	25.8	7%	24.1
Fxd. Chgs. Cov.	4.4	1%	4.4	8%	4.0	-3%	4.2
Constr. Credits	1.6	-43%	2.8	-38%	4.5	18%	3.8
Eff. Tax Rate	36%	—	35%	—	34%	—	33%
Net Inc.	102	-3%	105	2%	103	-10%	115

Balance Sheet & Other Fin. Data (Million $)

	1994	1993	1992	1991	1990	1989
Gross Prop.	2,303	2,222	2,146	2,080	2,006	1,967
Cap. Exp.	92.0	92.0	73.0	80.0	50.0	46.0
Net Prop.	1,508	1,480	1,448	1,429	1,401	1,410
Capitalization:						
LT Debt	506	523	513	520	520	564
% LT Debt	40	41	40	40	41	43
Pfd.	72.7	72.7	99	100	101	102
% Pfd.	5.70	5.70	7.60	7.70	7.90	7.90
Common	696	689	679	674	656	635
% Common	55	54	53	52	51	49
Total Cap.	1,621	1,540	1,538	1,529	1,505	1,532

Ratio Analysis

	1994	1993	1992	1991	1990	1989
Oper. Ratio	83.4	82.6	81.6	79.3	81.1	81.2
% Earn. on Net Prop.	9.4	9.6	9.6	10.6	10.4	10.6
% Ret. on Revs.	12.0	13.0	13.7	15.8	15.5	13.5
% Ret. On Invest.Cap	9.0	9.5	9.5	10.5	11.1	10.5
% Return On Com.Eqty	14.0	14.5	14.2	16.2	17.3	15.9

Dividend Data —Dividends have been paid since 1942. A dividend reinvestment plan is available. A "poison pill" stock purchase rights plan was adopted in 1991.

Amt. of Div. $	Date Decl.	Ex-Div. Date	Stock of Record	Payment Date
0.550	Oct. 25	Nov. 08	Nov. 15	Dec. 01 '94
0.550	Jan. 11	Feb. 09	Feb. 15	Mar. 01 '95
0.550	Apr. 25	May. 09	May. 15	Jun. 01 '95
0.550	Jul. 25	Aug. 11	Aug. 15	Sep. 01 '95

Data as orig. reptd.; bef. results of disc opers. and/or spec. items. Per share data adj. for stk. divs. as of ex-div. date. E-Estimated. NA-Not Available. NM-Not Meaningful. NR-Not Ranked.

Office—SPS Tower, 6th and Tyler Sts., Amarillo, TX 79101. **Tel**—(806) 378-2121. **Chrmn & CEO**—B. D. Helton. **Pres & COO**—D. M. Wilks. **VP & CFO**—D. R. Bunch II. **Secy-Treas**—R. D. Dickerson. **Group Mgr.-Fin & Investor Contact**—Jim Steinhilper. **Dirs**—G. H. Bishop, C. C. Burgess, J. C. Chambers, D. H. Conklin, G. M. Forbess, B. D. Helton, R. R. Hemminghaus, D. Maddox, J. H. Mock, S. B. Perry, D. M. Wilks, G. W. Wolf. **Transfer Agent & Registrar**—Society National Bank. **Incorporated** in New Mexico in 1921. **Empl**-2,000. **S&P Analyst:** Jane Collin

STANDARD & POOR'S

STOCK REPORTS

Standard Register

NASDAQ Symbol **SREG**

In S&P MidCap 400

21-AUG-95 **Industry:** Office Equipment

Summary: This company is a leading provider of business forms, pressure sensitive labels, business equipment and systems, direct mail marketing materials and materials management software.

Quantitative Evaluations

Outlook
(1 Lowest—5 Highest)
• **4+**

Fair Value
• **22¾**

Risk
• **Average**

Earn./Div. Rank
• **A**

Technical Eval.
• **Bearish** since 6/95

Rel. Strength Rank
(1 Lowest—99 Highest)
• **82**

Insider Activity
• **NA**

Recent Price • 22½ Yield • 3.2%

52 Wk Range • 22½-14½ 12-Mo. P/E • 14.0

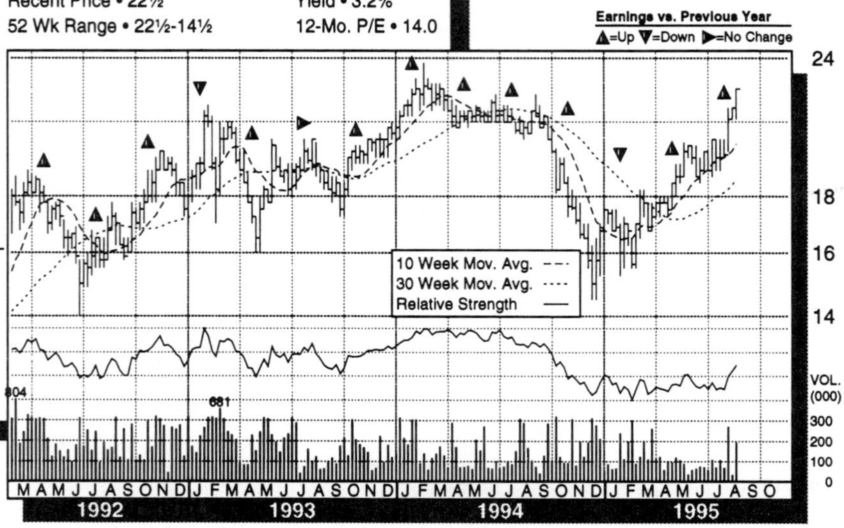

Business Profile - 11-AUG-95

SREG is a business information management company that provides business forms, business equipment and systems, direct mail marketing materials and materials management software. Its traditional business forms products, which have experienced flat to declining demand, now constitute only 39% of total sales. The company entered into a strategic alliance with F3 Software Corp., a developer of electronic forms software, in July 1995. Other alliances with electronic forms companies are pending.

Operational Review - 17-AUG-95

The 16% year-to-year increase in sales in the first half of 1995 reflected strong shipments in all major product groups and higher business forms prices prompted by rising paper costs. The price increases failed to match the rise in paper costs, though, leading to a narrowing of margins. Net income rose only 11%. SREG's financial position is solid, with current assets nearly four times current liabilities, and long-term debt only 2% of shareholders' equity.

Stock Performance - 18-AUG-95

In the past 30 trading days, SREG's shares have increased 11%, compared to a 0.51% rise in the S&P 500. Average trading volume for the past five days was 37,880 shares, compared with the 40-day moving average of 22,605 shares.

Key Stock Statistics

Dividend Rate/Share	0.72	Shareholders	3,200
Shs. outstg. (M)	28.7	Market cap. (B)	$0.645
Avg. daily vol. (M)	0.028	Inst. holdings	71%
Tang. Bk. Value/Share	13.94	Insider holdings	0%
Beta	1.21		

Value of $10,000 invested 5 years ago: $ 17,610

Fiscal Year Ending Dec. 31

	1995	% Change	1994	% Change	1993	% Change
Revenues (Million $)						
1Q	204.5	11%	183.9	9%	169.3	NM
2Q	222.5	21%	184.3	5%	174.7	1%
3Q	—	—	190.0	6%	179.1	5%
4Q	—	—	209.2	5%	199.0	3%
Yr.	—	—	767.4	6%	722.1	2%
Income (Million $)						
1Q	10.78	8%	10.02	7%	9.37	7%
2Q	12.04	14%	10.56	11%	9.55	1%
3Q	—	—	10.31	6%	9.75	12%
4Q	—	—	12.99	-4%	13.52	8%
Yr.	—	—	43.88	4%	42.19	7%
Earnings Per Share ($)						
1Q	0.38	9%	0.35	6%	0.33	10%
2Q	0.42	14%	0.37	12%	0.33	NM
3Q	—	—	0.36	6%	0.34	10%
4Q	—	—	0.45	-4%	0.47	9%
Yr.	—	—	1.53	4%	1.47	7%

Next earnings report expected: mid October

Standard Register

Business Summary - 18-AUG-95

The Standard Register Company provides a wide range of products and services that facilitate the recording, storage and communication of business transactions and information. It believes it is the second largest company in the U.S. forms industry, which includes roughly 500 firms. Major divisions include Forms, Business Equipment and Systems, Communicolor and Advanced Medical Systems (AMS).

The Forms division focuses on customized paper and electronic-based products providing users with value-added solutions. SREG has experienced increased sales of value-added products including cut sheets, form and label combinations, variable imaged products, forms management and document automation.

In 1994, SREG doubled the size of its Imprinting Services Group, which assists customers with quick turnaround of forms imprinted with variable information, bar codes and MICR and provides complete fulfillment services. The Business Equipment & Systems division's field service and third party service operations were also expanded.

Communicolor provides personalized direct mail production, while the AMS division provides materials management software to hospitals. In 1994, the company invested significantly in the AMS division to incorporate new technology and add functionality to the product. It also purchased a direct mail operation in Kansas to increase Communicolor's capacity to serve the growing direct response market.

The Advanced Medical Systems division develops and markets expense management application software used by hospitals.

The Stanfast unit's 19 print centers make business forms for customers requiring relatively small quantities on a quick-turnaround basis. Two new Stanfast centers were opened in 1994.

Important Developments

Jul. '95—In reporting second quarter earnings, the company said there will be continued growth in all operating divisions in 1995. Also, SREG formed a strategic alliance with F3 Software Corp., a developer and marketer of electronic forms software. Standard Register invested $3.5 million and agreed to take an equity position in F3.

Capitalization

Long Term Debt: $7,835,000 (7/95).

Per Share Data ($) (Year Ended Dec. 31)

	1994	1993	1992	1991	1990	1989
Tangible Bk. Val.	13.42	12.59	11.78	11.49	10.92	10.71
Cash Flow	2.42	2.30	2.15	1.89	1.44	1.98
Earnings	1.53	1.47	1.37	1.14	0.74	1.35
Dividends	0.68	0.64	0.60	0.56	0.56	0.52
Payout Ratio	44%	44%	44%	49%	76%	38%
Prices - High	23¾	21¾	19¾	15⅝	18	19¾
- Low	14½	16	13¾	9½	8⅝	14¾
P/E Ratio - High	16	15	14	14	24	15
- Low	9	11	10	8	12	11

Income Statement Analysis (Million $)

	1994	%Chg	1993	%Chg	1992	%Chg	1991
Revs.	767	6%	722	2%	705	2%	694
Oper. Inc.	100	4%	95.3	7%	89.3	18%	75.4
Depr.	25.5	7%	23.9	7%	22.3	4%	21.4
Int. Exp.	1.1	-4%	1.1	-46%	2.1	-30%	3.0
Pretax Inc.	72.9	4%	70.2	13%	61.9	21%	51.0
Eff. Tax Rate	40%	—	40%	—	36%	—	36%
Net Inc.	43.9	4%	42.2	7%	39.4	20%	32.7

Balance Sheet & Other Fin. Data (Million $)

	1994	1993	1992	1991	1990	1989
Cash	55.2	79.0	86.2	61.7	41.4	56.2
Curr. Assets	321	328	312	293	289	301
Total Assets	526	502	482	464	454	459
Curr. Liab.	89.7	84.2	81.0	75.1	74.1	67.9
LT Debt	11.1	17.5	24.5	35.2	41.9	48.7
Common Eqty.	384	361	338	329	313	319
Total Cap.	411	394	377	389	380	391
Cap. Exp.	52.1	31.1	22.7	28.0	24.7	33.8
Cash Flow	69.4	66.1	61.7	54.1	42.5	59.1

Ratio Analysis

	1994	1993	1992	1991	1990	1989
Curr. Ratio	3.6	3.9	3.9	3.9	3.9	4.4
% LT Debt of Cap.	2.7	4.5	6.5	9.1	11.0	12.5
% Net Inc.of Revs.	5.7	5.8	5.6	4.7	3.0	5.7
% Ret. on Assets	8.5	8.6	8.3	7.1	4.9	8.9
% Ret. on Equity	11.8	12.1	11.8	10.2	7.0	13.2

Dividend Data —Cash has been paid each year since 1927.

Amt. of Div. $	Date Decl.	Ex-Div. Date	Stock of Record	Payment Date
0.170	Jul. 21	Aug. 15	Aug. 19	Sep. 02 '94
0.170	Oct. 21	Nov. 14	Nov. 18	Dec. 02 '94
0.180	Dec. 15	Feb. 17	Feb. 24	Mar. 10 '95
0.180	Apr. 19	May. 15	May. 19	Jun. 02 '95
0.180	Jul. 25	Aug. 16	Aug. 18	Sep. 01 '95

Data as orig. reptd.; bef. results of disc. opers. and/or spec. items. Per share data adj. for stk. divs. as of ex-div. date. E-Estimated. NA-Not Available. NM-Not Meaningful. NR-Not Ranked.

Office—600 Albany St., Dayton, OH 45401. **Tel**—(513) 443-1000. **Chrmn**—P. H. Granzow. **Pres & CEO**—P. S. Redding. **SVP-Fin, Treas & CFO**—C. J. Brown. **Secy**—R. A. Kagan. **Dirs**—R. W. Begley, Jr., R. R. Burchenal, F. D. Clarke, III, J. K. Darragh, P. H. Granzow, M. C. Nushawg, P. S. Redding, D. Rediker, J. J. Schiff, Jr., C. F. Sherman, J. Q. Sherman, II. **Transfer Agent & Registrar**—Wachovia Bank of North Carolina, Winston-Salem. **Incorporated** in Ohio in 1912. **Empl-** 6,201. **S&P Analyst:** Stephen Madonna, CFA

STANDARD & POOR'S
STOCK REPORTS

Stanhome Inc.

NYSE Symbol **STH**
In S&P MidCap 400

30-AUG-95 **Industry:** Retail merchandiser

Summary: Stanhome is a global marketer of high quality consumer products, including giftware, collectibles, home care and personal care items.

Quantitative Evaluations
Outlook
(1 Lowest—5 Highest)
• **2+**
Fair Value
• **29¾**
Risk
• **Low**
Earn./Div. Rank
• **A-**

Technical Eval.
• **Bullish** since 12/94
Rel. Strength Rank
(1 Lowest—99 Highest)
• **23**
Insider Activity
• **NA**

Recent Price • 31
52 Wk Range • 35⅞-26⅞
Yield • 3.4%
12-Mo. P/E • 14.2

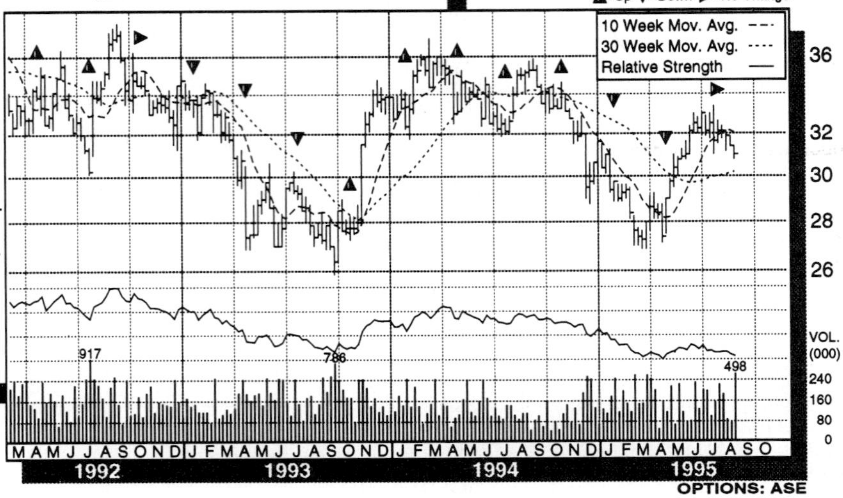

Business Profile - 30-AUG-95

The operating units of this global marketer of consumer products include: Enesco Worldwide Giftware Group, which produces and markets quality designed giftware and collectibles; Hamilton Worldwide Direct Response Group, which markets collectible dolls, plates and figurines; and the Stanhome Worldwide Direct Selling Group, which sells home care, personal care, cosmetics and giftware items. Stanhome has placed increased emphasis on global markets due to a mature domestic marketplace.

Operational Review - 30-AUG-95

Net sales in the first half of 1995, advanced 9.4%, year to year. Operating income rose 2.7%, as record sales and earnings at Enesco Worldwide Giftware were offset by an operating loss for Hamilton Direct Response (due to higher expenses) and continued softness in sales for Worlwide Direct Selling (which exited the U.S. direct selling business). After net interest expense, versus income, and higher amortization expenses, net income declined.

Stock Performance - 25-AUG-95

In the past 30 trading days, STH's shares have declined 5%, compared to a 0.04% rise in the S&P 500. Average trading volume for the past five days was 99,500 shares, compared with the 40-day moving average of 38,782 shares.

Key Stock Statistics

Dividend Rate/Share	1.06	Shareholders	3,700
Shs. outstg. (M)	18.8	Market cap. (B)	$0.578
Avg. daily vol. (M)	0.037	Inst. holdings	79%
Tang. Bk. Value/Share	7.30	Insider holdings	NA
Beta	0.64		

Value of $10,000 invested 5 years ago: $ 14,069

Fiscal Year Ending Dec. 31

	1995	% Change	1994	% Change	1993	% Change
Revenues (Million $)						
1Q	184.9	8%	171.8	4%	165.0	-2%
2Q	209.5	11%	188.6	NM	187.2	1%
3Q	—	—	193.3	6%	182.5	NM
4Q	—	—	236.6	9%	216.5	4%
Yr.	—	—	790.2	5%	750.7	NM
Income (Million $)						
1Q	6.45	-21%	8.13	30%	6.27	-24%
2Q	11.17	-4%	11.61	NM	-1.22	NM
3Q	—	—	13.12	10%	11.90	2%
4Q	—	—	11.20	-31%	16.19	5%
Yr.	—	—	44.06	33%	33.13	-29%
Earnings Per Share ($)						
1Q	0.34	-17%	0.41	32%	0.31	-24%
2Q	0.59	NM	0.59	NM	-0.06	NM
3Q	—	—	0.67	12%	0.60	3%
4Q	—	—	0.58	-30%	0.83	9%
Yr.	—	—	2.26	35%	1.68	-28%

Next earnings report expected: late October

Stanhome Inc.

Business Summary - 30-AUG-95

Stanhome is a worldwide marketer of consumer products. Its key product segments include quality-designed giftware and collectibles sold to retailers; collectible dolls, plates and figurines sold through direct response; and household, personal care and giftware items marketed through direct selling. Business segment contributions in 1994 were:

	Sales	Profits
Giftware	53%	69%
Direct response	17%	9%
Direct selling	30%	22%

In 1994, international operations (principally in Europe) accounted for 35% of sales.

Giftware operations are led by the Enesco unit, a leading importer and distributor of giftware items, including licensed lines and collectibles. Products include porcelain and cold cast figurines, musicals and music boxes, hand-painted cottages, dolls, ornaments, waterballs, decoupage, miniatures, jack-in-the-boxes, tinware, gift bags and other giftware. Company-owned businesses operate in the U.S., Canada, Germany, Hong Kong, Mexico and the U.K.

The direct response segment (established in 1989 through an acquisition) consists of the Hamilton Collection unit, which sells collectible plates, dolls and figurines directly to consumers through advertising and direct-mail marketing in the U.S., the U.K. and Canada.

The direct selling division makes a broad line of home care, personal care and giftware items, sold and distributed by independent representatives worldwide. In January 1995, an agreement was reached to license domestic operations. Sales of products generally result from the "Party Plan," under which a hostess invites friends and neighbors to her home to view a product demonstration by an independent Stanhome dealer, who subsequently solicits orders.

Important Developments

Aug. '95—The company said that Enesco had record sales and earnings in 1995's second quarter. Hamilton reported an operating loss for the quarter on sharply higher expenses. Sales and earnings were lower at Worldwide Direct, reflecting STH's exit from the U.S. direct selling business and weakness in Mexico and Italy. STH plans to expand licensed product offerings, review pricing strategies and control costs at Hamilton; and has implemented management and organizational changes at Worldwide Direct, which it believed would yield positive results in 1995's second half.

Jun. '95—Directors authorized the repurchase of 2.0 million STH common shares, to be used for general corporate purposes or employee benefit plans.

Capitalization

Long Term Debt: None (6/95).

Per Share Data ($)

(Year Ended Dec. 31)

	1994	1993	1992	1991	1990	1989
Tangible Bk. Val.	7.72	10.88	10.96	10.20	9.14	7.07
Cash Flow	2.79	2.18	2.80	2.67	2.98	2.60
Earnings	2.26	1.68	2.32	2.22	2.55	2.23
Dividends	1.03	1.00	0.96	0.92	0.83	0.71
Payout Ratio	46%	60%	41%	40%	32%	31%
Prices - High	37	34¾	41⅝	44¾	35¼	35½
- Low	28¾	25⅞	30⅛	30¾	25⅝	18⅜
P/E Ratio - High	16	21	18	20	14	16
- Low	13	15	13	14	10	8

Income Statement Analysis (Million $)

	1994	%Chg	1993	%Chg	1992	%Chg	1991
Revs.	790	5%	751	NM	744	5%	710
Oper. Inc.	88.2	-2%	90.1	NM	91.0	5%	86.4
Depr.	10.4	6%	9.8	NM	9.8	7%	9.2
Int. Exp.	2.0	NM	2.0	-40%	3.3	-33%	5.0
Pretax Inc.	80.7	22%	66.1	-24%	87.0	7%	81.1
Eff. Tax Rate	45%	—	50%	—	46%	—	45%
Net Inc.	44.1	33%	33.1	-29%	46.7	4%	45.1

Balance Sheet & Other Fin. Data (Million $)

	1994	1993	1992	1991	1990	1989
Cash	19.4	60.7	42.3	52.2	51.8	43.8
Curr. Assets	323	314	298	294	271	219
Total Assets	512	430	416	419	392	335
Curr. Liab.	220	155	143	159	162	150
LT Debt	Nil	Nil	0.9	1.2	1.4	1.4
Common Eqty.	269	254	257	241	211	170
Total Cap.	269	254	258	242	213	172
Cap. Exp.	16.8	6.5	6.9	7.8	10.9	5.1
Cash Flow	54.5	43.0	56.5	54.3	59.6	52.4

Ratio Analysis

	1994	1993	1992	1991	1990	1989
Curr. Ratio	1.5	2.0	2.1	1.8	1.7	1.5
% LT Debt of Cap.	Nil	Nil	0.4	0.5	0.7	0.8
% Net Inc.of Revs.	5.6	4.4	6.3	6.3	7.6	7.8
% Ret. on Assets	9.4	7.9	11.2	11.0	14.0	14.8
% Ret. on Equity	16.9	13.1	18.8	19.8	26.6	27.6

Dividend Data —Cash has been paid each year since 1943. A dividend reinvestment plan is available. A "poison pill" stock purchase rights plan was adopted in 1988.

Amt. of Div. $	Date Decl.	Ex-Div. Date	Stock of Record	Payment Date
0.265	Sep. 07	Sep. 15	Sep. 21	Oct. 01 '94
0.265	Dec. 07	Dec. 13	Dec. 19	Jan. 01 '95
0.265	Mar. 01	Mar. 09	Mar. 15	Apr. 01 '95
0.265	Jun. 06	Jun. 16	Jun. 20	Jul. 01 '95

Data as orig. reptd.; bef. results of disc. opers. and/or spec. items. Per share data adj. for stk. divs. as of ex-div. date. E-Estimated. NA-Not Available. NM-Not Meaningful. NR-Not Ranked.

Office—333 Western Ave., Westfield, MA 01085. **Tel**—(413) 562-3631. **Chrmn**—H. L. Tower. **Pres & CEO**—G. W. Seawright. **EVP & CFO**—A. G. Keirstead. **Treas**—C. J. Mascaro. **VP & Secy**—B. H. Wyatt. **Asst Treas & Investor Contact**—Gerald W. Tower. **Dirs**— J. F. Cauley, Jr., J. M. Clarke, C. W. Elliott, J. R. Haberkorn, T. R. Horton, A. G. Keirstead, H. G. Perkins, G. W. Seawright, H. L. Tower, A. L. Verville. **Transfer Agent & Registrar**—Mellon Securities Trust Co., East Hartford, CT. **Incorporated** in Massachusetts in 1931. **Empl**-4,940. **S&P Analyst:** Philip D. Wohl

STANDARD & POOR'S

STOCK REPORTS

Staples, Inc.

NASDAQ Symbol **SPLS**
In S&P MidCap 400

22-AUG-95 **Industry:** Retail Stores

Summary: Staples is one of the nation's leading operators of office products superstores.

Quantitative Evaluations
Outlook
(1 Lowest—5 Highest)
• **5**
Fair Value
• **32¾**
Risk
• **Average**
Earn./Div. Rank
• **NR**

Technical Eval.
• **Bullish** since 6/95
Rel. Strength Rank
(1 Lowest—99 Highest)
• **91**
Insider Activity
• **Neutral**

Recent Price • 25
52 Wk Range • 26-9⅞
Yield • Nil
12-Mo. P/E • 47.2

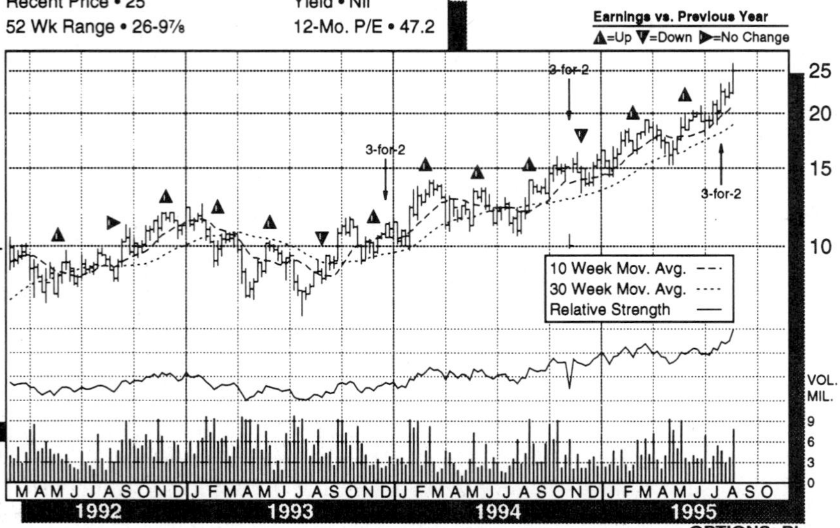

OPTIONS: Ph

Business Profile - 22-AUG-95

This operator of office products superstores has been aggressively expanding its operating base and had 386 units in operation as of August 1995. Staples also entered the contract stationer business through the acquisition of four stationers in fiscal 1994-95 and one in June 1995. Earnings have risen substantially in recent years, and analysts' estimates call for strong growth to continue into fiscal 1996-97. The shares reached an all-time high in August 1995.

Operational Review - 22-AUG-95

Net sales for the 26 weeks ended July 29, 1995, rose 63%, year to year, reflecting more stores in operation, a 20% increase in same-store sales, and acquisitions. Margins widened, due to the leveraging of fixed costs over a larger sales base and improved buying costs. Net income was up 157%, to $16,896,000 ($0.17 a share, based on 9.5% more average shares) from $6,568,000 ($0.07, as adjusted for the July 1995 three-for-two split).

Stock Performance - 18-AUG-95

In the past 30 trading days, SPLS's shares have increased 30%, compared to a 0.51% rise in the S&P 500. Average trading volume for the past five days was 1,556,100 shares, compared with the 40-day moving average of 953,350 shares.

Key Stock Statistics

Dividend Rate/Share	Nil	Shareholders	4,100
Shs. outstg. (M)	104.6	Market cap. (B)	$ 2.6
Avg. daily vol. (M)	0.951	Inst. holdings	76%
Tang. Bk. Value/Share	3.53	Insider holdings	2%
Beta	1.63		

Value of $10,000 invested 5 years ago: $ 69,823

Fiscal Year Ending Jan. 31

	1996	% Change	1995	% Change	1994	% Change
Revenues (Million $)						
1Q	668.8	68%	398.0	59%	251.0	34%
2Q	605.0	57%	385.8	60%	241.3	25%
3Q	—	—	552.1	83%	301.1	25%
4Q	—	—	664.7	102%	328.4	25%
Yr.	—	—	2,000	78%	1,122	27%
Income (Million $)						
1Q	7.88	140%	3.29	42%	2.32	77%
2Q	9.02	175%	3.28	NM	-4.03	NM
3Q	—	—	11.99	-12%	13.58	162%
4Q	—	—	21.38	59%	13.48	28%
Yr.	—	—	39.94	58%	25.35	57%
Earnings Per Share ($)						
1Q	0.08	125%	0.04	14%	0.03	50%
2Q	0.09	154%	0.04	NM	-0.05	NM
3Q	—	—	0.13	-23%	0.16	142%
4Q	—	—	0.21	33%	0.16	26%
Yr.	—	—	0.43	37%	0.31	41%

Next earnings report expected: mid November

Staples, Inc.

Business Summary - 22-AUG-95

Staples, Inc., as of January 28, 1995, was operating 350 high-volume office superstores in 19 states, the District of Columbia and five Canadian provinces, primarily in California (63), New York (49), New Jersey (33), Ontario (30), Massachusetts (26) and Pennsylvania (23). Sales by major product category in recent fiscal years were:

	1994-95	1993-94
Office supplies & services	53.7%	59.0%
Equipment & business machines	21.7%	20.4%
Computers & related products	16.2%	12.9%
Office furniture	8.4%	7.7%

Stores operate under the names Staples--The Office Superstore, Staples Express, Business Depot and Bureau en Gros. The prototype superstore is approximately 20,000 sq. ft. of sales area, carries 6,200 stock items, employs a no-frills format and generally is located in a suburban area. Express stores are generally 7,000 to 8,000 sq. ft., stock about 3,800 items and are located in downtown business areas. Items are priced at discounts ranging from 30% to 70% below manufacturer suggested list prices. The contract and commercial division operates a mail order delivery operation and a contract stationer business.

In August 1994, SPLS exercised its option to acquire the remaining 58% of The Business Depot Ltd. it did not already own. Business Depot superstores (including Bureau en Gros) offer substantially the same product selection as the Staples suburban superstores but are slightly larger than the typical superstore.

The company targets what it considers the four major end-user groups in the office product market: households, home offices and students; small businesses and organizations with fewer than 20 office workers; medium-size businesses and organizations with between 20 and 100 office workers; and large businesses with more than 100 office workers.

The company opened 36 stores in 1995-96's first half. SPLS plans to open between 85 to 90 stores in all of 1995-96, and over 100 stores in 1996-97. A total of 90 new stores were opened in 1994-95.

Important Developments

Jul. '95—SPLS redeemed virtually all of its $115 million 5% convertible subordinated debentures due November 1, 1999. Each $1,000 of debentures was converted into 75 common shares (as adjusted for the July 1995 3-for-2 split) of Staples.

Capitalization

Long Term Debt: Approx. $225,000,000 (7/95).
Options: To purchase 14,181,541 shs. at $0.001 to $16.50 ea. (1/95; adj.).

Per Share Data ($)

(Year Ended Jan. 31)

	1995	1994	1993	1992	1991	1990
Tangible Bk. Val.	2.90	3.14	2.73	1.84	1.04	1.22
Cash Flow	0.73	0.56	0.43	0.31	0.15	0.12
Earnings	0.43	0.31	0.22	0.14	0.07	0.09
Dividends	Nil	Nil	Nil	Nil	Nil	Nil
Payout Ratio	Nil	Nil	Nil	Nil	Nil	Nil
Cal. Yrs.	1994	1993	1992	1991	1990	1989
Prices - High	16½	12½	12¼	9⅛	5¼	5⅛
- Low	9¾	6⅞	7⅜	2⅞	2⅝	2⅞
P/E Ratio - High	39	39	55	64	72	58
- Low	23	22	33	20	36	32

Income Statement Analysis (Million $)

	1995	%Chg	1994	%Chg	1993	%Chg	1992
Revs.	2,000	78%	1,122	27%	883	61%	547
Oper. Inc.	110	62%	67.7	39%	48.8	77%	27.5
Depr.	28.7	44%	19.9	28%	15.5	70%	9.1
Int. Exp.	8.4	18%	7.1	39%	5.1	-20%	6.3
Pretax Inc.	63.9	58%	40.4	46%	27.7	115%	12.9
Eff. Tax Rate	38%	—	37%	—	42%	—	39%
Net Inc.	39.9	57%	25.4	58%	16.1	103%	7.9

Balance Sheet & Other Fin. Data (Million $)

	1995	1994	1993	1992	1991	1990
Cash	71.0	112	111	52.4	58.9	16.2
Curr. Assets	640	374	346	177	138	52.0
Total Assets	1,008	581	494	286	204	84.0
Curr. Liab.	350	159	116	54.4	53.1	16.5
LT Debt	249	122	120	80.9	79.2	4.0
Common Eqty.	385	282	247	145	69.0	63.0
Total Cap.	634	405	367	226	148	67.0
Cap. Exp.	64.7	52.1	27.5	29.5	21.9	12.0
Cash Flow	68.6	45.2	31.6	17.0	7.7	5.6

Ratio Analysis

	1995	1994	1993	1992	1991	1990
Curr. Ratio	1.8	2.4	3.0	3.2	2.6	3.2
% LT Debt of Cap.	39.3	30.2	32.6	35.9	53.5	5.9
% Net Inc.of Revs.	2.0	2.3	1.8	1.5	1.2	2.3
% Ret. on Assets	4.7	4.7	3.7	3.0	2.5	5.1
% Ret. on Equity	11.1	9.5	7.4	6.9	5.5	7.0

Dividend Data —No cash dividends have been paid, and Staples does not expect to pay any in the foreseeable future. A shareholder rights plan was adopted in February 1994. 3-for-2 stock splits were effected in December 1993, October 1994 and July 1995.

Amt. of Div. $	Date Decl.	Ex-Div. Date	Stock of Record	Payment Date
3-for-2	Jun. 29	Jul. 25	Jul. 14	Jul. 24 '95

Data as orig. reptd.; bef. results of disc. opers. and/or spec. items. Per share data adj. for stk. divs. as of ex-div. date. E-Estimated. NA-Not Available. NM-Not Meaningful. NR-Not Ranked.

Office—100 Pennsylvania Ave., P.O. Box 9328, Framingham, MA 01701-9328. **Tel**—(508) 370-8500. **Chrmn & CEO**—T. G. Stemberg. **Pres & COO**—M. Hanaka. **EVP & CFO**—J.B. Wilson. **VP & Treas**—R. K. Mayerson. **VP & Secy**—P. M. Schwarzenbach. **Investor Contact**—S. J. Levenson. **Dirs**—M. E. Burton, W. L. Heisey, L. Kahn, D. G. Lubrano, R. T. Moriarty, R. C. Nakasone, W. M. Romney, T. G. Stemberg, M. Trust, P. F. Walsh, S. J. Westerfield. **Transfer Agent**—First National Bank of Boston. **Incorporated** in Delaware in 1985. **Empl**-14,566. **S&P Analyst:** Michael V. Pizzi

STANDARD & POOR'S

STOCK REPORTS

State Street Boston

NYSE Symbol **STT**

In S&P MidCap 400

08-OCT-95 **Industry:** Banking

Summary: This bank holding company, with $1.6 trillion in assets under custody and $160 billion in assets under management, is a leading servicer of financial assets worldwide.

S&P Opinion: Hold (★★★)

Recent Price • 40⅛ | 52 Wk Range • 41½-27⅝ | Yield • 1.7% | 12-Mo. P/E • 14.3

Quantitative Evaluations

Outlook (1 Lowest—5 Highest)
• **5-**

Fair Value
• **47⅜**

Risk
• **Low**

Earn./Div. Rank
• **A+**

Technical Eval.
• **Bullish** since 9/95

Rel. Strength Rank (1 Lowest—99 Highest)
• **79**

Insider Activity
• **Neutral**

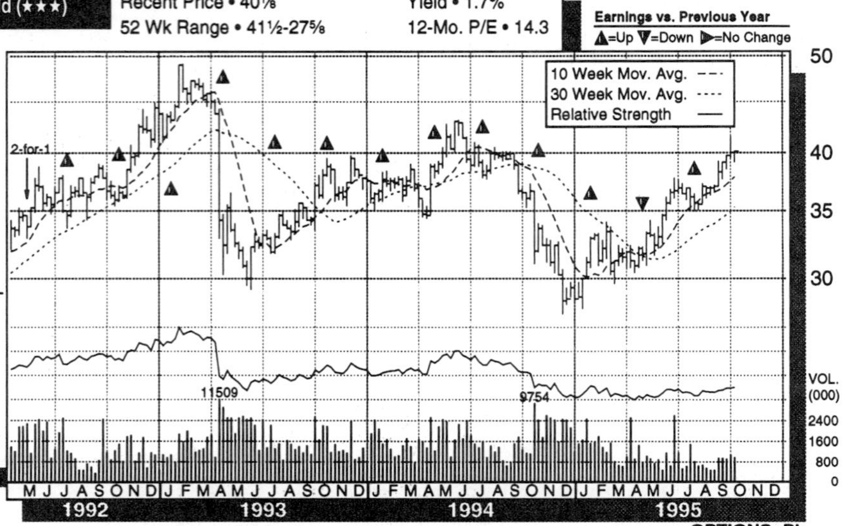

OPTIONS: Ph

Overview - 06-OCT-95

Revenue growth improved in the second quarter of 1995, aided by an increase in non-U.S. assets under custody and thriving U.S. equity and bond markets that led to growth in mutual fund servicing and investment management revenues. Still, the rate of future growth in fiduciary compensation remains under pressure from certain customers internalizing functions and pricing adjustments to retain large customers. The company's growth strategy includes selective expansion and careful control of operating expenses. Recently announced acquisitions will substantially expand the corporate trust business. STT's expectation for double-digit earnings growth in 1995 is based on continued favorable market conditions, further penetration of world markets, a resumption of growth in global investing and stable short-term interest rates.

Valuation - 05-OCT-95

The shares rebounded in the second quarter of 1995 but remain well below highs reached in 1993. A surging equity market and strong mutual fund activity led to higher than expected revenues in the second quarter of 1995. However, future revenue growth remains a challenge given price concessions and certain large customers internalizing various services. STT has reiterated its double-digit earnings growth target for 1995, which will be difficult given a weak first half performance. While we would not add to current positions, the company's dominant industry position and longer term prospects make the shares worthwhile to hold.

Key Stock Statistics

S&P EPS Est. 1995	2.95	Tang. Bk. Value/Share	18.05
P/E on S&P Est. 1995	13.6	Beta	1.55
S&P EPS Est. 1996	3.25	Shareholders	6,000
Dividend Rate/Share	0.68	Market cap. (B)	$ 3.3
Shs. outstg. (M)	82.7	Inst. holdings	71%
Avg. daily vol. (M)	0.193	Insider holdings	NA

Value of $10,000 invested 5 years ago: $ 22,362

Fiscal Year Ending Dec. 31

	1995	% Change	1994	% Change	1993	% Change
Revenues (Million $)						
1Q	580.5	32%	440.7	23%	357.4	2%
2Q	380.5	-14%	442.7	17%	377.1	7%
3Q	—	—	479.6	24%	388.3	7%
4Q	—	—	522.8	28%	409.5	16%
Yr.	—	—	1,886	23%	1,532	8%
Income (Million $)						
1Q	54.34	6%	51.29	20%	42.66	18%
2Q	62.66	23%	51.04	18%	43.22	12%
3Q	—	—	51.82	12%	46.27	11%
4Q	—	—	53.27	12%	47.68	9%
Yr.	—	—	207.4	15%	179.8	12%
Earnings Per Share ($)						
1Q	0.66	-1%	0.67	20%	0.56	17%
2Q	0.75	14%	0.66	16%	0.57	12%
3Q	E0.75	12%	0.67	10%	0.61	11%
4Q	E0.80	14%	0.70	13%	0.62	9%
Yr.	E2.95	9%	2.70	14%	2.36	12%

Next earnings report expected: mid October

State Street Boston

Business Summary - 06-OCT-95

State Street Boston Corp. is the holding company for State Street Bank and Trust, the 23rd largest U.S. commercial bank. It is the leading U.S. mutual fund custodian, providing securities custody and record-keeping services to about 2,200 U.S. mutual funds with assets totaling $675 billion at December 31, 1994 (down from $683 billion a year earlier). STT is also the largest servicer of tax-exempt assets for U.S. corporations and public funds and the largest global custodian for U.S. pension assets, servicing $664 billion for North American customers. It also provides global and domestic custody-related services for $72 billion in assets for customers outside the U.S. An additional $210 billion of bonds under trusteeship brought total assets under custody to $1.6 trillion at 1994 year-end. The company also provides corporate banking services, primarily to New England middle-market companies, and specialized lending on a national basis and international banking services.

In 1994, average earning assets of $19.2 billion (up 18% from 1993) were divided: commercial and financial loans 12%; real estate, consumer and other loans 6%; investment securities 35%; trading account assets 2%; interest-bearing deposits 27%; and federal funds sold and securities purchased under resale agreements 18%. Average sources of funds were: noninterest-bearing deposits 19%; other domestic deposits 9%; other foreign deposits 34%; short-term debt 27%; long-term debt 2%; shareholders' equity 5%; and other 4%.

At year-end 1994, nonperforming assets amounted to $27.4 million (0.71% of total loans) versus $37.9 million (1.00%) a year earlier. The allowance for loan losses was 1.80% of loans, down from 2.03%. Net chargeoffs in 1994 came to 0.23% of average loans versus 0.63% in 1993.

Important Developments

Oct. '95—The company said it acquired the corporate trust business of Bank of Boston, including more than 1,400 corporate accounts, providing trusteeship, paying and escrow agent services for $60 billion in assets. Earlier, in May, State Street acquired the corporate trust business of Bay Banks, serving 260 corporate accounts with $4.4 billion in assets under trusteeship. Together, the acquisitions represent a nearly 30% increase in the company's corporate trust business.

Jun. '95—Directors reaffirmed an authorization to repurchase up to 2 million common shares, to be used for employee benefit plans.

Capitalization

Long Term Debt: $127,086,000 (6/95), incl. $3.4 million of sub. debs. conv. into com. at $5.75 a sh.

Per Share Data ($)

(Year Ended Dec. 31)

	1994	1993	1992	1991	1990	1989
Tangible Bk. Val.	16.10	14.56	12.70	10.97	9.51	8.29
Earnings	2.70	2.36	2.10	1.86	1.59	1.42
Dividends	0.60	0.52	0.46	0.39	0.34	0.30
Payout Ratio	22%	22%	22%	21%	21%	21%
Prices - High	43⅛	49⅛	44⅞	32⅛	21⅝	20½
- Low	27⅝	29¼	29¼	15½	11	12¾
P/E Ratio - High	16	21	21	17	14	14
- Low	10	12	14	8	7	9

Income Statement Analysis (Million $)

	1994	%Chg	1993	%Chg	1992	%Chg	1991
Net Int. Inc.	367	15%	318	13%	282	3%	274
Tax Equiv. Adj.	23.8	18%	20.2	49%	13.6	-28%	18.8
Non Int. Inc.	982	20%	818	18%	691	12%	617
Loan Loss Prov.	11.6	2%	11.3	-7%	12.2	-80%	60.0
% Exp/Op Revs.	74%	—	75%	—	73%	—	67%
Pretax Inc.	320	16%	277	8%	257	14%	225
Eff. Tax Rate	35%	—	35%	—	38%	—	38%
Net Inc.	207	15%	180	13%	160	15%	139
% Net Int. Marg.	NA	—	2.08%	—	2.14%	—	2.89%

Balance Sheet & Other Fin. Data (Million $)

	1994	1993	1992	1991	1990	1989
Earning Assets:						
Money Mkt.	7,615	7,763	8,224	8,113	4,278	3,262
Inv. Securities	8,414	5,701	4,092	3,250	2,842	2,515
Com'l Loans	2,522	2,215	1,771	1,623	1,738	1,632
Other Loans	711	466	233	282	803	833
Total Assets	21,730	18,720	16,490	15,046	11,651	9,983
Demand Deposits	4,212	5,450	4,374	3,564	3,236	3,263
Time Deposits	9,691	7,568	6,687	5,168	4,422	2,915
LT Debt	128	129	146	147	112	115
Common Eqty.	1,231	1,105	953	817	695	597

Ratio Analysis

	1994	1993	1992	1991	1990	1989
% Ret. on Assets	1.0	1.0	1.0	1.2	1.1	1.3
% Ret. on Equity	NA	17.4	18.1	18.0	18.1	18.7
% Loan Loss Resv.	1.8	2.0	2.9	3.5	2.0	2.0
% Loans/Deposits	23.3	20.6	18.1	21.8	33.2	39.9
% Equity to Assets	NA	5.7	5.7	6.7	6.3	6.9

Dividend Data —Cash has been paid each year since 1910.

Amt. of Div. $	Date Decl.	Ex-Div. Date	Stock of Record	Payment Date
0.150	Sep. 15	Sep. 27	Oct. 03	Oct. 17 '94
0.160	Dec. 15	Dec. 23	Jan. 02	Jan. 16 '95
0.160	Mar. 16	Mar. 28	Apr. 03	Apr. 17 '95
0.170	Jun. 15	Jun. 29	Jul. 03	Jul. 17 '95
0.170	Sep. 21	Sep. 28	Oct. 02	Oct. 16 '95

Data as orig. reptd.; bef. results of disc opers. and/or spec. items. Per share data adj. for stk. divs. as of ex-div. date. E-Estimated. NA-Not Available. NM-Not Meaningful. NR-Not Ranked.

Formed—in 1970; bank incorporated in Massachusetts in 1891. **Office**—225 Franklin St., Boston, MA 02110. **Tel**—(617) 786-3000. **Chrmn & CEO**—M. N. Carter. **Vice Chrmn, CFO & Treas**—D. A. Spina. **Secy**—J. R. Towers. **SVP & Investor Contact**—Susanne G. Clark. **Dirs**—T. E. Albright, J. A. Baute, I. M. Booth, M. N. Carter, J. I. Cash, Jr., T. S. Casner, N. F. Darehshori, L. D. Juliber, C. F. Kaye, J. M. Kucharski, C. R. LaMantia, D. B. Perini, D. J. Picard, A. Poe, B. W. Reznicek, D. A. Spina, R. E. — Weissman. **Transfer Agent**—State Street Bank & Trust Co., Boston. **Empl-** 11,127. **S&P Analyst:** Stephen R. Biggar

STANDARD & POOR'S

Sterling Chemicals

STOCK REPORTS

NYSE Symbol **STX**
In S&P MidCap 400

22-AUG-95 **Industry:** Chemicals

Summary: Sterling is a major manufacturer of commodity chemicals, the most important of which is styrene monomer. It also produces chemicals and equipment for the pulp and paper industry.

S&P Opinion: Hold (★★★) | Recent Price • 10⅝ | 52 Wk Range • 14⅛-9¾ | Yield • Nil | 12-Mo. P/E • 3.9

Quantitative Evaluations

Outlook (1 Lowest—5 Highest)
• 5+

Fair Value
• 16¾

Risk
• High

Earn./Div. Rank
• NR

Technical Eval.
• Bearish since 9/94

Rel. Strength Rank (1 Lowest—99 Highest)
• 11

Insider Activity
• Unfavorable

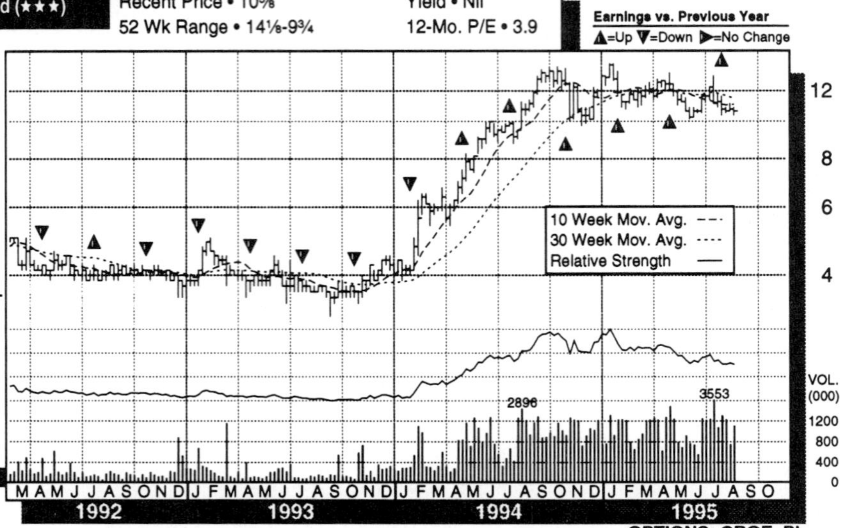

OPTIONS: CBOE, Ph

Overview - 22-AUG-95

Following exceptionally strong second and third quarters, revenues in the fourth quarter of fiscal 1995 will be hurt by reduced styrene sales. In addition to a scheduled three week unit maintenance shutdown, results will be affected by weak spot prices for styrene in the Far East, due to the recent slowdown in imports from China. Acrylonitrile prices have also softened from their recent peak, but, with markets tight, should still stay strong. Although the costs of raw materials has trended downward, lower prices will narrow margins in the near term. The pulp chemical operations will continue to benefit from the increased demand for sodium chlorate, and STX's 30% expansion of its sodium chlorate capacity should help to soften the next cyclical downturn. Results should remain strong in fiscal 1996, but will probably fall somewhat below the current cyclical peak.

Valuation - 22-AUG-95

After having tripled from their 1994 low, propelled by the dramatic turnaround in the petrochemicals market, the shares have declined more than 20% from their 1995 high. The market remained remarkably indifferent to the earnings reports for the second and third quarters (which came in well above expectations) and has instead seemed to focus on the belief that STX is now at the peak of its current cycle, and will continue to trade at the low end of its historic P/E range.

Key Stock Statistics

S&P EPS Est. 1995	3.05	Tang. Bk. Value/Share	2.93
P/E on S&P Est. 1995	3.5	Beta	0.42
S&P EPS Est. 1996	2.95	Shareholders	15,000
Dividend Rate/Share	Nil	Market cap. (B)	$0.585
Shs. outstg. (M)	55.7	Inst. holdings	36%
Avg. daily vol. (M)	0.282	Insider holdings	0%

Value of $10,000 invested 5 years ago: $ 18,843

Fiscal Year Ending Sep. 30

	1995	% Change	1994	% Change	1993	% Change
Revenues (Million $)						
1Q	240.6	84%	130.6	-5%	137.8	19%
2Q	304.0	96%	154.8	37%	113.1	27%
3Q	298.5	46%	204.7	55%	132.3	9%
4Q	—	—	210.9	55%	135.7	30%
Yr.	—	—	700.8	35%	518.8	21%
Income (Million $)						
1Q	22.26	NM	-3.49	NM	0.10	-86%
2Q	56.08	NM	1.83	NM	-2.60	NM
3Q	59.80	NM	5.54	NM	-0.45	NM
4Q	—	—	15.20	NM	-2.47	NM
Yr.	—	—	19.13	NM	-5.42	NM
Earnings Per Share ($)						
1Q	0.40	NM	-0.06	—	Nil	—
2Q	1.01	NM	0.03	NM	-0.05	NM
3Q	1.07	NM	0.10	NM	-0.01	NM
4Q	E0.57	111%	0.27	NM	-0.04	—
Yr.	E3.05	NM	0.34	NM	-0.10	NM

Next earnings report expected: late October

Sterling Chemicals

Business Summary - 22-AUG-95

Sterling Chemicals is a major producer of seven commodity petrochemicals used in the manufacture of other goods or in other chemical processes. The company also manufactures pulp chemicals and related equipment. Contributions by segment in fiscal 1994 were:

	Sales	Profits
Petrochemicals	83%	70%
Pulp chemicals	17%	30%

Export sales accounted for 46% of total sales in fiscal 1994, versus 31% in fiscal 1993 and 43% in fiscal 1992.

Styrene monomer is the major product Sterling manufactures, accounting for more than one-third of the company's total capacity (about 13% of total U.S. domestic capacity). End-uses for styrene include disposable cups, building products, tires, audio and video cassettes, toys and carpet backing. Sterling is the second largest domestic producer (25%) of acrylonitrile, the principal raw material for synthetic fibers. It is also a major producer of acetic acid (16%), which is used in a variety of pharmaceuticals, adhesives and coatings, and of plasticizers, which are used to make flexible plastics, such as shower curtains, floor coverings and cable insulation. It is the only U.S. producer of synthetic lactic acid, used in food additives and preservatives, pharmaceuticals and surface coatings, and of TBA, used in silicone caulk, tires and hoses. The company operates a 100-million-lb.-per-year sodium cyanide project owned by duPont; sodium cyanide is used in precious metals recovery and electroplating. Manufacturing facilities are in Texas City, Texas.

The Albright & Wilson pulp chemicals business was acquired in August 1992. It produces sodium chlorate, which is used to produce chlorine dioxide (sold primarily as a bleaching agent for kraft pulp manufacturing), and sodium chlorite (used primarily as an antimicrobial agent and disinfectant). Sterling owns 20% of North American sodium chlorate capacity.

Important Developments

Jul. '95—Sterling said earnings in the fourth quarter would be adversely affected by the recent weakness of styrene prices in the Far East, reflecting the slowdown in imports from China that followed the recent government crackdown on the local non-payment of import duties.

May '95—STX and BP Chemicals Inc., a unit of British Petroleum, agreed to construct a methanol plant at Sterling's Texas City petrochemical facility. The company and BP Chemicals will share capital investment costs and the completed plant's 150 million gallon annual capacity.

Capitalization

Long Term Debt: $115,300,000 (6//95).

Per Share Data ($) (Year Ended Sep. 30)

	1994	1993	1992	1991	1990	1989
Tangible Bk. Val.	1.61	1.27	1.59	1.95	1.96	1.97
Cash Flow	0.96	0.50	0.53	1.03	1.41	2.01
Earnings	0.34	-0.10	0.08	0.67	1.07	1.77
Dividends	Nil	0.06	0.24	0.65	1.00	0.75
Payout Ratio	Nil	NM	297%	97%	93%	40%
Prices - High	13⅞	5	5⅛	7⅛	8⅝	18¾
- Low	3⅞	3⅛	3½	3⅞	5¼	6⅞
P/E Ratio - High	41	NM	64	11	8	11
- Low	11	NM	44	6	5	4

Income Statement Analysis (Million $)

	1994	%Chg	1993	%Chg	1992	%Chg	1991
Revs.	701	35%	519	20%	431	-21%	543
Oper. Inc.	82.0	71%	48.0	14%	42.0	-48%	81.0
Depr.	34.3	4%	32.9	34%	24.5	22%	20.1
Int. Exp.	22.3	-2%	22.7	144%	9.3	22%	7.6
Pretax Inc.	28.0	NM	-7.0	NM	9.0	-84%	55.0
Eff. Tax Rate	32%	—	NM	—	51%	—	33%
Net Inc.	19.0	NM	-5.0	NM	5.0	-86%	37.0

Balance Sheet & Other Fin. Data (Million $)

	1994	1993	1992	1991	1990	1989
Cash	2.0	1.4	2.6	3.0	0.2	0.4
Curr. Assets	212	145	172	118	124	108
Total Assets	575	540	600	361	352	329
Curr. Liab.	191	114	115	89.0	91.0	72.0
LT Debt	187	257	292	71.0	64.0	66.0
Common Eqty.	90.0	70.0	87.0	112	108	110
Total Cap.	315	363	423	224	214	211
Cap. Exp.	12.0	12.0	138	35.0	20.0	58.0
Cash Flow	53.0	27.0	29.0	57.0	78.0	118

Ratio Analysis

	1994	1993	1992	1991	1990	1989
Curr. Ratio	1.1	1.3	1.5	1.3	1.4	1.5
% LT Debt of Cap.	59.2	70.7	69.1	31.7	29.8	31.6
% Net Inc.of Revs.	2.7	NM	1.1	6.8	12.0	17.9
% Ret. on Assets	3.4	NM	0.9	10.3	17.5	34.4
% Ret. on Equity	23.9	NM	4.5	33.4	54.5	106.6

Dividend Data —Payments were omitted in July 1993, after having been initiated in 1989.

Data as orig. reptd.; bef. results of disc. opers. and/or spec. items. Per share data adj. for stk. divs. as of ex-div. date. E-Estimated. NA-Not Available. NM-Not Meaningful. NR-Not Ranked.

Office—1200 Smith St., Suite 1900, Houston, TX 77002. **Tel**—(713) 650-3700. **Chrmn**—G. A. Cain. **Pres & CEO**—J. V. Waggoner. **VP-CFO & Investor Contact**—Jim P. Wise. **Secy**—F. M. Evans. **Dirs**—G. A. Cain, J. J. Kerley, R. R. Knowland, W. A. McMinn, F. J. Pizzitola, G. M. A. Portal, J. V. Waggoner. **Transfer Agent & Registrar**—Society National Bank, Houston. **Incorporated** in Delaware in 1986. **Empl**-1,210. **S&P Analyst:** Justin McCann

STANDARD & POOR'S

STOCK REPORTS

Stewart & Stevenson Services

NASDAQ Symbol **SSSS**

In S&P MidCap 400

16-OCT-95 **Industry:** Machinery

Summary: This leading manufacturer of custom diesel and gas turbine power systems and tactical military vehicles is also a distributor of industrial equipment.

S&P Opinion: Hold (★★★)

Recent Price • 29¾
52 Wk Range • 41¼-28
Yield • 1.1%
12-Mo. P/E • 14.2

Quantitative Evaluations

Outlook (1 Lowest—5 Highest)
• **5−**

Fair Value
• **38⅞**

Risk
• **Average**

Earn./Div. Rank
• **B**

Technical Eval.
• **Bearish** since 8/95

Rel. Strength Rank (1 Lowest—99 Highest)
• **12**

Insider Activity
• **NA**

OPTIONS: P

Overview - 16-OCT-95

We expect an 11% increase in sales for fiscal 1995-96 as continued growth in engineered power systems, the acquisition of PAMCO and an increase in distribution sales offset a decline in tactical vehicles. Sales will advance at a lower rate than in 1994-95 because of the decrease in truck deliveries and revenue per vehicle versus fiscal 1994-95. Margins will be about even with 1994-95 as greater overall volume and continued high operating rates in engineered power offsets the absence of LIFO income in the distribution unit and lower margins in tactical vehicles. Assuming stable business conditions worldwide, sales and earnings should rise again in 1996-97. Long-term sales and earnings growth will benefit from a worldwide trend toward smaller-scale production of electric power.

Valuation - 16-OCT-95

Through mid October, SSSS has underperformed the market, falling 13% versus a 27% gain in the S&P 500. Because there are no companies that fit SSSS's business profile, we can not measure it relative to peers. SSSS appears attractive on our 1996-97 estimate and may have turned the corner in tactical vehicles, but we are maintaining our neutral opinion. It is difficult to calculate what the appropriate P/E valuation should be because of the absence of peers. Thus, SSSS may be fairly valued on 1996-97 earnings given the less rapid earnings growth. Until earnings resume their former growth rate, SSSS only warrants a hold rating.

Key Stock Statistics

S&P EPS Est. 1996	2.25	Tang. Bk. Value/Share	13.56
P/E on S&P Est. 1996	13.2	Beta	0.72
S&P EPS Est. 1997	2.50	Shareholders	900
Dividend Rate/Share	0.32	Market cap. (B)	$0.983
Shs. outstg. (M)	33.0	Inst. holdings	70%
Avg. daily vol. (M)	0.268	Insider holdings	NA

Value of $10,000 invested 5 years ago: $ 22,238

Fiscal Year Ending Jan. 31

	1996	% Change	1995	% Change	1994	% Change
Revenues (Million $)						
1Q	289.0	12%	259.0	18%	220.1	21%
2Q	319.8	11%	287.0	11%	257.9	29%
3Q	—	—	304.3	17%	259.1	25%
4Q	—	—	287.8	18%	244.7	10%
Yr.	—	—	1,138	16%	981.9	21%
Income (Million $)						
1Q	16.02	7%	15.03	24%	12.09	36%
2Q	16.93	3%	16.49	20%	13.79	32%
3Q	—	—	17.60	25%	14.07	22%
4Q	—	—	18.44	10%	16.83	28%
Yr.	—	—	67.56	19%	56.78	29%
Earnings Per Share ($)						
1Q	0.49	7%	0.46	24%	0.37	32%
2Q	0.51	2%	0.50	19%	0.42	27%
3Q	E0.61	15%	0.53	23%	0.43	19%
4Q	E0.64	14%	0.56	10%	0.51	28%
Yr.	E2.25	10%	2.05	18%	1.73	28%

Next earnings report expected: mid November

Stewart & Stevenson Services

16-OCT-95

Business Summary - 13-OCT-95

Stewart & Stevenson Services, Inc. manufactures custom diesel and gas turbine power systems and tactical military vehicles, and distributes industrial equipment.

Revenue and profit contributions in 1994-95 were:

	Revs.	Profits
Engineered power systems	57%	71%
Distribution	30%	21%
Tactical vehicle sytems	13%	8%

Engineered power systems (EPS) engineers and sells generator sets and mechanical drive packages that are driven by diesel or gas turbine engines supplied by independent manufacturers and are designed to meet specific requirements of customers in various applications. The gas turbine generator sets range from 20 Mw to 52 Mw and are sold to independent power producers and public utilities. Gas turbine-driven products and services accounted for 47.6% of 1994-95 sales. EPS also includes the manufacture of well simulation and other diesel equipment for the oilfield service industry, aircraft ground support equipment, and generator sets ranging in size from 20 kw to 12,700 kw.

The distribution division markets industrial equipment and related parts manufactured by others and provides in-shop and on-site repair services for such products. Principal products include Detroit Diesel engines, General Motors Electro-Motive diesel engines, Allison automatic transmissions, Thermo King transport refrigeration units, and John Deere equipment.

The Tactical Vehicle Systems unit manufactures tactical vehicles, primarily 2 1/2 and 5-ton trucks under contract with the U. S. Army. The division has a contract to produce 7,738 2 1/2 -ton trucks and 3,105 5-ton trucks over a five-year period beginning in 1992. The contract is valued at $1.2 billion.

Important Developments

Sep. '95—SSSS announced that it would begin mass production of 14 types of trucks for the U. S. Army as part of a $1.2 billion contract. The company will begin delivering the 10,843 trucks in mid December.

Aug. '95—SSSS reported share earnings of $0.51 on an 11% increase in sales for fiscal 1995's second quarter, versus $0.50 a year earlier. The gain in sales mostly reflected a 24% rise in the distribution unit; engineered power's sales rose 6.8% while tactical vehicle sales were virtually unchanged. The gain in earnings for the quarter trailed the rise in sales due to margin pressure in the engineered power segment.

Capitalization

Long Term Debt: $116,858,000 (7/95).

Per Share Data ($)

(Year Ended Jan. 31)

	1995	1994	1993	1992	1991	1990
Tangible Bk. Val.	12.70	10.89	9.33	8.40	6.09	5.22
Cash Flow	2.78	2.37	1.73	1.46	1.25	1.23
Earnings	2.05	1.73	1.35	1.18	0.99	0.97
Dividends	0.33	0.22	0.19	0.14	0.11	0.07
Payout Ratio	16%	13%	14%	12%	11%	8%
Cal. Yrs.	1994	1993	1992	1991	1990	1989
Prices - High	53¾	52½	34¾	33⅝	20¼	16¼
- Low	28	28	22	16⅛	12⅜	7
P/E Ratio - High	26	30	25	28	21	17
- Low	14	16	16	14	13	7

Income Statement Analysis (Million $)

	1995	%Chg	1994	%Chg	1993	%Chg	1992
Revs.	1,138	16%	982	21%	813	19%	686
Oper. Inc.	131	20%	109	40%	77.8	21%	64.3
Depr.	24.0	13%	21.2	72%	12.3	49%	8.3
Int. Exp.	6.9	108%	3.3	-10%	3.7	-47%	7.0
Pretax Inc.	102	20%	84.8	31%	64.6	23%	52.5
Eff. Tax Rate	34%	—	33%	—	32%	—	32%
Net Inc.	67.6	19%	56.8	29%	44.0	23%	35.7

Balance Sheet & Other Fin. Data (Million $)

	1995	1994	1993	1992	1991	1990
Cash	4.0	7.8	21.9	6.5	3.3	7.4
Curr. Assets	714	541	436	413	344	261
Total Assets	876	693	573	478	394	311
Curr. Liab.	311	241	199	166	166	122
LT Debt	117	68.0	44.5	27.9	38.0	23.5
Common Eqty.	419	359	306	272	182	155
Total Cap.	544	433	356	309	225	186
Cap. Exp.	33.4	30.6	75.1	26.2	11.6	7.7
Cash Flow	91.5	78.0	56.3	44.0	37.2	34.7

Ratio Analysis

	1995	1994	1993	1992	1991	1990
Curr. Ratio	2.3	2.2	2.2	2.5	2.1	2.1
% LT Debt of Cap.	21.5	15.7	12.5	9.0	16.9	12.6
% Net Inc.of Revs.	5.9	5.8	5.4	5.2	4.6	4.5
% Ret. on Assets	8.6	8.9	8.3	7.9	8.3	9.2
% Ret. on Equity	17.4	17.1	15.1	15.2	17.4	20.4

Dividend Data —Cash dividends, which had been paid in each year since 1976, were omitted in 1983 and resumed in 1988.

Amt. of Div. $	Date Decl.	Ex-Div. Date	Stock of Record	Payment Date
0.070	Sep. 14	Oct. 25	Oct. 31	Nov. 15 '94
0.070	Dec. 19	Jan. 25	Jan. 31	Feb. 14 '95
0.070	Apr. 11	Apr. 24	Apr. 28	May. 12 '95
0.080	Jun. 13	Jul. 27	Jul. 31	Aug. 11 '95
0.080	Sep. 13	Oct. 27	Oct. 31	Nov. 15 '95

Data as orig. reptd.; bef. results of disc. opers. and/or spec. items. Per share data adj. for stk. divs. as of ex-div. date. E-Estimated. NA-Not Available. NM-Not Meaningful. NR-Not Ranked.

Office—2707 North Loop West, P.O. Box 1637, Houston, TX 77008. **Tel**—(713) 868-7700. **CEO & CFO**—R. L. Hargrave. **VP & Secy**—L. E. Wilson. **Investor Contact**—David R. Stewart (713-868-7657). **Dirs**—O. C. Clay, J. T. Currie, R. L. Hargrave, J. W. Lander, J. C. Manning, B. H. O'Neal, R. H. Parsley, B. H. Rowe, D. E. Stevenson, C. J. Stewart II, R. R. Stewart, R. S. Sullivan. **Transfer Agent & Registrar**—Bank of New York, NYC. **Incorporated** in Texas in 1947. **Empl**-4,300. **S&P Analyst:** Leo Larkin

STANDARD & POOR'S

Stock Reports

Storage Technology

NYSE Symbol **STK**
In S&P MidCap 400

07-AUG-95 **Industry:** Data Processing

Summary: Storage Technology manufactures and markets high-performance, computer information storage and retrieval disk and tape subsystems.

S&P Opinion: Hold (★★★)

Recent Price • 24⅞
52 Wk Range • 39⅛-17⅞
Yield • Nil
12-Mo. P/E • 33.6

Quantitative Evaluations
Outlook (1 Lowest—5 Highest) • **4-**
Fair Value • **27⅜**
Risk • **High**
Earn./Div. Rank • **C**

Technical Eval. • **Bearish** since 7/95
Rel. Strength Rank (1 Lowest—99 Highest) • **57**
Insider Activity • **NA**

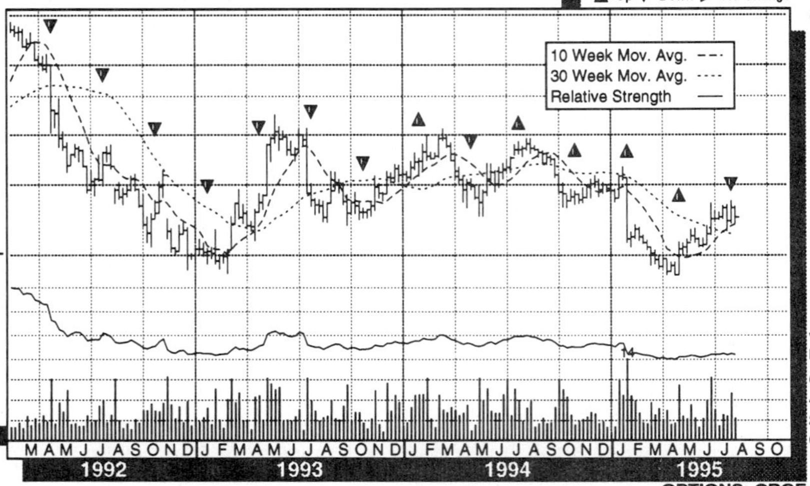

OPTIONS: CBOE

Overview - 07-AUG-95

Revenue should continue to rise through 1996, aided by strong demand for the company's tape and DASD storage products and contributions from the acquisition of Network Systems Corp. Demand for the current mainstay of tape libraries remains strong, and sales of the Iceberg data storage subsystem should improve with recent enhancements in performance and functionality. New product introductions are expected to further strengthen STK's competitive position. Operating margins should be maintained, as a more favorable product mix, manufacturing cost reductions and continued expense controls offset competitive price pressures.

Valuation - 07-AUG-95

Earnings in 1996 are expected to advance over 20% above the levels projected for 1995. The company's competitive position remains solid and should improve further with the roll out of additional storage offerings and enhancements to existing products. While the multiple attached to the projected earnings is low, the stock appears fairly valued in light of the potential risk of an earnings disappointment, stemming from competitive product and pricing pressures, as well as uncertainties related to the smooth integration of acquired Network Systems. The stock is expected to track the market in the months ahead.

Key Stock Statistics

S&P EPS Est. 1995	1.80	Tang. Bk. Value/Share	20.64
P/E on S&P Est. 1995	13.8	Beta	1.67
S&P EPS Est. 1996	2.20	Shareholders	19,600
Dividend Rate/Share	Nil	Market cap. (B)	$ 1.3
Shs. outstg. (M)	52.5	Inst. holdings	58%
Avg. daily vol. (M)	0.586	Insider holdings	NA

Value of $10,000 invested 5 years ago: $ 21,170

Fiscal Year Ending Dec. 31

	1995	% Change	1994	% Change	1993	% Change
Revenues (Million $)						
1Q	450.2	34%	335.6	NM	339.0	1%
2Q	480.7	33%	360.9	NM	358.5	-7%
3Q	—	—	412.3	34%	307.1	-21%
4Q	—	—	516.2	29%	400.2	-3%
Yr.	—	—	1,625	16%	1,405	-8%
Income (Million $)						
1Q	-8.91	NM	-19.59	NM	4.02	-68%
2Q	11.86	-17%	14.36	NM	-5.28	NM
3Q	—	—	18.55	NM	-122.9	NM
4Q	—	—	28.11	NM	6.35	NM
Yr.	—	—	41.44	NM	-117.8	NM
Earnings Per Share ($)						
1Q	-0.23	NM	-0.52	NM	0.08	-73%
2Q	0.17	-35%	0.26	NM	-0.19	NM
3Q	E0.46	—	0.35	NM	-2.94	NM
4Q	E1.40	—	0.56	NM	0.08	NM
Yr.	E1.80	—	0.66	NM	-2.98	NM

Next earnings report expected: late October

Business Summary - 07-AUG-95

Storage Technology is engaged in the design, manufacture, marketing and service of information storage and retrieval subsystems for high-performance and midrange computer systems, as well as for computer networks. Revenue sources in recent years were:

	1994	1993	1992
Serial access subsystems	64%	62%	62%
Random access subsystems	16%	9%	11%
Midrange systems	16%	22%	21%
Other	5%	7%	6%

International sales accounted for 39% of total revenue in 1994, compared with 37% in 1993.

The company's serial access (or tape) subsystems are based on its automated cartridge system (ACS) library, which automates the process of locating, transporting and mounting storage tapes in STK cartridge drives. Products include the Powderhorn 9310, a second generation ACS library; Wolfcreek 9360, a smaller, high-performance, lower cost library; and Timberline and Silverton, 36-track cartridge subsystems. STK's tape products operate in mainframe and other computer environments.

Random access subsystems consist of online random access DASD products including Iceberg 9200, a fault-tolerant disk array subsystem for the IBM compatible mainframe environment, and Arctic Fox 9800, a high performance shared access facility.

STK also offers software enhancement products for data management and access. The company sold the lease assets of its Distributed Systems Division, which served the midrange storage market, in June 1995.

Important Developments

Jul. '95—Revenues and earnings in the second quarter of 1995 were below original expectations, which the company attributed to customer anticipation of certain important feature enhancements to Iceberg.

Jun. '95—The company sold the lease assets of its Storagetek Distributed Systems Division (DSD) to a unit of AT&T Corp. STK said it would continue to serve its mid-range and open-systems customers via marketing and customer services activities and sell its storage solutions in these marketplaces through the integration of DSD into its core operations.

Apr. '95—During the first quarter of 1995, STK recorded \$20.7 million (\$0.35 a share) in charges including \$14.4 million for costs related to the acquisition of Network Systems Corp., a supplier of networking products with annual sales of \$250 million.

Capitalization

Long Term Debt: \$261,856,000 (6/95), incl. \$30.3 million of nonrecourse borrowings.

\$3.50 Conv. Exch. Preferred Stock: 3,450,000 shs. (liquid. pref. \$50).

Per Share Data (\$) (Year Ended Dec. 31)

	1994	1993	1992	1991	1990	1989
Tangible Bk. Val.	19.52	19.34	22.25	21.80	16.14	13.12
Cash Flow	5.29	0.52	3.58	5.05	4.78	4.39
Earnings	0.66	-2.98	0.37	2.33	2.22	1.40
Dividends	Nil	Nil	Nil	Nil	Nil	Nil
Payout Ratio	Nil	NM	Nil	Nil	Nil	Nil
Prices - High	41½	45	78	51½	35¼	22½
- Low	25	18	18⅜	17¾	11	9¼
P/E Ratio - High	63	NM	NM	22	16	16
- Low	38	NM	NM	8	5	7

Income Statement Analysis (Million \$)

	1994	%Chg	1993	%Chg	1992	%Chg	1991
Revs.	1,625	16%	1,405	-8%	1,521	-4%	1,585
Oper. Inc.	277	174%	101	-33%	150	-24%	198
Depr.	206	37%	150	11%	135	24%	109
Int. Exp.	40.7	-7%	43.7	-8%	47.6	-7%	51.4
Pretax Inc.	58.0	NM	-112	NM	34.0	-68%	106
Eff. Tax Rate	29%	—	NM	—	55%	—	12%
Net Inc.	41.0	NM	-117	NM	15.0	-84%	93.0

Balance Sheet & Other Fin. Data (Million \$)

	1994	1993	1992	1991	1990	1989
Cash	206	271	118	175	64.0	61.0
Curr. Assets	923	874	768	866	515	478
Total Assets	1,890	1,793	1,710	1,700	1,048	977
Curr. Liab.	449	406	413	439	300	276
LT Debt	357	362	370	372	216	360
Common Eqty.	902	833	919	884	530	337
Total Cap.	1,442	1,387	1,297	1,261	748	698
Cap. Exp.	131	68.0	105	111	141	240
Cash Flow	236	22.0	150	202	152	114

Ratio Analysis

	1994	1993	1992	1991	1990	1989
Curr. Ratio	2.1	2.2	1.9	2.0	1.7	1.7
% LT Debt of Cap.	24.8	26.1	28.5	29.5	28.9	51.5
% Net Inc.of Revs.	2.5	NM	1.0	5.9	6.2	3.7
% Ret. on Assets	2.2	NM	0.9	6.2	6.1	3.8
% Ret. on Equity	3.3	NM	1.7	12.1	14.7	11.1

Dividend Data (No common dividends have ever been paid. A "poison pill" stock purchase rights plan was renewed in 1990.)

Data as orig. reptd.; bef. results of disc. opers. and/or spec. items. Per share data adj. for stk. divs. as of ex-div. date. E-Estimated. NA-Not Available. NM-Not Meaningful. NR-Not Ranked.

Office—2270 South 88th St., Louisville, CO 80028-4309. **Tel**—(303) 673-5151. **Chrmn & Pres**—R. R. Poppa. **VP & CFO**—D. E. Lacey. **Investor Contact**—Michael Klatman. **Dirs**—J. E. N. Albino, W. L. Armstrong, R. A. Burgin, P. Friedman, W. R. Hoover, S. J. Keane, R. E. LaBlanc, R. E. Lee, R. R. Poppa, H. Shull, R. C. Steadman, R. C. Wilson. **Transfer Agent**—American Stock Transfer, NYC. **Incorporated** in Delaware in 1969. **Empl**-11,157. **S&P Analyst:** Peter C. Wood, CFA

STANDARD & POOR'S

STOCK REPORTS

Stratus Computer

NYSE Symbol **SRA**
In S&P MidCap 400

31-AUG-95 **Industry:** Data Processing

Summary: This company offers a broad range of continuously available computer platforms, application software, middleware and professional services for critical on-line computing.

S&P Opinion: Accumulate (★★★★) | Recent Price • 25¾ | Yield • Nil | 52 Wk Range • 39⅞-23 | 12-Mo. P/E • 14.1

Quantitative Evaluations

Outlook (1 Lowest—5 Highest)
• **1-**

Fair Value
• **22⅝**

Risk
• **High**

Earn./Div. Rank
• **B+**

Technical Eval.
• **Bullish** since 8/93

Rel. Strength Rank (1 Lowest—99 Highest)
• **46**

Insider Activity
• **Neutral**

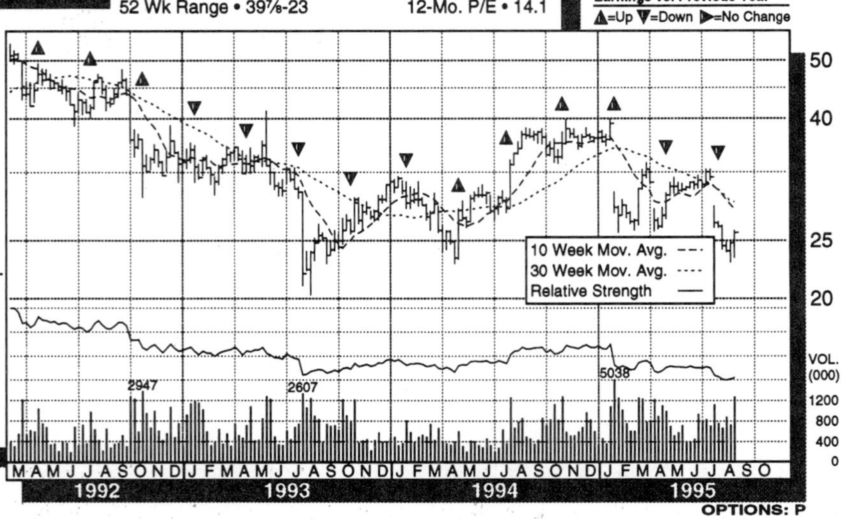

OPTIONS: P

Overview - 31-AUG-95

Revenues are projected to decline about 2% in 1995, as strong service revenue growth outweighs depressed product sales. Transition issues related to a new product line led to a 17% and 14% drop in product revenues, in the first two quarters of 1995 respectively. We are expecting further but moderating product revenue declines for the balance of the year, offset by continued 20%+ growth in service revenues. Gross margins are expected to narrow further, although at a much slower rate than seen in the first half, as cost cuts temper the lower margins on the new product line. Further cost cutting in R&D and SG&A categories should lead to a rebound in EPS from the depressed first half levels. Our EPS projection of $1.65 for 1995 excludes a $20 million restructuring charge to be taken in the third quarter.

Valuation - 31-AUG-95

We have upgraded our opinion on the shares to accumulate from hold, due to recently announced workforce reductions that are expected to save $60 million annually. We are encouraged by these aggressive actions in light of the lower gross margins on SRA's new product line. Just as importantly, these cuts should provide substantial operating leverage, as underscored by our sharply higher EPS projection for 1996. With the shares trading at a low multiple to this estimate and because we believe there is additional upside to this projection if revenue growth accelerates, we now recommend that investors accumulate the shares for their above-average appreciation potential.

Key Stock Statistics

S&P EPS Est. 1995	1.65	Tang. Bk. Value/Share	19.59
P/E on S&P Est. 1995	15.6	Beta	2.08
S&P EPS Est. 1996	3.10	Shareholders	1,600
Dividend Rate/Share	Nil	Market cap. (B)	$0.653
Shs. outstg. (M)	23.5	Inst. holdings	88%
Avg. daily vol. (M)	0.298	Insider holdings	NA

Value of $10,000 invested 5 years ago: $ 11,195

Fiscal Year Ending Dec. 31

	1995	% Change	1994	% Change	1993	% Change
Revenues (Million $)						
1Q	128.5	-5%	135.4	18%	114.6	4%
2Q	140.3	-3%	144.4	16%	124.1	6%
3Q	—	—	145.8	15%	126.8	2%
4Q	—	—	151.0	2%	148.1	10%
Yr.	—	—	576.6	12%	513.7	6%
Income (Million $)						
1Q	6.41	-44%	11.39	29%	8.82	-22%
2Q	6.09	-65%	17.37	29%	13.50	NM
3Q	—	—	18.81	66%	11.36	-24%
4Q	—	—	13.42	NM	-17.07	NM
Yr.	—	—	60.98	NM	16.61	-71%
Earnings Per Share ($)						
1Q	0.26	-43%	0.46	24%	0.37	-24%
2Q	0.26	-63%	0.71	25%	0.57	-2%
3Q	E0.45	-41%	0.76	58%	0.48	-24%
4Q	E0.70	30%	0.54	NM	-0.72	NM
Yr.	E1.65	-33%	2.47	NM	0.70	-71%

Next earnings report expected: late October

Stratus Computer

Business Summary - 31-AUG-95

Stratus Computer manufactures fault-tolerant computer systems designed for normal and continuous operation despite failure of hardware or software components. It also provides application software, middleware and professional services. Revenues by product line/sales channel in recent years were:

	1994	1993
Direct product sales	60%	63%
Distributors	7%	6%
OEM	6%	8%
Services/Education	27%	23%

International revenues accounted for 46% of the total in 1994, up from 44% in each of the three prior years.

SRA systems are used primarily for on-line transaction processing (OLTP) and other interactive applications in which data integrity, system availability and rapid, high-volume processing are critical. Vertical industry markets targeted include telecommunications (22% of 1994 revenues), banking (11%), retail (7%), securities/trading (5%), gaming (4%) and travel (3%).

The company's proprietary architecture uses comparative circuitry, duplication of inexpensive off-the-shelf microprocessors, and a proprietary Virtual Operating System (VOS) designed specifically for OLTP or Stratus FTX, a UNIX System V.4-based operating system. The multiprocessor architecture allows the system to handle heavy transaction loads efficiently, with multiple users accessing data simultaneously. SRA's XA/R hardware family consists of 12 fully compatible software systems from entry-level models through powerful mainframe-class platforms.

In January 1995, SRA acquired London-based AST/Transact LTD., a provider of retail bank application software and professional services. In November 1994, TCAM Systems, a software and consulting firm targeting the securities industry, was purchased. Three companies were acquired in late 1993: Shared Financial Systems (software and professional services); BellSouth Systems Integration (communications middleware and services); and Isis Distributed Systems (advanced middleware products).

Important Developments

Aug. '95—SRA said that it was reducing its workforce by 18% (500 people), resulting in a one-time charge against third quarter earnings of $20 million. The company took this action to bring its cost structure in line with the economic reality of lower gross profit margins experienced in recent quarters.

Jul. '95—The company announced that it renewed its reseller agreement with Oracle Corp., under which it will distribute Oracle products worldwide.

Capitalization

Long Term Obligations: $7,991,000 (7/2/95).

Per Share Data ($)

(Year Ended Dec. 31)

	1994	1993	1992	1991	1990	1989
Tangible Bk. Val.	20.31	17.95	17.03	14.18	11.15	9.12
Cash Flow	4.11	2.18	3.78	3.51	2.72	2.52
Earnings	2.47	0.70	2.43	2.22	1.77	1.71
Dividends	Nil	Nil	Nil	Nil	Nil	Nil
Payout Ratio	Nil	Nil	Nil	Nil	Nil	Nil
Prices - High	39⅞	41¼	54¼	51½	29	35¼
- Low	22⅞	20¼	29½	20⅜	14⅝	19¼
P/E Ratio - High	16	59	22	23	16	21
- Low	9	29	12	9	8	11

Income Statement Analysis (Million $)

	1994	%Chg	1993	%Chg	1992	%Chg	1991
Revs.	577	12%	514	6%	486	8%	449
Oper. Inc.	118	17%	101	1%	100	10%	91.0
Depr.	40.4	15%	35.1	10%	31.8	10%	28.9
Int. Exp.	1.1	86%	0.6	-43%	1.0	-46%	1.9
Pretax Inc.	77.1	151%	30.7	-57%	72.1	10%	65.4
Eff. Tax Rate	21%	—	46%	—	21%	—	24%
Net Inc.	61.0	NM	16.6	-71%	56.9	14%	49.7

Balance Sheet & Other Fin. Data (Million $)

	1994	1993	1992	1991	1990	1989
Cash	230	191	135	98.0	43.0	32.0
Curr. Assets	438	416	351	306	242	197
Total Assets	613	559	467	385	321	274
Curr. Liab.	113	109	73.6	64.1	71.9	60.7
LT Debt	7.8	6.4	0.5	2.6	14.3	29.4
Common Eqty.	490	436	390	314	230	184
Total Cap.	498	442	390	317	245	213
Cap. Exp.	53.9	33.7	60.8	31.5	27.4	37.0
Cash Flow	101	51.7	88.7	78.6	56.9	52.3

Ratio Analysis

	1994	1993	1992	1991	1990	1989
Curr. Ratio	3.9	3.8	4.8	4.8	3.4	3.2
% LT Debt of Cap.	1.6	1.5	0.1	0.8	5.8	13.8
% Net Inc.of Revs.	10.6	3.2	11.7	11.1	9.2	10.4
% Ret. on Assets	10.4	3.2	13.2	13.6	12.3	14.8
% Ret. on Equity	13.1	3.9	16.0	17.7	17.7	21.7

Dividend Data —No dividends have been paid. A "poison pill" stock purchase rights plan was adopted in 1990.

Data as orig. reptd.; bef. results of disc. opers. and/or spec. items. Per share data adj. for stk. divs. as of ex-div. date. E-Estimated. NA-Not Available. NM-Not Meaningful. NR-Not Ranked.

Office—55 Fairbanks Blvd., Marlborough, MA 01752. **Tel**—(508) 460-2000. **Chrmn & CEO**—W. E. Foster. **Pres**—G. E. Haroian. **VP-Fin & CFO**—R. E. Donahue. **Clerk**—F. S. Prifty. **Investor Contact**—Peter Christiana. **Dirs**—A. V. d'Arbeloff, A. Carr, P. J. Ferri, W. E. Foster, G. E. Haroian, G. C Hendrie, R. M. Morrill, C. M. Obourn. **Transfer Agent**—First National Bank of Boston. **Incorporated** in Massachusetts in 1980. **Empl**-2,878. **S&P Analyst:** John D. Coyle, CFA

STANDARD & POOR'S
STOCK REPORTS

Structural Dynamics Research

NASDAQ Symbol **SDRC**
In S&P MidCap 400

05-AUG-95

Industry:
Data Processing

Summary: This company supplies mechanical design automation software and services used for the design, analysis, testing and manufacture of sophisticated mechanical products.

S&P Opinion: Hold (★★★)

Recent Price • 13⅛
52 Wk Range • 15-3⅝
Yield • Nil
12-Mo. P/E • NM

Quantitative Evaluations
Outlook
(1 Lowest—5 Highest)
• **5+**
Fair Value
• **14**
Risk
• **High**
Earn./Div. Rank
• **C**

Technical Eval.
• **Bearish** since 3/95
Rel. Strength Rank
(1 Lowest—99 Highest)
• **76**
Insider Activity
• **Unfavorable**

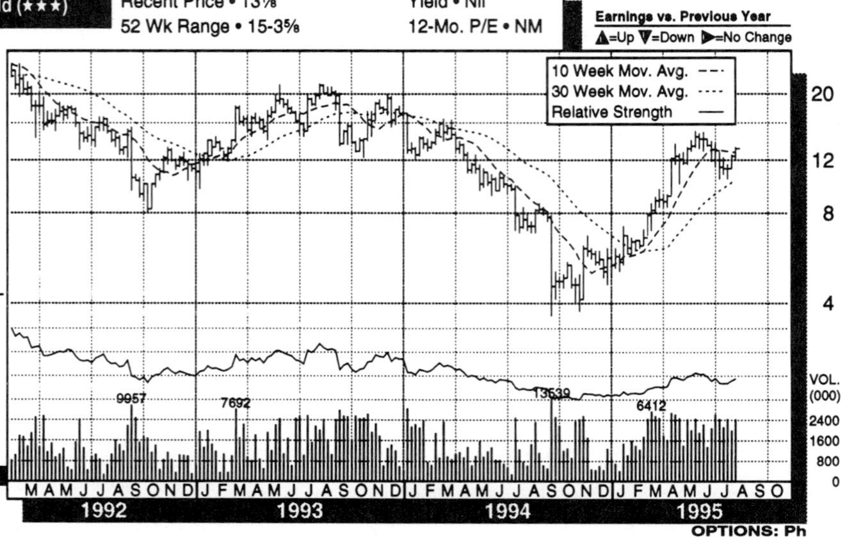

Overview - 03-AUG-95

Revenues through 1996 are expected to increase, reflecting continued demand for the company's flagship I-DEAS mechanical design automation software product and related services. Operations should be increasingly profitable, aided by the higher volume and well controlled expenses. The demand for mechanical design related products is associated with general business conditions; therefore, a general strengthening in the economies of such key markets as Germany and Japan as well as the U.S. would be beneficial.

Valuation - 03-AUG-95

Following a year-long slide, the shares of this mechanical design automation software vendor rebounded sharply off the lows reached in late 1994, and currently trade close to their 52-week high. The shares have benefited from the final resolution of certain accounting irregularities and the restatement of prior years' financial statements, together with a general uptick in business. The company has returned to profitability, and strong earnings growth is expected even though the mechanical design automation software market is very competitive and somewhat tied to the general economy, which currently seems lackluster. We expect the shares to track the market in the coming months.

Key Stock Statistics

S&P EPS Est. 1995	0.30	Tang. Bk. Value/Share	2.55
P/E on S&P Est. 1995	43.8	Beta	2.24
S&P EPS Est. 1996	0.60	Shareholders	4,900
Dividend Rate/Share	Nil	Market cap. (B)	$0.390
Shs. outstg. (M)	29.7	Inst. holdings	54%
Avg. daily vol. (M)	0.462	Insider holdings	NA

Value of $10,000 invested 5 years ago: $ 17,796

Fiscal Year Ending Dec. 31

	1995	% Change	1994	% Change	1993	% Change
Revenues (Million $)						
1Q	43.81	19%	36.80	—	--	—
2Q	46.78	10%	42.70	—	--	—
3Q	—	—	42.50	—	--	—
4Q	—	—	45.54	—	--	—
Yr.	—	—	167.6	14%	147.6	NM
Income (Million $)						
1Q	0.27	NM	-4.30	—	—	—
2Q	3.06	91%	1.60	—	—	—
3Q	—	—	0.10	—	—	—
4Q	—	—	-6.29	—	—	—
Yr.	—	—	-9.00	NM	-11.70	NM
Earnings Per Share ($)						
1Q	0.01	NM	-0.14	—	--	—
2Q	0.10	100%	0.05	—	--	—
3Q	E0.09	—	Nil	—	--	—
4Q	E0.10	—	-0.22	—	--	—
Yr.	E0.30	—	-0.31	NM	-0.39	NM

Next earnings report expected: late October

Structural Dynamics Research

Business Summary - 04-AUG-95

Structural Dynamics Research Corporation (SDRC) is a leading international supplier of mechanical design automation software and engineering services used by automotive, aerospace and industrial manufacturers for the design, analysis, testing and manufacturing of sophisticated mechanical products.

The company's software and services are intended to reduce product development time and costs, and to improve product quality by enabling customers to optimize product designs prior to production.

I-DEAS, SDRC's flagship mechanical design automation software system, provides design engineers with solid modeling, finite-element modeling and analysis, computer-aided testing, drafting and manufacturing. The I-DEAS system, which allows all members of a product development team to evaluate multiple designs and manufacturing processes before final production, is available on leading engineering workstations, minicomputers and mainframes.

Software products are sold to end-users primarily through a direct sales force. The company also markets its products by means of original equipment manufacturers, distributors, value added resellers and hardware suppliers.

SDRC's engineering services division provides mechanical engineering consulting services to improve the design of its customers' products, as well as its customers' engineering and manufacturing processes. The company also offers its clients advanced training and technology transfer services. Engineering services are offered in the areas of design audits, product design, engineering process development and troubleshooting.

Important Developments

Jul. '95—Revenues in the three months ended June 30, 1995, rose 9.5%, year to year, as gains in maintenance and engineering services outweighed a fractional decline in software product and services revenue. Margins widened on well controlled expenses, and following lower equity losses of affiliates, net income nearly doubled.

Jan. '95—The company restated its financial results for the first half of 1994 and the years 1993, 1992 and 1991; pretax income was reduced by about $31.4 million for the period, owing to invalid sales transactions in Far East operations. An additional $30.4 million reduction of pretax income was recorded for the period upon examination of the company's business practices and internal controls.

Capitalization

Long Term Debt: None (6/95).

Per Share Data ($) (Year Ended Dec. 31)

	1994	1993	1992	1991	1990	1989
Tangible Bk. Val.	2.50	2.95	3.29	2.97	2.67	2.11
Cash Flow	-0.07	NA	NA	NA	0.70	0.57
Earnings	-0.31	-0.39	0.29	0.33	0.49	0.37
Dividends	Nil	Nil	Nil	Nil	Nil	Nil
Payout Ratio	Nil	Nil	Nil	Nil	Nil	Nil
Prices - High	17⅛	21⅝	30	29¼	13⅞	7½
- Low	3⅝	9⅝	8	11⅞	6⅞	4¼
P/E Ratio - High	NM	NM	NM	89	29	20
- Low	NM	NM	NM	34	14	11

Income Statement Analysis (Million $)

	1994	%Chg	1993	%Chg	1992	%Chg	1991
Revs.	168	14%	148	NM	149	15%	130
Oper. Inc.	4.9	—	NA	—	NA	—	NA
Depr.	7.0	—	NA	—	NA	—	NA
Int. Exp.	Nil	—	Nil	—	Nil	—	0.1
Pretax Inc.	-5.2	NM	-7.4	NM	13.9	-4%	14.5
Eff. Tax Rate	NM	—	NM	—	37%	—	36%
Net Inc.	-9.0	NM	-11.7	NM	8.8	-5%	9.3

Balance Sheet & Other Fin. Data (Million $)

	1994	1993	1992	1991	1990	1989
Cash	39.2	45.5	52.4	47.8	43.2	36.0
Curr. Assets	88.0	77.1	91.8	79.1	79.0	61.8
Total Assets	143	135	136	119	107	86.0
Curr. Liab.	60.3	49.6	43.3	33.9	29.5	25.2
LT Debt	Nil	Nil	Nil	Nil	2.6	2.8
Common Eqty.	72.0	84.6	92.4	80.4	68.4	52.5
Total Cap.	72.0	84.6	92.4	80.4	77.0	61.0
Cap. Exp.	5.0	6.4	9.1	11.3	7.0	6.8
Cash Flow	-2.0	NA	NA	NA	19.2	15.0

Ratio Analysis

	1994	1993	1992	1991	1990	1989
Curr. Ratio	1.5	1.6	2.1	2.3	2.7	2.5
% LT Debt of Cap.	Nil	Nil	Nil	Nil	3.4	4.5
% Net Inc.of Revs.	NM	NM	5.9	7.1	11.2	10.4
% Ret. on Assets	NM	NM	6.9	NA	13.6	12.5
% Ret. on Equity	NM	NM	10.2	NA	21.7	20.7

Dividend Data (No cash dividends have been paid. A "poison pill" stock purchase rights plan was adopted in 1988.)

Data as orig. reptd.; bef. results of disc. opers. and/or spec. items. Per share data adj. for stk. divs. as of ex-div. date. E-Estimated. NA-Not Available. NM-Not Meaningful. NR-Not Ranked.

Office—2000 Eastman Dr., Milford, OH 45150. **Tel**—(513) 576-2400. **Chrmn**— W. P. Conlin. **Pres & CEO**—A. F. Peter. **VP & Secy**—J. A. Mongelluzzo. **Dirs**—W. P. Conlin, R. P. Henderson, B. B. Hudson, T. H. McCourtney, Jr., J. E. McDowell, J. W. Nethercott, A. F. Peter, A. B. Sims, G. R. Whitaker, Jr. **Transfer Agent**—Fifth Third Bank, Cincinnati. **Empl**- 1,166. **S&P Analyst:** Peter C. Wood, CFA

STANDARD & POOR'S

STOCK REPORTS

Stryker Corporation

NASDAQ Symbol **STRY**

In S&P MidCap 400

05-SEP-95 **Industry:** Medical equipment/ supply

Summary: Stryker makes specialty surgical and medical products such as orthopedic implants, endoscopic items and hospital beds, and operates a chain of physical therapy clinics.

S&P Opinion: Hold (★★★)

Recent Price • 43⅞ | Yield • 0.2%
52 Wk Range • 48⅞-32¾ | 12-Mo. P/E • 26.8

Quantitative Evaluations

Outlook (1 Lowest—5 Highest)
• 3⁻

Fair Value
• 43⅝

Risk
• Average

Earn./Div. Rank
• A-

Technical Eval.
• Bullish since 7/95

Rel. Strength Rank (1 Lowest—99 Highest)
• 56

Insider Activity
• Neutral

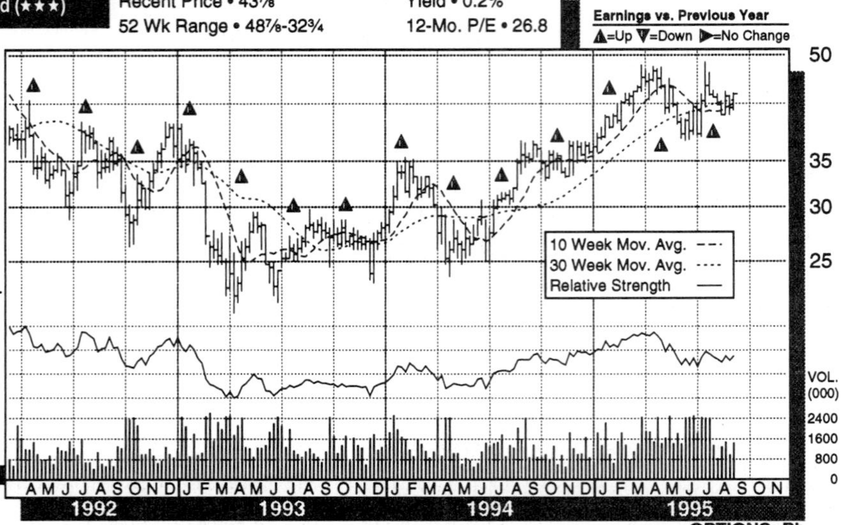

OPTIONS: Ph

Overview - 05-SEP-95

Stryker has historically been able to grow through market penetration and new product development. Sales are projected to rise about 15%, to $1 billion, in 1996, paced by gains for orthopedic implants, powered surgical instruments, endoscopic products and specialty hospital stretchers and beds. Another strong advance is also indicated for outpatient rehabilitation center revenues, aided by an aggressive acquisition program. Despite recent increases in the ratio of SG&A to sales, overall margins should be well maintained for the balance of 1995 and through 1996. The company is expected to maintain its long-term 20% annual earnings growth goal in 1996.

Valuation - 05-SEP-95

The shares have been erratic performers in recent months, following a strong rise in the 12 months through March 1995. Investor concerns included competition in the orthopedic market, and the impact of likely cuts in Medicare and Medicaid on future hospital spending. Hospital markets are also under pressure from rising managed care cost containment presures. In addition, medical device markets remain subject to risks of obsolescence resulting from technological advances. However, Stryker has chalked up an outstanding record (1994 marked its 18th consecutive year of 20% annual earnings growth), and should continue to produce above-average earnings growth in coming years. The shares remain a long-term hold.

Key Stock Statistics

S&P EPS Est. 1995	1.80	Tang. Bk. Value/Share	7.79
P/E on S&P Est. 1995	24.4	Beta	1.78
S&P EPS Est. 1996	2.15	Shareholders	2,900
Dividend Rate/Share	0.08	Market cap. (B)	$ 2.1
Shs. outstg. (M)	48.4	Inst. holdings	37%
Avg. daily vol. (M)	0.255	Insider holdings	NA

Value of $10,000 invested 5 years ago: $ 35,708

Fiscal Year Ending Dec. 31

	1995	% Change	1994	% Change	1993	% Change
Revenues (Million $)						
1Q	214.0	44%	148.8	10%	135.0	19%
2Q	228.5	48%	154.2	10%	140.0	20%
3Q	—	—	174.3	27%	136.9	17%
4Q	—	—	204.6	41%	145.2	12%
Yr.	—	—	681.9	22%	557.3	17%
Income (Million $)						
1Q	20.80	20%	17.34	20%	14.45	31%
2Q	20.41	20%	17.01	22%	14.00	27%
3Q	—	—	16.37	17%	13.99	27%
4Q	—	—	21.32	20%	17.77	22%
Yr.	—	—	72.40	20%	60.21	26%
Earnings Per Share ($)						
1Q	0.43	19%	0.36	20%	0.30	30%
2Q	0.42	20%	0.35	21%	0.29	26%
3Q	E0.42	20%	0.35	21%	0.29	26%
4Q	E0.53	20%	0.44	19%	0.37	19%
Yr.	E1.80	20%	1.50	20%	1.25	25%

Next earnings report expected: mid October

Stryker Corporation

Business Summary - 05-SEP-95

Stryker Corporation produces a wide range of specialty surgical and medical products, which are sold in over 100 countries. In 1994, international sales accounted for 41% of revenues and 16% of operating profits.

In the area of surgical products (80% of 1994 sales), Stryker's principal specialty is orthopedics. Artificial joint replacements (primarily hips and knees), medical video cameras, arthroscopes, heavy-duty powered instruments, and pulsating irrigation systems are produced and sold for use by orthopedic surgeons. The company also designs and manufactures spinal implant systems.

The company's broad line of drills, saws, fixation and reaming equipment and other powered surgical instruments is used primarily by orthopedic surgeons; its small "micro" powered tools are used in oral and maxillofacial surgery, otology, neurosurgery, spinal surgery, podiatry and plastic surgery. Endoscopic systems, used in less-invasive surgery such as arthroscopy and laparoscopy, include miniature video cameras, a light source, endoscopes, and powered and manual instruments.

Other products include the CBC-Constavac system, a post-operative wound drainage and blood repurfusion device that enables joint replacement patients to receive their own blood rather than donor blood; the Haemocell system, an intraoperative blood filtration system to recover and reinfuse patient blood lost during surgery; and the High Vacuum Cement Injection System, used to mix and inject cement for implant applications.

The medical product line (20%) consists primarily of specialty stretchers and beds that facilitate the transportation, transfer and treatment of patients within the hospital. In addition, the Physiotherapy Associates subsidiary operates 135 outpatient rehabilitation centers in 14 states offering physical, occupational and speech therapy to patients with orthopedic or neurological injuries.

Important Developments

Jul. '95—A federal district court judge awarded Stryker $52.7 million, plus attorney's fees, in its patent suit against Intermedics Orthopedics Inc. Certain Intermedics hip products were found to have infringed on the company's patent on its Omniflex Hip system. Intermedics is expected to appeal the decision. Stryker is seeking to obtain an injunction to stop Intermedics from marketing the hip systems that were found to infringe on company patents.

Capitalization

Long Term Debt: $121,944,000 (6/95).
Minority Interest: $126,142,000.

Per Share Data ($)

(Year Ended Dec. 31)

	1994	1993	1992	1991	1990	1989
Tangible Bk. Val.	7.05	5.80	4.61	3.69	3.25	2.30
Cash Flow	1.93	1.58	1.24	0.94	0.65	0.54
Earnings	1.50	1.25	1.00	0.70	0.50	0.41
Dividends	0.08	0.07	0.06	0.05	Nil	Nil
Payout Ratio	5%	6%	6%	7%	Nil	Nil
Prices - High	37½	39¾	52¼	52¼	16⅞	12½
- Low	23¾	21	26¼	13¾	9⅝	6½
P/E Ratio - High	25	32	52	75	34	30
- Low	16	17	26	20	19	16

Income Statement Analysis (Million $)

	1994	%Chg	1993	%Chg	1992	%Chg	1991
Revs.	682	22%	557	17%	477	31%	365
Oper. Inc.	141	31%	108	27%	85.1	34%	63.4
Depr.	20.9	29%	16.2	42%	11.4	-3%	11.8
Int. Exp.	3.7	NM	1.1	161%	0.4	-38%	0.7
Pretax Inc.	128	33%	96.1	25%	76.9	44%	53.3
Eff. Tax Rate	40%	—	37%	—	38%	—	38%
Net Inc.	72.4	20%	60.2	26%	47.7	44%	33.1

Balance Sheet & Other Fin. Data (Million $)

	1994	1993	1992	1991	1990	1989
Cash	202	153	91.8	80.0	54.1	19.3
Curr. Assets	541	344	270	229	176	125
Total Assets	768	454	340	270	210	152
Curr. Liab.	179	130	101	88.0	58.0	36.0
LT Debt	95.3	31.3	1.4	1.4	1.9	2.7
Common Eqty.	358	288	232	180	148	112
Total Cap.	556	321	234	182	152	117
Cap. Exp.	29.2	20.2	31.6	16.6	11.9	7.1
Cash Flow	93.3	76.4	59.1	44.9	30.7	25.5

Ratio Analysis

	1994	1993	1992	1991	1990	1989
Curr. Ratio	3.0	2.6	2.7	2.6	3.0	3.5
% LT Debt of Cap.	17.1	9.8	0.6	0.8	1.3	2.3
% Net Inc.of Revs.	10.6	10.8	10.0	9.1	8.4	8.5
% Ret. on Assets	11.9	15.1	15.5	13.8	13.0	13.8
% Ret. on Equity	22.4	23.1	23.0	20.2	18.2	18.9

Dividend Data —In December 1994, a year-end cash dividend of $0.08 a share was declared, payable January 31, 1995, to shareholders of record December 30, 1994.

Amt. of Div. $	Date Decl.	Ex-Div. Date	Stock of Record	Payment Date
0.080	Dec. 15	Dec. 23	Jan. 30	Jan. 31 '95

Data as orig. reptd.; bef. results of disc. opers. and/or spec. items. Per share data adj. for stk. divs. as of ex-div. date. E-Estimated. NA-Not Available. NM-Not Meaningful. NR-Not Ranked.

Office—2725 Fairfield Rd., P.O. Box 4085, Kalamazoo, MI 49003-4085. **Tel**—(616) 385-2600. **Chrmn, Pres & CEO**—J. W. Brown. **VP, Secy & CFO**—D. J. Simpson. **Treas**—J. M. Paradine-Rice. **Contr**—D. H. Bergy. **Dirs**—J. W. Brown, H. E. Cox, Jr., D. M. Engelman, J. H. Grossman, J. S. Lillard, W. U. Parfet, R. E. Stryker. **Transfer Agent & Registrar**—First National Bank of Chicago. **Incorporated** in Michigan in 1946. **Empl**-4,221. **S&P Analyst:** Robert M. Gold

STANDARD & POOR'S

STOCK REPORTS

Sundstrand Corp.

NYSE Symbol **SNS**
In S&P MidCap 400

27-AUG-95 **Industry:** Aerospace

Summary: This major manufacturer of aircraft components also produces transmissions, heavy-duty gears, pumps and compressors for a broad range of industries.

S&P Opinion: Hold (★★★) | Recent Price • 68⅜ | Yield • 1.8% | 52 Wk Range • 69⅞-41¼ | 12-Mo. P/E • 32.7

Quantitative Evaluations
Outlook (1 Lowest—5 Highest) • 2+
Fair Value • 63¾
Risk • Low
Earn./Div. Rank • B

Technical Eval. • Bullish since 8/95
Rel. Strength Rank (1 Lowest—99 Highest) • 75
Insider Activity • Neutral

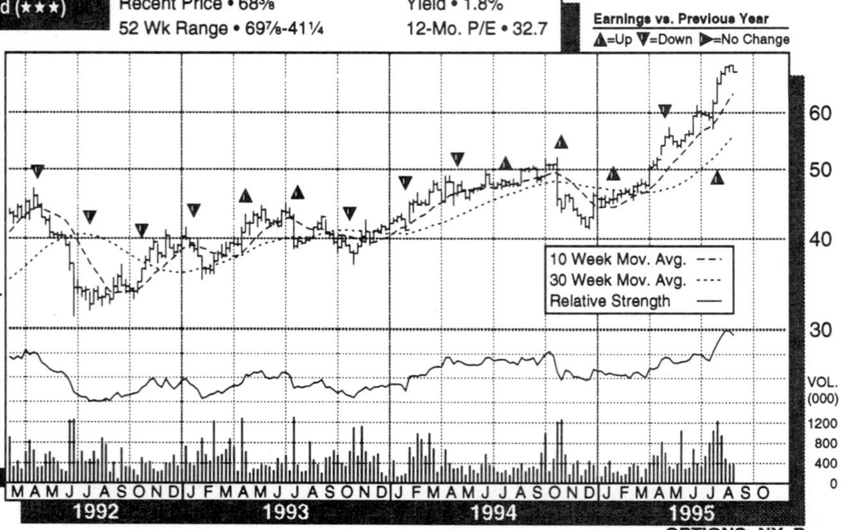

OPTIONS: NY, P

Overview - 25-AUG-95

Sales for 1995 are projected to climb about 10% from those of 1994. Aerospace sales may be up slightly, despite a continuing decline in military business, due to the recovery in the commercial markets. The restructuring of the Lima facility and the absence of some less-profitable non-core business units should boost aerospace margins. Industrial sales are forecast to advance between 15% and 20%, reflecting strong demand in the European markets for all three business units: Falk, Sullair and Milton Roy. Margin expansion is anticipated, on higher volume and a more favorable product mix. Results will be penalized by $61 million of restructuring charges.

Valuation - 25-AUG-95

A substantial rise in the shares since late 1994 reflects improvement in the airline industry and anticipation that 1995 will mark the end of four years of declining orders. Since SNS's electric power generating systems are used in virtually every jet plane manufactured in the Western Hemisphere, aerospace contributions would rebound. While the plant restructuring and the pickup in commercial aircraft orders should lift earnings, we are cautious about other factors. Results may be limited by the downsizing of certain commercial aerospace operations. In addition, weak domestic industrial sales may signal a cyclical slowing at Milton Roy and Sullair.

Key Stock Statistics

S&P EPS Est. 1995	2.30	Tang. Bk. Value/Share	6.23
P/E on S&P Est. 1995	29.7	Beta	1.21
S&P EPS Est. 1996	4.35	Shareholders	4,100
Dividend Rate/Share	1.20	Market cap. (B)	$ 2.1
Shs. outstg. (M)	31.3	Inst. holdings	83%
Avg. daily vol. (M)	0.107	Insider holdings	NA

Value of $10,000 invested 5 years ago: $ 24,799

Fiscal Year Ending Dec. 31

	1995	% Change	1994	% Change	1993	% Change
Revenues (Million $)						
1Q	346.0	7%	324.3	-5%	340.7	-11%
2Q	377.0	14%	331.1	-3%	341.8	-17%
3Q	—	—	339.7	5%	324.7	-22%
4Q	—	—	377.6	NM	375.9	-18%
Yr.	—	—	1,373	NM	1,383	-17%
Income (Million $)						
1Q	-18.00	NM	17.80	-29%	25.20	40%
2Q	27.00	41%	19.10	-1%	19.30	NM
3Q	—	—	23.70	53%	15.50	-41%
4Q	—	—	35.00	14%	30.70	-22%
Yr.	—	—	95.60	5%	90.70	9%
Earnings Per Share ($)						
1Q	-0.59	NM	0.54	-23%	0.70	40%
2Q	0.88	52%	0.58	7%	0.54	NM
3Q	E0.94	31%	0.72	64%	0.44	-40%
4Q	E1.05	-3%	1.08	23%	0.88	-19%
Yr.	E2.30	-21%	2.92	14%	2.56	11%

Next earnings report expected: mid October

Sundstrand Corp.

Business Summary - 25-AUG-95

Sundstrand is a major manufacturer of aircraft and aerospace components and industrial parts and equipment. Contributions by segment in 1994 were:

	Sales	Profits
Aerospace	52%	45%
Industrial	48%	55%

In 1995, sales outside the U.S. represented 36% of total revenues. Military sales (primarily to the U.S. government) accounted for 20%.

The aerospace group produces electrical, mechanical and hydraulic components used in commercial and military jets, including constant-speed drives and electric power regulators, actuation systems, fuel pumps and air valves, and other products used in engine starting and environmental control systems. The segment's largest product line, electric power systems, accounted for 62% of segment revenues in 1994 (60% in 1993). A substantial portion of sales is to the aftermarket.

The industrial group produces a broad range of products for the world's basic industries. It consists of three businesses. Milton Roy Co. produces precision pumps and analytical instruments. The Falk Corp. manufactures mechanical power transmissions, couplings, stationary fluid power drives and marine drives. Sullair Corp. makes rotary screw air and gas compressors, pneumatic tools, dryers and filters.

Important Developments

Jul. '95—The company said aerospace sales in the second quarter of 1995 rose 6.0%, year to year, and industrial sales increased 22%. Operating income, including $3 million of restructuring charges, jumped 33% in both divisions.

Jul. '95—Total backlog at June 30, 1995, was $946 million, versus $685 million a year earlier and $747 million at the end of 1994. Separately, SNS said that to date it had repurchased some 5.4 million of its common shares under a 1993 authorization to buy-back up to 10 million shares.

Jun. '95—Sundstrand sold its Spectronic Instruments, Inc. business for $19 million. The analytical instruments business had 1994 sales of $31 million.

Apr. '95—Sundstrand said that in the first 1995 quarter, it received a $172 million long-term contract to provide the propulsion system for the U.K.'s Royal Navy heavyweight torpedo program.

Capitalization

Long Term Debt: $243,000,000 (3/95).

Per Share Data ($) (Year Ended Dec. 31)

	1994	1993	1992	1991	1990	1989
Tangible Bk. Val.	6.57	7.11	6.19	13.03	13.76	12.63
Cash Flow	4.78	4.52	4.34	4.90	5.19	5.43
Earnings	2.92	2.56	2.31	3.02	3.15	3.09
Dividends	1.20	1.20	1.17	1.10	1.10	0.90
Payout Ratio	41%	47%	51%	37%	34%	29%
Prices - High	52	44¾	47¼	37	39⅞	41¾
- Low	41	35	31⅛	23⅜	21¾	25⅛
P/E Ratio - High	18	17	20	12	13	14
- Low	14	14	13	8	7	8

Income Statement Analysis (Million $)

	1994	%Chg	1993	%Chg	1992	%Chg	1991
Revs.	1,373	NM	1,383	-17%	1,673	NM	1,669
Oper. Inc.	238	-4%	248	-13%	286	-4%	299
Depr.	60.6	-13%	69.3	-5%	73.2	8%	67.7
Int. Exp.	30.0	-25%	40.0	-37%	63.0	-19%	78.0
Pretax Inc.	149	12%	133	2%	130	-25%	174
Eff. Tax Rate	36%	—	32%	—	36%	—	38%
Net Inc.	96.0	5%	91.0	10%	83.0	-24%	109

Balance Sheet & Other Fin. Data (Million $)

	1994	1993	1992	1991	1990	1989
Cash	65.8	15.4	5.2	8.4	5.9	18.0
Curr. Assets	735	693	915	945	897	895
Total Assets	1,587	1,512	1,804	1,720	1,582	1,503
Curr. Liab.	432	328	425	301	326	438
LT Debt	236	247	400	455	370	234
Common Eqty.	494	512	530	692	625	573
Total Cap.	730	759	939	1,340	1,189	1,033
Cap. Exp.	53.0	56.0	81.0	72.0	93.0	81.0
Cash Flow	156	160	157	177	181	201

Ratio Analysis

	1994	1993	1992	1991	1990	1989
Curr. Ratio	1.7	2.1	2.2	3.1	2.7	2.0
% LT Debt of Cap.	32.3	32.5	42.6	33.9	31.1	22.7
% Net Inc.of Revs.	7.0	6.6	5.0	6.5	7.2	7.6
% Ret. on Assets	6.3	5.7	4.7	6.6	7.6	7.9
% Ret. on Equity	19.5	18.1	13.6	16.5	19.6	21.4

Dividend Data —Dividends have been paid since 1940. A dividend reinvestment plan is available. A poison pill stock purchase rights plan was adopted in 1986.

Amt. of Div. $	Date Decl.	Ex-Div. Date	Stock of Record	Payment Date
0.300	Jun. 21	Aug. 30	Sep. 06	Sep. 20 '94
0.300	Nov. 15	Nov. 30	Dec. 06	Dec. 20 '94
0.300	Feb. 21	Mar. 01	Mar. 07	Mar. 21 '95
0.300	Apr. 18	May. 31	Jun. 06	Jun. 20 '95
0.300	Jun. 20	Aug. 31	Sep. 05	Sep. 19 '95

Data as orig. reptd.; bef. results of disc. opers. and/or spec. items. Per share data adj. for stk. divs. as of ex-div. date. E-Estimated. NA-Not Available. NM-Not Meaningful. NR-Not Ranked.

Office—4949 Harrison Ave., P.O. Box 7003, Rockford, IL 61125-7003. **Tel**—(815) 226-6000. **Chrmn & CEO**—D. R. O'Hare. **EVP & CFO**—P. Donovan. **VP & Secy**—R. M. Schilling. **Investor Contact**—Craig Watson (815-226-2136). **Dirs**—J. P. Bolduc, G. Grinstein, C. Marshall, K. H. Murmann, D. E. Nordlund, D. R. O'Hare, T. G. Pownall, J. A. Puelicher, W. Smith, R. J. Smuland, B. G. Wallin. **Transfer Agent & Registrar**—Harris Trust & Savings Bank, Chicago. **Incorporated** in Illinois in 1910; reincorporated in Delaware in 1966. **Empl-** 9,200. **S&P Analyst:** Joe Victor Shammas

STANDARD & POOR'S

STOCK REPORTS

Superior Industries Int'l

NYSE Symbol **SUP**

In S&P MidCap 400

15-SEP-95

Industry: Auto parts/equipment

Summary: This company is a leading maker of cast aluminum road wheels for automotive OEMs, as well as a producer of automotive aftermarket products.

S&P Opinion: Buy (★★★★★)

Recent Price • 28¼ | Yield • 0.8%

52 Wk Range • 35¾-23⅞ | 12-Mo. P/E • 14.0

Quantitative Evaluations

Outlook (1 Lowest—5 Highest)
• **4-**

Fair Value
• **30¾**

Risk
• **Average**

Earn./Div. Rank
• **A**

Technical Eval.
• **Bearish** since 7/95

Rel. Strength Rank (1 Lowest—99 Highest)
• **3**

Insider Activity
• **Unfavorable**

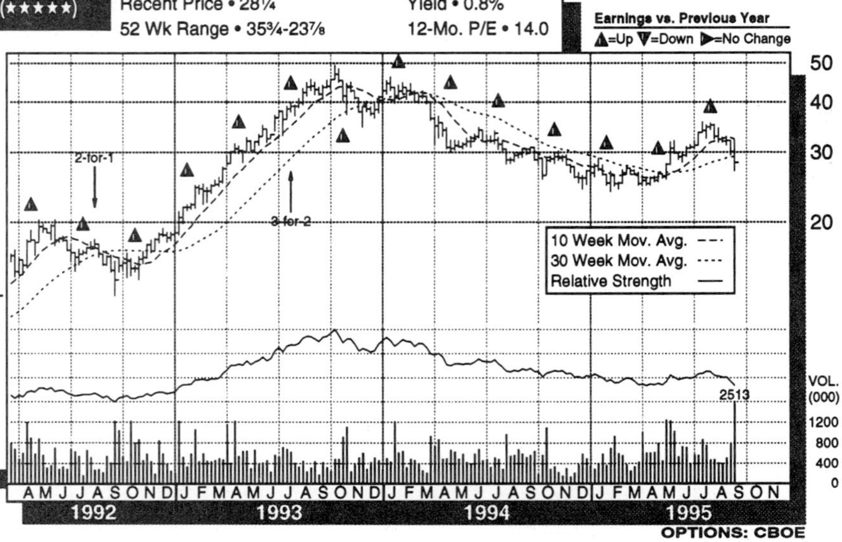

Overview - 15-SEP-95

Sales of cast aluminum automotive road wheels should continue to grow in 1996, reflecting improved production at recently opened plants, higher worldwide demand for aluminum wheels, new contracts with Japanese automakers, growing volume of chrome-plated aluminum wheels, and full operation of SUP's Mexican plant. Market penetration should also rise in 1996, as vehicle buyers opt for aesthetically pleasing aluminum wheels in place of traditional steel wheels. Changes in the price of aluminum should not affect overall profits because of cost pass-throughs in most contracts, and with expected resolution of issues which have slowed the start-up of a new chrome-plating facility we expect earnings to rise strongly in 1996. A stock repurchase program should continue to boost EPS.

Valuation - 15-SEP-95

We view the recent pullback in the shares on news of expected weak third quarter earnings as an opportunity to add to positions. The various factors affecting operations are temporary and should be resolved shortly. Overlooked are recent positive steps which will benefit future years. These include a contract with GM that seems to secure 40% of SUP's current business for the intermediate term, the start of construction of a plant in Hungary to supply the European market, and completion of development work with Alcoa on a line of medium-duty truck and bus wheels. The shares, trading at a significant discount to the S&P MidCap 400, are a favorite for capital appreciation.

Key Stock Statistics

S&P EPS Est. 1995	1.85	Tang. Bk. Value/Share	6.76
P/E on S&P Est. 1995	15.3	Beta	1.06
S&P EPS Est. 1996	2.25	Shareholders	1,300
Dividend Rate/Share	0.20	Market cap. (B)	$0.789
Shs. outstg. (M)	29.6	Inst. holdings	49%
Avg. daily vol. (M)	0.246	Insider holdings	NA

Value of $10,000 invested 5 years ago: $ 55,495

Fiscal Year Ending Dec. 31

	1995	% Change	1994	% Change	1993	% Change
Revenues (Million $)						
1Q	134.4	27%	105.9	8%	98.12	34%
2Q	142.8	18%	120.7	13%	106.9	24%
3Q	—	—	107.4	30%	82.81	13%
4Q	—	—	122.6	17%	105.2	14%
Yr.	—	—	456.6	16%	393.0	21%
Income (Million $)						
1Q	15.73	26%	12.52	24%	10.07	80%
2Q	16.70	8%	15.40	16%	13.25	75%
3Q	—	—	12.64	36%	9.29	51%
4Q	—	—	15.76	25%	12.58	36%
Yr.	—	—	56.32	25%	45.18	58%
Earnings Per Share ($)						
1Q	0.53	29%	0.41	24%	0.33	77%
2Q	0.56	10%	0.51	19%	0.43	74%
3Q	E0.30	-29%	0.42	40%	0.30	45%
4Q	E0.46	-12%	0.52	27%	0.41	34%
Yr.	E1.85	NM	1.85	26%	1.47	55%

Next earnings report expected: mid October

Superior Industries Int'l

Business Summary - 14-SEP-95

Superior Industries International produces cast aluminum road wheels for original equipment manufacturers (OEMs) (91% of sales in 1994 and 1993) and a variety of automotive aftermarket products (9%).

SUP is the leading supplier of aluminum wheels to Ford and General Motors which together accounted for 88% of sales in 1994. Industrywide aluminum wheel installations on North American vehicles have increased greatly in recent years, and SUP has benefited from a 40% share of the North American market. In 1994, unit shipments of OEM aluminum wheels climbed 15.5% from the level of 1993, which in turn was up 25% from 1992's level.

SUP's long-term goal is to broaden its customer base. Through a joint venture with Topy Industries Ltd., Japan's largest wheel producer, the company is developing sales in the U.S. and abroad to Japanese automakers, who are expected to account for 10% of sales in three to five years. Separately, contracts have been obtained from Jaguar and BMW. A joint project under way with Alcoa to develop a line of aluminum wheels for medium duty trucks and buses was nearing completion in mid-1995.

SUP operates six OEM casting plants with combined annual capacity of over 10 million aluminum wheels. Expansion projects will boost capacity to over 12 million wheels in 1995. An aluminum wheel chrome-plating facility was added to the flagship Fayetteville plant in late 1994 and could ultimately add $100 million to sales.

For the aftermarket, SUP produces one-piece cast aluminum, all-steel, composite steel and aluminum, and chrome-plated aluminum wheels, in styles to fit most vehicles. Related items include chrome-plated and locking lug nuts, hub covers and wire baskets. SUP also makes steering wheel covers, suspension and other accessories.

Important Developments

Sep. '95—SUP expects third quarter 1995 earnings to be 25% to 30% below the same 1994 period. The drop is primarily due to technical problems at the new chrome-plating facility and the depressed economy in Mexico which has caused the new plant in Chihuahua, Mexico to only produce for the U.S. market. The technical problems relating to waste processing will be resolved shortly with the installation of more processing capacity. Costs were also incurred to eliminate 400 employees due to transfer of some production from Fayetteville to Chihuahua, Mexico which is SUP's lowest cost plant. SUP expects at least a $0.26 a share positive swing in earnings in 1996 just from resolution of the chrome-plating problems. Based on orders, SUP expects shipments to rise by between 1.0 million and 1.5 million wheels in 1996 even with flat North American motor vehicle production.

Capitalization

Long Term Debt: $22,919,000 (6/30/95).

Per Share Data ($) (Year Ended Dec. 31)

	1994	1993	1992	1991	1990	1989
Tangible Bk. Val.	6.75	5.88	4.56	3.58	3.02	2.70
Cash Flow	2.73	2.14	1.65	1.07	0.84	0.82
Earnings	1.85	1.47	0.95	0.63	0.43	0.56
Dividends	0.15	0.08	0.10	0.09	0.08	0.08
Payout Ratio	8%	6%	10%	14%	19%	13%
Prices - High	$46\frac{1}{4}$	$49\frac{3}{8}$	$20\frac{3}{8}$	$11\frac{1}{8}$	$7\frac{3}{4}$	$7\frac{3}{8}$
- Low	$24\frac{1}{4}$	$18\frac{5}{8}$	$10\frac{3}{4}$	$5\frac{1}{4}$	$4\frac{1}{2}$	$4\frac{1}{4}$
P/E Ratio - High	25	34	21	18	18	13
- Low	13	13	11	8	10	8

Income Statement Analysis (Million $)

	1994	%Chg	1993	%Chg	1992	%Chg	1991
Revs.	457	16%	393	21%	325	19%	273
Oper. Inc.	120	26%	95.2	37%	69.3	58%	44.0
Depr.	26.6	29%	20.6	-4%	21.5	73%	12.4
Int. Exp.	4.8	2%	4.7	-16%	5.6	-17%	6.8
Pretax Inc.	90.3	24%	72.6	60%	45.4	59%	28.5
Eff. Tax Rate	38%	—	38%	—	37%	—	36%
Net Inc.	56.3	25%	45.2	58%	28.6	57%	18.2

Balance Sheet & Other Fin. Data (Million $)

	1994	1993	1992	1991	1990	1989
Cash	27.0	36.6	39.8	63.6	28.1	37.2
Curr. Assets	161	141	134	147	121	109
Total Assets	358	310	267	271	234	218
Curr. Liab.	107	76.0	63.3	91.9	70.2	59.5
LT Debt	23.1	34.0	44.1	53.3	63.2	67.8
Common Eqty.	200	177	137	104	86.0	77.0
Total Cap.	234	223	195	173	161	156
Cap. Exp.	60.2	53.8	28.1	25.0	18.6	64.0
Cash Flow	82.9	65.8	50.1	30.6	23.8	23.6

Ratio Analysis

	1994	1993	1992	1991	1990	1989
Curr. Ratio	1.5	1.9	2.1	1.6	1.7	1.8
% LT Debt of Cap.	9.9	15.2	22.6	30.8	39.3	43.6
% Net Inc.of Revs.	12.3	11.5	8.8	6.7	4.6	6.6
% Ret. on Assets	17.0	15.6	10.4	7.2	5.5	8.5
% Ret. on Equity	30.1	28.8	23.4	19.0	15.1	22.9

Dividend Data —Dividends have been paid since 1984.

Amt. of Div. $	Date Decl.	Ex-Div. Date	Stock of Record	Payment Date
0.045	Aug. 01	Oct. 03	Oct. 07	Oct. 21 '94
0.045	Dec. 12	Jan. 09	Jan. 13	Jan. 27 '95
0.045	Mar. 24	Apr. 07	Apr. 14	Apr. 28 '95
0.050	May. 19	Jul. 05	Jul. 07	Jul. 21 '95
0.050	Jul. 31	Oct. 11	Oct. 13	Oct. 27 '95

Data as orig. reptd.; bef. results of disc. opers. and/or spec. items. Per share data adj. for stk. divs. as of ex-div. date. E-Estimated. NA-Not Available. NM-Not Meaningful. NR-Not Ranked.

Office—7800 Woodley Ave., Van Nuys, CA 91406. **Tel**—(818) 781-4973. **Chrmn & Pres**—L. L. Borick. **VP-Fin, Treas & Investor Contact**—R. Jeffrey Ornstein. (818) 771-5906. **Secy**—C. E. Barrantes. **Dirs**—S. I. Ausman, L. L. Borick, S. J. Borick, R. C. Brown, P. W. Colburn, V. B. Evans, R. J. Ornstein, J. H. Parkinson. **Transfer Agent & Registrar**—Chemical Trust Co. of California. **Incorporated** in Delaware in 1969; reincorporated in California in 1994. **Empl**-4,500. **S&P Analyst:** Joshua M. Harari, CFA

STANDARD & POOR'S

STOCK REPORTS

Surgical Care Affiliates

NYSE Symbol **SCA**
In S&P MidCap 400

03-OCT-95 **Industry:** Health Care Centers

Summary: This company operates more than 65 outpatient surgery centers in 24 states.

Quantitative Evaluations

Outlook (1 Lowest—5 Highest) • **5-**

Fair Value • **26¾**

Risk • **Average**

Earn./Div. Rank • **B**

Technical Eval. • **Bullish** since 8/95

Rel. Strength Rank (1 Lowest—99 Highest) • **72**

Insider Activity • **NA**

Recent Price • 23¼ | 52 Wk Range • 24⅞-17⅞ | Yield • 0.9% | 12-Mo. P/E • 25.8

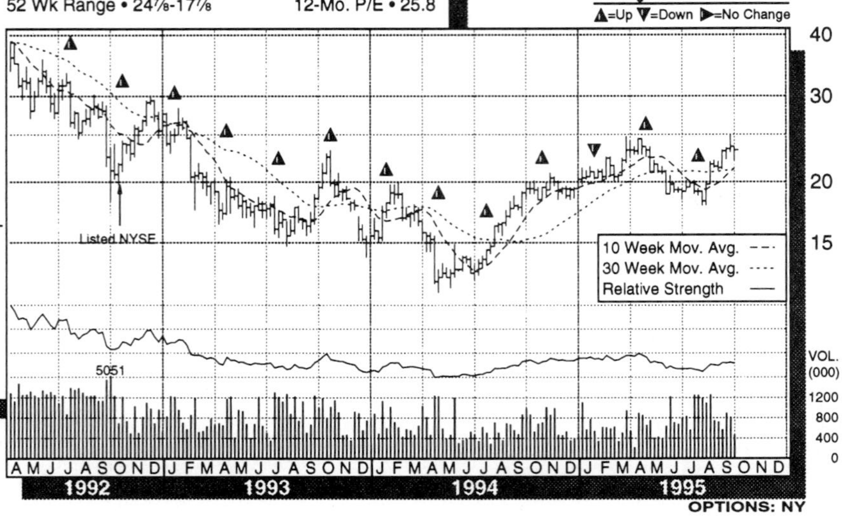

Business Profile - 03-OCT-95

SCA is adapting to an increasingly competitve health-care environment by offering lower prices for outpatient surgery than those of comparable hospital departments, expanding its services, and providing greater convenience and efficiency to surgeons and patients. The company plans to add 10 to 12 new facilities during 1995. It is also creating joint ventures with local hospitals and physicians.

Operational Review - 03-OCT-95

Revenues, which have been rising in recent periods, continued to advance in the first half of 1995, reflecting an increase in the total number of surgical cases and higher pricing. Costs and expenses rose less rapidly, and income continued to climb. During 1994, the company sold all of its Medical Care America stock, realizing a $7.7 million gain, with $5.2 million realized in the first half of 1994.

Stock Performance - 29-SEP-95

In the past 30 trading days, SCA's shares have increased 7%, compared to a 5% rise in the S&P 500. Average trading volume for the past five days was 91,200 shares, compared with the 40-day moving average of 177,505 shares.

Key Stock Statistics

Dividend Rate/Share	0.20	Shareholders	3,000
Shs. outstg. (M)	38.5	Market cap. (B)	$0.881
Avg. daily vol. (M)	0.139	Inst. holdings	47%
Tang. Bk. Value/Share	2.43	Insider holdings	NA
Beta	1.27		

Value of $10,000 invested 5 years ago: NA

Fiscal Year Ending Dec. 31

	1995	% Change	1994	% Change	1993	% Change
Revenues (Million $)						
1Q	65.11	25%	52.15	14%	45.70	-11%
2Q	65.68	12%	58.52	20%	48.60	-10%
3Q	—	—	59.30	21%	48.92	-12%
4Q	—	—	66.75	22%	54.70	-15%
Yr.	—	—	236.7	20%	198.0	-12%
Income (Million $)						
1Q	10.40	29%	8.08	-5%	8.53	31%
2Q	11.35	18%	9.63	24%	7.75	10%
3Q	—	—	11.15	36%	8.17	10%
4Q	—	—	2.52	-71%	8.67	10%
Yr.	—	—	31.31	-3%	32.22	12%
Earnings Per Share ($)						
1Q	0.27	29%	0.21	5%	0.20	11%
2Q	0.29	16%	0.25	25%	0.20	5%
3Q	—	—	0.29	32%	0.22	10%
4Q	—	—	0.06	-74%	0.23	10%
Yr.	—	—	0.80	-6%	0.85	9%

Next earnings report expected: mid October

Surgical Care Affiliates

Business Summary - 02-OCT-95

Surgical Care Affiliates primarily develops, owns and operates outpatient surgical care centers. HMO operations were spun off in late 1993.

About 20% of the company's patients are covered by commercial insurance, 31% by Medicare, 11% by Blue Cross, and 7% self pay. SCA estimates that 21% of its patients in 1994 were members of an HMO or preferred provider organization, and that approximately 10% are covered by Medicaid, workers' compensation and CHAMPUS.

An outpatient or ambulatory surgical care center is a facility that is designed, equipped and staffed to perform surgical procedures that generally do not require overnight hospitalization and that the treating physician chooses not to or cannot perform in the office. Approximately 500 types of surgical procedures can be performed in SCA's centers. The company believes that outpatient surgical care centers help control health care costs. SCA believes that in the area in which it operates, fees charged by its outpatient surgical centers are lower than those charged by hospitals for similar services performed on an outpatient basis.

As of July 1995, the company was operating 67 centers in 24 states, up from 26 centers at the end of 1989. SCA's ownership interest in surgical care centers typically consists of all the capital stock of corporations that are general partners of a limited or general partnership that owns and operates a center. The other general or limited partners of the partnerships are physicians who practice in the communities where the surgical care center is located or, in the case of joint ventures, other local health care providers. The company and participating partners share the center's operating income or loss and depreciation deductions, and receive quarterly distributions of excess cash. At the end of 1994, 25% of SCA centers were joint ventured with community hospitals. The company's goal was to have between 35% and 40% of its centers joint ventured by the end of 1995.

Important Developments

Jun. '95—SCA acquired four surgery centers from Vivra, Inc.

Feb. '95—SCA said it had recorded a $9.4 million charge in the 1994 fourth quarter for the closing of three centers, the writedown of goodwill, and the writedown of certain assets of a medical office building.

Capitalization

Long Term Debt: $71,959,190 (6/95), incl. $4,798,301 of capital lease obligs.
Minority Interest: $30,502,636.

Per Share Data ($)

(Year Ended Dec. 31)

	1994	1993	1992	1991	1990	1989
Tangible Bk. Val.	2.26	2.18	1.93	1.73	1.38	1.01
Cash Flow	1.25	1.27	1.02	0.74	0.45	0.29
Earnings	0.81	0.85	0.78	0.57	0.33	0.19
Dividends	0.16	0.16	0.15	0.09	0.04	0.01
Payout Ratio	20%	19%	19%	16%	13%	3%
Prices - High	$20\frac{7}{8}$	$28\frac{3}{8}$	46	$45\frac{1}{4}$	$15\frac{7}{8}$	$7\frac{1}{2}$
- Low	$11\frac{7}{8}$	14	$18\frac{1}{4}$	$11\frac{7}{8}$	$5\frac{5}{8}$	$2\frac{7}{16}$
P/E Ratio - High	26	33	59	79	48	39
- Low	15	16	23	21	17	13

Income Statement Analysis (Million $)

	1994	%Chg	1993	%Chg	1992	%Chg	1991
Revs.	237	20%	198	-12%	225	32%	170
Oper. Inc.	105	13%	92.6	14%	81.1	33%	60.9
Depr.	17.4	9%	16.0	78%	9.0	43%	6.3
Int. Exp.	NA	—	3.6	6%	3.4	-14%	4.0
Pretax Inc.	78.8	4%	75.5	3%	73.1	31%	55.7
Eff. Tax Rate	32%	—	27%	—	24%	—	23%
Net Inc.	31.4	-2%	32.2	12%	28.8	39%	20.7

Balance Sheet & Other Fin. Data (Million $)

	1994	1993	1992	1991	1990	1989
Cash	31.5	42.5	52.6	61.0	47.8	32.4
Curr. Assets	81.6	80.7	82.1	83.1	64.4	44.9
Total Assets	340	300	248	188	131	107
Curr. Liab.	56.5	30.0	42.1	32.1	25.4	19.7
LT Debt	49.7	62.2	35.4	40.0	36.8	38.3
Common Eqty.	197	167	136	89.0	53.0	38.0
Total Cap.	284	270	206	156	106	87.0
Cap. Exp.	30.1	47.4	34.8	25.3	13.5	11.6
Cash Flow	48.8	48.2	37.8	27.0	16.0	9.7

Ratio Analysis

	1994	1993	1992	1991	1990	1989
Curr. Ratio	1.4	2.7	2.0	2.6	2.5	2.3
% LT Debt of Cap.	17.5	23.0	17.2	25.7	34.8	44.1
% Net Inc.of Revs.	13.3	16.3	12.8	12.2	9.3	7.7
% Ret. on Assets	9.8	11.6	13.0	12.7	9.4	6.6
% Ret. on Equity	17.2	21.0	25.3	28.8	24.9	20.0

Dividend Data —Cash dividends were initiated in late 1989.

Amt. of Div. $	Date Decl.	Ex-Div. Date	Stock of Record	Payment Date
0.040	Oct. 20	Nov. 21	Nov. 28	Dec. 09 '94
0.040	Feb. 22	Feb. 24	Mar. 02	Mar. 10 '95
0.050	Apr. 24	May. 22	May. 26	Jun. 09 '95
0.050	Jul. 21	Aug. 18	Aug. 22	Sep. 08 '95

Data as orig. reptd.; bef. results of disc. opers. and/or spec. items. Per share data adj. for stk. divs. as of ex-div. date. E-Estimated. NA-Not Available. NM-Not Meaningful. NR-Not Ranked.

Office—102 Woodmont Blvd., Suite 610, Nashville, TN 37205. **Tel**—(615) 385-3541. **Chrmn & CEO**—J. C. Gordon. **Pres & COO**—W. J. Hamburg. **SVP, CFO, Treas, Secy & Investor Contact**—Tarpley B. Jones. **Dirs**—D. E. Bruhl, Jr., L. Burch III, R. J. Fraiman, J. C. Gordon, W. J. Hamburg, K. J. Melkus, A. W. Miller, E. J. Nighbert, M. J. Schaeffer. **Transfer Agent & Registrar**—Trust Co. Bank, Atlanta. **Incorporated** in Tennessee in 1982; reincorporated in Delaware in 1986. **Empl**-2,300. **S&P Analyst:** Philip J. Birbara

STANDARD & POOR'S

STOCK REPORTS

Symantec Corp.

NASDAQ Symbol **SYMC**

In S&P MidCap 400

17-OCT-95

Industry: Data Processing

Summary: Symantec provides application and system software products designed to enhance individual and workgroup productivity, as well as manage networked computing environments.

S&P Opinion: Hold (★★★)

Recent Price • 25⅞ | 52 Wk Range • 33¼-15 | Yield • Nil | 12-Mo. P/E • 25.1

Quantitative Evaluations

Outlook
(1 Lowest—5 Highest)
• **5+**

Fair Value
• **30⅝**

Risk
• **Average**

Earn./Div. Rank
• **C**

Technical Eval.
• **Bullish** since 7/95

Rel. Strength Rank
(1 Lowest—99 Highest)
• **10**

Insider Activity
• **Neutral**

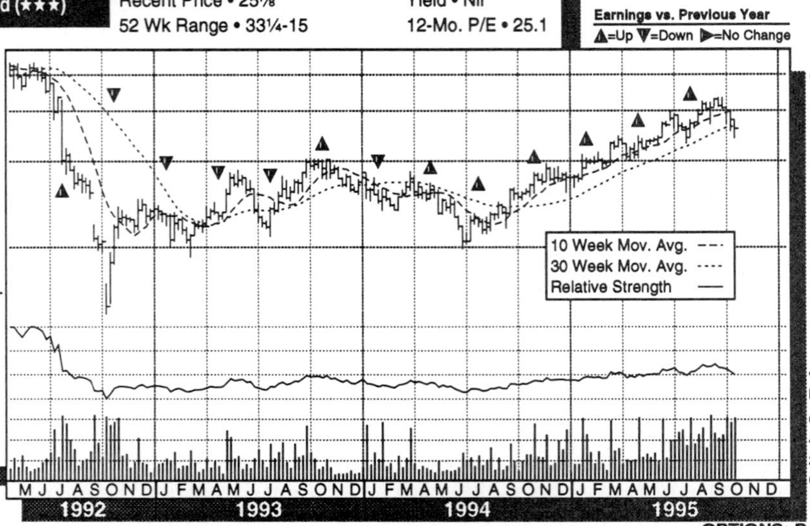

OPTIONS: P

Overview - 17-OCT-95

Revenues are expected to rise in fiscal 1995-96, reflecting acquisition-related gains and contributions from new products, including development tools and network utilities. The company has focused on the Windows market for new product development and is offering more products for the enterprisewide environment of networked computers. A new product cycle tied to the release of the Windows 95 operating system is expected to further benefit results. Operating margins should widen on progressively higher volume, a more favorable revenue mix and well-controlled costs. Earnings are expected to be aided by the increased revenues and wider margins.

Valuation - 16-OCT-95

The shares of this major vendor of software utilities and development tools have soared over the past 12 months, aided by success in developing and marketing products for the networked environment of enterprisewide computing. The release of new products developed for the Windows 95 operating system is also expected to positively impact earnings. While a premium valuation is deserved in light of the company's growth prospects, the P/E multiple the shares currently command leaves little room for further expansion in the near term. In addition, there are uncertainties related to Symantec's pending acquisition of Delrina Corp. We expect the stock to track the market in the months ahead.

Key Stock Statistics

S&P EPS Est. 1996	1.20	Tang. Bk. Value/Share	3.40
P/E on S&P Est. 1996	21.6	Beta	2.08
Dividend Rate/Share	Nil	Shareholders	800
Shs. outstg. (M)	38.6	Market cap. (B)	$0.970
Avg. daily vol. (M)	1.254	Inst. holdings	80%
		Insider holdings	NA

Value of $10,000 invested 5 years ago: $ 33,387

Fiscal Year Ending Mar. 31

	1996	% Change	1995	% Change	1994	% Change
Revenues (Million $)						
1Q	90.11	8%	83.11	24%	67.20	9%
2Q	—	—	79.08	24%	63.60	43%
3Q	—	—	84.13	25%	67.05	38%
4Q	—	—	88.55	27%	69.87	36%
Yr.	—	—	334.9	25%	267.7	30%
Income (Million $)						
1Q	11.70	NM	1.05	NM	-7.09	NM
2Q	—	—	7.98	NM	2.42	NM
3Q	—	—	9.06	NM	-9.19	NM
4Q	—	—	10.42	45%	7.21	NM
Yr.	—	—	28.50	NM	-11.11	NM
Earnings Per Share ($)						
1Q	0.29	NM	0.03	NM	-0.32	NM
2Q	E0.30	36%	0.22	NM	0.01	NM
3Q	E0.30	20%	0.25	NM	-0.31	NM
4Q	E0.31	15%	0.27	17%	0.23	NM
Yr.	E1.20	56%	0.77	NM	-0.37	NM

Next earnings report expected: late October

Symantec Corp.

Business Summary - 17-OCT-95

Symantec Corporation designs, markets and supports a line of microcomputer software products designed to enhance individual and workgroup productivity, as well as manage networked computing environments. Approximately 80% of fiscal 1994-95 revenues came from products that operate on MS-DOS or MS-Windows operating systems; other software products utilize the Apple Macintosh and IBM's OS/2 operating systems. Products are organized into seven groups: advanced utilities, security utilities, network/communications utilities, contact management, development tools, project management/productivity applications, and client/server technology.

Utilities software includes offerings (many sold under the Norton brand name) designed to provide disk and data recovery, security, performance optimization, preventive maintenance, virus protection, storage backup, ASCII editing and remote computing capabilities.

Contact management products manage and integrate contacts, calendar and communication through the use of E-mail messaging.

Development tools include professional programming tools for the C++ environment and other software development tools.

Project management/productivity applications include Q&A, an integrated database management and word processing program with report-generation capabilities; and Time Line, a project organizing, scheduling and resource allocation program.

Client/server technology consists of client/server application development tools for creating complex distributed database applications.

International revenues accounted for 35% of the total in 1994-95, versus 33% in 1993-94.

Important Developments

Jul. '95—Symantec announced that it had signed a definitive agreement to acquire Delrina Corp., a developer of fax, data, voice communications and electronic forms software products, for about 15 million SYMC shares. The transaction was valued at about $415 million when first announced.

Jul. '95—The company said that in the first quarter of fiscal 1995-96, sales of its enterprise software products rose 30%, year to year, and made up over one-third of total revenues. During the first quarter of 1994-95, Symantec recorded charges of $9.5 million ($0.19 a share) for costs associated with the acquisitions of utility software vendors Central Point Software and SLR Systems.

Capitalization

Long Term Obligs.: $15,293,000 (6/95), incl. $15 million of 7.75% sub. notes due 2001, conv. into com. at $12 a sh.

Per Share Data ($) (Year Ended Mar. 31)

	1995	1994	1993	1992	1991	1990
Tangible Bk. Val.	2.77	2.23	2.91	3.35	2.10	1.77
Cash Flow	1.12	Nil	-0.05	0.98	0.63	0.65
Earnings	0.77	-0.37	-0.49	0.77	0.47	0.53
Dividends	Nil	Nil	Nil	Nil	Nil	Nil
Payout Ratio	Nil	Nil	Nil	Nil	Nil	Nil
Cal. Yrs.	1994	1993	1992	1991	1990	1989
Prices - High	19⅝	20½	51	44¾	14¾	9
- Low	9⅞	9¼	5⅞	13	7½	5½
P/E Ratio - High	25	NM	NM	46	32	17
- Low	13	NM	NM	13	16	10

Income Statement Analysis (Million $)

	1995	%Chg	1994	%Chg	1993	%Chg	1992
Revs.	335	25%	268	30%	206	-5%	217
Oper. Inc.	60.0	99%	30.2	NM	4.6	-89%	40.2
Depr.	13.3	20%	11.1	7%	10.4	100%	5.2
Int. Exp.	2.4	4%	2.3	—	NA	—	0.5
Pretax Inc.	38.3	NM	-16.0	NM	-17.2	NM	28.8
Eff. Tax Rate	26%	—	NM	—	NM	—	35%
Net Inc.	28.5	NM	-11.1	NM	-11.5	NM	18.7

Balance Sheet & Other Fin. Data (Million $)

	1995	1994	1993	1992	1991	1990
Cash	105	51.5	53.3	31.9	24.9	21.5
Curr. Assets	180	120	110	95.7	52.5	30.7
Total Assets	221	158	142	123	65.0	38.0
Curr. Liab.	84.5	52.7	45.9	45.5	22.8	10.8
LT Debt	25.4	25.6	26.2	1.6	1.6	6.1
Common Eqty.	111	80.1	69.6	75.6	41.0	21.3
Total Cap.	137	106	95.8	77.3	42.6	27.4
Cap. Exp.	17.7	7.3	15.4	12.7	5.5	2.8
Cash Flow	41.8	-0.1	-1.1	23.9	12.7	8.3

Ratio Analysis

	1995	1994	1993	1992	1991	1990
Curr. Ratio	2.1	2.3	2.4	2.1	2.3	2.8
% LT Debt of Cap.	18.6	24.2	27.4	2.1	3.8	22.3
% Net Inc.of Revs.	8.5	NM	NM	8.6	8.1	13.4
% Ret. on Assets	13.9	NM	NM	18.8	14.8	15.7
% Ret. on Equity	32.5	NM	NM	30.4	24.9	NM

Dividend Data —No cash dividends have been paid.

Data as orig. reptd.; bef. results of disc. opers. and/or spec. items. Per share data adj. for stk. divs. as of ex-div. date. E-Estimated. NA-Not Available. NM-Not Meaningful. NR-Not Ranked.

Office—10201 Torre Ave., Cupertino, CA 95014-2132. **Tel**—(408) 253-9600. **Chrmn**—C. D. Carman. **Pres & CEO**—G. E. Eubanks Jr. **Exec VP-Fin & CFO**—R. R. B. Dykes. **Secy**—G. K. Davidson. **Dirs**—C. Boesenberg, W. W. Bregman, C. D. Carman, G. E. Eubanks Jr., R. Miller, L. L. Vadasz. **Transfer Agent**—Bank of Boston. **Incorporated** in Delaware in 1988. **Empl**-1,442. **S&P Analyst:** Peter C. Wood, CFA

STANDARD & POOR'S

STOCK REPORTS

Symbol Technologies

NYSE Symbol **SBL**
In S&P MidCap 400

22-AUG-95 **Industry:** Data Processing

Summary: This company develops, makes and sells portable bar-code scanning equipment that uses laser technology to read data encoded in bar-code symbols.

S&P Opinion: Accumulate (★★★★)

Recent Price • 37⅛
52 Wk Range • 40⅝-24⅜

Yield • Nil
12-Mo. P/E • 23.3

Quantitative Evaluations

Outlook
(1 Lowest—5 Highest)
• **4+**

Fair Value
• **37⅝**

Risk
• **Average**

Earn./Div. Rank
• **B-**

Technical Eval.
• **Bullish** since 2/95

Rel. Strength Rank
(1 Lowest—99 Highest)
• **40**

Insider Activity
• **Neutral**

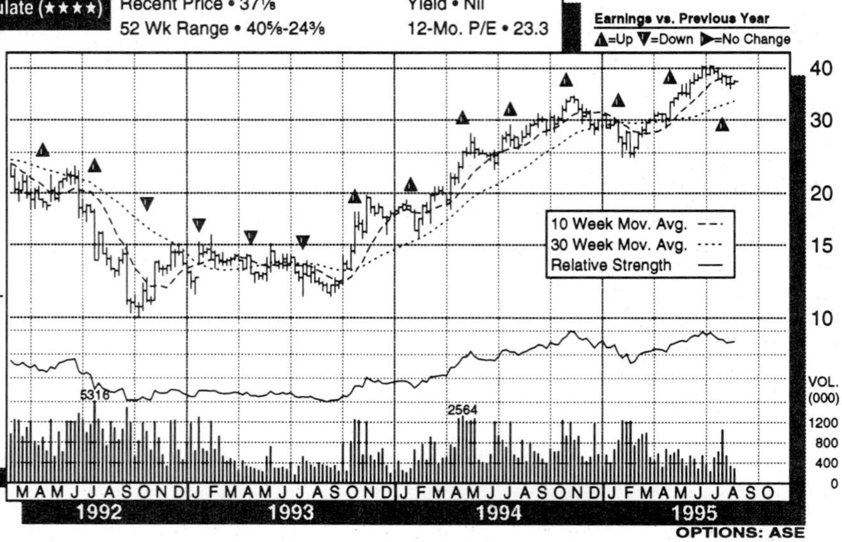

Overview - 22-AUG-95

Revenues should climb about 15% in 1995, on improved domestic and international economic conditions, and greater product line diversity. The domestic market for Symbol's products is broadening, as large retail customers insist on bar coding technology from suppliers and vendors. The affordability of the company's scanner products has let it penetrate smaller retail chains and individual businesses. A sharp uptrend in European sales should continue. In addition, Symbol recently entered the Asia-Pacific market, which could spur long-term growth. Margins should widen modestly, as cost cutting efforts offset an increased percentage of sales of lower-margin terminal products. A strong cash positon could allow for a share repurchase program.

Valuation - 22-AUG-95

The shares have rebounded since the beginning of 1995, reflecting earnings gains and anticipated strong overseas growth. The increasing popularity of products in Europe and Asia should spur double-digit sales growth in 1995. New product launches, expected in the second half of 1995, are expected to aid long-term sales growth. In the near-term, gross margins could flatten, as a less favorable product mix offsets cost cutting efforts. Although the shares are volatile, a long-term uptrend continues.

Key Stock Statistics

S&P EPS Est. 1995	1.72	Tang. Bk. Value/Share	8.45
P/E on S&P Est. 1995	21.6	Beta	2.15
S&P EPS Est. 1996	2.00	Shareholders	2,200
Dividend Rate/Share	Nil	Market cap. (B)	$0.972
Shs. outstg. (M)	26.0	Inst. holdings	91%
Avg. daily vol. (M)	0.100	Insider holdings	1%

Value of $10,000 invested 5 years ago: $ 22,846

Fiscal Year Ending Dec. 31

	1995	% Change	1994	% Change	1993	% Change
Revenues (Million $)						
1Q	131.3	27%	103.7	24%	83.72	-6%
2Q	137.6	21%	113.4	26%	89.94	-5%
3Q	—	—	124.4	35%	92.38	18%
4Q	—	—	123.8	32%	93.95	14%
Yr.	—	—	465.3	29%	360.0	4%
Income (Million $)						
1Q	10.75	61%	6.66	NM	0.73	-87%
2Q	11.78	40%	8.40	NM	2.25	-64%
3Q	—	—	10.30	122%	4.63	NM
4Q	—	—	9.64	99%	4.84	NM
Yr.	—	—	34.98	181%	12.45	NM
Earnings Per Share ($)						
1Q	0.40	54%	0.26	NM	0.03	-86%
2Q	0.43	34%	0.32	NM	0.09	-64%
3Q	E0.45	15%	0.39	105%	0.19	NM
4Q	E0.44	22%	0.36	89%	0.19	NM
Yr.	E1.72	28%	1.34	168%	0.50	NM

Next earnings report expected: mid October

Symbol Technologies

Business Summary - 22-AUG-95

Symbol Technologies, Inc. designs, makes and markets bar code reading equipment, portable data collection systems, and radio frequency data communications products. Its products are used in data collection systems in retail, parcel delivery and postal service, warehousing and distribution, factory automation and other applications.

Bar code scanning products employ laser technology to read data encoded in bar-code symbols and transmit data. The largest-selling hand-held laser scanner is the LS 2000, sold primarily to point-of-sale customers and for use in conjunction with portable data collection terminals. During 1994, Symbol introduced the LS 9100 omnidirectional bar code scanner developed specifically for a broad range of retail applications. The LT 1700 LaserTouch family of visible laser-based bar code scanners combines the performance and accuracy of laser-based bar code technology with scanning for applications, where near contact scanning and touch ergonomics are sufficient. The company's portable bar-code scanning equipment is compatible with a wide variety of data collection systems, including computers, electronic cash registers and portable data collection terminals. Bar code scanning products accounted for 40% of total revenues in 1994, down from 45% in 1993 and 50% in 1992.

Portable data collection systems (50% of revenues in 1994, and 40% in each of 1993 and 1992) consist of portable data collection devices, peripheral devices, software and programming tools and are designed to provide solutions to specific customer needs in data collection. Based on spread spectrum RF technology, the Spectrum One cellular RF network provides real-time wireless data communications with a host computer for hundreds of portable and fixed computers and radio-integrated scanners.

International sales accounted for 36%, 31% and 35% of total revenues in 1994, 1993 and 1992, respectively.

Important Developments

May '95—The company introduced two new series of bar code scanners, the LS 2600 and LS 3600, incorporating new technologies for improved performance. They are the industry's first scanners to incorporate fuzzy logic, allowing accurate digitation and decoding of bar codes that had been considered unreadable. They also assure maximum scanning efficiency, even with poor quality or damaged bar codes. In addition, they use Symbol's patented Beam Management Optical Technology, which allows them to read information up to 4.5 feet away.

Capitalization

Long Term Debt: $63,852,000 (6/95).

Per Share Data ($) (Year Ended Dec. 31)

	1994	1993	1992	1991	1990	1989
Tangible Bk. Val.	12.29	10.78	5.95	11.12	10.14	9.83
Cash Flow	2.03	1.13	0.10	1.51	0.87	1.37
Earnings	1.34	0.50	-0.65	0.91	0.33	0.91
Dividends	Nil	Nil	Nil	Nil	Nil	Nil
Payout Ratio	Nil	Nil	Nil	Nil	Nil	Nil
Prices - High	34$\frac{3}{8}$	19$\frac{3}{4}$	26$\frac{1}{2}$	29$\frac{3}{8}$	16$\frac{5}{8}$	25$\frac{5}{8}$
- Low	15$\frac{5}{8}$	11$\frac{1}{4}$	10	10$\frac{3}{4}$	5$\frac{3}{8}$	15$\frac{1}{8}$
P/E Ratio - High	26	39	NM	32	50	28
- Low	12	22	NM	12	16	17

Income Statement Analysis (Million $)

	1994	%Chg	1993	%Chg	1992	%Chg	1991
Revs.	465	29%	360	4%	345	8%	319
Oper. Inc.	81.3	108%	39.0	-1%	39.5	-26%	53.7
Depr.	18.0	16%	15.5	-13%	17.9	19%	15.1
Int. Exp.	5.3	14%	4.7	125%	2.1	-27%	2.8
Pretax Inc.	58.3	NM	19.4	NM	-22.5	NM	36.7
Eff. Tax Rate	40%	—	36%	—	NM	—	38%
Net Inc.	35.0	182%	12.4	NM	-15.5	NM	22.8

Balance Sheet & Other Fin. Data (Million $)

	1994	1993	1992	1991	1990	1989
Cash	31.4	7.5	6.9	17.3	19.0	21.9
Curr. Assets	266	220	185	171	146	134
Total Assets	474	420	379	354	315	294
Curr. Liab.	74.3	78.5	96.2	48.2	46.7	39.6
LT Debt	59.9	62.1	14.6	21.7	24.8	23.7
Common Eqty.	316	259	245	263	226	217
Total Cap.	386	328	260	284	251	241
Cap. Exp.	24.8	18.1	15.0	17.2	15.3	14.1
Cash Flow	53.0	27.9	2.4	37.8	19.9	28.6

Ratio Analysis

	1994	1993	1992	1991	1990	1989
Curr. Ratio	3.6	2.8	1.9	3.5	3.1	3.4
% LT Debt of Cap.	15.5	18.9	5.6	7.6	9.9	9.9
% Net Inc.of Revs.	7.5	3.5	NM	7.1	3.3	8.5
% Ret. on Assets	7.6	3.1	NM	6.6	2.5	8.3
% Ret. on Equity	11.8	4.9	NM	9.0	3.4	10.8

Dividend Data —No cash dividend has ever been paid.

Data as orig. reptd.; bef. results of disc. opers. and/or spec. items. Per share data adj. for stk. divs. as of ex-div. date. E-Estimated. NA-Not Available. NM-Not Meaningful. NR-Not Ranked.

Office—116 Wilbur Place, Bohemia, NY 11716. **Tel**—(516) 563-2400. **Chrmn & CEO**—J. Swartz. **Vice Chrmn**—R. R. Martino. **Pres & COO**—J. Lindelow. **SVP & CFO**—T. G. Amato. **SVP & Secy**—L. H. Goldner. **Investor Contact**—Michael G. Archambault (516-244-4632). **Dirs**—G. Bugliarello, L. C. Freiberg, F. P. Heiman, J. Lindelow, H. P. Mallement, R. R. Martino, S. P. Steinberg, J. Swartz, C. B. Wang. **Transfer Agent & Registrar**—Continental Stock Transfer & Trust Co., NYC. **Incorporated** in New York in 1973; reincorporated in Delaware in 1987. **Empl**-2,387. **S&P Analyst:** Steven A. Jaworski

STANDARD & POOR'S
STOCK REPORTS

TCA Cable TV

NASDAQ Symbol **TCAT**
In S&P MidCap 400

29-JUN-95 **Industry:** Broadcasting

Summary: This cable system operator owns or manages systems located primarily in smaller markets in Texas, Louisiana and Arkansas, which as of June 1995 served 573,000 subscribers.

S&P Opinion: Accumulate (★★★★) | Recent Price • 27¼ | Yield • 1.8%
52 Wk Range • 28⅛-20⅞ | 12-Mo. P/E • 25.2

Quantitative Evaluations
Outlook (1 Lowest—5 Highest)
• **4+**
Fair Value
• **28⅞**
Risk
• **Low**
Earn./Div. Rank
• **A-**

Technical Eval.
• **Bearish** since 3/95
Rel. Strength Rank (1 Lowest—99 Highest)
• **63**
Insider Activity
• **Neutral**

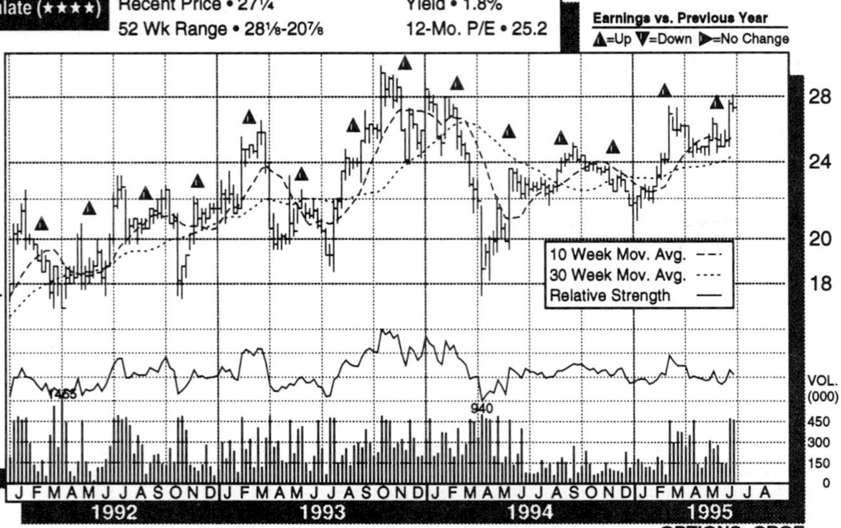

OPTIONS: CBOE

Overview - 29-JUN-95

Revenues and cash flow should advance more than 10% in fiscal 1995, aided by rate increases allowed on regulated services under new FCC guidelines. Subscriber growth will also contribute to the improvement, boosted by acquisitions. Profit comparisons should benefit from the revenue gains, ongoing efficiencies, and the absence of unusual charges. Net income will also benefit from continuing reductions in debt. Fewer shares outstanding will boost share earnings. Revenues in fiscal 1996 are expected to rise another 12%-15% or more, aided by the same factors that influenced growth in fiscal 1995, augmented by further relaxation of price restraints anticipated later in the year. Profitability will benefit from the revenue momentum, growth in higher margined business, and operating efficiencies.

Valuation - 29-JUN-95

TCAT's long-term attraction lies in its strategy to remain a viable player in the cable TV universe in spite of its relatively small size. TCAT has carved out a lucrative niche in serving small markets in the South, and it is strengthening its position through strategic acquisitions. The company is well into the second year of a five-year plan to upgrade channel capacity and provide state-of-the-art telecommunications and data transmission capabilities. The $100 million project, funded internally, bodes well from a competitive stance and promises new revenue streams. Although insiders own 32% of TCAT, the stock is an attractive takeover candidate.

Key Stock Statistics

S&P EPS Est. 1995	1.30	Tang. Bk. Value/Share	NM
P/E on S&P Est. 1995	21.0	Beta	0.90
S&P EPS Est. 1996	1.65	Shareholders	2,200
Dividend Rate/Share	0.48	Market cap. (B)	$0.653
Shs. outstg. (M)	24.5	Inst. holdings	49%
Avg. daily vol. (M)	0.072	Insider holdings	NA

Value of $10,000 invested 5 years ago: $ 17,355

Fiscal Year Ending Oct. 31

	1995	% Change	1994	% Change	1993	% Change
Revenues (Million $)						
1Q	43.30	10%	39.28	7%	36.65	9%
2Q	43.95	10%	39.85	5%	37.84	9%
3Q	—	—	41.08	7%	38.31	9%
4Q	—	—	42.10	7%	39.49	11%
Yr.	—	—	162.3	7%	152.3	10%
Income (Million $)						
1Q	7.74	34%	5.76	21%	4.77	39%
2Q	7.72	34%	5.76	13%	5.08	37%
3Q	—	—	5.35	7%	4.99	35%
4Q	—	—	6.09	9%	5.61	49%
Yr.	—	—	22.98	12%	20.45	36%
Earnings Per Share ($)						
1Q	0.31	35%	0.23	21%	0.19	36%
2Q	0.31	29%	0.24	14%	0.21	31%
3Q	E0.33	—	0.21	5%	0.20	25%
4Q	E0.35	—	0.25	9%	0.23	53%
Yr.	E1.30	—	0.93	12%	0.83	36%

Next earnings report expected: mid September

TCA Cable TV

29-JUN-95

Business Summary - 29-JUN-95

Formed in 1981, TCA Cable TV, Inc. develops, operates and manages cable television systems. As of June 1995, TCA owned or managed cable systems serving over 573,000 basic subscribers. The systems are located primarily in smaller markets in Arkansas, Louisiana and Texas where over-the-air television reception is unsatisfactory.

Basic service includes signals of nearby over-the-air TV stations carrying the commercial networks; independent, specialty and educational stations; sports and educational programming; and additional satellite programming such as signals of distant independent stations and continuous time, news and weather information. Expanded basic service includes a variety of packaged programming, purchased from independent suppliers and combined in different formats to appeal to different tastes. TCA also offers premium services such as The Movie Channel, HBO, Showtime, and The Disney Channel. During fiscal 1994, the company derived 68.5% of revenues from basic or expanded basic subscriptions, 18% from premium subscriptions, 8.5% from advertising, and 5% from other sources such as home shopping channels, "pay-per-view" services and other sources.

TCA's operating plan calls for geographically clustered cable systems in medium density markets. Clustering allows for lower costs through operating efficiencies as well as a future for connected markets large enough to offer "pay-per-view" and other non-regulated ancillary services.

In September 1993, TCA announced plans to spend $100 million over the next three to five years to complete an extensive system upgrade. Capital expenditures for fiscal 1995 are budgeted at about $30 million, up from $28.5 million spent in fiscal 1994 and $21.7 million in fiscal 1993.

Important Developments

Jun. '95—TCA finalized the acquisition of cable systems in Texas serving 32,800 subscribers. In May, TCA acquired systems in Arkansas serving 44,700 subscribers.
Nov. '94—In its "going forward" rules, the FCC announced that cablers will be allowed to raise monthly rates on regulated service beginning in 1995. Certain other restrictions were also eased.
Aug. '94—TCA said that it was continuing to move aggressively in rebuilding its existing 40-channel systems into high capacity, interactive plans capable of many more entertainment channels, data and telephone applications. TCA also said that it is continuing to pursue acquisitions of systems to add to its geographic market clusters.

Capitalization

Long Term Debt: $122,744,095 (4/95).

Per Share Data ($) (Year Ended Oct. 31)

	1994	1993	1992	1991	1990	1989
Tangible Bk. Val.	-2.62	-3.41	-4.15	-4.91	-5.57	-5.66
Cash Flow	2.30	2.18	1.95	1.27	1.06	1.19
Earnings	0.93	0.83	0.61	0.35	0.20	0.45
Dividends	0.44	0.40	0.34	0.28	0.24	0.20
Payout Ratio	47%	48%	56%	80%	120%	44%
Prices - High	28⅜	30⅛	23¼	19	17½	21⅜
- Low	17½	18½	17	13½	9⅞	15⅝
P/E Ratio - High	31	36	38	54	88	48
- Low	19	22	28	39	49	34

Income Statement Analysis (Million $)

	1994	%Chg	1993	%Chg	1992	%Chg	1991
Revs.	162	7%	152	9%	139	9%	127
Oper. Inc.	79.6	2%	77.7	10%	70.4	31%	53.9
Depr.	33.6	NM	33.3	2%	32.8	46%	22.5
Int. Exp.	9.7	-12%	11.0	-17%	13.2	-26%	17.9
Pretax Inc.	37.9	12%	33.7	36%	24.7	78%	13.9
Eff. Tax Rate	39%	—	39%	—	39%	—	39%
Net Inc.	23.0	13%	20.4	36%	15.0	76%	8.5

Balance Sheet & Other Fin. Data (Million $)

	1994	1993	1992	1991	1990	1989
Cash	2.5	1.5	0.8	1.0	0.7	1.0
Curr. Assets	NA	NA	NA	NA	NA	NA
Total Assets	286	288	290	306	325	328
Curr. Liab.	48.3	45.3	48.8	40.5	27.9	22.2
LT Debt	99	118	130	165	205	216
Common Eqty.	99	90.3	78.0	70.8	64.9	65.8
Total Cap.	238	243	241	265	297	305
Cap. Exp.	28.5	23.4	16.5	11.9	20.2	49.9
Cash Flow	56.6	53.8	47.8	31.0	25.6	28.9

Ratio Analysis

	1994	1993	1992	1991	1990	1989
Curr. Ratio	NA	NA	NA	NA	NA	NA
% LT Debt of Cap.	41.6	48.4	54.0	62.0	69.1	70.8
% Net Inc.of Revs.	14.2	13.4	10.8	6.7	4.2	13.7
% Ret. on Assets	8.0	7.1	5.0	2.7	1.5	4.7
% Ret. on Equity	24.3	24.3	20.1	12.4	7.3	17.3

Dividend Data (Cash has been paid each year since 1982.)

Amt. of Div. $	Date Decl.	Ex-Div. Date	Stock of Record	Payment Date
0.110	Jun. 21	Jun. 29	Jul. 06	Jul. 20 '94
0.110	Sep. 22	Sep. 29	Oct. 05	Oct. 19 '94
0.120	Dec. 07	Dec. 19	Dec. 23	Jan. 10 '95
0.120	Apr. 04	Apr. 07	Apr. 13	Apr. 27 '95
0.120	Jun. 07	Jun. 23	Jun. 27	Jul. 11 '95

Data as orig. reptd.; bef. results of disc. opers. and/or spec. items. Per share data adj. for stk. divs. as of ex-div. date. E-Estimated. NA-Not Available. NM-Not Meaningful. NR-Not Ranked.

Office—3015 SSE Loop 323, Tyler, TX 75701. **Tel**—(903) 595-3701. **Chrmn & CEO**—R. M. Rogers. **Pres & COO**—F. R. Nichols. **VP, CFO, Treas & Investor Contact**—Jimmie F. Taylor. **Secy**—Martha Sue Hensley. **Dirs**—J. F. Ackerman, B. R. Fisch, K. S. Gunter, W. J. McKinney, F. R. Nichols, A. W. Riter, Jr., R. K. Rogers, R. M. Rogers. **Transfer Agent & Registrar**—First National Bank of Chicago. **Incorporated** in Texas in 1981. **Empl**-772. **S&P Analyst:** William H. Donald

Tambrands Inc.

NYSE Symbol **TMB**
In S&P MidCap 400

27-SEP-95

Industry: Cosmetics/Toiletries

Summary: This company manufactures and markets tampons in about 150 countries worldwide. It is the leading tampon producer in the U.S.

S&P Opinion: Avoid (★★)

Recent Price • 44¾
52 Wk Range • 48⅛-36¼
Yield • 4.0%
12-Mo. P/E • 19.5

Quantitative Evaluations

Outlook
(1 Lowest—5 Highest)
• **1**⁻

Fair Value
• **36**

Risk
• **Low**

Earn./Div. Rank
• **B+**

Technical Eval.
• **Bullish** since 1/95

Rel. Strength Rank
(1 Lowest—99 Highest)
• **26**

Insider Activity
• **NA**

Earnings vs. Previous Year
▲=Up ▼=Down ▶=No Change

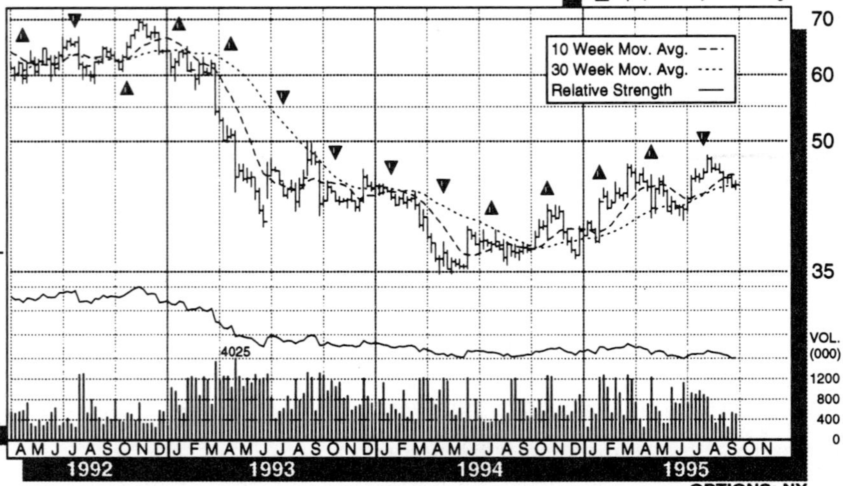

OPTIONS: NY

Overview - 27-SEP-95

Sales should advance about 10% in 1995, reflecting favorable responses to new product introductions and product relaunches in late 1994 and 1995. Despite intense competition, sales in the U.S. and Europe should be boosted by strong marketing initiatives, promotions, and greater overall demand for tampons. Volume in untapped growth markets, such as the People's Republic of China and Russia, should be significantly higher, reflecting expansion efforts. While gross margins should widen slightly on the higher volume, operating margins will narrow on higher promotional spending in the U.S. and Europe to maintain or increase market share, and on expenses related to educating consumers to use tampons in developing countries. Share earnings will hurt by a one-time $0.23 charge related to litigation.

Valuation - 27-SEP-95

The shares have been trading in a fairly narrow range since the beginning of 1995. We attribute this to the highly competitive worldwide tampon business, and its negative effect on TMB's margins. In order to protect or grow its market share, TMB has been steadily increasing its marketing expenses, discounting product prices, and employing many other promotional tactics. The severe competition seen in the U.S. and Europe is expected to continue. Costs to educate consumers to use tampons in developing markets are also high. Despite the appeal of the nearly 4% dividend yield, we recommend investors avoid this stock for now.

Key Stock Statistics

S&P EPS Est. 1995	2.30	Tang. Bk. Value/Share	2.16
P/E on S&P Est. 1995	19.3	Beta	1.02
S&P EPS Est. 1996	2.50	Shareholders	7,200
Dividend Rate/Share	1.76	Market cap. (B)	$ 1.6
Shs. outstg. (M)	36.6	Inst. holdings	67%
Avg. daily vol. (M)	0.088	Insider holdings	NA

Value of $10,000 invested 5 years ago: $ 15,064

Fiscal Year Ending Dec. 31

	1995	% Change	1994	% Change	1993	% Change
Revenues (Million $)						
1Q	166.9	20%	139.2	-10%	154.4	-12%
2Q	176.3	6%	165.6	11%	149.0	-12%
3Q	—	—	175.3	9%	161.4	-7%
4Q	—	—	164.4	12%	146.7	-11%
Yr.	—	—	644.5	5%	611.5	-11%
Income (Million $)						
1Q	22.82	4%	22.04	-32%	32.19	10%
2Q	13.04	-35%	20.01	NM	-3.39	NM
3Q	—	—	25.02	5%	23.82	-29%
4Q	—	—	22.65	7%	21.07	-32%
Yr.	—	—	89.73	22%	73.70	-40%
Earnings Per Share ($)						
1Q	0.62	7%	0.58	-29%	0.82	12%
2Q	0.36	-33%	0.54	NM	-0.09	NM
3Q	E0.69	1%	0.68	10%	0.62	-27%
4Q	E0.63	2%	0.62	13%	0.55	-31%
Yr.	E2.30	-5%	2.43	27%	1.91	-38%

Next earnings report expected: mid November

Tambrands Inc.

Business Summary - 27-SEP-95

Tambrands Inc. (formerly Tampax Inc.) is the leading international manufacturer and marketer of tampons. As part of a restructuring program announced in 1989, TMB has divested various divisions in order to focus on its global tampon business. Between 1989 and the end of 1993, TMB sold its cosmetics, diagnostics and Maxithins pad and panty shield businesses; its headquarters in Lake Success, N.Y.; its non-tampon business in Spain; its interest in a joint venture in Turkey; its disposable diaper and external pad business in Brazil; and its alcohol and external pad business in Mexico. Contributions to sales and pretax earnings by region in 1994:

	Sales	Profits
U.S.	59%	79%
Europe	30%	15%
Other foreign	10%	6%

TMB's largest selling product is the Tampax flushable applicator tampon, which became commercially available in 1936. TMB also sells Tampax tampons with plastic applicators in the U.S. and Canada; Tampax Compak tampons, with a compact all-plastic applicator, in the U.S., Canada and parts of Europe; and Tampax comfort shaped flushable applicator tampons, with an all-paper rounded-end applicator and a slimmer design than the company's standard product, in North America, Australia, parts of Europe and in several other countries.

TMB is increasing its emphasis on the development and marketing of new products. Recent new products include the Tampax Satin Touch tampon, which offers the ease and comfort of a plastic applicator but has an all-paper applicator that is flushable and biodegradable; Tampax Lites, designed for use on days of light menstruation; and Tampax Tampets non-applicator tampons.

TMB sells its products in the U.S. and some 150 other countries. In the U.S., TMB believes it has the leading market position in tampons: 50.0% in dollars and 53.1% in units. Wal-Mart accounted for about 10.3% of 1994 sales. Foreign subsidiaries and joint ventures operate in Canada, Europe and the U.K., Eastern Europe, Latin America and Ukraine. TMB owns 80% of a joint venture in the People's Republic of China.

Important Developments

Aug. '95—TMB announced that, in line with its strategy to grow through product innovation via new products and ongoing upgrades of existing products, it was relaunching its original Tampax tampon line in the fall of 1995.

Capitalization

Long Term Debt: $65,543,000 (6/95).

Per Share Data ($)

(Year Ended Dec. 31)

	1994	1993	1992	1991	1990	1989
Tangible Bk. Val.	2.03	2.79	4.09	5.22	5.74	5.69
Cash Flow	3.06	2.36	3.49	2.26	2.56	0.33
Earnings	2.43	1.91	3.09	1.92	2.30	0.04
Dividends	1.70	1.56	1.40	1.24	1.11	1.04
Payout Ratio	70%	82%	45%	64%	47%	NM
Prices - High	44½	65	70½	66⅞	45½	38¼
- Low	34¾	39½	58⅝	38⅝	33¾	26⅜
P/E Ratio - High	18	34	23	35	20	NM
- Low	14	21	19	20	15	NM

Income Statement Analysis (Million $)

	1994	%Chg	1993	%Chg	1992	%Chg	1991
Revs.	645	6%	611	-11%	684	3%	661
Oper. Inc.	175	7%	164	-22%	210	20%	175
Depr.	23.5	34%	17.6	12%	15.7	11%	14.1
Int. Exp.	7.6	55%	4.9	-43%	8.6	-3%	8.9
Pretax Inc.	142	19%	119	-38%	192	45%	132
Eff. Tax Rate	37%	—	38%	—	36%	—	40%
Net Inc.	90.0	22%	74.0	-39%	122	54%	79.0

Balance Sheet & Other Fin. Data (Million $)

	1994	1993	1992	1991	1990	1989
Cash	14.0	16.0	24.0	73.0	100	115
Curr. Assets	177	174	197	234	250	249
Total Assets	379	362	373	390	381	411
Curr. Liab.	203	186	184	153	117	113
LT Debt	60.0	30.5	1.0	2.1	2.4	Nil
Common Eqty.	82.0	115	168	223	249	284
Total Cap.	163	163	189	237	264	298
Cap. Exp.	38.5	45.6	55.1	46.0	43.7	14.9
Cash Flow	113	91.0	138	93.0	109	15.0

Ratio Analysis

	1994	1993	1992	1991	1990	1989
Curr. Ratio	0.9	0.9	1.1	1.5	2.1	2.2
% LT Debt of Cap.	36.7	188.0	0.5	0.9	0.9	Nil
% Net Inc.of Revs.	13.9	12.1	17.9	12.0	15.5	0.3
% Ret. on Assets	24.7	20.3	32.7	20.7	25.5	0.4
% Ret. on Equity	93.4	52.7	63.9	33.9	37.8	0.5

Dividend Data —Dividends have been paid since 1942. A new "poison pill" stock purchase rights plan was adopted in 1989. A dividend reinvestment plan is available.

Amt. of Div. $	Date Decl.	Ex-Div. Date	Stock of Record	Payment Date
0.440	Nov. 09	Nov. 29	Dec. 05	Dec. 15 '94
0.440	Jan. 31	Feb. 27	Mar. 03	Mar. 15 '95
0.440	Apr. 25	May. 26	Jun. 02	Jun. 15 '95
0.440	Jul. 25	Aug. 30	Sep. 01	Sep. 15 '95

Data as orig. reptd.; bef. results of disc. opers. and/or spec. items. Per share data adj. for stk. divs. as of ex-div. date. E-Estimated. NA-Not Available. NM-Not Meaningful. NR-Not Ranked.

Office—777 Westchester Ave., White Plains, NY 10604. **Tel**—(914) 696-6000. **Chrmn**—H. B. Wentz, Jr. **Pres & CEO**—E. T. Fogarty. **SVP-CFO & Treas**—R. F. Wright. **Investor Contact**—Kathy Makrakis. **Dirs**—L. H. Affinito, P. S. Doherty, E. T. Fogarty, F. Hall, R. P. Kiley, J. Loudon, R. M. Manton, J. A. Meyers, H. L. Tower, H. B. Wentz Jr., R. M. Williams. **Transfer Agent & Registrar**—First Chicago Trust Co. of New York, NYC. **Incorporated** in Delaware in 1936. **Empl**-3,400. **S&P Analyst:** E.A. Vandeventer

TECO Energy

NYSE Symbol **TE**
In S&P MidCap 400

22-AUG-95 **Industry:** Utilities-Electric

Summary: TECO Energy owns Tampa Electric Co., a utility serving the Tampa Bay region in west central Florida. It also has significant diversified operations related to its core business.

S&P Opinion: Hold (★★★)

Recent Price • 21⅝
52 Wk Range • 22¾-18⅛
Yield • 4.9%
12-Mo. P/E • 14.3

Quantitative Evaluations
Outlook
(1 Lowest—5 Highest)
• 1+
Fair Value
• 16⅛
Risk
• Low
Earn./Div. Rank
• A

Technical Eval.
• Bullish since 12/94
Rel. Strength Rank
(1 Lowest—99 Highest)
• 36
Insider Activity
• NA

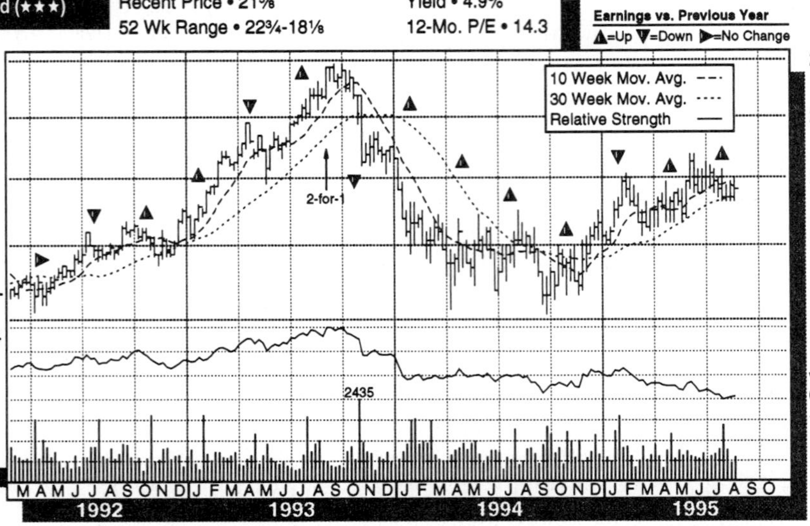

Overview - 17-AUG-95

Share earnings for 1995 should reflect somewhat higher earnings from Tampa Electric on continued growth in energy sales, the absence of a one-time charge from a corporate restructuring, and cost savings from work force reductions stemming from the restructuring. Results should benefit further from additional cost controls, higher construction-related credits, and slightly higher profit contributions from the nonregulated businesses. We expect increasing profitability for the diversified segment and growth in energy sales to enhance long-term prospects. Also, TE appears relatively well insulated from increasing competition within the electric utility industry since industrial customers comprise a relatively small portion of its customer base.

Valuation - 22-AUG-95

The shares have risen just over 6% thus far in 1995, well below the broader S&P 500 average. The shares peaked, along with most utility stocks, during a rally in May, and are currently selling near the high end of their trading range over the past 18 months. With an eye to deregulated markets looming in the near- to mid-term, the company intends to maintain the dividend payout ratio at 60% to 70% of earnings, a range that should allow substantial pricing flexibility as competition in the industry heats up. While the stock is yielding less than that of the average electric utility, TE's ability to raise the dividend over the next few years should significantly exceed that of its peers.

Key Stock Statistics

S&P EPS Est. 1995	1.55	Tang. Bk. Value/Share	9.33
P/E on S&P Est. 1995	14.0	Beta	0.37
S&P EPS Est. 1996	1.65	Shareholders	32,700
Dividend Rate/Share	1.06	Market cap. (B)	$ 2.5
Shs. outstg. (M)	116.5	Inst. holdings	39%
Avg. daily vol. (M)	0.123	Insider holdings	0%

Value of $10,000 invested 5 years ago: $ 18,878

Fiscal Year Ending Dec. 31

	1995	% Change	1994	% Change	1993	% Change
Revenues (Million $)						
1Q	319.1	4%	307.0	9%	282.0	7%
2Q	349.7	NM	353.0	12%	315.0	11%
3Q	—	—	366.6	NM	365.0	7%
4Q	—	—	324.3	NM	322.0	9%
Yr.	—	—	1,351	5%	1,284	9%
Income (Million $)						
1Q	36.50	9%	33.60	35%	24.82	-6%
2Q	46.38	11%	41.86	10%	38.21	10%
3Q	—	—	54.57	5%	51.83	-3%
4Q	—	—	23.15	-35%	35.45	3%
Yr.	—	—	153.2	2%	150.3	NM
Earnings Per Share ($)						
1Q	0.31	7%	0.29	38%	0.21	-9%
2Q	0.40	11%	0.36	9%	0.33	6%
3Q	E0.50	6%	0.47	4%	0.45	-4%
4Q	E0.34	70%	0.20	-35%	0.31	3%
Yr.	E1.55	17%	1.32	2%	1.30	NM

Next earnings report expected: mid October

TECO Energy

Business Summary - 22-AUG-95

TECO Energy's principal subsidiary is Tampa Electric, which serves Tampa, Fla., and adjacent communities. TECO has diversified extensively into nonregulated businesses, including transportation, energy production and real estate. Contributions to operating income in recent years:

	1994	1993	1992
Regulated utility	74%	73%	77%
Energy services	24%	25%	21%
Other	2%	2%	2%

Tampa Electric serves some 477,000 customers in west central Florida, including Hillsborough, Polk, Pasco and Pinellas counties. In 1994, Tampa sold 13.93 million megawatt hours (mwh) of power, versus 13.45 million mwh sold in 1993. TE's customer mix in 1994 (based on revenues) was: residential (46%); commercial (29%); industrial (10%); and other (15%), including bulk power sales for resale. TE derives about 99% of its power needs from coal. The total generating capability of TE's 19 power units at 1994 year end was 3,393 mw, while peak usage in 1994 was 2,754 mw.

TE's diversified operations include: TECO Coal, whose subsidiaries sold about 40% of their 1994 production to Tampa Electric from properties in Kentucky and Tennessee containing 175 million tons of coal; TECO Coalbed Methane, which participates in the production of natural gas from coalbeds located in Alabama's Black Warrior Basin; TECO Transport, which consists of four subsidiaries that transport, store and transfer coal and other bulk commodities to Tampa Electric (54%) and other customers (46%); and TECO Power Services, which seeks opportunities both in and outside Florida to develop, own and operate cogeneration and independent power projects. TE also has interests in real estate development and financial investments.

Important Developments

Jul. '95—TE reported earnings of $0.71 a share for the 1995 first half, versus $0.65 a year earlier. The 9% increase stemmed from 3% growth in retail energy sales, and a 9% reduction in non-fuel operating and maintenance expense. TECO Coal and TECO Transport & Trade saw higher operating income as a result of increased third-party sales, better pricing in the second quarter, and lower operating costs.

Capitalization

Long Term Debt: $997,173,000 (6/95).
Subsidiary Preferred Stock (Tampa Electric Co.): $54,956,000.

Per Share Data ($) (Year Ended Dec. 31)

	1994	1993	1992	1991	1990	1989
Tangible Bk. Val.	9.33	8.89	8.32	7.81	7.31	7.73
Earnings	1.32	1.30	1.30	1.28	1.23	1.18
Dividends	0.99	0.95	0.90	0.85	0.80	0.75
Payout Ratio	76%	73%	69%	67%	65%	63%
Prices - High	22 5/8	25 7/8	21 1/8	20 7/8	17	14 3/4
- Low	18 1/8	20 1/4	18	15 3/4	13 1/8	11
P/E Ratio - High	17	20	16	16	14	13
- Low	14	16	14	12	11	9

Income Statement Analysis (Million $)

	1994	%Chg	1993	%Chg	1992	%Chg	1991
Revs.	1,351	5%	1,284	9%	1,183	3%	1,154
Depr.	174	5%	165	16%	142	7%	133
Maint.	101	2%	99	5%	94.3	5%	89.4
Fxd. Chgs. Cov.	3.5	-3%	3.6	-11%	4.0	3%	3.9
Constr. Credits	5.7	54%	3.7	NM	1.1	NM	1.1
Eff. Tax Rate	23%	—	26%	—	27%	—	26%
Net Inc.	153	2%	150	NM	149	3%	145

Balance Sheet & Other Fin. Data (Million $)

	1994	1993	1992	1991	1990	1989
Gross Prop.	4,096	3,846	3,639	3,286	2,881	2,669
Cap. Exp.	309	271	255	410	253	157
Net Prop.	2,620	2,483	2,382	2,219	1,945	1,815
Capitalization:						
LT Debt	1,024	1,043	1,048	908	763	675
% LT Debt	49	50	52	51	48	44
Pfd.	NA	NA	NA	NA	NA	NA
% Pfd.	NA	NA	NA	NA	NA	NA
Common	1,084	1,028	956	891	831	877
% Common	51	50	48	50	521	57
Total Cap.	2,620	2,588	2,583	2,367	2,156	2,107

Ratio Analysis

	1994	1993	1992	1991	1990	1989
Oper. Ratio	83.4	81.7	82.0	81.9	82.2	82.7
% Earn. on Net Prop.	8.8	9.7	9.2	10.0	10.3	10.2
% Ret. on Revs.	11.3	11.7	12.6	12.6	12.7	12.6
% Ret. On Invest.Cap	8.9	8.8	8.6	9.3	9.3	9.2
% Return On Com.Eqty	14.5	15.2	16.1	16.9	16.3	15.7

Dividend Data —Dividends have been paid since 1900. A dividend reinvestment plan is available. A "poison pill" stock purchase rights plan was adopted in 1989.

Amt. of Div. $	Date Decl.	Ex-Div. Date	Stock of Record	Payment Date
0.253	Oct. 19	Oct. 26	Nov. 01	Nov. 15 '94
0.253	Jan. 17	Jan. 26	Feb. 01	Feb. 15 '95
0.265	Apr. 19	Apr. 25	May. 01	May. 15 '95
0.265	Jul. 18	Jul. 28	Aug. 01	Aug. 15 '95

Data as orig. reptd.; bef. results of disc opers. and/or spec. items. Per share data adj. for stk. divs. as of ex-div. date. E-Estimated. NA-Not Available. NM-Not Meaningful. NR-Not Ranked.

Office—702 North Franklin St., Tampa, FL 33602. **Tel**—(813) 228-4111. **Chrmn & CEO**—T. L. Guzzle. **Pres & COO**—G. F. Anderson. **SVP-Fin & Treas**—A. D. Oak. **VP-Secy**—R. H. Kessel. **Investor Contact**—Sandra Callahan. **Dirs**—G. F. Anderson, C. D. Ausley, S. L. Baldwin, H. L. Culbreath, J. L. Ferman Jr., E. L. Flom, H. R. Guild Jr., T. L. Guzzle, C. H. Ross Jr., R. L. Ryan, J. T. Touchton, J. A. Urquhart, J. O. Welch Jr. **Transfer Agent & Registrar**—First National Bank of Boston. **Incorporated** in Florida in 1899; reincorporated in 1949. **Empl**-4,440. **S&P Analyst:** Jane Collin

STANDARD & POOR'S

STOCK REPORTS

Tecumseh Products

NASDAQ Symbol **TECUA**

In S&P MidCap 400

31-JUL-95

Industry: Building

Summary: This company manufactures a broad range of hermetic compressors for air-conditioning and refrigeration products, gasoline engines for lawn and garden applications, and pumps.

S&P Opinion: Hold (★★★)

Recent Price • 48

52 Wk Range • 55½-40⅜

Yield • 2.1%

12-Mo. P/E • 8.3

Quantitative Evaluations

Outlook (1 Lowest—5 Highest)
• NA

Fair Value
• NA

Risk
• Low

Earn./Div. Rank
• B+

Technical Eval.
• Bearish since 4/95

Rel. Strength Rank (1 Lowest—99 Highest)
• 47

Insider Activity
• NA

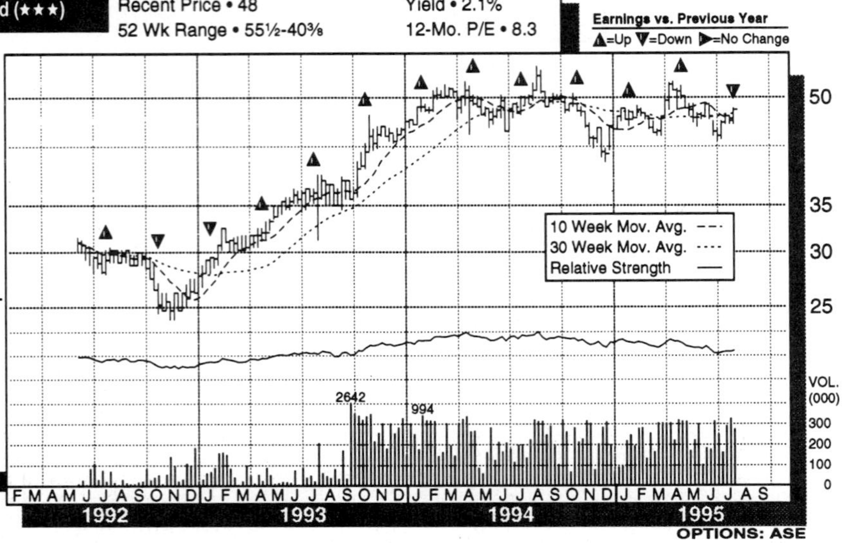

Overview - 31-JUL-95

Sales should rise moderately in 1995, with very strong sales of compressor products (as global shortages reflect depleted room air-conditioner inventory levels) outweighing lower engine and power train and pump products revenues. However, the industry is trending toward the use of scroll compressors, which are in development but will not contribute significantly to revenues until 1996. Overall profits should advance on continued improvement at two European operations and contributions from the company's high-margin Brazilian business, SICOM (although profits may be hurt by currency translations). Long-term growth should come from new product introductions, including a commercial compressor using R-134a, an alternative to CFC refrigerants, which the U.S. Government has required to be phased out by the end of 1995.

Valuation - 31-JUL-95

In late April, we downgraded the shares to hold, as earnings growth has slowed in recent quarters, primarily reflecting ongoing weakness in the engine and power train segment. Snowthrower sales stalled as heavy snowfalls expected for the winter of 1994-5 did not materialize. In addition, the inclement weather this past spring caused a slowing of lawn mower sales, and inventory has built up in both areas. Although compressor sales remain very strong, we believe the shares are currently fairly valued.

Key Stock Statistics

S&P EPS Est. 1995	5.70	Tang. Bk. Value/Share	34.93
P/E on S&P Est. 1995	8.4	Beta	0.32
S&P EPS Est. 1996	5.80	Shareholders	1,000
Dividend Rate/Share	1.00	Market cap. (B)	$ 1.1
Shs. outstg. (M)	21.9	Inst. holdings	65%
Avg. daily vol. (M)	0.070	Insider holdings	NA

Value of $10,000 invested 5 years ago: NA

Fiscal Year Ending Dec. 31

	1995	% Change	1994	% Change	1993	% Change
Revenues (Million $)						
1Q	483.4	25%	386.0	13%	342.0	3%
2Q	467.3	10%	424.8	15%	369.0	2%
3Q	—	—	355.0	18%	302.0	4%
4Q	—	—	367.2	22%	302.0	11%
Yr.	—	—	1,533	17%	1,314	4%
Income (Million $)						
1Q	34.90	20%	29.00	62%	17.90	26%
2Q	35.30	-2%	35.90	48%	24.30	19%
3Q	—	—	26.90	46%	18.40	75%
4Q	—	—	28.50	37%	20.80	193%
Yr.	—	—	120.3	48%	81.40	56%
Earnings Per Share ($)						
1Q	1.59	20%	1.32	61%	0.82	12%
2Q	1.62	-1%	1.64	48%	1.11	10%
3Q	E1.23	—	1.23	46%	0.84	53%
4Q	E1.26	—	1.31	38%	0.95	188%
Yr.	E5.70	—	5.50	48%	3.72	56%

Next earnings report expected: late October

Tecumseh Products

31-JUL-95

Business Summary - 31-JUL-95

Tecumseh Products Company believes it is the world's largest independent producer of hermetically sealed compressors and among the world's leading makers of small gasoline engines and power train products used in lawn and garden applications. It also makes submersible and centrifugal-type pumps. Contributions in 1994 were:

	Sales	Profits
Compressor products	57%	48%
Engine & power train products	37%	44%
Pump products	6%	8%

Sales outside of North America accounted for 28% of net sales and 30% of pretax income in 1994.

Compressor products, ranging from fractional-horsepower units used in small refrigerators and dehumidifiers to large units used in commercial air-conditioning applications, are sold to four major markets: household refrigerators and freezers; room air conditioners; commercial and residential unitary central air-conditioning systems; and commercial devices. During 1994, there was a significant increase in production of compressor products using R134-a, a non-CFC refrigerant, and other non-ozone depleting refrigerants. In late 1994, the company began commercial production of a new line of smaller room air-conditioning rotary compressors for use primarily in portable window units and recreational vehicles. Its customers have begun receiving samples of its new scroll compressors, but this line is not expected to contribute significantly to revenues before 1996.

Engine products consist of two- and four-cycle gasoline engines for use in a variety of lawn and garden chores, including lawn mowers, snow blowers and small lawn and garden tractors, small power devices used in outdoor chore products and certain self-propelled vehicles. Power train products include transmissions and transaxles used in lawn and garden tractors and riding lawn mowers.

Tecumseh markets small submersible pumps and related products through its Little Giant Pump Co. unit and heavy-duty centrifugal pumps through its MP Pumps Inc. subsidiary under the names Jaeger and MP Pumps.

Important Developments

Jun. '95—The company announced the purchase and planned expansion of a manufacturing facility in Douglas, Ga., where Tecumseh will build reduced exhaust emission engines and carburetors, with limited production expected to begin in February 1996. Total investment of $40 million is planned for the facility.

Capitalization

Long Term Debt: $8,000,000 (6/95).
Class A Common Stock: 16,410,438 shs. ($1 par); nonvoting.
Class B Common Stock: 5,470,146 shs. ($1 par).

Per Share Data ($)

(Year Ended Dec. 31)

	1994	1993	1992	1991	1990	1989
Tangible Bk. Val.	33.25	28.90	26.46	29.44	28.37	28.23
Cash Flow	8.04	6.04	4.84	4.23	2.92	5.76
Earnings	5.50	3.72	2.39	1.95	0.65	3.78
Dividends	1.35	1.15	0.80	0.80	0.80	1.11
Payout Ratio	25%	31%	33%	41%	124%	29%
Prices - High	55½	47¼	33	26½	34¼	37¼
- Low	40⅜	26¾	25¼	20	19½	33¼
P/E Ratio - High	10	13	13	14	53	10
- Low	7	7	10	10	30	9

Income Statement Analysis (Million $)

	1994	%Chg	1993	%Chg	1992	%Chg	1991
Revs.	1,533	17%	1,314	4%	1,259	5%	1,197
Oper. Inc.	221	36%	163	31%	124	13%	110
Depr.	55.7	10%	50.8	-5%	53.6	7%	49.9
Int. Exp.	6.5	63%	4.0	-33%	6.0	-8%	6.5
Pretax Inc.	192	50%	128	45%	88.0	16%	76.0
Eff. Tax Rate	37%	—	36%	—	41%	—	44%
Net Inc.	120	47%	81.4	56%	52.3	23%	42.5

Balance Sheet & Other Fin. Data (Million $)

	1994	1993	1992	1991	1990	1989
Cash	283	313	264	256	240	186
Curr. Assets	756	684	628	636	638	666
Total Assets	1,290	1,133	1,079	1,055	1,032	1,034
Curr. Liab.	252	210	207	233	224	269
LT Debt	9.1	11.2	14.4	17.9	23.6	19.9
Common Eqty.	786	687	640	713	692	682
Total Cap.	795	698	654	765	748	736
Cap. Exp.	136	53.0	56.6	85.8	64.8	57.5
Cash Flow	176	132	106	92.0	64.0	126

Ratio Analysis

	1994	1993	1992	1991	1990	1989
Curr. Ratio	3.0	3.3	3.0	2.7	2.9	2.5
% LT Debt of Cap.	1.1	1.6	2.2	2.3	3.2	2.7
% Net Inc.of Revs.	7.8	6.2	4.2	3.6	1.1	5.5
% Ret. on Assets	9.9	7.4	4.9	4.1	1.4	8.5
% Ret. on Equity	16.3	12.3	7.7	6.0	2.1	12.7

Dividend Data (Dividends have been paid each year since 1940 on Class B shares.)

Amt. of Div. $	Date Decl.	Ex-Div. Date	Stock of Record	Payment Date
0.200	Aug. 24	Sep. 12	Sep. 16	Sep. 30 '94
0.500	Nov. 23	Dec. 05	Dec. 09	Dec. 23 '94
0.250	Nov. 23	Dec. 05	Dec. 09	Dec. 23 '94
0.250	Feb. 22	Mar. 13	Mar. 17	Mar. 31 '95
0.250	May. 24	Jun. 14	Jun. 16	Jun. 30 '95

Data as orig. reptd.; bef. results of disc. opers. and/or spec. items. Per share data adj. for stk. divs. as of ex-div. date. E-Estimated. NA-Not Available. NM-Not Meaningful. NR-Not Ranked.

Office—100 E. Patterson St., Tecumseh, MI 49286. **Tel**—(517) 423-8411. **Chrmn**—K. G. Herrick. **Pres & CEO**—T. W. Herrick. **VP, Treas & CFO**—J. H. Foss. **Secy**—D. P. McDonald. **Investor Contact**—Sherry L. Cogswell (517) 423-8455. **Dirs**—P. M. Banks, J. E. Barfield, J. H. Foss, J. R. Fowler, J. W. Gelder, K. G. Herrick, T. W. Herrick, S. L. Hickman, E. C. Levy Jr., D. E. Richardson. **Transfer Agent & Registrar**—State Street Bank & Trust Co. **Incorporated** in Michigan in 1930. **Empl**-15,000. **S&P Analyst:** Alan Aaron

STANDARD & POOR'S

STOCK REPORTS

Teleflex Inc.

NYSE Symbol **TFX**
In S&P MidCap 400

22-AUG-95 **Industry:** Electronics/Electric

Summary: This company designs, manufactures and distributes engineered products and services for the automotive, marine, industrial, medical and aerospace markets worldwide.

S&P Opinion: Accumulate (★★★★) | Recent Price • 38⅞ | 52 Wk Range • 45¾-31¾ | Yield • 1.6% | 12-Mo. P/E • 15.0

Quantitative Evaluations

Outlook
(1 Lowest—5 Highest)
• **5+**

Fair Value
• **44⅞**

Risk
• **Low**

Earn./Div. Rank
• **A+**

Technical Eval.
• **Bearish** since 8/95

Rel. Strength Rank
(1 Lowest—99 Highest)
• **12**

Insider Activity
• **Unfavorable**

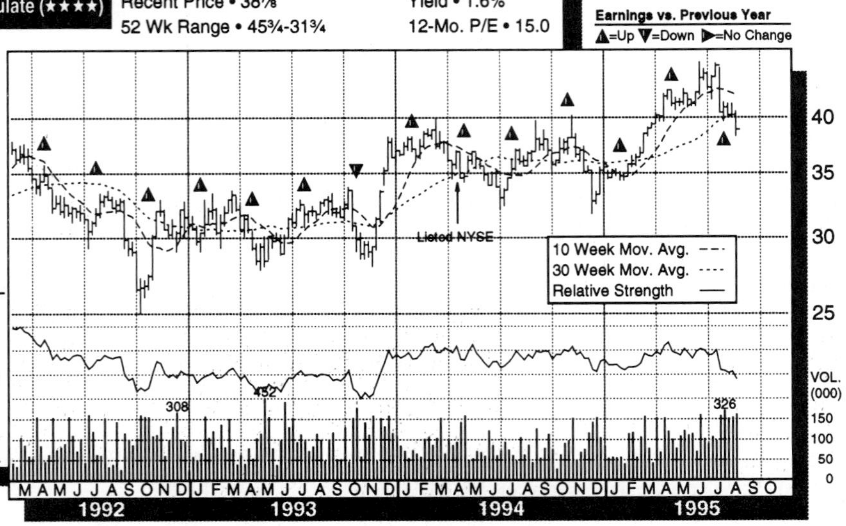

Overview - 17-AUG-95

Revenues for 1995 are expected to advance about 10% from those of 1994. The commercial sector should benefit from marine exports and increased penetration in the automotive market. The medical segment is projected to continue its international expansion, aided by new products and increased selling efforts. Gains from the aerospace group will be limited by lower aircraft build rates; nonetheless, surging cargo operations and strong turbine refurbishment and repair operations may result in increased revenues for the year. Margins could widen slightly, as improved aerospace profitability should offset higher medical product expenses.

Valuation - 22-AUG-95

The expected recovery in the aviation industry lifted TFX shares in the first half of 1995, but underperformance by the medical products group has pulled the stock back in recent weeks. Given the nature of the setback -- two unprofitable acquisitions and increased new product development expenses -- we are not overly concerned that underperformance will persist, and we therefore view the stock price pullback as a buying opportunity. Strong profit growth continues for the commercial segment. In addition, the company is shifting the focus of its aerospace operations away from government work and toward commercial work, in which it can compete effectively. With TFX trading at around 14 times our estimate of 1995 earnings, we view the stock as attractive.

Key Stock Statistics

S&P EPS Est. 1995	2.85	Tang. Bk. Value/Share	17.89
P/E on S&P Est. 1995	13.6	Beta	1.09
Dividend Rate/Share	0.62	Shareholders	2,000
Shs. outstg. (M)	17.4	Market cap. (B)	$0.685
Avg. daily vol. (M)	0.048	Inst. holdings	58%
		Insider holdings	0%

Value of $10,000 invested 5 years ago: $ 20,111

Fiscal Year Ending Dec. 31

	1995	% Change	1994	% Change	1993	% Change
Revenues (Million $)						
1Q	226.9	19%	191.1	21%	157.6	19%
2Q	233.9	12%	209.5	20%	174.9	18%
3Q	—	—	193.4	23%	156.9	14%
4Q	—	—	218.8	23%	177.4	18%
Yr.	—	—	812.7	22%	666.8	17%
Income (Million $)						
1Q	12.33	24%	9.97	16%	8.56	8%
2Q	13.30	19%	11.18	21%	9.26	8%
3Q	—	—	7.40	25%	5.90	-4%
4Q	—	—	12.66	27%	9.96	7%
Yr.	—	—	41.20	22%	33.69	5%
Earnings Per Share ($)						
1Q	0.70	23%	0.57	14%	0.50	6%
2Q	0.75	17%	0.64	19%	0.54	8%
3Q	E0.53	26%	0.42	24%	0.34	-6%
4Q	E0.86	19%	0.72	26%	0.57	6%
Yr.	E2.85	21%	2.35	21%	1.95	4%

Next earnings report expected: mid October

Teleflex Inc.

Business Summary - 22-AUG-95

Teleflex Inc., originally a manufacturer of push/pull controls for military aircraft, has diversified over the years in specific market niches in the aerospace, commercial and medical markets. Contributions by business segment in 1994 were:

	Sales	Profits
Commercial products	44%	59%
Medical products	31%	36%
Aerospace products	25%	6%

Foreign operations, principally in Europe, provided 27% of total sales in 1994 (28% in 1993); export sales accounted for 11% (10%).

Commercial products made for the automotive industry include automatic and manual transmission shift controls, accelerator and cruise controls, trunk and hood release cables, and fuel system hose. Marine products include mechanical and hydraulic steering systems, electrical gauges and instrumentation, and electronic navigation systems. Industrial products include cables for outdoor power equipment and flexible hose used in fluid transfer and other applications.

The aerospace products and services segment consists of the aerospace/defense group and Sermatech International Inc. The aerospace/defense group designs and makes mechanical and electromechanical controls for application on commercial and military aircraft, missiles, ground support equipment and ordnance. Sermatech provides a variety of sophisticated protective coatings and other services for gas turbine engine components; highly specialized repairs for critical components; and manufacturing and finishing of airfoils.

The medical products segment operates three businesses: Pilling Weck makes and distributes, primarily through its own sales force, instruments used in both traditional (open) and minimally invasive surgical procedures; Rusch International makes disposable and reusable invasive devices used primarily in urology and anesthesiology; and TFX OEM produces standard and customer designed semi-finished components for other medical devices.

Important Developments

Jul. '95—The company reported that operating income for the aerospace products segment almost doubled in the second quarter of 1995, despite a 2.3% decline in sales. Income for commercial products climbed 13% on a 12% sales increase, but medical products income fell 2.9% on 23% higher sales.

Capitalization

Long Term Debt: $190,672,000 (6/95).

Per Share Data ($) (Year Ended Dec. 31)

	1994	1993	1992	1991	1990	1989
Tangible Bk. Val.	17.89	15.79	14.25	12.73	11.45	9.87
Cash Flow	4.23	3.47	3.13	2.81	2.72	2.38
Earnings	2.35	1.95	1.87	1.77	1.73	1.63
Dividends	0.52	0.45	0.42	0.39	0.35	0.31
Payout Ratio	22%	23%	22%	22%	20%	19%
Prices - High	40¼	38¼	39½	34⅜	24⅛	25⅞
- Low	31¾	27¾	25	19⅝	16⅝	18¾
P/E Ratio - High	17	20	21	19	14	16
- Low	14	14	13	11	10	11

Income Statement Analysis (Million $)

	1994	%Chg	1993	%Chg	1992	%Chg	1991
Revs.	813	22%	667	18%	567	18%	480
Oper. Inc.	114	23%	92.9	13%	82.5	13%	73.1
Depr.	33.0	26%	26.1	21%	21.6	23%	17.5
Int. Exp.	18.4	27%	14.5	-6%	15.5	12%	13.8
Pretax Inc.	63.0	20%	52.3	7%	48.7	8%	45.3
Eff. Tax Rate	35%	—	36%	—	34%	—	34%
Net Inc.	41.2	22%	33.7	5%	32.0	7%	29.8

Balance Sheet & Other Fin. Data (Million $)

	1994	1993	1992	1991	1990	1989
Cash	24.1	11.3	36.3	24.5	44.3	18.4
Curr. Assets	390	322	290	255	237	194
Total Assets	711	641	535	478	425	367
Curr. Liab.	170	151	123	123	103	82.0
LT Debt	190	184	135	119	113	106
Common Eqty.	309	270	240	212	188	160
Total Cap.	529	478	402	342	311	275
Cap. Exp.	25.3	92.8	19.3	42.4	17.5	64.8
Cash Flow	74.2	59.8	53.6	47.3	44.7	39.1

Ratio Analysis

	1994	1993	1992	1991	1990	1989
Curr. Ratio	2.3	2.1	2.4	2.1	2.3	2.4
% LT Debt of Cap.	36.0	38.4	33.5	34.9	36.4	38.6
% Net Inc.of Revs.	5.1	5.1	5.6	6.2	6.5	7.5
% Ret. on Assets	6.1	5.7	6.3	6.6	7.2	8.5
% Ret. on Equity	14.2	13.1	14.1	14.8	16.3	18.0

Dividend Data —Quarterly dividends have been paid since 1977.

Amt. of Div. $	Date Decl.	Ex-Div. Date	Stock of Record	Payment Date
0.135	Aug. 05	Aug. 19	Aug. 25	Sep. 15 '94
0.135	Nov. 07	Nov. 18	Nov. 25	Dec. 15 '94
0.135	Feb. 06	Feb. 17	Feb. 24	Mar. 15 '95
0.155	Apr. 28	May. 19	May. 25	Jun. 15 '95
0.155	Aug. 07	Aug. 23	Aug. 25	Sep. 15 '95

Data as orig. reptd.; bef. results of disc. opers. and/or spec. items. Per share data adj. for stk. divs. as of ex-div. date. E-Estimated. NA-Not Available. NM-Not Meaningful. NR-Not Ranked.

Office—630 W. Germantown Pike, Plymouth Meeting, PA 19462. **Tel**—(610) 834-6301. **Fax**—(610) 834-8228. **Chrmn**—L. K. Black. **Pres & CEO**—D. S. Boyer. **VP & CFO**—H. L. Zuber, Jr. **VP & Secy**—S. K. Chance. **Investor Contact**—Janine Dusossoit (610-834-6362). **Dirs**—D. Beckman, L. K. Black, D. S. Boyer, J. S. Gonnella, L. E. Hatch, Jr., P. Hutchinson, S. W. W. Lubsen, J. H. Remer, P. E. Retzlaff, J. W. Stratton. **Transfer Agent & Registrar**—American Stock Transfer & Trust Co., NYC. **Incorporated** in Delaware in 1943. **Empl**-9,000. **S&P Analyst:** Joe Victor Shammas

STANDARD & POOR'S

Telephone and Data Systems

STOCK REPORTS

ASE Symbol **TDS**
In S&P MidCap 400

05-SEP-95 **Industry:** Telecommunications

Summary: TDS, the 17th largest telephone holding company in the U.S., provides local telephone service in 29 states, as well as cellular telephone and paging services.

S&P Opinion: Hold (★★★)

Recent Price • 41
52 Wk Range • 49⅞-36
Yield • 0.9%
12-Mo. P/E • 29.3

Quantitative Evaluations

Outlook (1 Lowest—5 Highest)
• **4-**

Fair Value
• **42**

Risk
• **Low**

Earn./Div. Rank
• **B+**

Technical Eval.
• **Bullish** since 3/95

Rel. Strength Rank (1 Lowest—99 Highest)
• **58**

Insider Activity
• **Neutral**

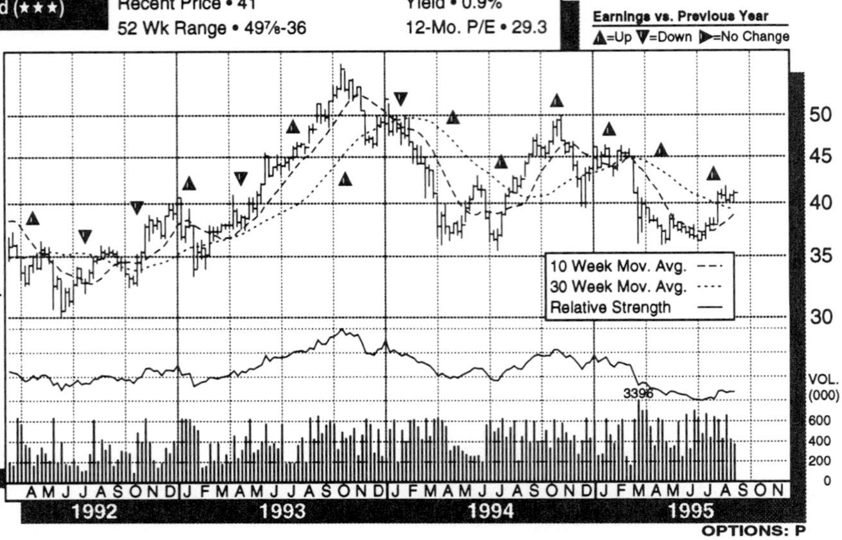

Overview - 05-SEP-95

Telephone revenue growth is expected to be in the high single digits in 1995, aided by internal growth and acquisitions. Higher depreciation charges should be offset by greater operating efficiencies. Cellular revenues should grow rapidly, and contributions from paging operations should improve. TDS also recently won eight broadband personal communications services licenses in an FCC auction. The company anticipates that within five years over 50% of revenues will come from wireless services. Economies and efficiencies from a clustering strategy should contribute to improved operating results, but earnings gains will be restricted by higher interest costs and more shares outstanding as a result of an aggressive acquisition program. Our 1995 EPS estimate of $1.40 includes $0.15 of nonrecurring gains.

Valuation - 05-SEP-95

The shares have fallen in 1995, reflecting investor concern regarding the company's successful $289 million bid for personal communication services (PCS) licenses. Although the average cost per potential customer of $10.35 was below the $15.54 average paid by all bidders, the total bid, together with capital spending needed to build the PCS network, indicates a substantial investment by TDS. In the long-term, PCS operations should further strengthen the company's rapidly growing cellular operations. We expect the shares to be only market performers until the PCS network begins to generate revenues.

Key Stock Statistics

S&P EPS Est. 1995	1.40	Tang. Bk. Value/Share	27.99
P/E on S&P Est. 1995	29.3	Beta	1.65
S&P EPS Est. 1996	1.70	Shareholders	3,800
Dividend Rate/Share	0.38	Market cap. (B)	$ 2.4
Shs. outstg. (M)	57.8	Inst. holdings	64%
Avg. daily vol. (M)	0.121	Insider holdings	NA

Value of $10,000 invested 5 years ago: $ 9,253

Fiscal Year Ending Dec. 31

	1995	% Change	1994	% Change	1993	% Change
Revenues (Million $)						
1Q	210.0	32%	158.8	25%	126.7	26%
2Q	232.1	34%	173.6	20%	144.8	30%
3Q	—	—	193.1	22%	158.7	34%
4Q	—	—	205.3	28%	160.6	27%
Yr.	—	—	730.8	24%	590.7	30%
Income (Million $)						
1Q	23.19	127%	10.22	50%	6.80	-48%
2Q	22.58	58%	14.32	60%	8.97	28%
3Q	—	—	17.62	48%	11.89	79%
4Q	—	—	18.38	195%	6.24	-47%
Yr.	—	—	60.54	79%	33.90	-12%
Earnings Per Share ($)						
1Q	0.39	117%	0.18	29%	0.14	-60%
2Q	0.38	46%	0.26	44%	0.18	13%
3Q	E0.38	23%	0.31	29%	0.24	60%
4Q	E0.25	-22%	0.32	191%	0.11	-58%
Yr.	E1.40	31%	1.07	60%	0.67	-26%

Next earnings report expected: mid October

Telephone and Data Systems

Business Summary - 05-SEP-95

Telephone and Data Systems (TDS) is a diversified telecommunications holding company. Contributions to revenues in recent years were:

	1994	1993	1992
Telephone	42%	45%	52%
Cellular	45%	42%	36%
Paging	13%	13%	12%

As of June 30, 1995, TDS provided local telephone service through 416,000 access lines in rural and suburban areas in 29 states. Operations have been expanded through an aggressive acquisition program.

Paging services are offered through American Paging, Inc. (APP, ASE). At June 30, 1995, 738,600 pagers were in service in 14 states and Washington, D.C. APP is expanding geographic coverage of its paging systems and initiating new services, such as voice mail, as they become practical. In APP's February 1994 initial public offering, 3.5 million shares were sold at $14 each. TDS retained an 82.5% interest in APP.

Virtually all cellular operations are conducted through 81.3%-owned United States Cellular Corp. (USM, ASE). The company and USM own or have the right to acquire cellular interests in metropolitan rural service areas representing 25.2 million population equivalents. As of June 30, 1995, USM served 550,000 customers in 137 majority-owned and managed systems. During 1994, USM agreed to acquire or trade for 13 markets with a total population of 2.3 million. The purpose of these transactions is to add to the company's existing clusters, thereby increasing the local areas in which customers can receive the company's wireless services.

Important Developments

Aug. '95—PCS Development Corp. signed a memorandum of understanding with American Paging for development and marketing of voice messaging services for the PCS network.
Jun. '95—U.S. Cellular and AT&T's McCaw Cellular closed transactions under which they exchanged interests in certain cellular markets.
May '95—The company agreed to acquire Camden Telephone Co. of Indiana. Camden's assets include a substantial cellular interest in Indiana Rural Services Area No. 4 north of Indianapolis.

Capitalization

Long Term Debt: $646,389,000 (3/95).
Minority Interest: $295,616,000.
Red. Preferred Stock: $1,666,000.
Nonred. Preferred Stock: $29,557,000.
Series A Common Stock: 5,879,661 shs. ($1 par); conv. sh.-for-sh. into com. About 96% is closely held.

Per Share Data ($) (Year Ended Dec. 31)

	1994	1993	1992	1991	1990	1989
Tangible Bk. Val.	26.87	24.15	21.27	18.42	14.17	12.00
Cash Flow	4.06	3.36	3.44	2.91	2.93	2.29
Earnings	1.07	0.67	0.91	0.59	0.86	0.35
Dividends	0.36	0.34	0.32	0.30	0.28	0.26
Payout Ratio	34%	51%	35%	51%	33%	74%
Prices - High	51½	57	41¼	40⅜	48	46½
- Low	35½	33¼	30⅛	28½	21¾	26⅞
P/E Ratio - High	48	85	45	68	56	NM
- Low	33	50	33	48	25	NM

Income Statement Analysis (Million $)

	1994	%Chg	1993	%Chg	1992	%Chg	1991
Revs.	731	24%	591	30%	456	29%	354
Depr.	162	27%	128	29%	99	29%	76.8
Maint.	NA	—	50.3	7%	46.9	10%	42.5
Constr. Credits	Nil	—	Nil	—	Nil	—	Nil
Eff. Tax Rate	40%	—	44%	—	44%	—	41%
Net Inc.	60.5	78%	33.9	-12%	38.5	82%	21.1

Balance Sheet & Other Fin. Data (Million $)

	1994	1993	1992	1991	1990	1989
Gross Prop.	2,783	2,111	1,571	1,225	831	706
Net Prop.	2,003	1,624	1,178	898	564	463
Cap. Exp.	311	209	162	169	152	157
Total Cap.	2,410	2,071	1,511	1,232	789	694
Fxd. Chgs. Cov.	3.3	2.4	2.9	1.6	2.0	1.4
Capitalization:						
LT Debt	537	514	405	381	255	256
Pfd.	315	266	174	156	54.4	40.5
Common	1,473	1,224	877	645	430	355

Ratio Analysis

	1994	1993	1992	1991	1990	1989
% Ret. on Revs.	8.3	5.7	8.4	6.0	9.2	4.6
% Ret. On Invest.Cap	4.5	4.0	5.2	5.0	6.8	5.4
% Return On Com.Eqty	4.4	3.0	4.8	3.6	6.6	3.6
% Earn. on Net Prop.	3.7	3.1	2.3	3.5	6.0	4.8
% LT Debt of Cap.	23.1	25.6	27.8	32.2	34.5	39.3
Capital. % Pfd.	13.6	13.3	12.0	13.2	7.4	6.2
Capital. % Common	63.3	61.1	60.2	54.6	58.1	54.5

Dividend Data —Dividends have been paid since 1974.

Amt. of Div. $	Date Decl.	Ex-Div. Date	Stock of Record	Payment Date
0.090	Dec. 06	Dec. 12	Dec. 16	Dec. 30 '94
0.095	Mar. 07	Mar. 13	Mar. 17	Mar. 31 '95
0.095	May. 25	Jun. 14	Jun. 16	Jun. 30 '95
0.095	Aug. 31	Sep. 13	Sep. 15	Sep. 29 '95

Data as orig. reptd.; bef. results of disc. opers. and/or spec. items. Per share data adj. for stk. divs. as of ex-div. date. E-Estimated. NA-Not Available. NM-Not Meaningful. NR-Not Ranked.

Office—30 North LaSalle St., Chicago, IL 60602. **Tel**—(312) 630-1900. **Chrmn**—L. T. Carlson. **Pres & CEO**—L. T. Carlson, Jr. **EVP-Fin & CFO**—M. L. Swanson. **VP & Treas**—R. D. Webster. **Secy**—M. G. Hron. **Investor Contact**—Julie Mathews. **Dirs**—J. Barr III, D. R. Brown, L. T. Carlson, L. T. Carlson, Jr., W. C. D. Carlson, R. J. Collins, R. E. Hornacek, L. O. Johnson, D. C. Nebergall, M. L. Swanson, H. S. Wander. **Transfer Agent**—Harris Trust & Savings Bank, Chicago. **Incorporated** in Iowa in 1968. **Empl**-5,322. **S&P Analyst:** Kevin J. Gooley

STANDARD & POOR'S

STOCK REPORTS

Teradyne, Inc.

NYSE Symbol **TER**
In S&P MidCap 400

11-SEP-95 **Industry:** Electronics/Electric

Summary: This manufacturer of automatic test equipment used primarily by the semiconductor and telecommunications industries also makes backplane connectors.

S&P Opinion: Hold (★★★)

Recent Price • 40⅝
52 Wk Range • 42⅞-12⅞
Yield • Nil
12-Mo. P/E • 28.0

Quantitative Evaluations

Outlook
(1 Lowest—5 Highest)
• **3+**

Fair Value
• **37½**

Risk
• **Average**

Earn./Div. Rank
• **B-**

Technical Eval.
• **Bullish** since 7/94

Rel. Strength Rank
(1 Lowest—99 Highest)
• **80**

Insider Activity
• **Unfavorable**

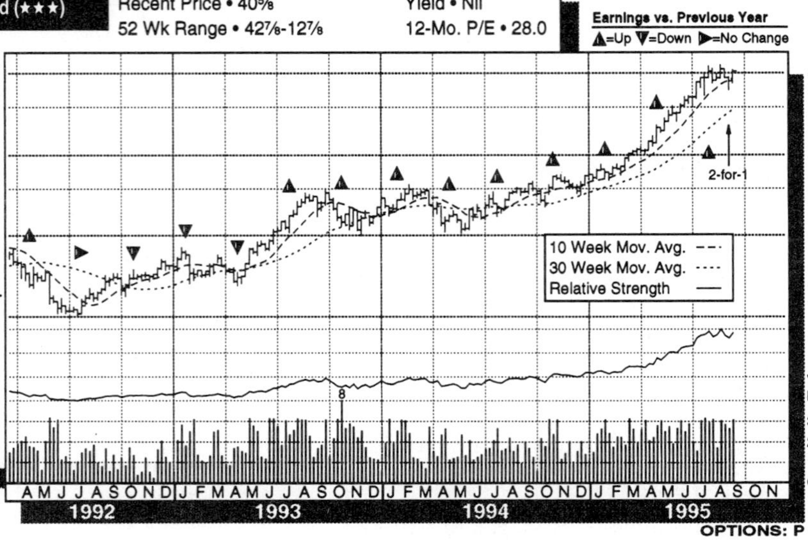

Overview - 11-SEP-95

Revenues are expected to rise sharply in 1995's second half, as TER enters the third quarter with some $640 million in backlog and order momentum from continued strong semiconductor demand. TER is experiencing order strength in all product lines and also in key telecommunications and military end-markets. Gross margins, which were up significantly in the second quarter, should widen further on the greater volume and manufacturing efficiencies. While TER is expected to ramp up R&D as a percent of sales for the balance of the year, the ratio for sales and marketing expenses is expected to fall, resulting in significant operating leverage. Our $1.80 EPS estimate for 1995 is up 89% from 1994's $0.95. We are forecasting 25% EPS growth in 1996, which assumes minimal dilution from the pending Megatest acquisition.

Valuation - 11-SEP-95

Teradyne's strong financial performance is expected to continue through the balance of 1996, which should provide a solid underpinning for the shares. The stock has run up dramatically in 1995, owing to the EPS gains and future visibility, and now trades at a relatively high P/E multiple. However, the P/E valuation on 1996 projected earnings is still below our 20%-25% projected two-to-three year growth rate for TER. Based on current fundamentals, we believe the shares could trade at 20X our 1996 estimate, which would yield a price of $45. We view this return, based on the current price range, as an average performance. Thus we recommend holding the shares.

Key Stock Statistics

S&P EPS Est. 1995	1.80	Tang. Bk. Value/Share	7.85
P/E on S&P Est. 1995	22.6	Beta	2.38
S&P EPS Est. 1996	2.25	Shareholders	3,100
Dividend Rate/Share	Nil	Market cap. (B)	$ 3.1
Shs. outstg. (M)	75.6	Inst. holdings	47%
Avg. daily vol. (M)	0.619	Insider holdings	NA

Value of $10,000 invested 5 years ago: $ 73,863

Fiscal Year Ending Dec. 31

	1995	% Change	1994	% Change	1993	% Change
Revenues (Million $)						
1Q	213.3	40%	152.0	19%	127.8	-5%
2Q	256.1	64%	156.5	12%	139.3	3%
3Q	—	—	178.8	27%	140.3	7%
4Q	—	—	190.1	29%	147.3	14%
Yr.	—	—	677.4	22%	554.7	5%
Income (Million $)						
1Q	28.73	113%	13.47	150%	5.39	-24%
2Q	38.75	165%	14.65	91%	7.66	68%
3Q	—	—	20.36	101%	10.11	76%
4Q	—	—	22.47	76%	12.78	148%
Yr.	—	—	70.94	97%	35.92	59%
Earnings Per Share ($)						
1Q	0.38	111%	0.18	125%	0.08	-24%
2Q	0.50	150%	0.20	90%	0.10	50%
3Q	E0.50	82%	0.28	96%	0.14	65%
4Q	E0.43	42%	0.30	71%	0.17	133%
Yr.	E1.80	89%	0.95	90%	0.50	49%

Next earnings report expected: mid October

Teradyne, Inc.

Business Summary - 11-SEP-95

Teradyne, Inc. is a manufacturer of electronic systems and software and backplane connection systems used in the electronics and telecommunications industries. Contributions by product line in 1994 were:

	Sales	Profits
Electronic test systems and software	84%	83%
Backplane connection systems	19%	17%

Exports contributed 46% of sales in 1994, up from 41% in 1993. Sales to Motorola were 10% of revenues in both 1994 and 1993.

TER designs, manufacturers, markets and services electronic test systems and related software used by component manufacturers in the design and testing of their products and by electronic manufacturers for the inspection of components and for the design and testing of circuit boards and other assemblies. Electronic systems and software are also used by telephone operating companies for testing and maintenance.

Electronic systems and software produced by the company include test systems for a wide variety of semiconductors, including digital and analog integrated circuits, test systems for circuit boards and other assemblies, and test systems for telephone lines and networks. The company's test systems are all controlled by computers, and programming and operating software is supplied both as an integral part of the product and as a separately priced enhancement. Prices range from below $100,000 to over $5 million.

TER also makes backplane connection systems, principally for the computer, telecommunications, and military/aerospace industries. A backplane is a panel that supports the circuit boards in an electronic assembly and carries wiring. The company has begun to shift from the manufacture of backplane connection systems to the manufacture of fully integrated electronic assemblies.

Engineering and development expenditures amounted to $70.4 million (10% of sales) in 1994, versus $62.4 million (11%) in 1993.

Important Developments

Sep. '95—TER agreed to acquire Megatest Corp., a maker of semiconductor test equipment with estimated revenues of $150 million for the fiscal year ended August 31, 1995. Under terms of the agreement, TER will issue about 6,650,000 common shares (between 0.8333 and 0.9091 of its shares for each Megatest share). The transaction, which is expected to be completed in January 1996, had a value of $245 million as of September 1.

Jul. '95—TER acquired Hammer Technologies, a supplier of test systems for mission-critical telecommunication providers.

Capitalization

Long Term Debt: $9,284,000 (7/2/95).

Per Share Data ($) (Year Ended Dec. 31)

	1994	1993	1992	1991	1990	1989
Tangible Bk. Val.	6.78	5.81	5.21	4.89	4.63	5.01
Cash Flow	1.38	0.93	0.79	0.80	0.29	0.82
Earnings	0.96	0.50	0.33	0.29	-0.36	0.17
Dividends	Nil	Nil	Nil	Nil	Nil	Nil
Payout Ratio	Nil	Nil	Nil	Nil	Nil	Nil
Prices - High	17⅞	14⅞	10¼	8½	5⅝	7⅜
- Low	10¼	6½	5	3⅛	1⅞	5
P/E Ratio - High	18	30	30	29	NM	42
- Low	11	13	15	11	NM	28

Income Statement Analysis (Million $)

	1994	%Chg	1993	%Chg	1992	%Chg	1991
Revs.	677	22%	555	5%	530	4%	509
Oper. Inc.	130	59%	82.0	40%	58.7	4%	56.2
Depr.	31.5	2%	30.8	NM	31.1	-3%	32.1
Int. Exp.	1.7	-53%	3.6	-12%	4.1	-21%	5.2
Pretax Inc.	103	101%	51.3	97%	26.1	29%	20.3
Eff. Tax Rate	31%	—	30%	—	14%	—	10%
Net Inc.	70.9	97%	35.9	60%	22.5	23%	18.3

Balance Sheet & Other Fin. Data (Million $)

	1994	1993	1992	1991	1990	1989
Cash	203	144	67.4	35.4	7.4	3.9
Curr. Assets	447	341	261	218	173	194
Total Assets	656	544	461	421	389	418
Curr. Liab.	139	107	92.4	86.9	84.9	75.2
LT Debt	8.8	9.1	23.6	24.3	25.0	38.4
Common Eqty.	493	420	345	306	275	293
Total Cap.	517	438	369	331	301	339
Cap. Exp.	29.6	20.6	19.5	14.6	23.9	28.3
Cash Flow	102	66.7	53.6	50.3	17.0	48.0

Ratio Analysis

	1994	1993	1992	1991	1990	1989
Curr. Ratio	3.2	3.2	2.8	2.5	2.0	2.6
% LT Debt of Cap.	1.7	2.1	6.4	7.3	8.3	11.3
% Net Inc.of Revs.	10.5	6.5	4.3	3.6	NM	2.1
% Ret. on Assets	11.7	6.9	5.0	4.4	NM	2.4
% Ret. on Equity	15.4	9.1	6.8	6.1	NM	3.5

Dividend Data —Dividends have never been paid. A two-for-one stock split was effected August 30, 1995. A "poison pill" stock purchase rights plan was adopted in 1990.

Amt. of Div. $	Date Decl.	Ex-Div. Date	Stock of Record	Payment Date
2-for-1	Jul. 25	Aug. 30	Aug. 08	Aug. 29 '95

Data as orig. reptd.; bef. results of disc. opers. and/or spec. items. Per share data adj. for stk. divs. as of ex-div. date. E-Estimated. NA-Not Available. NM-Not Meaningful. NR-Not Ranked.

Office—321 Harrison Ave., Boston, MA 02118. **Tel**—(617) 482-2700. **Chrmn & Pres**—A. V. d'Arbeloff. **EVP-Fin**—O. W. Robbins. **Clerk**—R. J. Testa. **VP & Investor Contact**—Frederick T. Van Veen. **Dirs**—A. V. d'Arbeloff, E. L. Artzt, A. Carnesale, D. S. Gregory, D. H. Hibbard, F. P. Johnson, Jr., J. P. Mulroney, J. Prestridge, O. Robbins, R. J. Testa. **Transfer Agent & Registrar**—Bank of Boston. **Incorporated** in Massachusetts in 1960. **Empl**-4,000. **S&P Analyst:** John D. Coyle, CFA

STANDARD & POOR'S

STOCK REPORTS

Thermo Electron

NYSE Symbol **TMO**
In S&P MidCap 400

27-AUG-95 **Industry:** Manufacturing/Distr

Summary: This company makes analytical instruments, biomedical equipment, cogeneration systems and process equipment. Minority interests have been sold in publicly traded subsidiaries.

S&P Opinion: Accumulate (★★★★)

Recent Price • 41¼ | Yield • Nil
52 Wk Range • 45-27⅛ | 12-Mo. P/E • 26.8

Quantitative Evaluations

Outlook
(1 Lowest—5 Highest)
• **4+**

Fair Value
• **43⅛**

Risk
• **Low**

Earn./Div. Rank
• **B+**

Technical Eval.
• **Bullish** since 7/94

Rel. Strength Rank
(1 Lowest—99 Highest)
• **41**

Insider Activity
• **NA**

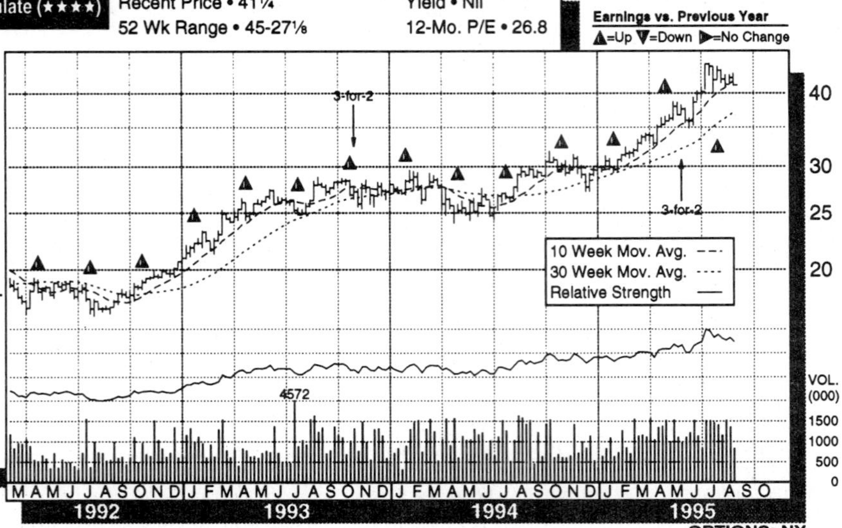

OPTIONS: NY

Overview - 25-AUG-95

Revenues grew 24% (versus restated 1994 results) in the first half of 1995 and should pass $2 billion for the full year. Thermo Instrument completed its spinoff of ThermoSpectra and is developing seven additional spinoffs. Expect Thermo Fibertek to maintain 20% growth in its paper-recycling business and to see ThermoCardiosystems start benefiting from its air-driven ventricular assist system. Thermedics, now in a product transition stage, should emerge with strong growth in 1996. ThermoTrex is seeing strong demand for its X-ray systems, and ThermoLase will soon open its first hair-removal treatment center. Demand should stay strong for Thermo Power and Thermo Process Systems (including Thermo Remediation), while Thermo Voltek and Thermo Ecotek are also expected to improve on earnings. Overall, we expect operating income, up 25% in the first half, to grow about 28% for the full year.

Valuation - 25-AUG-95

TMO has benefited from the market's awareness of its success in creating spinoffs with high growth potential and of its substantial equity interest in that growth. The shares have advanced approximately 40% in 1995 and have grown about 75% since the spring of 1994. Momentum was enhanced by the FDA approval for ThermoLase's hair-removal system, and the new level has been generally sustained by a strong first half. Given TMO's compelling growth prospects, the shares remain attractive at about 21 times our 1996 earnings estimate of $1.95.

Key Stock Statistics

S&P EPS Est. 1995	1.60	Tang. Bk. Value/Share	4.91
P/E on S&P Est. 1995	25.8	Beta	1.45
S&P EPS Est. 1996	1.95	Shareholders	6,400
Dividend Rate/Share	Nil	Market cap. (B)	$ 3.4
Shs. outstg. (M)	83.1	Inst. holdings	65%
Avg. daily vol. (M)	0.246	Insider holdings	NA

Value of $10,000 invested 5 years ago: $ 30,305

Fiscal Year Ending Dec. 31

	1995	% Change	1994	% Change	1993	% Change
Revenues (Million $)						
1Q	478.5	37%	350.5	20%	292.8	43%
2Q	528.7	34%	395.0	31%	300.5	43%
3Q	—	—	406.5	28%	318.4	31%
4Q	—	—	433.5	28%	338.1	16%
Yr.	—	—	1,585	27%	1,250	32%
Income (Million $)						
1Q	29.55	31%	22.54	46%	15.45	22%
2Q	32.58	35%	24.15	37%	17.61	27%
3Q	—	—	27.74	33%	20.92	35%
4Q	—	—	28.98	28%	22.66	22%
Yr.	—	—	103.4	35%	76.63	26%
Earnings Per Share ($)						
1Q	0.37	18%	0.31	24%	0.25	19%
2Q	0.39	17%	0.33	15%	0.29	25%
3Q	E0.41	10%	0.37	24%	0.30	16%
4Q	E0.43	13%	0.38	19%	0.32	4%
Yr.	E1.60	14%	1.40	20%	1.17	16%

Next earnings report expected: early November

Thermo Electron

Business Summary - 25-AUG-95

Thermo Electron Corporation has developed businesses from existing technologies and through acquisition and has sold minority positions in subsidiaries judged able to provide long-term growth. Segment contributions in 1994 were:

	Sales	Profits
Instruments	41%	52%
Alternative-energy systems	18%	17%
Process equipment	12%	10%
Biomedical products	11%	9%
Environmental services	9%	7%
Advanced technologies	9%	5%

Thermo Instrument Systems Inc. (83% owned) makes instruments to detect and measure air pollution, nuclear radioactivity and toxic substances. In August 1994, it formed privately held ThermoSpectra Corp. to focus on promising technologies. Thermo Power (60%) develops and makes packaged cogeneration and cooling systems fueled principally by natural gas. Thermo Fibertek (81%) makes processing machinery for the paper-making and recycling industries. Thermo Process Systems (80%) produces custom-engineered thermal processing systems to treat primary metals and metal parts, and, with TMO, owns 65% of Thermo Remediation, which remediates petroleum-contaminated soils.

Thermedics Inc. (51%) makes biomedical products and instruments used to detect explosives and narcotics. It owns, with TMO, 58% of Thermo Cardiosystems, a producer of ventricular-assist devices, and 71% of Thermo Voltek, a maker of high-voltage equipment. Thermotrex Corp. (50%) conducts research in advanced laser and electro-optical systems, thermodynamics and advanced parallel and signal processing. It owns, with TMO, 69% of ThermoLase, which is developing a long-term hair removal system. Thermo Ecotek (formerly Thermo Energy Systems), spun off in February 1995, operates alternative-energy power systems and is 83% owned by TMO.

Important Developments

Aug. '95—TMO said the termination date for Thermo Instrument System's planned acquisition of Fisons plc's Scientific Instruments division was extended to September 30 1995, to allow for further negotiations with the FTC. Separately, Thermo Cardiosystems received European Conformity Mark approval to market its electric LVAS. Earlier, TMO commenced a cash tender offer for the shares of Bird Medical Technologies, a manufacturer of respiratory care equipment, with sales of $53.8 million in 1994.

Capitalization

Long Term Debt: $1,072,027,000 (7/1/85), incl. $568,037,000 of sr. conv. obligs.
Minority Interest: $367,870,000.

Per Share Data ($)

(Year Ended Dec. 31)

	1994	1993	1992	1991	1990	1989
Tangible Bk. Val.	12.95	11.95	9.10	8.28	6.52	3.49
Cash Flow	2.25	1.81	1.49	1.31	1.14	0.91
Earnings	1.40	1.17	1.01	0.88	0.73	0.60
Dividends	Nil	Nil	Nil	Nil	Nil	Nil
Payout Ratio	Nil	Nil	Nil	Nil	Nil	Nil
Prices - High	31⅞	28⅞	21⅛	20⅞	15⅝	16⅞
- Low	24	20⅞	16⅝	11½	9⅝	8½
P/E Ratio - High	23	25	21	24	21	28
- Low	17	18	17	13	13	14

Income Statement Analysis (Million $)

	1994	%Chg	1993	%Chg	1992	%Chg	1991
Revs.	1,585	27%	1,247	32%	947	18%	805
Oper. Inc.	242	48%	163	71%	95.5	46%	65.3
Depr.	62.3	47%	42.4	45%	29.2	25%	23.4
Int. Exp.	61.7	54%	40.0	27%	31.4	72%	18.3
Pretax Inc.	204	56%	131	28%	102	29%	79.0
Eff. Tax Rate	34%	—	26%	—	27%	—	31%
Net Inc.	103	34%	76.6	26%	60.6	29%	47.1

Balance Sheet & Other Fin. Data (Million $)

	1994	1993	1992	1991	1990	1989
Cash	998	700	369	422	178	210
Curr. Assets	1,683	1,245	830	763	494	416
Total Assets	3,020	2,474	1,818	1,199	898	624
Curr. Liab.	537	416	326	297	254	153
LT Debt	1,050	790	694	255	210	172
Common Eqty.	990	859	553	481	307	211
Total Cap.	2,426	1,989	1,451	869	614	450
Cap. Exp.	60.0	60.0	193	33.0	24.0	20.0
Cash Flow	166	119	89.8	70.4	52.6	37.3

Ratio Analysis

	1994	1993	1992	1991	1990	1989
Curr. Ratio	3.1	3.0	2.5	2.6	1.9	2.7
% LT Debt of Cap.	43.3	39.7	47.8	29.4	34.2	38.2
% Net Inc.of Revs.	6.5	6.1	6.4	5.8	4.8	4.2
% Ret. on Assets	3.7	3.3	3.9	4.1	4.2	4.3
% Ret. on Equity	10.9	10.1	11.5	10.9	12.3	12.3

Dividend Data —No cash dividends have been paid. A shareholder rights plan was adopted in 1988.

Amt. of Div. $	Date Decl.	Ex-Div. Date	Stock of Record	Payment Date
3-for-2	Mar. 31	May. 25	Apr. 26	May. 24 '95

Data as orig. reptd.; bef. results of disc. opers. and/or spec. items. Per share data adj. for stk. divs. as of ex-div. date. E-Estimated. NA-Not Available. NM-Not Meaningful. NR-Not Ranked.

Office—81 Wyman St., P.O. Box 9046, Waltham, MA 02254-9046. **Tel**—(617) 622-1000. **Chrmn, Pres & CEO**—G. N. Hatsopoulos. **CFO & Investor Contact**—John N. Hatsopoulos (617) 622-1111. **VP-Fin**—P. F. Kelleher. **Secy**—Sandra L. Lambert. **Dirs**—J. M. Albertine, P. O. Crisp, E. P. Gyftopoulos, G. N. Hatsopoulos, F. Jungers, R. A. McCabe, F. E. Morris, D. E. Noble, H. S. Olayan, R. D. Wellington. **Transfer Agent & Registrar**—Bank of Boston. **Incorporated** in Delaware in 1956; reincorporated in 1960. **Empl-** 10,234. **S&P Analyst:** Justin McCann

STANDARD & POOR'S

STOCK REPORTS

Thiokol Corp.

NYSE Symbol **TKC**
In S&P MidCap 400

27-AUG-95

Industry:
Aerospace

Summary: Thiokol is the leading maker of solid rocket propulsion systems used in the Space Shuttle, other space vehicles and missiles. It also produces aerospace and industrial fasteners.

S&P Opinion: Hold (★★★)

Recent Price • 34½
52 Wk Range • 34¾-22¾

Yield • 2.0%
12-Mo. P/E • 12.4

Quantitative Evaluations

Outlook
(1 Lowest—5 Highest)
• **2+**

Fair Value
• **30⅞**

Risk
• **Low**

Earn./Div. Rank
• **NR**

Technical Eval.
• **Bullish** since 11/94

Rel. Strength Rank
(1 Lowest—99 Highest)
• **69**

Insider Activity
• **NA**

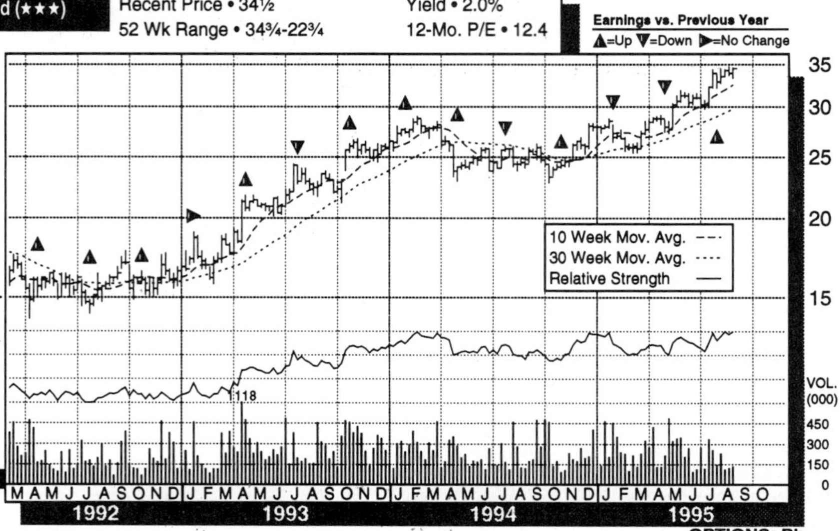

OPTIONS: Ph

Overview - 25-AUG-95

Fiscal 1996 revenues are expected to decline slightly from those of fiscal 1995. Strategic, tactical and ordnance sales are projected to drop substantially, reflecting lower government spending on a number of defense programs, including the Trident and Standard Missile. Space activities are expected to remain almost the same, as revenues from one less shuttle launch should be mostly offset by sales of other engines. Fastener sales should grow about 15%, reflecting the market recovery and acquisitions. Comparisons will benefit without $61.4 million of restructuring charges (despite the absence of a $43.5 million tax refund).

Valuation - 25-AUG-95

TKC shares have climbed in recent periods partially in response to cost cutting moves that should boost margins and competitiveness. However, we still have concerns about further budget reductions at NASA and the department of defense. Thiokol appears to be particularly susceptible to such cuts. With few defense/space programs likely to increase revenues, Thiokol is attempting to boost its program content. Otherwise, we would only expect long-term gains to be derived from greater demand for satellite launch vehicles and the expanding fastener operations. Recent problems with the space shuttle (which has delayed shuttle launches) will likely penalize NASA incentive award fees.

Key Stock Statistics

S&P EPS Est. 1996	3.00	Tang. Bk. Value/Share	16.60
P/E on S&P Est. 1996	11.5	Beta	0.09
Dividend Rate/Share	0.68	Shareholders	8,500
Shs. outstg. (M)	18.5	Market cap. (B)	$0.638
Avg. daily vol. (M)	0.029	Inst. holdings	88%
		Insider holdings	NA

Value of $10,000 invested 5 years ago: $ 29,811

Fiscal Year Ending Jun. 30

	1995	% Change	1994	% Change	1993	% Change
Revenues (Million $)						
1Q	238.1	-8%	257.7	-11%	289.0	NM
2Q	218.6	-9%	240.7	-22%	307.5	-7%
3Q	232.6	-13%	266.1	-4%	277.9	-19%
4Q	267.4	-4%	279.4	-15%	327.3	-7%
Yr.	956.8	-8%	1,044	-13%	1,202	-8%
Income (Million $)						
1Q	14.29	2%	14.03	4%	13.47	2%
2Q	11.29	-24%	14.80	1%	14.60	NM
3Q	-35.11	NM	15.37	NM	15.43	2%
4Q	61.77	NM	16.13	-21%	20.30	2%
Yr.	52.25	-13%	60.32	-5%	63.80	1%
Earnings Per Share ($)						
1Q	0.76	12%	0.68	1%	0.67	2%
2Q	0.60	-18%	0.73	1%	0.72	NM
3Q	-1.87	NM	0.77	1%	0.76	1%
4Q	3.29	NM	0.84	-14%	0.98	-1%
Yr.	2.78	-8%	3.02	-4%	3.13	NM

Next earnings report expected: late October

Thiokol Corp.

Business Summary - 25-AUG-95

Thiokol Corp. consists of the aerospace operations of the former Morton Thiokol, following the spinoff of nonaerospace businesses in 1989. The company also produces fastening systems. Contributions by segment (preliminary; excluding restructuring charges) in fiscal 1995 were:

	Sales	Profits
Space	49%	57%
Defense	27%	25%
Fastening systems	24%	18%

Space operations consist of the development and production of solid propellant rocket motor systems for space vehicles, such as the booster motors for the Space Shuttle and the Delta, Scout and other launch vehicles. Placement motors are produced for satellites such as Westar, Telesat Satcom and Intelsat.

Strategic systems include propulsion for the submarine-launched Trident. Tactical missile propulsion systems include the Maverick, HARM, Sidewinder, Standard (MK-70 and MK-104) and Patriot. With 40% of the market, TKC is the largest producer of solid rocket propulsion systems in the U.S.

Gas generator operations consist of the production of generator components for missile applications, including thrust vector control actuators, launch eject systems, attitude control and ordnance dispensers.

Ordnance operations consist of production of air- and ground-launched flares, munitions simulators for training, and conventional artillery munitions, mines and mine clearing and demolition charges.

Fastening systems include specialty fasteners used in aerospace and other transportation and industrial markets.

Services include launch and recovery operations for the Space Shuttle.

Important Developments

Aug. '95—TKC reported income of $3.03 for fiscal 1995 before the effect of nonrecurring charges. The year included a $61.4 million restructuring charge ($2.62 a share, after taxes) to close its Huntsville, Ala., facility, divest its Omneco, Inc. subsidiary, consolidate facilities, and write down goodwill. In addition, there was income of $43.5 million ($2.37) related to an IRS refund. In March, TKC retired $85.5 million of private placement debt, resulting in an extraordinary loss of $0.25 a share.

Feb. '95—The company acquired certain assets of the Automatic Fastener Corp. Automatic Fastener, with annual sales of about $17 million, produces a broad line of blind and specialty rivets for the automotive and light truck markets.

Capitalization

Long Term Debt: $2,637,000 (3/95).

Per Share Data ($) (Year Ended Jun. 30)

	1995	1994	1993	1992	1991	1990
Tangible Bk. Val.	NA	16.63	18.09	15.31	13.57	11.01
Cash Flow	NA	5.06	5.02	5.06	4.64	4.19
Earnings	2.78	3.02	3.13	3.12	2.75	2.15
Dividends	0.68	0.68	0.47	0.36	0.30	0.30
Payout Ratio	24%	23%	15%	11%	11%	14%
Prices - High	34½	29	26¾	17¾	21¼	14½
- Low	25⅜	22⅞	15¾	13⅝	12⅛	9⅛
P/E Ratio - High	12	10	9	6	8	7
- Low	9	8	5	4	4	4

Income Statement Analysis (Million $)

	1994	%Chg	1993	%Chg	1992	%Chg	1991
Revs.	1,044	-13%	1,202	-8%	1,312	5%	1,255
Oper. Inc.	140	-11%	158	2%	155	17%	133
Depr.	41.0	6%	38.6	-1%	39.0	6%	36.7
Int. Exp.	14.4	-44%	25.5	5%	24.2	9%	22.3
Pretax Inc.	98.0	-4%	102	NM	102	16%	88.0
Eff. Tax Rate	38%	—	37%	—	38%	—	39%
Net Inc.	60.3	-5%	63.8	1%	63.0	18%	53.4

Balance Sheet & Other Fin. Data (Million $)

	1994	1993	1992	1991	1990	1989
Cash	40.1	31.4	136	198	113	15.0
Curr. Assets	362	400	499	490	468	378
Total Assets	801	841	962	849	816	729
Curr. Liab.	145	184	360	134	150	120
LT Debt	87.9	87.9	123	220	220	220
Common Eqty.	385	443	387	326	274	238
Total Cap.	489	594	547	672	621	568
Cap. Exp.	21.0	20.0	37.0	41.0	30.0	37.0
Cash Flow	101	102	102	90.0	81.0	58.0

Ratio Analysis

	1994	1993	1992	1991	1990	1989
Curr. Ratio	2.5	2.2	1.4	3.7	3.1	3.2
% LT Debt of Cap.	18.0	14.8	22.5	32.7	35.5	38.7
% Net Inc.of Revs.	5.8	5.3	4.8	4.3	3.5	1.5
% Ret. on Assets	7.4	7.0	6.9	6.4	5.3	1.3
% Ret. on Equity	14.6	15.3	17.5	17.7	16.1	2.7

Dividend Data —Dividends were initiated following the 1989 spinoff of Morton International. A poison pill stock purchase rights plan was adopted in 1989.

Amt. of Div. $	Date Decl.	Ex-Div. Date	Stock of Record	Payment Date
0.170	Aug. 18	Aug. 25	Aug. 31	Sep. 14 '94
0.170	Oct. 26	Nov. 23	Nov. 30	Dec. 14 '94
0.170	Jan. 26	Feb. 22	Feb. 28	Mar. 14 '95
0.170	Apr. 20	May. 24	May. 31	Jun. 14 '95
0.170	Aug. 17	Aug. 29	Aug. 31	Sep. 14 '95

Data as orig. reptd.; bef. results of disc. opers. and/or spec. items. Per share data adj. for stk. divs. as of ex-div. date. E-Estimated. NA-Not Available. NM-Not Meaningful. NR-Not Ranked.

Office—2475 Washington Blvd., Ogden, UT 84401-2398. **Tel**—(801) 629-2052. **Chrmn**—U. E. Garrison. **Pres & CEO**—J. R. Wilson. **SVP & CFO**—R. L. Corbin. **Secy**—E. M. North. **Treas**—N. J. Iuanow. **Investor Contact**—Mark W. Hunt (801-629-2091). **Dirs**—N. A. Armstrong, J. R. Burnett, M. P. C. Carns, E. D. Dunford, U. E. Garrison, L. D. Kozlowski, C. S. Locke, J. M. Ringler, D. C. Trauscht, J. R. Wilson. **Transfer Agent & Registrar**—First Chicago Trust Co. of New York, NYC. **Incorporated** in New York in 1890; reincorporated in Delaware in 1969. **Empl-** 8,000. **S&P Analyst:** Joe Victor Shammas

STANDARD & POOR'S

STOCK REPORTS

Tidewater Inc.

NYSE Symbol **TDW**
In S&P MidCap 400

08-SEP-95 **Industry:** Oil and Gas

Summary: Tidewater operates the largest fleet of vessels serving the international offshore energy business. It also supplies compression equipment and services for a number of industries.

S&P Opinion: Hold (★★★)

Recent Price • 26¾
52 Wk Range • 27-16½
Yield • 1.9%
12-Mo. P/E • 31.1

Quantitative Evaluations
Outlook
(1 Lowest—5 Highest)
• **2+**
Fair Value
• **24½**
Risk
• **Average**
Earn./Div. Rank
• **B-**

Technical Eval.
• **Bearish** since 4/95
Rel. Strength Rank
(1 Lowest—99 Highest)
• **66**
Insider Activity
• **Neutral**

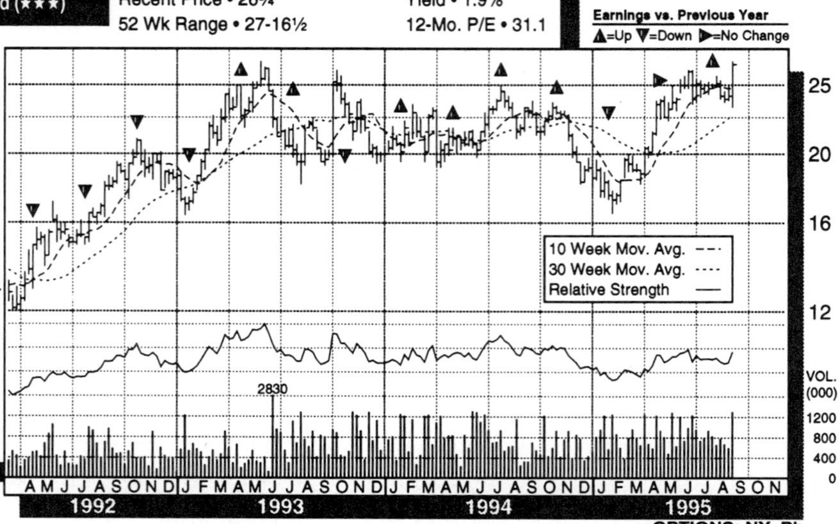

OPTIONS: NY, Ph

Overview - 06-SEP-95

The company should continue on its path of improving earnings in fiscal 1995-96. Marine operations have been restructured, with corporate streamlining and the withdrawal of older vessels; estimated savings range up to $7 million annually. Recent improvements in the U.S Gulf of Mexico point to increased rig count and a higher supply vessel utilization rate. The overseas fleet can be redeployed to meet demand in more lucrative operating areas, as oil prices have risen from their 1994 lows. The recent acquisitions of the Halliburton and Mitchell Energy fleets of gas compressors, which tripled the size of TDW's fleet, making it the largest in the U.S., have already improved results (an initial 100% increase in revenues was recorded) and should continue to do so going forward.

Valuation - 06-SEP-95

The company's shares have continued their upward trend, which began in early 1995. The market has reacted favorably to the expansion of TDW's gas compression fleet, and its consequent positive impact on revenues. Although the new, combined fleet does not have the same utilization rate as the old, earnings are projected to rise. The demand for oil support services has also improved from last year. However, the yield on the stock is relatively low and recent prices have been in excess of fair value. Selling at about 25 times estimated fiscal 1995-96 earnings, the shares can only be considered a hold.

Key Stock Statistics

S&P EPS Est. 1996	1.05	Tang. Bk. Value/Share	11.10
P/E on S&P Est. 1996	25.5	Beta	1.18
S&P EPS Est. 1997	1.25	Shareholders	2,400
Dividend Rate/Share	0.50	Market cap. (B)	$ 1.4
Shs. outstg. (M)	53.3	Inst. holdings	77%
Avg. daily vol. (M)	0.319	Insider holdings	NA

Value of $10,000 invested 5 years ago: $ 19,760

Fiscal Year Ending Mar. 31

	1996	% Change	1995	% Change	1994	% Change
Revenues (Million $)						
1Q	141.0	6%	133.3	3%	129.2	17%
2Q	—	—	131.3	-2%	134.2	12%
3Q	—	—	135.9	2%	133.0	7%
4Q	—	—	138.3	10%	125.8	5%
Yr.	—	—	538.8	3%	522.1	10%
Income (Million $)						
1Q	16.50	23%	13.44	64%	8.20	23%
2Q	—	—	12.33	35%	9.10	-20%
3Q	—	—	11.70	-14%	13.54	85%
4Q	—	—	5.16	NM	5.20	111%
Yr.	—	—	42.63	18%	36.13	30%
Earnings Per Share ($)						
1Q	0.31	24%	0.25	67%	0.15	15%
2Q	E0.29	26%	0.23	35%	0.17	-19%
3Q	E0.28	27%	0.22	-12%	0.25	79%
4Q	E0.17	70%	0.10	NM	0.10	100%
Yr.	E1.05	31%	0.80	19%	0.67	26%

Next earnings report expected: mid October

Tidewater Inc.

Business Summary - 07-SEP-95

Tidewater is an international energy service company that provides various support services, engineered products and technical services to the oil and gas industry. The company's two principal divisions are Tidewater Marine and Tidewater Compression. The company owns and operates the world's largest fleet of vessels primarily serving the international offshore energy industry, and is one of the leading suppliers of compression services in the U.S. Business segment contributions in fiscal 1994-95 were:

	Revs.	Profits
Marine services	85%	83%
Compression services	15%	17%

Marine service and support functions include towing and anchor-handling for mobile drilling rigs and equipment; transporting supplies necessary to sustain drilling, workover and production activities; and supporting pipelaying and construction activities. At March 31, 1995, TDW's fleet, including joint-venture holdings, consisted of approximately 570 vessels, down from 594 at 1993-94 year-end. In 1994-95, the company derived 54% of marine equipment revenues from foreign marine operations, down from 58% in 1993-94. Vessel utilization in 1994-95 declined to 75% from 78% in 1993-94. Quality Shipyards, Inc., a wholly-owned subsidiary, operates two shipyards in Houma, La., which build, repair, modify and drydock vessels.

The company provides gas and air compression equipment and services for a variety of industries. With 2,876 compressors, TDW operates the largest rental fleet of gas compressors in the U.S. The compressors are used to boost natural gas from the wellhead to feed it into nearby gas processing plants or into high pressure pipelines. Compression equipment also is used in production of coalbed methane, and enhanced recovery projects. During fiscal 1994-95, the company acquired the natural gas compression assets of Halliburton Co. and one of its affiliated companies and Brazos Compressing Co., a subsidiary of Mitchell Energy & Development Corp. Utilization rates in 1994-95 were 82%, down from 86% in 1993-94.

Tidewater Marine generally has its highest utilization rates in the warmer weather months when the weather is more favorable for offshore exploration, development and construction work. Tidewater Compresssion has its best results in the winter months when natural gas is in greater demand.

Important Developments

Jul. '95—TDW's earnings advanced in the first quarter of fiscal 1996, reflecting the company's expanded compressor fleet and increased average day rates, while utilization rose for towing supply/supply vessels.

Capitalization

Long Term Debt: $60,000,000 (6/95).

Per Share Data ($) (Year Ended Mar. 31)

	1995	1994	1993	1992	1991	1990
Tangible Bk. Val.	10.90	10.50	10.36	10.22	9.03	7.90
Cash Flow	2.42	2.25	2.03	2.01	2.50	1.42
Earnings	0.80	0.67	0.53	0.50	1.11	-0.38
Dividends	0.40	0.40	0.32	Nil	Nil	Nil
Payout Ratio	50%	60%	43%	Nil	Nil	Nil
Cal. Yrs.	1994	1993	1992	1991	1990	1989
Prices - High	25	27	21	18½	22¼	14⅞
- Low	18	16⅜	11⅜	9⅞	12⅜	7¼
P/E Ratio - High	31	40	40	37	20	NM
- Low	23	24	21	20	11	NM

Income Statement Analysis (Million $)

	1995	%Chg	1994	%Chg	1993	%Chg	1992
Revs.	539	3%	522	10%	476	-13%	547
Oper. Inc.	147	5%	140	8%	130	-8%	141
Depr.	86.6	3%	83.7	5%	79.9	NM	79.6
Int. Exp.	4.7	-41%	7.9	-36%	12.3	-34%	18.6
Pretax Inc.	68.9	15%	59.7	40%	42.7	NM	43.0
Eff. Tax Rate	36%	—	36%	—	29%	—	39%
Net Inc.	42.6	18%	36.1	30%	27.8	6%	26.3

Balance Sheet & Other Fin. Data (Million $)

	1995	1994	1993	1992	1991	1990
Cash	15.0	107	109	113	54.0	45.0
Curr. Assets	201	286	297	289	147	125
Total Assets	902	810	839	846	391	370
Curr. Liab.	101	130	96.0	111	44.0	45.0
LT Debt	100	2.0	96.0	124	84.0	92.0
Common Eqty.	580	557	548	536	257	224
Total Cap.	738	615	699	718	341	317
Cap. Exp.	300	53.3	52.4	39.0	42.0	17.0
Cash Flow	129	120	108	106	72.0	32.0

Ratio Analysis

	1995	1994	1993	1992	1991	1990
Curr. Ratio	2.0	2.2	3.1	2.6	3.3	2.8
% LT Debt of Cap.	13.5	0.3	13.7	17.3	24.5	29.1
% Net Inc.of Revs.	7.9	6.9	0.8	4.8	12.9	NM
% Ret. on Assets	5.0	4.4	3.3	3.4	8.3	NM
% Ret. on Equity	7.5	6.5	5.1	5.2	13.2	NM

Dividend Data —Dividends, omitted in 1986, were resumed in 1992. A "poison pill" stock purchase rights plan was adopted in 1990.

Amt. of Div. $	Date Decl.	Ex-Div. Date	Stock of Record	Payment Date
0.100	Oct. 20	Oct. 28	Nov. 03	Nov. 17 '94
0.100	Jan. 04	Jan. 13	Jan. 20	Feb. 03 '95
0.100	Apr. 26	May. 02	May. 08	May. 18 '95
0.125	Jul. 20	Jul. 28	Aug. 01	Aug. 11 '95

Data as orig. reptd.; bef. results of disc. opers. and/or spec. items. Per share data adj. for stk. divs. as of ex-div. date. E-Estimated. NA-Not Available. NM-Not Meaningful. NR-Not Ranked.

Office—1440 Canal St., New Orleans, LA 70112. **Tel**—(504) 568-1010. **Chrmn, Pres & CEO**—W. C. O'Malley. **EVP, CFO & Investor Contact**—Ken C. Tamblyn. **VP & Secy**—V. I. Koock. **Dirs**—R. H. Boh, D. T. Bollinger, A. R. Carlson, H. J. Kelly, J. P. Laborde, P. W. Murrill, W. C. O'Malley, L. Pollack, J. H. Roff, Jr. **Transfer Agent & Registrar**—First National Bank of Boston. **Incorporated** in Delaware in 1956. **Empl**-6,870. **S&P Analyst:** Michael C. Barr

STANDARD & POOR'S
STOCK REPORTS

Tiffany & Co.

NYSE Symbol **TIF**
In S&P MidCap 400

12-SEP-95

Industry: Jewelry, silverware, time pieces, china

Summary: This company is an international retailer, designer, manufacturer and distributor of fine jewelry and gift items.

Quantitative Evaluations

Outlook (1 Lowest—5 Highest)
• **5+**

Fair Value
• **51⅛**

Risk
• **Average**

Earn./Div. Rank
• **NR**

Technical Eval.
• **Bearish** since 6/95

Rel. Strength Rank (1 Lowest—99 Highest)
• **78**

Insider Activity
• **Neutral**

Recent Price • 42⅞
52 Wk Range • 43⅝-29
Yield • 0.6%
12-Mo. P/E • 21.7

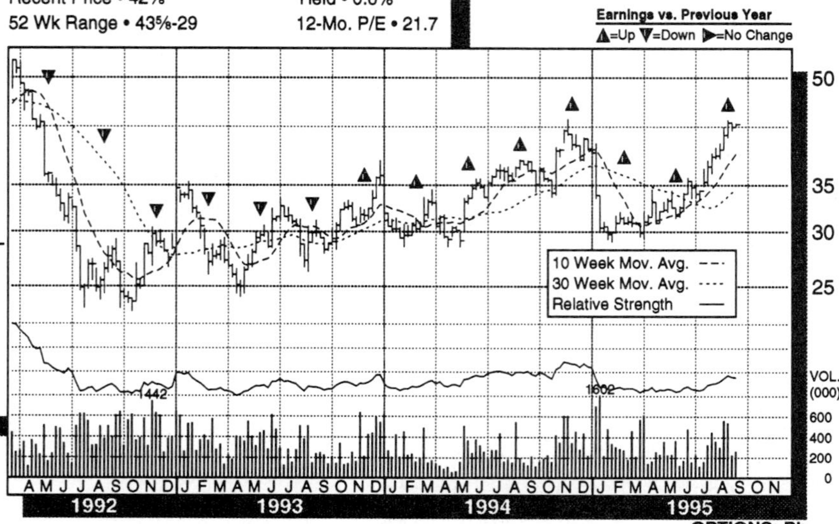

OPTIONS: Ph

Business Profile - 12-SEP-95

The company hopes to pursue sales and earnings growth through increasing its accessibility in key global markets, offering superior products and heightening consumer awareness of its competitive attributes. In 1994-5, TIF opened stores in Illinois, Hawaii and Sydney, Australia. International retail sales, the fastest growing segment of the company's operations, accounted for 45% of total sales in the first half of 1995-6.

Operational Review - 12-SEP-95

Net sales for the six months ended July 31, 1995, rose 18%, year to year, paced by strong growth in international retail sales, which were helped by the weaker dollar. U.S. comparable-store sales rose 12%. The higher volume and improved gross profit margins helped profitability in the second quarter. Net income increased 54% in the second quarter and 40% in the first half of 1995-6.

Stock Performance - 08-SEP-95

In the past 30 trading days, TIF's shares have increased 11%, compared to a 2% rise in the S&P 500. Average trading volume for the past five days was 63,700 shares, compared with the 40-day moving average of 76,090 shares.

Key Stock Statistics

Dividend Rate/Share	0.28	Shareholders	2,300
Shs. outstg. (M)	15.7	Market cap. (B)	$0.679
Avg. daily vol. (M)	0.082	Inst. holdings	61%
Tang. Bk. Value/Share	14.71	Insider holdings	NA
Beta	0.58		

Value of $10,000 invested 5 years ago: $ 9,577

Fiscal Year Ending Jan. 31

	1996	% Change	1995	% Change	1994	% Change
Revenues (Million $)						
1Q	150.1	14%	131.2	20%	109.5	2%
2Q	184.7	21%	152.3	33%	114.2	-5%
3Q	—	—	160.1	19%	134.8	27%
4Q	—	—	239.3	15%	208.0	36%
Yr.	—	—	682.8	21%	566.5	16%
Income (Million $)						
1Q	2.16	15%	1.88	81%	1.04	-66%
2Q	5.31	54%	3.45	NM	-32.55	NM
3Q	—	—	4.72	45%	3.26	NM
4Q	—	—	19.30	7%	18.02	108%
Yr.	—	—	29.34	NM	-10.24	NM
Earnings Per Share ($)						
1Q	0.14	17%	0.12	71%	0.07	-65%
2Q	0.33	50%	0.22	NM	-2.06	NM
3Q	—	—	0.30	43%	0.21	—
4Q	—	—	1.21	6%	1.14	107%
Yr.	—	—	1.85	NM	-0.65	NM

Next earnings report expected: mid November

Tiffany & Co.

Business Summary - 12-SEP-95

Tiffany & Co. is engaged in the design, manufacture and distribution of fine jewelry, gift and fashion accessory items.

Jewelry (67% of sales in 1994-5) is offered in an extensive selection at a wide range of prices. All jewelry products are constructed of gold, platinum or sterling silver, with or without precious gems or colored stones.

TIF is well known for its sterling silver merchandise such as flatware, hollowware, trophies, key holders, picture frames and desk accessories. Other products include decorative crystal, serving pieces, vases, decanters, glassware, china and other tableware, watches, clocks, handbags, wallets, scarves, ties and fragrances.

The company produced 26% of the merchandise offered for sale in 1994-5; 74% was purchased from other sources. About 43% of purchased merchandise was made outside the U.S.

Products are sold through three channels of distribution: U.S. retail, direct marketing and international retail. U.S. retail consists primarily of the New York flagship store, branch stores (17 at the end of 1994-5) and a network of selected independent retailers authorized under TIF's wholesale trade program. The New York flagship store accounted for 19% of total sales in 1994-5, down from 21% in 1993-4.

Direct marketing involves the sale of products and services to businesses (through business-to-business selling specialists, advertising and special catalogs) and to nonbusiness customers (through catalog mailings).

International business includes sales of merchandise at retail through Mitsukoshi Ltd. in Hong Kong, Taipei, Hawaii and Guam; at wholesale to Lotte Trading Co., Ltd. in Korea; and at wholesale to independent distributors in Japan, Europe, the Middle East, Korea, the Philippines and Saipan. The company also sells at retail through stores in London, Munich, Zurich, Frankfurt, Milan, Florence, Hong Kong, Taipei, Singapore, Toronto and Sydney. In 1993, TIF assumed full marketing and merchandising responsibility for retail activities at 29 boutiques operated by Mitsukoshi Ltd. in Japan. The company and Mitsukoshi entered into an agreement that expires October 15, 2001.

Important Developments

May '95—In reporting results for 1995-6's second quarter, TIF announced that U.S. retail sales rose 21%, year to year, with comparable-store sales up 15%. International retail sales increased 29%, including an 11% increase in comparable-store sales in Japan, and direct marketing catalog sales rose 2%.

Capitalization

Long Term Debt: $101,500,000 (7/95).

Per Share Data ($) (Year Ended Jan. 31)

	1995	1994	1993	1992	1991	1990
Tangible Bk. Val.	13.70	11.63	12.64	12.37	11.06	8.48
Cash Flow	2.88	0.21	1.72	2.52	2.69	2.36
Earnings	1.85	-0.65	1.00	2.01	2.34	2.13
Dividends	0.28	0.28	0.28	0.28	0.26	0.18
Payout Ratio	15%	NM	28%	14%	11%	8%
Cal. Yrs.	1994	1993	1992	1991	1990	1989
Prices - High	43⅝	38	52⅞	57½	53¾	61¼
- Low	28½	24⅛	23	32⅝	27½	26
P/E Ratio - High	24	NM	53	29	23	29
- Low	15	NM	23	16	12	12

Income Statement Analysis (Million $)

	1995	%Chg	1994	%Chg	1993	%Chg	1992
Revs.	683	20%	567	17%	486	-1%	493
Oper. Inc.	81.2	33%	61.1	60%	38.2	-45%	69.2
Depr.	16.5	21%	13.6	19%	11.4	40%	8.1
Int. Exp.	12.9	35%	9.6	32%	7.2	14%	6.3
Pretax Inc.	51.6	NM	-18.0	NM	19.9	-64%	55.1
Eff. Tax Rate	43%	—	NM	—	21%	—	42%
Net Inc.	29.3	NM	-10.2	NM	15.7	-51%	31.8

Balance Sheet & Other Fin. Data (Million $)

	1995	1994	1993	1992	1991	1990
Cash	44.3	5.0	6.7	4.0	4.6	2.6
Curr. Assets	402	365	292	282	234	187
Total Assets	551	504	418	395	307	237
Curr. Liab.	167	153	92.0	122	103	74.0
LT Debt	102	102	102	50.0	18.2	18.2
Common Eqty.	222	189	205	200	176	136
Total Cap.	326	297	310	258	201	161
Cap. Exp.	19.0	18.0	22.8	41.4	24.8	14.0
Cash Flow	45.8	3.3	27.1	39.9	42.1	36.8

Ratio Analysis

	1995	1994	1993	1992	1991	1990
Curr. Ratio	2.4	2.4	3.2	2.3	2.3	2.5
% LT Debt of Cap.	31.1	34.1	32.7	19.4	9.0	11.3
% Net Inc.of Revs.	4.3	NM	3.2	6.5	8.0	8.7
% Ret. on Assets	5.6	NM	3.9	9.0	13.4	16.6
% Ret. on Equity	14.3	NM	7.7	16.8	23.4	28.2

Dividend Data —Dividends were initiated in 1988. A "poison pill" stock purchase right was adopted in 1988.

Amt. of Div. $	Date Decl.	Ex-Div. Date	Stock of Record	Payment Date
0.070	Aug. 22	Sep. 14	Sep. 20	Oct. 11 '94
0.070	Nov. 17	Dec. 14	Dec. 20	Jan. 10 '95
0.070	Feb. 16	Mar. 15	Mar. 21	Apr. 11 '95
0.070	May. 18	Jun. 16	Jun. 20	Jul. 10 '95
0.070	Sep. 07	Sep. 18	Sep. 20	Oct. 10 '95

Data as orig. reptd.; bef. results of disc. opers. and/or spec. items. Per share data adj. for stk. divs. as of ex-div. date. E-Estimated. NA-Not Available. NM-Not Meaningful. NR-Not Ranked.

Office—727 Fifth Ave., New York, NY 10022. **Tel**—(212) 755-8000. **Chrmn & CEO**—W. R. Chaney. **Sr VP-Fin & CFO**—J. N. Fernandez. **Sr VP & Secy**—P. B. Dorsey. **Investor Contact**—Mark L. Aaron (212) 605-4016. **Dirs**—W. R. Chaney, J. Dudley, S. L. Hayes III, M. J. Kowalski, C. K. Marquis, J. E. Quinn, Y. Sakakura, W. A. Shutzer, G. Stutz. **Transfer Agent & Registrar**—Chemical Bank, NYC. **Incorporated** in Delaware in 1984. **Empl**-3,306. **S&P Analyst:** Stephen Madonna, CFA

STANDARD & POOR'S

STOCK REPORTS

Topps Co.

NASDAQ Symbol **TOPP**
In S&P MidCap 400

01-AUG-95 **Industry:** Leisure/Amusement

Summary: Topps produces baseball picture cards and "Bazooka" bubble gum products, as well as other collectible picture, gum and candy items and creates and markets high-quality comic books.

Quantitative Evaluations

Outlook (1 Lowest—5 Highest) • **5**

Fair Value • **9⅞**

Risk • **High**

Earn./Div. Rank • **B+**

Technical Eval. • **Bullish** since 12/94

Rel. Strength Rank (1 Lowest—99 Highest) • **37**

Insider Activity • **Favorable**

Recent Price • 6⅛ | 52 Wk Range • 7¼-4⅛ | Yield • Nil | 12-Mo. P/E • 30.6

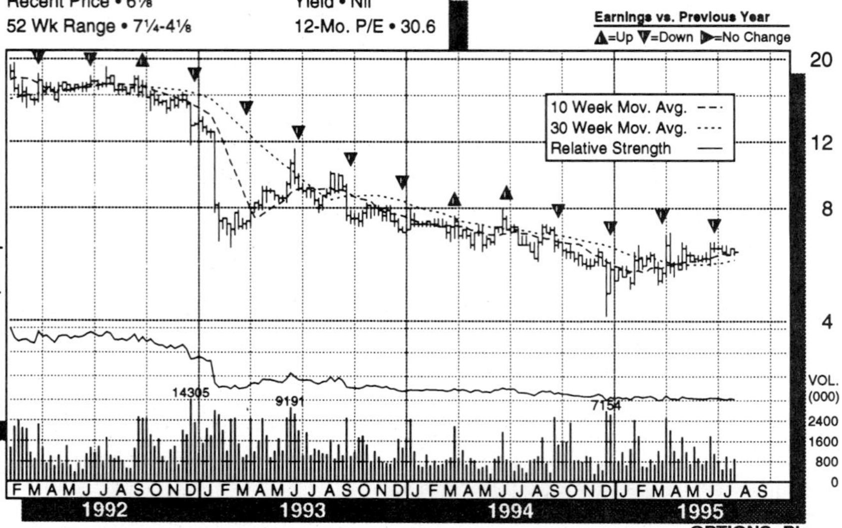

Business Profile - 01-AUG-95

Topps has continued to be hurt by a contraction of the sports card market, most recently by the lingering impact of labor disputes in professional baseball and hockey. The stock, which has recovered from the six-year low hit in late 1994, is still well-below the all-time high. However, Topps has diversified its product line to offset the weak sports card market through the July 1995 acquisition of U.K.-based Merlin Publishing, and its confectionery business showed continued growth.

Operational Review - 01-AUG-95

Net sales for the 13 weeks ended May 27, 1995, fell 29%, year to year, reflecting lower shipments of sports card products, principally baseball cards stemming from the lingering effects of the baseball strike. Profitability was hurt by the lower sales volume, and pretax income plunged 57%. After taxes at 43.0% in both periods, net income also plunged 57%, to $4,640,000 ($0.10 a share), from $10,746,000 ($0.23).

Stock Performance - 28-JUL-95

In the past 30 trading days, TOPP's shares have declined 2%, compared to a 4% rise in the S&P 500. Average trading volume for the past five days was 173,020 shares, compared with the 40-day moving average of 185,456 shares.

Key Stock Statistics

Dividend Rate/Share	Nil	Shareholders	6,300
Shs. outstg. (M)	47.0	Market cap. (B)	$0.294
Avg. daily vol. (M)	0.148	Inst. holdings	65%
Tang. Bk. Value/Share	1.19	Insider holdings	NA
Beta	1.13		

Value of $10,000 invested 5 years ago: $ 6,101

Fiscal Year Ending Feb. 28

	1996	% Change	1995	% Change	1994	% Change
Revenues (Million $)						
1Q	67.43	-29%	94.50	24%	76.27	NM
2Q	—	—	61.35	-12%	69.93	-17%
3Q	—	—	52.94	-9%	57.98	-7%
4Q	—	—	56.60	-12%	64.05	59%
Yr.	—	—	265.4	NM	268.0	2%
Income (Million $)						
1Q	4.64	-57%	10.75	14%	9.44	-24%
2Q	—	—	2.49	-68%	7.85	-52%
3Q	—	—	1.48	-68%	4.66	-59%
4Q	—	—	1.03	-78%	4.64	NM
Yr.	—	—	15.75	-41%	26.59	40%
Earnings Per Share ($)						
1Q	0.10	-57%	0.23	15%	0.20	-23%
2Q	—	—	0.05	-71%	0.17	-51%
3Q	—	—	0.03	-70%	0.10	-58%
4Q	—	—	0.02	-80%	0.10	NM
Yr.	—	—	0.33	-42%	0.57	43%

Next earnings report expected: mid September

Topps Co.

Business Summary - 01-AUG-95

The Topps Company, Inc. was incorporated as a holding company in February 1987 as the successor to Topps Chewing Gum Inc. The company is best known for its Topps Baseball Bubble Gum picture cards and its "Bazooka" bubble gum. It is also the leader in marketing other collectible picture products, primarily picture cards, featuring sports figures, popular television, movie and comic book characters, significant events of national interest and parodies of popular trends or recognized products. In addition, Topps manufactures and distributes lollipops, candy and candy-coated bubble gums, usually in packaging that has entertainment value, and creates and markets high-quality comic books. Sales contributions in recent fiscal years were:

	1994-95	1993-94
Collectible picture products	68%	72%
Confectionery products	32%	28%

The company's sports and entertainment collectible picture products are sold in packages with or without bubble gum. It also markets picture cards in various size packages for distribution through a variety of trade channels and distributes complete sets for direct sales to consumers. The most popular sports packages currently contain 12 cards and a promotional insert card. Topps has exclusive license arrangements with virtually every major league baseball and professional football, basketball and hockey player, while it also holds a variety of licenses with the entertainment media. License royalties and fees paid or accrued in 1994-95 approximated $36.0 million.

Topps Comics, Inc., creates and markets high-quality color comic books for distribution in specialy shops and newsstands. In 1994-95, Topps Comics published more than 60 different comic books and four graphic novels featuring well-known titles such as Jurassic Park, The X-Files and MARS ATTACKS. TOPP also publishes and distributes fan magazines featuring subjects of current interest in the entertainment field.

In December 1992, directors authorized the repurchase of up to five million Topps common shares. Through 1994-95 year-end, a total of 455,000 shares had been acquired (all in 1992-3's fourth quarter).

Important Developments

Jul. '95—Topps announced it completed the acquisition of U.K.-based Merlin Publishing International plc, one of the world's leading publishers and marketers of sticker and album collections, for approximately $46.2 million in cash. Merlin's products feature the U.K. Premier League Football, the Power Rangers action heroes and a variety of other entertainment properties. Previously, in June 1995, TOPP entered into a $65 million credit agreement to finance the Merlin acquisition and provide a working capital facility.

Capitalization

Long Term Debt: None (5/95).

Per Share Data ($) (Year Ended Feb. 28)

	1995	1994	1993	1992	1991	1990
Tangible Bk. Val.	1.08	0.89	0.57	0.56	-0.41	-1.48
Cash Flow	0.45	0.67	0.50	1.29	1.28	0.98
Earnings	0.33	0.57	0.40	1.15	1.15	0.80
Dividends	0.21	0.28	0.28	0.24	0.19	0.15
Payout Ratio	64%	49%	70%	21%	17%	19%
Cal. Yrs.	1994	1993	1992	1991	1990	1989
Prices - High	8	14	20¼	19	17¼	12½
- Low	4⅛	6¼	11¾	12	8½	5½
P/E Ratio - High	24	25	51	17	15	16
- Low	13	11	29	10	7	7

Income Statement Analysis (Million $)

	1995	%Chg	1994	%Chg	1993	%Chg	1992
Revs.	268	-1%	271	1%	268	-13%	309
Oper. Inc.	32.0	-37%	50.9	36%	37.5	-62%	97.6
Depr.	5.2	4%	5.0	7%	4.7	-28%	6.5
Int. Exp.	Nil	—	Nil	—	Nil	—	1.9
Pretax Inc.	27.4	-41%	46.1	41%	32.8	-63%	89.3
Eff. Tax Rate	43%	—	42%	—	42%	—	39%
Net Inc.	15.7	-41%	26.6	40%	19.0	-65%	54.5

Balance Sheet & Other Fin. Data (Million $)

	1995	1994	1993	1992	1991	1990
Cash	17.8	27.7	13.8	10.9	7.7	6.7
Curr. Assets	79.9	85.6	86.5	87.2	64.3	57.9
Total Assets	136	142	142	143	125	121
Curr. Liab.	49.0	61.9	80.9	80.8	65.5	63.7
LT Debt	Nil	Nil	Nil	Nil	40.0	85.0
Common Eqty.	73.9	67.0	54.4	55.1	11.4	-35.5
Total Cap.	83.5	76.3	58.5	60.3	56.8	54.5
Cap. Exp.	4.9	4.2	3.8	2.2	3.9	2.7
Cash Flow	21.0	31.6	23.7	61.0	60.4	45.9

Ratio Analysis

	1995	1994	1993	1992	1991	1990
Curr. Ratio	1.6	1.4	1.1	1.1	1.0	0.9
% LT Debt of Cap.	Nil	Nil	Nil	Nil	70.4	156.0
% Net Inc.of Revs.	5.9	9.8	7.1	17.6	18.7	15.2
% Ret. on Assets	11.3	18.7	13.4	40.6	43.9	30.8
% Ret. on Equity	22.4	43.8	34.9	163.6	NM	NM

Dividend Data (Cash payments, made in each year since 1987, were omitted in December 1994. The company attributed the omission to uncertainty in the sports card market, due in part to the baseball strike and hockey lockout, as well as TOPP's belief that the reinvestment of earnings could build greater shareholder value over the long term. The most recent quarterly payment was a $0.07-a-share distribution on November 1, 1994. A "poison pill" stock purchase rights plan was adopted in December 1991.)

Amt. of Div. $	Date Decl.	Ex-Div. Date	Stock of Record	Payment Date
0.070	Sep. 21	Oct. 12	Oct. 18	Nov. 01 '94

Data as orig. reptd.; bef. results of disc. opers. and/or spec. items. Per share data adj. for stk. divs. as of ex-div. date. E-Estimated. NA-Not Available. NM-Not Meaningful. NR-Not Ranked.

Office—One Whitehall St., New York, NY 10004. **Tel**—(212) 376-0300. **Chrmn & CEO**—A. T. Shorin. **Pres & COO**—J. J. Langdon. **VP-CFO & Contr**—J. Perillo. **Dirs**—S. P. Berger, A. A. Feder, T. J. Forstmann, S. D. Greenberg, J. J. Langdon, W. B. Little, J. H. Nusbaum, A. T. Shorin, S. Tulchin. **Transfer Agent & Registrar**—Chemical Bank, NYC. **Incorporated** in Delaware in 1987. **Empl**-800. **S&P Analyst:** Michael V. Pizzi

STANDARD & POOR'S

STOCK REPORTS

Tosco Corp.

NYSE Symbol **TOS**

In S&P MidCap 400

16-AUG-95

Industry:
Oil and Gas

Summary: Tosco, which is in the midst of a major acquisition program, is an independent refiner, wholesaler and retail marketer of petroleum products, mostly on the East and West Coasts.

S&P Opinion: Accumulate (★★★★)

Recent Price • $32\frac{1}{8}$

52 Wk Range • $36\frac{1}{2}$-$26\frac{3}{4}$

Yield • 2.0%

12-Mo. P/E • 26.1

Quantitative Evaluations

Outlook
(1 Lowest—5 Highest)
• **2⁻**

Fair Value
• **30**

Risk
• **Low**

Earn./Div. Rank
• **B**

Technical Eval.
• **Bearish** since 5/95

Rel. Strength Rank
(1 Lowest—99 Highest)
• **16**

Insider Activity
• **NA**

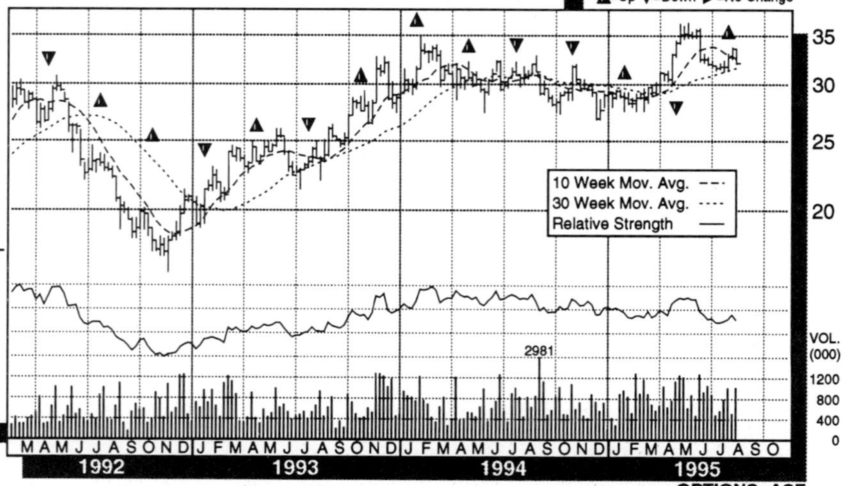

OPTIONS: ASE

Overview - 16-AUG-95

Tosco is one of the largest independent oil companies in the U.S., with three refineries producing over 500,000 bbl. per day. Revenues are expected to benefit from recent acquisitions and diversification efforts, especially in the retail business. In 1994, while production costs were contained, refining margins were poor, and with maintenance turnarounds, income growth was restrained. Profits in 1995 should trend slightly higher, as evidenced by second quarter results, reflecting wider product margins and improved refinery performance, the latter being a key company objective as programs to reduce operating costs are being accelerated. Also boosting returns should be the company's plan to expand its retail operations in the western U.S. over the course of the next three years at an estimated cost of $200 million.

Valuation - 16-AUG-95

The company's shares spurted earlier in the year on announced plans to reduce California personnel, but have since retreated. Results improved in the second quarter on improved refining margins and lack of scheduled maintenance, allowing full capture of margins, while retail business continued to perform well. TOS has committed resources to boosting its retail line over the next three years, while containing present refining operating costs. Consequently, while upward stock movement in the immediate future will be limited, growth prospects are favorable, and the stock should be acquired as a long-term investment.

Key Stock Statistics

S&P EPS Est. 1995	2.33	Tang. Bk. Value/Share	14.22
P/E on S&P Est. 1995	13.8	Beta	1.28
S&P EPS Est. 1996	2.95	Shareholders	11,900
Dividend Rate/Share	0.64	Market cap. (B)	$ 1.2
Shs. outstg. (M)	37.0	Inst. holdings	83%
Avg. daily vol. (M)	0.170	Insider holdings	NA

Value of $10,000 invested 5 years ago: $ 16,284

Fiscal Year Ending Dec. 31

	1995	% Change	1994	% Change	1993	% Change
Revenues (Million $)						
1Q	1,696	13%	1,496	NM	416.1	25%
2Q	1,904	36%	1,400	46%	956.3	100%
3Q	—	—	1,672	60%	1,044	102%
4Q	—	—	1,799	57%	1,143	114%
Yr.	—	—	6,366	79%	3,559	91%
Income (Million $)						
1Q	-4.27	NM	38.87	163%	14.80	NM
2Q	20.72	43%	14.45	-35%	22.14	-36%
3Q	—	—	9.68	-65%	27.93	182%
4Q	—	—	20.85	33%	15.71	NM
Yr.	—	—	83.84	4%	80.58	166%
Earnings Per Share ($)						
1Q	-0.12	NM	1.11	164%	0.42	NM
2Q	0.55	49%	0.37	-45%	0.67	-37%
3Q	E1.20	NM	0.25	-71%	0.86	NM
4Q	E0.70	25%	0.56	30%	0.43	NM
Yr.	E2.33	3%	2.27	-5%	2.38	NM

Next earnings report expected: late October

Tosco Corp.

Business Summary - 16-AUG-95

Tosco Corp., through divisions and subsidairies, is a large independent refiner, wholesaler and retail marketer of petroleum products, principally on the East and West Coasts of the U.S. Tosco has extensive distribution facilities and also engages in related commercial activities throughout the U.S and internationally.

Through three major facilities, Tosco currently processes approximately 525,000 bbl. per day of crude oil and other feedstocks into various petroleum products, consisting chiefly of light transportation fuels and heating oil. The Tosco Refining Co. division operates the Avon refinery, located in the San Francisco Bay area, which is the largest independently owned refinery on the West Coast, with daily crude oil distillation capacity of 160,000 bbl. Bayway Refining Co., an indirect subsidiary, owns and operates the Bayway Refinery in Linden, N.J., which is the largest refinery, as measured by distillation capacity, on the East Coast. It can process in excess of 275,000 bbl. per day, and its facilities include hydrodesulfurization units and the largest catalytic cracking unit in the world. The Tosco Northwest Co. division operates the Ferndale refinery on Puget Sound, 100 miles north of Seattle. It is connected by the Olympic pipeline to its major retail markets, has crude oil distillation capacity of approximately 90,000 bbl. per day, and is equipped with thermal catalytic cracking and hydrodesulfurization units, as well as modern marine facilities.

Tosco sells unbranded refined products to wholesale purchasers. During 1994, 1993 and 1992, wholesale gasoline products accounted for approximately 44%, 57% and 68%, respectively, of TOS's revenues, while during the same periods distillates accounted for approximately 29%, 31% and 25%, respectively, of revenues.

During 1994, TOS continued the expansion of its retail petroleum fuel marketing business. Tosco's current sales volume through its retail system is approximately 67,000 bbl. per day. In 1993, TOS acquired from BP its retail marketing system in Washington and Oregon, consisting of 500 retail locations. In 1994, the company acquired BP's California retailing system of approximately 370 locations. Also in 1994, TOS completed the acquisition of Exxon Company USA's retail marketing assets in Arizona, including 83 company controlled stores. In May 1995, the company announced a $200 million program to add 50 retail outlets in the western U.S. by 1998.

Important Developments

Jul. '95—TOS announced the public sale of $125 milion of 7% notes due 2000. The issue is non-callable, and the proceeds were used to repay existing short term, floating rate bank debt.

Capitalization

Long Term Debt: $454,519,000 (3/95).

Per Share Data ($)

(Year Ended Dec. 31)

	1994	1993	1992	1991	1990	1989
Tangible Bk. Val.	15.53	12.60	9.10	12.78	11.15	7.00
Cash Flow	3.78	3.58	1.55	4.04	7.52	4.32
Earnings	2.27	2.38	0.68	2.39	5.37	1.71
Dividends	0.62	0.60	0.60	0.60	0.60	0.30
Payout Ratio	27%	25%	87%	25%	15%	21%
Prices - High	35	32¾	30¾	25⅞	24⅝	26¼
- Low	26¾	18⅞	16⅜	14⅝	14½	15⅝
P/E Ratio - High	15	14	45	11	5	15
- Low	12	8	24	6	3	9

Income Statement Analysis (Million $)

	1994	%Chg	1993	%Chg	1992	%Chg	1991
Revs.	6,366	79%	3,559	91%	1,861	-6%	1,980
Oper. Inc.	228	NM	229	91%	120	-23%	155
Depr.	51.9	46%	35.6	39%	25.7	-48%	49.6
Int. Exp.	58.3	19%	48.9	141%	20.3	-53%	43.2
Pretax Inc.	134	2%	132	159%	51.0	-35%	78.0
Eff. Tax Rate	37%	—	39%	—	41%	—	3.80%
Net Inc.	84.0	4%	81.0	170%	30.0	-60%	75.0

Balance Sheet & Other Fin. Data (Million $)

	1994	1993	1992	1991	1990	1989
Cash	55.0	85.0	103	50.7	53.2	30.1
Curr. Assets	859	671	439	273	291	232
Total Assets	1,797	1,493	963	970	949	938
Curr. Liab.	480	311	168	171	188	143
LT Debt	687	603	357	266	398	496
Common Eqty.	575	407	266	382	333	112
Total Cap.	1,265	1,128	745	778	743	778
Cap. Exp.	160	74.0	69.0	60.0	29.0	24.0
Cash Flow	129	106	46.0	121	162	58.0

Ratio Analysis

	1994	1993	1992	1991	1990	1989
Curr. Ratio	1.8	2.2	2.6	1.6	1.5	1.6
% LT Debt of Cap.	54.3	53.5	47.9	34.2	53.6	63.7
% Net Inc.of Revs.	1.3	2.3	1.6	3.8	5.7	2.8
% Ret. on Assets	4.8	6.3	3.2	7.9	9.1	4.0
% Ret. on Equity	14.9	20.1	6.3	20.0	42.7	23.2

Dividend Data —Payments in the past 12 months:

Amt. of Div. $	Date Decl.	Ex-Div. Date	Stock of Record	Payment Date
0.150	Jun. 10	Jun. 14	Jun. 20	Jun. 30 '94
0.160	Aug. 26	Sep. 14	Sep. 20	Sep. 30 '94
0.160	Dec. 09	Dec. 14	Dec. 20	Dec. 30 '94
0.160	Mar. 13	Mar. 15	Mar. 21	Mar. 31 '95
0.160	Jun. 09	Jun. 16	Jun. 20	Jun. 30 '95

Data as orig. reptd.; bef. results of disc. opers. and/or spec. items. Per share data adj. for stk. divs. as of ex-div. date. E-Estimated. NA-Not Available. NM-Not Meaningful. NR-Not Ranked.

Office—72 Cummings Point Rd., Stamford, CT 06902. **Tel**—(203) 977-1000. **Chrmn, CEO & Pres**—T. D. O'Malley. **EVP, CFO & Treas**—J. F. Allen. **VP & Secy**—W. McClave III. **Investor Contact**—Joseph D. Watson. **Dirs**—J. F. Allen, J. B. Carr, H. I. Flournoy, C. G. Frame, E. A. Hajim, J. P. Ingrassia, C. J. Luellen, T. D. O'Malley. **Transfer Agent & Registrar**—First Interstate Bank, LA. **Incorporated** in Nevada in 1955. **Empl**-3,613. **S&P Analyst:** Michael C. Barr

STANDARD & POOR'S

Transatlantic Holdings

STOCK REPORTS

NYSE Symbol **TRH**

In S&P MidCap 400

17-OCT-95 **Industry:** Insurance

Summary: Transatlantic Holdings provides property-casualty reinsurance worldwide through Transatlantic Reinsurance and Putnam Reinsurance Cos. American International Group owns 46% of TRH.

S&P Opinion: Accumulate (★★★★)

Recent Price • 66¾ | Yield • 0.6%

52 Wk Range • 70⅜-47¾ | 12-Mo. P/E • 12.9

Quantitative Evaluations

Outlook (1 Lowest—5 Highest)
• **2+**

Fair Value
• **60¾**

Risk
• **Low**

Earn./Div. Rank
• **NR**

Technical Eval.
• **Bearish** since 9/95

Rel. Strength Rank (1 Lowest—99 Highest)
• **55**

Insider Activity
• **Neutral**

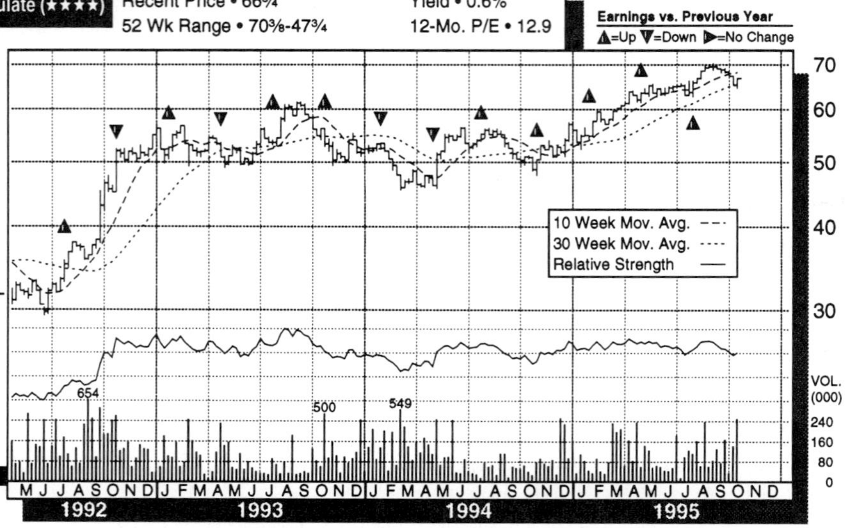

Overview - 13-OCT-95

Written premium growth in 1995 will likely top 20%, reflecting increased demand for and better pricing of certain property coverage in the U.S. and expansion into certain overseas markets. Although much of the casualty lines reinsurance market remains competitive, TRH is well positioned to benefit from the "flight to quality" and consolidation trends driving the reinsurance market today, as primary insurers eschew financially marginal reinsurers in favor of high-quality, financially sound companies. Since 1987, primary insurers have been retaining a larger portion of their risks. These higher retention levels have hampered reinsurers' premium growth, but TRH's refusal to write subpar business for the sake of near-term premium growth leaves it better positioned to benefit from an array of growth opportunities in select overseas markets.

Valuation - 13-OCT-95

Despite trading close to their 52-week high, the shares of this high-quality reinsurer remain attractive at about 13 times our 1995 operating earnings estimate of $5.20 a share (compared with $4.02 a share of operating earnings in 1994), given the company's above-average premium and earnings growth prospects. Thanks to a conservative strategy, its underwriting record is superior to that of the overall industry. Though reinsurance stocks tend to trade at higher P/E multiples than those of primary insurers, TRH is currently trading at the lower end of its historical range.

Key Stock Statistics

S&P EPS Est. 1995	5.20	Tang. Bk. Value/Share	38.97
P/E on S&P Est. 1995	12.8	Beta	1.24
S&P EPS Est. 1996	6.25	Shareholders	2,500
Dividend Rate/Share	0.40	Market cap. (B)	$ 1.6
Shs. outstg. (M)	22.9	Inst. holdings	87%
Avg. daily vol. (M)	0.041	Insider holdings	NA

Value of $10,000 invested 5 years ago: NA

Fiscal Year Ending Dec. 31

	1995	% Change	1994	% Change	1993	% Change
Revenues (Million $)						
1Q	304.6	39%	219.8	34%	163.7	—
2Q	275.5	22%	225.9	34%	169.1	—
3Q	—	—	250.1	39%	180.4	—
4Q	—	—	309.0	49%	206.7	32%
Yr.	—	—	1,005	40%	720.0	18%
Income (Million $)						
1Q	30.51	59%	19.20	NM	19.35	-12%
2Q	32.59	21%	26.87	24%	21.65	18%
3Q	—	—	26.87	17%	23.03	NM
4Q	—	—	28.70	26%	22.71	-8%
Yr.	—	—	101.6	17%	86.74	21%
Earnings Per Share ($)						
1Q	1.33	58%	0.84	-1%	0.85	-11%
2Q	1.42	21%	1.17	24%	0.94	17%
3Q	—	—	1.17	16%	1.01	NM
4Q	—	—	1.26	27%	0.99	-7%
Yr.	E5.20	17%	4.44	17%	3.79	21%

Next earnings report expected: late October

Transatlantic Holdings

Business Summary - 13-OCT-95

Transatlantic Holdings, Inc. provides property and casualty reinsurance, directly and through brokers, to insurance and reinsurance companies in both the domestic and international markets through its wholly owned subsidiaries--Transatlantic Reinsurance Co. and Putnam Reinsurance Co. Contributions to net premiums earned by line of reinsurance in recent years were:

	1994	1993	1992
General liability	29%	40%	48%
Fire	16%	12%	9%
Auto liability	13%	11%	12%
Medical malpractice	11%	11%	14%
Homeowners multi peril	6%	5%	Nil
Allied lines	5%	3%	2%
Other	20%	18%	15%

Based upon 1994 statutory net premiums written of $868 million, Transatlantic Reinsurance and Putnam Reinsurance together would have ranked as the fourth largest domestic reinsurer.

About 21% of 1994 gross premiums written resulted from reinsurance business with American International Group, Inc. (AIG), which has informed the company that it intends to continue to provide TRH with a right of first acceptance to participate in substantially all property and casualty reinsurance purchased by AIG through at least 1995. Non-U.S. business accounted for 28% of 1994 net premiums written.

TRH seeks to focus a significant part of its business on the reinsurance of more complex risks within the broad range of insurance lines it writes, requiring a relatively high degree of underwriting, actuarial and claims expertise.

Important Developments

Oct. '95—TRH opened a branch office in Paris, France, as part of a plan to further expand its overseas operations. The 24% growth in TRH's net premiums written during the first half of 1995 largely reflected continued growth in certain overseas markets, (particularly London) and in certain specialty classes of casualty coverage (like medical malpractice). Underwriting results were aided by much lower catastrophe losses. As a result, the combined ratio improved to 103.2%, from 108.5% in 1994's first half. Underwriting results included $4.5 million of losses from the Kobe, Japan earthquake in the 1995 interim, versus losses totaling $20 million from the Northridge, California earthquake in the 1994 interim.

Capitalization

Long Term Debt: None (6/95).

Per Share Data ($)

(Year Ended Dec. 31)

	1994	1993	1992	1991	1990	1989
Tangible Bk. Val.	33.30	33.67	24.52	21.80	18.38	16.28
Oper. Earnings	4.02	3.63	2.74	2.96	NA	NA
Earnings	4.44	3.79	3.13	3.09	2.71	2.44
Dividends	0.36	0.28	0.24	0.20	0.05	Nil
Payout Ratio	8%	7%	8%	6%	2%	Nil
Prices - High	57⅞	61½	56¾	39⅜	29⅛	NA
- Low	45⅝	49	29⅜	25	18⅞	NA
P/E Ratio - High	13	16	18	13	11	NA
- Low	10	13	9	8	7	NA

Income Statement Analysis (Million $)

	1994	%Chg	1993	%Chg	1992	%Chg	1991
Premium Income	851	46%	581	22%	478	-4%	497
Net Invest. Inc.	154	11%	139	7%	130	7%	121
Oth. Revs.	14.9	161%	5.7	-49%	11.1	NM	3.7
Total Revs.	1,020	40%	726	17%	619	NM	623
Pretax Inc.	119	27%	93.6	12%	83.8	NM	84.1
Net Oper. Inc.	96.2	16%	83.1	32%	62.8	-7%	67.5
Net Inc.	102	17%	86.7	21%	71.7	2%	70.5

Balance Sheet & Other Fin. Data (Million $)

	1994	1993	1992	1991	1990	1989
Cash & Equiv.	114	120	155	111	126	99
Premiums Due	26.4	7.7	Nil	21.2	22.1	13.6
Inv Assets Bonds	2,260	2,108	1,768	1,604	1,383	1,177
Inv. Assets Stock	161	171	124	107	57.0	63.0
Inv. Assets Loans	13.5	10.8	19.7	13.6	20.8	8.9
Inv. Assets Total	2,434	2,289	1,912	1,725	1,461	1,249
Deferred Policy Cost	37.3	30.4	21.7	21.5	26.4	26.8
Total Assets	3,458	3,170	2,432	2,204	1,993	1,735
Debt	Nil	Nil	Nil	Nil	Nil	Nil
Common Eqty.	763	772	562	500	421	374

Ratio Analysis

	1994	1993	1992	1991	1990	1989
Prop&Cas Loss	80.1	80.1	86.0	81.4	79.8	79.7
Prop&Cas Expense	25.6	27.3	25.6	26.2	25.9	27.2
Prop&Cas Comb.	105.7	107.4	111.6	107.6	105.7	106.9
% Ret. on Revs.	10.0	12.0	11.6	11.3	10.7	9.6
% Return on Equity	13.2	13.0	13.5	15.3	15.6	16.0

Dividend Data —Dividends have been paid since 1990.

Amt. of Div. $	Date Decl.	Ex-Div. Date	Stock of Record	Payment Date
0.090	Sep. 23	Nov. 30	Dec. 06	Dec. 20 '94
0.100	Nov. 30	Mar. 01	Mar. 07	Mar. 21 '95
0.100	Apr. 03	May. 31	Jun. 06	Jun. 20 '95
0.100	May. 26	Aug. 31	Sep. 05	Sep. 19 '95
0.100	Sep. 22	Dec. 01	Dec. 05	Dec. 19 '95

Data as orig. reptd.; bef. results of disc. opers. and/or spec. items. Per share data adj. for stk. divs. as of ex-div. date. E-Estimated. NA-Not Available. NM-Not Meaningful. NR-Not Ranked.

Office—80 Pine St., New York, NY 10005. **Tel**—(212) 770-2000. **Chrmn**—M. R. Greenberg. **Pres**—R. F. Orlich. **Secy**—E. M. Tuck. **VP & Investor Contact**—David W. Smith. **Dirs**—J. Balog, A. A. Barnard, J. M. Fowler, M. R. Greenberg, J. J. Mackowski, E. E. Matthews, J. F. Murphy, R. F. Orlich, Y. Sato, H. I. Smith, T. R. Tizzio. **Transfer Agent & Registrar**—Harris Trust Co. of New York, NYC. **Incorporated** in Delaware in 1986. **Empl**-245. **S&P Analyst:** Catherine A. Seifert

STANDARD & POOR'S STOCK REPORTS

Trinity Industries

NYSE Symbol **TRN**
In S&P MidCap 400

31-JUL-95

Industry:
Rail Equipment

Summary: This company is a leading railcar manufacturer, a major producer of marine vessels, a metal products fabricator and an important supplier of construction materials.

S&P Opinion: Hold (★★★)

Recent Price • 33⅝
52 Wk Range • 40⅜-30⅜
Yield • 2.0%
12-Mo. P/E • 14.0

Quantitative Evaluations

Outlook
(1 Lowest—5 Highest)
• 5

Fair Value
• 40⅜

Risk
• Low

Earn./Div. Rank
• B+

Technical Eval.
• Bearish since 6/95

Rel. Strength Rank
(1 Lowest—99 Highest)
• 14

Insider Activity
• Neutral

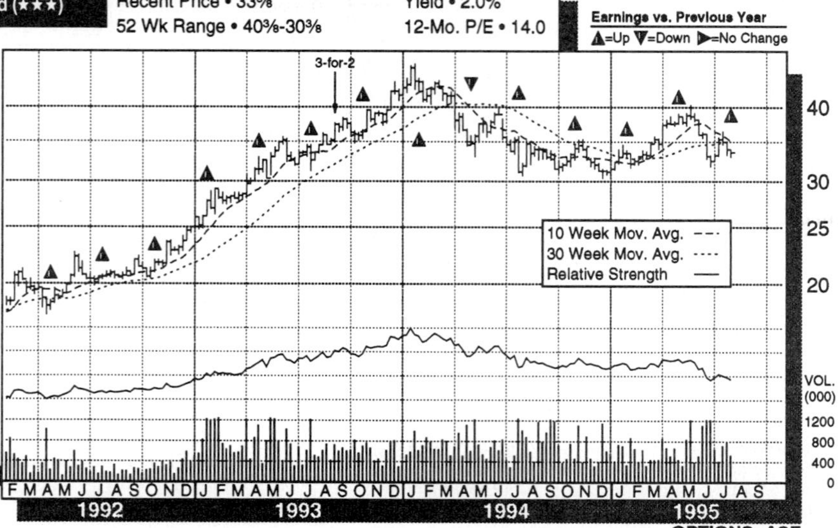

OPTIONS: ASE

Overview - 31-JUL-95

Profits in fiscal 1995-96 will benefit from increased demand to replace older railcars plus expansion of fleets to meet higher traffic levels. Margins will benefit from higher railcar prices and increased operating efficiencies at higher production levels. Profits for the marine segment may slip as increased work for military and specialty vessels is outweighed by the absence of a large gain on the sale of TRN's barge fleet in fiscal 1994. The container group will benefit from the acquisiton of Grupo Tatsa and a rebound in the residential housing market. Metal components will benefit from rising capital spending by the chemical industry. The construction segment will benefit from increased infrastructure spending and the acquisition of concrete and aggregate producers. Leasing profits should increase moderately.

Valuation - 31-JUL-95

After failing to sustain the gains posted in early 1995, shares of this leading railcar builder have slipped back to the lower end of their 12-month trading range. Investors have shunned TRN, first because railcar orders looked too strong to be sustained and later because railcar orders did turn down. Though there are signs that the mid-1995 lull in rail traffic is ending, we advise not abandoning a cautious posture just yet. We consider TRN a well-managed firm, and a leader in the markets that it competes in. With TRN's earnings multiple now more in line with that of other cyclical firms, we think a buying opportunity may be close at hand.

Key Stock Statistics

S&P EPS Est. 1996	2.90	Tang. Bk. Value/Share	15.95
P/E on S&P Est. 1996	11.6	Beta	1.07
S&P EPS Est. 1997	3.20	Shareholders	2,700
Dividend Rate/Share	0.68	Market cap. (B)	$ 1.4
Shs. outstg. (M)	40.2	Inst. holdings	79%
Avg. daily vol. (M)	0.124	Insider holdings	NA

Value of $10,000 invested 5 years ago: $ 19,389

Fiscal Year Ending Mar. 31

	1996	% Change	1995	% Change	1994	% Change
Revenues (Million $)						
1Q	604.7	11%	544.3	35%	402.0	10%
2Q	—	—	555.5	20%	463.6	18%
3Q	—	—	576.9	24%	466.4	19%
4Q	—	—	638.2	41%	452.7	16%
Yr.	—	—	2,315	30%	1,785	16%
Income (Million $)						
1Q	27.50	49%	18.50	10%	16.80	102%
2Q	—	—	22.20	25%	17.80	84%
3Q	—	—	22.70	23%	18.50	50%
4Q	—	—	25.70	69%	15.20	3%
Yr.	—	—	89.10	30%	68.30	52%
Earnings Per Share ($)						
1Q	0.66	43%	0.46	10%	0.42	75%
2Q	E0.70	—	0.55	25%	0.44	57%
3Q	E0.75	—	0.56	22%	0.46	31%
4Q	E0.79	—	0.63	66%	0.38	-5%
Yr.	E2.90	—	2.20	30%	1.69	33%

Next earnings report expected: mid October

Trinity Industries

Business Summary - 31-JUL-95

Contributions by business segment to operating profits (in million $) in recent fiscal years were:

	1994-95	1993-94	1992-93
Railcars	$88.5	$53.2	$26.9
Containers	9.7	9.8	15.0
Construction products	35.6	35.6	22.6
Marine products	30.3	28.9	30.8
Metal components	14.9	11.7	13.8
Leasing	23.6	15.3	7.5

The company is the largest railcar manufacturer in the U.S. It produces a variety of car types including pressure and non-pressure tank cars, hoppers and intermodal freight cars, as well as rail components, and performs repair services.

The container group produces heavy pressure vessels and other welded products, including industrial silencers, desalinators, evaporators and gas processing systems, used to store and transport liquefied petroleum gas. TRN also producers LPG containers and industrial heat transfer equipment custom vessels, kettles and cookers.

The construction group produces highway guardrail and barrier systems, beams, girders, and columns, ready-mix concrete, aggregates and passenger loading bridges and baggage handling systems.

TRN is a leading fabricator of marine vessels for inland waterways and offshore applications. Its product line includes tug boats, barges, military vessels, patrol and service vessels and commercial and private transport and pleasure vessels.

Metal components include elbow, flanges and other weld fittings, as well as forges, used by the petrochemical, process and power industries.

Trinity Industries Leasing controls a fleet of 9,066 specialized railcars. TRN disposed of its fleet of river hopper barges in fiscal 1995.

Important Developments

May '95—TRN acquired Grupo Tatsa S.A. for 1.2 million TRN common shares. Based in Mexico, Grupo Tatsa manufactures various steel products including those use in the storage and transportation of liquified petroleum products. Grupo Tatsa's annual revenues are approximately $50 million.

Dec. '94—TRN completed the purchase from Lafarge Corp. of 29 concrete plants in Texas and five sand and gravel plants in Texas and Louisiana for an undisclosed sum.

Nov. '94—TRN acquired Gulf Coast Fabrication Inc., a Biloxi, MI shipbuilder, for an undisclosed amount. Other recent acquisitions include Port Allen Marine Service, a barge construction concern and Houston-based Platzer Shipyard, a provider of tank barge cleaning services.

Capitalization

Long Term Debt: $242,900,000 (3/95).

Per Share Data ($)

(Year Ended Mar. 31)

	1995	1994	1993	1992	1991	1990
Tangible Bk. Val.	15.95	14.37	12.97	10.91	10.74	9.79
Cash Flow	3.65	3.10	2.95	2.19	2.26	2.67
Earnings	2.20	1.69	1.27	0.69	0.95	1.37
Dividends	0.68	0.61	0.53	0.53	0.53	0.43
Payout Ratio	31%	35%	46%	76%	56%	33%
Cal. Yrs.	1994	1993	1992	1991	1990	1989
Prices - High	47⅜	44⅛	26½	21⅛	21⅞	30⅝
- Low	30⅜	24¾	17⅛	12⅛	10⅜	19⅛
P/E Ratio - High	22	26	21	30	23	22
- Low	14	15	13	18	11	14

Income Statement Analysis (Million $)

	1995	%Chg	1994	%Chg	1993	%Chg	1992
Revs.	2,315	30%	1,785	16%	1,540	29%	1,192
Oper. Inc.	237	20%	197	22%	162	43%	113
Depr.	58.6	3%	56.8	-4%	59.3	25%	47.4
Int. Exp.	33.3	14%	29.3	-10%	32.6	NM	32.9
Pretax Inc.	148	29%	114	58%	72.1	99%	36.3
Eff. Tax Rate	40%	—	40%	—	38%	—	39%
Net Inc.	89.1	30%	68.3	52%	45.0	104%	22.1

Balance Sheet & Other Fin. Data (Million $)

	1995	1994	1993	1992	1991	1990
Cash	15.3	8.7	7.5	4.5	5.9	7.4
Curr. Assets	NA	NA	NA	NA	NA	NA
Total Assets	1,420	1,307	1,089	975	929	875
Curr. Liab.	NA	NA	NA	NA	NA	NA
LT Debt	206	238	257	326	291	333
Common Eqty.	641	571	507	346	340	285
Total Cap.	892	883	850	754	721	702
Cap. Exp.	93.4	83.0	111	112	91.0	57.0
Cash Flow	148	125	104	70.0	72.0	74.0

Ratio Analysis

	1995	1994	1993	1992	1991	1990
Curr. Ratio	NA	NA	NA	NA	NA	NA
% LT Debt of Cap.	23.1	27.0	30.2	43.2	40.3	47.4
% Net Inc.of Revs.	3.8	3.8	2.9	1.9	2.4	2.9
% Ret. on Assets	6.5	5.7	3.9	2.3	3.2	4.2
% Ret. on Equity	14.7	12.6	9.6	6.4	9.3	14.4

Dividend Data (Dividends have been paid since 1964. A "poison pill" stock purchase right was adopted in 1989.)

Amt. of Div. $	Date Decl.	Ex-Div. Date	Stock of Record	Payment Date
0.170	Sep. 08	Oct. 07	Oct. 14	Oct. 31 '94
0.170	Dec. 08	Jan. 09	Jan. 13	Jan. 31 '95
0.170	Mar. 09	Apr. 07	Apr. 14	Apr. 28 '95
0.170	Jun. 08	Jul. 12	Jul. 14	Jul. 31 '95

Data as orig. reptd.; bef. results of disc. opers. and/or spec. items. Per share data adj. for stk. divs. as of ex-div. date. E-Estimated. NA-Not Available. NM-Not Meaningful. NR-Not Ranked.

Office—2525 Stemmons Freeway, Dallas, TX 75207-2401. **Tel**—(214) 631-4420. **Chrmn & Pres**—W. R. Wallace. **Secy**—J. J. French, Jr. **Treas**—N. O. Shoop. **Investor Contact**—Michael Conley. **Dirs**—D. W. Biegler, B. J. Galt, D. P. Guerin, J. T. Hay, E. M. Hoffman, R. J. Pulley, T. R. Wallace, W. R. Wallace. **Transfer Agent & Registrar**—Bank of New York, NYC. **Incorporated** in Texas in 1933; reincorporated in Delaware in 1987. **Empl**-16,500. **S&P Analyst:** Stephen R. Klein

STANDARD & POOR'S

STOCK REPORTS

Tyson Foods

NASDAQ Symbol **TYSNA**
In S&P MidCap 400

02-AUG-95 **Industry:** Food

Summary: Tyson is the world's largest fully integrated producer, processor and marketer of poultry-based food products. Sales are roughly split 55% foodservice and 45% retail.

S&P Opinion: Accumulate (★★★★)

Recent Price • 24⅝ | Yield • 0.3%
52 Wk Range • 25-20⅝ | 12-Mo. P/E • 16.3

Quantitative Evaluations

Outlook (1 Lowest—5 Highest)
• 4⁻

Fair Value
• 24⅜

Risk
• Low

Earn./Div. Rank
• A

Technical Eval.
• **Bullish** since 3/94

Rel. Strength Rank (1 Lowest—99 Highest)
• 62

Insider Activity
• **Favorable**

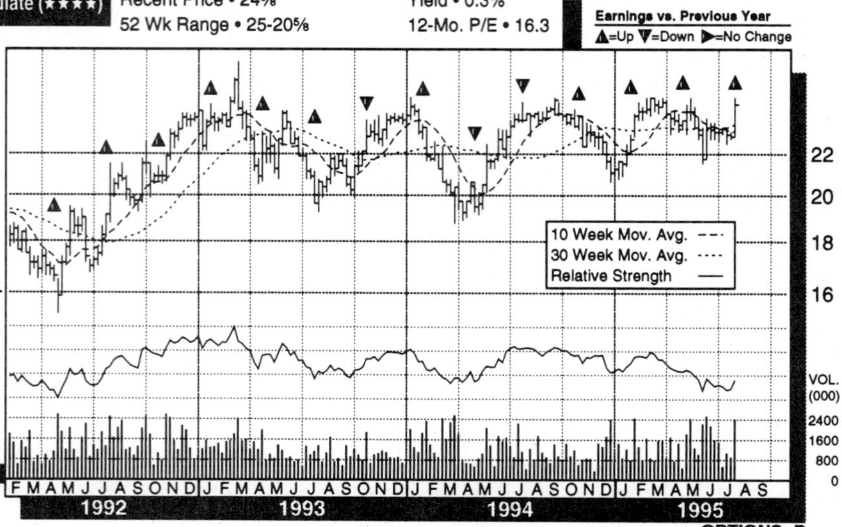

OPTIONS: P

Overview - 02-AUG-95

Sales are expected to rise at an approximate 10% annual pace through fiscal 1996, driven primarily by consumer poultry product volume growth and acquisition contributions. Lower feed costs enhanced operating margins in fiscal 1995's first nine months, but recent increases in the cost of feed may restrict full-year margins. Near-term earnings may also be further penalized by the devalued peso. With higher acquisition related interest and depreciation expense, net income may rise at a rate only modestly greater than that of sales. Nevertheless, assuming 2% to 3% fewer shares outstanding in both years, we anticipate earnings per share of $1.55 for fiscal 1995, and $1.75 for fiscal 1996.

Valuation - 02-AUG-95

Based on our projection of low double-digit earnings per share growth over the next two years, we view these shares as attractive at current levels. Although rising feed costs may restrict profitability levels over the near term, we expect that further product mix enhancements will help support operating margins. The stock has traded in a narrow range since late 1992, held down in part by difficulties related to the company's seafood operations. Trading at only about the P/E level of the overall market, we expect this high quality, low-risk stock to be an above-average performer over the next 12 months.

Key Stock Statistics

S&P EPS Est. 1995	1.55	Tang. Bk. Value/Share	4.32
P/E on S&P Est. 1995	15.9	Beta	0.99
S&P EPS Est. 1996	1.75	Shareholders	5,900
Dividend Rate/Share	0.08	Market cap. (B)	$ 3.6
Shs. outstg. (M)	144.2	Inst. holdings	20%
Avg. daily vol. (M)	0.305	Insider holdings	NA

Value of $10,000 invested 5 years ago: $ 20,047

Fiscal Year Ending Sep. 30

	1995	% Change	1994	% Change	1993	% Change
Revenues (Million $)						
1Q	1,326	15%	1,153	6%	1,083	13%
2Q	1,343	6%	1,262	8%	1,170	12%
3Q	1,362	4%	1,308	7%	1,217	19%
4Q	—	—	1,388	12%	1,237	8%
Yr.	—	—	5,110	9%	4,707	13%
Income (Million $)						
1Q	52.24	18%	44.38	13%	39.40	24%
2Q	50.44	17%	43.12	-6%	46.09	25%
3Q	57.71	NM	-148.4	NM	53.71	21%
4Q	—	—	58.77	43%	41.14	-13%
Yr.	—	—	-2.13	NM	180.3	12%
Earnings Per Share ($)						
1Q	0.36	20%	0.30	11%	0.27	17%
2Q	0.35	21%	0.29	-6%	0.31	15%
3Q	0.40	NM	-1.00	NM	0.36	13%
4Q	E0.44	—	0.40	43%	0.28	-18%
Yr.	E1.55	—	-0.01	NM	1.22	5%

Next earnings report expected: mid November

Tyson Foods

Business Summary - 02-AUG-95

Tyson Foods, the largest poultry processor in the U.S., produces fresh, frozen and precooked poultry, as well as pork, beef, seafood and other foods.

Contributions to sales in recent fiscal years were:

	1994	1993
Value-enhanced poultry	65%	67%
Basic poultry	10%	8%
Beef, pork, Mexican food & other prepared foods	18%	17%
Seafood	5%	5%
Animal foods & other	2%	3%

Value-enhanced poultry products include chicken patties and nuggets, pre-cooked chicken, individually quick-frozen chicken segments, pre-packaged and pre-priced poultry, and cornish game hens. Basic poultry includes chilled and prepackaged fresh chicken. Products are sold primarily to foodservice, retail and wholesale club markets under labels including Tyson, Holly Farms and Weaver.

Other value-enhanced items include beef and pork products such as portion controlled steaks, chops and roasts, ground beef, chicken-fried steaks, meatloaf, hams, bacon and sausages; flour and corn tortillas, corn chips, taco shells and filled tortilla specialty items; and premium frozen dinners.

Export sales accounted for 10.5% of the total in fiscal 1994.

Important Developments

Jul. '95—During fiscal 1995's first nine months, operating income (before amortization & depreciation expenses and nonrecurring items) climbed 16%, year to year, on an 8.3% sales rise, primarily reflecting an increase in consumer poultry sales tonnage and lower feed costs. Management also cited company cost reduction and aggressive marketing programs as contributing factors. Separately, TYSNA signed an agreement in principle to purchase McCarty Farms, Inc., a chicken processor (annual sales of $320 million) for an undisclosed amount of cash, which is to be finalized on or about September 1, 1995. The announcement followed TYSNA's July 14 agreement to acquire Cargill's domestic broiler operations ($300 million) in exchange for cash and TYSNA's Marshall, Missouri swine processing facility.

Capitalization

Long Term Debt: $1,498,747,000 (7/95).
Class B Common Stock: 68,454,738 shs. ($0.10 par); 10 votes per sh.; 99.9% owned by the Tyson family.
Class A Common Stock: 75,735,869 shs. ($0.10 par).
Officers and directors control 9.5%.
Institutions hold 37%.
Shareholders of record: 36,030 (10/94).

Per Share Data ($) (Year Ended Sep. 30)

	1994	1993	1992	1991	1990	1989
Tangible Bk. Val.	3.77	2.96	1.72	0.43	-0.89	-2.31
Cash Flow	1.06	2.41	2.24	2.04	1.78	1.43
Earnings	-0.01	1.22	1.16	1.05	0.91	0.78
Dividends	0.07	0.04	0.04	0.03	0.02	0.02
Payout Ratio	NM	3%	3%	3%	2%	3%
Prices - High	25	27⅛	24⅞	23¼	17¾	13⅛
- Low	18¾	19¼	15¼	14	11⅜	7⅜
P/E Ratio - High	NM	22	21	22	20	17
- Low	NM	16	13	13	13	10

Income Statement Analysis (Million $)

	1994	%Chg	1993	%Chg	1992	%Chg	1991
Revs.	5,110	9%	4,707	13%	4,169	6%	3,922
Oper. Inc.	568	3%	552	15%	481	3%	469
Depr.	159	-10%	177	19%	149	10%	136
Int. Exp.	88.0	19%	74.0	-5%	78.0	-20%	97.0
Pretax Inc.	119	-62%	310	19%	261	7%	243
Eff. Tax Rate	102%	—	42%	—	39%	—	40%
Net Inc.	-2.0	NM	180	12%	161	11%	145

Balance Sheet & Other Fin. Data (Million $)

	1994	1993	1992	1991	1990	1989
Cash	27.0	22.0	27.0	25.0	17.0	56.0
Curr. Assets	1,261	812	680	662	586	750
Total Assets	3,668	3,254	2,618	2,646	2,501	2,586
Curr. Liab.	540	527	466	550	483	470
LT Debt	1,381	920	727	846	950	1,319
Common Eqty.	1,289	1,361	980	822	663	448
Total Cap.	3,128	2,727	2,152	2,096	2,018	2,116
Cap. Exp.	232	447	108	214	164	129
Cash Flow	156	357	309	281	237	185

Ratio Analysis

	1994	1993	1992	1991	1990	1989
Curr. Ratio	2.3	1.5	1.5	1.2	1.2	1.6
% LT Debt of Cap.	44.2	33.8	33.8	40.4	47.1	62.3
% Net Inc.of Revs.	NM	3.8	3.9	3.7	3.1	4.0
% Ret. on Assets	NM	6.0	6.1	5.6	4.6	5.8
% Ret. on Equity	NM	15.0	17.8	19.5	21.1	25.3

Dividend Data (Cash has been paid each year since 1976.)

Amt. of Div. $	Date Decl.	Ex-Div. Date	Stock of Record	Payment Date
0.020	Nov. 15	Feb. 23	Mar. 01	Mar. 15 '94
0.020	Aug. 26	Nov. 25	Dec. 01	Dec. 15 '94
0.020	Nov. 18	Feb. 23	Mar. 01	Mar. 15 '95
0.020	Jan. 13	May. 25	Jun. 01	Jun. 15 '95
0.020	Apr. 21	Aug. 30	Sep. 01	Sep. 15 '95

Data as orig. reptd.; bef. results of disc. opers. and/or spec. items. Per share data adj. for stk. divs. as of ex-div. date. E-Estimated. NA-Not Available. NM-Not Meaningful. NR-Not Ranked.

Office—2210 W. Oaklawn Dr., P.O. Drawer E, Springdale, AR 72764. **Tel**—(501) 290-4000. **Chrman & CEO**—L. E. Tollett. **Pres & COO**—D. Wray. **EVP-Fin**—G. Johnston. **Treas**—D. Leatherby. **Secy & Investor Contact**—Mary Rush. **Dirs**—N. Cassady, L. V. Hackley, S. D. Massey, J. F. Starr, L. E. Tollett, B. Tyson, D. Tyson, J. H. Tyson, F. Vorsanger, D. E. Wray. **Transfer Agent**—First Chicago Trust Co. of New York, Jersey City, NJ. **Incorporated** in Arkansas in 1947; reincorporated in Delaware in 1986. **Empl**-55,800. **S&P Analyst:** Kenneth A. Shea

STANDARD & POOR'S

STOCK REPORTS

UJB Financial

NYSE Symbol **UJB**
In S&P MidCap 400

28-JUL-95 **Industry:** Banking

Summary: This bank holding company, the third largest in New Jersey, operates member banks with 278 offices in New Jersey and eastern Pennsylvania.

S&P Opinion: Accumulate (★★★★) | Recent Price • 34⅝ | Yield • 3.3% | 52 Wk Range • 36¼-22½ | 12-Mo. P/E • 12.5

Quantitative Evaluations
Outlook (1 Lowest—5 Highest) • 3-
Fair Value • 34¼
Risk • Low
Earn./Div. Rank • A-

Technical Eval. • **Bullish** since 2/95
Rel. Strength Rank (1 Lowest—99 Highest) • 82
Insider Activity • **Neutral**

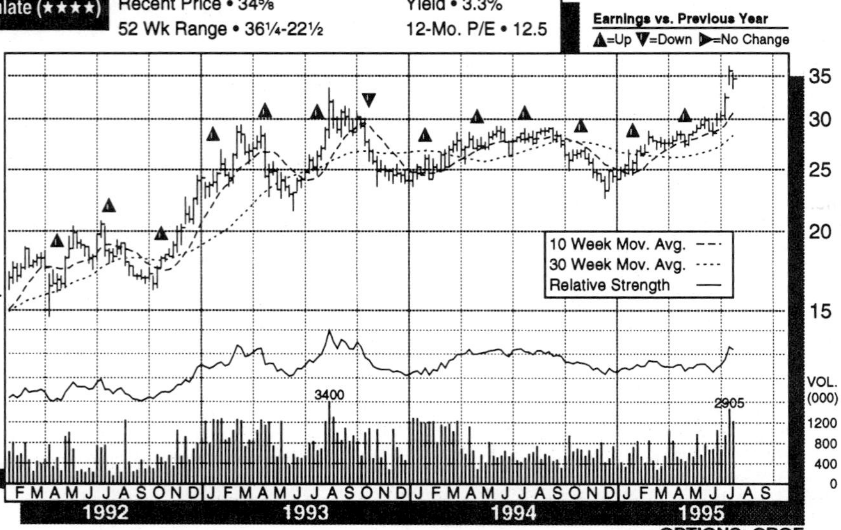

OPTIONS: CBOE

Overview - 28-JUL-95

Earnings in 1995 should continue to benefit from cost savings related to a recently completed restructuring plan that focused on profitable core businesses and consolidation of statewide member banks. Results should also be aided by modest loan growth, relatively stable net interest margins, new products, cross-selling opportunities, and reductions in the loan loss provision made possible by further declines in nonperforming loans (which fell 15% to $192.2 million at June 30, 1995, from a year earlier). An improving economic environment and acquisitions have led to a stronger mortgage and consumer loan market in recent periods, but commercial loan demand has slowed in the past few months.

Valuation - 28-JUL-95

Regional bank stocks have performed well in 1995 in the wake of banking merger activity and the apparent stabilization of interest rates. UJB's shares recently moved higher on takeover speculation after the July 1995 merger agreeement between its New Jersey rival, Midlantic Corp., and PNC Bank Corp. UJB has a solid franchise in some of the highest per capita income counties in the nation, and would make an inviting target. Management is currently focusing on boosting noninterest income and squeezing out additional operating expenses. The shares, trading near their 52-week high and about 10X our 1996 EPS estimate, are recommended for investors seeking conservative growth.

Key Stock Statistics

S&P EPS Est. 1995	3.10	Tang. Bk. Value/Share	19.97
P/E on S&P Est. 1995	11.2	Beta	1.24
S&P EPS Est. 1996	3.40	Shareholders	20,300
Dividend Rate/Share	1.16	Market cap. (B)	$ 2.0
Shs. outstg. (M)	57.3	Inst. holdings	45%
Avg. daily vol. (M)	0.337	Insider holdings	NA

Value of $10,000 invested 5 years ago: $ 24,801

Fiscal Year Ending Dec. 31

	1995	% Change	1994	% Change	1993	% Change
Revenues (Million $)						
1Q	313.3	3%	305.3	13%	270.7	-6%
2Q	317.6	8%	293.3	10%	266.6	-7%
3Q	—	—	276.3	4%	265.6	-4%
4Q	—	—	263.4	1%	259.6	-6%
Yr.	—	—	1,138	7%	1,062	-6%
Income (Million $)						
1Q	39.99	32%	30.29	83%	16.53	73%
2Q	40.34	41%	28.70	28%	22.43	119%
3Q	—	—	38.57	NM	11.84	-27%
4Q	—	—	34.32	46%	23.44	32%
Yr.	—	—	131.9	78%	74.24	38%
Earnings Per Share ($)						
1Q	0.72	41%	0.51	59%	0.32	60%
2Q	0.72	38%	0.52	21%	0.43	105%
3Q	E0.80	—	0.70	NM	0.22	-33%
4Q	E0.75	—	0.62	38%	0.45	29%
Yr.	E3.10	—	2.38	68%	1.42	30%

Next earnings report expected: mid October

UJB Financial

Business Summary - 28-JUL-95

UJB Financial Corp. is a bank holding company with 278 banking offices in New Jersey and eastern Pennsylvania. It owns two subsidiary banks and nine active non-bank subsidiaries engaged in securities brokerage, venture capital, commercial finance, lease finance and credit insurance. In 1994, UJB restructured the company along core lines of business. In March 1994, three Pennsylvania banks were merged as First Valley Bank, and in July 1994 three New Jersey banks were consolidated into United Jersey Bank. At December 31, 1994, United Jersey Bank was the company's largest subsidiary, with total assets of $12.6 billion.

Average earning assets in 1994 of $13.6 billion (up 6.2% from 1993) were divided: commercial loans 33%, mortgage loans 19%, instalment loans 16%, and investment securities 32%.

Average sources of funds were savings deposits 38%, other time deposits 23%, borrowed funds 11%, demand deposits 20%, shareholders' equity 7%, and other 1%.

The average yield on interest earning assets in 1994 was 7.17% (7.20% in 1993), while the average cost of interest-bearing liabilities was 3.23% (3.22%), for a net interest rate spread of 3.94% (3.98%).

At year-end 1994, nonperforming loans were $167.6 million (1.74% of total loans), down from $254.3 million (2.91%) a year earlier. The reserve for loan losses was $214.2 million (2.22%), against $244.2 million (2.79%). Net charge-offs in 1994 were $78.9 million (0.86% of average loans), down from $129.0 million (1.46%) in 1993.

Important Developments

Jul. '95—The company reported that it had completed its acquisition of Bancorp New Jersey ($506 million in assets), which operates 12 New Jersey Savings Bank offices, for cash and stock valued at about $91 million. The acquisition enhances UJB's presence in central New Jersey, especially in Somerset County.

Feb. '95—UJB Commercial Corp., UJB's asset-based lending affiliate, entered the Connecticut market, opening an office in Stamford.

Sep. '94—UJB acquired Palisade Savings Bank, Ridgefield Park, N.J. ($324 million in assets), for $42.2 million in cash.

Jul. '94—VSP Bancorp ($379 million in assets) was acquired in exchange for 2,628,912 common shares. Separately, the company completed the consolidation of its New Jersey operations into a single bank, which is expected to result in annual savings and incremental revenues of over $40 million in 1995.

Capitalization

Long Term Debt: $204,486,000 (6/95).
Adjust. Rate Cum. Preferred Stock: 600,166 shs. ($50 stated value).

Per Share Data ($) (Year Ended Dec. 31)

	1994	1993	1992	1991	1990	1989
Tangible Bk. Val.	18.66	17.77	16.88	16.26	16.45	18.28
Earnings	2.38	1.42	1.09	0.45	-0.17	2.62
Dividends	0.94	0.69	0.60	0.60	1.16	0.82
Payout Ratio	39%	49%	55%	133%	NM	31%
Prices - High	29¼	33½	24½	17½	20	28⅞
- Low	22½	21½	14	6⅞	6½	18
P/E Ratio - High	12	24	23	39	NM	11
- Low	9	15	13	15	NM	7

Income Statement Analysis (Million $)

	1994	%Chg	1993	%Chg	1992	%Chg	1991
Net Int. Inc.	616	9%	563	5%	538	10%	491
Tax Equiv. Adj.	15.3	-8%	16.7	-13%	19.1	-17%	23.0
Non Int. Inc.	175	-2%	178	13%	158	16%	136
Loan Loss Prov.	84.0	-13%	96.0	-31%	139	-17%	167
% Exp/Op Revs.	63%	—	73%	—	70%	—	69%
Pretax Inc.	204	106%	99	38%	71.9	188%	25.0
Eff. Tax Rate	35%	—	25%	—	25%	—	11%
Net Inc.	132	78%	74.2	38%	53.8	145%	22.0
% Net Int. Marg.	4.63%	—	4.64%	—	4.52%	—	4.22%

Balance Sheet & Other Fin. Data (Million $)

	1994	1993	1992	1991	1990	1989
Earning Assets:						
Money Mkt.	97.0	149	270	72.0	95.0	156
Inv. Securities	4,294	3,619	3,515	3,377	2,944	2,589
Com'l Loans	4,627	4,236	3,314	4,586	3,358	3,327
Other Loans	5,029	4,371	5,468	4,183	5,325	5,032
Total Assets	15,429	13,411	13,771	13,378	12,818	12,172
Demand Deposits	3,261	2,802	2,587	2,097	2,008	2,043
Time Deposits	9,307	8,654	9,200	9,217	8,621	7,293
LT Debt	205	208	216	66.6	72.2	81.1
Common Eqty.	1,074	946	890	782	777	823

Ratio Analysis

	1994	1993	1992	1991	1990	1989
% Ret. on Assets	0.9	0.6	0.4	0.2	NM	1.0
% Ret. on Equity	12.6	8.2	6.3	2.6	NM	14.3
% Loan Loss Resv.	2.2	2.8	3.1	3.3	3.0	1.5
% Loans/Deposits	76.8	75.1	74.5	77.5	81.5	89.3
% Equity to Assets	7.1	6.8	6.1	5.9	6.6	7.1

Dividend Data (Dividends have been paid since 1935. A dividend reinvestment plan is available. A "poison pill" stock purchase rights plan was adopted in 1989.)

Amt. of Div. $	Date Decl.	Ex-Div. Date	Stock of Record	Payment Date
0.260	Aug. 17	Sep. 30	Oct. 06	Nov. 01 '94
0.260	Dec. 21	Dec. 29	Jan. 05	Feb. 01 '95
0.290	Feb. 15	Mar. 31	Apr. 06	May. 01 '95
0.290	Jun. 21	Jul. 11	Jul. 13	Aug. 01 '95

Data as orig. reptd.; bef. results of disc opers. and/or spec. items. Per share data adj. for stk. divs. as of ex-div. date. E-Estimated. NA-Not Available. NM-Not Meaningful. NR-Not Ranked.

Office—301 Carnegie Center, P.O. Box 2066, Princeton, NJ 08543-2066. **Tel**—(609) 987-3200. **Chrmn, Pres & CEO**—T. J. Semrod. **EVP & Secy**—R. F. Ober, Jr. **SVP-Fin & Treas**—J. R. Haggerty. **VP & Investor Contact**—William J. Healy (609-987-3220). **Dirs**—R. L. Boyle, J. G. Collins, T. J. D. Dunphy, A. E. Estabrook, E. J. Ferdon, F. G. Harvey, J. R. Howell, F. J. Mertz, G. L. Miles, Jr., H. S. Patterson II, T. J. Semrod, R. Silverstein, J. M. Tabak. **Transfer Agents**—First Chicago Trust Co. of New York, NYC; United Jersey Bank, Hackensack. **Registrar**—First Chicago Trust Co. of New York, NYC. **Incorporated** in New Jersey in 1969. **Empl**-6,143. **S&P Analyst:** Robert Schpoont

U.S. Robotics

NASDAQ Symbol USRX Options on ASE & CBOE (Incl. in Nat'l Market)

Price	Range	P-E Ratio	Dividend	Yield	S&P Ranking	Beta
Aug. 28'95	1995					
139	161¾–39¼	65	None	None	NR	NA

Summary

This company designs, manufactures, markets and supports high performance data communications products and systems, including dial-up modems, local area network access products and wide area network hubs. Revenues for the first nine months of fiscal 1995 rose sharply, although the gain in net income was limited by an acquisition-related charge and a higher effective tax rate. A two-for-one stock split was recently declared.

Business Summary

U.S. Robotics Corp. designs, manufactures, markets and supports high performance data communications products and systems for business, professional and personal users worldwide. Its products include a broad line of dial-up modems, local area network (LAN) access products and wide area network hubs.

The company markets its products under five different brands: Sportster, WorldPort and Courier modems; Share Access LAN access products; and Total Control Wide Area Network Hubs. Sportster, the company's largest selling brand, is an entry-level dial-up modem targeted at home office and professional users. Sportster products range from 2,400 to 28.8 Kbps in transmission speed and are available in internal, external and PCMCIA (a mechanical standard adopted for a majority of laptop computers) formats.

WorldPort modems are designed for use with portable, laptop and palmtop computers and are targeted to the traveling professional. WorldPort products range from the 2,400 to the WorldPort Dual Standard FAX PCMCIA. Courier products, targeted to corporate users, range from the Courier 2,400 to the Courier V. Everything, which provides universal compatibility at the highest available standard transmission speed.

The Shared Access line of LAN access products (introduced in 1994) include NETServer/2, a two-port product used for LAN access and connecting smaller office sites, and FAXserver, a two-port device that supports unlimited users and provides inbound and outbound network-based fax capabilities. Other Share Access products, COMserver and LAN modem 2.0, allow remote and LAN-based users to transfer files with remote devices, access E-mail, connect to remote bulletin boards and hosts, connect to other remote LANs, participate in workgroup software applications and run applications remotely.

Total Control Wide Area Network Hubs are networking products that combine high speed

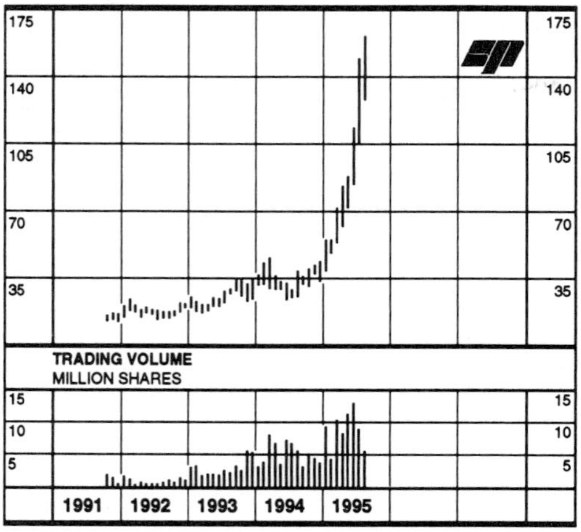

modems including the V.34 standard, X.25 PADs, terminal servers, CSU/DSUs and network interfaces into one centrally managed platform. Products include the Enterprise Network Hub and the Transaction Processing Hub, which use a common architecture to integrate digital and analog communications.

During fiscal 1994, the company's largest distributor, Ingram Micro, accounted for 16% of net sales (23% in fiscal 1993). Sales outside of North America, primarily in Europe, accounted for 18% and 22% of net sales in fiscal 1994 and 1993, respectively.

Important Developments

Aug. '95— The company acquired privately-held ISDN Systems Corp., which develops board-level integrated services digital network and frame relay-based client and server products, for about $40 million in common stock.

Next earnings report expected in late October.

Per Share Data ($)

Yr. End Sep. 30	1994	[1]1993	1992	[1]1991	[1]1990
Tangible Bk. Val.	**11.30**	8.64	6.06	2.66	1.45
Cash Flow	**2.60**	1.72	1.19	0.92	0.53
Earnings	**[2]2.06**	[2]1.42	1.00	0.78	0.44
Dividends	**Nil**	Nil	Nil	Nil	Nil
Payout Ratio	**Nil**	Nil	Nil	Nil	Nil
Prices[3]—High	**46**	35¼	24¼	16¾	NA
Low	**24**	17	13⅜	12¼	NA
P/E Ratio—	**22–12**	25–12	24–13	21–16	NA

Data as orig. reptd. **1.** Refl. merger or acquisition. **2.** Ful. dil.: 2.05 in 1994, 1.40 in 1993. **3.** Cal. yr. NA-Not Available.

Income Data (Million $)

Year Ended Sep. 30	Revs.	Oper. Inc.	% Oper. Inc. of Revs.	Cap. Exp.	Depr.	Int. Exp.	Net Bef. Taxes	Eff. Tax Rate	Net Inc.	% Net Inc. of Revs.	Cash Flow
1994	**379**	**49.6**	**13.1**	**15.9**	**6.99**	**1.82**	**40.5**	**34.7%**	**26.4**	**7.0**	**33.4**
[1]1993	189	28.4	15.0	18.5	3.56	0.35	25.9	34.3%	17.0	9.0	20.6
1992	112	19.6	17.4	6.6	2.01	0.36	17.6	38.2%	10.9	9.7	12.9
[1]1991	77	12.3	15.9	3.3	1.35	0.72	12.1	39.5%	7.3	9.5	8.7
[1]1990	56	9.4	16.7	1.7	0.88	0.56	7.8	39.6%	4.7	8.4	5.6

Balance Sheet Data (Million $)

Sep. 30	Cash	Curr. Assets	Curr. Liab.	Curr. Ratio	Total Assets	% Ret. on Assets	Long Term Debt	Common Equity	Total Cap.	% LT Debt of Cap.	% Ret. on Equity
1994	**37.5**	**197**	**47.5**	**4.2**	**251**	**13.1**	**60.3**	**141**	**203**	**29.7**	**21.0**
1993	12.3	110	39.5	2.8	147	14.5	0.3	106	107	0.3	19.2
1992	23.5	60	14.5	4.1	75	17.9	0.2	60	60	0.3	25.1
1991	1.9	24	11.0	2.2	35	26.2	3.2	20	24	13.5	46.5
1990	3.1	16	7.8	2.0	24	NA	3.4	13	17	20.6	NA

Data as orig. reptd. **1.** Refl. merger or acq. NA-Not Available.

Revenues (Million $)

Quarter:	1994–95	1993–94	1992–93	1991–92
Dec.	---	82.7	33.1	24.9
Mar.	[1]358.6	90.6	38.5	27.9
Jun.	237.3	99.3	48.2	28.5
Sep.		106.1	69.4	31.1
		378.7	189.2	112.4

Net sales for the nine months ended July 2, 1995, advanced 62%, year to year (1993-94 restated), reflecting continued solid worldwide demand for information access systems and products. Gross margins were unchanged, but with operating expenses up 81%, mostly related to a $29.4 million charge for the early 1995 acquisition of Megahertz, the gain in pretax income was limited to 19%. After taxes at 43.0%, versus 34.3%, net income was up 3.3%, to $31,733,000 ($1.57 a share), from $30,729,000 ($1.61, restated).

Common Share Earnings ($)

Quarter:	1994–95	1993–94	1992–93	1991–92
Dec.	---	0.46	0.30	0.22
Mar.	[1]0.38	0.49	0.31	0.24
Jun.	1.19	0.53	0.36	0.26
Sep.		0.57	0.44	0.28
		2.06	1.42	1.00

Dividend Data

No cash dividends have been paid. The company intends to retain its earnings for use in its business and does not anticipate paying cash dividends for the foreseeable future. On August 10, 1995, directors declared a two-for-one stock split, payable September 8, 1995.

Finances

In May 1995, underwriters completed a public offering of 2,500,000 USRX common shares at $85.50 a share. Of the 2,500,000 shares, 1,500,000 were sold by the company and 1,000,000 by certain shareholders. Net proceeds will be used for general corporate purposes.

At April 2, 1995, the company had no balances outstanding under either a three-year, $50 million credit facility or two uncommitted bank lines of credit totaling $25 million.

In February 1995, the company acquired Megahertz Holding Corp., which designs, manufactures, markets and supports mobile and wireless information access products, for about 6,187,000 common shares. In connection with the acquisition, the company recorded nonrecurring charges of $27.3 million and $29.4 million in the first quarter and first six months, respectively, of fiscal 1995, mostly related to the writedown of inventory and goodwill due to the elimination of overlapping product lines, transaction costs and the consolidation of certain facilities and personnel.

Capitalization

Long Term Debt: $65,138,000 (7/2/95).

Common Stock: 18,293,105 shs. ($0.01 par).
Officers & directors own about 18%.
Institutions hold approximately 79% (includes some closely held shares).
Shareholders of record: 385 (12/94).

Options: To purchase 3,228,617 shs. at $0.93 to $42.75 (10/94).

1. Six mos., restated to reflect pooling-of-interests acquisition of Megahertz Holding Corp.

Office—8100 N. McCormick Blvd., Skokie, IL 60076. **Tel**—(708) 982-5010. **Chrmn, Pres & CEO**—C. G. Cowell. **VP-Fin & CFO**—M. O. Remissong. **VP & Secy**—G. A. Vinyard. **Treas**—C. D. Hall. **Dirs**—C. G. Cowell, J. E. Cowie, G. M. Fulgoni, P. I. Mason, J. McCartney, P. G. Yovovich, J. Zakin. **Transfer Agent**—Harris Trust and Savings Bank, Chicago. **Incorporated** in Delaware in 1983. **Empl**—1,451.

 Stephen R. Biggar

STANDARD & POOR'S

STOCK REPORTS

Unifi, Inc.

NYSE Symbol **UFI**
In S&P MidCap 400

14-SEP-95

Industry: Textiles

Summary: Unifi is one of the world's largest producers of textured polyester and nylon yarns, and also processes yarns through spinning of cotton and cotton blend fibers.

Quantitative Evaluations

Outlook (1 Lowest—5 Highest)
• **5⁻**

Fair Value
• **29¼**

Risk
• **Low**

Earn./Div. Rank
• **B+**

Technical Eval.
• **Bearish** since 9/95

Rel. Strength Rank (1 Lowest—99 Highest)
• **22**

Insider Activity
• **Unfavorable**

Recent Price • 25¼
52 Wk Range • 29⅛-22⅝

Yield • 2.1%
12-Mo. P/E • 15.1

Earnings vs. Previous Year
▲=Up ▼=Down ▶=No Change

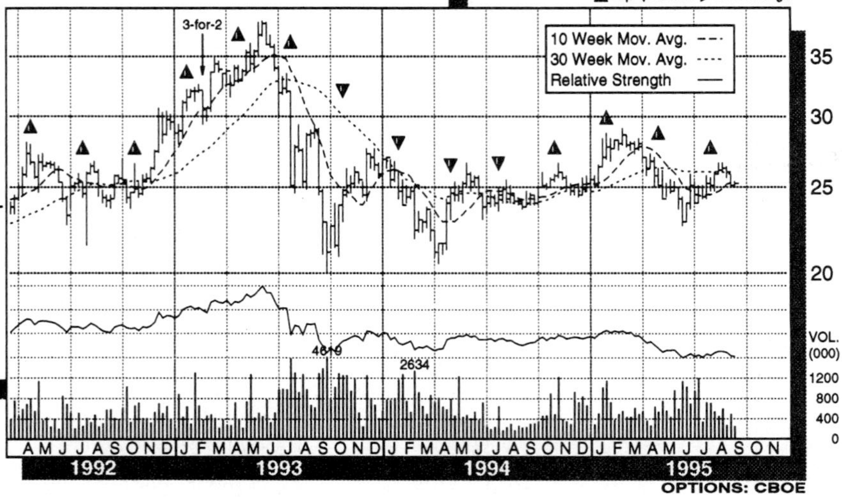

Business Profile - 14-SEP-95

This company, one of the world's largest producers of textured polyester and nylon yarns, also processes yarns through the spinning of cotton and cotton blend fibers. It plans to continue to reduce costs in response to upward pressure on prices of raw materials and packaging supplies. Unifi also plans over the next two years to build management information systems and to improve internal business control and customer service.

Operational Review - 14-SEP-95

Net sales advanced 12% in the fiscal year ended June 25, 1995, primarily reflecting unit increases in polyester and cotton yarn products. Gross margins were essentially unchanged, and following sharply higher other income and in the absence of a $13.4 million charge from the sale of UFI's French nylon operation, pretax income climbed 36%. After taxes at 37.4%, versus 44.1%, net income increased 52%.

Stock Performance - 08-SEP-95

In the past 30 trading days, UFI's shares have increased 0.50%, compared to a 2% rise in the S&P 500. Average trading volume for the past five days was 60,275 shares, compared with the 40-day moving average of 100,892 shares.

Key Stock Statistics

Dividend Rate/Share	0.52	Shareholders	800
Shs. outstg. (M)	68.1	Market cap. (B)	$ 1.7
Avg. daily vol. (M)	0.068	Inst. holdings	68%
Tang. Bk. Value/Share	8.36	Insider holdings	NA
Beta	1.35		

Value of $10,000 invested 5 years ago: $ 38,980

Fiscal Year Ending Jun. 30

	1995	% Change	1994	% Change	1993	% Change
Revenues (Million $)						
1Q	359.2	10%	325.4	3%	316.0	21%
2Q	387.3	10%	351.5	7%	328.0	26%
3Q	403.0	16%	346.1	NM	344.0	23%
4Q	405.1	12%	361.9	5%	344.5	19%
Yr.	1,555	12%	1,385	4%	1,332	22%
Income (Million $)						
1Q	22.69	15%	19.81	-28%	27.37	NM
2Q	28.12	15%	24.36	-19%	29.95	71%
3Q	31.05	36%	22.75	-37%	36.19	65%
4Q	34.31	NM	9.57	-72%	34.54	34%
Yr.	116.2	52%	76.49	-40%	128.1	105%
Earnings Per Share ($)						
1Q	0.32	14%	0.28	-30%	0.40	NM
2Q	0.40	18%	0.34	-23%	0.44	52%
3Q	0.45	41%	0.32	-40%	0.53	47%
4Q	0.50	NM	0.14	-72%	0.50	16%
Yr.	1.67	55%	1.08	-42%	1.87	80%

Next earnings report expected: late October

Unifi, Inc.

Business Summary - 14-SEP-95

Unifi, Inc. is one of the world's largest texturizers and dyers of polyester and nylon filament fibers, and is also engaged in the spinning of cotton and cotton blend fibers.

Texturizing involves the purchase of partially oriented yarn (POY), either raw polyester or nylon filament fiber, and the use of high speed machines to draw, heat and twist the POY to produce yarns. Company yarns have physical characteristics that depend upon their intended end-use.

Spinning operations involve the spinning of cotton, cotton and undyed synthetic blends, and cotton and pre-dyed polyester blends, into yarns of different strengths and thicknesses. Spinning is done on either open-end or ring spindles.

The company's business, which had consisted solely of texturizing and producing polyester yarn, was expanded into the areas of nylon texturizing, dyed yarns and spandex yarns through the August 1991 acquisition of Macfield, Inc., which doubled the revenue base at that time. Unifi expanded into the production of spun yarns through the April 1993 acquisition of Vintage Yarns. Spun yarn operations were further enlarged through the August 1993 acquisition of the Pioneer group of companies.

Unifi sells its products, both domestically and internationally, to weavers and knitters that produce fabrics for the apparel, industrial, hosiery, home furnishings, auto upholstery and other end-use markets.

In fiscal 1994, the largest customer accounted for 12% of total sales. International subsidiaries, operating mainly in Europe, contributed 13% of fiscal 1994 sales.

Important Developments

Jul. '95—Unifi reported that its sales reached a record level in fiscal 1995, aided by unit increases in its polyester and cotton yarn products. The company said it is looking to reduce costs in an environment of upward pressure on prices of raw materials and packaging supplies.

Capitalization

Long Term Debt: $230,000,000 (6/95) of sub. notes due 2002, conv. into com. at $29.67 a sh.

Per Share Data ($) (Year Ended Jun. 30)

	1995	1994	1993	1992	1991	1990
Tangible Bk. Val.	NA	8.36	7.83	6.79	4.29	4.15
Cash Flow	NA	2.06	2.69	1.67	1.59	1.15
Earnings	1.67	1.08	1.87	1.04	1.08	0.71
Dividends	0.40	0.56	0.50	0.36	0.21	Nil
Payout Ratio	24%	52%	27%	34%	18%	Nil
Prices - High	29⅛	27	38⅜	30⅝	24⅛	9⅞
- Low	22⅝	20½	20	21⅜	9⅜	6½
P/E Ratio - High	17	25	21	29	22	14
- Low	14	19	11	21	9	9

Income Statement Analysis (Million $)

	1994	%Chg	1993	%Chg	1992	%Chg	1991
Revs.	1,385	4%	1,332	22%	1,091	147%	442
Oper. Inc.	229	-14%	266	58%	168	140%	70.0
Depr.	70.1	25%	56.0	50%	37.4	109%	17.9
Int. Exp.	18.2	-22%	23.2	140%	9.7	NM	0.9
Pretax Inc.	137	-33%	205	99%	103	84%	56.0
Eff. Tax Rate	44%	—	38%	—	39%	—	31%
Net Inc.	76.0	-41%	128	104%	62.6	63%	38.3

Balance Sheet & Other Fin. Data (Million $)

	1994	1993	1992	1991	1990	1989
Cash	152	189	262	17.0	36.0	2.0
Curr. Assets	457	491	505	120	129	109
Total Assets	1,003	970	805	197	208	187
Curr. Liab.	152	177	132	52.0	47.0	59.0
LT Debt	230	230	251	Nil	4.0	Nil
Common Eqty.	589	529	404	140	152	121
Total Cap.	851	794	673	145	161	128
Cap. Exp.	105	135	66.9	17.3	19.8	41.3
Cash Flow	147	184	100	56.0	43.0	42.0

Ratio Analysis

	1994	1993	1992	1991	1990	1989
Curr. Ratio	3.0	2.8	3.8	2.3	2.8	1.8
% LT Debt of Cap.	27.0	29.0	37.3	Nil	2.7	Nil
% Net Inc.of Revs.	5.5	9.6	5.7	8.7	6.6	6.7
% Ret. on Assets	7.6	13.6	10.8	20.0	13.3	15.3
% Ret. on Equity	13.5	25.9	19.0	27.7	19.3	22.4

Dividend Data —UFI limits dividend payments to about 30% of the preceding fiscal year's earnings.

Amt. of Div. $	Date Decl.	Ex-Div. Date	Stock of Record	Payment Date
0.100	Oct. 20	Oct. 28	Nov. 03	Nov. 10 '94
0.100	Jan. 24	Jan. 30	Feb. 03	Feb. 10 '95
0.100	Apr. 20	May. 01	May. 05	May. 12 '95
0.130	Jul. 20	Aug. 02	Aug. 04	Aug. 11 '95

Data as orig. reptd.; bef. results of disc. opers. and/or spec. items. Per share data adj. for stk. divs. as of ex-div. date. E-Estimated. NA-Not Available. NM-Not Meaningful. NR-Not Ranked.

Office—7201 West Friendly Ave., P.O. Box 19109, Greensboro, NC 27419. **Tel**—(910) 294-4410. **Chrmn**—G. A. Mebane. **Pres & CEO**—W. T. Kretzer. **EVP, CFO & Investor Contact**—Robert A. Ward. **Secy**—C. C. Frazier, Jr. **Dirs**—W. J. Armfield IV, C. R. Carter, J. W. Eller, W. T. Kretzer, K. G. Langone, G. A. Mebane, D. F. Orr, G. R. Perkins, Jr., T. R. Pohl, R. A. Ward, G. A. Webster. **Transfer Agent & Registrar**—First Union National Bank, Charlotte, NC. **Incorporated** in New York in 1969. **Empl**-6,000. **S&P Analyst:** Philip D. Wohl

STANDARD & POOR'S

STOCK REPORTS

Universal Corp.

NYSE Symbol **UVV**
In S&P MidCap 400

15-AUG-95 **Industry:** Tobacco

Summary: Universal is the holding company for the world's largest independent leaf tobacco dealer, as well as agriproducts and lumber products businesses.

S&P Opinion: Hold (★★★)

Recent Price • 22¼ | Yield • 4.5%
52 Wk Range • 24¾-18⅞ | 12-Mo. P/E • 30.5

Quantitative Evaluations
Outlook (1 Lowest—5 Highest) • **1+**
Fair Value • **17**
Risk • **Average**
Earn./Div. Rank • **B+**

Technical Eval. • **Bearish** since 6/95
Rel. Strength Rank (1 Lowest—99 Highest) • **43**
Insider Activity • **NA**

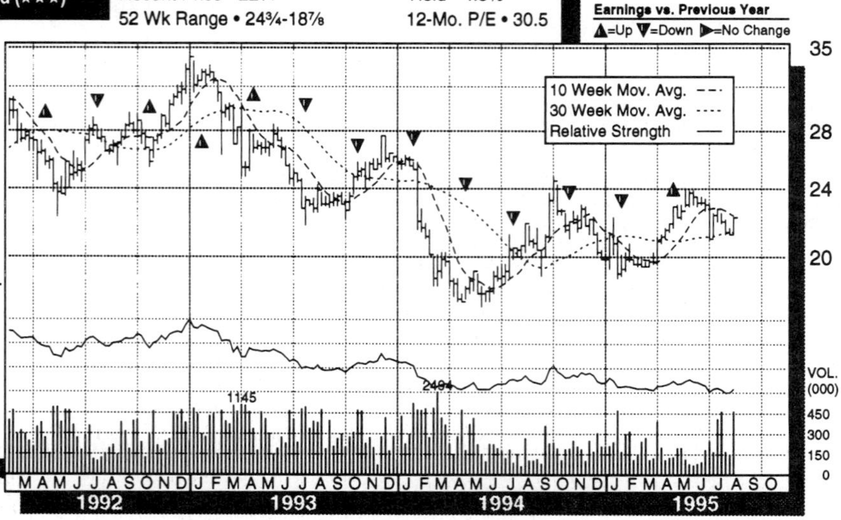

Overview - 15-AUG-95

We expect profits in fiscal 1996 to recover steadily from the lower earnings recorded over the past two years, principally reflecting the gradual drawdown of recently oversupplied global leaf markets. Also, recent restructuring actions aimed at rationalizing and consolidating international operations should help enhance international margins, while an improving domestic mix toward higher profit business would also support domestic profitability. Earnings should also trend upward for both the agri-products and lumber & building products groups, aided by acquisitions. U.S. tobacco marketings may be somewhat disrupted by a possible increase in near-term regulatory burdens on U.S. cigarette manufacturers.

Valuation - 15-AUG-95

Given our expectation of gradually improving per share earnings in fiscal 1996 (from fiscal 1995's $1.04, excluding special charges), coupled with a fairly secure, approximate 4% dividend yield, the shares appear to be a worthwhile holding for total return. Also, tobacco-related stocks may benefit from their relatively defensive characteristics in a slow U.S. economy. Investors should note, however, that these shares are sensitive to the fortunes of the U.S. cigarette manufacturers, who come under constant scrutiny from various governmental agencies. Also, UVV's earnings from non-tobacco interests are subject to a high level of variability, owing to the constantly changing market conditions for the products and services UVV provides.

Key Stock Statistics

S&P EPS Est. 1996	1.60	Tang. Bk. Value/Share	6.81
P/E on S&P Est. 1996	13.9	Beta	1.04
Dividend Rate/Share	1.00	Shareholders	4,100
Shs. outstg. (M)	35.0	Market cap. (B)	$0.784
Avg. daily vol. (M)	0.078	Inst. holdings	77%
		Insider holdings	NA

Value of $10,000 invested 5 years ago: $ 15,786

Fiscal Year Ending Jun. 30

	1995	% Change	1994	% Change	1993	% Change
Revenues (Million $)						
1Q	656.0	-5%	690.7	-16%	827.0	19%
2Q	963.8	12%	863.7	-3%	888.0	2%
3Q	974.9	30%	749.6	-10%	837.0	-11%
4Q	—	—	671.1	35%	495.6	4%
Yr.	3,281	10%	2,975	-2%	3,047	2%
Income (Million $)						
1Q	5.89	-68%	18.46	-22%	23.78	18%
2Q	14.95	-26%	20.21	-43%	35.25	22%
3Q	10.30	10%	9.34	-51%	19.08	1%
4Q	—	—	-9.40	NM	2.14	-26%
Yr.	25.60	-34%	38.56	-52%	80.24	13%
Earnings Per Share ($)						
1Q	0.17	-67%	0.52	-28%	0.72	18%
2Q	0.43	-25%	0.57	-47%	1.08	21%
3Q	0.29	12%	0.26	-55%	0.58	2%
4Q	—	—	-0.27	NM	0.06	-25%
Yr.	0.73	-33%	1.09	-54%	2.39	11%

Next earnings report expected: late October

Universal Corp.

Business Summary - 14-AUG-95

Universal Corporation is the holding company for Universal Leaf Tobacco Co., the world's largest independent leaf tobacco dealer. Through other subsidiaries, it is engaged in the agriproducts and lumber and buildings products businesses. Contributions in fiscal 1994 were:

	Revs.	Profits
Tobacco	73%	75%
Lumber & building products	12%	17%
Agriproducts	15%	8%

In fiscal 1994, the U.S. accounted for 51% of revenues, Europe for 37% and South and Central America for 7%.

Tobacco operations involve selecting, buying, shipping, processing, packing, storing and financing leaf tobacco in the U.S. and other tobacco-growing countries for the account of, or resale to, manufacturers of tobacco products throughout the world. UVV estimates that in fiscal 1994 it purchased or processed about 33% of the flue-cured and burley tobacco produced in the aggregate in the U.S., Brazil, Zimbabwe and Malawi.

Agriproducts involve the selection, buying, shipping, processing, storing, financing, distribution, importing and exporting of a number of products, including tea, rubber, sunflower seeds, nuts, dried fruit, canned meats, spices and seasonings.

UVV is also engaged in the lumber and building products business in the Netherlands and Belgium, where its subsidiaries distribute and sell lumber and related building products mainly to the construction market.

Important Developments

Aug. '95—UVV attributed the 10% decline in operating profits (before an after-tax restructuring charge of $10.7 million, or $0.31 per share) primarily to lingering effects of the worldwide oversupply of leaf that began in late 1993. Domestic tobacco operations improved slightly on increased volume in 1995, but a shift in processing toward lower margin business partially offset such benefits. Agri-products operating profits improved, reflecting contributions by all product groups and the absence of recently terminated coffee trading activities in 1994. Lumber and building products profits also improved, led by increased volumes and margins in the wholesale sector, and from acquisitions. Management said tobacco market conditions were beginning to produce benefits for the company, and expected improved company earnings in fiscal 1996.

Capitalization

Long Term Debt: $285,325,000 (3/95).
Minority Interest: $5,673,000.

Per Share Data ($) (Year Ended Jun. 30)

	1995	1994	1993	1992	1991	1990
Tangible Bk. Val.	NA	6.55	7.81	8.75	11.43	11.10
Cash Flow	NA	2.13	3.36	3.04	2.51	1.92
Earnings	0.73	1.09	2.39	2.15	1.72	1.11
Dividends	0.98	0.92	0.84	0.79	0.76	0.73
Payout Ratio	134%	84%	37%	37%	44%	65%
Prices - High	24	26¼	33¾	34¼	34	18⅛
- Low	18⅞	17½	21¾	22¼	11⅞	11
P/E Ratio - High	33	24	14	16	20	16
- Low	26	16	9	10	7	10

Income Statement Analysis (Million $)

	1994	%Chg	1993	%Chg	1992	%Chg	1991
Revs.	2,975	-2%	3,047	2%	2,989	3%	2,896
Oper. Inc.	157	-24%	206	14%	180	13%	160
Depr.	37.1	13%	32.8	12%	29.2	13%	25.8
Int. Exp.	58.4	27%	46.1	-7%	49.8	-14%	58.0
Pretax Inc.	50.5	-59%	123	16%	106	31%	81.0
Eff. Tax Rate	23%	—	35%	—	33%	—	30%
Net Inc.	38.6	-52%	80.2	13%	70.7	25%	56.4

Balance Sheet & Other Fin. Data (Million $)

	1994	1993	1992	1991	1990	1989
Cash	165	120	82.7	59.5	50.8	68.4
Curr. Assets	1,186	1,087	970	877	717	639
Total Assets	1,667	1,562	1,261	1,276	1,171	1,062
Curr. Liab.	868	786	697	654	453	438
LT Debt	298	282	190	160	144	85.0
Common Eqty.	377	418	302	390	397	386
Total Cap.	687	735	522	578	576	505
Cap. Exp.	23.7	37.5	47.1	44.6	31.8	37.7
Cash Flow	75.7	113	100	82.2	64.2	79.7

Ratio Analysis

	1994	1993	1992	1991	1990	1989
Curr. Ratio	1.4	1.4	1.4	1.3	1.6	1.5
% LT Debt of Cap.	43.3	38.3	36.4	27.7	25.1	16.9
% Net Inc.of Revs.	1.2	2.6	2.4	1.9	1.3	1.9
% Ret. on Assets	2.3	5.5	5.6	4.6	3.4	5.2
% Ret. on Equity	9.6	21.5	20.4	14.4	9.6	14.6

Dividend Data —Dividends have been paid since 1927. A dividend reinvestment plan is available. A "poison pill" stock purchase rights plan was adopted in 1989.

Amt. of Div. $	Date Decl.	Ex-Div. Date	Stock of Record	Payment Date
0.240	Aug. 04	Oct. 04	Oct. 11	Nov. 07 '94
0.250	Dec. 01	Jan. 03	Jan. 09	Feb. 06 '95
0.250	Feb. 02	Apr. 04	Apr. 10	May. 08 '95
0.250	May. 04	Jul. 06	Jul. 10	Aug. 07 '95
0.250	Aug. 03	Oct. 05	Oct. 10	Nov. 06 '95

Data as orig. reptd.; bef. results of disc. opers. and/or spec. items. Per share data adj. for stk. divs. as of ex-div. date. E-Estimated. NA-Not Available. NM-Not Meaningful. NR-Not Ranked.

Office—150 No. Hamilton St., Richmond, VA 23230. **Tel**—(804) 359-9311. **Chrmn & CEO**—H. H. Harrell. **Pres**—A. B. King. **VP & Secy**—J. M. White III. **VP & CFO**—H. H. Roper. **VP, Treas & Investor Contact**—Karen M. L. Whelan. **Dirs**—W. W. Berry, R. E. Carrier, W. L. Chandler, L. S. Eagleburger, J. Godthelp, E. T. Gray, H. H. Harrell, R. G. Holder, A. B. King, J. D. Munford, H. R. Stallard, T. R. Towers. **Transfer Agent & Registrar**—Wachovia Bank of North Carolina, Winston-Salem. **Incorporated** in Virginia in 1918. **Empl**-25,000. **S&P Analyst:** Kenneth A. Shea

STANDARD & POOR'S

STOCK REPORTS

Universal Foods

NYSE Symbol **UFC**
In S&P MidCap 400

24-JUL-95 **Industry:** Food

Summary: UFC produces primarily for the food processing industry food ingredient products such as flavors, colors, yeast products, and dehydrated vegetables.

S&P Opinion: Accumulate (★★★★)

Recent Price • 31⅞
52 Wk Range • 34¼-26⅛
Yield • 3.0%
12-Mo. P/E • 11.8

Quantitative Evaluations

Outlook
(1 Lowest—5 Highest)
• **5⁻**

Fair Value
• **36⅛**

Risk
• **Low**

Earn./Div. Rank
• **A**

Technical Eval.
• **Bearish** since 4/95

Rel. Strength Rank
(1 Lowest—99 Highest)
• **34**

Insider Activity
• **Neutral**

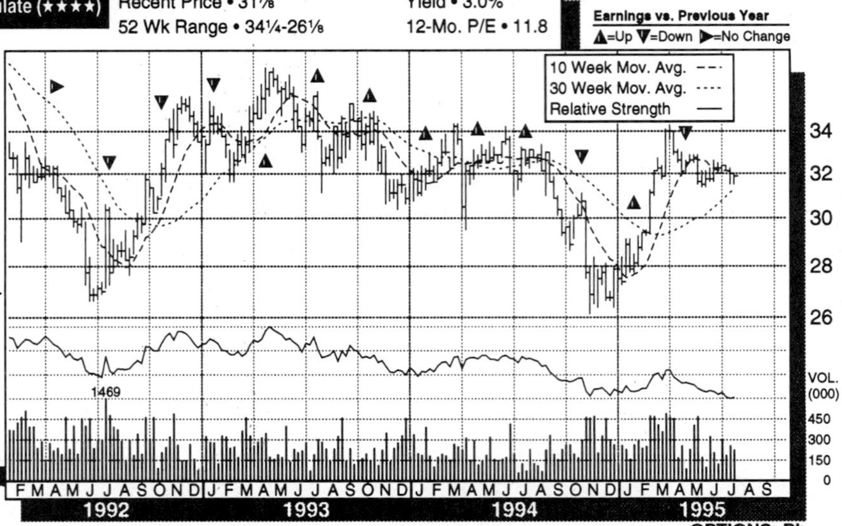

OPTIONS: Ph

Overview - 24-JUL-95

Revenues from ongoing operations (excluding the $270 million frozen foods division sold in August 1994) are expected to advance at a near 20% pace in fiscal 1995, driven primarily by recent acquisitions and good internal growth. Beginning in fiscal 1996, sales growth will moderate to about 10% annually, paced mostly by internal growth. Gross margins should continue to benefit from recent restructuring actions and an improving product mix, and allow operating margins to expand moderately. In all, earnings per share in fiscal 1996 are projected to climb to $2.40 a share from the estimated $2.15 (exclusive of a one-time $0.90 gain) in fiscal 1995. Longer term prospects are bright, reflecting growing worldwide demand for the company's products.

Valuation - 24-JUL-95

Based on our forecast of steady, low double-digit earnings per share growth from ongoing operations over the next few years, we view the shares as attractive at current levels. Although having rebounded sharply from late 1994's $26 low, this high quality, low-risk stock trades at a multiple only at about the level of the overall market. We expect that investors will become increasingly confident of the company's prospects as earnings growth trends are re-established following the August 1994 sale of the frozen foods segment, and push the stock's relative valuation higher. Sporting a generous 3% dividend yield, the shares are a compelling choice for above-average total return.

Key Stock Statistics

S&P EPS Est. 1995	3.05	Tang. Bk. Value/Share	8.07
P/E on S&P Est. 1995	10.5	Beta	0.85
S&P EPS Est. 1996	2.40	Shareholders	6,800
Dividend Rate/Share	0.96	Market cap. (B)	$0.831
Shs. outstg. (M)	26.1	Inst. holdings	70%
Avg. daily vol. (M)	0.049	Insider holdings	NA

Value of $10,000 invested 5 years ago: $ 15,491

Fiscal Year Ending Sep. 30

	1995	% Change	1994	% Change	1993	% Change
Revenues (Million $)						
1Q	187.7	-15%	220.8	5%	209.4	2%
2Q	191.8	-19%	237.1	9%	217.0	-3%
3Q	207.5	-17%	249.5	9%	228.0	2%
4Q	—	—	222.5	-6%	237.5	3%
Yr.	—	—	929.9	4%	891.6	NM
Income (Million $)						
1Q	35.58	146%	14.46	7%	13.52	-7%
2Q	13.65	-6%	14.57	9%	13.41	6%
3Q	14.56	-5%	15.31	7%	14.34	13%
4Q	—	—	6.57	-57%	15.33	12%
Yr.	—	—	50.91	-10%	56.60	36%
Earnings Per Share ($)						
1Q	1.37	149%	0.55	8%	0.51	-7%
2Q	0.52	-7%	0.56	10%	0.51	9%
3Q	0.56	-5%	0.59	7%	0.55	15%
4Q	E0.60	—	0.25	-57%	0.58	NM
Yr.	E3.05	—	1.95	-9%	2.15	37%

Next earnings report expected: mid November

Universal Foods

Business Summary - 24-JUL-95

Universal Foods makes and distributes a wide range of food products. International operations accounted for 20% and 22% of revenues and profits, respectively, in fiscal 1994. Revenues by segment in fiscal 1994 were:

Frozen Foods	26%
Flavor	28%
Red Star Yeast & Products	18%
Color	15%
Dehydrated Products	9%
Red Star BioProducts	4%

The frozen food products division was sold to ConAgra, Inc. in August 1994.

Flavor products are sold as ingredients to the dairy, beverage and food processor industries worldwide. UFC operates in the marketplace as Universal Flavors.

The yeast division specializes in the production of compressed, active dry and nutritional yeast products for sale to industrial, institutional and retail accounts under the Red Star and Quick-Rise names.

Food color products, sold under the brand names of Red Seal and Spectracoat, are used by producers of soft drinks, bakery products, processed foods, confections, pet foods, alcoholic beverages and pharmaceuticals.

Dehydrated onion and garlic products are marketed under the Rogers Foods trademark and private labels. UFC also produces and distributes chili powder and pepper, paprika and dehydrated vegetables.

The Red Star BioProducts division creates products with unique nutritional or savory properties, or fermentation growth characteristics. Markets served include food processors, pharmaceuticals, and agriculture.

Important Developments

Jul. '95—UFC said share earnings from continuing operations in fiscal 1995's first nine months increased 14.8%, year to year, to $1.55 (excluding the one-time gain of $0.90 on the sale of the frozen foods division), from $1.35 in the fiscal 1994 period, driven by existing business growth and acquisition contributions. Flavor division (35% of revenues) revenues and profits were higher, as strong international sales and U.S. beverage flavor sales offset weakness in the U.S. dairy flavors market and the negative impact of conditions in Mexico. Color division (19%) revenues and profits were higher, as an improved business mix in the U.S. offset the impact of conditions in Mexico. Revenues for Dehydrated products (13%) and Red Star BioProducts were higher, while revenues for Red Star Yeast & Products were modestly below year-earlier levels.

Capitalization

Long Term Debt: $156,142,000 (6/95).

Per Share Data ($) (Year Ended Sep. 30)

	1994	1993	1992	1991	1990	1989
Tangible Bk. Val.	6.89	7.49	7.42	7.38	6.10	5.19
Cash Flow	3.14	3.47	2.62	3.09	2.99	2.42
Earnings	1.95	2.15	1.57	2.18	1.95	1.60
Dividends	0.92	0.88	0.84	0.76	0.68	0.53
Payout Ratio	47%	41%	54%	35%	35%	34%
Prices - High	34⅜	37¼	39½	40⅝	33⅞	26¼
- Low	26⅛	30⅜	26⅝	28⅝	23¼	21⅜
P/E Ratio - High	18	17	25	19	17	16
- Low	13	14	17	13	12	13

Income Statement Analysis (Million $)

	1994	%Chg	1993	%Chg	1992	%Chg	1991
Revs.	930	4%	892	1%	883	6%	834
Oper. Inc.	140	NM	141	8%	131	NM	130
Depr.	31.0	-11%	34.9	24%	28.1	16%	24.2
Int. Exp.	15.9	5%	15.2	-11%	17.1	16%	14.8
Pretax Inc.	81.1	-10%	90.6	35%	67.0	-27%	92.3
Eff. Tax Rate	37%	—	38%	—	38%	—	37%
Net Inc.	50.9	-10%	56.6	36%	41.7	-28%	57.8

Balance Sheet & Other Fin. Data (Million $)

	1994	1993	1992	1991	1990	1989
Cash	43.4	11.4	11.0	13.2	8.2	3.9
Curr. Assets	328	312	300	284	226	214
Total Assets	764	730	702	653	549	489
Curr. Liab.	192	175	185	157	135	121
LT Debt	172	172	168	152	117	126
Common Eqty.	327	305	303	292	243	203
Total Cap.	517	498	495	466	374	352
Cap. Exp.	95.0	54.0	51.5	54.8	69.6	46.6
Cash Flow	81.9	91.5	69.8	81.9	75.9	60.6

Ratio Analysis

	1994	1993	1992	1991	1990	1989
Curr. Ratio	1.7	1.8	1.6	1.8	1.7	1.8
% LT Debt of Cap.	33.3	34.6	33.9	32.6	31.3	35.6
% Net Inc.of Revs.	5.5	6.3	4.7	6.9	5.9	4.8
% Ret. on Assets	6.9	7.9	6.2	9.4	9.5	8.9
% Ret. on Equity	16.2	18.6	14.1	21.1	22.0	20.8

Dividend Data (Dividends have been paid since 1934. A dividend reinvestment plan is available. A "poison pill" stock purchase right was adopted in 1988.)

Amt. of Div. $	Date Decl.	Ex-Div. Date	Stock of Record	Payment Date
0.240	Oct. 10	Oct. 27	Nov. 02	Dec. 01 '94
0.240	Jan. 27	Feb. 02	Feb. 08	Mar. 01 '95
0.240	Apr. 17	May. 04	May. 10	Jun. 01 '95
0.240	Jun. 13	Aug. 01	Aug. 03	Sep. 01 '95

Data as orig. reptd.; bef. results of disc. opers. and/or spec. items. Per share data adj. for stk. divs. as of ex-div. date. EPS in fiscal 1995 1Q incl. one-time gain of 0.90. E-Estimated. NA-Not Available. NM-Not Meaningful. NR-Not Ranked.

Office—433 East Michigan St., Milwaukee, WI 53202. **Tel**—(414) 271-6755. **Chrmn & CEO**—G. A. Osborn. **Pres & COO**—K. P. Manning. **VP & CFO**—M. Fung. **VP & Secy**—T. M. O'Reilly. **Investor Contact**—Mary E. Brevard (414-347-3827). **Dirs**—M. E. Batten, J. F. Bergstrom, J. L. Forbes, O. D. Forker, L. T. Kendall, J. H. Keyes, K. P. Manning, C. S. McNeer, J. L. Murray, G. A. Osborn, W. U. Parfet, C. I. Waslien-Ghazaii, E. Whitelaw. **Transfer Agent & Registrar**—Firstar Trust Co., Milwaukee. **Incorporated** in Wisconsin in 1882. **Empl**-4,063. **S&P Analyst:** Kenneth A. Shea

STANDARD & POOR'S

STOCK REPORTS

UtiliCorp United

NYSE Symbol **UCU**

In S&P MidCap 400

08-SEP-95 **Industry:** Util.-Diversified

Summary: This electric and gas utility, based in Kansas City, serves 1.2 million customers in eight states and one Canadian province.

Quantitative Evaluations

Outlook (1 Lowest—5 Highest)
• **2⁻**

Fair Value
• **26⅛**

Risk
• **Low**

Earn./Div. Rank
• **A-**

Technical Eval.
• **Bullish** since 9/94

Rel. Strength Rank (1 Lowest—99 Highest)
• **21**

Insider Activity
• **NA**

Recent Price • 27⅛ Yield • 6.3%

52 Wk Range • 29½-25⅛ 12-Mo. P/E • 14.3

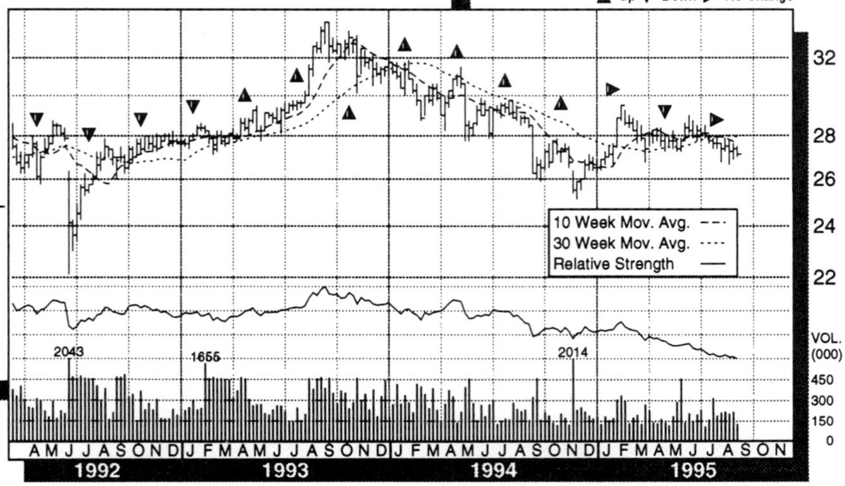

Business Profile - 08-SEP-95

In December 1994, UCU adopted a new strategy designed to make it the first national utility in the U.S. The plan includes EnergyOne, a brand name under which UCU's energy products and services will be marketed nationwide. EnergyOne is currently participating in an experimental one-year program in Rocky Valley, Iowa, that will enable residential customers to choose their own natural gas supplier. In August 1995, UCU agreed to sell Aquila Energy Resources to Apache Corp. for $198 million in cash.

Operational Review - 08-SEP-95

Earnings fell in 1995's first half, reflecting lower sales volume to electric and gas utility customers due to milder-than-normal weather, partially offset by customer growth, cost reductions and acquisitions. The Aquila subsidiary showed income improvement due to increased gas throughput, increased natural gas liquids prices and lower depreciation, depletion and amortization. Interest expense was up significantly, and share earnings were hurt by a 3.7% increase in common shares outstanding.

Stock Performance - 01-SEP-95

In the past 30 trading days, UCU's shares have declined 2%, compared to a 2% rise in the S&P 500. Average trading volume for the past five days was 24,400 shares, compared with the 40-day moving average of 40,188 shares.

Key Stock Statistics

Dividend Rate/Share	1.72	Shareholders	37,200
Shs. outstg. (M)	44.9	Market cap. (B)	$ 1.2
Avg. daily vol. (M)	0.037	Inst. holdings	22%
Tang. Bk. Value/Share	20.54	Insider holdings	NA
Beta	0.75		

Value of $10,000 invested 5 years ago: $ 17,262

Fiscal Year Ending Dec. 31

	1995	% Change	1994	% Change	1993	% Change
Revenues (Million $)						
1Q	463.8	-7%	497.3	3%	480.9	31%
2Q	328.5	5%	311.6	-5%	329.4	30%
3Q	—	—	315.1	-5%	330.1	20%
4Q	—	—	390.6	-9%	431.2	7%
Yr.	—	—	1,515	-4%	1,572	21%
Income (Million $)						
1Q	32.20	-17%	39.00	12%	34.80	22%
2Q	7.20	-3%	7.40	1%	7.30	NM
3Q	—	—	14.50	32%	11.00	124%
4Q	—	—	33.60	NM	33.30	30%
Yr.	—	—	94.40	9%	86.40	63%
Earnings Per Share ($)						
1Q	0.71	-19%	0.88	1%	0.87	13%
2Q	0.15	NM	0.15	15%	0.13	NM
3Q	—	—	0.31	41%	0.22	120%
4Q	—	—	0.76	NM	0.76	12%
Yr.	—	—	2.08	7%	1.95	48%

Next earnings report expected: late October

UtiliCorp United

Business Summary - 31-AUG-95

UtiliCorp United (formerly Missouri Public Service) is an energy company that consists of electric and natural gas utility operations, gas marketing, exploration and production, and independent power generation projects. The company operates in eight states and one Canadian province. Nonregulated businesses are Aquila Energy Corp., which has units that market, transport and process natural gas; and UtilCo Group, which holds interests in 16 independent power projects throughout the U.S. and Jamaica. In 1995, UCU sold the assets of its Aquila Energy Resources unit to Apache Corp. for $198 million in cash. The company also markets natural gas in the U.K. through several joint ventures, and owns a joint venture interest in an electric utility in New Zealand. Segment contributions in 1994 were as follows:

	Revenues	Profit
Electric	37%	54%
Gas	41%	27%
Nonregulated	22%	19%

In 1994, 45% of electricity was generated from coal, 14% from hydro sources, 6% from natural gas and oil, and 36% was purchased from other utilities. At the end of 1994, total system capability was 2,682 mw, and the company had 426,414 electric customers. Residential sales acounted for 44% of total electric revenues in 1994, commercial 28%, industrial 14%, and other 14%.

UCU serves some 779,630 natural gas customers in eight states. Residential sales accounted for 58% of total gas revenues in 1994, commercial 25%, industrial 11%, and other 6%. Total gas sales in 1994 were 128,019,000 Mcf versus 145,193,000 Mcf in 1993.

In January 1995, the company purchased a Missouri intrastate natural gas pipeline system from Edisto Resources Corp. for $75 million. In September 1994, UCU purchased the Kansas gas distribution system and selected pipeline properties from NorAm Energy Corp. for about $23.0 million. In February 1993, UtiliCorp purchased the Nebraska gas distribution system of NorAm Energy Corp. for about $106 million.

Important Developments

Aug. '95—UCU entered into a definitive agreement to sell substantially all of the assets of Aquila Energy Resources Corp., a wholly-owned subsidiary of Aquila Energy Corp., to Apache Corp. for about $198 million in cash. The assets include oil and natural gas reserves in the Gulf of Mexico, Texas, Oklahoma, Louisiana and New Mexico and about 141,000 net acres of developed and undeveloped oil and gas properties. The sale is expected to close by the end of September 1995.

Capitalization

Long Term Debt: $1,073,700,000 (6/95).
Subsid. Preferred Stock: $400,000.
Preference Stock: $25,000,000.

Per Share Data ($)

(Year Ended Dec. 31)

	1994	1993	1992	1991	1990	1989
Tangible Bk. Val.	20.33	20.27	18.66	19.45	17.49	16.58
Earnings	2.08	1.95	1.32	2.23	2.13	2.04
Dividends	1.70	1.62	1.60	1.54	1.46	1.41
Payout Ratio	82%	83%	121%	69%	69%	69%
Prices - High	31⅞	34	29	29⅜	22⅜	22¼
- Low	25⅛	27⅛	22⅛	20⅛	17⅜	17½
P/E Ratio - High	15	17	22	13	11	11
- Low	12	14	17	9	8	9

Income Statement Analysis (Million $)

	1994	%Chg	1993	%Chg	1992	%Chg	1991
Revs.	1,515	-4%	1,572	21%	1,299	21%	1,075
Depr.	140	4%	135	10%	123	128%	53.9
Maint.	49.3	4%	47.2	17%	40.5	9%	37.1
Fxd. Chgs. Cov.	2.4	13%	2.1	21%	1.7	-21%	2.2
Constr. Credits	NA	—	NA	—	NA	—	NA
Eff. Tax Rate	34%	—	26%	—	37%	—	36%
Net Inc.	94.4	9%	86.4	63%	52.9	-28%	73.5

Balance Sheet & Other Fin. Data (Million $)

	1994	1993	1992	1991	1990	1989
Gross Prop.	2,557	2,445	2,221	2,088	1,591	1,479
Cap. Exp.	132	141	150	134	119	98.0
Net Prop.	1,634	1,580	1,454	1,366	1,084	1,003
Capitalization:						
LT Debt	977	1,010	891	928	668	438
% LT Debt	50	52	54	55	53	48
Pfd.	53.8	83.9	95.1	97.1	86.8	97.4
% Pfd.	2.80	4.30	5.80	5.70	6.90	11
Common	907	852	661	670	491	378
% Common	47	44	40	40	23	41
Total Cap.	2,238	2,227	1,830	1,873	1,415	1,059

Ratio Analysis

	1994	1993	1992	1991	1990	1989
Oper. Ratio	88.0	92.2	89.4	86.3	87.1	88.1
% Earn. on Net Prop.	11.3	8.1	9.7	12.0	11.1	9.6
% Ret. on Revs.	6.2	5.5	4.1	6.8	6.6	6.6
% Ret. On Invest.Cap	9.0	6.1	8.2	9.4	9.5	10.4
% Return On Com.Eqty	10.4	10.0	7.0	11.3	11.8	12.2

Dividend Data —Dividends have been paid since 1939. A dividend reinvestment plan is available.

Amt. of Div. $	Date Decl.	Ex-Div. Date	Stock of Record	Payment Date
0.430	Aug. 03	Aug. 15	Aug. 19	Sep. 12 '94
0.430	Nov. 02	Nov. 14	Nov. 18	Dec. 12 '94
0.430	Feb. 01	Feb. 13	Feb. 17	Mar. 12 '95
0.430	May. 03	May. 15	May. 19	Jun. 12 '95
0.430	Aug. 02	Aug. 16	Aug. 18	Sep. 12 '95

Data as orig. reptd.; bef. results of disc opers. and/or spec. items. Per share data adj. for stk. divs. as of ex-div. date. E-Estimated. NA-Not Available. NM-Not Meaningful. NR-Not Ranked.

Office—3000 Commerce Tower, 911 Main, Kansas City, MO 64105. **Tel**—(816) 421-6600. **Chrmn, Pres & CEO**—R. C. Green, Jr. **VP & Secy**—D. J. Wolf. **Investor Contact**—Phil Hermanson (816-691-3541). **Dirs**—D. R. Armacost, J. R. Baker, H. Cain, R. C. Green, Jr., R. K. Green, I. O. Hockaday, Jr., S. O. Ikenberry, R. F. Jackson, Jr., L. P. Kline, A. G. Tucker. **Transfer Agent & Registrar**—First Chicago Trust Co. of New York, NYC., UMB Bank, Kansas City. **Incorporated** in Missouri in 1950; reincorporated in Delaware in 1986. **Empl**-4,683. **S&P Analyst:** Ronald J. Gross

STANDARD & POOR'S

STOCK REPORTS

Valero Energy

NYSE Symbol **VLO**
In S&P MidCap 400

10-AUG-95 **Industry:** Oil and Gas

Summary: VLO primarily refines and markets unleaded gasoline and other petroleum products. It also conducts natural gas pipeline operations in Texas, and markets natural gas liquids.

Quantitative Evaluations

Outlook
(1 Lowest—5 Highest)
• **2-**

Fair Value
• **20½**

Risk
• **Average**

Earn./Div. Rank
• **B**

Technical Eval.
• **Bearish** since 5/95

Rel. Strength Rank
(1 Lowest—99 Highest)
• **69**

Insider Activity
• **NA**

Recent Price • 23
52 Wk Range • 23¼-16
Yield • 2.3%
12-Mo. P/E • 34.8

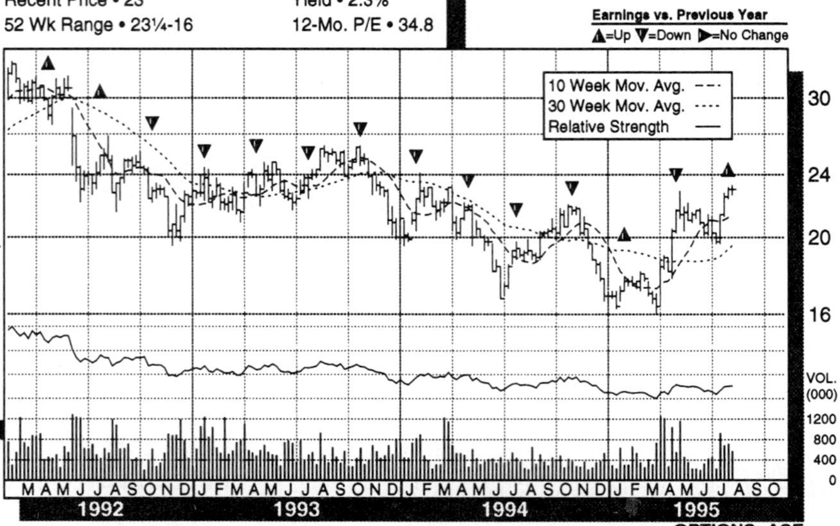

OPTIONS: ASE

Business Profile - 10-AUG-95

This diversified energy company is engaged in the production, transportation and marketing of fuels. Its May 1994 merger with Valero Natural Gas Partners significantly increased cash flow and boosted operating earnings. VLO is now better balanced with regard to assets and earnings in the natural gas and natural gas liquids businesses. It continues to make capital commitments and pursue strategic alliances.

Operational Review - 10-AUG-95

Revenues have risen dramatically in recent periods, reflecting the May 1994 consolidation of Valero Natural Gas Partners. Refining margins improved significantly in the second quarter, aided by MTBE and a premium for reformulated over conventional gasoline. Natural gas results reflected the absence of a litigation settlement. Natural gas liquids operating income was boosted by higher production volumes and lower prices for natural gas.

Stock Performance - 04-AUG-95

In the past 30 trading days, VLO's shares have increased 10%, compared to a 2% rise in the S&P 500. Average trading volume for the past five days was 111,780 shares, compared with the 40-day moving average of 107,903 shares.

Key Stock Statistics

Dividend Rate/Share	0.52	Shareholders	7,500
Shs. outstg. (M)	43.6	Market cap. (B)	$0.998
Avg. daily vol. (M)	0.117	Inst. holdings	79%
Tang. Bk. Value/Share	19.00	Insider holdings	NA
Beta	0.68		

Value of $10,000 invested 5 years ago: $ 17,060

Fiscal Year Ending Dec. 31

	1995	% Change	1994	% Change	1993	% Change
Revenues (Million $)						
1Q	690.5	145%	281.3	-5%	295.8	8%
2Q	744.6	79%	416.1	30%	321.1	NM
3Q	—	—	577.4	79%	323.4	-4%
4Q	—	—	562.6	99%	282.0	-7%
Yr.	—	—	1,837	50%	1,222	-1%
Income (Million $)						
1Q	3.76	-40%	6.28	-60%	15.61	-22%
2Q	20.50	NM	4.22	-83%	24.68	-10%
3Q	—	—	12.53	11%	11.29	-60%
4Q	—	—	3.84	NM	-15.16	NM
Yr.	—	—	26.88	-26%	36.42	-57%
Earnings Per Share ($)						
1Q	0.02	-85%	0.13	-64%	0.36	-25%
2Q	0.40	NM	0.03	-95%	0.56	-11%
3Q	—	—	0.22	-15%	0.26	-60%
4Q	—	—	0.02	NM	-0.36	NM
Yr.	—	—	0.40	-51%	0.82	-58%

Next earnings report expected: mid October

Valero Energy

Business Summary - 10-AUG-95

Valero is a diversified energy company engaged in the producton, transportation and marketing of environmentally clean fuels and products. Its three core businesses are specialized refining, natural gas and natural gas liquids. The company owns a specialized petroleum refinery, a network of about 8,000 miles of natural gas transmission and gathering lines in Texas, and 11 natural gas processing plants in Texas.

Business segment contributions in 1994 (profits in million $) were:

	Revs.	Profits
Refining and marketing	57%	$78.7
Natural gas	25%	26.7
Natural gas liquids	16%	35.2
Other	2%	- 14.7

Refining operations at VLO's Corpus Christi, Tex., refinery process high-sulfur atmospheric tower bottoms, a type of residual fuel oil, into products including unleaded gasoline and middle distillates. Refining and marketing sales volumes averaged 140,000 bbl. per day in 1994 (133,000 bbl. in 1993); average sales price per bbl. was $21.13, versus $21.23. Refinery throughput averaged 146,000 bbl. per day (136,000 bbl.) and throughput margin per bbl. was $5.36 ($5.99). Productos Ecologicos S.A. de C.V. (35% owned) is proceeding with plans to construct a plant in Mexico with capacity to produce 17,000 bbl. per day of methyl tertiary butyl ether (MTBE); the plant is expected to cost $450 million.

The company's natural gas business includes a strategically located pipeline system accessing most major producing and consuming regions nationwide, with a daily throughput capacity of over three billion cubic feet. VLO is the sixth largest producer of natural gas liquids in the U.S.; its plants are capable of producing 90,000 bbl. per day.

In December 1994, VLO and Hoechst Celanese Corp. formed a joint venture to renovate a 13,000 bbl. per day methanol plant owned by Hoechst Celanese in Clear Lake, Tex. The company was to contribute $75 million, with Hoechst Celanese to provide the methanol unit and the plant infrastructure and serve as operator of the facility.

Important Developments

Jul. '95—VLO said it anticipates that refining margins will be supported by strong product demand, lower gasoline inventories and lower levels of gasoline imports. Throughput volumes should be higher in the second half of the year.

Capitalization

Long Term Debt: $946,114,000 (3/95).
$3.125 Conv. Preferred Stock: 3,450,000 shs. ($50 liq. val.); conv. into com. at $27.03 a sh.
Red. Preferred Stock, Series A: $12,650,000.

Per Share Data ($) (Year Ended Dec. 31)

	1994	1993	1992	1991	1990	1989
Tangible Bk. Val.	19.51	19.45	19.09	16.90	15.20	13.16
Cash Flow	2.34	2.13	3.07	3.19	3.25	2.17
Earnings	0.40	0.82	1.94	2.28	2.31	0.98
Dividends	0.52	0.46	0.42	0.34	0.26	0.15
Payout Ratio	130%	56%	22%	15%	12%	19%
Prices - High	$24\frac{1}{8}$	$26\frac{1}{8}$	$33\frac{3}{8}$	31	$20\frac{1}{4}$	$19\frac{5}{8}$
- Low	$16\frac{1}{2}$	$19\frac{5}{8}$	$19\frac{1}{2}$	$14\frac{1}{4}$	$13\frac{1}{2}$	$8\frac{7}{8}$
P/E Ratio - High	60	32	17	14	9	20
- Low	41	24	10	6	6	9

Income Statement Analysis (Million $)

	1994	%Chg	1993	%Chg	1992	%Chg	1991
Revs.	1,837	50%	1,222	-1%	1,235	22%	1,012
Oper. Inc.	210	59%	132	-27%	182	17%	156
Depr. & Depl.	84.0	48%	56.7	18%	48.2	32%	36.6
Int. Exp.	79.0	58%	50.0	9%	46.0	21%	38.0
Pretax Inc.	43.0	-37%	68.0	-48%	131	-10%	146
Eff. Tax Rate	37%	—	47%	—	36%	—	33%
Net Inc.	26.9	-26%	36.4	-57%	83.9	-15%	99

Balance Sheet & Other Fin. Data (Million $)

	1994	1993	1992	1991	1990	1989
Cash	61.7	7.3	8.2	13.9	51.7	15.1
Curr. Assets	533	235	305	288	315	247
Total Assets	2,831	1,764	1,759	1,481	1,254	1,018
Curr. Liab.	461	153	175	168	149	122
LT Debt	1,022	486	482	380	247	222
Common Eqty.	849	842	821	687	618	472
Total Cap.	2,311	1,574	1,544	1,269	1,064	849
Cap. Exp.	81.0	137	283	230	138	37.0
Cash Flow	NA	92.0	131	129	123	63.0

Ratio Analysis

	1994	1993	1992	1991	1990	1989
Curr. Ratio	1.2	1.5	1.7	1.7	2.1	2.0
% LT Debt of Cap.	44.2	30.8	31.2	29.9	23.2	26.1
% Ret. on Assets	1.2	2.1	5.0	7.2	7.9	3.6
% Ret. on Equity	2.1	4.2	10.7	14.2	15.2	5.9

Dividend Data (Common dividends, omitted in late 1984, were resumed in 1989. A poison pill stock purchase rights plan was adopted in 1985.)

Amt. of Div. $	Date Decl.	Ex-Div. Date	Stock of Record	Payment Date
0.130	Oct. 20	Oct. 25	Oct. 31	Dec. 07 '94
0.130	Jan. 19	Feb. 06	Feb. 10	Mar. 10 '95
0.130	Mar. 23	May. 03	May. 09	Jun. 09 '95
0.130	Jul. 20	Aug. 04	Aug. 08	Sep. 08 '95

Data as orig. reptd.; bef. results of disc opers. and/or spec. items. Per share data adj. for stk. divs. as of ex-div. date. E-Estimated. NA-Not Available. NM-Not Meaningful. NR-Not Ranked.

Office—530 McCullough Ave., San Antonio, TX 78215. **Tel**—(210) 246-2000. **Chrmn & CEO**—W. E. Greehey. **SVP & CFO**—D. M. Heep. **Secy**—R. C. Schmidt. **VP & Investor Contact**—Keith Booke (800-531-7911). **Dirs**—J. Becraft, E. C. Benninger, R. G. Dettmer, A. R. Dudley, R. M. Escobedo, W. E. Greehey, J. L. Johnson, L. H. Lebermann, S. K. Purcell. **Transfer Agent & Registrar**—Harris Trust and Savings Bank, Chicago. **Incorporated** in Delaware in 1955. **Empl**-1,658. **S&P Analyst:** Michael C. Barr

Value Health

NYSE Symbol **VH**
In S&P MidCap 400

27-SEP-95

Industry:
Health Care Centers

Summary: Value Health is a leading independent provider of specialty managed care benefit programs and health care information systems.

S&P Opinion: Accumulate (★★★★)

Recent Price • 27¾
52 Wk Range • 48½-26¾
Yield • Nil
12-Mo. P/E • 19.0

Quantitative Evaluations

Outlook
(1 Lowest—5 Highest)
• **NA**

Fair Value
• **NA**

Risk
• **Average**

Earn./Div. Rank
• **NR**

Technical Eval.
• **Bullish** since 9/95

Rel. Strength Rank
(1 Lowest—99 Highest)
• **1**

Insider Activity
• **NA**

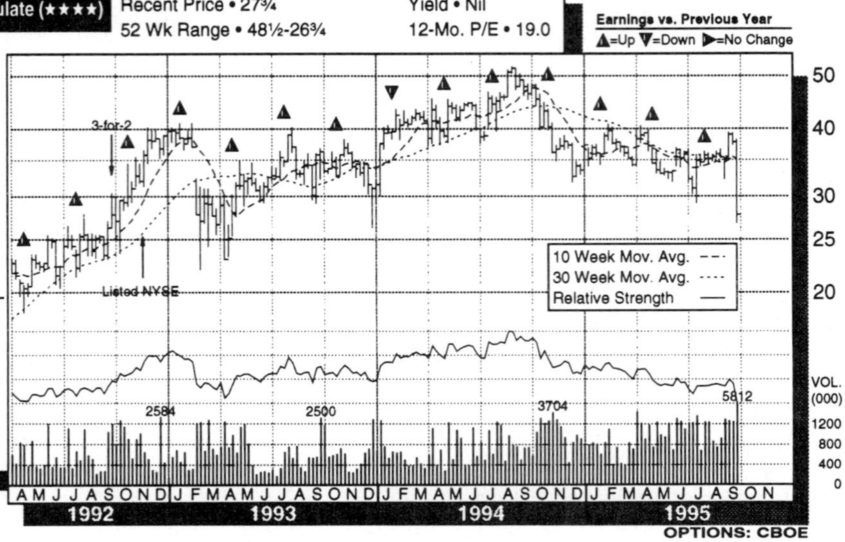

Overview - 27-SEP-95

Revenues in 1995 should exceed $1.4 billion, boosted by the acquisition of Diagnostek, demand from existing customers and new client additions. Soft business conditions at Diagnostek will force VH to focus on improving these operations at least for the next few quarters. In addition, the company is seeking to streamline its pharmacy benefits management and mental health operations in order to improve its chances when bidding on lower margin government and HMO contracts. Restructuring charges of up to $80 million will be incurred in the fourth quarter.

Valuation - 27-SEP-95

The shares fell sharply following VH's September comments regarding unexpected weakness at Diagnostek and a shifting business focus at the pharmacy benefits and mental health segments. Although the long-term outlook remains bright, and the company continues to guide analysts toward a 1996 EPS estimate of $2.25, investors sold the stock based on what appears to be a more clouded profit outlook. We are confident that VH can generate 20% annual profit gains, paced by its strong market presence and solid fundamentals of the pharmacy benefits management segment, but have lowered our opinion on the shares pending indications that problems at Diagnostek will be quickly resolved.

Key Stock Statistics

S&P EPS Est. 1995	1.75	Tang. Bk. Value/Share	7.66
P/E on S&P Est. 1995	15.9	Beta	NA
S&P EPS Est. 1996	2.20	Shareholders	NA
Dividend Rate/Share	Nil	Market cap. (B)	$ 1.4
Shs. outstg. (M)	53.5	Inst. holdings	52%
Avg. daily vol. (M)	0.691	Insider holdings	NA

Value of $10,000 invested 5 years ago: NA

Fiscal Year Ending Dec. 31

	1995	% Change	1994	% Change	1993	% Change
Revenues (Million $)						
1Q	276.1	28%	216.4	58%	137.0	138%
2Q	281.6	18%	238.3	61%	147.8	139%
3Q	—	—	252.3	61%	156.8	145%
4Q	—	—	269.5	56%	172.6	120%
Yr.	—	—	976.4	59%	614.2	134%
Income (Million $)						
1Q	16.58	54%	10.78	43%	7.52	179%
2Q	17.51	43%	12.21	43%	8.52	148%
3Q	—	—	11.03	22%	9.04	133%
4Q	—	—	15.61	NM	-16.54	NM
Yr.	—	—	49.62	NM	8.61	-41%
Earnings Per Share ($)						
1Q	0.40	54%	0.26	37%	0.19	58%
2Q	0.42	45%	0.29	32%	0.22	57%
3Q	E0.45	73%	0.26	8%	0.24	50%
4Q	E0.48	26%	0.38	NM	-0.43	NM
Yr.	E1.75	47%	1.19	NM	0.22	-64%

Next earnings report expected: early November

Value Health

Business Summary - 27-SEP-95

Value Health Inc. is a leading provider of specialty managed care benefit programs and health care information services, with programs designed to manage costs and maintain quality in health care sectors including prescription drugs, mental health and substance abuse and workers' compensation.

ValueRx (67% of 1994 revenues) provides outpatient prescription drug plans that incorporate benefit plan design services, a network of retail pharmacies, utilization review, claims processing, a mail service prescription option and member support services. VH's prescription drug preferred provider organization includes a national network of more than 37,000 chain and independent pharmacies serving more than 8 million people.

Value Behavioral Health (VBH; 20%) offers mental health and substance abuse programs that incorporate preferred provider networks, clinically based utilization review and case management, benefit design, member support and claims administration services. The primary clients for these programs are large self-insured employers who contract with VBH to provide the plan on a "carved out" basis separate from the balance of the customer's healthcare programs.

Value Health Insurance Services Group (7%) provides managed workers' compensation and group health services. Programs include comprehensive utilization management, claims administration, disability management and health care data analysis.

The company also develops comprehensive programs that improve patient outcomes and control costs by organizing managed care initiatives around diseases. VH also develops and sells software and services designed to assist in the identification and elimination of inappropriate medical services and the profiling of provider practices.

Important Developments

Sep. '95—The company said it would focus on reducing operating expenses of its prescription benefit management and mental health operations by 10% to 15% in order allow for more competitive bidding on HMO and government business. it added that weaker than expected results at Diagnostek would likely lead to charges of up to $80 million in the third or fourth quarter.

Jul. '95—VH acquired Diagnostek Inc., the third largest U.S. provider of mail order pharmacy services, for about $450 million in common stock. The integration of Diagnostek into the ValueRx subsidiary will produce the largest independent U.S. pharmacy benefits manager, covering 32 million individuals.

Capitalization

Long Term Debt: $3,310,000 (3/95).

Per Share Data ($) (Year Ended Dec. 31)

	1994	1993	1992	1991	1990	1989
Tangible Bk. Val.	7.05	6.26	7.26	1.95	-0.09	NA
Cash Flow	1.67	0.57	0.61	0.52	0.19	-0.22
Earnings	1.19	0.22	0.61	0.40	0.10	-0.47
Dividends	Nil	Nil	Nil	Nil	Nil	Nil
Payout Ratio	Nil	Nil	Nil	Nil	Nil	Nil
Prices - High	52	41	40¼	20	NA	NA
- Low	30⅛	22	18⅜	9⅞	NA	NA
P/E Ratio - High	44	NM	66	50	NA	NA
- Low	25	NM	30	25	NA	NA

Income Statement Analysis (Million $)

	1994	%Chg	1993	%Chg	1992	%Chg	1991
Revs.	976	59%	614	138%	258	66%	155
Oper. Inc.	109	51%	72.1	NM	22.0	93%	11.4
Depr.	19.7	44%	13.7	150%	5.5	142%	2.3
Int. Exp.	0.5	-2%	0.5	-52%	1.1	183%	0.4
Pretax Inc.	82.6	NM	19.5	-3%	20.0	130%	8.7
Eff. Tax Rate	40%	—	56%	—	27%	—	11%
Net Inc.	49.6	NM	8.6	-41%	14.6	87%	7.8

Balance Sheet & Other Fin. Data (Million $)

	1994	1993	1992	1991	1990	1989
Cash	114	116	141	12.3	6.5	8.0
Curr. Assets	302	244	185	37.3	16.0	14.5
Total Assets	537	471	295	92.0	35.6	26.0
Curr. Liab.	139	144	47.3	24.9	16.4	11.4
LT Debt	3.4	4.9	3.2	1.6	3.0	0.3
Common Eqty.	392	319	243	64.8	-16.7	-18.6
Total Cap.	395	324	246	66.3	18.3	13.7
Cap. Exp.	36.9	35.5	3.7	1.7	3.1	0.8
Cash Flow	69.3	22.3	20.1	10.0	2.9	-2.9

Ratio Analysis

	1994	1993	1992	1991	1990	1989
Curr. Ratio	2.2	1.7	3.9	1.5	1.0	1.3
% LT Debt of Cap.	0.9	1.5	1.3	2.4	16.4	1.9
% Net Inc.of Revs.	5.1	1.4	5.7	5.0	1.6	NM
% Ret. on Assets	9.6	1.9	7.0	6.2	5.0	NM
% Ret. on Equity	13.6	2.6	8.0	NM	NM	NM

Dividend Data —Cash dividends have never been paid.

Data as orig. reptd.; bef. results of disc. opers. and/or spec. items. Per share data adj. for stk. divs. as of ex-div. date. E-Estimated. NA-Not Available. NM-Not Meaningful. NR-Not Ranked.

Office—22 Waterville Rd., Avon, CT 06001. **Tel**—(203) 678-3400. **Chrmn, CEO & Pres**—R.E. Patricelli. **VP, Treas & CFO**—D.M. Wurzer. **Dirs**—D.J. McDonnell, W.J. McNerney, R.W. Moorhead III, C. Newman, R.E. Patricelli, S.J. Shulman, J.L. Vogelstein, H.B. Waldron. **Transfer Agent & Registrar**—Mellon Securities Transfer Services, E. Hartford, CT. **Incorporated** in Delaware in 1987. **Empl**-4,200. **S&P Analyst:** Robert M. Gold

STANDARD & POOR'S

STOCK REPORTS

Vanguard Cellular Systems

NASDAQ Symbol **VCELA**

In S&P MidCap 400

01-OCT-95 **Industry:** Telecommunications

Summary: The largest independent, nonwireline cellular operator in the U.S., Vanguard has expanded its population base through an ongoing acquisition program.

S&P Opinion: Accumulate (★★★★)

Recent Price • 25⅝ | Yield • Nil
52 Wk Range • 29⅝-21½ | 12-Mo. P/E • NM

Quantitative Evaluations

Outlook
(1 Lowest—5 Highest)
• **1**⁻

Fair Value
• **14⅜**

Risk
• **Average**

Earn./Div. Rank
• **NR**

Technical Eval.
• **Bearish** since 9/95

Rel. Strength Rank
(1 Lowest—99 Highest)
• **27**

Insider Activity
• **Unfavorable**

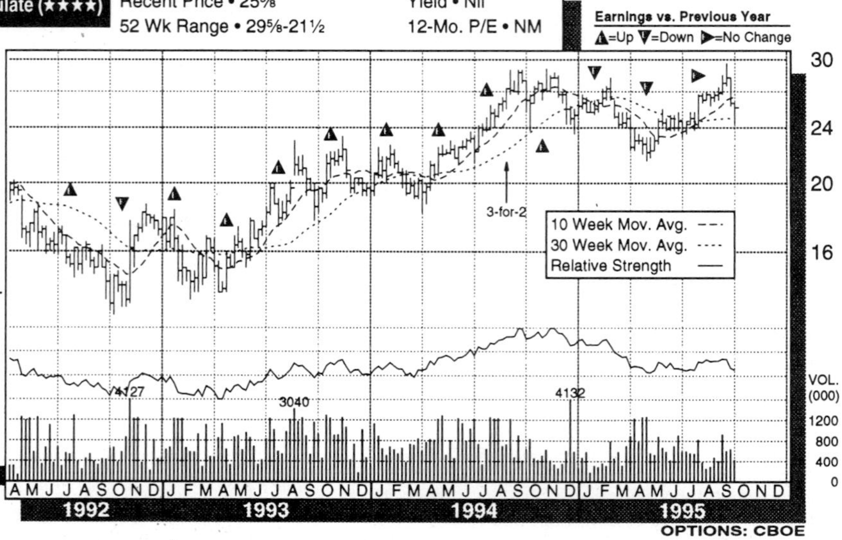

OPTIONS: CBOE

Overview - 28-SEP-95

Revenue growth is expected to be in the 30% range for the next several quarters, reflecting rapid subscriber growth; however, average revenue per subscriber is expected to decline, although at a lesser rate than the industry average. Operating profits should expand, benefiting from growth in the revenue base and efforts to control marketing costs. Interest charges are likely to rise on higher debt levels associated with VCELA's aggressive acquisition program; share earnings will reflect additional shares outstanding. Vanguard also owns 2.5 million shares of Geotek Communications, which it purchased in early 1994 for $30 million; an option agreement to buy more shares is to be amended as part of a recent agreement to buy preferred stock of Geotek, which is building an advanced digital wireless communications system.

Valuation - 28-SEP-95

The shares, which have retreated somewhat after trading near the high end of their 52 week range earlier in September, offer one of the few pure plays in the fast-growing cellular industry. While the larger players are facing the threat of increased competition from new personal communications services (PCS) networks, Vanguard has the advantage of operating primarily in smaller markets. PCS providers are expected to initially target larger, more populous metropolitan areas. Although PCS will eventually surface in Vanguard's markets, that new competitive threat is not expected to materialize for several years.

Key Stock Statistics

S&P EPS Est. 1995	-0.21	Tang. Bk. Value/Share	0.80
P/E on S&P Est. 1995	NM	Beta	1.94
S&P EPS Est. 1996	0.40	Shareholders	1,200
Dividend Rate/Share	Nil	Market cap. (B)	$ 1.1
Shs. outstg. (M)	41.2	Inst. holdings	61%
Avg. daily vol. (M)	0.130	Insider holdings	NA

Value of $10,000 invested 5 years ago: $ 10,943

Fiscal Year Ending Dec. 31

	1995	% Change	1994	% Change	1993	% Change
Revenues (Million $)						
1Q	49.82	51%	33.09	35%	24.43	32%
2Q	58.75	44%	40.76	35%	30.12	34%
3Q	—	—	44.72	31%	34.04	40%
4Q	—	—	49.44	40%	35.40	46%
Yr.	—	—	168.0	35%	124.0	38%
Income (Million $)						
1Q	-7.16	NM	-3.06	NM	-5.44	NM
2Q	-1.33	NM	-1.24	NM	-4.00	NM
3Q	—	—	-0.26	NM	-1.83	NM
4Q	—	—	-9.38	NM	-4.02	NM
Yr.	—	—	-13.94	NM	-15.28	NM
Earnings Per Share ($)						
1Q	-0.18	NM	-0.08	NM	-0.15	NM
2Q	-0.03	NM	-0.03	NM	-0.11	NM
3Q	E0.05	NM	-0.01	NM	-0.05	NM
4Q	E-0.05	NM	-0.24	NM	-0.11	NM
Yr.	E-0.21	NM	-0.36	NM	-0.40	NM

Next earnings report expected: late October

Vanguard Cellular Systems

Business Summary - 28-SEP-95

Vanguard Cellular Systems owns and operates cellular telephone systems, primarily in the eastern U.S. The company believes it is the largest independent, nonwireline U.S. cellular service provider, with operations covering 7.5 million pops (the population of a market area multiplied by the company's percentage ownership of the cellular system serving that market). At June 30, 1995, it had 314,000 subscribers in its majority-owned markets.

Vanguard's growth strategy has been to expand the scope of operations through the acquisition of some or all of the assets of corporations or partnerships owning cellular telephone license interests. Its goal has been to obtain controlling interests in cellular markets that can be efficiently managed and easily integrated into existing operations within concentrated geographic areas. The company has concentrated on acquiring licenses adjacent to its existing markets in order to build market clusters; VCELA has created five regional metro-clusters in the Mid-Atlantic states, Florida, the Carolinas, New England and West Virginia.

Vanguard offers customers several pricing options, most of which consist of a fixed monthly access charge plus additional variable charges per minute of telephone or airtime usage. The company has also implemented automatic roaming agreements with other cellular operators throughout the U.S. With automatic roaming, subscribers are preregistered in other cellular systems and receive service automatically while they are outside their home system for a daily fee and usage charges.

Important Developments

Sep. '95—VCELA filed a shelf registration with the SEC relating to $250 million of common stock, debentures, warrants, and preferred stock which it may offer from time to time. The filing was intended to provide Vanguard flexibility to pursue a variety of possible future financings if market conditions are considered favorable.

Jul. '95—The company added 34,000 net subscribers during the second quarter.

Apr. '95—Vanguard and Toronto Dominion Investments reached an agreement in principle to invest $10 million in Geotek Communications Inc. Each company will purchase $5 million of Geotek's convertible preferred shares.

Capitalization

Long Term Debt: $459,146,000 (6/95).
Minority Interest: $2,688,000.
Cl. A Common Stock: 41,192,158 shs. ($0.01 par).
Officers & directors control 14%.
Institutions hold about 60%.
Shareholders: 1,180 of record (3/95).

Per Share Data ($)

(Year Ended Dec. 31)

	1994	1993	1992	1991	1990	1989
Tangible Bk. Val.	0.97	0.57	0.80	1.41	0.30	1.16
Cash Flow	0.26	0.13	-0.25	-0.53	-0.61	0.08
Earnings	-0.36	-0.40	-0.72	-0.96	-0.95	-0.21
Dividends	Nil	Nil	Nil	Nil	Nil	Nil
Payout Ratio	Nil	Nil	Nil	Nil	Nil	Nil
Prices - High	29⅛	23⅜	21⅝	20⅜	23⅝	27⅞
- Low	18⅛	13⅝	13	12	8½	13⅜
P/E Ratio - High	NM	NM	NM	NM	NM	NM
- Low	NM	NM	NA	NA	NA	NA

Income Statement Analysis (Million $)

	1994	%Chg	1993	%Chg	1992	%Chg	1991
Revs.	168	35%	124	38%	89.6	29%	69.4
Oper. Inc.	35.9	75%	20.5	123%	9.2	—	NM
Depr.	24.1	19%	20.3	17%	17.3	18%	14.7
Int. Exp.	22.8	46%	15.6	-5%	16.4	-18%	20.0
Pretax Inc.	-13.8	NM	-15.1	NM	-27.0	NM	-33.0
Eff. Tax Rate	NM	—	NM	—	NM	—	NM
Net Inc.	-13.9	NM	-15.3	NM	-26.7	NM	-32.7

Balance Sheet & Other Fin. Data (Million $)

	1994	1993	1992	1991	1990	1989
Cash	5.7	9.1	9.5	11.0	12.7	15.8
Curr. Assets	39.5	26.6	19.6	22.2	26.2	31.6
Total Assets	432	284	252	256	237	202
Curr. Liab.	41.3	22.0	20.7	14.3	24.8	18.6
LT Debt	349	238	195	184	198	146
Common Eqty.	39.2	21.9	30.3	51.7	9.3	35.6
Total Cap.	390	262	231	241	212	183
Cap. Exp.	51.0	21.0	18.2	16.5	37.4	21.2
Cash Flow	10.1	5.0	-9.3	-18.0	-18.9	2.5

Ratio Analysis

	1994	1993	1992	1991	1990	1989
Curr. Ratio	1.0	1.2	0.9	1.5	1.1	1.7
% LT Debt of Cap.	89.3	90.7	84.4	76.1	93.2	79.6
% Net Inc.of Revs.	NM	NM	NM	NM	NM	NM
% Ret. on Assets	NM	NM	NM	NM	NM	NM
% Ret. on Equity	NM	NM	NM	NM	NM	NM

Dividend Data —No cash dividends have been paid. Three-for-two stock splits were effected in March 1989 and in August 1994.

Data as orig. reptd.; bef. results of disc. opers. and/or spec. items. Per share data adj. for stk. divs. as of ex-div. date. E-Estimated. NA-Not Available. NM-Not Meaningful. NR-Not Ranked.

Office—2002 Pisgah Church Rd., Suite 300, Greensboro, NC 27455. **Tel**—(910) 282-3690. **Chrmn**—S. S. Richardson. **Pres & CEO**—H. G. Griffin. **Vice Chrmn, EVP & Treas**—L. R. Preyer Jr. **EVP, COO & Secy**—S. R. Leeolou. **SVP & CFO**—S. L. Holcombe. **Investor Contact**—Stanley Haines. **Dirs**—F. C. Brantley, D. R. Bray, R. M. DeMichele, H. G. Griffin, S. R. Leeolou, L. R. Preyer Sr., L. R. Preyer Jr., S. S. Richardson, R. A. Silverberg. **Transfer Agent**—First Union National Bank of North Carolina, Charlotte. **Reincorporated** in North Carolina in 1987. **Empl-** 1,050. **S&P Analyst:** Kevin J. Gooley

STANDARD & POOR'S

STOCK REPORTS

Varco International

NYSE Symbol **VRC**
In S&P MidCap 400

25-SEP-95 **Industry:** Oil and Gas

Summary: Varco manufactures products used in the oil and gas drilling industry that are focused on enhancing the safety and productivity of the drilling process.

Quantitative Evaluations

Outlook (1 Lowest—5 Highest)
• **NA**

Fair Value
• **NA**

Risk
• **Average**

Earn./Div. Rank
• **B-**

Technical Eval.
• **Bearish** since 4/95

Rel. Strength Rank (1 Lowest—99 Highest)
• **56**

Insider Activity
• **Neutral**

Recent Price • 10¾
52 Wk Range • 11⅞-5⅞
Yield • Nil
12-Mo. P/E • 23.4

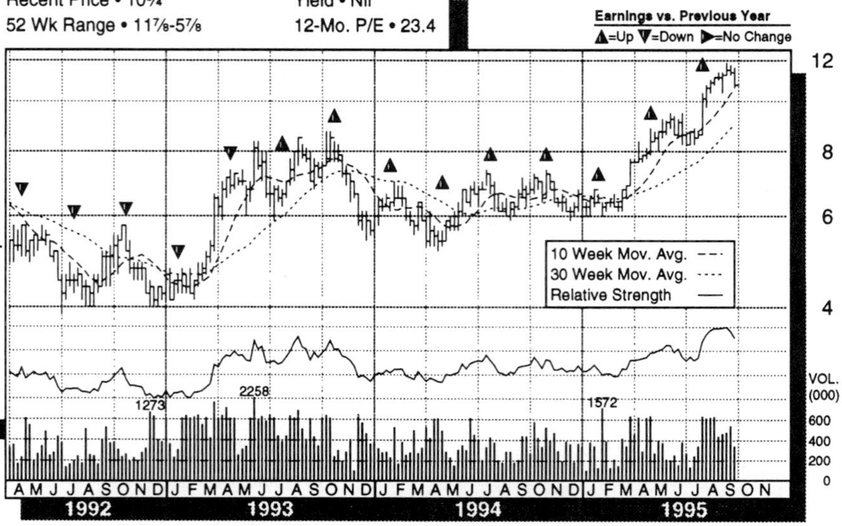

Business Profile - 25-SEP-95

VRC is focused on developing new products that enhance the productivity and safety of the drilling process and extend its line to cover more parts of a drilling rig, and boosting quality to meet rising customer expectations. Products are supplied for new rigs and to upgrade existing ones. VRC has made modest acquisitions to further its goals, and excess cash has been used to repurchase shares including 3,150,560 shares purchased for $8.00 each through a Dutch Auction tender offer in April 1995.

Operational Review - 25-SEP-95

Revenues for the six months ended June 30, 1995 rose 24%, year to year, primarily reflecting increases at the Drilling Systems Division. Margins widened and pretax income climbed 57%. After taxes at 36.1%, against 36.3%, net income advanced 58%, to $8,316,000 from $5,262,000.

Stock Performance - 22-SEP-95

In the past 30 trading days, VRC's shares have declined 1%, compared to a 5% rise in the S&P 500. Average trading volume for the past five days was 67,420 shares, compared with the 40-day moving average of 119,405 shares.

Key Stock Statistics

Dividend Rate/Share	Nil	Shareholders	2,100
Shs. outstg. (M)	30.4	Market cap. (B)	$0.326
Avg. daily vol. (M)	0.092	Inst. holdings	46%
Tang. Bk. Value/Share	3.65	Insider holdings	NA
Beta	1.30		

Value of $10,000 invested 5 years ago: $ 14,827

Fiscal Year Ending Dec. 31

	1995	% Change	1994	% Change	1993	% Change
Revenues (Million $)						
1Q	57.65	12%	51.31	12%	45.81	-3%
2Q	76.79	34%	57.52	18%	48.66	30%
3Q	—	—	54.25	24%	43.69	16%
4Q	—	—	60.52	9%	55.32	10%
Yr.	—	—	223.6	16%	193.5	12%
Income (Million $)						
1Q	2.91	23%	2.36	75%	1.35	-44%
2Q	5.40	86%	2.90	104%	1.42	NM
3Q	—	—	3.01	192%	1.03	NM
4Q	—	—	3.89	18%	3.29	8%
Yr.	—	—	12.16	71%	7.10	NM
Earnings Per Share ($)						
1Q	0.09	29%	0.07	75%	0.04	-43%
2Q	0.17	89%	0.09	125%	0.04	NM
3Q	—	—	0.09	NM	0.03	NM
4Q	—	—	0.11	10%	0.10	11%
Yr.	—	—	0.36	71%	0.21	NM

Next earnings report expected: late October

Varco International

Business Summary - 25-SEP-95

Varco International, Inc. is a leader in the design and manufacture of drilling tools, equipment and integrated systems and rig instrumentation for oil and gas drilling worldwide. It is widely recognized for the development of equipment and systems that enhance the safety and productivity of the drilling process. In 1994, Varco Drilling Systems accounted for 34% of revenues, Martin-Decker/TOTCO Instrumentation for 24%, Shaffer for 23%, and Varco BJ Oil Tools for 19%.

Products are sold for use in about 84 countries, and international sales contributed about 68% of revenues in 1994, versus 71% in 1993.

Varco Drilling Systems designs and manufactures drilling equipment that mechanizes or automates drilling and pipe handling operations and enhances their efficiency and safety. Principal products are Top Drive Drilling Systems, pipe racking and handling systems, and the Automated Roughneck, which combines the functions of the spinning wrench and torque wrench in a single tool.

Varco BJ Oil Tools produces a wide variety of conventional tools and equipment used on drilling rigs, including pipe handling tools, hoisting equipment and rotary equipment. Replacement and spare parts represent a substantial portion of sales.

Martin-Decker/TOTCO designs, manufactures and sells or rents instrumentation, primarily for use in oil and gas well drilling operations; to a lesser extent, instrumentation is also provided to certain industrial markets and for use in non-drilling oilfield applications.

Shaffer designs, manufactures, sells and distributes pressure control equipment, including blowout preventers and compensators.

The Thule Rigtech Division designs, sells and rents equipment and systems used in the handling, mixing, transport and conditioning of drilling fluids. The division, formerly known as Scotland-based Rig Technology Ltd., was acquired in November 1994 for about $9 million.

Sales of VRC's drilling equipment, and sales and rentals of instrumentation products, depend on the level of construction of new drilling rigs and the replacement and upgrading of equipment for existing rigs. The activity in these markets is ultimately dependent on the price of oil and natural gas.

Important Developments

May '95—In April, VRC completed a "Dutch Auction" cash tender offer by purchasing 3,150,560 of its shares at $8.00 each. In May, the company increased its stock buy-back program by authorizing the repurchase of up to 1.5 million shares for a maximum of $11 million. To date, VRC has repurchased 267,200 common shares at an average price of about $6.28 each.

Capitalization

Long Term Debt: $30,350,000 (6/95).

Per Share Data ($) (Year Ended Dec. 31)

	1994	1993	1992	1991	1990	1989
Tangible Bk. Val.	3.62	3.38	3.26	3.18	2.11	2.31
Cash Flow	0.69	0.46	0.28	0.73	0.55	0.26
Earnings	0.36	0.21	0.01	0.45	0.33	0.09
Dividends	Nil	Nil	Nil	Nil	Nil	Nil
Payout Ratio	Nil	Nil	Nil	Nil	Nil	Nil
Prices - High	7⅜	8¾	7⅝	12½	13¾	7½
- Low	5⅛	4⅛	3⅞	5⅝	5⅝	2⅞
P/E Ratio - High	20	42	NM	28	42	83
- Low	14	20	NM	12	17	32

Income Statement Analysis (Million $)

	1994	%Chg	1993	%Chg	1992	%Chg	1991
Revs.	221	15%	192	12%	172	-20%	216
Oper. Inc.	32.9	46%	22.6	26%	18.0	-40%	29.8
Depr.	10.8	33%	8.1	-9%	8.9	2%	8.7
Int. Exp.	4.9	-1%	5.0	28%	3.9	-13%	4.5
Pretax Inc.	18.9	75%	10.8	NM	0.9	-95%	16.9
Eff. Tax Rate	36%	—	34%	—	62%	—	17%
Net Inc.	12.2	72%	7.1	NM	0.3	-98%	14.0

Balance Sheet & Other Fin. Data (Million $)

	1994	1993	1992	1991	1990	1989
Cash	38.6	53.3	26.9	4.8	4.1	23.4
Curr. Assets	159	153	136	118	98.0	65.0
Total Assets	258	248	232	204	186	101
Curr. Liab.	96.4	39.3	33.5	36.1	39.7	13.6
LT Debt	39.3	49.2	52.4	25.6	51.8	26.5
Common Eqty.	164	152	144	141	94.0	60.0
Total Cap.	204	204	199	167	146	87.0
Cap. Exp.	8.6	4.0	4.6	7.9	4.0	2.5
Cash Flow	23.0	15.2	9.2	22.7	14.5	6.6

Ratio Analysis

	1994	1993	1992	1991	1990	1989
Curr. Ratio	3.4	3.9	4.1	3.3	2.5	4.7
% LT Debt of Cap.	19.3	24.1	26.3	15.3	35.5	30.3
% Net Inc.of Revs.	5.5	3.7	0.2	6.5	6.7	2.8
% Ret. on Assets	4.8	2.9	0.1	6.8	5.8	2.3
% Ret. on Equity	7.7	4.8	0.2	11.3	10.7	4.2

Dividend Data —Common stock dividends were omitted in late 1982 after having been paid since 1974.

Data as orig. reptd.; bef. results of disc. opers. and/or spec. items. Per share data adj. for stk. divs. as of ex-div. date. E-Estimated. NA-Not Available. NM-Not Meaningful. NR-Not Ranked.

Office—743 North Eckhoff St, Orange, CA 92668. **Tel**—(714) 978-1900. **Chrmn**—W. B. Reinhold. **Pres & CEO**—G. Boyadjieff. **VP-Fin, CFO & Investor Contact**—Richard A. Kertson. **Treas & Secy**—D. L. Stichler. **Dirs**—G. Boyadjieff, T. R. Embry, A. R. Horn, M. E. Jacques, J. W. Knowlton, L. J. Pircher, W. B. Reinhold, C. W. Suggs, R. A. Teitsworth, E. R. White, J. D. Woods. **Transfer Agent & Registrar**—Harris Trust Co. of California, Los Angeles. **Incorporated** in California in 1911. **Empl**-1,410. **S&P Analyst:** J.M.H.

STANDARD & POOR'S

STOCK REPORTS

Varian Associates

NYSE Symbol **VAR**
In S&P MidCap 400

08-SEP-95

Industry:
Electronics/Electric

Summary: Varian produces a broad line of medical equipment, analytical instruments, and semiconductor production equipment. Electron tube operations were sold in August 1995.

S&P Opinion: Hold (★★★)

Recent Price • 54
52 Wk Range • 57⅜-30⅞

Yield • 0.5%
12-Mo. P/E • 17.6

Quantitative Evaluations

Outlook
(1 Lowest—5 Highest)
• **3+**

Fair Value
• **53**

Risk
• **Low**

Earn./Div. Rank
• **B+**

Technical Eval.
• **Bullish** since 11/92

Rel. Strength Rank
(1 Lowest—99 Highest)
• **55**

Insider Activity
• **Neutral**

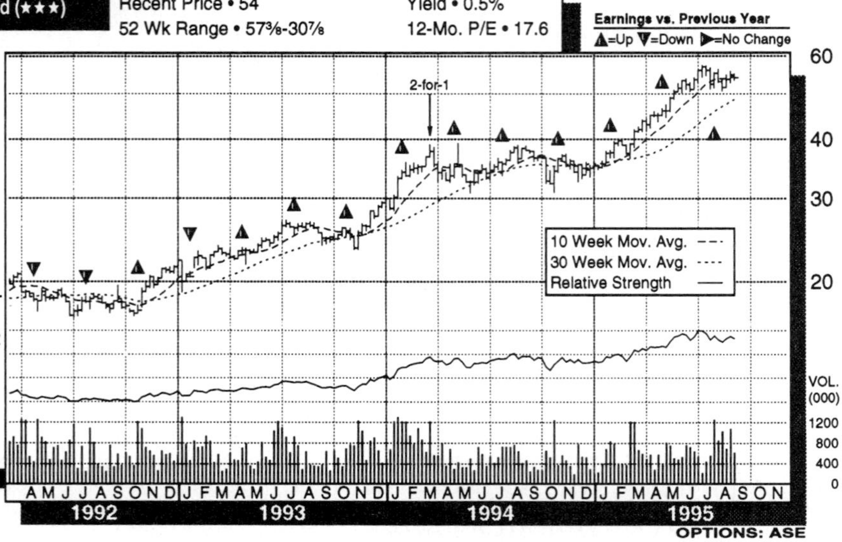

Overview - 08-SEP-95

Sales are projected to rise approximately 15% in fiscal 1996, which excludes the sale of the company's Electron Devices unit sold in August 1995. Demand for semiconductor production equipment should continue to benefit from strong conditions in the industry and particularly brisk sales of iron implantation and thin film coating equipment. Health care sales are projected to experience another year of solid growth, due largely to strong demand for radiation therapy equipment to treat cancer. Instrument demand should moderate. Operating costs should remain well controlled and the EPS gain should approximate the growth in revenues.

Valuation - 08-SEP-95

Shares of this company appear fairly valued and are likely to perform in line with the market over the next 12 months. We believe the semiconductor industry will continue to enjoy strong growth over the next several years and VAR should be a leading beneficiary. However, we believe the company's long-term EPS growth rate is approximately 15%, which is roughly equivalent to the current P/E valuation on our 1996 estimate. Absent a financial performance much better than our current projection, the shares should be only an average performer.

Key Stock Statistics

S&P EPS Est. 1995	3.30	Tang. Bk. Value/Share	14.14
P/E on S&P Est. 1995	16.4	Beta	1.16
S&P EPS Est. 1996	3.75	Shareholders	7,200
Dividend Rate/Share	0.28	Market cap. (B)	$ 1.9
Shs. outstg. (M)	33.9	Inst. holdings	81%
Avg. daily vol. (M)	0.140	Insider holdings	NA

Value of $10,000 invested 5 years ago: $ 52,136

Fiscal Year Ending Sep. 30

	1995	% Change	1994	% Change	1993	% Change
Revenues (Million $)						
1Q	401.1	24%	323.8	11%	291.0	-4%
2Q	490.4	24%	394.5	21%	325.0	3%
3Q	458.9	17%	393.0	20%	327.9	5%
4Q	—	—	441.1	20%	366.5	2%
Yr.	—	—	1,552	18%	1,312	2%
Income (Million $)						
1Q	20.75	78%	11.66	77%	6.60	-13%
2Q	29.69	62%	18.34	97%	9.30	19%
3Q	31.74	42%	22.43	87%	12.00	19%
4Q	—	—	26.93	50%	18.00	37%
Yr.	—	—	79.36	73%	45.80	18%
Earnings Per Share ($)						
1Q	0.59	82%	0.32	81%	0.18	-10%
2Q	0.85	67%	0.51	96%	0.26	27%
3Q	0.90	43%	0.63	85%	0.34	26%
4Q	E0.95	25%	0.76	50%	0.51	42%
Yr.	E3.30	49%	2.22	76%	1.26	24%

Next earnings report expected: mid October

Varian Associates

Business Summary - 08-SEP-95

Varian Associates produces equipment and components for communications, scientific, medical, industrial and defense markets. Segment contributions (profits in millions) in fiscal 1994, including the recently sold Electron devices unit, were:

	Sales	Profits
Healthcare systems	27%	$86
Instruments	24%	33
Semiconductor equipment	31%	36
Electron devices	18%	18
Eliminations & other	---	-9

International business accounted for 29% of sales and 20% of pretax income in fiscal 1994.

The company is one of the world's leading suppliers of equipment and services for treating cancer with high-energy radiation therapy. Products include medical linear accelerators, which generate the radiation, simulators for treatment planning and ancillary equipment aimed at therapy management and enhanced precision.

The instruments group supplies analytical instruments for the determination of chemical structure, chemical composition or both. The instruments are used in industrial, academic and government laboratories.

The semiconductor equipment group makes semiconductor fabrication equipment, with leadership positions in ion implantation and sputtering systems.

In August 1995, the company sold its Electron Devices unit, which manufactured microwave, power-grid and X-ray tubes and related equipment such as amplifiers and power supplies.

Important Developments

Aug. '95—The company authorized a "Dutch Auction" self tender offer for up to 3 million common shares. Under terms of the auction, shareholders can tender shares at prices ranging from $51 to $58, with the final price and allocation of shares tendered determined by the company. The company is using the $200 million in proceeds from the August sale of its Electron Devices business for the repurchases.

Jul. '95—VAR and Samsung Electronics announced the commencement of Phase 3 of their joint venture program to develop advanced process technologies for next generation dynamic random access memory (DRAM) semiconductor devices.

Jun. '95—The company received clearance from the Food and Drug Administration (FDA) to market a capability on its radiation therapy equipment. This capability, called dynamic multileaf collimation, is designed to improve cancer care by destroying tumors more aggressively and accurately than prior treatments.

Capitalization

Long Term Debt: $60,300,000 (6/95).

Per Share Data ($)

(Year Ended Sep. 30)

	1994	1993	1992	1991	1990	1989
Tangible Bk. Val.	13.23	12.17	11.79	11.36	10.38	10.74
Cash Flow	3.70	2.63	2.31	2.64	1.40	1.80
Earnings	2.22	1.26	1.02	1.48	0.32	0.77
Dividends	0.23	0.19	0.17	0.15	0.13	0.13
Payout Ratio	10%	14%	16%	10%	40%	16%
Prices - High	39¼	30	22⅜	25⅛	17⅜	15¼
- Low	28¼	19	16¾	14⅞	10	10
P/E Ratio - High	18	24	22	17	54	20
- Low	13	15	16	10	31	13

Income Statement Analysis (Million $)

	1994	%Chg	1993	%Chg	1992	%Chg	1991
Revs.	1,552	18%	1,311	2%	1,288	-7%	1,378
Oper. Inc.	183	43%	128	12%	114	-22%	146
Depr.	52.5	6%	49.7	2%	48.9	8%	45.4
Int. Exp.	6.3	-5%	6.6	12%	5.9	-30%	8.4
Pretax Inc.	128	73%	73.9	18%	62.4	-33%	92.8
Eff. Tax Rate	38%	—	38%	—	38%	—	38%
Net Inc.	79.4	73%	45.8	18%	38.7	-33%	57.5

Balance Sheet & Other Fin. Data (Million $)

	1994	1993	1992	1991	1990	1989
Cash	78.9	73.3	67.0	54.0	26.0	Nil
Curr. Assets	669	605	604	595	668	643
Total Assets	962	893	893	884	924	931
Curr. Liab.	432	382	384	350	408	414
LT Debt	60.4	60.5	49.7	68.0	76.8	54.9
Common Eqty.	449	422	428	434	400	427
Total Cap.	531	511	509	535	516	517
Cap. Exp.	62.6	45.1	48.6	59.7	54.9	49.4
Cash Flow	132	95.0	88.0	103	55.0	74.0

Ratio Analysis

	1994	1993	1992	1991	1990	1989
Curr. Ratio	1.5	1.6	1.6	1.7	1.6	1.6
% LT Debt of Cap.	11.4	11.8	9.8	12.7	14.9	10.6
% Net Inc.of Revs.	5.1	3.5	3.0	4.2	1.0	2.3
% Ret. on Assets	8.6	5.2	4.5	6.4	1.4	3.7
% Ret. on Equity	18.4	11.0	9.2	13.8	3.1	7.5

Dividend Data —Dividends were initiated in 1973. A dividend reinvestment plan is available. A "poison pill" stock purchase rights plan was adopted in 1986.

Amt. of Div. $	Date Decl.	Ex-Div. Date	Stock of Record	Payment Date
0.060	Aug. 19	Oct. 17	Oct. 21	Nov. 01 '94
0.060	Nov. 18	Dec. 05	Dec. 09	Jan. 03 '95
0.070	Feb. 17	Mar. 06	Mar. 10	Apr. 03 '95
0.070	May. 19	Jun. 06	Jun. 09	Jul. 03 '95
0.070	Aug. 18	Sep. 28	Oct. 02	Oct. 20 '95

Data as orig. reptd.; bef. results of disc. opers. and/or spec. items. Per share data adj. for stk. divs. as of ex-div. date. E-Estimated. NA-Not Available. NM-Not Meaningful. NR-Not Ranked.

Office—3100 Hansen Way, Palo Alto, CA 94304. **Tel**—(415) 493-4000. **Chrmn & CEO**—J. T. O'Rourke. **VP-Fin & CFO**—R. A. Lemos. **VP & Secy**—J. B. Phair. **Investor Contact**—Allen Jones. **Dirs**—R. M. Davis, S. Hellman, T. R. Lautenbach, A. A. MacNaughton, D. W. Martin Jr., J. G. McDonald, W. F. Miller, G. E. Moore, D. E. Mundell, J. T. O'Rourke, D. O. Pederson, P. J. Quigley, B. Richter, P. G. Stern, R. W. Vieser. **Transfer Agent & Registrar**—First National Bank of Boston. **Incorporated** in California in 1948; reincorporated in Delaware in 1976. **Empl**-8,100. **S&P Analyst:** John D. Coyle, CFA

VeriFone, Inc.

NYSE Symbol VFI Options on CBOE In S&P MidCap 400

Price	Range	P–E Ratio	Dividend	Yield	S&P Ranking	Beta
Sep. 14'95	1995					
30⅝	31⅜–19¾	24	None	None	B	1.98

Summary

This company is the leading supplier of transaction automation systems for the payment processing market, with more than 4.4 million systems sold worldwide. Following a 31% increase in 1994, share earnings continued to advance strongly in the first half of 1995 on higher sales.

Business Summary

VeriFone, Inc. designs, manufactures, markets and supports transaction automation solutions used by retailers, petroleum service station and convenience store operators, healthcare providers and government agencies to electronically automate the processing of payments, benefits and information transactions. The company played a major role in expanding transaction automation in the payment processing market by offering the first low-cost systems for electronic credit card authorization and is now the leading supplier of transaction automation systems for the payment processing market.

VeriFone has shipped systems to over 2,400 customers in more than 90 countries. A majority of the shipments were to retailers. In 1994, sales outside the U.S. represented 32% of consolidated revenue, up from 25% in 1993.

The company manufactures and markets a comprehensive line of transaction automation solutions, including transaction system platforms, system and application software, peripheral products, communications options for both local-area and wide-area networking and interface options for connectivity with other point-of-sale devices such as displays, scanners, electronic cash registers and personal computers. VeriFone also provides a wide range of support services to help customers and end-users implement and maintain their systems in the most efficient and cost-effective manner.

VFI classifies its business into three distinct markets: the U.S. financial retail market, the U.S. emerging market and the international market. The U.S. financial market consists of the company's payment processing distribution channels used to reach retail merchants. The emerging market is an extension of the retail market and consists of petroleum/convenience retailing, multi-lane retailers and the healthcare/government markets. The international market is potentially larger than the U.S. market and is less penetrated.

Since 1989, products have been manufactured primarily at a VeriFone facility in Taiwan. The company markets its products mainly through resellers, such as banks, independent sales organizations, industry service providers, distributors and systems integrators.

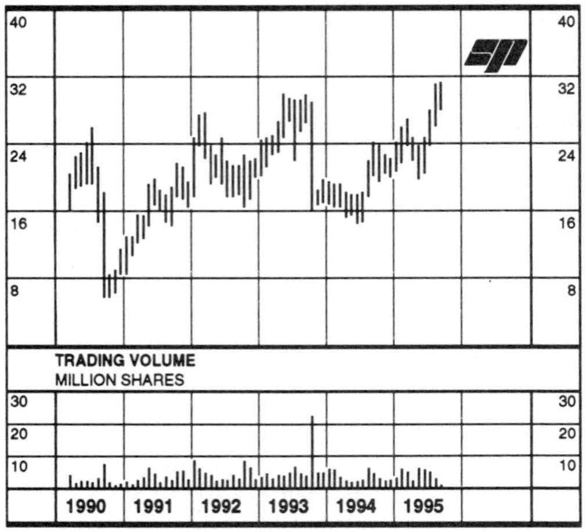

Important Developments

Aug. '95— VeriFone announced an agreement to acquire Enterprise Integration Technologies (EIT), a leading independent provider of software and consulting services for electronic commerce on the Internet, for VFI stock and stock options valued at about $28 million.

Feb. '95— VFI announced the introduction of a low-cost, add-on solution aimed at multi-lane retailers such as mass merchandisers and supermarkets. The system has a built-in card reader and keypad that allows customers to initiate their own card transactions. Earlier, the company announced the fulfillment of two major orders in the Persian Gulf region, a move consistent with the company's international expansion.

Next earnings report expected in late October.

Per Share Data ($)

Yr. End Dec. 31	1994	1993	1992	1991	1990	1989	1988	1987	1986	1985
Tangible Bk. Val.	[1]**9.37**	8.37	7.48	[1]6.37	[1]5.53	[1]2.29	[1]NA	[1]NA	[1]NA	[1]NA
Cash Flow	**1.58**	1.36	1.32	1.09	0.73	0.60	0.43	NA	NA	NA
Earnings	**1.18**	0.90	1.02	0.82	0.55	0.50	0.36	0.01	NM	0.13
Dividends	**Nil**	Nil	Nil	Nil	Nil	Nil	Nil	Nil	Nil	Nil
Payout Ratio	**Nil**	Nil	Nil	Nil	Nil	Nil	Nil	Nil	Nil	Nil
Prices—High	**24¼**	30	27¾	21¾	26	NA	NA	NA	NA	NA
Low	**14½**	16	16½	8½	5¾	NA	NA	NA	NA	NA
P/E Ratio—	**21–12**	33–18	27–16	27–10	47–11	NA	NA	NA	NA	NA

Data as orig. reptd. 1. Incl. intangibles. NA-Not Available. NM-Not Meaningful.

Income Data (Million $)

Year Ended Dec. 31	Oper. Revs.	Oper. Inc.	% Oper. Inc. of Revs.	Cap. Exp.	Depr.	Int. Exp.	Net Bef. Taxes	Eff. Tax Rate	Net Inc.	% Net Inc. of Revs.	Cash Flow
1994	**309**	**46.6**	**15.1**	**12.3**	**9.3**	**0.61**	**39.7**	**28.6%**	**27.7**	**9.0**	**37.0**
1993	259	40.8	15.8	12.3	11.0	0.48	32.4	27.1%	21.5	8.3	32.5
1992	226	38.2	16.9	6.7	7.2	0.84	33.3	28.0%	24.0	10.6	31.2
1991	188	29.8	15.9	11.2	6.2	0.51	27.1	31.0%	18.7	10.0	24.9
1990	155	19.9	12.9	10.9	4.2	0.75	18.3	33.5%	12.2	7.8	16.3
1989	123	16.4	13.3	8.5	2.1	0.65	15.8	36.5%	10.1	8.1	12.0
1988	73	10.7	14.5	1.9	1.1	0.57	10.3	38.0%	6.4	8.7	7.5
1987	44	1.7	3.9	1.1	0.9	0.70	0.1	25.9%	0.1	0.2	NA
1986	31	NA	NA	NA	NA	NA	NM	NM	NM	NM	NA
1985	15	NA	NA	NA	NA	NA	0.9	4.7%	0.9	5.6	NA

Balance Sheet Data (Million $)

Dec. 31	Cash	Curr. Assets	Curr. Liab.	Curr. Ratio	Total Assets	% Ret. on Assets	Long Term Debt	Common Equity	Total Cap.	% LT Debt of Cap.	% Ret. on Equity
1994	**86.9**	**254**	**73.0**	**3.5**	**328**	**9.0**	**7.5**	**217**	**255**	**2.9**	**13.5**
1993	73.1	222	54.5	4.1	291	8.1	12.2	194	236	5.2	11.7
1992	82.5	197	43.0	46.0	240	11.1	2.2	[1]174	197	1.1	14.9
1991	74.0	153	31.2	4.9	189	10.8	2.4	[1]144	158	1.5	13.9
1990	61.9	124	23.9	5.2	151	6.4	1.4	[1]119	127	1.1	14.4
1989	20.2	71	21.2	3.4	93	12.2	1.2	[1]68	72	1.7	16.3
1988	35.9	68	13.8	4.9	73	12.1	NM	[1]55	59	0.1	17.3
1987	NA	NA	NA	NA	33	0.4	0.1	[1]19	19	0.5	0.7
1986	NA	NA	NA	NA	23	NM	0.6	[1]11	12	5.1	NM
1985	NA	NA	NA	NA	8	NA	0.2	[1]5	5	4.1	NA

Data as orig. reptd. 1. Refl. conv. of pfd. stk. upon public offering. NA-Not Available. NM-Not Meaningful.

Net Revenues (Million $)

13 Weeks:	1995	1994	1993	1992
Mar.	77.6	64.7	54.7	46.9
Jun.	92.8	77.7	65.5	58.7
Sep.		82.1	70.2	58.0
Dec.		84.7	68.5	62.6
		309.1	258.9	226.2

Net revenues for the six months ended June 30, 1995, rose 20%, year to year, reflecting strong growth in both the domestic and international markets. Margins narrowed slightly, due to a less favorable product mix, but in the absence of a minority interest deduction, pretax income increased 20%. After taxes at 29.0% in both periods, net income also advanced 20%, to $13,873,000 ($0.60 a share, based on 1.8% fewer shares), from $11,593,000 ($0.49).

Common Share Earnings ($)

13 Weeks:	1995	1994	1993	1992
Mar.	0.22	0.18	0.18	0.15
Jun.	0.38	0.31	0.26	0.26
Sep.		0.34	0.22	0.29
Dec.		0.35	0.25	0.32
		1.18	0.90	1.02

Dividend Data

No cash dividends have been paid on the common shares, and VeriFone does not expect to pay any dividends in the foreseeable future.

Finances

In January 1995, directors approved the repurchase of 750,000 common shares on the open market to be used for its stock option and employee stock purchase program. A total of 600,000 shares were purchased during the first quarter of 1995. In 1994, 451,000 shares were repurchased for $9.3 million as part of a previous repurchase program.

The company completed the acquisition of VeriFone Finance, which offers flexible financing and leasing exclusively for VeriFone systems, in 1994. Beginning in the second quarter of 1993, VeriFone Finance's results were consolidated with those of the company.

Capitalization

Long Term Debt: $5,081,000 (6/95).

Common Stock: 22,840,388 shs. ($0.01 par).
Officers & directors own 7.4%.
Institutions hold about 57%.
Shareholders: 1,438 of record (12/94).

Options: To buy 1,989,352 shs. at $7.50 to $29.50 ea. (12/94).

Office—Three Lagoon Dr., Suite 400, Redwood City, CA 94065. **Tel**—(415) 591-6500. **Chrmn, Pres & CEO**—H. A. Tyabji. **VP-Fin & CFO**—J. M. Zaelit. **VP-Secy**—W. G. Barmeier. **Dirs**—H. H. Haight IV, J. R. Harcharik, W. N. Melton, J. R. C. Porter, A. M. Spence, H. A. Tyabji, R. E. White. **Transfer Agent & Registrar**—First National Bank of Boston. **Incorporated** in Delaware in 1986. **Empl**—1,900.

 Alan Aaron

STANDARD & POOR'S

STOCK REPORTS

Vishay Intertechnology

NYSE Symbol **VSH**

In S&P MidCap 400

03-OCT-95

Industry: Electronics/Electric

Summary: VSH is a leading manufacturer and supplier in the U.S. and Europe of a wide range of passive electronic components, including resistors, inductors and capacitors.

Quantitative Evaluations

Outlook (1 Lowest—5 Highest)
• **4+**

Fair Value
• **42¾**

Risk
• **Average**

Earn./Div. Rank
• **B+**

Technical Eval.
• **Bullish** since 5/94

Rel. Strength Rank (1 Lowest—99 Highest)
• **44**

Insider Activity
• **NA**

Recent Price • 42

52 Wk Range • 44⅜-20⅞

Yield • Nil

12-Mo. P/E • 27.6

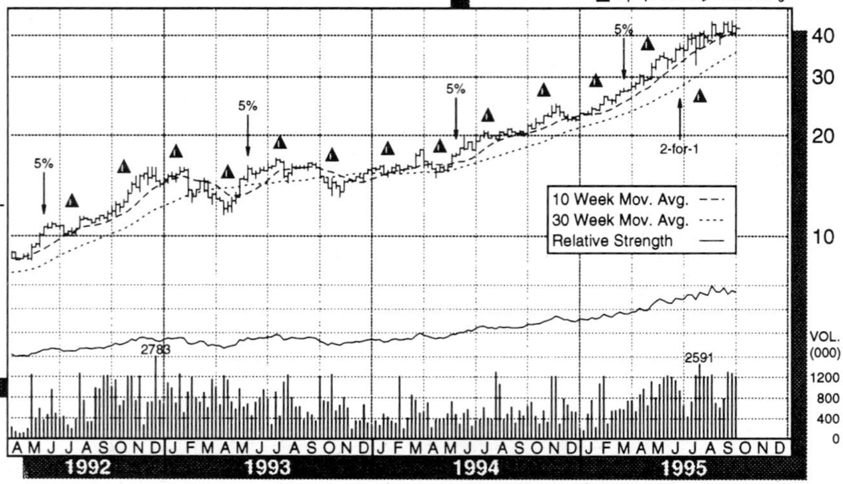

Business Profile - 06-SEP-95

The passive components (PCs) sector has been experiencing strong demand, sparked by the robust semiconductor market. As integrated circuits become increasingly sophisticated, the need for PCs rises significantly. A leader in surface mounted PC devices, VSH is in a position to capitalize on the capacity constraint which is affecting that niche. The company continues to expand its capacity through an aggressive capital spending program and strategic acquisitions.

Operational Review - 06-SEP-95

Sales have risen sharply in recent periods, led by the continued strength of the electronics industry and the Vitramon acquisition (1994). Bookings outpaced shipments for the past six quarters, a trend that is expected to continue. Gross margins have widened, aided by higher margin Vitramon products and larger investment grants from the Israeli government. The recent investment in Nikkohm Co. (49% ownership) should accelerate VSH's entry into the multi-billion dollar Japanese components market.

Stock Performance - 29-SEP-95

In the past 30 trading days, VSH's shares have declined 3%, compared to a 5% rise in the S&P 500. Average trading volume for the past five days was 255,160 shares, compared with the 40-day moving average of 276,790 shares.

Key Stock Statistics

Dividend Rate/Share	Nil	Shareholders	1,400
Shs. outstg. (M)	57.7	Market cap. (B)	$ 2.3
Avg. daily vol. (M)	0.332	Inst. holdings	53%
Tang. Bk. Value/Share	7.81	Insider holdings	NA
Beta	1.00		

Value of $10,000 invested 5 years ago: $ 66,216

Fiscal Year Ending Dec. 31

	1995	% Change	1994	% Change	1993	% Change
Revenues (Million $)						
1Q	310.3	37%	226.0	NM	227.5	32%
2Q	315.5	39%	226.7	NM	224.6	34%
3Q	—	—	261.0	30%	200.2	21%
4Q	—	—	274.2	34%	203.9	29%
Yr.	—	—	987.8	15%	856.3	29%
Income (Million $)						
1Q	22.03	74%	12.66	15%	11.04	55%
2Q	24.72	74%	14.23	18%	12.08	42%
3Q	—	—	14.56	36%	10.70	44%
4Q	—	—	17.50	98%	8.83	19%
Yr.	—	—	58.95	38%	42.65	40%
Earnings Per Share ($)						
1Q	0.42	56%	0.27	14%	0.24	25%
2Q	0.47	52%	0.31	20%	0.26	17%
3Q	—	—	0.29	28%	0.23	17%
4Q	—	—	0.33	76%	0.19	10%
Yr.	—	—	1.20	32%	0.91	17%

Next earnings report expected: early November

Vishay Intertechnology

Business Summary - 03-OCT-95

Vishay Intertechnology is a leading manufacturer of a wide range of passive electronic components (ECs) (resistors, capacitors and inductors) in the U.S. and Europe, and the leading producer of printed circuit boards in France. The company's products are used in consumer and industrial goods, telecommunications systems, medical equipment, computers, automotive systems, aerospace and defense. Customers are primarily other manufacturers. About 50% of Vishay's revenues come from outside the U.S.

Resistors, inductors and capacitors are classified as "passive" ECs. They are used to perform various control functions in an electronic circuit, such as reducing current or voltage and storing electric energy. They are called "passive" because they do not amplify DC current or DC voltage as opposed to "active" ECs, such as semiconductors, which amplify DC currents.

All electronic circuits use resistors which usually represent- by a considerable margin -the most common circuit component. Resistors regulate the flow of electricity to meet circuit performance requirements. Capacitors, the next most common component found in ECs, perform energy storage, filtering functions and frequency control. Inductors impede the flow of AC current while offering negligible resistance to DC current. As the complexity of integrated circuits increases, the demand for passive ECs rises.

Traditionally, ECs were mounted and interconnected on printed circuit boards (PCB) using conventional through-hole mounting of components with leads. Within the last ten years, the electronics industry has rapidly moved to surface mount devices (SMDs), which are components without leads. SMDs make it possible to design PCBs that are much smaller and allow for highly automated mounting procedures as well as mounting on both sides of the board. These features reduce assembly costs and satisfy the growing demand for smaller products such as laptop computers, cellular phones and pagers. Vishay's family of SMDs comprise 17 different technologies. The company believes that no other passive ECs manufacturer produces so many types of SMDs.

Over the past several years, Vishay's sales base has been expanded significantly through acquisitions. It has about 60 manufacturing facilities located worldwide. Vishay is aggressively expanding its operations in Israel where it receives investment-related tax incentives and government-sponsored investment grants.

Important Developments

Sep. '95—Vishay sold a total of 5,750,000 common shares at $41.75 each in an underwritten public offering. Net proceeds of over $230 million are earmarked for debt reduction, capital expansion and possible future acquisitions.

Capitalization

Long Term Debt: $444,707,000 (6/95).

Per Share Data ($) (Year Ended Dec. 31)

	1994	1993	1992	1991	1990	1989
Tangible Bk. Val.	6.71	8.05	5.81	3.85	3.32	1.92
Cash Flow	2.34	1.91	1.49	1.26	1.19	1.23
Earnings	1.20	0.91	0.78	0.57	0.67	0.56
Dividends	Nil	Nil	Nil	Nil	Nil	Nil
Payout Ratio	Nil	Nil	Nil	Nil	Nil	Nil
Prices - High	25	17⅛	16⅛	9⅜	9⅛	7¾
- Low	14⅞	11½	6¾	4¾	3⅞	5⅛
P/E Ratio - High	21	19	21	16	14	14
- Low	12	13	9	8	6	9

Income Statement Analysis (Million $)

	1994	%Chg	1993	%Chg	1992	%Chg	1991
Revs.	988	15%	856	29%	664	50%	442
Oper. Inc.	154	31%	118	37%	85.9	19%	71.9
Depr.	55.9	19%	46.8	40%	33.4	31%	25.4
Int. Exp.	24.8	20%	20.6	8%	19.1	26%	15.2
Pretax Inc.	74.1	46%	50.9	34%	37.9	39%	27.3
Eff. Tax Rate	21%	—	16%	—	20%	—	23%
Net Inc.	58.9	38%	42.6	40%	30.4	45%	20.9

Balance Sheet & Other Fin. Data (Million $)

	1994	1993	1992	1991	1990	1989
Cash	26.9	10.9	16.0	14.2	16.1	27.8
Curr. Assets	561	394	288	207	205	202
Total Assets	1,334	948	662	449	441	420
Curr. Liab.	232	188	142	78.0	85.0	86.0
LT Debt	402	267	140	128	140	186
Common Eqty.	565	377	347	201	178	118
Total Cap.	1,007	670	496	340	318	304
Cap. Exp.	83.0	190	144	31.0	34.0	24.0
Cash Flow	115	89.4	63.8	46.3	47.1	38.8

Ratio Analysis

	1994	1993	1992	1991	1990	1989
Curr. Ratio	2.4	2.1	2.0	2.6	2.4	2.4
% LT Debt of Cap.	39.9	39.9	28.1	37.6	44.1	61.2
% Net Inc.of Revs.	6.0	5.0	4.6	4.7	5.2	4.3
% Ret. on Assets	5.0	5.3	4.9	4.7	5.0	5.9
% Ret. on Equity	12.1	11.8	10.1	11.0	14.7	16.8

Dividend Data —Vishay does not pay cash dividends, but annual stock distributions have been frequent.

Amt. of Div. $	Date Decl.	Ex-Div. Date	Stock of Record	Payment Date
5%	Mar. 03	Mar. 13	Mar. 17	Mar. 31 '95
2-for-1	May. 19	Jun. 19	Jun. 02	Jun. 16 '95

Data as orig. reptd.; bef. results of disc. opers. and/or spec. items. Per share data adj. for stk. divs. as of ex-div. date. E-Estimated. NA-Not Available. NM-Not Meaningful. NR-Not Ranked.

Office—63 Lincoln Highway, Malvern, PA 19355-2120. **Tel**—(610) 644-1300. **Chrmn & Pres**—F. Zandman. **SVP-Treas & CFO**—R. N. Grubb. **Investor Contact**—Robert A. Freece. **VP-Secy**—W. J. Spires. **Dirs**—D. G. Alfson, A. D. Eden, R. A. Freece, R. N. Grubb, E. Hurvitz, G. Paul, E. B. Shils, L. B. Slaner, M. I. Solomon, J.-C. Tine, F. Zandman. **Transfer Agent & Registrar**—American Stock Transfer & Trust Co., NYC. **Incorporated** in Delaware in 1962. **Empl**-17,800. **S&P Analyst:** Steven A. Jaworski

STANDARD & POOR'S

STOCK REPORTS

Vons Companies

NYSE Symbol **VON**
In S&P MidCap 400

11-AUG-95 **Industry:** Retail Stores

Summary: One of the largest supermarket and drug store chains in Southern California, this company operates over 325 stores under the names Vons and Pavilions.

Quantitative Evaluations

Outlook (1 Lowest—5 Highest) • **5+**

Fair Value • **24⅞**

Risk • **Low**

Earn./Div. Rank • **B-**

Technical Eval. • **Bullish** since 9/94

Rel. Strength Rank (1 Lowest—99 Highest) • **71**

Insider Activity • **Neutral**

Recent Price • 22⅜ | 52 Wk Range • 22½-15⅛ | Yield • Nil | 12-Mo. P/E • 23.6

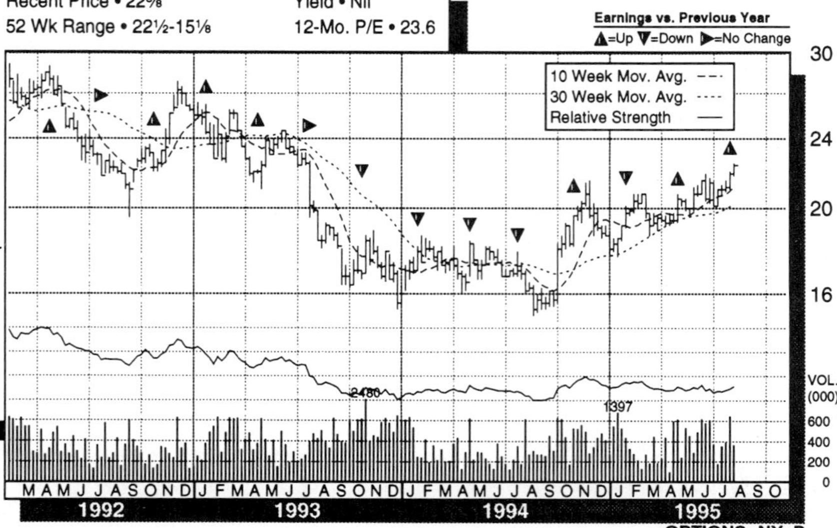

OPTIONS: NY, P

Business Profile - 11-AUG-95

In 1993's third quarter, this company embarked upon a cost-containment and strategic repositioning program, which has resulted in some $90 million of related charges to date. Vons has reduced prices throughout its stores, eliminated some 700 administrative personnel, outsourced its delicatessen kitchen and meat grinding facility and closed 26 underperforming stores. With the closure of its San Diego distribution facility in 1995's third quarter, the restructuring program will be complete.

Operational Review - 11-AUG-95

Lower year-to-year sales in 1995's first half primarily reflected the impact of 18 fewer stores in operation, partially offset by a 1.7% gain in same-store sales. Gross margins benefited from lower product costs as a result of better utilization of category management, more effective promotional offerings and increased private brand sales. A reduction in administrative expenses helped to reduce the impact of higher store payroll costs due to a union wage rate increase.

Stock Performance - 04-AUG-95

In the past 30 trading days, VON's shares have increased 5%, compared to a 2% rise in the S&P 500. Average trading volume for the past five days was 72,080 shares, compared with the 40-day moving average of 100,728 shares.

Key Stock Statistics

Dividend Rate/Share	Nil	Shareholders	7,200
Shs. outstg. (M)	43.5	Market cap. (B)	$0.990
Avg. daily vol. (M)	0.105	Inst. holdings	46%
Tang. Bk. Value/Share	2.11	Insider holdings	NA
Beta	0.92		

Value of $10,000 invested 5 years ago: $ 11,474

Fiscal Year Ending Dec. 31

	1995	% Change	1994	% Change	1993	% Change
Revenues (Million $)						
1Q	1,143	NM	1,144	-4%	1,194	-6%
2Q	1,140	-2%	1,160	-1%	1,175	-9%
3Q	—	—	1,516	-1%	1,535	-9%
4Q	—	—	1,176	NM	1,171	-14%
Yr.	—	—	4,997	-2%	5,075	-9%
Income (Million $)						
1Q	14.00	56%	9.00	-43%	15.90	6%
2Q	14.50	NM	4.50	-75%	17.70	3%
3Q	—	—	4.00	NM	-19.50	NM
4Q	—	—	9.10	-52%	18.90	-32%
Yr.	—	—	26.60	-19%	33.00	-60%
Earnings Per Share ($)						
1Q	0.32	52%	0.21	-43%	0.37	6%
2Q	0.33	NM	0.10	-75%	0.40	NM
3Q	—	—	0.09	NM	-0.45	NM
4Q	—	—	0.21	-52%	0.44	-30%
Yr.	—	—	0.61	-20%	0.76	-60%

Next earnings report expected: early November

Vons Companies

Business Summary - 04-AUG-95

The Vons Companies, Inc., one of the largest supermarket chains in Southern California, owned and operated 326 stores under the Vons and Pavilions names as of July 20, 1995. Store data for recent years (in operation as of year-end) was:

	1994	1993	1992	1991
Opened or acquired	6	12	26	6
Closed or sold	17	12	1	6
In operation	334	345	345	320

The company's traditional supermarkets offer dry groceries, produce, meat, fish, dairy products wine and liquor and limited assortments of general merchandise and health and beauty aids. Many Vons supermarkets also have in-store bakeries, service floral, service delicatessens with fresh and prepared foods and service seafood departments. Approximately one-third of the Vons stores offer full-service pharmacies and an expanded health and beauty care section.

Pavilions stores are targeted to a clientele conscious of food trends, who typically spend more discretionalry income for food and food-related items. Stores offer expanded selections of food products and a variety of service departments. Many stores offer extensive general merchandise emphasizing food-related products of department store quality. Selected stores offer a party shop, sausage and smoke shop, bagel shop, sushi bar, and high quality prepared Chinese food. The company intends to open approximately 15 new Pavilions stores over the next three years.

Introduced in June 1993, EXPO stores combined a traditional supermarket with a deep discount drug store and a warehouse food store, offering low prices with limited service departments. As part of the company's strategic restructuring program, all eight EXPO stores were closed in January 1995.

The company also operates a fluid milk processing facility, an ice cream plant, a central bakery, and distribution facilities for meat, grocery, produce and general merchandise.

In 1988, Vons acquired the Southern California operations of Safeway Stores, consisting of 162 stores (net of stores sold to comply with FTC requirements), plus distribution and processing operations. In January 1992, Vons acquired 18 Williams Bros. supermarkets.

Important Developments

Jul. '95—Vons opened three new stores, closed two stores, and completed seven remodels in the second quarter of 1995, ending the period with 326 stores in operation. The company expected to open approximately eight new stores during the third quarter. An additional 30 stores are scheduled to be remodeled.

Capitalization

Long Term Debt: $743,400,000 (6/95), incl. lease obligs.

Per Share Data ($) (Year Ended Dec. 31)

	1994	1993	1992	1991	1990	1989
Tangible Bk. Val.	12.73	12.11	11.38	11.05	7.04	4.91
Cash Flow	3.30	3.19	3.97	3.40	3.08	1.19
Earnings	0.61	0.76	1.89	1.56	1.28	-0.65
Dividends	Nil	Nil	Nil	Nil	Nil	Nil
Payout Ratio	Nil	Nil	Nil	Nil	Nil	Nil
Prices - High	21½	26⅜	29⅛	34⅛	23⅞	23¾
- Low	15⅛	15⅝	19½	19¾	14¾	11⅞
P/E Ratio - High	35	35	15	22	19	NM
- Low	25	20	10	13	12	NM

Income Statement Analysis (Million $)

	1994	%Chg	1993	%Chg	1992	%Chg	1991
Revs.	4,997	-2%	5,075	-9%	5,596	5%	5,350
Oper. Inc.	276	-8%	299	-4%	310	12%	276
Depr.	1.7	-98%	106	17%	90.6	19%	76.2
Int. Exp.	71.0	8%	66.0	-8%	72.0	-16%	86.0
Pretax Inc.	55.0	-21%	70.0	-53%	148	31%	113
Eff. Tax Rate	52%	—	53%	—	44%	—	43%
Net Inc.	26.6	-19%	33.0	-60%	82.1	26%	65.0

Balance Sheet & Other Fin. Data (Million $)

	1994	1993	1992	1991	1990	1989
Cash	9.0	8.5	8.3	6.7	6.4	6.9
Curr. Assets	468	473	465	448	428	419
Total Assets	2,222	2,250	2,066	1,803	1,713	1,655
Curr. Liab.	564	543	557	523	549	511
LT Debt	804	882	788	691	775	839
Common Eqty.	552	525	493	478	273	190
Total Cap.	1,478	1,518	1,375	1,169	1,047	1,029
Cap. Exp.	128	269	261	157	126	64.0
Cash Flow	144	139	173	141	120	46.0

Ratio Analysis

	1994	1993	1992	1991	1990	1989
Curr. Ratio	0.8	0.9	0.8	0.9	0.8	0.8
% LT Debt of Cap.	54.4	58.1	57.3	59.1	74.0	81.5
% Net Inc.of Revs.	0.5	0.7	1.5	1.2	0.9	NM
% Ret. on Assets	1.2	1.5	4.2	3.5	3.0	NM
% Ret. on Equity	4.9	6.5	16.9	16.6	21.5	NM

Dividend Data (No common dividends have been paid since 1970.)

Data as orig. reptd.; bef. results of disc. opers. and/or spec. items. Per share data adj. for stk. divs. as of ex-div. date. E-Estimated. NA-Not Available. NM-Not Meaningful. NR-Not Ranked.

Office—618 Michillinda Ave., Arcadia, CA 91007. **Tel**—(818) 821-7000. **Chrmn & CEO**—L. A. Del Santo. **Pres & COO**—R. E. Goodspeed. **EVP & CFO**—P. K. Knous. **SVP & Secy**—T. J. Wallock. **Investor Contact**—Mary M. McAboy (818-821-7897). **Dirs**—S. A. Burd, W. S. Davila, L. A. Del Santo, F. L. Duda, J. H. Greene, Jr., J. M. Lillie, R. I. MacDonnell, P. A. Magowan, C. E. Rickershauser, R. E. Stangeland, W. Y. Tauscher. **Transfer Agent**—Bank of New York, NYC. **Incorporated** in Delaware in 1926. **Empl**-28,000. **S&P Analyst:** Maureen C. Carini

STANDARD & POOR'S

STOCK REPORTS

Vulcan Materials

NYSE Symbol **VMC**
In S&P MidCap 400

14-SEP-95 **Industry:** Building

Summary: Vulcan Materials is the foremost U.S. producer of construction aggregates and a leading maker of a wide variety of industrial chemicals.

S&P Opinion: Accumulate (★★★★)

Recent Price • 54⅜ | Yield • 2.7%
52 Wk Range • 60⅜-46 | 12-Mo. P/E • 14.9

Quantitative Evaluations

Outlook (1 Lowest—5 Highest) **• 4-**

Fair Value **• 54¾**

Risk **• Low**

Earn./Div. Rank **• A-**

Technical Eval. **• Bullish** since 9/95

Rel. Strength Rank (1 Lowest—99 Highest) **• 23**

Insider Activity **• Favorable**

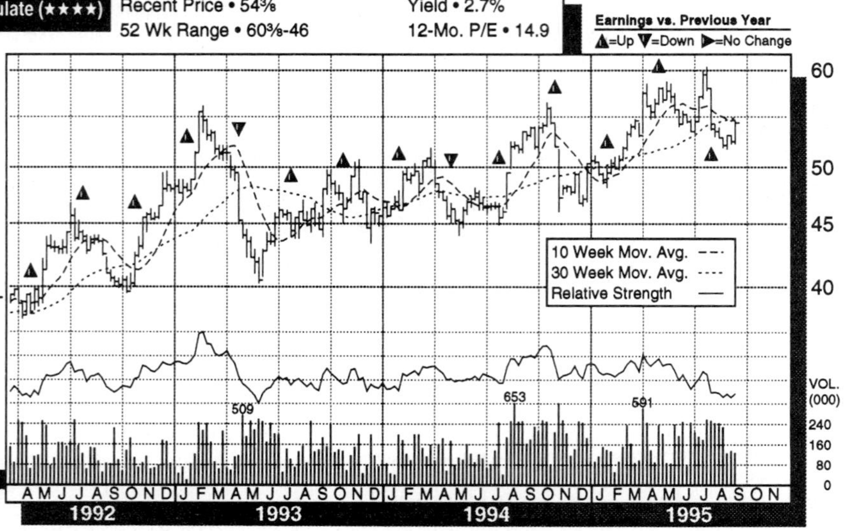

Overview - 14-SEP-95

We anticipate a 12% gain in sales in 1996, reflecting acquisitions, increases in volume and prices in construction aggregates and continued strength in volume and prices for the chemical unit. High operating rates and modest price gains will boost profits for aggregates; firm prices for caustic soda, a favorable product mix, only small increases in raw material costs and lower acquisition related costs should enable the chemical unit to record another solid gain in 1996. Assuming flat interest expense, an unchanged tax rate and a larger contribution from the Mexican joint venture, earnings should rise again in 1996. Acquisitions, gains in market share in aggregates and a product mix shift toward specialty chemical products should boost longer term sales and profit growth.

Valuation - 14-SEP-95

Although shares of this financially strong aggregates/chemical manufacturer have underperformed the market through mid-September 1995, we are maintaining our accumulate rating on VMC based on its attractive valuation and the prospect for accelerating earnings in 1996. Currently selling at around 11X our $4.90 earnings estimate for 1996 and 7.9X our 1996 estimate for cash flow per share, we believe VMC is undervalued. VMC deserves to sell at a higher multiple based on the company's solid growth prospects, its very solid balance sheet, comparatively stable earnings for a cyclical company and its long-standing practice of buying back its own shares.

Key Stock Statistics

S&P EPS Est. 1995	4.25	Tang. Bk. Value/Share	21.30
P/E on S&P Est. 1995	12.8	Beta	0.26
S&P EPS Est. 1996	4.90	Shareholders	4,500
Dividend Rate/Share	1.46	Market cap. (B)	$ 1.9
Shs. outstg. (M)	35.9	Inst. holdings	58%
Avg. daily vol. (M)	0.030	Insider holdings	NA

Value of $10,000 invested 5 years ago: $ 14,400

Fiscal Year Ending Dec. 31

	1995	% Change	1994	% Change	1993	% Change
Revenues (Million $)						
1Q	294.4	36%	216.9	1%	214.0	1%
2Q	382.8	17%	326.7	7%	305.9	8%
3Q	—	—	360.4	9%	331.5	6%
4Q	—	—	349.4	24%	282.0	4%
Yr.	—	—	1,253	11%	1,133	5%
Income (Million $)						
1Q	15.96	NM	-5.23	NM	-0.53	NM
2Q	47.73	42%	33.73	7%	31.64	5%
3Q	—	—	37.60	3%	36.56	2%
4Q	—	—	31.87	55%	20.55	NM
Yr.	—	—	97.98	11%	88.23	-3%
Earnings Per Share ($)						
1Q	0.44	NM	-0.14	NM	-0.01	NM
2Q	1.32	43%	0.92	10%	0.84	5%
3Q	E1.35	32%	1.02	3%	0.99	5%
4Q	E1.14	31%	0.87	53%	0.57	4%
Yr.	E4.25	59%	2.67	12%	2.39	NM

Next earnings report expected: late October

Vulcan Materials

Business Summary - 13-SEP-95

Vulcan Materials is engaged in the production of construction materials and chemicals. Contributions (profits in millions $) in 1994:

	Sales	Profits
Construction materials	67%	$162.5
Chemicals	33%	-7.3

VMC's construction materials unit is the nation's foremost producer of construction aggregates, consisting of crushed stone, sand, gravel, crushed slag, rock asphalt and expanded shale. Crushed stone comprised some 75% of the dollar volume of this unit's 1994 sales, as compared with 81% in 1993 and 78% in 1992. VMC, directly or through joint ventures, operates 127 permanent plants in 14 states for the production of crushed limestone and granite, with estimated reserves of some 7.7 billion tons. Shipments of all construction aggregates totaled 133 million tons in 1994, versus 126.6 million tons in 1993; crushed stone accounted for 125 million tons, versus 116.6 million tons in 1993.

Sales by end use in 1994 were: highway, road and airport 39%; nonresidential, commercial and industrial facilities 31%; residential buildings 16%; dams, sewers and water supply systems 8%; railroad ballast 3%; and nonconstruction use 3%.

Through its chloralkali unit (85% of 1994's sales) VMC produces chlorine, muriatic acid, caustic soda, caustic potash, chlorinated hydrocarbons and calcium chlorine. VMC makes process aids for the pulp and paper, textile and water treatment markets through its performance systems unit (15% of 1994's sales). Products made by performance systems include sodium chlorite and sodium hydrosulfite.

Sales by end use in 1994 were: process and intermediate chemicals 58%; industrial durables and nondurables 24%; and consumer nondurables 18%.

Important Developments

Jul. '95—In its second quarter earnings release VMC said that it expected to achieve record sales, net income and earnings per share in 1995. The company noted that net cash from operations for the first half of 1995 rose to $68.1 million from $37.8 million a year earlier. Separately, it disclosed that it purchased 58,600 shares of its common stock in 1995's second quarter at an average price of $54.29 a share. For 1995's first half, the company purchased 106,300 shares at an average cost of $52.24 a share.

Jun. '95—VMC completed the acquisition of Rio Linda Chemical Co. from Albright & Wilson's Americas Inc. Rio Linda manufactures small-scale chlorine dioxide generators for the water treatment, food processing and pulp and paper industries. Rio Linda had sales of $12.1 million in 1994.

Capitalization

Long Term Debt: $91,927,000 (6/95).

Per Share Data ($) (Year Ended Dec. 31)

	1994	1993	1992	1991	1990	1989
Tangible Bk. Val.	20.38	19.34	18.81	17.98	17.85	16.80
Cash Flow	5.58	5.30	5.28	4.43	5.84	5.67
Earnings	2.67	2.39	2.41	1.38	3.10	3.30
Dividends	1.32	1.26	1.20	1.20	1.20	1.12
Payout Ratio	49%	53%	49%	87%	38%	33%
Prices - High	56½	56⅛	49⅝	40	46¾	48½
- Low	44	40¼	36	30⅜	29⅜	40½
P/E Ratio - High	21	23	21	29	15	15
- Low	16	17	15	22	9	12

Income Statement Analysis (Million $)

	1994	%Chg	1993	%Chg	1992	%Chg	1991
Revs.	1,253	11%	1,133	5%	1,078	7%	1,007
Oper. Inc.	244	3%	238	-4%	247	11%	223
Depr.	107	NM	108	NM	109	-7%	117
Int. Exp.	10.7	5%	10.2	-2%	10.4	-8%	11.3
Pretax Inc.	146	17%	125	-5%	131	79%	73.0
Eff. Tax Rate	33%	—	30%	—	30%	—	28%
Net Inc.	98.0	11%	88.0	-3%	91.0	72%	53.0

Balance Sheet & Other Fin. Data (Million $)

	1994	1993	1992	1991	1990	1989
Cash	8.0	14.0	16.0	19.0	19.0	84.0
Curr. Assets	337	303	305	285	295	333
Total Assets	1,181	1,079	1,084	1,073	1,118	1,003
Curr. Liab.	211	141	135	135	234	141
LT Debt	97.0	102	107	111	45.0	55.0
Common Eqty.	732	703	700	683	680	664
Total Cap.	912	879	880	864	810	792
Cap. Exp.	100	101	98.0	86.0	222	147
Cash Flow	205	196	200	169	227	229

Ratio Analysis

	1994	1993	1992	1991	1990	1989
Curr. Ratio	1.6	2.1	2.3	2.1	1.3	2.4
% LT Debt of Cap.	10.7	11.6	12.2	12.9	5.5	7.0
% Net Inc.of Revs.	7.8	7.8	8.4	5.2	10.9	12.4
% Ret. on Assets	8.7	8.3	8.5	4.8	11.5	13.8
% Ret. on Equity	13.7	12.7	13.3	7.7	18.2	20.9

Dividend Data —Dividends have been paid since 1934. A dividend reinvestment plan is available.

Amt. of Div. $	Date Decl.	Ex-Div. Date	Stock of Record	Payment Date
0.330	Sep. 28	Nov. 17	Nov. 23	Dec. 09 '94
0.365	Feb. 16	Feb. 21	Feb. 27	Mar. 10 '95
0.365	May. 22	May. 24	May. 31	Jun. 10 '95
0.365	Jul. 14	Aug. 23	Aug. 25	Sep. 08 '95

Data as orig. reptd.; bef. results of disc. opers. and/or spec. items. Per share data adj. for stk. divs. as of ex-div. date. E-Estimated. NA-Not Available. NM-Not Meaningful. NR-Not Ranked.

Office—One Metroplex Drive, Birmingham, AL 35209. **Tel**—(205) 877-3000. **Chrmn, Pres & CEO**—H. A. Sklenar. **VP-Fin**—D. F. Sansone. **VP-Secy**—W. F. Denson III. **Investor Contact**—E. Starke Sydnor. **Dirs**—M. H. Antonini, L. D. DeSimone, J. K. Greene, R. H. Leet, D. J. McGregor, A. D. McLaughlin, J. V. Napier, D. B. Rice, H. A. Sklenar, O. R. Smith. **Transfer Agents**—AmSouth Bank, Birmingham; First Chicago Trust Co. of New York, NYC. **Registrars**—Trust Co. Bank, Atlanta; First Chicago Trust Co. of New York, NYC. **Incorporated** in New Jersey in 1956. **Empl**-6,753. **S&P Analyst:** Leo Larkin

WPL Holdings

NYSE Symbol WPH In S&P MidCap 400

Price	Range	P-E Ratio	Dividend	Yield	S&P Ranking	Beta
Oct. 9'95	1995					
29½	31–27¼	17	1.94	6.6%	A	0.61

Summary

WPL Holdings is the holding company for Wisconsin Power and Light, which supplies electric, gas and water service in south-central Wisconsin. The fuel that WP&L most relies on for electric power generation is coal, with nuclear used to a much lesser extent. WPH also owns Heartland Development Corp., which is engaged in nonutility operations. Following a small gain in 1994, share earnings fell in the first half of 1995, reflecting lower revenues, nuclear plant refueling maintenance and overhaul costs, much lower other income, and higher interest expenses.

Business Summary

WPL Holdings, Inc. is the holding company for Wisconsin Power and Light (WP&L) and Heartland Development Corp. (HDC). Electric sales accounted for 65% of operating revenues in 1994, gas sales 17%, and fees, rents and other 18%.

WP&L is a public utility predominantly engaged in the transmissin and distribution of electric energy and the generation and bulk purchase of electric energy for sales. WP&L also transports, distributes, and sells natural gas purchased from gas suppliers. Nearly all of WP&L's retail customers are located in South and Central Wisconsin. WP&L's principal consolidated subsidiary is South Beloit Water, Gas and Electric Co.

Electric revenues by class of customer in recent years:

	1994	1993	1992	1991
Residential/rural	37%	37%	36%	37%
Industrial	26%	26%	27%	25%
Commercial	19%	19%	19%	19%
Wholesale	16%	16%	14%	14%
Other	2%	2%	4%	5%

Electric generation by fuel source in 1994 was as follows: 81% coal, 17% nuclear, and the balance hydro and gas.

HDC and its principal subsidiaries are engaged in business development in three major areas: 1) environmental services through Environmental Holding Company, the parent company of RMT, Jones and Neuse, and QES; 2) affordable housing and historic rehabilitation through Heartland Properties; and 3) energy services, which includes ENSERV, A&C Enercom Consultants Consultants, and Entec Consulting.

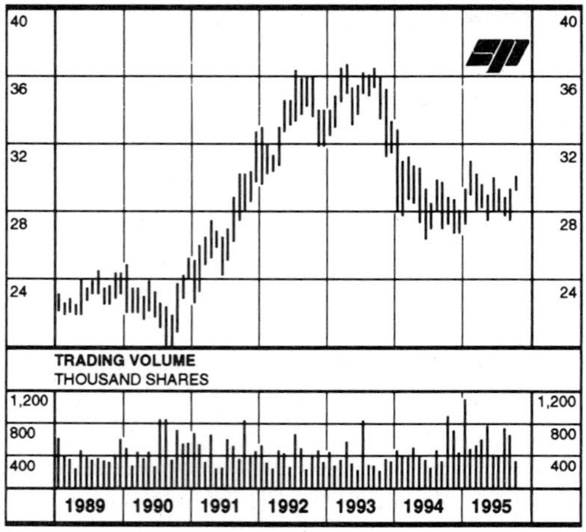

Important Developments

Aug. '95— WPL Holdings said it is exploring options to exit the energy conservation business. The company had noted that the market for its energy conservation and consulting business has continued to soften.

Jun. '95— WP&L filed an application with the Wisconsin Public Service Commission's for the sale, sometime in 1995, of $60 million of first mortgage bonds. Proceeds would be used in part to repay short-term debt incurred in June 1995 to repurchase in private transactions $18 million of WP&L 9.30% first mortgage bonds, Series V, due December 1, 2025. The remainder of proceeds would be used to repay other short-term debt incurred to finance utility construction spending and for general corporate purposes.

Next earnings report expected in late October.

Per Share Data ($)

Yr. End Dec. 31	1994	1993	1992	1991	1990	1989	1988	1987	1986	1985
Tangible Bk. Val.	**18.77**	18.44	17.55	17.02	16.31	15.85	15.59	14.98	14.44	13.76
Earnings	**2.13**	2.11	2.11	2.43	2.23	1.93	2.18	2.08	2.14	2.13
Dividends	**1.92**	1.90	1.86	1.80	1.74	1.68	1.62	1.54	1.45	1.35
Payout Ratio	**90%**	90%	88%	74%	78%	87%	74%	74%	68%	63%
Prices—High	**32⅞**	36¾	36⅜	32¾	25¼	24½	23⅞	27⅜	30⅛	20¼
Low	**26⅜**	31¼	29⅝	22⅝	20	21⅞	21⅜	21¼	19½	14⅝
P/E Ratio—	**15–12**	17–15	17–14	13–9	11–9	13–11	11–10	13–10	14–9	10–7

Data as orig. reptd. Adj. for stk. div. of 100% Sep. 1988.

Income Data (Million $)

Year Ended Dec. 31	Revs.	Depr.	Maint.	Oper. Ratio	[1]Fxd. Chgs. Cover.	Constr. Credits	Eff. Tax Rate	Net Inc.	% Return On Revs.	% Return On [2]Invest. Capital	% Return On Com. Equity
1994	**816**	**81.5**	**41.2**	**88.4%**	**3.96**	**4.04**	**34.1%**	**65.3**	**8.0**	**7.9**	**11.0**
1993	773	69.1	44.8	86.9%	3.14	4.00	27.4%	62.5	8.1	8.2	11.7
1992	652	59.5	45.1	85.6%	2.92	3.70	28.4%	57.0	8.7	8.6	12.1
1991	649	53.0	42.9	84.7%	3.51	2.00	32.9%	64.9	10.0	9.6	14.5
1990	618	55.3	41.7	84.2%	3.45	1.30	32.4%	59.5	9.6	9.1	13.8
1989	605	54.6	40.6	85.2%	3.67	1.80	34.3%	51.5	8.5	9.4	12.2
1988	601	52.3	39.8	85.1%	3.69	1.60	35.0%	57.9	9.6	10.7	14.2
1987	549	58.7	36.3	84.0%	3.50	1.00	38.3%	55.0	10.0	10.5	14.1
1986	569	58.6	34.8	84.4%	3.59	1.30	43.5%	60.5	10.6	11.0	15.1
1985	589	63.5	33.7	86.3%	4.68	5.80	44.7%	60.7	10.3	10.2	15.9

Balance Sheet Data (Million $)

Dec. 31	[3]Gross Prop.	Capital Expend.	Net Prop.	% Earn. on Net Prop.	Total Cap.	Capitalization LT Debt	% LT Debt	Pfd.	% Pfd.	Com.	% Com.
1994	**2,075**	**123**	**1,266**	**8.5**	**1,371**	**448**	**40.5**	**60**	**5.4**	**598**	**54.1**
1993	1,984	150	1,221	8.6	1,324	425	39.8	60	5.6	583	54.6
1992	1,853	125	1,133	8.5	1,184	418	43.5	60	6.3	481	50.2
1991	1,747	93	1,072	9.4	1,098	367	41.5	60	6.8	458	51.7
1990	1,682	74	1,041	9.4	1,076	360	42.0	60	7.0	437	51.0
1989	1,622	97	882	10.3	857	321	39.9	60	7.4	424	52.7
1988	1,549	103	853	10.7	855	323	40.4	60	7.5	417	52.1
1987	1,465	80	821	10.8	838	398	51.0	60	7.7	323	41.3
1986	1,404	85	809	11.1	837	333	42.9	60	7.7	384	49.4
1985	1,336	88	791	10.3	822	333	43.9	60	7.9	366	48.2

Data as orig. reptd. **1.** Times int. exp. & pfd. divs. covered (pretax basis). **2.** Based on income before interest charges. **3.** Utility plant.

Operating Revenues (Million $)

Quarter:	1995	1994	1993	1992
Mar.	225	234	204	178
Jun.	183	181	169	140
Sep.		194	174	151
Dec.		210	216	182
		816	773	652

Operating revenues for the first half of 1995, declined 2.8%, year to year, reflecting decreases in both electric and gas sales. The lower sales, expenses for the Kewaunee nuclear power plant refueling and maintenance overhaul, and greater depreciation/amortization charges led to a drop in operating profit of 6.5%. Following sharply reduced other income and higher interest expenses net income dropped 27%, to $0.86 a share, from $1.20.

Common Share Earnings ($)

Quarter:	1995	1994	1993	1992
Mar.	0.64	0.87	0.71	0.69
Jun.	0.22	0.33	0.24	0.26
Sep.		0.50	0.44	0.45
Dec.		0.43	0.73	0.71
		2.13	2.11	2.11

Finances

WPL estimated capital spending for 1995 at about $129 million, up from $123 million spent in 1994, with around $104 million projected for 1996.

In October 1993, WPL sold 599,460 shares of 6.50% preferred stock at $25 per share through Robert W. Baird & Co. Proceeds were used to redeem 149,865 shares of 8.48% preferred stock.

Dividend Data

Dividends have been paid since 1946. A dividend reinvestment plan is available. A "poison pill" stock purchase rights plan was adopted in 1989.

Amt. of Divd. $	Date Decl.	Ex-divd. Date	Stock of Record	Payment Date
0.48½	Jan. 18	Jan. 25	Jan. 31	Feb. 15'95
0.48½	Apr. 12	Apr. 24	Apr. 28	May 15'95
0.48½	Jul. 12	Jul. 27	Jul. 31	Aug. 15'95

Capitalization

Long Term Debt: $431,027,000 (6/95).

Subsid. Cum. Preferred Stock: $59,963,000.

Common Stock: 30,773,588 shs. ($0.01 par). Institutions hold about 17%. Shareholders of record: 37,049.

Office—222 West Washington Ave., Madison, WI 53703. **Tel**—(608) 252-3311. **Pres & CEO**—E. B. Davis Jr. **VP-Treas & Secy**—E. M. Gleason. **Investor Contact**—Susan J. Kosmo (608-252-4851). **Dirs**—L. D. Carley, E. B. Davis Jr., R. G. Flowers, D. R. Haldeman, K. C. Lyall, A. M. Nemirow, M. E. Neshek, H. C. Prange, J. D. Pyle, C. T. Toussaint. **Transfer Agent & Registrar**—WPL Holdings, Inc. **Incorporated** in Wisconsin in 1917. **Empl**—3,835.

 N.J. DeVita

Waban Inc.

NYSE Symbol **WBN**
In S&P MidCap 400

23-AUG-95

Industry:
Retail Stores

Summary: This company is a major participant in warehouse merchandising through its 78 HomeBase home improvement outlets and 65 BJ's Wholesale Club membership warehouses.

S&P Opinion: Buy (★★★★★)

Recent Price • 18⅝
52 Wk Range • 20⅜-13½

Yield • Nil
12-Mo. P/E • 9.2

Quantitative Evaluations

Outlook
(1 Lowest—5 Highest)
• **4-**

Fair Value
• **20¼**

Risk
• **Average**

Earn./Div. Rank
• **NR**

Technical Eval.
• **Bullish** since 7/95

Rel. Strength Rank
(1 Lowest—99 Highest)
• **84**

Insider Activity
• **NA**

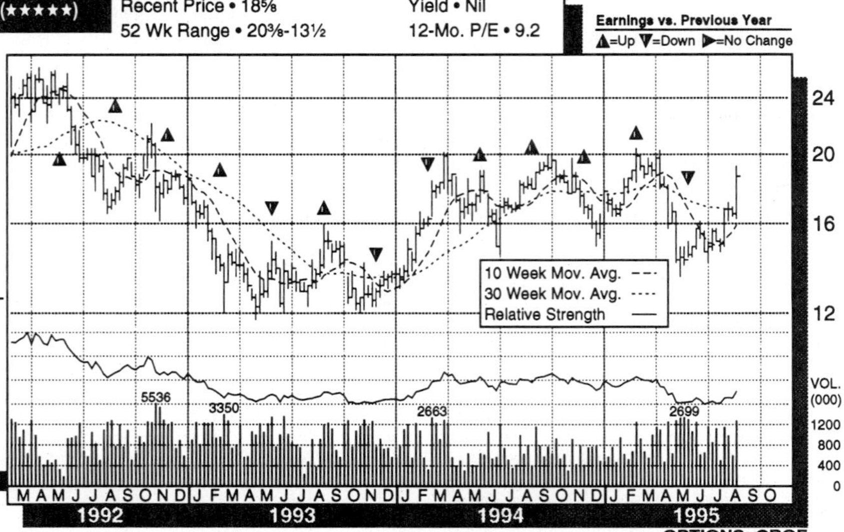

OPTIONS: CBOE

Overview - 23-AUG-95

Sales for fiscal 1995-96 will benefit from new openings, and same-store sales gains of 3% at BJ's. Operating income at BJ's should increase strongly, reflecting an improved product mix, logistical efficiencies and cost controls. Operating income at HomeBase should increase only moderately after 1994-95's 21% gain, excluding the $101 million restructuring charge for store closings and writedown of discontinued merchandise. The closing of unprofitable units will give operating income a boost, but profitability of newly remodeled stores will still be tempered by strong competition from Home Depot. By contrast, BJ's will benefit from less competition over time as the warehouse club industry continues to consolidate. Interest expense will be boosted by borrowings to fund new store openings.

Valuation - 23-AUG-95

The shares rallied when second quarter 1995-96 earnings were higher than expected; at that time we upgraded our recommendation. We believe that in spite of continued softness in sales at HomeBase units, the company's marketing and merchandising strategies will continue to strengthen the regional standing of both HomeBase and BJ's. BJ's operations are strong and improving and HomeBase looks like a viable second place to Home Depot in the do-it-yourself market in the sharply competitive West Coast trade area.

Key Stock Statistics

S&P EPS Est. 1996	2.15	Tang. Bk. Value/Share	14.95
P/E on S&P Est. 1996	8.7	Beta	1.49
S&P EPS Est. 1997	2.35	Shareholders	4,500
Dividend Rate/Share	Nil	Market cap. (B)	$0.612
Shs. outstg. (M)	33.3	Inst. holdings	97%
Avg. daily vol. (M)	0.239	Insider holdings	0%

Value of $10,000 invested 5 years ago: $ 15,520

Fiscal Year Ending Jan. 31

	1996	% Change	1995	% Change	1994	% Change
Revenues (Million $)						
1Q	888.5	8%	821.0	-2%	834.2	13%
2Q	1,052	11%	951.8	-2%	967.2	12%
3Q	—	—	905.6	NM	897.7	9%
4Q	—	—	972.0	9%	890.3	-5%
Yr.	—	—	3,650	2%	3,589	7%
Income (Million $)						
1Q	8.26	-10%	9.13	106%	4.43	-28%
2Q	24.40	15%	21.14	54%	13.70	7%
3Q	—	—	13.40	66%	8.09	-28%
4Q	—	—	21.32	NM	-44.90	NM
Yr.	—	—	64.99	NM	-18.69	NM
Earnings Per Share ($)						
1Q	0.25	-7%	0.27	108%	0.13	-32%
2Q	0.74	17%	0.63	62%	0.39	3%
3Q	E0.44	10%	0.40	67%	0.24	-31%
4Q	E0.72	13%	0.64	NM	-1.36	NM
Yr.	E2.15	10%	1.95	NM	-0.56	NM

Next earnings report expected: mid November

Waban Inc.

Business Summary - 23-AUG-95

Waban Inc. consists of HomeBase (formerly HomeClub), one of the leading U.S. merchandisers of home improvement products at everyday low prices, and BJ's Wholesale Club, a chain of membership warehouse clubs. The company was spun off to shareholders of Zayre Corp. (now TJX Companies) in June 1989 as part of a corporate restructuring.

HomeBase sells home improvement products in warehouse outlets targeted to the contractor and the do-it-yourselfer. The company has launched a number of customer service programs and promotional campaigns designed to enhance its appeal to casual do-it-yourselfers. In the spring of 1991, HomeBase discontinued its membership program, under which members paid annual fees and non-members paid a 5% surcharge on all purchases. In 1992, HomeBase changed its name from HomeClub to eliminate any remaining perception that it maintained a membership program. As of January 28, 1995, HomeBase operated 79 units in 10 states in the West and Southwest, including 47 in California.

BJ's is a membership warehouse club for food and general merchandise. Shopping is limited to members only. BJ's membership fees are generally $30 per annum for business and individual members; supplemental business memberships are available for $15 a year. The company's ability to achieve profitability while selling merchandise at low prices depends on high sales volume and efficient operations. BJ's buys virtually all of its merchandise at volume discounts from manufacturers for shipment either directly to BJ's warehouse clubs or to a consolidation/deconsolidation facility. As a result, many of the costs associated with the normal distribution channels are eliminated.

Important Developments

Aug. '95—Management said that HomeBase's second quarter 1995-96 sales continued to reflect the slowdown in housing turnover and a weak economy in southern California. Despite this difficult environment, the division achieved operating income slightly greater than last year. Same-store sales at BJ's rose 3.0% in the second quarter; operating income increased 29%. The marketing program initiated at the beginning of the quarter attracted many prospective members; BJ's is working to convert these trial members to paid members in the next few months. WBN plans to open 10 new BJ's in 1995-96 and three HomeBase units. Over the next year, some 31 HomeBase units have been earmarked for remodeling. Waban repurchased 371,500 shares in the second quarter at an average cost of $14.73 a share.

Capitalization

Long Term Debt: $245,990,000 (7/29/95), incl. $108.6 million of 6.5% debs. due 2002, conv. into com. at $24.75 a sh.

Per Share Data ($) (Year Ended Jan. 31)

	1995	1994	1993	1992	1991	1990
Tangible Bk. Val.	14.71	12.71	13.23	11.87	9.94	9.29
Cash Flow	3.16	0.53	2.23	1.75	1.28	1.54
Earnings	1.95	-0.56	1.33	1.01	0.64	1.01
Dividends	Nil	Nil	Nil	Nil	Nil	Nil
Payout Ratio	Nil	Nil	Nil	Nil	Nil	Nil
Cal. Yrs.	1994	1993	1992	1991	1990	1989
Prices - High	20⅛	18⅜	26½	24⅝	12	20
- Low	13	11¾	16⅛	9½	4⅝	10
P/E Ratio - High	10	NM	20	24	19	20
- Low	7	NM	12	9	7	10

Income Statement Analysis (Million $)

	1995	%Chg	1994	%Chg	1993	%Chg	1992
Revs.	3,650	2%	3,589	7%	3,358	21%	2,784
Oper. Inc.	162	36%	119	14%	104	25%	83.2
Depr.	40.4	11%	36.3	22%	29.8	35%	22.1
Int. Exp.	23.0	37%	16.8	24%	13.5	75%	7.7
Pretax Inc.	106	NM	-34.0	NM	68.3	40%	48.9
Eff. Tax Rate	39%	—	NM	—	35%	—	39%
Net Inc.	65.0	NM	-18.7	NM	44.2	47%	30.0

Balance Sheet & Other Fin. Data (Million $)

	1995	1994	1993	1992	1991	1990
Cash	129	20.0	53.0	116	13.0	15.0
Curr. Assets	737	634	638	556	400	362
Total Assets	1,242	1,073	1,007	786	580	537
Curr. Liab.	445	430	352	288	246	224
LT Debt	259	174	193	87.0	29.0	31.0
Common Eqty.	488	420	437	389	284	265
Total Cap.	751	595	639	485	323	305
Cap. Exp.	112	133	165	68.6	35.8	41.8
Cash Flow	105	17.6	74.1	52.1	36.5	43.7

Ratio Analysis

	1995	1994	1993	1992	1991	1990
Curr. Ratio	1.7	1.5	1.8	1.9	1.6	1.6
% LT Debt of Cap.	34.4	29.3	30.2	17.9	9.0	10.3
% Net Inc.of Revs.	1.8	NM	1.3	1.1	0.8	1.4
% Ret. on Assets	5.6	NM	4.9	4.1	3.3	5.8
% Ret. on Equity	14.3	NM	10.7	8.4	6.7	18.4

Dividend Data —No dividends have been paid. A "poison pill" stock purchase rights plan was adopted in 1989.

Data as orig. reptd.; bef. results of disc. opers. and/or spec. items. Per share data adj. for stk. divs. as of ex-div. date. E-Estimated. NA-Not Available. NM-Not Meaningful. NR-Not Ranked.

Office—One Mercer Rd., P. O. Box 9600, Natick, MA 01760. **Tel**—(508) 651-6500. **Chrmn**—S. L. Feldberg. **Pres & CEO**—H. J. Zarkin. **CFO**—E. J. Weisberger. **VP-Treas**—G. Freeman. **Secy**—Sarah M. Gallivan. **Investor Contact**—Catherine E. Woods. **Dirs**—S. J. Coppersmith, S. H. Feldberg, S. L. Feldberg, K. L. Hamilton, A. L. Levy, A. F. Loewy, T. J. Shields, L. R. Waxlax, H. J. Zarkin. **Transfer Agent & Registrar**—First Chicago Trust Co. of New York, NYC. **Incorporated** in California in 1983; reincorporated in Delaware in 1985. **Empl**-16,000. **S&P Analyst:** Karen J. Sack, CFA

STANDARD & POOR'S

Wallace Computer Services

STOCK REPORTS

NYSE Symbol **WCS**

In S&P MidCap 400

20-OCT-95

Industry:
Office Equipment

Summary: This leading maker of business forms, mainly continuous forms for computer applications, is the object of a hostile tender offer at $60 a share.

S&P Opinion: Avoid (★★)

Recent Price • 59

52 Wk Range • 60-25⅞

Yield • 1.5%

12-Mo. P/E • 24.0

Quantitative Evaluations

Outlook
(1 Lowest—5 Highest)
• **3+**

Fair Value
• **58⅝**

Risk
• **High**

Earn./Div. Rank
• **A**

Technical Eval.
• **Bullish** since 1/95

Rel. Strength Rank
(1 Lowest—99 Highest)
• **82**

Insider Activity
• **Favorable**

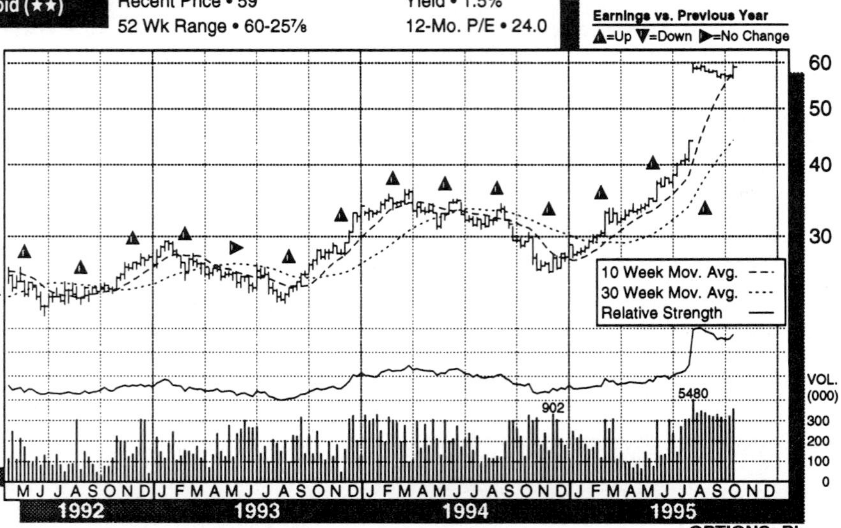

OPTIONS: Ph

Overview - 20-OCT-95

Wallace's growth prospects helped make it a target for acquisition. Sales should continue to increase through fiscal 1996, as backlogs are at record levels. The company continues to gain market share in the declining paper business forms industry, aided by its value added Wallace Information Network. Paper forms account for 39% of total sales. Solid growth prospects exist for Wallace's label business, and the company acquired two label manufacturers in fiscal 1995. Revenues should also increase at the Tops office products business and at Colorforms direct mail and printing services. Income will grow with the higher volume, and potential widening of gross margins. Gross profit was squeezed by higher paper prices in fiscal 1995.

Valuation - 20-OCT-95

The shares were recently trading slightly below Moore Corps.'s sweetened tender offer of $60 a share, which was rejected by Wallace directors. We believe that Moore's offer, at 19X estimated fiscal 1996 EPS, is fair, and doubt that a significantly higher bid will emerge. The company has reiterated its desire to remain independent, and if no transaction is consummated, the shares could drop dramatically. As the risk/reward factors of owning the shares are not favorable, we recommend avoiding the stock. Investors should note that Wallace's officers and directors own less than 2% of the shares.

Key Stock Statistics

S&P EPS Est. 1996	3.20	Tang. Bk. Value/Share	18.35
P/E on S&P Est. 1996	18.4	Beta	1.47
Dividend Rate/Share	0.86	Shareholders	4,300
Shs. outstg. (M)	22.5	Market cap. (B)	$ 1.3
Avg. daily vol. (M)	0.242	Inst. holdings	79%
		Insider holdings	NA

Value of $10,000 invested 5 years ago: $ 21,315

Fiscal Year Ending Jul. 31

	1996	% Change	1995	% Change	1994	% Change
Revenues (Million $)						
1Q	—	—	158.4	10%	144.5	8%
2Q	—	—	176.2	15%	153.1	11%
3Q	—	—	180.1	27%	141.5	7%
4Q	—	—	198.2	33%	149.1	5%
Yr.	—	—	712.8	21%	588.2	8%
Income (Million $)						
1Q	—	—	11.64	6%	10.99	11%
2Q	—	—	13.44	5%	12.83	10%
3Q	—	—	14.45	25%	11.58	20%
4Q	—	—	15.77	33%	11.87	20%
Yr.	—	—	55.30	17%	47.27	15%
Earnings Per Share ($)						
1Q	E0.78	50%	0.52	4%	0.50	14%
2Q	E0.75	25%	0.60	3%	0.58	12%
3Q	E0.80	25%	0.64	23%	0.52	21%
4Q	E0.87	24%	0.70	32%	0.53	18%
Yr.	E3.20	30%	2.46	15%	2.13	16%

Next earnings report expected: late November

Wallace Computer Services

Business Summary - 20-OCT-95

Wallace Computer Services makes and supplies business forms, industrial and consumer catalogs, directories and price lists, pressure-sensitive labels, computer and business machine ribbons, a standard line of office products forms and direct-mail promotional printing. It also markets computer accessories, office supplies and computer hardware and software. Sales by product category in recent fiscal years were:

	1994	1993	1992
Printed products	90%	89%	89%
Other	10%	11%	11%

The Business Forms division produces customized and standard forms primarily for use on computers. Major products include custom continuous forms, unit set forms and mailer forms. The company offers value-added services such as W.I.N. (Wallace Information Network) and Select Services, which let customers better manage forms inventories and ordering. It also offers an electronic business forms software program, PLATFORMS.

The TOPS Business Forms division is a leading manufacturer of office forms and systems, offering more than 1,000 products manufactured and distributed from four U.S. locations.

The Label division has four units: Datamark, a manufacturer of computer-generated pressure-sensitive labels; Continental Ribbon & Carbon, which makes computer ribbons; Business Data, a supplier of computer hardware and proprietary software; and Apollo Labeling Systems, a producer of prime pressure-sensitive labels.

Visible Computer Supply Corp. sells computer supplies and office products via catalogs mailed directly to users. The catalogs carry over 8,000 items for order by telephone, fax or mail.

The Wallace Press division produces a wide variety of catalogs, price guides and directories using computerized typesetting and page makeup.

The Colorforms division (acquired in 1991) provides printing, personalization and mailing services to the direct-mail advertising industry.

Important Developments

Oct. '95—The company rejected an offer by Moore Corp. (MCL) to buy all Wallace common shares for $60 a share in cash. It had previously rejected a $56 offer from MCL. The new tender offer expires November 3, 1995. The company also said it anticipates sharply higher earnings for the fiscal 1996 first quarter and full year.

Capitalization

Long Term Debt: $25,600,000 (7/95).

Per Share Data ($) (Year Ended Jul. 31)

	1995	1994	1993	1992	1991	1990
Tangible Bk. Val.	NA	17.61	15.95	15.00	14.15	12.97
Cash Flow	NA	3.62	3.20	3.03	2.67	2.65
Earnings	2.46	2.13	1.84	1.76	1.63	1.86
Dividends	0.71	0.63	0.57	0.53	0.49	0.44
Payout Ratio	29%	29%	31%	30%	30%	24%
Prices - High	60	36¼	33⅞	28	29⅛	31½
- Low	27½	30⅞	22⅞	21¾	19	15⅞
P/E Ratio - High	24	17	18	16	18	17
- Low	11	14	12	12	12	9

Income Statement Analysis (Million $)

	1994	%Chg	1993	%Chg	1992	%Chg	1991
Revs.	588	8%	545	6%	512	12%	459
Oper. Inc.	105	17%	89.8	8%	83.4	16%	71.6
Depr.	33.0	9%	30.3	6%	28.6	27%	22.5
Int. Exp.	2.3	17%	2.0	-24%	2.6	42%	1.8
Pretax Inc.	73.9	18%	62.4	4%	59.8	11%	53.9
Eff. Tax Rate	36%	—	34%	—	34%	—	35%
Net Inc.	47.3	15%	41.2	4%	39.5	13%	35.0

Balance Sheet & Other Fin. Data (Million $)

	1994	1993	1992	1991	1990	1989
Cash	77.0	46.9	55.1	52.3	54.4	60.9
Curr. Assets	248	213	205	184	187	179
Total Assets	539	481	467	399	375	332
Curr. Liab.	64.8	55.2	53.0	42.9	49.0	40.9
LT Debt	23.5	25.2	26.0	19.8	20.2	20.5
Common Eqty.	410	368	356	309	279	244
Total Cap.	456	416	405	349	320	286
Cap. Exp.	34.2	31.8	33.5	40.5	49.8	30.7
Cash Flow	80.3	71.5	68.0	57.5	56.3	52.3

Ratio Analysis

	1994	1993	1992	1991	1990	1989
Curr. Ratio	3.8	3.9	3.9	4.3	3.8	4.4
% LT Debt of Cap.	5.2	6.1	6.4	5.7	6.3	7.2
% Net Inc.of Revs.	8.0	7.5	7.7	7.6	8.8	8.6
% Ret. on Assets	9.3	8.8	8.9	9.0	11.1	11.8
% Ret. on Equity	12.1	11.5	11.7	11.8	15.0	16.1

Dividend Data —Dividends have been paid since 1933. A poison pill stock purchase rights plan was adopted in 1990.

Amt. of Div. $	Date Decl.	Ex-Div. Date	Stock of Record	Payment Date
0.185	Nov. 09	Nov. 25	Dec. 01	Dec. 20 '94
0.185	Jan. 26	Feb. 23	Mar. 01	Mar. 20 '95
0.185	Mar. 08	May. 25	Jun. 01	Jun. 20 '95
0.185	Jun. 14	Aug. 30	Sep. 01	Sep. 20 '95
0.215	Sep. 07	Nov. 29	Dec. 01	Dec. 20 '95

Data as orig. reptd.; bef. results of disc. opers. and/or spec. items. Per share data adj. for stk. divs. as of ex-div. date. E-Estimated. NA-Not Available. NM-Not Meaningful. NR-Not Ranked.

Office—4600 West Roosevelt Rd., Hillside, IL 60162. **Tel**—(312) 626-2000. **Chrmn**—T. Dimitriou. **Pres & CEO**—R. J. Cronin. **VP & CFO**—M. J. Halloran. **Secy**—M. Laudizio. **Investor Contact**—Brad Samson (708)-449-8600. **Treas**—M. T. Quane. **Dirs**—F. F. Canning, R. J. Cronin, T. Dimitriou, R. F. Doyle, R. D. Ewers, W. N. Lane III, W. E. Olsen, N. E. Stearns, Jr. **Transfer Agent & Registrar**—State Street Bank & Trust, Boston. **Incorporated** in Illinois in 1908; reincorporated in Delaware in 1963. **Empl**-3,530. **S&P Analyst:** Stephen Madonna, CFA

STANDARD & POOR'S

STOCK REPORTS

Washington Gas Light

NYSE Symbol **WGL**

In S&P MidCap 400

16-OCT-95 **Industry:** Utilities-Gas

Summary: Through its three divisions and two distribution subsidiaries, this company provides natural gas service to Washington, D.C. and areas of Maryland and Virginia.

Quantitative Evaluations

Outlook (1 Lowest—5 Highest) • **2+**

Fair Value • **18**

Risk • **Low**

Earn./Div. Rank • **A**

Technical Eval. • **Bullish** since 9/95

Rel. Strength Rank (1 Lowest—99 Highest) • **68**

Insider Activity • **NA**

Recent Price • 20⅛ | Yield • 5.6%

52 Wk Range • 21-16 | 12-Mo. P/E • 14.3

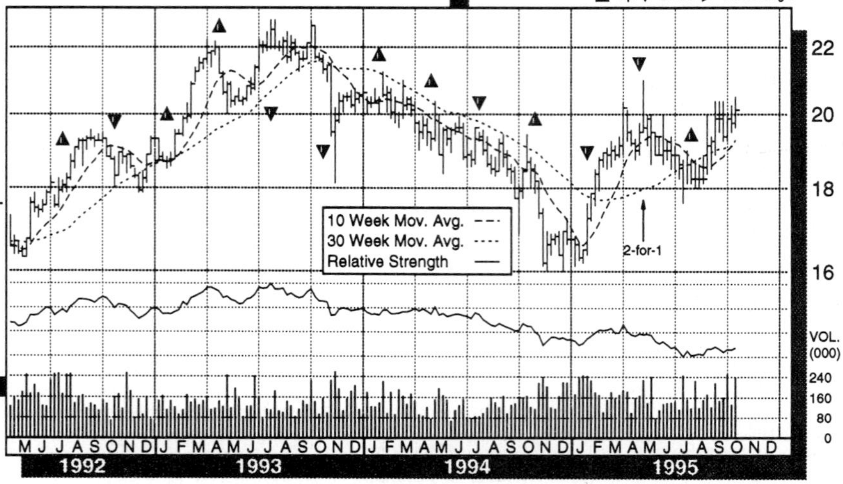

Business Profile - 16-OCT-95

This natural gas distributor serves Washington, D.C., and adjoining areas of suburban Maryland and northern Virginia. A distribution subsidiary also serves a portion of West Virginia. WGL is focusing on its gas distribution business and discontinuing or selling most non-utility operations. Seasonal quarterly losses have narrowed, reflecting greater control of operating and maintenance costs. A two-for-one stock split was effected in May 1995.

Operational Review - 16-OCT-95

Revenues in the nine months ended June 30, 1995, dropped 10%, year to year, as the impact of mild weather outweighed more customer meters and a rate increase. Margins widened, due to lower injury and damage provisions, labor costs and expenses for uncollectible accounts; operating profit declined 3.0%. Following gains of $0.04 a share from the sale of a subsidiary, net income rose marginally, to $75,723,000 ($1.76 a share after preferred dividends) from $75,081,000 ($1.77, adjusted).

Stock Performance - 13-OCT-95

In the past 30 trading days, WGL's shares have increased 5%, compared to a 4% rise in the S&P 500. Average trading volume for the past five days was 47,400 shares, compared with the 40-day moving average of 39,364 shares.

Key Stock Statistics

Dividend Rate/Share	1.12	Shareholders	24,800
Shs. outstg. (M)	42.8	Market cap. (B)	$0.861
Avg. daily vol. (M)	0.044	Inst. holdings	22%
Tang. Bk. Value/Share	11.48	Insider holdings	NA
Beta	0.34		

Value of $10,000 invested 5 years ago: $ 18,092

Fiscal Year Ending Sep. 30

	1995	% Change	1994	% Change	1993	% Change
Revenues (Million $)						
1Q	242.9	-10%	271.2	NM	273.1	18%
2Q	353.6	-14%	410.2	7%	383.8	26%
3Q	131.9	NM	130.9	-6%	139.8	21%
4Q	—	—	102.6	5%	97.53	2%
Yr.	—	—	914.9	2%	894.3	20%
Income (Million $)						
1Q	27.73	-8%	30.25	8%	27.98	11%
2Q	53.44	-3%	54.96	12%	49.28	14%
3Q	-5.44	NM	-10.13	NM	-6.11	NM
4Q	—	—	-14.62	NM	-16.07	NM
Yr.	—	—	60.46	10%	55.08	5%
Earnings Per Share ($)						
1Q	0.65	-10%	0.72	6%	0.68	10%
2Q	1.25	-5%	1.31	10%	1.20	12%
3Q	-0.14	NM	-0.25	NM	-0.15	NM
4Q	—	—	-0.36	NM	-0.39	NM
Yr.	—	—	1.42	8%	1.31	4%

Next earnings report expected: late October

Washington Gas Light

Business Summary - 16-OCT-95

Washington Gas Light provides natural gas service to metropolitan Washington, D.C., and to adjoining areas of suburban Maryland and northern Virginia. Portions of West Virginia are served by a distribution subsidiary. The population of the total area served is 4.4 million; at the end of fiscal 1994, 725,960 customer meters were being served. Breakdown by customer category of the 1,465 million therms sold in fiscal 1994 (up from 1,358 million therms in fiscal 1993) was:

Firm residential	46%
Firm commercial & industrial	30%
Interruptible commercial & industrial	16%
Interruptible electric generating facility	6%
Transportation	2%

WGL has several wholly owned active subsidiaries.

Shenandoah Gas Co. is engaged in the distribution and sale of natural gas at retail in the Shenandoah Valley, including Winchester, Middletown, Strasburg, Stephens City and New Market, Va.; and Martinsburg, West Va.

Frederick Gas Co. distributes and sells natural gas at retail in Frederick County, Maryland, in and near the city of Frederick. It also provides propane gas service in Frederick County.

Hampshire Gas Co. operates an underground gas storage field in the vicinity of Augusta, West Va., under a cost of service trariff regulated by the Federal Energy Regulatory Commission.

Washington Resources Group, Inc. (WRG) holds and manages the company's non-utility investments, except for Crab Run Gas Co. Its operations have been scaled back significantly, as WGL focuses on natural gas distribution operations. The subsidiaries of WRG include: Washington Gas Energy Systems, an energy conservation company slated for sale in fiscal 1995; Brandywine Estates, Inc., a partnership with land development interests in Maryland; Advanced Marketing Concepts, Inc., provider of energy-related home improvements; and Crab Run Gas Co., which explores for and produces natural gas.

Important Developments

May '95—A hearing examiner appointed by the Virginia regulatory commission recommended a retail rate increase for the company of $6.9 million and return on equity of 11.50%. A final decision on the rate increase is subject to the commission's review.

Capitalization

Long Term Debt: $379,040,000 (6/95).
Serial Preferred Stock: $28,477,000.

Per Share Data ($) (Year Ended Sep. 30)

	1994	1993	1992	1991	1990	1989
Tangible Bk. Val.	11.48	11.01	10.64	10.30	10.13	9.81
Earnings	1.42	1.31	1.27	1.14	1.26	1.21
Dividends	1.10	1.08	1.06	1.04	1.00	0.96
Payout Ratio	78%	82%	84%	91%	80%	79%
Prices - High	21¼	22⅞	19⅝	17¼	16¼	15⅞
- Low	16	18⅛	15⅝	13¾	13¼	11⅞
P/E Ratio - High	15	17	15	15	13	13
- Low	11	14	12	12	11	10

Income Statement Analysis (Million $)

	1994	%Chg	1993	%Chg	1992	%Chg	1991
Revs.	915	2%	894	20%	746	7%	698
Depr.	43.5	9%	39.8	7%	37.2	3%	36.1
Maint.	35.8	7%	33.5	7%	31.4	2%	30.9
Fxd. Chgs. Cov.	3.9	NM	3.9	2%	3.8	9%	3.5
Constr. Credits	0.2	NM	0.0	-88%	0.2	-68%	0.5
Eff. Tax Rate	38%	—	38%	—	37%	—	37%
Net Inc.	60.5	10%	55.1	6%	52.2	13%	46.4

Balance Sheet & Other Fin. Data (Million $)

	1994	1993	1992	1991	1990	1989
Gross Prop.	1,516	1,405	1,313	1,240	1,186	1,109
Cap. Exp.	120	101	88.0	82.0	94.0	116
Net Prop.	995	921	865	821	783	729
Capitalization:						
LT Debt	342	348	294	263	280	297
% LT Debt	40	42	39	37	40	42
Pfd.	28.5	28.5	28.6	28.6	28.6	28.6
% Pfd.	3.30	3.40	3.80	4.10	4.00	4.10
Common	486	458	433	412	399	381
% Common	57	55	57	59	56	54
Total Cap.	997	930	852	783	776	779

Ratio Analysis

	1994	1993	1992	1991	1990	1989
Oper. Ratio	89.9	90.4	89.0	89.9	89.7	90.9
% Earn. on Net Prop.	9.6	9.6	9.8	8.8	10.0	10.0
% Ret. on Revs.	6.6	6.2	7.0	6.6	6.8	6.3
% Ret. On Invest.Cap	9.6	9.4	9.8	9.5	10.1	9.9
% Return On Com.Eqty	12.5	12.1	12.0	11.1	12.5	13.0

Dividend Data —Dividends have been paid since 1852. A two-for-one stock split was effected in May 1995. A dividend reinvestment plan is available.

Amt. of Div. $	Date Decl.	Ex-Div. Date	Stock of Record	Payment Date
0.555	Dec. 14	Jan. 04	Jan. 10	Feb. 01 '95
0.560	Mar. 29	Apr. 04	Apr. 10	May. 01 '95
2-for-1	—	May. 02	Apr. 20	May. 01 '95
0.280	Jun. 20	Jul. 06	Jul. 10	Aug. 01 '95
0.280	Sep. 26	Oct. 05	Oct. 10	Nov. 01 '95

Data as orig. reptd.; bef. results of disc opers. and/or spec. items. Per share data adj. for stk. divs. as of ex-div. date. E-Estimated. NA-Not Available. NM-Not Meaningful. NR-Not Ranked.

Office—1100 H St., NW, Washington, DC 20080. **Tel**—(703) 750-4440. **Chrmn & CEO**—P. J. Maher. **Pres & COO**—J. H. DeGraffenreidt, Jr. **SVP & CFO**—J. M. Schepis. **Secy**—D. V. Pope. **Treas**—Elizabeth M. Arnold. **Investor Contact**—Maria Frazzini. **Dirs**—M. Barnes, F. J. Brinkman, D. J. Callahan III, O. W. Darden, J. H. DeGraffenreidt Jr, M. J. Estrin, S. W. Fantle, P. J. Maher, K. H. Williams, S. G. Yeonas. **Transfer Agent & Registrar**—Bank of New York, NYC. **Incorporated** in Washington, D.C., in 1848, and in Virginia in 1953. **Empl**-2,647. **S&P Analyst:** M.E.P.

STANDARD & POOR'S

STOCK REPORTS

Washington Post

NYSE Symbol **WPO**
In S&P MidCap 400

16-OCT-95 **Industry:** Publishing

Summary: WPO publishes The Washington Post and Newsweek magazine, operates TV stations and cable systems, provides education and database services, and has interests in newsprint.

S&P Opinion: Accumulate (★★★★)

Recent Price • 302
52 Wk Range • 315-237½
Yield • 1.5%
12-Mo. P/E • 17.5

Quantitative Evaluations

Outlook
(1 Lowest—5 Highest)
• **2+**

Fair Value
• **285⅞**

Risk
• **Low**

Earn./Div. Rank
• **B+**

Technical Eval.
• **Bearish** since 11/94

Rel. Strength Rank
(1 Lowest—99 Highest)
• **69**

Insider Activity
• **Neutral**

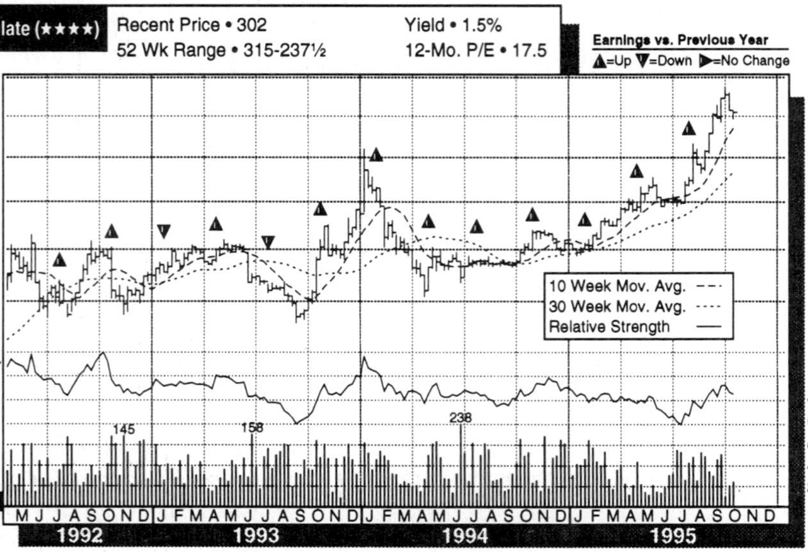

Overview - 16-OCT-95

Revenues are expected to rise 8% in 1995, boosted by gains in TV advertising. Newspaper, magazine and cable revenues should also improve, but the gains from these segments are expected to be modest. Ongoing cost controls, combined with the improved revenues, will bolster profitability. Newspaper and magazine margins will be pressured by higher paper prices, but the firmer pricing should lead to another significant advance in equity contributions. A stronger rise in share net will reflect fewer average shares outstanding. The pace of earnings growth should slow in 1996, due to a less dramatic improvement in equity earnings and continuing pressure on newspaper margins from high newsprint prices and a lackluster operating climate for the flagship newspaper.

Valuation - 16-OCT-95

Although the stock has outperformed the market, advancing nearly 13% since our last appraisal at the end of July, there appears to be room for further gains. Operating prospects are favorable, although magazine and newspaper earnings gains will be relatively modest going forward. The P/E ratio of nearly 18 on trailing 12-month earnings is not out of line with historical averages. Management is building value through additions to WPO's TV and cable holdings. The cable industry is undergoing a period of rapid consolidation, and WPO may eventually decide to sell. The stock's price does not yet reflect the true value of the company's cable assets, which could bring over $87 a share.

Key Stock Statistics

S&P EPS Est. 1995	17.65	Tang. Bk. Value/Share	53.10
P/E on S&P Est. 1995	17.1	Beta	0.76
S&P EPS Est. 1996	18.75	Shareholders	1,500
Dividend Rate/Share	4.40	Market cap. (B)	$ 3.3
Shs. outstg. (M)	11.0	Inst. holdings	51%
Avg. daily vol. (M)	0.005	Insider holdings	NA

Value of $10,000 invested 5 years ago: $ 11,945

Fiscal Year Ending Dec. 31

	1995	% Change	1994	% Change	1993	% Change
Revenues (Million $)						
1Q	401.5	12%	358.5	NM	362.0	10%
2Q	437.0	8%	404.8	7%	376.7	NM
3Q	—	—	399.8	10%	364.1	4%
4Q	—	—	450.9	14%	395.7	NM
Yr.	—	—	1,614	8%	1,498	3%
Income (Million $)						
1Q	43.90	52%	28.81	1%	28.51	45%
2Q	51.51	25%	41.26	9%	37.99	-17%
3Q	—	—	47.45	6%	44.84	63%
4Q	—	—	52.15	23%	42.48	22%
Yr.	—	—	169.7	10%	153.8	20%
Earnings Per Share ($)						
1Q	3.91	59%	2.46	2%	2.42	46%
2Q	4.65	31%	3.54	10%	3.23	-17%
3Q	E3.99	-3%	4.13	8%	3.82	64%
4Q	E5.10	12%	4.56	26%	3.63	23%
Yr.	E17.65	20%	14.65	12%	13.10	21%

Next earnings report expected: late October

Washington Post

Business Summary - 16-OCT-95

Contributions by business segment in 1994 were:

	Sales	Profits
Newspaper publishing	45%	49%
Magazine publishing	21%	5%
Broadcasting	16%	39%
Cable television	11%	15%
Other	7%	-8%

The Newspaper division publishes The Washington Post, the largest newspaper in Washington, D.C., with an average circulation of 821,956 daily and 1,152,441 Sunday in 1994; the Washington Post national weekly edition; the Gaithersburg Gazette (84%-owned), which publishes 14 weeklies in Maryland; and the Everett Herald (Everett, Wash.). The division also includes newspaper feature syndication and other publications and a 94%-owned newsprint warehousing firm.

The Magazine division publishes Newsweek, with weekly average circulation of about 3.1 million. It also publishes three international editions.

The Broadcast division operates six VHF network-affiliated television stations: WFSB in Hartford, WDIV in Detroit, WPLG in Miami, WJXT in Jacksonville, KPRC in Houston and KSAT in San Antonio. The Cable Television division includes 53 systems serving over 500,000 subscribers in 15 midwestern, western and southern states. The company also owns the Stanley H. Kaplan Educational Centers and Legi-Slate, a database service. Significant interests are owned in two newsprint concerns, a timberlands company, The International Herald Tribune (50%), the Los Angeles Times-Washington Post News Service (50%) and Cowles Media (28%).

Important Developments

Aug. '95—WPO agreed to acquire four cable systems from Time Warner and from Cox Communications serving 65,000 subscribers for about $120 million. WPO noted that the acquisition is part of its long-range strategy to increase cable holdings in classic, non-urban markets.

May '95—WPO announced plans to build a new printing plant for The Washington Post in Maryland that will replace its Virginia presses. The $250 million project will provide full-color printing by 1998.

Capitalization

Long Term Debt: None (6/95).
Class A Common Stock: 1,843,250 shs. ($1 par); conv. sh.-for sh.-into Class B com.; elects 70% of directors; owned by the Graham family (57%) & related trusts.
Class B Common Stock: 9,160,023 shs. ($1 par); limited voting rights.
Berkshire Hathaway Inc. owns 17%.
Institutions hold a total of 51%.
Shareholders of record: 1,467.

Per Share Data ($) (Year Ended Dec. 31)

	1994	1993	1992	1991	1990	1989
Tangible Bk. Val.	54.16	66.44	56.58	51.02	48.16	49.14
Cash Flow	22.19	19.55	17.09	16.23	20.12	20.12
Earnings	14.65	13.10	10.80	10.00	14.45	15.50
Dividends	4.20	4.20	4.20	4.20	4.00	1.84
Payout Ratio	29%	32%	39%	42%	27%	12%
Prices - High	284	256½	246	251	295½	311
- Low	221¾	212	191½	169	167	204
P/E Ratio - High	19	20	23	25	20	20
- Low	15	16	18	17	12	13

Income Statement Analysis (Million $)

	1994	%Chg	1993	%Chg	1992	%Chg	1991
Revs.	1,614	8%	1,498	3%	1,451	5%	1,380
Oper. Inc.	362	15%	315	3%	306	12%	273
Depr.	87.3	15%	75.9	2%	74.3	NM	74.1
Int. Exp.	5.6	12%	5.0	-22%	6.4	-64%	17.8
Pretax Inc.	287	9%	263	17%	224	18%	190
Eff. Tax Rate	41%	—	42%	—	43%	—	38%
Net Inc.	170	10%	154	20%	128	8%	119

Balance Sheet & Other Fin. Data (Million $)

	1994	1993	1992	1991	1990	1989
Cash	142	430	328	280	277	365
Curr. Assets	376	626	525	472	472	553
Total Assets	1,697	1,623	1,568	1,488	1,497	1,532
Curr. Liab.	273	259	282	288	296	270
LT Debt	50.0	52.0	52.0	52.0	127	152
Common Eqty.	1,127	1,087	993	924	905	942
Total Cap.	1,206	1,173	1,092	1,024	1,114	1,166
Cap. Exp.	75.0	80.0	59.0	56.0	72.0	81.0
Cash Flow	257	230	202	193	243	260

Ratio Analysis

	1994	1993	1992	1991	1990	1989
Curr. Ratio	1.4	2.4	1.9	1.6	1.6	2.0
% LT Debt of Cap.	4.2	4.4	4.7	5.1	11.4	13.0
% Net Inc.of Revs.	10.5	10.3	8.8	8.6	12.1	13.7
% Ret. on Assets	10.4	9.7	8.4	8.0	11.8	13.6
% Ret. on Equity	15.6	14.8	13.3	13.0	19.4	22.2

Dividend Data —Cash has been paid each year since 1956.

Amt. of Div. $	Date Decl.	Ex-Div. Date	Stock of Record	Payment Date
1.050	Sep. 08	Oct. 03	Oct. 07	Nov. 11 '94
1.100	Jan. 12	Jan. 17	Jan. 23	Feb. 10 '95
1.100	Mar. 09	Apr. 03	Apr. 07	May. 12 '95
1.100	Jul. 13	Jul. 20	Jul. 24	Aug. 11 '95
1.100	Sep. 14	Oct. 04	Oct. 06	Nov. 10 '95

Data as orig. reptd.; bef. results of disc. opers. and/or spec. items. Per share data adj. for stk. divs. as of ex-div. date. E-Estimated. NA-Not Available. NM-Not Meaningful. NR-Not Ranked.

Office—1150 15th St., N.W., Washington, D.C. 20071. **Tel**—(202) 334-6000. **Chrmn & CEO**—D. E. Graham. **Pres**—A. G. Spoon. **VP & Secy**—D. M. Daniels. **VP-Fin & Investor Contact**—John B. Morse (202) 334-6662. **Dirs**—J. E. Burke, M. Cohen, G. J. Gillespie III, R. E. Gomory, D. E. Graham, K. Graham, D. R. Keough, B. S. Preiskel, W. J. Ruane, R. D. Simmons, A. G. Spoon, G. W. Wilson. **Transfer Agent & Registrar**—First Chicago Trust Co. of New York, NYC. **Incorporated** in Delaware in 1947. **Empl**-6,800. **S&P Analyst:** William H. Donald

Watts Industries

NYSE Symbol WTS In S&P MidCap 400

Price	Range	P–E Ratio	Dividend	Yield	S&P Ranking	Beta
Sep. 27'95	1995					
24½	25⅝–19¾	16	0.25	1.0%	A–	1.24

Summary

This company makes an extensive line of valves for the water safety and flow control, water quality, industrial and other markets. Acquisitions are an important element in the company's growth strategy. Earnings have been in a steady uptrend since fiscal 1993. Sales and earnings should increase again in fiscal 1996. Trading in the Class A common shares moved to the NYSE from The Nasdaq Stock Market in July.

Current Outlook

Earnings for the fiscal year ending June 30, 1996, are estimated at $1.70 a share, up from fiscal 1995's $1.54.

The $0.06¼ quarterly dividend may be increased in fiscal 1996.

Sales for fiscal 1996 are expected to rise, reflecting acquisitions, an upturn in demand from aerospace, growth in oil and gas business and a rebound in plumbing and water quality products. Gross margins should expand somewhat on an improvement at Jameco Industries, better pricing, and more stable raw material costs. Assuming well-controlled SG&A expense, and only small increases in interest expense and the tax rate, earnings should increase again in fiscal 1996.

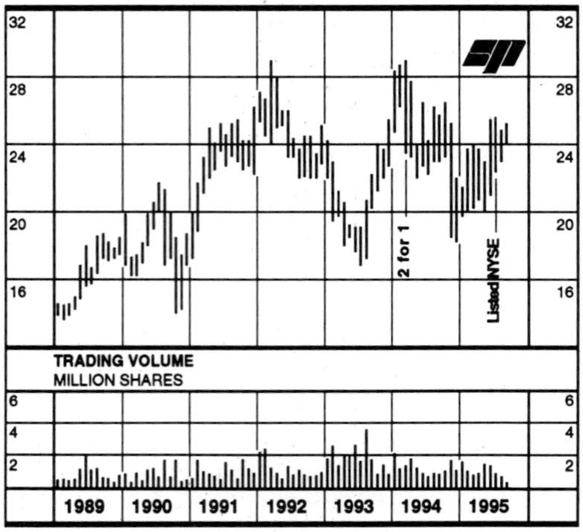

Net Sales (Million $)

Quarter:	1994–95	1993–94	1992–93	1991–92
Sep.	153	131	110	94
Dec.	159	128	114	108
Mar.	174	134	120	110
Jun.	172	127	123	111
	658	519	466	424

Sales for the fiscal year ended June 30, 1995 (preliminary), rose 27% from those of fiscal 1994. Margins narrowed, and the gain in net income was held to 11.5%. Share earnings (fully diluted) were $1.54, versus $1.38.

Common Share Earnings ($)

Quarter:	1994–95	1993–94	1992–93	1991–92
Sep.	0.38	0.36	0.33	0.33
Dec.	0.38	0.36	0.17	0.33
Mar.	0.43	0.37	0.29	0.36
Jun.	0.35	0.30	0.23	0.28
	1.54	1.38	1.01	1.30

Important Developments

Jul. 5'95— Trading in the Class A common shares moved to the NYSE from The Nasdaq Stock Market.

Apr. '95— Watts said it had agreed to form a joint venture (60% owned) with the Suzhou Valve Factory of the People's Republic of Chine (PRC). Suzhou Valve Factory, which had 1994 sales of $30 million, makes valve products that are sold primarily to the petrochemical and industrial markets in China and for export. The transaction is the company's second joint venture in China. Closing, subject to Chinese governmental approval, was expected in May.

Mar. '95— The company acquired Palmsdale, Calif.-based Anderson-Barrows, a manfacturer of valves and pipe products to home repair markets, with 1994 sales of $21 million.

Next earnings report expected in mid-October.

Per Share Data ($)

Yr. End Jun. 30	1995	1994	1993	[1]1992	[1]1991	[1]1990	1989	1988	[1]1987
Tangible Bk. Val.	**NA**	9.23	8.29	8.60	7.56	5.88	5.32	4.75	4.08
Cash Flow	**NA**	2.14	1.70	1.81	1.74	1.51	1.24	1.02	0.80
Earnings[2]	**1.54**	1.38	1.01	1.30	1.22	1.09	0.91	0.75	0.58
Dividends	**0.24**	0.20	0.15	0.13	0.11	0.09	0.07	0.05	0.03
Payout Ratio	**16%**	14%	15%	11%	9%	8%	8%	7%	5%
Prices[3]—High	**25⅝**	29	25½	29	26¼	21¾	18¾	14½	11⅞
Low	**19¾**	18¼	16⅞	22	17¼	14	13⅝	9¼	6⅞
P/E Ratio—	**17–13**	21–13	25–17	22–17	22–14	20–13	21–15	19–12	21–12

Data as orig. reptd. Adj. for stk. div. of 100% Mar. 1994. **1.** Refl. merger or acq. **2.** Bef. spec. item(s) of -0.11 in 1993. **3.** Cal. yr. NA-Not Available.

Income Data (Million $)

Year Ended Jun. 30	Revs.	Oper. Inc.	% Oper. Inc. of Revs.	Cap. Exp.	Depr.	Int. Exp.	Net Bef. Taxes	Eff. Tax Rate	[2]Net Inc.	% Net Inc. of Revs.	Cash Flow
1994	**519**	**97.0**	**18.7**	**19.9**	**22.4**	**8.78**	**67.3**	**39.1%**	**41.0**	**7.9**	**63.0**
1993	466	82.7	17.8	25.8	20.6	9.15	49.1	38.1%	30.4	6.5	51.0
[1]1992	424	79.2	18.7	29.4	14.7	7.88	59.9	38.9%	36.6	8.6	51.3
[1]1991	351	67.8	19.3	14.1	13.6	5.85	51.3	38.3%	31.7	9.0	45.3
[1]1990	292	57.3	19.6	33.1	10.7	5.92	44.2	37.4%	27.7	9.5	38.4
1989	224	46.5	20.8	16.5	8.4	3.06	37.8	39.0%	23.0	10.3	31.4
1988	181	38.9	21.5	15.4	6.8	2.13	31.1	39.1%	18.9	10.4	25.7
[1]1987	146	33.4	23.0	11.4	5.4	1.84	27.6	48.2%	[3]14.3	9.8	19.7
1986	137	28.4	20.7	11.7	4.4	1.86	24.2	47.2%	12.8	9.3	16.9

Balance Sheet Data (Million $)

Jun. 30	Cash	Curr. Assets	Curr. Liab.	Curr. Ratio	Total Assets	% Ret. on Assets	Long Term Debt	Common Equity	Total Cap.	% LT Debt of Cap.	% Ret. on Equity
1994	**65**	**321**	**74.3**	**4.3**	**559**	**7.5**	**97.0**	**362**	**475**	**20.5**	**11.8**
1993	83	301	78.5	3.8	536	6.0	101.0	335	450	22.5	9.3
1992	109	295	54.9	5.4	469	8.6	95.6	315	412	23.2	12.8
1991	76	230	44.8	5.1	353	9.6	65.3	236	307	21.3	15.1
1990	42	181	42.4	4.3	287	10.4	65.4	171	243	26.9	17.6
1989	79	175	30.0	5.8	247	10.9	65.2	144	216	30.2	17.3
1988	40	119	23.2	5.1	177	11.6	23.7	123	153	15.5	16.6
1987	42	100	15.2	6.6	148	10.4	22.7	105	133	17.1	15.3
1986	17	72	12.8	5.6	115	NA	22.9	76	102	22.4	NA

Data as orig. reptd. **1.** Refl. merger or acq. **2.** Bef. spec. item(s). **3.** Refl. acctg. change. NA-Not Available.

Business Summary

Watts Industries, Inc. designs, makes and sells an extensive line of valves for the plumbing and heating, water quality, flow control, steam, industrial and oil and gas markets.

Product lines include: 1) safety relief valves, regulators, ball valves and flow control valves for water service primarily in residential and commercial environments and specialty bronze valves and fittings used in underground water service connections; 2) backflow preventers to prevent contamination of potable water; 3) steam regulators and control devices for industrial HVAC and naval/marine applications; 4) ball valves, pneumatic and electric actuators, relief valves, check valves and butterfly valves for industrial applications; 5) valves for the oil and gas industry; and 6) butterfly valves used in water distribution, treatment and wastewater management.

Water service and water quality valve products account for over 50% of total sales. Foreign sales in fiscal 1994 provided 29% of the total, and 16% of operating income.

Watts operates its own automated foundries for casting bronze component parts and has extensive facilities for machining bronze, brass, iron and steel components and assembling them into finished valves. It operates manufacturing plants, warehouses, product development facilities or sales offices at 20 locations in the U.S., four in Canada, 12 in Europe, and one in Asia through a 60% interest in a joint venture in China.

An important element in Watts' growth strategy is to acquire companies in related businesses. Since 1984, the company has acquired 28 valve companies or product lines. These acquisitions accounted for 60% of total sales in fiscal 1994.

Dividend Data

Cash dividends have been paid since 1986.

Amt of Divd. $	Date Decl.	Ex-divd. Date	Stock of Record	Payment Date
0.05½	Nov. 4	Nov. 28	Dec. 2	Dec. 16'94
0.06¼	Jan. 24	Feb. 23	Mar. 1	Mar. 15'95
0.06¼	Apr. 25	May 25	Jun. 1	Jun. 15'95
0.06¼	Aug. 8	Aug. 30	Sep. 1	Sep. 15'95

Capitalization

Long Term Debt: $128,791,000 (3/95).

Class A Common Stock: 18,071,022 shs. ($0.10 par); one vote per sh.
Institutions hold about 94%.
Shareholders of record: 295 (9/94).

Class B Common Stock: 11,472,470 shs. ($0.10 par); conv. sh.-for-sh. into Cl. A; 10 votes per sh. Officers & directors control about 85% of the company's voting power.

Office—815 Chestnut St., North Andover, MA 01845. **Tel**—(508) 688-1811. **Chrmn, Pres & CEO**—T. P. Horne. **VP, CFO, Secy, Treas & Investor Contact**—Kenneth J. McAvoy. **Dirs**—D. A. Bloss Sr., N. T. Herndon, F. B. Horne, T. P. Horne, W. E. Lane, K. J. McAvoy, G. W. Moran, D. J. Murphy III. **Registrar & Transfer Agent**—First National Bank of Boston. **Incorporated** in Delaware in 1985. **Empl**—4,850.

 Leo Larkin

STANDARD & POOR'S

STOCK REPORTS

Wausau Paper Mills

NASDAQ Symbol **WSAU**

In S&P MidCap 400

20-JUL-95

Industry: Paper/Products

Summary: Wausau manufactures writing and printing paper at two mills located in Wisconsin and New Hampshire, and specialty paper at another Wisconsin mill.

S&P Opinion: Hold (★★★)

Recent Price • 23¼

52 Wk Range • 25-19¾

Yield • 1.1%

12-Mo. P/E • 20.2

Quantitative Evaluations

Outlook (1 Lowest—5 Highest)
• 3−

Fair Value
• 22⅞

Risk
• Average

Earn./Div. Rank
• A

Technical Eval.
• Bullish since 6/95

Rel. Strength Rank (1 Lowest—99 Highest)
• 24

Insider Activity
• NA

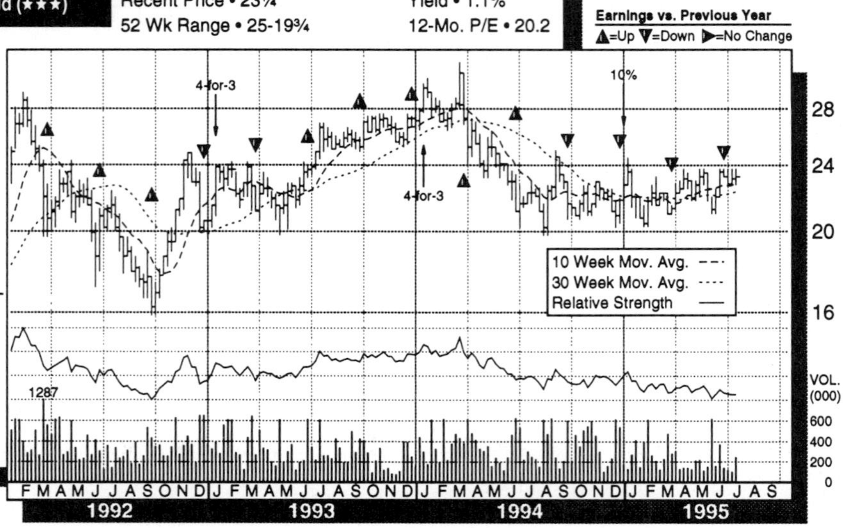

Overview - 20-JUL-95

Solid sales growth should continue through fiscal 1996, boosted by increased shipment volume and higher product prices. The gain in shipment volume will be related to strong demand for printing and writing paper, geographic expansion stemming from the April 1993 acquisition of a paper mill in Groveton, N.H., and product line introductions, extensions and upgrades. Although sales have started to slow in the specialty paper area, the sector should benefit from the recent drop in interest rates, which is likely to spark the economy. Despite overall favorable sales trends, an earnings decline is anticipated in fiscal 1995, as excessive pulp prices should continue to far outweigh cost control efforts. Earnings should begin to turn around in fiscal 1996, given our assumption of stabilizing pulp prices in that period.

Valuation - 20-JUL-95

Wausau's shares have far underperformed the market since early 1994, as investor sentiment deteriorated on increases in pulp prices and the resultant decline in WSAU's earnings. Given those operating difficulties, the stock might seem richly priced at about 16X our fiscal 1996 estimate, but we would hold the shares based on the company's longer term prospects. We expect Wausau's earnings to turn around once pulp prices begin to ease, even if industry trends slow. Sales should remain solid in slower times, on further geographic expansion, product line introductions, and WSAU's wide ranging status as a supplier of choice.

Key Stock Statistics

S&P EPS Est. 1995	1.10	Tang. Bk. Value/Share	7.85
P/E on S&P Est. 1995	21.1	Beta	1.28
S&P EPS Est. 1996	1.40	Shareholders	1,900
Dividend Rate/Share	0.25	Market cap. (B)	$0.655
Shs. outstg. (M)	29.5	Inst. holdings	53%
Avg. daily vol. (M)	0.034	Insider holdings	NA

Value of $10,000 invested 5 years ago: $ 35,138

Fiscal Year Ending Aug. 31

	1995	% Change	1994	% Change	1993	% Change
Revenues (Million $)						
1Q	126.3	16%	108.7	15%	94.79	-2%
2Q	119.1	22%	97.71	12%	87.27	NM
3Q	135.6	25%	108.7	8%	100.3	6%
4Q	—	—	111.4	12%	99.5	7%
Yr.	—	—	426.5	12%	381.8	3%
Income (Million $)						
1Q	8.60	-22%	11.06	38%	8.04	-21%
2Q	7.12	-22%	9.11	7%	8.54	NM
3Q	8.74	-30%	12.52	6%	11.85	11%
4Q	—	—	9.36	-12%	10.68	1%
Yr.	—	—	42.05	10%	38.37	-4%
Earnings Per Share ($)						
1Q	0.29	-22%	0.38	38%	0.27	-21%
2Q	0.24	-22%	0.31	8%	0.29	-2%
3Q	0.30	-28%	0.42	4%	0.40	12%
4Q	E0.27	—	0.32	-12%	0.36	NM
Yr.	E1.10	—	1.42	9%	1.30	-4%

Next earnings report expected: late September

Wausau Paper Mills

20-JUL-95

Business Summary - 20-JUL-95

Wausau Paper Mills Company manufactures and sells paper through its printing and writing division and its Rhinelander Paper Co. subsidiary. In addition, wholly owned Wausau Papers International Inc. acts as a foreign sales corporation and markets company products outside the U.S.

The printing and writing division produces fine printing, writing and specialty papers at mills in Brokaw, Wis., and Groveton, N.H. The April 1993 acquisition of the Groveton facility boosted the division's production capacity 50% and recycled capacity sixfold. Papers are sold to a large network of paper distributors and converters, which in turn sell these products to commercial printers, in-plant print shops and quick print copy centers. End uses include printed advertising, corporate reports, office papers and converted products such as envelopes and announcements. About 70% of the division's fine printing and writing paper is colored paper.

The Rhinelander Paper Co. subsidiary manufactures lightweight, dense, technical specialty papers, sold directly to converters and end users. Rhinelander is the leading U.S. maker of backing papers for the pressure-sensitive labeling industry, its largest product category. Other products include lightweight papers used for sterilized medical packaging, and specialty papers used in food packaging such as microwaveable popcorn, cereal and other convenience food packaging.

About 55% of pulp consumed by the Brokaw mill is produced internally from aspen, which is in abundant supply. The balance used by Wausau is purchased from pulp mills throughout the U.S. and Canada. Recycled, de-inked fiber with a high content of post-consumer waste is also purchased from domestic suppliers.

Important Developments

Jun. '95—The company reported that on the benefits of higher paper prices and very brisk order levels for printing and writing products, sales were ahead 25% on a year over year basis in fiscal 1995's third quarter, reaching an all-time record for WSAU. The record sales and shipment performance (shipments up 15% to 103,300 tons) was achieved despite a marked slowdown in orders for Rhinelander's specialty technical products, which forced the curtailment of production schedules at two of the unit's four machines. However, despite the overall favorable sales performance, excessive increases in pulp costs over the past year caused a 30% year over year decline in Wausau's earnings for the quarter.

Capitalization

Long Term Debt: $41,092,000 (5/95).

Per Share Data ($) (Year Ended Aug. 31)

	1994	1993	1992	1991	1990	1989
Tangible Bk. Val.	7.27	6.18	5.60	4.40	3.53	3.14
Cash Flow	2.02	1.81	1.81	1.48	0.92	0.96
Earnings	1.42	1.30	1.35	1.03	0.54	0.71
Dividends	0.16	0.19	0.17	0.15	0.17	0.11
Payout Ratio	12%	15%	13%	15%	32%	15%
Prices - High	31⅞	27⅝	29⅜	20¾	9⅛	8⅛
- Low	19¾	19¾	15⅞	7½	6	5¾
P/E Ratio - High	22	21	22	20	17	11
- Low	14	15	12	7	11	8

Income Statement Analysis (Million $)

	1994	%Chg	1993	%Chg	1992	%Chg	1991
Revs.	427	12%	382	3%	371	6%	350
Oper. Inc.	87.6	12%	78.3	3%	76.1	20%	63.2
Depr.	17.6	14%	15.4	12%	13.7	5%	13.1
Int. Exp.	2.2	62%	1.4	5%	1.3	-68%	4.1
Pretax Inc.	68.1	10%	61.8	NM	61.3	30%	47.0
Eff. Tax Rate	38%	—	38%	—	35%	—	35%
Net Inc.	42.1	10%	38.4	-4%	40.0	31%	30.5

Balance Sheet & Other Fin. Data (Million $)

	1994	1993	1992	1991	1990	1989
Cash	3.2	2.6	2.0	3.5	2.0	1.9
Curr. Assets	106	99	72.5	63.3	54.8	49.4
Total Assets	361	330	267	240	217	178
Curr. Liab.	46.1	41.9	38.2	43.7	31.3	28.4
LT Debt	30.3	42.7	22.7	30.7	55.4	37.5
Common Eqty.	215	183	166	130	104	92.0
Total Cap.	277	254	222	189	181	148
Cap. Exp.	44.0	51.0	59.0	53.0	98.0	108
Cash Flow	59.7	53.8	53.7	43.5	27.2	28.3

Ratio Analysis

	1994	1993	1992	1991	1990	1989
Curr. Ratio	2.3	2.4	1.9	1.5	1.8	1.7
% LT Debt of Cap.	10.9	16.8	10.2	16.3	30.5	25.3
% Net Inc.of Revs.	9.9	10.0	10.8	8.7	4.7	6.6
% Ret. on Assets	12.2	12.9	15.8	13.3	8.0	13.2
% Ret. on Equity	21.2	22.0	27.0	26.0	16.1	25.0

Dividend Data (Cash has been paid each year since 1960.)

Amt. of Div. $	Date Decl.	Ex-Div. Date	Stock of Record	Payment Date
0.060	Aug. 15	Sep. 12	Sep. 16	Oct. 03 '94
0.063	Dec. 19	Dec. 28	Jan. 04	Jan. 17 '95
10%	Dec. 19	Dec. 28	Jan. 04	Jan. 17 '95
0.063	Feb. 15	Mar. 07	Mar. 13	Apr. 03 '95
0.063	May. 30	Jun. 14	Jun. 16	Jul. 03 '95

Data as orig. reptd.; bef. results of disc. opers. and/or spec. items. Per share data adj. for stk. divs. as of ex-div. date. E-Estimated. NA-Not Available. NM-Not Meaningful. NR-Not Ranked.

Office—One Clark's Island, P.O. Box 1408, Wausau, WI 54402-1408. **Tel**—(715) 845-5266. **Chrmn & CEO**—S. W. Orr, Jr. **Pres & COO**—D. D. King. **VP-Fin, Secy, Treas & Investor Contact**—Steven A. Schmidt. **Dirs**—H. R. Baker, D. D. King, S. W. Orr, Jr., D. B. Smith, Jr., S. F. Staples, Jr. **Transfer Agent**—Harris Trust & Savings Bank, Chicago. **Incorporated** in Wisconsin in 1899. **Empl-** 1,695. **S&P Analyst:** Michael W. Jaffe

STANDARD & POOR'S

Weatherford Enterra Inc.

STOCK REPORTS

NYSE Symbol **WII**
In S&P MidCap 400

19-OCT-95

Industry:
Oil and Gas

Summary: Weatherford Enterra (formerly Weatherford International) is a diversified international energy service and manufacturing company serving the oil and gas industry.

Quantitative Evaluations

Outlook
(1 Lowest—5 Highest)
• **4**

Fair Value
• **30⅛**

Risk
• **Average**

Earn./Div. Rank
• **B-**

Technical Eval.
• **Bullish** since 11/94

Rel. Strength Rank
(1 Lowest—99 Highest)
• **28**

Insider Activity
• **NA**

Recent Price • 26¼
52 Wk Range • 52¼-16¼

Yield • Nil
12-Mo. P/E • 26.3

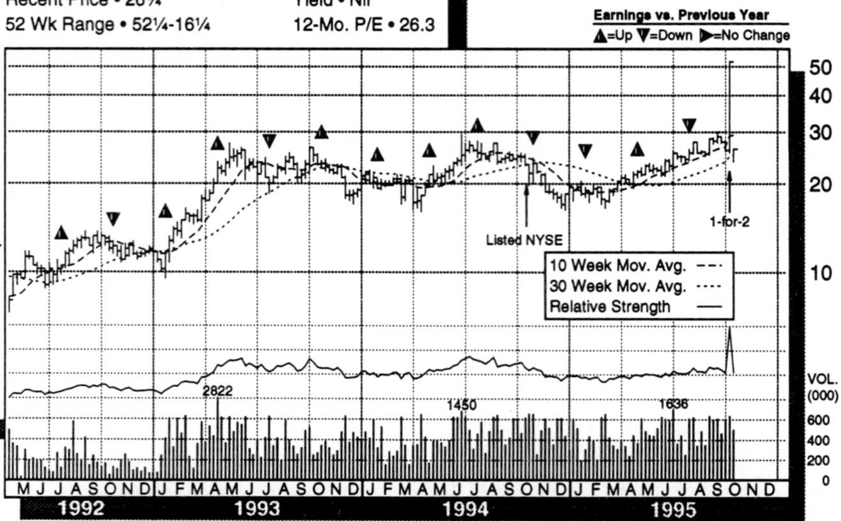

OPTIONS: ASE, CBOE

Business Profile - 18-OCT-95

WII significantly expanded its operations through its recent pooling-of-interests acquisition of oilfield services concern Enterra Corp. This represents the largest in a series of acquisitions in recent years, which have added more than 18 businesses since November 1991. Demand for WII's services and products depends primarily on drilling activity, which in turn is dependent on the level and volatility of oil and natural gas prices.

Operational Review - 18-OCT-95

Revenues in the 1995 first half rose 10%, year to year, despite the absence of rig growth. Results benefited from recent acquisitions, especially those with an international impact, where the most growth was seen. SG&A expenses were well controlled, and equity in income of affiliates and other income both rose. Net income advanced 8.7%, to $18,382,000 ($0.68 a share), from $16,903,000 ($0.62). Per-share figures are as adjusted for the October 1995 one-for-two reverse split.

Stock Performance - 13-OCT-95

In the past 30 trading days, WII's shares have declined 8%, compared to a 4% rise in the S&P 500. Average trading volume for the past five days was 99,100 shares, compared with the 40-day moving average of 131,385 shares.

Key Stock Statistics

Dividend Rate/Share	Nil	Shareholders	3,100
Shs. outstg. (M)	50.7	Market cap. (B)	$ 1.4
Avg. daily vol. (M)	0.132	Inst. holdings	36%
Tang. Bk. Value/Share	9.77	Insider holdings	NA
Beta	0.35		

Value of $10,000 invested 5 years ago: $ 26,250

Fiscal Year Ending Dec. 31

	1995	% Change	1994	% Change	1993	% Change
Revenues (Million $)						
1Q	101.0	14%	88.79	59%	55.69	15%
2Q	98.05	7%	91.60	7%	85.58	73%
3Q	—	—	94.60	13%	83.60	61%
4Q	—	—	97.31	8%	89.82	60%
Yr.	—	—	372.3	18%	314.7	53%
Income (Million $)						
1Q	9.16	28%	7.18	80%	4.00	50%
2Q	9.23	-5%	9.72	NM	1.29	-63%
3Q	—	—	5.00	-29%	7.00	115%
4Q	—	—	7.56	-7%	8.14	86%
Yr.	—	—	29.46	44%	20.44	48%
Earnings Per Share ($)						
1Q	0.34	31%	0.26	44%	0.18	50%
2Q	0.34	-6%	0.36	NM	0.04	-75%
3Q	—	—	0.18	-31%	0.26	86%
4Q	—	—	0.28	-13%	0.32	60%
Yr.	—	—	1.08	32%	0.82	32%

Next earnings report expected: late October

Weatherford Enterra Inc.

Business Summary - 19-OCT-95

Weatherford Enterra (formerly Weatherford International Inc.) is a diversified international manufacturing and energy service company that provides tubular running and fishing tool services, sells cementation products and other equipment, and rents specialized equipment and fishing tools to the oil and gas industry. It operates in two industry segments-oilfield services and rentals, and oilfield products and equipment. The company serves customers from over 200 locations worldwide. Revenue and operating profit contributions in 1994:

	Revs.	Profits
Services & rentals	44%	89%
Products & equipment	56%	11%

Historically, WII supplied tubular running services and cementation products, with extensive international operations. Beginning in 1991, it focused on improving its domestic market position and expanding in related oilfield service businesses. Since 1991, 18 businesses have been acquired, including eight in 1994.

Since April 1993, revenues have been balanced between domestic and international operations. International revenues accounted for 50% of the 1994 total, including 19% from Europe, 9% from Africa and 22% from other international markets, and contributed $28,157,000 of operating income.

WII focuses on tubular services (services and equipment used to "make up" threaded tubular connections and run tubulars), specialized rental tools such as drill pipe and tubing used in drilling and workover of wells, fishing tools to retrieve obstructions from wells, and cementation products used in well casing. A number of products are expendable. The company also makes and sells hydraulic pedestal mounted cranes, power tongs, kelly spinners and other tools.

WII also holds a 49% interest in three affiliates: Weatherford (Saudi Arabia), Ltd.; Weatherford/Al Rushaid, Ltd.; and Weatherford/Bin Hamoodah. WII's 1994 equity in the earnings of these affiliates was $1.2 million.

Important Developments

Oct. '95—WII completed its pooling-of-interests acquisition of oilfield services concern Enterra Corp. for approximately 24 million WII common shares (after giving effect to a one-for-two reverse stock split effected as part of the transaction) and changed its name from Weatherford International to Weatherford Enterra. Pro forma 1994 revenues, net income, and cash flow for the combined entities would have been $903 million, $70 million and $158 million, respectively.

Capitalization

Long Term Debt: $53,692,000 (3/95).

Per Share Data ($) (Year Ended Dec. 31)

	1994	1993	1992	1991	1990	1989
Tangible Bk. Val.	9.14	9.10	5.40	5.18	4.68	2.74
Cash Flow	2.48	1.86	1.34	0.48	0.92	0.58
Earnings	1.08	0.82	0.62	-0.42	0.40	-0.38
Dividends	Nil	Nil	Nil	Nil	Nil	Nil
Payout Ratio	Nil	Nil	Nil	Nil	Nil	Nil
Prices - High	29½	27½	13¾	14½	21¾	10¼
- Low	16	9½	7	8	8½	3½
P/E Ratio - High	27	34	22	NM	54	NM
- Low	15	12	11	NM	21	NM

Income Statement Analysis (Million $)

	1994	%Chg	1993	%Chg	1992	%Chg	1991
Revs.	372	18%	315	53%	206	NM	206
Oper. Inc.	81.1	38%	58.9	76%	33.4	-3%	34.3
Depr.	37.9	53%	24.7	72%	14.4	-19%	17.7
Int. Exp.	5.8	70%	3.4	73%	2.0	-25%	2.6
Pretax Inc.	40.2	38%	29.2	47%	19.9	NM	-0.3
Eff. Tax Rate	27%	—	30%	—	31%	—	NM
Net Inc.	29.5	45%	20.4	48%	13.8	NM	-6.8

Balance Sheet & Other Fin. Data (Million $)

	1994	1993	1992	1991	1990	1989
Cash	24.4	23.2	18.0	20.2	9.3	7.9
Curr. Assets	190	168	120	122	89.0	75.0
Total Assets	454	337	201	203	134	114
Curr. Liab.	100	71.3	44.0	47.9	30.4	44.3
LT Debt	55.7	15.7	23.4	24.7	15.7	10.1
Common Eqty.	282	234	108	102	62.0	31.0
Total Cap.	340	250	155	152	101	67.0
Cap. Exp.	51.0	107	18.1	22.0	8.6	5.5
Cash Flow	67.4	44.0	26.6	9.3	11.7	3.6

Ratio Analysis

	1994	1993	1992	1991	1990	1989
Curr. Ratio	1.9	2.4	2.7	2.5	2.9	1.7
% LT Debt of Cap.	16.4	6.3	15.1	16.3	15.6	15.1
% Net Inc.of Revs.	7.9	6.5	6.7	NM	4.5	NM
% Ret. on Assets	7.3	6.9	6.8	NM	4.9	NM
% Ret. on Equity	11.1	10.4	11.6	NM	10.4	NM

Dividend Data —Cash was last paid on the common in December 1982.

Data as orig. reptd.; bef. results of disc. opers. and/or spec. items. Per share data adj. for stk. divs. as of ex-div. date. E-Estimated. NA-Not Available. NM-Not Meaningful. NR-Not Ranked.

Office—1360 Post Oak Blvd., Suite 1000, Houston, TX 77056; P.O. Box 27608, Houston, TX 77227-7608. **Tel**—(713) 439-9400. **Chrmn, Pres & CEO**—P. Burguieres. **SVP, CFO, Treas & Investor Contact**—Norman W. Nolen. **SVP & Secy**—H. Suzanne Thomas. **Dirs**—T. N. Amonett, P. Burguieres, W. E. Greehey, J. A. Hill, J. W. Johnson, W. E. Macaulay, R. K. Moses, Jr., R. L. Parker, Sr., R. Rudolph Reinfrank, Roger M. Widmann. **Transfer Agent & Registrar**—American Stock Transfer and Trust Co., NYC. **Incorporated** in Delaware in 1970. **Empl-**6,000. **S&P Analyst:** Michael C. Barr

STANDARD & POOR'S

STOCK REPORTS

Wellman, Inc.

NYSE Symbol **WLM**
In S&P MidCap 400

22-SEP-95

Industry: Textiles

Summary: Wellman manufactures polyester textile fibers under the Fortrel brand name and recycled polyester fibers and plastic resins. The company is the world's largest plastics recycler.

S&P Opinion: Hold (★★★)

Recent Price • 26⅜ | Yield • 1.1%
52 Wk Range • 34½-23⅜ | 12-Mo. P/E • 10.9

Quantitative Evaluations

Outlook (1 Lowest—5 Highest)
• **5−**

Fair Value
• **32⅜**

Risk
• **Average**

Earn./Div. Rank
• **B+**

Technical Eval.
• **Bullish** since 10/92

Rel. Strength Rank (1 Lowest—99 Highest)
• **16**

Insider Activity
• **Neutral**

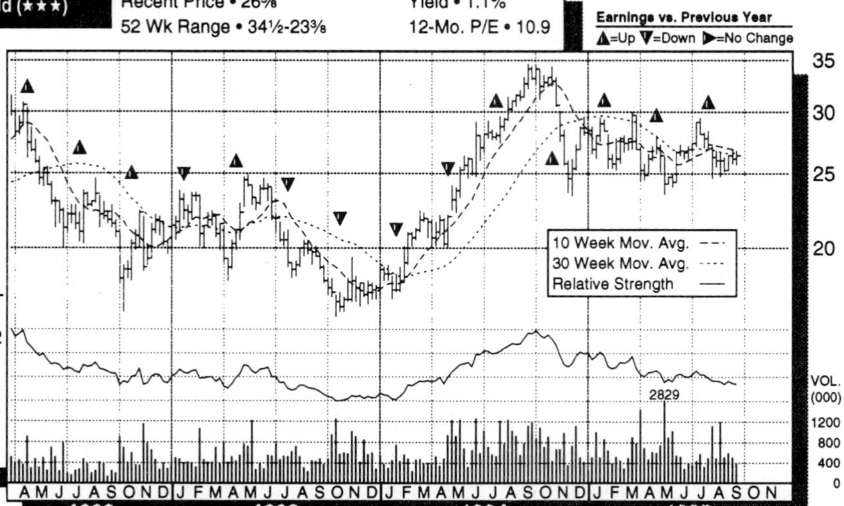

OPTIONS: NY

Overview - 22-SEP-95

We see sales and profits rising in 1995 and 1996, due mainly to price increases for polyester fibers and PET resins since 1994, in response to very strong industry demand and higher raw material costs. The startup of a 140-million-lb. expansion of PET resin capacity in mid-1995 and the pending acquisition of an European PET business will be positives. WLM should also achieve modest fiber volume growth as a result of a multi-year capacity expansion program announced in 1994, offsetting the curtailment of recycled polyester fiber production by 10% due to decreased availability of raw material. Capital spending could aggregate about $1 billion over the next five years, with a major portion for the construction by late 1998 of a major U.S. production facility for polyester fiber and PET resins. WLM plans to double its combined fiber and PET capacity by the year 2000.

Valuation - 22-SEP-95

The shares have been a poor performer in 1995, due to concerns regarding possible increased competition to polyester fiber from cotton and the impact of higher raw material costs. The company's strategy to aggressively expand PET capacity over the next few years is positive in view of the product's long-term growth of more than 10% per year, though other PET producers also plan major expansions. We recommend maintaining current holdings in view of the stock's modest P/E multiple.

Key Stock Statistics

S&P EPS Est. 1995	2.55	Tang. Bk. Value/Share	9.84
P/E on S&P Est. 1995	10.3	Beta	0.95
S&P EPS Est. 1996	3.00	Shareholders	1,200
Dividend Rate/Share	0.28	Market cap. (B)	$0.842
Shs. outstg. (M)	33.3	Inst. holdings	83%
Avg. daily vol. (M)	0.095	Insider holdings	NA

Value of $10,000 invested 5 years ago: $ 7,837

Fiscal Year Ending Dec. 31

	1995	% Change	1994	% Change	1993	% Change
Revenues (Million $)						
1Q	276.1	24%	222.6	7%	208.0	NM
2Q	294.0	28%	229.8	7%	214.0	4%
3Q	—	—	233.0	11%	210.2	-1%
4Q	—	—	250.8	25%	200.9	NM
Yr.	—	—	936.1	11%	842.1	2%
Income (Million $)						
1Q	22.74	101%	11.30	-48%	21.80	75%
2Q	21.60	34%	16.09	26%	12.80	-11%
3Q	—	—	17.32	147%	7.00	-45%
4Q	—	—	20.10	NM	-1.20	NM
Yr.	—	—	64.80	60%	40.45	-23%
Earnings Per Share ($)						
1Q	0.67	97%	0.34	-48%	0.66	74%
2Q	0.64	33%	0.48	23%	0.39	-11%
3Q	E0.62	19%	0.52	148%	0.21	-46%
4Q	E0.62	3%	0.60	NM	-0.04	NM
Yr.	E2.55	31%	1.94	58%	1.23	-23%

Next earnings report expected: late October

Wellman, Inc.

Business Summary - 19-SEP-95

Wellman manufactures polyester textile fibers and also produces recycled polyester and nylon fibers and plastic resins. WLM is the largest U.S. recycler of postconsumer plastics and the largest producer of polyester stable fiber made from recycled feedstocks consisting of postconsumer polyethylene terephthalate (PET) soft-drink bottles and fiber producer wastes. Contributions to sales in recent years were:

	1994	1993
Fibers	77.9%	77.8%
Manufactured products	19.2%	19.4%
CRInc.	2.9%	2.8%

Western Europe accounted for 12% of sales and 15% of operating profits in 1994.

The Fibers division produces from petrochemicals polyester textile staple in Darlington, S.C. (annual capacity of 465 million lbs.), and partially oriented yarn (130 million lbs.) in Fayetteville, N.C. These are marketed under the Fortrel brand name and used in apparel, home furnishings and industrial applications. WLM also recycles fiber wastes to produce polyester and nylon staple fibers at plants in Johnsonville (250 million lbs.) and Marion (30 million lbs.), S.C., for fiberfill, furniture, home furnishings, carpet and industrial uses. Wellman International Ltd. (Ireland) conducts a similar business serving the U.K. and Western Europe with annual capacity of 154 million lbs.

WLM also produces PET resin (240 million lbs.) for bottles and packaging uses and makes recycled nylon engineering resins for automobile, consumer and industrial uses. It converts polyester fiber into high-loft nonwoven batting used as filling for home furnishings and manufactures geotextile fabrics. WLM also processes raw wool to produce wool blends. Creative Forming, Inc. produces thermoformed plastics packaging products and PET sheet.

In September 1995, WLM sold New England CRInc., which designs, builds and operates materials recycling facilities for mixed recyclables.

Important Developments

Jun. '95—WLM announced a significant expansion of its PET resin and polyester fiber businesses, which will more than double its capacity of these products by the year 2000. WLM will build a plant in North America with combined PET resin and polyester fiber capacity of 600 million pounds by the end of 1998. The plant will cost almost $500 million. WLM will also expand its European PET capacity to between 400 and 500 million pounds by the end of the decade. WLM plans to have 175 million pounds of European PET capacity by the end of 1995 as a result of the planned acquisition of Akzo Nobel's PET business located in the Netherlands.

Capitalization

Long Term Debt: $228,047,000 (6/95).

Per Share Data ($) (Year Ended Dec. 31)

	1994	1993	1992	1991	1990	1989
Tangible Bk. Val.	17.40	15.45	14.86	13.44	12.11	9.97
Cash Flow	3.72	2.99	3.18	2.71	2.80	2.21
Earnings	1.94	1.23	1.60	1.39	1.90	1.84
Dividends	0.23	0.18	0.12	0.12	0.12	0.11
Payout Ratio	12%	15%	7%	9%	6%	7%
Prices - High	34⅝	24⅞	31½	29	36	43
- Low	17⅛	16¼	16½	17¼	12¾	18½
P/E Ratio - High	18	20	20	21	19	23
- Low	9	13	10	12	7	10

Income Statement Analysis (Million $)

	1994	%Chg	1993	%Chg	1992	%Chg	1991
Revs.	936	11%	842	2%	828	3%	806
Oper. Inc.	181	21%	149	-9%	163	6%	154
Depr.	59.5	3%	57.9	12%	51.7	20%	43.1
Int. Exp.	16.7	-8%	18.1	-21%	23.0	-22%	29.4
Pretax Inc.	108	48%	73.0	-17%	88.0	7%	82.0
Eff. Tax Rate	40%	—	45%	—	41%	—	45%
Net Inc.	64.8	60%	40.5	-23%	52.3	15%	45.3

Balance Sheet & Other Fin. Data (Million $)

	1994	1993	1992	1991	1990	1989
Cash	21.6	18.8	1.7	0.7	5.4	7.8
Curr. Assets	272	254	252	232	227	221
Total Assets	1,041	1,015	997	865	891	861
Curr. Liab.	84.0	98.0	110	111	109	121
LT Debt	256	294	300	270	342	396
Common Eqty.	578	507	483	435	392	319
Total Cap.	834	801	783	705	734	714
Cap. Exp.	74.0	111	62.0	26.0	31.0	246
Cash Flow	124	98.0	104	88.0	101	68.0

Ratio Analysis

	1994	1993	1992	1991	1990	1989
Curr. Ratio	3.2	2.6	2.3	2.1	2.1	1.8
% LT Debt of Cap.	30.7	36.7	38.3	38.2	46.6	55.4
% Net Inc.of Revs.	6.9	4.8	6.3	5.6	7.4	12.4
% Ret. on Assets	6.3	4.0	5.6	5.2	7.0	9.6
% Ret. on Equity	11.9	8.1	11.4	10.9	17.2	22.3

Dividend Data —Dividends were initiated in 1988. A "poison pill" stock purchase rights plan was adopted in 1991.

Amt. of Div. $	Date Decl.	Ex-Div. Date	Stock of Record	Payment Date
0.060	Nov. 15	Nov. 25	Dec. 01	Dec. 15 '94
0.060	Feb. 17	Feb. 23	Mar. 01	Mar. 15 '95
0.070	May. 18	May. 25	Jun. 01	Jun. 15 '95
0.070	Aug. 16	Aug. 30	Sep. 01	Sep. 15 '95

Data as orig. reptd.; bef. results of disc. opers. and/or spec. items. Per share data adj. for stk. divs. as of ex-div. date. E-Estimated. NA-Not Available. NM-Not Meaningful. NR-Not Ranked.

Office—1040 Broad St., Suite 302, Shrewsbury, NJ 07702. **Tel**—(908) 542-7300. **Fax**—(908) 542-9344. **Pres & CEO**—T. M. Duff. **VP, CFO & Treas**—K. R. Phillips. **Secy**—D. K. Duffell. **Investor Contact**—Jill M. Rea (908) 935-7319. **Dirs**—J. B. Baker, C. W. Beckwith, P. H. Conze, A. R. Dragone, T. M. Duff, R. F. Heitmiller, J. M. Nelson, J. E. Rogers, R. C. Tower, R. A. Vandenberg. **Transfer Agent & Registrar**—Continental Stock Transfer & Trust Co., NYC. **Incorporated** in Delaware in 1985. **Empl**-3,600. **S&P Analyst:** Richard O'Reilly, CFA

STANDARD & POOR'S
STOCK REPORTS

West One Bancorp

NASDAQ Symbol **WEST**
In S&P MidCap 400

14-AUG-95 **Industry:** Banking

Summary: This Idaho-based regional multibank holding company, which in May 1995 agreed to merge with U.S. Bancorp, operates more than 250 offices in Idaho, Utah, Oregon and Washington.

Quantitative Evaluations
Outlook (1 Lowest—5 Highest) • **5-**
Fair Value • **40⅛**
Risk • **Average**
Earn./Div. Rank • **A-**

Technical Eval. • **Bearish** since 7/95
Rel. Strength Rank (1 Lowest—99 Highest) • **64**
Insider Activity • **Neutral**

Recent Price • 36⅛
52 Wk Range • 37⅛-24¼
Yield • 2.4%
12-Mo. P/E • 11.8

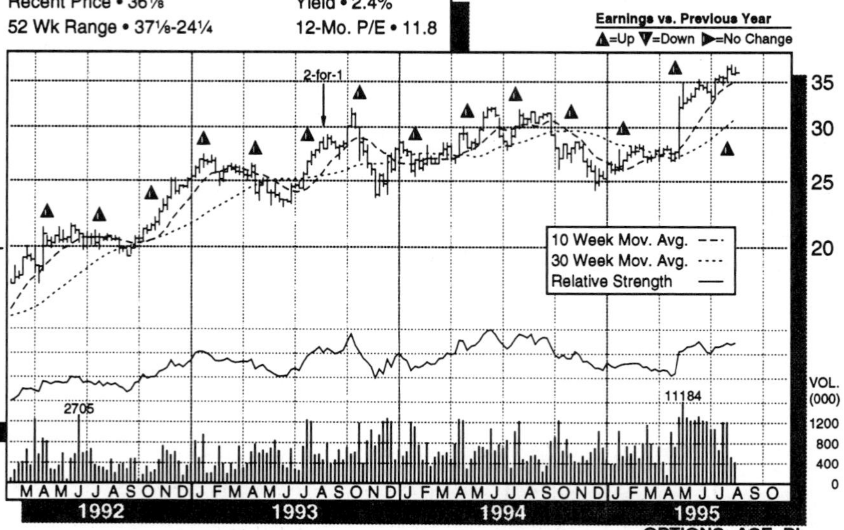

OPTIONS: ASE, Ph

Business Profile - 14-AUG-95

In May 1995, West One Bancorp and U.S. Bancorp signed an agreement to merge under the U.S. Bancorp name. The combined institution will have about $30 billion in assets and $21 billion in deposits, ranking it among the 30 largest U.S. banking organizations. Earnings continued their upward trend in the second quarter of 1995, as a strong regional economy helped fuel 13% loan growth. Asset quality continued to improve, with nonperforming assets at the lowest level since 1981.

Operational Review - 14-AUG-95

Net interest income for the six months ended June 30, 1995, advanced 9.9%, year to year, as increased earning assets outweighed a narrowing in the net interest margin. The loan loss provision declined 17%, to $6,470,000. With 11% higher noninterest income and 9.0% greater noninterest expense, pretax income climbed 15%. After taxes at 29.8%, versus 30.6%, net income was up 17%, to $57,016,000 ($1.55 a share; $1.47 fully diluted), from $48,838,000 ($1.38; $1.31).

Stock Performance - 11-AUG-95

In the past 30 trading days, WEST's shares have increased 8%, compared to a 2% rise in the S&P 500. Average trading volume for the past five days was 82,860 shares, compared with the 40-day moving average of 197,431 shares.

Key Stock Statistics

Dividend Rate/Share	0.88	Shareholders	7,000
Shs. outstg. (M)	36.9	Market cap. (B)	$ 1.3
Avg. daily vol. (M)	0.171	Inst. holdings	59%
Tang. Bk. Value/Share	20.25	Insider holdings	NA
Beta	0.96		

Value of $10,000 invested 5 years ago: $ 37,381

Fiscal Year Ending Dec. 31

	1995	% Change	1994	% Change	1993	% Change
Revenues ()						
1Q	192.4	26%	152.3	7%	142.6	16%
2Q	206.0	24%	166.1	11%	149.2	23%
3Q	—	—	173.7	13%	153.1	19%
4Q	—	—	184.4	19%	154.9	7%
Yr.	—	—	676.4	13%	599.8	16%
Income ()						
1Q	28.27	23%	22.92	26%	18.17	28%
2Q	28.75	11%	25.92	25%	20.81	36%
3Q	—	—	27.06	24%	21.78	32%
4Q	—	—	27.27	22%	22.43	29%
Yr.	—	—	103.2	24%	83.19	31%
Earnings Per Share ()						
1Q	0.76	17%	0.65	18%	0.55	10%
2Q	0.79	8%	0.73	16%	0.63	19%
3Q	—	—	0.76	17%	0.65	25%
4Q	—	—	0.75	14%	0.66	23%
Yr.	—	—	2.88	15%	2.50	20%

Next earnings report expected: late October

West One Bancorp

Business Summary - 14-AUG-95

West One Bancorp is a regional bank holding company that serves four western states through more than 250 offices, mainly in Idaho and in Utah, Oregon and Washington. Its lead bank is West One Bank, Idaho, the largest in that state.

Loans totaled $6.1 billion (net of unearned income) at the end of 1994, up from $5.4 billion a year earlier, divided as follows:

	1994	1993
Real estate	42%	40%
Commercial & agricultural	36%	37%
Consumer	19%	20%
Leases	3%	3%

The allowance for credit losses was $81,757,000 (1.35% of loans outstanding) at the end of 1994, versus $74,923,000 (1.40%) a year earlier. Net loan chargeoffs totaled $10,277,000 (0.18% of average loans) in 1994, against $7,053,000 (0.14%) in 1993. At December 31, 1994, nonperforming assets (including nonaccrual loans and restructured loans and other real estate owned) totaled $25,799,000 (0.42% of loans and other real estate owned), compared with $28,401,000 (0.53%) a year earlier.

At December 31, 1994, deposits totaled $6.81 billion, comprised of noninterest-bearing 21%, interest-bearing demand 11%, regular and money-market savings 31%, time certificates 26% and time certificates of $100,000 and more 12%.

Interest on loans provided 70% of total income for 1994, interest on investment securities 13%, trust fees and commissions 2%, service charges on deposit accounts 6%, other service charges, fees and commissions 7% and other noninterest income 2%.

The average yield on total interest-earning assets was 7.97% in 1994 (7.80% in 1993), while the average rate paid on total interest-bearing liabilities was 3.67% (3.46%), for a net spread of 4.30% (4.34%).

Important Developments

May '95—A merger agreement was signed that calls for U.S. Bancorp to exchange 1.47 shares of its common stock for each West One Bancorp common share. The combined institution, retaining the U.S. Bancorp name, would have about $30 billion in assets and $21 billion in deposits and would rank among the 30 largest banking organizations in the U.S. Subject to shareholder and regulatory approvals, the merger is expected to be completed by the end of 1995.

Capitalization

Long Term Debt: $321,970,000 (6/95).

Per Share Data () (Year Ended Dec. 31)

	1994	1993	1992	1991	1990	1989
Tangible Bk. Val.	19.48	17.96	15.14	13.08	12.10	10.98
Earnings	2.88	2.50	2.09	1.46	1.67	1.36
Dividends	0.76	0.65	0.52	0.48	0.44	0.41
Payout Ratio	26%	25%	25%	33%	26%	30%
Prices - High	32⅛	32	25½	17⅞	12⅞	13⅝
- Low	24¼	22⅞	15½	11⅝	8⅞	9¾
P/E Ratio - High	11	13	12	12	8	10
- Low	8	9	7	8	5	7

Income Statement Analysis ()

	1994	%Chg	1993	%Chg	1992	%Chg	1991
Net Int. Inc.	342	13%	304	27%	239	21%	198
Tax Equiv. Adj.	20.9	13%	18.5	41%	13.1	7%	12.2
Non Int. Inc.	115	13%	102	25%	81.8	16%	70.5
Loan Loss Prov.	13.3	NM	13.4	-6%	14.3	-52%	29.7
% Exp/Op Revs.	62%	—	64%	—	65%	—	65%
Pretax Inc.	147	22%	121	32%	91.3	59%	57.5
Eff. Tax Rate	30%	—	31%	—	31%	—	28%
Net Inc.	103	24%	83.2	31%	63.4	54%	41.2
% Net Int. Marg.	4.95%	—	4.87%	—	4.76%	—	4.48%

Balance Sheet & Other Fin. Data ()

	1994	1993	1992	1991	1990	1989
Earning Assets:						
Money Mkt.	113	15.0	191	205	102	192
Inv. Securities	1,721	1,626	1,657	1,220	998	996
Com'l Loans	2,366	2,165	1,923	1,521	1,411	1,246
Other Loans	3,699	3,190	2,609	1,976	1,576	1,353
Total Assets	8,793	7,671	7,134	5,417	4,587	4,350
Demand Deposits	1,398	1,261	1,136	669	692	656
Time Deposits	5,413	4,676	4,500	3,375	2,847	2,585
LT Debt	253	116	118	112	71.0	62.0
Common Eqty.	716	624	490	367	309	272

Ratio Analysis

	1994	1993	1992	1991	1990	1989
% Ret. on Assets	1.3	1.1	1.1	0.8	1.0	0.8
% Ret. on Equity	15.6	14.9	14.9	11.8	14.7	13.1
% Loan Loss Resv.	1.4	1.4	1.5	1.5	1.5	1.8
% Loans/Deposits	89.1	90.2	80.4	86.5	84.4	80.2
% Equity to Assets	8.2	7.5	7.3	6.8	6.6	6.4

Dividend Data (Cash has been paid each year since 1935. A dividend reinvestment plan is available.)

Amt. of Div. $	Date Decl.	Ex-Div. Date	Stock of Record	Payment Date
0.220	Oct. 20	Dec. 23	Dec. 31	Jan. 19 '95
0.220	Jan. 20	Mar. 27	Mar. 31	Apr. 20 '95
0.220	Apr. 20	Jun. 28	Jun. 30	Jul. 20 '95
0.220	Jul. 21	Sep. 27	Sep. 29	Oct. 19 '95

Data as orig. reptd.; bef. results of disc opers. and/or spec. items. Per share data adj. for stk. divs. as of ex-div. date. E-Estimated. NA-Not Available. NM-Not Meaningful. NR-Not Ranked.

Office—101 S. Capitol Blvd., Boise, ID 83733. **Tel**—(208) 383-7000. **Chrmn & CEO**—D. R. Nelson. **Pres**—D. M. Jones. **Exec VP & CFO**—S. M. Hayes. **Sr VP & Secy**—D. V. Board. **VP & Investor Contact**—Linda Blount-Strauss (208) 383-7474. **Dirs**—H. Bettis, N. D. Cugini, W. J. Deasy, J. B. Fery, S. A. Hall, D. M. Jones, J. B. Little, W. E. McCain, D. W. McCallum, D. R. Nelson, A. T. Noble, P. B. Soulen. **Transfer Agent & Registrar**—West One Bank. **Incorporated** in Idaho in 1981. **Empl**-4,778. **S&P Analyst:** Brad Ohlmuller

STANDARD & POOR'S

STOCK REPORTS

Western Publishing Group

NASDAQ Symbol **WPGI**

In S&P MidCap 400

20-JUL-95

Industry: Publishing

Summary: This company is the largest U.S. publisher of children's books, largely under the "Golden" trademark, and produces other leisure-time and commercial products.

S&P Opinion: Accumulate (★★★★)

Recent Price • 11 | Yield • Nil

52 Wk Range • 14⅛-8 | 12-Mo. P/E • NM

Quantitative Evaluations

Outlook (1 Lowest—5 Highest)
• **NA**

Fair Value
• **NA**

Risk
• **Average**

Earn./Div. Rank
• **NR**

Technical Eval.
• **Bearish** since 5/95

Rel. Strength Rank (1 Lowest—99 Highest)
• **41**

Insider Activity
• **NA**

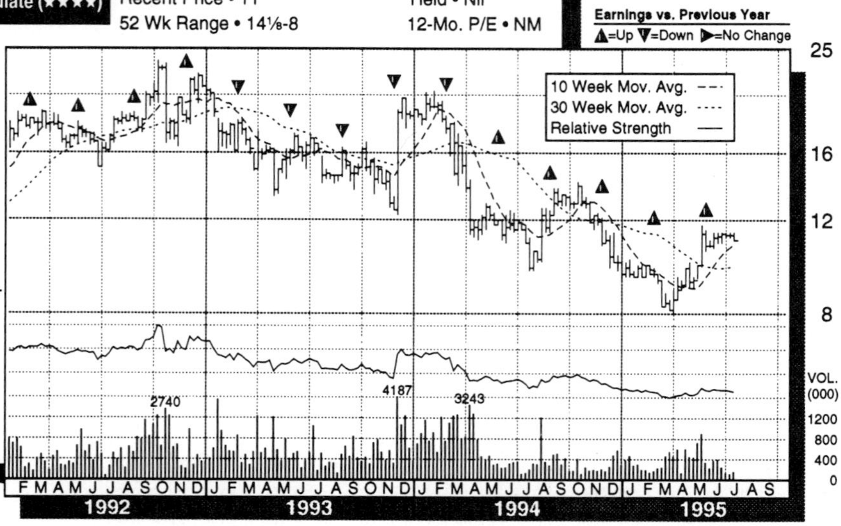

Overview - 18-JUL-95

Sharply higher revenues from ongoing operations are anticipated in fiscal 1995-96. Profitability should improve dramatically in the absence of the operating upheavals and costs stemming from the downsizing and restructuring actions undertaken in calendar year 1994. A roughly 28% reduction in personnel, and a sharp drop in interest expenses will be instrumental in returning the company to profitability. Western's strategy to focus on its core competencies in publishing, printing, party paper goods, gifts and stationery is contributing to strong across-the-board sales growth. In addition, the company is continuing to hold its costs down. Start-up problems with a new computerized operating system, that hurt sales and profits in the fiscal first quarter, should be resolved by the start of the busy season in the third quarter.

Valuation - 18-JUL-95

Western's stock price is recovering from the low reached in December 1994. Healthy ongoing revenue and earnings gains from continuing businesses will partly reflect recovery of some market share that was lost during 1993 and 1994 and partly from new business and expanded distribution. Results in fiscal 1996 and 1997 will also benefit from tax loss carryforwards, and implementation of additional operating efficiencies. A new president and CEO should also help to breathe vitality into WPGI's operations. These positive factors, combined, should help to strengthen the market's perception of the stock.

Key Stock Statistics

S&P EPS Est. 1996	0.55	Tang. Bk. Value/Share	5.55
P/E on S&P Est. 1996	20.0	Beta	1.56
Dividend Rate/Share	Nil	Shareholders	NA
Shs. outstg. (M)	21.0	Market cap. (B)	$0.226
Avg. daily vol. (M)	0.028	Inst. holdings	60%
		Insider holdings	NA

Value of $10,000 invested 5 years ago: $ 5,605

Fiscal Year Ending Jan. 31

	1996	% Change	1995	% Change	1994	% Change
Revenues (Million $)						
1Q	85.94	26%	68.10	-39%	111.0	-9%
2Q	—	—	105.5	-20%	131.3	6%
3Q	—	—	130.3	-35%	201.9	-12%
4Q	—	—	98.67	-43%	172.5	-3%
Yr.	—	—	402.6	-35%	616.7	-5%
Income (Million $)						
1Q	-13.31	NM	-14.02	NM	-30.31	NM
2Q	—	—	-2.93	NM	-3.97	NM
3Q	—	—	5.38	121%	2.43	-81%
4Q	—	—	-6.01	NM	-9.17	NM
Yr.	—	—	-17.58	NM	-41.03	NM
Earnings Per Share ($)						
1Q	-0.64	NM	-0.68	NM	-1.45	NM
2Q	E0.16	—	-0.15	NM	-0.20	NM
3Q	E0.79	—	0.25	127%	0.11	-82%
4Q	E0.24	—	-0.30	NM	-0.45	NM
Yr.	E0.55	—	-0.88	NM	-1.99	NM

Next earnings report expected: mid September

Western Publishing Group

Business Summary - 19-JUL-95

Western Publishing Group, Inc. is the nation's largest publisher of children's story books, (primarily under the "Golden" trademark), and produces other leisure-time and commercial products. Contributions (profits in million $) by business segment in 1993-4 were:

	Sales	Profits
Consumer products	87.3%	$0.19
Commercial products	12.7%	-2.56

Western creates and publishes story books, coloring books, and activity books for children, as well as special-interest books for adults. Products are marketed primarily through mass merchandising chains, bookstores and toy stores.

About half of consumer product sales are from juvenile products using characters and properties from the company's five largest licensors: The Walt Disney Co., Children's Television Workshop (Sesame Street), Mattel Inc., International Design Workshop Inc. and Warner Brothers Inc.

The Diversified Products division provides printing and creative publishing services. During the second and third quarters of fiscal 1994-5, Western sold its advertising specialties, games and puzzles, and school book club businesses. Western, in partnership with Sierra On-Line Inc., launched a line of children's interactive and multi-media software products in April 1994.

Important Developments

Nov. '94—Western completed the restructuring plan announced on April 7, 1994. Five business units were sold for about $130 million, which effectively provided for the repayment of all bank debt. Western sold its games and book puzzles business, its school book and direct marketing continuity clubs, and the Ritepoint, Adtrend, Vitronic and K-Studio businesses of the Advertising Specialty Division. The overall restructuring plan was aimed at focusing Western on publishing, paper party goods, stationery and printing businesses, improving its competitive position and reducing its ongoing operating cost structure, which should be helped by the sale of a manufacturing facility and staff reductions of roughly 28%. It expects to accrue a pretax net gain of about $20 million (including operating losses) from the combined asset sales.

Capitalization

Long Term Debt: $149,832,000 (4/95).
Preferred Stock: 19,970 shs. (no par); ea. conv. into 28 com. shs.; entitled to cum. divds. at annual rate of $42.50 per sh.; red. at $500 per sh. no later than Mar. 31'96.

Per Share Data ($) (Year Ended Jan. 31)

	1995	1994	1993	1992	1991	1990
Tangible Bk. Val.	NA	6.92	8.23	7.76	7.06	6.72
Cash Flow	NA	-1.19	1.43	1.25	0.97	1.71
Earnings	-0.88	-1.99	0.80	0.62	0.36	1.05
Dividends	Nil	Nil	Nil	Nil	Nil	Nil
Payout Ratio	Nil	Nil	Nil	Nil	Nil	Nil
Cal. Yrs.	1994	1993	1992	1991	1990	1989
Prices - High	20⅞	21	23¾	16⅛	19⅞	23½
- Low	9¼	12¼	14⅝	9¼	9⅛	16⅝
P/E Ratio - High	NM	NM	30	26	55	22
- Low	NM	NM	18	15	25	16

Income Statement Analysis (Million $)

	1994	%Chg	1993	%Chg	1992	%Chg	1991
Revs.	616	-5%	651	18%	553	12%	492
Oper. Inc.	-3.0	NM	50.7	25%	40.7	22%	33.4
Depr.	17.0	28%	13.3	NM	13.3	4%	12.8
Int. Exp.	16.3	57%	10.4	65%	6.3	-16%	7.5
Pretax Inc.	-63.3	NM	28.4	27%	22.3	63%	13.7
Eff. Tax Rate	NM	—	38%	—	39%	—	39%
Net Inc.	-41.0	NM	17.5	28%	13.7	65%	8.3

Balance Sheet & Other Fin. Data (Million $)

	1994	1993	1992	1991	1990	1989
Cash	9.6	10.4	8.8	7.5	8.2	5.8
Curr. Assets	412	375	282	232	206	208
Total Assets	505	509	391	339	310	311
Curr. Liab.	79.0	93.0	176	129	109	131
LT Debt	230	180	Nil	Nil	Nil	Nil
Common Eqty.	159	215	199	190	183	163
Total Cap.	398	414	213	207	199	178
Cap. Exp.	37.4	22.8	11.9	14.4	13.2	9.8
Cash Flow	-24.9	30.0	26.2	20.3	34.3	42.0

Ratio Analysis

	1994	1993	1992	1991	1990	1989
Curr. Ratio	5.2	4.0	1.6	1.8	1.9	1.6
% LT Debt of Cap.	57.7	43.4	Nil	Nil	Nil	Nil
% Net Inc.of Revs.	NM	2.7	2.5	1.7	4.4	5.4
% Ret. on Assets	NM	3.9	3.8	2.5	7.0	9.8
% Ret. on Equity	NM	8.0	6.6	3.9	12.1	19.6

Dividend Data (No cash dividends have been paid on the common shares.)

Data as orig. reptd.; bef. results of disc. opers. and/or spec. items. Per share data adj. for stk. divs. as of ex-div. date. E-Estimated. NA-Not Available. NM-Not Meaningful. NR-Not Ranked.

Office—444 Madison Ave., New York, NY 10022. **Tel**—(212) 688-4500. **Chrmn**—R. A. Bernstein. **Pres & CEO**—J. F. Moore. **EVP, CFO & Treas**—S. M. Grossman. **VP & Secy**—J. A. Cohen. **Dirs**—R. A. Bernhard, R. A. Bernstein, S. B. Fortenbaugh III, A. S. Gordon, J. Morgenthau, M. A. Pietrangelo. **Transfer Agent & Registrar**—First Chicago Trust Co. of New York, NYC. **Incorporated** in Delaware in 1984. **Empl-** 4,200. **S&P Analyst:** William H. Donald

STANDARD & POOR'S

STOCK REPORTS

Wilmington Trust

NASDAQ Symbol **WILM**

In S&P MidCap 400

01-OCT-95 **Industry:** Banking

Summary: This bank holding company, through its Wilmington Trust Co. subsidiary, operates over 60 branches offering a broad variety of financial services, mainly in Wilmington, Del.

S&P Opinion: Accumulate (★★★★)

Recent Price • 29½ | 52 Wk Range • 31½-22 | Yield • 4.1% | 12-Mo. P/E • 12.1

Quantitative Evaluations

Outlook (1 Lowest—5 Highest)
• **3-**

Fair Value
• **29½**

Risk
• **Low**

Earn./Div. Rank
• **A+**

Technical Eval.
• **Bearish** since 7/95

Rel. Strength Rank (1 Lowest—99 Highest)
• **44**

Insider Activity
• **NA**

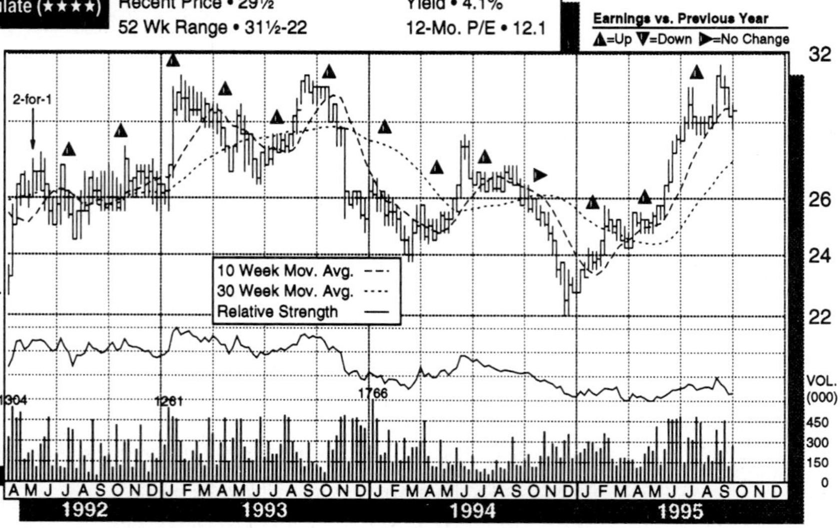

Overview - 29-SEP-95

Loans grew 10% in the second quarter of 1995, year to year, driven by continued growth in the commercial loan portfolio. The net interest margin narrowed five basis points (4.49% from 4.54%) during the quarter, as a decline in the level of deposits forced the bank to use short term borrowings to fund balance sheet growth. WILM has instituted a number of marketing initiatives designed to resume growth in the deposit base. Trust and investment management fees were up 6% in the second quarter and, looking forward, should benefit from the opening of a new trust office in Philadelphia in 1995's second quarter and WILM's expansion into Florida in May. Year to date results have produced, on an annualized basis, a return on assets and return on equity of 1.83% and 20.77%, respectively, which ranks WILM among the top banks in the nation in these key measures of profitability.

Valuation - 29-SEP-95

So far this year, the shares, which are up approximately 32%, have outpaced the broader market and performed in line with those of other regional banks. The stock currently trades at a valuation of about 10 times our earnings estimate for 1996. With earnings expected to rise 9%, the shares should continue to outperform the overall market over the next 6 to 12 months and, with a dividend yield of about 4.0%, remain attractive for above average total return prospects.

Key Stock Statistics

S&P EPS Est. 1995	2.65	Tang. Bk. Value/Share	12.38
P/E on S&P Est. 1995	11.1	Beta	0.82
S&P EPS Est. 1996	2.90	Shareholders	9,100
Dividend Rate/Share	1.20	Market cap. (B)	$ 1.0
Shs. outstg. (M)	35.3	Inst. holdings	37%
Avg. daily vol. (M)	0.060	Insider holdings	NA

Value of $10,000 invested 5 years ago: $ 19,207

Fiscal Year Ending Dec. 31

	1995	% Change	1994	% Change	1993	% Change
Revenues (Million $)						
1Q	116.5	15%	101.1	NM	100.6	-9%
2Q	126.0	20%	104.7	4%	100.2	-6%
3Q	—	—	104.3	4%	100.5	-4%
4Q	—	—	110.8	7%	103.3	NM
Yr.	—	—	420.9	4%	404.6	-5%
Income (Million $)						
1Q	20.97	NM	20.86	6%	19.71	10%
2Q	22.50	4%	21.67	6%	20.39	5%
3Q	—	—	21.25	-3%	21.82	5%
4Q	—	—	21.40	3%	20.85	NM
Yr.	—	—	85.17	3%	82.76	5%
Earnings Per Share ($)						
1Q	0.60	3%	0.58	9%	0.53	13%
2Q	0.64	7%	0.60	9%	0.55	8%
3Q	E0.68	15%	0.59	NM	0.59	7%
4Q	E0.73	22%	0.60	5%	0.57	2%
Yr.	E2.65	12%	2.37	6%	2.24	7%

Next earnings report expected: late October

Wilmington Trust

Business Summary - 21-JUN-95

Wilmington Trust Corporation conducts commercial banking, savings, trust, investment management and other financial activities through its Wilmington Trust Co. subsidiary, which operates 61 full-service branches, mainly in Delaware. The company also has offices in Maryland (three), Pennsylvania (five) and Florida (four).

Gross loans outstanding were $3.28 billion at year-end 1994, compared with $3.04 billion a year earlier. Loans were divided as follows:

	1994	1993
Mortgage	41%	42%
Commercial, financial & agricultural	31%	30%
Consumer	25%	24%
Construction	3%	4%

The reserve for possible loan losses at December 31, 1994, was $48.7 million ($51.4 million a year earlier), equal to 1.57% (1.75%) of average loans outstanding. Net chargeoffs in 1994 amounted to $7,244,000 ($8,153,000 in 1993), equal to 0.23% (0.28%) of average loans. Nonaccruing loans, restructured loans and loans past due 90 days or more totaled $45,702,000 (1.39% of loans outstanding) at 1994 year-end, compared with $33,767,000 (1.11%) a year earlier.

Total deposits at 1994 year-end amounted to $3.31 billion, of which noninterest-bearing demand deposits represented about 21%, savings 11%, interest checking 15%, money market 18%, certificates of under $100,000 31%, and certificates of $100,000 and more 4%.

On a tax-equivalent basis, the average yield on total interest-earning assets was 7.59% in 1994 (7.73% in 1993), while the average rate paid on total interest-bearing liabilities was 3.55% (3.56%), for a net interest spread of 4.04% (4.17%).

Important Developments

Apr. '95—In the quarter ended March 31, 1995, Wilmington recorded, on an annualized basis, a return on average assets of 1.82% (1.87% in the year-ago period) and a return on equity of 20.41% (21.23%), ranking it among the highest in the industry for banks of comparable or larger size.

Apr. '95—Directors increased the quarterly dividend 11%, from $0.27 a share to $0.30 a share, raising the annual rate to $1.20. This marks the fourteenth consecutive year in which the dividend has been raised.

Capitalization

Long Term Debt: None (3/95).

Per Share Data ($)

(Year Ended Dec. 31)

	1994	1993	1992	1991	1990	1989
Tangible Bk. Val.	11.80	10.87	10.12	9.72	8.41	7.45
Earnings	2.37	2.24	2.09	2.04	1.90	1.70
Dividends	1.06	0.98	0.88	0.79	0.72	0.59
Payout Ratio	45%	44%	42%	39%	38%	35%
Prices - High	28 1/2	31	29	29 3/8	22 1/2	23 1/8
- Low	22	24 3/4	22 5/8	18	15 1/8	13 1/4
P/E Ratio - High	12	14	14	14	12	14
- Low	9	11	11	9	8	8

Income Statement Analysis (Million $)

	1994	%Chg	1993	%Chg	1992	%Chg	1991
Net Int. Inc.	184	5%	175	6%	165	16%	142
Tax Equiv. Adj.	10.5	-7%	11.3	-7%	12.1	-25%	16.1
Non Int. Inc.	115	2%	113	5%	108	13%	96.0
Loan Loss Prov.	4.6	-52%	9.5	-27%	13.0	-2%	13.3
% Exp/Op Revs.	55%	—	54%	—	54%	—	51%
Pretax Inc.	121	3%	117	7%	109	16%	94.0
Eff. Tax Rate	30%	—	29%	—	28%	—	24%
Net Inc.	85.2	3%	82.8	5%	78.8	10%	71.9
% Net Int. Marg.	4.64%	—	4.76%	—	4.62%	—	4.47%

Balance Sheet & Other Fin. Data (Million $)

	1994	1993	1992	1991	1990	1989
Earning Assets:						
Money Mkt.	132	190	147	141	117	237
Inv. Securities	985	1,093	802	828	835	793
Com'l Loans	1,006	923	867	842	791	739
Other Loans	2,277	2,117	2,142	1,932	1,824	1,642
Total Assets	4,742	4,638	4,285	4,061	3,834	3,703
Demand Deposits	696	587	528	424	392	452
Time Deposits	2,613	2,804	2,746	2,623	2,461	2,162
LT Debt	Nil	Nil	Nil	Nil	Nil	Nil
Common Eqty.	418	395	377	346	296	258

Ratio Analysis

	1994	1993	1992	1991	1990	1989
% Ret. on Assets	1.9	2.0	1.9	1.9	1.9	1.9
% Ret. on Equity	20.8	21.1	21.5	22.7	24.5	24.4
% Loan Loss Resv.	1.5	1.7	1.6	1.5	1.5	1.5
% Loans/Deposits	99.1	89.6	91.5	90.7	91.3	90.8
% Equity to Assets	9.0	9.3	8.9	8.4	7.7	7.8

Dividend Data —Cash has been paid each year since 1914. A dividend reinvestment plan is available. A shareholder rights plan was adopted in January 1995.

Amt. of Div. $	Date Decl.	Ex-Div. Date	Stock of Record	Payment Date
0.270	Oct. 20	Oct. 26	Nov. 01	Nov. 15 '94
0.270	Jan. 20	Jan. 26	Feb. 01	Feb. 15 '95
0.300	Apr. 20	Apr. 25	May. 01	May. 15 '95
0.300	Jul. 20	Jul. 28	Aug. 01	Aug. 15 '95

Data as orig. reptd.; bef. results of disc opers. and/or spec. items. Per share data adj. for stk. divs. as of ex-div. date. E-Estimated. NA-Not Available. NM-Not Meaningful. NR-Not Ranked.

Office—Rodney Sq. North, Wilmington, DE 19890. **Tel**—(302) 651-1000. **Chrmn, Pres, & CEO**—L. W. Quill. **EVP, CFO & Investor Contact**—T. T. Cecala (302) 651-1897. **EVP & Treas**—R. V. A. Harra, Jr. **VP & Secy**—T. P. Collins. **Dirs**—R. H. Bolling Jr., C. S. Burger, J. E. Burris, R. R. Collins, Jr., H. E. Cosgrove, C. S. Crompton, Jr., H. S. Dunn, Jr., E. B. duPont, E. P. Fairman, R. C. Forney, T. L. Gossage, A. B. Kirkpatrick, Jr., R. L. Mears, W. D. Mertz, H. E. — Miller, S. J. Mobley, G. B. Pearson, Jr., L. W. Quill, D. P. Roselle, T. P. Sweeney, B. J. Taylor, II, M. J. Theisen, R. W. Tunnell, Jr. **Transfer Agent & Registrar**—Co. itself. **Incorporated** in Delaware in 1901; reincorporated in 1985. **Empl-** 2,303. **S&P Analyst:** Brad Ohlmuller

STANDARD & POOR'S

STOCK REPORTS

Wisconsin Energy

NYSE Symbol **WEC**

In S&P MidCap 400

11-OCT-95 **Industry:** Util.-Diversified

Summary: This electric and gas utility holding company and Northern States Power Co. have agreed to merge and form a new company, Primergy Corp., with completion expected in late 1996.

S&P Opinion: Hold (★★★)

Recent Price • 28⅝ | 52 Wk Range • 29-24½ | Yield • 5.1% | 12-Mo. P/E • 13.6

Quantitative Evaluations

Outlook (1 Lowest—5 Highest)
• 1⁻

Fair Value
• 23⅛

Risk
• Low

Earn./Div. Rank
• A

Technical Eval.
• Bullish since 9/95

Rel. Strength Rank (1 Lowest—99 Highest)
• 83

Insider Activity
• NA

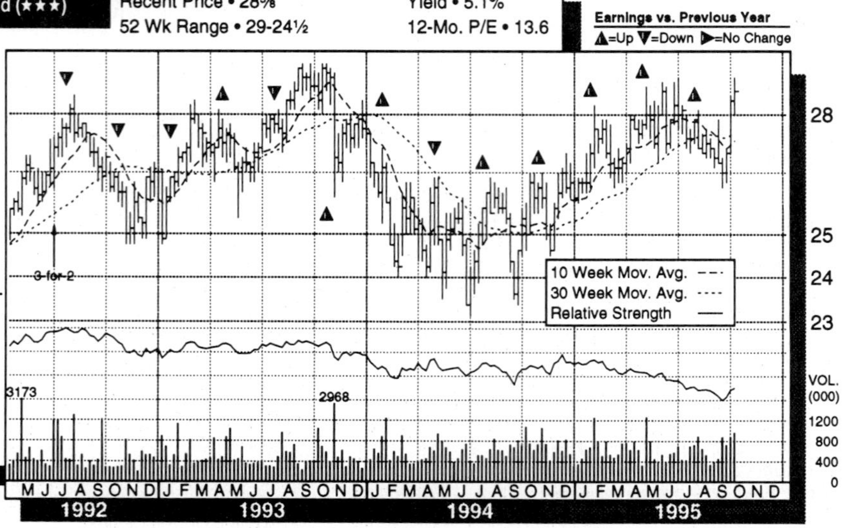

Overview - 11-OCT-95

Share earnings for 1995 should reflect increases in sales of both electricity and gas as the economy within WEC's service territory continues to grow. Results should also benefit from cost savings from its restructuring program that included an 18% reduction in the workforce. WEC's balance sheet is healthy, with a strong cash flow, and long term debt at 42% of total capital as of 1994 year-end. Longer term, WEC's shareholders should benefit from a strengthened position in the industry after the proposed merger with Northern States Power, expected to be completed in late 1996. Combined, the companies would lower costs by some $2 billion over 10 years, allowing a more competitive rate structure going forward.

Valuation - 11-OCT-95

In both 1994 and 1995 to date, the shares have performed considerably better than the average electric utility, as dividend-paying issues such as WEC were hurt in the latter part of 1993 and much of 1994 by rising interest rates. Further dampening investor enthusiasm for electric utility stocks has been the spectre of increasing competition within the industry, which has generated a flight to quality, aiding such issues as WEC. As a result of this and the pending merger, the stock appears reasonably valued at a P/E ratio of 13 (based on estimated 1995 earnings). If the merger is approved, the dividend rate for Primergy would be $1.62 a share.

Key Stock Statistics

S&P EPS Est. 1995	2.20	Tang. Bk. Value/Share	15.81
P/E on S&P Est. 1995	13.0	Beta	0.51
S&P EPS Est. 1996	2.30	Shareholders	85,300
Dividend Rate/Share	1.47	Market cap. (B)	$ 3.2
Shs. outstg. (M)	109.9	Inst. holdings	36%
Avg. daily vol. (M)	0.164	Insider holdings	NA

Value of $10,000 invested 5 years ago: $ 17,822

Fiscal Year Ending Dec. 31

	1995	% Change	1994	% Change	1993	% Change
Revenues (Million $)						
1Q	471.1	-8%	509.7	15%	443.3	5%
2Q	405.1	1%	400.3	7%	375.5	5%
3Q	—	—	400.5	2%	393.2	10%
4Q	—	—	431.7	NM	431.7	4%
Yr.	—	—	1,742	6%	1,644	6%
Income (Million $)						
1Q	62.53	174%	22.82	-61%	57.92	7%
2Q	51.59	19%	43.43	52%	28.60	-6%
3Q	—	—	51.49	8%	47.71	27%
4Q	—	—	63.13	16%	54.26	14%
Yr.	—	—	180.9	-4%	188.5	11%
Earnings Per Share ($)						
1Q	0.57	171%	0.21	-63%	0.56	6%
2Q	0.47	17%	0.40	43%	0.28	-7%
3Q	E0.52	8%	0.48	4%	0.46	24%
4Q	E0.64	10%	0.58	12%	0.52	12%
Yr.	E2.20	32%	1.67	-8%	1.81	8%

Next earnings report expected: late October

Wisconsin Energy

Business Summary - 11-OCT-95

Wisconsin Energy is the holding company for Wisconsin Electric Power and Wisconsin Natural Gas, which supply electricity (80% of 1994 revenues), gas (19%) and steam service (1%) in Milwaukee, northern Wisconsin and the Upper Peninsula of Michigan. It also owns five nonregulated businesses. Electric revenues by customer class in recent years were:

	1994	1993	1992	1991
Residential	36%	35%	34%	35%
Small comm'l & ind'l	30%	29%	29%	28%
Large comm'l & ind'l	29%	28%	30%	29%
Other	5%	8%	7%	8%

According to recent figures, some 64% of generating capability is derived from coal, 27% from nuclear, and 7% purchased power, and 2% from other sources. WEC's nuclear capacity consists of the two-unit Point Beach nuclear station. Peak load in 1994 was 4,950 mw, and capability at peak totaled 5,288 mw, for a capacity margin of 6%. Gas deliveries in 1994 totaled 811,219,000 therms, versus 809,348,000 therms in 1993, as adjusted for the merger of Wisconsin Southern Gas Co. in early 1994. WEC anticipates electric kilowatt-hour sales will grow at a compound annual rate of 1.0% a year over the next five years; growth in natural gas therm deliveries is forecast at about 2.2% compounded annually over the same period.

Capital outlays over the last three years were $1.2 billion, including $984 million to build the new Concord Generating Station, a four-unit, 300 mw natural gas fired combustion turbine facility completed in 1994, and the Paris Generating Station, a four-unit 300 mw combustion turbine facility to be completed in the summer of 1995. Conservation expenditures were $87 million; payments to a trust for eventual decommissioning of the Point Beach Nuclear Plant totaled $42 million.

Important Developments

Sep. '95—WEC shareholders approved a merger (originally announced May 1, 1995) with Northern States Power Co. (NYSE; NSP) into a new holding company, Primergy Corp. WEC shareholders will receive one common share of the new corporation for each of the 109.3 million WEC common shares owned; NSP shareholders will receive 1.626 common shares of Primergy for each of the 67.3 million NSP shares outstanding. The preferred stock of WEC will remain outstanding after the transaction, which is expected to be completed in late 1996, subject to shareholder and regulatory approvals, and other conditions.

Capitalization

Long Term Debt: $1,253,148,000 (6/95).
Subsid. Preferred Stock: $30,451,000.

Per Share Data ($) (Year Ended Dec. 31)

	1994	1993	1992	1991	1990	1989
Tangible Bk. Val.	15.81	15.67	14.78	14.25	13.63	13.41
Earnings	1.67	1.81	1.67	1.87	1.85	1.92
Dividends	1.40	1.34	1.29	1.22	1.16	1.09
Payout Ratio	84%	74%	77%	65%	63%	57%
Prices - High	27½	29⅜	28½	26½	21¾	21½
- Low	23⅛	24¾	23¾	20	17¾	16¾
P/E Ratio - High	16	16	17	14	12	11
- Low	14	14	14	11	10	9

Income Statement Analysis (Million $)

	1994	%Chg	1993	%Chg	1992	%Chg	1991
Revs.	1,742	6%	1,644	6%	1,552	NM	1,539
Depr.	178	8%	165	1%	163	11%	147
Maint.	125	-19%	155	3%	150	6%	142
Fxd. Chgs. Cov.	3.6	-3%	3.7	NM	3.7	-11%	4.2
Constr. Credits	10.1	-31%	14.7	21%	12.1	-10%	13.4
Eff. Tax Rate	35%	—	34%	—	34%	—	34%
Net Inc.	181	-4%	188	11%	170	-10%	189

Balance Sheet & Other Fin. Data (Million $)

	1994	1993	1992	1991	1990	1989
Gross Prop.	5,019	4,773	4,463	4,170	3,977	3,805
Cap. Exp.	322	388	344	268	238	230
Net Prop.	2,941	2,809	2,629	2,466	2,374	2,060
Capitalization:						
LT Debt	1,284	1,286	1,210	1,094	990	1,004
% LT Debt	42	43	42	41	40	41
Pfd.	30.0	36.0	98.0	100	100	100
% Pfd.	1.00	1.20	3.50	3.80	4.10	4.20
Common	1,745	1,651	1,543	1,450	1,384	1,314
% Common	57	56	54	55	56	54
Total Cap.	3,628	3,547	3,402	3,180	3,003	2,585

Ratio Analysis

	1994	1993	1992	1991	1990	1989
Oper. Ratio	85.0	84.0	84.6	83.7	83.3	82.3
% Earn. on Net Prop.	9.1	9.7	9.4	10.4	10.3	12.9
% Ret. on Revs.	10.4	11.5	10.9	12.3	12.9	13.0
% Ret. On Invest.Cap	8.1	8.5	8.1	9.1	9.3	11.1
% Return On Com.Eqty	10.6	11.8	11.3	13.4	13.8	15.2

Dividend Data —Dividends have been paid since 1939. A dividend reinvestment plan is available.

Amt. of Div. $	Date Decl.	Ex-Div. Date	Stock of Record	Payment Date
0.353	Oct. 26	Nov. 02	Nov. 08	Dec. 01 '94
0.353	Jan. 26	Feb. 02	Feb. 08	Mar. 01 '95
0.368	Apr. 27	May. 02	May. 08	Jun. 01 '95
0.368	Jul. 26	Aug. 04	Aug. 08	Sep. 01 '95

Data as orig. reptd.; bef. results of disc opers. and/or spec. items. Per share data adj. for stk. divs. as of ex-div. date. E-Estimated. NA-Not Available. NM-Not Meaningful. NR-Not Ranked.

Office—231 West Michigan St. (P.O. Box 2949), Milwaukee, WI 53201. **Tel**—(414) 221-2345. **Chrmn & Pres**—R. A. Abdoo. **VP & Secy**—J. H. Goetsch. **Treas & CFO**—J. G. Remmel. **Investor Contact**—Tim Hennig (414-221-3239). **Dirs**—R. A. Abdoo, J. F. Ahearne, J. F. Bergstrom, J. W. Boston, R. A. Cornog, R. R. Grigg, Jr., G. B. Johnson, F. P. Stratton, Jr., J. G. Udell. **Transfer Agent & Registrar**—First National Bank of Boston, Boston, MA. **Incorporated** in Wisconsin in 1896; reincorporated in Wisconsin in 1986. **Empl**-4,801. **S&P Analyst:** Jane Collin

STANDARD & POOR'S

STOCK REPORTS

Witco Corp.

NYSE Symbol **WIT**
In S&P MidCap 400

13-SEP-95 **Industry:** Chemicals

Summary: This company produces a wide range of specialty chemical and petroleum products for industrial and consumer use.

S&P Opinion: Accumulate (★★★★) Recent Price • $33\frac{5}{8}$ Yield • 3.2%
52 Wk Range • $34\frac{3}{4}$-$24\frac{1}{4}$ 12-Mo. P/E • 12.3

Quantitative Evaluations

Outlook
(1 Lowest—5 Highest)
• **1-**

Fair Value
• **$27\frac{1}{4}$**

Risk
• **Low**

Earn./Div. Rank
• **B**

Technical Eval.
• **Bullish** since 2/95

Rel. Strength Rank
(1 Lowest—99 Highest)
• **67**

Insider Activity
• **Neutral**

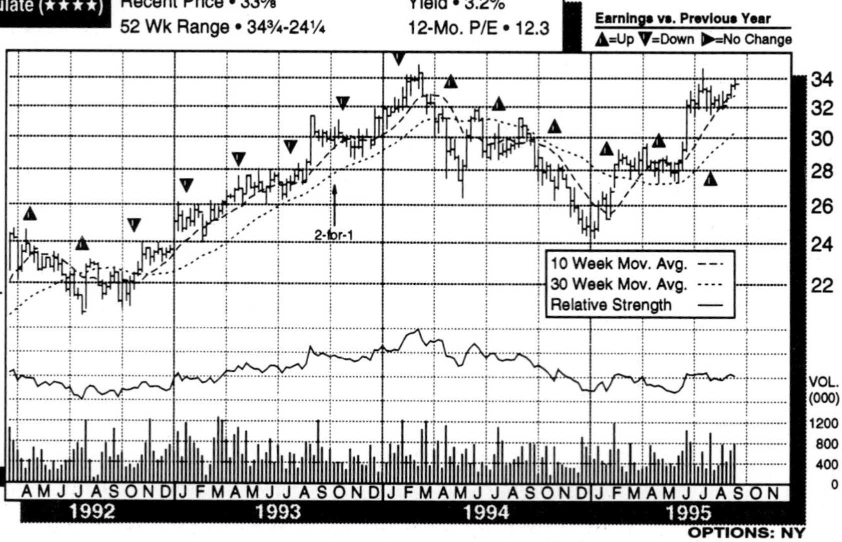

Overview - 13-SEP-95

S&P expects that sales will rise moderately in 1996, reflecting stronger demand and higher selling prices in the ongoing core chemical and petroleum segments. The pending purchase of OSi Specialties will offset the loss of sales resulting from the planned sale of the lubricant business and the recent sale of the diversified segment. Additional acquisitions related to the core businesses would also boost revenues. Profitability should improve, aided by a better product mix and cost reductions resulting from a downsizing of salaried staff and a plant consolidation program. A possible stock repurchase program would also boost EPS comparisons.

Valuation - 13-SEP-95

This stock has performed well in 1995, up 40% year to date, largely on the anticipation of a major acquisition and further divestitures. We are positive about the pending purchase of OSi Specialties, which should make an earnings contribution in 1996, as well as the planned sale of the lackluster lubricants business. We also see Witco's profit margins recovering in 1996 as selling price increases catch up with raw material costs. The shares are attractive at current levels based on the long term growth prospects of the company; internal growth and additional acquisitions will accelerate global expansion of the core businesses. Dividends have been raised for the past 22 consecutive years and provide an above average yield.

Key Stock Statistics

S&P EPS Est. 1995	2.65	Tang. Bk. Value/Share	13.22
P/E on S&P Est. 1995	12.7	Beta	0.93
S&P EPS Est. 1996	2.30	Shareholders	5,000
Dividend Rate/Share	1.12	Market cap. (B)	$ 2.0
Shs. outstg. (M)	56.4	Inst. holdings	80%
Avg. daily vol. (M)	0.163	Insider holdings	NA

Value of $10,000 invested 5 years ago: $ 22,081

Fiscal Year Ending Dec. 31

	1995	% Change	1994	% Change	1993	% Change
Revenues (Million $)						
1Q	602.5	9%	553.4	NM	553.2	32%
2Q	586.7	4%	565.6	3%	549.5	29%
3Q	—	—	564.2	4%	540.6	27%
4Q	—	—	541.5	8%	499.3	10%
Yr.	—	—	2,225	4%	2,143	24%
Income (Million $)						
1Q	29.78	35%	22.04	17%	18.81	NM
2Q	71.35	120%	32.38	117%	14.90	-17%
3Q	—	—	27.00	98%	13.63	-28%
4Q	—	—	25.65	NM	-27.57	NM
Yr.	—	—	107.1	NM	19.76	-63%
Earnings Per Share ($)						
1Q	0.53	29%	0.41	3%	0.40	-2%
2Q	1.26	121%	0.57	97%	0.29	-26%
3Q	E0.43	-10%	0.48	78%	0.27	-33%
4Q	E0.43	-7%	0.46	NM	-0.47	NM
Yr.	E2.65	38%	1.92	NM	0.46	-61%

Next earnings report expected: late October

Witco Corp.

Business Summary - 12-SEP-95

Witco Corp. (formerly Witco Chemical) produces a wide range of specialty chemical and petroleum products. The company completed the divestiture of its diversified products segment in mid-1995 and plans to sell its lubricant business. Contributions by industry segment in 1994 were:

	Sales	Profits
Chemicals	60%	63%
Petroleum	34%	28%
Diversified	6%	9%

Foreign operations accounted for 30% of sales and 35% of profits in 1994.

Chemicals include oleochemicals (fatty acids, glycerines, amines, amides, esters), surfactants (surfactants, emulsifiers, detergents and cleaners), plastic additives (stabilizers, plasticizers, lubricants, anti-oxidants, catalysts, stearates, organic peroxides), and polyester and urethanes resins (polyols, urethane chemicals, epoxy resins, polyamide and polyamine resins, and curing agents).

Petroleum consists of petroleum specialties (white mineral oils, petrolatums, sulfonates, microcrystalline waxes, refrigeration and ink oils, cable fillers) and lubricants (lubricants, greases and equipment, naphthenic oils, asphalt, road treatment products, and Kendall and Amalie brand motor oils and lubricants) produced from refined or semi-refined oils.

In order to focus on its core chemicals and petroleum segments, WIT has divested its diversifed products segment. WIT sold its carbon black business in June 1995. A unit which produced plastic and hard rubber battery containers and parts was sold in March 1995. Allied-Kelite (metal cleaning, plating and corrosion resistant products) was sold in 1994. A producer of conveyor belts and industrial diaphragms was sold in 1993.

Important Developments

Sep. '95—WIT agreed to acquire OSi Specialties Inc. for $486 million. OSi, a leading producer of silane and other silicone derivatives, is projected to have sales in 1995 of $450 million with close to 50% outside the U.S. WIT also announced its intention to sell its lubricants group (sales of $404 million in 1994). In July 1995, WIT completed the Diversified Products Group divestiture program with the sale of its carbon black unit for $122 million, resulting in a gain of $27 million ($0.48 a share) in the second quarter. The sale of the battery parts business in March resulted in a first quarter gain of $6.2 million ($0.11 a share). WIT announced a salaried work force reduction and plans for a rationalization of manufacturing facilities.

Capitalization

Long Term Debt: $351,601,000 (6/95).
$2.65 Conv. Preferred Stock: 7,000 shs. ($1 par); red. at $66; conv. into 8.4037 com.

Per Share Data ($) (Year Ended Dec. 31)

	1994	1993	1992	1991	1990	1989
Tangible Bk. Val.	13.32	9.82	8.19	12.76	12.55	12.27
Cash Flow	3.76	1.89	2.43	2.71	2.48	1.73
Earnings	1.92	0.46	1.19	1.61	1.48	0.80
Dividends	1.06	0.96	0.92	0.90	0.86	0.83
Payout Ratio	55%	NM	77%	56%	55%	107%
Prices - High	35	32¼	25⅜	22	20	22⅝
- Low	24⅜	24	20	14½	10⅞	17⅜
P/E Ratio - High	18	70	21	14	14	28
- Low	13	52	17	9	7	22

Income Statement Analysis (Million $)

	1994	%Chg	1993	%Chg	1992	%Chg	1991
Revs.	2,225	4%	2,143	24%	1,729	6%	1,631
Oper. Inc.	280	15%	244	40%	174	NM	173
Depr.	105	25%	83.8	25%	67.1	13%	59.6
Int. Exp.	31.9	-14%	36.9	113%	17.3	NM	17.2
Pretax Inc.	165	NM	33.0	-60%	82.0	-25%	110
Eff. Tax Rate	35%	—	41%	—	34%	—	33%
Net Inc.	107	NM	19.8	-63%	53.9	-27%	73.5

Balance Sheet & Other Fin. Data (Million $)

	1994	1993	1992	1991	1990	1989
Cash	197	183	134	139	116	213
Curr. Assets	897	793	747	577	563	636
Total Assets	1,919	1,839	1,812	1,198	1,179	1,139
Curr. Liab.	345	341	769	256	204	180
LT Debt	347	496	173	179	230	236
Common Eqty.	840	713	614	625	587	571
Total Cap.	1,368	1,284	896	878	878	858
Cap. Exp.	107	104	72.6	74.3	90.8	70.4
Cash Flow	212	104	121	133	123	88.0

Ratio Analysis

	1994	1993	1992	1991	1990	1989
Curr. Ratio	2.6	2.3	1.0	2.3	2.8	3.5
% LT Debt of Cap.	25.3	38.6	19.3	20.4	26.2	27.4
% Net Inc.of Revs.	4.8	0.9	3.1	4.5	4.2	2.2
% Ret. on Assets	5.4	1.0	3.5	6.2	6.0	3.1
% Ret. on Equity	12.4	2.8	8.6	12.1	12.0	6.1

Dividend Data —Dividends have been paid since 1950. A dividend reinvestment plan is available. A "poison pill" stock purchase rights plan was adopted in 1995.

Amt. of Div. $	Date Decl.	Ex-Div. Date	Stock of Record	Payment Date
0.280	Sep. 01	Sep. 09	Sep. 15	Oct. 04 '94
0.280	Dec. 01	Dec. 09	Dec. 15	Jan. 03 '95
0.280	Mar. 02	Mar. 06	Mar. 10	Apr. 04 '95
0.280	Jun. 01	Jun. 08	Jun. 12	Jul. 05 '95
0.280	Sep. 05	Sep. 14	Sep. 18	Oct. 03 '95

Data as orig. reptd.; bef. results of disc. opers. and/or spec. items. Per share data adj. for stk. divs. as of ex-div. date. E-Estimated. NA-Not Available. NM-Not Meaningful. NR-Not Ranked.

Office—One American Lane, Greenwich, CT 06831-2559. **Tel**—(203) 552-2000. **Chrmn & CEO**—W. R. Toller. **EVP & CFO**—M. D. Fullwood. **VP & Secy**—D. McCoy. **SVP & Investor Contact**—C. R. Soderlind. **Dirs**—W. J. Ashe, S. Brinberg, W. G. Burns, W. R. Grant, R. M. Hayden, H. G. Hohn, W. E. Mahoney, L. J. Polite Jr., D. J. Samuel, W. R. Toller, B. F. Wesson, W. Wishnick. **Transfer Agent & Registrar**—First Chicago Trust Co. of New York, Jersey City, N.J. **Incorporated** in Delaware in 1968. **Empl**-7,955. **S&P Analyst:** Richard O'Reilly, CFA

STANDARD & POOR'S

STOCK REPORTS

WorldCom Inc.

NASDAQ Symbol **WCOM**

In S&P MidCap 400

18-OCT-95

Industry: Telecommunications

Summary: WorldCom (formerly LDDS Communications) is the fourth largest long distance carrier in the U.S., providing service throughout the nation and to over 220 foreign countries.

S&P Opinion: Accumulate (★★★★)

Recent Price • 32⅝
52 Wk Range • 34⅛-16⅜
Yield • Nil
12-Mo. P/E • NM

Quantitative Evaluations

Outlook (1 Lowest—5 Highest) • **2**

Fair Value • **30¾**

Risk • **Average**

Earn./Div. Rank • **B**

Technical Eval. • **NA**

Rel. Strength Rank (1 Lowest—99 Highest) • **73**

Insider Activity • **NA**

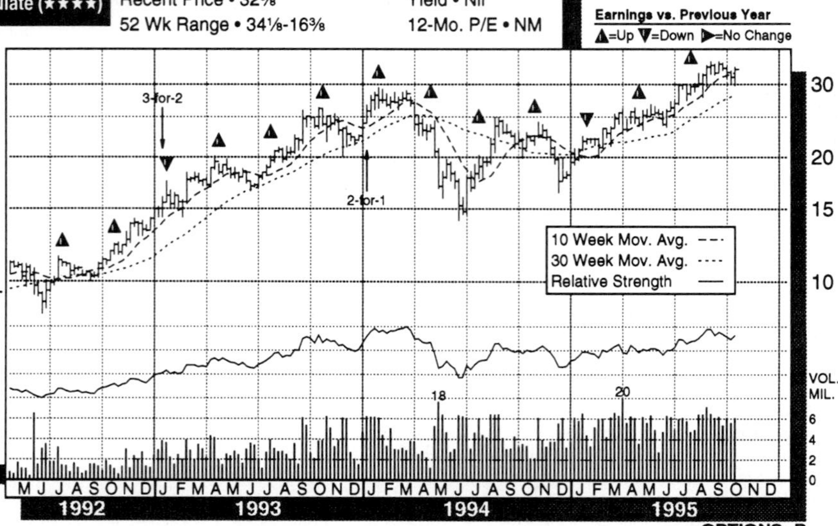

OPTIONS: P

Overview - 18-OCT-95

Revenues should continue to grow rapidly in coming periods reflecting the company's aggressive acquisition strategy as well as strong internal growth. The acquisition strategy will help WorldCom strengthen its competitive position as regulators move to allow additional competitors into the long-distance market. Meanwhile, margins will benefit from economies of scale; the addition of Wiltel is expected to result in additional cost savings from owning a nationwide network rather than leasing facilities. In addition the acquisition of global service provider IDB Communications is a key part of WorldCom's goal of increasing its international presence. Separately, Metromedia recently sold its entire minority stake in WCOM, based on its policy of not holding minority interests for the long term.

Valuation - 18-OCT-95

The shares soared 65% through September 30, 1995, far outpacing both the S&P Telecommunications (long distance) index, which rose 32%, and the S&P 500, which climbed 27%. This reflects both continued strong earnings growth and speculation that the company may be an attractive acquisition candidate for some of the large telecommunications carriers. Future growth will be fueled by strong internal growth and the recent acquisitions of WilTel and IDB. The company will benefit in particular from the addition of IDB given the industry growth in international calling volumes. The shares remain attractive for long term appreciation.

Key Stock Statistics

S&P EPS Est. 1995	1.38	Tang. Bk. Value/Share	NM
P/E on S&P Est. 1995	23.6	Beta	1.85
S&P EPS Est. 1996	1.75	Shareholders	7,200
Dividend Rate/Share	Nil	Market cap. (B)	$ 6.2
Shs. outstg. (M)	191.1	Inst. holdings	41%
Avg. daily vol. (M)	1.219	Insider holdings	NA

Value of $10,000 invested 5 years ago: $ 144,422

Fiscal Year Ending Dec. 31

	1995	% Change	1994	% Change	1993	% Change
Revenues (Million $)						
1Q	865.0	110%	411.3	88%	219.0	19%
2Q	894.7	111%	424.5	69%	251.5	27%
3Q	—	—	439.8	56%	281.8	37%
4Q	—	—	573.0	46%	392.4	84%
Yr.	—	—	2,221	94%	1,145	43%
Income (Million $)						
1Q	53.96	86%	29.00	69%	17.19	40%
2Q	54.88	67%	32.85	54%	21.32	55%
3Q	—	—	42.93	51%	28.44	97%
4Q	—	—	-77.24	NM	37.23	NM
Yr.	—	—	-122.2	NM	104.2	NM
Earnings Per Share ($)						
1Q	0.28	22%	0.23	44%	0.16	28%
2Q	0.33	27%	0.26	30%	0.20	48%
3Q	E0.37	32%	0.28	12%	0.25	79%
4Q	E0.40	NM	-0.49	NM	0.24	NM
Yr.	E1.38	NM	-0.95	NM	0.85	NM

Next earnings report expected: mid November

WorldCom Inc.

Business Summary - 05-OCT-95

WorldCom Inc. (formerly LDDS Communications) is the fourth largest long-distance carrier in the U.S., providing long-distance services throughout the U.S. and to numerous foreign countries. The company offers a variety of service options, including "one plus" dialing, inbound "800" service, "800" travel service, operator, private line network and data services.

Customers are charged on the basis of minutes of usage at rates that vary with the distance, duration and time of day of the call. Marketing is directed primarily toward commercial customers, who are typically higher volume users than residential customers, with usage concentrated during peak hours, when rates are highest.

Domestically, traffic is transmitted over a 1,300 mile digital fiber optic network that serves Florida and Georgia, a 400 mile digital microwave network in Texas and a 2,678 mile digital microwave network running from New York City to Houston. When combined with the recent acquisition of WilTel, the company's network now consists of more than 15,000 miles of fiber optic cable and microwave equipment with access to an additional 40,000 miles of fiber optic network through lease agreements with other carriers. Internationally, the company owns fiber optic facilities on most major international cable systems in the Pacific and Atlantic Ocean regions, providing fiber optic cable connections between the United States and the Pacific Rim and the United States and Europe. WCOM also owns fiber optic cable for services to the former Soviet Union and to Latin America.

The company follows a four point expansion strategy, consisting of internal growth, selective acquisitions of smaller interexchange carriers with limited geographic service areas and market shares, the consolidation of certain third-tier carriers with larger market shares and international expansion. Operations were significantly expanded with the September 1993 three-way merger with Metromedia Communications Corp. and Resurgens Communications Group, Inc.

Important Developments

Aug. '95—Metromedia Co. sold its entire stake of 30,855,983 common shares. Included in the sale were 21,876,976 shares issued to Metromedia upon conversion of series 1 preferred shares.

Jan. '95—WorldCom completed the acquisition of WilTel Network Services for $2.5 billion in cash. WilTel operates one of only four national digital telecommunications networks in the U.S. Earlier, WCOM acquired IDB Communications Group, Inc. in a stock transaction valued at about $687 million.

Capitalization

Long Term Debt: $3,393,600,000 (6/95, as adjusted).

Per Share Data ($) (Year Ended Dec. 31)

	1994	1993	1992	1991	1990	1989
Tangible Bk. Val.	-1.53	-1.01	-1.12	-2.77	-1.98	-1.99
Cash Flow	0.09	1.57	0.53	0.79	0.52	0.38
Earnings	-0.95	0.85	-0.03	0.42	0.26	0.13
Dividends	Nil	Nil	Nil	Nil	Nil	Nil
Payout Ratio	Nil	Nil	Nil	Nil	Nil	Nil
Prices - High	29½	26⅜	15⅛	9⅞	4⅛	3⅜
- Low	14	14¼	8⅜	3⅞	2	1⅛
P/E Ratio - High	NM	31	NM	23	16	26
- Low	NM	17	NM	9	8	9

Income Statement Analysis (Million $)

	1994	%Chg	1993	%Chg	1992	%Chg	1991
Revs.	2,221	94%	1,145	43%	801	NM	263
Oper. Inc.	341	23%	278	62%	172	196%	58.2
Depr.	164	105%	79.9	48%	53.9	NM	15.4
Int. Exp.	47.3	75%	27.0	13%	23.8	82%	13.1
Pretax Inc.	-48.0	NM	175	NM	8.2	-74%	31.1
Eff. Tax Rate	NM	—	41%	—	102%	—	43%
Net Inc.	-121	NM	104	NM	-0.2	NM	17.7

Balance Sheet & Other Fin. Data (Million $)

	1994	1993	1992	1991	1990	1989
Cash	20.3	6.2	4.2	4.1	1.1	0.6
Curr. Assets	589	322	178	56.0	22.6	16.4
Total Assets	3,430	2,515	870	337	169	129
Curr. Liab.	711	309	164	72.0	28.4	21.4
LT Debt	788	526	334	151	94.0	77.0
Common Eqty.	1,827	1,621	296	100	39.0	29.0
Total Cap.	2,615	2,148	704	263	140	108
Cap. Exp.	192	35.6	57.7	19.0	13.1	9.5
Cash Flow	14.0	174	51.6	33.1	19.2	10.7

Ratio Analysis

	1994	1993	1992	1991	1990	1989
Curr. Ratio	0.8	1.0	1.1	0.8	0.8	0.8
% LT Debt of Cap.	30.1	24.5	47.4	57.2	67.0	71.2
% Net Inc.of Revs.	NM	9.1	NM	6.7	6.3	3.9
% Ret. on Assets	NM	5.8	NM	6.6	6.1	NA
% Ret. on Equity	NM	9.4	NM	24.0	26.4	NA

Dividend Data —No cash has been paid. The company has periodically distributed stock splits to shareholders; a two-for-one split was effected in January 1994, and three-for-two splits were effected in each of January 1993, July 1990 and June 1991.

Data as orig. reptd.; bef. results of disc. opers. and/or spec. items. Per share data adj. for stk. divs. as of ex-div. date. E-Estimated. NA-Not Available. NM-Not Meaningful. NR-Not Ranked.

Office—515 East Amite Street, Jackson, MS 39201-2702. **Tel**—(601) 360-8600. **Chrmn**—J. W. Kluge. **Pres & CEO**—B. J. Ebbers. **CFO & Treas**—S. D. Sullivan. **Secy**—C. J. Aycock. **Investor Contact**—Charles T. Cannada. **Dirs**—C. J. Aycock, M. E. Bobbit, D. M. Dunnaway, B. J. Ebbers, F. Galesi, S. A. Kellett Jr., S. Kessel, J. W. Kluge, J. A. Porter, S. Subotnick. **Transfer Agent & Registrar**—First Union National Bank of North Carolina, Charlotte. **Incorporated** in Mississippi in 1983; reincorporated in Georgia in 1993. **Empl**-7,500. **S&P Analyst:** Kevin J. Gooley

STANDARD & POOR'S

STOCK REPORTS

Xilinx, Inc.

NASDAQ Symbol **XLNX**

In S&P MidCap 400

29-JUL-95

Industry: Data Processing

Summary: Xilinx is the world's leading supplier of programmable logic and related development system software.

S&P Opinion: Accumulate (★★★★)

Recent Price • 121
52 Wk Range • 127⅛-33¾

Yield • Nil
12-Mo. P/E • 57.1

Quantitative Evaluations

Outlook (1 Lowest—5 Highest) **• 5**

Fair Value **• 125⅜**

Risk **• High**

Earn./Div. Rank **• B**

Technical Eval. **• Bullish** since 8/94

Rel. Strength Rank (1 Lowest—99 Highest) **• 94**

Insider Activity **• Neutral**

Earnings vs. Previous Year
▲=Up ▼=Down ▶=No Change

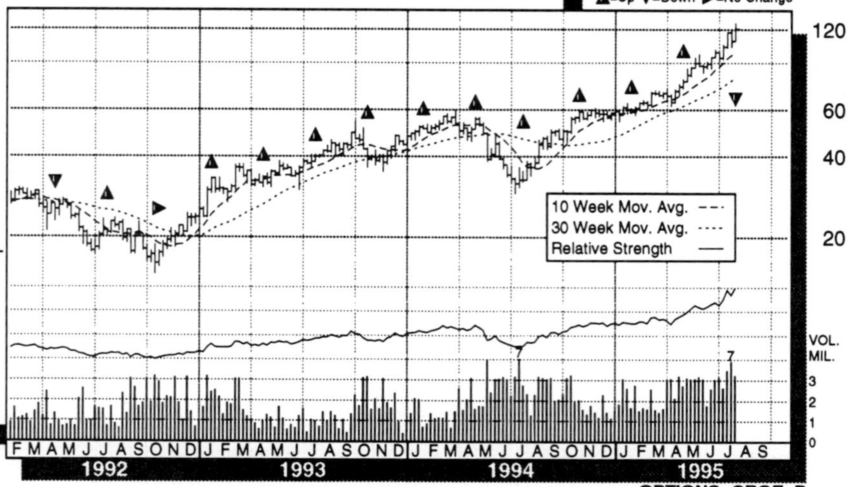

OPTIONS: CBOE, P

Overview - 27-JUL-95

Sales are expected to rise more than 50% in 1995-6, reflecting continued strong growth of the programmable logic market, fueled by broadening applications for the products and an estimated 15%-18% increase in sales by the semiconductor industry. An aggressive new product introduction program will also assist growth. Demand in the U.S. should be led by the networking and telecommunications markets, while telecommunications markets should lead European sales. The Japanese market is beginning to rebound after prolonged weakness. Gross margins, among the highest in the industry, are expected to flatten as the company seeks additional market share through price reductions.

Valuation - 27-JUL-95

We recommend accumulation of Xilinx on the continued bright outlook for semiconductor manufacturers. First-quarter sales rose 67%, year to year, and 15% sequentially. This increase was largely attibutable to the XC4000 product line, which had 30% higher sales than in the prior period. Gross margins climbed to a record 61.4% of sales, while total operating costs, excluding acquistion-related charges, fell to an all-time low of 31.7% of sales. A record backlog of orders at the end of the first quarter, coupled with the new XC5200 product line, should aid near-term growth. A pending three-for-one stock split should indirectly benefit the share price as the stock's liquidity is increased.

Key Stock Statistics

S&P EPS Est. 1996	3.52	Tang. Bk. Value/Share	10.42
P/E on S&P Est. 1996	34.4	Beta	1.71
S&P EPS Est. 1997	5.50	Shareholders	500
Dividend Rate/Share	Nil	Market cap. (B)	$ 2.8
Shs. outstg. (M)	23.5	Inst. holdings	90%
Avg. daily vol. (M)	1.061	Insider holdings	NA

Value of $10,000 invested 5 years ago: NA

Fiscal Year Ending Mar. 31

	1996	% Change	1995	% Change	1994	% Change
Revenues (Million $)						
1Q	125.8	67%	75.15	38%	54.43	40%
2Q	—	—	79.51	32%	60.07	41%
3Q	—	—	91.28	37%	66.50	44%
4Q	—	—	109.2	45%	75.44	50%
Yr.	—	—	355.1	38%	256.5	44%
Income (Million $)						
1Q	5.55	-54%	12.01	35%	8.87	49%
2Q	—	—	11.82	23%	9.60	52%
3Q	—	—	15.57	46%	10.67	53%
4Q	—	—	19.87	64%	12.14	52%
Yr.	—	—	59.28	44%	41.28	52%
Earnings Per Share ($)						
1Q	0.21	-57%	0.49	32%	0.37	48%
2Q	E1.02	—	0.49	22%	0.40	54%
3Q	E1.10	—	0.62	41%	0.44	47%
4Q	E1.19	—	0.79	58%	0.50	47%
Yr.	E3.52	—	2.40	40%	1.71	49%

Next earnings report expected: mid October

Xilinx, Inc.

Business Summary - 28-JUL-95

Xilinx, Inc. is the leading supplier of field programmable gate arrays (FPGAs) and related development system software. Xilinx products are standard integrated circuits that are programmed by Xilinx customers to perform desired logic operations. These products provide high levels of integration and significant time and cost savings for electronic equipment manufacturers in the computer peripherals, telecommunications, industrial control and instrumentation, and military markets.

Net revenues in recent fiscal years were derived as follows:

	1994-1995	1993-1994
FPGAs	96%	95%
Development system software	4%	5%

U.S. export revenue from shipments to Europe represented 19% of product revenue in 1994-5, while exports to Japan and the Pacific Rim accounted for 10%.

The company's FPGAs are proprietary integrated circuits designed by Xilinx; they provide a unique combination of the high logic density usually associated with custom gate arrays, the time-to-market advantages of programmable logic and the availability of a standard product. The company offers three families of FPGAs, ranging from 500 to 25,000 usable gates.

To implement the FPGA solution, system designers use proprietary Xilinx development system software, together with industry standard CAE software, to develop FPGA applications. At the end of 1994-5, Xilinx had shipped more than 21,000 development systems to over 5,000 companies.

The company's product line was expanded in April 1995 with the $35 million acquisition of NeoCAD, a private firm engaged in FPGA software design tools for programmable electronic technologies.

In 1994-5, research and development outlays totaled $45.3 million (12.8% of revenues), compared with $34.3 million (13.4%) in 1993-4.

Important Developments

Jul. '95—Xilinx reported a nonrecurring charge of $19.4 million ($0.75 per share) related to the April 1995 acquisition of NeoCAD, a developer of high-performance design software for field programmable gate arrays. The purchase price for NeoCAD was $35 million. The remaining $15.4 million, primarily representing acquired developed technology, will be amortized over six years.

May '95—The company announced that it amended a two-for-one split of its common stock and approved a three-for-one split. The split is effective August 11, 1995, to shareholders of record July 28.

Capitalization

Long Term Debt: $738,000 of lease obligs. (7/1/95).

Per Share Data ($) (Year Ended Mar. 31)

	1995	1994	1993	1992	1991	1990
Tangible Bk. Val.	10.42	7.56	5.50	4.73	3.68	-0.01
Cash Flow	2.90	2.16	1.52	1.12	0.83	0.40
Earnings	2.40	1.71	1.15	0.89	0.70	0.33
Dividends	Nil	Nil	Nil	Nil	Nil	Nil
Payout Ratio	Nil	Nil	Nil	Nil	Nil	Nil
Cal. Yrs.	1994	1993	1992	1991	1990	1989
Prices - High	62	54½	31	32½	17	NA
- Low	29	23½	14½	12½	9½	NA
P/E Ratio - High	26	32	27	37	24	NA
- Low	12	14	13	14	14	NA

Income Statement Analysis (Million $)

	1995	%Chg	1994	%Chg	1993	%Chg	1992
Revs.	355	39%	256	44%	178	31%	136
Oper. Inc.	107	41%	76.0	51%	50.2	28%	39.2
Depr.	12.2	13%	10.8	25%	8.6	55%	5.6
Int. Exp.	10.3	NM	0.5	-18%	0.7	2%	0.6
Pretax Inc.	94.8	41%	67.4	55%	43.6	29%	33.8
Eff. Tax Rate	38%	—	39%	—	38%	—	37%
Net Inc.	59.3	44%	41.3	52%	27.2	28%	21.3

Balance Sheet & Other Fin. Data (Million $)

	1995	1994	1993	1992	1991	1990
Cash	123	116	84.8	81.3	71.8	13.1
Curr. Assets	256	194	137	121	100	29.0
Total Assets	321	226	163	147	112	35.0
Curr. Liab.	76.1	51.1	35.7	33.0	24.6	9.8
LT Debt	0.9	2.2	3.9	5.0	3.8	2.0
Common Eqty.	244	173	123	109	83.0	23.0
Total Cap.	245	175	127	114	87.0	25.0
Cap. Exp.	26.2	12.3	9.8	7.2	4.1	2.0
Cash Flow	71.5	52.1	35.9	26.8	19.1	7.5

Ratio Analysis

	1995	1994	1993	1992	1991	1990
Curr. Ratio	3.4	3.8	3.8	3.7	4.1	3.0
% LT Debt of Cap.	0.4	1.3	3.1	4.4	4.4	8.0
% Net Inc.of Revs.	16.7	16.0	15.3	15.7	16.3	12.2
% Ret. on Assets	21.5	21.0	17.6	16.4	10.8	21.2
% Ret. on Equity	28.2	27.0	23.5	22.0	30.1	33.2

Dividend Data (No cash dividends have been paid, and Xilinx does not expect to pay any in the foreseeable future.)

Amt. of Div. $	Date Decl.	Ex-Div. Date	Stock of Record	Payment Date
2-for-1	May. 24	Aug. 14	Jul. 28	Aug. 11 '95

Data as orig. reptd.; bef. results of disc. opers. and/or spec. items. Per share data adj. for stk. divs. as of ex-div. date. E-Estimated. NA-Not Available. NM-Not Meaningful. NR-Not Ranked.

Office—2100 Logic Dr., San Jose, CA 95124. **Tel**—(408) 559-7778. **Fax**—(408) 559-7114. **CEO**—B. V. Vonderschmitt. **Pres**—C. Wozniak. **VP-Fin & CFO**—G. M. Steel. **Secy**—R. C. Hinckley. **Investor Contact**—Maria Quillard (408) 879-4988. **Dirs**—J. L. Doyle, P. T. Gianos, B. V. Vonderschmitt. **Transfer Agent & Registrar**—First National Bank of Boston. **Incorporated** in Delaware in 1990. **Empl-** 868. **S&P Analyst:** Steven A. Jaworski

STANDARD & POOR'S

STOCK REPORTS

York International

NYSE Symbol **YRK**
In S&P MidCap 400

06-AUG-95 **Industry:** Building

Summary: This full-line, global manufacturer of heating, ventilating, air-conditioning and refrigeration products derives about 50% of sales from service, repairs and replacement parts.

S&P Opinion: Hold (★★★) | Recent Price • 45 | 52 Wk Range • 48½-33⅞ | Yield • 0.5% | 12-Mo. P/E • 17.4

Quantitative Evaluations
Outlook
(1 Lowest—5 Highest)
• NA
Fair Value
• NA
Risk
• Low
Earn./Div. Rank
• NR

Technical Eval.
• Bearish since 5/95
Rel. Strength Rank
(1 Lowest—99 Highest)
• 50
Insider Activity
• Neutral

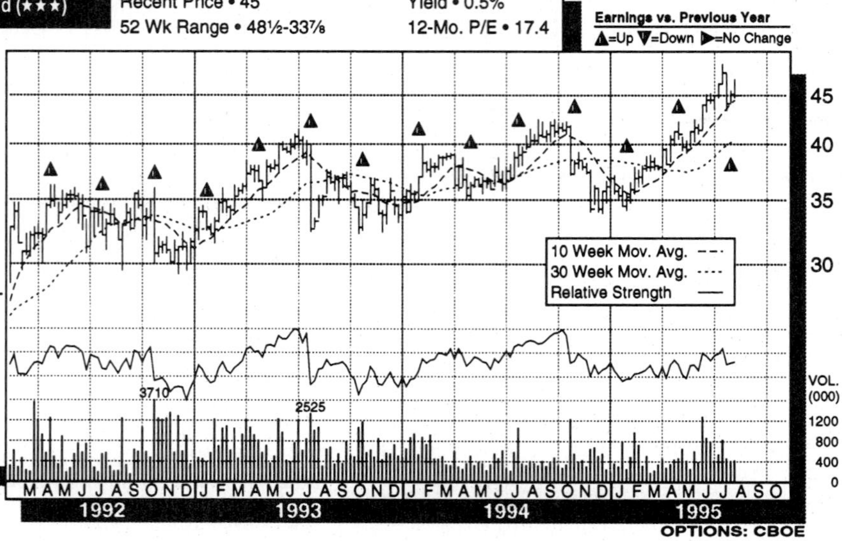

Overview - 04-AUG-95

Sales from existing businesses in 1995 and 1996 are expected to advance 10%, which is YRK's stated annual goal, and with contributions from acquisitions, a stronger overall sales rise is likely. Gains will be driven by booming U.S. demand and economic growth in Europe. Sales will benefit from increased capital spending for commercial air conditioning and refrigeration modernization projects, particularly for conversion of existing systems to environmentally friendly refrigerants. Demand for residential products should remain strong, even with a downturn in housing starts, since 75% of residential air-conditioning sales are replacements. Reduction of debt with proceeds from a recent 4.3 million share offering will lower interest expense, but equity dilution will negate the impact on share earnings.

Valuation - 04-AUG-95

The leader in its industry, YRK is an excellent example of a balanced industrial concern. Its business is derived from a blend of domestic and international customers in commercial and residential markets, purchasing new equipment and servicing existing installations. Prospects for the stable service business are enhanced by the need to update existing installations to operate with environmentally friendly refrigerants. The shares, trading at about 17X trailing 12-month EPS and at about 15X projected 1996 EPS, are adequately valued, and should be average performers in the coming year.

Key Stock Statistics

S&P EPS Est. 1995	2.85	Tang. Bk. Value/Share	3.09
P/E on S&P Est. 1995	15.8	Beta	1.31
S&P EPS Est. 1996	3.10	Shareholders	800
Dividend Rate/Share	0.24	Market cap. (B)	$ 1.9
Shs. outstg. (M)	41.9	Inst. holdings	82%
Avg. daily vol. (M)	0.104	Insider holdings	NA

Value of $10,000 invested 5 years ago: NA

Fiscal Year Ending Dec. 31

	1995	% Change	1994	% Change	1993	% Change
Revenues (Million $)						
1Q	604.3	14%	531.2	19%	446.8	2%
2Q	775.0	22%	636.8	20%	531.2	3%
3Q	—	—	598.6	23%	488.7	3%
4Q	—	—	655.3	16%	565.3	11%
Yr.	—	—	2,422	19%	2,032	5%
Income (Million $)						
1Q	18.78	23%	15.22	17%	13.03	20%
2Q	35.55	17%	30.49	16%	26.19	10%
3Q	—	—	22.49	21%	18.54	2%
4Q	—	—	21.57	22%	17.71	7%
Yr.	—	—	89.77	19%	75.46	9%
Earnings Per Share ($)						
1Q	0.50	22%	0.41	17%	0.35	6%
2Q	0.91	11%	0.82	17%	0.70	11%
3Q	E0.79	—	0.60	22%	0.49	2%
4Q	E0.65	—	0.57	21%	0.47	7%
Yr.	E2.85	—	2.40	19%	2.01	6%

Next earnings report expected: mid October

York International

06-AUG-95

Business Summary - 04-AUG-95

York International is a full-line manufacturer of heating, ventilating, air-conditioning and refrigeration products. It believes that it is the third largest U.S. maker of such products, and one of the leaders internationally. Its air-conditioning systems range from a one-ton small residence unit to the 59,000-ton system installed in New York's World Trade Center. Products are sold in 120 countries through over 700 sales and distribution centers. Contributions by geographic segment in 1994 were:

	Sales	Profits
U.S.	66.0%	80.8%
Europe	19.7%	13.3%
Other	13.0%	5.6%
Canada	1.3%	0.3%

Products fall into three categories: commercial (48% of sales in 1994), including heating, air-conditioning, process cooling and thermal storage equipment for commercial applications in stores, buildings, malls, manufacturing plants, airports and ships; residential (33%), consisting of central air-conditioning and heat pumps, furnaces and hermetic compressors; and refrigeration and gas compression equipment (19%), for use in food, beverage, chemical and petrochemical processing.

YRK's 2,500 company technicians, stationed worldwide, generate 48% of revenues through the sale of replacement parts and by providing routine and emergency service for equipment made by the company and its competitors.

Residential products are marketed throughout the U.S. and internationally through 43 exclusive distributors, 10 company-owned distribution centers, and more than 200 nonexclusive distributors and wholesalers. Other products are marketed directly to contractors, distributors, architects, engineers and building owners. YRK's products are used in such locations as the British Houses of Parliament, NASA's Vehicle Assembly Building at Cape Canaveral, the Los Angeles International Airport, the Jeddah Airport, the Overseas Union Bank Centre in Singapore, the Sydney Opera House, the National Library Complex in Beijing, the Hong Kong Exposition Centre, and the English Channel Tunnel.

Important Developments

Jun. '95—YRK announced that it had completed the sale of 4.3 million newly issued common shares at $42 each through underwriters. In addition, the underwriters were granted an option to purchase an additional 645,000 shares at the same price. With full exercise of the overallotment option, net proceeds after expenses should approximate $200 million.

Capitalization

Long Term Debt: $439,858,000 (3/95).

Per Share Data ($) (Year Ended Dec. 31)

	1994	1993	1992	1991	1990	1989
Tangible Bk. Val.	3.07	2.09	2.10	-4.17	NA	NA
Cash Flow	3.31	2.84	2.72	1.83	2.18	NA
Earnings	2.40	2.01	1.90	0.56	1.21	NA
Dividends	0.16	0.08	0.04	0.01	NA	NA
Payout Ratio	7%	4%	2%	2%	NA	NA
Prices - High	42½	41½	36¼	27¼	NA	NA
- Low	33⅞	31½	25¾	22⅝	NA	NA
P/E Ratio - High	18	21	19	49	NA	NA
- Low	14	16	14	40	NA	NA

Income Statement Analysis (Million $)

	1994	%Chg	1993	%Chg	1992	%Chg	1991
Revs.	2,422	19%	2,032	5%	1,939	17%	1,653
Oper. Inc.	219	13%	194	-5%	204	15%	177
Depr.	34.0	9%	31.3	5%	29.9	NM	30.0
Int. Exp.	31.0	29%	24.0	-43%	42.0	-58%	99
Pretax Inc.	144	13%	127	3%	123	NM	36.8
Eff. Tax Rate	38%	—	41%	—	44%	—	65%
Net Inc.	89.8	19%	75.5	9%	69.3	NM	13.0

Balance Sheet & Other Fin. Data (Million $)

	1994	1993	1992	1991	1990	1989
Cash	5.9	3.4	5.1	2.5	NA	NA
Curr. Assets	851	703	579	612	NA	NA
Total Assets	1,588	1,335	1,164	1,206	1,172	NA
Curr. Liab.	614	522	414	432	NA	NA
LT Debt	281	204	227	458	488	NA
Common Eqty.	527	457	455	254	214	NA
Total Cap.	808	661	699	723	NA	NA
Cap. Exp.	81.6	30.6	37.0	37.7	21.8	NA
Cash Flow	124	107	99	42.6	67.2	NA

Ratio Analysis

	1994	1993	1992	1991	1990	1989
Curr. Ratio	1.4	1.3	1.4	1.4	NA	NA
% LT Debt of Cap.	34.8	30.9	32.5	63.4	NA	NA
% Net Inc.of Revs.	3.7	3.7	3.6	0.8	2.3	NA
% Ret. on Assets	6.1	6.0	5.1	0.9	NA	NA
% Ret. on Equity	18.2	16.5	17.7	NM	NA	NA

Dividend Data (Quarterly dividends were initiated in 1991.)

Amt. of Div. $	Date Decl.	Ex-Div. Date	Stock of Record	Payment Date
0.040	Sep. 08	Sep. 14	Sep. 20	Sep. 30 '94
0.040	Dec. 06	Dec. 12	Dec. 16	Dec. 27 '94
0.060	Mar. 06	Mar. 08	Mar. 14	Mar. 24 '95
0.060	Jun. 08	Jun. 15	Jun. 19	Jun. 29 '95

Data as orig. reptd.; bef. results of disc. opers. and/or spec. items. Per share data adj. for stk. divs. as of ex-div. date. E-Estimated. NA-Not Available. NM-Not Meaningful. NR-Not Ranked.

Office—631 South Richland Ave., York, PA 17403. **Tel**—(717) 771-7890. **Chrmn, Pres & CEO**—R. N. Pokelwaldt. **VP & CFO**—D. T. DuCray. **VP & Secy**—Jane G. Davis. **Investor Contact**—Helen S. Marsteller (717-771-7451). **Dirs**—M. W. Gambrill, R. F. B. Logan, G. C. McDonough, R. N. Pokelwaldt, D. M. Roberts, J. A. Urry, J. E. Welsh III, W. B. Wriston. **Transfer Agent & Registrar**—Chemical Bank, NYC. **Incorporated** in Delaware in 1988. **Empl-** 17,000. **S&P Analyst:** Joshua M. Harari, CFA